Bill 'n' Anne Campbell
1221 Littlebrook Lane
Birmingham, AL 35235
Phone: (205)853-8227
FAX: (205)853-9951
e-mail: acamp10720@aol.com
THE FLASH
FASTEST MAN ALIVE
WONDER WOMAN
SENSATION COMICS
SUPERMEN OF AMERICA
ACTION COMICS
RANCH BOSS
Radio and Box Top Premiums
(Rings, Badges, Decoders, Manuals)
Character Watches, Boxes, Inserts, Bands, Parts, Hands, Dials
Western Hero Items Including Cap Guns and Holsters
Comics, Big Little Books, Pop-Ups
Capt. Marvel, Capt. Midnight, Capt. Video, Buck Rogers, Tom Corbett Space Cadet, Doc Savage, Shadow, Tom Mix, Lone Ranger, Superman, Batman, Little Orphan Annie, Mickey Mouse, Donald Duck, Popeye, Howdy Doody, Hopalong Cassidy, Roy Rogers, G-Man, Gene Autry, Jack Armstrong, Davy Crockett, Paladin, Rin Tin Tin, Sgt. Preston, Zorro, Green Hornet, Sky King, Straight Arrow, Buster Brown, Flash Gordon
For personal collection: Capt. Marvel items wanted. Also especially need Whistle Bomb Ring, Big Bad Wolf and Donald Duck 1934 Wrist Watches with leather bands.
www.billnannecampbell.qpg.com

**Bruce Hamilton, one of the most experienced collectors and historians in the business, is selling his personal inventory! Don't miss out on this key opportunity to pick up the items you've been looking for OR the chance to start your collection out right!**

Contact:
Another Rainbow
160 Desert Holly Drive
Sedona, AZ 86336
(928) 204-0086
Fax (928) 204-1858

c Books ★ Carl Barks Figurines
ks ★ Other Original Art

INTRODUCING POCKET-SIZED FIGURES OF THE ENTIRE DC UNIVERSE!
DC COMICS POCKET SUPER HEROES™ SERIES 1
The exciting new line of DC Comics Pocket Super Heroes features pocket-sized figures of DC's greatest heroes and villains.
Each 2-figure set contains related characters complete with their own backdrop story card and stand.
$9.95 US / $16.95 CAN for each 2-figure set
Figures are approximately 3.25" tall.
DC COMICS POCKET SUPER HEROES SERIES 1
GREEN LANTERN VS. SINESTRO
COLLECT THEM ALL! PLACE YOUR ORDER AT YOUR FAVORITE COMICS SHOP!
FOR MORE INFORMATION GO TO: dcdirectonline.com and dccomics.com
CALL 1-888-COMIC BOOK FOR YOUR NEAREST COMICS SHOP
DC DIRECT™
DC Comics Pocket Super Heroes and all related characters, and elements are trademarks of and © DC Comics. All rights reserved. Product may vary from image shown. (S02)

WOW
...is what everyone is saying when they see the prices that Jay Parrino's The Mint is paying for the finest Golden-Age, Silver-Age and Bronze-Age comic books in the marketplace today. If you want the top offer for your collection, come deal with the people who are as serious about these gems as you are. Professionals with over 50 years of combined experience and who share the same passion for vintage comic books. Call Today. You will be glad you did.
The Rarest and The Finest
CGC
Comics Guaranty, LLC
© DC
Jay Parrino's
The MINT L.L.C.

## ABOUT THE AUTHOR

Ted Hake founded Hake's Americana & Collectibles in 1967, the first auction house to specialize in 20th century American popular culture. His early initiatives in hundreds of collecting areas contributed significantly to establishing collectibles as a major pastime for millions of Americans. Over the years, Hake has shared his expertise by writing sixteen reference/price guides covering such subjects as television collectibles, presidential campaigns, advertising, comic characters, and cowboy characters. These books are recognized by collectors and dealers as informative, useful, and accurate. Hake produces his books, sales lists, and auction catalogues from his hometown of York, Pennsylvania. •

## OTHER BOOKS BY TED HAKE:

**The Button Book**
(out of print)

**Buttons in Sets**
with Marshall N. Levin

**Collectible Pin-Back Buttons 1896-1986: An Illustrated Price Guide**
with Russ King

**The Encyclopedia of Political Buttons 1896-1972; Political Buttons Book II 1920-1976; POLITICAL BUTTONS BOOK III 1789-1916**

**The Encyclopedia of Political Buttons: 1998 REVISED PRICES FOR BOOKS I, II AND III**

**Hake's Guide to Advertising Collectibles 100 Years of Advertising from 100 Famous Companies**

**Hake's Guide to Comic Character Collectibles An Illustrated Price Guide to 100 Years of Comic Strip Characters**

**Hake's Guide to Cowboy Character Collectibles An Illustrated Price Guide Covering 50 Years of Movie & TV Cowboy Heroes**

**Hake's Guide to Presidential Campaign Collectibles An Illustrated Price Guide to Artifacts from 1789-1988**

**Hake's Guide to TV Collectibles: An Illustrated Price Guide**

**Non-Paper Sports Collectibles: An Illustrated Price Guide**
with Roger Steckler

**Sixgun Heroes: A Price Guide to Movie Cowboy Collectibles**
with Robert Cauler

**A Treasury of Advertising Collectibles**
(out of print)

For ordering information write the author at P.O. Box 1444-PG York, PA 17405

THE OFFICIAL

# Hake's Price Guide to Character Toys

## 4th Edition

## by TED HAKE

FOR GEMSTONE PUBLISHING

J. C. Vaughn, **Executive Editor**
Arnold T. Blumberg, **Editor** • Brenda Busick, **Creative Director**
Mark Huesman, **Pricing Coordinator**
Jamie David, **Office Manager**
Kimberly Grover, **Administrative Assistant**

THE CROWN PUBLISHING GROUP
NEW YORK

HOUSE OF COLLECTIBLES

GEMSTONE PUBLISHING

GEMSTONE PUBLISHING, INC.

NOTICE: Values for items pictured in this book are based on author's experience, consultations with a network of advisors including collectors specializing in various categories, and actual prices realized for specific items sold through private sales and auctions, including the catalogs of Hake's Americana & Collectibles mail and telephone bid auctions. The values offered in this book are approximations influenced by many factors including condition, rarity and demand, and they should serve as only guidelines, presenting an average range of what one might expect to pay for the items. In the marketplace, knowledge and opinions held by both sellers and buyers determine prices asked and prices paid. This is not a price list of items for sale or items wanted by the author or publisher. The author and the publisher shall not be held responsible for losses that may occur in the purchase, sale or other transaction of property because of information contained herein. Efforts have been made to present accurate information, but the possibility of error exists. Readers who believe they have discovered an error are invited to mail corrective information to the author, Ted Hake, at P.O. Box 1444-PG, York, PA 17404. Verified corrections will be incorporated into future editions of this book.



**THE OFFICIAL® HAKE'S PRICE GUIDE TO CHARACTER TOYS** (4th Edition) is an original publication of Gemstone Publishing, Inc. and House of Collectibles. Distributed by The Crown Publishing Group, a division of Random House, Inc., New York and simultaneously in Canada by Random House of Canada Limited, Toronto. This edition has never before appeared in book form.

House of Collectibles
The Crown Publishing Group
299 Park Ave.
New York, New York 10171

www.randomhouse.com

HOUSE OF COLLECTIBLES

House of Collectibles is a registered trademark and the H colophon is a trademark of Random House, Inc.

Published by arrangement with Gemstone Publishing.

ISBN: 0-609-80822-2
ISSN: 1538-9634

Printed in the United States of America

10 9 8 7 6 5 4 3 2 1

Fourth Edition: June 2002

Dark Horse brings you...
CLASSIC
DARK HORSE COMICS®
COMIC
CHARACTERS™
Don't miss your shot at owning these limited-edition collectibles. Place your orders NOW before they sell out!
Mandrake
Item #19-294
Daisy Mae
Item #19-403
Li'l Abner
Item #19-390
Little Orphan Annie
Item #19-543
Dick Tracy
Item #19-502
Olive Oyl
Item #19-380
Bluto
Item #10-214
Wimpy
Item #10-203
Albert
Item #10-212
Dragon Lady
Item #19-531
Flash Gordon
Item #10-046
Nancy
Item #00-246
Sluggo
Item #00-249
Beetle Bailey
Item #19-436
Sarge
Item #19-444
Smokey Stover
Item #19-546
Terry
Item #19-529
Fearless Fosdick
Item #19-502
SOLD OUT!
Dagwood
Blondie
Krazy Kat
Popeye
Prince Valiant
The Phantom
Ignatz
Felix The Cat
Each statue stands approx. 5"- 6-1/2" tall and comes packaged in a collector's tin with pin!
$49.99 U.S. each ($74.95 Canada)
Wholesale inquiries! Inquiries please contact Rachelle Calloway, (503) 652-8815, ext. 346
AVAILABLE AT YOUR LOCAL COMICS SHOP OR BOOKSTORE
To find a comics shop in your area, call 1-888-266-4226
For more information or to order direct:
On the web: www.darkhorse.com • E-mail: mailorder@darkhorse.com •
Phone: 1-800-862-0052 or (503) 652-9701
Mon.-Sat. 9 A.M. to 5 P.M. Pacific Time
Blondie, Beetle Bailey™, Bluto, Dagwood, Flash Gordon, Ignatz, Krazy Kat, ,Mandrake the Magician, Olive Oyl, The Phantom, Popeye, Prince Valiant, Sarge™, Wimpy™2002 King Features Syndicate, Inc. TM Hearst Holdings, Inc. Daisy Mae, Fearless Fosdick, Li'l Abner ® & © 2002 Capp Enterprises, Inc. Dick Tracy , Dragon Lady , Little Orphan Annie, Smokey Stover, Terry & the Pirates ® & © 2002 Tribune Media Services, Inc. Felix the Cat ® & © 2000 Felix the Cat Productions, Inc. Nancy and Sluggo © 2002 United Features Syndicate, Inc. Albert ™ by Walt Kelly © 2002 OGPI. Dark Horse Comics ® and the Dark Horse logo are trademarks of Dark Horse Comics, Inc., registered in various categories and countries. All rights reserved.



063266

# ACKNOWLEDGEMENTS

We want to express our gratitude to the collectors, dealers and advertisers whose continued support has made this fourth edition possible. Both original and first-time contributors submitted new items and information to further our goal of presenting accurate facts and previously un-catalogued collectibles. We appreciate collectors sharing their expertise and special items with the collecting fraternity and invite new readers to submit their special items for our future editions.

Marshall Levin researched and wrote the majority of the category histories for our first edition, with subsequent updating by the staffs at Hake's Americana and Gemstone Publishing. The entire Hake's organization contributed in many ways, and I wish to thank my wife Jonell and staff members Vonnie Burkins, Joan Carbaugh, Russ King, Charlie Roberts, Jeff Robison, Deak Stagemyer and Alex Winter.

A special word of thanks goes to Steve Geppi, President and Chief Executive Officer of Gemstone Publishing, Inc. Steve's personal enthusiasm and devotion to both our hobby and this book has been critical in sustaining us through four editions.

The challenges of a guide with 13,000 photos accompanied by descriptions and values is immense. Always rising to the occasion is Bob Overstreet and staff at Gemstone Publishing. We appreciate Bob's willingness to share pricing information that also appears in his price guide to comic books. Joe McGuckin photographed or scanned 3,000 new items for this edition. Mark Huesman devotes hundreds of hours to laying out the items in their chronological order, and Editor Arnold T. Blumberg brings order out of chaos with the touch of a master magician. Creative Director Brenda Busick designed our cover and interior format. Executive Editor J.C. Vaughn, with Administrative Assistants Kimberly Grover and Jamie David, heads the advertising and marketing aspects of the book and provides additional support for the production team. My sincere thanks and congratulations to everyone at Gemstone for producing our largest and best edition.

The support of our advertisers goes a long way to keeping the cost of this massive book affordable. A big thanks to our repeat advertisers and those joining us for the first time. We encourage our readers to mention this guide when conducting business with these leading firms and individuals.

The collectibles pictured in the guide come from many sources. We thank everyone who contributed. Additional rare items are included in this edition from the archive files of Gordon Gold. Mr. Gold, along with his father Sam Gold, known as the "premium king," created thousands of toy premiums from the 1930s through the 1970s. The Golds maintained an archive, with usually only one example of each creation, for their in-house use. Over the past few years, Gordon Gold has made these available to collectors through Hake's Americana & Collectibles auctions. We enjoy documenting these toy premiums and unique prototypes. Items from this archive carry the notation "Gordon Gold Archives."

Our gratitude to those people who contributed many items or aided our research for this edition. John K. Snyder provided vintage rarities as well as many recent issues we've included. Gene Seger found new items for our extensive Buck Rogers section. Joe Cywinski helped update many category histories. Other major contributors are Bill Campbell, Ken Chapman, Tom Gordon III and Jim Scancarelli. The efforts of these people and the following contributors to this and earlier editions are sincerely appreciated. •

Gary Alexander
Bob Allison
Andy Anderson
Dave Anderson
Graeme Atkinson
Bob Baker
Bob Barrett
Robert R. Barrett
Howard Bender
Arnold T. Blumberg
Robert Bruce
Scott Bruce
John Bruszewski
Terry Bruszewcki
Jane Byrd
Joel S. Cadbury
Brian Callahan
Bill Campbell
Joe Caro
Bob Cauler
Ken Chapman
Mike Cherry
Tom Claggett
Jerry Cook
Dan Coviello
Charles Crane
Lory Curtis
Joe Cywinski
Jimmy Dempsey
Larry Doucet
Jerry Doxey
Mark Drennen
Bob Dziadosz
Tony Evangelista
Joe Fair
John Fawcett
Lee Felbinger
Ada L. Fitzsimmons
Don Flanagan
Matt Flynn
Keif Fromm
Danny Fuchs
Everett Gamble
John Gilman
S. Harlan Glassman
Gordon Gold
Tony Goodstone
Tom Gordon, III
Ralph Gould
Gary Greenberg
David Grisez
Rick Gronquist
Al Grossman
Bill Hagen
Robert Hall
Bruce Hamilton
Jim Harmon
Phil Hecht
S. Leonard Hedeen
Joe Hehn
Robert Heide
Bob Hencey
John Hintz
John Hone
David J. Howe
Bob Hritz
Mark Huesman
Steve Ison
Tom Kage
Stephen A. Kallis, Jr.
Harvey Kamins
Bruce Kaufman
Fred L. King
Walter Koenig
Ray La Briola
John C. La Monte
Bob Lesser
Richard Leibner
Andy Levison
Randy Lieberman
Don Lineberger
Larry Lowery
Howard Lowry
Hy Mandelowitz
Don Maris
Barry Martin
Bill Mastro
Harry Matetsky
Walter V. Matishak
Jack Melcher
Richard Merkin
Peter Merolo
Rex Miller
Vall Miller
John Mlachnik
Pat Morgan
Michael Naiman
DeWayne Nall
M. G. 'Bud' Norris
Richard Olson
Bob Overstreet
Ralph Perry
Don Phelps
Ralph Plumb
Ron Plotkin
Ed Pragler
Benn Ray
Tony Raymond
Roger Reed
Harry Rinker
Robert Rogovin
Herb Rolfes
Scott Rona
Bruce Rosen
Frank Salacuse
Michael Saler
Joe Sarno
Jim Scancarelli
Jay Scarfone
Russ Sears
Gene Seger
Tony Seger
Joel Siegel
Jim Silva
Joel Smilgis
Eugene M. Smith
Herb Smith
John K. Snyder, Jr.
Larry Stidham
William Stillman
Dale Stratton
John Szuch
George Thomas
Harry Thomas
Chalres Travis
Ernest Trova
Paul Troyer
Tom Tumbusch
Jim Ungerman
Jim Wagner
David Walsh
Jon R. Warren
Frank Weidner
Howard C. Weinberger
Jerry Weist
David Welch
Lizabeth West
Mike West
Mike Wilbur
Evelyn Wilson
Alex Winter
Jim Wojtowicz
Joe Young
Larry Zdeb
Marco Zorrilla
Paul Zubritzky

Welcome to our fourth edition. You hold the most comprehensive reference devoted to character-themed toys. Cherished memories are the rationale for this book; the tangible objects documented within these pages reinforce and give life to those memories.

Thirty-five years ago, I discovered the significance of toys and the memories they embody. For several years, I had been selling presidential campaign buttons to members of a small, but organized, collecting fraternity. Occasionally, my modest catalogues would include an item related to Buck Rogers, Little Orphan Annie, Hopalong Cassidy or Superman. To my surprise, on a priced sale list I would receive five to ten orders for these items, or if it was an auction catalogue, these pieces would receive bids outpacing my offerings of Teddy Roosevelt, FDR or Truman politicals. The decision was obvious. Hake's Americana & Collectibles began specializing in character toys, and memories, in 1967.

While most twenty-year olds focus on the future, those of us with a few more growth rings and still in touch with our roots come to appreciate the memories that make us both unique as individuals and capable of sharing past experiences with others. Toys, in their many forms, are among the most potent objects that can embody and inspire our fondest memories. I learned this truth in the early years of my business as I began to receive letters from collectors who were truly grateful for my role in helping them obtain some toy that held great significance. What I could not have predicted in 1967 is how the interest in character toys evolved and expanded over thirty-five years to reach millions of people.

This growth is evidenced by price guides, shows, publications, clubs and auctions devoted to toys in general and character toys in particular. In recent years, the incredibly fast growth of internet auctions and success of television programs such as Antiques Roadshow demonstrate the appeal of collectibles to vast segments of the American public.

Like many things in life, the toy collectibles which represent our personal memories and popular cultural history come with price tags. Our market report on actual sales of items since our third edition was published in 2000 is filled with record-setting transactions. Also, two major events occurred since 2000: the stock market peaked and terrorists attacked America. While both events severely impacted segments of the economy, the marketplace for character toys, remarkably, was not adversely affected.

For much of the 1990s, the growth in stock market values drained dollars away from the collectibles market and slowed its explosive growth. However, studies document that market turmoil, recessions and wars throughout the 20th century actually increased competition and values in the fine art market. The fine art and collectibles markets generally attract different audiences, but do move in tandem. Today's low interest rates are a powerful magnet to attract new money to collectibles. Likewise, the aftermath of the terrorist attacks caused many people to focus on American values, the home, the family and those most cherished memories. We are determined that terrorist-inspired adversity will not divert or dilute our passion for the things we love. The character toy market is robust and poised for a leap forward.

Reviewing the last two years confirms the important relationship between condition and value. The difference in value for items in Fine versus Near Mint condition is substantial. Our prices reflect most collectors' desire to own high grade examples of their favorite character toys. To use the guide values properly, the condition of an item must be accurately evaluated. Each type of item has its unique set of standards detailed in our Condition Definitions section. Condition importance is clearly demonstrated in those hobby areas which have evolved to the point of having businesses devoted to evaluating and certifying the condition of collectibles, such as coins, comic books, sports and non-sports cards. Many "slabbed" items will bring three to five times their guide value just because their condition has been certified by experts in the field.

Over the past two years, we've also noticed growing interest in some of the earliest character toys. From 1890s cast-iron character toys to early 1900s books that reprinted comic strips of the era, the historical importance of older characters is being recognized, and quite frequently by younger collectors.

## INTRODUCTION TO THE FOURTH EDITION

Whether a collector comes to character toy collecting to recapture cherished memories, to build a collection of related or themed objects, or to preserve the history of an art form, most collectors bring a passion to the quest. To aid that quest, our fourth edition presents over 13,000 toys of all types, and every one is pictured and evaluated. There are 364 fascinating histories detailing the development and background of each character, personality, movie, radio broadcast, TV show, product and publication. A checklist feature accompanies each entry to help collectors maintain a record of acquisitions.

Our first edition was published in 1996 with a "mere" 5,000 entries. John K. Snyder, President of Diamond International Galleries, with the enthusiastic backing of Steve Geppi, CEO of Diamond Comic Distributors, Inc., convinced me of the importance of documenting the character toys so avidly collected by thousands of Americans across many generations.

Since that first edition, each subsequent edition has added new categories, expanded others, and seen constant refinement of both the historical information and evaluations. During this time, well over one hundred contributors provided photos and information, making this a truly collaborative effort. Whether you use this guide as a reference for buying and selling or as a spark to bring old memories to life, we hope you find this book both useful and enjoyable.

Ted Hake
May, 2002

## USING THIS GUIDE

This guide is composed of 364 categories from the collecting areas related to advertising characters, cereal companies, comic books, comic strip and cartoon characters, movies, music, pulps, radio and television. The categories are arranged in alphabetical order by name of the character, company, person, product, program or publication. The most basic name form is used. This applies to character names in particular, because a given character often appears in several mediums, frequently with a variety of titles.

Each category is introduced by a brief history of the subject. Within each category, each item is illustrated and given a brief descriptive title. Quotation marks in the title denote words actually appearing on the item. Where possible, the exact name assigned by the sponsor to the item is used in the descriptive title, although these are not indicated by quotation marks unless the words actually appear on the item.

All items in a category are arranged in chronological order, with minor exceptions due to photo layout restrictions. The item's title is followed by an exact year of issue, an approximate year of issue, an exact decade of issue or an approximate decade of issue. Accordingly, within each category, items with the earliest specific year of the earliest decade come first. These are followed by items approximated to the earliest specific year. Following all items with an exact or approximate specific year come those items dated exactly or approximately to the earliest decade. The sequence begins anew with items dated to the earliest specific year of the next decade.

Date information is followed by the name of the sponsor or issuer, if known, for the majority of the toys. However, this information is not listed for certain categories where it would merely be redundant. For example, Cracker Jack items are all issued by Cracker Jack and Ovaltine issued all Captain Midnight premiums between 1941-1989, with a few exceptions which are specified. In categories where sponsors are not noted, refer to the historical information introducing that category. Some items saw use both as store items and premiums. Where known, this type of information is included in the description.

Following the date and sponsor information, any descriptive text necessary to explain the item is included. The description ends with three values for the item in Good, Fine and Near Mint condition, with a few exceptions where Near Mint examples

do not exist. It is most important to read the section defining these condition terms to properly understand and use the values specified for each item.

### TYPES OF ITEMS

For this guide book, the terms "Comic" and "Premiums" are broadly defined.

"Comic" includes not only characters from newspapers, comic books, animated cartoons but also a gamut of entertainment-related personalities--created or actual—ranging from animated Speedy Alka-Seltzer to live-action Zorro.

"Premiums" includes items by sponsors given away directly—as package insert or loosely—plus items requested and obtained by mail, sometimes requiring small payment and/or purchase proof of the sponsor's product.

Webster's New World Dictionary (3rd College Edition) defines a toy as any article to play with, expecially playthings for children. Since all of the entries in this guide fit this description, whether they are premiums or store-bought toys, we include both categories of items under the title of Hake's Price Guide to Character Toys.

Almost all of the items in this book are of U.S. origin, with some notable exceptions, such as those included in the "Doctor Who" category (most of which originated in Great Britain). There are also foreign items issued under authorized U.S. copyright; prominent examples are the popular 1930s bisque character figures made in Germany or Japan.

This book's listings are comprehensive but not all-inclusive. Omitted items should not be assumed to be either common and inexpensive or rare and costly.

### DATING

Toys of each category are listed chronologically. The majority of toys are specifically dated by (a) copyright year on the item, (b) dated source such as a toy catalogue, newspaper or comic book ad, or similar period source. General references of films or broadcast dates were also consulted. In a few instances, an item's patent date (not the copyright date) is used to document its age, when the patent date only is indicated.

Toys offered in overlapping years, for more than one year, or re-issued in later years are dated to the earliest year the item was available. Conversely, a few toys are known to have a copyright year earlier than the actual issue of the item. In these limited examples, the exact or approximate issue date is indicated rather than the copyright year.

If an exact year could not be determined, the item is dated to an approximate year or the known exact decade. When an exact year or decade specification is open to question, the date is denoted by the abbreviation c. for circa to indicate an approximation of issue date.

Using these criteria, the sequence of items within each category is: earliest specific year of the earliest decade followed by earliest approximate year of the earliest decade. After all items with an exact or approximate year are listed, the remaining items dated exactly or approximately to the earliest decade are listed. The sequence begins anew with items dated to the earliest specific year of the next decade.

### ABBREVIATIONS

Three abbreviations are used very frequently for recurring descriptive purposes:

c. = circa. An approximate date.

cello. = celluloid. Usually referring to a pinback button or other small collectible having a protective covering of this substance. The term and abbreviation are also used for convenience to indicate similar latter day substances, such as acetate or thin plastic, which gradually replaced the use of flammable celluloid coverings after World War II.

litho. = lithographed process. Usually referring to a pinback button or other small collectible with the design printed directly on metal, usually tin, rather than "cello" version wherein the design is printed on paper with a celluloid protective covering.

ADDITIONAL ABBREVIATIONS:

ABC=American Broadcasting Companies, Inc.
BLB=Big Little Book series by Whitman Publishing Co.
BTLB = Better Little Book series by Whitman Publishing Co.
CBS = Columbia Broadcasting System, Inc.
KFS = King Features Syndicate
K.K.Publications = Kay Kamen Publications
MGM = Metro-Goldywn-Mayer Studios, Inc.
NBC = National Broadcasting Co.
NPP = National Periodical Publications, Inc.
RCA = Radio Corporation of America
WDE = Walt Disney Enterprises
WDP = Walt Disney Productions

### SIZES

For the majority of items, sizes are not specified with these exceptions. Sizes are specified for pinback buttons measuring two inches in diameter or larger, as well as some select buttons measuring less than two inches. Sizes are also specified for display signs, maps, posters, standees, items produced in more than one size, and items where size was deemed an important distinguishing factor.

### DEFINITIONS

Physical condition and appearance of a toy are primary factors in determining its value, along with rarity, demand and packaging (see next two sections). Condition judgments are certain to have some subjective nuances between individuals. Still, general criteria exist in the collecting community.

Only a small fraction of items, unless recently produced or stored away at time of issue, can properly be termed Mint, i.e. in original new condition with absolutely no flaws. Items evaluated in this guide will very seldom be encountered in Mint condition.Therefore, the highest grade evaluated for each item is Near Mint, i.e. nearly perfect like new condition with only the slightest detectable wear on close inspection. Additional values are provided for each item in the grades of Fine and Good.

Condition concerns vary according to an item's basic material, and the items in this guide fall into four basic categories. Accurately determining an item's condition is the crucial step in arriving at a price equitable to both the seller and buyer. Because of the wide value gap, particularly for rarer items, between Near Mint condition and the lower grades, it's essential for the proper use of this book to understand and apply the following condition definitions, in the complete absence of wishful thinking.

### PAPER/ CARDBOARD

Near Mint: Fresh, bright, original crisply-inked appearance with only the slightest perceptible evidence of wear, soil, fade or creases. The item should lay flat, corners must be close to perfectly square and any staples must be rust free.

Fine: An above average example with attractive appearance but moderately noticeable aging or wear including: small creases and a few small edge tears; lightly worn corners; minimal browning, yellowing, dust or soiling; light staple rust but no stain on surrounding areas, no more than a few tiny paper flakes missing, small tears repaired on blank reverse side are generally acceptable if the front image is not badly affected.

Good: A complete item with no more than a few small pieces missing. Although showing obvious aging, accumulated flaws such as: creases, tears, dust and other soiling, repairs, insect damage, mildew, and brittleness must not combine to render the item unsound and too unattractive for display.

### METAL

Near Mint: Item retains 90% or more of its original bright finish metallic luster as well as any accent coloring on the lettering or design. Badges must have the original pin intact and rings must have near perfect circular bands. Any small areas missing original luster must be free of rust, corrosion, dark tarnish or any other defect that stands out enough to render the naked eye appearance of the piece less than almost perfect.

Fine: An above average item with moderate wear to original luster but should retain at least 50%. There may be small, isolated areas with pinpoint corrosion spotting, tarnish or similar evidences of aging. Badges must have the original pin, although perhaps slightly bent, and rings must have bands with no worse than minor bends. Although general wear does show, the item retains an overall attractive appearance with noticeable luster.

Good: An average well-used or aged item missing nearly all luster and color accents. Badges may have a replaced pin and ring bands may be distorted or obviously reshaped. There may be moderate, not totally defacing, evidence of bends, dents, scratches, corrosion, etc. Aside from a replaced pin, completeness is still essential.

### CELLULOID OR LITHOGRAPHED TIN PINBACK BUTTONS

Near Mint: Both celluloid and lithographed tin pinbacks retain the original, bright appearance without visual defect. For celluloid, this means the total absence of stain (known as foxing to button collectors). There can be no apparent surface scratches when the button is viewed directly; although when viewed at an angle in reflected light, there may be a few very shallow and small hairline marks on the celluloid surface. The celluloid covering must be totally intact with no splits, even on the reverse where the button paper and celluloid covering are folded under the collet. Lithographed tin buttons may have no more than two or three missing pinpoint-size dots of color and no visible scratches. Even in Near Mint condition, a button image noticeably off-center, as made, reduces desirability and therefore value to some price below Near Mint depending on the severity of the off-centering.

Fine: Both styles of buttons may have a few apparent scattered small scratches. Some minor flattening or a tiny dent noticeable to the touch, but not visually, is also acceptable. Celluloids may have a very minimal amount of age spotting or moisture stain, largely confined to the rim area, not distracting from the graphics and not dark in color. There may be a small celluloid split on the reverse by the collet, but the celluloid covering must still lay flat enough not to cause a noticeable bump on the side edge. Lithographed tin buttons may have only the slightest traces of paint roughness, or actual rust, visible on the front.

A variation of the celluloid pinback is the celluloid covered pocket mirror which holds a glass mirror on the reverse rather than a fastener pin. Condition definitions for pocket mirrors match those for celluloid buttons except a fine condition item may have a clouded or smoked mirror and some streaks on the silvering. A cracked mirror typically reduces desireability to the level of Good condition.

Good: Celluloid pinbacks may have moderately dark spotting or moisture stain not exceeding 25% of the surface area. There could be some slight evidence of color fade, a small nick on the front celluloid, or a small celluloid split by the reverse collet causing a small edge bump. Dark extensive stain, deep or numerous scratches and extensive crazing of the celluloid covering each render the button to a condition status of less than good and essentially unsalable. Lithographed tin buttons must retain strong color and be at least 75% free of noticeable surface wear or they too fall into the likely unsalable range.

#### OTHER MATERIALS

(Ceramic, Glass, Wood, Fabric, Composition, Rubber, Plastic, Vinyl, Etc.)

Near Mint: Regardless of the substance, the item retains its fresh, original appearance and condition without defect. Only the slightest traces of visually non-distracting wear are acceptable.

Fine: Each material has its inherent weakness in withstanding age, typical use or actual abuse.

Ceramic, porcelain, china, bisque and other similar clay-based objects are susceptible to edge chips. These are acceptable if minimal. Glazed items very typically develop hairline crazing not considered a flaw unless hairlines have also darkened.

Glass is fragile and obviously susceptible to missing chips, flakes or hairline fractures but acceptable in modest quantity.

Wood items, as well as the faithful likeness composition wood, generally withstand aging and use well. Small stress fractures or a few small missing flakes are acceptable if the overall integrity of the item is not affected.

Fabric easily suffers from weave splits or snags plus stain spots are frequently indelible. Weaving breaks are generally acceptable in limited numbers but fabric holes are not. Stains may not exceed a small area and only a blush of color change.

Composition items, typically dolls or figurines, tend to acquire hairline cracks of the thin surface coating. This is commonly expected and normally acceptable to the point of obvious severity. Color loss should not exceed 20% and not involve critical facial details.

Rubber items, either of solid or hollow variety, tend to lose original pliability and evolve into a rigid hardness that frequently results in a warped or deformed appearance. Some degree of original flexibility is preferred or, at least, minimal distortion.

Plastic and vinyl items have a tendency to split at areas of high stress or frequent use. This is frequently expected and excused by collectors up to the point of distracting from overall appearance or function.

Good: Items of any material are expected to be complete and/or functional. Obvious wear is noticeable, but the item retains its structural soundness. Wear or damage must not exceed the lower limits of being reasonably attractive for display purposes.

### RARITY & DEMAND DETERMINE VALUE

A toy's value rests largely on its degree of rarity plus collector demand. Rarity is a constant–either few examples of a given object were produced originally or few are known to remain.

Demand, however, is influenced by a number of variables. An item must have popular appeal, otherwise rarity is not a salient consideration. Appeal is typically based on the subject matter of the item or the type of item. Superman appeals to more collectors than Rocky Jones, Space Ranger and more collectors specialize in rings than pedometers.

Following popular appeal, with rarity being equal, the condition of an item is the primary factor in determining value. Whatever the rarity factor may be, only a very small percentage of known specimens of any item will still exist in high grade condition. The desire to own items in close-to-new condition is a commonly-shared trait among collectors. The resulting competition accounts for the wide gap in value between an example in Fine condition and one in Near Mint condition. The rarer the item, the greater this value differential is likely to be. Collectors willing to forego top condition examples and the inherent competition-driven high prices may add much purchasing power to available funds if lesser grade examples are acceptable.

Among the remaining factors that create value are cross-over interest, emotional factors and geographic variation.

Cross-over interest occurs when a toy has the same appeal but for a different reason to various collectors. A Lone Ranger Frontier Town cereal box may appeal to a cereal box collector, a generalist premium collector, a Lone Ranger collector and a collector specializing in cut-out toys. Cross-over interest frequently increases demand and therefore prices for those kinds of items.

Emotional factors include the determination to acquire a toy once owned and lost, the desire to finally own an item never acquired during childhood or the desire to "complete" a particular collection. For others, collecting may spring from aesthetic considerations or perceived investment potential. Emotions play the role of a wild card in the factors establishing value.

Geographical factors also play some role in determining values. Toys and radio premiums of the 1930s were likely offered and distributed in larger numbers in the most populous areas, frequently in the Eastern United States. Even today, items may be offered on a regional or local basis generating a sense of scarcity and increased value among those outside the distribution area. Ultimately, geographic differences diminish as old and new toys and premiums are distributed among collectors by sales lists and auctions, publications with buy and sell advertising, and collectibles shows attended by collectors and dealers from all points.

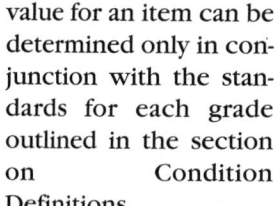

### VALUATIONS IN THIS BOOK

Values in this guide are based on the author's 35 years experience in auctioning toys. Also considered were results of other auctions, sales lists, show prices, known transactions between individuals and advice from collectors with various specialties. The values listed are for retail sales, not prices paid by dealers (See "Selling A Collection" on page 24).

The Good, Fine, and Near Mint condition grades used in this book cover the vast majority of toys. The value for an item can be determined only in conjunction with the standards for each grade outlined in the section on Condition Definitions.

For items falling between the three grades, i.e. Very Fine or Very Good, an approximate value is the midpoint value between the two grades closest to the condition of the item under consideration.

Truly Mint items, like new and with absolutely no wear or defect, could command a price 10% or even greater than the Near Mint listed value. Conversely, an item with severe damage or missing parts may lose 50% or more of the Good listed value.

The final consideration in establishing valuations is packaging. Most collectors highly value items complete with original packaging, box or carton, when applicable.

Earlier toys of the 1930s to mid-1950s-before the collectibles era we know now--were generally saved by the recipient without regard to packaging or other contents. This is particularly true of mail order premiums. Mailing boxes and envelopes from this era were seldom graphic but frequently held instruction sheets, other paper inserts such as a premium catalogue, or an order form for re-ordering another of the premium at hand. A "complete" premium package—assuming acceptable condition—can command between 25-75% more value than the actual premium item alone. Many of the most desirable instruction sheets, or similar papers, are included and priced in this guide. Many items are also assigned a separate value for an example boxed and complete with papers, all in Near Mint condition.

The value of store bought toys of any era are also enhanced approximately 50-100% in value if all original packaging is present.

The range of items covered by this guide is vast and assigned values are as low as a few dollars to as high as many thousands. Within this collecting universe are subjects and areas of specialization to match any collecting budget.

## RESTORED ITEMS

Original toys damaged and restored are marketable, particularly scarcer examples, due to continuing demand as available examples leave the marketplace and enter private collections.

Restoration takes many forms depending on the material substance of the toy. Examples range from simply cleaning an item to completely refinishing one. In between, typical restorations include book rebinding, refilling minor chips or flakes, color or scratch retouching, replacement of missing part(s).

Responsible dealers and collectors volunteer full disclosure on restorations at the time offered for sale. Even an expertly restored item will seldom exceed the value of another example in unrestored Fine condition.

Proper restoration is a delicate process often overlooked by the well-meaning but inexperienced restorer. Countless items drop dramatically in value by a devout scrubbing that removes not only soiling but age patina as well. Paint restorations may be neatly done but in a color hue so unfaithful to the original that distracting appearance results. Repairs using improper tapes or glues usually turn brown, radically diminishing the appearance and value of the "restored" toy.

Wisdom will leave repairs and restorations to proven professionals unless an individual is confident of his or her restoration skills and willing to accept the marketplace judgment of these skills.

## REPRODUCTIONS AND FANTASIES

Every hobby with valuable items attracts thieves who operate by deception. Toys and popular culture collectibles in general are not exempt from this immoral practice. A collector may avoid being deceived by acquiring some basic knowledge about the chosen specialty, by exercising reasoned judgment when faced with an apparent bargain and by patronizing dealers who unconditionally guarantee their merchandise as authentic.

Deceptive items usually take the form of reproductions and fantasies.The fantasy item is an object, never licensed by the copyright owner, that did not even exist during the time period that produced original and authorized collectibles. Fantasy collectibles are produced after the fact, typically when a person, character, movie, etc. is the subject of collector interest. The people making fantasy items intend them to appeal to, or intentionally defraud, collectors unaware of the item's unauthorized status and relative newness. Frequently such items bear illegitimate copyright notices and spurious dates. The best defenses are familiarity with authentic items issued in a particular category or a guarantee from a reputable dealer.

Reproductions, undated and unmarked as such, will undoubtedly be encountered by active collectors. Unlike a fantasy item, the reproduction has its original, authentic counterpart. In some circumstances, a questionable item may be compared directly to a known original to determine any difference. Producing reproductions doesn't require ethics, but it does require some care and skill to produce a copy with most, if not all, of the distinguishing features of the original. Careful observation of originals, some appreciation of the materials and manufacturing techniques in use when the original was produced and a healthy degree of skepticism are potent weapons against reproductions. Copied items very seldom match all the characteristics of the original. If any doubts surface, postpone the purchase and get a second opinion, or at least obtain a written receipt with the seller's money-back guarantee of authenticity.

Here are a few basic warnings and tips to keep in mind regarding reproductions:

Tin Signs–many authentic signs have been reproduced and many fantasy signs created. The reproductions are frequently executed in a size different than the originals. Buyers need personal expertise or the guarantee of a reputable dealer knowledgeable in this area.

Framed Items–covering an item with glass, or even shrink wrap, may hide a multitude of problems. A generous layer of grime or highly reflective glare may obscure the image enough to hide what proves to be a photocopy, color laser copy or printed reproduction.

Printed Items–small single sheet paper items and cards are easy to reproduce. Color laser copies are particularly deceptive, but detectable on close inspection. Sometimes this technology is put to use to reproduce wrist or pocket watch dials as well as other deceptions. Both color and black/white reproductions of paper items sometimes reproduce small tears, creases or other flaws on the paper of the original item being copied. These defects may show on the copy while the paper used to produce the copy is actually not torn, not creased or otherwise flawed.

Pinback Buttons–very few buttons were made in both celluloid and lithographed tin varieties. However, a small number of lithographed tin buttons have been reproduced as celluloids. Nearly all buttons described in this guide as lithographed tin (litho.) should be regarded with much suspicion if encountered as a celluloid version. Most button reproductions are celluloid copies made by photographing celluloid originals. This sometimes results in a slightly blurred appearance, sometimes the dot screen fills in on the reproduction and sometimes the covering of plastic is noticeably different than the celluloid of the 1950s and earlier. A shiny metal back doesn't prove much. The metal used now may quickly oxidize while the metal used in the 1960s and earlier may retain its shine.

Metal Badges--these are more costly to copy than paper items or buttons but a limited number have been subject to reproduction. These are typically very exact copies of the front image. However, most originals had a soldered bar pin on the reverse. Most reproductions feature a small oval metal plate with two small raised areas used to anchor the bottom bar of the pin.

Reproductions and fantasies are an annoying aspect of nearly all hobbies, but not cause for despair. In the normal course of enjoying and learning about a particular specialization, the ability to discern the small number of deceptive items is acquired almost automatically. Just proceed with a bit of caution at the outset and rely on fellow collectors for advice concerning reputable dealers.

## BUILDING A COLLECTION

Any dedicated collector will attest to the joys and satisfaction of being one. Even the most experienced were newcomers at the outset and most will admit to mistakes and judgment errors along the way. Most are still driven by the exciting possibility of a "new find" regardless of the years and depth of their collection.

Beginning collectors often explore various fields of interest, casually or intensely, before generally settling into a specific choice of collectible within financial means. This guide book will hopefully demonstrate to beginning collectors the wide range of specialization options to fit any budget.

Needless to say, unseasoned collectors can benefit by purchasing from dealers who guarantee their collectibles as authentic and have a clear return policy in the event of an error in representation.

The first step in collection building is to acquire the appropriate reference books. References show at least a segment of the universe of collectibles in a given area and often provide the author's opinion regarding value.

Armed with some basic knowledge, the next step is to see, handle and price the collectibles of interest. Typically, this occurs at a local flea market, a more specialized collectibles show, or via the Internet. This participation in the marketplace, whether as a buyer or merely as an observer, brings the new collector in contact with the collecting fraternity. Meeting collectors and dealers with a shared interest, learning about collector clubs and discovering any relevant specialized publications will provide the information necessary to focus collecting interests. This focus must be acquired to minimize the number of errors that occur in every learning process.

When collection building begins in earnest there are many sources. Locally, successful finds can occur at estate auctions, garage sales, flea markets, general line antiques shops and collectibles co-operative stores. An advertisement in the local newspaper could yield a bonanza–or nothing.

Regional sources likely include larger flea markets and general line antiques shows. Hopefully, for a greater concentration of interesting items, there may be some shows of a specialized nature such as paper Americana, sport and non-sport cards, comic books, toys and advertising memorabilia.

National sources for collectibles include many magazines and newspaper format publications that carry display and classified advertising. There are also catalog and Internet auctions such as we offer at Hake's Americana & Collectibles (www.hakes.com), specialists in comic artifacts and premiums such as Diamond International Galleries (www.diamondgalleries.com), and any of the dealers advertising in this book.

## SELLING A COLLECTION

The collectibles marketplace necessarily relies on sellers as well as buyers. The prices in this book are retail values. Dealers will pay a percentage of these prices based on their own business practices, operational costs and assessment of value.

Sellers with a collection, as opposed to a few random items, must decide whether to wholesale to a dealer in a single transaction or whether to invest the time, energy and financial costs inherent in retailing the collection piece by piece to collectors. Each approach has advantages and disadvantages. Prospective sellers can well use the resources described in the section Building A Collection for the opposite purpose of selling a collection.

If selling to a dealer, the sale price will likely be maximized by selling all the items–the good with the bad–all at once, all for one price. The dealer's offer, or reaction to a price asked by the seller, will be based on quantity, quality, condition and the dealer's instincts as to how easily and quickly the items may be marketed to his clientele.

An in-person transaction is ideal–it becomes the dealer's responsibility to evaluate exactly what he is buying. Conversely, a transaction by mail will require the seller to list, photograph, photocopy and/or video tape the items as well as to evaluate and make representations regarding condition. The dealer cannot react to a price or make an offer without this essential information. A tentative price agreement still leaves the seller the chore of packing and shipping. The dealer will want to see what he is buying before accepting the transaction as complete and making payment.

Should a seller aspire to full retail prices, the role of "dealer" is assumed by necessity. The choices become in-person sales, mail order, or Internet auctions.

A seller may elect to become a vendor at local, regional or national shows. Assuming the size of the collection warrants this option, the seller must balance hopes of obtaining retail prices against the costs of personal time, transportation expense, booth rental fee, lodging and food; all the while assuming adequate show publicity or tradition and acceptable weather, when a factor, for crowd turnout. In addition are sales tax and income tax reporting requirements.

If a seller chooses the mail order or Internet option, travel and booth expenses trade place with advertising costs. Personal time costs likely increase and certainly extend into weeks and months as the process unfolds: advertising copy preparation with descriptions and perhaps photos, mail, telephone and e-mail inquiries with attendant correspondence, packing, shipping and fielding complaints from some percentage of customers dissatisfied with a purchase. Taxes remain a constant.

The novice seller, aiming for retail prices, faces a final hurdle. Whether selling in-person, by mail, or the Internet, don't count on a sell-out. The highest quality items and obviously under-priced items will sell quickly. The seller will soon be left with an inventory, probably the bulk of the collection, comprised of average, damaged and low grade items. To move this material will require repeated offerings. Offering a dealer what remains of the "collection" at this point will probably be met with a polite "I'll pass" response.

In summation, selling an intact collection to a dealer offers immediate cash in a single payment and elimination of time and expenses required for retailing. A higher profit could be realized by retailing to collectors, if the time and expenses required are accurately calculated with regard to the collection's realistic retail value. •

**by John K. Snyder Jr.**

The market for character toys enjoyed steady and sometimes surprising growth in the two years since our last edition. Increased activity on the auction scene and eBay's growing influence propelled another round of record prices, and the increased exploration of pop culture history has kept interested authors and researchers working on an increasing number of new reference works on toys of all types. Character toys, though, seem to be leading the way.

*1933 King Kong Puzzle brings $2,957.*

Through TV specials, newspaper articles, Internet sites and other outlets, the search for the story behind the toys carries on. The ongoing release of information, coupled with the impact of high profile movie remakes, exciting new TV shows, and celebrations and rediscoveries of perennial favorite characters continues to foster keen interest in our hobby. The Learning Channel, A&E, Discovery, History Channel, AMC, Turner Classic Movies and other cable outlets have helped greatly to revive our interest in the past and to expose whole new generations to things gone by.

The power of nostalgia is not limited to those who experienced something the first time around. Kids are continuing to follow the path of adults in collecting toys like never before. In the next five years almost 20 million young people will enter adulthood. Collectibles are definitely not news to this group, and their effect on the marketplace should be as positive as it is substantial.

Universities and learning institutions across the country are teaching courses on the history of entertainment. New toys are being churned out each month and the producers of these products are getting smarter about design and quality of productions. The level of workmanship in some of the newer products is awe-inspiring. When one looks at the wide array of great material, including the Classic Comics Characters line of Syroco-like figures from Dark Horse Comics, the fabulous Marvel Comics mini-busts from sculptor Randy Bowen, the Popeye statues from Leblon et Delienne, the numerous superhero props from DC Direct, the character cars in the Johnny Lightning line, and many others, it's hard not to feel like a kid again.

*1941 U.S. Jones button sells for $6,785.*

*Examples of Dark Horse figures– Krazy Kat & Ignatz.*

It is estimated that toys surpassed $25 billion in sales last year. Included in that figure are the significant numbers connected to the fast food industry's continued support of new films and TV shows with toys in kids' meals, and the return of giveaways to gas stations, once a very familiar source of such prizes.

In surveying the last two years in our market, four principle areas of positive change come to mind:

1. Vintage toys in high grade are drying up; new collections are not surfacing like they did in the '90s or earlier.

2. The toy business has become a dynamic market with significant, established players from other markets, such as The Mint, Heritage Comics, and MastroNet, entering the field. Consignors are now in the driver's seat since there is more

## Character rings sparkle in auction!

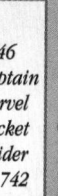

*1946 Captain Marvel Rocket Raider $1,742*

*1941 Valric of the Vikings $7,000*

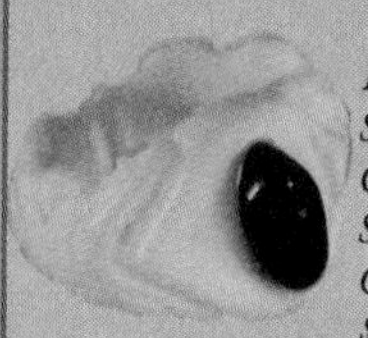

*1945 Shadow Carey Salt Complete $1,500*

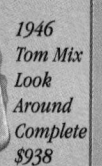

*1946 Tom Mix Look Around Complete $938*

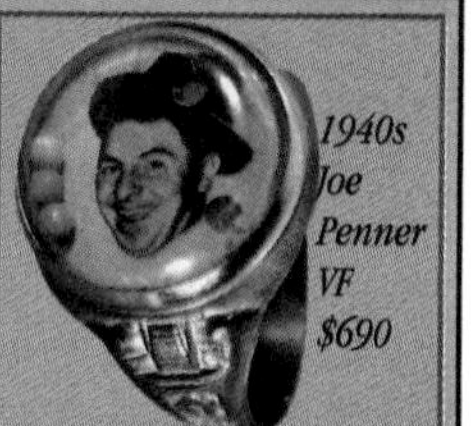

*1940s Joe Penner VF $690*

money competing for their items.

3. The sales force in our hobby has continued to grow across the U.S., particularly with antique stores and malls popping up next to interstate highways. This is allowing collections from local areas to be displayed and sold in more accessible locations. Magazines, newspapers and related guides continue to pound out articles about our hobby. As we know, for most collectors the desire to know about their collectibles is only surpassed by the desire to own them.

1930s Donald Duck musters $10,525.

4. The impact of the independent grading service, CGC, has definitely been felt. Many observers have keenly noted the effect that encapsulation has had in the areas of coins, trading cards and comic books. Standardization of grading and grading terminology, accessibility to laymen, and the level of confidence in one's purchases are all enhanced. With the increasing likelihood that the near future will bring independent authentication and grading of pinbacks, buttons, and rings, the prospects for this area of collecting continue to look bright.

1933 variation of Mail Pilot BLB sold for $5,090, a new record for a BLB.

1934 Tarzan badge in VG brings $1,415.

In conclusion, our market has all the right ingredients for growth. New collectors, new dealers and the expanding development of new toys, coupled with continued interest in the old characters from the last one hundred years, combine to equal fun and enjoyment for all of us who love this game.

1935 Tarzan pop-up book sells for $805.

Listed below are some of the documented sales in the last two years. This is, as you might expect, a drop in the bucket of the vast amount of sales that took place, but it does represent some of the true highlights:

Tom Mix Stetson Hat ..........$2,750
Roy Rogers Personal Touring Saddle ............................$412,000
Marvel Comics #1 9.0 ....$350,000
Donald Duck 1930s Doll ..$10,525
Creature from Black Lagoon 1 sheet ............................$16,000
Diamond Planet Robot ......$26,437
Pelham Puppet-Steve Zodiac XL5 ..........................................$1,938
Batman Cowl-1989 Film Prop ..........................................$1,988
Parker Puppet from "Thunderbirds"- Original ..$53,960
Post Toasties Cardboard Sign ..........................................$1,437
The Day the Earth Stood Still one sheet ..........................$25,000
Joe Penner Ring......................$690
Sergeant Preston Badge..........$558
Captain Midnight Whistle Ring ..........................................$1,011
Tarzan Pop Up Book .............$805
Mary Marvel, Kerr Plastic Figure with Box ......$3,750
#1 Barbie Doll-Ponytail........$4,700
Munster Card Game 1964 ......$493
Jackie Robinson 41"x 61" Poster ..........................................$2,220
1966 Lone Ranger Holster Set in Box .......................................$552
1960 Barbie #3 with Box ......$742
Superman Ad Flyer-Horlick Milk ..........................................$1,169
Lone Ranger Chalk Carnival Figural ...........$448

1939 MPFW Promo reaps $88,000.

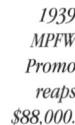

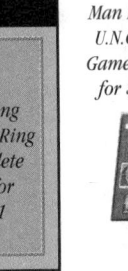

1965 Man From U.N.C.L.E. Game sells for $990.

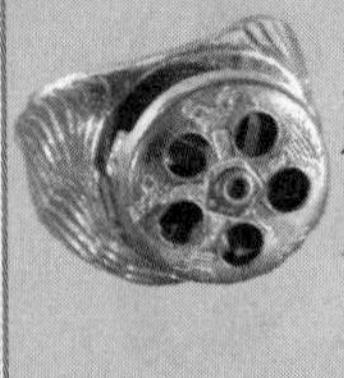

1941 Captain Midnight Whistle Ring Complete $1,011

1952 Space Patrol Ring Cosmic Glow sold for $1,522

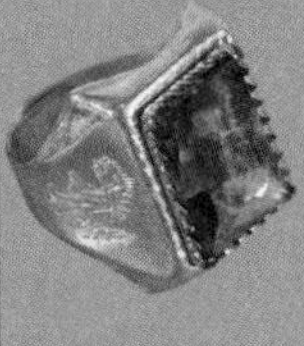

1951 Sky King Aztec Ring complete sells for $1,501

Sergeant Preston Hartland in Box ....................................$900
Colonel Ranald Mackenzie Hartland in Box ....................................$2,018
1964-Outer Limits Card Set Mostly PSA 7 ..........................$991
1966-Batman Set of Cards Mostly PSA 7 ..........................$731
1966-Green Hornet Button Set (9) ........................$139
1956-Elvis 1956 Card Set EX-MT ..............................................$612
1951-Hoppy Post Cereal 8 Different Cards-PSA 8..........$303
Man From U.N.C.L.E Game Mint in Box 1965 .................$990
Man From Uncle Napoleon Solo Gun in Box-1965 ........$2,304
Tom Mix Pocket Watch-1934 ...........................................$2,590
Detective #27-VF-Comic..$278,189
Snow White Banner For Club-1938......................$6,567
U.S. Jones Comic Premium Button..................$6,785
1954-Sunday-Peanuts-Original Art........................$17,046
1940 Double Action #2 Comic ................................$35,186
1939 Motion Pictures Funnies Weekly Comic 9.0 ...........$88,000
Spiderman #1-White Mountain copy- 9.4-Comic-1963........$67,304
Carl Barks-Treasure Island Painting ....$67,501
Tom Mix Autograph Photo ...........................................$3,515
Flash Gordon Movie Club Button ...........................................$1,708
Space Patrol Rocket Gun in Box ...........................................$1,069
Carey Salt Shadow Ring with Mailer..........................$1,500
Son of Tarzan Movie Mirror ...........................................$1,323
Captain Marvel Rocket Raider Ring.............$1,742
Li'l Abner Vending Machine....$900
Goofy Helbros Backwards Watch ...........................................$1,150

Collection of 12 Different Dime Banks ....$2,922
Superman Poster School at War-1942.............$2,036
1960s Popeye Flashlight Display with 12 small flashlights ........$900
1941-Captain Battle Boys Brigade Pin & Card-VF ........$1,937
Charlie Chaplin Signed Photo ...........................................$1,599
Three Stooges Signed Contract-1934..........$5,768
Centaur, Vernon Kiln Figure 10" ......$1,995
Roy Rogers Bobbin Head Doll in Box ...................................$493
1933 King Kong 3-Sheet Poster....................$64,715
King Kong-1933 Puzzle with Envelope ....................$2,957
"Score Against Hitler – Lift Ban on Negro Players" baseball button ....................$1502
"Judy Garland – El Mago De Oz" 1939 Spanish title button ....$3150
"Lee Powell – Original Motion Picture Lone Ranger" 1930s button ...................................$549
Buck Rogers "Sylvania" glowing light bulb 1950s ring............$1217
"The Green Hornet" glow-in-the-dark secret compartment 1947 ring ......$1136
"Sergeant Preston of the Yukon" 1949 lithograph button........$2315
"Sergeant Preston of the Yukon" 1956 celluloid button ..........$1200
Space Patrol Cosmic Glow 1952 ring.............................$1522
Sabu doll wearing "Sabu Club – Sabu in the Thief of Bagdad" 1940 button ...................................$689
Our Gang member "Jay Smith" 1930s portrait dish ...............$582
"Mickey Mouse in the Flood" 1930s 8-pager booklet...........$535
"Mickey Mouse Book" 1930 first version (Fine).................$534
Mickey Mouse "Germany" figural perfume vial with

1934 Chicago World's Fair sticker ..................................................$571
Mickey Mouse & Friends 1930s Italian 28-piece miniature china tea set .................................$1555
Disney characters "Ohio Art" 1930s tin tea set, 23 pieces ....$777
Disney characters "Ohio Art" 1930s tin sand pail (Fine) ......$662
Disney characters "Ferrero Chocolate" Italian 1940s set of 100 cards......................$506
"Donald Duck Handcar" 1930s Lionel Corp. Wind-up toy ..............................................$700
"Dick Tracy's Scrap Book of Adventure" 1950s Tip-Top Bread prototype. From the Gold Premium Archives ................$1200
Popeye "Harry Welch" (cartoon voice) photos, 1962 signed album ..............................................$546
"The Lone Ranger Western and Fun Book" 1950s Morton's Salt prototype. From the Gold Premium Archives .............$1043
"Roy Rogers" 1950s child leather saddle (Very Good) ......................... $640
"Flash Gordon Foundry Casting Set" boxed, 1934 ....................$750
"The Adventures of Superman" 1942 Random House book with dust jacket......................$900
"Batman and Robin Full Color Transfers" Detective Comics 1944 packet...........................$705
"Amos" and "Andy" 1930s composition wood 2.75" figure set ..............................$817
"Sky King Aztec Emerald Calendar Ring" 1951 Peter Pan Peanut Butter mailer, instructions and ring ...............................$1501
Rudolph Reindeer "32 Page Fun Book" 1950s Montgomery Ward prototype. From the Gold Premium Archives .................$626
"James Bond Action Figure" with accessories boxed 1965

Gilbert set ............................$585
"I Saw Buck Rogers 25th Century Show Did You?-A Century of Progress 1934" litho button....$526
"Supermen of America" 7/8" DC Comics 1940s button (Very Good)..........................$518
"Tarzan Radio Club – Drink More Milk" 1930s enameled metal badge (Very Good)..........................$1415
"Shirley Temple Box of Books" Saalfield boxed set of nine books, 1940....................................$1208
"Dionne Quints Let's Play House" set of five 1940 paperdoll books ..............................................$794
Li'l Abner Dogpatch Band 1946 Unique Art Co. wind-up toy ..$600
"The Milton Berle Car" 1950s boxed Marx Toys wind-up......$529
"Peanuts" 1977 original art for daily comic strip .................$2741
Disneyland 1955 Opening original artwork by Al Konetzni ........$1852
"Mickey Mouse Magazine" Volume 1 Number 1, November 1933 (Fine) .........................$1667
"Mickey Mouse Magazine" Volume 1 Number 4, February 1934 .......................$569
"Mickey Mouse Magazine" Volume 1 Number 9, June 1936 ..........$632
Mickey Mouse – Pluto the Pup 1928-1930 Japanese painted bisque figure .........................$675
Mickey Mouse 1931 jointed wood figure with 'lollipop' hands ....$525
Mickey Mouse 1930s string-climbing toy by Dolly Toy Co ..............................................$600
"Three Little Pigs" boxed 1934 pocket watch by Ingersoll ..$1984
"Donald Duck Duet" with Goofy 1946 Marx wind-up toy..........$695
"Sears 1947 Back-To-School Give-Away Plan" promotion folder. From the Gold Premium Archives.. ..............................................$616
Dick Tracy & Tracy Jr. 1936 "Libby's Tomato Juice" 16x24" paper poster. From the Gold Premium Archives .................$775
"Dick Tracy Detective De-Coder and Clue Finder" 1950s prototype original art. From the Gold Premium Archives .................$929
"Popeye the Pilot" airplane 1940 Marx wind-up toy .................$777
Popeye's Eugene "Jeep" 1935 jointed composition 13" figure ..............................................$950
Lone Ranger 1957 General Mills life-sized standee VG ...........$1500
"Hopalong Cassidy Trading Cards" 1951 Post Cereals 13x26" paper store sign. From the Gold Premium Archives .................$575
"Buck Rogers 3 Board Games" 1934 boxed set ...................$1415
Superman tank 1940 Marx wind-up toy .........................$1131
"Kellogg's Pep Real Photos" 1947 paper poster 22x32". From the Gold Premium Archives..........$816
"Batmobile Corgi" 1966 boxed first issue...........$526
"Big Toy Comic Circus" original art prototype 1930s book. From the Gold Premium Archives..........$600
"Elvis Presley" autographed 1958 military service snapshot ..............................................$1234
"Frank Morgan/M-G-M's Wizard of Oz" 1939 button .................$1000
"Jack Haley/M-G-M's Wizard of Oz" 1939 button.........................$2168
"Bert Lahr/M-G-M's Wizard of Oz" 1939 button.........................$1000
"Minnie Mouse – Evening Ledger Comics" 1930s button ..........$1011
"Mickey Mouse – Evening Ledger Comics" 1930s button ...........$500
Donald Duck "Icy-Frost Twins Club of America" 1950s button ......$603
Dick Tracy & Little Orphan Annie "Shop At Genung's and Save" 1930s button .......................$1241
"Dick Tracy Secret Service Patrol – Inspector General" Quaker Cereals 1938 badge ...........................$658
Dick Tracy "Patrol Leader" Quaker Cereals 1939 bar pin ..............................................$600
"Valric of the Vikings" 1941 Kellogg's ring .............$7000
Davey Adams Shipmates Club 1939 ring ..............................$500
"The Untouchables" 1961 Marx complete boxed playset ..............................................$1750
"The Yellow Kid in McFadden's Flats" 1890s book order form ..............................................$630
"Alley Oop" 1930s boxed board game ......$811
"Felix" 1920s jointed wood 8" doll ..................................$500
"Walt Disney's Silly Symphony Calendar," 1938 ...................$1009
"Mickey Mouse Magazine" Volume 1 Number 7, April 1936..........$708
Mickey Mouse 1930s Knickerbocker Toys 9" composition doll .................$1058
"Mickey Mouse Helter Skelter" 1930s English boxed game ..............................................$1383
Mickey Mouse 1930s figural pencil box by Dixon .............$600
Mickey Mouse 1930s Ingersoll English wristwatch .............$1000
Mickey Mouse/Bread Company 1930s promotional mailer ......$762
"Mickey's Mousemovers" 1950s Line Mar truck toy ......$700
"Mickey Mouse" 1954 Adco-Liberty lunch bottle .......................$1080
Three Little Pigs 1930s "Wade Heath-England" pitcher ..............................................$1660
"Tarzan Series" School Paper Products 1939-1940 salesman's folio (fair).............................$709
"Phantom" 1942 child's four-piece costume ...............$991
"Superman" 1940s school bag ..............................................$1397
"Lost In Space" 1967 American Thermos Co. lunch box......$1754
"Lost In Space Roto-Jet Gun"

1960s Mattel toy .................$500
"Carey's Salt Presents The Shadow" 1945 dealer's promotional campaign book .................$6082
"Don Winslow" c. 1939 New Haven Co. pocket watch ....$1628
Donald Duck "Wanna Fight" 1930s button ........................$575
"I Am A Member of Buck Rogers' Gang" 1930s button ..............$686
Operator 5 pulp magazine 1930s ring ..........................$5249
"The Three Stooges Magic Re-Color Book," 1959 ............$633
"Pore Lil Mose – His Letter To His Mammy" 1902 comic strip reprint book, restored ........$3523
Kellogg's Pep set of 86 comic character 1945-1947 buttons................................$1748
"Porky's Lunch Box" with bottle, 1959 .................$609
"Alley Oop" 1937 daily comic strip original art ........$700
"Peanuts" 1953 daily comic strip original art ......$4412
"Mickey Mouse Candy Store" box prototype art 1955 by Al Konetzni ........................$1720
Mickey Mouse "A Handful of Fun" 1930s diecut premium booklet from the Gold Premium Archives ..........................................$1725
"Mickey Mouse Magazine" 1937 gift subscription card ....$588
"Mickey Mouse Magazine" Volume 1 number 5, February 1936....................................$1079
"Popeye Song Folio" licensed 1936 by E.C. Segar and King Features .................................$628
Howdy Doody ceramic bust figure bank, early 1950s....................$534
"Annie Oakley" 1950s drawstring vinyl lunch box ..$1175
Lone Ranger/Merita Bakers Club 1946 letter with Tonto map, mailing envelope .................$1079
"Buck Rogers Solar Scouts Spaceship Commander" 1936 badge with leaflet, mailing envelope .................$1045
"Buck Rogers Whistling Rocket Ship" original art 1930s prototype. From Gold Premium Archives ............................................$1140
Superman artist/creator Joe Shuster 1960 concept art for "Skybolt" character ...............$708
Superman/Tim "Franco Club 1946" fabric patch .................$861
Superman/Skippy Peanut Butter 1940s "Overseas Cap" ..........$3560
"Junior Justice Society of America" 1948 complete kit of four items and mailing envelope ..........$1674
"Howie Wing's Adventures on the Canadian Lake" 1930s Kellogg's of Canada map.........................$1175
"Swift's Space Trading Cards" proof sheet with sign proof c. 1958. From the Gold Premium Archives ..............................................$500
"Underdog and His TV Friends Tattoo Transfers" 1966 display box ..............................................$920
"The Six Million Dollar Man Venus Space Probe" 1978 Kenner Toys accessory set boxed .............$695
"Judy Garland/M-G-M's Oz" 1939 button.........................$1280
Mickey Mouse 1930s store clerks 3-1/2" button .......................$1577
1955 Superman Sugar Smacks Cereal Box ...........................$5000
Superman Australian button, excellent (McDowells) ........$1063
"The Phantom's Club Member" Australian button ...................$762
"The Flash Fastest Man Alive" comic book premium button ...........................................$1193
"Our Gang Fun Kit" booklet ..$594
"Bob Hope" figurine, ceramic on star-shaped base 1950s......$529
"Bing Crosby" figurine, ceramic on star-shaped base 1950s......$529
Disney "War Insignia Stamp Album" Volume 1 series 2 with unused sheet - .....................$525
"The Fighting Yank/The Black Terror" prototype art. From the Gold Premium Archives ........$828
Donald Duck dancing toy art prototype. From the Gold Premium Archives .................$526
Mickey Mouse "Kiddie Malt" salesman's sample book. From the Gold Premium Archives........$5000
Mickey Mouse wallpaper section – Canadian – Mickey and Minnie in center ...................................$685
Three Little Pigs pocket watch – Ingersoll 1934 .......................$748
Donald Duck Knickerbocker compo doll – 8" tall circa 1935 ...... ..............................................$695
Maleficent 2" Hagen-Renaker figure ............$675
Captain Midnight 1945 "Secret Squadron" manual/badge/leaflet/ mailer Very Fine.....................$510
"3-D Howdy Doody Comic Strips" with viewer and envelope......$694
Tom Mix Look-Around Ring with folder and mailer. Folder excellent, ring Near Mint ........................$938
The Lone Ranger and Tonto Little Golden Book title page art ...............................$1865

*1940 Double Action #2 in CGC holder brings $35,186.*

"Hopalong Cassidy" boxed wristwatch (on saddle) ..................$839
"Buck Rogers Sylvania TV" retailers sales catalogue and roster. From the Gold Premium Archives ..................................$529
Star Wars Boba Fett 13" tall boxed figure ..........................$534
"Junior Justice Society of America" complete 1945 club kit ........$1476
"Adventures Of Og Son Of Fire" map Very Fine ......................$1030
Terry And The Pirates "Victory Airplane Spotter" store display. From the Gold Premium Archives .. ...............................................$900
"Terry And The Pirates Terryscope." From the Gold Premium Archives..........$564
"Post Honey-Comb Chitty Chitty Bang Bang Model Car" premium with box flat. From the Gold Premium Archives ..................$500
"Funny Face" finger puppet set. From the Gold Premium Archives .. .............................................$2035
"Funny Face" paper mask set of six. From the Gold Premium Archives ...............................$1200
"Beatles Sneakers by Wing Dings." Box Fine, shoes Mint ............$1085
"Jack Johnson Heavyweight Champion" button 1-3/4" circa 1908-1915 ............................$1079

Lindbergh flight commemorative clock - Fine ..........................$1101
Willard Mullin original art J. Mize/Brooklyn Bum ............$801
Willard Mullin original art Cletis Boyer ............................$534
Shirley Temple real photo 1-1/8" pin ....................$526
"Mickey Mouse Aviation Department" brass badge - 1-5/8" .....................................$575
The Lone Ranger rare prototype secret compartment ring......$3249
"The Wizard of Oz" game by Whitman, 1939 ..................$658
Golden Age costumed hero 1940 "Comicscope" projector with six picture strips ..................$1910
Felix large size 3-1/2" tall Japan cello figure....................$1021
Betty Boop large 7-3/4" cello jointed figure - Very Fine ....$1380
Comic strip character "Profit Parade"art prototype display. From the Gold Premium Archives ...............................................$526
"S. Jack/S. Stover/O. Annie/Smitty" original art for vacuform patches. From the Gold Premium Archives ...............................................$500
"Peanuts" Oct. 22, 1977 original daily strip art ..........$3307
Frazetta "Buck Rogers" limited edition watercolored print with small original art ............$3000
"Silly Symphonies" Dell Giant #5 cover rough original art ........$500
"Motion Picture Herald" with Mickey, Shirley Temple, Lone Ranger 10/2/1937..........$632
"Mickey Mouse Magazine" Volume 1 number 10 - Very Fine......$1213
"Donald Duck" Jack-In-The-Box toy late 1940s ...........................$1007
Snow White 1939 Emerson radio ..............................................$2000
Disneyland Dutch Boy paint large display ..................$939
ROA "Captain Sparks Airplane Pilot Training Cockpit" kit with envelope and booklet. From the Gold Premium Archives ..................$526
Buck Jones on bronc figural cast metal ashtray ..................$778
The Lone Ranger preliminary comic book cover art 1950s .......................................$658
"Buck Rogers/Muffets" rocketship art prototype sign. From the Gold Premium Archives ..................$750
"Buck Rogers Whistling Sky Rocket" lot of three concept sketches. From the Gold Premium Archives ..................$526
"Buck Rogers Space Ranger Kit" unpunched from Sylvania TV ...............................................$535
Golden Age Superman artist Fred Ray Superman art with 20 letters .. ...............................................$587
Moldoff large "Batman" with smoking gun art ............$690
"Post Grape-Nuts Flakes Jet Fighter" prototype art. From the Gold Premium Archives..........$750
"Funny Face Drink Stand" mini 3-D prototype art display. From the Gold Premium Archives ...........................................$2172
"Kellogg's Apple Jack/H.R. Pufnstuff Hand Puppets" cereal box. From the Gold Premium Archives .................................$500

*Collection of 12 different dime banks sells for $2,922.*

PREVIEWS Exclusive
Collectible Toys
Want to build the ULTIMATE collection?
TOMB RAIDER
SPIDER-GIRL
Turn to *PREVIEWS*— the Expert on Exclusives!
Looking for the latest and greatest in the world of white-hot collectible toys? Head to your local specialty shop and check out the newest issue of *PREVIEWS*! Each month, you'll find not just a ton of pop culture-based toys and collectibles – including imports at unbeatable prices – but also some that are unavailable *anywhere* else!
Only the Best! Only in *PREVIEWS*!
*Available at specialty shops everywhere!*
www.diamondcomics.com
RETAILERS: To order, or for more information on Diamond's selection of toys and other products, and on becoming a Diamond customer, please call Ryan Hadfield at (410) 560-7112, ext. 336, or (410) 308-2800 outside the continental U.S. & Canada.
COMIC SHOP LOCATOR SERVICE
888-COMIC-BOOK
888-266-4226
PREVIEWS
9-11
002 Diamond Comic Distributors and respective copyright holders.

# GENESIS OF TH

## How Fantasy and Reality Merge

***We all need heroes. That was never more apparent than when our illusions of American security were shattered on September 11, 2001 and heroes emerged from all walks of life to rescue and rebuild in the wake of those horrible events. For too long beforehand we seemed to be in the business of deconstructing our heroes, dragging them down into the dirt and leaving them behind as we trampled forward without them to guide and protect us. But we as Americans and as human beings have now rediscovered the value of heroes, real heroes, and we're lucky that they bear no grudges. They're back to help us through once again - in fact, they never really left.***

But what of the fictional heroes that once meant so much to us? They never left either, and for comic book fans, they have remained a potent vehicle for taking endless flights of fantasy into the stratosphere. At a time like this, it behooves us to look back at the dawn of an important heroic age - a time when our desperation and imagination merged and the resulting chemical reaction produced a type of character never before seen but inspired by generations of storytelling stretching back to the days when men gathered around the campfires and spun tales of adventure and allegory. It was the 1930s in the United States, and the superhero was about to fly into view.

### A LONG LINE OF HEROES

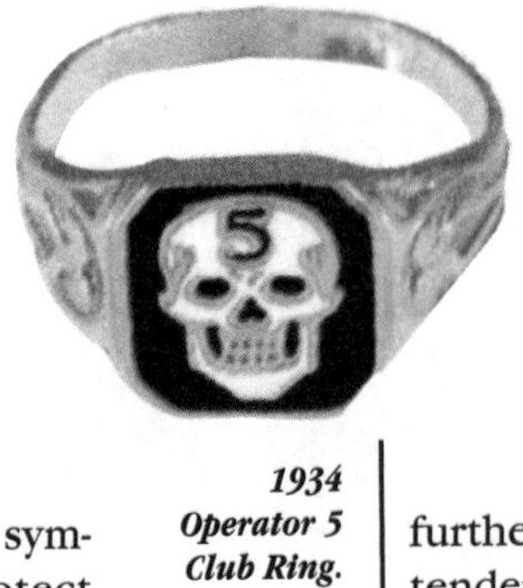

*1934 Operator 5 Club Ring.*

For as long as humans have shared stories and longed for a better world, heroic characters have existed to symbolize and protect our highest ideals. In the ancient world, Gilgamesh, perhaps the world's first true "superhero," served as an icon of power and wisdom. Predating the epics of Homer and the Bible itself, the tale of Gilgamesh, ruler of Uruk, chronicles the adventures of the first god/hero or superhero and lays the groundwork for the comic book superheroes millennia later by conferring divine abilities and faculties onto a human being. The superheroes of today merely draw on the mythical archetypes of the past, and Gilgamesh is the first and greatest of these hybrid heroes, a human with a mortal father and a goddess mother.

Many centuries later, Robin Hood (first referred to in the writings of William Langland in 1377) offered a very different - but very significant - twist on the notion of a hero, operating outside the law but honoring a higher set of morals as he battled tyranny with his band of merry men. His outlaw status is something we shall examine further in a moment, as well as our tendency to envision him in a particular, consistent mode of dress. While Robin did not maintain a "secret identity" per se, that con-

# SUPERHEROES

## to Create a Legend

by
Arnold T. Blumberg

cept would enter the vernacular by 1903, when Baroness Orczy introduced the world to Sir Percy Blakeney, also known as the Scarlet Pimpernel. Ostensibly a perfect English gentleman of means and morals, Blakeney hid another face which he donned to combat the forces of evil. This familiar device would become commonplace soon enough, but it would take a special medium to provide the fertile ground wherein all of these individual elements could germinate and blossom into the prototype superheroes of the post-WWI era.

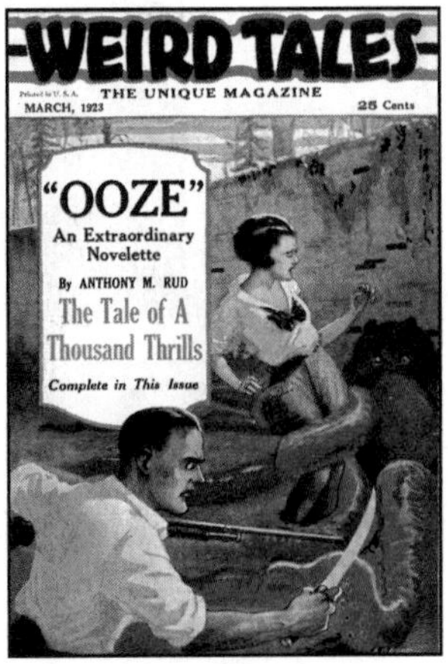

*1923 Weird Tales #1 pulp.*

In the early 1900s, a strong sense of morality, instilled by generations of fiercely religious communities fervently upholding their cherished ideals, began to give way as the country witnessed the return of the battle-weary veterans of WWI. Confronted with the most incredible horrors ever seen at that time, Americans found themselves slowly inured to ugliness and evil, and a tougher sense of justice replaced the old morality.

Street-wise, city-bred kids growing up on US streets in the 1910s and '20s wanted something more potent than the arrested adventures of previous fantasy characters. They wanted action, a quick and dirty solution to the hardships of the time, and a more honest depiction of the terrors that lurked around every corner. The Roaring Twenties brought with them a new education in the power of evil and the profit in crime. The horrors of war were all too vividly remembered; gangsters defied Prohibition by running liquor under the noses of the federal authorities; a booming stock market and a runaway economy led to a wanton hedonism that spread across the nation's burgeoning urban centers with abandon. The New Immorality kicked the door wide open for a different kind of medium

*1930s "Doc Savage Award" Bronze Medallion - Less than 10 have survived.*

with a rough-hewn sort of hero. The pulps were born.

### PULP FICTION

Today, many believe that the pulps were the predecessors of the comic books of the 1930s and beyond, but the two storytelling forms existed side by side for many years. The blending of the two is the

*1937 Vol. 13 #2 G-8 and His Battle Aces pulp.*

crux of our exploration, but at this point, the pulps were a unique entity unto themselves, depicting adventure, violence, racial intolerance and misogyny in equal measure. The detective stories that were in vogue years before gave way to heroes who plied their trade in the seedy back alleys of the early American cities, mingling with the very sordid types they fought in an effort to make the streets safe for law-abiding citizens. Many of these so-called heroes were actually thieves and swindlers who disguised themselves as wealthy men and infiltrated the upper classes to steal from corrupt millionaires and outwit the forces of "good." In a clever reversal of the formula, these rogue heroes resembled that crusading Robin and his merry band, and their adventures certainly inspired the heroes that followed a decade or so later.

*1933 Doc Savage pulp #1.*

While the heroes of the pulps and the rogue offshoots represented aspects of the superheroic world to come, there is little doubt who might have served as the single most important template for all that was to follow. As heroes traded in their fedoras and six-shooters for masks and capes, writer Frank Lucius Packard conceived a costumed crime fighter who would infiltrate the ranks of the underworld to overthrow the plans of evildoers. The Adventures of Jimmie Dale, first appearing in novel form in 1917 though serialized years earlier, followed the adventures of Dale's alter ego, The Gray Seal, and offered a blueprint for superhero success.

While not possessing the superhuman powers once seen in the mythological epics of old, The Gray Seal did maintain a secret identity and even a hideout known as "Sanctuary," a clear precursor to the Fortress of Solitude

*1930s Premium photo of Shadow Unmasked.*

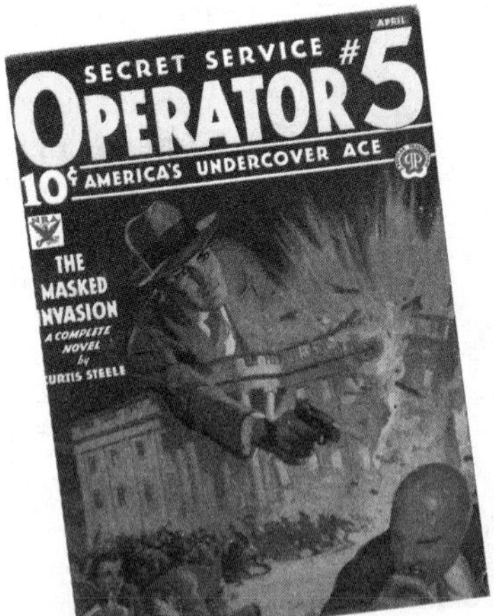


*1934 Operator 5 pulp #1.*

*1934 Spider Club Ring.*

*1934 "Tarzan and His Mate" Lobby Card.*

favored by pulp star Doc Savage (and later a certain Kryptonian immigrant), the Sandman's hidden lab and, of course, the legendary Batcave. The Gray Seal was a direct ancestor of Bruce Wayne's shadowy persona in many ways, utilizing his trademark facility with disguise to defeat an ever-expanding rogues' gallery of colorful villains. Add a dash of Zorro to the mix, with his millionaire resources and recurring iconography, and you have the Dark Knight himself.

And the march of heroes continued. As the protean comic books focused on cartoonish characters and light-hearted tales, the pulps generated excitement with a never-ending parade of illustrious adventurers all jockeying for their moment in the spotlight. Lester Dent crafted the "grandfather" of the superheroes in Doc Savage, whose gadget-filled, globe-trotting adventures set the groundwork for decades of stories to come. Grant Stockbridge's Spider, another playboy turned vigilante meted out a vicious, bloodthirsty justice with his wits and twin .45 pistols. Curtis Steele sent Jimmy Christopher, AKA Operator #5, on assignments that culminated in a pre-superhero epic dubbed "The Purple Invasion Saga," heralding the massive super-story arcs of the future.

The jungle lord Tarzan swung onto the newspaper pages in 1929 from the pages of Edgar Rice Burroughs' novel. Hal Foster, later the creator of Prince Valiant, lent Tarzan's adventures a realistic tone. A new decade arrived, bringing with it a radio show that, in 1930, marked the debut of "The Shadow!" William Gibson wrote the first Shadow tales in pulp form, describing the fearsome foe of crime as a master of disguise with two .45s ever at the ready (shades of the Spider).

The superhero era was still a decade away, but pulp heroes and adventurers like The Gray Seal, Zorro and the Scarlet Pimpernel exhibited many of the familiar aspects of the archetypal superhero, pushing the boundaries of fantasy by adopting costumed identities and battling criminals with style. No one had ever seen their like before, but there was still an infusion of power, of raw energy, lacking in these early characters. Before the superhero would be born, pulps would blend together with their comic book cousins, and the divine spark of the mythological heroes would lift their pulp descendents to loftier heights, up to the clear blue skies where a real, living hero named Charles Lindbergh was waiting to bring about the dawn of a new era in fantasy and reality. It was time to fly.

## PARALLELITIES

In such a troubled time, parents must have wondered who their children could look up to, only to have the answer zip out of the clouds as kids of all ages craned their necks to catch a glimpse of their new hero. By the time their eyes turned earthward again, their world had changed. Newspapers, radio, film - all media were consumed with flying, the men who dared the skies and the airplanes that took them there. And with the arrival of a real-world hero who could reach the lofty heights and inspire children to dream, the fictional heroes of the pulps and comics took to their planes and braved the air currents as well. What else could they do? A "normal" human being had bested them at their own game.

Even Dick Tracy, an unlikely choice for a pilot, leapt into the cockpit for a while as fantasy characters and their eager creators desperately tried to cash in on the airplane craze. Where the heroes of the pulps offered a distraction from a world weighed down with fear

***1937 Red Falcon Air Ranger 8 page comic premiums. Shown are #1 & #6 sponsored by Seal Right and used as a giveaway located in the top of each ice cream cup.***

*1933 Funnies on Parade comic book.*

and anxiety, along with the reassurance that justice would inevitably prevail, the high-flying heroes of the '30s and '40s provided a potent escape from those concerns, a chance to utterly ignore the pull of gravity and soar to a happier, more exciting world. These adventurers enthralled their youthful readers, whether they were truly young or merely young at heart, and delighted a generation desperate to turn away from the worsening world situation threatening to engulf them. Children dreamed of flying like Lindbergh, piloting a gleaming plane and finding the answers to all of life's problems, and the flying heroes had those answers. Their escapades not only entertained but inspired the next generation of creators, some of whom would take the next logical step - eliminate the airplane - ironically bringing about the end of their own heroes' reign.

But to do that, the worlds of the pulps and the comics would have to merge. The pulps had been restrained for years, unable to expand distribution due to resistance to their flagrant flaunting of the New Immorality. The "Bible" mentality still guided the newspaper syndicates, and most importantly the advertisers, both in print and on radio. They were enjoying a boom in interest thanks to the cartoon characters who were perceived by many adult purchasers of the newspapers as free "extras" to entertain their children (and themselves as well).

While the newspapers and the cartoons enjoyed such success, the comic book reprints were sinking fast. Steadily dropping the cover prices hadn't turned the tide. Why should anyone spend a quarter on a reprint comic filled with cartoons they could get in the paper for free? William Gaines found a partial answer in 1933 by introducing 10 cent comics for eager young readers, and when the comics decided they were no longer going to pay the royalties necessary to secure the cartoon characters from the papers, two parallel forms found their point of convergence. As the notion of independently sold comic books took

*1932 Popeye comic book sold for 25¢.*

*1944 Archie in Army Uniform.*

*1944 Tillie in War Uniform.*

1944 *Barney Google in Navy Uniform.*

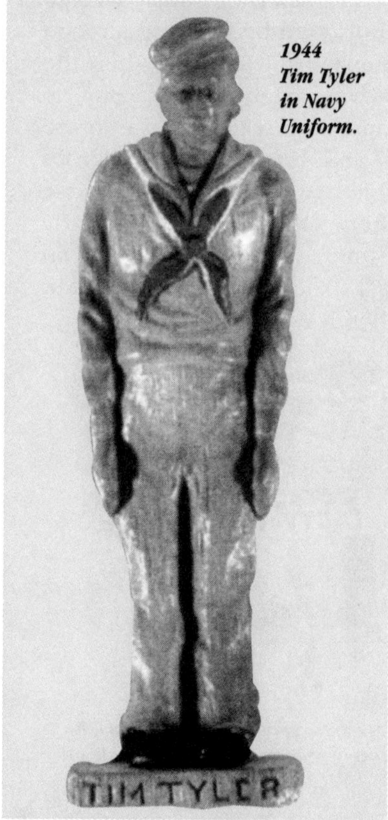


*1944 Tim Tyler in Navy Uniform.*

hold and grew throughout the 1930s, the pulps moved in for the kill, converting their material to comic book form after the Depression and its aftermath had left yet another door wide open.

## SELLING A DREAM ➪

"In olden days, a glimpse of stocking was looked on as something shocking, but now, God knows, anything goes," sang Cole Porter in 1934. Times had indeed changed, as had the pulps, and now they were freed from their restrictive moral prison. All of the elements introduced in decades of heroic tales blended into one, and the genesis of the superheroes was nearly complete. There is one factor left to consider, however - merchandising.

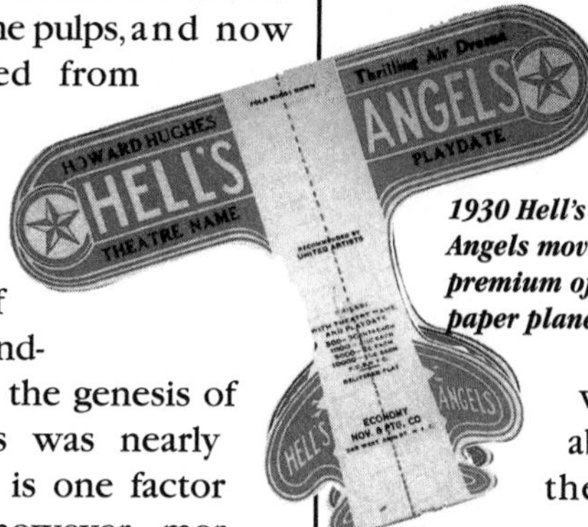


*1930 Hell's Angels movie premium of paper plane.*

The explosion of character toys between the 1900s and the 1930s was no accident. Savvy marketers had an established path to travel in the years after the debut of The Brownies. Along with other early comic characters, their creation can rightfully be considered a watershed event in pop culture, as it linked comic characters and merchandising.

There was at the time a small but eager number of entrepreneurs hungry for the opportunity to turn characters that previously existed only on paper into three-dimensional products made of plastic, balsa wood, celluloid, metal and other materials. They understood that if a character worked in one medium, such as pulps, that character could also work on radio or films or comics, and a character that was used to sell cereal could also sell bread or milk. Whether it was The Shadow, Mickey Mouse or some other character, by the time such a creation first appeared to the public, some businessman was eager to produce the toy rings, yo-yos, dolls, decoders, and hundreds of other types of toys based upon it, looking for that one special item that would hit the big time. For these enterprising individuals, there could be no better character to exploit to its fullest marketing potential than the superheroes who were now, finally, about to appear on the scene.

## A SUPERHERO ARRIVES ➪

1938 saw the arrival of costumed heroes to the comic book pages. In *Ace Comics* #11, published in February, the Phantom - created by Lee Falk - appeared for the first time (not yet in purple togs, but in a brown outfit). Debuting two years earlier in the

*1938 Ace Comic #11, first appearance of Phantom in comic book.*

*1940 "Sky Blazers" large sign promoting radio show.*

newspapers, the Phantom fought evil in much the same way as Zorro and The Gray Seal before him. He was human, but possessed of enhanced abilities and unwavering bravery. He was a masked hero that still lacked that one magic spark...and, of course, the ability to fly. In June 1938, two young men provided that spark, bringing their vision of a super-powerful guardian of justice and morality to the pages of *Action Comics* #1. Is it any wonder that this strange visitor from another planet arrived by hurtling through the air in a rocket, faster than any airplane could or would travel?

Superman was introduced to the world that day, and in the months and years to come, he would be joined by an ever-growing universe of superheroes, each more colorful and inventive than the last, each offering readers both young and old for generations to come the chance to slip those surly bonds and join their favorite heroes in the skies. And so the children flew. They were primed for it in 1938, inundated with the very notion of Superman, and ready to fuel his career and his accompanying merchandising empire.

As America marched inexorably toward war, superheroes burst onto the landscape in a plethora of guises, just as so many had copied Lindbergh and his image of heroism years before. The Superman juggernaut carried children (and adults) ever farther from the woes of reality into a fantasy that was too enticing to ignore...until reality asserted itself once more. 1941 brought terror into the hearts of Americans, and anger as well - an anger that even a Superman could not defeat.

But then too, superheroes served their purpose. It was as if they were created just in time to perform a most important duty, to shore up our nation's flagging confidence, to fire our patriotic fervor and inspire children to believe in freedom and justice. Soon, superheroes and super-teams - favorite heroes banding together for a common cause (and a tidy profit) - would turn their efforts to fighting the Axis forces both at home and abroad. The superheroes grounded us in reality even as they carried us to the skies, the ultimate wish fulfillment in a time of need, the greatest catharsis in a time of sorrow and fear. By the close of the war, Americans would seek to bury their memories of war, turning their attentions and their clocks back to a frontier long since forgotten. The superhero would be swept away in favor of the cowboy and his trusty steed, and the country would force itself back down to earth once again.

But that was still to come. For now, the superhero was here to stay, bolstered by war into an icon of unimaginable power. When the need was so great, the desire so profound, we reached up into the skies and brought down heroes capable of defending us. Then we let them catch the wind and fly once more, beckoning us to join them as they soared higher than Lindbergh ever dreamed.

***1941 Superman Bread Shield worn by grocery employees to promote sale of new bread product.***

Now that youve tracked down the greatest toys from the past...
COMIC SHOP LOCATOR SERVICE
COMICS
888-COMIC-BOOK
csls.diamondcomics.com
...here's how to find the hottest collectibles of the future!
Today's comics shops are your source for the latest toys and collectibles, and for nearly seven years, the Comic Shop Locator Service (CSLS) has been making it as easy as possible for serious collectors like you to find the comics specialty shops nearest them! Just call 1-888-COMIC-BOOK, or direct your Internet browser to http://csls.diamondcomics.com, and you'll never have to worry about missing a must-have collectible again!
The Comic Shop Locator Service -
FAST, FUN, AND FREE!
http://csls.diamondcomics.com
COMIC SHOP LOCATOR SERVICE
888-COMIC-BOOK
csls.diamondcomics.com

# It's a bird, it's a plane...

# No, it's *really* a

*By John K. Snyder, Jr.*

## IMAGINATION TAKES FLIGHT

***As a dream, as a calling, it may be as old as mankind. Who among us, if only as a child, hasn't looked up toward the sky and wondered what it would be like to fly like a bird? From the legend of Icarus in the days of myth to the Chinese kites of 1000 B.C., and from the ambitious drawings of Leonardo Da Vinci to Apollo 17 and the last footprints left by man on the moon, people have yearned, to closely paraphrase the words of John Gillespie Magee, Jr., to slip the surly bonds of earth and dance the skies on laughter-silvered wings.***

And for their efforts, until not all that long ago in human history, most of the dreamers died trying. Then on November 21, 1783, the Montgolfier brothers followed up their unmanned experiments with a successful manned balloon flight in Paris. During the next 120 years, many soared higher and stayed up in the air longer, but no one had a controlled, motorized flight until December 17, 1903, when Orville Wright took off in a contraption dubbed the Wright Flyer. His flight, at Kitty Hawk, North Carolina, covered 852 feet at the blazing speed of thirty-four miles per hour. After that, many other flyers tried and were successful.

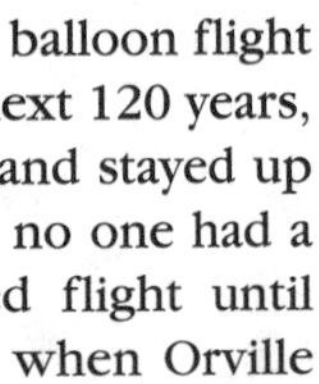


There were, of course, casualties, but danger and the dream of flight were no longer synonymous. It would not always remain that way.

World War I demonstrated that airplanes had a place in the skies as weapons, though they were used exclusively as observation platforms at the outset. In 1915 alone, however, the world experienced the first aerial bombardment (of Great Britain from a Zeppelin), the first air-to-air combat (a Frenchman shot down a German plane), and the flight of the first all-metal airplane (the Junkers J.1).

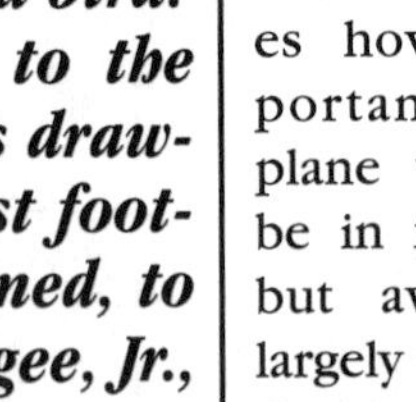

***Above- Better Little Book #1464.***

***Left-1930s pinback.***

In 1921, after the war, General Billy Mitchell demonstrated to our armed services how important the plane would be in future wars, but aviation was largely returned to the purview of adventurous souls and entrepreneurs.

***1934 Admiral Byrd in Little America Book.***

Throughout the next few years both men and women became stunt flyers. They performed at carnivals and circuses, putting on daredevil shows of aerial acrobatics. The first airlines and airmail routes had been organized during the war, and their development continued. In 1926, Richard Byrd and Floyd Bennett circled the North Pole and created public interest in just how far someone could fly.

### A FLIGHT FOR THE AGES

In 1927, a prize of $25,000 was offered by New York hotel owner Raymond Orteig for the first person to fly across the Atlantic from New York to Paris. The race was on and many of the

top aviators prepared for the challenge. The general public was fascinated. The national press, feeding on the curiosity, portrayed the feat as impossible, almost fatal for anyone to try. Bad weather, fuel capacity, speed of the aircraft, and endurance of the pilots were just a few of the reasons suggested as to why it couldn't be done. The failed attempts were as plentiful as the excuses.

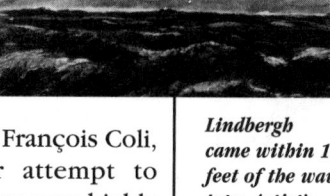

*Lindbergh came within 10 feet of the wave tops. Artist's rendering.*

On May 8, 1927, the then-famous French aviator Charles Nungesser took off from France with François Coli, his navigator. Their attempt to reach the United States was highly publicized, but they disappeared en route and were never found.

More than ever, the naysayers said it couldn't be done.

What followed now seems like a fairy tale, but the hard work to make this "fairy tale" come true had been going on behind the scenes for months. A dark horse candidate, little known outside aviation circles, came forward. On May 20, 1927 at 7:52am, a monoplane christened "The Spirit of St. Louis" took off from the damp ground runway of Roosevelt Field, Long Island. Its destination, Paris, was some 3,000 miles and thirty-three hours away. At times the pilot reportedly came within ten feet of the wave tops of the Atlantic Ocean as he struggled to stay awake for more than a day. He succeeded, though, and landed in France at 10:22pm on May 21.

His name was Charles Lindbergh, a 25-year-old quintessential mid-westerner with the face of a young high school student. Seventy-five years later, it's difficult to picture a world without highly paid athletes, entertainers and media superstars, but this is precisely the world that "Lindy" found himself in after his flight. To the waiting multitude who were on hand to greet him in Paris, and to millions more around the world, he was an instant hero. He not only landed in France, he landed in a different world. After touring Europe and being celebrated in country after country, he returned to the United States. He went first to Washington, D.C. for a ceremony with President Coolidge and then to New York City, where he received the largest ticker-tape

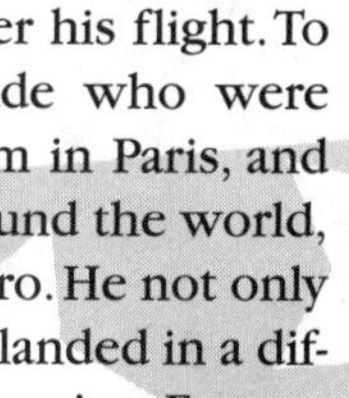


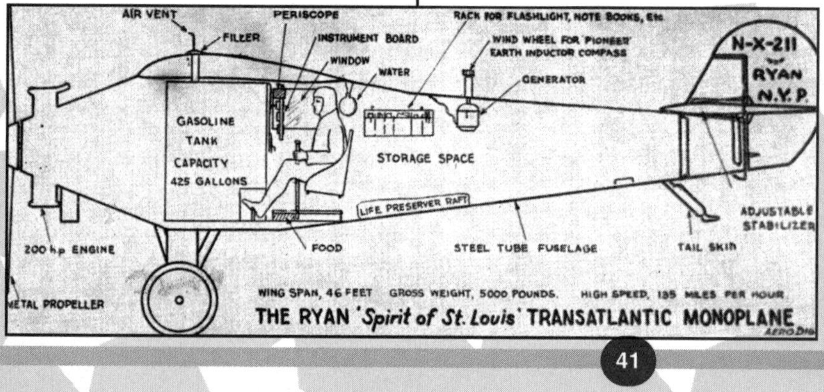

parade in the city's history.

Even prior to the grief of the Great Depression, the '20s had been a turbulent decade: a tough period with increased crime, a booming stock market, and declining morality associated with an unrestrained economy, incredible population concentrations in major urban areas, and the aftermath of the first World War. All of a sudden, the youth of America had someone to look up to, someone their parents were happy for them to look up to. The press jumped on the news of Lindbergh's heroics and continued to feed the public's adoration with article after article about "The Lone Eagle," as he was now being called.

## PROMOTING THE DREAM (AND PRODUCTS, TOO)

The kids of America wanted to learn how to fly like Lindy, and consumers were game for anything associated with the intrepid aviator. Products of all kinds were being produced with his photo and the likeness of his plane. Plates, maps, rings, bracelets, books, buttons and even bread were sold with his image. Lionized at every stop, he was indeed the world's first living superhero.

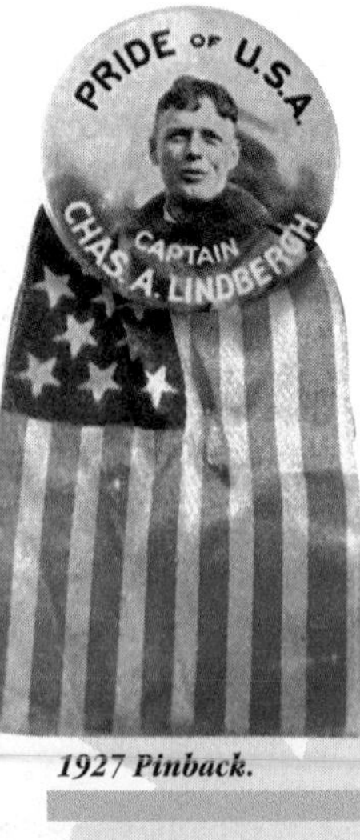


*1927 Pinback.*

Between 1927 and 1937 the entertainment industry jumped on the aviation band-wagon with movies, comic strips and radio shows about aerial adventures. Many clubs were formed to help kids learn more about flying and, of course, to get mom and dad to buy the products offered by the companies that promoted these clubs. Some of the best-known clubs were the Air Juniors, Sky Climbers, Sky Roads, Sky Blazers, Flying Aces, and Junior Birdmen of America. A plethora of premiums were produced for these organizations and others, including flying lessons, maps, rings, certificates, buttons, decals, patches, letters, and pins signifying various ranks such as pilot, lieutenant, captain. All were generally awarded for a few cents and some box tops. Hollywood wasn't slow to catch on either. Mickey Mouse's first appearance came in the animated short, *Plane Crazy*, which was directly inspired by Lindbergh-mania. Mickey, with

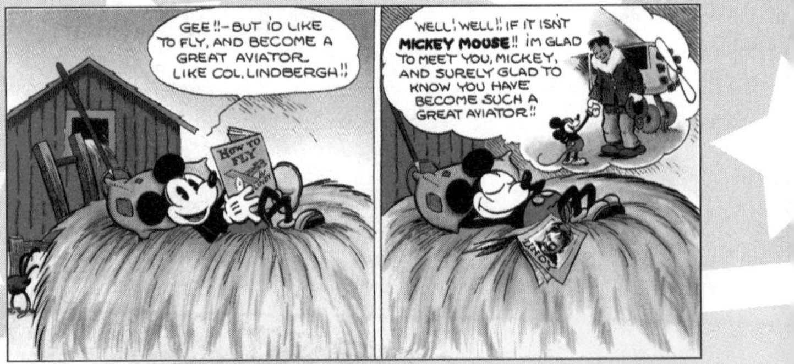


***The "Plane Crazy" story was also featured as Mickey's first appearance in the newspaper.***

***1929 Radio sponsored pin for Air Juniors Club.***

***1929-34 Club Memorabilia Items.***

girlfriend Minnie in tow, is a first-time pilot who takes a roller coaster-like ride in his new home-built airplane. The silent *Plane Crazy* was actually produced prior to the talkie (and more famous) *Steamboat Willie*, but ended up being the third cartoon Disney released.

The first Academy Award for Best Picture, presented in 1929 for a film released in late 1927, was about the young World War I warriors of the skies, titled *Wings*. Howard Hughes' first film, *Hell's Angels* (1930), staring newcomer Jean Harlow, was about flying, and the first paper airplane movie premium was given away to promote this film at theatres. Even poor old King Kong was no match for the airplane, gunned down from atop the Empire State Building.

And the heroes of aviation and the children they inspired were in no way limited to the male persuasion. Girls and young women had their heroes, too, in the likes of pilots Elinor Smith, Ruth Nichols, Laura Ingalls, Lilian Gatlin, Laura Brown-

well, Beryl Markham and, of course, the great Amelia Earhart.

Other pilots who gained notoriety from all the interest in flying were Earl Ortman, Capt. Frank Hawks, Jimmy Doolittle, Jimmy Mattern, and (now) Admiral Byrd.

***Above - 1935 Big Little Book #1164, Below- 1930s Ruth Nichols pinback.***

The radio shows and movies gave us characters like Jimmie Allen, Speed Robertson, Tailspin Tommy, Speed Gibson, and Ace Drummond. The pulps gave us Bill Barnes and his cadets and host of other flying venues including *War Aces*, *Sky Raiders*, *Flying Aces*, *Air Action*, *Flying Stories*, *Air Adventures*, *Airplane Stories*, *Air Stories*, *Air Trails*, *Air War*, *Wings*, *Air Wonder Stories*, and *War Birds*.

***Above - 1935 Captain Frank Hawks Photo, Post Cereal sponsored.***

***1930s James Mattern pinback.***

In 1935, Jimmy Cagney starred in *Devil Dogs of the Air*, a film significant for its double success in initial release and re-release preceding America's entry into World War II. From a collector's perspective, though, its importance was established when it became the first film to tie in a major film promotion with a cereal manufacturer. Quaker Oats, the sponsor, produced an array of quality merchandise that only served to further fuel kids' interest in aviation.

***1930s Premiums - pin & patch for Young Sky Birds and Flying Aces clubs.***

With the stock market crash in 1929 and the worldwide economic depression that followed, it's not a stretch of the imagination to surmise that many people – particularly kids – were eager for escapism. Buck Rogers and Flash Gordon answered their call. Great characters like Tarzan, the Phantom, and other heroes free of the confines of everyday reality also enjoyed great popularity, as did *New Adventure Comics* and the Federal Men Club. It was the flying heroes, though, who sparked the sense of wonder in a cadre of young kids, among them budding writers and artists who were dreaming up the next generation of characters. Jerry Siegel was a teen writer in the early '30s. He loved the comic strip *Sky Roads* and was amazed by the talent of its artist, Russell Keaton. He had his own thoughts on flying, but that's a super secret story for another time. Maybe one day the person who has the information will let it be known.

With the seemingly unending

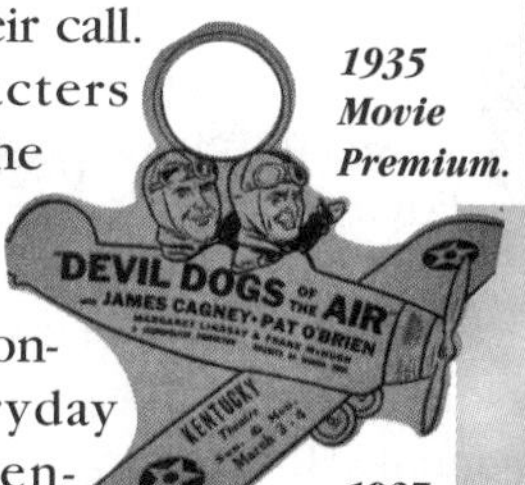


***1935 Movie Premium.***

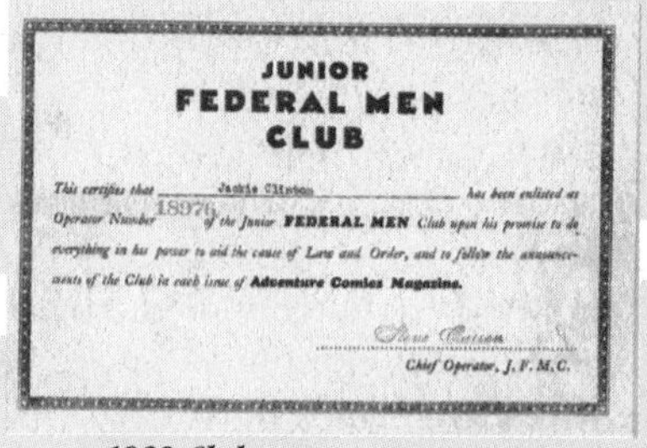
JUNIOR
FEDERAL MEN
CLUB

This certifies that Jackie Clinton has been enlisted as Operator Number 18976 of the Junior **FEDERAL MEN** Club upon his promise to do everything in his power to aid the cause of Law and Order, and to follow the announcements of the Club in each issue of **Adventure Comics Magazine.**

Chief Operator, J. F. M. C.

***1939 Club Certificate, Adventure Comics Premium.***

***Phantom, Better Little Book #1468, 1937 newspaper story in this 1945 book.***

***1927 Photo of Charles Lindbergh after his historic flight.***

***1929 Fan Card Newspaper Premium art drawn by Dick Calkins . . . of Buck Rogers, not Lindbergh.***

celebration and promotion of Lindbergh's triumph a decade earlier in newspapers, magazines, radio and film, the characters and stories it spawned had enlivened a generation of enthusiasts. They, in turn, had grown up with flight as far more than just a reality. It had become an adventure, and now the collective imagination of the nation's young people was ready to fly on its own. As the world headed for war, Siegel finally got his big break when a comic book company published his adventure story about a man from another world who could fly. Illustrated by Siegel's boyhood friend, Joe Shuster, Superman had arrived.

**1936**
***Buck Rogers* patch, *Cream of Wheat* Premium.**

*Action Comics #1* and its star character were instant hits. Armed with badges, buttons and rankings from all the flying clubs, kids flocked to the newsstands by the thousands to buy copies of the comic. Other superheroes were created in short order, many of them thinly-veiled Superman copies.

## REALITY RETURNS✈

However powerful the fantasy, the real world was not to be held at bay for very long. The war in Europe was quickly expanding. The attack on Pearl Harbor ended any speculation that the U.S. could stay out of the conflict, and the generation that had grown up idolizing aviators and airplanes was quickly turned into a generation of flyers. In 45,000 fighter aircraft with names like "Thunderbolt," "Mustang," "Tomahawk," "Lightning," "Corsair," "Hurricane" and "Spitfire," American, British, and allied pilots took to the skies of Britain, the European continent, Africa, the middle east, the south Pacific, and China. In 25,000 bombers with names like "Liberator," "Marauder," "Mitchell," "Lancaster," "Flying Fortress," and "Super Fortress," their comrades flew raids against enemy formations, cities, installations and equipment. How many of these young fliers were influenced by the sheer volume of aviation-based entertainment available throughout 1927 to 1940? While we'll never know for certain, we do know this generation grew up and saved our country.

***Better Little Book #1958.***

***Smilin' Jack Better Little Book #1973.***

During 1940 to 1945, characters with a slightly more realistic bent like Hop Harrigan and Captain Midnight and his Secret Squadron took to the skies to defend America. Comic books like *Captain Aero*, *Airboy*, *True Aviation*, *Air Ace*, *Black Hawk*, *Bill Barnes*, *Air Fighters*, *Skyrocket*, *Wings*, *Flying Cadet*, *Flying Aces* and *Skyman* filled the racks.

**1944 *Military Comics #34.***

Other characters had their styles of storytelling changed to promote flying as well. Dick Tracy and Jack Armstrong headed for the sky and Radio Orphan Annie teamed with Captain Sparks to form the Secret Guard and produced a number of inspired giveaways. Of course all of this was accomplished with the "club" concept, established so well in the '30s, firmly in place. It's not too surprising then that the Supermen of America Club was a rousing success. First advertised in 1939, it lasted until 1965.

***1938 Dick Tracy Air Detective wing bracelet.***

***1944 Hop Harrigan Promo.***

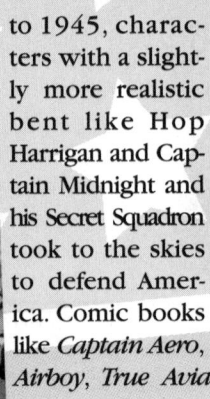

Other comic book character clubs got into the act as well. Patriotic-themed characters from Fox were created for The "U.S Jones Cadets" and the "American Eagle Defenders." DC added one of their most successful clubs, the "Junior Justice Society" of America [*see page 48*]. Timely added Captain America's "Sentinels of Liberty," and Gleason added "Captain Battle's Boys Brigade."

By the end of 1945, the activities of many clubs originating as far back as 1927 came to an end. Many of the characters, both real and fictional, faded into memory. The overwhelming bulk of the memorabilia produced for these clubs during that period was destroyed, either deliberately thrown away or set aside and forgotten like the youthful innocence of the real life aviators who flew in the war.

***1939 Sky Blazer, balsa wood toy plane.***

***Roscoe Turner pinback.***

## AFTERMATH

Today, only a handful of these pop culture artifacts survive, thanks to the kids who loved them so much or those rare moms who didn't throw them away. In this edition of *Hake's Price Guide To Character Toys*, we've taken special pride in documenting the history of these aviators, flying heroes, and marketing pioneers through our pictures and descriptions of the items and the events, radio shows, comic strips, movies and even celebrities they were created to promote.

These aviation characters, and the superheroes and spacemen who followed them, are like any other aspect of collecting; they're part of the bigger picture, that unique puzzle we only truly understand when we dig deeply into our past to understand not only the fun an item brought its original owner but the marketing effort behind it and the time and culture in which it was produced. They sprang from the accolades for Charles Lindbergh and other pioneers. They inspired a generation of dreamers, some who in turn flew to the defense of the civilized world and some of whom dreamt up their successors, the superheroes. They were both from and of real life. They became memories where they still reside, waiting to inspire us once more.

Lindbergh's triumphs, of course, remain as pivotal moments in history. As we celebrate his 100th birthday and the 75th anniversary of his famous flight, you might take a moment to contemplate what he started. His legacy in aviation is unquestioned, but if you love aviation adventurers, superheroes, or space heroes, give a nod to Charles Lindbergh in this year of celebration. He was the real deal, and he inspired them all.

***1941 Better Little Book #1417.***

*Editor's Note: A brief index of these characters and their location in this guide follows this article. If you have any additional items not pictured or other information regarding children's flying clubs, please contact us so we can include them in our next edition.*

# AVIATION CHARACTER INDEX

***Never before have collectibles related to flying been so highly sought after! Below is a list of categories included in this book that feature clubs related to flying. Many collectors have worked hard over the years to document this information.***

*1929 Air Scouts Pin.*

*1948 Sky King secret compartment belt buckle.*

*1943 Better Little Book #1438.*

*1933 Big Little Book #731.*

*1930s Hi Speed Photo Card.*

*1940 Bill Barnes #1 Comic Book.*

*1941 Captain Midnight Flight Commander Ring Offer Card.*

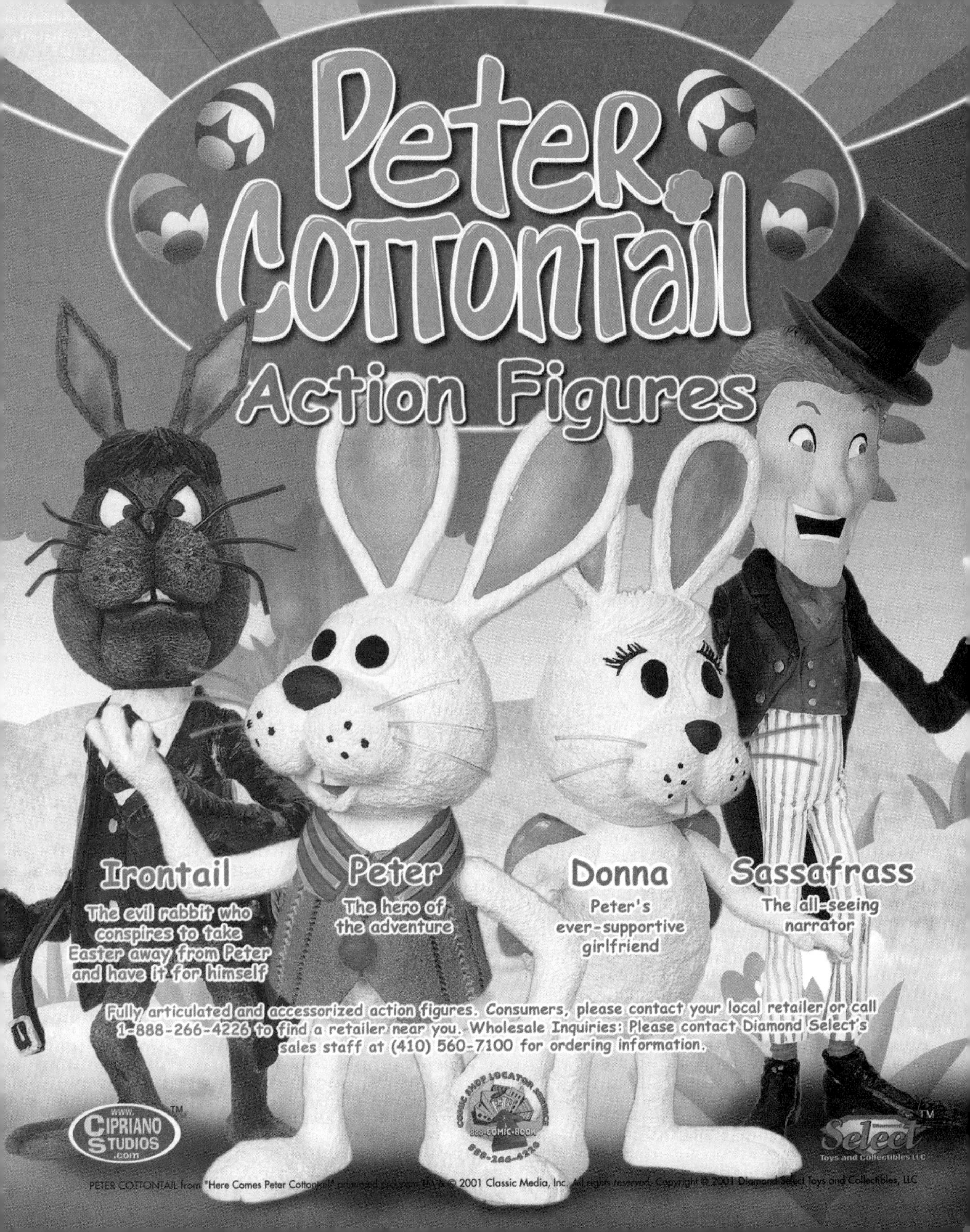
Peter Cottontail
Action Figures
Irontail
The evil rabbit who conspires to take Easter away from Peter and have it for himself
Peter
The hero of the adventure
Donna
Peter's ever-supportive girlfriend
Sassafrass
The all-seeing narrator
Fully articulated and accessorized action figures. Consumers, please contact your local retailer or call 1-888-266-4226 to find a retailer near you. Wholesale Inquiries: Please contact Diamond Select's sales staff at (410) 560-7100 for ordering information.
www.Cipriano Studios.com™
Comic Shop Locator Service
888-COMIC-BOOK
888-266-4226
Diamond Select™
Toys and Collectibles LLC
PETER COTTONTAIL from "Here Comes Peter Cottontail" animated program TM & © 2001 Classic Media, Inc. All rights reserved. Copyright © 2001 Diamond Select Toys and Collectibles, LLC

# ...And JUS

***It might not seem like the men behind the Junior Justice Society of America were taking a big risk. After all, they were following their highly successful formula of combining their top characters into the appropriately named All-Star Comics and the equally profitable concept of their Supermen of America club. Between a world at war and corporate in-fighting, though, things weren't as easy as they looked.***

## GATHERED TOGETHER ☆

When the superhero tide started, it took no time at all for it to become a deluge of super-powered, mystically charged, and flat-out weirdly attired crime fighters to become the norm in comics publishing. From the first appearance of Superman in *Action Comics #1* (June 1938) until the emergence of the Justice Society of America, the children of America found newsstands suddenly awash in superheroes.

Prior to the group's first appearance in *All-Star Comics #3* (November 1940) none of the publishers had cobbled their characters into a super team. In hindsight it's easy to wonder how it actually took someone so long to think of it. Numerous times during the preceding months publishers had put more than one feature character on the cover. By June 1940, Timely's Human Torch and Sub-Mariner, their two main mainstays, had done battle in a story, but it wasn't even close to the congregation of characters gathered together witnessed in *All-Star*.

The Flash, Green Lantern, Sandman, Hourman, Spectre and Hawkman had already appeared in other comics and were off to a rousing start (Flash and Green Lantern even had their own titles). Dr. Fate and The Atom appeared for the first time in the same issue that featured the team's debut, but by then there was a solid formula in place. If they weren't "can't miss" characters, they were at least close cousins.

Following the aviation-kindled boom in characters and character toys, Superman had been the logical extension of the collective imagination when he debuted two years earlier. Here was a man-like being who could throw automobiles, stop airplanes as they flew, and who was faster than a locomotive. That those three icons of the age's technology could be so easily bested by the Man of Steel was no coincidence. Through comic strips and pulps, in science fiction, adventure and crime stories, the fantasy characters frequently represented the pinnacle of development. Man, in whatever form, almost always succeed against the odds. Good most often triumphed over evil. Only the forces of nature were not subservient to man, at least not usually.

Compared to the times in which

*The first appearance of the Justice Society of America, in All-Star Comics #3.*

# TICE *for all!*

**by J.C. Vaughn**

they were created, this particular era of escapism makes sense. The prime consumers of this fare were children. The Great Depression notwithstanding, kids want to be reassured of their place in the world and the general order of things.

Like their predecessors in just about every other creative, fictional form of communication, the original superheroes lent themselves toward a child's interpretation of such archetypical struggles. It would not be so simple for very long.

Though replete with standard fantasy elements, superhero comics were among the vanguard in beginning to address the dark clouds then looming over America's future in 1940. Many yarns were filled with spies, saboteurs, action, adventure and patriotism. There were also numerous thinly disguised tales about the treatment of those trapped under the Nazi control. While the real world accounts that inspired such stories were often discounted or entirely ignored by the general media, they began to find a home in comics very quickly. Though played delicately at the time, this would soon play an important role in the Junior Justice Society of America.

As 1940 progressed, Belgium, Czechoslovakia, Denmark, Holland, Luxembourg, Norway, Romania, and a large portion of Poland had fallen to the Germans. Estonia, Latvia, Lithuania and the remainder of Poland had been overwhelmed by the Soviet Union, then Germany's ally. France, which with Britain had declared war on Germany after the invasion of Poland, was forced to surrender in less than 11 months. Germany, Italy and Japan signed the Tripartite Pact, officially creating the Axis alliance.

At home, the isolationist movement, though still vocal, was increasingly marginalized as war spread across the European continent. Conscription had begun in September of that year.

The escapism so prevalent in the years since Charles Lindbergh's Transatlantic flight and so vital in creating the entertainment giants of the Great Depression would now have to adapt to the new situation or find itself being perceived as entirely out of touch with the real world.

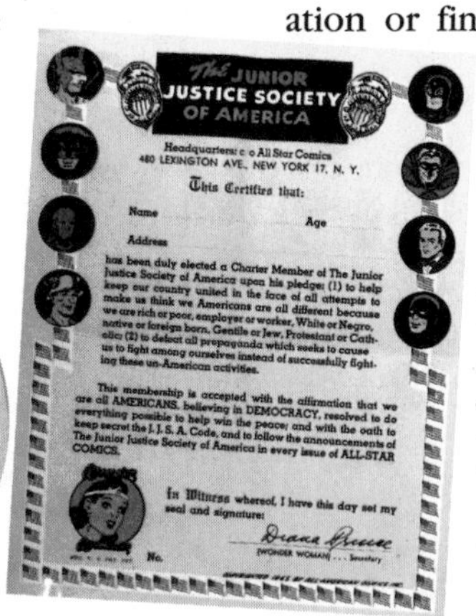


*All-Star Comics #12 (far left) featured the first ad for the Junior Justice Society of America. Each edition of the club kit featured variations of the decoder and membership certificate (left).*

### TWO COMPANIES, ONE FACE? ☆

Toward the end of 1938, comics pioneer M.C. Gaines entered into an agreement with DC Comics' Harry Donnefeld. Their bargain created a marketing arrangement that presented one public face to two distinct companies. DC and its new counterpart, All-American, both displayed the DC logo on their comics. Advertising cross-promoted the lines in each other's titles, and there was little to distinguish for readers that they were in fact not one company but two.

It has been noted that *All-Star Comics* came about following on the heels of DC's *New York World's Fair Comics* annuals in 1939 and 1940 (precursor of their *World's Finest Comics* title), particularly since the 1940 edition featured Superman, Batman and Robin on the cover. Whatever the actual genesis of the notion, it's not a huge series of leaps to go from co-cover features to team-ups to a permanent team-up.

Regardless of their direct or indirect inspirations, writer Gardner Fox and editor Sheldon Mayer are credited with coming up with the team. Through the DC/AA relationship, they were permitted to choose both DC and All-American characters to populate

## ☆☆☆☆☆☆☆☆ TIMELINE ☆☆☆☆☆☆☆☆

***It's difficult for collectors today to put themselves in the shoes of the late '30s and early '40s. With newspaper headlines and radio broadcasts forming an ominous portent of what was to come, an explosion of superhero comics flooded newsstands. By the time All-Star Comics #3 was published in November 1940, sizeable chunks of real world bad news had begun to add up.***

May 1936 –
Italian forces take Ethiopia

October 1938 –
German troops occupy Sudentenland, Czechoslovakia

March 1939 –
Germany takes Czechoslovakia

August 1939 –
Germany and Italy sign "Pact of Steel"

August 1939 –
Germany and Soviet Union sign non-aggression pact

September 1939 –
Germany invades Poland

September 1939 – Britain, France, Australia, New Zealand declare war on Germany

September 1939 –
U.S. proclaims neutrality

September 1939 –
Soviets invade Poland

September 1939 –
Germans, Soviets divide Poland

November 1939 –
Soviets invade Finland

March 1940 –
Finland signs peace treaty with Soviets

April 1940 –
Germans invade Denmark, Norway

May 1940 –
Germans invade France, Beglium, Luxembourg, Holland

May 1940 –
Holland, Belgium fall

June 1940 –
Norway falls

June 1940 –
France signs armistice with Germany

July 1940 –
Battle of Britain begins

July 1940 –
Soviets take Estonia, Latvia, Lithuania

August 1940 –
Hitler declares blockcade of British Isles

September 1940 –
Italy invades Egypt

September 1940 –
Conscription begins in the U.S.

September 1940 –
Tripartite ("Axis") Pact signed by Germany, Italy and Japan

October 1940 –
Germans enter Romania

October 1940 –
Italians invade Greece

November 1940 -
Hungary joins Axis powers

November 1940 –
Greece defeats Italian invasion force

November 1940 – Romania joins Axis powers

the comic. They did so, and the Justice Society was born.

Almost any thorough account of the period's incredible dynamic between publishers and their creators, as well as between publishers and their competitors, reads like pulp fiction. That might be why Michael Chabon's well-researched novel, *The Amazing Adventures of Cavalier and Klay*, wrung so true and eventually won the Pulitzer Prize in 2001. The relationship between All-American and DC was not as seamless as its public face, and there would be difficulties later.

## THE CLUB CONCEPT ☆

By the time the Justice Society of America was born, comic character clubs for children were no longer a new idea. While the exploitation of the information they generated was limited by today's standards, they must be considered not only as pioneering efforts, but by and large as incredible successes.

The reader participation concept for comic characters can in some sense be dated back to the Yellow Kid, noted as the first regular comic strip, which appeared in the *New York World* and subsequently the *New York Journal*. Created by R.F. Outcault, who also created Buster Brown, the Yellow Kid inspired theatrical productions, songs, and dozens of licensed products. The images on these items in turn directed readers back to the newspapers or the strip itself. A series of celluloid buttons in particular made the Yellow Kid part of a consumer's apparel and helped to create an early sort of brand identification generally associated with much more sophisticated marketing programs decades later.

The evolutionary course of the club concept became associated with comic characters as it developed through the newspaper comic strips, the pulps, comic books, and radio shows. A series of significant manifestations of the club concept corresponds directly with the marketing of aviation heroes (both real and fictitious) in the late '20s and through the '30s [*see the article "It's a Bird, it's a Plane... No, it's REALLY a Plane!" on page 40*].

The Junior Birdmen of America, one of those aviation-themed clubs, was one of the most successful. Starting in 1934, Hearst Newspapers successfully invited the participation of the nation's youth through at least 22 of their papers. By the time DC's Supermen of America club rolled around there was already an art, if not a science, to getting kids involved.

On the trailing edge of the Great Depression, before America's involvement in the Second World War, the Supermen of America was simultaneously marketing at its most cynical and most inspired. The readers of the Superman comic books, unlike the readers of the newspaper strip or listeners to the radio show, were overwhelmingly children. This club recruited Superman fans and enlisted them to recruit others. In other words, it took the standard advertising tactic of going straight to the kids and getting them to pester the parents into buying a product one better: it got kids to not only work on their own beleaguered parents, it got them to get their friends to work on their own parents, too. For successfully recruiting others, members received the Supermen of America patch, today one of the most highly prized Superman collectibles. This successful club continued into the 1960s.

## IDEALS IN A HOSTILE ENVIRONMENT ☆

*Text of the 1942 Junior Justice Society Certificate:*

This Certifies that: [Name, Age, Address] has been duly elected a charter member of this organization upon his or her pledge to help keep our country united in the face of enemy attempts to make us think we Americans are all different, because we are rich or poor; employer or worker; native or foreign-born; Gentile or Jew, Protestant or Catholic. And makes the further pledge to defeat this Axis propa ganda, seeking to get us to fight among ourselves, so we cannot suc cessfully fight our enemies – knowing that are all AMERICANS believing in DEMOCRACY and are resolved to do everything possible to help win the war!

It's next to impossible to understand the historic significance of the Junior Justice Society of America without placing it in its proper historic context. Rather than espousing a generic albeit genuine patriotism of many of their contemporaries, the JJSA certificate asked a few specifics of its members. Six months after the first class of Tuskegee Airmen graduated and six years before President Harry Truman ordered the integration of the U.S. military, the writers, editors, marketing men and their publisher all made a small but very significant stand. Half a year before race riots broke out in Detroit and more than two years before American troops came face-to-face with the realities of Hitler's "final solution" when they liberated the Buchenwald concentration camp, the folks behind the club not only wrapped themselves in the spirit of the flag, the Constitution and the Declaration of Independence, they asked America's kids to do the same.

What All-American Comics and DC did with the Junior Justice Society changed what could have been perceived as a cynical promotional ploy into something far more altruistic. And in doing so they took at least some risk, if not a great deal of it.

At that time and for decades to come it would not have been a prudent business decision in many parts of the country to suggest that "rich or poor; employer or worker; native or foreign-born; Gentile or Jew, Protestant or Catholic" would be on the same team. In an age when many of the men who created *All-Star Comics* could not gain access to a country club on Long Island, New York, let alone one in Mobile, Alabama, they decided that in order to "provide for the common defense, promote the general Welfare, and secure the Blessings of Liberty to ourselves and our Posterity," we had to be better than what was being thrown at us from across the Atlantic and Pacific oceans. In the form of this simple certificate intended for children, they held that "with liberty and justice for all" meant something, even

## ☆☆ TEN NOTABLE DIFFERENCES ☆☆ BETWEEN THE JJSA CLUB KITS

**1.**

The badge first appeared in 1942. It was replaced after two months by the first cloth patch. A second version of the cloth patch was issued in 1945 only. A second version of the badge, recognizable from its smaller lettering, appeared in 1948.

**2.**

The text in each of the letters changes to reflect the items included with the membership.

**3.**

Characters portrayed on the certificates change after the first two.

**4.**

Text changes on each of the certificates.

**5.**

There were three versions of the decoder, 1942, 1945 and 1948.

**6.**

The pamphlet, "Youth and the War Effort" existed in two versions with different fonts and layout. The second version was created for first 1945 kit.

**7.**

"The Minute Man Answers The Call" was a four-page color comic included in the kits. Two versions, 1942 and 1945 were produced (the latter including a reference to 1945).

**8.**

Neither "The Minute Man Answers The Call" nor "Youth and the War Effort," appear in the second 1945 or the 1948 kits.

**9.**

The War Savings Bond stamp album became a Defense Savings Bond stamp album for the 1945 kits. It was omitted from the 1948 kit.

**10.**

On the first 1945 kit, the return address on the mailers, letters and certificates changes, corresponding with the fall-out between All-American and DC.

if we as a nation hadn't quite worked out exactly what it meant.

They had a roadmap, a great one, in the guise of Supermen of America. They went another direction. Thousands of kids joined. The Junior Justice Society of America was a smash hit.

## THE CLUB KITS ☆

Over the years the kits themselves have been documented and re-documented, researched, photocopied, theorized upon and written about. They've been the subjects of many "definitive" articles and much discussion amongst comic book fans and other collectors. Each of the kits had differences, some distinct, some subtle. While it's relatively easy to theorize about the reasons behind the changes in each of the editions, one thing is certain:

There were five of them.

While it's been common to report otherwise, there were at least five distinct JJSA kits [Editor's note: You will find all five listed in our Justice Society of America section beginning on Page 484].

The original 1942 kit was issued for just two months before the membership badge fell victim to wartime metal shortages. It was replaced by a cloth patch featuring the JSA shield emblem. The original certificate was also modified. The phrase "White or Negro" was added to the pledge after "employer or worker" and before "native or foreign-born." It might not seem so huge today, but that was cutting edge stuff in pre-Jackie Robinson America. The letter was also changed to correspond with the membership items. Both versions distinctly mention Axis propaganda, and both were produced with DC's 480 Lexington Avenue return address.

The third variation of the JJSA kit was produced in 1945. On May 7, Germany had surrendered, but the Allies remained at war with Japan. In addition to the substitution of "enemy" for "Axis" in the wording, the certificate, letter and mailer from this kit are easily distinguishable because they used All-American's 225 Lafayette Street return address.

There have been numerous theories postulated about the ins and outs of the relationship between DC and All-American, ranging from the wild to the entirely plausible (including Gaines' ownership of vital paper contracts during the wartime rationing years making him an attractive partner to any publisher). While vagaries of the business dealings may be unproven, their effects can definitely be seen.

*The recent JSA pin and an example of the membership letter included in the JJSA kits.*

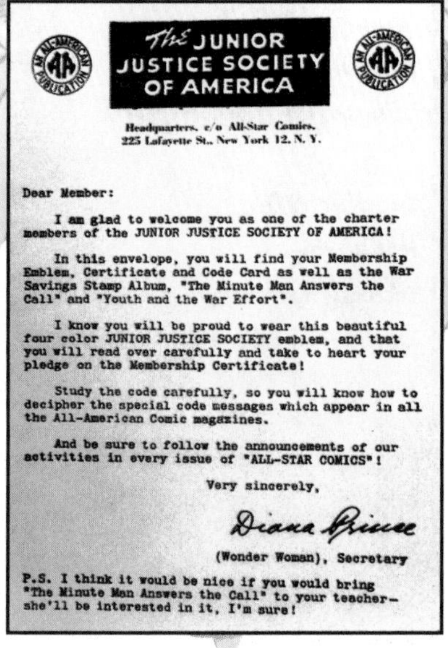

The JUNIOR JUSTICE SOCIETY OF AMERICA

Headquarters, c/o All-Star Comics,
225 Lafayette St., New York 12, N. Y.

Dear Member:

I am glad to welcome you as one of the charter members of the JUNIOR JUSTICE SOCIETY OF AMERICA!

In this envelope, you will find your Membership Emblem, Certificate and Code Card as well as the War Savings Stamp Album, "The Minute Man Answers the Call" and "Youth and the War Effort".

I know you will be proud to wear this beautiful four color JUNIOR JUSTICE SOCIETY emblem, and that you will read over carefully and take to heart your pledge on the Membership Certificate!

Study the code carefully, so you will know how to decipher the special code messages which appear in all the All-American Comic magazines.

And be sure to follow the announcements of our activities in every issue of "ALL-STAR COMICS"!

Very sincerely,

Diana Prince

(Wonder Woman), Secretary

P.S. I think it would be nice if you would bring "The Minute Man Answers the Call" to your teacher—she'll be interested in it, I'm sure!

With the first 1945 kit, it's clear that All-American had pulled back from their close relationship with DC. The use of the All-American return addresses on the certificate, mailer and letter, and the All-American logo on the comics themselves are readily apparent.

Later that year, following Japan's surrender on August 14, another version of the kit was produced. Among other considerable changes, the certificate's text about winning the war was replaced by the phrase "win the peace" and DC's 480 Lexington Avenue address reappeared for the remainder of the kits. In 1946 Gaines sold All-American to Donnefeld, and what had been one company in the public perception became one in reality.

Advertised in late 1947, the last documented rendering of the JJSA club kit was issued in 1948 and remained in use until the club was discontinued in 1951. For this version the certificate's text was completely re-written to eliminate references to war and included admonishments to follow the Golden Rule and to "never be guilty of prejudice or discrimination against a fellow human being because of race, creed or color!" It also included fewer items than the previous editions, discarding the war-related pamphlets and exchanged the cloth patch for the return of a silver badge.

## THE LONG, LEAN YEARS ☆

With only Superman, Batman and handful of others surviving during the next very lean decade for superheroes, it would have been easy enough for the idea of a super-team to fade away as well. Superhero clubs and club kits quickly went the way of the superhero in post war years, which is to say they almost entirely disappeared. *All-Star Comics* #57 was the last issue featuring the Justice Society. Following the then-current craze, the title became All-Star Western with the next issue.

In 1960, DC debuted the Justice League of America in the pages of *Brave & The Bold* #28. After a three-issue smash hit run there, they got their own title. Clearly inspired by the Justice Society, it took less than three years for the Justice League to feature their elder counter-parts as guest-stars. This cross-time crossover was a big hit with the fans and became a regular event. Comics from the '60s and '70s featuring these crossovers are among the most fondly remembered of the period for many collectors, and the early Justice Society appearances in Justice League of America sparked not only fan interest, but eventually a great deal of research into the history of the comics and the people behind them.

In 1976, DC took an odd step and revived *All-Star Comics* featuring the Justice Society. The oddity was not in the revival of the characters, but the numbering of the series. They started with *All Star Comics* #58, as if the 61 subsequent issues of *All-Star Western* never happened. This series lasted until 1978. The JSA appeared briefly in *Adventure Comics*, then was relegated to only the Justice League crossovers, one-shots, mini-series and other guest appearances until 1999.

## AFTERMATH & REBIRTH ☆

In the intervening years, those collectors with copies of these kits should have started sending thank-you notes to all of the mothers and kids who discarded their kits. In many of the cases, particularly with the later kits, less than 10 copies are known to exist.

When the 1997 re-launch of the Justice League, entitled simply *JLA*, proved to be a major hit, it spawned the 1999 introduction of *JSA*, the first on-going title to feature the Justice Society in more than 20 years.

With the creation of their DC Direct label, DC Comics launched a line of toys based on their comic characters. They included many different Justice Society items featuring the team, its villains, and a number of the individual characters. It had been a half-century since the last JSA collectibles other than comics themselves had been produced, which just might be the longest inactive period for any presently active characters depicted in this book.

Since the early DC Direct toys saw distribution limited to comic book specialty shops, many of these items will prove a worthy challenge to track down for JSA collectors who are only now becoming aware that their collection will no longer be complete if it ends with the club kits for Junior Justice Society of America.

## ☆ IMPORTANT DATES IN JUSTICE SOCIETY HISTORY ☆

| | | |
|---|---|---|
| November 1940 | All-Star Comics #3 | Justice Society of America formed |
| June/July 1941 | All-Star Comics #5 | Debut of Hawkgirl (1st costumed female) |
| December 1941/January 1942 | All-Star Comics #8 | Debut of Wonder Woman |
| | All-Star Comics #12 | Wonder Woman JSA secretary |
| December 1942 | All-Star Comics #14 | Junior Justice Society Advertised |
| March 1951 | All-Star Comics #57 | Last JSA issue |
| February/March 1960 | Brave & The Bold #28 | Debut of the Justice League |
| October/November 1960 | Justice League of America #1 | First issue |
| August 1963 | Justice League of America #21 | JSA appears for first time in JLA |
| January/February 1976 | All-Star Comics #58 | Revived series begins featuring JSA |
| September/October 1978 | All-Star Comics #74 | Last issue of revived series |
| 1986 | Last Days of the Justice Society | One-shot special |
| August 1992 | Justice Society of America #1 | Ten-issue mini-series |
| August 1999 | JSA #1 | New series debuts |

WE WANT YOU
© MARVEL
LEGENDS of AMERICA
AUCTION 2002

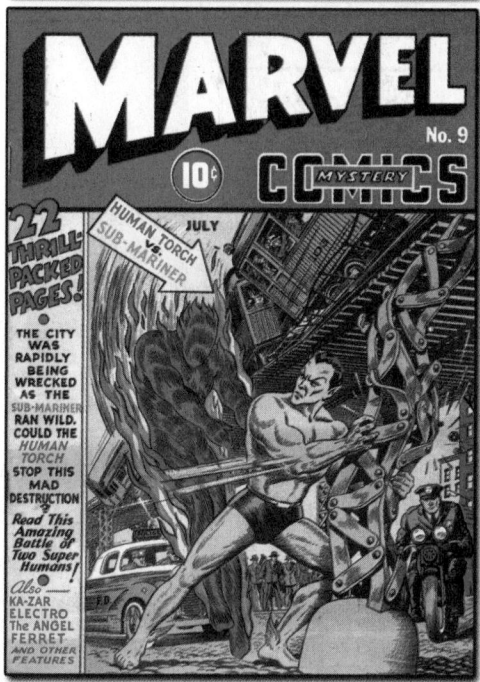

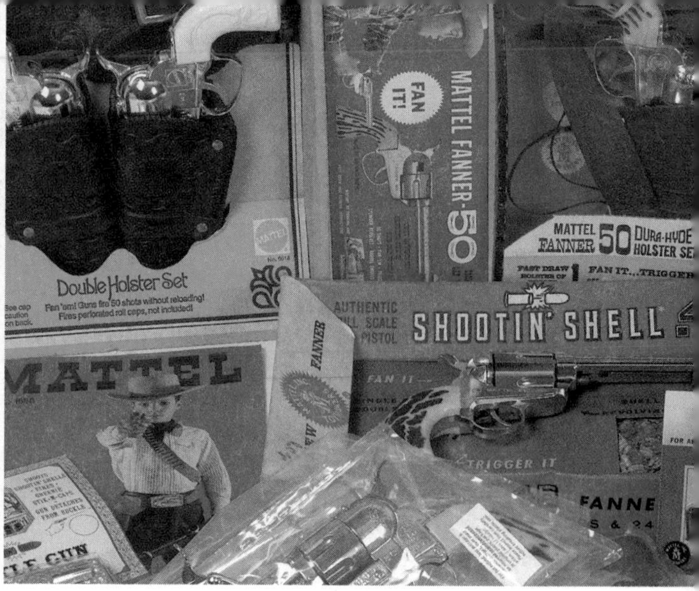

# Auction Your Vintage Toys With The Finest Auction House In The World.

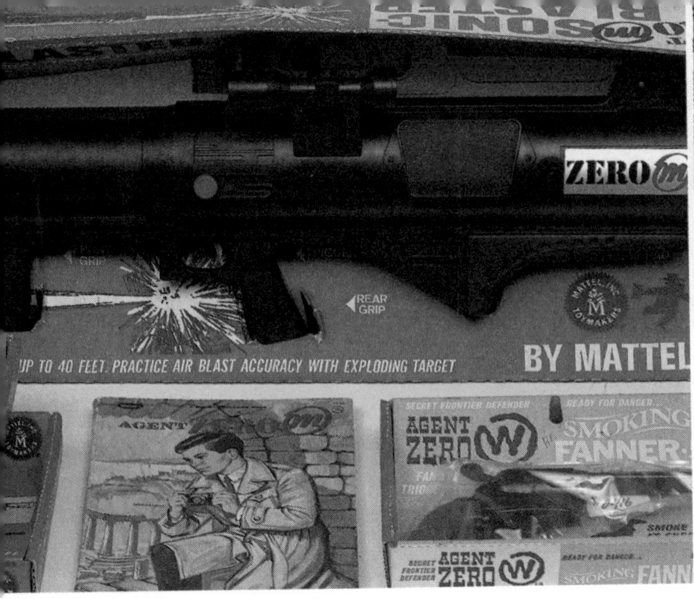

# MastroNet, Inc. Your Premier Source For Fine Collectibles

**No auction house can market your significant, high value collectibles like MastroNet, Inc.**

We offer the most ideal forum in which to bring high quality individual items and significant collections to the marketplace. MastroNet not only helps you realize the highest possible prices for your valuable material, we offer you the peace of mind that your consignments will be treated with the utmost care and that every aspect of the auction process will be executed with the greatest attention to every detail. MastroNet even offers generous cash advances for significant collections. And to provide the unparalleled service of a MastroNet auction event, we invest not just money, but the time your material deserves. Our goal is your total satisfaction with the presentation of your fine collectibles. We do whatever it takes.

**It's all in the presentation.**

Your material will be featured in the most beautifully designed catalogs with the largest circulation for any auction catalog devoted to any specialty field of collectibles. Every item is photographed in full color and accompanied by an in depth historical description. MastroNet has created the most sophisticated, secure, and user-friendly website in the auction world, the first to ever offer internet-telephone integrated real-time bidding. It has by far the largest traffic for any website devoted to any specialty field of collectibles. Catalog recipients and bidders include all museums, institutions, and collectors devoted to a given field of

collectibles who might be interested in your item(s). And MastroNet's highly regarded research and authentication services make us the favorite auction house among sophisticated and discriminating collectors.

## Man does not live by sports alone.

MastroNet specializes in the very best in all areas of collectibles, including: Baseball Cards and Memorabilia; Political and Campaign Material; Autographs and Manuscripts; Classic Original Illustration Art; Significant Comic Books and Original Comic Art; Significant Vintage Posters; Classic Toys, Banks and Games; Cigar Store Figures; Civil War and Abraham Lincoln Material; Significant Coin, Currency and Stamp Collections; Cause and Civil Rights Related Material; Disney and Character Items; Significant Movie Posters; Hollywood and Television Memorabilia; Music and Popular Icon Items–Elvis, Beatles, Marilyn Monroe, etc.; Photography; Significant Items and Collections In All Areas of Americana and Popular Culture; Single items and collections of all types of significance and value. Whatever high value collectible you want to sell, we can handle it for you.

## Generous cash advances. The finest presentation. Highest prices realized.

Whether you have the world's most valuable baseball card, a Norman Rockwell Painting, or the Rosa Parks Bus, no one can market your significant high value collectibles like MastroNet. Our only concerns are to offer your material in the most ideal manner possible and to make sure that the value of your material is maximized. Furthermore, MastroNet is a consignment auction house. Many other auctions are run by dealers offering material *they* own, exposing consignors to numerous unreconcilable conflicts of interest. *We* succeed when we do the best possible job for *you*. If you have material you think might be of interest, call us today at **630-472-1200** or visit us at ***www.mastronet.com*** and click on ***Consignments***.

MASTRONET inc.

**Your Premier Source For Fine Collectibles**

1515 W. 22nd Street Suite 125 Oak Brook, IL 60523
630.472.1200 fx.630.472.1201 www.mastronet.com

# Collector Buying Most Pre-1967 Comic Memorabilia

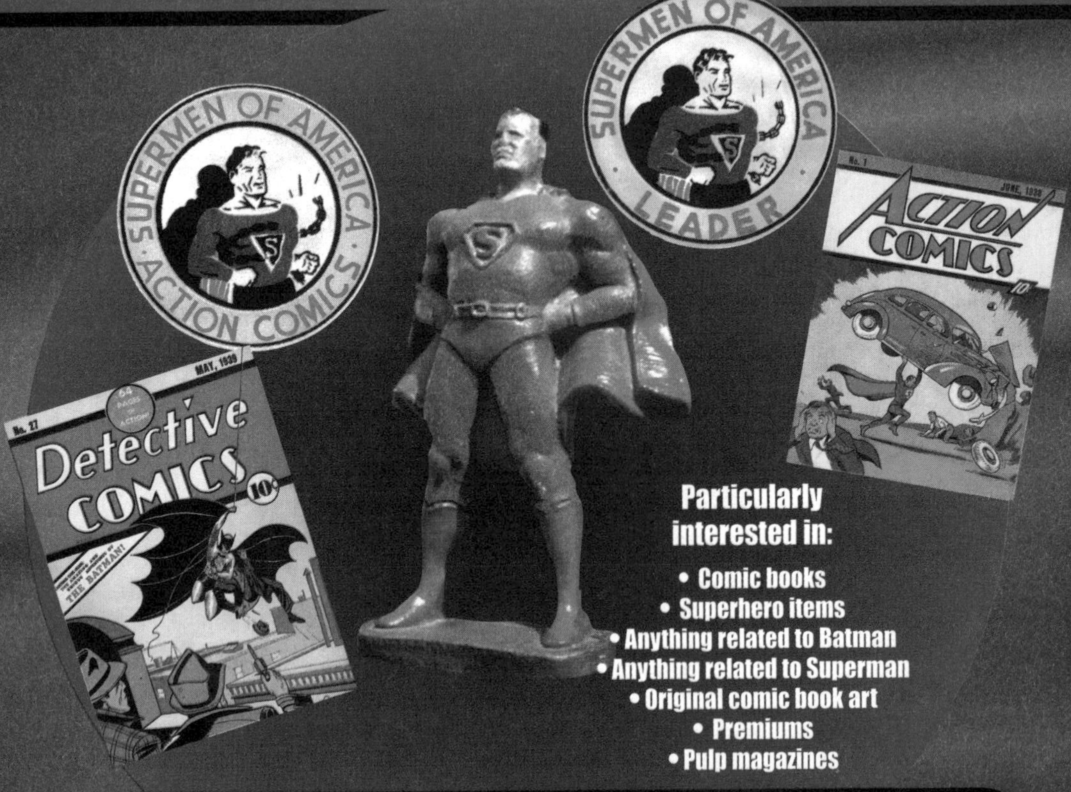


**Particularly interested in:**

- Comic books
- Superhero items
- Anything related to Batman
- Anything related to Superman
- Original comic book art
- Premiums
- Pulp magazines

## Why Sell To Me?

**This is a hobby, not a business. Therefore, I can and will pay more.**
**I will buy entire collections or individual pieces.**
**Immediate cash is always available for purchases!**

**Dr. David J. Anderson, D.D.S. • 5192 Dawes Avenue**
**Seminary Professional Village • Alexandria, VA 22311**
**Tel (703) 671-7422 • Fax (703) 578-1222**
**dja@erols.com**

# WANTED

## "The Snow White Gang"

### (Have You Seen These Characters?)

Snow White, aka The Little Princess, Dwarfs' Housekeeper

Evil Queen, aka Witch, Evil Step Mother, The Old Hag

The Seven Dwarfs, aka The Little Men, The Miniature Miners

## WANTED FOR THE FOLLOWING:

Cuteness, Innocence(?), High pitched singing

Attempted murder!

Mining without a permit

**If you have seen any of these animated characters in the form of concept art, drawings, storyboards, layouts, cels, or production backgrounds, please contact:**

**Steve Ison**
**317-872-0660(Phone) • 317-872-1480 (Fax)**
**SIson@sprintmail.com (Email)**

# HIGHEST REWARDS PAID!

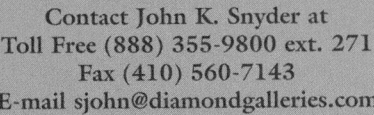

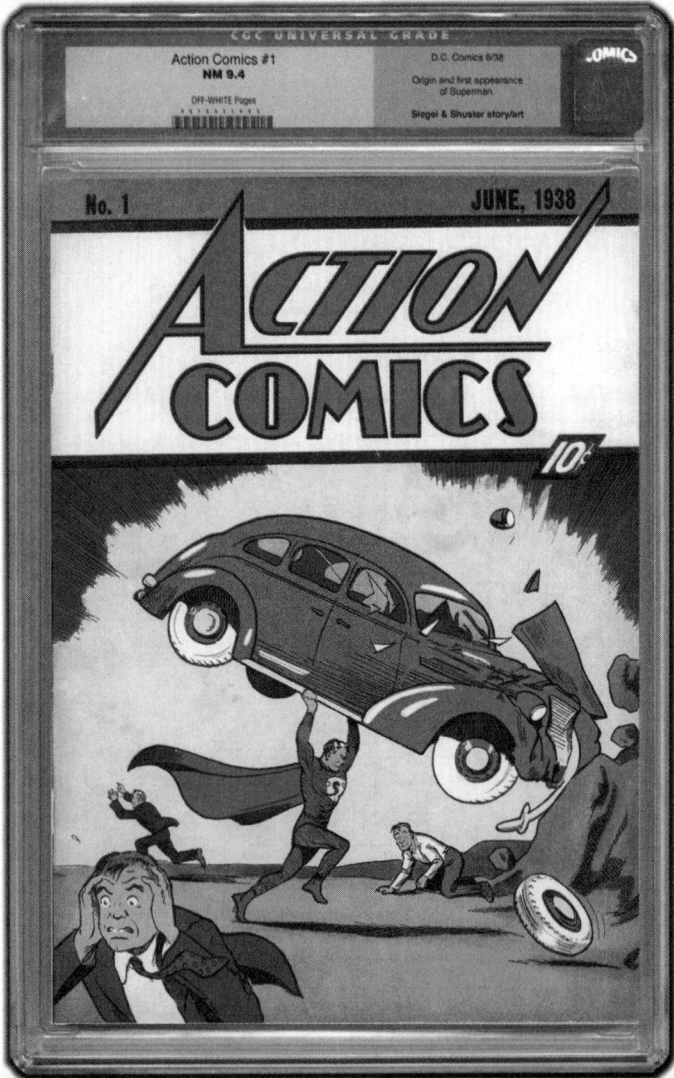

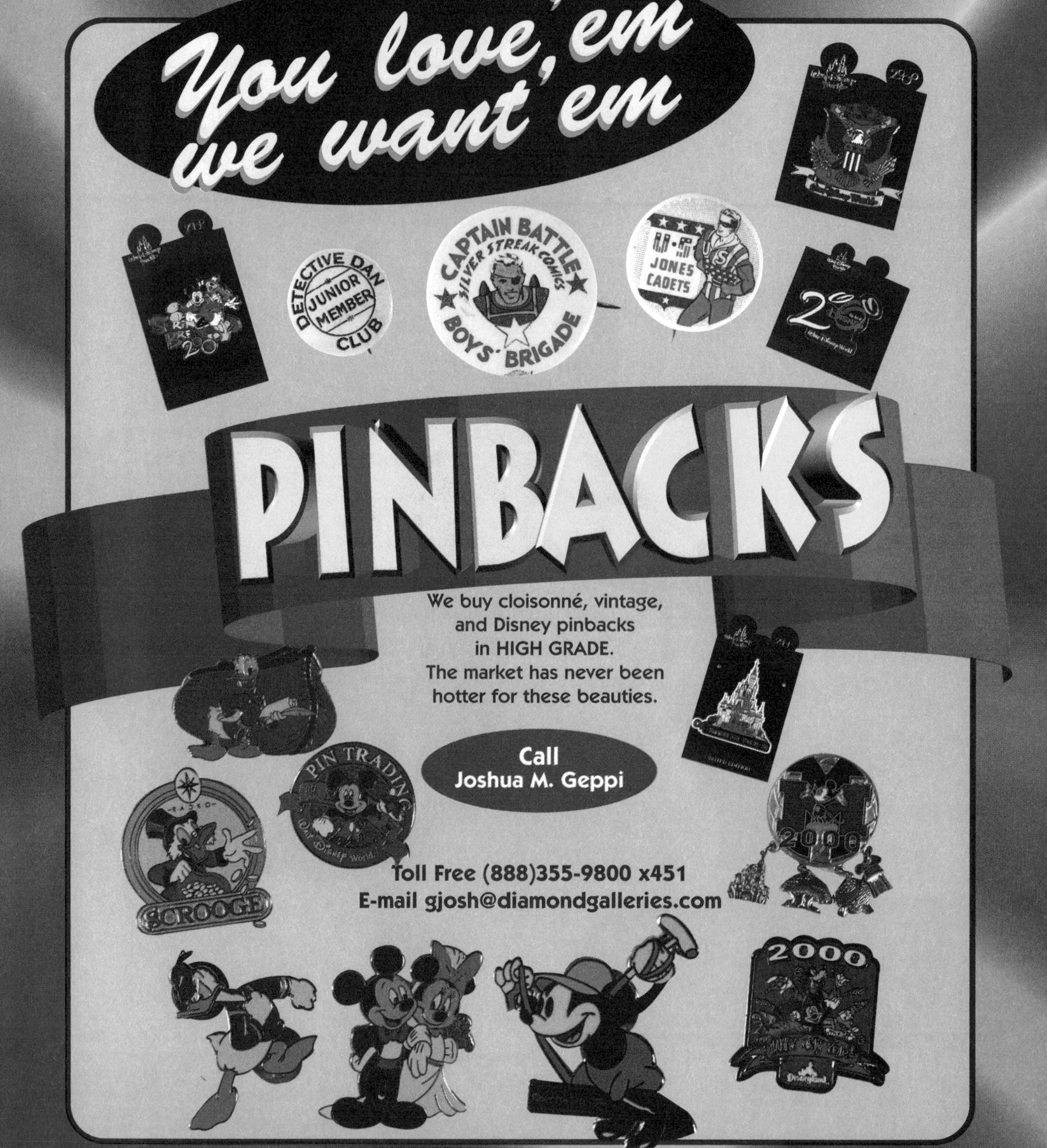
You love 'em
we want 'em
DETECTIVE DAN
JUNIOR MEMBER
CLUB
CAPTAIN BATTLE
SILVER STREAK COMICS
BOYS' BRIGADE
JONES CADETS
PINBACKS
We buy cloisonné, vintage, and Disney pinbacks in HIGH GRADE. The market has never been hotter for these beauties.
Call
Joshua M. Geppi
PIN TRADING
SCROOGE
Toll Free (888)355-9800 x451
E-mail gjosh@diamondgalleries.com
2000
2000

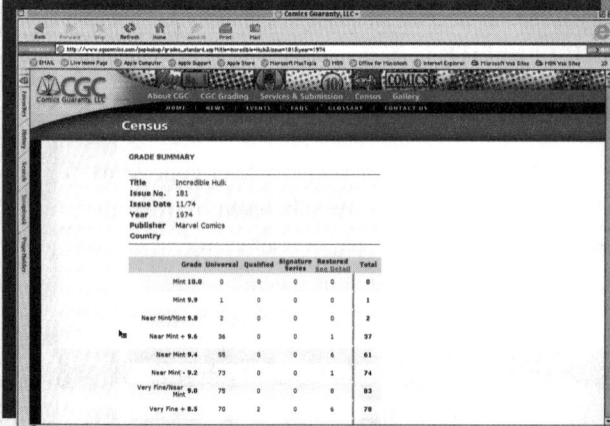

# CGC Offers the Most Services in the

Steve Borock

Mark Haspel

Paul Litch

## CGC Offers the Most Trusted Grading

CGC maintains a steadfast commitment to a standard of consistent and accurate grading. Our grading team is made up of the most experienced and widely recognized experts in the field.

## CGC Has the Most Innovative Holder

The innovative holder design is the most reliable means of safe storage for your comic books. Through extensive research and development we feel the CGC holder provides the most effective barrier from harmful elements.

## CGC Holds the Most Respected Endorsements

"CGC has made the grading debate at conventions disappear. As a dealer in the high-end market, I no longer spend hours debating on who's the better grader, because CGC has now set the industry standard."

**Bob Storms • Highgradecomics.com**

"So far CGC has shown integrity, good intentions, and above all, the desire to improve by listening to the people they serve."

**Matt Nelson • Classic Conservation**

"I am going to keep purchasing via mailorder and let CGC do my grading for me. Let me tell you mate, I have been burnt more than once in the past with overgraded and restored books. CGC is a godsend in that regard-thanks for your efforts."

**Ben Teoh • Collector (Australia)**

"I could go on and on about why I like Comics Guaranty, but the bottom line is that they are going to make this hobby a lot safer and a lot more fun."

**Mike Grissmer • Collector**

"The last 6 months the level of commitment to customer service and turnaround on graded comics has surpassed all of my expectations. The future of comic book collecting is CGC."

**Vincent Zurzolo • Metropolis**

"The level of accuracy, consistency, professionalism and beauty of the end product at CGC has revolutionized, energized and stabilized this hobby, lifting it to a height that would have otherwise been impossible."

**Mark Wilson • PGC Mint**

**For information on submitting your comic books call us or visit our website at CGCcomics.com!**

CGC
Comics Guaranty, LLC

1-877-NM-COMIC • P.O. Box 4738 • Sarasota, FL 34230 • fax: 941-360-2558 • www.CGCcomics.com

# THE COMIC ART PRICE GUIDE

- ▾ Pulp Price Guide
- ▾ Fanzine Price Guide
- ▾ Monster Magazine Price Guide
- ▾ Market Reports
- ▾ Huge Science Fiction & Pulp Artist Listing
- ▾ Special Color Insert
- ▾ Articles on how to bid at auction, buy rare original comic art and more
- ▾ Collectible Alex Ross cover art

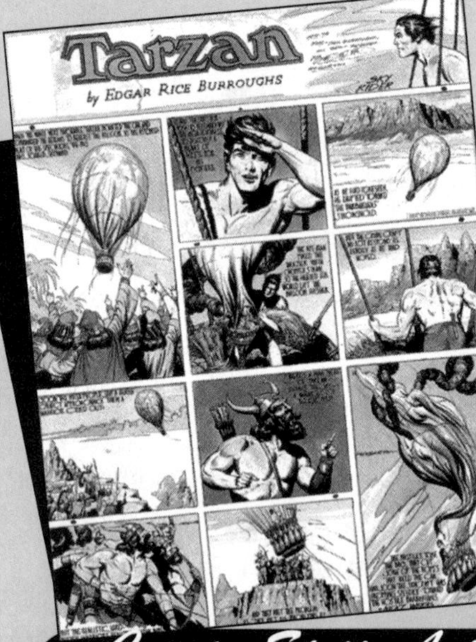


Tarzan ©2002 United Features Syndicate/Edgar Rice Burroughs, Inc.

*Comic Strip Art*
1942 Tarzan Sunday page hand-colored by Burne Hogarth.

Spider-Man ©2002 Marvel Characaters, Inc.

*Comic Book Art*
Jack Kirby's pencil recreation of *Amazing Fantasy #15.*

*pulps*

*fanzines*

*monster mags*

**Second Edition · By Jerry Weist · $26.95 Soft Cover · Hardcover $45.00**
**ISBN 0-9700922-0-2 · Available at a comic shop or bookstore near you!**

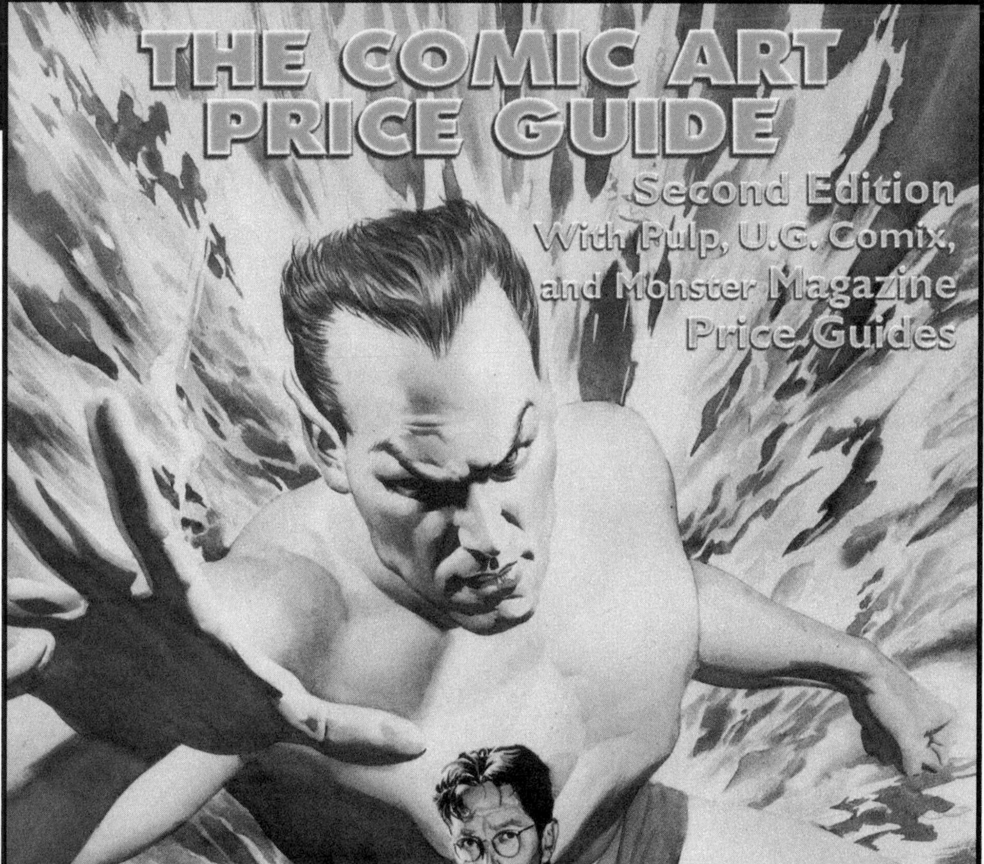
THE COMIC ART PRICE GUIDE
Second Edition
With Pulp, U.G. Comix, and Monster Magazine Price Guides
Jerry Weist

# Listen Up Y'All! There's A New Sheriff In Town...

# And His Name Is MastroNet, Inc.
# Your Premier Source For Fine Collectibles

**No auction house can market your significant, high value collectibles like MastroNet, Inc.**

We offer the most ideal forum in which to bring high quality individual items and significant collections to the marketplace. MastroNet not only helps you realize the highest possible prices for your valuable material, we offer you the peace of mind that your consignments will be treated with the utmost care and that every aspect of the auction process will be executed with the greatest attention to every detail. MastroNet even offers generous cash advances for significant collections. And to provide the unparalleled service of a MastroNet auction event, we invest not just money, but the time your material deserves. Our goal is your total satisfaction with the presentation of your fine collectibles. We do whatever it takes.

**It's all in the presentation.**

Your material will be featured in the most beautifully designed catalogs with the largest circulation for any auction catalog devoted to any specialty field of collectibles. Every item is photographed in full color and accompanied by an in depth historical description. MastroNet has created the most sophisticated, secure, and user-friendly website in the auction world, the first to ever offer internet-telephone integrated real-time bidding. It has by far the largest traffic for any website devoted to any specialty field of collectibles. Catalog recipients and bidders include all museums, institutions, and collectors devoted to a given field of collectibles who might be interested in your item(s). And MastroNet's highly regarded research and authentication services make us the favorite auction house among sophisticated and discriminating collectors.

**Man does not live by sports alone.**

MastroNet specializes in the very best in all areas of collectibles, including: Baseball Cards and Memorabilia; Political and Campaign Material; Autographs and Manuscripts; Classic Original Illustration Art; Significant Comic Books and Original Comic Art; Significant Vintage Posters; Classic Toys, Banks and Games; Cigar Store Figures; Civil War and Abraham Lincoln Material; Significant Coin, Currency and Stamp Collections; Cause and Civil Rights Related Material; Disney and Character Items; Significant Movie Posters; Hollywood and Television Memorabilia; Music and Popular Icon Items–Elvis, Beatles, Marilyn Monroe, etc.; Photography; Significant Items and Collections In All Areas of Americana and Popular Culture; Single items and collections of all types of significance and value. Whatever high value collectible you want to sell, we can handle it for you.

**Generous cash advances.**
**The finest presentation.**
**Highest prices realized.**

Whether you have the world's most valuable baseball card, a Norman Rockwell Painting, or the Rosa Parks Bus, no one can market your significant high value collectibles like MastroNet. Our only concerns are to offer your material in the most ideal manner possible and to make sure that the value of your material is maximized. Furthermore, MastroNet is a consignment auction house. Many other auctions are run by dealers offering material *they* own, exposing consignors to numerous unreconcilable conflicts of interest. *We* succeed when we do the best possible job for *you*. If you have material you think might be of interest, call us today at **630-472-1200** or visit us at ***www.mastronet.com*** and click on ***Consignments***.

**MASTRONET inc.**

***Your Premier Source For Fine Collectibles***

**1515 W. 22nd Street Suite 125 Oak Brook, IL 60523**
**630.472.1200 fx.630.472.1201 *www.mastronet.com***

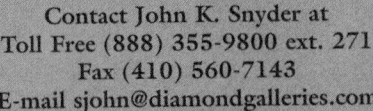

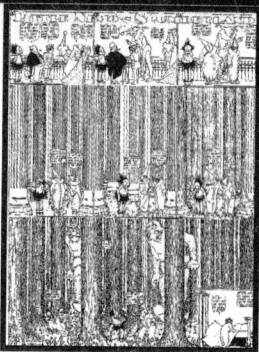

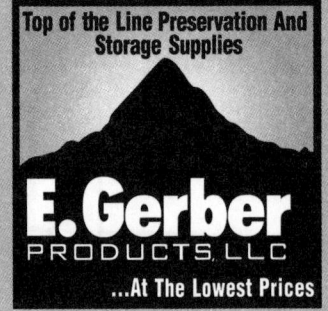

# SHOWCASE NEW ENGLAND

# $PAID$

**$400,000 PAID** in Canada, 1997

**$460,000 PAID** in California, 1998

**$140,000 PAID** in California, 1999

**$320,000 PAID** in Florida, 1999

**$157,000 PAID** in Milwaukee, 2000

## We pay amounts from

# $1,000 to $50,000

## EVERY WEEK

## for books we need.

**Call today for immediate response, no nonsense response!**

**BOOKS SHOWN BY APPOINTMENT ONLY • WEEKDAYS 9:30 a.m. - 5:30 p.m. E.S.T.**

**CALL DANIEL GREENHALGH TODAY**

*CGB Customer Service Award 1994, 1995, 1996,1997, 1998, 1999, 2000*
*Member AACBC Authenticity, Certification, & Grading Committee*
*Christie's 1994, 1995, 1996, 1997, 1998 Sotheby's 1995, 1996, 1997, 1998, 1999*
*Senior Advisor to Overstreet Annual Price Guide 1995, 1996, 1997, 1998, 1999, 2000, 2001*

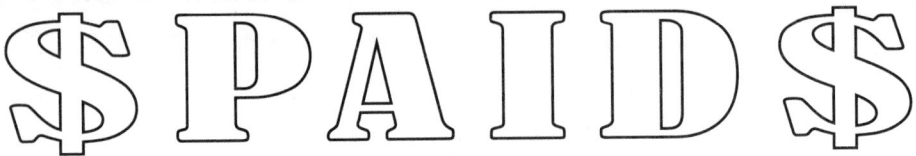

**67 Gail North • Northford, CT 06472 • (203) 484-4579 • Fax (203) 484-4837 • Email: comics@showcasene.com**

QUEEN & COUNTRY
BATMAN
ORPHEUS
RISING
ULTIMATE
SPIDER-MAN
mark ricketts'
NOWHERESVILLE
HAMMER of the GODS
MICHAEL AVON OEMING
MARK OBIE WHEATLEY
STAR WARS
TAG & BINK
ARE DEAD
RUBIO
MARANGON
SHUM

# *The* Magazine for Serious Collectors!

**CBM** is your gateway to the nostalgic past and the exciting world of popular collectibles! Get the inside story on the rarest, the highest-demand and the most undervalued **Platinum Age, Golden Age, Silver Age** and **Bronze Age** collectibles. **Comic Book Marketplace**... the magazine for advanced collectors!

CBM

A GEMSTONE PUBLICATION

*Ask for CBM at your local comic shop!*

Comic Book Marketplace • PO Box 469 • West Plains • MO • 65775 • (800) 322-7978



**www.ECcrypt.com**

# RUSS COCHRAN'S COMIC ART AUCTION

**Russ Cochran's Comic Art Auction**, which has been published regularly since 1973, specializes in the finest comic strip art, comic book art, and illustrations by artists such as Frank Frazetta and Carl Barks.

If you collect (or would like to start a collection of) classic strips such as **Krazy Kat, Tarzan, Flash Gordon, Prince Valiant, Dick Tracy, Terry and the Pirates, Gasoline Alley, Li'l Abner, Pogo, Mickey Mouse, Donald Duck**, or comic book art from **EC Comics**, then you need to subscribe to this auction!

To subscribe to **Russ Cochran's Comic Art Auction**, send $20.00 (Canada $25.00; other international orders, $30.00) for a four-issue subscription. These fully illustrated catalogs will be sent to you by first class mail prior to each auction. If you're still not sure about subscribing and would like a sample issue from a past auction, send $1.00 to **Gemstone Publishing, P.O. Box 469, West Plains, MO 65775**, or call **Toll Free (800) 322-7978.**

MD residents must ad 5% sales tales; MO residents add 6.475% sales tax.

Bill Hughes Paid You How Much?

# TAKE TWO!
## GET BOTH COVERS!

### THE OVERSTREET® COMIC BOOK PRICE GUIDE THIRTY-SECOND EDITION

SPIDER-MAN IN THE MOVIES • SUPERMAN GETS PATRIOTIC
ARCHIE AT SIXTY
MARKET REPORTS, KEY SALES & MUCH MORE!
The MOST COMPLETE LISTING of COMICS
from the 1800s to Present!

These covers available at your local comic book shop
or call (888) 375-9800 ext. 249 to order



GEMSTONE PUBLISHING

COMIC SHOP LOCATOR SERVICE 888-COMIC-BOOK 888-266-4226

# THE OVERSTREET INDIAN ARROWHEADS IDENTIFICATION AND PRICE GUIDE #7

By Robert M. Overstreet

- More than 8,000 photo images!
- Dazzling color section!
- Expert's guide on how to buy!
- Regional market reports!
- 1,136 pages!
- Much, much more!

**$24 SOFT COVER**

MD & MO residents must add applicable sales tax. Shipping & handling charges extra. Discounts available for quantity purchase. Please call for details.

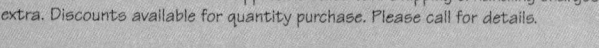

*Tales of Terror!* is a fully illustrated visual checklist, creator index, guidebook and more! Celebrate the legend of EC's "New Trend" titles with this full-color, exhaustively researched and meticulously detailed book! It's the perfect addition to any comics or pop culture library, and it's an absolute "must have" for even the casual EC enthusiast.

**Hardcover $39.95**
**Soft Cover $24.95**

GEMSTONE PUBLISHING

FANTAGRAPHICS BOOKS

COMIC SHOP LOCATOR SERVICE 888-COMIC-BOOK 888-266-4226

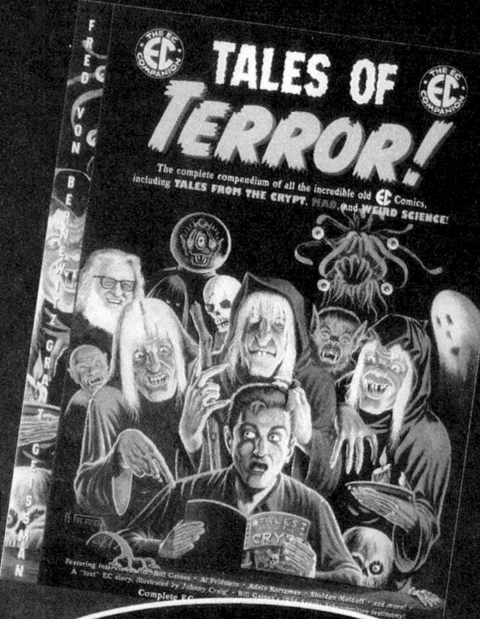




MD & MO residents must add applicable sales tax. Shipping & handling charges extra. Discounts available for quantity purchase. Please call for details

Available at a comic book shop or bookstore near you, or call Toll Free (800) EC-CRYPT (322-7978) to order direct from Gemstone Publishing.

# EC COMICS!

## SEND TODAY FOR YOUR FREE CATALOG!

VISIT US ON THE WEB AT
**WWW.ECCRYPT.COM**

ALL THE GREAT EC TITLES REPRINTED IN A VARIETY OF FORMATS! ACES HIGH · CRIME PATROL · CRIME SUSPENSTORIES · EXTRA! · FRONTLINE COMBAT · HAUNT OF FEAR · IMPACT · INCREDIBLE SCIENCE-FICTION · M.D. · PANIC! · PIRACY · PSYCHOANALYSIS · SADDLE JUSTICE · SHOCK SUSPENSTORIES · TALES FROM THE CRYPT · TWO-FISTED TALES · VALOR · VAULT OF HORROR · WAR AGAINST CRIME · WEIRD FANTASY · WEIRD SCIENCE · WEIRD SCIENCE-FANTASY AND MORE!

© DIS

© DC

© FAW

© DC

# COMIC BOOKS WANTED

**NO COLLECTION TOO LARGE OR TOO SMALL!**

**NO ONE PAYS MORE!**

**IF YOU HAVE COMIC BOOKS TO SELL, CONTACT US!**

**WE WILL TRAVEL TO VIEW LARGE COLLECTIONS!**

## Call Toll Free
## 1-800-229-6387

phone: (212) 260-4147
fax: (212) 260-4304
buying@metropoliscomics.com
www.metropoliscomics.com
By Appointment Only

---

- **Accurate Grading**
- **Competitive Pricing**
- **Large Selection of Golden and Silver Age**
- **Complete Want List Service**
- **New Approval Policy**
  (available to Want List customers only)

Will ship all books under $5000 to any want list customer without prepayment.

Payment due within 7 days unless other arrangements are made.
Time payments possible.

© MEG

© DC

© FAW

© MEG

# METROPOLIS

873 Broadway, Suite 201, New York, NY 10003
Toll Free: (800) 229-6387 or call (212) 260-4147 • Fax: (212) 260-4304
buying@metropoliscomics.com • www.metropoliscomics.com
By Appointment Only

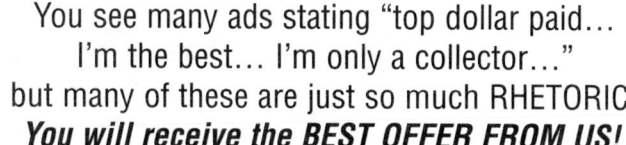

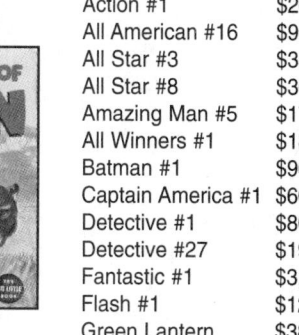

CROSSGEN
RUSE
1 $2.95

DC
GREEN ARROW
QUIVER

DAWN
Pin-Up Goddess

POWERS
BRIAN MICHAEL BENDIS
MICHAEL AVON OEMING
POWERS IS HIGHLY RECOMMENDED!

THOMAS YEATES
2001

BUYING
I WILL TRAVEL ANY-WHERE TO VIEW YOUR COLLECTION
HIGHEST PRICES PAID
IMMEDIATE CASH
NO COLLECTION TOO BIG OR TOO SMALL
COMPLETE CUSTOMER SATISFACTION
EXPERIENCED, PROFESSIONAL SERVICE
SENIOR ADVISOR TO OVERSTREET PRICE GUIDE
OVER 14 YEAR EXPERIENCE BUYING
SENIOR ADVISOR TO
OVERSTREET PRICE GUIDE
PROMPT, PROFESSIONAL SERVICE
SPECIALIZING IN GOLDEN AND SILVER AGE
CALL, WRITE OF FAX:
HARLEY YEE
P.O. BOX 51758
LIVONIA, MI 48151-5758
PHONE: 800.731.1029 OR 734.421.7921
FAX: 734.421.7928
WWW.HARLEYYEECOMICS.COM
CALL OR WRITE FOR A FREE CATALOG

# THE DEFINITIVE VISUAL GUIDE AND CHECKLIST!

**Gemstone Publishing is proud to present the Fourth Edition of the book the Maine Antique Digest called "...without a doubt the most informative price guide written." Hake's Price Guide To Character Toys is "The Definitive Visual Price Guide & Checklist,"™ - a veritable phonebook full of toy treasures from the past century right up through this year. Don't you know a fellow collector who would love this book?**

Hake #1

Hake #2

Hake #3

**First Edition - $24.95**
**Second Edition - $24.95**
**Third Edition $35.00**

**You can also get the historic previous editions of Hake's Price Guide for your collection. These remarkable volumes unfold the story of comic character collectibles before your eyes. Don't miss out as they become collector's items themselves!**

**Also available as sets!**
**Set A: Hake's Price Guide #1, 2 & 3 - $75.00 (regularly $84.90)**
**Set B: Hake's Price Guide #1, 2, 3 & 4 - $100 (regularly $119.90)**

Prices do not include shipping & handling.

# THE COMIC ART PRICE GUIDE

**Pulp Price Guide : Fanzine Price Guide : Monster Magazine Price Guide Market Reports : Huge Science Fiction & Pulp Artist Listing : Special Color Insert : Articles on how to bid at auction & buy rare original comic art**

## Collectible Alex Ross cover art

*Comic Book Art*
Jack Kirby's pencil re-creation of *Amazing Fantasy #15.*

*Comic Strip Art*
1942 Tarzan Sunday page hand-colored by Burne Hogarth.



EXPLORE THE HISTORY OF COMIC ART IN THE COMIC ART PRICE GUIDE!

*pulps*

*fanzines*

*monster mags*

**To order by phone call Toll Free (888) 375-9800 ext. 249**
You can also order by mail. Write to: Comic Art Price Guide, Gemstone Publishing, Inc., 1966 Greenspring Drive, Timonium, MD 21093.

Visa, MasterCard, Checks & Money Orders accepted.
MD & MO residents must add applicable sales tax. Shipping & Handling charges extra.
Discounts available for quantity purchase.

**Second Edition**
**By Jerry Weist**
**Softcover $26.95**
**Hardcover $45**
**ISBN 0-9700922-0-2**
**Available at a comic shop or bookstore near you!**

# BUYING ALL COMICS

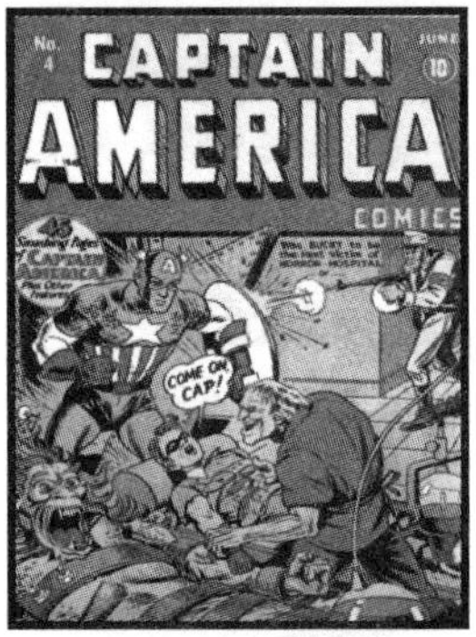

## with 10 and 12¢ cover prices

## TOP PRICES PAID!

## IMMEDIATE CASH PAYMENT

**Stop Throwing Away
Those Old Comic Books!**

I'm always paying top dollar
for any pre-1966 comic.
No matter what title or
condition, whether you have
one comic or a warehouse full.

***Get my bid,
you'll be glad you did!***

I will travel anywhere to view large
collections, or you may box them up
and send for an expert appraisal and
immediate payment of
my top dollar offer.
Satisfaction guaranteed.

**For a quick reply
Send a List
of What You Have
or Call Toll Free**

**1-800-791-3037**

**or**

**1-608-277-8750**

**or write**

**Jef Hinds**
**P.O. Box 44803**
**Madison, WI 53744-4803**

Also available for
Insurance & Estate Appraisals, Strictly Confidential.

Animation Art ~ Comic Art ~ Character Collectibles

Original Ink/Board Cover Art for Walt Disney's Comics & Stories #309 *

We buy, sell, and trade vintage and contemporary art and collectibles from all major studios.

Gifted Images Gallery, Inc.

7A North Park Avenue Rockville Centre, NY 11570

516-536-6886

*Price upon request

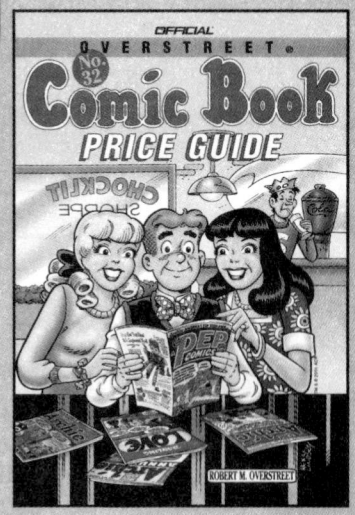

THE BIG BIG OVERSTREET® COMIC BOOK PRICE GUIDE #32
At a comic shop near you in May!
the BIG! BIG!
OVERSTREET® COMIC BOOK #32 PRICE GUIDE
ROBERT M. OVERSTREET
COVER BY ALEX ROSS
SPECIAL LIMITED EDITION!
8.5" X 11"!
STAY-FLAT SPIRAL BINDING!
LARGER PRINT!
ESSENTIAL FOR ALL COMIC BOOK SPECIALISTS!
For more information, or to order direct from Gemstone Publishing, call toll free (888) 375-9800 ext. 249
$35.00
Spider-Man ©2001 Marvel Characters, Inc. Overstreet ® is a Registered Trademark of Gemstone Publishing, Inc. All rights reserved.

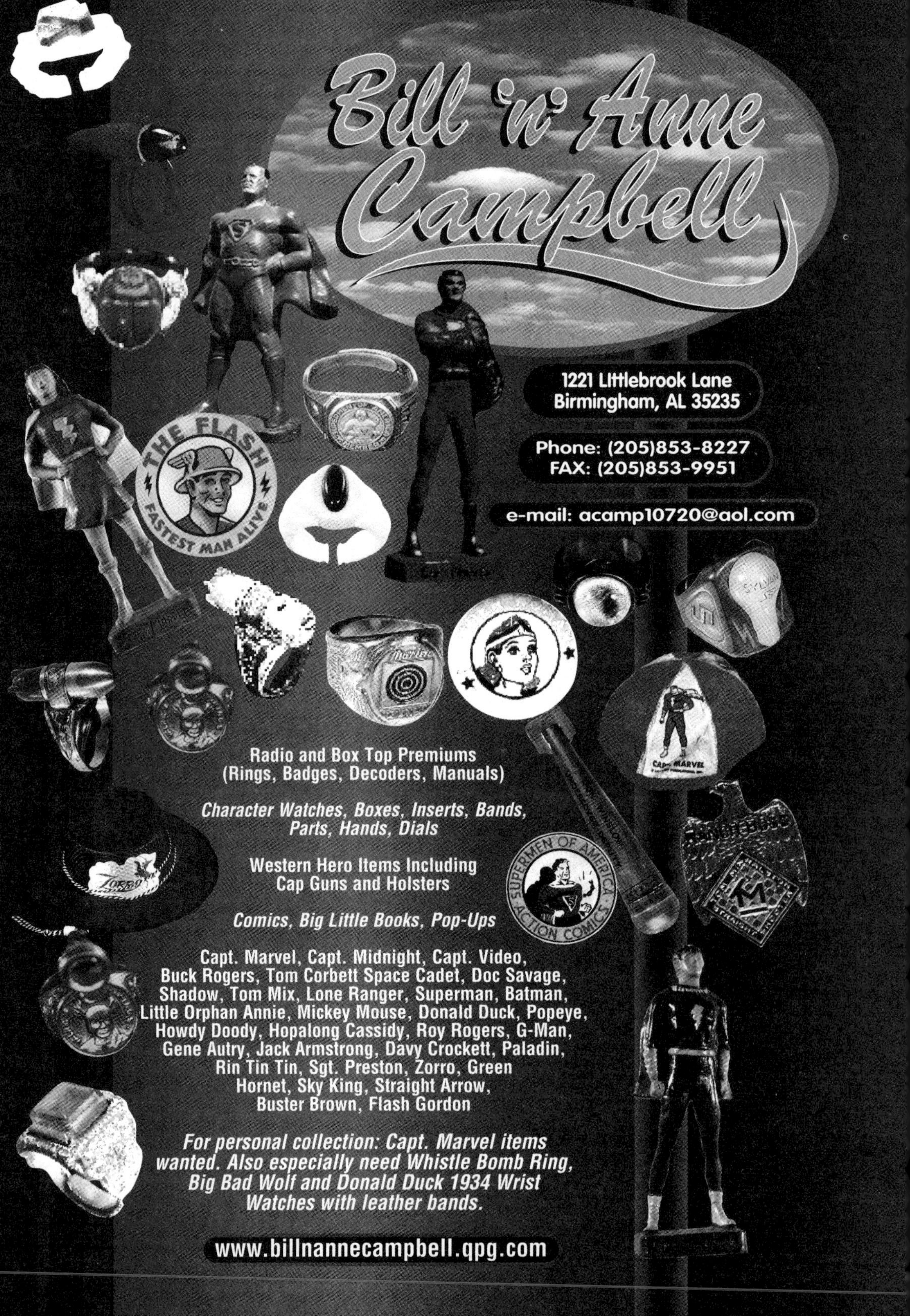

Bill 'n' Anne Campbell
1221 Littlebrook Lane
Birmingham, AL 35235
Phone: (205)853-8227
FAX: (205)853-9951
e-mail: acamp10720@aol.com
THE FLASH
FASTEST MAN ALIVE
Radio and Box Top Premiums
(Rings, Badges, Decoders, Manuals)
Character Watches, Boxes, Inserts, Bands,
Parts, Hands, Dials
Western Hero Items Including
Cap Guns and Holsters
Comics, Big Little Books, Pop-Ups
SUPERMEN OF AMERICA
ACTION COMICS
Capt. Marvel, Capt. Midnight, Capt. Video,
Buck Rogers, Tom Corbett Space Cadet, Doc Savage,
Shadow, Tom Mix, Lone Ranger, Superman, Batman,
Little Orphan Annie, Mickey Mouse, Donald Duck, Popeye,
Howdy Doody, Hopalong Cassidy, Roy Rogers, G-Man,
Gene Autry, Jack Armstrong, Davy Crockett, Paladin,
Rin Tin Tin, Sgt. Preston, Zorro, Green
Hornet, Sky King, Straight Arrow,
Buster Brown, Flash Gordon
For personal collection: Capt. Marvel items
wanted. Also especially need Whistle Bomb Ring,
Big Bad Wolf and Donald Duck 1934 Wrist
Watches with leather bands.
www.billnannecampbell.qpg.com

Bill Hughes Paid You How Much?

**Monumental Collectibles**

Specializing in Vintage Character Collectibles

MONUMENTAL COLLECTIBLES

P.O. Box 287
Westminster, MD 21158
www.monumentalcollectibles.com
sales@monumentalcollectibles.com
Phone: (410) 848-0275

Tom Gordon III

---

NOBLESVILLE IN RANDY'S TOY SHOP EST. 1987

REPAIR & RESTORATION
ON ANTIQUE TOYS
PARTS FOR TIN & CELLULOID
MECHANISMS REPAIRED
BOX & CARDBOARD
RESTORATION

WWW.RANDYSTOYSHOP.COM
RANDY@RANDYSTOYSHOP.COM
PHONE – 317-776-2220

165 N. 9TH ST.
NOBLESVILLE, IN 46060
FAX – 317-776-9007

---

*James F. Payette*
*Rare Books & Comics*

**P.O. Box 750**
**Bethlehem, NH 03574**

*Dealing in Old & New*
*Rare Comic Books*

**Big Little Books • 1st Ed. Books • Pulp Magazines**
**Sci-Fi Fantasy Material • Old Coins • Baseball Cards**
**TELEPHONE: (603) 869-2097**

---

**SPECIAL OFFER!**

Order **Hake's Price Guide to Character Toys #1-4, and save almost $20!**

These volumes include highly informative articles about the history of collectibles. Huge color sections.

**$100** (+s&h) **/ Save almost $20!**

**Call Toll Free (888) 375-9800 ext. 249**

---

**I'm Buying!** THE SIMPSONS

• Items in their original packaging •
• Foreign and Domestic •

**Michael Naiman**

PO Box 151029 San Diego, CA 92175-1029
(619) 698-6666 • E-mail mnaiman1@cox.net

---

**COMIC BOOK MARKETPLACE**

The monthly magazine for serious comics collectors!

CBM

www.eccrypt.com

---

**1116 N. Rolling Road**
**Baltimore, MD 21228**
**(410) 788-0900**

GEPPI'S COMIC WORLD

Comics, Games, Magazines & More!
New and Back Issues
Subscription Service
Special Orders

---

DIAMOND INTERNATIONAL GALLERIES

Always interested in high grade pre-1965 comics!

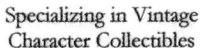

**Fax your list to (410) 560-7143 or**
**e-mail sjohn@diamondgalleries.com**

(PAID ADVERTISING - STORE LISTINGS)

The following businesses are paid advertisers in this edition of Hake's Price Guide To Character Toys and this list is provided for information only. When planning trips, it is advisable to make appointments in advance.

You can have your store listed in this directory for a very reasonable rate! For more information, write
Hake's Price Guide
Gemstone Publishing, Inc.,
1966 Greenspring Drive
Timonium, MD 21093

Fax (410) 560-7143,
call (410) 560-5806 ext. 249
or e-mail ads@gemstonepub.com

## ALABAMA

**Bill 'N' Anne Campbell**
1221 Littlebrook Lane
Birmingham, AL 35235
PH: (205) 853-8227
FAX: (205) 853-9951
E-MAIL: acamp10720@aol.com
WEB:
www.billnannecampbell.qpg.com
Online or by appointment only

## ARIZONA

**Key Comics: Discount Back-Issues**
P.O. Box 5035
Mesa, AZ 85211
PH: (480) 890-0055
E-MAIL: keycomics@hotmail.com

**Bruce Hamilton/
Another Rainbow**
160 Desert Holly Drive
Sedona, AZ 86336
PH: (520) 204-0086
Online or by appointment only

## CALIFORNIA

**21st Century Comics**
124 W. Commonwealth Ave.
Fullerton, CA 92832
PH: (714) 992-6649
WEB: www.21stcenturycomics.com

**Mile High Comics**
12591 Harbor Blvd.
Garden Grove, CA 92840
PH: (714) 741-2096
E-MAIL: gardengrove
@milehighcomics.com
WEB: www.milehighcomics.com

## COLORADO

**Mile High Comics**
Market Square Shopping Center
1155 South Havana Unit 45
Aurora, CO 80012
PH: (303) 695-9664
WEB: www.milehighcomics.com

**Mile High Comics**
760 S. Colorado Blvd.
Denver, CO 80246
PH: (303) 691-2212
WEB: www.milehighcomics.com

**Mile High Comics**
98 Wadsworth Blvd.
Lakewood, CO 80226
PH: (303) 238-8125
WEB: www.milehighcomics.com

**RTS Unlimited Inc.**
P.O. Box 150412
Lakewood, CO 80215-0412
PH: (303) 403-1840
FAX: (303) 403-1837
E-MAIL: rtsunlimited@earthlink.net

**Mile High Comics**
60 W. Littleton Blvd. #105
Littleton, CO 80120
PH: (303) 730-8160
WEB: www.milehighcomics.com

**Mile High Comics**
9201 N. Washington
Thornton, CO 80229
PH: (303) 457-2612
E-MAIL: thornton
@milehighcomics.com
WEB: www.milehighcomics.com

## CONNECTICUT

**The Bookie**
155 Burnside Ave.
E. Hartford, CT 06108
PH: (860) 289-1208

**Showcase New England**
67 Gail North
Northford, CT 06472
PH: (203) 484-4579
FAX: (203) 484-4837
E-MAIL: comics@showcasene.com
Online or by appointment only

**D-J Cards & Comics**
1 Lincoln Street
Corner Washington Ave.
North Haven, CT 06473
PH: (203) 234-2989
FAX: (203) 234-2103

## GEORGIA

**Heroes Ink**
2500 Cobb Pkwy NW, Suite A-3
Kennesaw, GA 30152
PH: (770) 428-3033

**Odin's Comic Bookshelf**
Killian Hill Crossing
360 Killian Hill Rd., Suite #G5
Lilburn, GA 30047
PH: (770) 923-0123

## ILLINOIS

**Graham Crackers Comics Ltd.**
120 N. Bolingbrook Dr.
(Rt. 53)
Bolingbrook, IL 60440
PH: (630) 739-6810

**Chicago Comics**
3244 North Clark St.
Chicago, IL 60657
PH: (773) 528-1983
PH: (800) 509-0333
WEB: www.chicagocomics.com

**Graham Crackers Comics Ltd.**
69 E. Madison
Chicago, IL 60603
PH: (312) 629-1810

**Graham Crackers Comics Ltd.**
2652 North Clark St.
(Lincoln Park)
Chicago, IL 60614
PH: (773) 665-2010

**Graham Crackers Comics Ltd.**
901C Lucinda Ave.
Dekalb, IL 60115
PH: (815) 748-3883

**Graham Crackers Comics Ltd.**
5223 S. Main St.
Downers Grove, IL 60515
PH: (630) 852-1810

**Graham Crackers Comics Ltd.**
2047 Bloomingdale Rd.
Glendale Heights, IL 60108
PH: (680) 894-8810

**Graham Crackers Comics Ltd.**
1271 Rickert Dr. 135
Naperville, IL 60540
PH: (630) 355-4310

**Graham Crackers Comics Ltd.**
610 S. Randall Rd.
(at Rt 38)
St. Charles, IL 60174
PH: (630) 584-0610

**Jaster Collectibles**
P.O. Box 30
St. Charles, IL 60174
PH: (630) 762-9350
FAX: (630) 762-9351
E-MAIL: ed@nearmint.com
WEB: www.nearmint.com

**Graham Crackers Comics Ltd.**
1207 Butterfield Rd. (Rt. 56)
Wheaton, IL 60187
PH: (630) 668-1350

## MARYLAND

**Geppi's Comic World**
1116 N. Rolling Rd.
Baltimore, MD 21228
PH: (410) 298-1758
FX: (410) 298-1727

**Cards, Comics & Collectibles**
100-A Chartley Drive
Reisterstown, MD 21136
PH: (410) 526-7410
FAX: (410) 526-4006
E-MAIL: cardscomicscollectibles
@yahoo.com

**Diamond International Galleries**
1966 Greenspring Drive, Suite 401
Timonium, MD 21093
PH: (410) 560-7112 ext. 271
FAX: (410) 560-7143
E-MAIL:
sjohn@diamondgalleries.com
WEB: www.diamondgalleries.com

## MASSACHUSETTS

**Bill Cole Enterprises**
P.O. Box 60, Dept.00
Randolph, MA 02638
PH: (781) 986-2653
FAX: (781) 986-2656
E-MAIL:
bcemylar@cwbusiness.com
WEB: www.neponset.com/
bcemylar

## MICHIGAN

**Harley Yee**
P.O. Box 51758
Livonia, MI 48151-5758
PH: (800) 731-1029
PH: (734) 421-7921
FAX: (734) 421-7928

## NEW HAMPSHIRE

**James F. Payette**
Rare Books & Comics
P.O. Box 750
Bethlehem, NH 03574
PH: (603) 869-2097
FAX: (603) 869-3475

## NEW JERSEY

**Legend Numismatics**
P.O. Box 9
Lincroft, NJ 07738
PH: (800) 743-2646
FAX: (732) 935-1807

**All-Star Auctions**
122 West End Avenue
Ridgewood, NJ 07450
PH: (201) 652-1305
FAX: (201) 445-3371
E-MAIL: allstarauctions
@mindspring.com
Online or by appointment only

## NEW YORK

**Metropolis Collectibles, Inc.**
873 Broadway, Suite 201
New York, NY 10003
PH: (800) 229-6387
FAX: (212) 260-4304
E-MAIL: buying@metropolis-
comics.com
WEB: www.metropoliscomics.com

**Philip Weiss Auctions**
1 Neal Court
Oceanside, NY 11572
PH: (516) 594-0731
FAX: (516) 594-9414
WEB:
www.philipweissauctions.com
WEB: www.appraisalforfree.com

**Gifted Images Gallery, Inc.**
7A North Park Avenue
Rockville Centre, NY 11570
PH: (516) 536-6886
Please call for appointment

**Four Color Comics**
P.O. Box 1399
Scarsdale, NY 10583
PH: (914) 722-4696
FAX: (914) 722-7656
WEB: www.fourcolorcomics.com

**ComicLink**
PH: (718) 423-6079
E-MAIL: buysell@comiclink.com
WEB: www.comiclink.com

## OHIO

**Bookery Fantasy**
16 W. Main St.
Fairborn, OH 45324
PH: (937) 879-1408
FAX: (937) 879-9327
E-MAIL: bookeryfan@aol.com
WEB: www.bookeryfantasy.com

## OKLAHOMA

**Want List Comics**
(Appointment only)
Box 701932
Tulsa, OK 74170-1932
PH: (918) 299-0440
E-MAIL: *wlc777@cox.net*

## PENNSYLVANIA

**The Comic Store**
28 McGovern Ave., Station Square
Lancaster, PA 17602
PH: (717) 397-8737
FAX: (717) 397-8903
E-MAIL: comicstorepa@juno.com
WEB: www.comicstorepa.com

**Duncan Comics, Books, and Accessories**
1047 Perry Highway
Pittsburgh (North Hills), PA 15237
PH: (412) 635-0886
WEB:
www.duncancomics.ohgolly.com

**Ted Hake**
**Hake's Americana & Collectibles**
541 West Market St
York, PA 17404
PH: (717) 843-3731
FAX: (717) 852-0344
E-MAIL: Hake@Hakes.com

## TEXAS

**Lone Star Comics**
**Books & Games**
504 East Abram St.
Arlington, TX 76010
PH: (817) Metro 265-0491

**Lone Star Comics**
**Books & Games**
511 East Abram St.
Arlington, TX 76010
PH: (817) 860-7827
FAX: (817) 860-2769
E-Mail: lonestar@
lonestarcomics.com
Web: www.mycomicshop.com/

**Lone Star Comics**
5720 Forest Bend Dr., Suite 101
Arlington, TX 76017
PH: (817) 563-2550

**Lone Star Comics**
**Books & Games**
11661 Preston Rd. #151
Dallas, TX 75230
PH: (214) 373-0934

**Lone Star Comics**
**Books & Games**
6312 Hulen Bend Blvd.
Ft. Worth, TX 76132
PH: (817) 346-7773

**Bedrock City Comic Company**
6517 Westheimer
Houston, TX 77057
PH: (713) 780-0675
FAX: (713) 780-2366
E-MAIL: bedrock@flash.net
WEB: www.bedrockcity.com

**Lone Star Comics**
**Books & Games**
931 Melbourne
Hurst, TX 76053
PH: (817) 595-4375

**Lone Star Comics**
**Books & Games**
2550 N. Beltine Rd.
Irving, TX 75062
PH: (972) 659-0317

**Lone Star Comics**
**Books & Games**
3600 Gus Thomasson, Suite 107
Mesquite, TX 75150
PH: (972) 681-2040

**Lone Star Comics**
**Books & Games**
3100 Independence Pkwy.,
Suite 219
Plano, TX 75075
PH: (972) 985-1593

## VIRGINIA

**Atlas Comics**
1750 Rio Hill Center
Charlottesville, VA 22901
PH: (434) 974-7512

**Trilogy Shop 1**
5773 Princess Anne Rd.
Virginia Beach, VA 23462
PH: (757) 490-2205
FAX: (757) 671-7721
E-MAIL:
trilogy1@trilogycomics.com
WEB: www.trilogycomics.com

To have your shop listed here in future editions, write Hake's Price Guide, Gemstone Publishing, Inc., 1966 Greenspring Drive, Timonium, MD 21093, fax (410) 560-7143, call (410) 560-5806 ext. 249 or e-mail ads@gemstonepub.com for more information!

# PRICING section

USC-50
(page 887)

The 21st century. Once that sounded like such an unattainable goal, such a sci-fi concept. But here we are, standing on the other side of the divide, in the realm of the future. There are no flying cars, no weather control machines, no amazing leaps in technology like we all thought there would be decades ago. Ah, but wait a minute...there are! Super-powerful home computer systems, DVD players, personal data assistants, a plethora of electronic gadgets for work, home and outdoor play. Many of them, particularly in the case of entertainment formats like DVDs, merely recycle old aspects of familiar pop culture for audiences both new and old. We haven't left the past behind at all - we've tricked it up with Dolby sound and digital resolution and brought it along with us.

This book is all about the past-all those characters, television shows, radio programs and films that meant something to us as we traveled the path from the 20th century to the 21st. It's about the artifacts that were left behind, the tangible things that are now bought and sold and traded, that remind us of happier times, or a joke that made us laugh, or a smile that warmed our heart. It's about joy, pure and simple.

There are those, however, who find this sort of fixation on the past a bit troubling. They worry that those of us who consider ourselves collectors-caretakers of our shared pop culture past-are focusing on the ephemera and not the more important emotions underlying the compulsion to collect. But as anyone who has read the articles in previous editions of this book can tell you, we've never been more aware or more appreciative of those feelings and the drive to seek out the artifacts that remind us where those feelings came from.

So is it wrong for us to cling so tightly to our childhoods and the childhoods of our predecessors? Those same naysayers and psychological experts would tell you that collecting is a peculiar phenomenon usually inspired by some sort of deep-seated trauma or lack of completion in one's formative years. A collector continually seeks fulfillment in objects in order to address some unresolved issue in his or her youth. A sad portrait of the collector indeed.

But perhaps it isn't about psychological damage or emotional gaps. Perhaps it's just as we stated before-collectors merely seek to accumulate things that remind them of the joys of childhood, all those simple pleasures that adults too often leave behind as they take up the larger responsibilities of life. In an age where children often grow up too fast, buffeted by images and experiences that force them to grow up before they are truly ready, retaining that youthful outlook or rediscovering it in our later years may not be such a bad idea. Age, as many have said before, is only a state of mind. Collectors hold one key secret to slowing down the inexorable march of time-surround yourself with reminders of what it was like to be happy and carefree.

So enjoy the fourth edition of Hake's Price Guide, and then go collect something you love. You'll live longer.

Arnold T. Blumberg
May 2002

---

TYPES OF MATERIALS CHARACTER COLLECTIBLES HAVE BEEN MADE FROM: Cardboard, Celluloid, Ceramic, Cloth, Glass, Leather, Metal, Paper, Plaster, Plastic, Resin, Rubber, Soap, String, Wood.

TYPES OF ITEMS INCLUDED IN THIS BOOK:

Action figures
Ads
Airplanes
Albums
Ash trays
Awards
Badges
Balloons
Balls
Bandannas
Banks
Battery toys
Bean bags
Beanie Babies
Beanies
Belts
Big Little Books
Billfolds
Binoculars
Blotters
Bobbing head dolls
Bookmarks
Books
Bottle caps
Bottles
Bowls
Boxes
Bracelets
Bubble bath soakies
Buses
Buttons
Calendars
Cameras
Candles
Candy
Candy containers
Candy machines
Car emblems
Cards
Cars
Casting sets
Catalogues
Cereal box premiums
Cereal boxes
Certificates
Chains
Charms
Christmas cards
Christmas lights
Circus premiums
Clickers
Clocks
Club kits
Coasters
Code books
Coins
Colorform sets
Coloring books
Coloring sets
Comic book stands
Comic books
Compasses
Concert programs
Cookie cutters
Cookie jars
Costumes
Coupons
Cracker Jack toys
Crayon sets
Cups
Cut-out books
Decals
Decoders
Detective kits
Dishes
Doll patterns
Dolls
Drawings
Envelopes
Eyeglasses
Fans
Fast food premiums
Figurines
Films
Fishing kits
Flashlights
Flickers
Flip books
Folders
Footwear
Forks
Friction toys
Games
Gasoline premiums
Glasses
Globes
Gloves
Golden books
Greeting cards
Gum cards
Gum wrappers
Gun holsters
Guns
Gyroscopes
Hair accessories
Handbags
Handbills
Handbooks
Handkerchiefs
Hats
Helmets
Ice cream lids
Ingots
Instructions
Jackets
Kaleidoscopes
Key chains
Kites
Knives
Labels
Lamps
Lariats
Leaflets
Letter openers
Letters
License plates
Lighters
Lithographs
Lobby cards
Locks
Lunch bottles

Lunch boxes
Magazines
Magic answer boxes
Magic sets
Magic slates
Magnets
Magnifiers
Mailers
Make-up kits
Manuals
Maps
Marbles
Marionettes
Masks
Matches
Mechanical toys
Medals
Membership cards
Merchandise catalogs
Microscopes
Mirrors
Mobiles
Model kits
Money clips
Movie premiums
Movie programs
Movie viewers
Mugs
Musical instruments
Napkins
Necklaces
Necktie slides
Neckties
Newsletters
Newspaper premiums
Newspapers
Nightlights
Noise makers
Notepaper
Original art
Ornaments
Package seeds
Paddles
Paint sets
Paper money
Paperbacks
Paper dolls
Paperweights
Party supplies
Patches
Pedometers
Pen holders
Pencil boxes
Pencil erasers
Pencil holders
Pencil sharpeners
Pencils
Pennants
Pens
Periscopes
Pez
Phonographs
Photo frames
Photos
Pillows
Pin Wheels
Pinbacks
Pinball Machines
Pins
Pitchers
Placemats
Planters
Plaques
Plates
Playsets
Pocket watches
Pop-up books
Post cards
Posters
Pottery
Press books
Printing sets
Prints
Product containers
Projection equipment
Prototypes
Pull toys
Pulps
Punch-out sets
Punching bags
Puppets
Puzzles
Radio guides
Radio premiums
Radios
Records
Ribbons
Rings
Robots
Rockets
Rugs
Rulers
Salt & pepper shakers
Sandbox toys
Scales
Scarves
School bags
Science kits
Scissors
Scrapbooks
Scripts
Sewing kits
Sheet music
Shirts
Show tickets
Signs
Sirens
Skates
Sleds
Snow domes
Soap
Song books
Spaceships
Sparklers
Spinners
Spoons
Sporting goods
Spurs
Squeeze toys
Stamps
Standees
Star finders
Stickers
Stools
Straws
Suspenders
Sweaters
Swords
Tags
Targets
Tattoos
Telephones
Telescopes
Thermometers
Tie bars
Tin containers
Toothbrush holders
Toothbrushes
Tote bags
Toy boats
Toy chests
Toy televisions
Trains
Transfers
Trays
Trucks
TV guides
TV premiums
Umbrellas
Valentines
Videos
Viewers
Walkie talkies
Wastebaskets
Whistles
Wind-up toys
Wrappers
Wrapping paper
Wrist watches
Writing paper
Yearbooks
Yo-yos

## A SPECIAL NOTE ABOUT TOY-RELATED ARTWORK:

In most of the categories listed above, original artwork featuring comic characters was commissioned and used in packaging, displaying, and advertising the toys. These unique and often highly collectible pieces of art should be considered as very closely related to the products they were created to market. Among these types of art are advertising, animation (in numerous forms), comic book, comic strip, packaging, poster, and puzzle art. Examples of packaging art can range from book covers, such as the much sought after Big Little Book or Golden Book covers, to the actual package in which a toy is sold. Several types appear throughout the book.

**Unless otherwise noted, prices listed for all items represent GOOD, FINE, and NEAR MINT conditions.**

## Ace Drummond

**World War I air ace Eddie Rickenbacker created the story line for this aviation strip, with illustrations by Clayton Knight, for King Features in 1934. The strip was not a major success and was dropped in the late 1930s. A 13-episode adventure serial based on the strip was produced by Universal Pictures in 1936, with John King as Drummond and Noah Beery, Jr., as Jerry, his mechanic. The serial was released to TV in 1949.**

ACE-1

ACE-2

❑ **ACE-1. Big Little Book,**
1935. Store item by Whitman Publishing Company. - **$15 $30 $60**

❑ **ACE-2. "Ace Drummond" Cello. Button,**
1936. Universal Pictures. For 13-chapter movie serial "Ace Drummond" with added inscription "Capt. Eddie Rickenbacker's Junior Pilot's Club". - **$50 $150 $275**

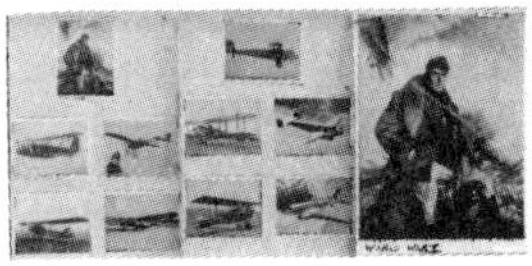

ACE-3

❑ **ACE-3. Movie Theater Giveaway Cards,**
1936. Universal Pictures. Ten shown from unnumbered set of 12. Each 2-3/8x3-1/4" browntone photo card. One depicts "Captain Eddie Rickenbacker" while others depict "Air Transport Progress." Examples seen have red ink stamp on reverse with theater name and starting date of serial. Each **- $3 $10 $20**

## Admiral Byrd

**Richard E. Byrd (1888-1957), American aviator and preeminent polar explorer, flew to the North Pole and back in 1926, made a spectacular transatlantic flight in 1927, and starting in 1928, led several important expeditions to Antarctica. The second such expedition featured weekly on-site short wave broadcasts--*The Adventures of Admiral Byrd*--over the CBS network from November 1933 to January 1935. The program was sponsored by Grape-Nuts Flakes.**

ADM-1

❑ **ADM-1. "Conquerers Of The North Pole" Pamphlet,**
c. 1927. Issued by John Wanamaker stores. Opens to 7-1/2x13-1/2". **- $15 $25 $40**

ADM-2

❑ **ADM-2. Antarctic Expedition Medal,**
1928-1930. Features Admiral Byrd on front and an image of his plane with #NX4542 on wing. This was the plane that flew over the South Pole. - **$10 $20 $30**

ADM-3

ADM-4

❑ **ADM-3. Commander Byrd Cello. Button,**
c. 1928. Identified "Commander Richard E. Byrd". - **$10 $25 $35**

❑ **ADM-4. Admiral Byrd Cello. Button,**
c. 1930. Profile picture inscribed "Rear Admiral Richard Evelyn Byrd, U.S.N." - **$15 $30 $45**

ADM-5

❑ **ADM-5. "Commander Byrd's 'Floyd Bennett'" Cello. Buttons,**
1931. Bond Bread. 1-1/4" blue, black and white from set of six buttons picturing airplanes of famous aviators. One set has blank top rims while the second set has slogans promoting the virtues of bread. Second set is scarcer and images are the same as on the first set except button #4 pictures an autogiro.
Byrd Blank Rim - **$5 $15 $25**
Byrd Slogan Rim - **$8 $20 $35**

ADM-6

❑ **ADM-6. "Famous Flyers" Book with Dust Jacket,**
1931. Features Admiral Byrd on the cover and has a 46 page story of his life. - **$20 $40 $60**

ADM-7

❑ **ADM-7. Admiral Byrd Radio Promo,**
1933. Scarce. Radio promo for gift map offered when you send 2 tops from Grape-Nuts packages. - **$20 $40 $75**

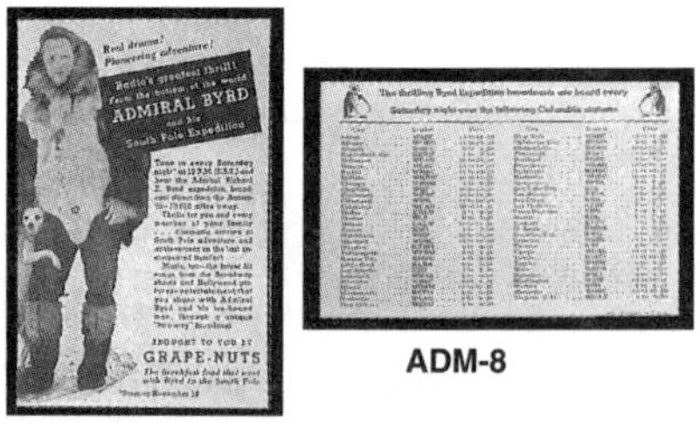


ADM-8

❑ **ADM-8. Radio Station Schedule Flyer,**
c. 1933. Grape-Nuts. 3-1/2x5" with reverse listing of many cities, station call letters and times when the broadcasts were heard over Columbia stations. - **$10 $25 $50**

ADM-9

❑ **ADM-9. "Authorized Map Of The Second Byrd Antarctic Expedition",**
c. 1933. General Foods. 18x24" opened. - **$25 $70 $100**

ADM-10

❑ **ADM-10. "Little America Aviation & Exploration Club" Member's Card,**
1933. Sponsor unknown. Card is dated 1933-34 and has facsimile signature of "C. A. Abele Jr., President/With Byrd, At The South Pole." - **$15 $30 $50**

(FRONT ENLARGED)

ADM-11

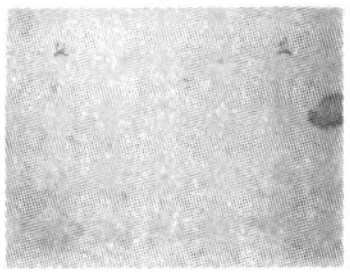
(BACK)

❑ **ADM-11. Byrd Map Hard Cardboard Version,**
c. 1933. Thick cardboard back with two hangers. - **$50 $100 $150**

ADM-12

❑ **ADM-12. "Trail Blazers" Watch,**
c. 1933. - **$250 $450 $700**

ADM-13

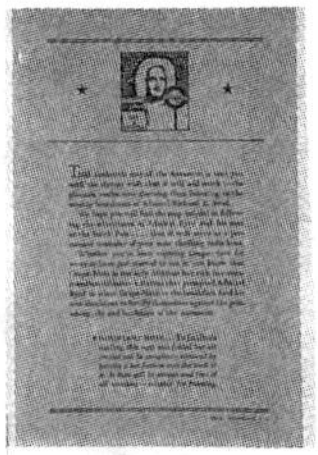
ADM-14

❑ **ADM-13. "South Pole Radio News" Photo Newspaper,**
c. 1933. Grape-Nuts, "The Cereal Byrd Took To Little America". Issue #3 shown. At least three issues known.
Each - **$20 $40 $75**

❑ **ADM-14. Map Flyer,**
1933. Grape Nuts Cereal premium. Talks about receiving and using the map. - **$5 $15 $25**

ADM-15

❑ **ADM-15. "To The South Pole With Byrd" Booklet,**
1933. Ralston Purina Co. - **$15 $25 $35**

ADM-16

❑ **ADM-16. South Pole Radio News #2,**
1933. Grape Nuts Cereal premium. - **$15 $35 $70**

ADM-17

❑ **ADM-17. "South Pole Picture Book,"**
1934. Softcover with 32 pages. Carries copyright of Capt. Ashley McKinley, third-in-command of the expedition. - **$5 $15 $30**

ADM-18

❑ **ADM-18. "The Romance Of Antarctic Adventure" Expedition Summary Book,**
1935. 48 pages. Includes numerous ads for food and household products. - **$10 $20 $35**

ADM-19

ADM-20

❑ **ADM-19. Byrd Expedition-Guernsey Club Award Medal,**
1935. 2-1/2" bronze with reverse text "For Distinguished Service To The Dairy Industry-In Commemoration By The American Guernsey Cattle Club May, 1935." Depicted cow was born December 19, 1933 during the second expedition, the farthest south recorded birth of any dairy animal. - **$20 $35 $60**

❑ **ADM-20. Magazine Cover Article,**
1936. May issue of "The Open Road For Boys" with article and photos from his 1929 expedition to Little America of South Pole. - **$10 $15 $25**

ADM-21

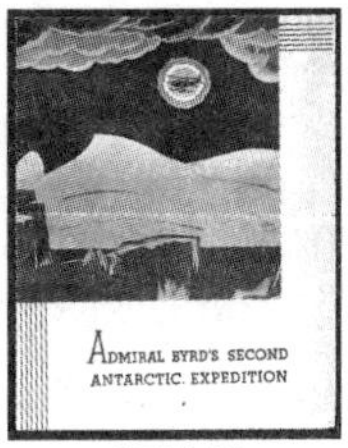

ADM-22

❑ **ADM-21. Blotter,**
1930s. Golden Guernsey Milk premium. - **$30 $50 $85**

❑ **ADM-22. Admiral Byrd Grape Nuts Booklet,**
1930s. - **$20 $40 $60**

ADM-23

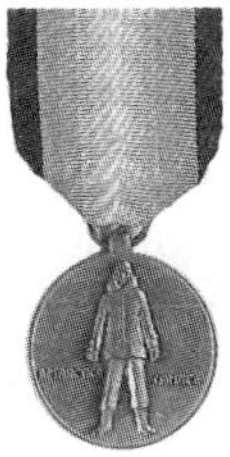
ADM-24

❑ **ADM-23. "Welcome Home" Cello. Button,**
1930s. Black and white 1-1/4". - **$15 $30 $50**

❑ **ADM-24. "Antarctica Service" Award Medal,**
1930s. Bar pin holds ribbon in shades of blue joined to 1-1/4" brass metal inscribed on reverse "Courage/Sacrifice/Devotion." - **$40 $70 $125**

## Adventure Comics

**Major Malcolm Wheeler-Nicholson got into the comic book publishing business in early 1935 with *New Fun*. Although sales weren't very good, he decided to try a second title. *New Comics* #1 appeared in late 1935 with paper covers and 80 pages of color and black and white stories and art. Siegel and Shuster did Federal Men and Sheldon Mayer and Walt Kelly also contributed. Starting with issue #12, the title became *New Adventure* and finally *Adventure Comics* with issue #32. Like *New Fun*, *Adventure Comics* was part of the foundation of DC Comics. DC cancelled the title in 1983.**

ADC-1

ADC-2

ADC-3

❑ **ADC-1. "Special Operator" Cello. Button,**
c. 1937. New Adventure Comics magazine. - **$50 $100 $250**

❑ **ADC-2. Club Member Cello. Button,**
c. 1937. Inscribed "Special Operator/Junior Federal Men Club/New Adventure Comics Magazine." - **$50 $100 $250**

❑ **ADC-3. "Special Operator" Cello. Button,**
c. 1939. Adventure Comics magazine. - **$100 $200 $450**

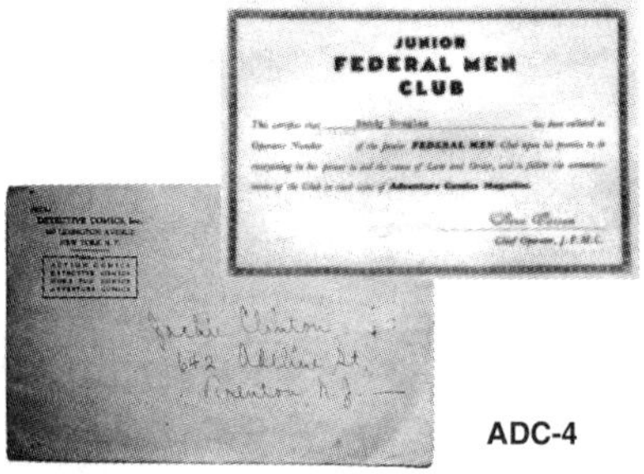


ADC-4

❑ **ADC-4. "Junior Federal Men Club" Member Certificate and Mailer,**
c. 1939. Adventure Comics magazine. Ink stamped Chief Operator's name "Steve Carson". Certificate - **$100 $200 $300**
Mailer - **$25 $50 $100**

## Advertising Misc.

**Literally thousands of product makers in the past century have offered premiums in token or sporadic fashion. An absolute listing of all known advertising premiums would necessitate a massive set of volumes in book form while still leaving gaps of information lost in time. This section offers an overview of advertising premiums and similar items of established appeal to collectors. Represented are some of the most famous trademark characters of our popular culture. A more comprehensive listing is contained in *Hake's Guide To Advertising Collectibles/100 Years of Advertising From 100 Famous Companies* published in 1992.**

ADV-1

❑ **ADV-1. Hires Easel Card,**
1892. 5x6-1/2" diecut small counter sign with full color image. - **$50 $100 $175**

ADV-2

ADV-3

❑ **ADV-2. Friends Oats Promo Booklet,**
1800s. Uses children to promote cereal products. - **$20 $40 $60**

❑ **ADV-3. J & P Coats Promo Calendar,**
1888. Thread ad shows dogs reading paper. Classic example of animals being used to promote products. - **$8 $15 $28**

ADV-4

ADV-5

❑ **ADV-4. J & P Coats Promo Card,**
1880s. Thread ad shows captured lion. Early use of animals, later used cartoon characters. - **$8 $15 $28**

❑ **ADV-5. J & P Coats Promo Card,**
1880s. Thread ad shows mice dressed up on front. Calendar on back. - **$8 $15 $28**

ADV-6

ADV-7

❑ **ADV-6. Quaker Oats Card,**
1890. - **$10 $30 $50**

❑ **ADV-7. Calendar Card,**
1891. Promotes Lucto Cereal on back of card. Sponsored by Reed & Carnrick. - **$20 $40 $60**

ADV-8

❑ **ADV-8. Roasted Oats Promo Card,**
1899. - **$10 $30 $50**

ADV-9

❑ **ADV-9. Friends Oats Promo Booklet,**
1890s. Front and back shown. - **$20 $40 $60**

(FRONT)

(BACK)

ADV-10

❑ **ADV-10. Frogs Thread J & P Coats Trade Card,**
1890s. - **$15 $30 $50**

(CLOSED) ADV-11 (OPEN)

❑ **ADV-11. Mother Goose Series - Mother in Shoes Trade Card,**
1890s. Nestle's Chocolate. - **$30 $60 $110**

(FRONT) (BACK)

ADV-12

❑ **ADV-12. Spider's Spool Cotton Trade Card,**
1890s. - **$15 $30 $50**

ADV-13 ADV-14

❑ **ADV-13. Promo Card,**
1900. Domestic sewing machine ad card shows elves climbing trees. - **$15 $25 $50**

❑ **ADV-14. Wheatlet Cereal Standee,**
1900. Cereal and Flour Premium. 6" standee of girl in a long pink dress. - **$25 $50 $75**

ADV-15 ADV-16

❑ **ADV-15. Buffalo Bill Photo,**
c. 1900. Circus premium of famous star. - **$35 $65 $90**

❑ **ADV-16. Star Nursery Rhymes Book,**
1901. Star Soap premium. Twenty page book in color with beautiful art. - **$25 $50 $75**

ADV-17

❑ **ADV-17. Mapl-Flake Promo,**
1902. - **$15 $30 $50**

ADV-18

❑ **ADV-18. Mother Goose Series - Mother in Shoes Trade Card,**
1900s. Nestle's Food. - **$10 $30 $50**

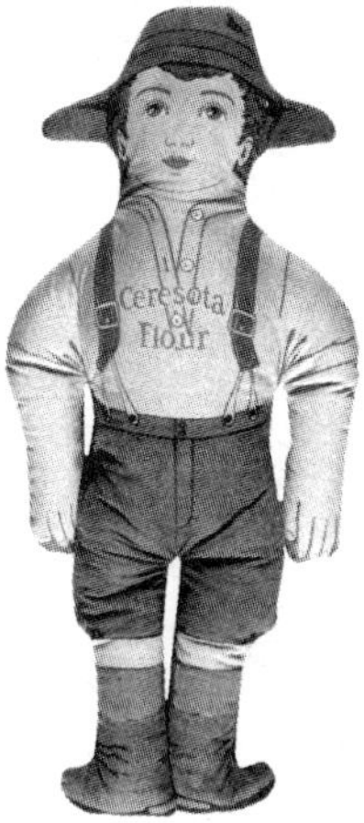


ADV-19

❑ **ADV-19. Ceresota Mill Worker Cloth Doll,**
1912. 12" premium for Ceresota flour. - **$50 $100 $175**

ADV-20

❑ **ADV-20. The Ad-ven-tur-ous Billy And Betty,**
1923. VanCamp Products. Fairy tales, 30 pages. Beautifully illustrated stories of Billy and Betty VanCamp. - **$30 $60 $100**

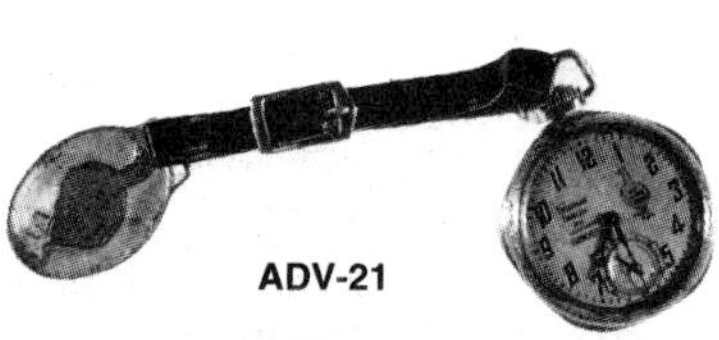

ADV-21

ADV-22

❑ **ADV-21. Red Goose Pocket Watch & Fob,**
1927. Watch - **$200 $450 $700**
Fob - **$60 $135 $190**

❑ **ADV-22. Red Goose Alarm Clock,**
1920s. - **$200 $400 $750**

ADV-23

❑ **ADV-23. "Red Goose Shoes" Card Toy,**
1920s. "Mov-I-Graff." 3-1/2x6-1/2" card featuring fine chain mounted on character face to form various facial images when card is jiggled or tapped. - **$10 $18 $30**

ADV-24

❑ **ADV-24. Boy Scout Pocket Watch in Box,**
1933. Has scout motto on hour and minute hands. Has scout badge as second hand and the words of the Scout Code of Honor around the dial. Scarce.
Watch - **$250 $600 $850**
Box - **$175 $275 $375**

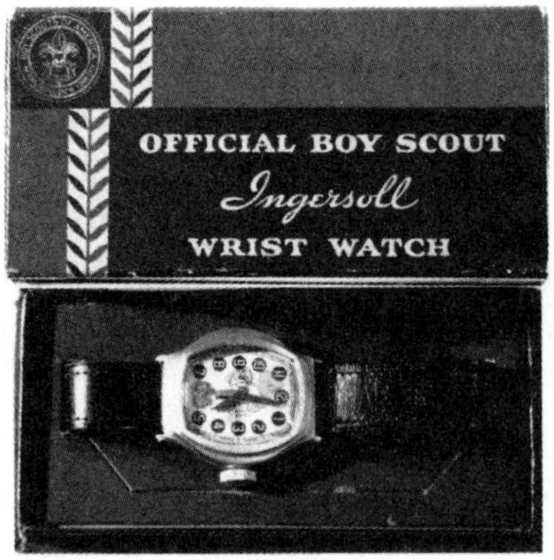


ADV-25

❑ **ADV-25. Boy Scout Wrist Watch in Box,**
1933. Has same make-up on dial as the pocket watch. Rare.
Watch - **$225 $600 $800**
Box - **$175 $275 $400**

ADV-26

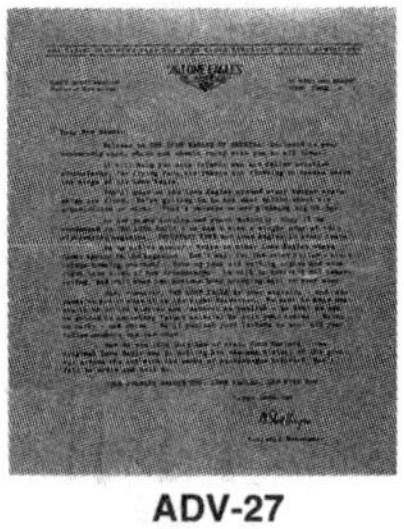

ADV-27

❑ **ADV-26. Lone Eagles Club Card,**
1934. Lone Eagles Magazine. -
**$20 $60 $100**

❑ **ADV-27. Lone Eagles Of America Club Letter,**
1934. National Lone Eagle Magazine. -
**$15 $30 $50**

ADV-28

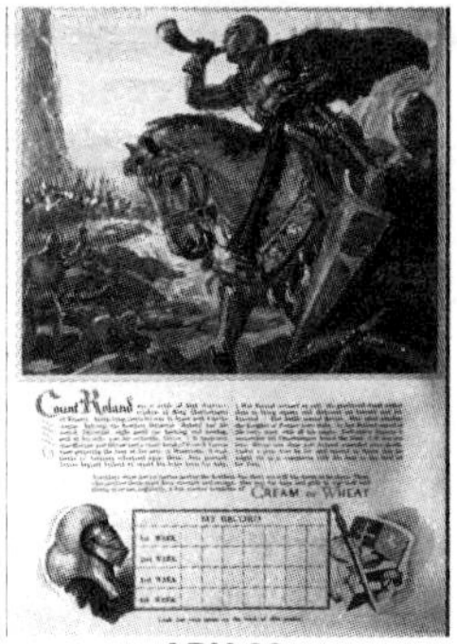

ADV-29

❑ **ADV-28. H. C. B. (Hot Cereal Breakfast) Club Grand Award Certificate,**
1935. Cream-of-Wheat premium. -
**$20 $40 $60**

❑ **ADV-29. H. C. B. (Hot Cereal Breakfast) Club Letter/Poster-on-Back,**
1935. Cream-of-Wheat premium. -
**$20 $40 $60**

ADV-30

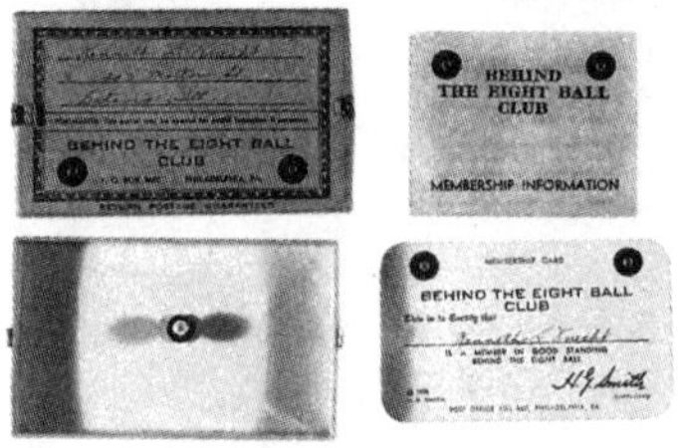


ADV-31

❑ **ADV-30. Kool-Aid Membership Card,**
1938. Kool-Aid Drink. Club card for Junior Aviation Corps. - **$15 $25 $40**

❑ **ADV-31. Behind The Eight Ball Club Kit,**
1938. National Salesman Club. Has rules, membership card, small plastic eight ball, and box. Complete - **$30 $65 $125**

ADV-32

ADV-33

❑ **ADV-32. Miller Wheat Flakes Cereal Sign 13x16 1/2"**
1930s. Wheat Flakes promotional for free punch-out rubberband gun. - **$50 $100 $150**

❑ **ADV-33. Butter-Nut Bread Beanie,**
1930s. Beanie type hat given away by bakeries. - **$20 $35 $55**

ADV-34

❑ **ADV-34. Richfield Puzzle,**
1930s. Richfield Oil. India golf puzzle with mailer. - **$25 $50 $75**

ADV-35

❑ **ADV-35. Richfield Puzzle,**
1930s. Richfield Oil. Chinese golf puzzle with mailer. - **$25 $50 $75**

ADV-36

ADV-37

❑ **ADV-36. Airplane Model League Of America Coupon,**
1930s. American Boys Magazine. Coupon for joining club. - **$5 $10 $15**

❑ **ADV-37. Airplane Model League Of America Membership Card,**
1930s. American Boys Magazine. Club card. - **$15 $30 $50**

ADV-38

❑ **ADV-38. "Light Up A Kool" Willie Penguin Iron Cigarette Lighter,**
1930s. - **$100 $250 $350**

ADV-39

❑ **ADV-39. Rippled Wheat - Jack Dempsey 6" Standee,**
1930s. - **$50 $175 $275**

ADV-40

ADV-41

❑ **ADV-40. "RCA" Cardboard Fan,**
1930s. Radio Corp. of America. - **$35 $60 $100**

❑ **ADV-41. RCA Nipper Salt & Pepper Shaker Set,**
1930s. By Lenox, 3" tall white china. - **$30 $60 $100**

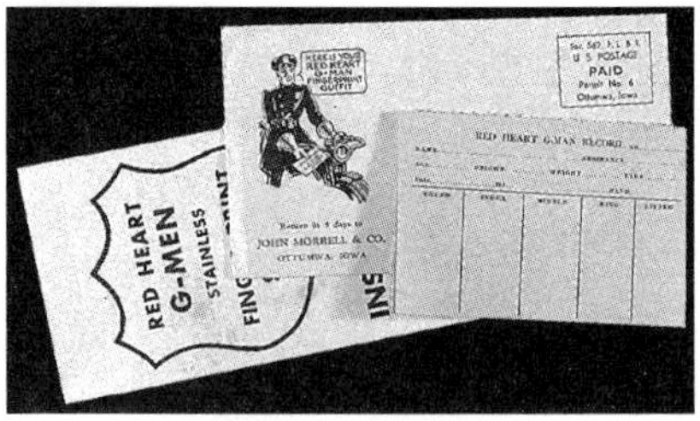


ADV-42

**❑ ADV-42. G-Men Fingerprint System (Red Heart),**
1930s. Instruction book. G-Man records and mailer. Gives children instructions on how to obtain fingerprints. Talks about capture of John Dillinger and gives advice from #1 G-Man J. Edgar Hoover. - **$50 $100 $150**

ADV-43

ADV-44

**❑ ADV-43. "Michelin" Plastic Ashtray,**
1930s. Likely produced into 1950s. -
**$35 $70 $100**

**❑ ADV-44. Nipper Papier Mache Store Display,**
1930s. Victor Talking Machine Co. -
**$200 $400 $600**

ADV-45

**❑ ADV-45. Heinz Aristocrat Tomato Composition Figure,**
1930s. White base or black base. -
**$65 $100 $150**

ADV-46

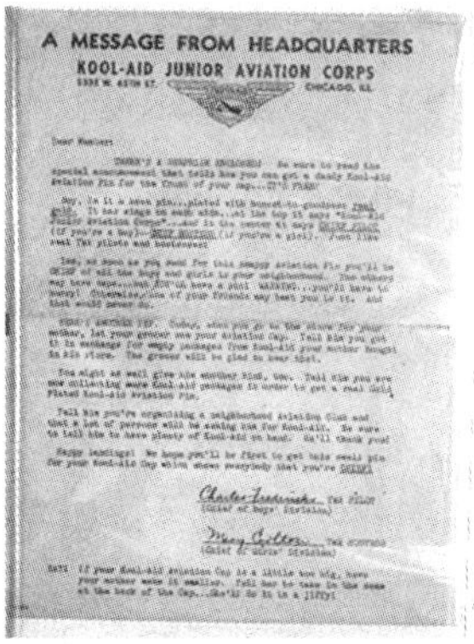


ADV-47

ADV-48

**❑ ADV-46. Kool-Aid 10x12" Sign,**
1930s. Has attached membership certificate for Junior Aviation Corps. - **$50 $100 $200**

**❑ ADV-47. T.W.A. Kool-Aid Club Instruction Form,**
1930s. - **$20 $40 $60**

**❑ ADV-48. Kool-Aid Aviation Club Cap,**
1930s. - **$30 $75 $90**

ADV-49

**❑ ADV-49. "Knot Hole League Of America" Patch and Card,**
1930s. Goudey Gum fabric patch plus member card for "Lou Gehrig" baseball club.
Patch - **$100 $200 $350**
Card - **$50 $125 $200**

ADV-50

**❑ ADV-50. Kraft 17" Standee,**
1930s. Promotes Malted Milk and offers free 28" model of S.S. Normandie. From the Gordon Gold Archives. - **$125 $225 $375**

ADV-51

ADV-52

**❑ ADV-51. Sunny Jim Cloth Doll,**
1930s. Force Cereal premium. - **$50 $75 $100**

**❑ ADV-52. Holsum Ranger Badge,**
1930s. Bread giveaway. - **$50 $100 $150**

ADV-53

**❑ ADV-53. Curtiss Candy Premium Puzzle,**
1930s. Puzzle titled "Singing in the Rain" shows kids eating Baby Ruth candy bars. With mailer.
Complete - **$30 $75 $150**

ADV-54

❑ **ADV-54. "Firestone" Plantation Worker Figurine,**
1930s. 5-3/4" tall painted hard rubber figurine on 3" diameter base. Issued to promote company's world-wide activities. - **$50 $125 $175**

ADV-55

❑ **ADV-55. Earl Ortman's Model Planes Die Cut Standee,**
1930s. Promotes Allsweet oleo and offers 4 different model planes. - **$175 $350 $575**

ADV-56

ADV-57

❑ **ADV-56. ESKO-GRAM Sign,**
1930s. With promo list that promotes premiums. - **$30 $80 $125**

❑ **ADV-57. Stamp Album For 48 Stamps,**
1940. Tydol Oil. - **$15 $30 $50**

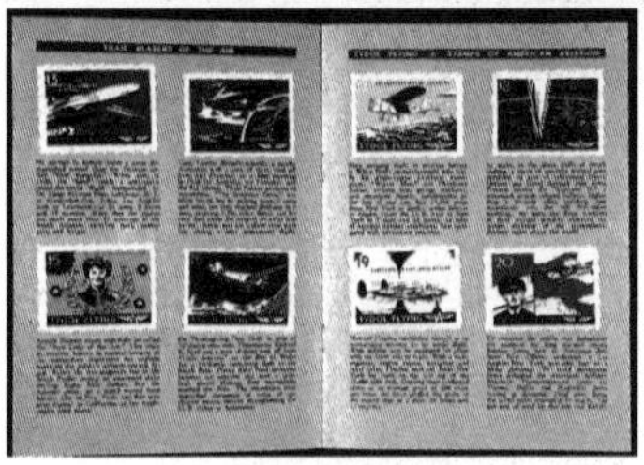

ADV-58

❑ **ADV-58. Stamps For Album,**
1940. Tydol Oil.
Each Loose or Mounted - **$1 $2 $4**

ADV-59

ADV-60

❑ **ADV-59. Flibbity Jibbit Book Premium,**
1943. Junkets Dessert premium. 32 pages. Vernon Grant art. - **$25 $50 $75**

❑ **ADV-60. Chiquita Banana Fabric Doll Pattern With Envelope,**
c. 1944. Kellogg's Corn Flakes. First version offered. Near Mint Packaged - **$150**
Loose Uncut - **$30 $50 $75**

ADV-61

❑ **ADV-61. "RCA Victor Little Nipper" Cello. Button,**
c. 1948. "Club Member" designation for children's records series. - **$35 $60 $125**

ADV-62

❑ **ADV-62. Fearless Fosdick Matches,**
1949. Unused - **$10 $20 $30**

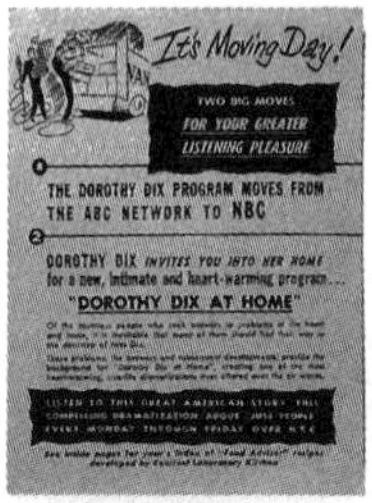

ADV-63

ADV-64

❑ **ADV-63. Dorothy Dix Food Advisor Booklet,**
1949. Sealtest. Four page radio premium. - **$15 $25 $35**

❑ **ADV-64. Macy's Red Star Club Badge,**
1940s. Scarce. - **$30 $60 $100**

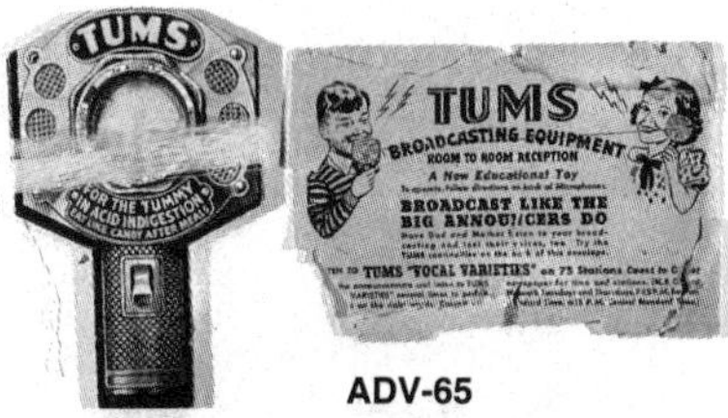


ADV-65

❑ **ADV-65. Tums Broadcasting Equipment,**
1940s. Radio premium with mailer. - **$25 $50 $75**

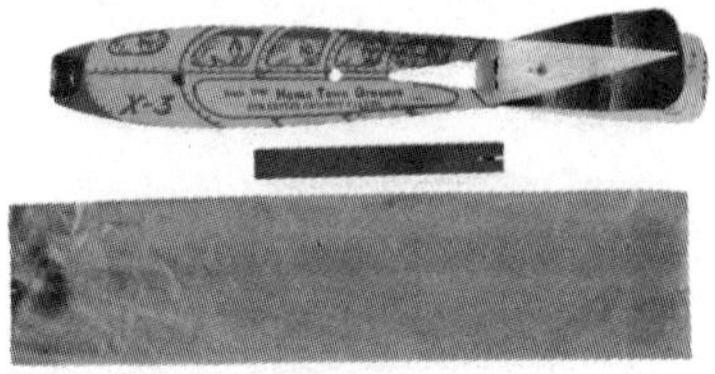


ADV-66

❑ **ADV-66. Rocket Gyro X-3 with Mailer,**
1940s. Sponsor Hometown Grocers. - **$30 $75 $110**

ADV-67

ADV-68

- ❑ **ADV-67. Red Goose Tin Whistle,** 1940s. Shoe premium. - **$10 $30 $45**

- ❑ **ADV-68. War Bond Matchbook Promo,** 1940s. Striking surface on Hitler's rear end. - **$30 $75 $150**

ADV-69 (DETAIL)

ADV-70

- ❑ **ADV-69. Pepsi-Cola Policemen Tin Sign,** 1940s. Lightly embossed litho. tin in red, white and blue, 3-1/2x21". - **$50 $125 $250**

- ❑ **ADV-70. "Pal" Cello. Button With Design By Al Konetzni, Prior To Career With Disney,** 1940s. 3" showing trademark man with lathered face. Design includes artist's "Alko" signature. - **$25 $50 $90**

ADV-71

- ❑ **ADV-71. Zoom Bullet Pen And Mailer,** 1940s. Premium bullet yellow pen from Zoom Cereal for Future Flyers. - **$20 $40 $75**

ADV-72

ADV-73

ADV-74

- ❑ **ADV-72. Tip-Top Bread Dial,** 1940s. Select Presidents of U.S. - **$10 $20 $35**

- ❑ **ADV-73. Good Humor "Captain" Safety Club button,** 1940s. Scarce - **$50 $85 $150**

- ❑ **ADV-74. "Junior Adventures" Club button,** 1940s. Premium from Marshall Field and Company. - **$25 $50 $75**

ADV-75

ADV-76

- ❑ **ADV-75. Philip Morris 12" Tall Standee,** 1940s. 4" wide. Classic picture of Johnny , who always called out, "Call for Philip Morris." - **$100 $175 $250**

- ❑ **ADV-76. "Dr. Kool" Plaster Figure Paperweight,** 1940s. - **$50 $85 $150**

ADV-77

- ❑ **ADV-77. Fleer Gum Promo Booklet,** 1950. 12 pages with colorful pictures throughout. Front & back cover shown. - **$15 $40 $60**

ADV-78

- ❑ **ADV-78. Dubble Bubble Doodle Diary** 1950. Fleer. - **$10 $15 $30**

ADV-79

- ❑ **ADV-79. "Lennie Lennox" Figural Salt & Pepper Set,** c. 1950. Each is 4-1/2" tall painted ceramic. Warren Products, Columbus, Ohio. - **$65 $125 $200**

ADV-80

- ❑ **ADV-80. Kool Plastic Salt & Pepper Set,** 1951. Boxed - **$30 $60 $100**
Loose - **$15 $25 $35**

ADV-81

ADV-82

❑ **ADV-81. 7up "Fresh Up Freddie" Litho. Button,**
c. 1959. - **$10 $20 $35**

❑ **ADV-82. 7up "Fresh-Up Freddie" Soft Rubber Doll,**
c. 1959. - **$65 $125 $250**

ADV-83

❑ **ADV-83. Royal Crown Cola Postcard,**
1950s. Card offer for free carton of Royal Crown Cola. - **$10 $20 $30**

ADV-84

ADV-85

❑ **ADV-84. "Oscar Mayer" Plastic Weinermobile,**
1950s. "Little Oscar" figure rises and lowers. - **$75 $200 $300**

❑ **ADV-85. "RCA" Victor Plastic Salt & Pepper Set,**
1950s. RCA Victor Corp. - **$35 $55 $90**

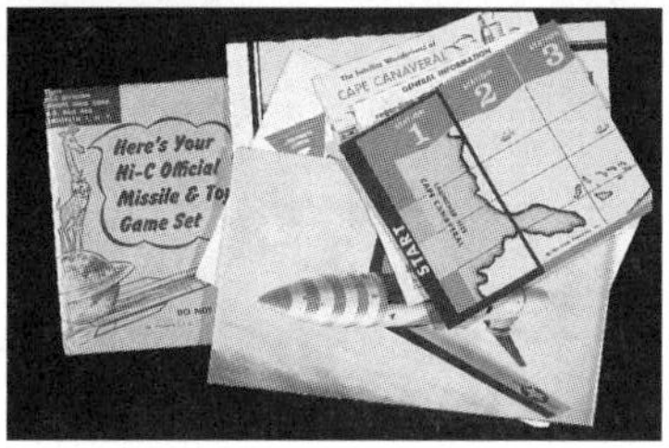

ADV-86

❑ **ADV-86. Missile Game Set,**
1950s. Consists of map, punch-outs, manual, instructions, game board, and mailer. Hi-C Minute Maid premium. - **$35 $75 $125**

ADV-87

❑ **ADV-87. Bardahl Detective Club 10x15" Sign,**
1950s. Rare. Shows all the villains. - **$75 $250 $450**

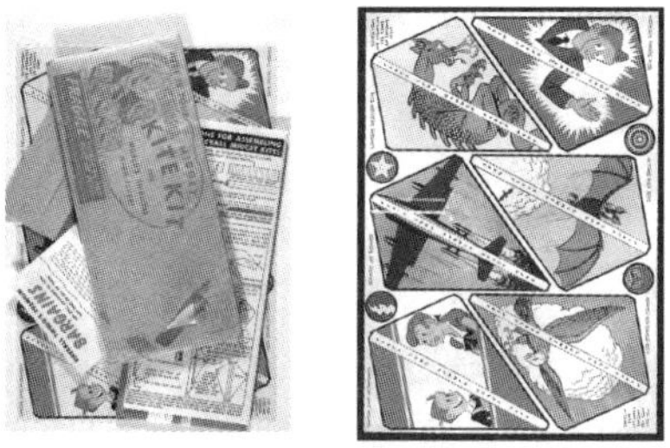

ADV-88

ADV-89

❑ **ADV-88. Fireball Twigg Midget Kite Kit with Mailer,**
1950s. 6 Kites. - **$30 $65 $100**

❑ **ADV-89. Grape-Nuts Flakes Fireball Twigg Kite Premium Sign,**
1950s. - **$30 $60 $125**

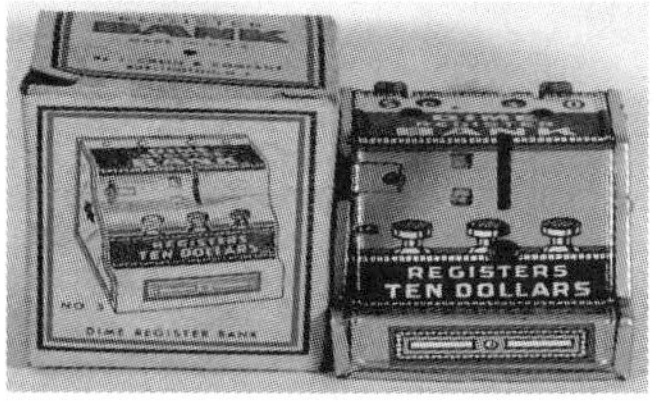

ADV-90

❑ **ADV-90. Register Dime Bank with Box,**
1950s. This was a very popular item used by children in the 1950s. Bankers used toys and TV characters to help entice children to save money, a habit they would take into adulthood.
Bank - **$15 $30 $50**
Box - **$25 $50 $85**

ADV-91

❑ **ADV-91. Red Goose Shoe,**
1950s. St. Louis Zoo punch-outs. - **$30 $75 $100**

ADV-92

❑ **ADV-92. Flap Happy Bird with Mailer,**
1950s. Post Toasties premium. - **$20 $40 $70**

ADV-93

❑ **ADV-93. Wild West Candy Box,**
1950s. Has Wild Bill Hickok card on back of box. - **$30 $65 $90**

ADV-94

ADV-95

ADV-96

ADV-97

ADV-98

❑ **ADV-94. Cheerio Yo-Yo Company Patch,**
1950s. Large Champion patch. - **$40 $75 $125**

❑ **ADV-95. Cheerio Junior Instructor Patch,**
1950s. - **$10 $20 $35**

❑ **ADV-96. Cheerio Bronze Award Patch,**
1950s. - **$10 $20 $35**

❑ **ADV-97. 9 Trick Bronze Award Patch,**
1950s. - **$10 $20 $35**

❑ **ADV-98. 18 Trick Silver Award Patch,**
1950s. - **$15 $35 $65**

ADV-99

❑ **ADV-99. Esso Space Captain Sign (Silver Wings),**
1950s. Canada. - **$30 $60 $100**

ADV-100

❑ **ADV-100. Dubble Bubble Gum Premium Paddle Ball,**
1950s. By Fleer. - **$20 $40 $60**

ADV-101

ADV-102

ADV-103

❑ **ADV-101. Bardahl Club Shield Litho. Tab,**
1950s. - **$15 $25 $40**

❑ **ADV-102. Red Goose Display Goose,**
1950s. Scarce. Goose lays plastic golden eggs. - **$400 $750 $1100**

❑ **ADV-103. Red Goose Gold Plastic Egg-Bank,**
1950s. Bank contained prize, connected to previous item. - **$10 $25 $40**

ADV-104

❑ **ADV-104. Bert And Harry Piel Ceramic Salt And Pepper Set,**
1950s. Piel's Beer. Bert is 3" tall salt, Harry is 4" tall pepper. - **$50 $90 $140**

ADV-105

❑ **ADV-105. "Toppie" Large Doll Premium,**
1950s. Top Value Stores. 11" tall by 14" long oilcloth. - **$50 $100 $175**

ADV-106

ADV-107

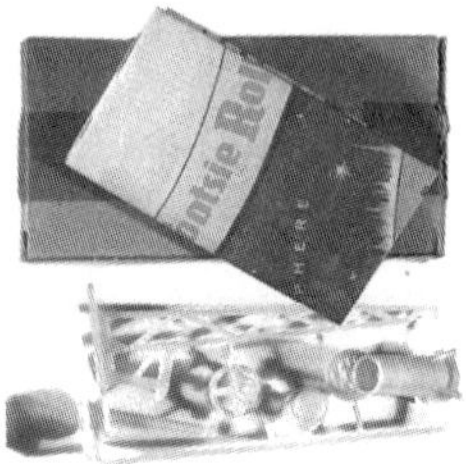

ADV-108

❑ **ADV-106. Mr. Clean Vinyl Doll,**
c. 1961. Procter & Gamble. - **$30 $65 $100**

❑ **ADV-107. Marky Maypo Vinyl Figure,**
1961. Maypo Cereal. Came with unmarked 5" styrene bowl and 5" styrene spoon for $1 and box top. - **$30 $60 $100**

❑ **ADV-108. Astronaut -Orbit - Target Game,**
1962. Tootsie Roll premium. Plastic rocket with man and paper targets. Shows statistics of seven U.S. and Russian men who have been in space. Instruction and mailer enclosed. Near Mint Boxed Unassembled - **$125**
Assembled With Target - **$20 $40 $60**

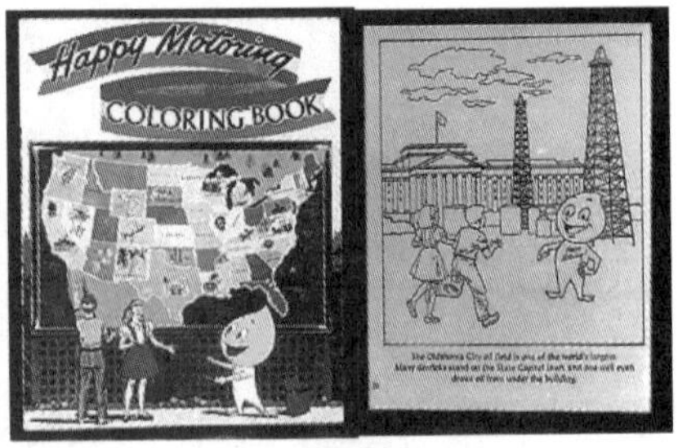

ADV-109

❑ **ADV-109. Esso "Happy Motoring" Coloring Book,**
1963. Esso/Humble Oil. 24 pages picturing national landmarks described by "Happy" Oil Drop character. - **$10 $20 $30**

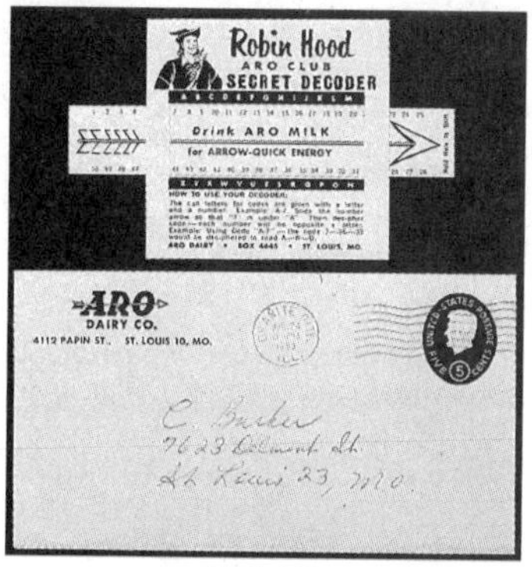


ADV-110

❑ **ADV-110. Robin Hood Decoder and Mailer,**
1963. ARO Milk premium. - **$30 $80 $135**

ADV-111

❑ **ADV-111. "Naugahyde" Doll,**
1967. Issued by Uniroyal for naugahyde vinyl fabric. Many different color variations. - **$15 $30 $50**

ADV-112

ADV-113

❑ **ADV-112. "Bud Man" Ceramic Stein,**
c. 1969. Re-issued in 1990s. Original marked under base. Ceramarte made in Brazil. - **$100 $150 $250**

❑ **ADV-113. Football Movie Viewer And Slides,**
1969. Chiquita. 26 slides of photos of All Star football players like Bubba Smith, Mercury Morris, Joe Greene, Bob Lilly, and others. Also includes mailer and yellow plastic viewer. - **$75 $150 $225**

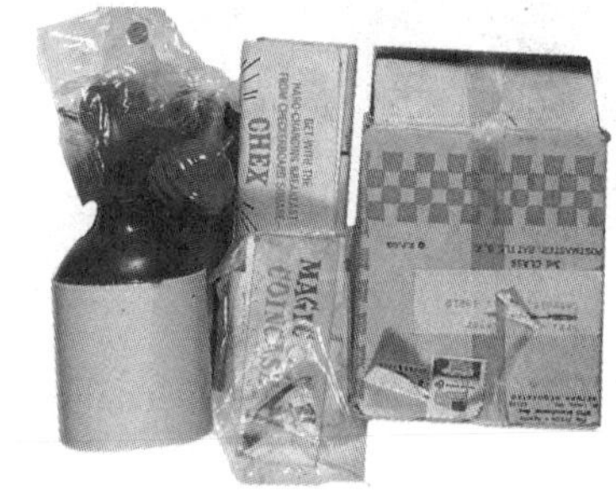


ADV-114

❑ **ADV-114. Wheat Chex Magic Kit,**
1960s. 24 trick instruction book, includes items: 7 paper, 1 ring, 8 plastic, 3 wood, 3 metal. - **$25 $50 $85**

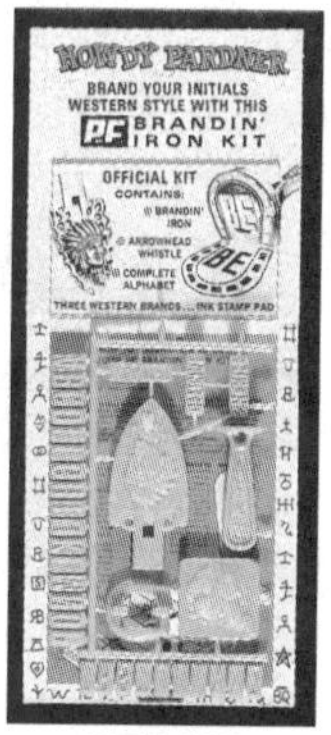


ADV-115

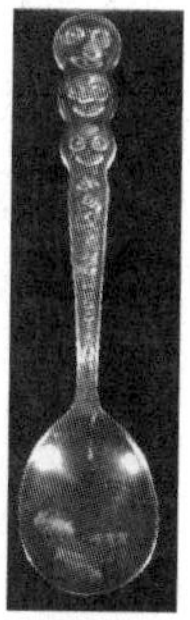

ADV-116

❑ **ADV-115. P.F. Branding Iron Kit With Whistle On Card,**
1960s. Scarce. B.F. Goodrich premium. Plastic kit with membership card on back. - **$40 $75 $125**

❑ **ADV-116. SpaghettiOs Spoon Premium,**
1960s. - **$10 $20 $30**

ADV-117

ADV-118

❑ **ADV-117. Maypo Cello. Button,**
1960s. Classic cereal promotion with slogan, "I want my Maypo." Pinback shown from the promotion - **$15 $25 $50**

❑ **ADV-118. Colonel Sanders Composition Bobbing Head,**
1960s. - **$60 $125 $215**

ADV-119

ADV-120

❑ **ADV-119. Bud Man Foam Rubber Doll,**
c. 1970. - **$30 $65 $100**

❑ **ADV-120. "Chicken Hungry" Flexible Plastic Ring,**
1972. Red Barn System. - **$10 $20 $35**

ADV-121

ADV-122

❑ **ADV-121. Indian Sticker Badges,**
1972. Ovaltine premium. 6 different. Each - **$4 $8 $12**

❑ **ADV-122. "Bazooka Joe" Cloth Doll,**
c. 1973. Bazooka Gum. 19" tall. - **$15 $40 $65**

ADV-123

❑ **ADV-123. "M&M's" Wall Clock,**
1979. Scarce. 15 1/2" tall. Wall clock has early version of the M&M boys. Premium offer. With box - **$60 $100 $150**

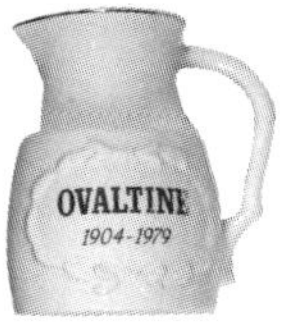


ADV-124

ADV-125

ADV-126

❑ **ADV-124. Ovaltine Premium Pitcher,**
1979. Celebrates 75 years (1904-1979) in business. - **$10 $25 $45**

❑ **ADV-125. Colonel Sanders 100 Club Award,**
1970s. Quality Service Club Award, approx. 4" in diameter. - **$20 $40 $60**

❑ **ADV-126. Eskimo Pie Cloth Doll,**
1970s. 12" premium. - **$15 $30 $50**

ADV-127

ADV-128

ADV-129

❑ **ADV-127. Ben Franklin Stuffed Doll,**
1970s. Franklin Life Insurance Premium. - **$15 $30 $50**

❑ **ADV-128. "Burger Chef" Hand Puppet,**
1970s. Soft vinyl head with fabric chef hat and body. - **$15 $30 $60**

❑ **ADV-129. Tastykake Cloth Doll,**
1970s. Scarce. Tastykake Bakery. - **$15 $30 $50**

ADV-130

❑ **ADV-130. "Where's the Beef?" Puzzle,**
1984. Wendy's Restaurants. 18"x 24" with box. 551 pieces. - **$10 $30 $60**

ADV-131

ADV-132

❑ **ADV-131. Raid Bug Plastic Wind-Up,**
1980s. - **$25 $60 $100**

❑ **ADV-132. Raid Battery Operated Plastic Robot With Remote Control,**
1980s. - **$125 $250 $300**

ADV-133

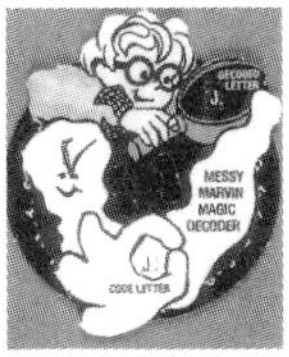


ADV-134

❑ **ADV-133. "Heinz" Talking Plastic Alarm Clock,**
1980s. Battery operated. - **$60 $125 $225**

❑ **ADV-134. Hershey "Messy Marvin Magic Decoder",**
1980s. Hershey's Chocolate Syrup. Mechanical cardboard with two diecut letter openings. - **$5 $12 $20**

ADV-135

❑ **ADV-135. Twinkie the Kid Anniversary Standee,**
1990. 4 ft. tall. - **$30 $85 $150**

ADV-136

❑ **ADV-136. "Oscar Mayer" Weinermobile,**
c. 1991. Re-issue without Little Oscar figure. - **$10 $15 $25**

ADV-137

❑ **ADV-137. A&W Root Beer Bean Bear Figures,**
1997. Orange shirt and hat. - **$18**
1998. Green shirt and hat. - **$15**

ADV-138

ADV-139

❑ **ADV-138. "Barnum Animals" Lion Bean Figure,**
1998. In box with tag. - **$12**

❑ **ADV-139. "Barnum Animals" Tiger Bean Figure,**
1998. In box with tag. - **$12**

ADV-140

ADV-141

❑ **ADV-140. Energizer Bunny Bean Bag,**
1998. - **$15**

❑ **ADV-141. "Hawaiian Punch" Doll,**
1998. With 2 tags. - **$20**

ADV-142

❑ **ADV-142. Pepsi Man Action Figure,**
1998. Japanese product has "Head Change" action. Sold in vending machines to promote the soft drink. - **$30**

ADV-143 ADV-144

❑ **ADV-143. Orioles Bear Beanie,**
1999. - **$10**

❑ **ADV-144. Taco Bell Bean Bag Dog,**
1999. With unbent tag - **$10**

ADV-145 ADV-146

❑ **ADV-145. FAO Schwarz Paddle Ball,**
1999. - **$10**

❑ **ADV-146. M&M's Sports Dispenser Figure,**
1999. Includes candy. - **$20**

ADV-147

❑ **ADV-147. Joe Camel Party Member Button,**
Early 1990s. Very colorful 2 1/2" button shows probably the last cartoon-type character to ever promote cigarettes. - **$5 $10 $25**

ADV-148

❑ **ADV-148. Hot Wheels M&M's Racing Team Transporter,**
2001. In box. - **$20**

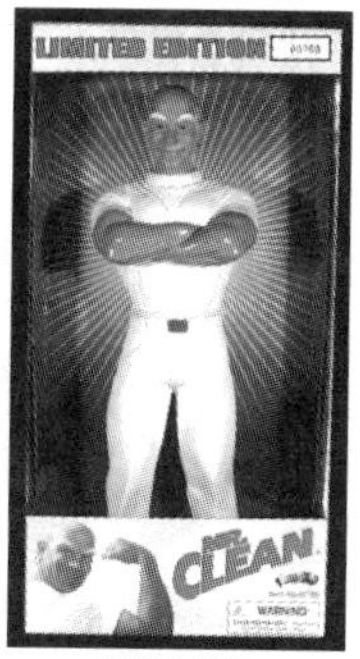


ADV-149 ADV-150

❑ **ADV-149. Colonel Sanders Wacky Wobbler Figure,**
2001. - **$15**

❑ **ADV-150. Mr. Clean Figure,**
2001. Limited edition in box. - **$25**

## Air Juniors

**One of the earliest radio clubs designed to encourage happy boys and girls to learn about flying airplanes and aspire to become pilots when they grew up, the *Air Juniors* club was formed in 1929. It was sponsored by the Commonwealth Edison Electric Shops. The project was promoted on the WENR Radio station broadcasting out of Chicago. The idea for the club piggy-backed on the popularity of Charles Lindbergh's flight from New York to Paris in May of 1927.**

AIR-1

AIR-2

❑ **AIR-1. Member's Card,**
1929. See AIR-3. - **$20 $60 $95**

❑ **AIR-2. Club Member Pin,**
1929. Scarce. - **$90 $135 $210**

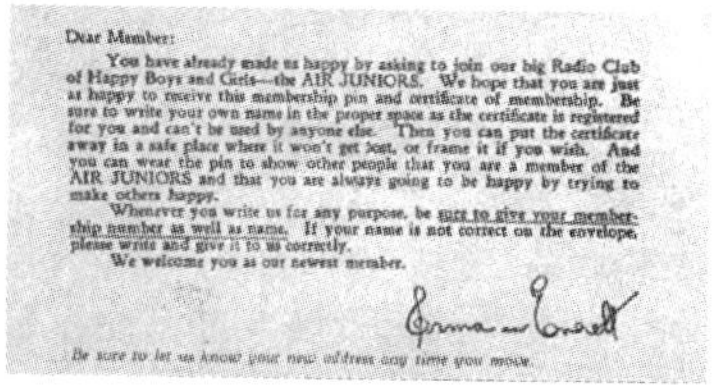

Dear Member:

You have already made us happy by asking to join our big Radio Club of Happy Boys and Girls—the AIR JUNIORS. We hope that you are just as happy to receive this membership pin and certificate of membership. Be sure to write your own name in the proper space as the certificate is registered for you and can't be used by anyone else. Then you can put the certificate away in a safe place where it won't get lost, or frame it if you wish. And you can wear the pin to show other people that you are a member of the AIR JUNIORS and that you are always going to be happy by trying to make others happy.

Whenever you write us for any purpose, be sure to give your membership number as well as name. If your name is not correct on the envelope, please write and give it to us correctly.

We welcome you as our newest member.

*Be sure to let us know your new address any time you move.*

AIR-3

❑ **AIR-3. Club Letter,**
1929. Membership card and letter came as a single piece for member to separate on perforated line. - **$15 $25 $40**

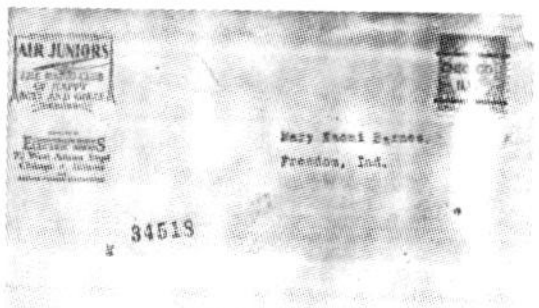


AIR-4

AIR-5

❑ **AIR-4. Mailer For Membership Card And Letter,**
1929. - **$15 $30 $50**

❑ **AIR-5. "Air Scouts" Member's Brass Pin,**
c. 1929. Same design as 1929 member's pin. Uncertain if title represents change in club's name or member's advancement to higher club rank. - **$90 $135 $210**

## Alphonse and Gaston

**"You first, my dear Gaston!" "After you, my dear Alphonse!" The Frederick Opper (1857-1937) pair of acutely polite Frenchmen and their friend Leon first appeared in the Hearst Syndicate Sunday pages in 1902. The strip was a hit with readers, but after 1904 the characters appeared only occasionally in Opper's other strips, particularly *Happy Hooligan* and *And Her Name Was Maud.* An early collection of color reprints was published by the *N.Y. American & Journal.***

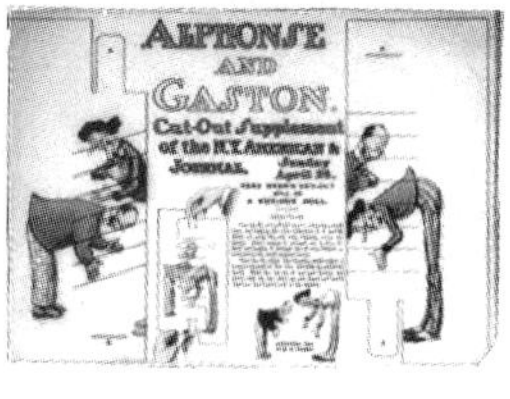


ALP-1

❑ **ALP-1. "Alphonse and Gaston" Cut-Out Supplement,**
1902. New York American & Journal newspaper. Uncut - **$40 $75 $125**

ALP-2

ALP-3

❑ **ALP-2. Cello. Button,**
c. 1903. Advertises South Dakota State Fair. - **$15 $35 $65**

❑ **ALP-3. Cello. Button,**
1903. Advertises Omaha Grocers and Butchers picnic. - **$20 $40 $75**

ALP-4

❑ **ALP-4. Early Hankerchief,**
c. 1903. - **$15 $30 $60**

ALP-5

❑ **ALP-5. Handkerchief,**
c. 1903. Probable store item. - **$15 $30 $60**

ALP-6

ALP-7

❑ **ALP-6. Cello. Button Without Imprint,**
c. 1903. - **$25 $50 $85**

❑ **ALP-7. Gaston Tinted White Metal Charm,**
c. 1904. There is a matching Alphonse. Each - **$5 $12 $25**

ALP-8

❑ **ALP-8. Aluminum Cartoon Card,**
c. 1904. Store item set of 10 aluminum cards, only one featuring Alphonse & Gaston. Card pictures lady waiting at her bed as they deliberate who should go first. - **$20 $40 $60**

ALP-9

❑ **ALP-9. Postcard,**
1906. American Journal Newspapers. - **$8 $15 $25**

## American Bandstand

**It started in 1952 on WFIL, a Philadelphia ABC affiliate, and went on to become one of television's longest-running and most successful shows. Dick Clark brought *American Bandstand* to prime-time ABC in 1957, where it ran for 13 weeks from October through December. Since then, under various names and in different formats and time slots, Clark's program showcased thousands of contemporary bands, singers and dancers. He was inducted into the Rock and Roll Hall of Fame in 1993. Promotional items associated with the show typically carry an American Broadcasting Co. copyright.**

AME-1

❑ **AME-1. Bandstand Yearbook,**
1955. WFIL-TV Philadelphia. Local program hosted by Bob Horn, pre-dating Dick Clark era. - **$25 $50 $75**

AME-2

❑ **AME-2. "Dick Clark Yearbook",**
1957. - **$10 $30 $50**
Mailer - **$5 $10 $20**

AME-3

AME-4

❑ **AME-3. "This Week Magazine" Cover Article,**
November 16, 1958. Sunday supplement magazine of various newspapers. - **$8 $12 $20**

❑ **AME-4. "Dick Clark Yearbook",**
c. 1959. - **$15 $25 $50**

AME-5

AME-6

❑ **AME-5. "Dick Clark"/"IFIC" 3" Litho. Buttons,**
1950s. Beech-Nut Gum, TV show sponsor. "Ific" is from slogan "Beech-Nut Gum Is Flavor-Ific."
Picture Version - **$15 $25 $35**
Initials Version - **$10 $15 $25**

❑ **AME-6. Dick Clark Doll,**
1950s. Store item by Juro. - **$150 $225 $350**

AME-7

❑ **AME-7. Store Display With Jewelry,**
1950s. Scarce. Displays 17 pieces including necklace, cuff links and tie clasps.
Complete - **$600 $1200 $2000**
Sign (without jewelry) - **$200 $300 $400**

AME-8

AME-9

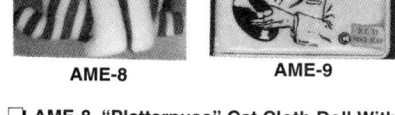

❑ **AME-8. "Platterpuss" Cat Cloth Doll With Tag,**
1950s. Store item. 14" tall with tag inscription "Official Autograph Mascot/Dick Clark American Bandstand". - **$50 $100 $150**

❑ **AME-9. "Secret Diary",**
1950s. Store item. - **$20 $40 $75**

AME-10

AME-11

❑ **AME-10. American Bandstand Patch of Dick Clark,**
1950s. - **$5 $12 $25**

❑ **AME-11. American Bandstand Ad Promo Display,**
1950s. Promotes Vicks Cough Drops. - **$40 $75 $125**

AME-12

AME-13

❑ **AME-12. Cello. Button,**
1950s. WFIL-TV (Philadelphia). - **$15 $35 $60**

❑ **AME-13. Cardboard Record Case,**
1950s. Store item. - **$25 $60 $100**

AME-14

❑ **AME-14. "Dick Clark's Blinker Badge,"**
1950s. Battery operated store item by Emenee musical toys. Near Mint Packaged **- $50**
Badge Only - **$10 $20 $35**

AME-15

AME-16

❑ **AME-15. "American Bandstand" Dick Clark Autographed Card,**
1950s. Color photo front with text on reverse, 2-1/4x3-1/2". - **$20 $50 $75**

❑ **AME-16. "Because They're Young" Window Card,**
1960. Columbia Pictures Corp. 14x22" card with images of Clark, Tuesday Weld and James Darren. - **$15 $30 $60**

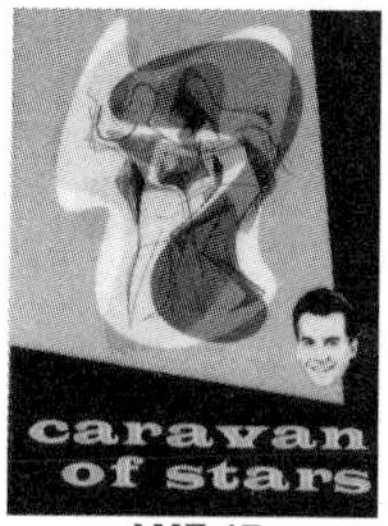

AME-17

AME-18

❑ **AME-17. "Caravan Of Stars" Program,**
c. 1964. - **$15 $20 $40**

❑ **AME-18. "Where The Action Is" TV Show Program,**
c. 1966. - **$15 $25 $50**

AME-19

AME-20

❑ **AME-19. "Caravan Of Stars" Concert Program,**
1967. - **$15 $25 $45**

❑ **AME-20. "20 Years Of Rock And Roll Yearbook",**
1973. - **$12 $20 $35**

AME-21

❑ **AME-21. 20th Anniversary Dick Clark's American Bandstand Promotional Ashtray,**
1977. - **$5 $12 $20**

## Amos 'n' Andy

**Amos Jones and Andrew H. Brown, rustic blacks striving to succeed in the big city, were born in the imaginations of Freeman Gosden and Charles Correll, two white show business producers. Amos and Andy ran the Fresh Air Taxicab Co. and--together with George Stevens, the Kingfish of the Mystic Knights of the Sea Lodge--enchanted and entranced a huge radio audience in the 1930s. The program, probably the most successful radio series ever, was aired locally in Chicago beginning in March 1928 and went to the NBC network in August 1929. Sponsors included Pepsodent toothpaste until 1937, Campbell's soup until 1943, and Rinso soap, Rexall drugs and Chrysler automobiles. *The Amos and Andy Music Hall* ran on CBS radio from 1954 to 1960, and a prime-time television series with a black cast appeared on CBS from 1951 to 1953.**

AMO-1

❑ **AMO-1. "Sam 'n' Henry Original Stories Of Amos 'n' Andy,"**
c. 1928. Softbound giveaway with 1926 Chicago Tribune copyright, published by Shrewsbury Publishing Co., Chicago. - **$25 $50 $75**

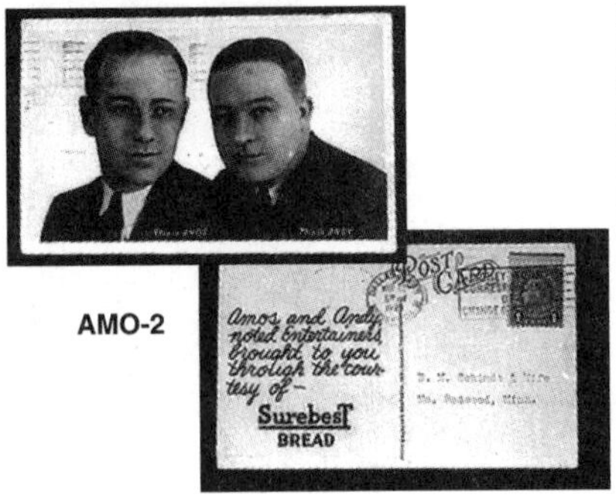


AMO-2

❑ **AMO-2. Fan Postcard,**
1929. Surebest Bread. Photo pictures actual portrayers of radio broadcast Amos and Andy. - **$20 $40 $60**

AMO-3

AMO-4

❑ **AMO-3. "All About Amos 'n' Andy And Their Creators" Hardbound Book,**
1929. Store item published by Rand McNally & Co. Striking black, white and orange dust jacket.
With Jacket **$40 $75 $150**
Without Jacket **$15 $30 $75**

❑ **AMO-4. Cast Photo & Mailer,**
1929. Pepsodent Co. Photo Only - **$12 $25 $60**
With Mailer And Letter - **$40 $85 $140**

AMO-5

AMO-6

❑ **AMO-5. Gosden & Correll Biography Folder,**
1930. Accompanied Pepsodent cardboard standup figure set of two. - **$10 $20 $30**

❑ **AMO-6. Pepsodent Cardboard Standup Figure Set,**
1930. Each - **$30 $60 $100**

AMO-7

❑ **AMO-7. "Amos 'N' Andy On The Screen" Movie Herald,**
1930. R-K-O Radio Pictures. Double-fold leaflet, photos show front cover and both sides opened. - **$30 $50 $85**

AMO-8

❑ **AMO-8. Cardboard Candy Box,**
1930. Williamson Candy Co. - **$100 $175 $350**

AMO-9

❑ **AMO-9. "Amos" and "Andy" Litho. Tin Wind-Up Toys,**
1930. Store items by Marx. 11" tall.
Each - **$300 $800 $1300**

AMO-10

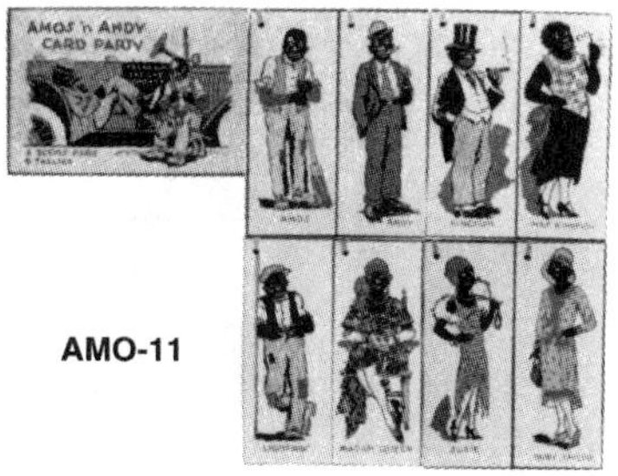


AMO-11

❑ **AMO-10. "Amos 'n' Andy" Pencil Tablet,**
c. 1930. From series available through store.
Each - **$25 $65 $100**

❑ **AMO-11. "Amos 'n' Andy Card Party" Boxed Set,**
1930. Store item by A. M. Davis Co.
Near Mint Complete Unused **$150**
Complete Used **$25 $50 $100**

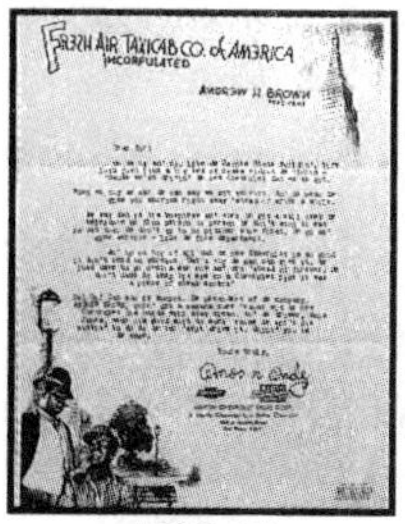


AMO-12

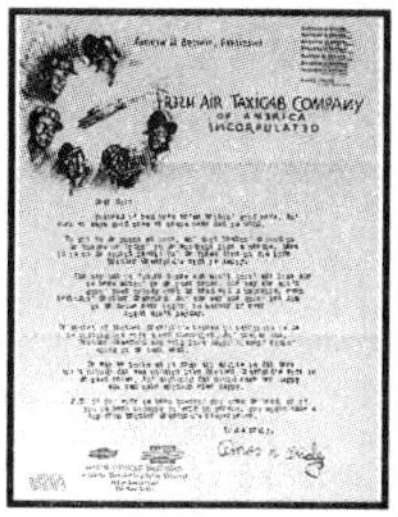


AMO-13

❑ **AMO-12. Chevrolet Car Dealer Promotion Letter,**
1931. Martin Chevrolet Sales Corp. Promotes products in dialect text on Fresh Air Taxicab Co. letterhead. - **$40 $85 $150**

❑ **AMO-13. Chevrolet Car Promotion Letter,**
1931. Martin Chevrolet Sales Corp. Similar to preceding item but different text and illustrations. - **$40 $85 $150**

AMO-14

AMO-15

❑ **AMO-14. Ford Automobile Promotion Letter,**
1931. Ford Motor Co. local dealers. Promotion letter for Ford products in dialect text on Fresh Air Taxi Cab Co. letterhead. - **$40 $85 $150**

❑ **AMO-15. Sheet Music,**
1931. Check and Double Check movie theme. - **$20 $35 $70**

AMO-16

❑ **AMO-16. Christmas Card,**
1931. Hall Brothers. - **$20 $40 $65**

AMO-17

❑ **AMO-17. "Here They Are Amos 'n' Andy" Hardcover Book,**
1931. Store item published by Ray Long & Richard R. Smith, Inc., N ew York.
With Jacket - **$40 $75 $150**
Without Jacket - **$15 $30 $75**

AMO-18

❑ **AMO-18. Cardboard Standup Figures With Letters And Envelope,**
1931. Set of six figures with two letters promoting Pepsodent toothpaste and urging dental visit. Near Mint In Envelope - **$300**
Each Standup - **$15 $30 $40**

AMO-19

AMO-20

❑ **AMO-19. Candy Display Box,**
1931. Williamson Candy Company. Candy bars held in box on Amos' back. - **$150 $300 $550**

❑ **AMO-20. Puzzle,**
1932. Pepsodent Co. - **$35 $80 $140**

AMO-21

❑ **AMO-21. Radio Episode Script,**
December 25, 1935. Pepsodent. For episode "Amos' Wedding". - **$5 $20 $30**

AMO-22

❑ **AMO-22. Radio Theme Song Sheet Music,**
1935. Pepsodent Toothpaste, also store item.
Pepsodent Imprint - **$15 $30 $60**
Store Item - **$20 $35 $70**

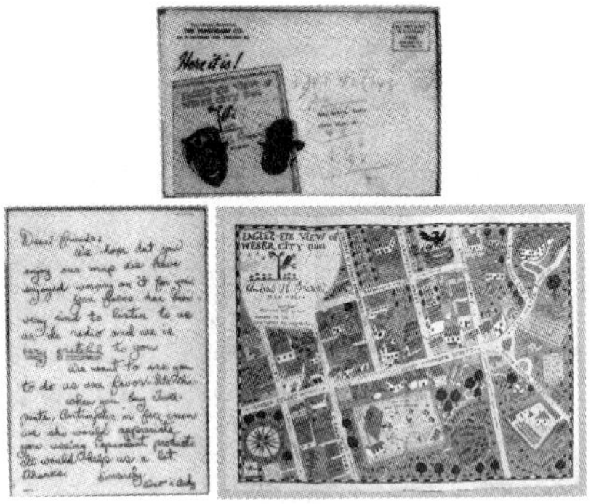

AMO-23

❑ **AMO-23. "Eagle's-Eye View Of Weber City (Inc.)" Map,**
1935. Pepsodent Co. Prize to each entrant of "Why I Like Pepsodent Toothpaste" contest.
Near Mint In Envelope - **$100**
Map Only - **$15 $30 $50**

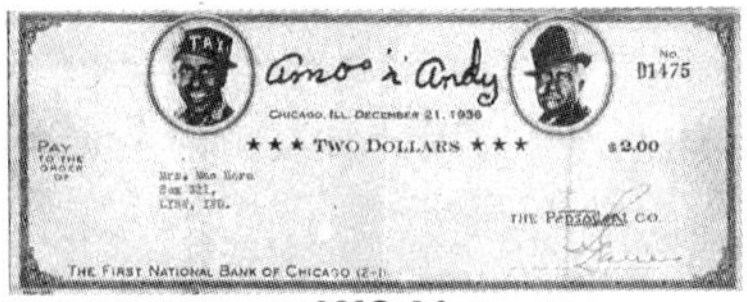


AMO-24

❑ **AMO-24. Pepsodent Contest Winner Check,**
1936. Rare. - **$450 $800 $950**

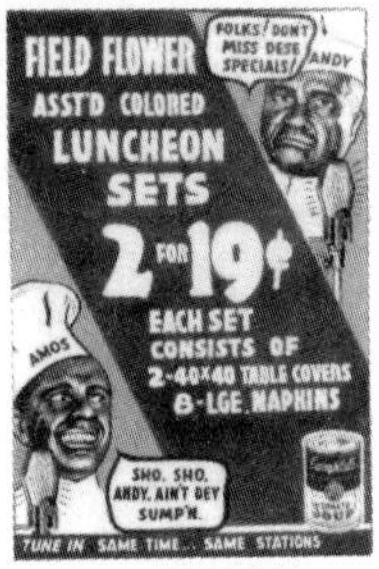


AMO-25

❑ **AMO-25. "Campbell's Soup" 13x20" Paper Poster,**
c. 1938. - **$20 $50 $100**

AMO-26

AMO-27

❑ **AMO-26. "Amos" Wood Jointed Doll,**
1930s. Store item. - **$100 $200 $300**

❑ **AMO-27. "Andy" Wood Jointed Doll,**
1930s. Store item. - **$100 $200 $300**

AMO-28

❑ **AMO-28. Detroit Sunday Times Supplement Photo,**
1930s. - **$20 $35 $60**

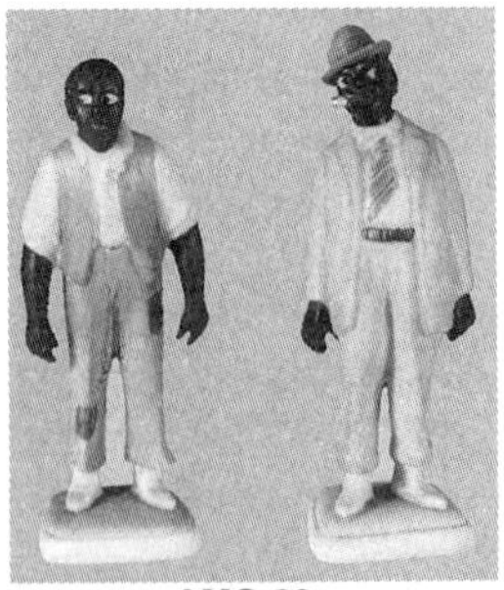

AMO-29

❑ **AMO-29. Bisque Figurines,**
1930s. Store item. Pair - **$150 $250 $400**

AMO-30

❑ **AMO-30. Wood Composition Figure Set,**
1930s. Probable store item. Beautifully colored 2x2x2-3/4" tall fully dimensional figures each with a 3/8" diameter cylindrical opening running vertically through the entire figure which may have held tube cigarette lighters. Only example we've seen so we are uncertain about the purpose of this opening which is only seen from the top or underneath views.
Value As Described Pair **$300 $600 $1000**

AMO-31

AMO-32

❑ **AMO-31. Portrait Button,**
1930s. Issuer unknown. 13/16" black and gray. Scarce. - **$60 $125 $250**

❑ **AMO-32. Promotional Sticker,**
1930s. "Shell 400, The 'Dry' Gas." 4-1/2" black and white including radio station call letters "KFRC." Diecut in shape of sponsor's logo. - **$20 $50 $85**

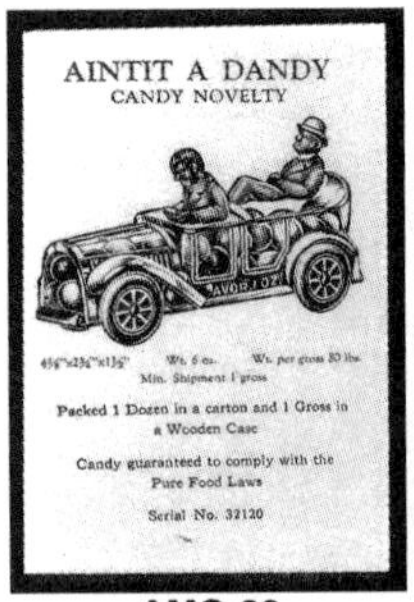


AMO-33

AMO-34

❑ **AMO-33. Glass Candy Container,**
1930s. Store item usually identified as Amos 'n' Andy is actually an unlicensed candy novelty called "Aintit A Dandy." Painted with Amos in blue suit, brown hair; Andy in red suit, brown derby. Value for example with tin cover on underside. - **$150 $300 $600**

❑ **AMO-34. Photo Card,**
1930s. Exhibit card from numbered set of about 20. Each - **$8 $15 $25**

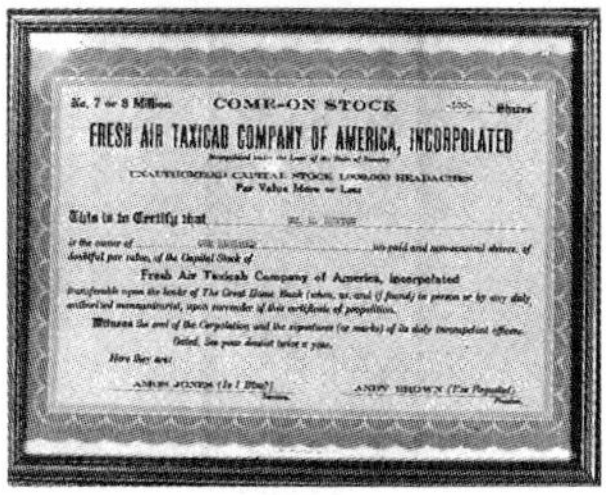

AMO-35

❑ **AMO-35. "Fresh Air Taxicab Company" Stock Certificate,**
1930s. Seen with advertising on bottom margin for "Ford Furniture Stores In Northwestern New Jersey." - **$75 $125 $225**

AMO-36

❑ **AMO-36. "Fresh Air Taxicab Company" Stock Certificate,**
1930s. - **$75 $125 $225**

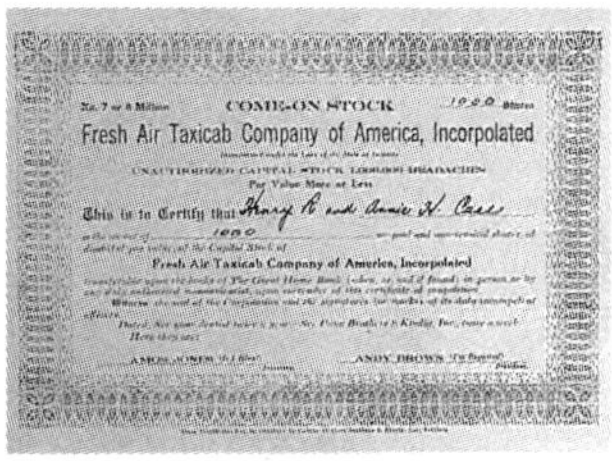


AMO-37

❑ **AMO-37. "Fresh Air Taxicab Company" Stock Certificate,**
1930s. Cann Brothers & Kindig, Inc., Printers. - **$75 $125 $225**

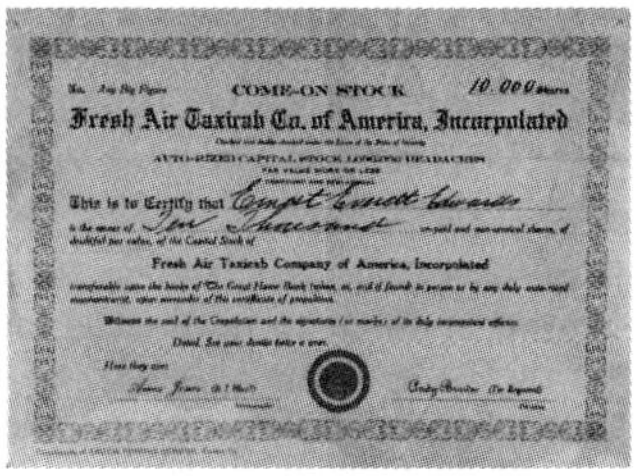


AMO-38

❑ **AMO-38. "Come-On" Stock Certificate,**
1930s. For the Fresh Air Taxicab Company. One of at least 3 varieties. - **$75 $125 $225**

AMO-39

❑ **AMO-39. Amos 'N' Andy Candy Wrapper,**
1930s. Store item. Williamson Candy Co. "An Oh Henry Product." - **$50 $90 $175**

AMO-40

AMO-41

❑ **AMO-40. Lead Ashtray,**
1930s. Store item. - **$125 $260 $500**

❑ **AMO-41. "Free Ride In Fresh Air Taxi" Litho. Button,**
1930s. Amos 'N Andy Fresh Air Candy. From known series of 19 with different slogan on each, including one example picturing the taxi. Each - **$15 $30 $55**

AMO-42

❑ **AMO-42. Amos and Andy Record Album,**
1947. Contains four 78 rpm records. Inside the front and back covers are write-ups of contents and a history of the radio show. Great picture of Amos and Andy on the inside front cover. Scarce. - **$75 $150 $200**

AMO-43

❑ **AMO-43. Paper Store Sign,**
1940s. Rexall drugstores. 11-1/2x36" in red, black and white. - **$50 $100 $150**

AMO-44

AMO-45

❑ **AMO-44. Amos and Andy Broadcast Sign,**
1940s. - **$100 $200 $400**

❑ **AMO-45. Amos and Andy Plenamins Promo Band,**
1940s. - **$25 $50 $75**

(Front) AMO-46 (Back)

❑ **AMO-46. "The Best of Amos 'N' Andy" CD Box set,**
2001. Set is packaged in a box facsimile of an old style radio- **$15**

## Annie Oakley

**Born in a log cabin in Ohio, Annie Oakley (1860-1926) was a skilled marksman even as a child. Nicknamed "Little Sure Shot," she joined the Buffalo Bill Wild West Show in 1885 and toured the world for 17 years. Her trick shooting was a consistent sensation and she continued setting and breaking records as late as 1920.**

**Hollywood began producing romanticized versions of the Annie Oakley legend as early as 1935. On the big screen she has been portrayed by--among others--Barbara Stanwyck,**

Betty Hutton, Gail Davis, and Geraldine Chaplin; on Broadway by Ethel Merman in *Annie Get Your Gun*; on television by Jamie Lee Curtis in a made-for-TV movie; and, memorably, by Gail Davis. Produced by Gene Autry Flying A Productions, the *Annie Oakley* television series with Davis (1925-1997) aired originally on ABC from 1954 to 1956, sponsored by Canada Dry, TV Time popcorn and Wonder bread. There was a brief revival in 1964-1965. *Annie Oakley* comic books appeared in the 1940s and 1950s. An annual Annie Oakley festival is staged in Greenville, Ohio.

ANN-1

❑ **ANN-1. Movie Version "Annie Oakley" Dixie Ice Cream Picture,**
1935. Pictures Barbara Stanwyck in title role from RKO Radio Pictures release. -
**$15 $30 $60**

ANN-2

(ENLARGED VIEW)

❑ **ANN-2. Movie "Annie Oakley" Lobby Hanger,**
1935. RKO Radio Pictures. 17" tall diecut stiff paper string hanger assembled into rectangle bottom. Pictured is title star Barbara Stanwyck. -
**$75 $125 $200**

ANN-3

❑ **ANN-3. Canada Dry Ginger Ale "Free Carton" Coupon,** 1954. Carton insert paper offering free carton for six bottle caps mailed to bottlers with offer expiring June 30. -
**$10 $20 $30**

ANN-4

ANN-5

❑ **ANN-4. "Annie Oakley And Tagg" Cello. Button,**
c. 1955. Club issue by unknown sponsor. Also inscribed "Gail Davis/Member/Sharpshooter." -
**$40 $75 $125**

❑ **ANN-5. Annie Oakley Litho. Button,**
c. 1955. - **$10 $20 $35**

ANN-6

ANN-7

❑ **ANN-6. Annie Oakley Cello. Button,**
c. 1955. Pictures Gail Davis. Australian issue. -
**$30 $60 $90**

❑ **ANN-7. Annie Oakley Cello. Button,**
c. 1955. Pictures Gail Davis. - **$25 $50 $85**

ANN-8

❑ **ANN-8. "Hostess Surprise Party" Puzzle Folder,**
c. 1955 Hostess Cupcakes. Leaflet with diecut strip panels to be arranged properly to reveal her as surprise hostess and her Hostess products. - **$15 $30 $50**

ANN-9

ANN-10

❑ **ANN-9. Wonder Bread Flipper Badge,**
c. 1955. Two-sided cardboard with pin fastener plus pull string for completion of front and back message "Annie Oakley Says Eat Wonder Bread." - **$10 $25 $50**

❑ **ANN-10. Wonder Bread Coloring Contest Store Sign,**
c. 1955. 6-1/2x12" cardboard placard for contest offering prize of tickets to live rodeo performance. - **$25 $50 $75**

ANN-11

❑ **ANN-11. Wonder Bread Cardboard Badge,**
c. 1955. 4" cardboard urging TV viewership. Back is blank with fastener pin at top margin, probable design for store clerk. - **$20 $40 $75**

ANN-12

ANN-13

❑ **ANN-12. Bread Loaf End Label,**
c. 1955. Issued by Wonder Bread with b&w photo of Gail Davis as Annie Oakley.
Each - **$20 $40 $75**

❑ **ANN-13. Wonder Bread Rodeo Announcement,**
c. 1955. Waxed paper bread loaf insert strip for live performance in "Days Of '47 Rodeo" believed titled by commemorative nature year. - **$5 $10 $15**

ANN-14

❑ **ANN-14. Cowgirl Outfit,**
c. 1955. Store item. Both vest and skirt have applied full color portrait patches.
Box (Not Shown) - **$35 $75 $125**
Playsuit - **$40 $85 $150**

ANN-15

ANN-16

❑ **ANN-15. TV Show Promo Drinking Cup,**
c. 1955. KTTV 11 Annie Oakley 7 P.M. Tues. co-sponsored by Laura Scutter Fine Foods. Thin paper cup is 3-1/4" tall. - **$5 $15 $25**

❑ **ANN-16. Drawstring Lunch Box,**
c. 1955. Issued by Aladdin. Vinyl over metal. Comes in blue or red background versions. - **$400 $1000 $1500**

ANN-17

❑ **ANN-17. "Watch For Annie" Button,**
c. 1955. 3" black, white and red target design with six simulated bullet holes. - **$10 $25 $50**

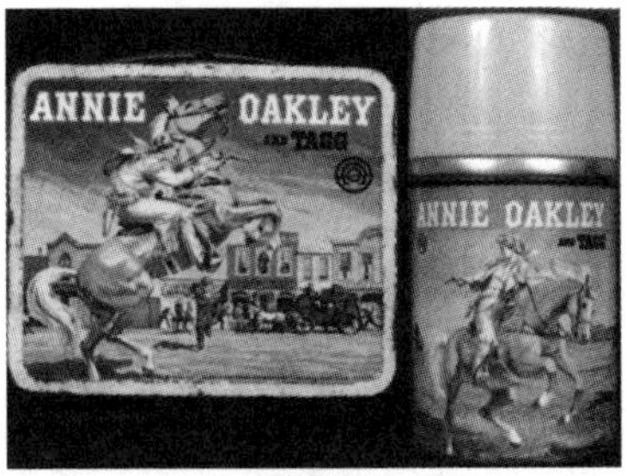


ANN-18

❑ **ANN-18. "Annie Oakley And Tagg" Lunch Box And Bottle,**
1955. Store item by Aladdin.
Box - **$75 $175 $350**
Bottle - **$25 $60 $100**

ANN-19

ANN-20

❑ **ANN-19. "Annie Oakley Cut-Out Dolls" Portfolio With Pocket Sleeves H olding Fashions And Diecut Dolls,**
1956. Whitman #1960. Uncut **$25 $50 $100**
Cut Complete - **$20 $35 $50**

❑ **ANN-20. Annie Oakley Hat,**
1950s. Store bought. - **$30 $65 $140**

## Archie

**Archie Andrews, typical American teen, first appeared in December 1941 in *Pep Comics* and in more than 60 years has not yet aged a day. Artist Bob Montana created Archie, his girlfriends Betty and Veronica, his pal Jughead, his rival Reggie, and dozens of other students at Riverdale High. They have appeared in comic books, a syndicated newspaper strip, paperback books, 15-and 30-minute radio shows (from 1943 to 1953 on the Mutual and NBC networks), and, starting in 1968, a continuing succession of TV cartoons on CBS or NBC. Archie became a merchandising success as well as a cartoon phenomenon: his bubble gum rock band even produced three hit songs.**

**The mid-1990s and early 21st century marked yet another upswing for the character and some of his more successful spin-offs. *Sabrina The Teenage Witch* debuted on ABC TV September 27, 1996, later moving to WB, and *Josie and the Pussycats* was released theatrically in 2001. Archie himself appears headed back to TV or the silver screen with both live action and animated projects in development. New music groups based on The Archies and Josie and the Pussycats are also being formed. 2002 marks the 60th anniversary of Archie's appearance in his own comic title.**

ARC-1

❑ **ARC-1. Final July Issue Of "Hi" Magazine Before Becoming Archie Magazine,**
1948. Diamond Sales Corporation. Clothing store promotion announcing forthcoming title change plus picturing cast members of radio show. - **$30 $60 $100**

ARC-2

❑ **ARC-2. First Issue "Archie" Title Magazine,**
August 1948. Archie Comics Publications. Various store sponsor imprints on back. - **$40 $75 $150**

ARC-3

❑ **ARC-3. Magazines,**
1948. Archie Comics Publications Inc. Each - **$15 $25 $45**

ARC-4

❑ **ARC-4. "Archie Pin-Up Calendar,"**
1952. 6x9" calendar sheet obtained by mail coupon in back of Archie comic books. - **$15 $30 $65**

ARC-5

❑ **ARC-5. Bob Montana Personal Family Christmas Card,**
1956. Limited issue. - **$10 $20 $35**

ARC-6

❑ **ARC-6. Comic Book Club Kit,**
1950s. Includes envelope, letter, card, cello. button. Set - **$30 $65 $100**

ARC-7

❑ **ARC-7. "Archie's Girls Betty And Veronica Doll Book,"** 1964. Store item by Lowe Publishing Co. Unpunched **- $20 $40 $65**

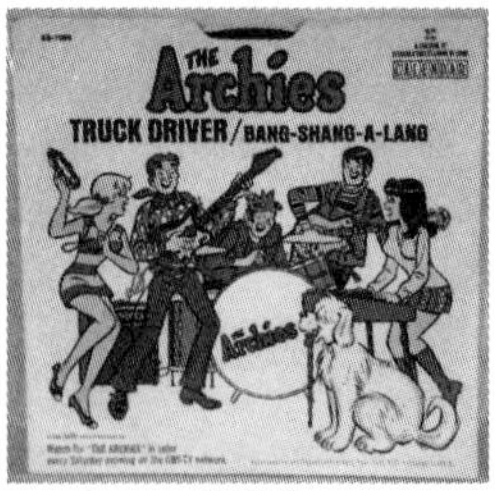


ARC-8

❑ **ARC-8. Archies TV Show Record,**
1968. Came with colorful sleeve holder. Distributed by RCA Records. - **$30 $50 $90**

ARC-9

❑ **ARC-9. Archie's Car Model Kit in Box,**
1968. Aurora. - **$150**

ARC-10

❑ **ARC-10. Archie Spring-Loaded Plastic Head,**
1969. Post Cereals. - **$10 $20 $30**

ARC-11

❑ **ARC-11. "Post Super Sugar Crisp" Box With "The Archies Record",**
1969. Example from set of 4 boxes. Each - **$25 $65 $100**

ARC-12

❑ **ARC-12. "Archie's Car" Premium Offer Cereal Box Flat,**
1969. Box held one of three Archie cars. Gordon Gold Archives. Near Mint Flat - **$350** Used Complete - **$50 $150 $250**

ARC-13

❑ **ARC-13. Jughead's Hat Felt Beanie,**
1969. Post Raisin Bran and Toasties. -
**$25 $60 $120**

ARC-14

❑ **ARC-14. Club Member Cello. Button,**
1960s. Version without accent border. -
**$5 $10 $20**

ARC15

ARC-16

ARC-17

❑ **ARC-15. "Archie" Doll,**
c. 1969. Issuer unknown but possibly a Post Cereals premium. Stuffed cloth 19" tall. -
**$20 $30 $60**

❑ **ARC-16. "Official Member Archie Club" Cello. Button,**
c. 1960s. For comic book club. - **$8 $15 $25**

❑ **ARC-17. Club Member Cello. Button,**
c. 1960s. One of at least two versions accented by rim color. - **$5 $12 $20**

ARC-18

❑ **ARC-18. Picture Or Slogan Litho. Buttons,**
1970. Store item vending machine set of 16.
Each Picture - **$2 $4 $8**
Each Slogan - **$1 $3 $5**

ARC-19

ARC-20

❑ **ARC-19. "Archies Gang!" Vending Machine Paper,**
1970. Archie Comic Publications Inc. Advertises vending items including 16 buttons and five booklets. - **$10 $15 $25**

❑ **ARC-20. Welch's Jelly Glasses,**
1971. Set of eight. Each - **$5 $8 $12**

ARC-21

ARC-22

❑ **ARC-21. Archie Doll with Original Tag,**
1987. - **$15 $40 $80**

❑ **ARC-22. Jughead Doll with Original Tag,**
1987. - **$10 $30 $70**

## Aunt Jemima

**Aunt Jemima Pancake Flour was formulated in 1889 in St. Joseph Missouri, but it was the 1892 Columbian Exposition in Chicago that made Jemima a national figure. The R.T. Davis Mill & Manufacturing Co. hired Nancy Green, a black cook from Kentucky to stand outside its exposition booth and cook pancakes--more than a million, it is claimed--during the course of the fair. Ms. Green traveled the country making personal appearances as Aunt Jemima for the next 30 years until her death in 1923. Quaker Oats bought the product and name in 1924, and today there are over three dozen Aunt Jemima breakfast products. Various Aunt Jemima variety programs ran on CBS between 1929 and 1953 in either 5-minute or 15-minute versions. The trademark face has been redrawn a number of times to cosmetically update the character's features.**

AUN-1

❑ **AUN-1. Cello. Button,**
c. 1896. First issue is not inscribed "Pancake Flour."
Without Inscription - **$40 $110 $175**
With Inscription - **$30 $85 $125**

AUN-2

❑ **AUN-2. "Aunt Jemima Pancake Flour" Paper Puzzle,**
c. 1900. R. T. Davis Co. 3x4" diecut paper portrait card with string holding miniature paper pancake flour box. Reverse offers premium titled "Life History Of Aunt Jemima And A Set Of Her Pickaninny Dolls." - **$50 $100 $200**

AUN-3

❑ **AUN-3. Needle Book With Doll Offer,**
c. 1910. Davis Milling Co. Diecut paper folder holding sewing needles and related plus panel ad for "Aunt Jemima Rag Doll Family." - **$40 $90 $150**

AUN-4

❑ **AUN-4. Aunt Jemima, Uncle Mose, Wade and Diana Doll Fabrics With Envelope,**
c. 1915. Scarce. Aunt Jemima Mills Co.
Near Mint Uncut In Mailer - **$2000**
Aunt Jemima Cut Or Assembled - **$150 $250 $650**
Others Cut Or Assembled - **$100 $200 $350**

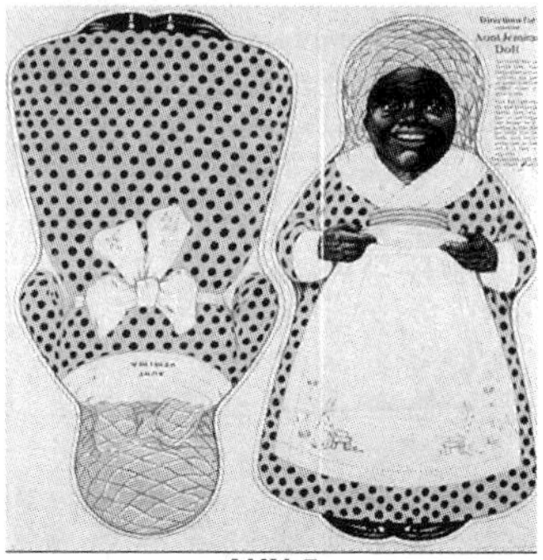

AUN-5

❑ **AUN-5. Cloth Doll,**
1929. Scarce. Near Mint Uncut - **$600**
Assembled - **$75 $175 $350**

AUN-6

❑ **AUN-6. Premium Doll (unstuffed) and Instructions,**
1948. - **$60 $125 $200**

AUN-7

❑ **AUN-7. Vinyl Stuffed Doll Set,**
1948. Set of four - **$75 $175 $375**

AUN-8

❑ **AUN-8. Recipe Booklet Pair,**
1948-1949. Each 4x6" with 20 pages.
Each - **$8 $12 $25**

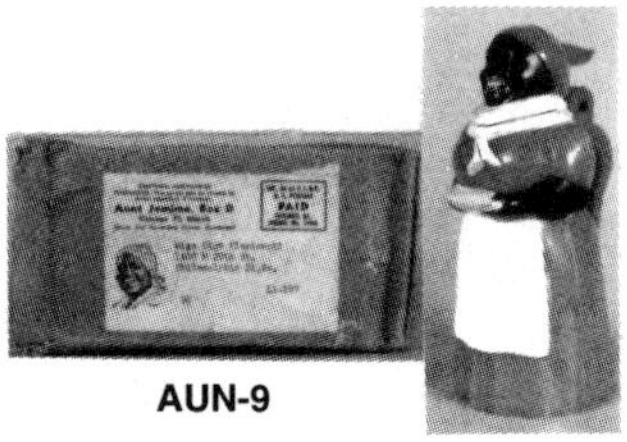

AUN-9

❑ **AUN-9. Plastic Syrup Pitcher With Box,**
c. 1949. Boxed - **$30 $75 $135**
Loose - **$15 $50 $85**

AUN-10

❑ **AUN-10. Hard Plastic Salt & Pepper Set,**
c. 1949. - **$15 $25 $50**

AUN-11

❑ **AUN-11. "Aunt Jemima Doll Family/Fun Book" Original Art Prototype Ad,**
1940s. 9-1/4x14-1/2" from the Gordon Gold Archives. Unique. - **$350**

AUN-12

AUN-13

❑ **AUN-12. "Pancake Days" Cardboard Pin-Back,**
c. 1952. Color portrait on rigid 4" cardboard. - **$20 $30 $60**

❑ **AUN-13. Promotional Pinback,**
1950s. - **$15 $25 $40**

AUN-14

❑ **AUN-14. "Store Promotions Of The Quaker Oats Company" Fold-Out,**
1953. Color folder 7-1/2x11" opens to length of 34-1/2". Promotes "Circus Action Wild Animals" inserts with Muffets Shredded Wheat. Reverse promotes Aunt Jemima cream and sugar set. Gordon Gold Archives. - **$40 $60 $125**

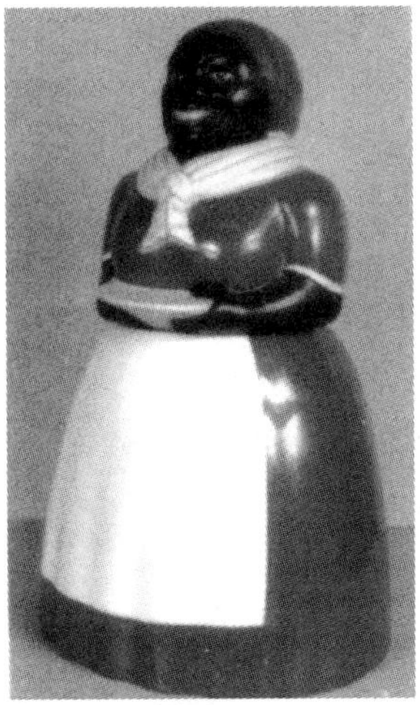

AUN-15

❑ **AUN-15. Plastic Cookie Jar,**
1950s. - **$100 $300 $450**

AUN-16

❑ **AUN-16. "Pastry Mix Set",**
1950s. Store item by Junior Chef. Complete - **$40 $70 $140**

AUN-17

❑ **AUN-17. Chrome Metal Cigarette Lighter,**
1960s. - **$25 $50 $85**

AUN-18

AUN-19

❑ **AUN-18. "Breakfast Club" 4" Litho Button,**
1960s. - **$15 $30 $45**

❑ **AUN-19. Litho. Tab With Color Portrait,**
1960s. - **$10 $15 $20**

## *Aunt Jenny*

**Known under a number of names--*Aunt Jenny, Aunt Jenny's Real Life Stories, Aunt Jenny's Thrilling Real Life Stories, Aunt Jenny's True-Life Stories*, and in Canada as *Aunt Lucy*--this 15-minute serial drama ran five times a week on CBS radio for almost 20 years, from 1937 to 1956. Jenny, played by Edith Spencer and Agnes Young, was assisted by her announcer Danny, played by Dan Seymour, in relating the troubles of her friends and neighbors, providing a golden thought of the day, and offering cooking tips, invariably involving Spry, her longtime sponsor.**

AJR-1

❑ **AJR-1. Cast Member Photo With Mailer Envelope,**
c. 1937. Lever Brothers. Facsimile signature "Best Wishes/Dan Seymour-Sincerely Jennifer F. Wheeler (Aunt Jenny)". Mailer - **$5 $10 $15**
Photo - **$10 $20 $40**

AJR-2

❑ **AJR-2. Fan Photo With Mailer,**
c. 1937. Lever Bros. 8x10" black and white with facsimile signature "Jennifer F. Wheeler (Aunt Jenny)". Mailer - **$5 $10 $15**
Photo - **$20 $40 $75**

AJR-3

AJR-4

❑ **AJR-3. Cook Book,**
1942. Spry Cooking Oil. Fifty pages of recipes. - **$10 $20 $35**

❑ **AJR-4. Cake Knife With Advertising On Cardboard Cover,**
c. 1940s. Scarce. - **$30 $90 $150**

AJR-5

AJR-6

❑ **AJR-5. Recipe,**
1940s. Spry Cooking Oil. Green premium card-board disc - Coconut cake. - **$10 $20 $30**

❑ **AJR-6. "Complete Birthday Kit" With Mailer Box,**
1940s. Spry Cooking Oil. Contents include small candles, candle holders, cake frosting tints, cake recipe leaflet, birthday scroll piece for cake. - **$8 $12 $20**

AJR-7

AJR-8

❑ **AJR-7. "Old Home Recipes" Folder,**
1940s. Spry cooking oil. Unfolds to 3-1/2x13" sheet printed on both sides. - **$3 $6 $10**

❑ **AJR-8. "Favorite Recipes" Booklet,**
1940s. Spry cooking oil. 6x7" with 52 pages. - **$5 $12 $20**

AJR-9

❑ **AJR-9. "Aunt Jenny's Recipe Book-12 Pies Husbands Like Best",**
1952. Lever Brothers. - **$5 $12 $25**

AJR-10

❑ **AJR-10. Recipe,**
1950s. Spry Cooking Oil. Yellow premium card-board disc - Cherry rolls. - **$10 $20 $30**

## Babe Ruth

**George Herman "Babe" Ruth (1895-1948), baseball legend and American national hero, began playing professionally in 1914 for the old Baltimore Orioles before being purchased by the Boston Red Sox. He was a formidable pitcher, but it was his bat that propelled him to greatness. He led the major leagues in home runs in 10 of the 12 years between 1919 and 1930, and in 1927 he hit a record 60. He played in the outfield for the New York Yankees from 1920 to 1935 and Yankee Stadium became known as "The House That Ruth Built." The Babe appeared on several network radio shows: *Play Ball* and *The Adventures of Babe Ruth* sponsored by Quaker cereals in 1934, the *Sinclair Babe Ruth Program* in 1937, *Here's Babe Ruth* in 1943 and *Baseball Quiz* in 1943 and 1944. Eleven issues of *Babe Ruth Sports Comics* were published by Harvey Publications from 1949 to 1951. Ruth was the subject of two feature films, *The Babe Ruth Story* (1948) and *The Babe* (1992). The Babe Ruth Birthplace & Official Orioles Museum in Baltimore, Maryland showcases his early years, playing career, and great moments in baseball history.**

BAB-1

❑ **BAB-1. "Babe Ruth Song" Litho. Button,**
1928. Promotes sheet music for song following his 1927 record-breaking year of 60 home runs in season. - **$35 $75 $125**

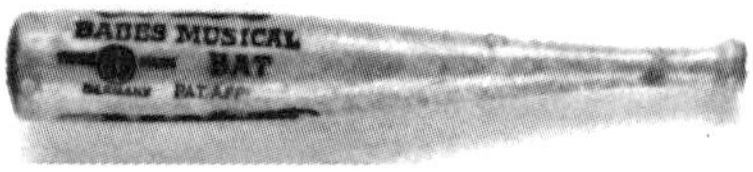


BAB-2

❑ **BAB-2. "Babe's Musical Bat",**
c. 1930. German made store item. 4" long wood replica bat with insert harmonica reeds. - **$75 $125 $225**

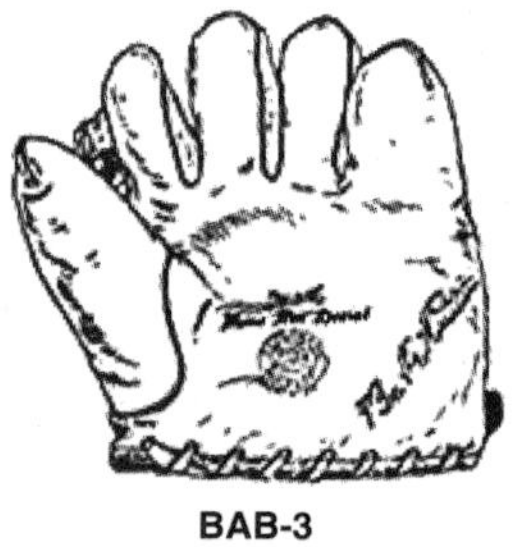

BAB-3

BAB-4

❑ **BAB-3. "Babe Ruth's Baseball Club" Contest Prize,**
1934. Quaker Puffed Wheat. Second prize in weekly contests of Babe Ruth model Spalding fielder glove with facsimile Ruth signature. - **$200 $400 $600**

❑ **BAB-4. "Babe Ruth's Baseball Club" Contest Prize,**
1934. Quaker Puffed Wheat, also store item. Weekly contest third prize boxed Spalding "Babe Ruth Home Run Special" baseball.
Box - **$150 $300 $450**
Baseball - **$100 $250 $450**

BAB-5

❑ **BAB-5. Baseball Scorer,**
c. 1934. Quaker Cereals. Cardboard mechanical disk card. - **$40 $90 $150**

BAB-6 BAB-7

❑ **BAB-6. Quaker Cereal "How To Throw Curves" Booklet,**
1934. - **$15 $30 $85**

❑ **BAB-7. Quaker Cereal "How To Knock Home Runs" Booklet,**
1934. Two additional "How To" booklets (not shown) are "Play The Infield" and "Play The Outfield". Each - **$15 $30 $85**

BAB-8 BAB-9

BAB-10

❑ **BAB-8. Cello. Baseball Scorer Fob,**
1934. Quaker Cereals. Pictures him in Boston cap, back has scoring wheel. - **$50 $150 $350**

❑ **BAB-9. Cello. Baseball Scorer Fob,**
1934. Quaker Cereals. Pictures him in Yankee cap, back has scorer wheel. - **$50 $100 $300**

❑ **BAB-10. Quaker Cello. Club Button,**
1934. - **$30 $60 $100**

BAB-11

❑ **BAB-11. Quaker Oats Patches and Mailer,**
1934. The offer for the Babe Ruth patch included 2 other patches for your initials.
Babe Ruth Patch - **$250**
Two Initial Patches - **$125**
Mailer - **$100**
Complete - **$475**

BAB-12

❑ **BAB-12. Premium Photo,**
c. 1934. Quaker Oats. 8x10" black and white photo with facsimile inscription "To My Pal From 'Babe' Ruth." Bottom margin reads "Presented To Members Of Babe Ruth Base Ball Club By The Quaker Oats Company, Makers Of Quaker Puffed Wheat And Puffed Rice." -
**$50 $125 $250**

BAB-13

❑ **BAB-13. "Babe Ruth In The 'Home Run' A Miniature Movie" Flip-Book,**
c. 1934. Lion Brand, probable coffee product. 1-3/4x2-1/2" with black and white pages. -
**$125 $250 $400**

BAB-14

BAB-15

❑ **BAB-14. "Ask Me" 3" Cello. Button,**
c. 1934. Store employee button promoting Quaker premium card game "Ask Me-The Game Of Baseball Facts". See BAB-16. -
**$125 $275 $400**

❑ **BAB-15. Quaker Oats "Babe Ruth Hitting A Homer" Flip Booklet,**
1934. Pages flip for batting sequence. -
**$125 $250 $400**

BAB-16

❑ **BAB-16. Ask Me Game,**
c. 1934. Scarce. Quaker Cereals. Includes mailer, cards and instructions. See BAB-14.
Complete - **$125 $350 $550**

BAB-17 BAB-18

❑ **BAB-17. Quaker "Babe Ruth Champions" Brass Club Badge,**
1935. - **$25 $50 $85**

❑ **BAB-18. Quaker "Babe Ruth Champions" Cello. Club Button,**
1935. Pictures him in Boston cap. -
**$50 $100 $175**

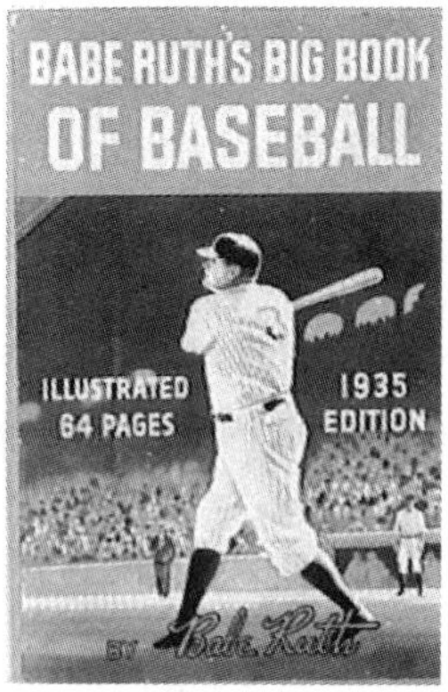


BAB-19

❑ **BAB-19. "Babe Ruth's Big Book Of Baseball",**
1935. Quaker Puffed Wheat And Puffed Rice. 5x7-1/2" with 64 pages of instructions on all facets of playing the game. - **$75 $150 $275**

FREE
Photo-Statuettes of your favorite Movie Stars
WITH TWO BOX TOPS FROM PUFFED WHEAT OR PUFFED RICE
MAIL THIS COUPON NOW!
SEND TWO BOX TOPS FROM EITHER PACK- AGE FOR EACH PHOTO-STATUETTE

BABE RUTH Offers
FREE BASEBALL GIFTS!
MAIL THIS COUPON NOW!

BAB-20

❑ **BAB-20. Mail Order Premium Insert Sheet,**
1936. Quaker Cereals. 8x9" folded insert with one side showing six Babe Ruth premiums with expiration date of July 31, 1936. Opposite side offers "Photo-Statuettes Of Your Favorite Movie Stars." - **$30 $60 $100**

BAB-21

BAB-22

❑ **BAB-21. Babe Ruth Brass Ring,**
1935. Quaker Cereals. No inscriptions but Babe Ruth Club premium picturing baseball symbols. - **$50 $125 $200**

❑ **BAB-22. Babe Ruth Brass Baseball Charms Bracelet,**
1935. Quaker Cereals. - **$50 $125 $200**

BAB-23

❑ **BAB-23. Club 3" Fabric Patch,**
1930s. Possibly Quaker Cereals. - **$25 $50 $85**

BAB-24

BAB-25

❑ **BAB-24. "Babe Ruth" Cello./Steel Bat Replica Pocketknife,**
1930s. Name inscribed on one side plus tiny baseball depiction. - **$50 $85 $150**

❑ **BAB-25. "Babe Ruth" Brass Belt Buckle,**
1930s. Store item by "Harris Belts" marked on reverse. - **$65 $150 $240**

BAB-26

BAB-27

❑ **BAB-26. "Esso Boys Club" Silvered Metal Badge,**
1930s. Figural baseball accented in red/blue with inscription "Charter Member". - **$25 $50 $100**

❑ **BAB-27. "Play Ball With Babe Ruth" Cello. Button,**
1930s. Universal Pictures. Promotion for "Christy Walsh All America Sports Reels" movie feature. - **$85 $160 $350**

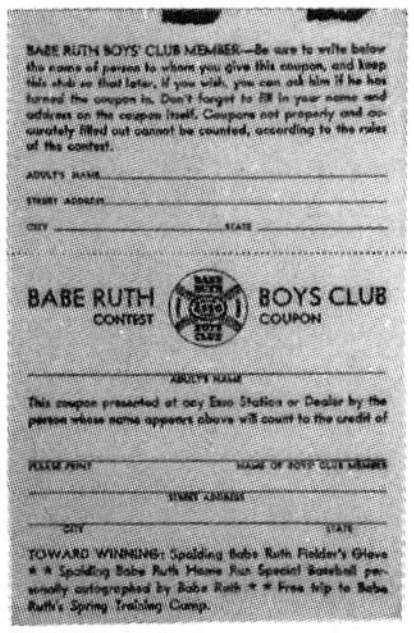
BABE RUTH CONTEST
BOYS CLUB COUPON

BAB-28

BAB-29

❑ **BAB-28. Esso Gasoline "Babe Ruth Boys Club" Contest Coupon,**
1930s. Offers premium for acquiring new members. See BAB-26. - **$15 $25 $50**

❑ **BAB-29. "Bambino/The Real Ball Game" 4" Cello. Button,**
1930s. For mechanical batting practice game based on Babe Ruth popular nickname by unidentified maker. - **$75 $175 $350**

BAB-30

❑ **BAB-30. "Babe Ruth" Plastic Ring,**
c. 1950. Inset picture of him swinging bat. From Kellogg's set of sixteen picturing sports and movie stars, airplanes and 19th century western personalities. - **$30 $60 $85**

(BOX)

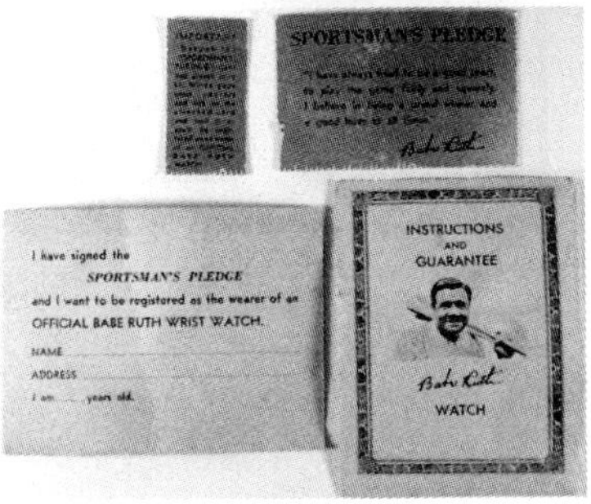


BAB-31

❑ **BAB-31. "Official Babe Ruth Wrist Watch" With Display Case,**
1949. Store item by Exacta Time. Plastic display case is replica baseball.
Near Mint In Case With Box, Coupons, Instructions, Pledge and Postcard - **$2500**
Watch Only - **$250 $600 $1000**

BAB-32

❑ **BAB-32. Look 'N See Gum Card,**
1952. Issued by Topps. This is the stand-out card in the set and the only one to feature a sports figure. **- $25 $50 $125**

BAB-33

❑ **BAB-33. "Hall Of Fame" Boxed Statuette,**
1963. From series of 20 players.
Near Mint Boxed - **$85**
Loose - **$15 $25 $40**

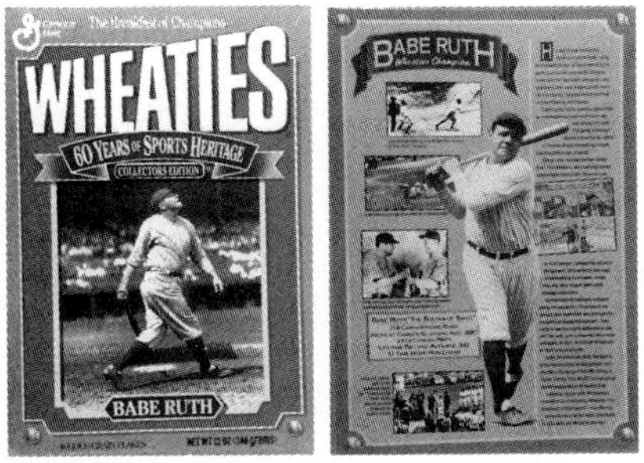


BAB-34

❑ **BAB-34. Wheaties Cereal Box,**
1992. From the set featuring "60 Years of Sports Heritage". Babe Ruth appears on front. Back has pictures and a write-up.- **$5 $10 $25**

BAB-35

❑ **BAB-35. Commemorative Bank Car,**
1995. 100th Anniversary product. Model car's window notes the Babe's 60 home runs hit in 1927.- **$50**

BAB-36

BAB-37

❑ **BAB-36. Commemorative Baseball in Box,**
1995. 100th Anniversary baseball.- **$25**

❑ **BAB-37. Christmas Ornament with Tag,**
1998. - **$12**

(THE BALL)

BAB-38

(3 VIEWS OF THE BOX)

❑ **BAB-38. Babe Ruth Baseball in Box,**
1999. Dark Horse Comics limited edition of 714. Signed by artist Monty Sheldon. - **$50**

BAB-39

BAB-40

❑ **BAB-39. Figure on Card,**
Late 1990s. Starting Lineup figure includes baseball card in package. - **$30**

❑ **BAB-40. Raisin Bran Cereal Box**
2001. Post Raisin Bran box features a "Babe Ruth Hall of Fame" card. - **$20**

# Baby Snooks

**Baby Snooks was a 7-year-old brat and America's radio listeners loved her. Born in the imagination of Ziegfeld Follies star Fanny Brice, the irrepressible imp was introduced to the world on February 29, 1936, in *The Ziegfeld Follies of the Air,* a lavish 60-minute extravaganza on CBS. The program had a brief life, but Baby Snooks was to appear continuously on one network program or another for the next 15 years until Fanny Brice's death in 1951. Sponsors included Maxwell House coffee, Post Toasties cereal, Sanka, Jell-O and Tums.**

BSN-1

BSN-2

❑ **BSN-1. "Radio Guide" Magazine With Fannie Brice Cover,**
1938.- **$8 $12 $25**

❑ **BSN-2. "Fanny Brice's Baby Snooks Pops" Lollipop Pail,**
c. 1938. Store item by E. Rosen Co. 3" tall by 3-1/4" diameter litho. tin featuring three different images around perimeter. - **$50 $85 $150**

BSN-3

❑ **BSN-3. Composition/Wood/Wire "Flexy" Doll With Outfit And Tag,**
1939. Store item by Ideal Toy & Novelty Co. - **$100 $200 $350**

BSN-4

❑ **BSN-4. Ad for "Baby Snooks" Doll,**
1940. From the back cover of Blue Bolt #1 comic book. Was not offered after the first issue. - **$75 $100 $200**

BSN-5

❑ **BSN-5. Whitman Cut-Out Doll Book,**
1940. Store item. Designs by Queen Holden. - **$100 $200 $350**

BSN-6

BSN-7

❑ **BSN-6. "My Second Childhood" Cover Article,**
1944. May issue of "Tune In" national radio magazine including three-page article about "Baby Snooks" radio portrayal by Fannie Brice. - **$10 $15 $25**

❑ **BSN-7. Plastic Figure On Metal Bar Pin,**
c. 1940s. Figure finished in gold color. - **$20 $40 $75**

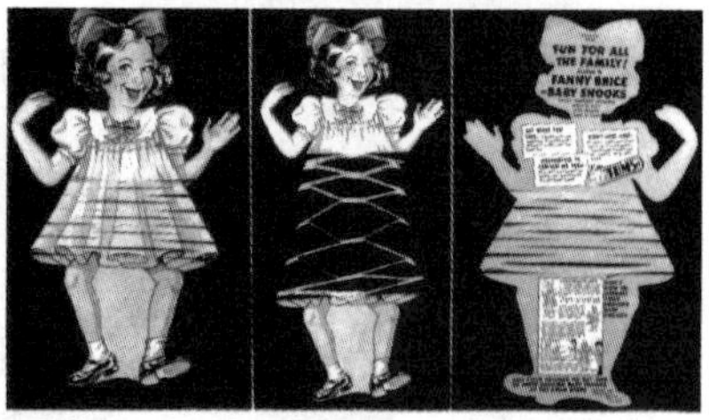

BSN-8

❑ **BSN-8. Cardboard Dancing Puppet,**
1950. Tums. Flexible diecut paper mid-section. - **$30 $75 $150**

BSN-9

❑ **BSN-9. Paper Store Sign With "Dancing Baby Snooks" Offer,**
1950. Tums. Full color 10x16". Gordon Gold archives. - **$50 $100 $150**

BSN-10

❑ **BSN-10. Cardboard Display Card With "Dancing Baby Snooks" Offer,**
1950. Tums. 3-1/2x6-1/2" with reverse instructions for inserting into display carton of product. Gordon Gold Archives. - **$25 $50 $75**

## Bachelor's Children

**Radio's beloved serial, *Bachelor's Children* tells the story of Dr. Bob Graham and the twin teenage girls he promised to raise. In true soap opera form, he eventually marries one of them. The popular series, which won awards for "realism," aired on CBS from 1936 to 1946, sponsored by Old Dutch cleanser, Wonder bread, and Colgate.**

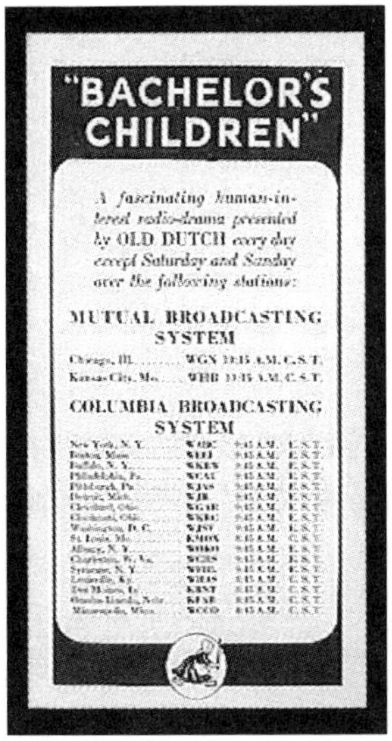
"BACHELOR'S CHILDREN"

A fascinating human-interest radio-drama presented by OLD DUTCH every day except Saturday and Sunday over the following stations:

MUTUAL BROADCASTING SYSTEM

COLUMBIA BROADCASTING SYSTEM

BCH-1

❑ **BCH-1. Story Synopsis Booklet With Station Listings,**
1937. Old Dutch Cleanser. 3-1/4x6-1/4" with 20 pages. - **$8 $15 $25**

BCH-2

❑ **BCH-2. "Bachelor's Children" Story Synopsis Book With Mailer,**
1939. Old Dutch Cleanser. 25-page hardcover including cast member photo plates.
Near Mint With Mailer - **$35**
No Mailer - **$5 $12 $20**

BCH-3

❑ **BCH-3. Wonder Bread Fan Newsletter,**
c. 1945. - **$10 $20 $40**

## Bambi

**One of Disney's most endearing creatures, *Bambi* debuted as a Technicolor feature cartoon at New York City's Radio City Music Hall on August 21, 1942. Since then, Bambi the deer, Thumper the rabbit, Flower the skunk and the Wise Old Owl have continued to enchant young and old audiences alike. Based on the Felix Salten story, Disney's Bambi was also published as a Better Little Book in 1942 and in comic book form several times in the early 1940s and as recently as 1984.**

BAM-1

❑ **BAM-1. "Bambi Woodland Playset,"**
c. 1942. Store item by The Bronfield Publishers. - **$75 $150 $250**

BAM-2

❑ **BAM-2. Big Little Book #1469,**
1942. - **$20 $75 $160**

BAM-3

❑ **BAM-3. "Thumper" Glass Tumbler,**
c. 1942. Probably a dairy product container. Reverse has descriptive verse. - **$75 $150 $225**

BAM-4

BAM-5

❑ **BAM-4. "Prevent Forest Fires" 14x20" Poster,**
1943. U.S. Forest Service. - **$100 $225 $400**

❑ **BAM-5. Paper Bookmark,**
c. 1943. U.S. Department of Agriculture-Forest Service.- **$8 $15 $25**

BAM-6

❑ **BAM-6. "Bambi's Children" Book,**
1943. Better Little Book #1497. - **$20 $75 $160**

BAM-7

❑ **BAM-7. Bambi Glazed Ceramics,**
c. 1947. Store items by American Pottery Co. Each is about 7" tall. One shows him looking forward and the other shows him looking over his shoulder at butterfly on his tail.
Each - **$25 $50 $75**

BAM-8

BAM-9

❑ **BAM-8. Wristwatch,**
1949. Store item by US Time. - **$50 $125 $200**

❑ **BAM-9. Bambi Planter,**
1949. - **$10 $25 $50**

BAM-10

BAM-11

❑ **BAM-10. Signed Studio Fan Card,**
1940s. Signed by Disney staff artist. -
**$50 $75 $135**

❑ **BAM-11. Bambi And Thumper Figurine,**
1950s. 3-1/4" tall. Issued by Goebel. -
**$65 $150 $225**

BAM-12

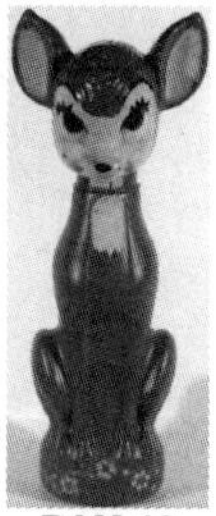

BAM-13

❑ **BAM-12. Bambi And Thumper Goebel Figurines,**
1950s. Store item. Underside of each has full bee marking. Each - **$20 $45 $75**

❑ **BAM-13. Bambi Soaky Toy,**
1965. - **$10 $30 $50**

BAM-14

❑ **BAM-14. Bambi And Thumper Salt And Pepper Set,**
1960s. Store item by Enesco. Set is from series that included generic wood grain plastic tray.
Pair - **$35 $65 $115**

BAM-15

BAM-16

❑ **BAM-15. Limited Edition Watch,**
1993. With die-cut image and box. - **$125**

❑ **BAM-16. Bambi and Thumper Bean Figures in Display Box,**
1990s. - **$18**

BAM-17

❑ **BAM-17. Musical Water Globe,**
1999. Includes all the major characters. Bambi moves up and down as music plays. - **$55**

## The Banana Splits

**This imaginative live-action show consisted of four people wardrobed in outfits of Fleegle the dog, Bingo the gorilla, Drooper the lion and Snorky the baby elephant. The group was musically inclined in addition to adventuresome and appeared in 60-minute shows produced by Hanna-Barbera on NBC, sponsored by Kellogg's, from 1968 to 1970. The show's official title was a lengthy *Kellogg's of Battle Creek Presents The Banana Splits Adventure Hour.* Characters were voiced by Paul Winchell (Fleegle), Daws Butler (Bingo), Allan Melvin (Drooper) and Don Messick (Snorky).**

BSP-1

❑ **BSP-1. Thin Plastic Premium Hand Puppets,**
1968. Kellogg's Chocolate Flavored Kombos. Set consists of Fleegle, Bingo, Drooper and (not shown) Snorky. Each - **$5 $10 $30**

BSP-2

BSP-3

❑ **BSP-2. Record In Sleeve,**
1968. Kellogg's. Includes song "Doin' The Banana Split" and three others. With Mailer - **$25 $50 $85**
No Mailer - **$15 $40 $65**

❑ **BSP-3. Record With Sleeve,**
1968. Kellogg's. Song "Tra-La-La Song" and three others.
With Mailer - **$25 $50 $85**
No Mailer - **$15 $40 $65**

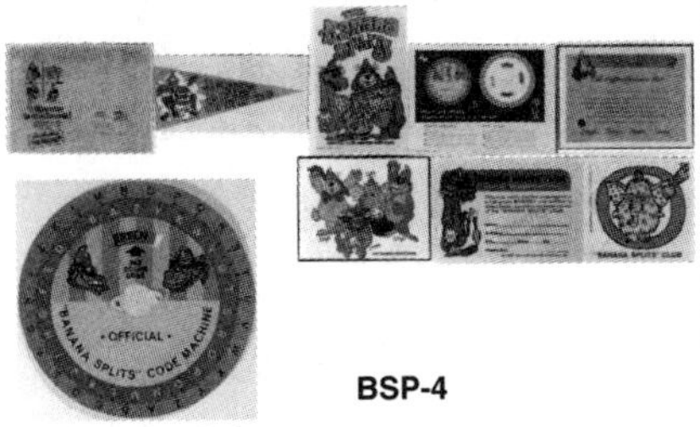

(enlarged coder)

BSP-4

❑ **BSP-4. Club Kit,**
1968. Mailing envelope plus pennant, membership book, code machine, certificate, group portrait, membership card, sticker.
Complete - **$125 $375 $550**
Code Card Only - **$50 $100 $175**

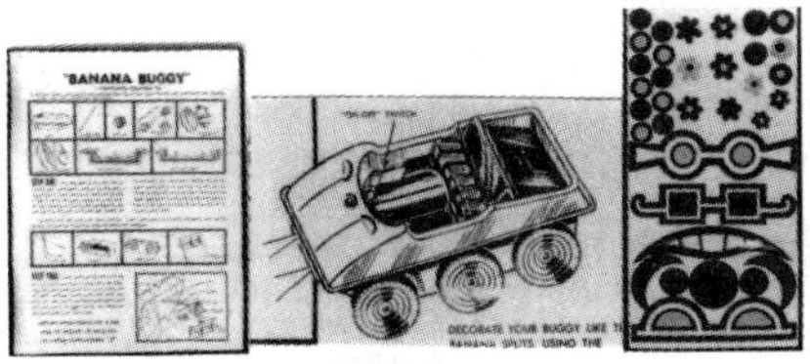

BSP-5

❑ **BSP-5. "Banana Buggy" Model Kit,**
c. 1968. Kellogg's. Yellow vinyl with motor and sticker sheet.
Mint Boxed - **$600**
Assembled - **$100 $200 $400**

BSP-6

❑ **BSP-6. Banana Splits Character Stamp Pad Set,**
c. 1968. Kellogg's. Plastic case holding six character image ink stamp blocks plus instruction slip. - **$25 $60 $125**

BSP-7

❑ **BSP-7. Fleegle Plastic Mug,**
1969. Came with red plastic cereal bowl picturing the characters. Each - **$10 $20 $35**

BSP-8

❑ **BSP-8. "Breakfast Set" Premium Offer Cereal Box,**
1969. Gordon Gold Archives.
Near Mint Flat - **$425**
Used Complete - **$100 $200 $300**

BSP-9

❑ **BSP-9. NBC Promo Transparency,**
c. 1969. 4x5". - **$10 $15 $25**

BSP-10

❑ **BSP-10. Banana Buggy Aurora Model Kit,**
1969. Store item. Set consists of instructions, decal sheet, buggy, bench, figures of Fleegle, Bingo, Snorky, Drooper, along with eyeglasses and tails.
Near Mint Boxed Unassembled - **$350**
Built Model - **$50 $100 $150**
Box Only - **$30 $60 $100**

BSP-11

❑ **BSP-11. Cereal Box With "Banana Splits Pin-Up Posters" Offer,**
1969. This box held "Kellogg's Froot Loops" although offer was made on various Kellogg's product boxes. Gordon Gold archives.
Near Mint Flat - **$425**
Used Complete - **$75 $150 $250**

BSP-12

❑ **BSP-12. Fleer Gum "Tattoo" Vending Machine Card,**
1969.- **$5 $10 $15**

BSP-13

❑ **BSP-13. "Banana Splits Snorky" Large Stuffed Plush Doll,**
1970. Store item. 25" tall. - **$75 $150 $250**

BSP-14

BSP-15

❑ **BSP-14. Drooper Vinyl Figure,**
1971. Store item by Sutton.
Bagged - **$40 $60 $115**
Loose - **$15 $35 $70**

❑ **BSP-15. Fleegle Vinyl Figure,**
1971. Store item by Sutton.
Bagged - **$40 $60 $115**
Loose - **$15 $35 $70**

BSP-16

❑ **BSP-16. Button Set,**
1972. Hanna-Barbera copyright. Full color 1-1/4" buttons showing the group: Bingo, Drooper, Fleegle, and Snorky. Each - **$8 $15 $25**

BSP-17

❑ **BSP-17. 7-Eleven Plastic Cups,**
1976. Each - **$10 $20 $30**

## Barbie

**Until 1959, when Barbie first appeared, dolls were pretty much the same for hundreds of years. They were baby dolls to be mothered and nurtured by their youthful owners who would probably be mothers with their own real babies someday. Dolls came on the market with eyes that opened, movable arms and legs and finally dolls that wet and needed to be fed and changed--not too exciting. Barbie started a revolutionary trend; she wasn't a baby doll, but a young lady out in the world with fashionable clothes, cars, and boyfriends...and she had a bosom! Ruth Handler, Barbie's creator, has been quoted as saying "Barbie was originally created to project every little girl's dream of the future."**

**Barbie's boyfriend Ken came along in 1961; her best friend Midge arrived in 1963. Little sister Skipper was introduced in 1964 as were her male friend Ricky and girlfriend Skooter. The Barbie product line by Mattel continues to rank among the most successful offerings of the toy industry.**

BAR-1

BAR-2

❑ **BAR-1. "Barbie Play Ring" On Card,**
1962. Store item by Mattel. 4x6-1/2" card holds gold luster metal ring featuring Barbie profile surrounded by rhinestones.
Near Mint On Card - **$200**
Ring Only - **$25 $50 $100**

❑ **BAR-2. Metal Lunch Bottle,**
1962. Store item by King-Seeley. This bottle came with several different vinyl lunch boxes. - **$15 $30 $60**

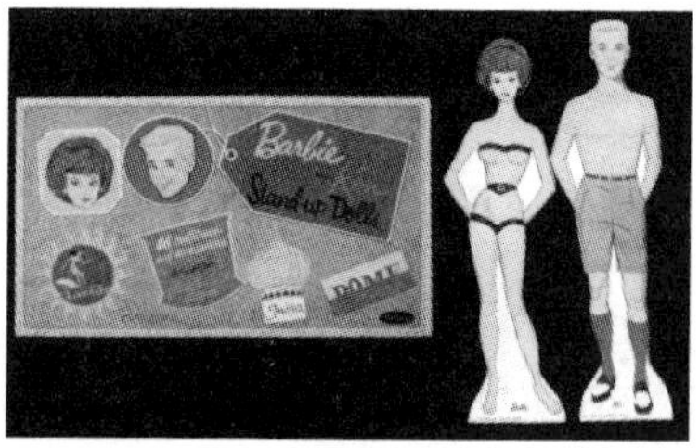

BAR-3

❑ **BAR-3. "Barbie & Ken Standup Dolls" Kit,**
1962. Store item by Whitman under Mattel copyright. Carrying case holds two diecut cardboard 9-1/2" tall figures. - **$30 $50 $85**

BAR-4

❑ **BAR-4. "Barbie's Keys To Fame" Game,**
1963. Store item by Mattel. - **$20 $40 $60**

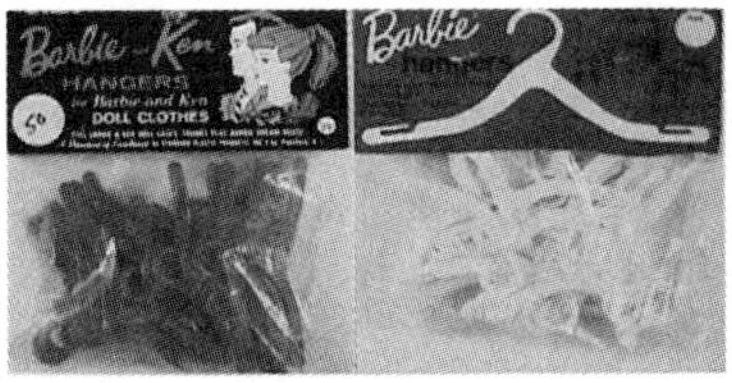


BAR-5

❑ **BAR-5. Barbie And Ken Clothing Hanger Packs,**
c. 1963. Store item by Mattel. Barbie and Ken pack has red plastic hangers with 1963 copyright. Second pack has 1965 copyright with white plastic hangers for Barbie, Francie, Skipper and Scooter.
Each Sealed Pack - **$5 $15 $30**

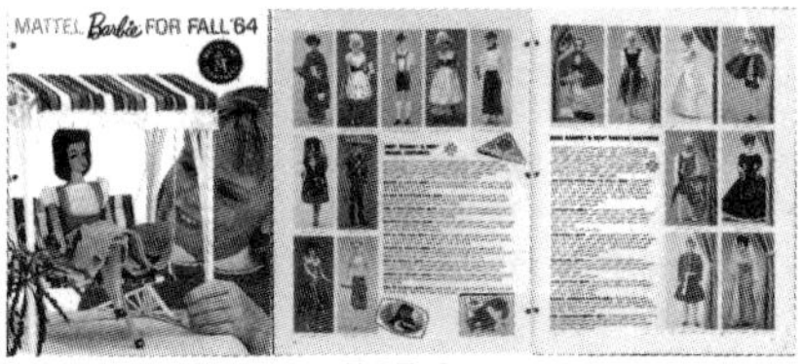


BAR-6

❑ **BAR-6. "Mattel Dolls For Fall '64" Retailer's Catalogue,**
1964. - **$40 $75 $125**

BAR-7

BAR-8

❑ **BAR-7. Fan Club Membership Card,**
1964.- **$10 $20 $40**

❑ **BAR-8. Wristwatch,**
1964. Store item. - **$35 $65 $130**

BAR-9

❑ **BAR-9. "Skipper" Vinyl Wallet,**
1964. Store item by Standard Plastics Products under license from Mattel. Comes with yellow or blue background. Each - **$15 $30 $50**

BAR-10

❑ **BAR-10. "Barbie For Fall" Catalogue,**
1964. Store item by Mattel. - **$40 $75 $125**

BAR-11

❑ **BAR-11. "Barbie" Magazine,**
March-April, 1965. One of a series by Mattel.
Each - **$5 $10 $20**

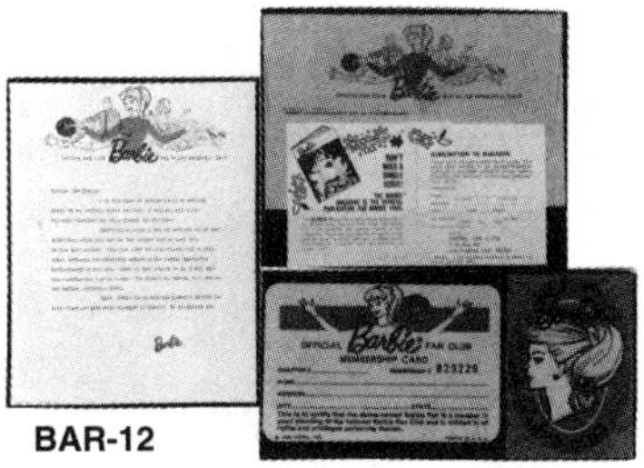


BAR-12

❑ **BAR-12. Club Kit,**
1965. Mailing envelope holding cover letter, Barbie Magazine subscription coupon, club chapter application form, membership card, fabric peel-off sticker.
Near Mint Complete - **$125**

BAR-13

❑ **BAR-13. "World Of Fashion" Game,**
1967. Store item by Mattel - **$10 $20 $40**

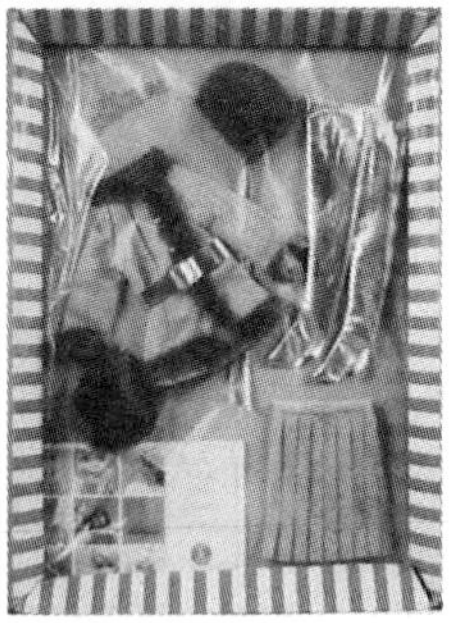

BAR-14

❑ **BAR-14. "Barbie & Stacey" Packaged Fashion Outfit,**
1967. Store item by Mattel. 9x11-1/2x1" deep package holds outfit for Barbie or "Barbie's British Friend." Sealed - **$30 $60 $90**

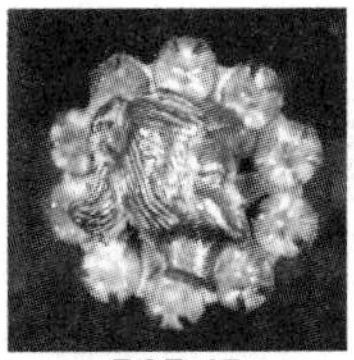

BAR-15

❑ **BAR-15. Silvered Metal Adjustable Ring,**
1960s. Rhinestones around Barbie's profile in brass. - **$25 $50 $100**

BAR-16

❑ **BAR-16. Barbie & Friends 6x10x30" Glass And Metal Mattel Electrical Display Sign,**
1960s. Florescent lighted. - **$100 $200 $325**

BAR-17

❑ **BAR-17. Special Edition of 1959 Barbie,**
1993. Boxed. - **$20**

BAR-18

❑ **BAR-18. Barbie and Ken Star Trek Gift Set,**
1996. Boxed. - **$80**

BAR-19

❑ **BAR-19. Space Camp Barbie in Box,**
1998. Boxed. - **$20**

BAR-20

❑ **BAR-20. "Barbie Loves Elvis" Gift Set,**
1999. - **$75**

BAR-21

❑ **BAR-21. "Barbie Loves Frankie Sinatra" Gift Set,**
1999. - **$80**

BAR-22

❑ **BAR-22. Becky Doll in Box,**
1999. Boxed. - **$20**

BAR-23

❑ **BAR-23. Barbie Ring and Earrings,**
1999. On card - **$5**

BAR-24

❑ **BAR-24. Becky Paralympic Champion Doll in Box,**
2000. Promotes races at Sydney 2000 Paralympic Games. - **$25**

BAR-25

❑ **BAR-25. President Barbie Doll in Box,**
2000. Toys 'R' Us Exclusive. Came in both a red box and a blue box. Each - **$25**

BAR-26

❑ **BAR-26. Barbie as Wonder Woman Collector Edition in Box,**
2000. DC Comics product. - **$55**

BAR-27

❑ **BAR-27. Barbie as Samantha from Bewitched - Collector Edition in Box,**
2001. From the 1960s TV show. - **$43**

## Barney Google

***"Barney Google, with his Goo-Goo-Googly Eyes,"* the 1923 hit song by Billy Rose and Con Conrad, was about a feisty little sport in a top hat, the cartoon creation of Billy De Beck (1890-1942) that has been called one of the 10 greatest American comic strips of all time. The daily Barney strip first appeared in 1919 on the sports page of the Chicago Herald-Examiner, where he was soon joined by his pitiful racehorse Spark Plug. Readers loved them. Snuffy Smith, a mountain hillbilly, was introduced to the strip in 1934; his name was added to the title a few years later and by the mid-1940s he had taken full title. Fred Lasswell continued the strip after De Beck's death in 1942. A series of movie shorts was produced in the 1920s and a few animated TV cartoons were produced in the 1960s.**

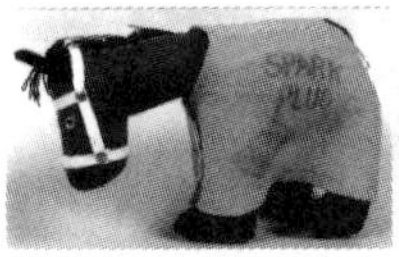

BNG-1

BNG-2

❑ **BNG-1. Fabric Doll,**
1922. Store item. - **$50 $125 $250**

❑ **BNG-2. "Spark Plug" Glass Candy Container,**
1923. Store item. Saddle blanket area originally had orange paint. - **$75 $150 $300**

BNG-3

BNG-4

❑ **BNG-3. "Barney Google" Sheet Music,**
1923. Store item by Jerome Remick. -
**$10 $25 $75**

❑ **BNG-4. "Barney Google And His Faithful Nag Spark Plug" Comic Strip Reprint Book,**
1923. First Barney Google title in Cupples & Leon series. - **$100 $200 $300**

BNG-5

❑ **BNG-5. "Spark Plug" Wooden Pull Toy,**
1923. Store item. - **$65 $125 $200**

BNG-6

BNG-7

❑ **BNG-6. Cello. Button,**
1924. The L.A. Examiner. 7/8" with color portrait. - **$25 $50 $100**

❑ **BNG-7. Barney Google Riding Spark Plug Tin Litho. Wind-Up Toy,**
c. 1925. Store item by Nifty, made in Germany. - **$600 $1200 $2200**

BNG-8

BNG-9

BNG-10

❑ **BNG-8. "Official Song Of The Secret And Mysterious Order Of Billygoats" Sheet Music,**
1928. - **$20 $40 $75**

❑ **BNG-9. Brotherhood Of Bulls Membership Card,**
1920s. Scarce. Chicago Herald and Examiner. - **$30 $60 $125**

❑ **BNG-10. Brotherhood Of Billy Goats Membership Card,**
1920s. Scarce. Chicago Herald and Examiner. - **$30 $60 $125**

BNG-11

BNG-12

❑ **BNG-11. "The Atlanta Georgian's Silver Anniversary" Litho. Button,**
1937. Named newspaper. From set of various characters. - **$40 $125 $275**

❑ **BNG-12. "Sunday Herald And Examiner" Litho. Button,**
1930s. Chicago newspaper. From "30 Comics" set of various characters. - **$15 $25 $50**

BNG-13

BNG-14

❑ **BNG-13. Enamel On Silvered Brass Pin,**
c. 1930s.- **$ 50 $75 $150**

❑ **BNG-14. "Barney Google/Detroit Times" Cello. Button,**
1930s. Newspaper contest serial number issue from comic character series. - **$15 $30 $60**

BNG-15

BNG-16

❑ **BNG-15. Newspaper Contest Cello. Button,**
1930s. New York Sunday American. 1-1/4" in black, white and shades of red. - **$20 $35 $60**

❑ **BNG-16. Boston Sunday Advertiser 11x17" Cardboard Display Sign,**
1930s. - **$75 $150 $275**

BNG-17

❑ **BNG-17. "Barney Google/Snuffy Smith" Hand-Painted Plaster Salt & Pepper Set,**
c. 1943. Each is 2-3/4" tall. - **$15 $30 $50**

BNG-18

❑ **BNG-18. "Buy War Stamps" 14x18" Poster,**
c. 1944. U.S. Government. - **$50 $100 $175**

BNG-19

❑ **BNG-19. Snuffy Smith Hand Puppet,**
c. 1955. Store item by Gund. - **$15 $30 $60**

# Batman

**The legendary Batman--and the huge Bat-industry he was to spawn--was introduced in *Detective Comics* #27 of May 1939. Since then, the Caped Crusader and his sidekick, Robin the Boy Wonder, have battled crime and the forces of evil in comic strips, in live-action and animated cartoon TV series, on the radio, on prime-time network television, in comic books, movie serials, feature films and in the hearts of millions of fans, young and old. Artists Bob Kane and Jerry Robinson, and writer Bill Finger also produced an array of notable knaves, among them the Joker, Penguin, the Riddler and Catwoman. Batman's two greatest successes were the 1966-1968 ABC television series with Adam West and Burt Ward as the Dynamic Duo and a string of famous actors as the various villains (which also spawned its own feature film--and the famous line "Some days you just can't get rid of a bomb."--starring the same regular cast of heroes and villains); and the 1989 blockbuster film starring Michael Keaton, Jack Nicholson, and Kim Basinger. This hit movie, directed by Tim Burton, was followed by three sequels: *Batman Returns* (1992), *Batman Forever* (1995), which handed the Bat-cowl from Keaton to Val Kilmer and featured Jim Carrey as the Riddler, and the lackluster *Batman and Robin*, starring George Clooney as the latest Batman, with Alicia Silverstone as Batgirl. These productions generated hundreds of toys, premiums, posters, games, models, dolls, etc. Holy Merchandise, Batman!**

**Batman presently stars in four monthly titles: *Batman*, *Detective Comics*, *Batman: Legends of the Dark Knight*, and *Batman: Gotham Knights*. A fifth monthly title, *Batman: Gotham Adventures*, was created as a stylistic companion to the character's animated adventures (see below).**

**Batman is currently featured with Superman and other Justice League characters in *JLA*, and appears frequently in such related titles as *Azreal: Agent of the Bat*, *Batgirl*, *Birds of Prey*, *Catwoman*, *Harley Quinn*, *Nightwing*, and *Robin*, as well as in numerous specials and one-shots.**

**Debuting on Fox in 1992, *Batman–The Animated Series* featured a "Dark Deco" style and a superb voice cast including Kevin Conroy (Batman/Bruce Wayne), Mark Hamill (The Joker), and Efrem Zimbalist, Jr. (Alfred). The series ran for 85 episodes, the final season of which was under the title *The Adventures of Batman & Robin*. Two animated films, *Batman: Mask of the Phantasm* (theatrical release, 1993) and *Batman: Sub-Zero* (direct-to-video release, 1998), were also released. Episodes of a successor series, *The New Batman Adventures*, aired with re-broadcast episodes of the series as part of *The New Batman-Superman Adventures* on WB. Numerous lines of popular licensed toys were produced in conjunction with this succession of animated incarnations.**

**A spin-off cartoon set in a darker future, *Batman Beyond*, debuted in 1999 and saw an elderly Bruce Wayne (again voiced by Kevin Conroy) guiding his young replacement, Terry McGinnis (Will Friedle), against a variety of new and old villains. It ran 52 episodes over three seasons on WB and spawned one direct-to-video film, *Return of the Joker* (which featured the returning voice of Mark Hamill). The series also inspired comic book limited series, an on-going monthly that ran 24 issues, and numerous toys.**

BAT-1

❑ **BAT-1. Paper Mask,**
1943. Scarce. Philadelphia Record newspaper, probably others. Back announces new daily and Sunday comic strips. - **$300 $1200 $2000**

BAT-2

❑ **BAT-2. Paper Mask,**
1943. Same front and back design as BAT-1 except front has green type announcing start of movie serial at "State Theatre" and references feature movie "Deanna Durbin In 'Her's To Hold.'" - **$300 $1200 $2000**

BAT-3

❑ **BAT-3. Batplane Movie Promo,**
1943. Various sponsors. - **$850 $1600 $2800**

BAT-4

❑ **BAT-4. "Full Color Transfers",**
1944. Rare. Not a premium but earliest known merchandise (10 cents) item for Batman. Back of sheet has ad for Detective Comics. -
**$300 $650 $1250**

BAT-5

❑ **BAT-5. "Batman's Last Chance" One-Sheet,**
1949. Columbia Pictures serial. -
**$600 $1400 $2000**

BAT-6

❑ **BAT-6. "New Adventures of Batman & Robin Three-Sheet,**
1949. Columbia Pictures serial. -
**$2000 $6000 $9000**

(1943 FRONT)

(1947 FRONT)

BAT-7

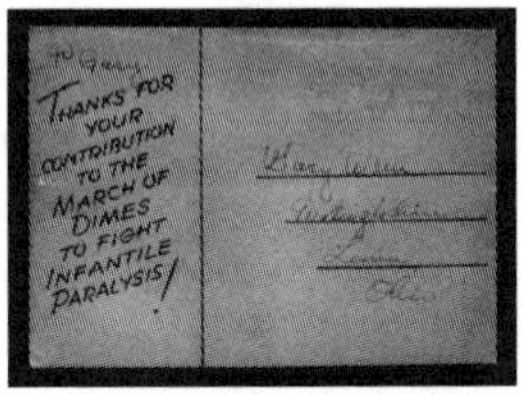


(BACK)

❑ **BAT-7. Batman Infantile Paralysis Card,**
1940s. Scarce. March of Dimes premium. Small version offered in 1943, large version in 1947.
1943 version - **$100 $200 $500**
1947 version - **$75 $150 $400**

BAT-8

❑ **BAT-8. Batman Sportsmanship Promo,**
1949. Scarce. National Comics Pub., Inc. -
**$75 $150 $250**

BAT-9

❑ **BAT-9. Batman/Superman Christmas Card,**
1940s. Rare. - **$500 $1500 $2000**

BAT-10

❑ **BAT-10. DC Comics Fan Card,**
1960. - **$30 $60 $125**

BAT-11

BAT-12

❑ **BAT-11. "Crimefighter" 1-3/8" Litho. Button,**
1966.- **$5 $10 $15**

❑ **BAT-12. "Batman And Robin Deputy Crimefighter,**
1966. Cello. button 3-1/2", store item. -
**$12 $25 $35**

BAT-13

❑ **BAT-13. Batmobile Model Kit in Box,**
1966. Aurora. With instructions.
Complete - **$400**

BAT-14

❑ **BAT-14. Batplane Model Kit in Box,**
1966. Aurora. With instructions.
Complete - **$300**

BAT-15

❑ **BAT-15. Batmobile Tin Car with Box,**
1960s. Complete - **$350**

BAT-16

BAT-17

❑ **BAT-16. Batman Beanie,**
1966. - **$10 $20 $30**

❑ **BAT-17. "Batman" Litho. Button,**
1966. From red, white and blue set of 14 in 7/8" size, also issued in similar set colored red, green, yellow, black.
Each - **$3 $8 $12**

BAT-18

❑ **BAT-18. Batman Kellogg's OKs Cereal Box (Flat),**
1966. features Yogi Bear on front, Batman on back. Promotes Batman periscope premium. - **$400 $950 $1500**

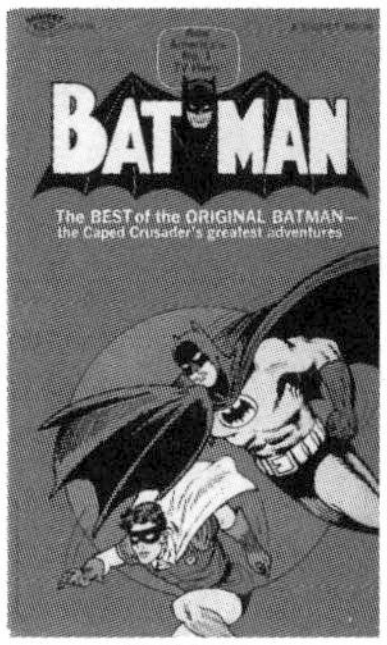


BAT-19

BAT-20

❑ **BAT-19. Batman Periscope,**
1966. Kellogg's OKs cereal premium. -
**$30 $60 $90**

❑ **BAT-20. "Batman" Paperback Book,**
1966. TV related. - **$10 $25 $35**

(FRONT) BAT-21 (BACK ENLARGED)

❑ **BAT-21. Batman Kellogg's Frosted Flakes Box (Flat),**
1966. promotes Batman printing set premium. -
**$300 $800 $1200**

BAT-22

❑ **BAT-22. "Batman Golden Records" Boxed Set,**
1966. N.P.P. Inc. Includes comic book, LP record, "Batman Official Member" gold and black litho. button, one of twelve different flicker rings and membership card with secret code.
Near Mint Boxed Set - **$125**
Comic - **$7 $21 $70**
Button - **$2 $3 $5**
Ring - **$8 $15 $25**
Card - **$5 $12 $20**

BAT-23

❑ **BAT-23. "Batman Print Set,"**
1966. Kellogg's Sugar Frosted Flakes. Plastic case holding six different plastic stamps and ink pad. Stamps picture Batman, Robin, Joker, Penguin, Riddler, Batmobile.
Near Mint Boxed - **$150**
Unboxed - **$20 $40 $60**

BAT-24

BAT-25

❑ **BAT-24. "Batman And Robin Buttons" Vending Machine Display Paper,**
1966. - **$5 $8 $16**

❑ **BAT-25. "Batman" Lucky Charm Ad,**
1966. Used in gumball display and machines.- **$10 $25 $35**

BAT-26

❑ **BAT-26. Batman 1" Size Litho. Button Set,**
1966. Vending machines but scarcer than 7/8" size. 14 different.
Red/White/Blue Style Each - **$15 $25 $50**
Red/Green/Yellow Style Each - **$15 $30 $55**

BAT-27

❑ **BAT-27. Contest Card With Three Picture Playing Pieces,**
1966. Safeway Or Merit Gasoline. Shows both TV and comic book characters. - **$75 $150 $300**

BAT-28

❑ **BAT-28. "Batman Coins" On Card,**
1966. Store item by Transogram.
Complete On Card - **$20 $40 $75**
Loose Coin - **$1 $2 $3**

BAT-29

BAT-30

❑ **BAT-29. Fan Photo,**
1966. Adam West and Burt Ward with facsimile signatures. - **$25 $40 $85**

❑ **BAT-30. All Star Dairies 24x44" Cardboard Sign,**
1966.- **$100 $200 $300**

BAT-31

❑ **BAT-31. "Batman Ring Club" 4x5" Flicker Display Card,**
1966. Showing both images. - **$75 $100 $125**

BAT-32

BAT-33

❑ **BAT-32. Metal License Plate,**
1966. Store item by Groff Signs. - **$10 $20 $40**

❑ **BAT-33. Metal License Plate,**
1966. Store item by Groff Signs. - **$10 $20 $40**

BAT-34

BAT-35

❑ **BAT-34. Robin Flexible Rubber Ring,**
1966. Vending machine issue. - **$12 $20 $35**

❑ **BAT-35. "Batman Fudge Crusader-Sundae" Wrapper,**
1966. Parallelogram waxed paper. - **$5 $10 $20**

BAT-36

BAT-37

❑ **BAT-36. Metal License Plate,**
1966. Store item. - **$10 $20 $35**

❑ **BAT-37. "Flicker Pictures" Vending Machine Display Paper,**
1966. - **$10 $20 $35**

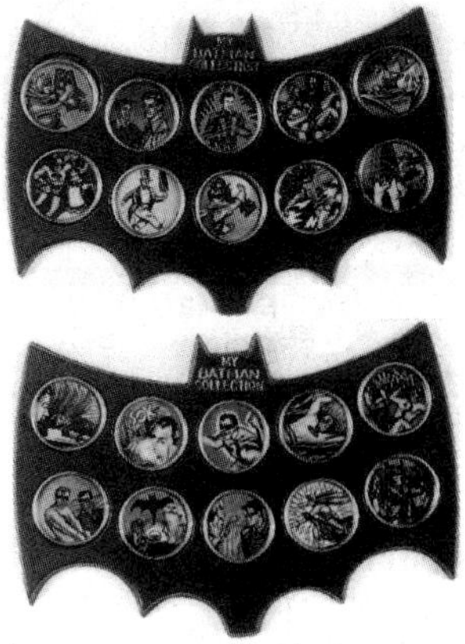

BAT-38

❑ **BAT-38. "My Batman Collection" Metal Coin Set With Plastic Holders,**
1966. Set of 20 coins.
Set In Holders - **$100 $200 $325**
Each Coin - **$3 $7 $12**

BAT-39

BAT-40

**❑ BAT-39. Batman Poster 27x40",**
1966. Toothpaste premium for TV show. -
**$50 $125 $250**

**❑ BAT-40. Robin Poster 27x40",**
1966. Toothpaste premium for TV show. -
**$50 $125 $250**

BAT-41

BAT-42

**❑ BAT-41. Cardboard Mask,**
1966. General Electric television. One mask on front, other on reverse. - **$5 $10 $15**

**❑ BAT-42. "Batman & Robin Mask" Appliance Store Kit,**
1966. Issued to promote General Electric television. Envelope originally held 50 thin cardboard flip masks printed on both sides plus pictured example 33x40" wall poster.
Envelope - **$5 $10 $20**
Poster - **$75 $175 $300**

BAT-43

BAT-44

**❑ BAT-43. Batman/Magazine Promotion 3-1/2" Cello. Button,**
1966. Authorized issue for Electronic Industries magazine. Probably a trade show item. -
**$50 $125 $200**

**❑ BAT-44. Batman/Robin Clock Face Flicker Ring,**
c. 1966. Vending machine issue. - **$20 $30 $40**

BAT-45

BAT-46

**❑ BAT-45. Batman Mug,**
1966. - **$10 $20 $35**

**❑ BAT-46. Batman & Robin Glass Mug,**
1966. Made in England. - **$25 $50 $75**

BAT-47

**❑ BAT-47. "All Star Ice Cream" Large Store Sign,**
1966. 24x44". - **$100 $200 $400**

BAT-48

**❑ BAT-48. "Corgi Batmobile" Complete Boxed First Issue,**
1966. Store item. Near Mint Boxed - **$500**
Car With Figures Only - **$50 $100 $150**

BAT-49

**❑ BAT-49. "Life" Magazine With Batman Cover Article,**
1966. March 11 issue. - **$8 $15 $30**

BAT-50

**❑ BAT-50. TV Guide With Batman Cover Article,**
1966. Has five-page article "Batty Over Batman?" - **$15 $25 $40**

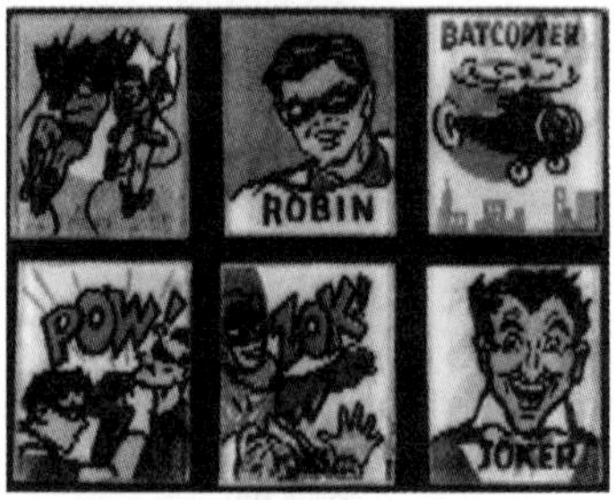


BAT-51

**❑ BAT-51. Flicker Miniature Pictures,**
1966. Vending machine set of six.
Each- **$5 $12 $18**

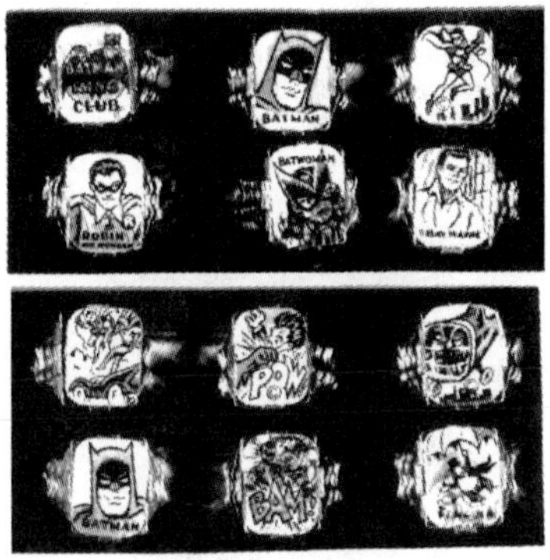

BAT-52

❑ **BAT-52. Plastic Flicker Rings,**
1966. Set of 12 in either silver or blue base.
Silver Base Each - **$8 $15 $25**
Blue Base Each - **$5 $15 $20**

BAT-53

❑ **BAT-53. "Batman Candy & Toy" Boxes,**
1966. Store item by Phoenix Candy Co. Set of eight with front and back numbered pictures (1-16). Each Box - **$15 $30 $45**

BAT-54

❑ **BAT-54. Holloway Candies 17x22" Cardboard Store Sign,**
1966. Milk Duds, Black Cow, Slo-Poke candies. Offered three different coloring books with six-pack candy purchase. - **$100 $175 $250**

BAT-55 BAT-56

❑ **BAT-55. "Batman" English Cello. Button,**
1966. A&BC Chewing Gum Ltd. In addition to Robin (next item), the set includes an image of Batman flying through the air and one of Batman on a batwing design.
Each - **$15 $30 $50**

❑ **BAT-56. "Robin" English Cello. Button,**
1966. A&BC Chewing Gum Ltd. - **$15 $30 $50**

BAT-57 BAT-58

❑ **BAT-57. Batman Glass Tumbler,**
1966. - **$8 $12 $20**

❑ **BAT-58. Robin Glass Tumbler,**
1966. Same reverse side as Batman tumbler.- **$8 $12 $20**

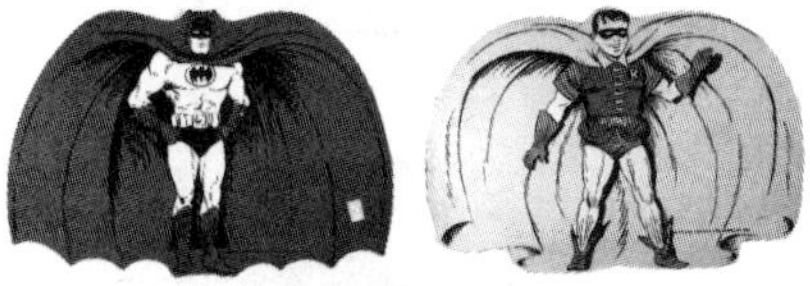

BAT-59

❑ **BAT-59. Rubber Place Mats,**
1966. 18 3/4" wide and 13" tall.
Each - **$25 $50 $75**

(Front) BAT-60 (Back)

❑ **BAT-60. Coloring Book,**
1966. Holloway Candy. 4-1/4x4-3/4" 16 pages on newsprint. - **$30 $60 $90**

BAT-61

BAT-62

❑ **BAT-61. Pop Tarts Comic Booklet,**
1966. "The Mad Hatter's Hat Crimes" from set of six. - **$3 $9 $30**

❑ **BAT-62. Pop Tarts Comic Booklet,**
1966. "The Penguin's Fowl Play" from set of six. - **$3 $9 $30**

BAT-63

BAT-64

❑ **BAT-63. Pop Tarts Comic Booklet,**
1966. "The Catwoman's Catnapping Caper" from set of six. - **$3 $9 $30**

❑ **BAT-64. Pop Tarts Comic Booklet,**
1966. "The Man In The Iron Mask" from set of six. - **$3 $9 $30**

BAT-65

❑ **BAT-65. Large Plastic Free-Wheeling Airplane,**
c. 1966. Store item by Irwin. 19" long by 21" wide by 5" tall with name and image logo stickers. - **$100 $250 $400**

BAT-66

BAT-67

❑ **BAT-66. Composition Bobbing Head Figure,**
c. 1966. Store item. - **$100 $350 $650**

❑ **BAT-67. "The Joker And His Pals Candy & Toy" Box,**
1967. Store item by Phoenix Candy Co. Eight different boxes in set.
Each Box - **$40 $90 $150**

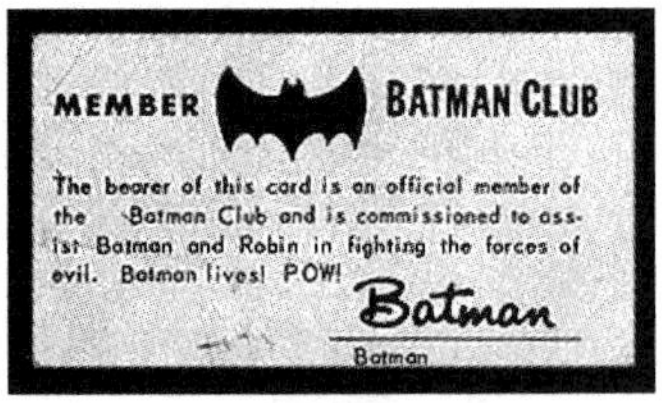
MEMBER BATMAN CLUB

The bearer of this card is an official member of the Batman Club and is commissioned to assist Batman and Robin in fighting the forces of evil. Batman lives! POW!

Batman
Batman

BAT-68

❑ **BAT-68. Club Card,**
1966. Membership card for TV show. -
**$10 $20 $30**

(STICKER, CARD, BUTTON SHOWN)
BAT-69

❑ **BAT-69. "Batman Club" Items,**
c. 1966. Ron Riley's Batman Club of WLS/WBKB-TV, Chicago. Includes 2" litho. button, 3-1/2" sticker plus card.
Button - **$3 $6 $10**
Sticker - **$5 $10 $15**
Card - **$8 $12 $20**

BAT-70

BAT-71

BAT-72

❑ **BAT-70. Batman 6 Ft. Standee,**
1966.- **$50 $125 $175**

❑ **BAT-71. "Batman's Buddy" Cello. Button,**
c. 1966. Hy Vee grocery chain. - **$5 $12 $25**

❑ **BAT-72. "Curly Wurly/Blam" Litho. Button,**
c. 1966. English product. - **$8 $12 $20**

BAT-73

❑ **BAT-73. High Relief Plastic 33x48" Store Display Sign,**
1969. Issued to promote Aurora Batmobile kit offered as premium by Burry's cookies. -
**$250 $600 $1200**

BAT-74

❑ **BAT-74. Photo And Record,**
1960s. DC Comics. Photo reads "To All My Batman Fans-'Bats' Wishes Bob Kane." Record co-written by Kane titled "Have Faith In Me".
Pair - **$50 $85 $150**

BAT-75

❑ **BAT-75. "Batman And, Of Course, Robin" Movie Serial Re-Release 27x41 " Poster,**
1960s. Columbia Pictures. For reissue of original 1943 serial. - **$50 $100 $200**

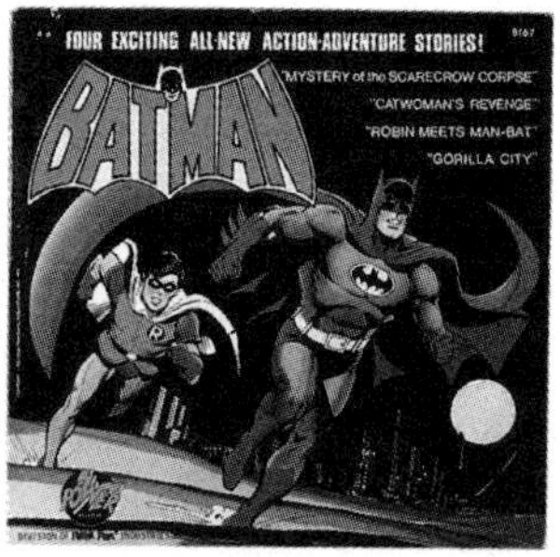


BAT-76

❑ **BAT-76. Batman Record,**
1975. Power Records, a division of Peter Pan Industries. Features "4 Exciting All-New Adventure Stories!" - **$3 $5 $8**

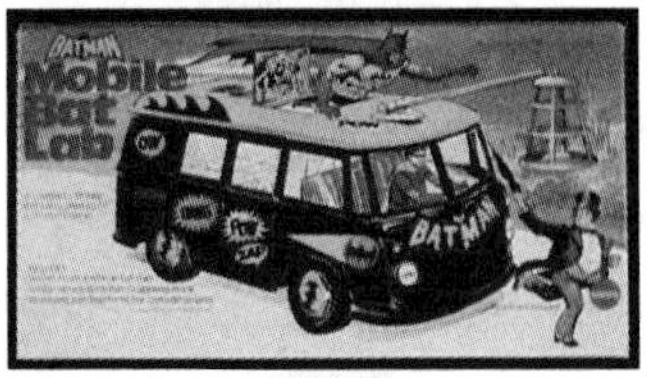


BAT-77

❑ **BAT-77. "Batman Mobile Bat Lab" Boxed Vehicle Set,**
1975. Store item by Mego. Large 8x14x7" tall hard plastic vehicle. Near Mint Boxed - **$250**
Used Complete - **$50 $100 $150**

BAT-78

**❑ BAT-78. Batman Diecut Enameled Brass Ring,**
1976. Store item made by Aviva. - **$5 $12 $20**

BAT-79

BAT-80

**❑ BAT-79. Batman Enameled Brass Ring,**
1976. Store item made by Aviva. - **$5 $12 $20**

**❑ BAT-80. Batman Enameled Brass Ring,**
1976. Store item made by Aviva. - **$5 $12 $20**

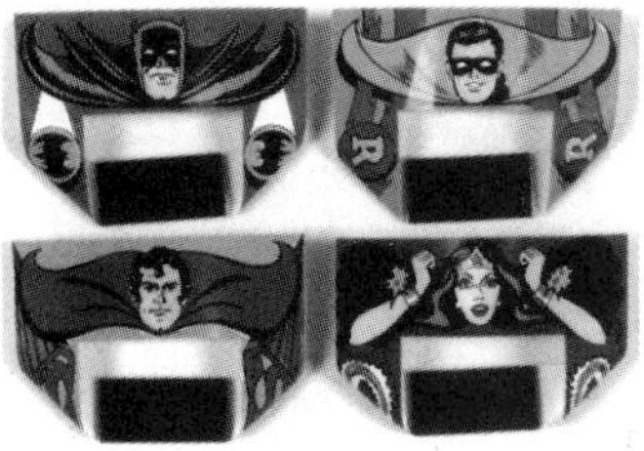

BAT-81

**❑ BAT-81. "Super Heroes Magnetic Dart Game",**
1977. Cheerios. - **$10 $25 $50**

BAT-82

**❑ BAT-82. Batman and Robin Yo-Yo,**
1978. Duncan. Sold in special container. - **$15 $30 $60**

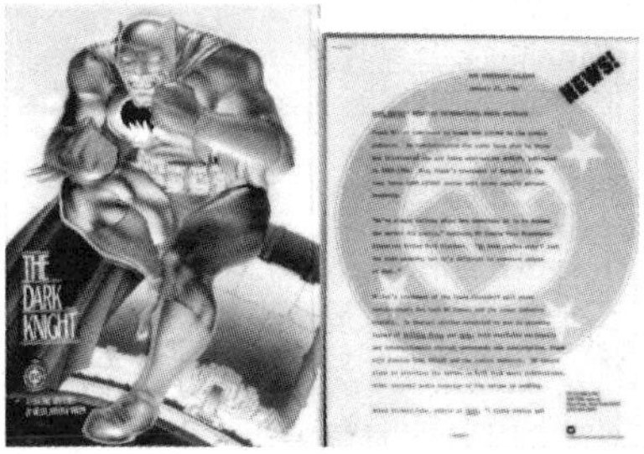


BAT-83

**❑ BAT-83. "The Dark Knight" Plastic Display Sign With Press Release,**
1986. Promotes mini-series by Frank Miller.
Display - **$20 $35 $60**
Press Release - **$3 $5 $10**

BAT-84

BAT-85

**❑ BAT-84. Batman Button Collection,**
1989. Four on card. - **$20**

**❑ BAT-85. Large Button,**
1989. On card. - **$10**

BAT-86

BAT-87

**❑ BAT-86. Warner Brothers Limited Edition Batman Statue,**
1989. Offered only on the opening day of the Batman movie. Limited to 50, these were sculpted and hand-painted by Kent Melton. - **$750 $1700 $2750**

**❑ BAT-87. Warner Brothers Limited Edition Joker Statue,**
1989. Offered only on the opening day of the Batman movie. Limited to 50, these were sculpted and hand-painted by Kent Melton. - **$750 $1700 $2750**

BAT-88

**❑ BAT-88. Ralston Batman Cereal Box,**
1989. With plastic bank attached to box front. - **$15 $35 $50**

BAT-89

**❑ BAT-89. "Battery Operated Batman Motorcycle,"**
1980s. Tam Toys.
Near Mint Boxed - **$200**
Unboxed - **$35 $75 $125**

BAT-90

**❑ BAT-90. "Batman Returns" Promo Badge,**
1992. Each - **$2 $4 $10**

BAT-91

BAT-92

❑ **BAT-91. McDonald's Happy Meals 14x14" Plastic Translight Panel,**
1992. Depicts eight figures and vehicles. - **$25 $60 $100**

❑ **BAT-92. McDonald's Happy Meals 14x14" Plastic Translight Panel,**
1992. Depicts six cups. - **$10 $20 $30**

BAT-93

❑ **BAT-93. McDonald's Happy Meals 14x14" Plastic Translight Panel,**
1992. Depicts four vehicles. - **$10 $20 $30**

BAT-94

❑ **BAT-94. Batman Standee With Cups,**
1992. - **$100 $200 $320**

BAT-95

BAT-96

❑ **BAT-95. "Batman Returns" Movie Cards,**
1992. Depicts 8 scenes. - **$20**

❑ **BAT-96. "Batman Returns" Print Portfolio,**
1992. Contains eight 11"x14" prints. - **$20**

(BOX FRONT)

(PUZZLE #1)

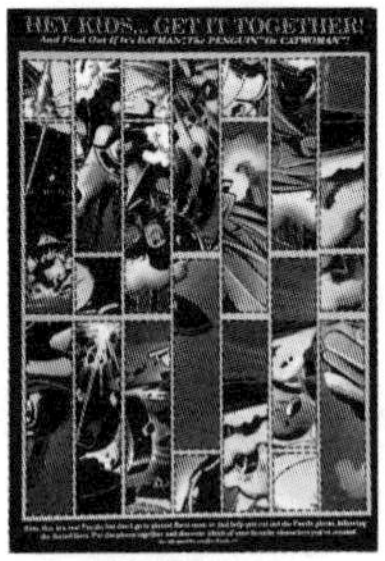


(PUZZLE #2)

(PUZZLE #3)

BAT-97

❑ **BAT-97. "Batman Returns" Cereal Box with Puzzle Box Back,**
1992. Three different puzzle backs.
Each - **$2 $8 $20**

BAT-98

BAT-99

❑ **BAT-98. "Batman Returns" Cereal Box with Glow-In-The Dark Stickers Premium,**
1992. 4 differnet stickers.
Box - **$2 $8 $20**

❑ **BAT-99. "Batman Returns" Catch Game,**
1992. Back of box shown. - **$2 $4 $10**

BAT-100

BAT-101

❑ **BAT-100. "Robin" Resin Statue,**
1994. Limited to 3,900. Miniature version released in 1997. Boxed - **$285**

❑ **BAT-101. "The Joker" Resin Statue,**
1995. Limited to 4,650. Miniature version released in 1998. Boxed - **$250**

BAT-102

BAT-103

❑ **BAT-102. "Batman Forever" Promo Badge,**
1995. - **$2 $4 $10**

❑ **BAT-103. "Batman Forever" 3-D Viewer,**
1995. Has 21 3-D scenes from the movie on 3 discs. Projector is 7 1/2" tall. Stars of the movie are pictured on the back and sides of the box. - **$10 $25 $40**

BAT-104

BAT-105

❑ **BAT-104. "Batman Forever" Statue,**
1995. 14" tall with base. - **$100**

❑ **BAT-105. "Batman Forever" Robin Statue,**
1995. Warner Bros. Store exclusive. - **$85**

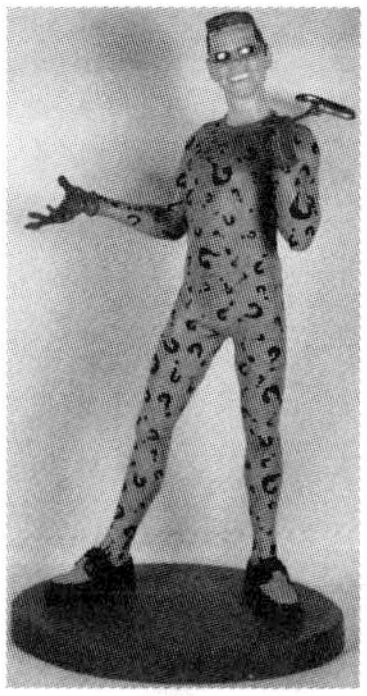

BAT-106

BAT-107

❑ **BAT-106. "Batman Forever" Riddler Statue,**
1995. - **$110**

❑ **BAT-107. "Batman Forever" Two Face Statue,**
1995. Warner Bros. Store exclusive by Kent Melton. - **$110**

BAT-108

BAT-109

❑ **BAT-108. Kellogg's Corn Pops Cereal Box,**
1995. 10.9 oz. box has offer for a "Batman Forever" baseball-style cap. - **$2 $4 $10**

❑ **BAT-109. "Batman Forever" Kellogg's Corn Pops 15 oz. Cereal Boxes,**
1995. 4 different boxes promote the movie. Each - **$5 $10 $20**

(Box front)

(Figures with reversed Bat logos)

(Corrected set)

BAT-110

❑ **BAT-110. "The History of Batman" Collection,**
1995. 3 figures in a display box. First set mistakenly reversed the colors of the yellow and black chest logos. Boxed- **$300**
Later corrected set boxed - **$120**

BAT-111

BAT-112

❑ **BAT-111. Batman "The Dark Knight Returns" Anniversary Resin Statue,**
1996. 10th Anniversary statue of Batman and Robin. Miniature version released in 1999. Limited to 5,500. - **$350**

❑ **BAT-112. "Poison Ivy" Ceramic Figure,**
1996. Warner Bros. catalog exclusive for promoting the next year's "Batman and Robin" movie. Limited edition of 1,250. - **$180**

BAT-113

BAT-114

❑ **BAT-113. Batgirl Resin Statue,**
1997. Limited to 3,600. Miniature version released in 1999. Boxed - **$210**

❑ **BAT-114. Catwoman Resin Statue,**
1997. Limited to 3,700. Boxed- **$260**

BAT-115

❑ **BAT-115. Batman Movie Resin Statue,**
1997. From "Batman & Robin" movie. Cape is easily chipped. Figure is slightly off-balance because of the weight of the cape. 13 1/2" high counting the base. - **$150**

BAT-116

BAT-117

❑ **BAT-116. Robin Movie Resin Statue,**
1997. From "Batman & Robin" movie. Harder to find than the 1995 movie statue. - **$100**

❑ **BAT-117. Batgirl Movie Resin Statue,**
1997. From "Batman & Robin" movie. - **$120**

BAT-118

❑ **BAT-118. Mr. Freeze 13" Movie Resin Statue,**
1997. Has removable gun. This is tough to find, as many were broken in shipping from China. The base was not balanced correctly, causing the ankles to break. The gun handle also breaks easily. Warner Brothers stores did not reorder. Do not confuse with different Mr. Freeze made later. That statue is different in size and stance. - **$175**

BAT-119

❑ **BAT-119. Batman Movie Batarang Prop,**
1997. From "Batman & Robin" movie. Batarang is made of chrome plated spin cast metal. In display case of Mr. Freeze ice.
Limited edition of 500. - **$600**

BAT-123

❑ **BAT-123. Cocoa Krispies Cereal Box,**
1997. Promotes "Batman & Robin" movie. Herovision poster puzzle on back. - **$2 $8 $15**

BAT-124

❑ **BAT-124. Mr. Freeze Freezer Bars Box,**
1997. Promotes "Batman & Robin" movie. Limited edition box holds 24 bars. - **$5 $10 $20**

(TOP OF BOX) BAT-125 (FRONT OF BOX)

❑ **BAT-125. Mr. Freeze Freezer Bars Box,**
1997. Promotes "Batman & Robin" movie. Limited edition box holds 72 bars. - **$6 $15 $30**

BAT-128

❑ **BAT-128. Promotional Display Box,**
1998. For the Charlotte Motor Speedway contest sponsored by Ford Credit. - **$5 $20 $40**

BAT-120

❑ **BAT-120. "Batman & Robin" Movie Watches in Case,**
1997. Two watches feature photos of Batman and Mr. Freeze. Also includes limited metal cards of each character. Watches are in a silver metal presentation case with insert.
Limited edition of 500. - **$350**

BAT-129

BAT-130

BAT-121

BAT-122

❑ **BAT-121. Kellogg's Smacks Cereal Box,**
1997. Promotes "Batman & Robin" movie. Robin on front. - **$2 $4 $10**

❑ **BAT-122. Kellogg's Apple Jacks Cereal Box,**
1997. Promotes "Batman & Robin" movie. Mr. Freeze on front. - **$2 $4 $10**

BAT-126

BAT-127

❑ **BAT-126. Batman Maquette,**
1998. From Superman/Batman Adventures animated series. Limited to 2,500. - **$225**

❑ **BAT-127. Robin Maquette,**
1998. Resin. From Superman/Batman Advs. animated series. Limited to 2,500. - **$185**

❑ **BAT-129. Classic Batman Figure with Card,**
1998. Has dark blue cape and card depicting cover of Batman #1. - **$20**

❑ **BAT-130. Classic Batman Figure with Card,**
1998. Has light blue cape and card depicting cover of Batman #4. - **$20**

BAT-131 BAT-132

❑ **BAT-131. Batman Bean Bag Figure,**
1998. Warner Bros. Store Exclusive. - **$8**

❑ **BAT-132. Robin Bean Bag Figure,**
1998. Warner Bros. Store Exclusive. - **$8**

BAT-133 BAT-134

❑ **BAT-133. Joker Bean Bag Figure,**
1998. Warner Bros. Store Exclusive. - **$8**

❑ **BAT-134. Penguin Bean Bag Figure,**
1998. Warner Bros. Store Exclusive. - **$8**

BAT-135

BAT-136

❑ **BAT-135. Catwoman Bean Bag Figure,**
1998. Warner Bros. Store Exclusive. - **$8**

❑ **BAT-136. Batman Resin Statue,**
1999. Warner Bros. Store Exclusive. - **$85**

BAT-137 BAT-138 BAT-139

❑ **BAT-137. Riddler Bean Bag Figure,**
1999. Warner Bros. Store Exclusive. - **$8**

❑ **BAT-138. Poison Ivy Bean Bag Figure,**
1999. Warner Bros. Store Exclusive. - **$8**

❑ **BAT-139. Harley Quinn Bean Bag Figure,**
1999. Warner Bros. Store Exclusive. - **$8**

BAT-140 BAT-141

❑ **BAT-140. Batgirl Bean Bag Figure,**
1999. Warner Bros. Store Exclusive. - **$8**

❑ **BAT-141. "Baman Beyond" Bean Bag Figure,**
1999. Warner Bros. Store Exclusive. - **$8**

BAT-142 BAT-143 BAT-144

❑ **BAT-142. Batman Miniature Figure,**
1999. In package. - **$20**

❑ **BAT-143. Robin Miniature Figure,**
1999. In package. - **$20**

❑ **BAT-144. Batgirl Miniature Figure,**
1999. In package. - **$20**

BAT-145 BAT-146 BAT-147

❑ **BAT-145. Joker Miniature Figure,**
1999. In package. - **$20**

❑ **BAT-146. Harley Quinn Miniature Figure,**
1999. In package. - **$20**

❑ **BAT-147. Penguin Miniature Figure,**
1999. In package. - **$20**

BAT-148 BAT-149 BAT-150

❑ **BAT-148. Riddler Miniature Figure,**
1999. In package. - **$20**

❑ **BAT-149. Mr. Freeze Miniature Figure,**
1999. In package. - **$20**

❑ **BAT-150. Poison Ivy Miniature Figure,**
1999. In package. - **$20**

BAT-151 BAT-152

❑ **BAT-151. Batman Walkie Talkies,**
2000. Warner Brothers Store exclusive. - **$35**

❑ **BAT-152. Batman 24" Statue on Base,**
2000. Warner Bros. Store Exclusive, sold only in New York City store which has since closed. Only a few were made. - **$75 $150 $200**

BAT-153

❑ **BAT-153. Batman Beyond Batmobile,**
2000. In box; from TV show. Fires 6 discs. - **$25**

BAT-154

BAT-155

❑ **BAT-154. Batgirl Resin Statue,**
2001. Styled from the animated series. Edition of 5,000. Boxed - **$100**

❑ **BAT-155. Batmite Resin Statue,**
2001. Edition of 1,400. Boxed - **$50**

BAT-156

❑ **BAT-156. Poison Ivy Porcelain Statue,**
2001. Limited edition of 2100. Designed by Bruce Timm based on the animated series version. Boxed - **$90**

BAT-157

❑ **BAT-157. Batman Resin Statue,**
2001. Golden Age figure. Boxed - **$40**

# The Beatles

**The Beatles were Paul McCartney, John Lennon, George Harrison, and Ringo Starr (Richard Starkey), four lads from Liverpool, England, who became the dominant musical force of the turbulent 1960s and have remained cultural icons to this day. The Fab Four burst onto the American scene in an explosive live appearance on the Ed Sullivan Show on CBS-TV in February 1964, and though their last public concert was less than three years later, Beatles records and tapes still sell in the millions. Their movies--*A Hard Day's Night* (1964), *Help!* (1965) and the psychedelic animated feature *Yellow Submarine* (1968)--an animated Saturday morning series produced by King Features (1965-1969) and sponsored primarily by the A. C. Gilbert toy company, and comic books all added to the luster; but it was the brilliance and charm of the music that revolutionized rock and roll.**

**Half of the Fab Four have passed away; John Lennon on December 8, 1980 and George Harrison on November 29, 2001. In terms of lasting influence, The Beatles continue to sway not only music but pop culture in general. *A Hard Day's Night* is commonly considered to be one of the best rock and roll films ever made, while *Help!* is widely thought of as a precursor to the modern music video and a direct inspiration for the Monkees (see their category elsewhere in this book). With the release of *The Beatles Anthology I-III* (three 2-CD sets) and the companion video tape set, the surviving Beatles again set sales records around the world. These releases were accompanied by a large amount of Beatles merchandise, as well as the first new Beatles songs in years, mixing recently discovered Lennon vocals with new backing tracks by the surviving band members. Beatles memorabilia of all sorts, both original issues and later reproductions, are usually copyrighted NEMS Enterprises or SELTAEB.**

BEA-1

❑ **BEA-1. Ashtray From "The Cavern" Early Beatles Venue,**
c. 1962-63. About 5-1/2" square by 5/8" deep glazed ceramic with 2-1/2x4" center scene inscribed "The 'Cavern'-Home Of The Mersey Sound." Group on stage resembles The Beatles and readable words on stage backdrop include "The Mersey Beet/Rolling/The Fourmost/The Beatles." Marked on reverse "Prince William Warranted 22 Carat Gold/Made In England." - **$150 $350 $600**

BEA-2

❑ **BEA-2. Vinyl Doll Set,**
1964. Store item by Remco Plastics. Each has life-like hair.
Each - **$50 $85 $125**

BEA-3

❑ **BEA-3. "Beatle Dolls" 7x18" Paper Store Poster,**
1964. Remco Industries. - **$125 $225 $350**

BEA-4

❑ **BEA-4. "The Bobb'n Head Beatles" Boxed Set,**
1964. Store item. Composition figures by Car Mascots Inc.
Boxed Set - **$400 $700 $1300**
Each Loose - **$75 $150 $225**

BEA-5

❑ **BEA-5. "The Beatles" Charm Bracelet,**
c. 1964. Store item. - **$25 $50 $90**

BEA-6

❑ **BEA-6. "Beatles Sneakers By Wing Dings,"**
c. 1964. Near Mint Boxed - **$1000**
Box - **$100 $200 $300**
Sneakers - **$150 $300 $500**

BEA-7

❑ **BEA-7. "The Beatles" Pillow,**
1964. 12x12x2-1/2" deep store item by Nordic House. One of three designs. Each - **$50 $100 $150**

BEA-8

❑ **BEA-8. "The Beatles A Hard Day's Night" Movie Ticket,**
1964. Embassy Theater. - **$50 $100 $175**

BEA-9 BEA-10

❑ **BEA-9. "The Beatles" Linen Wall Hanging,**
c. 1964. Store item marked "Pure Irish Linen/Alster." 20x31" with black and white portraits of them wearing dark burgundy suits against lavender background with white border. - **$100 $200 $300**

❑ **BEA-10. Vinyl Overnight Case With Zippered Front And Handle,**
1964. Store item by Air Flite. Large item 12x13x5" deep.
Black Variety - **$150 $250 $450**
Red Variety - **$200 $400 $650**

BEA-11

❑ **BEA-11. Calendar Cards,**
1964. Various advertisers.
Each - **$8 $12 $25**

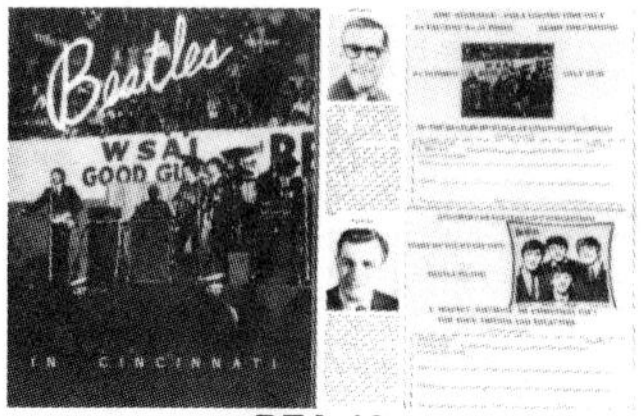


BEA-12

❑ **BEA-12. Cincinnati Concert Program,**
1964. - **$15 $30 $70**

BEA-13 BEA-14

BEA-15

BEA-16 BEA-17

❑ **BEA-13. First Series G**
1964. Topps. Set of 60 num
Set - **$25 $60 $125**

❑ **BEA-14. Second Series**
1964. Topps. Set of 55 numbe
Set - **$25 $60 $125**

❑ **BEA-15. Third Series Gum**
1964. Topps. Set of 50 numbere
Set - **$25 $60 $125**

❑ **BEA-16. "Beatles Diary" Gum**
1964. Topps. Set of 60. Set - **$35**

❑ **BEA-17. "Beatles Color Cards" Set,**
1964. Topps. Set of 64. Set - **$25 $6**

BEA-18

❑ **BEA-18. Topps Gum Wrapper,**
1964. - **$10 $20 $35**

BEA-19

❑ **BEA-19. "A Hard Day's Night" Movie Poster,**
1964. One sheet poster from the first Beatles film. Measures 41"x27". Produced by United Artists. - **$600 $750 $800**

BEA-20

**BEA-20. "Color Oil Portraits" Set Of 4,**
64. Store item. Cut-out "Buddies Club" card header.
ackaged With Uncut Card - **$50 $75 $125**

BEA-21

BEA-22

❑ **BEA-21. "Free/One Beatle Button" Ad Paper,**
c. 1964. 5x7" glossy paper pennant printed on both sides including back offer for Beatles bill-fold. - **$50 $125 $225**

❑ **BEA-22. "I'm A Official Beatles Fan" Button,**
1964. Authorized issue in several variations all marked on rim curl "Copyright NEMS Ent. Ltd. 64" and Green Duck Co., Chicago-Made In U.S.A."
Litho. 4" Size - **$15 $25 $50**
Cello. 3-1/2" Size - **$10 $20 $40**
Litho. 1-3/8" Size - **$20 $40 $75**

BEA-23

❑ **BEA-23. "Official Fan Club News Bulletin",**
c. 1964. Includes six stapled photo pages. - **$25 $50 $90**

BEA-24

BEA-25

BEA-26

❑ **BEA-24. Vending Machine Litho. Button,**
1964. Set of nine (four pictures/five slogans) either in black/white/red, blue/orange, red/white/blue, or black/white/blue.
Pictures - **$3 $8 $15**
Slogans- **$3 $6 $10**

❑ **BEA-25. "Life Member" Fan Club Patch,**
c. 1964. - **$15 $30 $70**

❑ **BEA-26. "I Love" 3-1/2" Cello. Buttons,**
c. 1964. Each - **$8 $15 $30**

BEA-27

BEA-28

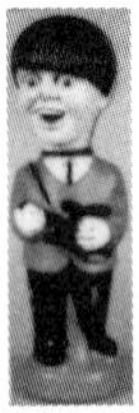

BEA-29

❑ **BEA-27. Flicker Ring Set,**
c. 1964. Set of four.
Silver Base Each - **$10 $15 $25**
Blue Base Each - **$8 $12 $15**

❑ **BEA-28. "Ringo Starr" Soaky Bottle,**
1965. Colgate-Palmolive. Only Ringo and Paul were produced. - **$40 $75 $140**

❑ **BEA-29. "Paul McCartney" Soaky,**
1965. Colgate-Palmolive. Only Paul and Ringo were produced. - **$40 $75 $140**

BEA-30

❑ **BEA-30. "The Beatles" Bracelet On Card,**
c. 1965. Store item by Randall.
Near Mint Carded - **$125**
Bracelet Only - **$20 $40 $75**

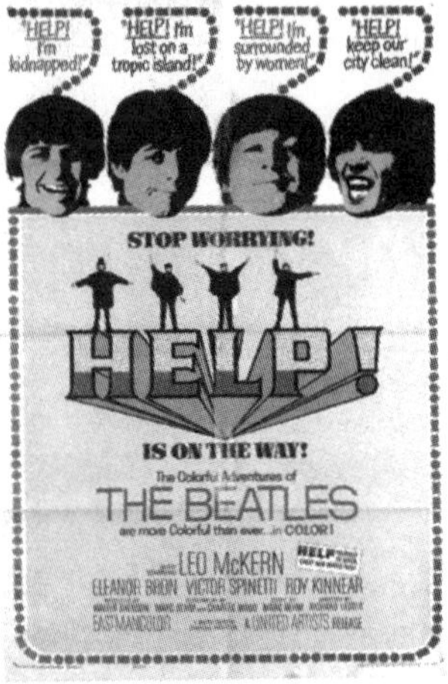


BEA-31

❑ **BEA-31. "Help!" Movie Poster,**
1965. One sheet poster from the Beatles' 2nd film. Measures 41"x27". - **$600 $750 $800**

BEA-32

❑ **BEA-32. Embossed Metal Lunch Box,**
1965. Store item by Aladdin Industries Inc. - **$150 $350 $600**

BEA-33

BEA-34

❑ **BEA-33. Metal Lunch Box Bottle,**
1965. Aladdin Industries Inc. Came with previous lunch box. - **$75 $200 $300**

❑ **BEA-34. Bracelet With Celluloid Charms,**
c. 1965. Store item. 6" long in brass luster with black and white celluloid portraits. - **$35 $75 $125**

BEA-35

BEA-36

❑ **BEA-35. "Help" Packaged Bandage,**
c. 1965. Movie promotion on Curad bandage. -
**$10 $20 $40**

❑ **BEA-36. Nestle's Quik Container,**
1966. Has offer for inflatable doll set. -
**$200 $400 $650**

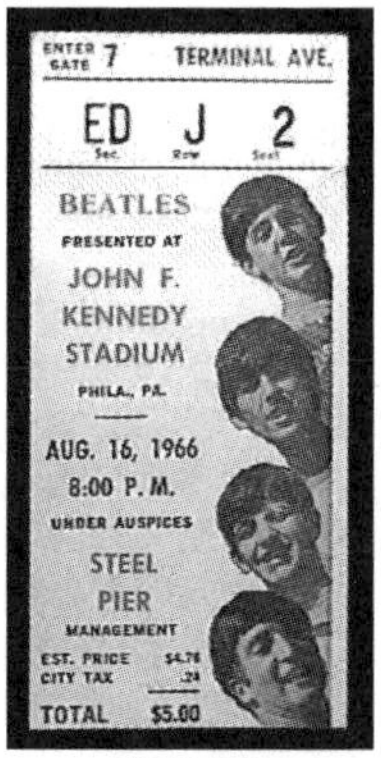

BEA-37

❑ **BEA-37. Ticket Stub For JFK Stadium, Philadelphia,**
1966. Black and white with red lettering. -
**$75 $150 $300**

BEA-38

❑ **BEA-38. "The Beatles Disk-Go-Case" Plastic 45 RPM Record Holder,**
1966. Store item by Charter Industries. Issued in various colors. - **$50 $125 $250**

BEA-39

❑ **BEA-39. Fan Club Christmas Record Postcard,**
1966. The Beatles Bulletin/Official Publication Of The National Beatles Fan Club. 7x8-1/2" stiff cardboard with record on front inscribed "1966 Season's Greetings From The Beatles." -
**$20 $40 $85**

BEA-40

❑ **BEA-40. "Go Go Beatles" Japanese Tote Bag,**
c. 1966. Tag Only - **$50 $75 $125**
Bag Only - **$25 $60 $90**

BEA-41

❑ **BEA-41. Beatles Inflatable Vinyl Dolls Set,**
1966. Store item, also Nestle's Quik and Lux Soap. Each - **$15 $30 $60**

BEA-42

❑ **BEA-42. "Lux" Soap Box With "Inflatable Beatles" Offer,**
1967. Lux Beauty Soap by Lever Brothers Co. 2-1/4x4x2-1/2" deep box has back panel offering set of four 15" tall inflatable vinyl dolls.
Near Mint Sealed - **$500**
Opened Box - **$75 $150 $275**

BEA-43

❑ **BEA-43. "Magical Mystery Tour" Poster,**
1967. 31" tall and 23" wide. Promotes the TV special filmed in England. - **$250 $375 $525**

BEA-44

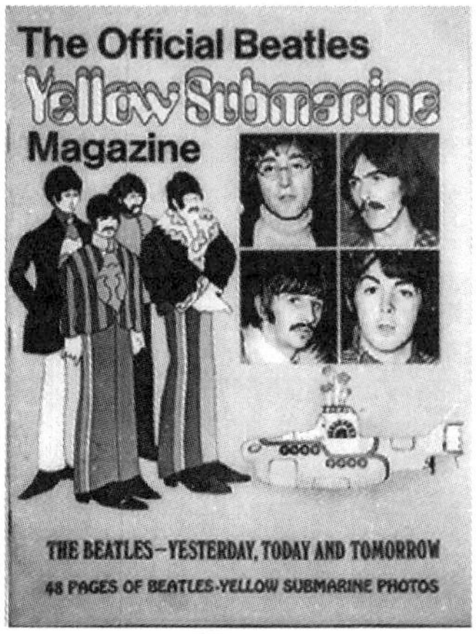

BEA-45

❑ **BEA-44. "Sgt. Pepper's Lonely Hearts Club Band" 2-1/8" Litho. Button,**
c. 1967. Great Britain issue for original record release although no copyright or company name. - **$10 $25 $50**

❑ **BEA-45. "Yellow Submarine Magazine",**
1968. Store item published jointly by Pyramid Publications and King Features. - **$20 $40 $85**

BEA-46

❑ **BEA-46. "Yellow Submarine" Movie Poster,**
1968. Earlier version of the one sheet poster. With its great graphics, it's one of the most sought after posters of the 60s. The apple at the left center mentions 11 Beatles songs.
United Artists. - **$800 $1000 $1200**

BEA-47

❑ **BEA-47. "Yellow Submarine" Movie Poster,**
1968. Later version of the one sheet poster has the apple moved to the center, now promoting a dozen Beatles songs. The pointing glove with a face was also added.
United Artists. - **$800 $1000 $1200**

BEA-48

❑ **BEA-48. "Yellow Submarine" Lunch Box,**
1968. Store item by King-Seeley Thermos Co.
Box - **$150 $350 $700**
Thermos - **$100 $250 $475**

BEA-49

❑ **BEA-49. "Yellow Submarine" Blue Meanie Boxed Costume,**
1968. Store item by Collegeville Costumes.
Near Mint Boxed - **$400**
Costume and Mask Only - **$75 $150 $275**

BEA-50

❑ **BEA-50. "Yellow Submarine Inc." Straw,**
1968. No official copyright but art is 100% identical to that of the Beatles' Yellow Submarine. Issued by Sweetheart Straws.
Unopened **- $5 $15 $30**

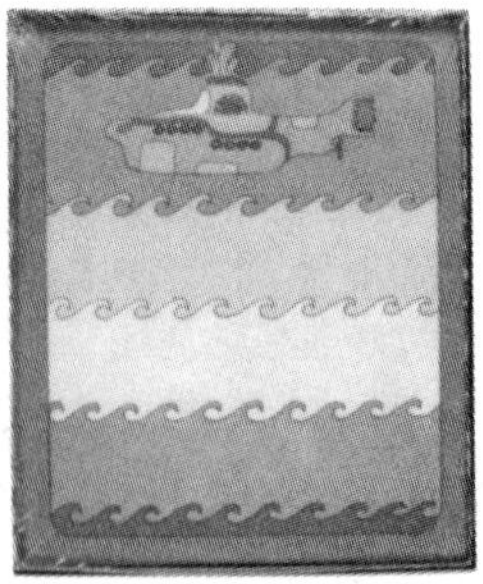

BEA-51

❑ **BEA-51. Yellow Submarine Stationery Set,**
1968. Store item by Unicorn Creations Inc. 18 different sets. Each Complete - **$25 $45 $80**

BEA-52

❑ **BEA-52. "The Beatles Yellow Submarine Phantom Pocket Picture Puzzle,**
1968. Store item by Jaymar. **- $40 $100 $200**

BEA-53

❑ **BEA-53. Yellow Submarine Pin Set,**
1968. Store item. Set **- $100 $200 $300**

BEA-54

❑ **BEA-54. Yellow Submarine European Movie Theater Mobile,**
c. 1968. Two diecut thick cardboard pieces 17x25" and 6x10" for forming ceiling dangle mobile. Each piece is printed identically both sides with tiny inscriptions for French theater and possibly disco entertainment spot. -
**$150 $300 $600**

BEA-55

❑ **BEA-55. Corgi "Yellow Submarine" Replica,**
1968. Near Mint Boxed - **$700**
Loose - **$150 $300 $450**

BEA-56

❑ **BEA-56. Yellow Submarine Rub-Ons,**
1969. Nabisco Wheat (Or Rice) Honeys. Set of eight. Each - **$15 $25 $50**

BEA-57

❑ **BEA-57. "The Swingers Music Set,"**
1960s. Unlicensed. Four figures, two standing microphones and drum set.
Boxed Complete - **$35 $75 $150**

BEA-58

BEA-59

❑ **BEA-58. Australian Fan Club Cello. Button,**
1960s. - **$30 $60 $100**

❑ **BEA-59. Rubber Figure Charms,**
1960s. Believed vending machine issue. Set of four, each 2-1/2" tall. Each - **$8 $12 $20**

BEA-60

❑ **BEA-60. "Let It Be" Poster,**
1970. Six sheet poster for the last of the Beatles' films. United Artists. - **$600 $750 $800**

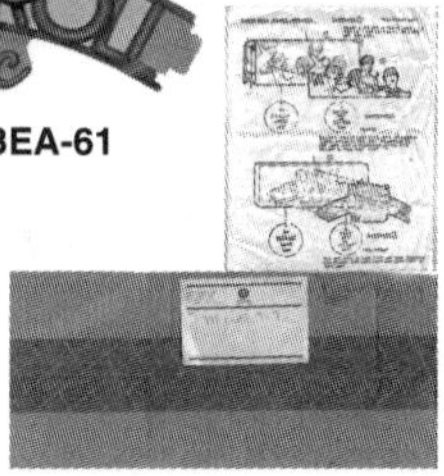

BEA-61

❑ **BEA-61. Promotional Mobile Set,**
1971. Capital Records promo. 5-piece mobile advertising a 2-record set. Comes with instructions and mailer.
5-Piece Mobile - **$100 $225 $400**
Instructions and Mailer - **$10 $25 $50**

BEA-62

❑ **BEA-62. Anti-Vietnam War Button,**
c. 1972. 3" full color reflecting their support of the "Give Peace A Chance" movement. - **$65 $150 $300**

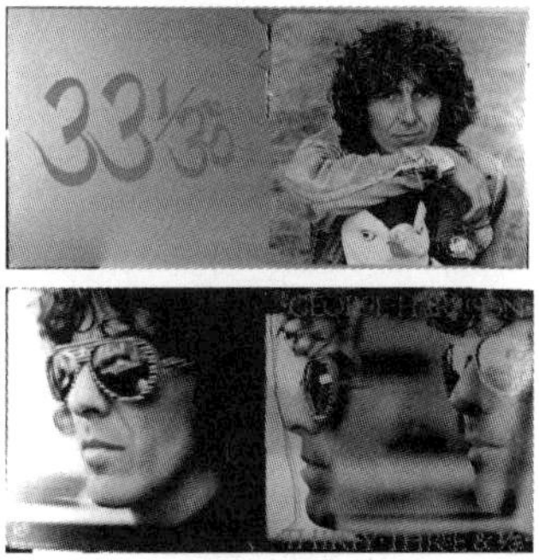

BEA-63

❑ **BEA-63. George Harrison Promotional Mobile,**
1976. Ganga Distributors. 8-sided ad piece promotes new album. Scarce - **$90 $180 $250**

BEA-64

❑ **BEA-64. "John Lennon" Figural Memorial Boxed Radio,**
c. 1980. Store item marked only "Made In Hong Kong." 8" vinyl figure in fabric outfit stands on 3-1/2x5x1-1/2" deep plastic base. He holds a silver microphone with white cord in one hand.
Near Mint Boxed - **$100**
Radio Only - **$25 $50 $75**

## Betty Boop

**Max Fleischer created the Boop-Oop-a-Doop girl as an animated cartoon in 1931. The sexy little flirt, modeled on singer Helen Kane and actress Mae West, was an immediate success and became Paramount's leading cartoon feature. Along with her dog Bimbo and her pal Koko the clown, Betty vamped and sang her way through comedies and adventures throughout the 1930s. Several actresses provided Betty's voice but Mae Questel is most closely identified with the character. A Sunday comic strip was distributed by King Features (1935-1938) and published as an Avon paperback in 1975. A children's show, *Betty Boop Fables*, had a brief run on NBC radio in 1932-1933, and the cartoons were packaged for TV in 1956 and re-released in color in 1971. Many merchandised items appeared in the 1930s at the height of Betty's popularity. Her continuing appeal has produced an even wider range of licensed items in the 1980s to the present.**

BTY-1

❑ **BTY-1. Movie Theater Premium Flip Movie Booklet,**
1932. Russell Theater Maysville, KY. 1-5/8x2-1/4" with 40 black and white pages. - **$50 $125 $200**

BTY-2

BTY-3

❑ **BTY-2. Betty Boop/Gus Gorilla Fan Card,**
1933. Fleischer Studios. Autographed by Max Fleischer. Text refers to Paramount Pictures and NBC. - **$35 $75 $150**
Unsigned - **$15 $40 $75**

❑ **BTY-3. Fleischer Studios Fan Card,**
c. 1933. Autographed by Max Fleischer. Text refers to Paramount, not NBC. - **$35 $75 $150**

BTY-4

BTY-5

❑ **BTY-4. "Betty Boop in Snow White" Big Little Book #1119,**
1934. From the Fleischer cartoon. -
**$35 $70 $150**

❑ **BTY-5. "Betty Boop in Miss Gulliver's Travels" Big Little Book #1158,**
1934. From the Fleischer cartoon. -
**$30 $60 $130**

BTY-6

❑ **BTY-6. "Betty Boop's Movie Cartoon Lessons By Max Fleischer" Book,**
c. 1935. Store item. Softcover 32-page illustrated guide "How To Make Movie Cartoons." -
**$200 $400 $700**

BTY-7

BTY-8

❑ **BTY-7. Large Celluloid Jointed Figure,**
c. 1935 Store item marked on reverse "Made In Japan." 7-3/4" tall with movable head and arms. -
**$350 $700 $1250**

❑ **BTY-8. Enamel On Silver Luster Pin With Charm,**
1939. Store item. 1-1/2" tall issued with the enamel on her dress in various single colors. Example shown has "New York World's Fair 1939" charm but also issued with other charms generally of a tourist destination nature.
With World's Fair Charm - **$40 $75 $175**
With Other Charm - **$35 $65 $150**
Version With Ankle-Length Dress and 1939 NYWF Charm - **$65 $150 $250**

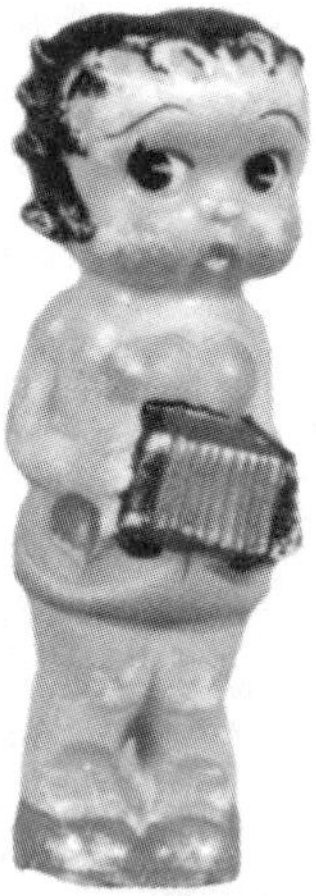
BTY-9

❑ **BTY-9. "Betty Boop" Playing Accordion Bisque Figure,**
1930s. Store item. Several different with various instruments. Each - **$40 $85 $150**

BTY-10

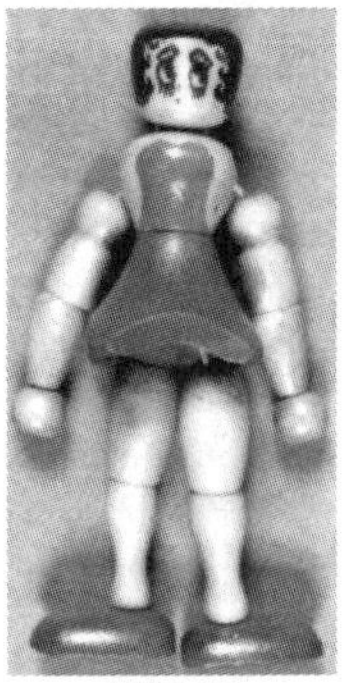
BTY-11

❑ **BTY-10. Composition/Wood Jointed Doll,**
1930s. Scarce in high grade. Store item by Cameo Products. 12-1/2" tall. -
**$400 $1000 $1800**

❑ **BTY-11. Wood Jointed Doll,**
1930s. Store item, 4-1/2" tall.- **$65 $125 $225**

BTY-12

BTY-13

❑ **BTY-12. China Wall Pocket,**
1930s. Store item. - **$75 $150 $225**

❑ **BTY-13. Bisque Figure,**
1930s. Store item. 3" size. - **$50 $100 $200**

BTY-14

❑ **BTY-14. Mask,**
1930s. "Bob-O-Link Shoes" ad on reverse. -
With ad - **$30 $60 $135**
Blank reverse - **$25 $50 $100**

BTY-15

❑ **BTY-15. China Ashtray,**
1930s. Store item. - **$75 $150 $250**

BTY-16

❑ **BTY-16. Spanish Envelope,**
1930s. Held transfer.
Envelope Only - **$10 $20 $35**
Complete - **$15 $30 $75**

BTY-17

❑ **BTY-17. Betty Boop Postcard with Mickey Rooney,**
1930s. - **$30 $75 $150**

BTY-18

❑ **BTY-18. "Socks Appeal By Bimbo" Booklet,**
1930s. Given with pair of Bimbo socks. -
**$50 $90 $150**

BTY-19

BTY-20

BTY-21

❑ **BTY-19. "Saturday Chicago American" Litho. Button,**
1930s. From set of 10 various characters. -
**$75 $150 $250**

❑ **BTY-20. "Ko-Ko/Max Fleischer's Talkatoons" Litho. Button #25,**
1930s. Western Theater Premium Co. From numbered set of 50 either black, white, red or with additional yellow accent. - **$25 $50 $90**

❑ **BTY-21. "Betty Boop" Cello. Button,**
1930s. 1-1/4" in bright yellow, black and white with small copyright symbol "Fleischer Studios." Rare. - **$150 $300 $850**

BTY-22

BTY-23

❑ **BTY-22. "Bimbo" Cello. Button,**
1930s. Inscribed "A Paramount Star Created By Fleischer Studios". - **$30 $50 $100**

❑ **BTY-23. Cello. Button,**
1930s. Rim inscription "A Paramount Star Created By Fleischer Studios".- **$40 $85 $175**

BTY-24

❑ **BTY-24. "Koko" Clown Figure,**
1990s. - **$30**

BTY-25

BTY-26

❑ **BTY-25. Ceramic Figure,**
2000. - **$20**

❑ **BTY-26. Wacky Wobbler Figure,**
2000. Black and white edition, limited to 3,000. -
**$30**

## Big Boy

**In 1936 Bob Wian, running a little diner called Bob's Pantry in Glendale, California, added a double-decker cheeseburger to his menu. A few weeks later, according to legend, a chubby little neighborhood boy named Richard Woodruff walked in wearing oversized pants and suspenders. Wian was enchanted, dubbed him Big Boy, changed the name of the diner and began using an image of the boy as his advertising logo. Wian sold his first franchise to the Elias Brothers in Michigan in 1952, and other franchises quickly followed. The Elias Brothers of Warren, Michigan currently operates over 600 Big Boy restaurants in the US, Japan, Saudi Arabia, Thailand and Brazil. A giveaway comic book was started in 1956 and continued to 1996.**

BIG-1

❑ **BIG-1. Big Boy Die-Cut Menu,**
1949. - **$20 $40 $80**

BIG-2

BIG-3

❑ **BIG-2. Big Boy Ad Card,**
1956. For Free comic. - **$10 $25 $60**

❑ **BIG-3. "Adventures Of The Big Boy" Comic Book #1,**
1956. Art by Bill Everett. - **$150 $475 $1000**

BIG-4

BIG-5

❑ **BIG-4. Ceramic Figural Ashtray,**
c. 1950s. 3-3/4" diameter tray with 3" tall figure on rear edge. Marked only "Made In Japan." - **$75 $150 $225**

❑ **BIG-5. "Big Boy" Salt & Pepper Set,**
1950s. Pair of 4" tall ceramic figures. - **$75 $125 $175**

BIG-6

BIG-7

BIG-8

❑ **BIG-6. Early Litho. Button,**
1950s. Light green rim. - **$15 $35 $60**

❑ **BIG-7. "Nat'l Big Boy Club" Litho. Member Button,**
c. 1960. - **$10 $20 $40**

❑ **BIG-8. Bobbing Head Figure,**
1960s. Painted composition figure with spring-mounted head. - **$250 $500 $900**

BIG-9

❑ **BIG-9. Ceramic Salt & Pepper Set,**
1960s. - **$60 $150 $300**

BIG-10

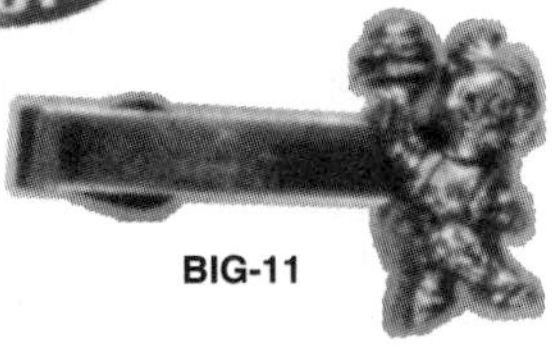

BIG-11

❑ **BIG-10. Club Member Litho. Button,**
c. 1960s. - **$8 $15 $25**

❑ **BIG-11. Silvered Metal Tie Bar,**
c. 1960s. "Big Boy" name on miniature figure. - **$10 $20 $35**

BIG-12

❑ **BIG-12. Frame Tray Puzzle With Envelope,**
1960s. 6-1/4x9-1/4" with both sides in full color.
Near Mint With Envelope - **$100**
Puzzle Only - **$15 $30 $60**

BIG-13

BIG-14

❑ **BIG-13. Vinyl Figure By Dakin,**
1970. - **$60 $120 $225**

❑ **BIG-14. "Adventures Of The Big Boy" Comic Book,**
1978. See The Overstreet Comic Book Price Guide for values of Issues #2 through #466.

BIG-15

❑ **BIG-15. Cloth Dolls,**
c. 1978. Dolls are Big Boy, Dolly and Nugget. Each - **$5 $10 $25**

BIG-16

BIG-17

❑ **BIG-16. Vinyl Figure,**
1970s. - **$15 $30 $50**

❑ **BIG-17. Watch,**
c. 1970s. - **$35 $60 $125**

BIG-18

BIG-19

❑ **BIG-18. Vinyl Figure Night Light,**
1970s. Electrical. - **$35 $75 $150**

❑ **BIG-19. Cloth Body Figure,**
1980. - **$15 $30 $45**

BIG-20

❑ **BIG-20. Limited Edition 50th Anniversary Watch in Box,**
1980. Produced by La Marque. Box snaps open and has "Big Boy" marked inside top. Big Boy name is on the dial. Boxed - **$150**

BIG-21

BIG-22

❑ **BIG-21. Limited Edition 5" Metal Figure,**
1980s. - **$20 $40 $80**

❑ **BIG-22. Big Boy Figure,**
1980s. - **$10 $20 $35**

BIG-23

BIG-24

❑ **BIG-23. Plastic Figure,**
1980s. - **$10 $20 $35**

❑ **BIG-24. Commemorative Figure,**
1980s. - **$10 $20 $35**

BIG-25

BIG-26

❑ **BIG-25. Big Boy Figure,**
1990s. - **$8 $16 $32**

❑ **BIG-26. Bobbing Head Figure,**
1999. In box. - **$25**

## Bill Barnes

**Street and Smith began publication of its pulp *Bill Barnes Air Trails* in the early 1930s and shortened the name of the magazine to *Air Trails* around 1937. Issues contained Bill Barnes air adventure stories, aviation news and features, and information on model planes. Barnes made his comic book debut in issue #1 of *Shadow Comics* in 1940 and had his own book from 1940 to 1943 under various titles: *Bill Barnes Comics, America's Air Ace Comics* and *Air Ace*.**

BBR-1

BBR-2

BBR-3

❑ **BBR-1. "Bill Barnes Air Adventurer" Pulp Magazine,**
September 1935. Published by Street & Smith. - **$20 $40 $80**

❑ **BBR-2. "Bill Barnes/Air Adventurer" Gummed Paper Envelope Sticker,**
1930s. Street & Smith Co., publisher of Bill Barnes pulp magazine. - **$20 $40 $85**

❑ **BBR-3. "Bill Barnes/Air Adventurer" 11x14" Window Card,**
1930s. Street & Smith Publications. Pictures example pulp magazine cover. - **$75 $150 $275**

BBR-4

❑ **BBR-4. "Air Warden Cadets" Club Kit,**
c. 1943. Cello. Button - **$30 $60 $125**
Airplane Spotting Booklet - **$15 $25 $50**
Group Of Six Related Sheets - **$20 $30 $40**

## Billy and Ruth

**Billed as America's Famous Toy Children, Billy and Ruth and their dog Terry were the fictional stars of annual pre-Christmas toy catalogues published for the toy industry as early as 1936. Created by Philadelphia-based L.A. Hoeflich, the catalogues promoted the toys of different participating manufacturers. Retailers who subscribed to the service printed their own store information on the front cover and thus had a ready-made catalogue for their customers. In the late 1950s, as independent toy retailers went out of business, Billy and Ruth became casualties of the new marketplace.**

BLR-1

❑ **BLR-1. Toy Catalogue,**
c. 1932. Various store imprints. 8-3/4x12" with 20 pages including Steelcraft, Lionel, Fisher-Price, Shoenhut, etc. - **$15 $30 $50**

BLR-2

❑ **BLR-2. "In Toy World With Billy And Ruth" Catalogue,**
1936. 32 pages of illustrated and priced period toys. - **$50 $100 $150**

BLR-3

BLR-4

BLR-5

❑ **BLR-3. Club Member's Cello. Button,**
c. 1936. Red on white 1-1/2". - **$10 $20 $40**

❑ **BLR-4. Promotional Cello. Button,**
c. 1936. - **$15 $30 $60**

❑ **BLR-5. Club Member Button,**
1940s. - **$15 $30 $45**

BLR-6

❑ **BLR-6. Christmas Toy Catalogue,**
1951. - **$20 $35 $60**

BLR-7

❑ **BLR-7. Christmas Toy Catalogue,**
1952. - **$20 $35 $60**

BLR-8

BLR-9

❑ **BLR-8. Christmas Toy Catalogue,**
1954. - **$15 $25 $50**

❑ **BLR-9. Christmas Toy Catalogue,**
1955. - **$12 $25 $50**

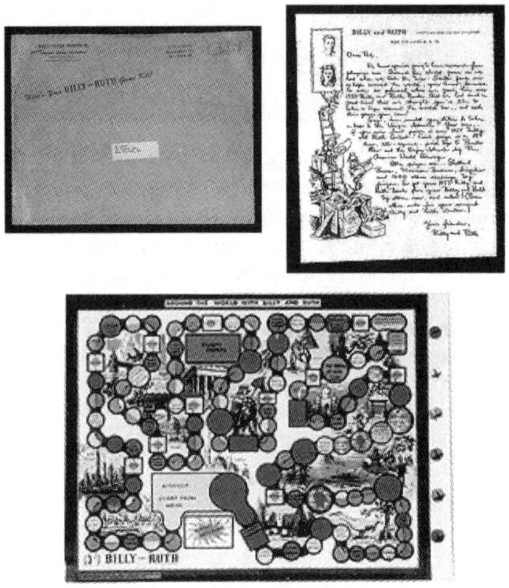

BLR-10

❑ **BLR-10. "Around The World With Billy And Ruth" Game Kit,**
1955. Billy And Ruth Promotion, Inc., Philadelphia. Mail envelope holding cover letter, instruction sheet, playing piece sheets to be scissored, paper playing board map opens to 13-1/2x17". Near Mint In Mailer - **$100**
Game - **$15 $25 $60**
Letter - **$5 $10 $25**

## Billy Bounce

**Little is known of this comic strip rotund youngster other than he briefly had his own strip in 1905 based on various youthful characters created by C. W. Kahles (1878-1931). Apparently Billy Bounce earned some syndication beyond home base of the *New York World*, as known premiums are mostly a few newspaper advertising pin-back buttons. A *Billy Bounce* hardcover book exists crediting W.W. Denslow, noted for his *Wizard of Oz* illustrations, as both author and illustrator.**

BYB-1

BYB-2

❑ **BYB-1. "Compliments Of Billy Bounce" Cello. Button,**
1904. Pictured is W. W. Denslow character with copyright by T. C. McClure. - **$100 $225 $350**

❑ **BYB-2. "Philadelphia Press" Cello. Button,**
c. 1905. - **$85 $150 $250**

BYB-3

BYB-4

❑ **BYB-3. "Billy Bounce In The Sunday Sentinel" Cello. Button,**
c. 1905. Also comes with "Washington Times" imprint. - **$75 $150 $275**

❑ **BYB-4. "Billy Bounce" Hardcover Book,**
1906. Store item published by Donohue Co. Story by Denslow & Bragdon with pictures by Denslow (noted "Oz" artist). - **$60 $125 $250**

## Black Flame of the Amazon

**This radio adventure series was produced in California but apparently found air time only in the Midwest on the Mutual network. The syndicated program dramatized the adventures of explorer Harold Noice in the jungles of South America. Accompanied by his young friends Jim and Jean Brady, his aide Pedro, and the native guide Keyto, Noice did battle with lawless types and dealt with wild animals and strange savage customs. Sponsors included Mayrose processed meats and Hi-Speed Gasoline. In Detroit the series aired on station WXYZ from February to May 1938, sponsored by Hi-Speed Gasoline.**

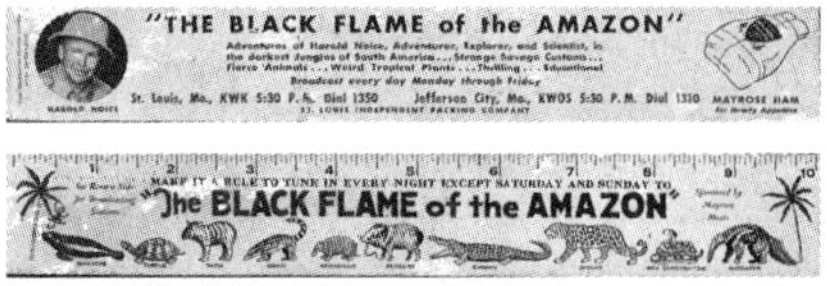


BLF-1

❑ **BLF-1. Cardboard Ruler,**
1930s. Rare. Mayrose Meats. - **$40 $100 $185**

BLF-2

(ENLARGED VIEW)

❑ **BLF-2. Map 21 1/2 x 17",**
1930s. Rare. Radio show sign sponsored by Hi-Speed Gas. - **$150 $350 $550**

BLF-3

BLF-4

❑ **BLF-3. Stamp,**
1930s. Rare. Shows picture of Amazon warriors. One of 24 in set. Each - **$15 $30 $50**

❑ **BLF-4. Paper Mask,**
1930s. Hi-Speed Gasoline. - **$20 $60 $100**

BLF-5

BLF-6

BLF-7

❑ **BLF-5. "Hi-Speed Explorer" Litho. Button,**
1930s. Hi-Speed gasoline. - **$10 $15 $30**

❑ **BLF-6. "Hi-Speed Explorer" Brass Compass Ring,**
1930s. - **$100 $225 $400**

❑ **BLF-7. "Paco Explorer" Litho. Club Button,**
1930s. - **$12 $25 $50**

## Blondie

**One of the world's most popular comic strips, Blondie was created by Chic Young (1901-1973) for King Features in 1930. This family comedy centers on the hectic misadventures of the Bumsteads--Blondie and Dagwood, their children Cookie and Alexander (originally Baby Dumpling), their dog Daisy and her pups, the neighbors Herb and Tootsie Woodley, Dagwood's boss Mr. Dithers and his wife Cora and the indestructible mailman Mr. Beasley. The strip has been continued since 1950 by at least five subsequent artists, including Denis Lebrun. Hollywood turned out more than two dozen Blondie films with Penny Singleton and Arthur Lake in the lead roles and a half-hour radio program ran from 1939 to 1950, sponsored by Camel cigarettes, Super Suds and Colgate. Two TV series, in 1957 and again in 1968, failed to match the success of the strip or the movies.**

BLD-1

BLD-2

❑ **BLD-1. "Sunday Examiner" Newspaper Contest Litho. Button,**
1930s. Part of a set of various characters. - **$10 $25 $50**

❑ **BLD-2. "Blondie and Bouncing Baby Dumpling" Better Little Book #1476,**
1940. - **$10 $35 $75**

BLD-3

❑ **BLD-3. Daisy The Dog Stuffed Knickerbocker Doll With Original Tag,**
c. 1940. Store item. 8" tall with plastic strap collar. Text on tag refers to Columbia Pictures movie.
Doll - **$35 $75 $150**
Tag - **$10 $20 $30**

BLD-4

❑ **BLD-4. Esso Ad Folder,**
1940. - **$15 $30 $60**

BLD-5

❑ **BLD-5. Gasoline Promo Folder,**
1940. Esso Oil. Closed 5x7-1/2" sheet with full color cover and inner comic story that opens to final 10x15" with photo ad for lubrication services on reverse. - **$20 $40 $75**

BLD-6

❑ **BLD-6. "Blondie Goes To Leisureland" Paper Game,**
1940. Westinghouse Co. - **$20 $40 $75**

BLD-7

BLD-8

❑ **BLD-7. Blondie Playing Card Game,**
1941. King Features. Boxed. - **$25 $75 $110**

❑ **BLD-8. "Blondie, Cookie And Daisy's Pups" Better Little Book,**
1941. Whitman #1491. - **$20 $50 $110**

BLD-9

BLD-10

❑ **BLD-9. "Blondie Or Life Among The Bumsteads" Better Little Book,**
1944. Whitman #1466. - **$15 $25 $60**

❑ **BLD-10. "Blondie 100 Selected Top-Laughs" Book,**
1944. Store item published by David McKay Co. Reprint of 100 daily strips from late 1930s through early 1940s. - **$20 $35 $60**

BLD-11

BLD-12

❑ **BLD-11. "Blondie- Papa Knows Best" Big Little Book #1490,**
1945. - **$10 $30 $60**

❑ **BLD-12. "Blondie and Dagwood in Hot Water" Big Little Book #1410,**
1946. - **$10 $30 $60**

BLD-13

BLD-14

❑ **BLD-13. "Comic Togs" Litho. Button,**
1947. From clothing maker series of various characters. - **$40 $60 $125**

❑ **BLD-14. "Blondie- Count Cookie in Too!" Big Little Book #1430,**
1947. - **$10 $30 $60**

BLD-15

BLD-16

❑ **BLD-15. "The Dagwood Sandwich" Boxed Tin Litho Kazoo,**
1947. Store item by Midwest Corp.
Near Mint Boxed - **$250**
Toy Only - **$20 $40 $75**

❑ **BLD-16. "Blondie No Dull Moments" Better Little Book,**
1948. Whitman #1450. - **$10 $30 $60**

BLD-17

BLD-18

❑ **BLD-17. "Blondie- Fun For All" Big Little Book #1463,**
1949. - **$10 $30 $60**

❑ **BLD-18. "Blondie" Paint Book,**
1949. King Features copyright. - **$10 $40 $110**

BLD-19

BLD-20

❑ **BLD-19. "Blondie and Dagwood- Everybody's Happy" Big Little Book #1438,**
1948. - **$10 $30 $60**

❑ **BLD-20. Dagwood Cello. Button,**
c. 1948. Philadelphia Inquirer newspaper. 1-1/4" dark red and cream from small set of comic character buttons issued to promote "Rotocomic" section. - **$50 $125 $200**

BLD-21

BLD-22

❑ **BLD-21. "Penny Singleton" Photo,**
1940s. Radio and films Blondie portrayer. -
**$5 $20 $30**

❑ **BLD-22. "Blondie" Coloring Book,**
1950. King Features copyright. - **$10 $40 $110**

(Box)

(Blocks)

BLD-23

❑ **BLD-23. "Blondie and Dagwood" Interchangable Blocks,**
1951. With instructions in box. Family pictured on the front of the very colorful box. -
**$75 $150 $225**

BLD-24

BLD-25

❑ **BLD-24. Refrigerators Advertising Cello. Button,**
1960s. Westinghouse. 1-1/4" with Dagwood in red, white and blue patriotic outfit. -
**$15 $30 $65**

❑ **BLD-25. Refrigerators Advertising Cello. Button,**
1960s. Westinghouse. 1-1/4". Blondie wears red, white and blue patriotic outfit. -
**$15 $30 $65**

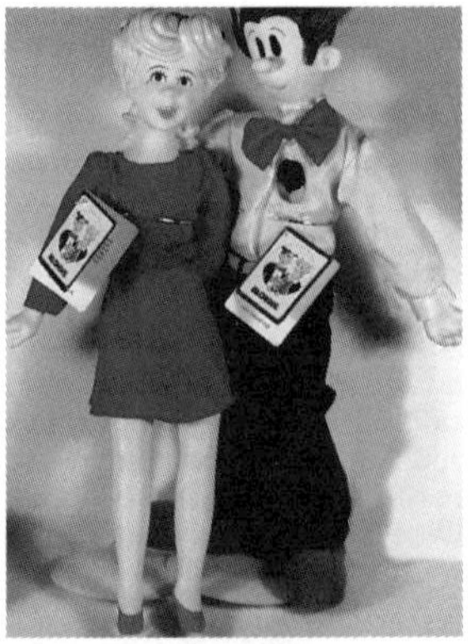
BLD-26

❑ **BLD-26. Blondie and Dagwood Figures,**
1983. 17" dolls have tags. Each - **$10 $35 $85**

BLD-27

❑ **BLD-27. Daisy the Dog Plush Doll with Tag,**
1985. - **$10 $25 $55**

## Bob Hope

**From a small-time vaudeville comic, Bob Hope went on to become one of the world's most beloved performers. His *Pepsodent Show*, which premiered on NBC in 1938, was one of radio's biggest hits for a dozen years. He made a series of successful "Road" movies with Bing Crosby and Dorothy Lamour from 1940 to 1962. He has made countless TV appearances since 1950, slowed only in later years by an age approaching the century mark. He has also devoted much time and energy entertaining American troops all over the world. Hope was given a special Academy Award on five occasions, won the Kennedy Center Honors for Lifetime Achievement in the Arts (1985) and was accorded Honorary Knighthood (1998) by Queen Elizabeth II. He is the sponsor of the Bob Hope Desert Classic, an annual golf event for charity. Thanks for the memories, Bob.**

BOB-1

BOB-2

❑ **BOB-1. Post Card,**
1930s. NBC Radio. - **$20 $40 $80**

❑ **BOB-2. "They Got Me Covered" Book,**
1941. Pepsodent toothpaste.
Book - **$5 $15 $35**
Mailer - **$10 $20 $30**

BOB-3

❑ **BOB-3. "Moonlight Becomes You" Song Sheet,**
1942. Featured in the movie hit "Road to Morocco" starring Bob Hope, Bing Crosby and Dorothy Lamour. - **$12 $20 $40**

BOB-4

❑ **BOB-4. "So This Is Peace" WWII Memoirs Book,**
1946. Simon and Schuster. Includes cartoon comparison of flying a P-38 plane to riding a bicycle pedaled by Superman. - **$10 $20 $40**

BOB-5

BOB-6

❑ **BOB-5. Hair Pin Card,**
1940s. Store item. - **$8 $12 $25**

❑ **BOB-6. Framed Photo,**
1940s. From the war years. - **$15 $25 $50**

BOB-7

❑ **BOB-7. Hope-Lamour Birthday Card,**
1940s. Store item. - **$8 $15 $40**

BOB-8

❑ **BOB-8. Bob Hope And Bing Crosby Figurines,**
c. 1950s. Each is 7-1/2" tall hollow ceramic figure standing on star-shaped base. From rare series of celebrity figures by unknown maker. Each - **$150 $300 $500**

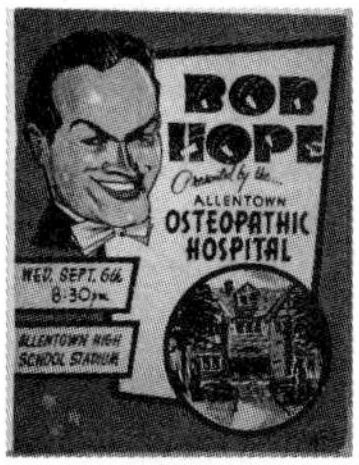


BOB-9

BOB-10

❑ **BOB-9. Hospital Visit Program,**
1950. Promotes a Bob Hope visit to a hospital. 78 pages containing several photos of Hope and a write-up. - **$10 $30 $45**

❑ **BOB-10. "Buttons and Bows" Song Sheet,**
1958. From the movie "Paleface" starring Bob Hope and Jane Russell. - **$10 $25 $45**

BOB-11

BOB-12

❑ **BOB-11. Cigarette Lighter With 14K Gold Plate Finish,**
c. 1950s. Issuer unknown but made by "Florentine." - **$10 $20 $45**

❑ **BOB-12. Biography Booklet,**
c. 1960. NBC/Chrysler Corp. For Chrysler Theater series on NBC-TV. - **$8 $15 $30**

BOB-13

❑ **BOB-13. "Popsicle" 8x20" Contest Poster,**
1961. Joe Lowe Corp. Pictures water recreation prizes including grand prize of a swimming pool. - **$25 $40 $90**

BOB-14

BOB-15

BOB-16

❑ **BOB-14. Bob Hope Veterans' Cause Photo,**
c. 1970. 3-1/2x3-1/2" card picturing him autographing veteran's leg cast with reverse inscription about craft kits given to hospitalized Vietnam veterans. - **$5 $10 $20**

❑ **BOB-15. "Vote Bob Hope" 3" Cello. Button,**
1976. NBC-TV. - **$10 $20 $35**

❑ **BOB-16. Plaster Statue,**
1979. Store item by Esco Products. 17" tall painted plaster from a series of personality statues. - **$15 $40 $75**

## Bobby Benson

**Bobby was the 12-year-old owner of a ranch in south Texas. With his cowgirl pal Polly and a cast of regulars, *Bobby Benson's Adventures* started riding the airwaves on CBS in 1932. As long as the show was sponsored by H-O (Hecker's Oats) cereal, the ranch was called the H-Bar-O. When H-O dropped out as sponsor in 1936, the ranch became the B-Bar-B and the show continued briefly. It was revived as *Bobby Benson and the B-Bar-B Riders* on the Mutual network from 1949 to 1955. Among the early cast members were Dead-End Kid Billy Halop as Bobby and Tex Ritter, Don Knotts and Al Hodge. A series of comic books was published by Magazine Enterprises from 1950 to 1953.**

BNS-1

BNS-2

❑ **BNS-1. Fan Club Photo,**
c. 1932. - **$10 $20 $40**

❑ **BNS-2. Bobby Benson Star Badge,**
1932. 1st badge. Silver finish. Rare in any grade. - **$75 $150 $200**

BNS-3

BNS-4

❑ **BNS-3. "H-Bar-O Transfer Book",**
1933. Paper cover holding strip of 12 sheets of transfer pictures to be cut apart and applied by water. - **$15 $60 $110**

❑ **BNS-4. H-Bar-O Ranger Belt,**
1933. H-O Cereals. Cowhide leather companion belt to BNS-7, unmarked and offered separately. - **$15 $35 $50**

BNS-5

❑ **BNS-5. H-Bar-O News,**
1933. Hecker H-O Co. 11x15" color print 16-page club newsletter edition including two center pages picturing 15 premiums. Pictured example is Vol. 1 #2. - **$15 $25 $50**

BNS-6

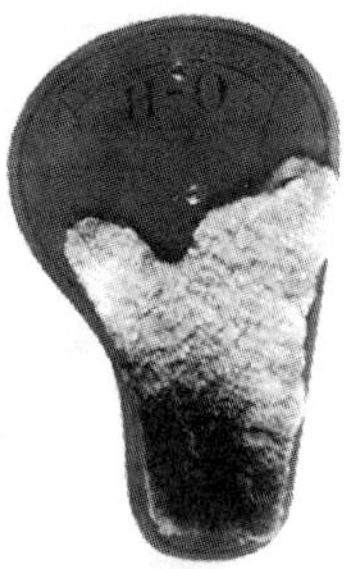

BNS-7

❑ **BNS-6. "H-Bar-O Ranger" Enameled Brass Star Badge,**
1933. Scarce. - **$50 $100 $200**

❑ **BNS-7. "H-Bar-O Ranger" Holster,**
1933. H-O Cereals. 7-1/2" long cowhide leather with wool cover panel, rear leather belt loop. See separately offered belt BNS-4. - **$35 $75 $140**

BNS-8

❑ **BNS-8. "H-Bar-O Herald" Vol. 1 #1 Newspaper,**
September 1933. Contents mention Benson radio broadcasts to begin September 18. - **$15 $30 $70**

BNS-9

❑ **BNS-9. "H-Bar-O Rangers Club" Neckerchief,**
c. 1933. 20x32" issued by H-O Cereal. - **$15 $30 $65**

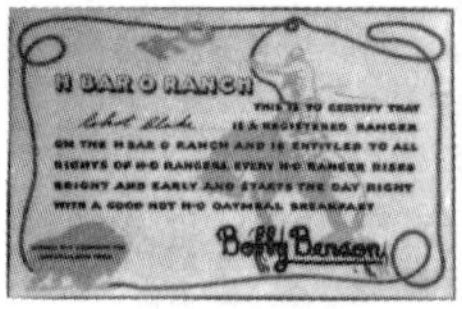


BNS-10

BNS-11

❑ **BNS-10. Certificate,**
1933. Hecker H-O Cereal. - **$15 $30 $50**

❑ **BNS-11. Catalog,**
1933. Hecker Oats Cereals. Six page color catalog. - **$30 $70 $100**

BNS-12

BNS-13

❑ **BNS-12. "H-Bar-O Rangers Club" Cello. Button,**
1933. - **$10 $15 $25**

❑ **BNS-13. "H-O" Cast Iron Cap Gun,**
c. 1934. 7" long with cereal initials inscription on one side, offered in Bobby Benson premium folder of that year. - **$50 $125 $225**

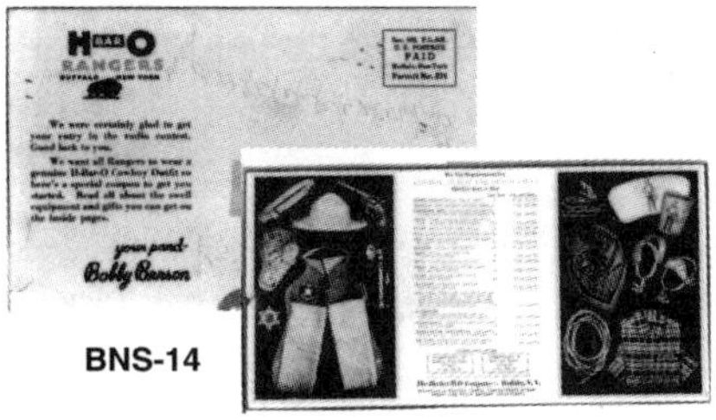

BNS-14

❑ **BNS-14. "H-Bar-O Rangers/Bobby Benson" Premium Offer Folder,**
1934. - **$25 $50 $85**

BNS-15

❑ **BNS-15. H-Bar-O Newspaper Vol. 1 #3,**
1934. Hecker Oats cereal. - **$10 $20 $40**

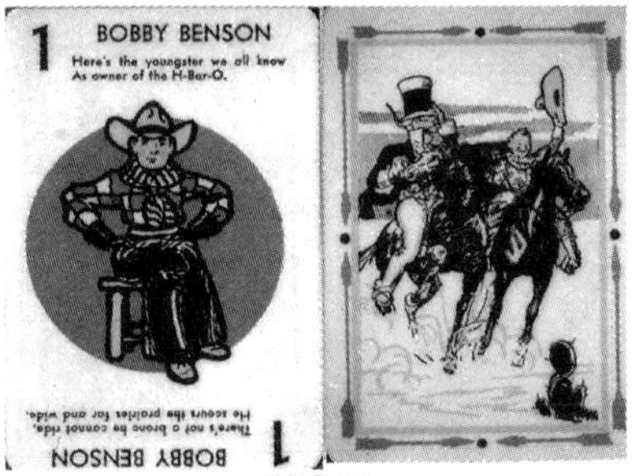

BNS-16

❑ **BNS-16. "Bobby Benson's Game Circus,"**
1934. Deck of 32 playing cards and instruction leaflet for 18 games.- **$20 $35 $60**

BNS-17

❑ **BNS-17. Code Rule,**
1935. - **$20 $35 $75**

BNS-18

❑ **BNS-18. Code Book,**
1935. - **$15 $30 $60**

BNS-19

BNS-20

❑ **BNS-19. "Bobby Benson In The Tunnel Of Gold" Booklet,**
1936. Hecker Cereals. - **$10 $30 $60**

❑ **BNS-20. "Bobby Benson And The Lost Herd" Book,**
1936. Hecker Cereals. - **$10 $30 $60**

BNS-21

❑ **BNS-21. Glass Bowl,**
1930s. Comes in green, yellow or red.
Each - **$10 $20 $35**

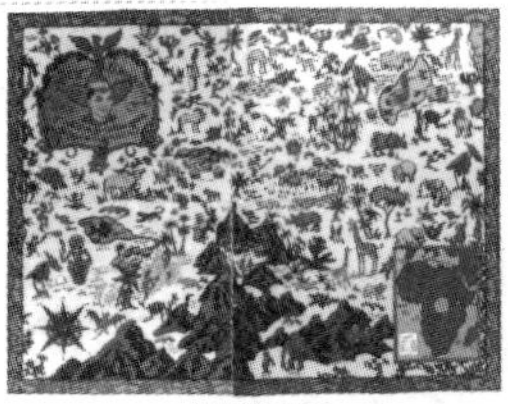
BNS-22

❑ **BNS-22. "Bobby Benson And The H-O Rangers In Africa" 19x25" Map,**
1930s. Map - **$100 $200 $325**
Envelope - **$30 $60 $120**

BNS-23

BNS-24

❑ **BNS-23. Star Junior Police Badge,**
1930s. Scarce. Gold badge with #808 which is number used on Bobby Benson premiums. - **$65 $150 $225**

❑ **BNS-24. "Special Captain" Cello. Club Rank Button,**
1930s. - **$25 $50 $75**

BNS-25

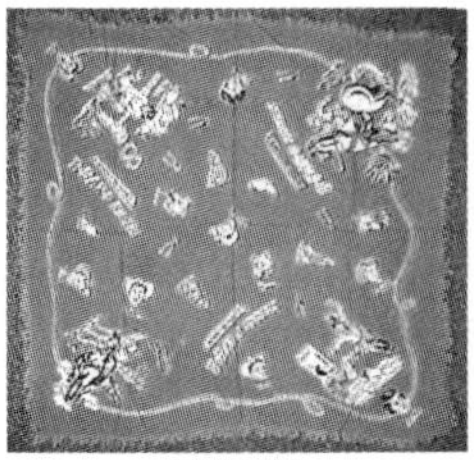
BNS-26

❑ **BNS-25. "Bobby Benson Ranger/H-Bar-O" Foil On Metal Badge,**
1930s. - **$20 $40 $85**

❑ **BNS-26. Fabric Scarf,**
1930s. Pictures and names the show's characters in white, dark brown and green on rose-colored background. - **$25 $50 $100**

BNS-27

❑ **BNS-27. Photos With Envelope,**
1930s. Ten different known. Photo not shown depicts Bart.
Envelope Or Each Photo - **$5 $12 $20**

BNS-28

❑ **BNS-28. Store Display Box With Glass Tumblers,**
1930s. Tumblers were obtained with two boxes of Force Toasted Wheat Flakes, six different characters.
Boxed Display - **$100 $200 $350**
Each - **$8 $12 $20**

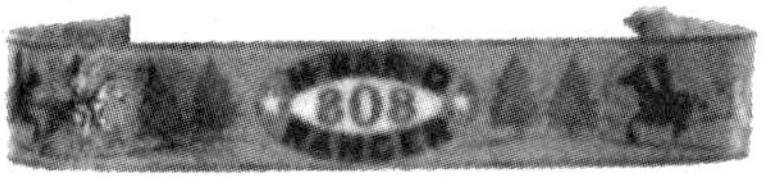


BNS-29

BNS-30

❑ **BNS-29. "H-Bar-O Ranger" Enameled Brass Bracelet,**
1930s. - **$75 $125 $250**

❑ **BNS-30. "H-Bar-O Ranger/808" 2" Long Enamel Brass Tie Clip,**
1930s. Near Mint On Card With Mailer - **$300**
Tie Clip Only - **$35 $75 $125**

BNS-31

❑ **BNS-31. "20 Decals For You!" Mailing Folder,**
c. 1949. Folder text promotes program on Mutual Network. Folder holds four-panel strip of brilliant color decals. Complete - **$20 $40 $95**

BNS-32

❑ **BNS-32. B-Bar-B Riders Club Kit With Mailer Envelope,**
c. 1949. Contents of Bobby Benson humming lariat, photo, membership certificate.
Each Item - **$20 $45 $90**

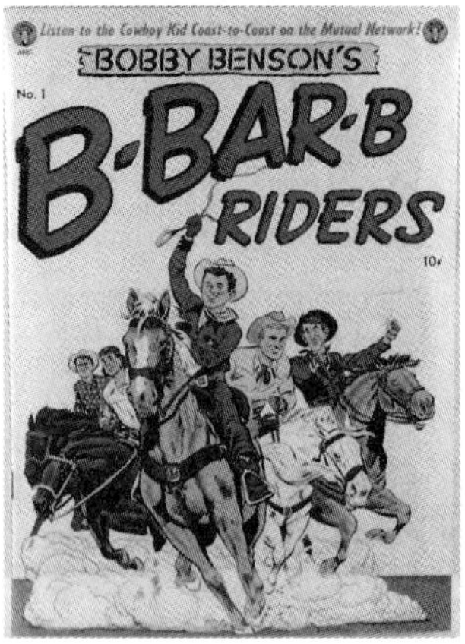


BNS-33

❑ **BNS-33. "Bobby Benson's B-Bar-B Riders #1" Comic Book,**
1950. Scarce. - **$43 $128 $340**

## *Bonanza*

**The story of the Cartwright family, set on their Ponderosa Ranch in Nevada in the 1860s, premiered on NBC in September 1959 and aired weekly until 1973--the second-longest Western series on television. One of the nation's most popular shows during most of the 1960s, it was also the first Western to be televised in color. The Ponderosa was a man's world, with Lorne Greene as the widowed father Ben and Pernell Roberts, Dan Blocker and Michael Landon as his sons Adam, Hoss and Little Joe. The program often focused on the relationships between the characters rather than on typical Western violence. As of early 1999, *Bonanza* was still being shown somewhere in the world every day. Special made-for-TV movie sequels including Michael Landon Jr. as a cast member are *Bonanza: The Return* (1993), *Bonanza: Under Attack* (1995) and *Bonanza: The Next Generation* (1998).**

BON-1

BON-2

❑ **BON-1. "Bonanza Booster" 2-1/4" Cello. Button,**
c. 1960. - **$40 $85 $150**

❑ **BON-2. "TV Guide Cover Portrait",**
1961. Large high quality color matted photo from series sent to television stations. -
**$25 $50 $125**

BON-3

❑ **BON-3. Arkansas Expo Sheet With "Bonanza" Stars,**
1962. 9x12" sheet printed on each side. -
**$10 $20 $40**

BON-4

BON-5

❑ **BON-4. Fort Madison Iowa 2-1/4" Rodeo Button,**
1964. From series of event buttons beginning in 1957. - **$30 $60 $125**

❑ **BON-5. "Bonanza Days" 3" Cello. Button,**
1964. For celebration in site city of series, picturing all four original cast members. - **$25 $50 $75**

BON-6

BON-7

❑ **BON-6. 33 RPM Record,**
1964. Chevrolet. - **$5 $10 $20**

❑ **BON-7. "Adam" And "Joe" European Litho. 2-1/2" Stickpin Buttons,**
c. 1965. Each - **$15 $30 $70**

BON-8

BON-9

❑ **BON-8. "Ponderosa Ranch" Tin Cup,**
c. 1965. Store item. Pictures all four original stars. - **$8 $15 $30**

❑ **BON-9. "Bonanza" Enamel Diecut Brass Stickpin,**
c. 1965. European made, depicts Ben Cartwright on horseback. - **$15 $30 $50**

BON-10

❑ **BON-10. "The Ponderosa Ranch Story" Booklet,**
1969. Ranch souvenir. - **$15 $25 $40**

BON-11

❑ **BON-11. "Ponderosa Ranch" Commemorative Beam Bottle,**
1969. 7" tall issued by James Beam Distilling Co. - **$15 $30 $60**

BON-12

BON-13

❑ **BON-12. Badge,**
1960s. Premium for TV series. Red stone in middle. - **$25 $50 $85**

❑ **BON-13. "Michael Landon/Little Joe" Fan Photo,**
1960s. - **$15 $25 $40**

BON-14

BON-15

❑ **BON-14. "Bonanza" Cello. Button,**
c. 1960s. Australian issue picturing Lorne Greene. - **$25 $50 $80**

❑ **BON-15. Cast Members Premium Photo,**
1960s. Inscribed "Compliments Of Your Local Authorized Chevrolet Dealer." 8x10" glossy black and white. - **$5 $15 $30**

BON-16

❑ **BON-16. Bonanza Cast Restaurant Matches,**
1960s. Various franchises. Full color portrait of cast member on front with restaurant location on back.
Near Mint Unused Lorne Greene **- $15**
Near Mint Unused Michael Landon - **$25**
Near Mint Unused Dan Blocker **- $18**

BON-17

❑ **BON-17. Ben And Hoss Cartwright Sheriff Badges,**
c. 1970. Unmarked store item.
Each **- $15 $25 $45**

BON-18

BON-19

❑ **BON-18. Portrait Pins Made In Spain,**
1970s. Store items. 1" tall brass pin, each with mounted black and white glossy photo with color tinting on faces and outfits. Pictured are Lorne Greene, Michael Landon, Dan Blocker, Pernell Roberts. Each - **$8 $15 $25**

❑ **BON-19. "I Met Hoss Cartwright" Litho. Tin Tab,**
c. 1970s. Nickey Chevrolet, with backwards "K." - **$8 $15 $35**

## Bozo the Clown

**Bozo began his clowning around in 1946 on a kid's record album created by Alan Livingston, a former Capitol Records executive. Bozo's TV debut came in 1949 on Los Angeles television with Pinto Colvig, the voice on the records, playing the role. Numerous Capitol Record albums and Dell comic books built Bozo's reputation in the 1950s, and by the 1960s, syndicated television shows were hosted by nearly 200 Bozos**

**in the U.S. and around the world. Larry Harmon, an early Bozo, acquired the character rights in 1956 and licensed products since then carry his name. By the 1990s, Bozo shows were in steep decline. Chicago's station WGN, once home to the show with the most extensive production values, abandoned the successful weekday time slot in 1994 for Sunday morning at 7 A.M. and began mixing educational themes with pure clowning around. WGN taped the last Bozo show June 12, 2001.**

BOZ-1

❑ **BOZ-1. "Bozo's Jungle Jingles" 78 RPM Record,**
1951. Capitol Records. Comes with colorful 4-page sleeve. - **$25 $50 $75**

BOZ-2

❑ **BOZ-2. "I Am A Bozo Pal" Cello. Button,**
c. 1950s. Serial number club button sponsored by WDSM-TV, Superior, Wisconsin. - **$8 $12 $25**

BOZ-3

❑ **BOZ-3. "Bozo The Clown" Hassock,**
1950s. 10" tall store item by Knickerbocker. - **$20 $40 $75**

BOZ-4

BOZ-5

❑ **BOZ-4. Bread Wrapper,**
c. 1950s. Colorful wrapper. - **$25 $50 $90**

❑ **BOZ-5. Soaky Toy,**
1965. - **$10 $35 $75**

BOZ-6

❑ **BOZ-6. Glass With Lid,**
1965. Held peanut butter. Set of five.
Each - **$5 $10 $25**
Lid - **$5 $10 $15**

BOZ-7

BOZ-8

❑ **BOZ-7. Mirror,**
1966. Promo for "Bozo Show." - **$10 $25 $45**

❑ **BOZ-8. "Bozo The Clown" Half Gallon Milk Carton,**
1968. London's Farm Dairy Inc. - **$10 $20 $40**

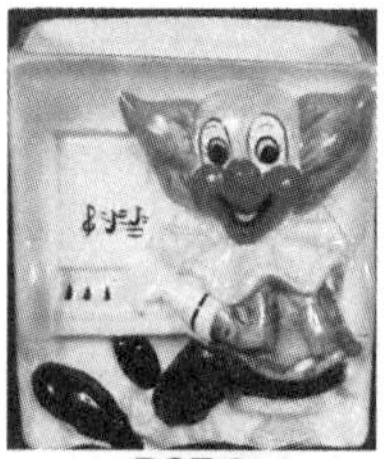

BOZ-9

❑ **BOZ-9. Glazed Ceramic Planter,**
1960s. Store item. 5" tall depicting Bozo at piano. - **$15 $25 $50**

BOZ-10

❑ **BOZ-10. "Bozo The Clown" Litho. Tin Button,**
1960s. Large, 3-1/2", colorful and scarce. - **$25 $50 $75**

BOZ-11

❑ **BOZ-11. "Bozo The Clown Dancing Toy" Vinyl Wind-Up,**
1960s. Store item by Lakeside Toys. 5" tall in box with cellophane window.
Box - **$5 $15 $20**
Toy - **$15 $25 $40**

BOZ-12

BOZ-13

❑ **BOZ-12. Patch And Membership Card,**
1960s. TV promo for "Bozo Show." Store bought. - **$10 $20 $30**

❑ **BOZ-13. Plastic Push Puppet,**
c. 1960s. Store item by Kohner. - **$12 $20 $40**

BOZ-14

BOZ-15

❑ **BOZ-14. Plastic Portrait Ring,**
1960s. - **$20 $50 $80**

❑ **BOZ-15. "I Visited Bozo's Circus" Litho. Button,**
c. 1970s. WGN-TV (Chicago). - **$5 $10 $15**

BOZ-16

BOZ-17

❑ **BOZ-16. Illuminated Plastic Snow Dome,**
c. 1970s. Store item, battery operated. -
**$40 $75 $150**

❑ **BOZ-17. "Bozo Is Love" 3" Cello. Button,**
c. 1970s. Various TV stations. Pictured example from Grand Rapids, Michigan. - **$3 $8 $15**

BOZ-18

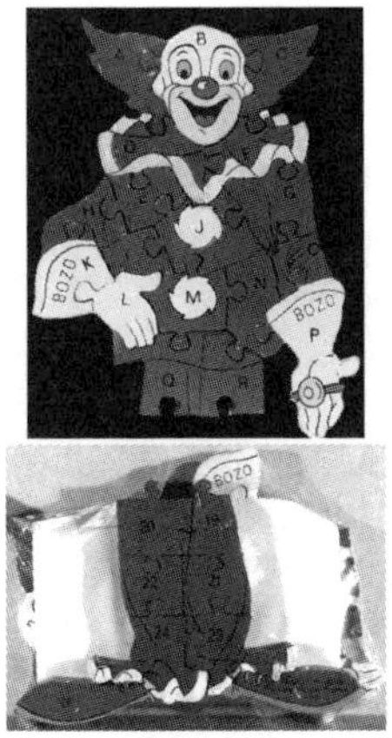

BOZ-19

❑ **BOZ-18. Bozo Valentines in Box,**
1996. 48 valentines with 3 cards on back of box. -
**$20**

❑ **BOZ-19. Bozo Block Puzzle,**
1997. © Larry Harmon Pictues Corp. Figure is 11 1/2" tall when completed. - **$10 $20 $35**

BOZ-20

BOZ-21

❑ **BOZ-20. Talking Bozo Bean Figure,**
1999. 18" tall. Unstable printing on gloves. Ink rubs off easily. Ink rubs off nose too.
With tag and label - **$25**

❑ **BOZ-21. Wacky Wobbler Figure,**
2001. In box. - **$15**

BOZ-22

BOZ-23

❑ **BOZ-22. Die-Cast Metal Car,**
2000. Team Lightning. - **$8**

❑ **BOZ-23. Bozo Plush Doll,**
2001. With tag. - **$24**

## Breakfast Club

**Don McNeill's *Breakfast Club*, a happy blend of Midwestern corn and audience participation, ruled morning radio for most of its 24 years on the air (1933 to 1968)--one of the longest-running network radio shows ever. The program, broadcast from Chicago, was essentially spontaneous and unrehearsed, combining contributions sent in by listeners, songs, prayers, marches around the breakfast table, poetry, anecdotes and occasional interviews with guest stars. There were many sponsors over the years. McNeill's familiar closing line--"Be good to yourself"--typified the warmth and charm of this popular and successful program. A TV simulcast in 1954 did not catch on.**

BRK-1

❑ **BRK-1. Club Member Folder Kit,**
c. 1944. Folder has contest and new member forms, comes with "Victory Garden" card.
Folder - **$15 $35 $55**
Card - **$5 $12 $20**

BRK-2

BRK-3

❑ **BRK-2. Don McNeill Club Book,**
1944. Says "Good Morning Breakfast Clubber & Good Morning to Ya" on cover. Contest rules & large photo of radio show cast & band. -
**$15 $35 $55**

❑ **BRK-3. "Don's Other Life..." Hardcover Book,**
1944. 7-7/8x9-1/4" with 64 pages credited as "By The First Lady Of The Breakfast Club Kay McNeill." - **$10 $25 $40**

BRK-4

BRK-5

❑ **BRK-4. "Don McNeill For President" Litho. Button,**
c. 1948. ABC Breakfast Clubs. - **$5 $10 $20**

❑ **BRK-5. "Don McNeill For President" Litho. Button,**
c. 1948. 2 1/2". Scarcer version. - **$10 $20 $40**

BRK-6

BRK-7

❑ **BRK-6. Paper Sticker,**
1948. Full color 2x2-7/8" sticker gummed on reverse showing Woody Woodpecker carrying campaign sign. - **$5 $10 $15**

❑ **BRK-7. Don McNeill Featured In Radio Mirror Magazine,**
1948. July, 1948 issue features Don McNeill and family on cover with photos and major story about him on the inside. The Radio Mirror Magazine was to radio as TV Guide is to television. This issue is also important because it was one of the transition mags to also include television material. On the cover, note the small words after "Radio." Inside are the first photos of Buffalo Bob and Howdy Doody with a picture of the 1st 20-seat Peanut Gallery. The Howdy Doody marionette is the same as the one pictured on the pinback when Howdy was running for President and the Howdy photo is totally different than the one we are used to seeing. - **$25 $50 $75**

BRK-8

BRK-9

❑ **BRK-8. Club Charter Member Card,**
1940s.- **$10 $25 $45**

❑ **BRK-9. Fan Club Folder,**
1940s. - **$5 $20 $35**

BRK-10

❑ **BRK-10. Don McNeill Club Card,**
1940s. Postcard premium from the radio show. - **$15 $30 $45**

BRK-11

BRK-12

❑ **BRK-11. Don McNeill's Breakfast Club Sign 12x36",**
1940s. Promotes radio show and victory bond drive in drug stores. - **$50 $125 $175**

❑ **BRK-12. "Don McNeill Sent Me" Litho. Button,**
c. 1950. Apparently to be worn to grocery or other retail store. - **$5 $12 $20**

BRK-13

BRK-14

❑ **BRK-13. Don McNeill's Breakfast Club Book,**
1953. Radio premium. "Twenty Years of Memory Time." - **$15 $40 $70**

❑ **BRK-14. "20 Years Of Corn" Booklet,**
c. 1953. - **$10 $20 $35**

BRK-15

BRK-16

❑ **BRK-15. "Kiddie Party Ideas" Booklet,**
c. 1950s. Fritos. - **$20 $80 $125**

❑ **BRK-16. "Don McNeill/Himself Hide-Away" 2-1/4" Cello. Button,**
1950s. - **$8 $15 $25**

BRK-17

**BRK-17. Various Yearbooks,**
1940s-1950s. Issued annually.
❑ 1942 - **$10 $20 $45**
❑ 1947 - **$8 $15 $35**
❑ 1948 - **$8 $15 $35**
❑ 1949 - **$8 $15 $35**
❑ 1950 - **$7 $15 $35**
❑ 1954 - **$7 $12 $30**

## Breakfast in Hollywood

**Radio veteran Tom Breneman was the host of *Breakfast at Sardi's* on the Blue network until he bought his own restaurant in 1943 and started broadcasting *Breakfast with Breneman.* The program, a variety show with audience participation, soon changed its name to *Breakfast in Hollywood* and aired on the ABC network with Breneman as host until his untimely death in 1948. Kellogg's cereals sponsored the show from 1945 to 1948. A United Artists film version was released in 1946 featuring Breneman, Bonita Granville, Beulah Bondi, Spike Jones, the King Cole Trio, and other Hollywood notables.**

BHL-1

BHL-2

❑ **BHL-1. Tom Breneman's Book,**
1943.Fifty page premium for breakfast. Pictures Orson Welles, Jimmy Durante, Lum & Abner, Xavier Cugat and others. - **$20 $35 $50**

❑ **BHL-2. Premium Postcard,**
1943. Features Tom Breneman and Bob Hope.- **$10 $20 $30**

BHL-3

❑ **BHL-3. Tom Breneman's Booklet,**
1945. Ivory Flakes. Eight page premium features Hedda Hopper, Lum & Abner and others. Has "Breakfast in Hollywood" song on back. Has 25¢ cover. - **$15 $25 $45**

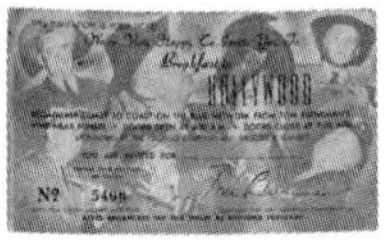

BHL-4

BHL-5

❑ **BHL-4. Tom Breneman's Ticket Postcard,**
1945.Premium ticket that can be used as postcard after attendance at show. - **$10 $20 $35**

❑ **BHL-5. "Tom Breneman's Magazine" First Issue,**
1948. Farrell Radio Magazine Inc. Volume 1 #1 from January with 128 pages. - **$8 $15 $25**

BHL-6

BHL-7

❑ **BHL-6. Tom Breneman's Peeks Book,**
1940s. Kellogg's Cereal. Photos of famous stars and a behind the scenes look at a movie breakfast in Hollywood - **$15 $35 $60**

❑ **BHL-7. Tom Breneman's Peeks Book Mailer,**
1940s. Kellogg's Cereal. - **$5 $10 $15**

## The Brownies

**Palmer Cox (1840-1924) tried cartooning in San Francisco in the 1860s and early 1870s then set up a studio in 1875 in New York City. He had some success being published in early *Life* humor magazines but his main claim to fame grew out of cartoons of Brownieland beginning in the *St. Nicholas* monthly children's magazine. Cox had been inspired by Scottish immigrant folk tales he heard as a boy in Granby, Canada. The frontispiece in the first book *The Brownies: Their Book* from 1887 reads: "Brownies, like fairies and goblins, are imaginary little sprites who are supposed to delight in harmless pranks and helpful deeds. They work and sport while weary households sleep and never allow themselves to be seen by mortal eyes." The Brownies world was a microcosm of society at its best and worst, all portrayed most skillfully through the mind and pen of Palmer Cox and his intricate work throughout the Victorian era and into the early 20th century. Brownieland complemented the times and most probably influenced the creation of *Little Nemo, Kewpies, Teenie-Weenies, Bucky Bug, Raggedy Ann* and other characters set in the world of fantasy.**

H. G. PERRY,
Dealer in the CELEBRATED
Estey Organs and Pianos,
And in Sewing Machines,
CANAJOHARIE, N. Y.

BRW-2

❑ **BRW-2. Estey Organs and Pianos Trade Card,**
1890. - **$12 $25 $45**

BRW-3

❑ **BRW-3. "Palmer Cox's Brownie Paper Dolls",**
1892. Brownies Chocolate Cream Drops. Each - **$15 $30 $55**

BRW-1

❑ **BRW-1. Original Pen and Ink Brownies Art by Palmer Cox,**
1880s. 46 characters shown, including Cox's favorite "The Dude" on the far left. Pen and ink originals are scarce; even rarer with his signature (found in the bottom left corner on this piece.) - **$2750**

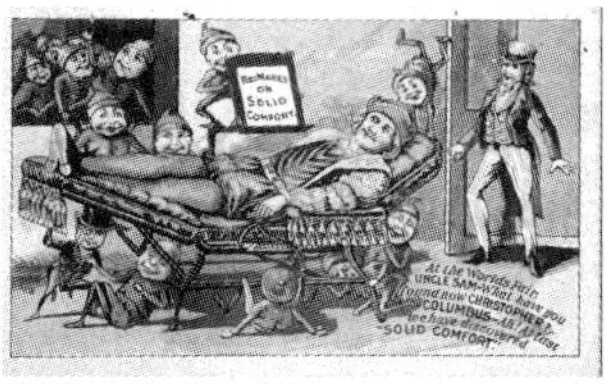


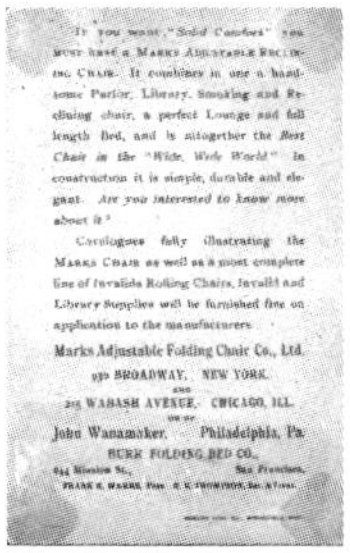


BRW-4

❑ **BRW-4. World's Fair Trade Card - Chairs,**
1892. - **$15 $30 $60**

BRW-5

❑ **BRW-5. World's Fair Pin, Needle & Thread Booklet,**
1892. - **$15 $30 $60**

BRW-6

❑ **BRW-6. World's Fair Trade Card - Stoves/Furnaces,**
1893. Scarce. - **$25 $60 $110**

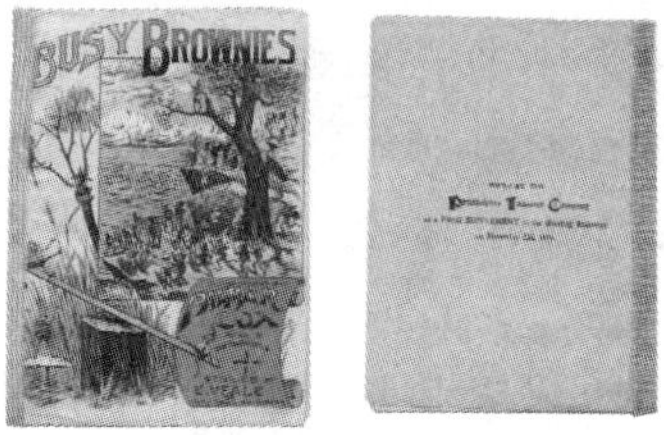


BRW-7

❑ **BRW-7. "Busy Brownies" Comic Giveaway,**
1896. Rare. 6 1/2 x 9". Various sponsors - this one sponsored by the **Philadelphia Inquirer** newspaper. - **$100 $200 $300**

BRW-8

❑ **BRW-8. "Palmer Cox Primers" Booklets,**
1897. Jersey Coffee and others. Set of 11. Each - **$25 $45 $75**

BRW-9

❑ **BRW-9. Hand-Painted Porcelain Lapel Stud,**
c. 1890s. Issuer unknown. 1-3/8" tall white porcelain with Brownie wearing a tam depicted in shades of brown. - **$25 $50 $100**

BRW-10

❑ **BRW-10. "See-Saw" Dexterity Puzzle,**
1890s. Imprinted for Parkhurst-Duker Co. clothing, Quincy, Illinois . 1/2x1-1/2x3-1/2" cardboard frame holding glass over cardboard playing surface picturing three Brownies. Inner surface tilts adding to difficulty of placing three balls in holes. - **$50 $100 $210**

BRW-11

❑ **BRW-11. "Brownies and the Farmer" Hardback Book by Palmer Cox,**
1890s. Rare. The title was appropriate for the time as 85% of the U.S. population lived in rural areas. - **$100 $225 $400**

BRW-12

❑ **BRW-12. Luden's Cough Drop 6x9" Sign,**
1890s. Rare. Earliest known character die-cut sign ad. - **$250 $750 $1200**

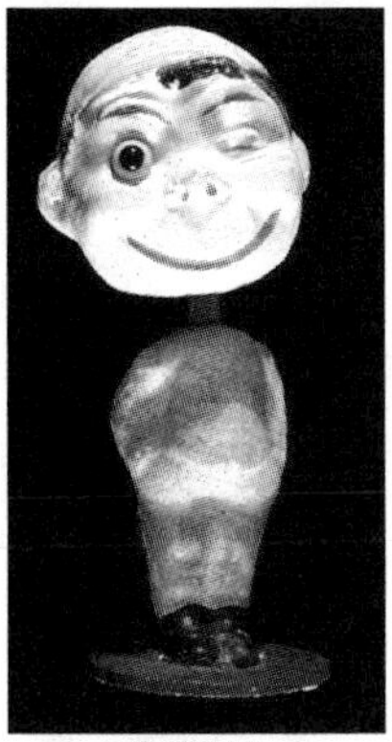

BRW-13

BRW-14

❑ **BRW-13. Brownie Type Bobbing Head with Glass Eye,**
1890s. Made in Germany. - **$125 $250 $400**

❑ **BRW-14. Candy Fig Box,**
1890s. - **$40 $140 $225**

BRW-15

❑ **BRW-15. "Brownie Member" Pinback,**
1890s. Rare. - **$25 $40 $85**

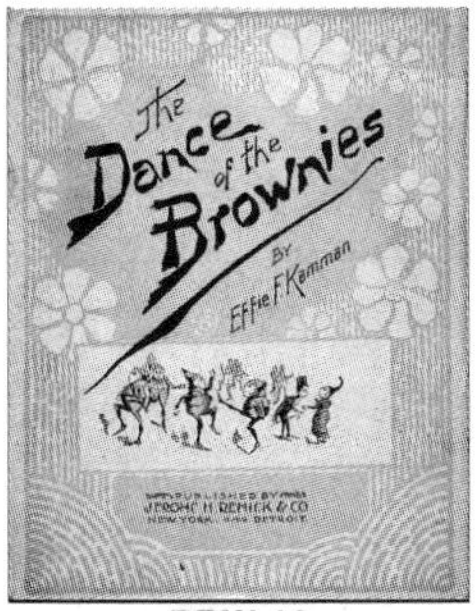


BRW-16

❑ **BRW-16. Brownies Song Book,**
1890s. - **$25 $60 $125**

BRW-17

❑ **BRW-17. Lion's Coffee Cut-Outs,**
1890s. Each - **$10 $30 $60**

BRW-18

❑ **BRW-18. Advertising Cards,**
1890s. Buttermilk Toilet Soap.
Each - **$10 $25 $50**

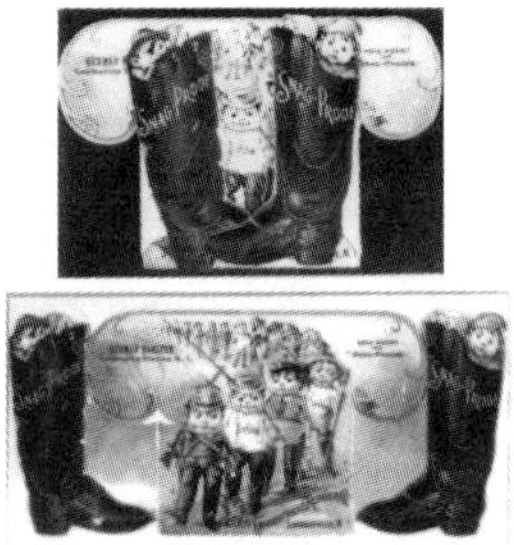

BRW-19

❑ **BRW-19. Advertising Trade Card,**
1890s. Snag-Proof Boots. Card opens to Brownies as sportsmen using boots. - **$15 $30 $75**

BRW-20

❑ **BRW-20. "Merry Christmas From The Brownies" Cardboard Box,**
1890s. Probably held candy or dates. -
**$25 $50 $75**

BRW-21

❑ **BRW-21. Defender Jar,**
Late 1890s. These were done for Palmer Cox's popular Brownie characters. Scarce. -
**$120 $350 $550**

BRW-22

BRW-23

❑ **BRW-22. Metal Figure Stickpin,**
1890s. Tinted luster. - **$12 $20 $35**

❑ **BRW-23. Brownie Policeman Stickpin,**
c. 1900. 3/4" diecut brass figure accented in black and red on 2" brass stickpin. - **$15 $25 $50**

BRW-24

❑ **BRW-24. Brownies Pair Of Stuffed Dolls,**
c. 1900. First is 6-3/4", second is 6-1/2" tall. Maker unknown.
Each In Series **- $65 $100 $175**

BRW-25

❑ **BRW-25. Brownie Camera,**
1901. In 1901, Kodak introduced the first boxed camera. In order to promote it to all age groups they called it the Brownie. Palmer Cox's Brownies were very popular at the time and the camera bacame an overnight success. The original box features many Brownies on the top of the box. The camera shown is a 1940s version.
Camera - **$30 $60 $90**
Box With Characters Shown - **$75 $100 $150**

BRW-26

❑ **BRW-26. "Libretto Of Palmer Cox's Brownies" Booklet,**
c. 1904. 16-page song folio from stage production. - **$25 $60 $125**

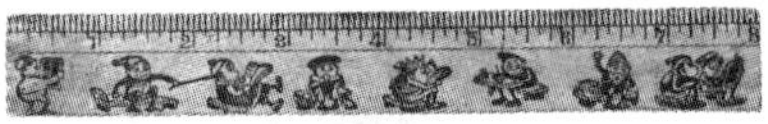

BRW-27

❑ **BRW-27. Brownie Ruler,**
1900s. Mrs. Winslow Syrup premium. 8" long. - **$75 $100 $150**

## Buck Jones

**Movie serials, known then as chapter plays, blossomed in the 1930s, drawing countless thousands of youngsters to local movie palaces every Saturday to find out how their hero would save himself from the perilous predicament at the end of the previous episode. Buck Jones was king of the Western serials. Charles Gebhart (1889-1942) was a cowpuncher, a mechanic, a soldier and a trick rider. Around 1917 he found work as a Hollywood stuntman. Three years later, as Buck Jones, he had his first starring role. In all, Buck Jones was to make more than 125 movies, but it was as the hero of six chapter plays released between 1933 and 1941 that he was to find his greatest success. Kids everywhere waited breathlessly for the next Buck Jones serial. A radio series, *Hoofbeats*, sponsored by Grape-Nuts Flakes, ran for 39 episodes in 1937-1938. In the early 1940s Buck Jones starred with Tim McCoy and Raymond Hatton in Monogram Pictures' *Rough Riders* movies.**

BKJ-1

❑ **BKJ-1. "Rangers Club Of America" Cowboy Outfit,**
c. 1931. Hat - **$20 $35 $70**
Bandanna. - **$25 $40 $80**
Chaps, Includes Metal Rivet Accents And Club Logo - **$75 $150 $325**

BKJ-2

❑ **BKJ-2. Club Booklet,**
1931. Columbia Pictures Corp. 4x6" black and white with 32 pages on bugle and harmonica playing along with information on club rank insignias and pledge text. - **$20 $40 $90**

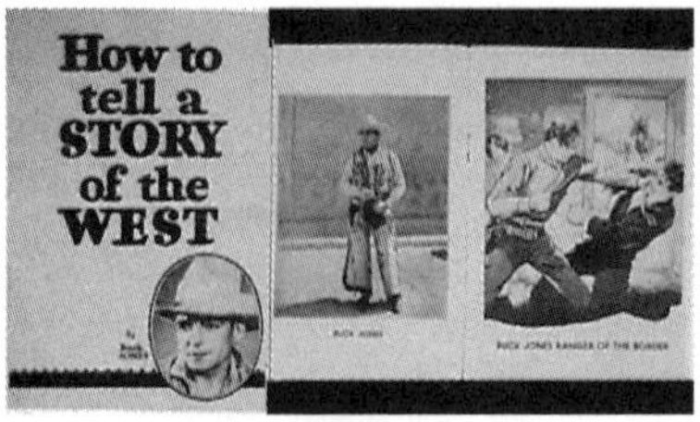


BKJ-3

❑ **BKJ-3. Club Booklet,**
1931. Columbia Pictures Corp. Similar to song booklet but devoted to storytelling techniques. - **$20 $40 $90**

BKJ-4

❑ **BKJ-4. Rangers' Club Newsletter,**
c. 1931. Columbia Pictures. - **$25 $60 $125**

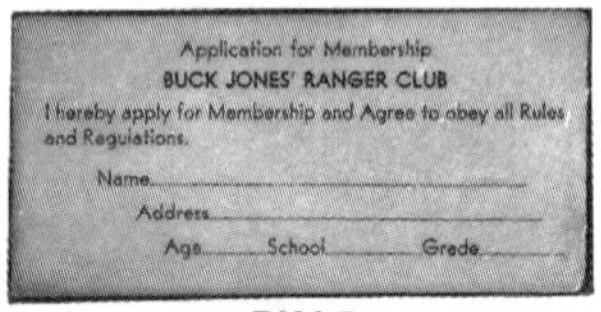
Application for Membership
BUCK JONES' RANGER CLUB
I hereby apply for Membership and Agree to obey all Rules and Regulations.
Name
Address
Age School Grade

BKJ-5

❑ **BKJ-5. Ranger's Club Member Application Card,**
c. 1931. - **$10 $15 $35**

BKJ-6

BKJ-7

❑ **BKJ-6. "Rangers' Club Of America" Cello. Button,**
c. 1931. Columbia Pictures. - **$15 $30 $60**

❑ **BKJ-7. "Buck Jones Rangers' Club Of America" Cello. Button,**
c. 1931. Version of blue photo with red rim. - **$15 $35 $65**

BKJ-8

❑ **BKJ-8. Ranger Club Card With Fabric Patch,**
c. 1931. Card - **$10 $20 $40**
Patch - **$20 $40 $80**

BKJ-9

❑ **BKJ-9. "Buck Jones' Ranger Club" Movie Cards,**
c. 1931. Columbia Pictures Corp. Black and white photo cards, each with club membership coupon on reverse.
Each - **$10 $20 $35**

BKJ-10

BKJ-11

❑ **BKJ-10. "Buck Jones Ranger" Enameled Brass Badge,**
c. 1931. Scarce. - **$50 $125 $225**

❑ **BKJ-11. "Buck Jones Rangers Club Of America" Leather Holster With Belt,**
c. 1931. Photo pictures embossed club symbol on holster cover panel. - **$75 $125 $225**

BKJ-12

BKJ-13

❑ **BKJ-12. Club Member's Large Brass Badge,**
c. 1931. Columbia Pictures. 1-1/2" with brass luster plus red and black enamel paint. -
**$50 $100 $200**

❑ **BKJ-13. Club Member's Button,**
c. 1931. Columbia Pictures. Similar to previous item but different photo and bolder type. -
**$20 $35 $70**

BKJ-14

❑ **BKJ-14. Song Folio/Club Manual,**
1932. Published by Bibo-Lang. Copyright "Book No. 1" with club ranks, pledge, etc. -
**$20 $60 $125**

BKJ-15

BKJ-16

❑ **BKJ-15. Dixie Ice Cream Picture,**
1932. Movie scenes on reverse from "White Eagle." - **$15 $30 $60**

❑ **BKJ-16. "White Eagle" Movie Promo Card,**
1932. - **$25 $50 $75**

BKJ-17

❑ **BKJ-17. Big Thrill Gum Booklet,**
1934. Goudey Gum. Six in series.
Each - **$10 $25 $50**

BKJ-18

BKJ-19

❑ **BKJ-18. "The Red Rider" Cello. Button,**
1934. Universal Pictures. For 15-chapter movie serial "The Red Rider". - **$60 $125 $225**

❑ **BKJ-19. Dixie Ice Cream Picture,**
1935. - **$15 $30 $60**

BKJ-20

BKJ-21

❑ **BKJ-20. "Buck Jones In Ride 'Em Cowboy" Big Little Book,**
1935. Whitman Movie Edition #1116. -
**$20 $45 $90**

❑ **BKJ-21. "Buck Jones In The Fighting Rangers" Big Little Book,**
1936. Whitman #1188. - **$20 $45 $90**

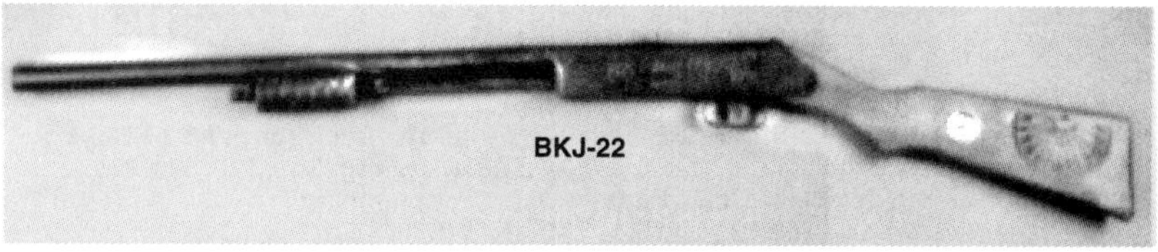
BKJ-22

❑ **BKJ-22. "No. 107 Daisy Buck Jones Special" Air Rifle,**
c. 1936. Store item by Daisy Mfg. Co., also used as premium. Compass and sundial on stock, sundial pointer often missing. - **$125 $250 $600**

BKJ-23

❑ **BKJ-23. Photo-Statuette And Mailer Insert,**
1936. Quaker Cereals. 7x7-1/2" black and white stiff cardboard standup with fold-backs on lower corners. 20 stars were in the set and these are listed on the folder. Reverse of folder offers six Babe Ruth Premiums (see Babe Ruth section).
Buck Jones Statuette - **$10 $20 $45**
Insert - **$15 $25 $45**

BKJ-24

❑ **BKJ-24. "The Phantom Rider Club" Cello. Button,**
1936. Scarce. Universal Pictures. For 15-chapter movie serial "The Phantom Rider". - **$75 $200 $350**

BKJ-25

BKJ-26

❑ **BKJ-25. Horseshoe Brass Badge,**
1937. Grape-Nuts Flakes. - **$15 $25 $50**

❑ **BKJ-26. "Buck Jones Club" Brass Ring,**
1937. Grape-Nuts Flakes. - **$60 $110 $175**

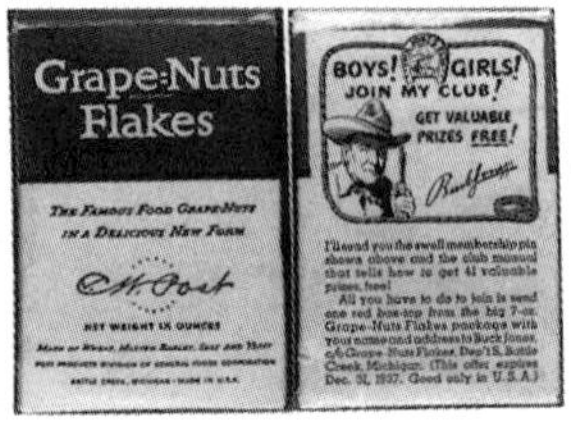


BKJ-27

❑ **BKJ-27. Club Membership Offer "Grape-Nuts Flakes" Sample Box,**
1937. 4" tall "New Package Adopted In 1936" with back panel ad expiring December 31, 1937. - **$50 $175 $325**

BKJ-28

BKJ-29

❑ **BKJ-28. Grape-Nuts Flakes Premium Catalogue Folder Sheet,**
1937. Offers about 40 premiums with expiration date December 31. - **$15 $35 $65**

❑ **BKJ-29. Prize Folder,**
1937. Four page Grape-Nuts Flakes premium prize list - **$15 $40 $70**

BKJ-30

❑ **BKJ-30. Cello. Over Brass 3-1/4" Bullet Holder For Pencil,**
c. 1937. Grape-Nuts Flakes. Inscription "From Buck Jones To His Pal" followed by personalized name designated by orderer. - **$30 $60 $100**

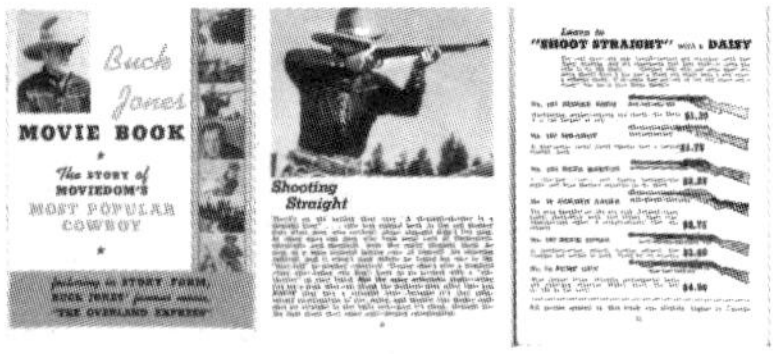


BKJ-31

❑ **BKJ-31. "Buck Jones Movie Book",**
1938. Daisy Mfg. Co. - **$20 $40 $75**

BKJ-33

BKJ-34

❑ **BKJ-33. "Buck Jones and the Killers of Crooked Butte" Better Little Book #1451,**
1938. - **$10 $30 $60**

❑ **BKJ-34. "Buck Jones and the Rock Creek Cattle Wars" Better Little Book #1461,**
1938. - **$10 $30 $60**

BKJ-35

BKJ-36

❑ **BKJ-35. "Buck Jones In The Cowboy Masquerade" Booklet,**
1938. Ice cream cone premium, Buddy Book #8. - **$15 $30 $65**

❑ **BKJ-36. Buck Jones Framed Photo,**
1938. Columbia Pictures. From his movie "Stranger From Arizona" co-starring Dorothy Fay. - **$15 $25 $45**

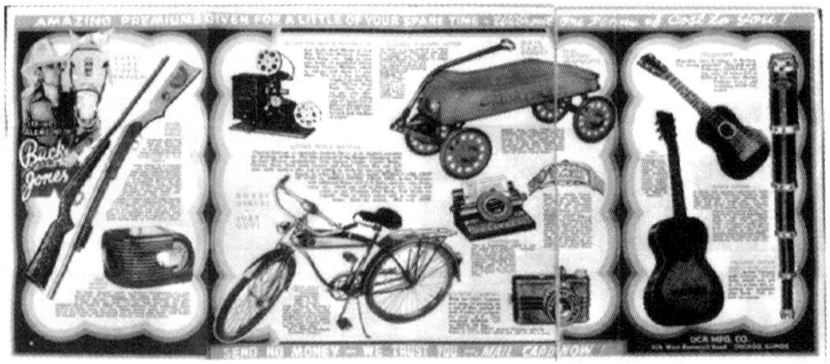

BKJ-32

❑ **BKJ-32. "UCA Salve" Premium Catalogue Folder Sheet,**
c. 1938. Has endorsement of Buck Jones and opens to 9x20" with air rifle only related premium to him. - **$20 $50 $80**

BKJ-37

BKJ-38

❑ **BKJ-37. "Chicago Stadium Rodeo" Cello. Button,**
1930s. Single event issue. - **$50 $150 $350**

❑ **BKJ-38. Australian Issue Movie Cello. Button,**
1930s. Black and white real photo without dot pattern, 1". Two versions. Bottom rim reads "A Universal Star" or "The Red Rider."
Each - **$40 $100 $175**

BKJ-39

BKJ-40

BKJ-41

❑ **BKJ-39. Photo,**
1930s. Sepia of him and horse Silver with facsimile autograph. - **$10 $20 $35**

❑ **BKJ-40. "For U.S. Marshal/Buck Jones" Cello. Button,**
1930s. - **$50 $90 $200**

❑ **BKJ-41. "Buck Jones Club" Cello. Button,**
1930s. Probably movie serial club. -
**$35 $70 $125**

BKJ-42

BKJ-43

❑ **BKJ-42. Fan Photo,**
1930s. - **$8 $15 $30**

❑ **BKJ-43. Portrait Photo,**
1930s. Probably a premium. - **$10 $25 $40**

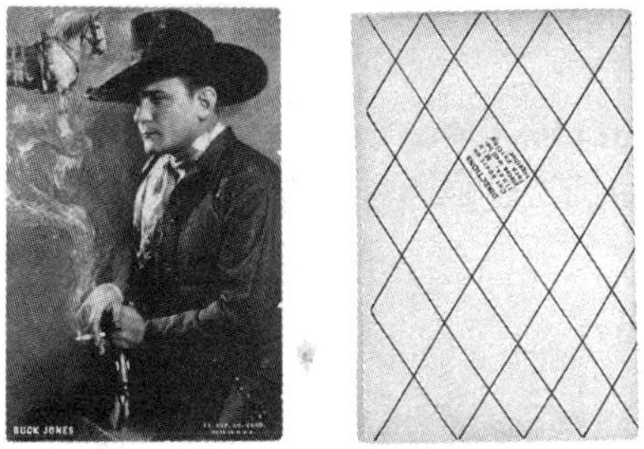

(FRONT) (BACK)

BKJ-44

❑ **BKJ-44. Photo Puzzle Card,**
1930s. Scarce. Movie premium. Very odd photo of Buck in deep thought, his cigarette smoke forming into the shape of his horse. Also note that his gun is pointed up towards him. Card is meant to be cut apart at lines on back and used as a puzzle. - **$25 $60 $100**

BKJ-45

❑ **BKJ-45. "Buck Jones Columbia Star" Figural Cast Metal Ashtray,**
1930s. Probable promotional item. 4-1/2" diameter by 6" tall. - **$250 $500 $750**

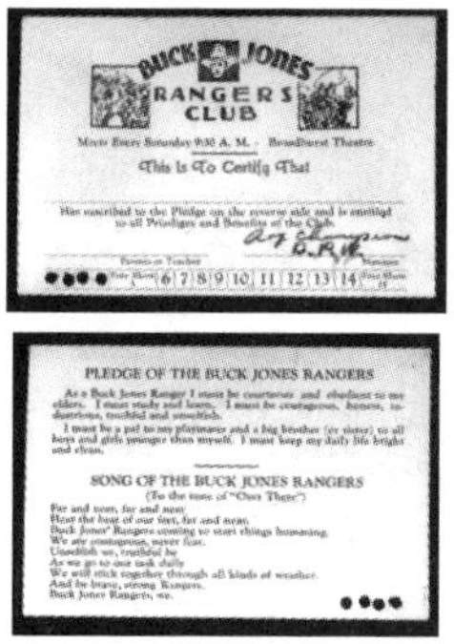
BUCK JONES RANGERS CLUB
This Is To Certify That
PLEDGE OF THE BUCK JONES RANGERS
SONG OF THE BUCK JONES RANGERS

BKJ-46

❑ **BKJ-46. "Ranger's Club" Movie Serial Ticket,**
1930s. Front is designed for punching admittance to 15-chapter serial, back has Buck Jones Rangers Pledge and song lyrics. - **$20 $35 $60**

BKJ-47

BKJ-48

❑ **BKJ-47. Movie Serial Promotion Plaster Ashtray,**
1941. Universal. Issued for "Riders Of Death Valley", its stars listed on the 4x6" back panel from which an ashtray extends outward 3-1/2" at the bottom. - **$60 $125 $200**

❑ **BKJ-48. "Riders Of Death Valley Club" Cello. Button,**
1941. Universal Pictures. For 15-chapter movie serial "Riders Of Death Valley". - **$50 $80 $150**

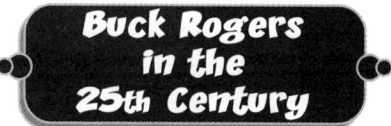

# Buck Rogers in the 25th Century

**Buck Rogers was the first American comic strip to plunge into science fiction and it enjoyed great success after it was introduced in January 1929. The story was adapted by Phil Nowlan from his futuristic novel, illustrated by Dick Calkins and syndicated by the John F. Dille Co. Buck wakes after 500 years of suspended animation and, along with young Wilma Deering and the old scientist Dr. Huer, battles to save America and the earth from various enemies, in particular Killer Kane and Ardala Valmar, who want to conquer the world. The strip ran until 1967 (a companion Sunday strip appeared from 1930 to 1965) and both were revived in 1979 to 1983. A successful radio adaptation was broadcast from 1932 to 1947, sponsored first by Kellogg, then Cocomalt, Cream of Wheat, Popsicle and General Foods. A TV version had a brief run in 1950-1951 and a revised series, produced by Glen Larson and starring Gil Gerard and Erin Gray, debuted in 1979 and lasted two seasons. Movie adaptations appeared in 1939, with Buster Crabbe, and 1979 (released theatrically but also serving as the pilot for the Larson series). Crabbe had a memorable cameo in one episode of the '80s series. There have also been a variety of Big Little Books and comic books over the years.**

**The Buck Rogers exhibit building at the 1934 Chicago World's Fair in the Enchanted Island area.**

BRG-1

❑ **BRG-1. "Amazing Stories" Pulp Magazine With First Buck Rogers Story ,**
1928. Vol. 3 #5, August issue with story "Armageddon-2419 A.D." The cover illustration does not picture Buck Rogers, but a flying scientist from the magazine's lead story, "The Skylark of Space," by Edward Elmer Smith and Lee Hawkins Garby. (Sequel "Airlords of Han" appeared here May, 1929.) - **$500 $1000 $2750**

BRG-2

❑ **BRG-2. "With My Very Best Regards" Fan Picture,**
1929. Newspaper premium, black on green paper 6x9". Large 11-1/2x17-1/2" black on orange paper version appeared 1932.
Each - **$150 $300 $500**

BRG-3

❑ **BRG-3. Blotter In Full Color,**
1930. Detroit Free Press. 3-1/2x8-1/2". - **$75 $200 $350**

BRG-4

❑ **BRG-4. "The Planet Venus" Coloring Sheet,**
1931. Newspaper offer in black and white with art by Russell Keaton.
Uncolored - **$250 $500 $1000**
Colored - **$150 $350 $650**

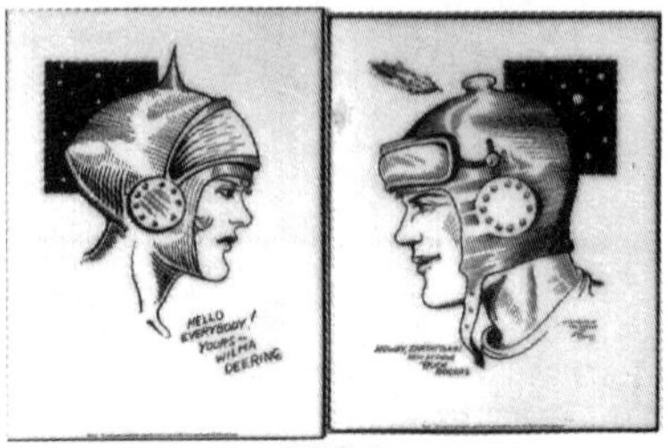

BRG-5

❑ **BRG-5. Newspaper Comic Strip Portraits Premiums,**
1932. Black and white, each about 8x10-1/2". Printed on buff paper. Both were reprinted in 1969 on white paper as part of promotion for book *The Collected Works of Buck Rogers.*
Each - **$100 $200 $400**

BRG-6

❑ **BRG-6. "Pep" Leaflet With Radio Show Ad,**
1932. Kellogg's. - **$20 $40 $75**

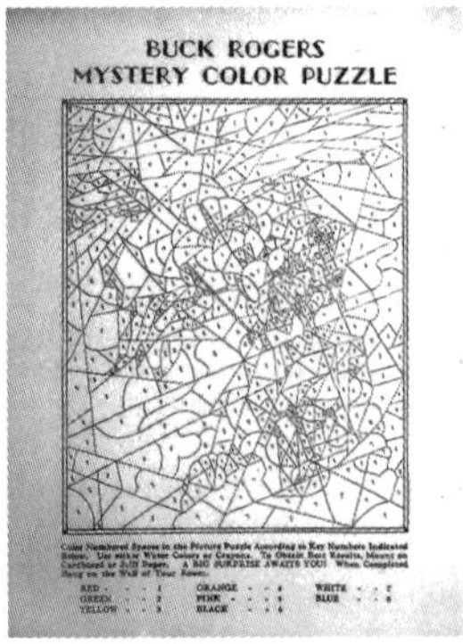


BRG-7

❑ **BRG-7. "Mystery Color Puzzle" Paper Sheet,**
1932. Newspaper offer in black and white 8-1/4x10-3/4". Reveals a giant bird.
Uncolored - **$150 $300 $550**
Colored - **$100 $250 $450**

BRG-8

❑ **BRG-8. "Bucktoy" Set Of Six Cut-Out Cards,**
1932. Newspaper offer of set of six issued from 1932 to 1934. Stiff paper 2-3/8x5-5/8" in black and white (except Dr. Huer in green) to cut and color. Six others were used for Baltimore promotion, and of these, only 3 have been seen.
Each Uncut And Uncolored - **$100 $200 $400**
Each Uncut And Colored - **$75 $150 $250**
Each Cut And Colored - **$50 $75 $150**

BRG-9

❑ **BRG-9. Radio Broadcast Publicity Leaflet,**
1932. Kellogg's Corn Flakes. Sponsorship indicated for Buck Rogers and Singing Lady programs. - **$20 $50 $85**

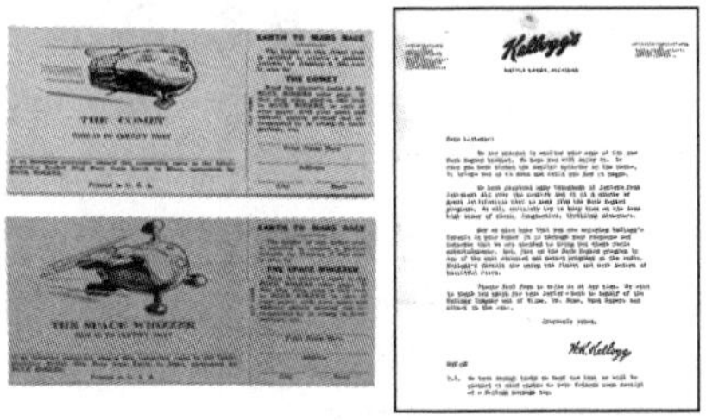

BRG-10

**❑ BRG-10. "Earth To Mars" Contest Cards,** 1933. Various newspapers. Pair of 2-1/2x5-1/2" cards for competing rocketships named "The Comet" and "The Space Whizzer." Card also issued for third ship "The Rocket Flash" (the eventual winner). Those holding card for winning ship signed and mailed the stub to receive "Picture Suitable For Framing" and winner's name would be printed in "The Buck Rogers Color Page." Each - **$100 $250 $400**

BRG-11

**❑ BRG-11. "The Rocket Flash" Contest Prize Picture,**
1933. Newspaper giveaway reading "Congratulations to YOU as one of the Buck Rogers fans who picked the winning ship in the race to Mars." 6x9" black and white with art by Russell Keaton. Three different tickets, black on single card color stock, were issued; each pictures a different ship. Contest entrants selecting "The Rocket Flash" ship to win the Earth to Mars race received this picture.-
**$350 $750 $1500**

BRG-12

**❑ BRG-12. Origin Storybook,**
1933. Kellogg's. Reprinted in 1995 but no Kellogg's ad on back cover.
Near Mint With Envelope - **$600**
Loose - **$75 $150 $400**
White Paper Letter (2 Versions) Each -
**$40 $80 $125**

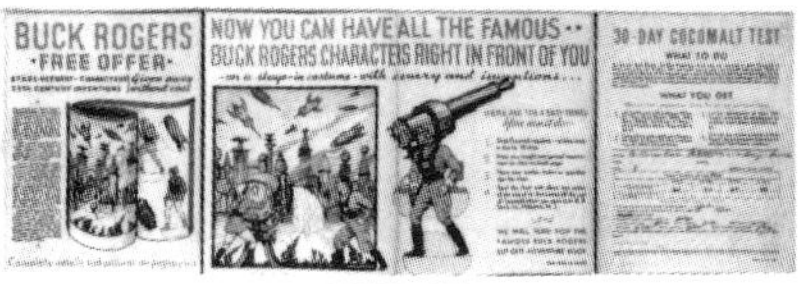


BRG-13

**❑ BRG-13. Cocomalt "Buck Rogers Cut-Out Adventure Book" Order Folder,**
1933. Full color 9x13" Sent with BRG-16 and BRG-20. Also see BRG-19. - **$75 $150 $400**

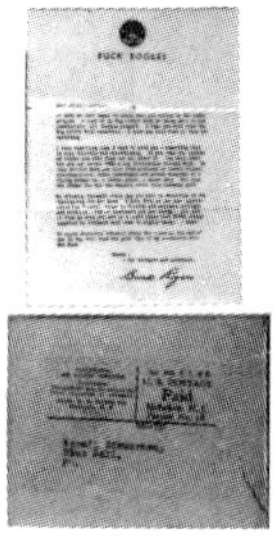

BRG-14

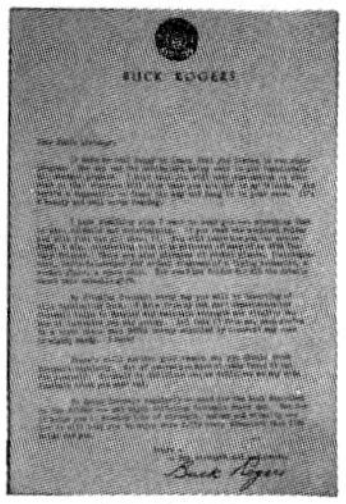


BRG-15

**❑ BRG-14. Mailer And Letter For Cocomalt BLB,**
1933. Accompanied BRG-20.
Mailer - **$20 $50 $85**
Yellow Paper Letter - **$40 $80 $165**

**❑ BRG-15. "Solar System Map" Letter,**
1933. Cocomalt. Deep yellow paper. The text refers to fabric patch (see BRG-88) and map being sent separately and promotes the Cut-Out Adventure Book offer. - **$35 $75 $165**

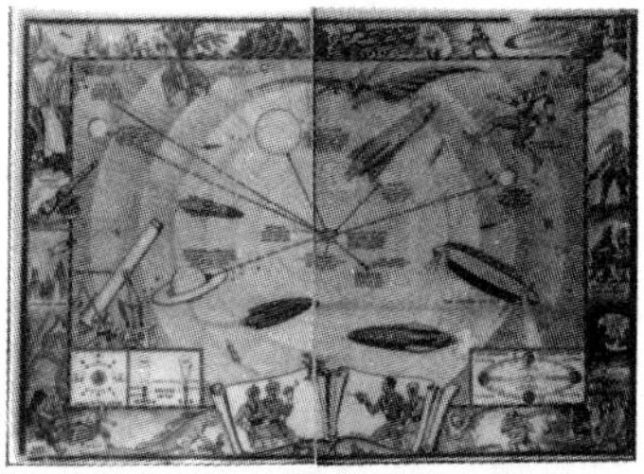

BRG-16

(ENLARGED VIEW)

**❑ BRG-16. Solar System Map 18x25",**
1933. Cocomalt. Sent rolled in a tube. Beware of 1970s color reproductions on glossy paper or color photo-copies. - **$200 $400 $1200**

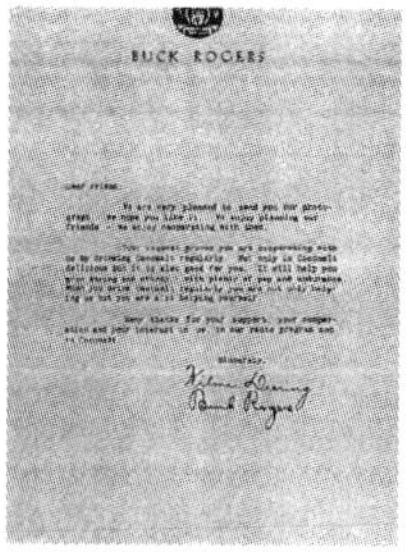

BRG-17

BRG-18

**❑ BRG-17. Buck And Wilma Cocomalt Browntone Picture,**
1933. Size 7-1/2" by 10". - **$65 $125 $200**
Blue Paper Letter **$35 $75 $135**

**❑ BRG-18. Buck and Wilma Paper Masks,**
1933. Cocomalt. Made by Einson-Freeman. Note curly hair design on Wilma. An unlicensed store item marked "Made in Japan" without curly hair and on less slick paper was also issued. See BRG-131. Each - **$100 $200 $400**

BRG-19

**❑ BRG-19. Cocomalt "Buck Rogers Cut-Out Adventure Book",**
1933. Rare. Came with letter and separate cardboard sheet for theater stage. Has 20 stand-ups. See order form BRG-13.
Complete Uncut - **$2500 $5000 $7500**
Complete, Figures Cut - **$600 $1200 $2000**

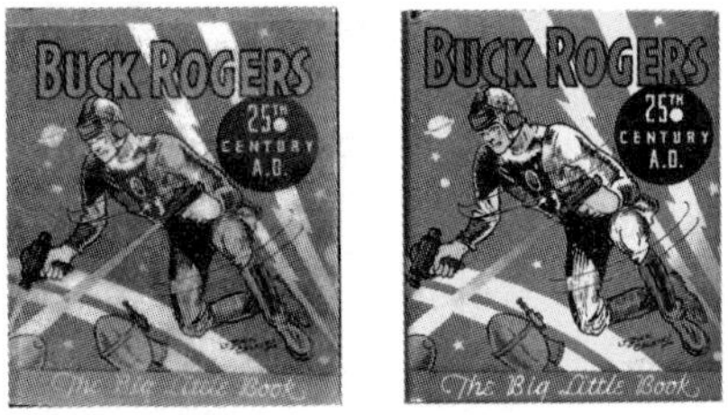


(Softcover) BRG-20 (Hardcover)

❑ **BRG-20. "Buck Rogers 25th Century A.D." BLB,**
1933. Softcover has Cocomalt ad on back cover. Sent boxed. The text for all BLBs were written by Dick Calkins and Rick Yager. See BRG-14.
Softcover - **$20 $60 $175**
Hardcover - **$20 $60 $175**

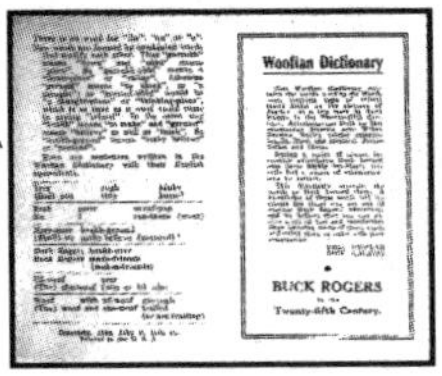


BRG-21

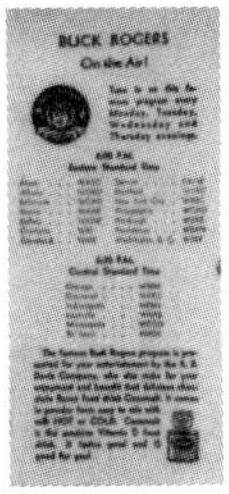


BRG-22

❑ **BRG-21. "Woofian Dictionary" Folder,**
1933. Newspaper offer containing words used by "Woofs," amazing animals living on the plateaus of Jupiter. Shown open. Beige paper. - **$125 $250 $500**

❑ **BRG-22. "Buck Rogers On The Air" Radio Station Listing Sheet,**
c. 1933. Cocomalt. Three versions or more on blue or white paper, sizes vary.
Each - **$25 $60 $100**

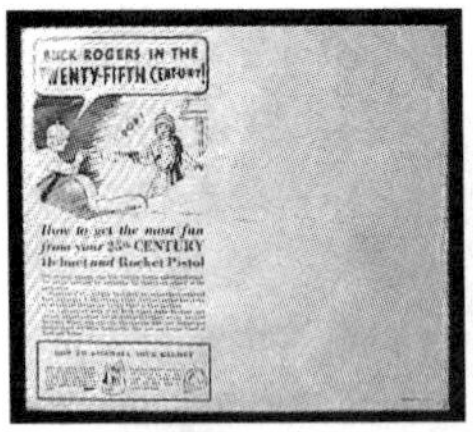


BRG-23

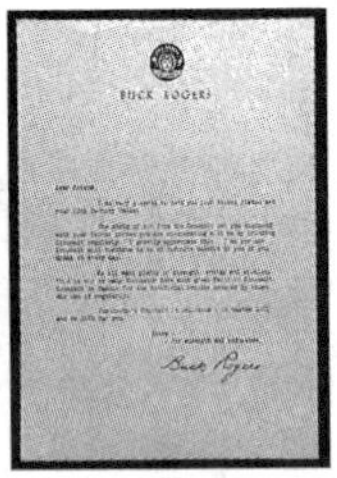

BRG-24

❑ **BRG-23. Mailer For Buck Or Wilma Helmet And Rocket Pistol,**
1934. Cocomalt. Two variations. See pistol BRG-30. - **$25 $75 $150**

❑ **BRG-24. Letter Enclosed With Buck Or Wilma Helmet And Rocket Pistol,**
1934. Cocomalt. Blue paper letter. - **$35 $75 $150**

BRG-25

❑ **BRG-25. "Buck Rogers" Cardboard Helmet,**
1934. Cocomalt. Helmet - **$75 $150 $300**

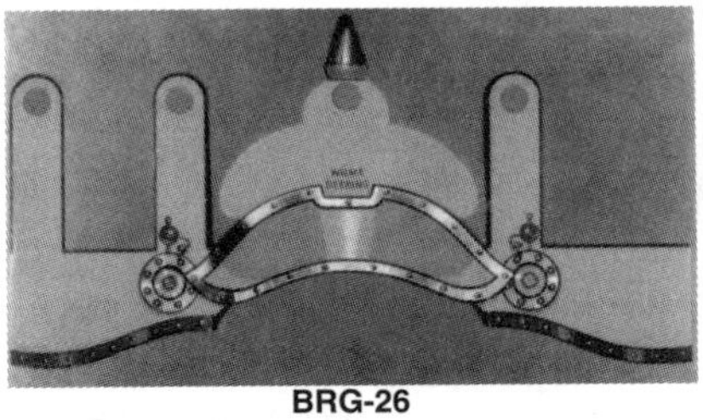

BRG-26

❑ **BRG-26. "Wilma Deering" Cardboard Helmet,**
1934. Cocomalt. Helmet - **$75 $150 $300**

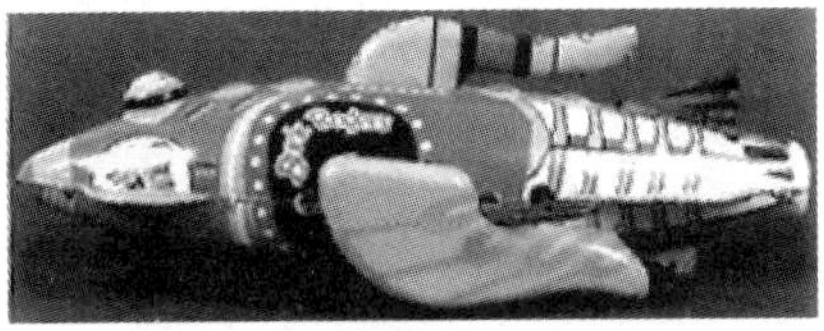

BRG-27

❑ **BRG-27. "Buck Rogers" Tin Wind-Up Rocketship,**
1934. Store item by Marx Toys. Flint cover often missing. Toy came in illustrated box.
Toy only - **$350 $750 $1500**
Box - **$350 $750 $1500**

BRG-28

❑ **BRG-28. Buck Rogers Painted Lead Figure,**
1934. Cocomalt. Wilma and Killer Kane also issued. Each in full color packaged individually with leaflet in a cellophane bag.
Each With Leaflet - **$100 $200 $300**
Each Figure Only - **$40 $75 $125**

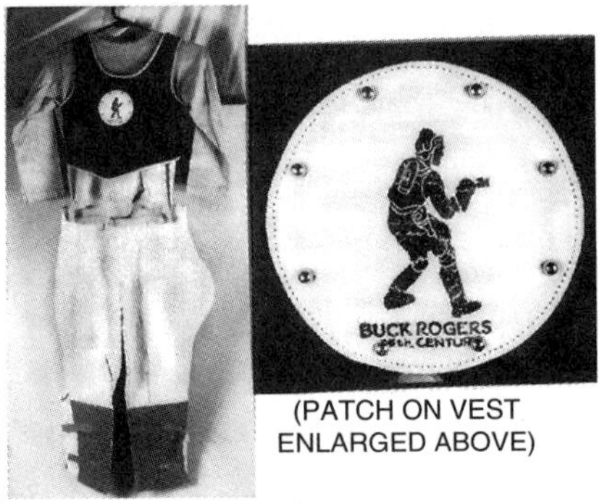


(PATCH ON VEST ENLARGED ABOVE)

BRG-29

❑ **BRG-29. Child's Playsuit,**
1934. Scarce. Store item and Cream of Wheat. Came with suede cloth helmet XZ-42. Jersey is orange. Sizes 4 to 14 made by Sackman Brothers. Playsuit also made for girls with khaki skirt.
Uniform, Complete Except Helmet - **$400 $1000 $2000**
Vest Only With Patch - **$200 $450 $650**
Store Box Only - **$200 $500 $800**

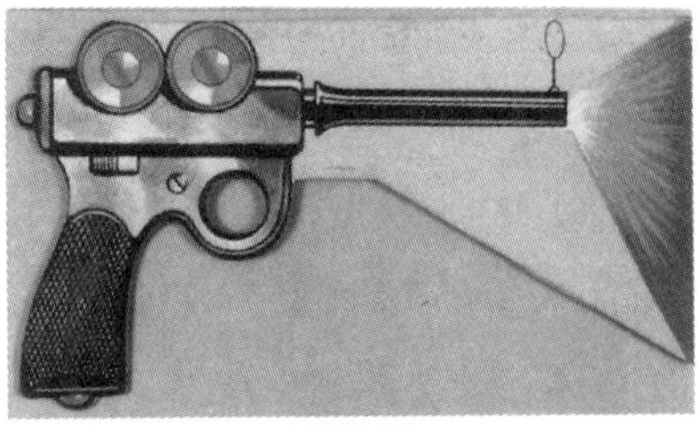

BRG-30

❑ **BRG-30. Cardboard Pop Gun,**
1934. Cocomalt. Came with Buck or Wilma paper helmet. See BRG-23-26.
Gun - **$75 $125 $250**
Mailer (Two styles) - **$25 $50 $100**

(BOX FRONT)

(SIDE PANEL)

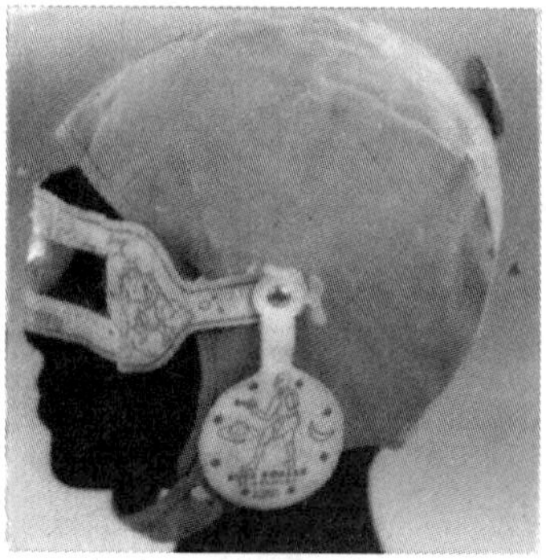

BRG-31

❑ **BRG-31. "Buck Rogers 25th Century" Navigation Helmet by Daisy,**
1934. Store item (brown suede cloth version) and Cream of Wheat (leather version). Suede version XZ-42 was included with previous item and came unboxed in three sizes. Leather version XZ-34 issued in 1935 came boxed in three sizes. Suede version has white cloth visor with metal ear flaps. Leather version came with metal visor and flaps.
Each Helmet - **$250 $600 $1000**
XZ-34 Store Box - **$300 $600 $1200**

BRG-32

❑ **BRG-32. Buck Rogers Gum Booklets,**
1934. Big Thrill Chewing Gum. Six Buck Rogers titles from set of 24 booklets. 2-3/8x3" with eight pages. Color covers with black and white scenes inside. Buck is shown on one corner of the Goudey Co. wrapper. Booklets are usually brittle from age. Each - **$25 $50 $100**

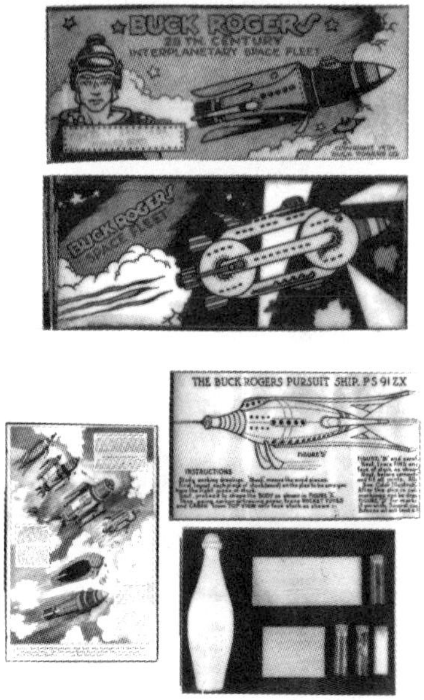


BRG-33

❑ **BRG-33. Rocketship Balsa Wood Model,**
1934. Six in set (#6 shown), each boxed ready-made or unfinished with color/bw instruction sheet. Sold in stores (Sears offered #1,3,and 4) or as newspaper premium. Only #4 "Super Dreadnought" was available (unfinished) as Cream of Wheat premium. The full set of models was completed by late 1935. Instruction sheets 11x17" were still available into the early 1940s. Each Boxed - **$200 $500 $750**
Instruction Sheet - **$100 $200 $300**

BRG-34

❑ **BRG-34. Scientific Laboratory,**
1934. Store item by Porter Chemical Co. Pictured are box, envelope that holds instruction manuals (three) and envelope for slide covers. Many other items came in boxed set. No complete sets known. See BRG-45.
Empty Box - **$500 $1000 $2000**
Other Items Shown - **$100 $250 $400**

(COMBAT SET BOX)

(GUN BOX)

(HANDLE ENLARGED)

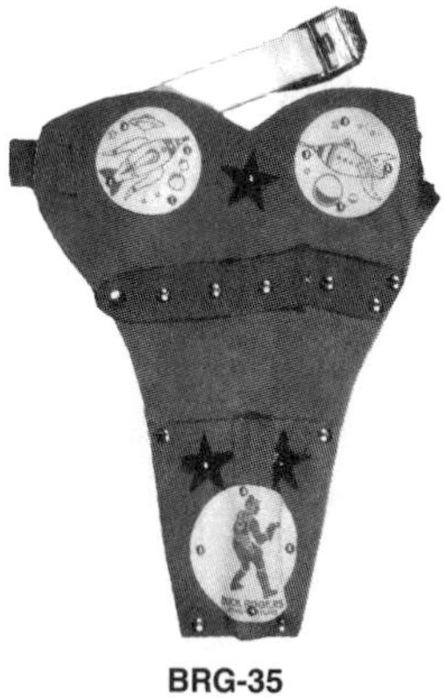

BRG-35

❑ **BRG-35. Rocket Pistol XZ-31 and Holster XZ-33 by Daisy,**
1934. Store item. Gun is 9-1/2" long with black finish and cocking handle. The three-color suede cloth holster and belt came unboxed or boxed with the gun, sold as "25th Century Combat Set." This box pictures Buck firing his pistol.
Gun - **$95 $175 $375**
Holster - **$50 $150 $300**
Gun Box - **$200 $400 $600**
Combat Set XZ-32 Box - **$200 $400 $800**

BRG-36

BRG-37

**❑ BRG-36. "Buck Rogers In The City Below The Sea" BLB,**
1934. Cocomalt. Softcover premium version but has no Cocomalt advertising. - **$50 $150 $300**

**❑ BRG-37. "Buck Rogers On The Moons Of Saturn" BLB,**
1934. Cocomalt. Softcover premium version but has no Cocomalt advertising. - **$75 $175 $325**

BRG-38

BRG-39

**❑ BRG-38. "Buck Rogers On The Moons Of Saturn" BLB #1143,**
1934. - **$50 $100 $250**

**❑ BRG-39. Saturday Chicago American Litho. Button,**
c. 1934. Multicolor on white 1-1/8" by Greenduck Co. - **$40 $100 $175**

BRG-40

**❑ BRG-40. Walgreen Drugstores World's Fair 2 For 1 Ticket,**
1934. For use at Chicago's "Island Midway" attractions including the "Buck Rogers Show." Upper portion of ticket stub with perforated coupons shown. - **$40 $75 $125**

BRG-41

**❑ BRG-41. "The Adventures Of Buck Rogers" Big Big Book,**
1934. Published by Whitman. -
**$100 $200 $400**

BRG-42

**❑ BRG-42. "A Century Of Progress-I Was There" Brass Key Fob,**
1934. From Buck Rogers exhibit at the fair during 1934 season. 1" holed as made. Giveaways included a pad and pencil set and a generic jigsaw puzzle. - **$200 $400 $850**

BRG-43

BRG-44

**❑ BRG-43. "A Century Of Progress" Chicago World's Fair Litho. Button,**
1934. Blue, orange and white 1-1/8" by Greenduck Co. - **$125 $300 $500**

**❑ BRG-44. Birthstone Initial Ring,**
1934. Cocomalt. Unmarked brass Buck Rogers tie-in issue and other non-Buck offers, top has personalized single initial designated by orderer. Also offered by Popsicle, 1939. - **$150 $325 $475**

(ENLARGED VIEW OF LABEL ABOVE)

BRG-45

**❑ BRG-45. "Buck Rogers Telescope",**
1934. Store item, part of Scientific Laboratory set. See BRG-34. 14" long, not the later Cream of Wheat or Popsicle versions. -
**$100 $275 $500**

(CASTER SET LID)

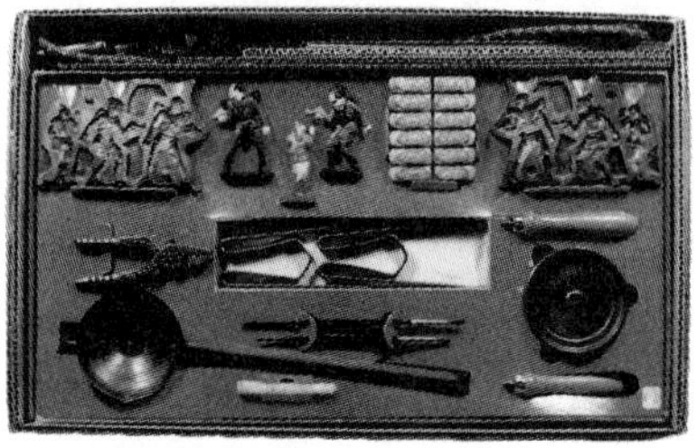

(CASTER SET OPEN)

(RAPAPORT CATALOG)

BRG-46

**❑ BRG-46. Electric Caster Set and Catalog,**
1934. Caster sets were store items by Rapaport Brothers. Sets were also made in 1933 for total of 3 different. Box size is 10x19". Pliers came with only one set and are scarce. There are only three catalog versions; one includes eight daily strips and photos of caster and mold sets. Caster sets were sold with one of eight molds. Two of the eight are rare. Of these, the Amphibian Squadron of Neptune (3 figures) is known, but the Martian Stratosphere Patrol is unknown except for published pictures.
Caster Set - **$300 $800 $1750**
Catalog - **$75 $200 $300**
Typical Mold (Both Sides) - **$50 $85 $125**

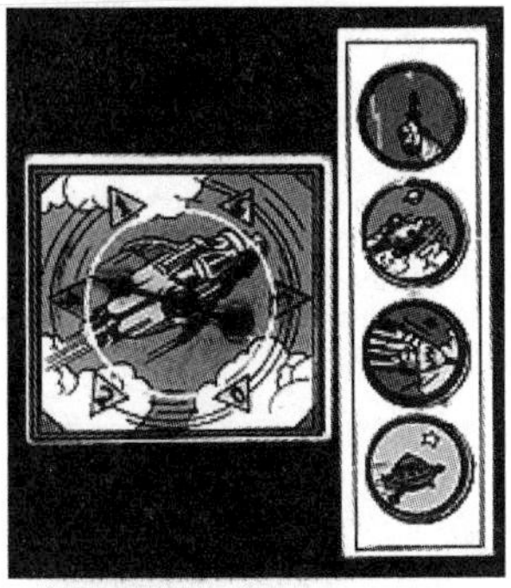

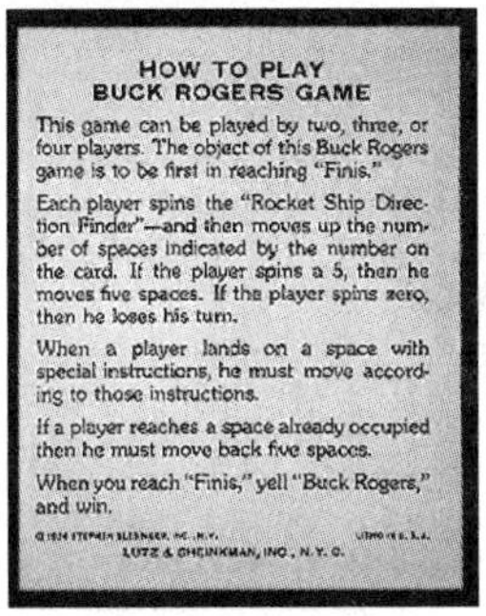
HOW TO PLAY
BUCK ROGERS GAME

This game can be played by two, three, or four players. The object of this Buck Rogers game is to be first in reaching "Finis."

Each player spins the "Rocket Ship Direction Finder"—and then moves up the number of spaces indicated by the number on the card. If the player spins a 5, then he moves five spaces. If the player spins zero, then he loses his turn.

When a player lands on a space with special instructions, he must move according to those instructions.

If a player reaches a space already occupied then he must move back five spaces.

When you reach "Finis," yell "Buck Rogers," and win.

LUTZ & SHEINKMAN, INC., N. Y. C.

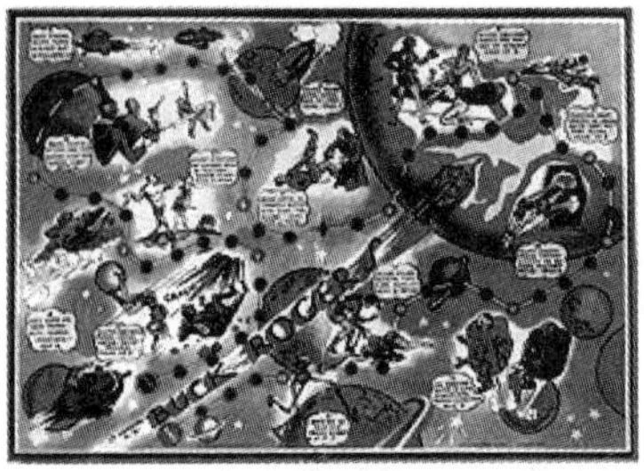

BRG-47

❑ **BRG-47. "Buck Rogers Game Of The 25th Century A.D.",**
1934. Store item by Lutz and Sheinkman, Inc. with Stephen Slesinger copyright. Box holds 13x18" board with cardboard spinner, four cardboard markers in a punch-out frame, and instruction sheet. Complete - **$200 $400 $800**
Board Only - **$125 $250 $350**

BRG-48

❑ **BRG-48. Set of Three Board Games,**
1934. Store item and Cream of Wheat premium. Came with 40 cards and 12 miniature bowling pin-shaped wood markers. Made by Lutz & Sheinkman. Instructions printed on game boards. Box size was 8-1/2"x17".
Complete Boxed Set - **$400 $800 $1300**
Each Board - **$85 $200 $350**

BRG-49

❑ **BRG-49. "Buck Rogers In The 25th Century" Cello. Button,**
1935. Cream of Wheat. Full color on dark blue 1" with Whitehead & Hoag Co. back paper. - **$40 $75 $125**

BRG-50

BRG-51

❑ **BRG-50. "Rocket Ship Knife" Box,**
1935. Scarce. Cream of Wheat and store item. Box Only - **$200 $400 $600**

❑ **BRG-51. "Buck Rogers" Steel/Cello. Pocketknife,**
1935. Scarce. Store item produced by Adolph Kastor with manufacturer's name, Camillus Cutlery Co., on one of the two blades. Also a premium from Cream of Wheat. Same image on both grips in red, green or blue styles. Color easily worn off. - **$300 $800 $1600**

BRG-52

BRG-53

❑ **BRG-52. "Buck Rogers In The City Of Floating Globes" BLB,**
1935. Cocomalt. Issued only as softcover with Cocomalt ad on back. - **$100 $250 $500**

❑ **BRG-53. "Tarzan Cups" Premium Booklet Featuring Buck Rogers,**
1935. Tarzan Ice Cream Cups or Lily Tulip brand. In the Big Little Book style, 1/2" thick, softcover only. From Whitman set of six different characters, each obtained for 12 cup lids. - **$100 $250 $500**

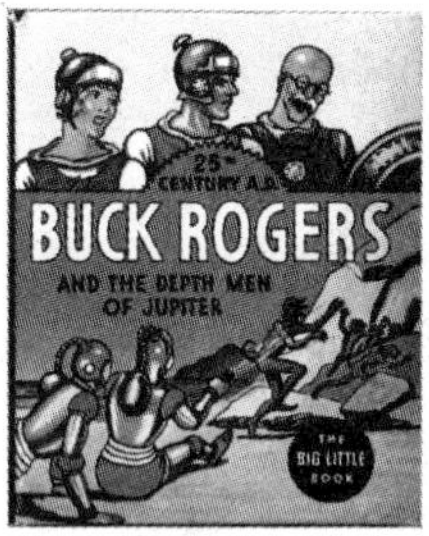


BRG-54

❑ **BRG-54. "Buck Rogers and the Depth Men Of Jupiter" BLB #1169,**
1935. - **$20 $85 $185**

BRG-55

❑ **BRG-55. "Buck Rogers and the Doom Comet" BLB #1178,**
1935. - **$20 $85 $180**

(COMBAT SET BOX)

(GUN BOX)

BRG-56

❑ **BRG-56. Rocket Pistol XZ-35 and Holster XZ-36 by Daisy,**
1935. Store item. Gun is 7-1/2" long with black finish and cocking handle. Leather holster with round hole on holster front straps. Holster came with 30" leather belt. No box for holster alone, but gun, holster and belt were sold boxed as Combat Set XZ-37.
Gun - **$100 $250 $475**
Holster - **$35 $75 $175**
Gun Box - **$100 $200 $350**
Combat Set XZ-37 Box - **$200 $400 $650**

BRG-57

❑ **BRG-57. Dille Syndicate Stationery,**
1935 and later. Buck Rogers scenes in black on red and rocket image in black and white. - **$50 $125 $200**

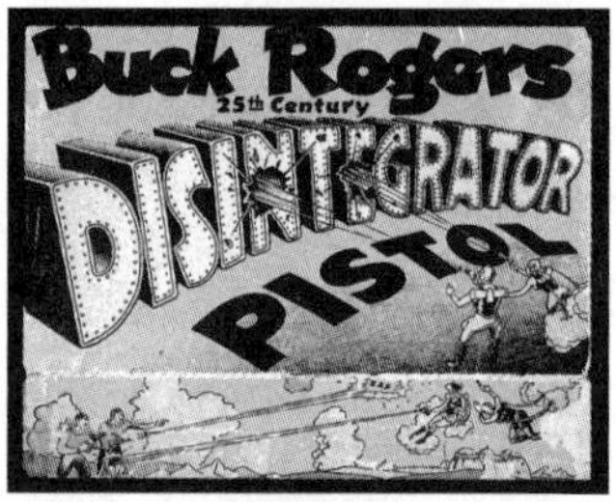

**(GUN BOX)**

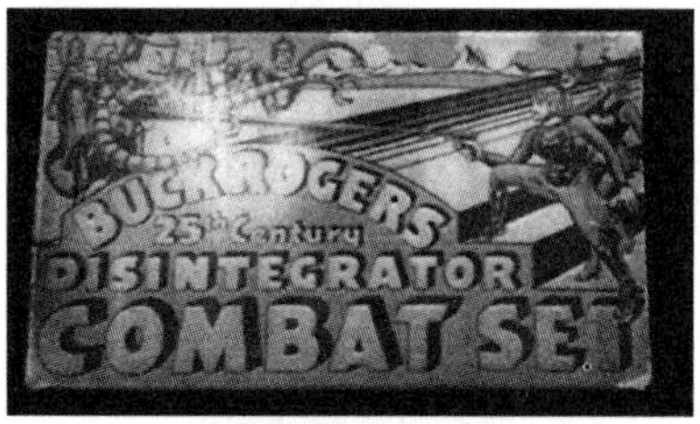

**(COMBAT SET BOX)**

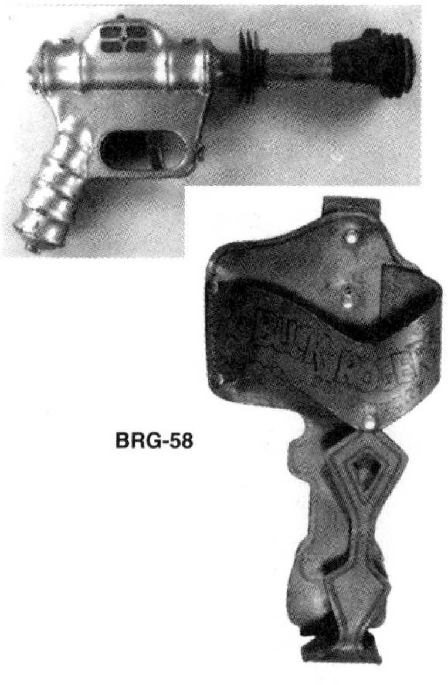
BRG-58

❑ **BRG-58. Disintegrator Pistol XZ-38 and Holster XZ-39 by Daisy,**
1935. Store item and Cream of Wheat. Used in 1939 as Popsicle premium. Copper finish. Flint produces spark. Leather holster with diamond-shaped hole on front straps. Holster came with 30" leather belt. No box for holster alone, but gun, holster and belt were sold boxed as Disintegrator Combat Set XZ-40.
Gun - **$150 $300 $650**
Holster - **$75 $150 $350**
Gun Box - **$200 $400 $600**
Combat Set XZ-40 Box - **$250 $500 $800**

BRG-59

❑ **BRG-59. "Punch-O-Bag",**
1935. Morton's Salt premium by Lou Fox, Chicago. Came in 3"x5" envelope done in two design styles. Various colors each showing a different character. Balloon typically missing or disintegrated. Envelope Only - **$35 $65 $90**

BRG-60

BRG-61

❑ **BRG-60. "Buck Rogers 25th Century Adventures" Printing Set,**
1935. Store item and Cream of Wheat. Set No. 4080 by StamperKraft Co. Includes 14 character stamps. - **$200 $500 $900**

❑ **BRG-61. "Cosmic Conquests" Boxed Printing Set,**
1935. Store item by StamperKraft Co. Set #4090 with 22 character stamps. A set with 15 character stamps and alphabet was issued as #4090-S. Each Set - **$225 $550 $950**

BRG-62

❑ **BRG-62. Pocketwatch,**
1935. Store item by Ingraham Co. Lightning bolt hands in copper color and case back pictures Comet Man. A 1971 version has brass hands and a blank case back.
Watch Only - **$300 $800 $1600**
Box With Golden Cardboard Insert - **$600 $1200 $2000**
Complete - **$900 $2000 $3600**

BRG-63

BRG-64

❑ **BRG-63. "Buck Rogers On The Air For Cream Of Wheat" Gummed Back Paper Sticker,**
c. 1935. Dark blue and yellow. 1-3/4x2-3/4". - **$50 $100 $175**

❑ **BRG-64. "Buck Rogers 25th Century Catalog,"**
1935. John Dille folder catalog of items available from company by mail order. Some items shown were also used as premiums. Black and white folder opens to 9x12". - **$100 $250 $450**

BRG-65

❑ **BRG-65. School Kit Bag With Strap,**
1935. Store item and Cream of Wheat premium made of suede cloth. - **$500 $1200 $2500**

BRG-66

❑ **BRG-66. Dixie-Style Ice Cream Cup Lid,**
c. 1935. C.B.S. Radio. Red lettering on tan cardboard. Reads "Listen To Buck Rogers In The 25th Century On CBS!" - **$75 $150 $300**

BRG-67

❑ **BRG-67. Pencil Box No. 35228,**
1935. Store item and Cream of Wheat premium. Red and blue, issued with contents. Between 1934 and 1938 at least 40 different boxes were made in various sizes and colors. - **$75 $150 $275**

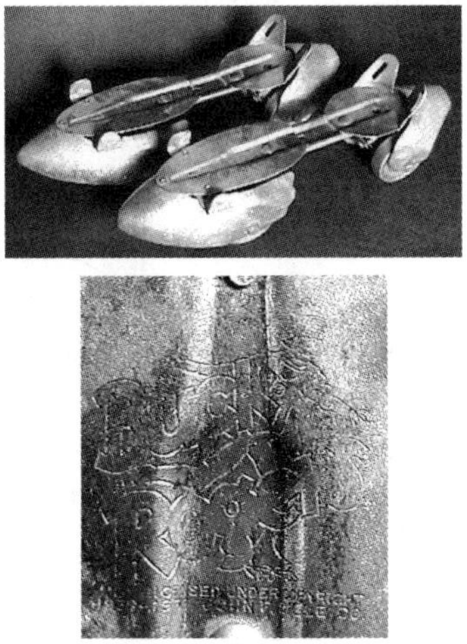

(ENLARGED VIEW OF FOOT PLATE)

BRG-68

❑ **BRG-68. Buck Rogers Rocket Skates,**
1935. Store item by Louis Marx. Pair of 11-1/2" long heavy steel roller skates with wheel coverings simulating a rocketship design. Shown in our photo without leather straps. Rear end of skates hold a 1" red jeweled reflector. Front of each foot plate has impressed image of Buck and his name "Buck Rogers" in large letters. Rare. - **$1000 $2000 $3500**

BRG-69

❑ **BRG-69. "Astral Heroes" Printing Set,**
1935. Store item by StamperKraft Co. Set number 4070 with seven character stamps.
Complete Boxed - **$250 $600 $1000**

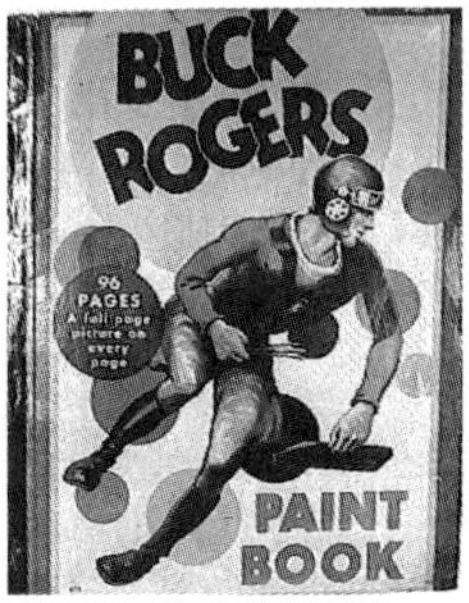


BRG-70

❑ **BRG-70. "Buck Rogers Paint Book",**
1935. Store item by Whitman Publishing Company. Whitman No. 679. Large 11-1/4x14" format. Has eight red and green pages with others in black and white. - **$150 $300 $650**

BRG-71

❑ **BRG-71. "Ardala" Metal Alloy Figure By Britains,**
1936. Cream of Wheat. Full color paint. Each with moveable arm. Set (with name under base) of Buck, Wilma, Killer Kane, Ardala, Dr. Huer, Robot. Reproductions in metal made by DP Miniatures in 1989 do not have name under base.
Robot - **$300 $650 $1300**
Others, Each - **$200 $400 $700**

BRG-72

❑ **BRG-72. "Buck Rogers 25th. Century" Cello. Button,**
1936. Issuer unknown. 1-1/2" black on dark blue picturing Buck with Dr. Huer peering over Buck's left shoulder. Only a couple examples known, both with staining. - **$250 $750 $1750**

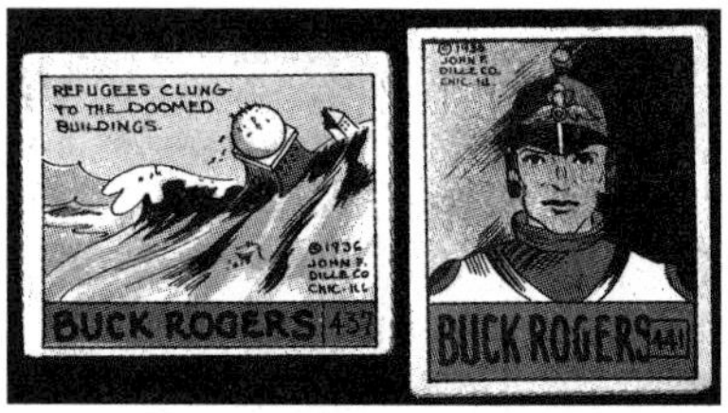


BRG-73

❑ **BRG-73. Cartoon Adventures Perforated Strip Cards,**
1936. Store item. Set of 24 (#425-448) from a larger set of 48 that includes other newspaper comic characters. Cards are 2-1/4x2-3/4".
Each In Buck Rogers Set - **$50 $100 $175**

BRG-74

❑ **BRG-74. Buck Rogers Standing On North America Picture,**
1936. Newspaper premium offered as "Dandy Picture Of Buck Rogers." Black and white 5-1/2x8-1/2" stiff paper. Example shown was later signed by the artist Dick Calkins. Scarce.
Unsigned - **$200 $400 $650**

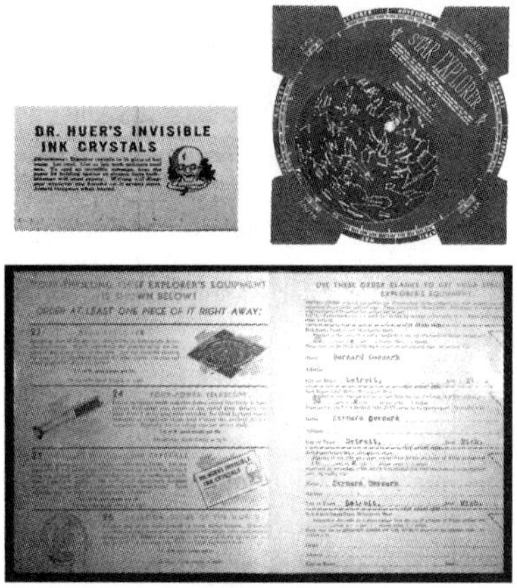


BRG-75

❑ **BRG-75. "Chief Explorer" Leaflet, "Star Explorer" Dial Device, and Dr. Huer's Ink Crystals**
1936. Cream of Wheat. Offers Chief Explorer badge (See BRG-91), Star Explorer (star finder device), Four-Power Telescope (smaller than one with Scientific Laboratory and not Popsicle version), Dr. Huer's Invisible Ink Crystals and Balloon Globe of the World. Leaflet - **$100 $250 $400**
Dial - **$100 $200 $300**
Crystals Envelope - **$100 $200 $300**

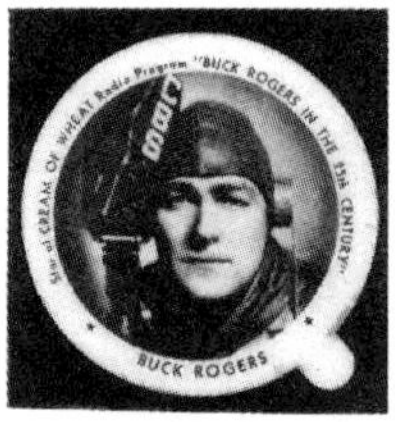


BRG-76

BRG-77

❑ **BRG-76. Dixie Ice Cream Lid,**
1936. Browntone photo. Inscribed for Cream of Wheat radio series. Lid also issued with Breyers Ice Cream imprint and others. A generic three-fold album with slots to hold the lids was available. - **$25 $60 $100**

❑ **BRG-77. "Lite-Blaster" Flashlight,**
1936. Cream of Wheat. Design in four colors. - **$300 $600 $1200**

BRG-78

❑ **BRG-78. Dixie Ice Cream Picture,**
1936. Photo of Matthew Crowley, radio portrayer. Full color, 8"x10", obtained by redeeming lids. - **$50 $100 $200**

BRG-79

❑ **BRG-79. "Irwin Projector" With Comic Character Films,**
1936. Unmarked but offered as premium with six Buck Rogers film loops of 16mm black and white cartoon art (from group of 13 titles) in Cream of Wheat Buck Rogers Solar Scouts Club Manual. Films also issued on reels of four different lengths in 2-1/2" or 4" boxes.
Boxed Projector - **$50 $80 $150**
Each Boxed Film - **$5 $10 $15**

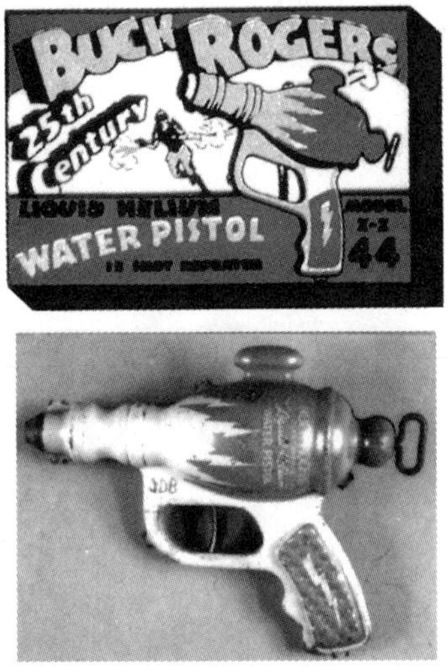


BRG-80

❑ **BRG-80. Liquid Helium Water Pistol XZ-44 And Box By Daisy,**
1936. Store item. Used in 1939 as Popsicle premium. No holster made. Gun examples are now non-functional due to aging of bladder. A red, yellow and black promotional flier was issued.
Red and Yellow Version - **$300 $800 $1600**
Copper Colored Version - **$350 $900 $1800**
Box Only - **$350 $750 $1500**

BRG-81

❑ **BRG-81. Water Pistol Promotional Flyer,**
1936. Daisy Mfg. Co. Full color 5-1/2x8-1/2" folder. Shown open, front and back. -
**$100 $200 $400**

BRG-82 BRG-83

❑ **BRG-82. "Buck Rogers and the Planetoid Plot" Big Little Book #1197,**
1936. - **$25 $100 $175**

❑ **BRG-83. Decal Probably From Cream Of Wheat,**
1936. Black on gold, 1x1-1/4" with blue serial number on backing paper.
Unused - **$75 $150 $300**

BRG-84

❑ **BRG-84. "Solar Scout" Premium Pennant,**
1936. Rare. Ony 2 known. Has tag on back. 11x18" red and white cloth. -
**$1000 $2750 $4000**

BRG-85

❑ **BRG-85. "Solar Scouts" Radio Club Manual,**
1936. Cream Of Wheat. Offers 18 premiums. Color cover with black and red illustrations. -
**$100 $300 $650**

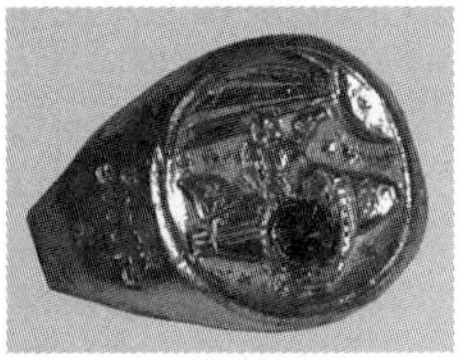

BRG-86

BRG-87

❑ **BRG-86. Repeller Ray Brass Ring With Green Stone,**
1936. Scarce. Cream Of Wheat and newspaper premium offer. Original stone is faceted. Beware of replacements. Within Buck Rogers Solar Scouts club, also known as "Supreme Inner Circle" ring. Offered again in 1939. -
**$600 $1750 $3500**

❑ **BRG-87. Solar Scouts Member Brass Badge,**
1936. Cream of Wheat and newspaper premium offer. Facsimile Buck Rogers signature on reverse. Offered again in 1939. - **$35 $75 $125**

BRG-88

❑ **BRG-88. "Solar Scouts" Sweater Emblem,**
1936. Cream of Wheat. Rare. Less than 10 known. Offered first with BRG-15. 3-1/2" red and blue on yellow felt. - **$1500 $4500 $6500**

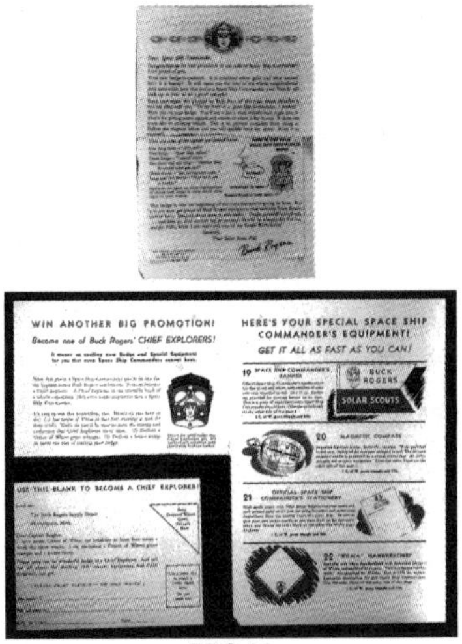


BRG-89

❑ **BRG-89. "Spaceship Commander" Leaflet,**
1936. Cream of Wheat. Offers badge, banner, magnetic compass, stationery, Wilma handkerchief. Leaflet - **$75 $150 $300**

BRG-90

BRG-91

❑ **BRG-90. "Spaceship Commander/Buck Rogers Solar Scouts" Silvered Brass Badge,**
1936. Cream of Wheat and newspaper premium offer. Metallic blue accent paint, holed at bottom to serve as whistle. Offered again in 1939. - **$85 $225 $325**

❑ **BRG-91. "Chief Explorer/Buck Rogers Solar Scouts" Brass Badge,**
1936. Cream of Wheat and newspaper premium offer. Red enamel paint background. Badge inscribed on back "Awarded For Distinguished Achievement" with facsimile Buck Rogers signature. Offered again in 1939. - **$100 $250 $400**

BRG-92

BRG-93

❑ **BRG-92. "Chief Explorer" Brass Badge,**
1936. Scarce. Cream of Wheat and newspaper premium offer. Variety with gold luster and no red enamel paint. - **$150 $350 $600**

❑ **BRG-93. Wilma Deering Brass Pendant With Chain,**
1936. Rare. Cream of Wheat and newspaper premium offer. Back inscription "To My Pal In The Solar Scouts". Offered again in 1939. - **$300 $1100 $1650**

BRG-94

❑ **BRG-94. Boxed Card Game,**
1936. Store item by All-Fair. Box comes in two sizes, larger one shown. 35 full-color cards plus instruction card. Cards are in pairs except for Killer Kane. - **$200 $450 $650**

BRG-95

❑ **BRG-95. "Buck Rogers Rocketship" Balsa Flying Toy With Mailer Envelope,**
1936. Rare. Mrs. Karl's Bread by Spotswood Specialty Co., also Cream of Wheat premium. Envelope is plain, comes with wood stick and rubber band launcher. - **$150 $300 $600**

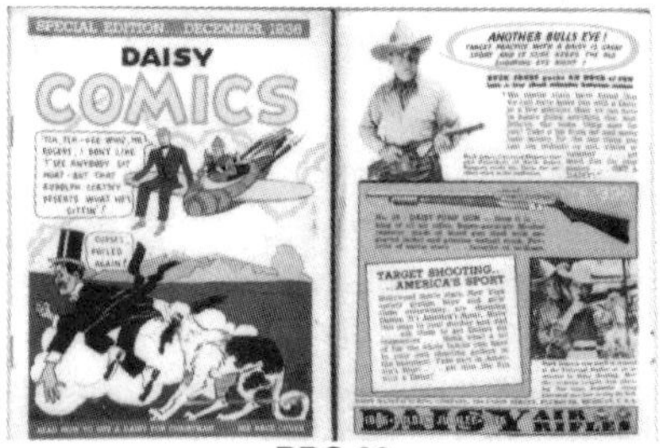


BRG-96

❑ **BRG-96. "Daisy Comics",**
1936. Daisy Mfg. Co. Contents include Buck Rogers comic story and shows guns for him plus features on cowboys Buck Jones and Tim McCoy. Thinner and smaller format than a standard comic book. - **$34 $103 $240**

BRG-97

❑ **BRG-97. "25th Century Acousticon Jr." 2-1/4" Cello. Button,**
1936. Rare. Hearing aid device by Dictograph Products Co. Black, blue, red and fleshtone on white background. - **$400 $1500 $3000**

BRG-98

❑ **BRG-98. "Buck Rogers" Silver Luster Belt Buckle,**
1937. Store item by Reliable Belt Co. Came attached to brown leather belt, see next item. Buckle Only - **$75 $150 $250**

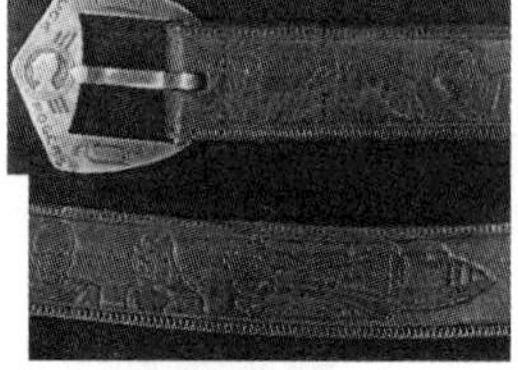

BRG-99

❑ **BRG-99. "Buck Rogers" Buckle With Brown Leather Belt,**
1937. Store item by Reliable Belt Co. Buckle is the same as preceding item but this example is attached to dark brown leather belt impressed with repeating images of Buck Rogers and other characters of the comic strip. 36" long. Buckle And Belt - **$150 $300 $500**

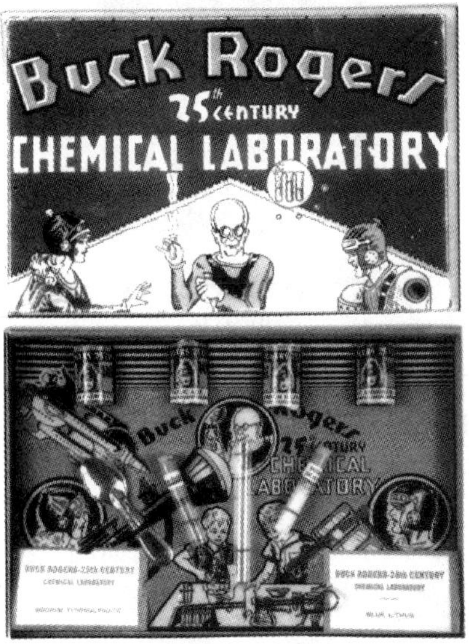


(SMALL SET)

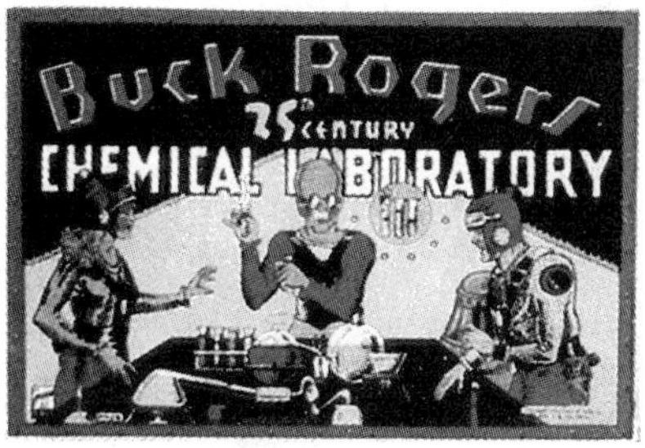


(LARGE SET BOX LID)

BRG-100

**❑ BRG-100. Chemical Laboratory Boxed Set,**
1937. Store item in two sizes with four-section 6x16" instruction folder. By Gropper Mfg. Co.
Small Set - **$400 $800 $1500**
Large Set - **$550 $1100 $1750**

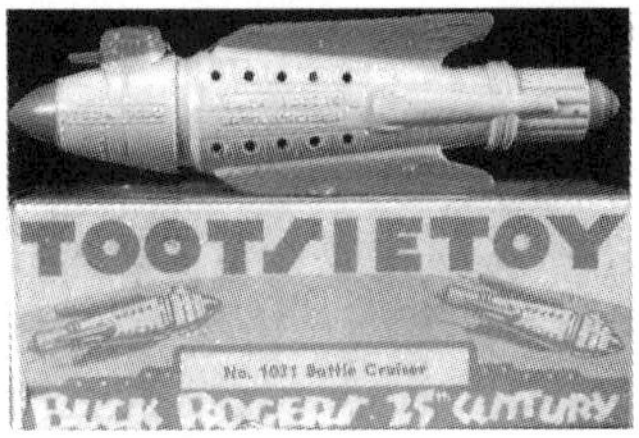


BRG-101

**❑ BRG-101 Tootsietoy #1031 "Battle Cruiser",**
1937. Metal "Buck Rogers Battle Cruiser TSDDM3030." Used as Popsicle premium in 1939. Came in several color variations over the years. Reissued in early 1950s by Dowst in silver color with U.S. Air Force insignia but without Buck Rogers name. The reissue is scarce. Again reissued in 1960s, this time without Air Force insignia. Slides on string.
Near Mint Boxed - **$500**
Loose - **$75 $175 $300**
1950s Reissue Loose - **$125 $200 $350**
1950s Reissue NM on Blister Card - **$400**
1960s Reissue NM on Blister Card - **$350**

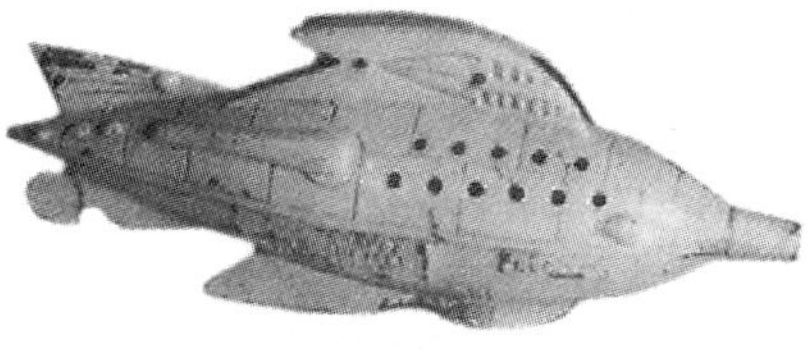

BRG-102

**❑ BRG-102. "Earth Jupiter Transport NNS36" Metal Spaceship,**
1937. Tootsietoy, perhaps intended as fourth rocketship in their series but may exist as prototype only. Slides on string. -
**$500 $1000 $1600**

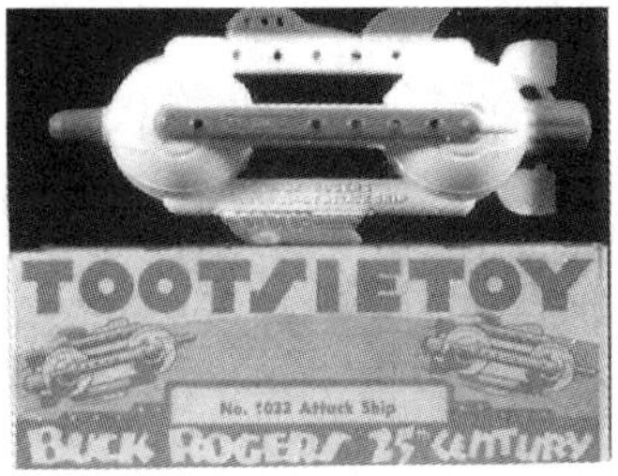


BRG-103

**❑ BRG-103. Tootsietoy #1033 "Attack Ship",**
1937. Metal "Buck Rogers Flash Blast Attack Ship TS 310 Z". Used as Popsicle premium in 1939. Came in several color variations over the years. Reissued in early 1950s by Dowst in silver color with U.S. Air Force insignia but without Buck Rogers name. The reissue is scarce. Again reissued in 1960s, this time without Air Force insignia. Slides on string. Near Mint Boxed - **$500**
Loose - **$75 $175 $300**
1950s Reissue Loose - **$125 $200 $350**
1950s Reissue NM on Blister Card - **$400**
1960s Reissue NM on Blister Card - **$350**

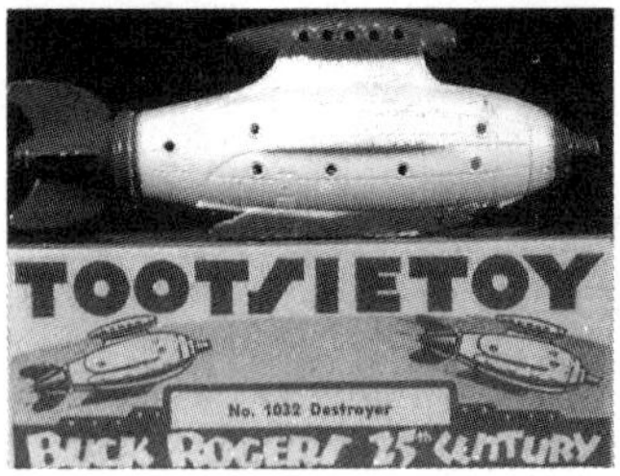


BRG-104

**❑ BRG-104. Tootsietoy #1032 "Destroyer" With Box,**
1937. Metal "Buck Rogers Venus Duo-Destroyer MK 24 L". Used as Popsicle premium in 1939. Came in several color variations over the years. Reissued in early 1950s by Dowst in silver color with U.S. Air Force insignia but without Buck Rogers name. The reissue is scarce. Again reissued in 1960s, this time without Air Force insignia. Slides on string. Near Mint Boxed - **$500**
Loose - **$75 $175 $300**
1950s Reissue Loose - **$125 $200 $350**
1950s Reissue NM on Blister Card - **$400**
1960s Reissue NM on Blister Card - **$350**

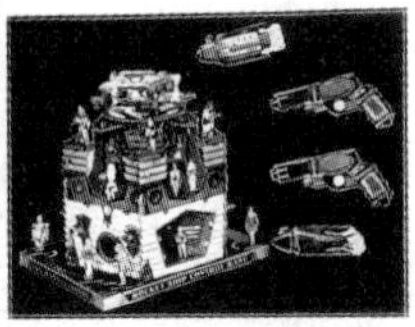

BRG-105

**❑ BRG-105. "Combat Game!",**
1937. Store item by Warren Paper Products Co. Set No. 110. Many full color pre-cut stiff thin cardboard pieces to form Rocket Ship Control Base with accessories of spaceships, guns and 11 standup characters. Total of 65 pieces plus instructions.
Boxed Complete - **$500 $1500 $2150**
Complete No Box - **$300 $700 $1300**

BRG-106

**❑ BRG-106. "Buck Rogers Rocket Rangers" Cello. Button,**
1937. Issuer unknown. 1-1/2" dark blue on white. Only a couple of examples known and the two examples we know about are both heavily stained. - **$400 $800 $1600**

BRG-107

BRG-108

❑ **BRG-107. Canadian Club Member Cello. Button,**
1937. Issuer unknown but 1" in blue/white/orange. Curl reads "Shaw Mfg. Toronto." - **$300 $750 $1600**

❑ **BRG-108. Buck Rogers Metal Figure 1-3/4" Tall,**
1937. Packaged with Tootsietoy rocketships. Sold with boxed set #5450 only. Buck (Silver Color) Or Wilma (Gold Color) with respective name under base. Each - **$100 $200 $350**

BRG-109

❑ **BRG-109. "Buck Rogers Rocket Rangers" Member's Card,**
1937. Black and white card with yellow burst, same design as BRG-106. -
**$50 $100 $165**

BRG-110

❑ **BRG-110. "Rocket Rangers" Enlistment Sheet,**
c. 1939. Various newspapers. 7x11" black on yellow with text stating membership card will be sent upon receipt of this enlistment application. Also see BRG-118 and BRG-119. -
**$75 $150 $275**

BRG-111

❑ **BRG-111. Vicks And Other Premium Comic Books,**
c. 1938. Vicks Chemical Co. shown with their logo and same comic with local store imprint. These thin books reprinted stories from earlier Famous Funnies comic books. Three additional similar thin versions were produced: two by Pure Oil and one by Salerno.
Each - **$65 $175 $325**

BRG-112

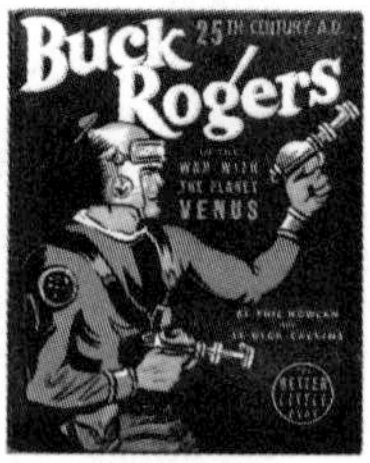


BRG-113

❑ **BRG-112. "Vicks Comics" Comic Book,**
1938. Vicks Chemical Co. published by Eastern Color Printing Co. 64 pages of stories printed earlier in Famous Funnies. Five pages relate to Buck Rogers, the others feature various characters. - **$75 $225 $600**

❑ **BRG-113. "Buck Rogers in the War with the Planet Venus" BLB #1437,**
1938. - **$25 $80 $175**

BRG-114

❑ **BRG-114. "Buck Rogers" Story Pencil Tablet,**
c. 1939. Store item. At least five in numbered series. Each - **$100 $250 $350**

BRG-115

❑ **BRG-115. "Buck Rogers Whistling Rocket Ship" Prototype Original Art,**
c. 1939. 16-1/4x21-1/2" in colored pencil. For a premium rocketship that was to be given away at movie theaters but was altered slightly and became the Muffets premium. Gordon Gold Archives. Unique. - **$1750**

BRG-116

❑ **BRG-116. "Buck Rogers/Muffets" Premium Rocketship Original Art Prototype Sign,**
c. 1938. Produced for 1939 Whistling Rocketship premium issued by Muffets Cereal. 15-3/4x20-1/2". Gordon Gold Archives. Unique.
**- $1200**

BRG-117

❑ **BRG-117. "Buck Rogers Rocket Police Patrol" Tin Wind-Up,**
1939. Store item by Marx Toys. Flint cover often missing. Toy Complete - **$400 $850 $1750**

BRG-118

❑ **BRG-118. "Rocket Rangers" Club Member Card,**
1939. Pictures "Inter-Planetary Battle Cruiser" on yellow card. Each card acquired by sending offer coupon clipped from newspaper comic strip. Five later versions were on blue or white cards, the last issued in 1978. See cards for years 1944, 1946, 1952, 1958 and 1978.
First Version - **$75 $150 $300**
Later Versions - **$20 $50 $125**

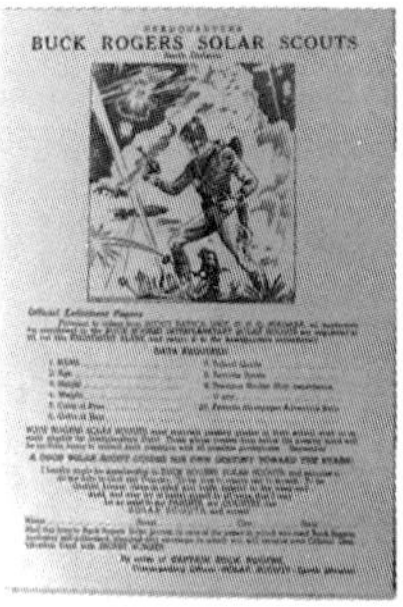


BRG-119

❑ **BRG-119. Solar Scouts Enlistment Form,**
1939. Newspaper issue. Art by Dick Calkins. Club was in name transition. Enlistment form uses "Solar Scouts" name but member's card uses "Rocket Rangers" name. 7-1/4x10-1/2". - **$100 $200 $325**

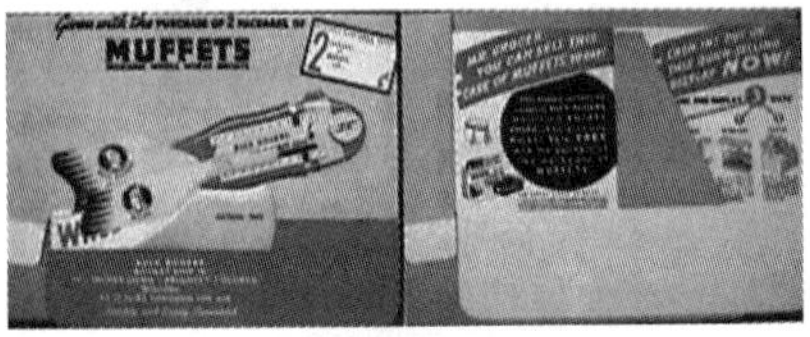


BRG-120

❑ **BRG-120. "Buck Rogers Whistling Rocketship" Premium Store Display,**
1939. Muffets cereal. Flattened size of 13-1/2x16-3/4" plus a 4" wide top panel missing from our illustrated example. This panel read "Free Buck Rogers Whistling Rocketship." Reverse shows how to assemble into three-dimensional form. See BRG-124. Gordon Gold Archives. - **$200 $400 $850**

BRG-121

❑ **BRG-121. Movie Serial Press Book,**
1938-1939. Universal Studios. Eight pages printed in purple, green and white. Includes separate proof sheet with ads for all 12 chapters. Rare. - **$250 $500 $850**

BRG-122

❑ **BRG-122. Vintage Photostat Of Prototype Art,**
c. 1939. 5-1/2x8-1/2" pair of photostats mounted back to back picturing prototype artwork with reverse rocketship resembling the premium actually offered by Muffets. Gordon Gold Archives. Probably Unique. - **$300**

BRG-123

❑ **BRG-123. "Strange World Adventures Club" Serial Club Cello. Button,**
1939. Universal. Made by Philadelphia Badge Co. in blue and silver 1-1/4" design. Offered with a membership card by various theaters. One of the rarest and most desirable movie serial club buttons.
Button - **$350 $1000 $1750**
Card - **$200 $400 $600**

BRG-124

❑ **BRG-124. "Whistling Rocketship" Cardboard Punch-Out Assembly Kit With Envelope,**
1939. Scarce. Muffets cereal. Example photo shows portrait details from tail fins. See BRG-120.
Unused With Envelope - **$250 $500 $800**
Assembled - **$200 $400 $600**

BRG-125

❑ **BRG-125. "Gift List Radio News" Catalog,**
1939. Popsicle. Full color 7-1/2x10" with four pages. A different version was issued in 1940.
Each - **$75 $150 $325**

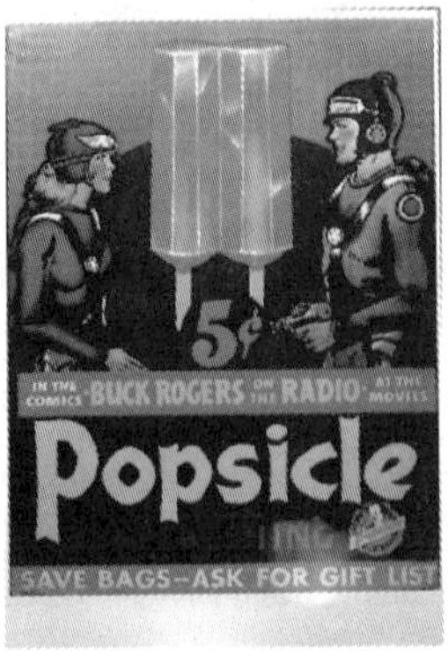


BRG-126

❑ **BRG-126. Diecut Standup Of Buck And Wilma,**
1939. Popsicle store display. 11x14" in superb color. - **$500 $1200 $2000**

BRG-127

❑ **BRG-127. Creamsicle Gifts Dealer Instruction Card,**
1939. Two versions: 1939 and 1940, each 8-1/4x12". 1939 issue is shown. - **$100 $300 $600**

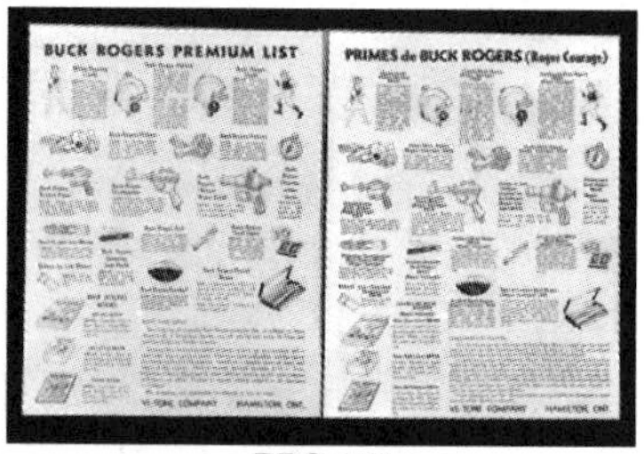


BRG-128

❑ **BRG-128. Canadian "Buck Rogers Premium List,"**
1930s. Vi-Tone Company Hamilton, Ont. 8-1/2x11" sheet in English o n one side and French on the opposite side showing 19 premiums obtained by saving Vi-Tone and Egg-O Baking Powder coupons. Included are Buck and Wilma outfits, holsters, guns, Light Blaster, books, camping knife, Directoscope, card game, football game, pencil box. The French side has Buck Rogers name in English and identifies him as "Roger Courage." **- $50 $300 $550**

BRG-129

❑ **BRG-129. School Map,**
1930s. Rare. Probable Dixon Pencil Co. Yellow-tone, 8-1/2"x11" paper sheet came folded with Buck Rogers art in red border scenes on map of North America. - **$200 $500 $750**

BRG-130

❑ **BRG-130. Newspaper Contest 1-1/4" Cello. Buttons,**
1930s. "Buffalo Evening News" example pictures aviator character from early Buck Rogers daily newspaper strip. "Pittsburgh-Post Gazette" example pictures Buck Rogers. Both blue with flesh tone accent on white.
Buffalo - **$50 $100 $175**
Pittsburgh - **$75 $150 $250**

BRG-131

BRG-132

❑ **BRG-131. Wilma Unlicensed Mask,**
1930s. Store item, marked "Made In Japan". Unlike 1933 Cocomalt premium, hair is not curly and less slick paper stock resulted in duller color. See item BRG-18. - **$50 $125 $250**

❑ **BRG-132. "Buck Rogers Gang" Club Member Cello. Button,**
1930s. Issuer unknown. 1-1/2" red on cream. - **$200 $400 $700**

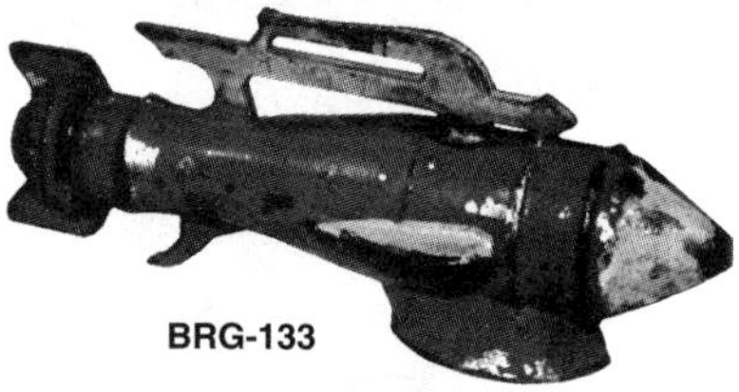

BRG-133

BRG-134

❑ **BRG-133. Buck Rogers Style Rocketship,**
1930s. Store item by Barclay in red, blue and yellow similar to Tootsietoy rockets. - **$100 $175 $350**

❑ **BRG-134. "Lucky Coin",**
1930s. Issuer unknown. 1-1/2" in the style of a "wooden nickel." - **$100 $250 $450**

BRG-135

❑ **BRG-135. "Follow Buck Rogers" Cello. Button,**
1930s. Washington Herald newspaper. Red type and blue image on white 1-1/4" from a set that includes other comic character strips appearing in the newspaper. - **$400 $1000 $1800**

BRG-136

❑ **BRG-136. "The Hecht Co.'s Toy Land Funnies" Comic Book,**
1930s. Hecht Department Store, Washington, D.C. 32 pages reprinting stories from earlier Famous Funnies comic books. - (value will be based on future reported sales)

BRG-137

BRG-138

❑ **BRG-137. Matchbook,**
1940. Popsicle/Creamsicle. May 4th version for new radio sponsorship. Also issued with April 6th date for southern states.
Empty or Incomplete - **$10 $20 $40**
Complete With All Matches - **$20 $40 $80**

❑ **BRG-138. Matchbook,**
1940. Popsicle. May 4th version for new radio sponsorship. Also issued with April 6th date for southern states.
Empty or Incomplete - **$10 $20 $40**
Complete With All Matches - **$20 $40 $80**

BRG-139

❑ **BRG-139. "Onward School Supplies" 18x24" Paper Hanger Sign,**
1940. Printed on both sides. A larger 18"x50" version came rolled on a wood dowel.
Small Version - **$150 $350 $600**
Large Version - **$250 $600 $1000**

BRG-140

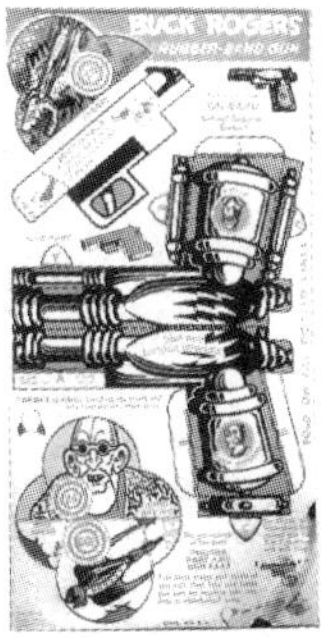


BRG-141

❑ **BRG-140. School Supplies 11x16" Paper Store Poster,**
1940. Onward School Supplies. Announces rubber band gun free with school supply purchase.- **$175 $400 $800**

❑ **BRG-141. Cardboard Punch-Out Rubber Band Gun,**
1940. Onward School Supplies. Punch-out sheet includes standup targets of Sea Monster, Wing Bat Wu, Spaceship. 5"x10", red and black art. Unpunched - **$75 $200 $300**

BRG-142

❑ **BRG-142. "School Sale" Newspaper-Size Circular,**
1940. Photo examples show top half of front cover plus two illustration details. -
**$35 $60 $100**

BRG-143

❑ **BRG-143. "Buck Rogers and the Overturned World" Better Litttle Book #1474,**
1941. - **$30 $85 $175**

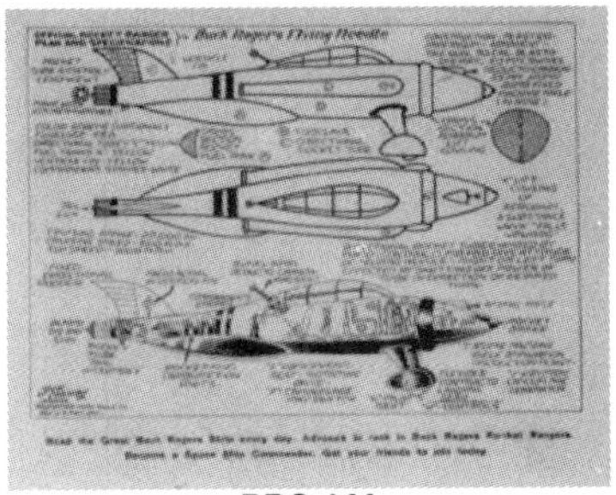

BRG-144

❑ **BRG-144. "Flying Needle" Airship Diagram Sheet,**
1941. Daily comic strip offer. For "Buck Rogers Rocket Rangers" club of aspiring "Spaceship Commander" readers. 8-1/2"x11", red on white, not a punch-out. - **$100 $225 $400**

BRG-145

❑ **BRG-145. "Buck Rogers Ranger" Aluminum Dog Tag With Chain,**
c. 1942. Rare. Item has 1935 copyright but probably issued a few years later. Black details wear off easily. - **$400 $1200 $1750**

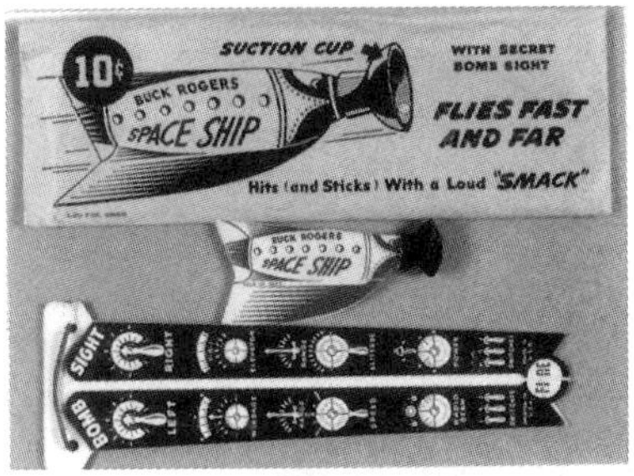


BRG-146

❑ **BRG-146. Cardboard Spaceship With Envelope,**
1942. Morton's Salt. Includes cardboard "Secret Bomb Sight". Suction cup nose stiffens with age.
Complete With Envelope - **$50 $100 $250**

BRG-147

BRG-148

❑ **BRG-147. "Buck Rogers and the Super-Dwarf of Space" Better Little Book #1490,**
1943. - **$30 $85 $175**

❑ **BRG-148. "Rocket Rangers" Club Member Card,**
1944. Various newspapers. Same design as 1939 card but on blue card stock. -
**$35 $75 $125**

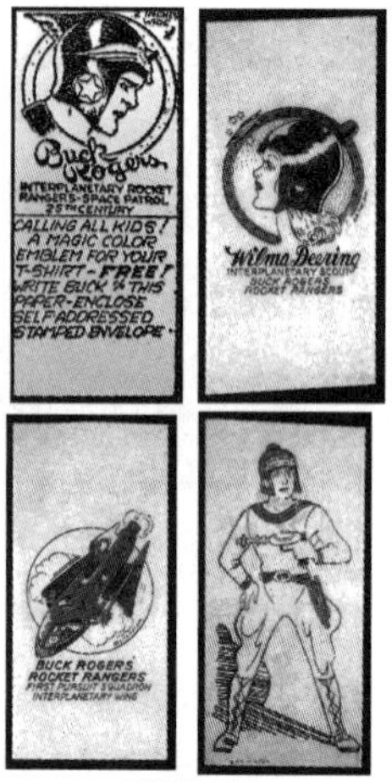


BRG-149

**❑ BRG-149. Rocket Rangers Iron-On Transfers,**
1944. Newspaper premium. Set of three sent individually for Buck, Wilma and Rocketship. Photos show offer and two transfers. Transfers are red and blue on 3x6" tissue paper. Last photo is example of tranfers with outlined image of Buck in green or blue, with or without orange details (4 versions), c. 1940 by Jitterprints.
Each Ranger Transfer - **$50 $85 $140**
Each Older Transfer - **$10 $25 $50**

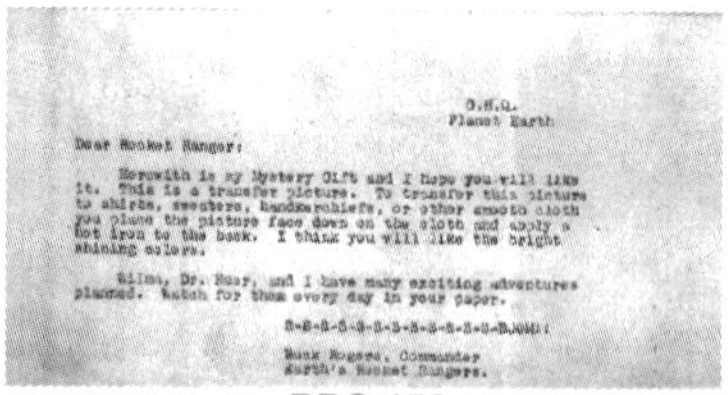

G.H.Q.
Planet Earth

Dear Rocket Ranger:

Herewith is my Mystery Gift and I hope you will like it. This is a transfer picture. To transfer this picture to shirts, sweaters, handkerchiefs, or other smooth cloth you place the picture face down on the cloth and apply a hot iron to the back. I think you will like the bright shining colors.

Wilma, Dr. Huer, and I have many exciting adventures planned. Watch for them every day in your paper.

S-S-S-S-S-S-S-S-S-S-S-S-BOOM!

Buck Rogers, Commander
Earth's Rocket Rangers.

BRG-150

**❑ BRG-150. Transfer Picture Instruction Sheet,**
1944. Newspaper "Mystery Gift" addressed to "Dear Rocket Ranger." 4-1/4x8-1/2" white paper. - **$35 $65 $90**

BRG-151

**❑ BRG-151. Newspaper Strip Promotional Brochure,**
1944. John Dille Co. and National Newspaper Service. Text calls the strip "Public Fascinator No. 1-A" reverse lists ranks in the "Buck Rogers Rocket Rangers Club." Opens to 19x24". Various brochures were issued throughout the run of the strip. - **$75 $175 $350**

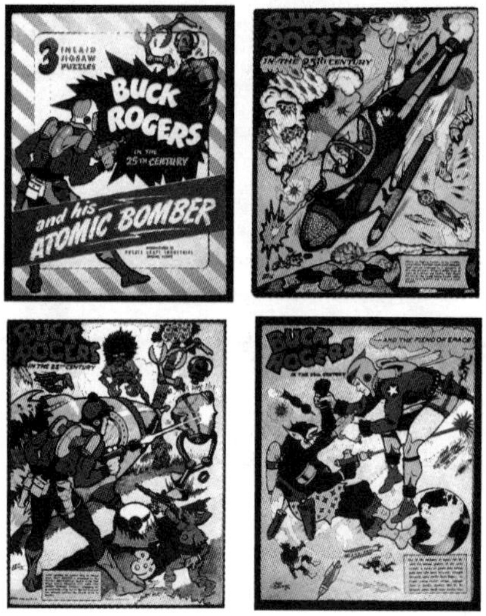


BRG-152

**❑ BRG-152. "Atomic Bomber" Jigsaw Puzzle Boxed Set,**
1945. Store item by Puzzle Craft Industries, Chicago. Each puzzle is 8-1/2x11" with art by Dick Calkins. Two versions of box lid. Exceptionally colorful. For color photo see the second edition of this book, page 711.
Each Puzzle Or Box - **$100 $250 $400**

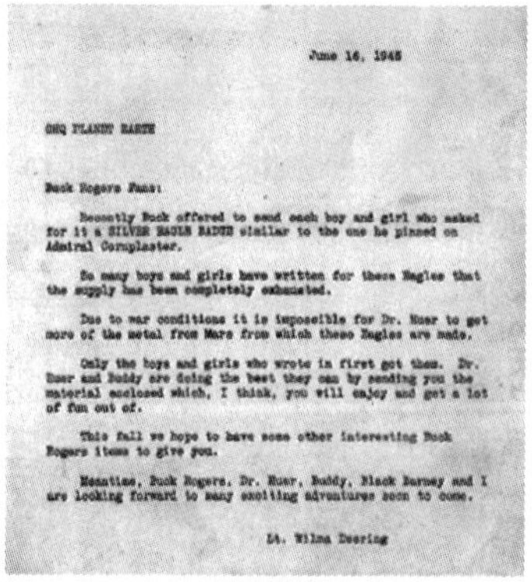

June 16, 1945

GHQ PLANET EARTH

Buck Rogers Fans:

Recently Buck offered to send each boy and girl who asked for it a SILVER EAGLE BADGE similar to the one he pinned on Admiral Corruplaster.

So many boys and girls have written for these Eagles that the supply has been completely exhausted.

Due to war conditions it is impossible for Dr. Huer to get more of the metal from Mars from which these Eagles are made.

Only the boys and girls who wrote in first got them. Dr. Huer and Buddy are doing the best they can by sending you the material enclosed which, I think, you will enjoy and get a lot of fun out of.

This fall we hope to have some other interesting Buck Rogers items to give you.

Meantime, Buck Rogers, Dr. Huer, Buddy, Black Barney and I are looking forward to many exciting adventures soon to come.

Lt. Wilma Deering

BRG-153

**❑ BRG-153. Silver Eagle Badge Letter,**
1945. Yellow paper letter 6-1/4x7" dated June 16, 1945. Text explains supply of badge is exhausted as "Due To War Conditions It Is Impossible For Dr. Huer To Get More Of The Metal From Mars From Which These Eagles Are Made." Letter says boys and girls will enjoy the (unknown) substituted item sent with this letter. Badge is extremely rare. No photo available.
Letter - **$75 $150 $300**
Badge-Undetermined

BRG-154

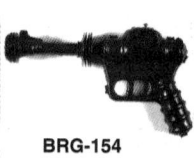

**❑ BRG-154. Atomic Pistol U-235 By Daisy,**
1945. Store item. Silver or black color finish. Flint produces spark. No holster made. A red, black and yellow promotional flyer was issued.
Gun - **$75 $225 $450**
Box - **$75 $200 $400**
3-Page Story Folder - **$50 $100 $200**

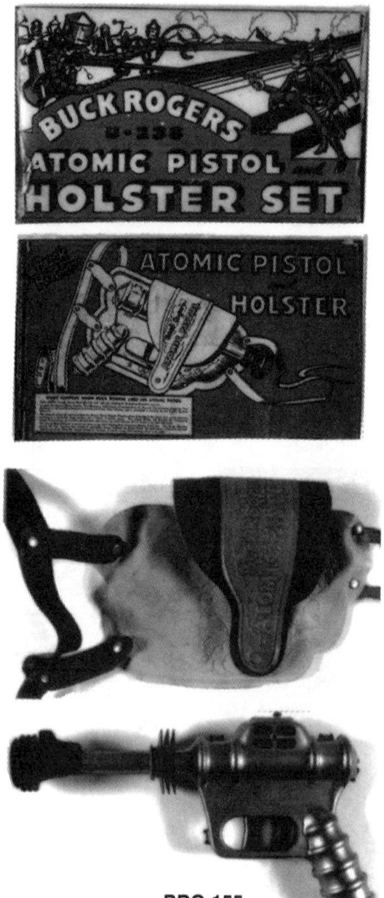


BRG-155

**❑ BRG-155. Atomic Pistol U-238 By Daisy,**
1946. Store item. Gold color finish. Flint produces spark. Gun - **$100 $275 $500**
Leather Holster - **$100 $250 $450**
Box - **$75 $200 $400**
3-Page Story Folder **$50 $100 $200**

BRG-156

❑ **BRG-156. Atomic Pistol Promotional Flyer,**
1946. Daisy Mfg. Co. Three-fold full color 8-1/2x11" flyer. Both sides shown open. - **$75 $175 $350**

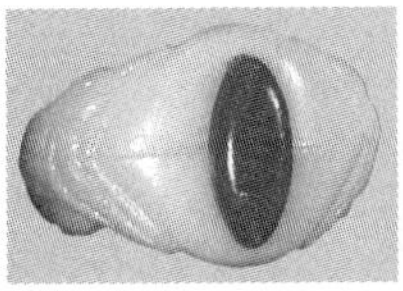

BRG-157

BRG-158

❑ **BRG-157. Glow-In-Dark Ring Of Saturn,**
1946. Post's Corn Toasties radio premium. White plastic topped by red plastic stone. - **$100 $200 $500**

❑ **BRG-158. "Ring Of Saturn" Instruction Folder,**
1946. Came with ring. Post's Corn Toasties radio premium. Red and black on white. Opens to 5-1/2"x9-1/4". - **$75 $175 $250**

BRG-159

❑ **BRG-159. "Rocket Rangers" Club Member Card,**
1946. Various newspapers. Shows flying ship on blue card stock. - **$45 $100 $150**

BRG-160

❑ **BRG-160. "Adventure Book,"**
1946. Daisy three-section folder issued with boxed guns Atomic Pistol U-235 and Atomic Pistol U-238. Folder in black and white reprints six daily newspaper comic strips. 3x15". - **$50 $100 $200**

BRG-161

❑ **BRG-161. Full Color Blotter,**
c. 1946. Chicago Herald-American. 3-1/2x8-1/2" newspaper promotional. - **$100 $200 $350**

BRG-162

❑ **BRG-162. Post's Corn Toasties Cereal Box,**
1946. Rare. Post Cereal. Advertises radio program on The Mutual Network.
Complete Box - **$400 $800 $1600**
Back Panel Only - **$200 $300 $500**

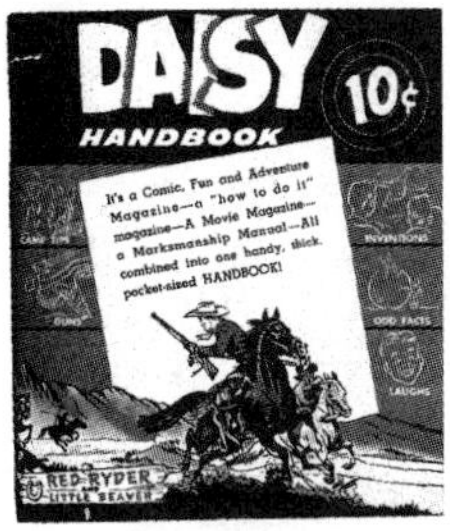


BRG-163

BRG-164

❑ **BRG-163. "Daisy Handbook,"**
1946. Daisy Mfg. Co. The first of several booklets promoting Daisy products. Contents include 10 Buck Rogers daily newspaper strip reprints. 4-1/2"x5-1/4", 128 pages. - **$50 $125 $300**

❑ **BRG-164. John Larkin Fan Card,**
c. 1947. Issuer unknown. 3-1/2x5-1/2" black and white. Larkin portrayed Buck Rogers on radio 1946-1947. - **$25 $50 $85**

BRG-165

❑ **BRG-165. Supersonic Two-Way Trans-Ceiver,**
1948. Store item made by Da-Myco. Box art by Rick Yager. Box 8x13-1/2". - **$175 $325 $550**

BRG-166

❑ **BRG-166. Drawing Of Pluton,**
1948. Newspaper premium with Rick Yager art in dark red on tan paper 8-1/2x11". Sent to readers who mailed in their own conception drawing.- **$125 $300 $600**

BRG-167

BRG-168

❑ **BRG-167. Rocket Rangers Application Form,**
c. 1948. Newspaper issue. Art by Murphy Anderson. 8-1/2x11". - **$50 $150 $225**

❑ **BRG-168. Pittsburgh "Post-Gazette Sunday Funnies" Comic Book,**
1949. Newspaper insert 16 page comic including Buck Rogers and other characters. - **$300 $550 $800**

BRG-169

❑ **BRG-169. Buck Rogers And Flame D'Amour Trading Cards,**
1949. Store item by Comic Stars, Inc. Full color 2-1/4x3-1/2" part of a set including other characters. Art by Murphy Anderson.
Buck - **$15 $35 $65**
Flame - **$10 $30 $55**

BRG-170

❑ **BRG-170. "Punch-O-Bag,"**
1940s. Store item from late 1940s by Lee-Tex Rubber Products Corp. Glassine bag 5x7" in red and blue held balloon usually missing or disintegrated. Bag Only - **$60 $125 $250**

BRG-171

BRG-172

❑ **BRG-171. Cardboard "Flying Saucer",**
c. 1940s. Store item by unknown maker marked S. P. Co. Has metal rim and two convex surfaces, unlike a frisbee. - **$45 $100 $175**

❑ **BRG-172. Amoco Gasoline Penny Cards,**
1940s. Black on cream thin cardboard 3x3". Many in series that include non-Buck Rogers characters. Images are pages out of Big Little Books. Display board was also available.
Each Buck Rogers - **$75 $125 $200**

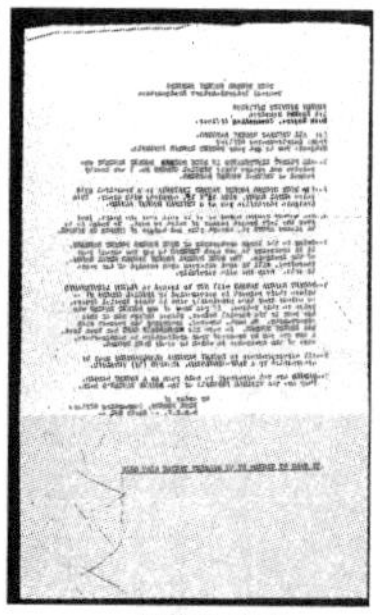
BRG-173

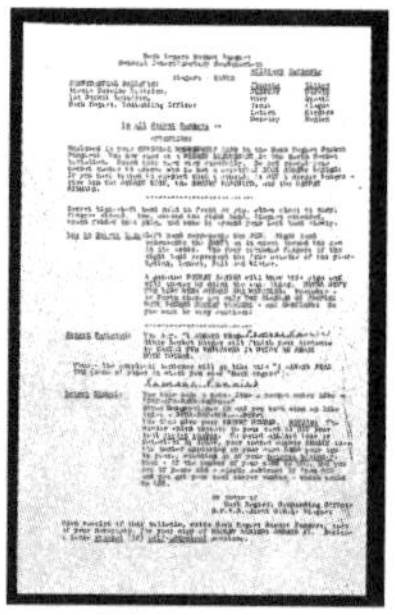
BRG-174

❑ **BRG-173. Letter - How To Get Rocket Ranger Insignia,**
1940s. Newspaper Premium. Have to hold up to mirror to read message. This letter, the following four items, and many others not shown, were offered in series by newspapers running the Buck Rogers daily strip and its associated club, the Rocket Rangers. All were sent folded. These letters were offered to young readers in 1939 through 1942, 1944, 1946, 1948 through 1950, 1952, and 1954. - **$30 $40 $60**

❑ **BRG-174. Letter - How To Get Secret Signals,**
1940s. Newspaper Premium. Came with membership card. - **$30 $40 $60**

BRG-175

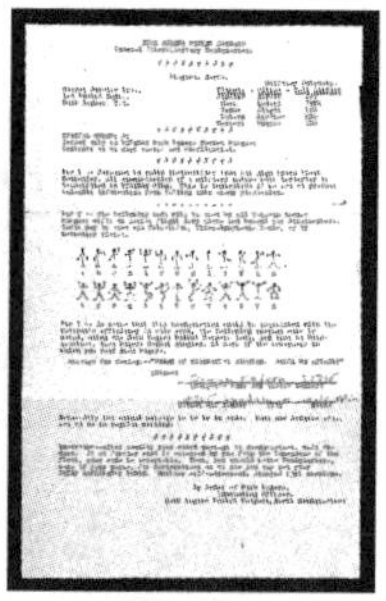
BRG-176

❑ **BRG-175. Letter - Special Orders #1,**
1940s. Newspaper Premium. Mars fighting globes described. - **$30 $40 $60**

❑ **BRG-176. Letter - Special Orders #2,**
1940s. Newspaper Premium. Shows secret code system. - **$40 $80 $100**

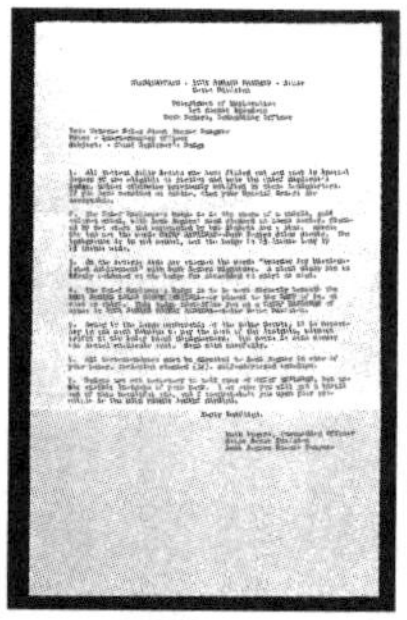
BRG-177

❑ **BRG-177. Letter - Chief Explorer,**
1940s. Newspaper premium. Talks about badge and Solar Scouts club information. See BRG-91. - **$50 $100 $175**

BRG-178

❑ **BRG-178. Rick Yager Personal Stationery,**
c. 1950. Scenes in blue. - **$40 $75 $125**

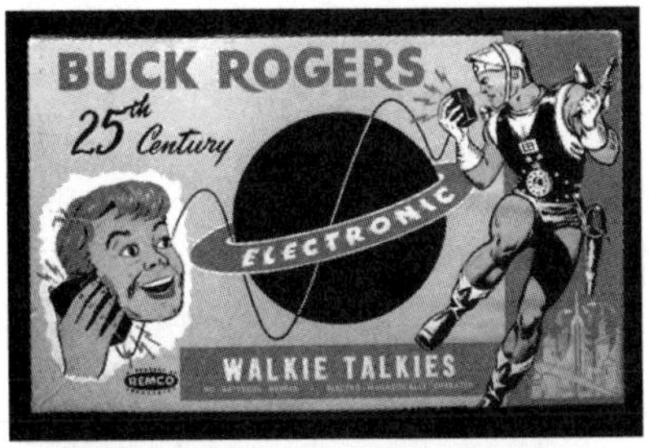

BRG-179

❑ **BRG-179. Electronic Walkie-Talkies,**
c. 1950. Store item made by Remco. Box art by Murphy Anderson. 8-1/2x13x2" deep box holds "walkie talkie" units and box insert features cardboard secret decoder. - **$125 $250 $450**

BRG-180

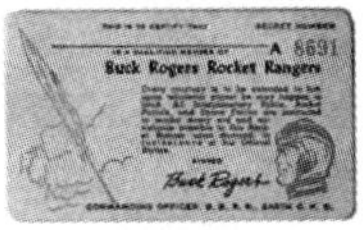

BRG-181

❑ **BRG-180. "Rocket Rangers" Member Litho. Tin Tab,**
1952. Newspaper premium made by L.J. Imber, Chicago. 3/4x1-1/2" red, white and blue. - **$25 $60 $125**

❑ **BRG-181. "Rocket Rangers" Club Member Card,**
1952. Various newspapers. White card with red profile of Buck. - **$20 $50 $100**

BRG-182

❑ **BRG-182. Space Ranger Kit,**
1952. Sylvania Electric Products Inc. Six full color punch-out sheets, each 10-1/2x14-1/2". Kit includes string. One punch-out is a membership card. Unpunched In Envelope - **$75 $150 $300**

BRG-184

❑ **BRG-184. "Buck Rogers Sylvania Space Ranger Kit" Promotional Flyer,**
1952. 8x10-3/4". Issued to promote premium kit by Sylvania Electric Products Inc. - **$25 $75 $125**

BRG-185

BRG-183

❑ **BRG-183. Large Die-Cut Sign,**
1952. Promotes Sylvania and shows Space Ranger Kit pieces. From the Gordon Gold Archives. - **$1000 $2000 $3000**

❑ **BRG-185. Sales Book for Space Ranger Kit,**
1952. Rare. From the Gordon Gold Archives. - **$500**

BRG-186

❑ **BRG-186. "Sylvania TV Buck Rogers Space Ranger Kit" Large Sales Promotion Folder,**
1952. Issued by Sylvania Electric Products Inc. Gordon Gold Archives. - **$65 $135 $225**

BRG-187

❑ **BRG-187. Space Ranger Kit Flyer,**
1952. Sylvania TV. Red and black on tan newsprint 8x10-3/4", printed only on one side. - **$25 $50 $100**

BRG-188

❑ **BRG-188. Ranger Kit Promo Photo,**
1952. From the Gordon Gold Archives. - **$75**

BRG-189

❑ **BRG-189. Large Display Poster,**
1952. Promotes Space Ranger Kit premium from Sylvania. See BRG-182. From the Gordon Gold Archives. - **$500 $1200 $1800**

BRG-190

❑ **BRG-190. Sylvania TV Retailer's Sales Catalogue And Roster,**
1952. 8-1/2x11" catalogue promotes use of the premium "Buck Rogers Space Ranger Kit." Roster is used to record names and addresses of children and parents visiting the store and given a kit. Gordon Gold Archives.
Catalogue - **$100 $250 $400**
Roster - **$25 $50 $75**

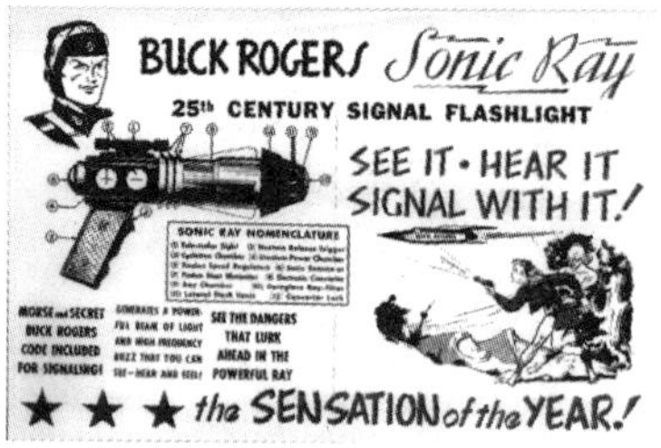


BRG-191

❑ **BRG-191. Sonic Ray Signal Flashlight (Gun Style) Flyer,**
c. 1952. Store item by Norton-Honer Mfg. Co. 11x17" full color. Several other flyer styles exist. - **$50 $100 $175**

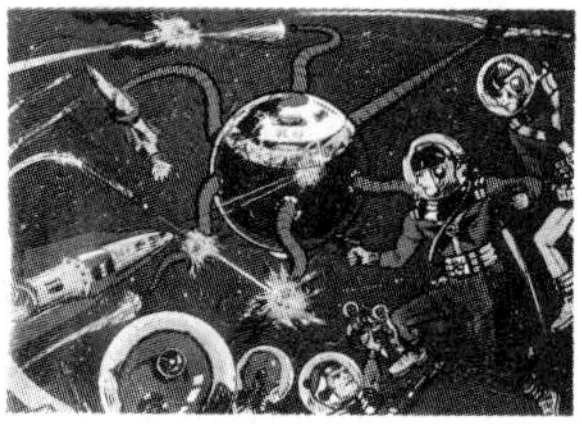

BRG-192

❑ **BRG-192. Octopus Space Station Tray Puzzle,**
1952. Store item by Milton Bradley. 10x14" originally sold with paper sleeve. Full color.
Sleeve - **$25 $50 $85**
Puzzle - **$35 $60 $125**

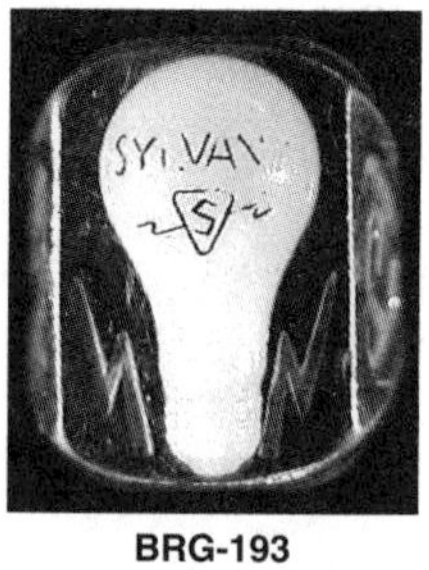

BRG-193

❑ **BRG-193. Sylvania Glow-In-Dark Light Bulb Ring,**
c. 1953. Sylvania was a Buck Rogers licensee around this time and used the character to promote their Halolight televisions. Although we've seen no paperwork linking this ring to Buck Rogers, the ring is accepted in the hobby as a Buck Rogers item. Bulb is white plastic mounted on brass base with adjustable bands. - **$250 $500 $1000**

BRG-194

❑ **BRG-194. Super Sonic Ray Gun Flyer,**
1955. Store item by Norton-Honer Mfg. Co. 8-1/2x11" full color. Reverse shows three accessories. Two versions are known.
Each - **$25 $75 $140**

BRG-195

BRG-196

❑ **BRG-195. "Buck Rogers/Satellite Pioneers" Litho. Tin 2" Tab,**
1957. Shown with stem unbent. Red and black on white made by Greenduck Co. This club lasted until 1967. - **$25 $50 $90**

❑ **BRG-196. "Buck Rogers Satellite Pioneers" Member's Card,**
1958. Used from 1958 through 1967. Various newspapers. White card with red scenes. 2-1/2x4-1/4". - **$20 $50 $100**

BRG-197

❑ **BRG-197. "Satellite Pioneers Cadet Commission" Bulletin Folder,**
1958. Various newspapers. Sent folded. 5-1/2x8-1/2". - **$30 $60 $100**

BRG-198

❑ **BRG-198. Starfinder Folder,**
1958. Newspaper premium. Satellite Pioneers Club. Guide to major constellations. 5-1/2x8-1/2". Sent folded. See BRG-200. - **$25 $60 $75**

BRG-199

❑ **BRG-199. Satellite Pioneers Club Bulletin,**
c. 1958. Various newspapers. Cover portrait faces right. Includes "Map of the Solar System." 5-1/2x8-1/2". Sent folded. - **$20 $30 $60**

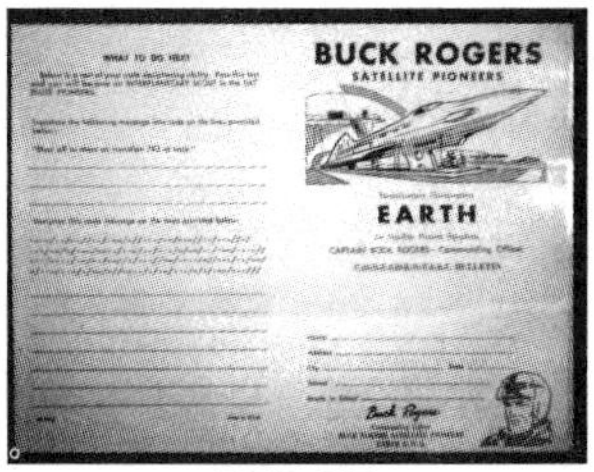


BRG-200

❑ **BRG-200. "Satellite Pioneers" Bulletin,**
1958. Newspaper premium. Secret Order No. 1 on pink paper mailed with Star Finder folder. 5-1/2x8-1/2". Sent folded. See BRG-198. -
**$25 $50 $85**

BRG-201

❑ **BRG-201. "Satellite Pioneers" Picture Card,**
1960. Offered by various newspapers. 3-1/2x5". Black and white. - **$20 $40 $65**

BRG-202

❑ **BRG-202. Captain Action & Action Boy Small Format Comic,**
1967. Ideal Toy & Novelty Co. Features Buck Rogers and other character accessory sets for use with Captain Action 12" figure. -
**$20 $60 $125**

BRG-203

❑ **BRG-203. Captain Action/Buck Rogers Plastic Flicker Ring,**
1967. Ideal Toys. Silver base marked "Hong Kong" came with boxed figure.
Silver "Hong Kong" Base - **$30 $45 $60**
Blue Base with "Disney" Name - **$10 $20 $30**
Silver "China" Modern Base - **$5 $10 $15**

BRG-204

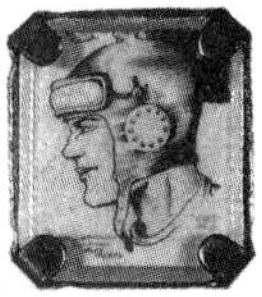

BRG-205

❑ **BRG-204. Captain Action Card Game,**
1967. Kool-Pops/Kool-Aid. Buck Rogers and other characters on 36 card game. Full color cards came in separate mailing box.
Complete - **$25 $50 $75**

❑ **BRG-205. Buck Rogers Profile Ring,**
1960s. Issuer unknown. Brass base with black and white paper image under beveled edge plastic top. First example surfaced in late 1960s. No documentation known and possibly a fantasy creation but uncommon. - **$150 $325 $500**

BRG-206

❑ **BRG-206. Warren Paper Co. Promotional Items,**
1971. Color poster, stiff paper zap pistol and postcard. Poster 24x36".
Poster - **$20 $40 $85**
Pistol - **$20 $40 $85**
Postcard - **$10 $20 $40**

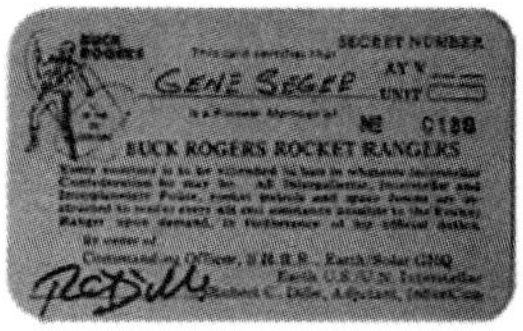


BRG-207

❑ **BRG-207. "Rocket Rangers" Club Member Card,**
1977. Red figure of Buck standing on blue card. Not offered through newspapers. -
**$20 $50 $100**

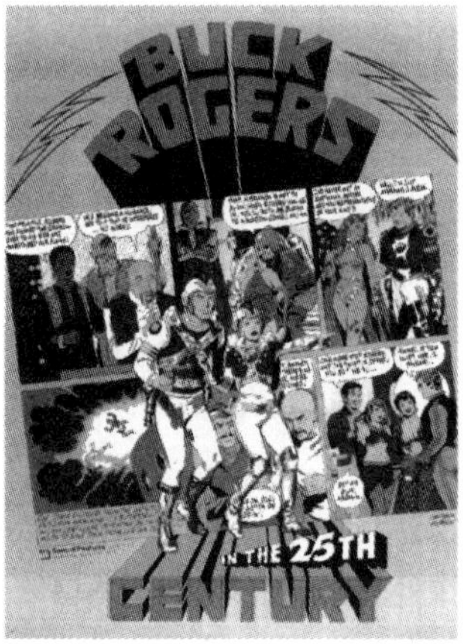


BRG-208

❑ **BRG-208. New York Times Special Features Sunday Strip Promotional Poster,**
1979. 16-1/2x21-1/2" full color on yellow paper. Art by Gray Morrow. - **$15 $30 $60**

BRG-209

❑ **BRG-209. Television Series Promotional Poster,**
1979. Burger King. 17x22" color paper giveaway poster. - **$15 $30 $50**

BRG-210

❑ **BRG-210. Television Series Plastic Cup Promotional Poster,**
1979. Burger King issue advertising Coca-Cola. 13x19" color paper poster advertising set of eight tumblers. - **$25 $50 $75**

BRG-211

❑ **BRG-211. "Buck Rogers Walking Twiki Robot,"**
1979. Store item by Mego.
Near Mint Boxed - **$65**
Loose - **$10 $20 $35**

BRG-212

❑ **BRG-212. "Buck Rogers Galactic Playset,"**
1979. Store item by HG Toys.
Near Mint Boxed - **$90**

BRG-213

❑ **BRG-213. "Buck Rogers" Cards/Sticker Set,**
1979. Issued by Topps. 88 cards and 22 stickers. Near Mint Set **- $15**

BRG-214

BRG-215

❑ **BRG-214. Coca-Cola Plastic Tumblers,**
1979. Distributed in theaters playing Buck Rogers movie. Eight different smaller size and five different larger size, each showing one character from the movie. Full color.
Small - **$5 $10 $15**
Large - **$15 $30 $50**

❑ **BRG-215. Coca-Cola Glass Tumblers,**
1979. Two sizes for four different characters. These may exist as test or prototypes only. Full color. Near Mint Each - **$200**

BRG-216

BRG-217

❑ **BRG-216. "Adventures Of Big Boy" Comic Book,**
1979. Restaurant giveaway issue No. 270 with Buck Rogers movie skit. Various local restaurant logos used. - **$5 $10 $20**

❑ **BRG-217. "Star Of The '80s" 3" Metal Button,**
1979. Gottlieb pinball game advertising button, probably distributed at industry trade show. White and blue on black background. A 19" by 28" poster and a four page folder were also available. - **$15 $35 $65**

BRG-218

❑ **BRG-218. TV Board Game,**
1979. - **$30 $60 $90**

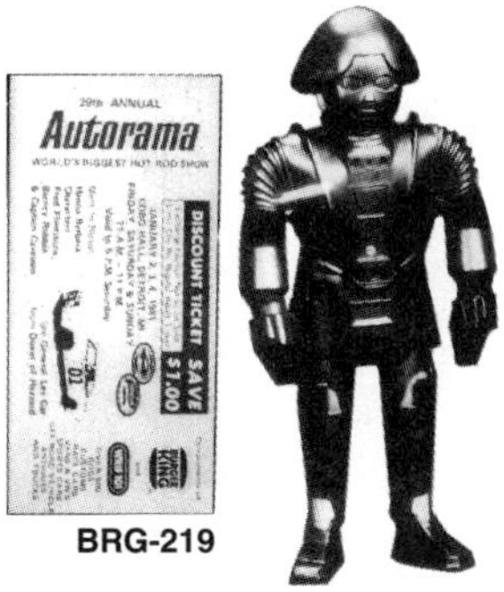

BRG-219

❑ **BRG-219. Twiki Photo,**
1981. Detroit 29th Annual Autorama show giveaway 8x10" black and white photograph. Shown with admission discount ticket. - **$10 $20 $30**

BRG-220

BRG-221

❑ **BRG-220. Color Postcard,**
1981. Quick Fox 5x8" promo for Gray Morrow Buck Rogers book. - **$10 $20 $35**

❑ **BRG-221. Buck Rogers Slurpee Video Game Plastic Tumbler,**
1982. Southland Corporation. 1982 version has blue scene while 1983 version has red scene.
1982 Issue - **$10 $20 $30**
1983 Issue (Shown) - **$5 $10 $15**

BRG-222

❑ **BRG-222. Cardboard Mobile,**
1988. Issued by TSR. Full color packaged unassembled in 17x21" stiff envelope. -
**$10 $20 $35**

BRG-223

❑ **BRG-223. Movie/TV Show Armband Patch,**
1980s. Issuer unknown. 4"x4" blue and black on white cloth. Band was worn on Buck and Wilma's right arm during 1979-81 TV series. -
**$5 $12 $25**

BRG-224

BRG-225

❑ **BRG-224. Bookmark,**
1991. Issued by TSR. Full color 2-1/8x7-3/4". - **$3 $6 $10**

❑ **BRG-225. Metal Badge and Cloth Insignia,**
1994 (Badge, 1988). Both issued by TSR. Badge is 1-1/2" long in three colors; insignia is 1-3/4x3-3/8" silver and red on blue cloth. Each - **$5 $10 $15**

BRG-226

❑ **BRG-226. Cardboard Pog,**
1995. Issued by Ektek Inc. 1-5/8" full color. Shows painting "War Against The Han" by Dennis Beauvais. - **$1 $2 $3**

BRG-227

❑ **BRG-227. Wall Clock in Box,**
1990s. Ingraham. - **$25 $50 $75**

## Bugs Bunny

**Probably the world's best-known rabbit, Bugs Bunny evolved into the brash character we know in the late 1930s in the Leon Schlesinger cartoon studios at Warner Brothers, dubbed "Termite Terrace" by its employees. He first uttered his memorable "Eh, what's up, Doc?" to Elmer Fudd in *The Wild Hare* in 1940, and the mischievous wabbit has been asking it ever since in the voice made famous by Mel Blanc. (Following Blanc's death, Jeff Bergman has occasionally voiced the wise-cwacking wabbit).**

**Until 1969 the cartoons were released or produced by Warner Brothers. Bugs' first comic book appearance was in 1941 in the first issue of *Looney Tunes and Merrie Melodies* and a Sunday newspaper strip started in 1943. Many cartoons, comic books and animated TV specials in the years since have been accompanied by a seemingly endless parade of merchandise, usually copyrighted by Warner Brothers.**

BUG-1

❑ **BUG-1. Animator Bob Clampett Personal Christmas Card,**
c. 1942. Inner design includes art of Clampett boiled in kettle stirred by Bugs. - **$60 $150 $240**

BUG-2

BUG-3

❑ **BUG-2. "Bugs Bunny All Picture Comics/Tall Comic Book,"**
1943. Whitman #530. 3-3/4x8-3/4" tall format with early comic book reprints. - **$20 $45 $100**

❑ **BUG-3. Bugs Bunny Paint Book,**
1944. Scarce in high grade and uncolored. - **$20 $60 $150**

BUG-4

BUG-5

❑ **BUG-4. Bugs Bunny All Pictures Comics,**
1944. Big Little Book #1435. - **$10 $40 $75**

❑ **BUG-5. "Bugs Bunny and His Pals" All Pictures Comics,**
1945. Big Little Book #1496. - **$10 $40 $75**

BUG-6

BUG-7

❑ **BUG-6. Figural Metal Bank,**
c. 1946. Store item. - **$60 $125 $190**

❑ **BUG-7. Bugs Bunny and the Pirate Loot,**
1947. Big Little Book #1403 - **$10 $35 $70**

BUG-8

BUG-9

❑ **BUG-8. Bugs Bunny and Klondike Gold,**
1948. Big Little Book #1455 - **$10 $35 $70**

❑ **BUG-9. "Bugs Bunny in Risky Business" All Pictures Comics,**
1948. Big Little Book #1440. - **$10 $35 $70**

BUG-10

BUG-11

BUG-12

❑ **BUG-10. "Bugs Bunny And The Giant Brothers" New Better Little Book,**
1949. Whitman #706-10. - **$15 $30 $60**

❑ **BUG-11. Bugs Bunny The Masked Marvel,**
1949. Big Little Book #1465 - **$10 $35 $70**

❑ **BUG-12. Color 8"x10" Picture,**
1940s. Comic book premium from Dell. - **$30 $60 $100**

BUG-13

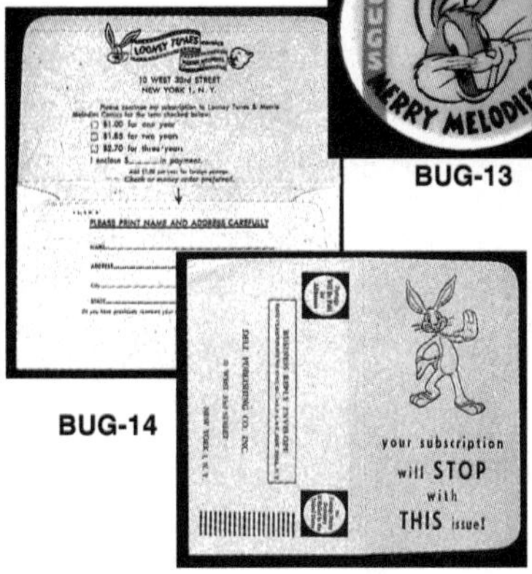

BUG-14

❑ **BUG-13. Warner Bros. Cartoon Promotion Button,**
1940s. 1-1/4" in red, gray, black and white. - **$15 $30 $60**

❑ **BUG-14. Mailer,**
1940s. Subscription mailer for Looney Tunes comic. - **$15 $30 $50**

BUG-15

❑ **BUG-15. Bugs, Sniffles Cardboard Plaques,**
1940s. Store items. Glows in the dark. Each - **$15 $25 $50**

BUG-16

BUG-17

❑ **BUG-16. Rubber Squeaker Figure,**
1940s. Store item by Oak Rubber Co. - **$25 $50 $100**

❑ **BUG-17. Dell Comics Picture,**
1940s. - **$15 $30 $60**

BUG-18

❑ **BUG-18. Dell Comics Christmas Card,**
1940s. - **$20 $50 $80**

BUG-19

❑ **BUG-19. Dell Looney Tunes Comic Book Character Picture Strip,**
1951. Dell Publishing Co. with Warner Bros. Cartoon Inc. copyright . Folder strip of five pictures, each about 6x8". - **$25 $50 $85**

BUG-20

❑ **BUG-20. Original Comic Book Cover Art,**
1951. 11 1/2"x16" Front and back cover art for Christmas Funnies #2. Early painted covers for Warner Bros. characters are rare. - **$2200**

BUG-21

BUG-22

❑ **BUG-21. "What's Up Doc?" Litho. Button,**
1959. Came on doll. - **$20 $40 $65**

❑ **BUG-22. "Help Crippled Children" Litho. Tin Tab,**
c. 1950s. - **$3 $8 $12**

BUG-23

❑ **BUG-23. Bugs Bunny Beanie,**
1950s. - **$40 $100 $200**

BUG-24

BUG-25

❑ **BUG-24. "Bugs Bunny" Largest Version Stuffed Felt Doll,**
1950s. 19" tall toes to ears. - **$65 $125 $250**

❑ **BUG-25. Bugs Bunny Ceramic Planter,**
1950s. - **$10 $35 $50**

BUG-26

❑ **BUG-26. "Magic Paint Book",**
1961. Post Sugar Coated Corn Flakes. Includes offer for Kool-Aid "Smiling Pitcher." -
**$8 $15 $35**

BUG-27

❑ **BUG-27. "March Of Comics" #273,**
1965. Various sponsors. - **$5 $10 $20**

BUG-28

❑ **BUG-28. Talking Alarm Clock,**
1974. 17 1/2" tall. Says "Eh, Wake Up Doc." -
**$15 $30 $60**

BUG-29

❑ **BUG-29. Club Member's Litho. Tin Button,**
1976. Has Warner Bros. copyright but no club sponsor indicated. Colorful 2-1/4". - **$10 $20 $35**

BUG-30

❑ **BUG-30. Mug and Premium Offer,**
1988. Mug comes with premium offer coupon for Bugs Bunny Vitamins.
Mug - **$5 $10 $30**
Paperwork - **$5**

(SERIES 1 BOX)

BUG-31

BUG-32

❑ **BUG-31. Comic Ball Cards Box,**
1990. Series 1 box with 34 packs of cards. Each silver-colored pack holds 12 cards. Each card has new artwork and stories from Chuck Jones. Each pack - **$5**
Box - **$5 $10 $25**

❑ **BUG-32. Comic Ball Cards Box with Display,**
1990. Series 2 box with 34 packs of cards. Each silver-colored pack holds 12 cards.
Each pack - **$5**
Box - **$5 $10 $25**
Display - **$100**

BUG-33

❑ **BUG-33. Commemorative Figurine,**
1991. By Ron Lee. Bugs and Daffy shown in a scene from the cartoon "The Adventures of Robin Hood Bugs." Edition of 1250. - **$150**

BUG-34

❑ **BUG-34. "Space Jam" Cookie Jar,**
1996. With Bugs and Michael Jordan. - **$175**

BUG-35

BUG-36

❑ **BUG-35. "Space Jam" Figure with Tag,**
1996. Sold at theaters. - **$5 $15 $35**

❑ **BUG-36. U.S. Olympic 13" Resin Figure,**
1996. U.S. Olympic team special edition with official 4 1/2" x 3 1/2" Red, White and Blue tag. Made in China however! - **$10 $35 $50**

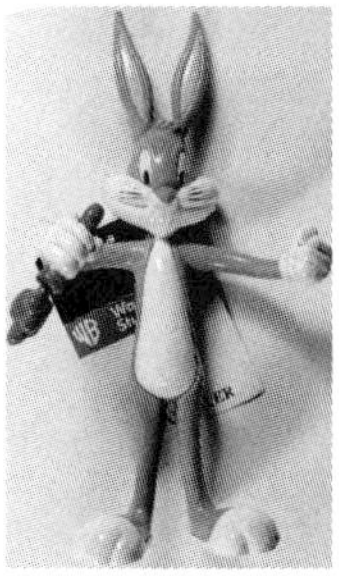

BUG-37

BUG-38

❑ **BUG-37. Bugs Flexible Figure with Tag,**
1997. 8" Warner store exclusive. Paint rubs off easily. - **$20**

❑ **BUG-38. Bugs Bunny Bobbing Head Figure,**
1997. Warner Brothers store. - **$5 $10 $35**

BUG-40

BUG-41

❑ **BUG-40. Bugs Bean Figure with 2 Tags,**
1997. - **$10**

❑ **BUG-41. Bugs Bunny Pencils on Card,**
1998. WIth free Bugs bookmark. - **$1 $2 $4**

BUG-42

BUG-43

❑ **BUG-42. Bugs Bunny Easter Bean Figure,**
1998. With tag. - **$20**

❑ **BUG-43. Bugs Bunny Stars and Stripes Bean Figure,**
1998. With tag. - **$18**

(BOX)

**(Two views of the action)**

BUG-39

❑ **BUG-39. Large Electric Christmas Display,**
1997. Boxed. 2' 4" tall. Shows Bugs as Santa and the "Taz" as his reindeer. When working, characters spin in circle. - **$150**

BUG-44

BUG-45

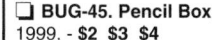

❑ **BUG-44. Snowman Bugs Bunny "Peace on Earth" Bean Figure,**
1998. With tag. - **$28**

❑ **BUG-45. Pencil Box,**
1999. - **$2 $3 $4**

# Bullwinkle and Rocky

**Rocky the flying squirrel and his pal Bullwinkle the moose were created by Jay Ward in one of television's successful early animated cartoons. From 1959 to 1963 they battled the evil little Mr. Big and his cohorts Boris and Natasha in *Rocky and His Friends* on ABC, in *The Bullwinkle Show* from 1961 to 1964 on NBC and then back to ABC until 1973. Other regulars included Mr. Peabody the time-traveling beagle, his human friend Sherman, the inept Mountie Dudley Do-Right, his criminal foe Snidely Whiplash, and to a lesser degree, aliens Cloyd and Glidney. *Fractured Fairy-Tales*, offering skewed send-ups of classic folk and fairy-tales, was another regular feature of the show. Comic books started appearing in the early 1960s. A feature film starring Robert DeNiro (!) as Fearless Leader, Jason Alexander as Boris Badanov, and Rene Russo as Natasha had a disappointingly brief appearance in theatrical release in 2000 and has since made the leap to home video. Toys, games and other merchandise usually carry the copyright of P.A.T.-Ward Productions.**

BUL-1

BUL-2

❑ **BUL-1. "P-F Flyers" Bullwinkle & Rocky 12x21" Cardboard Store Sign,**
c. 1959. B. F. Goodrich Co. Also promotes Rin-Tin-Tin, The Lone Ranger, Captain Gallant. - **$50 $100 $200**

❑ **BUL-2. "Rocky and His Friends" Little Golden Book #408,**
1960. - **$10 $25 $50**

BUL-3

❑ **BUL-3. Original Cover Art for "Rocky and His Friends" Little Golden Book,**
1960. 12 1/2" x 10 1/2" painting. - **$2500**

BUL-4

BUL-5

BUL-6

❑ **BUL-4. Rocky The Flying Squirrel Glazed Ceramic Figure,**
1960. 4-3/4" tall store item. - **$65 $150 $250**

❑ **BUL-5. "Mr. Peabody" Glazed Ceramic Figural Bank,**
1960. Store item. 5-3/4" tall. - **$100 $250 $350**

❑ **BUL-6. "Mr. Sherman" Glazed Ceramic Figural Bank,**
1960. Store item. 5-7/8" tall. Japan. - **$100 $250 $350**

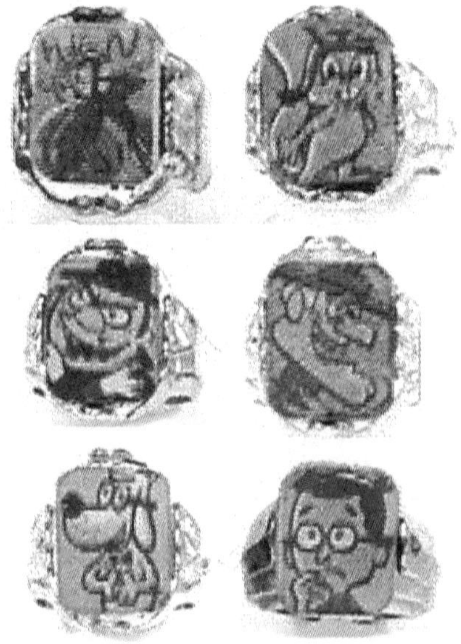
BUL-7

❑ **BUL-7. Jay Ward Character Flicker Rings Set,**
1961. Scarce rings distributed through vending machines. Each is on silvered plastic base although flickers have also been seen on modern bases marked "China." Two views of each character: Bullwinkle, Rocky, Boris, Dudley Do-Right, Sherman, Mr. Peabody.
Original Base Each - **$125 $250 $350**
Modern Base - **$75 $125 $200**

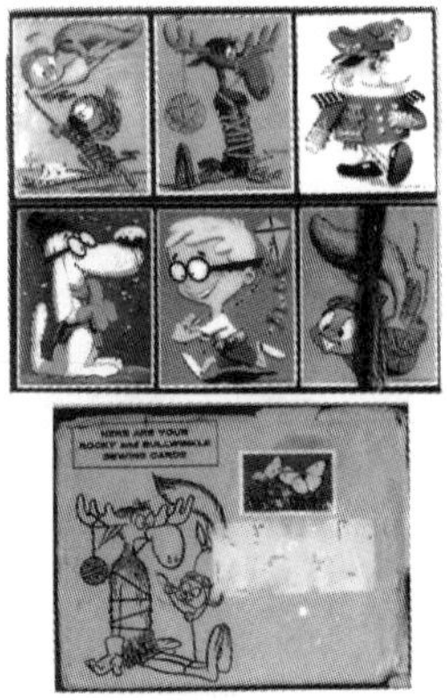
BUL-8

❑ **BUL-8. "Sewing Cards" Kit With Envelope,**
1961. Set of six cards for yarn threading.
Near Mint In Mailer - **$150**
Each Card- **$5 $10 $20**

BUL-9

BUL-10

❑ **BUL-9. "March Of Comics" Booklet,**
1962. Child Life Shoes. Comic #233. - **$15 $35 $80**

❑ **BUL-10. "Moosylvania" Litho. Tab And Decal,**
1962. Issuer unknown. 1-1/4" tall unfolded tab reads "The 52nd State" while 3-1/2" decal proclaims "Statehood." Each - **$3 $8 $12**

BUL-11

❑ **BUL-11. "Bullwinkle" Three Reel View-Master Pack With Story Booklet,**
1962. #B515. - **$10 $20 $35**

BUL-12

❑ **BUL-12. "Electric Quiz Fun Game",**
1962. General Mills. Battery operated. - **$25 $40 $85**

BUL-13

❑ **BUL-13. Bullwinkle's Safety Coloring Book,**
1963. General Mills. - **$10 $25 $50**

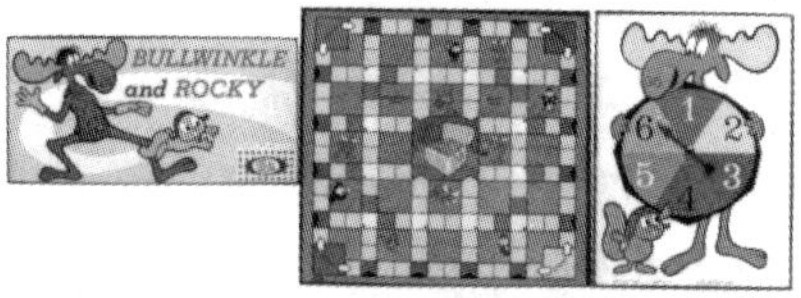


BUL-14

❑ **BUL-14. "Bullwinkle And Rocky" Boxed Game,**
1963. Ideal #2216-0-200. - **$25 $60 $100**

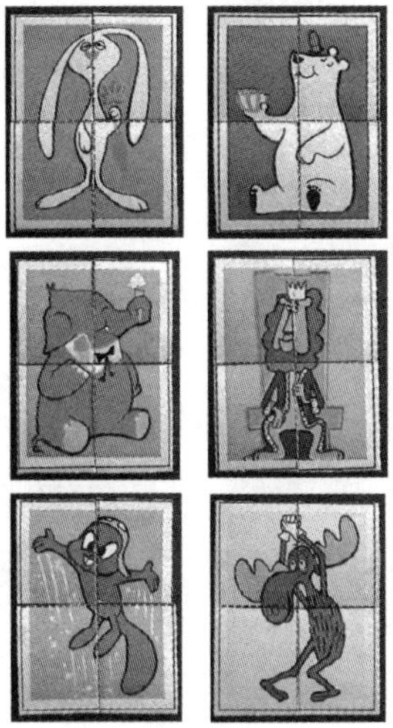

BUL-15

❑ **BUL-15. Bullwinkle's Mix 'N Match Game,**
1964. Cheerios. Set of six character cut-outs which comprised one of eight cut-out games on the back panels of the cereal boxes.
Each Box Used Complete - **$50 $100 $150**
Each Game Cut Complete - **$10 $20 $30**

(CLOSE-UP)

BUL-16

❑ **BUL-16. Cheerios 21x28" Double-Sided Paper Sign,**
c. 1963. - **$40 $75 $140**

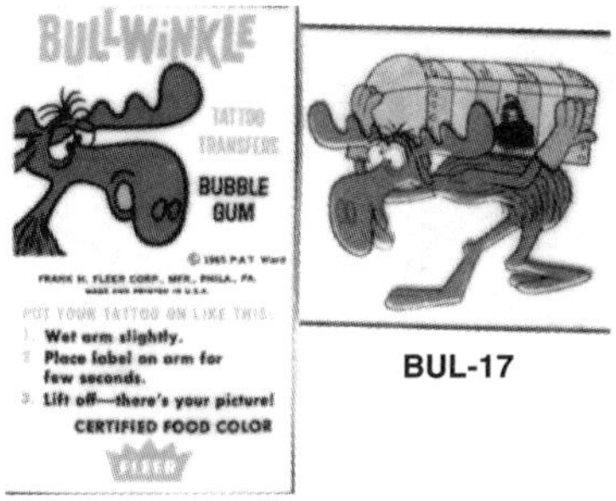


BUL-17

BUL-18

❑ **BUL-17. "Tattoo" Fleer Gum Wrapper,**
1965. Example from set with different tattoo images. - **$8 $15 $25**

❑ **BUL-18. "Bullwinkle" Follow The Colors Portrait,**
1966. Cheerios box back.
Used Complete Box - **$50 $85 $175**
Panel Only - **$10 $20 $35**

BUL-19

❑ **BUL-19. Bullwinkle With Cheerios Kid Drink Cup,**
1969. Cheerios premium made of Melmac. Other pieces in set believed to be plate and bowl. Each - **$5 $10 $25**

BUL-20

BUL-21

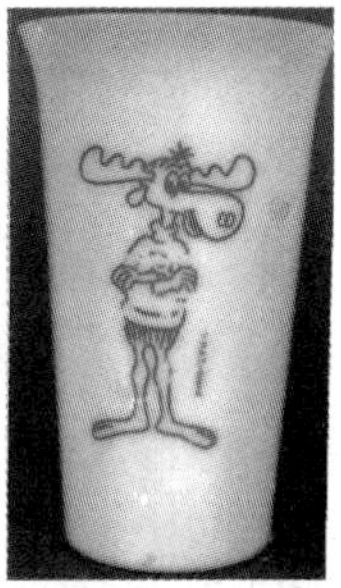

BUL-22

❑ **BUL-20. Bullwinkle And Cheerios Kid Store Clerk Cello. Button,**
1960s. 3" full color. - **$100 $200 $300**

❑ **BUL-21. Bullwinkle Trading Coin,**
1960s. Old London Dipsy Doodles and Corn Doodles. Numbered set of 60 plastic coins with paper inserts picturing Bullwinkle and other Jay Ward characters.
Each - **$5 $10 $15**

❑ **BUL-22. Plastic Tumbler,**
1960s. Issuer unknown. - **$15 $25 $40**

(BOTH PICTURED IN ADS)

BUL-23 BUL-24

**BUL-23. T-Shirt,**
1970. Charlton Comics. - **$35 $75 $150**

**BUL-24. Sweatshirt,**
1970. Charlton Comics. - **$50 $100 $175**

BUL-25

BUL-26

❑ **BUL-25. Fan Club Membership Card,**
1970. Charlton Comics. Part of fan club kit. - **$5 $10 $15**

❑ **BUL-26. Bullwinkle Pez Dispenser,**
1970s. Issued with yellow antlers and either brown or yellow body. - **$40 $150 $225**

BUL-27

❑ **BUL-27. Bullwinkle And Rocky Dakin Figures In Cartoon Theater Boxes,**
1976. Each Near Mint Boxed **- $65**
Each Loose **- $10 $20 $35**

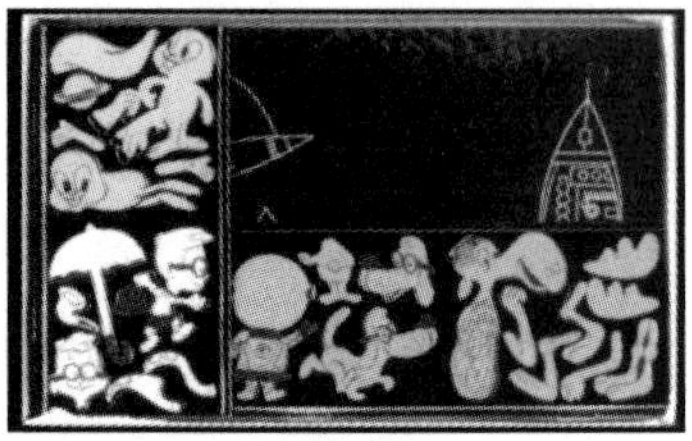
BUL-28

❑ **BUL-28. Colorforms Set ,**
1970s. Interior shown. - **$25 $50 $75**

BUL-29

❑ **BUL-29. Pepsi Collector Series Glasses,**
1970s. Each - **$8 $12 $18**

BUL-30

BUL-31

❑ **BUL-30. Rocky Plush Figure,**
1982. From Wallace Berrie & Company. With cloth hat and tag. - **$15 $40 $75**

❑ **BUL-31. Bullwinkle Plush Figure,**
1982. From Wallace Berrie & Company.
17" tall with tag. - **$15 $35 $65**

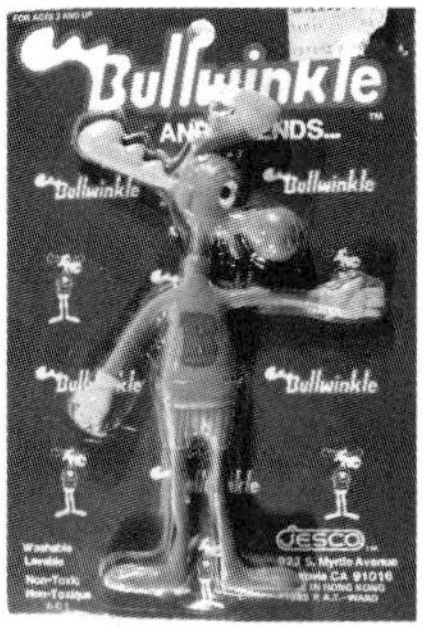

BUL-32

BUL-33

❑ **BUL-32. Bullwinkle Bendy on Card,**
1985. - **$5 $10 $25**

❑ **BUL-33. Rocky Ceramic Figure,**
1980s. 2 1/2" tall. - **$5 $15 $35**

BUL-34

❑ **BUL-34. Bullwinkle Bobbing Head Figure,**
1996. Ward Productions. - **$10 $30 $45**

BUL-35

❑ **BUL-35. Rocky & Bullwinkle Christmas Ornament,**
1996. Carlton Cards. - **$30**

BUL-36

❑ **BUL-36. Hot Wheels Car-Toon Friends Die-Cut Car Series,**
1998. Set includes Natasha's "Saltflat Racer," Rocky's "XT-3," Bullwinkle's "Double Vision," and Boris' "Lakester." On card. Each - **$7**

BUL-37

❑ **BUL-37. Mr. Peabody Plastic Figure,**
1999. Comes with tag. - **$10 $15 $20**

BUL-38

❑ **BUL-38. Mr. Peabody and Sherman Plush Dolls,**
1999. Large - **$30** each.
Small - **$15** each.

BUL-39

❑ **BUL-39. TV Ad 2-1/2" Cello. Button,**
c. 1990s. Channel 5, unidentified location. By Reno, Nevada maker without copyright. - **$5 $10 $15**

BUL-40

❑ **BUL-40. "The Adventures of Rocky and Bullwinkle" Flying Playset,**
2000. Promotes movie. Store bought. - **$20**

BUL-41 BUL-42

❑ **BUL-41. "The Adventures of Rocky and Bullwinkle" Plush Rocky Doll on Card,**
2000. Promotes movie. - **$20**

❑ **BUL-42. "The Adventures of Rocky and Bullwinkle" Talking Rocky Doll,**
2000. On card-type box. - **$20**

## Burns and Allen

**Longtime vaudeville stars, George Burns (1896-1996) and Gracie Allen (1906-1964) made a successful transition to radio in 1932 and broadcast continuously on CBS or NBC until Gracie decided to retire in 1958. George was the straight man, Gracie the scatterbrain and the show ranged from standup gags to situation comedy. The program also introduced Mel Blanc's Happy Postman character. Sponsors over the years included Robert Burns and White Owl cigars, Campbell's soup, Grape-Nuts Flakes, Chesterfield cigarettes, Hinds lotion, Hormel Packing Co., Swan soap, Maxwell House coffee and Block Drugs. A popular half-hour TV show aired from 1950 to 1958 on CBS. "Say goodnight, Gracie."**

BUR-1 BUR-2

❑ **BUR-1. "Gracie Allen's Anniversary Gift To Guy Lombardo" Booklet,**
1933. General Cigar Co., maker of Robert Burns cigars. Humor dialogue between Gracie and George Burns on what to buy orchestra leader Lombardo for his fourth anniversary of radio broadcasts.- **$10 $18 $30**

❑ **BUR-2. Photo,**
1937. Philadelphia Record newspaper premium. - **$10 $25 $45**

BUR-3 BUR-4

❑ **BUR-3. Grape-Nuts 12x18" Sign,**
1930s. Scarce. Printed on both sides and with hanging cord. - **$300 $600 $1200**

❑ **BUR-4. Fan Photo,**
1930s. Campbell's Soups. - **$15 $25 $40**

BUR-5

BUR-6

❑ **BUR-5. Fan Photo,**
1930s. Columbia Broadcasting System. - **$10 $20 $30**

❑ **BUR-6. Radio Broadcast Listing Folder,**
1930s. Grape-Nuts. - **$15 $30 $45**

BUR-7

BUR-8

❑ **BUR-7. "Gracie Allen's Missing Brother" Boxed Jigsaw Puzzle,**
1930s. Store item by Commanday-Roth Co. Comes with leaflet describing the search for him in pictured crowd scene. Boxed - **$15 $30 $50**
Loose - **$8 $15 $30**

❑ **BUR-8. Gracie Allen "How To Become President" Cello. Button,**
c. 1940s. - **$35 $75 $125**

BUR-9

❑ **BUR-9. "George Burns And Gracie Allen/Swan Soap" Display Sign,**
1940s. 11x14". - **$15 $30 $75**

BUR-10

❑ **BUR-10. "Motorola TV Coffee Servers" Boxed Set,**
1950s. Motorola, maker of TV sets. Offered at 99 cents per set, glass items by Pyrex. Boxed - **$25 $40 $65**

## Buster Brown

**Buster Brown was the creation of R. F. Outcault (1863-1925). The color strip first appeared in the Sunday New York Herald of May 4, 1902, a half-dozen years after Outcault's first great strip, *The Yellow Kid*, appeared in the New York World. Buster was a pint-size prankster, constantly bedeviling those around him, then resolving to behave better in the future. His ever-present companion was Tige, a Boston terrier with an evil toothy grin. The strip was a huge success and ran until 1920. A number of newspaper strip reprint books and advertising booklets featuring cartoon panels appeared in the early part of the century. Outcault sold merchandising rights to the Buster Brown character to more than 50 manufacturers of everything from bread to soap to harmonicas; today we can still buy Buster Brown shoes and children's clothes. A weekly drama based on the strip ran on CBS in 1929 and was revived as *Smilin' Ed McConnell's Buster Brown Gang* for NBC. It aired from 1943 to 1953, when it transferred to television, retaining Buster Brown Shoes as sponsor. On McConnell's death in 1954, Andy Devine took his place and the show was renamed *Andy's Gang*. The star of the show was Froggy the Gremlin. Buster Brown has been a rich source of toys, comic books and premiums for about a century and still going strong. "Plunk your magic twanger, Froggy!"**

BWN-1

❑ **BWN-1. "New York Herald/Young Folks" Cello. Button,**
c. 1902. Early newspaper issue. -
**$75 $150 $300**

BWN-2

❑ **BWN-2. "Buster Brown And His Bubble" Postcard,**
1903. From numbered set of 10. The Yellow Kid appears on cards 3, 6, 8, 9, and 10.
Each - **$15 $30 $50**

BWN-3

❑ **BWN-3. "Brown's Blue Ribbon Book Of Jokes And Jingles",**
1904. Scarce. Brown Shoe Co. Considered the first comic book premium. This is the first of four books in a series titled *Jokes and Jingles*. This first book came in four versions. Earliest printings include Pore Li'l Mose, while later printings replace him with the Yellow Kid. See BWN-13 and BWN-21. - **$300 $1200 $2400**

BWN-4

❑ **BWN-4. Bloomingdale's Christmas Postcard,**
1904. One of the most sought-after of all Buster Brown cards. - **$50 $75 $150**

BWN-6

BWN-5

❑ **BWN-5. "Buster Brown's Experiences With Pond's Extract" Booklet,**
1904. - **$125 $250 $500**

❑ **BWN-6. "Buster Brown Bread" Cello. Button,**
c. 1905. Issued in both yellow and gray rim variations. - **$15 $25 $50**

BWN-7

BWN-8

❑ **BWN-7. "Buster Brown Drawing Book,"**
1904. Issued by Collins Bread. 3x4-7/8" with eight pages. - **$50 $100 $300**

❑ **BWN-8. "Buster Brown Bread" Ad Cards,**
1904. Back has imprint of baker in Lancaster, Pa. Each card is 3-1/2x5-3/8".
Each - **$10 $20 $50**

BWN-9

BWN-10

❑ **BWN-9. "Buster Brown Shoes" Cello. Pocket Mirror,**
c. 1905. - **$75 $175 $325**

❑ **BWN-10. Enamel And Brass Stickpin,**
c. 1905. Initials on bottom edge stand for 'Buster Brown Blue Ribbon Shoes'. -
**$60 $150 $225**

BWN-11

❑ **BWN-11. "Quick Meal Steel Ranges" Booklet,**
c. 1905. - **$35 $125 $250**

BWN-12

❑ **BWN-12. "Buster Brown's Pranks" Comic Strip Reprint Book,**
1905. Published by Frederick A. Stokes Co. -
**$375 $1300 $2000**

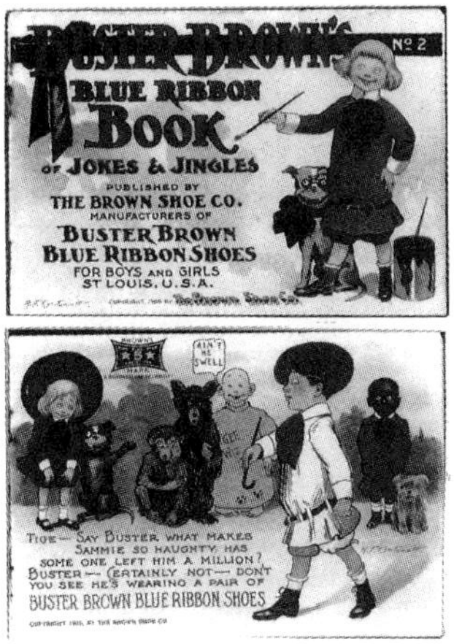


BWN-13

❑ **BWN-13. "Buster Brown's Blue Ribbon Book Of Jokes & Jingles No. 2",**
1905. One of earliest premium comic books. See BWN-3 and BWN-21. - **$150 $400 $800**

BWN-14

❑ **BWN-14. Original Watercolor of "Tige",**
Early 1900s. A small picture of Buster's sidekick Boston Terrier, signed by RF Outcault. - **$500**

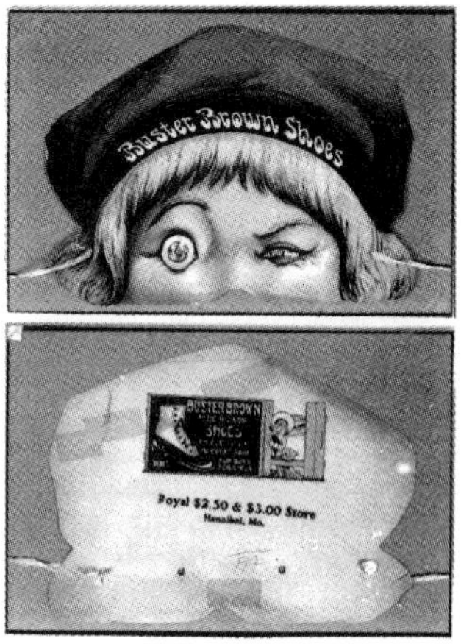


BWN-15

❑ **BWN-15. Paper Mask,**
c. 1905. - **$50 $100 $200**

BWN-16

❑ **BWN-16. "Buster Brown Stocking Magazine",**
1906. - **$25 $50 $100**

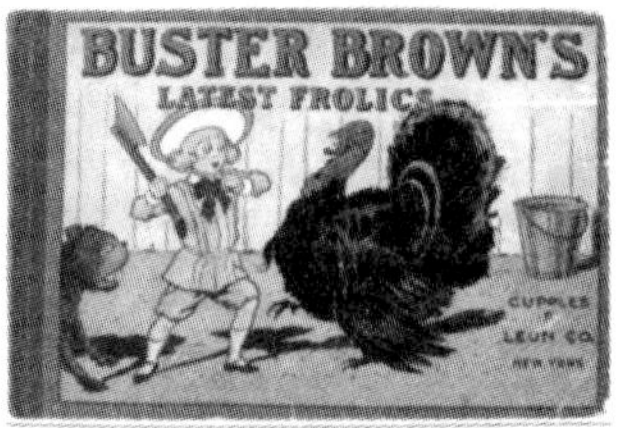


BWN-17

❑ **BWN-17. "Buster Brown's Latest Frolics",**
1907. Comic strip reprint book published by Cupples & Leon Co. - **$160 $550 $950**

BWN-18

BWN-19

❑ **BWN-18. "Buster Brown's Amusing Capers" Comic Strip Reprint Book,**
1908. Cupples & Leon Co. - **$125 $450 $750**

❑ **BWN-19. Buster Brown Mirror,**
1900s. Shoe Premium. - **$40 $80 $160**

BWN-20

❑ **BWN-20. Assortment of Postcards from several series,**
1900s. Buster Brown and his dog Tige.-
**$10 $20 $40**

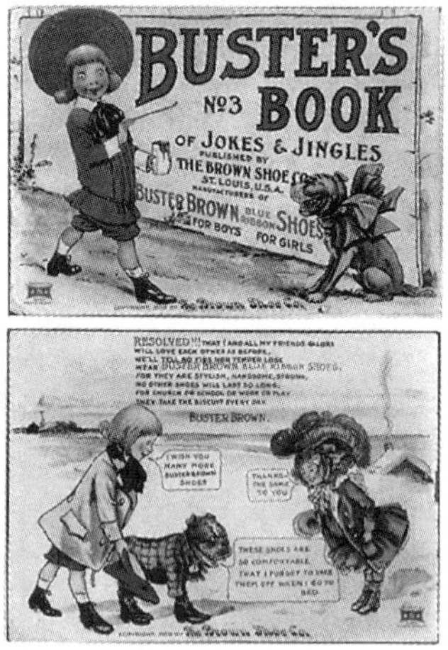


BWN-21

❑ **BWN-21. "Buster's Book Of Jokes And Jingles No. 3",**
1900s. Third of four in series. See BWN-3 and BWN-13. - **$150 $400 $800**

BWN-22

BWN-23

❑ **BWN-22. "Buster Brown Shoes" Cello. Button,**
c. 1910. Red background. - **$60 $150 $225**

❑ **BWN-23. Black Background Version Cello. Button,**
c. 1910. - **$75 $175 $250**

BWN-24

❑ **BWN-24. "You Can't 'Buster Brown' Hose Supporter" Advertising Cello. Buttons,**
c. 1910. Buster Brown Hosiery. Examples also known with Buster hugging Tige and Buster falling down. Each - **$12 $20 $40**

BWN-25

❑ **BWN-25. "Buster Brown Blue Ribbon Shoes" Watch Fob,**
c. 1910. Silvered white metal, 1-3/4" oval. - **$100 $200 $300**

BWN-26

BWN-27

❑ **BWN-26. "Buster Brown Shoes" Store Ad Fan,**
c. 1910. Diecut cardboard with wooden rod. Imprinted for various stores. - **$75 $150 $275**

❑ **BWN-27. Cigar Tin,**
c. 1910 Store item. Price includes lid. -
**$400 $1000 $1600**

BWN-28

BWN-29

❑ **BWN-28. Entry Card For Pocketwatch Premium,**
c. 1912. - **$20 $40 $80**

❑ **BWN-29. Buster And Tige Pocketwatch,**
c. 1912. - **$200 $400 $700**

BWN-30

❑ **BWN-30. "Buster Brown's Book Of Travels",**
1912. Brown Shoe Co. 12 pages 3-1/2x5". -
**$125 $250 $500**

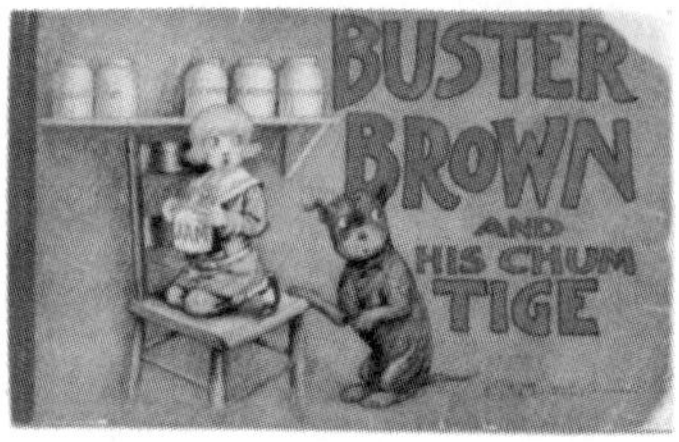


BWN-31

❑ **BWN-31. "Buster Brown And His Chum Tige" Comic Strip Reprint Book,**
1915. Published by Frederick A. Stokes Co. -
**$150 $525 $900**

BWN-32

BWN-33

❏ **BWN-32**. **Celluloid Oval With Stickpin,**
c. 1917. Buster Brown Shoes. 1-3/8" tall with color portrait of Buster in Army uniform on red, white and blue background. - **$35 $75 $150**

❏ **BWN-33. Wood Whistle,**
1910s. Shoe Premium - **$25 $50 $75**

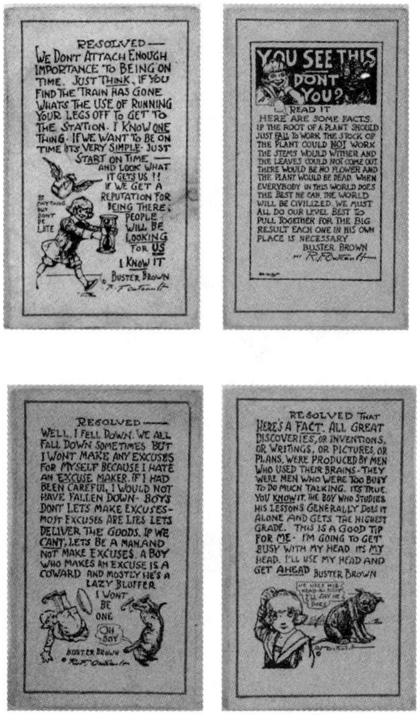


BWN-34

❏ **BWN-34. Bread Premium Cards,**
1910s. Scarce.
Each - **$15 $30 $50**

BWN-35

BWN-36

❏ **BWN-35. Buster Brown 4" Bisque Figure,**
1910s. With movable arms. - **$125 $350 $500**

❏ **BWN-36. Buster Brown 2" Bisque Figure,**
1920s. Arms do not move. - **$50 $100 $150**

BWN-37

❏ **BWN-37. "Buster Brown Walking Club" Oval Cello. Button,**
c. 1920s. Includes "Tread Straight" trademark arrow symbol. - **$20 $40 $85**

BWN-38

❏ **BWN-38. Magic Kit,**
1934. Includes "Magic Ball, My Magic Ink, My Secret Ink, Trick Hospital Bandage".
In Mailer - **$15 $25 $60**

BWN-39

❏ **BWN-39**. **Jointed Celluloid Seated Figure,**
1930s. Issuer unknown. Beautifully colored figure with movable arms and legs but with legs molded in seated position. Comes in two sizes, either 3-1/4" tall or 5-1/4" tall as measured seated. Marked "Made In Japan" on reverse and may have Japan paper sticker under seat.
Each - **$50 $150 $300**

BWN-40

BWN-41

❏ **BWN-40. Cello. Fob,**
1930s. - **$25 $75 $150**

❏ **BWN-41. Litho. Tin Clicker,**
1930s. - **$15 $25 $45**

BWN-42

BWN-43

❑ **BWN-42. Felt Patch,**
1930s. - **$10 $20 $35**

❑ **BWN-43. Buster Brown Blotter,**
1930s. - **$20 $40 $65**

BWN-44

BWN-45

❑ **BWN-44. Tin Whistle,**
1930s. Shoe Premium - **$30 $70 $100**

❑ **BWN-45. Tin Whistle,**
1930s. - **$20 $40 $65**

BWN-46

❑ **BWN-46. Buster Brown Comics #1,**
1945. Scarce. Brown Shoe Co. No number and no date, covers refer to various shoe stores. - **$62 $187 $600**

BWN-47

BWN-48

❑ **BWN-47. Slide,**
1940s. Premium slide for neckerchief. - **$30 $60 $100**

❑ **BWN-48. Card,**
1940s. Buster Brown Shoes premium. When folded, eyes and mouth move when pulled. - **$20 $40 $60**

BWN-49

❑ **BWN-49. Toy Currency,**
c. 1940s. Various denominations collected for prizes. Each -**$3 $8 $12**

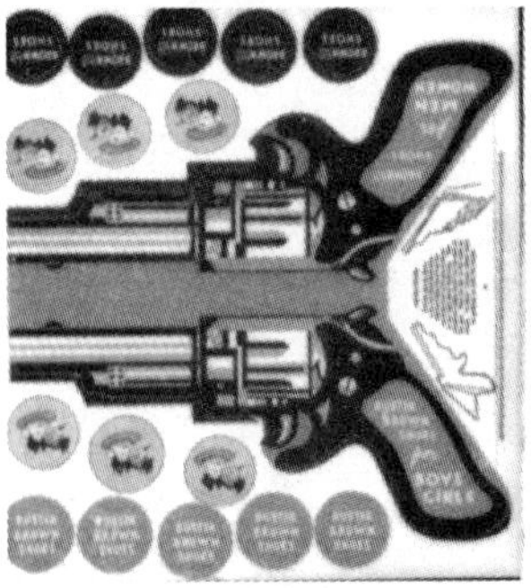

BWN-50

❑ **BWN-50. Punch-Out Gun Sheet,**
1940s. Unpunched - **$15 $25 $50**

BWN-51

❑ **BWN-51. Buster Brown Knife,**
1940s. Shoe premium, rare. - **$50 $100 $175**

BWN-52

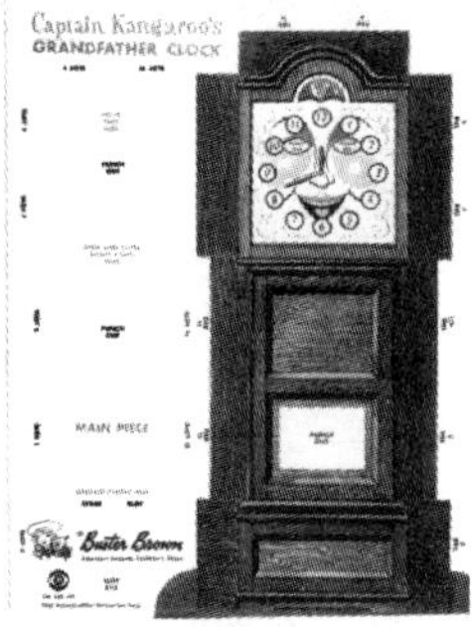


BWN-53

❑ **BWN-52. 50th Anniversary Commemorative Coin,**
1954. Gold plastic medalet inscribed on both sides by text for 50 years of children's shoes. - **$5 $10 $15**

❑ **BWN-53. "Captain Kangaroo's Grandfather Clock" Punch-Out Sheet,**
1956. Buster Brown Shoes, copyright Keeshan-Miller Enterprises. Unpunched - **$10 $30 $50**

BWN-54

❑ **BWN-54. Buster Brown Beanie,**
1950s. - **$15 $25 $50**

BWN-55

❑ **BWN-55. "Buster Brown Textiles Inc." Figural Cast Metal Award Bank,**
1964. 5" tall. - **$50 $100 $150**

BWN-56

❑ **BWN-56. Buster Brown Secret Agent Periscope,**
1960s. - **$20 $40 $65**

BWN-57

❑ **BWN-57. Buster Brown/Capt. Kangaroo Hat Punch-out,**
1960s. - **$20 $30 $50**

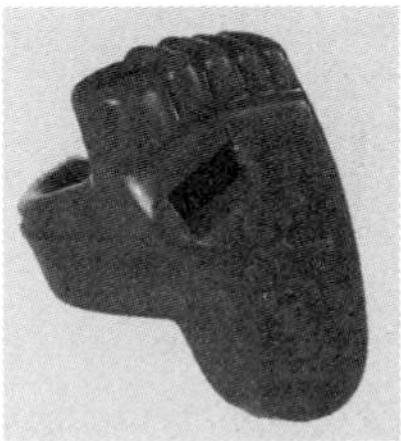

BWN-58 BWN-59

❑ **BWN-58. Plastic Flicker Ring,**
1960s. Image changes from Buster and Tige to "Stop" and "Go" signs. - **$15 $25 $40**

❑ **BWN-59. "Buster Brown Big Foot" Plastic Whistle Ring,**
c. 1960s. Blowing into big toe creates whistling sound. - **$10 $15 $20**

BWN-60 BWN-61

❑ **BWN-60. Palm Puzzle,**
1960s. - **$5 $12 $25**

❑ **BWN-61. Child's Watch,**
1975. - **$20 $45 $85**

## California Raisins

**In the mid-1980s much of America was captivated by a bunch of cool raisins with an irresistable beat--the California Raisins had arrived. Created in clay by Will Vinton for the California Raisin Advisory Board (CALRAB) and animated for musical television commercials by the Claymation process, these diminutive sports were anything but dry. The commercials began in 1986, featuring the raisins' signature song *I Heard It Through The Grapevine.* Small vinyl figures of the raisins were widely promoted as premiums or giveaways by CALRAB.**

CAL-1

❑ **CAL-1. Musical Sandwich Toy,**
1987. Del Monte Fruit Snacks. Figural plastic with push button to play "Grapevine" song.
Boxed - **$15 $30 $60**
Unboxed - **$10 $20 $30**

CAL-2

❑ **CAL-2. Large Plaster Figure Bank,**
c. 1987. Unauthorized store or carnival item. 15" tall with 10" diameter. - **$15 $30 $75**

CAL-3 CAL-4

❑ **CAL-3. Vinyl Bank,**
1987. - **$5 $15 $30**

❑ **CAL-4. Figure Keychain,**
1987. 3 1/4" tall. - **$3 $6 $12**

CAL-5 CAL-6

❑ **CAL-5. California Raisins "Duet" Music Toys On Card,**
1987. Store item by Imperial Toy Corp. - **$5 $10 $15**

❑ **CAL-6. "California Raisins Fan Club" Watch Set,**
1987. Nelsonic. Packaged - **$10 $20 $30**

CAL-7

❑ **CAL-7. Store Display,**
1988. Hardee's Food Systems. Came with six vinyl figures. Complete - **$40 $75 $135**

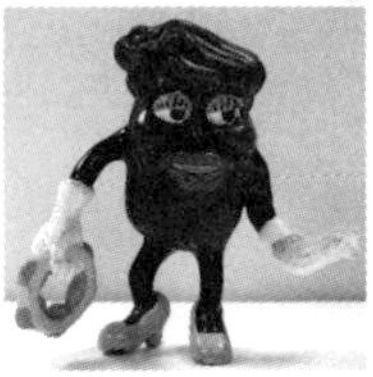

CAL-8 CAL-9

❑ **CAL-8. Girl Figure with Tambourine,**
1988. 2 3/4" tall. - **$2 $5 $10**

❑ **CAL-9. Figure with Bass Fiddle,**
1988. 2 3/4" tall. - **$2 $5 $10**

CAL-10 CAL-11

❑ **CAL-10. Valentine Boy Figure,**
1988. 2 3/4" tall. - **$2 $5 $10**

❑ **CAL-11. Valentine Girl Figure,**
1988. 2 3/4" tall. - **$2 $5 $10**

CAL-12

CAL-13

❑ **CAL-12. Vinyl Tote Bag,**
1988. - **$5 $10 $20**

❑ **CAL-13. Plastic Radio,**
1988. Flexible rubber arms and legs, microphone in hand. -**$15 $25 $45**

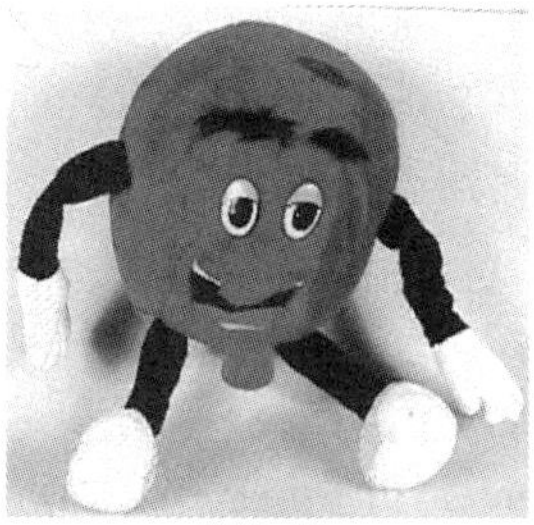
CAL-14

❑ **CAL-14. Large Plush And Fabric Stuffed Doll,**
1980s. Store item with no apparent CALRAB licensing. Torso is about 8" diameter of maroon soft plush. - **$10 $20 $35**

## Campbell Kids

**Philadelphia artist Grace Drayton (1877-1923) created the Campbell Kids to promote the company's canned soup in 1904. She called them Roly-Polys, and after initial use in cards on Philadelphia streetcars the kids greeted the world at large in advertising in the *Ladies' Home Journal* in 1905. Since then the kids have had a long and distinguished promotional career in various forms, such as dolls, salt & pepper shakers, lunch boxes, etc., and in print advertising. In 1976 the kids were dressed in colonial costumes to mark the nation's bicentennial. Today's kids are a bit taller and thinner than the originals, but they're still easily recognized and still selling soup.**

CAM-1

❑ **CAM-1. Early Postcards,**
1910. Jos. Campbell Co. Four numbered cards apparently published in a strip as small perforations mark the margins. Superb color art, probably by Grace Drayton but unsigned.
Each - **$10 $20 $45**

CAM-2

CAM-3

❑ **CAM-2. "Campbell's Menu Book,"**
1910. Softcover 48-page booklet of recipes for 30 days of the month based on 21 varieties of soups. Campbell Kids are pictured on cover and title page. - **$10 $20 $45**

❑ **CAM-3. "The Optimist" Booklet,**
1932. Published monthly c. 1932-1940. Superb color cover. Each - **$10 $20 $35**

CAM-4

CAM-5

❑ **CAM-4. Place Cards With Envelope,**
c. 1930s. Set of three to be divided into six bridge tally place cards. Set - **$15 $25 $40**

❑ **CAM-5. "Campbell's Kid Club" Cello. Button,**
c. 1930s. 1-1/2" "Official Badge". -
**$35 $100 $175**

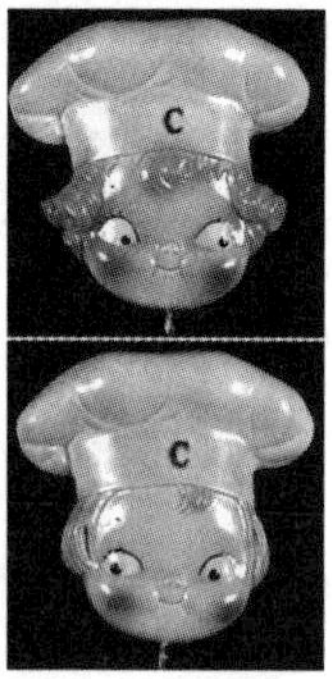
CAM-6

CAM-7

❑ **CAM-6. Hot Pad Holders,**
c. 1940s. Set of 5x5" painted plaster wall plaques with embedded wire hook hanger.
Each - **$15 $35 $60**

❑ **CAM-7. Campbell Kid Plaster Wall Plaque With Thermometer,**
c. 1940s. - **$60 $100 $160**

CAM-8

CAM-9

❑ **CAM-8. "I'm A Campbell Kid" Cello. Button,**
c. 1950s. Variation of girl kid in western outfit. -
**$15 $40 $75**

❑ **CAM-9. "I'm A Campbell Kid" Cello. Button,**
c. 1950s. Version of girl kid as milkmaid. -
**$15 $40 $75**

CAM-10

CAM-11

❑ **CAM-10. "I'm A Campbell Kid" Cello. Button,**
c. 1950s. Version of boy kid as chef. -
**$15 $40 $75**

❑ **CAM-11. "I'm A Campbell Kid" Cello. Button,**
c. 1950s. Version of boy kid as strongman. -
**$15 $40 $75**

CAM-12

CAM-13

❑ **CAM-12. Squeaker Doll,**
1950s. 7" tall painted soft hollow rubber chef doll. - **$60 $100 $200**

❑ **CAM-13. Tomato Soup And Fruit 17x22" Paper Store Sign,**
c. 1950s. Design includes chalkboard motif held by Campbell Kids. - **$20 $40 $75**

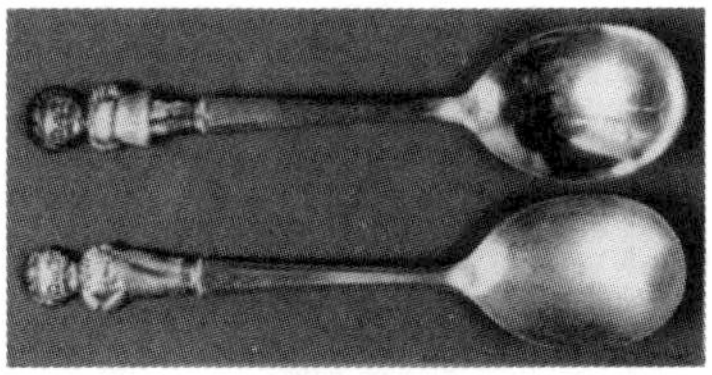

CAM-14

CAM-15

❑ **CAM-14. Campbell Kids Silver Plate Spoons,**
1950s. Each - **$8 $12 $15**

❑ **CAM-15. "Toy Electric Mixer,"**
1950s. Store item. Battery operated 5-1/2" tall tin toy. Boxed **- $20 $40 $75**

CAM-16

❑ **CAM-16. "Campbell's Tomato Soup" Pillow With Mailer,**
1960s. Made by U.S. Pillow Corp.
Near Mint Bagged - **$30**
Loose - **$5 $10 $15**

CAM-17

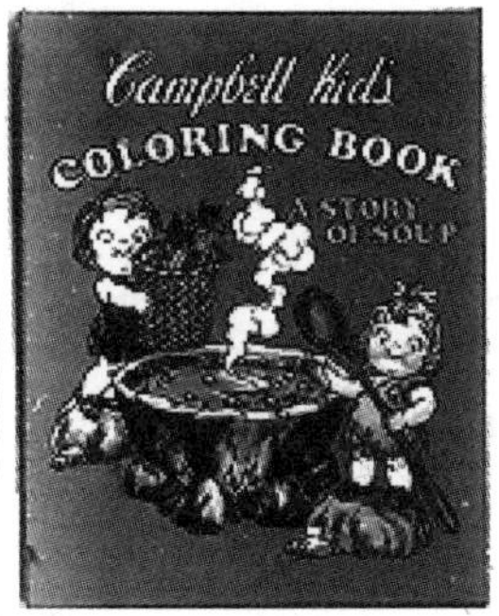


CAM-18

❑ **CAM-17. Campbell Kid Plastic Salt & Pepper Set,**
1960s. - **$15 $25 $45**

❑ **CAM-18. "A Story Of Soup" Coloring Book,**
1976. 11x14" official publication with 24 pages featuring Campbell Kids illustrating soup use from prehistoric times through present. - **$10 $20 $30**

CAM-19

❑ **CAM-19. Bicentennial Doll Set,**
1976. Pair of 10" vinyl dolls in fabric outfits offered as mail premium. Each - **$15 $30 $60**

CAM-20

❑ **CAM-20. Boxed Dolls,**
c. 1970s. Made by Product People. 7" tall painted soft vinyl boy and girl dolls in identical display carton.
Each Near Mint Boxed - **$85**
Each Loose - **$15 $30 $50**

CAM-21

❑ **CAM-21. Cookie Jar,**
1990s. - **$60**

## Cap'n Crunch

**Cap'n Crunch, a sweetened breakfast cereal that is supposed to stay crunchy down to the bottom of the bowl, was introduced in 1963 by Quaker Oats. In an unusual twist, the name of the cereal was also the name of the cartoon character created to promote it. The Cap'n was created in-house by Quaker and the TV ad campaign was designed by Jay Ward Productions, best known for Bullwinkle and Rocky animated cartoons. Other characters include Seadog, Jean LaFoote, Wilma the White Whale, Harry S. Hippo and Soggie. There have been many premium offers and giveaways.**

CRN-1

❑ **CRN-1. "I'm Dreaming Of A Wide Isthmus" Comic Booklet,**
1963. From set of three. Other titles are "Fountain of Youth" and "The Picture Pirates."
Each - **$8 $20 $50**

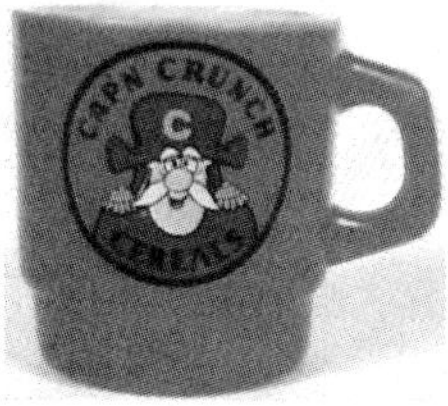


CRN-2

❑ **CRN-2. Corporate Gift Mug,**
1963. 3-1/2" tall red glass mug with color logo never available to the general public. -
**$25 $50 $85**

CRN-3

❑ **CRN-3. Cereal Box Featuring Nine Rings Packaged One Per Box,**
1964. Clockwise rings are titled: Compass Ring, Treasure Chest Ring, Pirate Gold Ring, Ship's Cannon Ring, Cutlass Ring, Pirate Puzzle Ring, Ship-In-Bottle Ring, Whistle Ring, Cap'n Crunch Statue Ring. Gordon Gold Archives.
Used Complete - **$200 $400 $650**

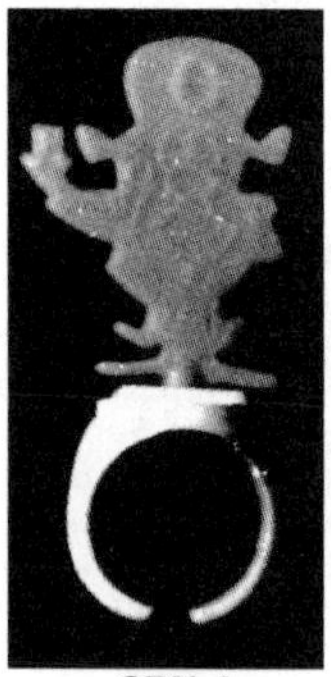

CRN-4

CRN-5

❑ **CRN-4. Cap'n Crunch Statue Plastic Ring,**
c. 1964. - **$50 $100 $150**

❑ **CRN-5. Ship's Cannon Plastic Ring,**
c. 1964. - **$30 $50 $75**

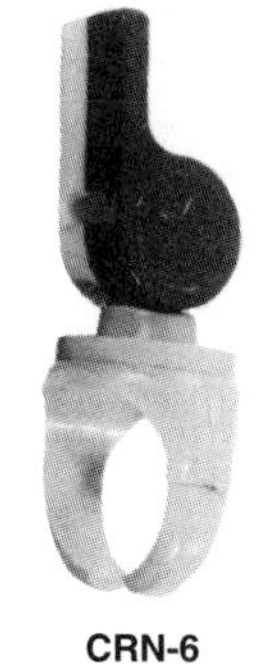

CRN-6

CRN-7

❑ **CRN-6. Whistle Plastic Ring,**
c. 1964. - **$30 $45 $60**

❑ **CRN-7. Ship-In-Bottle Plastic Ring,**
c. 1964. - **$30 $45 $60**

CRN-8

❑ **CRN-8. Cereal Box With "Sea Battle Game" Back Panel,**
c. 1964. Gordon Gold Archives. -
**$100 $200 $350**

CRN-9

❑ **CRN-9. Cereal Box With "Treasure Hunt Game" Back Panel,**
c. 1964. Gordon Gold Archives.
Used Complete - **$125 $250 $450**

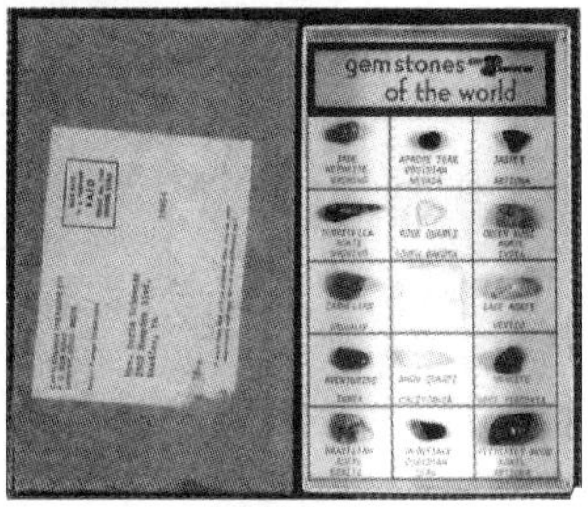


CRN-10

❑ **CRN-10. "Treasure Kit",**
c. 1965. Contains 14 "Gemstones Of The World." - **$10 $25 $40**

CRN-11

❑ **CRN-11. Plastic Treasure Chest Bank,**
1966. Came with padlock and key, 5 plastic pirate coins, insert tray useable as cereal bowl, pirate shovel (spoon), and treasure map.
Near Mint Complete - **$100**
As Bank, No Contents - **$10 $20 $35**

CRN-12

❑ **CRN-12. Cereal Box With "Hat" Offer,**
1968. Gordon Gold Archives.
Used Complete - **$150 $300 $550**

CRN-13

❑ **CRN-13. "Wiggle Figures" Offer Cereal Box,**
1969. Figures came one per box and offer pictures Cap'n Crunch and Seadog but additional figures were added to the series later. Gordon Gold Archives.
Box Used Complete - **$75 $150 $300**
Figures Assembled Each - **$15 $25 $40**

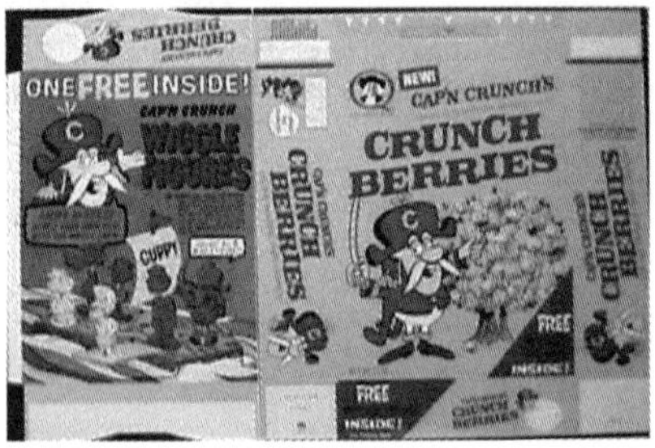

CRN-14

❑ **CRN-14. "Wiggle Figure" Offer Cereal Box Flat,**
1969. Gordon Gold Archives.
Near Mint Flat - **$450**
Used Complete - **$50 $150 $275**

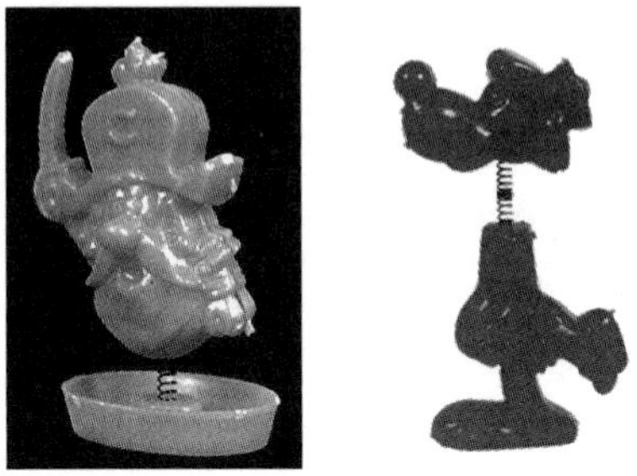
CRN-15

❑ **CRN-15. Cap'n Crunch Wiggle Figure,**
1969. Cap'n Crunch Berries. Six in set: Cap'n Crunch, Seadog, Jean LaFoote (pirate), Alfie (big boy with glasses), Little Boy (no glasses), Brunhilde (girl).
Cap'n Crunch, Seadog Near Mint Unassembled Each - **$60**
Others Near Mint Unassembled Each - **$40**
Cap'n Crunch, Seadog Assembled Each - **$15 $25 $40**
Others Assembled Each - **$10 $15 $25**

CRN-16

❑ **CRN-16. "Cap'n Crunch Coloring Book",**
1968. - **$10 $20 $35**

CRN-17

❑ **CRN-17. "Play Putty" Offer Cereal Box,**
1969. Silly Putty-like item was available free with three purchase seals.
Used Complete - **$50 $100 $165**

CRN-18

❑ **CRN-18. Cap'n Crunch Daily Log,**
1969. A combo desk calendar, engagement diary, and reference book. 120 pages. Quaker Oats gift to those who promoted cereal during 1968.- **$25 $75 $110**

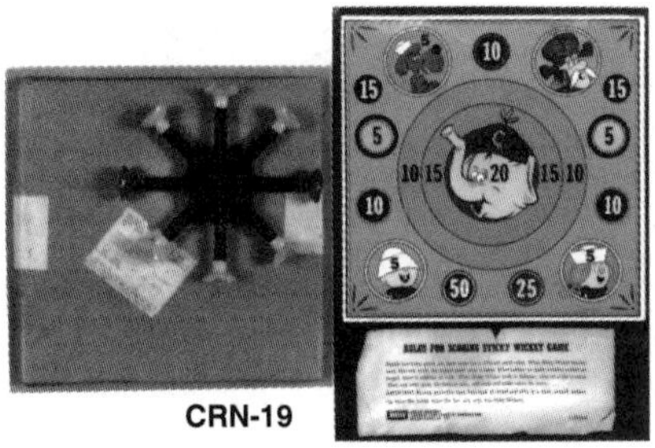
CRN-19

❑ **CRN-19. "Sticky Wicket" Target Game,**
1970. - **$10 $20 $40**

CRN-20

CRN-21

❑ **CRN-20. "Jean LaFoote" Vinyl Bank,**
1972. - **$30 $50 $100**

❑ **CRN-21. Vinyl Bank,**
1972. - **$25 $50 $75**

CRN-22

❑ **CRN-22. Seadog Spy Kit,**
1974. Kit - **$10 $20 $35**
Instructions - **$5 $10 $15**

CRN-23

❑ **CRN-23. Fabric Doll,**
1976. - **$15 $30 $40**

CRN-24

❑ **CRN-24. Plastic Sea Cycle Model,**
1970s. Near Mint Boxed - **$35**
Assembled - **$10 $20 $30**

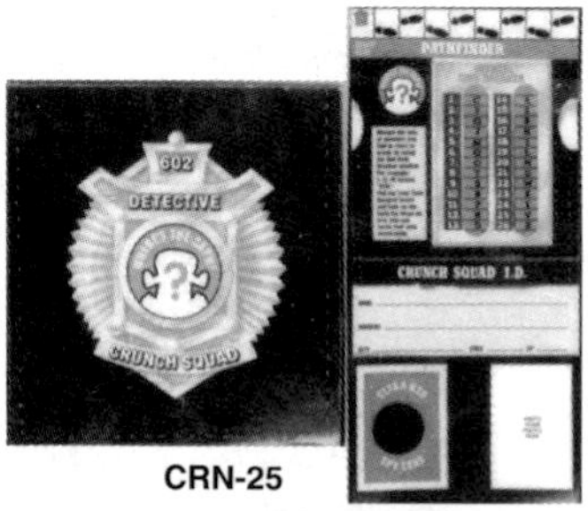


CRN-25

CRN-26

❑ **CRN-25. "Detective Crunch Squad" Paper Wallet,**
1970s. - **$8 $12 $25**

❑ **CRN-26. Finger Tennis Game,**
1970s. Plastic agility toy for two players. - **$5 $10 $15**

CRN-27

❑ **CRN-27. "La Foote" Miniature Plastic Vehicles,**
1970s. Balloon operated for movement.
Each - **$5 $10 $15**

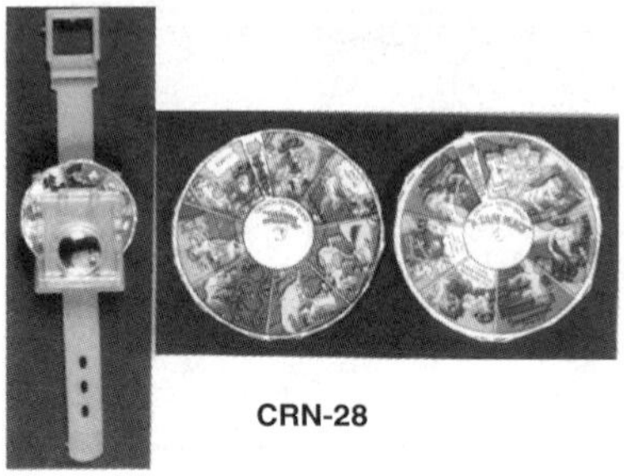

CRN-28

❑ **CRN-28. Story Scope With Disks,**
1970s. At least three disks cut from box backs.
Scope Unit - **$8 $15 $30**
Each Disk - **$2 $5 $10**

CRN-29

❑ **CRN-29. Cap'n Crunch Four Plastic Rings,**
c. 1970s. Our photo shows illustration off cereal box back panel.
Guided Missile Ring - **$50 $100 $150**
I-Spy Glass Ring - **$40 $85 $125**
Brunhilde's Spin-It-Ring - **$50 $100 $150**
Carlyle's Rocket Ring (With Shooting Missile) - **$50 $100 $150**

CRN-30

❑ **CRN-30. Cap'n Crunch Box Inserts,**
c. 1981. Plastic mechanical toys of flying saucer and tennis game plus booklet "Crunch Berry Beast's Farm Animals Stamp Album."
Saucer Toy Near Mint Packaged - **$20**
Loose - **$5 $10 $15**
Tennis Game Toy Near Mint Packaged - **$20**
Loose - **$3 $8 $12**
Stamp Album - **$5 $10 $15**

CRN-31

❑ **CRN-31. "Surfer" Cereal Box With Premium,**
1983. Three different figures, each 1-1/2" tall with 3-1/2" long plastic foam "Surfboard" were packaged one per box.
Used Complete Box - **$35 $70 $125**
Premium Assembled Each - **$5 $10 $15**

CRN-32

CRN-33

❑ **CRN-32. "Cap'n Crunch" 15x17x21" Treasure Chest Toy Box,**
1987. Awarded as a contest prize. - **$25 $50 $90**

❑ **CRN-33. Frame Tray Puzzle,**
1987. - **$3 $5 $8**

CRN-34

❑ **CRN-34. Crunch The Soggie Target Game,**
1987. Came with three balls covered with velcro strips. - **$5 $8 $12**

CRN-35

❑ **CRN-35. Flicker Button 2-1/4",**
1980s. - **$8 $12 $20**

CRN-36

❑ **CRN-36. Cap'n Crunch Island Adventure Board Game,**
1980s. Includes four 2" figures. - **$25 $50 $75**

CRN-37

❑ **CRN-37. TV Commercial Animation Cel With Matching Pencil Drawing,**
1980s. Similar Age And Quality Near Mint **- $75**

## Captain Action

**The Ideal Toy Company produced a series of jointed, posable dolls of Captain Action, his protégé Action Boy, and the villainous Dr. Evil in 1966-1968. The dolls were outfitted with costumes, boots, and assorted weaponry. Also offered were boxed character costumes and accessories, including flicker rings of Captain Action and his alter-ego superheroes Aquaman, Batman, Buck Rogers, Captain America, Flash Gordon, the Green Hornet, the Lone Ranger, the Phantom, Sgt. Fury, Spider-Man, Steve Canyon, Superman or Tonto. Kool-Pops offered a deck of Captain Action playing cards as a mail-order premium, and National Periodical published five Captain Action comic books in 1968-1969.**

**In 1998, Playing Mantis restarted the Captain Action line. They produced the Captain Action and Dr. Evil dolls, along with costumes for Green Hornet, Kato, Flash Gordon and Ming. Later, they entered into an exclusive deal with Diamond Select Toys, and recently produced the Lone Ranger costume and the Kid Action doll. Soon to be released are costumes and accessories for Speed Racer, Racer X and Captain Terror. While they are similar to the old line, each is different with completely new packaging. In the future, all accessories will be marked so that they will be easy to distinguish from the 1960s originals. All of this activity can only help the market and create new interest in Captain Action products.**

CAC-1

❑ **CAC-1. "Captain Action" Store Sign,**
c. 1966. 12x19" glossy paper. -
**$250 $500 $1500**

CAC-2

❑ **CAC-2. Catalogue Folder,**
1966. Ideal Toy Corp. Opens to 9x12" picturing Captain Action nine different outfit sets. -
**$20 $40 $75**

CAC-3

❑ **CAC-3. Captain Action Doll,**
1966. Ideal Toys. Store bought.
Boxed With Accessories - **$950**
Loose Figure - **$275**

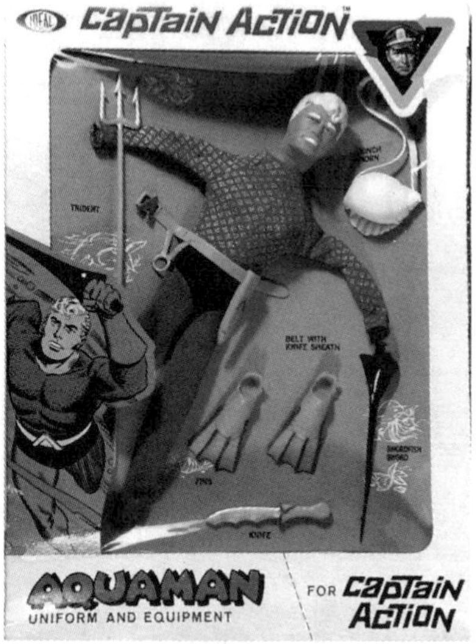


CAC-4

❑ **CAC-4. Captain Action "Aquaman" Set,**
1966. Uniform and equipment.
Boxed With Accessories - **$800**
Loose - **$140**

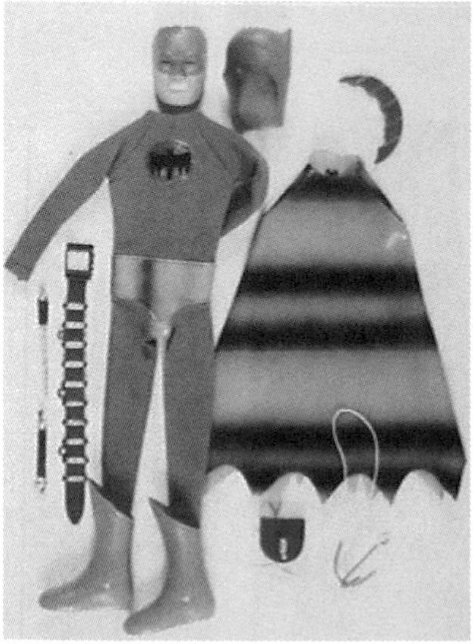

CAC-5

❑ **CAC-5. Batman Accessory Set,**
1966. Store item by Ideal.
Near Mint Boxed - **$1450**
Loose Complete - **$225**

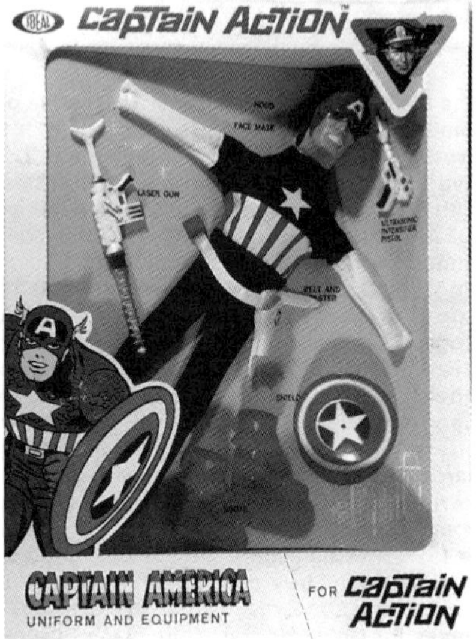


CAC-6

❑ **CAC-6. Captain Action "Captain America" Set,**
1966. Uniform and equipment.
Boxed With Accessories - **$1200**
Loose - **$225**

CAC-7

❑ **CAC-7. Captain Action "Flash Gordon" Set,**
1966. Uniform and equipment.
Boxed With Accessories - **$1450**
Loose - **$225**

CAC-8

❑ **CAC-8. Captain Action "The Phantom" Set,**
1966. Uniform and equipment.
Boxed With Accessories - **$950**
Loose - **$150**

CAC-9

❑ **CAC-9. Captain Action "Superman" Set,**
1966. Uniform, equipment and caped Krypto the dog. The 1967 version came with a flasher ring as a bonus. Boxed With Accessories - **$1750**
Loose - **$200**

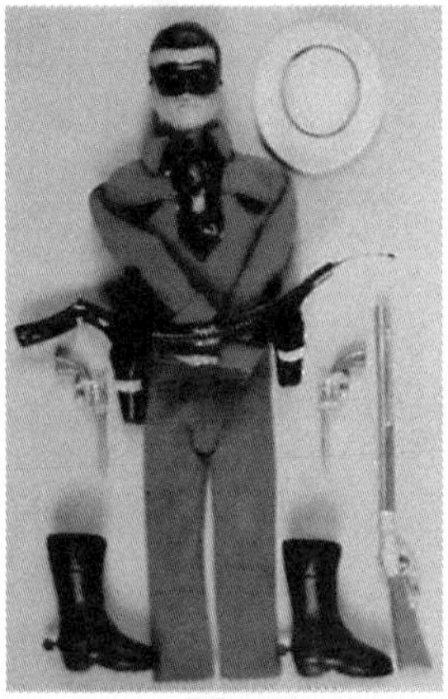

CAC-10

❑ **CAC-10. Lone Ranger Accessory Set,**
1966. Store item by Ideal. Set with red rather than blue shirt. Near Mint Boxed - **$1750**
Loose Complete - **$500**

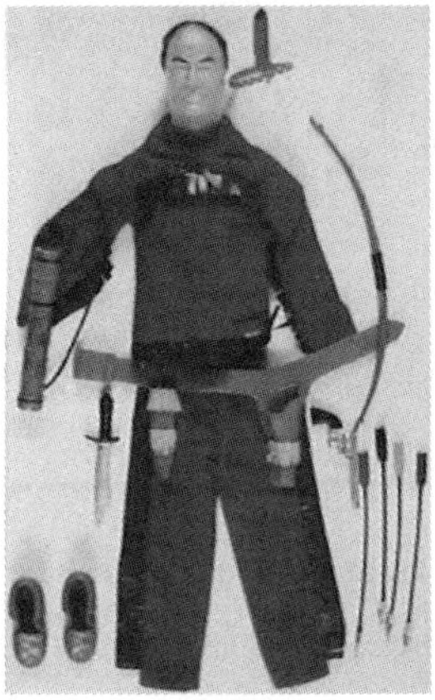

CAC-11

❑ **CAC-11. Tonto Accessory Set,**
1966. Store item by Ideal.
Near Mint Boxed - **$2000**
Loose Complete - **$400**

CAC-12

❑ **CAC-12. Comic Book Style Catalogue,**
1967. Ideal Toy Corp. packaged with store bought items. 3-1/2x7", 32 pages in full color. - **$20 $60 $125**

CAC-13

❑ **CAC-13. Action Boy Boxed Figure,**
1967. Store item by Ideal.
Near Mint Boxed - **$1000**
Loose Complete - **$300**

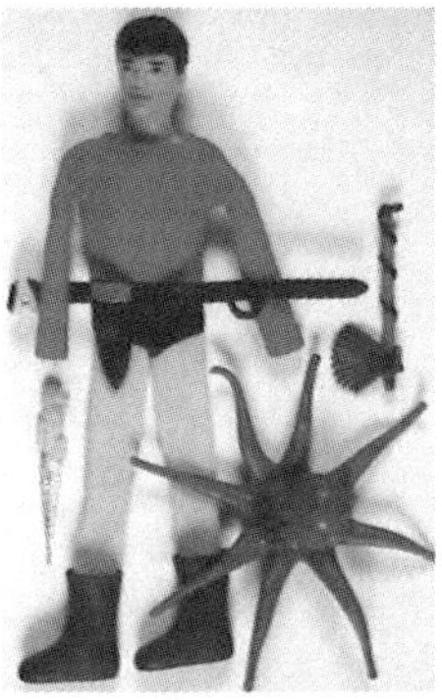

CAC-14

❑ **CAC-14. Action Boy Aqualad Accessories,**
1967. Store item by Ideal.
Near Mint Boxed - **$1200**
Loose Complete - **$400**

CAC-15

❑ **CAC-15. Robin Accessory Set,**
1967. Store item by Ideal.
Near Mint Boxed - **$1400**
Loose - **$400**

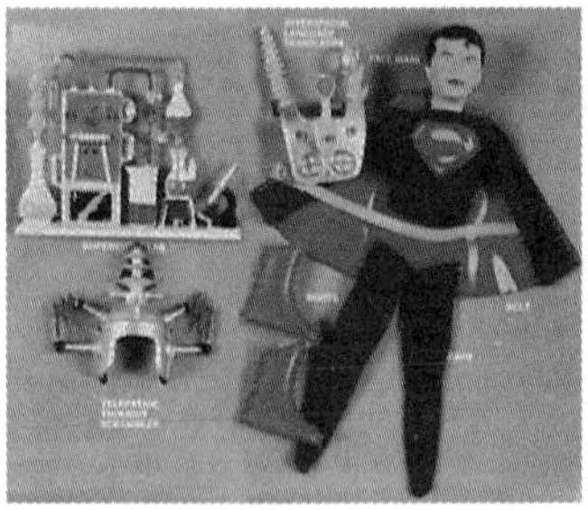

CAC-16

❑ **CAC-16. Superboy Accessory Set On Card,**
1967. Store item by Ideal.
Near Mint Boxed - **$2500**
Loose Complete - **$750**

CAC-17

❑ **CAC-17. Captain Action "Buck Rogers" Set,**
1967. Uniform and equipment.
Boxed With Accessories - **$3000**
Loose - **$450**

CAC-18

❑ **CAC-18. Dr. Evil Doll,**
1967. Ideal Toys. Store bought. Arch-enemy of Capt. Action. Boxed With Accessories - **$1400**
Loose Figure - **$450**

CAC-19

CAC-20

CAC-21

CAC-22

❑ **CAC-19. Captain Action/The Lone Ranger Flicker Ring,**
1967. Ideal Toys. Silver base marked "Hong Kong" came with boxed figure. Silver "Hong Kong" Base - **$30 $45 $60**
Blue Base - **$10 $20 $30**
Silver "China" Modern Base - **$5 $10 $15**

❑ **CAC-20. Captain Action/Tonto Flicker Ring,**
1967. Ideal Toys. Silver base marked "Hong Kong" came with boxed figure. Silver "Hong Kong" Base - **$30 $45 $60**
Blue Base - **$10 $20 $30**
Silver "China" Modern Base - **$5 $10 $15**

❑ **CAC-21. Captain Action/The Phantom Flicker Ring,**
1967. Ideal Toys. Silver base marked "Hong Kong" came with boxed figure. Silver "Hong Kong" Base - **$20 $35 $50**
Blue Base - **$10 $20 $30**
Silver "China" Modern Base - **$5 $10 $15**

❑ **CAC-22. Captain Action/Batman Flicker Ring,**
1967. Ideal Toys. Silver base marked "Hong Kong" came with boxed figure. Silver "Hong Kong" Base - **$20 $35 $50**
Blue Base - **$10 $20 $30**
Silver "China" Modern Base - **$5 $10 $15**

CAC-23

❑ **CAC-23. Uncut Flicker Ring Strip,**
1967. Vari-Vue Co. Strip of 16 flicker images alternating between Captain Action and other different action character outfits made for his use. - **$15 $25 $40**

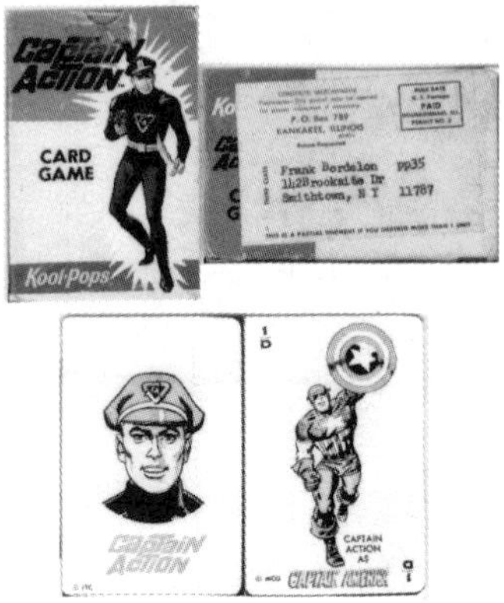


CAC-24

❑ **CAC-24. Kool-Pops "Captain Action" Card Game With Mailer Box,**
1967. - **$25 $50 $75**

CAC-25

❑ **CAC-25. "Captain Action" First Issue Comic Book,**
1968. Issue #1 for October-November by National Periodical Publications featuring his origin plus appearance by Superman. - **$12 $36 $140**

CAC-26

❑ **CAC-26. Ming Costume for Dr. Evil Doll,**
1998. New series for return of Captain Action. Products in box. - **$30**

CAC-27

❑ **CAC-27. Lone Ranger Red Costume for Captain Action Doll,**
1998. Cover box has Carmine Infantino art. - **$30**

CAC-28

❑ **CAC-28. Kabai Singh Costume for Dr. Evil Doll,**
1999. Products in box. - **$20**

CAC-29

❑ **CAC-29. Kato Costume for Captain Action Doll,**
1999. - **$20**

CAC-30

❑ **CAC-30. Lone Ranger Blue Costume for Captain Action Doll,**
2000. Diamond Exclusive from Playing Mantis. - **$20**

# Captain America

**World War II had begun but direct U.S. involvement was still nine months away when Captain America debuted in Captain America Comics in March 1941. Steve Rogers, a 4-F desperate to serve his country in the conflict looming on the horizon, volunteered to take the "Super Soldier Formula" which turned him into the one-man army known as Captain America. With his teenage sidekick, Bucky, he battled the Nazi hordes (usually commanded by the nefarious Red Skull) and numerous other villains until January 1950, when his title was canceled. The comic was revived for a brief, three-issue run in 1954, then went dormant until Marvel Comics' Stan Lee brought Cap into the modern era in The Avengers #4 (1964), and launched a string of solo stories in Tales of Suspense #59 which culminated in the title switching its name to Captain America with issue #100. That series ended with #454 and was followed immediately by a 13-issue mini-series. Currently an ongoing Captain America comic is published monthly,and he can also be found in the Avengers title. Cap's partners have included Bucky (WWII era) and the Falcon ('70s & '80s), as well as many other Marvel characters for shorter periods. The Overstreet Comic Book Price Guide carries a list of Captain America's other appearances. While the character is an integral part of Marvel's continuity, he has not enjoyed nearly the mainstream success of Spider-Man, the Hulk or The X-Men.**

**A 15-episode Republic Pictures serial starring Dick Purcell appeared in 1944 (and was re-released in 1953), followed by two TV movies starring Reb Brown (1979). In 1989, a would-be feature film starring Matt Salinger (son of author J.D. Salinger) went straight to home video. None of these productions had any lasting impact, nor did the original 13-episode animated series (1966). Fox debuted a short-lived new *Avengers* cartoon in 1999 that featured Captain America as a guest star.**

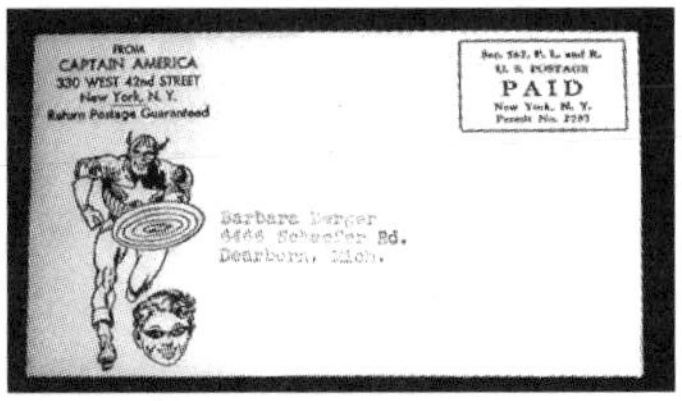


CAP-1

❑ **CAP-1. Mailing Envelope Version One,**
1941. "A" on helmet is below "G" of Guaranteed.- **$175 $375 $575**

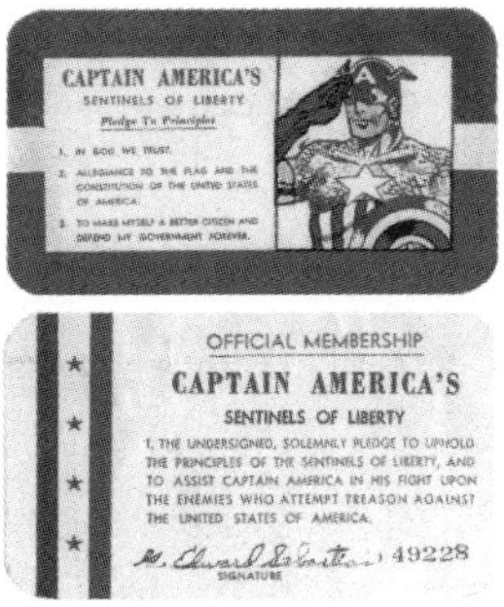


CAP-2

❑ **CAP-2. Membership Card Version One,**
1941. "A" on helmet is pointed. Blue color much lighter than version two, plus other differences in size and placement of type and words as well as amount of white shading on helmet. Design changed sometime between issuance of membership numbers 50,105 and 56,623. Art is by Joe Simon. - **$250 $650 $900**

CAP-3

CAP-4

❑ **CAP-3. "Captain America/Sentinels of Liberty" Enameled Brass Badge (Version One),**
1941. - **$200 $400 $800**

❑ **CAP-4. Enameled Copper Member's Badge (Version Two),**
1941. Same size and inscription as CAP-3, but in copper rather than brass luster. - **$250 $450 $850**

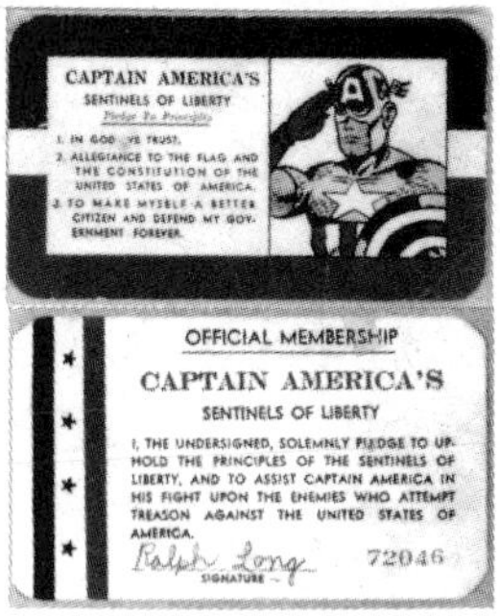


CAP-5

❑ **CAP-5. Membership Card Version Two,**
1941. "A" on helmet is squared off at the top. Blue color much darker than version one and other small differences. (See CAP-2). Art is by Al Avison. - **$250 $650 $900**

CAP-6

❑ **CAP-6. Mailing Envelope Version Two,**
1941. "A" on helmet is below "g" of postage. - **$175 $375 $575**

CAP-7

❑ **CAP-7. Mailing Envelope Version Three,**
1941. "A" on helmet is below the spacing between the words "Postage Guaranteed." Also, in the address the "W" of "west" is formed by two "V"s that overlap and form a tiny "V" at the center. At this time, it is not clear if this envelope was used with the Version One or the Version Two membership card and badge. - **$175 $375 $575**

CAP-8

❑ **CAP-8. Three-Sheet Movie Poster,**
1944. Scarce. Republic Pictures serial. 41" by 81". - **$2000 $4000 $6500**

CAP-9

❑ **CAP-9. "Return Of Captain America" 27x41" Movie Poster,**
1953. Republic Pictures. Example is 1953 re-issue of 1944 serial. - **$150 $300 $500**

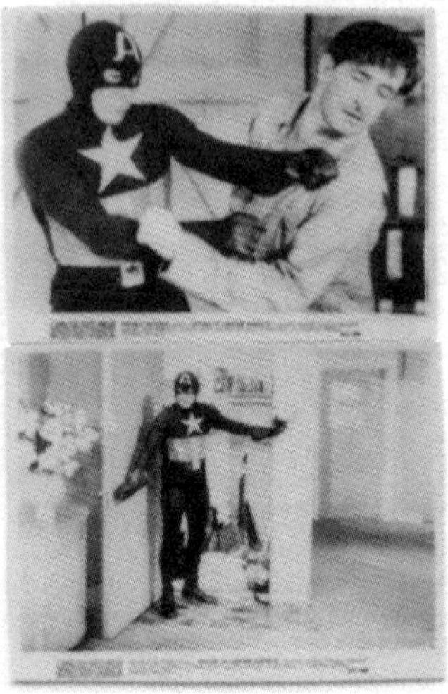
CAP-10

❑ **CAP-10. "Return Of Captain America" Movie Still Set,**
1953. Re-release of original 1944 serial with original title "Captain America."
Set - **$75 $150 $225**

CAP-11

❑ **CAP-11. "Captain America Game,"**
1966. Store item by Milton Bradley. -
**$15 $30 $60**

CAP-12

CAP-13

❑ **CAP-12. "Captain America" 3-1/2" Cello. Button,**
1966. Store item. #3 from numbered series.
Near Mint Bagged - **$45**
Loose - **$10 $15 $30**

❑ **CAP-13. Litho. Metal Bicycle Attachment Plate,**
1967. Store item by Marx Toys. - **$12 $30 $60**

CAP-14

CAP-15

❑ **CAP-14. Captain America Ring,**
1978. Store item by Marvel Comics Group. Part of a set marked with copyright symbol and "1978 MCG." Each - **$25 $50 $100**

❑ **CAP-15. "Keep Saving Energy" 2-1/2" Cello. Button,**
1980. Marvel Comics. - **$10 $20 $40**

CAP-16

❑ **CAP-16. "Captain America And The Campbell Kids" Comic Book,**
1980. Copyright by Marvel Comics and Campbell Soup Co. - **$1 $4 $10**

CAP-17

CAP-18

❑ **CAP-17. Pillow,**
1984. Captain America pictured on a large white pillow. Satin cloth. Very colorful. - **$10 $30 $60**

❑ **CAP-18. Watch on Card,**
1980s. - **$20 $35 $60**

CAP-19

❑ **CAP-19. Captain America Ring,**
1980s. Vitamins premium. - **$60 $120 $175**

CAP-20

❑ **CAP-20. Gum Ball Machine,**
1980s. Superior Toy Inc. Copyright Marvel. Plastic machine is 10" tall. Cap's upper body can be adjusted. - **$30 $50 $85**

CAP-21

CAP-22

❑ **CAP-21. 50th Anniversary Pin Set,**
1990. 1500 produced. Three in a holder. Mint - **$80**

❑ **CAP-22. Limited Edition Of Badge In Holder,**
1990. Reverse inscribed "Captain America Is A Registered Trademark TM & ©1990 Marvel." Mint - **$35**

CAP-23

❑ **CAP-23. Store Poster,**
1991. Marvel Entertainment Group, Inc. 11x17" red, white and blue poster promoting "A New Bookshelf Format Series This August From Marvel." - **$5 $10 $15**

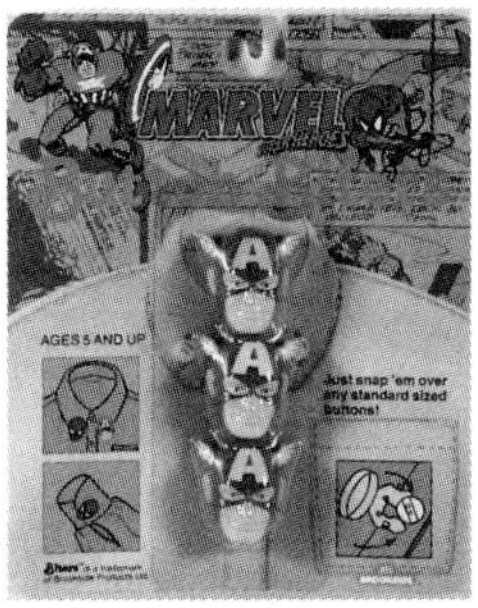


CAP-24

❑ **CAP-24. Button Biters,**
1990s. Produced by Brookside. - **$5**

CAP-25

❑ **CAP-25. Wastebasket,**
1999. - **$15**

CAP-26

❑ **CAP-26. Golden Age Resin Statue,**
1999. Limited to 2,000. - **$200**

CAP-27

❑ **CAP-27. Modern Age Resin Statue,**
1999. Limited to 4,000. Miniature version released in 2001. - **$150**

CAP-28

❑ **CAP-28. "Red Skull" Mini-Bust,**
1999. Limited to 3,000. With clear base. - **$80**

## Captain Battle

Captain Battle had a brief run as a superpatriot comic book hero in the early 1940s. He made his first appearance in *Silver Streak Comics* #10 in May 1941, then in Captain Battle Comics from 1941 to 1943. Readers who promised to uphold the principles of Americanism and the Constitution could join the Captain Battle Boys' Brigade. Two issues of *Captain Battle Jr.* were published in 1943-1944.

CBT-1

❑ **CBT-1. "Captain Battle Boys' Brigade" Cello. Button,**
1941. Scarce. Silver Streak Comics. - **$400 $1000 $2000**

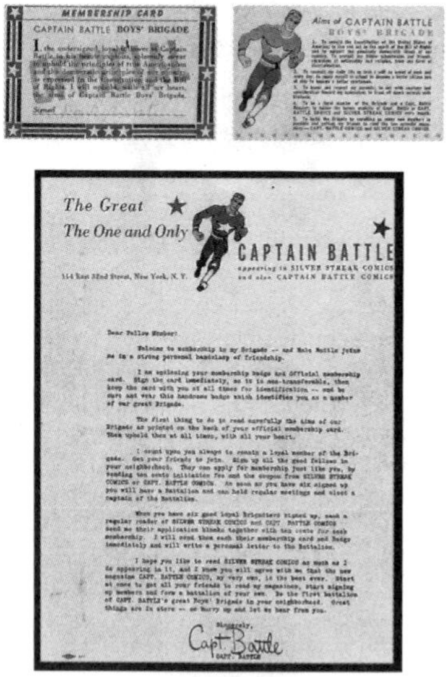


CBT-2

❑ **CBT-2. Membership Kit Mailer, Letter and Card,**
1941. The 1-3/4" cello. club button came as part of this kit. The membership card has a list of 5 "Aims" printed on the reverse.
Mailer - **$50 $150 $350**
Letter - **$150 $300 $650**
Membership Card - **$150 $300 $600**

## Captain 11

Following the success of Captain Video and Space Patrol, the Rocket Ranger Club was formed in 1955. This club was designed to encourage children to watch Channel 11, a Midwestern station. Premiums issued for the club were only produced and distributed on a regional basis and are quite rare. The creed of the club focused on telling children to obey the laws and their parents at all times. The kit included a variety of decoders and planet credits, which enabled the young listeners to receive special messages and follow the exploits of the Rocket Ranger.

CVN-1

CVN-2

❑ **CVN-1. Membership Card,**
1955. - **$15 $30 $75**

❑ **CVN-2. Mailer,**
1955. - **$10 $20 $40**

CVN-3

❑ **CVN-3. Membership Certificate And Creed,**
1955. - **$20 $50 $100**

CVN-4

CVN-5

❑ **CVN-4. Super Zoom Decoder,**
1955. Rare. - **$75 $200 $325**

❑ **CVN-5. Zoom Code Card,**
1955. - **$40 $80 $120**

CVN-6

❑ **CVN-6. Venus Credits Play Money,**
1955. Six different. Each - **$3 $10 $20**

CVN-7

❑ **CVN-7. Martian Credits Play Money,**
1955. Seven different. Each - **$3 $10 $20**

## Captain Ezra Diamond

*Captain Diamond's Adventures* aired on the NBC Blue radio network from 1932 to 1937, offering weekly tales of sea adventures as related by Captain Diamond in his lighthouse. Al Swenson played the Captain, and his young visitor each week was Tiny Ruffner. Diamond Salt was the sponsor.

CEZ-1

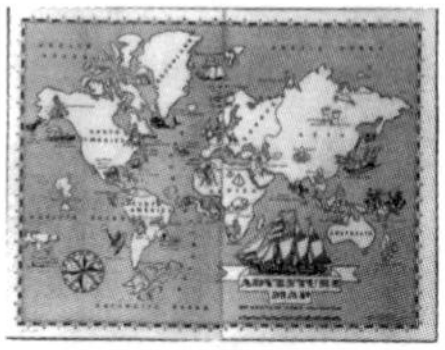

CEZ-2

❑ **CEZ-1. "Adventure Map Of Captain Ezra Diamond" 17x22",**
1932. - **$15 $25 $60**

❑ **CEZ-2. "Adventure Map Of Captain Ezra Diamond" 16x22",**
1933. - **$15 $25 $60**

CEZ-3

CEZ-5

CEZ-4

❑ **CEZ-3. Cast Member Fan Photo,**
c. 1933. White background version. - **$5 $10 $20**

❑ **CEZ-4. Fan Photo Of Cast,**
c. 1933. Black background version. - **$5 $10 $20**

❑ **CEZ-5. Weather Forecast Card,**
c. 1933. Lighthouse window area holds litmus paper. - **$20 $40 $60**

## Captain Frank Hawks

**Frank Hawks (1897-1938) was a skilled pilot and an air instructor for the army during World War I. He set a number of speed records, including two in nonstop flights from Los Angeles to New York in 1929 and 1933. As a spokesman for Post cereals in the 1930s he made guest appearances on the radio and was always available to speak to the press. Boys and girls were urged to join Capt. Hawks' Sky Patrol to win free prizes. Ironically, Hawks was killed in an airplane crash.**

CFH-1

CFH-2

❑ **CFH-1. Photo With Achievement Inscription,**
c. 1935. Facsimile signature includes "Snapped Over The Andes At 19,000 Feet Altitude On May 4 1935". - **$15 $40 $75**

❑ **CFH-2. Club Manual,**
1935. Post's 40% Bran Flakes. - **$15 $30 $70**

CFH-3

❑ **CFH-3. Sky Patrol Propeller Badge,**
1935. Three ranks. Member - **$10 $15 $30**
Flight Lieutenant - **$15 $25 $60**
Flight Captain (scarce) - **$25 $45 $100**

CFH-4

❑ **CFH-4. "Capt. Hawks Moon Rocket" Toy,**
c. 1936. Label on mailing tube reads "General Foods/The Makers Of Post Cereals." 10-3/4" long stiff cardboard tube with silver and blue paper covering, pair of aluminum tail fins and small wood plug inside tail end. Plug is removable and apparently blowing into the tube was meant to launch a red rubber ball from the front of the tube although the example we have seen was dried out. Front underside of tube has small wire loop for unknown purpose.
Mailer - **$25 $50 $10**
Rocket - **$75 $200 $300**

CFH-5

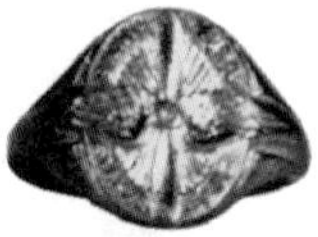

CFH-6

❑ **CFH-5. "Capt. Hawks Sky Patrol" Brass Ring,**
1936. Depicts portrait, cloud and propeller design. - **$50 $100 $200**

❑ **CFH-6. "Capt. Frank's Air Hawks" Brass Ring,**
1936. - **$35 $75 $125**

CFH-7

❑ **CFH-7. Air Hawks Wings Badge,**
1936. Three ranks.
Silver - "Member" - **$10 $15 $30**
Brass - "Squadron Leader" - **$15 $25 $60**
Bronze - "Flight Commander" - **$20 $45 $100**

CFH-8

CFH-9

❑ **CFH-8. "Air Hawks" Club Folder,**
1936. Post's 40% Bran Flakes. Eight pages of contents include illustrated premium offers, contest information on how to get 28 prizes. - **$15 $25 $50**

❑ **CFH-9. Fan Photo,**
c. 1936. - **$10 $25 $40**

CFH-10

❑ **CFH-10. Goggles,**
1936. Rare. Circular goggles. Premium obtained with 4 Post Bran Flakes box tops. - **$50 $75 $100**

CFH-11

❑ **CFH-11. One Sheet Poster,**
1937. For "The Mysterioius Pilot," Chapter 3 of the Columbia Pictures serial "Enemies of the Air" starring Frank Hawks. - **$400**

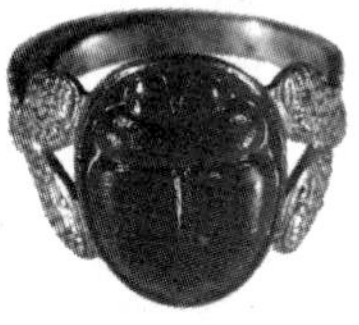

CFH-12

CFH-13

❑ **CFH-12. Sacred Scarab Ring,**
1937. Post's Bran Flakes. Scarab in green. Also issued for Melvin Purvis. - **$300 $600 $1400**

❑ **CFH-13. Sky Patrol Premium Booklet,**
1937. Post's 40% Bran Flakes. Offers eight premiums including club badge, manual, ring, ID bracelet. - **$15 $25 $60**

CFH-14

❑ **CFH-14. "Sacred Scarab Ring" Newspaper Ad,**
1937. Post's Bran Flakes. Ring offer expiration date December 31. Scarab in green, also issued for Melvin Purvis. Newspaper Ad. - **$8 $15 $30**

CFH-15

❑ **CFH-15. "Air Ace and the League of Twelve" BLB #1444,**
1938. - **$10 $35 $80**

CFH-16

CFH-17

❑ **CFH-16. Bracelet With Photo Picture,**
1930s. Rare. Assumed to be related to Capt. Hawks cereal campaign. - **$100 $200 $400**

❑ **CFH-17. Brass Paperweight and Perpetual Calendar,**
1940. - **$100 $200 $350**

## Captain Gallant

**Two-fisted Captain Gallant, played by Olympic gold medalist and seasoned actor Buster Crabbe (1907-1983), premiered in a black-and-white series on NBC-TV in February 1955. Filmed originally in Morocco and later in Libya and Italy, the show was essentially a Western in Arab garb, with the Captain chasing camel thieves rather than cattle rustlers. Crabbe's son Cullen was featured as Cuffy Sanders, his ward. The show was sponsored by Heinz Foods until 1957, then by General Mills in repeats from 1960 to 1963. The following year the show was syndicated to local stations as *Foreign Legionnaire*. Items are usually copyrighted by Frantel Inc.**

CGL-1

❑ **CGL-1. Captain Gallant #1 Comic Book,**
1955. Heinz Foods. Membership certificate on back cover. Near Mint. - **$6**
See The Overstreet Comic Book Price Guide for values of other issues.

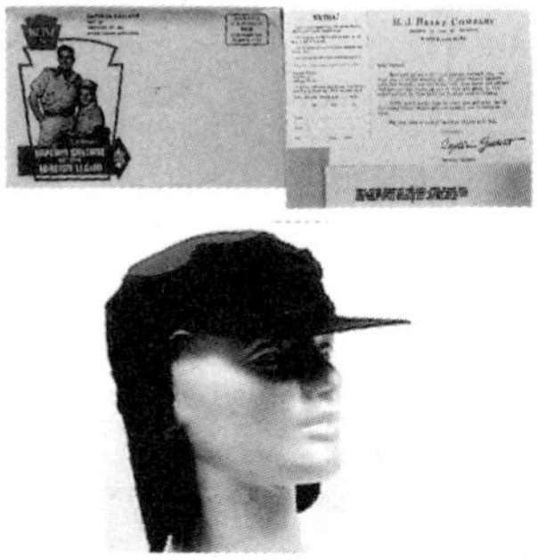

CGL-2

❑ **CGL-2. "Captain Gallant Hat" With Mailer,**
c. 1955. H. J. Heinz Co. Fabric hat with cover letter, instructions and order coupon. Near Mint In Mailer - **$300**
Mailer Or Letter Only Each - **$15 $25 $50**
Hat Only - **$50 $100 $200**

CGL-3

❑ **CGL-3. "Captain Gallant Of The Foreign Legion" Boxed Playset,**
1955. Store item by Marx. 14-3/4x23x3-1/4" deep box holds tin litho. building and wall sections with many hard plastic accessories including character figures of Captain Gallant and Cuffy. Complete - **$300 $650 $1000**

CGL-4

❑ **CGL-4. "Tim Magazine For Boys" Cover Article,**
June 1957. - **$15 $25 $40**

CGL-5

❑ **CGL-5. Captain Gallant And Cuffy Photos,**
1950s. Each - **$10 $25 $40**

CGL-6

❑ **CGL-6. "Junior Legionnaires" Club Card,**
1950s. - **$20 $40 $85**

CGL-7

CGL-8

❑ **CGL-7. "Junior Legionnaire" Litho. Tab,**
1950s. - **$12 $25 $50**

❑ **CGL-8. TV Sponsor Paper Store Pennant,**
1950s. P.F. footwear of B.F. Goodrich. -
**$20 $50 $75**

CGL-9

CGL-10

❑ **CGL-9. "Captain Gallant" Cuffy Cello. Button,**
1950s. Holsum Bread. - **$25 $60 $125**

❑ **CGL-10. "Captain Gallant Junior Legionnaire" Silvered Metal Badge,**
1950s. Cardboard insert photo. Probably came with store bought gun set and was sold off store display card or on individual card. -
**$25 $50 $100**

CGL-11

CGL-12

❑ **CGL-11. Heinz Diecut Embossed Metal Member Badge,**
1950s. "57" numeral under flame image. For mounting on Heinz premium Legionnaire's hat. Scarce. - **$50 $100 $250**

❑ **CGL-12. "The Italy Star" Metal And Fabric Award Medal,**
1950s. Back has Captain Gallant logo and name. - **$15 $35 $85**

CGL-13

❑ **CGL-13. "Captain Gallant" Holster,**
1950s. Came with belt in boxed set by Halco.
Boxed Complete - **$50 $125 $250**
Holster Only - **$20 $50 $75**

CGL-14

CGL-15

❑ **CGL-14. Foreign Legion Replica Award Medal,**
1950s. Fabric ribbon holding gold luster metal pendant with military motifs and "GRI" inscription. - **$15 $35 $85**

❑ **CGL-15. Foreign Legion Replica Award Medal,**
1950s. Fabric ribbon suspending silver luster metal pendant depicting cat-like animal killing dragon-like creature with commemorative date 1939-1945. - **$15 $35 $85**

## Captain Marvel

**Young Billy Batson, a homeless orphan, only had to utter the name of the wizard Shazam to be transformed into Captain Marvel, the World's Mightiest Mortal. Created by artist C. C. Beck and writer Bill Parker, Captain Marvel was introduced in *Whiz Comics* #2 in February 1940. It was a huge success, outselling all its competition and generating a Mary Marvel, Captain Marvel Jr., Uncle Marvel, several Lt. Marvels and Hoppy the Marvel Bunny. The Captain Marvel club was announced in *Whiz Comics* #23, on October 31st, 1941.**

**The Captain subdued criminals and mad scientists for 13 years until a costly lawsuit for copyright infringement of the Superman character ended his run in 1954, but not before dozens of toys, novelties and premiums had been issued. Several comic book revivals and spinoffs have been published over the years. *The Adventures of Captain Marvel*, a 12-episode chapter play starring Tom Tyler as the Captain and Frank Coghlan Jr. as Billy was released by Republic Pictures in 1941. In 1974 a television series with Michael Gray as Billy was produced by Filmation Studios.**

**Ironically, Captain Marvel is now owned by DC Comics, publishers of *Superman*, and has enjoyed a recent resurgence. *The Power of Shazam!*, a 1994 hard cover graphic novel and 1995 monthly series of the same name, relaunched the character. Mary Marvel has appeared with Supergirl and in a solo story in *Showcase '96*. Captain Marvel, Jr. joined the Teen Titans, a group of other young heroes, marking his first regular incorporation into the mainstream of DC's continuity in *Teen Titans* #17 (1998).**

**The Marvel Family of characters continues to appear throughout the DC Universe, with Captain Marvel himself playing big roles in the mini-series *Kingdom Come* (1996) and *The Dark Knight Strikes Again* (2002).**

CMR-1

❑ **CMR-1. Promotional Poster For Republic Pictures 12 Episode Captain Marvel Serial,**
1941. 27"x41". Advertised in press book. - **$1700 $3000 $4500**

CMR-2

❑ **CMR-2. Advs. of Captain Marvel Title & Scene Cards**
1941. Each chapter has 8 cards--one title card and seven scene cards (portraying action images from the film). The cards for Chapter 1 were in full color, while Chapters 2-12 were in duotone. Three of the seven scene cards for each chapter featured Captain Marvel and are considered more desirable. All 96 are rare.

❑ **Captain Marvel Title Card Chapter 1 - Color**
Scarce. Less than 10 known. -
**$600 $900 $1500**

❑ **Captain Marvel Title Cards Chapters 2-12 - Duotone**
Scarce. - **$100 $250 $400**

❑ **Captain Marvel Scene Card Chapter 1 - Color**
With Captain Marvel - **$150 $300 $450**
Without Captain Marvel - **$50 $100 $150**

❑ **Captain Marvel Scene Cards Chapters 2-12 - Duotone**
With Captain Marvel - **$100 $200 $250**
Without Captain Marvel - **$50 $75 $100**

CMR-3

❑ **CMR-3. Adventures of Captain Marvel Six-Sheet Movie Poster,**
1941. Six-sheet and three-sheet posters were commonly created to span the entire run of a serial. Whereas a theater might have displayed a one-sheet for only the week that particular chapter was playing, the six-sheet would be displayed for the length of the serial. The Adventures of Captain Marvel Six-Sheet is rare, with less than 10 known. Full color. -
**$2500 $6000 $8000**

CMR-4

❑ **CMR-4. Adventures of Captain Marvel One-Sheet Movie Posters**
1941. Like most serials, the Captain Marvel one-sheets were created to promote the individual chapters of the serial.

❑ **Chapter 1**
Rare. Full color. Less than 10 known. Chapter 1 one-sheet does not have insert box as do Chapters 2-12; one, full poster image. -
**$2500 $5500 $7000**

❑ **Chapters 2-12**
Scarce. Full color. One-sheets for Chapters 2-12 have insert boxes. Those with inserts featuring Captain Marvel are considered more desirable.With Capt. Marvel Insert -
**$1000 $2000 $3000**
Without Capt. Marvel Insert -
**$500 $1000 $1500**

CMR-5

❑ **CMR-5. Flyer for Spanish "Aventuras del Capitan Maravillas" Serial,**
1941. Features the villain The Scorpion. -
**$25 $50 $100**

CMR-6

❑ **CMR-6. Blotter 6",**
1941. Rare. Promotes "The Adventures of Captain Marvel" 12 chapter serial. -
**$250 $500 $800**

CMR-7

❑ **CMR-7. "Captain Marvel Club/Shazam" Club Litho. Button,**
1941. - **$30 $60 $90**

(PUZZLE BOX)

(PUZZLE IMAGE)

CMR-8

❑ **CMR-8. Boxed Picture Puzzle,**
1941. Store item. 7-1/4x9-3/4x2" deep box contains puzzle that assembles to 13x17-1/2" titled "Captain Marvel Rides The Engine Of Doom" originally featured on the cover of Whiz #12
Box - **$50 $100 $125**
Puzzle - **$50 $120 $175**
Complete Box and Puzzle - **$100 $220 $300**

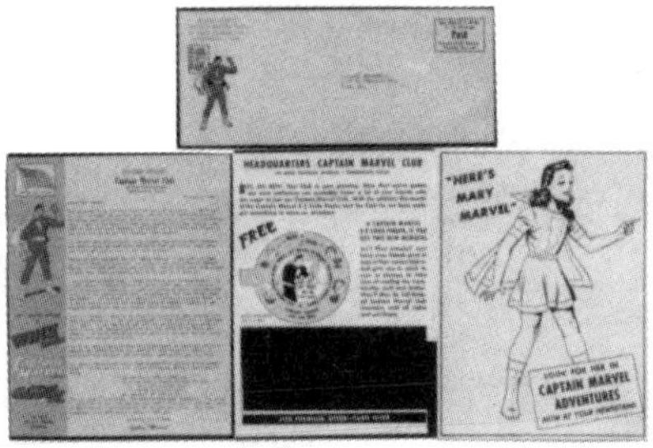


CMR-9

❑ **CMR-9.Club Letter With Inserts,**
1942. November 1942 letter with order form for "E-Z Code Finder" and promo picture of Mary Marvel. Near Mint Complete **- $250**

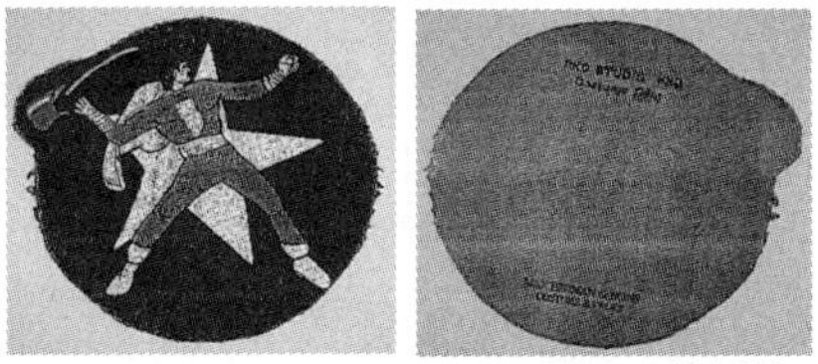

(FRONT) CMR-10 (BACK)

❑ **CMR-10. Studio Prop Patch For Jacket,**
c. 1942. RKO Studio Costume Dept. Reverse also reads "Max Berman & Sons Costume & Props." About 6" diameter. - **$250 $500 $750**

CMR-11

CMR-12

❑ **CMR-11. "Captain Marvel Comic Hero Punch-Outs Book",**
1942. Store item by Samuel Lowe Co. -
**$75 $150 $225**

❑ **CMR-12. "Flying Captain Marvel" Punch-Out With Envelope,**
c. 1942. Store item and club premium.
Unused - **$20 $40 $60**

CMR-13

❑ **CMR-13. Captain Marvel Jr. #1 Promotional Kit,**
1942. Rare. Elaborate kit of 12 separate pieces plus mailing envelope. Includes full-color picture of front cover of **Capt. Marvel Jr.** #1.
Complete - **$500 $1200 $1500**
Capt. Marvel Jr. Cover Promo Only -
**$300 $600 $900**

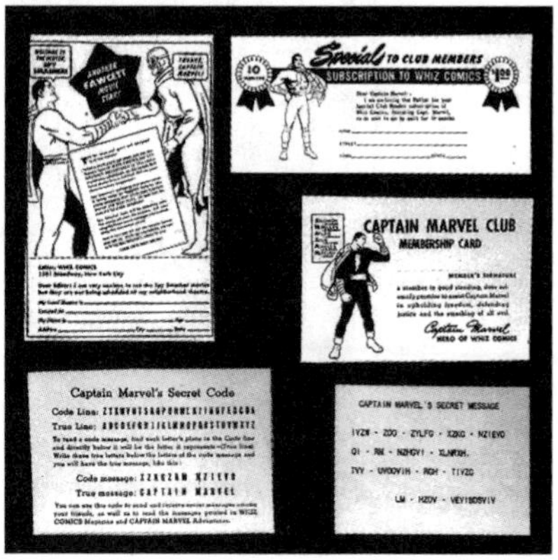


CMR-14

❑ **CMR-14. Membership Kit With Spy Smasher Tie-In,**
1942. Kit includes envelope with "Remember Pearl Harbor" imprint, club member's cello. button, Whiz Comics subscription form, insert promoting Spy Smasher movie, membership card with secret code on reverse, insert with Captain Marvel's Secret Message which decodes as "Read all about Capt. Marvel Jr. in Master Comics. Gee Fellers it's great. On sale everywhere."
Near Mint Complete - **$500**
Button - **$20 $40 $65**
Subscription Form - **$20 $35 $50**
Membership Card - **$25 $50 $100**
Spy Smasher Insert - **$50 $75 $150**
Secret Message - **$20 $40 $60**

CMR-15

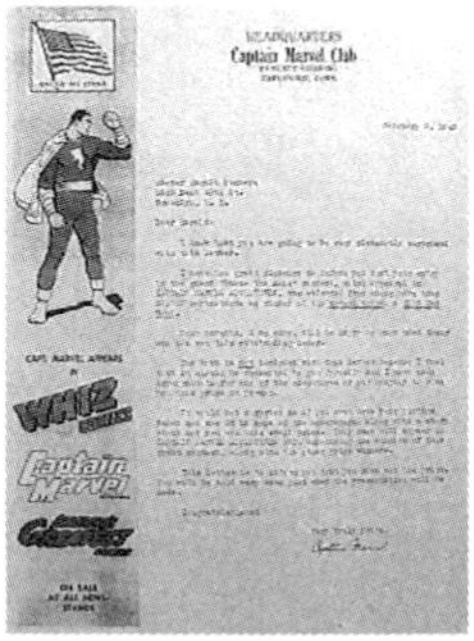

CMR-16

❑ **CMR-15. "Captain Marvel Club/Shazam" Cello. Club Button,**
1942. - **$30 $65 $110**

❑ **CMR-16. "Paste The Axis" Letter To Second Prize Winner,**
1943. Announces award of "$100 War Bond" and "Captain Marvel" states "I Have Made Arrangements For One Of The Executives Of Our Company To Give You This Prize In Person." - **$75 $150 $250**

CMR-17

CMR-18

❑ **CMR-17. "Secret Message Postcard",**
1943. Scarce. - **$75 $175 $275**

❑ **CMR-18. "E.-Z. Code Finder",**
c. 1943. Scarce. - **$200 $350 $500**

CMR-19

CMR-20

❑ **CMR-19. "Captain Marvel Comic Story Paint Book",**
c. 1943. Store item by Samuel Lowe Co. -
**$60 $180 $400**

❑ **CMR-20. "Magic Lightning Box" Punch-Out Paper Toy In Envelope,**
c. 1943. Store item and club premium. Captain Marvel figure moves up and down inside box, scarcest item in punch-out series. -
**$50 $100 $150**

CMR-21

CMR-22

❑ **CMR-21. Yellow Rectangular Patch,**
c. 1943. Rare. Fawcett premium. -
**$75 $200 $350**

❑ **CMR-22. Blue Rectangular Patch,**
c. 1943. Fawcett premium. - **$35 $60 $120**

CMR-23

❑ **CMR-23. Club Mailing February,**
1943. Included Spy Smasher litho. button to make recipient an honorary member of Spy Smasher Victory Batallion, cover letter, sheet with new items including figure by Multi-Products, subscription offer coupon, Captain Marvel tie coupon, envelope.
Five Paper Items - **$100 $200 $300**
Spy Smasher Button **$20 $40 $65**

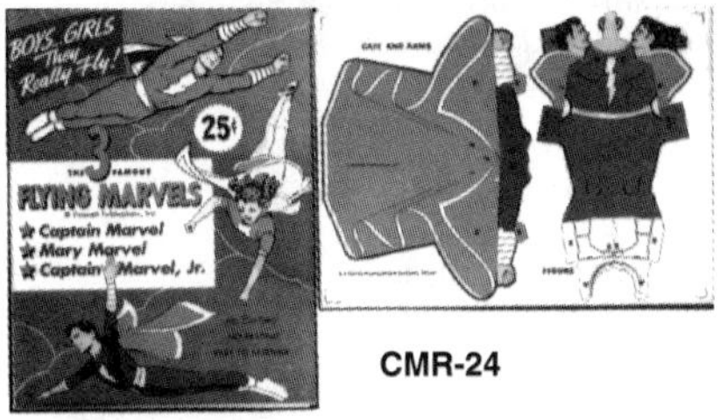


CMR-24

❑ **CMR-24. "The Three Famous Flying Marvels" Punch-Outs,**
c. 1943. Store item and club premium.
Unused - **$25 $50 $75**

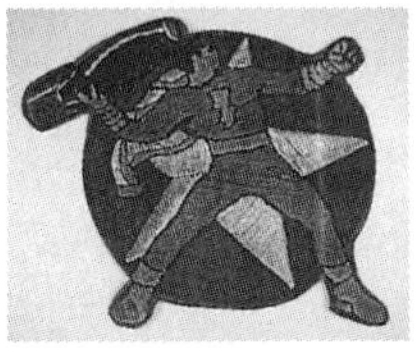

CMR-25

CMR-26

❑ **CMR-25. World War II Navy Jacket Chest Patch,**
1943. About 5-1/2" diameter featuring same design as cover of Captain Marvel #27. - **$300 $700 $1600**

❑ **CMR-26. "Captain Marvel's Fun Book",**
1944. Store item and also available from Fawcett for 25¢. - **$36 $108 $330**

CMR-27

❑ **CMR-27. "Hoppy The Flying Marvel Bunny" Punch-Out Toy,**
c. 1944. Issued by Reed & Associates Inc.
Unpunched - **$25 $50 $75**

CMR-28

CMR-29

❑ **CMR-28. "Captain Marvel Well Known Comics" Booklet,**
1944. Bestmaid give-away published by Samuel Lowe Co. - **$25 $75 $175**

❑ **CMR-29. "Captain Marvel's Rocket Raider" Paper Toy Kit,**
c. 1944. Store item and club premium.
Unused - **$20 $40 $60**

CMR-30

CMR-31

❑ **CMR-30. "Fawcett's Comic Stars",**
c. 1944. Store item with three metal stars depicting Captain Marvel, Hoppy The Marvel Bunny, Sherlock Monk.
Near Mint With Envelope - **$250**
Each Star - **$20 $40 $60**

❑ **CMR-31. "Captain Marvel Painting Book",**
c. 1944. Store item by L. Miller & Sons, London, England. - **$100 $150 $200**

CMR-32

❑ **CMR-32. Christmas Letter To Members,**
1944. Cover letter plus sheet showing official items for 1945. Letter - **$25 $50 $75**
Premium Sheet - **$15 $35 $60**

CMR-33

CMR-34

❑ **CMR-33. Magic Picture,**
1944. Billy Batson's broadcast on front, says "Can you help Billy Batson". - **$75 $125 $175**

❑ **CMR-34. Punch-Out "Magic Eyes" Picture With Envelope,**
c. 1944. Store item and club premium.
Unused - **$20 $40 $60**

CMR-35

CMR-36

❑ **CMR-35. "Captain Marvel Club/Shazam" Litho. Button,**
1944. - **$50 $80 $125**

❑ **CMR-36. "Captain Marvel Club/Shazam" Cello. Button,**
1944. Background around figure is blue rather than white as on 1942 version. - **$40 $80 $120**

CMR-37

❑ **CMR-37. "One Against Many" Picture Puzzle,**
c. 1944. Store item and club premium. -
**$20 $40 $60**

CMR-38

❑ **CMR-38. "Hoppy And Millie In Musical Evening" Cardboard Toy,**
c. 1944. Store item and club premium.
Unused - **$20 $40 $60**

CMR-39

❑ **CMR-39. "Buzz Bomb" Punch-Out Toy,**
c. 1944. Store item and club premium.
Unused - **$20 $40 $60**

CMR-40

❑ **CMR-40. "Shazam" Punch-Out Game With Envelope,**
c. 1944. Store item and club premium.
Unused - **$25 $50 $75**

CMR-41

❑ **CMR-41. "Magic Picture" Cardboard Toy,**
c. 1944. Store item and club premium. Scarcer than others in series. Unused - **$50 $75 $125**

CMR-42 CMR-43

❑ **CMR-42. "Captain Marvel, Jr. Ski Jump" Paper Assembly Toy In Envelope,**
c. 1944. Store item and club premium. -
**$20 $40 $60**

❑ **CMR-43. Toss Bag,**
1945. Five varieties: Captain Marvel or Mary Marvel either flying or standing plus Hoppy.
Each - **$25 $60 $100**

CMR-44

❑ **CMR-44. "Captain Marvel" Canadian Comic Book Glow-In-Dark Patch,**
c. 1945. Anglo-American Publishing Co. Set of ten "Glo-Crests."
Captain Marvel - **$200 $600 $800**

Others: Commander Steel, Crusaders, Dr. Destiny, Freelance, Hurri-Kane, Kip Keene, Purple Rider, Red Rover, Terry Kane.
Each - **$35 $75 $150**

CMR-45

❑ **CMR-45."Captain Marvel Club" Christmas Letter With Order Form,**
1945. Mentions first issue of "Marvel Family Comics." Offers 16 different premiums. -
**$25 $50 $100**

CMR-46

❑ **CMR-46. Skull Cap,**
1945. Scarce. Fawcett Premium. No brim. -
**$100 $200 $400**

CMR-47 CMR-48

❑ **CMR-47. Girl's Pink Felt Beanie,**
1945. Rare. Marked Capt. Marvel with figure on front and back. Fawcett premium. -
**$150 $400 $450**

❑ **CMR-48. Boy's Felt Beanie,**
1945. Fawcett premium.
Black - **$150 $300 $500**
Blue - **$100 $175 $350**

CMR-49 CMR-50

❑ **CMR-49. "Captain Marvel" Four Color Felt Patch,**
1945. - **$75 $150 $250**

❑ **CMR-50. "Mary Marvel" Four Color Felt Patch,**
1945. - **$75 $150 $250**

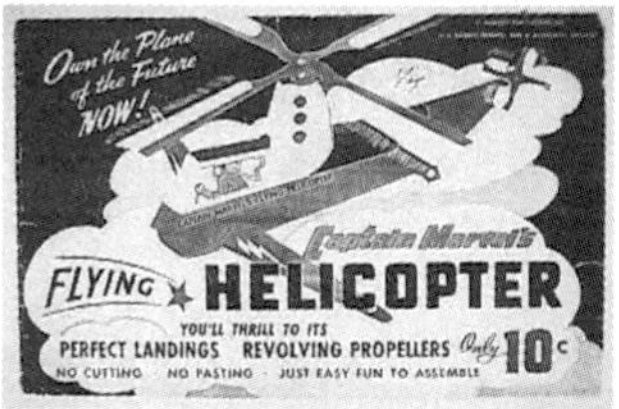

CMR-51

❑ **CMR-51. "Flying Helicopter" Punch-Out Toy,**
1945. Store item and probable premium by Reed & Associates.
Unpunched - **$75 $125 $200**

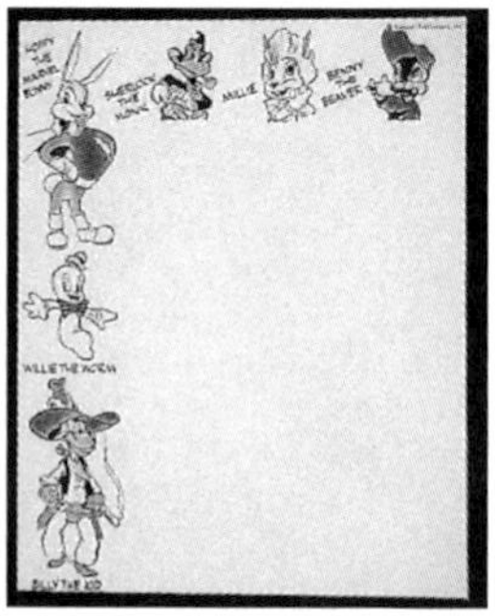
CMR-52

❑ **CMR-52. Hoppy The Marvel Bunny Note Paper,**
1946. Store item. From the same series as the Captain Marvel and Mary Marvel examples.
Scarce. Each Sheet - **$25 $50 $75**

CMR-53

**❏ CMR-53. "Mary Marvel Notepaper" Boxed Set,**
1946. Store item by Hobby Notes. Holds 18 sheets with envelopes.
Near Mint Boxed - **$600**
Each Sheet - **$10 $20 $35**

CMR-54

**❏ CMR-54. "Mary Marvel Club" Member's Card,**
1946. Card is captioned "Heroine Of Wow Comics." - **$125 $225 $350**

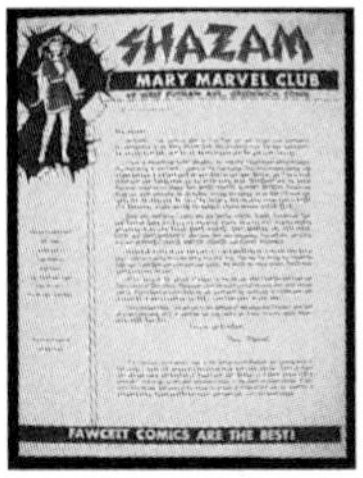


CMR-55

CMR-56

**❏ CMR-55. "Mary Marvel Club" New Member Letter,**
1946. Welcome letter acknowledging application receipt. Specifically mentions cardboard flip-style club badge and membership card was probably part of the package but is not mentioned. - **$75 $150 $200**

**❏ CMR-56. "Mary Marvel" Fabric Scarf,**
1946. Probable store item, maker unknown. - **$75 $150 $300**

CMR-57

**❏ CMR-57. "Mary Marvel Club Official Badge" Cardboard Flip-Pin,**
1946. 1-7/8" stiff cardboard with bar pin and string so piece can be flipped to show each side. A scarce badge for Mary's club members. - **$125 $250 $350**

CMR-58

CMR-59

**❏ CMR-58. Whiz Wheaties Comic,**
1946. Thirty-two pages. Captain Marvel premium. Issued taped to Wheaties box. - **$100 $400 $ - (not found in Mint condition)**

**❏ CMR-59. Flute With Balloon,**
1946. - **$40 $80 $120**

CMR-60

CMR-61

**❏ CMR-60. Magic Flute With Whistle on Card,**
1946. End piece in green or grey plastic.
Near Mint On Card - **$200**
Loose - **$30 $60 $90**

**❏ CMR-61. "Shazam" Paper Pop-Up String Toy,**
1946. Fawcett Publications. - **$80 $150 $225**

CMR-62 CMR-63 CMR-64 CMR-65 CMR-66

**❏ CMR-62. Captain Marvel Syroco-Style 5" Figure,**
1943. Rare. Fawcett premium by Multi Products, Chicago. "Captain" spelled out on base. No box produced. 12 known. - **$1500 $3500 $5000**

**❏ CMR-63. Captain Marvel 5" Figure,**
1946. Rare. Fawcett premium by Kerr Co. of unknown blend of resin-like materials. "Capt." on base. No box produced. Less than 10 known. - **$1500 $3500 $5000**

**❏ CMR-64. Captain Marvel Jr. 5" Figure,**
1946. Fawcett premium by Kerr Co. of unknown blend of resin-like materials. No box produced. - **$775 $1500 $2000**

**❏ CMR-65. Mary Marvel 5" Figure,**
1946. Fawcett premium by Kerr Co. of unknown blend of resin-like materials. Light color hair. No box produced. - **$775 $1500 $2000**

**❏ CMR-66. Mary Marvel 5" Figure,**
1946. Rare. Similar to previous item. Hair may be light or dark. Wearing red dress with red belt and red lightning bolt. - **$1200 $2400 $3650**

CMR-67

CMR-68

**❏ CMR-67. Marvel Bunny 4 3/4" Figure,**
1946. Fawcett premium by Kerr Co. Rare. No box produced. - **$1200 $3000 $4500**

**❏ CMR-68. Marvel Bunny 6" Figure,**
1946. Fawcett premium by Kerr Co. of plastic. 20 known. Most examples have damaged or repaired ears. For C.C. Beck designed box in Near Mint, add $750. - **$1000 $3000 $4400**

CMR-69 CMR-70 CMR-71

❑ **CMR-69. Captain Marvel 6-1/2" Figure,**
1946. Scarce. Fawcett premium by Kerr Co. of plastic. For C.C. Beck designed box in Near Mint add $750. - **$1000 $2500 $4000**

❑ **CMR-70. Captain Marvel Jr. 6-1/2" Figure,**
1946. Scarce. Fawcett premium by Kerr Co. of plastic. For C.C. Beck designed box in Near Mint add $750. - **$900 $1800 $2500**

❑ **CMR-71. Mary Marvel 6-1/2" Figure,**
1946. Scarce. Fawcett premium by Kerr Co. of plastic. For C.C. Beck designed box in Near Mint add $750. - **$1000 $2000 $3000**

CMR-72

❑ **CMR-72. Statuettes Store Sign,**
1946. Rare. R. W. Kerr Co. Art by C. C. Beck. 6 known. - **$1200 $2700 $4200**

CMR-73

❑ **CMR-73. "Mary Marvel" Diecut Fiberboard Figure Badge,**
1946. Full color litho. paper front. -
**$100 $200 $350**

CMR-74

❑ **CMR-74. "Captain Marvel Adventures" Vol. 10 #55,**
1946. Scarce. Atlas Theater, Detroit. Theater replaced original cover of issue #55 with their own cover picturing generic heroes. -
**$100 $300 $500**

CMR-75

❑ **CMR-75. Tie-Clip,**
1946. On Card - **$35 $75 $125**
Clip Only - **$25 $50 $75**

CMR-76

CMR-77 CMR-78

❑ **CMR-76. Captain Marvel Glow-In-The-Dark Picture,**
1946. - **$75 $150 $300**

❑ **CMR-77. Captain Marvel Jr. Glow-In-The-Dark Picture,**
1946. - **$75 $150 $250**

❑ **CMR-78. Mary Marvel Glow-In-The-Dark Picture,**
1946.- **$75 $150 $250**

CMR-79 CMR-80

❑ **CMR-79. Hoppy Glow-In-The-Dark Picture,**
1946. Came unframed. - **$50 $75 $150**

❑ **CMR-80. "Captain Marvel Adventures" Wheaties Comic Book,**
1946. Copies were taped to box. Good - **$75**
About Fine - **$250**

CMR-81

❑ **CMR-81. "Note Paper" Boxed Set,**
1946. Held 18 sheets and envelopes.
Near Mint Boxed - **$400**
Each Sheet - **$5 $15 $25**

CMR-82 CMR-83

❑ **CMR-82. "Captain Marvel" Litho. Button,**
1946. From set of 10 picturing Fawcett characters. - **$50 $125 $200**

❑ **CMR-83. "Mary Marvel" Litho. Button,**
1946. From set of 10 picturing Fawcett characters. - **$40 $110 $175**

CMR-84 CMR-85

❑ **CMR-84. "Captain Marvel Jr." Litho. Button,**
1946. From set of 10 picturing Fawcett characters. -**$50 $125 $200**

❑ **CMR-85. "Billy Batson" Litho. Button,**
1946. From set of 10 picturing Fawcett characters. - **$40 $110 $175**

CMR-86 CMR-87

❑ **CMR-86. "Hoppy The Marvel Bunny" Litho. Button,**
1946. From set of 10 picturing Fawcett characters. - **$30 $60 $100**

❑ **CMR-87. "Bulletman" Litho. Button,**
1946. From set of 10 picturing Fawcett characters. - **$20 $50 $80**

CMR-88 CMR-89

❑ **CMR-88. "Golden Arrow" Litho. Button,**
1946. From set of 10 picturing Fawcett characters. - **$20 $50 $80**

❑ **CMR-89. "Ibis" Litho. Button,**
1946. From set of 10 picturing Fawcett characters. - **$20 $50 $80**

CMR-90 CMR-91

❑ **CMR-90. "Nyoka" Litho. Button,**
1946. From set of 10 picturing Fawcett characters. - **$20 $50 $80**

❑ **CMR-91. "Radar" Litho. Button,**
1946. From set of 10 picturing Fawcett characters. - **$20 $50 $80**

CMR-92

❑ **CMR-92. "Mary Marvel" Felt Patch,**
1946. Scarce. Fawcett Publications. -
**$75 $200 $325**

CMR-93

❑ **CMR-93. Captain Marvel Felt Club Patch,**
1946. - **$30 $60 $100**

CMR-94

❑ **CMR-94. Captain Marvel Jr. Felt Patch,**
1946. Blue - **$25 $50 $100**
Dark Green (Scarce) - **$50 $150 $275**

CMR-95

❑ **CMR-95. Felt Pennant,**
1946. Blue - **$40 $80 $150**
Yellow - **$50 $100 $200**

CMR-96 CMR-97

❑ **CMR-96. Plastic Keychain Fob,**
1946. Back inscription "This Certifies That The Holder Of This Key Ring Is A Bonafied Member Of The Captain Marvel Club". - **$30 $75 $150**

❑ **CMR-97. Rocket Raider Compass Ring,**
c. 1946. Red and black enamel paint on brass, unmarked but attributed to Captain Marvel. -
**$300 $800 $1600**

CMR-98

**❑ CMR-98. Captain Marvel Club Premiums Ad,**
1946. Fawcett Publications. Comic book page offering six premiums including set of 10 character litho. buttons picturing Marvels and other Fawcett adventure characters. - **$2 $6 $10**

Box side

CMR-99

**❑ CMR-99. Capt. Marvel and Mary Marvel Illustrated Soap Box,**
1947. Illustrated Soap Co., Brooklyn, N.Y. Rare. Box only - **$200 $400 $600**

CMR-100

**❑ CMR-100. "Mary Marvel Illustrated Soap" Boxed,**
1947. Probable store item by Illustrated Soap Inc., Brooklyn, N.Y. This box holds three soap bars, each with different color decal. Also issued was three-bar set with Captain, Jr. and Mary.
Each Complete Box - **$200 $400 $750**

CMR-101

**❑ CMR-101. Box Set of Race Cars,**
1947. Store item by Automatic Toy Co. Numbered set of four.
Boxed With Keys - **$1250 $2500 $3500**
Each Car Loose, No Keys - **$125 $250 $450**

CMR-102

**❑ CMR-102. Sweater,**
1947. Store item by Somerset Knitting Mills, Philadelphia. - **$100 $300 $400**

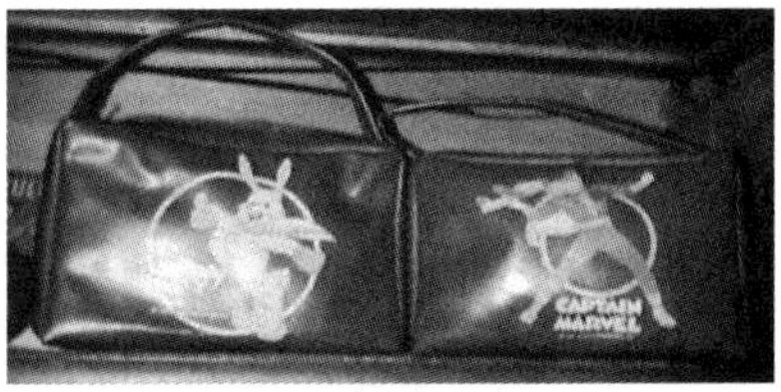

CMR-103

**❑ CMR-103. Hoppy And Captain Marvel Brunch Bags,**
1947-48. Store items. Captain Marvel has color image on red and is from 1947 while Hoppy has color image on dark green and is from 1948. Both are scarce.
Captain Marvel - **$500 $750 $1000**
Hoppy - **$500 $1000 $1500**

CMR-104

**❑ CMR-104. "Captain Marvel" Watch,**
1948. Store item and probable premium. Made in two sizes. Boxed - **$225 $650 $950**
Watch Only - **$125 $250 $500**

CMR-105

❑ **CMR-105. "Mary Marvel" Wristwatch,**
1948. Fawcett Publications copyright.
Boxed - **$200 $500 $800**
Watch Only - **$100 $200 $425**

CMR-106

CMR-107

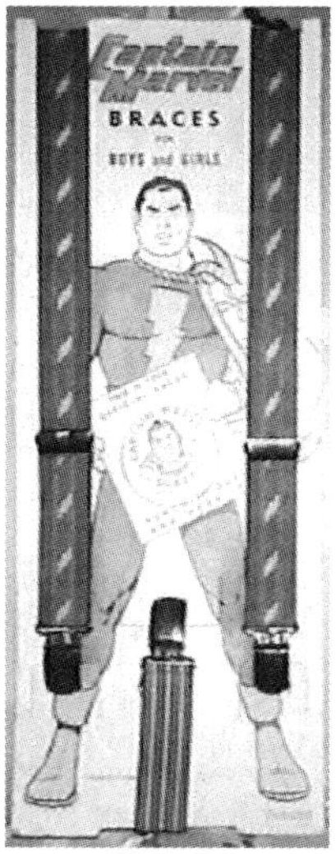


CMR-108

❑ **CMR-106. "Capt. Marvel Jr." Wristwatch,**
1948. Scarce. Offered by the Fawcett Club and not known with a box. Luminous hands and blue, green, or red plastic strap. - **$300 $600 $1000**

❑ **CMR-107. "Shazam-Captain Marvel Club" Litho. Button,**
1948. Fawcett Publications. - **$40 $85 $150**

❑ **CMR-108. Captain Marvel Braces" On Display Card,**
1948. Store item by Dunhill. Card includes punch-out "Official Badge" reading "Captain Marvel Shazam." Complete - **$200 $400 $800**

CMR-109

(CLOSE-UP OF THE CAPT. MARVEL CORNER IMAGE)

(A ?NECESSARY? WARNING IN THE FINE PRINT)

❑ **CMR-109. Captain Marvel Play Cape,**
1948. Only one known. This one shown is in Fine + condition. - **$500 $1000 $1500**

CMR-110

❑ **CMR-110. Captain Marvel & Others Blotter Pad,**
1948. Imprinted for J. T. Flagg Knitting Co. by publisher Brown & Bigelow Co. Cello. cover also pictures Red Ryder, Little Beaver, Gene Autry. - **$75 $150 $250**

CMR-111

❑ **CMR-111. "Hoppy The Marvel Bunny An Animated Novelty Book",**
c. 1948. Store item by John Martins House Inc., Kenosha, Wis. Spiral binding with four pop-ups. Rare. - **$200 $400 $600**

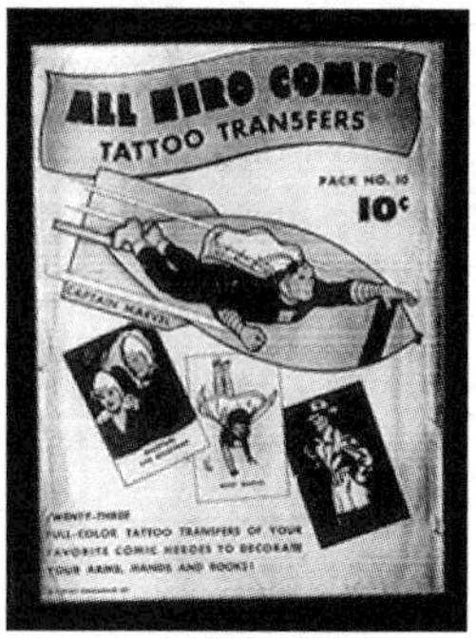


CMR-112

CMR-113

❑ **CMR-112. "All Hero Comic" Tattoo Transfers Pack,**
c. 1948. Fawcett Publications. Retail packet of 23 with envelope sample images of Captain Marvel, Bulletgirl and Bulletman, Mary Marvel, Radar. - **$75 $150 $250**

❑ **CMR-113. Captain Marvel Club Button,**
1949. English Club. 1 1/4" cello. button. - **$250 $500 $750**

CMR-114

CMR-115

❑ **CMR-114. "Captain Marvel" Polo Shirt,**
1949. Store item by Flagg Polo Shirt. Rare, particularly near mint with company and Good Housekeeping labels. - **$150 $350 $800**

❑ **CMR-115. Portrait Picture,**
1940s. Comes with blank bottom margin or with "Capt. Marvel Appears Monthly In Whiz Comics." A third variety is known with text on reverse promoting movie serial.
Blank Margin - **$40 $75 $125**
Text Margin - **$50 $100 $150**
Text Reverse - **$75 $125 $175**

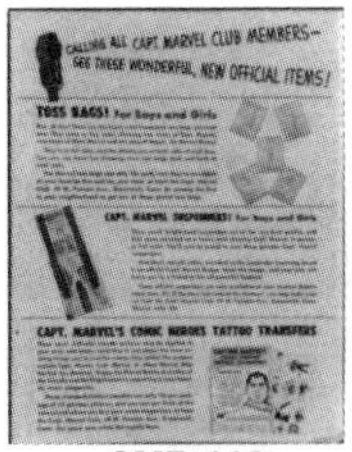

CMR-116

CMR-117

❑ **CMR-116. Merchandise Sheet,**
1940s. Regularly issued by Captain Marvel Club. - **$15 $30 $45**

❑ **CMR-117. Captain Marvel Club Membership Ad,**
1940s. Fawcett Publications. Comic book page ad offering Secret Code Finder, Magic Membership Card, Official Club Button. - **$10 $20 $30**

CMR-118

❑ **CMR-118. Captain Marvel Club Button,**
1940s. English Club. 1"Cello. - **$150 $300 $500**

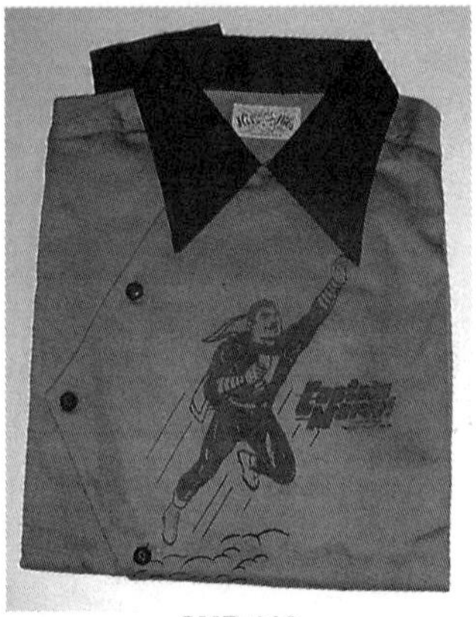


CMR-119

❑ **CMR-119. Captain Marvel Shirt,**
1940s. - **$300 $600 $900**

CMR-120

CMR-121

❑ **CMR-120. "Mechanix Illustrated" Subscription Offer,**
1940s. Fawcett Publications. Comic book page ad utilizing Captain Marvel as promoter for sister publication by Fawcett. - **$10 $20 $30**

❑ **CMR-121. "Captain Marvel's Radar Racer" Punch-Out In Envelope,**
1940s. From series by Reed & Associates copyright by Fawcett Public ations. Assembly parts are for race car pictured on envelope.
Unpunched - **$50 $125 $200**

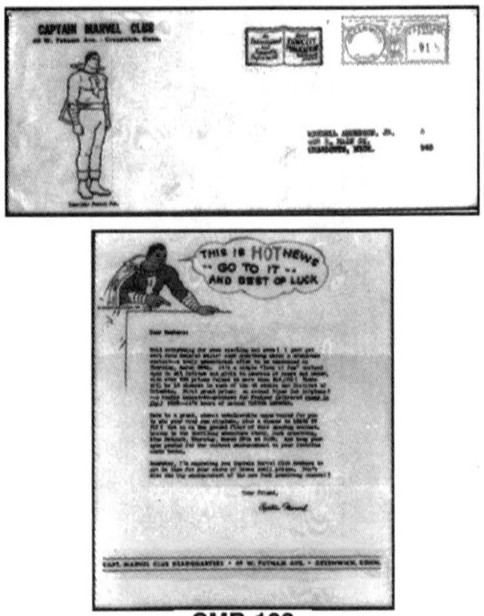


CMR-122

❑ **CMR-122. Club Letter With Envelope,**
1940s. Text for Jack Armstrong contest by Wheaties offering actual Piper Cub airplane as grand prize.
Envelope - **$25 $50 $75**
Letter- **$30 $60 $100**

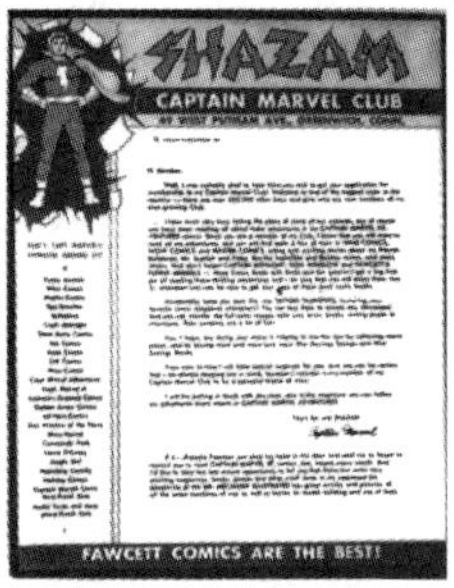


CMR-123

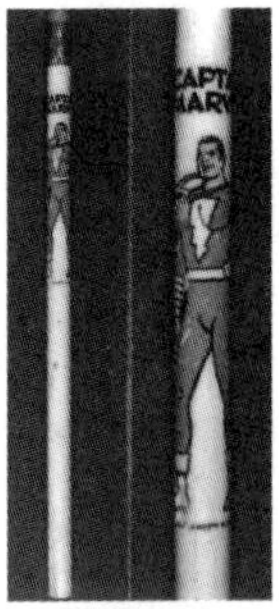

CMR-124

❑ **CMR-123. Club Letter,**
1940s. Example of many sent to club members. - **$15 $30 $60**

❑ **CMR-124. Pencil,**
1940s. Scarce. - **$35 $125 $225**

CMR-125

❑ **CMR-125. "Comic Heroes Iron-Ons" Packet,**
1940s. Envelope held 24 transfers.
Complete In Envelope - **$100 $150 $200**

CMR-126

❑ **CMR-126. "War Stamps Savings Book" Envelope,**
1940s. Held World War II savings stamp booklet. Included with mailings to club members. - **$100 $200 $300**

CMR-127

❑ **CMR-127. "Jig-Saw" Puzzle #1,**
1940s. Store item by L. Miller & Son Ltd., England. Boxed - **$35 $75 $150**

CMR-128

❑ **CMR-128. "Magic Membership Card",**
1940s. - **$40 $100 $175**

CMR-129

❑ **CMR-129. "Mechanix Illustrated" Magazine Subscription Handbill,**
1940s. Captain Marvel pictorial endorsement for magazine subscription. Included with mailings to club members. - **$20 $40 $75**

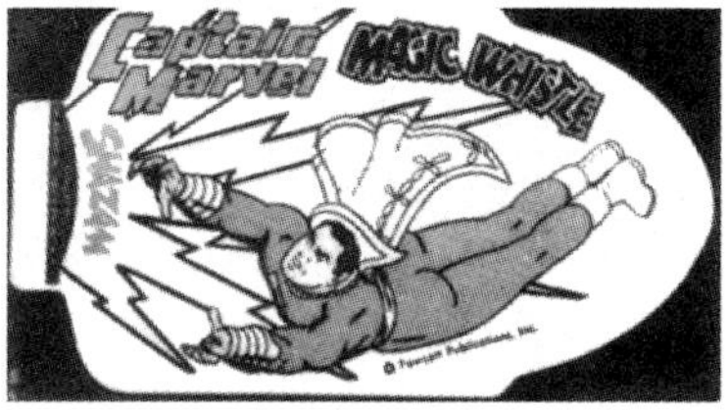


CMR-130

❑ **CMR-130. "Magic Whistle" Diecut Cardboard,**
1940s. American Seed Co., Lancaster, Pennsylvania. Working whistle that opens to show premiums earned by selling seed products. - **$30 $80 $120**

CMR-131

❑ **CMR-131. "Magic Whistle" Envelope,**
1940s. Reverse depicts generic premiums. Envelope Only - **$60 $120 $180**

CMR-132

❑ **CMR-132. Club Christmas Kit In Mailer Envelope,**
1940s. Came with cover letter and sheet of 20 Fawcett character gummed stamps.
Near Mint In Mailer - **$150**
Letter - **15 $35 $60**
Stamp Sheet - **$15 $35 $60**

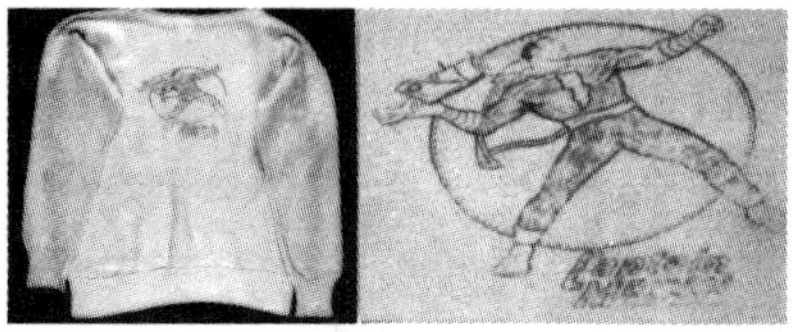

CMR-133

❑ **CMR-133. Child's Sweatshirt,**
1940s. Scarce. - **$75 $150 $250**

CMR-134

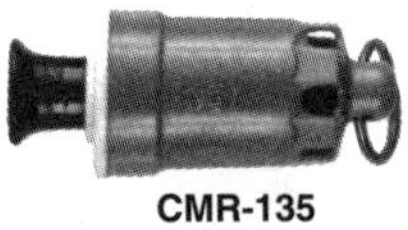

CMR-135

❑ **CMR-134. "Captain Marvel/Shazam" Cello. On Silvered Brass Pencil Clip ,**
1940s. - **$40 $85 $135**

❑ **CMR-135. "Captain Marvel" Power Siren,**
1940s. Store item. Red plastic siren whistle with metal loop ring. - **$50 $100 $150**

CMR-136

CMR-137

❑ **CMR-136. "Captain Marvel And The Good Humor Man" Movie Comic,**
1950. Jack Carson on cover. - **$47 $142 $500**

❑ **CMR-137. "Captain Marvel And The Lieutenants Of Safety" Comic Book #1 ,**
1950. Rare. Fawcett Publications/Ebasco Services. - **$233 $700 $1400**

CMR-138

❑ **CMR-138. "The Boy Who Never Heard Of Captain Marvel" Comic Booklet,**
1950. Bond Bread. Pocket size comic with 24 pages. Two other titles in series are "Captain Marvel And The Stolen City" and "Captain Marvel Meets The Weatherman."
Each - **$37 $110 $240**

CMR-139

CMR-140

❑ **CMR-139. "Captain Marvel And The Lieutenants Of Safety" Comic Book #2 ,**
1950. Rare. Fawcett Publications/Ebasco Services. - **$183 $550 $1000**

❑ **CMR-140. "Captain Marvel And The Lieutenants Of Safety" Comic Book #3 ,**
1951. Rare. Fawcett Publications/Ebasco Services. - **$183 $550 $1000**

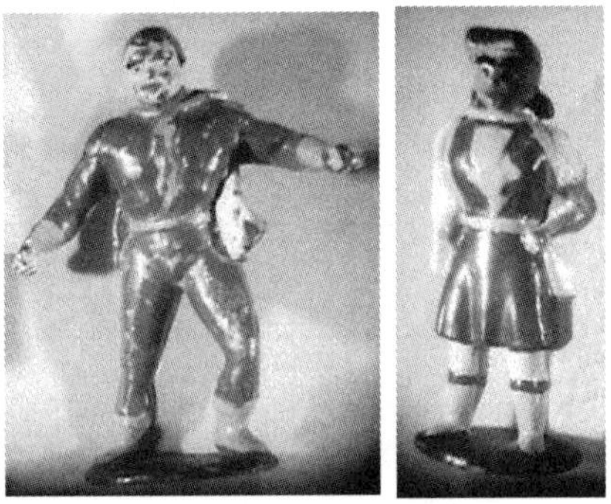

CMR-141

❑ **CMR-141. Captain Marvel And Mary Marvel Lead Figures,**
1954. Store item by Timpo. Captain Marvel Jr. was also issued. Originals by this English firm have hollow bodies but reproductions are known with solid bodies. Each - **$25 $75 $150**

CMR-142

❑ **CMR-142. Tattoo Transfers,**
1955. Pack Number 2 shown. - **$25 $55 $100**

CMR-143

❑ **CMR-143. Coco-Wheats "Tattoo Transfers" Kit With Mailer Envelope,**
1956. Mailer - **$10 $20 $30**
Illustrated Inner Envelope With Two Sheets - **$25 $55 $100**

CMR-144

CMR-145

❑ **CMR-144. "Captain Marvel Club" Cello. Button,**
c. 1968. Mostly red, yellow and black 1-3/4". Button first appeared in the late 1960s and carries no sponsor or maker information. Several years later, Captain Marvel resurfaced in 1973 in DC Comics' *Shazam* #1. - **$10 $25 $50**

❑ **CMR-145. "Shazam Is Coming" 4" Cello. Button,**
1972. N.P.P. Inc. - **$10 $25 $50**

CMR-146

❑ **CMR-146. "Shazam!" Puzzle,**
1978. - **$10 $20 $40**

CMR-147

CMR-148

❑ **CMR-147. "Power of Shazam" Sign,**
1994. 19x35" sign promoting the return of Captain Marvel to comics. - **$20 $35 $50**

❑ **CMR-148. Bean Bag Figure,**
1999. Warner Bros. Store Exclusive. - **$8**

CMR-149

CMR-150

❑ **CMR-149. Action Figure,**
1999. DC Super-Heroes Collection. Display stand is included. - **$20**

❑ **CMR-150. "Kingdom Come" Resin Statue,**
1999. Sculpted by Alex Ross, based on his rendition of Capt. Marvel in the comic mini-series. Statue is copper-colored. Boxed - **$250**

CMR-151

❑ **CMR-151. Billy Batson/Captain Marvel Action Figures,**
2000. With sound chip in box. - **$50**

CMR-152

❑ **CMR-152. Full Color Resin Statue,**
2001. 9 1/2" tall. Full color hand painted statue from the Kingdom Come comic series. Designed and sculpted by Alex Ross. - **$150**

## Captain Midnight

**A shadowy plane and a mysterious pilot...diving furiously from the night sky...Captain Midnight and his Secret Squadron battled the sinister forces of evil on radio during most of the 1940s. The program originated in 1939 over WGN in Chicago, sponsored by the Skelly Oil Co. and broadcast in the Midwest. The following year it went national on the Mutual network sponsored by Ovaltine, which had just dropped Little Orphan Annie. Captain Midnight's Secret Squadron was one of radio's major producers of premiums. For an Ovaltine seal and a dime kids became Secret Squadron members. Decoder badges, pins, patches, mugs, maps, booklets, wings and rings followed in great profusion until the show closed in 1949.**

**The Captain made his first comic book appearance in *The Funnies* #57 in July 1941, moved to *Popular Comics* a year later and had his own book from September 1942 to September 1948. A 15-episode chapter play was released by Columbia Pictures in 1942. The *Captain Midnight* TV series premiered in 1953, starring Richard Webb as the American superhero and aired for four years on ABC and CBS, still sponsored by Ovaltine, still offering Secret Squadron mugs and decoder badges. The Secret Squadron logo, SS, was changed to SQ.**

**In the late 1950s, after Ovaltine declined to give up the copyrighted Captain Midnight name, the show was syndicated in reruns as *Jet Jackson, Flying Commando*. In 1988 Ovaltine offered a Captain Midnight SQ Secret Squadron watch in exchange for a proof-of-purchase seal.**

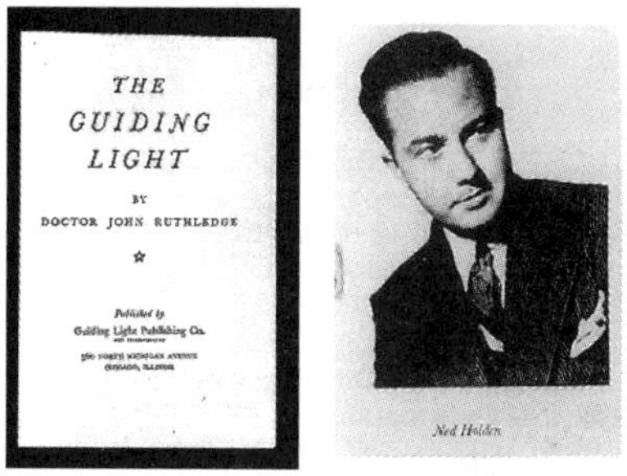


CMD-1

❑ **CMD-1. Radio Portrayer Photo In "The Guiding Light" Booklet,**
1938. Guiding Light Publishing Co./Ovaltine. Radio program synopsis booklet picturing Ed Prentiss, the radio voice of Captain Midnight on Mutual Network although identified by "Ned Holden" name of Guiding Light character. - **$35 $75 $160**

CMD-2

❑ **CMD-2. Skelly Large 36x84" Cardboard Display Sign,**
1939. Rare. Has three brass grommet holes to aid in displaying. - **$800 $1600 $3200**

CMD-3

CMD-4

❑ **CMD-3. Skelly Oil "Flight Patrol Reporter" Vol. 1 #1 Newspaper,**
Spring 1939. Six issues between Spring 1939 and March 1940. First Issue - **$40 $125 $225**
Other 5 Issues - **$25 $85 $150**

❑ **CMD-4. Skelly Oil "Flight Patrol Reporter" Vol. 1 #2 Newspaper,**
June 15, 1939. - **$25 $85 $150**

CMD-5

❑ **CMD-5. "Trick And Riddle Book",**
1939. Skelly Oil Co. - **$10 $40 $75**

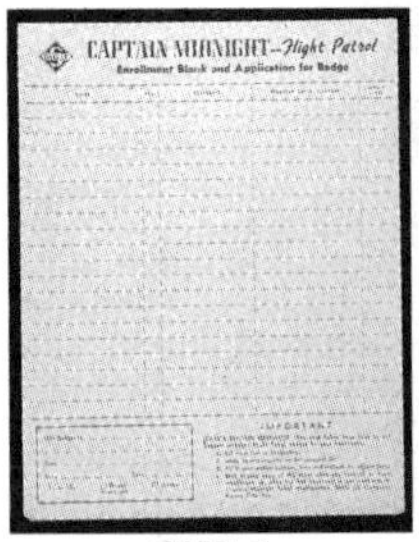


CMD-6

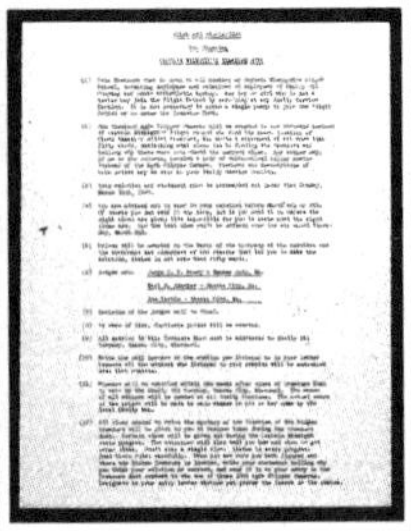

CMD-7

❑ **CMD-6. Flight Patrol Badge Application,**
1939. Skelly Oil Co. - **$30 $75 $140**

❑ **CMD-7. Treasure Hunt Rules,**
1939. Skelly Oil Co. - **$20 $40 $75**

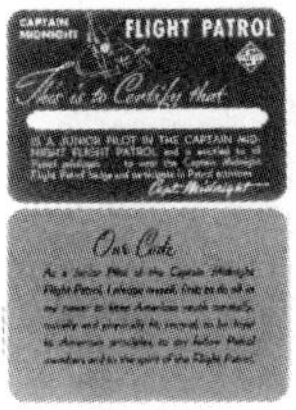


CMD-8

CMD-9

❑ **CMD-8. Membership Card,**
1939. Skelly Oil Co. - **$20 $75 $140**

❑ **CMD-9. "Air Heroes" Stamp Album,**
1939. Skelly Oil. Holds 16 stamps.
Empty - **$10 $20 $50**
Complete - **$25 $65 $100**

CMD-10

CMD-11

❑ **CMD-10. Portrait Photo,**
1939. Skelly Oil Co. - **$25 $70 $125**

❑ **CMD-11. "Happy Landings" Photo,**
1939. Skelly Oil Co. Captain Midnight with Patsy and Chuck. Bottom left margin says "Compliments of Skelly Oil Co." A reproduction exists. On the reproduction, both letter "i"s in "Compliments" and "Oil" are missing the dot. Also, the tonal contrast of the photo is much lighter than the original. - **$20 $60 $90**

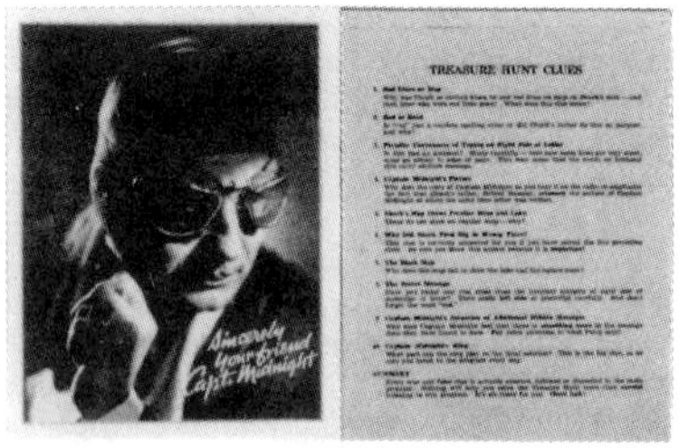


CMD-12

❑ **CMD-12. Portrait Photo With Treasure Hunt Back,**
1939. Skelly Oil Co. - **$60 $125 $200**

CMD-13

CMD-14

❑ **CMD-13. "Chuck Ramsey" Portrait Photo,**
1939. Skelly Oil Co. - **$20 $50 $90**

❑ **CMD-14. Unmarked Known As 'Chuck's Treasure Map' 9x11".**
1939. Skelly Oil Co. - **$50 $165 $275**

CMD-15

CMD-16

❑ **CMD-15. Mysto-Magic Weather Forecasting Flight Wings Badge,**
1939. Skelly Oil Co.
With litmus paper - **$15 $30 $60**
Without litmus paper - **$10 $20 $35**

❑ **CMD-16. "Flight Patrol Commander" Brass Badge,**
1939. Rare. Skelly Oil Co. One of the rarest Captain Midnight badges. - **$400 $1200 $1800**

CMD-17

CMD-18

❑ **CMD-17. Skelly Oil "Fly With Captain Midnight" Radio Sponsorship Announcement Brochure,**
1940. Pictures Captain Midnight, Chuck, Patsy, Steve, Ivan Shark. Skelly president announces show with list of midwest stations. -
**$100 $275 $475**

❑ **CMD-18. Skelly Flight Patrol Member Card,**
1940. - **$35 $85 $165**

CMD-19

❑ **CMD-19. Membership Card,**
1940. Skelly Oil Co. - **$20 $75 $140**

(FRONT) (BACK)

CMD-20

❑ **CMD-20. Skelly Flight Patrol Brass Spinner Medal,**
1940. Spinner disk pictures Captain Midnight, Patsy Donovan, Chuck Ramsey, propeller design. - **$10 $15 $30**

CMD-21

CMD-22

❑ **CMD-21. "Mexican Jumping Beans" Paper Bag,**
1940. Skelly Oil Co. For premium game utilizing jumping beans. - **$75 $175 $275**

❑ **CMD-22. "Mexican Ringo-Jumpo" Game Sheet,**
1940. Skelly Oil Co. For jumping bean game. - **$100 $225 $400**

CMD-23

❑ **CMD-23. "Captain Midnight's Flight Patrol Reporter" Vol. 1 #6 Newspaper,**
1940. Skelly Oil Co. Last issue. - **$25 $85 $150**

(ENLARGED VIEW)

CMD-24

❑ **CMD-24. Skelly Oil "Flight Patrol" Airline Map,**
1940. Scarce. 11x17" opened. - **$125 $300 $550**

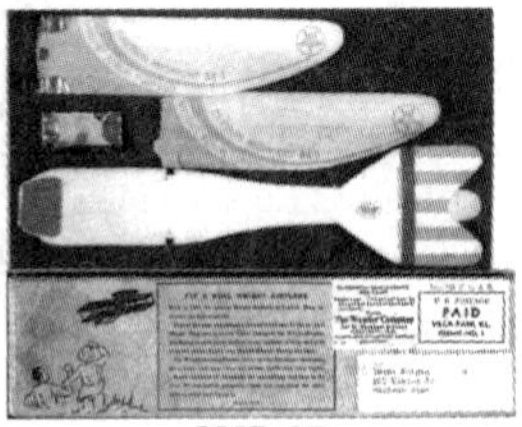

CMD-25

CMD-26

❑ **CMD-25. "Wright Airplane" Balsa/Paper Assembly Kit With Box ,**
1941. Scarce. Wings inscribed "Captain Midnight SS-1" and "Wright Aerial Torpedo".
Near Mint Boxed - **$400**
Assembled - **$75 $175 $275**

❑ **CMD-26. Mystery Dial Code-O-Graph Brass Decoder,**
1941. First Captain Midnight decoder. - **$40 $80 $140**

CMD-27

❑ **CMD-27. "Detect-O-Scope",**
1941. Cardboard tube holds metal piece to judge altitudes. Also see item CMD-31. - **$35 $75 $165**

CMD-28

❑ **CMD-28. Club Manual With Member Papers,**
1941. With card and parents letter.
Complete Near Mint - **$275**
Manual Only - **$70 $140 $225**

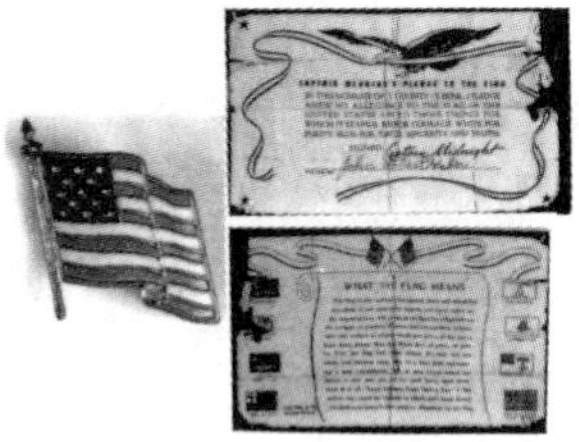

CMD-29

❑ **CMD-29. American Flag Loyalty Pin With Paper,**
1941. Patriotic text paper held in tube on pin reverse.
Badge - **$25 $70 $100**
Paper - **25 $50 $100**

CMD-30

❑ **CMD-30. "Flight Commander" Handbook,**
1941. - **$75 $200 $325**

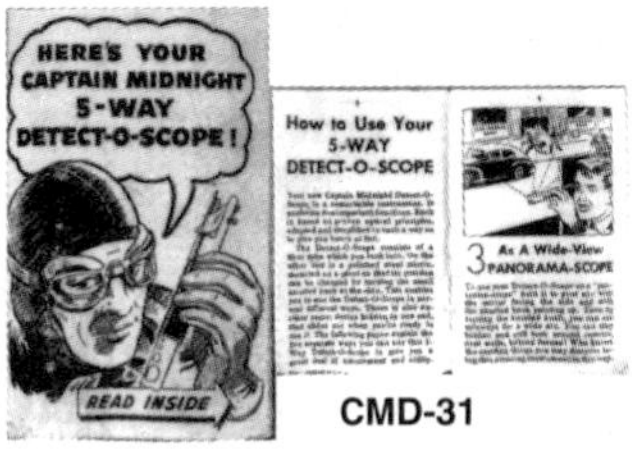


CMD-31

❑ **CMD-31. "Detect-O-Scope" Instruction Leaflet,**
1941. - **$35 $85 $150**

CMD-32

CMD-33

❑ **CMD-32. Whirlwind Whistling Brass Ring,**
1941. No Captain Midnight markings. - **$150 $400 $800**

❑ **CMD-33. "Whirlwind Whistling Ring" Instruction Sheet,**
1941. - **$75 $125 $175**

CMD-34

CMD-35

❑ **CMD-34. Flight Commander Brass Decoder Ring,**
1941. Inner side has "Captain Midnight Super Code 3". -**$125 $300 $500**

❑ **CMD-35. "Super Book Of Comics" Comic Book #3,**
1941. Various sponsors. - **$31 $93 $290**

CMD-36

CMD-37

❑ **CMD-36. Club Manual,**
1942. - **$60 $125 $200**

❑ **CMD-37. Manual Insert,**
1942. Paper sheet. Owner was instructed to "Tear Out and Destroy After Reading!" Explains how instructions to use "Master Code 6" are to fool outsiders and to actually use "Master Code 2." Loose Insert - **$10 $20 $35**

CMD-38

❑ **CMD-38. "Flight Commander" Club Manual,**
1942. Leaflet including "Official Commission" certification panel. - **$75 $175 $325**

CMD-39

CMD-40

CMD-41

❑ **CMD-39. Photomatic Decoder Brass Badge,**
1942. Original glossy black and white photo usually missing or replaced as club manual instructed owner to insert a photo of themselves.
With Original Photo - **$75 $150 $300**
Without Original Photo - **$35 $65 $100**

❑ **CMD-40. Flight Commander Flying Cross Brass Badge,**
1942. - **$50 $100 $200**

❑ **CMD-41. Mystic Eye Detector Look-In Brass Ring,**
1942. Brass eagle cover over viewer mirror, issued by Captain Midnight, Radio Orphan Annie, The Lone Ranger. - **$40 $80 $150**

CMD-42

CMD-43

❑ **CMD-42. Sliding Secret Compartment Brass Ring,**
1942. Also offered as Kix Pilot's Ring in 1945. - **$75 $100 $200**

❑ **CMD-43. Marine Corps Insignia Brass Ring,**
1942. - **$100 $275 $500**

CMD-44

❑ **CMD-44. "Magic Blackout Lite-Ups" Kit With Envelope,**
1942. Near Mint In Mailer - **$500**
Illustrated Folder Only - **$75 $150 $250**

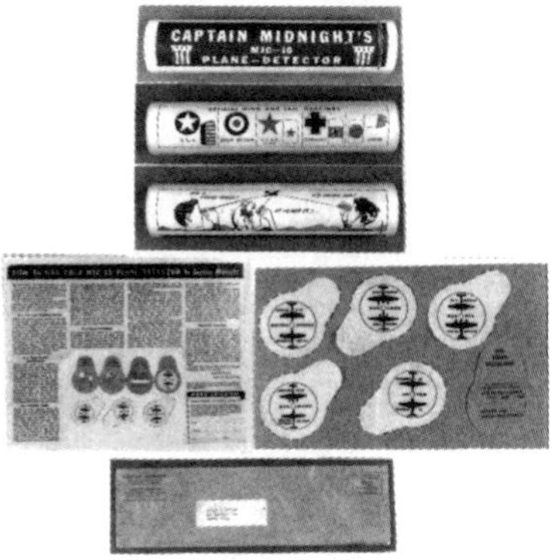


CMD-45

❑ **CMD-45. MJC-10 Plane-Detector Set,**
1942. Rare. Tube with seven disk inserts and 12 airplane silhouettes.
Complete - **$200 $600 $1000**
Tube Only - **$50 $200 $300**

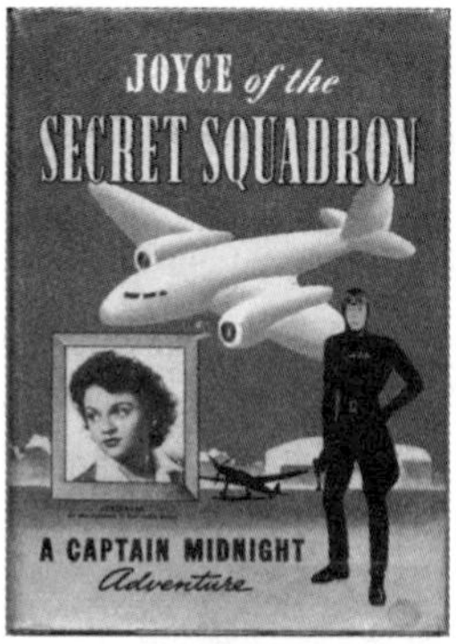


CMD-46

❑ **CMD-46. "Joyce Of The Secret Squadron" Hardback Book,**
1942. Store item by Whitman. A Captain Midnight Adventure with Joyce Ryan
With Dust Jacket - **$10 $25 $40**
No Dust Jacket - **$5 $10 $15**

CMD-47

CMD-48

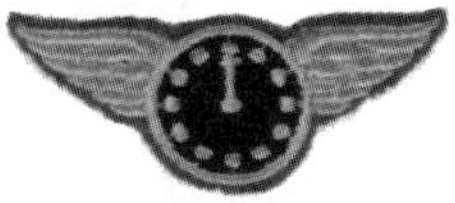
CMD-49

❑ **CMD-47. First Issue Comic Book,**
1942. Store item from Fawcett Publications September 30, 1942. - **$300 $900 $3500**

❑ **CMD-48. Newspaper Comic Strip Introduction Page,**
1942. Full page ad from Chicago Sun edition of Sunday, July 5. - **$25 $60 $125**

❑ **CMD-49. Shoulder Insignia 3-1/2" Wide Fabric Patch,**
1943. - **$60 $125 $200**

CMD-50

❑ **CMD-50. "Captain Midnight and the Moon Woman" Better Little Book,**
1943. - **$15 $45 $90**

CMD-51

❑ **CMD-51. Army "Sleeve Insignia" Folder With Envelope,**
1943. Came with Captain Midnight insignia.
Folder - **$60 $125 $200**
Envelope - **$10 $30 $50**

CMD-52

CMD-53

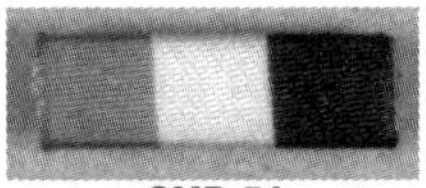
CMD-54

❑ **CMD-52. "Pilot's Badge" With Order Sheet,**
c. 1943. Brass wings badge. In 1933, National Chicle Company offered wings of the same design but finished in silver as a Sky Birds Chewing Gum premium available for 50 wrappers.
Sky Birds Silver Finish - **$20 $40 $85**
Capt. Midnight Gold Finish - **$50 $125 $225**
Capt. Midnight Coupon - **$25 $50 $100**

❑ **CMD-53. Pilot's Badge "Award Of Merit" Certificate,**
c. 1943. - **$75 $150 $300**

❑ **CMD-54. Distinguished Service Ribbon,**
1944. - **$75 $175 $275**

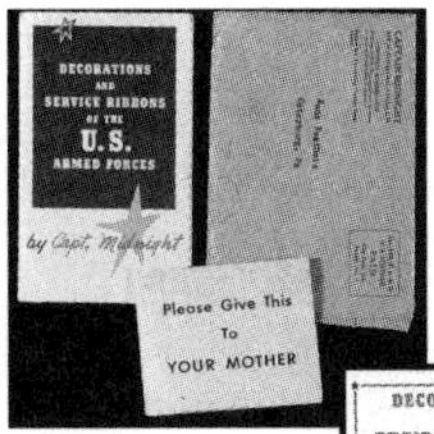

CMD-55

(BOOKLET INTERIOR)

❑ **CMD-55. Service Ribbon Booklet,**
1944. Radio premium.
Booklet - **$50 $100 $150**
Mailer - **$15 $30 $45**
Mother's Letter - **$15 $30 $40**

CMD-56

CMD-57

❑ **CMD-56. "Invention Patent" Acknowledgement Postcard,**
1944. Fawcett comic book premium. Assigns registration number for unknown invention by youthful fan. - **$50 $100 $200**

❑ **CMD-57. Club Manual,**
1945. - **$40 $100 $175**

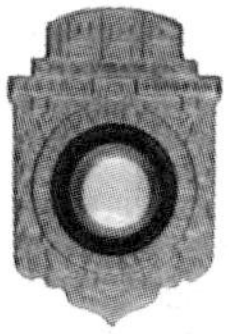
CMD-58

CMD-59

CMD-60

❑ **CMD-58. Magni-Matic Decoder Metal Badge,**
1945. - **$40 $100 $200**

❑ **CMD-59. Mirro-Flash Code-O-Graph Brass Decoder,**
1946. - **$40 $100 $175**

❑ **CMD-60. Mystic Sun God Ring,**
1946. - **$350 $700 $1500**

CMD-61

CMD-62

❑ **CMD-61. Mystic Sun-God Ring Leaflet,**
1946. - **$75 $125 $250**

❑ **CMD-62. Club Manual,**
1946. - **$50 $100 $175**

CMD-63

❑ **CMD-63. "Captain Midnight and Sheik Jomak Khan" Better Little Book #1402,**
1946. - **$10 $40 $80**

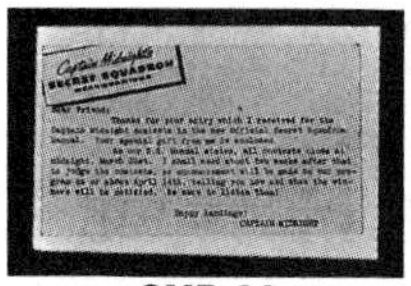
CMD-64

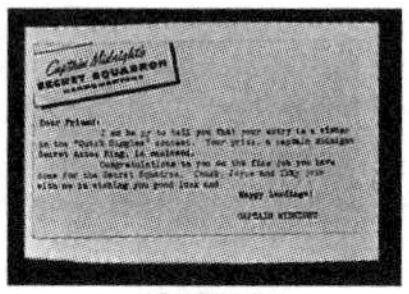
CMD-65

❑ **CMD-64. Contest Entry Acknowledgement,**
1947. Thank you card to entrant of contest closing March 31 with winners to be announced on radio program on or about April 14. -
**$25 $70 $115**

❑ **CMD-65. "Quick Giggles" Contest Winner Notification,** 1947. Winner's notice including prize "Secret Aztec Ring" (Mystic Sun God Ring). - **$20 $60 $100**

CMD-66

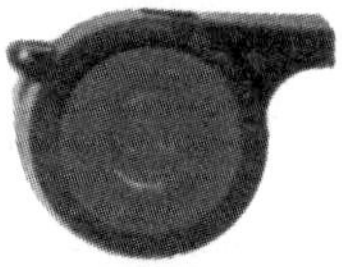
CMD-67

❑ **CMD-66. Shake-Up Mug,**
1947. Portrait on orange plastic with blue lid. A variation is known, perhaps a manufacturing test or error, with a blue top on a creamy white cup.
Orange Version - **$40 $85 $175**
White Version - **$150 $300 $500**

❑ **CMD-67. Whistling Code-O-Graph Plastic Decoder,**
1947. Whistle with movable code wheel. -
**$40 $75 $125**

CMD-68

❑ **CMD-68. Manual,**
1947. First of smaller format. - **$50 $100 $150**

CMD-69

❑ **CMD-69. Ed Prentiss Publicity Photo,**
1947. The Mutual Broadcasting System. Glossy 8x10" with back label noting "Ninth Year On Radio" now "As A New Mutual Program." -
**$30 $75 $125**

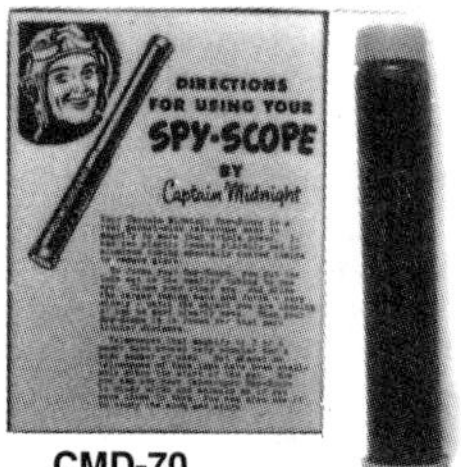

CMD-70

CMD-71

CMD-72

❑ **CMD-70. "Spy-Scope" With Instructions,**
1947. Plastic small telescope in two varieties of plastic rims. Rare Blue Rims - **$40 $85 $175**
Orange Rims - **$30 $75 $125**
Instructions - **$15 $25 $40**

❑ **CMD-71. Mirro-Magic Brass/Plastic Decoder,**
1948. Red plastic reverse usually warped and often missing. - **$125 $200 $325**

❑ **CMD-72. Initial Printing Ring,**
1948. Brass ring with personalized single initial designated by orderer. - **$100 $200 $400**

CMD-73

❑ **CMD-73. Manual,**
1948 - **$50 $100 $160**

CMD-74

CMD-75

❑ **CMD-74. Iron-On Transfer With Mailer Envelope,**
1948. Scarce. Cellophane transfer on tissue sheet with reverse lettering for application to fabric.
Envelope - **$15 $25 $50**
Transfer - **$35 $85 $175**

❑ **CMD-75. "Tattoo Transfers" Kit,**
c. 1948. "Pack No. 8" with both Fawcett and Wander Co. (Ovaltine) copyright. Two sheets with 22 transfers. - **$20 $50 $100**

CMD-76

❑ **CMD-76. Club Manual,**
1949. - **$50 $125 $250**

CMD-77

CMD-78

❑ **CMD-77. Key-O-Matic Code-O-Graph Brass Decoder,**
1949. Without key. - **$40 $85 $150**

❑ **CMD-78. Key-O-Matic Code-O-Graph Brass Key,**
1949. Used with decoder to set letter and number combinations. - **$75 $100 $150**

**CMD-79**

❑ **CMD-79. Three-Sheet,**
1940s. Scarce. Columbia Pictures serial. 41" by 81". - **$2000 $4500 $6500**

**CMD-80**

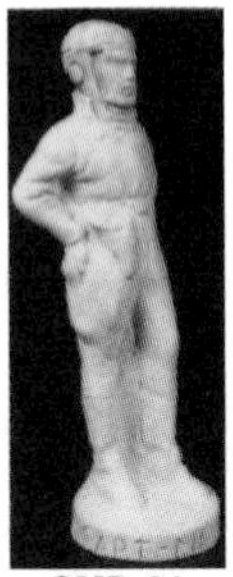

**CMD-81**

❑ **CMD-80. "Captain Midnight" Litho. Button,**
1940s. Scarce. Issuer unknown. Pictures him at radio microphone, no identification other than his name. - **$250 $500 $750**

❑ **CMD-81. Plaster Figure,**
1940s. Store item from series of characters (76 known). Issued between 1941-1947 in white plaster to be painted.
Captain Midnight - **$50 $100 $150**
Most Others- **$5 $10 $15**

**CMD-82**

❑ **CMD-82. "Hot Ovaltine Mug" Leaflet And Related Papers,**
1953. Three pieces included in the box which held the 1953 plastic mug.
Mug Brochure - **$15 $30 $50**
"Mother" Folder - **$5 $10 $15**
"Caution" Slip - **$3 $5 $10**

**CMD-83**

**CMD-84**

❑ **CMD-83. Plastic Mug With Decal,**
1953. - **$20 $40 $60**

❑ **CMD-84. Membership Card,**
1955-56. - **$40 $75 $125**

**CMD-85**

❑ **CMD-85. Manual,**
1955-56. Scarce. - **$60 $200 $350**

**CMD-86**

❑ **CMD-86. Flight Commander Kit,**
1955-56. Envelope - **$10 $20 $30**
Certificate - **$75 $125 $225**
Handbook - **$100 $200 $350**

**CMD-87**

**CMD-88**

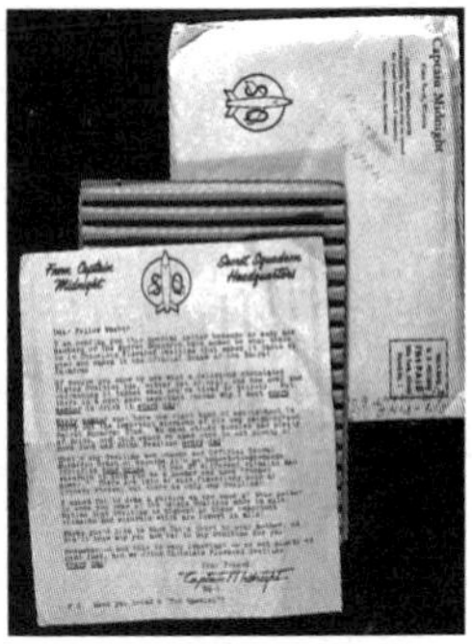

**CMD-89**

❑ **CMD-87. "SQ" Plane Puzzle Decoder Plastic Badge,**
1955-56. Near Mint Decoder With Mailer And Cardboard Holder- **$550**
Decoder Only - **$100 $300 $450**

❑ **CMD-88. "SQ" Cloth Peel-Off Patch,**
1955-56. Unused - **$10 $25 $50**

❑ **CMD-89. Mailer and Letter,**
1955. Mailer and cardboard insert for 1955 decoder. Letter descibes the rocket power of Ovaltine and its benefits.
Letter - **$10 $20 $40**
Mailer - **$20 $40 $60**

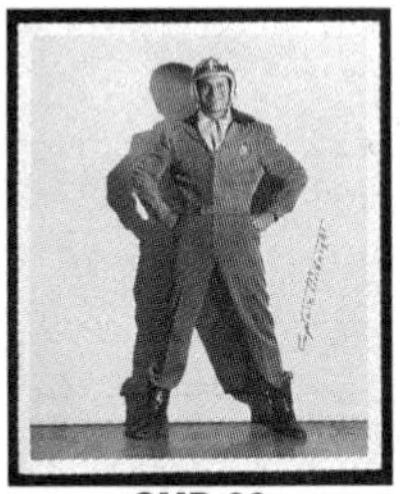

**CMD-90**

**CMD-91**

❑ **CMD-90. Photo,**
1955. Scarce. TV promotion premium. - **$75 $150 $250**

❑ **CMD-91. Richard Webb Photo,**
c. 1955. Issuer unknown. 4x4-1/2" photo. No inscriptions. - **$20 $50 $75**

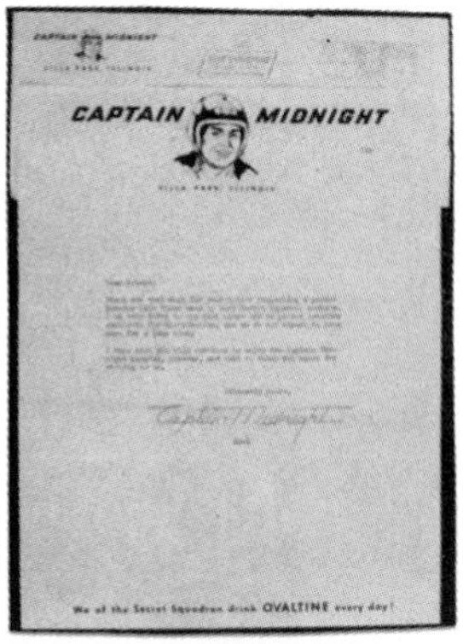


CMD-92

❑ **CMD-92. Ovaltine Premium Letter Of Apology With Envelope,**
1956. Explains "pocket locators" are no longer available. Envelope **- $5 $15 $30**
Letter - **$50 $100 $175**

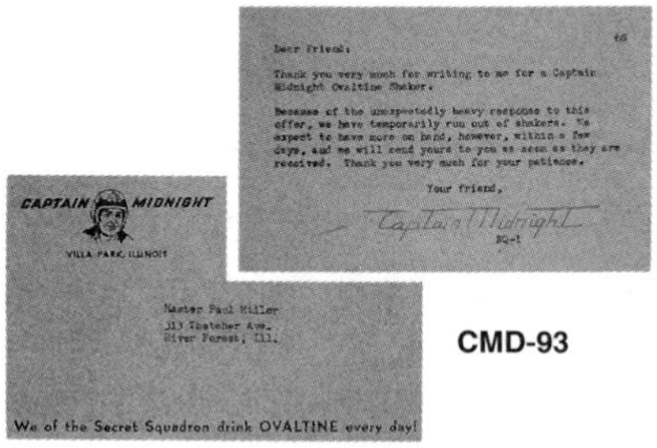


CMD-93

❑ **CMD-93. Postcard Notice,**
1957. Rare. Notice that Ovaltine ran out of shakers and will send when new shipments arrive. -
**$50 $100 $150**

CMD-94

❑ **CMD-94. "Secret Squadron" Membership Kit,**
1957.
Complete With Envelope - **$150 $350 $650**
Club Manual - **$60 $150 $250**
Member Card - **$30 $50 $75**
Silver Dart Decoder - **$50 $150 $300**

CMD-95

CMD-96

❑ **CMD-95. Peel-Off Cloth Patch,**
1957. Unused - **$10 $20 $40**

❑ **CMD-96. Silver Dart "SQ" Jet Plane Decoder Plastic Badge,**
1957. - **$50 $150 $300**

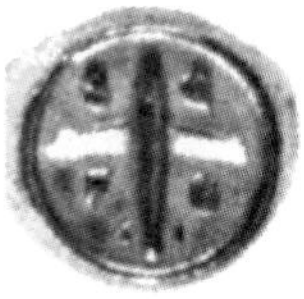

CMD-97

CMD-98

❑ **CMD-97. Flight Commander Signet Ring,**
1957. Silvered plastic depicting jet plane inscribed "SQFC". - **$200 $400 $800**

❑ **CMD-98. Plastic Shake-Up Mug,**
1957. - **$25 $45 $75**

CMD-99

❑ **CMD-99. "Flight Commander's Handbook",**
1957. - **$100 $225 $375**

CMD-100

❑ **CMD-100. Flight Commander Commission Reproduction Certificate,**
c. 1970. Longines Symphonette Society. Accompanied vinyl records re-issue of radio programs. - **$10 $18 $30**

CMD-101

CMD-102

❑ **CMD-101. Flexible Record With Sleeve,**
c. 1970. Longines Symphonette Society. Set of eight radio show program recordings.
Each - **$3 $5 $8**

❑ **CMD-102. Punch-Out Decoder,**
c. 1970. Longines Symphonette Society.
Unpunched - **$8 $12 $20**

CMD-103

❑ **CMD-103. Record,**
1972. Ovaltine premium with sleeve. -
**$15 $25 $50**

CMD-104

❑ **CMD-104. Ovaltine Action Book,**
1977. Ovaltine Products Inc. Published by Marvel Comics Group about 8x10-1/2" with 128 pages. Includes offers for cash and Ovaltine labels of two Captain Midnight records, an Orphan Annie record and an Ovaltine collector's mug showing a Swiss village. - **$25 $50 $75**

CMD-105

❑ **CMD-105. Captain Midnight Record,**
1977. Contains four adventures from the radio show. - **$15 $25 $50**

CMD-106

❑ **CMD-106. "Secret Squadron Watch" Promo Kit,**
1988. Ovaltine store promotion. - **$15 $30 $50**

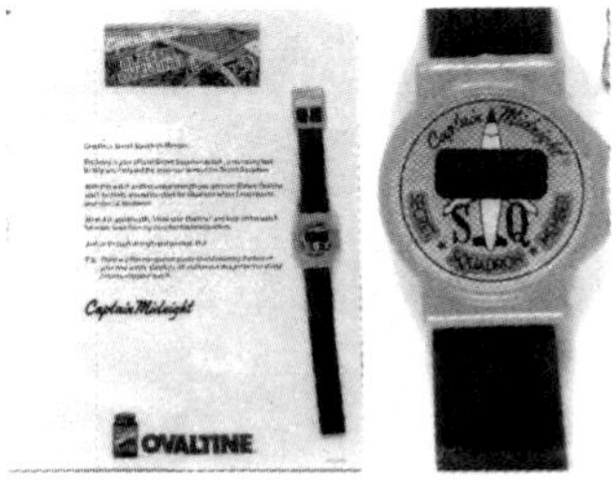


CMD-107

❑ **CMD-107. Cover Letter And Watch,**
1987. Offered for Ovaltine 30th anniversary year of 1988. Letter - **$10 $12 $25**
Watch- **$20 $50 $100**

CMD-108

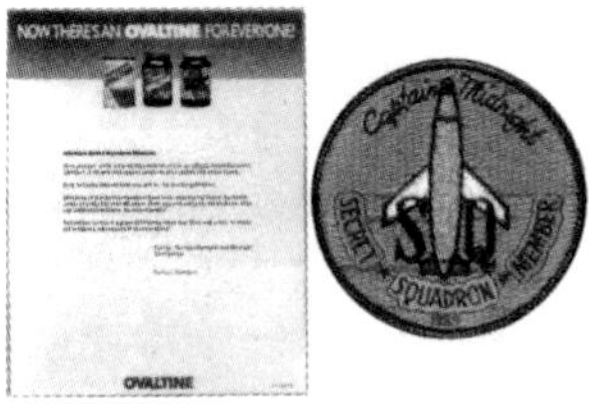


CMD-109

❑ **CMD-108. Cover Letter And T-Shirt,**
1988. Ovaltine 30th Anniversary Premium.
Letter - **$3 $6 $12**
T-Shirt- **$5 $20 $35**

❑ **CMD-109. Cover Letter And Patch,**
1989. Ovaltine offer from preceding 30th anniversary year of 1988. Letter - **$3 $5 $8**
Patch - **$5 $15 $25**

## Captain Tim Healy

**Kids interested in collecting postage stamps in the 1930s and 1940s could tune in their radios to the Tim Healy programs. From 1934 to 1945 under a variety of names--*Stamp Club, Ivory Stamp Club, Captain Tim's Adventures, Calling All Stamp Collectors* and *Captain Tim Healy's Adventure Stories*--and sponsored by Ivory soap or Kellogg's Pep cereal, Tim Healy described the romance of stamps and encouraged kids to become collectors. The few premiums offered were, naturally, stamp-related.**

CTH-1

CTH-2

❑ **CTH-1. Ivory Soap Stamp Club Album With Letter And Envelope,**
1934. Cover Letter - **$10 $20 $30**
Album - **$5 $20 $25**

❑ **CTH-2. Member's Stamp-Shaped Brass Pin,**
1934. Ivory Soap.
Red Background - **$10 $20 $35**
Black Background - **$10 $30 $50**

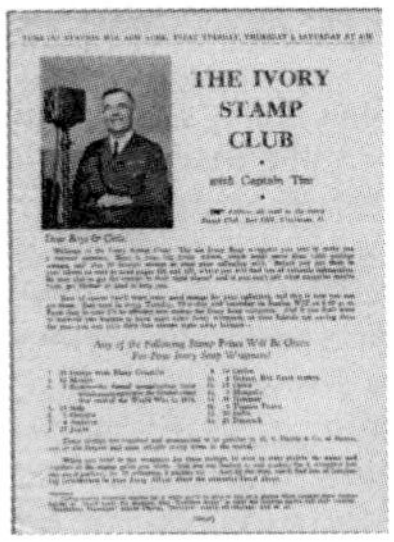


CTH-3

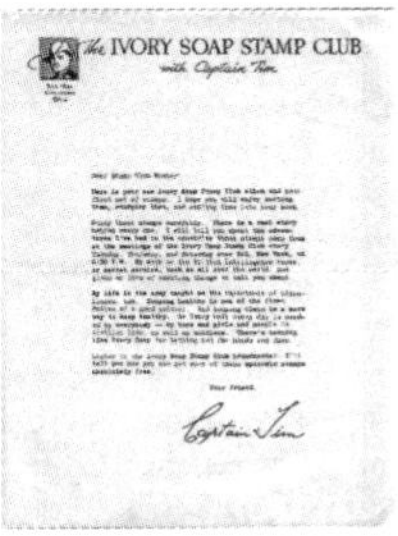


CTH-4

❑ **CTH-3. "Ivory Stamp Club" Ad,**
1934. - **$10 $20 $30**

❑ **CTH-4. "Ivory Stamp Club" Letter,**
1934. - **$10 $20 $30**

CTH-5

❑ **CTH-5. Packet of Stamps,**
1934. Offered on WJZ radio Tuesdays, Thursdays and Saturdays - 16 stamps for 4 Ivory Soap wrappers. Stamps were guaranteed by a Boston firm to be genuine. Stamps were displayed in albums also offered on the show. Each packet - **$15 $30 $45**

CTH-6

❑ **CTH-6. "Ivory Stamp Club" Folder,**
1934. Ivory Soap. Closed 4x6" sheet that opens to four panels printed in color on both sides to illustrate 68-page stamp album offered by Captain Tim Healy. - **$8 $15 $30**

CTH-7

CTH-8

❑ **CTH-7. Stamp Club Book,**
1934. Ivory Soap. Features pictures of Stamps of the World.- **$15 $30 $45**
Mailer - **$5 $10 $15**

❑ **CTH-8. Ivory Stamp Club Album With Envelope,**
c. 1935. Ivory Soap. - **$5 $20 $25**

CTH-9

CTH-10

❑ **CTH-9. "Spies I Have Known" Booklet,**
1936. Ivory Soap. Photo-illustrated stories about famous spies known by Captain Tim Healy. - **$10 $20 $40**

❑ **CTH-10. Autographed Captain Tim Healy Photo,**
c. 1938. Ivory Soap. - **$10 $20 $40**

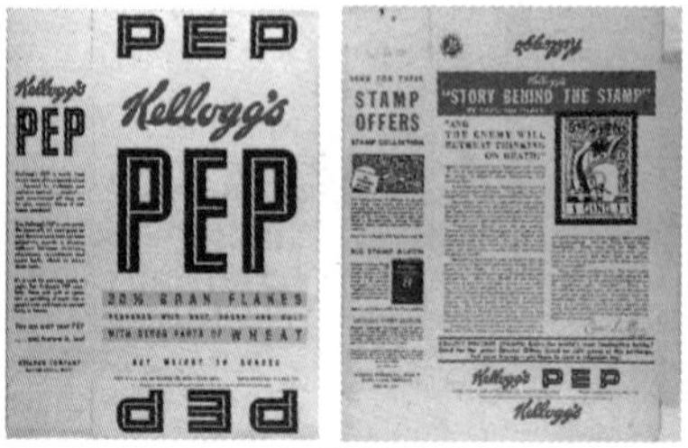


CTH-11

❑ **CTH-11. Kellogg's Pep Cereal Box Flat,**
1938. 10 oz. box has Captain Tim Healy stamp offer and story about stamps, the usual focus of the radio show. - **$20 $40 $100**

CTH-12

❑ **CTH-12. "Capt. Tim Healy" Dixie Ice Cream Picture,**
c. 1939. Reverse has biography and radio broadcast scenes. - **$12 $20 $40**

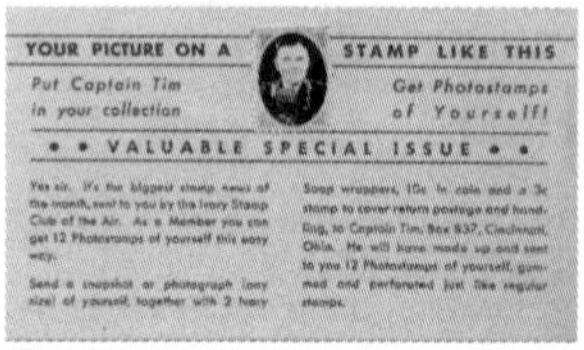


(Front)

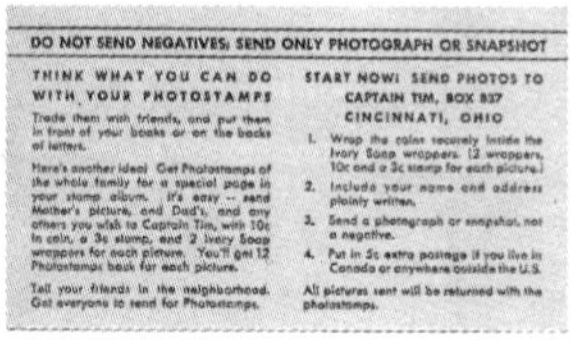


CTH-13 (Back)

❑ **CTH-13. "Captain Tim Photostamp" Card,**
1930s. Ivory Stamp Club. 3-1/4x5-1/2" card with photo stamp of Captain Tim telling club members how to receive set of 12 "Photostamps" picturing themselves. Laminated stamp shows him at the microphone. Ivory Soap sponsored this promotion. Two wrappers, 10¢ and a 3¢ stamp were sent with your photo to get 12 photo stamps. - **$40 $80 $120**

CTH-14

❑ **CTH-14. Dixie Ice Cream Picture,**
c. 1940. - **$12 $20 $45**

## Captain Video

***Captain Video*** **was television's first venture into the solar system, beating Buck Rogers by a year. The show premiered on the Dumont network in June 1949 with Richard Coogan as the super cop, a role taken over in 1951 by Al Hodge. The series, one of the most popular children's shows of its time, was notoriously low-budget, with props made of cardboard or household items, but it featured such futuristic devices as an Opticon Scillometer, a Radio Scillograph, an Atomic Rifle, a Discatron and a Cosmic Ray Vibrator. Sponsors such as Post cereals and Power House candy bars offered many premiums--rings, a plastic ray gun, a Captain Video helmet, a Rite-O-Lite flashlight and Luma-Glo card for writing secret messages. The series ended its network run in 1955, went local in New York City in 1956 and finally dissolved in 1957. The Captain appeared in comic books in 1949-1951 and a 15-episode chapter play with Judd Holdren in the title role was released by Columbia Pictures in 1951.**

CVD-1

CVD-2

❑ **CVD-1. Picture Ring,**
c. 1950. Power House candy bars. Brass holding plastic dome over black/white photo of Richard Coogan holding ray gun. - **$75 $150 $250**

❑ **CVD-2. "Picture Ring" Instruction Leaflet,**
c. 1950. Power House candy bars. - **$25 $75 $110**

CVD-3

❑ **CVD-3. Captain Video #1 Comic Book,**
1951. Fawcett Publications. - **$114 $342 $1250**

CVD-4

❑ **CVD-4. "Captain Video" Original Art Prototype Sign,**
1951. 14x21" for proposed premium tie-in campaign between Post's Raisin Bran and local theaters for 1951 Columbia Pictures Captain Video serial. Gordon Gold Archives. Unique. - **$550**

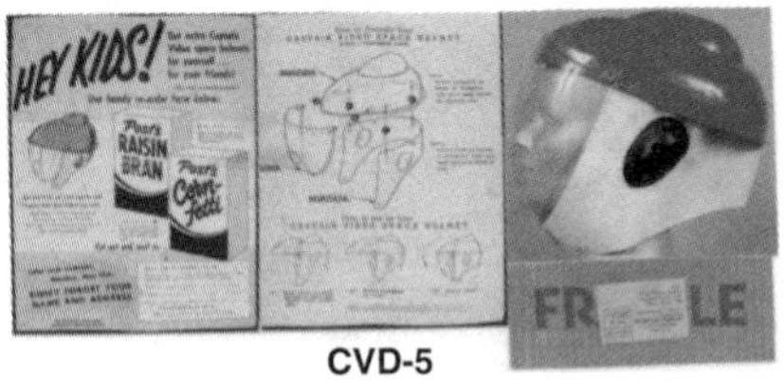


CVD-5

❑ **CVD-5. "Official Captain Video Space Helmet" Boxed Premium,**
c. 1951. Post's Raisin Bran. Fragile thin plastic. Near Mint Boxed **- $500**

CVD-6

❑ **CVD-6. Post Toasties "Flying Saucer Ring" Set,**
1951. Saucers of metal or plastic, non-glow or glow-in-dark. Near Mint Boxed - **$1100**
Ring And Two Saucers - **$300 $600 $900**

CVD-7

❑ **CVD-7. "Flying Saucer Ring" Instruction Sheet,**
1951. Post Toasties. Includes order coupon for additional rings with expiration date March 31, 1952. - **$120 $135 $160**

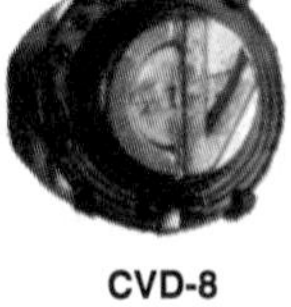

CVD-8

CVD-9

❑ **CVD-8. "CV" Secret Seal Brass Ring,**
1951. Two-piece top is designed to emboss in paper "CV" initials, but top cover frequently snapped off. Rim pictures tiny rocketship and four stars. - **$150 $375 $650**

❑ **CVD-9. "Secret Seal Ring" Leaflet And Card,**
1951. Power House candy bar. Instructions plus identification card. - **$150 $225 $300**

CVD-10

❑ **CVD-10. "Flying Saucer Ring" Instruction Sheet,**
1951. Power House Candy Bar. Different design than Post Toasties version. - **$40 $75 $150**

CVD-11

❑ **CVD-11. Original Art Prototype For Newspaper Ad,**
c. 1951. Post's Raisin Bran Cereal. 11x16" colorful original art titled "Join Captain Video's Ranger's Club And Get A Complete Membership Kit." Gordon Gold Archives. Unique. - **$650**

CVD-12

❑ **CVD-12. Original Art Prototype Movie Theater Sign,**
1951. Prepared for proposed premium tie-in campaign between Post's Raisin Bran and local theaters for the 1951 Columbia Pictures Captain Video serial. Gordon Gold Archives. Unique. - **$650**

CVD-13

CVD-14

❑ **CVD-13. "Captain Video" Ink Signed Photo,**
c. 1951. Black and white 5-1/2x6-1/2". - **$25 $60 $125**

❑ **CVD-14. Cast Photo,**
c. 1951. Facsimile signatures of Al Hodge and Don Hastings. - **$15 $40 $85**

CVD-15

❑ **CVD-15. "Captain Video" Spaceship Set,**
1951. Lido Toy Product. Sets #2101 and #2102 were produced, containing different spaceships and accessories. Great packaging graphics! - **$125 $250 $400**

CVD-16

CVD-17

❏ **CVD-16. Radio Scillograph Set,**
1952. TV premium advertised in comics. - **$100 $225 $400**

❏ **CVD-17. "Ranger" Cardboard Badge,**
1952. Badge came with pin on back. Came with Radio Scillograph set advertised in comics. TV premium. - **$75 $125 $175**

CVD-18

❏ **CVD-18. Mock-Up Test Photos For Proposed Premium,**
c. 1952. Issuer unknown. Pair of 4x5" black and white photos to test concept of including child's photo with Captain Video in rocketship cockpit. Only two examples we've seen.
Each Near Mint - **$250**

CVD-19

❏ **CVD-19. Captain Video Space Man,**
1953. Post's Raisin Bran. Hard plastic set of 12.
Each - **$12 $25 $35**

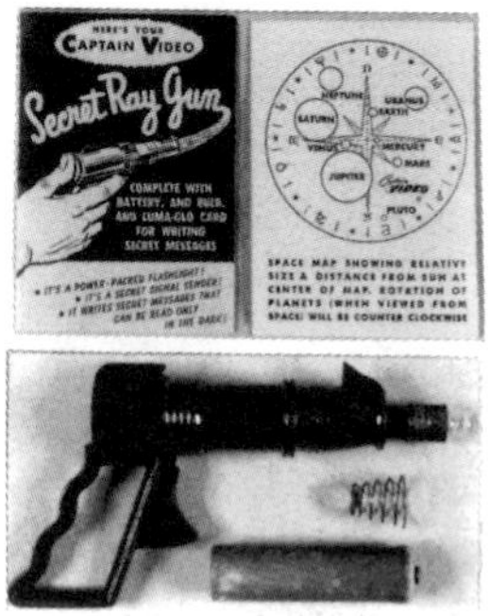


CVD-20

❏ **CVD-20. "Secret Ray Gun",**
1950s. Power House candy bars. Includes instruction sheet and "Luma-Glo" card. Instruction sheet also seen with gun, titled as "Rite-O-Lite."
Complete - **$40 $75 $175**
Gun Only - **$25 $40 $85**

CVD-21

❏ **CVD-21. "Captain Video" Suspenders,**
1950s. Store item. - **$25 $50 $90**

CVD-22

CVD-23

❏ **CVD-22. "Electronic Video Goggles" With Envelope,**
1950s. Power House candy bars.
In Envelope - **$100 $150 $300**
Loose - **$75 $150 $250**

❏ **CVD-23. "Video Ranger" Club Member Card,**
1950s. Scarce. Probable Post's Cereals. - **$60 $100 $200**

CVD-24

CVD-25

❏ **CVD-24. Purity Bread Litho. Tin Tab,**
1950s. - **$15 $35 $75**

❏ **CVD-25. Mysto-Coder Brass Decoder With Clip Fastener,**
1950s. Front has red plastic removable dome over Captain Video photo, back has two plastic code wheels. - **$75 $200 $350**

CVD-26

❏ **CVD-26. Plastic Rocket Ring/Pendant With Keychain,**
1950s. Rocketship includes glow portrait of Captain Video, magnifying glass and whistle. - **$250 $400 $800**

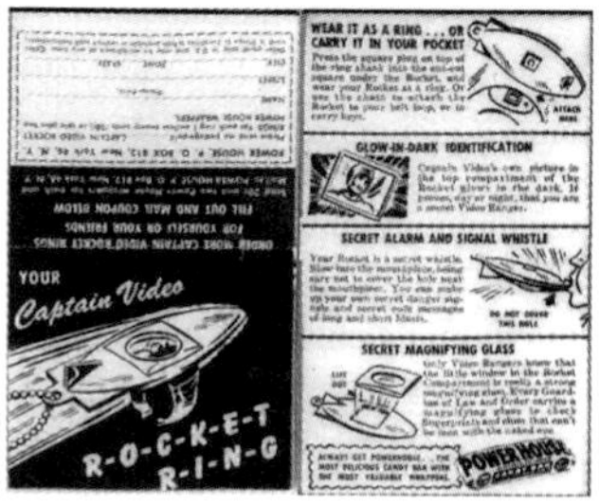


CVD-27

❏ **CVD-27. "Rocket Ring" Instruction Sheet,**
1950s. Scarce. Power House candy bars. - **$60 $125 $200**

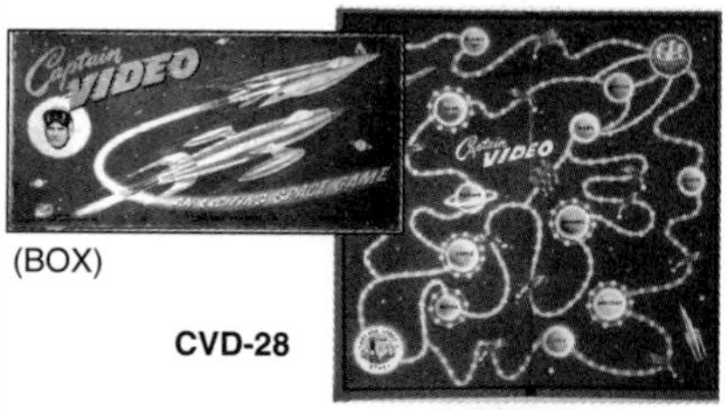


(BOX)

CVD-28

(GAME BOARD)

❏ **CVD-28. "Captain Video" Space Game,**
1950s. Scarce. Milton Bradley product.
Complete - **$100 $250 $400**
Board only - **$50 $100 $150**

# Casey, Crime Photographer

**Flashgun Casey, Press Photographer, Crime Photographer--under whatever name, "the ace cameraman who covers the crime news of a great city" for the Morning Express was first broadcast on CBS in 1943. With Staats Cotsworth as the crusading crime fighter, the program ran until 1950, then was revived from 1953 to 1955. Sponsors included the Anchor Hocking Glass Co., Toni Home Permanents and Philip Morris cigarettes. A television adaptation for CBS (1951-1952) featured Richard Carlyle, then Darren McGavin, in the title role. A brief run of comic books appeared in 1949-1950.**

CCP-1

❑ **CCP-1. Photo Of Cast,**
1940s. - **$25 $50 $85**

## Casper the Friendly Ghost

**Casper, The Friendly Ghost, created by Seymour Reit and Joe Oriolo, made his debut in animated cartoons in 1945 and has grown over the years into a merchandising giant through films, comic books, and television series. Between 1950 and 1959 Paramount/Famous Studios produced 62 *Casper* cartoons telling the simple story of the ghost who just wanted to make friends, not scare people. ("A g-g-ghost!") Casper made his first television appearance in 1959 on ABC in *Matty's Funday Funnies*, sponsored by Mattel toys. Other series followed in 1963, 1969, and *1979 (Casper and the Angels*, NBC). Two NBC specials, *Casper's Halloween* and *Casper's First Christmas*, also aired in 1979. The cartoons have been in syndication since 1963. A $50 million *Casper* film produced by Steven Spielberg was released in the summer of 1995, with a direct-to-video sequel that recently followed.**

**Casper made his first comic book appearance in 1949, then started again in 1950, and again in 1953, this time from Harvey Comics, which has also produced a wide variety of spin-off comic books and magazines. Harvey also acquired the television rights from Famous/Paramount in 1958. The merchandising of Casper has been extensive, including everything from costumes to candy dispensers to jewelry, records, toys, etc. Casper has also been an official recruiter for the Boy Scouts of America, and in 1972 he flew to the moon (painted on the side of Apollo 16).**

CSP-1

CSP-2

❑ **CSP-1. Sliding Tile Puzzle On Card,**
c. 1961. Store item by Roalex Co. Plastic puzzle for forming images of Casper, Katnip, Baby Huey, Little Audrey. On Card - **$25 $60 $85**
Loose - **$10 $20 $40**

❑ **CSP-2. Talking Doll Made Of Terrycloth Fabric With Plastic Face,**
1962. Store item by Mattel. 16" tall.
Talking - **$75 $125 $175**
Not Talking - **$25 $50 $75**

CSP-3

❑ **CSP-3. Diecut Cardboard Standee,**
c. 1963. ABC-TV. Colorful 20x20" picturing "Stars Of The New Casper Cartoon Show." - **$100 $200 $400**

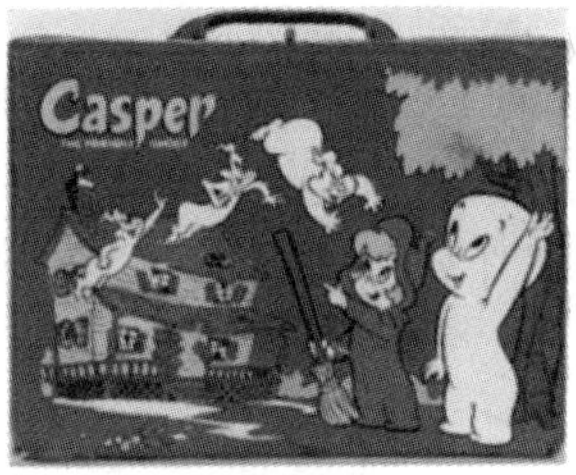


CSP-4

❑ **CSP-4. Vinyl Lunch Box,**
1966. Store item by Thermos. - **$75 $175 $300**

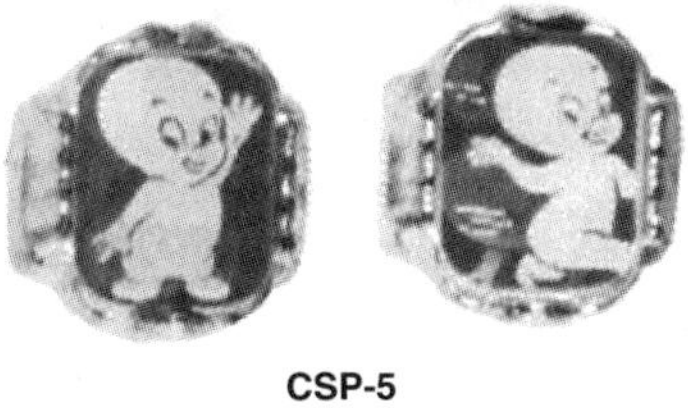

CSP-5

❑ **CSP-5. Casper Flicker Rings,**
1960s. Vending machine issue. Believed set of two with one ring showing him peeking from left edge and then as full figure with name below in green and the second showing him flying through space and then walking to the right. Both on silver luster plastic bases.
Each - **$10 $20 $35**

CSP-6

CSP-7

❑ **CSP-6. "Casper" Soaky Bottle,**
1960s. Colgate-Palmolive Co. store item. Hard plastic container for liquid soap. - **$10 $25 $50**

❑ **CSP-7. "Wendy" Soaky Bottle,**
1960s. Colgate-Palmolive Co. store item. Hard plastic container for liquid soap. - **$10 $25 $50**

CSP-8

CSP-9

❑ **CSP-8. "Casper's Ghostland Trick Or Treat" 12x12" Store Sign,**
1960s. Thin plastic with Harvey Famous Cartoons copyright. - **$15 $30 $50**

❑ **CSP-9. Vending Machine Display Paper,**
1960s. Depicts Casper and shows three monsters appearing on flicker rings. - **$30 $45 $60**

CSP-10

❑ **CSP-10. Mugs**
1971. In blue, red, yellow, and green colors.
Each - **$8 $15 $35**

CSP-11

CSP-12

❑ **CSP-11. "Casper Day BSA Cub Scouts Equipment Center" 3" Cello. Button,**
1975. - **$8 $15 $25**

❑ **CSP-12. Cub Scouts Recruitment Litho. Button,**
1976. Boy Scouts of America (BSA). Harvey Comics copyright. - **$5 $10 $15**

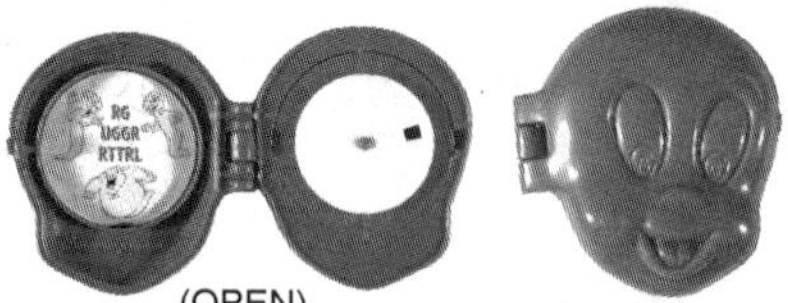
(OPEN) (CLOSED)

**CSP-13**

❑ **CSP-13. Plastic Decoder (Blue),**
1997. Boston Chicken premium. - **$5 $10 $20**

## Cereal Boxes

**See entries by name of company, program and character.**

## Chandu, the Magician

**Chandu was actually Frank Chandler, an American secret agent who used ancient occult powers he learned from a Hindu yogi to combat evil. The 15-minute program originated on Los Angeles radio station KHJ in 1932 and ran on Mutual until 1936, sponsored in the west by White King soap and in the east by Beech-Nut products. The series was revived in 1948, based on the original scripts, with White King again as sponsor. It had a final run as a half-hour weekly show on the ABC network in 1949-1950.**

**CHA-1**

❑ **CHA-1. "Chandu Book Of Magic,"**
1932. Rio Grande Oil Co. Twelve-page booklet of illustrated tricks plus sponsor ad on back cover. - **$35 $75 $125**

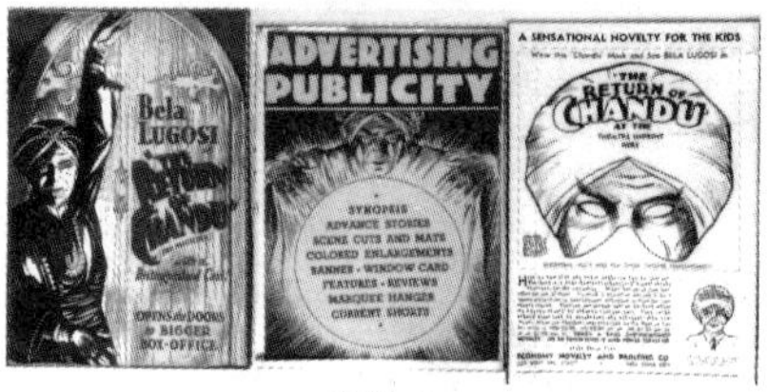


**CHA-2**

**CHA-3**

❑ **CHA-2. "The Return Of Chandu" Movie Serial Pressbook,**
1934. Principal Distributing Corp. - **$200 $400 $650**

❑ **CHA-3. "The Return Of Chandu" 27x41" Movie Serial Poster,**
1934. Principal Distributing Corp. - **$150 $300 $600**

**CHA-4**

**CHA-5**

❑ **CHA-4. Fan Photo,**
1930s. Pictures four unidentified cast members.- **$60 $125 $200**

❑ **CHA-5. Radio Listing Folder,**
1930s. White King Soap. Contents include listing of stations in Central and Western United States carrying Chandu broadcasts. - **$75 $140 $225**

**CHA-6**

❑ **CHA-6. Paper Mask,**
1930s. Possible Beech-Nut Gum. Probable give-away. - **$50 $100 $200**

**CHA-7**

**CHA-8**

❑ **CHA-7. "Beech-Nut's King Of Magic" Leaflet,**
1930s. Contents include radio cast photo, magic trick offer. -**$20 $40 $75**

❑ **CHA-8. Magic Slate,**
1930s. Ernst Kerr Co., Detroit department store radio sponsor on WJR. Comes with wood stylus marker. - **$50 $175 $300**

**CHA-9**

**CHA-10**

❑ **CHA-9. Chandu Club Cello Button,**
1930s. - **$75 $175 $350**

❑ **CHA-10. "Chandu Magicians Club" Cello. Member Button,**
1930s. - **$75 $175 $300**

**CHA-11**

**CHA-12**

❑ **CHA-11. "Beech-Nut Holiday Trick" Greeting Postcard,**
1930s. Back lists radio cast members with holiday message. - **$25 $50 $75**

❑ **CHA-12. Beech-Nut Galloping Coin Trick,**
1930s. Boxed Set - **$25 $60 $100**

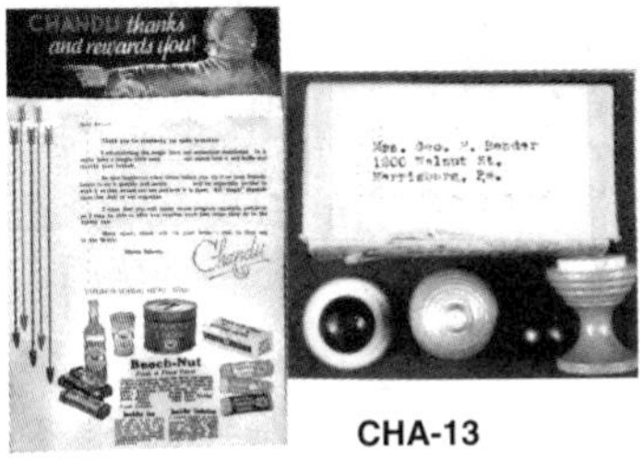


CHA-13

❑ **CHA-13. "Chandu Ball And Base" Boxed Trick,**
1930s. Beech-Nut Gum. With letter and instruction leaflet. - **$25 $60 $100**

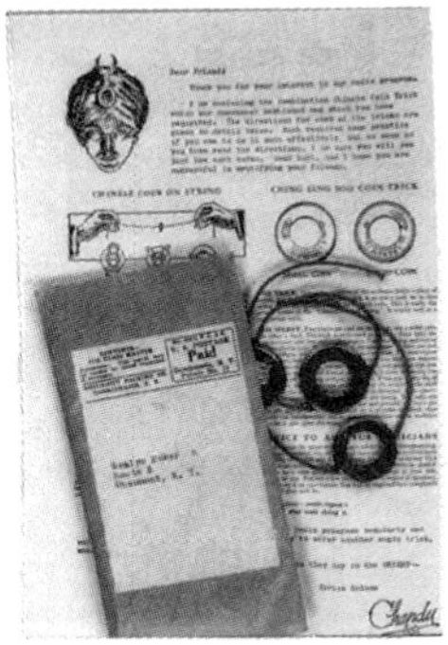

CHA-14

❑ **CHA-14. "Chinese Coin On String" Trick With Mailer Envelope,**
1930s. Beech-Nut Gum. - **$25 $60 $100**

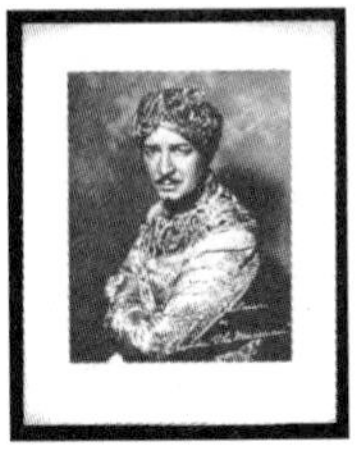

CHA-15

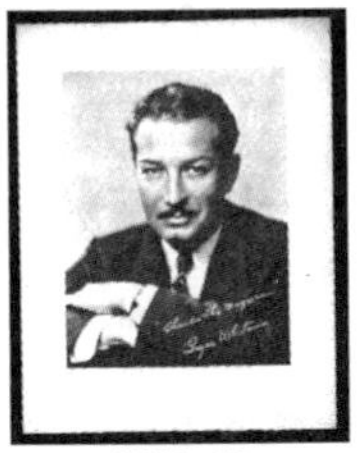

CHA-16

❑ **CHA-15. Photo - Gayne Whitman in Costume,**
1930s. Beech-Nut Gum. - **$35 $75 $135**

❑ **CHA-16. Photo - Gayne Whitman in Business Suit,**
1930s. Beech-Nut Gum. - **$35 $75 $135**

CHA-17

CHA-18

❑ **CHA-17. "Betty Lou Regent" Portrait Print,**
1930s. Probably Beech-Nut Gum. 8-1/2x11" textured paper black and white photo also identifying Betty Webb as the portrayer. - **$15 $30 $50**

❑ **CHA-18. "Bob Regent" Portrait Print,**
1930s. Probably Beech-Nut Gum. 8-1/2x11" textured paper black and white photo also identifying Bob T. Bixby as the portrayer. -
**$15 $30 $50**

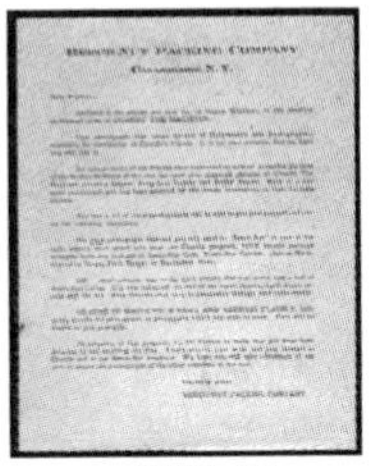

CHA-19

CHA-20

❑ **CHA-19. Letter,**
1930s. For costume photo. With color photos of products on back. - **$10 $20 $40**

❑ **CHA-20. Letter,**
1930s. For Bobby Regent photo. With color photos of products on back. - **$10 $20 $40**

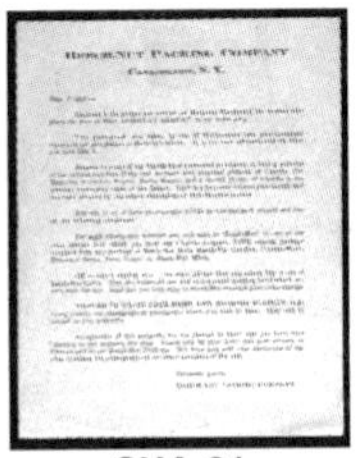

CHA-21

CHA-22

❑ **CHA-21. Letter,**
1930s. For Mrs.Bobby Regent photo. With color photos of products on back. - **$10 $20 $40**

❑ **CHA-22. Radio Broadcasts Guide 11x21" Cardboard Sign,**
1930s. Beech-Nut Gum. - **$125 $275 $500**

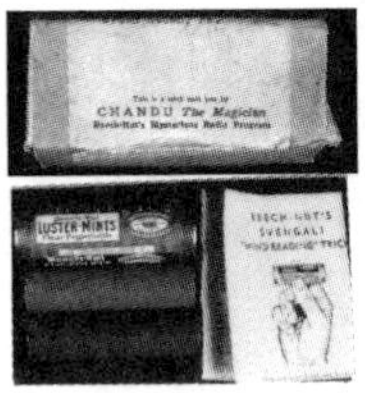

CHA-23

CHA-24

❑ **CHA-23. "Svengali Mind Reading Trick",**
1930s. Beech-Nut Gum. Boxed - **$25 $60 $100**

❑ **CHA-24. "The Great Beech-Nut Buddha Money Mystery" Packet,**
1930s. Magic trick based on Chandu radio series. -**$20 $40 $70**

CHA-25

CHA-26

❑ **CHA-25. "Hypnotized Silver Sphere" Trick With Box And Order Sheet,**
1930s. Beech-Nut Gum. - **$25 $50 $75**

❑ **CHA-26. "Chandu White King Of Magic" Boxed Trick Set,**
1930s. White King Soap.
Complete - **$100 $175 $300**

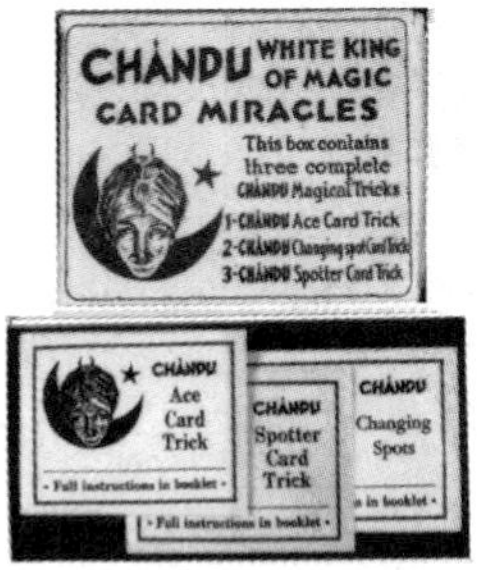


CHA-27

❑ **CHA-27. "Card Miracles" Boxed Set,**
1930s. White King Soap. - **$25 $50 $75**

CHA-28

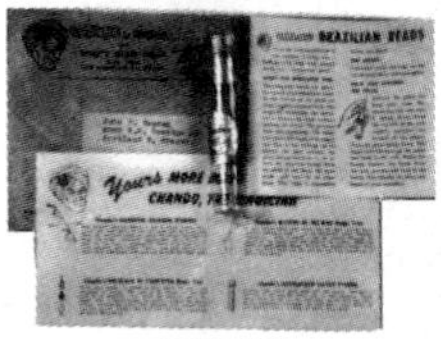

CHA-29

❑ **CHA-28. "Assyrian Money Changer" Trick With Mailer Envelope,**
1930s. White King Soap. With instruction card, wooden block, two metal bands for holding penny. - **$25 $50 $75**

❑ **CHA-29. "Brazilian Beads" Trick With Mailer Envelope,**
1930s. White King Soap. Comes with instructions, glass vial containing beads and cork. -
**$25 $50 $75**

# Charles Lindbergh

**Charles Augustus Lindbergh (1902-1974), Midwestern farm boy, barnstorming stunt flier and airmail pilot, flew into history on May 21, 1927, when he completed the first nonstop solo flight across the Atlantic in his monoplane Spirit of St. Louis. America's Lone Eagle--Lucky, Plucky Lindy--became an instant international hero, with banner headlines, medals, awards, receptions, banquets, and a ticker tape parade up Broadway in New York City. Souvenirs and commemorative memorabilia followed in great profusion. James Stewart starred in the 1957 biographical movie *The Spirit of St. Louis.***

CLD-1

CLD-2

❑ **CLD-1. "Welcome Lindy" Cello. Button,**
1927. Depicts and names his aircraft "Spirit Of St. Louis." - **$30 $85 $150**

❑ **CLD-2. Transatlantic Flight Commemorative Plate,**
1927. Store item. 8-1/2x8-1/2" limoges china plate by "Golden Glow" process of somewhat irridescent quality on outer margin around full color Lindbergh portrait. Pictured example has imprint for local sponsor. - **$20 $35 $70**

CLD-3

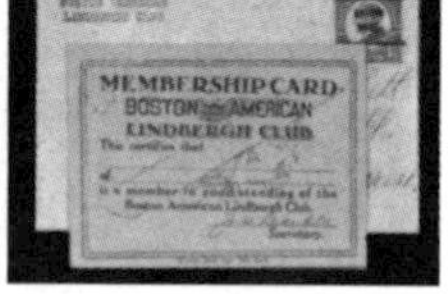


CLD-4

❑ **CLD-3. "Lindy" Sheet Music,**
1927. - **$20 $40 $75**

❑ **CLD-4. "Boston American Lindbergh Club" Member Card With Mailer,**
c. 1927. Sponsored by Boston Evening American newspaper. Mailer - **$5 $10 $15**
Card - **$15 $25 $50**

CLD-5

❑ **CLD-5. "Lindbergh Flight Commemorative Cigar Box Labels,**
c. 1927. Photo shows lid label and one end panel only. Lid Label - **$10 $15 $25**
End Panel Label - **$3 $5 $10**

CLD-6

❑ **CLD-6. Spirit Of St. Louis Pin,**
1927. Brass pin on card - **$50 $75 $165**

CLD-7

CLD-8

❑ **CLD-7. Flight School 13x15" Poster,**
1927. U.S. Army Flying Schools. Recruiting poster with Lindbergh tributes concluding "The Army Trained Him." - **$30 $60 $125**

❑ **CLD-8. Flight Celebration Cap,**
1927. Fabric over cardboard headband holding fabric crown. Pictured example has stamped name of local sponsor on headband rear. - **$25 $50 $100**

CLD-9

❑ **CLD-9. "Welcome Home" Felt Pennant,**
1927. 8x26". - **$40 $80 $175**

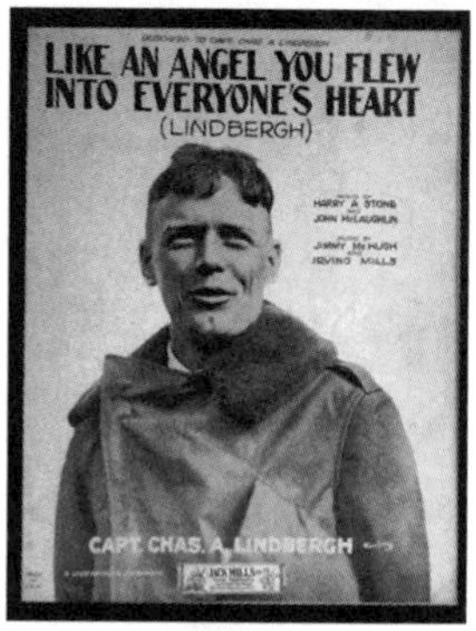


CLD-10

❑ **CLD-10. Song Sheet,**
1927. "Like An Angel You Flew Into Everyone's Heart, " a song dedicated to Capt. Lindbergh. - **$35 $70 $100**

CLD-11

CLD-12

❑ **CLD-11. "Our Hero" Cello. Button,**
1927. Red, white and blue rim surrounds black and white photo, 1-1/4". - **$25 $40 $75**

❑ **CLD-12. Transatlantic Flight Commemorative Glass,**
1927. White opaque glass with red illustrations. - **$20 $40 $85**

CLD-13

CLD-14

❑ **CLD-13. Commemorative Ring,**
1927. New York to Paris. - **$35 $75 $150**

❑ **CLD-14. "The Lone Eagle" Lindbergh/Bulova Endorsement Plaque,**
c. 1927. Bulova watches. 9x12" walnut wood plaque with mounted metal photo portrait plate including endorsement statement for sponsor plus facsimile Lindbergh signature. - **$50 $125 $200**

**CLD-15**

**CLD-16**

❑ **CLD-15. "Our National Hero Col. Lindbergh" China Ashtray,**
c. 1927. Full color portrait on glazed pastel yellow. - **$20 $35 $70**

❑ **CLD-16. "Mystery Picture" Card,**
c. 1927. Majestic Radio, "Mighty Monarch Of The Air." 3-1/2x5-1/2" black and white optical illusion card with instructions for causing Lindbergh image to enlarge, disappear, reappear. - **$8 $15 $30**

**CLD-17**

**CLD-18**

❑ **CLD-17. Lindbergh High School Tribute Album,**
1928. Little Falls High School, Little Falls, Minnesota. Tribute photo folio by his high school alma mater with 24 pages including numerous youth photos in addition to those from his adult flying career. - **$150 $300 $500**

❑ **CLD-18. "Two Great Flyers" Cello. Button,**
c. 1928. Flexible Flyer Sleds. - **$12 $20 $35**

**CLD-19**

❑ **CLD-19. "Lindy Bread" Bullet Pencil Holder,**
c. 1928. - **$25 $65 $115**

**CLD-20**

❑ **CLD-20. "Lindy Bread" Wrapper,**
c. 1928. Cottage Bakery, Springfield, Ohio. 10-1/2x15" waxed glassine loaf wrapper. Photo shows entire wrapper and detail from it. - **$25 $60 $100**

**CLD-21**

**CLD-22**

❑ **CLD-21. Parachute Product Endorsement Photo,**
c. 1928. Irvin Air Chutes. 8x10" black and white with product inscription on margin "He has saved his life on four different occasions by using Irvin Air Chutes." - **$10 $20 $50**

❑ **CLD-22. "His Story in Pictures" Book,**
1929. 320 pages by Francis Trevelyan Miller. Elaborate and well-documented book about one of America's greatest heroes. With dust jacket. - **$25 $50 $100**

**CLD-23**

❑ **CLD-23. Premium Map 31-1/2"x 42",**
1935. Heinz 57. Map of famous aviator flights. Shows 25 famous pilots and 25 different planes. Photos could be cut out and used as cards. - **$75 $150 $240**

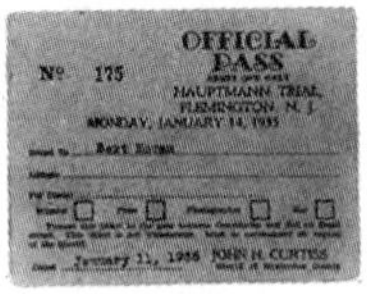


**CLD-24**

❑ **CLD-24. Hauptmann Trial Official Pass,**
1935. Single day authorization pass for January 14 day of trial for accused Lindbergh baby kidnapper and slayer Richard Bruno Hauptmann. - **$150 $250 $500**

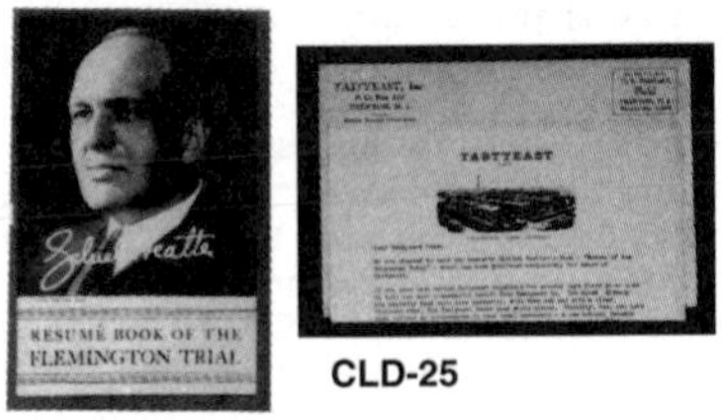


**CLD-25**

❑ **CLD-25. Lindbergh Infant Kidnapping Murder Trial Summary,**
c. 1936. Tastyeast, Inc. Cover letter and 24-page photo and text booklet summarizing evidence and trial of accused kidnapper and slayer. Contents include editorial by newscaster Gabriel Heatter.
Near Mint Complete - **$100**
Booklet Only - **$15 $40 $70**
Letter Only - **$5 $10 $15**

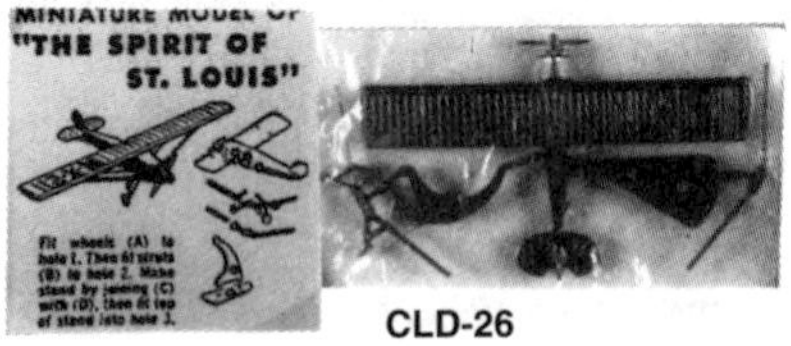


**CLD-26**

❑ **CLD-26. "The Spirit Of St. Louis" Miniature Model,**
c. 1956. Kellogg's. Cellophane pack holding assembly parts for 2x3" replica aircraft.
Cereal Box With Offer - **$40 $75 $125**
Model Kit - **$25 $50 $75**

# Charlie Chaplin

**Charles Spencer Chaplin (1889-1977) was born in London and spent most of his early years in homes and institutions. By 1898 he was working on stage, and in 1913 he signed a contract to make comic movies with Mack Sennett's Keystone Studios. The next year, in *Kid Auto Races at Venice*, Chaplin unveiled his screen persona as "The Little Tramp" in baggy pants, floppy shoes, bowler hat and bamboo cane--a role he was to play in more than 70 films and one that brought him international acclaim as a true comic genius. Chaplin took The Tramp from Keystone to Essanay in 1915, to Mutual in 1916, and to First National in 1917. In 1919 he helped form United Artists so he could produce and distribute his films independently. From *The Tramp* in 1915 to *Limelight* in 1952, Chaplin's fame and box-office appeal continued to grow.**

**The Tramp was adapted in a newspaper comic strip, *Charlie Chaplin's Comic Capers*, for the *Chicago Record-Herald* and national syndication in 1915-1917, and *Baggy Pants*, an animated cartoon, aired on NBC in 1977-1978, but the humor and pathos of Chaplin's character proved impossible to capture in either medium.**

**In the late 1940s and 1950s Chaplin was wrongfully accused of "Communist leanings" by the American Legion and other right-wing organizations. He moved to Switzerland, returning only in 1972 to receive a special Academy Award. He was knighted in 1975, and his Little Tramp remains to this day the universal embodiment of the eventual triumph of the individual.**

CPN-1

❑ **CPN-1. Early Water Shooting White Metal Novelty,**
c. 1915. 1-3/4" tall figure has tiny hole at waist with small metal tube on reverse originally affixed to a rubber tube and squeeze ball. The rubber disintegrated over time. - **$15 $25 $45**

CPN-2

CPN-3

CPN-4

❑ **CPN-2. Charlie Chaplin Composition/Cloth Doll,**
c. 1915. Scarce. Store item by Louis Amberg & Son. - **$100 $250 $500**

❑ **CPN-3. "Chas. Chaplin" Statuette,**
1915. Includes wire cane. Store item. - **$50 $75 $150**

❑ **CPN-4. "Chas. Chaplin" Statuette,**
1915. 9" tall painted plaster figurine with underside token insert "Sold By Mark Hampton Co. Inc." with New York City address and copyright year. - **$35 $75 $150**

CPN-5

❑ **CPN-5. Movie Promo,**
1934. National Theatre Premium. 16 pages, shows coming attraction. - **$10 $25 $35**

CPN-6

❑ **CPN-6. "Charlie Chaplin's Comic Capers" Book,**
1917. Store item published by M. A. Donohue & Co. Softcover 9-1/2x16" with 16 black and white pages reprinting daily comic strips. -
**$200 $600 $900**

CPN-7

❑ **CPN-7. "Charlie Chaplin in The Movies" Book,**
1917. Store item published by M. A. Donohue & Co. Softcover 9-1/2x16" with 16 black and white pages reprinting daily comic strips. -
**$200 $600 $900**

CPN-8

CPN-9

❑ **CPN-8. Portrait Stickpin In Brass,**
c. 1917. - **$15 $25 $50**

❑ **CPN-9. "The Kid" Handbill,**
1920. Paper sheet for silent film starring Chaplin and "The Wonder Boy" Jackie Coogan in his first role. - **$10 $20 $40**

CPN-10

CPN-11

❑ **CPN-10. Early Portrait Button,**
c. 1920. 7/8" black and white, one of the earliest buttons to picture him. - **$30 $60 $125**

❑ **CPN-11. "The Gold Rush" Movie Promotion Mask,**
1924. Diecut stiff paper for silent film release. -
**$50 $125 $250**

CPN-12

CPN-13

❑ **CPN-12. "The Gold Rush" Movie Program,**
1925. From world premiere at Grauman's Egyptian Theater, Hollywood for dramatic comedy written, directed and starring Chaplin. -
**$35 $75 $125**

❑ **CPN-13. Chaplin Image Party Favor,**
c. 1920s. Store item. 7-1/2" crepe paper and confetti table marker with 3" figure of him formed by glossy paper and fabric. - **$10 $20 $30**

CPN-14

CPN-15

❑ **CPN-14. Charlie Chaplin Candy Container Bank,**
1920s. Store item. Glass plus metal lid. -
**$75 $150 $250**

❑ **CPN-15. Charlie Chaplin Cello. Button,**
1920s. Sampeck Suits. - **$15 $30 $50**

CPN-16

❑ **CPN-16. Condiment Jar,**
c. 1920s. Glazed ceramic jar and lid. #4628 stamped on underside, probably of European or Japanese origin. - **$50 $100 $175**

CPN-17

CPN-18

❑ **CPN-17. Mask,**
1920s. Made in England. Possible premium. -
**$20 $40 $80**

❑ **CPN-18. Cardboard 9" Puppet With Mailer and Instructions,**
1920s. Made in England. Possible premium.
Puppet - **$25 $50 $75**
Mailer - **$10 $20 $30**
Instructions - **$5 $10 $15**

CPN-19

CPN-20

❑ **CPN-19. "Modern Times" Movie Button,**
1936. 7/8" blue on orange. - **$15 $30 $60**

❑ **CPN-20. "The Great Dictator" Movie Promotion Mask,**
1940. Diecut stiff paper for United Artists film release. This mask was used as a promotion for Chaplin's films during the 1920s-1940s. For each new film, the title was displayed on the hat. -
**$50 $125 $250**

CPN-21

CPN-22

❑ **CPN-21. Charlie Chaplin Hat-Tipper Figure,**
1960s. Store item. Italian-made, hard plastic upper torso with flexible fabric over spring base. - **$35 $75 $125**

❑ **CPN-22. Charlie Chaplin Figural Ashtray,**
1970s. Store item by Lego, Japan. High gloss finish hollow ceramic. - **$25 $50 $90**

CPN-23

❑ **CPN-23. "Silent Star" Ornament in Box,**
1997. - **$25**

## Charlie McCarthy

**Edgar Bergen (1903-1978) and Charlie McCarthy accomplished the seemingly impossible--a successful ventriloquist act on radio. After years of knocking around vaudeville, Bergen and Charlie broke into radio with a guest appearance on Rudy Vallee's show in 1936. They were an instant hit and five months later they were stars on the Chase & Sanborn Hour. Week after week Charlie feuded with W. C. Fields and flirted with Dorothy Lamour and America loved him. Another dummy, Mortimer Snerd, was added in 1939 and Effie Klinker joined the crew in 1944 but Charlie ruled supreme. Chase & Sanborn's sponsorship ended in 1948 and other sponsors (Coca-Cola, Hudnut, Kraft cheese) carried the show until it ended in 1956. Charlie made an early TV appearance on the *Hour Glass* variety show in 1946 and, along with Bergen, hosted *Do You Trust Your Wife?* in 1956-1957 and *Who Do You Trust?* on daytime TV from 1957-1963. A comic strip had a brief run in the late 1930s and comic books were published in the late 1940s and early 1950s.**

CHE-1

CHE-2

❑ **CHE-1. "Chase & Sanborn Radio News" Newsletter,**
c. 1937. - **$25 $50 $90**

❑ **CHE-2. "Adventure Pops" Cardboard Folder,**
1938. Held six lollipops by E. Rosen Co. From a set of five. Each - **$25 $60 $110**

CHE-3

CHE-4

❑ **CHE-3. "Radio Party" Game,**
1938. Chase & Sanborn Coffee. Includes spinner and 21 figures. Complete - **$20 $40 $75**

❑ **CHE-4. Animated Alarm Clock,**
1938. Store item by Gilbert. - **$300 $600 $1200**

CHE-5

CHE-6

❑ **CHE-5. "Charlie McCarthy" Wooden Figure With Rope Arms,**
c. 1938. Store item. 5-1/4" tall. -
**$50 $100 $200**

❑ **CHE-6. "The Adventures Of Charlie McCarthy And Edgar Bergen" Fast Action Book,**
1938. 4x5-3/8" in BLB format. - **$25 $60 $150**

CHE-7

❑ **CHE-7. "Charlie McCarthy Valentine Pops" Lollipop Holder/Valentine Card,**
1938. Held six lollipops by E. Rosen Company from a set of five. Each - **$25 $60 $100**

CHE-8

❑ **CHE-8. Flying Hats Game,**
1938. Contains 4 games of chance and skill. -
**$30 $60 $120**

CHE-9

CHE-10

❑ **CHE-9. Cardboard Figure,**
c. 1938. Chase & Sanborn Coffee. -
**$25 $75 $150**

❑ **CHE-10. Mortimer Snerd Cardboard Figure,**
c. 1938. Chase & Sanborn Coffee. -
**$40 $100 $200**

CHE-11

CHE-12

❑ **CHE-11. Effanbee Doll "Edgar Bergen's Charlie McCarthy" Cello. Button,**
c. 1938. For "An Effanbee Play-Product". -
**$30 $60 $100**

❑ **CHE-12. Photo,**
1938. Philadelphia Record newspaper premium. -
**$10 $20 $30**

CHE-13

❑ **CHE-13. Ventriloquist Doll Detective Outfit,**
c. 1938. Store item believed to be Effanbee. -
**$200 $400 $700**

CHE-14

❑ **CHE-14. Ventriloquist Doll In Tuxedo,**
c. 1938. Store item believed to be Effanbee. -
**$200 $400 $700**

CHE-15

❑ **CHE-15. "Radio Guide" Magazines With McCarthy Covers,**
1938-1939. Issues for July 9, 1938 and February 25, 1939. Each - **$10 $15 $25**

CHE-16

❑ **CHE-16. "Edgar Bergen's Mortimer Snerd Ideal Flexy Doll,"**
c. 1939. 12-1/2" tall composition.
Doll - **$100 $250 $500**
Tag - **$20 $40 $75**

CHE-17

❑ **CHE-17. "Meet My Friend Mortimer Snerd" Tin Litho Wind-Up Toy,**
1939. Marx Toys. - **$100 $225 $400**

CHE-18

CHE-19

❑ **CHE-18. "Speaking For Myself On Life And Love" Book,**
1939. Chase & Sanborn Coffee. - **$10 $20 $40**

❑ **CHE-19. Painted Plastic Portrait Pin,**
c. 1939. - **$15 $30 $60**

CHE-20

❑ **CHE-20. Figural Soap In Diecut Box,**
c. 1939. Store item by Kerk Guild Inc., N.Y. 5-1/4" tall figure with small color accents.
Near Mint Boxed - **$100**
Soap Only - **$20 $40 $60**

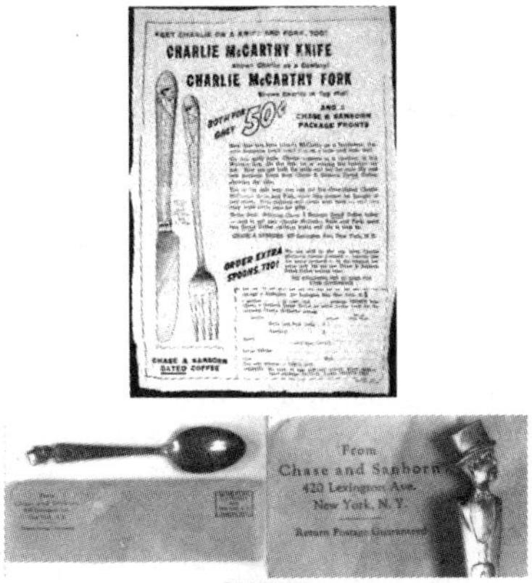

CHE-21

❑ **CHE-21. Silver Plate Spoon With Mailer,**
c. 1939. Mailer Only - **$10 $15 $25**
Standard Tuxedo Design Spoon - **$5 $10 $15**
Order Form For Knife and Fork - **$25 $50 $75**

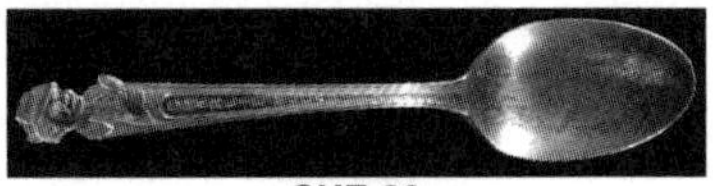
CHE-22

❑ **CHE-22. Detective Outfit Design Spoon,**
c. 1939. - **$10 $20 $40**

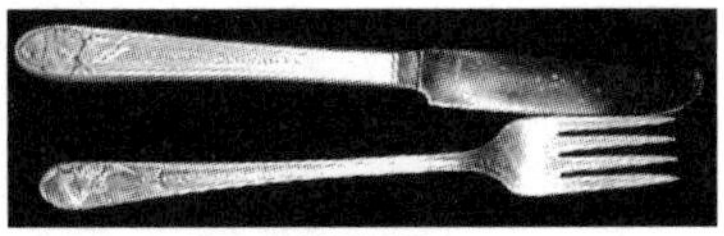
CHE-23

❑ **CHE-23. Silver Plate Knife And Fork,**
c. 1939. Each - **$15 $30 $50**

CHE-24

❑ **CHE-24. Wind-Up Litho. Tin Car,**
1930s. Store item by Marx. - **$200 $400 $700**

CHE-25

CHE-26

❑ **CHE-25. "Goldwyn Follies Club" Cello. Button,**
1930s. Metro-Goldwyn-Mayer. - **$15 $30 $50**

❑ **CHE-26. Bust Portrait Brass Ring,**
1940. Chase and Sanborn coffee. -
**$150 $240 $375**

CHE-27

❑ **CHE-27. "Gold-Plated Ring" Coupon Sheet,**
1940. Scarce. Clipping from can wrapper of Chase & Sanborn Coffee offering ring for 10 cents plus the clipping. - **$10 $20 $40**

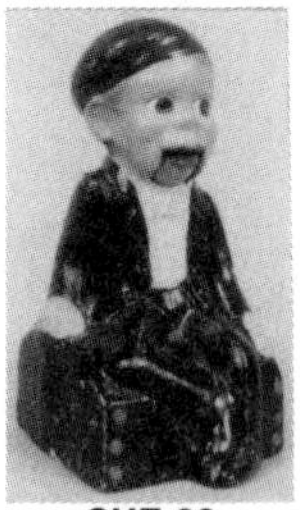
CHE-28

CHE-29

❑ **CHE-28. Composition Bank,**
c. 1940. Store item. - **$50 $100 $175**

❑ **CHE-29. Bergen/McCarthy Glass,**
c. 1940. - **$25 $60 $100**

CHE-30

❑ **CHE-30. Contest Card,**
1944. - **$12 $25 $60**

CHE-31

❑ **CHE-31. Record Album,**
1947. Contains four 78 RPM records. Inside are write-ups about the radio show. - **$30 $75 $150**

## Charlie the Tuna

**Charlie is the out-of-luck character created for Star-Kist Foods in the 1960s. Charlie's ambition was to impress Star-Kist (and viewers) with his demonstrations of esthetic "good taste," inevitably rejected by "Sorry, Charlie. Star-Kist doesn't want tuna with good taste. Star-Kist wants tuna that tastes good." Despite--or because of--his loser image, Charlie became a winner in premium popularity.**

CTU-1

CTU-2

❑ **CTU-1. Talking Cloth Doll,**
1969. - **$20 $40 $75**

❑ **CTU-2. Metal Alarm Clock,**
1969. - **$20 $50 $100**

CTU-3

CTU-4

❑ **CTU-3. "Charlie For President" Litho. Button,**
1960s. - **$8 $15 $25**

❑ **CTU-4. Charlie The Tuna Predecessor Premium,**
1960s. Sponsored by Star-Kist. Mailer with inflatable 24x40" "Loona The Star-Kist Tuna" swim toy. Mailer - **$3 $8 $12**
Toy - **$10 $20 $40**

CTU-5

CTU-6

❑ **CTU-5. Plastic Radio,**
1970. Battery operated, base often missing.
Complete - **$40 $60 $90**
No Base - **$15 $25 $40**

❑ **CTU-6. Watch With Mailer & Paper,**
1971. Sponsored by Star-Kist Foods.
Mailer And Paper - **$5 $12 $20**
Watch - **$20 $40 $60**

CTU-7

CTU-8

❑ **CTU-7. Plastic Figural Camera,**
1971. - **$25 $50 $85**

❑ **CTU-8. Oval Bathroom Scale,**
1972. - **$20 $40 $75**

CTU-9

CTU-10

❑ **CTU-9. Charlie The Tuna Electric Clock,**
1972. Star-Kist Foods. 4x4x4" plastic cube with color paper images on all inner panels. -
**$35 $70 $100**

❑ **CTU-10. Metal Wristwatch,**
1973. - **$25 $40 $65**

CTU-11

CTU-12

❑ **CTU-11. Mug,**
1977. - **$5 $15 $30**

❑ **CTU-12. "25th Anniversary" Wristwatch,**
1986. Authorized Star-Kist limited edition metal case watch accompanied by paper slips for Charlie the Tuna history and other mail premiums. Near Mint Boxed - **$65**
Watch Only - **$20 $35 $50**

CTU-13

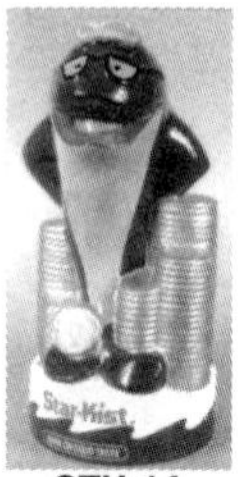
CTU-14

❑ **CTU-13. "Charlie The Tuna" Telephone,**
1987. Star-Kist Foods premium found in some quantity in late 1990s . Near Mint Boxed - **$50**

❑ **CTU-14. Ceramic Bank,**
1988. - **$25 $50 $75**

## Cheerios Misc.

**Cheerios ready-to-eat oat cereal was introduced by General Mills as Cheerioats in 1941 and has remained a perennial favorite with kids and adults ever since. Over the years the Cheerios box has carried cutout toys and promotions for a wide variety of merchandisers, notably the Lone Ranger, Wyatt Earp, Superman, the Muppets, Bugs Bunny, Snoopy and Peanuts, Star Trek, Star Wars and Mickey Mouse. Disney comic books and 3-D glasses were featured giveaways in the 1940s and 1950s. The items in this section are primarily a selection of Cheerios non-character premiums.**

CEE-1

CEE-2

❑ **CEE-1. "Hall Of Fun/Groucho Marx" 3-D Picture,**
c. 1942. Assembled from box back. Set of eight.
Box Panel Or Assembled - **$25 $40 $60**

❑ **CEE-2. "Hall Of Fun/Joe E. Brown" 3-D Picture,**
c. 1942. Assembled from box back. Set of eight.
Box Panel Or Assembled - **$25 $40 $60**

CEE-3

❑ **CEE-3. "Cheerios Hall Of Fun" Box Back 3-D Pictures,**
1940s. Famous comedians include Jack Oakie, Hugh Herbert, Jerry Colonna, Joe E. Brown, Mischa Auer, Groucho Marx, and two others.
Each Complete Panel - **$25 $40 $60**

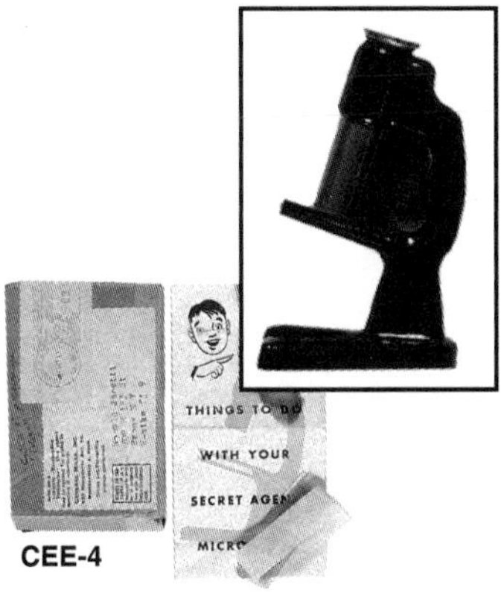

CEE-4

❑ **CEE-4. Secret Agent Microscope,**
1950. Secret Agent black microscope with six slides. Eight page instruction booklet and mailer. - **$30 $60 $100**

CEE-5

❑ **CEE-5. "Confederate Currency" Album With Envelope,**
1954. Reproductions of Confederate money. - **$40 $80 $160**

CEE-6

❑ **CEE-6. "Confederate Money" Box,**
1954. Front panel pictures one of nine different designs of replica currency bills of Confederate States of America issued individually as box insert. Complete Box - **$25 $75 $150**

CEE-7

❑ **CEE-7. "American Airlines Air Travel Game" Box Panel With Game Sheet,**
1955. Game designed by Milton Bradley.
Back Panel - **$5 $10 $20**
Game Sheet - **$5 $10 $20**

CEE-8

❑ **CEE-8. "Cheerios Airport Missile Control Center" Box Flat,**
1958. From a series of five different boxes with side panel offer of 39 piece set including missile launchers and airplanes as well as a "Full Color Layout Sheet." Gordon Gold Archives.
Each Near Mint Flat - **$125**
Each Used Complete - **$20 $40 $65**

CEE-9

❑ **CEE-9. "'Rocky' The Walking Horse" Cereal Box Flat,**
1950s. Canadian offer of small plastic ramp walker toy packaged in the box with cut-outs on back for "Rocky's Ranch." Gordon Gold Archives. Near Mint Flat - **$100**
Used Complete - **$20 $40 $65**

CEE-10

❑ **CEE-10. 3D Wiggle Picture Display,**
1950s. Cheerios Cereal. Features Cheerio Kid and Donald Duck. - **$20 $40 $65**
Each of 4 Extra Pictures - **$3 $6 $9**

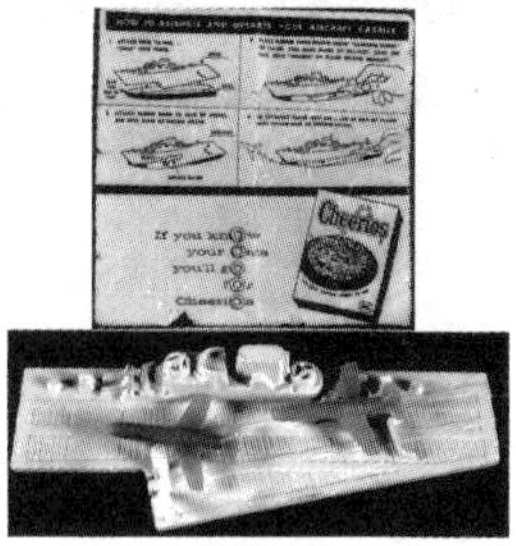
CEE-11

❑ **CEE-11. Aircraft Carrier And Planes Plastic Toy With Instructions And Box,**
1960s. Planes are launched by rubber band.
Near Mint In Mailer - **$100**

CEE-12

❑ **CEE-12. "Cape Cheerios Rocket Base" Box Panel Set,**
1960s. Completed by parts from five box backs.
Uncut Backs Each - **$15 $30 $50**

CEE-13

❑ **CEE-13. "Cape Cheerios Rocket Base",**
c. 1960s. Premium by Marx.
Complete Boxed - **$30 $50 $90**

CEE-14

❑ **CEE-14. "Cheerios Kids Snack Time Dispenser",**
2001. Eat your cereal from the back of his head. Cool! - **$5**

## Chick Carter

**Like father, like son, for detective work done. Nick Carter, a sleuth of considerable prominence to readers of pulp magazines and hardbound novels of the 1930s, fathered a son in his image--at least for purposes of radio and movie serial producers. The elder Carter, by name, was avoided for reasons unknown in broadcast and screen versions. *Chick Carter, Boy Detective* began as a radio drama on the Mutual network July 5, 1943 and ran until July 6, 1945. *Chick Carter, Detective*, a 1946 Columbia Pictures 15-episode serial, dropped all pretense that Chick was a youngster. Chick was an instant adult, portrayed by Lyle Talbot, a veteran actor of gangster and crime movie roles.**

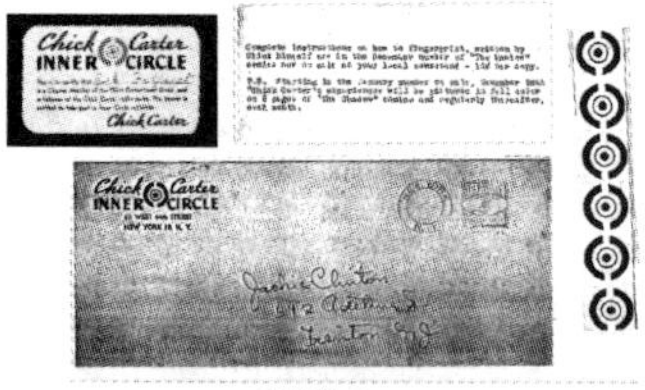

CCK-1

❑ **CCK-1. Chick Carter Club Kit,**
1944. Envelope - **$35 $75 $100**
Club Card - **$50 $100 $150**
"The Shadow" Comic Promo Insert - **$20 $40 $60**
Club Logo Long Strip of Stickers - **$20 $40 $60**

CCK-2

❑ **CCK-2. Radio Club Promo Booklet,**
1945. - **$20 $50 $100**

CCK-3

❑ **CCK-3. Club Kit Folder,**
1945. - **$30 $80 $165**

CHICK CARTER INNER CIRCLE

This is to certify that ... is a Charter Member of the CHICK CARTER INNER CIRCLE, and a regular listener to the CHICK CARTER radio program. The bearer may participate in all INNER CIRCLE activities and is entitled to use the INNER CIRCLE INSIGNIA.

1945 Chick Carter BOY DETECTIVE

CCK-4

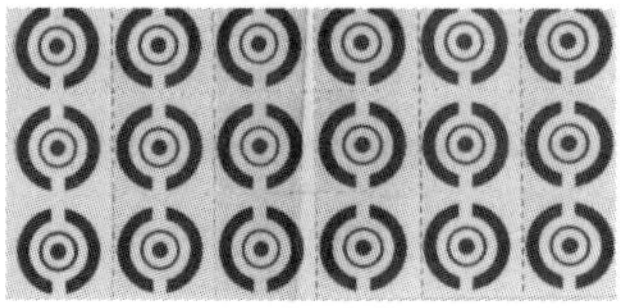
CCK-5

❑ **CCK-4. Club Kit Card,**
1945. Rare. - **$15 $55 $80**

❑ **CCK-5. Set of 24 Inner Circle Logo Stickers,**
1945. - **$10 $20 $48**
Each - **$2**

## China Clipper

**In spite of the early 1930s Depression years, air travel demand continued almost unabated. The enterprising Pan American Airways offered a challenge based on need: a transport aircraft capable of 2,500 mile non-stop flight to span the Pacific. Aircraft makers responded quickly. On November 22, 1935 the first of the romantically-named "China Clipper" flights began to the Orient. The selected aircraft, one by Martin and one by Boeing, were masterpieces of huge payload capacity, incredible size and magnificent interior elegance for crew and passengers. So remarkable was this advance in aviation technology, a 1936 movie starring Pat O'Brien detailed the account of the initial flight that compared in public stature to Lindbergh's earlier solo flight of the Atlantic. The "China Clipper" mystique and adulation resulted in several tribute premiums issued by Quaker Oats.**

CLP-1

CLP-2

❑ **CLP-1. China Clipper Brass Ring,**
1935. Quaker Puffed Wheat and Rice. - **$40 $80 $120**

❑ **CLP-2. China Clipper 2" Brass Bar Badge,**
1935. Quaker Puffed Wheat and Rice. - **$20 $40 $75**

CLP-3

❑ **CLP-3. Quaker "China Clipper" Balsa Model,**
1935. Quaker Puffed Wheat and Rice. 12" wing span. Assembled - **$25 $75 $125**

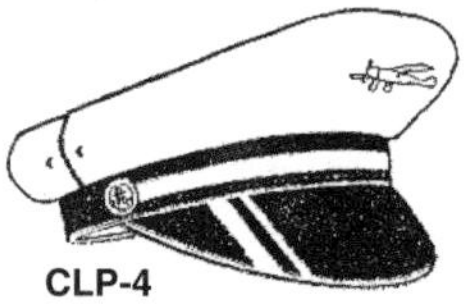
CLP-4

CLP-5

❑ **CLP-4. Pilot's Cap,**
1936. Quaker Puffed Wheat/Puffed Rice. White twill with gilt braid, brass buttons, black bill, metal airplane ornament. - **$50 $100 $200**

❑ **CLP-5. Girl's Bracelet,**
1936. Quaker Puffed Wheat/Puffed Rice. Gold luster metal with personalized single initial on wing design. - **$25 $60 $100**

CLP-6

CLP-7

❑ **CLP-6. Boys Life Magazine - Feature And Picture On Cover,**
1936. China Clipper pictures on cover with story about Pan-American Clippers. - **$15 $25 $50**

❑ **CLP-7. "Flying the Sky Clipper" Big Little Book #1108,**
1936. - **$10 $30 $60**

CLP-8

❑ **CLP-8. Standee 10x14",**
1939. Rare. Kraft Malted Milk. Promo for China Clipper model plane - **$100 $250 $375**

CLP-9

❑ **CLP-9. China Clipper Promo Wraparound Label for National Dairy Malted Milk,**
1939. Shows pictures of China Clipper model plane. Gordon Gold Archives. -
**$25 $50 $100**

CLP-10

❑ **CLP-10. Free China Clipper Model Store Sign,**
1939. Kraft Malted Milk. 18x24-1/2" full color sign with same image printed on each side. Has lightly scored top margin allowing it to be hung over a string so either side can be viewed. Advertises "Giant 22" Model." Gordon Gold Archives. - **$100 $200 $350**

CLP-11

❑ **CLP-11. Poster,**
1939. Rare. 32x44". Beautiful colorful poster for grocery stores which shows how to get free photos and models of the China Clipper.-
**$100 $275 $500**

CLP-12

❑ **CLP-12. Model Mailer,**
1939. Kraft Malted Milk. - **$30 $60 $100**

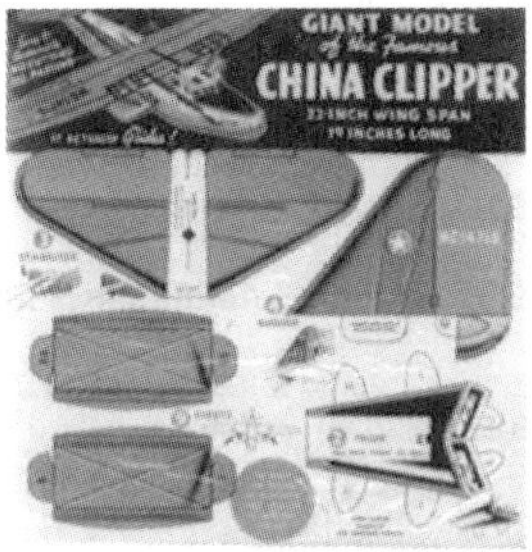

CLP-13

❑ **CLP-13. "Giant Model Of The Famous China Clipper" Cardboard Punch-Out Folder,**
1939. Pan-American Airways. Folder opens to 11x30". - **$40 $100 $200**

## The Cinnamon Bear

**First aired in 1937, *The Cinnamon Bear* was a syndicated children's Christmas tale broadcast five times a week between Thanksgiving and Christmas. In 26 chapters it followed the adventures of Judy and Jimmy Barton and Paddy O'Cinnamon as they travel through Maybe Land in search of their stolen Silver Star--across the Root Beer Ocean, face-to-face with the Wintergreen Witch and Captain Taffy the Pirate. The show was sponsored by department stores, principally Wieboldt's of Chicago, and ran annually for many years.**

CIN-1

CIN-2

CIN-3

❑ **CIN-1. Wieboldt's Litho. Tin Tab,**
1940s. Rare. - **$75 $275 $525**

❑ **CIN-2. Foil Silver Star Picturing Paddy,**
c. 1940s. - **$50 $100 $200**

❑ **CIN-3. "TV Club" Litho. Button With Cardboard Bear Attachment,**
1950s. Wieboldt's department store. -
**$50 $125 $200**

## The Cisco Kid

**The beloved bandito and his sidekick Pancho were created by O. Henry in a short story, *The Caballero's Way*, in the early 1900s and have lived a long entertainment life. They appeared in several silent movies and in 23 sound features between 1929 and 1950, starring either Warner Baxter (who won an Oscar for *In Old Arizona* in 1929), Cesar Romero, Duncan Renaldo (1904-1980) or Gilbert Roland. A radio series aired on Mutual from 1942 to 1956 and a popular television version with Renaldo and Leo Carrillo (1880-1961) was syndicated between 1950 and 1956. Over 150 half-hour episodes were filmed by ZIV Television--in color, though at the time TV could broadcast only in black and white. Comic books appeared in the 1940s and 1950s and a daily comic strip ran from 1951 to 1968. Most premiums date from the successful broadcast period of the 1950s. A 1994 telefilm brought Cisco and Pancho back to TV audiences in the forms of Jimmy Smits and Cheech Marin, respectively. "Oh Pancho! Ooooh Ceesco!"**

CIS-1

CIS-2

❑ **CIS-1. "Safety Club Member" Cello. Button,**
c. 1948. - **$25 $50 $90**

❑ **CIS-2. "I'm A Cisco Kid Fan!" Cello. Button,**
1949. ZIV Co. Radio Productions. Issued to show sponsors for promotional purposes. -
**$10 $20 $35**

(FRONT)

(BACK)

CIS-3

❑ **CIS-3. Cisco Kid Paper Mask,**
1949. Various sponsors. Pictured example for Cisco Kid cookies, Cisco Kid sweet buns by Schofer's Bakery. - **$15 $25 $45**

CIS-4

CIS-5

❑ **CIS-4. "Wrigley's Cisco Kid Club" Cello. Button,**
c. 1949. Wrigley's Gum, Canadian issue. - **$25 $65 $100**

❑ **CIS-5. Pancho Paper Mask,**
1949. Various bakeries. - **$15 $25 $45**

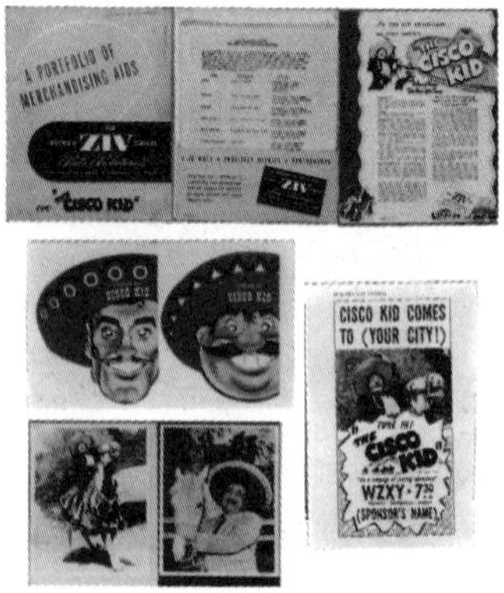


CIS-6

❑ **CIS-6. Merchandising Portfolio,**
1949. ZIV Co. Radio Productions . Contains over 25 promotional items such as bw photos, sample ads, source list for premiums.
Complete - **$100 $300 $500**

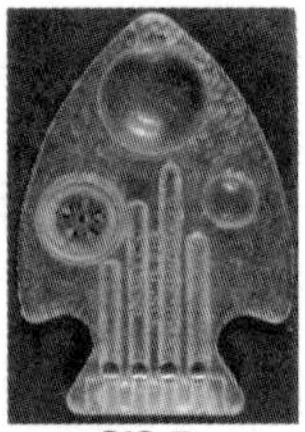

CIS-7

CIS-8

CIS-9

❑ **CIS-7. "Wrigley's Cisco Kid Signal Arrowhead",**
c. 1949. - **$125 $250 $450**

❑ **CIS-8. "Cisco Kid" Ring,**
c. 1950. Name appears on each side. - **$75 $150 $250**

❑ **CIS-9. "Cisco Kid" Aluminum Saddle Ring,**
1950. Name in raised letters on saddle seat. - **$100 $325 $525**

CIS-10

CIS-11

❑ **CIS-10. Cisco Kid Humming Lariat,**
1950. Eddy's Bread. Cardboard rectangle with string and streamer roll of crepe paper to "Execute The Thrilling Rope Tricks Done By The Famous Cisco Kid". - **$30 $75 $120**

❑ **CIS-11. Secret Compartment Photo Ring,**
c. 1950. Rare. Brass bands holding plastic compartment with brass lid over bw picture. - **$1500 $6000 $10000**

CIS-12

❑ **CIS-12. "Arden Milk" Black Fabric Bandanna,**
c. 1950. Opens to 16x16". - **$25 $50 $75**

CIS-13

❑ **CIS-13. Freihofer's Bread Labels,**
c. 1950. From a set. Each - **$15 $25 $35**

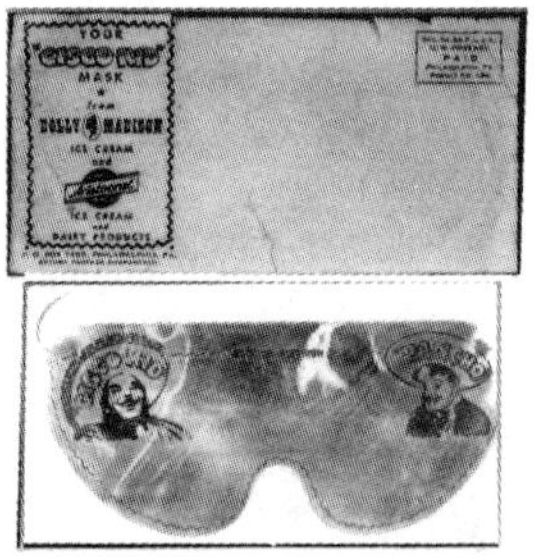

CIS-14

❑ **CIS-14. Thin Plastic Reflective Mask With Envelope,**
c. 1950. Scarce. Dolly Madison Ice Cream.
In Envelope - **$75 $160 $250**
Loose - **$25 $60 $100**

CIS-15

CIS-16

CIS-17

❑ **CIS-15. Cello. Button,**
c. 1950. Possibly for rodeo appearance. - **$30 $65 $125**

❑ **CIS-16. "Cisco Kid On TV-Radio" Litho. Tin Tab,**
c. 1950. Various sponsors. Various hat colors. - **$10 $25 $45**

❑ **CIS-17. TV-Radio Pancho Litho. Tab,**
c. 1950. Various sponsors. Various hat colors. - **$10 $25 $45**

CIS-18

CIS-19

❑ **CIS-18. Glass,**
c. 1950. Probably held dairy product. Seen in lime green/black or yellow/brown.
Each - **$25 $60 $125**

❑ **CIS-19. Kern's Bread Postcard,**
1951. - **$12 $20 $40**

CIS-22

CIS-23

❑ **CIS-22. Triple "S" Club Litho. Button,**
c. 1951. - **$15 $25 $60**

❑ **CIS-23. Kern's Bread "Triple S Club" Clothing Transfer,**
c. 1951. Tissue paper with reverse image to be applied by warm iron on fabric. - **$15 $40 $60**

CIS-28

❑ **CIS-28. Paper Masks Set,**
1953. Tip-Top Bread. Each - **$15 $25 $45**

CIS-20

❑ **CIS-20. Comic Strip Announcement Portfolio,**
1951. Nine picture prints and three comic strip prints with art by Jose Luis Salinas. Issued by King Features Syndicate. - **$150 $300 $500**

CIS-24

CIS-25

❑ **CIS-24. Bread Label Folder,**
1952. Freihofer's Bread. Holds 36 different bread labels. - **$50 $75 $175**

❑ **CIS-25. Pancho Photo,**
1952. Butter-Nut Bread. Shows Pancho and horse Loco. Promotes radio and TV show. - **$10 $20 $35**

CIS-29

❑ **CIS-29. Tip-Top Bread Puzzle,**
1953. With Envelope - **$20 $50 $75**
Puzzle Only - **$8 $15 $35**

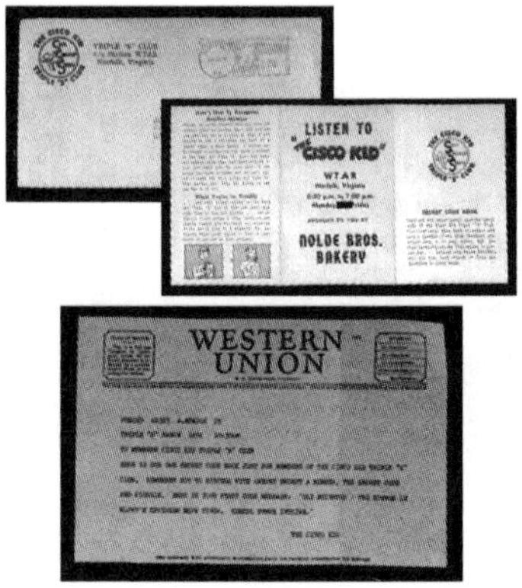

CIS-21

❑ **CIS-21. "Triple 'S' Club" Papers With Envelope,**
1951. Imprinted for Nolde Bros. Bakery and WTAR Radio, Norfolk, Virginia. Contents are replica "Western Union" transmittal telegram plus Code Book leaflet.
Near Mint In Envelope - **$100**
Folder - **$15 $25 $40**
Telegram - **$10 $20 $30**

CIS-30

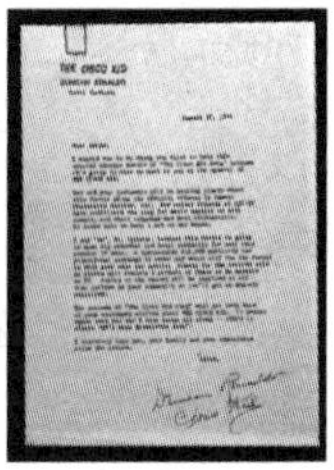
CIS-31

❑ **CIS-30. Record With Sleeve,**
1956. - **$25 $50 $100**

❑ **CIS-31. Letter For Record Promotion,**
1956. - **$25 $50 $100**

CIS-26

CIS-27

❑ **CIS-26. Portrait Photo,**
1952. Butter-Nut Bread. - **$10 $20 $35**

❑ **CIS-27. Cisco Photo,**
1952. Butter-Nut Bread. Shows Cisco riding Diablo. Promotes radio and TV show. - **$10 $20 $35**

CIS-32

CIS-33

❑ **CIS-32. Photo,**
1950s. Farm Crest Bakery. - **$15 $30 $75**

❑ **CIS-33. Tip-Top Labels,**
1950s. Tip-Top Bread. Bread labels were cut in shape of star to fit folder. Each - **$10 $20 $35**

CIS-34

CIS-35

❑ **CIS-34. Plastic Tumbler,**
1950s. Leatherwood Dairy. - **$15 $30 $85**

❑ **CIS-35. Glass Bowl,**
1950s. Dairy product container. - **$10 $15 $25**

CIS-36

❑ **CIS-36 Tip-Top Bread Labels,**
1950s. At least 28 in set. Each - **$8 $15 $25**

CIS-37

CIS-38

❑ **CIS-37. Store Poster,**
1950s. Nolde's Bread and possibly others. 17x21" black on yellow. - **$40 $75 $150**

❑ **CIS-38. "Cisco Kid" Salesman's Sample Combination Comb And Shoe Horn ,**
1950s. 5-1/2" long ivory hard plastic reading "The Cisco Kid On Television/Sponsor's Imprint Here." - **$20 $45 $100**

CIS-39

❑ **CIS-39. Tip-Top Bread Folder,**
1950s. Tip-Top Bread. Eight pages. Holds 16 star bread labels. Large photo inside of Cisco holding gun. Bread labels tell story of Bolders & Bullet when completed. - **$50 $75 $150**

CIS-40

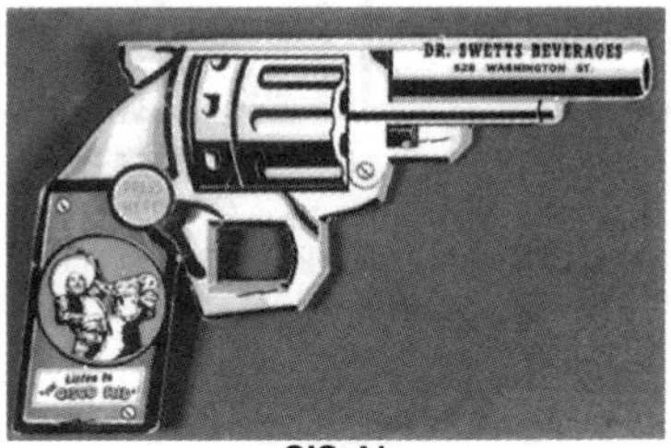

CIS-41

❑ **CIS-40. Photo Cards,**
1950s. Tip-Top Bread but various sponsors. Each - **$5 $15 $25**

❑ **CIS-41. Cardboard Clicker Gun,**
1950s. Dr. Swetts beverages but various sponsors. -**$20 $35 $75**

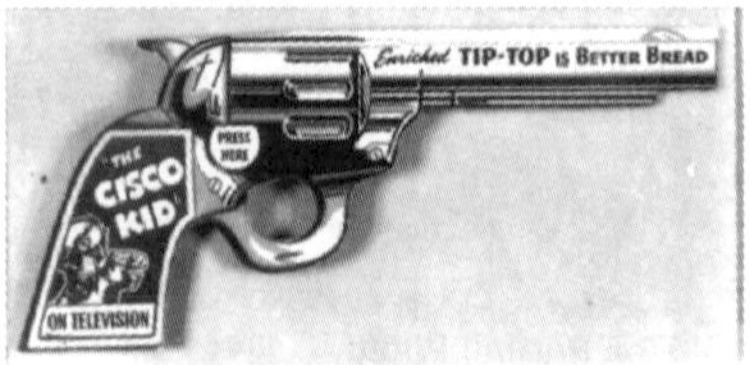

CIS-42

❑ **CIS-42. Cardboard Clicker Gun,**
1950s. Tip-Top Bread. - **$15 $30 $75**

CIS-43

CIS-44

❑ **CIS-43. "Cisco Kid's Choice Tip Top Bread" Bread Labels,**
1950s. Black and white center star design on white with red accents. Label back says "48 Pictures In All." Each - **$8 $15 $25**

❑ **CIS-44. Milk Bottle,**
1950s. Harrisburg (Pa.) Dairies. Company name plus "WTPA Channel 71" every Wednesday 6 P.M. - **$50 $75 $125**

CIS-45

❑ **CIS-45. TV "Sponsor's Name" 10x18" Cardboard Sample Store Sign,**
1950s. - **$40 $90 $150**

CIS-46

CIS-47

❑ **CIS-46. Shopping Mall Photo,**
1950s. Printed for "Thruway Plaza," likely various mall sponsors. - **$12 $20 $40**

❑ **CIS-47. "Cisco Kid" Silvered Brass Hat Ring,**
1950s. Name on brim. - **$100 $300 $500**
Without Name - **$10 $20 $30**

CIS-48

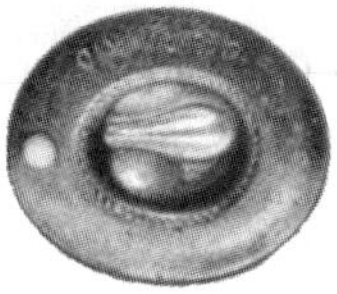

CIS-49

CIS-50

❑ **CIS-48. "TV Channel 10" Member Cello. Button,**
1950s. Dolly Madison and Aristocrat. Comes with beige or green background.
Green - **$25 $50 $75**
Beige - **$40 $90 $140**

❑ **CIS-49. "Cisco Kid" Silvered Brass Keychain Fob,**
1950s. Store item stamped "Japan". - **$15 $25 $40**

❑ **CIS-50. "Cisco Kid"-type Doll,**
1950s. Probably unlicensed. - **$75 $150 $250**

CIS-51

❑ **CIS-51. "Cisco Kid" Advertising Press Book,**
1950s. Has info on Duncan Renaldo's sessions as a performer at fairs, stadiums and auditoriums. Has 13" full figure photo of Cisco printed on press book. - **$55 $110 $225**

CIS-52

❑ **CIS-52. "Cisco Kid Ranchers Club" Member Kit,**
1956. Probable various breads. Includes two certificates, manual, application, "Cattle Brand" card. Complete - **$75 $200 $350**

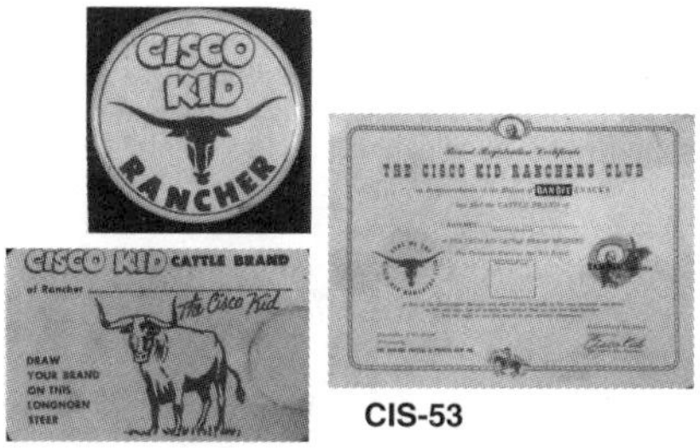


CIS-53

❑ **CIS-53. "Cisco Kid Ranchers Club" Kit,**
1956. Dan-Dee Pretzel And Potato Chip Co.
Certificate - **$15 $40 $75**
Card - **$10 $20 $30**
Button - **$10 $25 $50**
Letter - **$15 $40 $75**

CIS-54

❑ **CIS-54. "Cisco Kid Ranchers Club" Kit,**
1956. Issued locally by Leatherwood Dairy, Bluefield, West Virginia. Mailer - **$5 $10 $15**
Photo - **$10 $20 $35**
Button - **$10 $25 $50**
Certificate - **$20 $50 $75**

CIS-55

❑ **CIS-55. "Ranchers Club" Card,**
1956. Pro-tek-tiv' Shoes. - **$15 $25 $45**

CIS-56

❑ **CIS-56. Honorary Citizenship Certificate,**
1956. Premium. - **$25 $50 $100**

CIS-57

❑ **CIS-57. Ranchers Club Plan Book,**
1956. 28 pgs. including front and back covers. - **$100 $200 $300**

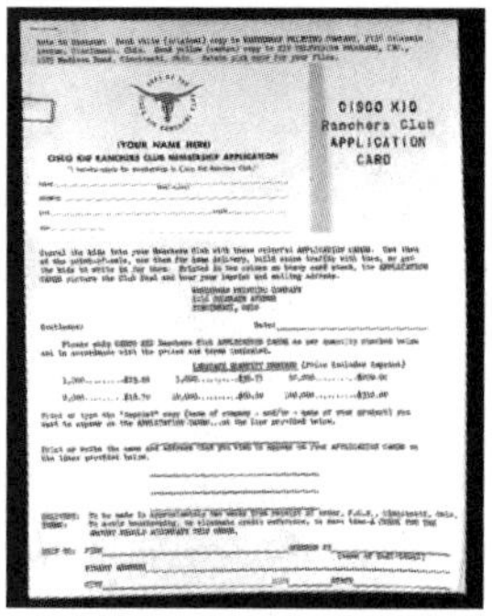


CIS-58

❑ **CIS-58. Ranchers Club Membership Application,**
1956. 3 pgs. of order blanks.
Each - **$25 $50 $75**

CIS-59

❑ **CIS-59. Range War Manual,**
1957. With cardboard back cover. Has two applications with pictures of game, one letter example and eight pages explaining game rules and distribution information. - **$100 $200 $300**

CIS-60

❑ **CIS-60. Range War Game With Punch-Outs,**
1957. Rare. Show was cancelled shortly after release of this game. Few were produced. - **$300 $850 $1300**

CIS-61

❑ **CIS-61. "Cisco & Pancho In '84" Video Release Promotional Cello. Button,**
1984. Blair Entertainment. 3-1/2" full color button used when TV programs became available on video. - **$10 $25 $60**

## Clara, Lu 'n' Em

**This low-key comedy about three gossipy housewives was created by three Northwestern University coeds to amuse their sorority sisters. After graduation they took it to Chicago radio station WGN, which ran it locally in 1930-1931 and then as an evening program on NBC until 1932 when it became the nation's first daytime soap opera. The sponsor was Colgate. The program ran until 1936 and was revived for a short run on CBS in 1942 for Pillsbury flour.**

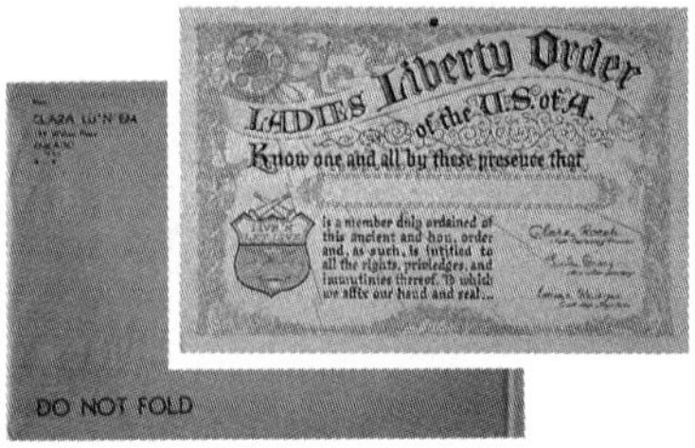


CLN-1

❑ **CLN-1. Certificate and Mailer,**
1932. Radio premium. Beautiful cardboard membership certificate for Ladies Liberty Order.
Certificate - **$25 $50 $115**
Mailer - **$10 $20 $30**

CLN-2

CLN-3

❑ **CLN-2. Cast Member Photo,**
c. 1932. Fan photo 5x7" black and white with facsimile first name signature of each. - **$15 $25 $45**

❑ **CLN-3. Newspaper,**
1932. Radio premium. The Ladies Clarion Blast - Vol. #1. - **$20 $50 $85**

CLN-4

**CLN-4. "Clara, Lu' n' Em" Radio Show Promotion Page,**
1932. Featured in Ladies' Home Journal - **$5 $15 $20**

CLN-5

**CLN-5. "Clara, Lu' n' Em" Puzzle,**
c. 1933. Colgate. Envelope - **$5 $10 $25**
Puzzle - **$20 $50 $85**

## Clyde Beatty

**Clyde Beatty (1903-1965), world-famous wild animal trapper and trainer, played himself in two chapter plays: *The Lost Jungle* for Mascot in 1934 and *Darkest Africa* for Republic in 1936. In both he defeats hostile forces, human and animal, and wins the girl. His *Clyde Beatty Show* on radio, on the other hand, was said to dramatize actual incidents from his life in the wild and at his circus. The program was syndicated in the late 1940s and ran on the Mutual network from 1950 to 1952, sponsored by Kellogg's cereal. Scattered comic book appearances included a 1937 giveaway by Malto-Meal and a 1956 giveaway by Richfield Oil.**

CLY-1

❑ **CLY-1. "Lions And Tigers With The Sensational Dare-Devil Clyde Beatty" Big Little Book,**
1934. Whitman #653. - **$20 $50 $100**

CLY-2

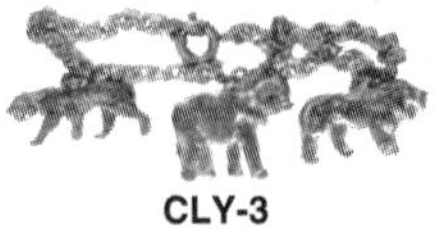

CLY-3

❑ **CLY-2. Gold-Plated Lion Head Ring,**
1935. Quaker Wheat Crackels. Our photo is taken from published ad showing the ring. Ring has adjustable bands with large open-mouth lion head on the top with lion displaying four large fangs. There are no jewels in the eyes or mouth. Ring may have been issued in a jeweled version but we've seen no paperwork identifying such rings as Clyde Beatty premiums. -
**$200 $350 $500**

❑ **CLY-3. Jungle Animal Brass Link Charm Bracelet,**
1935. Scarce. Quaker Wheat Crackels. Unmarked Clyde Beatty premium. -
**$75 $200 $400**

CLY-4

❑ **CLY-4. "Clyde Beatty & His Wild Animal Act" Punch-Out Album,**
1935. Scarce. Quaker Wheat Crackels. Made by Fold-A-Way Toys.
Unpunched - **$100 $250 $425**

CLY-5

❑ **CLY-5. Quaker Oats Circus Book,**
1935. Inside front offers punch-out animal act, lion head ring, jungle bracelet, bullwhip. -
**$20 $50 $75**

CLY-6

CLY-7

❑ **CLY-6. "Cole Bros. Circus" Cello. Button,**
1930s. - **$12 $25 $40**

❑ **CLY-7. Circus Souvenir Cello. Button,**
1930s. - **$15 $30 $50**

CLY-8

❑ **CLY-8. "Hingees" Punch-Out Kit In Envelope,**
1945. Store item. Unused - **$25 $40 $75**

CLY-9

❑ **CLY-9. "Richfield Presents Clyde Beatty's African Jungle Book,"**
1956. Issued by Richfield Oil. 16 pages. Has Disneyland back cover ad. - **$15 $25 $50**

## Coca-Cola

**Since the mid-1890s, Coca-Cola has distributed premiums in staggering numbers and almost every conceivable material and variety. What started as a patent medicine tonic soon evolved into a soda fountain or bottled drink sold in more than 160 countries globally. Coca-Cola premiums never lack for distinct self-advertising but over the years have frequently been related to war, entertainment and comic characters, sports, toy trucks, educational materials and much more. Hundreds of items intended originally as only convenience items to stores and customers now swell the ranks of advertising collectibles. The quantity of Coca-Cola premiums issued in the past century have resulted in several reference books devoted solely to this output.**

COC-1

❑ **COC-1. Cello. Note Pad,**
1902. Front cover has full color portrait, back has art illustrating sales growth 1886-1901. -
**$150 $350 $600**

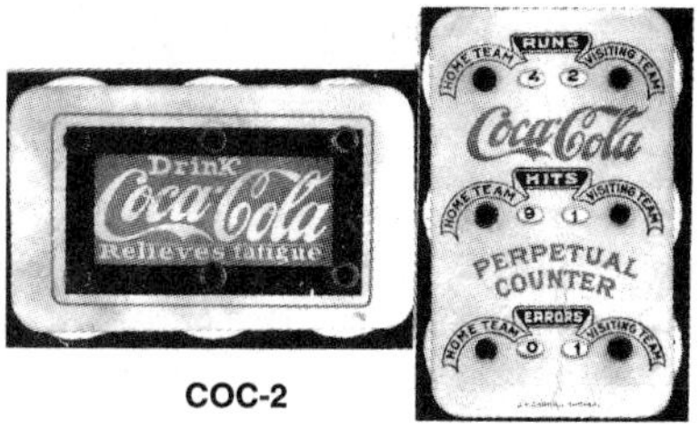


COC-2

❑ **COC-2. Cardboard Baseball Score Counter,**
c. 1907. - **$65 $125 $175**

COC-3

COC-4

❑ **COC-3. Cello. Pocket Mirror,**
1909. Illustration by Hamilton King. -
**$150 $250 $500**

❑ **COC-4. Cello. Pocket Mirror,**
1917. Pictures World War I era girl. -
**$150 $250 $500**

COC-5

❑ **COC-5. "Toonerville Refreshment Palace" Leaflet,**
1931. From a series for distribution by salesman. - **$15 $30 $50**

COC-6

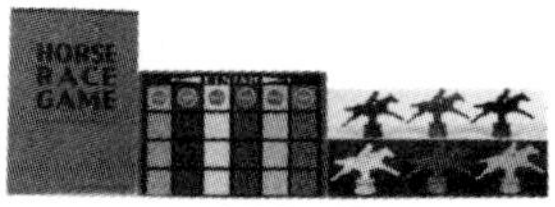


COC-7

❑ **COC-6. Coca-Cola Tin Thermometer,**
c. 1935. 7x16" litho tin. - **$75 $125 $200**

❑ **COC-7. "Horse Race Game,"**
c. 1930s. Milton Bradley. - **$75 $150 $250**

COC-8

COC-9

❑ **COC-8. Cleveland Press "Big Wheels Club" Cello. Button,**
1930s. - **$15 $25 $40**

❑ **COC-9. "Bottlers Club" Cello. Button,**
1930s. - **$40 $85 $150**

COC-10

❑ **COC-10. Warplane 13x15" Cardboard Sign,**
1943. From series bordered in white and gold. Each - **$20 $40 $75**

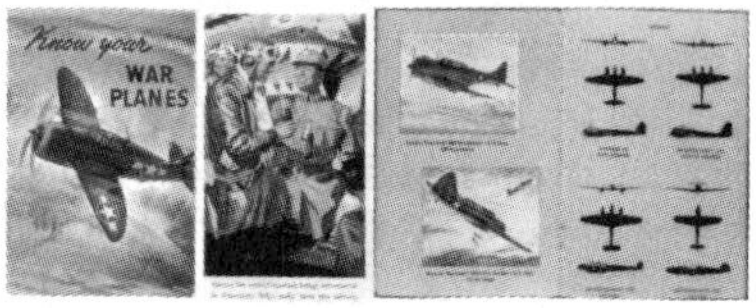


COC-11

❑ **COC-11. "Know Your War Planes" Booklet,**
c. 1943. Coca-Cola. - **$20 $50 $75**

COC-12

❑ **COC-12. Warplane Cards,**
1943. Set of 20. Set - **$40 $80 $150**

COC-13

❑ **COC-13. Newspaper Ads For Premium Booklet "Know Your War Airplanes",**
c. 1943. Our photos show three different ads, each featuring a different warplane. Each - **$5 $10 $15**

COC-14

❑ **COC-14. Warplane 13x15" Cardboard Sign,**
1943. From series bordered in simulated wood. Each - **$20 $40 $75**

COC-15

COC-16

❑ **COC-15. Felt Fabric Beanie,**
1940s. - **$20 $50 $75**

❑ **COC-16. "hi fi Club" Member Litho. Button,**
c. 1959. - **$12 $18 $30**

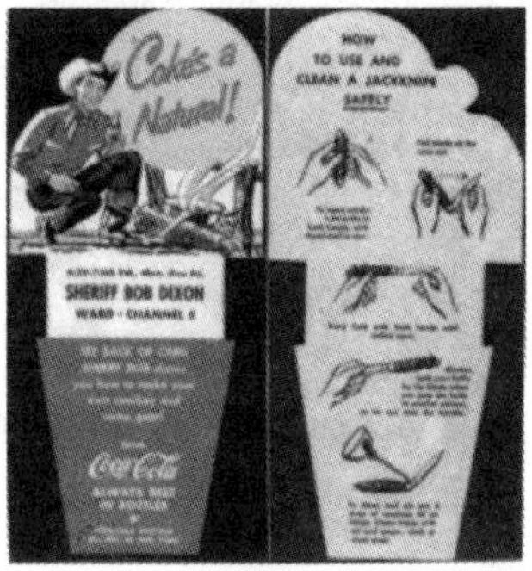


COC-17

❑ **COC-17. "Sheriff Bob Dixon" Insert,**
1950s. Promotes TV show on local station. - **$5 $10 $25**

COC-18

COC-19

❑ **COC-18. Celluloid 9" Wall Sign,**
1950s. - **$40 $65 $150**

❑ **COC-19. Plastic Cooler Replica,**
c. 1950s. 4x4x5" wide. - **$35 $75 $110**

COC-20

❑ **COC-20. Diecut 5' Standee,**
1960s. - **$75 $200 $400**

COC-21

❑ **COC-21. Coca-Cola Dispenser And Bank,**
1960s. Store item by C&G Toys. Comes with two miniature mugs. Holds 6-1/2 ounces of soda. Near Mint Boxed - **$90**
Toy Only - **$20 $40 $65**

COC-22

❑ **COC-22. Red Vinyl Lunch Box,**
c. 1980. Issued with unmarked styrofoam lunch bottle. Made by Aladdin Industries.
Box - **$35 $60 $100**
Bottle - **$5 $10 $25**

COC-23

❑ **COC-23. "Bring Home the Classics" Poster Prize,**
1988. 17"x24". 2nd prize from Coca-Cola/Disney sweepstakes promotion. - **$40 $60 $120**

COC-24

COC-25

❑ **COC-24. Christmas Elf Cloth Doll,**
1980s. - **$15 $25 $35**

❑ **COC-25. Canadian 3" Cello. Endorsement Button,**
1980s. By Coca-Cola Ltd. of Canada picturing Bill Cosby. - **$5 $10 $15**

COC-26

❑ **COC-26. Coca-Cola International Bean Bag Standee Sign and Bean Bags,**
1999. There are 5 different signs for 5 sets of 10 bean bags. Series 2 sign shown here.
Each sign - **$5 $20 $35**

The 50 Bean Bags and the countries they represent:

| | | |
|---|---|---|
| ❑ **Ardi The Aardvark** | **Nigeria** | **$10** |
| ❑ **Badgey The Badger** | **Czech Rep.** | **$10** |
| ❑ **Baltic The Reindeer** | **Sweden** | **$10** |
| ❑ **Barris The Brown Bear** | **Russia** | **$12** |
| ❑ **Barrot The Parrot** | **Brazil** | **$10** |
| ❑ **Blubby The Pot Bellied Pig** | **Vietnam** | **$12** |
| ❑ **Can Can The Pelican** | **Cuba** | **$10** |
| ❑ **Clomp The Elephant** | **Kenya** | **$12** |
| ❑ **Croon The Baboon** | **Pakistan** | **$10** |
| ❑ **Crunch The Crocodile** | **Sudan** | **$12** |
| ❑ **Curry The Tiger** | **India** | **$10** |
| ❑ **Dover The Bulldog** | **England** | **$15** |
| ❑ **Fannie The Fox** | **Germany** | **$10** |
| ❑ **Gourmand The Moose** | **Canada** | **$10** |
| ❑ **Heeta The Cheetah** | **Nambia** | **$10** |
| ❑ **Hopps The Coki Frog** | **Puerto Rico** | **$12** |
| ❑ **Howls The Wolf** | **Romania** | **$10** |
| ❑ **Kelp The Kiwi** | **New Zealand** | **$10** |
| ❑ **Key Key The Snow Monkey** | **Japan** | **$15** |
| ❑ **Laffs The Llama** | **Bolivia** | **$10** |
| ❑ **Locks The Rabbit** | **Scotland** | **$10** |
| ❑ **Lors The Wild Boar** | **Italy** | **$10** |
| ❑ **Masa The Lion** | **Mozambique** | **$12** |
| ❑ **Masha The Ostrich** | **South Africa** | **$10** |
| ❑ **Meeska The Hippo** | **Zambia** | **$12** |
| ❑ **Nardie The St. Bernard** | **Switzerland** | **$15** |
| ❑ **Neppy The Proboscis Monkey** | **Thailand** | **$10** |
| ❑ **Oppy The Octopus** | **Greece** | **$12** |
| ❑ **Orany The Orangutan** | **Singapore** | **$10** |
| ❑ **Paco The Iguana** | **Mexico** | **$10** |
| ❑ **Peng The Penguin** | **Chile** | **$10** |
| ❑ **Pok The Peacock** | **Sri Lanka** | **$10** |
| ❑ **Quala The Koala Bear** | **Australia** | **$15** |
| ❑ **Ramel The Camel** | **Egypt** | **$12** |
| ❑ **Reegle The Eagle** | **USA** | **$20** |
| ❑ **Rhiny The Black Rhinoceros** | **Tanzania** | **$10** |
| ❑ **Rif Raff The Giraffe** | **Somalia** | **$10** |
| ❑ **Rilla The Gorilla** | **Rwanda** | **$12** |
| ❑ **Salty The Sea Turtle** | **Bahamas** | **$12** |
| ❑ **Streak The Jackal** | **Tunisia** | **$10** |
| ❑ **Strudel The Poodle** | **France** | **$10** |
| ❑ **Taps The Tapir** | **Venezuela** | **$10** |
| ❑ **Toolu The Toucan** | **Honduras** | **$10** |
| ❑ **Topus The Zebra** | **Nigeria** | **$10** |
| ❑ **Toro The Bull** | **Spain** | **$12** |
| ❑ **Vaca The Long Horned Cow** | **Argentina** | **$12** |
| ❑ **Waks The Yak** | **Nepal** | **$10** |
| ❑ **Waller The Walrus** | **Greenland** | **$10** |
| ❑ **Woolsey The Sheep** | **Ireland** | **$10** |
| ❑ **Zongshi The Panda Bear** | **China** | **$15** |

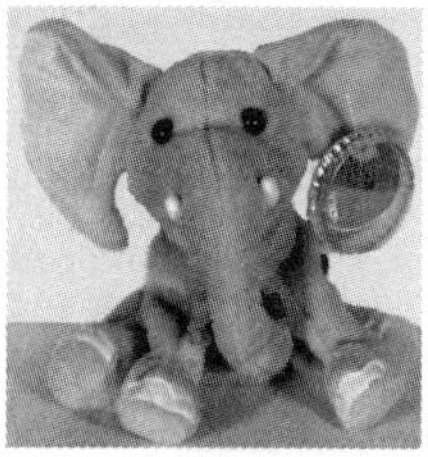
Clomp

Dover

Gourmand

Key Key

Masha

Nardie

Quala

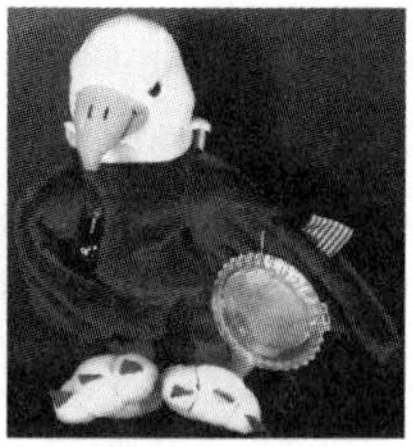
Reegle

Woolsy

Zongshi

# Comic Character Misc.

**Comic strip characters, particularly prior to World War II and the following early years of television, could almost be considered "family" to readers. No surprise, then, that advertisers sensed that premiums based on such familiar and well-loved characters would boost sales. Historically, the Yellow Kid and Buster Brown led the way. These and 73 others of intense popularity are listed in *Hake's Guide To Comic Character Collectibles* published in 1993, as well as other pages of this book. This section is devoted to comic characters that may have a large number of associated collectibles but relatively few offered as actual premiums.**

COM-1

COM-2

❏ **COM-1. "New York Five Cent Library #87" Book,**
June 30, 1894. Rare. High grade copies are rarely found. Comic paper.- **$25 $60 $110**

❏ **COM-2. "Comic Library #136" Softcover,**
April 10, 1896. Rare. Soft cover comic with staples. Comic paper. - **$75 $150 $220**

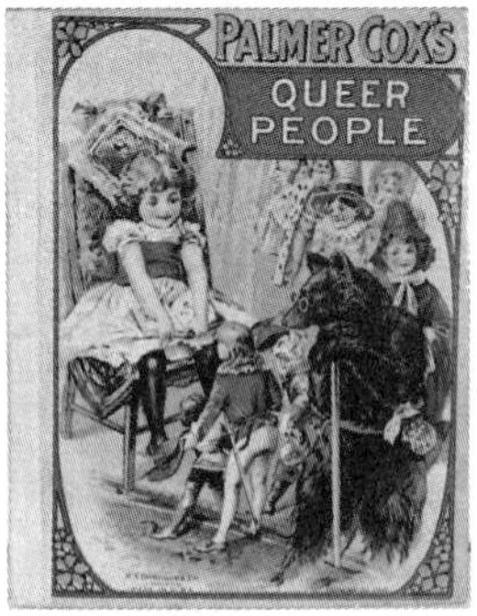


COM-3

❏ **COM-3. "Palmer Cox's Queer People" Book,**
Late 1800s. Rare. Donohue and Co., Chicago. Illustrates many famous fairy tales with Brownie-like characters.- **$100 $200 $400**

COM-4

COM-5

❏ **COM-4. "Punch's Book of Comical Pictures and Stories" Hardcover Book,**
Late 1800s. Rare. Published by Hurst & Co., New York. - **$100 $200 $360**

❏ **COM-5. "Sleeping Beauty" Hardcover Book,**
Early 1900s. Published by Hurst & Co., New York. - **$50 $125 $175**

COM-6

❏ **COM-6. "Pore Lil Mose His Letters To His Mammy" Comic Strip Reprint Book,**
1902. Published by Grand Union Tea Company, copyright New York Herald. Good - **$1429**
Fine - **$5000**

COM-7

❏ **COM-7. "Little Sammy Sneeze" Book,**
1905. Rare. By Winsor McCay. Rarely found better than very good. Good - **$971**
Fine - **$3400**

COM-8

COM-9

❏ **COM-8. Tad Dorgan "Tad's Joke Book",**
1911. New York Sunday American. 10x12" Sunday supplement with 16 pgs. - **$10 $30 $60**

❏ **COM-9. T. E. Powers "The Little Hatchet Joke Book",**
c. 1911. New York Sunday American. 10x12" Sunday supplement with 16 pgs. - **$10 $30 $60**

COM-10

COM-11

❏ **COM-10. T. E. Powers "Joy & Gloom Joke Book",**
c. 1911. New York Sunday American. 10x12" Sunday supplement with 16 pgs. - **$10 $30 $60**

❏ **COM-11. Gus Mager "The Monkey Joke Book",**
1912. New York Sunday American. 10x12" Sunday supplement with 16 pgs. - **$10 $30 $60**

COM-12

COM-13

❏ **COM-12. Jimmy Swinnerton "Swinnerton's Joke Book",**
1912. New York Sunday American. 10x12" Sunday supplement with 16 pgs. - **$10 $30 $60**

❏ **COM-13. T. E. Powers "Married Life Joke-Book",**
1912. New York Sunday American. 10x12" Sunday supplement with 16 pgs. - **$10 $30 $60**

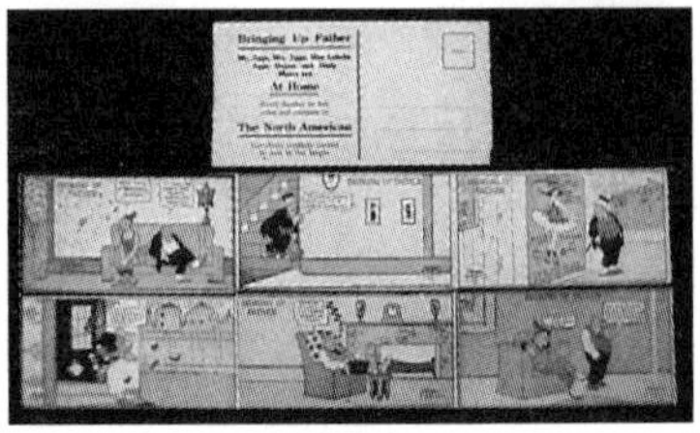


COM-14

❏ **COM-14. "Bringing Up Father At Home Every Sunday In The North American" Postcards,**
1919. The Star Co. promoting newspaper. Full color 3-5/8x6-5/8" with at least six known. Each - **$5 $15 $25**

COM-15

❑ **COM-15. "Snookums" Ceramic Figures,**
1920. Came in two sizes.
Large 4" - **$75 $210 $300**
Small 3" - **$60 $180 $225**

(FRONT) COM-16 (BACK)

❑ **COM-16. Pamphlet,**
1922. Philadelphia Bulletin. 12 page premium."Jerry Muskrat Wins Respect." Harrison Cady art. - **$25 $50 $75**

COM-17

❑ **COM-17. "Mutt And Jeff Crayon Drawing Book" Boxed Set With Comic Strip Reprint Book,**
1924. Cupples And Leon Company. -
**$125 $250 $500**

COM-18

❑ **COM-18. "All The Funny Folks" King Features Syndicate Comic Character Hardback Book,**
1926. Promoted through Sunday comic sections and published by The World Today Inc. 9-1/2x11-3/4" hardbound with 112-page story of choice color specialty art by Louis Biederman, noted KFS staff artist. Theme of story is horse race with Barney Google on Spark Plug and Jiggs on Maud the Mule. Scarce in top condition. - **$100 $200 $400**

COM-19

❑ **COM-19. "Ella Cinders" Song Sheet,**
1927. Featured strip in comic newspapers.
Scarce - **$25 $50 $85**

COM-20

❑ **COM-20. Little Jimmy Writing Tablet,**
1920s. Scarce. - **$20 $40 $100**

COM-21

❑ **COM-21. Sunday Comic Section 7x11" Cardboard Sign With Jiggs,**
1920s. Boston Sunday Advertiser. -
**$35 $65 $125**

COM-22

❑ **COM-22. "Winnie Winkle" Boxed Board Game,**
c. 1930. Store item by Milton Bradley #4269. -
**$65 $150 $250**

COM-23

❑ **COM-23. Marx Merrymakers Band,**
1931. Came in three versions. Two were without marquees: one with a mouse holding a violin sitting on top of the piano and one with a conductor mouse on top. The third version has a marquee and a violin mouse.
Each version - **$600 $1200 $2000**

COM-24

COM-25

❑ **COM-24. "Bringing Up Father" Puzzle Box with 4 Puzzles,**
1932. Each Puzzle - **$10 $30 $40**
Box - **$30 $65 $75**

❑ **COM-25. "Reg'lar Fellers" BLB,**
1933. - **$10 $25 $60**

COM-26

❑ **COM-26. "Tillie The Toiler" Jigsaw Puzzle,**
1933. Various newspapers supplement. - **$10 $20 $35**

COM-27

COM-28

❑ **COM-27. "Funnies on Parade" #1,**
1933. Scarce. Probably the 1st regular format comic book. Proctor & Gamble giveaway. - **$1160 $3480 $14500**

❑ **COM-28. "Century of Comics" #1,**
1933. Scarce. 100 pages. Probably the third comic book. Wheatena/Malt-O-Milk giveaway. - **$3670 $11000 $22000**

COM-29

❑ **COM-29. "Houdini's BLB of Magic",**
1933. Cocomalt Premium. - **$10 $40 $80**

COM-30

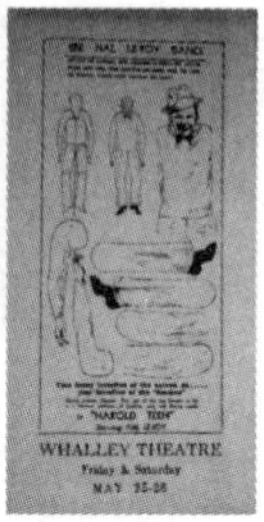

COM-31

❑ **COM-30. "Big Little Mother Goose" Book,**
1933. BLB #725. 576 pages. One of the top 3 rarest BLBs.
Hardcover - **$110 $600 $1200**
Softcover - **$75 $400 $800**

❑ **COM-31. Harold Teen Movie Premium,**
1934. Pieces were cut out to make a dangle puppet. - **$25 $50 $110**

COM-32

COM-33

❑ **COM-32. "Smitty Golden Gloves Tournament" BLB,**
1934. Cocomalt. - **$10 $25 $60**

❑ **COM-33. Top-Line Comic,**
1935. From a Whitman series similar to Big Little Books done in softcover with 160 pages. - **$40 $60 $110**

COM-34

❑ **COM-34. Sears, Roebuck "Funny Paper Puppets" Punch-Out Sheet,**
1935. Also seen with Marshall Field & Co. imprint. Unpunched - **$75 $200 $400**

COM-35

COM-36

❑ **COM-35. "Tailspin Tommy In The Famous Pay-Roll Mystery" BLB,**
1933. #747. - **$15 $50 $125**

❑ **COM-36. "Tailspin Tommy In The Great Air Mystery/A Universal Picture " Cello. Button,**
1935. For movie serial picturing cast members Clark Williams, Noah Beery, Jr., Jean Rogers. - **$50 $85 $175**

COM-37

COM-38

❑ **COM-37. "Tailspin Tommy Club" Cello. Button,**
c. 1935. Evening Sun newspaper. - **$50 $85 $150**

❑ **COM-38. "Tailspin Tommy" Cello. Button,**
c. 1935. Newark Star-Eagle. From series of newspaper contest buttons, match number to win prize. - **$10 $20 $35**

COM-39

❑ **COM-39. "Tailspin Tommy In The Great Air Mystery" BLB,**
1936. #1184. - **$12 $30 $75**

COM-40

❑ **COM-40. "Tailspin Tommy" Wings Badge,**
1930s. Scarce. - **$25 $50 $90**

COM-41

❑ **COM-41. "Scrappy's Puppet Theater" Standee,**
1936. Has die-cut front to hold Pillsbury's pupput punchouts kit. - **$100 $250 $400**

COM-42

❑ **COM-42. "Alley Oop" Boxed Jungle Game,**
c. 1936. Whitman #2091. One of the first non-book Alley Oop items made**. - $200 $400 $800**

COM-43

❑ **COM-43. "Scrappy's Animated Puppet Theater" Punch-Out Kit,**
1936. Pillsbury's Farina cereal.
Unpunched - **$30 $75 $125**

COM-44

❑ **COM-44. "Big Top Comic Circus" Original Art Prototype Punch-Out Book ,**
c. 1936. Similar to Orphan Annie punch-out circus book but also includes other Chicago Tribune comic strip characters. Gordon Gold archives. Unique**. - $800**

COM-45

❑ **COM-45. "The Game of Alley Oop",**
1937. - **$30 $60 $120**

COM-46

❑ **COM-46. Red Falcon Adventures,**
1937. Rare. 8 page comic premium, Seal Right Ice Cream.
Issue #1 - **$110 $265 $450**
Issues #2-#5 - **$65 $155 $300**
Issues #6-#10 - **$55 $135 $200**
Issues #11-#50 - **$30 $90 $150**

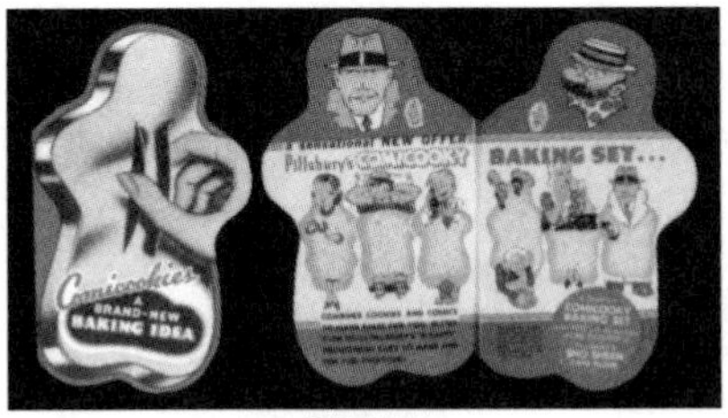


COM-47

❑ **COM-47. Comicookie Die-cut Promo Booklet,**
1937. - **$50 $100 $200**

COM-48

❑ **COM-48. "Smokey Stover" Ice Cream Premium Buddy Book,**
1938. Whitman Publishing Co. used by various sponsors as giveaway. This example is marked #1 in the series and was obtained for 12 ice cream cone coupons. - **$50 $100 $150**

COM-49

❑ **COM-49. Federal Agent Fingerprint Outfit,**
1938. Gold Medal toy. - **$30 $75 $150**

COM-50 COM-51

❑ **COM-50. Harold Teen Dummy Punchout 11x20",**
1938. Rare. Malt-O-Meal Cereal premium. - **$150 $300 $500**

❑ **COM-51. Moon Mullins Dummy Punchout 11x20",**
1938. Pure Oil premium. - **$75 $175 $350**

COM-52 COM-53 COM-54

❑ **COM-52. Harold Teen Bat-O-Ball,**
1938. Morton Salt premium. - **$15 $30 $50**

❑ **COM-53. Lillums Bat-O-Ball,**
1938. Morton Salt premium. - **$15 $30 $50**

❑ **COM-54. Shadow Bat-O-Ball,**
1938. Morton Salt premium. - **$15 $30 $50**

COM-55

❑ **COM-55. "Merry Christmas From Sears Toyland" Comic Book,**
1939. Scarce. Features Chicago Tribune Syndicate characters. - **$100 $375 $750**

COM-56

COM-57

❑ **COM-56. Smilin' Jack Fan Photo,**
c. 1939. Has inked-in recipient's name and "Zack Mosley" autograph.
Signed - **$30 $60 $100**

❑ **COM-57. Oswald Enamel On Brass Pin,**
1930s. Store item. About 1" tall with ears and pants in coppertone enamel and other areas in green enamel. - **$75 $125 $200**

COM-58

COM-59

❑ **COM-58. Junior G-Man Badge,**
1930s. Large bronze color shield premium. - **$25 $50 $85**

❑ **COM-59. "Ella Cinders Spinner",**
1930s. United Features Syndicate. Cello. over metal disk that has underside center bump for spinning. - **$50 $100 $185**

COM-60

COM-61

❑ **COM-60. "Moon Mullins" Pocketknife,**
1930s. Imprinted for local sponsor. Cello. grip also pictures comic strip sidebar characters Little Egypt and Mushmouth. - **$50 $100 $225**

❑ **COM-61. "Read America's Greatest Comics" Newsboy Apron With Jiggs,**
1930s. Philadelphia Sunday Ledger. 13-1/2x18" canvas fabric with neck strap and tie strings. - **$50 $150 $300**

COM-62

❑ **COM-62. "Winnie Winkle" Cigar Ad Sign,**
1930s. - **$50 $75 $140**

COM-63

❑ **COM-63. "Winnie Winkle" Cigar Box,**
1930s. - **$50 $75 $150**

COM-64

COM-65

❑ **COM-64. Sky Pilot Pin Brass Wings,**
1930s. - **$15 $40 $70**

❑ **COM-65. Aviation Department Boy Flight Commander Brass Badge,**
1930s. - **$20 $50 $85**

COM-66

❑ **COM-66. "All Star Comics" Boxed Playing Card Game,**
1930s. Store item. 35 full color cards including Krazy Kat. - **$50 $100 $150**

COM-67

❑ **COM-67. Sky Rangers Wings,**
1930s. For childrens' club - **$20 $50 $85**

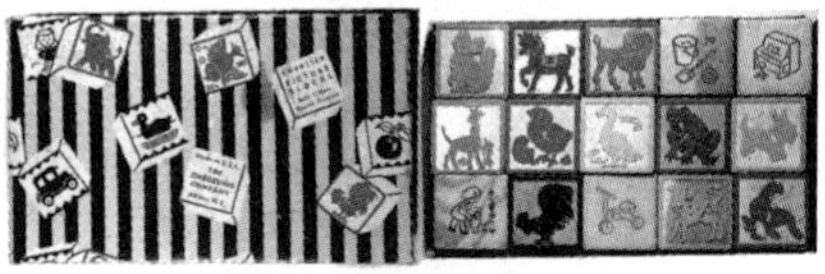

COM-68

❑ **COM-68. Embossed Blocks,**
1930s. Boxed set of wood blocks from the Embossing Company. - **$35 $65 $90**

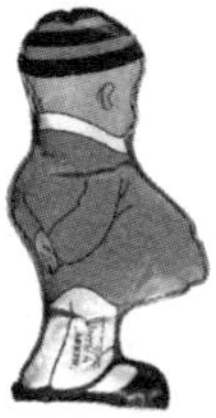

COM-69

COM-70

COM-71

❑ **COM-69,70,71. Herby, Moon Mullins and Smitty Cloth Dolls,**
1930s. Starched fabric from set believed issued by unknown cereal sponsor. Back view of Herby illustrates artist's facsimile signature on each. Also known in set are Kayo, Little Orphan Annie and Sandy.
Annie - **$75 $150 $200**
Sandy - **$50 $85 $150**
Others - **$40 $80 $125**

COM-72

COM-73

❑ **COM-72. Eagle Shield Pin,**
1930s. For airplane children's club.-
**$25 $50 $75**

❑ **COM-73. Boy Chief of Police Brass Badge,**
1930s. - **$20 $50 $85**

COM-74

COM-75

❑ **COM-74. Fire Department Boy Chief Brass Badge,**
1930s. - **$20 $50 $85**

❑ **COM-75. Junior Sheriff Brass Badge,**
1930s. - **$15 $25 $60**

COM-76

COM-77

❑ **COM-76. Ranger Pinback,**
1930s. For I-Spy show.- **$15 $25 $40**

❑ **COM-77. "Winds" Junior Police Children's Club Pinback,**
1930s. Probably a bread sponsor. - **$25 $45 $80**

COM-78

❑ **COM-78. Original Art for Standee,**
1930s. Ivory Soap. Promotes Moon Mullins comic dummy giveaway. - **$275**

COM-79

❑ **COM-79. Sam Gold Comic Character Promotion Circular,**
c. 1940. Black and white 8-1/2x11" designed by Sam Gold for Alfred Loewenthal, President, Famous Artists Syndicate to encourage product advertisers to license the use of syndicate characters including Dick Tracy, Little Orphan Annie, Terry & The Pirates, Captain Midnight and 15 others listed on the sheet. - **$20 $50 $100**

COM-80

❑ **COM-80. Great Comics Victory Club Pinback,**
1941. Comic book premium. Features the Great Zarro. - **$300 $600 $850**

COM-81

❑ **COM-81. World War II Promotion Civil Defense Book,**
1942. Features Flash Gordon, Phantom, Blondie & others. "Eat Right To Work And Win." - **$30 $75 $120**

COM-82

❑ **COM-82. "Smilin' Jack's Victory Bombers" Assembly/Play Game,**
c. 1943. Store item by Plane Facts, Inc. - **$75 $250 $400**

COM-83

❑ **COM-83. "Santa's Christmas Comic Variety Show" Book,**
1943. Sears, Roebuck & Co. Features Dick Tracy, Orphan Annie, Terry and the Pirates, many others. - **$75 $300 $600**

COM-84

❑ **COM-84. Captain Ben Dix Member Card,**
1943. Entitled child to receive copy of a premium comic book. Scarce. - **$20 $45 $60**

COM-85

❑ **COM-85. King Features Stationery Sheet,**
1944. - **$10 $25 $60**

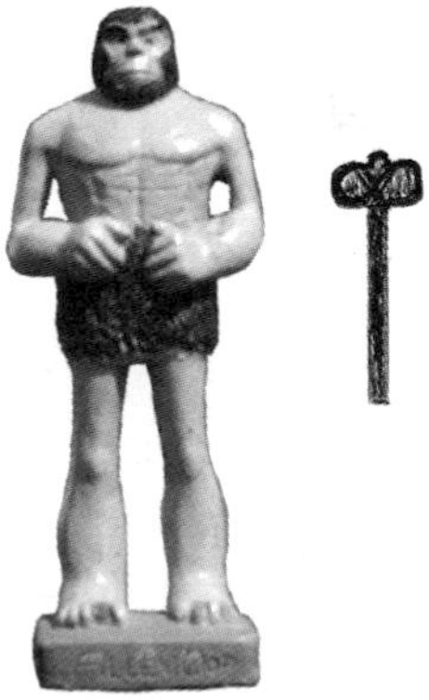
COM-86

❑ **COM-86. Alley Oop (Test) Product Statuette,**
1945. Rare. - **$750 $1500 $2850**
With club/handle that fits inside arm - add **$100 $200 $350**

COM-87

COM-88

❑ **COM-87. "Pete the Tramp" Hardback,**
1944. With dust jacket - **$35 $80 $160**
Dust jacket alone - **$15 $35 $70**

❑ **COM-88. "Magic Is Fun" Book,**
1946. #1 issue with feature on Houdini. Includes photos and a pin-up picture of Houdini (1874-1926) - **$10 $25 $60**

COM-89

❑ **COM-89. "Sears 1947 Back-To-School Giveaway Plan" Promo Folder,**
1947. Promotion offers comic character bookmarks, bookplates, pencil holder. Gordon Gold Archives. - **$150 $300 $600**

COM-90

COM-91

❑ **COM-90. Joe Palooka Matchbook,**
1948. - **$10 $20 $40**

❑ **COM-91. "Black Cat" Comic Book Ad Matchbook,**
1940s, Harvey Comics. - **$10 $20 $40**

COM-92

COM-93

❑ **COM-92. Royal Northwest Mounted Police Brass Badge,**
1940s. Scarce. - **$30 $60 $120**

❑ **COM-93. Prince Valiant Dime Bank,**
Late 1940s. One of the harder metal banks to find. - **$75 $180 $350**

COM-94

COM-95

❑ **COM-94. "New Funnies/Andy Panda" Cello. Button,**
c.1940s. New Funnies Comics. - **$50 $75 $160**

❑ **COM-95. "Denny Dimwit" Candy Box,**
1940s. Ma & Pa Winkle card on back of box. - **$30 $110 $150**

COM-96

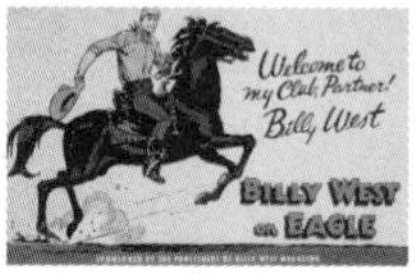

COM-97

❑ **COM-96. "C99 Ranch Gang" Code Book,**
1940s. Eight pages with decoder. Sponsor unknown. - **$15 $25 $45**

❑ **COM-97. Billy West Promo Card,**
1950. Scarce. - **$20 $50 $85**

COM-98

❑ **COM-98. Children's Puzzles,**
1950. Two jigsaw puzzles featured elves.
Each puzzle - **$5 $10 $15**
Box - **$10 $15 $20**

(MAILER FOR #4) COM-99 (MAILER FOR #5)

❑ **COM-99. Katy Keene Paper Dolls & Mailer,**
1951. Comic premiums for Katy Keene #4 & #5.
Each - **$50 $75 $125**

COM-100

❑ **COM-100. Metro Sunday Promo,**
1951. Rare. Features 29 comic characters from Metro Sunday newspapers. - **$200 $400 $800**

COM-101

❑ **COM-101. Funny Paper Hour Card,**
1954. Denver Post. Birthday card premium. - **$10 $25 $40**

COM-102

❑ **COM-102. Sparky's Fire Dept. Inspector Silvered Brass Badge,**
1950s. - **$20 $40 $60**

COM-103 COM-104

❑ **COM-103. Beetle Bailey Bobbing Head Doll,**
1950s. - **$40 $75 $150**

❑ **COM-104. Sgt. Snorkel Bobbing Head Doll,**
1950s. - **$40 $75 $150**

COM-105

COM-106

❑ **COM-105. Snuffy Smith Adult-Sized Over The Head-Style Costume,**
1960. Store item by Collegeville. 25" wide by 50" tall. Near Mint Carded - **$350**
Uncarded - **$75 $150 $250**

❑ **COM-106. Tasmanian Devil Plush Doll,**
1971. Scarce early figure. With original tags. - **$20 $60 $120**

COM-107

❑ **COM-107. Garfield Die-Cut Sign with Lapel Pins,**
1978. Sign - **$20 $40 $60**
Each pin - **$1 $2 $3**

COM-108 COM-109

❑ **COM-108. Wile E. Coyote Plush Doll,**
1978. 14" tall. - **$20 $40 $65**

❑ **COM-109. "Opus" Plush Doll,**
1982. 8 1/2" tall. From the newspaper strip "Bloom County." When sold, some of the proceeds went to the Greenpeace Foundation. Figure with tag - **$50**

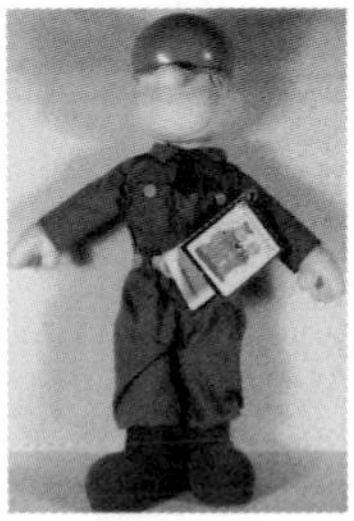

COM-110 COM-111

❑ **COM-110. Beetle Bailey 14" Doll,**
1984. King Features copyright.
With original tag - **$125**

❑ **COM-111. Sgt. Snorkel Doll,**
1984. King Features copyright.
With original tag - **$125**

COM-112

COM-113

❑ **COM-112. "Teenage Mutant Ninja Turtles" Cereal Box with Cereal Bowl Attached,**
1989. - **$10 $25 $40**

❑ **COM-113. "The Tick" Neckerchief,**
1990s. - **$2 $4 $10**

COM-114

❑ **COM-114. Wile E. Coyote and Road Runner Bronze Sculpture,**
1990. Hand painted, 25" long. Limited edition. Warner Bros. exclusive product sold through their catalog. - **$2400**

COM-115

❑ **COM-115. Mt. Yosemite Sculpture,**
1991. Ron Lee's clever presentation of the four presidents and Yosemite Sam. - **$375**

COM-116

❑ **COM-116. Taz "No Pain No Gain" Figurine,**
1992. Warner Bros. copyright. Figure and base are 12" tall. Only 950 were made, and they sold out in 60 days. - **$300**

COM-117

❑ **COM-117. Pepe Le Pew and Penelope Sculpture,**
1992. Warner Brothers Store exclusive figures by Ron Lee. - **$150**

COM-118

❑ **COM-118. "The Jetsons" Watch and Pin in Small Tin Lunch Box,**
1993. Fossil product. Limited edition watch pictures the family. Pin shows Astro the dog. Complete - **$100**

COM-119

❑ **COM-119. "Spawn The Game" Boardgame,**
1994. Over 110 total pieces. Spawn has made a successful leap to TV and movies. Complete - **$50**

COM-120

❑ **COM-120. "Fone Bone" Resin Figure,**
1994. Dark Horse product, limited to 3,000. Map is a separate piece. In box - **$100**

COM-121

❑ **COM-121. Carl Barks Pocket Watch,**
1994. Gifted Images product. Watch features a Barks self portrait. Limited edition of 65. - **$150**

COM-122

❑ **COM-122. "Grendel" Resin Statue,**
1994. Character by Matt Wagner. Sculpted by Randy Bowen. Boxed - **$350**
1999 2nd Edition Boxed - **$185**

COM-123

COM-124

COM-125

❑ **COM-123. "Cerebus" Drinking Glass Mug,**
1994. - **$5 $10 $15**

❑ **COM-124. Taz Pin on Card,**
1995. - **$5 $10 $20**

❑ **COM-125. "Lady Death" Statue,**
1995. Resin on wood base. Limited to 3,200. Miniature version released in 2000. - **$350**

COM-126

❑ **COM-126. Carl Barks "The Barkster" Commemorative Figure,**
1995. Painted resin figure by Randy Bowen. Only 10 produced. - **$1500**

COM-127

❑ **COM-127. "The Maxx" Bust,**
1996. From MTV Networks. Limited to 2,500. Boxed - **$150**

COM-128

COM-129

❑ **COM-128. Carl Barks Treasury Bill,**
1997. City of Ducksburg paper $100 dollar bill featuring Carl Barks and his signature. - **$25**

❑ **COM-129. Scooby Doo Race Car Replica,**
1997. Revell. - **$8**

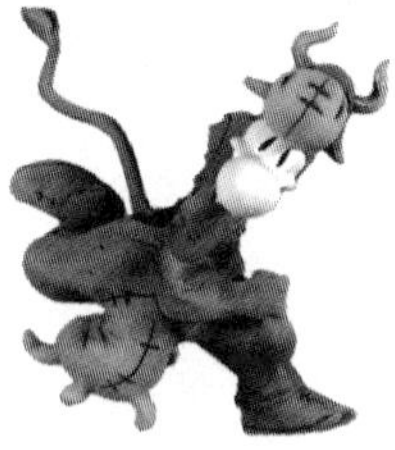

COM-130

❑ **COM-130. "Smiley Bone" Resin Figure,**
1997. Graphitti Designs product. Limited edition of 2,500. In box - **$80**

COM-131

COM-132

❑ **COM-131. "Evel Knievel" X-2 Replica,**
1998. Johnny Lightning replica of the X-2 rocket with bonus snapshot picture. On card - **$10**

❑ **COM-132. "Father Time" Dragster,**
1998. Limited edition of 15,000. On card - **$15**

COM-133

❑ **COM-133. Raggedy Ann and Andy Bean Dolls,**
1998. With tags. - **$40**

COM-134 COM-135

❑ **COM-134. Alvin Singing Bean Bag,**
1998. Gund product. - **$2 $5 $10**

❑ **COM-135. Alvin Singing Bean Bag,**
1999. Gemme product. - **$2 $5 $10**

COM-136 COM-137

❑ **COM-136. Simon Singing Bean Bag,**
1998. Gund product. - **$2 $5 $10**

❑ **COM-137. Simon Singing Bean Bag,**
1999. Gemme product. - **$2 $5 $10**

COM-138 COM-139

❑ **COM-138. Theodore Singing Bean Bag,**
1998. Gund product. - **$2 $5 $10**

❑ **COM-139. Theodore Singing Bean Bag,**
1999. Gemme product. - **$2 $5 $10**

COM-140

COM-141

❑ **COM-140. "Tweety" Leprechaun Bean Bag,**
1999. With tag. - **$20**

❑ **COM-141. "Tweety" Skeleton Bean Bag,**
1999. With tag. - **$20**

COM-142

❑ **COM-142. Scooby Doo Bean Bag,**
1999. - **$15**

COM-143

COM-144

COM-145

❑ **COM-143. "Astro" Bean Bag,**
1998. With tag.Came out 1 year earlier than the rest of the Jetsons figures. - **$25**

❑ **COM-144. "George Jetson" Bean Bag,**
1999. With tag. - **$12**

❑ **COM-145. "Jane Jetson" Bean Bag,**
1999. With tag. - **$10**

COM-146

COM-147

COM-148

❑ **COM-146. "Elroy Jetson" Bean Bag,**
1999. With tag. - **$10**

❑ **COM-147. "Judy Jetson" Bean Bag,**
1999. With tag. - **$10**

❑ **COM-148. The Jetsons "Rosie" Bean Bag,**
1999. Warner Bros. copyright. 8 1/2" tall. - **$10**

COM-149

❑ **COM-149. "Big Guy and Rusty the Boy Robot" Statue,**
1999. Produced by Dark Horse. Limited to 1,500. Sculpted by Kent Melton. - **$125**

COM-150

COM-151

❑ **COM-150. Danger Girl Action Figure,**
1999. Abby Chase with accessories on card. - **$15**

❑ **COM-151. Danger Girl Action Figure,**
1999. Natalia Kassle w/accessories on card. - **$15**

COM-153

COM-154

❑ **COM-153. Danger Girl Action Figure,**
1999. Sydney Savage w/accessories on card. - **$15**

❑ **COM-154. Danger Girl Action Figure,**
1999. Major Maxim w/accessories on card. - **$15**

COM-155

❑ **COM-155. "Cowboy Droopy" Resin Figure,**
1999. On his trusty horse. - **$100**

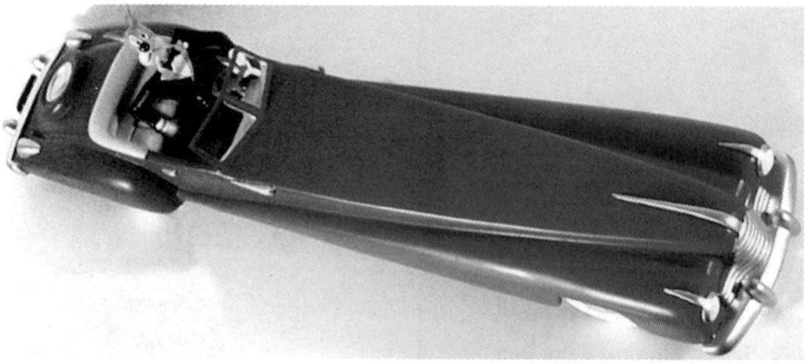
COM-152

❑ **COM-152. "Driving Wolfie" Resin Figure,**
1999. Tex Avery character. In box. - **$50**

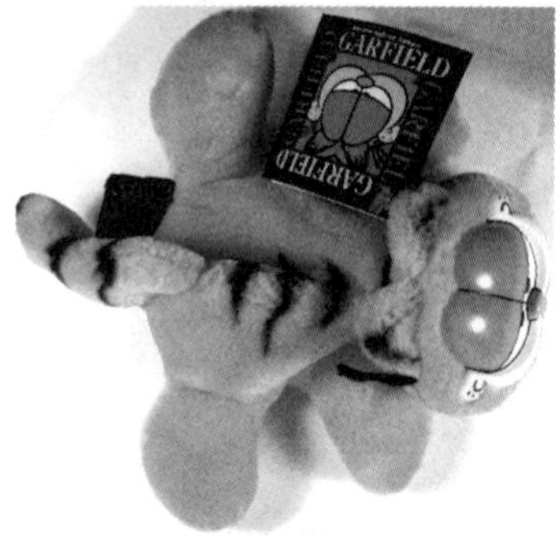

COM-156

❑ **COM-156. "Garfield" Bean Bag,**
1999. - **$10**

COM-157

COM-158

**❑ COM-157. "Flaming Carrot" Action Figure,**
1990s. On card. - **$7**

**❑ COM-158. "Marvin the Martian" Yo-Yo,**
1990s. Glows in the dark. - **$10**

COM-159

COM-160

**❑ COM-159. "Badrock" Action Figure,**
1990s. Deluxe ed. Spawn on card. - **$15**

**❑ COM-160. "Violator" Action Figure,**
1990s. With special edition comic book. - **$12**

COM-161

**❑ COM-161. Garfield Figure with Watch,**
1990s. Limited Edition. Glass globe covers items. Complete - **$100**

COM-162

COM-163

**❑ COM-162. "Madman" Lunch Box,**
2000. Mike Allred artwork. - **$20**

**❑ COM-163. "Cy-Gor 2" Action Figure,**
2000. 12" figure boxed. - **$20**

COM-164

**❑ COM-164. Beetle Bailey PVC Set,**
2000. Copyright King Feature Syndicate. This seven figure set from Dark Horse features Beetle, Sarge, Otto, General Halftrack, Miss Buxley, Cookie and Lt. Flap. - **$40**

COM-165

**❑ COM-165. Beetle Bailey Resin Figure with Flag,**
2000. Limited Edition, 6 1/2" tall figure from Equity Marketing Inc. Boxed. - **$25**

COM-166

**❑ COM-166. Garfield Playing Cards in Collector Tin,**
2001. Contains two decks of cards. Boxed - **$10**

COM-167

**❑ COM-167. Bone 10th Anniversary Figure,**
2001. PVC figure came with purchase of 10th Ann. Special Edition comic. Boxed - **$10**

COM-168

COM-169

**❑ COM-168. "Hot Stuff" Wacky Wobbler,**
2001. In box. - **$15**

**❑ COM-169. "Richie Rich" Wacky Wobbler,**
2001. In box. - **$15**

## Counter-Spy

**Washington calling David Harding, Counter-Spy! In 1942, with the nation at war, the call was answered. One of radio's long-running adventure series, *Counter-Spy* aired on ABC, NBC or Mutual from 1942 to 1957. With Don MacLaughlin as the ace agent, Counter-Spy fought Axis enemies during the war and other security threats once the war was won. Sponsors over the years included Mail Pouch chewing tobacco, Schutter Candies, Pepsi-Cola and Gulf Oil.**

COU-1

**❑ COU-1. Pepsi-Cola 8x19" Paper Store Sign,**
1949. - **$50 $100 $160**

COU-2

❑ **COU-2. Large Outdoor Sign,**
c. 1949. Pepsi-Cola. 40x60" starched white fabric with red and blue printing advertising show on ABC radio station WJZ. - **$50 $100 $225**

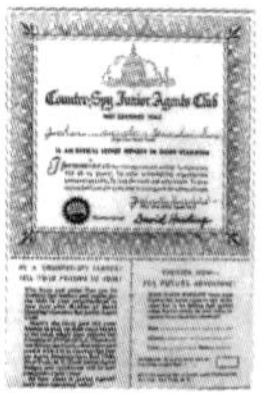

COU-3

COU-4

❑ **COU-3. Club Member Certificate,**
1949. Scarce. Pepsi-Cola. For "Counter-Spy Junior Agents Club". - **$15 $50 $90**

❑ **COU-4. Junior Agent Glow-In-Dark Brass Badge,**
1949. Pepsi-Cola. Centered by plastic lens over bw glow portrait. - **$30 $60 $110**

COU-5

❑ **COU-5. Matchbook,**
1940s. Old Nick candy bars. - **$10 $30 $60**

COU-6

❑ **COU-6. "Junior Counter-Spy" Activity Booklet,**
1951. Gulf Oil. Story pages feature David Harding, Counterspy. - **$10 $25 $50**

## Cracker Jack

**This blend of popcorn, peanuts and molasses candy has been a best-selling snack food for about 100 years. F. W. Rueckheim, a German immigrant, had opened a small popcorn stand in Chicago in 1872. He sold the first version of his candy combination at the 1893 Columbian Exposition; the product proved to be popular, but the kernels stuck together. By 1896 the company had found not only a process to keep the kernels separate, but also a name--cracker jack was a new slang term for excellent or superior, and F. W. promptly trademarked it for his sweet.**

**By 1899 Cracker Jack was being packaged in a waxed-sealed box to keep it fresh, by 1902 it was listed in the Sears catalogue and in 1908 it became part of sports Americana in the song *Take Me Out to the Ball Game.* A happy customer is said to have contributed the company slogan, The More You Eat, The More You Want. In 1910 the company started inserting coupons in the packages to be traded in for prizes and two years later the coupons were replaced by the prizes themselves.**

**Since 1912 every package has contained a toy surprise inside. Sailor Jack, modeled after F. W.'s grandson, appeared in advertisements in 1916 with his dog Bingo and made it onto the box in 1919. The company was sold to Borden in 1972 and then to Frito Lay in 1997. Today Cracker Jack, still with a toy in every box, is marketed worldwide.**

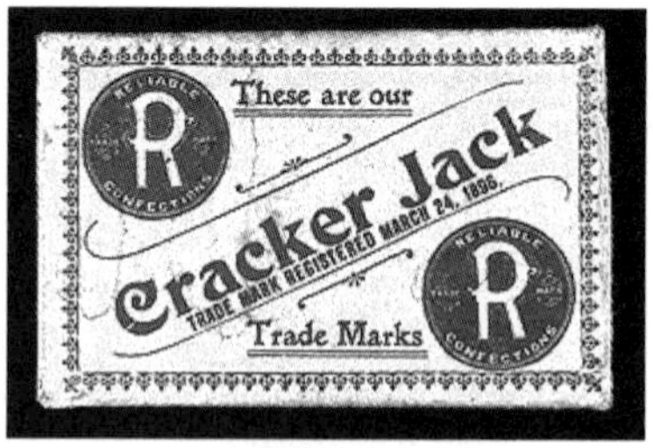


CRJ-1

❑ **CRJ-1. Early Sample Box,**
c. 1896. 1x1-3/4x2-3/4" long sample container for "Reliable Confections" by "F. W. Rueckheim & Bro.," Chicago. Trademark registration date is March 24, 1896 and precedes the added "Eckstein" partnership designation of 1902. - **$125 $250 $525**

CRJ-2

CRJ-3

CRJ-4

❑ **CRJ-2. "The Cracker Jack Bears" Postcard,**
1907. Example from set of 16. - **$12 $20 $35**

❑ **CRJ-3. Portrait Cello. Button,**
c. 1908. With "Cracker Jack" back paper. One of a series also issued by tobacco companies. - **$30 $50 $85**

❑ **CRJ-4. "Cracker Jack" Wagon In White Metal,**
c. 1910. Scarce. Metal has gold luster and wagon interior has cardboard insert floor. Horse's legs are usually broken. - **$75 $150 $250**

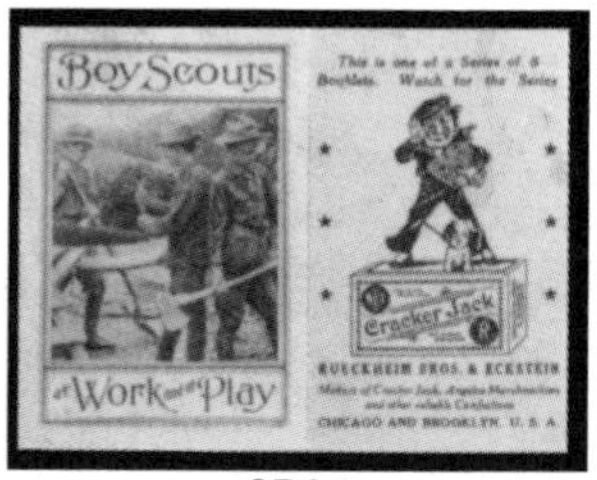


CRJ-5

❑ **CRJ-5. "Boy Scouts At Work And At Play" Booklet,**
c. 1923. 2-1/2x3-1/2" with 12 pages. Reverse reads "Series Of 8 Booklets."
Each - **$125 $200 $300**

CRJ-6

❑ **CRJ-6. "Cracker Jack Riddles" Booklet,**
c. 1920s. - **$15 $30 $70**

CRJ-7

CRJ-8

❑ **CRJ-7. "Cracker Jack Drawing Book",**
c. 1920s. - **$20 $30 $70**

❑ **CRJ-8. Miniature Litho. Tin Wagon,**
c. 1920s. - **$25 $65 $120**

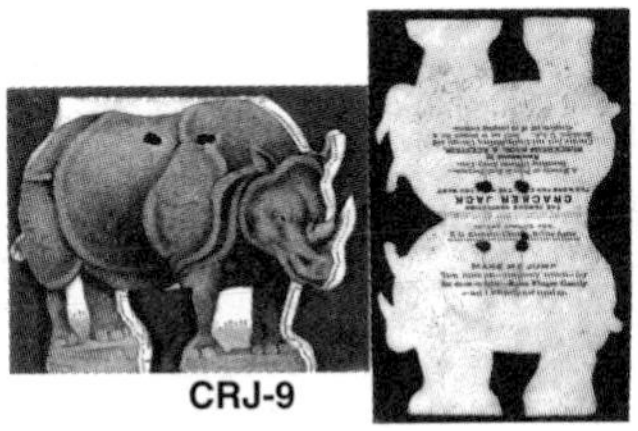

CRJ-9

CRJ-10

❑ **CRJ-9. Rhinoceros Paper Prize,**
c. 1920s. From set of 16 "Jumping Animals" to fold. Each - **$35 $75 $125**

❑ **CRJ-10. "Cracker Jack/The Famous Confection" Top,**
c. 1920s. Silver finish with incised lettering and slightly thicker metal than later versions. - **$40 $75 $140**

CRJ-11

❑ **CRJ-11. Cardboard String Toy,**
c. 1920s. - **$25 $60 $90**

CRJ-12

❑ **CRJ-12. Chicago World's Fair Miniature Booklet,**
1933. Ten pictures. - **$40 $80 $175**

CRJ-13

❑ **CRJ-13. "Tune In With Cracker Jack" Litho. Tin Miniature Desk Radio Replica,**
1930s. Scarce. - **$65 $140 $200**

CRJ-14

CRJ-15

❑ **CRJ-14. Queen Of Spades Litho. Tin Whistle,**
1930s. About 1-3/4" tall unmarked except "Japan." - **$35 $75 $150**

❑ **CRJ-15. Andy Gump Miniature Bisque Figure,**
1930s. 2-1/8" tall unmarked except for "FAS" (Famous Artists Syndicate) copyright and "Japan" on reverse. Similar Cracker Jack give-aways include: Chester Gump, Herby, Kayo, Little Orphan Annie, Sandy, Smitty.
Each - **$15 $35 $60**

CRJ-16

CRJ-17

❑ **CRJ-16. Litho. Tin Spinner Top,**
1930s. Red, white and blue with thin wooden dowel at center. - **$15 $30 $50**

❑ **CRJ-17. "Ambulance" Litho. Tin Miniature,**
1930s. About 1-1/2" long with Red Cross symbol on each side. - **$30 $60 $100**

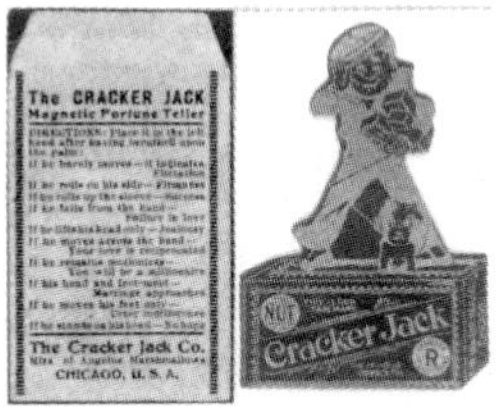


CRJ-18

CRJ-19

CRJ-20

❑ **CRJ-18. "Magnetic Fortune Teller" With Envelope,**
c. 1930s. Gold printing on thin cellophane of various solid colors. - **$15 $25 $50**

❑ **CRJ-19. Litho. Tin Spinner Top,**
c. 1930s. - **$15 $25 $40**

❑ **CRJ-20. Litho. Tin Top,**
c. 1930s. - **$10 $20 $35**

CRJ-21

CRJ-22

❑ **CRJ-21. Toy Cart,**
c. 1930s. Litho. tin with wood shaft. - **$10 $20 $30**

❑ **CRJ-22. Beanie,**
1930s. Rare. Wool Beanie with bell on spring. - **$50 $100 $175**

CRJ-23

CRJ-24

CRJ-25

❑ **CRJ-23. Tin Litho. Pocketwatch Replica,**
c. 1930s. - **$20 $40 $75**

❑ **CRJ-24. Aluminum Snapper,**
1930s. - **$10 $25 $35**

❑ **CRJ-25. Tin Litho. Standup,**
1930s. From a set of 10: Chester, Harold Teen, Herby, Kayo, Moon Mullins, Orphan Annie, Perry, Skeezix, Smitty, Uncle Walt.
Each - **$35 $65 $125**

CRJ-26

CRJ-27

❑ **CRJ-26. "The Cracker Jack Line" Litho. Tin Train Engine,**
1930s. - **$45 $90 $150**

❑ **CRJ-27. Litho. Tin Delivery Truck,**
1930s. - **$40 $75 $125**

CRJ-28

❑ **CRJ-28. "Free Comic Valentine" 9x26" Paper Store Sign,**
1930s. Pictures examples from believed set of 25 given individually by purchase of individual boxes. - **$75 $150 $300**

CRJ-29

CRJ-30

❑ **CRJ-29. "Cracker Jack Shows" Tin Circus Wagon,**
c. 1930s. Depicts caged lion on each side. - **$30 $60 $100**

❑ **CRJ-30. Diecut Paper Frog,**
1930s. - **$20 $40 $75**

CRJ-31 CRJ-32 CRJ-33

❑ **CRJ-31. Tin Miniature Book Bank,**
1930s. - **$50 $80 $150**

❑ **CRJ-32. Tin Bank,**
c. 1930s. Brass luster. - **$25 $50 $75**

❑ **CRJ-33. Litho. Tin Diecut Bookmark,**
1930s. One of scarcer in series. - **$15 $25 $45**

CRJ-34 CRJ-35

❑ **CRJ-34. Litho. Tin Fortune Wheel,**
1930s. Reveals fortune words by revolving upper disk to spell name of fortune-seeker. - **$15 $25 $40**

❑ **CRJ-35. Paper Fortune Wheel,**
c. 1930s. Similar design and function to litho. tin version. - **$10 $20 $35**

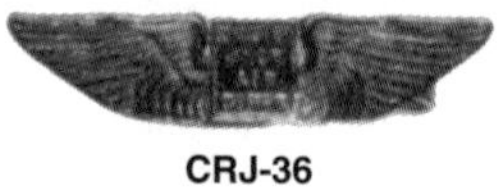

CRJ-36

CRJ-37

❑ **CRJ-36. "Cracker Jack Air Corps" Dark Metal Wings,**
1930s. Lapel stud reverse. - **$15 $30 $50**

❑ **CRJ-37. Oval Litho. Tin American Flag Stand-Ups,**
1940-1949. Unfolded 2-1/4" tall red, white and blue unmarked with Cracker Jack name but distributed by them and made by Cosmo Manufacturing Company. Primary titles of four examples issued in the 1940s read "Long May It Wave!, God Bless America, Stars And Stripes Forever!, The Flag Of Freedom."
Each - **$8 $15 $25**

CRJ-38

❑ **CRJ-38. "Razz Zooka" Paper Whistle Toy,**
1949. Cloudcrest Creations. - **$10 $15 $25**

CRJ-39

CRJ-40

❑ **CRJ-39. "Cracker Jack" Transfer Sheet Set,**
1940s. 25 in set. - **$50 $125 $200**

❑ **CRJ-40. "Midget Auto Race" Paper Prize,**
1940s. - **$15 $25 $40**

CRJ-41

❑ **CRJ-41.Box Insert Papers,**
c. 1965. Set of 20. Each is 4-1/4x6". Gordon Gold Archives. Near Mint Set - **$200**
Each - **$1 $3 $5**

CRJ-42 CRJ-43

❑ **CRJ-42. Cracker Jack Tin Wastebasket,**
1980s. - **$5 $15 $30**

❑ **CRJ-43. Baseball Card Sheet 8x11",**
1991. Uncut 36 card sheet with miniature replicas of Topps Gum "40 Years Of Baseball" cards. Uncut - **$25 $50 $75**

CRJ-44

❑ **CRJ-44. "Cracker Jack" Wacky Wobbler,**
2001. With box. - **$25**

# Dan Dunn

***Detective Dan*** **began in 1933, and after the first issue sold poorly, the title was changed. Norman Marsh created this popular comic strip, now called *Dan Dunn, Secret Operative 48*, for the Publishers' Syndicate. Offered as a low-cost alternative to *Dick Tracy*, the strip ran daily and Sunday for 10 years, appearing in as many as 135 newspapers. The hard-boiled Dunn, along with his sidekick Irwin Higgs, his dog Wolf, and an orphan girl named Babs, fought urban crime and such arch-fiends as Wu Fang and Eviloff. At the height of its popularity in the 1930s the strip was reprinted in *Big Little Books* and in several comic books. Two issues of *Dan Dunn*, a dime novel pulp, were published in 1936, and a radio version of *Dan Dunn, Secret Operative 48* was syndicated in 1944.**

DUN-1

DUN-3

DUN-2

❑ **DUN-1. Detective Dan Button,**
1933. Rare. First comic book character club premium. The club was canceled after the first issue of *Detective Dan* failed. -
**$600 $850 $1250**

❑ **DUN-2. "Dan Dunn Secret Operative 48 Crime Never Pays" Big Little Book,**
1934. Whitman #1118. - **$20 $50 $110**

❑ **DUN-3. "Dan Dunn Detective Magazine" First Issue,** 1936. Vol. 1 #1 monthly issue for September. - **$50 $100 $200**

DUN-4

DUN-5

❑ **DUN-4. "Dan Dunn On the Trail of The Counterfeiters" Big Little Book #1125,**
1936. 432 pages. Art by Norman Marsh. -
**$11 $45 $100**

❑ **DUN-5. "Dan Dunn On the Trail of Wu-Fang" Big Little Book #1454,**
1938. - **$11 $45 $100**

DUN-6

DUN-7

❑ **DUN-6. "Dan Dunn/Secret Operative 48 And The Counterfeiter Ring" Booklet,**
1938. From "Buddy Book" ice cream cone series printed by Whitman. Also seen as give-away from Stern & Co. with "Merry Christmas" on back cover. 126 pages in Big Little Book format with page art reprinted from comic strips. -
**$20 $50 $90**

❑ **DUN-7. "Dan Dunn Plays A Lone Hand" Whitman Penny Book,**
1938. - **$12 $20 $50**

DUN-8

DUN-9

❑ **DUN-8. "Dan Dunn Secret Operative 48 And The Zeppelin Of Doom" Fast -Action Book,**
1938. Dell Publishing. 3-7/8x5-1/4" format. -
**$40 $90 $160**

❑ **DUN-9."Dan Dunn Secret Operative 48" Penny Book,**
1938. Published by Whitman. - **$12 $20 $50**

DUN-10

DUN-11

❑ **DUN-10. "Dan Dunn Junior Operative" Cello. Button,** 1930s. - **$75 $150 $275**

❑ **DUN-11. Dan Dunn "I'm Operative 48" Cello. Button,**
1930s. Philadelphia Evening Ledger Comics. From colorful series depicting Ledger comic strip characters. - **$50 $85 $150**

DUN-12

DUN-13

❑ **DUN-12. "Dan Dunn Detective Corps/Secret Operative 48" Badge,**
1930s. Probably a newspaper promotion item. Silvered tin shield with embossed lettering. -
**$20 $40 $70**

❑ **DUN-13. Fan Club Membership Card,**
c. 1980s. Issuer unknown. Unknown if Dan Dunn item or perhaps local radio/TV personality club card. - **$5 $10 $15**
Pinback - **$10 $20 $30**

## Daniel Boone

**Dan'l Boone (1734-1820), legendary Kentucky frontiersman, hunter, farmer and wilderness scout, was brought to life by 20th Century-Fox in a successful adventure series on CBS-TV from 1964 to 1970. The show starred Fess Parker, who a decade earlier had found fame playing Davy Crockett on the *Disneyland* series. The stories were centered on Boone's Kentucky settlement days, his expeditions and his struggles with the Indians. Other featured actors included Patricia Blair, Ed Ames, Albert Salmi and Roosevelt Grier. Merchandised items are usually copyrighted by 20th Century-Fox TV. An hour-long animated TV special sponsored by Kenner toys premiered on CBS in 1981 with Richard Crenna as the voice of Boone.**

DNL-1

DNL-2

❑ **DNL-1. Picture,**
1963. Cut-out premium found on back of Frosted Flakes box. - **$10 $25 $40**

❑ **DNL-2. Fess Parker As Daniel Boone 5" Hard Plastic Doll,**
1964. American Tradition Co. Store item. Accessories of fur hat, plastic rifle and strap with bag and powder horn. -
**$35 $60 $135**

DNL-3

❑ **DNL-3. Trail Blazers Game,**
1964. N.B.C. tie-in with Milton Bradley. Includes Trail Blazers Club application. - **$20 $40 $75**

DNL-4

❑ **DNL-4. Vinyl Zippered Pencil Case,**
1964. Fess Parker/Daniel Boone Trail Blazers Club. Includes NBC premium leaflet offering wallet, ring binder, kaboodle kit, etc. -
**$10 $20 $40**

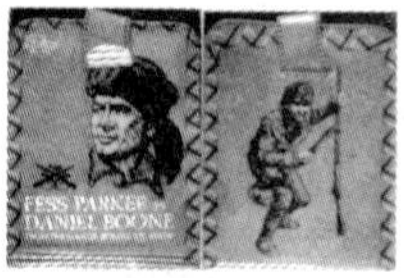

DNL-5 DNL-6

❑ **DNL-5. "Fess Parker As Daniel Boone" Vinyl Wallet,**
1964. N.B.C. Holds miniature magic slate and four photos from TV series. - **$15 $30 $60**

❑ **DNL-6. "Official Daniel Boone Fess Parker Woodland Whistle",**
c. 1964. Autolite. - **$20 $40 $75**

DNL-7

❑ **DNL-7. "Fess Parker As Daniel Boone" Coonskin Cap,**
1964. Store item by American Tradition Co. -
**$10 $20 $40**

DNL-8

❑ **DNL-8. "Daniel Boone" Boxed Card Game,**
1965. Store item by Ed-U-Cards. Boxed Complete - **$8 $15 $30**

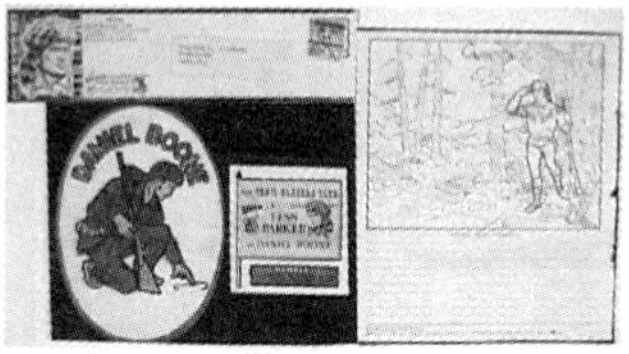


DNL-9

❑ **DNL-9. "Trail Blazers Club" Box With Contents,**
1965. American Tradition Co. Mailer contains fabric patch, water transfer decal, puzzle contest entry sheet requiring proof of purchase of store products by American Tradition Co.
Near Mint Boxed - **$85**
Patch - **$5 $10 $20**
Decal - **$3 $8 $12**
Form - **$3 $8 $12**

DNL-10

DNL-11

❑ **DNL-10. Fess Parker As Daniel Boone On "Fort Madison, Iowa" Rodeo Cello. Button,**
1966. 2-3/16" from a series issued annually. -
**$15 $30 $50**

❑ **DNL-11. "TV Channels" Cover Article,**
1969. Weekly issue for July 6 of schedule guide supplement to Baltimore News American. -
**$5 $10 $15**

## Davey Adams, Son of the Sea

**Details on this pre-World War II radio drama starring Franklin Adams are scarce but the program offered listeners membership in the DASC, the Davey Adams Shipmates Club, along with such premiums as a siren ring, a secret compartment members badge and a manual showing sailor knots and marine codes. Lava soap was the sponsor of this short-lived 1939 series.**

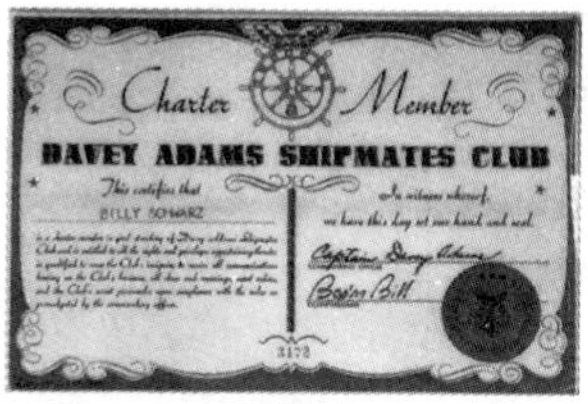


DVM-1

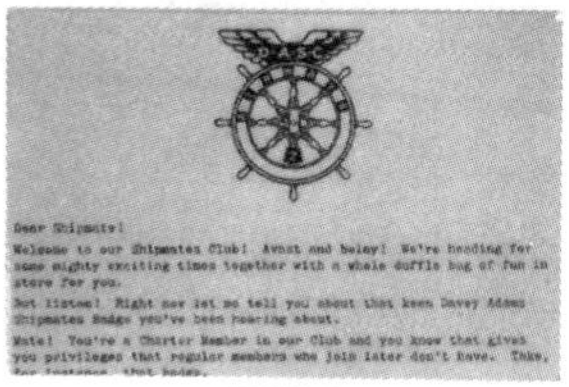

DVM-2

❑ **DVM-1. Club Charter Member Certificate,**
1939. Scarce. Lava soap. - **$25 $50 $90**

❑ **DVM-2. Club Letter,**
1939. Lava soap. Offers Secret Compartment Shipmate's Badge. - **$10 $20 $40**

DVM-3 DVM-4

❑ **DVM-3. "D.A.S.C." Siren Ring,**
1939. Scarce. Initials for "Davey Adams Shipmates Club." -**$175 $325 $500**

❑ **DVM-4. Shipmates Club Brass Decoder Badge,**
1939. Lava Soap. Decoder wheel front, back has secret compartment. - **$60 $125 $250**

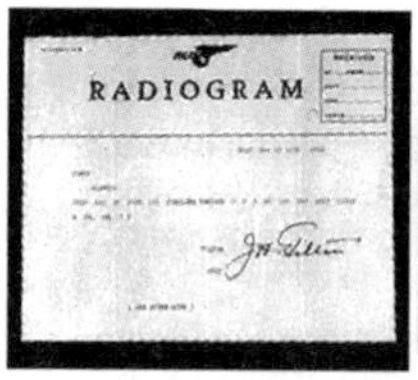


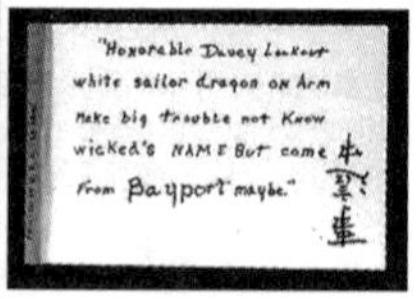

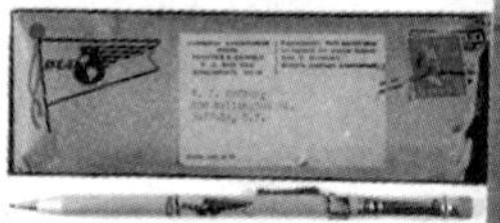

DVM-5

❑ **DVM-5. "Davey Adams Shipmates" Club Kit With Pencil,**
c. 1939. Pan American Airways. Mailing envelope containing Radiogram bulletin, Secret Flying Orders booklet, mechanical pencil with secret compartment, all identified by sponsor name. Near Mint Complete - **$575**
Pencil - **$50 $100 $160**
Each Paper Item - **$25 $50 $80**

## Davy Crockett

**Frontier scout, Indian fighter, bear killer, congressman, statesman, martyred at the Alamo--Davy Crockett (1786-1836) was a natural for television. Five fictionalized episodes from his life were broadcast on the *Disneyland* series on ABC in 1954 and 1955, starring Fess Parker in a coonskin cap and carrying his trusty rifle Old Betsy. Parker became an instant star, Crockett became an idol to an estimated 40 million viewers, *The Ballad Of Davy Crockett* landed on the *Hit Parade* and a merchandising mania swept the country. Some 500 products were licensed by Disney--toys, games, rifles, books, lunch boxes, costumes, coonskin caps--and unlicensed merchandise capitalizing on the craze followed in great profusion. Disney re-edited the films and released them to theaters as *Davy Crockett, King of the Wild Frontier* in 1955 and *Davy Crockett and the River Pirates* in 1956 and the original episodes were rebroadcast a half-dozen times over the next 20 years. An animated TV special sponsored by Kenner toys aired on CBS in 1976.**

DVY-1

❑ **DVY-1. "Davy Crockett's Boy Hunter" Book,**
1908. Store item. 5x7" paperback pulp published by Arthur Westbrook Company, Cleveland. #11 from series of 100 western titles. - **$10 $25 $50**

DVY-2

❑ **DVY-2. Davy Crockett Watch in Box,**
1954. WIth plastic gunpowder horn. Musical piece on top of horn that makes it blow is sometimes missing. Also has rawhide string that attaches to each end of the horn.
Complete - **$450**

DVY-3

❑ **DVY-3. "Davy Crockett King Of The Wild Frontier" TV Tray,**
1955. Store item, Disney Productions. 12-1/2x17". - **$35 $75 $140**

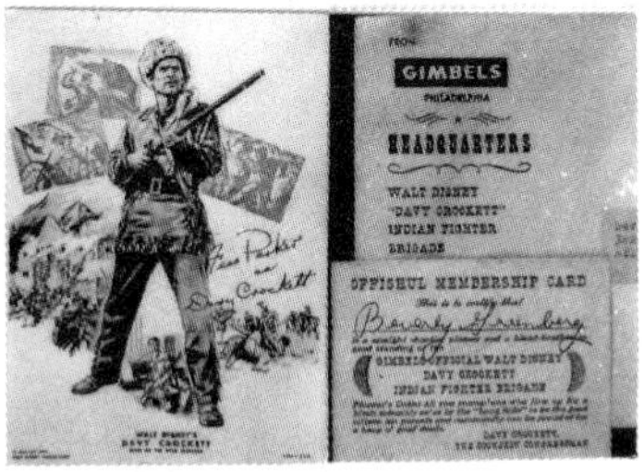

DVY-4

❑ **DVY-4. Gimbel's Club Kit In Mailer Envelope,**
1955. Gimbel's department store. Disney authorized contents include photo and member card.
Near Mint In Mailer - **$100**
Photo - **$15 $25 $50**
Card - **$8 $15 $30**

DVY-5

DVY-6

❑ **DVY-5. "Davy Crockett In The Raid At Piney Creek" Comic,**
1955. American Motors give-away. -
**$10 $20 $50**

❑ **DVY-6. "Yaller Yaller Gold" Song Sheet,**
1955. Featured in TV's "Davy Crockett and Mike Fink" production. - **$15 $30 $50**

(ENLARGED VIEW)
DVY-7

❑ **DVY-7. "Frontier Action Ring" On Card,**
1955. Karo Syrup. Plastic ring holds flicker portrait.
On Card - **$100 $200 $350**
Loose - **$50 $85 $150**

DVY-8

❑ **DVY-8. Cloverbloom Box With Magic Viewer,**
c. 1955. Armour Co. Premium for "Cloverbloom '99' Oleomargarine." Eight different viewers with four 3-D scenes issued. Gordon Gold Archives.
Boxed - **$25 $50 $125**
Each Viewer - **$10 $15 $25**

DVY-9

❑ **DVY-9. Plastic Bank,**
c. 1955. Various local sponsors. - **$10 $20 $35**

DVY-10

❑ **DVY-10. Frosted Glass,**
c. 1955. Farmers Dairy Milk Ice Cream. -
**$8 $15 $25**

DVY-11

❑ **DVY-11. Honey Grahams Box,**
c. 1955. Promotes Davy Crockett free cloth patches. All 12 pictured on back of box. - **$50 $100 $150**

DVY-12

❑ **DVY-12. "Free Cloth Patches" Store Display,**
c. 1955. Flavor Kist Honey Grahams. 17x20-1/2" thick diecut cardboard designed as back panel of a store display bin. Gordon Gold Archives. - **$150 $300 $450**

DVY-13

❑ **DVY-13. "Free Cloth Patches" Shelf Hanger Sign,**
c. 1955. Flavor Kist Honey Grahams. 5-1/2x10-1/4". Gordon Gold Archives. - **$100 $200 $300**

DVY-14

❑ **DVY-14. Davy Crockett Cloth Patches Set,**
c. 1955. Flavor Kist Honey Grahams. Set of 12 in five different shapes, each about 3x3". Reverse has paper covering over adhesive back. Gordon Gold Archives.
Each - **$10 $20 $35**

DVY-15

DVY-16

❑ **DVY-15. Ceramic Cookie Jar,**
c. 1955. Store item. - **$150 $250 $425**

❑ **DVY-16. "Davy Crockett Hero Of The Alamo" Gold Finish White Metal Badge,**
c. 1955. "Tootsietoy" name appears on reverse. - **$35 $75 $150**

DVY-17

❑ **DVY-17. Canadian Lunch Box,**
1955. Store item by Kruger Mfg. Co. Ltd. - **$100 $200 $400**

DVY-18

❑ **DVY-18. "Candies And Toy" Box,**
c. 1955. Super Novelty Candy Co. with Disney copyright. Cut-out cards on box back.
Uncut Box - **$10 $50 $100**

DVY-19

DVY-20

❑ **DVY-19. Pocketknives With Fess Parker,**
c. 1955. Store items by Imperial. Three varieties. 2-1/4" With Hatchet - **$25 $50 $90**
2-1/4" Single Blade - **$20 $40 $80**
3-1/2" Three Blades - **$15 $25 $60**

❑ **DVY-20. "Davey Crocket" Frontier Gun Set On Store Card,**
c. 1955. Store item by John Henry Products. - **$35 $75 $150**

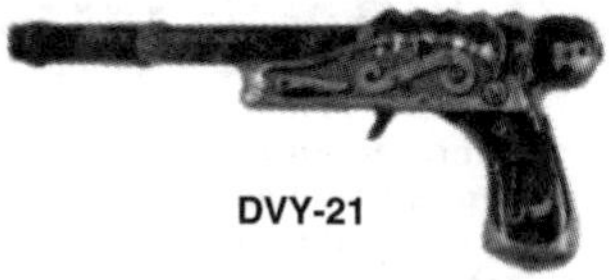

DVY-21

❑ **DVY-21. "Davy Crockett" Clicker Gun,**
c. 1955. Store item by Marx Toys. - **$75 $150 $250**

DVY-22

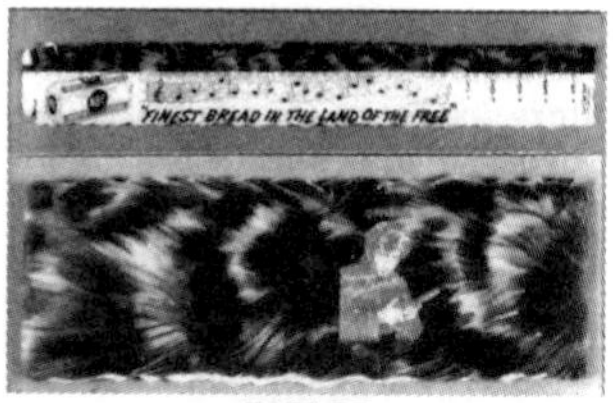


DVY-23

❑ **DVY-22. "Frontier Bread" Waxed Paper Bread Wrapper,**
1950s. - **$15 $30 $50**

❑ **DVY-23. Coonskin Cap Punch-Out Sheet,**
1950s. Nabisco. With simulated fur design.
Unused With Tail - **$15 $30 $60**

DVY-24

❑ **DVY-24. "Davy Crockett Cookies" Box,**
1950s. Federal Sweets & Biscuit Co. - **$25 $60 $125**

DVY-25

DVY-26

❑ **DVY-25. Deed of Land,**
1950s. Scarce. - **$30 $75 $110**

❑ **DVY-26. "Jackson Daily News Fan Club" 2-1/4" Cello. Button,**
1950s. - **$35 $75 $140**

DVY-27

❑ **DVY-27. Cardboard Money Saver,**
1950s. Various sponsors. - **$12 $20 $50**

DVY-28

DVY-29

❑ **DVY-28. "Davy Crockett Frontier Club" Cello. Button,**
1950s. - **$20 $35 $75**

❑ **DVY-29. "Big Yank Frontiersman" Litho. Button,**
1950s. Clothing company. - **$15 $30 $60**

DVY-30

DVY-31

❑ **DVY-30. "Pfeifers Davy Crockett Fan Club" Litho. Button,**
1950s. - **$20 $40 $80**

❑ **DVY-31. "King Of The Wild Frontier" Cello. Button,**
1950s. Disney authorized. - **$15 $30 $50**

DVY-32

DVY-33

❑ **DVY-32. "Frontiersman" Litho. Button,**
1950s. Disney authorized. - **$15 $35 $55**

❑ **DVY-33. "Walt Disney's Davy Crockett" Metal Compass Ring,**
1950s. Peter Pan Peanut Butter. -
**$65 $140 $225**

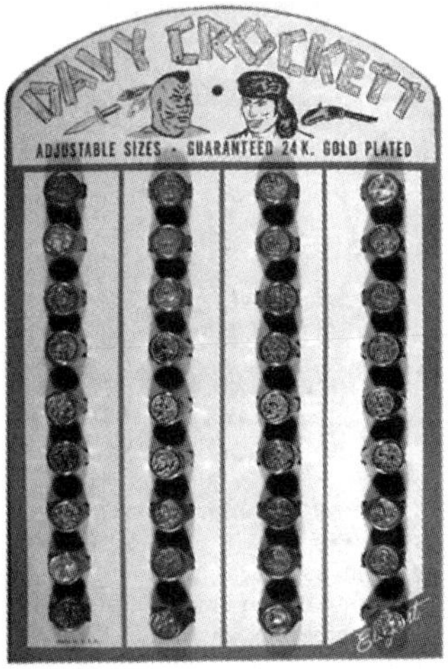


DVY-34

❑ **DVY-34. Davy Crockett Card with Rings,**
1950s. Card holds 36 rings, 24K gold plated.
Complete - **$800**
Each gold ring - **$20**
Similar ring in silver - **$25**

DVY-35

❑ **DVY-35. "Davy Crockett Indian Scout Badge" On Store Card,**
1950s. Carded - **$15 $30 $50**
Badge Only - **$10 $20 $30**

DVY-36

DVY-37

DVY-38

❑ **DVY-36. "Frontier Club" Litho. Tab,**
1950s. - **$15 $30 $45**

❑ **DVY-37. Fess Parker/Crockett English Metal Badge,**
1950s. Store item by "DCMT Ltd." of England. Silver finish, red lettering, black/white insert photo. - **$20 $50 $85**

❑ **DVY-38. Composition Bobbing Head,**
1950s. Store item. - **$75 $125 $225**

DVY-39

❑ **DVY-39. Play Suit in Box,**
1950s. - **$150 $300 $600**

DVY-40

❑ **DVY-40. Leatherette Jacket,**
1950s. Store bought. TV merchandise. -
**$50 $150 $300**

## DC Comics

**Former pulp magazine writer and army cavalry officer Major Malcolm Wheeler Nicholson published the first issue of *New Fun* (subsequent issues became *More Fun*) in 1935. Tabloid size with a full color cover and 32 black and white pages, it was the first comic book with original material in a Sunday comic page format. Although he wasn't making any money, the Major added *New Comics* (later to become *Adventure Comics* late in 1935). Most notable is that these two titles featured art by Walt Kelly as well as stories by Jerry Siegel and Joe Shuster in their pre-Superman days.**

**Next came *Detective Comics* in early 1937. The Major was so broke by now he was forced to take a partner, his printer. The new company was called Detective Comics, Inc. or DC Comics. Nicholson left soon afterwards. The new owners decided to add another title, *Action Comics*. Editor Vincent Sullivan was looking for new material when he saw samples of Superman by co-workers**

**Siegel and Shuster. He decided to use the character. *Action Comics* #1 debuted in June 1938 and the comic book world was changed forever.**

**Sullivan also edited *Detective Comics* and after he suggested artist Bob Kane come up with something, Batman debuted in issue #27 in 1939. Within one year editor Vincent Sullivan oversaw the beginnings of the two greatest comic book characters to ever see print. These characters are covered in their own sections while this section touches on additional DC characters.**

**The addition of their own toy imprint, DC Direct, has greatly enhanced the number of character toys DC has generated and increased the number of characters represented in statues, action figures, plush toys and props. This trend can be expected to continue. Their toys are generally only available in comic book specialty shops.**

DCM-1

❑ **DCM-1. Advertising Flyer for Boy Commandos #1,**
1942. Sign is 11 1/2" high, 8 1/2" wide. Also pictures other DC comics from that year. Rare. -
**$150 $300 $525**

DCM-2

❑ **DCM-2. DC Publication Promo**
1942. Features top selling comics that are among the first 25 in newsstand sales. Note they refer to them as magazines and not comic books. - **$100 $200 $325**

DCM-3

❑ **DCM-3. "Boy Commandos" Transfers Pack,**
1948. DC Comics copyright. Store packet of transfer pictures based on comic book military cartoon characters. - **$50 $125 $225**

DCM-4

❑ **DCM-4. Flyer for The National Jamboree for Boy Scouts,**
1950. Features Superman, Batman and Robin. Also promotes DC's line of comics. -
**$100 $200 $325**

DCM-5

❑ **DCM-5. "DC" Promotional Glass,**
1950s. This is a 5-5/8" glass and there is a similar 6-3/4" glass with slightly different character designs. Characters on this example are Superman, Batman, Mutt, Wonder Woman, Tomahawk, The Crow (from Fox and The Crow), Judy (from A Date With Judy). Larger version features illustration of The Flash in place of Mutt.
Each version - **$60 $125 $200**

DCM-6 DCM-7 DCM-8

❑ **DCM-6. "Green Lantern" 3-1/2" Cello. Button,**
1966. #13 from series. Near Mint Bagged - **$45**
Loose - **$10 $15 $30**

❑ **DCM-7. "Aquaman" 3-1/2" Cello. Button,**
1966. #15 from series. Near Mint Bagged - **$45**
Loose - **$10 $15 $30**

❑ **DCM-8. "Hawkman" 3-1/2" Cello. Button,**
1966. #16 from series. Near Mint Bagged - **$45**
Loose - **$10 $15 $30**

DCM-9

❑ **DCM-9. Advertising Poster for 48-Page Issues,**
1971. Shows Superman and Batman. -
**$5 $15 $35**

DCM-10

❑ **DCM-10. Promotional 3 1/2"x 8" Sticker,**
1975. Shows Superman and Batman. -
**$15 $30 $45**

DCM-11

❑ **DCM-11. Display Box and Mini-Comics,**
1981. The display box holds 8 packs, each containing a secret origin comic and candy. Origins include Superman, Batman, Hawkman, Flash, Aquaman, Wonder Woman, Green Arrow, and the Justice League.
Box - **$10 $25 $50**
Each Comic with Candy - **$1 $2 $5**

DCM-12

❑ **DCM-12. "DC/Keebler President's Drug Awareness Campaign" Kit,**
1983. Various paper items including those with facsimile endorsement signature of Nancy Reagan. Complete - **$5 $10 $20**

DCM-13

DCM-14

❑ **DCM-13. Super Powers Metal Lunch Box,**
1983. Aladdin Industries, Inc. Features Superman, Batman and Wonder Woman. - **$20 $40 $75**

❑ **DCM-14. "The Sandman" Statue,**
1991. Graphitti Designs. Limited to 1,800. Based on designs from artist Kelley Jones. Miniature version released in 1998.
Boxed - **$950**

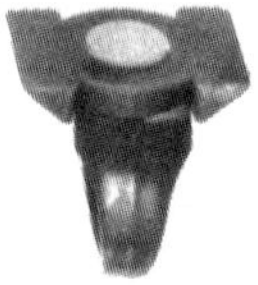

DCM-15

DCM-16

DCM-17

❑ **DCM-15. Green Lantern Glow-In-Dark Plastic Ring,**
1992. - **$3 $5 $10**

❑ **DCM-16. Zero Hour Litho. Tin Tab,**
1994. From mini series.
Unbent - **$1 $2 $3**

❑ **DCM-17. "The Sandman Arabian Nights" Statue,**
1994. Graphitti Designs. Limited to 7,200. Based on character designs in Sandman #50 from artist P. Craig Russell.
Boxed - **$175**

DCM-18

DCM-19

❑ **DCM-18. Justice League Of America Litho. Button,**
1997. - **$1 $2 $3**

❑ **DCM-19. "U.S." (Uncle Sam) Comics Cello. Promo Button,**
1997. DC/Vertigo mini series. - **$1 $2 $3**

DCM-20

DCM-21

❑ **DCM-20. Modern Age Green Lantern Resin Statue of Kyle Rayner,**
1997. Limited to 2,200. 13" tall including base. The base of this figure and the 2 other Green Lanterns fit together. All 3 sculpted by William Paquet. Figure with box - **$215**

❑ **DCM-21. Green Lantern 5" Figure,**
1998. Limited to 2,500. - **$80**

DCM-22

DCM-23

❑ **DCM-22. Silver Age Green Lantern Resin Statue of Hal Jordan,**
1998. Limited to 2,500. 12" tall including base. Figure with box - **$210**

❑ **DCM-23. Golden Age Green Lantern Resin Statue of Alan Scott,**
1999. Limited to 2,000. 13" tall including base. Figure with box - **$225**

DCM-24

❑ **DCM-24. "Super Heroes" Die Cast Metal Figures in Box,**
1998. Warner Bros. Store exclusive. Features Supergirl, Superman, Green Lantern, Captain Marvel and Batman. Set sold out quickly and is hard to find on the secondary market. - **$50**

**DCM-25**

**DCM-26**

❑ **DCM-25. Green Lantern Bean Bag Figure,**
1998. Warner Bros. Store exclusive. - **$8**

❑ **DCM-26. Aquaman Bean Bag Figure,**
1999. Warner Bros. Store exclusive. - **$8**

**DCM-27**

**DCM-28**

❑ **DCM-27. Supergirl Bean Bag Figure,**
1999. Animated series version. Warner Bros. Store exclusive. - **$8**

❑ **DCM-28. Supergirl Resin Statue,**
2000. Limited to 2,000. 12" tall including base. Figure with box - **$195**

**DCM-29**

**DCM-30**

❑ **DCM-29. Martian Manhunter Bean Bag Figure,**
2000. Warner Bros. Store exclusive. - **$8**

❑ **DCM-30. "Legion of Super-Heroes" PVC Set,**
2000. From DC Direct. 7 figures in box shaped like the Legion's clubhouse. - **$40**

**DCM-31**

**DCM-32**

❑ **DCM-31. Silver Age Green Lantern Figure with Ring on Card,**
2000. - **$20**

❑ **DCM-32. Plastic Man Figure on Card,**
2000. Variant version - **$30**

**DCM-33**

❑ **DCM-33. Green Lantern Power Battery Prop with Ring and Box,**
2000. Limited to 2,200. 11 3/4" tall and 9 3/4" wide. Lights up when ring touches it. - **$400**

**DCM-34**

❑ **DCM-34. "The New Teen Titans" PVC Set,**
2000. From DC Direct. 7 figures in box. - **$40**

**DCM-35**

❑ **DCM-35. Sgt. Rock Resin Statue,**
2000. Only 750 produced. Figure has removable helmet. Boxed with signed print by longtime Sgt. Rock artist Joe Kubert. - **$195**

**DCM-36**

**DCM-37**

❑ **DCM-36. Plastic Man Watch,**
2000. On card. - **$40**

❑ **DCM-37. Green Lantern PVC Set,**
2000. Seven figure set in box - **$40**

**DCM-38**

**DCM-39**

❑ **DCM-38. Golden Age Green Lantern Bust with Removable Power Ring,**
2001. Limited to 2,500. - **$90**

❑ **DCM-39. Sinestro Action Figure on Card,**
2001. Comes with yellow power ring. - **$18**

DCM-40

❑ **DCM-40. Hal Jordan Green Lantern Bust with Removable Power Ring,**
2001. Limited to 2,500. - **$90**

DCM-41

❑ **DCM-41. Aquaman Water Globe,**
2001. Limited edition of 2,000. With box - **$80**

DCM-42

❑ **DCM-42. Hawkman Statue,**
2001. Limited edition of 1,350. DC Direct product came with signed print by Joe Kubert. With box - **$195**

DCM-43

❑ **DCM-43. Green Arrow Resin Statue,**
2002. Limited edition of 2,200. Designed by Matt Wagner. With box - **$195**

## Death Valley Days

**One of the earliest radio dramas, *Death Valley Days* premiered on NBC in 1930. The stories of miners and homesteaders in the California desert, told by a character called the Old Ranger, were based on actual happenings and the show earned a reputation for historical accuracy. The program moved to CBS in 1941 and evolved into *Death Valley Sheriff* and then *The Sheriff* in 1945 when it aired on ABC. It ended its long radio life in 1951, sponsored from the beginning by 20 Mule Team Borax and Boraxo soap products. A syndicated television adaptation ran for 558 episodes, from 1952 to 1975, with Ronald Reagan, Robert Taylor, Dale Robertson or Merle Haggard playing the Old Ranger. The series has been rerun under a variety of titles.**

DTH-1

DTH-2

❑ **DTH-1. "Radio Stars" Leaflet,**
1930. Pictures John White, Old Ranger, Virginia Gardiner. - **$8 $15 $30**

❑ **DTH-2. "Death Valley Days" Storybook,**
1931. - **$5 $15 $30**

DTH-3

DTH-4

❑ **DTH-3. "Old Ranger's Yarns Of Death Valley" Magazine,**
1933. - **$5 $15 $30**

❑ **DTH-4. "Hauling 20 Mule Team Borax Out Of Death Valley" Puzzle,**
1933. - **$15 $30 $75**

DTH-5

❑ **DTH-5. "Picture Sheet" Newspaper Style Folder Promoting Radio Show,**
1933. - **$12 $25 $40**

DTH-6

DTH-7

❑ **DTH-6. "Death Valley Days" Charles Marshall Song Book,**
1934. - **$5 $15 $30**

❑ **DTH-7. "Cowboy Songs As Sung By John White...",**
1934. - **$5 $15 $30**

DTH-8

❑ **DTH-8. "Death Valley Tales" Storybook,**
1934. - **$5 $15 $25**

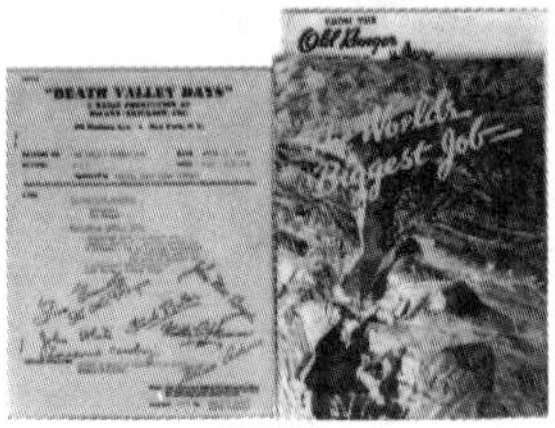

DTH-9

❑ **DTH-9. "The World's Biggest Job" Radio Broadcast Script With Cover Folder And Envelope,**
1935. For April 11 episode about construction of Boulder Dam. - **$10 $20 $40**

DTH-10

❑ **DTH-10. "High Spots Of Death Valley Days" Vol. 1 #1 Booklet With Envelope,**
1939. Includes six previous broadcast stories plus radio script for May 19, 1939 episode.
Booklet - **$10 $20 $40**
Envelope - **$3 $10 $15**

DTH-11

❑ **DTH-11. Old Ranger Seed Packets With Mailer,**
1939. Pacific Coast Borax Co.
Each - **$20 $40 $65**
Mailer - **$25 $50 $75**

DTH-12

DTH-13

❑ **DTH-12. "Old Ranger" Fan Postcard,**
1930s. Pacific Coast Borax Co. Text for weekly broadcasts on NBC Blue Network in East and Red Network in West with back text for "Death Valley Days" program title. - **$5 $10 $15**

❑ **DTH-13. "20 Mule Team" Model Kit,**
1950s. Borax. Issued for many years from the 1950s through 1970s. Packaged in one or two boxes. Near Mint In Box - **$35**

# Dell Comics

**Dell Publishing Company founder George Delacorte started in the comic book business in 1929 with *The Funnies*, a 24-page weekly tabloid with eight pages in color, all original features and a ten cent price. 36 issues appeared, then Delacorte tried a few black and white titles in the early 1930s. Late in 1935 he introduced *Popular Comics*, the first Sunday comic page reprint title to compete with *Famous Funnies*. This proved successful enough for Delacorte to begin *The Funnies*, using the title a second time, the summer of 1936. Both titles used original material in conjunction with reprints. Next came *The Comics* in March 1937. The Four Color series began in 1939. Delacorte really began rolling in 1940 as Dell published *Walt Disney's Comics and Stories,* followed by *Looney Tunes and Merrie Melodies* in 1941 and original stories featuring Captain Midnight and Andy Panda in *The Funnies* of 1942. *Four Color* #9 (the first Donald Duck comic with original story and art) appeared in 1942. Carl Barks, Walt Kelly, *Marge's Little Lulu, The Lone Ranger, Roy Rogers, Gene Autry, Tarzan* and a host of others appeared in comics with the Dell logo. Many paper premiums to promote comic book subscriptions are listed in this book under sections for specific characters.**

DEL-1

DEL-2

❑ **DEL-1. Dell Characters 8x10" Color Print,**
1950. - **$50 $125 $225**

❑ **DEL-2. "KE" Plastic Puzzle Game,**
1952. Played by pegs with "Secret Formula" instruction sheet.
Complete Puzzle Only - **$20 $50 $90**

DEL-3

❑ **DEL-3. Comic Book Rack 6x15" Litho. Tin Sign,**
c. 1950. Display attachment picturing 13 Dell Comics characters. - **$100 $250 $400**

DEL-4

❑ **DEL-4. Club Membership Card,**
1952. - **$10 $20 $50**

DEL-5

❑ **DEL-5. Dell Comic Club Promo & Club Card,**
1953. Scarce. Barks cover.
Folder - **$50 $125 $200**
Card - **$10 $30 $60**

DEL-6

DEL-7

❑ **DEL-6. "Walt Disney Comics And Stories" Christmas Gift Subscription Certificate,**
c. 1950s. - **$20 $75 $125**

❑ **DEL-7. "Official Dell Comics Club/Member" Aluminum Cased Lincoln Penny,**
1950s. Pictured example has 1953 penny, rim inscription "Keep Me And You Will Have Good Luck". - **$10 $20 $30**

# Dennis the Menace

**Mischief-maker supreme, Dennis the Menace made his first appearance as a daily cartoon panel in 1951 and as a Sunday page the following year. Based on cartoonist Hank Ketcham's own son, Dennis, trailed by his dog Ruff, has been harassing his suburban neighborhood ever since. Frequent victims include his parents, Henry and Alice Mitchell and their neighbor, cantankerous George Wilson. The strip has been a consistent winner, so much so that the title itself has entered the language. Many paperback and hardcover reprints have been published and the first of many Dennis comic books appeared in 1953. A prime-time television series starring Jay North as Dennis ran on CBS from 1959 to 1963 and was rerun on NBC from 1963 to 1965. Most merchandised items are related to the comic strip; those based on the TV series are usually copyrighted by Screen Gems Inc.**

DNS-1

DNS-2

❑ **DNS-1. "Dennis The Menace On Safety" Booklet,**
1956. National Safety Council. - **$5 $10 $25**

❑ **DNS-2. "Dennis The Menace Takes A Poke At Poison",**
1961. Food and Drug Administration.
Original 1961 Edition - **$1 $3 $6**
Later Reprints - **$1 $2 $4**

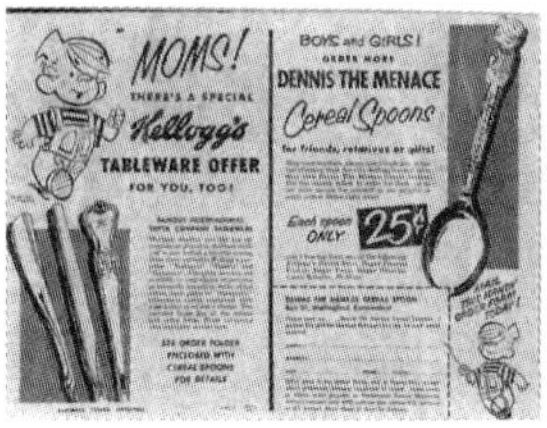


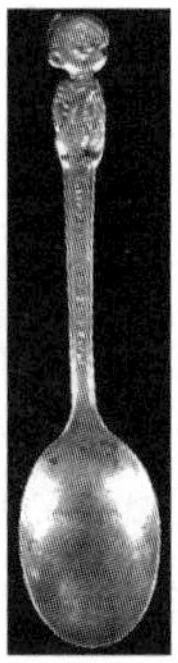

DNS-3

❑ **DNS-3. Spoon Ad Paper With Silver Plate Spoon,**
1961. Kellogg's Rice Krispies. Ad - **$3 $5 $8**
Spoon - **$5 $10 $20**

DNS-4

❑ **DNS-4. Spoon Offer Kellogg's Sugar Pops Cereal Box,**
1961. - **$40 $100 $200**

DNS-5

DNS-6

❑ **DNS-5. Silver Luster Metal Pin,**
c. 1962. Probable Kellogg's premium. 1-1/2" tall. - **$5 $12 $25**

❑ **DNS-6. Three-Reel View-Master Pack With Story Booklet,**
1967. - **$8 $15 $25**

DNS-7

❑ **DNS-7. "Cast Your Ballot" Litho. Button,**
1968. Sears. - **$12 $20 $35**

DNS-8

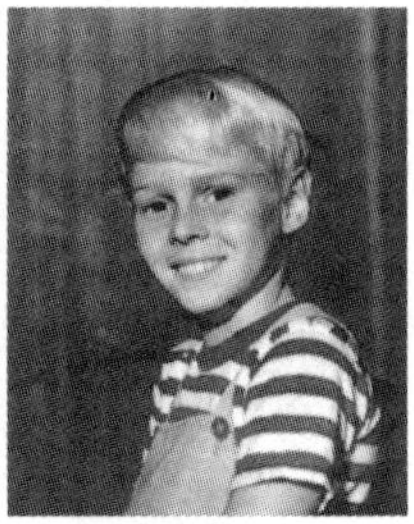

DNS-9

❑ **DNS-8. Cloth And Vinyl Hand Puppet,**
1960s. Store item. - $50

❑ **DNS-9. Fan Photo,**
1960s. - **$5 $10 $20**

DNS-10

DNS-11

❑ **DNS-10. "..And Away We Go!" Comic Book,**
1970. Caladryl medication. - **$1 $3 $6**

❑ **DNS-11. Joey From Dennis The Menace 2-1/4" Cello. Ad Button,**
1972. Dairy Queen. - **$5 $10 $15**

DNS-12

DNS-13

❑ **DNS-12. Dennis The Menace Plastic Assembly Ring,**
1970s. Dairy Queen. From same series as next three items picturing characters from "Ketcham" copyright comic strip. Parts separate for ring assembly.
Near Mint Unfolded On Tree - **$50**
Assembled - **$10 $20 $30**

❑ **DNS-13. Joey From Dennis The Menace Plastic Assembly Ring,**
1970s. Dairy Queen. Near Mint Unfolded On Tree - **$50**
Assembled - **$10 $20 $30**

DNS-14

DNS-15

❑ **DNS-14. Margaret From Dennis The Menace Plastic Assembly Ring,**
1970s. Dairy Queen.
Near Mint Unfolded On Tree - **$50**
Assembled - **$10 $20 $30**

❑ **DNS-15. Ruff From Dennis The Menace Plastic Assembly Ring,**
1970s. Dairy Queen. Near Mint Unfolded On Tree - **$50**
Assembled - **$10 $20 $30**

DNS-16

DNS-17

❑ **DNS-16. Dennis Doll with Tag,**
1987. 9 1/4" tall. - **$10 $30 $50**

❑ **DNS-17. Joey Doll with Tag,**
1987. 9 1/4" tall. - **$10 $20 $40**

## Detectives Black and Blue

***Adventures of Detectives Black and Blue*, an early syndicated comedy crime show from Los Angeles radio station KHJ, aired from 1932 to 1934. The series followed the adventures of a pair of shipping clerks/amateur sleuths in their bumbling attempts at criminology. "Detec-a-tives Black and Blue, good men tried and true."**

DTC-1

❑ **DTC-1. Fabric Double-Billed Detective Cap,**
c. 1932. Iodent toothpaste. Front bill names radio show and sponsor. - **$20 $40 $85**

DTC-2

DTC-3

❑ **DTC-2. "Detectives Black & Blue/Iodent Toothpaste" Brass Badge,**
c. 1932. - **$20 $50 $90**

❑ **DTC-3. "Detectives Black & Blue/Folger's Coffee" Brass Badge,**
c. 1932. - **$20 $50 $90**

## Devil Dogs of the Air

**The combination early in 1935 of a Warner Brothers real life U.S. Marine Flying Corps action adventure movie *Devil Dogs of the Air* and James Cagney in the starring role was quickly seized by Quaker Oats as a likely basis for premiums. A March 3, 1935 Sunday newspaper ad by Quaker offered Devil Dog ring, emblem badge and model airplane kit premiums based specifically on the movie plus closely related premiums of aviator goggles and leatherette flying helmet. Quaker Oats was thoroughly identified as Cagney's favorite cereal and the premium offer expiration date was May 15, 1935.**

DVL-1

DVL-2

❑ **DVL-1. Quaker Oats Cardboard Sign,**
1935. Rare. Displays the premiums and pictures James Cagney. - **$1000 $1850 $2500**

❑ **DVL-2. Ad Sign for Premiums,**
1935. Scarce. Regular paper, color. -
**$50 $125 $225**

DVL-3

DVL-4

❑ **DVL-3. Quaker Cereals "Man's Wings/How To Fly" Booklet,**
1935. Scarce. Includes photo strip with James Cagney plus flight instruction pages. Has a 1931 copyright by Reilly & Lee Co. - **$30 $100 $150**

❑ **DVL-4. Quaker Oats Premium Order Blank,**
1935. - **$15 $35 $70**

DVL-5

DVL-6

❑ **DVL-5. "Devil Dogs" Brass Badge,**
1935. Quaker Cereals premium. - **$20 $40 $85**

❑ **DVL-6. "Military Order Of Devil Dogs" Brass Identification Tag,**
c. 1935. Probably Quaker Cereals premium. -
**$30 $75 $150**

DVL-8

DVL-7

❑ **DVL-7. Brass Ring,**
1935. Quaker Cereals premium. Gold-plated with initial. - **$25 $75 $125**

❑ **DVL-8. Promo Card,**
1935. - **$100 $175 $225**

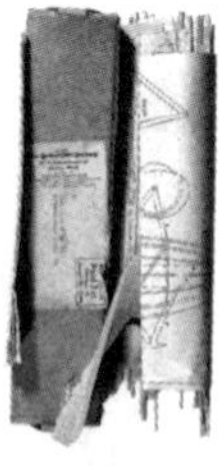
DVL-9

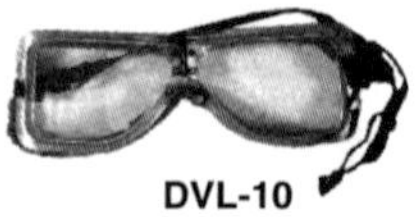
DVL-10

❑ **DVL-9. Plane With Mailer and Instructions,**
1935. Quaker Oats premium plane. -
**$25 $75 $150**
Mailer - **$20 $40 $60**
Instructions - **$20 $40 $60**

❑ **DVL-10. Plane Goggles,**
1935. Quaker Oats premium. Rare. -
**$30 $75 $150**

# Dick Daring's Adventures

**Merrill Fugit played Dick Daring and Donald Briggs was Coach Greatguy in this 15-minute afternoon adventure series that had a brief run in 1933 on the NBC Blue network. Quaker Oats sponsored the show and offered merchandised and generic premiums in exchange for boxtops.**

DDA-1

DDA-2

❑ **DDA-1. "Bag Of Tricks" Book,**
1933. Quaker Oats. - **$5 $20 $60**

❑ **DDA-2. Quaker Underground Cavern Headquarters Map, Matching Puzzle,**
c. 1933. Paper map and cardboard puzzle with identical design. Each - **$20 $100 $225**

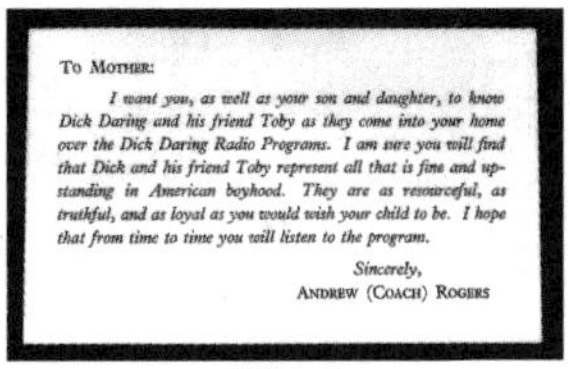

To MOTHER:

*I want you, as well as your son and daughter, to know Dick Daring and his friend Toby as they come into your home over the Dick Daring Radio Programs. I am sure you will find that Dick and his friend Toby represent all that is fine and upstanding in American boyhood. They are as resourceful, as truthful, and as loyal as you would wish your child to be. I hope that from time to time you will listen to the program.*

*Sincerely,*
ANDREW (COACH) ROGERS

DDA-3

❑ **DDA-3. "Coach" Rogers Card "To Mother",**
c. 1933. Promotes "Dick Daring Radio Programs" starring him and his friend Toby. - **$5 $10 $20**

DDA-4

DDA-5

❑ **DDA-4. Quaker Jigsaw Puzzle,**
c. 1933. Puzzle scene of headquarters beneath city. - **$20 $100 $225**

❑ **DDA-5. "New Bag Of Tricks" Book,**
1934. Quaker Oats. - **$8 $25 $60**

# Dick Steel, Boy Reporter

**Fresh from his role as Dick Daring, Merrill Fugit moved on to portray boy reporter Dick Steel in another 15-minute adventure series aired on NBC in 1934. The Educator Biscuit company was the sponsor and premiums included membership badges, booklets revealing secrets of police reporting and how to start a newspaper and such detective paraphernalia as a false mustache, invisible ink and handcuffs.**

DST-1

DST-2

❑ **DST-1. "Secrets Of Police Reporting" Manual,**
1934. Scarce. Educator Hammered Wheat Thinsies. - **$30 $100 $175**

❑ **DST-2. "Neighborhood News" Vol. 1 #1 Newspaper,**
Feb. 15, 1934. Newspaper - **$50 $125 $175**
Envelope Mailer - **$5 $10 $15**

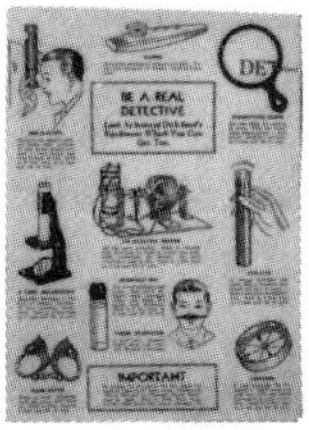


DST-3

❑ **DST-3. Premium Order Sheet,**
c. 1934. Hammered Wheat Thinsies and Toasted Cheese Thins. Ten premiums offered. - **$15 $35 $60**

DST-4

DST-5

DST-6

❑ **DST-4. "Chief Editor" Silvered Metal Badge,**
c. 1934. Rare. Awarded to "Reporter" advancing in rank. - **$50 $150 $300**

❑ **DST-5. "Reporter" Badge only,**
c. 1934. - **$10 $20 $40**

❑ **DST-6. "Dick Steel News Service/Special Police Reporter" Brass Badge,**
c. 1934. Design includes radio front, lightning bolts, portrait, eagle. - **$30 $75 $125**

DST-7

❑ **DST-7. Radio Cast Photo,**
c. 1934. Shown entering United Airlines airplane. - **$20 $40 $75**

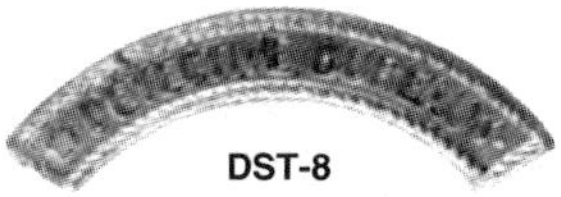


DST-8

❑ **DST-8. "Detective Bureau" Curved Brass Badge,**
c. 1934. Rare. Awarded to "Special Police Reporter" as advancement in rank. Ownership of original badge was required. Kids collected three Wheat Thinsies labels and three names from friends, and sent them in with a form to receive this badge. - **$30 $65 $100**

DST-9

DST-10

❑ **DST-9. Dick Steel Whistle,**
1934. Scarce. - **$20 $75 $100**

❑ **DST-10. Press Card,**
1934. Rare. Membership card for Radio Reporters Club. - **$50 $100 $150**

DST-11

❑ **DST-11. News Service Pamphlet,**
1934. Hammered Wheat Thinsies. Four page premium "How to publish your own newspaper." - **$25 $60 $75**

# Dick Tracy

**October 4, 1931 saw the birth of *Dick Tracy* in the Sunday Chicago Tribune. Eight days later the first daily strip appeared. So began Chester Gould's (1900-1985) continuing saga of crime and violence that has produced a collection of appropriately named rogues and villains from Boris Arson to the Brow, Pruneface to Littleface, Flattop to the Mole, Gravel Gertie and B.O. Plenty and many others. Teamed with Tracy were his sidekicks Pat Patton and Sam Catchem and his enduring fiancee Tess Trueheart.**

**Despite the fanciful characters, the strip has been recognized for its realism and attention to details of police procedure and crime prevention. Tracy's popularity spread out into other media as well. Radio series ran on the CBS, Mutual and NBC networks from 1935 to 1939 sponsored by Sterling Products and Quaker cereals. The majority of early premiums came from Quaker in 1938-39. The show was revived on ABC from 1943 to 1948 sponsored by Tootsie Rolls candy.**

**Four 15-episode chapter plays with Ralph Byrd as Tracy were released between 1937 and 1941, followed by four full-length films between 1945 and 1947, and ultimately the 1990 Disney blockbuster with Warren Beatty, Madonna as Breathless Mahoney and Al Pacino as Big Boy Caprice. A live-action television series with Ralph Byrd again in the title role ran for a season (1950-1951) on ABC and was syndicated throughout the 1950s, and 130 five-minute animated comic cartoons were released in the 1960s. Tracy cartoons were also reprised as segments of *Archie's TV Funnies* (1971-1973) on CBS.**

**The fearless crimefighter's first comic book appearance of many was in 1936 in *Popular Comics* #1. *The Celebrated Cases of Dick Tracy*, a hardbound anthology, was published in 1970. There have been countless Dick Tracy premiums over the years.**

DCY-1

❑ **DCY-1. Paper Mask,**
1933. Text on back tab reads "Free with one package of Handi-Tape." Published by Einson-Freeman Co. - **$75 $150 $325**

DCY-2

DCY-3

❑ **DCY-2. "Dick Tracy And Dick Tracy, Jr." Book,**
1933. Perkins Products Co. - **$25 $75 $150**

❑ **DCY-3. "Comic Section" Promotion Poster,**
c. 1933. Sunday News, N.Y.C. 10x16" in full color. Early and rare. - **$250 $500 $750**

DCY-4

DCY-5

❑ **DCY-4. "Dick Tracy/Junior" Cello. Button,**
c. 1933. Unknown sponsor but made by Parisian Novelty Co. - **$100 $200 $400**

❑ **DCY-5. Belt Attachment With Link Chain And Loop,**
1934. Scarce. Dated and inscribed "Dick Tracy Detective Agency." - **$100 $250 $350**

DCY-6

❑ **DCY-6. "Dick Tracy And The Stolen Bonds" Big Little Book,**
1934. Whitman #1105. - **$50 $100 $200**

DCY-7

DCY-8

❑ **DCY-7. "Big Thrill" Chewing Gum Booklets,**
1934. Goudey Gum Co. Set Of Six,
Each - **$10 $20 $60**

❑ **DCY-8. Dick Tracy Playing Card Game,**
1934. - **$30 $60 $110**

DCY-9

❑ **DCY-9. "The 'Pop-Up' Dick Tracy 'Capture Of Boris Arson'",**
1935. Store item by Blue Ribbon Press. Contains three pop-ups. - **$125 $250 $450**

DCY-10

DCY-11

❑ **DCY-10. "Dick Tracy on the Trail of Larceny Lu" Big Little Book #1170,**
1935. - **$15 $60 $130**

❑ **DCY-11. "Dick Tracy and the Racketeer Gang" Big Little Book #1112,**
1936. - **$15 $60 $130**

DCY-12

❑ **DCY-12. "Libby's Tomato Juice" Poster,**
1936. 15-1/4x23-1/4". Gordon Gold Archives. - **$300 $700 $1000**

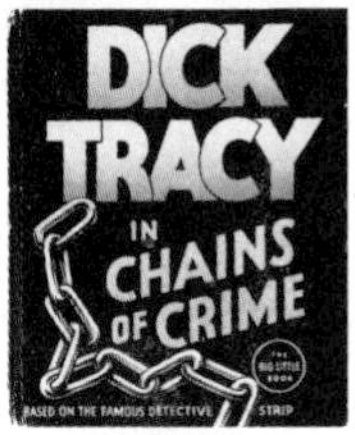

DCY-13

DCY-14

❑ **DCY-13. "Dick Tracy in Chains of Crime" Big Little Book #1185,**
1936. 432 pages. - **$15 $60 $130**

❑ **DCY-14. "Dick Tracy and the Hotel Murders" Big Little Book #1420,**
1937. - **$15 $60 $130**

DCY-15

DCY-16

❑ **DCY-15. "Dick Tracy Detective Club" Brass Shield Badge,**
c. 1937. Reverse has leather cover slotted to wear on belt. - **$40 $75 $150**

❑ **DCY-16. "Dick Tracy Detective Club" Brass Shield Badge,**
c. 1937. Reverse has leather coin pouch with snap shut flap.- **$30 $65 $125**

DCY-17

DCY-18

❑ **DCY-17. "Diamond Theatre Dick Tracy Club" Cello. Badge,**
c. 1937. - **$65 $125 $250**

❑ **DCY-18. "Dick Tracy and the Spider Gang" Big Little Book #1446,**
1937. Story of the movie serial. - **$20 $80 $170**

DCY-19

❑ **DCY-19. "Dick Tracy Detective Game,"**
1937. Store item by Whitman. - **$40 $75 $150**

DCY-20

❑ **DCY-20. "Comicooky Baking Set" Premium Offer Poster,**
1937. 14x21" issued by Pillsbury's Sno Sheen cake flour. Gordon Gold Archives. -
**$100 $250 $400**

DCY-21

DCY-22

DCY-23

❑ **DCY-21. Club Manual,**
1938. - **$40 $80 $125**

❑ **DCY-22. "Secret Service Patrol" Litho. Club Button,**
1938. Quaker Cereals. - **$15 $25 $60**

❑ **DCY-23. "Secret Service Patrol" Cello. Button,**
1938. Rare celluloid version, probably for Canadian membership. - **$80 $200 $400**

DCY-24

❑ **DCY-24. Quaker Two-Sided Sign,**
1938. Rare. Shows the 1938 premiums. -
**$250 $450 $700**

DCY-25

❑ **DCY-25. Quaker Silvered Brass Initial Ring,**
1938. No Tracy inscriptions, personalized initials designated by orderer. Sent in Tracy mailer. -
**$100 $200 $400**

DCY-26

(ENLARGED VIEW)

❑ **DCY-26. Newspaper Premium Ad,**
1938. Quaker Cereals. - **$8 $15 $30**

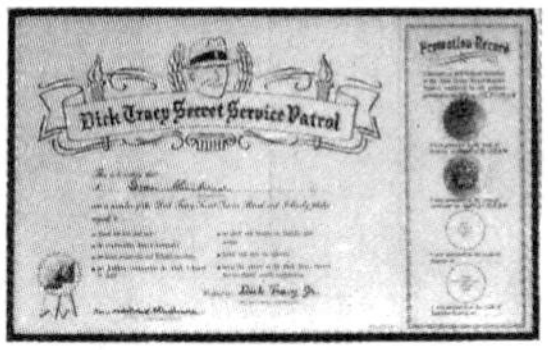

DCY-27

❑ **DCY-27. "Secret Service Patrol Promotion Certificate",**
1938. Quaker Cereals. Add $20 for each applied promotion foil sticker.
Without Stickers - **$15 $30 $50**

DCY-28

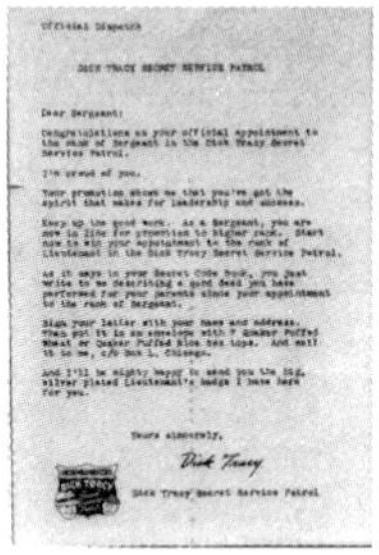
DCY-29

❑ **DCY-28. Sergeant 2-3/4" Tall Brass Badge,**
1938. - **$40 $75 $150**

❑ **DCY-29. Sergeant Promotion Letter,**
1938. Congratulatory letter also listing qualification for next rank of Lieutenant. - **$15 $35 $85**

DCY-30

DCY-31

❑ **DCY-30. Lieutenant Silvered Brass Badge,**
1938. - **$50 $125 $250**

❑ **DCY-31. "Captain" 2-1/2" Brass Rank Badge,**
1938. - **$75 $175 $375**

DCY-32

DCY-33

❑ **DCY-32. "Inspector General" 2-1/2" Brass Badge,**
1938. Scarce. - **$250 $450 $900**

❑ **DCY-33. Secret Service Secret Compartment Brass Ring,**
1938. -**$50 $125 $250**

DCY-34

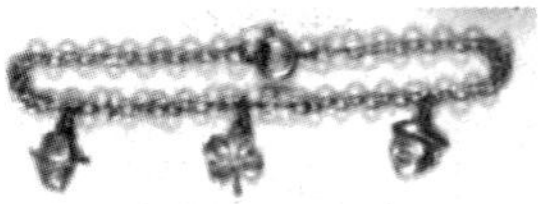

DCY-35

❑ **DCY-34. Patrol Leader Brass Bar,**
1938. Rare. Awarded after "Inspector General" rank. - **$200 $450 $725**

❑ **DCY-35. Lucky Bangle Brass Bracelet,**
1938. Scarce. Charms of Tracy, Junior and four-leaf clover. - **$60 $125 $225**

DCY-36

❑ **DCY-36. "Dick Tracy Air Detective" Brass Wings Badge,**
1938. - **$25 $50 $100**

DCY-37

❑ **DCY-37. Dick Tracy Penny Books,**
1938. Whitman. Each - **$15 $30 $50**

DCY-38

❑ **DCY-38. Rocket Gyro X-3 with Mailer,**
1938. Rare. - **$100 $275 $475**

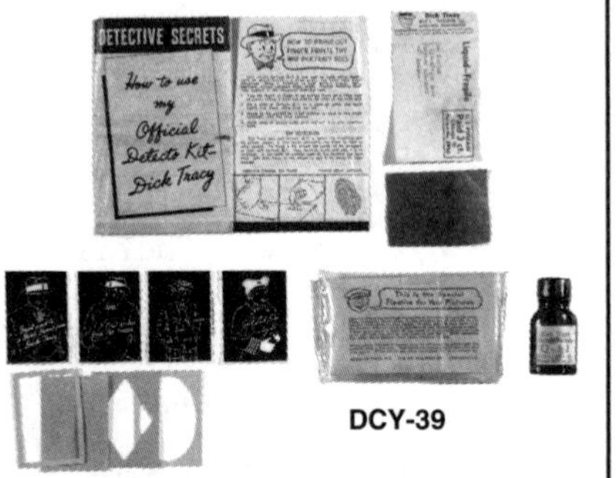


DCY-39

❑ **DCY-39. Official Detecto Kit,**
1938. Scarce. Quaker Cereals. Includes mailer, bottle of "Q-11 Secret Formula", four negative-like black photos and instructions.
Complete - **$100 $300 $425**

DCY-40

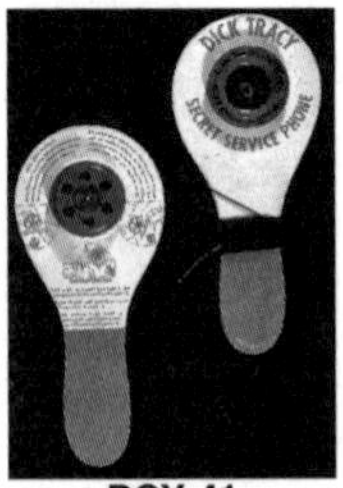


DCY-41

❑ **DCY-40. "Dick Tracy Air Detective" Brass Wing Bracelet,**
1938. Scarce. Top of bracelet opens to place on wrist. - **$125 $325 $650**

❑ **DCY-41. Secret Service Cardboard And Metal Phones,**
1938. Scarce. Quaker Cereals.
Pair - **$75 $200 $350**

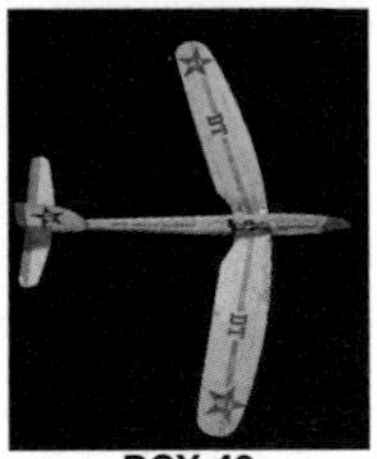

DCY-42

DCY-43

❑ **DCY-42. Dick Tracy Flagship Balsa Wood Plane,**
1938. Scarce. - **$100 $350 $450**

❑ **DCY-43. "Dick Tracy Returns" Movie Serial Promo Photo,**
1938. Republic. About 8x10" black and white. - **$25 $65 $125**

DCY-44

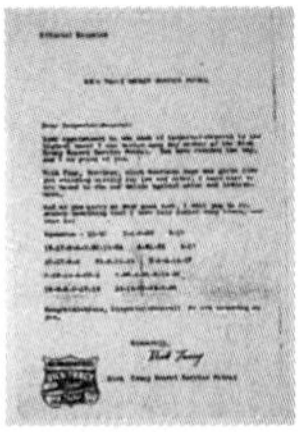

DCY-45

❑ **DCY-44. "Dick Tracy Detective" Large Silver Luster Badge,**
c. 1938. Inscribed "The Vindicator," a probable newspaper publication . - **$40 $75 $150**

❑ **DCY-45. "Inspector-General" Rank Notification Letter,**
1938. 5x7-1/2" "Official Dispatch" notifying recipient this appointment is "The Highest Honor I Can Bestow Upon Any Member Of The Dick Tracy Secret Service Patrol. You Have Reached The Top And I Am Proud Of You." - **$40 $85 $150**

DCY-46

❑ **DCY-46. "Dick Tracy Siren Plane" Assembly Parts With Mailer,**
1938. Issued by Quaker Cereals.
Mailer - **$25 $50 $75**
Plane - **$100 $300 $400**

DCY-47

DCY-48

DCY-49

❑ **DCY-47. "Dick Tracy Returns" Movie Serial Handbill,**
1938. Republic Pictures. - **$20 $45 $85**

❑ **DCY-48. "Secret Code Book Revised Edition",**
1939. Quaker Puffed Wheat & Puffed Rice. - **$30 $60 $110**

❑ **DCY-49. Quaker Radio Play Script,**
1939. "Dick Tracy And The Invisible Man" first of two booklets. - **$20 $50 $130**

DCY-50

DCY-51

❑ **DCY-50. Quaker "Dick Tracy's Ghost Ship" Booklet,**
1939. By Whitman with actual radio broadcast script. - **$30 $75 $150**

❑ **DCY-51. "Dick Tracy Returns" Better Little Book #1495,**
1939. Based on the Republic Movie Serial. Chester Gould art. - **$15 $60 $115**

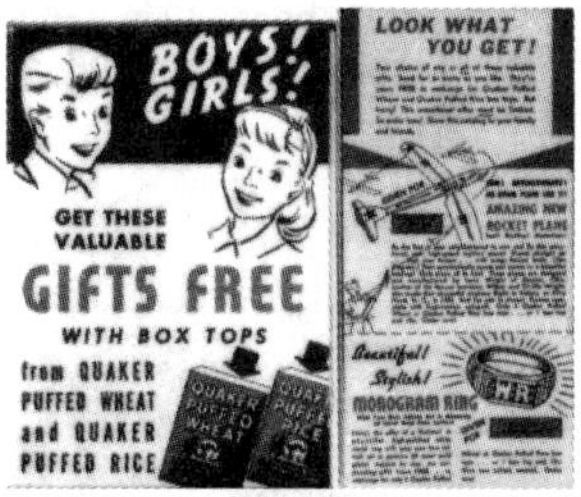

DCY-52

❑ **DCY-52. Quaker Fold-Out Premium Sheet,**
1939. Pictures 11 premiums including Tracy Flag Ship Rocket Plane, Pocket Flashlight, Radio Adventures Booklet, Siren Code Pencil. - **$30 $60 $110**

DCY-53

❑ **DCY-53. Quaker "Secret Detective Methods And Magic Tricks" Booklet,**
1939. Picture example shows both covers. - **$30 $60 $120**

DCY-54

DCY-55

❑ **DCY-54. "Dick Tracy Secret Service" 3" Pen Light,**
1939. Metal tube and plastic end cap. Seen with green or red tube - **$25 $60 $120**

❑ **DCY-55. "Dick Tracy Junior Secret Service" Brass Attachment,**
1939. Originally attached by cord to Dick Tracy pen light. - **$15 $30 $75**

DCY-56

DCY-57

❑ **DCY-56. "Member" Brass Badge,**
1939. - **$15 $30 $60**

❑ **DCY-57. "Second Year Member" Brass Badge,**
1939. - **$20 $40 $75**

DCY-58

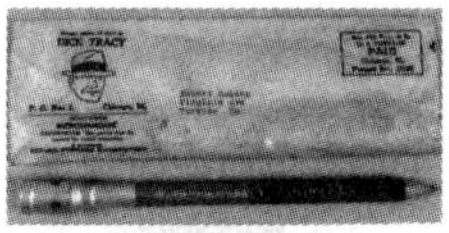
DCY-59

❑ **DCY-58. "Dick Tracy Secret Service Patrol/Girls Division" Brass Badge,**
1939. - **$20 $40 $60**

❑ **DCY-59. Signal Code Siren Cap Pencil With Envelope,**
1939. Near Mint In Mailer - **$175**
Pencil Only - **$50 $100 $150**

DCY-60

❑ **DCY-60. "Girls Dick Tracy Club" Silvered Brass Chain Link Bracelet,**
c. 1939. Shield charm has red enamel accents (shown without chain). - **$40 $100 $175**

DCY-61

❑ **DCY-61. Wood Pencil And Wood Pen,**
c. 1939. Each - **$20 $40 $85**

DCY-62

❑ **DCY-62. Chinese Checkers Game,**
1939. No Dick Tracy or Quaker identification on game but comes in envelope with Tracy pictured on mailing label. 13x13" cardboard playing board plus paper marker pieces.
Complete In Envelope - **$50 $100 $175**
Game Only - **$25 $50 $100**

DCY-63

❑ **DCY-63. "Dick Tracy Siren Pistol,"**
1930s. Store item by Marx Toys. 8-1/2" long metal. - **$75 $150 $275**

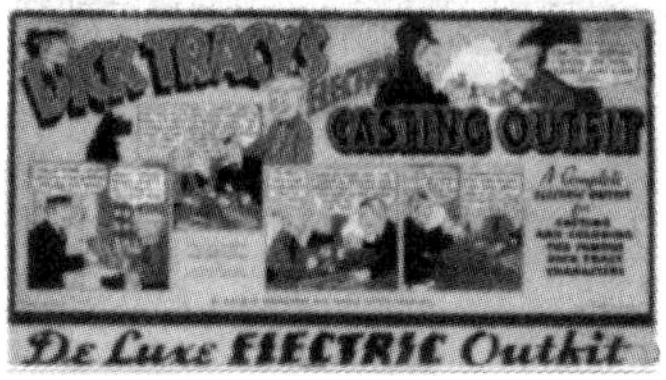

DCY-64

❑ **DCY-64. "Electric Casting Outfit,"**
1930s. Store item by Allied Mfg. Co. - **$200 $500 $1000**

DCY-65 DCY-66

❑ **DCY-65. "Dick Tracy/Detective" Metal Lapel Stud,**
1930s. Unknown sponsor. Brass finish over white metal version. - **$15 $25 $50**

❑ **DCY-66. Picture Card,**
1930s. Retailer incentive candy premium. Retailers received a few of these cards at the bottom of display boxes containing smaller individually wrapped cards with caramel candies. The larger premium cards could be distributed to favorite customers. 6x8" full color. -
**$50 $125 $225**

DCY-67

❑ **DCY-67. Diecut Paper Mask,**
1930s. Imprinted for Philadelphia Inquirer. Published by Einson-Freeman Co. -
**$60 $110 $200**

DCY-68

DCY-69

❑ **DCY-68. Caramels Waxed Wrapper,**
1930s. Store item by Walter H. Johnson Candy Co., Chicago. 6x7" with red and blue design. -
**$50 $100 $150**

❑ **DCY-69. "Dick Tracy Caramels" Wrapper For Cardboard Box,**
1930s. Store item by Walter H. Johnson Co., Chicago. 12-1/4x19" wrapper from box which held 100 caramel candy bars. Gordon Gold Archives. - **$500 $1000 $1500**

DCY-70

❑ **DCY-70. "The Ace Of Sleuths" Candy Store Sign,**
1930s. Walter H. Johnson Co., Chicago. 8-1/4x19" red, white and blue sign referring to caramel candy bars. Gordon Gold Archives. -
**$750 $1500 $2000**

DCY-71

❑ **DCY-71. Detective Set,**
1930s. Store item. Two sizes: 7 x 12-1/2", no number on lid; 9-1/2 x 15" with #119 on lid, same contents. Includes tin badge.
Small - **$50 $100 $175**
Large - **$75 $125 $225**

DCY-72 DCY-73 DCY-74

❑ **DCY-72. "Detective" Cello. Button Facing Left, No Gun,**
1930s. Back paper advertises comic strip in "The Chicago Tribune" or sometimes with name of New York City newspaper. - **$20 $40 $85**

❑ **DCY-73. "Detective" Cello. Button Facing Left With Gun,**
1930s. Promoted newspaper comic strip with various newspapers indicated on back paper. -
**$15 $35 $65**

❑ **DCY-74. "Detective" Cello. Button Facing Forward,**
1930s. Chicago Tribune back paper. Promotes comic strip appearing in that newspaper. -
**$15 $35 $65**

DCY-75

❑ **DCY-75. Genung's Store Advertising Cello. Button With Dick Tracy/Little Orphan Annie,**
1930s. Rare. Considered one of the rarest and most desirable comic character buttons. -
**$400 $1000 $1750**

DCY-76 DCY-77

❑ **DCY-76. "Dick Tracy/A Republic Picture" Enameled Brass Shield Badge,**
1930s. - **$25 $60 $90**

❑ **DCY-77. "Detective/Dick Tracy Club/Sun Papers" Silvered Embossed Tin Badge,**
1930s. Probably Baltimore newspaper. -
**$25 $60 $125**

DCY-78 DCY-79

❑ **DCY-78. "Boy's Police Automatic" Cardboard Noisemaker Gun,**
1930s. Philadelphia Inquirer. - **$20 $40 $70**

❑ **DCY-79. Pocketknife,**
1930s. Celluloid grips on steel made by Imperial Co. - **$50 $125 $275**

DCY-80 DCY-81

❑ **DCY-80. "Cleveland News Dick Tracy Club" Brass Badge,**
1930s. - **$25 $50 $90**

❑ **DCY-81. "Dick Tracy and the Phantom Ship" Better Little Book #1434,**
1940. - **$15 $60 $130**

DCY-82

❑ **DCY-82. "Family Fun Book",**
1940. Tip-Top Bread radio premium. 14 pages with no super-heroes inside. - **$50 $150 $450**

DCY-83

❑ **DCY-83. Plaster Figures,**
c. 1941. Store item. From a set of at least 76 characters which we believe started as early as 1941 and still appeared in catalogues as late as 1951. Catalogue carries name Professional Art Products, but we believe the maker was Plasto Mfg. Co. of Chicago. Sold unpainted. Unpainted or nicely painted examples.
Tracy - **$15 $40 $75**
Tess - **$12 $30 $60**

DCY-84

DCY-85

❑ **DCY-84. "Dick Tracy Detective Club" Enameled Brass Diecut Tab,**
1942. - **$25 $60 $100**

❑ **DCY-85. Junior Dick Tracy Crime Detection Folio Offer Sign,**
c. 1942. Miller Bros. Hat Co. 11x14" stiff cardboard easel sign offering premium for purchase of hat. Gordon Gold Archives. -
**$150 $250 $500**

DCY-86

❑ **DCY-86. "Junior Dick Tracy Crime Detection Folio",**
c. 1942. Includes detective's notebook, jigsaw puzzle, cardboard code finder, etc.
Near Mint Set - **$325**

DCY-87

DCY-88

❑ **DCY-87. Christmas Giveaway Promotion To Toy Department Managers,**
1943. Sears. 8-1/2x11" black and white flyer promoting use of giveaway comic. Gordon Gold Archives. - **$50 $100 $150**

❑ **DCY-88. Promotional Flyer To "Mr. Store Manager",**
1943. Sears. 8-1/2x11" black and white with Dick Tracy stating he is "Mystified" why manager has not yet ordered Christmas comic giveaway comic. Gordon Gold Archives. -
**$60 $125 $175**

DCY-89

❑ **DCY-89. Hardback Book with Dust Jacket,**
1943. Whitman Publishing Co. - **$10 $20 $35**

DCY-90

❑ **DCY-90. Junior Detective Kit Newspaper Advertisement,**
1944. Tootsie V-M Chocolate Drink Mix. -
**$8 $12 $20**

DCY-91

❑ **DCY-91. Junior Detective Kit,**
1944. Tootsie V-M Chocolate Drink Mix and Miller Bros. Hat Co. Includes manual, decoder, membership card, suspect sheets, ruler, line-up chart, badge. Two manual varieties: Type 1 includes anti-Japanese propaganda, Type 2 eliminates this and has different mailer. See color section for other differences.
Type 1 Near Mint Complete - **$575**
Type 2 Near Mint Complete - **$425**

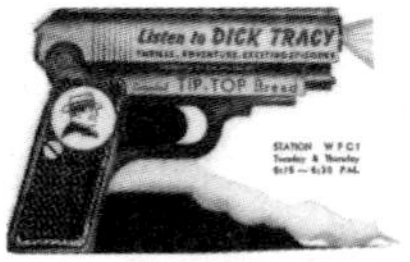

DCY-92

DCY-93

❑ **DCY-92. Tip-Top Bread Cardboard Noisemaker Gun,**
1944. Urges radio broadcast listenership. -
**$20 $45 $85**

❑ **DCY-93. "Dick Tracy's G Men" Cardboard Blotter/Ruler Card,**
1945. Local theaters for 15-week movie serial. -
**$35 $75 $175**

DCY-94

❑ **DCY-94. "Dick Tracy And The Wreath Kidnapping Case" Better Little Book,**
1945. Whitman #1482. **- $20 $50 $110**

DCY-95

(Enlarged view of puzzle)

❑ **DCY-95. Dick Tracy Jigsaw Puzzle in Box,**
1946. - **$40 $100 $175**

DCY-96

❑ **DCY-96. Color Portrait,**
1946. Pillsbury Farina. 7x10". Cost was 10 cents plus box top and included Orphan Annie, Skeezix, Harold Teen, Shadow, Andy Gump, Winnie Winkle, Smitty.
Tracy And Annie Each - **$25 $50 $75**
Others Each - **$5 $15 $25**

DCY-97 DCY-98

❑ **DCY-97. "Dick Tracy and Yogee Yamma" Big Little Book #1412,**
1946. Chester Gould art. - **$11 $45 $100**

❑ **DCY-98. "Dick Tracy and the Mad Killer" Big Little Book #1436,**
1947. - **$11 $45 $100**

DCY-99

❑ **DCY-99. "Flare-Top" Ice Cream Cone Sign,**
1947. Full color about 18x24". Gordon Gold archives. - **$75 $150 $275**

DCY-100

❑ **DCY-100. Tracy Villain "Influence" Eyes On Card,**
c. 1948. Store item by Mac Novelty Co.
Carded **- $35 $75 $125**

DCY-101

❑ **DCY-101. Dick Tracy Watch in Box with Insert,**
1948. Chester Gould art. - **$700**

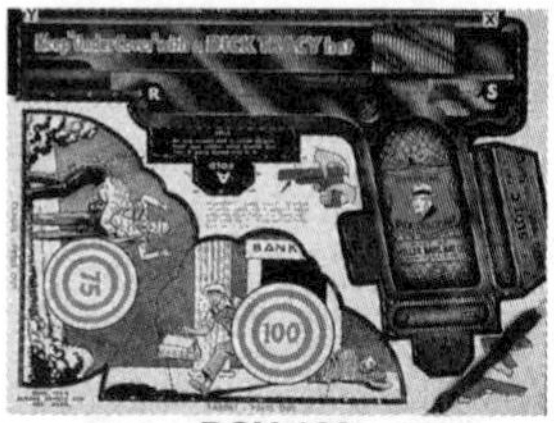


DCY-102

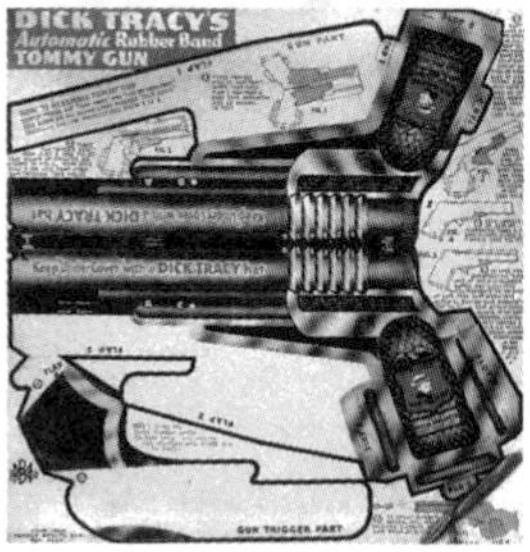


DCY-103

❑ **DCY-102. Cardboard Rubber Band Pistol,**
1949. Miller Brothers Hats.
Unpunched - **$50 $100 $175**

❑ **DCY-103. Cardboard Tommy Gun,**
1949. Rare. Miller Brothers Hats. From the Gordon Gold Archives.
Unpunched - **$150 $300 $600**

DCY-104

❑ **DCY-104. "Straight From The Shoulder" Anti-Crime Booklet,**
c. 1949. Crime Prevention Council of Illinois. Chester Gould art, printed in Illinois Penitentiary. - **$25 $50 $90**

DCY-105 DCY-106

❑ **DCY-105. "Dick Tracy and The Tiger Lilly Gang" Big Little Book #1460,**
1949. - **$11 $45 $100**

❑ **DCY-106. Dick Tracy Candy Box,**
1940s. Cartoon strips on back of box. - **$35 $125 $185**

DCY-107

DCY-108

❑ **DCY-107. "Hatfull O' Fun!" Game Book,**
1940s. Miller Brothers Hats. - **$20 $60 $125**

❑ **DCY-108. "Dick Tracy Jr./Detective Agency" Silvered Brass Tie Clip,**
1940s. Store item. - **$40 $65 $110**

DCY-109

DCY-110

❑ **DCY-109. Kit Die-Cut Sign,**
1940s, Miller Bros. Hat Corp. Dick Tracy Hat promo shows pieces of Junior Detective kit. - **$150 $250 $500**

❑ **DCY-110. "Dick Tracy Braces" Box,**
1940s. Store item by Strum & Schenberg Inc. Held 12. - **$100 $200 $300**

DCY-111

DCY-112

❑ **DCY-111. Hat Box,**
1940s. Store item by Miller Bros. Hat Corp. Brown box with large red, white and blue label. - **$150 $300 $500**

❑ **DCY-112. Cardboard Original Art Prototype Mask,**
c. 1940s. 11" tall by 13" wide with accordion-like paper ears. Reverse notation "Made For Sam Gold. Neuman Rudolph Litho. Co. 844 W. Jackson, Chicago." From archive of former Gold employee. Unique. - **$600**

DCY-113

❑ **DCY-113. Sparkle Plenty Plaster Bank,**
1940s. Store item by Jayess Co. -
**$150 $300 $600**

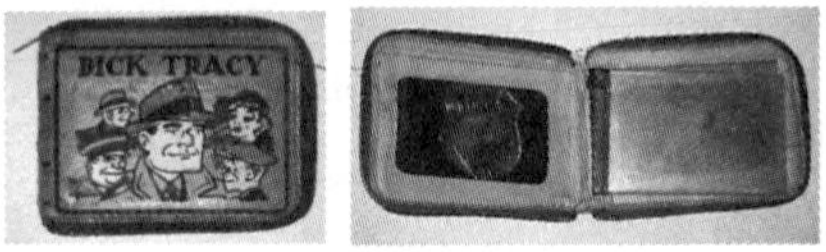

DCY-114

❑ **DCY-114. Wallet With Foil Shield,**
c. 1940s. Store item. Leather wallet with color portraits containing gold foil shield inscribed "Dick Tracy Badge/Junior Detective First Grade." Wallet **- $35 $75 $150**
Foil Badge - **$25 $50 $100**

DCY-115

DCY-116

❑ **DCY-115. "Dick Tracy Hat" Store Window Ad Card With Mailer,**
1940s. Miller Bros. Hat Co. 12x15-1/2" tan envelope holds 11x14" yellow, red, black and white sign offering free ring with hat purchase. -
**$75 $125 $225**

❑ **DCY-116. "Dick Tracy" Enameled Brass Hat Ring,**
1940s. Miller Brothers Hat Corp. -
**$50 $100 $200**

DCY-117

**(Enlarged view of gun decal)**

DCY-118

❑ **DCY-117. Dick Tracy Rapid-Fire Tommy Gun,**
1940s. Advertised in Sunday comic pages for - $3.79 from Parker Johns, Chicago. 20" all metal gun is gray with brown stock featuring full color Tracy decal on one side. Gun was issued with canvas shoulder strap, missing in our photo and a brass "Dick Tracy Detective Club" shield badge. - **$100 $250 $500**

❑ **DCY-118. "Detective Club" Brass Shield Badge,**
1940s. Issued with the Dick Tracy Tommy Gun and used for many other licensed promotions as well. - **$10 $25 $50**

DCY-119

DCY-120

❑ **DCY-119. "Dick Tracy Hatfull O' Fun!" Book Offer Sign,**
1940s. Miller Bros. Hat Co. 11x14" easel sign offering activity book for purchase of hat. Gordon Gold Archives. - **$150 $250 $500**

❑ **DCY-120. "Dick Tracy" and "Junior" Salt and Pepper Shakers,**
1940s. Plaster shakers are a store item from a series of different characters. - **$25 $40 $75**

DCY-121

❑ **DCY-121. "Dick Tracy Detective De-Coder And Clue Finder" Prototype Original Art,**
c. 1950. 3x12" decoder bar with 3-1/4" tall sliding thin cardboard sleeve. Gordon Gold Archives. Unique**. - $1000**

DCY-122

DCY-123

❑ **DCY-122. Chester Gould Personal Christmas Card,**
c. 1950. 6x9-1/2" stiff paper picturing and naming 10 characters. - **$30 $60 $100**

❑ **DCY-123. "Dick Tracy Crimestopper" Tin Shield Badge,**
c. 1950. Lettering in black and red. - **$35 $70 $150**

DCY-124

❑ **DCY-124. Dick Tracy Full Color Original Art Prototype Book Created By Sam Gold For Tip Top Bread,**
c. 1950. 8x10-3/4" with 24 pages of color original art. Gordon Gold Archives. Unique**. - $1200**

DCY-125

DCY-126

❑ **DCY-125. "Sunday Post-Gazette" 3" Cello. Button,**
c. 1950. - **$50 $100 $150**

❑ **DCY-126. Dick Tracy And B.O. Plenty Knife,**
c. 1950. Store item includes whistle, magnifier and grips that glow in the dark. Grips usually cracked by rivet. - **$20 $40 $95**

DCY-127

❑ **DCY-127. "Dick Tracy" Fully Three-Dimensional Plaster Lamp,**
1951. Store item by Plasto Mfg. Co., Chicago. Sold unpainted to be painted by purchaser, Tracy stands 9" tall and with the shade, which has two identical images of Sparkle Plenty on the reverse, the total height is 16".
Base Only - **$200 $400 $600**
Shade Only - **$100 $200 $400**

DCY-128

DCY-129

❑ **DCY-128. Dick Tracy Wrist Watch with Box,**
1951. Produced by New Haven Corp.
Boxed - **$625**

❑ **DCY-129. "Dick Tracy TV Detective Club" Member Certificate,**
1952. © Chicago Tribune. - **$20 $30 $50**

DCY-130

❑ **DCY-130. Dick Tracy Movie Serial Re-Release Poster,**
1952. Re-issue of 1941 Republic serial originally titled "Dick Tracy Vs. Crime Inc." - **$40 $60 $125**

DCY-131

(FRONT VIEW)

❑ **DCY-131. Dick Tracy Police Station with Car in Original Box,**
1952. Original Box - **$75 $150 $325**
Police Station and Squad Car - **$150 $300 $600**

DCY-132

❑ **DCY-132. Cardboard Flip Badge,**
1952. Ward's Tip-Top Bread. - **$20 $50 $125**

DCY-133

❑ **DCY-133. Coco-Wheats Iron-On Transfers Set With Mailer Envelope,**
1956. Inner envelope holding two transfer sheets picturing Tracy friends and villains.
Mailer - **$10 $15 $25**
Illustrated Envelope With Two Sheets - **$25 $50 $75**

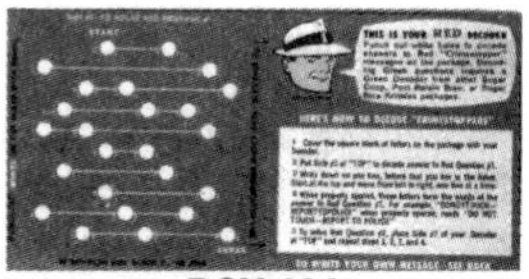

DCY-134

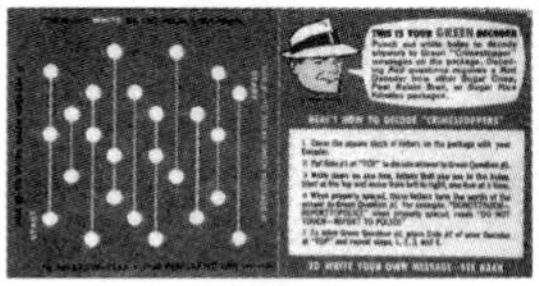

DCY-135

❑ **DCY-134. Post's Cereals "Red" Decoder Card,**
1957. To decode answers to red "Crimestopper" messages on cereal box. - **$15 $25 $50**

❑ **DCY-135. Post's Cereals "Green" Decoder Card,**
1957. Decodes green "Crimestopper" messages on cereal box. - **$15 $25 $50**

DCY-136

❑ **DCY-136. "Dick Tracy Squad Car" With Tracy And Sam Catchem Plastic Fi gures,**
1950s. Marx Toys. 20" long tin litho friction with battery operated light.
Near Mint With Figures - **$400**
No Figures - **$75 $150 $300**

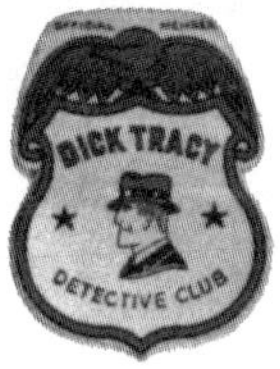


DCY-137

DCY-138

❑ **DCY-137. Detective Club 2-1/4" Tall Fabric Sticker Patch,**
c. 1950s. - **$40 $85 $150**

❑ **DCY-138. Cracker Jack Giveaway,**
c. 1950s. From a series of comic characters, each 1-5/8" made of thin plastic with high relief portrait. Additional Tracy characters were also issued. Each - **$10 $20 $35**

DCY-139

❑ **DCY-139. "Dick Tracy Crime Stoppers Lab" Boxed Set,**
1950s. Store item by Porter Chemical Co., Hagerstown, Md. 12x19x3" deep set designated "No. 3" on lid panels. Holds wide variety of equipment and chemicals used in crime detection. Scarce. - **$300 $750 $1500**

DCY-140

DCY-141

❑ **DCY-140. "Dick Tracy Crime Stoppers" Litho. Tin Tab,**
1950s. Sponsored by Mercury Records. - **$75 $150 $250**

❑ **DCY-141. "Dick Tracy Detective Club" Brass Clip Shield,**
1950s. Slotted gripper from set of store bought elastic suspenders. - **$15 $25 $60**

DCY-142

❑ **DCY-142. "Dick Tracy Costume with Mask,**
1950s. Includes instructions. Shirt/jacket piece was worn like a tunic. Complete - **$150**

DCY-143

DCY-144

❑ **DCY-143. Enameled Brass Suspender Gripper,**
c. 1950s. From set of elastic fabric suspenders, store item. - **$10 $20 $40**

❑ **DCY-144. "Dick Tracy/Crimestopper" Silvered Metal Badge,**
1961. Came with next item. - **$5 $12 $20**

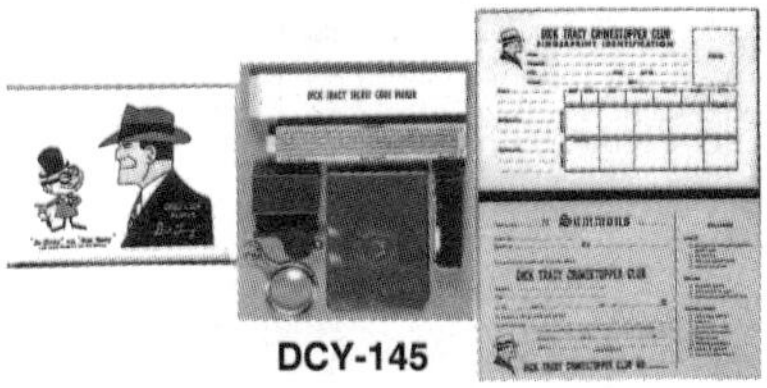


DCY-145

❑ **DCY-145. Crimestopper Club Kit,**
1961. Sponsor unknown. Many contents including badge (see previous item). Fairly common due to warehouse find in the 1980s.
Near Mint Boxed - **$50**

DCY-146

❑ **DCY-146. Sweepstakes Contest Packet,**
1962. Procter & Gamble. Includes leaflet, instruction sheet, store purchase coupons. - **$30 $60 $90**

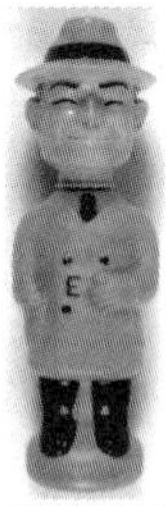

DCY-147

DCY-148

❑ **DCY-147. Soaky Bottle,**
1965. Colgate-Palmolive. - **$15 $35 $60**

❑ **DCY-148. "WGN-TV" Crimestopper Litho. Tin Tab,**
1960s. Chicago TV station. - **$15 $30 $70**

DCY-149

❑ **DCY-149. Dick Tracy Space Coupe Model,**
1968. Aurora model Kit in Box. - **$50 $75 $160**

DCY-150

❑ **DCY-150. Tracy Villains Stationery Sample Kit,**
c. 1971. Boise Cascade Paper Group. Six 11x14" posters, stationery sheets and envelope. - **$20 $35 $50**

DCY-151

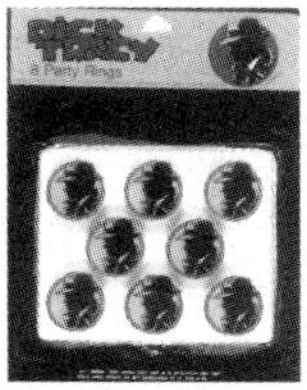

DCY-152

DCY-153

❑ **DCY-151. Dick Tracy/Detective Badge On Card,**
1990. Store item. Carded - **$10**
Loose - **$1 $2 $4**

❑ **DCY-152. "Dick Tracy Party Rings" On Card,**
1990. Total of eight. Store Item.
Carded Set - **$20**
Each Ring - **$1 $2 $3**

❑ **DCY-153. Comic Book Giveaway,**
1990. Gladstone published Dick Tracy Rogues Gallery book made for bakeries. Sixteen pages, featuring Blank, Flattop, Brow, Pruneface and other villains. - **$5 $10 $25**

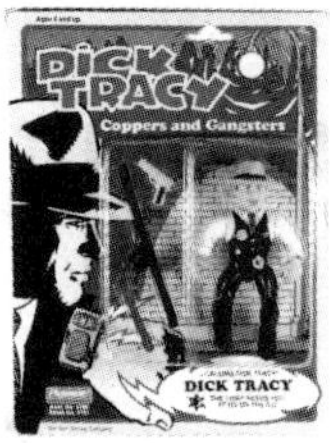


DCY-154

DCY-155

❑ **DCY-154. Dick Tracy Movie Figure on Card,**
1990. - **$25**

❑ **DCY-155. Influence Figure on Card,**
1990. - **$12**

DCY-156

DCY-157

❑ **DCY-156. Lips Manlis Figure on Card,**
1990. - **$12**

❑ **DCY-157. Mumbles Figure on Card,**
1990. - **$12**

DCY-158

DCY-159

❑ **DCY-158. Pruneface Figure on Card,**
1990. - **$12**

❑ **DCY-159. The Rodent Figure on Card,**
1990. - **$12**

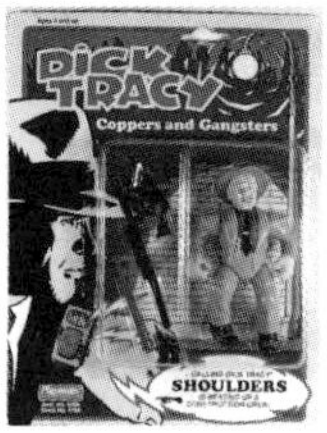


DCY-160

DCY-161

❑ **DCY-160. Shoulders Figure on Card,**
1990. - **$12**

❑ **DCY-161. Clip-On Magnet on Card,**
1990. Features Steve the Tramp. - **$2 $4 $12**

DCY-162

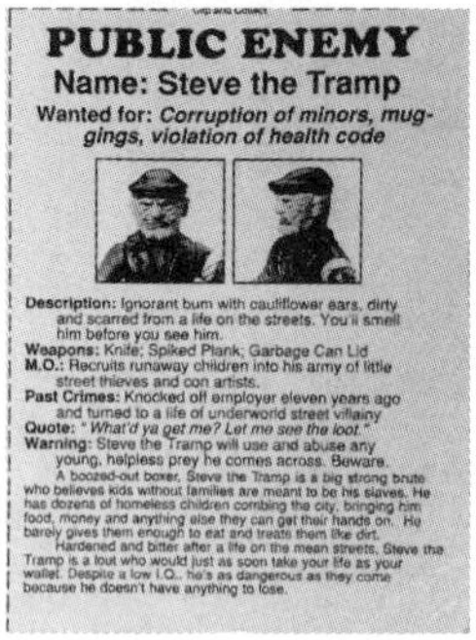

**PUBLIC ENEMY**
**Name: Steve the Tramp**
**Wanted for:** ***Corruption of minors, muggings, violation of health code***

**Description:** Ignorant bum with cauliflower ears, dirty and scarred from a life on the streets. You'll smell him before you see him.
**Weapons:** Knife; Spiked Plank; Garbage Can Lid
**M.O.:** Recruits runaway children into his army of little street thieves and con artists.
**Past Crimes:** Knocked off employer eleven years ago and turned to a life of underworld street villainy
**Quote:** *"What'd ya get me? Let me see the loot."*
**Warning:** Steve the Tramp will use and abuse any young, helpless prey he comes across. Beware.

A boozed-out boxer, Steve the Tramp is a big strong brute who believes kids without families are meant to be his slaves. He has dozens of homeless children combing the city, bringing him food, money and anything else they can get their hands on. He barely gives them enough to eat and treats them like dirt.

Hardened and bitter after a life on the mean streets, Steve the Tramp is a lout who would just as soon take your life as your wallet. Despite a low I.Q., he's as dangerous as they come because he doesn't have anything to lose.

❑ **DCY-162. The Tramp Figure on Card,**
1990. When this Steve the Tramp Figure appeared, associations and support groups for the homeless complained, convincing Disney to conduct a well-publicized recall of this product. The content of his rap sheet raises the question, "What was the Disney brass thinking?" - **$20**

DCY-163

❑ **DCY-163. Cap'n Crunch Crunch Berries Cereal Box with Door Hanger Promo,**
1990. Premium door hanger came inside 19 oz. value pack box. - **$5 $10 $25**

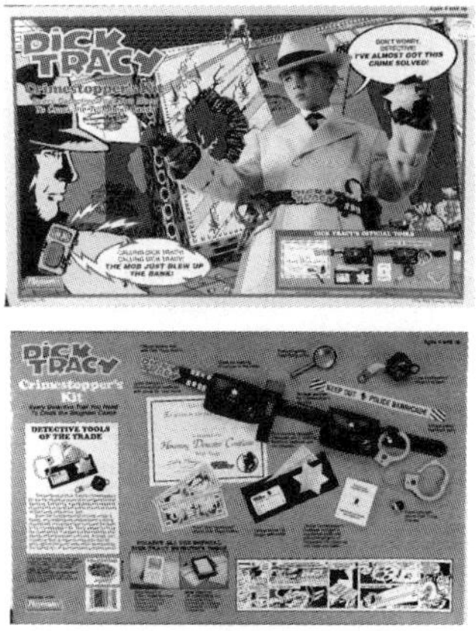


DCY-164

❑ **DCY-164. Dick Tracy Crimestopper's Kit,**
1990. Everything a kid needs to stop crime. The Kit's designers benefitted from using many Dick Tracy items from previous sets for inspiration. Includes a secret-compartment ring.
Boxed - **$20 $50 $100**
Ring Only - **$10 $20 $45**

DCY-165

❑ **DCY-165. Dick Tracy and Breathless Mahoney Movie Dolls with Tags,**
1990. Dick Tracy is 10" tall, Breathless 9 1/2".
Set - **$30**

DCY-166

DCY-167

❑ **DCY-166. Movie Promo Pinback,**
1990. - **$2 $4 $10**

❑ **DCY-167. Movie Promo Neckerchief,**
1990. - **$5 $15 $30**

## Dionne Quintuplets

**Their names were Annette, Cecile, Emilie, Marie and Yvonne and their combined weight at birth was less than 10 pounds. They were born on May 28, 1934, in Callander, Ontario. They were the Dionne quintuplets and they created an international sensation as the first documented set of quints to survive beyond a few days. Tourists and entrepreneurs flocked to see them, they were made wards of the government to protect them from exploitation, it was said, and a promotional and merchandising bonanza was born. The Quints appeared in three films between 1936 and 1938 with Jean Hersholt as Dr. Allan Roy Dafoe, the country doctor who delivered and cared for them and they earned fees in exchange for lending their names and images to promote a wide range of products, from soup to margarine to Karo syrup. Marketers took full advantage of the age of these charming little girls. Palmolive beauty soap, for example, offered adult purchasers a Dionne quintuplets cutout book--especially for the children. Their promotional appeal continued into their early teen years. Emilie and Marie died in 1954 and 1970 respectively.**

DIO-1

❑ **DIO-1. Quaker 15x32" Paper Store Poster,**
1935. Photo portrait set offer. - **$50 $100 $175**

DIO-2

DIO-3

❑ **DIO-2. Ink Blotter,**
1935. Various sponsors. - **$10 $20 $35**

❑ **DIO-3. Cardboard Fan,**
1935. Various advertisers. - **$8 $20 $30**

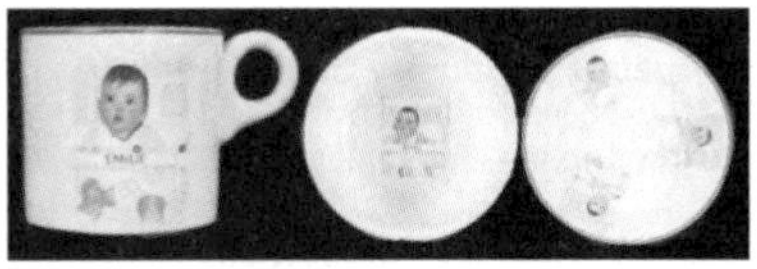

DIO-4

❑ **DIO-4. Three Piece China Set,**
c. 1935. Store item, no maker's mark. Emile on mug, Marie on bowl, others on plate.
Set - **$60 $150 $225**

DIO-5

❑ **DIO-5. Large 11-1/2" Platter,**
c. 1935. Printed with maple leaf design, their names, place and date of birth, "Niagara Falls." Underside marked "Photo Copyright N.E.A."
**$75 $150 $225**

DIO-6

❑ **DIO-6. "Quintland",**
c. 1935. Canadian published visit souvenir in mailer cover. - **$10 $35 $50**

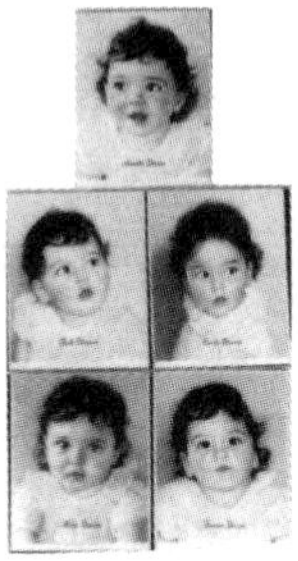

DIO-7

DIO-8

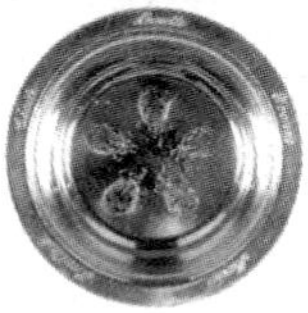

DIO-9

❑ **DIO-7. Quaker Cereals Color Photo Portrait Set,**
1935. - **$15 $30 $60**

❑ **DIO-8. China Mug,**
c. 1935. Probable store item. - **$20 $40 $75**

❑ **DIO-9. Chrome Finish Metal Cereal Bowl,**
1935. Quaker Oats. - **$10 $30 $50**

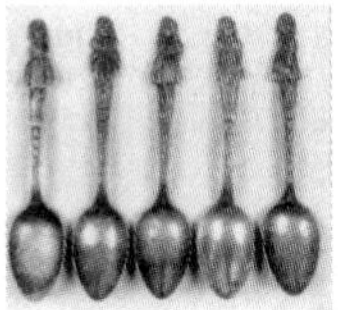

DIO-10

DIO-11

❑ **DIO-10. Silver Plate Spoons,**
c. 1935. Probably Quaker Cereals. Set of five.
Each - **$8 $15 $30**

❑ **DIO-11. "Dionne Pops" Display Box,**
1936. Vitamin Candy Co. - **$40 $100 $225**

DIO-12

❑ **DIO-12. "Dionne Quins" Quaker Contest Sign,**
1936. 10-1/2x13" diecut cardboard. -
**$50 $100 $175**

DIO-13

DIO-14

❑ **DIO-13. Portrait Fan,**
1936. Various advertisers. - **$10 $25 $40**

❑ **DIO-14. Cardboard Fan,**
1936. Various advertisers. - **$8 $20 $30**

DIO-15

DIO-16

❑ **DIO-15. Dionne Quintuplet Bread 3-1/2" Cello. Button,**
c. 1936. - **$15 $40 $85**

❑ **DIO-16. "Quintuplet Bread" Paper Hanger,**
c. 1936. Schulz Baking Co. Went on door knob. - **$20 $40 $75**

DIO-17

❑ **DIO-17. Ink Blotter Pad,**
c. 1936. Various advertisers. Clear plastic cover. - **$12 $20 $50**

DIO-18

❑ **DIO-18. Shirley Temple/Dionnes 9x12" Store Card,**
1937. Modern Screen magazine. - **$50 $125 $225**

DIO-19

❑ **DIO-19. "Dionne Quin Cutout Book",**
1937. Palmolive Soap.
With Mailer - **$50 $100 $175**
No Mailer - **$35 $75 $115**

DIO-20

DIO-21

❑ **DIO-20. The Country Doctor Booklet,**
1937. Lysol. Radio premium. 32 page story about the Dionne Quintuplets. - **$25 $50 $75**

❑ **DIO-21. Cardboard Wall Calendar,**
1938. Published by Brown & Bigelow with local imprints. - **$10 $20 $35**

DIO-22

❑ **DIO-22. Movie Promo Photo,**
1938. For "The Dionne Quintuplets - Five of a Kind" movie. - **$20 $40 $60**

DIO-23

DIO-24

❑ **DIO-23. "Souvenir Of Callander" China Tray,**
c. 1938. Birthplace souvenir. - **$25 $75 $115**

❑ **DIO-24. "Lysol Vs. Germs" Booklet,**
1938. Lehn & Fink Products. - **$12 $25 $40**

DIO-25

DIO-26

❑ **DIO-25. Dionne Quintuplets Wood Pin,**
c. 1938. Birthplace souvenir. - **$25 $50 $100**

❑ **DIO-26. Dexterity Puzzle,**
1930s. Store item made by Bar Zim Toy Mfg. Co. Unauthorized but based on the Dionnes with caption "Place The Quintuplets In The Carriage." - **$15 $30 $60**

DIO-27

❑ **DIO-27. "Let's Play House" Paperdoll Book Set,**
1940. Merrill Publishing Co. Books are numbered 1-5 for each Quint.
Uncut Each - **$50 $90 $150**

DIO-28

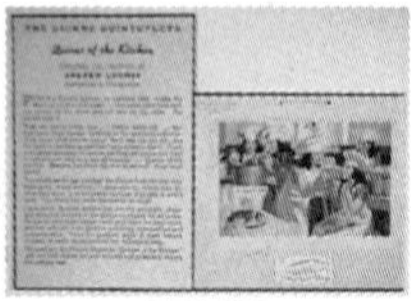

DIO-29

❑ **DIO-28. "Baby Ruth" Candy Box,**
1941. Curtiss Candy Co. 8x11-1/2x2" deep display box which held individual bars. - **$50 $125 $225**

❑ **DIO-29. "Queens Of The Kitchen" Calendar,**
1946. Various sponsors. 8-3/4x11" with tipped-on 5x7-1/4" color print of painting by Andrew Loomis. Pictures them when 12 years old, one of the last calendars in the series. - **$15 $30 $50**

## Disney Characters Misc.

**Walter Elias Disney (1901-1966) and his talented skills dominated the animation field throughout his working career and established the monumental success of the current Disney international empire. Entering animation shortly after World War I, Disney and his associates created dozens of household name animated characters headed, of course, by Mickey Mouse, but including Oswald The Rabbit, Donald Duck, Goofy, Pluto, Snow White and The Seven Dwarfs, Dumbo, Bambi, Cinderella, Alice In Wonderland, Peter Pan and Sleeping Beauty to name only the most obvious. Disney was the leader in creating full-length animated films--*Snow White* (1937), *Pinocchio* and *Fantasia* (1940)--and joined these successes with live-action films starting in the late 1940s including classics *Treasure Island, 20,000 Leagues Under The Sea, Davy Crockett* and *Mary Poppins*. Children's TV**

entertainment during the 1950s-1960s was dominated by ***Disney's Mickey Mouse Club*** and ***Zorro*** in addition to the popular family series beginning under the ***Disneyland*** title. Over the years, the quantity and beloved quality of Disney characters have prompted more premiums than any other single source.

DIS-1

❑ **DIS-1. "Silly Symphony" Cardboard Fan,**
c. 1935. Various sponsors. - **$60 $150 $250**

DIS-2

DIS-3

❑ **DIS-2. Department Store 18x25" Christmas Hanger Sign,**
c. 1935. Various stores for toy departments. Paper printed identically both sides. -
**$150 $400 $750**

❑ **DIS-3. Walt Disney Cigarette Card,**
1935. Imperial Tobacco Premium from England. Tells on back that in 1920 Disney was a hack artist making only 5 pounds a week, then says today he is making 80,000 pounds a year. -
**$35 $75 $100**

(BOX FRONT)

(MELVIS PURVIS AD ON SIDE OF BOX)

(ENLARGED VIEW OF THE BOX BACK)

DIS-4

❑ **DIS-4. Post Toasties Cereal Box with Movie Promo,**
1936. Promotes the Walt Disney Silly Symphony "Cock O' The Walk" on back and the Melvin Purvis Junior G-Man Corps and Badge on side.-
**$250 $500 $825**

DIS-5

❑ **DIS-5. Goofy Ink Blotter,**
1939. Sunoco. Igloo and polar bear. -
**$15 $35 $65**

DIS-6

❑ **DIS-6. Fantasia Game Premium,**
1940. This is the rarest of all "Fantasia" promotional items for the RKO/Disney film. Given out on opening night to children and adults by theaters that purchased the item to promote the film. Complete game - **$350 $450 $550**

DIS-7

❑ **DIS-7. Morrell Hams "Walt Disney Calendar",**
1942. 12 Disney character scenes. -
**$100 $250 $400**

DIS-8

❑ **DIS-8. "Combat Insignia Stamps Of The United States Army & Navy Air Corps",**
1942. Volume 1 from a set of four albums designed to hold 50 different full color numbered stamps many designed by the Disney Studios. Usually found with the name of a newspaper on the front cover.
Complete With Stamps Unmounted Or Neatly Mounted - **$35 $60 $125**

DIS-9

❑ **DIS-9. "War Insignia Stamp Album" Volume 2,**
1942. Holds stamps #51-101.
Complete With Stamps Unmounted Or Neatly Mounted - **$35 $60 $125**

DIS-10

❑ **DIS-10. "War Insignia Stamp Album" Volume 3,**
1942. Holds stamps #102-151. Complete With Stamps Unmounted Or Neatly Mounted. Same Value For Book 4 #152-201 (Not Shown) Each - **$45 $85 $150**

DIS-11

DIS-12

❑ **DIS-11. "Mickey's Dog Pluto" All Picture Comics BLB,**
1943. © Walt Disney. Tall Comic Book format. - **$30 $90 $180**

❑ **DIS-12. Firestone Giveaway Comic,**
1943. Features Carl Bark art. - **$75 $225 $825**
1944-1949 issues - See the Overstreet Comic Book Price Guide for values.

DIS-13

❑ **DIS-13. War Bond Certificate,**
1944. United States Treasury Finance Committee. Also see Donald Duck items DNL-49 & 50. - **$40 $75 $150**

DIS-14

❑ **DIS-14. "Winter Draws On" Safety Booklet,**
c. 1944. Safety Education Division Flight Control Command. - **$25 $50 $80**

DIS-15

❑ **DIS-15. "The Flying Donkey and Gauchito" Dolls,**
1945. Cloth-stuffed dolls featured in the animated segment "The Flying Gauchito" from the Disney film "The Three Caballeros." Made in Mexico. - **$150 $300 $500**

DIS-16

❑ **DIS-16. Cheerios 7 oz. Cereal Box with Comic Book Offer on Back,**
1946. Brer Rabbit pictured on front. - **$200 $400 $650**

DIS-17

❑ **DIS-17. Mickey Mouse Library of Games,**
1946. Comes with 6 card games, holder and instructions for each game. - **$75 $200 $300**

DIS-18

❑ **DIS-18. "Walt Disney's Comics And Stories" Subscription Christmas Card,**
c. 1948. - **$25 $60 $110**

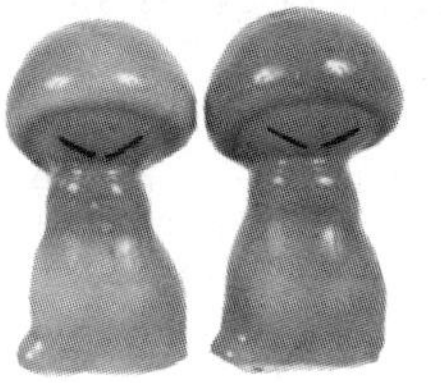

DIS-19

DIS-20

❑ **DIS-19. Fantasia Mushroom Salt & Pepper Set,**
1940s. Two versions.
Vernon Kiln - **$50 $100 $200**
American Pottery - **$35 $65 $125**

❑ **DIS-20. Insignia Cards With Disney Designs,**
1940s. Two shown from a set of nine. - **$5 $12 $20**

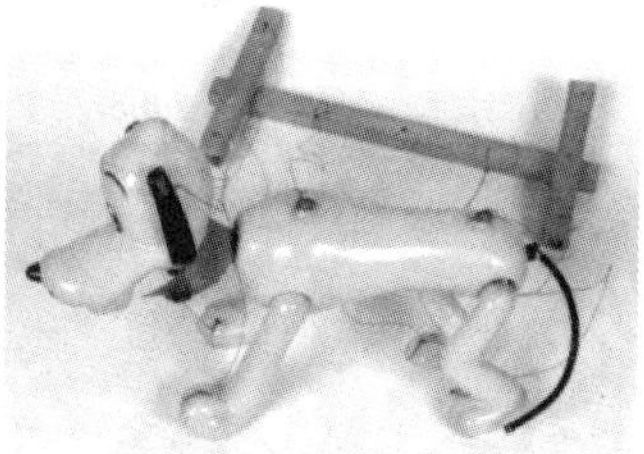

DIS-21

❑ **DIS-21. Madame Alexander Marionette,**
1940s. Store item and also offered in Mickey Mouse Magazine as a contest prize. Composition 8" long with fabric collar and fabric covered rubber tail. - **$150 $300 $500**

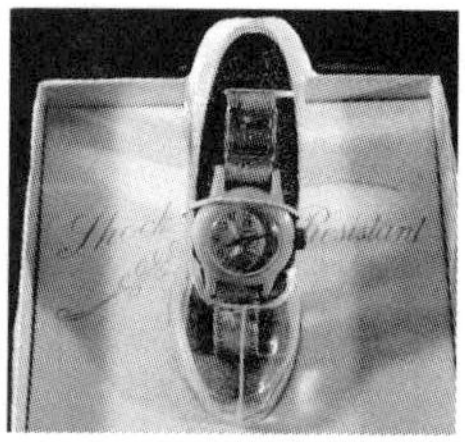

DIS-22

DIS-23

❑ **DIS-22. Cinderella Watch on Glass Slipper in Box,**
1950. - **$100 $250 $375**

❑ **DIS-23. "Cinderella" Movie Promotion 6" Cello. Button,**
1950. RKO movie theaters. - **$25 $50 $100**

DIS-24

❑ **DIS-24. "Wheaties" Box With "Walt Disney Comic Books" Ad,**
1950. 32 comics offered 1950-1951.
Complete Box - **$85 $225 $350**

DIS-25

❑ **DIS-25. Wheaties Comic Set A,**
1950. Set of eight. #8 not shown.
Donald Duck issues each - **$9 $27 $70**
Mickey Mouse issues each - **$6 $18 $40**
Other issues each - **$5 $15 $35**

DIS-26

❑ **DIS-26. Wheaties Comic Set B,**
1950. Set of eight.
Donald Duck issues each - **$9 $27 $70**
Mickey Mouse issues each - **$6 $18 $40**
Other issues each - **$5 $15 $35**

DIS-27

❑ **DIS-27. "Oh Sing Sweet Nightingale" Song Sheet,**
1950. Featured in the movie "Cinderella."
Artist copy in black & white - **$15 $30 $45**
Regular issue - **$7 $14 $28**

DIS-28

❑ **DIS-28. Wheaties Comic Set C,**
1951. Set of eight.
Donald Duck issues each - **$9 $27 $70**
Mickey Mouse issues each - **$6 $18 $40**
Other issues each - **$5 $15 $35**
(Set D, Not Shown, Same Values)

DIS-29

❑ **DIS-29. "Walt Disney's Comics And Stories" Gift Subscription Christmas Card,**
c. 1951. Dell Publishing Co. - **$35 $60 $115**

DIS-30

❑ **DIS-30. "Robin Hood Flour" Store Sign,**
1952. 9-1/2x17" promoting company's product and Disney movie. - **$25 $50 $85**

DIS-31

❑ **DIS-31. Cheerios 3-D Comics,**
1954. 24 in set. Each - **$10 $30 $75**

DIS-32

❑ **DIS-32. "Lady And The Tramp" Store Poster And Premium Set,**
c. 1955. Scotch Tape. 14-1/2x30" sign advertises set of eight plastic dog premiums issued one per tape dispenser. Figures punch out and stand up. Set includes Lady, Tramp, Bull, Trusty, Peg, Pedro, Jock, Dachy. Gordon Gold Archives. Sign - **$50 $100 $150**
Each Unpunched Premium - **$5 $10 $15**

DIS-33

DIS-34

❑ **DIS-33. Brer Rabbit "Ice Cream For The Party As Told By Uncle Remus" Comic Booklet,**
1955. American Dairy Assoc. - **$50 $150 $375**

❑ **DIS-34. Lady And The Tramp "Butter Late Than Never" Comic Booklet,**
1955. American Dairy Assoc. - **$10 $30 $85**

DIS-35

❑ **DIS-35. Plastic Dogs Newspaper Advertisement,**
1955. Scotch Tape. Set of 7. Each - **$3 $5 $10**

DIS-36

❑ **DIS-36. Hardy Boys Secret Compartment Doubloon Ring,**
1956. Weather-Bird Shoes. Holds pop-out plastic coin picturing them on one side and 1808 Spanish coin on other side. Second content is cardboard disk printed by treasure map directions on one side and sponsor logo on other. - **$75 $125 $175**

DIS-37

❑ **DIS-37. "Walt Disney's Magazine" Vol. 4 #1,**
1958. Example issue. Published 6/57 - 10/59. Continuation of Walt Disney's Mickey Mouse Club Magazine. Each - **$10 $20 $40**

DIS-38

DIS-39

❑ **DIS-38. Sleeping Beauty Prince Philip Ring,**
1959. Plastic topped by sword on shield inscribed "Truth/Virtue". - **$20 $40 $60**

❑ **DIS-39. Maleficent Figurine,**
c. 1959. Store item by Hagen-Renaker. Raven often missing or damaged. 2-1/2" tall painted and glazed. - **$250 $500 $750**

DIS-40

❑ **DIS-40. Pluto Drum Major Wind-Up,**
1950s. Store item by Line Mar. 7" tall with baton and bell in hands and horn in mouth.
Box - **$100 $200 $300**
Toy - **$100 $250 $400**

DIS-41

❑ **DIS-41. Goofy Cyclist Wind-Up,**
1950s. 7-1/4" tall tin litho store item by Line Mar. - **$250 $500 $1000**

(Front)

(Back)

DIS-42

❑ **DIS-42. Tiny Golden Books Library Set,**
1950s. "Tiny Golden Theater" box holds 12 tiny Golden Library books. - **$75 $150 $225**

DIS-43

❑ **DIS-43. Disneykins Boxed Set,**
c. 1961. RCA Victor. - **$35 $60 $125**

DIS-44

❑ **DIS-44. Studio Christmas Card,**
1962. - **$40 $75 $150**

DIS-45

❑ **DIS-45. Sword In The Stone Mechanical Plastic Ring,**
1963. Miniature sword withdraws from holder. - **$10 $20 $35**

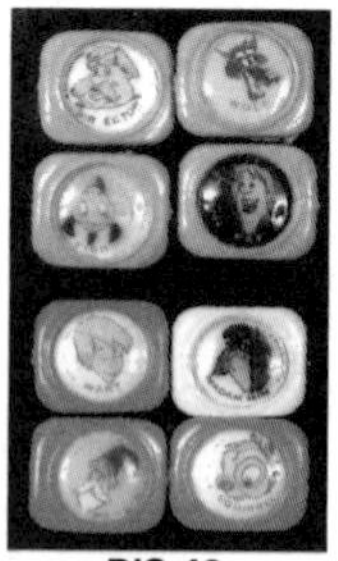
DIS-46

❑ **DIS-46. Sword In The Stone Plastic Ring Set,**
1963. Sponsor unknown, set of eight. Fish, Kay, Madam Min, Merlin, Sir Ector, Squirrel, Wart, Wolf. Each - **$10 $15 $30**

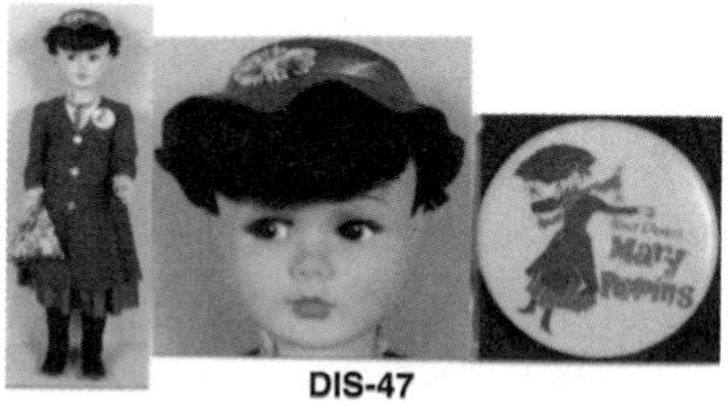

DIS-47

❑ **DIS-47. "Mary Poppins" Giant Doll With Button,**
1964. 35" tall store item by Horsman.
Doll - **$75 $150 $225**
Button - **$15 $30 $50**

DIS-48

❑ **DIS-48. "Mary Poppins Pop-Up" Cereal Box,**
1964. Nabisco Rice or Wheat Honeys. Back panel pictures and describes box insert plastic toy. Bert the Chimney Sweep was also issued.
Each Box - **$50 $125 $225**
Each Pop-Up - **$15 $25 $45**

DIS-49

❑ **DIS-49. "Mary Poppins Whirling Toy" Plastic Wind-Up,**
1964. Store item by Marx. 8" tall hard plastic.
Box - **$25 $50 $75**
Toy - **$50 $75 $125**

DIS-50

❑ **DIS-50. Jungle Book Swingers Plastic Figures,**
1967. Nabisco Wheat and Rice Honeys.
Set of six: Mowgli, Baloo, King Louie, Buzzy, Bagheera, Kaa.
Each - **$3 $8 $12**

DIS-51

❑ **DIS-51. "Jungle Book Swap Cards",**
1967. Nabisco. Australian numbered set of 24.
Set - **$15 $30 $60**

DIS-52

❑ **DIS-52. "The Love Bug Coloring Book",**
1969. Hunt's Ketchup. - **$5 $8 $15**

DIS-53

❑ **DIS-53. "Crazy College Pennant Collector's" 17x22" Poster With Pennants,**
1975. Wonder Bread. Poster Only - **$5 $8 $15**
Complete - **$20 $40 $60**

DIS-54

❑ **DIS-54. "Crazy License Plates Collectors'" 22x26" Poster With Stickers,**
1975. Wonder Bread. Poster Only - **$5 $8 $15**
Complete - **$20 $40 $60**

DIS-55

DIS-56

❑ **DIS-55. "NSDA Convention/Anaheim, California" Glass Soda Bottle,**
1977. National Soft Drink Association. - **$8 $15 $35**

❑ **DIS-56. "The Jungle Book Fun Book",**
1978. Baskin-Robbins Ice Cream. - **$5 $8 $12**

DIS-57

❑ **DIS-57. Corn Flakes Cereal Box with "Black Cauldron" Movie Premium,**
1985. Canadian box . Offers a model in each package. - **$20 $40 $100**

DIS-58

DIS-59

❑ **DIS-58. Roger Rabbit 17" Plush Doll in Benny the Car Cardboard Box,**
1988. - **$10 $25 $50**

❑ **DIS-59. Roger Rabbit 13 3/4" Super Flex Figure on Card,**
1988. - **$10 $25 $50**

DIS-60

❑ **DIS-60. "Who Framed Roger Rabbit" Movie Board Game,**
1988. Hard to find due to low production run.
Boxed - **$25 $50 $100**

DIS-61

❑ **DIS-61. "Alice at the Mad Hatter's Tea Party",** Late 1980s. Crafted by master sculpturor Enzo Arzenton. Edition 322. - **$3500**

DIS-62

DIS-63

❑ **DIS-62. Daisy Duck 13" Porcelain Doll,** 1991. Limited edition from the Franklin Mint. - **$75 $150 $250**

❑ **DIS-63. Dewey 9" Porcelain Figure,** 1991. Limited edition from the Franklin Mint. - **$40 $80 $150**

DIS-64

DIS-65

❑ **DIS-64. Huey 9" Porcelain Figure,** 1991. Limited edition from the Franklin Mint. - **$40 $80 $150**

❑ **DIS-65. Louie 9" Porcelain Figure,** 1991. Limited edition from the Franklin Mint. - **$40 $80 $150**

DIS-66

❑ **DIS-66. "Minnie on the Beach" Figure,** 1993. Very unusual Capodiamonte figure; a sold out edition of only 197. - **$600**

DIS-67

DIS-68

❑ **DIS-67. "Simba" Bean Bag Figure,** 1998. From the Broadway Lion King set of 10. Simba shown with 2 tags - **$20**
Other 9 figures each - **$15**

❑ **DIS-68. "Cruella" Hat with 2 Tags,** 1999. From the "101 Dalmations" movie. Has badge on front. - **$10**

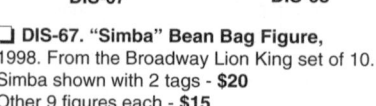

DIS-69

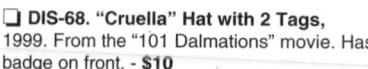

❑ **DIS-69. "Roger Rabbit" Snow Globe,** 1999. - **$65**

DIS-70

❑ **DIS-70. "Villains" Snow Globe,** 1999. Features all the nasty Disney character crew. - **$75**

DIS-71

❑ **DIS-71. "Cinderella" Snow Globe,** 1990s. Has working clock on top. - **$75**

DIS-72

❑ **DIS-72. "Pecos Bill" Statue,**
1990s. From the Disney Classic collection. Limited to 10,462. - **$475**

DIS-73

❑ **DIS-73. "Slue Foot Sue" Statue,**
1990s. From the Disney Classic collection. - **$550**

DIS-74

❑ **DIS-74. "Happy 2000" Bean Bags,**
1999. Mickey, Donald and Goofy bean bags in top hat designed to celebrate the Year 2000. With tag. - **$10 $20 $30**

DIS-75

❑ **DIS-75. "The Tortoise and the Hare" Movie Figures,**
2000. Two figures from the Disney Classic collection. Each - **$100**

DIS-76

DIS-77

❑ **DIS-76. Goofy Paddle Ball,**
2000. From Tootsietoy. - **$20**

❑ **DIS-77. "Walt and Mickey 2000" Coin and Card,**
2000. Last in series of 55 different. - **$30**

## Disneyana Convention

**In 1992, The Walt Disney Company hosted the very first convention solely for the collectors of Disney memorabilia. This signaled that Disney corporately recognized the importance of collectors in the secondary market and their tie in with the promotion of new Disney toys. This set the stage for the production of limited edition material to be offered only to attendees at the convention. The extravaganza is held each year at Walt Disney World in Orlando. The operation at the convention falls under the Park Division of The Walt Disney Company and the staff for the meetings are employees of that section. A substantial fee is charged for attendance.**

**If you are a Disney collector, this show is for you. Each year special buttons and badges are given out as part of your arrival kit, and some are sold at a special store open to attendees only. The theme of the event is changed every year and a limited edition resin figure is produced to support that theme. It is sold through a lottery drawing. This means there is a shortage, which creates demand on the secondary market. Even at the show, the buttons, badges and resins can bring a high percentage over the original value because of the limited supply. Disney also presents an auction each year of older material from their archives at the gathering. Some of the prices realized are astonishing. This category of character merchandise will expand with each new edition of our book as long as the convention continues. We have selected the event-themed resins, badges and buttons to be shown in this edition.**

DSA-1

❑ **DSA-1. "Steamboat Mickey" Figure,**
1990. First resin Convention figure produced, with only 600 made. Mickey is featured as the star of the 1928 cartoon *Steamboat Willie*. It sold out at the convention and is always in high demand in the secondary market because of it being the 1st in the series and the low number of figures produced. - **$1600**

DSA-2

DSA-3

❑ **DSA-2. "1st Convention" Pin on Card,**
1992. Pin is 1 1/2" high.
On original card - **$80-$100**

❑ **DSA-3. "1st Convention" Badge,**
1992. Badge has 4" diameter. - **$20-$30**

DSA-4

DSA-5

❑ **DSA-4. "1st Convention" Badge,**
1992. Shaped like Mickey's head. - **$10-$15**

❑ **DSA-5. "1st Convention" Badge,**
1992. Limited edition badge sold out at the first Convention. 2 3/4" long. - **$8-$10**

DSA-6

DSA-7

❑ **DSA-6. "Sorcerer's Apprentice" Figure,**
1993. Convention resin. Edition of 2,000. - **$250**

❑ **DSA-7. "Band Concert" Figure,**
1993. Mickey Mouse as conductor in this limited resin figure of 1,200. Sold out at the 1993 convention. - **$300**

DSA-8

❑ **DSA-8. 1993 Convention Flicker Badge,**
1993. Features Mickey and Donald. Badge has 4" diameter. - **$15-$20**

DSA-9

❑ **DSA-9. "40th Anniversary of Disneyland",**
1994. Convention resin of Mickey and Minnie, limited to 1,500. - **$225**

DSA-10

DSA-11

❑ **DSA-10. "40 Years of Adventure" Pin,**
1995. On card. - **$15-$25**

❑ **DSA-11. "40 Years of Adventure" Flicker Badge,**
1995. 4" diameter. - **$10-$15**

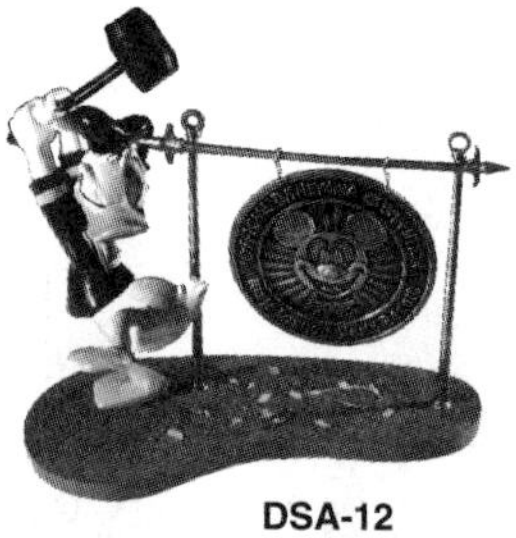

DSA-12

❑ **DSA-12. Donald Duck with Gong,**
1995. Convention resin. - **$75 $100 $200**

DSA-13

DSA-14

❑ **DSA-13. "Mickey Mouse Club" Pin,**
1995. Limited edition pin promotes the anniversary of the show. On card. - **$14-$18**

❑ **DSA-14. Employees Pin**
1995. Used only by staff assigned to Convention duties. Scarce. - **$15 $25 $50**

DSA-15

DSA-16

❑ **DSA-15. "Mickey Mouse Club" Figure,**
1995. Resin limited edition of 2,000. Sold out at the 1995 convention. - **$350**

❑ **DSA-16. "Brave Little Tailor" Figure,**
1996. Mickey Mouse featured in this limited resin figure of 1,500. Sold out at the 1996 convention. - **$250**

DSA-17

DSA-18

❑ **DSA-17. "5th Convention" Pin on Card,**
1996. Theme of "Mickey and the Beanstalk." - **$12-$15**

❑ **DSA-18. " '96 Convention" Pin on Card,**
1996. Theme of "Mickey and the Beanstalk." - **$12-$15**

DSA-19

DSA-20

❑ **DSA-19. 1996 Convention Flicker Badge,**
1996. 4" diameter. - **$10-$15**

❑ **DSA-20. 1996 Convention Badge,**
1996. Theme of "Mickey and the Beanstalk." 4" diameter. - **$10-$15**

DSA-21

DSA-22

❑ **DSA-21. 1997 Official Pin,**
1997. Proclaims "I am a Convention Ear." 1 1/4" diameter. - **$18-$25**

❑ **DSA-22. 1997 Convention Badge,**
1997. 3" diameter. - **$10-$15**

DSA-23

DSA-24

❑ **DSA-23. Disney Catalog Badge,**
1997. Convention theme was "Disney Villains." - **$5-$8**

❑ **DSA-24. Disney Villains Pinback,**
1997. 4" diameter pinback with Convention theme. - **$10-$15**

DSA-25

DSA-26

❑ **DSA-25. Villains Flicker Badge,**
1997. 4" diameter badge shows Chernobog from *Fantasia*. - **$10-$15**

❑ **DSA-26. "Black Pete" Pin,**
1997. Promotes the Convention's Villain theme. - **$12-$15**

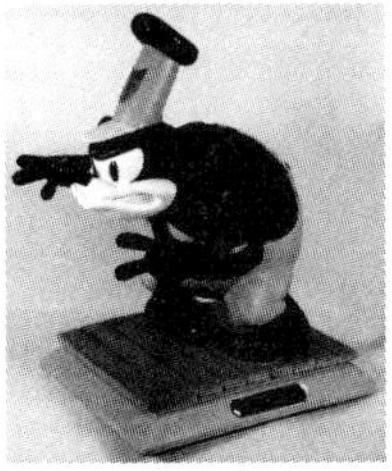
DSA-27

❑ **DSA-27. "Peg Leg Pete" Figure,**
1997. Limited (1,000 made) resin figure of villain from cartoon *Steamboat Willie*. Sold out at the 1997 convention. - **$225**

DSA-28

DSA-29

DSA-30

❑ **DSA-28. Official Convention Pin,**
1998. 1 1/2" pin promotes "75 Years of Love and Laughter." - **$12-$15**

❑ **DSA-29. Convention Flicker Badge,**
1998. 3" diameter. - **$8-$10**

❑ **DSA-30. Badge with Hanging Pin on Card,**
1998. Features the whole gang: Mickey and Minnie, Donald and Daisy, Goofy and of course, Pluto. - **$18-$25**

DSA-31

DSA-32

❑ **DSA-31. Safari Adventure Flicker Badge,**
1999. - **$5-$7**

❑ **DSA-32. "Serengeti Seminars" Pin,**
1999. Special pin for those who attended Walkabout Workshops. Had *Lion King* theme. - **$8-$10**

DSA-33

DSA-34

❑ **DSA-33. Safari Adventure Party Program,**
1999. By Disney Art Classics. - **$2 $4 $6**

❑ **DSA-34. Donald Duck *Fantasia 2000* Pin,**
1999. Promotes movie. Limited to 2,500.
On card - **$40**

DSA-35

❑ **DSA-35. "The Pointer" Figure,**
1999. Mickey Mouse resin honoring the 1939 film *The Pointer*. Limited to 1,500. Sold out at the 1999 convention. - **$250**

DSA-36

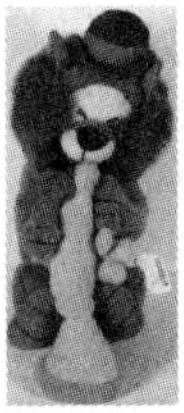
DSA-37

DSA-38

❑ **DSA-36. "Chinese Cat" Bean Figure,**
1999. 7" tall. From the set of 5 "Aristocat" bean figures. - **$15**

❑ **DSA-37. "Scat Cat" Bean Figure,**
1999. 8 1/2" tall "Aristocat" bean figure. - **$15**

❑ **DSA-38. "English Cat" Bean Figure,**
1999. 8" tall "Aristocat" bean figure. - **$15**

DSA-39

DSA-40

❑ **DSA-39. "Italian Cat" Bean Figure,**
1999. 8" tall "Aristocat" bean figure. - **$15**

❑ **DSA-40. "Russian Cat" Bean Figure,**
1999. 8" tall "Aristocat" bean figure. - **$15**

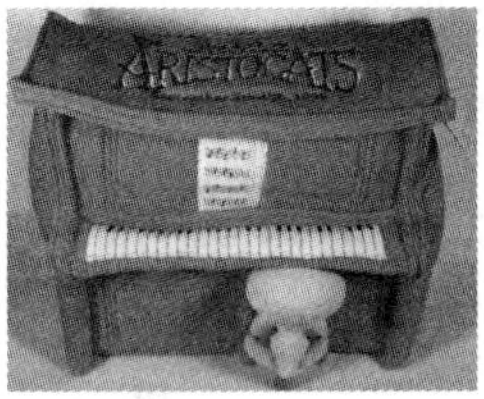

DSA-41

❑ **DSA-41. "Aristocats" Plush Piano,**
Sept. 7-11, 1999. Special event product offered only at the 1999 Convention. The Piano is the holder for the "Aristocat" bean figures. - **$30**

DSA-42

DSA-43

DSA-44

❑ **DSA-42. "Mickey" Bean Figure,**
1999. With tag. 1999 Convention. - **$20**

❑ **DSA-43. "Minnie" Bean Figure,**
1999. With tag. 1999 Convention. - **$20**

❑ **DSA-44. "Mickey" Bean Figure,**
2000. With tag. 2000 Convention. - **$20**

DSA-45

DSA-46

❑ **DSA-45. Convention Badge,**
2000. - **$15**

❑ **DSA-46. Convention Badge,**
2000. - **$20**

DSA-47

DSA-48

❑ **DSA-47. Flicker Badge,**
2000. - **$20**

❑ **DSA-48. "It's a Small World" Badge With Pin Hanging,**
2000. On card. - **$25 $30**

DSA-49

DSA-50

❑ **DSA-49. Convention Pin,**
2000. - **$25**

❑ **DSA-50. "It's a Small World" Resin Figure,**
2000. Only 1,000 made. - **$200**

DSA-51

DSA-52

❑ **DSA-51. Family Reunion Pin,**
2001. Has die-cut face of Mickey on top. - **$15**

❑ **DSA-52. Family Reunion Pin,**
2001. Shows Mickey taking pictures. - **$15**

DSA-53

DSA-54

❑ **DSA-53. Cloth Holder with Badge,**
2001. Premium for each registered guest. - **$20**

❑ **DSA-54. California Adventure Pin Badge,**
2001. A Disney Family Reunion theme. - **$20**

DSA-55

DSA-56

❑ **DSA-55. Disneyana Pin,**
2001. Features shadow of Walt Disney in window telling Mickey to have fun at Walt's 100th Birthday Reunion Celebration. - **$15**

❑ **DSA-56. Walt's Workshop Pin,**
2001. Has photo image of Walt. - **$15**

**(Stickers)**

(Box)
DSA-57

❑ **DSA-57. Premium Sticker Set,**
2001. 12 stickers in box. - **$15**

DSA-58

(Back)

❑ **DSA-58. Promotional Plush,**
2001. Donald and his nephews take a ride to Walt's 100th Anniversary Reunion. Plush figures with tag. - **$60**

## Disneyland

**Sunday, July 17, 1955 began a new concept in Disney entertainment. The day officially opened Disneyland, a 230-acre complex in Anaheim, California on ground that was flat orange groves only a year before. The park's major components--Main Street U.S.A., Fantasyland, Frontierland, Adventureland, Tomorrowland--have been continuously refined and expanded annually to assure fresh entertainment year by year. Disneyland shops, of course, retail a virtually endless array of souvenir items with ceramics and jewelry quite popular. Giveaway premiums of paper items, buttons and the like, are quite frequent. Similar memorabilia is offered at Disneyland parks in France and Tokyo as well as Disney World, Epcot Center, and the MGM Studios Theme Parks.**

DIY-1

DIY-2

DIY-3

❑ **DIY-1. "The Story Of Disneyland" Guide Book,**
1955. The first guide book. - **$50 $100 $200**

❑ **DIY-2. "The Disneyland News" Vol. 1 #1,**
1955. - **$50 $100 $200**

❑ **DIY-3. "Fly TWA To Disneyland" Schedule Book,**
1955. Effective July 1 for July 17 opening day. - **$35 $75 $150**

DIY-4

❑ **DIY-4. Disney Studio Christmas Card,**
1955. Features illustrated aerial view of Disneyland with 1956 calendar. - **$75 $125 $250**

DIY-5

DIY-6

❑ **DIY-5. Souvenir Menu,**
1955. Carnation Ice Cream Parlor, Disneyland. Overall size of 4-3/4x9-3/4" but designed to be folded and mailed. Near Mint Unfolded - **$60**
Folded - **$10 $20 $30**

❑ **DIY-6. Leather Coin Purse,**
1955. - **$20 $35 $75**

DIY-7

DIY-8

❑ **DIY-7. Guide Book,**
1956. Second annual issue. - **$40 $75 $150**

❑ **DIY-8. Disneyland Guide Book,**
1957. Third annual issue with year printed on top right cover corner. - **$40 $85 $160**

DIY-9

DIY-10

❑ **DIY-9. "Tom Sawyer Island" Map Folder,**
1957. Mostly green and brown 4x9" opening to 9x12". - **$15 $25 $65**

❑ **DIY-10. "Sleeping Beauty Castle" Souvenir Book,**
1957. Sold at Disneyland. - **$15 $30 $65**

DIY-11

❑ **DIY-11."Disneyland/Dutch Boy" Large Display,**
c. 1957. Store display by Dutch Boy Paints. 8x32-1/2x18-1/2" tall. - **$250 $500 $1000**

DIY-12

❑ **DIY-12. Flicker Picture Card,**
c. 1958. 2x2-1/2" "Souvenir From The Art Corner At Disneyland" picturing Tinkerbell at castle. - **$15 $25 $40**

DIY-13

❑ **DIY-13. "Chesterfriend Chocolate Cigarettes" Plastic Pack,**
1950s. Disneyland Candy Palace. Park souvenir. - **$15 $30 $70**

DIY-14

DIY-15

❑ **DIY-14. "Disneyland And Santa Fe" Brochure,**
1950s. Park brochure with Santa Fe advertising. - **$10 $20 $40**

❑ **DIY-15. "Butter Mints" Tin Container,**
1950s. Disneyland Candy Palace. Park souvenir. - **$20 $40 $85**

DIY-16

❑ **DIY-16. "Walt Disney's Guide To Disneyland" Book,**
1960. Sold at Disneyland. - **$15 $35 $75**

DIY-17

DIY-18

❑ **DIY-17. "Win A Trip To Disneyland" Donald Duck Contest Form,**
1960. - **$5 $12 $20**

❑ **DIY-18. "Disneyland Hotel" Match Pack,**
c. 1960. - **$5 $10 $15**

DIY-19

DIY-20

❑ **DIY-19. "Disneyland Adventureland View-Master" Set,**
c. 1962. - **$35 $75 $125**

❑ **DIY-20. "Disneyland Tomorrowland View-Master" Set,**
c. 1962. - **$35 $75 $125**

DIY-21

❑ **DIY-21. "Disneyland" Map,**
1968. Park souvenir. 30x45". - **$35 $65 $100**

DIY-22

DIY-23

❑ **DIY-22. "Disneyland/General Electric" Sheet Music,**
1968. Theme song for Electric Carousel of Progress. - **$10 $20 $30**

❑ **DIY-23. Souvenir Guide,**
1968. Park souvenir. - **$10 $25 $40**

DIY-24

❑ **DIY-24. "Pirate Party Kit",**
1960s. Chicken of the Sea. Based on Pirate Ship Restaurant in Disneyland. Many pieces including eight place mats, paper game, hats, eye patches, etc.
Complete In Envelope - **$25 $50 $85**

DIY-25

DIY-26

❑ **DIY-25. Pepsi "I've Been To The Golden Horseshoe" 2" Litho. Button,**
1960s. - **$15 $25 $50**

❑ **DIY-26. "Club 55" Employee 10K Gold Award Ring,**
1975. Awarded to 92 employees of continuous service since Disneyland opening in 1955. Images on band include Disneyland castle, inner band has award date and initials of recipient. - **$250 $500 $1000**

DIY-27

❑ **DIY-27. "The Disneyland Railroad" Poster,**
c. 1977. 18x24" stiff paper. - **$15 $40 $60**

DIY-28

DIY-29

❑ **DIY-28. "Disneyland 25th Birthday Party" 2-1/4" Cello. Button,**
1980. - **$5 $12 $20**

❑ **DIY-29. 40th Anniversary Cookie Jar,**
1995. Nestle Products. 11" tall large three-dimensional ceramic limited edition replica of Sleeping Beauty castle. - **$25 $75 $150**

## Dixie Ice Cream

**The disposable paper drinking cup, called the Health Cup, had been around for 15 years when the Individual Drinking Cup Company changed its name to the Dixie Cup and began offering ice cream franchises in Cleveland in 1923. Dixie Cup has since become part of the language. Lithographed photographs printed on the underside of the cup lids helped sell the five-cent ice cream. The first were a set of 24 animals featured on the *Dixie Circus* radio program (Blue network, 1929-1930, and CBS, 1930-1931 and 1934). In the early 1930s a set of 24 MGM movie stars followed, with an offer of enlarged photographs in exchange for a number of lids. A "Defend America" lid series in the early 1940s featured pictures of tanks and battleships, also available as enlarged full color pictures in exchange for lids. The company continued offering lids and picture sets into the early 1950s.**

DIX-1

❑ **DIX-1. Early Waxed Cardboard Lid,**
c. 1920. Scarce. Patent date of 1918. Lid reads "This Lunch Box Dixie Made By The Individual Drinking Cup Co., Inc." - **$10 $25 $50**

DIX-2

❑ **DIX-2. Circus Punch-Out Set,**
1929. Stage and cut-outs in Series A-F and possibly more. Art by illustrator Dan Smith.
Stage - **$25 $60 $125**
Each Cut-Out - **$5 $10 $15**

DIX-3

DIX-4

❑ **DIX-3. "Animal Heroes Of Dixie's Circus Radio Stories" Lids,**
c. 1930. Waxed cardboard set of 24 numbered cup lids, each 2-1/4" diameter. Each - **$2 $4 $6**

❑ **DIX-4. First Series Movie Star Dixie Lids,**
1933. From set of 24 with M-G-M stars only.
Each **$5 $10 $15**

DIX-5

❑ **DIX-5. "Portraits" 12x17" Cardboard Store Sign,**
c. 1935. Easel sign picturing example of Barbara Stanwyck from "Annie Oakley" 1935 movie. - **$75 $175 $300**

DIX-6

❑ **DIX-6. Dixie Lid Album,**
1935. Breyers Ice Cream. 6x7" stiff paper which unfolds to 18" long with diecut slots to hold 15 lids which could then be exchanged for larger full color picture. - **$20 $50 $90**

DIX-7

❑ **DIX-7. "Movie Stars Ice Cream Dixie Lids" 6x18" Paper Sign,**
c. 1930s. - **$50 $125 $175**

DIX-8

❑ **DIX-8. "Defend America" Dixie Picture Covers,**
1941. Front and back covers are 8x10" and inside back cover lists the 24 pictures in the series. Pair - **$10 $20 $40**

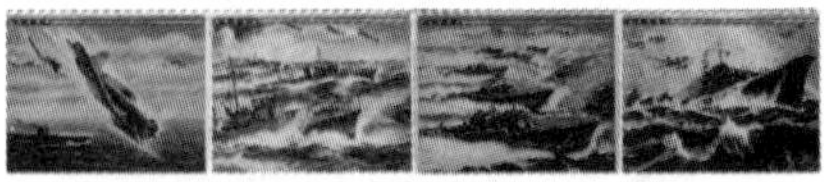

DIX-9

❑ **DIX-9. "America's Fighting Forces" Dixie Pictures,**
c. 1942. Four examples from set.
Each - **$8 $12 $20**

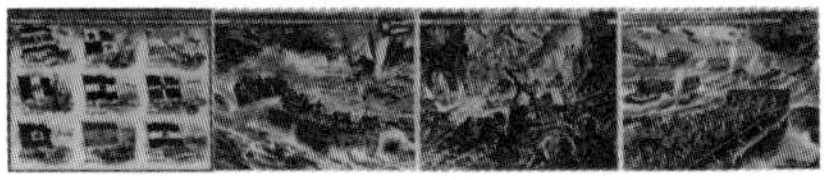

DIX-10

❑ **DIX-10. "United Nations At War" Dixie Pictures,**
c. 1944. Four examples from set.
Each - **$8 $12 $20**

DIX-11

DIX-12

❑ **DIX-11. "United Nations At War" Lid Set,**
c. 1944. Set of 24. Each - **$3 $5 $12**

❑ **DIX-12. Al "Lash" LaRue Dixie Picture,**
1947. - **$20 $40 $75**

DIX-13

❑ **DIX-13. "William 'Bill' Elliott" Dixie Picture,**
1948. - **$10 $20 $40**

DIX-14

❑ **DIX-14. Covers For Celebrity Dixie Pictures,**
c. 1950. Titled "My Picture Book Of Movie, Cowboy And TV Stars" with front and back cover size of 8x10". Pair - **$15 $30 $50**

## Dizzy Dean

**Baseball's Jerome Herman Dean or Jay Hanna Dean (1911-1974), known to all as "Dizzy," was an outstanding pitcher for the St. Louis Cardinals from 1932 to 1938 and then for the Chicago Cubs (1938-1940). He was named the National League's Most Valuable Player in 1934, when his win-loss record of 30-7 helped carry the Cardinals to the World Championship. In 1952 his life story was the basis of the movie *Pride of St. Louis* and he was elected to the Baseball Hall of Fame in 1953. Dean did the radio broadcasts of St. Louis games from 1941 to 1949, where his grammar proved to be as challenging as his pitching--"he slud into third!" In 1948 Dean did a dozen weekly shows on NBC radio for Johnson Wax. His *Dizzy Dean Winners*, sponsored by Post cereals in the 1930s and promoted in Sunday comic sections, offered pins, rings and other premiums to young fans.**

DZY-1

❑ **DZY-1. Dizzy Dean Watch with Box,**
1933. Watch has either metal band or leather strap. Comes in colorful box. Rare.
Boxed - **$2000**

DZY-2

DZY-3

❑ **DZY-2. Dizzy Dean Watch Newspaper Ad,**
1933. From the Everbrite Watch Company. Leather strip band is shown. Even in 1933, you could still get time payments. - **$35**

❑ **DZY-3. Photo Baseball Card,**
1933. Tattoo Orbit. - **$60 $290 $625**

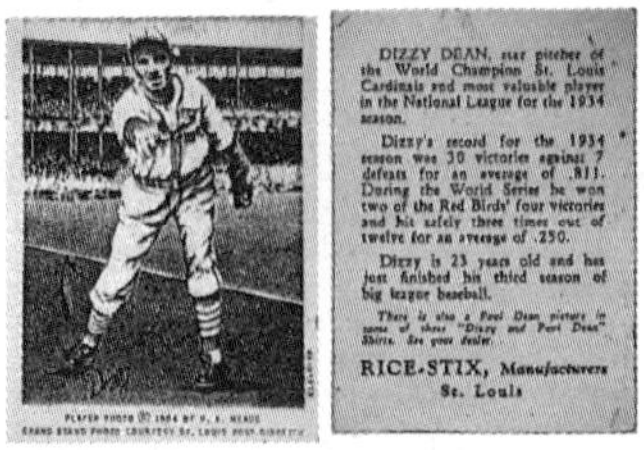


DZY-4

❑ **DZY-4. Premium Photo Card,**
1934. Rice-Stix, St. Louis. This and a matching Paul Dean picture were included with "Some Of These 'Dizzy And Paul Dean' Shirts." Cards are 2-1/4x3-1/4" in red and white.
Each - **$50 $125 $200**

DZY-5

DZY-6

❑ **DZY-5. Sepiatone Facsimile Autographed Portrait,**
1935. - **$40 $100 $150**

❑ **DZY-6. Grape-Nuts Booklet,**
1935. - **$25 $50 $100**

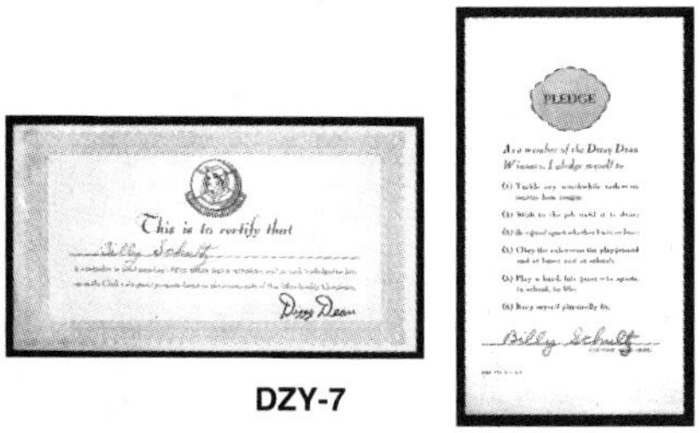


DZY-7

❑ **DZY-7. "Dizzy Dean Winners" Club Certificate,**
1935. Post Cereals. Both front and back pictured. This sample belonged to the Mayor of Cleveland, Tenn., Billy Schultz from his childhood. - **$15 $40 $85**

DZY-8

❑ **DZY-8. Post's "Dizzy Dean Winners" Brass Club Badge,**
1935. Figural baseball with profile portrait. - **$10 $20 $40**

DZY-9

DZY-10

DZY-11

❑ **DZY-9. Post's "Dizzy Dean Winners" Brass Bat Figural Pin,**
1935. - **$15 $40 $80**

❑ **DZY-10. "Win With Dizzy Dean" Brass Ring,**
1935. Raised portrait and other baseball symbols. - **$75 $150 $250**

❑ **DZY-11. "Dizzy Dean Winners" Brass Baseball Charm,**
1935. - **$15 $40 $75**

DZY-12

DZY-13

❑ **DZY-12. "Dizzy Dean-Good Luck" Brass Token,**
1935. Portrait in horseshoe, back has short inspirational sports text. - **$25 $50 $100**

❑ **DZY-13. Post's "Dizzy Dean Winners" Brass Ring,**
1936. - **$100 $200 $350**

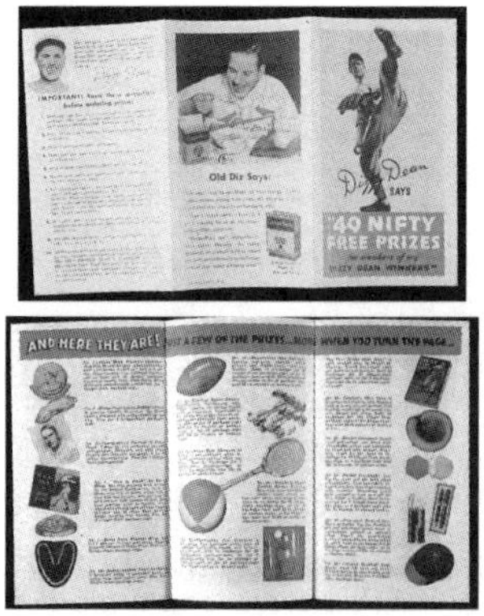


DZY-14

❑ **DZY-14. "Dizzy Dean Winners" Premium Leaflet,**
1936. Grape-Nuts. Pictures "49 nifty free prizes." - **$20 $50 $100**

DZY-15

DZY-16

❑ **DZY-15. "Dizzy Dean Helmet" Leaflet,**
1930s. Store item. Folder including "His Life Story" as supplement to safari-like pith helmet purchase. - **$10 $20 $50**

❑ **DZY-16. Pinback with Small Pennant,**
1939. Small Chicago Cubs pennant is attached. Rare. - **$75 $150 $300**

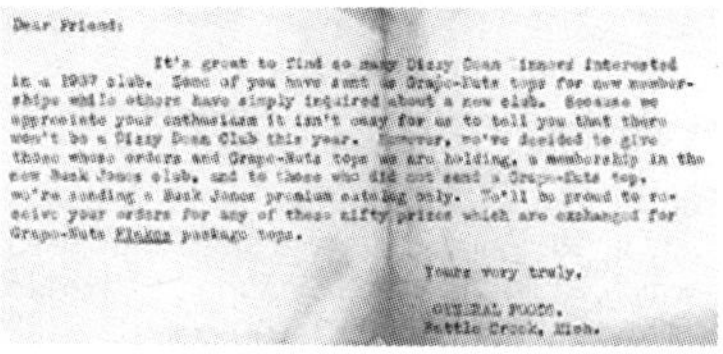

Dear Friend:

It's great to find so many Dizzy Dean fans interested in a 1937 club. Some of you have sent us Grape-Nuts tops for new memberships while others have simply inquired about a new club. Because we appreciate your enthusiasm it isn't easy for us to tell you that there won't be a Dizzy Dean Club this year. However, we've decided to give those whose orders and Grape-Nuts tops we are holding, a membership in the new Buck Jones club, and to those who did not send a Grape-Nuts top, we're sending a Buck Jones premium catalog only. We'll be proud to receive your orders for any of these fifty prizes which are exchanged for Grape-Nuts Flakes package tops.

Yours very truly,

GENERAL FOODS.
Battle Creek, Mich.

DZY-17

❑ **DZY-17. "Dizzy Dean Club" Cancellation Letter,**
1937. Sent to those who sent in a Grape-Nuts box top. A membership in the new Buck Jones Club was given in place of the Dizzy Dean Club. - **$10 $20 $35**

## Doc Savage

**Doc Savage was the superhero of popular pulp magazine stories by Lester Dent and others, published by Street & Smith starting in March 1933. He made his first comic appearance in *Shadow Comics* #1 of March 1940. Two months later he had his own comic book, which lasted only until October 1943, but he continued to show up occasionally in *Shadow Comics* until 1949. There were brief excursions into radio in 1934-1935 and 1942-1943, Warner Brothers made a film--*Doc Savage, Man of Bronze*--starring Ron Ely in 1975 and there have been comic book revivals into the 1990s, but nothing equaled the success of the original pulps. Fans who joined the Doc Savage Club and followed the membership code could obtain badges and other premiums.**

DOC-1

DOC-2

❑ **DOC-1. "The Man Of Bronze" Hardcover Book,**
1933. Store item from Street & Smith Co. Ideal Library Series. - **$40 $80 $175**

❑ **DOC-2. "Quest Of The Spider" Hardcover Book,**
1933. Store item from Street & Smith Co. Ideal Library Series. - **$40 $80 $175**

DOC-3

❑ **DOC-3. "Doc Savage Magazine" 11x14" Cardboard Window Poster,**
1930s. Scarce. Promotes "Doc Savage Radio Program Sponsored By Cystex". - **$125 $400 $650**

DOC-4

DOC-5

DOC-6

❑ **DOC-4. Pulp Magazine Ad Sticker,**
1930s. Example shown has trimmed margins. - **$40 $75 $150**

❑ **DOC-5. Pulp Subscriber Portrait,**
1930s. Doc Savage Magazine. Color print of painting by Robert G. Harris especially for magazine. - **$125 $150 $350**

❑ **DOC-6. Pulp Subscriber Portrait,**
1930s. Scarce. Doc Savage Magazine. Print of painting believed by Walter M. Baumhofer especially for magazine. - **$75 $140 $225**

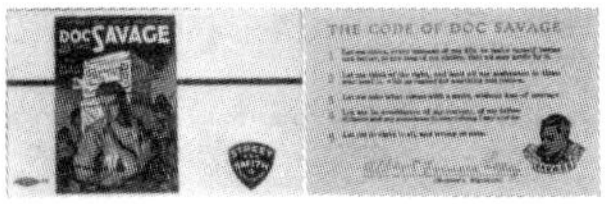


DOC-7

❑ **DOC-7. "The Code Of Doc Savage" Wallet Card,**
1930s. Street & Smith Publishing Co. - **$40 $125 $250**

DOC-8

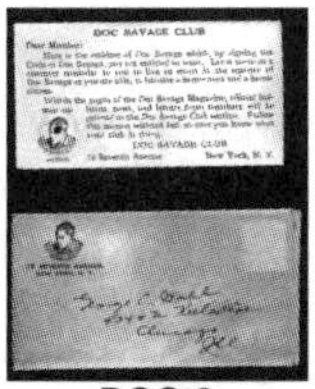


DOC-9

❑ **DOC-8. "Doc Savage Club" Member's Bronze Lapel Stud,**
1930s. - **$75 $150 $250**

❑ **DOC-9. Lapel Stud Card With Envelope,**
1930s. Pair - **$150 $450 $600**

DOC-10

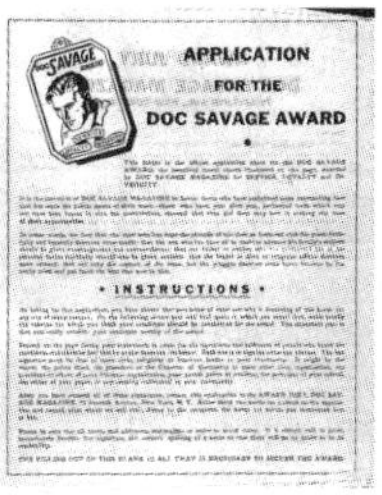


DOC-11

❑ **DOC-10. "Doc Savage Award" Bronze Medallion,**
1930s. Rare. Less than 10 known. Doc Savage pulp magazine. Inscribed "Service-Loyalty-Integrity" below portrait. - **$500 $2000 $3500**

❑ **DOC-11. Application For Doc Savage Award,**
1930s. Scarce. - **$100 $225 $375**

DOC-12

DOC-13

❑ **DOC-12. "Doc Savage Club/Member" Rubber On Wood Stamp Block,**
1930s. Photo example includes image of ink stamped picture. - **$200 $400 $700**

❑ **DOC-13. Movie Card,**
1975. Warner Bros. - **$5 $10 $20**

DOC-14

❑ **DOC-14. "Doc Savage" Hardbacks,**
1975. Published by Golden Press. Set of six. Each **- $2 $5 $8**

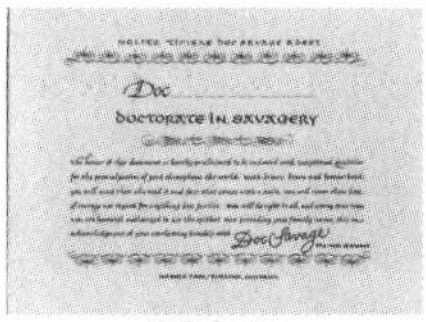

DOC-15

❑ **DOC-15. Commemorative Certificate,**
1975. Warner Bros. From "The Man Of Bronze" film kit. - **$10 $25 $40**

DOC-16

❑ **DOC-16. "Doc Savage/Brotherhood Of Bronze" Fan Club Kit,**
1975. Issued by comic artist Jim Steranko. Contents consist of Bulletin #1 (#2 and #3 followed), membership card, button.
Near Mint Complete - **$75**
Each Piece - **$5 $10 $15**

DOC-17

DOC-18

❑ **DOC-17. First Issue Magazine,**
1975. Store item. 8x11" with 76 pages. Volume 1 #1, August. - **$1 $4 $10**

❑ **DOC-18. Boxed Jigsaw Puzzle,**
1975. Store item by Whitman. 8-1/4x10" box holds parts for 14x18" puzzle. - **$5 $10 $30**

DOC-19

❑ **DOC-19. Doc Savage Bust,**
1991. By Graphitti Designs, limited to 543. Bronze in color, 9 1/4" tall. Difficult to find on the secondary market. - **$750**

# Doctor Who

**_Doctor Who_ was the longest-running science-fiction television series in history, airing on the BBC from 1963 to 1989. The show chronicled the adventures of a Time Lord from the planet Gallifrey who stole a time machine called a TARDIS (Time And Relative Dimension In Space) and left to explore the universe. The Doctor was capable of "regenerating" when near death, allowing the production to replace the lead actor when necessary. Seven actors played the Doctor regularly before the show's cancellation in 1989: William Hartnell, Patrick Troughton, Jon Pertwee, Tom Baker, Peter Davison, Colin Baker, and Sylvester McCoy.**

**Stories were aired in serialized form, with several half-hour episodes comprising a complete adventure. The second story, titled "The Daleks," introduced the Doctor's most popular adversaries and made the series a hit. Two feature films starring Peter Cushing as a human "Dr. Who" were released in the mid-'60s. Starting in the mid-'70s, the series was syndicated in the US largely through PBS stations.**

**A 1996 TV-movie co-produced by the BBC and Universal aired on the Fox network, starring Paul McGann as the Eighth Doctor. New prose, audio and comic book adventures insure the continuation of the Doctor's travels well beyond his 40th anniversary in 2003. Most items are copyright BBC. "It's a mistake to clutter one's pockets, Harry."**

(CEREAL BOX) DWH-1 (BADGES)

(POSTER)
DWH-1

DWH-2

❑ **DWH-1. Kellogg's Sugar Smacks Badges,**
1971. Cereal offered 6 different celluloid badges. Sample box with promotional artwork (which continued to run after the end of the offer) and advertisement also shown. Boxes came in 'standard' and 'mini' sizes.
Each Badge - **$7 $10 $15**
Complete Set - **$150 $225 $300**
Unopened Small Box - **$75 $90 $150**
Unopened Large Box - **$105 $135 $225**

❑ **DWH-2. Radio Times 10th Anniversary Special,**
1973. Features photos, interviews, and story synopses. - **$35 $75 $150**

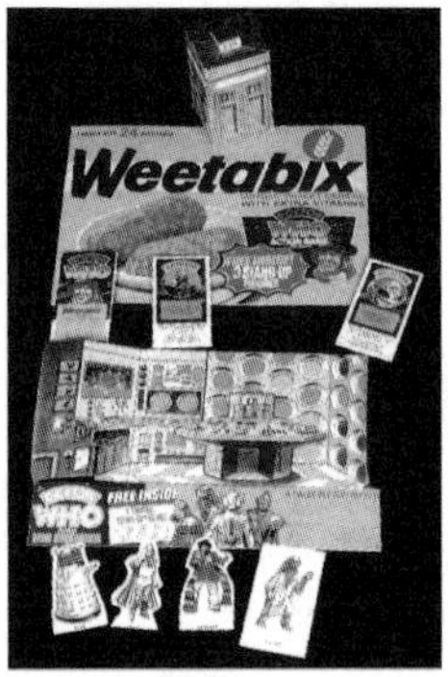


DWH-3

❑ **DWH-3. Weetabix Cards,**
1975. Cereal offered 6 different sets of 2 cards each for use as playing pieces with board game on back of box. There were two Weetabix sets offered in 1975 and 1977.
SET 1 (1975)
Each Unpressed Figure - **$15**
Complete Figures - **$30**
Complete Set - **$105 $200 $300**
Each Box-Back - **$10**
Unopened Box - **$60**

SET 2 (1977)
Each Unpressed Figure - **$10**
Complete Figures - **$22**
Complete Set - **$75 $120 $225**
Each Box-Back - **$7**
Unopened Box - **$45**

DWH-4

DWH-5

❑ **DWH-4. Ty-Phoo Tea Cards,**
1976. Offered with tea bags, accompanied by poster and book of comic book reprints.
12 cards in set.
Each Card - **$1 $2 $3**
Complete Set - **$105**
Book - **$15 $22 $45**
Poster - **$35 $60 $105**
Opened Box - **$22**
Unopened Box - **$75**
Complete Set of All Items - **$450**

❑ **DWH-5. Promotional Poster,**
1977. Produced for Crosse & Blackwell baked beans. - **$45 $75 $105**

DWH-6 DWH-7

❑ **DWH-6. Doctor Who Weekly #1,**
October 17, 1979. Marvel Comics. Newsprint magazine featured articles, interviews, and an ongoing comic strip starring the current Doctor and a variety of companions, many of whom were original to the strip. The magazine has undergone substantial design improvements, and is still published continuously by Panini under the title Doctor Who Magazine.
With Free Gift - **$11**
Without Free Gift - **$7**

❑ **DWH-7. "Terry Nation's Dalek 1979 Annual,"**
1979. UK hardcover. - **$20 $30 $50**

DWH-8

❑ **DWH-8. Radio Times 20th Anniversary Special,**
1983. Features photos, an original story, and a pull-out poster. Also available in a United States edition from Starlog. - **$7 $15 $35**

DWH-9

❑ **DWH-9. Dalek Model Kit,**
1984. Sevans Models.
Complete and Unassembled in Box - **$75**

DWH-10

❑ **DWH-10. Doctor Who Gloves,**
1985. PeshawearUK Ltd. Available in a variety of sizes in black and silver with the neon logo on the back of the hand. - **$7 $18 $30**

DWH-11

❑ **DWH-11. Golden Wonder Snacks Comic Book Giveaway,**
1986. Snack packages offered reprint comic books and also advertised 1987 Doctor Who calendar. Sample packages and comic shown.
Unopened Packets - **$7**
Opened Packets - **$4**
Each Comic - **$1**
Complete Set - **$15**

DWH-12

❑ **DWH-12. Doctor Who Slippers,**
1989. Mothercare. A matching pair of pajamas were also produced. - **$15 $35 $60**

DWH-13

❑ **DWH-13. Bally Pinball Machine,**
1991. Bally Midway. Features a second playing field activated by game play, a built-in video monitor for additional play, and specially recorded material by Seventh Doctor Sylvester McCoy. A number of plastic promotional disks were released for use at game locations and are also sought-after collectibles. - **$3500**

DWH-14

DWH-16

DWH-15

❑ **DWH-14. Weapons Gunner Dalek Figure,**
2000. Product Enterprise Ltd. In box on card. One of an extensive series of Dalek Rolykins, based on a 1960s line of Dalek ball-bearing toys. Now discontinued. - **$10**

❑ **DWH-15. Promo Pen,**
2000. - **$5**

❑ **DWH-16. Dalek Figure on Card,**
2000. Dapol. Dalek figures were mass produced in a variety of color schemes, but this crystal plastic version was limited to 2,000.
Crystal figure (shown) - **$25**
Colored figures Each - **$10**

# Don Winslow of the Navy

**Don Winslow was conceived by Lt. Commander Frank V. Martinek (1895-1971) in the early 1930s as the hero of a series of novels written to promote navy recruiting. A Bell Syndicate comic strip, also originally written by Martinek and drawn by Leon Beroth and Carl Hammond, premiered in March 1934 and ran until July 1955. Winslow made his comic book debut in *Popular Comics* #1 of February 1936 and appeared in various Dell and Fawcett comics, among others, into the 1950s. Don Terry starred in two chapter plays, *Don Winslow of the Navy* in 1942 and *Don Winslow of the Coast Guard* in 1943, both of which were released to television in 1949. Winslow, along with his pal Lt. Red Pennington and his girlfriend Mercedes Colby, also fought the forces of evil on the radio from 1937 to 1943. His Squadron of Peace first did battle with the international Scorpia spy network, then turned its attention to the Axis menace of World War II. The series originated on WMAQ in Chicago and was aired on the NBC Blue network from 1937 to 1939 sponsored by Kellogg's cereals and Iodent toothpaste, and on ABC in 1942-1943 sponsored by Post cereals and Red Goose shoes.**

DON-1

DON-2

❑ **DON-1. Secret Code Book,**
1935. 20 page premium from Metropolitan newspaper. - **$75 $150 $250**

❑ **DON-2. "Lieutenant Commander Don Winslow U.S.N." Big Little Book,**
1935. Whitman #1107. - **$20 $50 $120**

DON-3

DON-4

❑ **DON-3. "Don Winslow U.S. Navy" Penny Book,**
1938. Published by Whitman. - **$10 $25 $40**

❑ **DON-4. "Squadron Of Peace" Brass Ring,**
1938. Kellogg's. Each ring serially numbered. See DON-7. - **$300 $750 $1500**

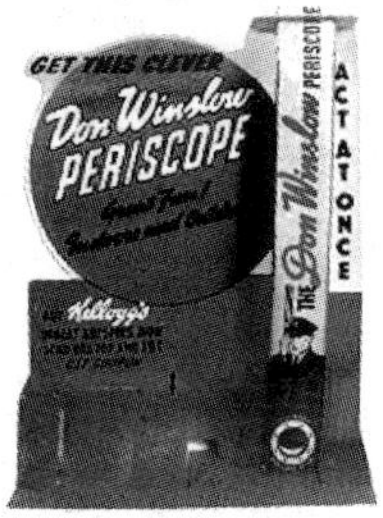

DON-5

DON-6

❑ **DON-5. "Don Winslow Periscope" Countertop Display,**
1939. Kellogg's Wheat Krispies. Diecut cardboard 5x13x17" tall holding example periscope plus order coupons tablet.
With Periscope - **$200 $400 $700**
Without Periscope - **$100 $200 $400**

❑ **DON-6. Periscope Order Coupon,**
1939. Kellogg's Wheat Krispies. - **$15 $25 $50**

DON-7

❑ **DON-7. Guide Book,**
1939. Iodent Toothpaste. This booklet (folded) and the serially-numbered membership ring came in the mailer which has typed notation "Ring" on the label.
Mailer - **$25 $50 $100**
Booklet - **$60 $125 $250**

DON-8

DON-9

❑ **DON-8. "The Don Winslow Creed" Certificate,**
c. 1939. Iodent toothpaste and tooth powder. 9x12" parchment-like paper. - **$50 $125 $200**

❑ **DON-9. "Squadron Of Peace" Member Card,**
1939. Kellogg's Wheat Krispies. - **$40 $70 $140**

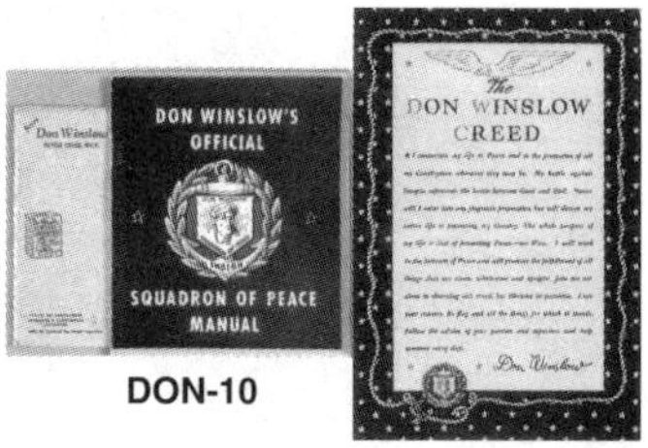

DON-10

❑ **DON-10. Club Manual And Creed,**
1939. Kellogg's. Near Mint In Mailer - **$275**
Manual - **$25 $60 $125**
Creed - **$10 $20 $50**

DON-11

DON-12

DON-13

❑ **DON-11. Honor Coin,**
c. 1939. Kellogg's. Center has spinner disk, back inscription is "Take Me For Luck". - **$50 $100 $150**

❑ **DON-12. "Ensign/Squadron Of Peace" Silvered Brass Badge,**
1939. Kellogg's. - **$10 $20 $40**

❑ **DON-13. "Lt. Commander/Squadron Of Peace" Silvered Brass Badge,**
1939. Kellogg's. Scarce. Highest rank of series.- **$250 $750 $1100**

DON-14

❑ **DON-14. Kellogg's Cardboard Periscope,**
1939. Scarce. Slanted mirrors in each end. See DON-5. - **$100 $200 $300**

(FRONT) **DON-15** (BACK)

❑ **DON-15. Pocket Watch,**
c. 1939. Store item by New Haven. Reverse has colorful decal portrait. Rare. -
**$500 $1500 $2500**

DON-16

❑ **DON-16. "Guardians Of Peace" Cereal Box Backs,**
c. 1939. Kellogg's Wheat Krispies.
Each Back - **$8 $12 $20**

DON-17

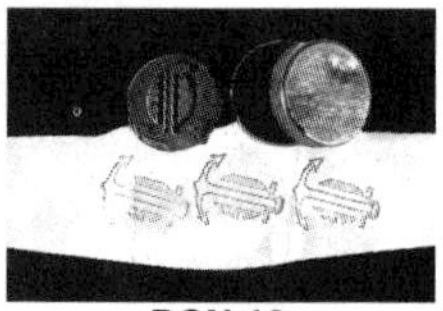
DON-18

❑ **DON-17. "Don Winslow's Secret And Private Code" Paper Sheet,**
c. 1939. Includes Creed and decipher instructions. - **$20 $40 $75**

❑ **DON-18. Identification Stamp Miniature Kit,**
c. 1940. 1" tin container holding ink pad and rubber stamp personalized by initials designated by orderer with anchor design. - **$50 $100 $200**

DON-19

DON-20

❑ **DON-19. "Group Leader" Cello. Button,**
1940. Scarce. Fleer's Dubble Bubble Gum. Radio club premium for League For Defense. -
**$100 $200 $350**

❑ **DON-20. Premium Photo,**
c. 1940. Duquesne Baking Co. Black and white 5x7" with blue inscription. - **$30 $60 $115**

DON-21

❑ **DON-21. "League For Defense" Kit,**
1940. Fleer's Dubble Bubble Gum. Includes pencil autograph of "Don And Red" on card with Navy text plus member card.
Each - **$20 $50 $85**

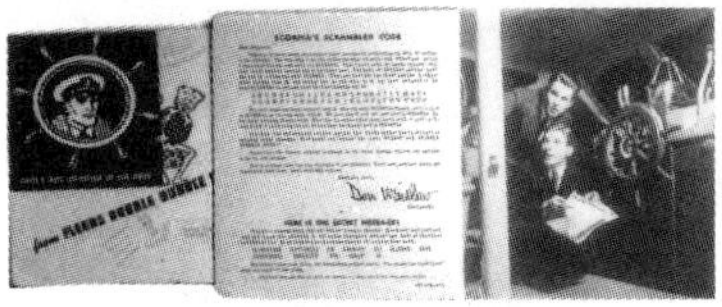

DON-22

❑ **DON-22. "Scorpia's Scrambled Code" Cardboard Sheet and Photo With Mailer Envelope,**
1940. Scarce. Fleer's Dubble Bubble Gum. Explains code system with secret message to be deciphered. Mailer - **$15 $40 $75**
Code Sheet - **$20 $65 $100**
Winslow and Red Pennington Photo - **$30 $75 $100**

DON-23

❑ **DON-23. Catapult Bomber,**
1942. Scarce. Post Toasties. - **$150 $350 $450**

DON-24

❑ **DON-24. Golden Torpedo Decoder,**
1942. Rare. Post Toasties. Came in two pieces, with wood top, cardboard side and metal fin. One of the toughest premiums to find. - **$400 $1200 $2000**

(FRONT)

DON-25 (BACK)

❑ **DON-25. Undercover Deputy Certificate With Instructions,**
1942. Scarce. Post Toasties. Goes with Golden Torpedo Decoder. - **$100 $250 $350**

DON-26

DON-27

❑ **DON-26. "Don Winslow Navy Intelligence Ace" Big Little Book #1418,**
1942. 432 pages. Flip pictures. - **$10 $40 $85**

❑ **DON-27. "Don Winslow Red Goose Shoes" Portrait Picture,**
c. 1942. 8-1/2x11" black and white. The only Red Goose premium known for the show. - **$75 $150 $250**

DON-28

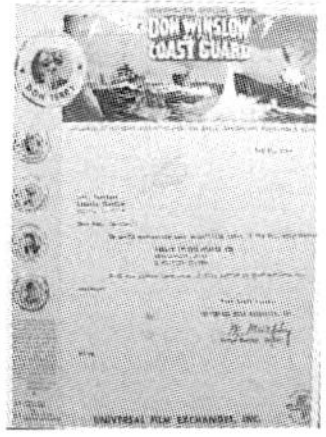


DON-29

❑ **DON-28. "Don Winslow Of The Navy And The Secret Enemy Base" Better Little Book,**
1943. Whitman #1453. - **$20 $45 $110**

❑ **DON-29. "Don Winslow Of The Coast Guard" Serial Letterhead,**
1943. Universal Film Exchanges, Inc. Colorful illustrations on 8-1/2x11" sheet. - **$25 $50 $85**

DON-30

DON-31

❑ **DON-30. "Flare-Top" Ice Cream Cone Store Sign,**
1947. Full color about 18x24". Gordon Gold archives. - **$50 $125 $200**

❑ **DON-31. Don Winslow & Red Pennington Plaster Salt & Pepper Set,**
1940s. Store item. From series of character sets. - **$25 $50 $90**

DON-32

DON-33

❑ **DON-32. Coco-Wheats "Tattoo Transfers" With Mailer Envelope,**
1956. Transfer sheets picture 22 characters.
Mailer - **$10 $15 $25**
Illustrated Inner Envelope With Two Sheets - **$25 $50 $75**

❑ **DON-33. Secret Code Booklet with Shirt/Box,**
1950s. Set - **$50 $100 $175**

## Donald Duck

**Donald Duck was born in 1934 as a minor character in *The Wise Little Hen*, a Disney animated short and comic strip. By his second cartoon appearance he was a star. Clarence Nash, a milk salesman, was the voice of Donald and Dick Lundy did the animation. The irascible duck's first solo performance in the comics was in a Sunday feature in August 1936, drawn by Al Taliaferro and written by Bob Karp and a daily strip started in 1938. Nephews Huey, Louie and Dewey were introduced in 1937. Comic books, reprints of the strip, 64-page comic magazines as well as three decades of animated films and cartoons in theaters and on television have kept Donald a major Disney star. *Donald Duck's 50th Birthday*, a 60-minute spectacular on CBS-TV in 1984, reviewed his illustrious career.**

DNL-1

❑ **DNL-1. Donald Duck Snapshots Book,**
1935. Scrap picture book with hinges, in original box. Rare. - **$100 $200 $350**

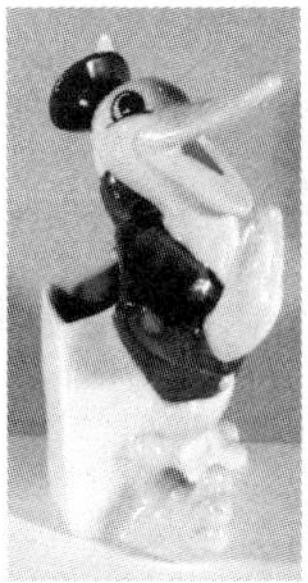

DNL-2 (Side view)

❑ **DNL-2. Toothbrush Holder Figurine,**
1935. From S. Maw & Sons, London. This glazed ceramic item was one of the first Donald Duck toy figures. - **$300 $750 $900**

DNL-3

DNL-4

❑ **DNL-3. Donald Duck Figurine,**
1935. Carnival style figure- possibly a prototype for a German doll. Rare. - **$300 $750 $1000**

❑ **DNL-4. Donald Duck Figurine,**
1935. Large-billed ceramic figure. Rare. - **$125 $250 $425**

DNL-5

DNL-6

❑ **DNL-5. Donald Duck Linen Book,**
1935. 16 pgs. First book devoted to Donald Duck. Scarce in Near Mint, common in lower grades. - **$350 $1050 $3500**

❑ **DNL-6. "Donald Duck Jackets" Cello. Button,**
c. 1935. Scarce. Norwich Knitting Co. - **$200 $400 $700**

DNL-7

❑ **DNL-7. Donald's First Birthday Specialty Piece,**
1936. New York Mirror, Sunday Mirror magazine section. 11-1/2x15-1/2" 20-page section with back cover illustration of Donald and the Funny Bunnies preparing Easter eggs. Text notes just after one year Donald has "usurped the ranking position of his college and playmate Mickey Mouse." Art was exclusive to this newspaper. - **$40 $85 $150**

DNL-8

❑ **DNL-8. Donald And Pluto Handcar Wind-Up,**
1936. Store item which came with generic train track. Box - **$500 $1000 $1500**
Toy - **$400 $900 $1750**

DNL-10

❑ **DNL-10. Donald Duck Story Book,**
1937. Story about Donald writing a book. Printed on unstable paper. - **$50 $150 $225**

DNL-11

❑ **DNL-11. Butter Creams 11x14" Cardboard Advertising Sign,**
1937. - **$100 $250 $500**

DNL-9

**(Original box - boxes from the '30s are extremely rare.)**

❑ **DNL-9. Donald Duck and Donna Duck Fisher-Price Pull Toy ,**
1937. The first Fisher-Price Disney Toy to tie-in with a film. This is perhaps the most sought after of any of the early Fisher-Price toys. Extremely rare. Labeled #160 by the company. To our knowledge, this is only the 2nd time this item has been pictured in a price guide. The film this toy promotes, "Don Donald," was Donald Duck's first solo feature. Donna Duck probably was the inspiration for Donald's next girlfriend Daisy. - **$1200 $3000 $4200**

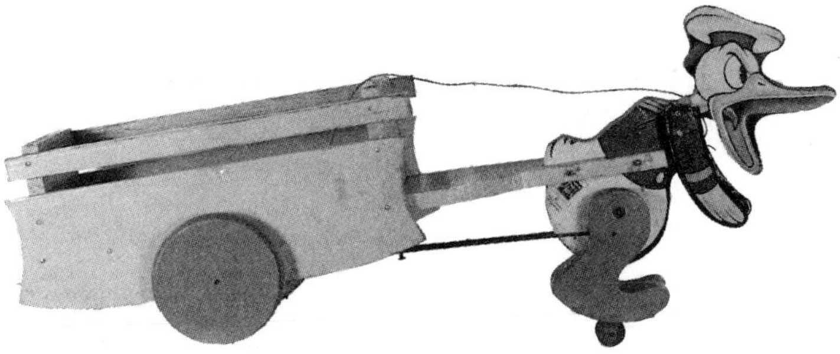

DNL-12

❑ **DNL-12. Donald Duck Angry Face Trotter Fisher-Price Pull Toy ,**
1937. Labeled #741 by the company. This item was produced as an Easter toy only. It is one of two "angry face Donald" toys, the other made in 1936. Both of these are extremely rare. To our knowledge, this is the 1st time an original has been pictured in a price guide. The toy was sold without a box. - **$1000 $2500 $3500**

DNL-18

DNL-19

❑ **DNL-18. "Donald Duck Says Such Luck" Flip Picture Book,**
1939. 432 pages. Taliaferro art. -
**$20 $70 $135**

❑ **DNL-19. "Donald Duck Forgets To Duck" Big Little Book #1434,**
1939. 432 pages. - **$15 $65 $120**

DNL-13

❑ **DNL-13. Donald Duck Happy Face Trotter Fisher-Price Pull Toy,**
1937. Labeled #500. This item was produced as an Easter toy only. Yellow cart variety with rubber insert wings. - **$500 $950 $1300**

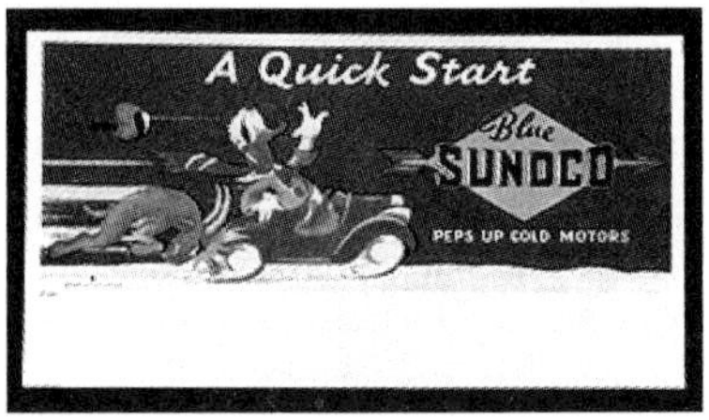


DNL-14

❑ **DNL-14. "Blue Sunoco" Cardboard Ink Blotter,**
1938. - **$20 $40 $65**

DNL-15

❑ **DNL-15. "Walt Disney's 1939 All Star Parade" Announcement Folder,**
1939. Sheffield Cottage Cheese. Pictures 10 glass tumblers distributed over 10 weeks picturing total of 45 Disney characters. -
**$40 $75 $140**

DNL-16

❑ **DNL-16. Pint Milk Bottle,**
c. 1939. Various milk companies. -
**$75 $150 $250**

DNL-17

❑ **DNL-17. Donald Duck Pocket Watch,**
1939. Ingersoll product. Box (not pictured) is blue with Donald pictured on the left holding the watch, showing it to a head shot of Mickey. Box is rare and watch is scarce.
Mickey Decal Back - **$650 $1750 $2250**
Plain Metal Back - **$400 $1000 $1500**
Box - **$200 $500 $750**

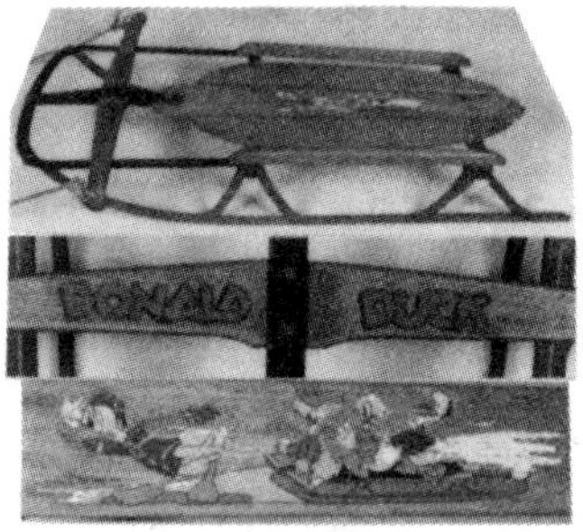

DNL-20

❑ **DNL-20. "Donald Duck" Sled,**
1930s. Store item by S. L. Allen & Co. -
**$200 $500 $750**

DNL-21

DNL-22

❑ **DNL-21. Donald Duck 4 1/2" Bisque Figurine,**
1930s. Borgfeldt & Co. bisque figure of Donald. -
**$100 $250 $400**

❑ **DNL-22. Donald Duck 5 1/2" Bisque Figurine,**
1930s. Borgfeldt & Co. bisque figure of Donald. Both arms are movable. - **$500 $1000 $1500**

DNL-23

DNL-24

❑ **DNL-23. Donald Duck 4 1/2" Bisque Figurine,**
1930s. 4 1/2" tall Borgfeldt & Co. product. - **$100 $200 $350**

❑ **DNL-24. Donald Duck Oil Cloth Doll,**
1930s. Rare. 6" x 7" x 13 1/2". One sold in near mint at auction in 2001 for $10,525.

DNL-25

❑ **DNL-25. Double Figure Ashtray,**
1930s. Japanese-made ashtray featuring double head Donald Duck. Several other Disney characters appeared in this series. This is one of the hardest to find. - **$150 $400 $650**

DNL-26

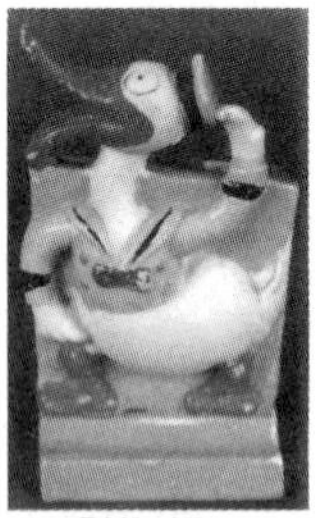

DNL-27

❑ **DNL-26. Plastic Bowl,**
1930s. Post Grape Nuts Flakes. Beetleware bowl in various colors with alphabet and numbers around bowl. Donald Duck pictured in center. - **$25 $50 $75**

❑ **DNL-27. Long-Billed Donald Bisque Toothbrush Holder,**
1930s. Store item. - **$80 $250 $500**

DNL-28

DNL-29

❑ **DNL-28. Long-Billed Double Figure Toothbrush Holder,**
1930s. Store item. - **$125 $400 $625**

❑ **DNL-29. Mickey And Minnie With Donald Toothbrush Holder,**
1930s. Store item. - **$100 $250 $425**

DNL-30

DNL-31

❑ **DNL-30. "Wanna Fight" Cello. Button,**
1930s. Scarce. Image of exuberant long-billed Donald. - **$200 $400 $600**

❑ **DNL-31. Donald Duck Squeaker Toy,**
1930s. Rubber hardens over time, so toy is hard to find in high grade. - **$75 $200 $450**

DNL-32

DNL-33

❑ **DNL-32. "Donald Duck Gets Fed Up" Better Little Book #1462,**
1940. Taliaferro art. - **$15 $60 $120**

❑ **DNL-33. Dell Comic Book Promo,**
1940. - **$30 $75 $125**

DNL-34

❑ **DNL-34. "Donald Duck Fisher-Price Pull Toy #185,**
1940-43. Walt Disney Production version. Rare. - **$500 $850 $1200**

(FRONT) DNL-35 (BACK)

❑ **DNL-35. "Donald Duck Out Of Luck" Fast Action Book,**
1940. Reprints newspaper strips. Notable for back cover ad for rare Four Color Comics #4. Scarce in high grade. - **$40 $150 $300**

DNL-36

DNL-37

❑ **DNL-36. "Donald Duck Takes It On The Chin" Fast-Action Book,**
1941. Scarce in high grade. - **$40 $150 $300**

❑ **DNL-37. "Donald Duck Headed For Trouble" Flip Picture Book,**
1942. 432 pages. - **$20 $70 $135**

DNL-38

❑ **DNL-38. Sunoco Ink Blotter,**
1942. Donald with adding machine. - **$15 $25 $60**

DNL-39

❑ **DNL-39. Sunoco Ink Blotter,**
1942. Donald driving from garage. - **$15 $25 $50**

DNL-40

❑ **DNL-40. Dell Comics/K.K. Publications Pictures With Envelope,**
c. 1942. Set of 10. 7x10" pictures in color, with art likely by Walt Kelly.
Near Mint In Mailer - **$600**
Each - **$15 $30 $50**

DNL-41

❑ **DNL-41. "This Is A Victory Garden" 12x18" Sign,**
c. 1942. Printed masonite board with wood rod pole for insertion in World War II home produce garden. - **$200 $400 $600**

DNL-42

❑ **DNL-42. "Donald Duck Off The Beam" Flip Picture Book,**
1943. 432 pages. Taliaferro art. -
**$20 $70 $135**

DNL-43

❑ **DNL-43. "The Spirit Of '43" 27x41" Government Movie Poster,**
1943. Donald war-time patriotic cartoon used as added attraction to featured films. -
**$200 $500 $1050**

DNL-44

DNL-45

❑ **DNL-44. "USCG Patrol" Booklet,**
1943. U.S. Coast Guard. - **$25 $50 $100**

❑ **DNL-45. Goodyear "Donald Duck Says:" Booklet,**
c. 1943. Donald demonstrates how to make synthetic rubber. - **$25 $40 $85**

DNL-46

DNL-47

❑ **DNL-46. "Saludos" Studio Fan Card,**
c. 1943. - **$30 $60 $90**

❑ **DNL-47. War Bond Poster,**
1944. Scarce. - **$100 $225 $425**

DNL-48

❑ **DNL-48. Apron,**
1944. Has World War 2 image. - **$30 $75 $150**

(FRONT)

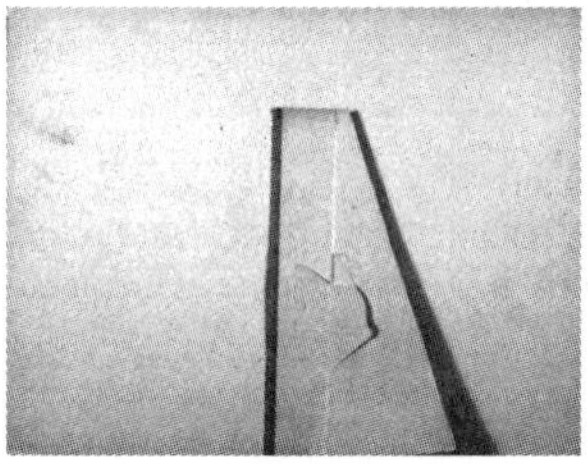

DNL-49
(BACK)

❑ **DNL-49. War Bond Promo with Cardboard Stand-Up,**
1944. Scarce. - **$40 $100 $200**

DNL-50

❑ **DNL-50. War Bond Certificate with Paper Frame,**
1944. United States Treasury War Bond Committee. - **$60 $100 $200**
Certificate Only - **$40 $75 $150**

DNL-51

❑ **DNL-51. Three Caballeros Studio Fan Card,**
c. 1945. - **$15 $35 $85**

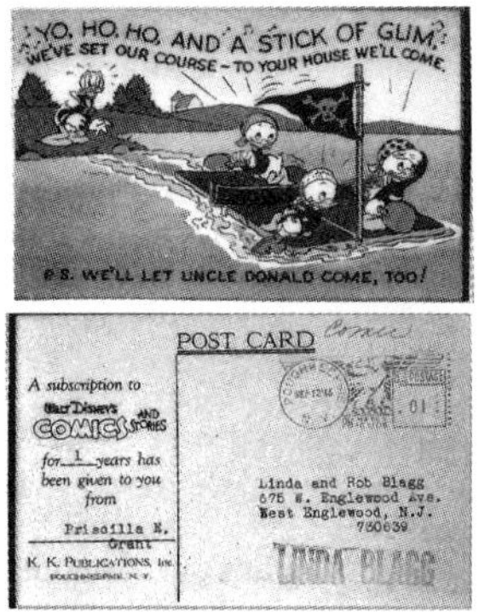


DNL-52

❑ **DNL-52. "Walt Disney's Comics And Stories" Comic Book Gift Subscription Postcard,**
1946. - **$30 $60 $100**

DNL-53

DNL-54

❑ **DNL-53. Donald Duck and Ghost Morgan's Treasure BLB #1411,**
1946. All Pictures Comics, reprints Carl Barks' first work from Four Color Comics #9.-
**$25 $100 $175**

❑ **DNL-54. Donald Duck and The Green Serpent BLB #1432,**
1947. All Pictures Comics, reprints Carl Barks' art from Four Color Comics #108.-
**$20 $75 $150**

DNL-55

❑ **DNL-55. Donald Duck Wristwatch in Box,**
1947. U.S. Time watch. Boxed - **$650**

DNL-56

❑ **DNL-56. "Donald Duck" Cookie Jar By Leeds,**
c. 1947. 12" tall. - **$75 $165 $300**

DNL-57

❑ **DNL-57. Dell Comics Christmas Mailer,**
1947. Inner panels picture comic book cover faced by subscription offer. - **$25 $65 $125**

DNL-58

❑ **DNL-58. "Donald Duck's Atom Bomb" Pocket-Sized Comic,**
1947. Cheerios. Features Carl Barks art and the scarcest by far of 16 giveaway comics issued four to a set with the sets lettered "W" through "Z." This is book "Y1" apparently withdrawn shortly after the set was issued and Disney currently bans reprinting of this title. U.S.A. Edition -
**$90 $270 $900**

DNL-59

❑ **DNL-59. Canadian Quaker Cereal Version "Donald Duck's Atom Bomb" Pocket-Sized Comic,**
1947. Quaker Corn Flakes. Same book as "Cheerios U.S.A." edition but back cover pictures Quaker box and request is directed to "Donald Duck, Box 100, Peterborough, Ont. Or Saskatoon, Sask." Also U.S.A. book is 6-3/4" while this Canadian is 7" long although that may be unique to this example. - **$150 $350 $950**

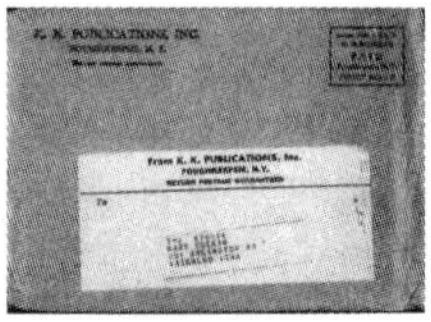


DNL-60

❑ **DNL-60. "Donald Duck In Bringing Up The Boys" Book,**
1948. Store item and K.K. Publications premium. With Mailer - **$18 $72 $125**
Book Only - **$14 $43 $100**

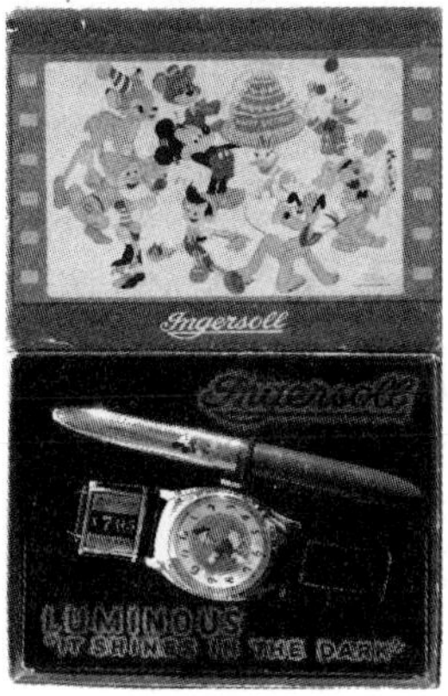


DNL-61

❑ **DNL-61. Donald Duck Luminous Watch and Pen in Box,**
1949. Ingersoll product. Comes with instructions. Boxed - **$650**

DNL-62 DNL-63

❑ **DNL-62. "Donald Duck and The Mystery of the Double X" Book,**
1949. Barks art. - **$15 $45 $85**

❑ **DNL-63. "Donald Duck in Volcano Valley" BLB #1457,**
1949. 288 pages. Barks art. - **$20 $70 $135**

DNL-64 DNL-65

❑ **DNL-64. Donald Duck "Living Toy" Ring,**
1949. Donald's head and miniature cereal box both have magnets for moving his head.
Complete - **$150 $225 $300**
Ring Only - **$40 $65 $100**

❑ **DNL-65. "Living Toy Ring" Instruction Sheet,**
1949. Kellogg's Pep. - **$50 $100 $200**

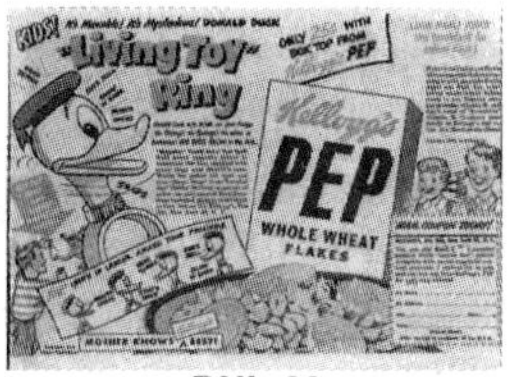


DNL-66

❑ **DNL-66. "Living Toy Ring" Newspaper Advertisement,**
1949. Kellogg's Pep. - **$10 $20 $40**

DNL-67

❑ **DNL-67. Donald Duck Boys Bike,**
1949. Shelby product features horn and Donald headlight. Bike is yellow with light blue highlights. Rare. - **$2500 $5000 $7500**

DNL-68 DNL-69

❑ **DNL-68. "Donald Duck Up in the Air" BLB #1486,**
1949. Barks art. - **$20 $75 $140**

❑ **DNL-69. "Walt Disney's Comics And Stories" Gift Subscription Card,**
1940s. - **$40 $80 $135**

DNL-70

❑ **DNL-70. Mustard Product Glass Jar/Bank,**
1940s. Nash Mustard.
With Label And Lid - **$50 $100 $150**
With Lid, No Label - **$20 $35 $60**

DNL-71

❑ **DNL-71. Figural Glass Jar With Metal Bank Lid,**
1940s. Donald Duck Peanut Butter - **$50 $85 $135**

DNL-72

DNL-73

❑ **DNL-72. "Nu-Blue Sunoco" Cardboard Blotter,**
1940s. Donald with smiling gasoline pump. - **$15 $35 $75**

❑ **DNL-73. Sylvania Radio Bulbs 18x28" Sign,**
1940s. Rare. This Version - **$500 $1500 $2000**
Smaller Version (scarce) - **$150 $300 $600**

DNL-74

❑ **DNL-74. Sunoco Ink Blotter,**
1940s. Donald being hit by punching bag. - **$15 $25 $50**

DNL-75

❑ **DNL-75. Sunoco "How's Your I.Q." Booklet,**
1940s. Automotive quiz. - **$35 $75 $135**

DNL-76 DNL-77

❑ **DNL-76. "Glow in the Dark" Picture,**
1940s. In a brown frame. - **$25 $50 $80**

❑ **DNL-77. "Glow in the Dark" Picture,**
1940s. In a yellow frame. - **$25 $50 $80**

DNL-78

❑ **DNL-78. Membership Card,**
1940s. West Coast Theatre, San Bernardino, Calif. - **$50 $100 $160**

DNL-79 DNL-80

❑ **DNL-79. Donald Duck Push Puppet,**
1940s. - **$35 $75 $140**

❑ **DNL-80. Book End Figure,**
1940s. Donald on his way to school. Figure used as a book end - **$75 $150 $200**

DNL-81 DNL-82

❑ **DNL-81. "Donald Duck Peanut Butter" Litho. Button,**
1940s. Sponsor inscription on reverse, probable set of eight also including Mickey Mouse, Minnie Mouse, Joe Carioca, Pinocchio, Snow White, Bambi, Dumbo.
Each - **$10 $20 $40**

❑ **DNL-82. "Ducky Dubble Club Of America/Member" Cello. Button,**
1950. Scarce. Depicts Donald eating Twin popsicle. Also issued with top imprint of "Icy-Frost Twins." Each - **$125 $250 $500**

DNL-83

❑ **DNL-83. Decal Window Sign,**
1950. Ice Cream Novelties, Inc. - **$20 $50 $85**

DNL-84

❑ **DNL-84. Premium Catalogue,**
1950. Ice Cream Novelties, Inc. - **$10 $20 $40**

DNL-85 DNL-86

❑ **DNL-85. Icy-Frost Beanie,**
1950. Rare. - **$100 $200 $425**

❑ **DNL-86. Icy-Frost Twins Cardboard Sign,**
1950. - **$50 $150 $275**

DNL-87

❑ **DNL-87. Wheaties 12oz. Cereal Box Flat,**
1953. Has Donald Duck record on front and offer for Mouseketeers records on back. - **$50 $100 $250**

DNL-88

❑ **DNL-88."Walt Disney's Comics And Stories" Subscription Postcard,**
1956. Dell Comics**. - $50 $85 $135**

DNL-89

❑ **DNL-89 "Donald Duck Coloring Book",**
1958. Dell #206. Square bound book promotes The Mickey Mouse Club. Has pictures of Duck clan throughout. Odd size 11 1/4" x 6 1/2". Scarce. - **$35 $70 $140**

DNL-90

❑ **DNL-90. Disneyland Original Art,**
1950s. 7 1/4" x 12" by the late Chet Marshall. Fine art shows scene of Donald Duck and commemorates his 1st appearance in *Wise Little Hen.* Used for a poster highlighting his performance in that film. - **$1200**

DNL-91

❑ **DNL-91. Line Mar Wind-Up Toy,**
1950s. 2-1/4x11x3-1/2" tall tin litho. - **$150 $300 $600**

DNL-92

DNL-93

❑ **DNL-92. "Donald Duck Wind-up Toy,**
1950s. Donald on a scooter. Scarce. - **$150 $350 $700**

❑ **DNL-93. "Donald Duck With Huey & Voice" Tin Toy,**
1950s. Store item by Line Mar. Huey attached to cord is pulled back and then toy walks and quacks. Boxed - **$300 $600 $1000**

DNL-94

❑ **DNL-94. "Walt Disney's Donald Duck Duet" Tin Wind-Up,**
1950s. Store item by Marx.
Boxed - **$350 $750 $1250**

DNL-95

❑ **DNL-95. "Walt Disney's Rocking Chair" Plastic And Tin Toy,**
1950s. Store item by Line Mar.
Boxed - **$500 $1000 $1500**

DNL-96

❑ **DNL-96. Donald Duck Bread Cardboard Bank,**
1950s. - **$25 $50 $85**

DNL-97

❑ **DNL-97. Bread Labels,**
1950s. Examples shown from state and country sets. Each - **$4 $8 $12**

DNL-98

DNL-99

❑ **DNL-98. Donald Duck Beverages Cola Glass,**
1950s. - **$10 $25 $60**

❑ **DNL-99. "Donald Duck Cola" Cardboard 9x10-1/2" Store Counter Sign,**
1950s. Printed in Canada.
This Example - **$50 $125 $250**
Larger Version - **$75 $200 $450**

DNL-100

DNL-101

❑ **DNL-100. Beverages Trade Show 2-1/2" Cello. Button,**
1950s. Canadian issue. Matte finish with center strip blank to write name. - **$200 $400 $600**

❑ **DNL-101. "Donald Duck Bread" 30x38" Cardboard Standee Sign,**
1950s. - **$125 $200 $350**

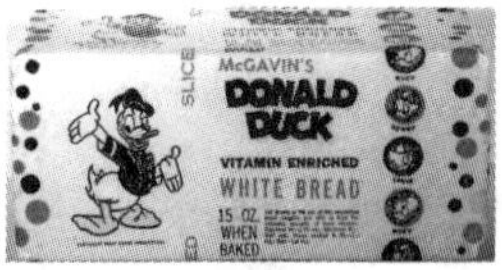


DNL-102

DNL-103

❑ **DNL-102. Bread Wrapper for Donald Duck Bread,**
1950s. McGavin Bread sponsor. Copyright Walt Disney Productions. Scarcer variety. - **$15 $30 $60**

❑ **DNL-103. Donald Duck Beverage,**
1950s. Unopened with cap intact. - **$75**

DNL-104

❑ **DNL-104. Donald Duck Ceramic Planter,**
c. 1950. Western scene. - **$35 $80 $125**

DNL-105

❑ **DNL-105. Orange Juice 6x13" Cardboard Display Sign,**
1950s. - **$40 $90 $175**

DNL-106

❑ **DNL-106. Donald & Ludwig Ceramic Mug Set,**
1961. RCA Victor. Each - **$10 $20 $30**

DNL-107

DNL-108

❑ **DNL-107. Place Mats & Offer,**
1964. RCA. Set - **$20 $40 $60**

❑ **DNL-108. Donald Duck Puppets Wheat Puffs Cereal Container/Bank,**
1966. Vinyl with metal lid by Nabisco. - **$8 $15 $30**

DNL-109

❑ **DNL-109. Donald Duck "Patter Pillow",**
1967. Mattel. Talking cloth doll in box. - **$60 $120 $240**

DNL-110

❑ **DNL-110. Cloth Figure,**
1968. Lars Company. 23" cloth figure made in Italy. Only 10 produced. - **$3000**

DNL-111

DNL-112

❑ **DNL-111. Metal Figure,**
1970s. Walt Disney Productions. Limited edition of 200. - **$150 $300 $450**

❑ **DNL-112. Rubber Figure,**
1970s. 2 1/2" tall. Made in Hong Kong. Copyright Walt Disney Productions. - **$10**

DNL-113

❑ **DNL-113. Bisque Candleholder,**
1970s. - **$10 $20 $35**

DNL-114

DNL-115

❑ **DNL-114. Tokyo Disneyland Patch,**
1983. Opening day patch used by employees; also sold at the Park. - **$75**

❑ **DNL-115. Donald Figure in Car,**
1983. Made by Burago in Italy. Car is 9" long, box is 14" long. - **$175**

DNL-116

❑ **DNL-116. Disneyworld Wood Figure,**
1984. Painted wood. - **$25 $50 $100**

DNL-117

❑ **DNL-117. Donald Duck 50th Birthday Scene,**
1984. From Disney Capodimonte Collection. Sculpted by retired master Enzo Arzenton. Editon size 540. - **$3000**

DNL-118

❑ **DNL-118. Donald Duck Puzzle,**
1984. Puzzle size is 11 1/2" x 15". 100 pieces with box. - **$15 $35 $50**

DNL-119

❑ **DNL-119. Set of Glasses**
1980s. Set of 6 glasses, made in France. With original box that can be cut out to form a mobile. - **$20 $50 $100**

DNL-120

DNL-121

❑ **DNL-120. Donald Duck Figure,**
1980s. Capodimonte figure of Donald reading a comic. Produced in limited editon of 1,090. - **$450**

❑ **DNL-121. Donald Duck Yo-Yo on Card,**
1980s. - **$30**

DNL-122

❑ **DNL-122. Donald Duck Porcelain Figure,**
1991. 13" figure has felt clothing. Very limited by the Franklin Mint. - **$75 $150 $300**

DNL-123

❑ **DNL-123. "Sixty Years Quacking" Statue,**
1994. Fine English Bone China. Figure and base is 14" tall. Comes with small lithograph with a matching image from the Carl Barks painting "Hi, I'm Donald Duck."
Limited editon of 100.
Editions no. 11-100 were issued at **$5300** each
Editions no. 1-10 were issued at higher prices.

(CLOSED)

(OPEN)

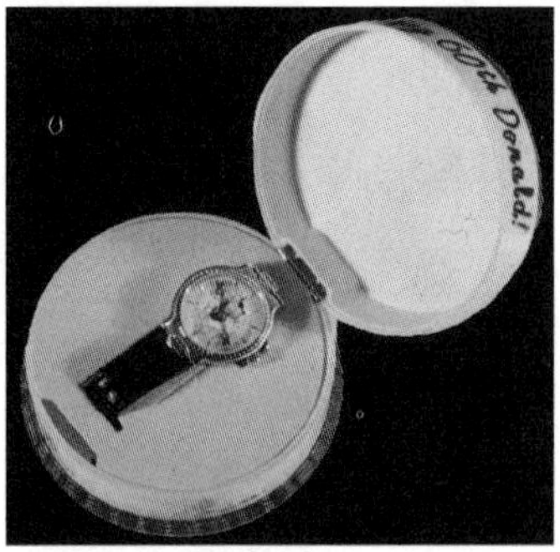

DNL-124

❑ **DNL-124. 60th Anniversary Watch,**
1994. Boxed - **$30 $60 $100**

DNL-125

❑ **DNL-125. Mechanical Moveable Christmas Figure,**
1994. Statue is 22" tall. - **$25 $85 $150**

DNL-126

❑ **DNL-126. "Sheriff of Bullet Valley" Statue,**
1995. Bronze statue is 13" tall. Adapted from famous comic story by Carl Barks.
Limited edition of 200. - **$3200**

DNL-127

❑ **DNL-127. "Admiral Duck" Statue,**
1995. From the Classic Disney Collection. Edition was retired in 1995. - **$135**

DNL-128

❑ **DNL-128. "Three Caballeros" Statue,**
1996. From the Classic Disney Collection. Edition was retired in 1996. - **$135**

DNL-129

❑ **DNL-129. "With Love From Daisy" Statue,**
1996. From the Classic Disney Collection. Edition was retired in 1996. - **$135**

DNL-130

❑ **DNL-130. "Mr. Duck Steps Out" Statue,**
1996. Donald and Daisy shown. From the Classic Disney Collection. Retired in 1996. - **$450**

DNL-131

❑ **DNL-131. Mechanical Moveable Christmas Figure with Box,**
1996. Statue is 24" tall. - **$15 $65 $125**

DNL-132

DNL-133

❑ **DNL-132. "Wise Little Hen" Figure,**
1997. Honors Donald Duck's debut cartoon. From the Classic Disney Collection. Golden Circle dealer event figure. 5 3/4" tall - **$225**

❑ **DNL-133. Armani 7" Figure,**
1998. Donald Duck holding an Armani briefcase. Limited edition made in Italy. - **$250**

DNL-134

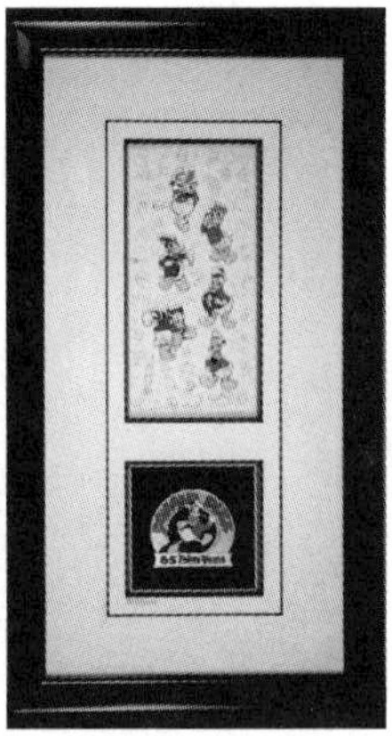

DNL-135

❑ **DNL-134. Mechanical Christmas Figure,**
1998. Very large statue with Donald's usual look of Christmas cheer. - **$80**

❑ **DNL135. Framed Pin Set,**
1999. Celebrates 65 Feisty Years with a framed set of 6 small pins and 1 large pin. Limited edition of 5000. - **$30 $75 $100**

DNL-136

❑ **DNL-136. Framed Pin Set,**
1999. Exclusive 3 pin set with Donald Duck model sheet. Framed in limited edition of 2,500. - **$25 $40 $60**

DNL-137

❑ **DNL-137. Framed Pin Set,**
1999. 65th Anniversary set of 6 pins in a 12" high frame with stamped matte. Third in the series and the hardest to find. Limited to 1,934, the year of Donald Duck's debut. - **$100**

DNL138

DNL-139

❑ **DNL-138. Musical Doll with Key,**
1998. Plays "Ducktales" theme song. Commemorates "The Prince and the Pauper" movie. Porcelain head and feet. 15" tall - **$100**

❑ **DNL-139. Anniversary Magnet,**
1999. - Commemorates 65 Feisty Years. - **$5**

DNL-140

❑ **DNL-140. 65th Anniversary Bisque,**
1999. Celebrates 65 Feisty Years as a movie star. Small figures of Donald represent appearances in successful cartoon features over 65 years. Sculpted by Bruce Lau. Limited to 2500. - **$100**

DNL-141

❑ **DNL-141. Anniversary Watch in Box,**
1999. 65th Anniversary watch comes in wooden box. Limited edition. Boxed - **$85**

DNL-142

❑ **DNL-142. Anniversary Watch and Yo-Yo Set in Box,**
1999. Limited edition 65th Anniversary set includes a watch, yo-yo, pin and instructions. Complete - **$100**

DNL-143

❑ **DNL-143. "Donald's Better Self" Statues,**
1999. From the Classic Disney Collection. Commemorates the original 1938 cartoon.
Set - **$450**
Each figure - **$150**

DNL-144

❑ **DNL-144. Donald "On Ice" Statue,**
1999. From the Classic Disney Collection. Donald on skates - **$150**

DNL-145

❑ **DNL-145. Donald Duck Resin Figure on Base,**
1999. Commemorates 65th Anniversary. First few statues created had the date "1928" on the base. The error was corrected to "1934". Limited edition of 1,999. - **$250**

DNL-146

❑ **DNL-146. Donald Duck Bean Bag Doll Set,**
1999. Promotes 65th Anniversary. Only offered in Japan for a short time. Each has its own tags.
Set - **$125**

DNL-147

❑ **DNL-147. Donald Duck Pocket Watch with Resin Display Holder,**
1999. Limited edition 65th Anniversary pocket watch with chain displayed in a resin holder featuring the old and new Donald. Boxed - **$125**

DNL-148

❑ **DNL-148. Donald Duck Bean Bag Figure,**
1999. Sold in Japan with 2 tags. - **$75**

DNL-149

DNL-150

❑ **DNL-149. Donald Duck White Plush,**
1999. From Tokyo Disneyland. With tag. Referred to as "Monochrome Donald." - **$50**

❑ **DNL-150. Donald Duck "Wacky Kingdom" Figure with Bells,**
1999. Tokyo Disneyland product with tag. - **$10 $20 $35**

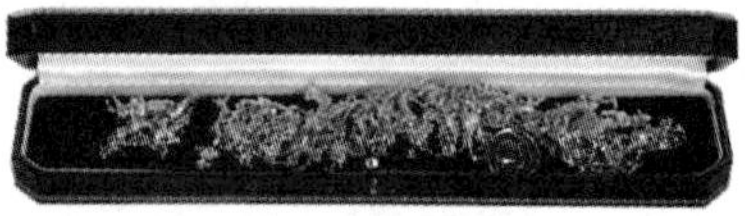

DNL-151

❑ **DNL-151. Charm Bracelet ,**
1999. Disney Store exclusive. 65th Anniversary item boxed. 65 small duck figure charms on the bracelet. Silver and Gold editions produced. Each - **$175**

DNL-152

❑ **DNL-152. 65th Anniversary Ornate Clock,**
1999. Clock base has numerous images from Donald Duck's lengthy movie career. - **$175**

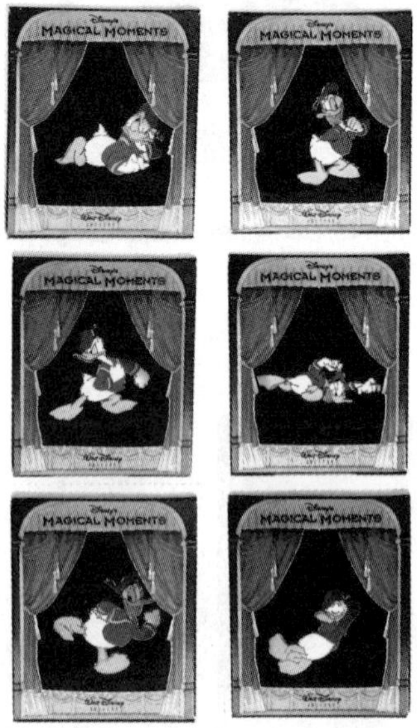


DNL-153

❑ **DNL-153. Magical Moments Pin Set,**
1999. Walt Disney Gallery exclusive. 65th Anniversary item. Set of 6 pins, each in a separate box. Each - **$10**
Set with boxes **- $60**

DNL-154

❑ **DNL-154. 65th Anniversary Marionette,**
1999. On stand. - **$100**

DNL-155

❑ **DNL-155. "Donald's Drum Beat" Ceramic Figure on Base,**
1990s. From the Classic Collection. - **$340**

DNL-156 DNL-157

❑ **DNL-156. Embroidered Patch,**
1990s. Walt Disney Productions. - **$25**

❑ **DNL-157. Donald as Native American Bean Bag Figure,**
2000. - **$75**

DNL-158

❑ **DNL-158. Alarm Clock,**
2000. Stands on plastic duck feet. - **$35**

DNL-159

❑ **DNL-159. "Debonair Donald" Figure,**
2000. From Lenox. - **$150**

## Dorothy Hart, Sunbrite Jr. Nurse Corps

***Junior Nurse Corps* was broadcast on CBS radio in 1936-1937 and on the Blue network in 1937-1938. The series, sponsored by Sunbrite cleanser and Quick Arrow soap flakes, both products of Swift and Company, centered on the activities of teen nursing student Dorothy Hart and her Aunt Jane. The program was aimed at an audience of teenage girls, focusing on the nurse's life and the importance of knowing first aid, as well as on historical events. There were many premiums offered in exchange for Sunbrite and Quick Arrow labels; most of the premiums were nursing-oriented.**

DOR-1 DOR-2

❑ **DOR-1. Nurse Pin Back,**
1937. Radio premium. Different photo in center. This photo variety is scarcer than next example. - **$20 $40 $75**

❑ **DOR-2. Cello. Club Button,**
1937. - **$15 $30 $50**

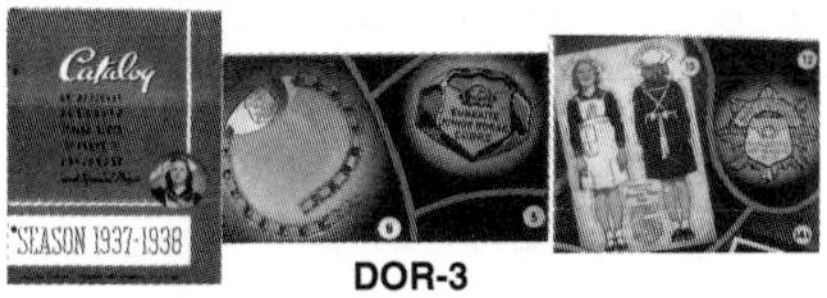

DOR-3

❑ **DOR-3. Club Premium Catalogue Fold-Out Sheet,**
1937. For 1937-1938 season. - **$35 $100 $150**

DOR-4 DOR-5

❑ **DOR-4. Club Newspaper,**
September 1937. - **$15 $30 $65**

❑ **DOR-5. Indian Princess Sa-ca-ja-wea Photo,**
1937. Radio cast member. - **$10 $25 $40**

DOR-6

❑ **DOR-6. Sa-ca-ja-wea Radio Premium,**
1937. Shows examples of Indian sign language throughout the 8 page booklet. Scarce. - **$30 $85 $130**

DOR-7

❑ **DOR-7. Cast Member Photo,**
1937. - **$15 $40 $70**

DOR-8 DOR-9

❑ **DOR-8. Sunbrite Junior Nurse Corps Card,**
1937. Rare. Membership card for radio show. - **$30 $75 $125**

❑ **DOR-9. "Sunbrite Junior Nurse Corps" Brass Ring,**
1937. - **$75 $200 $350**

DOR-10 DOR-11 DOR-12

❑ **DOR-10. "Sunbrite Junior Nurse Corps" Brass Badge,**
1937. - **$25 $40 $75**

❑ **DOR-11. "Graduate" Rank Brass Badge,**
1937. - **$25 $65 $135**

❑ **DOR-12. "Supervisor" Highest Rank Brass Badge,** 1937. - **$35 $75 $160**

DOR-13 DOR-14

❑ **DOR-13. Radio Program/Premiums Promo Card,**
1937. Cardboard ink blotter including imprint for radio stations WHK, Cleveland and WLW, Cincinnati. - **$8 $15 $30**

❑ **DOR-14. Membership Certificate,**
c. 1937. Design in green and tan with black text and gold seal on 8-1/2x11" sheet. Has text of Nurse's Creed. - **$25 $50 $85**

DOR-15

❑ **DOR-15. "Sunbrite Junior Nurse Corps" Silvered Brass Bracelet,**
1937. - **$30 $85 $135**

# Dr. Seuss

**Theodor Seuss Geisel (1904-1991), creator of verbally complex fantasies that have enchanted millions of children throughout the world for over 50 years, was born and raised in Springfield, Massachusetts, graduated from Dartmouth in 1925, and was soon contributing humor to magazines such as *Liberty* and *Judge*. After some success illustrating the "Quick Henry, the Flit!" insecticide ads, Geisel published the first of his nearly 50 books in 1937. Among the best-known: *Horton Hatches the Egg* (1940), *How the Grinch Stole Christmas* (1957), *The Cat in the Hat* (1957), *Yertle the Turtle* (1958), *Green Eggs and Ham* (1960) and *The Lorax* (1971). Television cartoon adaptations of some of the titles premiered on CBS or ABC between 1966 and 1994, winning Peabody and Emmy awards. Geisel also won Academy Awards for two documentary films (*Hitler Lives* in 1946 and *Design for Death* in 1947) and for his animated short *Gerald McBoing Boing* in 1951. Gerald also had a brief run in a series of comic books published by Dell in 1952-1953.**

DSU-1

DSU-2

❑ **DSU-1. "Flit Cartoons" Booklet,**
1929. Stanco Inc. 24-page booklet of Seuss art single cartoon panels illustrating use of "Flit" insecticide spray. - **$100 $200 $300**

❑ **DSU-2. "Secrets Of The Deep Or The Perfect Yachtsman" Booklet,**
1935. Essomarine Oils & Greases. 36 pages including 18 character cartoons by Dr. Seuss. - **$50 $100 $175**

DSU-3

**❑ DSU-3. "Moto Monster" Puzzle With Envelope,**
1930s. Essolube motor oil. 11-1/2x17" envelope and assembled 150-piece jigsaw puzzle picturing various named motoring villain monsters "Foiled By Essolube" use.
Near Mint With Envelope - **$200**
Puzzle Only - **$40 $85 $135**

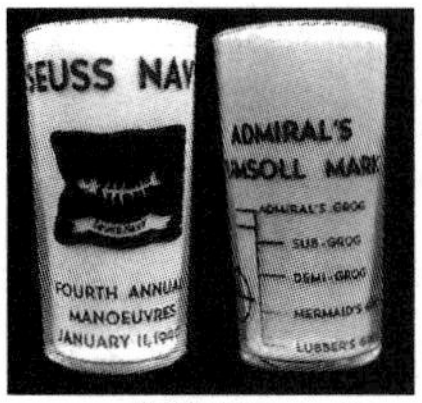


DSU-4

DSU-5

**❑ DSU-4. "Seuss Navy" Glass Tumbler,**
1940. Drinking glass designed for naval event gauged for minimum beverage consumption of Lubber to maximum consumption of Admiral. - **$35 $60 $100**

**❑ DSU-5. "Seuss Navy Fifth Annual Manoeuvres" Glass,**
1941. Red and blue image and text including "1941 Snag Tooth Annie's/Raincheck Alaska." - **$50 $150 $275**

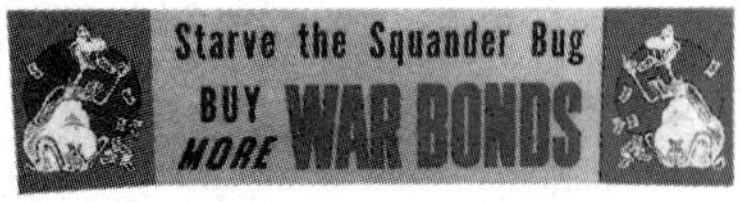


DSU-6

**❑ DSU-6. World War II Paper Poster,**
1943. U.S. Government Printing Office. Unsigned but Dr. Seuss art 8x32" anti-patriotic "Squander Bug" character for promotion of more War Bond purchases. - **$100 $250 $400**

DSU-7

**❑ DSU-7. Esso "Meet Gus!" Cello. Button,**
1940s. Esso/Standard Oil. Back paper has "Happy Motoring!" slogan plus logo.
With Back Paper - **$30 $50 $110**
Without Back Paper - **$20 $35 $75**

DSU-8

DSU-9

**❑ DSU-8. Beer Serving Tray With Dr. Seuss Art,**
c. 1940s. Narragansett Lager & Ale. Full color with 12" diameter and 1-3/8" tall rim. - **$50 $150 $250**

**❑ DSU-9. "Seuss Navy" Glass Tumbler,**
1940s. Esso products. Beverage glass with consumption gauge markings monitored by "Official When-Hen." - **$25 $50 $90**

DSU-10

**❑ DSU-10. "Gerald McBoing Boing Told By The Great Gildersleeve" Dr. Seuss Record With Sleeve,**
1950. Capitol Album CAS-304. Superflex Children's Series #5154. - **$100 $250 $400**

DSU-11

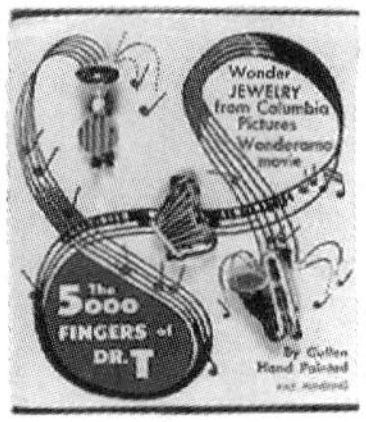


DSU-12

**❑ DSU-11. "The 5000 Fingers Of Dr. T" Hair Barrettes On Card,**
1953. Store item based on characters created by Dr. Seuss for Columbia Pictures Wonderama movie of same title. Two versions exist.
**Barrettes with gold luster**
Near Mint On Card - **$85**
Loose - **$15 $30 $40**

**Barrettes with silver luster**
Near Mint On Card - **$85**
Loose - **$15 $30 $40**

**❑ DSU-12. "The 5000 Fingers Of Dr. T" Pins On Card,**
1953. Figural miniature pins of horn, harp and trombone based on Dr. Seuss creations from Columbia Pict. Wonderama movie of same title.
Near Mint On Card - **$85**
Loose - **$15 $30 $40**

DSU-13

**❑ DSU-13. "Chief Gansett" Beer Coaster,**
c. 1950s. Narragansett Lager & Ale, Rhode Island. 4-1/4" diameter cardboard disk featuring sponsor character art by Seuss. - **$5 $12 $25**

DSU-14

**❑ DSU-14. Puzzle,**
1964. Premium with 18 characters pictured. - **$20 $30 $40**

DSU-15

**❑ DSU-15. Book,**
1968. Crest Toothpaste premium. 56 page story of "Horton Hatches the Egg". - **$20 $40 $60**

DSU-16

**❑ DSU-16. Original Concept Drawing,**
1960s. Hand colored pen and ink drawing of "The Cat in the Hat" by Maurice Noble for 1960s TV special about the Cat wearing different hats.- **$1500**

DSU-17

DSU-18

❑ **DSU-17. Large Litho. Tin Tab,**
1970. 2" diameter red on white reading "See Dr. Seuss 'Horton Hears A Who' On CBS-TV March 19." - **$10 $20 $40**

❑ **DSU-18. "The World Of Dr. Seuss" Vinyl Lunch Box,**
1970. Store item by Aladdin. - **$100 $200 $425**

DSU-19

❑ **DSU-19. "The World Of Dr. Seuss" Lunch Box With Bottle,**
1970. Store item by Aladdin Industries. Steel box and plastic bottle. Box - **$35 $75 $175**
Bottle - **$15 $30 $50**

DSU-20

❑ **DSU-20. "The Cat In The Hat" Boxed Plush Hand Puppet,**
1975. 20-1/2" tall store item by Douglas Co. Cuddle Toys. Near Mint Boxed - **$200**
Puppet Only - **$40 $100 $150**

DSU-21

❑ **DSU-21. "Sam I Am" Boxed Plush Hand Puppet,**
1975. 18" tall store item by Douglas Co. Cuddle Toys. Near Mint Boxed - **$200**
Puppet Only - **$40 $100 $150**

DSU-22

DSU-23

❑ **DSU-22. Cat In The Hat Alarm Clock,**
1978. Store item. Metal case and alarm bells, wind-up. - **$50 $100 $200**

❑ **DSU-23. Seuss Character Litho. Button,**
c. 1970s. Probable various stores for Christmas promotion of Dr. Seuss copyright items. - **$15 $30 $70**

DSU-24

DSU-25

❑ **DSU-24. Cat In The Hat 30th Birthday 2-1/2" Cello. Button,**
1987. - **$10 $20 $35**

❑ **DSU-25. "Cat In The Hat" 2-1/2x2-1/2" Cello. Button,**
1995. Macy's department store. For promotional use by store employee. - **$10 $25 $50**

DSU-26

❑ **DSU-26. Kix Cereal Box with Book Offer,**
1997. Celebrates 40 years of "The Cat in the Hat" with a mail-in offer. - **$2 $4 $8**

(Two views of the item)

DSU-27

❑ **DSU-27. "Cat In The Hat" in Car Bisque Figure,**
1999. TM Dr. Seuss Enterprises. Universal Studios, Islands of Adventure exclusive.- **$20**

DSU-28

DSU-29

❑ **DSU-28. "Cat In The Hat" Bean Figure,**
1999. Seuss Landing set. With tag. - **$15**

❑ **DSU-29. "Sam I Am" Bean Figure,**
1999. Seuss Landing set. With tag. - **$12**

DSU-30

DSU-31

❑ **DSU-30. "The Grinch" Bean Figure,**
1999. Seuss Landing set. With tag. - **$15**

❑ **DSU-31. "Yertle the Turtle" Bean Figure,**
1999. Seuss Landing set. With tag. - **$12**

DSU-32

❑ **DSU-32. "Thing #1" and "Thing #2" Bean Figures,**
1999. Seuss Landing set. With tag.
Set of 2 - **$15**

DSU-33 DSU-34

❑ **DSU-33. Cat In The Hat Yo-Yo,**
1999. Promotes Universal Studios Theme Park.
On card - **$5 $10 $15**

❑ **DSU-34. Dr. Seuss Fish Yo-Yo,**
1999. Promotes Universal Studios Theme Park.
On card - **$5 $10 $15**

DSU-35

❑ **DSU-35. The Grinch Resin Figure,**
1990s. With tag. - **$35**

DSU-36 DSU-37

❑ **DSU-36. Talking "Grinch" Doll,**
2000. 19" tall in box. - **$15 $25 $40**

❑ **DSU-37. "Cindy Lou Who" Doll,**
2000. From the movie; has Whobilation Hair.
17" tall in box. - **$10 $20 $35**

DSU-38 DSU-39

❑ **DSU-38. "Grinch" Walkie Talkies,**
2000. On card. - **$20**

❑ **DSU-39. "Grinch" Wacky Wobbler,**
2000. Resembles animated Grinch. - **$15**

DSU-40 DSU-41

❑ **DSU-40. "Grinch" Lunch Box,**
2000. - **$15**

❑ **DSU-41. "Whoville-opoly" Board Game,**
2000. From the Grinch movie. Boxed. - **$35**

## Dudley Do-Right

**The misadventures of the noble Mountie Dudley Do-Right began life as a segment of *The Bullwinkle Show* in 1961. The dedicated lawman appeared on his own in *The Dudley Do-Right Show*, which premiered on ABC in 1969 and started in syndication the following year. *Dudley Do-Right* comic books were published in 1970-1971. Square-jawed and bone-headed, the ever-chivalrous Dudley pursued his arch-enemy, Snidely K. Whiplash (voiced by Hans Conreid), in one melodramatic tale after another. His romantic interest in Nell, his boss's daughter, was not returned; she preferred his horse, Horse. Items are usually copyrighted P.A.T.-Ward Productions.**

DUD-1 DUD-2

❑ **DUD-1. Dudley Do-Right Figural Rubber Magnet,**
1960s. By "Magnetic Novelties" with "Ward" copyright. - **$3 $6 $10**

❑ **DUD-2. "Dudley Do-Right" Stuffed Fabric Pillow,**
1960s. - **$15 $25 $50**

DUD-3 DUD-4

❑ **DUD-3. T-Shirt,**
1970. Charlton Comics. - **$35 $75 $140**

❑ **DUD-4. Sweatshirt,**
1970. Charlton Comics. - **$50 $100 $160**

DUD-5 DUD-6

❑ **DUD-5. Dudley Do-Right Plastic Ring,**
1970. Charlton Comics. From membership kit. - **$20 $40 $80**

❑ **DUD-6. Portrait Wristwatch,**
c. 1971. Battery watch inscribed "Buren 17 Jewels" with Jay Ward Productions copyright. - **$75 $175 $250**

DUD-7

❑ **DUD-7. "Dudley Do-Right Emporium Catalogue,"**
1972. Jay Ward Productions. 24-page illustrated and priced listing of dozens of Ward character items including the Dudley Do-Right Mountie Stetson hat. - **$35 $75 $125**

DUD-8

DUD-9

DUD-10

❑ **DUD-8. Vinyl Lunch Box,**
1972. Store item by Ardee Industries. - **$250 $650 $1000**

❑ **DUD-9. "Snidely Whiplash" Cello. Button,**
c. 1972. P.A.T.-Ward copyright. - **$8 $15 $25**

❑ **DUD-10. "Nell" Cello. Button,**
c. 1972. P.A.T.-Ward copyright. - **$8 $15 $25**

DUD-11

DUD-12

❑ **DUD-11. "Pepsi Collector Series" Glass Tumblers,** 1973. Pepsi-Cola.
Each - **$5 $10 $15**

❑ **DUD-12. Dudley Do-Right Dakin Figure,**
1976. R. Dakin & Company. Store item. 6-3/4" tall. - **$10 $20 $30**

DUD-13

DUD-14

❑ **DUD-13. Patch On Card,**
1970s. - **$10 $20 $40**

❑ **DUD-14. "Dining With Dudley Do-Right" Plate, Soup, Cereal Bowl, Tumb ler Boxed Set,**
c. 1980. Store item by Libbey.
Near Mint Box - **$70**
Each Loose - **$5 $10 $15**

DUD-15

DUD-16

❑ **DUD-15. "Deputy Mountie" Plastic Badge,**
1980s. Bullwinkle's Restaurant. 2-3/4" tall plastic badge in two shades of gold with title and his hat and collar in red. - **$15 $30 $50**

❑ **DUD-16. "Bendee" Figure On Card,**
1985. Store item. Flexible figure on blister card by Jesco Products. Carded - **$15 $30 $60**
Loose - **$10 $20 $30**

## Duffy's Tavern

**"Where the elite meet to eat," *Duffy's Tavern* was the radio creation of actor/director Ed Gardner in 1940. Gardner played Archie, the manager and with Abe Burrows did most of the writing. Shirley Booth originated the role of Miss Duffy, daughter of the never-present proprietor. The program was a 30-minute comedy variety with show-business guests dropping by each week for banter with Archie. It premiered on CBS in March 1941, went to the Blue network in 1942, to NBC in 1944 and was last heard in 1951. Sponsors included Schick, Sanka, Ipana toothpaste and Blatz beer. A 1945 Paramount film was essentially a reprise of the radio show.**

DUF-1

❑ **DUF-1. "Duffy's First Reader By Archie" Booklet,**
1943. Bristol-Myers Co. - **$15 $25 $50**

DUF-2

DUF-3

❑ **DUF-2. Song Book,**
1944. Possible premium. Six pages. -
**$20 $60 $80**

❑ **DUF-3. "Etiket By Archie" Cover Article,**
1944. June issue of "Tune In" national radio magazine including three-page photo article by Ed Gardner, Archie of Duffy's Tavern. -
**$10 $20 $30**

DUF-4

❑ **DUF-4. "Ed (Archie) Gardner" Record Album,**
1947. Monitor, an appliance maker. Set of four 78 rpm records of actual broadcasts. Inside are write-ups about the radio show. -
**$30 $75 $150**

DUF-5

DUF-6

❑ **DUF-5. Ceramic Mug,**
1948. Probably a cast member item. -
**$50 $100 $160**

❑ **DUF-6. Ed Gardner As Archie Fan Photo,**
1940s. - **$5 $15 $30**

DUF-7

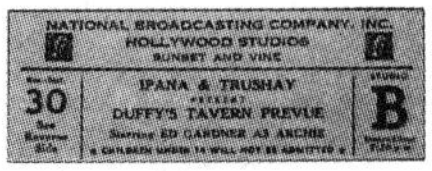


DUF-8

❑ **DUF-7. "Meet 'Archie' Thursday Night" Cello. Button,**
1940s. Promotion for Duffy's Tavern radio show. - **$10 $20 $40**

❑ **DUF-8. "Duffy's Tavern Preview" Radio Show Ticket,**
1940s. 1-1/2x4" ticket for NBC Hollywood Studios. - **$20 $40 $60**

## Dumbo

**The enchanting cartoon feature film of a baby circus elephant with big ears, Walt Disney's Dumbo was released in 1941 to great popular acclaim. Critics praised it and the public flocked to see the delightful tale of a flying elephant and his pal Timothy the Mouse. The musical score won Oscars for Frank Churchill and Oliver Wallace--most notable were the *Pink Elephants on Parade* dream sequence, the crows' song, and *When I See An Elephant Fly*. There have been a number of Dumbo comic-book presentations, including early giveaways by Weatherbird shoes (1941) and multiple issues of the *Dumbo Weekly* by Diamond D-X gas stations (1942). Other premiums and merchandised items followed.**

DMB-1

DMB-2

❑ **DMB-1. Song Book,**
1941. Various sponsors. - **$15 $35 $65**

❑ **DMB-2. "The Gossipy Elephants" Glass Tumbler,**
1941. Probably held dairy product. Set of six. Each - **$35 $65 $125**

DMB-3

DMB-4

❑ **DMB-3. Dumbo Cloth Beanie,**
1941. Probable premium. - **$100 $200 $300**

❑ **DMB-4. "Dumbo Song Book" 2-1/4" Litho. Button,**
1941. Various sponsors. - **$40 $80 $165**

DMB-5

❑ **DMB-5. D-X Gasoline Mask,**
1942. Rare. - **$30 $100 $175**

DMB-6

❑ **DMB-6. "The Adventures Of Walt Disney's Dumbo" Binder Folder With Issues,**
1942. Diamond D-X Gasoline. Folder for 16 "Dumbo Weekly" four-page color comics.
Folder - **$35 $100 $450**
First Issue - **$75 $225 $750**
Other Issues - **$23 $69 $210**

DMB-7

DMB-8

❑ **DMB-7. "D-X" Gasoline Station Cello. Button,**
1942. - **$15 $25 $40**

❑ **DMB-8. "D-X Dumbo Club" Member Card,**
1942. Diamond D-X Gasoline. Card includes chart to mark off first 16 copies of "Dumbo Weekly" obtained plus signature line for adult sponsor pledging a trial purchase of D-X products. - **$15 $60 $125**

DMB-9

❑ **DMB-9. Original Golden Book Art,**
1944. 7 3/4"x 17 1/2". - **$2400**

DMB-10

❑ **DMB-10. "Dumbo" Figurine By American Pottery,**
1940s. 5-1/4" tall. - **$25 $60 $115**

DMB-11

DMB-12

❑ **DMB-11. "Dumbo" Catalin Plastic Pencil Sharpener,**
1940s. 1-1/16" tall done in various colors with color decal. - **$30 $65 $125**

❑ **DMB-12. Cardboard Bookmark,**
1940s. Heath Publishing Co. - **$20 $40 $60**

DMB-13

❑ **DMB-13. Figurine By Hagen-Renaker,**
1950s. 2-1/2" tall. Near Mint With Original Feather - **$175**
No Feather - **$25 $50 $100**

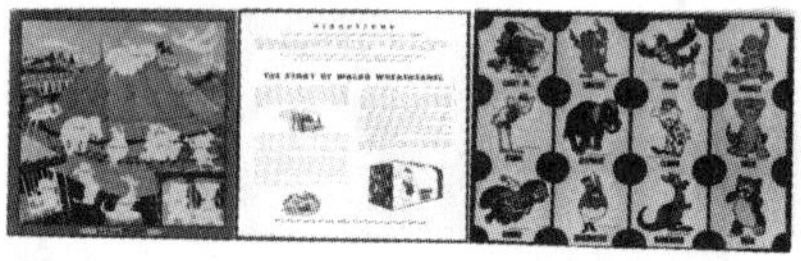
DMB-14

❑ **DMB-14. Bread Label Picture Set,**
1950s. Donald Duck Bread. 11x11" mounting sheet for 12 Dumbo character bread loaf labels.
Label Sheet - **$15 $30 $60**
Each Label - **$3 $6 $10**

DMB-15

❑ **DMB-15. Dumbo Bronze Prototype,**
1989. Disney copyright. Only 5 made. Never produced by Disney for mass release. The 10x10" sculpture by artist Paul Vought is hand colored on a marble base. - **$4000**

DMB-16

❑ **DMB-16. 50th Anniversary Watch in Case,**
1991. Case is leather-like with instructions. Watch features a minted 18KT gold electroplated dial. Limited and numbered. Exclusively sold at the Disney Stores. - **$125**

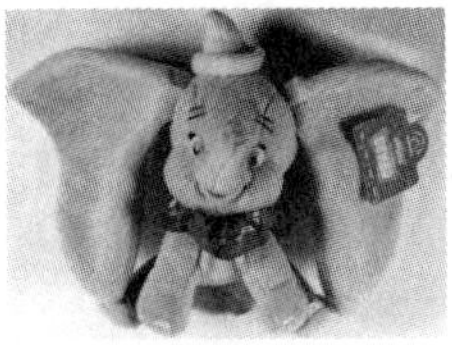

DMB-17

DMB-18

❑ **DMB-17. Dumbo Bean Figure,**
1998. Applause product. With tag. - **$15**

❑ **DMB-18. Dumbo 8" Bean Figure,**
1998. Disney store exclusive. With tag. - **$10**

DMB-19

DMB-20

❑ **DMB-19. Dumbo Lunch Box,**
1999. With thermos. - **$30**

❑ **DMB-20. Dumbo Holiday Ornament,**
1999. With clown face; in box. - **$10 $20 $30**

# The Eagle

**The first appearance of this patriotic hero was in issue #1 of *Science Comics* in February 1940. He then showed up in issue #8 of *Weird Comics*; in four issues of his own book, *The Eagle*, in 1941-1942; and in a second *Eagle* series of two issues in early 1945. The 1941-1942 membership club for fans was known as American Eagle Defenders.**

EAG-1

❑ **EAG-1. Member's Cello. Button,**
1942. Scarce. - **$300 $900 $1800**

# Ed Wynn

**Ed Wynn (1886-1966) came to radio after a long career as a headliner in vaudeville and on Broadway. He was reluctant to try radio but he successfully made the transition from the visual comedy of his stage character, *The Perfect Fool*, to his radio persona, *The Fire Chief*, sponsored by Texaco "Fire Chief" gasoline, on NBC from 1932 to 1935. Wynn had several other radio shows in the 1930s and a brief run on *Happy Island* in 1944-1945 for Borden's milk, did comedy variety shows on television in 1949-1950 and 1958-1959 and appeared in a number of dramatic roles on television in the 1950s and 1960s.**

EDW-1

❑ **EDW-1. Texaco Fire Chief Cardboard Mask,**
c. 1933. - **$40 $100 $160**

EDW-2

EDW-3

❑ **EDW-2. "The Chief" Movie Cello. Button,**
1933. Metro-Goldwyn-Mayer Pictures. -
**$20 $60 $100**

❑ **EDW-3. Wood Jointed Figure,**
c. 1935. Store item. - **$40 $75 $125**

EDW-4

❑ **EDW-4. "The Grab Bag" Movie Promotion,**
1930s. Cloth bag holding 10 paper figures based on movie "The Perfect Fool". -
**$40 $75 $125**

EDW-5

EDW-6

❑ **EDW-5. "All Star Radio Show-Plymouth Radio Broadcast" Folder,**
1930s. Plymouth Motors. - **$12 $20 $30**

❑ **EDW-6. "Ed Wynn Nut Crunch" Candy Box,**
1930s. Store item by Quaker City Chocolate and Confectionary Co. of Philadelphia. 8-3/4x11x2" deep red, white and blue box for countertop display. - **$100 $200 $300**

EDW-7

❑ **EDW-7. "Fire-Chief" Boxed Puzzle,**
1930s. Store item by Viking Mfg. Co., Boston. Assembles to 11x14-1/2" and includes facsimile autograph and nickname designation "The Perfect Fool." Boxed - **$15 $30 $70**

# Eddie Cantor

**Over a span of more than 50 years in show business, Eddie Cantor (1892-1964) went from singing waiter to radio superstar. Cantor juggled, sang, played in blackface in vaudeville and on the stage, made movies, hosted television series and toured Europe, but it was on the radio in the 1930s that the banjo-eyed comic achieved his greatest success. He premiered on the comedy-variety *Chase & Sanborn Hour* on NBC in September 1931 and during the next 20 years in various shows, mainly on NBC, he had a succession of major sponsors: Pebeco toothpaste (1935-1936), Texaco gasoline (1936-1938), Camel cigarettes (1938-1939), Sal Hepatica laxative (1940-1946), Pabst beer (1946-1949) and Philip Morris cigarettes (1951-1952). The manic comic often joked about his wife, Ida, and their five daughters, introduced many young performers and featured such accented characters as the Mad Russian and Parkyakarkas. On television he hosted *The Colgate Comedy Hour* (NBC, 1950-1954) and the *Eddie Cantor Comedy Theatre* (syndicated, 1954-1955).**

EDD-1

❑ **EDD-1. "I'd Love to Call You My Sweetheart" Song Sheet,**
1926. - **$10 $20 $40**

EDD-2

❑ **EDD-2. "How To Make Quack-Quack" Folder,**
1932. Standard Brands Inc. 9-1/4x12-1/4" folded single sheet with cartoon-style centerfold and text on back of "Dr. Cantor Examines Uncle Sam" radio sketch "For Which Chase & Sanborn Have Had The Greatest Number Of Requests." - **$8 $15 $30**

EDD-3

❑ **EDD-3. "Radio Stars And Stations" Booklet,**
1933. RCA Radiotron Co. Inc. 6x8" with 36 pages picturing many stars of the era. - **$10 $20 $35**

EDD-4

❑ **EDD-4. "Eddie Cantor's Picture Book",**
1933. Chase & Sanborn Coffee. - **$15 $35 $50**

EDD-5

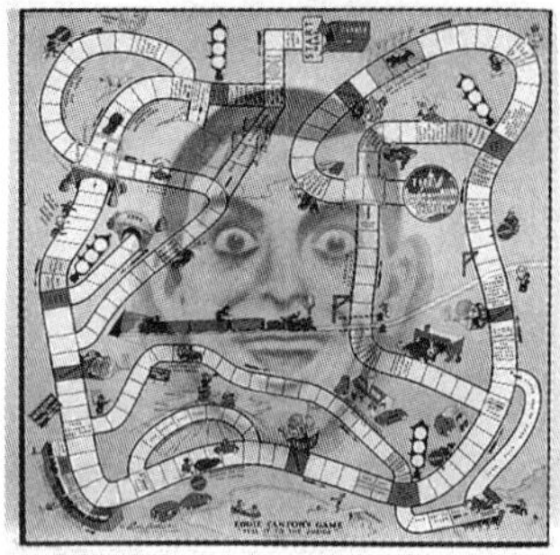

(Game board)

❑ **EDD-5. "Tell It To the Judge" Game,**
1933. Came with board, instructions and various cards and pieces. Complete - **$50 $100 $200**
Board only (scarce) - **$30 $60 $120**

EDD-6

EDD-7

❑ **EDD-6. Folder,**
1934. Chase and Sanborn radio premium. Includes 8 page foldout- **$15 $35 $50**

❑ **EDD-7. Ink Blotter,**
1934. Various advertisers. - **$5 $15 $25**

EDD-8

EDD-9

❑ **EDD-8. Calendar Postcard,**
1934. Various advertisers. - **$5 $15 $30**

❑ **EDD-9. "Eddie Cantor Magic Club" Enameled Brass Club Badge,**
1935. Pebeco toothpaste. - **$15 $40 $75**

EDD-10

EDD-11

❑ **EDD-10. Magic Club Book And Trick,**
1935. Pebeco Milk of Magnesia. Trick includes 12 cards and two instruction sheets.
Book - **$15 $35 $60**
Trick Packet - **$5 $20 $30**

❑ **EDD-11. Pebeco Toothpaste 12x19" Paper Store Sign,**
c. 1936. - **$50 $100 $150**

EDD-12

EDD-13

❑ **EDD-12. Jokes Booklet,**
1936. Pebeco Toothpaste. - **$15 $35 $60**

❑ **EDD-13. Photo,**
1937. Philadelphia Record newspaper premium. - **$5 $12 $20**

EDD-14

EDD-15

❑ **EDD-14. Magic Trick With Bag,**
1930s. Pebeco Toothpaste Club premium. Includes 13 cardboard pieces- **$25 $50 $85**

❑ **EDD-15. "Tune In" Magazine With Cover Article,** 1944. Monthly issue for August of "National Radio Magazine" including three-page article written by him and accompanied by photos. - **$5 $10 $15**

EDD-16

❑ **EDD-16. Calendar Card,**
1946. Pabst Blue Ribbon Beer. - **$10 $20 $30**

EDD-17

❑ **EDD-17. "Eddie Cantor" Record Album,**
1947. Set of 4 78rpm records. - **$20 $40 $75**

EDD-18

EDD-19

❑ **EDD-18. "Eddie Cantor For President" Litho. Button,**
1948. - **$10 $18 $35**

❑ **EDD-19. "The Eddie Cantor Comedy Theater" Clip,**
1955. Salesman's sample. 2x3" plastic. - **$5 $15 $25**

## Ellery Queen

**Sophisticated detective and mystery writer Ellery Queen was the hero of a number of popular novels written by Frederic Dannay and Manfred Lee. He had several incarnations on radio, beginning with Hugh Marlowe in *The Adventures of Ellery Queen* on CBS in 1939 and ending on ABC in 1948. Sponsors included Gulf Oil, Bromo-Seltzer and Anacin. Live-action TV series appeared on DuMont and ABC from 1950 to 1952 and on NBC 1958-1959 and 1975-1976. Queen's first comic book appearance was in *Crackajack Funnies* #23 in May 1940 and he had his own book in the late 1940s and early 1950s. A number of second-feature Ellery Queen films were released between 1935 and 1952, most starring Ralph Bellamy or William Gargan as the gentleman detective.**

ELL-1

ELL-2

❑ **ELL-1. "Ellery Queen Club Member" Cello. Button,**
c. 1939. - **$50 $135 $225**

❑ **ELL-2. "The Adventure Of The Last Man Club" BLB,**
1940. Store item. Whitman #1406. - **$15 $30 $60**

ELL-3

❑ **ELL-3. "Adventure Of The Murdered Millionaire" Better Little Book,**
1942. Store item by Whitman. - **$15 $30 $60**

## Elsie the Cow

**In the late 1930s the Borden Company ran a series of advertisements for its milk featuring a herd of cartoon cows. One, dubbed Elsie, became a star at the 1939 New York World's Fair when visitors to the Borden exhibit insisted on knowing which of the cows there was Elsie. Borden put Elsie to work during World War II touring the country to sell war bonds and promote its milk. Contests to name Elsie's calf in 1947 and twins in 1957 brought overwhelming public responses. Elsie is still appearing in Borden advertising and in bovine appearances around the country. Merchandising has included giveaway comic books, fun activity books and a wide variety of glass and ceramic items related to food and drink such as bowls, glasses and mugs.**

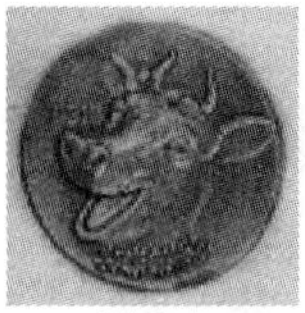
ELS-1

ELS-2

❑ **ELS-1. Brass 2-1/4" Badge,**
c. 1939. Likely issued during 1939 New York World's Fair. - **$15 $30 $75**

❑ **ELS-2. Mechanical Card,**
1940. 2x3-1/2" with action of Elsie opening and closing her eyes while her lower jaw moves back and forth. Reverse notes her appearance in RKO movie title "Little Men." - **$15 $40 $75**

ELS-3

❑ **ELS-3. Wood Pull Toy,**
1944. Store item by Wood Commodities Corp.
Boxed - **$100 $200 $350**
Loose - **$50 $100 $200**

ELS-4

ELS-5

❑ **ELS-4. Store Display Poster,**
1945. 30x45". - **$20 $50 $85**

❑ **ELS-5. Elsie And Baby China Lamp,**
c. 1947. Store item. - **$75 $150 $250**

ELS-6

❑ **ELS-6. "Borden's Cheese Comic Picture Book,"**
1940s. Sixteen-page booklet of single page Elsie cartoons related to use of various Borden cheese products. - **$18 $54 $125**

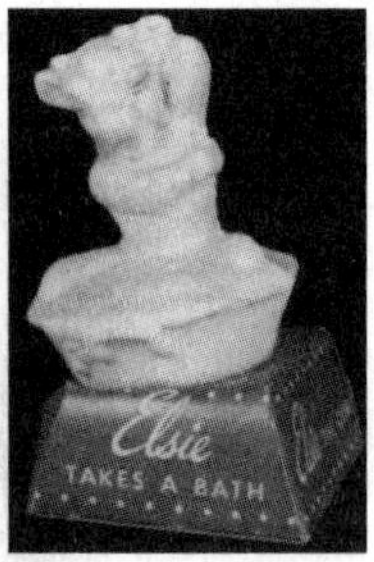

ELS-7

❑ **ELS-7. "Elsie Takes A Bath" Soap Figure,**
1940s. Store item by Lightfoot. 3" tall. - **$30 $65 $100**

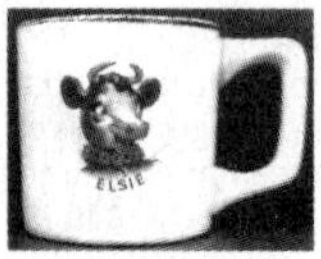
ELS-8

ELS-10

ELS-9

❑ **ELS-8. "Elsie" Ceramic Mug,**
1940s. - **$15 $30 $50**

❑ **ELS-9. "Beulah" Ceramic Mug,**
1940s. - **$15 $30 $50**

❑ **ELS-10. "Borden's" Glass Tumbler,**
1940s. - **$15 $25 $40**

ELS-11

❑ **ELS-11. "Elmer" Boxed China Mug,**
1950. Box Only - **$30 $50 $80**
Mug Only - **$15 $30 $50**

ELS-12

❑ **ELS-12. "Elsie's Good Food Line" Railroad Engineer Punch-Out Hat,**
1955. Blue and white 10x11-1/2" unpunched. Gordon Gold archives.
Hat Unpunched - **$25 $50 $85**
Order Sheet - **$10 $20 $30**

ELS-13

ELS-14

❑ **ELS-13. Activity Booklet,**
1957. 100th birthday fun book, 20 pages. - **$20 $50 $100**

❑ **ELS-14. Elsie Ceramic Mug,**
1950s. - **$15 $30 $50**

ELS-15

ELS-16

❑ **ELS-15. Fabric Uniform Patch,**
c. 1950s. Large 7" diameter. - **$10 $20 $40**

❑ **ELS-16. Elsie And Elmer Serving Set,**
1950s. Hard plastic by F&F Mold Co.
Each - **$15 $40 $85**

ELS-17

ELS-18

❑ **ELS-17. Elsie Diecut Sign,**
1950s. - **$50 $150 $275**

❑ **ELS-18. Plush Doll With Rubber Head,**
1950s. 15" tall. - **$25 $50 $100**

ELS-19

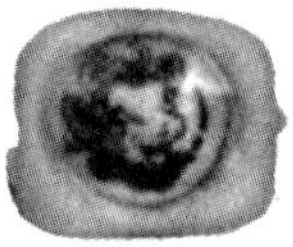
ELS-20

❑ **ELS-19. "Elsie's Fun Book",**
1950s. - **$15 $50 $100**

❑ **ELS-20. Plastic Ring,**
1950s. - **$15 $20 $30**

ELS-21

❑ **ELS-21. "A Trip Through Space" Booklet,**
1950s. - **$10 $30 $60**

ELS-22

❑ **ELS-22. Ceramic Cookie Jar,**
c. 1950s. - **$100 $150 $300**

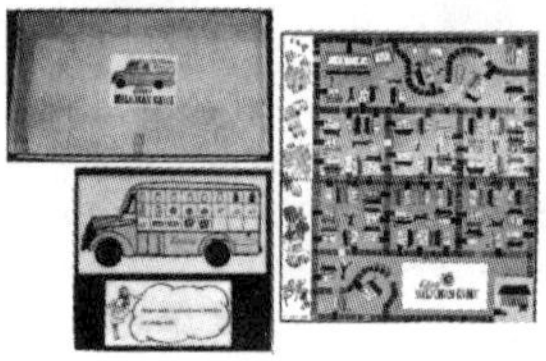
ELS-23

ELS-24

❑ **ELS-23. "Elsie's Milkman Game",**
1963. - **$25 $40 $75**

❑ **ELS-24. "Elsie The Borden Cow" Litho. Button,**
1960s. - **$5 $10 $20**

## Elvis Presley

**Elvis Presley (1935-1977) was born in a two-room house in Tupelo, Mississippi. He died in his Memphis, Tennessee mansion with an estate valued at more than $30 million. In his lifetime--and since his death--the rock 'n' roll legend spawned a merchandising cornucopia that has yet to subside. The national mania exploded in 1956 when Presley appeared on *The Ed Sullivan Show* and items from that period generate great collector interest. But the King lives on: in addition to frequent Elvis sightings at shopping malls and county fairs, Elvis Presley Enterprises continues to license countless memorial and commemorative items. *TV Guide*, in its January 1-7 2000 issue, named Elvis "The Entertainer of the Century."...thank you very much.**

ELV-1

ELV-2

❑ **ELV-1. Fan Photo,**
c. 1955. 5x7" glossy bw with facsimile signature, a personal giveaway by him at his home on Audubon Street in Memphis in addition to other forms of distribution. - **$25 $65 $110**

❑ **ELV-2. "Elvis Presley Complimentary Fan Club Membership Card",**
c. 1956. Fan club headquarters in Madison, Tenn. Includes facsimile Elvis signature as "Honorary President." - **$20 $40 $70**

ELV-3

ELV-4

❑ **ELV-3. Elvis Gum Card Set,**
1956. Bubbles Inc./Elvis Presley Enterprises. Set of 66. Each - **$3 $5 $10**

❑ **ELV-4. "Elvis Presley/Love Me Tender" Movie Theater Giveaway Wallet Card,**
1956. Various theaters. 2-1/8x3-1/4". - **$25 $60 $100**

ELV-5

ELV-6

❑ **ELV-5. "R.C.A. Records" National Fan Club Button,**
1956. Black on pink.
Litho. Variety - **$50 $75 $150**
Scarcer Cello. Variety - **$65 $125 $175**

❑ **ELV-6. Color Photo 3" Cello. Button,**
1956. Vendor Item. - **$20 $40 $75**

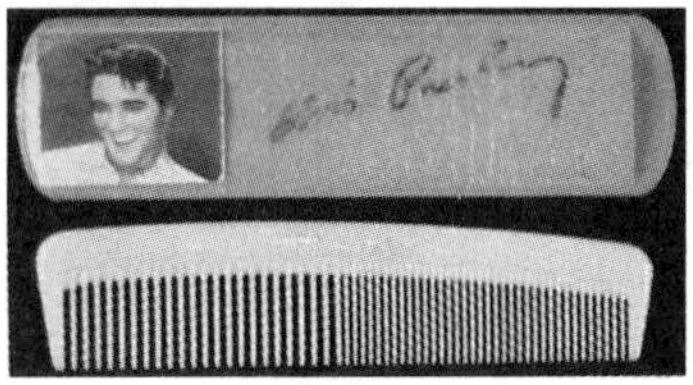

ELV-7

❑ **ELV-7. "Elvis Presley" Comb And Case,**
c. 1956. Store item. 5-1/2" long plastic case has color photo of Elvis and facsimile signature. Case holds a generic plastic "Dupont" comb. - **$50 $110 $165**

ELV-8

ELV-9

❑ **ELV-8. "TV Guide", September 8,**
1956. Issue has first part of three-part article. - **$50 $100 $200**

❑ **ELV-9. Brass Lipstick Tube,**
1956. Store item by Teen-Ager Lipstick Corp. Available in six colors. - **$50 $75 $175**

ELV-10

❑ **ELV-10. Five Buttons From Scarce Set,**
1956. Each is 7/8" litho with "1956 E.P.E." on curl. Issued in several different color combinations by Green Duck Co.
Each With Elvis Picture - **$20 $50 $75**
Each With Text Only - **$15 $30 $50**

ELV-11

ELV-12

❑ **ELV-11. Jeans Tag,**
1956. Elvis Presley Enterprises store item. - **$25 $75 $125**

❑ **ELV-12. Song Title T-Shirt,**
1956. Store item. Elvis Presley Enterprises copyright. -**$75 $200 $275**

ELV-13

❑ **ELV-13. Fabric Hat,**
1956. Store item by Magnet Hat & Cap Corp.
With Tag - **$60 $125 $200**
No Tag - **$40 $80 $125**

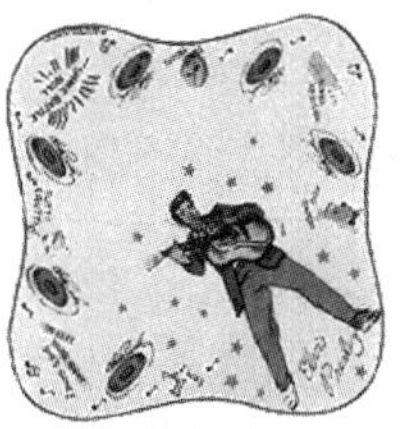

ELV-14

ELV-15

❑ **ELV-14. Song Titles Handkerchief,**
1956. Elvis Presley Enterprises. Includes song titles Hound Dog, Mystery Train, Blue Moon, Tutti Frutti. 13x13-1/2". - **$100 $250 $400**

❑ **ELV-15. Glass Tumbler,**
1956. Store item. Copyright Elvis Presley Enterprises. - **$50 $80 $150**

ELV-16

ELV-17

ELV-18

❑ **ELV-16. "Elvis Presley For President" Litho. Tin Tab,**
1956. - **$20 $40 $75**

❑ **ELV-17. "Love Me Tender" Litho. Button,**
1956. Elvis Presley Enterprises. From set of 10 with pictures, record titles or slogans.
Each - **$8 $15 $25**

❑ **ELV-18. "Love Me Tender" Paper Photo,**
1956. Theater hand-out. - **$5 $15 $30**

ELV-19

ELV-20

❑ **ELV-19. Metal Charm Bracelet,**
1956. Store item. Elvis Presley Enterprises copyright. - **$35 $60 $100**

❑ **ELV-20. Plastic Picture Frame Charm,**
c. 1956. Vending machine item. - **$10 $25 $50**

ELV-21

ELV-22

❑ **ELV-21. Metal Ring With Photo Under Plastic Dome,**
c. 1956. Elvis Presley Enterprises store item. Two different color photos.
Each - **$75 $175 $275**

❑ **ELV-22. Gold Record Litho. Button,**
c. 1956. Known with seven different record titles. Each - **$15 $25 $50**

ELV-23

❑ **ELV-23. "I Like/Hate Elvis" Buttons,**
c. 1956. Each is 3-1/2" diameter.
Each - **$10 $25 $40**

ELV-24

❑ **ELV-24. "Elvis Presley Photo Folio",**
1957. Elvis Presley Enterprises. From concert tour. - **$20 $50 $85**

ELV-25

ELV-26

❑ **ELV-25. Fabric And Paper 6" Badge,**
c. 1957. Pleated fabric border around paper disk portrait, possibly designed for movie usher use.- **$25 $60 $85**

❑ **ELV-26. RCA Promotional Photo,**
1958. 8x10" glossy black and white. - **$25 $50 $100**

ELV-27

❑ **ELV-27. "Welcome Back Elvis" Button,**
c. 1958. Vendor button by Emress Specialty Co. 3-1/2" issued for Elvis' return from the Army. - **$25 $65 $125**

ELV-28

❑ **ELV-28. Christmas Card,**
1958. Red, green and white 5-1/2x8-1/2" including inset photo of Colonel Parker as Santa. - **$15 $30 $50**

ELV-29

ELV-30

❑ **ELV-29. Elvis In Army Uniform 4" Cello. Button,**
c. 1958. No markings other than "U.S. Army" patch pictured above left pocket and part of "Presley" name patch visible above right pocket.- **$100 $250 $400**

❑ **ELV-30. "King Creole" Wallet Card,**
1958. Movie promotion. - **$25 $50 $90**

ELV-31

❑ **ELV-31. Christmas Postcard,**
1959. - **$15 $25 $50**

ELV-32

❑ **ELV-32. Photo Cube Bank,**
c. 1960s. Store item. 3-1/2" cube of hard plastic has removable circular disk panels on the sides and these hold color portraits of Elvis, John Wayne, two females models or actresses. - **$25 $50 $75**

ELV-33

❑ **ELV-33. "G.I. Blues" Paper Army Hat,**
1960. Advertises movie and record album. - **$15 $45 $85**

ELV-34

❑ **ELV-34. "Blue Hawaii" Movie Promotion Lei,**
1961. Tissue paper lei with 5" cardboard disk. - **$25 $65 $125**

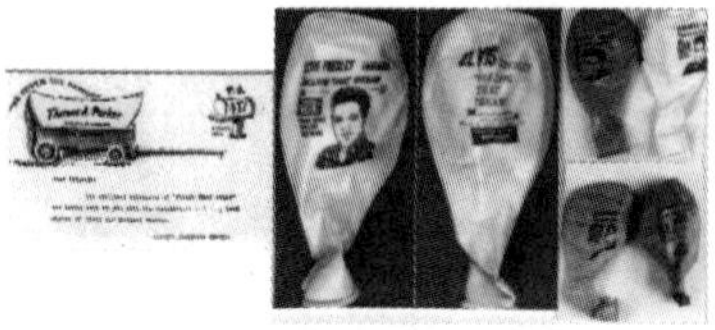

ELV-35

❑ **ELV-35. "Follow That Dream" Movie Balloons With Promotion Letter,**
1962. Rubber balloons with cover form letter from Thomas A. Parker, Elvis' manager.
Letter - **$15 $25 $50**
Each Balloon - **$3 $8 $15**

ELV-36

ELV-37

❑ **ELV-36. Movie Coloring Contest Sheet,**
1962. Paramount Pictures for local stores. Promotion for "Girls! Girls! Girls!" movie. - **$20 $40 $75**

❑ **ELV-37. Girls! Girls! Girls! Album Insert,**
1963. - **$10 $20 $30**

ELV-38

ELV-39

❑ **ELV-38. Fan Club Booklet,**
1967. - **$10 $20 $40**

❑ **ELV-39. "Elvis' Gold Car On Tour" RCA Postcard,**
1960s. - **$8 $12 $25**

ELV-40

ELV-41

❑ **ELV-40. "Something From Elvis' Wardrobe For You" Fabric Swatch In Envelope,**
1971. RCA Records. 3-1/2x5-1/2" window envelope holds 2x3" piece of fabric, sometimes a solid single color or sometimes with colorful pattern. - **$25 $60 $125**

❑ **ELV-41. Elvis Concert Program,**
1977. Souvenir Folio Concert Edition, Volume 6. Boxcar Enterprises. - **$10 $15 $25**

ELV-42

❑ **ELV-42. Post-Death Elvis Concert Ticket,**
1977. Unused ticket for concert to be held August 17, 1977 at Cumberland County Civic Center, Portland, Maine. Elvis died the previous day. - **$25 $50 $100**

ELV-43

ELV-44

❑ **ELV-43. "Elvis In Gold Suit" Doll In Box,**
1984. Includes guitar and microphone. - **$10 $30 $50**

❑ **ELV-44. "Elvis In Jumpsuit" Doll In Box,**
1984. Includes guitar and microphone. - **$10 $30 $50**

ELV-45

❑ **ELV-45. "Elvis' Lisa Marie" Airplane Pen,**
c. 1990. Plastic ballpoint with liquid in upper barrel around image of Elvis' jet plane that moves when pen is tilted. Other images include him and gates of Graceland. Possible souvenir from Graceland. - **$25 $50 $75**

ELV-46

❑ **ELV-46. "Teen Idol" Doll,**
1993. Hasbro. 11 1/2" doll in box. - **$45**

ELV-47

❑ **ELV-47. Matchbox Graceland Collection,**
2001. Vehicle #1 from the set. - **$15**

## E.T.

**Steven Spielberg's *E.T. The Extra-Terrestrial* opened in mid-1982 and was soon being touted as the most popular movie in Hollywood history. An endearing tale of a 10-year-old boy who befriends an alien creature stranded on earth, the film starred Henry Thomas, Dee Wallace, and Drew Barrymore. The phenomenal success of the movie was matched by a merchandising explosion. Universal City Studios licensed some 50 companies to produce E.T. products, including stuffed dolls (Kamar International), vitamins (Squibb), E.T. cereal (General Mills), trading cards and stickers (Topps), a tie-in promotion with Reese's Pieces (Hershey), and a flood of such items as video games (Atari), T-shirts, ice cream, candy, posters, pins, bed sheets, calendars, an animated alarm clock, a "power" tricycle from Coleco,**

and countless toys. A profusion of knock-offs and unlicensed items also appeared. An official E.T. Fan Club offered an "E.T. Speaks" record along with a photo, poster, newsletter, membership card and certificate. Entering the year 2002, *E.T. The Extra-Terrestrial* had grossed over $700 million worldwide, placing it seventh on the all time list . The film's 20th anniversary was marked by a March 2002 re-release in theaters, with new footage and improved special effects added to the classic.

ETT-1

❑ **ETT-1. "Reese's Pieces" 29x33" Cardboard Display Sign,**
1982. Reese Candy Co. Large diecut image of E.T. eating Reese's Pieces plus text for T-shirt and poster mail premiums. - **$25 $60 $110**

ETT-2

❑ **ETT-2. "E.T. Party Set,"**
1982. Store item by Shilton-Globe Inc. Contains 30 pieces. Near Mint Boxed **- $40**

ETT-3

ETT-4

❑ **ETT-3. "E.T. Card Set,"**
1982. Topps Gum. Set of 87, each with different film scene. Near Mint Set - **$25**

❑ **ETT-4. "E.T." 6" Glass Tumbler,**
1982. Imprinted for Army & Air Force Exchange Service. Illustration "I'll be right here" from series of four copyright by Universal City Studios. - **$3 $6 $12**

ETT-5

❑ **ETT-5. "E.T." Phone Book,**
1982. For phoning home. - **$5 $10 $20**

ETT-6

❑ **ETT-6. Lunch Box With Bottle,**
1982. Store item by Aladdin Industries Inc.
Box - **$10 $20 $40**
Bottle - **$5 $10 $25**

ETT-7

ETT-8

❑ **ETT-7. "E.T." Glass Tumblers,**
1982. Pizza Hut. From set of four.
Each - **$2 $5 $10**

❑ **ETT-8. Wristwatch,**
1982. Store item by Nelsonic. Metal case with vinyl straps. - **$15 $45 $90**

ETT-9

❑ **ETT-9. Figural Plastic Ring With Box,**
1982. Store item by Naum Bros. Plastic head on adjustable metal band. Boxed - **$25**
Ring Only - **$10 $15 $20**

ETT-10

❑ **ETT-10. "E.T." 20x28" Video Cassette Display Sign,**
1988. Pepsi-Cola sponsorship. Molded thin plastic for MCA Home Video Inc. designed for attachment to a light box or hung in window to enhance 3-D effect. - **$15 $30 $50**

ETT-11

❑ **ETT-11. Video Release Promo Items,**
1988. MCA Home Video. First item is 8-1/2x15x2" deep oversized cardboard display box designed like a video cassette box. Second item is 26x39" glossy poster. Both pieces include Pepsi-Cola ad for a rebate on the video.
Each - **$5 $10 $15**

## Fawcett Comics

**Fawcett Publications began with *Capt. Billy's Whiz Bang*, a digest-sized somewhat bawdy magazine of the 1920s. The mix of girlie photos, stories, and cartoons (later Donald Duck artist Carl Barks being a regular contributor) was successful enough that Fawcett would expand into a major magazine publisher in the 1930s. Titles included *True Confessions, Motion Picture*,and *Mechanix Illustrated.***

**Late in 1939 Roscoe Fawcett announced the company's entry into the comic book field with *Whiz Comics*, dated February, 1940. Captain Marvel was the lead feature, ably drawn by C.C. Beck and his assistants Pete Costanza and Kurt Schaffenberger. The success of Captain Marvel spawned a number of spin-offs including Captain Marvel Jr., Mary Marvel, and Hoppy the Marvel Bunny.**

**By 1943 Fawcett was also publishing *Captain Midnight, Bulletman, Spy Smasher*, and *Don Winslow.* In the later 1940s the line was expanded to westerns (including *Hopalong Cassidy, Tom Mix Western*, and**

*Gabby Hayes Western*) as well as romance, humor, sports, horror, and science fiction titles. Fawcett had become a major comic book publisher, with a yearly circulation of 50 million copies in the mid 1940s which grew to over 70 million by 1949. A 1941 DC Comics lawsuit alleging Captain Marvel was an imitation of Superman was settled in DC's favor in 1953. This, combined with lost sales due to the popularity of TV, brought an end to the Fawcett comic book empire. They re-entered the field with *Dennis the Menace* in 1958 and published that title until 1980.

FAW-1

**❑ FAW-1. "American Alphabet" Song Book,**
1944. Patriotism song pages with cover art of Hoppy the Marvel Bunny and other Fawcett characters. - **$15 $35 $60**

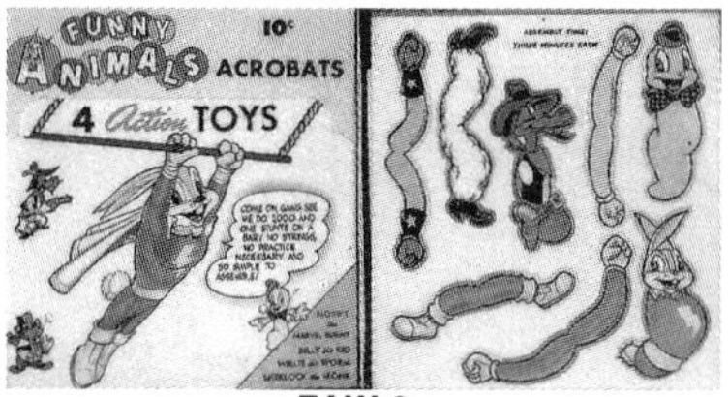

FAW-2

**❑ FAW-2. "Funny Animals Acrobats" Punch-Out,**
c. 1944. Store item and probable club issue. Unpunched - **$35 $50 $85**

FAW-3

FAW-4

**❑ FAW-3. "Tippy Toy" Punch-Out Sheet With Envelope,**
1945. Store item and club premium. For assembly of 3-D rocker toy featuring Hoppy the Marvel Bunny and Millie Bunny. Unused - **$15 $30 $50**

**❑ FAW-4. "Comic Stamps" Perforated Sheet,**
c. 1945. Pictures 24 Fawcett comic book characters. - **$15 $35 $60**

FAW-5

FAW-6

**❑ FAW-5. Captain Marvel Club Offer Sheet,**
c. 1945. Offers 18 action toys, games, puzzles, etc. for Captain Marvel and other Fawcett characters. 8-1/2x11" black on yellow printed both sides. - **$10 $20 $30**

**❑ FAW-6. "Funny Animals Coloring Book",**
1946. Store item by Abbott Publishing Co. Features Hoppy the Marvel Bunny and other Fawcett characters. - **$25 $40 $75**

FAW-7

**❑ FAW-7. "Funny Animal Paint Books" With Box,**
c. 1946. Store item by Abbott Publishing Co. Set of six including Hoppy the Marvel Bunny and five other Fawcett animals.
Boxed - **$50 $90 $150**
Hoppy Book - **$10 $25 $50**
Others Each - **$5 $10 $15**

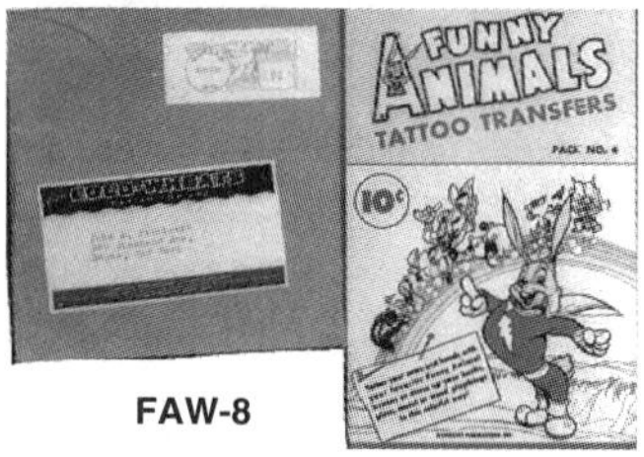

FAW-8

**❑ FAW-8. Coco-Wheats "Tattoo Transfers" Kit With Mailer Envelope,**
1956. Transfer sheets picture 22 Fawcett characters. Mailer - **$10 $15 $25**
Illustrated Inner Envelope With Two Sheets - **$25 $50 $75**

## Felix the Cat

**Felix has been called one of the great creations of comic art...a supercat...an animation superstar...the Charlie Chaplin of cartoon characters. Alienated, alone, a heroic and resourceful battler against fate, Felix was created by cartoonists Otto Messmer and Pat Sullivan shortly after World War I. His first animated appearance came in 1919 and by the mid-1920s he was an international star, most notably in England. Sullivan was quick to license the character and many early merchandised items were produced. A Sunday comic strip from King Features Syndicate debuted in August 1923 and a daily strip followed in May 1927. Comic book appearances began in the 1930s and Felix has had his own books from the 1940s into the 1990s. Hundreds of the silent shorts were distributed to television in 1953 by Pathe Films. New color episodes, produced for television by the Joe Oriolo Studios, appeared in 1960. Felix now had a magic bag of tricks to rely on in place of his talented and multifunctional tail.**

FLX-1

FLX-2

**❑ FLX-1. Schoenhut First Version Wood Jointed Doll,**
1924. Large 8" tall. Label under foot "Felix Copyright 1922, 1924 By Pat Sullivan Pat. Applied For." Most versions have label "Pat June 23, 1925." Nose on first version extends 1/2", second version only 1/4".
First Version - **$300 $500 $850**
Second Version - **$200 $350 $600**

**❑ FLX-2. "Felix The Cat" Ceramic Plate,**
1925. 7" diameter. German. - **$125 $300 $450**

FLX-3

FLX-4

**❑ FLX-3. "Felix Meets His Match" English Cartoon Booklet,**
c. 1925. Sportex clothing. Printed in England for distribution with clothing items locally and abroad. Eight-page story about Felix adopted by a tailor to dissatisfaction of both. -
**$50 $125 $200**

**❑ FLX-4. "Felix" Plaster Figure On Base,**
1920s. Store item. 1-1/2x3x3-1/2" tall figure in classic pose. - **$150 $300 $525**

FLX-5

FLX-6

❑ **FLX-5. Felix Large Size Japanese Celluloid Figure,**
1920s. Store item. 3-1/2" tall. - **$35 $75 $140**

❑ **FLX-6. "Felix" Wood-Jointed Doll,**
1920s. Store item by Schoenhut. 4" tall. - **$50 $125 $225**

FLX-7

❑ **FLX-7. English Cream Toffee Candy Tin,**
c. 1920s. Scarce. Store item. - **$300 $1200 $2000**

FLX-8

❑ **FLX-8. Spanish Candy Company Premium Card Set,**
1920s. San Fernando Chocolate, Barcelona, Spain. Full color set of 15 numbered cards comprise "Series C." Artist's name "Bofarull" appears on lower right corner.
Set - **$50 $85 $150**

FLX-9

FLX-10

❑ **FLX-9. Hand Puppet,**
c. 1930. Store item. 9-1/2" tall plush fabric by Steiff. With Ear Button - **$300 $650 $1000**
Button Removed - **$250 $500 $750**

❑ **FLX-10. "Felix" Tin Litho Sparking Toy,**
c. 1930. Store item. Pat Sullivan copyright. - **$125 $275 $500**

FLX-11

❑ **FLX-11. "Felix The Cat" Golfing Pillow Cover,**
c. 1930. Store item by Vogue Needlecraft #198. - **$40 $90 $150**

FLX-12

FLX-13

❑ **FLX-12. Tin Pull Toy,**
1930s. Store item by Nifty Toys. - **$150 $325 $650**

❑ **FLX-13. "Evening Ledger Comics" Cello. Button,**
1930s. Philadelphia newspaper. From set of 14 various characters. - **$60 $150 $300**

FLX-14

FLX-15

❑ **FLX-14. Felix Clicker,**
1930s. From Germany. Several in set. - **$35 $90 $135**

❑ **FLX-15. "Katz Kitten Klub" Cello. Button,**
1930s. Unknown sponsor. Felix image not identified. - **$40 $80 $165**

FLX-16

FLX-17

❑ **FLX-16. "Herald & Examiner" Litho. Button,**
1930s. Chicago newspaper. From "30 Comics" series featuring various characters. - **$10 $20 $40**

❑ **FLX-17. "Warner Bros. State" Theater Cello. Button,**
1930s. Obvious Felix image although "Krazy Kat Klub" designation. - **$30 $75 $165**

FLX-18

FLX-19

❑ **FLX-18. Aviation Shield Badge,**
1930s. Scarce. - **$100 $200 $300**

❑ **FLX-19. "Felix The Cat" Litho. Button,**
1950s. From set of various King Features Syndicate characters. - **$10 $20 $30**

FLX-20

❑ **FLX-20. "Felix The Cat Candies And Toy" Empty Box With Messmer Art,**
1952. Store item. Card on front punches out. - **$20 $60 $120**

FLX-21

❑ **FLX-21. Felix Board Game Set,**
1956. Includes a box, 1 die, a board, and 6 punch out markers. - **$25 $50 $85**

FLX-22

❑ **FLX-22. "Felix The Cat Candy And Toy" Product Box,**
1960. Phoenix Candy Co. - **$20 $50 $100**

FLX-23

FLX-24

❑ **FLX-23. Soaky Toy,**
1965. Colgate-Palmolive. Came in two colors - black and blue. Toy shown is blue version.
Black Variety - **$15 $25 $50**
Blue Variety - **$10 $20 $40**

❑ **FLX-24. Felix Plush Doll,**
1982. 23" tall with tag. - **$12 $40 $80**

FLX-25

FLX-26

❑ **FLX-25. Plush Doll,**
1982. 3" tall. Made in Korea. Hard to find. - **$10 $25 $35**

❑ **FLX-26. Felix Ceramic Bank,**
1980s. By Applause. 7 1/4" tall. - **$10 $30 $50**

FLX-27

FLX-28

❑ **FLX-27. Felix Beanie,**
1999. Beanie with tag. Heart on chest. - **$15**

❑ **FLX-28. Trophy Figure,**
1990s. Plastic figure with trophy stand that has revolving titles for Felix. Wendy's Premium. - **$5**

FLX-29

FLX-30

❑ **FLX-29. Felix Premium,**
1990s. From Wendy's Restaurants. Felix figure with a plastic fish in ball which you can catch when you turn Felix upside down. - **$2 $4 $10**

❑ **FLX-30. Felix Wacky Wobbler,**
2000. - **$15**

# Fibber McGee and Molly

**Jim and Marian Jordan were veterans of small-time vaudeville before they ventured into radio comedy in Chicago, first as *The O'Henry Twins* in 1924, then as *The Smith Family* in 1925, as *The Air Scouts* in 1927 and in *Smackout* from 1931 to 1935. Finally along with writer Don Quinn, they created *Fibber McGee and Molly* for Johnson's Wax. The show premiered on the NBC Blue network in April 1935 and developed into one of the most popular radio comedies of all time.**

**From their home at 79 Wistful Vista, McGee, the blundering windbag, and Molly, his long-suffering, forgiving wife, presided over one domestic disaster after another. Listeners waited each week for Fibber to open his closet door, whereupon the stacked contents would crash to the floor. The show featured a number of regular supporting characters: their neighbor Gildersleeve, Beulah the maid, henpecked Wallace Wimple, the Old Timer, Mayor La Trivia and Myrt, the telephone operator whose voice was never heard.**

**After Johnson's Wax dropped the show in 1950, Pet milk sponsored it until 1952, then Reynolds Aluminum until 1953, when the half-hour format was replaced by a 15-minute weekday series that ran until 1957. There was a comic book in 1949, the Jordans made some movies in the 1940s and a television series had a brief run on NBC in 1959-1960, but nothing equaled the McGee success on radio.**

FIB-1

❑ **FIB-1. Cast Photo,**
c. 1935. Shown at "NBC" microphone. - **$15 $30 $55**

FIB-2

FIB-3

❑ **FIB-2. Fibber Cello. Spinner Top On Wood Peg,**
1936. Scarce. Johnson's Wax Polishes. - **$50 $150 $300**

❑ **FIB-3. Molly Cello. Spinner Top With Wood Peg,**
1936. Scarce. Johnson's Wax Polishes. - **$50 $150 $300**

FIB-4

❑ **FIB-4. Party Game in Box,**
1936. NBC tie-in. - **$35 $70 $140**

FIB-5

❑ **FIB-5. "Johnson Glo-Coat Floor Polish" 8x14" Cardboard Display Sign ,**
1937. - **$50 $175 $275**

FIB-6

FIB-7

❑ **FIB-6. Cardboard 9x15" Store Display Sign,**
c. 1937. Designed for holding sample can of Johnson's Wax. - **$75 $150 $300**

❑ **FIB-7. Cardboard 11x16" Store Display Sign,**
c. 1937. Designed for holding sample can of Johnson's Wax. - **$60 $125 $250**

FIB-8

FIB-9

❑ **FIB-8. Johnson Products 11x15" Countertop Sign,**
c. 1937. Johnson's auto wax and cleaner. Diecut cardboard with easel back. - **$50 $125 $200**

❑ **FIB-9. Countertop Display Sign,**
1930s. Johnson's Wax Polishes. Full color 13x20". - **$100 $200 $300**

FIB-10

❑ **FIB-10. Cast Photo,**
1930s. - **$15 $30 $50**

FIB-11

FIB-12

❑ **FIB-11. Cardboard Advertising Blotter,**
1930s. Prudential Insurance. - **$15 $30 $60**

❑ **FIB-12. Fan Photo,**
c. 1940s. - **$15 $30 $50**

FIB-13

❑ **FIB-13. Record Album ,**
1947. Four 78 rpm rcords. - **$50 $100 $150**

FIB-14

❑ **FIB-14. "Fibber McGee And Molly" Record Set,**
c. 1940s. Store item. 10-1/4x12" cardboard album holds set of three 78 rpm records on the Capitol label. Mentions "Their First Appearance On Discs." - **$15 $30 $50**

## The Flash

**The fastest man alive, a superhero of the Golden Age of comic books, made his first appearance in *Flash Comics* #1 of January 1940. The book was discontinued in 1949 after 104 issues and was revived with issue #105 in March 1959. The speedster also appeared in *All-Flash* comics from 1941 to 1948 and showed up in early issues of *All-Star Comics* and *Comic Cavalcade* and in various DC Comics collections. He was revived in *Showcase* #4 of October 1956, with a new costume and a new secret identity. Among the colorful villains confronted by The Flash were The Fiddler and his magic Stradivarius, Mirror Master and Captain Cold, each with special evil powers. The Scarlet Speedster had his own live-action TV series on CBS during the 1990-91 season, and he currently appears in Cartoon Network's animated Justice League series. A 1946 giveaway comic book was distributed taped to boxes of Wheaties and a comics club offered a membership card and button as premiums.**

FLA-1

FLA-2

❑ **FLA-1. "The Flash/Fastest Man Alive" Litho. Button,**
1942. Rare. Flash Comics. Sent to everyone submitting a reader survey coupon printed in All-Flash #6 (July, 1942). The first thousand respondents also received a free copy of All-Flash #7. - **$300 $800 $2000**

❑ **FLA-2. "Flash Comics" Wheaties Purchase Comic Book,**
1946. As taped to two-box purchase, highest grade is fine. Good - **$325**
Fine - **$1400**

FLA-3

❑ **FLA-3. Flash Trading Cards,**
1980s. - **$25**

FLA-4

FLA-5

❑ **FLA-4. Modern Age Flash Resin Statue,**
1995. Limited to 2,870. Boxed - **$225**

❑ **FLA-5. Flash Keepsake Ornament in Box,**
1998. From Hallmark. - **$20**

FLA-6

FLA-7

❑ **FLA-6. Flash 5" Figure,**
1998. Limited to 2,500 - **$100**

❑ **FLA-7. Golden Age Flash Resin Statue,**
1998. Limited to 1,600. Hard to find on secondary market. Boxed - **$100**

FLA-8

FLA-9

❑ **FLA-8. Barry Allen Flash Ring,**
1999. Replica of ring in which the Flash's costume was compressed and stored. Cast in pewter and plated in 24-karat gold and metallic finish. Limited to 1,100. - **$100**

❑ **FLA-9. Flash Bean Bag Figure,**
1999. Warner Bros. Store exclusive. - **$8**

FLA-10

❑ **FLA-10. Flash Seven-Piece PVC Set,**
2000. DC DIrect. - **$40**

FLA-11

❑ **FLA-11. Flash and Kid Flash Action Figure Set,**
2001. DC DIrect. Set includes a miniature Cosmic Treadmill and a Flash ring with a secret costume compartment. - **$50**

## Flash Gordon

**Flash Gordon first blasted into space in January 1934 in a Sunday comic strip created by Alex Raymond for King Features. Since then, along with his companions Dale Arden and Dr. Zarkov, Flash has done violent battle with Ming the Merciless on the planet Mongo and with an assortment of interplanetary menaces in every possible medium. The Sunday strip, an immediate success, generated many comic book appearances--the first in *King Comics* #1 of April 1936; a radio series on the Mutual network in 1935-1936; an original novel published in 1936; three chapter plays for Universal starring Buster Crabbe between 1936 and 1940; a daily comic strip that ran from 1940 to 1944 and was revived in 1951; a syndicated live-action television series in 1953-1954; hardback reprints of early strips in 1967 and 1971; a Filmation animated cartoon for NBC in 1979-1980 and a lavish Technicolor movie in 1980. "Steady, Dale!"**

FGR-1

❑ **FGR-1. Home Foundry Casting Set,**
1934. Store item by Home Foundry Mfg. Co. Inc. 9x16x2" deep beautifully designed box holds instruction book/catalogue along with a two-part mold and equipment needed to produce lead figures.
Complete Set - **$300 $800 $1600**
Instruction Book Only - **$20 $40 $60**

FGR-2

FGR-3

❑ **FGR-2. "Flash Gordon" Litho. Button,**
1934. From set of seven showing various King Features Syndicate characters. - **$25 $65 $125**

❑ **FGR-3. "Dale Arden" Litho. Button,**
1934. From set of seven showing various King Features Syndicate characters. - **$25 $65 $125**

FGR-4

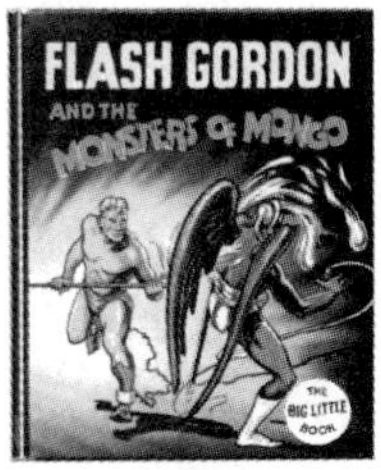


FGR-5

❑ **FGR-4. "Flash Gordon on the Planet Mongo" Big Little Book #1110,**
1934. - **$20 $75 $150**

❑ **FGR-5. "Flash Gordon and the Monsters of Mongo" Big Little Book #1166,**
1934. - **$20 $75 $150**

FGR-6

FGR-7

❑ **FGR-6. "Flash Gordon and the Tournaments of Mongo" Big Little Book #1171,**
1935. - **$20 $75 $150**

❑ **FGR-7. Buster Crabbe Dixie Ice Cream Lid,**
1936. - **$15 $25 $60**

FGR-8

❑ **FGR-8. "Flash Gordon Strange Adventure Magazine" Vol. 1 #1,**
1936. - **$200 $400 $800**

FGR-9

❑ **FGR-9. Movie Serial Club Member Card,**
1936. Scarce. Buster Crabbe pictured as Flash Gordon. - **$200 $500 $1000**

FGR-10

❑ **FGR-10. "Flash Gordon/Buster Crabbe Movie Club" Cello. Button,**
1936. - **$300 $850 $1700**

FGR-11

FGR-12

❑ **FGR-11. "Buster Crabbe" Dixie Ice Cream Picture,**
c. 1936. He is pictured as Flash Gordon from "New Universal Serial" described on reverse. - **$35 $100 $200**

❑ **FGR-12. "Buster Crabbe" Dixie Ice Cream Picture,**
c. 1936. He is pictured as Flash Gordon from "New Universal Serial" described on reverse. - **$35 $115 $225**

FGR-13

❑ **FGR-13. "Flash Gordon Vs. The Emperor Of Mongo" Book,**
1936. 4x5" hardcover otherwise similar format to Fast-Action Book. - **$75 $150 $200**

FGR-14

FGR-15

❑ **FGR-14. "Flash Gordon in the Water World Of Mongo" Big Little Book #1407,**
1937. By Alex Raymond. - **$20 $75 $150**

❑ **FGR-15. "Flash Gordon and the Witch Queen Of Mongo" Big Little Book #1190,**
1937. By Alex Raymond. - **$20 $75 $150**

FGR-16

❑ **FGR-16. "Flash Gordon's Trip to Mars" One Sheet Poster,**
1938. Universal Pictures serial stars Buster Crabbe. This duotone poster is for Chapter 4 of the 15 part serial- **$2500 $3200 $3750**

FGR-17

❑ **FGR-17. "Flash Gordon Adventure Club" Cello. Button,**
1938. Rare. Universal Pictures. For 12-chapter movie serial "Flash Gordon Conquers The Universe" starring Buster Crabbe and Carol Hughes, both pictured. - **$300 $750 $1300**

FGR-18

FGR-19

❑ **FGR-18. "Flash Gordon in the Forest Kingdom of Mongo" Better Little Book #1492,**
1938. - **$20 $75 $150**

❑ **FGR-19. "Chicago Herald And Examiner" Club Litho. Button,**
1930s. - **$75 $150 $300**

FGR-20

❑ **FGR-20. "Flash Gordon and the Perils of Mongo" Better Little Book #1423,**
1940. - **$20 $75 $150**

FGR-21

❑ **FGR-21. Feature Book No. 25,**
1941. Art by Austin Briggs, noted American illustrator who drew the daily newspaper series. - **$90 $270 $1170**

FGR-22

FGR-23

❑ **FGR-22. "Flash Gordon and the Tyrant of Mongo" Better Little Book #1484,**
1941. - **$20 $75 $150**

❑ **FGR-23. "Flash Gordon in The Ice World of Mongo" Better Little Book #1443,**
1942. - **$20 $75 $150**

FGR-24

FGR-25

❑ **FGR-24. "World Battle Fronts" World War II Folder Map,**
1943. Macy's department store "Flash Gordon Headquarters". Map opens to 20x27" sheet picturing global areas on both sides. - **$40 $75 $140**

❑ **FGR-25. "Flash Gordon and the Power Men of Mongo" Better Little Book #1469,**
1943. - **$15 $50 $110**

FGR-26

FGR-27

❑ **FGR-26. "Flash Gordon and the Red Sword Invaders" Better Little Book #1479,**
1945. - **$15 $50 $110**

❑ **FGR-27. "Flash Gordon in the Jungles of Mongo" Better Little Book #1424,**
1947. - **$10 $35 $70**

FGR-28

FGR-29

❑ **FGR-28. "Flash Gordon and the Fiery Desert of Mongo" Better Little Book #1447,**
1948. - **$10 $35 $70**

❑ **FGR-29. "S.F. Call-Bulletin" Cardboard Disk,**
c. 1940s. San Francisco newspaper. From series of contest disks, match number to win prize. - **$10 $25 $50**

FGR-30

❑ **FGR-30. "Flash Gordon Comics",**
1951. Gordon Bread Give-Away. Two issues of strip reprints. Each - **$2 $5 $10**

FGR-31

❑ **FGR-31. Inlaid Puzzle,**
1952. With sleeve. - **$75 $150 $200**

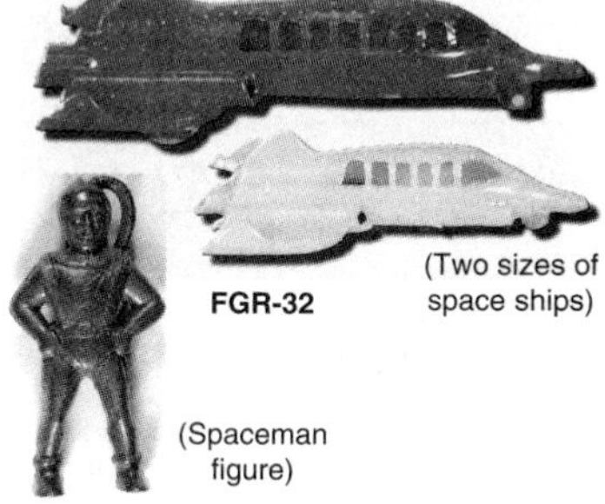
FGR-32
(Two sizes of space ships)
(Spaceman figure)

❑ **FGR-32. Solar Command Set,**
1952. Made by Premier. Set includes 2 space rockets (3 1/4" long) and 3 spaceman figures on card. Complete - **$395**
Space rockets (3 1/4") each - **$15 $30 $60**
Spaceman figures each - **$5 $15 $25**

Flash Gordon Space Rockets were also issued in different sizes on a separate card - 5 total.
Each 6 1/2" Rocket - **$50 $100 $150**
Each 4 3/4" Rocket - **$30 $60 $90**
Each 3 1/4" Rocket - **$15 $30 $60**

FGR-33

❑ **FGR-33. "March Of Comics No. 133" Booklet,**
1955. Poll-Parrot Shoes. From series by K.K. Publications. - **$10 $30 $85**

FGR-34

FGR-35

❑ **FGR-34. "Flash Gordon and the Baby Animals" Wonder Book,**
1955. - **$10 $20 $40**

❑ **FGR-35. "Puck" 10x10" Paper Store Sign,**
1950s. Puck The Comic Weekly and Sunday Comics. From series for drugstore use picturing various King Features characters. - **$25 $75 $135**

FGR-36

❑ **FGR-36. "Puck" 15x40" Paper Store Sign,**
1950s. Puck The Comic Weekly and Sunday Comics. For drugstore use picturing King Features characters. - **$35 $85 $150**

FGR-37

FGR-38

❑ **FGR-37. Litho. Button,**
1950s. 7/8" litho. from series picturing King Features Syndicate characters. Comes in several different color variations. - **$15 $30 $50**

❑ **FGR-38. Litho. Button,**
1950s. Issuer unknown but from a set of at least 30, each marked only by a tiny copyright symbol. 7/8" full color. - **$20 $40 $75**

FGR-39

FGR-40

❑ **FGR-39. Dale Arden Litho. Button,**
1960s. From set of King Features characters marked only by copyright symbol. -
**$15 $30 $60**

❑ **FGR-40. Medals and Insignia Pack,**
1978. Four medals and one insignia on card. -
**$25 $50 $75**

FGR-41

❑ **FGR-41. Candy Boxes,**
1978. Phoenix Candy Co. Set of eight.
Each - **$5 $10 $25**

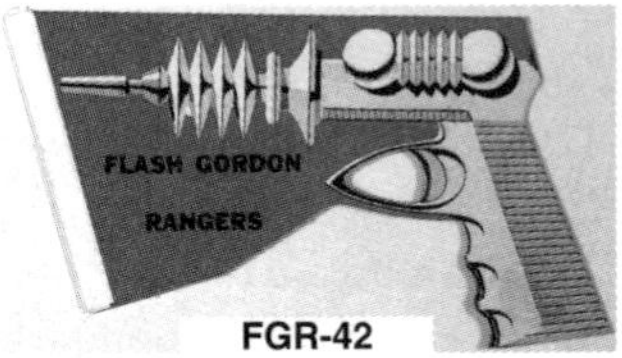


FGR-42

❑ **FGR-42. Flash Gordon Rangers Pop Gun,**
1970s.- **$25 $50 $75**

FGR-43

FGR-44

FGR-45

❑ **FGR-43. Ming the Merciless Figure on Card,**
1996. From the animated series. - **$8**

❑ **FGR-44. General Lynch Figure on Card,**
1996. From the animated series. - **$10**

❑ **FGR-45. Kobalt the Mercenary Figure on Card,**
1996. From the animated series. - **$8**

FGR-46

❑ **FGR-46. Ming's Jaws of Death Throne in Box,**
1996. From the animated series. Ming sold separately.- **$10**

FGR-47

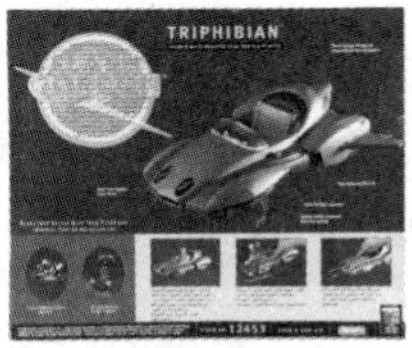


FGR-48

❑ **FGR-47. Flash Gordon Rebel Airbike in Box,**
1996. From the animated series. - **$10**

❑ **FGR-48. Flash Gordon Triphibian in Box,**
1996. Playmates. Multi purpose vehicle. - **$20**

FGR-49

❑ **FGR-49. Flash Gordon Lunch Box,**
2001. - **$20**

## The Flintstones

**Hanna-Barbera's Flintstones started life as the first adult prime-time television cartoon, went on to become the longest running such animated series in TV history (until *The Simpsons* came along) and spawned numerous reruns, specials, spinoffs and adaptations--as well as a merchandising bonanza. *The Flintstones* premiered on ABC in September 1960 and ran uninterrupted for six years, was rebroadcast on NBC Saturday mornings from 1967 to 1970 and has been around in one form or another ever since. A major film starring John Goodman was released in 1994. Another movie with a different cast, *Viva Rock Vegas*, was released in 2000. Scheduled for November 2001, the most recent animated feature, this time from the Cartoon Network, was titled *The Flintstones: On the Rocks*. The co-directors were Chris Savino and David Smith, with the characters based on the original designs of Ed Benedict.**

**Fred and Wilma Flintstone and their friends Barney and Betty Rubble are a prehistoric parody of the Kramdens and Nortons of *The Honeymooners,* complete with marital bickering, get-rich-quick schemes, bowling nights out and lodge membership. As added attractions, Dino, their pet dinosaur, was joined in 1963 by a baby daughter, Pebbles and by the Rubbles' adopted son, Bamm-Bamm. The kids spun off on their own show in 1971.**

**Comic book appearances began in 1961 and continued into the 1990s. The characters have been merchandised extensively, with several thousand tie-in items licensed. Post's Pebbles cereal and Flintstones chewable vitamins were promotional successes. "Yabba dabba doo!"**

FLN-1

❑ **FLN-1. "Stone Age Candy" Boxes,**
1962. Store item. Each - **$5 $10 $15**

FLN-2

❑ **FLN-2. "Welch's Fruit Drinks" Store Sign,**
1962. Full color 11x14". - **$50 $110 $160**

FLN-3

❑ **FLN-3. "Fred Flintstone Racing Kart" Plastic Friction Toy,**
1962. Store item by Marx.
Boxed - **$150 $300 $500**
Toy Only - **$100 $200 $300**

FLN-4

❑ **FLN-4. "Flintstone Pals On Dino" Litho. Tin Wind-Up Toy,**
1962. Store item by Marx. Available with either Fred or Barney riding. Each is 8-1/2" long.
Box - **$100 $200 $300**
Toy - **$125 $250 $350**

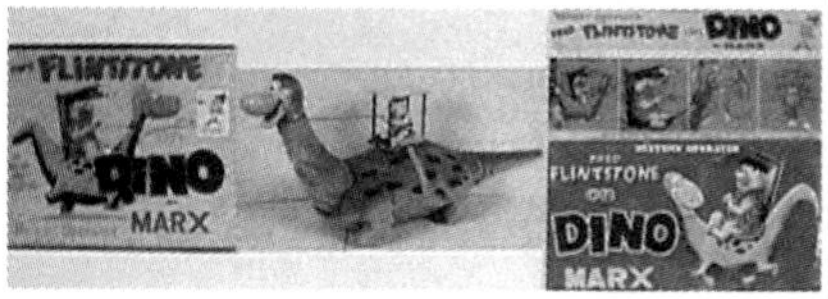

FLN-5

❑ **FLN-5. "Fred Flintstone On Dino" Battery Operated Toy,**
1962. Store item by Marx. Large vinyl and metal toy about 20" long with Dino covered in purple plush fabric very subject to color fading. Toy performs many functions specified on the box side panels. Near Mint Boxed - **$1350**
Toy Only - **$200 $450 $800**

FLN-6

❑ **FLN-6. "March Of Comics" #243,**
1963. Various retail sponsors. - **$8 $24 $60**

FLN-7

❑ **FLN-7. Pebbles On Dino Ramp Walker,**
c. 1963. Plastic store item by Marx Toys. - **$25 $60 $100**

FLN-8

❑ **FLN-8. "Pebbles-Wilma Pull Toy" In Plastic,**
1963. Store item by Transogram. 9" long by 10" tall. Boxed - **$125 $250 $400**

FLN-9

FLN-10

❑ **FLN-9. 1964-1965 New York World's Fair Comic Book,**
1964. Officially licensed souvenir published by JW Books With Hanna-Barbera copyright. - **$5 $15 $60**

❑ **FLN-10. Dino Litho. Button,**
1960s. Hanna-Barbera copyright. From 1960s Flintstone character set. - **$10 $20 $30**

FLN-11

FLN-12

❑ **FLN-11. "History Of Bedrock" 23x28" Poster,**
1970. Miles Laboratories. - **$25 $50 $85**

❑ **FLN-12. Flintstone Jewelry Display With 36 Character Rings,**
1972. Store item by Cartoon Celebrities Inc.
Complete - **$150 $250 $350**
Each Ring - **$3 $5 $8**

FLN-13

❑ **FLN-13. Cocoa Pebbles Box Flat And Premium,**
1972. Issued by Post. 13x17" flat. Example of three different "bird" kite premiums. Gordon Gold Archives. Near Mint Flat - **$225**
Each Near Mint Bagged Premium - **$10**

FLN-14

FLN-15

❑ **FLN-14. Fred Flintstone "Powell Valves" Pencil Eraser,**
1972. Wm. Powell Co. - **$15 $30 $50**

❑ **FLN-15. Vending Machine Litho. Button Set,**
1973. Set of 12, various color combinations.
**Each - $3 $5 $15**

FLN-16

❑ **FLN-16. Litho. Buttons,**
1973. Store item. Set of 10. Each - **$5 $12 $20**

FLN-17

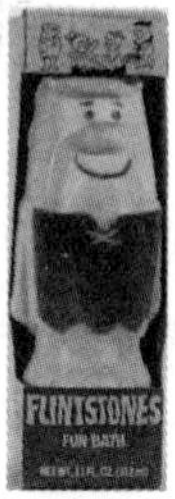


FLN-18

❑ **FLN-17. "Flint Cycle 16" Large Boxed Riding Toy,**
1974. Store item by AMF. Box - **$15 $30 $50**
Cycle - **$40 $65 $125**

❑ **FLN-18. Barney Fun Bath Bottle in Box,**
1977. Boxed - **$10 $25 $50**

FLN-19

FLN-20

❑ **FLN-19. Vending Machine Header Card,**
c. 1970s. Includes generic rings, generic Dino figure and rubber Flintstones figures.
Complete - **$75**

❑ **FLN-20. "Flintstick" Plastic/Metal Miniature Cigarette Lighter,**
c. 1970s. Flintstones Multiple Vitamins. -
**$50 $100 $150**

FLN-21

❑ **FLN-21. Flintstones Brand Multiple Vitamins Plastic Mugs,**
1970s. Each - **$5 $8 $15**

FLN-22

FLN-23

FLN-24

❑ **FLN-22. Flintstone Land/Sea Vehicle,**
1970s. Probable Post's Fruity Pebbles.
Unassembled In Cellophane Wrapper - **$20**
Assembled - **$5 $10 $20**

❑ **FLN-23. Fred On Dino Digger Toy,**
c. 1970s. Pebbles Cereal. Plastic mechanical action toy. - **$8 $15 $25**

❑ **FLN-24. Fruit Drinks Litho. Tab,**
c. 1970s. Yabba Dabba Dew. - **$8 $12 $20**

FLN-25

FLN-26

❑ **FLN-25. Fred Flintstone Bank Statue**
1993. 13" tall carnival statue. - **$30 $60 $120**

❑ **FLN-26. Barney Rubble Bank Statue**
1993. 12.5" tall carnival statue. - **$30 $60 $120**

FLN-27

❑ **FLN-27. "Post" Plastic Cereal Box Banks,**
1984. Cocoa Pebbles and Fruity Pebbles.
Each - **$8 $12 $20**

FLN-28

❑ **FLN-28. Fred & Barney Ceramic Figurines,**
1990. Post Cereals. Boxed - **$15 $30 $50**
Loose Pair - **$5 $15 $25**

FLN-29

❑ **FLN-29. Fruity Pebbles 17 oz. Cereal Box with Bendable Toys,**
1991. Post Cereals. Fred, Barney or Dino figures were packaged in the top of the box.
Each - **$5 $10 $20**

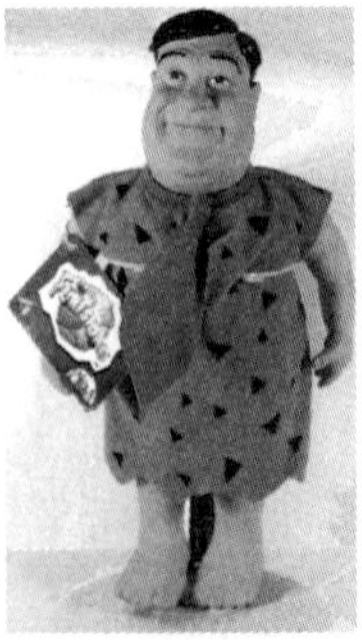

FLN-30

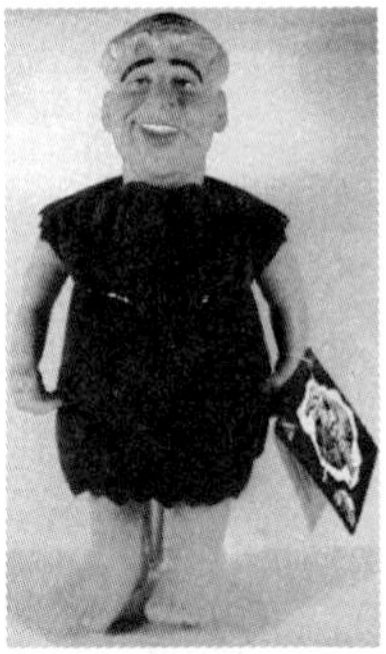

FLN-31

❑ **FLN-30. Fred Flintstone Movie Doll,**
1993. Dakin product. 13" tall with the likeness of actor John Goodman. - **$5 $15 $30**

❑ **FLN-31. Barney Rubble Movie Doll,**
1993. Dakin product. 12" tall with the likeness of actor Rick Moranis. - **$5 $15 $30**

(Lunch box)

FLN-32

(Box)

❑ **FLN-32. Flintstones Boxed Watch Set,**
1993. From Fossil. Watch and Barney pin come in a metal lunchbox picturing Fred and Barney.
Complete - **$125**

(Lunch box)

FLN-33

(Box)

❑ **FLN-33. Flintstones Boxed Watch Set,**
1993. From Fossil. Watch with 2 tags and Fred pin come in a metal lunchbox picturing Fred.
Complete - **$125**

FLN-34

FLN-35

FLN-36

❑ **FLN-34. Flintstones Movie Badge,**
1994. Giveaway badge. - **$2 $4 $10**

❑ **FLN-35. Replica Racing Car,**
1997. Features Flintstones on the car. - **$8**

❑ **FLN-36. Dino Bean Bag Figure,**
1998. Released a year before the other Flintstones Bean Bag figures. - **$25**

FLN-37

FLN-38

❑ **FLN-37. Fred Flintstone Bean Bag Figure,**
1999. With tag. - **$10**

❑ **FLN-38. Barney Rubble Bean Bag Figure,**
1999. With tag. - **$10**

FLN-39

❑ **FLN-39. Barney Rubble's Car on Card,**
1990s. Johnny Lightning series. - **$5**

## Flying Aces Club

**One of the many 1930s aviation-themed clubs inspired in part by the accomplishment of Charles Lindbergh. Sponsored by *Flying Aces Magazine*, most premiums carry the initials "FAC."**

FAC-1

FAC-2

❑ **FAC-1. Club Membership Card,**
1932. Logo of wings only, no propeller. - **$10 $40 $70**

❑ **FAC-2. Gold Cadet Wings,**
1932. - **$30 $60 $90**

FAC-3

FAC-4

❑ **FAC-3. Silver Pilot Wings,**
1932. - **$30 $60 $90**

❑ **FAC-4. "Pilot/FAC" Wings Badge,**
1932. Propeller on top of wings.
Silver version. - **$15 $25 $50**
Gold version - **$30 $60 $90**

FAC-5

FAC-6

❑ **FAC-5. "Cadet/FAC" Wings Rank Badge,**
1932. Propeller on top of wings.
Silver version. - **$15 $30 $50**
Gold version - **$30 $60 $90**

❑ **FAC-6. "Ace/FAC" Star Badge,**
1932. Scarce. - **$35 $75 $150**

FAC-7

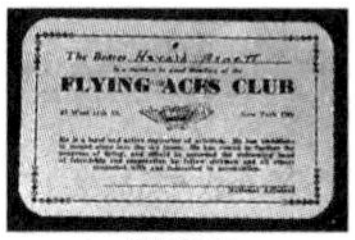

FAC-8

❑ **FAC-7. "Flying Aces" Silvered Brass Bracelet,**
1932. Link bands with top plate in wing and propeller design. - **$20 $60 $125**

❑ **FAC-8. Club Membership Card,**
1932. Logo of wings mounted by propeller. - **$10 $40 $70**

FAC-9

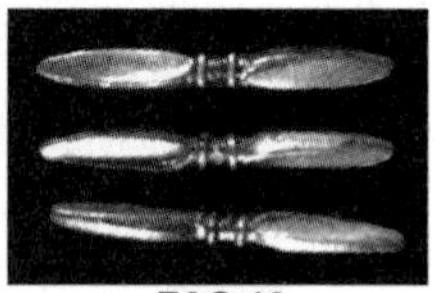
FAC-10

❑ **FAC-9. "F.A.C. Distinguished Service Medal" Brass Medal With Ribbon ,**
1932. Rare. Back inscription "Awarded By Flying Aces Club". - **$65 $150 $275**

❑ **FAC-10. FAC Propeller Pins,**
1932. Rare. For placement on "Service Medal" ribbon.
Each - **$15 $30 $50**

FAC-11

FAC-12

❑ **FAC-11. "FAC" Stitched Fabric Wings Patch,**
1932. Scarce. Flying Aces magazine. - **$30 $80 $125**

❑ **FAC-12. "Flying Aces" Large Cloth Patch,**
1930s. Flying Aces Magazine. 1-7/8x4-1/4" long with nice design of red, white and blue plus large gold wings all against white background. - **$30 $80 $125**

## The Flying Family

**This children's adventure program aired briefly on NBC in 1932-1933. The program dramatized the true-life story of Colonel George Hutchinson, his wife Blanche, and their daughters Kathryn and Janet. Accompanied by Sunshine, their lion cub mascot, the flying family found adventure in all parts of the country. Cocomalt sponsored the series, and young listeners could obtain their Flight Commander wings by drinking Cocomalt for at least 30 days and mailing in a statement witnessed and signed by a parent.**

FLY-1

❑ **FLY-1. Puzzle, Flight Commander Folder And Envelope,**
1932. Complete - **$15 $25 $45**

FLY-2

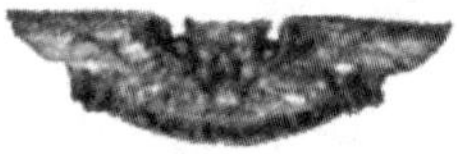
FLY-3

❑ **FLY-2. "Flight Commander/Flying Cubs" Brass Wings Rank Badge,**
1932. Highest rank depicting tiger head. - **$15 $30 $60**

❑ **FLY-3. "Flying Cubs" Brass Wings Badge,**
1932. Depicts tiger head. - **$15 $25 $50**

FLY-4

FLY-5

❑ **FLY-4. Family Picture Wheaties Box Back,**
c. 1932. - **$10 $20 $30**

❑ **FLY-5. Family Adventures Map,**
c. 1932. Cocomalt. Pictures various global regions plus listing of air times on NBC radio stations. - **$30 $65 $150**

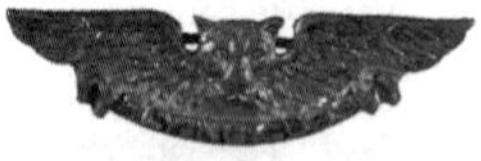
FLY-6

FLY-7

❑ **FLY-6. "Cub" Brass Wings Pin,**
c. 1932. Association with this program is uncertain. - **$10 $30 $50**

❑ **FLY-7. "Cub" Silvered Brass Lapel Stud,**
c. 1932. Association with this program is uncertain. - **$10 $30 $50**

## Foodini

**They started out in 1948 as the bumbling villains of the *Lucky Pup* series on CBS but Foodini and his dimwit accomplice Pinhead eventually took over the show and by 1951 were starring in their own series, *Foodini the Great*, on ABC. The hand puppets, created by Hope and Morey Bunin, were fated never to accomplish their swindling schemes, defeated by the Pup's pal Jolo the clown as well as by their own ineptitude. Sponsors of the two series (1948-1951) included Ipana toothpaste, Good and Plenty candy, Sundial shoes and Bristol-Myers. Licensed items are normally copyrighted R. P. Cox.**

FOO-1

❑ **FOO-1. Paper Portraits,**
c. 1948. Scarce. CBS-TV. Set of four: Doris Brown with Lucky Pup, Foodini, Pinhead, Jolo. Each - **$15 $25 $50**

FOO-2

FOO-3

❑ **FOO-2. "Jolo" Metal Pin On Card,**
1949. Store item. Pins or bracelets, also seen for Foodini. Each Carded - **$20 $40 $75**
Each Loose - **$10 $25 $50**

❑ **FOO-3. Plastic Microscope With Instructions,**
1950. Ipana Toothpaste. Includes six slides for microscope. Instruction Folder - **$10 $15 $25**
Microscope - **$15 $30 $50**
Slides Each - **$1 $3 $5**

FOO-4

❑ **FOO-4. Birthday Card,**
1950. Store item by The Daline. - **$15 $25 $50**

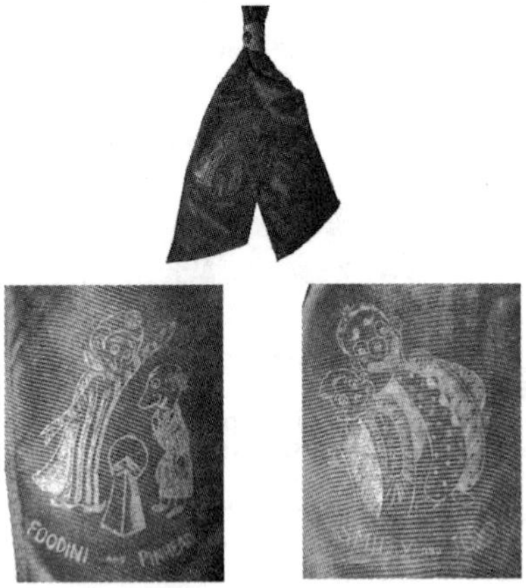
FOO-5

❑ **FOO-5. Foodini Fabric Scarf,**
c. 1950. Ipana Toothpaste. 19" long dark brown fabric with large gold illustration on each end picturing "Foodini And Pinhead" and "Smiley And Jolo." Front of Smiley's costume is inscribed "Ipana." Example shown has simulated brown leather slide accented by brass rivets and faceted emerald green stone but we're not certain this was actually part of the original item. - **$35 $75 $150**

FOO-6

❑ **FOO-6. Cardboard Mask,**
c. 1950. Scarce. Punch-out from unknown source. - **$50 $150 $250**

FOO-7

FOO-8

❑ **FOO-7. "Foodini" As Magician Dexterity Puzzle,**
1951. Plastic over tin frame puzzle. -
**$20 $50 $90**

❑ **FOO-8. "Jolo" Juggling Dexterity Puzzle,**
1951. Plastic over tin frame puzzle. -
**$20 $50 $90**

FOO-9

FOO-10

❑ **FOO-9. "Pinhead" Dexterity Puzzle,**
1951. Plastic over tin frame puzzle. -
**$20 $50 $90**

❑ **FOO-10. Cardboard Pop Gun,**
c. 1951. Sundial Bonnie Laddie Shoes. -
**$25 $65 $100**

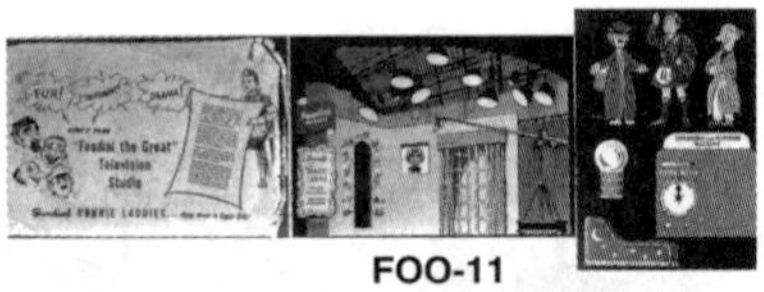
FOO-11

❑ **FOO-11. "Television Studio" Cardboard Kit With Mailer,**
c. 1951. Sundial Bonnie Laddie Shoes. Includes stage, figures and accessories.
Near Mint In Mailer - **$300**

# Foxy Grandpa

**Cartoonist C. E. Schultze (1866-1939) created his *Foxy Grandpa* comic strip for the Sunday New York Herald in 1900. The strip, which showed Grandpa consistently outwitting a pair of young tormentors, was an instant success with readers, but its popularity waned over the years. It moved to the New York American in 1902, then to the New York Press, where it ran until 1918. A series of nature tales, *Foxy Grandpa's Stories*, ran in newspapers during the 1920s. Hardcover reprints of the strip were published in the early years and a musical comedy based on the strip opened on Broadway in 1902. Schultze typically signed his drawings Bunny, with an appropriate sketch.**

FOX-1

FOX-2

❑ **FOX-1. Comic Strip Announcement 15x20" Paper Poster,**
1902. New York Sunday Journal. -
**$100 $200 $400**

❑ **FOX-2. "Foxy Grandpa's Grocery Store" Cut-Out Supplement,**
1902. New York American & Journal newspaper. Uncut - **$35 $60 $100**

FOX-3

FOX-4

❑ **FOX-3. "Six Months In New York" Cello. Button,**
1902. For theater version based on comic strip.-
**$15 $30 $50**

❑ **FOX-4. "Foxy Grandpa" Cello. Button,**
c. 1902. Hearst's Chicago American. Promotes start of comic strip by that newspaper. -
**$15 $30 $50**

FOX-5

❑ **FOX-5. Foxy Grandpa Song Sheet,**
c. 1902. Scarce. Newspaper supplement. -
**$20 $60 $120**

FOX-6

FOX-7

❑ **FOX-6. Foxy Grandpa Song Sheet,**
c. 1902. Scarce. Newspaper supplement. -
**$20 $60 $120**

❑ **FOX-7. "Foxy Grandpa/Chicago American" Diecut White Metal Stickpin,**
c. 1902. Lightly tinted, depicts him and both boys. - **$25 $40 $75**

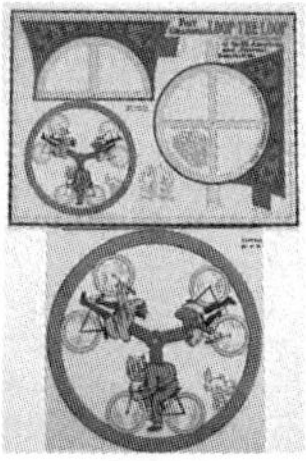
FOX-8

FOX-9

❑ **FOX-8. Foxy Grandpa's "Loop-The-Loop" Sunday Comic Cut-Out Supplement,**
1903. New York American and Journal. 10x14" stiff paper issued Sunday, May 10.
Uncut - **$35 $60 $100**

❑ **FOX-9. "Foxy Grandpa Second Year Of The Musical Comedy" Diecut Cello. Figure,**
c. 1903. 2-1/2" tall full color thin cello. figure by Whitehead & Hoag Co. - **$20 $40 $75**

FOX-10

❑ **FOX-10. Sunday Newspaper Comics Reprint Book,**
1905. Store item by M. A. Donohue & Co., Chicago. One of a series of books by various publishers published between 1901 and 1916 with at least 18 known.
Each Approximately - **$104 $365 $625**

FOX-11

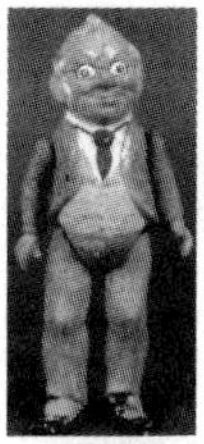
FOX-12

❑ **FOX-11. Bisque Figure,**
c. 1905. Store item. - **$50 $120 $200**

❑ **FOX-12. Composition Figure,**
c. 1905. Store item. Jointed arms and legs. -
**$50 $120 $200**

FOX-13

FOX-14

❑ **FOX-13. Flocked Composition Candy Container,**
c. 1905. Store item. - **$75 $150 $325**

❑ **FOX-14. Foxy Grandpa And The Boys Stickpin,**
c. 1905. About 1-1/2" tall in silver luster white metal. - **$10 $20 $40**

FOX-15

❑ **FOX-15. Figural Bisque Humidor,**
c. 1905. Unmarked but probably German. Our photo example is missing lid.
No Lid - **$65 $125 $175**
Near Mint With Lid - **$250**

FOX-16

❑ **FOX-16. Postcard,**
1906. Boston Sunday American premium. Has heat-applied tattoo transfer on front. -
**$8 $15 $25**

FOX-17

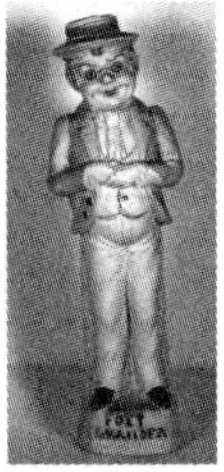
FOX-18

❑ **FOX-17. Bisque Figure,**
Early 1900s. - **$75 $200 $300**

❑ **FOX-18. Bisque Figure,**
1920s. - **$50 $100 $200**

## Frank Buck

**Animal hunter and trapper Frank Buck (1884-1950) achieved international fame after World War I as a jungle explorer whose claim that he never intentionally harmed a wild animal led to his motto "Bring 'Em Back Alive." Buck went around the world more than a dozen times collecting animals, giving lectures, making movies and writing magazine articles and books, and at one point owned the world's largest private zoo in Amityville, New York. He appeared as himself in two brief radio series: on NBC in 1932 sponsored by A. C. Gilbert toys and on the Blue network in 1934 sponsored by Pepsodent toothpaste. Buck and his animals were featured at the 1934 Century of Progress Exposition in Chicago and the 1939-1940 New York World's Fair. Items inscribed "Jungle Camp" are from the earlier exposition; those inscribed "Jungle Land" or "Jungleland" are from his 1939 exhibit. A 1932 documentary film followed him through the Malay jungles as he collected various animals and Buck played an adventurer in Columbia Pictures' first chapter play, *Jungle Menace*, in 1937. CBS-TV aired a *Bring 'Em Back Alive* fiction series in 1982-1983 starring Bruce Boxleitner as the legendary hunter.**

FRB-1

FRB-2

❑ **FRB-1. "Bring 'Em Back Alive" Book,**
1930. By Frank Buck. Published by Simon and Schuster.
Book - **$25 $50 $75**
With Dust Jacket - **$150**

❑ **FRB-2. A.C. Gilbert Christmas Ad Photo,**
1932. Frank Buck inscription "I Hope You Get An Erector Set For Christmas". - **$20 $40 $70**

FRB-3

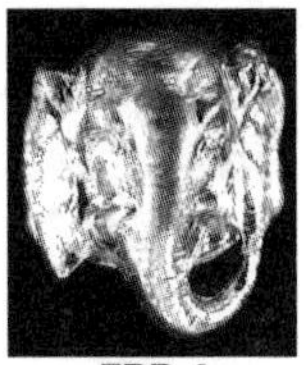
FRB-4

❑ **FRB-3. "Bring 'Em Back Alive" Button,**
c. 1932. 1-3/4" likely issued to promote the movie of this title. - **$25 $50 $95**

❑ **FRB-4. Movie Ring,**
1932. Silver luster with adjustable bands made by Uncas and issued to promote 1932 movie "Bring 'Em Back Alive." - **$75 $150 $300**

FRB-5

❑ **FRB-5. Chicago World's Fair Brochure,**
1934. Four pages. Promotes Jungleland exhibit. - **$20 $30 $45**

FRB-6

❑ **FRB-6. "Capturing Wild Elephants!" Book,**
1934. 28 page book, 12"x9". Merrill Publishing Co. - **$35 $70 $200**

FRB-7

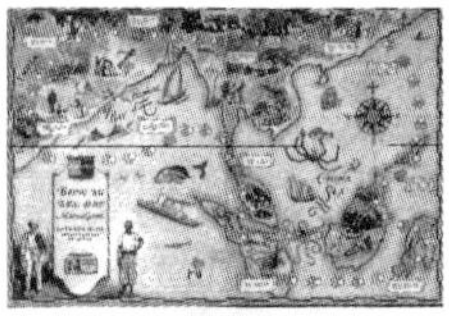
FRB-8

❑ **FRB-7. "Frank Buck's Jungle Camp" Cello. Button,**
1934. From exhibit at Chicago World's Fair. - **$20 $40 $75**

❑ **FRB-8. "Bring 'Em Back Alive" Map And Game 14x22",**
c. 1934. Two versions: premium from "Scott's Emulsion" or store item by "Funland Books & Games". - **$60 $150 $250**

FRB-9

❑ **FRB-9. Club Manual,**
1934. Pepsodent toothpaste. - **$35 $100 $175**

FRB-10

FRB-11

❑ **FRB-10. Mailer,**
1934. For Club manual. Rare. - **$35 $85 $130**

❑ **FRB-11. "Frank Buck" Brass Lucky Piece,**
1934. Pepsodent toothpaste. Back pictures leopard head with inscription "Tidak Hilang Berani". Copy of Hindu hunter's charm carried by Ali, Frank Buck's Number 1 Boy. -
**$30 $100 $150**

FRB-12

FRB-13

❑ **FRB-12. "A Century Of Progress" Chicago World's Fair Litho. Button,**
1934. From exhibit, dated for second year of fair. - **$35 $75 $140**

❑ **FRB-13. "Adventurers Club-Member" Brass Button,**
1934. Pepsodent toothpaste. - **$5 $12 $25**

FRB-14

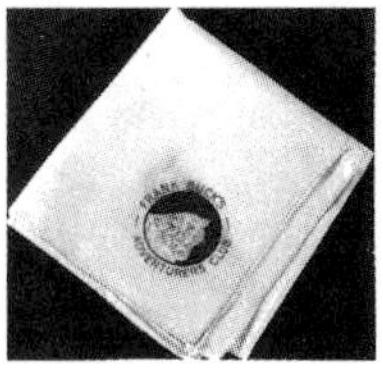

FRB-15

❑ **FRB-14. Film Supplement,**
1934. Sixteen page premium. Promotes the film "Wild Cargo." - **$25 $50 $75**

❑ **FRB-15. "Adventurers Club" Fabric Neckerchief,**
1934. Pepsodent toothpaste. - **$40 $80 $150**

FRB-16

❑ **FRB-16. "Young American News Weekly,"**
1935. Weekly issue with 16 pages. -
**$15 $30 $60**

FRB-17

FRB-18

❑ **FRB-17. Prize Checklist,**
1935. Pepsodent prize list. - **$10 $20 $30**

❑ **FRB-18. "Frank Buck Club" Cello. Button,**
1936. - **$25 $75 $150**

FRB-19

❑ **FRB-19. "Frank Buck's Adventure Club" Ring,**
1938. Bronze or silver color. -
**$800 $1200 $2400**

FRB-20

❑ **FRB-20. "Frank Buck's Jungleland" New York World's Fair Card,**
1939. Briefly described his exhibit in the amusement area. - **$8 $12 $25**

(CLOSE-UP)

FRB-21

❑ **FRB-21. "Jungle Camp" Metal Letter Opener/Bookmark,**
1939. From exhibit at New York World's Fair. -
**$25 $50 $100**

FRB-22

FRB-23

❑ **FRB-22. "Bring 'Em Back Alive" Ivory Initial Ring,**
1939. Ivory Soap. Brass with personalized initial ivory-colored insert. - **$100 $250 $400**

❑ **FRB-23. "Frank Buck's Jungleland" New York World's Fair Brass Ring,**
1939. Rare. Tiny "NYWF" initials rather than traditional Frank Buck's Adventurers Club inscription. - **$1000 $2500 $5000**

FRB-24

❑ **FRB-24. "New York World's Fair/Frank Buck's Jungleland" Leather Pennant,**
1939. 14-1/4" long. - **$75 $175 $300**

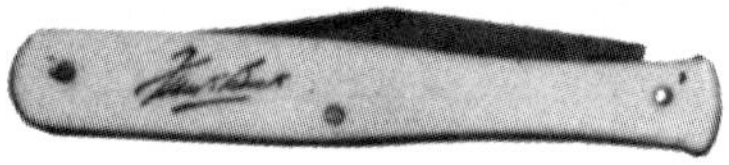

FRB-25

❑ **FRB-25. Cello./Steel Pocketknife,**
1939. Ivory Soap. White grips with facsimile signature on one. - **$65 $150 $250**

FRB-26

❑ **FRB-26. Pennant,**
1939. New York World's Fair Jungleland exhibit pennant. Scarce. - **$75 $175 $300**

FRB-28

FRB-27

FRB-29

❑ **FRB-27. World's Fair Promo,**
1939. New York World's Fair brochure. Eight pages. - **$25 $35 $50**

❑ **FRB-28. Coin,**
1939. Jungleland premium with hole for chain. New York World's Fair Coin. Scarce. -
**$35 $70 $125**

❑ **FRB-29. New York World's Fair Exhibit Cello. Button,**
1939. Black and white 1-1/4". - **$20 $45 $90**

FRB-31

FRB-30

❑ **FRB-30. Buckhorn Rifle Manual,**
1930s. Twelve page premium. Shows Frank testing the gun, as well as various photos of the gun. - **$15 $25 $50**

❑ **FRB-31. Postcard,**
1930s. Premium for exhibition in New York -
**$10 $25 $40**

FRB-32

(Back view)

❑ **FRB-32. "Jacaré" Movie Promo,**
1942. United Artists film. - **$20 $50 $75**

FRB-33

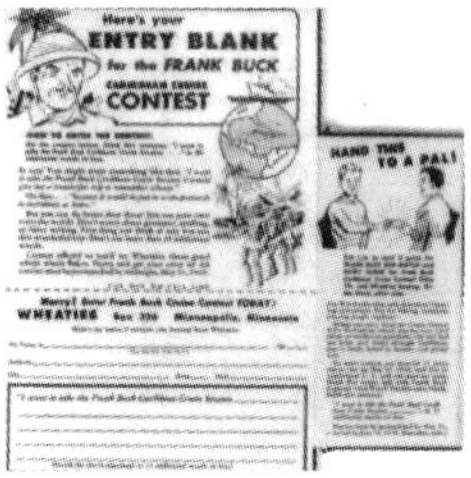


FRB-34

❑ **FRB-33. "Frank Buck Explorer's Sun Watch",**
1949. Jack Armstrong/Wheaties. - **$20 $35 $65**

❑ **FRB-34. Wheaties Caribbean Cruise Contest And Sun Watch Leaflets,**
1949. Contest Sheet - **$5 $15 $25**
Sun Watch Order Form - **$5 $10 $15**

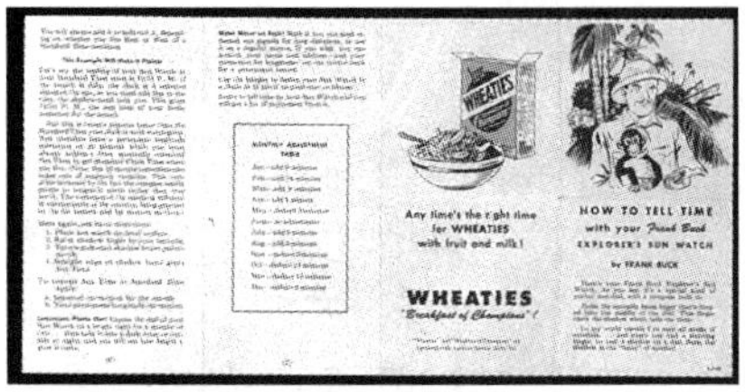


FRB-35

❑ **FRB-35. "Frank Buck Explorer's Sun Watch" Instruction Leaflet,**
1949. Wheaties. Folder opening to four panels w/instructions printed on both sides. -
**$10 $20 $35**

## Frank Merriwell

**Dime novels, the forerunner of pulp magazines, became popular in the 1880s. Colorful covers highlighted text stories embellished with daring deeds and the triumph of good over evil. Writer Gilbert Patten, under various pseudonyms, had been doing stories for several years when approached by the large publishing company Street & Smith to come up with a character for their new magazine *Tip Top Library*. Using "Frank" for frankness, "Merri" for happy disposition and "Well" for good health, he came up with Frank Merriwell.**

**Written under the pen name Burt L. Standish, Frank's first adventure was published on April 18, 1896. Author Patten imbued Frank Merriwell with a Yale education, a sharp mind, physical fitness, an honest demeanor and a penchant for hard work. Merriwell became an inspiration to boys and girls nationwide. He was not only a role model, but an imaginary friend they could trust. Patten went on to author 208 Frank Merriwell books, which sold over 100 million copies.**

**Merriwell's adventures remained popular well in the 1940s in a comic strip, a Big Little Book title, a movie serial and a radio program with Lawson Zerbe in the title role. Frank Merriwell's adventures and personality set the tone for one of radio's most popular characters, the next "All-American Boy," Jack Armstrong.**

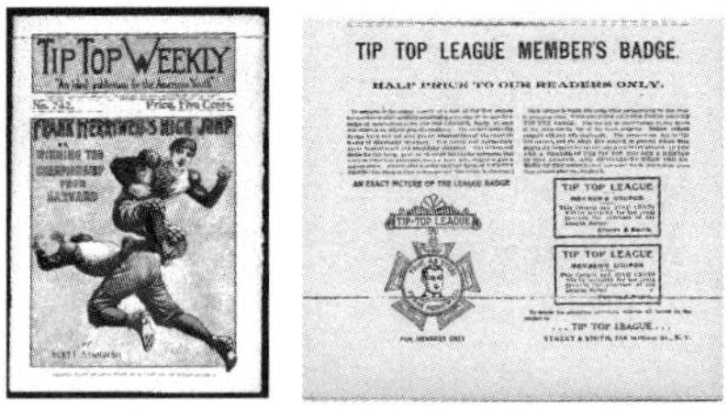


FRM-1

❑ **FRM-1. Tip Top Weekly #242,**
1900. Frank Merriwell's Tip Top League Badge pictured with application for 1st premium badge.-
**$25 $50 $75**

FRM-2

FRM-3

❑ **FRM-2. Frank Merriwell Tip Top League Brass Badge,**
1900. Tip Top Magazine premium. First character badge. Offered for 20¢ or a dime and two coupons from Tip Top Weekly. -
**$100 $250 $500**

❑ **FRM-3. "Frank Merriwell At Yale" BLB,**
1935. Store item. Whitman #1121. -
**$15 $30 $75**

FRM-4

FRM-5

❑ **FRM-4. "Club Member/Follow The Adventures Of Frank Merriwell" Cello . Button,**
1936. Scarce. Universal Pictures. For 12-chapter movie serial "The Adventures Of Frank Merriwell". - **$50 $125 $250**

❑ **FRM-5. "Follow Frank Merriwell" Cello. Button,**
1930s. Also reads "Daily In The Washington Herald." 1-1/4" blue and red on white from a scarce series of comic characters issued by this newspaper. - **$50 $125 $225**

## Freakies

**Ralston Purina Company introduced Freakies cereal--crunchy, sugary puffs--in 1973, along with a gang of seven creatures also called Freakies. The creatures, ugly little characters covered with bumps, were named Boss Moss, Cowmumble, Gargle, Goody-Goody, Grumble, Hamhose, and Snorkledorf. In-package premiums included PVC Freakies, stickers, holograms, and a set of rubber air bulb-powered vinyl race cars. The cereal was an initial success but failed to win repeat customers. An attempt to revive Freakies as Space Surfers in 1987 also failed.**

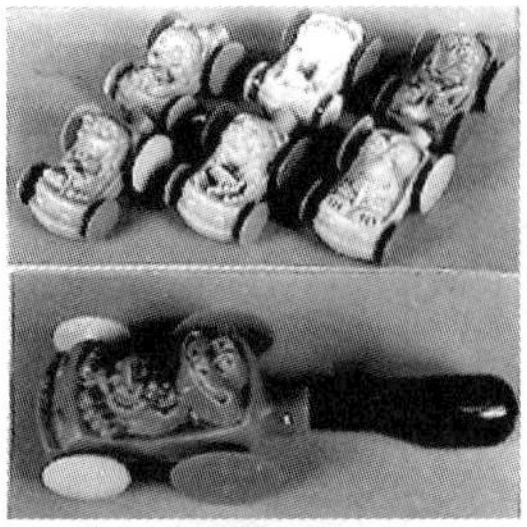

FRK-1

FRK-2

❑ **FRK-1. "Freakie Car" Set Of Seven Vinyl Racers,**
1974. Each is 2-1/2" long plus rubber air bulb to launch car. Top edge of front bumper names each as "Boss Moss, Goody Goody, Hamhose, Cowmumble, Snorkledorf, Gargle, Grumble."
Near Mint Boxed With Instructions - **$125**
Each With Air Bulb - **$5 $8 $12**

❑ **FRK-2. Fabric Iron-On Patches,**
1975. Pictured are Gargle, Cowmumble, Hamhose from probable set of seven.
Each - **$5 $10 $15**

FRK-3

FRK-4

FRK-5

❑ **FRK-3. Boss Moss Freakies Plastic Ring,**
1970s. Ralston Cereal. Orange plastic with 1-1/2" tall figure on top accented in black. - **$75 $150 $275**

❑ **FRK-4. Freakies Rubber Magnet,**
1970s. At least five different characters seen in a small version about 1" to 1-1/2" and a larger version about 1-1/2" to 2". Each - **$3 $6 $12**

❑ **FRK-5. Freakies Vinyl Figures,**
1970s. At least seven different in various single colors, each about 1-1/2" to 2".
Each - **$3 $5 $12**

FRK-6

❑ **FRK-6. Freakies Boats,**
1970s. Soft plastic figures of Hamhose, Cowmumble, Grumble, each designed to hold balloon to propel in water by air loss after inflation. Each - **$3 $10 $15**

FRK-7

❑ **FRK-7. Freakies Cereal Box,**
1987. - **$20 $60 $85**

# Fred Allen

**Fred Allen (1894-1956) was a vaudeville juggler and standup comic who became one of the legendary radio comedians of the 1930s and 1940s. From his first show on CBS in 1932 to his last on NBC in 1949, hardly a week went by without a Fred Allen program of one sort or another. Allen wrote his own material and his "feud" with Jack Benny was a successful running gag from 1936 to 1949. Also memorable was Allen's Alley, a mythical street he developed in 1942, inhabited by Mrs. Nussbaum, Titus Moody, Ajax Cassidy and Senator Claghorn. Sponsors over the years included Linit bath oil, Hellmann's mayonnaise, Sal Hepatica, Ipana toothpaste, Texaco gasoline, Tenderleaf tea and Ford automobiles. Allen made a number of television appearances in the 1950s on comedy and quiz shows but his biting wit and literate humor were better suited to radio.**

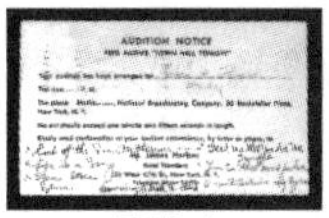
FRD-1

FRD-2

FRD-3

❑ **FRD-1. Fred Allen's "Town Hall Tonight" Audition Notice Postcard,**
1935. Notification to entertainer hopeful granting radio audition at NBC Studios, New York. - **$5 $10 $20**

❑ **FRD-2. "Town Hall Tonight" Fan Postcard,**
1937. Radio show title on back. - **$8 $15 $30**

❑ **FRD-3. Fred Allen & Portland Hoffa Fan Photo,**
c. 1937. Ipana toothpaste and Salhepatica Stomach Relief. Back names "Town Hall Tonight" radio show. - **$8 $15 $30**

# Friends of the Phantom

**Between 1933 and 1953 Richard Curtis Van Loan--alias the Phantom--solved over 150 crimes in the pages of the pulp magazine *Phantom Detective*. Created by D.L. Champion writing under the name Robert Wallace, the Phantom was a genius of disguise and a physical marvel. During the 1930s, readers who joined his crime-fighting club would receive a Friends of the Phantom badge.**

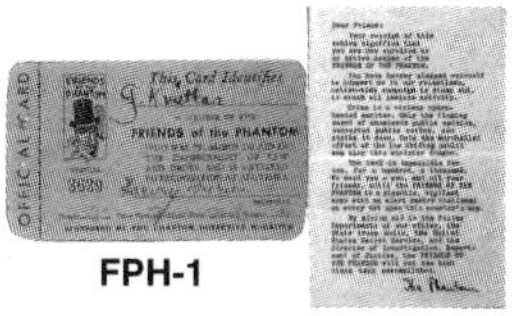
FPH-1

FPH-2

❑ **FPH-1. "Friends Of The Phantom" Letter And Membership Card,**
1930s. Phantom Detective magazine.
Card - **$75 $125 $250**
Letter - **$50 $100 $150**

❑ **FPH-2. "Friends Of The Phantom" Brass Shield Badge,**
1930s. Phantom Detective magazine. Phantom depicted in mask and top hat. - **$75 $150 $300**

# Fu Manchu

**Master scientist and brilliant prince of evil, Fu Manchu was created by novelist Sax Rohmer in 1911. He appeared in a series of silent films in the 1920s and in talkies from 1929 to 1980 played by Warner Oland, Boris Karloff, Henry Brandon, Christopher Lee or Peter Sellers. The evil oriental, who was either avenging the death of his wife and son or out to conquer or destroy the world, starred in several radio serials: on *The Collier Hour*, sponsored by Collier's magazine, on the Blue network in 1927; on CBS in 1932-1933 sponsored by Campana Balm and in *The Shadow of Fu Manchu*, a syndicated 1939-1940 serial. A syndicated television series had a brief run in 1956.**

FUM-1

FUM-2

❑ **FUM-1. "The Hand Of Fu Manchu" Hardback With Dust Jacket,**
1917. Published by A. L. Burt Co. With Jacket - **$20 $40 $75**

❑ **FUM-2. "The Mask Of Fu Manchu" Hardcover Book,**
1932. Published by A. L. Burt Co. with art by J. R. Flanagan. - **$20 $40 $65**

FUM-3

FUM-4

❑ **FUM-3. Paper Mask,**
1932. Rare. Various theaters. - **$75 $200 $325**

❑ **FUM-4. "Mask Of Fu Manchu" Movie Herald,**
1932. Folder for M-G-M movie starring Boris Karloff in title role. - **$25 $50 $80**

FUM-5

FUM-6

❑ **FUM-5. "Shadow Of Fu Manchu" Radio Promo Matchbook Cover,**
1939. - **$10 $40 $75**

❑ **FUM-6. "The Shadow Of Fu Manchu" Radio Serial Cello. Button,**
1939. - **$35 $75 $150**

FUM-7

FUM-8

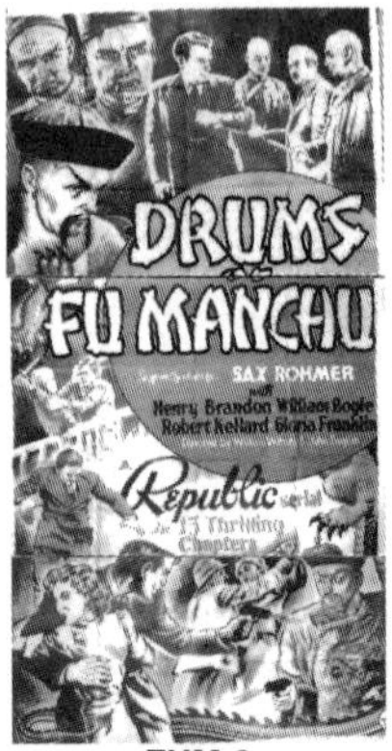


FUM-9

❑ **FUM-7. "Shadow Of Fu Manchu" Keys Trick With Envelope,**
c. 1939. Dodge Motors Co. "Mystic Keys" dexterity trick of two interlocking 2" metal keys in envelope imprinted for WFBR Radio, Baltimore.
Envelope - **$50 $100 $150**
Key Set - **$30 $60 $90**

❑ **FUM-8. "Drums Of Fu Manchu" Movie Serial Cello. Button,**
1940. Scarce. - **$40 $100 $250**

❑ **FUM-9. "Drums Of Fu Manchu" 41x77" Three-Sheet Poster,**
1940. Republic Pictures. 15-chapter movie serial. - **$200 $450 $800**

FUM-10

FUM-11

❑ **FUM-10. "Drums Of Fu Manchu" 27x41" Movie Serial Poster,**
1940. Republic Pictures. - **$150 $400 $650**

❑ **FUM-11. "Drums Of Fu Manchu" 14x22" Window Card,**
1940. Republic Pictures. - **$30 $50 $75**

FUM-12

❑ **FUM-12. Six-Sheet Poster,**
1940. Republic Pictures. Issued in folded size of 11x15" but assembles to 80x80". -
**$210 $500 $850**

## Fury

**Fury was a black stallion and the star attraction on NBC-TV's Saturday morning lineup from 1955 to 1966. His human co-stars in this extremely popular series were Bobby Diamond as a young orphan and Peter Graves as the rancher who adopted the boy and gave him the horse as a means of teaching him responsibility. The show received a number of awards from various civic and service groups for its non-violent handling of problems of right and wrong. Post cereals was an early sponsor but merchandising was not extensive. Items are normally copyrighted Vision Productions Inc., Television Programs of America Inc. or Independent Television Corp. The show has been syndicated under the title *Brave Stallion.* Dell published a series of *Fury* comic books between 1957 and 1962.**

FUR-1

❑ **FUR-1. Cast Member Photo,**
c. 1955. Glossy black and white with facsimile signatures of Bobby Diamond, Peter Graves, William Fawcett, Ann Robinson. - **$10 $20 $30**

FUR-2

❑ **FUR-2. "Fury Cowboy Neckerchief" Kit With Envelope,**
c. 1955. Mail premium of fabric bandanna, metal clasp, color photo. Near Mint In Mailer - **$100**
Photo - **$5 $10 $20**
Bandanna - **$5 $10 $15**
Clasp - **$15 $30 $65**

FUR-3

❑ **FUR-3. "Fury's Western Roundup" Party Kit,**
c. 1955. Borden Co. Extensive paper items including eight punch-out sheets.
Unused - **$20 $40 $75**

FUR-4

FUR-5

❑ **FUR-4. "Fury And The Lone Pine Mystery" Book,**
1957. Whitman #1537. - **$5 $10 $25**

❑ **FUR-5. "Fury And The Mystery At Trappers Hole" Book,**
1959. Whitman #1557. - **$5 $10 $25**

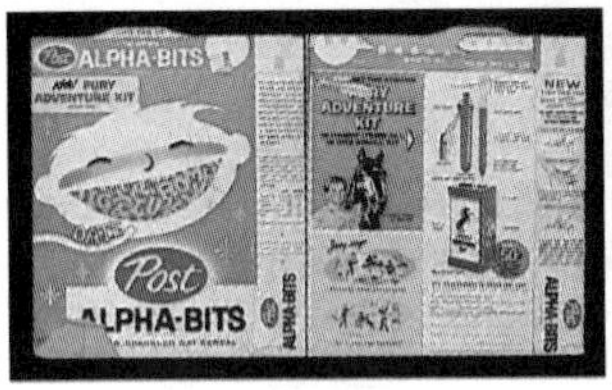


FUR-6

FUR-7

❑ **FUR-6. Cereal Box Offering Fury Adventure Kit,**
1960. Post Alpha-Bits.
Used Complete - **$35 $75 $125**

❑ **FUR-7. "Fury Adventure Kit",**
1960. Post Alpha-Bits. Multi-purpose plastic including weather indicator, flashlight, whistle, pen and miniature writing tablet. -
**$50 $100 $150**

## Gabby Hayes

**George "Gabby" Hayes (1885-1969) acted in a traveling repertory company and played burlesque and vaudeville before he went to Hollywood for a film career that spanned more than 30 years. Known as Windy, then Gabby, the whiskered, ornery, toothless geezer played sidekick to Hopalong Cassidy, Roy Rogers, Gene Autry, Bill Elliott, Randolph Scott and John Wayne in well over 100 Westerns. Hayes was a regular on radio's *Roy Rogers Show* in the 1940s and had his own program on the Mutual network in 1951-1952, sponsored by Quaker cereals. Adventure and Western comic books appeared between 1948 and 1957. On television, two separate series--both called *The Gabby Hayes Show*--ran concurrently. One was a weekly educational program about episodes in American history (NBC 1950-1951), the other a fictional series of tall tales and Western film clips (NBC 1950-1954 and ABC 1956). Sponsors were Quaker cereals and Peter Paul candy.**

GAB-1

GAB-2

❑ **GAB-1. Gabby Hayes Arcade Card,**
Early 1940s. Photo is from his early movie era. Note that Gabby is not wearing his prospector's hat. - **$5 $10 $20**

❑ **GAB-2. Dixie Picture,**
c. 1942. Thinner paper than typical Dixie picture. **- $50 $100 $150**

GAB-3

GAB-4

❑ **GAB-3. "George 'Gabby' Hayes" Dixie Ice Cream Picture,**
1947. - **$75 $150 $350**

❑ **GAB-4. "George 'Gabby' Hayes" Cello. Button,**
c. 1948. - **$20 $40 $75**

GAB-5

❑ **GAB-5. Fantasy Tales Storybook-Record Album,**
c. 1950. RCA Victor Little Nipper Series. -
**$15 $40 $75**

GAB-6

❑ **GAB-6. Hand Puppet,**
c. 1950. Store item. 9" tall. **- $60 $115 $150**

GAB-7

GAB-8

❑ **GAB-7. Record Album With Story,**
c. 1950. Store item from RCA Victor "Little Nipper" series. 10x10" paper folder holding single 78 rpm record "Allee Bamee And The Forty Horse Thieves." - **$25 $50 $85**

❑ **GAB-8. School Tablet,**
c. 1950. Store item. 5-1/2x9" with color cover. -
**$15 $25 $40**

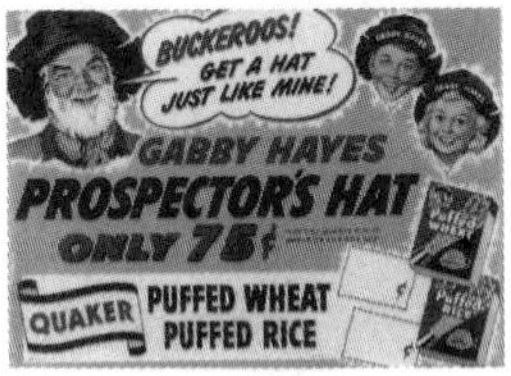


GAB-9

❑ **GAB-9. Prospector's Hat 16x21" Paper Store Sign,**
1951. Quaker Cereals. - **$50 $125 $250**

GAB-10

❑ **GAB-10. Prospector's Black Felt Hat,**
1951. Quaker Cereals. - **$25 $75 $150**

GAB-11

❑ **GAB-11. Quaker Cereal Comic Booklets With Mailing Envelopes,**
1951. Set of five.
Each Book Or Mailer - **$10 $30 $85**

GAB-12

GAB-13

❑ **GAB-12. Mother's Oats Container,**
1951. Offers set of 5 Gabby Hayes comic books. - **$50 $135 $185**

❑ **GAB-13. Quaker Cannon Ring,**
1951. Puffed Wheat & Puffed Rice. Large ring with brass base and spring-loaded barrel in either brass or aluminum. - **$100 $200 $300**

GAB-14

❑ **GAB-14. "Shooting Cannon Ring" Instruction Sheet,**
1951. Quaker Cereals. Opposite side offers Miniature Western Gun Collection. -
**$35 $75 $125**

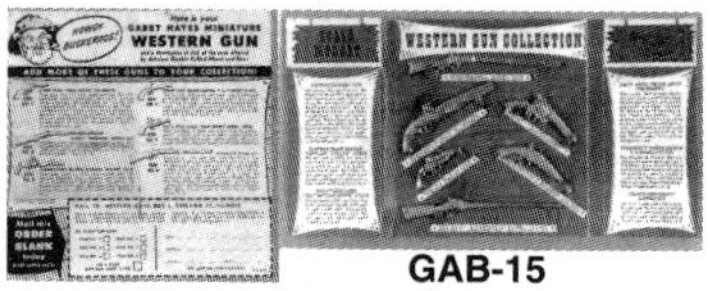


GAB-15

❑ **GAB-15. "Gabby Hayes Miniature Western Gun Collection",**
1951. Quaker Cereals. Set of six: Buffalo Rifle, Colt Revolver, Flintlock Dueling Pistol, "Peacemaker" Pistol, Remington Breech-Loader Rifle, Winchester 1873 Rifle.
Gun Set - **$25 $50 $100**
Display Folder - **$30 $75 $125**
Order Sheet - **$15 $30 $40**

GAB-16

❑ **GAB-16. Quaker "Five Western Wagons" Cereal Box,**
1952. Quaker Puffed Rice.
Complete Box - **$50 $200 $300**

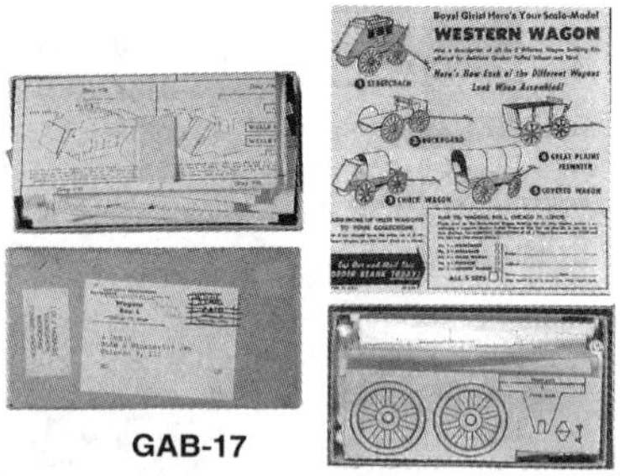


GAB-17

❑ **GAB-17. Gabby Hayes Western Wagon Kits,**
1952. Quaker Cereals. Five different kits: Buckboard, Chuck Wagon, Covered Wagon, Great Plains Freighter, Wells Fargo Stagecoach. Each Boxed - **$20 $50 $75**

GAB-18

❑ **GAB-18. "Tall Tales For Little Folks" Mechanical Book,**
1954. Inside front cover has diecut head and pair of boots that swing into position to create a 17" tall figure. Pages fold to give Gabby different outfits. Published by Samuel Lowe Co. -
**$10 $25 $50**

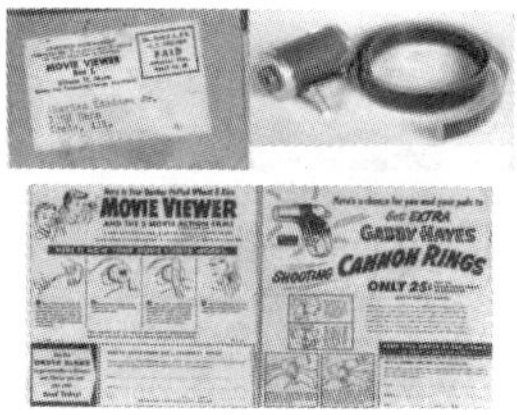


GAB-19

❑ **GAB-19. Movie Viewer Set,**
1952. Quaker Cereals. Filmstrip with five titles, instruction slip, mailer. Near Mint Boxed - **$250**

GAB-20

❑ **GAB-20. Quaker "Pocket-Sized Movie Viewer" Newspaper Ad,**
1952. - **$5 $10 $15**

GAB-21

❑ **GAB-21. Gabby Hayes Metal Automobiles,**
1952. Quaker Cereals. Set of five.
Near Mint Boxed - **$200**
Each - **$5 $15 $30**
Instructions - **$15 $25 $35**

GAB-22

❑ **GAB-22. Quaker "Clipper Ship in a Bottle" Cereal Box,**
Early 1950s. Quaker Puffed Wheat.
Complete Box - **$50 $200 $300**

## Gang Busters

**Marching against the underworld, proving each week that crime does not pay, *Gang Busters* was based on case files of the FBI and local police and proved so popular that it ran on network radio for 21 years. The show premiered on CBS in 1936 sponsored by Palmolive. Succeeding sponsors including Cue magazine (1939-1940), Sloan's liniment (1940-1945), Waterman pens (1945-1948), Tide soap (1948), Grape-Nuts cereal (1949-1954) and Wrigley's gum (1954-1955). The show was last aired in 1957. Descriptions of actual criminals, broadcast at the end of each program, apparently resulted in the capture of hundreds of fugitives. A television series with the same format had a nine-month run on NBC in 1952. *Gang Busters* comic books were published from 1938 to 1959.**

GNG-1

GNG-2

❑ **GNG-1. "Phillips H. Lord's Gang Busters" Badge,**
c. 1935. Brass luster on embossed tin. -
**$75 $150 $300**

❑ **GNG-2. Member's Badge,**
c. 1937. Comes with or without blue stars around edge. - **$25 $60 $90**

GNG-3

GNG-4

❑ **GNG-3. "Green's Gang Busters Crime Crusaders" Enameled Brass Badge,**
c. 1937. "Phillips H. Lord's" copyright. - **$50 $100 $150**

❑ **GNG-4. Enameled Belt Buckle,**
c. 1937. Rare. - **$65 $150 $250**

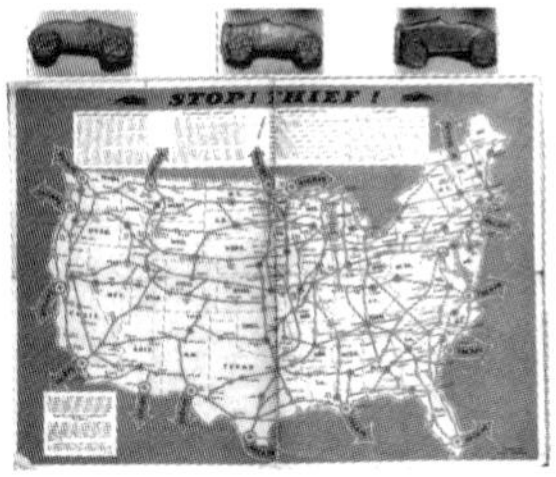

GNG-5

GNG-6

❑ **GNG-5. "Stop Thief" 22x30" Paper Game Board Map,**
1937. Palmolive. Came with nine metal cars.
Game - **$30 $75 $125**
Each Car - **$5 $10 $20**

❑ **GNG-6. Tie,**
1937. Scarce. - **$65 $150 $250**

GNG-7

GNG-8

❑ **GNG-7. "Gang Busters" Game,**
1938. Store item by Lynco Inc. - **$100 $200 $350**

❑ **GNG-8. "Gang Busters Step In" Better Little Book,**
1939. Based on radio program. - **$12 $40 $80**

GNG-9

❑ **GNG-9. Whitman Boxed Board Game,**
1939. Store item. - **$60 $100 $150**

GNG-10

❑ **GNG-10. "Gang Busters" Wind-Up Machine Gun,**
1930s. Store item by Marx. 23" long litho. tin with hand grip, missing from our photo example. Each side reads "Gang Busters/Crusade Against Crime." - **$150 $350 $600**

GNG-11

❑ **GNG-11. "Gang Busters" Wallet With Member Card,**
1930s. Store item. Wallet - **$25 $50 $85**
Card - **$25 $50 $85**

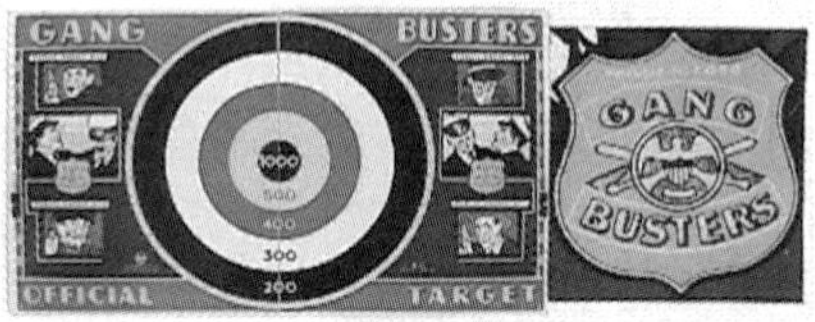

GNG-12

❑ **GNG-12. "Gang Busters" Litho. Tin Target,**
1940. Store item by Marx Toys with copyright of Phillips H. Lord. 16x27" full color litho. over rigid cardboard features "Public Enemy" pictorial targets designed to fall backwards when struck. - **$75 $175 $300**

## Gene Autry

**America's popular singing cowboy, Autry (1907-1998) was born on a small ranch in Texas and grew up in Oklahoma, where he worked as a railroad telegraph operator and began his career singing and composing. Local performances as a yodeling cowboy led to national radio spots on the *National Barn Dance* and *National Farm and Home Hour* programs in the 1930s. Autry began recording cowboy songs in 1929 and had phenomenal success both as a composer and as a singer. He moved to Hollywood in 1934 and a year later starred in *Phantom Empire*, a 12-episode chapter play for Mascot. Over the years Autry was to write more than 250 songs and act in more than 100 Westerns.**

***Gene Autry's Melody Ranch*, a program of Western songs and stories told around a campfire, premiered on CBS radio in 1940 and ran continually until 1956, interrupted only by Autry's service in the Army Air Corps from 1942 to 1945. The program, sponsored by Wrigley's gum, featured bearded sidekick Pat Buttram for comic relief, along with a variety of musical groups.**

**On television, also sponsored by Wrigley's gum, *The Gene Autry Show* aired on CBS from 1950 to 1956. Filmed at his 125-acre Melody Ranch and produced by his Flying A Productions company, the program put Autry back in the saddle again each week to do battle with assorted villains. Riding his wonder horse Champion and accompanied by saddle-partner Buttram, Autry set a consistently high moral tone for his young fans. A spinoff series, *The Adventures of Champion*, which ran for a season (1955-1956) on CBS, featured young Barry Curtis and his dog Rebel along with the hero horse.**

**A *Gene Autry* Sunday comic strip from General Features Syndicate was begun in 1940 and revived from 1952 to 1955, and Autry comic books from Dell and Fawcett--including giveaways from Pillsbury (1947) and Quaker Oats (1950)--appeared from 1941 through the 1950s. Autry and Champion made countless personal appearances at fairs, parades, Wild West shows, and rodeos, and Flying A Productions did extensive merchandising of Autry-related items ranging from 10-cent club membership cards to complete buckskin outfits.**

**In the 1950s Autry began a career in business that mirrored his show-business success. He invested in oil and real estate, bought a radio-TV chain and the California Angels baseball team, served as chairman of the Cowboy Hall of Fame, and created a Western Heritage Museum in Los Angeles.**

GAU-1

GAU-2

❑ **GAU-1. Movie Serial Club Member Button,**
1935. Rare. Name of club formed by kids in Mascot serial The Phantom Empire. -
**$200 $400 $750**

❑ **GAU-2. "Red River Valley" Song Sheet,**
1935. - **$20 $40 $60**

GAU-3

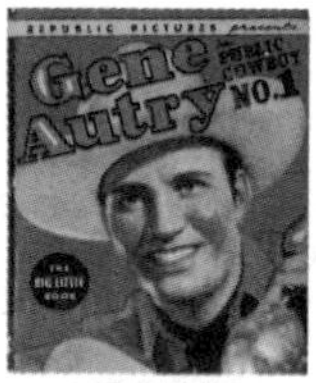


GAU-4

❑ **GAU-3. Wheaties Box Back,**
c. 1937. For Republic Picture "The Big Show" released late 1936. - **$10 $20 $40**

❑ **GAU-4. "Gene Autry In Public Cowboy #1" Big Little Book #1433,**
1937. Autry's 1st BLB. Has photo cover and movie scenes. - **$20 $75 $160**

GAU-5

GAU-6

❑ **GAU-5. "Gene Autry's Deluxe Edition Of Famous Original Cowboy Songs & Mountain Ballads" Song Folio,**
1938. - **$10 $20 $40**

❑ **GAU-6. "Gene Autry In Law Of The Range" Better Little Book,**
1939. Whitman #1483. - **$20 $60 $120**

GAU-7

GAU-8

❑ **GAU-7. "South of the Border" Song Sheet,**
1939. - **$12 $25 $40**

❑ **GAU-8. Photo,**
1930s. Radio premium shows Gene Autry in a business suit. - **$20 $40 $60**

GAU-9

GAU-10

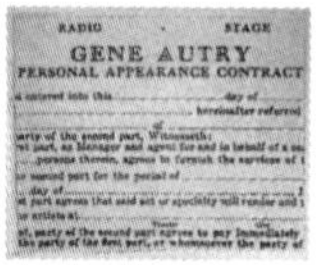


GAU-11

❑ **GAU-9. Photo,**
1930s. Radio premium shows Gene Autry playing guitar with foot on bench next to toy dog. -
**$20 $50 $80**

❑ **GAU-10. Composition Statue,**
c. 1930s. Rare. Store item. - **$200 $400 $700**

❑ **GAU-11. Personal Appearance Contract,**
1930s. Republic Studios, North Hollywood. 8-1/2x14" legal document printed in black on canary paper. Our photo shows detail from upper 3-1/2" of contract front page.
Signed - **$100 $200 $300**
Unsigned - **$25 $50 $75**

GAU-12

❑ **GAU-12. "Gene Autry The Screen Singing Cowboy In Person" Poster,**
c. 1940. Issued for Clovis, New Mexico appearance. 14x22". - **$50 $100 $150**

GAU-13

GAU-14

❑ **GAU-13. Fan Photo With Insert Sheet,**
1940. Republic Studio. Near Mint In Mailer - **$35**
Photo Only - **$8 $12 $20**

❑ **GAU-14. Rodeo Handbill,**
c. 1940. World Championship Rodeo, Boston Garden. - **$25 $50 $85**

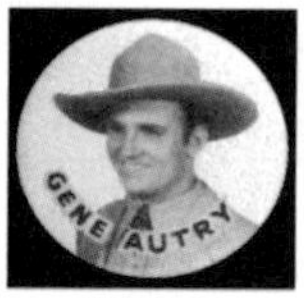


GAU-15

GAU-16

GAU-17

❑ **GAU-15. Cello. Button,**
c. 1940. 1-3/4" crisp black and white. -
**$15 $25 $50**

❑ **GAU-16. "Boston Garden Rodeo" Litho. Button,**
c. 1940. Single event issue. - **$25 $60 $125**

❑ **GAU-17. "Gene Autry" Friendship Ring,**
1941. Brass and silvered brass varieties issued by American Specialty Co. of Lancaster, PA for selling seed packs or Christmas cards. An aluminum variety with gold lustre on portrait is c. 1950, issuer unknown.
Brass or Silvered Brass - **$50 $90 $140**
Aluminum - **$85 $135 $200**

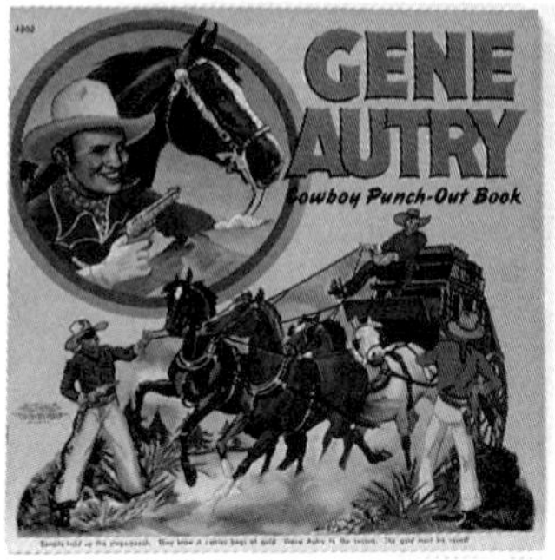


GAU-18

❑ **GAU-18. "Cowboy Punch-Out Book",**
1941. The 1st Gene Autry punch-out book. From Merrill Publishing Co. Has 5 pages of cardboard punch-outs. Odd sized 13 1/4" x 13". Rare. - **$150 $300 $450**

GAU-19

❑ **GAU-19. "Gene Autry's Flying A Ranch Rodeo" Program With Performance Insert Folder,**
1942. 16 pages with four-page insert for New Haven, Connecticut performance.
Program - **$15 $25 $50**
Insert - **$5 $10 $20**

GAU-20

GAU-21

❑ **GAU-20. "Gene Autry and the Hawk of the Hills" Big Little Book #1493,**
1942. Flip pictures. - **$15 $50 $90**

❑ **GAU-21. "Gene Autry and the Riders of the Range" Big Little Book #1409,**
1946. - **$10 $40 $75**

GAU-22

GAU-23

❑ **GAU-22. "Gene Autry and the Mystery of Paint Rock Canyon" Big Little Book #1425,**
1947. - **$10 $40 $75**

❑ **GAU-23. "Adventure Comics And Play-Fun Book",**
1947. Pillsbury Pancake Mix. - **$40 $120 $360**

GAU-24

❑ **GAU-24. "Gene Autry Adventure Comics And Play-Fun Book" Store Poster,**
1947. Pillsbury Pancake Mix. 9-1/2x26-1/2" full color showing premium activity book. Gordon Gold Archives. - **$50 $125 $250**

GAU-25

❑ **GAU-25. Pancake Mix Full Color Box Wrapper,**
1947. Pillsbury Pancake Mix. 3-1/2x18" segmented cardboard strip picturing the comic and play-fun book "Packed Between These Packages." Scarcer than the premium itself. - **$35 $75 $140**

GAU-26

❑ **GAU-26. Gene Autry Watch Box Set,**
1948. Comes with stand-up insert and instructions. Scarce. Boxed - **$800**

GAU-27

❑ **GAU-27. Gene Autry "Six Shooter" Watch Box Set,**
1948. New Haven Watch Co. Comes in box with instructions. Boxed - **$725**

GAU-28

GAU-29

❑ **GAU-28. Clothing Manufacturer Photo And Cover Note,**
1948. J. M. Wood Mfg. Co., maker of Autry shirts and jeans. Set - **$20 $35 $50**

❑ **GAU-29. "Gene Autry and the Land Grab Mystery" Big Little Book #1430,**
1948. - **$10 $40 $75**

GAU-30

GAU-31

❑ **GAU-30. Gene Autry Dixie Ice Cream Picture,**
1948. - **$20 $45 $85**

❑ **GAU-31. Gene Autry/Lone Ranger Plastic Ring,**
c. 1948. Dell Comics. U.S. flag pictured under plastic dome, offered for comic book subscription for each character. - **$50 $100 $150**

GAU-32

GAU-33

❑ **GAU-32. "Gene Autry/Champ Crackshot Cowboy" Metal Badge,**
c. 1948. Store item by Daniel Smilo & Sons, New York City. Hanger bar has "Deputy" inscription, linked pendant includes words "Valor/Honor Merit." Also issued with oval hangar bar reading "Expert Sharpshooter" around a target design.
Each Medal - **$75 $150 $300**
Card - **$25 $75 $150**

❑ **GAU-33. "Gene Autry and the Red Bandit's Ghost" Big Little Book #1461,**
1949. - **$10 $40 $75**

GAU-34

❑ **GAU-34. Dell Publishing Co. Picture Strip,**
1949. Folder strip of five color photos. - **$25 $50 $80**

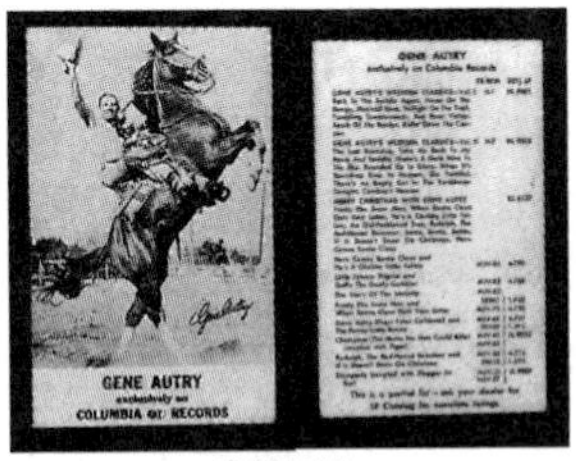

GAU-35

❑ **GAU-35. "Columbia Records" Listing Card,**
1940s. Black and white photo with facsimile signature, reverse lists album and individual record titles. - **$8 $15 $30**

GAU-36

GAU-37

❑ **GAU-36. Official Club Badge Cello. Button,**
1940s. - **$15 $30 $50**

❑ **GAU-37. "Republic's Singing Western Star" Cello. Button,**
1940s. - **$30 $100 $150**

GAU-38

GAU-39

❑ **GAU-38. Store Owner's 10x12" Cardboard Sign,**
1940s. Wrigley Doublemint Gum. Signifies sponsorship of "Doublemint Melody Ranch" radio show. - **$40 $60 $135**

❑ **GAU-39. "March Of Comics" #25,**
1940s. Various sponsors. - **$25 $75 $210**

GAU-40

GAU-41

GAU-42

❑ **GAU-40. Cello. Button,**
1940s. Probably a rodeo souvenir. - **$15 $25 $50**

❑ **GAU-41. Portrait Ring,**
c. 1940s. Brass frame holds black and white photo under clear plastic cover. - **$35 $65 $125**

❑ **GAU-42. "Minneapolis Aquatennial Rodeo" Cello. Button,**
1940s. Souvenir button. - **$50 $125 $175**

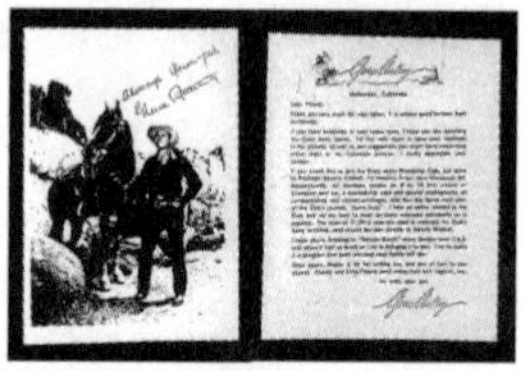

GAU-43

❑ **GAU-43. Fan Letter With Photo,**
c. 1950. Letter includes references to Columbia Pictures, Melody Ranch radio program, fan club address. Photo has facsimile signature.
Letter - **$5 $10 $15**
Photo - **$10 $15 $25**

GAU-44

❑ **GAU-44. Quaker Comic Booklets,**
1950. Puffed Wheat/Rice box inserts. Set of five. Each - **$15 $45 $130**

GAU-45

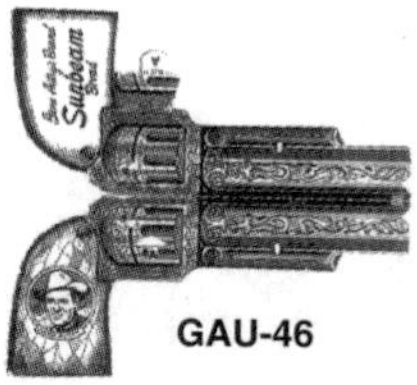


GAU-46

❑ **GAU-45. "Sunbeam Bread" Color Photo,**
c. 1950. - **$10 $18 $35**

❑ **GAU-46. "Sunbeam Bread" Cardboard Gun,**
c. 1950. - **$25 $40 $75**

GAU-47

GAU-48

GAU-49

❑ **GAU-47. Sunbeam Bread Litho. Button,**
c. 1950. 1-3/8" size, also as 1-1/4" cello.
Each - **$10 $15 $25**

❑ **GAU-48. Sunbeam Bread "Gene Autry Show" 3-1/2" Cello. Button,**
c. 1950. - **$25 $50 $100**

❑ **GAU-49. Plastic Ring,**
c. 1950. Store item. Gold finish with inset paper photo. - **$10 $15 $20**

GAU-50

GAU-51

❑ **GAU-50. Melody Ranch Cut-Out Dolls,**
1950. Photo cover. - **$75 $150 $250**

❑ **GAU-51. Three-Dimensional Ceramic Figure On Horseshoe-Shaped Base,**
c. 1950. Store item. 8-1/4" tall beautifully colored figure with his facsimile signature on the base. - **$200 $400 $800**

GAU-52

❑ **GAU-52. March of Comics #78,**
1951. This Gene Autry issue is the last sized like a regular comic book. - **$17 $51 $140**

GAU-53

❑ **GAU-53. "Jimmy And Jane Visit Gene Autry At Melody Ranch" Paperdoll Book,**
1951. Published by Whitman.
Uncut - **$60 $115 $185**

GAU-54

❑ **GAU-54. "Gene Autry/Melody Ranch" Lunch Box,**
1954. Store item by Universal. - **$150 $300 $500**

GAU-55

GAU-56

❑ **GAU-55. "March Of Comics No. 120",**
1954. Poll-Parrot Shoes. - **$10 $30 $85**

❑ **GAU-56. "Hit Show" Live Performance 14x22" Cardboard Poster,**
1955. - **$50 $125 $225**

GAU-57

❑ **GAU-57. Wallet With Inset Photo,**
c. 1956. Store item. Wallet front has black and white Autry photo under clear window cover. -
**$25 $65 $125**

GAU-58

❑ **GAU-58. Pair Of Litho. Buttons,**
1957. Probable vending machine issue. 7/8" with browntone photo on various single-color backgrounds. From a larger set depicting western TV stars, probably totaling 14 different.
Autry Or Champion Each - **$12 $25 $50**

GAU-59

GAU-60

❑ **GAU-59. Rodeo Souvenir Photo,**
1957. - **$5 $12 $20**

❑ **GAU-60. Flying A Cardboard Wrist Cuffs,**
1950s. Scarce. Probable premium. -
**$50 $175 $325**

GAU-61

❑ **GAU-61. Horseshoe Nail Ring On Card,**
1950s. Store item. Complete - **$200**
Ring Only - **$15 $35 $60**

GAU-62

❑ **GAU-62. School Tablet,**
1950s. Clothing stores. - **$15 $25 $50**

GAU-63

GAU-64

❑ **GAU-63. Plastic Ring With Photo,**
1950s. Store item, from card of rings featuring various personalities. Plastic cover over photo. -
**$10 $20 $35**

❑ **GAU-64. "Adventure Story Trail Map",**
1950s. Stroehmann's Bread. Large folder to hold 16 color photo bread end labels telling story of "Gene Autry And The Black Hat Gang!".
Folder - **$30 $65 $125**
Each Mounted Label - **$5 $10 $15**

GAU-65

GAU-66

❑ **GAU-65. Bread Labels,**
1950s. Various bread companies. Numbered photos in at least five different series.
Each - **$5 $10 $15**

❑ **GAU-66. Publicity Photo,**
1950s. Columbia Records. - **$5 $10 $20**

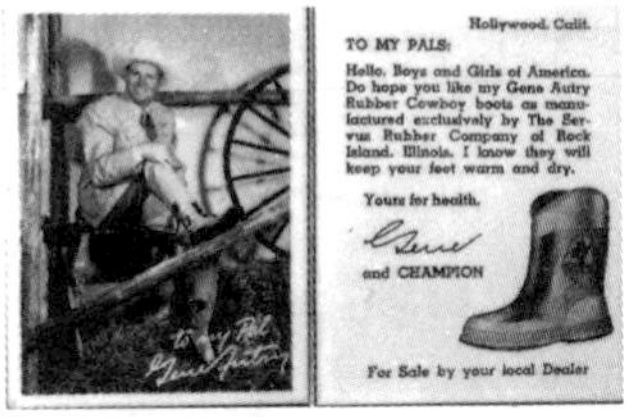

GAU-67

❑ **GAU-67. Rain Boots Merchandise Card,**
1950s. Servus Rubber Co. - **$10 $15 $30**

GAU-68

GAU-69

❑ **GAU-68. English Fan Club Badge On Card,**
1950s. Gene Autry Comics, Silvered tin with insert photo. Near Mint On Card - **$165**
Loose - **$25 $50 $100**

❑ **GAU-69. Second Variety Litho. Tin Club Tab,**
1950s. Same image as other version but design is of five-pointed star. 1-5/8" diameter in black and white with two shades of blue. -
**$15 $40 $75**

GAU-70

❑ **GAU-70. Dell Picture Strip,**
1950s. Unfolds with five photos. - **$25 $50 $75**

GAU-71

GAU-72

❑ **GAU-71. Litho. Tin Club Tab,**
1950s. - **$15 $40 $75**

❑ **GAU-72. "Gene Autry & Champion" Cello. Button,**
1950s. Star design in gold or silver. -
**$15 $25 $40**

GAU-73

GAU-74

❑ **GAU-73. Flying A Symbol Brass Wings Badge,**
1950s. - **$20 $45 $85**

❑ **GAU-74. Ranch Symbol Cigarette Lighter,**
1950s. Promotional item by Penguin. Chrome metal with plastic wrapper, other side has "Melody Ranch". - **$25 $50 $100**

GAU-75

GAU-76

❑ **GAU-75. Store Clerk's Or Bread Delivery Man's Cello. Badge,**
1950s. Stroehmann Bread. 2-1/4" with celluloid covering a paper bread loaf end label from their series meant to be collected and mounted in paper album. About five different seen.
Each - **$20 $40 $60**

❑ **GAU-76. Photo,**
1950s. Black & white premium photo of him playing guitar. - **$10 $20 $30**

GAU-77

GAU-78

❑ **GAU-77. Photo,**
1950s. Radio premium for radio show featuring Doublemints Melody Ranch on CBS. -
**$25 $50 $100**

❑ **GAU-78. "Gene Autry Deputy Sheriff",**
1950s. Issuer unknown. Large embossed brass badge. - **$50 $150 $275**

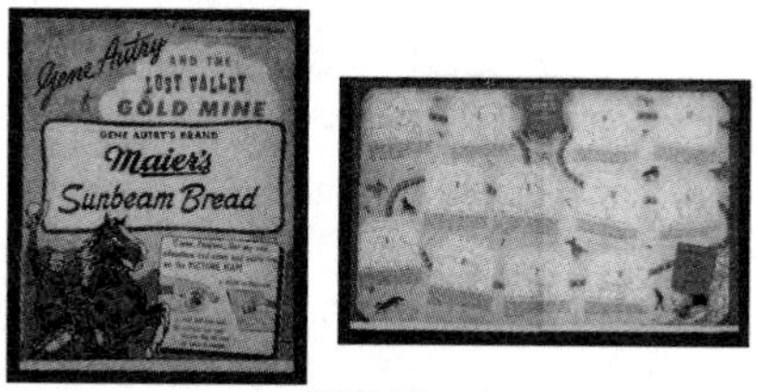


GAU-79

❑ **GAU-79. "Western Story Round-Up And Picture Map" Album,**
1950s. Sunbeam Bread. Paper folder for mounting 16 numbered bread loaf end pictures.
Album - **$40 $85 $135**
Each Mounted Label - **$5 $10 $15**

GAU-80

GAU-81

❑ **GAU-80. Gene Autry Small Photo Button,**
1950s. British Commonwealth. 1-1/4". Black on yellow with red accents on vest and bandanna. -
**$30 $75 $125**

❑ **GAU-81. Gene Autry Large Photo Button,**
1950s. US version. 1-3/4". Black and white photo, sometimes with red tint on various colored backgrounds.
Yellow Background - **$5 $15 $25**
Blue Background - **$15 $30 $50**
Purple Background - **$25 $50 $75**

# General Mills Misc.

**This mammoth food and related products company, born and still based in Minneapolis, was a mid-1920s pioneer in national radio advertising via a powerful transmitter provided jointly by an immediate preceding company, Washburn Crosby Co. and other business interests in the Minneapolis-St. Paul Twin Cities area. The first three programs--*Betty Crocker, The Wheaties Quartet, The Gold Medal Fast Freight*--were of homemaker nature and offered a few premiums in like style. The premium heyday for youngsters, however, began in the early 1930s through the *Skippy and His Pals* program based on the Percy Crosby comic strip. Skippy was followed in 1933 by *Jack Armstrong, The All-American Boy*. Both offered premiums by sponsor Wheaties, a very popular Depression era cereal that continues to the present. General Mills through the years has offered hundreds of premiums for purchase of food products, principally breakfast cereals. In 1949, Adelaide Hawley Cumming became television's original Betty Crocker, billed as "America's First Lady of Food." Various General Mills brands are represented in this section while Cheerios, Wheaties and major characters they sponsored are covered in separate sections.**

GEN-1

❑ **GEN-1. "Gen'l Mills/Five Star Hour" Plaster Figurine,**
c. 1938. Rare. Probably issued to retailers, base lists six radio programs. - **$250 $600 $1000**

GEN-2

❑ **GEN-2. Hedy Lamarr Key Pin And Photo,**
1946. Kix Cereal. Key - **$25 $50 $75**
Photo - **$10 $20 $35**

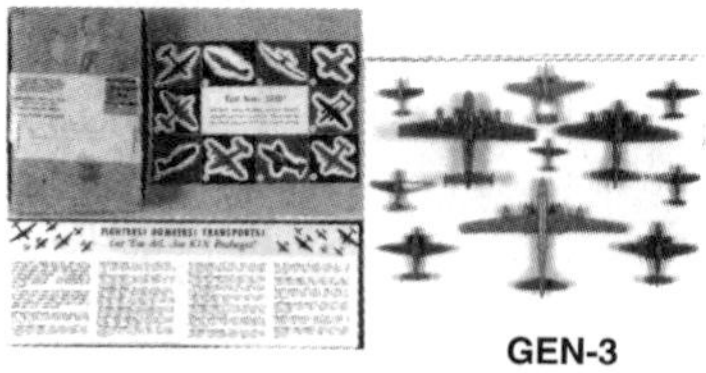

GEN-3

❑ **GEN-3. Kix Plastic Planes,**
1946. 22 planes in set. Booklet - **$20 $60 $100**
Each Plane - **$5 $10 $15**

GEN-4

❑ **GEN-4. Kix Cereal Box with Cut-outs,**
1948. Baldy the Regal Eagle cut-outs on back. 12 boxes in the series. - **$50 $100 $150**

GEN-5

❑ **GEN-5. "General Mills Map Of The Old West" 20x28",**
c. 1940s. - **$15 $60 $90**

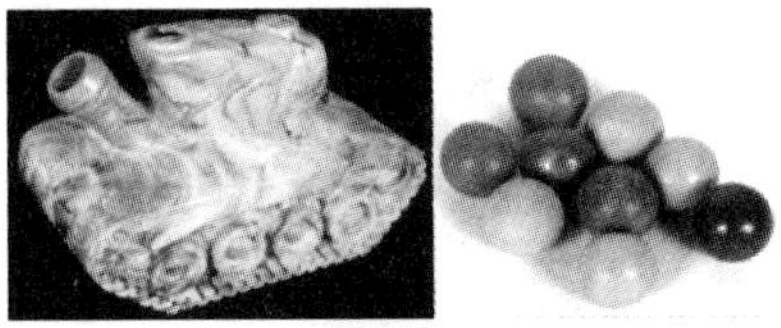
GEN-6

❑ **GEN-6. "10 Shooter Tank" With Mailer,**
c. 1956. 3-1/2" tall General Mills premium. Came with ten colored wood balls which fire from gun barrel as tank is pushed. 3x5x3-1/2" tall. - **$25 $40 $85**

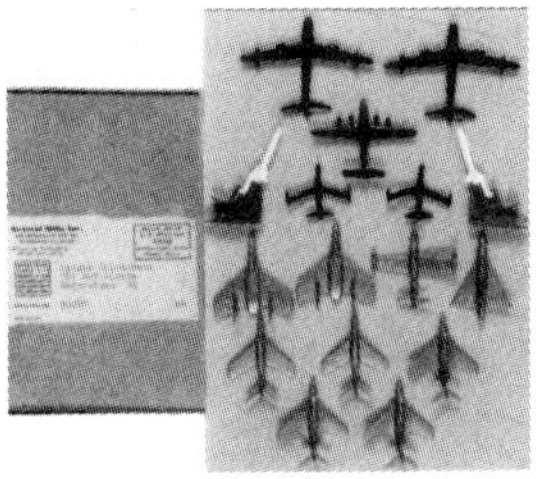
GEN-7

❑ **GEN-7. General Mills Airplanes/Missile Launchers,**
1950s. At least eight different planes in various colors and missile launchers. Each - **$2 $7 $10**

GEN-8

GEN-9

❑ **GEN-8. Toytimer,**
1950s. Stop watch with mailer. - **$30 $50 $75**

❑ **GEN-9. Tex-Son Cowhand Badge,**
1950s. General Mills premium. - **$20 $75 $150**

GEN-10

GEN-11

❑ **GEN-10. "Twinkles And Sanford's Boat" Book,**
1962. Whitman hardcover issued by General Mills. - **$8 $15 $30**

❑ **GEN-11. Franken Berry 2-3/4" Tall Figural Plastic Pencil Sharpener,**
1960s. - **$5 $10 $15**

GEN-12

❑ **GEN-12. "General Mills Cocoa Puffs Bobbing Cuckoo Bird" Box Flat With Premium,**
c. 1970. Gordon Gold Archives.
Near Mint Flat - **$350**
Used Complete - **$50 $125 $200**
Cuckoo Bird - **$8 $12 $25**

GEN-13

❑ **GEN-13. Cereal Box With "Monster Eraser" Offer,**
1972. Set of six consisting of Boo Berry, Count Chocula, Franken Berry, bat, owl and skull/crossbones. Gordon Gold archives.
Used Complete Box - **$100 $200 $300**
Each Eraser - **$3 $8 $20**

GEN-14

GEN-15

❑ **GEN-14. "Franken Berry" Vinyl Doll With Box,**
1975. Near Mint Boxed - **$160**
Loose - **$25 $40 $80**

❑ **GEN-15. "Count Chocula" Vinyl Doll With Box,**
1975. Near Mint Boxed - **$160**
Loose - **$25 $40 $80**

GEN-16

GEN-17

❑ **GEN-16. "Fruit Brute" Vinyl Squeeze Doll,**
1975. Near Mint Boxed - **$160**
Loose - **$25 $40 $80**

❑ **GEN-17. "Boo Berry" Vinyl Squeeze Doll,**
1975. Near Mint Boxed - **$175**
Loose - **$25 $40 $85**

GEN-18

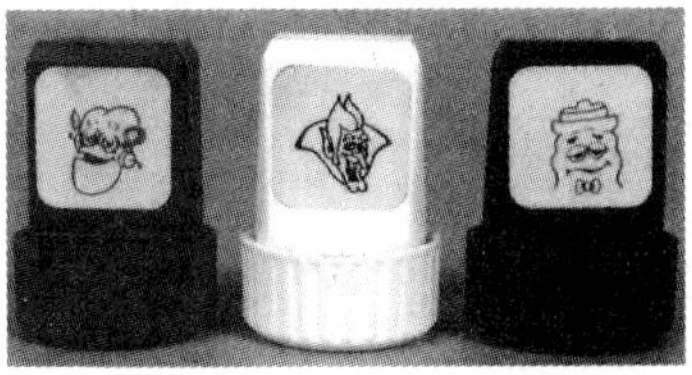
GEN-19

❑ **GEN-18. Secret Compartment Plastic Ring Set,**
1976. Four rings with Hasbro name in four colors depicting Franken Berry, Boo Berry, Count Chocula, Fruit Brute.
Each - **$25 $100 $150**

❑ **GEN-19. "Stampos" Printing Kit,**
1970s. Ink stampers with portraits of Franken Berry, Count Chocula, Boo Berry.
Each - **$15 $30 $50**

GEN-20

❑ **GEN-20. Big Monster Flicker Rings,**
1970s. Five of six shown: two feature the Count and Franken Berry, two feature the Count only, two feature Franken Berry only.
Each - **$25 $50 $100**

GEN-21

❑ **GEN-21. Count Chocula Original Art Prototype Ring,**
1970s. Made for presentation to General Mills. Hard plastic base like the six box insert flicker rings with a full color original art insert on the top. Gordon Gold archives. Unique - **$500**

GEN-22

❑ **GEN-22. Cereal Box With "Pop Rocket" Offer And Premium,**
1970s. Rockets came in three colors and consisted of base, center stage and nose cone. Gordon Gold Archives.
Near Mint Flat - **$350**
Used Complete - **$50 $100 $150**
Rocket - **$10 $20 $30**

GEN-23

❑ **GEN-23. "Count Chocula Monster Action Ring" Offer Cereal Box,**
1970s. Gordon Gold Archives.
Near Mint Flat - **$425**
Used Complete - **$50 $150 $250**

GEN-24

❑ **GEN-24. "Franken Berry Monster Action Ring" Offer Box Flat,**
1970s. Gordon Gold Archives.
Near Mint Flat - **$425**
Used Complete - **$50 $150 $250**

GEN-25

GEN-26

❑ **GEN-25. Count Chocula Vinyl Flat Figure,**
1970s. Finished image front and back, molded small base. - **$8 $15 $25**

❑ **GEN-26. Franken Berry Vinyl Flat Figure,**
1970s. Finished image front and back, molded small base. - **$8 $15 $25**

GEN-27

GEN-28

❑ **GEN-27. Count Chocula Toothbrush Holder,**
1970s. 3" tall soft plastic with raised portrait design looped on back to hold toothbrush. - **$10 $20 $30**

❑ **GEN-28. Character Card Games,**
1981. Two sets of cards featuring Lucky Charms, Cocoa Puffs, Trix, Franken Berry, Count Chocula, Boo Berry. Complete With Mailer - **$15 $25 $40**

GEN-29

❑ **GEN-29. "Raiders Of The Lost Ark" Packaged Action Figures,**
1982. Set of "Indiana Jones Four Pack" of him, Toht, Cairo Swordsman, Marian Ravenwood.
Near Mint Complete - **$175**

GEN-30

❑ **GEN-30. "Count Chocula" Cereal Box And Disguise Stickers,**
1987. Box art depicts necklace on Dracula's neck with design similar to Star of David. Box was quickly redesigned. Box - **$25 $75 $150**
Stickers - **$5 $15 $30**

GEN-31

❑ **GEN-31. "Count Chocula" Cereal Box,**
1987. Box art altered to remove Dracula's necklace that resembled Star of David. - **$25 $75 $150**

GEN-32

❑ **GEN-32. Franken Berry Cereal Box With Spooky Shape Maker Offer,**
1987. Three different to emboss paper with images of Franken Berry, Count Chocula, Fruity Yummy Mummy. Box - **$20 $35 $50**
Each Shape Maker - **$5 $10 $20**

GEN-33

❑ **GEN-33. Fruity Yummy Mummy Cereal Box,**
1987. Packaging introduces the character and the cereal to the public while back panel introduces the new character to the established monsters. - **$100 $150 $250**

GEN-34

❑ **GEN-34. Boo Berry Cereal Box With Monster Poster And Crayons Offer,**
1988. Last premium issued for monster cereals. Crayons shaped like monsters in their correct colors. Box - **$10 $25 $50**
Poster And Crayons - **$20 $35 $60**

GEN-35

❑ **GEN-35. Franken Berry Mask,**
1980s. Thin shell plastic with high relief design. - **$10 $20 $30**

GEN-36

❑ **GEN-36. Count Chocula Die-cast Car,**
2000. Team Lightning metal Road Rod. **- $5**

GEN-37

GEN-38

❑ **GEN-37. Count Chocula Wacky Wobbler,**
2001. - **$15**

❑ **GEN-38. Franken Berry Wacky Wobbler,**
2001. - **$15**

# G.I. Joe

**Hasbro's creative director of product development Don Levine was approached by independent toy designer Stanley Weston in March of 1962. Weston was selling merchandising rights to the TV show *"The Lieutenant,"* based on a Marine, and thought Hasbro would be interested in doing combat action figures for boys similar in design to what the Mattel Co. was doing with Barbie figures for girls. Levine and the people at Hasbro decided to go with a more universal appeal, basing the name on a 1945 Robert Mitchum war movie *The Story of G.I. Joe.* Hasbro claimed the trademark and christened the new product GI Joe.**

**Test marketing began in New York stores in August, 1964 and the figures sold out in one week. By early fall the figures were selling out nationwide. The GI Joe Club started in December and soon had 150,000 members. 1965 saw the introduction of a black action soldier into the line of American Army, Air Force, Navy and Marine figures.**

**1966 brought the introduction of Action Soldiers of the World, offering soldiers from six countries. In 1969 GI Joe's hard core military image was softened to an "Adventurer" concept which would expand the merchandising even further. 1975 saw the introduction of the 11-1/2" Atomic Man.**

**The oil shortage of 1976 halted production due to lack of petroleum used in manufacturing the figures. In 1982 Joe was re-introduced in a new 3 and 3/4" size. In 1991 Hasbro brought out the first original 12-inch action figure since 1976, Master Sergeant Duke, based on the *GI Joe, A Real American Hero* cartoon series. The same title was used for a 1982-1994 comic book series published by Marvel Comics. All 155 issues were written by Larry Hama and illustrated by some of the foremost comic book artists, including Todd (*Spawn*) McFarlane.**

**Over the years, the company has sold hundreds of millions of the ever-popular GI Joe dolls and associated figures, vehicles and gear.**

GIJ-1

❑ **GIJ-1. "GI Joe Action Soldier" Boxed,**
1964. Store item by Hasbro.
Near Mint Boxed - **$400**
Used Complete - **$35 $75 $125**

GIJ-2

GIJ-3

❑ **GIJ-2. GI Joe Sailor Action Figure With Shore Patrol Uniform,**
1964. Near Mint Boxed - **$750**
Loose Complete - **$200 $350 $550**

❑ **GIJ-3. "GI Joe" Action Sailor Deep Sea Diver Set,**
1965. Store item by Hasbro #7620. **-**
**$100 $250 $400**

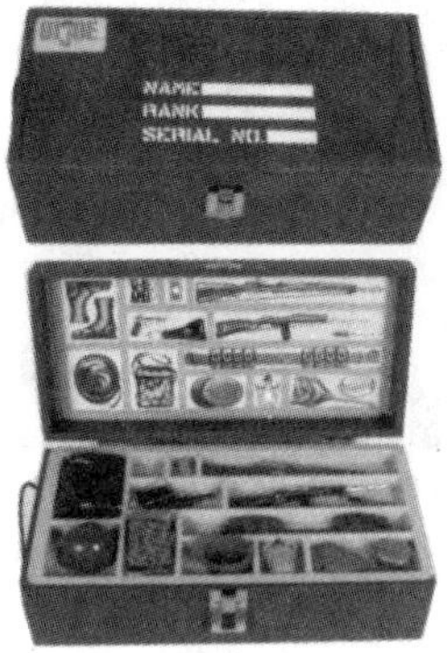

GIJ-4

❑ **GIJ-4. Footlocker With Equipment,**
c. 1965. Store item by Hasbro.
Near Mint Complete **- $200**
Without Accessories **- $10 $20 $35**

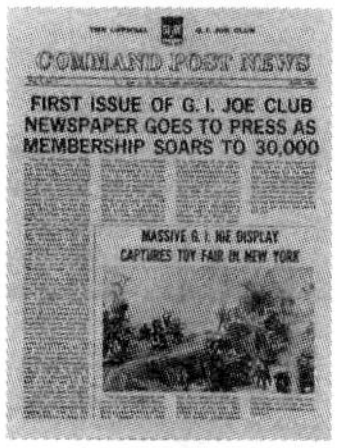


GIJ-5

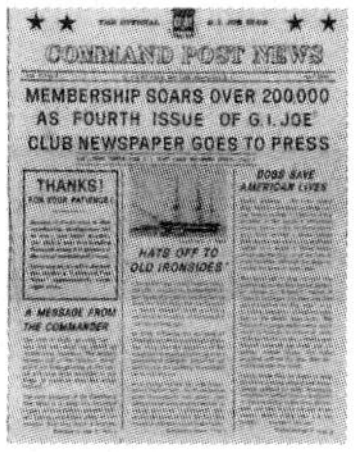


GIJ-6

❑ **GIJ-5. "Command Post News" Newspaper. Vol. 1 #1,**
April, 1965. - **$25 $40 $75**

❑ **GIJ-6. "Command Post News" #4,**
April, 1966. - **$5 $12 $25**

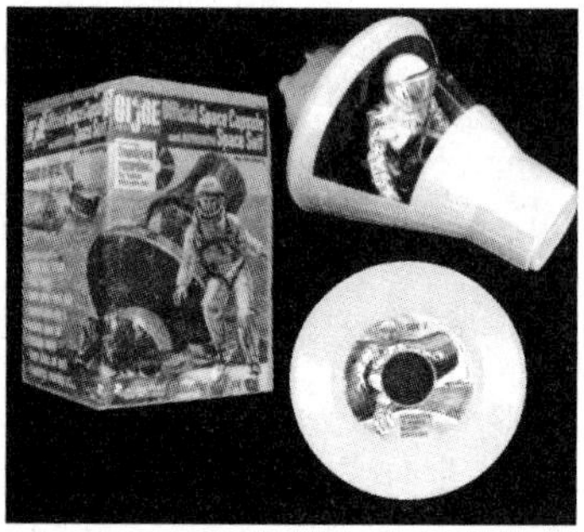

GIJ-7

❑ **GIJ-7. "GI Joe Space Capsule And Space Suit" Boxed Set,**
1966. Store item by Hasbro. Contents include 45 rpm record, stickers and instruction sheet. Small "handles" inside cockpit often snapped off. - **$150 $250 $400**

GIJ-8

GIJ-9

❑ **GIJ-8. Japanese Imperial Soldier Action Figure,**
c. 1966. Store item by Hasbro.
Near Mint Boxed - **$2000**
Loose - **$150 $300 $500**

❑ **GIJ-9. "Talking GI Joe Astronaut",**
1967. Store item by Ideal.
Near Mint Boxed - **$700**
Loose Complete - **$50 $100 $150**

GIJ-10

❑ **GIJ-10. "GI Joe At The Battle Of The Bulge" Record Album,**
1967. Store item by United Artists Records Inc. Certainly inspired by GI Joe but no Hasbro reference. - **$15 $30 $50**

GIJ-11

❑ **GIJ-11. "GI Joe Action Pilot Crash Crew Fire Truck",**
1967. Store item by Hasbro.
Near Mint Boxed - **$2000**
Loose Complete - **$200 $400 $750**

GIJ-12

GIJ-13

❑ **GIJ-12. Catalogue,**
1967. Came only with the 1967 series of talking GI Joe figures. - **$3 $8 $15**

❑ **GIJ-13. "Command Post Yearbook",**
1967. - **$20 $40 $75**

GIJ-14

❑ **GIJ-14. GI Joe Adventurer Action Figure,**
1969. Store item by Hasbro.
Near Mint Boxed - **$1000**
Loose - **$75 $200 $300**

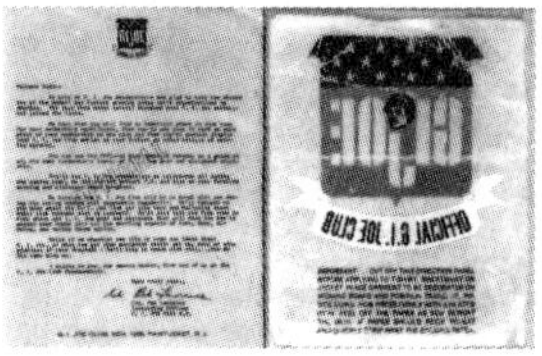

GIJ-15

❑ **GIJ-15. GI Joe Letter With Transfer,**
1960s. Letter - **$3 $6 $12**
Transfer - **$5 $10 $20**

GIJ-16

❑ **GIJ-16. "Combat Soldier" Pencil Case,**
1960s. Store item by Hasbro. 5-1/2x9" brown vinyl with zipper. - **$10 $20 $35**

GIJ-17

GIJ-18

❑ **GIJ-17. "GI Joe Sea Adventurer" Boxed,**
1970. Store item by Hasbro.
Near Mint Boxed - **$250**
Used Complete - **$15 $30 $50**

❑ **GIJ-18. "GI Joe Land Adventurer" Action Figure,**
1970. Store item by Hasbro.
Near Mint Boxed - **$225**
Complete Unboxed - **$20 $40 $65**

GIJ-19

❑ **GIJ-19. "Search For The Stolen Idol" Boxed,**
1971. Store item by Hasbro.
Near Mint Boxed - **$200**
Used Complete - **$25 $50 $75**

GIJ-20 GIJ-21

❑ **GIJ-20. Super Joe Commander With Power Vest Ring,**
1970s. Store item by Hasbro. Color photo under acrylic on non-adjustable brass base. Six to eight in set. Each - **$5 $10 $25**

❑ **GIJ-21. Cello. Button,**
c. 1970s. Probably Hasbro promotional button. - **$10 $25 $40**

GIJ-22 GIJ-23

❑ **GIJ-22. Official Commando Medal and Bar Pin,**
1982. On card. - **$20 $35 $50**

❑ **GIJ-23. Official Dog Tag with I.D. Sticker,**
1982. On card. - **$10 $20 $35**

GIJ-24 GIJ-25

❑ **GIJ-24. Official I.D. Bracelet,**
1982. On card. - **$10 $20 $40**

❑ **GIJ-25. Official Key Ring with Dog Tag and Bullet Charm,**
1982. On card. - **$15 $25 $40**

GIJ-26 GIJ-27

❑ **GIJ-26. Official Machine Gunner Medal and Sergeant Stripes Pin,**
1982. On card. - **$10 $20 $40**

❑ **GIJ-27. Official Ranger-Medal and Ranger Bar Pin,**
1982. On card. - **$25 $35 $60**

GIJ-28 GIJ-29

❑ **GIJ-28. Official G.I. Joe Ring and Bar Pin,**
1982. On card. - **$25 $40 $60**

❑ **GIJ-29. Official G. I. Joe Whistle,**
1982. On card. - **$10 $20 $40**

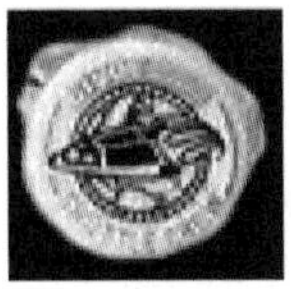

GIJ-30

GIJ-31

❑ **GIJ-30. "GI Joe Shuttle Crew" Plastic Ring,**
1980s. Image of space shuttle high above world globe. - **$5 $8 $10**

❑ **GIJ-31. "Cryo-Freeze Sgt. Savage" Figure on Card,**
1994. From Hasbro's Sgt. Savage series. With energy pack squirt ring on card. - **$20**

GIJ-32 GIJ-33

❑ **GIJ-32. "Urban Attack Dynamite" Figure on Card,**
1994. From the Sgt. Savage series. With decoder ring on card. - **$20**

❑ **GIJ-33. "Jet-Pack General Blitz" Figure on Card,**
1994. From the Sgt. Savage series. With working compass ring on card. - **$20**

GIJ-34

❑ **GIJ-34. G.I. Joe Action Astronaut Masterpiece Edition,**
1996. Limited edition from FAO Schwarz. Includes book and reproduction of a G.I. Joe astronaut doll. Boxed- **$125**

GIJ-35 GIJ-36

❑ **GIJ-35. Teddy Roosevelt G.I. Joe in Box,**
1999. 12" tall. From the G.I. Joe Classic Collection, commemorating 35 years. Set includes gun, flag and pin. Boxed - **$30**

❑ **GIJ-36. Resin Statue,**
1990s. 13 1/2" tall. Limited to 400. - **$150**

## The Goldbergs

***The Goldbergs*, the first memorable Jewish radio comedy, was the brainchild of Gertrude Berg, who wrote, produced, directed, and starred as Molly, the benevolent matriarch of a working-class family in the Bronx. With husband Jake, children Sammy and Rosalie, and Uncle David, Molly was a fixture on the NBC, CBS, or Mutual networks from 1929 to 1945 and again in 1949-1950. Sponsors included Pepsodent (1931-1934), Colgate (1936), Oxydol (1937-1945), and General Foods (1949-1950). A successful television series aired from 1949 to 1954, a Broadway play (*Molly and Me*) was produced in 1948, and a movie (*Molly*) was released in 1951. "Yoo-Hoo, Mrs. Bloom!"**

GLD-1

❑ **GLD-1. Goldbergs Puzzle,**
1932. Pepsodent Co. 8x10" full color jigsaw puzzle. - **$15 $40 $70**

GLD-2

GLD-3

❑ **GLD-2. Molly Goldberg Fan Photo,**
1930s. - **$8 $15 $30**

❑ **GLD-3. Gertrude Berg 11x14" Frame Tray Jigsaw Puzzle,**
1952. Store item by Jaymar. - **$15 $35 $50**

GLD-4

❑ **GLD-4. Molly Goldberg Store Sign,**
1954. - **$20 $60 $110**

## Gone With The Wind

**One of the most popular films of all time, *Gone with the Wind* premiered in Atlanta, Georgia, on December 15, 1939, won 10 Academy Awards, and remains a perennial smash in theaters, on television, and in video rentals. This Civil War saga, based on Margaret Mitchell's novel, starred Clark Gable, Vivien Leigh, an all-star cast--and the burning of Atlanta. Merchandising, including portrait dolls, collector plates, and porcelain figurines, continues to this day.**

GON-1

❑ **GON-1. Book Publishing House Summary Booklet,**
1936. Macmillan Co. - **$35 $75 $135**

GON-2

GON-3

❑ **GON-2. Pre-Movie Sheet Music,**
1937. Store item by Irving Berlin Inc. and Selznick International Pictures Inc. 9x12" captioned "Based Upon Margaret Mitchell's Novel, And The Forthcoming Greatest Of All Motion Pictures Gone With The Wind." - **$15 $30 $60**

❑ **GON-3. "Gone With The Wind" Souvenir Program,**
1939. Large numbers sold and saved so condition is critical to higher value. - **$20 $40 $100**

GON-4

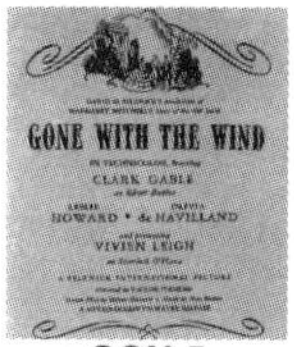


GON-5

❑ **GON-4. "Gone With The Wind" Curtain Fabric,**
c. 1940. Example shown is 34x51". Similar Size Near Mint - **$300**

❑ **GON-5. Movie Theater Herald,**
1940. Various theaters. - **$15 $30 $60**

GON-6

GON-7

❑ **GON-6. "I've Seen Gone With The Wind" Cello. Button,**
1940. - **$40 $80 $150**

❑ **GON-7. "Clark Gable/Gone With The Wind" Cigarette Series Card,**
c. 1940. Turf Cigarettes. Card #34 from series of 50 "Famous Film Stars" with photo head on illustrated body. - **$8 $15 $35**

GON-8

GON-9

❑ **GON-8. "Scarlett O'Hara" Handkerchief,**
c. 1940. Store item. Sheer fabric with design image repeated on all four quadrants. - **$40 $75 $125**

❑ **GON-9. "Scarlett O'Hara Perfume" Novelty Container,**
1940. Store item. - **$50 $85 $175**

GON-10

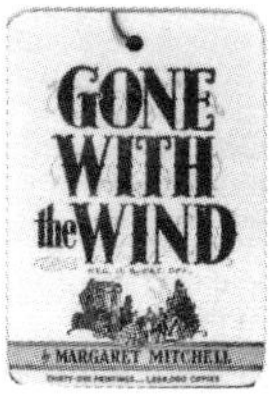


GON-11

❑ **GON-10. Scarlett O'Hara "Yesteryear" Perfume Glass Vial,**
1940. Babs Creations. Figure image within vertical dome. - **$60 $150 $250**

❑ **GON-11. Cardboard String Tag From Clothing Dress,**
1940. Mae Delli's Originals. - **$40 $100 $150**

GON-12

GON-13

❑ **GON-12. Brass Heart-Shaped Jewelry Pin,**
1940. Store item. - **$50 $125 $200**

❑ **GON-13. "Gone With The Wind" Brass Charm Locket Designed In Book Image,**
1940. Opens to hold two miniature pictures. - **$50 $100 $175**

GON-14

GON-15

❑ **GON-14. Gone With The Wind Brass/Cello. Cameo Brooch,**
1940. Lux Toilet Soap. Replica of brooch worn by Scarlett in movie, offered originally for 15 cents and three soap wrappers. -
**$35 $65 $125**

❑ **GON-15. Scarlett's Brooch,**
1940. Lux Soap. Movie jewelry replica in brass accented by simulated pearls around single simulated turquoise stone. - **$40 $75 $150**

GON-16

GON-17

❑ **GON-16. Cookbook,**
1940. Pebeco Toothpaste premium. -
**$35 $65 $100**

❑ **GON-17. Cookbook Store Display From Pebeco Toothpaste,**
1940. Scarce. - **$100 $150 $300**

GON-18

GON-19

❑ **GON-18. "Tara's Theme" Sheet Music,**
1941. Store item by Remick Music Corp. 9x12" with browntone illustration. Also seen with 1954 copyright date. First Printing - **$15 $25 $50**
Later Printing - **$5 $12 $20**

❑ **GON-19. Gone With The Wind Spanish Herald Sheet,**
1940s. 3-1/2x5-1/2" full color with Spanish text on reverse. - **$10 $20 $30**

GON-20

❑ **GON-20. Re-release Promo Poster,**
1998. 20" x 13". Promotes re-release of the movie in its original technicolor and with digital sound. - **$5 $10 $20**

# The Great Gildersleeve

**Throckmorton P. Gildersleeve started life as a character on the *Fibber McGee and Molly* radio series in the 1930s. Created and played by actor Harold Peary, Gildy was a pompous windbag who was spun off successfully to his own program on NBC in 1941. He was a small-town water commissioner, but the show centered on his life as the bachelor uncle of Leroy and Marjorie and his romantic encounters as the town's most prominent eligible man. Willard Waterman stepped into the role in 1950, and the program ran until 1958. Kraft Foods was the sponsor. There was a brief television series and a 1942 RKO movie of the same name.**

GIL-1

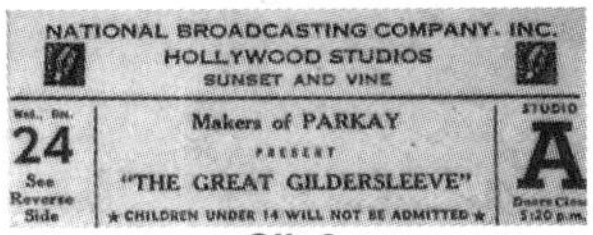


GIL-2

GIL-3

❑ **GIL-1. Kraft Foods Litho. Tin 2-1/4" Jar Lid,**
1946. - **$15 $25 $45**

❑ **GIL-2. Radio Show Studio Audience Ticket,**
1947. Parkay margarine. Pictured example for December 24 Christmas Eve broadcast. -
**$10 $20 $40**

❑ **GIL-3. Great Gildersleeve Record w/Sleeve,**
1940s. Radio premium. Titled "Name My Song Contest" part 1& 2. - **$20 $40 $80**

# Green Giant

**The Green Giant was born in 1925 as the trademark for a new variety of peas by the Minnesota Valley Canning Company. The original illustration of a giant wrapped in fur, created to satisfy trademark requirements, was redesigned 10 years later into the character we now recognize--a smiling green giant clothed in leaves. Little Sprout was added in the early 1970s, and the company has merchandised both characters.**

GNT-1

❑ **GNT-1. 20th Anniversary Birthday Record With Envelope,**
1949. In Mailer - **$5 $15 $30**
Loose - **$2 $7 $15**

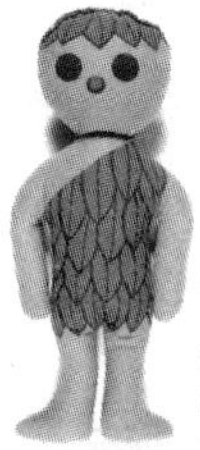

GNT-2

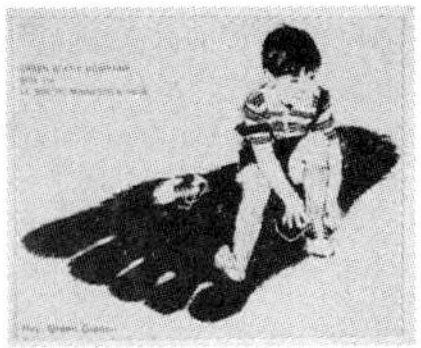

GNT-3

❑ **GNT-2. Earliest Cloth Doll,**
1966. - **$10 $20 $45**

❑ **GNT-3. "Footprint Rug" In Mailer,**
1967. Issued both as "Left Foot" and "Right Foot" versions, each about 22" wide by 42" long mailed in a 24" long green plastic sleeve.
Near Mint In Mailer - **$25**
Loose - **$5 $10 $15**

GNT-4

❑ **GNT-4. Campaign Kit,**
1968. Voter card, litho. badge, sticker, 26x38" poster.
Set - **$12 $20 $40**

GNT-5

GNT-6

❑ **GNT-5. Little Sprout Cloth Doll,**
c. 1970. - **$5 $12 $20**

❑ **GNT-6. "Speakin' Sprout" Talking Cloth Doll,**
1971. Contains battery operated tape recorder. - **$25 $50 $75**

GNT-7

GNT-8

❑ **GNT-7. "Little Sprout" Sleeping Bag With Mailer,**
1977. Mail order premium. - **$10 $20 $35**

❑ **GNT-8. Little Sprout Vinyl Doll,**
1970s. - **$10 $15 $35**

GNT-9

❑ **GNT-9. "Little Sprout Radio" With Box,**
1980s. Hard plastic battery operated figural radio 9-1/2" tall. Near Mint Boxed - **$60**
Loose - **$10 $20 $30**

# The Green Hornet

**Accompanied by his faithful valet Kato, the Green Hornet matched wits with the underworld on the radio from 1936 to 1952, first on WXYZ in Detroit, then on the Mutual network in 1938, on NBC in 1939, on the ABC Blue network in 1940, and finally back on Mutual in 1952. Sponsors included General Mills in 1948 and Orange Crush in 1952. Under his mask the Hornet was Britt Reid, crusading newspaper publisher and grand-nephew of the Lone Ranger, and his crime-fighting exploits in the big city resembled those of his relative in the West. (Both shows were created by George W. Trendle and written largely by Fran Striker.) Also featured was Miss Case, secretary and love interest, along with Black Beauty, the Hornet's super-charged limousine, and his non-lethal gas gun. Kato, originally Japanese, became a Filipino after Pearl Harbor.**

**Two Green Hornet chapter plays were released by Universal in 1940, with Keye Luke as Kato, and a souped-up television series aired for a season (1966-1967) on ABC, with Van Williams in the title role and Bruce Lee as Kato. Comic books appeared more or less regularly from 1940 to 1949, followed by a one-shot in 1953, three issues in 1966-1967 timed to coincide with the television series, and a revival in 1989.**

**Speculation about a new Green Hornet movie surfaces regularly, though no production has actually begun.**

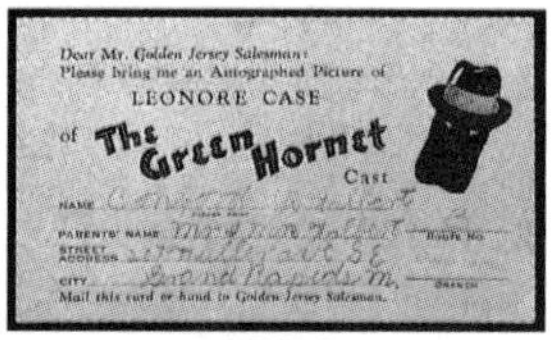

GRN-1

❑ **GRN-1. Postcard,**
1936. Golden Jersey Milk. Radio premium-
**$100 $225 $400**

GRN-2

❑ **GRN-2. Radio Fan Club Photo,**
1938. Golden Jersey Milk. Pictures Britt Reid (Al Hodge) as Green Hornet with back ad text. -
**$75 $225 $400**

GRN-3

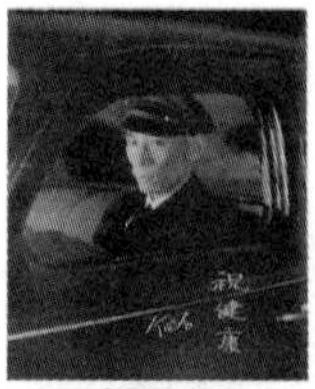
GRN-4

❑ **GRN-3. Radio Fan Club Photo,**
1938. Golden Jersey Milk. Pictures Miss Case (Lee Allman) with back ad text, from G-J-M Club photo series of several cast members. -
**$60 $150 $200**

❑ **GRN-4. "Kato" Portrait Photo,**
1938. Golden Jersey Milk. - **$50 $175 $250**

GRN-5

❑ **GRN-5. "Mike Oxford" Portrait Photo,**
1938. Golden Jersey Milk. - **$50 $150 $200**

GRN-6

❑ **GRN-6. Membership Card,**
1938. Golden Jersey Milk. - **$50 $200 $300**

GRN-7

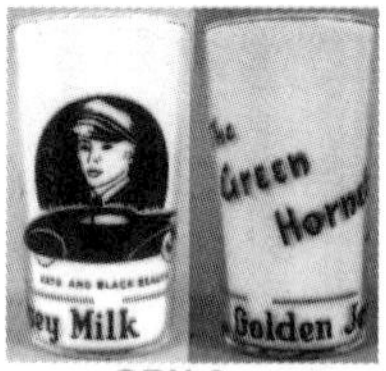
GRN-8

❑ **GRN-7. Green Hornet Glass,**
c. 1938. Scarce. Golden Jersey Milk. -
**$75 $250 $375**

❑ **GRN-8. Kato And Black Beauty Glass,**
c. 1938. Scarce. Golden Jersey Milk. -
**$75 $250 $375**

GRN-9

GRN-10

❑ **GRN-9. Radio Show Postcard,**
1939. - **$75 $175 $300**

❑ **GRN-10. "The Green Hornet Strikes" Better Little Book,**
1940. Whitman #1453. - **$30 $60 $160**

GRN-11

GRN-12

GRN-13

❑ **GRN-11. "The Green Hornet Adventure Club" Cello. Button,**
1940. Rare. Universal Pictures. For 13-chapter movie serial. - **$250 $600 $900**

❑ **GRN-12. "The Green Hornet Strikes Again" Movie Serial Cello. Button,**
1940. Rare. Universal Serial/Adventure Club. For 13-chapter serial. - **$250 $600 $900**

❑ **GRN-13. "Green Hornet Loyalty Club" Cello. Button,**
c. 1940. - **$150 $325 $700**

GRN-14

GRN-15

❑ **GRN-14. "The Green Hornet Returns" Better Little Book #1496,**
1941. 432 pages. Flip pictures. - **$25 $90 $190**

❑ **GRN-15. "The Green Hornet Cracks Down" Better Little Book,**
1942. Whitman #1480. - **$60 $135 $275**

GRN-16

GRN-17

❑ **GRN-16. Speed Comics/Green Hornet Comics News Vendor's Apron,**
c. 1945. Includes text "Nationally Distributed By Publisher's Distributing Corporation." Black and red type on tan fabric featuring three pockets for change. - **$250 $400 $700**

❑ **GRN-17. Secret Compartment Glow-In-Dark Ring,**
1947. General Mills. Brass with hinged lid over glow plastic compartment. - **$200 $400 $800**

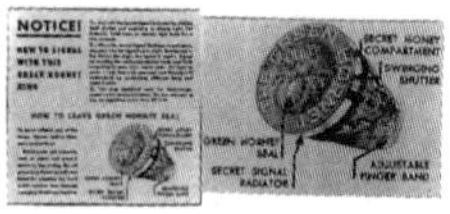
GRN-18

GRN-19

❑ **GRN-18. "Green Hornet Night Signaling Ring" Enclosure Slip,**
c. 1947. Betty Crocker Cereal Tray offer. Instructions are on one side, order coupon for additional rings on reverse. - **$100 $150 $225**

❑ **GRN-19. "Newspaper Reporter" Recruitment Letter,**
1940s. Union Biscuit Co. Offers reporter's kit described in full over radio broadcasts on KWK, St. Louis. - **$50 $150 $250**

GRN-20

GRN-21

❑ **GRN-20. Vernors Plastic "Trick Or Treat Bag",**
1966. Vernors Ginger Ale. - **$20 $40 $75**

❑ **GRN-21. "Agent" 4" Litho. Button,**
1966. Store item. - **$10 $25 $50**

GRN-22

❑ **GRN-22. "The Green Hornet" Hat With Mask,**
1966. Store item by Arlington. - **$75 $150 $250**

GRN-23

GRN-24

❑ **GRN-23. "The Green Hornet/Kato" Glass,**
1966. Probable food product container. - **$75 $150 $250**

❑ **GRN-24. TV Promo Postcard,**
1966. - **$25 $50 $75**

GRN-25

GRN-26

❑ **GRN-25. Pennant 28 1/2",**
1966. Promotes TV show. - **$25 $70 $125**

❑ **GRN-26. Green Hornet Character Plastic Flicker Rings,**
1966. Set of 12, each with double image when tilted.
Silver Base Each - **$10 $20 $30**
Blue Base Each - **$8 $15 $25**

GRN-27

GRN-28

❑ **GRN-27. Green Hornet Sting Whistle,**
1966. Scarce. Chicken Of The Sea Tuna (Required Two Labels). Two-piece plastic slide whistle with small name mark on handle.
Newspaper Ad - **$25 $50 $100**
Whistle - **$150 $350 $700**

❑ **GRN-28. Battery Operated "Signal Ray",**
1966. Store item by Colorforms. Display card is 10x11". Display With Toy - **$300 $600 $1000**

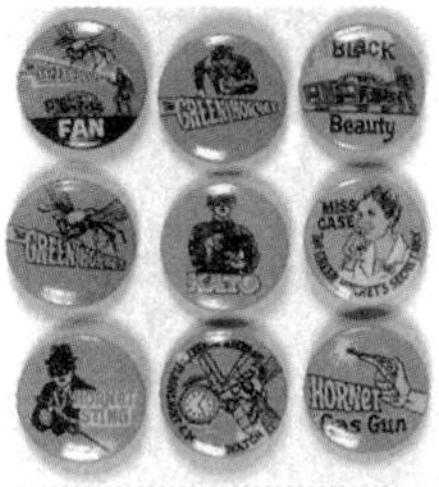

GRN-29

GRN-30

❑ **GRN-29. Litho. Buttons,**
1966. Vending machine set of nine. Two color styles, with or without yellow.
Each - **$8 $12 $20**

❑ **GRN-30. Rubber Figural Ring,**
1966. Vending machine issue. - **$5 $7 $10**

GRN-31

GRN-32

GRN-33

❑ **GRN-31. 3-1/2" Cello. Button,**
c. 1966. Store item by Button World Mfg. -
**$10 $20 $30**

❑ **GRN-32. "The Green Hornet" Drinking Glass,**
1966. Probable food product container. -
**$75 $150 $250**

❑ **GRN-33. Green Hornet Pez Dispenser,**
c. 1966. Several hat variations, grey & brown hats worth more. - **$75 $150 $250**

GRN-34

❑ **GRN-34. "Black Beauty" Car Boxed,**
1966. Store item by Corgi. 5-1/2" long die cast metal featuring missile-firing grille and trunk with spinner-firing mechanism. Issued with three orange saucers and single missile plus instruction paper. Near Mint Boxed - **$600**
Car With At Least One Saucer And One Missile - **$75 $150 $300**

GRN-35

❑ **GRN-35. "The Green Hornet Wallets" Store Display,**
1966. Store item by Standard Plastic Products Inc. 22" tall stiff cardboard countertop display with header card holding 12 wallets.
Near Mint Complete - **$1500**
Single Wallet - **$25 $50 $85**

GRN-36

GRN-37

❑ **GRN-36. "The Green Hornet" Charm Bracelet,**
1966. Store item. Card **- $10 $20 $40**
Bracelet **- $15 $30 $60**

❑ **GRN-37. "The Green Hornet Quick Switch Game,"**
1966. Milton Bradley**. - $50 $150 $250**

GRN-38

GRN-39

❑ **GRN-38. "The Green Hornet Ring,"**
1966. Vari-Vue. Flicker ring with silver base and full color flicker. Packaged **$150 $300 $450**

❑ **GRN-39. Hand Puppet,**
1966. Store item by Ideal. Photo example is missing hat. Complete - **$100 $200 $300**
Without Hat **- $75 $150 $200**

GRN-40

❑ **GRN-40. Metal Lunch Box,**
1967. Store item by King-Seeley. -
**$100 $250 $400**

GRN-41

❑ **GRN-41. Lunch Box Metal Bottle,**
1967. Store item by King-Seeley Thermos Co. Came with matching lunch box. -
**$50 $125 $200**

GRN-42

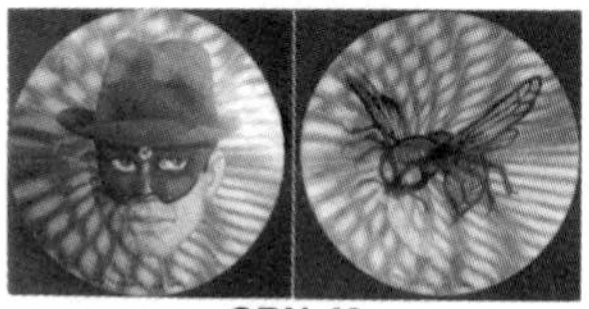
GRN-43

❑ **GRN-42. Flicker Button 3",**
1967. Store item. - **$10 $25 $50**

❑ **GRN-43. Flicker Disk 7",**
1967. Store item. - **$20 $40 $70**

GRN-44

❑ **GRN-44. Flicker Picture Plastic Ruler,**
1967. Store item by Vari-Vue. 6" length. -
**$50 $110 $165**

GRN-45

❑ **GRN-45. "The Green Hornet/American Motors" Record,**
1973. Mark 56 Records**. - $35 $75 $125**

GRN-46

❑ **GRN-46. "Bruce Lee/The Green Hornet" Movie Poster,**
1977. 27x41" for 20th Century Fox film. -
**$75 $150 $250**

GRN-47

GRN-48

❑ **GRN-47. "Green Hornet" Record,**
1977. With sleeve. Plays two complete radio programs from 1943. - **$50**

❑ **GRN-48. Green Hornet Large Rubber Ring,**
1970s. Vending machine issue. Thin band of green rubber attached to matching 2x2-1/4" hornet image. - **$7 $10 $15**

GRN-49

GRN-50

❑ **GRN-49. "Green Hornet" Die-cast Car,**
2000. Team Lightning metal Road Rod. - **$5**

❑ **GRN-50. "Black Beauty" Die-cast Car,**
2001. Johnny Lightning metal model. - **$5**

## The Green Lama

**The first appearance of the Green Lama was in *Prize Comics* #7 in 1940. He then appeared in his own book for eight issues from 1944 to 1946. For a dime readers could join the *Green Lama Club* and receive a membership card, the key to the Lama's secret code, and an Escapo folding trick that showed victory over Fascist rats. The character was revived on CBS radio for the summer of 1949 as a New York-based crime fighter with special powers acquired after 10 years of study in a Tibet monastery.**

(INSTRUCTIONS)

(CARD AND MAILER)

(VARIATION 2)

GLM-1

❑ **GLM-1. Club Kit,**
1945. Victory Game.
Club Card - **$75 $150 $300**
Mailer - **$20 $50 $125**
Escape Trick with Instructions, Two Variations,
Each - **$75 $200 $375**

GLM-2

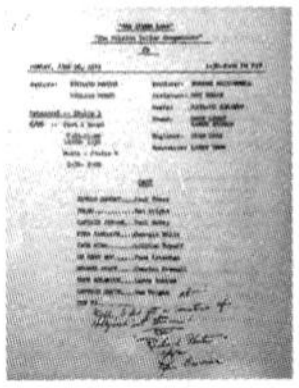

GLM-3

❑ **GLM-2. Code Letter,**
1940s. M.L.J. Magazines. Came with kit. "Green Lama Code Chart" with instructions concluding by translated "Buy Bonds" message. -
**$100 $250 $400**

❑ **GLM-3. Radio Episode Script,**
1949. For June 26 broadcast "Million Dollar Chopsticks". - **$50 $100 $150**

## Gulliver's Travels

**Jonathan Swift's masterpiece, published in 1726, has retained its satirical thrust and fairy-tale aura for almost three centuries. The voyages of Lemuel Gulliver to Lilliput, Brobdingnag, and the land of the Yahoos continue to enchant readers and viewers to this day. In addition to the many print editions of the classic, the tales have been adapted in various media, including: a full-length animated film by the Fleischer studios (1939); a Japanese animated feature that sent Gulliver into outer space (1966); a part live-action British film with Richard Harris (1977); *The 3 Worlds of Gulliver* (British, 1960); a Hanna-Barbera animated series, *The Adventures of Gulliver* (ABC, 1968-1970); a Hanna-Barbera feature for CBS, sponsored by Kenner toys (1979); Saban's *Gulliver's Travels*, syndicated in 1992; a Classic Comics edition first published in 1943; and Dell Comics editions in 1956 and again in 1965-1966. Ted Danson starred in a filmed version on NBC-television in 1996. Even the BBC tried its hand with a four-part adaptation for radio.**

GLL-1

❑ **GLL-1. "Gulliver's Travels" Booklet,**
1939. Macy's department store. - **$15 $50 $100**

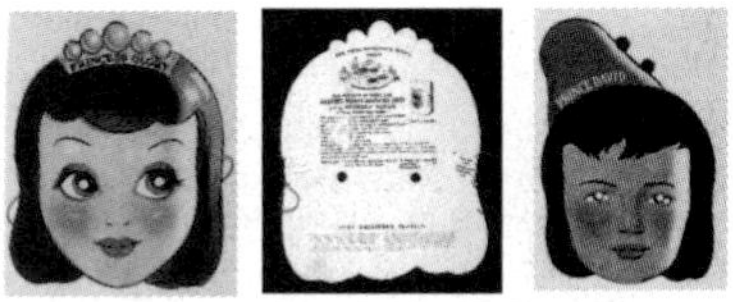

(BACK OF MASK)

GLL-2

❑ **GLL-2. Character Masks,**
1939. Hecker's Flour. Diecut stiff paper full color masks of Princess Glory, Prince David, King Bombo, Snitch, Gabby.
Each **$15 $40 $60**

GLL-3

❑ **GLL-3. "Gulliver's Travels" Tin Litho. Spinning Top,**
1939. Store item. 5" diameter by 4-3/4" tall with red wood handle on rod at center. -
**$50 $150 $200**

GLL-4

GLL-5

❑ **GLL-4. Boxed English Card Deck,**
1939. Store item copyright Paramount Pictures Inc., England. Set of 44 playing cards picturing various film scenes in color. - **$25 $50 $100**

❑ **GLL-5. Cereal Bowl,**
1939. White glass picturing characters from Fleischer animated film around perimeter. - **$20 $40 $75**

GLL-6

GLL-7

❑ **GLL-6. "Gulliver" Glass Tumbler,**
1939. Probably distributed as dairy product container. Reverse has descriptive verse. - **$10 $20 $30**

❑ **GLL-7. "King Little" Glass Tumbler,**
1939. Probably distributed as dairy product container. Reverse has descriptive verse. - **$10 $20 $30**

GLL-8

GLL-9

❑ **GLL-8. "Snoop" Glass Tumbler,**
1939. Probably distributed as dairy product container. Reverse has descriptive verse. - **$10 $20 $30**

❑ **GLL-9. "Snitch" Glass Tumbler,**
1939. Probably distributed as dairy product container. Reverse has descriptive verse. - **$10 $20 $30**

GLL-10

❑ **GLL-10. Child's China Cup,**
c. 1939. Pictures Gabby, Snitch and bird character from Fleischer animated cartoon movie. - **$15 $35 $75**

GLL-11

GLL-12

❑ **GLL-11. Gabby, Princess Glory And Prince David Glazed Ceramic Cup,**
c. 1939. Store item by Hammersley & Co., England. - **$40 $65 $125**

❑ **GLL-12. China Pitcher,**
c. 1939. Store item by Hammersley & Co., England. Pictures two scenes and five characters. - **$50 $110 $165**

GLL-13

❑ **GLL-13. Glazed Ceramic Creamer,**
c. 1939. Store item. 3-1/2" tall. Hammersley & Co., England**. - $50 $110 $165**

GLL-14

GLL-15

❑ **GLL-14. "Gulliver's Travels" Saalfield Book,**
1939. #1172, similar to Whitman Big Little Book**. - $20 $40 $95**

❑ **GLL-15. "Gulliver's Travels" Flip Movie Booklet With Four Scenes,**
1939. Issued by Kitchen Kleanzer. 2-1/2x4-7/8". **- $50 $100 $150**

## The Gumps

***The Gumps*, one of the most popular comic strips of the 1920s, was created by Sidney Smith (1887-1935) for the *Chicago Tribune*. The story of Andy and Min, son Chester, and rich Uncle Bim began as a daily strip in 1917 and as a Sunday feature in 1919, and lasted until 1959, some 24 years after Smith was killed in an automobile accident. Comic book reprints appeared from 1918 into the 1940s, and a radio series based on the strip and sponsored by Pebeco toothpaste was aired on CBS from 1934 to 1937. The popularity of the Gumps is reflected by the large variety of licensed items - toys, games, books, buttons, etc. "Oh Min!"**

GMP-1

GMP-2

❑ **GMP-1. "Andy Gump" Pictorial Sheet Music,**
1923. Store item. Words and music for novelty song illustrated by 15 characters from comic strip by Sidney Smith. - **$10 $20 $40**

❑ **GMP-2. "The Sunshine Twins" Book,**
1925. Sunshine Andy Gump Biscuits by Loose-Wiles Biscuit Co. Pictured example is designated fourth edition. - **$20 $40 $75**

GMP-3

❑ **GMP-3. "The Gumps At The Seashore" Boxed Game,**
c. 1930. Milton Bradley store item #4520**. - $60 $125 $200**

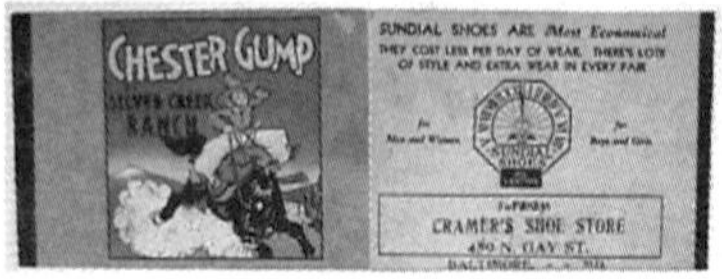


GMP-4

❑ **GMP-4. "Chester Gump At Silver Creek Ranch" Whitman Premium Book,**
1933. Sundial Shoes and others. Similar to a Big Little Book but 4x5-5/8" format and only 48 pages. - **$50 $100 $150**

GMP-5

GMP-6

❑ **GMP-5. "Chester Gump Finds Hidden Treasure" Premium Whitman Book,**
1934. Perkins Products (Korlix Pudding). Seen both with and without the Perkins name on the back cover. - **$50 $100 $150**

❑ **GMP-6. "Chester Gump And His Friends" Booklet,**
1934. Tarzan Ice Cream Cups. #5 from series of various character titles. - **$20 $50 $100**

GMP-7

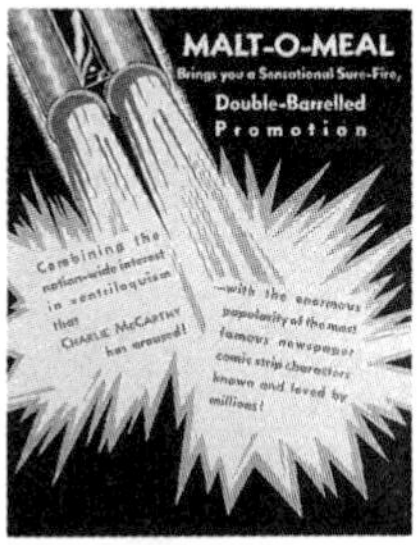


GMP-8

❑ **GMP-7. "The Gumps In Radio Land" Booklet,**
1937. Pebeco toothpaste. - **$25 $50 $100**

❑ **GMP-8. Malt-O-Meal Cereal Premium Folder,**
1938. Four pages of pictures of Andy Gump, Harold Teen, Herby, and cardboard Dummys. - **$30 $60 $120**

GMP-9

❑ **GMP-9. "Andy Gump" Die Cut Sign 14x16",**
1938. Rare. Malt-O-Meal promotional sign (standee.) Tells how to get comic character dummies. - **$500 $1200 $1600**

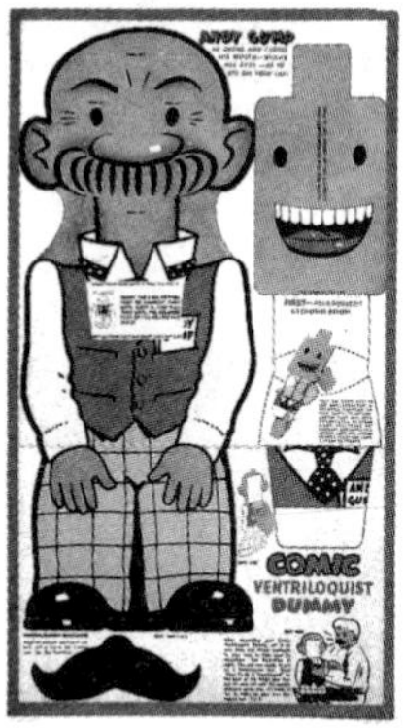


GMP-10

GMP-11

GMP-12

❑ **GMP-10. "Andy Gump" Dummy Punchout 11x20",**
1938. Rare. Malt-O-Meal Cereal premium. - **$150 $300 $500**

❑ **GMP-11. "Andy Gump" Wood Jointed Doll,**
1930s. Store item. - **$50 $75 $150**

❑ **GMP-12. "Andy Gump For Congress" Cello. Button,**
1930s. Various newspapers. - **$10 $20 $30**

GMP-13

GMP-14

❑ **GMP-13. "Investigator/Gump Charities/Use Solder Seal" Cello. Button,**
1930s. - **$20 $35 $65**

❑ **GMP-14. "Andy Gump For President" Cello. Button,**
1930s. Wonder Milk, various other food products. - **$20 $35 $65**

GMP-15

GMP-16

❑ **GMP-15. "Andy Gump For President" 2" Cello. Button,**
1930s. Good Humor Ice Cream Suckers. - **$50 $100 $200**

❑ **GMP-16. "The Gumps/Friendly Refreshment" Metal Cap For Soda Bottle,**
1930s. Bon-Ton Beverages, Chicago. - **$10 $20 $30**

GMP-17

**GMP-17. "Uncle Bim's Roll" Candy Wrapper,**
1930s. Voegele & Dinning Co. Waxed paper and design of currency money. - **$15 $25 $40**

## Gunsmoke

**Dodge City, Kansas, in the 1880s was the site of this adult Western that premiered on CBS radio in 1952 and on CBS television in 1955 for 20 years until the program ended in 1975. Starring James Arness as Matt Dillon, other continuing characters included the saloon keeper Miss Kitty, old Doc Adams, and the Marshal's deputy Chester, replaced by Festus in 1964. Radio sponsors included Post Toasties (1953), Chesterfield cigarettes (1954), and Liggett & Myers (1954-1957). L & M cigarettes was also a television sponsor. Related comic books appeared from the 1950s to 1970, and two Gunsmoke movies starring James Arness were released in 1987 and 1990. Items usually carry a copyright of CBS Television Enterprises or Columbia Broadcasting System.**

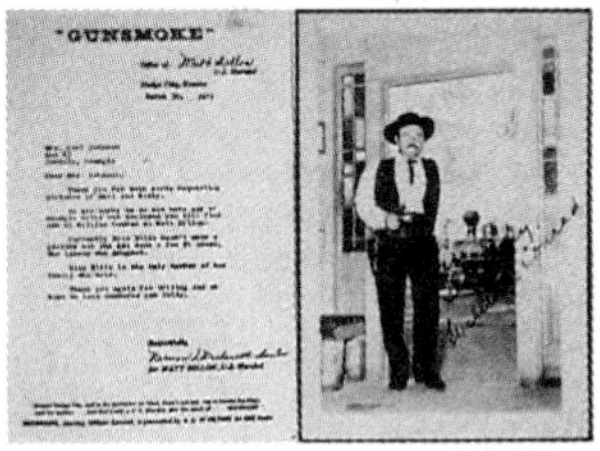


GUN-1

❑ **GUN-1. Radio Fan Letter With William Conrad Signed Photo,**
c. 1952. "L&M Filters on CBS Radio." 7-1/4x10-1/2" "Gunsmoke" letterhead sheet thanks fan for requesting "Pictures Of Matt And Kitty." Comes with 3-1/2x5-1/2" glossy black and white real photo autographed postcard.
Letter - **$30 $60 $100**
Photo - **$20 $40 $65**

GUN-2

GUN-3

❑ **GUN-2. "L&M Cigarettes" 21x22" Cardboard Store Sign,**
c. 1954. Liggett & Meyers. - **$35 $75 $150**

❑ **GUN-3. L&M Cigarettes Cast Card,**
c. 1954. - **$8 $15 $30**

GUN-4

GUN-5

❑ **GUN-4. Matt Dillon And Miss Kitty 21x21" Cigarette Sign,**
c. 1954. L&M Cigarettes of Liggett & Myers Tobacco Co. Stiff cardboard with full color photos. - **$35 $85 $160**

❑ **GUN-5. Big Little Book - TV Series,**
1958. Hard to find without cracks in the spine. Cover is laminated, which splits when opened repeatedly. One in a series of 6. - **$10 $25 $50**

GUN-6

❑ **GUN-6. Boxed Board Game,**
1958. Store item by Lowell Toy Corp. Has playing board along with four cardboard stand-up stockade structures. - **$25 $60 $90**

GUN-7

GUN-8

GUN-9

❑ **GUN-7. Matt Dillon Diecut Cardboard Standee,**
c. 1958. L&M Cigarettes. 8-1/2x25" tall with easel back. - **$50 $150 $250**

❑ **GUN-8. "James Arness Fan Club" Cello. Button,**
c. 1958. - **$15 $35 $75**

❑ **GUN-9. Packaged 3-1/2" Cello. Button,**
1959. Store item. From series of "Top Western T.V. Stars" packaged in cellophane bag with header card.
Near Mint Bagged - **$75**
Button Only - **$15 $30 $50**

GUN-10

❑ **GUN-10. "Matt Dillon-U.S. Marshal" Outfit,**
1959. Store item by Kaynee. - **$50 $100 $150**

GUN-11

GUN-12

❑ **GUN-11. "Matt Dillon/U.S. Marshal" Metal Badge,**
1959. Store item. On Card - **$20 $30 $50**
Loose - **$10 $15 $25**

❑ **GUN-12. "U.S. Marshal" Metal Badge,**
1959. Store item. Badge version omits "Matt Dillon" name. On Card - **$20 $30 $50**
Loose - **$10 $15 $25**

GUN-13

❑ **GUN-13. Personal Appearance Souvenir Folder With Photo,**
c. 1960. - **$15 $25 $50**

GUN-14

GUN-15

❑ **GUN-14. "All Star Dairies" Litho. Button,**
c. 1960. - **$8 $15 $25**

❑ **GUN-15. "Gunsmoke" Lunch Box,**
1962. Store item by Aladdin Industries. - **$75 $150 $250**

GUN-16

❑ **GUN-16. TV Show Commemorative Promotional Pocket Watch Encased As Paperweight,**
1968. Clear lucite block 2-3/4x4-1/2x3/4" thick holds actual pocket watch and fob depicting CBS-TV logo plus text "Gunsmoke Starts Its 13th Year September 11 New Day Monday New Time 7:30 PM." Watch hands point to 7:30. - **$50 $125 $200**

GUN-17

GUN-18

❑ **GUN-17. Metal Cuff Links With B&w Photo Inserts,**
1960s. Issuer unknown. - **$20 $40 $85**

❑ **GUN-18. "Matt Dillon's Favorite" Key Ring,**
1960s. Reverse of plastic star reads "Sanders Dairy/All Star". - **$20 $35 $70**

GUN-19

❑ **GUN-19. TV Publicity Stills,**
c. 1972. CBS-TV. 8x10" high gloss black and white photos of cast members. Each - **$2 $5 $10**

GUN-20

❑ **GUN-20. "Gunsmoke" Three-Reel View-Master Set With Color Story Booklet,**
1972. Complete - **$15 $25 $40**

## Happy Hooligan

**Happy Hooligan, the ever-innocent optimist, was created by Frederick Opper (1857-1937) for the Hearst Sunday comics in 1900 and continued, under a variety of titles, until 1932. The strip, considered a major classic comic, also involved Happy's pet dog Flip and his brothers Gloomy Gus and Lord Montmorency in a series of ill-fated adventures. Happy, with his tin-can hat, and Gus, with his battered top hat, were immensely popular characters, appearing in stage plays, silent animated cartoons, sheet music, and reprints of the strips in book form.**

HAP-1

HAP-2

❑ **HAP-1. "How To Make Happy Hooligan Dance" Cut-Out Supplement,**
1902. New York American & Journal newspaper. Uncut - **$35 $60 $100**

❑ **HAP-2. Postcard,**
1904. United States Card premium. Shows Happy facing left. Says "You have seen my face before 'Guess where". - **$10 $20 $30**

HAP-3

HAP-4

❑ **HAP-3. Valentine Postcard,**
1904. Shows Happy fishing. - **$10 $20 $30**

❑ **HAP-4. Valentine Postcard,**
1904. Shows Happy looking straight ahead. - **$10 $20 $30**

HAP-5

❑ **HAP-5. Bisque Match Holder,**
c. 1905. Probably German. 8-3/8" tall. - **$50 $100 $150**

HAP-6

HAP-7

❑ **HAP-6. "Shoemakers Fair" Cello. Button,**
1905. Figure back view although frontal head for slogan "Are You Goin' Or Comin'?" - **$20 $40 $85**

❑ **HAP-7. Happy Hooligan Song Sheet,**
c. 1905. Rare. Newspaper supplement. - **$20 $40 $100**

HAP-8

HAP-9

❑ **HAP-8. Figural White Metal Stickpin,**
c. 1905. Detailed image finished in black. - **$15 $25 $40**

❑ **HAP-9. Diecut Jointed Valentine,**
1906. Store item from series by Raphael Tuck & Sons Co. Ltd. 14-1/2" tall with pull string to make body parts move. - **$35 $75 $150**

HAP-10

HAP-11

❑ **HAP-10. Mechanical Postcard,**
1906. New York Sunday American & Journal newspaper. Shows picture of cops pulling Hooligan & others out of water. Card folds out to give a 3-D look. - **$30 $65 $100**

❑ **HAP-11. Postcard,**
1906. American Journal Examiner. Shows Happy watching the Moon. - **$10 $15 $25**

HAP-12

HAP-13

❑ **HAP-12. Postcard,**
1906. Boston Sunday American newspaper premium. - **$10 $15 $25**

❑ **HAP-13. Postcard,**
1906. Boston Sunday American newspaper premium. Egyptian police catch Happy & friend trying to steal the Sphinx. - **$10 $15 $25**

HAP-14

HAP-15

❑ **HAP-14. Composition Figure,**
c. 1910. Store item. Jointed arms and legs. - **$50 $80 $150**

❑ **HAP-15. Papier Mache Roly-Poly,**
c. 1910. Store item. - **$200 $300 $500**

HAP-16

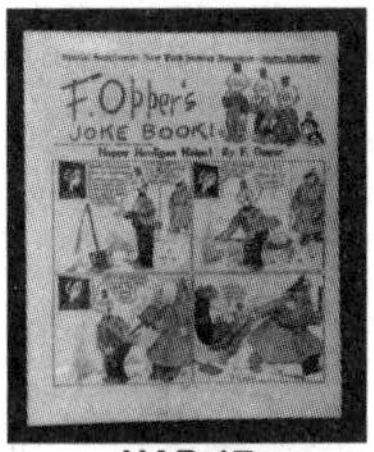

HAP-17

❑ **HAP-16. Happy Hooligan Figural White Metal Stickpin,**
c. 1910. - **$15 $25 $40**

❑ **HAP-17. "F. Oppers Joke Book,"**
1911. New York Sunday American. 10x12" Sunday supplement with 16 pages of Frederick Opper cartoons including Happy Hooligan, Alphonse and Gaston, And Her Name Was Maud. - **$15 $35 $70**

HAP-18

HAP-19

❑ **HAP-18. Cello. Button,**
c. 1915. - **$12 $25 $50**

❑ **HAP-19. Seated Bisque Nodder Figure,**
1920s. Store item. - **$50 $125 $250**

HAP-20

❑ **HAP-20. "The Story of Happy Hooligan" Feature Book #281,**
1932. 9 1/2" x 12". - **$64 $193 $450**

## Helen Trent

***The Romance of Helen Trent* reigned as the melodramatic queen of the daytime soap operas for over a quarter of a century on CBS radio from 1933 to 1960. Helen, remaining single and 35 through the years, was noble, pure, and pursued by dozens of suitors, most of whom came to a violent end. Sponsors included American Home Products, Affiliated Products, Whitehall Drugs, Pharmaco, Spry, Breeze, and Scott Waldorf tissue.**

HLN-1

HLN-2

❑ **HLN-1. Radio Replica Mechanical Brass Badge,**
1949. Five identified cast members are pictured in sequence through diecut opening by rear disk wheel. - **$20 $50 $85**

❑ **HLN-2. Silvered Brass Medallion,**
1949. Kolynos dental product. Design motifs on both sides including Sphinx, pyramids, other abstract symbols. - **$10 $18 $30**

## The Hermit's Cave

**Produced at Los Angeles radio station KMPC, this syndicated horror show aired from 1940 to 1944, offering ghost stories, weird stories, and mayhem and murders galore. Scary sound effects and the voice of Mel Johnson as the old hermit distinguished these weekly tales of carnage. Olga Coal was the sponsor.**

HER-1

❑ **HER-1. Cast Pictures,**
1940s. Scarce. Each - **$10 $25 $50**

HER-2

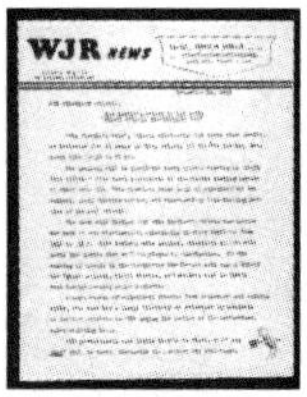


HER-3

❑ **HER-2. Promo Brochure,**
1940s. - **$30 $75 $150**

❑ **HER-3. Letter,**
1940s. - **$20 $40 $80**

HER-4

❑ **HER-4. Radio Show Promotion Mailer,**
1940s. Olga Coal of Carter Coal Company. Printed photos include "The Hermit With His Whiskers On." - **$30 $75 $150**

## Hobby Lobby

**From 1937 to 1949 on various networks this popular half-hour program highlighted listeners' unusual hobbies, everything from collecting elephant hairs to talking backwards. Dave Elman created the show, and each week a celebrity guest would show up to "lobby his hobby." Sponsors over the years included Hudson cars, Jell-O, Fels-Naptha soap, Colgate, and Anchor-Hocking glass. A television version with Cliff Arquette (Charley Weaver) as host was broadcast on ABC in 1959-60.**

HOB-1

HOB-2

❑ **HOB-1. Promotional Ad,**
c. 1940s. Rare. - **$30 $65 $125**

❑ **HOB-2. "Hobby Lobby" Rocking Horse Charm,**
c. 1940s. - **$20 $40 $60**

HOB-3

❑ **HOB-3. Merry Christmas And A Happy New Year Card,**
1940s. Fels-Naptha Soap Chips. 5x7-1/2" red, black and white card with inscription of "Dave Elman." - **$8 $20 $30**

## Hoot Gibson

**Edmund R. Gibson (1892-1962), known as Hoot because as a boy he liked to hunt owls, was born in Nebraska and learned to rope and ride on his father's ranch. He left home as a teenager and worked as a cowboy on the trail and in Wild West shows before arriving in Hollywood in 1910. His first minor film role was in 1911, but he became a star in the 1920s, ultimately appearing in well over 200 silent and talking movies. Gibson's popularity in the late 1920s was second only to Tom Mix. He retired in 1944, then had a few cameo film roles and a brief run as the host of a local television show in Los Angeles. Hoot Gibson comic books appeared in 1950.**

HGB-1

HGB-2

❑ **HGB-1. "Rope Spinning" Instruction Folder,**
1929. Came with Hoot Gibson Rodeo Ropes by Mordt Co., Chicago. - **$10 $20 $40**

❑ **HGB-2. Exhibit Cards,**
1920s. Vending machine cards by Exhibit Supply Co. Copyright year or movie titles from late 1920s.
Each - **$4 $8 $12**

HGB-3

HGB-4

❑ **HGB-3. Dixie Ice Cream Picture,**
1936. Title on reverse is "Frontier Justice." - **$25 $50 $100**

❑ **HGB-4. Dixie Ice Cream Picture,**
c. 1936. Reverse has four scenes from "Frontier Justice." - **$25 $50 $100**

HGB-5

❑ **HGB-5. Cello. Button,**
1930s. Black and white 1-3/4". - **$25 $65 $125**

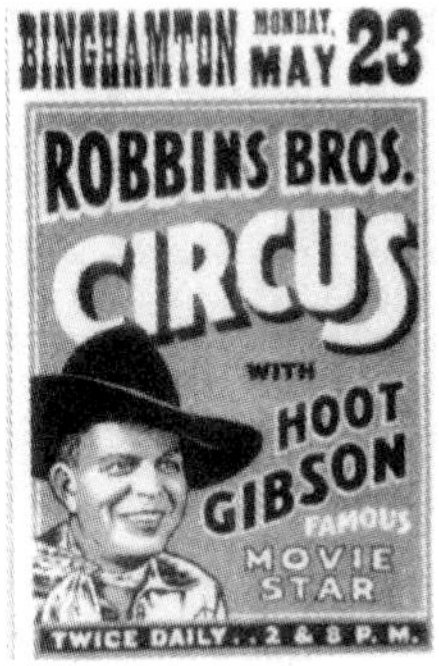

HGB-6

HGB-7

❑ **HGB-6. "Robbins Bros. Circus" 14x22" Cardboard Poster,**
1930s. - **$50 $125 $175**

❑ **HGB-7. Movie Felt Patch,**
1930s. - **$30 $75 $150**

HGB-8

HGB-9

HGB-10

❑ **HGB-8. Cello. Button,**
1930s. Probably circus souvenir. - **$35 $90 $175**

❑ **HGB-9. Litho. Button From Movie Star Set,**
1930s. - **$8 $12 $25**

❑ **HGB-10. "Ideal Moving Pictures" Flip Booklet,**
1930s. Flip sequence pictures Gibson lassoing two fistfighters. - **$20 $40 $75**

## Hop Harrigan

**America's ace of the airways, Hop Harrigan made his debut in *All-American Comics* #1 in 1939, complete with Flying Club wings, patch, and other membership paraphernalia. On the ABC and Mutual radio networks from 1942 to 1948, Hop and his mechanical pal Tank Tinker conquered the Axis powers during the war years and fought assorted American villains once the war ended. The program was locally sponsored for much of its run; network sponsors included Grape-Nuts Flakes (1944-1946) and Lever Brothers (1947-1948). Columbia Pictures released a 15-episode Hop Harrigan chapter play in 1946.**

HPH-1

❑ **HPH-1. "Hop Harrigan All American Flying Club" Copper Finish Brass Wings Badge,**
c. 1940. - **$25 $65 $125**

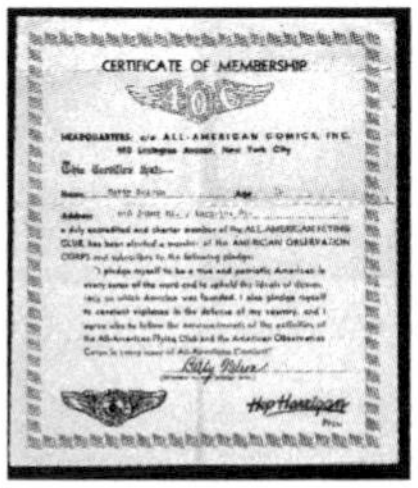

HPH-2

❑ **HPH-2. Certificate of Membership,**
1940. All American Comics premium-
**$75 $175 $300**

HPH-3

HPH-4

❑ **HPH-3. Photo,**
1940. All American Comics. DC premium - **$75 $100 $175**

❑ **HPH-4. Letter and Mailer For Badge,**
1940. All American Comics premium.
Letter - **$50 $75 $90**
Mailer - **$50 $60 $75**

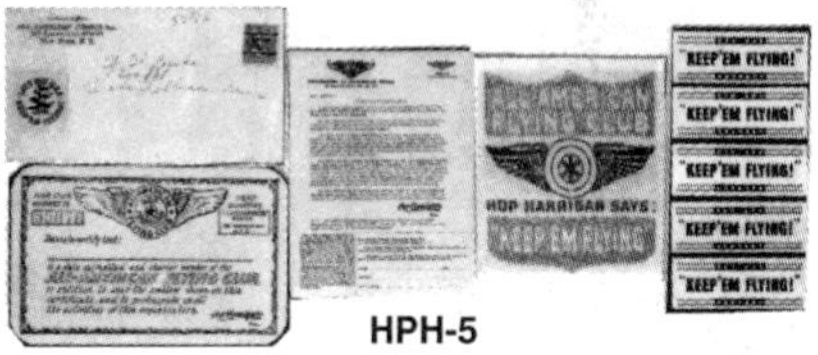

HPH-5

❑ **HPH-5. "All-American Flying Club" Kit.**
c. 1942. Membership letter, card, stickers, fabric patch. Near Mint In Mailer - **$250**
Patch - **$20 $60 $100**
Card - **$15 $35 $70**

HPH-6

❑ **HPH-6. Club Fabric Patch,**
c. 1942. - **$20 $60 $100**

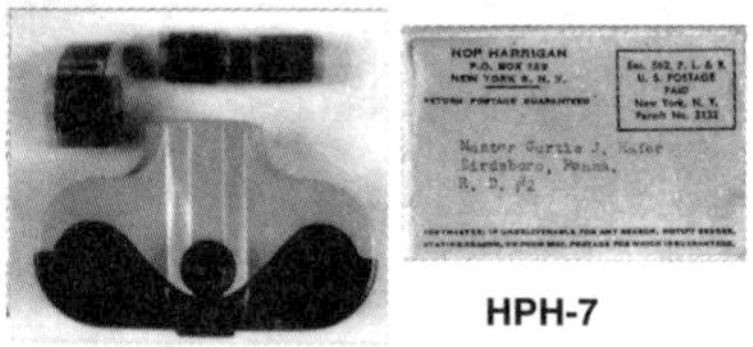

HPH-7

❑ **HPH-7. Plastic Movie Viewer With Films,**
c. 1942. Includes three films.
Near Mint Boxed - **$200**
Viewer And Films - **$40 $100 $150**

HPH-8 HPH-9

❑ **HPH-8. Jolly Junketeers Badge,**
1942. Jolly Junketeers Flying Club. Canada. - **$25 $50 $75**

❑ **HPH-9. Patch,**
1942. "Keep 'Em Flying" American Observation Corps patch. - **$20 $50 $85**

HPH-10

❑ **HPH-10. Grapenuts Flakes Sign 13x18",**
1944. Rare. Promotes radio show and shows Para-plane offer. - **$100 $275 $375**

HPH-11

❑ **HPH-11. "Para-Plane With Parachutists" 15x16" Diecut Cardboard Store Sign,**
1944. Rare. Grape-Nuts Flakes. Sign is three-dimensional and has open center to display cereal box. Sign **- $250 $500 $1200**

HPH-12

❑ **HPH-12. Superfortress Grape Nuts Flakes Sign,**
1944. Scarce. - **$200 $400 $500**

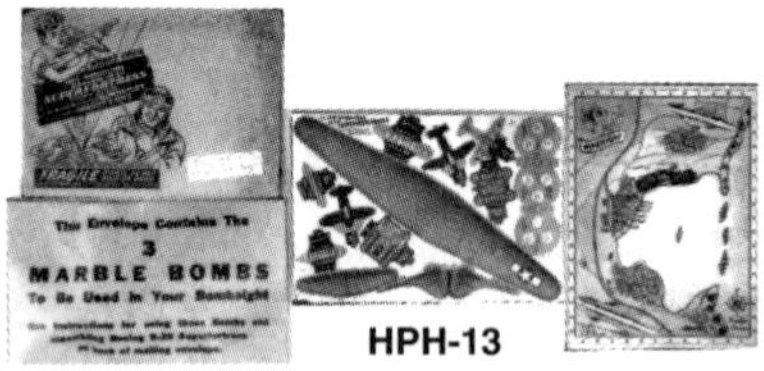


HPH-13

❑ **HPH-13. "Boeing B-29 Superfortress Model Plane And Target Game",**
1944. Scarce. Grape-Nuts Flakes. Includes target, two punch-out sheets, marbles. Complete - **$150 $350 $500**

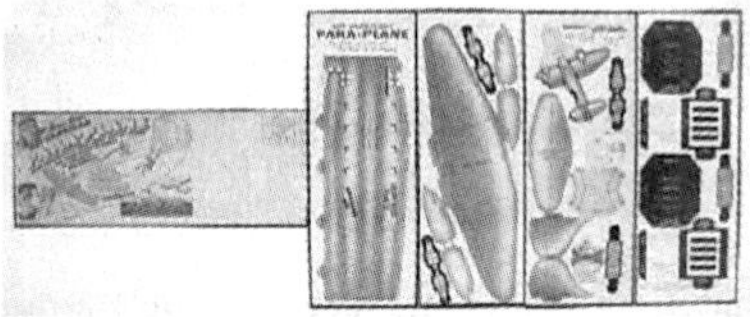

HPH-14

❑ **HPH-14. Hop Harrigan Para-Plane Punch-Out Premium,**
1944. Grape-Nuts Flakes. Consists of four punch-out sheets to form plane along with pair of "Code Signal Blinkers." An additional sheet forms the "Launching Tube" plus color sheet for "Rescue Helicopter." Comes with small wooden launching stick and red rayon fabric as parachute. Gordon Gold Archives.
Complete In Mailer - **$150 $300 $450**

HPH-15

❑ **HPH-15. "Fun Book Of Aviation" Original Art Prototype,**
1944. Prepared for Grape-Nuts Flakes but not produced. Twenty-eight pages of original art featuring various activities. Gordon Gold Archives. Unique - **$750**

# Hopalong Cassidy

**William Boyd (1898-1972) was born in Ohio, grew up in Oklahoma, and worked at odd jobs before he went to Hollywood in 1919 to look for work in the movies. By the mid-1920s he had become a major star of silent films. Boyd made his first cowboy movie in 1931, and his first as Hopalong Cassidy in 1935. (The original Cassidy character came from the pulp stories and novels of C.E. Mulford in the early 1900s). Dressed in black, with silver spurs and saddle, riding his white stallion Topper, with Andy Clyde or Gabby Hayes as sidekick, Hoppy battled outlaws in a series of movies among the most successful "B" Westerns ever made. Boyd became completely identified with the noble cowboy, and by the time he retired in 1959 he had made more than 100 theatrical and television Cassidy films.**

**Boyd bought the rights to the Hoppy character in 1948 and released edited versions of the films for syndication to Los Angeles television station KTLA, where they ran from 1948 to 1950. Barbara Ann bread and Wonder bread were sponsors. In 1950 the programs were leased to NBC, with General Foods as sponsor. *The Hopalong Cassidy Show*--the first major television Western series--was a sensation, airing on more than 60 stations and ranking consistently among the top three programs in the country. After two years a new series of half-hour made-for-TV films ran until 1954, with Edgar Buchanan in the sidekick role.**

**The television success spawned a radio series (1950-1952) on the Mutual and CBS networks, also sponsored by General Foods, and a comic strip drawn by Dan Spiegle that ran in more than 150 newspapers until 1955. Millions of Hoppy comic books appeared from 1943 through the 1950s, including give-aways by White Tower in 1946, Grape-Nuts Flakes in 1950, and several by Bond bread in 1951.**

**Hoppy's immense popularity with his young audience around the nation also generated an unprecedented merchandising cornucopia. Hundreds of endorsements and licensed products flooded the land, from roller skates to bicycles, watches, pocket knives, toy guns, cowboy outfits, pajamas, peanut butter, candy bars, cottage cheese, bread, cereal, cookies, milk, toothpaste, savings banks, wallpaper--even hair oil became part of the Hopalong Cassidy legend.**

HOP-1

HOP-2

❑ **HOP-1. "Bill Boyd" Dixie Ice Cream Picture,**
c. 1935. First in a series of five. 11" photo with movie info on back, highlighting films "Call of the Prairie", and "The Eagle's Brood". Text says to watch for 3 other films: "Bar 20 Rides Again", "Bar 23", and "Call of the Prairie". Scarce. - **$50 $100 $150**

❑ **HOP-2. "Bill Boyd" Dixie Ice Cream Picture,**
c. 1938. - **$25 $45 $90**

HOP-3

❑ **HOP-3. Dixie Ice Cream Picture,**
1938. - **$25 $45 $90**

HOP-4

HOP-5

❑ **HOP-4. "Bill Boyd" Dixie Ice Cream Picture,**
1939. Reverse scenes from movie "Silver On The Sage." - **$25 $45 $90**

❑ **HOP-5. Dixie Lid,**
c. 1939. - **$8 $15 $25**

HOP-6

HOP-7

❑ **HOP-6. Dixie Lid,**
1939. Includes Paramount movie title "Silver On The Stage." - **$10 $20 $30**

❑ **HOP-7. Premium Offer Store Sign,**
1940. 6-1/2x25" paper sign printed full color horizontally on front and black and white vertically on reverse. Both sides feature rubber band gun and second premium offered is "Linda Ware" standup paperdoll. Gordon Gold Archives. - **$100 $200 $400**

HOP-8

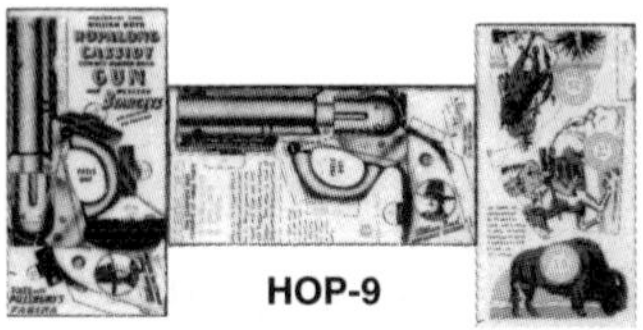

HOP-9

❑ **HOP-8. Pillsbury's Promotional 12x24" Sign,**
1940. Scarce. Advertises punch-out gun and targets. - **$200 $500 $750**

❑ **HOP-9. Punch-Out Gun And Targets Sheet,**
1940. Pillsbury's Farina. Boyd/Hoppy identified as "Paramount" star. Unpunched - **$50 $125 $250**

HOP-10

HOP-11

❑ **HOP-10. Postcard,**
1941.Chrysler Plymouth premium shows Hoppy in suit in front of car. Ads for cars on back. - **$20 $45 $65**

❑ **HOP-11. "Bill Boyd/For Democracy 100%" Cello. Button,**
c. 1942. Rare. From patriotism series picturing various cowboys. - **$100 $275 $450**

HOP-12

❑ **HOP-12. Fan Club Form Letter With Envelope,**
1946. Hopalong Cassidy Productions. Promotes new film series, photo on folder reverse.
With Envelope - **$50 $85 $175**
No Envelope - **$40 $75 $125**

HOP-13

❑ **HOP-13. Cole Bros. Circus Pennant,**
c. 1948. - **$20 $50 $95**

HOP-14

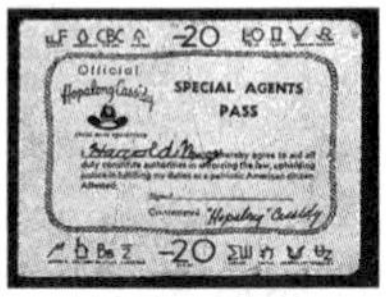


HOP-15

❑ **HOP-14. Round-Up Club "Special Agent Pass" Card,**
c. 1948. Probable movie theater give-away. - **$15 $30 $60**

❑ **HOP-15. Card,**
1948.Special Agents pass. - **$20 $40 $70**

HOP-16

HOP-17

❑ **HOP-16. Barclay Knitwear Co. Photo,**
1949. Given with sweater purchase. - **$15 $25 $40**

❑ **HOP-17. "Hopalong Cassidy Official Bar 20 T-V Chair",**
1949. Store item and Big Top Peanut Butter premium. Wood and canvas folding chair that opens to 16x16x22" tall. - **$200 $350 $600**

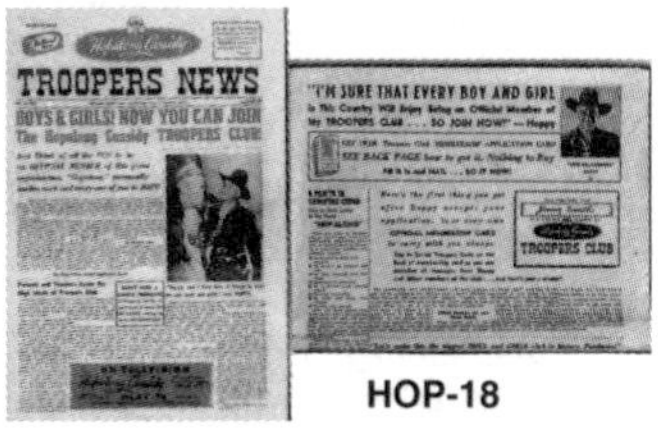


HOP-18

❑ **HOP-18. Butter-Nut Bread "Troopers News" Vol. 1 #1,**
1949. First issue of periodic newsletter. - **$75 $150 $275**

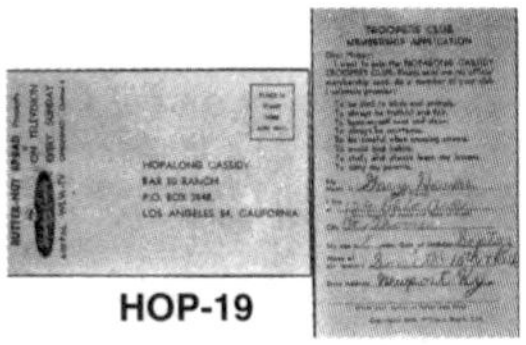

HOP-19

❑ **HOP-19. "Trooper's Club" Application Card,**
1949. Various sponsors. - **$15 $25 $40**

HOP-20

HOP-21

❑ **HOP-20. Troopers Club Card,**
1949. Barbara Ann Bread premium. Brown on yellow background with secret code on back. - **$25 $60 $95**

❑ **HOP-21. Photo,**
1940s. Rare. Early Bill Boyd movie premium with frame. - **$25 $50 $75**

HOP-22

HOP-23

❑ **HOP-22. Adult Hat,**
1950. Scarce. Premium and store item. Has white picture band and photo button. - **$100 $225 $475**

❑ **HOP-23. Child's Hat,**
1950. Premium and store item. - **$75 $150 $300**

HOP-24

❑ **HOP-24. Savings Club Brochure,**
1950. Worcester County Institution for Savings and others. Three-fold brochure, we show both sides open. - **$35 $65 $100**

HOP-25

❑ **HOP-25. "Hoppy" Arcade Photo Card,**
1950. - **$5 $10 $25**

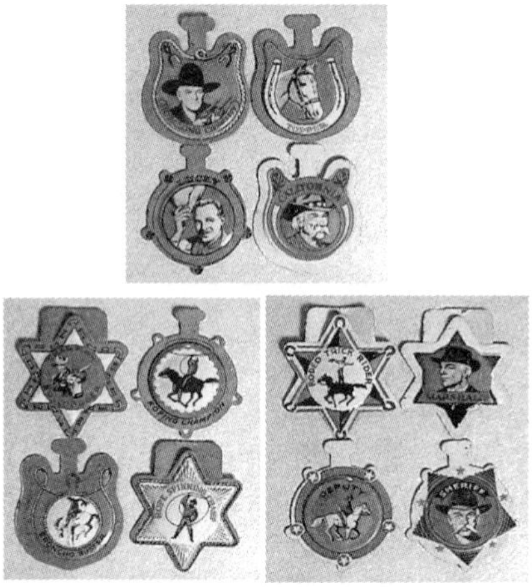

HOP-26

❑ **HOP-26. "Burry's Hopalong Cassidy Cookies" Litho. Tin Tabs,**
1950. 2" tall with 12 in set titled Hopalong Cassidy, Topper, Lucky, California, Champion Bulldogger, Rodeo Champion, Bronco Buster, Rope Spinning Champ, Rodeo Trick Rider, Marshal, Deputy, Sheriff. Reverse of each shows "Hoppy's Secret Code" with various symbols matching letters of the alphabet. Scarce. Each - **$20 $45 $85**

HOP-27

HOP-28

HOP-29

❑ **HOP-27. "Capitol Records" Premium Photo,**
c. 1950. Dealer's giveaway. 8x10" black and white. - **$20 $40 $75**

❑ **HOP-28. "Hopalong/Topper" Silver Luster White Metal Pin,**
c. 1950. Store item. 1-1/2" diameter. - **$30 $65 $100**

❑ **HOP-29. "Hopalong Cassidy" Silver Luster White Metal Pin,**
c. 1950. Store item. 1-1/8" tall. - **$15 $30 $50**

HOP-30

❑ **HOP-30. "Hopalong Cassidy And Smokey Bear" Radio Spots Brochure,**
c. 1950. Cooperative Forest Fire Prevention Campaign. 8x10-1/2" black and white 12-page folder captioned "Radio Platter #12." Contains scripts of various lengths with dialogue for announcer, Hoppy and Smokey. - **$30 $65 $110**

HOP-31

HOP-32

❑ **HOP-31. "Hoppy" Silver Luster Bracelet With Figural Charm,**
c. 1950. Store item. Charm is 1-1/4" tall. - **$20 $45 $85**

❑ **HOP-32. Employee's Large Litho. Tin Button,**
c. 1950. Used by Bond Bread delivery men and/or store clerks. Large 4" button with bw photo on red and black background. - **$100 $275 $525**

HOP-33

❑ **HOP-33. "Hopalong Cassidy Cookies" Box,**
1950. Burry Biscuit Corp. 12x16" waxed cardboard with back panel "Trading Post" ad as well as text for "Hopalong Cassidy's Creed For American Boys And Girls." Side panel pictures insert premiums set of 12 litho. tin badges. Gordon Gold Archives. Near Mint Flat - **$1200**
Used Complete - **$200 $400 $750**

HOP-34

HOP-35

❑ **HOP-34. Canadian Newspaper Cello. Button,**
c. 1950. Toronto Star. 1-1/4" white on dark blue. - **$100 $225 $325**

❑ **HOP-35. "Hopalong Cassidy In The Mirror" Cello. Button,**
c. 1950. Probably issued with names of various newspapers. - **$35 $85 $125**

HOP-36

❑ **HOP-36. Watch Paper Sign 6x24",**
1950. Scarce. US Time. - **$100 $250 $425**

HOP-37

❑ **HOP-37. Wrist Watch with Insert in Box,**
1950. Complete - **$110 $350 $600**

HOP-38

HOP-39

❑ **HOP-38. Bond Bread Loaf End Labels,**
1950. Photo style pictures, unnumbered series. Each - **$3 $6 $12**

❑ **HOP-39. Bond Bread Loaf End Labels,**
1950. Numbered with perforation around illustration, 16 in set (#17-32). Each - **$5 $8 $12**

HOP-40

❑ **HOP-40. Bond Bread "Hang-Up Album",**
1950. Folder wall poster for bread loaf end pictures for story "Hoppy Captures The Bank Robbers." Unused - **$30 $65 $100**

HOP-41

HOP-42

❑ **HOP-41. Wrist Watch on Saddle Display in Box,**
1950. Boxed - **$500**

❑ **HOP-42. "Timex" 16" Painted Latex Store Display,**
1950. Rare. Timex Watches. English made. - **$600 $1250 $1800**

HOP-43

HOP-44

❑ **HOP-43. Bond Bread Label Flyer 6x9",**
1950. - **$40 $75 $125**

❑ **HOP-44. Metal Pocketwatch,**
1950. Store item by US Time. -
**$200 $450 $650**

HOP-45

❑ **HOP-45. "Bond Bread" Store Hanger Sign 6x7",**
1950. - **$100 $175 $250**

HOP-46

❑ **HOP-46. Savings Club Thrift Kit,**
1950. Advertised in comic book and sponsored by various banks. Includes certificate, cover letter, color photo, postcard, folder showing club ranks. Near Mint In Mailer - **$300**
Certificate - **$30 $60 $100**
Letter - **$10 $20 $30**
Photo - **$5 $10 $15**
Postcard - **$5 $12 $20**
Folder - **$25 $50 $75**

HOP-47

❑ **HOP-47. Savings Club Membership Card,**
1950. Various sponsor banks. - **$35 $60 $90**

HOP-48

❑ **HOP-48. Savings Club Postcard,**
1950. Various sponsoring banks. -
**$15 $25 $40**

HOP-49

HOP-50

❑ **HOP-49. Plastic Bank,**
1950. Store item and Hopalong Cassidy Savings Club give-away.
Gold Plastic - **$25 $50 $85**
White Plastic - **$80 $185 $350**
Green - **$50 $125 $300**
Yellow - **$50 $125 $300**
Red - **$50 $125 $300**
Blue - **$75 $175 $350**

❑ **HOP-50. Bank Teller's 3" Litho. Button,**
1950. - **$15 $25 $50**

HOP-51

HOP-52

HOP-53

❑ **HOP-51. Saving Rodeo "Tenderfoot" Canadian Version Litho. Button,**
1950. Various Canadian banks. Smaller size than U.S. versions, first five ranks are 1-1/8" litho. while Straw Boss and Foreman versions are 1-3/8". - **$20 $50 $75**

❑ **HOP-52. Saving Rodeo "Tenderfoot" Litho. Button,**
1950. Various banks. Awarded for saving $2.00. -
**$15 $30 $50**

❑ **HOP-53. Saving Rodeo "Wrangler" Litho. Button,**
1950. Various banks. Awarded for saving $10.00. - **$10 $18 $25**

HOP-54

HOP-55

HOP-56

❑ **HOP-54. Saving Rodeo "Bulldogger" Litho. Button,**
1950. Various banks. Awarded for saving $25.00. - **$12 $25 $35**

❑ **HOP-55. Saving Rodeo "Bronc Buster" Litho. Button,**
1950. Various banks. Awarded for saving $50.00. - **$15 $35 $50**

❑ **HOP-56. Saving Rodeo "Trail Boss" Litho. Button,**
1950. Fifth highest of 7 ranks. - **$20 $40 $75**

HOP-57

HOP-58

❑ **HOP-57. Saving Rodeo "Straw Boss" 2-1/4" Litho. Button,**
1950. Scarce. Honor circle rating awarded for saving $250.00, also Canadian issue in smaller cello. version. - **$75 $150 $250**

❑ **HOP-58. Saving Rodeo"Foreman" 2-1/4" Litho. Button,**
1950. Scarce. Highest rank Honor Circle rating awarded for saving $500, also Canadian issue in smaller cello. version. - **$75 $175 $275**

HOP-59

❑ **HOP-59. Western Badges Box Wrapper,**
1950. Post's Raisin Bran. 11x17-1/2" picturing set of 12 litho. tin tabs. Near Mint Flat - **$750**
Used Complete - **$150 $250 $500**

HOP-60

❑ **HOP-60. Punch-Out Figure Sheet,**
c. 1950. Issuer unknown. Full color 7x7" sheet for forming Hoppy figure seated on Topper. Gordon Gold Archives.
Unpunched - **$50 $100 $150**

HOP-61

HOP-62

❑ **HOP-61. "Hopalong Cassidy's Western Magazine" First Issue,**
1950. Vol. 1 #1 quarterly pulp magazine. -
**$50 $150 $300**

❑ **HOP-62. Candy Bar Wrapper,**
1950. Foil paper with mail offer for "Hopalong Cassidy Cowboy Neckerchief With Stone Set Metal Steerhead Loop" expiring June 30. See HOP-170. - **$40 $100 $150**

HOP-63

HOP-64

HOP-65

❑ **HOP-63. "Timex Watches" Cello. Button,**
c. 1950. English made. - **$40 $85 $175**

❑ **HOP-64. Newspaper Strip Promotion Cello. Button,**
c. 1950. Sun-Telegram. - **$20 $60 $90**

❑ **HOP-65. Milk Bottle Cap,**
c. 1950. Jo-Mar Milk. Foil paper with inner card-board liner. - **$10 $25 $40**

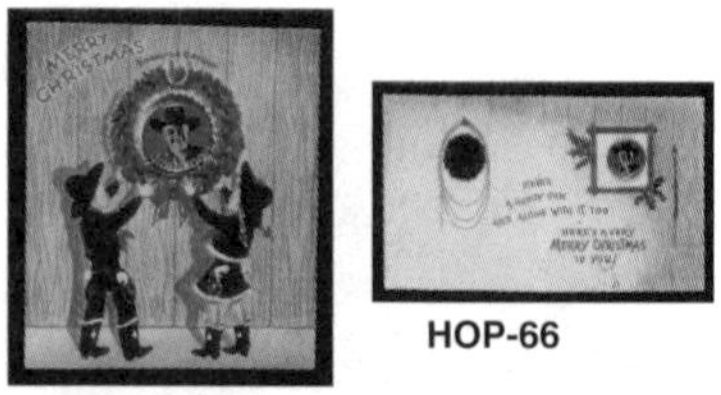

HOP-66

❑ **HOP-66. Christmas Card With Cello. Button,**
c. 1950. Store item. Folder card from authorized greeting card series by Buzza Cardozo, Hollywood. Inside button is visible through diecut opening on front cover.
With Button - **$25 $45 $80**
Card Only - **$15 $30 $50**

HOP-67

HOP-68

❑ **HOP-67. Christmas Card,**
1950. - **$25 $50 $100**

❑ **HOP-68. Die Cut Christmas Card,**
1950. Features Schmidt cap gun on front and inside card. - **$25 $50 $100**

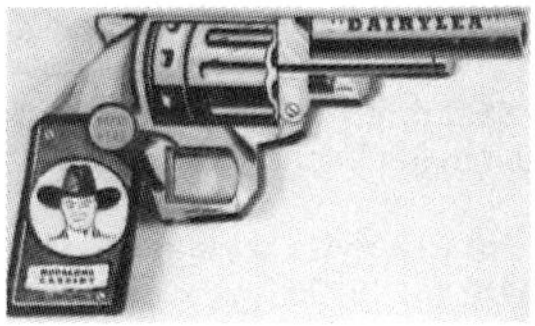


HOP-69

❑ **HOP-69. Cardboard Clicker Pistol,**
c. 1950. "Dairylea" and others. 7" long in blue, black and white. - **$25 $50 $75**

HOP-70

❑ **HOP-70. "Hoppy's Favorite Bond Bread" Shelf Sign,**
c. 1950. 6x9-1/2" slick paper in black, white and red. - **$25 $60 $85**

HOP-71

HOP-72

❑ **HOP-71. Card Set By Topps Gum Co.,**
1950. Store item. Set of 230 numbered cards done in various color combinations according to numbered sub-sets showing scenes from various Hopalong Cassidy movies.
Cards #1-186 Each - **$1 $3 $5**
Cards #187-230 Each - **$2 $5 $10**

❑ **HOP-72. Metallic Foil Card By Topps Gum Co.,**
1950. Store item. For each of the eight sub-sets in the Topps set of 230 cards, one "Header" card was produced with a metallic foil image. These eight cards were un-numbered.
Each - **$40 $75 $125**

HOP-73

HOP-74

❑ **HOP-73. Australian Candy Tin,**
c. 1950. Bester's Sweets Ltd., Melbourne. Litho. tin box and lid with color portrait. Side panels list eight rules of "Hopalong Cassidy's Troopers Creed For Boys And Girls." - **$100 $175 $350**

❑ **HOP-74. "Hopalong Cassidy" Large Doll,**
c. 1950. Store item and promotional award from Chicago Sun-Times news paper. 22" tall stuffed cloth and plush fabric body with thin vinyl boy image face with felt hat holding title headband. - **$250 $500 $750**

HOP-75

❑ **HOP-75. "Buzza Cardozo Greeting Cards" 15x27" Store Sign,**
c. 1950. Diecut cardboard for officially licensed Hoppy greeting card series. -
**$500 $1000 $1800**

HOP-76

HOP-77

❑ **HOP-76. "Hoppy's Favorite" Litho. Button,**
1950. Issued with names of various sponsors.
Each - **$10 $25 $50**

❑ **HOP-77. Postcard,**
1950.Beautiful color card of Hoppy with hands on gun. Bill Boyd write up on back. Says he started in films in 1919. - **$25 $50 $75**

HOP-78

❑ **HOP-78. Crayon Set In Box,**
1950.Crayons- 42 small, 28 large- with stencils and Hoppy pad. Promoted in Life Magazine. -
**$100 $250 $450**

HOP-79

❑ **HOP-79. Premium Catalogue With Order Form,**
1950. Big Top Peanut Butter. - **$50 $100 $200**

HOP-80

HOP-81

❑ **HOP-80. Metal Binoculars,**
1950. Store item and Big Top Peanut Butter premium. - **$25 $75 $125**

❑ **HOP-81. Boxed Camera,**
1950. Store item and Big Top Peanut Butter premium. Boxed - **$100 $150 $225**
Loose - **$40 $80 $150**

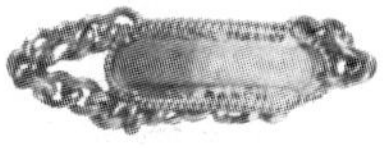

HOP-82

HOP-83

❑ **HOP-82. Silvered Brass Identification Bracelet,**
1950. Big Top Peanut Butter. Center plate edges have "Hopalong Cassidy-XX Ranch", center is designed for engraving owner's name. - **$50 $100 $150**

❑ **HOP-83. Silvered Brass Hair Barrette,**
1950. Store item and Big Top Peanut Butter premium. - **$20 $35 $60**

HOP-84

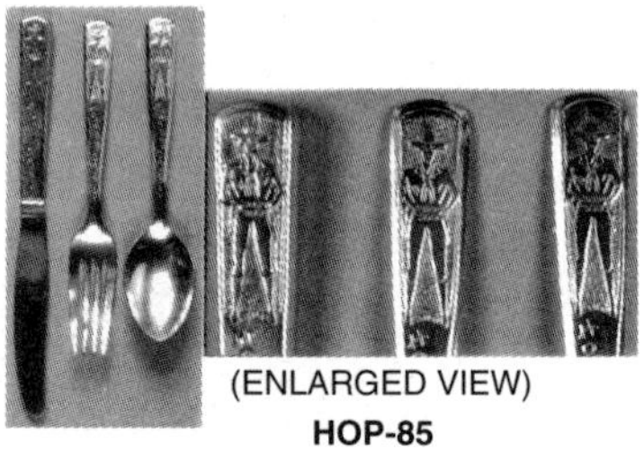
(ENLARGED VIEW)
HOP-85

❑ **HOP-84. "Junior Chow Set" Ad Sheet,**
1950. Big Top Peanut Butter. - **$15 $30 $60**

❑ **HOP-85. Stainless Steel Table Utensils,**
1950. Store item and Big Top Peanut Butter premium. Each - **$10 $20 $40**

HOP-86

❑ **HOP-86. "Bar 20 Chow Set" Boxed Glassware,**
1950. Store item and Big Top Peanut Butter premium. Set for "Gun Totin' Buckaroos".
Near Mint Boxed - **$350**
Each - **$30 $50 $75**

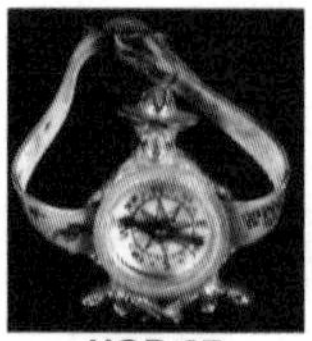
HOP-87

HOP-88

❑ **HOP-87. Plastic Wrist Compass,**
1950. Store item also used as Big Top Peanut Butter and Popsicle premium. - **$25 $50 $75**

❑ **HOP-88. Glass Mugs,**
1950. Big Top Peanut Butter. Set of four in black, green, blue, red on white.
Each - **$12 $20 $35**

HOP-89

HOP-90

HOP-91

❑ **HOP-89. Metal Thermos,**
1950. Store item by Aladdin Industries and Big Top Peanut Butter premium. - **$25 $70 $150**

❑ **HOP-90. Metal Lunch Box,**
1950. Store item by Aladdin Industries and Big Top Peanut Butter premium. Rectangular decal. - **$75 $150 $375**

❑ **HOP-91. Metal Lunch Box,**
1950. Store item by Aladdin Industries. Cloud-shaped decal. - **$75 $150 $375**

HOP-92

❑ **HOP-92. Wallet With Coin & Papers,**
1950. Store item and Big Top Peanut Butter premium. Complete - **$75 $125 $200**
Coin Only - **$8 $12 $20**

HOP-93

HOP-94

❑ **HOP-93. "Hopalong Cassidy Picture Card Gum" Waxed Paper Wrapper,**
1950. Topps Chewing Gum. Wrappers come with white, green or yellow backgrounds.
Each - **$20 $50 $100**

❑ **HOP-94. Candy Bag,**
1950. Topps Candy Division. - **$25 $50 $75**

HOP-95

HOP-96

❑ **HOP-95. Litho. Tin Potato Chips Can,**
1950. Kuehmann Foods Inc. - **$60 $165 $300**

❑ **HOP-96. Grape-Nuts Flakes Comic Book,**
1950. - **$15 $45 $130**

HOP-97

❑ **HOP-97. Boxed Drinking Straws,**
1950. Various pictures on reverse.
Complete - **$50 $80 $140**

HOP-98

HOP-99

❑ **HOP-98. "Good Luck From Hoppy" Aluminum Medal,**
1950. Earliest version with Hoppy image on each side was produced in 1948 for a Hoppy rodeo in Hawaii. The 1950 version for inclusion with wallets by Pioneer has a four-leaf clover within a horseshoe on the reverse. A heavy pewter-like version is a reproduction.
Rodeo Version - **$10 $20 $30**
Wallet Style - **$8 $12 $20**

❑ **HOP-99. Burry's Cookies Cut-Out Box Panel,**
1950. #1 panel from 24 different packages with "The Continued Story Of Hopalong Cassidy's Bar-20 Ranch Adventures".
Each Uncut Panel - **$20 $50 $75**

HOP-100

❑ **HOP-100. "Hair Trainer" 8x22" Paper Poster With Picture,**
1950. Poster - **$75 $175 $275**
Picture - **$5 $12 $18**

HOP-103

HOP-101 HOP-102

❑ **HOP-101. Vinyl Pocketknife Loop,**
1950. Store item. - **$25 $50 $100**

❑ **HOP-102. Pocketknife,**
1950. Store item by Hammer Brand. - **$30 $75 $140**

❑ **HOP-103. Cardboard Noisemaker Gun,**
1950. Capitol Records. - **$30 $70 $120**

HOP-104

❑ **HOP-104. Die-cut Birthday Card,**
1950. - **$25 $50 $110**

HOP-105 HOP-106

❑ **HOP-105. "Hopalong Cassidy and Lucky at Copper Gulch" Television Book,**
1950. - **$40 $80 $160**

❑ **HOP-106. "Hopalong Cassidy and Lucky at the 'Double X' Ranch" Book,**
1950. With 2 pop-ups. - **$45 $90 $180**

HOP-107

❑ **HOP-107. Bond Bread Promotional Sign,**
1950. Promotes the 32 Hoppy pictures on Bond Bread labels. Rare. - **$200 $400 $600**

(Front)

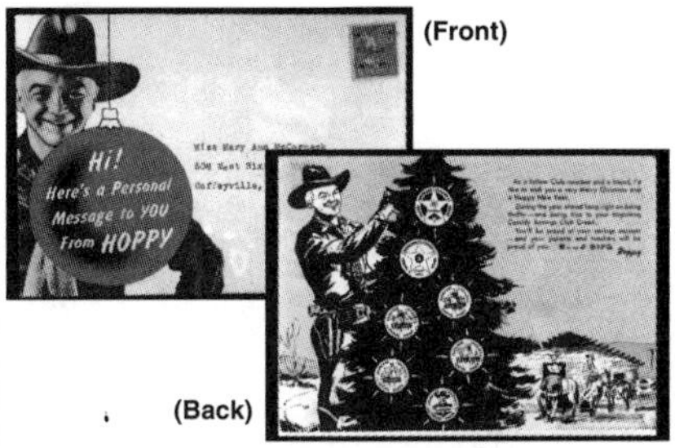


(Back)

HOP-108

❑ **HOP-108. Christmas Post Card,**
1950. Promotes the Hopalong Cassidy Savings Club. Pinbacks ae on other side of card. Rare. - **$60 $120 $180**

HOP-109

❑ **HOP-109. Hoppy "Clover Lake Ice Cream" Canister,**
c. 1950. 6-1/2" tall. - **$35 $65 $125**

HOP-110

❑ **HOP-110."Hopalong Cassidy's Favorite Ice Cream" Quart Container,**
c. 1950. 6" tall issued by O'Fallon Quality Dairy and others. - **$20 $45 $75**

HOP-111

❑ **HOP-111. "Hopalong Cassidy Lends A Helping Hand" Pop-Up Book,**
1950. A Bonnie Book from John Martin's House, published by Doubleday. - **$20 $35 $75**

HOP-112

❑ **HOP-112. "Hopalong-Aid" Drink Packet,**
1950. Bol Mfg. Co. 3-1/2x5". - **$25 $50 $100**

HOP-113

❑ **HOP-113. Full Color Bread Loaf End Label,**
1950. Sponsored by Mary Jane Bread. - **$25 $60 $100**

HOP-114

❑ **HOP-114. Camera With Box,**
1950. Box - **$35 $75 $150**
Camera - **$35 $75 $150**

HOP-115

❑ **HOP-115. Life Magazine With Hoppy Cover Article,**
1950. June 12 issue. - **$15 $30 $75**

HOP-116

❑ **HOP-116."Hopalong Cassidy Potato Chips" Bag,**
1950. Kuehmann Foods. - **$10 $20 $35**

HOP-117

❑ **HOP-117. Photo Images Child's Shirt,**
c. 1950. Store item by "The Little Champ Of Hollywood." Eight different repeating Hoppy photos in black and white plus inscriptions in red lettering. - **$75 $150 $250**

HOP-118

❑ **HOP-118. "Official Hopalong Cassidy Hang-Up Album" Bread Label Display Folder,**
1950. Issued by Bond Bread. Holds 16 different bread end labels. - **$30 $60 $100**

HOP-119

❑ **HOP-119. Hard Plastic Figures,**
1950. Store item by Ideal Corp.
Boxed - **$75 $150 $250**
Loose - **$30 $60 $100**

HOP-120

HOP-121

❑ **HOP-120. "Hopalong Cassidy Bikes And Skates" Ad Card,**
1950. Rollfast Co. - **$25 $60 $100**

❑ **HOP-121. "Hopalong Cassidy In The Daily News" 2" Cello. Button,**
1950. - **$15 $40 $65**

HOP-122

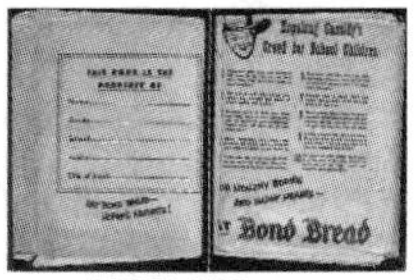


HOP-123

❑ **HOP-122. New York Daily News 10x13" Cardboard Poster,**
1950. Announces start of daily comic strip. - **$80 $175 $250**

❑ **HOP-123. Bond Bread Book Cover,**
c. 1950. - **$12 $20 $35**

HOP-124

❑ **HOP-124. Hoppy and Topper Die Cut Christmas Card with Envelope,**
1950. Various sponsors. - **$20 $50 $100**

HOP-125

HOP-126

HOP-127

❑ **HOP-125. Hopalong Cassidy Western Badge,**
1950. Post's Raisin Bran. From set of 12 including titles: Hopalong Cassidy, Calamity Jane, General Custer, Wild Bill Hickok, Rodeo Trick Rider, Sheriff, Ranch Boss, Bull Dogging Champ, Annie Oakley, Chief Sitting Bull, Roping Champ, Indian Scout. Also seen is "Ranger" with same border as Hopalong Cassidy but without "Post's Raisin Bran" on reverse.
Hopalong Cassidy or "Ranger" Tab - **$12 $25 $50**
Others Each - **$5 $12 $20**

❑ **HOP-126. Radio Show 9x11" Handbill,**
c. 1950. Grape-Nuts Flakes. Probable grocery bag insert. - **$40 $75 $140**

❑ **HOP-127. "Strawberry Preserves" Glass,**
c. 1950. Ladies Choice Foods.
With Label - **$35 $75 $125**

HOP-128

HOP-129

❑ **HOP-128. "Hoppy's Favorite" Bond Bread Cards,**
c. 1950. Some fronts advertise bread loaf seals. Reverse caption "Ways Of The West." Unnumbered, set of 16.
Each - **$5 $10 $15**

❑ **HOP-129. Bond Bread Postcard,**
c. 1950. - **$8 $15 $25**

HOP-130

HOP-131

❑ **HOP-130. Bond Bread Book Cover,**
c. 1950. - **$12 $20 $35**

❑ **HOP-131. "Ranch House Race" Game,**
c. 1950. Stroehmann's Sunbeam Bread. - **$35 $75 $125**

HOP-132

HOP-133

❑ **HOP-132. TV Show "Special Guest" 11x16" Cardboard Store Sign,**
c. 1950. Wonder Bread. - **$40 $125 $200**

❑ **HOP-133. Dairylea Milk 13x20" Paper Store Poster,**
c. 1950. Various dairies. - **$40 $100 $150**

HOP-134

❑ **HOP-134. Dairylea Ice Cream Carton,**
c. 1950. Offers neckerchief and t-shirt. - **$40 $75 $150**

HOP-135

HOP-136

❑ **HOP-135. "Dairylea Milk" Glass Inscribed "Do As Hoppy And Miss Dairylea Do/Drink Dairylea Milk",**
c. 1950. - **$75 $150 $300**

❑ **HOP-136. "1 Cent Play Money" Cardboard Milk Bottle Cap,**
c. 1950. - **$8 $12 $20**

HOP-137

❑ **HOP-137. Product Box And Premium Order Coupon,**
c. 1950. Scarce. Honey Roll Sugar Cones.
Box - **$200 $300 $450**
Coupon - **$20 $40 $75**

HOP-138

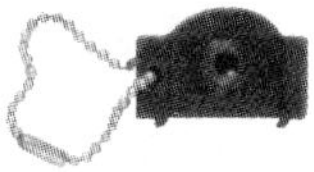

HOP-139

❑ **HOP-138. Waxed Cardboard Ice Cream "Hoppy Cup",**
c. 1950. - **$15 $30 $60**

❑ **HOP-139. Miniature Plastic TV With Hoppy Film,**
c. 1950. Hole on side for key chain, film has four color pictures of Hoppy. - **$35 $75 $110**

HOP-140

❑ **HOP-140. "Bob Atcher's Meadow Gold Song" TV Show Music Folder,**
c. 1950. Meadow Gold Butter. - **$20 $40 $75**

HOP-141

HOP-142

❑ **HOP-141. "All-Star Milk" Pint Glass Bottle,**
c. 1950. Local imprint for "McClellan's". - **$30 $65 $100**

❑ **HOP-142. Vinyl Tumbler,**
c. 1950. Cloverlake Cottage Cheese.
With Lid - **$25 $60 $100**
No Lid - **$20 $40 $70**

(FRONT)  (BACK)

HOP-143

❑ **HOP-143. Dinner Milk Glass,**
1950. Three different in set.
Each - **$20 $40 $60**

HOP-144

❑ **HOP-144. "Hopalong Cassidy" Black Leather Gloves,**
1950. Hard to find in high grade. White lettering rubs off easily. Pair - **$125 $250 $375**

HOP-145

HOP-146

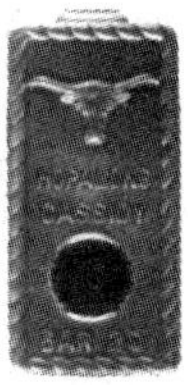

HOP-147

❑ **HOP-145. Popsicle "Hopalong Cassidy" Silvered Tin Badge,**
c. 1950. Various sponsors. Sold carded in stores. - **$20 $40 $75**

❑ **HOP-146. "HC" Silvered Metal Portrait Ring,**
c. 1950. Popsicle and various sponsors. - **$20 $40 $60**

❑ **HOP-147. "Hopalong Cassidy Bar 20" Vectograph Brass Clip,**
c. 1950. Hopalong Cassidy Ice Cream Bar and others. Plastic mechanical insert reveals Hoppy picture, although image almost always gone. Used as belt or pocket clip.
No Image - **$15 $40 $75**

HOP-148

❑ **HOP-148. "Dudin'-Up Kit",**
c. 1950. Fuller Brush Co. Hair treatment set with two trading cards on box back.
Complete - **$200 $350 $550**

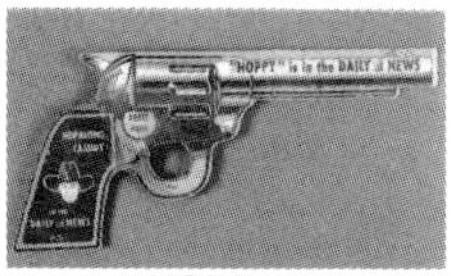

HOP-149

HOP-150

❑ **HOP-149. "Daily News" Cardboard Clicker Gun,**
c. 1950. Various sponsors. - **$30 $60 $125**

❑ **HOP-150. Color Photo,**
c. 1950. Came with gun to project filmstrips. - **$15 $25 $40**

HOP-151

HOP-152

HOP-153

❑ **HOP-151. "Hopalong Cassidy/Sheriff" Cello. Button,**
c. 1950. From Arizona radio station. For Mutual Network broadcasts. - **$30 $85 $150**

❑ **HOP-152. Double Sponsor Cello. Button,**
c. 1950. Filene's department store, Boston and Loew's State Theater. Dark red/black featuring Hoppy portrait. - **$100 $225 $350**

❑ **HOP-153. Encased Penny With Coded Message,**
1951. Reads "Member Hopalong Cassidy Savings Club/Security-First National Bank." Coded message and good luck symbols on rim. Code was printed on member's club card. - **$25 $75 $125**

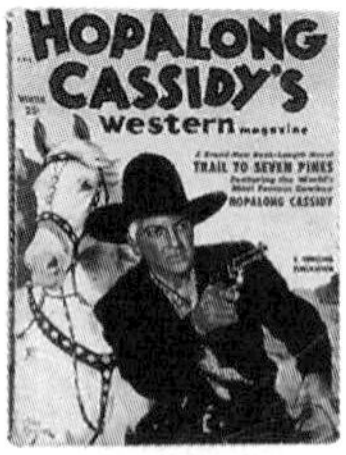


HOP-154

❑ **HOP-154. "Hopalong Cassidy's Western Magazine" Second Issue,**
1951. Vol. 1 #2 quarterly pulp magazine. Believed to be final issue. - **$75 $150 $300**

HOP-155

HOP-156

❑ **HOP-155. Wild West Trading Cards,**
1951. Post Cereals. Set of 36.
Each - **$10 $20 $40**

❑ **HOP-156. Bond Bread "The Strange Legacy" Comic Booklet,**
1951. 3-1/2x7" format. Titles also in series "The Mad Bomber" and "Meets The Brend Brothers, Bandits." Each - **$12 $36 $85**

HOP-157

❑ **HOP-157. Waxed Box Wrapper Promoting "Wild West Trading Cards",**
1951. Gordon Gold Archives.
Used Complete - **$250 $500 $800**

HOP-158

HOP-159

❑ **HOP-158. "Trading Cards" Store Sign,**
1951. Post Cereals. 13x26" full color promoting set of 36 cards. Gordon Gold Archives. - **$200 $500 $800**

❑ **HOP-159. "Trading Cards" Oversized Envelope For Promotion Materials,**
1951. Post Cereals. Likely held promotional posters for store use. Gordon Gold Archives. - **$200 $450 $750**

HOP-160

❑ **HOP-160. Concho/Branding Iron,**
c. 1951. Post's Grape-Nuts Flakes. Plastic steer head with tie slide loop on back, used as ring or tie clip. Front has steer head cover over "HC" initials for printing paper. See next item. - **$75 $150 $225**

HOP-161

❑ **HOP-161. Concho/Branding Iron Instruction Leaflet,**
c. 1951. Post's Grape-Nuts Flakes. See HOP-160. - **$30 $50 $75**

HOP-162

❑ **HOP-162. "Western Badges" 9x20" Paper Sign,**
1952. Shows set of 12 litho. tin tabs, but Hoppy is not pictured. Possibly the star design picturing a "Ranger" was never produced, or if it was, a "Hopalong Cassidy" image was soon substituted and produced using the identical border design of a horse head, four pistols and arrowhead. When the set with Hoppy was issued, the reverses were marked "Post's Raisin Bran," but the Post's name does not appear on this sign. - **$50 $100 $200**

HOP-163

HOP-164

❑ **HOP-163. Hoppy Savings Club "Honor Member" Litho. Button,**
c. 1952. Rare. Highest ranking award for early 1950s youthful bank savings program. Club folder from 1950 (HOP-46) does not show this button, which is likely the final in series. Rarest of all in series. See HOP-165. - **$100 $250 $400**

❑ **HOP-164. Hat/Compass Ring,**
1952. Post cereal. Brass bands, removable metal hat over plastic magnetic compass. - **$100 $150 $250**

HOP-165

❑ **HOP-165. "Savings Club Honor Member" Diecut Promo Folder For Bank Premium Wallet,**
c. 1952. Various banks. 3-3/8x4-1/8" four-section diecut paper folder in shape of wallet. Back cover illustrates "Honor Member" button and invites club membership. This is the only documentation we've seen showing the origin of the button. Wallet depicted is the high quality metal-covered example although we've never seen one inscribed with slogan "Honor Member Savings Club" as depicted in this artwork. Item is diecut in a parallelogram shape. See HOP-163. - **$150 $300 $500**

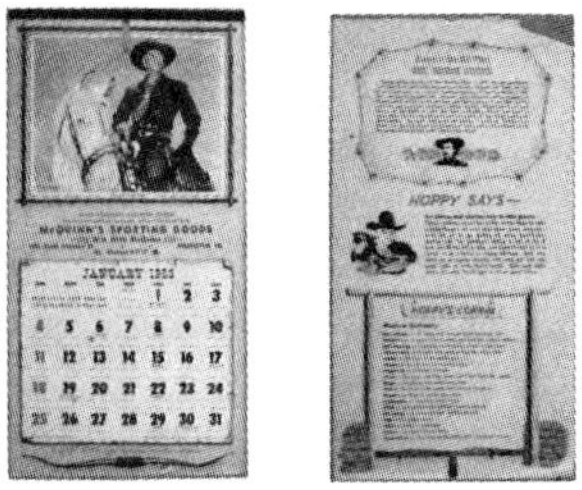

HOP-166

❑ **HOP-166. "Hopalong's Cowboy Calendar",**
1953. Issued with various sponsorship imprints. 6x11-1/2" with metal strip holding 12 monthly pages. Pages are in sepia hues with orange tint. Each page back features item of western lore followed by "Hoppy Says" advice to youngsters and "Hoppy's Corral" segment devoted to western history. - **$75 $150 $225**

HOP-167

❑ **HOP-167. "Crispo Cake Cone Co." Dealer Price Sheet,**
1953. 8-1/2x11" red, white and blue sheet showing eight product boxes, two of which are marketed as "Hopalong Cassidy's Favorite Brand." - **$15 $30 $50**

HOP-168

❑ **HOP-168. All-Star Dairy Products Folder,**
c. 1956. Pictured premiums include those for Hoppy as well as baseball stars Mickey Mantle and Stan Musial. - **$40 $80 $125**

HOP-169 HOP-170

❑ **HOP-169. Autographed Photo,**
1950s. Pictured holding supplement to Philadelphia Sunday Bulletin. - **$50 $100 $150**

❑ **HOP-170. Secretarial Autographed Photo,**
1950s. Signed by secretary or similar representative. - **$15 $30 $50**

HOP-171 HOP-172

❑ **HOP-171. Hopalong Cassidy 20 1/2" Doll,**
1950s. Has removable hat, metal star badge, removable belt with metal buckle inscribed with "Hopalong Cassidy." Has metal gun and holster, and a scarf with metal cowhead tie holder. - **$500 $1000 $1500**

❑ **HOP-172. Hopalong Cassidy Solid Core Carnival Statue,**
1950s. The second-most rare and valuable character carnival piece. Rare in any condition. - **$150 $400 $750**

HOP-173

❑ **HOP-173. Savings Club Pamphlet,**
1950s. "A New Plan" promotes Hoppy Savings Club Accounts with various promotional aids. Rare. - **$40 $80 $160**

HOP-174

HOP-175

❑ **HOP-174. "Hoppy's Bunkhouse Clothes Corral" Wood Rack,**
1950s. Northland Milk. - **$75 $150 $200**

❑ **HOP-175. Melville Milk 11x42" Cardboard Store Sign,**
1950s. Various dairies. Simulated wood grain. - **$60 $150 $250**

HOP-177

HOP-176 HOP-178

❑ **HOP-176. Photo Postcard,**
1950s. Shows Hoppy from the waist up in cowboy outfit. - **$15 $25 $35**

❑ **HOP-177. Pin Back,**
1950s. Scarce. Harmony Farms Dairies. - **$20 $40 $65**

❑ **HOP-178. Pin Back,**
1950s. Scarce. Med-O Pure Dairy. - **$20 $40 $65**

HOP-179

❑ **HOP-179. "Hopalong Cassidy's Favorite Grape Juice" Full Bottle,**
1950s. Store item by Betsy Ross California Pure Grape Juice. 8" tall. - **$50 $100 $150**

HOP-180 HOP-181

❑ **HOP-180. Pin Back,**
1950s. Promotes strip in the Detroit News. Uncommon. - **$35 $60 $90**

❑ **HOP-181. Paper Mask in Realistic Color,**
1950s. Gordon Gold Archives - **$100 $275 $425**

HOP-182

❑ **HOP-182. "Hopalong Cassidy Fan Club" English Black And White Photo Postcards,**
1950s. Each - **$10 $18 $30**

HOP-183

❑ **HOP-183. Premium Poster For Hoppy Bread Label Pictures,**
c. 1950s. Stroehmann's Sunbeam Bread. 11-1/2x14-3/8" Sunday comic strip-style format with 12-panel story "Stagecoach Robbery" with white silhouette areas for placement of numbered Hoppy images cut from bread loaf end labels. - **$75 $175 $275**

HOP-184

❑ **HOP-184. Picture Card Gum Box,**
1950s. Store item by Topps Chewing Gum. Held individual packs of six cards. - **$125 $275 $425**

HOP-185 HOP-186

❑ **HOP-185. Portrait Photo,**
1950s. Various sponsors. - **$12 $25 $40**

❑ **HOP-186. Restaurant Ad Postcard,**
1950s. Sherman Skipalong Club, Hotel Sherman, Chicago. Also pictures manager "Skipalong Tattler". - **$25 $40 $65**

HOP-187 HOP-188

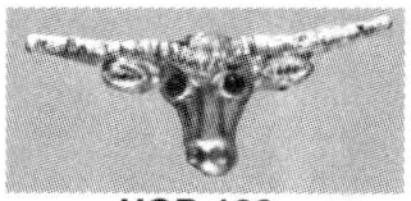

HOP-189

❑ **HOP-187. Quart Milk Carton,**
1950s. Various sponsors. - **$40 $75 $150**

❑ **HOP-188. Western Series Glass,**
1950s. Probably held food product. At least four in the set. - **$40 $80 $135**

❑ **HOP-189. "Hopalong Cassidy" Silvered Metal Kerchief Slide,**
1950s. Steer head has rhinestone eyes, his name is across the horns. See HOP-62. - **$15 $30 $60**

HOP-190

HOP-191

❑ **HOP-190. Sterling Silver Ring,**
1950s. Portrait framed by horseshoe, non-adjustable band. - **$60 $125 $250**

❑ **HOP-191. "Hopalong Cassidy Bar 20 Ranch" 2" Silvered Metal Badge,**
1950s. English made store item with "Sheriff" under inset b&w photo. - **$30 $50 $80**

HOP-192

❑ **HOP-192. Milk Promo Sign,**
1950s. Die Cut Bust sign was used to promote milk products. - **$75 $150 $250**

HOP-193

❑ **HOP-193. Newspaper Ad with Western Badge Offer,**
1950s. From the Gordon Gold Archives. - **$10 $25 $50**

HOP-194

HOP-195

❑ **HOP-194. Topper Bracelet,**
1950s. Scarce. Anson Jewelry, gold finish. - **$30 $60 $150**

❑ **HOP-195. Bar 20 Bracelet,**
1950s. Rare. Anson Jewelry, gold finish. - **$40 $80 $190**

HOP-196 HOP-197

❑ **HOP-196. "People and Places" Magazine,**
1950s. Scarce. Car premium. - **$30 $60 $120**

❑ **HOP-197. Poster,**
1980s. Promotes tapes of old films. - **$10 $20 $30**

HOP-198

❑ **HOP-198. Bar 20 Ranch Badge,**
1995. Store item, sold as party badges in blister-packs. Badge comes in gold and silver chrome on plastic. Gold - **$4 $8 $15**
Silver - **$5 $10 $20**

## *Howdy Doody*

**It aired on NBC-TV from 1947 to 1960, starting out as *The Puppet Playhouse*, created and hosted by Buffalo Bob Smith (1917-1998). It was one of television's all-time successes, winner of the first Peabody award, attracting millions of devoted young viewers and responsible for millions of dollars in licensed merchandise. It was *Howdy Doody Time*, a combination of fantasy, music, films, and slapstick played out by puppets and humans in front of a screaming studio audience of 40 kids for more than 2,300 performances.**

**Howdy, with voice supplied by Buffalo Bob, consorted with a long list of characters, including Clarabell the clown (played originally by Bob Keeshan); Mr. Bluster, the mayor of Doodyville; Flub-A-Dub, a fantastic animal crossbreed; Dilly-Dally, a big-eared carpenter; Indian Princess Summerfall-Winterspring; and many others. The original Howdy puppet was replaced with a new design in 1948.**

**Among the program's many sponsors: Wonder Bread, Colgate tooth powder, Ovaltine, Poll-Parrot shoes, Mars candy, Tootsie Rolls, Welch's grape juice, Marx and Ideal toys, Kellogg's and Nabisco cereals, and Royal pudding. Character licensees were barely able to meet the huge demand for toys, dolls, lunch boxes, clothes, marionettes, wristwatches, mugs, piggy banks, figurines, records, T-shirts, even a musical rocking chair. Items were copyrighted Bob Smith (1948-1951), Kagran Corp. (1951-1959), or NBC (1960 on).**

**A Sunday *Howdy Doody* comic strip appeared from 1950 to 1953, and Dell published comic books from 1950 to 1957. A radio version of the show aired on NBC from 1952 to 1958, and the TV series was revived briefly on NBC in 1976, but, sadly, it was no longer *Howdy Doody Time*.**

HOW-1

❑ **HOW-1. Photo Doody,**
Late 1940s. First advertising piece to sell for more than $100,000. This marionette was the third Howdy Doody to be created, and was used strictly for promotional purposes, It is virtually identical to the Howdy Doody we remember except for the lack of strings (to allow for easier use in photo shoots). Sold at Leland's 1997 auction for **$113,431**

HOW-2

HOW-3

❑ **HOW-2. "I'm For Howdy Doody" Cello. Button,**
1948. First item and premium offered March 23, 1948 as part of Howdy Doody for President campaign. Five stations carried the show and the offer was made seven times. NBC was astonished by 60,000 requests. Colgate, Continental Baking, Ovaltine and Mars candy quickly signed as sponsors. - **$30 $65 $125**

❑ **HOW-3. "The Billboard" Magazine With Cover Photo,**
November 27, 1948. Early item from second year of Howdy show. - **$20 $30 $60**

HOW-4

❑ **HOW-4."Hobby Reporter-Yankee Enterprise" Booklet With Review Article,**
1949. 6x9" issue for July-August. -
**$35 $75 $150**

HOW-5

❑ **HOW-5. Howdy Doody Newspaper #1,**
1950. Poll-Parrot. Scarce. - **$50 $175 $300**

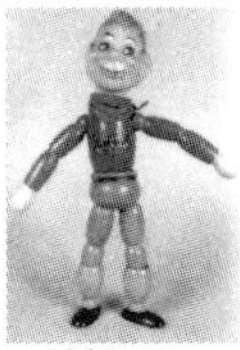

HOW-6

HOW-7

HOW-8

❑ **HOW-6. Wood Jointed Doll,**
c. 1950. Store item. Includes leather belt and fabric bandanna. - **$150 $300 $500**

❑ **HOW-7. Ovaltine Plastic Mug With Decal,**
c. 1950. - **$20 $45 $85**

❑ **HOW-8. Ovaltine Plastic Shake-Up Mug,**
c. 1950. - **$25 $50 $100**

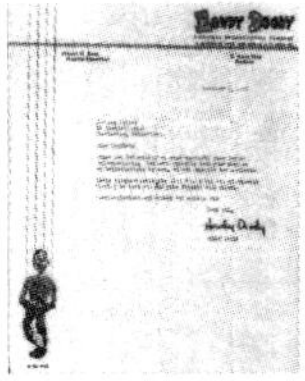

HOW-9

HOW-10

❑ **HOW-9. Thank-You Letter,**
1950. Rare. Recipient awarded box of Snickers for poem selected from a contest. -
**$75 $150 $250**

❑ **HOW-10. Poll-Parrot Coloring Book,**
c. 1950. - **$27 $82 $175**

HOW-11

HOW-12

❑ **HOW-11. Cardboard Store Sign,**
c. 1950. Colgate Dental Cream.
Large (About 24") Size - **$150 $300 $600**
Small (About 6") Size - **$25 $60 $100**

❑ **HOW-12. "Magic Trading Card" 14x21" Proof Sheet,**
1951. Issued individually in boxes of Burry's Howdy Doody Cookies. Uncut - **$80 $250 $400**
Each Card - **$3 $8 $12**

HOW-13

❑ **HOW-13. "Santa Visits Howdy Doody's House" Coloring Booklet,**
1951. 16 pages. Usually has store imprint. - **$15 $35 $70**

HOW-14

HOW-15

❑ **HOW-14. "Howdy Doody Talkin' Tag",**
1951. Wonder Bread/Hostess Cupcakes. Disk turns to form four mouth expressions. - **$20 $50 $75**

❑ **HOW-15. "Poll Parrot's" Comic Book #4,**
1951. Issues #2-#4. Each - **$22 $66 $140**

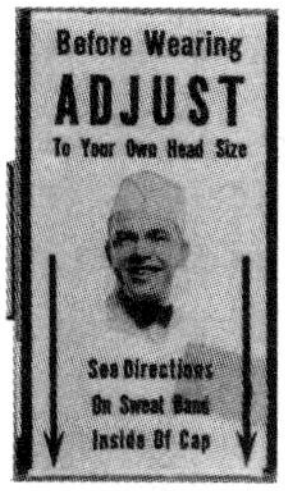

HOW-16

❑ **HOW-16. Store Clerk Paper Cap,**
c. 1951. Wonder Bread. - **$15 $30 $60**

HOW-17

❑ **HOW-17. "Circus Album" 5-1/2x8" Ad Sheet,**
c. 1951. Wonder Bread. - **$50 $100 $160**

HOW-18

HOW-19

❑ **HOW-18. "American History" Bread Label Album,** c.
1951. Wonder Bread. Holds 19 label cut-outs depicting Howdy Doody characters in historial situations such as "Landing Of The Pilgrims."
Album Only - **$20 $40 $70**
Each Uncut Label - **$10 $20 $30**
Each Cut Label - **$5 $10 $15**

❑ **HOW-19. Puppet Show Punch-out Book,**
1952. Book is 14 3/4" tall. Includes heavy cardboard punch-outs of Howdy, Clarabell, Mr. Bluster, Flub a Dub, Dilly Dally and the Inspector. - **$65 $150 $300**

HOW-20

❑ **HOW-20. T.V.-Merrimat Paper Place Mat,**
1952. Store item. Placematters, Inc. - **$20 $50 $85**

HOW-21

❑ **HOW-21. Sipping Straws Box And Premium Card,**
c. 1952. Colonial Paper Products. Cards are 2x2-3/4" from a set of 42 different picturing the image in color on the front while reverse has same image in black and white to be colored. Box offers both Howdy Doody Straw Holder as well as card set as mail-in premiums.
Box With Contents - **$30 $75 $125**
Each Of 42 Cards - **$5 $12 $20**

HOW-22

(Side of box)

❑ **HOW-22. Fifth Avenue Candy Box,**
1952. Rare. - **$175 $250 $325**

HOW-23

❑ **HOW-23. Rice Krispies Cereal Box,**
1952. 9 1/2 oz box. Crossover promotion for Wild Bill Hickok Show. Side panel has ad for Snap, Crackle, and Pop face rings premiums. - **$150 $300 $525**

HOW-24

HOW-25

❑ **HOW-24. T.V.-Merrimat Plastic Place Mat,**
1952. Store item. Placematters, Inc. -
**$20 $60 $100**

❑ **HOW-25. "Howdy Doody For President" Cello. Button,**
1952. Wonder Bread. - **$25 $60 $125**

HOW-26

HOW-27

❑ **HOW-26. "Campaign Cap",**
c. 1952. Poll-Parrot Shoes. Paper punch-out assembled by slots and tabs.
Unpunched - **$30 $75 $150**
Assembled - **$15 $50 $100**

❑ **HOW-27. Welch's Cookbook,**
1952. Welch's Grape Juice. - **$15 $50 $80**

(BOTTOM OF BOTTLE)

HOW-28

HOW-29

❑ **HOW-28. Welch's Grape Juice Glass Bottle,**
c. 1952. Various character portraits embossed on bottom. Each - **$10 $25 $40**

❑ **HOW-29. Welch's Grape Juice Tin Cap From Bottle,**
c. 1952. - **$5 $10 $15**

HOW-30

❑ **HOW-30. "Howdy Doody Ice Cream Circus" Puzzle,**
c. 1952. Howdy Doody Frozen Treat products. 10-1/2x14" jigsaw puzzle comprised of 42 numbered pieces obtained individually by product purchase. Complete - **$100 $200 $300**

HOW-31

HOW-32

❑ **HOW-31. Kellogg's "Free Cut-Out Masks" 15x20" Paper Store Sign,**
c. 1953. Corn Flakes and Rice Krispies. Offers masks on box rear panels. - **$30 $60 $100**

❑ **HOW-32. Kellogg's Howdy Doody Oversized Sample Mask,**
c. 1953. Diecut 12x15" paper promotion for masks offered on back panels of Corn Flakes and Rice Krispies boxes.
Howdy Doody - **$100 $150 $250**
Pirate, Witch Or Devil - **$35 $60 $85**

HOW-33

HOW-34

❑ **HOW-33. Kellogg's "Free Cut-Out Masks" 15x20" Paper Store Sign,**
c. 1953. Corn Flakes and Rice Krispies. Advertises pirate mask from series on box back panels. Howdy Doody - **$100 $150 $250**
Pirate, Witch Or Devil - **$35 $60 $85**

❑ **HOW-34. Welch's Grape Juice 3" Tin Lid From Glass Jelly Jar,**
1953. - **$8 $15 $25**

HOW-35

❑ **HOW-35. Welch's Grape Jelly Glasses,**
1953. Six designs, various colors, character faces on bottom. Each - **$8 $15 $25**

HOW-36

❑ **HOW-36. "Doodyville" Cardboard Houses,**
1953. Welch's Grape Juice. Set of eight.
Each Unused - **$20 $50 $85**
Each Assembled - **$10 $25 $50**

HOW-37

HOW-38

❑ **HOW-37. "Coloring Comics" Sheet #1,**
1953. Blue Bonnet Margarine. From numbered series of box inserts. Each - **$5 $10 $20**

❑ **HOW-38. "Snap-A-Wink" Target,**
1953. Poll-Parrot Shoes. - **$25 $50 $75**

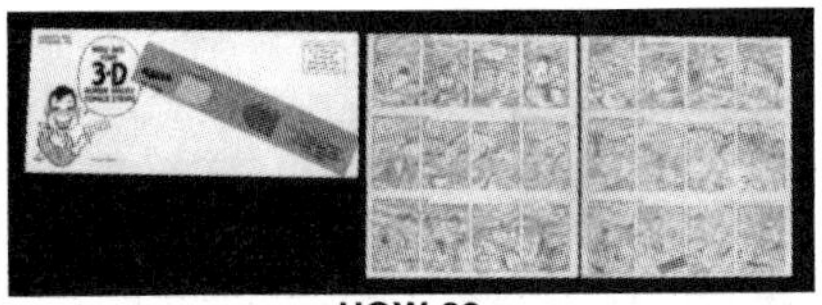


HOW-39

❑ **HOW-39. Luden's Cough Drops 3-D Comics,**
1953. With Mailer. - **$75 $150 $300**

HOW-40

❑ **HOW-40. Kellogg's Rice Krispies Flat,**
1953. Box (9 1/2 oz.) features Howdy on front and large mask of Howdy on back. -
**$300 $600 $1200**

HOW-41

❑ **HOW-41. Kellogg's Rice Krispies Flat,**
1953. Canadian issued. Offers free masks on back (the Princess pictured). - **$100 $200 $400**

HOW-42

❑ **HOW-42. "Cut-Out Masks" Store Sign,**
c. 1953. Issued by Kellogg's. 14-1/2x20-1/2". - **$100 $175 $275**

HOW-43

HOW-44

❑ **HOW-43. Kellogg's Rice Krispies Box Panel Masks,**
1953. One of a set: Howdy, Clarabell, Dilly Dally, The Princess.
Each Uncut Box Back - **$10 $25 $40**

❑ **HOW-44. "Comic Circus Animals" Picture Toy,**
1954. Poll-Parrot Shoes. - **$30 $75 $125**

HOW-45

❑ **HOW-45. "Big Prize Doodle List" Sheet,**
1954. Howdy Doody Ice Cream Club. Premium listing for 1954-1955. - **$10 $20 $30**

HOW-46

HOW-47

❑ **HOW-46. Wrist Watch with Die-Cut Display Box,**
1954. Display box had a mylar-like clear top which is usually damaged or missing. Instructions are included. - **$675**

❑ **HOW-47. TV Guide,**
1954. Weekly issue for June 25 with cover photo and related article. - **$30 $75 $125**

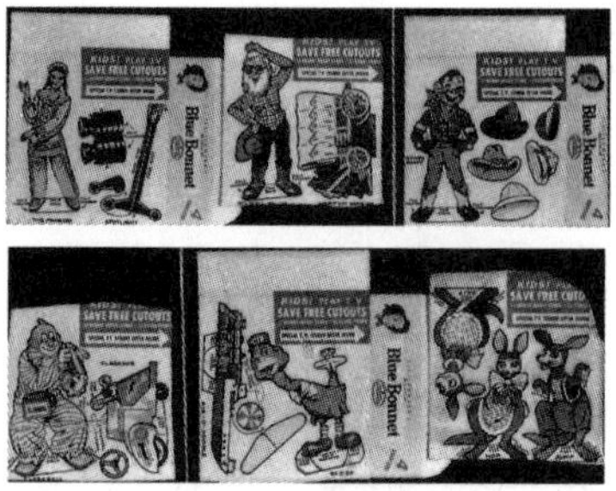

HOW-48

❑ **HOW-48. Blue Bonnet Margarine Box Panels,**
1954. Waxed cardboard set of 12 for "Play TV" stage offered separately as mail premium.
Each Uncut Panel - **$10 $25 $40**

HOW-49

❑ **HOW-49. "Howdy Doody TV Studio" Punch-Out Premium,**
1954. Blue Bonnet Margarine. Mailer holds 8-1/2x11" four-page instructions and six stiff paper 11x18" punch-out sheets to set up TV studio with Peanut Gallery and broadcasting accessories. Characters were depicted on product box panels as a set of 12 cut-outs. -
**$150 $300 $600**

HOW-50

❑ **HOW-50. Howdy Doody Characters Play Money/Coupon,**
1954. Ogilvie Flour Mills Co., Canada. Play money in at least eight denominations and picturing at least eight characters. When one million dollars was collected, a BSA bicycle was awarded. Each - **$5 $10 $15**

HOW-51

❑ **HOW-51. Merchandise Manual,**
1954. Rare. - **$100 $300 $600**
1955. Rare. - **$75 $250 $500**

HOW-52

HOW-53

❑ **HOW-52. Kellogg's Rice Krispies Box,**
1955. Features free Dangle-Dandies as a premium. - **$125 $250 $400**

❑ **HOW-53. Plastic Puppets on Card,**
1955. Figures have movable mouths which you can use by pressing lever on back.
Set with Card - **$75 $175 $250**

HOW-54

❑ **HOW-54. Tin Litho. Trapeze Toy,**
c. 1955. Store item made by Arnold of West Germany, imported by Novelty Toy Associates. 4x9x16" tall frame holding 9-1/2" tall figure of Howdy with composition head and cloth clothes. When vertical rod is pushed down, figure spins on horizontal bar. - **$150 $350 $550**

HOW-55

HOW-56

❑ **HOW-55. Ice Cream Cup Lid,**
1955. Doughnut Corp. of America. Lid and 25 cents used to order "Howdy Doody Magic Talking Pin." - **$10 $20 $40**

❑ **HOW-56. "Clarabell Dangle-Dandy" Box Back,**
c. 1955. Kellogg's. One of a series.
Uncut Each - **$20 $50 $75**
Assembled Each - **$10 $25 $50**

HOW-57

HOW-58

❑ **HOW-57. Jumble Joy Book,**
1955. Scarce. Poll Parrot shoe premium. 16 pages in color. - **$40 $100 $150**

❑ **HOW-58. "Twin-Pop" 7x14" Paper Store Sign,**
1956. - **$20 $60 $90**

HOW-59

HOW-60

HOW-61

❑ **HOW-59. Litho. Tab,**
c. 1956. Ten tabs were collected for free "Twin Pop Or Fudge Bar". - **$15 $40 $75**

❑ **HOW-60. Ice Cream Waxed Cardboard Cup,**
c. 1956. - **$20 $35 $50**

❑ **HOW-61. Packaged Wood Ice Cream Spoon,**
c. 1956. - **$5 $10 $20**

HOW-62

❑ **HOW-62. "Fudge Bar" Waxed Paper Bag,**
c. 1956. Offers talking pin and ice cream club membership. - **$5 $12 $20**

HOW-63

❑ **HOW-63. "Fudge Bar" Store Sign,**
c. 1956. Doughnut Corp. of America. 9x12" glossy paper with text "Save All Howdy Doody Bags For Swell Prizes." - **$30 $75 $115**

HOW-64

❑ **HOW-64. "Howdy Doody Smile Ballot",**
1957. 4x6" ballot to select best smile from among 10 competitors. - **$10 $20 $40**

HOW-65

HOW-66

❑ **HOW-65. "Jackpot Of Fun" Comic Book,**
1957. DCA Food Industries. - **$10 $30 $60**

❑ **HOW-66. Ceramic Piggy Bank,**
1950s. Store item. - **$100 $200 $350**

HOW-67

HOW-68

❑ **HOW-67. Four-Sided Mask,**
1950s. Philco TV. Scarce. Clarabell, Howdy, Gabby and Tom Corbett featured. -
**$50 $125 $200**

❑ **HOW-68. TV Set Instructions,**
1950s. Rare. Colgate premium. - **$35 $75 $100**

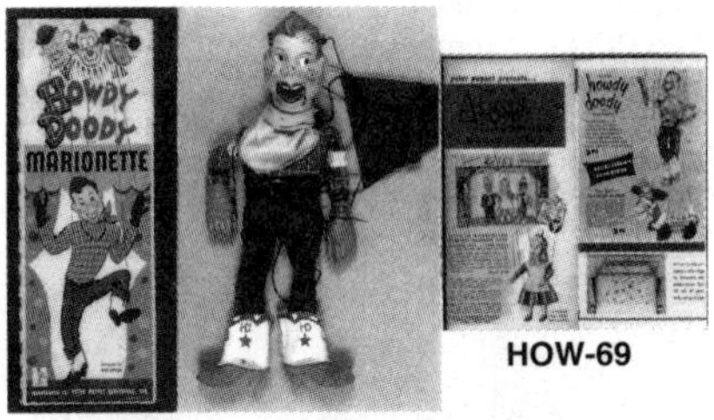


HOW-69

❑ **HOW-69. Composition Marionette,**
1950s. Store item by Peter Puppet Playthings.
Boxed - **$100 $150 $300**
Loose - **$50 $100 $150**

HOW-70

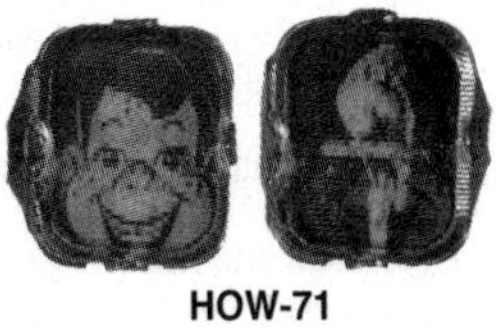

HOW-71

❑ **HOW-70. Photo Glow Ring,**
1950s. Ring name implies image glows in dark but all examples seen do not glow. -
**$50 $75 $150**

❑ **HOW-71. Flicker Picture Ring With Brass Base,**
1950s. Portrait of Howdy alternates with image of Poll Parrot on a perch. - **$50 $75 $100**

HOW-72

HOW-73

❑ **HOW-72. Large Glazed Ceramic Bust Bank,**
1950s. Store item. - **$250 $350 $700**

❑ **HOW-73. "Howdy Doody Climber" Store Poster,**
1950s. Welch's Frozen Grape Juice. 11x14" offering toy for 10 cents plus can top. Gordon Gold archives. - **$100 $200 $300**

HOW-74

❑ **HOW-74. Official Ice Cream Club "Fun And Prizes" Premium Catalogue,**
1950s. Catalogue directs points and money to Premium Associates Inc ., N.Y.C. 4x5" booklet includes club song and pictures eight premiums. - **$25 $60 $80**

HOW75

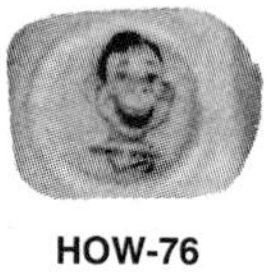

HOW-76

HOW-77

❑ **HOW-75. Poll-Parrot TV Plastic Ring With Flicker Picture,**
1950s. Frame image of TV screen, image alternates between Howdy and parrot. - **$50 $85 $125**

❑ **HOW-76. Plastic Ring With Paper Insert Picture,**
1950s. - **$50 $85 $125**

❑ **HOW-77. "Poll-Parrot" Plastic Ring,**
1950s. Raised portrait. - **$15 $25 $50**

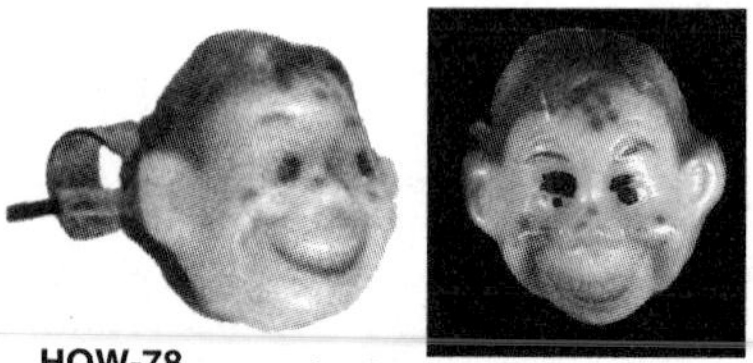

HOW-78 **(2 views of the ring)**

❑ **HOW-78. Illuminated Head Ring,**
1950s. Palmolive Soap. Brass bands holding plastic head lighted by bulb and battery. - **$75 $150 $250**

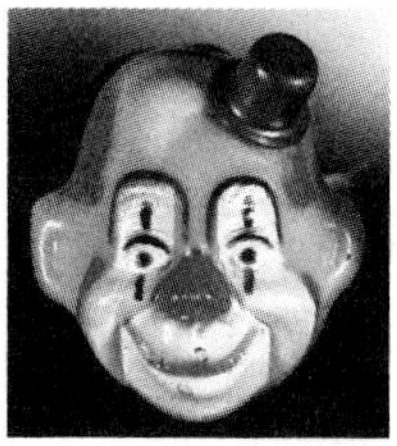

HOW-79

HOW-80

❑ **HOW-79. Clarabell Face/Hat Ring,**
1950s. Rare. - **$500 $1000 $2000**

❑ **HOW-80. Clarabell's Horn Ring,**
1950s. Scarce. Brass bands picture Clarabell and Howdy, top has aluminum horn that works by blowing. - **$100 $200 $350**

HOW-81

❑ **HOW-81. Sailor Style Hat,**
1950s. Store item. - **$15 $30 $50**

HOW-82

❑ **HOW-82. "Poll-Parrot's Howdy Doody Photo Album",**
1950s. Includes four blank pages to mount four photos. Complete - **$75 $150 $200**

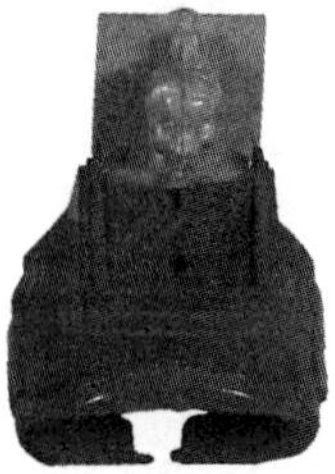

HOW-83

HOW-84

❑ **HOW-83. Jack-In-The-Box Plastic Ring,**
1950s. Poll-Parrot Shoes. Lid lifts, revealing miniature 3-D plastic Howdy head. - **$200 $500 $1000**

❑ **HOW-84. "Sunday Post-Dispatch" Litho. Button,**
1950s. Issued for newspaper comic strip. - **$30 $75 $150**

HOW-85

HOW-86

HOW-87

❑ **HOW-85. Newspaper Comic Strip Litho. Button,**
1950s. - **$25 $65 $125**

❑ **HOW-86. "Howdy Doody Safety Club/CBC" Cello. Button,**
1950s. Canadian Broadcasting Company. Canadian issue by Toronto maker. - **$35 $75 $125**

❑ **HOW-87. Jointed Cardboard Puppet,**
1950s. Wonder Bread. 13" tall. - **$20 $50 $85**

HOW-88

❑ **HOW-88. Tuk-A-Tab Mask,**
1950s. Poll-Parrot. Masks of Howdy and Clarabell.
Each Unpunched - **$20 $45 $75**

HOW-89

HOW-90

❑ **HOW-89. Jointed Cardboard Puppet,**
1950s. Wonder Bread. 7-1/2" tall. -
**$20 $50 $85**

❑ **HOW-90. Princess Cardboard Jointed Puppet,**
1950s. Wonder Bread. 7-1/2" tall. - **$20 $50 $85**

HOW-91

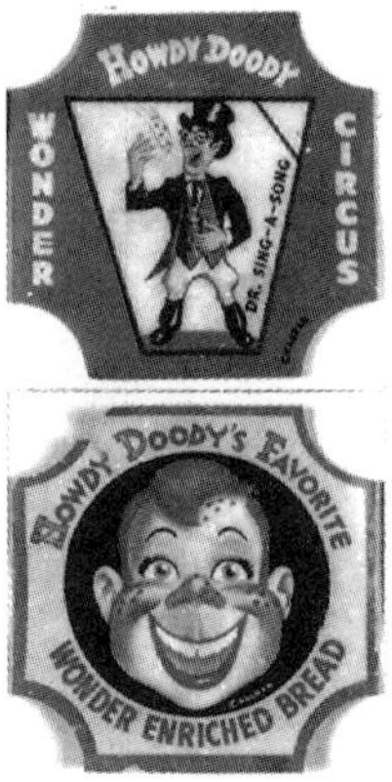


HOW-92

❑ **HOW-91. Howdy Doody Periscope,**
1950s. Rare. Wonder Bread. - **$150 $450 $750**

❑ **HOW-92. Bread Labels,**
1950s. Wonder Bread. From two different sets.
Each - **$5 $10 $15**

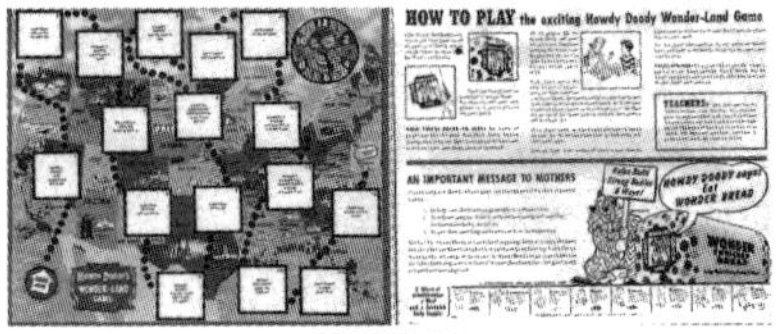


HOW-93

❑ **HOW-93. "Wonder-Land Game" Sheet,**
1950s. Wonder Bread. With spinner and 16 spaces for cut-outs from bread end labels.
Unused - **$25 $50 $100**
Complete - **$75 $150 $250**

HOW-94

❑ **HOW-94. "Wonder Bread Circus Album" Label Sheet,**
1950s. Unused - **$25 $50 $100**
Complete - **$75 $150 $250**

HOW-95

❑ **HOW-95. "Wonder Bread Balloon Parade" Label Sheet,**
1950s. Unused - **$25 $50 $100**
Complete - **$75 $150 $250**

HOW-96

❑ **HOW-96. Christmas Cards,**
1950s. Mars Candy. Set of 8 with 8 blank envelopes. Each - **$10 $15 $25**

HOW-97

HOW-98

❑ **HOW-97. "Howdy Doody's Favorite Doughnuts" Cellophane Package,**
1950s. Tom Thumb. - **$15 $40 $75**

❑ **HOW-98. "Wonder Bread Zoomascope",**
1950s. Opens to 3-1/2x51". - **$25 $60 $120**

HOW-99

HOW-100

❑ **HOW-99. Cardboard Disk Flipper Badge,**
1950s. Wonder Bread. Disk flips by pulling string to complete phrase "The Princess Says...Eat Wonder Bread". From set picturing various Howdy Doody characters.
Each - **$10 $20 $30**

❑ **HOW-100. "Hostess" Cupcake Package Tag,**
1950s. Continental Baking Co. - **$50 $75 $100**

HOW-101

HOW-102

❑ **HOW-101. "Mason Candy Words To The 'Howdy Doody' Song" Sheet,**
1950s. - **$10 $20 $35**

❑ **HOW-102. "Howdy Doody Animated Puppet" Punch-Out With Envelope,**
1950s. Three Musketeers/Mars candy bars.
Near Mint In Mailer - **$165**

HOW-103

❑ **HOW-103. "Royal Trading Card",**
1950s. Royal Pudding. Set of 16. Text on each card refers to "14 other pictures" but a sixteenth card designated on the card as "No. 16" exists. It pictures "Captain Scuttlebutt."
Each Complete Box - **$20 $45 $85**
Each Cut Card - **$10 $15 $20**

HOW-104

HOW-105

❑ **HOW-104. "Clarabell Animated Puppet" Punch-Out With Envelope,**
1950s. Mars Coconut Bar.
Near Mint In Mailer - **$165**

❑ **HOW-105. "E-Z DO Junior Space Saver" 2-1/4" Tin Tab,**
1950s. - **$20 $50 $100**

HOW-106

HOW-107

❑ **HOW-106. "Howdy Doody Climber" Cardboard Figure,**
1950s. Luden's Wild Cherry Cough Drops, Welch's Grape Juice and probably others.
Near Mint In Mailer - **$75**
Loose - **$10 $25 $50**

❑ **HOW-107. Princess Face Mask With Glassine Envelope,**
1950s. Royal Desserts. Issued for additional characters. With Envelope - **$20 $65 $125**
Loose - **$10 $25 $50**

HOW-108

HOW-109

❑ **HOW-108. Silver Plate Spoon,**
1950s. Sponsor unknown. - **$10 $20 $35**

❑ **HOW-109. "Magic Kit" With Envelope,**
1950s. Luden's, makers of Fifth Avenue candy bar. Tricks on punch-out sheets.
Near Mint In Mailer - **$150**

HOW-110

❑ **HOW-110. Four-Sided Mask,**
1950s. Philco TV depicting Howdy, Gabby Hayes and National/American League baseball players to promote World Series on Philco TV. - **$50 $125 $200**

HOW-111

HOW-112

❑ **HOW-111. "Howdy Doody Napkins" Trading Card Sheet,**
1950s. Colonial Paper Products Co. At least two different sheets. Each Uncut - **$20 $50 $85**

❑ **HOW-112. "Princess Summerfall Winterspring" Photo,**
1950s. Pictures Judy Tyler. - **$20 $50 $85**

HOW-113

HOW-114

❑ **HOW-113. Hat,**
1950s. Store bought. - **$15 $35 $70**

❑ **HOW-114. Large Postcard,**
1950s. - **$30 $75 $100**

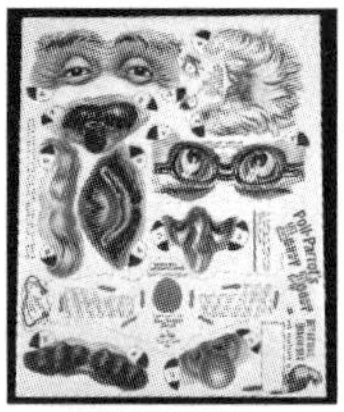
HOW-115

HOW-116

❑ **HOW-115. Detective Disguise Punch-Out Sheet,**
1950s. Poll-Parrot Shoes - **$20 $40 $60**

❑ **HOW-116. Air-O-Doodle Rocket Beanie with Mailer,**
1950s. Rare. Kellogg's Rice Krispies premium. - **$35 $125 $175**

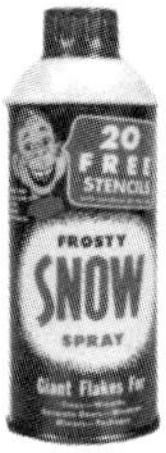

HOW-117

HOW-118

❑ **HOW-117. "Frosty Snow Spray" Can With Howdy Doody,**
1950s. Has offer "20 Free Stencils With Purchase Of This Can." - **$15 $35 $50**

❑ **HOW-118. "Howdy Doody Cookie-Go-Round" Canister,**
1950s. Store item by Luse Mfg. Co. 7" diameter by 7-1/2" tall. - **$50 $140 $250**

HOW-119

❑ **HOW-119. Salt & Pepper Set With Box,**
1950s. Store item by Doodlings Inc. Each is 3" tall plastic. Box - **$35 $85 $150**
Set UnBoxed - **$25 $65 $100**

HOW-120

❑ **HOW-120."Clarabell Double Doody Bar" Sign,**
1950s. Issued by Doughnut Corp. of America. 8-1/2x22". - **$75 $150 $250**

HOW-121

❑ **HOW-121. Howdy Doody And Santa Claus Christmas Light,**
1950s. Store item by Royal Electric Co. 10-1/4x14" Vaccu-Form thin plastic. - **$75 $125 $200**

HOW-122

❑ **HOW-122. Set Of Eight Flicker Rings,**
1960. Nabisco. Color images on gray plastic bases issued one per box. Each - **$7 $15 $30**

HOW-123

HOW-124

❑ **HOW-123. "Revival Show" Local Cello. Button,**
1971. Towson State College. Single day issue for May 5 event. - **$10 $20 $30**

❑ **HOW-124. "Howdy Doody For President" Litho. Tin Tab,**
c. 1976. National Broadcasting Corp. - **$10 $20 $30**

HOW-125

HOW-126

❑ **HOW-125. Buffalo Bob Smith "Tootsieroll" Personal Appearance Costume Patch,**
1970s. From personal collection of Bob Smith. - **$10 $20 $30**

❑ **HOW-126. "A 40-Year Celebration" 3" Cello. Button,**
1987. National Broadcasting Co. - **$5 $12 $25**

HOW-127

HOW-128

❑ **HOW-127. 40th Anniversary Watch With Box,**
1987. Store item with copyrights of NBC and King Features Syndicate.
Near Mint Boxed - **$75**
Watch Only - **$10 $20 $40**

❑ **HOW-128. Howdy Doody Cookie Jar,**
1980s. Made by Vandau. Produced in Japan. Very limited production. - **$500**

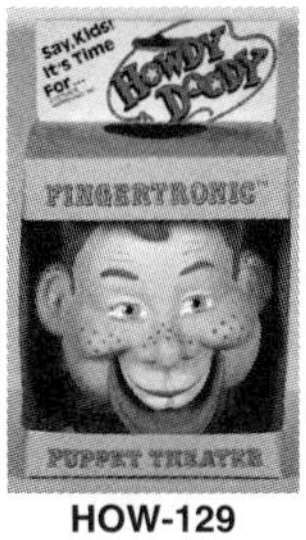

HOW-129

HOW-130

❑ **HOW-129. Howdy Doody Finger Puppet in Box,**
1980s. - **$20 $40 $75**

❑ **HOW-130. Christmas Ornaments,**
1998. Clarabell, Howdy and Buffalo Bob.
Set - **$50**

HOW-131

❑ **HOW-131. Lunch Box,**
2000. - **$35**

# Howie Wing

**The air adventures of ace Howie Wing were heard on CBS radio five times a week in 1938 and 1939, with William Janney battling evil as young Howie. Kellogg's cereals sponsored the program and issued a number of aviation-related premiums, including wings, a weather forecaster ring, decoder, model airplane kits, and membership paraphernalia for the Cadet Aviation Corps.**

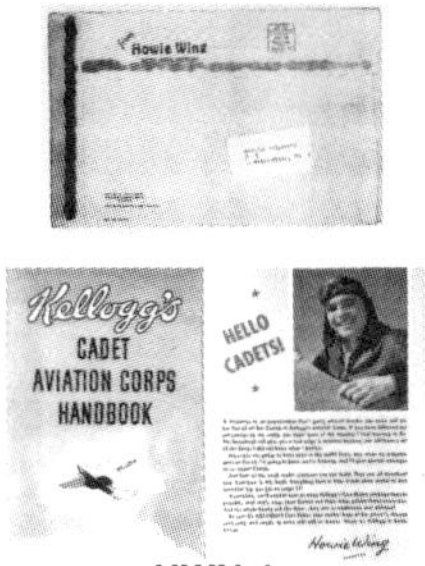


HWN-1

HWN-2

❑ **HWN-1. "Kellogg's Cadet Aviation Corps" Club Manual,**
1938. Mailer - **$5 $15 $25**
Manual - **$20 $50 $85**

❑ **HWN-2. Premium Order Sheet,**
c. 1938. Offers Cadet Aviation Corp. button, Flying Guide and Pilot Test Card. -
**$10 $20 $40**

HWN-3

HWN-4

❑ **HWN-3. "Kellogg's Rubber Band Pilot's Pistol And Targets",**
c. 1938. Unpunched - **$50 $125 $240**

❑ **HWN-4. "Kellogg's Moving Picture Machine",**
c. 1938. Unpunched - **$50 $125 $240**

HWN-5

❑ **HWN-5. Group Of Canadian Premiums,**
c. 1938. The Kellogg Co. of Canada. Group consists of: 8-1/2x10-3/4" "Howie Wing's Aviation Album," 8-1/2x10" folder with "Fellow Cadet" letter which folds out to chart of "Important Parts Of An Airplane...," 8-1/2x11" salesman's folder to grocery store owners which opens to a color store sign, 2-3/4x4-3/4" ad promoting radio program and "Planes Of All Nations" cereal boxes, 3-1/2x5-1/2" "Pilot Test Card." Gordon Gold Archives. Album - **$75 $125 $225**
Cadet Folder - **$15 $25 $60**
Salesman Folder/Sign - **$75 $125 $225**
"Listen" Flyer - **$10 $15 $30**
Pilot Card - **$10 $15 $30**

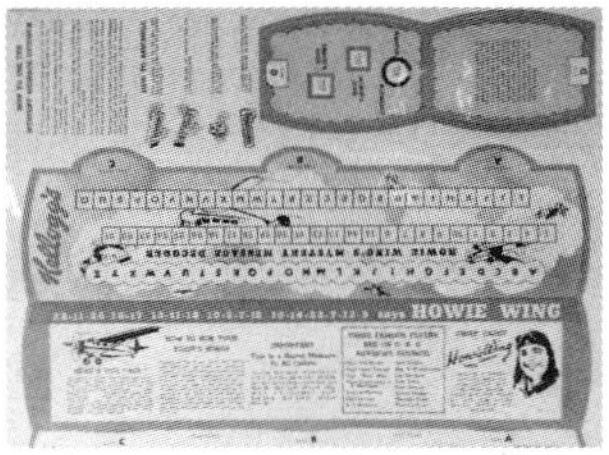

(DECODER)

(MAILER)

HWN-6

❑ **HWN-6. "Howie Wing Mystery Message Decoder" Punch-Out,**
c. 1938. Kellogg's marked "Printed In Canada." 9-1/2x13" mailer has image and text in orange. Punch-out decoder sheet has airplane illustrations and Howie Wing portrait. Gordon Gold Archives. Mailer - **$10 $20 $30**
Punch-Out - **$50 $125 $225**

HWN-7

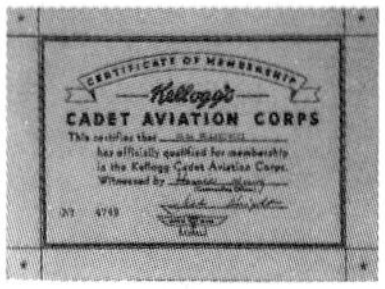


HWN-8

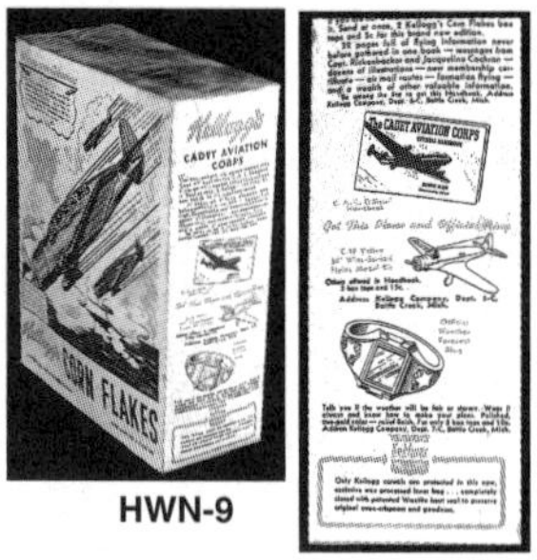


HWN-9

❑ **HWN-7. Cadet Aviation Corps News,**
c. 1938. - **$25 $50 $85**

❑ **HWN-8. "Kellogg's Cadet Aviation Corps" Club Member Certificate,**
1938. - **$10 $25 $40**

❑ **HWN-9. Kellogg's Corn Flakes Box - 8 oz.,**
1939. Cereal box features Wings Over America. Vultee V-12 plane pictured. Premium offer of ring, plane model kit, and handbook pictured on side of box. Complete - **$75 $175 $275**

HWN-10

HWN-11

❑ **HWN-10. Kellogg's Corn Flakes Box Back,**
1939. Wings Over America series. Brewster F2A-1 plane pictured. Premium offer for membership kit pictured on side of box. -
**$20 $30 $45**

❑ **HWN-11. Kellogg's Corn Flakes Box -13 oz.,**
1939. Wings Over America series. Curtiss SBC-40 plane pictured. Premium offer for club material on side of box. Shows badge at top. Complete - **$50 $125 $200**

HWN-12

❑ **HWN-12. "Official Handbook",**
1939. Kellogg's. Mailer - **$5 $15 $25**
Handbook - **$25 $50 $85**

HWN-13

HWN-14

❑ **HWN-13. "Howie Wing/Cadet Aviation Corps" Club Membership Card,**
1939. Kellogg's. - **$15 $30 $60**

❑ **HWN-14. Australian Club Member's Aluminum Wings Pin,**
1930s. Kellogg's in Australia. 1-5/8" long aluminum with red shield. - **$20 $50 $85**

HWN-15

❑ **HWN-15. "Howie Wing's Adventures On The Canadian Lakes" Map,**
1930s. Kellogg's of Canada. 11x16" opened. -
**$100 $225 $350**

HWN-16

HWN-17

❑ **HWN-16. Ventriloquist Dummy Cardboard Fold-Out,**
1930s. Kellogg's premium. - **$100 $200 $300**

❑ **HWN-17. Instructions For Dummy,**
1930s. Kellogg's premium. - **$10 $15 $25**

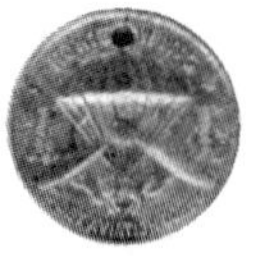

HWN-18

HWN-19

HWN-20

❑ **HWN-18. "Howie Wing/Kellogg's" Holed Aluminum Coin,**
1930s. - **$10 $15 $25**

❑ **HWN-19. "Howie Wing Cadet" Silvered/Enameled Brass Badge,**
1930s. - **$10 $20 $30**

❑ **HWN-20. "Pilot CAC" Aluminum Wings Badge,**
1930s. For Howie Wing Cadet Aviation Corps. Probably Canadian issue. - **$20 $50 $85**

HWN-21

HWN-22

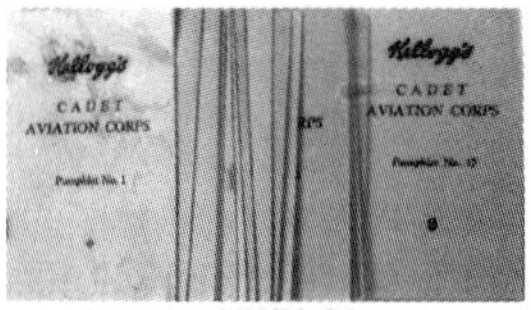


HWN-23

❑ **HWN-21. Weather Forecast Ring,**
1930s. Brass bands with metal clip holding slip of litmus paper. - **$100 $225 $350**

❑ **HWN-22. "Cadet" Cello. Button,**
1930s. Distributed to Canadian members. -
**$10 $20 $35**

❑ **HWN-23. "Kellogg's Cadet Aviation Corps" Pamphlet Set,**
1930s. Set of 17. Each - **$5 $10 $15**

# H.R. Pufnstuf

**This Saturday morning children's television series, which used both live actors and puppets, aired on NBC from 1969 to 1971 and was repeated on ABC from 1972 to 1974. The program told, with songs and dances, the adventures of young Jimmy and his golden talking flute Freddie as they try to escape the clutches of the wicked Witchiepoo on Living Island. A movie version was released by Paramount in 1970, and comic books appeared from 1970 to 1972.**

HPF-1

❑ **HPF-1. Peel-Off Patch,**
1969. Probably a Kellogg's premium and the eight we show are probably a set.
Each Unused On Card - **$5 $10 $15**

HPF-2

❑ **HPF-2. Soundtrack Record Album and Photo,**
1970. Kellogg's. With Mailer - **$40 $100 $150**
No Mailer - **$25 $75 $100**

HPF-3

❑ **HPF-3. "H.R. Pufnstuf Hand Puppets" Cereal Box,**
1970. Kellogg's Apple Jacks. Offers series of rare premium puppets that were available for $1 plus two "Puppet Stamps" from Kellogg's cereal boxes. Gordon Gold Archives.
Complete - **$200 $400 $600**

HPF-4

❑ **HPF-4. Fun Rings And Flute Premium Offer Cereal Box,**
1970. Back panel offers set of seven plastic character rings and side panel offers "Freddy The Flute" premium for 50 cents and one box top. Gordon Gold Archives.
Near Mint Flat - **$500**
Used Complete - **$100 $200 $300**

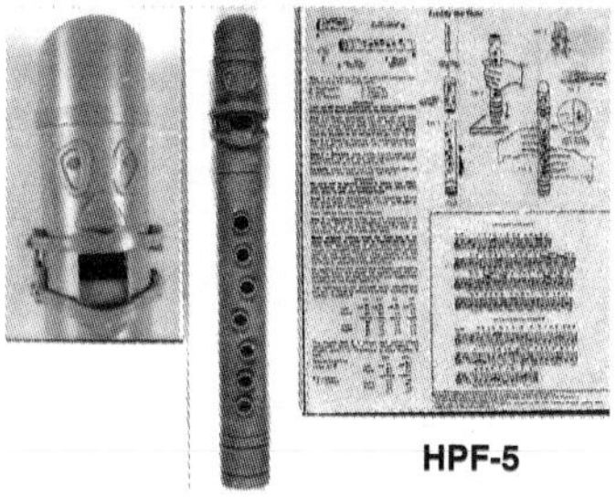

HPF-5

**HPF-5. "Freddie The Flute" Musical Toy With Instructions,**
1970. Kellogg's. Flute - **$100 $250 $350**
Instruction Sheet - **$25 $50 $75**

HPF-6

HPF-7

❑ **HPF-6. "Pufnstuf" Translucent Plastic Ring,**
1970. Copyright Sid & Marty Krofft Prod. Inc. Slightly raised character image from seven different versions also picturing Witchipoo, Cling and Clang, Jimmy and Freddie, Orson, two unknown. Each - **$40 $60 $80**

❑ **HPF-7. "Witchipoo" Translucent Plastic Ring,**
1970. Copyright Sid & Marty Krofft Prod. Inc. From series of seven different also picturing Pufnstuf, Cling and Clang, Jimmy and Freddie, Orson, two unknown.
Each - **$40 $60 $80**

HPF-8

❑ **HPF-8. Cereal Box With Pennants Offer,**
1970. The vinyl pennants were printed two per sheet with a total of eight character illustrations. Gordon Gold Archives.
Used Complete - **$100 $175 $250**

HPF-9

HPF-10

HPF-11

❑ **HPF-9. H.R. Pufnstuf Vinyl Hand Puppet,**
1970. Store item by Remco. - **$25 $50 $75**

❑ **HPF-10. Jimmy Vinyl Hand Puppet,**
1970. Store item by Remco. - **$25 $50 $75**

❑ **HPF-11. Cling Or Clang Vinyl Hand Puppet,**
1970. Store item by Remco. - **$25 $50 $75**

HPF-12

HPF-13

❑ **HPF-12. H.R. Pufnstuf Mayor Bean Figure,**
1999. - **$8**

❑ **HPF-13. "Pufnstuf" Signed Poster Reprint,**
1999. 11x17" reprint of 1970 one-sheet movie poster used for autographing purposes and signed by Marty Krofft and Jack Wild.
Near Mint - **$75**

HPF-14

❑ **HPF-14. Marty Krofft Signed "Blast" Program,**
1990s. For Sid & Marty Krofft theater production. Near Mint Signed - **$25**
Unsigned - **$5 $10 $15**

## Huckleberry Hound

***Huckleberry Hound*, the first animated cartoon to win an Emmy, was Hanna-Barbera's first major television hit and the source of hundreds of licensed products. The syndicated series, sponsored by Kellogg's cereals, aired from 1958 to 1962 and was watched by millions of viewers all over the world. Huck was a noble-hearted bloodhound who remained untroubled no matter what misfortunes plagued him. Other cartoon segments on the show: Pixie and Dixie, a pair of carefree mice who tormented the affable tomcat Mr. Jinks ("I hate those meeces to pieces!"); Yogi Bear, who debuted on the show and went on to his own major series in 1961; and Hokey Wolf, a Sgt. Bilko-**

like con artist whose pal was Ding-a-Ling, a fox. *Huckleberry Hound* comic books appeared from 1959 into the 1970s.

HUC-1

HUC-2

❑ **HUC-1. "Fun Cards" Box Back,**
1959. Kellogg's Corn Flakes. Back Panel Only - **$10 $20 $30**

❑ **HUC-2. Plush Doll With Vinyl Face,**
1960. Store item by Knickerbocker and Kellogg's premium. - **$25 $50 $85**

HUC-3

❑ **HUC-3. "Huck Hound Club" Kit,**
1960. Kellogg's. Includes letter, member card, two color pictures, club button, Breakfast Score Card (not shown). Complete - **$75 $150 $250**

HUC-4

HUC-5

❑ **HUC-4. "Huckleberry Hound For President" 3" Litho. Button,**
1960. - **$15 $30 $60**

❑ **HUC-5. "The Great Kellogg's TV Show" Record Album,**
c. 1960. - **$10 $20 $30**

HUC-6 HUC-7

❑ **HUC-6. "Huckleberry Hound" Glazed Ceramic Figure,**
1960. Store item by Ideas Inc., Des Moines, Iowa. 5-3/4" tall. - **$20 $50 $75**

❑ **HUC-7. Plastic Bank,**
c. 1960. Store item by Knickerbocker. - **$15 $25 $35**

HUC-8 HUC-9

❑ **HUC-8. "Huck Hound Club" Enameled Brass Ring,**
c. 1960. Kellogg's. - **$15 $50 $75**

❑ **HUC-9. "Huck Hound Club" Brass Ring Copyrighted,**
1961. Kellogg's. Variety without enamel paint accents. - **$15 $50 $75**

HUC-10

❑ **HUC-10. Club Card,**
1962. Scarce. Certified as TopDog. - **$20 $35 $60**

HUC-11

❑ **HUC-11. "Huckleberry Car" Vinyl And Litho. Tin Friction Car,**
1962. Store item by Marx.
Box - **$30 $60 $100**
Car - **$65 $125 $200**

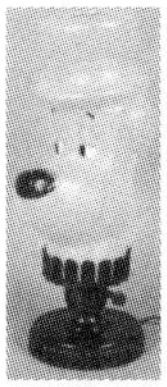

HUC-12

HUC-13

❑ **HUC-12. Vinyl/Plastic Figural Lamp,**
1962. 12" tall store item by Arch Lamp Mfg. Corp. - **$30 $75 $140**

❑ **HUC-13. Hanna-Barbera Cartoon Character Waste Can,**
c. 1962. 12-1/2" tall metal. - **$65 $125 $200**

HUC-14

HUC-15

❑ **HUC-14. Litho. Tin Wind-Up Toy,**
1962. Store item by Line Mar. 4" tall. - **$50 $125 $250**

❑ **HUC-15. March Of Comics,**
1962. Used as giveaway by various stores. Issue #235. - **$6 $18 $40**

HUC-16

HUC-17

❑ **HUC-16. "Kellogg's Special K" 17x41" Cardboard Hanger String Sign,**
1960s. - **$75 $125 $200**

❑ **HUC-17. Huck Hound/Mr. Jinks Plastic Flicker Ring,**
1960s. Kellogg's Cereal. Believed to be set of six. - **$45 $110 $175**

HUC-18

❑ **HUC-18. Cereal Box Plastic Figures,**
1960s. Kellogg's OK Cereal. Miniatures of Huck Hound, Pixie and Dixie, Mr. Jinks, Yogi Bear, Boo Boo Bear, Tony the Tiger.
Each - **$4 $8 $12**

## Inner Sanctum

The memorable squeaking door and the sinister voice of "Raymond, your host" introduced the macabre *Inner Sanctum* mysteries on radio from 1941 to 1952, first on the Blue network, then on CBS (1943-1950), and ABC. The morbid anthology featured such film veterans as Boris Karloff, Peter Lorre, and Claude Raines in ghostly tales of murder and mayhem. Sponsors included Carter's Little Liver Pills (1941-1943), Colgate-Palmolive shaving cream (1943-1944), Lipton tea and soup (1945), Bromo-Seltzer (1946-1950), and Mars candy (1950-1951). A number of second-feature Inner Sanctum movies were made in the 1940s by Universal, most starring Lon Chaney Jr.

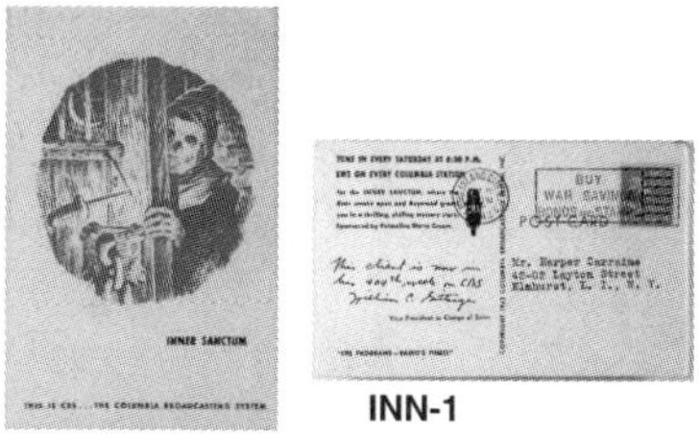

INN-1

❑ **INN-1. Promotional Postcard,**
1943. Rare. Sponsored by Palmolive Shave Cream. - **$75 $175 $350**

INN-2

INN-3

❑ **INN-2. Cardboard Ink Blotter,**
1945. Scarce. Lipton tea and soup. - **$50 $100 $175**

❑ **INN-3. Advertising Cello. Button With Radio Show Title Tie-In,**
1940s. Inner Sanctum Wallets. 2-1/8" issued in several different color combinations to promote wallets. We are uncertain if they were also sponsors of the show. - **$10 $20 $35**

## Inspector Post

General Foods created Post's Junior Detective Corps in 1932-1933 to promote its line of cereals. The club was advertised in Sunday newspaper comic sections and on the cereal boxes, offering its young members manuals edited by Inspector General Post and badges for detective ranks up to the level of Captain.

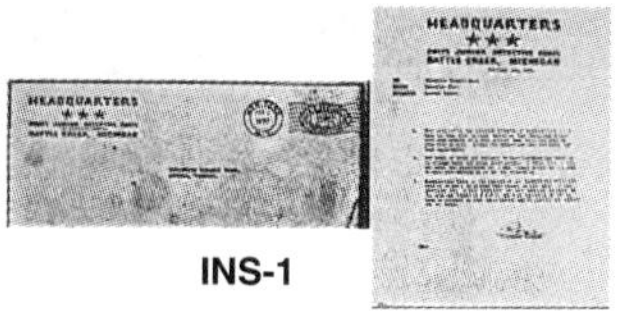


INS-1

❑ **INS-1. Club Letter With Envelope,**
1933. Text urges current club member to "Recruit New Members For The Corps."
Envelope - **$5 $10 $15**
Letter - **$10 $25 $40**

INS-2

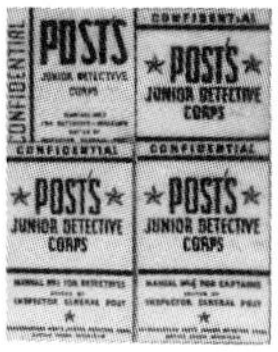


INS-3

INS-4

❑ **INS-2. "Inspector Post's Case Book" Manual,**
1933. Post Toasties. Includes 10 mysteries solved by answers on back. - **$15 $40 $60**

❑ **INS-3. Junior Detective Corps" Club Manuals,**
1933. Set of four. Each - **$15 $40 $60**

❑ **INS-4. Headquarters To Lieutenants Letter,**
1933. Announces lowering of requirements to advance from Sergeant to Lieutenant. - **$15 $25 $40**

INS-5

INS-6

❑ **INS-5. "Detective/Post's J.D.C." Silvered Tin Badge,**
1933. - **$15 $30 $50**

❑ **INS-6. "Detective Sergeant/Post's J.D.C." Brass Rank Badge,**
1933. - **$10 $30 $50**

INS-7

INS-8

❑ **INS-7. "Lieutenant Post's J.D.C." Silvered Brass Rank Badge ,**
1933. - **$15 $35 $60**

❑ **INS-8. "Captain/Post's J.D.C." Brass Rank Badge,**
1933. Scarce. - **$20 $50 $90**

## Jack Armstrong

Jack Armstrong hit the air in July 1933 and ruled the late-afternoon airwaves until 1951, one of the most popular and longest-running radio adventure series ever--and, thanks to Wheaties' sponsorship, one of the most bountiful sources of premiums. Jack started as a sports hero at Hudson High School, but within a year he and cousins Billy and Betty were seeking adventure with Uncle Jim in exotic spots all over the world. They were still waving the flag for Hudson High, but the intrepid four were tackling Tibet, searching out the elephants' graveyard in darkest Africa, recovering sunken uranium in the Sulu Sea, always looking for something lost or stolen or buried.

Jack Armstrong premiums were frequently linked to the program's story line--a Hike-O-Meter just like the one Jack used to measure how far he'd walked, a torpedo flashlight or explorer telescope, a signaling mirror or secret whistle ring to send messages, a bombsight, a bracelet just like Betty's, and, of course, club memberships. During World War II listeners were urged to buy war bonds, collect scrap, and write letters to servicemen, and to stay strong by eating their Wheaties. In 1950 the program was renamed *Armstrong of the SBI* and Jack, Billy, and Betty began working for the Scientific Bureau of Investigation. The series went off the air in 1951.

Jack Armstrong comic strips and a series of 13 comic books were published from 1947 to 1949, all drawn by Bob Schoenke. Also in 1947, Columbia Pictures released a 15-episode chapter play.

JAC-1

❑ **JAC-1. Wheaties Box With 1st Premium Offer On Back,**
1933. Rare. Offers hand exercise grips.
Complete - **$150 $400 $600**

JAC-2

JAC-3

JAC-4

❑ **JAC-2. "Johnny (Tarzan) Weissmuller" Photo,**
1933. Rare. One of earliest Jack Armstrong Wheaties premiums. - **$50 $175 $250**

❑ **JAC-3. Wheaties Babe Ruth "How To Hit A Home Run" Flip Booklet,**
1933. Scarce. Photo pages in sequence of batting stance, complete swing, follow-through. - **$100 $275 $425**

❑ **JAC-4. Armstrong On Horse Blackster Photo,**
1933. - **$10 $15 $25**

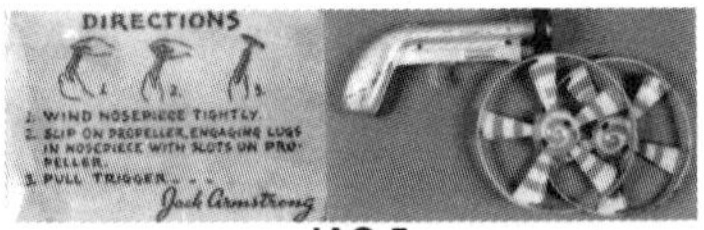

JAC-5

❑ **JAC-5. "Shooting Plane" With Directions And Mailer,**
1933. Made by Daisy Mfg. Co. Metal gun and two spinner wheels. Near Mint Boxed - **$250**
Gun - **$50 $75 $125**
Each Spinner - **$10 $40 $50**

JAC-6

❑ **JAC-6. "Wee-Gyro" Flying Ship, Instruction Paper,**
1934. Sheet came with a balsa model similar to autogyro. - **$25 $75 $135**

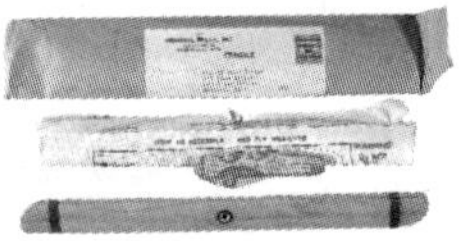
JAC-7

JAC-8

❑ **JAC-7. Jack Armstrong Wee-Gyro,**
1934. General Mills Cereal premium. Includes Wee gyro, mailer, and instructions.
Gyro - **$75 $125 $250**
Mailer - **$15 $30 $50**
Instructions - **$25 $75 $125**

❑ **JAC-8. All American Team Photo,**
1934. Radio premium. - **$10 $20 $30**

JAC-9

JAC-10

❑ **JAC-9. Jack Armstrong Photo,**
1934. Radio premium. - **$10 $20 $30**

❑ **JAC-10. Betty Fairfield Photo,**
1934. Radio premium. - **$10 $20 $30**

JAC-11

JAC-12

❑ **JAC-11. Box Back Panel,**
1935. - **$10 $30 $60**

❑ **JAC-12. Box Back Panel,**
1935. - **$10 $30 $60**

JAC-13

JAC-14

❑ **JAC-13. Betty Fairfield Box Back Panel,**
1935. - **$10 $30 $60**

❑ **JAC-14. Betty Fairfield Box Back Panel,**
1935. - **$10 $30 $60**

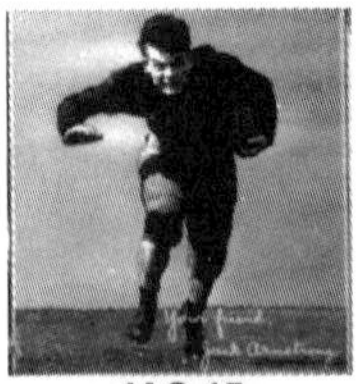
JAC-15

JAC-16

❑ **JAC-15. Box Back Panel,**
1935. - **$10 $30 $60**

❑ **JAC-16. Stamp Collecting Items,**
1935. Includes booklet and pamphlets about stamp collecting with offer of oriental stamps.
Each - **$10 $20 $40**

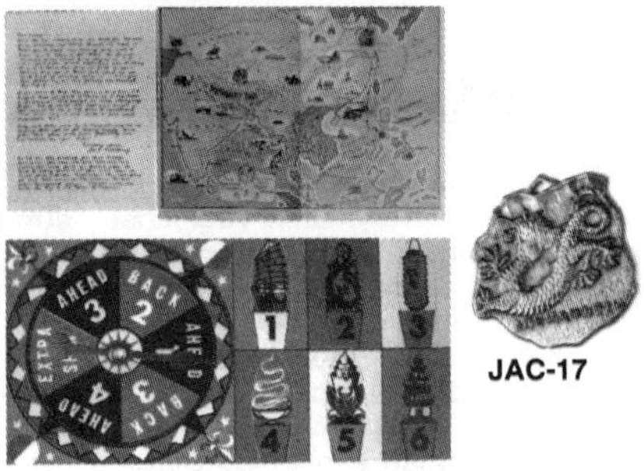
JAC-17

❑ **JAC-17. "Jack Armstrong's Chart Game/Adventures With The Dragon Talisman" Map Game,**
1936. The talisman inscription translated is: "China - The Key To The Door Of The Room Is Very Precious."
Map Game Only - **$35 $100 $175**
Spinner and Game Markers (4) - **$10 $20 $40**
Dragon Talisman - **$20 $40 $85**

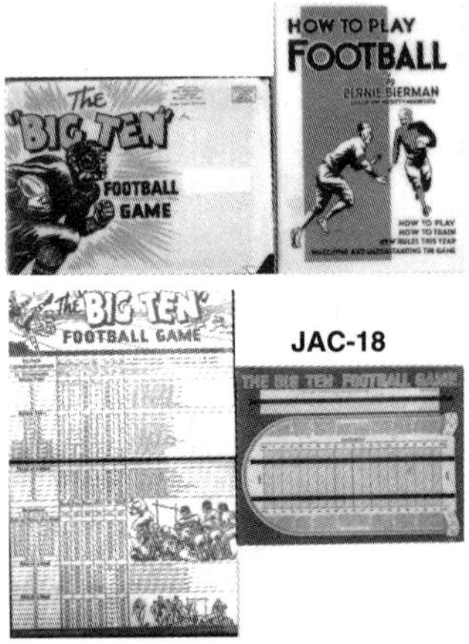

JAC-18

❑ **JAC-18. "Big Ten Football Game",**
1936. Near Mint In Mailer - **$250**
Board Only - **$10 $20 $50**
Booklet Only - **$10 $20 $30**

JAC-19

JAC-20

❑ **JAC-19. Milk Glass Bowl,**
1937. - **$10 $25 $40**

❑ **JAC-20. Movie Viewer With Filmstrip,**
1937. Film title is "Graveyard Of Elephants".
Box - **$10 $20 $35**
Viewer And Film - **$40 $75 $150**

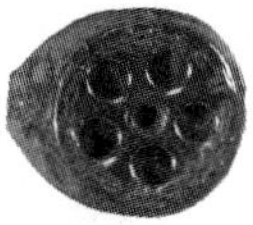

JAC-21

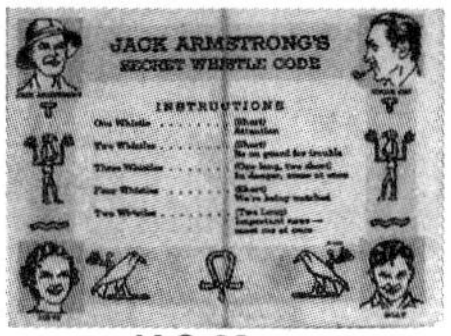


JAC-22

❑ **JAC-21. Secret Whistling Brass Ring,**
1937. Egyptian symbols on sides. -
**$40 $75 $140**

❑ **JAC-22. "Secret Whistle Code" Instruction Sheet,**
1937. Paper (not cardboard). For Egyptian Whistle Ring. - **$60 $70 $80**

JAC-23

❑ **JAC-23. "Treasure Hunt" Instruction Booklet,**
1938. Came with Hike-O-Meter pedometer. -
**$15 $25 $35**

JAC-24 JAC-25

❑ **JAC-24. "Baseball Centennial" Brass Ring,**
1938. Offered as Jack Armstrong premium by General Mills Wheaties and Corn Kix from 7/27/38-10/28/38. Company recorded 46,501 responses. Manufacturer's remainder offered by Quaker Puffed Rice in 1939. - **$125 $250 $400**

❑ **JAC-25. "Hike-O-Meter" Aluminum Pedometer,**
1938. Blue painted rim. - **$20 $40 $75**

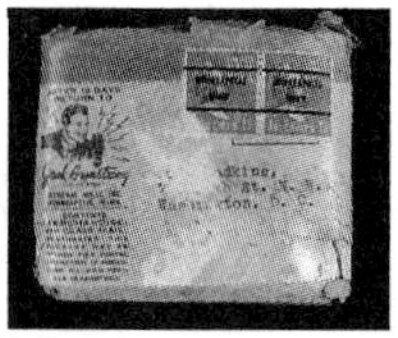

JAC-26

❑ **JAC-26. "Jack Armstrong Ped-O-Meter" Variety With Mailer,**
c. 1938. 2-5/8" dia. scarce version metal pedometer in chrome finish case rather than traditional blue rim plus title variation from traditional "Hike-O-Meter" title.
Near Mint In Mailer - **$125**
Ped-O-Meter Only - **$30 $50 $100**

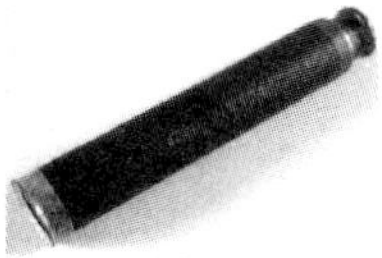

JAC-27 JAC-28

❑ **JAC-27. Explorer Telescope,**
1938. Cardboard tube with metal caps holding glass lenses. - **$8 $15 $30**

❑ **JAC-28. Heliograph And Distance Finder,**
1938. Scarce. Brass multi-function premium for land and water measurements, message sender, secret compartment, Morse Code. Scarce test premium. - **$250 $600 $1250**

JAC-29

❑ **JAC-29. "Jack Armstrong Magic Answer Box",**
1938. Complete Boxed - **$50 $75 $150**
Answer Box Only - **$30 $50 $75**

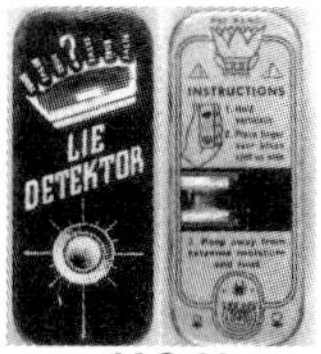


JAC-30

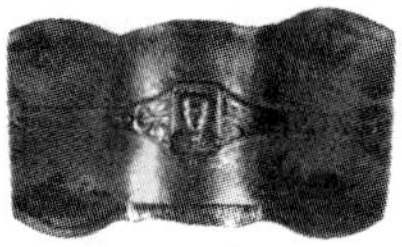

JAC-31

❑ **JAC-30. "Lie Detektor" Metal Answer Box,**
c. 1938. Supposed first version of "Magic Answer Box" quickly redesigned because parents objected to children telling lies. -
**$75 $150 $300**

❑ **JAC-31. All American Boy Ring Lead Proof,**
1939. Unique - **$2250**

JAC-32

❑ **JAC-32. "Adventures Of Jack Armstrong" Box Backs,**
1938. Wheaties. Set of six.
Each Back Panel - **$15 $30 $60**

JAC-33 JAC-34

❑ **JAC-33. Decoder Lead Proof,**
1939. Designed by Orin Armstrong for Robbins Company. Never produced. Unique - **$2000**

❑ **JAC-34. Pedometer,**
1939. Version with unpainted aluminum rim. See JAC-40. - **$15 $25 $40**

JAC-35

❑ **JAC-35. "Jack Armstrong" Original Art Prototype Book,**
c. 1939. 8-1/4x10-1/2" with four pages of art in lead and colored pencil for proposed 52-page book. Gordon Gold archives. Unique. - **$400**

JAC-36

❑ **JAC-36. "Jack Armstrong And The Mystery Of The Iron Key" Better Little Book,**
1939. Whitman #1432. - **$20 $50 $110**

JAC-37

JAC-38

❑ **JAC-37. Torpedo Flashlight Set,**
1939. Set of three in red, blue, or black cardboard barrels with metal nose and rear cap.
Blue - **$15 $25 $50**
Red - **$15 $30 $60**
Black - **$20 $35 $70**

❑ **JAC-38. Ad for the Torpedo Flashlight Wheaties Premium,**
1939. - **$10 $20 $35**

JAC-39

❑ **JAC-39. Serial - "Return To Mars,"**
1939. American Boy Magazine which features ad for Jack Armstrong promoting Wheaties and serial adventure "Return To Mars." Also shown is inside front cover featuring Armstrong ad. -
**$15 $30 $50**

JAC-40

JAC-41

❑ **JAC-40. Gold Rim Pedometer,**
c. 1939. Similar to JAC-34 but outer rim has bright gold luster and the word "Official" appears above the name "Jack Armstrong." In addition the center dial is red on cream rather than red, black and white. Scarce. -
**$50 $100 $150**

❑ **JAC-41. Windfair W. J. A. C. Club Lead Proof,**
1930s. Unique. - **$1300**

JAC-42

❑ **JAC-42. Sentinel Junior Ace First Aid Kit Complete with Mailer ,**
1930s. Complete With Mailer and Contents -
**$100 $300 $400**
Tin Box Only - **$30 $60 $100**

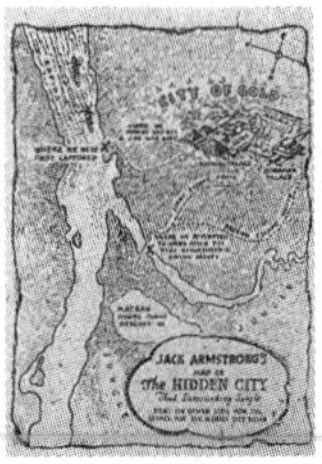

JAC-43

❑ **JAC-43. Map Of The Hidden City And Surrounding Jungle,**
1930s. 4x5-1/4" black on tan paper with perforated top edge. Reverse has story and lists several west coast radio stations. Probably the first Jack Armstrong overseas trip (to South America) because the reverse mentions he won a scholarship to make the trip. Rare. -
**$150 $300 $550**

JAC-44

❑ **JAC-44. Wheaties "Stampo" Game With Mailer Envelope,**
1930s. Two sheets to be cut and four leaflets for game devised by H. E. Harris Co., domestic and foreign postage stamps dealer of Boston. Uncut In Mailer - **$50 $100 $175**

JAC-45

JAC-46

❑ **JAC-45. Bicycle Safety Kit,**
c. 1930s. Booklet with generic light, battery, reflector and possibly more.
Complete - **$100 $200 $300**

❑ **JAC-46. Fan Card,**
1930s. "To My Friend" is imprinted followed by personalized inked first name of recipient above facsimile signature. - **$25 $60 $90**

JAC-47

JAC-48

❑ **JAC-47. "Lieutenant/Listening Squad" Brass Whistle Badge,**
1940. Scarce. Test premium, small quantity distributed. - **$150 $400 $850**

❑ **JAC-48. Lieutenant/Listening Squad Whistle Lead Proof,**
1940. Unique - **$1200**

JAC-49

JAC-50

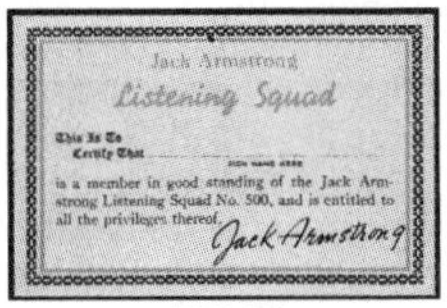


JAC-51

❑ **JAC-49. Betty's Luminous Gardenia Bracelet,**
1940. Rare. Glows in the dark. -
**$75 $150 $350**

❑ **JAC-50. Sky Ranger Plane,**
1940. - **$75 $200 $350**

❑ **JAC-51. Listening Squad Membership Card,**
1940. Rare. Test premium. - **$150 $300 $400**

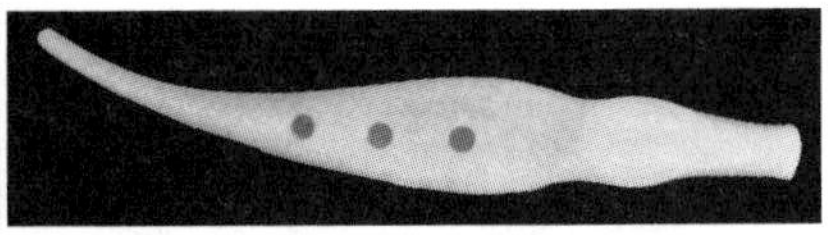

JAC-52

❑ **JAC-52. Crocodile Glow in the Dark Plastic Whistle,**
1940. Rare. Test premium with four known. -
**$1000 $3000 $4000**

JAC-53

JAC-54

❑ **JAC-53. "Captain/Listening Squad" Sample Brass Whistle Badge,**
1940. Rare. Test premium, even scarcer than Lieutenant version. - **$300 $1000 $1500**

❑ **JAC-54. Captain/Listening Squad Whistle Lead Proof,**
1940. Unique - **$1750**

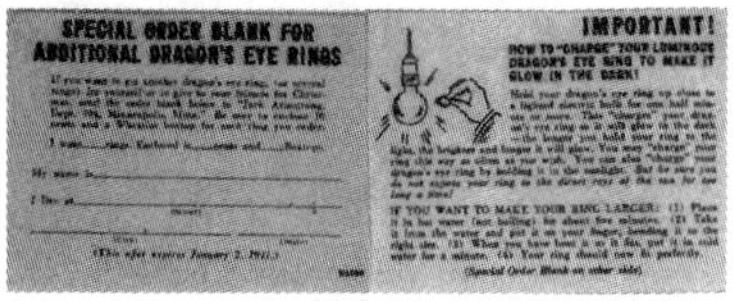


JAC-55

❑ **JAC-55. "Dragon's Eye Ring" Instructions/Order Blank Sheet,**
1940. Order coupon for additional rings expired January 2, 1941. - **$35 $75 $150**

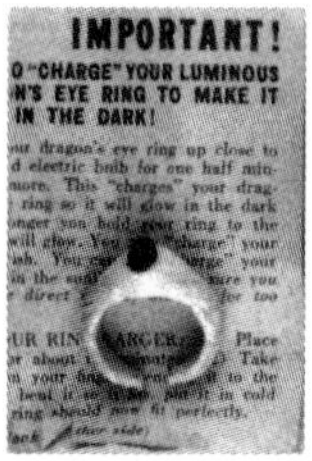


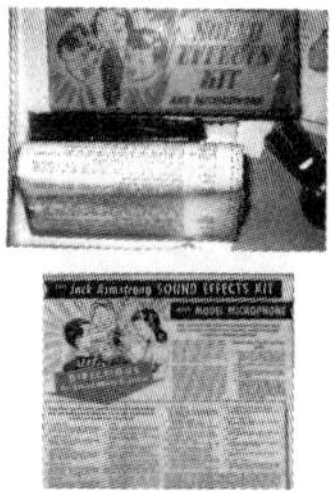


JAC-56 JAC-57

❑ **JAC-56. Dragon's Eye Ring With Instruction Paper,**
1940. White glow plastic ring topped by dark green stone. Yellow instruction sheet (shown folded) has expiration date of July 1, 1941.
Ring - **$150 $500 $1000**
Paper - **$35 $75 $150**

❑ **JAC-57. "Sound Effects Kit" and Instruction Sheet,**
1941. "Spy Hunt" mystery script utilizing sound effects.
Complete - **$150 $250 $400**

JAC-58 JAC-59

❑ **JAC-58. "Write A Fighter Corps" Kit,**
1942. Includes manual, stencils (6), star sticker sheets (6), insignia patches (6).
Near Mint In Mailer - **$250**
Manual Only - **$25 $50 $75**

❑ **JAC-59. Press Release Photo Picturing Wood Bombsight,**
1942. Mutual Broadcasting System. Pictures radio cast members Uncle Jim and Jack Armstrong holding Wheaties premium. - **$20 $50 $100**

JAC-60

❑ **JAC-60. Wheaties Secret Bombsight,**
1942. Wood/litho. paper bomb release holding three wooden bombs.
Bombsight Only - **$50 $100 $200**
Each Bomb - **$20 $30 $50**

JAC-61

❑ **JAC-61. "Secret Bomb Sight Instruction Manual",**
1942. Scarce. Includes cut-out ships for use with bomb sight. Uncut - **$60 $150 $300**

JAC-62 JAC-63

❑ **JAC-62. "Future Champions Of America" Club Manual,**
1943. - **$20 $40 $75**

❑ **JAC-63. "Future Champions Of America" Fabric Patch,**
1943. - **$5 $12 $20**

JAC-64

❑ **JAC-64. Model Planes 16x36" Paper Store Sign,**
1944. - **$100 $200 $350**

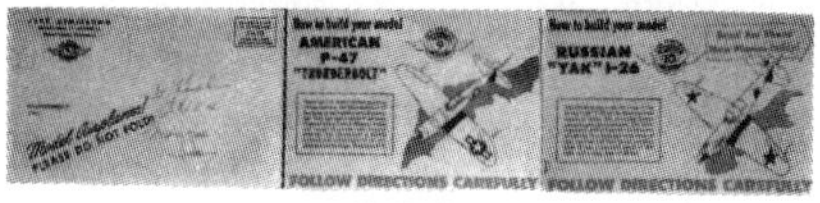


JAC-65

❑ **JAC-65. Wheaties Tru-Flite Warplane Paper Model Kit With Envelope,**
1944. Seven sets (A-G), each with two cut-out airplanes and instructions. Each Uncut Set In Mailer - **$25 $60 $90**

JAC-66 JAC-67

❑ **JAC-66. Tru-Flite News Vol. 1 #1 Newspaper,**
Sept. 1944. - **$15 $35 $75**

❑ **JAC-67. Tru-Flite News Vol. 1 #2 Newspaper,**
Oct. 1944. - **$15 $30 $65**

JAC-68

❑ **JAC-68. "Cub Pilot Corps" Contest Newspaper With I.D. Tag And Envelope,**
1945. Includes newspaper #3 and metal "G.I. Identification Tag". Near Mint In Mailer- **$250**
Newspaper - **$15 $35 $65**
Tag - **$25 $50 $100**

JAC-69

❑ **JAC-69. Jack Armstrong Sign,**
1945. Scarce. 17x22" sign promotes radio show and advertises joining Cub Pilots Corps. Talks about contest and how to get Piper Cub Pre-Flight Kit. Sponsored by Wheaties. - **$150 $300 $550**

JAC-70

❑ **JAC-70. Pre-Flight Training Kit,**
1945. Mailer holds "How To Fly" booklet, "Cub Pilot Corps. News" first issue newspaper, three-fold punch-out "Trainer" with short cardboard dowel "stick," and sheet of club logo transfers.
Complete Near Mint in Mailer - **$600**
Booklet - **$25 $50 $75**
Newspaper - **$15 $35 $60**
Punch-Out With Stick - **$100 $200 $300**
Transfers - **$10 $20 $30**

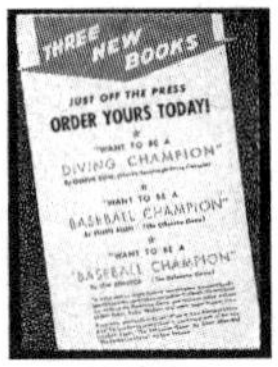


JAC-71

JAC-72

❑ **JAC-71. Announcement,**
1945. Announces 3 new books available for order from Library of Sports Books. -
**$10 $20 $30**

❑ **JAC-72. Book 1,**
1945. Wheaties. Library of Sports book premium. -
**$15 $30 $50**

JAC-73

JAC-74

❑ **JAC-73. Book 2 - Type 1 (Offense),**
1945. Wheaties. Library of Sports book premium. Features Bucky Walters, Bob Feller, Joe Cronin, the late Lou Gehrig and others. -
**$20 $45 $75**

❑ **JAC-74. Book 2 - Type 2 (Defense),**
1946. Wheaties. Library of Sports book premium. Cover and interior are different than 1945 edition. Also features Bucky Walters, Bob Feller, Joe Cronin, the late Lou Gehrig and others. -
**$20 $45 $75**

JAC-75

JAC-76

❑ **JAC-75. Book 3,**
1945. Wheaties. Library of Sports book premium. -
**$10 $20 $50**

❑ **JAC-76. Book 4,**
1945. Wheaties. Library of Sports book premium. -
**$10 $20 $50**

JAC-77

JAC-78

❑ **JAC-77. Book 5,**
1945. Wheaties. Library of Sports book premium. -
**$10 $20 $50**

❑ **JAC-78. Book 6,**
1945. Wheaties. Library of Sports book premium. -
**$10 $20 $50**

JAC-79

JAC-80

❑ **JAC-79. Book7,**
1945. Wheaties. Library of Sports book premium. -
**$10 $20 $50**

❑ **JAC-80. Book 8,**
1945. Wheaties. Library of Sports book premium. -
**$10 $20 $50**

JAC-81

JAC-82

❑ **JAC-81. Book 10,**
1945. Wheaties. Library of Sports book premium. -
**$10 $20 $50**

❑ **JAC-82. Book 11,**
1945. Wheaties. Library of Sports book premium. -
**$10 $20 $50**

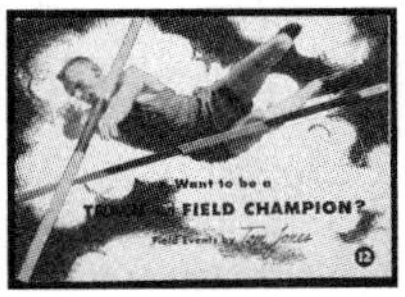


JAC-83

JAC-84

❑ **JAC-83. Book 12,**
1945. Wheaties. Library of Sports book premium. -
**$10 $20 $50**

❑ **JAC-84. Book14,**
1945. Wheaties. Library of Sports book premium. -
**$10 $20 $50**

JAC-85

JAC-86

❑ **JAC-85. Book 15,**
1945. Wheaties. Library of Sports book premium. Features Marty Marion, Johnny Mize, Mel Ott, Lou Boudreau and others. - **$20 $45 $75**

❑ **JAC-86. Book 16,**
1945. Wheaties. Library of Sports book premium. -
**$10 $20 $50**

JAC-87

❑ **JAC-87. Library Of Sports Mailer,**
1945. General Mills. - **$15 $25 $40**

JAC-88

❑ **JAC-88. "Parachute Ball" With Instructions And Mailer,**
1946. Aluminum ball with paper parachute.
Near Mint Boxed - **$250**
Ball And Parachute Only - **$35 $75 $150**

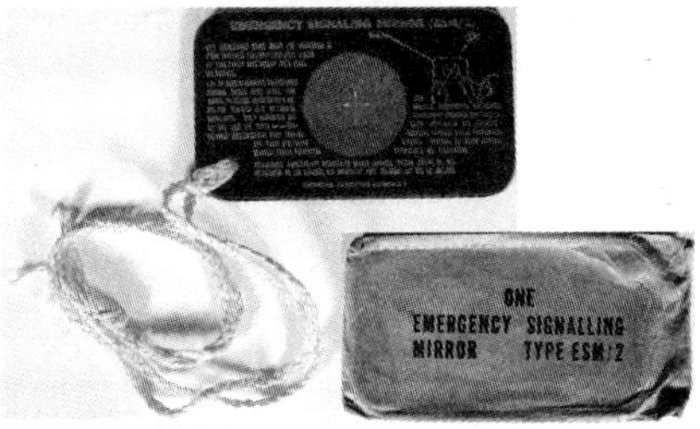


JAC-89 (Mailer)

❑ **JAC-89. Navy Emergency Signaling Mirror,**
1947. General Mills Premium. With braided cord. Obtained for 25¢ and 1 box top. - **$75 $125 $200**

JAC-90

❑ **JAC-90. Press Book for Movie Serial,**
1947. - **$50 $100 $125**

JAC-91 JAC-92

❑ **JAC-91. Jack Armstrong #1 Comic,**
1947. Odd size. - **$43 $129 $450**

❑ **JAC-92. "Explorer's Sun Watch" With Glow-In-Dark Dial,**
1948. Version without "Frank Buck" name with insert compass and movable pointer. Also offered by "Rocky" Lane, sponsored by Carnation Malted Milk, in 1951. - **$20 $30 $50**

JAC-93 JAC-94

❑ **JAC-93. Armstrong & Betty Fairfield Photo Cards,**
c. 1940s. Each - **$20 $40 $75**

❑ **JAC-94. Pictorial Pedometer,**
1940s. Metal with lt. green rim picturing six golfers. - **$50 $100 $200**

JAC-95

❑ **JAC-95. Record,**
1973. Wheaties. Volume One with sleeve. - **$15 $25 $50**

## Jack Benny

**Jack Benny (1894-1974) started in show business at the age of eight as a combination usher and violinist in a theater in Waukegan, Illinois. Thirty years later, when his program debuted on radio, he was a major star of stage and vaudeville. For 23 years on radio (1932-1955) and for 15 years on television (1950-1965) Benny was a Sunday night comic institution. His long-running feud with Fred Allen, his penny-pinching, his blue eyes, his ancient Maxwell car, his vault in the basement, his violin, his age--always 39--became part of the country's pop culture. Also featured over the years were his wife Mary Livingston, Rochester the valet, Don Wilson, Dennis Day, Phil Harris, Mel Blanc, and a host of others. Long-term radio sponsors were Jell-O (1934-1942) and Lucky Strike cigarettes (1944-1955); others included Canada Dry ginger ale (1932-1933), Chevrolet (1933-1934), General Tire (1934), and Grape-Nuts Flakes (1942-1944). Benny also appeared on numerous other television shows and made a number of movies.**

JBE-1 JBE-2

❑ **JBE-1. Fan Photo,**
c. 1934. Jell-O. - **$5 $12 $25**

❑ **JBE-2. Jell-O Recipe Book,**
1937. Inside covers have Jack Benny and Mary Livingston comic strips. - **$10 $20 $35**

JBE-3

JBE-4

❑ **JBE-3. Photo,**
1937. Philadelphia Record newspaper premium. - **$8 $15 $25**

❑ **JBE-4. "Benny Buck" Movie Theater Play Money,**
1939. Local theaters. For film "Buck Benny Rides Again" picturing supporting stars Ellen Drew and Andy Devine on back. - **$10 $20 $30**

JBE-5 JBE-6

❑ **JBE-5. Dixie Ice Cream Picture,**
1930s. - **$10 $20 $30**

❑ **JBE-6. "Grape-Nuts Flakes" Endorsement Box,** c. 1942. Back panel pictures him with balloon statement "Take It From Benny They're Better Than Any!" - **$30 $60 $120**

JBE-7

❑ **JBE-7. Radio Show Program,**
c. 1944. Lucky Strike cigarettes. - **$20 $40 $60**

JBE-8

❑ **JBE-8. "The Jack Benny Album" Record Set,**
1947. Set #2 from a numbered series of seven different featuring radio programs on the Top Ten Records label. Has four 78 rpm records, each featuring actual radio broadcast. - **$20 $50 $75**

JBE-9 JBE-10 JBE-11

❑ **JBE-9. "Rochester" Fan Photo,**
c. 1940s. Store item, probable sample from dime store picture frame. Pictured is Jack Benny's long-time valet on radio show, played by Eddie Anderson. - **$10 $20 $30**

❑ **JBE-10. "Friars Luncheon/Jack Benny" Gold Luster Metal Money Clip,**
c. 1950s. Dinner event souvenir. Raised design of his violin. - **$15 $25 $45**

❑ **JBE-11. Plaster Statue,**
c. 1979. Store item by Esco Products. 16-1/2" tall from series of personality statues. - **$20 $40 $60**

## The Jack Pearl Show

**A veteran comic of vaudeville and burlesque, Jack Pearl (1895-1982) brought his dialect character Baron Munchausen to radio in 1932. When straight man Cliff Hall expressed doubts about one of the Baron's tall tales, the inevitable response, "Vas you dere, Sharlie?" brought down the house. Sponsors of *The Jack Pearl Show* included Chrysler (1932), Lucky Strike cigarettes (1932-1933), Royal gelatin (1934), Frigidaire (1935), and Raleigh and Kool cigarettes (1936-1937). Comeback attempts in 1942 and 1948 were not successful.**

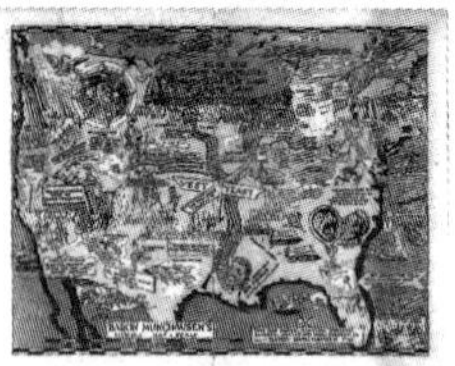

JPL-1

JPL-2

❑ **JPL-1. "Baron Munchausen" Map Of Radioland 19x24",**
c. 1932. Scarce. - **$50 $125 $250**

❑ **JPL-2. "Jack Pearl As Dectective Baron Munchausen" Book,**
1934. Store item published by Goldsmith Co. with endorsement of Juvenile Educators League. - **$10 $20 $40**

## Jack Westaway Undersea Adventure Club

**Membership in Jack Westaway's U.S.A.C. entitled young fans of the 1930s to wear the club badge (shaped like a diving helmet) and to a member's identification card that spelled out the club rules--including, whenever possible, eating a breakfast of Malt-O-Meal hot puffed wheat and puffed rice cereal.**

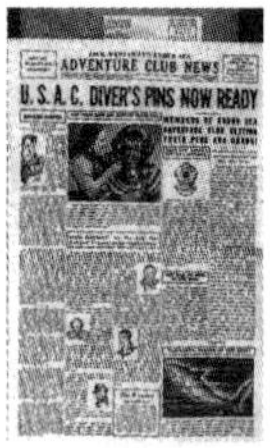


JWS-1

(FRONT)

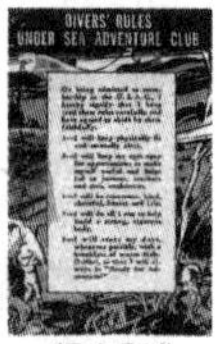


JWS-2

(BACK)

❑ **JWS-1. "Under Sea Adventure Club News" Vol. 1 #1 Newspaper With Envelope,**
1930s. Malt-O-Meal. Newspaper - **$15 $40 $75**
Mailer - **$3 $5 $10**

❑ **JWS-2. Club Membership Card,**
1930s. Malt-O-Meal. - **$20 $50 $100**

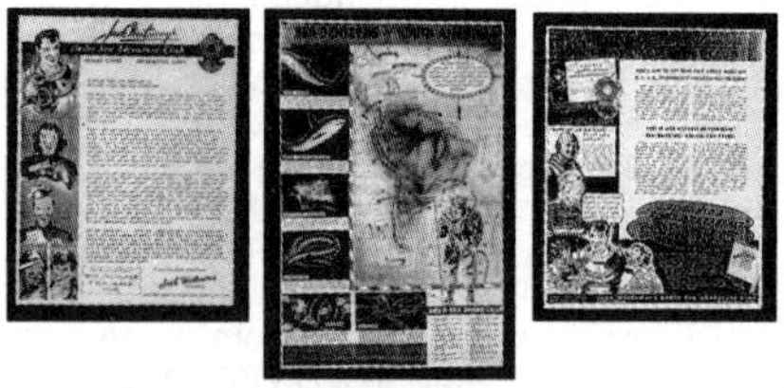

JWS-3

❑ **JWS-3. Member Recruitment Brochure,**
1930s. Malt-O-Meal. Cover features letter from Jack Westaway, center depicts "Sea Denizens of South America" with map and back cover tells how to order diver's badge and membership card. - **$35 $75 $150**

JWS-4

JWS-5

❑ **JWS-4. Shark's Tooth Story Letter,**
1930s. Malt-O-Meal. Front describes shark's tooth premium with coupon for a friend. Reverse recruits new member with coupon for diver's badge and membership card. - **$15 $25 $40**

❑ **JWS-5. "Jack Westaway Under The Sea/U.S.A.C." Brass Diver's Helmet Badge,**
1930s. - **$10 $25 $50**

## Jackie Robinson

**Born in Cairo, Georgia, John Roosevelt (Jackie) Robinson is well-remembered by baseball fans as the first black athlete admitted to Major League play in 1947. Fewer recall that he was previously a three-sport star at UCLA from 1939 to 1941, a US army lieutenant in WWII from 1942 to 1944, and a star shortstop and batter for the Kansas City Monarchs of the Negro League in 1945.**

**Robinson was selected personally as a Major League hopeful by Branch Rickey, venerable owner of the Brooklyn Dodgers. Rickey insisted that his candidate not only be a promising athlete but an individual of courage to withstand the expected insults and other abuse that might result from being the first black man in a white man's game. Robinson was signed to a 1946 contract with the Montreal farm club of the Dodgers and demonstrated his baseball ability through the batting championship that year for Montreal as well as the International League. Still, his Major League acceptance faced an obstacle–a 15-1 negative vote by club owners that was overridden by the single vote of Baseball Commissioner A.B. (Happy) Chandler.**

**Robinson thus became a Brooklyn Dodger in 1947, earning Rookie of the Year by talent alone, as well as the grudging admiration of players and fans alike. His subsequent career only added to his accomplishments as a fielder, batter, baserunner (National League's Most Valuable Player of 1949) and contributor to National League championships by Brooklyn in 1947, 1949, 1952, 1953, 1955 and 1956. Principally he is known as the pioneer who opened the Major Leagues to many other black players hitherto restricted to "their" leagues.**

**Robinson starred as himself in the 1950 film biography, The Jackie Robinson Story. After the 1956 season, at age 37, he was traded to the New York Giants but chose retirement instead. He was inducted into Baseball's Hall of Fame in 1962.**

**As a baseball retiree, Robinson continued as a highly-regarded spokesman for the NAACP and the YMCA in addition to business successes. Robinson suffered his second heart attack in 1972 at his Stamford, Connecticut home and died at age 53.**

JKR-1

❑ **JKR-1. Rookie of the Year Pinback,**
1947. - **$40 $100 $150**

JKR-2

❑ **JKR-2. "Slugger At The Bat" Record Album,**
1949. Two 78 rpm records featuring voices of Brooklyn Dodgers Pee Wee Reese and Jackie Robinson. Columbia Records. - **$35 $75 $150**

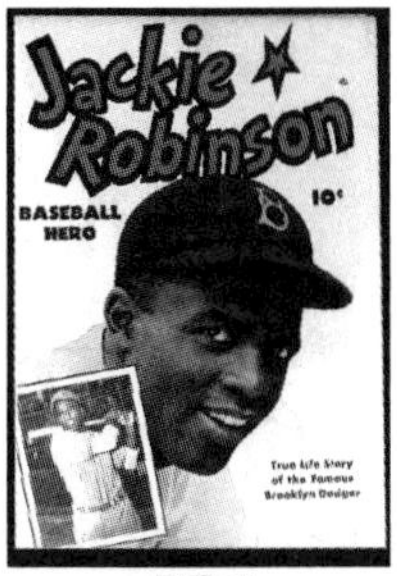


JKR-3

❑ **JKR-3. Jackie Robinson Baseball Hero Comic Book #1,**
1950. Fawcett Publications. Has photo cover and life story presented inside. Hard to find in high grade. - **$91 $273 $1000**

JKR-4

❑ **JKR-4. Metal Bust Bank,**
1950. Rare. Offered as a premium in Jackie Robinson comic books. - **$300 $600 $950**

JKR-5

❑ **JKR-5. Jointed Composition 13" Doll,**
c. 1950. Allied-Brand Doll Mfg. Co. Example shown missing Brooklyn Dodgers' uniform except for hat. Complete - **$300 $750 $2000**

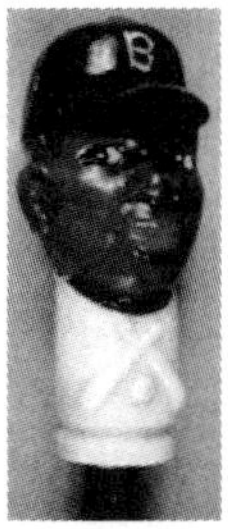

JKR-6

JKR-7

❑ **JKR-6. Cane With Plastic Handle,**
c. 1950. Store or vendor's item. 31-1/2" tall with 3-1/4" hard plastic hand grip inscribed "Jackie."
**$200 $350 $600**

❑ **JKR-7. Life Magazine,**
1950. May 8 issue subtitled "Star Ball Player Stars In A Movie." **$15 $30 $50**

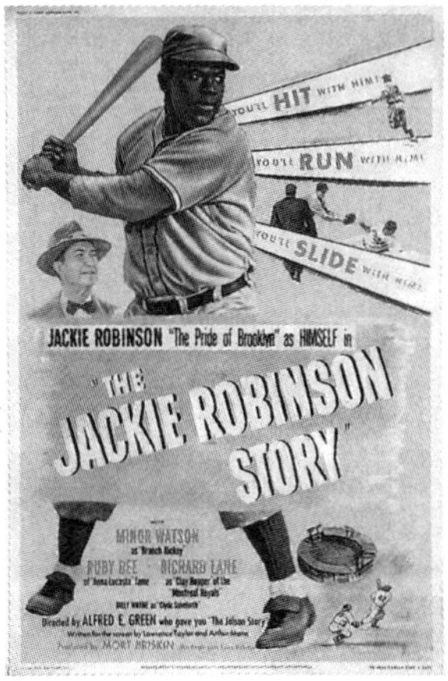


JKR-8

❑ **JKR-8. "The Jackie Robinson Story" Movie Poster,**
1950. Scarce. 41"x 61". One of the great baseball posters of the time. - **$1000 $1500 $2000**

JKR-9

❑ **JKR-9. Calendar Sample Photo,**
c. 1950. Full color 7-1/2x9-1/2" with 2x2" sticker upper right for unnamed publisher listing costs for using the photo on calendars. -
**$35 $65 $100**

JKR-10

❑ **JKR-10. Dime Bank,**
1950. Sold at stores and through ads in comic books. - **$150 $300 $500**

JKR-11

❑ **JKR-11. Quick Magazine,**
1952. October 6 issue subtitled "The World Series: Does The Best Team Win?" -
**$8 $15 $30**

JKR-12

❑ **JKR-12. Hoak-Robinson Topps Double Header Card,**
1955. From Topps Gum card set of folders designed with both player images sharing the same lower leg and foot artwork. -
**$25 $50 $125**

JKR-13

❏ **JKR-13. "Jackie Robinson" Figural Candy Container Cover,**
1950s. Plastic store item by Petitto Studio. - **$50 $125 $175**

JKR-14

JKR-15

❏ **JKR-14. "Team For Rockefeller" Endorsement Paper,**
c. 1962. 3-1/8" diecut to be made into a button.
Paper Unfinished - **$50 $100 $150**
Paper Finished Into Button - **$75 $125 $175**

❏ **JKR-15. "The Jackie Robinson Story" Hardback Book,**
1963. 254 page book with a 5 page photo gallery. - **$10 $20 $35**

JKR-16

❏ **JKR-16. Commemorative Coin,**
1997. $1 Silver and $5 gold coins, uncirculated and proofs. Official coins struck at the U.S. Mint to commemorate the 50th anniversary of Robinson's arrival in the Majors.
$1 Silver uncirculated - **$45**
$1 Silver proof - **$35**
$5 Gold uncirculated - **$975**
$5 Gold proof - **$375**

## James Bond

**English novelist Ian Fleming (1908-1964) created James Bond, the fabled Agent 007 of the British secret service, in a series of thrillers beginning with *Casino Royale* in 1953 and continuing until his death. But it was the film versions of the novels, starting with *Dr. No* in 1963, that made Bond an international hero. Sean Connery first embodied the cool but deadly Bond for millions of fans around the world. Licensed to kill, carrying a Baretta or Walther PPK, drinking his martinis shaken not stirred, and enjoying success with the ladies, Bond has defeated a string of unlikely villains in the most exotic of settings. Connery and Roger Moore each played Bond in seven films. Others who played the smooth commander: David Niven in the 1967 spoof (with Peter Sellers playing his replacement as James Bond and Woody Allen playing his evil nephew Jimmy), *Casino Royale*; George Lazenby in *On Her Majesty's Secret Service* (1969); Timothy Dalton in *The Living Daylights* (1987) and *Licence to Kill* (1989); and Pierce Brosnan in *Goldeneye* (1995), *Tomorrow Never Dies* (1997), and *The World is Not Enough* (1999).**

**Bond comic books appeared in the 1980s and 1990s, and the novels were adapted as a comic strip for the *London Daily Express* from 1957 into the 1960s. *James Bond Jr.*, a syndicated half-hour television cartoon, aired in 1991-1993. Merchandising of Bond items has been extensive, with most toys of the 1960s era produced by Gilbert and Corgi.**

JBD-1

JBD-2

❏ **JBD-1. "Agent 007" 3-1/2" Cello. Button,**
1964. Design includes image of woman painted gold from Goldfinger movie. - **$15 $30 $65**

❏ **JBD-2. Dell "James Bond 007" Magazine,**
1964. - **$20 $35 $70**

JBD-3

❏ **JBD-3. "Special Agent 007" Badge,**
1965. On card. - **$50 $75 $150**

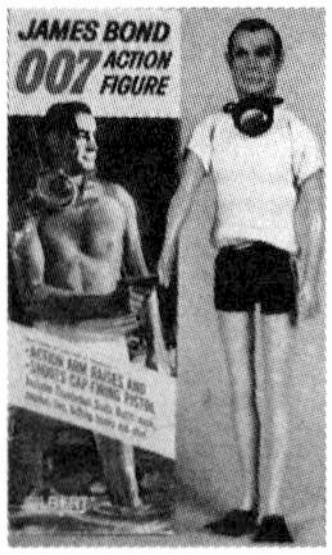


JBD-4

JBD-5

❏ **JBD-4. "James Bond Action Figure" Boxed,**
1965. Store item by Gilbert. 12-1/2" tall with complete accessories of shirt, shorts, fins, mask, snorkel, small metal cap-firing gun with holster in envelope plus instruction sheet.
Near Mint Boxed - **$250**
Complete Unboxed - **$50 $125 $175**

❏ **JBD-5. Odd Job Action Figure,**
1965. Store item by Gilbert. 10-1/4" tall in karate outfit plus black belt, elastic headband and with plastic derby. Near Mint Boxed - **$550**
Unboxed Complete - **$100 $200 $300**

JBD-6

❏ **JBD-6. Action Toys Display Sign,**
1965. Gilbert. 6x19-1/2" stiff cardboard sign originally held in a wire display rack. - **$75 $150 $250**

JBD-7

❏ **JBD-7. Gum Card Set,**
1965. Set of 66 issued by Philadelphia Chewing Gum Co. Set - **$50 $100 $175**

JBD-8

❏ **JBD-8. "James Bond's Aston-Martin" Toy Car With Box,**
1965. Store item by Gilbert Co. Battery operated metal replica including design feature that ejects passenger in addition to other mechanical features. Near Mint Boxed - **$600**
Loose - **$100 $250 $450**

(Original box)

JBD-9

(front view)

(side view)

❑ **JBD-9. "James Bond Secret Agent 007 Attaché Case,"**
1965. Store item by Multiple Products. Black plastic case holding gun and attachments, black flexible plastic dagger (frequently missing), code and decoder items, wallet with passport, business cards, play money. Case itself has trick-firing mechanism. Near Mint - **$700**
With original box, add **$500.**

JBD-10

❑ **JBD-10. "James Bond Thunderball" Gum Card Set,**
1966. Second set issued by Philadelpha Chewing Gum Co. Set of 66.
Set - **$60 $125 $200**

JBD-11

❑ **JBD-11."James Bond" Lunch Box,**
1966. Store item by Aladdin.
Box - **$125 $250 $450**
Bottle - **$85 $150 $250**

JBD-12

❑ **JBD-12. James Bond Spy Watch,**
1968. Made by Gilbert. Comes in display box with instructions.
Boxed - **$250**

JBD-13

JBD-14

JBD-15

❑ **JBD-13. "007 Coming Soon!" 3" Cello. Button,**
1960s. Probably worn by movie theater employees. - **$10 $25 $40**

❑ **JBD-14. "James Bond's Brew/007 Special Blend" 2-1/2" Cello. Button,**
1960s. For apparently unauthorized beverage. - **$8 $20 $35**

❑ **JBD-15. "Agent 0007" Bond-Inspired 3" Cello. Ad Button,**
1960s. "Wilton Vise Squad" issue picturing example bench vise. - **$10 $20 $35**

JBD-16

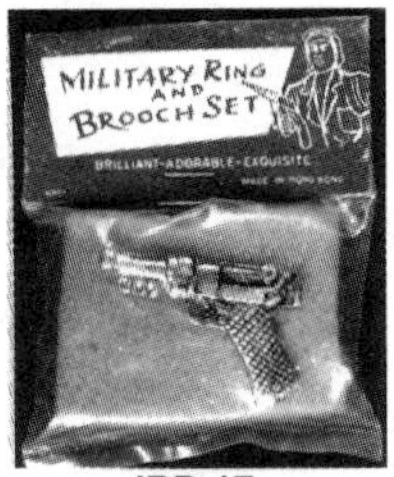


JBD-17

❑ **JBD-16. Sean Connery Fan Photo,**
1960s. - **$8 $15 $25**

❑ **JBD-17. "007" Replica Pistol Ring in Package,**
1960s. Store item, unauthorized. Gold luster or aluminum.
Packaged - **$10 $20 $30**
Loose - **$5 $15 $20**

JBD-18

JBD-19

JBD-20

❑ **JBD-18. James Bond Plastic Snow Dome,**
1960s. Store item. - **$50 $140 $225**

❑ **JBD-19. James Bond "Agent 007 Espionage" Litho. Button,**
1960s. Vending machine issue. - **$5 $10 $15**

❑ **JBD-20. James Bond "Goldfinger's Death Derby" Litho. Button,**
1960s. Vending machine issue. - **$5 $10 $15**

JBD-21

JBD-22

JBD-23

❑ **JBD-21. James Bond "Laser Beam/ Goldfinger's Ray Machine" Litho. Button,**
1960s. Vending machine issue. - **$3 $8 $12**

❑ **JBD-22. James Bond "Calling Agent 007" Litho. Button,**
1960s. Vending machine issue. - **$5 $10 $15**

❑ **JBD-23. James Bond "Agent 007" Plastic Ring,**
1960s. Vending machine issue. - **$10 $30 $50**

JBD-24

JBD-25

❑ **JBD-24. "007" Plastic Ring,**
1960s. Vending machine item depicting shield symbol. From set of five. Each - **$10 $20 $30**

❑ **JBD-25. "007" Plastic Ring,**
1960s. Vending machine item depicting face silhouette. From set of five. Each - **$10 $20 $30**

JBD-26

JBD-27

❑ **JBD-26. "007" Plastic Ring,**
1960s. Vending machine item picturing car. From set of five. Each - **$10 $20 $30**

❑ **JBD-27. "007" Plastic Flicker Ring,**
1960s. Vending machine issue from set of 12. Images are James Bond portrait and "007" numeral partially formed by image of pistol as the third numeral.
Each Silver Base - **$10 $22 $35**
Each Blue Base - **$5 $15 $25**

JBD-28

❑ **JBD-28. "Moonraker View-Master" Store Display,**
1979. 13-1/2x17" diecut. - **$20 $40 $60**

JBD-29

JBD-30

❑ **JBD-29. Movie Promotion Cello. English Buttons,**
1981. Eon Productions Ltd. For release of movie "For Your Eyes Only." Each - **$2 $4 $8**

❑ **JBD-30. "Michelin Dealers' 007 Sweepstakes" 3-1/2" Cello. Button,**
1985. Michelin tires. Art pictures Roger Moore as James Bond posed beside Michelin Man. - **$10 $25 $40**

JBD-31

JBD-32

❑ **JBD-31. James Bond Action Episode Game,**
1985. The Man With the Golden Gun. Boxed - **$50**

❑ **JBD-32. James Bond Action Episode Game,**
1985. You Only Live Twice. Boxed - **$50**

JBD-33

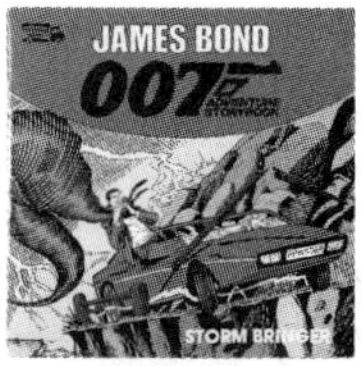


JBD-34

❑ **JBD-33. James Bond Adventure Storybook,**
1985. Blackclaw's Doomsday Plot. - **$5 $15 $25**

❑ **JBD-34. James Bond Adventure Storybook,**
1985. Storm Bringer. - **$5 $15 $25**

JBD-35

JBD-36

❑ **JBD-35. Movie Car Replica on Card,**
1998. Johnny Lightning series - For Your Eyes Only. - **$10**

❑ **JBD-36. Movie Car Replica on Card,**
1998. Johnny Lightning series - Goldeneye. - **$10**

JBD-37

JBD-38

❑ **JBD-37. Movie Car Replica on Card,**
1998. Johnny Lightning series - Goldfinger. - **$10**

❑ **JBD-38. Movie Car Replica on Card,**
1998. Johnny Lightning series - On Her Majesty's Secret Service. - **$10**

JBD-39

JBD-40

❑ **JBD-39. Movie Car Replica on Card,**
1998. Johnny Lightning series - The Living Daylights. - **$10**

❑ **JBD-40. Movie Car Replica on Card,**
1998. Johnny Lightning series - The Spy Who Loved Me. - **$10**

JBD-41

JBD-42

❑ **JBD-41. Movie Car Replica on Card,**
1998. Johnny Lightning series - Ford Mustang from Thunderball. - **$7**

❑ **JBD-42. Movie Car Replica on Card,**
1998. Johnny Lightning series - Aston Martin from Goldfinger. - **$7**

## James Dean

**The untimely and tragic death of this young actor (1931-1955) evoked an international outpouring of anguish and disbelief by his fandom. His brief acting career epitomized the moody, brooding, casual restlessness of young adulthood. Due to this brevity, related memorabilia from the 1950s is scarce. A few buttons were produced before his death but the most frequently encountered 1950s item is a memorial brass medalet offered by *Modern Screen Magazine* in October 1956.**

JDN-1

JDN-2

❑ **JDN-1. "James Dean's" Denim Jeans,**
1955. Store item by J.S.B. Adult sized, likened to those worn in his movies Rebel Without a Cause, East of Eden, Giant. With Tag - **$40 $75 $125**

❑ **JDN-2. Cello. 3-1/2" Photo Button,**
1955. Store item. Issued before his death. - **$15 $35 $75**

JDN-3

❑ **JDN-3. Premium Color Photo,**
1955. 8 x 10" color photo printed on unstable thin paper. Promotes "Rebel Without a Cause" movie. These were passed out at drive-in theaters. - **$10 $25 $50**

JDN-4

❑ **JDN-4. Die for First Promo Button,**
1955. - **$100**

JDN-5

JDN-6

JDN-7

❑ **JDN-5. Cello. 3-1/2" Button,**
c. 1955. Store item. Issued before his death. - **$15 $35 $75**

❑ **JDN-6. Color Portrait 2-1/2" Cello. Button,**
c. 1955. Photo with facsimile signature. - **$20 $40 $85**

❑ **JDN-7. "James Dean" Hanky,**
c. 1955. Store item totally unmarked but seems to be of the 1955-1956 era. 11x11-1/2" sheer fabric with color portrait of him in red shirt against blue background. - **$25 $60 $100**

JDN-8

❑ **JDN-8. Commemorative Brass Necklace Medallion,**
c. 1955. "Modern Screen" magazine. Inscription "In Memory Of James Dean 1931-1955". - **$5 $15 $30**

JDN-9

❑ **JDN-9. "This Then Is Texas" Song Sheet,**
1956. From "Giant" movie, Dean's last. - **$20 $35 $45**

JDN-10

JDN-11

❑ **JDN-10. Commemorative China Plate,**
c. 1956. Store item. - **$30 $50 $85**

❑ **JDN-11. "I, James Dean" Paperback Biography,**
1957. Store item published by Popular Library. First published biography after his death. - **$8 $15 $30**

JDN-12

❑ **JDN-12. James Dean And Tony Perkins Magazine Cut-Out Record,**
1957. Record was bound into an issue of "Hear, The Voice Of Hollywood" magazine. Label is inscribed "Rainbo Records." 7" diameter stiff cardboard. Gordon Gold archives.
Magazine Complete - **$25 $50 $100**
Record Only - **$10 $20 $35**

(Box)

(Certificate Booklet)

JDN-13

❑ **JDN-13. James Dean Doll with Tag in Box,**
1985. By Elegante Dolls. 17 3/4" tall doll has uncanny likeness of Dean. Hard to find.
Boxed - **$450**

JDN-14

**JDN-14. "Rebel Without a Cause" Movie Alarm Clock,**
1991. Turner product. - **$10 $25 $45**

JDN-15

JDN-16

**JDN-15. 100 Piece Photo Puzzle,**
1995. 8x10". Boxed - **$3 $6 $12**

**JDN-16. James Dean Ornament,**
1990s. Carlton ornament in box. - **$18**

JDN-17

**JDN-17. "1949 Mercury Coupe" Model Car,**
2000. Limited edition die-cast metal car. - **$40**

# Jimmie Allen

*The Air Adventures of Jimmie Allen* thrilled its young radio listeners from 1933 to 1943. Jimmie was a 16-year-old messenger at the Kansas City airport, taught to fly by veteran pilot Speed Robertson. Together they courted danger, searched for lost treasure, and competed in international air races. The series was syndicated, sponsored initially by the Skelly Oil company in the Midwest, then by Richfield Oil on the West Coast and by bakeries and many other companies eager to share in the show's large audience.

Premiums were an integral part of the program from the beginning, starting with a free jigsaw puzzle offer during the third week of broadcasting and available only at Skelly gas stations. The *Jimmie Allen Flying Club* and the *Weather-Bird Flying Club* attracted thousands of applicants, all of whom received membership cards, wings, emblems, patches, flight charts, and personal letters from Jimmie. Members could pick up weekly flying lessons and model airplane kits at their local gas stations.

Other promotional items followed in great profusion: photo albums, stamp albums, road maps, whistles, ID bracelets, model planes, Flying Cadet wings. Since sponsors were free to design and mark their own premiums, many varieties were produced. Jimmie Allen Air Races were held throughout the Midwest, with thousands of fans gathering to watch the young contestants piloting their model planes.

Paramount Pictures released a Jimmie Allen movie, *The Sky Parade*, in 1936. Transcriptions of the original broadcasts were re-released in 1942-1943.

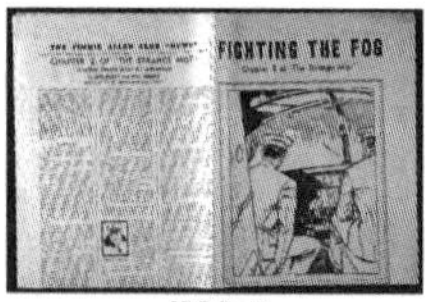

JMA-1

JMA-2

❑ **JMA-1. Club News Chapter 2 - "The Strange Mist",**
May 1933. Richfield Oil Co. Radio premium. At least six in series. Each - **$20 $40 $75**

❑ **JMA-2. Air Races Sterling Silver Wings Badge,**
1934. Skelly. 1-1/2" long marked on reverse "Sterling." Awarded only to participants. - **$150 $250 $400**

JMA-3

❑ **JMA-3. "She Sure Is A Honey-" Premium Photo,**
c. 1934. Richfield Oil Company of California. Shows Jimmie flying "Monsoon 800." - **$15 $30 $50**

JMA-4

❑ **JMA-4. Membership Application Postcard,**
1934. Richfield Oil Co. - **$10 $20 $35**

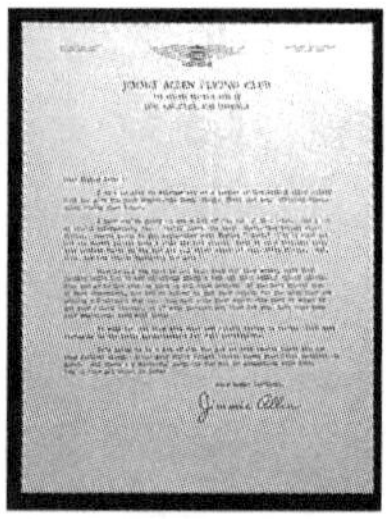
JMA-5

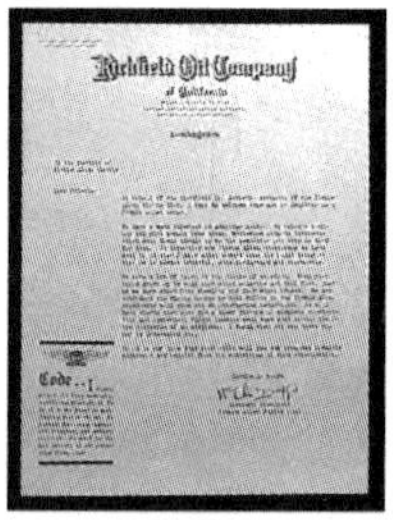

JMA-6

❑ **JMA-5. New Member Welcome Letter,**
c. 1934. Richfield Oil Co. Came with membership card, flight chart and wings. - **$10 $20 $40**

❑ **JMA-6. Welcome Letter To New Member's Parents,**
c. 1934. Richfield Oil Company of California. 8-1/2x11" black and white letter to new cadet's parents. - **$15 $30 $50**

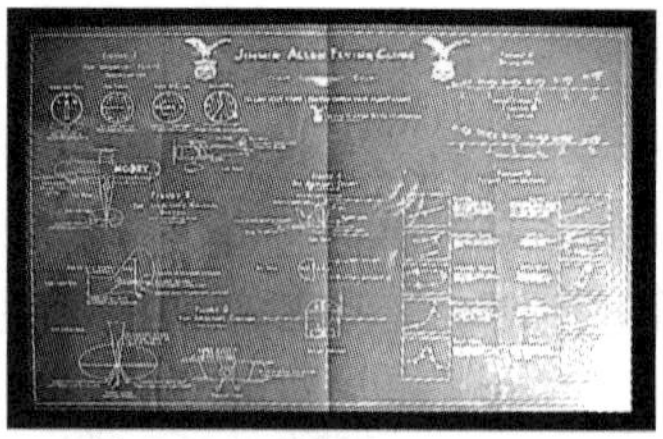

JMA-7

❑ **JMA-7. Flight Chart,**
c. 1934. Richfield Oil Co. 11x17" folder printed on one side white on blue like a blueprint. Used to follow the lessons heard over radio. - **$15 $30 $50**

JMA-8

❑ **JMA-8. Diecut Window Sticker,**
c. 1934. Richfield Oil Co. 2-1/2x5-1/2". - **$35 $75 $125**

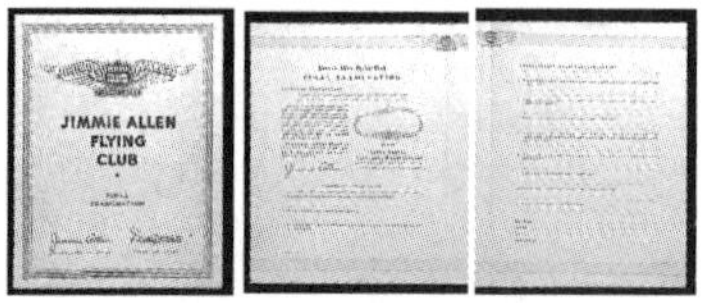

JMA-9

❑ **JMA-9. "Final Examination" Folder,**
1934. Richfield Oil Co. 8-1/2x11" folder in white, blue and yellow picturing "Pilot's Wristlet" to be sent when question and answer form is received by Jimmie Allen. - **$15 $30 $60**

JMA-10

❑ **JMA-10. "Map Of Countries Visited In 'Air Adventures Of Jimmie Allen ' 11x25",**
1934. Skelly Oil Co. - **$50 $175 $300**

JMA-11

❑ **JMA-11. Skelly Oil Holiday Newsletter,**
1934. - **$20 $40 $60**

JMA-12

JMA-13

❑ **JMA-12. "Flight Lesson" Sheet,**
1934. Various sponsors. Five lessons in set. Each - **$5 $10 $20**

❑ **JMA-13. "Merry Christmas" Photo,**
1934. Skelly Oil Co. - **$10 $20 $35**

JMA-14

❑ **JMA-14. "B-A Flying Cadet" Canadian Flight Wings Pin,**
c. 1934. British-American Oil. Embossed Brass. - **$25 $65 $125**

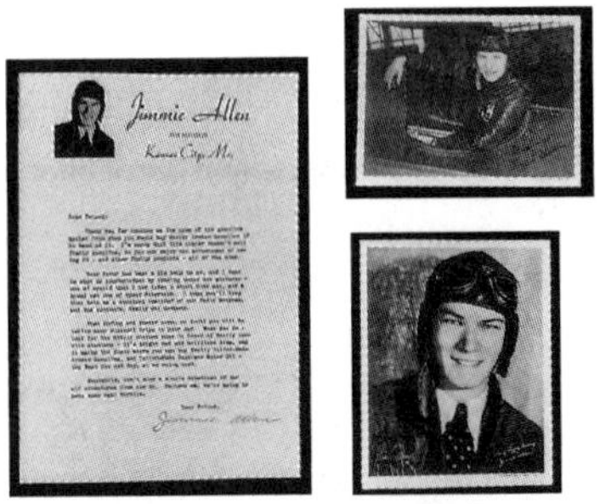


JMA-15

❑ **JMA-15. Radio Listener Letter With Photos,**
c. 1934. Skelly Oil Co. Letter thanks listener for name of gasoline dealer not handling Skelly products. Photos are Allen and Speed Robertson. Letter - **$15 $30 $50**
Each Photo - **$10 $20 $40**

JMA-16

JMA-17

❑ **JMA-16. Richfield Flight Wings,**
1934. - **$15 $25 $50**

❑ **JMA-17. Richfield I.D. Bracelet,**
1934. - **$15 $50 $75**

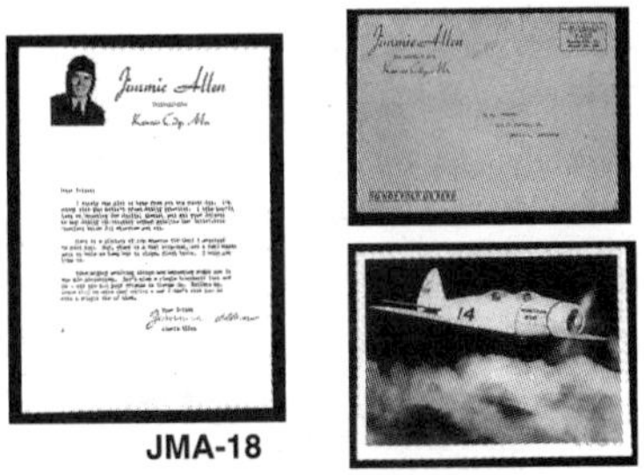


JMA-18

❑ **JMA-18. Radio Listener Letter With Picture And Mailer,**
c. 1934. Skelly Oil Co. Letter urges trial of Skelly products, picture is "Monsoon 800" aircraft.
Near Mint In Mailer - **$150**
Letter Only - **$15 $30 $60**
Picture Only - **$15 $30 $60**

JMA-19

JMA-20

❑ **JMA-19. "What's On The Air" Pacific Coast Schedule Book,**
1934. Richfield Oil Co. - **$15 $30 $60**

❑ **JMA-20. Skelly "Jimmie Allen Flying Cadet" Brass Airplane Badge,**
1934. - **$15 $30 $50**

JMA-21

❑ **JMA-21. Skelly Club Membership Card,**
c. 1934. - **$10 $30 $60**

JMA-22

JMA-23

❑ **JMA-22. Skelly "Jimmie Allen Flying Cadet" Bronze Luster Brass Wings Badge,**
c. 1934. - **$15 $25 $40**

❑ **JMA-23. "Jimmie Allen/Skelly Flying Cadet" Brass Wings Badge,**
c. 1934. - **$35 $75 $120**

JMA-24

JMA-25

❑ **JMA-24. "Jimmie Allen Cadet/Fairmont Air Corps" Brass Wings Badge,**
c. 1934. - **$60 $150 $225**

❑ **JMA-25. "B-A Flying Cadet" Canadian Flight Wings,**
c. 1934. British-American Oil. Red on silvered metal. - **$50 $100 $170**

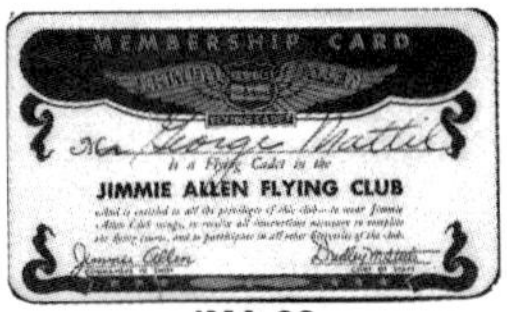


JMA-26

❑ **JMA-26. Membership Card,**
c. 1934. Richfield Oil Co. - **$15 $30 $60**

JMA-27

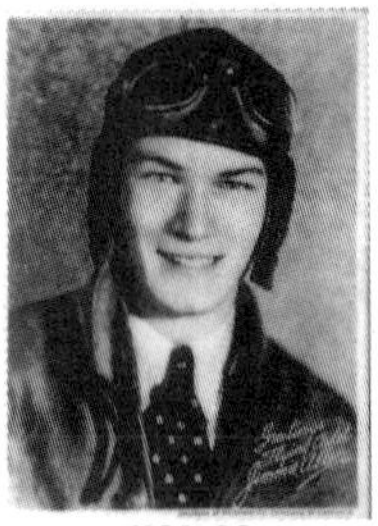

JMA-28

❑ **JMA-27. Club Creed Certificate,**
c. 1934. Richfield Oil. - **$15 $40 $60**

❑ **JMA-28. Photo,**
c. 1934. Richfield Oil. - **$10 $20 $35**

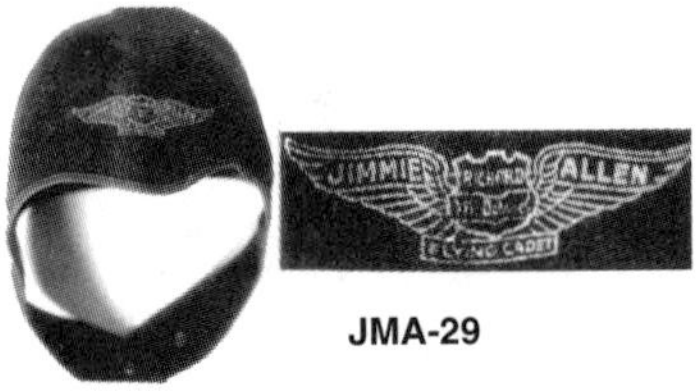


JMA-29

❑ **JMA-29. Felt Fabric Aviator Cap,**
c. 1934. Scarce. Richfield Oil. - **$35 $75 $150**

JMA-30

❑ **JMA-30. Postcard,**
c. 1934. Log Cabin Bread. - **$10 $20 $50**

JMA-31

JMA-32

❑ **JMA-31. "Jimmie Allen Flying Cadet/Log Cabin" Brass Wings Badge,**
c. 1934. Log Cabin Syrup. - **$20 $50 $80**

❑ **JMA-32. "Speed Robertson" Photo Card,**
c. 1934. Hi-Speed Gasoline of Hickok Oil Corp. Pictured is comrade aviator of Jimmie Allen. - **$12 $20 $35**

JMA-33

❑ **JMA-33. Richfield Oil Travel Map,**
1935. Paper folder that opens to 18x24" map of California with panel ad for Jimmie Allen radio show. - **$10 $35 $70**

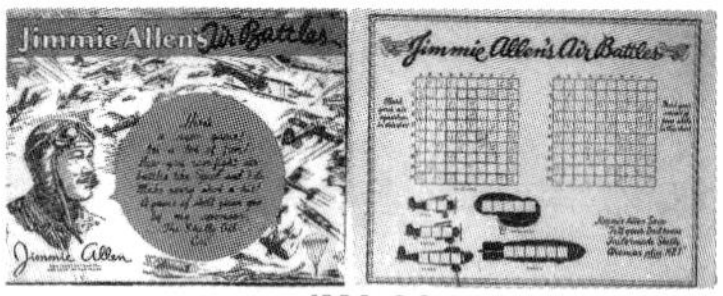

JMA-34

❑ **JMA-34. Skelly "Jimmie Allen's Air Battles" Booklet,**
1935. Contents include game pages plus comic strips. - **$20 $50 $85**

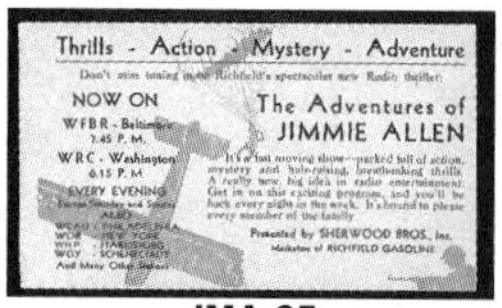

JMA-35

JMA-36

❑ **JMA-35. Postcard,**
1935. Richfield Oil Co. Radio premium. - **$15 $30 $50**

❑ **JMA-36. Road Map,**
1935. Skelly Oil Co. Map of U.S. and Kansas. - **$20 $40 $60**

JMA-37

JMA-38

❑ **JMA-37. "Jimmie Allen Air Races" Sterling Silver Bracelet With Silvered Brass Chain,**
c. 1935. Skelly Oil. - **$60 $150 $225**

❑ **JMA-38. "Jimmie Allen/Pilot" Silvered Brass Bracelet,**
c. 1935. Skelly Oil. - **$60 $150 $225**

JMA-39

JMA-40

❑ **JMA-39. "Jimmie Allen Air Races" Silvered Brass Bracelet,**
1935. Skelly Oil. - **$75 $200 $325**

❑ **JMA-40. Kansas City Air Races Enameled Bracelet,**
1935. Rare. Skelly Oil. - **$125 $375 $550**

JMA-41

❑ **JMA-41. "Jimmie Allen Club News,"**
1935. Sponsored by Richfield Oil. Numbered set of 11 with serialized "The Strange Mist" story. Each - **$10 $20 $30**

JMA-42

❑ **JMA-42. Browntone Photos,**
1936. Skelly Oil Co. Numbered set of six. Each - **$5 $10 $15**

JMA-43

JMA-44

❑ **JMA-43. Club Card,**
1936. Scarce. Skelly Oil Co. Membership card with pledge on back. Blue trim, plane on left. - **$15 $30 $50**

❑ **JMA-44. "Jimmie Allen in the Air Mail Robbery" Big Little Book #1143,**
1936. - **$15 $30 $60**

JMA-45

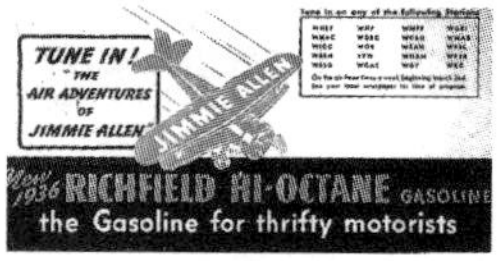

JMA-46

❑ **JMA-45. "Flying Club Stamp Album",**
1936. Richfield Oil Co.
Near Mint With Stamps - **$150**
Album Only - **$20 $50 $75**

❑ **JMA-46. Richfield Gasoline Cardboard Ink Blotter,**
1936. - **$12 $30 $50**

JMA-47

JMA-48

❑ **JMA-47. "Official Jimmie Allen Secret Signal" Brass Whistle,**
1936. - **$50 $85 $150**

❑ **JMA-48. "Jimmie Allen Air Races" Silvered Brass Pin,**
1936. Skelly Oil. - **$75 $175 $300**

JMA-49

JMA-50

❑ **JMA-49. Movie Cast Photo,**
1936. For movie "The Sky Parade" picturing Jimmie Allen, Grant Withers, Katherine DeMille, Kent Taylor. - **$15 $25 $50**

❑ **JMA-50. "Jimmie Allen In The Sky Parade" Movie Herald,**
1936. 6x9" issued by Paramount. - **$15 $35 $75**

JMA-51

❑ **JMA-51. "Jimmie Allen Flying Club" Letter/Membership Card,**
1937. Issued by Royal Baking Powder.
Mailer - **$3 $6 $10**
Card - **$15 $25 $50**
Letter - **$10 $20 $30**

JMA-52

❑ **JMA-52. "Flying B-A Cadet" Certificate,**
1939. British-American Oil. Canadian certificate received with Squadron Commander Badge. - **$25 $60 $125**

JMA-53

JMA-54

❑ **JMA-53. "Squadron Commander" Canadian Brass Badge,**
1939. British-American Oil. - **$75 $200 $325**

❑ **JMA-54. "Flying Cadet Be-Square Air Corps" Felt Patch,**
1930s. Sponsor unknown. 3" diameter white felt with design in blue. - **$100 $200 $300**

JMA-55

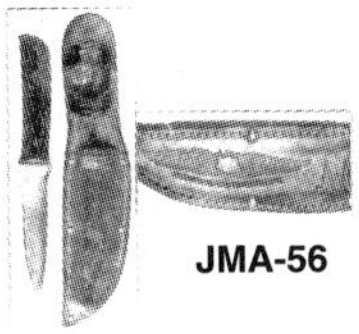

JMA-56

JMA-57

❑ **JMA-55. "Jimmie Allen" Bone Handle Pocketknife,**
1930s. Sponsor unknown. Grip has silvered metal club symbol. - **$50 $100 $200**

❑ **JMA-56. "Official Outing Knife" With Sheath,**
1930s. Sponsor unknown. - **$100 $200 $300**

❑ **JMA-57. "Jimmie Allen Model Builder Merit Award" Brass Badge,**
1930s. Scarce. Richfield Oil. Also designated "Richfield Hi-Octane Flying Cadet". - **$100 $200 $325**

JMA-58

JMA-59

❑ **JMA-58. Club Membership Card,**
1930s. Different text than previous item. - **$10 $25 $50**

❑ **JMA-59. Flying Club Membership Card,**
1930s. Skelly Oil Co. Blue trim on white with airplanes circling border. - **$25 $50 $75**

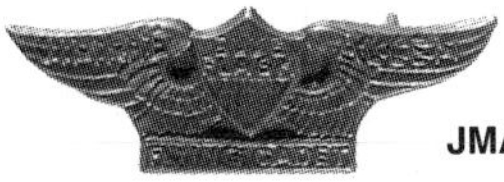

JMA-60

JMA-61

❑ **JMA-60. Blue Flash Brass Wings Badge,**
1930s. Blue Flash. Says "Jimmie Allen Flying Cadet". - **$35 $75 $120**

❑ **JMA-61. Certified Flying Cadet Brass Wings Badge,**
1930s. - **$35 $75 $120**

JMA-62

JMA-63

❑ **JMA-62. Cleo Cola Brass Wings Badge,**
1930s. Cleo Cola. - **$20 $45 $70**

❑ **JMA-63. Colonial Brass Wings Badge,**
1930s. Colonial. - **$15 $35 $55**

JMA-64

JMA-65

❑ **JMA-64. Duplex Brass Wings Badge,**
1930s. Duplex. - **$15 $35 $55**

❑ **JMA-65. Fair-Maid Brass Wings Badge,**
1930s. Fair-Maid. - **$20 $45 $85**

JMA-66

JMA-67

❑ **JMA-66. Rain-Bo Brass Wings Badge,**
1930s. Rain-Bo. - **$20 $50 $90**

❑ **JMA-67. Richfield Brass Wings Badge,**
1930s. Richfield. - **$15 $35 $50**

JMA-68

JMA-69

❑ **JMA-68. Richfield Silver Wings Badge,**
1930s. Richfield. - **$40 $80 $130**

❑ **JMA-69. Sawyer Brass Wings Badge,**
1930s. Sawyer. - **$40 $80 $130**

JMA-70

JMA-71

❑ **JMA-70. Skelly Gold Wings Badge,**
1930s. Skelly Oil. - **$35 $75 $120**

❑ **JMA-71. Town Talk Bread Brass Wings Badge,**
1930s. Town Talk Bread. - **$40 $80 $130**

JMA-72

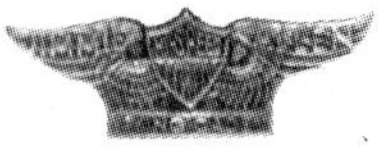

JMA-73

❑ **JMA-72. Weatherbird Brass Wings Badge,**
1930s. Weatherbird Shoes. - **$20 $45 $75**

❑ **JMA-73. "Jimmie Allen Hi-Speed Flying Cadet" Brass Wings Badge,**
1930s. - **$15 $30 $50**

JMA-74

JMA-75

❑ **JMA-74. Die-Cut Window Sticker,**
1930s. Hi-Speed Gasoline. - **$35 $75 $125**

❑ **JMA-75. Hi-Speed Photo Card,**
1930s. Hickok Oil Co. - **$10 $20 $35**

JMA-76

❑ **JMA-76. "Certificate In Aviation",**
1930s. Republic (Oil) Air Corps. Awarded for completion of advanced aviation course. - **$25 $60 $125**

JMA-77

❑ **JMA-77. "Jimmie Allen/Republic Pilot" Brass Wings Badge,**
1930s. - **$30 $60 $125**

JMA-78

JMA-79

❑ **JMA-78. Cloth "Mail Pouch",**
1930s. Cleo Cola. For saving bottle caps. - **$35 $75 $135**

❑ **JMA-79. Club Membership Card,**
1930s. Hi-Speed Gasoline. - **$10 $25 $50**

JMA-80

❑ **JMA-80. Flying Club Aviation Lesson Newspapers,**
1930s. Republic Motor Oil. Map inside lesson #1. Each - **$10 $20 $40**

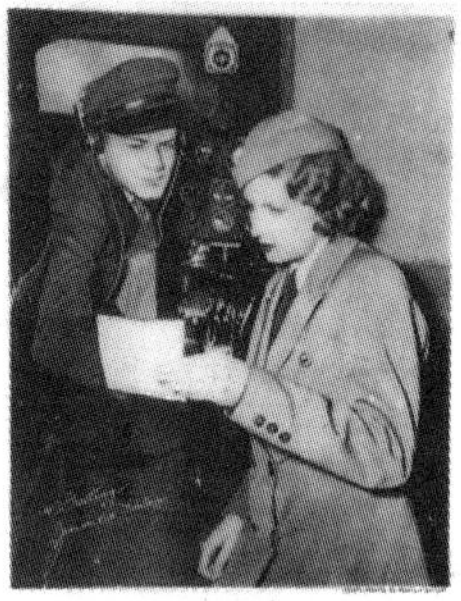

JMA-81

❑ **JMA-81. Jimmie & Barbara Photo,**
1930s. Skelly Oil. - **$10 $20 $35**

JMA-82

❑ **JMA-82. Skelly Oil Club Album,**
1930s. Booklet of photo pages.
Album Only - **$20 $45 $85**
Each Photo Page - **$5 $10 $15**

JMA-83

❑ **JMA-83. "Yellow Jacket" Model Airplane Construction Kit,**
1930s. Skelly Oil. Balsa parts with instructions and insignia cut-outs. - **$75 $125 $175**

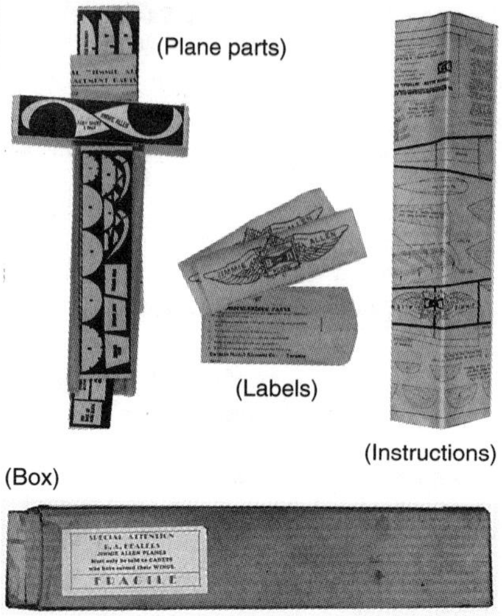


JMA-84

❑ **JMA-84. Official "Contest" Model Kit,**
1930s. B-A plane. Scarce. - **$75 $125 $175**

JMA-85

JMA-86

❑ **JMA-85. "Thunderbolt" Model Airplane Construction Kit,**
1930s. Skelly Oil. Balsa parts with instruction sheet and insignia cut-outs. - **$75 $125 $175**

❑ **JMA-86. "J.A. Air Cadets" Cello. Button,**
1930s. Canadian issue. - **$60 $125 $250**

JMA-87

JMA-88

❑ **JMA-87. Flying Club Membership Card,**
1930s. Skelly Oil Co. Brown trim on white. Propeller at top & bottom on front. - **$25 $50 $75**

❑ **JMA-88. Coin,**
1930s. Bond Bread premium. - **$50 $100 $150**

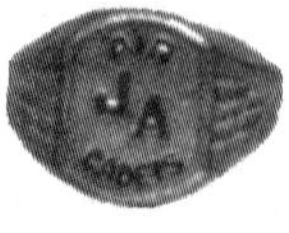


JMA-89

JMA-90

❑ **JMA-89. "J.A. Air Cadets" Brass Ring,**
1930s. Rare. Canadian issue. - **$150 $350 $600**

❑ **JMA-90. "J.A. Air Cadets" Brass Wings Badge,**
1930s. Canadian issue. - **$30 $75 $125**

JMA-91

❑ **JMA-91. Diploma,**
1930s. Hi-Speed Gasoline. - **$40 $80 $125**

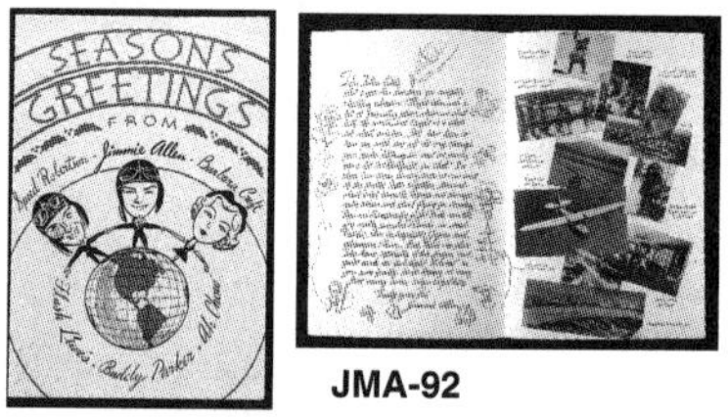


JMA-92

❑ **JMA-92. Season's Greetings Card,**
1930s. Richfield Oil Co. - **$30 $60 $125**

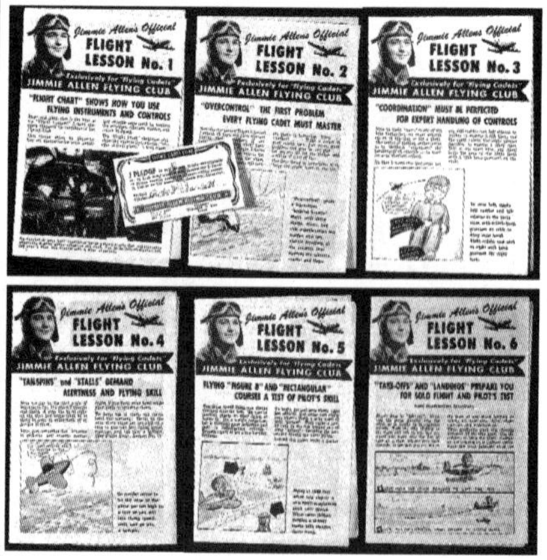


JMA-93

❑ **JMA-93. Flight Lesson #1-6 Lessons,**
1930s. Weather Bird Shoes.
Each - **$20 $50 $75**

JMA-94

JMA-95

❑ **JMA-94. Flight Lesson #4,**
1930s. Colonial Bread. - **$20 $30 $50**

❑ **JMA-95. Membership Card,**
1930s. Weather Bird Shoes. -
**$25 $60 $100**

JMA-96

❑ **JMA-96. Membership Certificate,**
1930s. Weather Bird Shoes. - **$40 $80 $125**

JMA-97

❑ **JMA-97. Air Corps Patch,**
1930s. Weather Bird Shoes. Rare. White design on red background. - **$100 $200 $300**

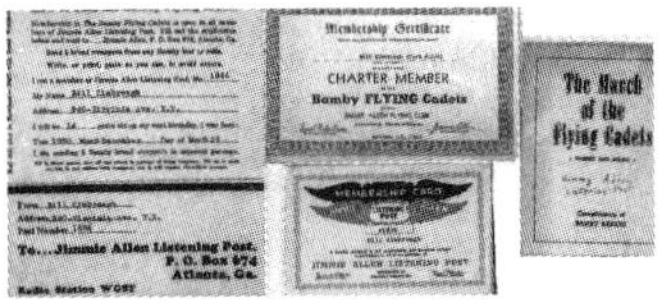

JMA-98

❑ **JMA-98. "Jimmie Allen Listening Post" Member Kit,**
1944. Re-broadcast of shows sponsored by Bamby Bread, Atlanta, Georgia. Includes cover letter, photo, member card, charter, song sheet, application, "Listening Post" tag.
Each Item - **$10 $20 $30**

## Jimmie Mattern

**An actual aviator in the early 1930s era of personal and mechanical endurance flying, Mattern is best remembered for his June 3 to August 3, 1933 solo flight around the world begun in his "Century of Progress" single engine aircraft (crashed en route) and finished by other borrowed planes. Premiums were typically aviation theme booklets and photo albums by sponsor Pure Oil.**

JMT-1

JMT-2

❑ **JMT-1. "The Diary Of Jimmie Mattern" Paper Folder,**
1935. Pure Oil Co. "Diary Sheet" insert pages issued separately, probably weekly.
Folder Only - **$10 $20 $35**
Each Insert Page - **$3 $5 $10**

❑ **JMT-2. "Air-E-Racer" Figural Rubber Eraser,**
c. 1936. Pure Oil Co., also marked "Tiolene Motor Oil". - **$20 $40 $75**

JMT-3

JMT-4

❑ **JMT-3. "Book One 'Cloud Country/Wings Of Youth'",**
1936. Pure Oil Co. hardcover. - **$5 $15 $35**

❑ **JMT-4. "Book 2 'Hawaii To Hollywood'",**
1936. Pure Oil Co. Hardcover. - **$5 $15 $35**

## Jimmy Durante

**At the age of 17 Jimmy Durante (1893-1980) was playing piano in a Coney Island beer garden. By his mid-thirties, after years in vaudeville and burlesque, he was playing Broadway and making movies. In 1943, when he and Gary Moore appeared together on NBC in the *Camel Comedy Caravan*, Durante was on the road to national stardom. With his joyful mangling of the language, his legendary nose, his mythical friends Umbriago and Mrs. Calabash, Durante charmed his radio audience for seven years, first for Camel cigarettes (1943-1945), then for Rexall drugs (1945-1948), then again for Camel (1948-1950). A couple of Durante comic books appeared in the late 1940s, and from 1950 to 1957 Durante was a regular on television for such sponsors as Buick, Colgate, and Texaco.**

JIM-1

JIM-2

❑ **JIM-1. "Schnozzle Durante/Vice-President" Cello. Button,**
1932. Paramount Pictures. Based on movie "Phantom President" that year. - **$20 $40 $75**

❑ **JIM-2. Song Book - Inka Dinka Doo,**
1933. Store bought. - **$15 $40 $50**

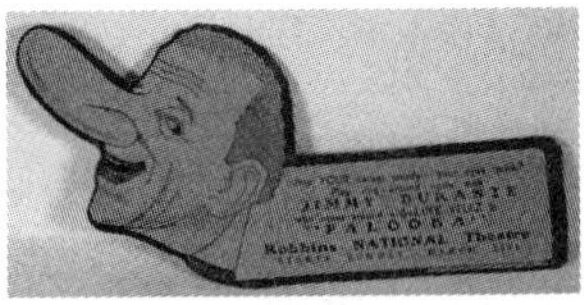

JIM-3

❑ **JIM-3. "Palooka" Movie Premium,**
1934. Die-cut book marker. - **$75 $150 $275**

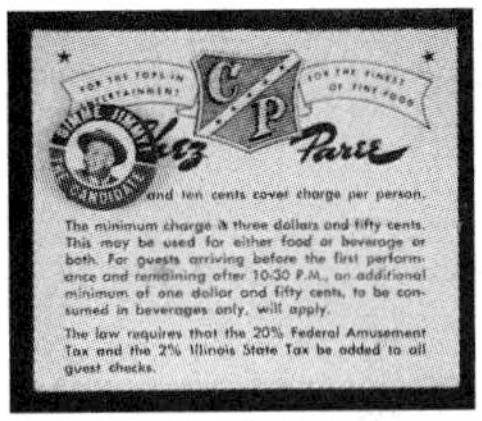

JIM-4

JIM-5

❑ **JIM-4. Cello. Button With Restaurant Card,**
1948. Chez Paree, Chicago. 1-1/4" button reads "Gimme Jimmy! The Candidate." Card from where he performed has no Durante reference but discusses cover charges per person.
Button - **$5 $12 $20**
Card - **$3 $5 $10**

❑ **JIM-5. "My Friend Umbriago" Litho. Button,**
c. 1940s. Durante holds hand puppet. -
**$8 $15 $25**

JIM-6

JIM-7

**JIM-6. "The Great Rupert" Movie Poster,**
1950. Pathe Industries. 27x41". - **$25 $50 $75**

**JIM-7. "The Candidate" Book,**
1952. Simon & Schuster. - **$8 $12 $18**

JIM-8

JIM-9

**JIM-8. "Gimme Jimmy! The Candidate" Button,**
1952. Issued with booklet of same title.
Cello. - **$5 $12 $20**
Litho. - **$5 $10 $15**

**JIM-9. Rubber/Fabric Hand Puppet,**
1950s. Store item. - **$15 $25 $ 50**

JIM-10

JIM-11

**JIM-10. "Children's Fund" Metal Portrait Pin On Card,**
1950s. - **$8 $15 $25**

**JIM-11. Portrait Pen,**
c. 1950s. Plastic and metal ballpoint with miniature bronze luster metal portrait attached on pocket clip. - **$10 $20 $30**

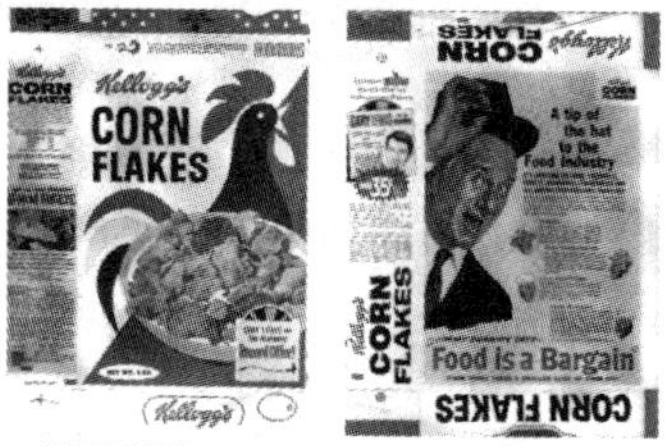

(FRONT) JIM-12 (BACK)

**JIM-12. Corn Flakes Box With Testimonial From Durante,**
1965. Gary Lewis and the Playboys record offer on side of box. Complete - **$30 $60 $140**

## Joe E. Brown

**Show-business veteran Joe E. Brown (1892-1973), noted for the contortions of his big mouth, started out as a circus acrobat at the age of 10, was a featured comedian in burlesque and vaudeville in his mid-twenties, graduated to musical comedies, and started making movies in 1927. He made dozens of films, with memorable roles in *You Said a Mouthful* (1932), *Alibi Ike* (1935), and *Some Like It Hot* (1959). Quaker Oats issued the *Joe E. Brown Bike Club* premiums in 1934. In 1936, Post cereal sponsored the *Joe E. Brown Club* through newspapers and packaging offers. On radio, the *Joe E. Brown Show*, a musical variety program, ran for a season (1938-1939) on CBS, sponsored by Post Toasties cereal.**

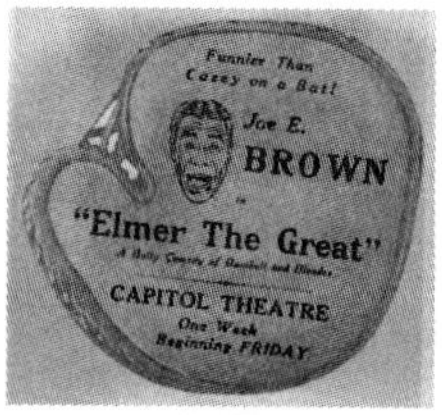

JOE-1

JOE-2

**JOE-1. Theatre Promo Baseball Glove,**
1933. Movie premium from baseball film "Elmer the Great." Lettering is printed on card shaped like a padded glove. Scarce. - **$60 $90 $130**

**JOE-2. Theatre Promo Card,**
1933. 8 1/2" tall movie premium of Joe E. Brown, starring in the film "Son of a Sailor." - **$50 $75 $160**

JOE-3

JOE-4

**JOE-3. "Joe E. Brown's Funny Bike Book",**
1934. Quaker Oats. - **$10 $30 $50**

**JOE-4. "Member/Joe E. Brown Bike Club" Cello. Button,**
1934. Quaker Oats. - **$5 $15 $25**

JOE-5

**JOE-5. Bicycle Contest 15x20" Store Sign,**
1934. Quaker Oats. Diecut cardboard display also picturing Joe E. Brown Bike Club button and book plus advertises his new film "6-Day Bike Rider." - **$75 $200 $325**

JOE-6

JOE-7

JOE-8

**JOE-6. Club Member Brass Badge With Three Award Bars,**
1936. Grape-Nuts Flakes. Bars in different colors individually marked by 1, 2, or 3 stars denoting club ranks of Sergeant, Lieutenant, or Captain.
Portrait Badge Only - **$5 $15 $25**
For Each Bar Add - **$5 $15 $30**

**JOE-7. Brass Club Member Ring,**
1936. Grape-Nuts Flakes. Features small portrait. - **$50 $100 $175**

**JOE-8. Radio Fan Photo,**
c. 1936. Probable Grape-Nuts Flakes. - **$8 $15 $25**

JOE-9

JOE-10

**JOE-9. Premium Folder Sheet,**
1936. Grape-Nuts Flakes. Offers about 30 premiums with expiration date December 31. - **$10 $20 $35**

**JOE-10. Fan Photo,**
1930s. Issuer unknown although possibly issued by Quaker Cereals. 8x10" browntone. - **$5 $10 $20**

JOE-11

JOE-12

❑ **JOE-11. "Smiler's Club" Cello. Button,**
1930s. - **$15 $40 $65**

❑ **JOE-12. "You Said A Mouthful" Booklet,**
1944. Doughnut Corp. of America with local dealer imprint. Contents include World War II tour photos plus mention of radio quiz show "Stop Or Go". - **$8 $15 $25**

JOE-13

❑ **JOE-13. Joe E. Brown "How To Play Baseball" Record Album,**
1940s. Store item by RCA Victor. -
**$20 $30 $60**

## Joe Louis

**Joe Louis (1914-1981) was born in Alabama but made Detroit his home for many years. Louis won the world heavyweight championship by knocking out James J. Braddock in 1937 and successfully defended the title 24 times in 12 years. Known as the "Brown Bomber," he won 68 of his 71 bouts, 54 by knockouts. He was elected to the Boxing Hall of Fame in 1954. Louis enlisted in the U.S. Army in 1942 and gave many exhibition bouts for troops around the world. He retired undefeated as champion in 1949, then returned to the ring the following year, without success. Louis is buried in Arlington Cemetery.**

JLO-1

JLO-2

❑ **JLO-1. "Braddock Or Louis" Puzzle In Envelope,**
1937. Green River Whiskey. Novelty cardboard puzzle based on upcoming June 22 bout between champion James J. Braddock and contender Joe Louis. Assembled puzzle is about 2-1/2x4" consisting of four pieces to form image pictured on envelope. - **$35 $60 $100**

❑ **JLO-2. "Louis-Schmeling Fight" 14x22" Tavern Poster,** 1938. Martin's Scotch Whiskey. Cardboard sign promoting radio listenership of return bout between Joe Louis and Max Schmeling of Germany with cartoon art by O. Soglow. - **$30 $60 $125**

JLO-3

JLO-4

❑ **JLO-3. Joe Louis "Heavyweight Sensation" Cello. Button,**
c. 1938. Sponsored by Valmor Products Co., Chicago. - **$40 $85 $175**

❑ **JLO-4. "Joe Louis Good Luck Club" Litho. Button,**
c. 1938. Bottom rim design includes tiny four-leaf clover symbol. - **$40 $100 $200**

JLO-5

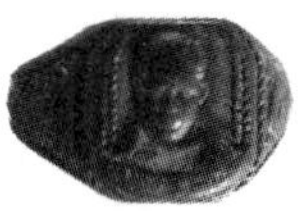
JLO-6

❑ **JLO-5. Real Photo Stickpin,**
1930s. Probable store item. 1" tall with black and white photo mounted on yellow celluloid. Reverse reads "Photo Pin Co. Chicago." - **$15 $30 $60**

❑ **JLO-6. "Joe Louis" Portrait Ring,**
1930s. Probable store item. Silvered brass non-adjustable with overlapping boxing gloves on each side. - **$75 $150 $500**

JLO-7

JLO-8

JLO-9

❑ **JLO-7. Premium Photo,**
1930s. Tie-in with premium ring giveaway. - **$25 $50 $85**

❑ **JLO-8. "Joe And Me For Willkie" Cello. Button,**
1940. Endorsement attributed to Joe Louis for U.S. Presidential candidate Wendell L. Willkie. - **$15 $30 $75**

❑ **JLO-9. "Joe Louis" Silver Top Variety Portrait Ring,**
c. 1940s. Probable store item. Non-adjustable heavy metal ring completely finished in silver luster. Ring sides depict overlapping boxing gloves. - **$250 $450 $850**

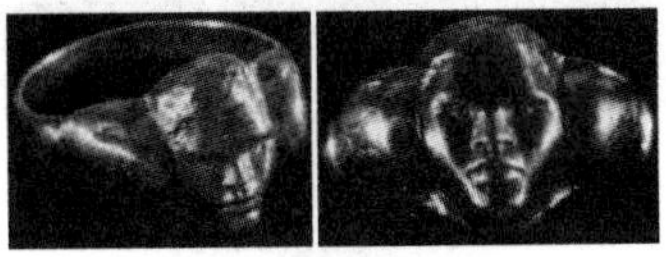
JLO-10

JLO-11

❑ **JLO-10. "Joe Louis" Ring,**
Early 1940s. Features Louis' face next to two boxing gloves with signature. Rare - less than 10 known. Silver color, non-adjustable. - **$750 $1500 $3000**

❑ **JLO-11. "Joe Louis" Ring Promo Sign,**
Early 1940s. - **$50 $100 $150**

JLO-12

JLO-13

JLO-14

❑ **JLO-12. "Joe Louis Punch" Cello. Button,**
c. 1940s. For soda beverage product also inscribed "It's A Knockout." - **$20 $45 $85**

❑ **JLO-13. "Joe Louis Punch" Soda Bottle Tin Cap,**
c. 1940s. For carbonated beverage. - **$15 $25 $40**

❑ **JLO-14. "Joe Louis Punch" Soda Bottle,**
c. 1940s. All American Drinks Corp. Reverse slogan is "It's A Knockout." - **$20 $40 $60**

JLO-15

❑ **JLO-15. "Joe Louis" Memoriam Badge,**
1981. 3-1/2" sold by vendors. - **$5 $15 $25**

# Joe Palooka

Ham Fisher (1901-1955) created the *Joe Palooka* comic strip, the most successful sports strip of all time. It started small, appearing in a handful of papers in 1928, but a decade later the strip was running in hundreds of papers. Joe was sweet, innocent, clean-cut, and given to uttering clichés about home, mother, and fair play. He was also a top boxer, winning the World Heavyweight Championship in 1931. Joe joined the army in 1940 and married his longtime girlfriend Ann Howe in 1949--two events that generated great reader interest and sent circulation soaring. Other characters included the Palooka's daughter Joan and Joe's sidekicks Humphrey Pennyworth and (mute) Little Max. The strip outlived Fisher, surviving until 1984.

A *Joe Palooka* radio series aired on CBS in 1932, sponsored by Heinz, with Ted Bergman as Joe. *Palooka*, a feature film based on the strip, was released in 1934 with Stu Erwin as Joe and Jimmy Durante as his manager Knobby Walsh. Two series of comic books were published, the first in 1942-1944, the second in 1945-1961. A live-action television series, *The Joe Palooka Story*, with Joe Kirkwood as Joe, was syndicated in 1952.

JPA-1

JPA-2

❑ **JPA-1. "Joe Palooka" Wood Jointed Doll,**
1930s. Store item. - **$40 $75 $140**

❑ **JPA-2. Anti-V.D. World War II Poster,**
1943. U.S. Government Printing Office. 14x20" designed like Sunday comic page with story warning that "Liquor An' Dames Don't Mix!" - **$50 $125 $225**

JPA-3

❑ **JPA-3. "Joe Palooka Lunch Kit",**
1948. Store item by Continental Can. 5x7x4" tall full color tin litho. box with handles. - **$50 $85 $150**

JPA-4

JPA-5

❑ **JPA-4. Red Cross Cartoon Booklet,**
1949. Softcover 12-page color booklet featuring Joe explaining work of American Red Cross. - **$10 $30 $60**

❑ **JPA-5. "Joe Palooka Championship Belt" Metal Buckle,**
1940s. Store item by Ham Fisher Belt Rite Leather Goods.
Buckle - **$25 $50 $75**
With Belt - **$40 $90 $150**

JPA-6

JPA-7

❑ **JPA-6. Joe Palooka "Tangle Comics" Cello. Button,**
1940s. Philadelphia Sunday Bulletin. - **$15 $30 $65**

❑ **JPA-7. Color Portrait Litho. Button,**
1940s. Reverse says "Manufactured Under Exclusive Rights By President's Novelty & Jewelry Co." - **$20 $50 $100**

JPA-8

JPA-9

❑ **JPA-8. "Joe Palooka Cap" Litho. Button,**
1940s. Sponsor not indicated. Pictures Joe as he appeared in early years of comic strip. - **$15 $35 $60**

❑ **JPA-9. Newspaper Strip Cello. Button,**
1940s. Philadelphia Bulletin. - **$25 $60 $125**

JPA-10

JPA-11

❑ **JPA-10. "Hi!-Humphrey" Cello. Button For Doll,**
1940s. Ideal Novelty & Toy Co. for character doll of Palooka sidekick Humphrey Pennyworth. - **$20 $50 $90**

❑ **JPA-11. Club Medal,**
1940s. New York Daily Mirror. Aluminum with portrait front and horseshoe/boxing glove design on reverse. - **$10 $20 $35**

JPA-12

❑ **JPA-12. Joe Palooka Candy Box,**
1940s. Boxing lesson card on back. - **$30 $110 $150**

JPA-13

❑ **JPA-13. Humphrey Doll,**
1940s. Came with removable (and usually missing) tag, pin back and apron. Made by Ideal. Rare when complete. - **$200 $500 $1000**

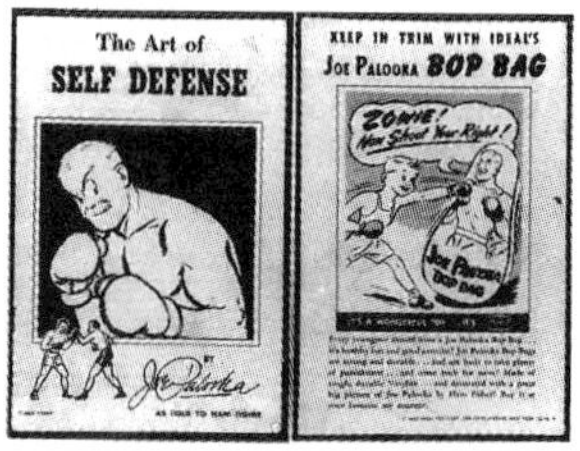


JPA-14

❑ **JPA-14. "The Art Of Self Defense" Booklet,**
1952. Store item by Ideal Toy Corp. Came with "Bop Bag" punching toy. - **$5 $15 $30**

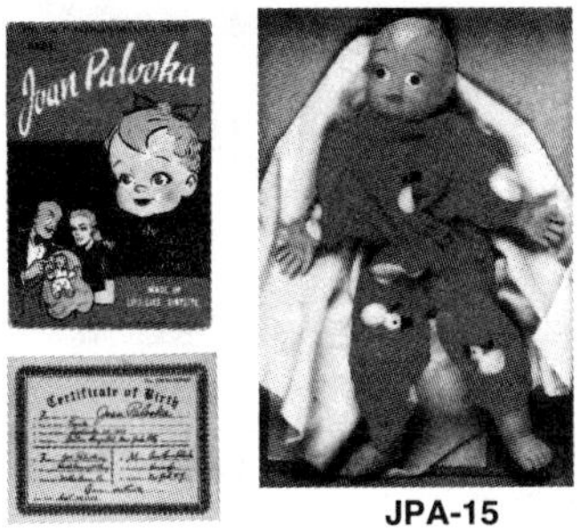

JPA-15

❑ **JPA-15. "Joan Palooka" Boxed Doll/Hand Puppet,**
c. 1952. Store item by National Mask & Puppet Corp. Replica doll of Joe and Ann's daughter plus flannel blanket, paper birth certificate and instruction sheet. Near Mint Boxed - **$150**
Doll - **$25 $50 $75**
Certificate - **$10 $15 $25**

JPA-16

❑ **JPA-16. "Little Max's Lunch" Boxed Plastic Bank,**
1950s. Store item by Comics Novelty Candy Corp. 4-1/2" tall. Box - **$10 $25 $40**
Bank - **$15 $30 $50**

## Joe Penner

**"Wanna buy a duck?" Perhaps no other comedian is so well remembered for such a single phrase as Joe Penner (1905-1941). Penner's trademark prop, of course, from vaudeville days into radio and 1930s to early 1940s films, was the inevitable live duck carried in a basket. His wacky repartee style ended with his death in 1941 at the early age of 37 years with his duck remaining unbought.**

JOP-1

❑ **JOP-1. "Wise Quacks" Fan Newsletter Vol. 1 #4,**
November 1934. - **$10 $15 $30**

JOP-2

JOP-3

❑ **JOP-2. "Stay As Sweet As You Are" Sheet Music,**
1934. From Penner's movie "College Rhythm". - **$15 $25 $40**

❑ **JOP-3. "Don't Never Do-o-o That" Sheet Music,**
1934. Six pages of words and music for novelty song subtitled "You Nasty Man" featuring cover art of Penner and his duck. - **$15 $25 $40**

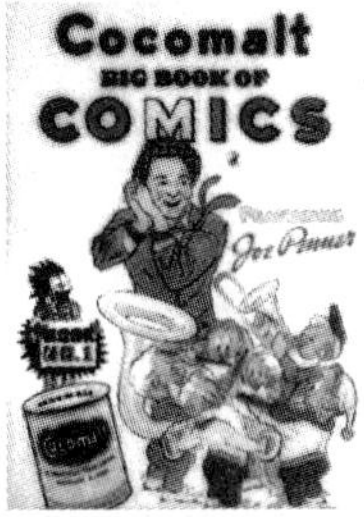

JOP-4

JOP-5

❑ **JOP-4. "Cocomalt Big Book Of Comics",**
1938. Featuring Joe Penner, various comic characters. - **$150 $400 $1000**

❑ **JOP-5. Premium Photo with Autograph,**
1938. - **$150**

JOP-6

JOP-7

JOP-8

❑ **JOP-6. Photo Promo,**
1934. 5"x7" photo from Penner's movie "I'm From the City". - **$10 $20 $30**

❑ **JOP-7. "Raisin Bread/Radio Special" Cello. Button,**
1930s. Unknown bakery or bakeries. From series listing various types of breads or rolls. - **$5 $15 $30**

❑ **JOP-8. "I'm A Joe Penner Quacker" Cello. Button,**
1930s. - **$10 $20 $40**

JOP-9

JOP-10

❑ **JOE-9. First Issue "Joe Penner Songs" Folio,**
1941. - **$10 $25 $40**

❑ **JOE-10. Photo/Dexterity Game Brass Ring,**
c. 1940s. Scarce. - **$300 $500 $800**

## John Wayne

**Born Marion Morrison in Iowa, John Wayne (1907-1979) was to grow from a football player at the University of Southern California to become one of the legendary giants of American film. After bit parts in silent films in the 1920s, he played the lead in *The Big Trail* (1930) and three chapter plays for Mascot Pictures (1932-1933). He achieved stardom with his role as the Ringo Kid in John Ford's *Stagecoach* in 1939. Wayne was to appear in more than 250 films over half a century, the most memorable directed by Ford or Howard Hawks, and most of them westerns. He won an Academy Award for *True Grit* (1969). The Duke, who came to symbolize the rugged courage of the American West, was one of the greatest box office attractions of all time. He was awarded a Congressional Medal of Freedom posthumously.**

***John Wayne Adventure Comics* was published from 1949 to 1955. Wayne made scattered appearances in other comic book series between 1948 and 1967, mostly associated with his movie roles, and in one of a set of six pocket-size giveaways from Oxydol-Dreft in 1950. Commemorative items appear to this day.**

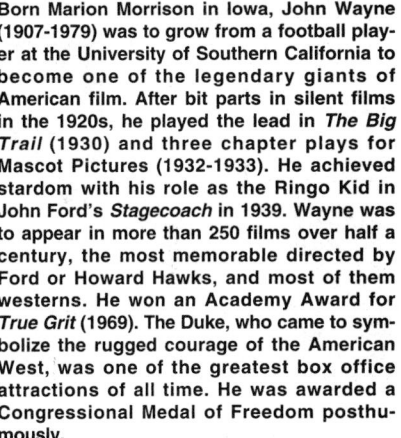

JWA-1

JWA-2

❑ **JWA-1. "Raoul Walsh's The Big Trail" Cello. Button,** 1930. Contest or club member promotion for movie of John Wayne's first starring role. - **$50 $100 $175**

❑ **JWA-2. Dixie Ice Cream Picture,** 1936. Four scenes on reverse from "King Of The Pecos." - **$50 $125 $175**

JWA-3

JWA-4

❑ **JWA-3. "John Wayne King Of The Pecos" Dixie Lid,** 1936. - **$8 $15 $25**

❑ **JWA-4. "The Song of the Seabees" Song Sheet,** 1944. Republic Pictures. From the movie "The Fighting Seabees."- **$15 $30 $60**

JWA-5

JWA-6

❑ **JWA-5. "The Fighting Seabees" Movie Postcard,** 1944. Republic Pictures. - **$10 $15 $30**

❑ **JWA-6. Ring With Photo Under Plastic,** 1940s. Store item. From series of movie star rings with black and white photo on brass base with adjustable bands. - **$20 $40 $85**

JWA-7

JWA-8

JWA-9

❑ **JWA-7. John Wayne Cello. Button,** 1940s. Black and white photo on blue background. - **$15 $40 $75**

❑ **JWA-8. John Wayne Photo Charm,** c. 1950. Vending machine item. Red plastic frame with black and white glossy photo. - **$5 $10 $15**

❑ **JWA-9. John Wayne Photo Charm,** c. 1950. Vending machine item. Silver plastic frame with black and white glossy photo. - **$5 $10 $15**

JWA-10

❑ **JWA-10. "John Wayne/The Cowboy Troubleshooter" Comic Booklet,** 1950. Procter & Gamble wrappers or boxtops from Dreft, Oxydol or Ivory Soap. - **$17 $51 $150**

JWA-11

JWA-12

JWA-13

❑ **JWA-11. John Wayne Photo Ring,** c. 1950. Silvered plastic base with inset glossy black and white paper photo. - **$20 $30 $50**

❑ **JWA-12. John Wayne Photo Charm,** c. 1950. Vending machine item. White plastic frame with glossy black and white photo. Example shown missing top edge loop. - **$5 $10 $15**

❑ **JWA-13. Dixie Ice Cream Picture,** c. 1952. Reverse has scenes from famous movies and promo text for "The Quiet Man." - **$50 $100 $150**

JWA-14

❑ **JWA-14. "The Searchers" 11x14" Cardboard Sign For Book Store,** c. 1956. Popular Library. Announces release of paperback novel by Alan Lemay "soon to be a great motion picture starring John Wayne." - **$25 $60 $115**

JWA-15

❑ **JWA-15. "She Wore A Yellow Ribbon" Lobby Card,** 1959. RKO Radio Pictures. 11x14" from set of eight. Title Card - **$50 $100 $150**
Other Cards With Wayne - **$30 $60 $100**

JWA-16

JWA-17

JWA-18

❑ **JWA-16. Transfer Picture Sheet,** 1950s. Store item. 4-1/2x5-1/2" paper with full color reverse image portrait for application to fabric. - **$10 $20 $40**

❑ **JWA-17. Leather Billfold,** c. 1950s. Store item. Zippered wallet with color portrait on front. - **$75 $150 $250**

❑ **JWA-18. John Wayne And Ronald Reagan Cello. Button,** c. 1968. Rim curl names "Big Little Store" of San Francisco. - **$15 $35 $65**

JWA-19

JWA-20

❑ **JWA-19. "McQ" Movie Mug,** 1974. Ceramic mug belived given to cast members of the film starring him as modern-day detective policeman. 3-1/2" tall with facsimile signature. - **$10 $20 $35**

❑ **JWA-20. Commemorative 3-1/2" Cello. Button,** 1979. - **$5 $10 $15**

JWA-21

❑ **JWA-21. Boxed Rifle Cartridges,** 1970s. Winchester. Each 32-40 cartridge has tiny "Duke" designation on firing cap. Boxed - **$15 $30 $65**

JWA-22

JWA-23

❑ **JWA-22. Plaster Statue,**
c. 1979. Store item by Esco. 18-1/2" tall from a series of personality statues. - **$25 $60 $100**

❑ **JWA-23. Boxed Commemorative Doll,**
1982. Store item by Effanbee Doll Corp. 18" vinyl in fabric cavalry outfit from limited "Legend Series." Near Mint Boxed - **$200**
Loose - **$35 $60 $100**

JWA-24

❑ **JWA-24. "Pick It Up Pilgrim" Replica Car,**
1999. Die cast replica at 1:64 scale. Features John Wayne on car and packaging. Issue #43. - **$10**

## Jonny Quest

***Jonny Quest*, a prime-time animated adventure series from the Hanna-Barbera studios, premiered on ABC in 1964 and aired for a year. The series was repeated on Saturday mornings on CBS (1967-1970), on ABC (1970-1972), and on NBC, first as part of the *Godzilla Power Hour* (1978), then on its own (1979-1981). Created by comic book artist Doug Wildey, Jonny and his scientist father traveled to exotic places in their supersonic plane, fought mythical beasts, confronted unsolved mysteries, and triumphed over danger wherever they found it.**

JNY-1

❑ **JNY-1. ABC TV Promo Photo With Text Information,**
1964. Black and white glossy promoting particular show "Calcutta Adventure" from October 23, 1964. - **$25 $50 $100**

JNY-2

❑ **JNY-2. Boxed Card Game,**
1965. Store item by Milton Bradley. - **$20 $40 $85**

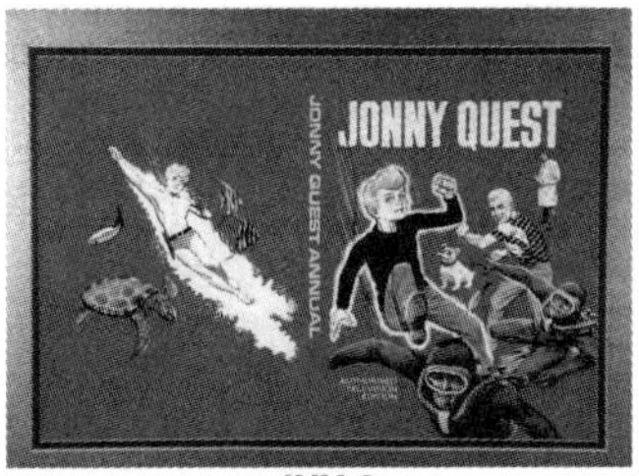


JNY-3

❑ **JNY-3. Original Cover Art for TV Edition Book,**
1965. Art is 12 1/2" x 17", acrylic on illustration board. Book was published in Great Britain. - **$1500**

JNY-4

JNY-5

❑ **JNY-4. "Magic Ring" 21x22" Cardboard Store Sign,**
1960s. P.F. footwear of B.F. Goodrich. Shows gold plastic decoder ring (Pictured in Rings, Miscellaneous section). - **$30 $75 $165**

❑ **JNY-5. Large Plastic Ring,**
1996. Issuer unknown. Blue plastic base has large oval top with color label. - **$3 $8 $12**

## Junior Birdmen of America

**Hearst newspapers sponsored this club for young aviation enthusiasts in the 1930s, offering membership cards and manuals along with pins and patches. Club activities included flying model airplanes, with medals awarded to contest winners.**

JRB-1

JRB-2

JRB-3

❑ **JRB-1. Champion Award Medal In Presentation Box,**
1934. Rare. Near Mint Boxed - **$300**
Unboxed - **$35 $100 $200**

❑ **JRB-2. Second Place Award Medal In Presentation Box,**
1934. Scarce. Near Mint Boxed - **$175**
Unboxed - **$35 $75 $125**

❑ **JRB-3. "Eagle Membership Test" Brochure And Membership Card,**
1938. Brochure - **$15 $30 $50**
Card - **$15 $30 $50**

JRB-4

❑ **JRB-4. "Flight Squadron Plan" Folder,**
1930s. Contents include depiction of rank insignia pins for Commander, Captain, Eagle. - **$15 $25 $50**

JRB-5

JRB-6

❑ **JRB-5. Club Manual,**
1930s. Folder explains how to form a squadron and advance in rank. - **$10 $25 $50**

❑ **JRB-6. Hearst Newspapers Club Card,**
1930s. For various newspapers of Hearst Syndicate with facsimile signature of George Hearst, National Commander. - **$15 $35 $60**

JRB-7

❑ **JRB-7. "Field Day" Felt Fabric Pennant,**
1930s. 22" long. - **$35 $100 $150**

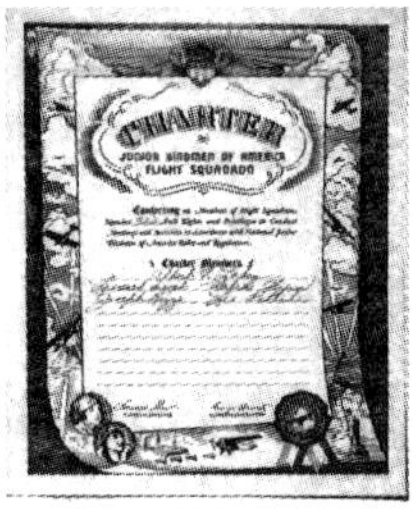

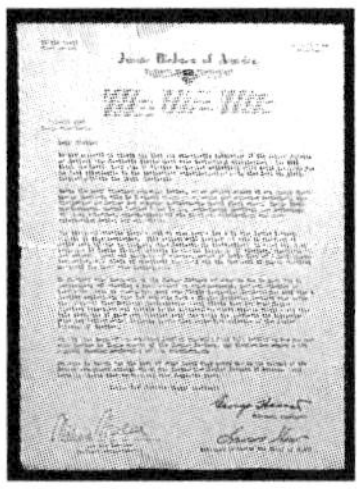

JRB-8 JRB-9

❑ **JRB-8. Hearst Newspapers "Flight Squadron" Charter Certificate,**
1930s. For various newspapers of Hearst Syndicate with facsimile signature of George Hearst, National Commander. - **$25 $50 $85**

❑ **JRB-9. Membership Approval Letter,**
1930s. Lists 22 different "Hearst Newspapers." Came with wings and membership card. -
**$8 $15 $30**

JRB-10

JRB-11

❑ **JRB-10. Membership Card,**
1930s. Shows boy and girl on front. -
**$25 $50 $85**

❑ **JRB-11. Rule Book,**
1930s. Also lists newspapers where Junior Birdmen column appears. - **$25 $50 $75**

JRB-12

❑ **JRB-12. Felt Fabric Emblem,**
1930s. Large 2-1/2x8" size. - **$35 $125 $200**

JRB-13 JRB-14

❑ **JRB-13. "Jr. Birdmen Of America" Enameled Brass Wings Badge,**
1930s. - **$15 $30 $50**

❑ **JRB-14. "Eagle" Enameled Brass Wings Badge With Rank Bar,**
1930s. Scarce. - **$35 $100 $175**

# Justice Society of America

**The first time superheroes ever got together and formed a team was when The Justice Society of America debuted in the pages of *All-Star Comics* #3, published in the fall of 1940. This collection of heroes, including at various times the Flash, Green Lantern, the Spectre, Wonder Woman, Hawkman, Hourman, Doctor Mid-Nite, Sandman and many others, set the stage for every super group that was to follow. Readers thrilled to the exploits of this first team until 1951, when trends led *All-Star* to change to *All-Star Western* with #58. The title would be revived in the '70s with old and new members, but it would not be until August 1999 that the JSA would receive its own title. Many interesting things happened in the meantime for Justice Society collectors and historians, though. Not the least of these was the creation of the Junior Justice Society of America.**

**The Junior Justice Society debuted in an ad in *All-Star Comics* #14, the December 1942 issue. Like many other clubs for young comic book readers, a membership kit was offered for a nominal charge, in this case 15¢. For their money, members received a welcome letter from Wonder Woman, a silver-plated membership badge (later replaced by a cloth sew-on patch), a cardboard decoder, a four-page War Bond comic entitled *The Minute Man Answers the Call*, and a four-color membership certificate. Though it has been theorized elsewhere that there were only four variations on this kit over the life of the Junior Justice Society, there were actually five distinct kits (see article elsewhere in this edition). The JJSA kits, including their mailers, have become among the most prized collectibles of this type.**

**The resurgence of superhero comics in the late '50s and early '60s owed a tremendous debt to their predecessors, particularly the Justice Society. Their spiritual successors, the Justice League of America, became their modern day counterparts and engaged with them in many cross-reality team-ups.**

**The modern incarnation of the JSA has established the team and its characters as contemporaries of the JLA and continues to open the world of the classic characters to new readers through DC's Archives series of hardcover collections and through DC Direct's line of JSA toys including PVCs and action figures.**

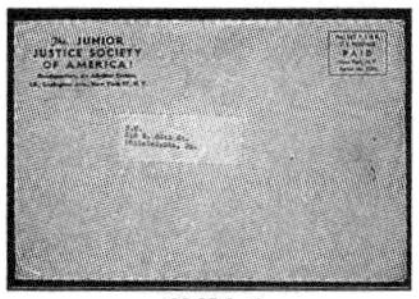

JUN-1

(CLOSE-UP)

JUN-2

(CLOSE-UP)

JUN-3

(CLOSE-UP)

JUN-4

(CLOSE-UP)

❑ **JUN-1. Club Kit Envelope,**
1942. - **$50 $75 $125**

❑ **JUN-2. 1943-1944 Club Kit Envelope,**
1943-44. - **$25 $50 $100**

❑ **JUN-3. 1945 Club Kit Envelope,**
1945. Scarce. - **$75 $100 $150**

❑ **JUN-4. Club Kit Envelope,**
1948. - **$50 $75 $125**

JUN-5

❑ **JUN-5. Solid Brass Badge,**
1942. Rare. In-house prototype with tie-tac fastener. The back of the badge is flat, unlike the later silver models. - **$750 $1500 $3000**

JUN-6 (BACK)

JUN-6
(CLOSE-UP)

❑ **JUN-6. Silver Finish Club Badge,** 1942. Large letter style only offered for two months. - **$175 $450 $900**

JUN-7 (BACK)

JUN-7
(CLOSE-UP)

❑ **JUN-7. Silver Finish Club Badge,** 1948. Small letter style. Badge also existed with variation of pin on back running across. - **$150 $350 $700**

JUN-8

**(1942-44)**

These similar looking patches can be distinguished by the differences in the stitching behind the shield. The red stitching stays within the circle on the 1942-44 patch.

JUN-9

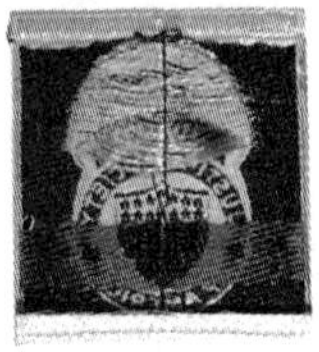
**(1945)**

❑ **JUN-8. Club Member Fabric Patch,** 1942-44. Replaced large letter badge because of metal shortage. - **$175 $500 $850**

❑ **JUN-9. Club Member Fabric Patch,** 1945. Scarce. Similar to 1942-44 patch but shield is 1/2" larger. - **$225 $550 $900**

JUN-10

❑ **JUN-10. Club Kit Decoder,** 1942-1944. - **$75 $175 $325**

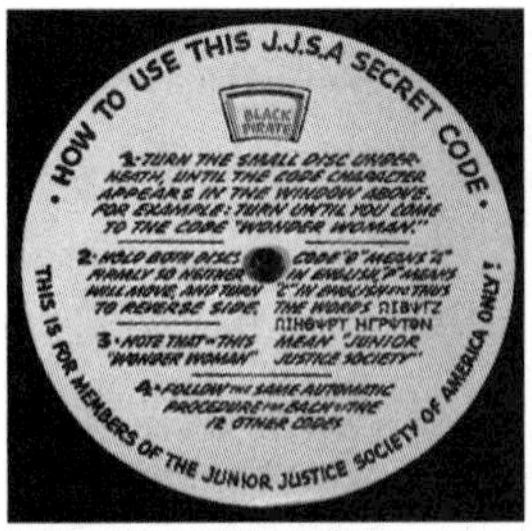

JUN-11

(CLOSE-UPS)

❑ **JUN-11. Club Kit Decoder,** 1945. Note different names in window. Rare. - **$160 $350 $500**

JUN-12

❑ **JUN-12. Club Kit Decoder,** 1948. Black rectangle design. - **$100 $225 $350**

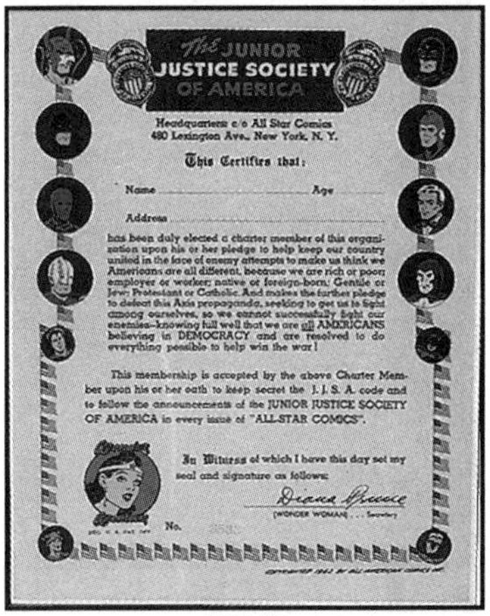

JUN-13

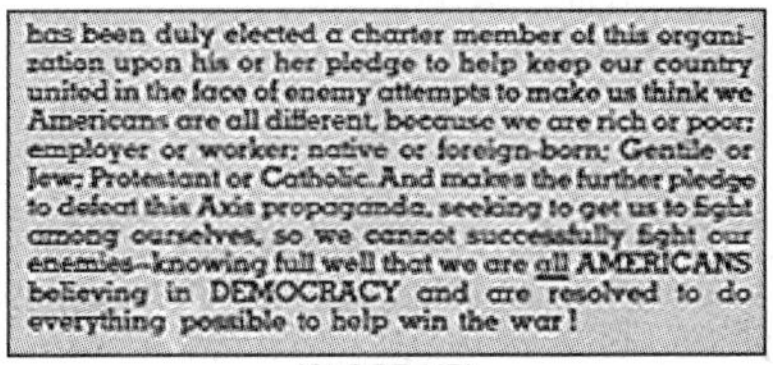
has been duly elected a charter member of this organization upon his or her pledge to help keep our country united in the face of enemy attempts to make us think we Americans are all different, because we are rich or poor; employer or worker; native or foreign-born; Gentile or Jew; Protestant or Catholic. And makes the further pledge to defeat this Axis propaganda, seeking to get us to fight among ourselves, so we cannot successfully fight our enemies—knowing full well that we are all AMERICANS believing in DEMOCRACY and are resolved to do everything possible to help win the war!

(CLOSE-UP)

❑ **JUN-13. Club Kit Certificate,** 1942. First certificate. - **$100 $275 $425**

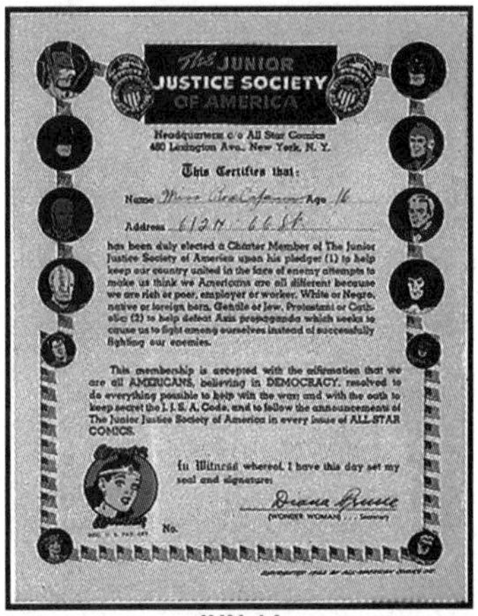

JUN-14

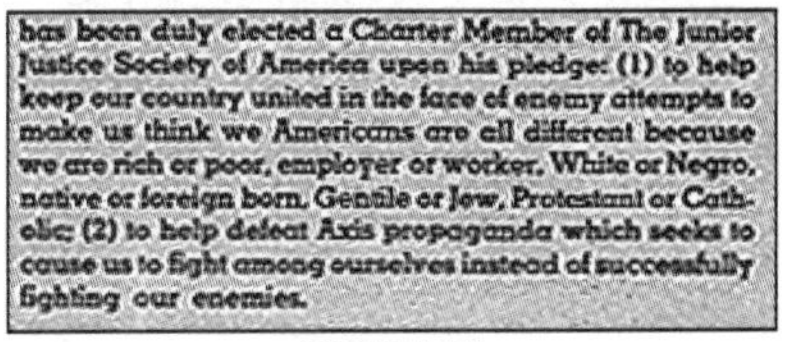
has been duly elected a Charter Member of The Junior Justice Society of America upon his pledge: (1) to help keep our country united in the face of enemy attempts to make us think we Americans are all different because we are rich or poor, employer or worker, White or Negro, native or foreign born, Gentile or Jew, Protestant or Catholic; (2) to help defeat Axis propaganda which seeks to cause us to fight among ourselves instead of successfully fighting our enemies.

(CLOSE-UP)

❑ **JUN-14. Club Kit Certificate,** 1942-44. - **$75 $250 $400**

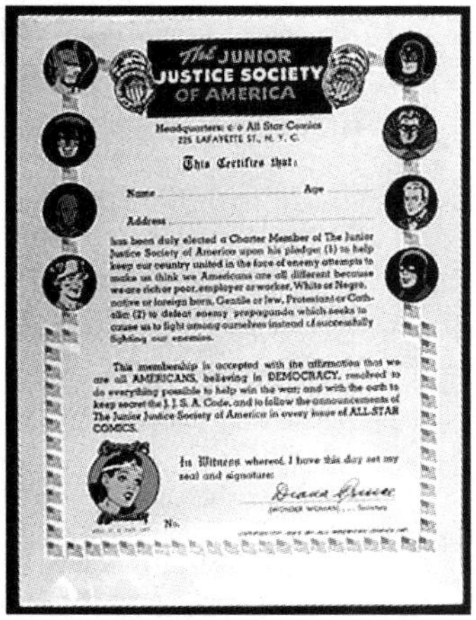

The JUNIOR JUSTICE SOCIETY OF AMERICA

Headquarters: c/o All Star Comics
225 LAFAYETTE ST., N. Y. C.

This Certifies that:

Name ______ Age ______

Address ______

has been duly elected a Charter Member of The Junior Justice Society of America upon his pledge: (1) to help keep our country united in the face of enemy attempts to make us think we Americans are all different because we are rich or poor, employer or worker, White or Negro, native or foreign born, Gentile or Jew, Protestant or Catholic; (2) to defeat enemy propaganda which seeks to cause us to fight among ourselves instead of successfully fighting our enemies.

This membership is accepted with the affirmation that we are all AMERICANS, believing in DEMOCRACY, resolved to do everything possible to help win the war; and with the oath to keep secret the J. J. S. A. Code, and to follow the announcements of The Junior Justice Society of America in every issue of ALL-STAR COMICS.

In Witness whereof, I have this day set my seal and signature:

Diana Prince

(WONDER WOMAN) ... Secretary

No.

JUN-15

This membership is accepted with the affirmation that we are all AMERICANS, believing in DEMOCRACY, resolved to do everything possible to help win the war; and with the oath to keep secret the J. J. S. A. Code, and to follow the announcements of The Junior Justice Society of America in every issue of ALL-STAR COMICS.

❑ **JUN-15. 1945 Club Kit Certificate,** 1945. Rare certificate with 225 Lafayette St. address at top. Note Wildcat photo is added. The Axis reference was deleted because Germany had already surrendered on May 7th. Japan had not, so the reference to war remained. Rare. - **$200 $500 $750**

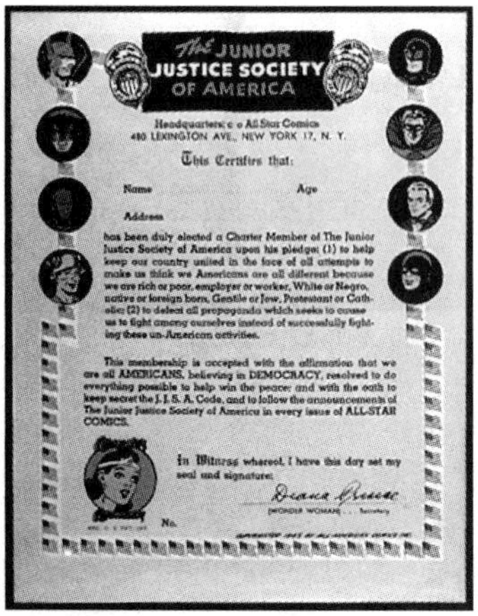

The JUNIOR JUSTICE SOCIETY OF AMERICA

Headquarters: c/o All Star Comics
480 LEXINGTON AVE., NEW YORK 17, N. Y.

This Certifies that:

Name ______ Age ______

Address ______

has been duly elected a Charter Member of The Junior Justice Society of America upon his pledge: (1) to help keep our country united in the face of all attempts to make us think we Americans are all different because we are rich or poor, employer or worker, White or Negro, native or foreign born, Gentile or Jew, Protestant or Catholic; (2) to defeat all propoganda which seeks to cause us to fight among ourselves instead of successfully fighting these un-American activities.

This membership is accepted with the affirmation that we are all AMERICANS, believing in DEMOCRACY, resolved to do everything possible to help win the peace; and with the oath to keep secret the J. J. S. A. Code, and to follow the announcements of The Junior Justice Society of America in every issue of ALL-STAR COMICS.

In Witness whereof, I have this day set my seal and signature:

Diana Prince

(WONDER WOMAN) ... Secretary

No.

JUN-16

This membership is accepted with the affirmation that we are all AMERICANS, believing in DEMOCRACY, resolved to do everything possible to help win the peace; and with the oath to keep secret the J. J. S. A. Code, and to follow the announcements of The Junior Justice Society of America in every issue of ALL-STAR COMICS.

(CLOSE-UP)

❑ **JUN-16. 1945 Club Kit Certificate,** 1945. Address is now 480 Lexington Ave. Text refers to "win the peace" following the surrender of Japan on August 14th. General MacArthur and U.S. troops had been put in charge of keeping peace in Japan. With the war over, the club was discontinued in Dec. 1945. Rare. - **$200 $500 $750**

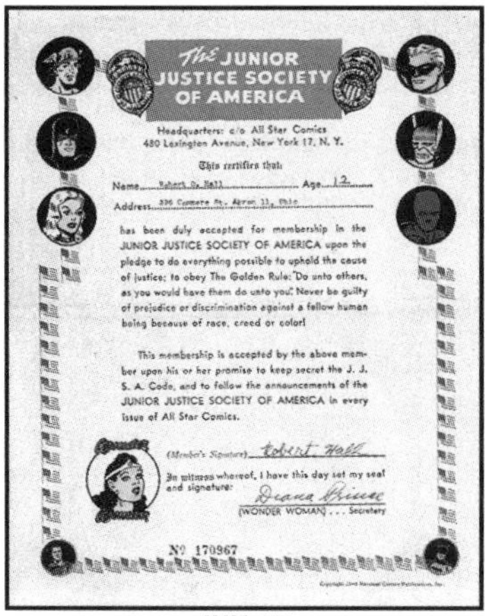

The JUNIOR JUSTICE SOCIETY OF AMERICA

Headquarters: c/o All Star Comics
480 Lexington Avenue, New York 17, N. Y.

This certifies that:

Name Robert D. Hall Age 12

Address 336 Commerce St., Akron 11, Ohio

has been duly accepted for membership in the JUNIOR JUSTICE SOCIETY OF AMERICA upon the pledge to do everything possible to uphold the cause of justice; to obey The Golden Rule: "Do unto others, as you would have them do unto you." Never be guilty of prejudice or discrimination against a fellow human being because of race, creed or color!

This membership is accepted by the above member upon his or her promise to keep secret the J. J. S. A. Code, and to follow the announcements of the JUNIOR JUSTICE SOCIETY OF AMERICA in every issue of All Star Comics.

(Member's Signature) Robert Hall

In witness whereof, I have this day set my seal and signature:

Diana Prince

(WONDER WOMAN) ... Secretary

No 170967

JUN-17

This membership is accepted by the above member upon his or her promise to keep secret the J. J. S. A. Code, and to follow the announcements of the JUNIOR JUSTICE SOCIETY OF AMERICA in every issue of All Star Comics.

(CLOSE-UP)

❑ **JUN-17. Club Kit Certificate,** 1948. Club kit was offered again in comics in late 1947. Earliest kit documented from this release was early 1948. The same materials were used up until 1951. Note Black Canary & Atom pictured. - **$125 $400 $500**

JUN-18

JUN-19

❑ **JUN-18. Club Kit Brochure,** 1942. - **$40 $60 $80**

❑ **JUN-19. Club Kit Brochure,** 1945. Newly printed for 1945. Rare. Brochure has different layout, a different font and the star on the cover is smaller. - **$80 $120 $160**

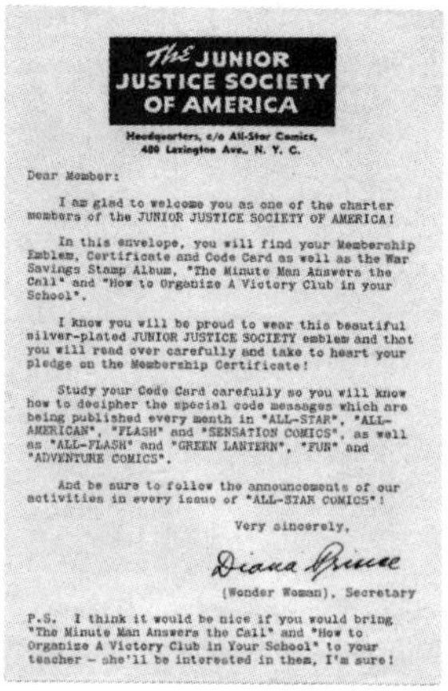

The JUNIOR JUSTICE SOCIETY OF AMERICA

Headquarters, c/o All-Star Comics,
480 Lexington Ave., N. Y. C.

Dear Member:

I am glad to welcome you as one of the charter members of the JUNIOR JUSTICE SOCIETY OF AMERICA!

In this envelope, you will find your Membership Emblem, Certificate and Code Card as well as the War Savings Stamp Album, "The Minute Man Answers the Call" and "How to Organize A Victory Club in your School".

I know you will be proud to wear this beautiful silver-plated JUNIOR JUSTICE SOCIETY emblem and that you will read over carefully and take to heart your pledge on the Membership Certificate!

Study your Code Card carefully so you will know how to decipher the special code messages which are being published every month in "ALL-STAR", "ALL-AMERICAN", "FLASH" and "SENSATION COMICS", as well as "ALL-FLASH" and "GREEN LANTERN", "FUN" and "ADVENTURE COMICS".

And be sure to follow the announcements of our activities in every issue of "ALL-STAR COMICS"!

Very sincerely,

Diana Prince

(Wonder Woman), Secretary

P.S. I think it would be nice if you would bring "The Minute Man Answers the Call" and "How to Organize A Victory Club in Your School" to your teacher - she'll be interested in them, I'm sure!

JUN-20

I know you will be proud to wear this beautiful silver-plated JUNIOR JUSTICE SOCIETY emblem and that you will read over carefully and take to heart your pledge on the Membership Certificate!

(CLOSE-UP)

❑ **JUN-20. 1942 Club Kit Member Letter,** 1942. This letter which lists the silver-plated emblem badge was only sent out for 2 months. The patch replaced the badge, noted in the following version. Rare. - **$70 $125 $175**

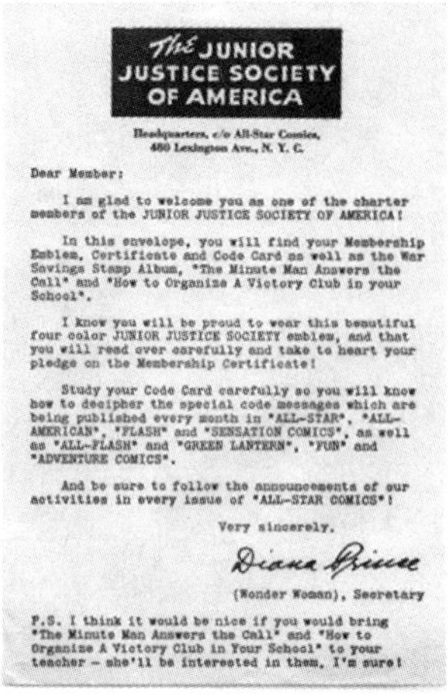

The JUNIOR JUSTICE SOCIETY OF AMERICA

Headquarters, c/o All-Star Comics,
480 Lexington Ave., N. Y. C.

Dear Member:

I am glad to welcome you as one of the charter members of the JUNIOR JUSTICE SOCIETY OF AMERICA!

In this envelope, you will find your Membership Emblem, Certificate and Code Card as well as the War Savings Stamp Album, "The Minute Man Answers the Call" and "How to Organize A Victory Club in your School".

I know you will be proud to wear this beautiful four color JUNIOR JUSTICE SOCIETY emblem, and that you will read over carefully and take to heart your pledge on the Membership Certificate!

Study your Code Card carefully so you will know how to decipher the special code messages which are being published every month in "ALL-STAR", "ALL-AMERICAN", "FLASH" and "SENSATION COMICS", as well as "ALL-FLASH" and "GREEN LANTERN", "FUN" and "ADVENTURE COMICS".

And be sure to follow the announcements of our activities in every issue of "ALL-STAR COMICS"!

Very sincerely,

Diana Prince

(Wonder Woman), Secretary

P.S. I think it would be nice if you would bring "The Minute Man Answers the Call" and "How to Organize A Victory Club in Your School" to your teacher - she'll be interested in them, I'm sure!

JUN-21

I know you will be proud to wear this beautiful four color JUNIOR JUSTICE SOCIETY emblem, and that you will read over carefully and take to heart your pledge on the Membership Certificate!

(CLOSE-UP)

❑ **JUN-21. Club Kit Member Letter,** 1943-44. This later version lists the four color embroidered patch. - **$50 $100 $125**

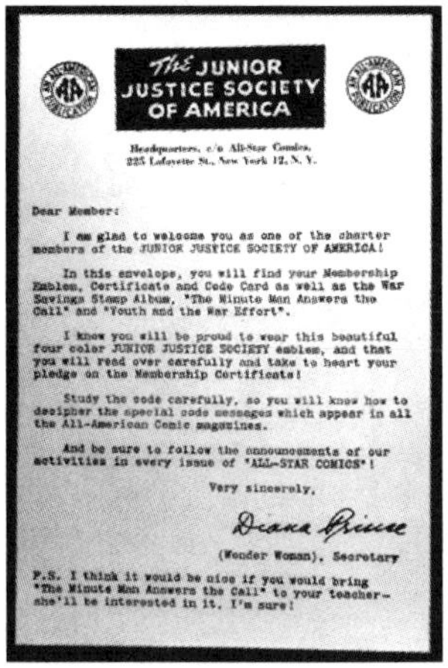

The JUNIOR JUSTICE SOCIETY OF AMERICA

Headquarters, c/o All-Star Comics,
225 Lafayette St., New York 12, N. Y.

Dear Member:

I am glad to welcome you as one of the charter members of the JUNIOR JUSTICE SOCIETY OF AMERICA!

In this envelope, you will find your Membership Emblem, Certificate and Code Card as well as the War Savings Stamp Album, "The Minute Man Answers the Call" and "Youth and the War Effort".

I know you will be proud to wear this beautiful four color JUNIOR JUSTICE SOCIETY emblem, and that you will read over carefully and take to heart your pledge on the Membership Certificate!

Study the code carefully, so you will know how to decipher the special code messages which appear in all the All-American Comic magazines.

And be sure to follow the announcements of our activities in every issue of "ALL-STAR COMICS"!

Very sincerely,

Diana Prince

(Wonder Woman), Secretary

P.S. I think it would be nice if you would bring "The Minute Man Answers the Call" to your teacher—she'll be interested in it, I'm sure!

JUN-22

**❏ JUN-22. Club Kit Letter,**
1945. Welcome letter for members has "An All-American Publication" stamps in top corners, a feature unique to this version. Rare. -
**$90 $150 $250**

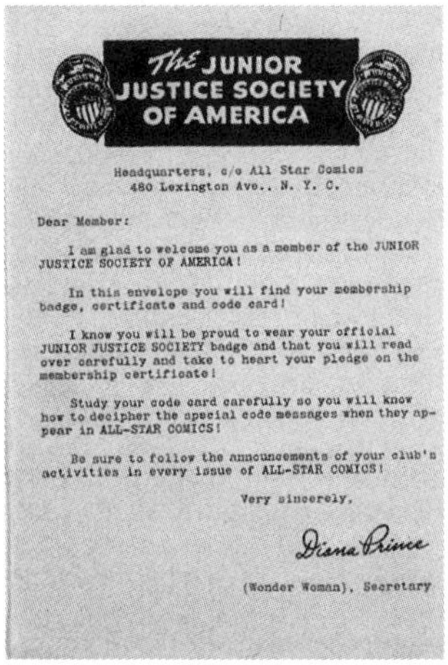

The JUNIOR JUSTICE SOCIETY OF AMERICA

Headquarters, c/o All Star Comics
480 Lexington Ave., N. Y. C.

Dear Member:

I am glad to welcome you as a member of the JUNIOR JUSTICE SOCIETY OF AMERICA!

In this envelope you will find your membership badge, certificate and code card!

I know you will be proud to wear your official JUNIOR JUSTICE SOCIETY badge and that you will read over carefully and take to heart your pledge on the membership certificate!

Study your code card carefully so you will know how to decipher the special code messages when they appear in ALL-STAR COMICS!

Be sure to follow the announcements of your club's activities in every issue of ALL-STAR COMICS!

Very sincerely,

Diana Prince

(Wonder Woman), Secretary

JUN-23

**❏ JUN-23. Club Kit Letter,**
1948. - **$70 $100 $150**

JUN-24

JUN-25

**❏ JUN-24. Stamp Album,**
1942-44. U.S. War Savings Bonds pamphlet which came with kits during 1942-44. -
**$10 $20 $40**

**❏ JUN-25. Defense Stamp Album,**
1945. Savings bonds promotional pamphlet that only came with the 1945 Kit. - **$20 $40 $80**

(Enlarged panel from back cover of 1942 issue)

JUN-26

**❏ JUN-26. "The Minute Man Answers the Call" Comic,**
1942. EC comic included in 1942-44 club kits. -
**$21 $64 $150**

(Enlarged panel from back cover of 1945 issue)

JUN-27

**❏ JUN-27. "The Minute Man Answers the Call" Comic,**
1945. Newer version with references to 1945. Rare. - **$50 $150 $300**

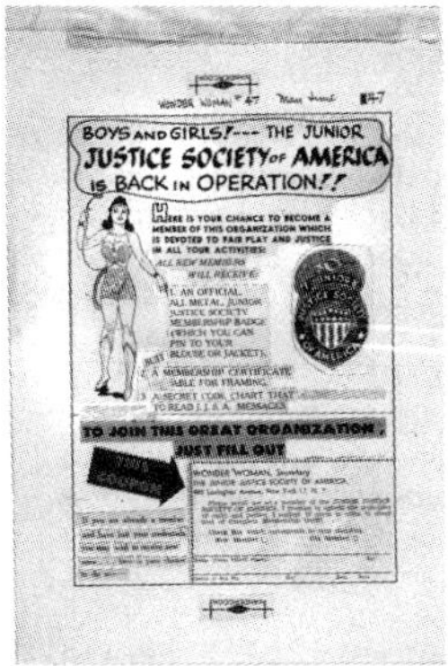


JUN-28

**❏ JUN-28. Comic Book Ad for Club,**
1947. Original art. Unique. - **$350**

JUN-29

**❏ JUN-29. JSA Badge with Plastic Case,**
2000. - **$25**

JUN-30

**❏ JUN-30. Justice Society of America Series 2 PVC Set,**
2000. DC Direct product in box. 7 figures. - **$40**

JUN-31

**❏ JUN-31. Justice Society of America Bookends,**
2001. DC Direct product. Hand painted cold-cast porcelain figures. Limited edition of 1,000. Boxed - **$295**

# Kate Smith

**Kate Smith (1909-1986) had a brief stage career on Broadway before she moved to radio and became a beloved American institution. Guided throughout by her partner and friend Ted Collins, she broadcast continually from 1931 to 1959, mainly on CBS. Known as the Songbird of the South, she was a large woman, with voice and personality to match. She made her opening theme, *When the Moon Comes Over the Mountain*, practically her own, and for a time she had exclusive rights to Irving Berlin's *God Bless America.* Audiences loved her, and sponsors followed: La Palina cigars (1931-1933), Hudson cars (1934-1935), Philip Morris (1947-1951), and Reader's Digest (1958-1959). During World War II her patriotic efforts sold millions of dollars in war bonds. On television, she had an afternoon show (1950-1954) and two evening variety programs, in 1951-1952 on NBC and in 1960 on CBS.**

KAT-1

KAT-2

❑ **KAT-1. "Crying Myself to Sleep" Song Sheet,**
1930. Features her hit song. - **$15 $30 $40**

❑ **KAT-2. Fan Photo,**
c. 1931. La Palina Cigars. - **$10 $15 $30**

KAT-3

KAT-4

❑ **KAT-3. "Kate Smith La Palina Club" Litho. Button,**
c. 1931. La Palina cigars. - **$12 $20 $40**

❑ **KAT-4. "Philadelphia A & P Party" 2-1/2" Cello. Button,**
1935. Great Atlantic & Pacific Tea Co. (grocery chain). Single day issue for November 4. - **$20 $35 $65**

KAT-5

KAT-6

❑ **KAT-5. "There's a Goldmine in the Sky" Song Sheet,**
1937. - **$10 $25 $40**

❑ **KAT-6. Photo,**
1937. Philadelphia Record newspaper premium. - **$10 $25 $45**

KAT-7

KAT-8

❑ **KAT-7. Recipe Folder - Christmas,**
1937. CBS. Radio premium. - **$15 $35 $50**

❑ **KAT-8. Recipe Folder - New Years,**
1938. CBS. Radio premium. - **$15 $35 $50**

KAT-9

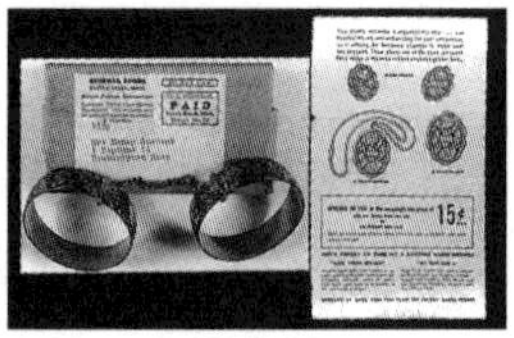
KAT-10

❑ **KAT-9. CBS Radio Card,**
1930s. - **$6 $12 $30**

❑ **KAT-10. Bracelets With Mailer And "Kate Smith Speaks" Reference,**
1940. Swan's Down Cake Flour and Calumet Baking Powder. Brass bracelets with enclosure slip naming Kate Smith program plus another sponsored daytime program "My Son And I." Near Mint Boxed - **$50**

KAT-11

KAT-12

❑ **KAT-11. "Violins Were Playing" Song Sheet,**
1943. - **$10 $15 $30**

❑ **KAT-12. Recipe Book - 16 pages,**
1945. Swans Down. Radio premium. - **$20 $40 $60**

KAT-13

❑ **KAT-13. Arcade Radio Card,**
1940s. - **$5 $10 $20**

# Katzenjammer Kids

**Considered by some to be the first true comic strip, *The Katzenjammer Kids* premiered in December 1897 in the *New York Journal.* The hell-raising kids, patterned after the similar 19th century story favorites Max and Moritz created by Wilhelm Busch (1832-1908), were introduced to Americans by Rudolph Dirks (1877-1968) as Hans and Fritz. Their debut has been called the single most important event in the history of the comic strip. Hans and Fritz, and their long-suffering Mamma, were joined by der Captain in 1902 and by der Inspector in 1905. As the result of a legal battle, Harold Knerr (1882-1949) took over the strip in 1914, while Dirks started a new strip, *The Captain and the Kids*, for the *New York World.* A stage adaptation appeared in 1903, and over the years the strips have been reprinted frequently in comic books. Both strips had their own comic books from the 1930s to the 1950s. Animated cartoon versions were directed by Gregory LaCava in 1916-1918 and by Friz Freleng for MGM in 1938-1939, and the Kids appeared on television in *MGM Cartoons* (ABC, 1960) and *The Fabulous Funnies* (NBC, 1978-1979).**

KAZ-1

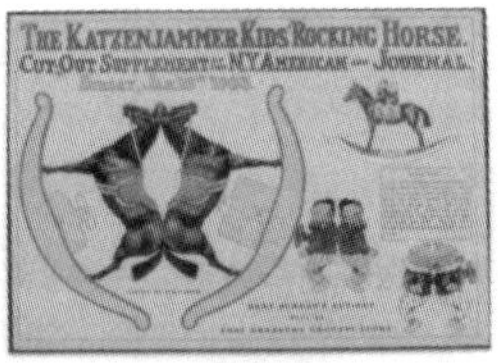

KAZ-2

❑ **KAZ-1. "Moritz" Dexterity Puzzle,**
c. 1900. 1-1/8" diameter with glass cover over compartment with three beads to place in recesses of color image. Max and Moritz were the German predecessors to the American Katzenjammer Kids. - **$30 $65 $125**

❑ **KAZ-2. "The Katzenjammer Kids' Rocking Horse" Early Newspaper Premi um Cut-Out Toy,**
1903. 10x14" stiff paper from Hearst Sunday newspaper. - **$15 $50 $100**

KAZ-3

❑ **KAZ-3. "The Katzies" Comic Strip Folder,**
1904. King Features copyright but no sponsor indicated. 2x3" folder that opens to 13-panel story. - **$15 $25 $50**

KAZ-4

KAZ-5

❑ **KAZ-4. Mama Spanking The Boys White Metal Stickpin,**
c. 1905. About 1-1/2" tall hand-colored with translucent reddish color wash. - **$10 $20 $40**

❑ **KAZ-5. Katzenjammers Heat Image Cartoon Postcard,**
1906. American Journal Examiner. Hidden image appears when heat is applied. - **$5 $10 $15**

KAZ-6

KAZ-7

❑ **KAZ-6. Katzenjammers Heat Image Postcard,**
1906. Hidden image appears when heat is applied. - **$5 $10 $15**

❑ **KAZ-7. Katzenjammer Heat Image Postcard,**
1906. Hidden image appears when heat is applied. - **$5 $10 $15**

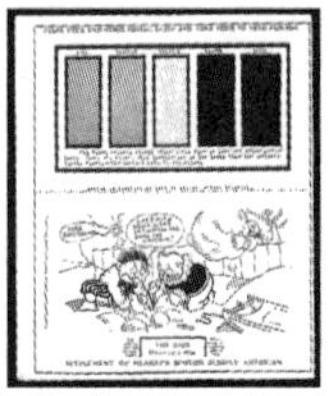
KAZ-8

KAZ-9

❑ **KAZ-8. Captain And The Kids Postcard,**
1907. Hearst's Boston Sunday American Newspaper Premium. Includes water color paint to paint comic. - **$20 $50 $90**

❑ **KAZ-9. "Jungle Joke Book" With R. Dirks Cover,**
1912. New York Sunday American. 10x12" Sunday supplement with cover cartoon by Katzenjammer artist Rudolph Dirks and 16 pages by various contemporary cartoonists. - **$15 $35 $70**

KAZ-10

KAZ-11

❑ **KAZ-10. Hot Air Balloon Picture Puzzle,**
c. 1915. Newspaper Feature Service. 4x4-1/2" cardboard jigsaw with eight interlocking pieces. - **$15 $30 $50**

❑ **KAZ-11. Mama And Kids Figurine,**
c. 1920. Store item. German made, hand-painted hollow bisque group figure. - **$60 $100 $175**

KAZ-12

❑ **KAZ-12. Hans German Bisque Figure,**
c. 1920. 3" tall. Fritz also likely produced. Each - **$75 $150 $250**

KAZ-13

❑ **KAZ-13. Comic Strip Reprint Book #2,**
1929. Store item by Saalfield Publishing Co. inscribed #193. 10x13-3/4" with color covers and 24 black and white pages. - **$40 $75 $150**

KAZ-14

KAZ-15

❑ **KAZ-14. "Comicaps" Bottle Caps,**
c. 1935. Golden Rod Beer. 1" diameter full color litho. tin. Each - **$10 $15 $30**

❑ **KAZ-15. "The Katzenjammer Kids" Fast Action Book,**
1942. Store item by Dell Publishing Company. #14 in series. - **$20 $60 $125**

KAZ-16

❑ **KAZ-16. Syroco Figures,**
1944. Store items. Painted wood composition.
Captain - **$30 $100 $150**
Hans - **$25 $75 $125**
Fritz - **$25 $75 $125**

KAZ-17

KAZ-18

❑ **KAZ-17. "Hingees" Punch-Out Kit With Envelope,**
1945. Store item. Contains two sheets of punch-out body parts for assembly into 3-D figures of major characters.
Unpunched In Envelope - **$15 $30 $65**

❑ **KAZ-18. Katzenjammer Character Litho. Buttons,**
1946. Kellogg's Pep. From box insert set picturing total of 86 comic characters.
Each - **$5 $15 $25**

# Kayo

**Frank Willard's *Moon Mullins*, one of the most successful comic strips of all time, first appeared in 1923. Four years later Moon was joined by kid brother Kayo, a brat in a derby hat. Together with Lord Plushbottom, Emmy, Uncle Willie, and Mamie, the Mullins boys were to hang out at carnivals and in pool rooms for decades. The Kayo name and character were licensed to promote a chocolate-flavored drink in the 1930s and 1940s. *Moon Mullins* comic books appeared from 1927 to 1933 and through the 1940s. After Willard's death in 1958 the strip was continued by long-time assistant Ferd Johnson.**

KAY-1

KAY-2

❑ **KAY-1. "Kayo And Moon Mullins-'Way Down South" Booklet,**
1934. Lemix & Corlix Desserts. Book #7 from Whitman series. - **$15 $40 $85**

❑ **KAY-2. "Kayo And Moon Mullins And The One Man Gang" Better Little Book,**
1939. Whitman #1415. - **$20 $50 $110**

KAY-3

KAY-4

❑ **KAY-3. "Moon Mullins" Original Art Premium Prototype Display,**
1930s. Designed for Ivory Soap. 12-1/8x21-1/2". Gordon Gold Archives. Unique. - **$300**

❑ **KAY-4. Yellow Mug,**
1930s. Mug pictures Kayo and promotes Kayo Hot Chocolate. - **$25 $50 $100**

KAY-5

❑ **KAY-5. Moon Mullins And Kayo Pair Of Jointed Wood Dolls,**
1930s. Store item by Jaymar. 5-1/2" and 4" tall respectively. Moon - **$40 $65 $125**
Kayo - **$50 $100 $175**

KAY-6

(FRONT) **KAY-7** (BACK)

❑ **KAY-6. Moon Mullins And Kayo Glazed Ceramic Figural Perfume Bottles ,**
1930s. Store item, unmarked but likely German-made. Moon is 8-1/4" tall with cigar in mouth and Kayo is 5-3/8" tall. Each - **$50 $115 $165**

❑ **KAY-7. Cloth Doll,**
1930s. Starched fabric from set believed issued by unknown cereal sponsor. Artist's facsimile signature on reverse. Six known.
Kayo, Moon Mullins, Herbie, Smitty Each - **$40 $80 $125**
Little Orphan Annie - **$75 $150 $200**
Sandy - **$50 $85 $150**

KAY-8

KAY-9

KAY-10

❑ **KAY-8. Club Member Cello. Button,**
1930s. Kayo Chocolate. - **$10 $20 $40**

❑ **KAY-9. "Kayo Comics Club" Litho. Button,**
1930s. San Francisco Chronicle newspaper. - **$20 $50 $100**

❑ **KAY-10. "Park Theater Kayo Club" Cello. Button,**
1930s. - **$20 $40 $85**

KAY-11

❑ **KAY-11. "Kayo/The Real Chocolate Malted Drink" Jigsaw Puzzle,**
1930s. - **$35 $75 $135**

(BOTTOM VIEW SHOWING DICE)

KAY-12

❑ **KAY-12. Statue with Dice Salesman's Premium,**
1930s. - **$200 $400 $800**

KAY-13

KAY-14

❑ **KAY-13. "Drink Kayo Chocolate" Transfer Picture,**
c. 1940s. Kayo Chocolate Drink. Image is reversed in unused condition. - **$20 $40 $75**

❑ **KAY-14. Promo Chocolate Drink Sign,**
1940s. Holed for display on bottle. - **$30 $90 $150**

KAY-15

❑ **KAY-15. Decal - Transfer Picture,**
1940s. Promotes chocolate drink. - **$20 $40 $75**

## Kellogg's Cereal Misc.

**Dr. John Harvey Kellogg (1852-1945) was at the center of a vegetarian health-food craze in Battle Creek, Michigan, in the late 19th century. The experimental kitchen at his Battle Creek Sanitarium created a number of meat substitutes for his patients, including Protose, Nuttose, Nuttolene, Granola, and Caramel Coffee. With his brother, W.K. Kellogg, he devised a wheat flake cereal in 1894 and, four years later, a variety made from corn, which he sold by mail as Sanitas Corn Flakes.**

**W.K. Kellogg struck out on his own in 1903, adding flavorings to the cereal, naming it Kellogg's Toasted Corn Flakes, and promoting it heavily with advertising and free samples. The cereal became, and remains, a breakfast staple in millions of homes. Over the years the company has used a variety of promotional symbols, starting with the Sweetheart of the Corn in 1907. With new cereals came the need for new personalities: Snap, Crackle, and Pop in 1933 to promote Kellogg's Rice Krispies, Tony the Tiger in 1953 for Kellogg's Sugar Frosted Flakes, and Toucan Sam in 1964.**

**Kellogg's sponsored many programs such as *Tom Corbett, Howdy Doody, Superman*, and *Huckleberry Hound* but the items in this section focus on characters specifically created for Kellogg's advertising and a sampling of the many non-character premiums they offered over the years. See separate sections devoted to Snap, Crackle, and Pop, as well as Tony the Tiger.**

KEL-1

❑ **KEL-1. "Kellogg's Funny Jungleland Moving-Pictures" Booklet,**
1909. Among the earliest premium booklets (3-1/2x4-3/4") but re-issued in 6x8" and available for many years.
Earliest Version - **$20 $40 $85**
Later Version - **$12 $20 $50**

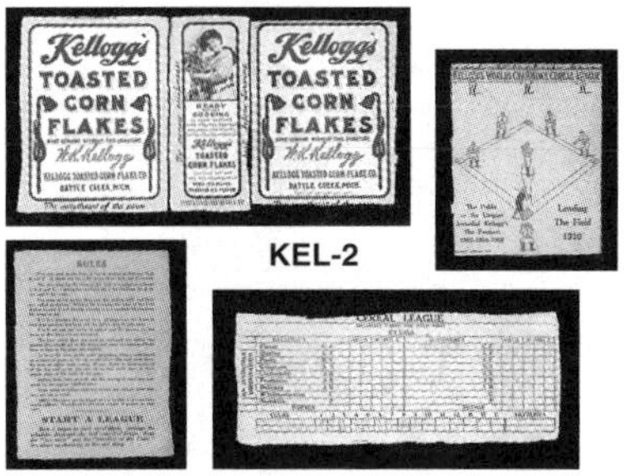


KEL-2

❑ **KEL-2. "Cereal League" Baseball Game Box Panels,**
1910. Three panels from same box of Kellogg's Toasted Corn Flakes, possibly the earliest cereal box game.
Complete - **$400**
As Shown - **$100 $200 $300**

KEL-3

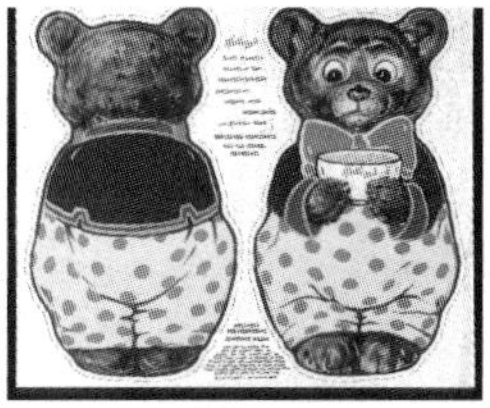

KEL-4

❑ **KEL-3. "My Visit To Kellogg's" Factory Visit Souvenir Book,**
c. 1924. - **$12 $20 $35**

❑ **KEL-4. Johnny Bear Uncut,**
1925. Kellogg's Corn Flakes premium. Goldilocks & The Three Bears cloth series. - **$40 $60 $100**

KEL-5

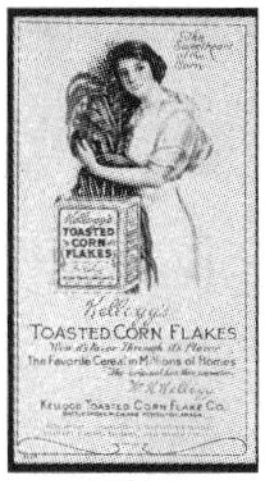


KEL-6

❑ **KEL-5. "Kellogg's Toasted Corn Flakes" Cello. Button,**
c. 1920s. - **$10 $25 $50**

❑ **KEL-6. Corn Flakes Blotter,**
1920s. Art deco blotter. Premium. - **$8 $15 $30**

KEL-7

KEL-8

❑ **KEL-7. Stamp Games #1,**
1931. 12 page book of fairy tales and games. Includes spinner and paper chips. -
**$25 $45 $60**

❑ **KEL-8. Stamp Games #3,**
1931. 12 page book of fairy tales and games. Includes spinner and paper chips. -
**$25 $45 $60**

KEL-9

KEL-10

❑ **KEL-9. Stamp Games #4,**
1931. 12 page book of fairy tales and games. Includes spinner and paper chips. -
**$25 $45 $60**

❑ **KEL-10. "Junior Texas Ranger Force" Member Certificate,**
1933. Facsimile signatures of commanding officer Colonel Louis and W. K. Kellogg. -
**$20 $50 $85**

KEL-11

❑ **KEL-11. Diet Book,**
1933. All Bran premium. 33 pages. "Keep On The Sunny Side Of Life." - **$10 $20 $30**

KEL-12

**❑ KEL-12. Corn Flakes Box Backs,**
1935. Features Kellogg's adventure stories on back. Tells plane stories about famous aviators like Admiral Byrd, Floyd Bennett, Cy Armstrong, Jack Traywick, and others.
Titles: Parachutes; Desperation and Science; Old Jonah
(1936 on); The Flying Dog; Bennett's Last Flight; Do-X The Flying Giant; Army Acrobatics; Mountain Mystery; An Unsung Hero; A Matter of Routine; The Red Dash Warning; Mid-AirTransfer; Night Wings.
Each - **$10 $25 $40**

KEL-13

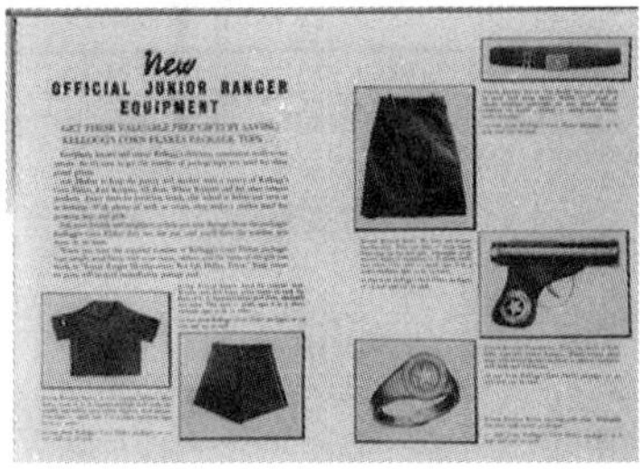


**❑ KEL-13. "Junior Texas Ranger" Club Kit,**
1936. Five paper items: Two premium folders, card that held badge, survey postcard, leaflet promoting Mother Goose stories by Kellogg's Singing Lady plus mailer.
Each - **$10 $25 $45**

KEL-14

**❑ KEL-14. "Vernon Grant Kellogg Town Kut-Outs,"**
1930s. Set of six. Each - **$5 $10 $15**

KEL-15

**❑ KEL-15. "Kellogg's 8 Model Planes" Store Display,**
1930s. 15x15x7" deep diecut cardboard.
Gordon Gold Archives. - **$150 $400 $600**

KEL-16

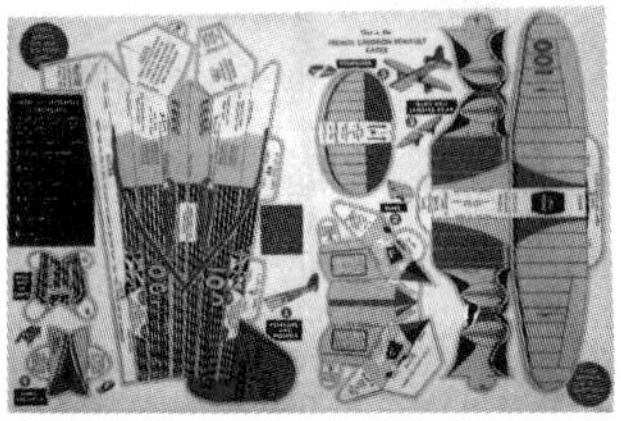

KEL-17

**❑ KEL-16. Die Cut Aeroplane Sign,**
1930s. Rare. Die cut standee promotes Corn Flakes and free planes. - **$175 $400 $600**

**❑ KEL-17. Premium Plane 13-1/2x20",**
1930s. Rare. Features Avion Cauldron cut-out plane. - **$50 $110 $175**

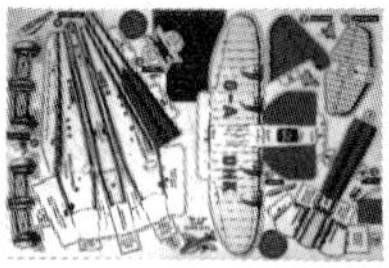

KEL-18

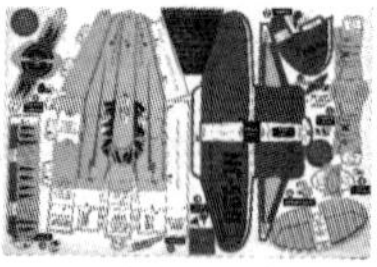

KEL-19

**❑ KEL-18. Premium Plane 13-1/2x20",**
1930s. Rare. Features Empire Flying Boat cut-out plane. - **$50 $110 $175**

**❑ KEL-19. Premium Plane 13-1/2x20",**
1930s. Rare. Features U.S. Stinson Reliant cut-out plane. - **$50 $110 $175**

KEL-20

KEL-21

**❑ KEL-20. Premium Plane 13-1/2x20",**
1930s. Rare. Features Brewster Scout Plane cut-out. - **$50 $110 $175**

**❑ KEL-21. Premium Plane 13-1/2x20",**
1930s. Rare. Features Seversky Convoy Fighter Plane cut-out. - **$50 $110 $175**

KEL-22

❑ **KEL-22. "Kellogg's Planes Of All Nations" Store Sign,**
1930s. Kellogg's All-Wheat. 18x25" in red, white, blue and yellow. Depicts the initial series of six designs on back panels of cereal boxes. Gordon Gold Archives. - **$50 $125 $225**

KEL-23

❑ **KEL-23. Fairy Tales Wall Plaques Premium Sign 12x18",**
1930s. Rare. Designed by Vernon Grant, picturing six plaques. Sign - **$200 $400 $600**
Each Plaque - **$25 $50 $100**

KEL-24

KEL-25

❑ **KEL-24. Baseball Hat with Mailer,**
1930s. - **$20 $45 $65**

❑ **KEL-25. Beamy Beanie with Mailer,**
1942. Scarce. - **$25 $75 $100**

KEL-26

❑ **KEL-26. "Kellogg's Pep Model Warplanes" 16x43" Advertising Poster,**
c. 1942. Scarce. - **$75 $250 $450**

KEL-27

❑ **KEL-27. "Kellogg's Pep Model Plane Kit" Store Sign,**
c. 1942. 10-1/2x14" stiff cardboard in red, green and white. Gordon Gold Archives. -
**$75 $150 $300**

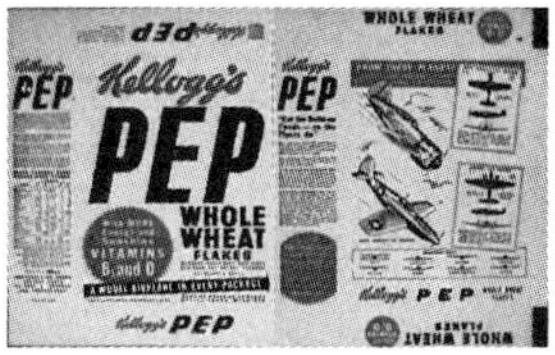


KEL-28

❑ **KEL-28. Cereal Box Flat Featuring Model Airplanes,**
c. 1942. 12x17-1/2" cardboard flat promotes punch-out planes and has pair of cut-out "Plane Spotter Cards." Gordon Gold Archives.
Near Mint Flat - **$300**
Used Complete - **$50 $125 $200**

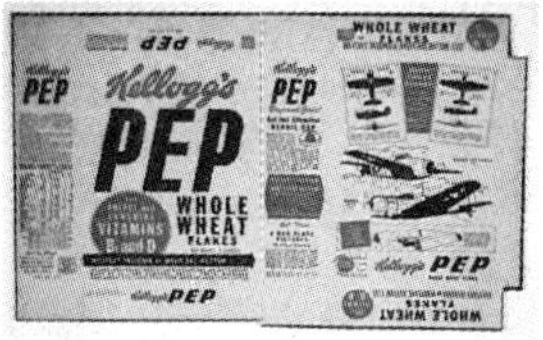


KEL-29

❑ **KEL-29. Cereal Box Flat,**
c. 1942. Front offers military insignia and warplane buttons. Side panel offers "Beanie Cap" and a set of six "Warplane Pictures." Back panel has cards #41 and #42 from series of at least 42 different. Gordon Gold Archives.
Near Mint Flat - **$300**
Used Complete - **$50 $125 $200**

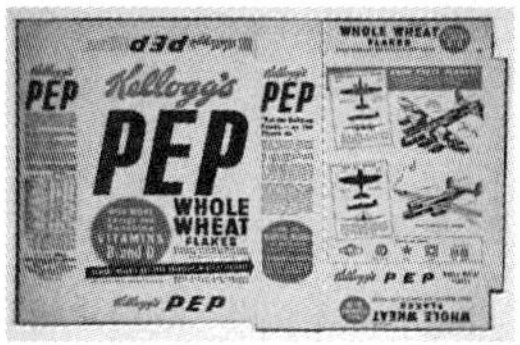


KEL-30

❑ **KEL-30. Cereal Box Flat,**
c. 1942. Promotes "Combat Insignia Hot Iron Transfers" included in each box while back panel has cards #3 and #4 from series of at least 42 different. Gordon Gold Archives.
Near Mint Flat - **$300**
Used Complete - **$50 $125 $200**

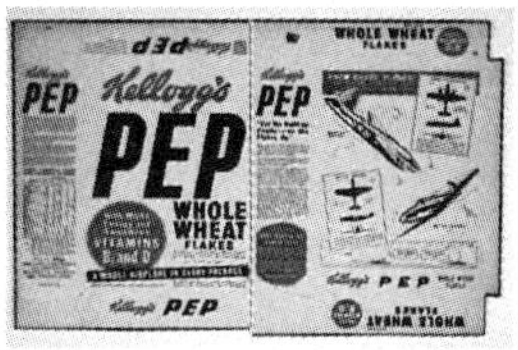


KEL-31

❑ **KEL-31. Cereal Box Flat,**
c. 1942. Front promotes series of color model warplane punch-outs while reverse has cut-out airplane cards #17 and #18 from a series of at least 42 different. Gordon Gold Archives.
Near Mint Flat - **$300**
Used Complete - **$50 $125 $200**

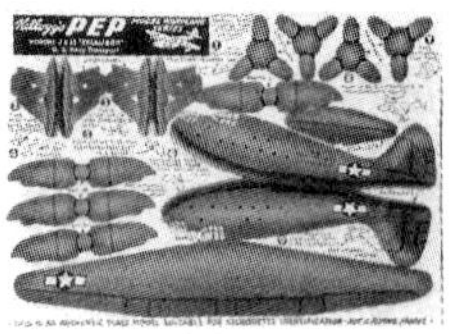

KEL-32

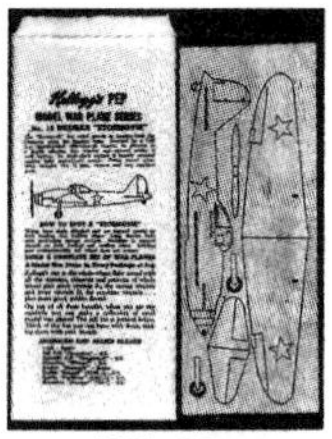

KEL-33

❑ **KEL-32. "Kellogg's Pep Model Warplane" Punch-Out,**
c. 1942. Set of 28 as follows:
Series "A":
❑ A1 - Vought SB2U "Vindicator" U.S. Dive Bomber
❑ A2 - Boulton Paul "Defiant" British Night Fighter
❑ A3 - Lockheed P-38 "Lightning" U.S. Fighter
❑ A4 - Sikorsky VS-300 U.S. Helicopter
❑ A5 - Douglas A-20C or A-20 "Havoc" U.S. Attack Bomber
❑ A6 - Grumman F6F "Hellcat" U.S. Fighter
❑ A7 - North American B-25 "Mitchell" U.S. Attack Bomber.
Series "B":
❑ B1 - Westland "Whirlwind" British Fighter
❑ B2 - YAK-4 Russian Fighter/Bomber
❑ B3 - Douglas A-24 "Dauntless" U.S. Dive Bomber
❑ B4 - Curtiss P-40F "Warhawk" U.S. Fighter
❑ B5 - Short "Sunderland" British Patrol Bomber
❑ B6 - Vought JR2S "Excalibur" U.S. Navy Transport
❑ B7 - Consolidated Vultee B-24 "Liberator" U.S. Heavy Bomber
Series "C":
❑ C1 - Boeing B-17E "Flying Fortress" U.S. Heavy Bomber
❑ C2 - De Havilland "Mosquito" British Medium Bomber
❑ C3 - Grumman F4F "Wildcat" U.S. Navy Fighter
❑ C4 - Republic P-47 "Thunderbolt" U.S. Fighter
❑ C5 - Doulgas A-17A U.S. Attack Bomber
❑ C6 - "Mosca" Russian Fighter
❑ C7 - Supermarine "Spitfire" British Fighter
Series "D":

❑ D1 - Lockheed C-69 "Constellation" U.S. Transport Plane
❑ D2 - Curtiss SB2C-1C "Helldiver" U.S. Dive Bomber
❑ D3 - Douglas C-54 "Skymaster" U.S. Transport
❑ D4 - Handley-Page "Hampden" British Bomber
❑ D5 - Avro "Lancaster" British Heavy Bomber
❑ D6 - Lockheed B-34 "Ventura" U.S. Bomber
❑ D7 - I-18 Russian Fighter
Each Unpunched - **$15 $25 $50**

❑ **KEL-33. "Pep Model Warplane" Balsa Sheet In Envelope,**
c. 1942. Numbered series, some envelopes mention Superman radio show. Believed to be a set of 21. Each In Envelope - **$15 $25 $50**

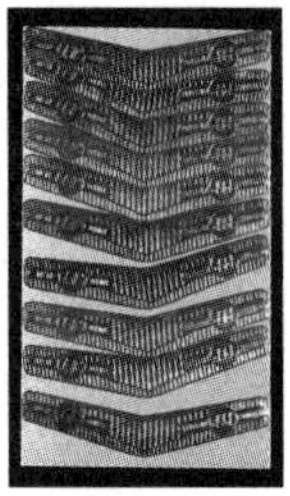

KEL-34

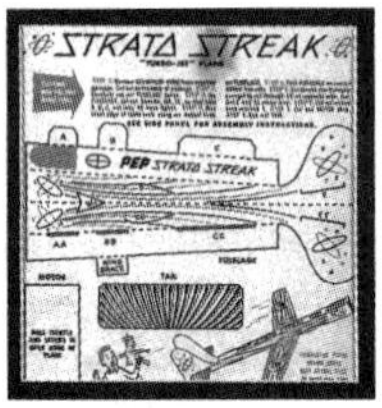


KEL-35

❑ **KEL-34. Pep Aluminum Wings,**
1943. Each Pep box contained an aluminum wing for turbo jet cut-out planes on back. Ten wings pictured for the ten plane set shown. Each - **$5 $10 $20**

❑ **KEL-35. Pep Cereal Back For Turbo Jet Plane Cut-Outs,**
1943. Strato Streak cut-out plane. - **$10 $25 $50**

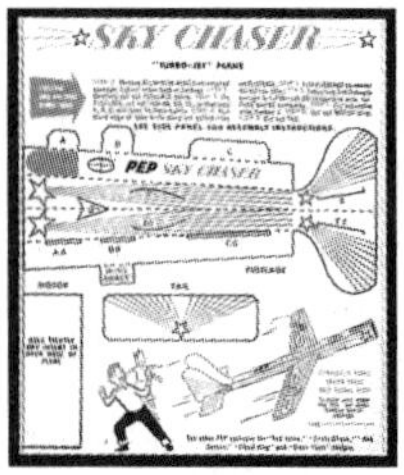


KEL-36

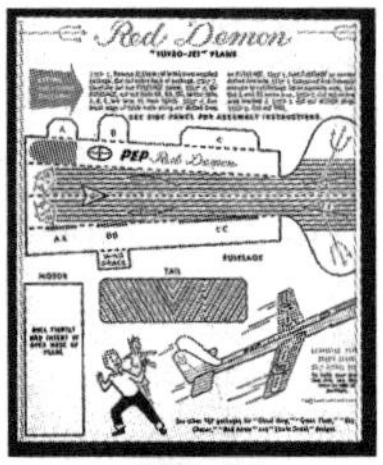


KEL-37

❑ **KEL-36. Pep Cereal Back For Turbo Jet Plane Cut-Outs,**
1943. Sky Chaser cut-out plane. - **$10 $25 $50**

❑ **KEL-37. Pep Cereal Back For Turbo Jet Plane Cut-Outs,**
1943. Red Demon cut-out plane. - **$10 $25 $50**

KEL-38

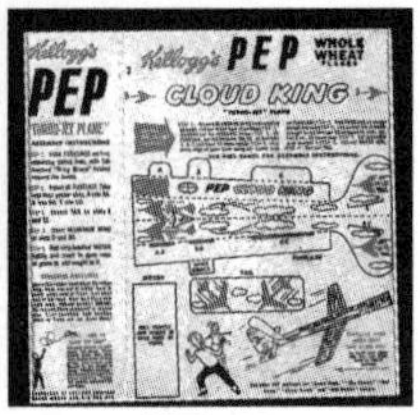


KEL-39

❑ **KEL-38. Pep Cereal Back For Turbo Jet Plane Cut-Outs,**
1943. Red Arrow cut-out plane. - **$10 $25 $50**

❑ **KEL-39. Pep Cereal Back For Turbo Jet Plane Cut-Outs,**
1943. Cloud King cut-out plane. - **$10 $25 $50**

KEL-40

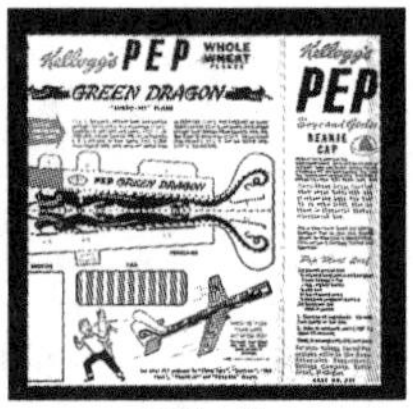


KEL-41

❑ **KEL-40. Pep Cereal Back For Turbo Jet Plane Cut-Outs,**
1943. Green Flash cut-out plane. -
**$10 $25 $50**

❑ **KEL-41. Pep Cereal Back For Turbo Jet Plane Cut-Outs,**
1943. Green Danger cut-out plane. -
**$10 $25 $50**

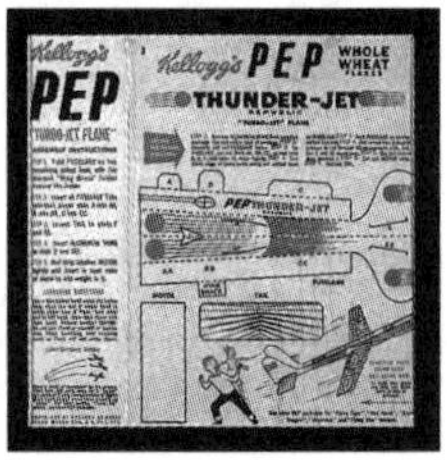


KEL-42

❑ **KEL-42. Pep Cereal Back For Turbo Jet Plane Cut-Outs,**
1943. Thunder-Jet cut-out plane. -
**$10 $25 $50**

KEL-43

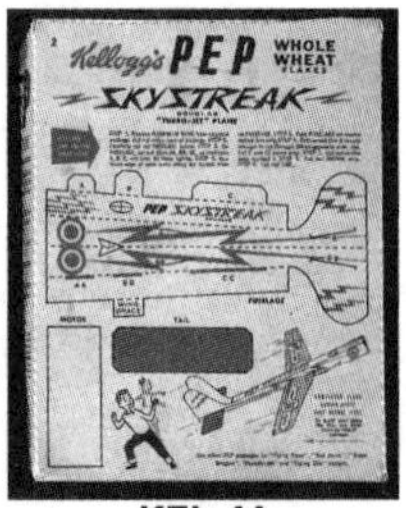


KEL-44

❑ **KEL-43. Pep Cereal Back For Turbo Jet Plane Cut-Outs,**
1943. Flying Tiger cut-out plane. - **$10 $25 $50**

❑ **KEL-44. Pep Cereal Box,**
1943. Promotes Turbo Jet Plane program. Each box shows cut-out. Sky Streak plane pictured. Complete Box - **$50 $100 $200**

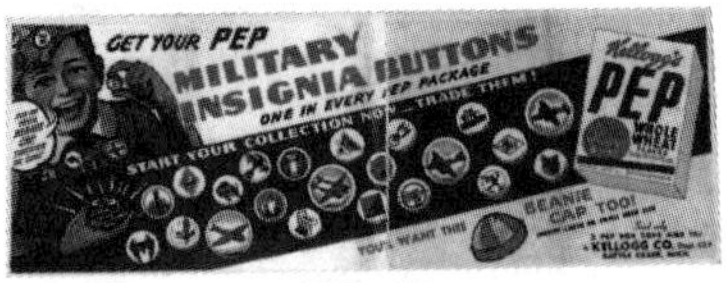


KEL-45

❑ **KEL-45. "Pep Military Insignia Buttons" 16x44" Paper Store Banner,**
1943. Scarce. Reverse offers beanie cap as mail premium for pinning box insert insignia and aircraft litho. buttons. - **$100 $300 $500**

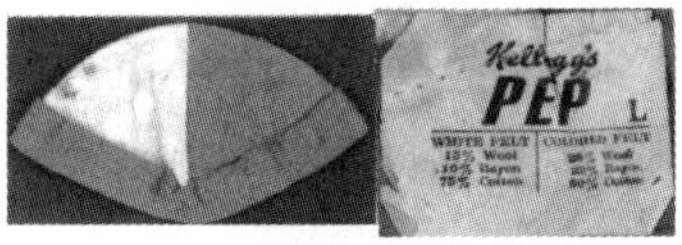


KEL-46

KEL-47

❑ **KEL-46. "Kellogg's Pep" Felt Beanie,**
1943. Orange and white.
With Tag - **$25 $60 $100**
Missing Tag - **$15 $25 $50**

❑ **KEL-47. Pep Beany/Military Insignia Buttons 16x44" Paper Store Poster,**
1943. Scarce. - **$100 $275 $450**

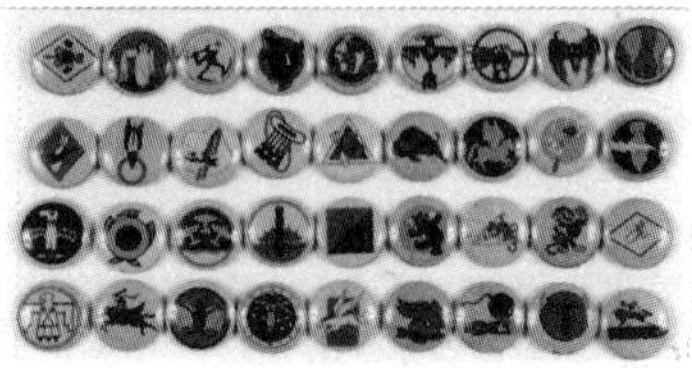

KEL-48

❑ **KEL-48. Pep Military Insignia Litho. Buttons,**
1943. Set of 36. Paint very susceptible to aging and wear, most examples grade fine or worse. Each - **$5 $12 $20**

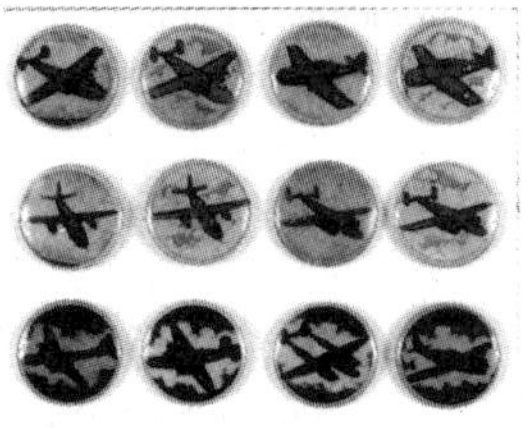

KEL-49

❑ **KEL-49. Pep Airplane Litho. Buttons,**
1943. Set of 12. Four planes in green, four planes in brown with photo-style artwork and same four planes in brown with hand illustrated style artwork. Paint very susceptible to wear. Each - **$30 $90 $140**

KEL-50

❑ **KEL-50. Pep "Plane Spotter" Box Card,**
c. 1944. Two cards on each back, at least 42 cards in set. Uncut Back - **$10 $15 $25**

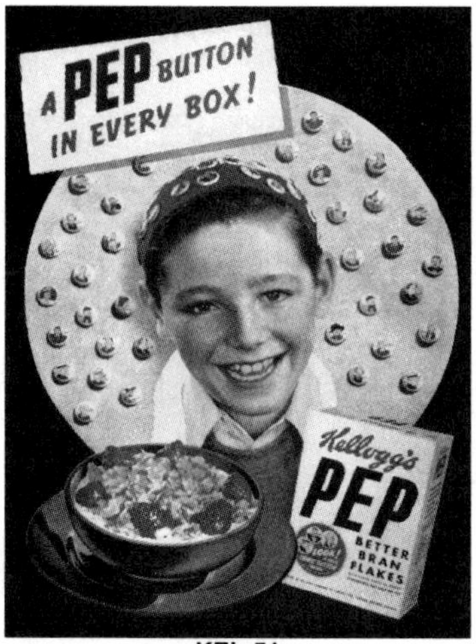


KEL-51

❑ **KEL-51. Pep Large Diecut Cardboard Sign,**
1945. 38" x 26". Features Pep buttons and boy wearing Pep beanie. Three known. - **$750 $2750 $4500**

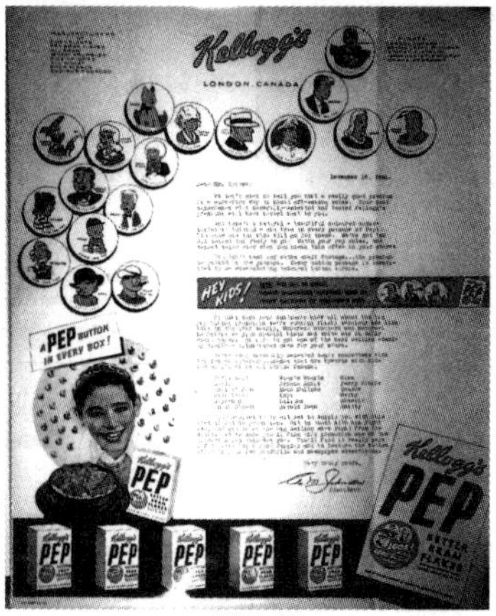


KEL-52

❑ **KEL-52. Pep Large Promo Letter Picturing Sign,**
1945. Letter to grocer explaining the value of the comic button program. Shows picture of the rare sign. Gold Archives. - **$200 $450 $625**

KEL-53

❑ **KEL-53. Pep Comic Character Litho. Button Set,**
1945. Complete set of 86. Issued in 1945-46 sealed in paper or cellophane packet inside specially marked boxes of Kellogg's Pep cereal. There were 5 sets each of 18 buttons, but Superman was included in each set, so the result is 86 different buttons.
Near Mint Set of 86 - **$2000**
Most Characters - **$8 $15 $25**
Felix - **$15 $30 $60**
Phantom - **$25 $50 $85**

KEL-54

❑ **KEL-54. Comic Character Error Litho. Button,**
1945. Manufacturing error caused by running the litho. tin sheet with images printed on both sides facing the wrong direction as it passed through the stamping machine. Reverse of this button has perfect color image of "Uncle Bim." Typically an error of this nature would have been discarded but somehow this example survived. Similar Examples - **$100 $200 $400**

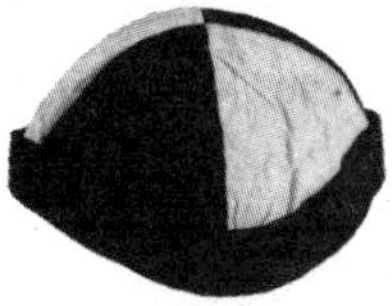

KEL-55

KEL-56

❑ **KEL-55. Pep Beanie,**
1945. Black and white.
With Tag - **$25 $60 $100**
Missing Tag - **$15 $25 $50**

❑ **KEL-56. "Metal Pin-On Comic Buttons" Ad,**
c. 1945. Comic book page ad for Kellogg's Pep box insert buttons although indicating complete set of 18 as opposed to eventual final set of 86. - **$3 $6 $10**

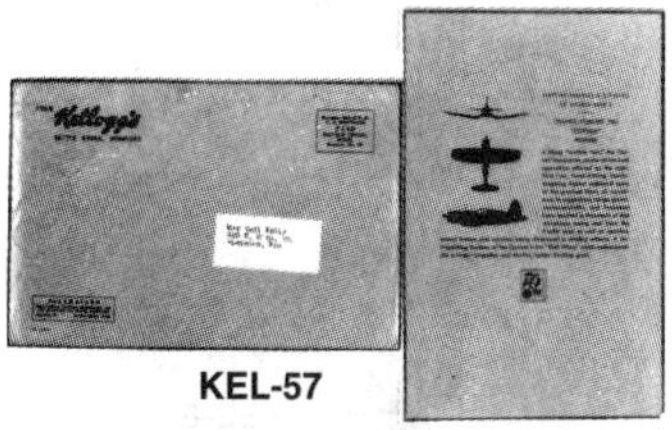


KEL-57

❑ **KEL-57. Pep Punch-Out Warplane Pictures With Envelope,**
c. 1945. Set of six. Near Mint In Mailer - **$325**

KEL-58

❑ **KEL-58. "Kellogg's Walky Talky" Punch-Out,**
c. 1945. Near Mint In Mailer - **$375**
Complete Assembled Pair - **$50 $125 $200**
Promotional Sign (Not Shown) -
**$100 $250 $375**

KEL-59

❑ **KEL-59. "Kellogg's Pep Real Photos" 16x20" Paper Sign,**
c. 1947. Pictures example movie and sports stars miniature photos offered individually as box inserts. - **$75 $150 $250**

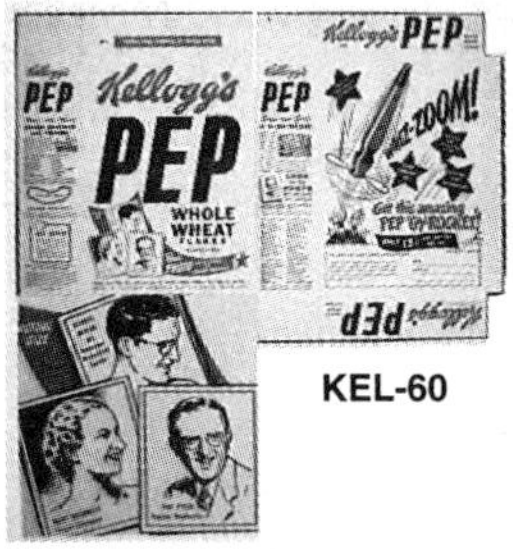


KEL-60

❑ **KEL-60. "Real Photo" And "Gy-Rocket" Cereal Box Flat,**
1947. Front panel promotes series of 66 photos with offer for a photo album. Reverse has offer for "Pep Gy-Rocket." Gordon Gold Archives.
Near Mint Flat - **$200**
Used Complete - **$30 $60 $100**

KEL-61

❑ **KEL-61. Pep Comic Character Buttons Ad Sheet,**
1947. Canadian issue. - **$75 $150 $250**

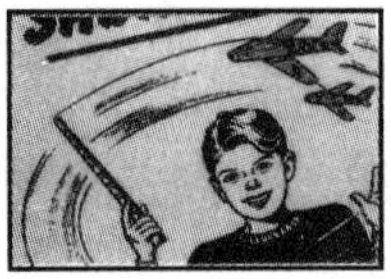

(CLOSE-UP)

KEL-62

❑ **KEL-62. "Flight Control Sabre Jet Plane",**
c. 1948. Unused In Mailer - **$20 $50 $100**

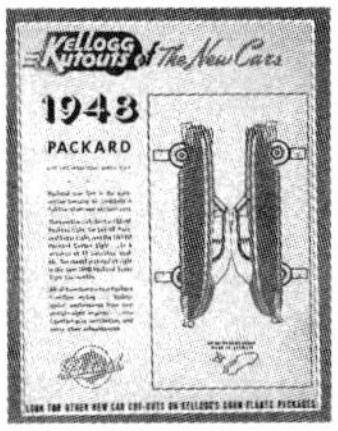


KEL-63

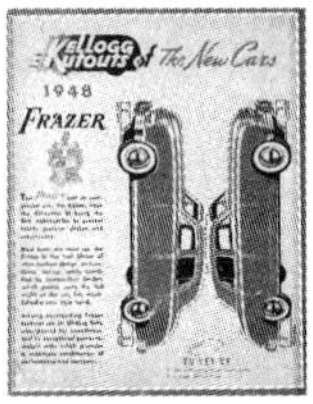


KEL-64

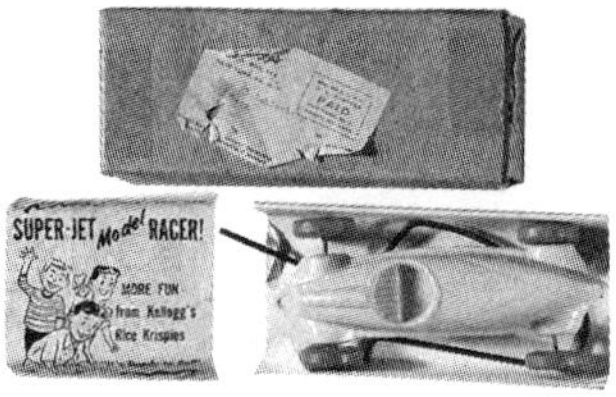


KEL-65

❑ **KEL-63. Auto Cut-Outs,**
1948. Corn Flakes box back shows cut-out of 1948 Packard. - **$25 $40 $50**

❑ **KEL-64. Auto Cut-Outs,**
1948. Corn Flakes box back shows cut-out of 1948 Frazer. - **$25 $40 $50**

❑ **KEL-65. Super Jet Racer**
1949. Rare. Yellow racer with red wheels, instructions, spring, mailer, and Rice Krispies ad. Complete - **$50 $75 $200**

KEL-66

KEL-67

KEL-68

❑ **KEL-66. Presidents Album,**
1949. Kellogg's Premium. 36 page stamp album. - **$10 $20 $40**

❑ **KEL-67. Presidents Album Mailer,**
1949. Kellogg's Premium. - **$5 $12 $20**

❑ **KEL-68. Presidents Album - The Stamps,**
1949. Kellogg's Premium. 32 different large stamps (cereal box contained 1 stamp).
Each - **$2 $4 $6**

KEL-69

❑ **KEL-69. "Warship Transfer" Cereal Box Flat,**
c. 1940s. Transfers came one per box. Back panel illustrates "L.S.T./Landing Ship, Tank" plus four "U.S. Navy Specialty Insignia" with panel marked "#9 Of A Series." Gordon Gold Archives. Near Mint Flat - **$125**
Used Complete - **$20 $40 $75**

KEL-70

❑ **KEL-70. Punch-Out Airport in Mailer,**
1940s. - **$30 $90 $150**

KEL-71

❑ **KEL-71. Kellogg's Pep "Photo Album",**
1940s. 10 pages for mounting miniature premium photos of sports and entertainment stars.
Near Mint With Mailer - **$150**
Album Only - **$35 $60 $100**

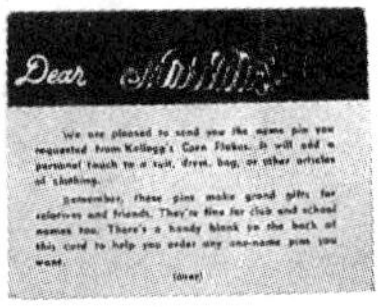

KEL-72

KEL-73

❑ **KEL-72. Pin Premium On Card,**
1940s. Metal name pin premium for 2 Corn Flakes box tops and10¢. - **$15 $25 $35**

❑ **KEL-73. Pennant ,**
1940s. Cereal premium, 17" long. - **$25 $60 $100**

**KEL-74**

❑ **KEL-74. College Prom Photo Sign,**
1940s. Pep On The Air - N.B.C. Blue Network. - **$15 $25 $50**

**KEL-75**

❑ **KEL-75. "Stagecoach" Toy With Mailer And Coupon,**
1950. Sugar Frosted Flakes, Sugar Smacks, Sugar Pops. 7" long replica plastic toy with order coupon in mailer carton. Near Mint Box - **$85**
Stagecoach - **$10 $25 $40**

**KEL-76**

❑ **KEL-76. Box Flat And Ad Proof For Picture Ring Premiums,**
1950. Cereal box promotes set of 16 plastic rings with domed inserts which were inserted one per box. Ad proof is 10x15" picturing example Wanda Hendricks ring. Gordon Gold Archives. Near Mint Flat - **$225**
Used Complete - **$40 $75 $125**
Ad Proof - **$10 $20 $40**

**KEL-77**

❑ **KEL-77. "Kellogg's Pep" Box With Ring Ads,**
1950. Complete Box - **$75 $175 $250**

**KEL-78**

**KEL-79**

❑ **KEL-78. Sugar Smacks Flat,**
1951. Soldier premium offer. Maxie the seal on front. - **$50 $200 $300**

❑ **KEL-79. Soldiers in Mailer,**
1951. 12 total. Complete - **$35 $100 $175**

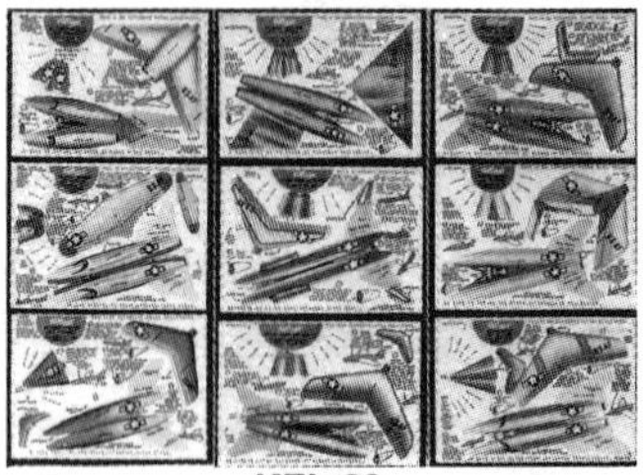

**KEL-80**

❑ **KEL-80. "Flying Model Jet Planes" Punch-Outs,**
1951. Ten in the set: Convair the Flying Triangle, Douglas Sky Rocket, Lockheed Fighter, Lockheed Shooting Star, Martin XB-51, North American Saber Jet, Northrop Flying Laboratory, Republic Interceptor, Republic Thunderjet (2 different). Unpunched Each - **$10 $15 $25**

**KEL-81**

❑ **KEL-81. "Free Comic Buttons" Store Sign,**
1952. Premium Specialties, Chicago, Ill. 9x20" sign pictures "18 Different Comics" buttons identical in design to the same characters in the Kellogg's Pep set of 86. However, this was a later offering unrelated to the Kellogg's promotion. Sign has blank area for sponsor's imprint. Gordon Gold Archives. - **$100 $200 $300**

**KEL-82**

❑ **KEL-82. Sugar Frosted Flake Insignia Box Back,**
1953. Armed Forces shoulder patch insignia. Box back with patch premium offer.
Each Patch - **$5 $10 $15**
Box Back - **$15 $30 $50**

**KEL-83**

❑ **KEL-83. Corn Flakes Cereal Box Flat,**
1953. Promotes Demon Dan mask on back of box. - **$35 $80 $200**

**KEL-84**

❑ **KEL-84. Rice Krispies Cereal Box Flat,**
1953. Canadian issued. Promotes free Atom Sub inside box. - **$50 $100 $225**

**KEL-85**

**KEL-86**

**KEL-87**

❑ **KEL-85. Baking Soda Frogman 3-1/2" Size,**
1954. Obstacles Scout. Depicts scuba diver holding knife. Various colors. - **$10 $30 $60**

❑ **KEL-86. Baking Soda Frogman 3-1/2" Size,**
1954. Demolitions Expert. Depicts diver holding mine. Various colors. - **$10 $30 $60**

❑ **KEL-87. Baking Soda Frogman 3-1/2" Size,**
1954. Torch Man. Depicts diver holding cutting torch. Various colors. - **$10 $30 $60**

**KEL-88**

❑ **KEL-88. U.S. Army Swamp Glider,**
1955. Sugar Frosted Flakes premium. Includes glider, instructions, and box. - **$30 $75 $150**

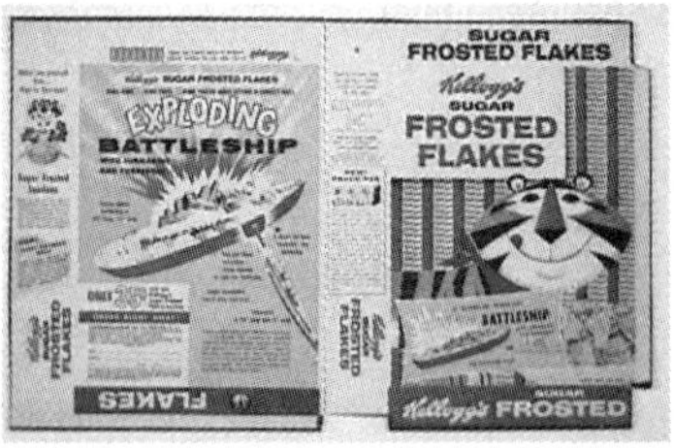

**KEL-89**

❑ **KEL-89. "Exploding Battleship" Cereal Box Flat,**
1958. Premium consisted of hard plastic battle-ship and submarine with torpedos. Gordon Gold Archives. Near Mint Flat - **$200**
Used Complete - **$30 $65 $110**

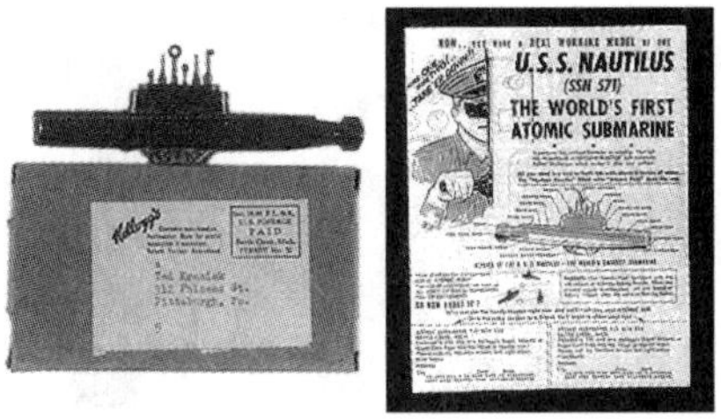

**KEL-90**

❑ **KEL-90. U.S.S. Nautilus Submarine Toy With Mailer,** 1950s. Sugar Smacks or Sugar Corn Pops. 4-1/2" toy powered by "Atomic Fuel" of baking powder. Pictured instruction sheet is earliest version. See KEL-103.
Near Mint Boxed - **$175**
Nautilus Only - **$10 $30 $60**

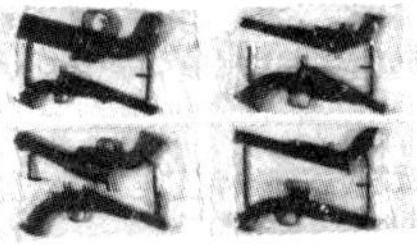
**KEL-91**

**KEL-92**

❑ **KEL-91. "Famous Guns of History" Sets,**
1950s. Pep Wheat Flakes premium. 8 different, 2 to a set. Each Set - **$10 $20 $40**

❑ **KEL-92. "Famous Guns of History" Box Back,**
1950s. Famous guns of history pictured. - **$10 $20 $30**

**KEL-93**

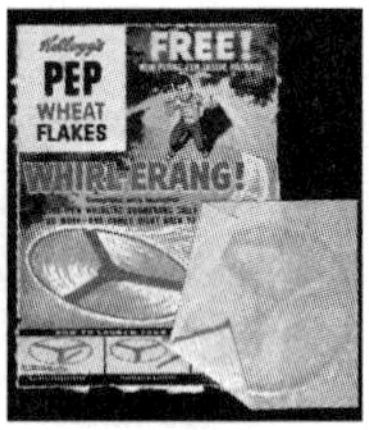

**KEL-94**

❑ **KEL-93. Jumbly Jungle Book with Mailer,**
1950s. - **$20 $30 $40**

❑ **KEL-94. Pep Whirl-Erang,**
1950s. Scarce. Discontinued because children were injured. - **$10 $20 $40**
Box Back with Ad - **$50**

**KEL-95**

❑ **KEL-95. Men Of The Wild West Cereal Box Back Panels,**
1963. Kellogg's. Set of 12: Cody, Custer, Carson, Bowie, Boone, "Yellowstone" Kelly, Houston, Sutter, Fremont, Slaughter, "Portugee" Phillips. Used Complete Box - **$25 $50 $100**
Each Cut Back - **$5 $10 $20**

**KEL-96**

❑ **KEL-96. Famous Indians Cereal Box Backs,**
c. 1963. No date or company name appears on the back panel cut-outs but these seem closely related to the Kellogg's "Men Of The Wild West" set. Probably set of 12. We have seen: Corn Planter, King Philip, Little Turtle, Logan, Osceola, Pontiac, Tecumseh.
Used Complete Box - **$25 $50 $75**
Each Cut Back - **$5 $10 $20**

**KEL-97**

❑ **KEL-97. "Corvette" Battery Operated Plastic Model Car,**
1965. Made by Ideal, issued by Kellogg's. 4-1/2" long. Near Mint Boxed - **$125**

**KEL-98**

❑ **KEL-98. Old West Trail Booklet,**
1968. Kellogg's premium. 16 pages history of the Old West.- **$15 $30 $50**

**KEL-99**

❑ **KEL-99. Robin Hood Premium Figures,**
1968. Kellogg's Sugar Smacks. About 2" tall plastic figures in various single colors with "Kellogg's" and character name under base. Set of 14 different. Each - **$8 $15 $25**

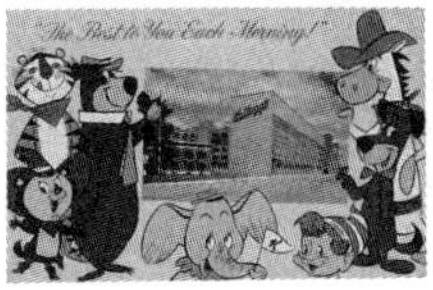

**KEL-100**

❑ **KEL-100. Postcard,**
1960s. Postcard features many cartoon and cereal characters like Yogi Bear and Tony the Tiger. - **$8 $15 $30**

KEL-101

❑ **KEL-101. "U.S. Navy PT Boat",**
c. 1960s. Includes boat, jet race way, package of propellant and instruction sheet.
Near Mint Boxed - **$175**
Boat Only - **$15 $30 $70**

KEL-102

❑ **KEL-102. Cereal Box With "Pin-Me-Ups" Back,**
1960s. Set of eight featuring Hanna-Barbera characters. Complete Box - **$20 $40 $75**

KEL-103

❑ **KEL-103. "U.S.S. Nautilus" Plastic Atomic Sub,**
c. 1960s. Later issue than KEL-90 with different box label and small differences on instructions.
Near Mint In Box - **$150**
Sub Only - **$10 $30 $60**

KEL-104

❑ **KEL-104. Sugar Pops 12 oz. Cereal Box Flat with Yo-yo Offer,**
1970. Offers free yo-yo in box.
Box - **$25 $50 $90**
Yo-yo - **$2 $4 $10**

KEL-105

KEL-106

❑ **KEL-105. "Dig 'Em" Metal Wind-Up Alarm Clock,**
1979. - **$15 $35 $60**

❑ **KEL-106. "Toucan Sam" Plastic Secret Decoder,**
1983. Movable disk code wheel. Comes in different colors - **$5 $12 $20**

KEL-107

❑ **KEL-107. Vanessa Williams 1984 Miss America Commemorative Corn Flakes Box,**
1984. These boxes hit the stores just before the scandal surfaced that cost her the crown. She has since moved on to become a successful actress and singer. - **$30 $75 $150**

KEL-108

❑ **KEL-108. Plastic Cereal Bowl Premiums,**
1995. Four bowls feature Corny, Rice Krispies' Snap, Crackle and Pop, Tony and Toucan Sam. Each bowl - **$20**

## Ken Maynard

**An all-around sagebrush hero, cowboy actor Maynard (1895-1973) was first an accomplished trick rider and rodeo championship rider. Pre-movie years included performances at King Ranch, Texas; Buffalo Bill's Wild West Show, Ringling Bros. Wild West Show, Tex Rickard's World's Champion Cowboy competition (first place in 1920). He was introduced into silent movies by Tom Mix and best remembered for his First National films of the mid-1920s and following decade, also featuring his talented horse Tarzan. He is credited by many as the first to introduce song to the western movie. His 1938-1948 years were mostly a return to live performances and he continued to draw audiences even into his fifties.**

KEN-1

KEN-2

KEN-3

❑ **KEN-1. "First National Films" Studio Matchbook,**
1929. Reverse lists six film titles from that year. - **$12 $20 $30**

❑ **KEN-2. "Ken Maynard Club/First National Pictures" Cello. Button,**
c. 1929. - **$15 $30 $60**

❑ **KEN-3. Paper Mask,**
1933. Einson-Freeman movie promo. - **$50 $125 $300**

KEN-4

KEN-5

❑ **KEN-4. Dixie Ice Cream Picture,**
1934. Title on reverse is "In Old Santa Fe." - **$20 $40 $75**

❑ **KEN-5. Dixie Ice Cream Picture,**
1934. Reverse pictures scenes from serial "Mystery Mountain." - **$20 $40 $60**

KEN-6

❑ **KEN-6. "Gun Justice Featuring Ken Maynard" Big Little Book,**
1934. Whitman #776. - **$20 $50 $100**

KEN-7

KEN-8

❑ **KEN-7. "Wheels Of Destiny Featuring Ken Maynard" Book,**
1934. Engel-Van Wiseman Five Star Library Book #5. Movie edition. - **$30 $60 $110**

❑ **KEN-8. "Ken Maynard in Western Justice" Big Little Book #1430,**
1938. - **$10 $35 $80**

KEN-9

KEN-10

❑ **KEN-9. "Ken Maynard" Penny Book,**
1938. Store item by Whitman. - **$10 $20 $40**

❑ **KEN-10. "Ken Maynard & Tarzan" Pinback,**
1930s. Large 1-3/4" with yellow background. Scarce. - **$35 $70 $125**

KEN-11

KEN-12

❑ **KEN-11. Movie Photo Card,**
1930s. Color card. Scarce. - **$10 $20 $40**
Black and white card - **$5 $10 $20**

❑ **KEN-12. "Round Up/Buckaroo Club" Card,**
1930s. Various radio stations. - **$15 $30 $60**

KEN-13

❑ **KEN-13. "Ken Maynard Western Star First Nat'l" Cigar Band,**
c. 1930s. Gold foil with black and white photo. - **$10 $20 $35**

KEN-14

KEN-15

❑ **KEN-14. Portrait Cello. Button,**
1930s. Probably circus souvenir. - **$30 $60 $125**

❑ **KEN-15. "Cole Bros. Circus" Cello. Button,**
1930s. - **$50 $125 $175**

KEN-16

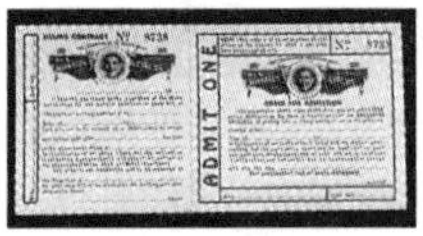


KEN-17

KEN-18

❑ **KEN-16. "Ken Maynard's Wild West And Indian Congress" Performance Ticket,**
1930s. Printed identically on both sides including small title for Diamond K Ranch. - **$10 $25 $40**

❑ **KEN-17. "Ken Maynard's Wild West Circus And Indian Congress" Contract Agreement Pass,**
1930s. Paper perforated into billing contract on left for right to post advertising, entitling free admission pass on right.
Complete - **$20 $40 $75**

❑ **KEN-18. Movie Press Book,**
1940. Colony Pictures Inc. 12x18" glossy eight-page exploitation manual. - **$15 $30 $70**

## King Features Misc.

**King Features Syndicate, the country's largest newspaper comic-strip syndicator, has been the agency of such legendary giants as Popeye, Flash Gordon, Felix the Cat, Krazy Kat, Beetle Bailey, Henry, Skippy, Betty Boop, Barney Google, and dozens of other major comic characters. In 1915 King Features became the sales agent for all the combined Hearst Newspapers syndicate operations. Over the years it has issued a number of items promoting various combinations of its comic characters.**

KIN-1

KIN-2

❑ **KIN-1. "Polar Lark" Metal Paperweight,**
1926. 10 King Features character heads form North Pole in homage to Commander Byrd's flight over pole. - **$150 $325 $650**

❑ **KIN-2. The Comic Club Stamps,**
1934. Wrigley's Gum. 18 stamps on sheet. - **$60 $125 $175**

KIN-3

❑ **KIN-3. Christmas Card Folder To Media Customers,**
1935. Authorized Hallmark Card publication with 24 full color pages featuring prominent King Features comic strip characters illustrating story theme "T'was The Night Before Christmas." - **$200 $400 $700**

KIN-4

❑ **KIN-4. King Features Syndicate Character Cloth Panel,**
1938. 12-3/4x16-7/8" premium offered as "Comic Flag." Issued by KFS via comic book ad. - **$40 $100 $200**

KIN-5

KIN-6

❑ **KIN-5. "Sunday Examiner" Newspaper Contest Litho. Button,**
1930s. Part of a set of various characters. - **$15 $35 $60**

❑ **KIN-6. "King Features Syndicate Blue Book,"**
1943. 11x15-1/2" with 80 slick pages of sample comic strips in black/white and full color. Limited distribution to newspaper editors. - **$100 $200 $300**

KIN-7

❑ **KIN-7. "A Christmas Carol Holiday Greetings" Book With Slipcase,**
1946. Christmas theme hardcover with 160 pages picturing virtually all King Features comic strip characters. Art is repeated on slipcase and book cover.
With Slipcase - **$75 $150 $225**
No Slipcase - **$50 $100 $150**

KIN-8

❑ **KIN-8. "Blue Book",**
1946 and other years before and after. King Features Syndicate. Sent annually to newspaper editors with black and white as well as beautiful color sample pages of the comic strips and features available to local newspapers. This Example - **$100 $200 $300**

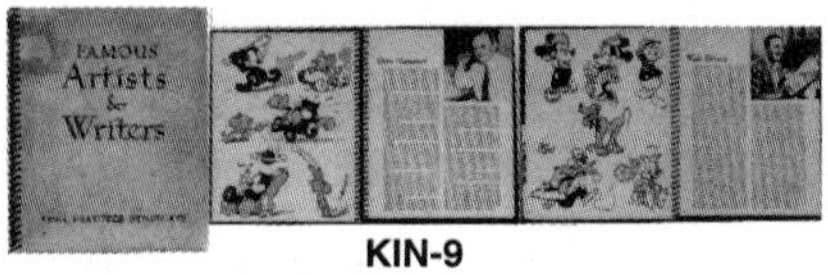


KIN-9

❑ **KIN-9. "King Features Syndicate Famous Artists & Writers" Book,**
1949. Biographies of those represented by K.F.S. - **$50 $85 $140**

KIN-10

❑ **KIN-10. "King Features Syndicate Blue Book,"**
1949. 9-1/2x12" spiral-bound with 140 black and white and color pages. Limited distribution to newspaper comic page editors. - **$100 $200 $300**

KIN-11

KIN-12

❑ **KIN-11. "Sing With King At Christmas" Book,**
1949. Pictures numerous Christmas carols sung by various syndicate characters. - **$50 $100 $150**

❑ **KIN-12. "Popular Comics" Boxed Christmas Cards,**
1951. Set of 16. - **$35 $90 $150**

KIN-13

❑ **KIN-13. "Merry Christmas From King Features Syndicate" Music Box Book With Character Fold-Out,**
1953. 3-3/4x5-1/2x1" thick with card on back that folds out to 39-1/2" with characters. Limited distribution. - **$50 $100 $150**

KIN-14

❑ **KIN-14. Merry Christmas/Happy New Year Comic Strip Character Table Cover With Mailer,**
1954. Mailer is 10x15" and holds folded 8-1/4x13-1/2" textured paper tablecloth which opens to 4-1/2' times 6'. Pictures many of the Syndicate's characters including Prince Valiant, The Phantom, Donald Duck, Popeye, Flash Gordon, others. Mailer - **$15 $25 $50**
Tablecloth - **$50 $125 $250**

KIN-15

❑ **KIN-15. Character Promo Pen/Pencil Holder,**
c. 1955. 2-3/4" diameter by 3-1/2" tall plastic. Limited issue. - **$20 $40 $75**

KIN-16

❑ **KIN-16. "King Features Syndicate Blue Book",**
1955. Full color sample pages of strips represented by K.F.S. - **$75 $150 $225**

KIN-17

❑ **KIN-17. Plastic Ornament Set Showing 12 Characters,**
c. 1950s. Boxed - **$50 $125 $200**

KIN-18

❑ **KIN-18. Comic Strip Character Lighter,**
1950s. Metal case cigarette lighter picturing total of eight characters on both sides. Probably an executive or salesman giveaway. -
**$20 $40 $70**

KIN-19

KIN-20

❑ **KIN-19. Glass Ashtray,**
1950s. Pictures 14 comic strip characters. -
**$15 $30 $60**

❑ **KIN-20. Plastic Pen Holder,**
1964. - **$20 $35 $60**

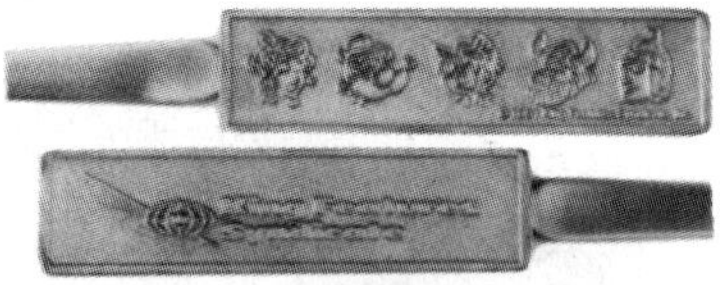

KIN-21

❑ **KIN-21. Character Promo Letter Opener,**
1981. 1x8-1/8" silvered metal with characters on handle. Limited issue. - **$10 $20 $35**

## KISS

**In 1971, Gene Simmons and Paul Stanley gave birth to a modern rock legend by playing their first show as Wicked Lester. In August of 1973, after a name change and the addition of new personnel, Kiss took the stage at the Grand Ballroom of the Diplomat Hotel in New York, shortly resulting in a record deal. Gene Simmons (bass player), Paul Stanley (guitarist), Ace Frehley (guitarist), and Peter Criss (drummer) had transformed themselves into The Demon, Starchild, Space Ace, and The Cat, respectively, through makeup. By mixing a hard rock edge with glam rock theatrics, Kiss took the world by storm as evidenced by their legion of followers, known as The Kiss Army. The group spawned best selling albums, action figures, a made-for-TV movie (*Kiss Meets the Phantom of the Park*—1978), a comic book, and scores of other merchandise.**

**In 1983, the group shed its makeup, and in the following years shuffled the lineup around mainstays Simmons and Stanley. In 1996, an appearance of the original Kiss in full makeup highlighted the Grammy Awards. The subsequent reunion tour was a huge success. Once again back on top, they launched new merchandise like best-selling action figures from McFarlane Toys, and a comic line, entertaining thousands of fans who only wanted to "rock 'n' roll all night and party every day."**

KIS-1

KIS-2

❑ **KIS-1. "Kiss Destroyer" Autographed Album,**
1976. Issued by Casablanca. Signed by members in gold ink.
Similar Examples - **$50 $100 $150**

❑ **KIS-2. "Kiss Custom Chevy Van" Model Kit,**
1977. AMT. Unbuilt - **$35 $75 $125**

KIS-3

KIS-4

❑ **KIS-3. Kiss Bracelet,**
1977. Aucoin. Gold with red logo on Love Gun display card. - **$10 $15 $25**

❑ **KIS-4. "Kiss Guitar",**
1977. Store item by Carnival Toys Inc. 11-1/2x30-1/2x3-1/2" deep box contains 29" long hard plastic guitar with photo label on front of body. Packaging includes instruction book.
Near Mint Boxed - **$750**
Guitar Only - **$150 $300 $500**

KIS-5

❑ **KIS-5. "Kiss Rockstics,"**
1978. Store item by Aucoin.
Each Unused Card - **$10 $20 $35**

KIS-6

❑ **KIS-6. "Kiss" Large Litho. Tin Waste Can,**
1978. Store item by P&K Products Co. Inc. 10" diameter by 19-1/2" tall. - **$75 $150 $250**

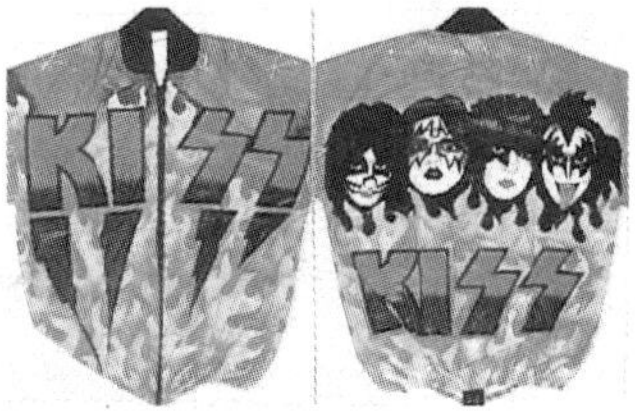

KIS-7

❑ **KIS-7. "Kiss" Jacket,**
1978. Store item by Rockrollium Corp. Brightly colored jacket made of thin fiberglass material. Originally packaged in plain plastic bag. -
**$20 $40 $75**

KIS-8

❑ **KIS-8. "Kiss On Tour Game",**
1978. Store item by American Publishing Corp.
Near Mint Sealed - **$100**
Open Complete - **$15 $25 $40**

KIS-9

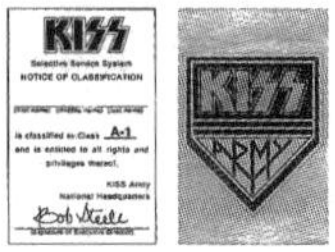

KIS-10

❑ **KIS-9. "Kiss Dynasty" Press Kit,**
1979. Issued by Casablanca Records. -
**$10 $20 $40**

❑ **KIS-10. Kiss Army Selective Service Notification,**
1970s. - **$10 $15 $25**

KIS-11

KIS-12

❑ **KIS-11. Colorform Set,**
1970s. Colorforms. - **$50 $75 $125**

❑ **KIS-12. "Destroyer" Puzzle,**
1970s. By Casse-tete. - **$25 $40 $55**

KIS-13

KIS-14

❑ **KIS-13. Kiss Make-Up Kit,**
1970s. By Remco. First issue. - **$75 $150 $225**

❑ **KIS-14. Window Sign,**
1970s. Blue Gene face. Creatures of the Night. - **$2 $5 $10**

KIS-15

KIS-16

KIS-17

❑ **KIS-15. View-Master Special Subjects Series,**
1970s. 21 3-D pictures on 3 reels in photo envelope. - **$10 $15 $20**

❑ **KIS-16. Rub 'N' Play Magic Transfer Set,**
1970s. 8 stand-up play figures by Colorforms. - **$50 $100 $175**

❑ **KIS-17. Kiss Signature Necklace,**
1970s. One of four featuring Ace, Gene, Paul, and Peter. Ace Frehely version pictured. Each - **$35 $65 $95**

KIS-18

KIS-19

❑ **KIS-18. Kiss Promo Card,**
1970s. 4x5" card says "Compliments of Kiss." - **$10 $20 $30**

❑ **KIS-19. "Kiss Meets the Phantom of the Park" Video,**
1986. World Vision Home Video. Tape of a 1978 Hanna Barbera production in association with Kiss/Aucoin Productions. 96 minute made-for-TV movie also starred Anthony Zerbe, Carmine Caridi, and Deborah Ryan. - **$50**

KIS-20

KIS-21

KIS-22

KIS-23

❑ **KIS-20. Kiss Toy Car - Paul Stanley,**
1996. Johnny Lightning Car Series - **$10**

❑ **KIS-21. Kiss Toy Car - Gene Simmons,**
1996. Johnny Lightning Car Series - **$10**

❑ **KIS-22. Kiss Toy Car - Ace Frehley,**
1996. Johnny Lightning Car Series - **$10**

❑ **KIS-23. Kiss Toy Car - Peter Criss,**
1996. Johnny Lightning Car Series - **$10**

KIS-24

❑ **KIS-24. Kiss Rings,**
1997. Three different plastic rings with a filigree metal base. Gene, Paul and the group. Each - **$5 $15 $30**

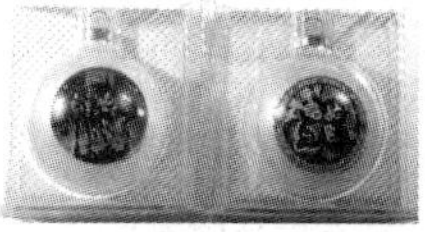

KIS-25

KIS-26

❑ **KIS-25. Kiss Christmas Ornaments,**
1997. Two different. Each - **$10**

❑ **KIS-26. Standee Promo for Neon Telephone,**
1998. 14 1/2" sign. - **$25 $40 $50**

KIS-27

**KIS-27. Kiss Bean Bag Collection,**
1999. First edition, limited to 25,000, with art deco open box - **$120**

# Krazy Kat and Ignatz

**George Herriman (1880-1944), creator of the comic strip *Krazy Kat*, has been ranked with Chaplin as one of the giants of American popular art. The strip, which began as a minor part of a daily strip called *The Dingbat Family* in the *New York Journal* in 1910, came into its own in 1913, and a Sunday page debuted in 1916. For the next 28 years the complex saga of Krazy Kat, the brick-throwing Ignatz Mouse, and Offissa Pupp unfolded against ever-changing backgrounds. Animated cartoons based on the strip were produced in the 1920s and 1930s and later as part of the King Features Trilogy and Screen Gems Theatrical Cartoon Package. Dell published a series of *Krazy Kat* comic books in the 1950s. The strip was retired upon Herriman's death.**

KRA-1

KRA-2

❑ **KRA-1. "Krazy Kat" Stuffed Doll,**
c. 1915. Store item by Averill Co. -
**$300 $600 $1000**

❑ **KRA-2. "Don't Be A Krazy Kat" Cello. Button,**
c. 1915. Cigarette purchase give-away. Art by character creator George Herriman. - **$20 $40 $75**

KRA-3

❑ **KRA-3. "Krazy Kat" Pin on Card,**
1927. Krazy votes "Yes" for the repeal of the Prohibition Bill. Rare. - **$45 $90 $140**

KRA-4

KRA-5

❑ **KRA-4. "Cats Pajamas" Enamel On Brass Pin,**
c. 1920s. - **$35 $75 $125**

❑ **KRA-5. "Krazy Kat Kiddies Klub" Member Card,**
c. 1920s. Art is unsigned, issuer is unknown. -
**$100 $250 $400**

KRA-6

KRA-7

❑ **KRA-6. "Ignatz" Flexible Figure,**
c. 1930. Store item. Composition/wood/wire by Cameo Doll Co. - **$150 $300 $500**

❑ **KRA-7. Animator Joe DeNat's Personal Christmas Card,**
1930. 5x7" also depicts cartoon character "Toby." - **$40 $100 $200**

KRA-8

❑ **KRA-8. "All Star Comics" Boxed Playing Card Game,**
1934. Store item by Whitman. Card characters also include those from "Just Kids" and "Captain And Kids" comic strips. - **$50 $100 $175**

KRA-9

KRA-10

❑ **KRA-9. "Krazy Kat" Wood Jointed Doll,**
1930s. Store item. No maker's name. Example shown possibly missing a hat. 5-3/4" tall. -
**$100 $250 $400**

❑ **KRA-10. "Archy Does His Part" Book With Art By Krazy Kat Creator Herriman,**
1935. Hardback published by Doubleday.
With Dust Jacket - **$65 $150 $250**

KRA-11

KRA-12

❑ **KRA-11. Krazy Kat Enameled Brass Figural Pin,**
1930s. Accents are four enamel colors and tiny rhinestone eyes. - **$15 $25 $50**

❑ **KRA-12. Krazy Kat Enameled Brass Figure Pin,**
1930s. Sign inscription is "If You Can Read This You're Too Darn Close." - **$20 $35 $60**

KRA-13

KRA-14

❑ **KRA-13. "Krazy Kat/New York Evening Journal" Cello. Button,**
1930s. From series of newspaper contest buttons, match number to win prize. - **$25 $60 $100**

❑ **KRA-14. "Krazy Kat/New York Evening Journal" Cello. Button,**
1930s. From series of newspaper contest buttons, match number to win prize. - **$15 $40 $75**

KRA-15

KRA-16

❑ **KRA-15. "Ignatz Mouse/New York Evening Journal" Cello. Button,**
1930s. From series of newspaper contest buttons, match number to win prize. - **$15 $40 $75**

❑ **KRA-16. "Kiddies Krazy Kat" Cello. Button,**
c. 1930s. State Theatre. 7/8" black on cream with red image of Krazy Kat. - **$40 $100 $175**

KRA-17

❑ **KRA-17. Krazy Kat Calendar,**
1999. - **$2 $8 $20**

# Kukla, Fran and Ollie

**Puppeteer Burr Tillstrom created Kukla, a chronic worrier, and Ollie, a one-tooth dragon, in Chicago in the late 1930s. Along with singer-actress Fran Allison, the Kuklapolitans were to produce one of early television's most beloved long-running successes, first as *Junior Jamboree* on WBKB (1947-1948), then as *Kukla, Fran & Ollie* on NBC (1948-1954), on ABC (1954-1957), again on NBC (1961-1962), on public television (1970-1971), and in syndication (1975-1976). Sponsors included RCA Victor, Sealtest, Ford and Pontiac automobiles, National Biscuit, Life magazine, Procter & Gamble, and Miles Laboratories. Promotional items are normally copyrighted Burr Tillstrom. A radio version aired on NBC in 1952-1953.**

KUK-1

❑ **KUK-1. "Kuklapolitan Courier" Newsletter With Envelope,**
1949. One of series sent to fans.
With Envelope - **$25 $75 $100**
Without Envelope - **$10 $35 $70**

KUK-2

❑ **KUK-2. Fan Postcard,**
1950. Announces August 8 starting day for third season of TV show. - **$15 $30 $75**

KUK-3

❑ **KUK-3. "Kuklapolitan Courier Year Book",**
1951. - **$25 $50 $125**

KUK-4 KUK-5

❑ **KUK-4. "TV Forecast" Cover Article,**
1953. - **$25 $50 $100**

❑ **KUK-5. "TV Guide" Cover Article,**
1953. Weekly issue for October 30 with two-page Kukla, Fran & Ollie article titled "Beulah Witch's Halloween." - **$10 $30 $60**

KUK-6 KUK-7

❑ **KUK-6. Tru-Vue Film Card,**
1953. Store item. Scenes of a wild west show. - **$8 $15 $25**

❑ **KUK-7. Vinyl On Cardboard Postcard Record,**
c. 1957. Curtiss Candy Co. Several versions. - **$15 $30 $60**

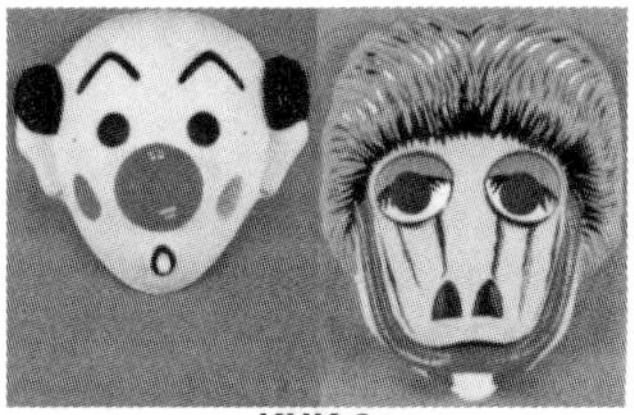
KUK-8

❑ **KUK-8. Kukla And Ollie Masks,**
1950s. Store items. Molded thin plastic.
Each - **$10 $20 $40**

KUK-9

❑ **KUK-9. "Kukla And Ollie Doddly Dolly" Boxed Set,**
1950s. Store item by H. Davis Toy Corp. 12x18x2" deep box contains yarn and fabric pieces for doll construction.
Unused - **$30 $65 $115**

KUK-10

❑ **KUK-10. Curtiss Candy Co. Vinyl Cardboard Record,**
1950s. - **$15 $50 $75**

(KUKLA) (OLLIE)
KUK-11

❑ **KUK-11. Spoon Set Of Two,**
1950s. Rare. - **$75 $150 $300**

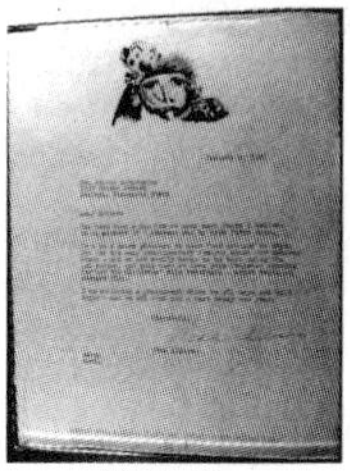
KUK-12

❑ **KUK-12. Personal Autographed Letter,**
1971. From the late Fran Allison on Kukla and Ollie stationery. - **$150**

# Lassie

**The story of the courageous, intelligent collie first appeared in Erick Knight's 1938 short story and 1940 best-selling novel *Lassie Come Home*--the start of an odyssey that was to continue for some 35 years: the 1943 MGM movie, followed by a half-dozen sequels over eight years; the radio serial sponsored by Red Heart dog food on ABC (1947-1948) and NBC (1948-1950); three decades of comic books beginning in 1949; and ultimately the CBS television saga, from 1954 to 1971, followed by three years of syndication under various titles (1972-1975), all sponsored by Campbell's soup. Lassie's human companions were played by Tommy Rettig (1954-1957) and Jon Provost (1957-1964), and by Robert Bray (1964-1969) as an adventurous forest ranger. *Lassie's Rescue Rangers*, an animated series, ran on ABC from 1973 to 1975. The 50th anniversary of the original movie was celebrated in 1994 with the release of a new movie (*Lassie*), a TV program, a new book (*Lassie: A Dog's Life*), and numerous deals for spinoff products. Items bear the copyright of Wrather Corp., Rankin & Bass Productions, or Jack Wrather Productions.**

LAS-1

LAS-2

❑ **LAS-1. Color Premium Picture - Red Heart, Large,**
1949. Scarce. - **$20 $50 $80**

❑ **LAS-2. Comic Book Premium - Red Heart,**
1949. Scarce. - **$33 $99 $300**

LAS-3

❑ **LAS-3. "M-G-M's Lassie" First Issue Comic Book,**
1950. Published by Dell. - **$14 $42 $180**

LAS-4

LAS-5

❑ **LAS-4. "Jeff's Collie Club" Member Card,**
c. 1954. Virginia Dairy Co., probable others. No direct Lassie reference but obviously based on early version of TV series. - **$10 $25 $50**

❑ **LAS-5. Lassie Friendship Silvered Brass Ring,**
c. 1955. Campbell Soup Company. Initial "L" on each side with high relief portrait on top. - **$75 $125 $175**

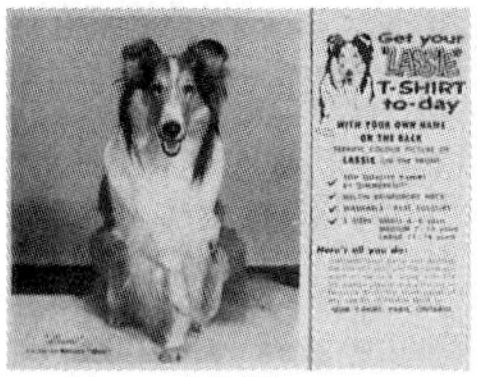


LAS-6

❑ **LAS-6. "'Lassie' T-Shirt" Offer And Photo,**
1956. Nestle's Quik. 8x10" full color photo with reverse ad for T-shirt available "With Your Own Name On The Back." - **$10 $20 $40**

LAS-7

LAS-8

LAS-9

❑ **LAS-7. "Lassie Club" Savings Bond Certificate,**
c. 1956. - **$20 $40 $60**

❑ **LAS-8. Postcard,**
1956. Thank you postcard for entering contest. - **$10 $25 $35**

❑ **LAS-9. "Tim Magazine For Boys" Issues With Lassie,**
1957-1958. Each has cover article featuring Tommy Rettig as youthful star of Lassie TV series. Issues are for September 1957 and November 1958 with imprint for local Tim store. Each - **$5 $15 $30**

LAS-10

❑ **LAS-10. "Lassie & Timmie Plastic Palette Coloring Set,"** c. 1958. Store item by Standard Toykraft. - **$30 $60 $100**

LAS-11

❑ **LAS-11. Wallet With Membership Card,**
1959. Campbell's Soups. Card reads "Lassie-Get-Up-And-Go Club". - **$15 $25 $60**

LAS-12

❑ **LAS-12. Western Series Card,**
1950s. Card #4 - **$10 $20 $35**

LAS-13

LAS-14

❑ **LAS-13. "Have You Voted For Lassie?" Cello. Button,**
1950s. 1-3/4" size. - **$10 $20 $40**

❑ **LAS-14. "I Voted For Lassie" Cello. Button,**
1950s. 1" version. - **$8 $12 $20**

LAS-15

❑ **LAS-15. "Lassie Forest Ranger" Vinyl Wallet With Contents,**
1964. Campbell's Soups. Includes white metal badge and Lassie photo.
Complete - **$20 $45 $75**

LAS-16

❑ **LAS-16. "Forest Ranger Handbook",**
1967. Authored by "Corey Stuart And Lassie." - **$10 $20 $35**

LAS-17

LAS-18

❑ **LAS-17. "Lassie" Watch,**
1968. Store item by Bradley. - **$25 $50 $75**

❑ **LAS-18. "Lassie Gold Award For Meritorious Action" Brass Medal,**
1960s. Champion Valley Farms, Inc. 1" with areas on reverse where dog's name and owner's name can be engraved along with text reading "For Giving Meaning To The Tradition That 'Man's Best Friend Is His Dog.'" - **$30 $75 $125**

LAS-19

LAS-20

❑ **LAS-19. TV Patch,**
1960s. - **$20 $40 $75**

❑ **LAS-20. Lassie/Corey Stuart TV Photo,**
1960s. - **$20 $40 $60**

LAS-21

LAS-22

❑ **LAS-21. Fan Card,**
1960s. Recipe Brand Dinners. Back has facsimile paw print of Lassie and signature of trainer Rudd Weatherwax. - **$10 $20 $30**

❑ **LAS-22. "A Friend Of Lassie" Brass Dog Tag,**
c. 1970s. Probable dog food sponsor. Back identification inscription to be completed by dog owner. - **$10 $20 $35**

LAS-23

LAS-24

❑ **LAS-23. Christmas Ornament,**
1999. From Carlton Cards. Boxed. - **$20**

❑ **LAS-24. Christmas Ornament,**
1990s. From Carlton Cards. Boxed. - **$30**

## Laugh-In

***Rowan & Martin's Laugh-In* was the psychedelic concoction of Dan Rowan and Dick Martin, a classic comic team of straight man and foil. The program, which aired on NBC television from 1968 to 1973 was a free-wheeling, frenetic mix of sight gags, low humor, and political satire. Among the supporting cast: Goldie Hawn, Lily Tomlin, Henry Gibson, Arte Johnson, Ruth Buzzi, and Judy Carne. Catch phrases from the show such as "You bet your bippy," "Look that up in your *Funk & Wagnall's*," and "Sock it to me," became part of the nation's vocabulary. *Laugh-In* was the No. 1 television show during its first two seasons, winning numerous awards. A dozen issues of *Laugh-In Magazine* were published in 1968-1969. Verrry interesting!**

LAU-1 LAU-2 LAU-3 LAU-4

❑ **LAU-1. Laugh-In Flicker Ring,**
1968. Store item made by L. M. Becker Co., Appleton, Wisconsin. This and the next 11 rings comprise a set of 12. Images are slogan "Here Comes The Judge" and photo of Pigmeat Markham. - **$10 $15 $25**

❑ **LAU-2. Laugh-In Flicker Ring,**
1968. Images are Henry Gibson as Indian and Priest. - **$10 $15 $25**

❑ **LAU-3. Laugh-In "Beauty/Beast" Flicker Ring,**
1968. Images are Dan Rowan and Ruth Buzzi. - **$10 $15 $25**

❑ **LAU-4. Laugh-In Joke Flicker Ring,**
1968. Text images are "If Minnehaha Married Don Ho/She'd Be Minne Ha Ha Ho." - **$10 $15 $25**

LAU-5 LAU-6 LAU-7 LAU-8

❑ **LAU-5. Laugh-In Phrase Flicker Ring,**
1968. Images are text "Flying Fickle Finger Of Fate Award" to winged hand featuring pointed index finger. - **$10 $15 $25**

❑ **LAU-6. Laugh-In Flicker Ring,**
1968. Alternate image is Dan Rowan and Dick Martin. - **$10 $15 $25**

❑ **LAU-7. Laugh-In Goldie Hawn Flicker Ring,**
1968. Images are close-up of her in black hat and as bikini dancer. - **$10 $15 $25**

❑ **LAU-8. Laugh-In Ruth Buzzi Flicker Ring,**
1968. Images are close-up of her in hair net and another in wig. - **$10 $15 $25**

LAU-9 LAU-10 LAU-11 LAU-12

❑ **LAU-9. Laugh-In "Good Night, Dick" Flicker Ring,**
1968. Images are Dan Rowan to Dick Martin with caption "Who's Dick?" - **$10 $15 $25**

❑ **LAU-10. Laugh-In Judy Carne Flicker Ring,**
1968. Images are "Sock It To Me" text to photo of her in striped sweater. - **$10 $15 $25**

❑ **LAU-11. Laugh-In Joanne Worley Flicker Ring,**
1968. Images are photo of her screaming to another with sad face. - **$10 $15 $25**

❑ **LAU-12. Laugh-In Arte Johnson Flicker Ring,**
1968. Images are "Verry Innteresting" slogan picturing him as German soldier to slogan "But Stupid" picturing him in different style German helmet. - **$10 $15 $25**

LAU-13

LAU-14

❑ **LAU-13. "Laugh-In Magazine" First Issue,**
1968. Laufer Publishing Co. Vol. 1 #1 for October. - **$10 $15 $25**

❑ **LAU-14. "Laugh-In" Gum Pack Box,**
1968. Topps Gum. Box Only - **$20 $50 $80**

LAU-15

❑ **LAU-15. Laugh-In Flicker Rings,**
1968. Vending machine issue. Photo shows 15 from set of 16 by Vari-Vue. Rings show the show stars and classic slogans on psychedelic-colored backgrounds.
Each On Original Base - **$10 $20 $30**
Each On "China" Base - **$5 $10 $15**

LAU-16

LAU-17

❑ **LAU-16. "Laugh-In View-Master" Set,**
1968. - **$10 $20 $30**

❑ **LAU-17. "Laugh-In" Paperdoll Book,**
1969. Saalfield Publishing Co.
Unpunched - **$8 $15 $25**

LAU-18

LAU-19

❑ **LAU-18. "Rowan And Martin's Laugh-In" Book,**
1969. Store item by World Publishing Co. Hardcover 160-page assortment of photos, fold-outs, sayings and jokes. - **$8 $15 $25**

❑ **LAU-19. "Laugh-In" 17x26" Fabric Banner,**
1970. Copyright by George Schlatter-Ed Friendly Productions and Romart Inc. -
**$10 $20 $40**

LAU-20

❑ **LAU-20. "Here Come The Judge" Pendants,**
c. 1970. Store items. Cast metal in silver or gold finish featuring one of the popular humor slogans from the show. Each - **$5 $10 $20**

LAU-21

LAU-22

❑ **LAU-21. "Rowan & Martin Laugh-In" Cello. Button,**
c. 1970. For "Westbury Music Fair" related appearance or event. - **$5 $10 $15**

❑ **LAU-22. Laugh-In Vending Machine Display,**
c. 1970. Paper insert on styrofoam with two plastic rings with Laugh-In slogans, other generic rings and novelties. - **$20 $50 $75**

## Laurel and Hardy

**Stan Laurel (1890-1965), the British-born thin one, and Oliver Hardy (1892-1957), the pompous fat one, teamed in 1926 to become one of the screen's finest comedy teams. In silent two-reelers, and in feature films between 1929 and 1950, the slapstick misadventures of Laurel, scratching his head, and Hardy, fiddling with his tie, found them in "one fine mess" after another. A British comic strip ran in *Film Fun* (1930-1942), and *Laurel and Hardy Comics* appeared in the U.S. from 1949 to 1956 and in 1962-1963. Vintage films were edited and cut for syndication to television in 1948 and ran locally for over three decades. Five-minute animated episodes based on the films, co-produced by Hanna-Barbera and Larry Harmon, were syndicated to television in 1966 with limited success. Merchandising in the 1960s and 1970s was extensive, with the pair used to promote a wide variety of products--toys, dolls, games, coloring books, watches, spray deodorants--and film clips used in television commercials in the 1970s. Items associated with the animated cartoons are usually copyrighted either by the co-producers or by Wolper Productions Inc.**

L&H-1

L&H-2

L&H-3

❑ **L&H-1. Laurel & Hardy "Old Gold Cigarettes" 31x42" Cardboard Sign,**
1934. - **$500 $800 $1500**

❑ **L&H-2. Laurel And Hardy Metal Figures,**
1930s. Store item by Mignot of France, maker of lead soldier toys. Paint and detailing on front and back of each figure standing on small base.
Pair - **$25 $50 $75**

❑ **L&H-3. Derby Hats Enameled Metal Pin,**
c. 1930s. English made without markings. -
**$15 $30 $50**

L&H-4

L&H-5

❑ **L&H-4. Figural Caricature Ceramic,**
c. 1930s. Store item made in Japan for use as pencil holder or planter . - **$35 $75 $135**

❑ **L&H-5. Salt And Pepper Set,**
1930s. China figural pair by Beswick of England. -
**$75 $125 $225**

L&H-6

❑ **L&H-6. "Mickey Mouse With The Movie Stars" Gum Card,**
1930s. Gum, Inc. Card #120 from series featuring Mickey and various stars. - **$50 $115 $200**

L&H-7

❑ **L&H-7. "The Big Noise" Movie Poster,**
1944. One sheet poster from the 20th Century Fox Pictures film. - **$300 $500 $750**

L&H-8

L&H-9

❑ **L&H-8. "Join The Laurel And Hardy Laff Club!" 3-1/2" Button,**
1960s. Larry Harmon's Pictures Corp. - **$15 $25 $45**

❑ **L&H-9. Donuts 9x13" Diecut Cardboard Store Signs,**
1960s. Various users. Depict Laurel and Hardy. Each - **$30 $50 $100**

L&H-10

❑ **L&H-10. Jack In The Box Cardboard, Vinyl And Fabric Toy,**
1960s. Store item by Larry Harmon Pictures Corp. 3-1/2" square by 4" tall with pop-up figure of Laurel. - **$25 $50 $75**

L&H-11

L&H-12

❑ **L&H-11. Esco Products Large Statuettes,**
1971. Set of 17" tall painted solid plaster figures colorfully painted. Each - **$15 $25 $60**

❑ **L&H-12. Stan Laurel Figural Bank,**
1972. 13-1/2" tall store item by Play Pal Plastics. **- $10 $20 $35**

L&H-13

❑ **L&H-13. Figure Set By Dakin,**
c. 1974. Store items by R. Dakin Co. Painted hard plastic figures with movable arms, soft vinyl movable heads, fabric jackets. Each is about 8". Each - **$15 $30 $60**

L&H-14

❑ **L&H-14. Pair Of Figural Steins,**
1970s. Each **- $20 $40 $65**

L&H-15

❑ **L&H-15. Bisque Figurine Set,**
1970s. Each is 6-1/2" tall on 2-1/2x3" base. Each **- $8 $15 $25**

L&H-16

❑ **L&H-16. "Laurel & Hardy '25T Roadster" Model,**
1970s. Store item by AMT.
Near Mint Boxed - **$65**
Complete Assembled - **$15 $30 $50**

L&H-17

L&H-18

L&H-19

❑ **L&H-17. Oliver Hardy "TV Pals" Plastic Candy Dispenser,**
1970s. - **$30 $60 $100**

❑ **L&H-18. "Ask Me About My Partner" 2-1/4" Cello. Button,**
c. 1980s. Ziyad Printers. - **$3 $8 $12**

❑ **L&H-19. "Together We're A Team" 2-1/2" Cello. Button,**
c. 1980s. Ziyad Printers. - **$3 $8 $12**

L&H-20

❑ **L&H-20. Keystone Cops Resin Figures,**
1999. Fully painted 6" figures. Limited edition of 5,000 sets promotes their 1930's movie.
Set - **$80**

# Lightning Jim

**U.S. Marshal Lightning Jim Whipple was the hero of a Western adventure radio series broadcast on the West Coast in the 1940s and syndicated in the 1950s. Meadow Gold dairy products sponsored the program. Membership in Lightning Jim's Special Reserve entitled the young listener to wear the Meadow Gold Round-Up Badge. Whitey Larsen served as Jim's sidekick and deputy.**

LGH-1

LGH-2

❑ **LGH-1. "Lightning" Jim Big Little Book #1441,**
1940. 432 pages. Based on the radio show. - **$10 $30 $60**

❑ **LGH-2. Special Reserve Pinback,**
1940. Sponsored by Meadow Gold Dairy. Children would send in their photo which would be paired with Jim's on the pinback. Very rare in high grade. - **$75 $175 $400**

LGH-3

❑ **LGH-3. "Lightning Jim Blackout Kit,"**
1942. Kix Cereal. Includes patch, "Pledge To The Flag" text, headband, four blank sheets of glow fabric, leaflet. **- $100 $250 $400**

LGH-4

❑ **LGH-4. "Meadow Gold Round-Up" Photo,**
1940s. - **$10 $20 $35**

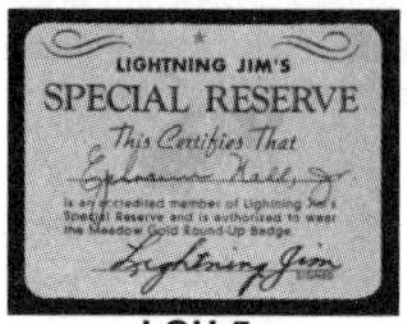


LGH-5

LGH-6

❑ **LGH-5. Membership Card,**
1940s. Scarce. - **$10 $50 $90**

❑ **LGH-6. Membership Brass Badge,**
1940s. Scarce. - **$30 $75 $135**

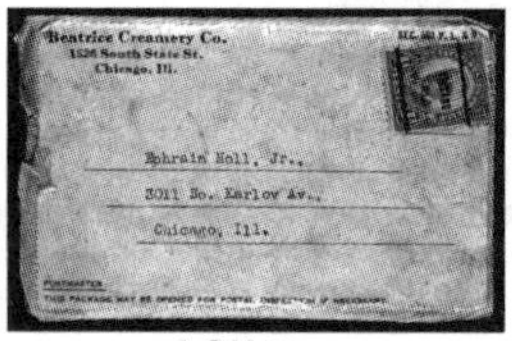


LGH-7

LGH-8

❑ **LGH-7. Mailer,**
1940s. Scarce. - **$10 $20 $40**

❑ **LGH-8. Drinking Glass,**
1940s. Rare. - **$40 $100 $200**

LGH-9

❑ **LGH-9. "Round-Up" Radio Broadcast Ad Paper,**
1940s. Meadow Gold Dairies. 3x5-1/2" imprinted for WMBC Radio, Columbus, Mississippi with text including names of Marshal "Lightning" Jim Whipple and his Deputy Whitey Larsen. - **$10 $20 $30**

LGH-10

LGH-11

❑ **LGH-10. "Lightning Jim Posse" Litho. Tin Tab,**
1950s. Sponsor is NuGrape Soda. Other inscriptions are "Learning-Justice-Power." - **$20 $40 $75**

❑ **LGH-11. Canadian Club Cello. Button,**
c. 1950s. Red image and blue text on white background, 1-1/4". - **$35 $75 $140**

## *Li'l Abner*

**Al Capp (1909-1979) created *Li'l Abner* for United Features as a daily comic strip in 1934 and as a Sunday page in 1935. Along with the handsome hillbilly from Dogpatch has come a string of unforgettable characters: Daisy Mae, Mammy and Pappy Yokum, Marryin' Sam, Sadie Hawkins, Sir Cecil and Lady Cesspool, Hairless Joe, Lonesome Polecat, Fearless Fosdick, the bountiful Shmoos, the Kigmys, Kickapoo Joy Juice, and many others. Comic books appeared from the 1930s into the 1950s. A *Li'l Abner* radio show on NBC in 1939-1940 featured John Hodiak as Abner; a brief run of five animated shorts was released in 1944-1945; a musical comedy ran on Broadway for almost 700 performances in 1956-1957; and a Paramount film was released in 1959.**

LIL-1

LIL-2

❑ **LIL-1. "Li'l Abner in New York" Big Little Book,**
1936. 432 pages by Al Capp. 1st Abner book. - **$15 $60 $120**

❑ **LIL-2. "Tip Top Comics" 11x14" Store Sign,**
c. 1938. - **$50 $100 $150**

LIL-3

LIL-4

❑ **LIL-3. "Li'l Abner Among The Millionaires" Better Little Book,**
1939. Whitman #1401. **- $20 $60 $120**

❑ **LIL-4. "Buy War Stamps" 14x18" Poster,**
c. 1944. U.S. Government. - **$50 $150 $250**

LIL-5

LIL-6

❑ **LIL-5. Li'l Abner And His Dogpatch Band Wind-Up,**
1946. By Unique Art Mfg. Co. Advertised in 1946 Playthings magazine as the first post-war metal wind-up toy. - **$250 $500 $850**

❑ **LIL-6. Li'l Abner Beanie with Tag,**
1948. Cereal premium. - **$30 $60 $100**

LIL-7

LIL-8

❑ **LIL-7. "Daisy Mae Needs You!" Cello. Button,**
c. 1948. Red, black and white 1-1/2". - **$20 $50 $125**

❑ **LIL-8. "Shmoo Club Member" Litho. Button,**
c. 1948. - **$25 $40 $75**

LIL-9

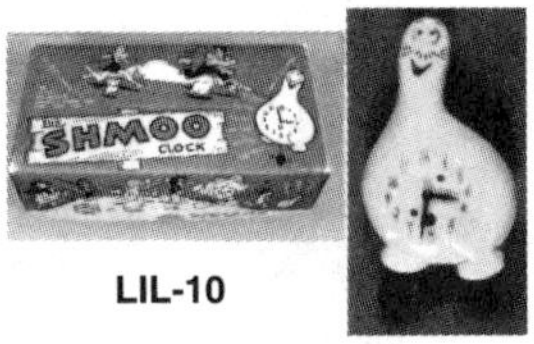


LIL-10

❑ **LIL-9. Shmoo Paddle Ball,**
1948. Scarce. - **$50 $100 $220**

❑ **LIL-10. Shmoo Plastic Wall Clock,**
c. 1948. Store item by Lux Clock Co.
Near Mint Boxed - **$500**
Loose - **$50 $125 $250**

LIL-11

❑ **LIL-11. Shmoo Carnival Bank,**
1948. Rare. - **$300 $600 $1200**

(Box) LIL-12 (Bag)

❑ **LIL-12. "Shmoo" Utility Bag,**
1948-49. Has small printed Shmoos on bag and large Shmoo figure on top of bag.
Boxed. - **$150 $300 $450**

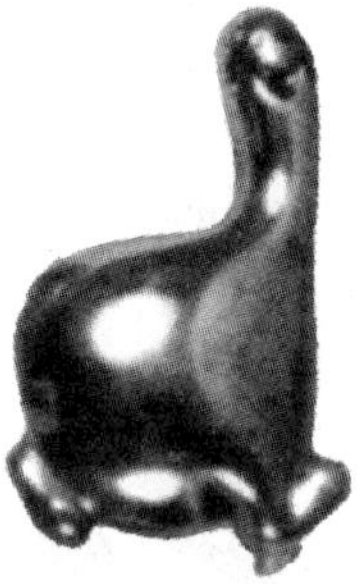

LIL-13

LIL-14

❑ **LIL-13. High Relief Brass Badge,**
c. 1948. - **$20 $35 $60**

❑ **LIL-14. Small Shmoo Pin,**
1949. - **$30 $60 $120**

LIL-15

LIL-16

❑ **LIL-15. Shmoo Soap in Box,**
1949. In black and white box. Unused. - **$150**

❑ **LIL-16. "Good Luck Shmoo" Coin,**
1949. Li'l Abner on back. - **$50 $100 $150**

LIL-17

❑ **LIL-17. Shmoo Figural Plaster Pin,**
c. 1949. - **$45 $90 $150**

LIL-18

❑ **LIL-18. "Shmoo Whistle Pencil Box,"**
c. 1949. Store item by Dixon. 10-3/4" long. - **$50 $125 $200**

LIL-19

❑ **LIL-19. Vending Machine,**
1949. 12-1/2" x 22-1/2" x 11-1/2". - **$275 $550 $900**

LIL-20

❑ **LIL-20. Shmoo Pocketbook,**
1949. Children's vinyl pocketbook with strap. Rare. - **$160 $320 $480**

LIL-21

❑ **LIL-21. Shmoo Bank on Card,**
1949. Yellow version. Scarce - **$60 $120 $180**
White version - **$30 $60 $90**
Lt. blue and dark blue versions. Scarce - **$50 $100 $150**

LIL-22

LIL-23

❑ **LIL-22. Shmoos Savings Bond Certificate,**
1949. - **$50 $100 $175**

❑ **LIL-23. Shmoo "Snow Week" Cello. Button,**
1949. University of Minnesota. Rim curl has 1948 copyright. - **$35 $75 $175**

LIL-24

❑ **LIL-24. "Shmoo Tumbler" Boxed Set Of Eight Glasses,**
1949. Fronts show Li'l Abner characters while reverses depict Shmoos in various outfits and activities. Probable dairy product container somehow offered for purchase as boxed full set.
Box - **$20 $40 $75**
Each Glass - **$5 $15 $25**

LIL-25

❑ **LIL-25. Figural Pencil Sharpener,**
c. 1949. Probable store item. 2-1/8" tall yellow plastic. - **$40 $75 $125**

LIL-26

LIL-27

LIL-28

❑ **LIL-26. Shmoo Club 2-1/4" Litho. Tab,**
1949. Sealtest ice cream. - **$10 $20 $35**

❑ **LIL-27. Shmoo Club 2-1/4" Litho. Tab,**
1949. Sealtest ice cream. - **$10 $20 $35**

❑ **LIL-28. Shmoo Club 2-1/4" Litho. Tab,**
1949. Sealtest ice cream. - **$10 $20 $35**

LIL-29

LIL-30

❑ **LIL-29. Shmoo Club 2-1/4" Litho. Tab,**
1949. Sealtest ice cream. - **$10 $20 $35**

❑ **LIL-30. Shmoo 2" Pinback,**
1949. - **$30 $75 $120**

LIL-31

❑ **LIL-31. Shmoo Character Litho. Buttons,**
c. 1949. United Features Syndicate copyrights. Pictured examples from series of about 12 are Captain Kidd, Sailor, Joe. Each - **$8 $15 $25**

(Figures inside)

LIL-32

❑ **LIL-32. Pet Shmoo 6 in 1 Figure,**
1940s. Large Shmoo figure contains 5 small Shmoo figures inside. Has plastic food products for "feeding" your Shmoo. On display card. Card and plastic food are both rare.
Shmoo 6 in 1 figure - **$50 $100 $150**
Card with food - **$150 $300 $450**

LIL-33

❑ **LIL-33. Decal Sheet With Envelope,**
1940s. Orange-Crush. - **$10 $20 $40**

LIL-34

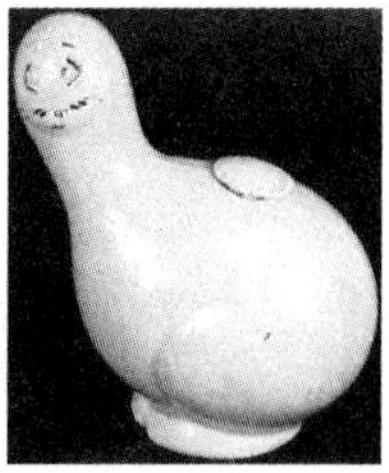

LIL-35

❑ **LIL-34. "Fearless Fosdick" Plaster Figure,**
1940s. 7-1/2" tall hand-painted figure atop base which has his name incised on front and copyright of "UFS" (United Features Syndicate) on reverse. Figure was apparently sold unpainted.
Near Mint Unpainted - **$400**
Painted - **$100 $200 $300**

❑ **LIL-35. Figural Ceramic Air Freshener Container,**
1940s. 5-1/2" tall pale green with color facial accents. Has rubber cap on back which pulls up to reveal air freshener. - **$40 $75 $140**

LIL-36

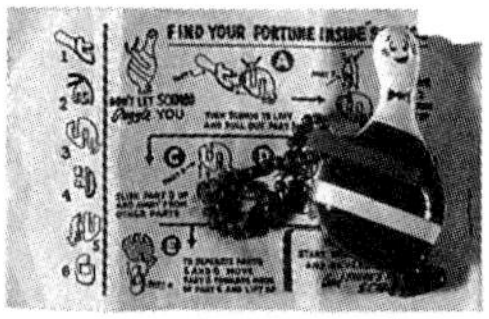


LIL-37

❑ **LIL-36. "Tangle Comics" Cello. Button,**
1940s. Philadelphia Sunday Bulletin. - **$20 $45 $75**

❑ **LIL-37. Shmoo Figure Puzzle,**
1940s. Red, white, and green puzzle with instructions. - **$15 $35 $60**

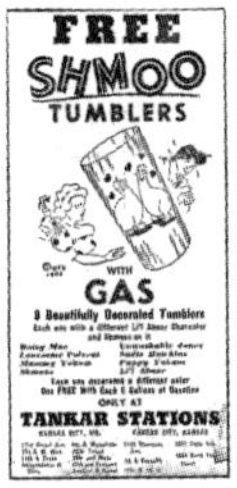


LIL-38

LIL-39

❑ **LIL-38. Shmoo Ad,**
Sept, 1940s. - **$5 $10 $20**

❑ **LIL-39. Shmoo Ad,**
Nov, 1940s. Shows 8 different glasses. - **$5 $10 $20**
Each Glass - **$5 $15 $25**

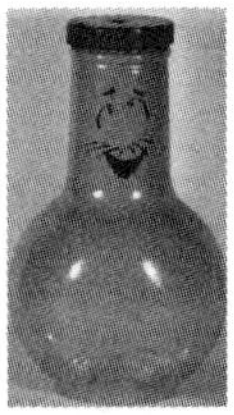

LIL-40

LIL-41

❑ **LIL-40. Boy Shmoo Bottle,**
Late 1940s. Blue bottle. - **$50 $100 $175**

❑ **LIL-41. Girl Shmoo Bottle,**
Late 1940s. Pink bottle shaped like a girl schmoo. Rarer than the boy model. - **$75 $125 $200**

LIL-42

LIL-43

❑ **LIL-42. "Shmoo Lucky Rings" 12x13" Cardboard Store Display Sign,**
c. 1950. Store item by Jarco Metal Products.
Empty Card - **$50 $125 $250**
Brass Ring - **$30 $45 $60**

❑ **LIL-43. "Li'l Abner" Cello. Button,**
c. 1950. - **$15 $30 $60**

LIL-44

❑ **LIL-44. "Al Capp's Sensational Comic Character Kigmy" Boxed Marble Game,**
1950. Store item by Milton Bradley. - **$150 $250 $500**

LIL-45

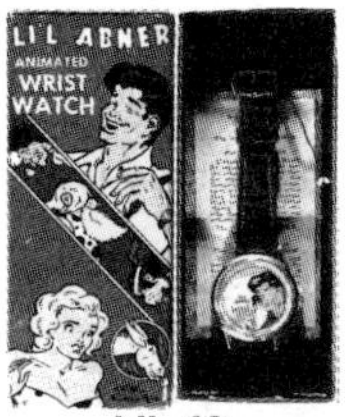


LIL-46

❑ **LIL-45. "Shmoo Girls" Felt Patch,**
c. 1950. 5x8" diecut fabric. - **$25 $60 $100**

❑ **LIL-46. L'il Abner Wrist Watch,**
1951. With flag second hand. In box with instructions. Boxed - **$550**

LIL-47

❑ **LIL-47. Metal Store Display Rack,**
1954. Wildroot Cream-Oil. All metal about four feet tall with red, black and white display sign. - **$150 $300 $500**

LIL-48

LIL-49

❑ **LIL-48. "Fearless Fosdick" Product Sticker,**
1954. Wildroot Cream-Oil Hair Dressing. 3x7" probable design for store window display. - **$20 $40 $75**

❑ **LIL-49. "Namely You" Song Sheet,**
1956. From the theater show. The cast list includes pre-fame Julie Newmar and Tina Louise. - **$10 $20 $35**

LIL-50

LIL-51

❑ **LIL-50. Li'l Abner Jointed Vinyl Doll,**
1950s. By Baby Barry. Daisy Mae, Mammy and Pappy Yokum also produced.
Each - **$40 $85 $150**

❑ **LIL-51. Civil Defense Comic Book,**
1956. Features Civil Defense comic figure created by Al Capp. - **$10 $50 $75**

LIL52

❑ **LIL-52. Fearless Fosdick 15x36" Standee,**
1950s. Scarce. Wildroot Hair Tonic. Five pieces attached to box. - **$500 $1000 $1500**

LIL-53

LIL-54

LIL-55

❑ **LIL-53. Kigmy Plastic Charm,**
1950s. Scarce. - **$30 $60 $90**

❑ **LIL-54. Dogpatch Mug,**
1974. Li'l Abner and Daisy Mae pictured. Scarce. - **$50 $100 $135**

❑ **LIL-55. Shmoo Pin,**
1997. From Kitchen Sink. - **$5**

## Little Lulu

**Mischievous Little Lulu Moppet, the brainchild of Marjorie H. Buell (Marge), started life as a single-panel cartoon in the *Saturday Evening Post* in 1935. She began her comic book career as a one-shot in 1945 and as a regular series in 1948, scripted by John Stanley. A newspaper strip ran from 1955 to 1967, and from 1944 to 1960 Lulu was featured in advertising campaigns for Kleenex tissues. She also appeared, along with boyfriend Tubby Tompkins and little Alvin, in an animated cartoon series from Paramount Pictures in 1944-1948. The series was syndicated on television in 1956, and other series were produced in the 1970s. A short-lived animated series with Tracey Ullman as the voice of Little Lulu debuted on HBO in 1995.**

LUL-1

❑ **LUL-1. "Little Lulu on Parade" Book,**
1941. Hardback book shows Marge art printed from "Saturday Evening Post" cartoons. - **$30 $90 $120**

LUL-2

❑ **LUL-2. Original Art,**
1944. Used for "Saturday Evening Post". - **$1000**

LUL-3

❑ **LUL-3. "Little Lulu, Alvin And Tubby" Better Little Book,**
1947. Whitman #1429. - **$20 $50 $100**

LUL-4

LUL-5

❑ **LUL-4. Boxed Crayons,**
1948. Store item by Milton Bradley. - **$20 $40 $80**

❑ **LUL-5. Stuffed Doll,**
1940s. Store item with label reading "Handmade By Hazel." 17" tall with yarn hair. - **$50 $125 $225**

LUL-6

❑ **LUL-6. "Little Lulu/Baldy" Glass,**
1940s. Dairy product container from set of six. - **$30 $60 $125**

LUL-7

LUL-8

❑ **LUL-7. "Tubby Tom And Flipper" Glass,**
1940s. Dairy product container, from set of six. - **$30 $60 $125**

❑ **LUL-8. Annie And Mops Glass,**
1940s. Dairy product container, from set of six. - **$25 $50 $85**

LUL-9

LUL-10

❑ **LUL-9. Wilbur Van Snobbe Glass,**
1940s. Dairy product container from set of six. - **$25 $50 $85**

❑ **LUL-10. Gloria And Tipper Glass,**
1940s. Dairy product container from set of six.- **$25 $50 $85**

LUL-11

❑ **LUL-11. Paint Book,**
1951. Kleenex. - **$15 $30 $60**

LUL-12

LUL-13

❑ **LUL-12. Little Lulu Mask,**
1952. Kleenex. - **$20 $40 $60**

❑ **LUL-13. Tubby Mask,**
1952. Kleenex. - **$25 $50 $75**

LUL-14

LUL-15

❑ **LUL-14. Kleenex Cut-Out Doll 11x14" Cardboard Store Sign,**
1952. - **$20 $40 $75**

❑ **LUL-15. March of Comics Booklet,**
1964. Various retail stores. - **$10 $35 $80**

LUL-16

LUL-17

❑ **LUL-16. Little Lulu Ceramic Figurine,**
1974. Western Publishing copyright on back of figure. - **$25 $75 $120**

❑ **LUL-17. Tubby Ceramic Figurine,**
1974. Western Publishing copyright on back of figure. - **$25 $75 $120**

LUL18

❑ **LUL-18. Little Lulu Comic Cover Recreation Art by John Stanley,**
1977-1989. Painting shown is 15 1/2" x 12 1/2". Stanley painted approximately 15 covers during the period of 1977-1989. Years later he was offered high prices to do more paintings for other collections, but he declined. His paintings have brought $3,500 - $5,000 in recent years. However, they are in collections now and none are for sale as of the publication of this book.

LUL19

❑ **LUL-19. Promo Glass,**
1982. 6-1/2" tall issued by Kleenex. -
**$10 $20 $30**

## Little Nemo

**Winsor McCay (1869-1934), widely considered the greatest of the comic strip artists, created his masterpiece, *Little Nemo in Slumberland,* out of dreams and visions, exploring the unconscious with grace and fairy-tale beauty through the dazzling nocturnal voyages of his little hero. The strip ran in the *New York Herald* from 1905 to 1911 and from 1924 to 1927. From 1911 to 1914 the adventures appeared as *The Land of Wonderful Dreams* in the Hearst newspapers. A musical with a score by Victor Herbert was produced in 1908, and the following year McCay started a parallel career in film cartoons with the release of a hand-colored version of *Nemo.* Scattered comic book reprints of the strips were published from 1905 to 1970.**

LNE-1

LNE-2

❑ **LNE-1. "Little Nemo" Bicycle Nameplate,**
c. 1905. Bicycle maker is Baker, Murray & Imbrie Inc., N.Y. 2x2-1/2" aluminum with accents in black, silver and orange. -
**$50 $100 $160**

❑ **LNE-2. "Little Nemo A Fairy Tale" Sheet Music,**
1906. Store item by Graul Publishing Company, Detroit, Mich. 10-1/4x13-1/4" mostly in blue and white with red accent. Covers hold a loose center sheet. - **$30 $60 $100**

LNE-3

❑ **LNE-3. "Little Nemo In Slumberland" First Comic Strip Reprint Book,**
1906. Store item by Duffield & Co. 11x16" with 58 pages of Winsor McCay strips printed one side to a page. - **$857 $3000 (No NM exist)**

LNE-4

❑ **LNE-4. "Little Nemo And His Bear" Sheet Music With Mention Of Wizard Of Oz,**
1907. Published by Jerome Remick & Co. Subtitled "Successfully Interpolated In The Wizard Of Oz." Cover also says "After Winsor McCay" with artist name appearing to be "Detakacs." **- $35 $75 $150**

LNE-5

❑ **LNE-5. "Won't You Be My Playmate" Sheet Music,**
1908. New York Herald Co. Words and music for song by Victor Herbert from "Little Nemo" stage play. From series of various song titles. Each - **$30 $60 $100**

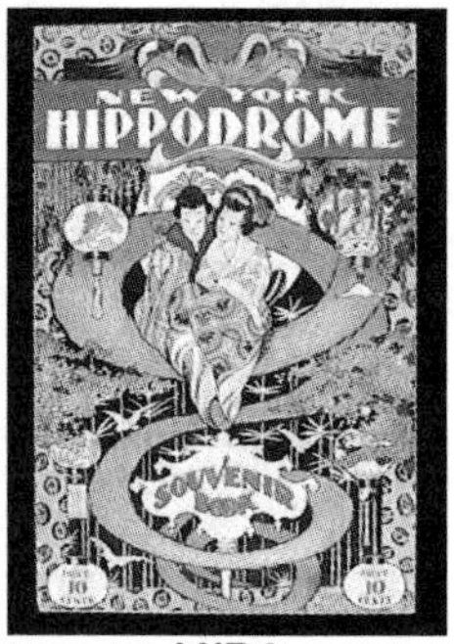

LNE-6

❑ **LNE-6. "New York Hippodrome Souvenir Book",**
1909. Unrelated to Little Nemo but 8x12" booklet has ornate color cover with art by Winsor McCay. Theatrical play was titled "A Trip To Japan." - **$50 $100 $150**

LNE-7

❑ **LNE-7. Little Nemo Postcard,**
1900s. From a series. Scarce. - **$30 $60 $120**

LNE-8

LNE-9

❑ **LNE-8. Dr. Pill Figural Bisque Toothbrush Holder,**
c. 1910. Store item. 5-1/4" tall holding bag with his name incised in his right hand while left hand rests atop hollow compartment for toothbrush. Made in Germany with #8317 on reverse. - **$600 $1200 $2200**

❑ **LNE-9. "Doctor Pill" Painted Bisque Figure,**
c. 1910. Store item. 4-3/4" tall figure from Little Nemo comic strip, one of the rarest comic character bisques. - **$600 $1200 $2200**

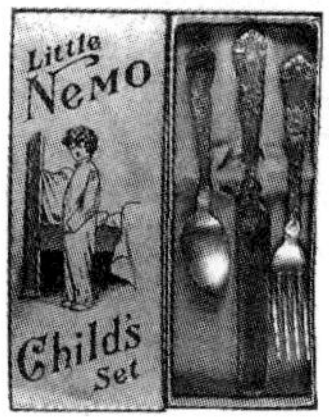

LNE-10

LNE-11

❑ **LNE-10. "Little Nemo Child's Set" Boxed Place Setting,**
c. 1910. Silver plate metal knife, fork and spoon with matching generic handle design. Box art is not attributed to Nemo creator Winsor McCay. Boxed - **$50 $125 $250**

❑ **LNE-11. "Little Nemo" Brass Clothing Buttons,**
c. 1910. 1/2" diameter with profile bust relief image of him. Each - **$10 $20 $30**

LNE-12

LNE-13

❑ **LNE-12. Flip Of Little Nemo Bobbing Head Figure,**
c. 1910. 6-1/2" tall painted composition with spring-mounted head on wooden rod neck. - **$100 $250 $550**

❑ **LNE-13. Bell Ringer Metal Toy,**
c. 1910. Pull or push toy on turning wheels causing ringing of bell chimes by figures of Nemo and Flip. - **$300 $600 $1000**

# Little Orphan Annie

**Orphan Annie was the life work of cartoonist/storyteller Harold Gray (1894-1968). From her comic strip debut in the *New York Daily News* in 1924 until Gray's death, the curly-haired pre-teen with blank eyes survived one thrilling adventure after another, accompanied by her faithful dog Sandy (Arf!), saved when necessary by billionaire Daddy Warbucks and his enforcers the Asp and Punjab.**

**The strip, consistently among the most popular of its time, gave rise to the classic radio serial that captivated its young fans on NBC from 1931 to 1942, sponsored by Ovaltine (1931-1940), then by Quaker Puffed Wheat and Rice Sparkies (1941-1942). With the new sponsor, Annie's pal Joe Corntassel was replaced by heroic combat pilot Captain Sparks, but the program could not survive the change and was soon dropped.**

**Merchandising of Annie premiums during the Ovaltine years was extensive, producing a seemingly endless stream of mugs, masks, decoders, games, books, pins, dolls, toys, dishes, rings, photos, whistles, and membership gear for *Radio Orphan Annie's Secret Society.* Premiums during the Puffed Wheat years included membership in the Secret Guard and the Safety Guard, along with aviation-related items.**

**A string of artists and writers continued the Annie comic strip after Gray's death, with little success, and in 1974 the strip was replaced by reprints of the original strip. Comic books, hardcover reprints of the newspaper strips, and giveaway books proliferated from 1926 through the 1940s.**
**Two movies added to the legend: the 1932 *Little Orphan Annie* from RKO and the 1982 *Annie* from Columbia Pictures, the latter based on the successful 1977 Broadway musical.**

LAN-1

LAN-2

❑ **LAN-1. "Little Orphan Annie/Her Story By Harold Gray" Convention Booklet,**
1927. Chicago Tribune Newspaper Syndicate. 32 pages of "Her Adventures To Date" given away at convention of American Newspapers Publishers Association. - **$75 $200 $400**

❑ **LAN-2. "Some Swell Sweater" Cello. Button,**
1928. Given with sweater purchase. - **$20 $40 $85**

LAN-3

❑ **LAN-3. "Little Orphan Annie" Storybook,**
1928. 4x5-1/2" paperback with 48 pages. Published by Whitman. - **$150 $300 $500**

LAN-4

LAN-5

❑ **LAN-4. Song Sheet Giveaway,**
1928. Scarce. Chicago Tribune. -
**$50 $100 $175**

❑ **LAN-5. "Some Swell Sweater" Cello. Button,**
1928. Given with sweater purchase. -
**$20 $50 $100**

LAN-6

❑ **LAN-6. "Little Orphan Annie Game,"**
c. 1930. Store item by Milton Bradley. -
**$35 $75 $150**

LAN-7

LAN-8

❑ **LAN-7. "Little Orphan Annie Candy Bar" Ad,**
1931. Monthly issue for September of "The Northwestern Confectioner" trade magazine for candy makers and retailers with cover art introducing new candy bar by Shotwell Mfg. Co., Chicago. - **$50 $100 $200**

❑ **LAN-8. "Little Orphan Annie" Candy Bar Wrapper,**
1931. Waxed paper cover for product of Shotwell Mfg. Co. also offering Orphan Annie doll and coloring book as mail premiums. -
**$60 $140 $275**

LAN-9

❑ **LAN-9. "Mitzie Green's Art Needlework Outfit" Set,**
1931. Store item by Standard Solophone Mfg. Co. She is titled "Paramount's Child Star, Appearing In Tom Sawyer And Skippy." A year later she starred in the Little Orphan Annie movie. Box is 13-1/2x18" holding fabrics, needles, snaps, scissors, thimble, embroidery hoops and a 7" tall jointed bisque doll. -
**$75 $150 $250**

LAN-10

❑ **LAN-10. "Little Orphan Annie's Song" Sheet Music,**
1931. Probably 1st Ovaltine Annie premium.
Near Mint in Mailer - **$85**
Music Only - **$15 $25 $50**

LAN-11

LAN-12

❑ **LAN-11. "Orphan Annie" Cello. Button,**
1931. Scarce. Known as Voter's Button issued as companion pair with Joe Corntassel version, awarded respectively for vote preferring Ovaltine with ice or Ovaltine with ice cream. -
**$200 $350 $600**

❑ **LAN-12. "Joe Corntassel" Cello. Button,**
1931. Known as Voter's Button with companion Orphan Annie button issued respectively for voters preferring Ovaltine with ice cream or simply ice. - **$100 $225 $400**

LAN-13

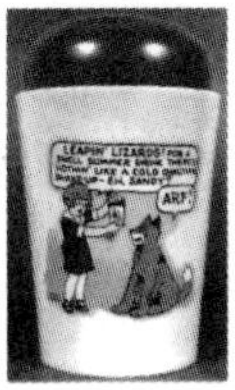

LAN-14

❑ **LAN-13. Joe Corntassel "Voters Button" Card,**
1931. Also issued for Annie.
Each - **$40 $100 $200**

❑ **LAN-14. Beetleware Shake-Up Mug,**
1931. - **$20 $50 $90**

LAN-15

❑ **LAN-15. "Shake-Up Game" Instruction Folder,**
1931. Came with Shake-Up mug. -
**$20 $40 $70**

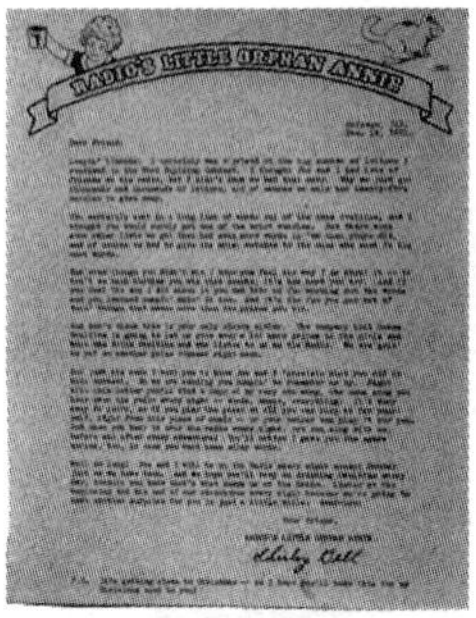


LAN-16

❑ **LAN-16. "Word Building Contest" Acknowledgement Letter,**
1931. Response to entrant in contest to see how many different words can be made from single word Ovaltine plus Christmas greeting from Shirley Bell, ROA portrayer. Dated Dec. 14, 1931. "P.S." reads "It's getting close to Christmas -- so I hope you'll take this as my Christmas card to you!" - **$20 $50 $100**

LAN-17

LAN-18

❑ **LAN-17. Ceramic Mug,**
1932. - **$25 $50 $85**

❑ **LAN-18. "Mitzi Green As Little Orphan Annie" Movie Photo,**
1932. Imprinted for local theaters. -
**$25 $60 $110**

LAN-19

❑ **LAN-19. RKO Film Promo,**
1932. Scarce. 4-page promo with Mitzi Green. - **$75 $150 $250**

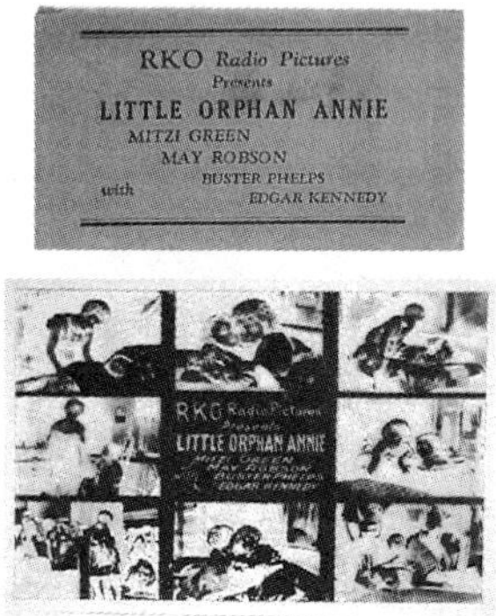


LAN-20

❑ **LAN-20. Sun Picture Negative And Envelope,**
1932. RKO Radio Pictures probable giveaway. 2-1/4x3-1/4" with scenes from movie starring Mitzi Green. - **$10 $20 $40**

LAN-21

LAN-22

❑ **LAN-21. "Shirley Bell" Radio Show Photo,**
1932. Pictured is Radio Orphan Annie portrayer. - **$20 $50 $70**

❑ **LAN-22. "Joe Corntassel/Allan Baruck" Radio Show Photo,**
1932. - **$15 $40 $60**

LAN-23

❑ **LAN-23. "Tucker County Fair" Jigsaw Puzzle With Mailer Box,**
1933. Near Mint In Mailer - **$135**
Loose - **$25 $50 $85**

LAN-24

LAN-25

❑ **LAN-24. Paper Face Mask,**
1933. - **$20 $60 $90**

❑ **LAN-25. Beetleware Plastic Cup,**
1933. - **$15 $30 $75**

LAN-26

❑ **LAN-26. "Treasure Hunt" Game With Paper Boats,**
1933. With Four Sailboats. Brown & yellow cover variations. Set - **$60 $125 $250**
Board Only - **$20 $30 $75**
Mailer - **$20 $40 $60**

LAN-27

LAN-28

❑ **LAN-27. Little Orphan Annie And Sandy Toothbrush Holder,**
c. 1933. Store item. Japan painted hollow bisque marked "S1565." - **$35 $85 $140**

❑ **LAN-28. "Little Orphan Annie Hair Brush,"**
c. 1933. Store item. - **$50 $125 $200**

LAN-29

❑ **LAN-29. "Little Orphan Annie Embroidery Set,"**
c. 1933. Store item by J. Pressman Company. - **$75 $150 $225**

LAN-30

❑ **LAN-30. Biscuit Box,**
c. 1933. Store item by Loose Wiles Biscuit Co. - **$150 $300 $500**

LAN-31

❑ **LAN-31. Ovaltine Cup Rare Color Variety,**
1933. Decal is identical to the standard 1933 issue but the Beetleware material is bright orange rather than standard cream color. Perhaps used briefly when supply of standard cups was temporarily exhausted. - **$150 $350 $600**

LAN-32

LAN-33

❑ **LAN-32. "Secret Society" Manual,**
1934. - **$20 $40 $80**

❑ **LAN-33. Secret Society Bronze Badge,**
1934. - **$10 $15 $25**

LAN-34

❑ **LAN-34. Adventure Books & Contest Winner Sheet,**
1934. One side lists winners of "Shake-Up Naming Contest". - **$15 $40 $60**

LAN-35

❑ **LAN-35. Bandanna Ring Slide Offer Sheet,**
1934. "Face" ring also used as bandanna holder. - **$20 $50 $80**

LAN-36

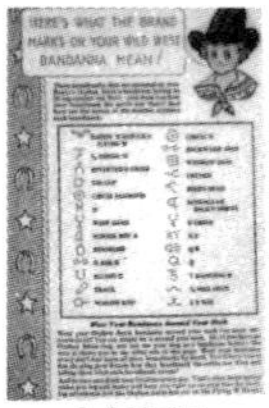
LAN-37

❑ **LAN-36. "Flying W" Bandanna,**
1934. - **$20 $50 $90**

❑ **LAN-37. "Flying W" Bandanna Explanation Card,**
1934. Explains the 26 brands pictured on bandanna. - **$25 $50 $80**

LAN-38

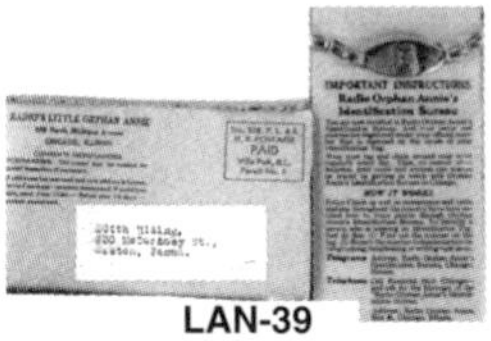
LAN-39

❑ **LAN-38. Annie Portrait Ring and Bandanna Slide,**
1934. - **$30 $60 $100**

❑ **LAN-39. "Identification Bureau" Bracelet With Mailer Envelope,**
1934. Silver finish, personalized with initial.
Near Mint In Mailer - **$175**
Bracelet Only - **$20 $50 $75**

LAN-40

LAN-41

❑ **LAN-40. Silver Star Club Badge,**
1934. Silvered brass. - **$15 $30 $50**

❑ **LAN-41. "Silver Star Member" Manual,**
1934. Near Mint In Mailer - **$100**
Loose - **$20 $50 $75**

LAN-42

LAN-43

❑ **LAN-42. "Good Luck" Brass Medal,**
1934. Includes "Ovaltine 3 Times A Day" with back "Good Luck" in several languages. - **$10 $20 $40**

❑ **LAN-43. Pronunciation Card For "Good Luck" Medal,**
1934. Offers correct phonetic pronunciation for each of the seven foreign language "Good Luck" inscriptions on medal reverse.
Slotted to hold medal. - **$20 $50 $100**

LAN-44

LAN-45

❑ **LAN-44. Club Manual,**
1935. - **$25 $60 $100**

❑ **LAN-45. Brass Decoder,**
1935. Silver flashing often worn off outer rim. - **$15 $35 $125**

LAN-46

❑ **LAN-46. Premium Catalogue Folder With Envelope,**
1935. Opens to 4x22" with May 15 expiration date, envelope has NRA symbol of Depression era.
Near Mint In Mailer - **$350**
Folder - **$75 $150 $275**

LAN-47

❑ **LAN-47. Magic Transfers and Instruction Sheet,**
1935 Scarce. - **$50 $150 $210**

LAN-48

LAN-49

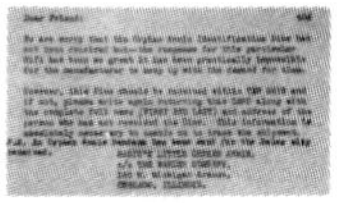
LAN-50

❑ **LAN-48. Beetleware Cup,**
1935. Green circle background. - **$15 $50 $90**

❑ **LAN-49. Beetleware Plastic Shake-Up Mug,**
1935. Orange lid. Shows Annie from waist up. - **$25 $50 $95**

❑ **LAN-50. Ovaltine Apology Postcard,**
1935. Form message for delay in shipment of Orphan Annie Identification Disk postmarked January 5. - **$25 $60 $85**

LAN-51

LAN-52

❑ **LAN-51. "Little Orphan Annie and the Ghost Gang" Big Little Book #1154,**
1935. - **$15 $60 $110**

❑ **LAN-52. "Little Orphan Annie and Punjab the Wizard" Big Little Book #1162,**
1935. - **$15 $60 $110**

LAN-53

❑ **LAN-53. Little Orphan Annie with Sandy Ashtray,**
Mid 1930s. One in a series of comic character ashtrays produced in Japan in the mid 1930s. - **$35 $85 $175**

LAN-54

LAN-55

❑ **LAN-54. Club Manual,**
1936. - **$15 $30 $75**

❑ **LAN-55. Secret Compartment Brass Decoder,**
1936. - **$15 $25 $85**

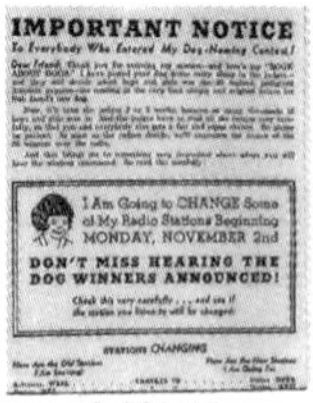


LAN-56

LAN-57

❑ **LAN-56. Dog-Naming Contest Notice,**
1936. Thank you notice for entering contest to name Bob Bond's new dog. - **$10 $25 $60**

❑ **LAN-57. "Book About Dogs",**
1936. Contents include Annie characters in various activities plus photo descriptions of various dog breeds. - **$15 $30 $70**

LAN-58

LAN-59

❑ **LAN-58. "Silver Star Member" Secrets Folder,**
1936. For Silver Star Ring, shown on cover. - **$25 $50 $85**

❑ **LAN-59. Silver Star Ring,**
1936. Silvered brass design of crossed keys over star. - **$100 $200 $300**

LAN-60

❑ **LAN-60. "Birthday Ring" With Folder And Envelope,**
1936. Birthstones in various colors. Offer appeared October, 1935.
Near Mint In Mailer - **$500**
Ring - **$100 $225 $400**
Folder - **$50 $55 $60**

LAN-61

❑ **LAN-61. "Welcome To Simmons Corners" 19x24" Paper Map,**
1936. - **$25 $60 $100**

LAN-62

❑ **LAN-62. "Little Orphan Annie And The Big Town Gunmen" Comic Strip Reprint Book,**
1936. Published by Whitman. 5-1/2x7-1/2" format. - **$50 $100 $165**

LAN-63

LAN-64

❑ **LAN-63. "Little Orphan Annie Circus" Punch-Out Book,**
1936. Six pages including more than 30 punch-outs. Unpunched - **$150 $300 $500**

❑ **LAN-64. Glassips Package In Mailer,**
1936. Rare. Contents are cellophane drinking straws. - **$100 $300 $425**

LAN-65

❑ **LAN-65. Club Manual with Mailer and Silver Star Ring Order Form,**
1937. Manual - **$20 $35 $70**
Other Items - **$5 $10 $20**

LAN-66

LAN-67

❑ **LAN-66. Sunburst Brass Decoder Badge,**
1937. - **$15 $50 $125**

❑ **LAN-67. "Silver Star Members" Folder With Mailer Envelope,**
1937. Includes code for Silver Star Ring.
Folder - **$65 $140 $235**
Envelope - **$10 $20 $30**

LAN-68

❑ **LAN-68. "Big Little Kit" Of Crayon Sheets,**
1937. Store item. Box holds 192 paper sheets. - **$75 $150 $300**

LAN-69

LAN-70

❑ **LAN-69. Silver Star Member Secret Message Ring,**
1937. Silvered brass with coded message to be decoded by that year's decoder. - **$75 $150 $250**

❑ **LAN-70. Rummy Cards,**
1937. - In a colorful box. - **$25 $65 $150**

LAN-71

❑ **LAN-71. Two Initial Signet Brass Ring,**
1937. Ring was customized with recipient's initials. Ring - **$35 $65 $115**
Instruction Sheet - **$15 $25 $60**

LAN-72

❑ **LAN-72. "Talking Stationery",**
1937. Diecut paper mouths open and close, came with 12 letter sheets and envelopes.
Near Mint Complete - **$275**
Each Sheet - **$5 $10 $20**

LAN-73

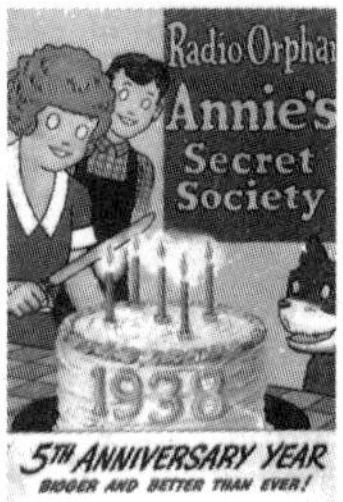


LAN-74

❑ **LAN-73. Foreign "Coin Collection" Folder,**
1937. - **$15 $30 $50**

❑ **LAN-74. Club Manual,**
1938. - **$20 $50 $85**

LAN-75

❑ **LAN-75. "Little Orphan Annie Saves Sandy" Penny Book,**
1938. Published by Whitman. - **$15 $35 $60**

LAN-76

LAN-77

❑ **LAN-76. Telematic Brass Decoder Badge,**
1938. - **$25 $60 $110**

❑ **LAN-77. Silver Star Manual,**
1938. - **$90 $300 $400**

LAN-78

❑ **LAN-78. Silver Star Triple Mystery Secret Compartment Ring,**
1938. Silvered brass with removable cap covering member's serial number.
Ring - **$250 $600 $1000**
Order Form - **$10 $18 $30**

LAN-79

LAN-80

❑ **LAN-79. Miracle Compass Sun-Watch,**
1938. - **$20 $50 $100**

❑ **LAN-80. School Brass Badge,**
1938. Customized with two initials. -
**$15 $40 $75**

LAN-81

LAN-82

❑ **LAN-81. Beetleware Shake-Up Mug,**
1938. Light blue with orange top, dancing scene. - **$35 $100 $185**

❑ **LAN-82. "Little Orphan Annie Gets Into Trouble" Booklet,**
1938. J. C. Penney Co. - **$15 $40 $70**

LAN-83

❑ **LAN-83. "Snow White And The Seven Dwarfs Cut-Out Book" With Envelope ,**
1938. Scarce. Ovaltine as Radio Orphan Annie premium, also store item. Published by Whitman with six punch-out sheets. See LAN-87.
Near Mint In Mailer - **$650**
No Mailer, Unpunched - **$150 $400 $500**

LAN-84

LAN-85

❑ **LAN-84. Silver Plated Foto-Frame,**
1938. Scarce. Metal base inscribed on front "To My Best Friend". - **$100 $250 $400**

❑ **LAN-85. Ann Gillis Photo,**
c. 1938. Little Orphan Annie radio portrayer of late 1930s. - **$20 $55 $75**

LAN-86

❑ **LAN-86. "Shadowettes" Mechanical Paper Portraits,**
1938. Set of six. Sandy, Annie, Warbucks, Joe Corntassel, Mr. Silo, Mrs. Silo.
Near Mint In Mailer - **$300**
Each Assembled - **$10 $20 $40**

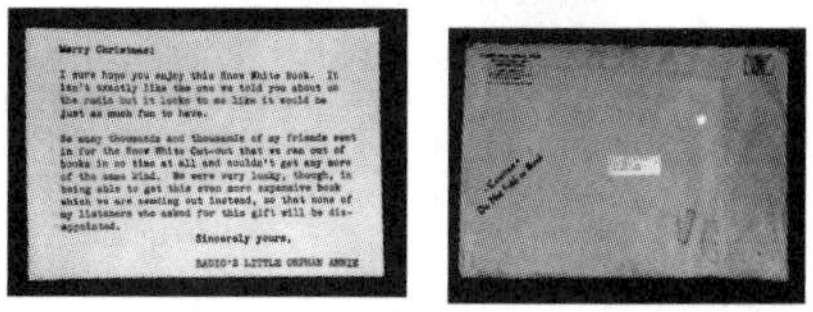

LAN-87

❑ **LAN-87. "Snow White And The Seven Dwarfs Paperdolls" Book With Envelope And Replacement Notice Slip,**
1938. Ovaltine Orphan Annie premium letter reads "even more expensive book" with full color cover sent as replacement due to depleted supply of lesser quality book originally offered as Christmas premium. Originally offered version had blue and yellow cover. Enclosed replacement slip explains details. Doll book is copyright Walt Disney Enterprises, 1938. See LAN-83.
Christmas Insert - **$25 $50 $100**
Unpunched Book - **$300 $750 $1100**
Mailer - **$50 $100 $150**

LAN-88

LAN-89

❑ **LAN-88. "Little Orphan Annie And The Ancient Treasure Of Am" Better Little Book,**
1939. Whitman #1468. - **$20 $50 $110**

❑ **LAN-89. "Little Orphan Annie And The Ancient Treasure Of Am" Better Little Book,**
1939. Whitman #1414. - **$20 $50 $110**

LAN-90

LAN-91

❑ **LAN-90. Manual with Mailer,**
1939. Manual - **$20 $40 $85**
Mailer - **$5 $10 $20**

❑ **LAN-91. Mysto-Matic Brass Decoder Badge,**
1939. - **$25 $50 $100**

LAN-92

LAN-93

❑ **LAN-92. "Goofy Gazette" First Issue,**
1939. Ovaltine. Vol. 1 #1 issue of eight-page newspaper including information on two contests closing June 15. - **$40 $80 $150**

❑ **LAN-93. Greater Boston Community Fund Campaign 13x22" Cardboard Poster,**
1939. Orphan Annie and Sandy art by Harold Gray. - **$40 $100 $175**

LAN-94

LAN-95

❑ **LAN-94. Code Captain Secret Compartment Badge,**
1939. Silvered finish. Sometimes found with link chain on back to fasten to that year's decoder badge. - **$35 $80 $125**

❑ **LAN-95. "Code Captain Secrets" Folder,**
1939. - **$50 $100 $200**

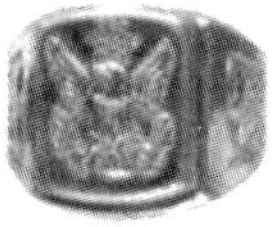

LAN-96

LAN-97

❑ **LAN-96. Mystic-Eye Detective (Look-Around) Ring,**
1939. Brass ring with American eagle cover cap over look-in mirror. Also issued for Captain Midnight and The Lone Ranger. -
**$40 $80 $125**

❑ **LAN-97. "Mystic-Eye Detective Ring" Instruction Sheet,**
1939. - **$15 $30 $60**

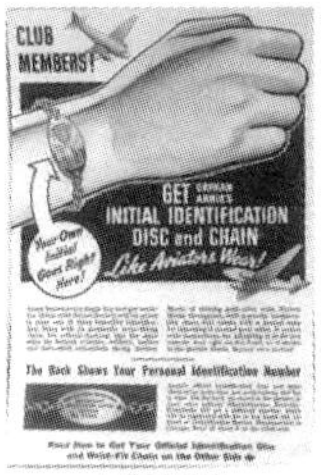


LAN-98

LAN-99

❑ **LAN-98. "Initial Identification Disc And Chain" Order Sheet,**
1939. Back explains how Identification Bureau works above order coupon. Brass finish. -
**$20 $50 $75**

❑ **LAN-99. Identification Bracelet,**
1939. Brass version with American flag in bow design, personalized by single initial designated by orderer. - **$25 $50 $100**

LAN-100

LAN-101

❑ **LAN-100. Beetleware Plastic Shake-Up Mug,**
1939. Brown mug with orange lid. -
**$50 $100 $185**

❑ **LAN-101. "Goofy Gazette" Newspaper #3 With Envelope,**
1939. Last of three issues.
Newspaper - **$35 $60 $100**
Mailer - **$5 $15 $25**

LAN-102

❑ **LAN-102. "Goofy Circus" Punch-Out Kit With Mailer Envelope,**
1939. Mailer - **$15 $50 $60**
Unpunched - **$200 $350 $650**

LAN-103

❑ **LAN-103. Greater Boston's 1939 Community Fund Campaign,**
1939. 7-1/2x10" with 16 pages featuring cover art by Harold Gray. - **$20 $40 $75**

LAN-104

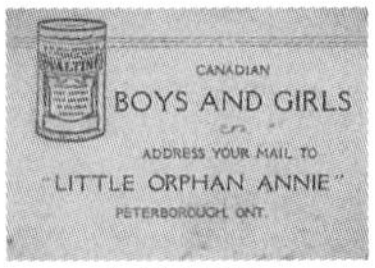


LAN-105

❑ **LAN-104. Rare Color Variety Shake-Up Mug,**
1939. Same decal design as the 1939 brown mug and the 1940 green mug but this has a light blue cup covered by a dark blue lid. Only a few examples known. - **$75 $150 $300**

❑ **LAN-105. Canadian Ovaltine Premium Insert Card,**
1930s. A. Wander Limited. 3x4-1/4" red on white providing "Canadian Boys And Girls" with address for letters. - **$10 $20 $40**

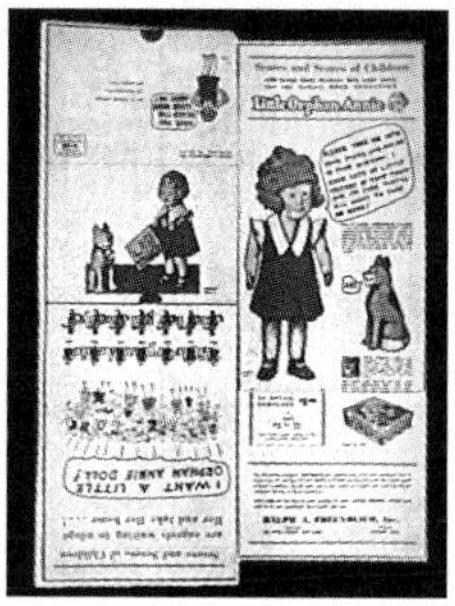

LAN-106

❑ **LAN-106. Doll Offer Sheet To Dealers,**
1930s. Ralph A. Freundlich Inc. Self-mailer opening to 8x21" printed on both sides offering composition 12" tall Annie doll and matching 7" tall Sandy doll. - **$50 $100 $150**

LAN-107 LAN-108

❑ **LAN-107. Little Orphan Annie Oilcloth Doll,**
1930s. Starched fabric from set believed issued by unknown cereal sponsor. Also in set are: Herby, Kayo, Moon Mullins, Smitty (see COM-67-69), and Sandy (see next item). - **$75 $110 $210**

❑ **LAN-108. Sandy Oilcloth Doll,**
1930s. See previous item. - **$50 $85 $150**

LAN-109

LAN-110

❑ **LAN-109. Cello. Button,**
1930s. Cunningham Ice Cream. - **$75 $125 $200**

❑ **LAN-110. Heart's Desire Dress Clip,**
1930s. Ovaltine. Offered as Orphan Annie unmarked premium with her name on order form of "Costume Jewelry Gifts" Ovaltine folder. Also issued by radio show "Girl Alone/Patricia Roberts" on a pink card. See LAN-113. - **$50 $125 $200**

LAN-111 LAN-112

❑ **LAN-111. "Pittsburgh Post-Gazette" Newspaper Contest Cello. Button,**
1930s. Part of a set showing other characters in the newspaper. - **$40 $75 $150**

❑ **LAN-112. "Funy Frostys Club" Cello. Button,**
1930s. Two styles: "Member" in straight or curved type. - **$75 $150 $275**

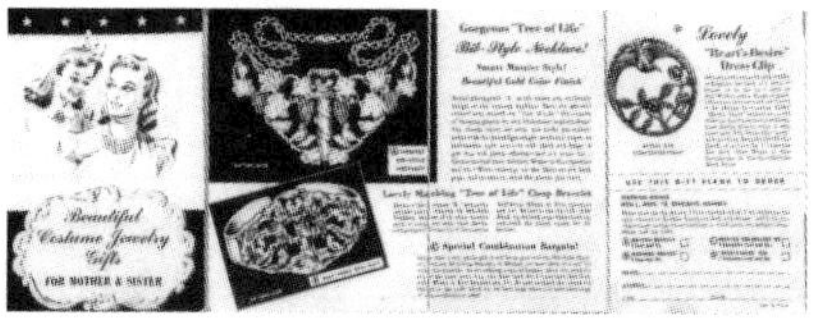

LAN-113

❑ **LAN-113. "Beautiful Costume Jewelry Gifts" Folder,**
1930s. Annie name on order coupon. See LAN-110. - **$50 $125 $175**

LAN-114

LAN-115

❑ **LAN-114. "Funy Frostys" Waxed Paper Wrapper,**
1930s. Funy Frostys Ice Cream. Bottom has cardboard finger hole card for holding ice confection bar. - **$25 $50 $100**

❑ **LAN-115. "Sunshine Biscuits" Box,**
1930s. Loose-Wiles Biscuit Co. - **$100 $300 $450**

LAN-116

LAN-117

❑ **LAN-116. "Los Angeles Evening Express" Cello. Button,**
1930s. From set of newspaper characters, match number to win prize. - **$30 $60 $100**

❑ **LAN-117. Bisque Toothbrush Holder,**
1930s. Store item. - **$60 $100 $185**

LAN-118

❑ **LAN-118. Club Manual,**
1940. - **$50 $80 $160**

LAN-119 LAN-120

❑ **LAN-119. Speed-O-Matic Brass Decoder Badge,**
1940. - **$30 $60 $125**

❑ **LAN-120. Beetleware Plastic Shake-Up Mug,**
1940. Green with red lid. - **$40 $90 $175**

LAN-121

LAN-122

LAN-123

❑ **LAN-121. Shake-Up Mug Leaflet,**
1940. Came with green mug. - **$25 $50 $75**

❑ **LAN-122. Sandy 3-Way Dog Whistle,**
1940. 3-1/4" brass tube whistle that extends to 5-1/4" length. - **$20 $35 $75**

❑ **LAN-123. "3 Way Mystery Dog-Whistle" Instruction Leaflet,**
1940. - **$20 $30 $50**

LAN-124

❑ **LAN-124. "Code Captain Secrets" Folder With Mailer,**
1940. Red, white and blue small paper folder that opens to 6-1/2x9-1/2". Describes club secrets including use of Code Captain Belt.
Mailer - **$15 $25 $40**
Folder - **$50 $125 $250**

LAN-125

LAN-126

LAN-127

❑ **LAN-125. Metal Puzzle,**
1940. Four metal ball puzzle tin. Store bought. - **$30 $90 $150**

❑ **LAN-126. "Code Captain" Brass Buckle With Fabric Belt,**
1940. Complete - **$100 $225 $350**
Buckle Only - **$50 $125 $200**

❑ **LAN-127. Card,**
1940. Card premium from the radio show. "How to Become a Code Captain." - **$20 $40 $90**

LAN-128

❑ **LAN-128. Watch with Box and Insert,**
1940. Watch was promoted as girls' watch. Also has a price tag and cardboard New Haven seal. Complete - **$200 $400 $700**

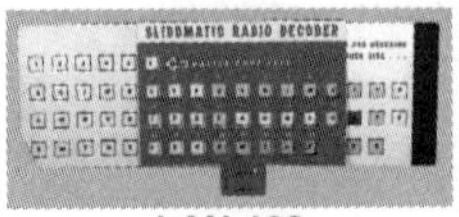

LAN-129

LAN-130

❑ **LAN-129. "Slidomatic Radio Decoder",**
1941. Quaker Cereals. Cardboard slide with instructions on back. - **$25 $75 $125**

❑ **LAN-130. "Safety Guard" Application Blank for Captain's Commission,**
1941. Quaker Cereals. Also see item LAN-146. - **$10 $20 $35**

LAN-131

❑ **LAN-131. Quaker Rice Sparkies Shipping Carton,**
c. 1941. 11x16x25" long corrugated cardboard box originally holding 24 boxes of cereal plus 12 comic books. - **$75 $150 $250**

LAN-132

LAN-133

❑ **LAN-132. Secret Guard Double-Sided Sign,**
1941. Gordon Gold Archives. - **$500 $800 $1200**

❑ **LAN-133. Club Manual,**
1941. Quaker Cereals. - **$60 $175 $250**

LAN-134

LAN-135

❑ **LAN-134. Secret Guard Mysto-Snapper,**
1941. Quaker Cereals. Litho. tin clicker. - **$25 $75 $110**

❑ **LAN-135. "Captain's Secrets" Folder Manual,**
1941. Quaker Sparkies. - **$50 $175 $325**

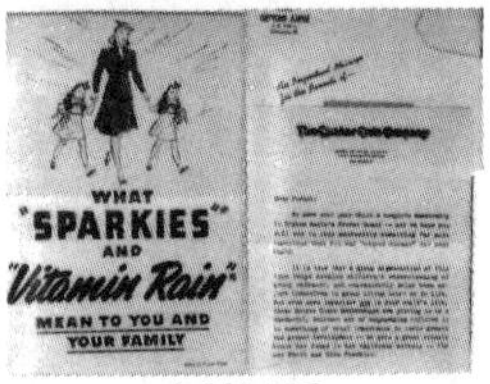

LAN-136

❑ **LAN-136. Secret Guard Member Letter With Quaker Cereal Leaflet,**
1941. Both explain "Vitamin Rain" additives to Quaker cereals. Each - **$10 $20 $40**

LAN-137

❑ **LAN-137. "The Adventures Of Little Orphan Annie" Comic Book,**
1941. Quaker Puffed Wheat & Rice Sparkies. "...Kidnappers/Magic Morro..." stories. - **$19 $58 $160**

(Back of booklet)

(Front of booklet)

LAN-138

❑ **LAN-138. Secret Guard 8 Page Promotional Booklet,**
1941. Large booklet displays all the info for the Secret Guard Club. The sponsor was Quaker Puffed Wheat Sparkies. This campaign was designed to tie "Little Orphan Annie" to the War effort. Captain Sparks was also created to help. Unfortunately, it didn't work and the show was cancelled in 1942. The premiums produced in 1941 and 1942 are very hard to find. Gordon Gold Archives. - **$200 $500 $850**

LAN-139 LAN-140

❑ **LAN-139. Secret Guard Wood Handle Rubber Stamp With Mailer,**
1941. Rare. Quaker Cereals.
Stamp Only - **$150 $300 $450**
Mailer - **$50 $100 $200**

❑ **LAN-140. Brass Slide Dog Whistle,**
1941. Scarce. Quaker Cereals. End has Orphan Annie head. - **$100 $200 $300**

LAN-141

LAN-142

❑ **LAN-141. "The Adventures Of Little Orphan Annie" Comic Book,**
1941. Quaker Puffed Wheat & Rice Sparkies. "...Rescue/Magic Morro..." stories. - **$19 $58 $160**

❑ **LAN-142. Quaker "How To Fly" Manual,**
1941. Came with Airplane Pilot Training Cockpit. - **$30 $75 $125**

LAN-143

❑ **LAN-143. "Captain Sparks Airplane Cockpit" Cardboard Assembly Kit,**
1941. Quaker Cereals. 6x27" assembled with him pictured at center.
Unassembled - **$150 $300 $500**
Assembled - **$100 $225 $350**

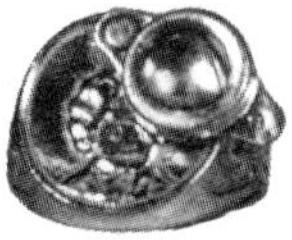

LAN-144 LAN-145

❑ **LAN-144. Secret Guard Magnifying Ring,**
1941. Quaker Cereals. Offered briefly in 1941 with 8/31/41 expiration date "before Orphan Annie comes back on the air next Fall". - **$450 $1000 $2300**

❑ **LAN-145. "SG" Secret Guard Brass Ring,**
1941. Scarce. Quaker Cereals. Also inscribed "Bravery/Health/Justice" and personalized with initial. - **$450 $1000 $2500**

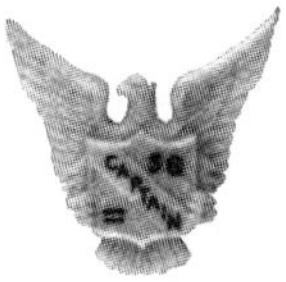

LAN-146 LAN-147

❑ **LAN-146. "SG/Captain" Glow-In-Dark Plastic Badge,**
1941. Quaker Cereals. Also see item LAN-130. - **$65 $250 $400**

❑ **LAN-147. "S.G." Secret Guard 3" Metal Flashlight,**
1941. Scarce. Quaker Cereals. - **$100 $200 $300**

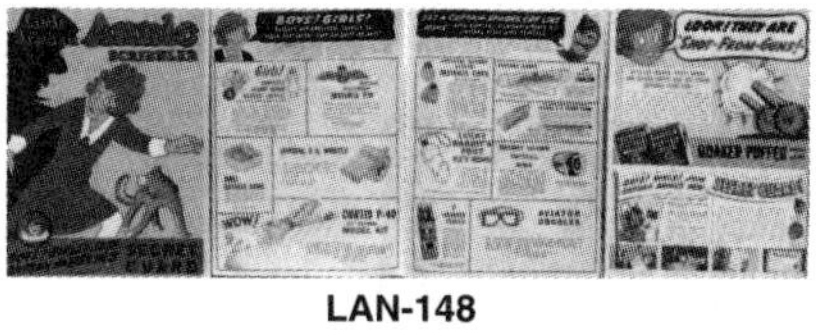


LAN-148

❑ **LAN-148. "Little Orphan Annie Scribbler" Canadian Booklet,**
1941. Quaker Puffed Wheat And Puffed Rice. Canadian issue. - **$35 $75 $125**

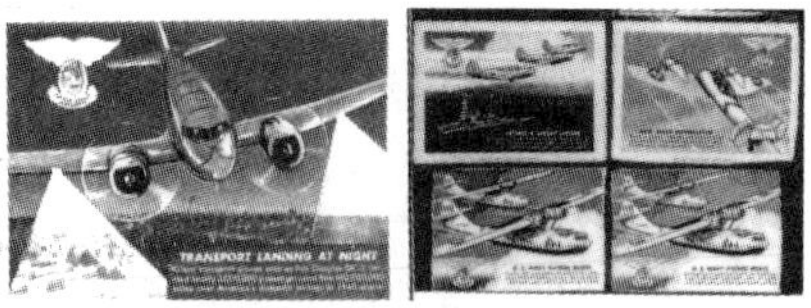

LAN-149

❑ **LAN-149. Captain Sparks Box Cut-Outs,**
c. 1941. Quaker Sparkies cereal. From "Home Defense Series" set of 12.
Each Panel Cut-Out - **$10 $20 $30**

LAN-150

❑ **LAN-150. "The Adventures Of Little Orphan Annie" Comic Book Offer Store Sign,**
1941. Quaker Puffed Rice 'Sparkies.' 12-3/4x19" red, black and white. Gordon Gold Archives. - **$250 $500 $850**

LAN-151

❑ **LAN-151. Secret Guard Store Display Sign With Application Blanks,**
1941. Flattened 11-1/2x23-1/2" diecut display designed to fold at mid-point. Lower center has area for tablet of application coupons. Pictured are handbook and both 1941 paper decoder and tin clicker member's badge. Gordon Gold Archives. Display - **$250 $500 $850**
Single Coupon - **$10 $20 $30**

LAN-152

❑ **LAN-152. "Captain Sparks' Airplane Pilot Training Cockpit" Paper Sign ,**
1941. Full color 13x21" sign. Gordon Gold Archives. - **$150 $300 $600**

LAN-153

❑ **LAN-153. Airplane Cockpit Offer Diecut Display Sign,**
1941. Flattened size of 14x25-1/2" designed to fold into dimensional display with holder for order blank coupons. Gordon Gold Archives. - **$150 $325 $650**

LAN-154

❑ **LAN-154. "Sparkies 2-Way Aviation Drive!" Dealer's Promo,**
c. 1941. Probable trade magazine advertising pages promoting cereal boxes with "Authentic U.S. Plane Pictures From Backs Of Sparkies Boxes." - **$15 $30 $50**

LAN-155

❑ **LAN-155. "Little Orphan Annie's Adventures In Fun-Land" Prototype Premium Activity Book,**
c. 1941. Prepared for Quaker Puffed Wheat Sparkies. 6x9" full color all original art prototype design for 16-page activity book. Gordon Gold Archives. Unique - **$1050**

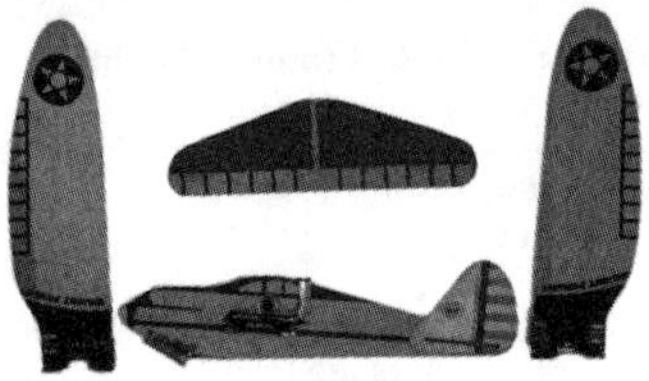
LAN-156

❑ **LAN-156. "Wright Pursuit" Balsa Plane,**
1941. Offered as giveaway pictured in Radio Orphan Annie comics. Shown in comic with "SG" on wings. The two letters on wing pictured appear to be rough design overlays and used for promo as only. Probably used as a Capt. Midnight giveaway as well. - **$50 $100 $175**

LAN-157

❑ **LAN-157. "ROA Cadet" Pendant,**
c. 1941. Possibly a Quaker premium used in Canada. Marked "Sterling" on reverse. - **$75 $200 $350**

LAN-158

❑ **LAN-158. "Little Orphan Annie And The Haunted Mansion" Better Little Book,**
1941. Whitman #1482. - **$20 $50 $110**

LAN-159

❑ **LAN-159. "Junior Commandos" Premium Comic Book,**
1942. Published by K.K. Publications, Inc., with back ad "Big Shoe Store." 16 pages reprinting strips from 9/7/42 to 10/10/42. - **$34 $102 $285**

(CLOSE-UP OF DECODER)

LAN-160

❑ **LAN-160. "Safety Guard" Membership Kit,**
1942. Quaker Cereals. Included tin whistle not shown (see item LAN-162).
Set Near Mint - **$600**
Decoder - **$50 $100 $150**
Whistle - **$20 $40 $85**
Handbook - **$60 $150 $300**

LAN-161

LAN-162

❑ **LAN-161. "Safety Guard" Captain Application Blank,**
1942. Quaker Cereals. Also see item LAN-167. - **$10 $20 $35**

❑ **LAN-162. "Safety Guard" Tri-Tone Signaler Badge,**
1942. Quaker Cereals. Litho. tin whistle from member's kit (see item LAN-160). - **$20 $40 $85**

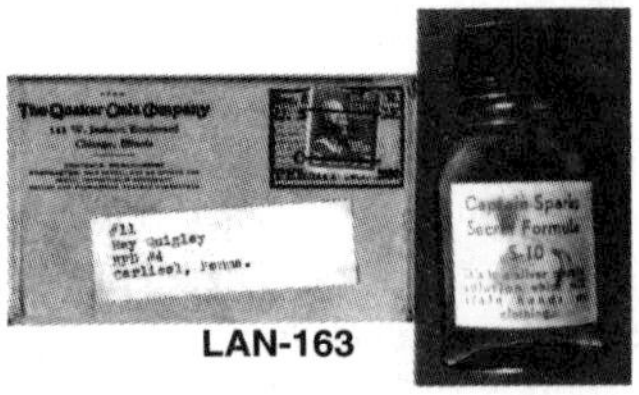

LAN-163

❑ **LAN-163. Quaker "Detector-Kit" With Mailer Box,**
1942. Many items for photo printing, "Captain Sparks Secret Formula S-10" on bottle label. Boxed - **$100 $150 $300**

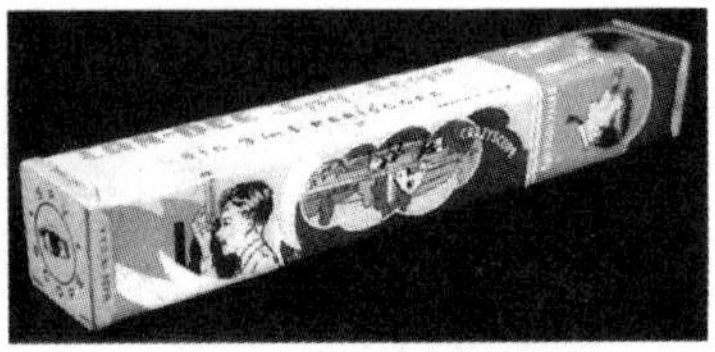
LAN-164

❑ **LAN-164. "3 In 1 Periscope",**
1942. Scarce. Quaker Cereals. No Annie name but offered in 1942 Safety Guard handbook. - **$100 $225 $400**

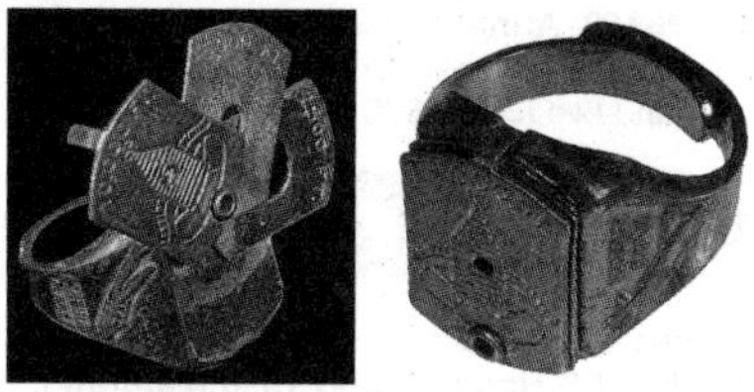

(OPEN) **LAN-165** (CLOSED)

❏ **LAN-165. Altascope Ring,**
1942. Rare. Quaker Cereals. Several moveable brass plates for sighting airplanes and estimating their altitudes. Nine known: two in good grade, three in very good, one in fine, two in very fine, and one in near mint.
Good - **$2500**
Fine - **$7000**
Very Fine - **$14500**

**LAN-166**

❏ **LAN-166."Little Orphan Annie And Her Junior Commandos" Better Little Book,**
1942. Whitman #1457. **- $35 $85 $200**

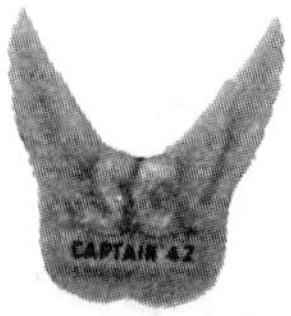

**LAN-167** **LAN-168**

❏ **LAN-167. "SG Captain" Safety Guard Magic Glow Bird Badge,**
1942. Rare. Quaker Cereals. Also see item LAN-161. **- $150 $300 $850**

❏ **LAN-168. "SG Captain" Glow-In-Dark Canadian Club Brass Badge,**
1942. Rare. Quaker Cereals. Design includes Canadian maple leaf symbol. -
**$150 $400 $800**

**LAN-169** **LAN-170**

❏ **LAN-169. "Super Book Of Comics-Little Orphan Annie",**
c. 1943. Pan-Am gasoline. Book #7 from numbered series featuring various characters. -
**$13 $39 $115**

❏ **LAN-170. Harold Gray Personal Christmas Card,**
1945. Choice color front cover art.
Limited issue. **- $35 $75 $125**

**LAN-171** **LAN-172**

❏ **LAN-171. "Little Orphan Annie And The Underground Hide-Out" Better Little Book,**
1945. Whitman #1461. **- $20 $75 $160**

❏ **LAN-172. "Super-Book Of Comics Featuring Little Orphan Annie",**
1946. Omar Bread. Book #23 from numbered series featuring various characters. -
**$8 $24 $60**

**LAN-173** **LAN-174**

❏ **LAN-173. Quaker Puffed Wheat Comic Book,**
1947. **- $4 $10 $20**

❏ **LAN-174. "Little Orphan Annie and the Gooneyville Mystery" Better Little Book,**
1947. #1435. **- $20 $50 $90**

**LAN-175**

❏ **LAN-175. "Little Orphan Annie And The Secret Of The Well" Better Little Book,**
1947. Whitman #1417. **- $20 $50 $110**

**LAN-176**

❏ **LAN-176. "Flare-Top" Ice Cream Cone Sign,**
1947. Full color about 18x24". Gordon Gold Archives. **- $50 $150 $250**

**LAN-177** **LAN-178**

❏ **LAN-177. Newspaper Comics Advertising Cello. Button,**
c. 1948. 1-1/4" light blue and maroon from small series of comic characters promoting "Rotocomic" Sunday section. **- $100 $250 $500**

❏ **LAN-178. Cracker Jack Giveaway,**
c. 1950s. From a comic character series of 1-5/8" diameter made of thin plastic with high relief portrait. An Orphan Annie and Daddy Warbucks are also known. Each **- $10 $20 $30**

**LAN-179**

**LAN-180**

❏ **LAN-179. "Orphan Annie's Parents Smoked" Litho. Tin Tab,**
1968. "Truth About Smoking" group. -
**$10 $20 $40**

❏ **LAN-180. Original Radio Broadcast Record Album,**
1972. Product of Mark 56 Records. "Ovaltine Presents..." unabridged radio broadcasts (with commercials.) Back of record jacket shows many premiums. **- $75**

LAN-181

❑ **LAN-181. Soundtrack Album for Musical,**
1977. CBS Records. Stars Dorothy Loudon as Annie. Has fold-out of 14 scenes that are explained in detail. - **$35**

LAN-182

LAN-183

❑ **LAN-182. Plastic Cup,**
1980. Ovaltine. - **$15 $25 $40**

❑ **LAN-183. Ceramic Anniversary Mug,**
1981. Ovaltine. - **$10 $20 $40**

LAN-184

❑ **LAN-184. Revival Era Lunch Box With Bottle,**
1981. Soft vinyl store item by Adi.
Box - **$15 $25 $45**
Generic Bottle - **$5 $10 $15**

LAN-185

❑ **LAN-185. Annie Motion Lamp,**
1982. Lamp fixture with shade. - **$30 $90 $150**

LAN-186

LAN-187

❑ **LAN-186. Movie Plastic Shake-Up Mug,**
1982. Ovaltine. - **$15 $30 $60**

❑ **LAN-187. Plastic 50-Year Anniversary Shake-Up Mug,**
1982. Ovaltine. - **$15 $30 $60**

LAN-188

LAN-189

❑ **LAN-188. "Annie" Cloth Doll With Order Form,**
1982. Ivory, Zest, Camay soaps and others. Offered April 15 to September 30.
Doll - **$5 $10 $25**
Order Form - **$2 $4 $6**

❑ **LAN-189. "In Person At Kennedy Center" Litho. Button,**
1980s. Related to stage play. - **$10 $20 $35**

LAN-190

❑ **LAN-190. Annie and Sandy Doll Set,**
2000. Madame Alexander product. Comes with locket and two toys. - **$75**

## Little Pinkies

**A series of product insert buttons made by Whitehead & Hoag around 1896 featured cartoon drawings of Little Pinkies in various guises. Including varieties, the set totals 21: The Actor, The Bad Boy, The Ball Player (with and without a period), the Boot Black, Boy Orator, The Clown, The Colonel, The Drum Major, The Dude, The Dunce, The Fireman, Greenie, Just Landed, The Letter Carrier, The News Boy, The Policeman, The Sailor, The Soldier (with sabre or with toy sword), and Uncle Sam. The buttons are usually found with back papers for American Pepsin gum, sometimes for Old Gold cigarettes or Whitehead & Hoag. Nothing else is known about Little Pinkies. They seem to be the briefly popular creation of an unknown Whitehead & Hoag staff artist, possibly inspired by Palmer Cox's Brownie characters.**

LPS-1

❑ **LPS-1. Little Pinkies Button Set,**
1896. American Pepsin Gum or less frequently Old Gold Cigarettes. Each - **$10 $15 $25**

## The Lone Ranger

**The legend of the Lone Ranger was born on Detroit radio station WXYZ in January 1933, the product of station owner George W. Trendle and writer Fran Striker. The program was a success from the start, and within a year was also being heard on WGN in Chicago and WOR in New York--in effect forming the nucleus of the new Mutual network. By 1937, "Hi-Yo Silver!" was echoing nationwide. Initially sustained by the station, the program was sponsored by Silver Cup bread starting in November 1933. Bond bread took over as sponsor in 1939 except in the Southeast states, where Merita bread retained its franchise. General Mills became the sponsor in 1941, tying the masked rider to such cereals as Kix and Wheaties until the radio series went off the air in 1955. Cheerios sponsored rebroadcasts until 1956, ending some 23 years and over 3,000 episodes of Western radio thrills and adventure.**

**Jack Deeds was the first actor to play the Lone Ranger, but only for the first six broad-**

casts. George Stenius, later a movie producer under the name George Seaton, assumed the role for the next three months. When Stenius quit, WXYZ station manager Brace Beemer took over the role for a few months, but then he left to open an advertising agency. Finally, in May 1933, Earl Graser became the Lone Ranger voice and he continued the role until his death in 1941. At this point, Brace Beemer was recruited to return to the role. He played the part from 1941 to 1955 and became the voice most closely associated with the character.

On television, the Lone Ranger rode for more than 30 years on the networks and in syndication. The series, sponsored by General Mills (and Merita bread), premiered on ABC in 1949 and aired in prime time until 1957. Reruns were shown on all three networks: CBS (1953-1960 and 1966-1969), ABC (1957-1961 and 1965), and NBC (1960-1961). Syndication began in 1961. Clayton Moore (1914-1999) played the lead for most of the series (John Hart covered the years 1952-1954) and Jay Silverheels (1919-1980), a Mohawk Indian, was Tonto, his faithful companion.

Republic Pictures released two 15-episode chapter plays; *The Lone Ranger* (1938), with Lee Powell as the lead, and *The Lone Ranger Rides Again* (1939), with Robert Livingston. Wrather Productions made three full-length films, *The Lone Ranger* (1955) and *The Lone Ranger and the Lost City of Gold* (1958), both with Clayton Moore and Jay Silverheels, and *The Legend of the Lone Ranger* (1981), with Klinton Spilsbury and Michael Horse.

A Saturday morning animated Lone Ranger series aired on CBS from 1966 to 1969, with the Ranger and Tonto battling mad scientists as well as conventional Western villains. The animated defenders of law and order surfaced again on CBS in 1980-1981 as part of *The Tarzan/Lone Ranger Adventure Hour*.

A Sunday comic strip distributed by King Features appeared from 1938 to 1971 and was revived from 1981 to 1984--one of the longest running of the Western strips. Comic books, including giveaways, novels, coloring books, photo albums, and scrapbooks appeared in great numbers from the 1940s on.

At press time, a pilot for a new television incarnation of the Lone Ranger was under consideration by the WB network. The series would focus on more youthful versions of the Lone Ranger and Tonto, and could debut in the fall of 2002.

It would be hard to overestimate the number of items licensed and merchandised in the name of the Lone Ranger, especially during the years the program ruled the air on radio and television. Items may be copyrighted by Lone Ranger Inc., Lone Ranger Television Inc., or, starting in 1954, Wrather Corp.

LON-1

LON-2

❑ **LON-1. Photo,**
1933. First premium photo for the Lone Ranger Show. Shows Lone Ranger on Silver with head tilted down. Michigan Radio Network printed on left and signed bottom right. - **$250 $400 $600**

❑ **LON-2. Photo On Horse,**
1934. Early Silvercup radio premium. - **$25 $35 $75**

LON-3

❑ **LON-3. Silvercup Bread "Chief Scout" Qualification Cards Set,**
1934. Scarce. Fifth card (shown first) came with "Chief Scout" brass badge, others denoted "Degree" rank advancements to the badge.
1st - **$30 $80 $145**
2nd - **$30 $80 $145**
3rd - **$40 $90 $180**
4th - **$50 $100 $220**
5th - **$60 $150 $300**

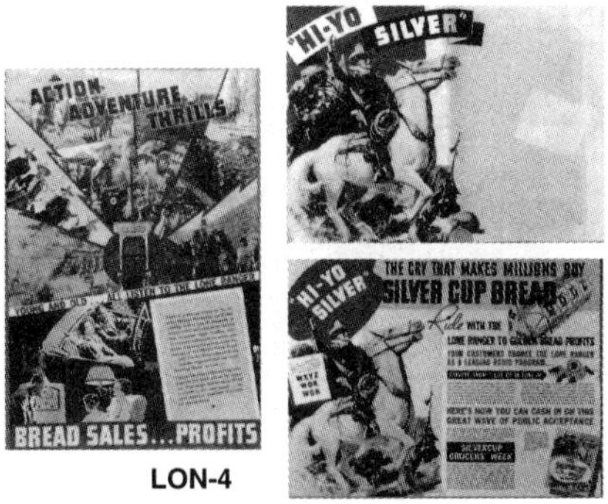


LON-4

❑ **LON-4. Radio Sponsorship Brochure Opens To 19x25",**
c. 1934. Silvercup Bread. - **$75 $175 $300**

LON-5

❑ **LON-5. Silvercup Bread Safety Club Folder,**
c. 1934. - **$50 $125 $225**

LON-6

LON-7

❑ **LON-6. Silvercup Bread "Chief Scout" Enameled Brass Badge,**
1934. Also inscribed "Lone Ranger Safety Scout/Silvercup". - **$100 $225 $375**

❑ **LON-7. "Oke Tonto" Photo Card,**
1934. Various bread company radio sponsors. - **$15 $40 $70**

LON-8

LON-9

❑ **LON-8. Safety Scout Member's Badge,**
1934. Silvercup Bread. - **$10 $20 $50**

❑ **LON-9. Safety Scout Badge Mailer,**
1934. Silvercup Safety Scout premium. Rare.- **$50 $75 $125**

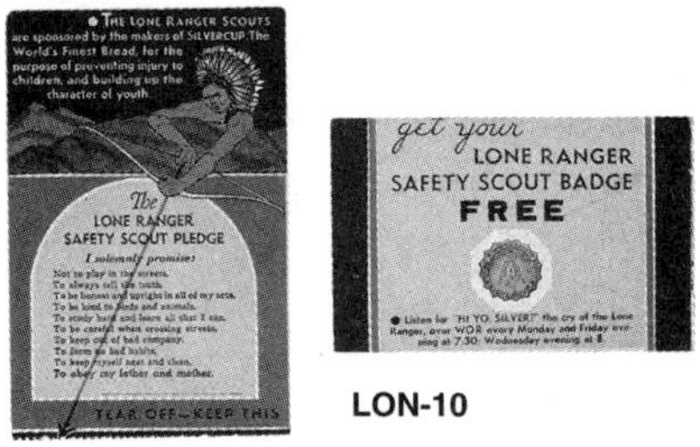

LON-10

❑ **LON-10. Scout Badge Offer Card With Pledge,**
1934. Silvercup Bread radio premium.-
**$35 $80 $135**

LON-11

❑ **LON-11. Campfire Photo,**
1935. Tonto and Lone Ranger at campfire with horses in background. - **$35 $85 $140**

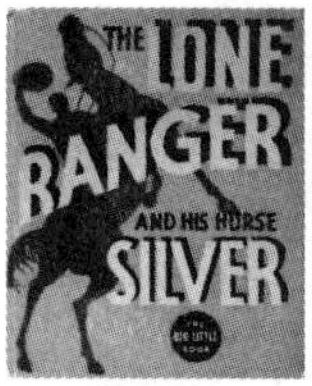

LON-12

LON-13

❑ **LON-12. "The Lone Ranger and His Horse Silver" Big Little Book #1181,**
1935. - **$15 $60 $130**

❑ **LON-13. Silvercup Bread Picture,**
1936. - **$15 $30 $50**

LON-14

❑ **LON-14. "How The Lone Ranger Captured Silver" Booklet,** 1936. Silvercup Bread. -
**$25 $75 $150**

LON-15

❑ **LON-15. "Lone Ranger Target Game",**
1936. Morton's Salt. Punch-out cardboard parts include gun and six targets.
Near Mint Unpunched - **$400**
Loose - **$100 $200 $300**

LON-16

❑ **LON-16. Cobakco Bread Story Booklet,**
c. 1936. "How The Lone Ranger Captured Silver" seven-page story collected over seven weeks. - **$60 $140 $250**

LON-17

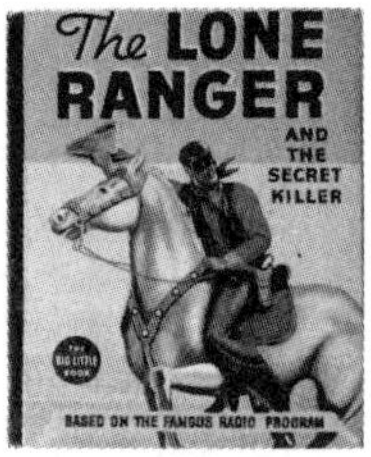

LON-18

❑ **LON-17. "The Lone Ranger and the Vanishing Herd" Big Little Book #1196,**
1936. - **$15 $50 $110**

❑ **LON-18. "The Lone Ranger and the Secret Killer" Big Little Book #1431,**
1937. H. Anderson art. 432 pages. -
**$15 $50 $110**

LON-19

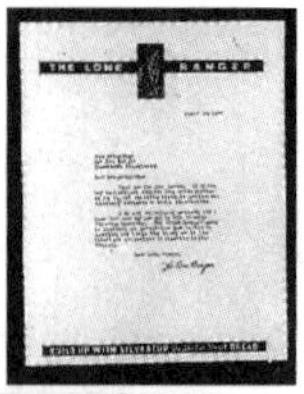

LON-20

❑ **LON-19. "The Lone Ranger Magazine" Vol. 1 #1,**
1937. Trojan Publishing Corp., Chicago. -
**$100 $300 $750**

❑ **LON-20. Silvercup Lone Ranger Personalized Letter,**
1937. Silvercup Bread. Response from Gordon Baking Co. to youngster who adopted kitten and wished Lone Ranger to know of it. -
**$25 $60 $125**

LON-21

LON-22

❑ **LON-21. "Lone Ranger News" Vol. 1 No. 1 Newspaper,**
1937. Weber's Bread. 11-1/2x17" four-page newspaper with black and red accents on newsprint. Contains seven black and white photos of "Frontier Scenes And People Familiar To The Lone Ranger." - **$50 $125 $175**

❑ **LON-22. "Hi-Yo, Silver! The Lone Ranger Every Week" Cello. Button,**
c. 1938. Boston American newspaper and others. 1" black and red on yellow. - **$30 $75 $115**

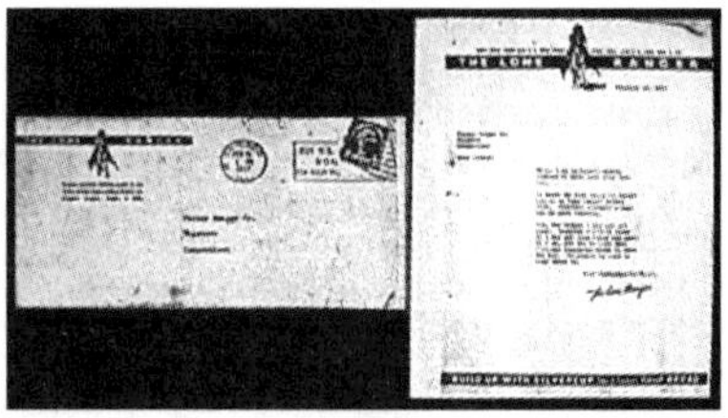
LON-23

❑ **LON-23. Silvercup Letter Noting Badge Supply Exhausted,**
1937. Letter assures new member that he is enrolled but states "Now, The Badges I Had Are All Gone. Sometime A Little Later On I May Get Some Brand New Ones. If I Do, You Can Be Sure That I'll Say Something About It Over The Air. So Always Be Sure To Keep Tuned In."
Letter - **$30 $70 $125**
Envelope - **$10 $20 $35**

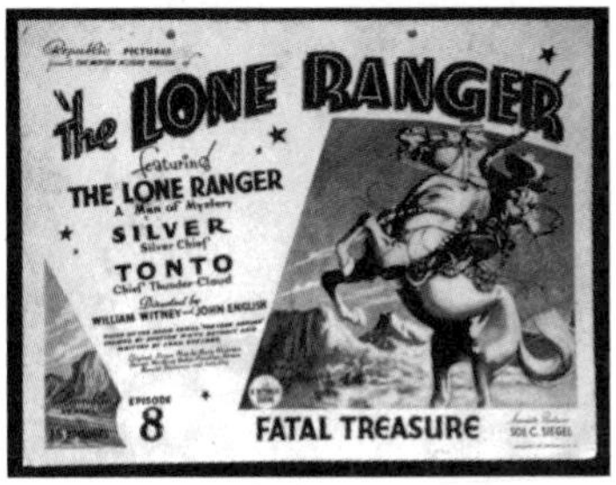


LON-24

❑ **LON-24. Fatal Treasure Serial Card,**
1938. Blue & white title card for Chapter 8. These cards are very rare. - **$250 $400 $600**

LON-25

❑ **LON-25. "The Lone Ranger" Cover On Radio Guide Magazine,**
1938. Vol. 7 #48 issue for September 17, 1938**. - $15 $35 $75**

LON-26 LON-27

❑ **LON-26. Silvercup Bread Photo,**
c. 1938. - **$15 $30 $75**

❑ **LON-27. Book Cover,**
c. 1938. Blue design on brown paper. Promotes Safety Club and program on "Mutual-Don Lee Stations." - **$35 $65 $100**

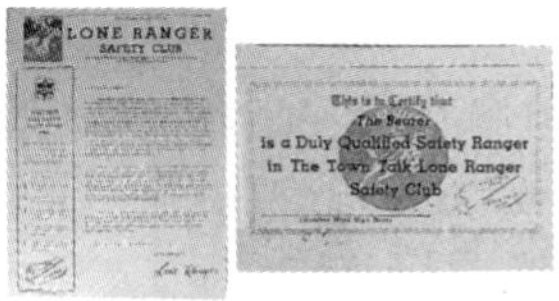


LON-28

❑ **LON-28. Club Membership Admission Letter And Card,**
1938. Town Talk Bread. Letter - **$20 $40 $80**
Card - **$15 $35 $75**

LON-29

❑ **LON-29. Membership Card,**
1938. Brown's Bread. Uncommon card with three illustrations. - **$25 $50 $85**

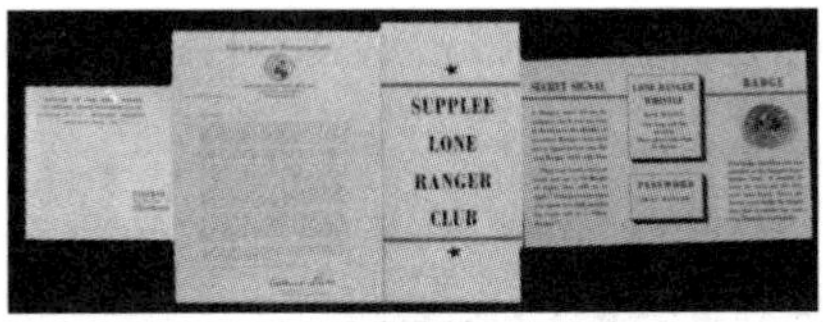


LON-30

❑ **LON-30. "Supplee" Club Member's Kit,**
c. 1938. Supplee-Wills-Jones Milk Co. Envelope has return address of "Office Of The Commander-Supplee Lone Ranger Club-Station WFIL." The folder is 3x6" and opens to 6x9" including secret signal, Lone Ranger whistle, password. The 8-1/2x11" letter is signed by "Colonel Bill, Commander Of Supplee Rangers."
Near Mint In Mailer **- $350**
Mailer **- $10 $15 $25**
Folder **- $35 $60 $100**
Letter **- $25 $50 $75**
Badge (see LON-97) - **$35 $75 $150**

LON-31

❑ **LON-31. "Butter-Nut Safety Club" Card,**
1938. 3-1/4x5" has individual Safety Ranger number. Card back has secret code**. - $35 $75 $150**

LON-32

❑ **LON-32. Postcard,**
c. 1938. Eddy's Bread. Reverse has club information. - **$15 $50 $85**

LON-33 LON-34

❑ **LON-33. Cramer's Enameled Brass Star Badge,**
c. 1938. Cramer's Bread. - **$35 $75 $135**

❑ **LON-34. Franz Enameled Brass Star Badge,**
c. 1938. Franz' Bread. - **$30 $65 $110**

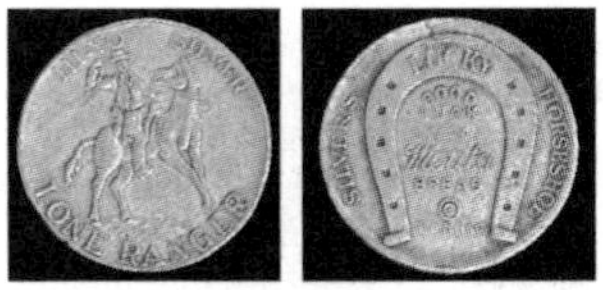

LON-35

❑ **LON-35. "Silver's Lucky Horseshoe" Sterling Silver Good Luck Piece,**
c. 1938. Merita Bread. 1-3/16" marked "Sterling" on side edge. Scarcer than similar versions described as "Solid Bronze." - **$35 $75 $125**

LON-36

❑ **LON-36. "Wear This Mask And Look Like The Lone Ranger,"**
1938. Issued by Schulze Butter-Nut Bread, Dolly Madison Cakes. Diecut stiff paper with list of five mid-west radio stations and Lone Ranger show times on reverse**. - $50 $100 $150**

LON-37 LON-38

❑ **LON-37. First Aid Kit,**
1938. American White Cross Labs Inc. Lithographed tin box, issued in at least two sizes, holding various basic medical supplies. The box included a 24-page "First Aid Guide" with Lone Ranger Safety Club Pledge and 10 Safety Rules.
Box With Contents Except Manual -
**$25 $40 $85**
Box Empty - **$15 $30 $50**

❑ **LON-38. Safety Club Member's Button,**
c. 1938. Black and white on bright yellow 1-1/2" probably from bread company sponsor, possibly Merita. - **$50 $100 $175**

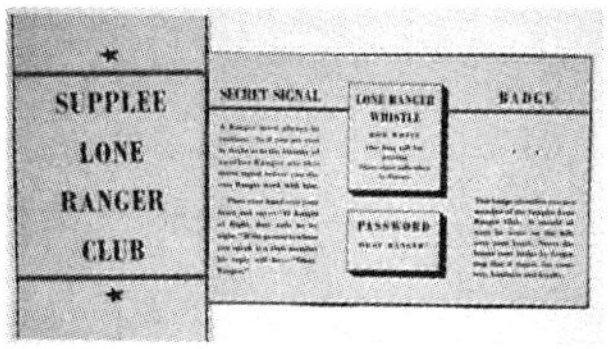

LON-39

❑ **LON-39. "Supplee Lone Ranger Club" Folder,**
c. 1938. Supplee milk and ice cream with Sealtest System logo. Folder opens to 6x9" with "Secret Signal" on left panel, "Whistling Code" on center panel, inscription on right panel which held circular brass club badge instructing new member "It Should Always Be Worn On The Left, Over Your Heart." See LON-30. - **$35 $60 $100**

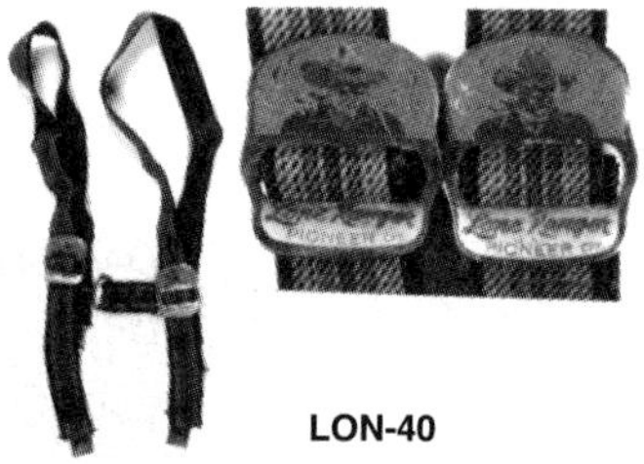
LON-40

❑ **LON-40. "Lone Ranger" Suspenders With Braces,**
1938. Store item by Pioneer. - **$75 $150 $275**

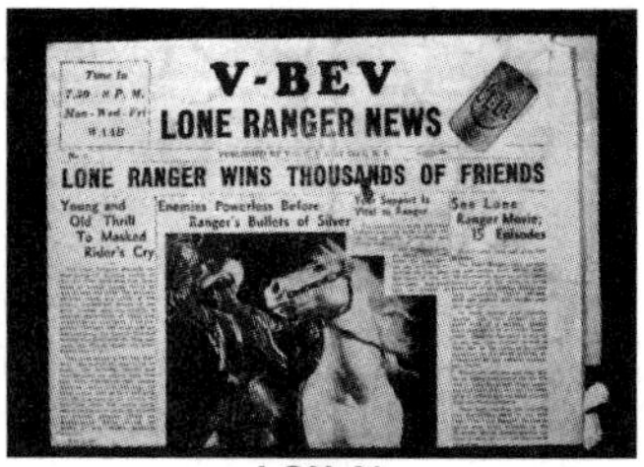

LON-41

❑ **LON-41. "V-Bev Lone Ranger News" First Issue,**
1938. V-Bev soda beverage. - **$60 $125 $200**

LON-42

LON-43

❑ **LON-42. Safety Club Membership Card,**
1938. Cobakco Bread. Back has code alphabet. - **$100 $200 $300**

❑ **LON-43. "Republic Picture" Horseshoe Enameled Brass Badge,**
1938. - **$40 $75 $125**

LON-44

LON-45

❑ **LON-44. Gately's Enameled Brass Star Badge,**
c. 1938. Gately's Bread. - **$35 $75 $140**

❑ **LON-45. Master Bread Enameled Brass Star Badge,**
c. 1938. - **$35 $75 $140**

LON-46

❑ **LON-46. "Merita" Bread Mask With Mailer,**
1938. Made of oilcloth-like material.
Mask - **$30 $65 $100**
Mailer - **$15 $30 $50**

LON-47

LON-48

❑ **LON-47. Merita "Lone Ranger Salesmen's Club" Badge,**
c. 1938. Merita Bread. White enamel and silvered brass. - **$100 $250 $500**

❑ **LON-48. Republic Serial Club Brass Badge,**
1938. Republic Pictures. Badges are serially numbered. - **$40 $75 $125**

LON-49

LON-50

❑ **LON-49. Movie Discount Card,**
1938. Republic Pictures. Admits child for 5 cents to Saturday matinee. - **$40 $75 $125**

❑ **LON-50. Strong Box Bank,**
1938. Sun Life Insurance. - **$100 $250 $450**

LON-51

LON-52

❑ **LON-51. Bat-O-Ball,**
1938. Scarce. Pure Oil premium. WOR Radio. - **$40 $125 $175**

❑ **LON-52. Bond Bread Promo,**
1938. Scarce. WOR Radio. - **$50 $100 $200**

LON-53

LON-54

❑ **LON-53. Glass,**
1938. - **$20 $50 $100**

❑ **LON-54. Republic Serial Promo,**
1938. Scarce. 15 episodes. - **$40 $100 $175**

LON-55

LON-56

❑ **LON-55. Detroit Sunday Times Comic Strip Announcement,**
1938. Strip began September 11. - **$40 $75 $125**

❑ **LON-56. Star Badge Used On Large Composition Doll,**
1938. Rare. Dollcraft Novelty Doll Co. See LON-60. - **$25 $75 $175**

LON-57

❑ **LON-57. Sign for Lone Ranger Gun Offer,**
1938. Gordon Gold Archives. -
**$200 $400 $800**

LON-58

❑ **LON-58. Lone Ranger Game in Box,**
1938. Includes 5 metal "Lone Ranger on horse" playing pieces, game board, instructions, 12 silver discs, 4 red discs, 2 spinning indicators, an insert and the game box.
Complete - **$75 $160 $325**

LON-59

LON-60

❑ **LON-59. Composition/Cloth Doll With Fabric Outfit,**
1938. Store item as well as premium. 16" tall.
Lone Ranger - **$500 $1200 $2200**
Matching Tonto - **$400 $1000 $1800**

❑ **LON-60. Lone Ranger Doll with Tag,**
1938. 16" tall. Comes with neckerchief, badge, gun and holster, belt, removable vest, hat, mask, shirt and pants. Used as a premium for Lone Ranger ice cream cones. See LON-56. -
**$500 $1200 $2200**

LON-61

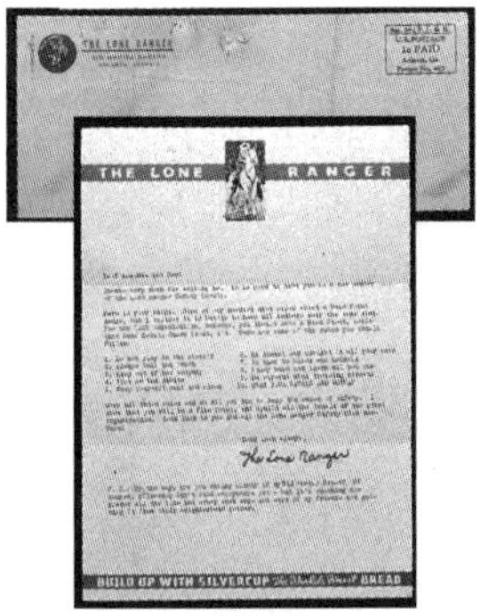

LON-62

❑ **LON-61. Radio WOR Promo,**
1938. - **$20 $40 $60**

❑ **LON-62. Safety Scouts Letter,**
1938. Silvercup Bread premium.
Mailer - **$25 $50 $75**
Letter - **$25 $60 $80**

LON-63

LON-64

❑ **LON-63. Certificate/Pledge,**
1938. Safety Club Bread premium. -
**$50 $150 $275**

❑ **LON-64. Tin Litho. Wind-Up,**
1938. Store item by Marx Toys.
"Silver" In White - **$100 $350 $500**
"Silver" In Silver - **$150 $400 $600**

LON-65

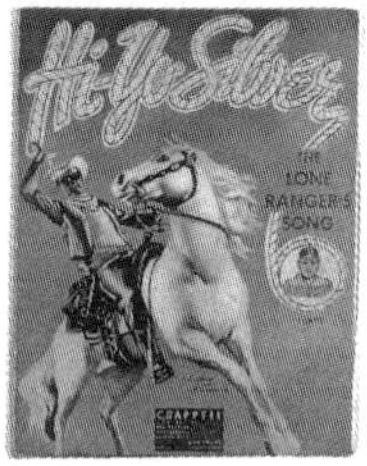

LON-66

❑ **LON-65. Silvercup Bread Picture,**
1938. - **$10 $20 $40**

❑ **LON-66. Sheet Music - Hi Yo Silver**
1938.Six pages. Store bought. - **$25 $50 $75**

LON-67

❑ **LON-67. Wright Bread Picture,**
1938. - **$20 $50 $75**

LON-68

LON-69

❑ **LON-68. Cellophane Picture Sheet,**
1938. Blue Ribbon Bread. Probably for window display.- **$50 $125 $250**

❑ **LON-69. High Gloss Photo,**
1938. Shown on horse with name at bottom right. Blank back. - **$25 $50 $75**

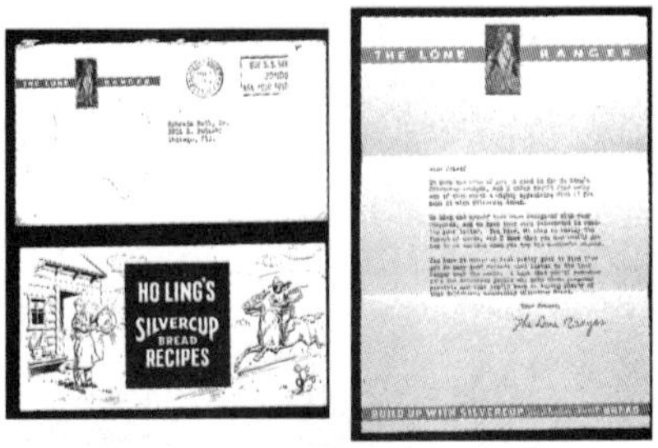

LON-70

❑ **LON-70. Ho-Ling Recipes Pamphlet and Letter,**
1938. Silvercup Bread. Mailer also shown.
Pamphlet - **$30 $75 $115**
Letter - **$25 $50 $75**
Mailer - **$20 $30 $40**

LON-71

❑ **LON-71. "Lone Ranger Safety Club" Membership Card,**
1938. Merita Bread. - **$15 $50 $75**

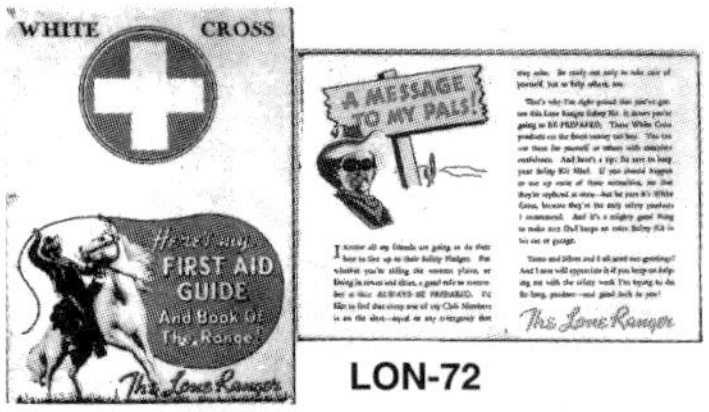

LON-72

❑ **LON-72. "White Cross" First Aid Booklet,**
1938. - **$25 $50 $125**

(CARD #1 WITHOUT MASK)

(CARD #1 WITH MASK)

LON-73

❑ **LON-73. Gum Wrappers Mail Picture,**
1938. Scarce. Lone Ranger Bubble Gum. Card #1 of five collected by sending wrappers. 8x10" size. Card #1 came with and without mask on Lone Ranger's face.
Card Without Mask - **$125 $250 $500**
Others - **$100 $200 $350**

LON-74

LON-75

LON-76

❑ **LON-74. Bond Bread 9x13" Paper Poster,**
1938. Scarce. Announces local radio broadcast times on WABY and WOR. - **$50 $100 $175**

❑ **LON-75. "Bond Bread Lone Ranger Safety Club" Enameled Brass Star Badge,**
1938. - **$10 $25 $40**

❑ **LON-76. "Lone Ranger Cones" Matchbook,**
1938. - **$10 $20 $40**

LON-77

LON-78

❑ **LON-77. "Silver's Lucky Horseshoe" Enameled Brass Badge,**
c. 1938. Smaller 1-1/4" size. - **$20 $40 $75**
Same design but lower panel reading "The May Co." - **$40 $85 $150**

❑ **LON-78. "Lone Ranger Cones" Paper Wrapper,**
1938. Offers comic book, bracelet, Lone Ranger Ring, Tonto Ring with October 31, 1940 expiration date. - **$20 $50 $75**

LON-79

❑ **LON-79. Lone Ranger Ice Cream Cones Enameled/Silvered Metal Picture Bracelet,**
1938. Rare. - **$300 $1000 $1600**

LON-80

LON-81

❑ **LON-80. Tonto Lucky Ring,**
1938. Rare. Lone Ranger Ice Cream Cones. Green plastic to simulate onyx with paper portrait, also issued for Lone Ranger.
Tonto - **$800 $1750 $3750**
Lone Ranger - **$1000 $2250 $5000**

❑ **LON-81. Blue Beanie With Red Trim,**
1938. Rare. Lone Ranger Ice Cream Cones. - **$100 $200 $450**

LON-82

LON-83

LON-84

❑ **LON-82. "Dr. West's Tooth Paste" Cello. Club Button,**
c. 1938. - **$35 $75 $140**

❑ **LON-83. Cobakco Bread "Your Friend Tonto" Picture Card,**
c. 1938. - **$25 $50 $85**

❑ **LON-84. Cobakco Bread Picture Card,**
c. 1938. - **$25 $50 $85**

LON-85

LON-86

❑ **LON-85. "Friend Of The Lone Ranger" Photo Card,**
c. 1938. Cobakco Bread. Pictured is "Your Friend, U.S. Marshal" from radio series. - **$25 $50 $85**

❑ **LON-86. Cobakco Bread "Chuck Livingston" Picture Card,**
c. 1938. Pictures "Outlaw On Lone Ranger Dramas". - **$25 $50 $85**

LON-87

LON-88

❑ **LON-87. "Cobakco Safety Club" Enameled Brass Badge,**
c. 1938. Cobakco Bread. - **$30 $75 $125**

❑ **LON-88. 7up Personalized Picture,**
c. 1938. Black/white print personalized in white ink "To" recipient's first name. - **$25 $50 $90**

LON-89

❑ **LON-89. Silvercup Bread 13x17" "Lone Ranger Hunt Map" With Envelope,**
c. 1938. With Envelope - **$75 $175 $300**
Map Only - **$50 $125 $200**

LON-90

LON-91

LON-92

❑ **LON-90. Merita Bread Photo,**
c. 1938. - **$20 $65 $110**

❑ **LON-91. Merita Enameled Brass Star Badge,**
c. 1938. Merita Bread. - **$20 $60 $100**

❑ **LON-92. "The Lone Ranger" Cello. Button,**
c. 1938. Possibly Merita Bread Safety Club. - **$50 $125 $200**

LON-93

❑ **LON-93. "Lone Ranger/Hi-Yo Silver" Brass Good Luck Medal,**
1938. Reverse design and inscription "Silver's Lucky Horseshoe". Sent in Detroit station WXYZ mailer with medal in red,white and blue stiff card.
Near Mint Complete - **$200**
Card Only - **$25 $50 $100**
Medal Only - **$15 $25 $50**

LON-94

LON-95

❑ **LON-94. "Silver's Lucky Horseshoe" Enameled Brass Badge,**
c. 1938. Larger 1-3/4" size. - **$20 $40 $75**

❑ **LON-95. "WFIL/Daily News Safety Club" Cello. Button,**
c. 1938. Philadelphia radio station. - **$40 $100 $175**

LON-96

LON-97

LON-98

❑ **LON-96. "Lee Powell/Original Motion Picture" Cello. Button,**
c. 1938. Scarce. Republic Pictures. - **$125 $300 $500**

❑ **LON-97. "Supplee Lone Ranger Club" Enameled Brass Badge,**
c. 1938. See LON-30. - **$35 $95 $175**

❑ **LON-98. "The Lone Ranger Radio Station" Cello. Button,**
c. 1938. WCSC, Charleston, South Carolina. - **$30 $100 $200**

LON-99

LON-100

LON-101

❑ **LON-99. Rath's Enameled Brass Star Badge,**
c. 1938. Rath's Bread. - **$35 $75 $135**

❑ **LON-100. Bestyett Enameled Brass Star Badge,**
c. 1938. Bestyett Bread. - **$35 $75 $135**

❑ **LON-101. A. B. Poe Enameled Brass Star Badge,**
c. 1938. Poe Bread. - **$35 $75 $135**

LON-102

LON-103

❑ **LON-102. "Sunday Herald And Examiner" Litho. Button,**
c. 1938. - **$10 $20 $40**

❑ **LON-103. Movie Serial Ticket With Sears Offer,**
c. 1938. Scarce. Ticket for 15-episode serial, reverse promotes cowboy suits at Sears, Roebuck. - **$75 $200 $350**

LON-104

❑ **LON-104. "Lone Ranger Safety Sentinel" Brass Badge,**
1939. Miami Maid Bread. - **$60 $150 $300**

LON-105

❑ **LON-105. "West's" Bread Wrapper,**
c. 1939. Sponsored by West's Yum Yum Sliced Twins. - **$40 $75 $150**

LON-106

❑ **LON-106. "Lone Ranger Special" Cap Pistol Box,**
1939. Store item by Kilgore. - **$100 $200 $300**

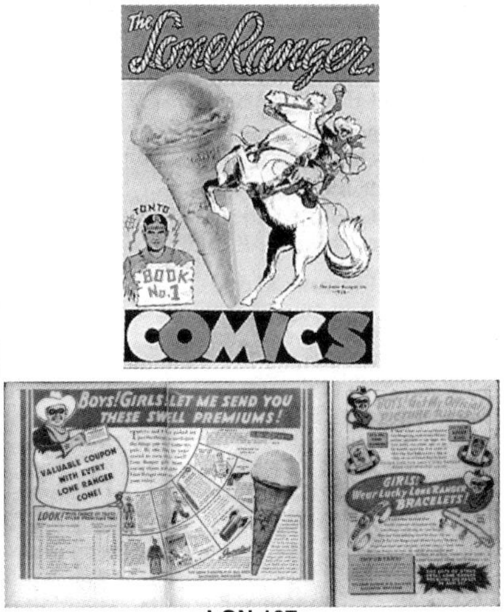


LON-107

❑ **LON-107. "The Lone Ranger Comic Book No. 1",**
1939. Rare. Lone Ranger Ice Cream Cones. - **$923 $3000 $6000**

LON-108

❑ **LON-108. "Ice Cream Cone Coupons" Envelope To Merchant,**
1939. Lone Ranger Cones. Originally held 100 mail coupons expiring Jan. 1, 1940.
Envelope Only - **$25 $60 $100**
Each Coupon - **$10 $20 $30**

LON-109

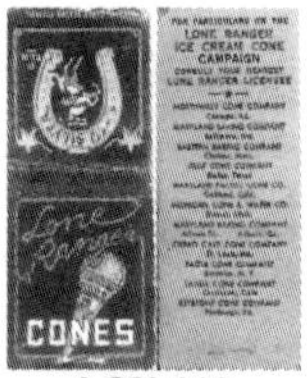


LON-110

LON-111

❑ **LON-109. "Lone Ranger Cake Cones" Matchbook,**
c. 1939. - **$10 $20 $50**

❑ **LON-110. "Lone Ranger Cones" Matchbook Cover,**
c. 1939. Inscribed "Lone Ranger Ice Cream Cone Campaign." - **$10 $20 $50**

❑ **LON-111. "Lone Ranger Ice Cream Cones" Dealer Sheet,**
1939. Reprinted ad from November issue of ice cream trade magazine for upcoming promotion in 1940. - **$40 $75 $125**

LON-112

❑ **LON-112. Large Feature Comic,**
1939. Whitman #715. - **$123 $369 $1350**

LON-113

LON-114

❑ **LON-113. Safety Club Letter,**
1939. Weber Bread premium. - **$70 $100 $135**

❑ **LON-114. Post Card,**
1939. Weber Bread. Back of postcard is an order form for 2 book covers.- **$25 $50 $75**

LON-115

❑ **LON-115. Bond Bread Safety Club "Lone Ranger Roundup" Vol. 1 #1 Newspaper,**
August 1939. Rare. At least nine issues through Vol. 2 #3. First Issue - **$100 $200 $300**
Other Issues - **$25 $100 $150**

LON-116

❑ **LON-116. Creed Postcard And Mailer,**
1939. Weber Bread premium. Postcard is used to join club.- **$60 $95 $110**

LON-117

❑ **LON-117. Photo,**
1939. Rare. Premium from New York World's Fair. Sponsored by Gimbel's Lone Ranger Show. - **$25 $50 $100**

LON-118

LON-119

❑ **LON-118. World's Fair Bond Bread Premium,**
1939. Rolled penny. - **$40 $85 $165**

❑ **LON-119. "Lone Ranger Secret Code" Cardboard Decoder,**
1939. Dr. West's Toothpaste. Came boxed with two bottles of "Invisible Writing Ink" and "Ink Developer" plus cotton swab. Complete Boxed - **$125 $250 $450**
Decoder Only - **$75 $150 $300**

LON-120

LON-121

❑ **LON-120. Membership Card,**
1939. Dr. West's Toothpaste. Came with club newsletter. - **$50 $100 $185**

❑ **LON-121. Membership Certificate,**
1939. Dr. West's Toothpaste. Came with club newsletter. - **$65 $150 $260**

LON-122

❑ **LON-122. "The Lone Ranger" Republic Serial Poster,**
1939. For a 15 episode serial.
Chapter 1 Stock Sheet - **$1500 $3000 $4500**
Chapter 2-15 each - **$500 $1000 $1500**

LON-123

❑ **LON-123. Dr. West's Lone Ranger News,**
1939. Dr. West's Toothpaste. Vol.1 #1 newsletter with 8 pages. Back cover offers Secret Writing Set that includes cardboard "Official Lone Ranger Automatic Decoder." (See LON-119). - **$100 $200 $425**

LON-124

❑ **LON-124. Weber's Bread Club Manual,**
1939. - **$50 $125 $250**

LON-125

LON-126

❑ **LON-125. Calendar,**
1939. Cobakco Bread. - **$75 $150 $325**

❑ **LON-126. Pony Contest 11x14" Cardboard Poster,**
c. 1939. Cobakco Bread. - **$50 $100 $225**

LON-127

LON-128

❑ **LON-127. Merita Safety Club Radio Card,**
1939. Merita Bakers. Card sent by WBT Radio, Charlotte, North Carolina. Code translates: "Be Sure To Obey My Ten Safety Rules Always And Remember That You Help To Make My Great Safety Drive Possible By Eating Merita Bread And Cakes. So Be Sure To Ask Mother To Always Buy Merita Products!" - **$60 $150 $300**

❑ **LON-128. Silver Club Bronze Pin,**
1939. Butter-Nut Bread. Rare. -
**$100 $225 $425**

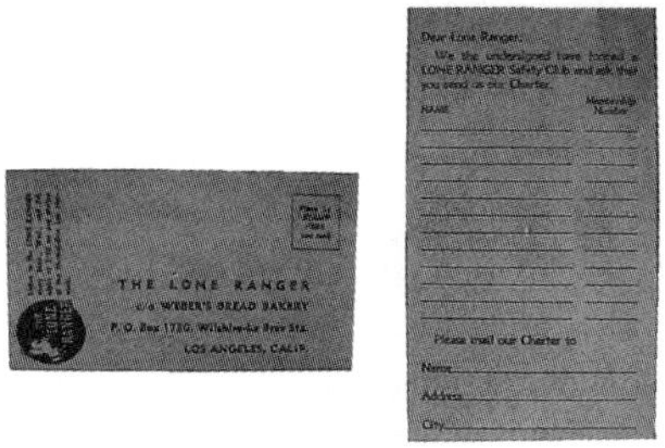

LON-129

❑ **LON-129. Request For Club Charter Card,**
1939. Weber's Bread/Lone Ranger Safety Club. Black on red with spaces to list 12 members with their membership number to acquire a charter certificate. - **$20 $50 $75**

LON-130

❑ **LON-130. Calendar Top,**
c. 1939. Merita Bread. Our photo shows 14x15" top while lower portion held calendar and pad of club applications. The Tonto image depicts Chief Thundercloud of the 1938-39 movie serials. Complete - **$350 $750 $1500**

LON-131

❑ **LON-131. "Lone Ranger Makeup Kit" On Card,**
1939. Store item by Miner's. - **$75 $150 $300**

LON-132

❑ **LON-132. Club Member's Kit,**
1939. Weber's Lone Ranger Safety Club.
Mailer - **$5 $15 $25**
Member Registration Letter - **$30 $65 $100**
Brass Badge - **$25 $50 $75**
Member Card With Code - **$20 $50 $75**

LON-133

LON-134

❑ **LON-133. Fabric Patch,**
1939. Probable club premium. 2-3/4" yellow and white on blue. - **$75 $125 $300**

❑ **LON-134. "Special School Pupil's Coupon",**
c. 1939. Wallace Bros. Circus. Used with 20 cents for admission with captioned redtone image on right "Lee Powell/The Original Talking Picture Lone Ranger Featured In Hi-Yo Silver." - **$50 $125 $200**

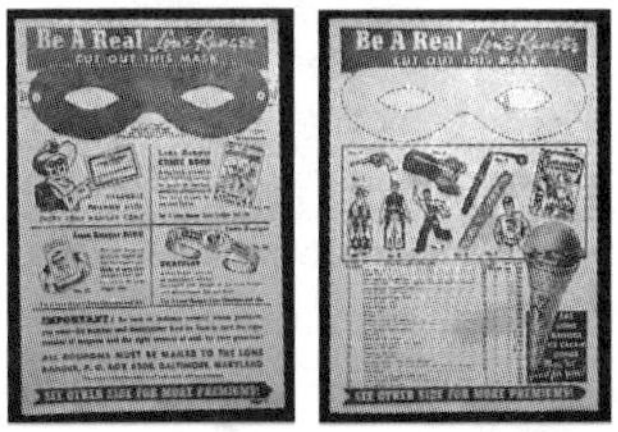

LON-135

❑ **LON-135. Lone Ranger Ice Cream Cones Premium Information Sheet,**
1939. 6x8-1/2" two-sided sheet in black and white which includes cut-out mask and list of 26 premiums along with combinations of coupons and cash needed to order. - **$100 $200 $300**

LON-136

LON-137

❑ **LON-136. "The Lone Ranger Comic Daily And Sunday Examiner" Cello. Button,**
c. 1939. Examiner newspaper. 1-1/4" with red lettering and blue and white image on white. - **$100 $250 $400**

❑ **LON-137. Horlick's Malted Milk Picture,**
1939. "Over Station WGN-Chicago". - **$20 $60 $100**

LON-138

LON-139

❑ **LON-138. Roundup Paper,**
1939. Bond Bread. Vol. 1 #2. 8 pages.-
**$25 $100 $150**

❑ **LON-139. Roundup Paper,**
1939. Bond Bread. Vol. 1 #3. 8 pages.-
**$25 $100 $150**

LON-140

❑ **LON-140. Leather Watch Fob Holster With Miniature Gun,**
1939. Came with some issues of New Haven pocketwatches. - **$35 $50 $120**

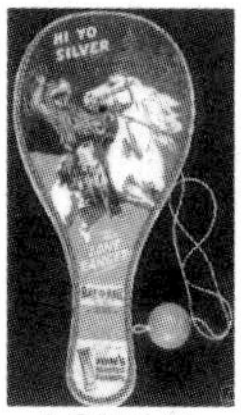


LON-141

LON-142

❑ **LON-141. "Bat-O-Ball" Toy,**
1939. Scarce. Tom's Toasted Peanuts. Cardboard paddle with rubber band and ball.
With Ball - **$40 $125 $175**
No Ball - **$30 $75 $150**

❑ **LON-142. Bond Bread Color Cellophane Picture Sheet,**
c. 1939. 6x9" probably for window display. -
**$50 $125 $250**

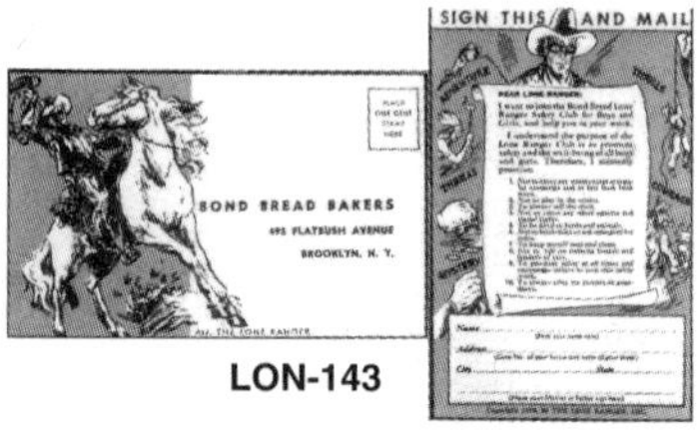


LON-143

❑ **LON-143. "Safety Club" Application Postcard,**
1939. Bond Bread. - **$10 $35 $60**

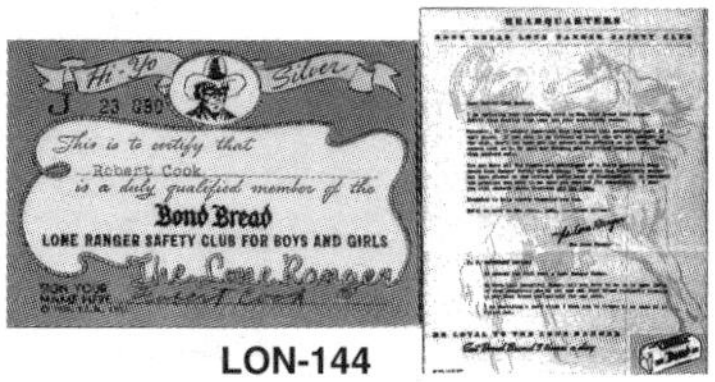


LON-144

❑ **LON-144. "Bond Bread Safety Club" Letter And Membership Card,**
1939. Card - **$15 $40 $100**
Letter - **$20 $50 $100**

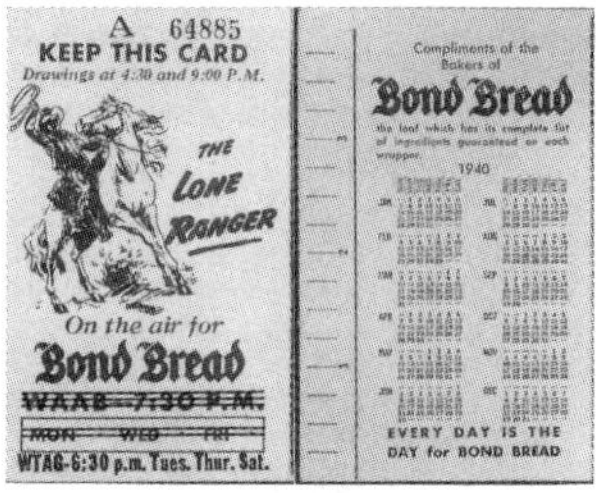


LON-145

❑ **LON-145. Bond Bread Contest Card Stub,**
c. 1939. - **$15 $40 $100**

LON-146

LON-147

❑ **LON-146. May Co. Activity Booklet,**
1939. May department store. Christmas issue. -
**$50 $150 $300**

❑ **LON-147. "The Lone Ranger and the Black Shirt Highwayman" Better Little Book #1450,**
1939. - **$20 $60 $110**

LON-148

❑ **LON-148. "Lapel Watch" Boxed Pocketwatch,**
1939. Store item by New Haven Time Co. as well as premium. Two different decal designs.
Near Mint Boxed - **$1250**
Watch Only - **$250 $450 $750**
Box Only - **$150 $300 $500**

LON-149

❑ **LON-149. Lone Ranger Wrist Watch,**
1939. Watch in colorful box with scarce stand-up display insert.
Watch with Box - **$250 $650 $1100**
Watch Only - **$100 $250 $450**
Box with Insert Only - **$250 $400 $650**

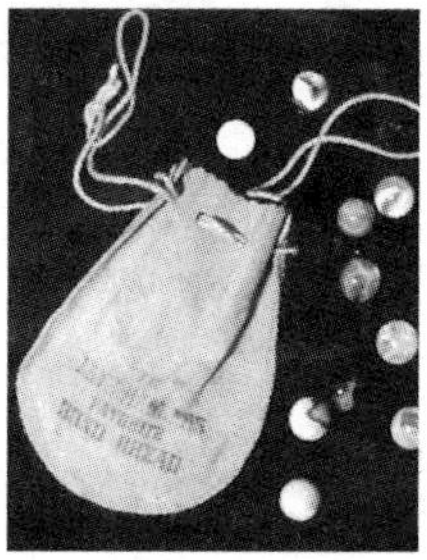

LON-150

❑ **LON-150. "The Lone Ranger's Favorite Bond Bread" Leather Pouch For Marbles,**
1930s. Bond Bread. 5" tall with cord drawstring.
Pouch Only - **$50 $125 $175**

LON-151

LON-152

❑ **LON-151. Lone Ranger Carnival Statue,**
1930s. Used as a bookend. Flat back. Scarce. -
**$75 $175 $275**

❑ **LON-152. Lone Ranger Carnival Statue,**
1940s. - **$40 $100 $225**

LON-153

❑ **LON-153. Bond Bread 8x12" Cardboard Store Sign,**
1940. Scarce. - **$100 $250 $400**

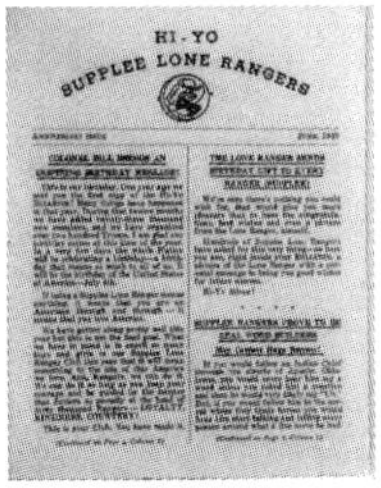


LON-154

LON-155

❑ **LON-154. "Hi-Yo Supplee Lone Rangers" Newsletter,**
1940. Supplee Milk. First anniversary issue. - **$25 $60 $125**

❑ **LON-155. "Orange Pops" 6x12" Cardboard Store Sign,**
1940. Scarce. - **$100 $300 $500**

LON-156

❑ **LON-156. "Cloverine Salve" Premium Catalogue With Watch Ads,**
c. 1940. - **$10 $25 $50**

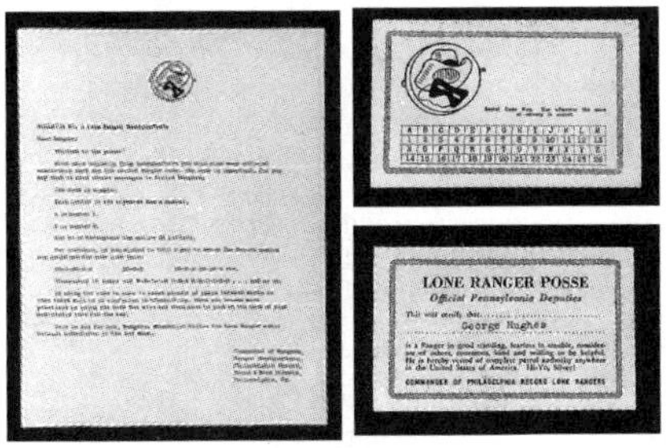


LON-157

❑ **LON-157. "Lone Ranger Posse" Club Papers,**
c. 1940. Philadelphia Record. Letter and membership card for comic strip promotion.
Letter - **$20 $50 $85**
Card - **$25 $60 $100**

LON-158

LON-159

❑ **LON-158. Bond Bread Wrapper,**
1940. - **$20 $50 $100**

❑ **LON-159. Color Photo,**
c. 1940. Bond Bread. - **$15 $25 $50**

LON-160

❑ **LON-160. Merita "The Life Of Tonto" Story Chapter,**
1940. Merita Bread of American Bakeries Co. 11-chapter newspaper ad/feature jointly sponsored by various radio stations. Pictured example is Chapter 10 co-sponsored by WDBJ, Roanoke, Virginia. Each - **$35 $65 $100**

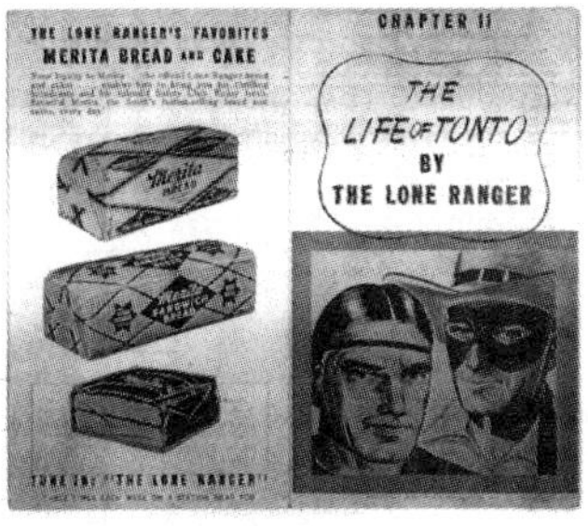


LON-161

❑ **LON-161. Merita "The Life Of Tonto" Story Folder,**
1940. Merita Bread. Set of 11 folders, about 4x7" (shown open). Same story text as version with photos but this version features cover illustration and no photo. Each - **$25 $50 $85**

Picture of Lone Ranger

Picture of Silver

LON-162

❑ **LON-162. Lone Ranger Prototype Secret Compartment Ring,**
1940. Rare Orin Armstrong designed ring has pictures of the Lone Ranger and Silver inside. The design was later modified by the Robbins Company and offered with smaller pictures and a sliding top in 1942.
**Sold at auction in April 2001 for $3,253 in near mint.**

(FRONT COVER)

(BACK COVER)

LON-163

❑ **LON-163. Punch-Out Book,**
1940. Rare. Less than 10 known. - **$200 $650 $1200**

LON-164

❑ **LON-164. Roundup Paper,**
1940. Bond Bread. Vol. 11 #3. 8 pages.- **$25 $100 $150**

LON-165

❑ **LON-165. "Lone Ranger Cones" Paper Wrapper,**
c. 1940. Offers same premiums as 1938 wrapper without expiration date. - **$20 $50 $75**

LON-166

❑ **LON-166. Kix Cereal "Name Silver's Son" 16x20" Contest Poster,**
1941. Rare. - **$1000 $2000 $3200**

LON-167

❑ **LON-167. Photo With Insert And Envelope,**
1941. Came with insert announcing Kix as new radio sponsor. Complete - **$40 $80 $160**
Photo Only - **$15 $25 $50**

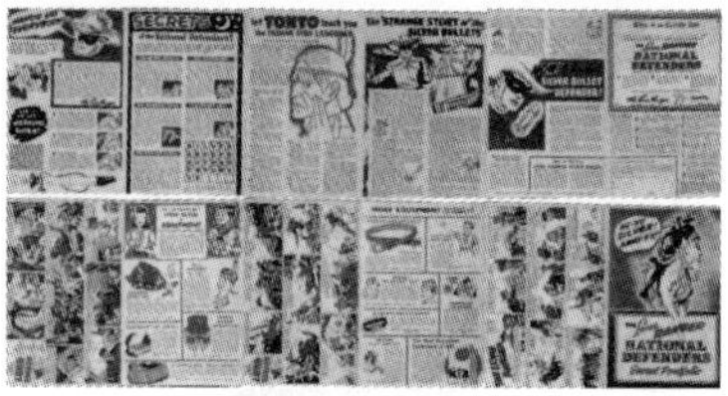

LON-168

❑ **LON-168. "National Defenders Secret Portfolio" Manual,**
1941. See "Whistling Jim" version in Premiums Misc. section. - **$75 $175 $300**
Mailer - **$20 $40 $75**

LON-169

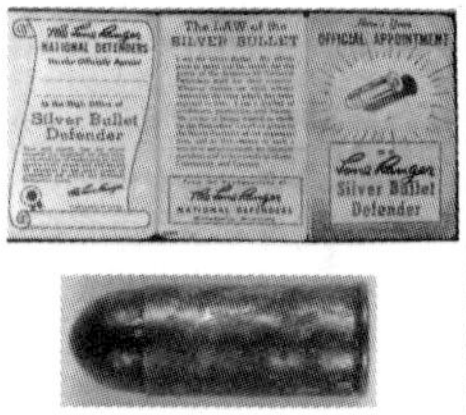

LON-170

❑ **LON-169. Glow-In-Dark Brooch 3" Plastic Pin,**
1941. General Mills. Offered in the Lone Ranger National Defenders Portfolio from Kix cereal as "something for mother" along with matching earrings. Also offered on soap operas sponsored by General Mills and in the southeastern states as a Whistling Jim premium. Not associated with Jack Armstrong as previously believed.
Brooch - **$50 $100 $150**
Earring Set - **$60 $125 $175**

**LON-170. "Silver Bullet Defender" Leaflet With 45-Caliber Silver Bullet,**
1941. Contains silver ore. Bullet - **$20 $40 $85**
Folder - **$25 $50 $90**

LON-171

❑ **LON-171. Kix Luminous Blackout Plastic Belt,**
1941. Near Mint Boxed With Insert Folder - **$250**
Belt Only - **$50 $75 $150**

LON-172

❑ **LON-172. "The Lone Ranger Follows Through" Better Little Book,**
1941. Whitman #1468. - **$15 $50 $110**

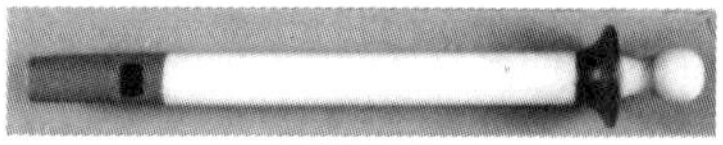

LON-173

❑ **LON-173. National Defenders Danger-Warning Siren,**
1941. Scarce. Came with carrying cord. Offered as bounce back premium with Gardenia Brooch. - **$150 $400 $800**
Tube Mailer - **$20 $40 $75**

LON-174

❑ **LON-174. "Danger-Warning Siren" Offer Ad,**
1941. Kix Cereal. Sunday comics one-half page color ad offering premium as part of Lone Ranger National Defenders Club kit. - **$15 $30 $75**

LON-175

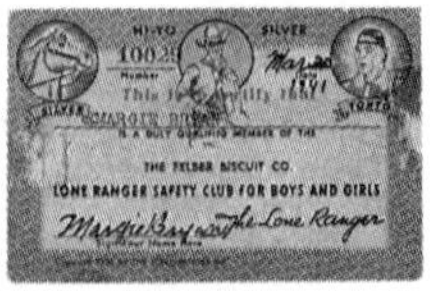


LON-176

❑ **LON-175. National Defenders Look-Around Brass Ring,**
1941. No inscription but offered in Lone Ranger premium advertisements. Also issued for Captain Midnight and Radio Orphan Annie. - **$40 $80 $125**

❑ **LON-176. Safety Club Card,**
1941. Rare. Felber Biscuit Co. Shows Silver, Lone Ranger, and Tonto on front.Secret code on back. - **$60 $85 $140**

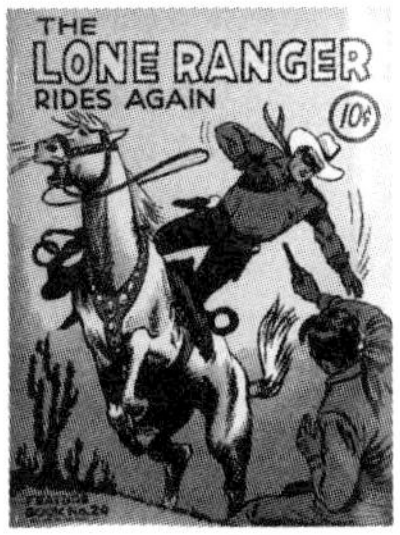

LON-177

❑ **LON-177."The Lone Ranger Rides Again",**
1941. Feature Book No. 24. - **$80 $240 $875**

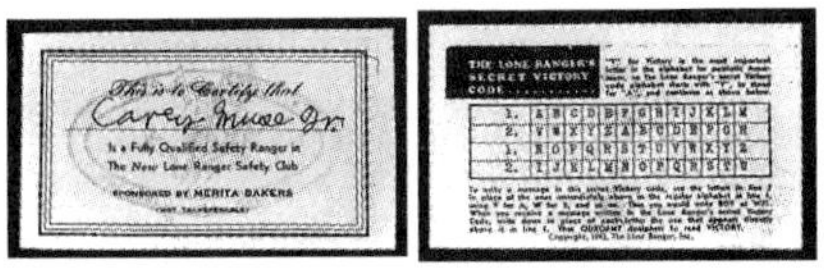

LON-178

❑ **LON-178. Merita Safety Club Card,**
1941 Merita Bakers. - **$20 $50 $75**

LON-179

LON-180

❑ **LON-179. Lone Ranger Contest Prize Award Poster,**
c. 1941. Awarded by Kix cereal as prize from contest to 'name Silver's son.' 22-1/2x31" in gray, black and white. - **$200 $500 $750**

❑ **LON-180. Brass Lucky Piece "From WXYZ Detroit",**
1941. Radio station where The Lone Ranger originated. Same design as the 1938 brass version but this piece has silvered finish plus incised WXYZ message within the design of Silver's horseshoe. - **$50 $100 $150**

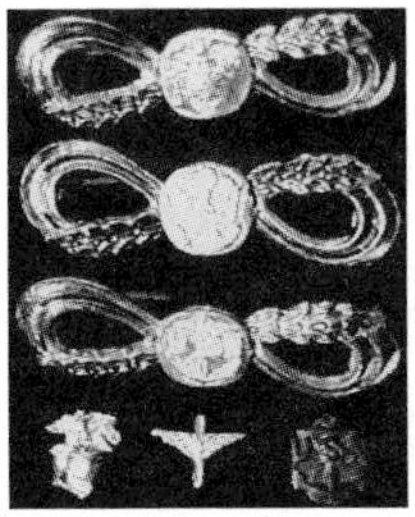
LON-181

❑ **LON-181. Military Sweetheart Pins,**
1941. General Mills, Korn Kix. Set of three large and three small brass luster pins depicting insignias of service branches. Verified by Evie Wilson, former General Mills archivist.
Near Mint In Original Case - **$400**

LON-182

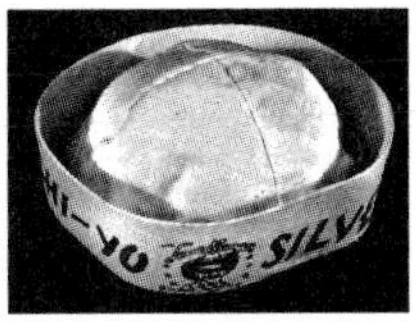
LON-183

❑ **LON-182. Victory Bread Wrapper,**
1942. Weber's White Bread. - **$20 $50 $100**

❑ **LON-183. Sailor Hat,**
1942. - **$50 $75 $140**

LON-184

❑ **LON-184. Victory Corps Club Promo,**
1942. - **$75 $175 $325**

LON-185

❑ **LON-185. Cardboard Standee,**
c. 1942. Merita Bread. 9-1/2x17-1/2" tall in full color. - **$500 $1000 $2000**

LON-186

LON-187

❑ **LON-186. Bread Loaf Wrapper,**
1942. Merita Bread. Small diamond designs between the company name diamonds say "Hi-Yo Silver/Lone Ranger." - **$20 $50 $100**

❑ **LON-187. "Lone Ranger Victory Corps" Brass Tab,**
1942. - **$15 $30 $65**

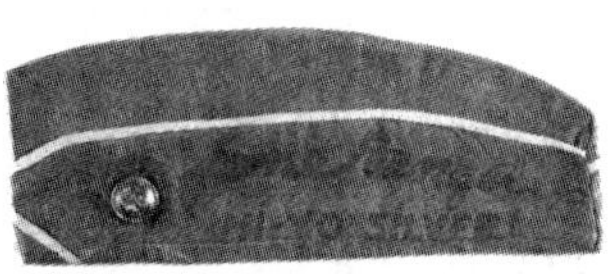
LON-188

❑ **LON-188. Military Hat with Metal Button,**
1942. Rare. - **$100 $300 $500**

LON-189

❑ **LON-189. "Victory Corps" Membership Kit,**
1942. Cheerios/Kix. Includes cover letter with membership/I.D. folder plus brass tab (see item LON-187). Envelope - **$20 $50 $85**
Letter - **$15 $60 $125**
Member Card Folder - **$30 $85 $125**

LON-190

❑ **LON-190. Safety Club Letter,**
1942. Merita Bread premium. - **$60 $85 $130**

LON-191

LON-192

❑ **LON-191. "Lone Ranger VC" Victory Corps Cello. Button,**
1942. - **$30 $60 $125**

❑ **LON-192. Kix Army Air Corps Ring,**
1942. Interior ring photos of Lone Ranger and Silver often missing.
Ring Complete - **$200 $400 $600**
Ring, No Photos - **$50 $100 $200**

LON-193

❑ **LON-193. Secret Compartment Ring Instruction Paper,**
1942. Leaflet opens to four panels with other Lone Ranger radio and club notes. -
**$50 $85 $165**

LON-194

❑ **LON-194. Marine Corps Brass Ring,**
1942. Two inside photos of Lone Ranger and Silver often missing.
Complete - **$200 $400 $600**
No Photos - **$50 $100 $200**

LON-195

LON-196

❑ **LON-195. Army Insignia Secret Compartment Brass Ring,**
1942. Two inside photos of Lone Ranger and Silver often missing.
Complete - **$200 $400 $600**
No Photos - **$50 $100 $200**

❑ **LON-196. "USN" Navy Photo Ring,**
1942. Brass, two inside photos of Lone Ranger and Silver often missing.
Complete - **$200 $400 $600**
No Photos - **$50 $100 $200**

LON-197

❑ **LON-197. "The Lone Ranger And The Great Western Span" Better Little Book,**
1942. Whitman #1477. - **$20 $60 $135**

LON-198

❑ **LON-198. Kix "Blackout Kit" With Envelope,**
1942. Contents include luminous paper items.
Near Mint In Mailer - **$300**

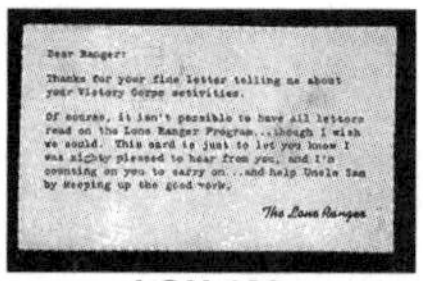

LON-199

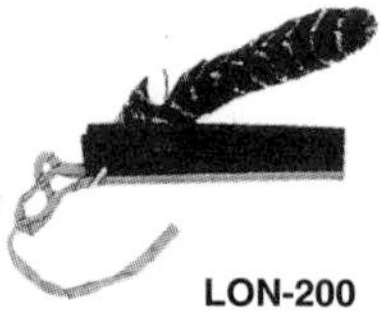

LON-200

❑ **LON-199. "Victory Corps" Postcard To Member,**
1942. Acknowledgement to "Dear Ranger" thanking member for letter describing Victory Corps activities. Pictured example has reverse August 5 postmark from Minneapolis. -
**$20 $40 $75**

❑ **LON-200. Merita "Tonto" Headband,**
1942. Merita Bakers. Tonto name on one side and "Merita" on other side of fabric band holding insert feather. - **$50 $125 $175**

LON-201

❑ **LON-201. "V" Toy Gun,**
c. 1942. 7" composition play gun with "Lone Ranger" name on right side and "V" letter symbol on both sides, symbolizing Lone Ranger Victory Corps. - **$100 $225 $350**

LON-202

❑ **LON-202. Merita Bread Standee,**
1942. 10x17-1/2" diecut cardboard shown framed with Merita Club Member's Application.
Standee - **$500 $1000 $2000**
Application - **$25 $50 $75**

LON-203

LON-204

❑ **LON-203. Lone Ranger Safety Club Calendar And Membership Application Pad Holder,**
1942. Merita Bread. 17x25". Boy shown wearing Lone Ranger Merita Bread Brass Club Badge. Example shown without application and calendar pads.
Complete - **$750 $1500 $2000**
Without Pads - **$500 $1000 $1500**

❑ **LON-204. Meteorite Ring,**
1942. Scarce. Kix bounce back offer with Lone Ranger military rings April, 1942. Company recorded 85 requests. Brass with plastic dome over tiny "meteorite" granules. Following General Mills (Kix) offer, also offered briefly by Kellogg's as Gold Ore ring. -
**$500 $1200 $3000**

LON-205

❑ **LON-205. Merita Safety Club Card,**
1943. Merita Bakers. - **$20 $50 $75**

LON-206

❑ **LON-206. Lone Ranger And Tonto Color Prints,**
1943. Merita Bread. Each about 9x11" with artist's name Sheffield. Each - **$75 $125 $250**

LON-207

❑ **LON-207. Weber's Decoder Folder,**
1943. Rare. - **$75 $200 $300**

LON-208

❑ **LON-208. World War II Ration Book Holder,**
1943. Merita Bread. 4-1/2x6" inscribed "Tune In The Lone Ranger." - **$35 $75 $150**

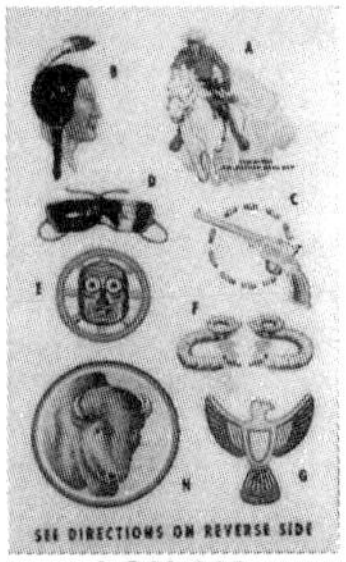

LON-209

❑ **LON-209. Kix Decal Sheet,**
1944. Set #5 sheet from series with water transfer decals of Lone Ranger and other western subjects. - **$15 $30 $50**

LON-210

❑ **LON-210. "War Album Of Victory Battles" With Mailer Envelope,**
1945. General Mills. No Lone Ranger mention but offered on radio show, came with battle scene stamps.
Complete With Mailer - **$35 $60 $100**
Complete Album - **$25 $40 $60**
Album No Stamps - **$10 $20 $30**

LON-211

❑ **LON-211. "Merita" Bread Loaf Label,**
c. 1945. Full color. - **$35 $75 $125**

LON-212

❑ **LON-212. "Kix Airbase" 27x27" Play Sheet Map With Envelope,**
1945. No Lone Ranger inscription but offered on his show. Used with 32 warplane cut-outs from four Kix cereal boxes.
With Envelope - **$60 $150 $300**
No Envelope - **$35 $75 $150**

LON-213

❑ **LON-213. Cereal Box With "Kix Atomic Bomb Ring" Offer,**
1946. Box has 1946 copyright of General Mills but company archive records indicate ring distribution began January 19, 1947. Gordon Gold Archives. Used Complete - **$300 $600 $1200**

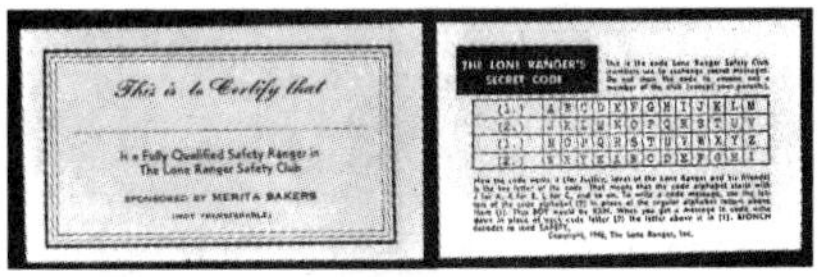

LON-214

❑ **LON-214. Merita Safety Club Card,**
1946. Merita Bakers. - **$15 $40 $65**

LON-215

❑ **LON-215. Lone Ranger Safety Club Calendar And Membership Application Pad Holder,**
1946. Merita Bread. 16-1/2x25-1/2" cardboard. Example shown without application and calendar pads. Complete - **$750 $1500 $2200**
Without Pads - **$500 $1000 $1500**

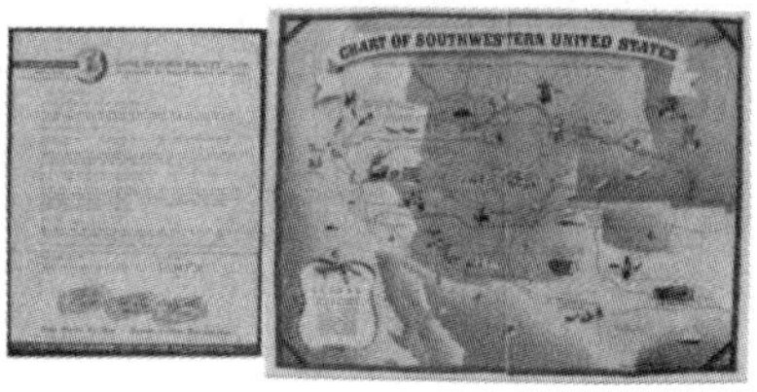

LON-216

❑ **LON-216. Merita Club Letter With Tonto Map And Envelope,**
1946. Merita Bakers. Map opens to 17x22" titled "Chart Of Southwestern United States."
Mailer - **$5 $15 $25**
Letter - **$25 $50 $100**
Chart - **$250 $600 $1000**

LON-217

❑ **LON-217. "The Lone Ranger and the Silver Bullets" Big Little Book #1498,**
1946. - **$10 $40 $90**

LON-218

LON-219

❑ **LON-218. Weather Forecasting Ring,**
1946. Brass with clear lucite cover over small litmus paper. - **$50 $90 $150**

❑ **LON-219. Merita Bread Portrait Picture,**
1946. Artist signature appears to be Frederic Myer. Also issued as a calendar.
Picture - **$100 $250 $500**

LON-220

LON-221

❑ **LON-220. Punch-Out Sheet,**
1947. American Bakeries Co. - **$50 $125 $225**

❑ **LON-221. "Lone Ranger .45" Secret Compartment Bullet,**
1947. Aluminum with removable cap. - **$20 $40 $75**

LON-222

LON-223

❑ **LON-222. "Atomic Bomb Ring" Newspaper Ad,**
1947. Kix Cereal. 10x14" clipping from Sunday newspaper comic section. - **$10 $20 $50**

❑ **LON-223. Atomic Bomb Ring,**
1947. Kix cereal. Brass with plastic bomb cap. A Kix cereal box dated 1946 with Atomic Bomb ring offer is known. However, most distribution began January 1947. - **$50 $100 $220**

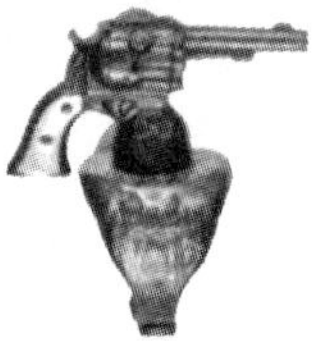
LON-224

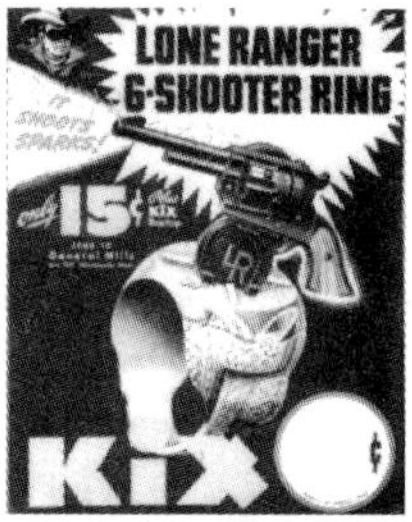

LON-225

❑ **LON-224. Six-Gun Ring,**
1947. Brass with plastic gun holding flint. - **$60 $110 $185**

❑ **LON-225. "Lone Ranger 6-Shooter Ring" 17x22" Store Poster,**
1947. - **$75 $125 $250**

LON-226

❑ **LON-226. Merita Bread Safety Club Calendar,**
1948. Rare. 16"x24". With calendar tablet pages and club application forms. - **$150 $1500 $2200**

(MAP)

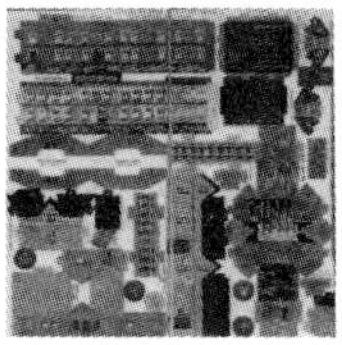
(BUILDING SECTION)

LON-227

❑ **LON-227. "Lone Ranger Frontier Town" Punch-Outs And Maps,**
1948. Four separate maps and four separate unpunched Building sections.
Each Unpunched Section With Mailer - **$425**
Complete Punched Section - **$275**
Each Map - **$75 $125 $225**

LON-228

❑ **LON-228. Merita Bread Safety Club Large Color Picture,**
1948. Smaller version of 1948 calendar, but without the calendar pages and application forms. Sent to new member. - **$100 $250 $500**

LON-229

LON-230

❑ **LON-229. Tonto Set Of Two Metal Bracelets,**
1948. Scarce. No character name on the bracelets, each has Indian symbols.
Complete With Mailer - **$50 $150 $275**

❑ **LON-230. Flashlight Ring,**
1948. Brass with lightbulb and battery. - **$25 $50 $100**

LON-231

❑ **LON-231. "Flashlight Ring" Instruction Sheet,**
1948. Cheerios. Reverse includes "Good Deed Order Blank" for friend. - **$25 $40 $65**

LON-232

LON-233

❑ **LON-232. Cheerios Aluminum Pedometer With Fabric Strap,**
1948. Near Mint Boxed - **$85**
Loose - **$15 $30 $50**

❑ **LON-233. Lone Ranger/Gene Autry Flag Ring,**
c. 1948. Dell Comics. Plastic with dome over flag image, for one-year subscription to comic book for either. - **$50 $100 $150**

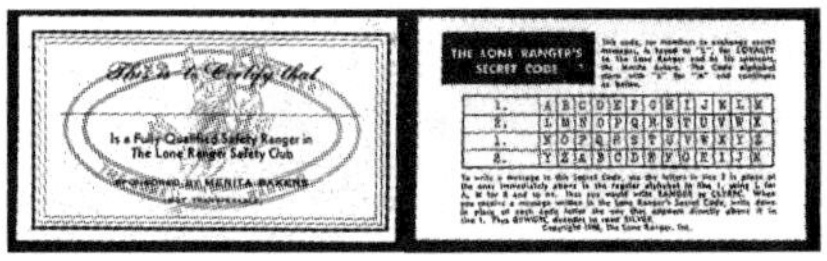

LON-234

❑ **LON-234. Merita Safety Club Card,**
1948. Merita Bakers. Dark blue or dark green variations. Either - **$15 $40 $65**

LON-235

❑ **LON-235. Christmas Card To Dell Comic Subscriber,**
1948. Photos show front and back of card.
Card - **$125 $250 $400**
Envelope - **$20 $40 $60**

LON-236

❑ **LON-236. "Lone Ranger Frontier Town" Newspaper Ad,**
1948. Cheerios. 10x14" clipping from Sunday newspaper comic section. - **$10 $20 $50**

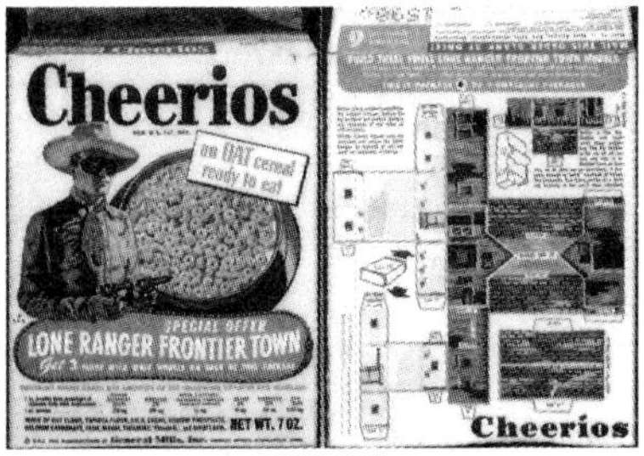


LON-237

❑ **LON-237. "Frontier Town" Cheerios Box,**
1948. Set of nine.
Complete Box Each - **$150 $375 $575**
Each Back Panel Used to Complete Lone Ranger Town - **$25 $50 $100**

LON-238

❑ **LON-238. "Movie Film Ring" Instruction Sheet,**
1949. Cheerios. Reverse has order blank and description of Marine Corps film. - **$50 $60 $75**

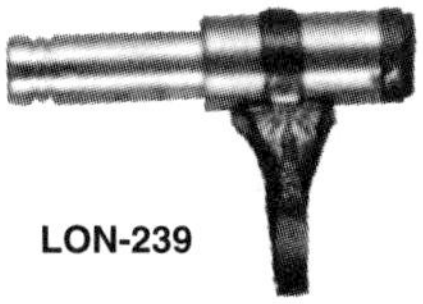

LON-239

❑ **LON-239. Lone Ranger Movie Film Ring,**
1949. Brass bands with aluminum viewing tube, came with 25-frame 8mm color filmstrip titled "U.S. Marines". Ring - **$50 $90 $125**
Film - **$40 $60 $85**

LON-240

❑ **LON-240. Flashlight Gun With Secret Compartment Handle and Lenses,**
1949. Battery operated with clear, red and green lenses. - **$50 $150 $220**

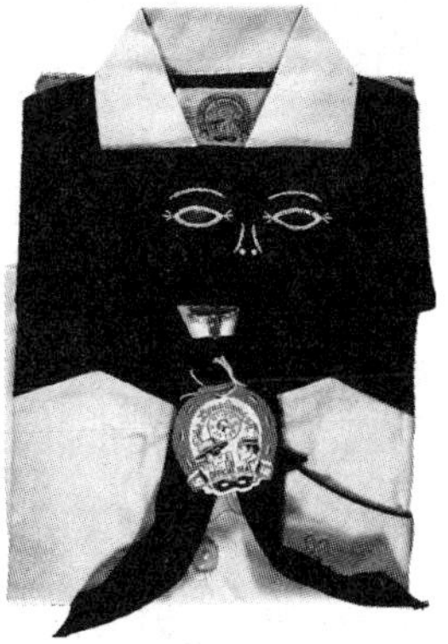

LON-241

❑ **LON-241. General Mills Outfit,**
1949. Rare. Includes shirt, mask, neckerchief, cardboard tag with official seal.
Set - **$150 $400 $700**

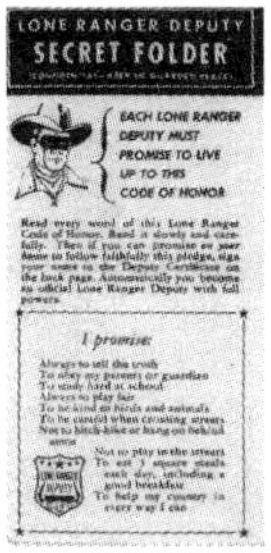


LON-242

LON-243

❑ **LON-242. Cheerios "Deputy Secret Folder",**
1949. - **$15 $30 $60**

❑ **LON-243. "Lone Ranger Deputy" 2" Brass Badge With Secret Compartment,**
1949. - **$25 $50 $100**

LON-244

LON-245

LON-246

❑ **LON-244. "Lone Ranger" Waxed Paper Bread Loaf Liner,**
1940s. Harris-Boyer Bakeries. - **$25 $50 $90**

❑ **LON-245. Child Labor Law Folder,**
1940s. New York State Department of Labor. Lone Ranger endorsement for labor laws affecting boys and girls aged 14-17. - **$20 $40 $85**

❑ **LON-246. Buchan's Bread Cello. Button,**
c. 1940s. 12 known in 7/8" size, various Lone Ranger slogans. Each - **$15 $30 $60**

LON-247

LON-248

LON-249

❑ **LON-247. Lone Ranger "Member" Star Button,**
1940s. Issued for "Buchen's (Bread) Lone Ranger Community Safety Club." - **$30 $75 $125**

❑ **LON-248. Lone Ranger "Captain" Star Button,**
1940s. - **$35 $85 $150**

❑ **LON-249. Lone Ranger "Deputy" Star Button,**
1940s. - **$35 $85 $150**

LON-250

LON-251

❑ **LON-250. Color Photo Card,**
1940s. Madison Square Garden promo (#A6181 at bottom.).Shows Lone Ranger riding horse. - **$25 $50 $75**

❑ **LON-251. Silver Bullet Offer,**
1940s. Kix Cereal. Explains how to order a silver bullet for 15¢ and 1 box top. - **$10 $25 $50**

LON-252

❑ **LON-252. "The Lone Ranger Rides Again!" Cardboard Punch-Out Figure Set,**
c. 1940s. Store item by DeJournette Mfg. Co., Atlanta. Consists of stiff cardboard punch-outs of unknown total quantity but including 5" tall Lone Ranger and Tonto plus 7-1/2" tall rearing horse, fence rails and small accessories such as gun, knife, dog, teepee, etc.
Complete - **$100 $225 $350**

LON-253

LON-254

❑ **LON-253. Note Paper,**
1940s (pre-1945). Rare. Test program for Victory Corps note paper. Shows 3 men firing cannon on left and says "Let's Go U.S.A." Put out during WWII. Each - **$25 $60 $100**

❑ **LON-254. Lone Ranger Official Hat,**
1940s. Lone Ranger name stamped on inside. - **$60 $125 $250**

LON-255

❑ **LON-255. "The Lone Ranger" Fabric Mask,**
c. 1940s. Issuer unknown. Possibly a movie theater giveaway or from a western costume set. - **$15 $30 $60**

LON-256

❑ **LON-256. Lone Ranger Calendar,**
1940s. Merita Bread. 16x28". Example shown without pad. Bread wrapper design includes children wearing masks and Indian headbands.
Complete - **$750 $1500 $2200**
Without Pad - **$500 $1000 $1500**

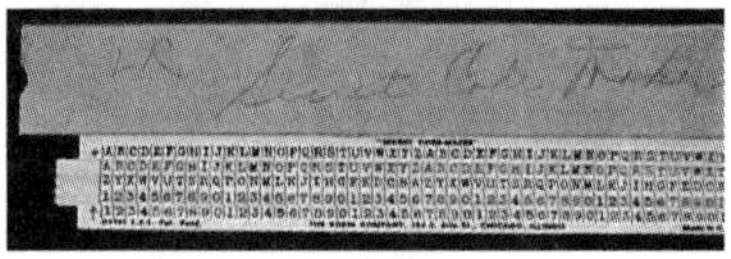
LON-257

❑ **LON-257. "Secret Code-Maker" Wooden Coding Device,**
1940s. General Mills. Item is marked "The Robin Company" Chicago with 1939 copyright. It does not carry the Lone Ranger name but its use was verified by Evie Wilson, former General Mills archivist. Also available as non-The Lone Ranger item. - **$30 $60 $100**

LON-258

❑ **LON-258. Pocketknife,**
1940s. Store item with grips in black, red or white. - **$35 $75 $110**

LON-259

❑ **LON-259. Dan Reid With Lone Ranger And Tonto Color Picture,**
1940s. Merita Bread. About 7x9". - **$50 $125 $200**

LON-260

LON-261

LON-262

❑ **LON-260. Seal Print Face Ring,**
1940s. Unmarked believed Lone Ranger premium tin ring designed to press face image into soft material. - **$75 $175 $300**

❑ **LON-261. "Lone Ranger Lucky Piece" Silvered Brass 17th Anniversary Key Ring Fob Medal,**
1950. Cheerios. - **$15 $25 $50**

❑ **LON-262. Merita Bread Safety Club 8x15" Cardboard Wall Calendar,**
1950. Scarce. - **$75 $200 $400**

**LON-263**

❑ **LON-263. "Merita Bread Cake" Floaty Mechanical Pencil,**
c. 1950. Brass barrel has text in red. Full figure Lone Ranger in blue outfit floats in chamber. Possibly a salesman's promotional giveaway. - **$50 $125 $200**

**LON-264**

❑ **LON-264. Shelf Hanger Or Topper,**
1950. Merita Bread. 8x18" in full color. - **$200 $400 $750**

**LON-265**

**LON-266**

❑ **LON-265. Bandanna Order Blank,**
1950. General Mills.- **$10 $15 $30**

❑ **LON-266. Fabric Bandanna,**
1950. Offered by Betty Crocker Soups. - **$25 $60 $100**

**LON-267**

**LON-268**

❑ **LON-267. Lone Ranger Calendar,**
1950. Merita Bread 16x28". Example shown without pad. Complete - **$500 $1000 $1600**
Without Pad - **$400 $800 $1200**

❑ **LON-268. Photo Card,**
1950. TV premium.- **$10 $20 $35**

**LON-269**

❑ **LON-269. Lone Ranger Original Art Prototype Book Created By Sam Gold For Morton Salt,**
c. 1950. "The Lone Ranger Western And Fun Book" with 48 pages of original art. Gordon Gold Archives. Unique. - **$1250**

**LON-270**

❑ **LON-270. Picture Strip Premium,**
1951. Subscription premium by Dell Publishing Co. 6-3/4x8-1/4" slick paper opens to 33-1/2" wide with five picture panels. - **$50 $80 $150**

**LON-271**

**LON-272**

❑ **LON-271. Cheerios Contest Postcard,**
1951. Back text for coloring contest. - **$8 $15 $35**

❑ **LON-272. Cheerios Crayon Offer Box Back,**
1951. #1 from set of four. - **$10 $20 $30**

**LON-273**

❑ **LON-273. Cheerios Crayon Offer Box Backs,**
1951. #2 and #4 shown, from set of four offering free crayon set for crayoned box picture sent to General Mills. - **$10 $20 $30**

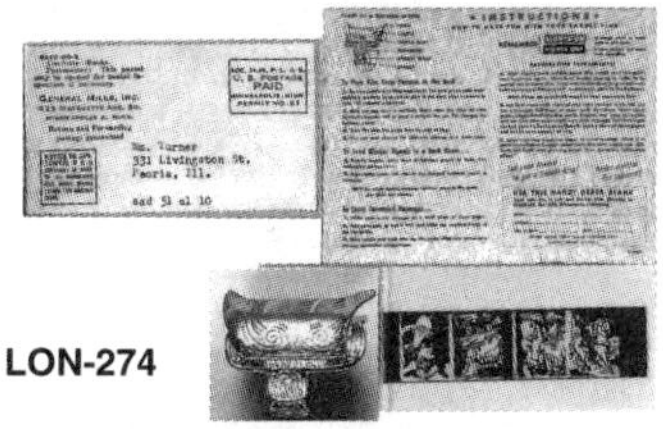

**LON-274**

❑ **LON-274. Cheerios Saddle Ring With Filmstrip, Paper And Box,**
1951. Near Mint Boxed - **$300**
Ring Only - **$75 $110 $150**
Film Only - **$20 $35 $50**

**LON-275**

❑ **LON-275. Cheerios Paper Mask,**
c. 1951. Back text "See The Lone Ranger And Silver In Person At Minneapolis Aquatennial". - **$30 $75 $125**

**LON-276**

❑ **LON-276. Calendar With Slot To Hold Club Application Blanks,**
1951. Merita Bread. Full color about 15x16" with additional text on reverse. With Or Without Application Blanks - **$400 $800 $1200**

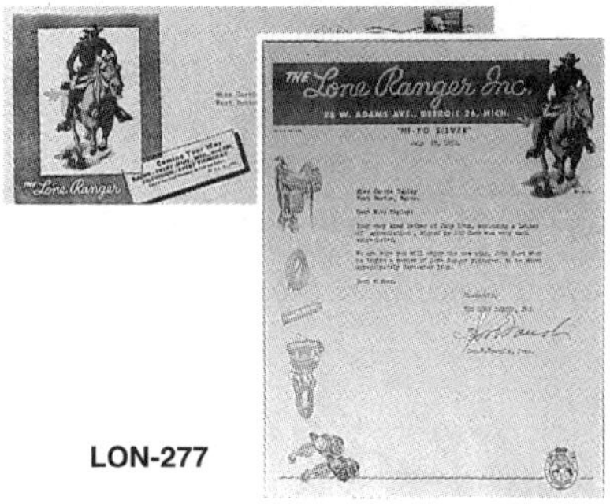


**LON-277**

❑ **LON-277. Fan Response Envelope With Letter Signed By "Geo. W. Trendle ",**
1952. Trendle acknowledges a letter of appreciation signed by 100 fans and says "We Are Sure You Will Enjoy The New Star, John Hart..."
Envelope - **$20 $40 $75**
Letter - **$75 $100 $150**

LON-278

❑ **LON-278. "The Lone Ranger" Wristwatch,**
1951. Store item, no maker specified. -
**$75 $125 $250**

LON-279

❑ **LON-279. Cheerios Box With Comic Book Advertising,**
1954. - **$150 $300 $600**

LON-280

❑ **LON-280. "The Lone Ranger, His Mask And How He Met Tonto" Comic Booklet,**
1954. 16-page full color newsprint issued by Cheerios. - **$20 $60 $140**

LON-281

❑ **LON-281. "The Lone Ranger And The Story Of Silver" Comic,**
1954. Cheerios. - **$20 $60 $140**

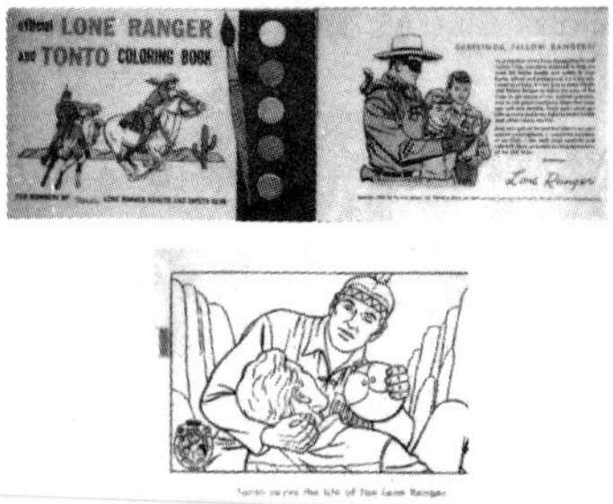


LON-282

❑ **LON-282. Merita Bread Coloring Book,**
1955. - **$10 $20 $50**

LON-283

❑ **LON-283. "Lone Ranger Rapid-Fire Revolver" Cereal Box,**
1955. Premium offer was 12" long plastic revolver with accessories.
Complete - **$75 $175 $300**

LON-284

❑ **LON-284. "Ride With The Lone Ranger" Premium Game And Mailer,**
1955. Merita Bakers. Cardboard folder opens to 11x17" with built-in spinner and four small bread loaf-shaped punch-outs as markers. These are titled "The Lone Ranger, Tonto" and two say "Outlaw." Mailer - **$10 $20 $30**
Game - **$75 $150 $300**

LON-285

❑ **LON-285. Merita Bread Safety Club "Branding" Booklet,**
1956. Cattle branding explained by Lone Ranger. - **$20 $75 $150**

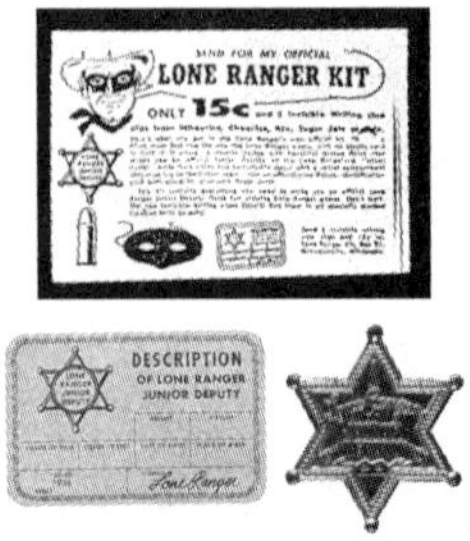


LON-286

❑ **LON-286. "Lone Ranger Junior Deputy" Kit,**
1956. Various General Mills cereals.
Copper luster tin star badge - **$20 $30 $45**
Identification Card - **$15 $25 $45**
Black Fabric Mask (unmarked) - **$5 $15 $25**
Bullet same or similar to 1947 issue -
**$20 $40 $75**
Descriptive Coupon - **$10 $15 $25**

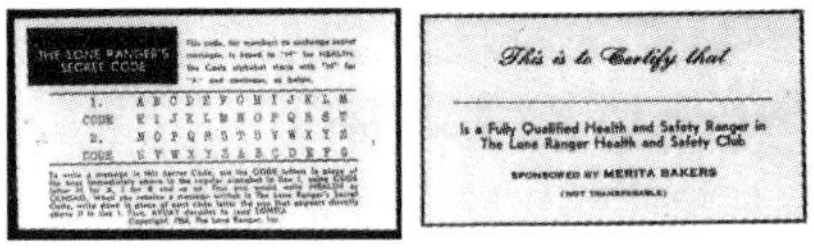


LON-287

❑ **LON-287. Merita Safety Club Card,**
1956. Merita Bakers. - **$10 $35 $60**

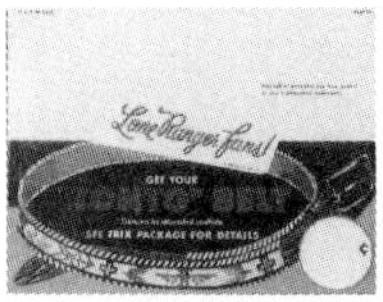

LON-288

LON-289

❑ **LON-288. Trix "Tonto Belt" Sign,**
1956. Diecut 6x8" paper display sign. -
**$25 $40 $60**
Belt with Mailer - **$30 $60 $120**

❑ **LON-289. Kix "Lone Ranger Branding Iron" Sign,**
1956. Diecut 6x8" paper display sign. -
**$30 $50 $75**

LON-290

LON-291

❑ **LON-290. Wheaties "Lone Ranger Hike-O-Meter" Sign,**
1956. Diecut 6x8" paper display sign. -
**$25 $40 $60**

❑ **LON-291. Sugar Jets "Lone Ranger Six-Shooter Ring" Sign,**
1956. Diecut 6x8" paper display sign. -
**$25 $40 $60**

LON-292

❑ **LON-292. "Lone Ranger Ranch Fun Book",**
1956. Cheerios. - **$25 $75 $160**

LON-293

LON-294

❑ **LON-293. Cheerios "Lone Ranger Fun Kit" Sign,**
1956. Diecut 6x8" paper display sign. -
**$30 $60 $100**

❑ **LON-294. Litho. Button,**
1957. Probable vending machine issue. 7/8" with browntone photo on various single-color backgrounds. From a larger set of western TV stars, probably totaling 14 different. -
**$20 $40 $75**

LON-295

❑ **LON-295. Lone Ranger With Guns 6' Standee,**
1957. Rare. General Mills. -
**$750 $2000 $3200**

LON-296

❑ **LON-296. Wheaties Box With Posters Offer,**
1957. Complete Box - **$200 $300 $525**
Box Back - **$20 $60 $85**

LON-297

❑ **LON-297. Wheaties Life-Sized Posters,**
1957. Set of two 25x75" paper posters.
Lone Ranger - **$80 $175 $300**
Tonto - **$80 $175 $300**

LON-298

❑ **LON-298. Life-Sized Uncut Poster Sheet (not separated),**
1957. Used in the lobby at General Mills headquarters. Unique - **$1300**

LON-299

❑ **LON-299. "Lone Ranger Movie Ranch Wild West Town" Box Panels,**
1957. Five in set.
Each Complete Box - **$75 $150 $250**
Each Uncut Back Pane - **$20 $40 $60**

LON-300

❑ **LON-300. Cheerios "Wild West Town" Figures With Sheet And Box,**
1957. Scarce. Set of 22 figures including Lone Ranger, Tonto, three horses, nine cowboys, eight Indians. Near Mint Complete - **$500**

LON-301

❑ **LON-301. Cheerios "Movie Ranch Wild West Town" Ad Sheet,**
1957. Box insert 3x4".
Sheet - **$15 $40 $60**

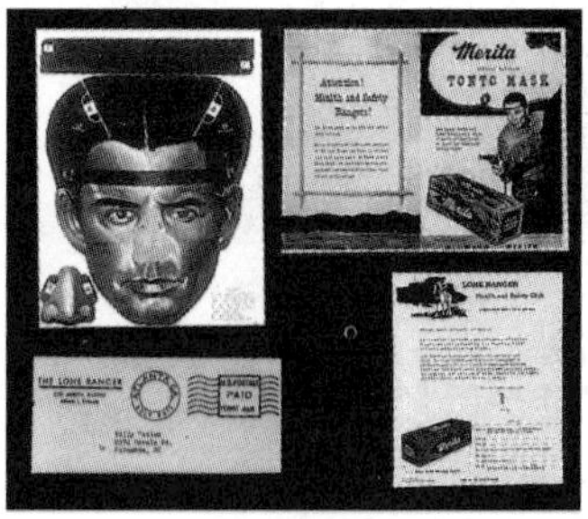


LON-302

❑ **LON-302. Merita "Tonto Mask" Kit,**
1957. Mailer with Lone Ranger Health And Safety Club letter including order form for Lone Ranger Growth Chart, punch-out face mask.
Near Mint In Mailer - **$400**
Letter - **$25 $50 $75**
Mask Unpunched - **$50 $100 $250**
Mask Assembled - **$35 $75 $150**

LON-303

❑ **LON-303. The Lone Ranger Large General Mills Standee,**
1957. 4x6' diecut with easel back. -
**$500 $1200 $2000**

LON-304

LON-305

❑ **LON-304. Photo Album,**
1957. General Mills, Nestle, Swift, and Merita Bread. Contains 12 black and white photos plus 2 front and back color photos. Has the history of the Lone Ranger and promotes the next year's 25th silver anniversary of his program. TV premium.- **$50 $100 $165**

❑ **LON-305. "T-Vue Time" Weekly Schedule Booklet,**
1957. Baltimore Sunday American. Issued for May 19 with front cover color photo and short article. - **$10 $20 $40**

LON-306

❑ **LON-306. Child's Stiff Cardboard Table ,**
c. 1958. - **$75 $150 $300**

LON-307

LON-308

❑ **LON-307. Calendar Card,**
1958. Premium calendar. Shaped like a loaf of bread. - **$25 $50 $75**

❑ **LON-308. Merita Bread "Lone Ranger Peace Patrol" Aluminum Token,**
1959. Sponsored in conjunction with U.S. Treasury Department. Promotion for savings bonds. - **$40 $85 $140**

LON-309

❑ **LON-309. "Peace Patrol" Member Card,**
c. 1959. U.S. Treasury Department. Encourages savings bond purchase, back has creed and pledge. - **$10 $20 $35**

LON-310

LON-311

❑ **LON-310. "Join The Peace Patrol" 11x14" Paper Poster,**
c. 1959. U.S. Treasury Department. Encourages savings bond purchase. - **$60 $150 $300**

❑ **LON-311. Full Color 1-1/4" Cello. Button,**
c. 1959. Unmarked but probably related to Treasury Department campaign to promote sales of U.S. Savings Bonds. - **$10 $20 $40**

LON-312

LON-313

❑ **LON-312. Litho. Button With B&W Photo On Lt. Blue,**
c. 1959. Same design as full color 1-1/4" cello. button but rare 1-3/8" litho. - **$75 $150 $350**

❑ **LON-313. Deputy Chief Badge,**
1950s. Rare. Detail of paper also shown. - **$100 $300 $450**

LON-314

❑ **LON-314. "The Lone Ranger Color Picture Cards" Ed-U-Cards Promo Card,**
1950s. 8-1/2x11" one-sided black and white sheet. - **$15 $25 $50**

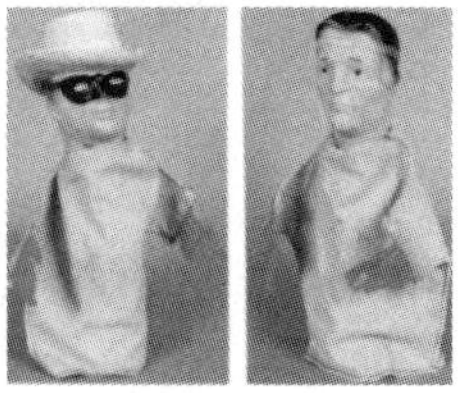

LON-315

❑ **LON-315. Lone Ranger And Tonto Hand Puppets,**
1950s. Store items. Each is 9" tall.
Each - **$25 $50 $100**

LON-316

LON-317

❑ **LON-316. "Merita Bread" Color Picture,**
1950s. - **$15 $30 $75**

❑ **LON-317. Merita Bread Aluminum Silver Bullet Pencil Sharpener,**
c. 1950s. - **$20 $50 $75**

LON-318

❑ **LON-318. Dell Comics Picture Strip,**
1950s. Strip folio of five pictures. -
**$50 $80 $150**

LON-319

❑ **LON-319. Smoking Click Plastic Pistol,**
1950s. Store item by Marx Toys.
Boxed - **$100 $250 $450**
Loose - **$65 $150 $325**

LON-320

❑ **LON-320. "Magic Lasso" With Brass Badge,**
1950s. Store item by Round-Up Products.
Near Mint Boxed - **$750**
Badge Only - **$125 $300 $600**

LON-321 LON-322

❑ **LON-321. "Lone Ranger Deputy" 2-1/4" Silvered Metal Badge,**
1950s. Red and black painted versions. Store Item. Card with 12 Badges - **$500**
Each - **$10 $20 $30**

❑ **LON-322. "Lone Ranger Deputy" Gold Finish Metal Badge,**
1950s. Store item. - **$15 $25 $40**

LON-323

LON-324

❑ **LON-323. Litho. Tin Tab Star Badge,**
1950s. Pictures Clayton Moore. - **$20 $50 $75**

❑ **LON-324. Lone Ranger and Silver Figure,**
1950s. Lone Ranger with chaps on Silver Hartland figure. Has two guns, saddle and hat as accessories. - **$75 $150 $275**

LON-325

❑ **LON-325. Western Series T.V. Card,**
1950s. Card #109 - **$10 $20 $35**

LON-326

❑ **LON-326. Canadian Color Photo Premium,**
1950s. Nestle's Quik. 9x10" with facsimile signature and "T.V. Star For Nestle's 'Quik' The 'Quick As A Wink' Chocolate Drink." -
**$20 $50 $110**

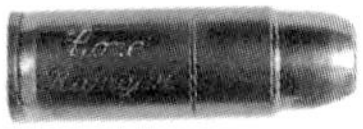

LON-327 LON-328

❑ **LON-327. Silver Bullet,**
1950s. Probably General Mills premium. 1-1/2" metal replica in silver finish with his name in cursive lettering on side. TLR Inc. copyright. -
**$15 $30 $50**

❑ **LON-328. "The Dodge Boys" Silver Bullet,**
c. 1950s. Dodge Motors Corp. 1-1/2" silver luster metal bullet issued for TV sponsor. -
**$20 $40 $60**

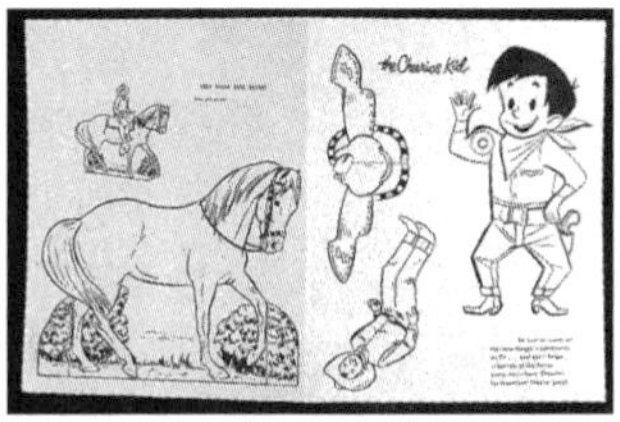

LON-329

❑ **LON-329. Coloring Book,**
1950s. Cheerios. Large two page premium featuring the Cheerios Kid and Tonto.-
**$10 $25 $50**

LON-330

❑ **LON-330. "27th Year" TV Networks Promotion Kit,**
1960-1961. Jack Wrather Productions. 9x12" with black and white image on red brochure holding extensive publicity and informational items issued for the 1960-1961 seasons on ABC-TV and NBC-TV. Includes Clayton Moore biography as Lone Ranger, TV fact sheet, Lone Ranger Creed, interview questions and more. -
**$125 $250 $400**

LON-331 LON-332

❑ **LON-331. English Cookie Tin,**
1961. Huntley & Palmers Biscuits. -
**$65 $150 $250**

❑ **LON-332. English Cookie Tin,**
1961. Huntley & Palmers Biscuits. Version pictures Tonto only. - **$65 $150 $250**

LON-333 LON-334

❑ **LON-333. "The Legend Of The Lone Ranger" Comic Book,**
1969. Chain restaurant promotion. Identifies him as "The Good Food Guy". - **$5 $12 $30**

❑ **LON-334. "The Good Food Guy" Cello. Button,**
c. 1969. Chain restaurant promotion. -
**$10 $18 $25**

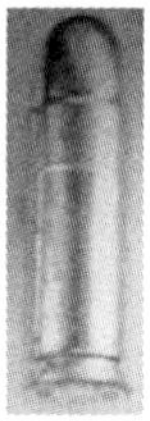

LON-335 LON-336

❑ **LON-335. "The Dodge Boys" TV Sponsor Card,**
1960s. 9x11" counter card for agency of Dodge Motors Corp. Facsimile Clayton Moore signature. - **$10 $20 $35**

❑ **LON-336. Railway Express Advertising Silver Bullet,**
c. 1960s. 1-3/4" long silver luster plastic with removable end cap inscribed "Hi-Yo REA Awaaay." - **$5 $10 $15**

LON-337 LON-338

❑ **LON-337. Record,**
1972. Coca Cola premium with sleeve. - **$15 $25 $60**

❑ **LON-338. Record,**
1977. Record album contains two famous radio episodes. - **$15 $25 $60**

LON-339

LON-340

❑ **LON-339. Autographed Clayton Moore Photograph,**
1977. Lynn Wilson's Convenient Fun Food. Design includes Lone Ranger Creed.
Signed - **$25 $60 $100**
Unsigned - **$8 $15 $30**

❑ **LON-340. Amoco Gas Station "Ride With Silver" 44x70" Vinyl Sign,**
1970s. "Amoco Silver" lead-free gasoline. - **$50 $100 $175**

LON-341

❑ **LON-341. "The Lone Ranger Wants You" Poster,**
1970s. Issued by The Lone Ranger Family Restaurant. 17-1/2x21-1/2" tan paper. - **$20 $40 $75**

LON-342

❑ **LON-342. "Lone Ranger Deputy Kit",**
1980. Cheerios. Contains Deputy certificate, "Legend" story folder, punch-out mask, 2-1/2" plastic Deputy badge and 17x22" color poster.
Complete - **$10 $20 $40**

LON-343

❑ **LON-343. Cheerios Box "Deputy Kit" Offer,**
1980. Promotion ran on identical 10 oz. and 15 oz. boxes. Box size is listed on the bottom.
Complete 10 oz. box - **$20 $40 $60**
Complete 15 oz. box - **$25 $50 $75**

LON-344

❑ **LON-344. "Legend of the Lone Ranger" Gun and Holster Set in Display Box,**
1980. Gabriel product. 6 piece set includes 2 guns, 2 holsters, a belt and a mask. Hard to believe this movie is already 20 years old.- **$35 $85 $150**

LON-345

LON-346

❑ **LON-345. Movie Press Kit,**
1981. Contains saddle bag mailer with 14 photos & script. - **$20 $75 $115**

❑ **LON-346. Movie Lone Ranger Rocking Book,**
1981. Lone Ranger on front cover, Tonto on back cover. - **$10 $20 $35**

(NECKERCHIEF)

(LUNCH BOX) LON-347 (BOX)

❑ **LON-347. Lone Ranger Watch Box Set,**
1994. Watch has vintage dial. It comes in a metal lunchbox with insert which pictures Clayton Moore as the Lone Ranger. Each box also contained a large neckerchief as a premium. The limited edition watch set sold out quickly and is hard to find on the secondary market.
Complete - **$175**

LON-348

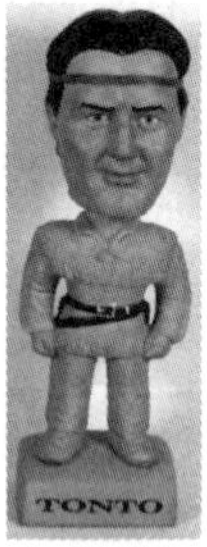


LON-349

❑ **LON-348. Lone Ranger 9 3/4" Bobbing Head Figure,**
1996. - **$60**

❑ **LON-349. Tonto 9 3/4" Bobbing Head Figure,**
1996. - **$60**

LON-350

❑ **LON-350. Hallmark Christmas Ornament,**
1997. Shaped like a Lone Ranger lunchbox. - **$35**

LON-351

❑ **LON-351. Porcelain Container,**
1999. Hinged container with a wooden "Silver bullet" inside. Golden Books product. - **$20**

(3 VIEWS OF THE RING)

(POUCH)

(MEMBERSHIP CARD)

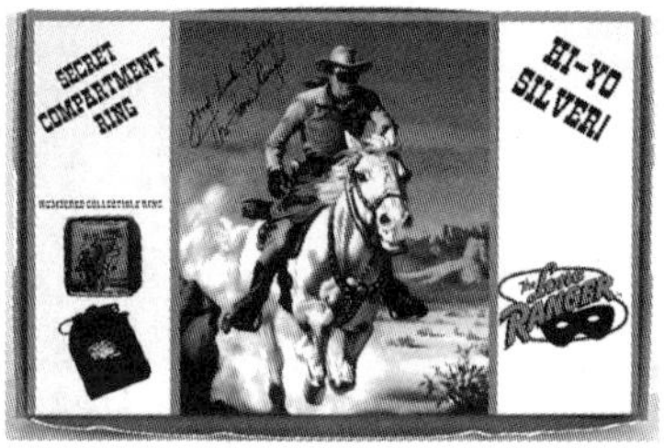

LON-352 (BOX)

❑ **LON-352. Secret Compartment Ring Set,**
2000. Ring comes in box with pouch and membership card. Complete - **$35**

LON-353

❑ **LON-353. Cheerios Then and Now Set,**
2001. 60th Anniversary set includes a 1941 design Cheerios box, a 2001 box and a retro lunch box. Complete near mint - **$20**

## Lone Wolf Tribe

**Wrigley's gum sponsored this children's program on CBS in 1932-1933. The series offered dramatized versions of the American Indian way of life, told by Chief Wolf Paw to the tribe members "with the voice that flies (radio)." Listeners could obtain premiums by sending in "wampum" (Wrigley's wrappers). Most premiums were marked with the imprint of a wolf paw. The club ring, sterling silver and non-adjustable, is considered the earliest issued premium ring.**

LWF-1

LWF-2

❑ **LWF-1. Wrigley's Chewing Gum Samples Folder,**
1932. Held three sticks of gum, reverse lists radio times and offers Lone Wolf Tribe Book.
With Gum - **$25 $100 $200**
Folder Only - **$15 $30 $75**

❑ **LWF-2. Club Manual,**
1932. Wrigley Gum. - **$15 $40 $85**

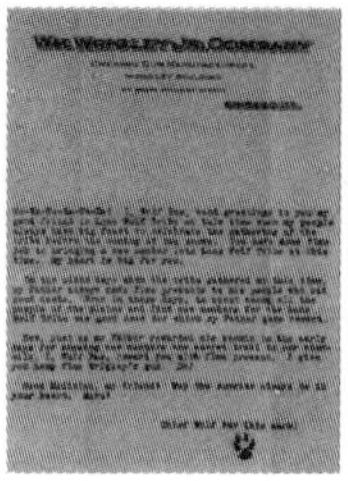
LWF-3

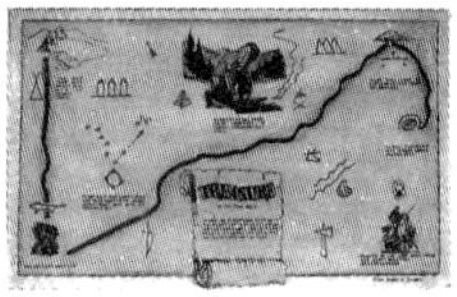
LWF-4

❑ **LWF-3. New Member Letter,**
1932. Wrigley Gum. - **$15 $25 $50**

❑ **LWF-4. "Treasure Of The Lone Wolf" 11x17" Paper Map,**
1932. Scarce. Wrigley Gum. - **$50 $150 $225**

LWF-5

❑ **LWF-5. "Lone Wolf Tribe Tom-Tom" Leather And Thin Rubber Drum With Beater Stick,**
c. 1932. Rare. Wrigley's Gum.
Boxed - **$50 $150 $225**
Loose - **$25 $80 $150**

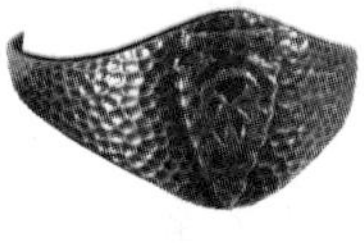
LWF-6

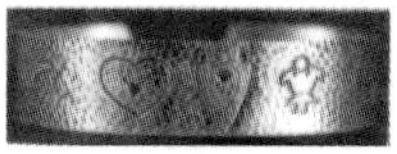
LWF-7

❑ **LWF-6. Chief Wolf Paw Sterling Ring,**
1932. Wrigley's Gum. Considered the first radio premium ring. - **$75 $150 $250**

❑ **LWF-7. Tribe Bracelet,**
1932. Wrigley Gum. Silvered metal expansion bracelet with tribal code symbols. - **$60 $125 $200**

LWF-8

❑ **LWF-8. Arrowhead Silvered Brass Member's Badge,**
1932. On Card - **$30 $75 $125**
Loose - **$15 $30 $50**

LWF-9

LWF-10

❑ **LWF-9. Lone Wolf Arrowhead Pin Mailer,**
1932. Wrigley's Gum. - **$20 $50 $85**

❑ **LWF-10. Lone Wolf Letter (Goes With Pin),**
1932. Wrigley's Gum. - **$10 $20 $40**

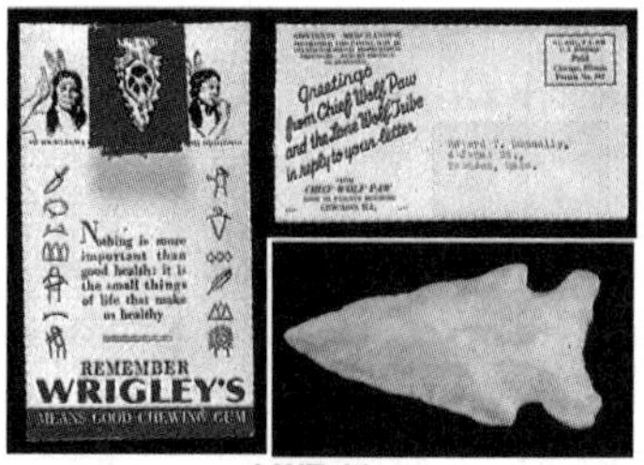

LWF-11

❑ **LWF-11. Chief Wolf Paw/Lone Wolf Tribe Arrowhead With Mailer,**
c. 1932. Wrigley's Gum. Stone arrowhead held in flap pocket of 3x5-1/2" mailer card.
Arrowhead With Mailer - **$35 $75 $150**

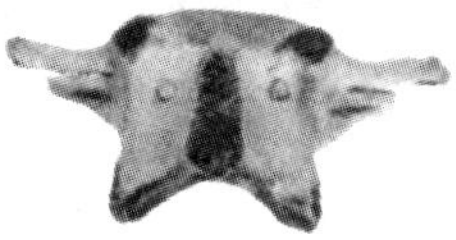

LWF-12

LWF-13

❑ **LWF-12. Cow Head Tie Holder,**
1932. Actual bone tie slide from "Vertebra Of A Range Animal". - **$20 $40 $60**

❑ **LWF-13. "Sitting Bull" Picture,**
c. 1932. Lone Wolf Tribe premium with back text "How Sitting Bull Got His Name". - **$15 $50 $85**

LWF-14

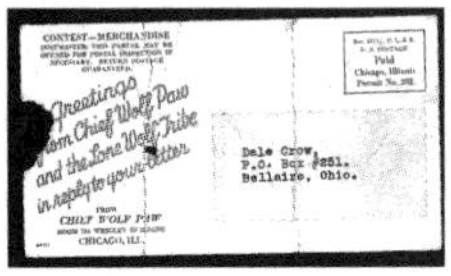

LWF-15

❑ **LWF-14. Tribe Necklace,**
1932. Scarce. - **$100 $250 $350**

❑ **LWF-15. Lone Wolf Tribe Postcard,**
1932. Wrigley's Gum. - **$40 $50 $60**

LWF-16

LWF-17

❑ **LWF-16. Chief Wolf Paw Arrowhead Fob,**
1932. Wrigley Gum. Thin silvered brass picturing paw and arrow designs. - **$20 $75 $110**

❑ **LWF-17. Lone Wolf Silvered Brass Pin,**
1932. Thunderbird broach. - **$25 $50 $85**

LWF-18

LWF-19

❑ **LWF-18. Lone Wolf Closing Mailer,**
1933. Wrigley's Gum. - **$20 $40 $60**

❑ **LWF-19. Lone Wolf Tribe Trading Post Closing Folder,**
1933. Wrigley's Gum. Four page folder with 3 sticks of gum. - **$100 $275 $425**

LWF-20

❑ **LWF-20. Lone Wolf Arrowhead Chain,**
1933. Unmarked - Hunt Buffalo sign. - **$20 $30 $50**

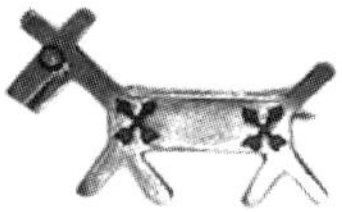

LWF-21

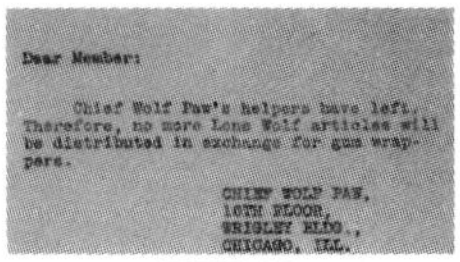

Dear Member:

Chief Wolf Paw's helpers have left. Therefore, no more Lone Wolf articles will be distributed in exchange for gum wrappers.

CHIEF WOLF PAW,
10TH FLOOR,
WRIGLEY BLDG.,
CHICAGO, ILL.

LWF-22

❑ **LWF-21. Lone Wolf Pin,**
1933. Unmarked - Horse symbol for journey. - **$20 $30 $50**

❑ **LWF-22. Out Of Business Paper,**
c. 1933. Wrigley Gum. Paper reads "Dear Member: Chief Wolf Paw's Helpers Have Left. Therefore, No More Lone Wolf Articles Will Be Distributed In Exchange For Gum Wrappers." - **$25 $50 $100**

# Lost In Space

**"Never fear, Smith is here!" This cult sci-fi TV series, created by Irwin Allen for 20th Century Fox Television and aired on CBS from 1965-1968, ran up against another memorable science fiction show with its own following--something called *Star Trek*. It was *Lost in Space* that was the first-run success, though, and to this day its three seasons remain popular in syndication and on the Sci-Fi Channel. Following the exploits of the intrepid Robinson family--Professor John Robinson, wife Maureen, daughters Judy and Penny, son Will, their pilot Major Don West, their Robot...called "Robot," and a stock villain stowaway known as Dr. Smith originally sent to sabotage the ship--the series was a campy hit that mixed cheap special effects, excessive over-acting, and a wild sense of fun to produce a show enjoyed by both children and adults.**

**Originally sent from Earth to colonize the nearby star system of Alpha Centauri, the family finds themselves encountering a bizarre collection of aliens thanks to the bumbling malevolence of Dr. Smith, who often attempts to exploit opportunities to return home at the expense of the family's safety. *Lost in Space* has now enjoyed a resurgence of popularity thanks to several anniversary celebrations, including a Sci-Fi Channel tribute aired on October 16th, 1997 (the date on which the Robinson's spacecraft, the Jupiter II, was supposedly launched) as well as the 1998 New Line feature film of the same name, starring William Hurt, Mimi Rogers, and Gary Oldman taking over for Jonathan Harris as Dr. Smith. Most items are copyright 20th Century Fox. "Oh the pain, the pain!"**

LIS-1

LIS-2

❑ **LIS-1. "March Of Comics" Booklet #352,**
1964. Various sponsors. "Space Family Robinson/Lost In Space" story. - **$9 $27 $110**

❑ **LIS-2. TV Guide Weekly Issue,**
1965. Volume 13 #45 for week of November 6.
Without Mailing Label - **$20 $40 $70**
With Mailing Label - **$15 $30 $50**

LIS-3

❑ **LIS-3. "Lost In Space" Model Kit,**
1966. Store item by Aurora.
Near Mint Boxed - **$1000**
Complete Assembled - **$100 $225 $350**

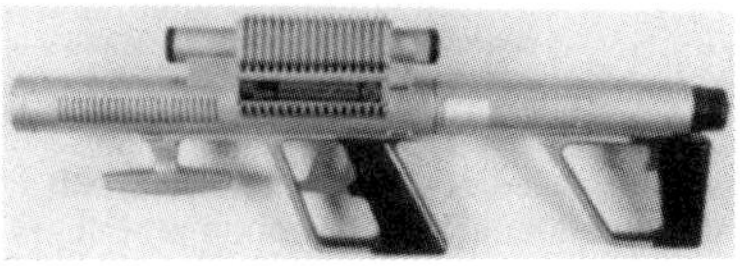

LIS-4

❑ **LIS-4. Roto Jet Gun,**
c. 1966. Mattel. Two main pieces transform to weapons. Came with two saucers and whistle attachment. Rare.
Complete - **$500 $1000 $1500**

LIS-5

❑ **LIS-5. "Lost In Space" Cast Photo,**
c. 1966. CBS-TV fan card. - **$20 $40 $75**

LIS-6

❑ **LIS-6. "Lost In Space" Battery Operated Robot,**
1966. Store item by Remco.
Boxed - **$200 $500 $750**
Loose - **$100 $250 $500**

LIS-7

❑ **LIS-7. Elaborate Press Kit,**
1967. 9-1/2x12" folder holds publicity materials for the third season. Primary contents are five glossy 8x10" photos and 35 fact sheets, cover letter has facsimile signature of Irwin Allen. - **$100 $250 $350**

LIS-8

❑ **LIS-8. Lost in Space Metal Lunch Box With Thermos,**
1967. King Seeley Thermos. - **$150 $450 $800**

LIS-9

❑ **LIS-9. "The Robot From Lost In Space",**
1968. Store item by Aurora.
Near Mint Boxed - **$800**
Complete Assembled - **$100 $200 $400**

LIS-10

❑ **LIS-10. "Lost In Space" Battery Operated Robot,**
1977. Store item by Ahi.
Boxed - **$75 $200 $325**
Loose - **$50 $150 $200**

LIS-11

❑ **LIS-11. "Lost In Space" Robot YM-3,**
1985. 16" talking figure in box by Masudaya.
Boxed - **$200**

LIS-12

❑ **LIS-12. Lost in Space 10" Talking Environmental Robot B-9,**
1997. Trendmasters, Inc. and Newline Productions. 10" tall Robot with two recorded sayings (delivered by the original Robot voice, Dick Tufeld): "Danger, Danger Will Robinson!" and "My sensors indicate an intruder is present." Comes with removable laser pistol, retractable arms, light-up dome and pull-back tread action. - **$40**

LIS-13 LIS-14

❑ **LIS-13. Lost in Space 7" Robot B-9,**
1997. Trendmasters, Inc. and Newline Productions. 7" tall Robot with two recorded sayings. - **$20**

❑ **LIS-14. Lost in Space Flashlight on Card,**
1997. - **$15**

LIS-15 LIS-16

❑ **LIS-15. Battle Ravaged Robot in Box,**
1997. 8" tall movie Robot. - **$15**

❑ **LIS-16. Motorized Robot,**
1997. 10" figure with remote control hacker deck. Box is approx. 13" wide. - **$25**

LIS-17

LIS-18

❑ **LIS-17. The Robot Model Kit in Box,**
1998. - **$25**

❑ **LIS-18. Movie Premium Pinback,**
1998. Large. - **$15**

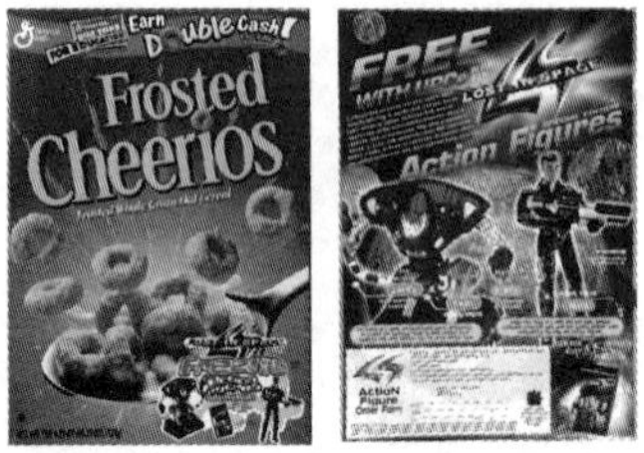


LIS-19

❑ **LIS-19. Frosted Cheerios Cereal Box with Action Figure Offer,**
1998. Movie action figures pictured on back of box. - **$2 $4 $10**

## Lucille Ball

**Lucille Ball (1911-1989) developed the character of the wacky housewife on radio in *My Favorite Husband*, which ran for three years (1948-1951) on CBS, sponsored by General Foods. But it was on CBS television that she became a comic star, first on *I Love Lucy* (1951-1957). The show, an instant hit, also featured Lucy's husband, Desi Arnaz, as bandleader Ricky Ricardo, and Vivian Vance and William Frawley as neighbors Ethel and Fred Mertz. The birth of little Ricky on the show in 1953--on the same night Lucille Ball was actually giving birth--was a major national event. A radio adaptation aired briefly in 1952, sponsored by Philip Morris cigarettes. Other television shows on CBS followed: *The Lucille Ball-Desi Arnaz Show* (1957-1959), *The Lucy Show* (1962-1968), *Here's Lucy* (1968-1974), and *Life With Lucy* on ABC in 1986. She received an Emmy Award as Best Comedy Actress for 1955, 1966 and 1967. Syndicated reruns are still being widely broadcast to this day.**

**Lucille Ball also appeared in a number of forgettable movies, including the title role in a disastrous *Mame* for Warner Bros. in 1974. Comic book versions of the television series include *I Love Lucy Comics* (1954-1962), *The Lucy Show* (1963-1964), and *I Love Lucy* (1990-1991). Licensed items are usually copyrighted Lucille Ball and Desi Arnaz or Desilu, the name of their production studio.**

LUC-1

LUC-2

❑ **LUC-1. Dixie Ice Cream Picture,**
c. 1940. - **$20 $40 $70**

❑ **LUC-2. Footwear 12x17" Countertop Display Sign,**
c. 1949. Summerettes Shoes by Ball-Band. Cardboard easel back with replica ad from Life magazine. - **$100 $200 $300**

LUC-3

❑ **LUC-3. "I Love Lucy" 3-D Picture Storybook,**
1953. Store item by 3 Dimension Publications Inc. 24-page photo magazine includes four pages printed in process for viewing by "Foto Magic 3-D Spex" eyeglasses.
With Glasses - **$100 $200 $300**
Without Glasses - **$75 $150 $250**

LUC-4

LUC-5

❑ **LUC-4. "TV Guide" Vol. 1 #1,**
April 3, 1953. First national issue with cover article "Lucy's Fifty Million Dollar Baby".
With label - **$200 $500 $1000**
No label - **$300 $750 $1500**

❑ **LUC-5. "TV Guide" Cover Article,**
1953. Weekly issue for July 17 with three-page article on Lucy and Desi movie "The Long-Long Trailer." - **$25 $60 $125**

LUC-6

LUC-7

❑ **LUC-6. "Philip Morris 1953 Football Schedule" Booklet,**
1953. Philip Morris Cigarettes. 3-3/4x6-1/2" booklet with 40 pages. Lucy is pictured on both the front cover and inside back cover. -
**$20 $40 $60**

❑ **LUC-7. Lucy & Desi Ad Postcard,**
1955. Pontiac Motors. - **$12 $20 $40**

LUC-8

LUC-9

❑ **LUC-8. "Pocket Encyclopedia Of Alaska" With Lucy/Desi Cover,**
1959. Westinghouse Corp. TV show sponsor folder opening to 20x25" featuring map and text about newly-admitted 49th state. - **$10 $20 $30**

❑ **LUC-9. "I Love Lucy" Cigarette Sponsor Display Card,** 1950s. Philip Morris Cigarettes. Cardboard hinge card for countertop or merchandise use with color photo lower half geared to Father's Day cigarette gifts. - **$75 $150 $275**

LUC-10

LUC-11

❑ **LUC-10. "Desi's Conga Drum",**
1950s. Store item by A&A American Metal Toy Co. Came with wooden beater. -
**$250 $475 $825**

❑ **LUC-11. "'I Love Lucy' Cupid" Boxed Squeeze Toy,**
1950s. Store item by Peter Puppet Playthings Inc. 9" tall colorful window box holds 7-1/2" tall molded soft rubber Cupid figure which squeaks. Side panel reads "Watch The Philip Morris 'I Love Lucy' Show On CBS."
Near Mint Boxed - **$550**
Doll Only - **$50 $100 $200**

LUC-12

LUC-13

❑ **LUC-12. "I Love Lucy" Doll With Apron,**
1950s. Store item. - **$150 $375 $575**

❑ **LUC-13. "How To Adjust And Service Your TV Set" Book,**
1950s. Store item by Popular Science Publishing Co. Inc. 6-1/2x9-1/4" with 160 pages. Lucy and Desi on cover but not in contents. - **$20 $40 $60**

LUC-14

LUC-15

❑ **LUC-14. "Lucille Ball Star-Cal" Pair Of Packaged Decals,**
1950s. Store item by The Meyercord Co. From a series picturing TV and movie personalities. Each - **$5 $10 $20**

❑ **LUC-15. "Lucy's Notebook",**
1950s. Philip Morris cigarettes. 40-page recipe booklet with Lucy/Desi photos. - **$20 $40 $60**

LUC-16

LUC-17

LUC-18

❑ **LUC-16. "Wildcat" Broadway Production 3" Cello. Button,**
c. 1961. For "Musical Smash Hit" at Alvin Theater. - **$20 $40 $60**

❑ **LUC-17. "Lucy Day" New York World's Fair 3-1/2" Cello. Button,**
1964. Macy's department store. Single day issue for August 31. - **$40 $80 $150**

❑ **LUC-18. "Lucy Day" New York World's Fair 3-1/2" Cello. Button,**
1964. Single day issue for August 31 event designated for "Press" representative. - **$40 $80 $150**

LUC-19

❑ **LUC-19. "Salesman's Opportunity Magazine" With Lucy Cover Article,**
1968. Trade publication has one-page article titled "Women Are Winners In Sales." - **$10 $20 $30**

LUC-20

❑ **LUC-20. "Home Painting And Color Guide,"**
1960s. Issued by Dupont. - **$10 $25 $40**

LUC-21

❑ **LUC-21. "Lucy" China Bust Bank,**
1998. - **$35**

## Lum and Abner

**For 22 years on various radio networks and for a long list of sponsors, Lum Edwards and Abner Peabody ran the Jot 'Em Down Store in the mythical town of Pine Ridge, Arkansas. The show was conceived by Chester Lauck and Norris Goff, boyhood friends in rural Arkansas who played not only the title roles but also most of the other characters in a continuing mixture of dialect comedy and rustic soap opera. The program premiered on Hot Springs station KTHS in 1931 and soon moved to Chicago and went national. Sponsors included Quaker Oats (1931), Ford automobiles (1933), Horlick's malted milk (1934-1938), Postum (1938-1940), Alka-Seltzer (1941-1948), and Frigidaire (1948-1949). The final broadcast was in 1953. (In 1936, in honor of the show, the town of Waters, Arkansas, officially changed its name to Pine Ridge).**

LUM-1

LUM-2

❑ **LUM-1. Horlick's Drink Mixer With Letter,**
1933. 6-1/2" tall glass and aluminum malted milk drink mixer prize with letter informing a contest winner. Letter - **$5 $15 $25**
Mixer - **$35 $70 $150**

❑ **LUM-2. "Pine Ridge News" Vol. 1 #1 Newspaper, November**
1933. Ford Motor Co. - **$25 $50 $80**

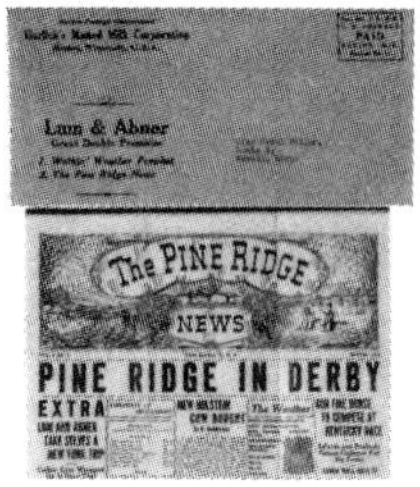


LUM-3

LUM-4

❑ **LUM-3. "The Pine Ridge News" Newspaper With Envelope,**
1936, Spring. Horlick's Malted Milk.
Near Mint In Mailer- **$75**
Loose - **$15 $25 $50**

❑ **LUM-4. "Lum And Abner's Almanac",**
1936. Horlick's Malted Milk. - **$5 $20 $40**

LUM-5

LUM-6

# LUM AND ABNER

❏ **LUM-5. Lum Edwards For President Cello. Button,**
1936. Horlick's Malted Milk. - **$10 $20 $30**

❏ **LUM-6. "Walkin' Weather Prophet" Brass Badge,**
1936. Horlick's Malted Milk. Litmus paper insert changes color with humidity but almost always inactive due to age. - **$10 $50 $85**

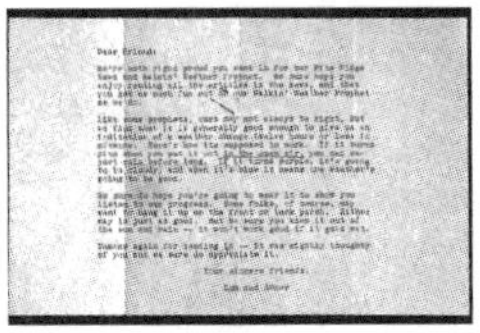

**LUM-7**

**LUM-8**

❏ **LUM-7. Letter,**
1936. Premium letter explains how the Weather Prophet Badge works.- **$5 $10 $15**

❏ **LUM-8. Glass Shake-Up Decanter With Aluminum Lid,**
c. 1936. For preparing Horlick's Malted Milk. Lid has pouring spout. - **$40 $75 $175**

**LUM-9**

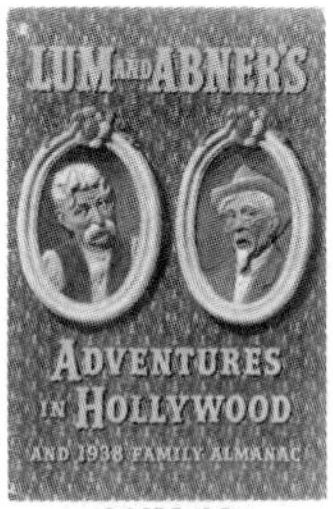


**LUM-10**

❏ **LUM-9. "Family Almanac",**
1937. Horlick's Malted Milk. - **$10 $25 $40**

❏ **LUM-10. "Lum And Abner's Family Almanac",**
1938. Horlick's Malted Milk. - **$10 $25 $40**

**LUM-11**

❏ **LUM-11. Postcard,**
1938. Shows Lum and Abner in and out of costume. Bottom card says "Mena, Arkansas Home of Lum and Abner." - **$10 $25 $40**

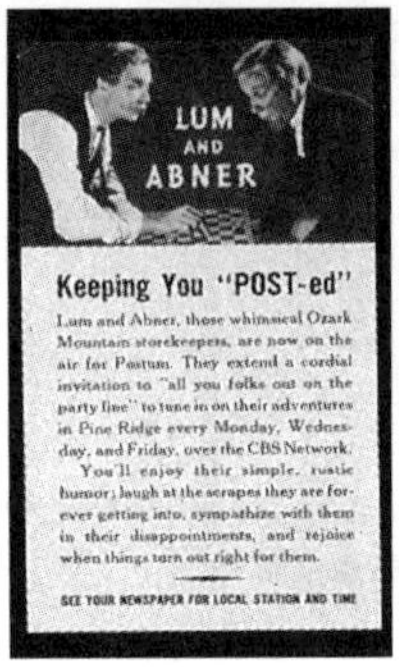


**LUM-12**

❏ **LUM-12. Promo,**
1930s. Postum Cereal. Promotes radio show.- **$10 $20 $30**

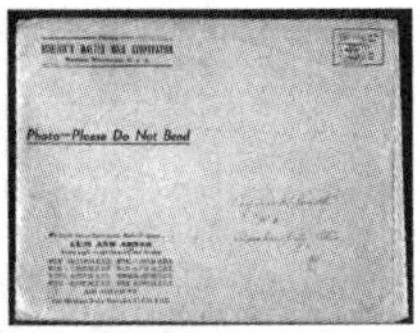


**LUM-13**

❏ **LUM-13. Mailer For Photo,**
1930s. Horlick's Malted Milk. - **$10 $20 $30**

**LUM-14**

**LUM-15**

❏ **LUM-14. Tour Book,**
1930s. Ten page premium. Gives a tour of the town. - **$15 $25 $35**

❏ **LUM-15. Fan Photo,**
1930s. 8x10" glossy b&w showing the characters in and out of costume and with facsimile signatures. - **$10 $20 $30**

**LUM-16**

**LUM-17**

❏ **LUM-16. Fan Photo,**
1930s. Inset photo of radio portrayers Chester Lauck and Norris Goff. - **$20 $35 $60**

❏ **LUM-17. Movie Postcard,**
1946. Various theaters. Announces upcoming movie "Partners In Time". - **$5 $20 $35**

**LUM-18**

❏ **LUM-18. Photo Card of Actors,**
1940s. Photo of radio portrayers Chester Lauck and Norris Goff without the usual character make-up. - **$8 $16 $32**

# Ma Perkins

**Beginning in 1933, Oxydol's own Ma Perkins solved her neighbors' problems and dished out her homespun philosophy from her lumber yard in Rushville Center for a total of 27 years. The program, first heard on Cincinnati radio station WLW, went national on NBC four months after its debut. From 1942 to 1948 it was broadcast on both the NBC and CBS networks, and from 1948 until it went off the air in 1960 it aired exclusively on CBS. Virginia Payne played the part of the widowed Ma for the entire run of over 7,000 episodes, and Procter & Gamble's Oxydol was the long-term sponsor.**

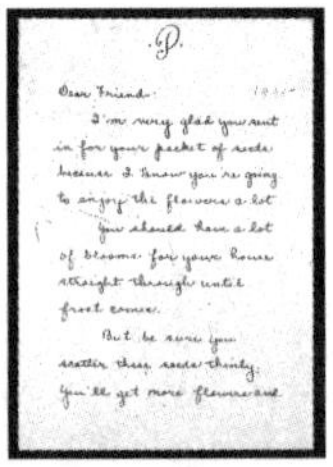

**MPK-1**

**MPK-2**

❏ **MPK-1. Garden Planner,**
1935. Oxydol. 3 pages. Letter came with flower seeds. Radio premium. - **$10 $25 $40**

❏ **MPK-2. Seeds and Mailer,**
1935. Oxydol.Cultivation instructions on packets. Radio premium. Seeds - **$5 $10 $25**
Mailer - **$5 $10 $25**

**MPK-3**

**MPK-4**

❑ **MPK-3. Oxydol Fan Photo,**
1930s. - **$12 $25 $35**

❑ **MPK-4. "Ma Perkins-Your Radio Friend" Photo,**
1930s. Oxydol. - **$8 $20 $30**

MPK-5

❑ **MPK-5. Seed Packs,**
1946. Oxydol. Zinnia, Morning Glory, Gourds and Sweet Alyssum. Each - **$10 $20 $30**

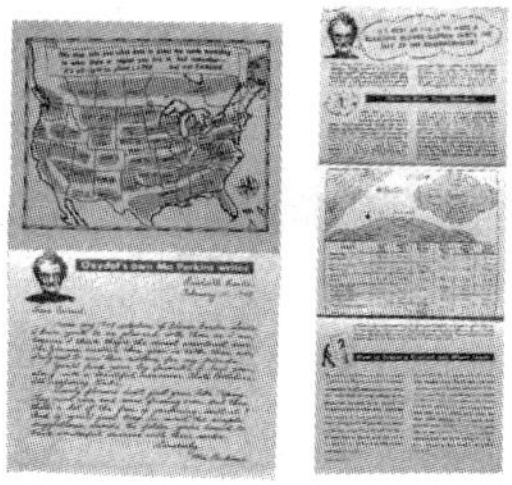

MPK-6

❑ **MPK-6. Garden Planner,**
1948. Oxydol. 6 pages. - **$10 $25 $40**

## *MAD Magazine*

**What started as an irreverent little comic book in August 1952 has grown into what was once the nation's leading humor magazine. Early issues, edited by Harvey Kurtzman, satirized popular comic strips with features such as *Little Orphan Melvin* and *Batboy and Rubin*. With issue #24 in 1955 publisher Bill Gaines changed the format from comic book to magazine. Alfred E. Neuman, a cartoon rendering of a 19th century icon, made his debut on the cover of issue #21 and has become the magazine's (What--Me Worry?) trademark. Annual issues of *More Trash from MAD* and *The Worst from MAD* appeared from 1958 to 1969, *MAD Follies* from 1963 to 1969, and *MAD Specials* from 1970 on. Licensed merchandise includes clothing, food products, games, trading cards, and greeting cards. *MAD TV*, a late-night comedy show, debuted on the Fox television network in October 1995. In 1997 *MAD* underwent an extensive editorial makeover with the addition of many new artists and writers. *Tales Calculated To Drive You MAD*, a limited series from DC Comics (now the publisher of *MAD*) reprinting *MAD*'s first 23 full-color issues in magazine format, ran for eight issues from 1997 to 1999.**

MAD-1

❑ **MAD-1. "Comfort Soap" Cello. Button,**
c. 1901. Very strong early character resemblance to later Alfred E. Neuman. -
**$200 $450 $950**

MAD-2

MAD-3

❑ **MAD-2. Birthday Card,**
c. 1930s. - **$50 $125 $200**

❑ **MAD-3. "Me Worry?" Cello. Button,**
1941. "Superior" unknown sponsor. -
**$100 $275 $450**

MAD-4

❑ **MAD-4. Get Well Card,**
c. 1940s. - **$25 $75 $125**

MAD-5

❑ **MAD-5. Robert Taft Presidential Hopeful Campaign Button,**
1952. 4" diameter with attached ribbon reading "Circus Saints And Sinners Jan. 25, 1952." Also issued without ribbon depicts character adopted a few years later as icon for MAD Magazine.
With Or Without Ribbon - **$100 $225 $350**

MAD-6

❑ **MAD-6. "EC Fan-Addict Club" Patch, Card And Bronze Badge,**
1953. Part of membership kit. Re-issue patch includes copyright symbol.
Original Patch - **$50 $150 $300**
Reissue Patch - **$25 $50 $75**
Card - **$50 $100 $150**
Badge - **$75 $200 $400**

(The Crypt-Keeper)

(The Vault-Keeper)

(The Old Witch)

MAD-7

❑ **MAD-7. "EC Fan-Addict Club" Kit Photographs,**
Early 1950s. Part of membership kit. Photos are posed by Johnny Craig.
Each - **$30 $60 $90**

MAD-8

❑ **MAD-8. "I Read MAD" T-Shirt,**
1958. Made by Champknit and first offered for sale on inside back cover of issue #39, May 1958. Reportedly three to four thousand were sold and now quite scarce. - **$200 $500 $800**

MAD-9

❑ **MAD-9. "Musically Mad" LP Album,**
1959. Issued by RCA. Monaural **- $10 $20 $30**
Stereo **- $15 $25 $40**

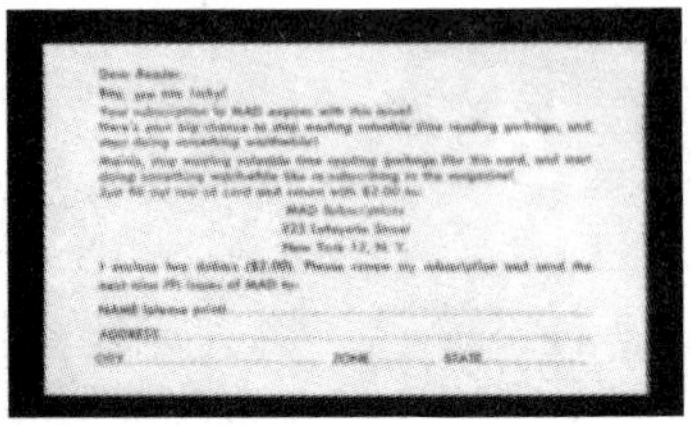

MAD-10

❑ **MAD-10. Subscription Card,**
1950s. **- $10 $15 $25**

MAD-11

❑ **MAD-11. "Me Worry??" Composition Bust Figure,**
c. 1960. Unlicensed. With Tag - **$75 $150 $250**
No Tag - **$50 $125 $200**

MAD-12

MAD-13

MAD-14

❑ **MAD-12. Figurine,**
1960. Glazed base with unglazed white bust to be painted by recipient.
Small 3-3/4" Size - **$75 $175 $300**
Large 5-1/2" Size - **$100 $250 $400**

❑ **MAD-13. "For President" 2-1/2" Cello. Button,**
1960. - **$30 $60 $100**

❑ **MAD-14. "What Me Worry" Adult-Sized Over The Head-Style Costume,**
1960. Collegeville. 25" wide by 50" tall.
Near Mint Carded - **$1500**
Uncarded - **$300 $600 $1000**

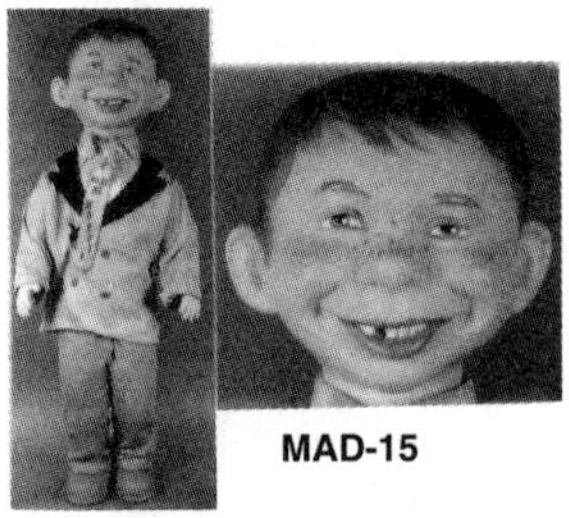

MAD-15

❑ **MAD-15. "What Me Worry?" Doll,**
1961. Unlicensed store item by Baby Barry. - **$350 $800 $1500**

MAD-16

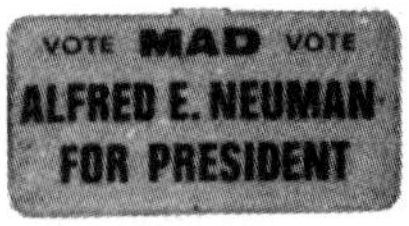


MAD-17

❑ **MAD-16. "For President" 2-1/2" Cello. Button,**
1964. - **$20 $40 $90**

❑ **MAD-17. "Alfred E. Neuman For President" Litho. Tin Tab,**
1964. - **$10 $15 $25**

MAD-18

❑ **MAD-18. "Alfred E. Neuman" Aurora Plastic Hobby Model Kit,**
1965. Store item. Boxed And Unbuilt - **$300**

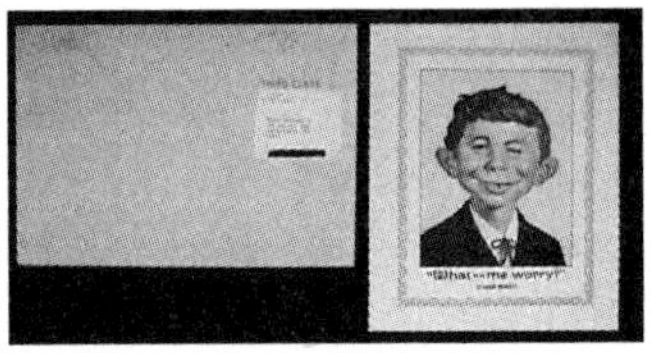

MAD-19

❑ **MAD-19. "What-Me Worry? I Read MAD!" Premium Picture,**
1960s. Full color 7x9".
Mailer - **$5 $10 $15**
Picture - **$15 $25 $40**

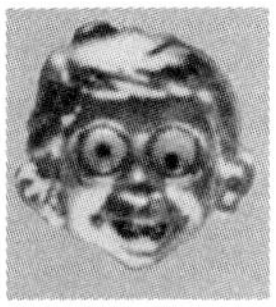

MAD-20

MAD-21

❑ **MAD-20. Alfred E. Neuman Plastic Portrait Pin,**
c. 1960s. Store item. Vending machine issue, unlicensed, marked "Hong Kong". - **$10 $25 $40**

❑ **MAD-21. "What Me Worry?" Dark Gold Luster Metal Necklace Pendant,**
c. 1960s. Store item. Depicts Alfred E. Neuman riding bomb. - **$40 $85 $150**

MAD-22

❑ **MAD-22. "Mad" Plastic Bookend Set,**
1970s. Issued in shrink wrap with five Mad paperbacks. Produced either in gold plastic with blue printing or red plastic with gold printing.
Set Without Books **- $15 $30 $60**

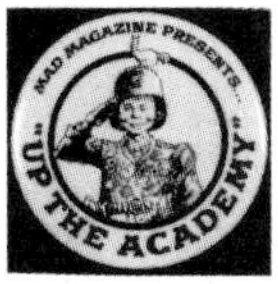


MAD-23

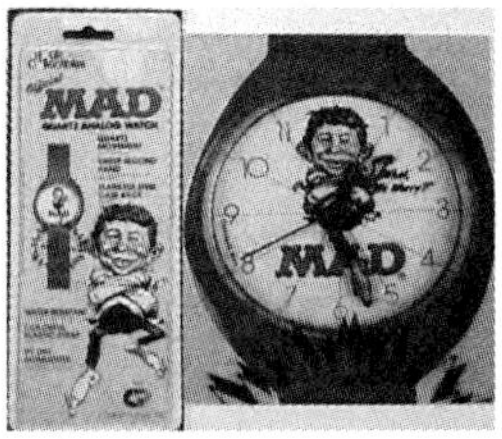


MAD-24

❑ **MAD-23. "Up the Academy" Movie Promotion 3" Cello Button,**
1980. Warner Brothers. MAD Magazine name was removed from the film after initial release but some versions now restore the full title and opening and closing cameo by a live-action Alfred E. Neuman. - **$8 $12 $20**

❑ **MAD-24. Official MAD 35th Anniversary Edition" Watch On Card,**
1987. Store item from E.C. Publications. Back of packaging shows three design varieties.
Near Mint Carded - **$25**

MAD-25

❑ **MAD-25. Magazine Subscription Promotion Buttons,**
1980s. E. C. Publishing Inc. Set of 24 cello. 1" pin-backs reproducing art from MAD Magazine covers 1950s-1980s. The set was used as a promotion for individuals who had subscribed to the magazine for 3 years. Each subscriber only received 3 pins. Many collectors did not know there were more than 3 styles. Rare to find in complete sets.
Complete set - **$250 $400 $600**
Each - **$10 $15 $25**

MAD-26

❑ **MAD-26. "What, Me Worry?" Pinback,**
1996. Alfred E. Neuman pictured. - **50¢ - $1**

MAD-27

MAD-28

❑ **MAD-27. Alfred E. Neuman Bobbing Head Figure,**
1999. With tag. - **$2 $5 $20**

❑ **MAD-28. Alfred E. Neuman Resin Statue,**
1990s. Limited to 900. Warner Bros. store exclusive. Boxed. - **$150**
During 1999, a second edition of the figure was produced. This version was slightly smaller and the "What--me worry?" slogan was printed using a different font and then pasted onto the base.
1999 Edition - **$75**

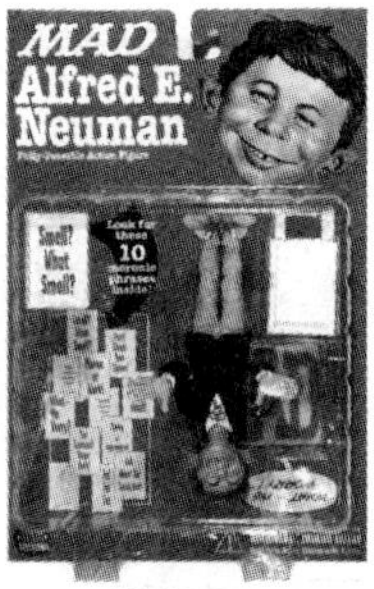


MAD-29

❑ **MAD-29. Poseable Action Figure,**
2000. On card - **$25**

MAD-30 (BOX)

❑ **MAD-30. "Alfred E. Neuman" Cookie Jar,**
2001. With box. - **$75**

MAD-31

MAD-32

❑ **MAD-31. Alfred E. Neuman as Batman Poseable Action Figure,**
2001. On card - **$20**

❑ **MAD-32. Alfred E. Neuman as Superman Poseable Action Figure,**
2001. On card - **$20**

## Major Bowes Original Amateur Hour

**Edward Bowes (1874-1946), a major in U.S. Army intelligence in World War I and a show-business veteran, introduced his amateur hour on New York radio station WHN in 1934. The following year, sponsored by Chase & Sanborn coffee, it aired on the NBC network, and from 1936 to 1946, sponsored by Chrysler automobiles, it was a Thursday night institution on CBS. 'Round and 'round she goes, and where she stops nobody knows--so went the wheel of fortune, each week drawing thousands of amateur performers looking for the big break. For most, it was a dream that didn't come true.**

MJB-1

MJB-2

❑ **MJB-1. First Fan Newsletter #1,**
1935. Chase & Sanborn Coffee. - **$15 $30 $50**

❑ **MJB-2. Second Fan Newsletter #2,**
1935. Chase & Sanborn Coffee. - **$12 $20 $30**

MJB-3

❑ **MJB-3. Fan Photo,**
1936. Chrysler Corp. Radio show title on back. - **$10 $15 $25**

MJB-4

MJB-5

❑ **MJB-4. "Major Bowes Amateur Parade" Photo Newsletter,**
June 1937. Chrysler Corp. - **$8 $25 $40**

❑ **MJB-5. Gong Alarm Clock,**
c. 1930s. Made by Ingersoll. - **$75 $150 $275**

MJB-6

MJB-7

❑ **MJB-6. Home Broadcasting Microphone With Box,**
1930s. Store item by Pilgrim Electric Corp. Metal actual working device for household radio set.
Boxed - **$100 $300 $400**
Loose - **$50 $175 $250**

❑ **MJB-7. Major Bowes Gong With Hammer Clasp,**
1930s. Prize from radio show. Sterling Silver. - **$50 $100 $150**

MJB-8

❑ **MJB-8. "Capitol Theatre Family" Fan Photo Card,**
1930s. Pictures Capitol Radio orchestra of radio broadcasts. - **$5 $12 $20**

MJB-9

❑ **MJB-9. Fan Postcards,**
1930s. Each - **$5 $8 $12**

## Major Jet

**A mid-1950s character created to promote Sugar Jets cereal of General Mills, Major Jet was an otherwise unidentified individual although always appearing in his jet-age flight helmet snappily accented by voltage bolt symbols centered by a "J" symbol denoting speed. His resemblance to an established comic strip jetting hero of the era, Milton Caniff's *Steve Canyon*, may have been more than coincidental. Actor Roger Pace portrayed Major Jet in TV commercials. His motto, "Jet Up And Go With Sugar Jets," accompanied premium offer--notably a mail premium Rocket-Glider kit of styrofoam and plastic but "made for high, jet-speed flying." The Rocket-Glider was offered by a May 1, 1955 Sunday comic section ad "while supplies last" and probably by cereal box as well.**

MAJ-1

❑ **MAJ-1. Magic Paint Set Booklet,**
1954. Sugar Jets cereal. #1 from set of three.
Each - **$8 $15 $25**

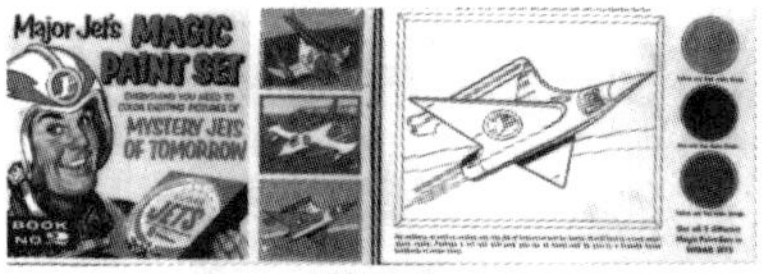


MAJ-2

❑ **MAJ-2. "Magic Paint Set" Book #2,**
1954. Sugar Jets cereal. From set of three.
Each - **$8 $15 $25**

MAJ-3

❑ **MAJ-3."Magic Paint Set" Book No. 3,**
1954. Sugar Jets Cereal. From set of three. - **$8 $15 $25**

MAJ-4

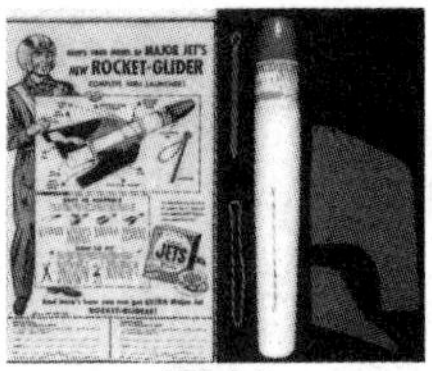


MAJ-5

❑ **MAJ-4. Sugar Jets "Filmo Vision" Box Back,**
1954. Cut-out parts for assembly of spaceship viewer for watching two cut-out films. Uncut Back - **$10 $20 $30**

❑ **MAJ-5. Rocket-Glider With Launcher,**
1955. Sugar Jets cereal.
Near Mint Boxed - **$50**
Loose - **$10 $15 $20**

MAJ-6

❑ **MAJ-6. Sugar Jets Cereal Box with Decoder,**
1955. On the front of the box is a Major Jet decoder which could be punched out and used to solve puzzles and comics on back. Rare.
Uncut Box with Decoder - **$50 $100 $200**

## Man From U.N.C.L.E.

**An admitted intentional television spoof of James Bond movies, *The Man From U.N.C.L.E.* was first telecast on September 22, 1964, continuing weekly on NBC until the death-gasp final episode on January 15, 1968. During those 3 and a half years, the U.N.C.L.E. (United Network Command for Law and Enforcement) team battled the persistent ne'er-do-well plots of the international crime syndicate known as THRUSH. U.N.C.L.E. was headed by Alexander Waverly (Leo G. Carroll), whose singular function was to hand out assignments and follow them up from the security of his secret office somewhere in New York City.**

**Assignments were doled out to agents Napoleon Solo (Robert Vaughn) and Ilya**

Kuryakin (David McCallum). Episodes were generally titled "The [specific name] Affair." Agent Solo was a borrowed name from the Bond movie *Goldfinger*. Solo and Kuryakin defeated THRUSH efforts through ingenuity, exotic weaponry and gadgets, and often with the aid of ordinary citizens.

The hour-long show spawned a one season spin-off series, *The Girl From U.N.C.L.E.* (September 13, 1966-August 29, 1967), starring Stefanie Powers in the title role of April Dancer. Her efforts were also directed by Mr. Waverly, but sans Solo and Kuryakin. The original U.N.C.L.E. series managed to make it into the Nielsen Top 20 only once, during its second season, but maintained a cadre of viewers to the end. The end was possibly due in part to NBC's numerous changes in evenings and time slots throughout the run of the series.

Vaughn and McCallum reunited for a 1983 made-for-TV movie, *The Return of the Man From U.N.C.L.E.*, on CBS. The movie also featured an amusing cameo by one-time James Bond, George Lazenby.

*The Man From U.N.C.L.E.* generated a surprising quantity of merchandise in comparison to other shows of higher-rated viewership in that era. *The Girl From U.N.C.L.E.* generated less due to its brevity.

MFU-1

❑ **MFU-1. "Theme From The Man From U.N.C.L.E." Autographed Sheet Music ,**
1964. Hastings Music Corp. M-G-M. Signed by Robert Vaughan. Near Mint Autographed **- $60**
Unsigned **- $10 $20 $30**

MFU-2

❑ **MFU-2. "The Man From U.N.C.L.E. Card Game,"**
1965. Milton Bradley. **- $15 $30 $75**

MFU-3

❑ **MFU-3. Man From U.N.C.L.E. Membership Kit,**
1965. Premium, sponsor unknown.
Instructions **- $10 $20 $30**
Card **- $15 $30 $50**
Photo **- $20 $40 $75**

MFU-4

❑ **MFU-4. Man From U.N.C.L.E. Illya Kuryakin Action Figure**
1965. Stands 12 1/4" tall with metal gun, metal gun holder, paper badge, club card and instructions. Boxed **- $350**

MFU-5

❑ **MFU-5. Man From U.N.C.L.E. Plastic Badge,**
1965. Store item that came with various sets by Ideal Toy Corp. **- $10 $20 $40**

MFU-6

❑ **MFU-6. Napoleon Solo Gun in Box,**
1965. Boxed with instructions. Box is rare. **- $750 $1500 $2000**

MFU-7

❑ **MFU-7. "The Man From U.N.C.L.E." Badge On Card,**
1965. Store item by Lone Star, England.
Near Mint Carded **- $75**
Badge Only **- $10 $25 $40**

MFU-8

❑ **MFU-8. "The Man From U.N.C.L.E. Playing Cards" Display Box With Deck,**
1965. Store item by Ed-U-Cards. Box is scarce.
Box **- $25 $50 $85**
Complete Cards **- $10 $20 $40**

MFU-9

❑ **MFU-9. "The Man From U.N.C.L.E." Board Game,**
1965. Ideal Toy Corporation. Rare in high grade. **- $40 $120 $480**

MFU-10

❑ **MFU-10. "The Man From U.N.C.L.E." Credentials and Secret Message Sender,**
1965. On card. - **$50 $100 $150**

MFU-11

MFU-12

❑ **MFU-11. "Napoleon Solo" 3-1/2" Cello. Button,**
1965. Store item. From "The Man From U.N.C.L.E." - **$10 $15 $25**

❑ **MFU-12. "The Men From U.N.C.L.E." 6" Cello. Button,**
1966. - **$20 $30 $50**

MFU-13

MFU-14

❑ **MFU-13. "The Girl From U.N.C.L.E." English Gum Card Wrapper,**
c. 1966. Store item by A. & B.C. Chewing Gum Ltd. - **$10 $20 $40**

❑ **MFU-14. "U.N.C.L.E. Secret Agent" Wristwatch,**
1966. Store item by Bradley. - **$50 $110 $175**

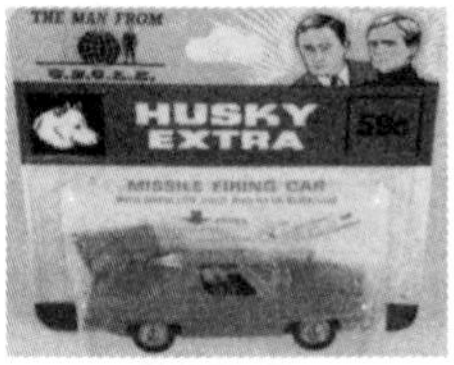


MFU-15

❑ **MFU-15. "The Man From U.N.C.L.E. Husky Extra" Die Cast Replica Car,**
1966. Carded - **$40 $75 $125**

MFU-16

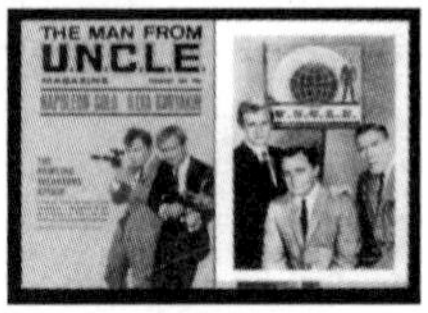


MFU-17

❑ **MFU-16. "The Man From U.N.C.L.E. Sweet Cigarettes" Candy Box,**
1966. English issue by Cadet Sweets. - **$50 $100 $135**

❑ **MFU-17. "The Man From U.N.C.L.E. Magazine" First Issue,**
1966. 144 pages. First Issue - **$20 $40 $65**
Other Issues - **$5 $10 $20**

MFU-18

MFU-19

❑ **MFU-18. "The Copenhagen Affair" Man From U.N.C.L.E. Paperback Book #3,**
1966. Ace Books. - **$5 $10 $20**

❑ **MFU-19. "The Vampire Affair" Man From U.N.C.L.E. Paperback Book #6,**
1966. Ace Books. - **$5 $10 $20**

MFU-20

MFU-21

❑ **MFU-20. "The Monster Wheel Affair" Man From U.N.C.L.E. Paperback Book #8,**
1967. - **$5 $10 $20**

❑ **MFU-21. "The Affair of the Gunrunners' Gold" Man From U.N.C.L.E. Hardcover Book,**
1967. 212 pages. - **$10 $20 $30**

# Mandrake the Magician

**Created by writer Lee Falk (1912-1999) and artist Phil Davis, Mandrake debuted as a daily comic strip in 1934 and as a Sunday page in 1935. Distributed by King Features, the adventures of the top-hatted magician with supernatural and hypnotic powers was an immediate success. Assisted by his faithful companion Lothar, an African king with enormous strength, and Princess Narda, Mandrake triumphed over earthly enemies and extraterrestrial invaders. He made his first comic book appearance in *King Comics* #1 in 1936 and has appeared in numerous collections in the decades since. Columbia Pictures released a 12-episode chapter play in 1939 with Warren Hull as Mandrake, and a syndicated radio series aired on the Mutual network from 1940 to 1942. A pilot made-for-TV movie was broadcast in 1979.**

MAN-1

MAN-2

❑ **MAN-1. "Member Mandrake's Magic Club" Litho. Button,**
1934. - **$50 $125 $225**

❑ **MAN-2. "Mandrake Magicians' Club/Taystee Bread" Enameled Brass Pin,**
1934. - **$30 $125 $200**

DEAR FRIEND—
I AM GLAD TO WELCOME YOU AS A MEMBER OF MY MAGICIAN'S CLUB FOR BOYS AND GIRLS. HERE IS YOUR OFFICIAL MEMBERSHIP CARD WITH SPACE PROVIDED FOR YOU TO PRINT YOUR NAME CLEARLY ON THE FRONT. ATTACHED TO THIS CARD IS A BEAUTIFUL CLUB BADGE WHICH I WANT YOU TO KEEP FOR YOUR VERY OWN. THIS IS VALUABLE SO GUARD IT CAREFULLY AND BE SURE IT IS SAFELY FASTENED ON YOUR COAT EVERY DAY. I AM ALSO PLACING IN THIS PACKAGE A SHEET OF MY SPECIAL MAGIC TRICKS FOR CLUB MEMBERS ONLY. I WANT TO REMIND YOU THAT ALL MAGICIANS OBSERVE A STRICT CODE OF HONOR. A MOST IMPORTANT RULE IS NEVER TO TELL ANY ONE WHO IS NOT A MEMBER OF THE CLUB, HOW TO DO THESE MAGIC TRICKS. PLEASE ALSO REMEMBER THAT IN JOINING MY

CLUB YOU GAVE ME YOUR WORD OF HONOR TO GET THREE LADIES TO TRY TAYSTEE BREAD FOR ONE WEEK. I AM COUNTING ON YOU TO KEEP THIS PLEDGE AND MAKE SURE, BY CHECKING THESE LADIES AGAIN AND AGAIN IF NECESSARY, THAT THEY DO GIVE TAYSTEE BREAD A FAIR ONE-WEEK TRAIL. OF COURSE EVERY LOYAL MEMBER OF MY MAGICIAN'S CLUB WILL WANT TO EAT TAYSTEE BREAD EVERY SINGLE DAY. BE SURE THAT YOUR MOTHER BUYS IT FOR YOU. I'LL HAVE MORE GOOD NEWS FOR YOU LATER—SO KEEP ON LISTENING TO MY RADIO PROGRAM EVERY MONDAY, WEDNESDAY, AND FRIDAY.

Sincerely your friend,

The secret sign of
MANDRAKE THE MAGICIAN

MAN-3

❑ **MAN-3. Club Kit Card,**
1934. Taystee Bread. Accompanied membership card and enameled brass member's pin. - **$35 $75 $125**

MAN-4

MAN-5

❑ **MAN-4. "Mandrake the Magician" Big Little Book #1167,**
1935. - **$15 $60 $110**

❑ **MAN-5. "Mandrake the Magician and the Midnight Monster" Better Little Book #1431,**
1939. - **$15 $60 $110**

MAN-6

MAN-7

❑ **MAN-6. "New Magic Tricks" Sheet,**
c. 1940. Taystee Bread and WOR (New York City). Sheet has earlier 1934 King Features copyright. - **$20 $50 $85**

❑ **MAN-7. "Mandrake the Magician Mighty Solver of Mysteries" Better Little Book #1454,**
1941. 432 pages. - **$15 $60 $110**

MAN-8

❑ **MAN-8. "Mandrake The Magician And The Flame Pearls" Better Little B ook,**
1946. Whitman #1418. - **$15 $40 $90**

MAN-9

MAN-10

❑ **MAN-9. Magic Kit Leaflet,**
1948. Suchard Chocolate Bars. Offers trick premiums with expiration date of January 31, 1949. - **$10 $15 $30**

❑ **MAN-10. Christmas Card,**
1950s. King Features Syndicate. From series featuring various syndicate characters. - **$10 $20 $40**

MAN-11

MAN-12

❑ **MAN-11. Plastic Gumball Charm,**
c. 1950s. Store item. Clear plastic with insert paper picture, from vending machine series. Second character on reverse. - **$8 $12 $20**

❑ **MAN-12. Boxed Game,**
1966. Store item by Transogram. - **$25 $60 $125**

MAJ-13

MAN-14

❑ **MAN-13. Mandrake Publisher's Response Card,**
1967. King Comics. 3-1/2x5-1/2" card with color portrait on front and blue text on back thanking writer for ideas and suggestions. - **$10 $20 $35**

❑ **MAN-14. Sponge,**
c. 1960s. Store item. - **$5 $12 $20**

## Marvel Comics

**Marvel began in 1939 with a firm known as Timely Publications operated by Martin Goodman who began publishing pulp magazines in 1932. Science fiction, western, crime and horror were steady sellers and Goodman became very astute at publishing and distribution. Superman had created quite a splash in 1938 and Goodman took notice. Funnies Inc. was a comic book shop, a business with artists, writers and editors who would produce comic books for others to publish. Their art director, Bill Everett, had created Prince Namor, The Sub-Mariner for another title and co-worker Carl Burgos came up with the Human Torch. Both characters made their debut in Goodman's *Marvel Comics* #1, October 1939. Martin Goodman was in the comic book business.**

**Joe Simon was Goodman's first editor and he and fellow artist Jack Kirby came up with *Captain America Comics*, the company's biggest seller. Super heroes waned in the 1950s but Goodman told editor Stan Lee that they should consider a revival in 1961. Shortly thereafter Jack Kirby's Fantastic Four appeared followed by Steve Ditko's Spider-Man, The Hulk, Daredevil and others. A risky venture into a new field in 1939 formed the foundation for what is today the best selling comic book company in the world.**

**Items in this section promote Marvel Comics in general and a variety of their superhero characters. Captain America, Spider-Man and the X-Men are in separate sections. Following the success of *The X-Men* motion picture and the build-up surrounding *Spider-Man*, *Blade 2*, *X-Men 2*, *The Incredible Hulk*, *Daredevil*, and other feature films, it can be expected that both the general Marvel category and the specific categories of their more notable heroes will continue to grow.**

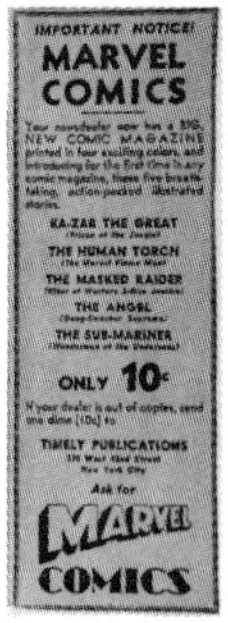

MAR-1

MAR-2

❑ **MAR-1. Newspaper Ad for 1st Issue of Marvel Comics,**
1939. Ka-Zar gets top billing in this ad for Marvel Comics #1. Notice it was called a magazine at the time. - **$100**

❑ **MAR-2. "Marvel Action Rings" Vending Machine Display Card,**
1966. Promotes set of 12 flicker rings and features Jack Kirby signed art. - **$40 $55 $75**

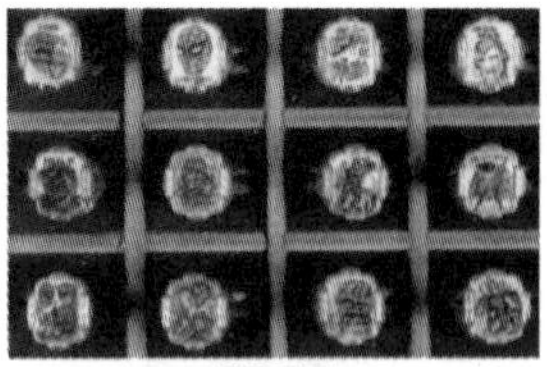
MAR-3

❑ **MAR-3. Vending Machine Flicker Rings,**
1966. Set of 12.
Each Silver or Gold Base - **$10 $18 $30**
Each Blue Base - **$8 $12 $20**

MAR-4

MAR-5

❑ **MAR-4. Marvel Pennant Iron Man,**
1966. 6 1/2" sold through comic books. -
**$10 $20 $40**

❑ **MAR-5. Marvel Pennant Thor,**
1966. 6 1/2" sold through comic book. -
**$10 $20 $40**

MAR-6

MAR-7

MAR-8

MAR-9

❑ **MAR-6. "The Avengers" 3-1/2" Cello. Button,**
1966. Store item. #10 from series.
Near Mint Bagged - **$50**
Loose - **$10 $15 $25**

❑ **MAR-7. "The Invincible Iron Man" 3-1/2" Cello. Button,**
1966. Store item. #7 from series.
Near Mint Bagged - **$50**
Loose - **$10 $15 $25**

❑ **MAR-8. "Sub-Mariner" 3-1/2" Cello. Button,**
1966. Store item. #8 from series.
Near Mint Bagged - **$50**
Loose - **$10 $15 $25**

❑ **MAR-9. "The Mighty Thor" 3-1/2" Cello. Button,**
1966. Store item. #9 from series.
Near Mint Bagged - **$50**
Loose - **$10 $15 $25**

MAR-10

❑ **MAR-10. "Merry Marvel Marching Society" Newsletter,**
1966. In addition to membership kit, member's received this mailing with first issue of "Merry Marvel Messenger" and a sheet for subscribing to various titles plus merchandise offers.
Mailer - **$5 $10 $20**
Newsletter - **$20 $40 $75**
Order Sheet - **$10 $20 $30**

MAR-11

MAR-13

MAR-12

❑ **MAR-11. "Daredevil" 3-1/2" Cello. Button,**
1966. Store item. #4 from numbered series.
Near Mint Bagged - **$50**
Loose - **$10 $15 $25**

❑ **MAR-12. "Mini-Books" Vending Machine Insert Paper,**
1966. Advertises tiny 1" tall, 48 page books for Captain America, Incredible Hulk, Millie the Model, Sgt. Fury, Spider-Man, Thor.
Insert Paper - **$8 $15 $30**
Each Book - **$5 $12 $35**

❑ **MAR-13. "The Incredible Hulk" 3-1/2" Cello. Button,**
1966. Store item. #5 from numbered series.
Near Mint Bagged - **$50**
Loose - **$10 $15 $25**

MAR-14

❑ **MAR-14. "Merry Marvel Marching Society" Membership Kit,**
1967. Envelope with letter, card, record, etc.
Complete Near Mint - **$350**
Each Paper Piece - **$15 $30 $85**
Record - **$10 $40 $85**

MAR-15

MAR-16

MAR-17

❑ **MAR-15. "Make Mine Marvel" 3-1/2" Cello. Button,**
1967. Issued with Marvel Marching Society club kit. - **$15 $35 $65**

❑ **MAR-16. Club Member 3" Cello. Button,**
1967. - **$10 $25 $50**

❑ **MAR-17. "Convention '75" 3" Cello. Button,**
1975. - **$10 $25 $45**

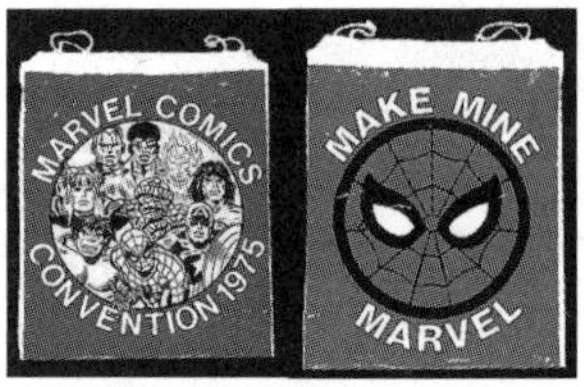


MAR-18

❑ **MAR-18. "Marvel Comics Convention" Shopping Bag,**
1975. 13x16" plastic bag with drawstring top given away at comic book collectors convention. -
**$3 $6 $15**

MAR-19

❑ **MAR-19. Marvel Super Heroes Ring Set,**
1977. Store or vending machine issue. Set of six. Each - **$3 $6 $10**

MAR-20

❑ **MAR-20. "7Eleven Marvel Comics Cup,"**
1977. Six cups, each 4-3/4" tall white plastic. Includes The Amazing Spider-Man, Captain America and The Falcon, The Mighty Thor, The Silver Surfer, Dr. Strange, The Incredible Hulk.
Each - **$2 $4 $8**

MAR-21

❑ **MAR-21. The Incredible Hulk Game with The Fantastic Four,**
1978. Milton Bradley. - **$15 $30 $60**

MAR-22

MAR-23

❑ **MAR-22. Cello. Button,**
1970s. 2" red and black on white. -
**$10 $20 $30**

❑ **MAR-23. Hulk Cloth Cover Football,**
1981. Marvel Comics Group. Mostly green with red and black highlights. - **$10 $25 $40**

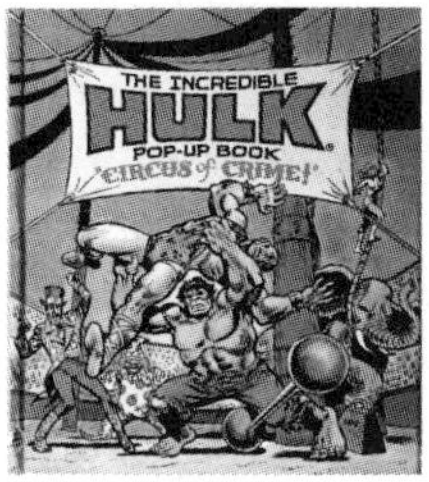


MAR-24

MAR-25

❑ **MAR-24. Hulk Pop-Up Book,**
1982. Hulk vs. Ringmaster. - **$10 $20 $35**

❑ **MAR-25. "Secret Wars" Decoder,**
1984. Secret messages set and hero shields. -
**$15 $35 $50**

MAR-26

❑ **MAR-26. "Marvel Super Heroes Secret Wars/Spider-Man" Radio System,**
1984. Three piece "Power Tronic" system by Nasta. Boxed - **$25 $50 $75**
UnBoxed - **$10 $20 $30**

MAR-27

MAR-28

❑ **MAR-27. "Avengers" Collector's Pin Set,**
1989. Six different on card. - **$25**

❑ **MAR-28. "The Punisher" Collector's Pin Set,**
1990s. Six different on card. - **$15**

MAR-29

MAR-30

❑ **MAR-29. "Disc Shooter Target Set,"**
1990. - **$5 $15 $30**

❑ **MAR-30. "Soft Darts Target Set,"**
1990. - **$5 $15 $30**

MAR-31

MAR-32

❑ **MAR-31. "Ball Blaster,"**
1990. - **$5 $15 $30**

❑ **MAR-32. "Sparkling Gun,"**
1991. - **$5 $15 $30**

MAR-33

❑ **MAR-33. "Flying Props" Toy Gun,**
1991. - **$5 $15 $30**

MAR-34

MAR-35

MAR-36

❑ **MAR-34. Hulk Mini-Gumball Machine,**
1996. Has bust figure on top. - **$5**

❑ **MAR-35. "Daredevil" Resin Statue,**
1998. Limited to 2,000. Sculpted by Randy Bowen. 14" tall including base. Miniature versions were released in 2001.
Yellow costume version - **$400**
Red costume version - **$250**

❑ **MAR-36. "Thor" Resin Statue,**
1999. Limited to 5,000. Sculpted by Randy Bowen. A miniature version was released in 2001. Boxed - **$400**

MAR-37

❑ **MAR-37. Avengers #1 Cover Figures Box Set,**
1999. Box contains six figures from the cover of the Avengers #1 comic, as well as flying ants. - **$25**

MAR-38

MAR-39

❑ **MAR-38. Hulk Lunch Box,**
1999. Circular format. One in a series of 3 different Marvel Lunch Boxes. - **$3 $10 $20**

❑ **MAR-39. Wonder Man Action Figure,**
1999. Comes with Avengers Ring. Figure lights up when you press his belt buckle. Animated Avengers series was cancelled after only a few airings, so these figures are hard to find on the secondary market. - **$15**

**MAR-40 MAR-41 MAR-42 MAR-43**

❑ **MAR-40. "Mole Man" Bust,**
1999. From Bowen Designs. - **$40**

❑ **MAR-41. "Scarlet Witch" Bust,**
1999. From Bowen Designs.
Limited to 5,000. - **$40**

❑ **MAR-42. "Hawkeye" Bust,**
2000. From Bowen Designs.
Limited to 5,000. - **$40**

❑ **MAR-43. "The Vision" Bust,**
2000. From Bowen Designs.
Limited to 5,000. - **$40**

**MAR-44**

**MAR-45**

❑ **MAR-44. "Iron Man" Statue,**
2000. Sculpted by Randy Bowen in two versions: gold color and grey color. Pose and base are identical for both versions. Limited to 2,000 in gold and 4,000 in grey. Each - **$140**

❑ **MAR-45. "The Thing" Statue,**
2000. Sculpted by Randy Bowen. Bases of the Fantastic Four statues are interlocking.
Limited to 4,000. - **$250**

**MAR-46**

❑ **MAR-46. "Dr. Doom" Statue,**
2000. Sculpted by Randy Bowen.
Limited to 5,000. - **$250**

**MAR-47**

**MAR-48**

❑ **MAR-47. "Black Widow" Statue,**
2001. Sculpted by Randy Bowen.
Limited to 4,000. - **$150**

❑ **MAR-48. "The Invisible Woman" Statue,**
2001. Sculpted by Randy Bowen.
Painted version, limited to 4,000, shown. - **$150**

**MAR-49**

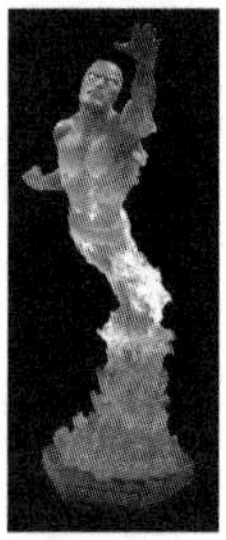

**MAR-50**

❑ **MAR-49. "Mr. Fantastic" Statue,**
2001. Sculpted by Randy Bowen.
Limited to 4,000. - **$150**

❑ **MAR-50. "The Human Torch" Statue,**
2001. Sculpted by Randy Bowen.
Limited to 4,000. - **$150**

**MAR-51**

**(With beard)**

**(Clean shaven)**

❑ **MAR-51. Thor "Change-O Head" Statue,**
2001. Has the basic body sculpt of the 1999 Randy Bowen figure. Statue has 2 interchangeable heads, one bearded and one shaven. Some costume details are different, and the rock base is a darker grey. Limited to 2,500. - **$200**

# McDonald's

**What began as a simple hamburger joint in southern California has become an international symbol of American initiative and drive. At last count there were more than 18,000 McDonald's fast-food restaurants in some 89 countries--the busiest of all in Pushkin Square, Moscow. It all started in 1937 when the McDonald brothers, Maurice and Richard, opened a small stand near Pasadena. Two years later they opened a second spot, fine-tuning their fast-food philosophy in a building with two yellow arches poking through the roof. A character called Speedee, with a hamburger for a head, courted drive-in customers atop another arch. Franchising the successful operation began in 1953, and Ray Kroc opened his first franchise in 1955. Six years later, with more than 200 stores licensed, Kroc bought out the entire operation. Speedee was retired in 1962 and replaced by the Ronald McDonald character in 1963. Other characters--Big Mac, the Hamburglar, Grimace, Mayor McCheese, Captain Crook, and the Professor--were introduced in the 1970s. Toys, games, premiums, licensed products, and promotional items continue to proliferate.**

**McD-1**

**McD-2**

❑ **McD-1. "Speedee" Litho. Button,**
c. 1955. Pictures trademark character used from beginnings until his retirement c. 1962. -
**$25 $60 $110**

❑ **McD-2. Cardboard Drive-In Punch-Out Sheet,**
c. 1962. Design intent of coin bank.
Unpunched - **$25 $50 $110**

**McD-3**

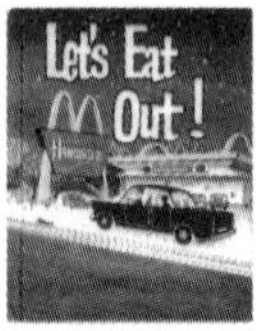


**McD-4**

❑ **McD-3. "Let's Go To McDonald's" Plastic/Tin Palm Puzzle,**
1964. Pictured is "Archie" serving character. -
**$20 $40 $80**

❑ **McD-4. "Let's Eat Out!" Storybook,**
1965. Issued for 10th anniversary, stiff covers. -
**$35 $75 $150**

McD-5

McD-6

❑ **McD-5. Philadelphia Area TV Show Cast Photo,**
1965. Pictures Gene London, Sally Starr, Lorenzo, Capt. Philadelphia, Bill Webber, Ronald McDonald, Happy the Clown, Rex Morgan. - **$15 $25 $50**

❑ **McD-6. "Ronald McDonald Goes To The Moon" Coloring Book,**
1967. Story and art about his victorious race to the moon against rival Mr. Muscle to establish a McDonald's restaurant there. - **$35 $65 $120**

McD-7

McD-8

❑ **McD-7. Premium Game Sheet,**
c. 1960s. Folded sheet 9x12" opens to 17-1/2x24" with nine numbered figures of Ronald to be cut out and used as game played blindfolded. Uncut - **$35 $75 $125**

❑ **McD-8. Ronald McDonald Christmas Record,**
1960s. Song "The Night Before Christmas" on both sides of 45 rpm record. - **$15 $25 $40**

McD-9

❑ **McD-9. Model Kit,**
c. late 1960s. Store item made by Life-Like Products (H.O. scale). - **$50 $125 $200**

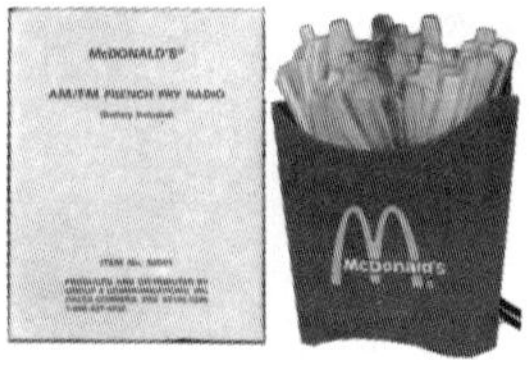
McD-10

❑ **McD-10. "McDonald's French Fry Radio,"**
1977. Near Mint Working **- $40**

McD-11

McD-12

❑ **McD-11. Captain Crook Bubble Boat,**
1979. Vacuum form plastic punch-out 2-1/2x2-1/2" toy that runs on baking powder. Near Mint Unassembled - **$75**
Assembled - **$10 $25 $50**

❑ **McD-12. Ronald Cloth Doll,**
1970s. First 1971 version designed with black zipper pull. Later 1970s versions have zipper design without pull.
First Style - **$8 $15 $35**
Later Style - **$5 $10 $15**

McD-13

❑ **McD-13. Ronald McDonald Bop Toy,**
1970s. 13" tall soft vinyl inflatable figure on 4-1/2" diameter base. - **$5 $15 $25**

McD-14

McD-15

❑ **McD-14. "Big Mac" Radio,**
1970s. Red plastic replica of hamburger carton 4x4x2-1/2" deep. - **$15 $25 $40**

❑ **McD-15. Ronald Wristwatch,**
1970s. - **$15 $35 $75**

McD-16

McD-17

❑ **McD-16. Ronald Litho. Tin Tab,**
c. 1970s. - **$3 $8 $15**

❑ **McD-17. Mayor McCheese Litho. Tin Tab,**
c. 1970s. - **$3 $8 $15**

McD-18

McD-19

❑ **McD-18. Employee Doll,**
c. 1970s. Jointed vinyl 11" doll in brown uniform. - **$20 $35 $50**

❑ **McD-19. Ronald McDonald Doll,**
1970s. With zip-up uniform. - **$10 $20 $40**

McD-20

McD-21

McD-22

❑ **McD-2. Employees Glasses Promotion 3-1/2" Cello. Button,**
c. 1970s. McDonald's and Coca-Cola Canadian issue. - **$8 $12 $20**

❑ **McD-21. Captain Crook Orange Vinyl Ring,**
c. 1980. - **$5 $7 $10**

❑ **McD-22. Big Mac Yellow Vinyl Ring,**
c. 1980. - **$5 $7 $10**

McD-23

McD-24

❑ **McD-23. Grimace Purple Vinyl Ring,**
c. 1980. - **$5 $7 $10**

❑ **McD-214. "Ronald McDonald" Alarm Clock,**
c. 1983. 6" tall metal. - **$40 $75 $125**

**McD-25**

**McD-26**

❑ **McD-25. Hamburglar Plastic Siren Whistle,**
1986. - **$5 $8 $12**

❑ **McD-26. Manager's Promotional Hamburgler Clock,**
1980s. 9x12". - **$40 $75 $125**

# Melvin Purvis

**The story of FBI agent Melvin Purvis (1903-1960) is a mixture of fact and legend. Purvis, a South Carolina lawyer, joined the FBI in 1927 and chased minor criminals in Texas and Oklahoma, eventually ending up in the Bureau's Chicago office. In 1934, with the help of a "woman in red," Purvis and other agents ambushed and killed the notorious John Dillinger as he left the Biograph movie theater in Chicago. Three months later Purvis, again acting on a tip, led a raid on an Ohio farm that ended in the killing of Pretty Boy Floyd. Purvis left the FBI in 1935, wrote a book about his experiences, and worked in law and broadcasting. In 1960, in poor health, he committed suicide.**

**As the embodiment of law and order and the implacable enemy of criminals, Purvis was heavily promoted in the 1930s by Post cereals in newspapers, on cereal boxes, and in magazine advertising. His *Junior G-Man Corps* and *Law and Order Patrol* enlisted kids by the thousands with a profusion of premiums--a variety of badges, ID cards, rings, flashlights, knives, fingerprint kits, manuals, pen and pencil sets, even separate badges for members of the Girls Division. Dale Robertson played Purvis in a 1974 television movie.**

**MLV-1**

❑ **MLV-1. Premium Photo,**
1936. Rare. - **$25 $50 $110**

**MLV-2**

❑ **MLV-2. "Melvin Purvis Secret Operator Fingerprint Set",**
1936. Made by New York Toy & Game Co. Used as a premium by various sponsors and was also likely a store item. Back cover of booklet offers "G-Men Club" membership in club sponsored by G-Men pulp magazine.
Version With Purvis Name - **$35 $110 $165**
Without Purvis Name - **$20 $50 $85**

**MLV-3**

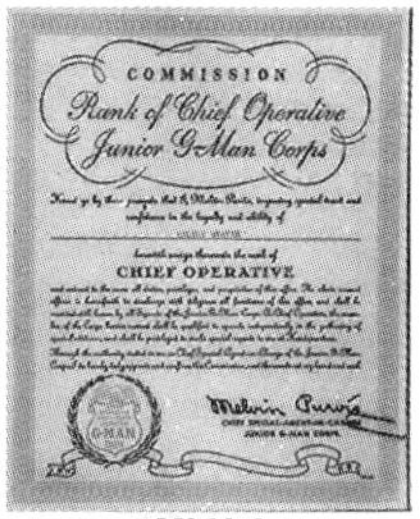


**MLV-4**

❑ **MLV-3. Club Manual Of Instructions,**
1936. - **$20 $35 $60**

❑ **MLV-4. Junior G-Man Corps "Chief Operative" Certificate,**
1936. - **$75 $150 $325**

**MLV-5**

**MLV-6**

❑ **MLV-5. Premium Folder,**
1936. - **$15 $40 $75**

❑ **MLV-6. "Junior G-Man Corps" Brass Badge,**
1936. - **$15 $30 $60**

**MLV-7**

**MLV-8**

**MLV-9**

❑ **MLV-7. "Roving Operative" Brass Badge,**
1936. - **$20 $45 $90**

❑ **MLV-8. "Chief Operative" Brass Shield Badge,**
1936. - **$20 $45 $90**

❑ **MLV-9. "Girls Division" Brass Club Badge,**
1936. - **$15 $40 $75**

**MLV-10**

**MLV-11**

❑ **MLV-10. "Melvin Purvis Junior G-Man Corps" Brass Ring,**
1936. - **$30 $60 $100**

❑ **MLV-11. "Special Agent" Metal Flashlight Gun,**
1936. Battery operated. - **$60 $150 $225**

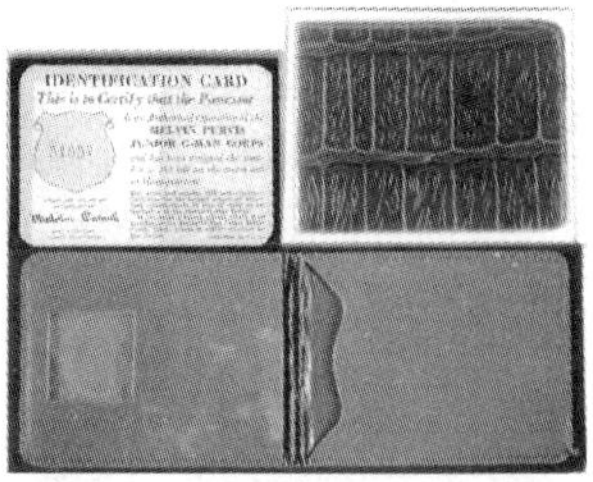


**MLV-12**

❑ **MLV-12. "Junior G-Man Corps" Member Card In Leather Wallet,**
1936. Wallet - **$30 $75 $140**
Card - **$15 $40 $75**

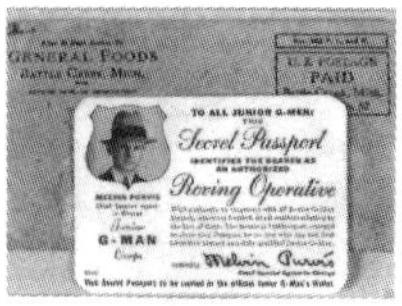


**MLV-13**

**MLV-14**

❑ **MLV-13. "Junior G-Men Secret Passport",**
1936. Envelope - **$5 $15 $30**
Card - **$20 $75 $100**

❑ **MLV-14. Junior G-Men Fingerprint Set With Mailer Envelope,**
1936. Cardboard folder containing fingerprint powder, ink pad, instruction booklet.
Mailer - **$10 $20 $30**
Set - **$35 $110 $165**

**MLV-15**

❑ **MLV-15. Wood Pencil With "G-Man" Metal Clip,**
c. 1936. Scarce. No Purvis markings.
Pencil - **$20 $50 $75**
Clip - **$20 $50 $75**

**MLV-16**

**MLV-17**

❑ **MLV-16. "G-Men" Brass Watch Fob,**
c. 1936. Unmarked for Purvis but pictured in his premium catalogues. Came with unmarked dark brown leather strap.
Fob Only - **$25 $50 $90**
With Correct Strap - **$50 $100 $250**

❑ **MLV-17. Club Manual,**
1937. Pictures 33 premiums. - **$15 $30 $75**

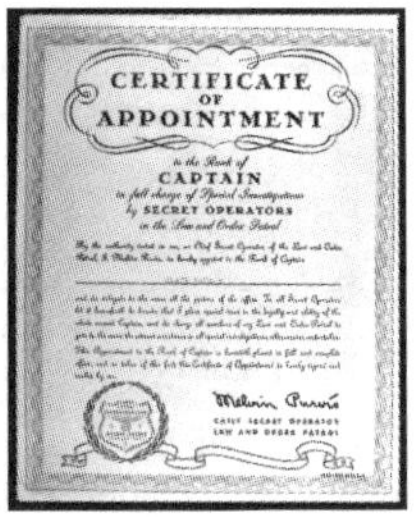

**MLV-18**

❑ **MLV-18. "Certificate of Appointment" with Mailer,**
1937. Rank of Captain. Rare. - **$125 $250 $425**

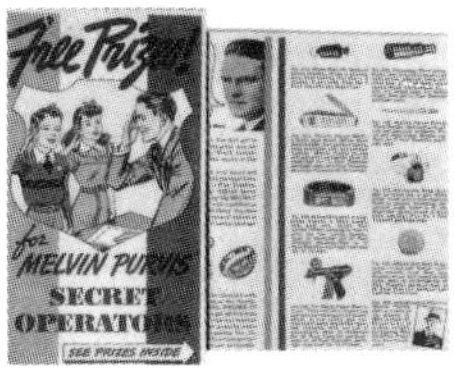

**MLV-19**

**MLV-20**

❑ **MLV-19. Premium Catalogue Folder Sheet,**
1937. Pictures 12 premiums. - **$15 $30 $50**

❑ **MLV-20. Scarab Ring,**
1937. Scarab in green. Also issued for Captain Frank Hawks. - **$300 $600 $1400**

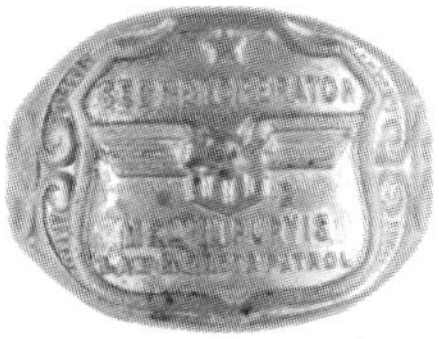
**MLV-21**

**MLV-22**

❑ **MLV-21. Secret Operator/Law & Order Patrol Brass Ring,**
1937. - **$75 $125 $175**

❑ **MLV-22. "Secret Operator" Brass Badge,**
1937. - **$20 $40 $80**

**MLV-23**

**MLV-24**

❑ **MLV-23. "Lieutenant" Brass Rank Badge,**
1937. - **$20 $40 $90**

❑ **MLV-24. "Captain" Brass Rank Badge,**
1937. - **$25 $50 $100**

**MLV-25**

❑ **MLV-25. "Secret Operator/Girls Division" Brass Badge,**
1937. - **$20 $60 $125**

**MLV-26**

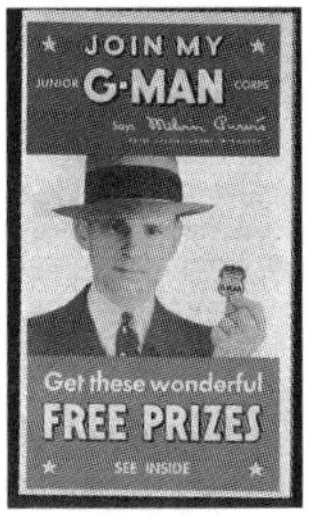

**MLV-27**

❑ **MLV-26. "Secret Operator" Grained Leather Wallet,**
1937. Inside has two slot pockets and small note pad. - **$35 $75 $150**

❑ **MLV-27. Prize Folder,**
1937. Junior G-Man premium folder. 4 pages. - **$25 $50 $85**

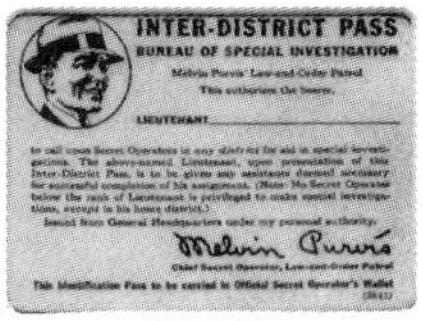

**MLV-28**

❑ **MLV-28. "Inter-District Pass" Club Card,**
1937. - **$20 $50 $100**

**MLV-29**

(CAP ON)

(CAP OFF)

**MLV-30**

❑ **MLV-29. "Melvin Purvis Official Secret Operator Pencil",**
1937. Scarce. 5-1/2" bakelite mechanical pencil with inscription plus portrait. - **$200 $400 $600**

❑ **MLV-30. "Melvin Purvis Official Secret Operator Combination" Bakelite Pen/Mechanical Pencil,**
1937. Rare. - **$200 $450 $800**

**MLV-31**

(Gun box)

(Front view)

❑ **MLV-31. "G-Man Squad" Gun,**
1937. Rare premium offered in the 1937 Junior G-Man Corps Prize Booklet by Post Toasties. You had to send in 69 Post Toasties box tops, or 36 Post Toasties box tops plus 50¢ in stamps or money order. Gun is 23" long and made of tin with a wood handle. Metal finish is red, yellow and black. This item was the hardest premium to get in all the offers presented by Melvin Purvis Chief Special Agent in charge. Made by Louis Marx & Co. Also sold in stores.
Gun - **$250 $500 $750**
Box for Gun - **$50 $75 $100**

MLV-32

MLV-33

❑ **MLV-32. "Secret Operator" Pocketknife,**
1937. Steel with cello. grips. Pictured in premium catalogue for Secret Operators. - **$50 $150 $300**

❑ **MLV-33. G-Man Tin Whistle,**
1930s. No Purvis markings. - **$20 $50 $90**

## Mickey Mantle

**Oklahoma-born Mickey Mantle (1931-1995) joined the New York Yankees in 1951 and soon succeeded Joe DiMaggio in center field. A powerful switch-hitter, Mantle hit 536 home runs in his 18 seasons with the team. The Mick won the Triple Crown in 1956, was voted the American League's Most Valuable Player in 1956, 1957, and 1962, and played in every All-Star game between 1951 and 1968, when he retired. He was elected to the Baseball Hall of Fame in 1974. One of the most popular athletes of his time, Mantle slugged his way into the hearts of sports fans everywhere.**

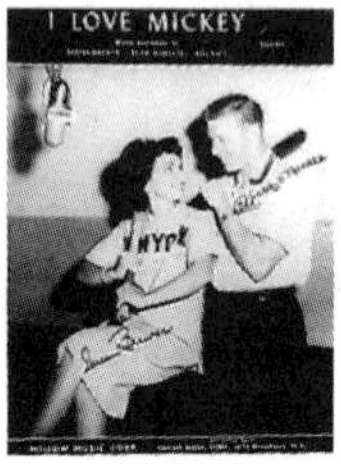


MKM-1

❑ **MKM-1. "I Love Mickey" Sheet Music,**
1956. Words and music for fan song popularized by songstress Teresa Brewer. - **$20 $40 $75**

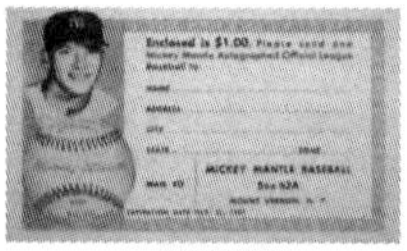

MKM-2

MKM-3

❑ **MKM-2. Baseball Offer Coupon,**
1957. Issuer unknown. 3x4-3/4" black and white coupon offering "Autographed Official League Ball" for $1.00. - **$20 $40 $70**

❑ **MKM-3. "Boys' Life" Cover Article,**
1959. Monthly issue for August with color photos cover for article "Star Of The Stadium" with 11 more photos. - **$10 $20 $50**

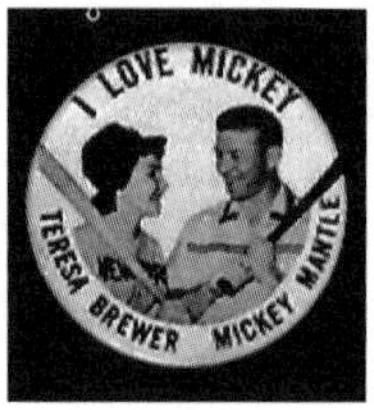


MKM-4

MKM-5

❑ **MKM-4. "I Love Mickey" Cello. Button,**
1950s. Promotion for tribute song to Mickey Mantle inspired and sung by songstress Teresa Brewer. - **$25 $70 $125**

❑ **MKM-5. Pale Blue Background 3-1/2" Button,**
1950s. Vendor button sold at stadiums. - **$15 $40 $75**

MKM-6

MKM-7

❑ **MKM-6. "Mickey Mantle" Cello. Button,**
1950s. Probable stadium souvenir with fabric ribbon and plastic charms. - **$40 $85 $160**

❑ **MKM-7. Mickey Mantle Cello. Button,**
1950s. Youthful photo image with attachments of fabric ribbon plus plastic charms on keychain. - **$75 $160 $275**

MKM-8

❑ **MKM-8. "Yoo-Hoo" Beverage Can,**
c. 1950s. Litho. metal 5-1/2" tall showing images on bottle caps of Yankees Skowron, Mantle, Berra, Kubek, Ford. - **$20 $50 $85**

MKM-9

MKM-10

❑ **MKM-9. Paper Decal,**
1950s. Issuer unknown. 3-1/2x4" full color positive image of Mantle as right-hand batter. Unused - **$15 $30 $50**

❑ **MKM-10. Mickey Mantle Official League Rawlings Baseball,**
c. 1950s. Issuer unknown but probable premium. - **$10 $20 $40**

MKM-11

❑ **MKM-11. "Playing Major League Baseball" Booklet,**
1950s. Karo Syrup. 6x9" with 32 pages including baseball tips attributed to Mickey Mantle plus similar tips from various other major league stars. - **$20 $40 $80**

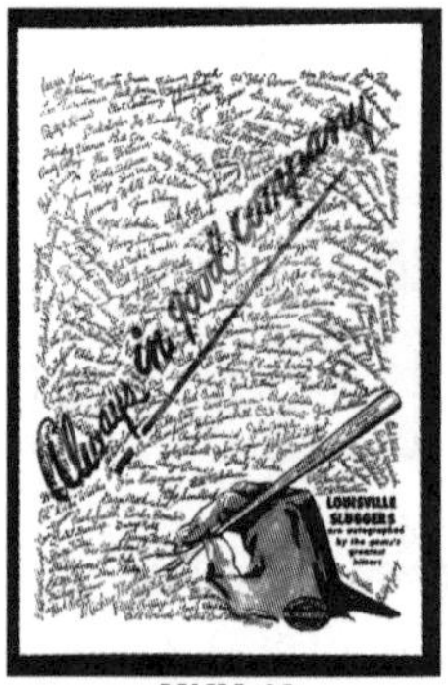


MKM-12

❑ **MKM-12. "Louisville Sluggers" 11x17" Paper Sign With Mantle And Others,**
1950s. Hillerich & Bradsby Co. Poster by bat maker company with facsimile signatures of dozens of well-known batters featuring "Mickey Mantle" signature on depicted baseball bat writing pen. - **$15 $30 $60**

MKM-13

❑ **MKM-13. Autographed Photo of Mantle, Pee Wee Reese and Duke Snider,**
1950s. Photo is 16 x 20". Mantle's signature is 5" long. - **$1200**

MKM-14

❑ **MKM-14. New York Yankees "World Champions" Photo Pennant,**
c. 1961. 28-1/2" wide. - **$20 $60 $90**

MKM-15

❑ **MKM-15. "Life" Magazine With Post Cereals Card Ad And Insert,**
1962. Weekly issue for April 13 with full page ad for cereal box cards plus example bound insert card picturing Mantle on one side and Roger Maris on other side.
Magazine With Insert Intact - **$25 $60 $100**

MKM-16

MKM-17

❑ **MKM-16. "Mickey Mantle" 3" Cello. Button,**
c. 1962. Full color photo with facsimile signature, image is 1955 Dormand postcard photo. - **$15 $30 $60**

❑ **MKM-17. Closeup Photo,**
1963. Phillies cigars. 6-1/2x9" black and white with facsimile signature. - **$15 $35 $60**

MKM-18

MKM-19

❑ **MKM-16. "The Baseball Life of Mickey Mantle" Paperback,**
1969. First printing. 176 pages. - **$20 $35 $50**

❑ **MKM-19. "All Star" Wristwatch With Mantle, Others,**
1960s. Store item. Dial face has facsimile signatures of Mickey Mantle, Roger Maris, Willie Mays. - **$50 $85 $175**

MKM-20

MKM-21

❑ **MKM-20. Mickey Mantle Guest Appearance Cello. Button,**
1982. For local mall visit in his retirement years. - **$5 $10 $20**

❑ **MKM-21. Mickey Mantle Personal Appearance Cello. Button,**
1982. For local mall visit in his retirement years. - **$5 $10 $20**

MKM-22

❑ **MKM-22. "Mickey Mantle" Hartland Statue With Box,**
1988. From 25th anniversary commemorative series. Near Mint Boxed - **$75**

MKM-23

❑ **MKM-23. "Mickey Mantle" Comic Book,**
1991. Magnum Comics. Features his life story. - **$3 $6 $18**

# Mickey Mouse

**Mickey Mouse has been called a legend, a national symbol, a worldwide celebrity, a work of art, a merchandising monarch, the successor to Charlie Chaplin, the keystone of the Walt Disney empire. Mickey's career took off in 1928 with *Steamboat Willie*, the first animated cartoon with synchronized sound. Ub Iwerks did the animation, Walt Disney did the voice of Mickey, and success was immediate.**

**Over the next 25 years the studio turned out some 120 cartoons starring Mickey. Supporting characters included Minnie Mouse, Pluto the Pup, Donald Duck, Goofy, Horace Horsecollar, and Clarabelle Cow. The Mickey daily comic strip, distributed by King Features, began in 1930 and the Sunday pages in 1932, scripted and drawn by Floyd Gottfredson for the next 45 years.**

**1930 also saw the first Mickey book published by Bibo and Lang followed by a continuing flood of magazines, collections, reprints, albums, specials, and hardbacks, along with feature appearances in other Disney books.**

**Mickey and his pals had a brief run on NBC radio in 1938, sponsored by Pepsodent toothpaste. *The Mickey Mouse Club*--the most popular afternoon children's network television series ever--was broadcast on ABC from 1955 to 1959, with reruns syndicated in 1962-1965, 1975-1976, and as *The New Mickey Mouse Club* in 1977-1978. The series, hosted by the Mouseketeers, was a mix of music, cartoons, serialized adventures, children's news features, and visits by guest celebrities. In 1995 *Runaway Brain*, the first Mickey cartoon short in more than 40 years, was released to theaters.**

**Mickey's popularity continues undiminished, as does the merchandising and licensing of Mickey Mouse items of all shapes and sizes.**

MCK-1

❑ **MCK-1. "Chief Mickey Mouse" 2-1/8" Cello. Button,** Copyright 1928-1930. High rank award from series of various officer ranks of Mickey Mouse Clubs organized in movie theaters. Copyright is by W. E. Disney. - **$650 $2000 $3000**

MCK-2

❑ **MCK-2. First "Mickey Mouse Book",**
1930. Published by Bibo & Lang, several printings. The first Disney publication, pages 9-10 often missing due to children cutting out game pieces. Complete - **$1200 $5400 $11000**
Missing Pages 9-10 - **$200 $800 $1500**

MCK-3

MCK-4

❑ **MCK-3. Movie Club Cello. Button,**
1930. Inscribed "Copy. 1928-1930 By W. E. Disney". - **$60 $110 $195**

❑ **MCK-4. "Mickey Mouse Club" Cello. Button,**
1930. 1928-1930 W. E. Disney copyright. - **$50 $100 $150**

MCK-5

MCK-6

❑ **MCK-5. "Meets Every Saturday" Club Member Cello. Button,**
1930. Standard image with 1930 Disney copyright and name on bottom edge but uncommon imprint. - **$75 $150 $250**

❑ **MCK-6. Mickey In Santa Outfit Cello. Button,**
c. 1930. Several imprints but usually "Meet Me At Hank's Toyland." - **$300 $600 $1300**

MCK-7

MCK-8

❑ **MCK-7. "Theme Song" Music Sheet,**
1930. Movie theater hand-out. Song title "Minnie's Yoo Hoo." - **$35 $75 $125**

❑ **MCK-8. "Mickey Mouse" Wood Jointed Figure,**
1930. Scarce. Store item. 4-1/2" tall with flat disk hands to allow balancing in various positions. - **$200 $450 $900**

MCK-9

❑ **MCK-9. "Mickey Mouse In Actual Motion Pictures" Flip Book,**
c. 1930. Movie Scope Corp. 1-3/4x2-1/2" captioned "Series A." - **$100 $225 $350**

MCK-10

❑ **MCK-10. Mickey Mouse Illustrated Movie Stories,**
1931. David McKay Co. Hardcover. Store item. 190 pages of black & white story pages with art taken from eleven of Mickey's earliest cartoons. 6-1/4x8-3/4."
With Dust Jacket. - **$400 $750 $1500**
Without Jacket. - **$250 $400 $850**
With 2" Red Wraparound Banner With Instructions add **$150**

MCK-11

❑ **MCK-11. First Newspaper Premium Picture Card,**
May 1931. Various newspapers. 3-1/2x5-1/2" b&w. - **$150 $425 $800**

MCK-12

❑ **MCK-12. Mickey Pendant With Chain,**
1931. Cohn and Rosenberger product. Black and green enameled pictured. Also comes in black with yellow. - **$50 $90 $150**

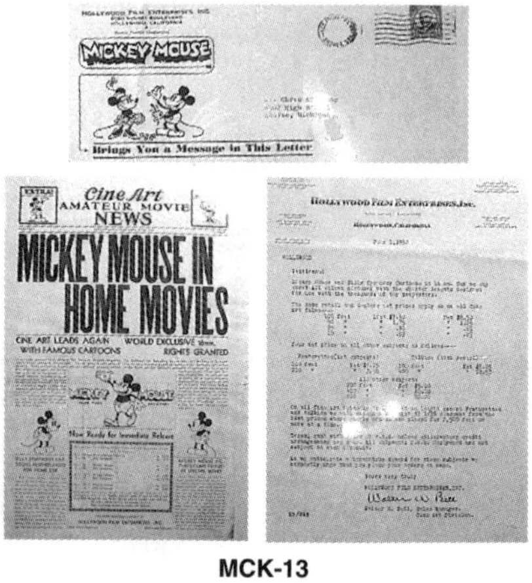


MCK-13

❑ **MCK-13. "Mickey Mouse In Home Movies" Dealer Promotion,**
1932. Hollywood Film Enterprises Inc. Envelope holds price lists for Mickey Mouse and Silly Symphony Cartoons in 16mm. Along with this is large sheet designed like a newspaper 12x18-1/2" inscribed "Volume 1/Number 1."
Envelope - **$15 $30 $50**
Price List - **$10 $20 $30**
Poster - **$75 $125 $250**

**MCK-14**

❑ **MCK-14. Puzzle Set,**
1933. Features the whole gang, except Donald who didn't arrive until the following year. Four different puzzles. Each - **$50 $80 $140**

**MCK-15**

❑ **MCK-15. Free Mask Store Sign,**
1933. Quaker Crackels 13"x22-1/2" in black white and red. **$100 $350 $650**

**MCK-16**

**MCK-17**

❑ **MCK-16. Mickey Mouse Paper Face Mask,**
1933. Store and theater give-away, published by Einson-Freeman Co. - **$25 $50 $80**

❑ **MCK-17. Minnie Mouse Paper Mask,**
1933. Store and theater give-away. - **$15 $25 $60**

**MCK-18**

❑ **MCK-18. "Mickey Mouse Magazine" V. 1 #1,**
January 1933. Rare #1. Various dairies, stores. "Published By Kamen-Blair, Inc." on front cover. Nine issues, first few had 5 cents on cover.
First Issue - **$533 $2132 $5000**
Other Issues - **$218 $545 $1250**

**MCK-19**

❑ **MCK-19. Mickey Mouse Big Little Book,**
1933. #717, 1st of series. Gottfredson story and art. Scarce in high grade. Two different covers were used. - **$120 $700 $1500**

(Cover) **MCK-20** (Back cover)

❑ **MCK-20. Mickey Mouse "The Mail Pilot" Big Little Book,**
1933. BLB #731. Cover picture is same as the 1st Mickey BLB, but with "The Mail Pilot" printed on front. Rare; only 1 known copy. 1933 cover was changed soon after. Lower left corner of back cover has small black box printed over the original BLB #717. The number 731 is printed next to it. Sold at auction in 2001 for **$5,090**.

**MCK-21**

❑ **MCK-21. Mickey Mouse, The Great Big Midget Book,**
1933. England version of 1st book. Scarce. - **$120 $600 $1300**

**MCK-22**

**MCK-23**

❑ **MCK-22. "Mickey Mouse Magazine",**
1933. #1 Rare. Various dairies, Nov. 1933-Oct. 1935. "Edited By Hal Horne" on cover.
1st Issue - **$240 $960 $1900**

❑ **MCK-23. "Mickey Mouse Magazine",**
1933. Various dairies, Nov. 1933-Oct. 1935.
Nos. 2-12 Each - **$80 $320 $650**

**MCK-24**

❑ **MCK-24. "Mickey Mouse Bubble Gum" Example Cards,**
1933. Gum Inc. #1-96 first series plus #97-120 titled "Mickey Mouse With The Movie Stars".
First Series Each - **$10 $20 $40**
Movie Stars Each - **$40 $90 $175**

**MCK-25**

❑ **MCK-25. Picture Card Album Vol. 1,**
1933. Mickey Mouse Bubble Gum. Has spaces for mounting the first 48 cards of the set.
Album Only - **$50 $150 $325**

**MCK-26**

❑ **MCK-26. Picture Card Album Vol. 2,**
1933. For cards #49-96. Volume 1 holds cards #1-48. Unused #2 - **$75 $150 $375**

**MCK-27**

**MCK-28**

❑ **MCK-27. "Mickey Mouse Bubble Gum" Waxed Paper Wrapper,**
1933. Store item, used for cards #1-96 of Gum Inc. card set. - **$60 $150 $220**

❑ **MCK-28. "Mickey Mouse With The Movie Stars" Gum Wrapper,**
1933. Gum Inc. Wrapper for cards #97-120. - **$150 $325 $625**

MCK-29

❑ **MCK-29.First Version Volume 1 "Picture Card Album,"** 1933. Mickey Mouse Bubble Gum. Briefly used for cards #1-48 and then replaced with cover featuring studio image of Mickey. Album Only - **$100 $250 $425**

MCK-30

❑ **MCK-30.German Mickey Mouse Figural Perfume Bottle,**
1933. 4-1/4" tall marked Germany on underside. Seen with foil sticker for Chicago's World's Fair. - **$150 $325 $600**

MCK-31

❑ **MCK-31. "Mickey Mouse Undies" Empty Box,**
c. 1933. 8-1/4x11-14/x2" deep. Nice graphics. - **$250 $425 $850**

MCK-32

MCK-33

❑ **MCK-32. "Mickey Mouse The Mail Pilot" BLB,**
1933. American Oil Co. Also used as Oxydol soap premium. Softcover version. - **$50 $150 $350**

❑ **MCK-33. Cello. Button 3-1/2",**
c. 1933. Worn by store employees. - **$300 $1250 $2500**

MCK-34

❑ **MCK-34. "Mickie Mouse Animal Crackers" Box,**
c. 1933. Rare. Apparent unauthorized item (or printing error) with misspelled name.
Near Mint Flat - **$1700**
Folded - **$200 $500 $1000**

MCK-35

❑ **MCK-35. "Micky Maus" 17x24" German Film Poster,**
1934. Rare. - **$500 $2500 $4000**

MCK-36

❑ **MCK-36."Mickey Mouse In Blaggard Castle" Big Little Book,**
1934. Whitman #726. - **$35 $85 $225**

MCK-37

❑ **MCK-37. Card Game,**
1934. Hoffman's Ice Cream. 24 cards. 8 page instruction sheet and box. - **$75 $150 $200**

MCK-38

❑ **MCK-38. Post Toasties Box,**
1934. Rare. Mickey pictured on front. Several versions.
Each Complete - **$750 $1800 $3000**

MCK-39

❑ **MCK-39. "Mickey Mouse and Minnie at Macy's" Big Little Book,**
1934. May be the rarest of all the premium type BLB's. Rarer than the 1935 version. - **$500 $1000 $2000**

MCK-40

❑ **MCK-40. "Mickey Mouse The Detective" Big Little Book,**
1934. Gottfredson art. 300 pages. -
**$25 $80 $175**

MCK-41

❑ **MCK-41. Post Toasties Box,**
1935. Scarce. Mickey pictured on front. Several versions. Each Complete - **$500 $1000 $2100**

MCK-42

❑ **MCK-42. First "Mickey Mouse Magazine" Vol. 1 #1,**
1935. Later became "Walt Disney's Comics & Stories". Kay Kamen Publications/Western Publishing Co., size 10-1/4x13-1/4". -
**$1120 $3360 $14500**

MCK-43

❑ **MCK-43. "USA Lite Mickey Mouse Battery,"**
c. 1935. 2-1/4" tall issued by United States Electric Mfg. Corp. **- $150 $300 $500**

MCK-44

❑ **MCK-44. "Mickey Mouse And The Magic Carpet" Book,**
1935. Various sponsors, and used as a Mickey Mouse Magazine premium as late as 1938. -
**$150 $300 $600**

MCK-45

❑ **MCK-45. "Mickey Mouse And Minnie March To Macy's" Booklet,**
1935. Rare. Macy's department store. Published by Whitman in format of Big Little Book. -
**$300 $750 $1500**

MCK-46

MCK-47

❑ **MCK-46. "Mickey Mouse Hose" Cello. Button,**
c. 1935. - **$50 $110 $200**

❑ **MCK-47. Litho. Button,**
c. 1935. Comes with back paper reading "Mickey Mouse Gloves And Mittens". -
**$75 $150 $375**

MCK-48

❑ **MCK-48. "A Handful Of Fun" Premium Booklet,**
c. 1935. Issued by Eisendrath Glove Co. 5-1/4x7-3/4" diecut with 12 pages. Rare**. -**
**$500 $1000 $2000**

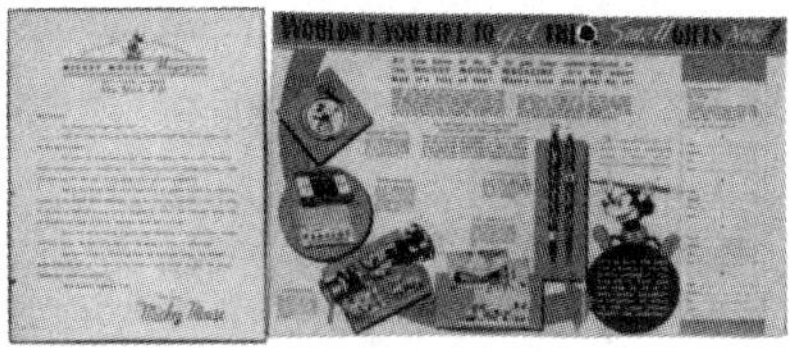
MCK-49

❑ **MCK-49. "Mickey Mouse Magazine" Contest Winner Folder,**
1935. 8-1/4x10-3/4" relating to premium contest in third issue of magazine**. - $200 $400 $600**

MCK-50

❑ **MCK-50. "Mickey Mouse Hoop-La Game,"**
c. 1935. Marks Brothers Co**. - $250 $400 $600**

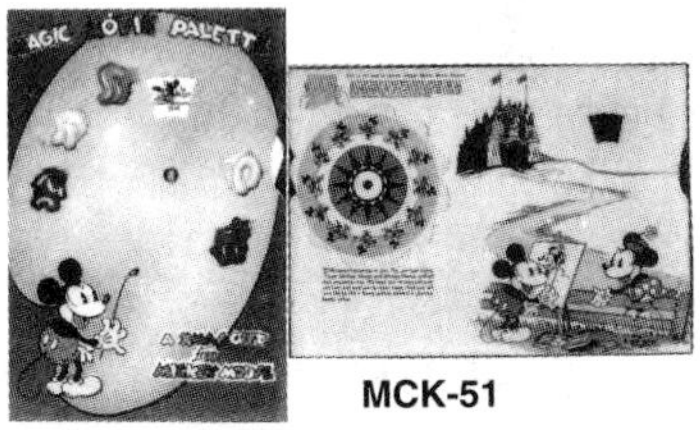
MCK-51

❑ **MCK-51. "Magic Movie Palette",**
1935. Store give-away. Mechanical paper. -
**$75 $175 $325**

MCK-52

❑ **MCK-52. Lionel Trains Promotional Folder,**
1935. Black, white and red 8-1/2x11" four-page folder including photos of Mickey Mouse Circus Train set as well as Mickey and Minnie and Santa with Mickey handcars. - **$50 $125 $175**

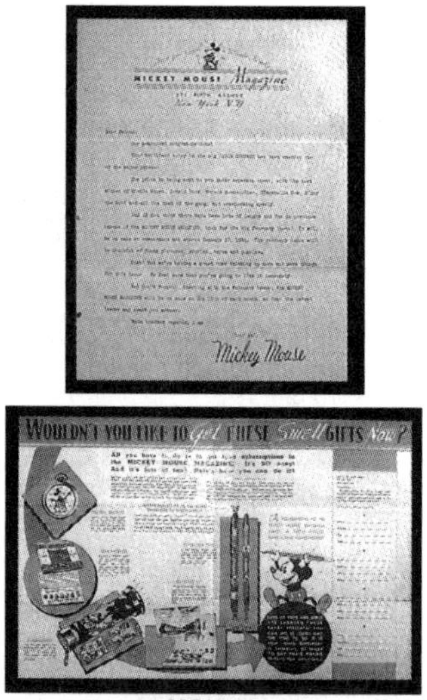


MCK-53

❑ **MCK-53. Mickey Mouse Magazine "Didja Contest" Award Announcement Letter And Folder,**
1935. Folder is 8-1/4x10-3/4" with letter on front cover announcing major prize is being sent under separate cover. Text promotes February 1936 issue and announces monthly publication schedule. Folder opens to red, black and white spread suggesting selling subscriptions as Christmas gifts and showing premiums awarded for four subscriptions. Disney-related premiums are Ingersoll pocket watch, Usa Lite flashlight and two styles of fountain pens. Rare. - **$150 $300 $500**

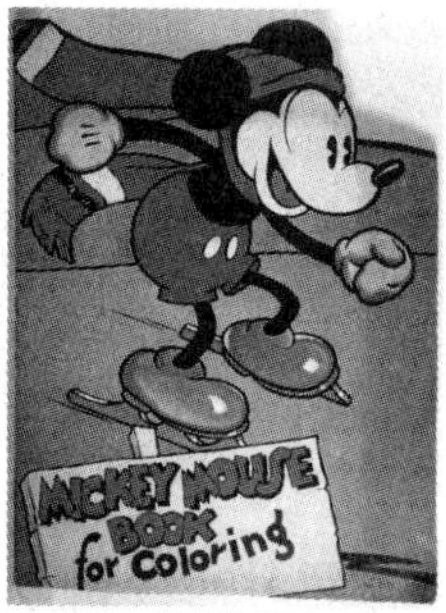


MCK-54

MCK-55

❑ **MCK-54. "Mickey Mouse Book for Coloring",**
1936. Fourth in a series of coloring books, but the first to be die-cut. Features early Mickey cartoons like *On Ice*, *Band Concert*, *The Pointer* and others. Has many great early pictures of Donald, Horace, Minnie, Tanglefoot, Pluto and the Goof. Usually found colored in. Book is 14" tall.- **$100 $250 $500**

❑ **MCK-55. Glazed Ceramic Toothbrush Holder,**
c. 1936. Store item by S. Maw & Son, London.- **$200 $400 $650**

MCK-56

MCK-57

❑ **MCK-56. Composition And Stuffed Cloth Doll,**
1936. Store item by Knickerbocker. 12" tall with composition shoes. Original eyes are thin diecut black oilcloth. - **$250 $600 $1200**

❑ **MCK-57. Minnie Mouse Stuffed Cloth Doll With Composition Shoes,**
1936. Store item by Knickerbocker. 12" tall. Eyes on original doll are thin diecut black oilcloth. - **$200 $600 $1200**

MCK-58

❑ **MCK-58. Italian Chocolate Bar Display Bin,**
c. 1936. Ciro Topolino. Mostly red and yellow with flattened size of 15x19-1/2". Front of bin is designed like a woven basket and opens to hold product. - **$200 $400 $700**

MCK-59

❑ **MCK-59. "Mickey Mouse Matinee Party" Movie Theater Herald,**
1936. Norwest Theater, Detroit, Mich. 9x18" announcing "Hallowe'en Big 4 Hour Mickey Mouse Matinee Party." - **$35 $75 $125**

MCK-60

❑ **MCK-60. Mickey Mouse Cookies Box,**
1937. Store item by National Biscuit Co. 5" long with fabric carrying strap. - **$200 $400 $650**

MCK-61

❑ **MCK-61. "The Atlanta Georgian's Silver Anniversary" Litho. Button,**
1937. Named newspaper. From set of various characters. - **$200 $400 $800**

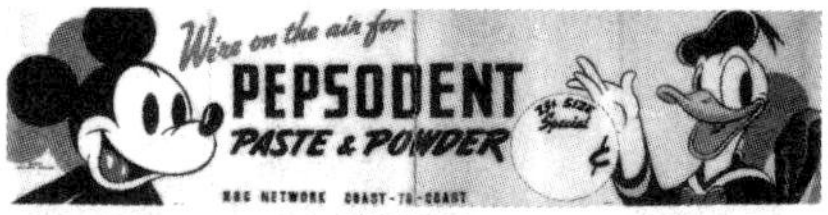


MCK-62

❑ **MCK-62. Pepsodent 10x40" Paper Poster,**
1937. For NBC radio show. - **$125 $300 $600**

MCK-63

❑ **MCK-63. Post Toasties Mickey Box,**
1937. - **$100 $300 $400**

MCK-64

❑ **MCK-64. "The Mickey Mouse Globe Trotter Weekly" Vol. 3 No. 3 Example ,**
1937. Various bakeries and dairies.
Each - **$20 $50 $100**

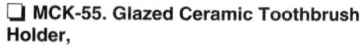

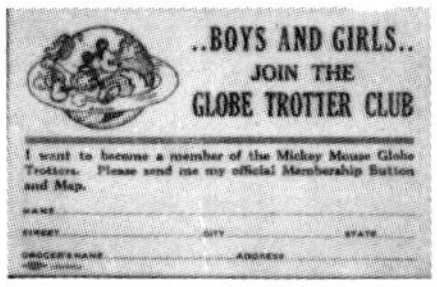

MCK-65

MCK-66

❑ **MCK-65. "Globe Trotter Club" Membership Card,**
1937. Various sponsors. - **$25 $50 $110**

❑ **MCK-66. "Mickey Mouse Globe Trotters/Member" Cello. Button,**
1937. Imprints of various bakeries and dairies.
Freihofer - **$15 $25 $40**
Others - **$25 $50 $100**

MCK-67

❑ **MCK-67. "Round The World" Map,**
1937. Issued by various bread companies. Opens to 20x27" for mounting 24 "Globe Trotters" picture cards.
Without Pictures - **$50 $175 $350**

MCK-68

❑ **MCK-68. "Mickey Mouse Globe Trotters" 11x23" Paper Store Sign,**
1937. Imprinted for Peter Pan Bread. Mickey is pictured holding May 1937 issue of Mickey Mouse Magazine. - **$200 $450 $800**

MCK-69

❑ **MCK-69. Sunoco Oil Advertising Booklet,**
1938. - **$40 $70 $150**

MCK-70

❑ **MCK-70. "Mickey Mouse Magazine" Gift Subscription Card With Envelope ,**
1938. With Envelope - **$50 $125 $250**
Loose - **$35 $75 $175**

MCK-71

❑ **MCK-71. Dental Appointment Envelope, Card And Certificate,**
c. 1938. Envelope - **$5 $10 $15**
Card - **$15 $25 $40**
Certificate - **$25 $75 $125**

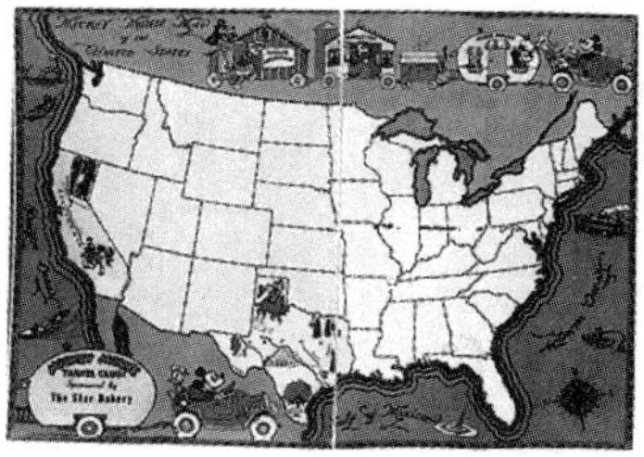
MCK-72

❑ **MCK-72. "Mickey Mouse Travel Club" Map,**
1938. Various sponsors, example is for Star Bakery. Opens to 16-1/2x24" from series featuring various states. - **$100 $300 $500**

MCK-73

MCK-74

❑ **MCK-73. "Mickey Mouse-Good Teeth" Cello. Button,**
c. 1938. Back paper for Bureau of Public Relations/American Dental Association. - **$50 $115 $190**

❑ **MCK-74. Christmas Giveaway for Shoes,**
1939. Rare. - **$315 $1260 $2800**

MCK-75

❑ **MCK-75. Mickey Mouse Cello. Button,**
1938. Offered for subscription to Mickey Mouse Magazine. - **$25 $40 $85**

MCK-76

❑ **MCK-76. Cereal Box,**
1939. Mickey not on front. - **$100 $300 $400**

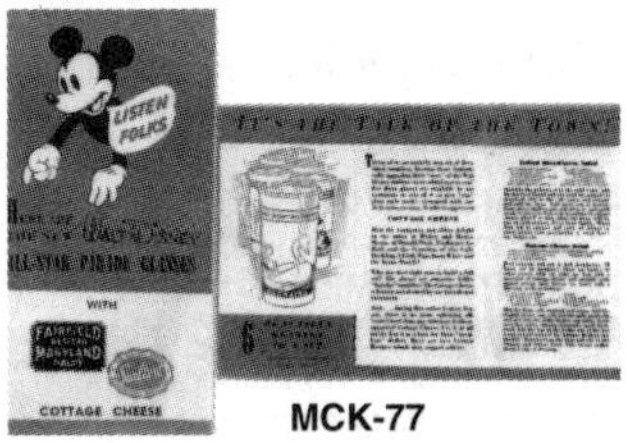

MCK-77

❑ **MCK-77. "All-Star Parade Glasses" Brochure,**
1939. Includes order blank for cottage cheese filled glasses. - **$40 $75 $150**

MCK-78

❑ **MCK-78. "Mickey's And Donald's Race To Treasure Island" 20x27" Paper Map.**
1939. Standard Oil of California. Pictures from "Travel Tykes" weekly newspapers go around border. Unused - **$125 $275 $525**

MCK-79

❑ **MCK-79. Sunoco Winter Oil Postcard,**
1939. Pictures Mickey as pilgrim. - **$20 $50 $85**

MCK-80

MCK-81

❑ **MCK-80. Blue Sunoco Cardboard Ink Blotter,**
1939. Pictures Minnie and Mickey as bride and groom. - **$25 $50 $75**

❑ **MCK-81. Pocket Mirror,**
1930s. Black/white/red printed on ribbed paper with satin-like finish. Only authentic 1930s design known, fantasy mirrors include Chicago 1933 and New York 1939 World's Fair reference. - **$75 $150 $300**

MCK-82

❑ **MCK-82. "Mickey Mouse Helter Skelter" English Game,**
1930s. Chad Valley Co. Ltd. store item with outstanding graphics. - **$250 $750 $1500**

MCK-83

❑ **MCK-83. Bread Company Promotional Mailer For Store Owners,**
1930s. Issued by A.B.C. Bread. 6-1/4x9" opens to 18-1/4x25-1/4". - **$200 $500 $750**

MCK-84

❑ **MCK-84. "Mickey Mouse Treasure Chest" Bank,**
1930s. 2x3x2-1/4" tall tin litho. Made in Japan. - **$200 $500 $750**

MCK-85

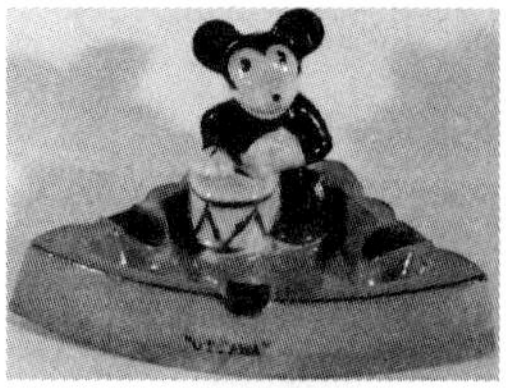

MCK-86

❑ **MCK-85. "Mickey Mouse Scrapbook",**
1930s. Various bakery imprints. The first bread card book. Designed to hold 24 large sized cards, see next item. - **$100 $225 $375**

❑ **MCK-86. Ashtray,**
1930s. Mickey Mouse playing drums. Scarce. - **$75 $275 $450**

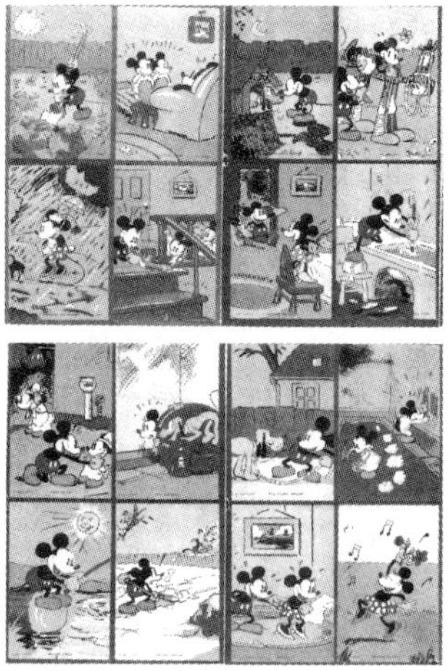

MCK-87

❑ **MCK-87. Large Recipe Cards,**
1930s. Photo shows 16 of 24 in set for previous item. Each - **$10 $18 $30**

MCK-88

❑ **MCK-88. "Mickey Mouse Recipe Scrapbook",**
1930s. Various bakery and dairy company imprints. Designed to hold 48 cards, see next item. - **$40 $75 $125**

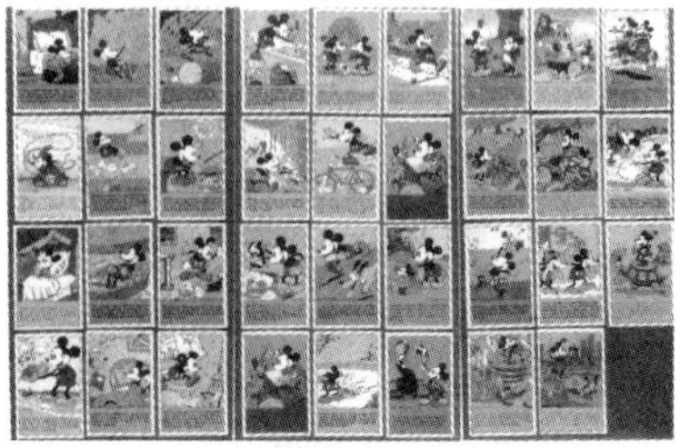

MCK-89

❑ **MCK-89. Small Recipe Cards,**
1930s. Photo shows 35 of 48 in set for previous item. Each - **$8 $15 $25**

MCK-90

MCK-91

MCK-92

❑ **MCK-90. Bread Loaf Waxed Paper Insert Band,**
1930s. Various breads. Offers free Recipe Scrapbook for bread pictures. - **$50 $125 $200**

❑ **MCK-91. Mickey Mouse 7-1/2" Bavarian China Plate,**
1930s. Used as movie theater give-aways, various designs. 7-1/2" Size - **$125 $200 $400**
6" Size - **$100 $175 $350**

❑ **MCK-92. Mickey Mouse Bavarian China Cream Pitcher,**
1930s. Used as movie theater give-aways, various designs. - **$100 $225 $425**

MCK-93

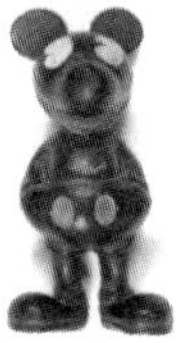

MCK-94

❑ **MCK-93. German Bisque Figures,**
1930s. Store item. Pair - **$150 $300 $600**

❑ **MCK-94. Hard Rubber Figure,**
1930s. Store item by Seiberling Rubber Co. Thin rubber tail usually gone.
No Tail - **$35 $75 $150**
With Tail - **$75 $150 $300**

MCK-95

MCK-96

❑ **MCK-95. Cardboard String Climbing Toy,**
1930s. Store item by Dolly Toy Co. -
**$250 $600 $800**

❑ **MCK-96. Cardboard Figural Pencil Case,**
1930s. Store item by Dixon Pencil Co. -
**$125 $275 $425**

MCK-97

❑ **MCK-97. "Dixon's Mickey Mouse Map Of The United States" 10x14",**
1930s. Came in pencil boxes. - **$25 $60 $115**

MCK-98

❑ **MCK-98. "Mickey Mouse Globe Trotters" Door Hanger,** 1930s. Pictured example imprinted for Pevely Dairy Co. Diecut stiff paper for door knob suspension including offer for membership button and world map. -
**$75 $150 $250**

MCK-99

❑ **MCK-99. "Mickey Mouse Beverages" Felt Cap,**
1930s. Fabric garrison-style cap with designated area on headband for mounting six bottle caps issued with brass pins. See MCK-111. -
**$75 $150 $275**

MCK-100

MCK-101

❑ **MCK-100. "Mickey Mouse Club" Cello. Button,**
1930s. W. E. Disney copyright plus back paper for Kay Kamen Distributorship. - **$50 $90 $150**

❑ **MCK-101. "Post Toasties" Stationery Sheet,**
1930s. Letterhead art offering "Mickey Mouse And Other Walt Disney Cut-Outs On Back And Sides Of Package." Pictured example is letterhead only of 8-1/2x11" sheet. - **$50 $125 $225**

MCK-102

MCK-103

❑ **MCK-102. Mickey Mouse Bread 9x16" Paper Poster,**
1930s. Advertises "A New Picture Card Every Day With Every Loaf." - **$250 $600 $1250**

❑ **MCK-103. Toasted Nut Chocolate Candy Wrapper,**
1930s. Wilbur-Suchard Chocolate Co. -
**$30 $60 $100**

MCK-104

MCK-105

❑ **MCK-104. Mickey & Minnie Bisque Toothbrush Holder,**
1930s. Store item. - **$75 $225 $350**

❑ **MCK-105. Paper Hat,**
1930s. Mickey Mouse Comic Cookies. -
**$50 $125 $250**

MCK-106

MCK-107

❑ **MCK-106. Play Money $1.00 Bill,**
1930s. Southern Dairies Ice Cream premium. -
**$10 $20 $35**

❑ **MCK-107. Play Money $10.00 Bill,**
1930s. Southern Dairies Ice Cream premium. -
**$10 $20 $35**

MCK-108

❑ **MCK-108. Mickey Mouse Circus Train,**
1930s. Six piece Lionel Train set in box includes a coal car with Mickey figure, Circus Dining Car, Mickey Mouse Band car, Mickey Mouse Circus car, train engine, a composition figure of Mickey with hand raised and a track. Plus die-cut cardboard pieces to create a circus location display. (Product #1536). - **$2500 $5000 $10,000**

MCK-109

MCK-110

❑ **MCK-109. Dixie Ice Cream Cup Lid,**
1930s. Southern Dairies. - **$25 $60 $100**

❑ **MCK-110. "Mickey And Oswald Shake Hands" Department Store Card,**
1930s. Boston store. Christmas "Toytown" give-away with unauthorized art. - **$25 $50 $80**

MCK-111

❑ **MCK-111. Mickey Mouse Bottle Cap Set Of Six,**
1930s. Stores supplied a felt hat for bottle caps that had brass pins for mounting. Usually found without the spring pins. See MCK-99.
Each - **$15 $30 $75**

MCK-112

❑ **MCK-112. Post Cereal Spoon,**
1930s.
Near Mint In Mailer With Instructions - **$250**
Spoon Only - **$8 $15 $35**

MCK-113

MCK-114

❑ **MCK-113. "Mickey Mouse's Midnight Adventure" Folder,**
1930s. Accompanied "USA Lites" flashlights. - **$35 $75 $150**

❑ **MCK-114. Dodge Motors Advertising Flip Booklet,**
1930s. Story title "Mickey Takes Minnie For A Ride". - **$50 $125 $225**

MCK-115

MCK-116

❑ **MCK-115. Movie Theater Club Card,**
1930s. Back has club creed. - **$50 $100 $175**

❑ **MCK-116. "Penney's For Back To School Needs" Cello. Button,**
1930s. - **$25 $50 $85**

MCK-117

MCK-118

MCK-119

❑ **MCK-117. Minnie Mouse "Good Teeth" Cello. Button,**
1930s. Kern County Health Department, California. - **$300 $800 $2000**

❑ **MCK-118. "Southern Dairies Ice Cream" Cello. Button,**
1930s. Scarce. - **$300 $800 $1750**

❑ **MCK-119. "California Mickey Mouse Club" Cello. Button,**
1930s. - **$60 $150 $225**

MCK-120

MCK-121

MCK-122

❑ **MCK-120. "Evening Ledger Comics" Cello. Button,**
1930s. Philadelphia newspaper. From set of 14 various characters. - **$250 $600 $1000**

❑ **MCK-121. "Evening Ledger Comics" Cello. Button,**
1930s. Philadelphia newspaper. From set of 14 various characters. - **$250 $600 $1000**

❑ **MCK-122. "Mickey Mouse Undies" Cello. Button,**
1930s. - **$50 $90 $150**

MCK-123

MCK-124

❑ **MCK-123. "Ask For Mickey Mouse Undies" Paper Tag,**
1930s. Stamp nature but example seen had ungummed back, other inscriptions "Make Children Happier" and "Undergarments Of Quality". - **$35 $75 $135**

❑ **MCK-124. Cardboard Coaster,**
1930s. Brock-Hall Milk and probably others. 4-1/4" diameter cardboard with red and black design. - **$25 $50 $75**

MCK-125

MCK-126

❑ **MCK-125. Mickey Mouse Vending Card Display Sign,**
1930s. Criss Cross Machines manufactured by Calex Mfg. Inc., Amityville, N.Y. Loose cards were distributed as an Amoco gas premium but apparently they were then also used as vending cards. Also see Phantom card sign PHN-2. - **$500 $750 $1000**

❑ **MCK-126. Steiff Small Size Mickey Mouse Doll,**
1930s. Store item. Stands only 4-3/4" tall.
Near Mint With Cardboard Tag And Metal Ear Button With Tag - **$2000**
Doll Without Tags And Button -
**$200 $500 $750**
Doll With Button But No Tags -
**$300 $650 $900**

MCK-127

❑ **MCK-127. Bread Picture And Scrapbook Promotional Store Window Sign,**
1930s. Bamby Bread and possibly others. 16x20" advertising color picture cards and 48-page scrapbook to hold them. -
**$300 $700 $1200**

MCK-128

❑ **MCK-128. First Version "Picture Card Album",**
1930s. Mickey Mouse Bubble Gum. Front cover has less refined image of Mickey and variations in text at lower left.
Album Only - **$160 $250 $425**

MCK-129

❑ **MCK-129. "Welcome To Toytown" Store Sign,**
1930s. Probably used by Macy's and others. 7x11" with same design on each side. -
**$100 $200 $400**

MCK-130

❑ **MCK-130. Chocolate Bar Candy Box,**
1930s. William Patterson Ltd., Canada. 4" long waxed cardboard box. - **$100 $225 $350**

MCK-131

❑ **MCK-131. Mickey Mouse "Nu-Blue Sunoco" Cardboard Ink Blotter,**
1940. Example pictures him in speeding car. -
**$20 $40 $60**

MCK-132

❑ **MCK-132. Goodyear Tires Mailing Brochure,**
1940. Canadian issue, opens to 11x20". -
**$35 $75 $140**

MCK-133

❑ **MCK-133. "Sunheat Furnace Oil" Cardboard Ink Blotter,**
c. 1940. Sun Oil Co. Mickey hanging wall plaque. - **$15 $35 $60**

MCK-134

❑ **MCK-134. "Liberty" Magazine Premium Card,**
c. 1940. 7x7-1/2" stiff paper designed like studio fan cards of the era but inscribed "To One Of The Grandest Boys In The World-A Liberty Boy Salesman" with Walt Disney facsimile signature. -
**$300 $600 $1200**

MCK-135

MCK-136

❑ **MCK-135. Sunoco Oil Cardboard Ink Blotter,**
c. 1940. Pictures Donald listening for motor knocks. - **$20 $40 $70**

❑ **MCK-136. Sunoco Oil Ink Blotter,**
1941. Depicts Mickey and Donald in military outfits. - **$40 $65 $100**

MCK-137

MCK-138

❑ **MCK-137. "Mickey Mouse on Sky Island" Book,**
1941. - **$20 $60 $135**

❑ **MCK-138. "Mickey Mouse and Pluto" Fast Action Book,**
1942. Scarce in high grade. - **$35 $140 $280**

MCK-139

❑ **MCK-139. Sunoco Oil Ink Blotter,**
1942. Mickey by artillery gun with oil bottle body. -
**$10 $20 $45**

MCK-140 MCK-141

❑ **MCK-140. "Mickey Mouse...On The Home Front" Newspaper,**
April 1944. Beechcraft Aviation Corp. -
**$35 $100 $175**

❑ **MCK-141. "Mickey Mouse" Weekly English Newspaper,**
1945. Long running publication, seldom better than Fine condition. 1930s Each - **$10 $20 $30**
1940s Each - **$8 $15 $25**

MCK-142 MCK-143

❑ **MCK-142. "Mickey Mouse Bell Boy Detective" Book,**
1945. - **$20 $60 $125**

❑ **MCK-143. "Mickey Mouse and the 'Lectro Box" Book,**
1946. - **$20 $60 $125**

MCK-144

❑ **MCK-144. Mickey Mouse Wrist Watch in Box,**
1946. US Time Corp. Has stand-up display insert. Much harder to find than 1st Mickey watch.
Boxed - **$750**
Loose with Original Straps - **$75 $150 $275**

MCK-145

❑ **MCK-145. "US Time" Comic With Mickey Watch Ad,**
c. 1947. - **$25 $50 $80**

MCK-146

❑ **MCK-146. Mickey Mouse Silver Bowl,**
1947. Sterling silver International Children's Bowl. - **$75 $200 $325**

MCK-147

❑ **MCK-147. "Walt Disney Character Merchandise" Catalogue,**
1947. Kay Kamen Ltd. 9x12" with 100 pages showing products of Disney merchandise licensees. - **$250 $500 $800**

MCK-148 MCK-149

❑ **MCK-148. "Mickey Mouse and the Desert Palace" Book,**
1948. BLB #1451. - **$20 $60 $125**

❑ **MCK-149. "Mickey Mouse in the World of Tomorrow" Book,**
1948. BLB #1444. - **$20 $60 $125**

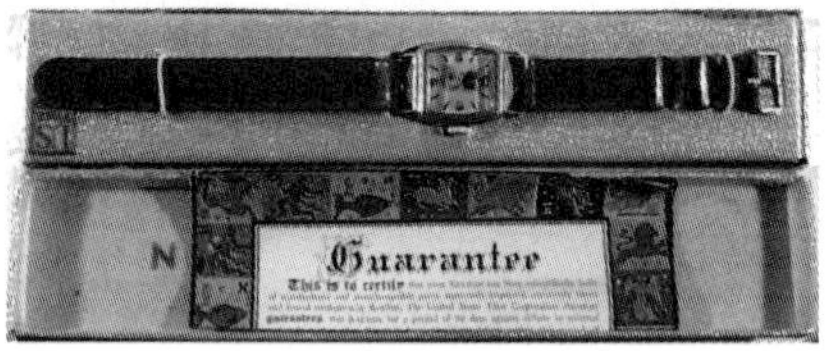


MCK-150

❑ **MCK-150. Mickey Mouse Watch,**
1940s. Kelton. With Guarantee card and instructions in original box. Has gold foil on bottom. Possibly the rarest of all the early pre-1950 Mickey watches. Original price was a steep $12.50, no doubt contributing to the watch's present-day rarity. - **$250 $600 $1000**

MCK-151

❑ **MCK-151. Mickey Mouse Cookies Box,**
1940s. Natinal Biscuit Co. Box is 5" long with a fabric carrying strap. Mickey pictured on back, Minnie and Pluto on sides. - **$150 $350 $550**

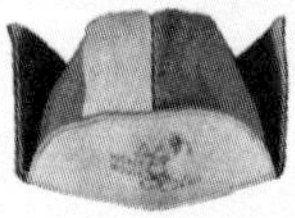

MCK-152 MCK-153

❑ **MCK-152. Beanie,**
1940s. Scarce. - **$100 $225 $325**

❑ **MCK-153. "March Of Comics" #60,**
1950. Various sponsors. - **$29 $87 $245**

MCK-154

❑ **MCK-154. 78 RPM Record,**
1956. General Mills, Inc. #3 from series of four.
Each With Sleeve - **$10 $15 $30**

MCK-155

❑ **MCK-155. Mickey Mouse And His Pals Plastic Rings,**
1956. Sugar Jets cereal. Peter Pan example from set of eight: Mickey, Minnie, Donald, Pluto, Snow White, Pinocchio, Dumbo, Peter Pan.
Each - **$15 $25 $40**

MCK-156

❑ **MCK-156. "Mickey's Mousekemovers" Truck,**
1950s. Store item by Line Mar. 12-1/2" long by 4-1/4" tall tin litho friction. - **$300 $700 $1200**

MCK-157

❑ **MCK-157. Picture Sheet For Bread Label Cut-Outs,**
1950s. NBC Bread. Blank - **$40 $60 $80**

MCK-158

❑ **MCK-158. "Mickey Mouse Club Magic Kit" Punch-Out Set,**
1950s. Mars candy. Near Mint In Mailer - **$90**

MCK-159

MCK-160

❑ **MCK-159. Mouseketeer Doll,**
1950s. Scarce. Mickey Mouse Club. Store bought marionette on roller skates. -
**$50 $175 $325**

❑ **MCK-160. Punch-Out Paper Puppet,**
1950s. Donald Duck Bread.
Unpunched - **$15 $30 $60**

MCK-161

❑ **MCK-161. Pillsbury "Mickey Mouse Club" Ring Offer Box,**
1950s. Offered set of five aluminum rings: Donald, Goofy, Jiminy, Bambi, Cinderella.
Box - **$25 $50 $75**
Each Ring - **$10 $20 $35**

MCK-162

❑ **MCK-162. "Special Deputy Mouseketeer" Large Badge,**
1950s. 4-1/4x4-3/4" originally came with Mouseketeers western outfit boxed set by L. M. Eddie Mfg. - **$25 $50 $100**

MCK-163

MCK-164

❑ **MCK-163. "KVOS-TV 12" Cello. Club Button,**
1950s. Unidentified but TV station of Bellingham, Washington. - **$15 $25 $50**

❑ **MCK-164. "Member Mickey Mouse Club" Litho. Tin Tab,**
1950s. - **$8 $15 $30**

MCK-165

❑ **MCK-165. Club Membership Card,**
1950s. Channel 12 TV premium. - **$15 $40 $65**

MCK-166

❑ **MCK-166. "Mars/Mickey Mouse Club Magic Manual" Booklet,**
1950s. - **$10 $20 $40**

MCK-167

❑ **MCK-167. "Mickey Mouse Club/Disneyland Headquarters" Membership Card And Litho. Tab,**
1963. Card - **$15 $30 $60**
Tab - **$20 $40 $75**

MCK-168

❑ **MCK-168. "Mickey Mouse Explorers Club Coloring Book",**
1965. Kroger food stores. - **$10 $25 $45**

MCK-169

❑ **MCK-169. Mickey Mouse Pocket Watch,**
1973. In plastic box with advertising overlay Train pictured on back of case. Bradley. Complete - **$30 $75 $150**

MCK-170

MCK-171

❑ **MCK-170. "Seed Shop" 3" Cello. Button,**
1976. Promotion for garden seeds in packages featuring Disney characters. - **$35 $100 $200**

❑ **MCK-171. "Around The World In 80 Days" Hardcover Book,**
1978. Crest Toothpaste. - **$5 $10 $20**

MCK-172

MCK-173

❑ **MCK-172. "The Magical Music of Walt Disney" Album Set,**
1978. Plays the 50 year history of Disney arranged movie music on 4 Long Playing records. Set includes a 52 page full color book.- **$25 $50 $90**

❑ **MCK-173. "Mickey And Goofy Explore The Universe Of Energy" Comic Book,**
1985. Exxon. - **$1 $3 $6**

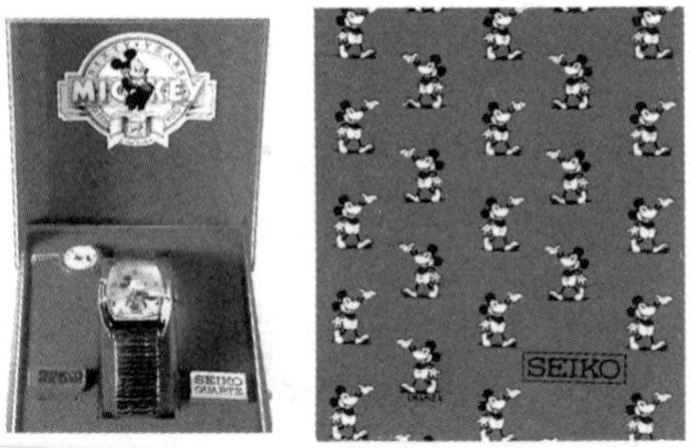


MCK-174

❑ **MCK-174. Sixtieth Anniversary Watch,**
1987. Limited edition watch with old-style box graphics and a plastic disc used as a label. Boxed - **$350**

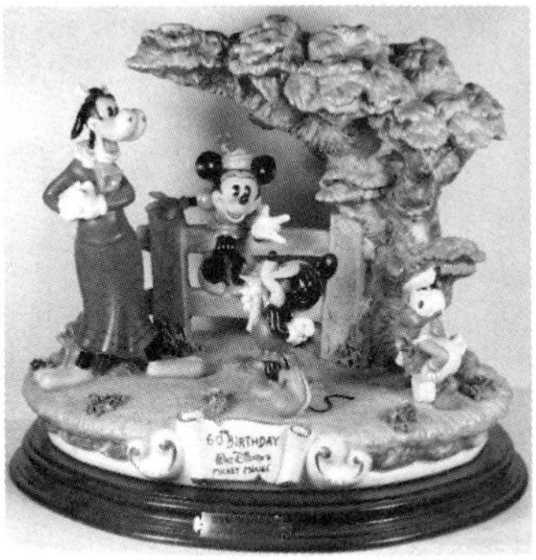

MCK-175

❑ **MCK-175. "Mickey's Sixtieth Birthday" Sculpture,**
1988. From the Disney Capodimonte Collection by retired sculptor Enzo Arzenton. Edition size of 192. - **$1750**

MCK-176

❑ **MCK-176. "Sorcerer's Apprentice" Figure,**
1980s. Fantasia Movie Figure from the "Capodimonte" collection. 955 made. - **$1000**

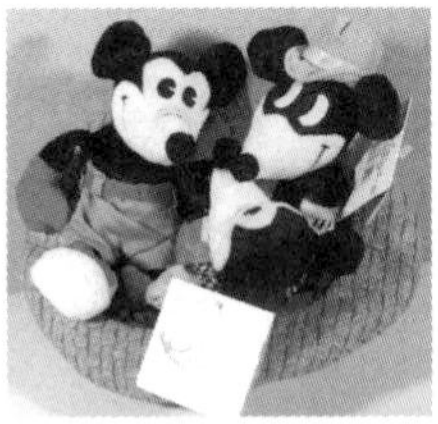

MCK-177

MCK-178

❑ **MCK-177. Mickey Bean Figures Set,**
1999. Disney Store exclusive shows 3 Mickeys from different eras. - **$40**

❑ **MCK-178. "Mickey Mouse Club" Resin,**
2000. Limited edition from Disney Store shows Donald ringing a gong. - **$75**

MCK-179

MCK-180

❑ **MCK-179. Mickey 4th of July Bean Figure,**
2000. Disney Store exclusive. - **$20**

❑ **MCK-180. Minnie 4th of July Bean Figure,**
2000. Disney Store exclusive. - **$20**

## Mighty Mouse

**The rodent equivalent of Superman, Captain Marvel and other humanoid cloaked flying heroes, Mighty Mouse was probably the best-known Terrytoons character and certainly one of the most prolific in animated episodes. Originally dubbed Supermouse in his 1942 creation year by Paul Terry, the battler of villainous cats was renamed Mighty Mouse in 1944. He starred in about 80 television episodes between 1955 and 1967, frequently saving girlfriend Pearl Pureheart from her perils. In addition to animated adventures, Mighty Mouse starred also in numerous comic books by various publishers, including Gold Key and Dell, from the mid-1940s into the early 1990s.**

MGH-1

❑ **MGH-1. Mighty Mouse 12" Stuffed Oilcloth Doll,**
1942. Rare. Rubber head, star designs on cape. - **$200 $600 $1000**

MGH-2

MGH-3

❑ **MGH-2. Vinyl/Plush/Fabric Doll,**
c. 1950. Store item by Ideal Toys. Tag inscriptions include "CBS". - **$50 $150 $250**

❑ **MGH-3. "Three Dimension Comics" Comic Book With 3-D Glasses,**
1953. Second printing, came with glasses. First printing says "World's First!" on cover.
First Printing - **$30 $90 $275**
Second Printing - **$27 $81 $245**

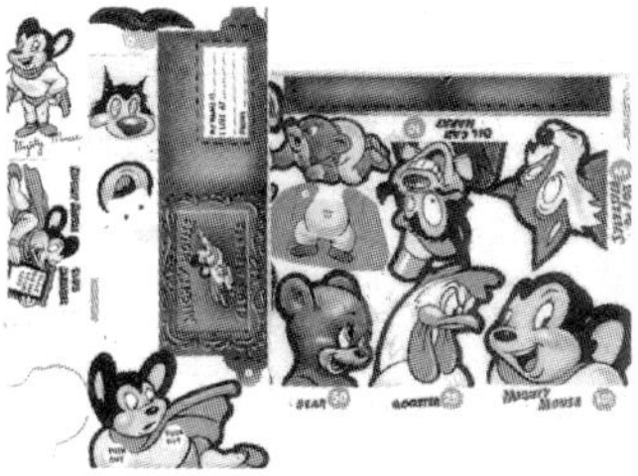

MGH-4

❑ **MGH-4. Post Cereals "Merry-Pack" Punch-Outs With Envelope,**
1956. Post Treat-Pak and Post Alpha-Bits. Consists of three sheets to form about 20 items.
Unpunched - **$15 $50 $75**

MGH-5

❑ **MGH-5. Club Member Paper Wallet,**
1956. Part of previous punch-out set. - **$5 $10 $15**

MGH-6

❑ **MGH-6. Cereal Box Wrapper With "Magic Mystery Picture" Offer,**
1957. Gordon Gold Archives.
Used Complete - **$50 $125 $225**

MGH-7

❑ **MGH-7. "Post Cereals Mighty Mouse Mystery Color Picture" Cards,**
1957. Set of six. Water makes invisible character appear. Unused Set - **$30 $50 $75**
Used Set - **$20 $35 $50**

MGH-8

❑ **MGH-8. Cereal Box With Cut-Out,**
c. 1957. Post Sugar Crisp. Back panel printed for cutting and assembly of action scene toy from set of four.
Uncut - **$50 $100 $150**

MGH-9

❑ **MGH-9. Cereal Pack Wrapper,**
1950s. Post. Advertises Naval Battles Trading Card. Back panel printed for cutting and assembly of action scene toy from set of four.
Uncut - **$50 $100 $150**

MGH-10

❑ **MGH-10. Terrytoons Store Hankies,**
1950s. Store item. Mighty Mouse opens display. Six hankies with all the Terrytoons characters featured. - **$50 $100 $200**

MGH-11

MGH-12

❑ **MGH-11. Rubber Squeaker Figure,**
1950s. Store item. Comes with red felt cape. - **$20 $60 $100**

❑ **MGH-12. Original Comic Book Cover Art,**
1950s. 20" x 13". - **$1500**

MGH-13

MGH-14

MGH-15

❑ **MGH-13. Terrytoons Fabric Scarf,**
1950s. Store item. - **$15 $25 $50**

❑ **MGH-14. "Mighty Mouse In Toyland" Record,**
1960. Store item by Peter Pan Records. - **$10 $20 $35**

❑ **MGH-15. Soaky Toy,**
1965. 10" tall. - **$20 $60 $90**

MGH-16

❑ **MGH-16. Vinyl/Cloth Hand Puppet,**
1960s. 9" tall. - **$15 $25 $40**

MGH-17

❑ **MGH-17. "Terrytoons" Characters Cereal Bowl,**
1977. Store item by Deka Plastic Inc., N.J. 5-1/2" diameter with many characters shown in color. - **$10 $20 $35**

MGH-18 MGH-19

❑ **MGH-18. Plush Doll,**
1981. 10" tall with tag. Hard to find. Beanie-like. Figure with tag - **$80**

❑ **MGH-19. Christmas Ornament in Box,**
1998. - **$15**

MGH-20

❑ **MGH-20. Tin Lunch Box,**
2001. - **$15**

## Mister Softee

**Sales of soft ice cream dispensed from a spigot blossomed in the 1950s, not only from ice cream trucks but also from drive-in retail outlets. Thousands of these outlets were opened on the nation's highways by such retail chains as Dairy Queen, Tastee Freeze, and Carvel. By the end of the decade hard ice cream was making a comeback, but the soft ice cream chains had established themselves as a continuing roadside fixture. Dairy Queen issued a few premiums (see Dennis the Menace rings), but Mister Softee was the leader, and issued premiums through the "Mister Softee Club," probably established in the late 1950s.**

MSF-1

❑ **MSF-1. Club Items With Sign,**
1960s. Kit Near Mint Complete - **$75**
Plastic Ring - **$5 $10 $15**
Membership Card - **$5 $10 $15**
Litho. Button - **$3 $8 $12**
Cloth Patch - **$5 $10 $15**
Iron-On Transfer Order Form - **$2 $5 $10**

MSF-2

MSF-3

❑ **MSF-2. "Mister Softee" Enameled Brass Keychain Tag,**
c. 1960s. - **$10 $25 $40**

❑ **MSF-3. "I Like Mister Softee" Logo Figure Plastic Ring,** 1960s. Mister Softee cones, shakes, sundaes. - **$25 $40 $75**

MSF-4

❑ **MSF-4. "Adventures Of Captain Chapel" Space Cards,**
1960s. Mister Softee. Cards 1-10 are numbered, following cards are unnumbered from unknown set total. - **$1 $2 $3**

## The Monkees

**Four "insane" boys--actors Mickey Dolenz (formerly Mickey Braddock of the TV series *Circus Boy*) and Davy Jones, and musicians Peter Tork and Mike Nesmith--picked from hundreds of hopefuls who answered an audition call, comprised the Monkees, a fictional rock group that nevertheless enjoyed considerable success on records and on network television. The show, inspired stylistically by the Beatles' 1964 film *A Hard Day's Night*, featured surrealistic camera work and comic or melodramatic story lines. The series ran on the three television networks, originally on NBC (1966-1968), and repeated on CBS (1969-1972) and ABC (1972-1973). *Monkees* comic books appeared from 1967 to 1969. Merchandising was extensive, and a custom-built Monkeemobile was created for appearances at automobile shows and shopping centers. After years of obscurity, a resurgence of popularity in Japan and a re-airing of the original television episodes on MTV in 1985 and 1986 sparked a 20th anniversary reunion that produced multiple live performances (a handful including Nesmith, now a successful video production entrepeneur) and a new album in 1987. In 1996, Mike reformed the group yet again to film a special 30th anniversay "episode" of the series and record another new album, and VH-1 produced a TV-movie about the history of the band in the summer of 2000. Items are usually copyrighted by Raybert Productions or Screen Gems. "Now crayon I can say!"**

MON-1

MON-2

❑ **MON-1. Celluloid 3-1/2" Button,**
1966. Vendor item. - **$15 $25 $50**

❑ **MON-2. "Official Monkees Fan" Cello. Button,**
1966. Raybert Productions. - **$15 $30 $50**

MON-3

MON-4

❑ **MON-3. First Gum Card Set,**
1966. Store item by Donruss Co. Set of 44 with sepia photo fronts and full color photo puzzle backs. Near Mint Set - **$100**

❑ **MON-4. "Series A" Card Set,**
1966. Store item by Donruss Co. Forty-four cards in set with color photo fronts and color photo puzzle backs. Near Mint Set - **$100**

MON-5

MON-6

❑ **MON-5. "Series B" Gum Card Set,**
1966. Store item by Donruss Co. Forty-four cards in set with color photo fronts and color photo puzzle backs with Monkee Questions and Answers. Near Mint Set - **$100**

❑ **MON-6. "Series C" Gum Card Set,**
1967. Store item by Donruss Co. Set of 44 with color photo fronts and color backs with photo puzzles and text. Near Mint Set - **$100**

MON-7

❑ **MON-7. Gum Card Display Box,**
1967. Store item by Donruss Co. Box held packs of "Series C" cards. - **$25 $50 $85**

MON-8

❑ **MON-8. Monkees Bracelet On Store Card,**
1967. Near Mint Carded **- $75**
Bracelet Only **- $15 $25 $40**

MON-9

❑ **MON-9. Fan Club Postcard,**
1967. - **$5 $8 $15**

MON-10

❑ **MON-10. Tour Sign 29x22",**
1967. Promotional sign for performance at the Cow Palace in San Francisco. -
**$200 $500 $700**

MON-11

MON-12

❑ **MON-11. Official Fan Club Button,**
1967. Litho. 2-1/4". - **$10 $20 $30**

❑ **MON-12. Monkees Litho. Button,**
1967. Vending machine issue set of six. Four with single portraits, two with group portraits. Each - **$3 $5 $10**

MON-13

❑ **MON-13. Kellogg's Flicker Rings,**
1967. Set of 12 silvered plastic with insert alternating picture of individual for group.
Each - **$20 $40 $65**

MON-14

❑ **MON-14. "Monkee Coins",**
1967. Kellogg's. Set of 12 color photos in yellow plastic frames. Canadian issue with reverse text in English and French. Each - **$10 $20 $30**

MON-15

❑ **MON-15. Photo Flip Booklets,**
1967. Store item. Set of 16. Each - **$10 $20 $35**

MON-16

MON-17

❑ **MON-16. "Talking Hand Puppet" Boxed,**
1967. Store item by Mattel, Inc.
Near Mint Boxed Talking - **$400**
Unboxed Talking - **$75 $150 $250**
Unboxed Not Talking - **$30 $60 $100**

❑ **MON-17. "Monkee-Mobile" Tin Friction Car,**
c. 1967. Store item, Japanese made. Has battery operated singing mechanism.
Box - **$125 $250 $400**
Car - **$125 $250 $400**

MON-18

MON-19

❑ **MON-18. Unopened Third Series Gum Card Pack,**
1967. Donruss. **- $15 $30 $50**

❑ **MON-19. Program,**
1967. 12x12" published by Raybert Prod. Inc. **-**
**$12 $25 $40**

MON-20

❑ **MON-20. "Monkees" Cereal Box Cut-Out Record,**
c. 1970. Kellogg's. Series of four box backs.
Each - **$5 $8 $15**

MON-21

❑ **MON-21. "Monkees" Summer Tour Program,**
1987. - **$15 $30 $50**

MON-22

❑ **MON-22. "Monkees" Wacky Wobblers,**
2002. - **$32**

## Monsters Misc.

**The monster and horror genre had its origins in late 18th and early 19th century British gothic novels. Theatrical adaptations, however, with their lighting and stage machinery, served as the inspiration and model for filmmakers, not the books themselves. In silent films, America and Europe took different approaches. European films suggested darker *possibilities with Das Cabinet des Dr. Caligari* (1919, German), which shows cinema's ability to transcend photographic realism, and *Nosferatu* (1921, German), which emphasized the sexual aspect of Bram Stoker's Dracula. Universal Studios led the way in the US with emphasis on fast-paced action and macabre chills and dominated the genre in the 1930s (more on their influence can be seen in the section devoted specifically to Universal Studios monster memorabilia).**

**Later in the 1930s, other studios like RKO added to the spectacle. *King Kong* (1933) made a mighty ape into a symbol of subversive power. RKO also produced a new version of *The Hunchback of Notre Dame* (1939) with Charles Laughton, which restored some of the complexity removed from the Lon Chaney version produced by Universal in 1923.**

**The genre declined in the 1940s and most films were routine and uninspired. By the late 1950s there was a rebirth, but these "modern" horror films were far removed from the innocent films of the '30s. Director Terence Fisher (Hammer Studios) led the way in Britain with his reinterpretation of the Frankenstein and Dracula stories. Fisher's *The Curse of Frankenstein* (1957) caused a protest about its sensuality. Fisher emphasized the Baron's character more than the creature's and used subtle characterizations and dramatic timing. He also made excellent use of color (this was the first British monster film in color). In *Horror of Dracula* (1958), Fisher created a film of subtle realism, with atmosphere and rhythm.**

**Beginning in the late 1950s, local television stations introduced "horror hosts" to spice up the telecasts of monster and horror movies. On the west coast, Maila Nurmi, a model and aspiring actress, went to a Hollywood costume ball dressed as a Charles Addams cartoon character which was at the time unnamed but now known as Morticia Addams. Los Angeles producer Hunt Stromberg, Jr. was struck by her macabre appearance and hired her as Vampira to host a Saturday night horror movie show on KBS-TV. Her popularity led to *Life* magazine coverage, guest appearances on TV shows and several films, including Ed Wood's cult classic Plan 9 From Outer Space. On the east coast, Philadelphia got its chills from Roland, played by John Zacherle, who later moved to haunt New York City as Zacherley.**

**On the publishing front, in 1958 Forrest J. Ackerman began to chronicle monster and horror history in *Famous Monsters of Filmland.* Warren Publishing Company introduced *Creepy* in 1964 and *Eerie* in 1965, which both featured the work of many excellent artists. Warren's *Vampirella* made her debut in September 1969 and to this day, she remains one of the premiere "Bad Girls" of the comic book world and a major success story with current comic books published by Harris Comics.**

**This section features an assortment of the monster items distinct from the Universal monsters, which are covered in their own section.**

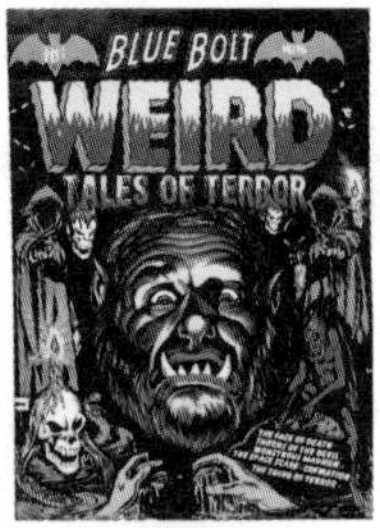


MNS-1

❑ **MNS-1. Cover Press Proof,**
1951. For Blue Bolt Weird Tales of Terror #111. Art by L.B. Cole. Blank on back side. - **$250**

MNS-2

❑ **MNS-2. "Charles Addams' Nightcrawlers" Hardcover With Dust Jacket,**
1957. With Dust Jacket **$20 $50 $85**

MNS-3

MNS-4

❑ **MNS-3. "Monster Mash" 45 RPM Record,**
1962. Store item on Garpax Records label. Black and white paper sleeve holds record by Bobby "Boris" Pickett and The Crypt-Kickers. - **$15 $40 $75**

❑ **MNS-4. The Hunchback Of Notre Dame Model Kit,**
1963. Store item by Aurora.
Near Mint Boxed - **$350**
Built No Box - **$15 $30 $60**

MNS-5

❑ **MNS-5. Godzilla Model Kit,**
1964. Store item by Aurora.
Near Mint Boxed - **$750**
Built No Box - **$65 $125 $200**

MNS-6

❑ **MNS-6. Aurora "The Witch" Model Kit,**
1965. Store item by Aurora.
Near Mint Boxed - **$275**
Built No Box - **$25 $50 $75**

MNS-7

❑ **MNS-7. Vampira Publicity Photo,**
1960s. Depicts her holding time bomb with her portrait plus text "I'm Dying To Meet You/Saturdays 10:30 On 7." - **$30 $60 $100**

MNS-8

❑ **MNS-8. Famous Monsters Magazine Flicker Ring,**
1960s. From set of five with flicker images that change from positive to negative. Set was advertised in the magazine. Silver luster plastic base. - **$15 $30 $50**

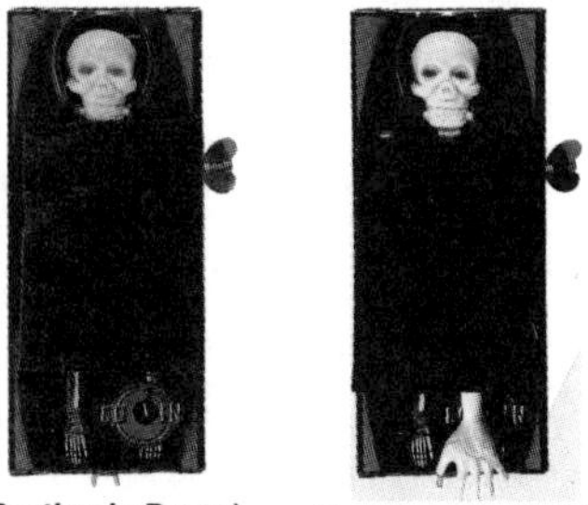

(Resting in Peace) (Grabbing the Coin)

MNS-9

❑ **MNS-9. Skeleton Wind-up Bank,**
1960s. Hand reaches out and grabs coin, pushing it into the tin box. - **$15 $35 $60**

MNS-10

MNS-11

❑ **MNS-10. "Vampirella Fan Club" Member's Button,**
1972. Warren Publishing Co. Membership cost was $2 and recipient received button and membership card. Button is full color 2-1/2". - **$30 $60 $100**

❑ **MNS-11. Magazine Fan Club Card,**
1972. Warren Pub. Co. Black and white on bright yellow. - **$25 $50 $75**

MNS-12

❑ **MNS-12. "Vampirella Giant Poster Puzzle" Boxed,**
1974. Store item by IPL. 9-1/4x13-1/2" box holds puzzle 15x21" assembled. - **$20 $40 $75**

MNS-13

MNS-14

❑ **MNS-13. "King Kong Colorforms Panorama Playset,"**
1976. Store item. - **$15 $40 $80**

❑ **MNS-14. Large Godzilla Figure,**
1977. 19" tall plastic figure by Mattel. Features spring-loaded fist that flies off. - **$35 $65 $125**

MNS-15

MNS-16

❑ **MNS-15. Dracula Figure,**
1980. - **$20 $40 $60**

❑ **MNS-16. Bride of Frankenstein Figure,**
1980. - **$20 $40 $60**

MNS-17

MNS-18

❑ **MNS-17. Addams Family Cereal Box with "Cousin It" Flashlight Premium,**
1991. - **$5 $10 $20**

❑ **MNS-18. Addams Family Cereal Box with "Uncle Fester" Flashlight Premium,**
1991. - **$5 $10 $20**

MNS-19

MNS-20

❑ **MNS-19. Addams Family Cereal Box with "Lurch" Flashlight Premium,**
1991. - **$5 $10 $20**

❑ **MNS-20. Addams Family Cereal Box with "Thing" Flashlight Premium,**
1991. - **$5 $10 $20**

MNS-21

❑ **MNS-21. Vampirella Statue,**
1993. Graphitti Designs. Limited edition of 350. Boxed - **$650**

MNS-22

❑ **MNS-22. Mecha-Ghidora Figure,**
1994. From Godzilla series. In box - **$20**

MNS-23 MNS-24 MNS-25

❑ **MNS-23. "Herman Munster" Bobbing Head Figure,**
1998. In motorcyclist outfit. - **$75**

❑ **MNS-24. "Grandpa" Bobbing Head Figure,**
1998. From Munsters TV show. - **$75**

❑ **MNS-25. Hot Wheels "Rodzilla",**
1999. Collectors' edition. - **$5**

MNS-26

MNS-27

❑ **MNS-26. Comic Book Fan Club Member's Cello. Button,**
1999. Harris Publications. 1-3/4" full color. - **$3 $5 $10**

❑ **MNS-27. Frankenstein Jr. Bean Bag,**
1999. Figure with tag. - **$15**

MNS-28 MNS-29

❑ **MNS-28. Comic Book Fan Club Member's Cello. Button,**
1990s. Harris Publications. 1" red, fleshtone, black and white. - **$3 $5 $10**

❑ **MNS-29. Comic Book Fan Club Member's Card,**
1990s. Harris Publications. Done in black and white. - **$3 $5 $10**

MNS-30

MNS-31

❑ **MNS-30. Bela Lugosi Resin Statue,**
1990s. Crafted by Randy Bowen. Limited edition of 1,000. Boxed - **$200**

❑ **MNS-31. "Dracula" Die-cast Metal Car,**
2000. Team Lightning. - **$5**

MNS-32

❑ **MNS-32. "Godzilla" Statue,**
2001. 12" tall polyester resin statue. Fully painted with deluxe base. Limited edition of 1,000. Sculpted by Yukifusa Shibata. - **$100**

## Movie Misc.

**The first known moving pictures on a public screen were shown at Koster and Bial's Music Hall in New York City April 23, 1896. The program included films of two blonde girls performing an umbrella dance, a comic boxing exhibition and a view of surf breaking on a beach. Movies remained only a novelty until shortly after the turn of the century. 1903 released two pioneer efforts, *The Passion Play* and *The Great Train Robbery* and movies as mass entertainment were born.**

**The 1920s added dimensions of sound plus color experimentation; full-length features were soon followed by the popular episode serial or "chapter play" that remained popular to the mid-1950s. Premiums followed individual stars of universal acclaim such as Charlie Chaplin, Our Gang, Shirley Temple.**

**Movies also produced souvenirs of non-premium original purpose, e.g., heralds and programs, lobby cards, posters and similar that since have matured to status paralleling premiums. Some classic films produced a greater selection of premiums in addition to the standard theater fare. These included *Gone With The Wind*, Disney creations from the early 1930s Mickey Mouse to the 1990s *Dick Tracy* version, other animated cartoons and the most popular of the adventure hero serials.**

**Movie premiums after the advent of television were very limited for a time but recent years have seen frequent tie-ins between movies aimed at family audiences and fast food restaurants.**

MOV-1 MOV-2

❑ **MOV-1. Movie Serial Promotional Button,**
1916. Universal. 7/8" naming stars Grace Cunard and Francis Ford. - **$10 $20 $30**

❑ **MOV-2. "Detective/The Purple Mask" Diecut Tin Star Badge Premium,**
1916. Universal. 2" tall, the earliest non-button movie serial giveaway designed to be worn that we have seen. - **$25 $50 $90**

MOV-3 MOV-4

❑ **MOV-3. "Civilization" Press Book,**
1916. Rare. 24 pages plus front and back covers. Includes 12 photo pages. Covers are color, insides are black & white. - **$75 $150 $300**

❑ **MOV-4. "Oh Helen!" Song Sheet,**
1918. Song is dedicated to Roscoe "Fatty" Arbuckle. - **$20 $40 $60**

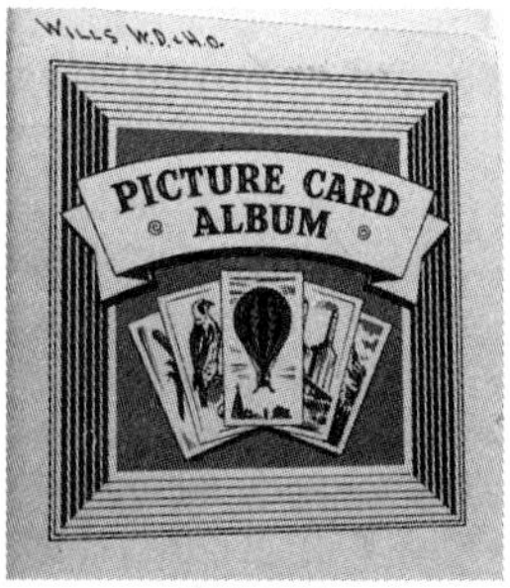


(COVER)

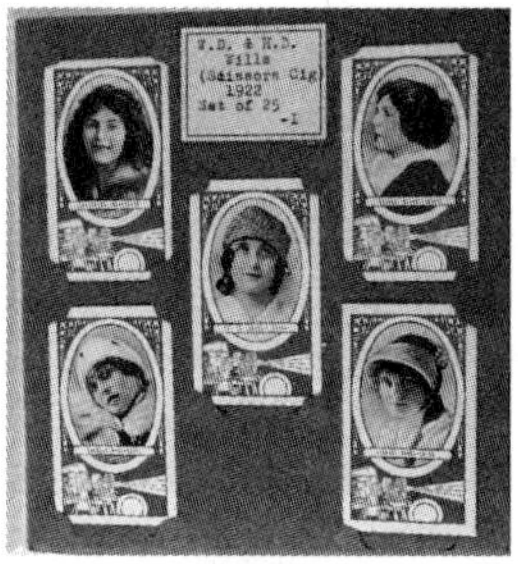

**MOV-5**

❑ **MOV-5. Silent Film Picture Card Album**
1922. Scissors Cigarettes premium. Shows notable stars like Ethel Barrymore, Pearl White, Mary Minter, Lucille Taft and 21 others.
Each Card - **$6**
Album - **$10 $25 $50**

**MOV-6**

❑ **MOV-6. "There's A New Star In Heaven To-Night" Song Sheet,**
1925. Rudolph Valentino on cover. - **$20 $40 $60**

**MOV-7** **MOV-8**

❑ **MOV-7. "Snookums" Cello. Button On Card,**
1927. Universal Exchange (Movie Publicity Agency). Pictured is toddler star of comedy based on "Newlyweds And Their Baby" comic strip. Button maker is Philadelphia Badge Co.
Complete - **$40 $90 $150**
Button Only - **$25 $60 $100**

❑ **MOV-8. "Oswald The Lucky Rabbit" Cello. Button,**
1927. Universal Exchange (Movie Publicity Agency). Pictured is animated cartoon character in Disney art. - **$200 $500 $750**

**MOV-9**

❑ **MOV-9. "Wings" Hardcover Book,**
1927. Feature story was based on the Paramount Pictures film "Wings." Starring Gary Cooper and Clara Bow, the film won the first Academy Award for Best Picture.
Book - **$50 $75 $150**
With Dust Jacket **- $75 $125 $200**

**MOV-10**

❑ **MOV-10. "The Ace of Scotland Yard" Club Button,**
1929. Billed as the 1st talking serial (10 chapters.) From Universal Pictures, starring Crawford Kent and Florence Allen. Rare. **- $50 $75 $100**

**MOV-11** **MOV-12**

❑ **MOV-11. "Jackie Coogan Club" Cello. Button,**
1920s. - **$15 $30 $60**

❑ **MOV-12. Roscoe "Fatty" Arbuckle Cello. Button,**
1920s. - **$15 $30 $50**

**MOV-13**

❑ **MOV-13. Movie Star Album,**
1920s. Cover has 54 pictures of silent film stars arranged like a fan. Book holds cards of stars like Theda Bara (the first major woman sex symbol in "The Vamp"), Ruth Roland, Douglas Fairbanks, Roscoe "Fatty" Arbuckle and others.
Album - **$35 $75 $100**
Theda Bara "The Vamp" card - **$25 $50 $75**
Arbuckle or Fairbanks cards - **$15 $35 $50**
Other cards - **$3 $5 $7**

**MOV-14**

❑ **MOV-14. Rudolph Valentino Cigar Box,**
1920s. Cardboard. - **$50 $100 $275**

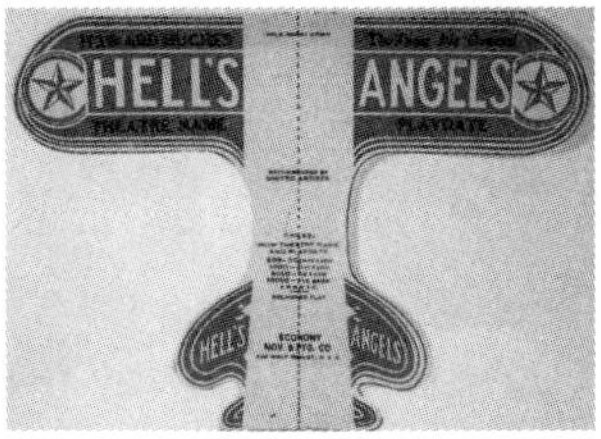

MOV-15

**❑ MOV-15. "Hell's Angels" Movie Promo,**
1930. Very rare promo airplane premium which was passed out at the movie. "Hell's Angels," produced by Howard Hughes for United Artists, was the breakthrough movie for platinum-tressed star Jean Harlow -
**$150 $350 $600**

MOV-16

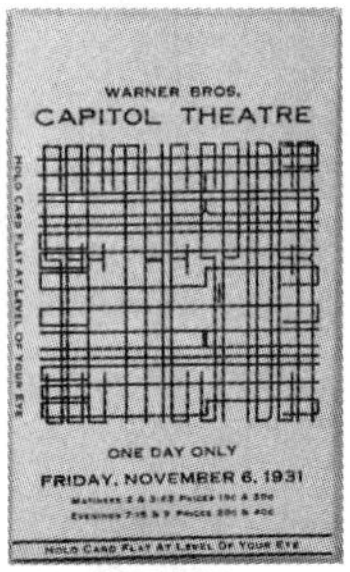

MOV-17

**❑ MOV-16. "Al Jolson In 'Mammy'" Button,**
1930. Warner Bros. 7/8" black, white and gray. -
**$50 $100 $175**

**❑ MOV-17. Promo Card for "The Spider",**
1931. Warner Brothers Theater premium for a Fox feature starring Edmund Lowe. When the card is held flat at eye-level, the design reads "See the Spider." How about those prices to get in the movies: Evenings 20¢ & 40¢. -
**$40 $85 $125**

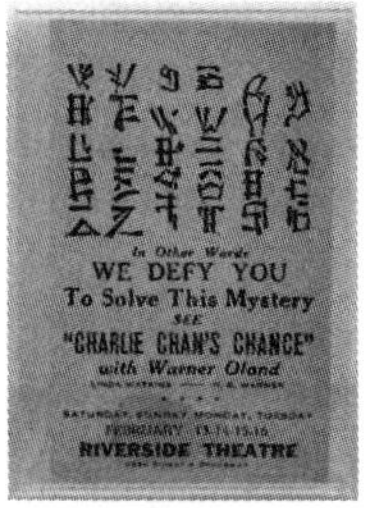

MOV-18

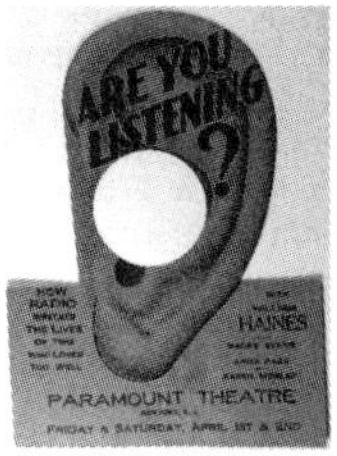

MOV-19

**❑ MOV-18. "Charlie Chan's Chance" Movie Premium Card,**
1931. Fox movie premium printed on unstable paper. This movie marked Warner Oland's 2nd appearance as Charlie Chan. -
**$150 $175 $200**

**❑ MOV-19. "Are You Listening?" Promo,**
1932. Premium for MGM film starring William Haines. - **$25 $60 $110**

MOV-20

**❑ MOV-20. "Horse Feathers" Sheet Music,**
1932. Music for "Ev'ryone Says 'I Love You' " from the Marx Brothers movie. Features Paramount Pictures promo on cover. -
**$25 $50 $90**

MOV-21

MOV-22

**❑ MOV-21. "Movie Crazy" Mechanical Sign,**
1932. Premium for Paramount film starring Harold Lloyd. When Lloyd's hand is moved to the right, the title of the film slowly disappears. Picture claims to be for kids as old as 60. -
**$75 $175 $275**

**❑ MOV-22. "Winner Take All" Promo,**
1932. Very Rare. Great Warner Brothers movie starring James Cagney. Item pictured was a boxing glove shaped premium. -
**$100 $225 $365**

MOV-23

MOV-24

**❑ MOV-23. "'Freaks' Metro-Goldwyn-Mayer's Amazing Picture" Cello. Button,**
1932. Scarce. Movie was quickly withdrawn from distribution. - **$300 $750 $1500**

**❑ MOV-24. "Tom Tyler/Clancy Of The Mounted" Movie Club Cello. Button,**
1933. Universal Pictures. For 12-chapter serial. -
**$75 $175 $300**

MOV-25

MOV-26

**❑ MOV-25. "Silver Dollar" Movie Premium,**
1933. Rare. Classic premium from 1st National Pictures. Ironically the silver dollar depicted is dated 1933, although there were no real silver dollars minted in 1933. - **$75 $150 $250**

**❑ MOV-26. "Meet The Baron" Movie Membership Certificate,**
1933. Rare. "Meet The Baron" starred Jimmy Durante. Certificate bestowed membership in the Baron Munchausen Club. - **$75 $120 $150**

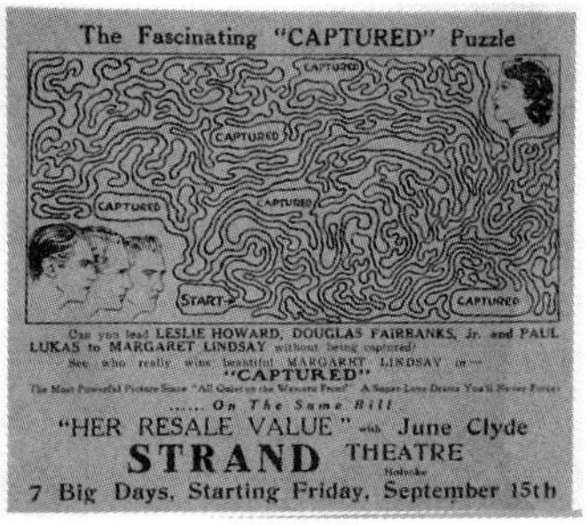

MOV-27

**❑ MOV-27. "Captured" Premium Puzzle,**
1933. Warner Bros.premium puzzle for Douglas Fairbanks, Jr. classic film. - **$50 $75 $100**

MOV-28

**❑ MOV-28. "Button Gum" Wrapper,**
c. 1933. Store item, no company specified on wrapper. Buttons in these sets are often credited to Cracker Jack, who possibly used them, but it seems this product is the original source. Wrapper states "Start A Collection Of 500 Buttons." Set titles are: Presidents, Ball Players, Movie Stars, Generals, Soldiers, Animals, Indians, Scouts, Birds, World's Fair. We've seen examples from all sets except World's Fair. Wrapper - **$50 $150 $250**

(COVER) (OPEN)

MOV-29

❑ **MOV-29. "I'm No Angel" 7 1/2 x3" Paper Premium Sign,**
1933. Rare. Paramount premium for movie starring the one and only Mae West. Standee card opens to display ad for the film. Cary Grant also starred. - **$150 $275 $400**

MOV-30

❑ **MOV-30. "Mae West" 17x30" Cardboard Store Sign,**
1934. Old Gold cigarettes. Text includes "Goin' To Town" movie title. - **$350 $750 $1300**

MOV-31

❑ **MOV-31. Mae West-Inspired China Ashtray,**
c. 1934. Store item. - **$35 $75 $150**

(COVER) MOV-32 (INSIDE)

❑ **MOV-32. "20 Million Sweethearts" Movie Premium,**
1934. Movie starred Dick Powell and Ginger Rogers. - **$25 $50 $85**

MOV-33

❑ **MOV-33. "Viva Villa" Movie Promo,**
1934. Wallace Beery art on cut out hat for MGM movie promo. 10 3/4" x 17". Rare. - **$175 $250 $325**

MOV-34

MOV-35

❑ **MOV-34. "The Crusades" Movie Mask,**
1935. Rare premium. 10x13". - **$35 $130 $200**

❑ **MOV-35. "Mutiny on the Bounty" Promo,**
1935. For MGM movie that won the Academy Award for best picture. This premium was used to hang on the doors of the parked cars of the theater patrons. Very rare. - **$100 $210 $375**

MOV-36

❑ **MOV-36. Hollywood Snapshots,**
1935. Booklet with actual photos of stars inside. Photos taken by an editor of the L.A. Evening Herald. - **$25 $50 $75**

MOV-37

❑ **MOV-37. Frankie Darro Stamp Album,**
1935. Tootsie Roll. Movie Club premium. Holds 24 stamps. - **$30 $60 $150**

MOV-38

❑ **MOV-38. Frankie Darro Stamps,**
1935. Large premium stamp given at each movie. Each - **$10 $20 $30**

MOV-39

MOV-40

MOV-41

❑ **MOV-39. "Gangster's Boy" BLB #1402,**
1936. Starring Jackie Cooper. - **$15 $45 $90**

❑ **MOV-40. "Bullets or Ballots" Promo,**
1936. Warner Bros. premium for Edward G. Robinson movie. Humphrey Bogart receives billing in the small print at bottom. Premium is bullet-shaped of course. - **$75 $150 $250**

❑ **MOV-41. "Captains Courageous" Bookmarker,**
1937. Die-cut premium for the MGM movie starring Spencer Tracy. He won a best actor Oscar for his role. - **$75 $150 $275**

MOV-42

❑ **MOV-42. "Boy of the Streets" Blotter,**
1937. Scarce. Jackie Cooper photo on premium '37 calendar, ruler and blotter. - **$25 $50 $110**

MOV-43

❑ **MOV-43. Rio Theatre Photo Folder,**
1938. Theatre premium. 16 photos (folder & two photos shown). Photos - **$2 $4 $10**
Folder - **$5 $10 $20**

MOV-44

MOV-45

❑ **MOV-44. Judy Garland Photo Promo,**
1938. 5"x7" photo for "Love Finds Andy Hardy". - **$10 $20 $30**

❑ **MOV-45. Wallace Beery Photo Promo,**
1938. 5"x7" photo for "Stablemates". - **$10 $20 $30**

MOV-46

❑ **MOV-46. "Motion Picture Funnies Weekly" Comic Book,**
1939. Only 8 known copies, one in near mint. First printed appearance of the Sub-Mariner. - **$4400 $11000 $24000**

MOV-47

MOV-48

❑ **MOV-47. Mickey Rooney and Judy Garland Fan Club Button,**
1939. Rare. Button is 1.25", black print on bright yellow. - **$50 $125 $200**

❑ **MOV-48. "The Black Falcon Of The Flying G-Men" Game,**
1939. Store item by Ruckelshaus Game Corp. Based on Columbia Pictures movie serial. - **$150 $300 $500**

MOV-49

MOV-50

❑ **MOV-49. "Blackmail" Movie Promo,**
1939. Glasses-shaped promo for MGM movie starring Edward G. Robinson. - **$75 $125 $200**

❑ **MOV-50. "Daredevils of the Red Circle" Promo Badge,**
1939. Silver cardboard movie premium badge outlined in red. Given to kids who attended the Republic Serial "Daredevils of the Red Circle" starring Herman Brix. Rare. - **$75 $125 $200**

MOV-51

❑ **MOV-51. Campaign Movie Button,**
1930s. For campaign to change Sunday Blue laws. Scarce.
7/8" size - **$15 $30 $45**
3 1/2" size - **$20 $40 $65**

MOV-52

❑ **MOV-52. Junior Cagney Club Litho. Buttons,**
1930s. Theater patrons collected set of 11, each with single letter of James Cagney name, to gain free admission. Each - **$8 $12 $25**

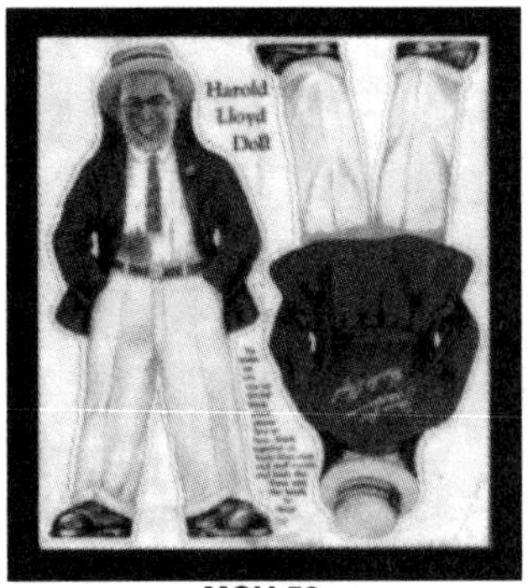


MOV-53

❑ **MOV-53. "Harold Lloyd Doll" Fabric Pattern,**
1930s. Fabric to form 12-1/2" tall doll.
Uncut - **$35 $75 $125**

MOV-54

MOV-55

❑ **MOV-54. Jackie Coogan Notes,**
1930s. 12 Note paper sheets and envelopes.
Each Note with Envelope - **$20**
Box - **$35 $70 $140**

❑ **MOV-55. Park Drive Album Series 1,**
1930s. Cigarette premium from England. Album for 48 cards. U.S. stars.
Album Only - **$5 $10 $20**

MOV-56

❑ **MOV-56. Park Drive Album Cards For Series 1 & 2 - Spencer,**
1930s. Cigarette premium from England. 96 total cards. Each Card - **$1 $3 $5**

MOV-57

❑ **MOV-57. Park Drive Album Series 2,**
1930s. Cigarette premium from England. Album for 48 cards. Each card - **$1 $3 $5**

MOV-58

MOV-59

❑ **MOV-58. Churchman's Card Album,**
1930s. Cigarette premium from England. Holds 50 cards. Album Only - **$10 $20 $30**

❑ **MOV-59. Churchman's Card Album - The Cards,**
1930s. Famous U.S. movie stars on cards.
Each Card - **$1 $3 $5**

MOV-60

❑ **MOV-60. Wallace Beery Photo,**
1930s. Autographed. - **$150**

MOV-61

❑ **MOV-61. Film Star Album,**
1930s. Cigarette premium from England. Holds cards for 53 stars from U.S. movies.
Album Only - **$10 $20 $30**

MOV-62

❑ **MOV-62. Film Star Album Cards,**
1930s. Cigarette premium from England. 53 different colorful cards. 3rd series.
Each Card - **$1 $3 $5**

MOV-63

MOV-64

❑ **MOV-63. "The Terrytooners Music And Fun Club" Cello. Button,**
1930s. Pictures Farmer Alfalfa and Little Wilbur. - **$25 $50 $100**

❑ **MOV-64. "George O'Brien Outdoor Club" Cello. Button,**
1930s. - **$20 $35 $75**

MOV-65

MOV-66

❑ **MOV-65. Wallace Beery Movie Pinback,**
1930s. One in a series of different stars. - **$10 $25 $50**

❑ **MOV-66. Bobby Breen Pinback on Card**
1930s. Promotes movie contest. - **$25 $50 $75**

MOV-67

❑ **MOV-67. Sabu Doll With "Thief Of Bagdad" Litho. Button,**
1940. Store item, maker unknown. Jointed composition doll 14" tall with fabric outfit and 1" black and white litho. button reading "Sabu Club/Sabu In 'The Thief Of Bagdad.'"
Doll - **$100 $200 $400**
Button - **$8 $12 $30**

MOV-68

MOV-69

❑ **MOV-68. "Flight Command" Premium,**
1940. Has small silver plane attached to promo card. Movie starred Robert Taylor. - **$75 $150 $180**

❑ **MOV-69. "Sky Raiders" Club Button,**
1941. Promotes 12-chapter serial by Universal starring Donald Woods and Billy Halop. - **$25 $75 $135**

MOV-70

❑ **MOV-70. Movie Star Premium Cards,**
1941. From J.C. Penney department stores.
Each - **$4 $8 $12**
Lucille Ball, Clark Gable, John Wayne, Roy Rogers and Gene Autry each - **$6 $10 $20**

MOV-71

MOV-72

❑ **MOV-71. "Keep 'Em Flying" Button,**
1941. 7/8" blue and white for their famous movie. - **$10 $20 $40**

❑ **MOV-72. "The Bad Man" Promo,**
1941. 7" movie premium of Wallace Beery starring in "The Bad Man." Rare. - **$35 $70 $150**

MOV-73

❑ **MOV-73. "Citizen Kane" Program,**
1941. Souvenir of RKO Radio Pictures classic film directed by and starring Orson Welles. - **$40 $80 $150**

MOV-74

❑ **MOV-74. Citizen Kane "Souvenir Of Xanadu" Card Deck,**
c. 1941. Playing cards with box art picturing seaside mansion Xanadu of William Randolph Hearst, the pattern for 1941 Orson Welles film "Citizen Kane." - **$100 $200 $300**

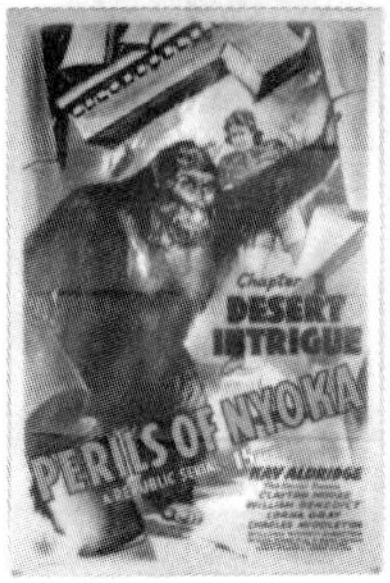


MOV-75

MOV-76

❑ **MOV-75. "Perils Of Nyoka" 27x41" Movie Serial Poster,**
1942. Republic Pictures. Poster is for Chapter 1. - **$200 $400 $750**

❑ **MOV-76. "Perils Of Nyoka" 27x41" Movie Serial Poster,**
1942. Republic Pictures. Same art for Chapters 2-15. Each - **$100 $250 $ 400**

MOV-77

❑ **MOV-77. "As Time Goes By" Song Sheet,**
1943. Features song from "Casablanca," starring Humphrey Bogart and Ingrid Bergman. - **$15 $30 $60**

MOV-78

MOV-79

❑ **MOV-78. Cardboard Stand-Up,**
1943. Two piece 6x9" promo from "The Outlaw" starring Jane Russell. - **$75 $125 $250**

❑ **MOV-79. "Secret Service In Darkest Africa" 27x41" Movie Serial Poster,**
1943. Republic Pictures. - **$50 $100 $175**

MOV-80

❑ **MOV-80. "International Reno Browne Fan Club" Newsletter And Membership Card,**
c. 1946. Issued by Canadian headquarters.
Near Mint In Mailer - **$65**
Newsletter - **$5 $10 $25**
Card - **$5 $10 $25**

MOV-81

(ENLARGED VIEW OF HOPPY STAMP)

❑ **MOV-81. Hollywood Star Stamps,**
1947. Set Q - 12 stamps on uncut sheet in mailer. Eleven Stamps - **$10 $25 $35**
Hoppy Stamp - **$10 $20 $35**

MOV-82

MOV-83

❑ **MOV-82. Hollywood Star Stamps,**
1947. Set Y - 12 stamps on uncut sheet in mailer. - **$10 $25 $35**

❑ **MOV-83. Hollywood Star Stamps,**
1947. Set H - 12 stamps on uncut sheet in mailer. - **$10 $25 $35**

MOV-84

❑ **MOV-84. Betty Grable Movie Promo,**
1947. Chunky Candy Premium. Ten pages of highlights of stars. - **$25 $60 $100**

MOV-85

MOV-86

❑ **MOV-85. "The Black Widow" 27x41" Movie Serial Poster,**
1947. Republic Pictures. - **$75 $250 $500**

❑ **MOV-86. "The Sea Hound Club" Movie Serial Card,**
1947. For admission to 15-episode Columbia Pictures serial starring Buster Crabbe. - **$50 $150 $225**

MOV-87

❑ **MOV-87. "King of the Rocket Men" Movie Serial 1 Sheet Poster,**
1949. Republic Pictures. - **$1750**

MOV-88

❑ **MOV-88. "Mighty Joe Young" Movie 3 Sheet Poster,**
1949. Promotes the classic RKO Pictures movie starring Terry Moore and Ben Johnson. - **$1800**

MOV-89

❑ **MOV-89. Martin & Lewis Fan Club Member Card And Cello. Button,**
1949. Card - **$15 $40 $75**
Button - **$10 $30 $60**

MOV-90

❑ **MOV-90. "The Adventures of Alan Ladd #1" Comic Book,**
1949. DC Comics. Shows highlights from his movie "Chicago Deadline." - **$95 $285 $1050**

MOV-91

MOV-92

❑ **MOV-91. Kirk Douglas Movie Photo,**
1940s. With frame. - **$15 $25 $45**

❑ **MOV-92. James Stewart Movie Photo,**
1940s. With frame. - **$15 $25 $45**

MOV-93

❑ **MOV-93. Susan Hayward Puzzle,**
1940s. Esquire Magazine premium includes puzzle and mailer. - **$25 $50 $125**

MOV-94

MOV-95

❑ **MOV-94. Claudette Colbert Photo,**
1940s. With original frame. - **$10 $35 $75**

❑ **MOV-95. "Reno Browne/Queen Of The Westerns" Cello. Button,**
1940s. - **$15 $30 $60**

MOV-96

❑ **MOV-96. Brass Luster Bracelet,**
1940s. Store item. Facsimile signatures in black of 13 stars including Bing Crosby, Nelson Eddie, Clark Gable, Tyrone Power and Spencer Tracy. - **$25 $50 $85**

MOV-97

MOV-98

❑ **MOV-97. Humphrey Bogart Then and Now Movie Card,**
1940s. Color tint. - **$6 $12 $30**

❑ **MOV-98. George Raft Movie Arcade Card,**
1940s. - **$5 $10 $25**

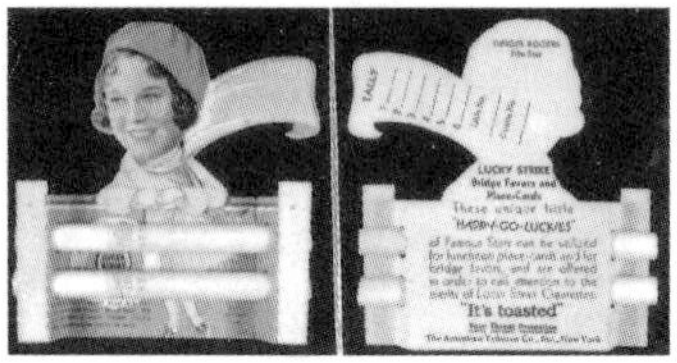


MOV-99

❑ **MOV-99. "Ginger Rogers" Cigarette Ad Paper Standup,**
1940s. Lucky Strike Cigarettes. Lunch place card holder also designed to hold two cigarettes, one of a series. - **$10 $18 $35**

MOV-100

❑ **MOV-100. "Little Women" Movie Premium Plastic Jewel Box with Mailer,**
1940s. Scarce. - **$40 $100 $160**

MOV-101

❑ **MOV-101. Elizabeth Taylor Lapel-Pin Perfume Atomizer,**
1950. Ralston. Near Mint Boxed - **$150**
Pin Only - **$15 $25 $50**

MOV-102 MOV-103

❑ **MOV-102. Esther Williams Coloring Book,**
1950. - **$20 $60 $150**

❑ **MOV-103. MGM Star Esther Williams Cut-Out Doll Book,**
1950. With "look thru" window. Has 2 dolls and 19 cut-out outfits. - **$75 $150 $200**

MOV-104

❑ **MOV-104. "Glance" Magazine With Monroe,**
May 1950. Features Marilyn Monroe by her original name, Norma Jean Dougherty. - **$50 $100 $175**

MOV-105 MOV-106

❑ **MOV-105. Betty Grable Coloring Book,**
1951. - **$50 $100 $150**

❑ **MOV-106. Betty Grable Paper Doll Book,**
1951. Paper dolls with outfits. - **$50 $100 $175**

MOV-107

❑ **MOV-107. "The Day The Earth Stood Still" 5' Standee,**
1951. Rare. - **$2000 $5000 $8000**

MOV-108

❑ **MOV-108. Martin & Lewis 21x22" Cardboard Sign,**
1951. Chesterfield cigarettes. - **$50 $100 $200**

MOV-109 MOV-110

❑ **MOV-109. "Jungle Drums Of Africa" Republic Serial, 27x41",**
1952. Starred Clayton Moore. - **$25 $50 $75**

❑ **MOV-110. "Radar Men From The Moon" 27x41" Movie Serial Poster,**
1952. Republic Pictures. - **$150 $275 $400**

MOV-111 MOV-112

❑ **MOV-111. Ann Blyth Coloring Book,**
1952. Universal Studios Movie Star large squarebound coloring book - **$30 $60 $100**

❑ **MOV-112. Ann Blyth Paper Doll Book,**
1952. Paper dolls with outfits. - **$35 $70 $110**

MOV-113

MOV-114

❑ **MOV-113. Betty Grable Paper Doll Book,**
1953. Has "look thru" window. - **$75 $125 $200**

❑ **MOV-114. Esther Williams Cutouts and Coloring Book,**
1953. Large size book. - **$50 $100 $150**

MOV-115

❑ **MOV-115. Marilyn Monroe Movie Postcard,**
1953. For movie "Niagara." - **$25 $60 $125**

MOV-116

❑ **MOV-116. "The War of the Worlds" Poster,**
1953. Original 1 sheet for the Paramount Pictures movie starring Gene Barry. - **$2400**

MOV-117

❑ **MOV-117. "The War of the Worlds" Movie Premium from Spain,**
1953. Has info on back with movie theater listings. Scarce. - **$75 $150 $220**

MOV-118

❑ **MOV-118. "Buster Crabbe Western Club" Photo Card And Button,**
1953. Black and white photo card with facsimile autograph plus litho. "Official Badge" pin-back button. Card - **$10 $15 $30**
Button - **$25 $65 $125**

MOV-119

MOV-120

❑ **MOV-119. Janet Leigh Cutouts and Coloring Book,**
1953. Large size book. - **$50 $100 $150**

❑ **MOV-120. Jane Russell Paper Doll Book,**
1955. Paper dolls with outfits. Photo cover. - **$75 $150 $300**

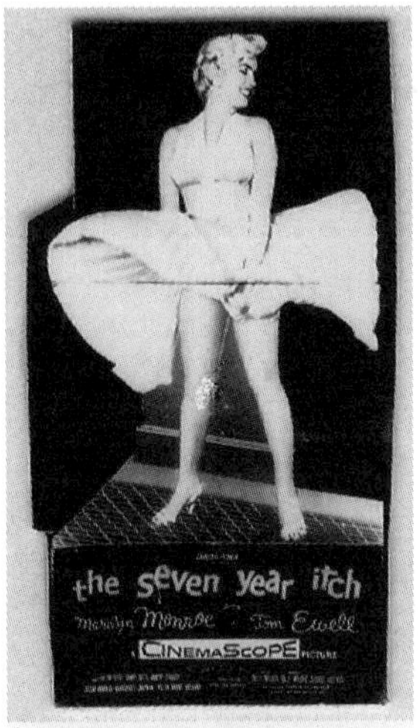


MOV-121

❑ **MOV-121. "The Seven Year Itch" 39x80" Theater Lobby Standee,**
1955. - **$750 $1500 $3500**

MOV-122

MOV-123

❑ **MOV-122. Doris Day Doll and Her Wardrobe of Magic Stay-On Clothes,**
1957. - **$45 $90 $180**

❑ **MOV-123. Dean Martin and Jerry Lewis Trade Card,**
1950s. Not common. - **$10 $20 $35**

MOV-124

MOV-125

❑ **MOV-124. Martin & Lewis Ceramic Salt & Pepper Set,**
1950s. Store item by Napco Ceramic Japan. - **$125 $250 $425**

❑ **MOV-125. Jerry Lewis Watch,**
1950s. Store item. - **$45 $85 $150**

MOV-126

MOV-127

❑ **MOV-126. Marilyn Monroe Pocket Mirror,**
1950s. Store item. Full color paper photo with cello. rim. - **$30 $65 $100**

❑ **MOV-127. Sunbeam Bread Movie Star Loaf End Labels,**
1950s. Each - **$8 $15 $25**

MOV-128

❑ **MOV-128. Robin Hood Watch,**
1950s. In open box with die-cut display. Mylar type top. - **$425**

MOV-129

MOV-130

❑ **MOV-129. Rock Hudson Fan Club Cello. Button,**
1950s. Black and white real photo button without dot pattern, 1-1/4". - **$10 $20 $35**

❑ **MOV-130. "Walkie-Talkie Set" Offer Folder,**
1950s. Campbell's tomato products. Promotional folder for distributors or retailers featuring endorsements of Abbott & Costello, Howdy Doody TV shows. - **$15 $25 $35**

MOV-131

❑ **MOV-131. "Melody Time" Promotional Brochure (Disney),**
1950s. - **$20 $40 $100**

MOV-132

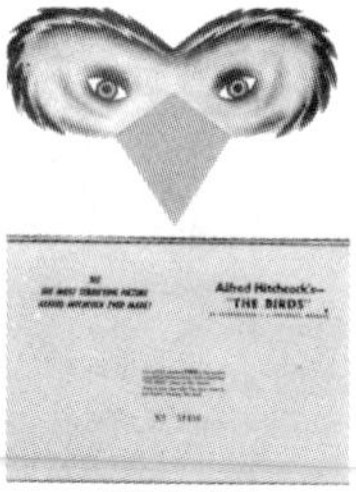


MOV-133

❑ **MOV-132. "Sal Mineo Fan Club" Button,**
1950s. - **$10 $20 $50**

❑ **MOV-133. "Alfred Hitchcock's The Birds" Movie Theater Mask,**
1963. - **$12 $25 $40**

MOV-134

MOV-135

❑ **MOV-134. "Tom Thumb" Standee,**
1960s. - **$20 $50 $120**

❑ **MOV-135. "Billy Jack For President" Pin,**
1976. 2 1/4" diameter. Black print on white. - **$15 $25 $50**

MOV-136

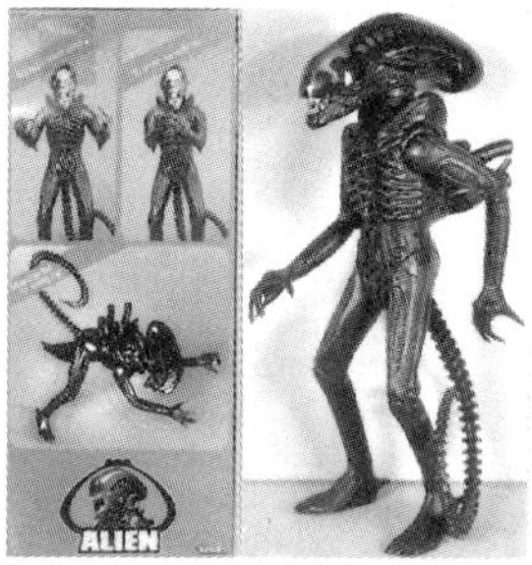


MOV-137

❑ **MOV-136. "Lou Costello" Plaster Statue,**
1979. 16 1/2" tall by Esco. - **$25 $50 $80**

❑ **MOV-137. "Alien" Poseable Plastic Figure,**
1979. Store item by Kenner. Came with poster in box. Often missing fangs from mouth.
Near Mint Boxed - **$500**
Figure Only - **$100 $200 $350**

MOV-138

❑ **MOV-138. Marx Brothers Figurines,**
1970s. Store items by Royal Crown. 6-1/2" to 7" tall hollow bisque. Each - **$10 $20 $30**

MOV-139

❑ **MOV-139. Robby the Robot Figure,**
1984. With instructions and box.
Complete - **$300**

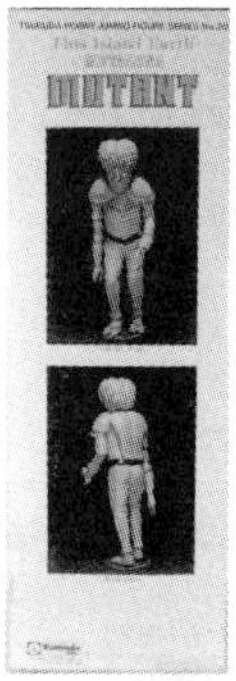


MOV-140

MOV-141

❑ **MOV-140. "This Island Earth" Metaluna Mutant Figure,**
1984. Tsukuda Model. Doll in box.
Complete - **$300**

❑ **MOV-141. "Gremlins" Stripe Figure,**
1984. 14" poseable figure in box. Boxed - **$85**

MOV-142

❑ **MOV-142. "Alien" Figure,**
1984. Tsukuda Model. Doll in box.
Complete - **$275**

MOV-143

MOV-144

❑ **MOV-143. Back To The Future Dream Truck,**
c. 1985. Toyota. 4-3/4" long black plastic truck with movie title on hood in red and yellow. Toy is battery operated and comes in mailing box with the name of the premium as part of the return address. Box - **$1 $3 $5**
Truck - **$5 $10 $15**

❑ **MOV-144. "Over the Top" Movie Figure,**
1986. 17" tall poseable figure of Lincoln Hawks, played by Sylvester Stallone.
Boxed - **$20 $50 $125**

MOV-145

MOV-146

❑ **MOV-145. "Ghostbusters Ectomobile" Die-Cast Vehicle,**
1988. Carded offer with two film rolls from Fuji Film. Carded - **$40 $75 $125**
Loose - **$10 $20 $30**

❑ **MOV-146. "Beetlejuice" Talking Figure,**
1989. Produced by Kenner. 12" talking figure. Head spins. Figure in original box - **$80**

MOV-147

❑ **MOV-147. "The Maltese Falcon" 50th Anniversary Figure,**
1991. Limited edition of 1250. The 4 1/4" figure celebrates the 50th anniversary of the 1941 film starring Humphrey Bogart. Very heavy. Copyright Warner Bros. - **$325**

MOV-148

MOV-149

❑ **MOV-148. "Rocketeer Thrill Club" Badge,**
1991. This hard-to-find badge was issued to promote the Disney film starring Billy Campbell and Jennifer Connelly. The Rocketeer character was created by Dave Stevens and first appeared in Starslayer #2 comic book in 1982. - **$25 $50 $75**

❑ **MOV-149. "Rocketeer" Watch,**
1991. Limited edition of 1,500. Giveaway to promote the movie. Shows the Rocketeer flying over Los Angeles. No box was made. - **$125**

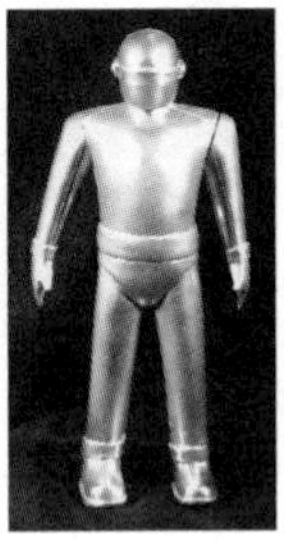

MOV-150

❑ **MOV-150. "Gort" Figure,**
1992. Limited edition boxed figure from the movie "The Day The Earth Stood Still." This was sculptor Randy Bowen's 3rd figure. Some assembly required. Two sets of arms were included. Box is scarce. Box - **$100**
Figure with extra set of arms - **$250**

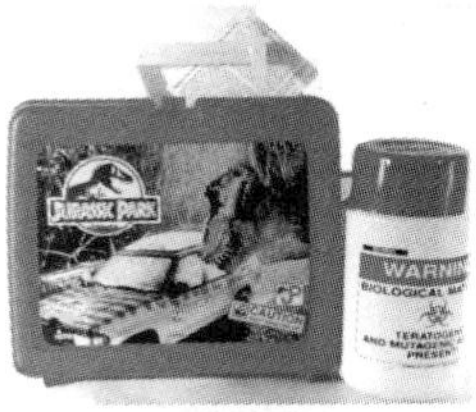


MOV-151

MOV-152

❑ **MOV-151. "Jurassic Park" Lunch Box,**
1993. Includes a thermos. - **$25 $50 $75**

❑ **MOV-152. "Back To The Future/Hill Valley High" Class Ring,**
1994. Universal Studios. Six rings in set with red, green or blue birthstones and done in gold or silver finishes. Each Near Mint - **$20**

MOV-153

MOV-154

❑ **MOV-153. "Waterworld" Watch,**
1995. Universal Studios premium tie-in for the video release. Nice wooden display box with map insert.
Boxed - **$50 $75 $100**

❑ **MOV-154. "Independence Day" Patch,**
1996. Premium notes "Restricted Access" to "Area 51." - **$150**

MOV-155

MOV-156

❑ **MOV-155. "Mars Attacks" Martian Supreme Commander Figure,**
1996. 11 3/4" tall figure talks and lights up.
In display box. - **$5 $10 $20**

❑ **MOV-156. "Mars Attacks" Supreme Martian Ambassador Figure,**
1996. Figure talks. - **$20**

MOV-157

MOV-158

❑ **MOV-157. "Mars Attacks" Martian Brain Disintegrator Gun,**
1996. In green display box. - **$40**

❑ **MOV-158. "Mars Attacks" Martian Brain Disintegrator Gun,**
1996. In blue display box. - **$45**

MOV-159

**MOV-159. "Mars Attacks" Martian Spy Girl Figure,**
1996. Two versions exist.
❑ Green gun version laughs and says "Mars will rule." - **$30 $50 $75**
❑ Red gun version is scarcer. It laughs and says "Trust me." - **$35 $65 $100**

(FRONT OF BOX)

(BACK OF BOX)

(3 DOLLS SHOWN INSIDE BOX)

MOV-160

**MOV-160. "James and the Giant Peach" Doll Set in Box,**
1996. Three dolls in the set. - **$60**

MOV-161

MOV-162

❑ **MOV-161. "Jack Frost" Snowman Bean Bag,**
1999. Distributed exclusively at Warner Bros stores. Promotes the movie which starred Michael Keaton. - **$25**

❑ **MOV-162. "Quack Nicholson" Bean Bag,**
1998. Infamous Meanies Series with tag. - **$8**

MOV-163

MOV-164

MOV-165

MOV-166

❑ **MOV-163. "Antz" Z Action Figure on Card,**
1999. From the computer animated film. Character was voiced by Woody Allen. - **$12**

❑ **MOV-164. "Antz" Princess Bala Action Figure on Card,**
1999. Bala was voiced by Sharon Stone. - **$10**

❑ **MOV-165. "Antz" Colonel Cutter Action Figure on Card,**
1999. Reconnaissance pilot. Character was voiced by Christopher Walken. - **$10**

❑ **MOV-166. "Antz" General Mandible Action Figure on Card,**
1999. Military leader of the colony. Character was voiced by Gene Hackman. - **$10**

MOV-167

MOV-168

❑ **MOV-167. "Austin Powers" Movie Car,**
1999. Replica of the "Shaguar." Johnny Lightning series on card. - **$10**

❑ **MOV-168. "The King and I" Promo Whistle**
1999. Premium whistle offered with video tape of animated movie. - **$5**

MOV-169

MOV-170

❑ **MOV-169. "The Iron Giant" Bean Bag,**
1999. Warner Bros. store exclusive. - **$15**

❑ **MOV-170. "The Iron Giant" 11" Figure,**
1999. With small Hogarth figure. - **$30**

MOV-171

❑ **MOV-171. "The Iron Giant" 20" Figure,**
1999. With small Hogarth figure. Unlike the 11" version, this has a remote control. Highly sought after and hard to find. Boxed - **$50**

MOV-172

MOV-173

❑ **MOV-172. "Nightmare Before Christmas" "Zero the Dog" Bean Bag,**
1999. With tag. First bean bag offered from the set. Hardest to find of the group. Sold at Disney Parks and Stores. - **$25**

❑ **MOV-173. "Nightmare Before Christmas" "Jack Skellington" Bean Bag,**
1999. With tag. - **$10**

MOV-174

MOV-175

❑ **MOV-174. "Nightmare Before Christmas" 11" "Sally" Bean Bag,**
1999. With tag. - **$22**

❑ **MOV-175. "Nightmare Before Christmas" "Mayor" Bean Bag,**
1999. With tag. - **$18**

MOV-176

MOV-177

❑ **MOV-176. "Nightmare Before Christmas" "Oogie Boogie" Bean Bag,**
1999. With tag. - **$15**

❑ **MOV-177. "Nightmare Before Christmas" "Santa" Bean Bag,**
1999. With tag. - **$18**

MOV-178

MOV-179

MOV-180

❑ **MOV-178. "Nightmare Before Christmas" 8" "Lock" Bean Bag,**
1999. With tag. Voiced in movie by Paul Reubens. - **$12**

❑ **MOV-179. "Nightmare Before Christmas" 8" "Shock" Bean Bag,**
1999. With tag. - **$12**

❑ **MOV-180. "Nightmare Before Christmas" 8" "Barrel" Bean Bag,**
1999. With tag. - **$20**

MOV-181

MOV-182

❑ **MOV-181. "Wild Wild West" Sunglasses,**
1999. Burger King premium. Artemus Gordon model has gold rims, with brown case. - **$10**

❑ **MOV-182. "Wild Wild West" Sunglasses,**
1999. Burger King premium. James West model has silver rims, with brown case. - **$10**

MOV-183

MOV-184

❑ **MOV-183. "Puppet Master" Totem Figure,**
1999. Previews exclusive. Has silver helmet mask and black body with cape. Stand is green with blue diamond on top. Scarcer of 2. - **$18**

❑ **MOV-184. "Puppet Master" Totem Figure,**
1999. Previews exclusive. Has gold helmet mask and brown body; no cape. Stand is red with orange diamond on top. - **$12**

MOV-185

MOV-186

❑ **MOV-185. "Puppet Master" Jester Figure,**
1999. Previews exclusive on card. Has purple hat and shirt, and green pants. - **$28**

❑ **MOV-186. "Puppet Master" Pinhead Figure,**
1999. Previews exclusive. Two versions. Gold Edition shown with gold shirt. - **$22**

MOV-187

MOV-188

❑ **MOV-187. "Puppet Master" Torch Figure,**
1999. Previews exclusive on card. Has dark green coat and green pants. - **$25**

❑ **MOV-188. "Puppet Master" Tunneler Figure,**
1999. Figure on card. - **$16**

MOV-189

❑ **MOV-189. "The Rocketeer" Resin Statue,**
1999. Sculpted by Kent Melton. 1,000 produced. There are also 50 bronze editions created a few years earlier. The resin version comes with a colorful box, but the bronze version does not.
Resin - **$125**
Bronze - **$2400**

MOV-190

MOV-191

❑ **MOV-190. "King Kong" Model Kit,**
2000. Aurora. Boxed - **$17**

❑ **MOV-191. "Ymir" Resin Statue ,**
2000. From the 1957 movie "20 Million Miles to Earth." 12" tall and fully painted. Sculpted by Hirokazu Tokugawa. Limited to 1,000. - **$85**

MOV-192

MOV-193

❑ **MOV-192. "Kali" Resin Statue,**
2000. From the movie "The Golden Voyage of Sinbad." 12" tall and fully painted with deluxe base. Limited to 1,000. - **$100**

❑ **MOV-193. "Minotaur" Resin Statue,**
2000. A Ray Harryhausen product from the movie "Sinbad and the Eye of the Tiger." Limited to 1,000. - **$100**

**MOV-194**

**MOV-195**

❑ **MOV-194. "Cyclops" Resin Statue ,**
2000. From the 1958 movie "7th Voyage of Sinbad." 12" tall and fully painted. Sculpted by Ryu Ohyama. Limited to 1,000. - **$100**

❑ **MOV-195. "Talos" Statue,**
2000. 16 1/2" high. From Sinbad movie. Limited to 1,000. Boxed - **$125**

**MOV-196**

**MOV-197**

❑ **MOV-196. "Dinosaur" Movie Lunch Box,**
2000. With Thermos and tag. Features Aladar from the Disney film. - **$35**

❑ **MOV-197. "The Crow" Lunch Box,**
2001. With Thermos. - **$21**

**MOV-198**

❑ **MOV-198. "Beetlejuice" Lunch Box,**
2001. With Thermos. - **$35**

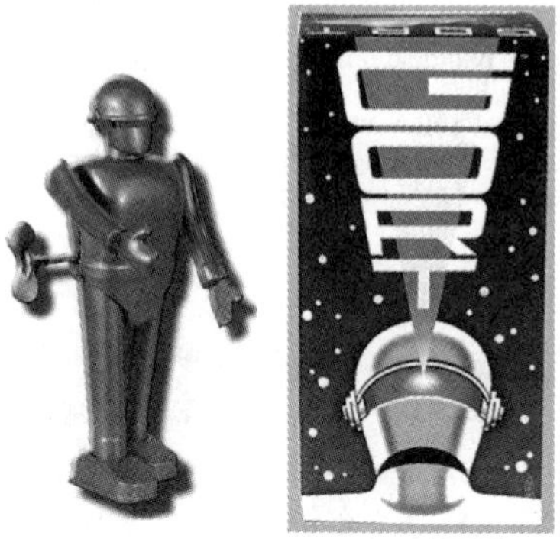

**MOV-199** (BOX)

❑ **MOV-199. "Gort" Wind-Up Toy,**
2001. 8-1/2" tall. In box. - **$22**

**MOV-200**

**MOV-201**

❑ **MOV-200. "Shrek" Doll in Box,**
2001. - **$25**

❑ **MOV-201. "Shrek" Donkey Figure in Box,**
2001. Figure stands on base; has 6 sound phrases. - **$20**

(Masks)
**MOV-202**

❑ **MOV-202. "Monsters, Inc. Masks and More!" Book,**
2001. Has 4 masks, game board and monster playing pieces. - **$5**

**MOV-203**

❑ **MOV-203. "Harry Potter" Tin Lunch Box,**
2001. - **$25**

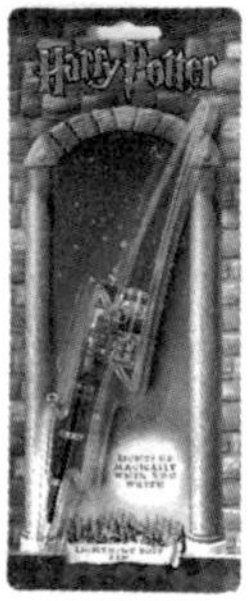
**MOV-204**

**MOV-205**

❑ **MOV-204. "Harry Potter" Lightning Bolt Pen,**
2001. On card. Lights up when used. - **$5**

❑ **MOV-205. "Harry Potter" Broom Pen,**
2001. On card. - **$5**

## Mr. Magoo

**Near-sighted, stubborn, crotchety Mr. Magoo first stumbled into view in 1949 in the UPA animated cartoon *Ragtime Bear*, and over the next 10 years he starred in more than 50 theatrical cartoons. He went to television on Los Angeles station KTTV in 1960 and to prime-time network television on NBC in *The Famous Adventures of Mr. Magoo* in 1964-1965. Other televised specials followed, and in 1977-1979 the old-timer reappeared in *What's New, Mister Magoo?* on CBS. A theatrical film, *1001 Arabian Nights*, was released by UPA in 1959. Jim Backus (1913-1989) was the voice of Magoo from the beginning. Comic books appeared between 1953 and 1965. General Electric has featured Mr. Magoo in various promotions, and Magoo films have been made for the National Heart Association, Timex, General Foods, Rheingold beer, Ideal toys, Dell Publishing, Colgate-Palmolive, and other advertisers. A 1997 Disney feature film starred Leslie Nielsen as Magoo.**

MGO-1

MGO-2

❑ **MGO-1. Figural Metal Badge,**
1960. GE Lightbulbs. On Card - **$15 $25 $50**
Badge Only - **$8 $15 $25**

❑ **MGO-2. General Electric Flicker Plastic Keychain Tag,**
1961. - **$15 $25 $40**

MGO-3

❑ **MGO-3. "The Official Mr. Magoo Battery Operated Car By Hubley",**
1961. Store item. Detailed litho. tin car with vinyl figure of Mr. Magoo and fabric roof.
Box - **$35 $75 $125**
Car - **$100 $250 $450**

MGO-4

MGO-5

❑ **MGO-4. Vinyl/Cloth Doll,**
1962. Store item. - **$40 $100 $175**

❑ **MGO-5. Hand Puppet,**
1962. Store item. Soft vinyl head with fabric body. - **$20 $40 $70**

MGO-6

❑ **MGO-6. "Mr. Magoo Tattoo Gum" Box Insert,**
1967. Store item by Fleer. 4-1/4x5-1/2" diecut. - **$10 $20 $40**

MGO-7

❑ **MGO-7. Boxed Double Deck Set Of Playing Cards,**
1960s. General Electric produced by Brown & Bigelow. - **$5 $15 $30**

MGO-8

MGO-9

❑ **MGO-8. Glass Ashtray,**
1960s. General Electric. - **$10 $20 $40**

❑ **MGO-9. Plastic Ring Kit,**
1960s. Store item. Comes with attachment heads of Magoo, Waldo or Charlie.
Near Mint Bagged - **$25**
Each Complete Ring - **$4 $6 $8**

MGO-10

❑ **MGO-10. "Big Pop Birthday Bash" Party Kit,**
1960s. GE/Hershey's numerous paper items of circus theme. Near Mint In Mailer - **$90**

MGO-11

❑ **MGO-11. Fabric Store Sign,**
1960s. General Electric. 15x25" white fabric with art in red and black. - **$30 $75 $125**

## Mr. Peanut

**The corporate symbol for the Planters Nut and Chocolate Company was the inspiration of a 13-year-old schoolboy in a 1916 company-sponsored contest. Decked out in top hat, monocle, and cane, Mr. Peanut has been promoting the products of this Suffolk, Virginia, company ever since. The design has been refined from the original figure, first in 1927 and again in 1962. Mr. Peanut has appeared in the form of a wide variety of promotional items, from lamps to salt and pepper sets, peanut dishes, banks, buttons, pins, bookmarks, figures and dolls of wood, plastic, bisque, and cloth, silverware, cigarette lighters, and mechanical pencils, as well as in a series of children's story and paint books first published in 1928 and available from the company in exchange for product wrappers.**

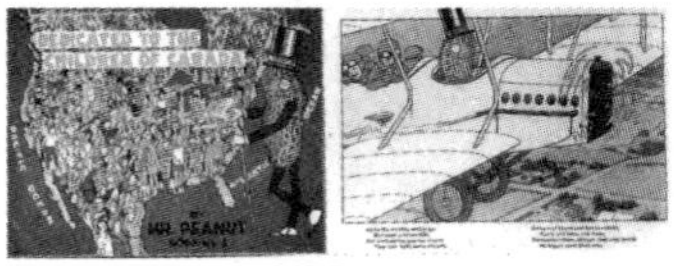
MRP-1

❑ **MRP-1. "Mr. Peanut Book No. 1" Canadian Version Coloring Book,**
c. 1928. Pictured example shows cover and sample coloring page. - **$40 $75 $150**

MRP-2

MRP-3

MRP-4

❑ **MRP-2. New York World's Fair Cardboard Bookmark,**
1939. - **$10 $20 $35**

❑ **MRP-3. Laminated Wooden Pin As Santa,**
c. 1939. - **$35 $75 $150**

❑ **MRP-4. Laminated Wood Pin,**
c. 1939. - **$20 $40 $75**

MRP-5

MRP-6

❑ **MRP-5. Wood Jointed Figure,**
1930s. Frequently missing his cane. -
**$125 $250 $400**

❑ **MRP-6. Bisque Ashtray,**
1930s. - **$35 $70 $125**

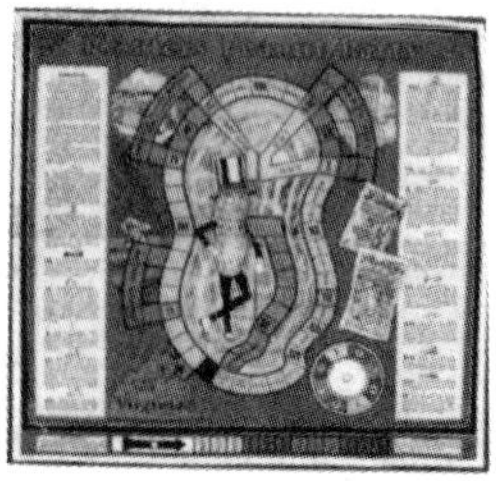

MRP-7

MRP-8

❑ **MRP-7. "Planters Peanut Party" Game Sheet,**
c. 1930s. 9x9-1/4" paper opens to 17-1/2x18-1/2". - **$35 $65 $140**

❑ **MRP-8. New York World's Fair Wood Figure Pin,**
1940. Dated on Trylon either 1939 or 1940. Each - **$25 $50 $90**

MRP-9

MRP-10

❑ **MRP-9. "Spooky Picture" Optical Illusion Card,**
c. 1940. Believed insert for Planter's Jumbo Block Bar. - **$5 $15 $30**

❑ **MRP-10. "The People's Choice" Litho. Button,**
c. 1940s. - **$10 $25 $40**

MRP-11

MRP-12

❑ **MRP-11. Serving Dish Set With Mailer,**
1940s. Distributed into 1950s.
Mailer - **$5 $10 $15**
Dish Set - **$5 $15 $25**

❑ **MRP-12. Paperweight Figure,**
c. 1940s. 7" tall painted metal figural weight with inscription on rear base "Compliments Planters Nut & Chocolate Co." - **$200 $400 $675**

MRP-13

MRP-14

❑ **MRP-13. "The Personal Story Of Mr. Peanut" Anniversary Comic Book,**
1956. Full color 7x10" with 16 pages. Back cover offers mail premiums of mechanical pencil, nut spoon, figural bank, drinking cup, presidents paint book. - **$25 $50 $90**

❑ **MRP-14. 50th Anniversary Metal Tray,**
1956. - **$20 $40 $75**

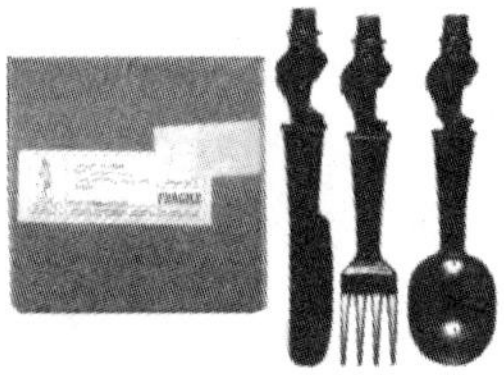

MRP-15

❑ **MRP-15. Knife/Fork/Spoon Sets With Mailer,**
1959. Nine plastic sets. Mailer - **$1 $3 $5**
Utensils - **$10 $15 $25**

MRP-16

❑ **MRP-16. "Mister Peanut Cocktail Glasses" Boxed Set,**
c. 1950s. Boxed - **$50 $100 $175**

MRP-17

MRP-18

❑ **MRP-17. Mr. Peanut Chopper With Mailer,**
1950s. Mailer - **$1 $3 $5**
Chopper - **$10 $15 $25**

❑ **MRP-18. Composition Bobbing Body Figure,**
1960s. - **$75 $125 $200**

MRP-19

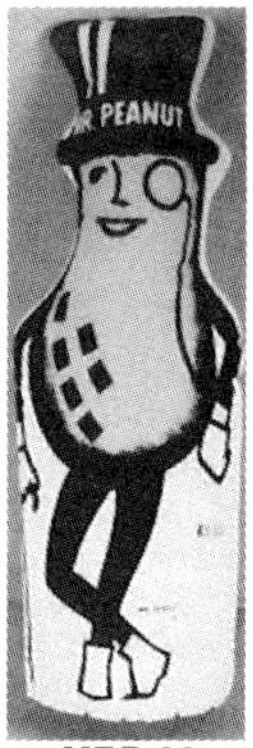


MRP-20

❑ **MRP-19. Mr. Peanut Metal Ring,**
c. 1960s. Gold luster with raised image of him. -
**$10 $20 $30**

❑ **MRP-20. Vinyl Inflatable Figure,**
c. 1970s. Image on each side. When inflated has 8" bottom diameter and stands 26" tall. -
**$10 $20 $30**

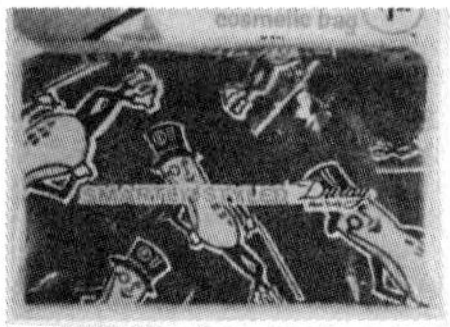

MRP-21

MRP-22

❑ **MRP-21. Fabric Cosmetic Bag,**
c. 1970s. Yellow and black images on blue denim. - **$10 $20 $30**

❑ **MRP-22. Mr. Peanut Silver Coin,**
1991. Limited edition 1 oz. coin came in box with certificate. Boxed - **$20**

MRP-23

MRP-24

❑ **MRP-23. Peanut Butter Maker,**
1996. Boxed. - **$30**

❑ **MRP-24. Stuffed Doll,**
1997. Modeled after the 1960's version of the character. - **$10 $25 $50**

MRP-25

MRP-26

❑ **MRP-25. Cookie Jar,**
1998. Nabisco premium from mail order offer. 10 1/4" tall. Black hat scuffs and chips easily. - **$25 $50 $100**

❑ **MRP-26. Beanie with Planters Tag,**
1999. - **$10 $15 $20**

MRP-27

MRP-28

❑ **MRP-27. Key Chain on Card,**
1990s. - **$5**

❑ **MRP-28. Vending Machine,**
1999. Boxed. - **$35**

MRP-29

❑ **MRP-29. Wall Clock,**
1990s. Modern quartz wall clock. TM Nabisco. 9 1/2 x 9 1/2" in box with instructions. - **$30**

## Mr. Zip

**The U.S. Post Office inaugurated its system of ZIP Codes (Zone Improvement Program) on July 1, 1963, to help speed delivery of increasing volumes of mail. A wide-eyed, cheerful character, Mr. ZIP was created to help popularize the program. He zipped along in advertising and at postal conventions between 1963 and July 1986, when he was officially retired.**

MRZ-1

MRZ-2

❑ **MRZ-1. Service Introduction 32x56" Paper Poster,**
1963. Large Mr. ZIP image on post office department poster issued in May. -
**$25 $50 $75**

❑ **MRZ-2. "Zip Code" Game,**
1964. Store item by Lakeside Toys. Game is based on actual post office and zip code operations. - **$15 $30 $60**

MRZ-3

MRZ-4

MRZ-5

❑ **MRZ-3. "Mr. ZIP" Cello. Button,**
1960s. U.S. Postal Service. - **$5 $10 $20**

❑ **MRZ-4. "Use Zip Code" Cello. Button,**
1960s. U.S. Postal Service. - **$5 $10 $20**

❑ **MRZ-5. "Mr. ZIP" Figure Pin,**
1960s. U.S. Postal Service. Gold luster figure image in salute pose with "US Mail" pouch over one shoulder. - **$8 $15 $35**

MRZ-6

MRZ-7

❑ **MRZ-6. Mail Box Bank,**
1960s. Store item. 6" tall litho. tin replica of mail drop box with coin savings chart on back panel. -
**$10 $20 $40**

❑ **MRZ-7. "Zip Code System" First Day Commemorative Cover,**
1974. Probably a 10th anniversary issue post-marked January 4 from Washington, D.C. -
**$10 $20 $30**

## Muhammad Ali

**He was born Cassius Clay in Louisville, Ky., in 1942, began amateur boxing at age 12, and burst into boxing prominence in 1960, when he won the Amateur Athletic Union light-heavyweight title, the National Golden Gloves heavyweight title, and an Olympic gold medal as a light-heavyweight. Then he turned professional, and four years later defeated Sonny Liston to win the world heavyweight championship. Clay changed his name to Muhammad Ali and embraced the Muslim religion. In 1967 he refused induction into the army as a conscientious objector and was stripped of his title and banned from boxing. In 1971 his refusal was upheld in a unanimous decision of the Supreme Court. Ali regained his title in 1974, knocking out George Foreman in "The Rumble in the Jungle" in Zaire, then lost it in 1978 to Leon Spinks, and won it back from Spinks seven months later. Ali retired in 1979, then returned to the ring and lost bouts in 1980 and 1981, after which he again retired.**

**Always a popular and beloved champion, Ali lent his name and image to a variety of commercial products, including shoe polish, potato chips, cookies, barbecue sauce,**

**candy bars, cologne, shaving cream, Knockout shampoo, roach traps, dolls and games. He played himself in a 1977 biographical movie, *The Greatest*, and provided his voice for the 1977 NBC-television animated series, *I Am the Greatest: The Adventures of Muhammad Ali*. In 1996, Ali lit the torch at the summer Olympics in Atlanta. Also, a 1997 documentary, *When We Were Kings*, about Ali's "Rumble in the Jungle" with Foreman, has garnered many awards and much critical praise. A biographical feature film, *Ali*, featuring Will Smith in the title role, opened strong in late 2001 but did not possess Ali's stamina at the box office.**

MUH-1

❑ **MUH-1. Cassius Clay "The Champ Sings!" Record,**
c. 1962. 7x7" sleeve holding 45 rpm record sung by him of song titles "Stand By Me" and "I Am The Greatest." - **$20 $40 $75**

MUH-2

❑ **MUH-2. "The Ring" Boxing Magazine Issues With Cassius Clay Covers,**
1964-1966. Each - **$5 $10 $15**

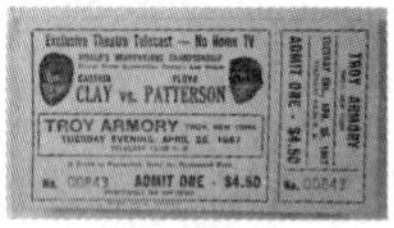


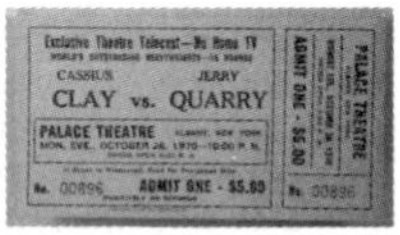


MUH-3 MUH-4

❑ **MUH-3. Cassius Clay vs. Floyd Patterson Theatre Telecast Ticket,**
Apr. 25, 1967. Complete ticket. - **$10 $25 $50**

❑ **MUH-4. Cassius Clay vs. Jerry Quarry Theatre Telecast Ticket,**
Oct. 26, 1970. Complete ticket. - **$10 $15 $35**

MUH-5 MUH-6

❑ **MUH-5. Cassius Clay vs. Bonavena Theatre Telecast Ticket,**
Dec. 7, 1970. Complete ticket. - **$5 $10 $30**

❑ **MUH-6. Ali-Joe Frazier Championship Fight Pennant,**
1971. 8x21" felt fabric for undated but March 8 bout at Madison Square Garden. -
**$20 $35 $65**

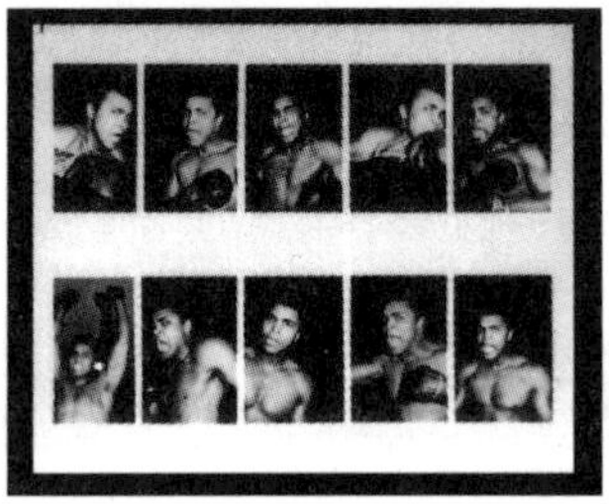

MUH-7

❑ **MUH-7. Ali-Jimmy Ellis Fight Promotion Photo,**
1971. 8x10" black and white print of 10 Ali facial expressions and contortions with inscriptions including upcoming July 26 closed circuit telecast bout from Houston Astrodome. -
**$10 $20 $35**

MUH-8 MUH-9

❑ **MUH-8. Ali-Joe Frazier 14x22" Fight Poster,**
1974. For closed circuit telecast of January 28 "Super Fight II" bout. - **$40 $80 $140**

❑ **MUH-9. Mr. Toothdecay Pinback,**
1974. 4" pin promotes St. John's toothpaste. -
**$50 $150 $350**

MUH-10 MUH-11

❑ **MUH-10. Ali-George Foreman Championship Fight Pennant,**
1974. 8-1/2x27" felt fabric for October 29 bout in Zaire, Africa. - **$15 $45 $65**

❑ **MUH-11. Foreman vs. Ali Theatre Telecast Ticket,**
Sept. 24, 1974. Complete ticket. - **$15 $30 $75**

MUH-12

❑ **MUH-12. "A Thrilla In Manila" Pennant,**
1975. 12" wide. - **$20 $40 $85**

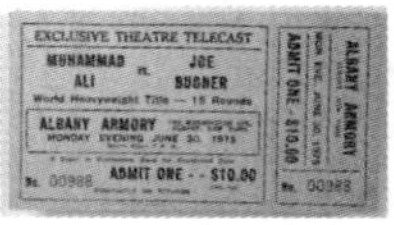

MUH-13 MUH-14

❑ **MUH-13. Ali vs. Joe Bugner Theatre Telecast Ticket,**
June 30, 1975. Complete ticket. - **$5 $10 $25**

❑ **MUH-14. Ali vs. Frazier Theatre Telecast Ticket,**
Sept. 30, 1975. Complete ticket. - **$15 $30 $70**

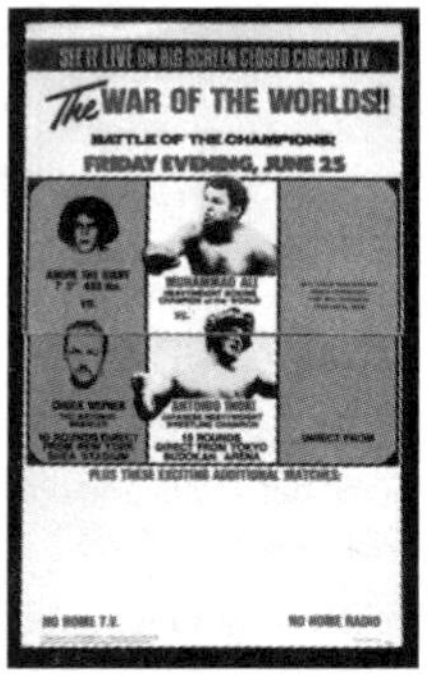


MUH-15

❑ **MUH-15. Ali vs. Inoki Exhibition Match 14x23" Paper Poster,**
June 25, 1976. For closed circuit TV 15-round specialty match between him and Antonio Inoki, Japanese heavyweight wrestling champion, televised from Tokyo. - **$25 $50 $75**

MUH-16 MUH-17

❑ **MUH-16. Ali vs. Inoki Exhibition Match Theatre Telecast Ticket,**
June 25, 1976. Complete ticket. - **$5 $10 $30**

❑ **MUH-17. Ali vs. Ken Norton Theatre Telecast Ticket,**
Sept. 28, 1976. Complete ticket. - **$10 $15 $35**

MUH-18

❑ **MUH-18. Ali-Norton Fight Poster,**
1976. 14-1/2x23" for closed circuit TV viewing of fight at Yankee Stadium September 28. -
**$40 $85 $135**

MUH-19

❑ **MUH-19. "Ali Bom-Ba-Ye!" Record,**
1977. 12" 45 rpm record on Arista label. -
**$10 $20 $30**

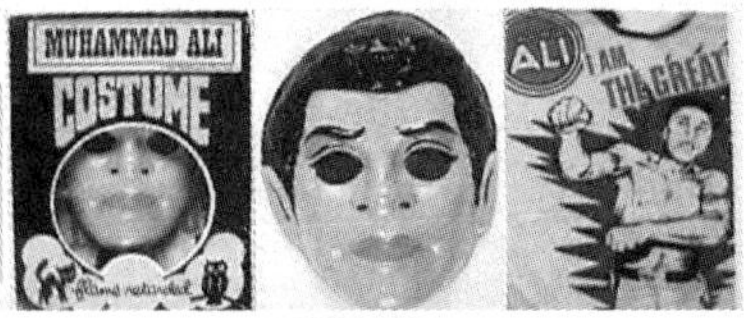

MUH-20

❑ **MUH-20. Boxed Costume By Collegeville,**
1977. Thin molded plastic mask with fabric costume including chest inscription "I Am The Greatest." Near Mint Boxed - **$100**
Complete No Box - **$15 $30 $50**

MUH-21

❑ **MUH-21. Ali-Spinks Fight Poster,**
1978. Budweiser beer. 21x28" high gloss tavern poster promoting fight in New Orleans September 15, 1978. - **$30 $60 $100**

MUH-22

MUH-23

❑ **MUH-22. Ali/Charity Event 3" Cello. Button,**
1979. Promotion for exhibition match between him and "The Urban Fighter" Mayor Tommie Smith of Jersey City, New Jersey. -
**$15 $30 $60**

❑ **MUH-23. Ali/Charity Event 3-1/2" Cello. Button,**
1979. For same event as preceding item also picturing New Jersey Governor Byrne and apparent Ali unnamed body guard to prevent thrashing by Mayor Smith. - **$15 $30 $60**

MUH-24

MUH-25

❑ **MUH-24. "Muhammad Ali" Belt Buckle,**
c. 1970s. Everlast boxing equipment. Bronze luster finish on thick metal with image and inscriptions in raised relief. - **$15 $40 $75**

❑ **MUH-25. Ali-Larry Holmes Championship Fight 4" Cello. Button,**
1980. For employee of hosting Caesar's Palace, Las Vegas prior to October 2 match. -
**$10 $20 $40**

MUH-26

❑ **MUH-26. Promotional Standee,**
1992. Promotes "His Life and Times" book by Thomas Hauser. - **$75 $150 $250**

MUH-27

MUH-28

❑ **MUH-27. Starting Lineup Figure on Card,**
1998. - **$25**

❑ **MUH-28. Starting Lineup Figure on Card,**
1998. - **$20**

MUH-29

MUH-30

❑ **MUH-29. Starting Lineup "Timeless Legend" Figure in Box,**
1998. - **$35**

❑ **MUH-30. Starting Lineup Figure in Box,**
1999. - **$25**

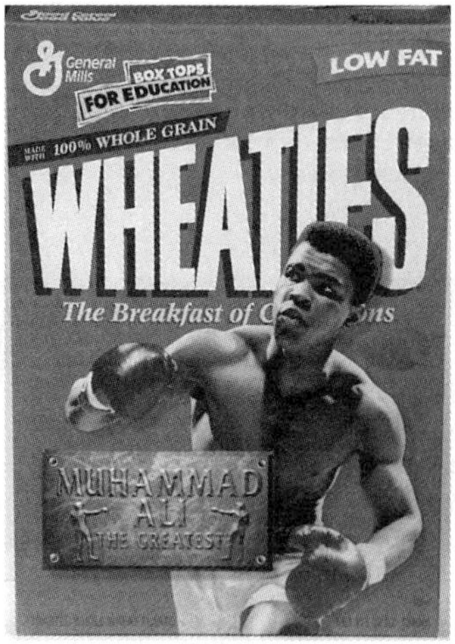

MUH-31

❑ **MUH-31. Wheaties Box,**
1999. - **$2 $4 $10**

## The Muppets

**Jim Henson (1936-1990) introduced his Muppets on local television in Washington, D.C. in 1955, with *Sam and Friends*. The creatures (the name is a combination of marionette and puppet) found use in commercials and gained national exposure in periodic guest appearances on a number of variety shows.**

**They debuted as regulars in 1969 on *Sesame Street*, the phenomenally successful children's television series, where Big Bird, Oscar the Grouch, Bert and Ernie, and the Cookie Monster have enchanted millions. *The Muppet Show* (syndicated, 1976-1981) was hosted by Kermit the Frog, who managed to avoid the persistent romantic advances of the divine Miss Piggy. The show garnered three Emmys. In 1975-1976, during the first season of *Saturday Night Live*, Jim Henson's creations—The Scred (lizard-like muppets that became the prototypes for the characters featured in the 1982 film *The Dark Crystal*)—appeared alongside the Not Ready For Prime Time Players. *Muppet Babies*, the animated series sponsored by Campbell soups and Sears, premiered on CBS in 1984 and went on to win numerous Emmy awards.**

**New Muppet characters were introduced on *Fraggle Rock* (cable, 1983). The creatures also made movies: *The Muppet Movie* (1979), *The Great Muppet Caper* (1981), *The Muppets Take Manhattan* (1984), and *Muppet Treasure Island* (1996). *Muppet-VIsion 3D* opened in 1991 at Walt Disney World's Disney/MGM Studios Theme Park. Kermit and pals also returned to TV, but less successfully than before. Jim Henson died on May 16, 1990. Despite the passing of this gifted man, his legacy lives on--Henson's son Brian continues to guide the Muppets through a variety of all-new adventures. Merchandising of the Muppet characters has become a multi-million-dollar industry.**

MUP-1

❏ **MUP-1. "The Muppet Show" Lunch Box With Bottle,**
1978. Store item by King-Seeley Co. Metal box and plastic bottle. Box - **$10 $20 $40**
Bottle - **$5 $10 $20**

MUP-2

❏ **MUP-2. Kermit The Frog Figural Container,**
1978. Store item. Ceramic holder and lid by Sigma. - **$25 $50 $100**

MUP-3

MUP-4

❏ **MUP-3. Fan Club Litho. Button,**
1978. 2-1/4" with color design on black. - **$5 $12 $20**

❏ **MUP-4. Miss Piggy Wristwatch,**
1979. Store item. By Picco with Henson Associates Inc. copyright. - **$10 $20 $40**

MUP-5

MUP-6

❏ **MUP-5. Fozzie Bear Enameled Brass Figure Pin,**
c. 1970s. Satchel inscription is "Jaycee Kids." - **$5 $10 $20**

❏ **MUP-6. Kermit Frog Enamel Brass Figure Pin,**
c. 1970s. Local sponsor is "NJ Jaycees." - **$5 $10 $20**

MUP-7

MUP-8

❏ **MUP-7. Miss Piggy Ceramic Mug,**
1970s. Store item by Sigma. - **$10 $20 $30**

❏ **MUP-8. Kermit The Frog Ceramic Mug,**
1970s. Store item by Sigma. - **$5 $15 $30**

MUP-9

MUP-10

❏ **MUP-9. Miss Piggy Ceramic Figural Bank,**
1970s. Store item by Sigma. - **$20 $40 $75**

❏ **MUP-10. Toy Promotion Litho. Button,**
c. 1970s. 2-1/4" inscribed "Bulletin Board Games." - **$5 $15 $25**

MUP-11

❏ **MUP-11. Muppets For President Pin-Back Buttons,**
1980. Store item. Each is 3-1/2" diameter with full color photo under acetate.
Each - **$5 $10 $15**

MUP-12

MUP-13

❏ **MUP-12. "The Great Muppet Caper" Glass Tumblers,**
1981. McDonald's. From set of four.
Each - **$2 $4 $6**

❏ **MUP-13. "Miss Piggy's Calendar Of Calendars" 2-1/4" Cello. Promo Button,**
1983. Alfred A. Knopf Publishing Co. with Henson Associates copyright. - **$8 $15 $25**

MUP-14

MUP-15

❑ **MUP-14. Kermit The Frog Telephone,**
1983. Store item by American Telecommunications Corp. copyright Henson Associates Inc. Hard plastic actual function telephone 8x8x11". - **$30 $65 $125**

❑ **MUP-15. "National Children's Dental Health Month" Litho. Button,**
1985. 2-1/4" with color portrait. - **$5 $15 $25**

## Music Misc.

**Great vocalists, instrumentalists or instruments do not necessarily great premiums make. Vocalists, other than Elvis and the Beatles, have created little furor in premiums throughout the years, other than a small flurry of pin-back buttons picturing crooner stars of the 1940s-1950s. Rock music groups beginning in the 1960s have inspired some very attractively designed buttons, although mainly of retail nature. Music instruments and premiums seldom mingle. Possibly a kazoo here, a harmonica there and--by considerable leeway - bird calls, sirens, etc. Still, music in its broadest sense has produced a modest assortment of premiums such as songbooks, records and novelty items.**

MUS-1

MUS-2

❑ **MUS-1. Rudy Vallée Song Sheet,**
1929. Features his song "I'm Just A Vagabond Lover." - **$10 $20 $30**

❑ **MUS-2. Frank Sinatra Song Sheet,**
1943. Features song "Close To You" and Sinatra photo on cover. - **$15 $30 $45**

MUS-3

MUS-4

❑ **MUS-3. "Lucky Strike Presents Your Hit Parade Starring Frank Sinatra" Cardboard Fan,**
1943. Scarce. Lucky Strike cigarettes. 12" tall diecut tobacco leaf replica inscribed on back "A Fan For My Fans-Frank Sinatra". - **$25 $75 $140**

❑ **MUS-4. Frank Sinatra Vendor Card,**
1940s. Pictured in front of an NBC mike. Not common. - **$10 $20 $35**

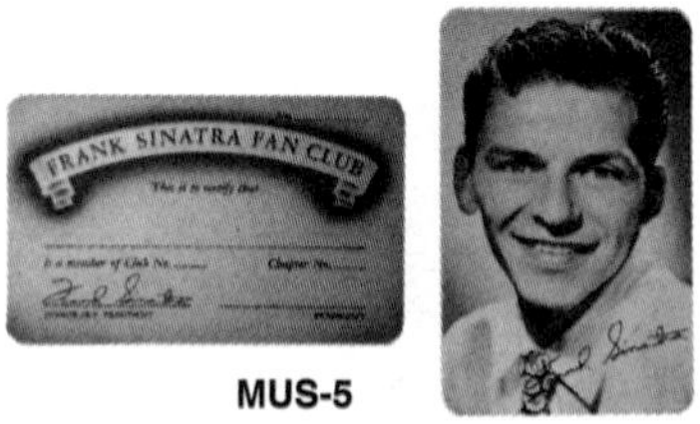


MUS-5

❑ **MUS-5. "Frank Sinatra Fan Club" Card**
1940s. - **$15 $30 $75**

MUS-6

MUS-7

❑ **MUS-6. "Four Aces" Cello. Button,**
c. 1940s. Philadelphia Fan Club. - **$10 $15 $30**

❑ **MUS-7. Tony Bennett "Bennett Tones Fan Club" Litho. Button,**
1940s. - **$10 $20 $35**

MUS-8

MUS-9

❑ **MUS-8. "Guy Lombardo" Record Brush,**
1940s. Decca Records. - **$10 $20 $30**

❑ **MUS-9. "Bing Crosby" Record Brush,**
1940s. Decca Records. - **$10 $20 $30**

MUS-10

MUS-11

❑ **MUS-10. "Woody Herman's Sweetwind" Litho. Advertising Button,**
1940s. Pioneer Musical Inst. Co. 1-5/8" black and white includes his endorsement signature. - **$10 $20 $30**

❑ **MUS-11. "Rock-Ola Leads Again!" Button,**
c. 1950. 3" diameter. - **$10 $20 $40**

MUS-12

MUS-13

❑ **MUS-12. "Liberace" Gold Luster Metal Link Charm Bracelet,**
c. 1956. Store item. Miniature framed photo plus charms depicting hands on keyboard, grand piano, candelabra, piano lid. - **$15 $35 $60**

❑ **MUS-13. Bill Haley and his Comets Program,**
1956. 32 pages & cover features photos and songs. - **$25 $50 $75**

MUS-14

MUS-15

❑ **MUS-14. "Eddie Cochran Fan Club" Pinback,**
1957. Rare. - **$50 $100 $200**

❑ **MUS-15. "Witch Doctor" Song Sheet,**
1958. From the hit record. - **$15 $35 $50**

MUS-16

MUS-17

❑ **MUS-16. "Chipmunks" Wallet,**
1959. Vinyl. - **$10 $15 $30**

❑ **MUS-17. "Chipmunks" Song Tote,**
1959. By Monarch Music Co. Vinyl holder for 10 records, with a separate record index. - **$15 $30 $60**

MUS-18 (Reverse side)

❑ **MUS-18. "Chipmunks" 45 Record,**
1959. With 2-sided sleeve.
Record - **$5 $10 $15**
Sleeve - **$10 $15 $25**

MUS-19

MUS-20

MUS-21

❑ **MUS-19. "Pat Boone/4th Anniversary" Litho. Button,**
1959. Dot Records. - **$5 $10 $15**

❑ **MUS-20. "Pat Boone Fan" Litho. Button,**
c. 1959. - **$5 $10 $15**

❑ **MUS-21. "Spike Jones" Pair Of Souvenir Programs,**
c. 1950s. Each has 16 pages issued by RCA. Each - **$8 $12 $20**

MUS-22

MUS-23

❑ **MUS-22. "Frank Sinatra" Record Store Sign,**
1950s. Capitol Records. 13-1/4x19" with black and white photo on yellow stiff paper. - **$50 $100 $150**

❑ **MUS-23. Pat Boone Brass Luster Jewelry Pin With Charms,**
1950s. Store item. 1" diameter frame has black and white photo under celluloid. - **$10 $20 $40**

MUS-24

❑ **MUS-24. "Picture Patches",**
1950s. Store item. Probable set of eight. Includes Ricky Nelson, Dave Nelson, Bobby Darin, Frankie Avalon, Tommy Sands, Jimmie Rodgers, Fabian. Each Packaged - **$3 $6 $12**

MUS-25

MUS-26

❑ **MUS-25. Fabian And Frankie Avalon 3-1/2" Cello. Buttons,**
1950s. Store item. Matching designs, possibly issued for others. Each - **$12 $25 $50**

❑ **MUS-26. "Everly Brothers Fan Club" Litho. Button,**
1950s. - **$12 $20 $40**

MUS-27

MUS-28

❑ **MUS-27. "Bill Haley And His Comets Fan Club" Cello. Button,**
1950s. - **$20 $50 $100**

❑ **MUS-28. Tony Bennett Fan Club 2" Cello. Button,**
1950s. - **$8 $15 $30**

MUS-29

MUS-30

❑ **MUS-29. Pat Boone Song Sheet,**
1950s. Features his hit "Love Letters in the Sand." - **$15 $30 $45**

❑ **MUS-30. "Pat Boone" Brass Heart Charm,**
1950s. Dot Records. Reverse inscription "Always Your Boy, Pat Boone." - **$5 $12 $20**

MUS-31

❑ **MUS-31. 'Teen Magazine,**
Jan. 1960. Features Alvin on cover with a story on David Seville, as well as other recoding stars like Fabian, Frankie Avalon, Bobby Darin, Nancy Sinatra and others. - **$5 $15 $25**

MUS-32

MUS-33

❑ **MUS-32. "The Alan Freed Show" Ticket,**
1960. For Carnegie Music Hall concert. - **$70**

❑ **MUS-33. "Beach Boys In Concert" Early Program,**
1965. 16 pages. - **$40 $100 $175**

MUS-34

MUS-35

❑ **MUS-34. "Herman's Hermits" 3-1/2" Cello. Button,**
c. 1965. Store item. - **$8 $15 $25**

❑ **MUS-35. "The Rolling Stones" 3-1/2" Cello. Button,**
c. 1966. Probably sold at concerts. - **$20 $35 $75**

MUS-36

❑ **MUS-36. "Freddie and the Dreamers" Photo Button,**
c. 1966. Known for single "I'm Telling You Now." - **$20 $40 $65**

MUS-37

MUS-38

❑ **MUS-37. "The Supremes Official Fan" 2-1/2" Cello. Button,**
1968. - **$15 $30 $60**

❑ **MUS-38. "Woodstock" Celebration Litho. Button,**
1969. Issued for 1970 live-action movie filmed during four-day concert. - **$10 $15 $25**

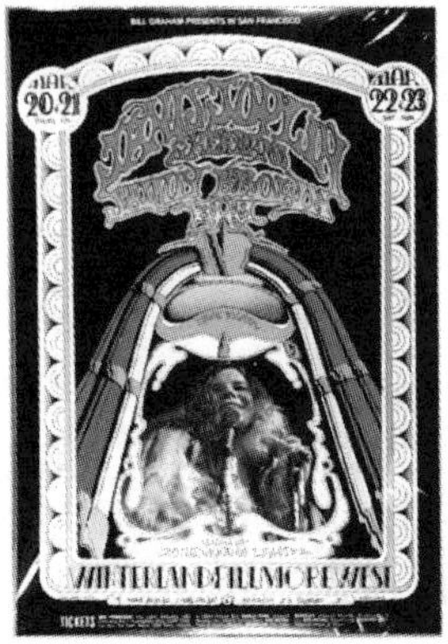

MUS-39

❑ **MUS-39. Janis Joplin Concert Poster,**
1969. - **$125 $250 $350**

MUS-40

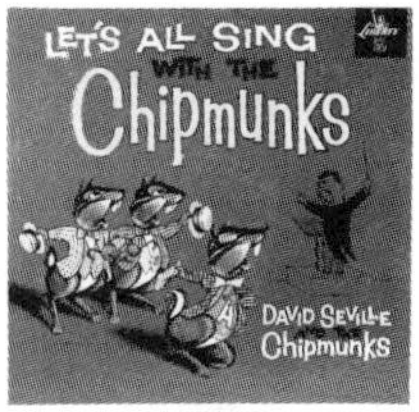

MUS-41

❑ **MUS-40. Frank Zappa Photo Button,**
c. 1969. 3". - **$25 $50 $75**

❑ **MUS-41. "Chipmunks" Album,**
1960s. Bright copper colored 33 1/3 rpm Hi-Fi record. - **$15 $35 $50**

MUS-42

❑ **MUS-42. Jackson 5 Groovie Push-Out Buttons,**
1970. Frosted Rice Krinkles. Strip of three 1-1/2" thin vacuum form sticker buttons. Set of 10 different titles. Each Near Mint Strip - **$10**
Each Used Button - **$1 $2 $3**

MUS-43

❑ **MUS-43. Fleetwood Mac Concert Poster,**
1977. For Oakland Stadium. - **$100 $175 $250**

MUS-44

❑ **MUS-44. David Bowie Pinback,**
1978. Promotes Madison Square Garden concerts. - **$10 $20 $30**

MUS-45

❑ **MUS-45. "The Who" Back Stage Pass Button Set,**
1979. Each is 1-1/2" diameter.
Each - **$10 $20 $35**

MUS-46

❑ **MUS-46. "The Police" Concert Badge,**
1979. 1st version has gold heads on silver background. 2nd version has solid gold color.
Each version - **$15 $25 $50**

MUS-47

❑ **MUS-47. "Bee Gees" Promo Button,**
1970s. 2 1/2" button is from the pre-"Saturday Night Fever" period. - **$10 $20 $45**

MUS-48

❑ **MUS-48. 5th Dimension Club Card,**
1970s. Card for official fan member. - **$5 $10 $25**

MUS-49

❑ **MUS-49. "Elton John" Ecology 3" Cello. Button,**
1980. Also inscribed "Central Park-Keep It Green." - **$10 $25 $50**

MUS-50

❑ **MUS-50. Solid Gold Dancers Promo on Super Sugar Crisp Cereal Box,**
1984. Box offers poster premiums for the Solid Gold Dancers, featured on their popular TV show "The Solid Gold Show." - **$10 $30 $60**
Each Poster **- $20**

MUS-51 MUS-52

❑ **MUS-51. "David Bowie" Moonlight Concert Pin,**
1985. Red, white and blue background with black color on outfit. - **$10 $20 $35**

❑ **MUS-52. "Cyndi Lauper" Promo Pin,**
1980s. Very ornate. - **$10 $20 $35**

MUS-53

❑ **MUS-53. "Freddie Mercury" Badge,**
1991. Commemorates lead singer of Queen. Badge has pin on back. - **$25 $50 $75**

MUS-54 MUS-55

❑ **MUS-54. "Mick Jaguar" Bean Bag,**
1998. Famous Meanies series with tag. - **$10**

❑ **MUS-55. Beach Boys Die-cast Car,**
1999. Racing Champions, Inc. Limited edition. On card. - **$6**

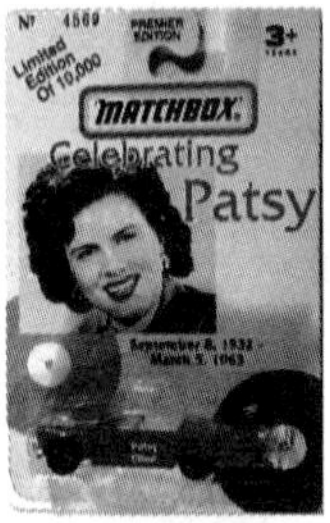

MUS-56 MUS-57

❑ **MUS-56. Patsy Kline Matchbox Car,**
1990s. Limited edition on card. - **$24**

❑ **MUS-57. 'N Sync Button Set,**
2000. Set of 5 on card. - **$5**

MUS-58 MUS-59

❑ **MUS-58. Janis Joplin Lunch Box,**
2000. - **$20**

❑ **MUS-59. Janis Joplin Figure on Card,**
2000. McFarlane Toys. - **$20**

## Mutt and Jeff

**Bud Fisher's *Mutt and Jeff*, the first continually published six-day-a-week comic strip, was to become one of the best known, funniest, and most popular strips in America. It started as a horseracing cartoon called *A. Mutt* in the *San Francisco Chronicle* in 1907. Jeff showed up the following year but it wasn't until 1916 that the strip was titled *Mutt and Jeff.* A Sunday color strip was added in 1918. There were many early collections of reprints starting around 1910, hardback books, and comic books into the 1960s. A series of *Mutt and Jeff* musicals toured the country from about 1911 to 1915, and from 1918 to 1923 Bud Fisher Productions turned out animated cartoons, typically at a pace of one a week.**

MUT-1 MUT-2

❑ **MUT-1. Postcard,**
1910. New York American newspaper premium. - **$25 $50 $75**

❑ **MUT-2. Mutt and Jeff #1 Hardcover Book,**
1910. 5 3/4" x 15 1/2". Shows photo of Bud Fisher on title page. Scarce in high grade. Reprints cartoon strips published prior to 1910.- **$186 $744 $1300**

MUT-3

❑ **MUT-3. Mutt and Jeff #2 Hardcover Book,**
1911. 5 3/4" x 15 1/2". Notice cover has been changed and title modified. Reprints cartoon strips published prior to 1911.- **$96 $384 $675**

MUT-4

❑ **MUT-4. Stage Show Cardboard Ink Blotter,**
1912. - **$10 $20 $40**

MUT-5

❑ **MUT-5. "Mutt And Jeff In Mexico" Cardboard Blotter,**
c. 1912. For musical comedy stage production. - **$10 $20 $40**

MUT-6

❑ **MUT-6. "Mutt And Jeff In College" Cardboard Blotter,**
c. 1913. For musical comedy stage production. - **$10 $20 $40**

MUT-7

❑ **MUT-7. "Mutt And Jeff In Panama" Song Album,**
1913. 20 pages, 10-1/4" x 13" book. Scarce. - **$15 $30 $50**

MUT-8

MUT-9

❑ **MUT-8. Mutt And Jeff Brass Stickpins,**
c. 1915. Issuer Unknown. Each - **$10 $20 $35**

❑ **MUT-9. Cast Iron Bank,**
c. 1915. Store item. - **$60 $150 $225**

MUT-10

MUT-11

❑ **MUT-10. "Join The Evening Telegraph" Cello. Button,**
c. 1915. Promotion for strip beginning and "Mutt & Jeff Club". - **$25 $50 $75**

❑ **MUT-11. "Cut That Stuff" Cartoon Litho. Button,**
c. 1916. Various cigarette sponsors. Example from set featuring art by Bud Fisher and other cartoonists. Paint easily worn.
Fisher Cartoons - **$5 $12 $20**
Other Artists - **$3 $8 $15**

MUT-12

❑ **MUT-12. German Bisques,**
c. 1920. Mutt is 3-1/8", Jeff is 3".
Each - **$40 $75 $125**

(CRAYON BOX)

MUT-13

❑ **MUT-13. Cupples And Leon Book Seven Boxed With Crayons As Set,**
1924. Store item. 10-1/4x12-1/4x1/2" deep box titled "Crayon Drawing Book." Interior holds book of strip reprints from 1920 along with six crayons. Apparently an effort to sell books from previous years. Boxed Set - **$125 $250 $500**

MUT-14

❑ **MUT-14. Mutt and Jeff Big Book,**
1926. By Bud Fisher. 144 pages.
Hardcover - **$114 $456 $800**
With Dust Jacket - **$193 $772 $1350**

MUT-15

❑ **MUT-15. "Mutt And Jeff Play Croquet" Dexterity Puzzle,**
1928. Tin and glass 2-1/2x4" skill game by Herbert Special Mfg. Co., Chicago with instructions on underside. - **$75 $125 $200**

MUT-16

MUT-17

❑ **MUT-16. Composition/Steel Jointed Flexible Figures,**
1920s. Store item. With fabric outfits.
Each - **$100 $250 $500**

❑ **MUT-17. Bronze Statue of Jeff,**
1920s. 5 3/4" - Premium /Award. - **$50 $125 $175**

MUT-18

MUT-19

❑ **MUT-18. "Meet Us At Forest Park" Cello. Button,**
c. 1920s. - **$25 $50 $100**

❑ **MUT-19. "I Am Mister Mutt/I Am Little Jeff" Pair Of Gas Station Premium Paper Masks,**
1933. Shell Oil Company. Each - **$20 $35 $75**

MUT-20

❑ **MUT-20. "Mutt And Jeff" Big Little Book,**
1936. Whitman #1113. - **$25 $50 $110**

MUT-21

MUT-22

❑ **MUT-21. "Buffalo Evening News" Cello. Button,**
1930s. From series of newspaper contest buttons, match number to win prize. - **$10 $20 $50**

❑ **MUT-22. "Tangle Comics" Cello. Button,**
1940s. Philadelphia Sunday Bulletin. -
**$20 $40 $65**

MUT-23

❑ **MUT-23. Jeff And Mutt Adult-Sized Over The Head-Style Costume,**
1960. Store item by Collegeville. 25" wide by 50" tall. Each Near Mint Carded - **$350**
Each Uncarded - **$75 $150 $200**

## Nabisco Misc.

**The giant National Biscuit Company was formed in 1898 by the merger of a number of smaller companies and independent bakers. The following year its sales totaled 70% of all the crackers and cookies sold in America. Adolphus Green, company chairman, set about to create a new product and a national brand. He named it the Uneeda biscuit, developed a carton (In-er-Seal) to keep it fresh, chose a picture of a boy wrapped in rain gear as a symbol, and invested heavily in advertising. In 1900 the company sold 100 million boxes of Uneeda biscuits. Then quickly came Oysterettes, Zu Zu ginger snaps, Fig Newtons, sugar wafers, and Barnum's Animal Crackers. Nabisco, always a heavy advertiser, issued a number of promotional items over the years and has sponsored such children's television classics as *The Adventures of Rin-Tin-Tin, Jabberwocky, Kukla, Fran & Ollie*, and *Sky King*. In the mid-1980s the company was acquired by R.J. Reynolds and became part of RJR Nabisco.**

NAB-1

NAB-2

❑ **NAB-1. Golden Anniversary Pinback,**
1948. Metallic gold with child icon which promoted the company. Scarce. - **$15 $25 $40**

❑ **NAB-2. Flying Circus Cards,**
1948. Shredded Wheat premium. Card set of 25 model planes and 12 card set of index and preparation of flight. Since cards were made of cardboard, they were to be cut out and assembled into planes and used like gliders. Cards were obtained in cereal boxes. The 12 card set tells how to fold, cut, and assemble the 25 card set of planes. Each - **$4 $8 $10**

NAB-3

NAB-4

❑ **NAB-3. Arthur Godfrey 6 1/2" Standee,**
1940s. Cardboard standee promoting his radio show for Nabisco. Scarce. - **$50 $85 $150**

❑ **NAB-4. Picture Story Album,**
1940s. Seven card set of classic fairy tales found in boxes of Shredded Wheat. Cards were used as a coloring book. Each - **$2 $4 $6**

NAB-5

NAB-6

❑ **NAB-5. Picture Story Album,**
1940s. 28 card set of boys and girls of all nations Each card tells the story of children in each foreign country. Each - **$2 $4 $6**

❑ **NAB-6. Toytown Cards,**
1940s. Rare. Shredded Wheat premiums. 36 card set which when assembled makes a toytown. Includes cut-outs of buildings like firehouses, stores, bank, church, general store, ice cream parlor and gas station. Also includes bus, car, trees, and of all things, an antique store. Yes, collecting was very popular in the 1940s. Each - **$4 $8 $10**

NAB-7

❑ **NAB-7. Box Promoting Jungle Beasts In 3-D,**
c. 1950. Complete - **$25 $50 $100**

NAB-8

❑ **NAB-8. "Nabisco Wheat Honeys/Prehistoric Beasts" Cereal Box,**
1957. Eight in set issued as companion to set of 10 dinosaurs. Gordon Gold Archives.
Complete Box **- $100 $225 $325**

NAB-9

❑ **NAB-9. Plastic Dinosaurs With Guide Folder And Box,**
1957. Near Mint In Mailer - **$175**

NAB-10

❑ **NAB-10. Wheat Honeys Store Promotional Box Replica Kit With Plastic Dinosaurs,**
1957. Stiff cardboard box with hinged cover and interior compartments. Set of 10.
Box Only - **$50 $150 $225**
Each Figure - **$5 $10 $15**

NAB-11

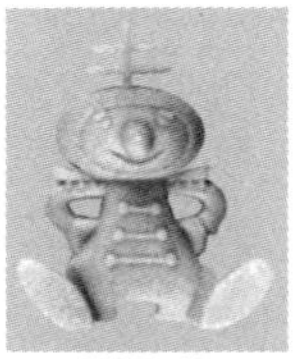

NAB-12

❑ **NAB-11. "Munchy The Spoonman" Pillow,**
1958. 3x9-1/2x15" stuffed fabric figure. -
**$75 $150 $300**

❑ **NAB-12. "Munchy" Vinyl Attachment For Spoon Handle,**
1959. One of three Nabisco Spoon Men. Three rows of buttons. - **$15 $25 $50**

NAB-13

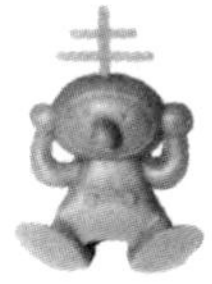

NAB-14

❑ **NAB-13. "Crunchy" Vinyl Attachment For Spoon Handle,**
1959. Two rows of buttons. - **$15 $25 $50**

❑ **NAB-14. "Spoon Size" Vinyl Attachment for Spoon Handle,**
1959. One row of buttons and smaller size than Munchy and Crunchy. - **$25 $35 $60**

NAB-15

❑ **NAB-15. "Rocket Man" Paper Mask,**
1950s. - **$15 $30 $60**

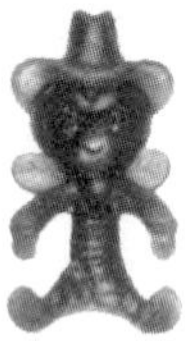

NAB-16

NAB-17

❑ **NAB-16. Buffalo Bee Breakfast Buddy,**
1961. Vinyl figure designed to perch on edge of cereal bowl. - **$5 $12 $20**

❑ **NAB-17. Jolly Clown Breakfast Buddy,**
1961. Vinyl figure designed to perch on edge of cereal bowl. - **$5 $12 $20**

NAB-18

**NAB-18. Defenders Of America Cards,**
1950s. Shredded Wheat. 24 cards in the set. 8 of the 24 are Rocket cards. 7 pictured. Full color.
Eight Rocket cards. Each - **$6 $12 $20**
Other sixteen cards. Each - **$4 $8 $12**

(FRONT) NAB-19 (BACK)

❑ **NAB-19. "Shredded Wheat" Cereal Box with Promo for 3-D Cut-outs on Back,**
Late 1950s. The Spoonmen appear on front. -
**$65 $130 $200**

NAB-20

❑ **NAB-20. Buffalo Bee Breakfast Buddy Cereal Box Flat,**
1961. Gordon Gold Archives.
Near Mint Flat - **$250**
Used Complete - **$60 $125 $175**

NAB-21

❑ **NAB-21. "Speedy Spaceman" Cereal Box Flat,**
1961. Back panel promotes 1-3/4" tall figure packaged in box. Came with a balloon to propel the toy. A matching toy called "Racing Robot" was packaged in Wheat Honeys cereal boxes.
Each Near Mint Flat - **$150**
Each Used Complete - **$25 $50 $75**

NAB-22

❑ **NAB-22. "Jolly Clown Breakfast Buddy" Cereal Box,**
1961. Gordon Gold Archives.
Near Mint Flat - **$250**
Used Complete - **$60 $125 $175**

NAB-23

❑ **NAB-23. "Comic Patch!" Cereal Box,**
1963. Four in set, inserted one per box: Little Orphan Annie, Smilin' Jack, Smitty, Smokey Stover. Gordon Gold Archives.
Used Complete - **$35 $75 $150**

NAB-24

❑ **NAB-24. Cereal Box With Dinosaur Figures Offer,**
1966. Promotes set of 12 "Kooky Spooky" figures packaged one per box. Gordon Gold Archives. Used Complete - **$75 $125 $225**

NAB-25

NAB-26

❑ **NAB-25. Football Premium Offers Box,**
1967. Nabisco Shredded Wheat. Gordon Gold Archives. Complete **- $25 $50 $100**

❑ **NAB-26. "Nabisco Wheat Honeys Jungle Pals" Box Flat With Premium Figure Set,**
1967. Figures are 3" long or tall in solid soft plastic. Gordon Gold Archives.
Near Mint Flat **- $300**
Used Complete **- $50 $100 $150**
Jungle Pals Each **- $3 $8 $12**

## Nancy and Sluggo

**Nancy, a stubby little girl with a perpetual hair arrangement resembling black steel wool held by a white bow, was created in 1933 by cartoonist Ernie Bushmiller, originally as a niece and periodic visitor to her aunt, the established Fritzi Ritz. By the late 1930s, niece and aunt had reversed their featured roles. Nancy's equally-stubby platonic boyfriend & sidekick, Sluggo, came into her life and the pair remains an inseparable cartoon strip duo to this day.**

NAN-1

NAN-2

❑ **NAN-1. "Fritzi Ritz Spinner",**
1930s. United Features Syndicate. Cello. over metal disk that has underside center bump for spinning. - **$50 $100 $175**

❑ **NAN-2. "Journal-Transcript Funnies Club" Litho. Button,**
c. 1930s. From set of various characters, also has radio call letters for station in Peoria, Illinois. - **$20 $40 $75**

NAN-3

❑ **NAN-3. "Nancy Has Fun" All Picture Comics,**
1944. Whitman #1487. **- $30 $75 $150**

NAN-4

NAN-5

❑ **NAN-4. "Nancy And Sluggo" BTLB,**
1946. Store item. Whitman Better Little Book #1400. - **$15 $40 $75**

❑ **NAN-5. Nancy 7-1/2" Hard Plastic Doll,**
1940s (late). Rare. Post Grape-Nuts Flakes. - **$250 $750 $1250**

NAN-6

NAN-7

❑ **NAN-6. Sluggo 7-1/2" Hard Plastic Doll,**
1940s (late). Rare. Post Grape-Nuts Flakes. - **$250 $750 $1250**

❑ **NAN-7. "Comic Capers Club" 2-1/8" Cello. Button,**
1940s. Sun-Times (newspaper). - **$400 $1000 $2000**

NAN-8

❑ **NAN-8. Stuffed Cloth Doll,**
1940s. Store item. 14" tall. - **$100 $200 $350**

NAN-9

NAN-10

❑ **NAN-9. Nancy Rubber/Vinyl Doll,**
1954. Store item by S&P Doll and Toy Co.
Near Mint Boxed - **$500**
Loose - **$75 $150 $300**

❑ **NAN-10. Sluggo Rubber/Vinyl Doll,**
1954. Store item by S&P Doll and Toy Co.
Near Mint Boxed - **$500**
Loose - **$75 $150 $300**

NAN-11

❑ **NAN-11. Punch-Out Paperdoll Book,**
1974. Store item by Whitman. 10x12-7/8" with 16 pages. Unpunched - **$10 $20 $35**

## New Fun Comics

**Former pulp magazine writer and cavalry officer Major Malcolm Wheeler-Nicholson came up with the idea of a comic book containing all original material in late 1934. The 10x15" tabloid size magazine *New Fun*, with color covers and black and white interiors, appeared on newstands with a cover date of February 1935. Pages were laid out in a Sunday comic page format with continuing stories, humor pages, text stories and games. Subsequent issues were titled *More Fun*. The magazine added more color and adapted to the standard comic book size and format by 1936. Historically, *More Fun* not only was one of the first comic books with original material but also the first to publish work by Walt Kelly of later *Pogo* fame and Siegel and Shuster of *Superman* fame. *New Fun* formed the cornerstone of the DC Comics publishing empire. The title ran through issue #127 dated November-December 1947.**

NEW-1

❑ **NEW-1. "New Fun Club" Cello. Button,**
1935. Rare. - **$250 $600 $1100**

## Newspaper Clubs

**During the 1930s newspapers reached out to younger readers by means of loosely organized clubs, usually associated with comic strip characters featured in their pages. Pinback buttons were a favored means of promotion; some papers offered buttons with a variety of different characters, while syndicated characters appeared with imprints from dozens of newspapers. Often the buttons were serially numbered for use in prize-winning contests designed to boost circulation.**

NES-1

NES-2

❑ **NES-1. Comic Strips Promotion Postcard,**
1929. Imprinted for Buffalo Courier-Express. For member of "Jolly Junior Sunshine Club" birthday greeting featuring group image of characters. - **$15 $30 $50**

❑ **NES-2. "Bud Billiken Club" Cello. Button,**
c. 1920s. Chicago Defender. - **$5 $10 $15**

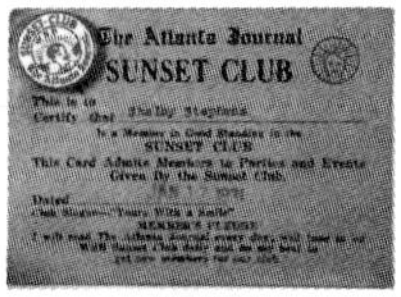


NES-3

(CLOSE-UP OF PIN)

❑ **NES-3. "Sunset Club" Pinback and Card,**
1931. Pinback - **$20 $40 $60**
Card - **$15 $35 $45**

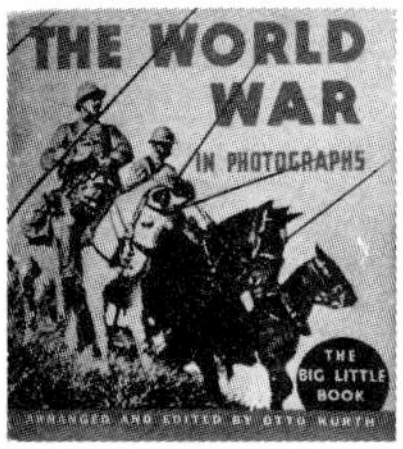


NES-4

NES-5

❑ **NES-4. "The World War" Big Little Book,**
1934. Shows newspaper photos of WW1. - **$10 $30 $75**

❑ **NES-5. Moon Mullins "Order Of The Fish" Litho. Button,**
1930s. No sponsor but probably a newspaper issue. - **$10 $20 $40**

NES-6

NES-7

❑ **NES-6. "Reg'lar Fellers Legion Of Honor" Litho. Button,**
1930s. No sponsor but probably a newspaper issue. - **$15 $30 $60**

❑ **NES--7. "Times Junior Pilot" Pinback,**
1930s. - **$20 $40 $60**

NES-8

(CLOSE-UP OF PIN)

❑ **NES-8. "Our Club" Pinback on Membership Card,**
1930s. A great example of one of the early children's clubs promoting the Milwaukee Journal.
Pinback - **$25 $50 $75**
Club Card - **$15 $30 $50**

NES-9

NES-10

NES-11

❑ **NES-9. Evening Ledger Comics "Relentless Rudolph" Cello. Button,**
1930s. Philadelphia Evening Ledger. From colorful series in 1-1/4" size with Evening Ledger promotional back paper. - **$30 $75 $150**

❑ **NES-10. Evening Ledger Comics "Connie" Cello. Button,**
1930s. Philadelphia Evening Ledger. - **$20 $45 $90**

❑ **NES-11. Evening Ledger Comics "Harold Teen" Cello. Button,**
1930s. Philadelphia Evening Ledger. - **$25 $50 $100**

NES-12

NES-13

NES-14

❑ **NES-12. Evening Ledger Comics "Bobby Thatcher" Cello. Button,**
1930s. Philadelphia Evening Ledger. - **$20 $45 $90**

❑ **NES-13. Evening Ledger Comics "Babe Bunting" Cello. Button,**
1930s. Philadelphia Evening Ledger. - **$15 $40 $60**

❑ **NES-14. Evening Ledger Comics "Smitty" Cello. Button,**
1930s. Philadelphia Evening Ledger. - **$20 $45 $85**

NES-15

NES-16

❑ **NES-15. "Just Kids Safety Club" Cello. Buttons,**
1930s. Imprinted for at least 48 different newspapers. Set includes 11 characters in 18 picture variations. Pictured examples are "Mush" and "Marjory." Each - **$12 $20 $35**

❑ **NES-16. Bronco Bill Litho. Button,**
1930s. Example is imprinted for media of Peoria, Illinois. From set of at least 15 different characters. - **$15 $35 $60**

# Nick Carter, Master Detective

**Nick Carter, hero of hundreds of dime novels, began life in 1886 in the pages of Street & Smith's *New York Weekly*. The stories, signed by "Nicholas Carter," were written by a number of different authors. Following decades of pulp magazine appearances, the master detective came to the Mutual radio network in 1943 and was broadcast until 1955. Sponsors included Lin-X Home Brighteners (1944-1945), Cudahy meats (1946-1951), and Old Dutch cleanser (1946-1952). Walter Pidgeon played Carter in a 1939 MGM movie. *The Nick Carter Club* was a 1930s Street & Smith promotion.**

NCK-1

NCK-2

❑ **NCK-1. "Nick Carter Magazine" Store Window 10x13" Ad Card,**
1933. Pictures cover of May issue. -
**$50 $100 $185**

❑ **NCK-2. "Nick Carter Magazine" Pulp Vol. 1 #3,**
May 1933. Published by Street & Smith. -
**$20 $40 $85**

NCK-3

❑ **NCK-3. "Nick Carter Fingerprint Set",**
1934. Store item by New York Toy & Game Co. Includes "Nick Carter 999 Club" instruction book with Street & Smith club enrollment form.
Complete - **$35 $75 $135**
Book Only - **$15 $30 $50**

NCK-4

NCK-5

NCK-6

❑ **NCK-4. Club Members Shield,**
c. 1934. Silver luster metal 1-1/16" tall. Issued with pin on reverse or with threaded post and screw-on cap to wear as a stud.
Pinback - **$50 $85 $140**
Stud - **$65 $100 $175**

❑ **NCK-5. Club Card,**
c. 1934. Nick Carter Magazine. Came with badge. - **$25 $60 $100**

❑ **NCK-6. "Nick Carter Magazine" Gummed Envelope Sticker,**
1930s. Street & Smith Publications. -
**$20 $40 $75**

NCK-7

❑ **NCK-7. "Mutual" Radio Program Sign,**
c. 1945. WFBR, Baltimore, Maryland. Photos of stars from Nick Carter, Bulldog Drummond, Sherlock Holmes. 10-1/2x27-1/2". -
**$75 $150 $300**

# Og, Son of Fire

**The prehistoric adventures of Og and his companions--Ru, Nada and Big Tooth--were broadcast for a year (1934-1935) on CBS radio, sponsored by Libby. Alfred Brown played the primeval hero of the series, written by Irving Crump, the author of the original Og stories.**

OGS-1

❑ **OGS-1. "Adventures Of Og, Son Of Fire" 15x20" Map,**
1935. Rare. Libby. - **$150 $350 $600**

OGS-2

OGS-3

❑ **OGS-2. "Og" 2-1/4" Painted Metal Figure,**
c. 1935. Marked under base "Made For Libby's Milk By Lincoln Logs USA." Six figures in set. For each mailing canister with metal lid add $10-20-30. - **$40 $60 $125**

❑ **OGS-3. "Ru" Metal Figure,**
c. 1935. Part of Og set. - **$40 $60 $125**

OGS-4

OGS-5

❑ **OGS-4. "Nada" Metal Figure,**
c. 1935. Part of Og set. - **$40 $60 $125**

❑ **OGS-5. "Big Tooth" Metal Figure,**
c. 1935. Part of Og set. - **$40 $75 $150**

OGS-6

OGS-7

❑ **OGS-6. "Three Horn" Metal Figure,**
c. 1935. Part of Og set. - **$60 $125 $175**

❑ **OGS-7. "Rex" Metal Figure,**
c. 1935. Part of Og set. - **$50 $100 $150**

OGS-8

❑ **OGS-8. "Og Son of Fire" BLB #115,**
1936. By Irving Crump. - **$15 $45 $100**

OGS-9

❑ **OGS-9. "Og, Son Of Fire" Adventure Game,**
1930s. Store item. Whitman game licensed by Stephen Slesinger Inc. "Based On The Famous Stories By Irving Crump" rather than radio premium by sponsor Libby Foods. - **$50 $150 $300**

## Omar the Mystic

**Also known as *Omar the Wizard*, this radio series ran for a year (1935-1936) on the Mutual radio network, sponsored by Taystee bread. M.H. Joachim played Omar.**

OMR-1

❑ **OMR-1. "The Secrets Of Omar The Mystic" Book,**
1936. Scarce. Taystee Bread. - **$35 $50 $100**

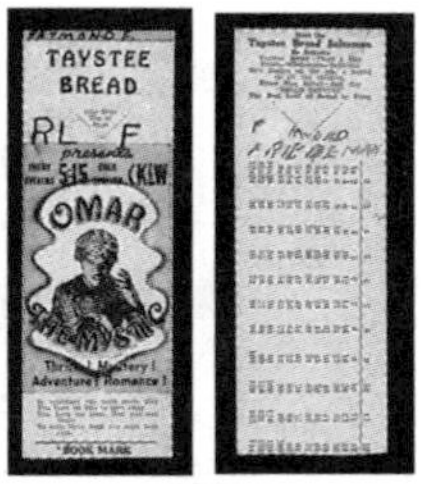


OMR-2 OMR-3

❑ **OMR-2. Taystee Bread Code Card,**
1936. Back has instructions for using "Mystic Wheel". - **$20 $40 $75**

❑ **OMR-3. Taystee Bread Code Bookmark,**
1936. Cardboard marker printed by code numerals on one side. - **$15 $30 $50**

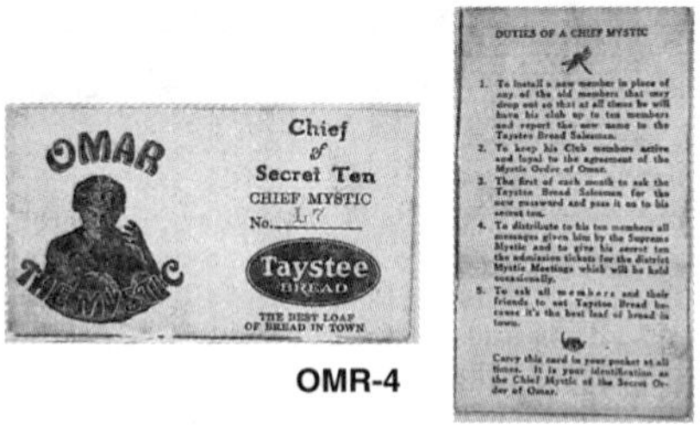


OMR-4

❑ **OMR-4. "Chief Of Secret Ten/Chief Mystic" Higher Rank Member's Card,**
1936. Reverse lists "Duties Of A Chief Mystic." - **$25 $50 $75**

OMR-5

❑ **OMR-5. "Mystic Omar Club" Cello. Member Button,**
1936. Blue and white 1" oval. - **$15 $30 $60**

OMR-6

❑ **OMR-6. "Secret 10 Membership Card",**
1936. Taystee Bread. Reverse lists 10 rules dealing with safety, obedience, school studies and related moral principles under the "Agreement Of The Secret Ten." - **$15 $30 $60**

OMR-7

❑ **OMR-7. Bread Wrapper,**
1930s. - **$20 $30 $60**

## One Man's Family

**The saga of the Barbour family, written lovingly by Carlton E. Morse, was the longest running serial drama in the history of radio. The program debuted in 1932 on NBC's San Francisco station KGO and a year later went to the NBC network, where it continued until 1959. The family tree series told the stories of Henry and Fanny Barbour, their five children (Paul, Hazel, the twins Claudia and Clifford, and Jack), and succeeding generations of Barbours as they lived and died, married, had children, and faced family crises against the backdrop of a changing world. Sponsors included Wesson Oil (1932-1933), Kentucky Winner tobacco (1933-1935), Royal gelatin (1935-1936), Tenderleaf tea (1936-1949), Miles Laboratories (1950-1954), and Toni Home Permanents (1954-1955). A television version ran on NBC prime time from 1949 to 1952 and as a daytime serial in 1954-1955.**

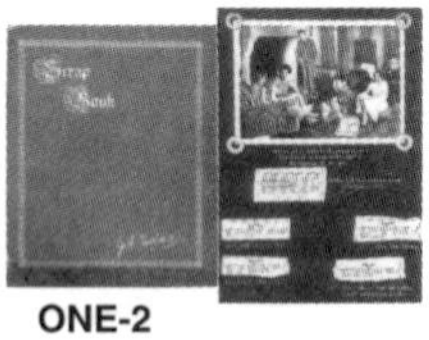

ONE-1 ONE-2

❑ **ONE-1. "One Man's Family History In Words And Pictures" Folder,**
1935. Standard Brands Foods. - **$12 $20 $35**

❑ **ONE-2. "Scrapbook" Yearbook,**
1936. Tenderleaf Tea. Published in graphic style of personally kept album. - **$10 $20 $30**

ONE-3 ONE-4

❑ **ONE-3. Teddy Barbour "Diary" Book,**
1937. Standard Brands Foods. Family events in simulated handwriting. - **$5 $20 $30**

❑ **ONE-4. "One Man's Family" Book,**
1938. Titled "Looks at Life." Has cast photos. Radio premium. - **$10 $20 $35**

ONE-5

ONE-6

❑ **ONE-5. Fanny Barbour "Memory Book",**
1940. Standard Brands Foods. Family photos, notes, etc. in simulated scrapbook form. - **$5 $20 $30**

❑ **ONE-6. "I Believe In America" Album,**
1941. Standard Brands Foods. Style of family scrapbook heavily emphasizing early war years. - **$20 $30 $60**

ONE-7

ONE-8

❑ **ONE-7. Barbour Family Scrapbook,**
1946. Standard Brands Foods. Format of simulated family photos, news clippings, telegrams, etc. - **$8 $25 $40**

❑ **ONE-8. "One Man's Family" Broadcast Highlights Record Album,**
c. 1947. Store item. Vol. 1 hardcover album of three 78 rpm records of selected excerpts from episodes between 1940-1946 on NBC Radio sponsored by Standard Brands Inc. - **$10 $20 $35**

ONE-9

❑ **ONE-9. TV Cast Photo,**
c. 1949. - **$8 $15 $25**

ONE-10

ONE-11

❑ **ONE-10. "Barbour Family Album",**
1951. Miles Laboratories. - **$10 $20 $35**

❑ **ONE-11. "Mother Barbour's Favorite Recipes" Booklet,**
c. 1951. Miles Laboratories. 20th anniversary souvenir picturing cast members over the years. - **$10 $20 $35**

## Open Road For Boys

***The Open Road for Boys*, a popular magazine of the 1920s and 1930s, organized The Open Road Pioneers Club in 1927 for boys and young men who loved the outdoor life and were willing to live up to the ideals of the old pioneers: courage, self-reliance, honesty, determination, endurance, progress, and meeting obstacles squarely. For 35¢ (in coins or stamps) sent to Deep-River Jim, members received a pin, certificate, and sweater emblem. The Club boasted over 3,000 chapters and lasted well into the 1950s.**

OPN-1

OPN-2

❑ **OPN-1. Open Road For Boys Magazine,**
1934. Has write-up for club & application for pin - **$8 $15 $30**

❑ **OPN-2. "Open Road Pioneers Club" Certificate,**
1935. - **$15 $30 $50**

THE OPEN ROAD PIONEERS' CLUB

OPN-3

❑ **OPN-3. Club Particulars Folder,**
c. 1938. Black and white 4-3/8x6-7/8" folder which opens to five panels 6-7/8x21-3/4". Details club aims and discusses various ranks which in order are Trailsman, Woodsman, Hunter, Explorer, Member of the Inner Circle. Text claims 85,000 registered boys and men as members. - **$10 $20 $35**

OPN-4

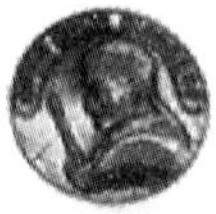

OPN-5

OPN-6

❑ **OPN-4. "Open Road Pioneers" Cello. Button,**
1930s. - **$5 $10 $15**

❑ **OPN-5. "Open Road Pioneers" Brass Badge,**
1930s. - **$8 $15 $25**

❑ **OPN-6. "Open Road Pioneers" 4-1/2" Fabric Patch,**
1930s. - **$25 $50 $85**

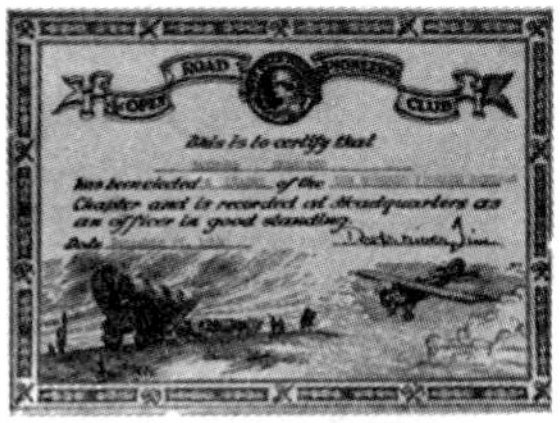

OPN-7

❑ **OPN-7. Leader's Certificate,**
1954. Different wording than member's certificate and "Deep-river Jim" no longer titled as "The Campfire Chief." - **$15 $30 $60**

## Operator #5

**America's Undercover Ace, handsome young Jimmy Christopher, fought spies and foreign agents from 1934 until the outbreak of World War II as Secret Service Operator #5 in the pages of the pulp magazine of the same name. His task, month after month, was to save the United States from destruction. A 1934 offer of a replica Operator #5 skull ring must have been short-lived as the ring is quite scarce.**

OPR-1

❑ **OPR-1. Enameled Silvered Metal Club Ring,**
1934. Rare. Operator 5 Magazine. Silvering easily worn off. Ten reported known: two in Good grade, three in Very Good, one in Fine, one in Very Fine, two in Near Mint, and one in Mint.
Good - **$1500**
Fine - **$5000**
Very Fine - **$9000**
Near Mint - **$13000**

OPR-2

❑ **OPR-2. "Secret Service Operator #5" Pulp Magazine,**
June-July 1936. Published by Popular Publications. - **$20 $40 $100**

# Our Gang

**Between 1922 and 1944 the Hal Roach Studios and MGM produced 221 *Our Gang* comedies. The short films, one- or two-reelers, were immensely successful, with the little rascals--Alfalfa, Farina, Buckwheat, Spanky, Darla Hood, Baby Jean, Mickey, Waldo, and their dogs Pete the Pup, Pal, and Von--joyfully getting into and out of mischief, playing hooky, putting on musicals, and generally doing no harm and having lots of fun. The films were syndicated on television as *The Little Rascals* (1955-1965), as *Our Gang Comedies* (1956-1965), and as *Mischief Makers* (1960-1970). *The Little Rascals* series was re-edited and televised again in the 1970s. A prime-time animated cartoon, *The Little Rascals Christmas Show*, aired on NBC in 1979. *Our Gang* comic books were published in the 1940s.**

OUR-1

OUR-2

❑ **OUR-1. "Pete" With Child Photo,**
c. 1920s. Child's souvenir of Steel Pier, Atlantic City. - **$15 $25 $60**

❑ **OUR-2. Cardboard Ad Blotter,**
1920s. Various sponsors. - **$15 $35 $75**

OUR-3

OUR-4

❑ **OUR-3. Joe Cobb China Mug,**
1920s. Store item by Sebring Pottery Co. - **$60 $125 $200**

❑ **OUR-4. Scooter Lowry China Mug,**
1920s. Store item by Sebring Pottery Co. - **$75 $125 $250**

OUR-5

❑ **OUR-5. "Jay Smith" Portrait Dish,**
1920s. The Seabring Pottery Co., probably used as movie theater premium. 5-1/4" diameter by 1" deep with color portrait. One of the scarcer pieces in a series picturing various Our Gang stars. - **$50 $100 $200**

OUR-6

OUR-7

❑ **OUR-6. "Hal Roach's Rascals" Photo,**
1920s. - **$20 $40 $75**

❑ **OUR-7. "Majestic Electric Radio" Cardboard Ink Blotter,**
1920s. - **$12 $35 $75**

OUR-8

❑ **OUR-8. Figure Mold Play Kit,**
1931. Store item by Gem Clay Forming Co. for Louis Wolf Co. Eight hollow plaster figures for painting plus backdrop panel.
Near Mint Boxed - **$400**
Each Painted Figure - **$8 $20 $35**

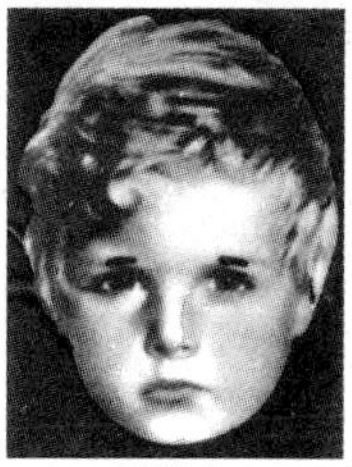

OUR-9

OUR-10

❑ **OUR-9. Dickie Moore Mask,**
c. 1932. U.S. Caramel Co. One of a set. - **$10 $25 $60**

❑ **OUR-10. "Pete" Cello. Button,**
c. 1932. From "Member Spanky Safety Club" series with Hal Roach copyright. - **$40 $85 $165**

OUR-11

OUR-12

OUR-13

❑ **OUR-11. "Buckwheat" Cello. Button,**
c. 1932. From "Member Spanky Safety Club" series with Hal Roach copyright. - **$40 $100 $200**

❑ **OUR-12. "Alfalfa" Cello. Button,**
c. 1932. From "Member Spanky Safety Club" series with Hal Roach copyright. - **$35 $90 $150**

❑ **OUR-13. "Darla Hood" Cello. Button,**
c. 1932. From "Member Spanky Safety Club" series with Hal Roach copyright. - **$30 $85 $140**

OUR-14

OUR-15

❑ **OUR-14. Puzzle,**
1932. McKesson's Milk of Magnesia. - **$40 $75 $125**

❑ **OUR-15. Puzzle Mailer,**
1932. McKesson's Milk of Magnesia. - **$15 $25 $50**

OUR-16

❑ **OUR-16. Fan Photo,**
1934. Hal Roach Studios. - **$10 $20 $45**

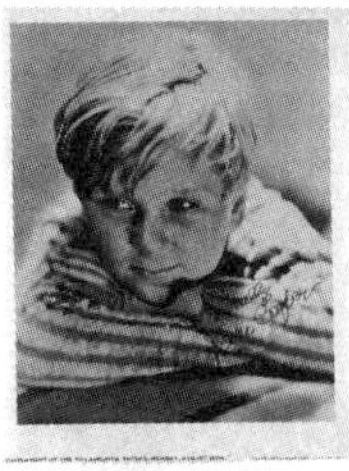

OUR-17

OUR-18

❑ **OUR-17. Jackie Cooper Photo,**
1936. Philadelphia Record newspaper premium. - **$8 $15 $25**

❑ **OUR-18. Fan Photo,**
1937. Hal Roach Studios. - **$10 $20 $45**

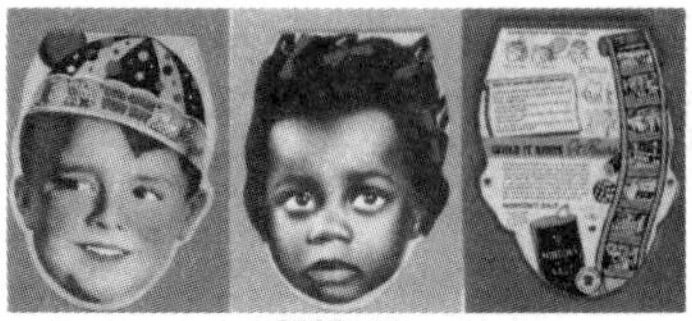

OUR-19

❑ **OUR-19. "Fun Kit" Diecut Booklet,**
1937. Morton's Salt. Features colored mask-like photos, activity pages, rules for their "Eagles Club". - **$50 $150 $225**

OUR-20

OUR-21

❑ **OUR-20. "Our Gang Painting Book",**
1937. Sears, Roebuck. Copyright by Hal Roach Studios. - **$30 $60 $100**

❑ **OUR-21. Spanky Fan Photo,**
c. 1937. Hal Roach Studios. - **$10 $18 $35**

OUR-22

OUR-23

OUR-24

❑ **OUR-22. "Spanky" Pencil Sharpener,**
1930s. 1-3/16" red catalin plastic. - **$40 $75 $125**

❑ **OUR-23. "Scottie" Pencil Sharpener,**
1930s. 1-3/16" green catalin plastic. - **$40 $75 $125**

❑ **OUR-24. "Pete" Pencil Sharpener,**
1930s. 1-3/16" red catalin plastic. - **$75 $140 $225**

OUR-25

❑ **OUR-25. "Our Gang" Pencil Box,**
1930s. Textured red cardboard. Eagle Pencil Co. - **$25 $50 $100**

OUR-26

OUR-27

❑ **OUR-26. Endorsement Poster For Boat Motors,**
1938. Evinrude-Elto Outboard Motors. 20x26" black and white with red borders. - **$75 $150 $250**

❑ **OUR-27. Our Gang Calendar,**
1939. Taystee bread. Cardboard sheet issued monthly. Each - **$20 $50 $100**

OUR-28

OUR-29

❑ **OUR-28. Litho Advertising Button,**
1930s. Sunfreze. 3/4" blue and white litho. Comes with and without sponsor's name. Each - **$10 $20 $35**

❑ **OUR-29. Movie Photo Including "Buster Brown",**
1930s. Probable premium. Shows kids and dog in boxing ring with caption "Buster Brown, Skinny, Tige & Kids." - **$20 $40 $60**

OUR-30

❑ **OUR-30. Our Gang Comedy Blatz Gum,**
1930s. - **$20 $50 $85**

OUR-31

OUR-32

❑ **OUR-31. "Contestant" Cello. Button,**
1930s. Probable theater or newspaper contest. - **$20 $40 $75**

❑ **OUR-32. "Our Gang Club" Cello. Button,**
1930s. Superba Theatre by Chicago button maker. Matinee inscription plus "Watch For Your Color". - **$25 $50 $85**

OUR-33

❑ **OUR-33. Bisque Nodders,**
1930s. German made store item. Set of six as shown: Pete, Chubby Chaney, Wheezer, Jackie Cooper, Farina, Mary Ann Jackson.
Each - **$75 $150 $250**

OUR-34

OUR-35

OUR-36

❑ **OUR-34. "Safety First" Cello. Button,**
1930s. Probable Our Gang member club button, rim curl copyright "Hal Roach Studios". - **$12 $25 $50**

❑ **OUR-35. "King Carl 'Alfalfa' Switzer" 2-1/2" Cello. Button,**
1930s. National Ice Cream Week. His name is followed by "Of Hal Roach's Our Gang-A MGM Release". - **$75 $150 $300**

❑ **OUR-36. "Spanky's Safety Patrol" 14x28" Sample Wall Calendar,**
1943. - **$50 $100 $150**

OUR-37

OUR-38

❑ **OUR-37. "Our Gang Adventures" Big Little Book #1456,**
1948. - **$12 $35 $75**

❑ **OUR-38. "The Little Rascals' Club" Member Card,**
c. 1955. WHUM-TV Channel 61. - **$15 $40 $60**

## Ovaltine Misc.

**Ovaltine was created in 1904 by Swiss physician Dr. George Wander as a flavored milk additive, and the original combination of malt, eggs, vitamins, and minerals is still in use in Europe. The Wander Company brought Ovaltine to the United States in 1905, using the same mix of ingredients except for the addition of sugar. Ovaltine found wide use as a tasty health food for children and adults. (The Red Cross shipped Ovaltine to Allied prisoner-of-war camps as a nutritional supplement during both World Wars.) The Sandoz Pharmaceutical Company acquired the Wander Company in 1967 and Ovaltine is now sold in "chocolate malt" (introduced in the 1960s) and "rich chocolate" (introduced in the 1980s) flavors, as well as the "original malt" version. In addition to the many premiums the company issued as the sponsor of such classic radio programs as *Radio Orphan Annie* and *Captain Midnight*, Ovaltine has produced promotional items not related to specific programs.**

OVL-1

❑ **OVL-1. "Lecture On Nutrition And Digestion By The Wonder Robot" Booklet,**
1934. Issued at Century of Progress Hall of Science. - **$40 $80 $150**

OVL-2

❑ **OVL-2. "Betty The Nail Biter" Sunday Comics Ad,**
1936. One-half page with coupon for Orphan Annie cup with green background decal. Text promotes Ovaltine as cure for nervousness. - **$5 $10 $15**

OVL-3

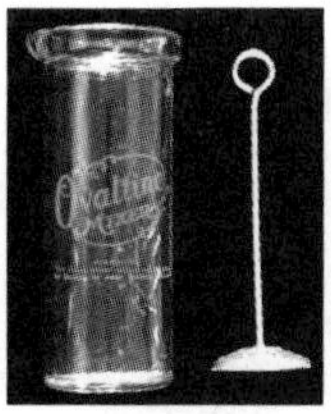
OVL-4

OVL-5

❑ **OVL-3. Litho. Tin Canister,**
1939. 9" tall "Hospital Size". - **$15 $25 $40**

❑ **OVL-4. Glass Shaker with Mixer,**
1930s. - **$20 $45 $85**

❑ **OVL-5. English "Delicious Ovaltine" China Mug,**
1930s. - **$15 $25 $45**

OVL-6

OVL-7

OVL-8

❑ **OVL-6. English "Delicious Ovaltine" China Mug Designed Without Handle,**
1930s. - **$15 $25 $50**

❑ **OVL-7. Sample Size Tin Container,**
1930s. Miniature 2-1/4" diameter by 2" tall. With Lid - **$15 $30 $60**

❑ **OVL-8. "School Size" Sample Tin Container,**
1930s. English issue miniature 1-1/2" diameter by 1-3/4" tall. Pictures Johnnie, Winnie, Elsie.
Complete - **$20 $35 $55**
Opened - **$15 $25 $40**

OVL-9

OVL-10

❑ **OVL-9. Plastic Mug,**
1940s. Sandy Strong. - **$20 $50 $75**

❑ **OVL-10. "Ding Dong School" Plastic Mug,**
1950s. Decal pictures "Miss Frances," the teacher on 1952-1956 TV educational series. - **$25 $50 $80**

OVL-11

❑ **OVL-11. Canadian "Ovaltine Trading Cards",**
c. 1960s. Made by Canada Decalcomania Co. Ltd. Distributed on Ovaltine jars with 12 in the set. Each - **$2 $4 $8**

OVL-12

❑ **OVL-12. Ovaltine Secret Decoder Ring,**
2000. - **$25**

## Peanuts

**Probably the most successful comic strip of all time, Charles Schulz's *Peanuts* appeared for a couple of years as *Li'l Folks* in the St. Paul *Pioneer Press* before it was syndicated under its new name by United Features in 1950. The antics of Charlie Brown, the strip's unlikely hero, Snoopy the wonder dog, Lucy van Pelt, Linus, Schroeder, and Pigpen have become part of American culture. There have been numerous reprint books, feature-length animated films, prime-time television specials, a musical comedy, and extensive merchandising and licensing of the major characters. Items are usually copyrighted Charles M. Schulz or United Features Syndicate. Copyright dates on items relate to character designs and are usually unrelated to the date an item was issued.**

PEA-1

PEA-2

❑ **PEA-1. College Football Homecoming 2-1/4" Litho. Button,**
1960. Minnesota Star and Sunday Tribune. For University of Minnesota vs. University of Illinois game with rim curl authorizations by Peanuts and United Features Syndicate. - **$10 $20 $40**

❑ **PEA-2. Daily Comic Strip Introduction 11x28" Promotion Card,**
c. 1960. United Features Syndicate. Imprinted for (New York) Daily News. - **$50 $100 $150**

PEA-3

❑ **PEA-3. "Peanuts" Child's Concert Wooden Piano,**
1962. Store item by Ely Mellow-Tone Chime Pianos. 18x18x11" tall black on white. -
**$75 $150 $250**

PEA-4

PEA-5

❑ **PEA-4. Charlie Brown 7 1/2" Vinyl Doll,**
1966. With removable hat, shirt and pants. Produced by Pocket Dolls in Hong Kong. -
**$15 $35 $60**

❑ **PEA-5. Charlie Brown's Reflections,**
1967. By Charles M. Schulz. Hallmark Product. 52 pages. - **$10 $20 $35**

PEA-6

❑ **PEA-6. Pre-School Child's Eye Exam Promotion Booklet,**
1967. Imprinted for Detroit Department of Health. Eight pages of comic strips illustrating vision information by members of Peanuts gang. -
**$10 $25 $50**

PEA-7

❑ **PEA-7. "Have Lunch With Snoopy" Dome Top Metal Lunch With Thermos,**
1968. Store item by Thermos.
Box - **$20 $50 $85**
Bottle - **$10 $25 $40**

PEA-8

❑ **PEA-8. Snoopy WWI Aviator Figural Music Box,**
1968. Wood/composition by Anri. Plays It's A Long Way To Tipperary. - **$50 $125 $175**

PEA-9

❑ **PEA-9. Snoopy Ceramic Figure,**
1968. Scarce. - **$40 $80 $125**

PEA-10

PEA-11

❑ **PEA-10. Charlie Brown Ceramic Figure,**
1968. 9" tall. - **$35 $80 $160**

❑ **PEA-11. "I'm On The Moon" Cello. Button,**
1969. Store item made by Simon Simple. 1-3/4" red, white and blue issued to commemorate moon landing. One of the nicest and most popular Snoopy buttons. - **$25 $50 $125**

PEA-12

PEA-13

❑ **PEA-12. Charlie Brown Composition Bobbing Head,**
1960s. Store item. Other characters also issued. - **$30 $100 $175**

❑ **PEA-13. Lucy Composition Bobbing Head,**
1960s. Store item, other characters also issued. - **$30 $100 $175**

PEA-14

PEA-15

❑ **PEA-14. Pig Pen Composition Bobbing Head,**
1960s. Most valuable of the series and hardest to find. - **$45 $150 $350**

❑ **PEA-15. Charlie Brown Enameled Metal Necklace Charm,**
1960s. Store item. United Features Syndicate copyright. From character series. - **$15 $30 $70**

PEA-16

PEA-17

PEA-18

❑ **PEA-16. Plastic Clip-On Badge,**
1970. Millbrook Bread. Five or more characters in set. Carded - **$5 $8 $12**
Loose - **$3 $5 $8**

❑ **PEA-17. "Snoopy's Spotters Club" 2" Litho. Tab,**
c. 1970. Millbrook Bread. - **$5 $10 $15**

❑ **PEA-18. Litho. Tab,**
c. 1970. Restaurant issue. - **$3 $5 $8**

PEA-19

PEA-20

❑ **PEA-19. "Peanuts Patches",**
1971. Interstate Brands. Set of five with envelope and order coupon.
Set With Mailer - **$10 $30 $60**

❑ **PEA-20. "Colonial Capers Cartoon Comics" 2-1/2" Cello. Button,**
1971. Probable newspaper issue. - **$5 $12 $25**

PEA-21

PEA-22

❑ **PEA-21. "It's The Great Pumpkin" Promo Button,**
1971. Promotes October 23 CBS TV program. 3". - **$20 $40 $75**

❑ **PEA-22. "Red Baron's Albatross" Punch-Out,**
1973. Coca-Cola. - **$25 $50 $75**

PEA-23

PEA-24

❑ **PEA-23. "Happy Birthday, America!" Cello. Button,**
1976. Bicentennial issue. - **$8 $12 $20**

❑ **PEA-24. Original Daily Comic Strip Art With Snoopy And Woodstock,**
1977. 7-1/2x29-1/2" black and white india ink art with four panels.
Similar Age With Snoopy **- $1500 $2000 $3000**

PEA-25

❑ **PEA-25. Linus Candle Figure,**
1970s. Hallmark. - **$15 $30 $75**

PEA-26

PEA-27

❑ **PEA-26. "Peanuts" Metal Lunch Box With Thermos,**
1980. Store item by Thermos.
Box - **$10 $30 $60**
Bottle - **$5 $10 $20**

❑ **PEA-27. "Snoopy and the Gang" Top**
1980s. Very colorful. - **$30 $50 $75**

PEA-28

PEA-29

❑ **PEA-28. Snoopy Bean Bag**
1998. With two tags. - **$20**

❑ **PEA-29. Snoopy as Frankenstein Stuffed Toy,**
1999. Halloween premium for Whitman's chocolates. - **$5**

PEA-30

❑ **PEA-30. Charles Schulz Final "Peanuts" Sunday Comic Strip,**
2000. Historic, and undoubtedly saved by many fans. Near Mint - **$2**

PEA-31

PEA-32

☐ **PEA-31. Snoopy Standee,**
2000. United Features Synd. Unusual die-cut standee which promotes the return of products after Charles Schulz's passing. - **$15 $30 $50**

☐ **PEA-32. Charlie Brown Ornament,**
2000. In box. - **$15**

PEA-33

☐ **PEA-33. Snoopy Ceramic Figure,**
2000. Made in Indonesia. - **$30**

PEA-34

☐ **PEA-34. Snoopy #1 Ace Pewter Figure,**
2000. Hallmark product in box. - **$35**

PEA-35

☐ **PEA-35. Peanuts Christmas Figures,**
2001. - **$20**

PEA-36

PEA-37

☐ **PEA-36. Snoopy Candy Container,**
2001. Plastic doghouse holds candy. Roof comes in blue, green or yellow. Each - **$10**

☐ **PEA-37. Playing Cards with Tin Box,**
2001. Two decks of cards in a collectors tin.
In box. - **$10**

## Pep Boys

**The Pep Boys--Manny, Moe and Jack--were three pals who opened an auto supply store in Philadelphia in 1921. The store prospered and eventually grew into a chain of operations in the Eastern states, watched over through the years by the smiling cartoon faces of the founders.**

PEP-1

☐ **PEP-1. U.S. Sesquicentennial Exposition 6x8" Decal,** 1926. Pep Auto Supply Co. copyright. Full color patriotic art water transfer decal with "Pep Boys" glassine envelope. Decal reverse inscription includes "All Over Philadelphia And Camden."
Near Mint With Envelope - **$100**
Loose - **$20 $40 $75**

PEA-2

☐ **PEP-2. Early Catalogue,**
c. 1926. 4-1/2x6-3/4" catalogue of 68 pages captioned "All Over Philadelphia And Camden!" - **$20 $40 $75**

PEP-3

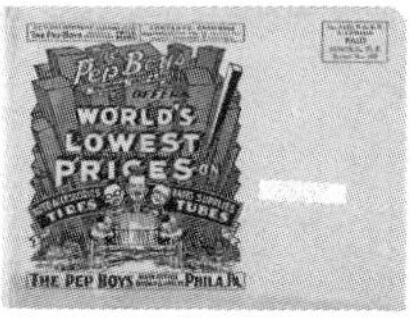


PEP-4

☐ **PEP-3. Manual,**
1930. 72 pages and front and back cover. - **$25 $50 $75**

☐ **PEP-4. Mailer For Manual,**
1930. - **$10 $20 $30**

PEP-5

PEP-6

☐ **PEP-5. Manual,**
1931. 96 pages and front and back cover. - **$25 $50 $75**

☐ **PEP-6. "Pep Boys Dawn Patrol" Postcard,**
1933. Response to listener over WIP Radio w/facsimile signature of announcer Fred Wood. - **$30 $60 $100**

PEP-7

PEP-8

❑ **PEP-7. Catalogue,**
1938. - **$20 $50 $75**

❑ **PEP-8. Catalogue,**
1939. - **$20 $50 $75**

**PEP-9**

**PEP-10**

❑ **PEP-9. Patch,**
1930s. Red outline with yellow background premium patch. - **$10 $20 $60**

❑ **PEP-10. Brass Match Cover Holder,**
1940s.Brass match holder which has opening for Pep Boy logo at bottom. - **$15 $35 $60**

**PEP-11**

**PEP-12**

❑ **PEP-11. Matches,**
1940s. No name printed at bottom. - **$5 $10 $15**

❑ **PEP-12. Matches,**
1940s. "Pep Boys" printed at bottom. - **$5 $10 $15**

**PEP-13**

**PEP-14**

❑ **PEP-13. Boxed Playing Cards,**
1940s. - **$50 $125 $175**

❑ **PEP-14. Catalogue,**
1954. Store premium. - **$10 $25 $40**

**PEP-15**

**PEP-16**

❑ **PEP-15. Catalogue,**
1955. Store premium. - **$20 $40 $60**

❑ **PEP-16. Plastic Cigarette Holder,**
c. 1950s. - **$25 $50 $85**

## Pete Rice

**Pistol Pete Rice was the sheriff of Buzzard Gap, Arizona, in a series of Street and Smith pulp westerns. Written by Ben Conlon under the name Austin Gridley, *Pete Rice Western Adventures* appeared from November 1933 to June 1936. For a dime, readers could get a *Pete Rice Club* deputy badge and a members' pledge card.**

**PTR-1**

❑ **PTR-1. "Pete Rice" Gummed Paper Envelope Sticker,**
c. 1934. Street & Smith Co., publishers of Pete Rice pulp magazine. - **$15 $30 $50**

**PTR-2**

❑ **PTR-2. Deputy Club Metal Badge,**
c. 1934. Badge - **$25 $50 $100**
Envelope - **$5 $10 $15**

## Peter Pan

**The story of Peter Pan, the boy who lived in Never-Never land and refused to grow up, was created in 1904 by British novelist and playwright Sir James M. Barrie (1860-1937). The fantasy of Peter, Wendy, Tinkerbell, and the evil Captain Hook was given new life in 1953 with the release of the full-length Disney animated feature, and in 1991 Tri-Star Pictures released *Hook*, a revised version of the beloved tale directed by Steven Spielberg and starring Dustin Hoffman and Robin Williams.**

**PAN-1**

❑ **PAN-1. "Animated Coloring Book",**
1943. Derby Foods. Non-Disney with punch-out sheet to animate the pictures. - **$15 $30 $60**

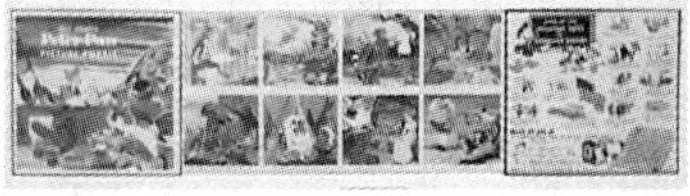

**PAN-2**

❑ **PAN-2. "Peter Pan Picture Puzzle" Bread Picture Album,**
1952. Various bread companies. 9x9" four-page folder depicting eight different scenes, each to be completed with three cut-outs per scene from bread end labels.
Near Mint Complete - **$175**
Album Only - **$15 $30 $50**
Single Uncut Label - **$3 $6 $10**

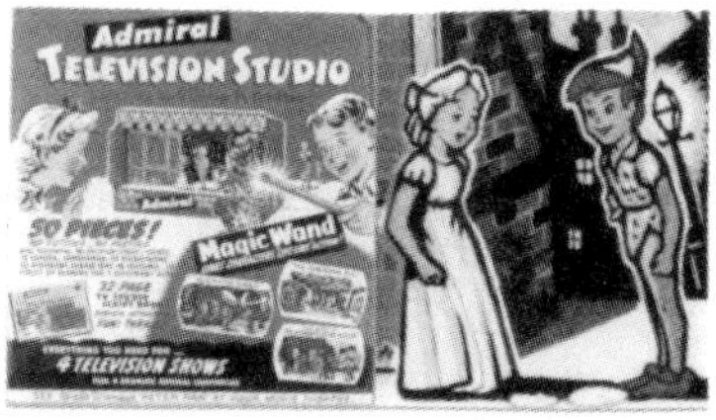


**PAN-3**

❑ **PAN-3. "Admiral Television Studio Featuring Walt Disney's Peter Pan " Punch-Out,**
1953. 50 piece set issued by Admiral dealers.
Unpunched **$35 $60 $125**

**PAN-4**

**PAN-5**

❑ **PAN-4. "Peter Pan" Studio Fan Card,**
1953. 8-1/8x10-1/8" stiff paper with color portrait. - **$35 $75 $125**

❑ **PAN-5. Soap Bar With 18x24" Paper Map,**
c. 1953. Colgate-Palmolive.
Map - **$35 $100 $200**
Soap Bar - **$5 $12 $25**

**PAN-6**

**PAN-7**

❑ **PAN-6. Coasters 11x14" Paper Store Sign,**
c. 1953. Peter Pan Peanut Butter. -
**$30 $60 $110**

❑ **PAN-7. "Peter Pan Peanut Butter" Tin Lids,**
c. 1953. Examples from set. Each - **$3 $8 $15**

**PAN-8**

**PAN-9**

❑ **PAN-8. "Get Your Peter Pan Picture Puzzle" Litho. Button,**
c. 1953. Disney copyright. - **$20 $50 $75**

❑ **PAN-9. Bread Labels,**
c. 1953. Various bread companies. Examples from set of 12. Each - **$5 $10 $15**

**PAN-10**

❑ **PAN-10. "Hallmark Pirate Ship" Kit With Mailer Envelope,**
c. 1953. Store item, Hallmark Cards. Includes 21x29" map and four punch-out sheets to assemble pirate ship.
Near Mint In Envelope - **$85**
Map Only - **$15 $25 $45**

**PAN-11**

**PAN-12**

❑ **PAN-11. Glazed Ceramic Figurine,**
1950s. Store item by Hagen-Renaker. 1-3/4" tall. - **$60 $125 $175**

❑ **PAN-12. Wendy Glazed Ceramic Figurine,**
1950s. Store item by Hagen-Renaker. 2" tall. - **$60 $125 $175**

**PAN-13**

❑ **PAN-13. Mermaid Ceramic Figurine,**
1950s. Store item by Hagen-Renaker. 2-3/4" long. - **$75 $150 $250**

**PAN-14**

**PAN-15**

❑ **PAN-14. Litho. Button,**
1950s. Hudson's department store, Detroit. No Disney copyright. - **$10 $20 $40**

❑ **PAN-15. Coloring Book,**
1963. Peter Pan Peanut Butter, non-Disney. -
**$5 $15 $25**

**PAN-16**

❑ **PAN-16. Tinkerbell Doll,**
2000. Part of Peter Pan ornament series. - **$25**

## Peter Rabbit

**The characters in Thornton Burgess's children's books were adapted by Harrison Cady for the *Peter Rabbit* Sunday comic strip, which appeared in the *New York Tribune* starting in 1920. The strip, however, soon became more Cady than Burgess, featuring an essentially new rabbit family and slapstick humor. Comic book reprints appeared in the 1940s and 1950s. The strip ceased publication in 1956.**

**PET-1**

❑ **PET-1. Celluloid Flip On Stickpin,**
c. 1915. Columbia Records. - **$50 $100 $150**

**PET-2**

❑ **PET-2. "Quaddy Note Paper" Box,**
1916. Store item. Stationery box copyright by Harrison Cady. - **$25 $60 $100**

**PET-3**

**PET-4**

❑ **PET-3. "Peter Rabbit Puts On Airs" Miniature Pamphlet,**
1922. Newspaper premium with Harrison Cady art. - **$30 $60 $90**

❑ **PET-4. "How Peter Rabbit Went to Sea" Miniature Hardback Book,**
1920s. From a series of hardbacks. Scarce. -
**$75 $125 $175**

PET-5

PET-6

❑ **PET-5. Peter Rabbit Child's Sterling Silver Ring,**
c. 1920s. Miniature figure image in clothing outfit. - **$50 $125 $250**

❑ **PET-6. Peter Rabbit "Bedtime Stories Club" Cello. Button,**
c. 1920s. Newspaper sponsor name specified. - **$40 $75 $125**

PET-7

PET-8

❑ **PET-7. Peter Rabbit "Bedtime Stories Club" Cello. Button,**
c. 1920s. Newspaper sponsor unspecified. - **$30 $65 $100**

❑ **PET-8. Newspaper Club Cello. Button,**
1920s. - **$40 $75 $125**

PET-9

❑ **PET-9. "Peter Rabbit" Tin Canister,**
c. 1920s. Store item. 4" dia. by 2" tall can and lid, both with full color Peter Rabbit family art. - **$50 $110 $165**

PET-10

PET-11

❑ **PET-10. Paint Book,**
1937. Store item. Whitman book with 36 pages of Harrison Cady art in comic strip panel format. - **$20 $40 $75**

❑ **PET-11. "Peter Rabbit Club" Cello. Button,**
c. 1930s. Sponsor "Wisconsin News." - **$60 $125 $225**

# Pez

**This peppermint candy originated in Austria in 1927. Edward Haas, the inventor, shortened the German word for peppermint, *pfefferminTz*, to Pez. Sales were slow until the company, Pez Candy Inc., entered the United States in 1952 targeting the children's market with a figural head on the dispenser and a cherry flavored candy. Collectors are now willing to spend four-figure amounts for a rare example. In addition to the classic dispensers featuring cartoon figures, animals, superheroes, and Disney characters, PEZ watches, jewelry, keychains, and clip-ons have been produced. Most dispensers are priced as Fine or Near Mint.**

PEZ-1

❑ **PEZ-1. Litho. Tin Clicker,**
c. 1955. - **$150 $300 $450**

PEZ-2

❑ **PEZ-2. Space Gun Display Sign,**
1956. Scarce. Cardboard sign that held the 6 candy-shooting guns. - **$200 $400 $700**

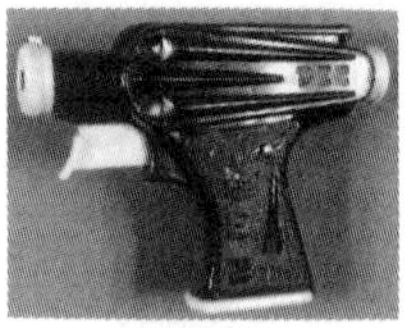

PEZ-3

❑ **PEZ-3. Space Gun,**
1950s. Candy shooter gun came in red, yellow, blue, green and black. - **$250 $400 $600**

PEZ-4

❑ **PEZ-4. Litho. Tin Yo-Yo,**
1950s. - **$125 $225 $300**

PEZ-5 (ENLARGED VIEW)

❑ **PEZ-5. Tin Rotating Store Rack,**
1950s. 16" tall. - **$300 $500 $1000**

PEZ-6

PEZ-7

PEZ-8

❑ **PEZ-6. Space Trooper Pez,**
1950s. Blue - **$250-$300**
Red - **$300-$400**
Yellow - **$350-$425**

❑ **PEZ-7. Pez Arithmetic,**
1962. Blue - **$600-$800**
Red or green - **$850-$1000**

❑ **PEZ-8. Pez Lions Club,**
1962. With 1962 stem - **$2500-$3000**
With generic stem - **$1800-$2200**

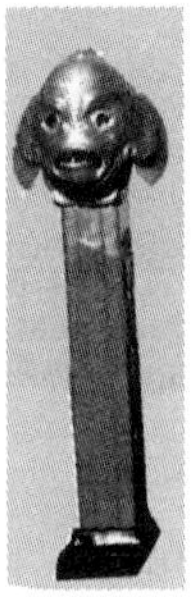

PEZ-9

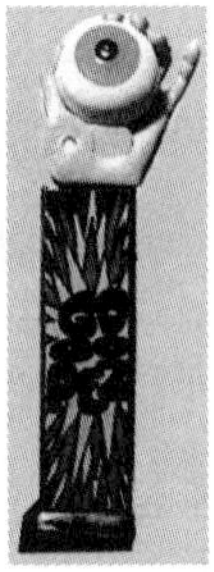

PEZ-10

PEZ-11

❑ **PEZ-9. Green Creature Pez,**
1965. - **$350-$400**

❑ **PEZ-10. Go-Pez,**
1968. Flesh - **$300-$400**
Black - **$500-$800**

❑ **PEZ-11. Tin Clicker,**
c. 1960s. - **$10 $15 $25**

PEZ-12

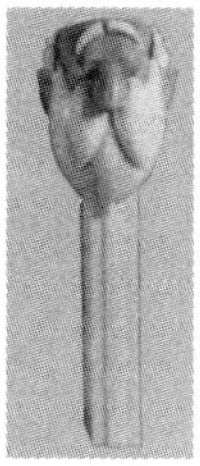

PEZ-13

PEZ-14

❑ **PEZ-12. Asterix Pez,**
1960s. Rare. Usually missing parts - **$1300-$1700**

❑ **PEZ-13. Müeslix Pez,**
1960s. Rare. - **$1650-$2000**

❑ **PEZ-14. Obelix Pez,**
1960s. Rare. - **$1400-$1800**

PEZ-15

❑ **PEZ-15. Disney Pez Dispenser Display Card,**
1970. Card fits into the back of a display box. - **$30 $45 $75**

PEZ-16

❑ **PEZ-16. Promotional Pocket Knife,**
c. 1970. 2-3/4" long with vinyl over metal case depicting Pez logo, the word "International" and stylized globe. - **$25 $50 $100**

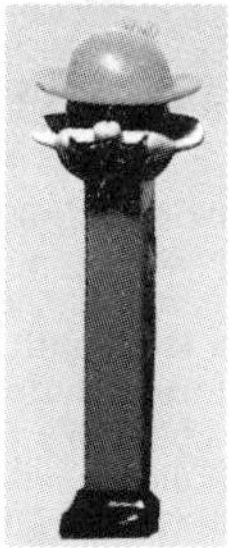

PEZ-17

PEZ-18 PEZ-19

❑ **PEZ-17. Pez Alpine,**
1972. - **$1600-$2000**

❑ **PEZ-18. Mary Poppins Pez,**
1972. - **$700-$900**

❑ **PEZ-19. Spare Froh Pez,**
1972. - **$1200-$1500**

PEZ-20

PEZ-21

❑ **PEZ-20. Pez Bride,**
1975. Red Hair - **$1500-$1800**
Brown Hair - **$1600-$2000**
Blonde Hair - **$1700-$2200**

❑ **PEZ-21. Olympic Snowman,**
1976. - **$400-$500**

PEZ-22

❑ **PEZ-22. Retailer's Sales Promotion Folder,**
1976. 8-1/2x11" promoting line of bicentennial dispensers. - **$30 $60 $100**

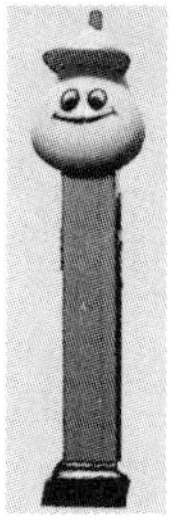

PEZ-23

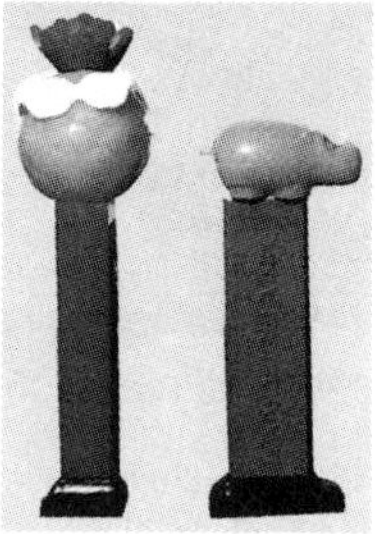

PEZ-24 PEZ-25

❑ **PEZ-23. Pez Pear,**
1979. - **$800-$1100**

❑ **PEZ-24. Pez Pineapple,**
1979. - **$2200-$2500**

❑ **PEZ-25. Pez Hippo,**
1970s. - **$850-$1100**

PEZ-26

❑ **PEZ-26. Make-A-Face on Card,**
1970s. German version. One of the most sought-after Pez dispensers.
Loose complete - **$2200-$2600**
Mint on card-USA Card - **$3500-$4000**
Mint on card-Foreign Card - **$3200-$3700**

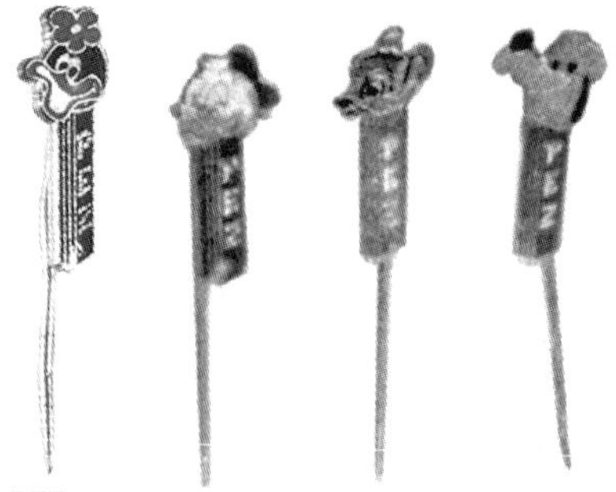

PEZ-27 PEZ-28 PEZ-29 PEZ-30

❑ **PEZ-27. Miniature Duck Plastic Dispenser Stick Pin,**
1970s. Premium. - **$10 $20 $30**

❑ **PEZ-28. Donald Duck Miniature Plastic Dispenser Replica On Brass Stickpin,**
1970s. From European made Disney character series. - **$10 $20 $35**

❑ **PEZ-29. Bambi Miniature Plastic Dispenser Replica On Brass Stickpin,** 1970s. From European made Disney character series. - **$10 $25 $40**

❑ **PEZ-30. Pluto Miniature Plastic Dispenser On Brass Stickpin,** 1970s. From European made Disney character series. - **$10 $20 $30**

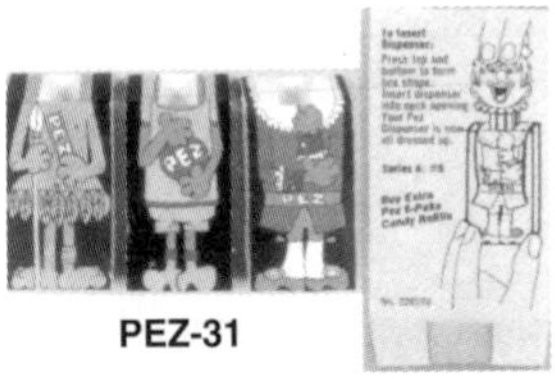

**PEZ-31**

❑ **PEZ-31. Dispenser Cardboard Costumes,** c. 1970s Three examples and one back panel from 12 in series "A". Each - **$12 $20 $35**

**PEZ-32**

❑ **PEZ-32. Insert Paper,** 1970s. Paper slip illustrating different dispensers plus reverse ad for Golden Glow candy dispenser and Pez Costume Fun Books. - **$20 $30 $50**

**PEZ-33**

❑ **PEZ-33. Pez Flag,** 1970s. 5.5x9" glossy paper on 15-1/2" wood rod. - **$10 $20 $35**

**PEZ-34**

❑ **PEZ-34. "Pez Premium Club" Paper,** 1970s. - **$20 $30 $50**

**PEZ-35**

**PEZ-36**

**PEZ-37**

❑ **PEZ-35. Spider-Man Cardboard Mask,** 1970s. - **$15 $25 $50**

❑ **PEZ-36. Hulk Cardboard Mask,** 1970s. - **$15 $25 $50**

❑ **PEZ-37. Silver Coin,** Late 1970s. Pez premium coin given to employees. Came in small red case attached to illustrated folder.
Coin only - **$100-$150**
Complete - **$150 $250 $450**

**PEZ-38**

❑ **PEZ-38. Donkey Kong Jr. Cereal Box with Pez Promo,** 1984. Has promotion and order form for Donkey Kong Jr. Pez Dispenser.
Complete - **$100 $200 $350**
With coupon missing - **$60 $100 $200**

**PEZ-39**

❑ **PEZ-39. Pez Promo Decal,** 1980s. 8 1/2" tall and 12" wide. Shows Donald and Mickey Pez holders. - **$25**

**PEZ-40** **PEZ-41**

❑ **PEZ-40. "Müeslix" Pez Dispenser,** 1997. On card. - **$20**

❑ **PEZ-41. "Roman" Pez Dispenser,** 1997. On card. - **$20**

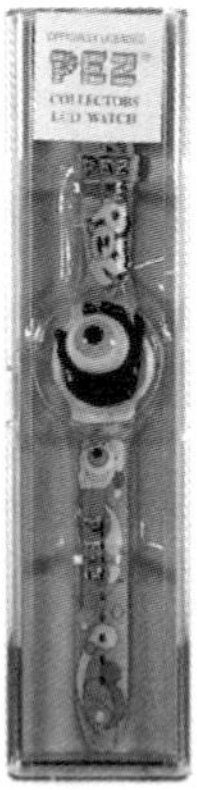

**PEZ-42**

**PEZ-43**

❑ **PEZ-42. Collectors Watch,** 1998. Limited edition watch has an eyeball held by a black hand. In box - **$25**

❑ **PEZ-43. Crystal Pumpkin Head Pez Dispenser,** 1999. From the Crystal Animals set. Head is blue-tinted. On card. - **$15**

**PEZ-44** **PEZ-45**

❑ **PEZ-44. Crystal Elephant Head Pez Dispenser,**
1999. Head is yellow-tinted. On blue card. - **$20**

❑ **PEZ-45. Crystal Hippo Head Pez Dispenser,**
1999. Head is blue-tinted. On blue card. - **$20**

PEZ-46

PEZ-47

PEZ-48

❑ **PEZ-46. Candy Phone on Card,**
1999. Came in several colors - yellow, green, blue, red and others. - **$10**

❑ **PEZ-47. Marvin the Martian Candy Hander,**
1999. On card. - **$5 $10 $20**

❑ **PEZ-48. Wile E. Coyote Candy Hander,**
1999. On card. - **$5 $10 $20**

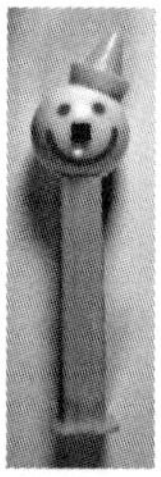

PEZ-49

PEZ-50

PEZ-51

❑ **PEZ-49. Jack In The Box Premium,**
1999. Comes in yellow, red and blue. Each - **$10**

❑ **PEZ-50. Johnny Lightning Car on Card,**
1999. One-time promotion run. - **$35**

❑ **PEZ-51. Tweety With Baseball Hat,**
1999. Dispenser. - **$2**

PEZ-52

PEZ-53

❑ **PEZ-52. Wolverine Pez on Card,**
1990s. Comes in yellow or black stem. - **$2**

❑ **PEZ-53. Pez Playworld,**
1990s. Set with dispenser, candy, outfit and pencils on card. - **$35**

PEZ-54

PEZ-55

❑ **PEZ-54. "Gyro Gearloose' Pez Dispenser,**
2000. On blue card. - **$7**

❑ **PEZ-55. "Webby" Pez Dispenser,**
2000. On blue card. - **$10**

PEZ-56

PEZ-57

❑ **PEZ-56. Eyewear Case,**
2000. Exclusive by A&A Optical in Dallas. - **$20**

❑ **PEZ-57. Eyewear Case,**
2000. Exclusive by A&A Optical in Dallas. - **$20**

PEZ-58

PEZ-59

❑ **PEZ-58. Valentine's Dispenser,**
2000. Heart is printed with "Happy Valentine's Day." Comes in red or pink. - **$7**

❑ **PEZ-59. Rocket Pen Candy Dispenser,**
2000. It lights, it writes and has a secret compartment. Comes in 6 different colors. - **$5**

PEZ-60

❑ **PEZ-60. Pez Card Game in Box,**
2000. Premiere edition. - **$10**

PEZ-61

❑ **PEZ-61. Bride & Groom Wacky Wobblers,**
2000. Limited to 5,000 sets. In colorful box - **$35**

PEZ-62

PEZ-63

❑ **PEZ-62. "Pez Policeman" Wacky Wobbler,**
2000. Limited to 5,000. In box - **$25**

❑ **PEZ-63. "Pez Fireman" Wacky Wobbler,**
2000. Limited to 5,000. In box - **$25**

PEZ-64

❑ **PEZ-64 General Mills Cereal Boxes with Mini-Pez on Box,**
2001. For Cocoa Puffs, Honey Nut Cheerios, Lucky Charms, and Trix. Each - **$20**

PEZ-65

❑ **PEZ-65. Smiley Face Pez Dispenser,**
2001. On card. - **$10**

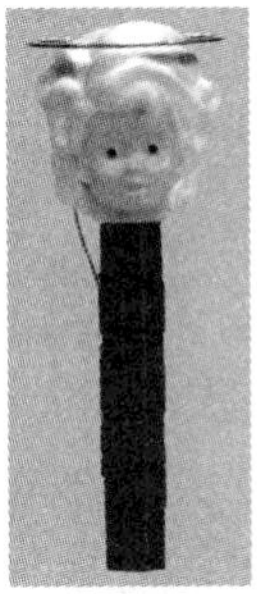

PEZ-66

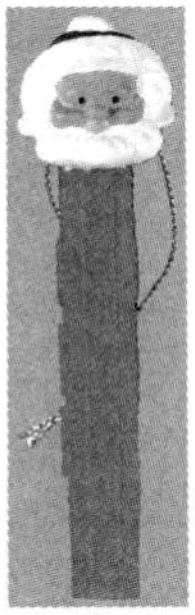

PEZ-67

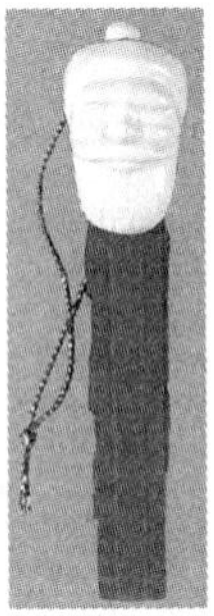

PEZ-68

❑ **PEZ-66. Pez "Angel" Christmas Ornament,**
2001. Boxed - **$15**

❑ **PEZ-67. Pez "Santa" Christmas Ornament,**
2001. Boxed - **$15**

❑ **PEZ-68. Pez "Old Style Santa" Christmas Ornament,**
2001. All white face. Boxed - **$15**

PEZ-69

PEZ-70

❑ **PEZ-69. "Giant Pez" Candy Roll Dispenser,**
2001. 12-1/2" tall in box. - **$25**

❑ **PEZ-70. "Fuzzy Friends" Dispenser,**
2001. With candy. 4 different. Each - **$5**

## The Phantom

**The legendary ghost-who-walks was created by writer Lee Falk (1912-1999) and artist Ray Moore as a daily comic strip for King Features in 1936. A Sunday page was added in 1939. Aided by Guran, the leader of the Bandar pygmies, and by his wolf Devil, the masked crime fighter with the sign of the skull has been battling evil and pursuing his fiancee Diana Palmer in comic strips in the U.S. and overseas ever since. Comic book reprints were first published in 1939, with new material added starting in 1951. A 15-episode chapter play starring Tom Tyler was released by Columbia Pictures in 1943. In 1996, Paramount Pictures released a big screen version of *The Phantom* staring Billy Zane. Despite an average box office showing, the film received favorable word of mouth from fans and has received good ratings on cable TV.**

PHN-1

❑ **PHN-1. "The Phantom And The Sign Of The Skull" Better Little Book,**
1939. Whitman #1474. - **$50 $100 $225**

PHN-2

PHN-3

❑ **PHN-2. Vending Machine Display Sign,**
1930s. Criss Cross Machines, manufactured by Calex Mfg. Co., Amityville, NY. Red on light yellow 10-1/2 x 14". Cards were used as Amoco gasoline give-aways but also sold via vending machines. Sign shows 5 Phantom cards. - **$500 $750 $1000**

❑ **PHN-3. Amoco Gas Station Premium Card,**
1930s. The earliest of all Phantom trading cards. On light cardboard, these 3"x3" black and white cards each depicted a different comic panel from the original Lee Falk/Ray Moore story from 1936. The reverse had an ink-stamped logo. Each - **$75 $100 $150**

PHN-4

❑ **PHN-4. "The Phantom And Desert Justice" Better Little Book,**
1941. Whitman #1421. - **$25 $75 $140**

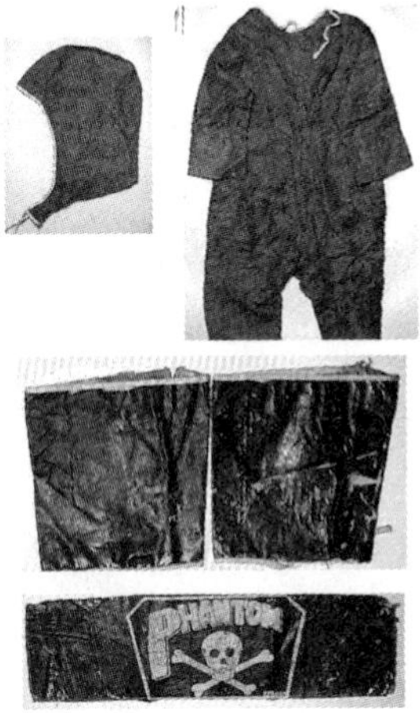


PHN-5

❑ **PHN-5. "Phantom" Child's Costume,**
1942. Store item with initials of "King Features Syndicate," a copyright symbol and a date of "42" on the waistband. Waistband is 5x25-1/2" with white illustration on black oilcloth. Photo shows black oilcloth leg cuffs. Matching wrist cuffs with a white stripe were also provided. The two fabric pieces are in deep purple and consist of a head covering along with a pull-on one-piece bodysuit. Came with a generic molded black fabric mask. As Illustrated - **$500 $1000 $1500**

PHN-6

❑ **PHN-6. One-Sheet Spanish Poster,**
1943. To coincide with the release of the Tom Tyler serial. - **$350 $500 $750**

PHN-7

PHN-8

❑ **PHN-7. "The Phantom and the Girl of Mystery" Big Little Book,**
1947. - **$15 $50 $100**

❑ **PHN-8. Comic Strip Characters Tattoo Pack,**
c. 1948. Classic Comics, published by Gilberton Co. Store item packet of 20 tattoo transfers with The Phantom and other examples pictured on envelope. - **$40 $80 $150**

PHN-9

PHN-10

❑ **PHN-9. Portrait Ring,**
c. 1948. Gold plastic bands with clear cover over color picture. - **$75 $115 $150**

❑ **PHN-10. Exhibit Card,**
1949. Postcard stock and size. Vending machine item sold for one penny. - **$50 $70 $90**

PHN-11

PHN-12

❑ **PHN-11. "The Phantom's Club Member" Australian Cello. Button,**
1940s. Scarce. - **$150 $400 $750**

❑ **PHN-12. "S.F. Call-Bulletin" Cardboard Disk,**
c. 1940s. San Francisco newspaper. From series of contest disks, match number to win prize. - **$10 $25 $50**

PHN-13

❑ **PHN-13. Three-Sheet,**
1940s. Columbia Pictures. 80" by 40". - **$2000 $4000 $6500**

PHN-14

❑ **PHN-14. Radio Show Billboard Poster,**
1940s. Produced in cooperation for the intended Phantom radio show to be heard on WEBR/Canada. One of two. - **$300 $600 $1200**

PHN-15

PHN-16

❑ **PHN-15. Australian Brass Stickpin,**
1953. Comic book premium. Embossed skull symbol with red eye accents. - **$50 $100 $150**

❑ **PHN-16. China Portrait Mug,**
1950s. Store item. - **$35 $75 $135**

PHN-17

PHN-18

PHN-19

❑ **PHN-17. Litho. Tab,**
1950s. - **$25 $60 $135**

❑ **PHN-18. "The Phantom" Litho. Button,**
1950s. From set of various King Features Syndicate characters. - **$15 $30 $60**

❑ **PHN-19. Plastic Frame Picture Charm,**
1950s. Store item. Gumball vending machine issue. - **$10 $20 $35**

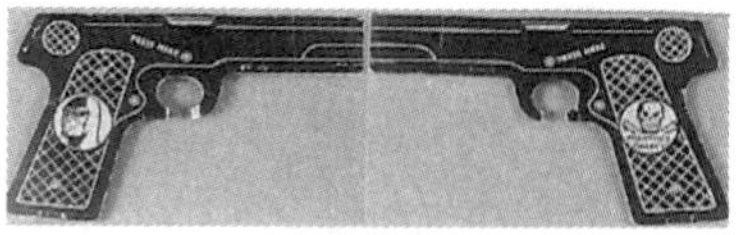
PHN-20

❑ **PHN-20. Australian Issue Cardboard Premium Gun,**
1950s. Possibly a comic book premium. Contains metal clicker. One grip has Phantom portrait while other has skull and crossbones captioned "Phantom's Mark." - **$50 $100 $150**

PHN-21

❑ **PHN-21. Litho. Buttons,**
1950s. Issuer unknown but from series of at least 30 different marked only with small copyright symbol. Each is 7/8" full color.
Phantom - **$30 $75 $125**
Phantom's Fiancee Diana Palmer - **$15 $30 $50**
Phantom's Wolf Dog, Devil - **$10 $15 $30**

**PHN-22**

❑ **PHN-22. Board Game With Plastic Skull Ring,**
1966. Store item by Transogram.
Near Mint Boxed With Ring - **$300**
Ring Only - **$50 $100 $150**

**PHN-23**

**PHN-24**

❑ **PHN-23. Comic Book Fan Reply Card,**
1967. King Features Syndicate. Color postcard with reverse message from King Comics thanking recipient for ideas and suggestions. - **$25 $60 $125**

❑ **PHN-24. Soda Cardboard Display,**
1960s. Swedish. Two-sided, for the promotion of carbonated lemon drink. - **$700 $1000 $1200**

**PHN-25**

**PHN-26**

**PHN-27**

❑ **PHN-25. Soda Lemon Drink Bottle,**
1960s. Store item. Phantom pictured in blue garb. - **$40 $50 $60**

❑ **PHN-26. Australian Ink Stamp Ring,**
1960s. Rubber with raised skull symbol as ink stamp, "Phantom" name on ring band. - **$500 $750 $1000**

❑ **PHN-27. Australian Brass Ring,**
1960s. Depicts raised skull symbol with red eye sockets. - **$200 $400 $600**

**PHN-28**

**PHN-29**

❑ **PHN-28. Sticker,**
1975. King Features. - **$5 $10 $20**

❑ **PHN-29. Figure with Two Rings on Card,**
1995. Great graphics on blister card. - **$50**

**PHN-30**

**PHN-31**

❑ **PHN-30. Movie Badge,**
1996. Given away at premiere. - **$2 $4 $10**

❑ **PHN-31. Movie Badge,**
1996. Given away at premiere. - **$2 $4 $10**

**PHN-32**

**PHN-33**

❑ **PHN-32. Slurpee Cardboard Promo Sign,**
1996. 7-11 store promo for free ring. - **$35**

❑ **PHN-33. Popcorn Bag,**
1996. Promo theater bag. - **$2 $4 $6**

**PHN-34**

❑ **PHN-34. Premium Ring And Tattoo Transfer Set,**
1996. Movie theater giveaway as well as 7-Eleven stores and Best Buy stores. Ring is heavy silver luster metal and set of five transfers are on 2x2" sheets. Ring - **$5 $10 $15**
Transfer Set - **$5 $10 $15**

**PHN-35**

**PHN-36**

❑ **PHN-35. Milk Promo 18" x 12" Poster,**
1996. Given away at theaters. - **$5 $10 $20**

❑ **PHN-36. Promo Movie Box,**
1996. Sponsored by Blockbuster Video and Visa. Has 6"x9" Phantom envelope showing him riding a horse. Has coupons inside; one with the Phantom on it. - **$20**

## Phantom Pilot Patrol

**Langendorf baked goods sponsored this regionally broadcast radio adventure series on the West Coast in the 1930s. We picture the items comprising the club membership kit. The club was headed by "Dennis O'Hara or Sparks - the operator of the radio station at the base of the Sierra Mountain."**

**PLT-1**

**PHN-2**

❑ **PLT-1. Black Enamel On Brass Member's Badge,**
1930s. - **$10 $25 $75**

❑ **PLT-2. Enrollment Card,**
1930s. 3-1/2x5-1/2" as shown with enrollment coupon removed from bottom edge. Reverse lists premiums. With Coupon - **$25 $40 $75**
Without Coupon - **$15 $25 $50**

PLT-3

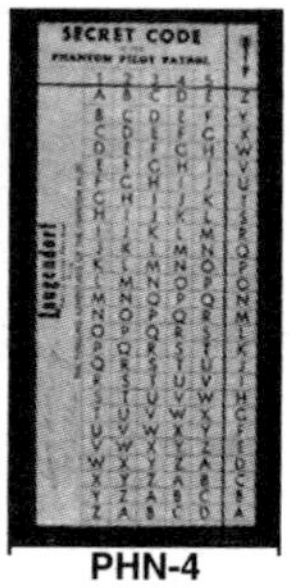

PHN-4

❑ **PLT-3. Official Orders Folder,**
1930s. Four pages, 8-1/2x11". Includes "A Personal Message From The Chief" (The Phantom Pilot), club secrets and instructions for decoding secret messages sent via radio. - **$25 $40 $75**

❑ **PLT-4. "Secret Code" Card,**
1930s. The "Chief" or club members began messages with "Langendorf" and a 3 digit number. The second digit specified which of the five columns shown on this card was the correct master code to use. 4x9-1/4" black on orange. - **$35 $65 $100**

## Pillsbury

**The Pillsbury Company was formed in 1869 when 27-year-old Charles Alfred Pillsbury bought a flour mill in Minneapolis and set about improving the milling process and producing a finer flour. Pillsbury's Best XXXX, a conversion of the historic bakers' XXX symbol for premium bread, was adopted as a company trademark in 1872. The Pillsbury Doughboy, created by animator Hal Mason, was introduced in television commercials in 1966 and named Poppin' Fresh in 1971. He was soon joined by Poppie Fresh, and the two characters have been successfully merchandised as corporate symbols.**

**In 1964, Pillsbury introduced the Funny Face products, a sugar-free drink mix for children. There were six flavors originally. The line went national in 1965 and more flavors were added throughout the 1970s. The brand faded in the late 1970s with stiff competition from market leader Kool-Aid. Pillsbury sold the line in 1980 to Brady Enterprises. The new owners test marketed Chug A Lug Chocolate in 1983 and offered the final plastic cup premium. Limited distribution makes this the scarcest of the nine cups in the Funny Face series.**

PLS-1

❑ **PLS-1. Pillsbury Products Ad Statuettes,**
1930s. Each is 3-1/4" tall diecut wood.
Each - **$10 $20 $35**

PLS-2

❑ **PLS-2. "Injun Orange" Unopened Drink Mix Pack,**
c. 1964. Store product depicts one of the six original characters whose name was later changed to Jolly Olly Orange.
Near Mint Sealed - **$250**
Open Pack - **$50 $100 $150**

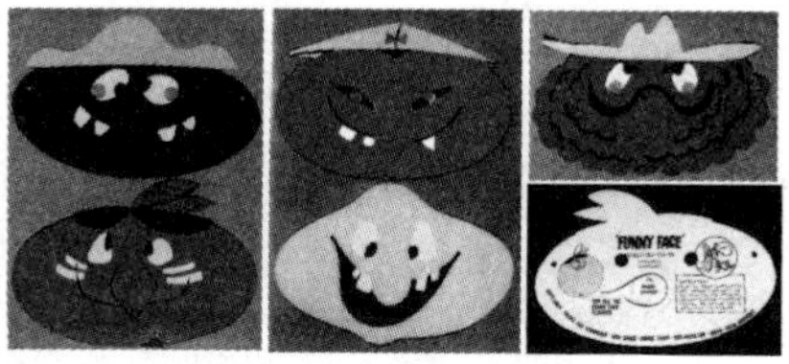
PLS-3

❑ **PLS-3. Funny Face Masks,**
c. 1964. Set of six diecut paper images of Freckle-Face Strawberry, Goofy Grape, Loud-Mouth Lime, Rootin' Tootin' Raspberry, Chinese Cherry, Injun Orange. Latter two were subsequently renamed Choo Choo Cherry and Jolly Olly Orange. Each - **$100 $200 $300**

PLS-4

❑ **PLS-4. Funny Face Finger Puppets,**
c. 1964. 2x4" plastic sheeting set of six: Chinese Cherry, Goofy Grape, Loud-Mouth Lime, Injun Orange, Rootin' Tootin' Raspberry and Freckle Face Strawberry. Each - **$50 $150 $300**

PLS-5

❑ **PLS-5. "Funny Face Fun Book",**
1965. Full color 5x7" self-mailer booklet with 20 pages of games, puzzles, jokes, rhymes, etc. - **$35 $75 $150**

PLS-6

❑ **PLS-6. Funny Face Contest Prize Wristwatch,**
c. 1965. A standard design "Lord Nelson" wristwatch with goldtone case and matching expansion band has on the inside of the crystal a 1-1/2" disk with image of Goofy Grape. 10,000 were produced and used as prizes. Gordon Gold Archives. - **$200 $400 $800**

PLS-7

❑ **PLS-7. "Funny Face Drink Stand" Miniature 3-D Premium Art Prototype ,**
c. 1965. Designed for Pillsbury. 1-1/2x3x6-1/2" tall. Gordon Gold Archives. Unique. - **$2500**

PLS-8

PLS-9

❑ **PLS-8. Litho. Tin Tab,**
c. 1965. 1-1/2" showing character in purple with yellow hat. - **$15 $30 $15**

❑ **PLS-9. "How Freckle Face Strawberry Got His Freckles" Book,**
1965. - **$25 $40 $75**

PLS-10

❑ **PLS-10. Entry Sheet For Drink Stand Contest,**
1965. Large 11x14" contest order form noting closing date of June 30, 1965. Ten thousand drink stands were awarded. - **$25 $60 $100**

PLS-11

❑ **PLS-11. Drink Stand Contest Prize,**
1965. Stand was shipped in a flat carton but when assembled was three feet wide, five feet three inches high, one foot four inches deep. Made of sturdy cardboard.
Near Mint Boxed - **$3000**
Unboxed - **$750 $1500 $2500**

PLS-12

❑ **PLS-12. "Funny Face" Contest Papers,**
1966-1967. First two photos are front and back of 5-1/2x8-1/2" coloring contest sheet. This has 1967 expiration date. Prizes included Matt Mason Deluxe Space Action Set and Twist-N Turn Barbie with house. Third image is of 14-1/4x21-1/2" Sunday comic section with picture to be colored and submitted. Expiration date of 1966. Grand prize was a giant "Funny Face Funhouse." Contest Sheet - **$20 $40 $60**
Newspaper Page - **$5 $10 $15**

PLS-13

PLS-14

❑ **PLS-13. "Crash Orange" Book,**
1967. - **$30 $60 $95**

❑ **PLS-14. Funny Face Mugs,**
1969. Nine in set. Chug A Lug Chocolate introduced in 1983. First Eight Each - **$10 $20 $35**
Chug A Lug - **$15 $25 $50**

PLS-15

❑ **PLS-15. Poppin' Fresh Salt & Pepper Set With Mailer,**
1970. Ceramic shakers issued by Pillsbury.
Mailer - **$1 $3 $5**
Set - **$5 $15 $20**

PLS-16

PLS-17

❑ **PLS-16. Choo Choo Cherry Cloth Pillow Doll,**
1970. Pillsbury Co. - **$15 $30 $65**

❑ **PLS-17. Lefty Lemon Cloth Pillow Doll,**
1970. Grape and Strawberry also issued.
Each - **$15 $30 $65**

PLS-18

❑ **PLS-18. Funny Face Plastic Walkers,**
1971. Set of four, each with plastic weight.
Each - **$50 $75 $125**

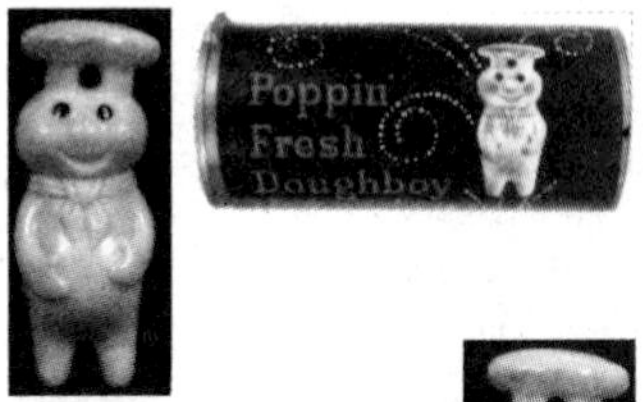


PLS-19

PLS-20

❑ **PLS-19. "Poppin' Fresh Doughboy",**
c. 1971. Full figure color label on plastic can holding vinyl figure. - **$20 $40 $80**

❑ **PLS-20. "Poppin' Fresh Doughboy",**
c. 1971. Closeup portrait label on plastic can holding vinyl figure. - **$20 $40 $80**

PLS-21

PLS-22

❑ **PLS-21. "Poppin' Fresh" & "Poppie" Plastic Salt & Pepper Shakers,**
1974. - **$12 $18 $25**

❑ **PLS-22. "Poppin' Fresh" Vinyl Playhouse,**
1974. Complete with four figures. -
**$60 $100 $150**

PLS-23

PLS-24

❑ **PLS-23. Goofy Grape Plastic Pitcher,**
1974. Pillsbury Co. Two versions: Single face or face on each side of pitcher. - **$20 $40 $85**

❑ **PLS-24. "Lefty Lemonade" Funny Face Iron-On Fabric Patch,**
1975. - **$10 $20 $30**

**PLS-25**

**PLS-26**

❑ **PLS-25. "Pillsbury" Cloth Doll,**
c. 1970s. - **$5 $10 $24**

❑ **PLS-26. "Goofy Grape Sings" Record,**
1970s. - **$15 $30 $50**

## The Pink Panther

**This slinky, bulgy-eyed pantomime creature first appeared in the opening credits of the 1964 live-action feature film of the same title starring actors David Niven and Peter Sellers. The catchy animated antics, abetted by Henry Mancini theme music, prompted a spin-off single cartoon short that evolved into a career of other performances in theaters, TV cartoons and comic books. Creators were animators DePatie-Freleng Enterprises. Early adventures typically pitted Pink Panther against his traditional inept, dim-witted foil Inspector Clouseau. Later animations added other characters and the 1985 *Pink Panther And Sons* (Pinky, Panky, Punkin) TV series was produced in association with Hanna-Barbera Studios.**

**PNK-1**

**PNK-2**

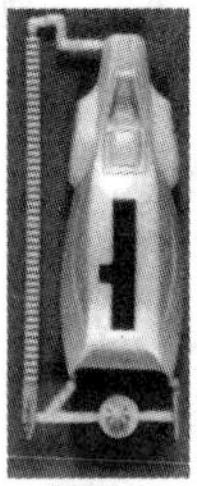

**PNK-3**

❑ **PNK-1. Inspector Clouseau 3" Cello. Button,**
c. 1965. Issued following original 1964 Pink Panther film starring Peter Sellers as Clouseau. - **$12 $20 $35**

❑ **PNK-2. Jointed Figure,**
1971. Store item by R. Dakin. 8" tall. - **$10 $20 $35**

❑ **PNK-3. RPX Race Car,**
1973. Pink Panther Cereal. Styled after George Barris car. - **$25 $50 $75**

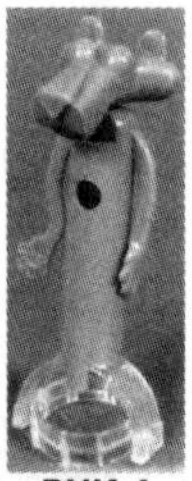

**PNK-4**

**PNK-5**

❑ **PNK-4. 5-1 Spy Kit,**
1973. Pink Panther Cereal. - **$50 $75 $125**

❑ **PNK-5. "Pink Panther Painless Pin" Litho. Tin Tab,** 1970s. Issued by Clean 'N Treat Medicated First Aid Pads. One of a series.
Each - **$5 $10 $15**

**PNK-6**

**PNK-7**

❑ **PNK-6. The Pink Panther In Swimsuit Animation Cel,**
1970s. Hand-inked.
Near Mint Similar Examples - **$75**

❑ **PNK-7. "One Man Band" Battery Toy With Box,**
c. 1980. Store item by Illco Toys.
Plush/vinyl/metal action movement toy.
Boxed - **$40 $75 $100**
Loose - **$25 $50 $75**

**PNK-8**

❑ **PNK-8. "The Pink Panther/The Inspector" Wind-up Plastic Figures On Store Cards,**
1981. Store items by Bandai.
Each Near Mint Carded - **$25**

**PNK-9**

**PNK-10**

❑ **PNK-9. Ceramic Figural Mug,**
1981. Store item by Royal Orleans. 4-1/4" tall. - **$5 $12 $20**

❑ **PNK-10. Albertson's 3-1/2" Cello. Button,**
1984. - **$5 $10 $15**

## Pinocchio

**Italian author Carlo Collodi wrote the children's tale *Pinocchio: the Story of a Puppet* in 1880. The classic adventure of a wooden marionette who wants to become a real boy was first translated into English in 1892 and given new life as a full-length animated feature by the Disney studio in 1940. The film was a huge success, and the characters were merchandised extensively. Pinocchio, his tiny conscience Jiminy Cricket, Figaro the cat, Cleo the goldfish, the Blue Fairy, Monstro the whale, and the other creations were produced in a great variety of materials and formats, and Pinocchio was licensed to a long list of manufacturers of foods, candy, gum, paint, salt, razors, mouthwash, clothing, watches, etc. Comic book appearances began in 1939, animated sequels were released in 1964 and 1987, and a television special using a stop-motion process was aired on ABC in 1980.**

**PCC-1**

**PCC-2**

❑ **PCC-1. "Walt Disney's Pinocchio" Book,**
1939. Store item and Cocomalt premium.
Premium Edition - **$20 $40 $100**
Store Edition - **$20 $40 $100**

❑ **PCC-2. Cocomalt "Walt Disney's Pinocchio" 10x16" Book Ad Poster,**
1939. - **$50 $150 $250**

**PCC-3**

❑ **PCC-3. Post Toasties Box,**
1939. Various boxes with cut-outs.
Each Complete - **$150 $325 $550**

PCC-4

❑ **PCC-4. Studio Christmas Card,**
1939. Total of 12 Pinocchio characters represented with back cover art of Mickey and friends. - **$75 $175 $275**

PCC-5

❑ **PCC-5. "Pinocchio Circus" 32x51" Linen Sign,**
1939. Various sponsors. - **$500 $1500 $2500**

PCC-6

❑ **PCC-6. "Pinocchio's Circus" Cut-Out Sheet,**
1939. Various bread companies. Came with 60 cards. Uncut Tent - **$50 $75 $100**
Each Uncut Card - **$1 $3 $5**

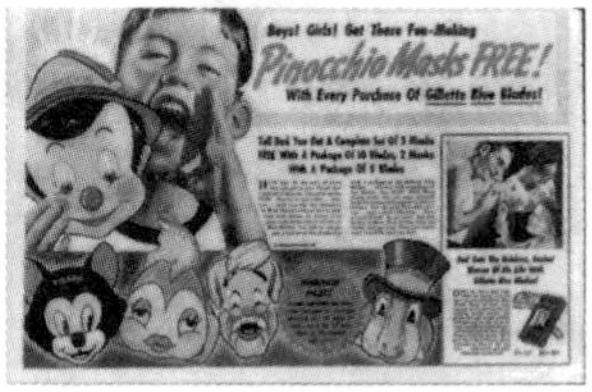

PCC-7

❑ **PCC-7. "Pinocchio Masks Free" Newspaper Ad,**
1939. Gillette Blue Blades. - **$10 $20 $35**

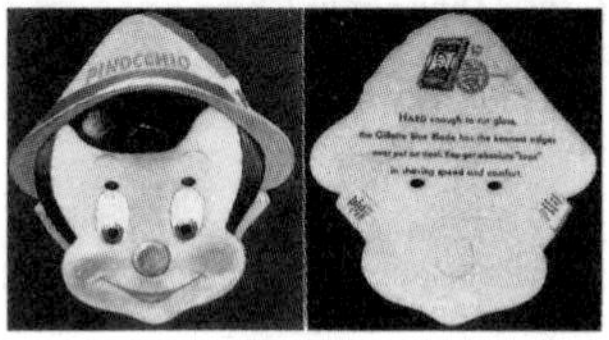

PCC-8

❑ **PCC-8. Pinocchio Paper Mask,**
1939. Gillette Blue Blades. From set of five characters: Pinocchio, Jiminy Cricket, Geppetto, Figaro, Cleo. Each - **$5 $12 $24**

PCC-9

❑ **PCC-9. "Save Pinocchio Lids From Ice Cream Cups" 6x18" Paper Sign,**
1939. - **$60 $100 $150**

PCC-10

❑ **PCC-10. "Pinocchio's Christmas Party" Department Store Give-Away Book,**
1939. Various stores. - **$15 $25 $50**

PCC-11

PCC-12

❑ **PCC-11. "Good Teeth Certificate",**
1939. American Dental Association. - **$25 $60 $100**

❑ **PCC-12. "Good Teeth" Cello. Button,**
1939. Back paper for Bureau of Public Relations/American Dental Association. - **$100 $250 $500**

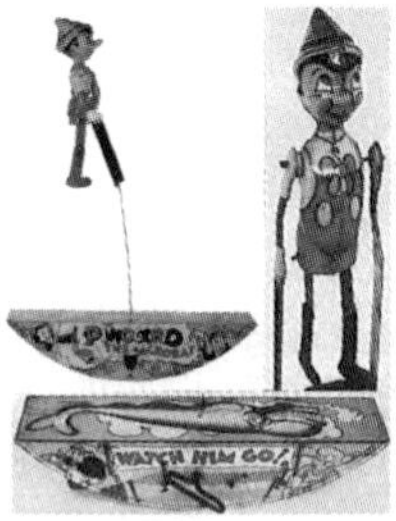

PCC-13

PCC-14

❑ **PCC-13. "Pinocchio The Acrobat" Litho. Tin Wind-Up Toy,**
1939. Store item by Marx. Overall size of 2x11x17" tall with 7" tall figure of Pinocchio who somersaults on top of spring-steel rod. - **$150 $350 $650**

❑ **PCC-14. Catalin Plastic Thermometer,**
1939. Store item. - **$50 $125 $200**

PLS-15

❑ **PCC-15. "Jiminy Cricket! It's A Monstro Soda" Store Sign,**
1939. 6x18" promoting ice cream soda float. - **$75 $150 $250**

PLS-16

PLS-17

❑ **PCC-16. "Pinocchio" Wood/Composition Jointed Doll,**
c. 1940. Store item by Ideal. Smallest 7-1/2" tall variety. - **$60 $125 $200**

❑ **PCC-17. Largest Doll,**
1940. Ideal Toy & Novelty Co. store item. 19-1/4" tall largest wood jointed and composition doll. Example shown is missing hat.
Figure - **$150 $300 $600**
Hat - **$25 $50 $75**

PCC-18

PLS-19

❑ **PCC-18. Studio Issued Fan Card,**
1940. - **$30 $50 $75**

❑ **PCC-19. Ice Cream Cup Lid,**
c. 1940. Erie County Milk Assn. "Fudgee Cup" lid 2-3/4" diameter. - **$12 $25 $40**

PCC-20

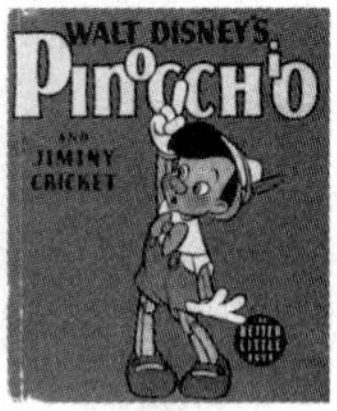

PCC-21

❑ **PCC-20. Theater Give-Away Sheet,**
1940. - **$35 $60 $125**

❑ **PCC-21. "Pinocchio and Jiminy Cricket" Better Little Book,**
1940. - **$20 $60 $125**

PCC-22

❑ **PCC-22. "Poster Stamps" Booklet,**
1940. Independent Grocers Alliance of America. Holds 32 stamps. Booklet - **$15 $60 $90**
Each Glued Stamp - **$2 $4 $6**

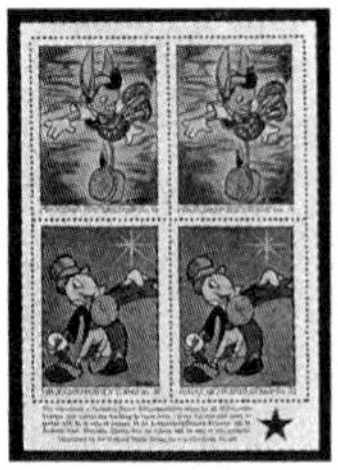
PCC-23

PCC-24

❑ **PCC-23. Stamp Set,**
1940. IGA premium. Set of 4 stamps. Not glued to book. - **$20 $40 $60**

❑ **PCC-24. Envelope,**
1940. IGA premium. Envelope for 4 stamps.- **$10 $20 $45**

PCC-25

❑ **PCC-25. "Jiminy Cricket Official Conscience Medal" Brass Badge,**
1940. Rare. Available for 5 Pinocchio candy bar wrappers and 10¢. Text on wrapper reads: "Medal is exactly like the one the Blue Fairy gave Jiminy Cricket." Issued by Schutter Candy Company. - **$50 $100 $200**

PCC-26

PCC-27

❑ **PCC-26. "Pinocchio Chewing Gum" Paper Wrapper,**
1940. Store item by Dietz Gum Co. - **$20 $35 $75**

❑ **PCC-27. "Pinocchio Candy Bar" Box,**
1940. Schutter Candy Co. Originally held 24 bars. - **$50 $150 $250**

PCC-28

PCC-29

❑ **PCC-28. "Walt Disney's Pinocchio" Cello. Button,**
1940. Back paper has Kay Kamen distributorship name. Used by toy stores and others as giveaway. - **$15 $30 $45**

❑ **PCC-29. Victor Records Cello. Button,**
1940. Phonograph record design inscribed "Pinocchio Comes To Town On Victor Records". - **$200 $600 $1100**

PCC-30

PCC-31

❑ **PCC-30. "Catch the Ring" Toy,**
1940. Premium die-cut from movie. - **$50 $100 $175**

❑ **PCC-31. Jiminy Cricket Wood Jointed Doll,**
c. 1940. Store item by Ideal. - **$150 $250 $450**

PCC-32

❑ **PCC-32. Jiminy Cricket Largest Size,**
1945. Store item by Multi Products, Chicago. 5-1/4" tall. - **$100 $225 $350**

PCC-33

PCC-34

PCC-35

❑ **PCC-33. Figaro 6" Figure,**
1945. Store item by Multi Products, Chicago. - **$40 $110 $200**

❑ **PCC-34. Geppetto Sitting 6" Figure,**
1945. Store item by Multi Products, Chicago. - **$60 $100 $200**

❑ **PCC-35. Geppetto Standing 6" Figure,**
1945. Store item by Multi Products, Chicago. - **$40 $90 $125**

PCC-36

PCC-37

PCC-38

❑ **PCC-36. Giddy 6" Figure,**
1945. Store item by Multi Products, Chicago. - **$40 $80 $200**

❑ **PCC-37. Honest John 7" Figure,**
1945. Store item by Multi Products, Chicago. Large 7" size. Scarce. - **$100 $200 $300**

❑ **PCC-38. Jiminy Cricket 6" Figure,**
1945. Store item by Multi Products, Chicago. - **$40 $110 $225**

PCC-39

PCC-40

PCC-41

❑ **PCC-39. Jiminy Cricket United Fund 6" Figure,**
1945. Award by Multi Products, Chicago. Issued in brown tones with or without red and green accents. Each - **$40 $125 $250**

❑ **PCC-40. Lampwick 6" Figure,**
1945. Store item by Multi Products, Chicago. - **$30 $100 $150**

❑ **PCC-41. Pinocchio 6" Figure With Hands Down,**
1945. Store item by Multi Products, Chicago. - **$40 $100 $200**

PCC-42

PCC-43

PCC-44

❑ **PCC-42. Figaro 2" Figure,**
1945. Store item by Multi Products, Chicago. - **$40 $125 $250**

❑ **PCC-43. Geppetto 2" Figure,**
1945. Store item by Multi Products, Chicago. - **$40 $110 $200**

❑ **PCC-44. Giddy 2" Figure,**
1945. Store item by Multi Products, Chicago. - **$40 $110 $200**

PCC-45

PCC-46

PCC-47

❑ **PCC-45. Lampwick 2" Figure,**
1945. Store item by Multi Products, Chicago. - **$40 $110 $200**

❑ **PCC-46. Pinocchio 2" Figure,**
1945. Store item by Multi Products, Chicago. - **$40 $110 $250**

❑ **PCC-47. Jiminy Cricket "United Way" Countertop Sign,**
1940s. Diecut cardboard 5x7" with easel back. - **$50 $85 $150**

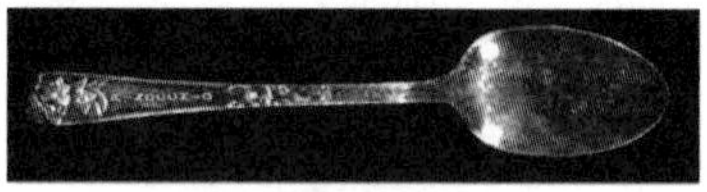

PCC-48

❑ **PCC-48. Pinocchio Silver Spoon Premium,**
1940s. - **$20 $40 $75**

PCC-49

PCC-50

❑ **PCC-49. Australian Club Badge,**
1940s. 1-1/8" die-cut aluminum with bar pin on reverse. - **$45 $90 $125**

❑ **PCC-50. Tell The Truth Ring,**
1954. Weather-Bird Shoes. Brass with rubber nose. - **$250 $450 $700**

PCC-51

❑ **PCC-51. "Tell The Truth Club" Membership Card,**
1954. Weather-Bird Shoes. - **$20 $40 $65**

PCC-52

❑ **PCC-52. "Jiminy Cricket" Premium Figure/Membership Card,**
1958. Issued by Bakers Instant Chocolate Flavored Mix. Dancing puppet is 8" tall diecut paper. Card - **$5 $10 $20**
Puppet **- $5 $10 $20**

PCC-53

❑ **PCC-53. Cardboard Punch-Out Puppet Sheets With Envelope,**
1950s. Campbell's Pork and Beans plus "Rex Allen" names on mailer.
Near Mint In Mailer - **$75**

PCC-54

PCC-55

❑ **PCC-54. "I've Seen Pinocchio At Hudson's" Cello. Button,**
1950s. Sponsored by Detroit department store. - **$25 $40 $75**

❑ **PCC-55. "United/Official Conscience" Litho. Button,**
c. 1950s. United Way. - **$20 $40 $75**

PCC-56

PCC-57

❑ **PCC-56. Wind-Up Toy,**
c. 1962. Line Mar. 5-1/2" tall tin litho. - **$100 $300 $500**

❑ **PCC-57. Soaky Toy,**
1965. 10" tall. - **$15 $50 $75**

PCC-58

❑ **PCC-58. "Pinocchio in Geppetto's Workshop" Sculpture,**
1984. Disney Capodimonte by master sculptor Enzo Arzenton. Edition 391. - **$2400**

PCC-59

❑ **PCC-59. Original Art for 1980s Poster,**
1980s. 21" x 17". This is the original watercolor painting designed as a theatrical poster for the 1980s rerelease of the 1941 Walt Disney film. This painting was designed and created by Mike Royer, head of character merchandising at Walt Disney Productions. - **$3000**

PCC-60

PCC-61

❑ **PCC-60. Talking Movie Doll in Box,**
1996. Promotes live action movie "The Adventures of Pinocchio". With 11x17" poster of Jonathan Taylor Thomas. - **$30**

❑ **PCC-61. Disney Artist Promotional Pin,**
2000. - **$20**

PCC-62

❑ **PCC-62. Pinocchio Water Globe,**
2000. - **$65**

## Planet of the Apes

**First released in 1968, the intensely popular sci-fi film *Planet of the Apes*, starring Charlton Heston, Roddy McDowall, and Kim Hunter, is appreciated by science fiction and pop culture fans worldwide, with Heston's hammy dialogue still quoted and parodied to this day. Heston's Colonel Taylor is a hapless astronaut who crash-lands on a planet ruled by talking apes, only to discover that it is in fact the Earth of the far future. The simple morality play with a *Twilight Zone*-like twist (no surprise, since it was scripted from the original Pierre Boulle novel by Rod Serling) also featured some heavy-handed political commentary, which would become a regular ingredient in the sequels: *Beneath the Planet of the Apes* (1970), with Heston in only a brief appearance at the beginning and end of the film, *Escape From the Planet of the Apes* (1971), *Conquest of the Planet of the Apes* (1972), and *Battle for the Planet of the Apes* (1973). All but *Beneath* featured Roddy McDowall as chimpanzee scientist Cornelius, and later Cornelius' son Caesar, the leader of the new ape civilization.**

**Thinly-veiled protests against the Vietnam war and racial tensions at home gave the films a political identity unusual for "sci-fi" films of the time. A short-lived TV series also starring McDowall as another chimpanzee named Galen aired in 1974, and a cartoon spin-off, *Return to the Planet of the Apes*, lasted one season as well. Today, the original movies and TV show are frequently aired on cable TV, contributing to strong collector interest and an attempt by the studio to jumpstart a new franchise. In 2001, 20th Century Fox and director Tim Burton released a new version of *Planet of the Apes* to mixed reviews and some box office success. The film was accompanied by a significant amount of hype and licensing. Also in 2001, the DVDs of the original films, the superb *Behind the Planet of the Apes* documentary, and the new feature were released. The DVDs of the television series were released in early 2002. Most items are copyright 20th Century Fox. "All the kids'll learn to talk."**

PLA-1

PLA-2

❑ **PLA-1. "Planet Of The Apes Playset,"**
1967. Store item by Multiple Toymakers. -
**$100 $200 $400**

❑ **PLA-2. Planet of the Apes Novel,**
1968. By Pierre Boulle. This edition was released with a photo cover to promote the film. -
**$8 $15 $25**

PLA-3

❑ **PLA-3. Movie Poster,**
1968. 27x41" issued by 20th Century Fox. -
**$25 $60 $125**

PLA-4

❑ **PLA-4. Original Soundtrack Album,**
1968. Inside shows scenes from the film and features some of the cast. - **$10 $25 $60**

PLA-5

PLA-6

❑ **PLA-5. Colorforms Adventure Set,**
1960s. Full color box with plastic clinging figures and coated color backgrounds. - **$10 $25 $60**

❑ **PLA-6. "Battle for the Planet of the Apes" Novelization,**
1973. Award Books. Written by David Gerrold, the book is one of several novelizing the five films in the series (see also PLA-2). -
**$5 $7 $10**

PLA-7

PLA-8

❑ **PLA-7. Planet of the Apes Coloring Book,**
1974. Authorized edition by Artcraft. One of several coloring and activity books. - **$10 $20 $35**

❑ **PLA-8. Planet of the Apes Press Book,**
1974. 14x8-1/2" U.S. press book. In 1974, all 5 films in the series were released on a marathon bill. Press books were supplied to theaters with ads, stories, photos, and mock newspaper front pages. Unclipped - **$15 $25 $50**

PLA-9

❑ **PLA-9. "Candy & Two Prizes" Box,**
c. 1974. Store item by Phoenix Candy Co. Inc. 2-1/2x5x1" deep box #3 from a series of 8. - **$10 $20 $40**

PLA-10

❑ **PLA-10. Playset,**
c. 1974. Store item by Multiple Toymakers, box text includes "Sears" and this was likely an exclusive to them. Contains four 2-1/2" Ape figures, five generic Army men, Army man with jeep, two horses, bridge, pair of trees that bridge attaches to plus bridge assembly instructions. Near Mint Boxed - **$75**
Used Complete - **$15 $25 $35**

PLA-11

❑ **PLA-11. "Planet Of The Apes" Game,**
1974. Store item By Milton Bradley. - **$15 $25 $50**

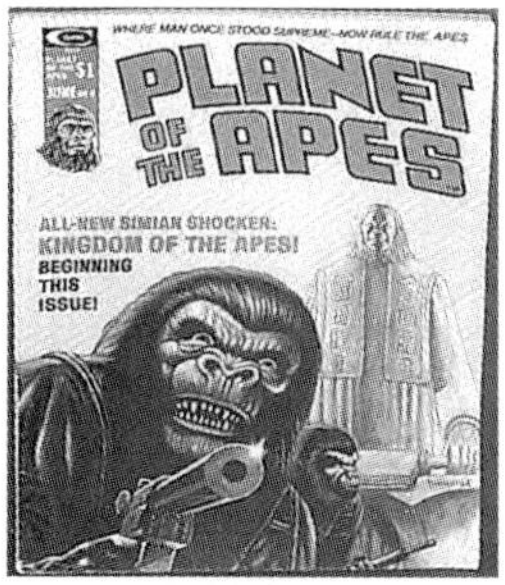

PLA-13

PLA-12

❑ **PLA-12. Planet of the Apes Magazine,**
1974. Volume 1 #9 shown. Published by Magazine Managment Co.
Volume 1 #1- **$3 $8 $26**
Later issues in Near Mint **- $10-$20**

❑ **PLA-13. Planet of the Apes Toy Rings,**
1975. Stan Toy Co., England. Scarce. 5 rings in set: Dr. Zaius, Galen, Zira, Urko, and Cornelius or Caesar. Galen and Dr. Zaius rings shown. Came in gold, silver, green or black on iodized aluminum base. Similar rings were made in Japan in recent years. Each - **$50 $100 $200**

PLA-14

PLA-15

❑ **PLA-14. Cornelius Figure Boxed,**
1998. 12" doll for the 30th Anniversary. - **$20**

❑ **PLA-15. Dr. Zaius Figure Boxed,**
1998. 12" doll for the 30th Anniversary. - **$20**

PLA-16

PLA-17

❑ **PLA-16. General Ursus Figure Boxed,**
1998. 12" doll for the 30th Anniversary. - **$30**

❑ **PLA-17. Gorilla Soldier Figure,**
2000. Collectors' Edition in circular box. - **$30**

PLA-18

❑ **PLA-18. Medicom Kubrick Set A,**
2000. First in a series of six 'Kubrick' playsets from Medicom based on the classic film series. Contains Lawgiver, Cornelius, Zira and Dr. Zaius figures. - **$35**

PLA-19

❑ **PLA-19. Medicom Kubrick Set B,**
2000. From Medicom. Contains General Ursus, two soldier apes and a horse. - **$35**

PLA-20

❑ **PLA-20. Medicom Kubrick Set C,**
2000. From Medicom. Contains Taylor, Nova, a horse, and the Statue of Liberty. - **$35**

PLA-21

❑ **PLA-21. Medicom Kubrick Set D,**
2000. From Medicom. Contains General Urko, a soldier ape, a horse, and a jail cart. - **$35**

PLA-22

❑ **PLA-22. Medicom Kubrick Set E,**
2000. From Medicom. Contains Caesar, a slave ape, General Aldo, and a bridge set piece. - **$35**

PLA-23

❑ **PLA-23. Medicom Kubrick Set F,**
2000. From Medicom. Contains Zira, Cornelius and Milo in spacesuits with variant helmet heads, and Taylor's spaceship. - **$35**

PLA-24

❑ **PLA-24. Medicom Kubrick Set G,**
2000. From Medicom. Contains soldier ape with jail cage, Taylor and Lucius. - **$35**

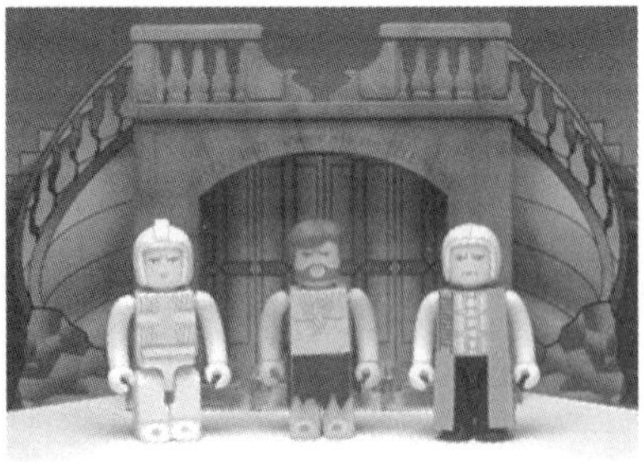

PLA-25

❑ **PLA-25. Medicom Kubrick Set H,**
2000. From Medicom. Contains Brent, two mutants, and a subway station set piece. - **$35**

PLA-26

❑ **PLA-26. Movie Lunch Box and Thermos,**
2001. Limited to 5,000. This features photos from the Tim Burton movie. - **$20**

Punchouts

PLA-27 Background

❑ **PLA-27. "Pop Out People" Punchouts,**
2001. Cardboard punchouts of movie photos with background. - **$3**

## Pogo

**Walt Kelly (1913-1973) chose the Okefenokee Swamp as home for his characters making their debut in *Animal Comics*, which ran briefly in the early 1940s. The strip then ran in the *New York Star* in 1948 and moved to the *New York Post* and syndication in 1949. Pogo the wise possum and his contrary pal Albert the alligator thrived for more than 25 years, dealing with the eccentricities of a cast of characters that included such creatures as Howland Owl, Churchy la Femme the turtle, Beauregard the retired veteran bloodhound, Porky Pine, and P.T. Bridgeport the scheming bear. Comic books appeared in the 1940s and 1950s and Simon & Schuster published more than 30 Pogo books between 1951 and 1976. An animated cartoon aired on NBC in 1969 and an animated "claymation" film was produced by Warner Brothers in 1980, starring the voices of Skip Hinnant, Vincent Price and Jonathan Winters. The strip itself was discontinued in 1975, but enjoyed a brief revival in the late 1980s.**

POG-1

❑ **POG-1. "The Little Fir Tree" Storybook,**
1942. W. T. Grant Co. Christmas giveaway with color cover and eight pages of bw unsigned Walt Kelly art. - **$200 $400 $800**

POG-2

❑ **POG-2. "Peter Wheat News" Comic Book With Kelly Art,**
1949. Peter Wheat Bread, Bakers Associates Inc. Issue #21 including cover and three pages of art by Walt Kelly, Pogo creator. -
**$8 $25 $50**

POG-3

❑ **POG-3. "Peter Wheat" Coloring Book With Kelly Art,**
1951. Peter Wheat Bread, Bakers Associates Inc. Sixteen pages including art examples by Walt Kelly, Pogo creator. - **$40 $75 $150**

POG-4

❑ **POG-4. "Peter Wheat" Cut-Out Circus,**
1951. Bakers Assoc. Designed by Walt Kelly.
Near Mint Uncut - **$250**
Cut - **$40 $100 $150**

POG-5

❑ **POG-5. "The Glob" Walt Kelly Hardcover With Dust Jacket,**
1952. With Jacket - **$15 $30 $65**

POG-6

POG-7

❑ **POG-6. "I Go Pogo" Litho. Button,**
1952. 7/8" version, similar button issued for 1956. - **$10 $15 $20**

❑ **POG-7. Pogomobile Kit,**
1954. Store item published by Simon and Schuster. Cardboard assembly parts for ceiling mobile. Near Mint In Envelope - **$250**

POG-8

POG-9

❑ **POG-8. 4" Diameter Litho. Button,**
1956. Probably sent by Post-Hall Syndicate to newspapers carrying the strip. - **$35 $75 $150**

❑ **POG-9. "I Go Pogo" Litho. Button,**
1956. 7/8" version. - **$5 $10 $18**

POG-10

❑ **POG-10. Walt Kelly Christmas Card,**
1958. His own personal issue.
Unsigned. - **$35 $75 $125**

POG-11

❑ **POG-11. Walt Kelly Christmas Card,**
1960. His own personal issue.
Unsigned - **$35 $75 $125**

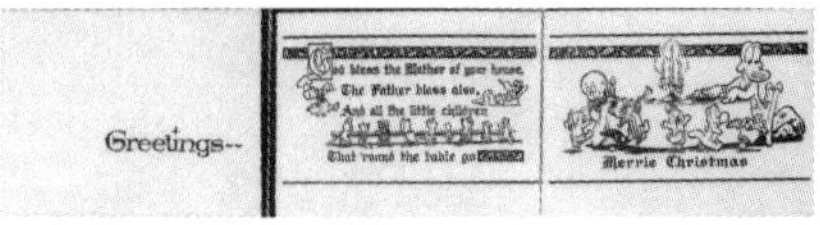

POG-12

❑ **POG-12. Walt Kelly Christmas Card,**
1961. His own personal issue.
Unsigned - **$35 $75 $125**

POG-13

❑ **POG-13. "Pogo Primer For Parents TV Division" Government Booklet,**
1961. U.S. Dept. of Health, Education and Welfare. 8x10" with 24 pages and theme of parents loving their children rather than letting television do that. - **$30 $60 $100**

POG-14

POG-15

❑ **POG-14. Advertising Cello. Button,**
1964. Crest Paperback Books. 1-1/4" black on yellow promoting 35 cents "Pogo For President" book. - **$50 $100 $150**

❑ **POG-15. Cello. Button,**
1968. One of 30 known designs with Walt Kelly facsimile signature on each. - **$20 $35 $65**

POG-16

POG-17

❑ **POG-16. Vinyl Figures,**
1968. Poynter Products, distributed exclusively by Montgomery Ward. Includes Beauregard, Albert, Churchy, Howland, Hepzibah, Pogo. Often missing are Pogo's hat and flowers, Howland's glasses, Beauregard's hat and cane, and Albert's cigar. Each - **$50 $100 $150**

❑ **POG-17. Okefenokee City Council Family Birthday Certificate,**
1969. Issuer unknown but has Walt Kelly copyright. 7-1/2x11-1/2" parchment-type paper with facsimile "Pogo" signature as "Curator Okefenokee Memorial Swamp." -
**$50 $100 $150**

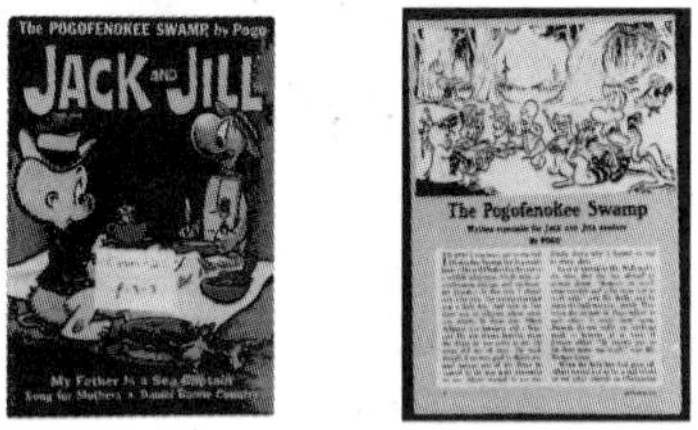

POG-18

❑ **POG-18. "Jack And Jill" Magazine With Cover Article,**
1969. Monthly issue of child's magazine for May with specialty cover art related to four-page historic article about Pogo plus promotion for NBC-TV Pogo cartoon. - **$10 $20 $35**

POG-19

❑ **POG-19. Vinyl Figures,**
1969. Procter & Gamble. Six in set: Pogo, Beauregard Hound, Churchy La Femme, Howland Owl, Albert Alligator, Porky Pine. Each - **$5 $10 $20**

POG-20

❑ **POG-20. Pogo Characters Plastic Mug Set,**
1969. Procter & Gamble. Set of six: Pogo, Albert, Churchy, Porky Pine, Howland, Beauregard. Each - **$5 $10 $20**

POG-21

❑ **POG-21. "Sunday Newsday" 2-1/2" Cello. Button,**
1972. Long Island newspaper promotion. Further inscribed "Try It/You'll Like It". -
**$35 $75 $150**

POG-22

POG-23

❑ **POG-22. Pogo Character Christmas Card,**
1975. Simon And Schuster. - **$15 $25 $40**

❑ **POG-23. "Vote Pogo For President" Campaign Poster,**
1979. Estate Of Walt Kelly. 14x22" red, white and blue slick paper. - **$10 $20 $30**

# Pokémon

Pokémon was created from a video game in Japan. In 1996, Nintendo took the Japanese game and developed Pocket Monsters, a Game Boy product. When it was introduced in 1998 in the U.S., it was marketed as Pokémon. In 1999, Wizards of the Coast issued a trading card game which was an instant success. To date there are over 250 Pokémon characters. Where it will end, one can only guess. The characters have an angular futuristic look to them which adds to their appeal. The classic old marketing scheme is at work here. Television shows, movies, videos, books, cards and of course an endless array of toys promote the series. The marketing staff has done a great job of packaging the toys as well. Listed below is a sampling of some of the products and their suggested values.

POK-1

POK-2

❑ **POK-1. Pikachu Figure Yo-Yo in Card,** 1999. Tiger Electronics. - **$5 $10 $15**

❑ **POK-2. Pikachu Talking Calculator,** 1999. In open front box. - **$22**

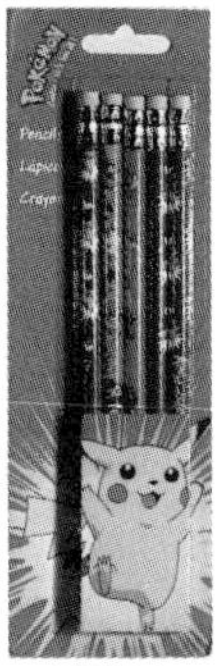

POK-3

POK-4

❑ **POK-3. 5 Pencil Set on Card,** 1999. - **$5**

❑ **POK-4. Cap'n Crunch Cereal Box with Pocket Camera Offer,** 1999. - **$3**

POK-5

POK-6

❑ **POK-5. Meowth Key Chain,** 1999. Part of a series. - **$2 $4 $8**

❑ **POK-6. Meowth Rubber Figure,** 1999. - **$3 $6 $12**

POK-7

❑ **POK-7. Poliwhirl Beanie-type Hat,** 1999. With tag. - **$8**

POK-8

POK-9

❑ **POK-8. Puzzle Featuring Meowth,** 1999. - **$2 $4 $10**

❑ **POK-9. Crayons,** 1999. Set of 16 crayons. Rose Art. - **$3**

POK-10

❑ **POK-10. Candy Dispenser on Card,** 1999. Set of 6. Each - **$6**

POK-11

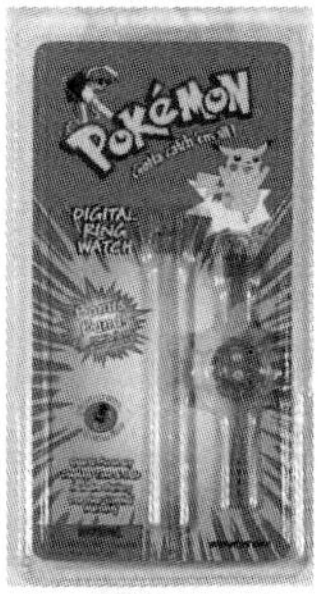


POK-12

❑ **POK-11. Pikachu Digital Ring Watch,** 1999. With Bonus Band. - **$12**

❑ **POK-12. Jigglypuff Digital Ring Watch,** 1999. With Bonus Band. - **$10**

POK-13

POK-14

❑ **POK-13. Gold Plated Trading Card,** 1999. Burger King premium - **$2 $4 $6**

❑ **POK-14. Trading Card Game Box,** 1999. - **$18**

POK-15

POK-16

❑ **POK-15. Trainers Figure with Poké Ball,** 1999. With Battle Disc. On card. - **$10**

❑ **POK-16. Water Toy on Card,** 1999. - **$8**

POK-17

POK-18

❑ **POK-17. Poké Ball,**
1999. Also called a Voltorb or Electrode. - **$3**

❑ **POK-18. Toy Holder,**
1999. - **$3**

POK-19

POK-20

❑ **POK-19. Butterfree (Batafuly) Figure,**
1999. - **$5**

❑ **POK-20. Figures,**
1999. Misty, Poliwrath (Nyolobon) and Ash.
Each - **$5**

**Various Pokémon Figures (and their Japanese Names)**
**$5 Each**

Pikachu (Pickachuu) | Golem (Golonya) | Rattata (Kolatta) | Alakazam (Fuudin)

Ponyta (Bonita) | Togepi (Togepee) | Spearow (Onisuzume) | Beedrill (Supier)

Venonat (Konpan) | Wartotortle (Kameeru) | Weezing (Matadogasu) | Ekans (Ahbo)

Scyther (Sutolaiku) | Omastar (Omster) | Clefable (Pikucy) | Venomoth (Molufon)

Vaporeon (Shawazu) | Arbok (Ahbock) | Tangela (Monjala) | Lapras (Lapulasu)

Venusaur (Fushigibana) | Abra (Keshy) | Gyarados (Gyalodosu) | Rhydon (Saidon)

POK-21

POK-22

❑ **POK-21. Marble Case with 8 Marbles,**
1999. 8 sets (Raichu shown). Each - **$10**

❑ **POK-22. Marble Pouch with 10 Marbles,**
1999. 8 sets in both Series 1&2 (Golem shown).
Each - **$10**

## Poll-Parrot Shoes

**Paul Parrot, owner of the Parrot Shoe Company, decided to christen his products Poll-Parrot Shoes in 1925. Extensive use of advertising and appropriate giveaways for boy and girl customers--carrying the parrot trademark--were successful marketing tools for the company's shoes and replacement parts. From 1947 to 1950 the company sponsored the *Howdy Doody* program on NBC television, resulting in a number of paper premiums and rings linking the puppet and the parrot.**

POL-1

POL-2

POL-3

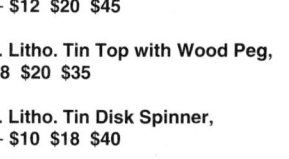

❑ **POL-1. Litho. Tin Spinner Top With Wood Peg,**
c. 1920s. - **$12 $20 $45**

❑ **POL-2. Litho. Tin Top with Wood Peg,**
1930s. - **$8 $20 $35**

❑ **POL-3. Litho. Tin Disk Spinner,**
c. 1930s. - **$10 $18 $40**

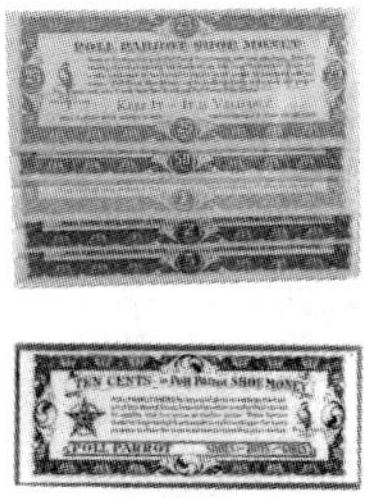

POL-5

POL-4

❑ **POL-4. Bracelet,**
1930s. - **$20 $40 $65**

❑ **POL-5. "Poll Parrot Shoe Money",**
1930s. Various denominations and colors.
10¢, 25¢ and 50¢ shoe money - **$3 $5 $10**
$1 and $2 shoe money - **$4 $6 $12**
$5 shoe money bill - **$5 $10 $15**

**(2 views of the whistle)**

POL-6

❑ **POL-6. "Poll Parrot Tin Whistle",**
1930s. - **$10 $20 $40**

POL-7

POL-8

POL-9

❑ **POL-7. "Pre-Tested Poll-Parrot Shoes" Litho. Button,** 1930s. - **$5 $12 $20**

❑ **POL-8. Litho. Tin Whistle,**
1930s. - **$10 $20 $40**

❑ **POL-9. Litho. Tin Clicker,**
1930s. - **$10 $15 $25**

POL-10

POL-11

❑ **POL-10. "The Cruise Of The Poll-Parrot" Radio Show Paper,** 1930s. Store hand-out slip imprinted for WSVA Radio, Harrisonburg, Virginia, also offering shoe purchase premium of magnetic compass. - **$5 $10 $15**

❑ **POL-11. "U KUZU" Tin Kazoo,** 1930s. - **$15 $30 $65**

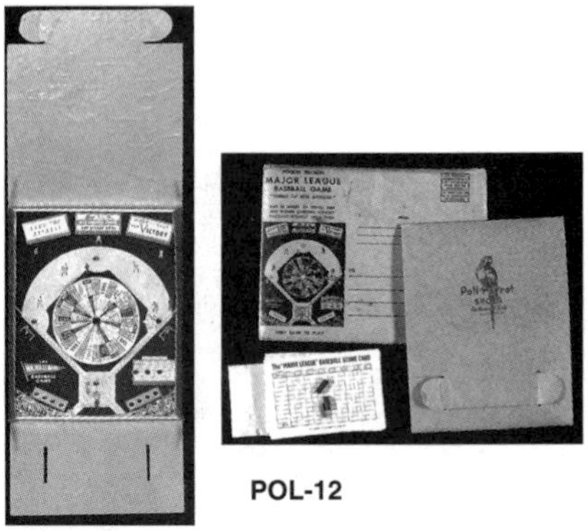

POL-12

❑ **POL-12. Baseball Game,** 1944. Premium includes cardboard baseball game with spinner, mailer, wooden pegs, holder, and scoreboards. Also promotes the War Bond drive. - **$50 $125 $200**

POL-13

❑ **POL-13. "Uncle Sam" Paper Over Tin Bank,** c. 1945. - **$25 $50 $85**

POL-14

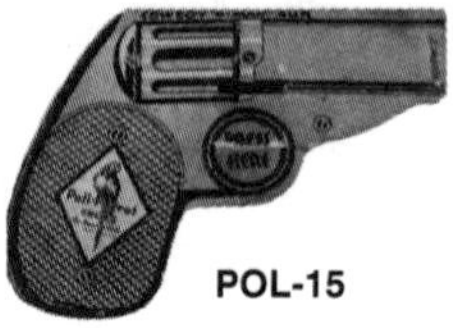

POL-15

❑ **POL-14. "Poll-Parrot Shoes" Solid Plaster Display Figure,** c. 1940s. Inscription on front base. 6x7x11-1/2" tall. - **$75 $150 $250**

❑ **POL-15. "Cowboy 'G-Man' Gun" Cardboard Premium,** c. 1940s. 4-1/2" long blue and gray with tin clicker mounted inside. - **$10 $30 $45**

POL-16

POL-17

❑ **POL-16. "G-Man" Premium Pop Gun,** 1940s. - **$10 $30 $45**

❑ **POL-17. Die-cut Standee,** 1950s. 10 1/2" tall. - **$25 $60 $100**

POL-18

POL-19

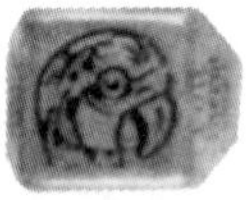

POL-20

❑ **POL-18. Flying Parrot Plastic Flicker Ring,** 1950s. - **$25 $50 $70**

❑ **POL-19. "Poll-Parrot Shoes" Symbol Brass Ring,** c. 1950s. - **$20 $30 $40**

❑ **POL-20. "Poll-Parrot Shoes" Symbol Aluminum Ring,** c. 1950s. - **$20 $30 $40**

## Popeye

**Popeye was introduced to the world in E.C. Segar's (1894-1938) *Thimble Theatre* comic strip in 1929 and within a year was the strip's most popular character. The adventures of the spinach-chomping sailor, Olive Oyl, the hamburger-mooching Wimpy, Jeep, Swee'pea, and a host of other characters proved to be a phenomenal success. Comic book reprints appeared as early as 1931, and in 1933 the Fleischer Studios released the first of what would eventually add up to more than 450 animated cartoon shorts for theaters and television. A *Popeye* radio series aired on NBC and CBS from 1935 to 1938, sponsored by Wheatena (1935-1937) and Popsicle (1938). Early cartoon shorts were syndicated on television starting in 1956, new films were added in 1961, plus a further series from Hanna-Barbera on CBS in 1978. Robin Williams and Shelley Duvall starred in the 1980 Paramount film. The Popeye characters have been merchandised extensively since the 1930s.**

PPY-1

❑ **PPY-1. Character Painted Cast Iron Figurines,** c. 1929. Store items. Each - **$60 $165 $275**

PPY-2

❑ **PPY-2. Popeye/Wimpy Glass Tumbler,** 1929. Probably held dairy product. From believed set of eight picturing two characters on each. - **$35 $75 $125**

PPY-3

PPY-4

❑ **PPY-3. "Thimble Theatre" Character Set To Paint,**
c. 1930. Copyrighted 1929 but issued in 1930s. Store item by Davidson Porcelain Co., Ohio. Early set predating Wimpy. Figures are 2" to 5" tall and came unpainted with watercolor pad and brush. Characters are: Popeye, Olive Oyl, Ham Gravy, Caster Oyl, Professor Kilph, The Bandit, Jack Snork, Tingaro, Whiffle Hen.
Boxed Unpainted - **$500 $1000 $1500**
Boxed Painted - **$300 $600 $1000**
Loose Figures Unpainted Or Nice Painted
Each - **$15 $25 $50**

❑ **PPY-4. Parrot Cages Wind-Up Toy,**
1932. Store item by Marx Toys. 7-1/2" tall tin litho. **- $150 $325 $650**

PPY-5

❑ **PPY-5. "Popeye Comic" Gum Folders,**
1933. Tattoo Gum by Orbit Gum Co. From numbered set. Each - **$10 $20 $40**

PPY-6

PPY-7

❑ **PPY-6. Popeye Musical Pipe Display Card With Pipes,**
1934. Store item by Northwestern Products. Full color card 11x17" originally holding one dozen metal and cardboard kazoos. Theater managers also gave away pipes to members of the Popeye Clubs.
Display Card Only - **$250 $500 $800**
Each Pipe - **$20 $40 $75**

❑ **PPY-7. Sheet Music For Cartoon "Popeye The Sailor",**
1934. Six pages. Store bought. - **$20 $40 $85**

PPY-8

❑ **PPY-8. Large Sign,**
1935. Promotes Magic Transfer picture premiums. IGA Rolled Oats sponsor. -
**$300 $550 $900**

PPY-9

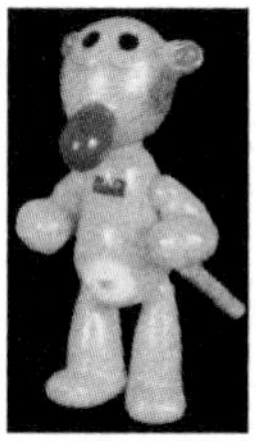

PPY-10

❑ **PPY-9. "Popeye Boat Fleet" Boxed Set,**
1935. Store item by Transogram. Contents are four numbered plastic sailboats depicting Popeye on each sail. - **$150 $250 $425**

❑ **PPY-10. Jeep Largest Size Jointed Composition Figure,**
1935. Store item sold in several sizes. The largest size is 13" tall. Other versions are 6", 7" and 8" tall. All are typically found with serious composition crazing.
Largest Unrestored - **$250 $800 $1600**
Largest Expertly Restored - **$1000**
Others Expertly Restored - **$750**
Others Unrestored - **$200 $600 $1000**

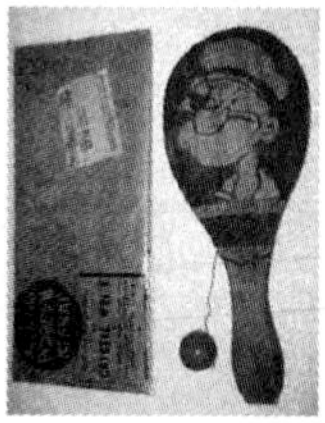

PPY-11

PPY-12

❑ **PPY-11. "Popeye Bifbat" With Mailer,**
c. 1935. Crystal White Soap and others. With Mailer - **$50 $115 $165**

❑ **PPY-12. Octagon Products Free Popeye Bifbat Cardboard Display,**
1935. Colgate Palmolive/Peet Co. 29-1/2" tall in red, black and white. - **$400 $800 $1200**

PPY-13

PPY-14

❑ **PPY-13. Tooth Brush On Card,**
1935. Store item by Lor-Dent Co., N.Y.C. Brush has Popeye decal and card is fleshtone, red, white and blue. Brush - **$30 $60 $115**
Card - **$50 $165 $275**

❑ **PPY-14. Pipe Toss Game,**
1935. Store item by Rosebud Art Co. Also used as Popsicle premium. - **$30 $75 $125**

PPY-15

❑ **PPY-15. "Popeye Magic Transfer Pictures" Store Sign With Premium,**
1935. IGA Rolled Oats. Store poster 10x21-1/2" along with 3-1/4" square decal sheet. Gordon Gold Archives. Sign - **$100 $300 $500**
Transfer Sheet - **$10 $20 $50**

PPY-16

PPY-17

❑ **PPY-16. "Penney's 'Back To School Days' With Popeye" Cello. Button,**
1935. J. C. Penney Co. - **$10 $20 $30**

❑ **PPY-17. Popeye/Jeep Glass Tumbler,**
1936. From same series as PPY-2 but later copyright year. - **$50 $100 $150**

PPY-18

❑ **PPY-18. "Make Your Own Popeye Family With Wood Parts" Boxed Set,**
1936. Store item by Jaymar. Holds wooden parts and elastic cords to make figures of Popeye, Olive, Wimpy and Jeep.
Complete - **$500 $1000 $1500**

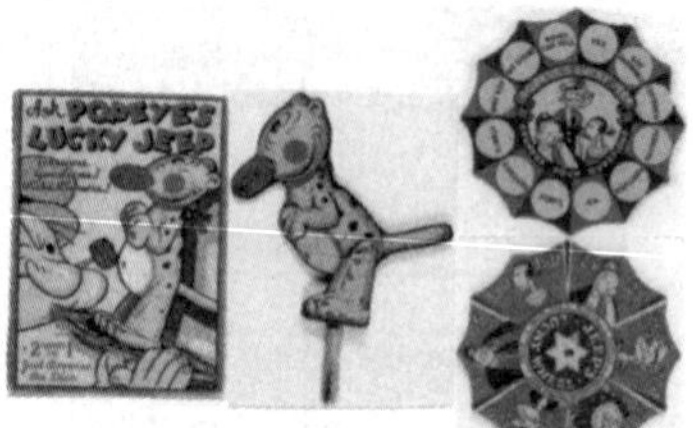

PPY-19

❑ **PPY-19. "Ask Popeye's Lucky Jeep" Fortune Toy,**
c. 1936. Store item by Northwestern Products. Cardboard with wood handle.
Box Only - **$100 $200 $300**
Toy Only - **$75 $150 $300**

PPY-20

❑ **PPY-20. "Popeye Cut-Outs" Premium Folder,**
1936. Popeye Fly Swatter. 2-1/2x6" stiff folder opens to 6x10". Apparent first issue as text refers to another "Group No. 2 Of The Popeye Family." Uncut - **$30 $60 $125**

PPY-21

PPY-22

❑ **PPY-21. "Ask The Jeep Lucky Spinner" On Store Card,**
1936. Store item. 3x4" card holds 1-1/2" plastic disk with a second 1" plastic disk depicting Jeep sniffing the gound with his tail in the air accented by a tiny arrow which will point at one of the numerals 1-12 when spun.
Card - **$50 $125 $175**
Spinner - **$100 $225 $325**

❑ **PPY-22. "Popeye The Sailor Man" 9x13" Cardboard Book Sign,**
c. 1937. Grosset & Dunlap. - **$125 $300 $600**

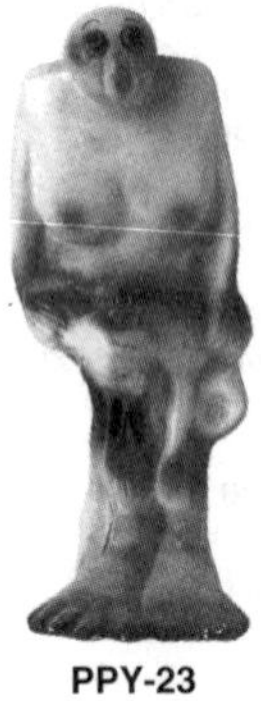
PPY-23

PPY-24

❑ **PPY-23. "Alice the Goon" Carnival Figure,**
1937. Figure is holding a knife. Rare. -
**$250 $500 $1000**

❑ **PPY-24. "Popeye And The Jeep" Big Little Book,**
1937. Whitman #1405. - **$30 $65 $135**

PPY-25

❑ **PPY-25. "Popeye In Quest Of His Poopdeck Pappy" Big Little Book,**
1937. Whitman #1450. - **$30 $65 $135**

PPY-26

(CLOSE-UP OF SEAL)

❑ **PPY-26. "State Theatre Popeye Club" Membership Certificate,**
1938. Paper document for theater in Kingsport, Tennessee with affixed foil paper seal. Local particulars are inked including member name and August 27 effective date of membership. -
**$30 $60 $110**

PPY-27

PPY-28

❑ **PPY-27. Popsicle-Fudgsicle-Creamsicle 13x18" Cardboard Store Sign,**
1938. Scarce. Pictures premiums and announces Popeye "On The Radio After May 1st". - **$125 $300 $600**

❑ **PPY-28. "Popeye All Pictures Comics,**
1939. Big Little Book #1406. - **$20 $65 $135**

PPY-29

❑ **PPY-29. "Popeye And The Deep Sea Mystery" Better Little Book,**
1939. Whitman #1499. - **$20 $65 $135**

PPY-30

PPY-31

❑ **PPY-30. Newsstand Apron,**
1930s. News-Sentinel. Red and white on dark blue fabric. - **$150 $250 $400**

❑ **PPY-31. "Popeye Navy/Admiral" Brass Badge,**
1930s. Store item. 1-1/2" tall in two shades of brass luster with red and black details. - **$100 $225 $375**

PPY-32

❑ **PPY-32. "Blow-Me-Down Handkerchiefs!" Boxed,**
1930s. Store item. Beautiful color box holds three hankies done in three colors on white.
Box Only - **$60 $150 $250**
Each Hanky - **$15 $30 $50**

PPY-33

PPY-34

❑ **PPY-33. Newsstand Vendor's Apron,**
1930s. Chicago American. Black and white on orange fabric with pockets for change. -
**$150 $300 $500**

❑ **PPY-34. Bisque Toothbrush Holder,**
1930s. Store item. Has moveable arm. -
**$75 $200 $350**

PPY-35

PPY-36

❑ **PPY-35. Painted White Metal Lamp With Pipe,**
1930s. Store item. - **$75 $200 $400**

❑ **PPY-36. Poll-Parrot Shoes Photo Ad Card,**
c. 1930s. Probable unauthorized use of Popeye character by local store owner. - **$12 $20 $35**

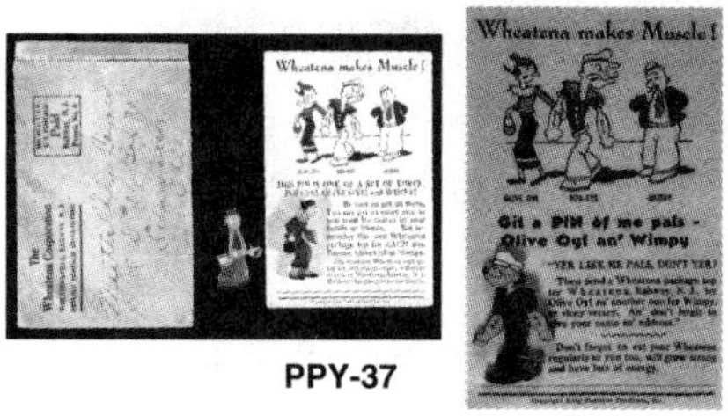

PPY-37

❑ **PPY-37. Enameled Metal Pin,**
1930s. Wheatena cereal. Set of three: Popeye, Olive Oyl, Wimpy. Each On Card (Two Varieties) - **$75 $150 $250**
Popeye Pin - **$20 $40 $80**
Olive Pin - **$30 $60 $100**
Wimpy Pin - **$30 $60 $100**

PPY-38

❑ **PPY-38. Theatre Club Card And Cello. Button,**
1930s. Various theaters.
Button - **$10 $20 $35**
Card - **$15 $60 $95**

PPY-39

PPY-40

PPY-41

❑ **PPY-39. Olive Oyl Enamel On Silvered Brass Pin,**
1930s. Wheatena cereal.
On Card - **$75 $150 $250**
Pin Only - **$30 $60 $100**

❑ **PPY-40. Jeep Enamel On Brass Pin,**
1930s. Apparent store item, similar to Wheatena giveaways and used as premium by Popsicle. Also comes with figure surrounded by a silvered brass horseshoe. - **$75 $175 $275**

❑ **PPY-41. Wimpy Color Picture Silvered Brass Ring,**
1930s. - **$75 $125 $175**

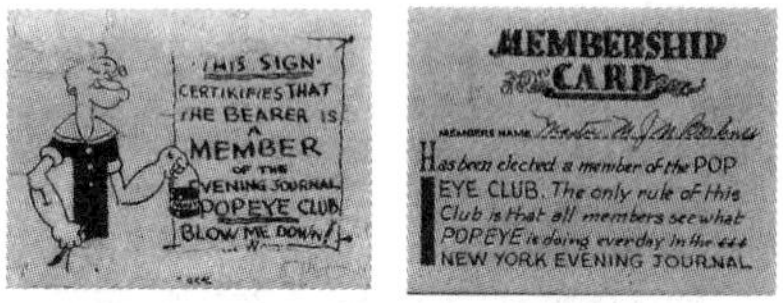

PPY-42

❑ **PPY-42. "New York Evening Journal" Club Card,**
1930s. - **$20 $50 $100**

PPY-43

❑ **PPY-43. "The Popeye Line Of Hats & Caps" Store Carton,**
c. 1930s. Unidentified clothing maker. 16x19x24" long carton with lid. -
**$200 $450 $650**

PPY-44

PPY-45

PPY-46

❑ **PPY-44. "I Yam Strong For King Comics" Cello. Button,**
1930s. One of earliest buttons to advertise comic books. - **$25 $60 $100**

❑ **PPY-45. "Sunday Examiner" Litho. Button,**
1930s. From "50 Comics" set of various newspaper characters, match number to win prize. - **$20 $40 $75**

❑ **PPY-46. "S. F. Examiner" Litho. Button,**
1930s. San Francisco newspaper. From set of various characters, match number to win prize. - **$25 $50 $100**

PPY-47

PPY-48

PPY-49

❑ **PPY-47. "Keep This Button" Cello. Button,**
1930s. Los Angeles Evening Herald & Express. Promotes cash prizes for contest. - **$15 $25 $50**

❑ **PPY-48. "New York Evening Journal" Button,**
1930s. Promotes Popeye strip. - **$20 $35 $75**

❑ **PPY-49. "Evening Ledger Comics" Button,**
1930s. - **$75 $150 $250**

PPY-50

PPY-51

❑ **PPY-50. "Popeye is in The News Bee" Pin,**
1930s. Promotes strip. - **$35 $75 $150**

❑ **PPY-51. Journal Pinback,**
1930s. Scarce. Promotes strip. - **$25 $50 $100**

PPY-52

❑ **PPY-52. "Popeye The Pilot" Airplane Wind-Up Toy,**
1940. Tin litho store item by Marx. - **$300 $750 $1250**

PPY-53

❑ **PPY-53. "Popeye And Caster Oyl The Detective" Better Little Book,**
1941. Whitman #1497. - **$20 $60 $120**

PPY-54

PPY-55

❑ **PPY-54. Coca-Cola Postcards With Wrapper,**
1942. Set of four.
Near Mint With Wrapper - **$100**
Each Card - **$5 $10 $20**

❑ **PPY-55. "Buy War Stamps" 14x18" Poster,**
c. 1944. U.S. Government. - **$75 $150 $300**

PPY-56

❑ **PPY-56. Popeye & Friends "Hingees" Kit,**
1945. Store item by Martin P. King & Son. Unpunched **- $20 $50 $85**

PPY-57

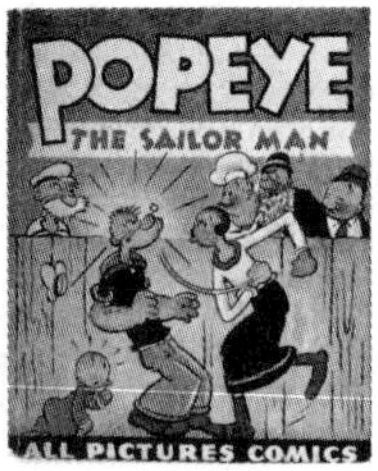


PPY-58

❑ **PPY-57. "Popeye The Spinach Eater" Book,**
1945. Big Little Book #1480. - **$20 $65 $125**

❑ **PPY-58. "All Pictures Comics" Book,**
1947. - **$20 $65 $125**

(enlarged view of puzzle)

PPY-59

❑ **PPY-59. Popeye Puzzle and Box,**
1949. - **$50 $125 $200**

PPY-60

PPY-61

❑ **PPY-60. "Popeye and Queen Olive Oyl",**
1949. Big Little Book #1458. - **$10 $40 $90**

❑ **PPY-61. Popcorn Bank,**
1949. Van Camp premium. 20 oz.popcorn can which converts into bank. - **$20 $50 $85**

PPY-62

❑ **PPY-62. Ruler,**
1940s. 7 inch ruler. Came with pencil box. Store bought. - **$10 $25 $50**

PPY-63

❏ **PPY-63. Popeye Sailor's Cap,**
1940s. Probable premium. - **$75 $150 $300**

PPY-64

PPY-65

❏ **PPY-64. Popeye Flashlight and Whistle,**
1940s. Came on display of 12 Magic Nite Glo flashlights with whistles.
Display Card (Not Shown) - **$50 $125 $250**
Each Glow In Dark Flashlight - **$20 $50 $85**

❏ **PPY-65. "Sunshine Popeye Cookies" Cardboard Tab,**
c. 1940s. - **$20 $50 $85**

PPY-66

PPY-67

❏ **PPY-66. Popeye Tin Bank,**
1949. Holds $5.00 worth of dimes. King Features copyright. - **$75 $150 $225**

❏ **PPY-67. "Popeye Bubble 'N Clean" Soap Box With Turtle Offer,**
c. 1950. Woolfoam Corp.
Complete Box **- $50 $100 $150**

PPY-68

❏ **PPY-68. Christmas Store Display,**
1952. King Features Syndicate. Pair of full color cardboard diecuts. Pair - **$100 $250 $400**

PPY-69

PPY-70

PPY-71

❏ **PPY-69. "Popeye: The First Fifty Years" 2-1/4" Cello. Button,**
1959. Workman Publishing Co. For book promotion with King Feautures copyright. -
**$5 $10 $15**

❏ **PPY-70. Popeye Cello. Button,**
1950s. Comes in 3-1/2" size and scarcer 1-3/4" size. Larger Size - **$10 $25 $45**
Smaller Size - **$25 $50 $75**

❏ **PPY-71. Cloth/Vinyl Doll,**
1950s. Store item by Gund Mfg. Co. -
**$50 $100 $165**

PPY-72

❏ **PPY-72. Popeye Soap Figure in Boat,**
1950s. In original box. - **$75 $200 $325**

PPY-73

❏ **PPY-73. Popeye Sports Roadster Friction Car,**
1950s. Store item by Line Mar. Tin with vinyl head. Popeye's car is known in yellow while a matching car for Olive, with simulated hair long ponytail, is known in red or yellow.
Boxed Popeye - **$400 $800 $1200**
Boxed Olive - **$300 $600 $900**

PPY-74

❏ **PPY-74. "Wooden Popeye" Pull Toy,**
1950s. Store item by Line Mar. About 10" tall designed to roll flat on the floor with parts including "Spinach" can which revolve.
Boxed - **$250 $500 $750**

PPY-75

❏ **PPY-75. "Pop Up Olive Oyl With Squeaker" Push Action Toy,**
1950s. Store item by Line Mar. Made of cloth with composition head and shoes. A matching Popeye was made.
Each Boxed - **$250 $600 $900**

PPY-76

PPY-77

❑ **PPY-76. "Juggling Popeye And Olive Oyl" Wind-Up,**
1950s. Store item by Line Mar. 9" tall with action of Popeye hitting Olive's chair with a metal rod which causes the chair to spin.
Boxed - **$1200 $2500 $3500**

❑ **PPY-77. "Popeye Lantern" Tin And Glass Light,**
1950s. Store item by Line Mar.
Boxed - **$150 $300 $500**

PPY-78

❑ **PPY-78. Tricycle Wind-Up Toy,**
1950s. Line Mar. 4-1/2" tall tin litho. - **$250 $500 $800**

PPY-79

❑ **PPY-79. Popeye And Eugene The Jeep Canadian Glass,**
1950s. Issuer unknown. 4-3/4" tall. #5 from rare Canadian series under King Features Syndicate copyright. - **$25 $50 $75**

PPY-80

PPY-81

❑ **PPY-80. Popeye Adult-Sized Over The Head-Style Costume,**
1960. Collegeville. 25" wide by 50" tall.
Near Mint Carded - **$350**
Uncarded - **$75 $150 $250**

❑ **PPY-81. Gasoline Pump Metal Sign,**
1960s. Crown Gas. Full color image on white. - **$75 $150 $300**

PPY-82

❑ **PPY-82. "Wooden Popeye" Figure,**
1960s. Store item by Line Mar.
Boxed - **$200 $400 $700**

PPY-83

PPY-84

❑ **PPY-83. Popeye Carpet Store Standee With Carpet,**
1970s. Bigelow Carpet. Diecut store display with seven feet tall Popeye holding actual carpet with many panels showing King Features Syndicate characters. Complete - **$300 $650 $1100**
Rug Alone - **$150 $300 $500**
Standee Alone - **$100 $250 $400**

❑ **PPY-84. Swee' Pea Ceramic Figure,**
1980. 6" tall. - **$30 $65 $130**

PPY-85

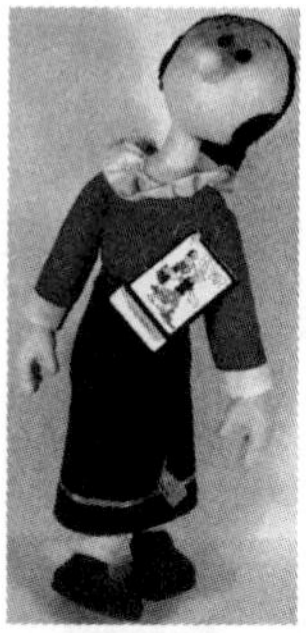

PPY-86

❑ **PPY-85. Popeye Doll with Tag,**
1985. 18 1/2" tall. King Features copyright. - **$10 $50 $110**

❑ **PPY-86. Olive Oyl Doll with Tag,**
1985. 18" tall. - **$10 $40 $95**

PPY-87

PPY-88

❑ **PPY-87. Brutus Doll with Tag,**
1985. 22" tall. King Features copyright. - **$10 $40 $95**

❑ **PPY-88. Poopdeck Pappy Doll with Tag,**
1985. 18" tall. - **$12 $55 $120**

PPY-89

❑ **PPY-89. "Crew Club" 16-Page Comic Booklets,**
1989. Instant Quaker Oatmeal. Photo shows set of 4 different plus one back. Each - **$2 $6 $15**

PPY-90

❑ **PPY-90. Popeye Tin Wastebasket,**
1985. Features Popeye and Olive on one side and a litho of the entire cast on the other. - **$5 $15 $50**

PPY-91 PPY-92

❑ **PPY-91. Popeye Limited Edition Figure,**
1999. 8" tall resin. Made in France. Sculpted by Leblon-Delienne. Only 999 made. - **$120**

❑ **PPY-92. Olive Oyl Limited Edition Figure,**
1999. 7 1/2" tall resin. Made in France. Sculpted by Leblon-Delienne. Only 999 made. - **$120**

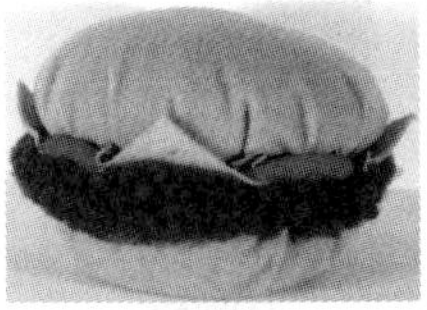

PPY-93 PPY-94

❑ **PPY-93. Swee' Pea Limited Edition Figure,**
1999. 4 1/2" tall resin. Made in France. Sculpted by Leblon-Delienne. Only 999 made. - **$60**

❑ **PPY-94. Wimpy Burger Bean Bag with Tag,**
1999. Exclusive from Universal Studios Island of Adventure Theme Park. - **$10**

PPY-95

❑ **PPY-95. Popeye Bronze Pin,**
1999. Very decorative. - **$30**

PPY-96 PPY-97

❑ **PPY-96. Popeye Bean Figure Set,**
2000. Sold at CVS Pharmacy. Limited set includes Popeye, Olive, Bluto, Swee'pea, Wimpy, and the Jeep.
Set of figures with tags - **$60**
Box - **$40**

❑ **PPY-97. "Popeye" Wacky Wobbler,**
2001. In box. - **$15**

PPY-98 PPY-99

❑ **PPY-98. Popeye Doll in Box,**
2001. Toys "R' Us exclusive. 14" tall. Boxed - **$25**

❑ **PPY-99. Popeye Maquette Figure,**
2001. Limited to 1,000. - **$75**

PPY-100 PPY-101

❑ **PPY-100. Bluto Maquette Figure,**
2001. Limited to 1,000. - **$75**

❑ **PPY-101. Olive Oyl Maquette Figure,**
2001. Limited to 1,000. - **$75**

## Popsicle

**Add some flavor and coloring to water, freeze it around a pair of flat sticks, and the result is a Popsicle, a popular alternative to ice cream promoted as a frozen drink on-a-stick. In addition to flavored ice, the producers created Popsicle Pete, a comic book character that started on a long run in *All-American Comics* in 1939. *The Popsicle Pete Fun Book* (1947) and *Adventure Book* (1948) contained stories, games, and cut-outs, and the company sponsored two short-lived television variety shows: *The Popsicle Parade of Stars* on CBS in 1950 and *Popsicle Five-Star Comedy* on ABC in 1957.**

PSC-1

PSC-2

❑ **PSC-1. Uncle Don Club Card Popsicle Premium,**
1932. Rare. - **$25 $50 $90**

❑ **PSC-2. "Popsicle" Premium Sheet,**
1937. - **$10 $20 $30**

PSC-3

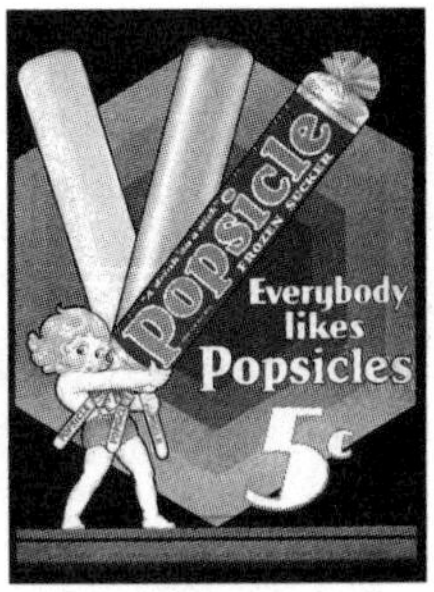


PSC-4

❑ **PSC-3. Store Sign Showing Premiums,**
c. 1937. Orange, black and white sheet 12-3/8x19-1/4". Only character premium shown is "Bob Burns Bazooka." - **$15 $30 $60**

❑ **PSC-4. Sign,**
1930s.Very early die-cut cardboard sign for Popsicle when they were offered one stick for 5¢. Young girl promoter was later replaced by Popsicle Pete. - **$50 $150 $250**

PSC-5

PSC-6

❑ **PSC-5. "Jo-Lo Creamsicles" Waxed Paper Bag,**
1930s. Popsicles with Joe Lowe Corp. copyright for various local retailers. Bags were saved for gifts. - **$8 $12 $20**

❑ **PSC-6. "Adventurer's Popsicle Club" Litho. Button,**
1930s. - **$10 $30 $50**

PSC-7

PSC-8

❑ **PSC-7. Popsicle Pete Cheerio Bag,**
1941. Cheerio bags were used as coupons to get gifts. - **$5 $10 $25**

❑ **PSC-8. Popsicle Pete Gift News,**
1941. 8 page flyer for gifts. Popsicle Pete pictured upper left. - **$15 $30 $50**

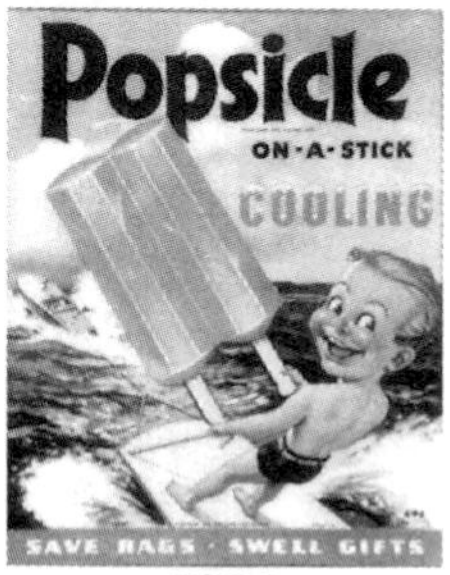


PSC-9

❑ **PSC-9. Paper Store Sign 11x14",**
1946. - **$30 $60 $100**

PSC-10

❑ **PSC-10. Paper Store Sign 9x19",**
1946. - **$30 $60 $100**

PSC-11

❑ **PSC-11. "Popsicle Pete Free Gift News",**
1947. - **$15 $30 $50**

PSC-12

PSC-13

❑ **PSC-12. "Giant Gift List" Catalogue,**
1949. - **$15 $40 $60**

❑ **PSC-13. "Popsicle Pete Jo-Lo-Fone",**
1940s. Assembled Pair - **$15 $25 $50**

PSC-14

PSC-15

❑ **PSC-14. Popsicle Pete's "Mystery Box With Mystery Prize",**
c. 1940s. Held prize and stick good for free Popsicle. Complete - **$100**
Empty - **$37 $56 $75**

❑ **PSC-15. Cowboy Boot Plastic Ring,**
1951. Popsicle. Top has magnifier lens, compass, secret compartment. Boot holds "Cowboy Ring Secret Code" symbols paper. Also offered by Bazooka Joe and shown in his premium catalog as late as 1966. - **$25 $60 $110**

PSC-16

PSC-17

❑ **PSC-16. Popsicle Pete Gift List,**
1952. Paper sheet opening to 11x15" printed on both sides including illustration of 34 premium offers for 1952-1953 years. - **$15 $25 $45**

❑ **PSC-17. "Giant Gift List" Sheet,**
1953. For 1953-1954 premium offers. - **$15 $25 $50**

PSC-18

❑ **PSC-18. Store Sign,**
1953. Issued by Joe Lowe Corp. 8x20". - **$15 $45 $75**

PSC-19

❑ **PSC-19. "Popsicle Music Maker Truck,"**
1954. Store item by Mattel. 5" tall hard plastic. - **$35 $75 $125**

PSC-20

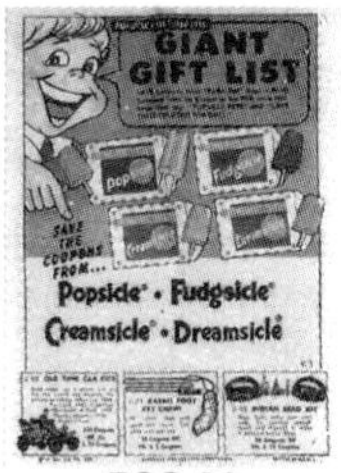


PSC-21

❑ **PSC-20. Abbott And Costello Paper Sign,**
1954. 11x15". - **$100 $200 $400**

❑ **PSC-21. "Giant Gift List" Sheet,**
1954. For 1954-1955 premium offers. - **$15 $25 $45**

PSC-22

PSC-23

❑ **PSC-22. "5 Star Comedy Party" 8x15" Paper Poster,**
1957. For short-lived May-July ABC-TV program. - **$35 $75 $125**

❑ **PSC-23. "Popsicle Gift List" Catalogue,**
1958. Eight-page color booklet picturing more than 40 premiums offered 1958-1959 for various coupon quantities. - **$10 $20 $40**

PSC-24

PSC-25

❑ **PSC-24. Popsicle Gift List,**
1959. 1959-1960 list of prizes. 8 pages. Children riding train on front. - **$10 $20 $30**

❑ **PSC-25. Popsicle Gift List,**
1961. 8 page premium. Has Bob Hope on the front and promotes his new film inside. - **$15 $25 $40**

PSC-26

❑ **PSC-26. "Popsicle 50th Anniversary" Promotional Paperweight,**
1973. Solid marble with enameled brass attachments on top. - **$10 $20 $30**

## Pop-Up Books

**What many collectors consider the most beautiful and imaginative children's books of the 1930s were produced by Pleasure Books Inc. of Chicago under the imprint "A Blue Ribbon Press Book." The word "Pop-Up" served as their registered trademark. Sam Gold, who created and produced *The Mickey Mouse Waddle Book* and *The Wizard of Oz Waddle Book* for Blue Ribbon Books, was also involved in the creative efforts, character licensing and marketing plan for the "Pop-Up" series. Most books in the series featured a licensed character, but a few were also done for nursery rhyme characters such as Mother Goose and Little Red Riding Hood.**

PUP-1

❑ **PUP-1. "Mickey Mouse In King Arthur's Court With 'Pop-Up' Illustrations",**
1933. Store item by Blue Ribbon Books. Contains four pop-ups. Originally issued with dust jacket. Dust Jacket Only - **$75 $150 $300**
Book Only - **$250 $500 $1000**

PUP-2

❑ **PUP-2. "Jack the Giant Killer" Book,**
1933. Blue Ribbon Books, Inc. Illustrated by Harold B. Lentz. - **$100 $250 $400**

PUP-3

❑ **PUP-3. "The 'Pop-Up' Silly Symphonies" Book With Dust Jacket,**
1933. Store item by Blue Ribbon Books. Story titles are "Babes In The Woods" and "King Neptune." Contains four pop-ups.
Dust Jacket - **$50 $125 $250**
Book - **$150 $325 $600**

PUP-4

❑ **PUP-4. "The Pop-Up Minnie Mouse" Book,**
1933. Store item by Blue Ribbon Books, Inc. Contains three pop-ups. - **$100 $250 $450**

PUP-5

❑ **PUP-5. "The Pop-Up Mickey Mouse" Book,**
1933. Store item by Blue Ribbon Books. Includes three pop-ups. - **$100 $250 $450**

PUP-6

❑ **PUP-6. "The Pop-Up Mother Goose" Hardcover Book,**
1933. Blue Ribbon Books Inc. Has four full color diecut pop-ups. - **$100 $225 $400**

PUP-7

❑ **PUP-7. "The 'Pop-Up' Popeye In Among The White Savages" Book,**
1934. Store item by Blue Ribbon Press. Small 4x5" format with single center pop-up. - **$150 $300 $550**

PUP-8

❑ **PUP-8. "The Wizard Of Oz Waddle Book",**
1934. Store item by Blue Ribbon Books. Not a pop-up but contains instructions and separate loose punch-out sheets for forming the characters Dorothy, Toto, Tin Man, Scarecrow, Lion and Wizard who when assembled walk down a cardboard ramp.
Dust Jacket Only - **$100 $200 $350**
Book Only - **$75 $125 $250**
Each Assembled Waddle - **$200 $400 $600**
Each Unpunched Waddle - **$500 $1100 $1750**
Near Mint Complete - **$11100**

PUP-9

❑ **PUP-9. "The 'Pop-Up' Buck Rogers In A Dangerous Mission" Book,**
1934. Blue Ribbon Press. Small 4x5" format with a single center pop-up. - **$175 $350 $700**

PUP-10

❑ **PUP-10. "The 'Pop-Up' Mickey Mouse In Ye Olden Days" Book,**
1934. Store item by Blue Ribbon Press. Small 4x5" format with single center pop-up. -
**$150 $325 $550**

PUP-11

❑ **PUP-11. "Little Red Riding Hood" Pop-Up Book,**
1934. Store item by Blue Ribbon Press. Contains three pop-ups. - **$75 $150 $300**

PUP-12

❑ **PUP-12. "Mickey Mouse Waddle Book",**
1934. Store item by Blue Ribbon Books. Not a pop-up but rear of book has instruction sheets and separate punch-out sheets for assembling characters of Mickey, Minnie, Pluto and Tanglefoot who when assembled will walk down a cardboard ramp.
Cover Slip Band - **$100 $250 $500**
Dust Jacket Only - **$75 $200 $400**
Book Only - **$75 $175 $350**
Each Assembled Waddle - **$300 $600 $1000**
Each Unpunched Waddle - **$500 $1100 $2900**
Near Mint Complete - **$12500**

PUP-13

❑ **PUP-13. "The 'Pop-Up' Terry And The Pirates" Book,**
1935. Store item by Blue Ribbon Press. Contains three pop-ups. - **$100 $250 $400**

PUP-14

PUP-15

❑ **PUP-14. "The 'Pop-Up' Little Orphan Annie And Jumbo The Circus Elephant" Book,**
1935. Blue Ribbon Press. Contains three pop-ups. - **$125 $275 $500**

❑ **PUP-15. "Popeye With The Hag Of The Seven Seas" Pop-Up Book,**
1935. Store item by Blue Ribbon Press. Contains three pop-ups. - **$125 $325 $550**

PUP-16

❑ **PUP-16. "Tim Tyler In The Jungle" Pop-Up Book,**
1935. Store item by Blue Ribbon Press, Pleasure Books Inc. Twenty pages including three double-page color pop-ups. -
**$100 $225 $375**

PUP-17

❑ **PUP-17. "Flash Gordon Tournament Of Death" Pop-Up Book,**
1935. Store item by Blue Ribbon Press. Contains three pop-ups. - **$150 $400 $750**

PUP-18

❑ **PUP-18. "The 'Pop-Up' Buck Rogers" Book,**
1935. Store item by Blue Ribbon Press. 8x9" with three pop-ups. Subtitled "Strange Adventures In The Spider-Ship." Reprinted in 1994 by Applewood Books, 8x9-1/2". -
Original - **$150 $400 $700**
Reprint - **$5 $10 $15**

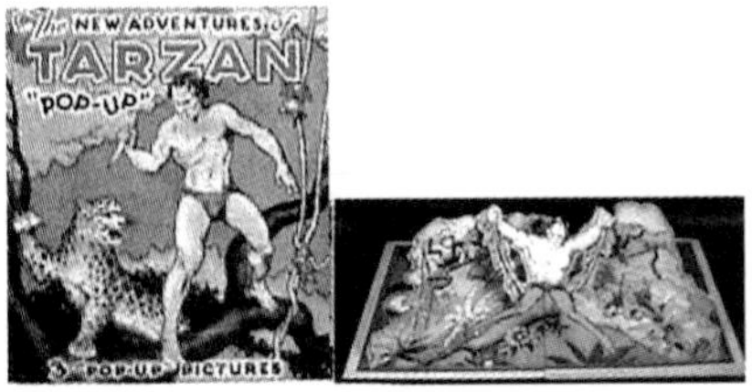


**PUP-19**

❑ **PUP-19. "The New Adventures Of Tarzan 'Pop-Up'" Book,**
1935. Store item by Blue Ribbon Press. 8x9-1/4" with three pop-ups. - **$150 $400 $700**

**PUP-20**

❑ **PUP-20. Buck Rogers In The 25th Century,**
1980. Store item by Random House. 6-3/4x9-1/4". Also published in Spanish by Editorial Norma. Each - **$5 $15 $30**

## Porky Pig

**Porky Pig, one of the star cartoon characters created by the Warner Brothers studio in the 1930s, made his screen debut in 1935 and had his first feature role the following year. From then until the mid-1960s the stuttering little porker appeared in more than 100 cartoon shorts, frequently paired with Daffy Duck, Sylvester the cat, or his girlfriend Petunia. Porky went through several early design changes, and from 1937 on was given voice by Mel Blanc. Porky made his comic book debut in issue #1 of *Looney Tunes & Merrie Melodies* in 1941, had his own book by 1943, and over the years has appeared in numerous special issues and as a guest star in other Warner character books. On television the *Porky Pig Show* aired on ABC from 1964 to 1967 and *Porky Pig and His Friends* was syndicated to local stations starting in 1971. "Tha- Tha- That's All Folks!"**

**PRK-1**

**PRK-2**

❑ **PRK-1. Bisque Bank,**
c. 1936. Store Item - **$30 $75 $165**

❑ **PRK-2. Coloring Book,**
1938. Store item by Saalfield Publishing Co. Probably first Porky coloring book. Sixteen pages of art by Ralph Wolfe involving Porky and Petunia in various activities. - **$50 $110 $160**

**PRK-3**

❑ **PRK-3. "Porky Pig Of Looney Tunes" Stationery Folder,**
1938. Store item by Mitchell Publishing Co. Very early appearance of Daffy and Elmer on a Warner Bros. merchandised item. -
**$25 $60 $100**

**PRK-5**

**PRK-4**

❑ **PRK-4. Early Linen-Like Book With First Daffy Duck Appearance,**
1930s. Store item. 9-3/4x12-1/2" with 12 linen-like textured pages. Porky goes on a duck hunt and runs into a wacky duck who later evolves into Daffy in Warner cartoons, although he is unnamed here. - **$60 $125 $300**

❑ **PRK-5. "Porky's Book Of Tricks" Activity Booklet,**
1942. K. K. Publications. - **$50 $225 $450**

**PRK-6**

**PRK-7**

❑ **PRK-6. All Pictures Comics #1408,**
1942. Reprints Four Color Comics #16 and Famous Gang Book of Comics. - **$15 $60 $125**

❑ **PRK-7. "Porky" Figural White Metal Bank,**
1947. Store item. From a series of banks, plant holders, and bookends. Series includes Porky Pig, Bugs Bunny, Elmer, Daffy Duck, Sniffles, Beaky. Each - **$65 $125 $200**

**PRK-8**

❑ **PRK-8. Porky Pig Wrist Watch,**
1949. Rare.
Watch with box insert. - **$200 $600 $1000**
Watch Only. - **$75 $150 $350**

**PRK-9**

❑ **PRK-9. "Petunia" Wood Jointed Doll,**
1940s. Store item. - **$50 $100 $175**

**PRK-10**

❑ **PRK-10. Warner Bros. Character Place Mats,**
c. 1940s. Probable store item. "Rhyme-A-Day Series" set of seven. Each - **$15 $40 $75**

**PRK-11**

❑ **PRK-11. Dell Comic Pictures,**
1940s. Version in top hat with Warner Bros. copyright, second version Leon Schlesinger copyright. Each - **$15 $30 $60**

PRK-12

❑ **PRK-12. "March Of Comics" #175,**
1958. Various sponsors. - **$4 $9 $18**

PRK-13

PRK-14

❑ **PRK-13. "Porky's Lunch Wagon" Dome Lunch Box With Matching Thermos,**
1959. Thermos. Box - **$100 $200 $450**
Bottle - **$35 $75 $150**

❑ **PRK-14. Porky Pig Adult-Sized Over The Head-Style Costume,**
1960. Store item by Collegeville. 25" wide by 50" tall. Near Mint Carded - **$350**
Uncarded - **$75 $150 $250**

PRK-15

❑ **PRK-15. Porky Pig Glazed Ceramic Figure,**
1975. Warner Bros. Inc., Japan. - **$5 $15 $30**

PRK-16

❑ **PRK-16. Porky and Petunia Salt & Pepper Shakers,**
1998. Warner Bros. Store exclusive. - **$25**

PRK-17

❑ **PRK-17. Model Car Kit,**
1999. In box. - **$20**

## Post Cereals Misc.

**Charles W. Post (1854-1914), a patient at Dr. John Kellogg's Battle Creek Sanitarium, was introduced to the benefits of a vegetarian diet in 1891. His enthusiasm for Kellogg's Caramel Coffee led him to develop his own formula and by 1895 he was marketing Postum Cereal Food Drink, a coffee substitute that "Makes Red Blood." Within two years he had created Grape-Nuts, a cold breakfast cereal that was also promoted as a health food. Post advertised his products as if they were medicines under the theme "There's a Reason." The company flourished, expanded, and took the name of General Foods in the late 1920s.**

PST-1

❑ **PST-1. "Post Toasties Movie Book" Folder,**
1920s. - **$10 $25 $40**

PST-2

❑ **PST-2. Classic Celebrity Photo Sign,**
1936. Rare 18" x42" sign. Features Jack Benny, Dizzy Dean, Joe E. Brown, Capt. Frank Hawks and Melvin Purvis. Benny was promoting Jello products and later in 1942 promoted Post cereals. The others were all bigger than life stars, and each had a children's club sponsored by Post cereals. Note - Melvin Purvis is holding the membership badge for his club. -
**$100 $200 $300**

PST-3

❑ **PST-3. Smiley Burnette Dixie Color Photo,**
1942. - **$10 $20 $40**

PST-4

❑ **PST-4. "Free Comic Rings" Store Sign,**
1948. 15-1/4x20" full color sign promoting set of 12 rings packaged one per box. Gordon Gold Archives. - **$100 $275 $450**

PST-5

❑ **PST-5. Cereal Box With "Comic Rings" Offer,**
1948. Gordon Gold Archives.
Complete - **$150 $275 $525**

PST-6

❑ **PST-6. Comic Rings Store Shelf Display,**
1948. Post's Raisin Bran. Cardboard assembly display for litho. tin ring box inserts. Twelve character rings are identified. -
**$100 $200 $375**

PST-7

❑ **PST-7. Andy Gump Litho. Tin Ring,**
1948. This and the next 11 rings are from the 1948 Post Raisin Bran set. The Near Mint price is for unbent examples with no rust. -
**$5 $20 $50**

PST-8

❑ **PST-8. Dick Tracy Litho. Tin Ring,**
1948. - **$20 $60 $125**

PST-9

❑ **PST-9. Harold Teen Litho. Tin Ring,**
1948. - **$5 $20 $50**

PST-10

❑ **PST-10. Herby Litho. Tin Ring,**
1948. - **$5 $20 $50**

PST-11

❑ **PST-11. Lillums Litho. Tin Ring,**
1948. - **$5 $20 $50**

PST-12

❑ **PST-12. Orphan Annie Litho. Tin Ring,**
1948. - **$10 $35 $80**

PST-13

❑ **PST-13. Perry Winkle Litho. Tin Ring,**
1948. - **$5 $20 $50**

PST-14

❑ **PST-14. Skeezix Litho. Tin Ring,**
1948. - **$5 $20 $50**

PST-15

❑ **PST-15. Smilin' Jack Litho. Tin Ring,**
1948. - **$10 $35 $75**

PST-16

❑ **PST-16. Smitty Litho. Tin Ring,**
1948. - **$5 $20 $50**

PST-17

❑ **PST-17. Smokey Stover Litho. Tin Ring,**
1948. - **$5 $20 $50**

PST-18

❑ **PST-18. Winnie Winkle Litho. Tin Ring,**
1948. - **$5 $20 $50**

PST-19

❑ **PST-19. Alexander Litho. Tin Ring,**
1949. This and the next 23 rings are from the 1949 Post Toasties set. The Near Mint price is for unbent examples with no rust. - **$5 $20 $50**

PST-20

❑ **PST-20. Blondie Litho. Tin Ring,**
1949. - **$5 $20 $60**

PST-21

❑ **PST-21. Captain Litho. Tin Ring,**
1949. - **$5 $20 $50**

PST-22

❑ **PST-22. Casper Litho. Tin Ring,**
1949. - **$5 $20 $50**

PST-23

❑ **PST-23. Dagwood Litho. Tin Ring,**
1949. - **$10 $30 $70**

PST-24

❑ **PST-24. Felix The Cat Litho. Tin Ring,**
1949. - **$20 $70 $175**

PST-25

❑ **PST-25. Flash Gordon Litho. Tin Ring,**
1949. - **$20 $70 $175**

PST-26

❑ **PST-26. Fritz Litho. Tin Ring,**
1949. - **$5 $20 $50**

PST-27

❑ **PST-27. Hans Litho. Tin Ring,**
1949. - **$5 $20 $50**

PST-28

❑ **PST-28. Henry Litho. Tin Ring,**
1949. - **$5 $20 $50**

PST-29

❑ **PST-29. Inspector Litho. Tin Ring,**
1949. - **$5 $20 $50**

PST-30

❑ **PST-30. Jiggs Litho. Tin Ring,**
1949. - **$5 $20 $50**

PST-31

❑ **PST-31. Little King Litho. Tin Ring,**
1949. - **$10 $30 $75**

PST-32

❑ **PST-32. Mac Litho. Tin Ring,**
1949. - **$5 $20 $50**

PST-33

❑ **PST-33. Maggie Litho. Tin Ring,**
1949. - **$5 $20 $50**

PST-34

❑ **PST-34. Mama Litho. Tin Ring,**
1949. - **$5 $20 $50**

PST-35

❑ **PST-35. Olive Oyl Litho. Tin Ring,**
1949. - **$10 $30 $65**

PST-36

❑ **PST-36. The Phantom Litho. Tin Ring,**
1949. - **$20 $70 $175**

PST-37

❑ **PST-37. Popeye Litho. Tin Ring,**
1949. - **$20 $70 $150**

PST-38

❑ **PST-38. Snuffy Smith Litho. Tin Ring,**
1949. - **$10 $30 $60**

PST-39

❑ **PST-39. Swee' Pea Litho. Tin Ring,**
1949. - **$10 $30 $75**

PST-40

❑ **PST-40. Tillie The Toiler Litho. Tin Ring,**
1949. - **$5 $20 $50**

PST-41

❑ **PST-41. Toots Litho. Tin Ring,**
1949. - **$10 $30 $60**

PST-42

❑ **PST-42. Wimpy Litho. Tin Ring,**
1949. - **$10 $30 $65**

PST-43

❑ **PST-43. "Turbo Jet Pilot" 3-1/2" Plastic Badge,**
1949. Center has built-in siren whistle. -
**$10 $30 $75**

PST-44

❑ **PST-44. Air Speed Indicator,**
1940s. Premium for bike with mailer. -
**$25 $50 $75**

PST-45

❑ **PST-45. "Free Comic Rings" Store Sign,**
1952. Premium Specialties, Chicago, Ill. 9x20" sign reads "12 Different Rings In The Series" and designs are the same as the rings used in the 1948 Post Raisin Bran set. However, this was a later use of the same rings unrelated to the Post promotion. Sign has blank area for sponsor's imprint. Gordon Gold Archives. - **$100 $200 $300**

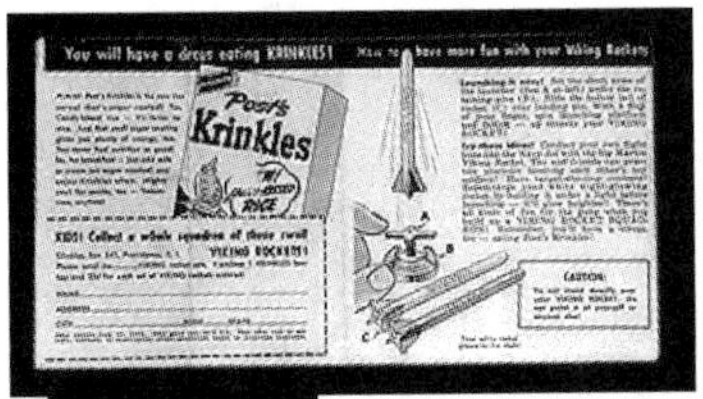


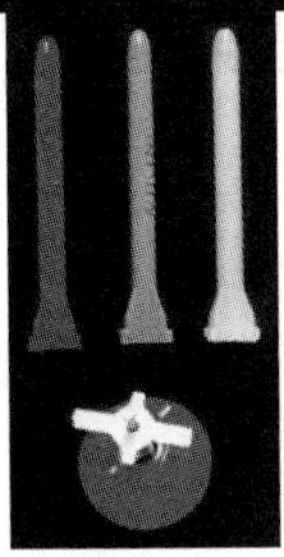

PST-46

PST-47

❑ **PST-46. "Viking Rockets" Toy With Instructions And Mailer,**
1952. Post's Krinkles. Set of plastic spring launcher and three 2-3/4" plastic rockets.
Near Mint Boxed - **$175**
Launcher and Three Rockets - **$25 $50 $75**

❑ **PST-47. Sugar Crisp Order Form for Puppets (Handy, Dandy, Candy),**
1953. Post Cereal. - **$10 $20 $30**

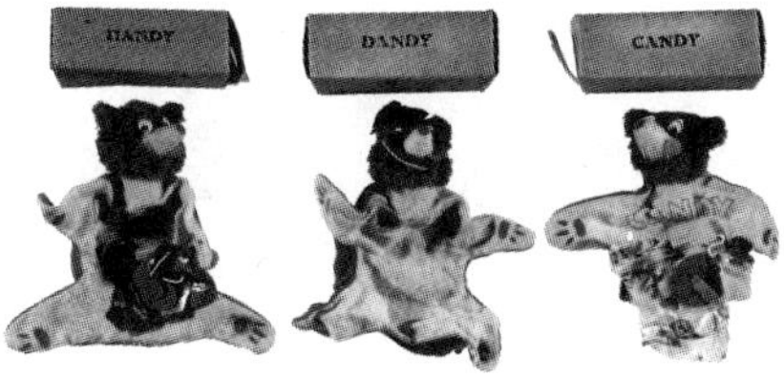


PST-48

❑ **PST-48. Sugar Crisp Puppets,**
1953. Post Cereal. With accesories add $20 each. - **$10 $20 $50**

PST-49

❑ **PST-49. Grape-Nuts Flakes Cars,**
1954. Plastic cars of models, Ford County Sedans, Ford Tudors, Ford Crown Victorias. Various colors: red, dark blue, turquoise, yellow, and brown. 8 cars pictured.
Each - **$8 $20 $50**

PST-50

❑ **PST-50. Sugar Crisp Bears Mug & Bowl Set,**
1954. With instructions & mailer. Blue & Pink. Post Cereal. - **$30 $50 $100**

PST-51

❑ **PST-51. Railroad Tin Signs,**
1954. 28 different tin signs of railroad companies logos and mailer.
Complete - **$150 $300 $740**
Each - **$5 $10 $25**

PST-52

PST-53

❑ **PST-52. Plastic Cars,**
1955. Eight different colors and models.
Each - **$8 $20 $50**

❑ **PST-53. Sugar Crisp Tractor Trailers,**
1955. Grey and orange color pictured. Freuhauf written on top of trailers. Each - **$10 $15 $30**

PST-54

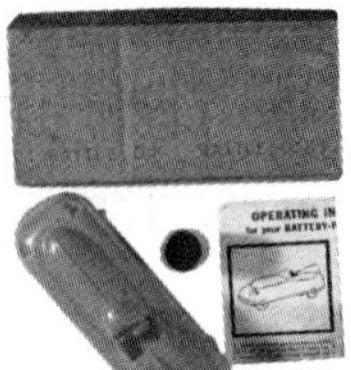

PST-55

❑ **PST-54. Grape-Nuts Flakes Plastic Tanker Set,**
1956. Ford/Freuhauf Oil. Set contained a red, yellow, orange, and grey tanker.
Each - **$15 $30 $50**

❑ **PST-55. Rocket Racer,**
1950s. Scarce. Orange battery powered plastic rocket racer. With mailer and instructions. - **$35 $75 $150**

PST-56

PST-57

❑ **PST-56. Post Race Car Premium (Speed Town) with Mailer,**
1950s. - **$30 $70 $100**

❑ **PST-57. Railroad Fun Book - Sugar Crisp,**
1950s. 36 page premium which promotes trains. - **$10 $35 $45**

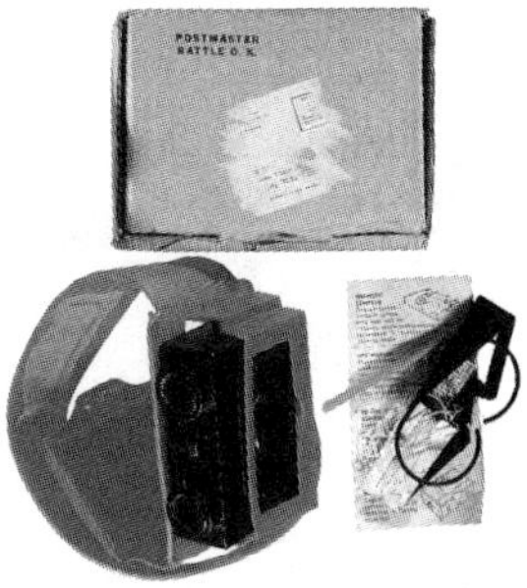

PST-58

❑ **PST-58. Spy Master Belt Set,**
1950s. Includes command belt which lights up, with camera, signal mirror, magnifying glass, sundial, compass, a measure with glasses and plastic mustache. With mailer and instructions. - **$35 $75 $135**

PST-59

❑ **PST-59. "Sugar Crisp Bear Jacket Patch" Waxed Box Wrapper,**
1950s. Promotes three different in box premiums. Gordon Gold Archives.
Uncut Flat Wrapper - **$200**
Used Complete Box - **$40 $80 $125**

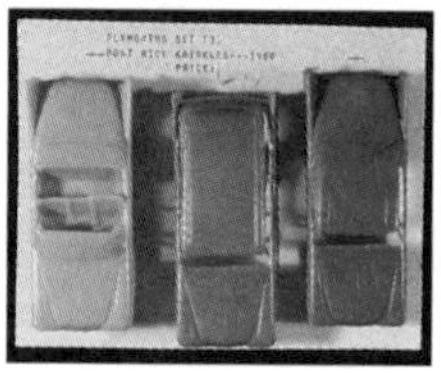
PST-60

❑ **PST-60. Plymouth Plastic Cars,**
1960. Post Rice Krinkles. Red, blue, and turquoise colors. Features convertible, hard top, and station wagon. Each - **$10 $25 $50**

PST-61

❑ **PST-61. Post Rice Krinkles Box With Baseball Trading Cards,**
1962. Back has five cards to cut out from total set of 200. Gordon Gold Archives.
Near Mint Flat - **$175**
Used Complete - **$25 $65 $100**

PST-62

❑ **PST-62. Football Booklet Set,**
1962. Each - **$3 $8 $15**

PST-63

❑ **PST-63. "3-Dimensional Jet Fighter" Cereal Box,**
1963. Numbered back panels of unknown total.
Near Mint Flat - **$175**
Used Complete - **$20 $40 $75**

PST-64

❑ **PST-64. Cereal Box with Football Trading Card on Back,**
Early 1960s. 7 cards from a set of 200 on each back. - **$50 $100 $200**

PST-65

❑ **PST-65. "Linus The Lion Fun Book" With Play Scene Card,**
1964. Near Mint In Mailer - **$100**
Book Only - **$20 $40 $75**

PST-66

❑ **PST-66. "Post's Crispy Critters Linus The Lion Card Game" Cereal Box ,**
c. 1963. Gordon Gold Archives.
Near Mint Flat - **$325**
Used Complete - **$50 $125 $200**

PST-67

❑ **PST-67. "Post Sugar Sparkled Rice Krinkles So-Hi Acrobat Toy" Box Flat With Premium,**
c. 1965. Gordon Gold Archives.
Near Mint Flat - **$275**
Used Complete - **$40 $100 $150**
So-Hi Premium - **$8 $12 $25**

PST-68

❑ **PST-68. Plastic Cars,**
1966. Ford Mustang, Ford hardtop, fastback and convertible. All yellow. Each - **$8 $20 $50**

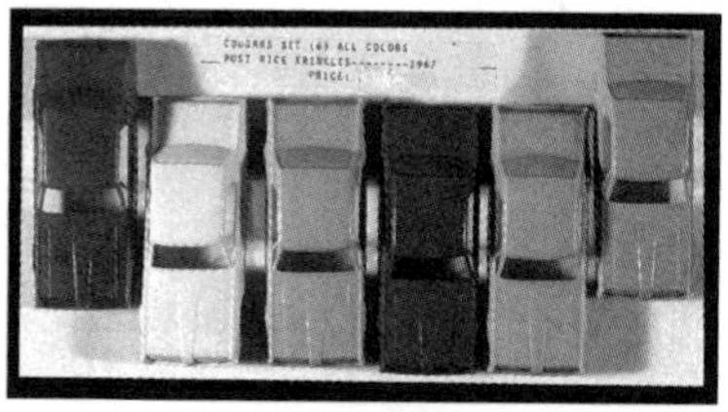
PST-69

❑ **PST-69. Rice Krinkles Plastic Cars,**
1967. Premium cars. Mercury Cougar. Green, dark blue, light blue, brown, red, and yellow. Each - **$8 $20 $50**

PST-70

❑ **PST-70. "Linus The Lion Fun Book" Cereal Box Flat,**
1967. Post Crispy Critters cereal.
Near Mint Flat - **$325**
Used Complete - **$50 $125 $200**

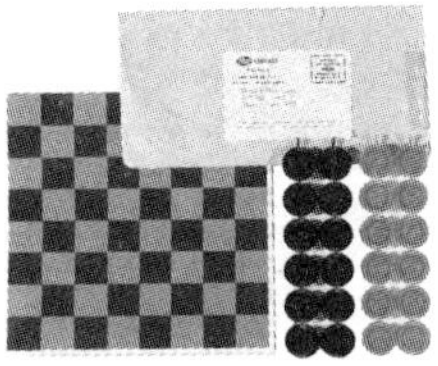

PST-71

PST-72

❑ **PST-71. Checkers Game and Mailer,**
1960s. Premium. Complete- **$10 $25 $40**

❑ **PST-72. 3-D Poster (Honeycomb Cereal),**
1970s. Kirby art. Premium with 3-D glasses. - **$15 $20 $40**

## Pot O' Gold

**A thinly-disguised lottery radio show hosted by Horace Heidt and sponsored by Tums from 1939-1941 on NBC, although briefly revived for one season by ABC in 1946. A "Wheel of Fortune" was spun three times during each broadcast to determine: (1) a telephone directory from a random city, (2) a page from it, and (3) a specific home telephone number from that page. The number, then called by Heidt, rewarded the answerer $1,000 by Western Union. Obviously people listened in hopes of being selected, probably with no concept of the millions-to-one odds against it. The wheel selections were interspersed by musical entertainment by Heidt's Musical Knights. The show left the air as a result of a ruling by the Federal Communications Commission.**

PGL-1

PGL-2

❑ **PGL-1. "Pot O' Gold" Game,**
1939. Store item. Large 13x20" box reading "America's Newest Radio Game Craze As Played Over NBC Network". - **$40 $80 $125**

❑ **PGL-2. "Tums Pot-O-Gold" 3" Metal Pocket Flashlight,**
c. 1939. Inscription continues "With Horace Heidt On Your Radio Thursday Night". - **$30 $60 $100**

PGL-3

(FRONT) (BACK)

PGL-4

❑ **PGL-3. Tums Metal Container With Show Logo,**
c. 1939. Rare. - **$50 $100 $200**

❑ **PGL-4. Metal Pencil With Logo On Attached Cello. Pencil Clip,**
c. 1939. - **$25 $50 $100**

PGL-5

❑ **PGL-5. Facsimile Money,**
c. 1939. Lists NBC show times and states "1,000 Or More Dollars Given Away." 2x4-1/2". - **$10 $20 $30**

## Powerpuff Girls

**The Powerpuff Girls, created by Craig McCracken, debuted on the Cartoon Network in 1998 and quickly gained a following among young and old alike. The series focused on the slightly skewed exploits of diminutive superheroines Bubbles, Blossom, and Buttercup as they defended Townsville with the help of their mentor, Professor Utonium. The series also mixed pop culture references and the sort of visual humor familiar from other sophisticated cartoon series like The Simpsons with cute character design and explosive action. An irreverent series suitable for all ages, The Powerpuff Girls has proliferated into a wide variety of merchandise, from videos and toys to fashion accessories. Most items are copyright the Cartoon Network.**

PPG-1

❑ **PPG-1. Pinback,**
2000. Colorful. - **$1 $2 $3**

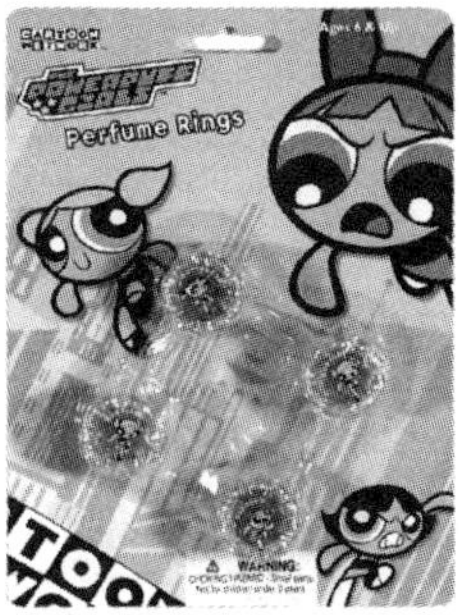


PPG-2

❑ **PPG-2. Perfume Rings,**
2000. Four rings on card. - **$15**

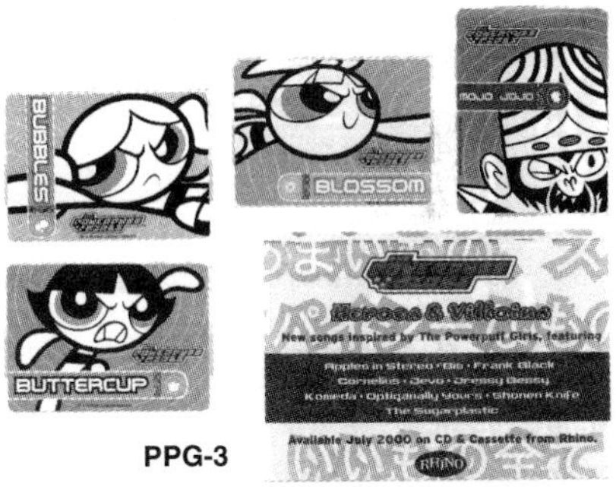


PPG-3

(Back enlarged)

❑ **PPG-3. Promo Decal Set,**
2000. Promotes the Rhino Records release of songs inspired by the show. Set - **$3**

PPG-4

❑ **PPG-4. Villains At Large Game,**
2000. Has 73 cards, 4 pawns with stands. - **$5**

PPG-5

PPG-6

❏ **PPG-5. Board Game,**
2001. From Milton Bradley. - **$30**

❏ **PPG-6. Kellogg's Pop-Tarts Box,**
2001. Limited edition. - **$1 $2**

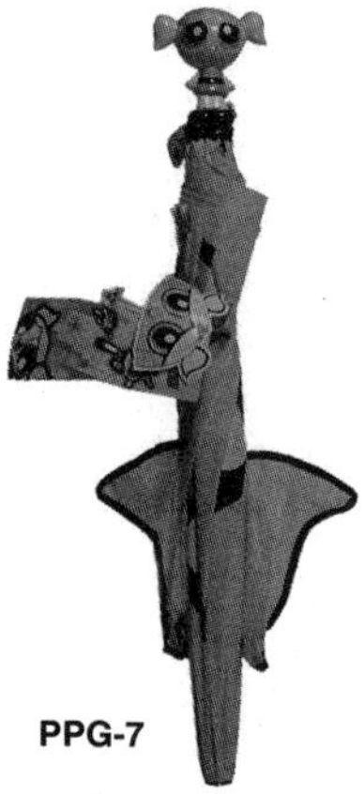

PPG-7

PPG-8

PPG-9

❏ **PPG-7. Umbrella with Tags,**
2001. - **$10**

❏ **PPG-8. Bandages,**
2001. Box of 25 bandages from Kidz Health. - **$3**

❏ **PPG-9. Pop-Up Book,**
2001. A 12 page Pop-Up adventure. - **$13**

## Premiums Misc.

**This brief category features interesting premiums which don't fit elsewhere. They are included because collectors are likely to encounter them or because of interesting graphics or subject matter. If readers have information about those items listed without an identifying sponsor, the author would appreciate receiving information about them.**

PRM-1

❏ **PRM-1. "Buffalo Bill Gun" 19th Century Personality Premium,**
1887. Farm and Fireside Newspaper. Advertisement offers 35-1/2" long wooden rifle with cast iron trigger. Text reads "Given As A Premium For 3 Subscribers To This Paper." Photo courtesy Jim Wojtowicz from his book Buffalo Bill Collectors Guide published by Collector Books. Gun - **$500 $1000 $2000**

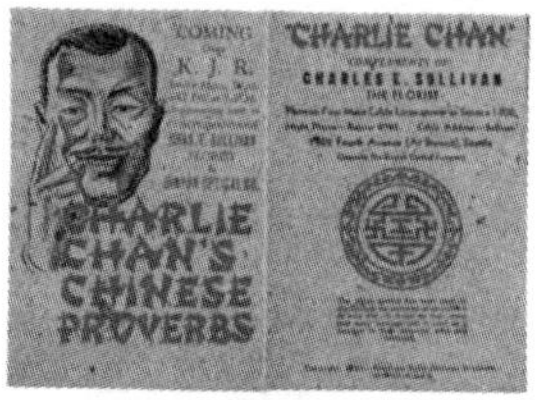


PRM-2

❏ **PRM-2. "Charlie Chan's Chinese Proverbs" Booklet,**
1935. Issued by American Radio Features Syndicate. 4x5-3/4" with 12 pages. - **$40 $85 $175**

PRM-3

PRM-4

❏ **PRM-3. "Eskimo Pie" Premiums Poster,**
1935. 22x28" cardboard and depicting Tracy wristwatch and penlight, Mickey Mouse wrist and pocket watches plus many generic premiums. Also issued as a flyer with coupon on bottom. Poster - **$125 $250 $400**
Flyer Intact - **$30 $60 $90**

❏ **PRM-4. "Tip Top Comics Booster" Cello. Button,**
c. 1936. Dark blue on bright gold 7/8" coinciding very closely to their first publications beginning April 1936. Button maker's back paper reads "Simon Co. 373-Fourth Ave. N.Y.C." - **$100 $225 $350**

PRM-5

❏ **PRM-5. Flying Model Airplanes Blueprint And Instruction Book,**
c. 1936. Curtiss Candy. 10x16" with 24 pages for construction of six different models and two pages picturing premiums. - **$35 $75 $150**

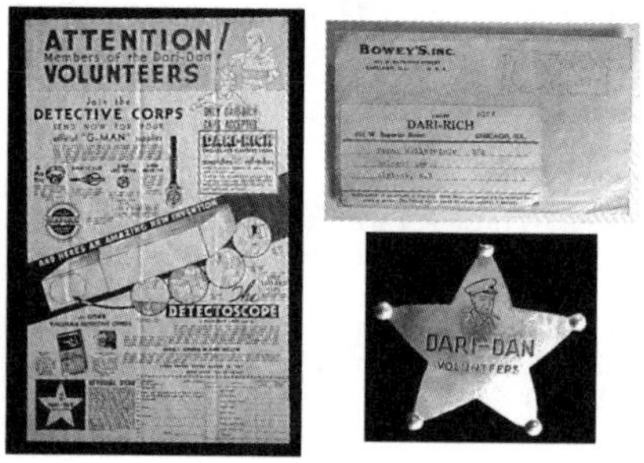


PRM-6

❏ **PRM-6. "Dari-Dan Volunteers" Official Silver Luster Star Badge With Mailer Insert,**
1937. Dari-Rich Chocolate Flavored Drink. Badge came with 11x17" folder promoting membership in "Detective Corps" and picturing "G-Man" supplies of ring, tie clasp, lapel button, watch fob, secret writing outfit, Jiu Jitsu book, Detectoscope and the badge we illustrate.
Mailer - **$5 $10 $15**
Badge - **$20 $50 $85**
Folder - **$25 $50 $75**

PRM-7

❏ **PRM-7. "Young Explorer's Club" Brass Shield Badge,**
1930s. Sponsor unknown. Two shades of brass luster with black accents. - **$20 $40 $75**

PRM-8

❏ **PRM-8. "Toddy" Shake-Up Mug And Map,**
1930s. Mug is 4-1/2" tall, map is 8-1/4x11-3/4". Issued by drink mix company.
Mug - **$10 $25 $40**
Map - **$15 $35 $75**

PRM-9

PRM-10

❏ **PRM-9. "Wings Of America" Club Wings Badge,**
1940. Wings Comics. About 1-1/2" long with red panel on chrome finish. Our photo illustrates the wings on an application for the club which appeared in comic books from late 1940 through at least March 1942. - **$100 $200 $300**

❏ **PRM-10. "Junior Flying Legion" Brass Wings Member's Badge,**
1940. United Feature Comic Group. About 2-1/2" long in brass. Our photo shows club application from inside back cover of Tarzan Single Series #20. Described as "A Great Nationwide Aviation Club..." - **$50 $100 $150**

PRM-11

PRM-12

❏ **PRM-11. "Whistling Jim's National Defenders Secret Portfolio",**
1941. General Mills. Similar to The Lone Ranger item in the same format but this has eight pages compared to 12. Used in states where General Mills did not have the rights to The Lone Ranger. - **$75 $175 $275**

❏ **PRM-12. "Sea Raiders Destroyer Club" Movie Serial Cello. Button,**
1941. 1-1/4" black and green. Cast members included Huntz Hall and Billy Halop. - **$65 $150 $200**

PRM-13

❏ **PRM-13. "Junior G-Men Of The Air" Movie Serial Brass Wings,**
1942. Universal. 2" long in brass luster with blue lettering and red, white and blue star design. - **$50 $100 $175**

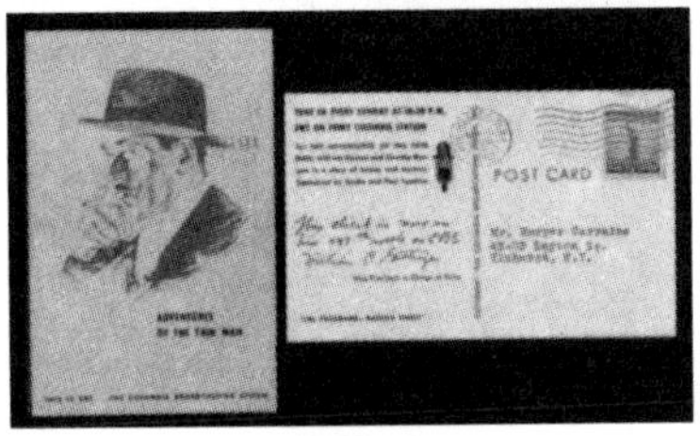


PRM-14

PRM-15

❏ **PRM-14. "The Adventures Of The Thin Man" Fan Postcard,**
1943. Sponsored by Sanka and Post Toasties. - **$30 $60 $120**

❏ **PRM-15. "Ato McBomb" Cello. Button,**
c. 1940s. Issuer unknown and we can find no references to this character. 1-1/4" beautifully designed button in black, red, yellow and flesh-tone. - **$50 $150 $300**

PRM-16

PRM-17

❏ **PRM-16. "Cowboy G-Men" Fan Card,**
1952. Issued by "Taystee Enriched Bread" for syndicated TV show. - **$20 $40 $65**

❏ **PRM-17. "3 In 1 Gift" Punch-Out Assembly Kit,**
1953. Sponsored by Nash Motors. 15-1/2x16-1/2" with parts to assemble show room, service area, three 1953 Nash cars and five early vintage Nash cars. Unpunched - **$75 $150 $250**

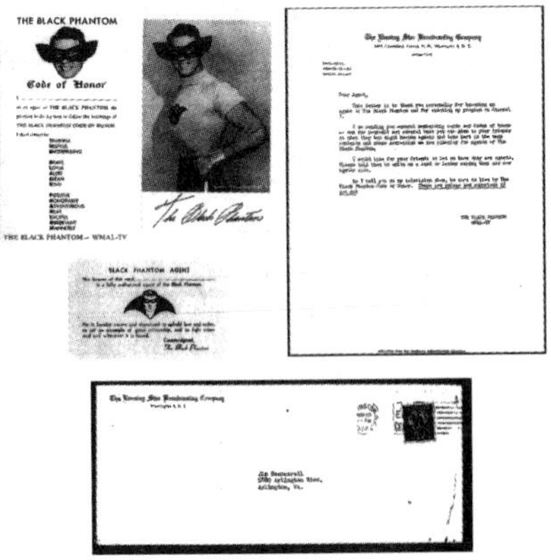


PRM-18

❏ **PRM-18. "The Black Phantom" TV Club Member's Kit,**
1954. The Evening Star Broadcasting Company. Issued by Washington, D.C. station WMAL-TV for local area show hosted by station personality who aired old movies. At first, membership cards were addressed on reverse and mailed separately. Later, membership card issued as part of three-piece club kit with cover letter.
Envelope - **$5 $10 $15**
Cover Letter - **$10 $15 $30**
Portrait Card - **$10 $20 $35**
Code Of Honor Card - **$10 $20 $35**
Member Card - **$10 $20 $35**

PRM-19

PRM-20

❏ **PRM-19. Bat Masterson Premium Cane With Leaflet And Mailer Tube,**
1959. Sealtest ice cream. 30" long black wood and silver plastic cane with mailer along with leaflet opening to 4-3/4x17" illustrated with instructions for cane twirling.
Tube - **$10 $20 $30**
Cane - **$25 $50 $85**
Leaflet - **$10 $20 $30**

❏ **PRM-20. "Junior Forest Fire Fighting Warden" Brass Badge,**
c. 1950s. Issuer unknown. 2-3/4" tall also reading "Jackie Davis Chief Warden/Protect Our Trees." - **$15 $30 $60**

PRM-21

❑ **PRM-21. "Official Paladin Kit" Hat Purchase Premium,**
c. 1960. Arlington Hat Co. 2-1/2x4-1/4" black and white envelope was attached to hat and holds 4" wide fake mustache and four "Have Gun Will Travel" business cards.
Complete - **$25 $65 $125**

PRM-22

❑ **PRM-22. Choo-Choo Charlie Sticker Sheet,**
c. 1970s. Good & Plenty. 7-1/2x10-1/2" sheet sent folded with 18 black, white and pink peel-off stickers. Mailer - **$1 $2 $3**
Sheet - **$5 $10 $15**

## Pretty Kitty Kelly

**The story of a young Irish immigrant girl who arrived in New York with amnesia, no friends, and charged with murder, aired on CBS radio from 1937 to 1940. Kitty managed to make friends and had a number of spirited adventures during her three-year run. Continental Baking Company's Wonder bread and Hostess cupcakes were sponsors.**

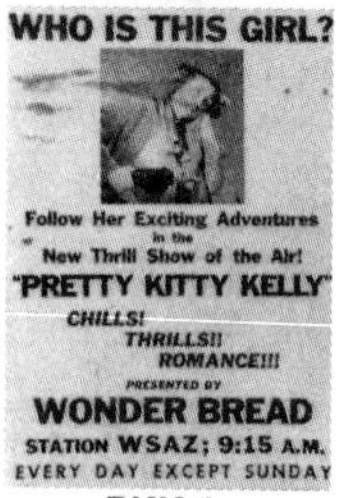


PKK-1

PKK-2

❑ **PKK-1. "Pretty Kitty Kelly" 12x17-1/2" Paper Store Sign,**
c. 1937. Wonder Bread. - **$10 $15 $35**

❑ **PKK-2. "Pretty Kitty Kelly Balloon" 11x15" Paper Store Sign,**
c. 1937. Wonder Bread. - **$5 $8 $20**

PKK-3

❑ **PKK-3. "Kitty Kelly" Enameled Brass "Perfume Pin" On Card,**
c. 1937. Wonder Bread.
Complete - **$25 $40 $70**
Pin Only - **$10 $25 $50**

PKK-4

PKK-5

❑ **PKK-4. Cello. Button,**
c. 1937. Columbia Broadcasting System. -
**$3 $5 $8**

❑ **PKK-5. Store Sign,**
c. 1937. Wonder Bread and Hostess Cake. 11x16-1/2" in black, white and red. -
**$10 $20 $30**

## Pulp Magazine Misc.

**Pictured is sampling of 1930s to 1940s membership cards. "Pulps" derived the name from inexpensive paper used for publication of fantasy and adventure magazines produced at low cost; very few pulps made the leap to producing a badge, ring or other premiums.**

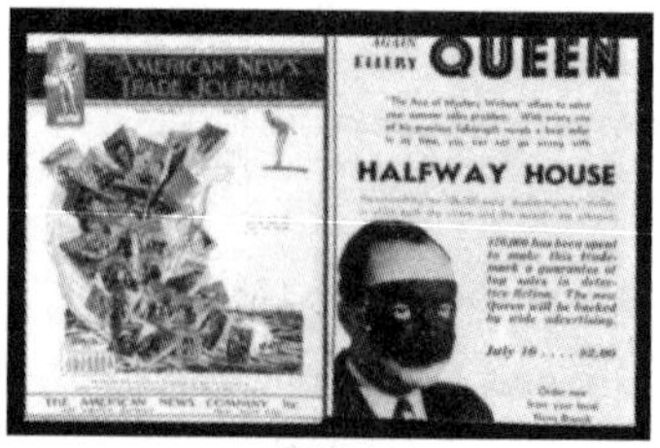


PUL-1

❑ **PUL-1. "The American News Trade Journal" Industry Magazine With Pulp Scene Cover,**
1936. Issue for July. - **$5 $20 $30**

PUL-2

❑ **PUL-2. "Boys' Magazine Detective Club" Badge,**
1930s. Has metal tab on back. First of a series of premiums from the popular pulp magazine.
Rare. - **$175 $385 $525**

PUL-3

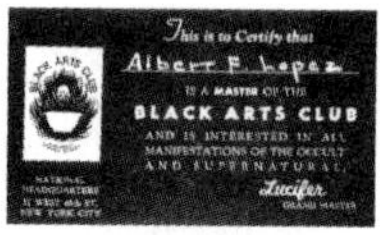


PUL-4

❑ **PUL-3. "Weird Tales Club" Member Card,**
1930s. - **$100 $250 $500**

❑ **PUL-4. "Black Arts Club" Member Card,**
1930s. - **$30 $100 $175**

PUL-5

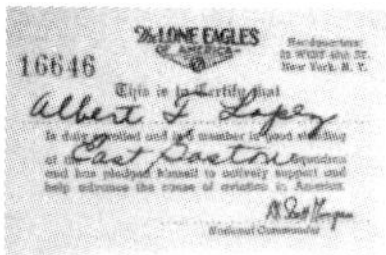


PUL-6

❑ **PUL-5. "The Futuremen" Club Card,**
1930s. Captain Future magazine. -
**$30 $100 $175**

❑ **PUL-6. "The Lone Eagles Of America" Member Card,**
1930s. Lone Eagle magazine. Back has club Ten Commandments. See ADV 27. -
**$30 $100 $175**

PUL-7

❑ **PUL-7. "Air Adventures" Pulp Magazine Premium, Badge,**
1930s. - **$75 $150 $300**

PUL-8

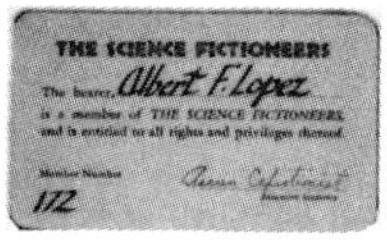


PUL-9

❑ **PUL-8. "Science Fiction League" Club Card With Metal Lapel Stud,**
1930s. Thrilling Wonder Stories magazine.
Card - **$30 $100 $175**
Lapel Stud - **$15 $75 $150**

❑ **PUL-9. "The Science Fictioneers" Club Card,**
1930s. Facsimile signature of executive secretary "Ascien Cefictionist". - **$30 $100 $175**

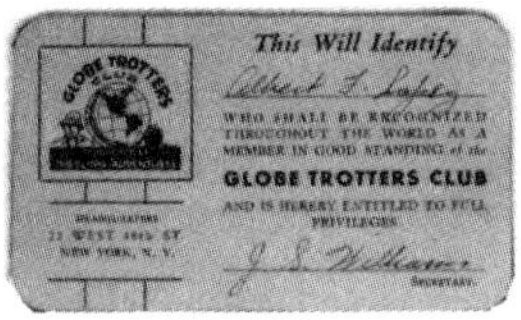


PUL-10

❑ **PUL-10. "Globe Trotters Club" Member Card,**
1930s. Thrilling Adventures magazine. - **$30 $100 $175**

PUL-11

PUL-12

❑ **PUL-11. "Breezy Stories" Store Window Card,**
1930s. C. H. Young Publishing Co., N.Y. 11x14". - **$50 $125 $200**

❑ **PUL-12. Carl Claudy Science Fiction Books Store Window Ad Card,**
1930s. 11x14" stiff paper advertising "New Thrilling Astounding Books by the Jules Verne Of Today." - **$30 $75 $125**

## Purple People Eater

**For six weeks in 1958 this novelty tune featuring a one-eyed, one-horned creature was the No. 1 record on the charts in America. The song was written by Sheb Wooley, a Western band leader with an MGM recording contract. Wooley also had an acting career, appearing in some 50 movies (he was the killer Ben Miller in *High Noon*) and on television as Pat Nolan in *Rawhide* (CBS, 1959-1965) and in the cast of *Hee Haw* (CBS, 1969) for which he also wrote the theme song.**

PUR-1

PUR-2

❑ **PUR-1. Stuffed Fabric Figure,**
1958. Store item copyright by Cordial Music Co. Features include jiggle eyeball in single eye. - **$20 $50 $75**

❑ **PUR-2. Plastic Figure,**
1950s. Store item by J. H. Miller Mfg. Co. 5" tall. - **$50 $125 $225**

PUR-3

❑ **PUR-3. Plastic Hat On Store Card,**
1950s. Store item by Spec-Toy-Ulars, Inc. Thin shell plastic purple hat designed with single eye on front plus markings "One-Eyed, One-Horned Purple People Eater."
Carded - **$20 $40 $75**
Hat Only - **$10 $20 $40**

PUR-4

PUR-5

❑ **PUR-4. "I'm A Purple People Eater" Litho. Button,**
1950s. Probably a vending machine issue. - **$3 $8 $12**

❑ **PUR-5. Cello. 3-1/2" Button,**
1950s. Store item. Purple and white art. - **$10 $20 $35**

PUR-6

❑ **PUR-6. Singing and Dancing Plush Doll,**
1999. In box. Doll plays the original 1950s song and dances. - **$25**

## Quaker Cereals Misc.

**The Quaker Oats Company got its start in 1877 when an oatmeal processor named Henry D. Seymour opened his Quaker Mills Company in Ravenna, Ohio, and registered a likeness of a somber Quaker as his trademark. The company was sold in 1879 and by 1890 was part of the giant American Cereal Company. With the Quaker as the symbol of its principal product, the company sold its rolled oats in cardboard boxes rather than in bulk, making it one of the first packaged foods. Heavy advertising and promotion--including cross-country trains distributing free samples--made Quaker Oats a national success. The company entered the cold cereal market with Puffed Wheat and Puffed Rice, "shot from guns." The Quaker logo was revised in 1945 and further modernized in 1971. This section shows Quaker premiums not associated with the many major characters they sponsored over the years.**

QKR-1

QKR-2

❑ **QKR-1. Trade Card,**
1883. Shows Quaker cereal assembly line. - **$20 $40 $60**

❑ **QKR-2. "Quaker Rolled White Oats" Cello. Button,**
c. 1905. - **$10 $20 $40**

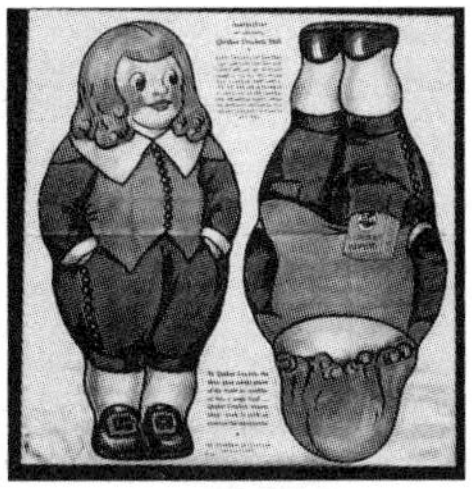

QKR-3

QKR-4

❑ **QKR-3. Quaker Oats Doll,**
1930. Rare. Cloth uncut mascot doll for Quaker Crackels Cereal. - **$75 $200 $300**
Assembled Doll - **$35 $75 $150**

❑ **QKR-4. "Phil Cook/The Quakerman" With Doll Photo,**
c. 1930. Quaker Crackels. Black and white photo of radio show host at NBC microphone while displaying 'Crackels Boy' assembled stuffed fabric cut-out premium doll.
Photo - **$10 $25 $50**

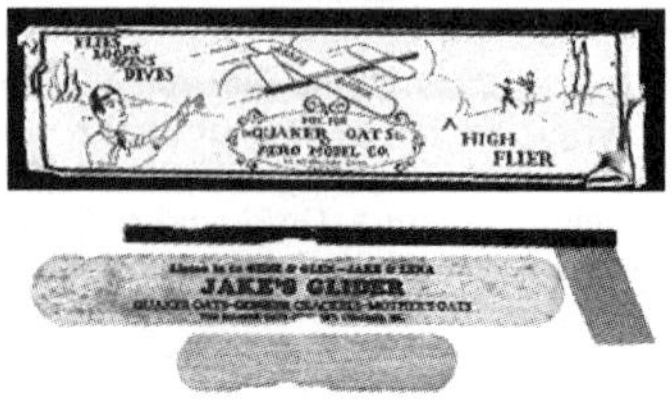

QKR-5

❑ **QKR-5. "Jake's Glider" Kit With Envelope,**
c. 1931. Quaker Oats/Quaker Crackels/Mother's Oats. Instructions envelope holding balsa assembly parts for 12x12" glider toy propelled by rubber band. Offered on "Quaker Early Birds" NBC radio program that began December 29, 1930. Envelope Only - **$10 $25 $40**
Glider Only - **$15 $30 $45**

QKR-6

QKR-7

❑ **QKR-6. Muffets Biscuits Humming Rocket Premium Sign 12x15",**
1930s. - **$40 $80 $175**

❑ **QKR-7. Muffets Biscuits Humming Rocket,**
1930s. - **$20 $40 $65**

QKR-8

❑ **QKR-8. Humming Rocket Ship Promo Manual,**
1930s. - **$30 $60 $90**

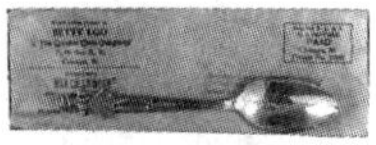
QKR-9

QKR-10

❑ **QKR-9. "Betty Lou" Silver Plate Spoon With Mailer,**
1930s. Quaker Oats. Handle tip is figural depiction of young girl in polka dot dress.
With Mailer - **$10 $20 $30**
Spoon Only - **$5 $10 $15**

❑ **QKR-10. "Milton Berle's Jumbo Fun Book",**
1940. Pre-TV era. - **$10 $15 $25**

QKR-11

QKR-12

❑ **QKR-11. "Maple Leaf Bantam Hockey Club" Certificate,**
1946. Canadian youth pledge certificate for club affiliated to professional Toronto Maple Leafs 1946-1947 season. - **$15 $25 $40**

❑ **QKR-12. "Veronica Lake" Litho. Button,**
1948. Quaker Puffed Wheat & Rice. From set of 20 movie stars, each including studio name in inscription. Each - **$5 $10 $15**

QKR-13

❑ **QKR-13. Movie Star Button Cereal Box,**
1948. Side panel shows 20 buttons in set distributed one per box. Each button is 13/16" tin litho. Gordon Gold Archives.
Used Complete - **$40 $100 $175**

QKR-14

QKR-15

❑ **QKR-14. Lizabeth Scott Litho. Button,**
c. 1948. Similar to photographic set of 20 distributed in America by Quaker Puffed Wheat & Rice but this is Canadian version with line drawings and back inscription "Quaker Puffed Wheat And Rice Sparkies." Eleven different known, all marked "A PARAMOUNT STAR".
Each - **$10 $20 $35**

❑ **QKR-15. Plastic Mug,**
c. 1950. - **$5 $10 $20**

QKR-16

❑ **QKR-16. "Space Flight To The Moon" Cereal Box**
1953. Quaker Puffed Rice. Last of a series of eight. Complete Box - **$50 $75 $175**

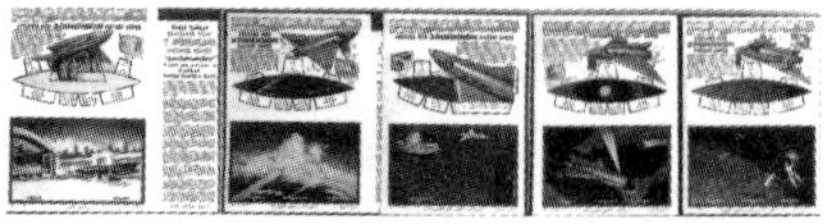
QKR-17

❑ **QKR-17. "Space Flight To The Moon" Box Backs #1-5,**
1953. Quaker Puffed Rice. From set of eight.
Each Complete Box - **$50 $75 $175**
Each Uncut Back - **$10 $25 $40**

QKR-18

❑ **QKR-18. Indian Picture Cards (18) & Mailer,**
1950s. - **$50 $100 $200**

QKR-19

❑ **QKR-19. "Quaker Stamps Of The Golden West Album" With Envelope,**
1950s. Mailer - **$3 $5 $10**
Album - **$10 $20 $30**

QKR-20

QKR-21

❑ **QKR-20. Shari Lewis Character Finger Puppets,**
1962. Quaker Oats. Each - **$2 $4 $8**

❑ **QKR-21. Indian Bead Rings Unassembled With Mailer,**
1962. Frosty-O's cereal premium. Rare. - **$50 $100 $150**

## Quisp and Quake

**Quaker Oats Company introduced a pair of competing new cereals in 1965--Quisp, for quazy energy, and earthquake-powered Quake. The Quisp character was a propeller-headed pink alien who promoted "the biggest selling cereal from Saturn to Alpha Centauri," and Quake was a spelunking superhero in a hard hat and logging boots who could swim through bedrock. Initial promotions included battery-operated helmets as premiums for grocers. Though the two cereals were virtually identical, Quake was dropped in the early 1970s, while Quisp still survives in selected areas.**

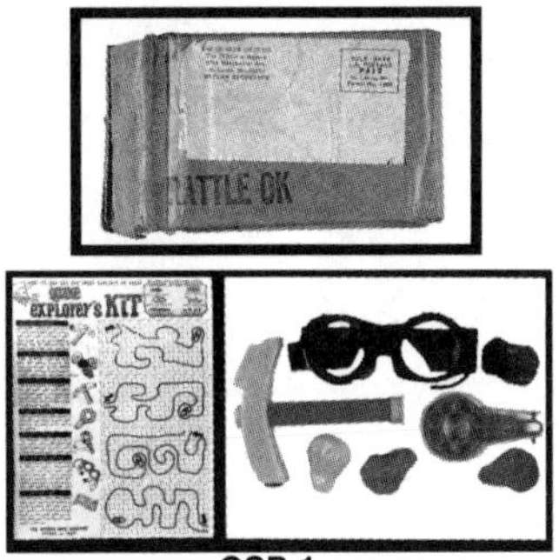


QSP-1

❑ **QSP-1. "Quake Explorer's Kit,"**
1965. Quaker Oats. Boxed mail premium of plastic play parts, paper maps and diagrams. Includes hammer, 4 color plastic rocks, Geiger counter, magnifying glass, tweezers and stand, goggles with mirrors, exploration maps, instructions and mailer. Near Mint Boxed - **$225**

QSP-2

❑ **QSP-2. "Cosmiclouder" Smoke Gun,**
1965. Plastic inscribed "Quisp" on each side. - **$75 $175 $325**

QSP-3

❑ **QSP-3. "Quispmobile" Offer Cereal Box,**
1965. Three-dimensional plastic flying saucer was packaged one per box. Back panel features four cut-out "United Monsters Of Outer Space Targets." Gordon Gold Archives.
Used Complete - **$300 $700 $1000**

QSP-4

❑ **QSP-4. "Mini-Movie Viewer" Offer Cereal Box,**
1965. In box premium was small plastic viewer and back panel features one of four different cardboard filmstrips. Viewers came in three different colors. Gordon Gold Archives.
Used Complete - **$200 $400 $700**

QSP-5

❑ **QSP-5. Cereal Box With "Mini-Movie Viewer" Offer,**
1965. Back panel pictures premium consisting of small figural plastic Quisp with attached viewing lens. Panel also has cut-out filmstrip from a series of four different. Gordon Gold Archives.
Used Complete - **$100 $200 $300**

QSP-6

❑ **QSP-6. "Adventures Of Quake And Quisp" Comic Book,**
1966. Three in series titled "Kite Tale," "Lava Come-Back," and "Plenty of Glutton."
Each - **$10 $20 $35**

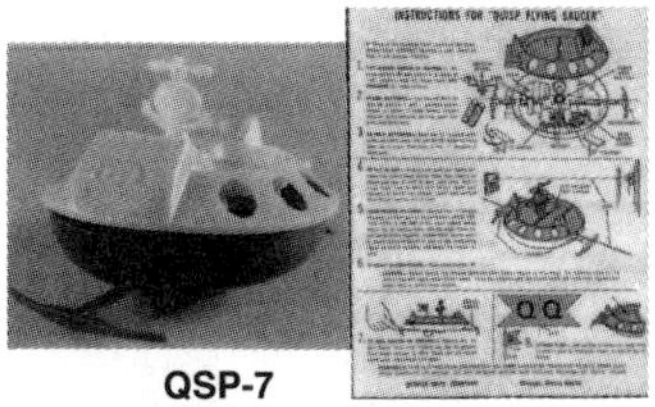

QSP-7

❑ **QSP-7. "Quisp Flying Saucer" With Instruction Sheet,**
1966. Battery operated plastic toy.
Near Mint In Generic Box - **$300**
Saucer Only - **$50 $125 $200**

QSP-8

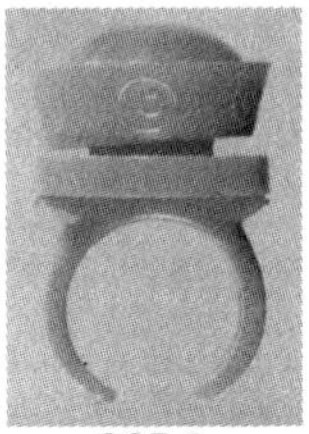

QSP-9

❑ **QSP-8. Quisp Friendship Figural Plastic Ring,**
1966. - **$200 $400 $800**

❑ **QSP-9. Quisp Space Disk Whistle Plastic Ring,**
1966. - **$100 $200 $300**

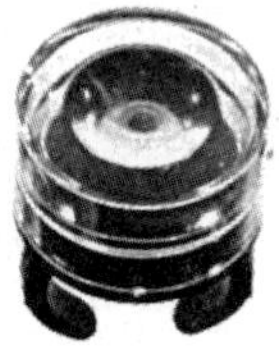

**QSP-10** **QSP-11**

❑ **QSP-10. Quisp Meteorite Plastic Ring,**
1966. - **$100 $200 $300**

❑ **QSP-11. Quisp Space Gun Plastic Ring,**
1966. - **$100 $200 $300**

**QSP-12**

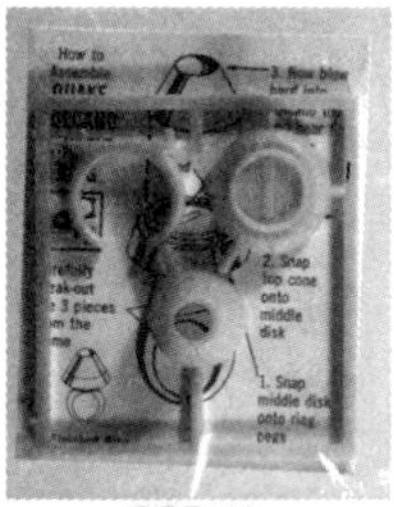

**QSP-13**

❑ **QSP-12. Quake Friendship Plastic Ring,**
1966. - **$125 $300 $500**

❑ **QSP-13. Quake Volcano Whistle Plastic Ring,**
1966. - **$100 $200 $300**

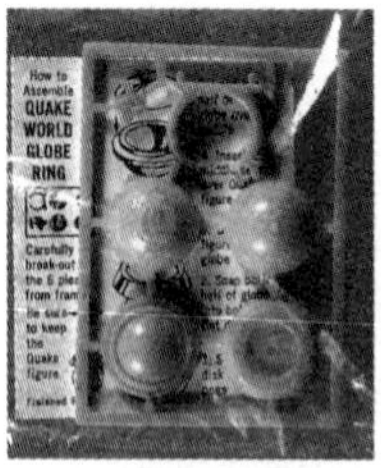

**QSP-14**

**QSP-15**

❑ **QSP-14. Quake World Globe Plastic Ring,**
1966. - **$100 $300 $500**

❑ **QSP-15. "Quake" Cavern Helmet,**
1967. Features include battery operated light bulb housing. - **$50 $100 $150**

**QSP-16** **QSP-17**

❑ **QSP-16. Quisp Playmate Cloth Doll,**
1968. - **$35 $100 $175**

❑ **QSP-17. Quake Playmate Cloth Doll,**
1968. - **$30 $90 $150**

**QSP-18**

❑ **QSP-18. "Quisp Space Beanie",**
1968. Battery operated plastic with turning propeller. - **$50 $100 $200**

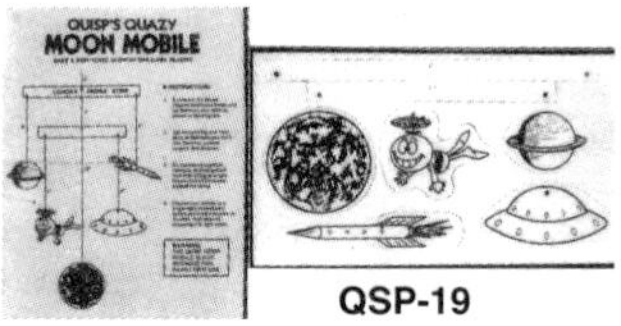


**QSP-19**

❑ **QSP-19. "Quazy Moon Mobile" Punch-Out Assembly Sheet,**
c. 1960s. Assembly parts glow in the dark.
Complete/Unpunched - **$50 $90 $135**

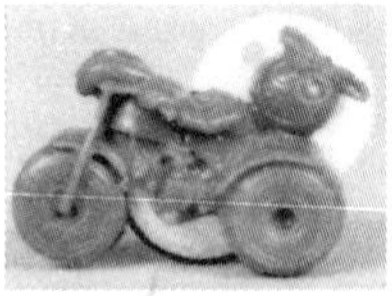

**QSP-20**

**QSP-21**

❑ **QSP-20. Quisp Gyro Trail Blazer,**
c. 1960s. - **$10 $20 $50**

❑ **QSP-21. Quisp Figural Composition Bank,**
c. 1970. 6-1/2" tall with rubber trap. -
**$150 $325 $650**

**QSP-22**

❑ **QSP-22. Quisp On Unicycle Toy,**
c. 1970. Issued by Quaker Oats. 2-1/2" tall.
Near Mint With Pull Cord - **$35**
Without Cord - **$5 $12 $20**

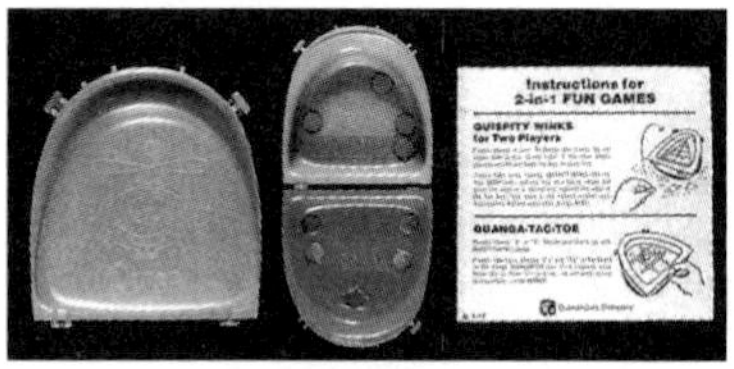

**QSP-23**

❑ **QSP-23. Quisp 2-In-1 Fun Bowl With Instructions,**
1972. Quaker Oats. Hinged plastic game bowl with four orange "X" and four blue "O" playing disks for game "Quispity Winks" or "Quanga-Tac-Toe." Near Mint Complete - **$200**
Bowl Only - **$25 $50 $100**

**QSP-24**

❑ **QSP-24. "Quake Super Spinner" Toy,**
1970s. Cellophane pack holds plastic disk ship and launcher with rubber band. Near Mint Sealed - **$40**
Loose - **$5 $15 $25**

**QSP-25**

❑ **QSP-25. Cereal Box,**
1985. Two panels have "Space Trivia" game parts. Complete Box - **$10 $15 $30**

QSP-26

❑ **QSP-26. "Quisp" Wristwatch In Colorful Illustrated Tin,**
1997. Offered to promote the re-entry of the cereal in the markets of Milwaukee, Chicago, parts of New York and Pennsylvania. Required proof of purchase and $16.95. Offer expired 12/31/97 but was reoffered the following year, this time in a plain tin without any graphics.
Near Mint Boxed Illustrated Tin - **$60**
Near Mint Boxed Plain Tin - **$40**

## Quiz Kids

**A panel of juvenile experts (from as young as 4 to as old as 16) answering questions submitted by listeners, the *Quiz Kids* had a successful 13-year run on network radio from 1940 to 1953. The program was heard initially on NBC, then on the Blue Network (1942-1946), and again on NBC (1946-1951)--sponsored throughout by Alka-Seltzer. For its final season it was sustained on CBS. The show was simulcast on television starting in 1949 and continued on NBC or CBS until 1953, sponsored by Alka-Seltzer (1949-1951) and Cat's Paws Soles (1952-1953). Show-business veteran Joe Kelly served as moderator and quizmaster. A brief television revival in 1956 was hosted by Clifton Fadiman.**

QIZ-1

❑ **QIZ-1. "Quiz Kids" Game,**
1940. Store item by Parker Brothers. - **$15 $25 $50**

QIZ-2

QIZ-3

❑ **QIZ-2. Red Book,**
1941. 31 page book of popular questions and answers from radio show. - **$25 $50 $85**

❑ **QIZ-3. Blue Book,**
1941. Blue cover. Popular questions and answers from radio show. - **$35 $85 $125**

QIZ-4

QIZ-5

❑ **QIZ-4. "Best Teacher Contest Certificate Of Honor",**
1947. Awarded to teachers nominated by their students. - **$15 $30 $60**

❑ **QIZ-5. Photo Postcard,**
c. 1949. Alka-Seltzer. - **$3 $6 $10**

QIZ-6

QIZ-7

❑ **QIZ-6. Photo Postcard,**
c. 1949. Alka-Seltzer. - **$3 $6 $10**

❑ **QIZ-7. "Quiz Kids" Cello. Button,**
1940s. - **$8 $12 $25**

QIZ-8

QIZ-9

QIZ-10

❑ **QIZ-8. "Quiz Kids" Cello. Button,**
1940s. Kaynee. - **$12 $20 $35**

❑ **QIZ-9. Tin Badge,**
1940s. - **$5 $20 $40**

❑ **QIZ-10. "Quiz Kids" Gold Finish Metal Figural Badge,**
1940s. Quiz Kid figure suspends miniature metal book that opens to pull-out paper listing questions and answers. - **$20 $60 $125**

## Radio Misc.

**Radio of the 1930s to early 1950s has little resemblance to the typical formats offered today's listeners. Newspapers and other periodicals could be perused as time or leisure allowed but radio program timing was firm if "live" household entertainment was desired. There was little casual listening, no lengthy spans of similar format. Program nature differed distinctively from one time slot to the next and the intervening commercial breaks could be as creative as the program itself. The earliest and infrequently offered radio premiums were usually tailored to adult listeners. The early 1930s ushered in premiums for youngsters--ever mindful that mom or other adult was still necessary for product purchase--and the subsequent flourishing of club badges, manuals, secret devices, etc. is a matter of record. This section is a sampling of shows, some admittedly obscure, whose sponsors issued at least one imaginative premium.**

RAD-1

RAD-2

❑ **RAD-1. Real Folks Radio Show,**
1925. Vaseline Hair Tonic. Thompkins' Corner Enterprise newspaper premium. - **$15 $25 $35**

❑ **RAD-2. "The Smile You Miss" Song Sheet,**
1929. Music by Raymond Hubbell broadcast on WJZ radio station. Autograph in center of sheet. - **$15 $30 $50**

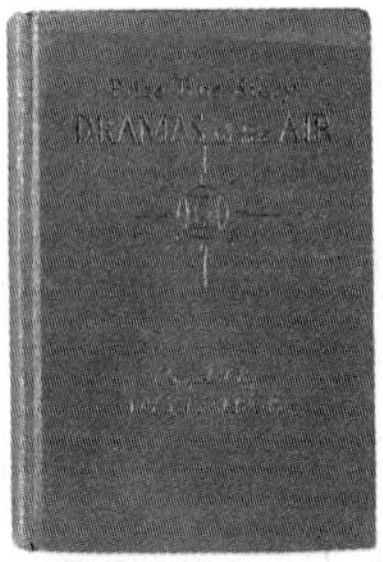

RAD-3

❑ **RAD-3. True Story Hour Book,**
1931. True Story hardcover. 196 pages. "Mary and Bob Radio Show" started in 1929. - **$25 $50 $75**

RAD-4

RAD-5

❑ **RAD-4. Old Time Songs & Mountain Ballads,**
1931. WLW Radio premium. - **$10 $15 $25**

❑ **RAD-5. Radio Pictorial Log Book, 34 Pages,**
1932. Photos of stars and listing of radio stations. - **$15 $30 $45**

RAD-6

❑ **RAD-6. "Just Plain Bill" Puzzle With Mailer Envelope,**
1933. Koloynos toothpaste. Puzzle pictures the three major radio cast members.
Envelope - **$3 $5 $10**
Puzzle - **$10 $15 $25**

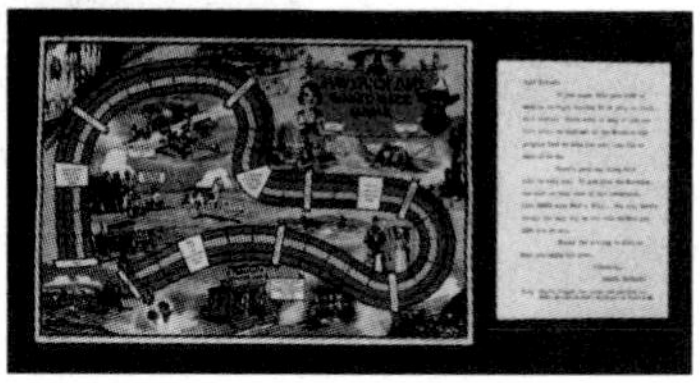

RAD-7

❑ **RAD-7. "Maverick Jim's Runko Race Game" With Letter,**
1934. Runkel Bros. Co. 14x20" full color map includes images of Maverick Jim, Amy, Sam, Aunt Sarah Hardy, Sackfull Wilkes. Map printer is Einson-Freeman Co. Letter urges listenership over WOR, New York City and sampling of new "Runko With Malt". Letter - **$5 $10 $15**
Game Sheet - **$20 $50 $85**

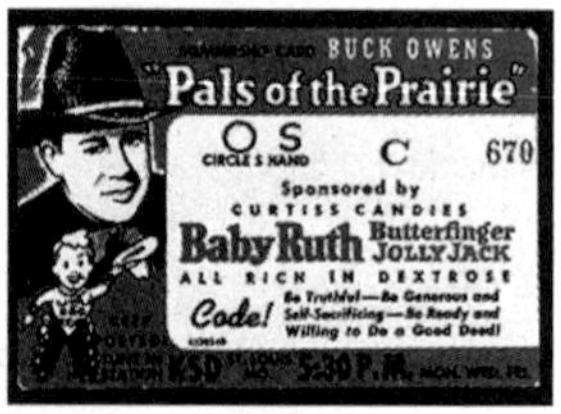


RAD-8

❑ **RAD-8. Buck Owens "Pals Of The Prairie" Membership Card,**
c. 1934. Curtiss Candies. Imprinted for KSD, St. Louis. - **$8 $15 $25**

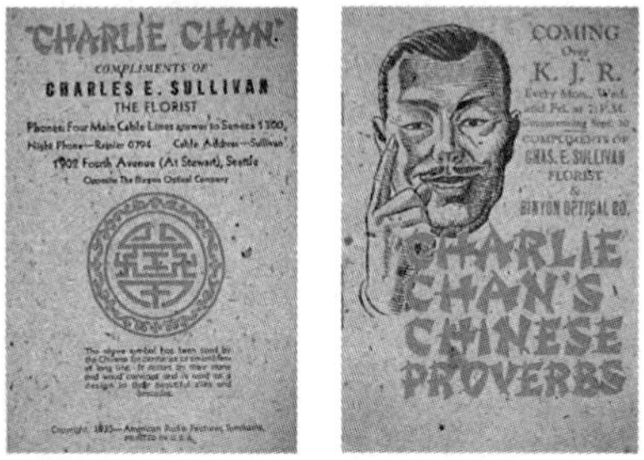


RAD-9

❑ **RAD-9. "Charlie Chan's Chinese Proverbs" Booklet,**
1935. American Radio Features Syndicate, with imprint of Seattle florist on the example pictured. 4x6" beautifully designed with 12 pages and stating "Coming Over K.J.R. Commencing Sept. 30." - **$40 $85 $175**

RAD-10

❑ **RAD-10. Congo Bartlett's "Ethiopia" 21x29" Paper Map,**
1935. Karl's White Bread. - **$40 $75 $150**

RAD-11

RAD-12

❑ **RAD-11. Radio Explorers Club Kit,**
1935. American-Bosch radios. Contents of certificate and folder sheet that opens to 17x22" including picture of Captain James P. Barker, master mariner and club commander.
Folder - **$15 $25 $35**
Certificate - **$10 $18 $30**

❑ **RAD-12. "Radio Explorers Club" Metal Globe,**
c. 1935. American-Bosch, made by J. Chein Co. - **$25 $60 $90**

RAD-13

RAD-14

❑ **RAD-13. Calling W-1-X-Y-Z Better Little Book #1412,**
1936. Jimmy Kean and the Radio Spies.- **$10 $40 $95**

❑ **RAD-14. Happy Hollow Promo With Mailer,**
1936. Network feature. Flyer with recipes. - **$10 $20 $30**

RAD-15

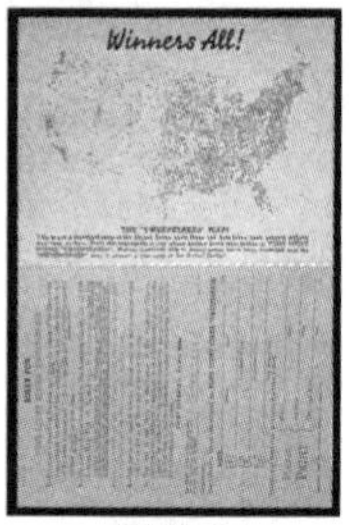


RAD-16

❑ **RAD-15. Lucky Strike Hit Parade Six Page Contest Flyer,**
1936. Radio premium which allowed you to pick hits for radio's Top 15 songs. Includes self addressed postcard still attached with 1¢ stamp. - **$35 $70 $100**

❑ **RAD-16. Lucky Strike Hit Parade Four Page Contest Flyer,**
1936. Radio contest flyer that was handed out with business reply card still attached. - **$25 $50 $75**

RAD-17

❑ **RAD-17. Monk And Sam Radio Show Kit,**
1936. Features photo, mailer, song book, and 1936 calendar called Monkalendar.
Complete - **$25 $50 $75**

RAD-18

❑ **RAD-18. Sara And Aggie's Cook Book,**
1936. 32 page radio premium from "The Tuttle Parlor Show." - **$10 $20 $30**

RAD-19 RAD-20 RAD-21

❑ **RAD-19. Mary Marlin Cast Photo Of David Post,**
1936. Kleenex. Radio premium from "The Story of Mary Marlin" show. - **$5 $10 $20**

❑ **RAD-20. Mary Marlin Cast Photo Of Joe Marlin,**
1936. Kleenex. Radio premium from "The Story of Mary Marlin" show. - **$5 $10 $20**

❑ **RAD-21. Mary Marlin Cast Photo Of Sally Gibbons,**
1936. Kleenex. Radio premium from "The Story of Mary Marlin" show. - **$5 $10 $20**

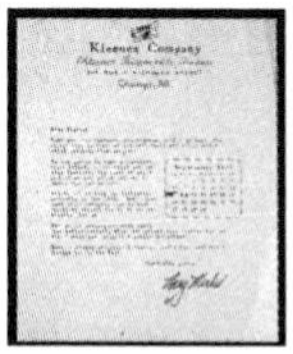

RAD-22 RAD-23 RAD-24

❑ **RAD-22. Mary Marlin Letter,**
1936. Kleenex. Talks about the cast pictures that were ordered. - **$10 $25 $35**

❑ **RAD-23. Mary Marlin Photo Of Actress Joan Gaine,**
1936. Kleenex. Radio premium from "The Story of Mary Marlin" show. - **$10 $20 $30**

❑ **RAD-24. Mary Marlin Photo Of Wedding,**
1936. Kleenex. - **$5 $10 $15**

RAD-25 RAD-26

❑ **RAD-25. Mary Marlin Photo With Station Attachment,**
1936. Kleenex. Holds letter and 5 cast photos from "The Story of Mary Marlin" show. -
**$25 $65 $125**

❑ **RAD-26. Thrilling Moments,**
1936. Sun Oil Co. Lowell Thomas - news voice on the air. - **$10 $20 $30**

RAD-27 RAD-28

❑ **RAD-27. Alka Seltzer Song Book,**
1937. 16 pages of songs featuring radio stars. -
**$10 $20 $30**

❑ **RAD-28. Stars Of Radio Book,**
1937. 16 pages of stars like Kate Smith, Orphan Annie and others. - **$15 $30 $50**

RAD-29 RAD-30

❑ **RAD-29. Rudy Vallee Photo,**
1937. Philadephia Record newspaper premium. -
**$8 $12 $20**

❑ **RAD-30. "The Woman In White" Photo Book,**
1938. Pillsbury Flour Co. 9-1/2x11-3/4" cast member and information promotion for hospital drama radio show beginning January 3 that year. - **$10 $20 $30**

RAD-31

❑ **RAD-31. "I Want A Divorce" Radio Show Game & Mailer,**
1938. Large colorful game with punch-outs and game spinner. Called S&W "Happy Marriage Game." - **$75 $150 $225**

RAD-32 RAD-33

❑ **RAD-32. Roi-Tan Cigars Contest Novelty,**
1939. Miniature metal car with mounted litho. tin sign for contest offering 1939 Chevrolet daily prize with added inscription for Sophie Tucker CBS radio show. - **$35 $125 $225**

❑ **RAD-33. "Voodoo Eye" Metal Pendant With Envelope,**
1930s. Wheato-Nuts. Pendant designed as look-around device. Envelope - **$50 $100 $150**
Pendant - **$75 $225 $350**

RAD-34 RAD-35

❑ **RAD-34. Jolly Joe's *Secret Code* and Radio Club Book,**
1930s. Co Co Wheat. Booklet for youth program utilizing partial code lettering. - **$10 $20 $30**

❑ **RAD-35. Promo Punchout Board,**
1930s. Promoted radio stations. Certain stations received more points than others. Prizes were offered when you reached high point totals. -
**$25 $50 $100**

RAD-36

❑ **RAD-36. "Charlie Chan" Skull Cap,**
1930s. Van Camp's Chili Sauce. 7" diameter with white lettering on black fabric accented by red felt-covered button on top. -
**$75 $150 $275**

RAD-37 RAD-38

❑ **RAD-37. "Adventures Of Frank Farrell" Bronze Luster Metal Badge,**
1930s. Poll Parrot shoes. This was a series of 35 syndicated radio programs. Badge features torch, winged foot along with various pieces of sporting equipment. - **$10 $25 $50**
Pinback with same design **- $15 $60 $75**

❑ **RAD-38. WLW Radio Photo Postcard Of Lullaby Boys,**
1930s. Big Ford & Little Glenn pictured. - **$5 $10 $15**

RAD-39

❑ **RAD-39. Rudy Vallée Jigsaw Puzzle,**
1930s. 200-piece puzzle in its original box. Store bought for 25¢. From a Radio Stars series. - **$40 $80 $120**

RAD-40

RAD-41

❑ **RAD-40. "Coco Wheats Radio Club" Brass Badge,**
1930s. About 1-1/4" tall depicting radio microphone. - **$10 $25 $50**

❑ **RAD-41. Radio Folks Brochure,**
1930s. Keystone Steel. Barn Dance Party, 16 pages, features George Gobel, Red Foley, and others. - **$10 $20 $35**

RAD-42

❑ **RAD-42. New Bachelor Cigar Cutter,**
1930s. Brass cutter premium for cigars. - **$20 $50 $75**

RAD-43

❑ **RAD-43. Fife - Musical Instruments In Mailer,**
1930s. Symphony Hour sponsored by Malt O'Meal. Includes instructions and mailer. - **$50 $75 $100**

RAD-44

RAD-45

❑ **RAD-44. Sohio Radio Puzzle,**
1930s. Boxed puzzle from "In Dutch" radio show. Bought at gas station. - **$15 $25 $50**

❑ **RAD-45. Rudy Vallee Photo,**
1930s. Fleischmann's Yeast. Radio premium with story of life folder.
Complete - **$20 $40 $75**

RAD-46

RAD-47

❑ **RAD-46. Uncle Bob Birthday Card,**
1930s. Hydrox premium for "Curb is the Limit Radio Show." Shows Mr. & Mrs. Uncle Bob on front. - **$10 $18 $30**

❑ **RAD-47. "Charlie Chan Mystery Midget" Premium Offer Original Art For Store Display,**
c. 1940. Prototype for Stokely's Tomato Juice. 12x19" stiff cardboard with tempera paint advertising "Mystery Midget 24 Inches High Including Complete Playlet And Instructions." Gordon Gold Archives. Unique - **$775**

RAD-48

❑ **RAD-48. Radio Personalities and Radio Log,**
1940. Celebrates 10 years of Philco Leadership. Has 144 photos of radio stars, 4 pages of radio logs and 2 pages of ads for radio products. Shows sponsor of each radio show. - **$20 $35 $50**

RAD-49

❑ **RAD-49. Family Hour of Stars Blotter,**
1940. Prudential. Radio premium from sponsor. - **$20 $40 $75**

RAD-50

❑ **RAD-50. Truth Or Consequences Brochure,**
1940. Thirty-two pages. Radio show premium. - **$25 $50 $75**

RAD-51

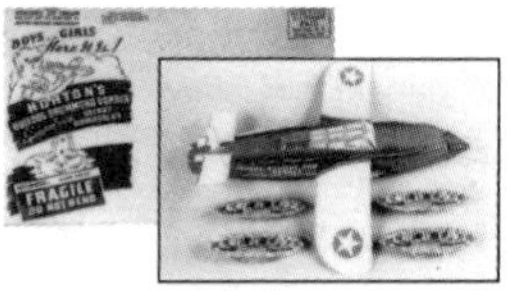

RAD-52

❑ **RAD-51. "The Aldrich Family" Schedule Sheet,**
c. 1940. Jell-O Puddings. Picture sheet of Ezra Stone as Henry Aldrich of NBC radio comedy series with listing on reverse of more than 75 stations coast to coast offering Thursday evening episode. - **$12 $20 $30**

❑ **RAD-52. "Horton's Bulldog Drummond Bomber",**
c. 1941. Cardboard punch-out that releases marble bombs onto four small battleships.
Near Mint In Mailer - **$400**
Used - **$75 $150 $225**

RAD-53

RAD-54

❑ **RAD-53. "The Sea Hound" Paper Map,**
1942. Blue Network. Pictures "Captain Silver's Sea Chart". - **$35 $75 $125**

❑ **RAD-54. "David Harum" Seed Packets,**
1943. Jermin Seed & Plant Co., Los Angeles. Contents are actual flower seeds "Packed For Season Of 1943". Each - **$5 $15 $25**

RAD-55

❑ **RAD-55. "Adventures of the Thin Man" Promo Postcard,**
1943. From CBS show. - **$30 $60 $120**

RAD-56

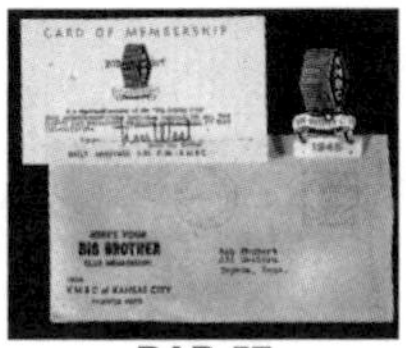


RAD-57

❑ **RAD-56. WFBL Radio Stars Cook Book With Mailer,**
1945. Featured Aunt Jenny, Lionel Barrymore, Milton Berle, Fanny Brice, Major Bowes, Burns & Allen, Danny Kaye, Frank Sinatra, and many others. - **$25 $40 $75**

❑ **RAD-57. Big Brother Radio Kit with Mailer,**
1945. KMBC radio, Kansas City, Kansas. - **$25 $50 $100**

RAD-58

❑ **RAD-58. Ruth Lyons Song Sheet,**
1946. Contains "The Nu-Maid Song" and "The Birthday Song" from Ruth Lyons, the star of "Morning Matinee" radio program on WLW and WINS stations. Nu-Maid was a sponsor of the show. - **$10 $20 $35**

RAD-59

❑ **RAD-59. "The Mel Blanc Show" Radio Program Ticket,**
1946. Sponsored by Colgate. - **$10 $20 $40**

RAD-60

❑ **RAD-60. "The Whistler" Blotter Card,**
1947. Household Finance Corp. Cardboard ink blotter for weekly drama suspense detective program. Pictured examples are imprinted for WBBM Radio, Chicago. - **$50 $120 $200**
CKAC Radio, Montreal. - **$75 $180 $290**

RAD-61

❑ **RAD-61. NBC "On The Air" Comic Book,**
1947. National Broadcasting Co. Full color 16-page illustrated description of network operations. Photo example shows front cover and final frame of story. - **$20 $60 $150**

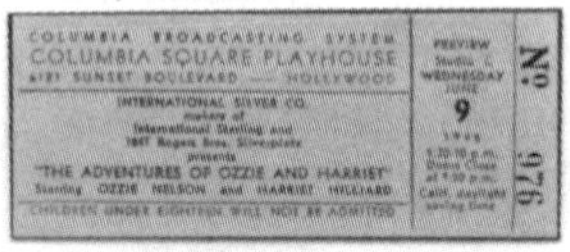


RAD-62

❑ **RAD-62. "The Adventures Of Ozzie And Harriet" Radio Program Ticket,**
1948. - **$10 $20 $50**

RAD-63

RAD-64

❑ **RAD-63. Texaco Star Theater Sign,**
1940s. 13x9-1/2" sign for ABC radio show featured famous stars. - **$25 $60 $100**

❑ **RAD-64. "Cowboy Thrills Club" Premium Pinback,**
1940s. Sponsored by Everybody's & Admiral radio products. Scarce. - **$15 $50 $100**

RAD-65

RAD-66

❑ **RAD-65. Spike Jones Souvenir Program,**
1949. 16 page program premium for RCA. - **$15 $25 $50**

❑ **RAD-66. "David Harum Handprint" Folder,**
c. 1940s. Bab-o Cleanser. Cover pictures "Homeville" community and cast members, inside "Handprint" is apparent clue to ongoing serial mystery. - **$10 $15 $25**

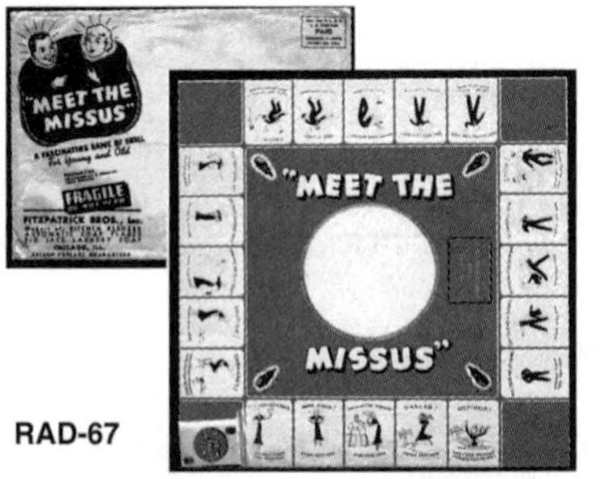


RAD-67

❑ **RAD-67. "Meet The Missus" Radio Game & Mailer,**
1940s. Automatic Soap Flakes. 48 cards and 19"x19" playing paper board with mailer. - **$65 $125 $200**

RAD-68

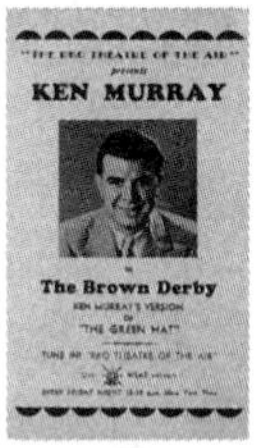


RAD-69

❑ **RAD-68. Dinah Shore Postcard,**
1940s. Promotes her RCA radio show "Up In Arms." - **$15 $30 $50**

❑ **RAD-69. Ken Murray Promo - NBC Radio,**
1940s. The Brown Derby. "RKO Theatre of the Air" program review. - **$15 $25 $35**

RAD-70

RAD-71

❑ **RAD-70. Radio Syd & Suzie's Scrapbook,**
1940s. Gas & Electric radio premium. Shows photo of cast. - **$10 $20 $30**

❑ **RAD-71. Captain Hal's Membership Card,**
1940s. Radio Rangers premium for radio show. - **$10 $20 $40**

RAD-72

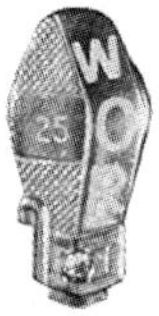
RAD-73

❑ **RAD-72. Big Jon Arthur & Sparkie Fan Card,**
1950s. American Broadcasting Corp. - **$15 $25 $50**

❑ **RAD-73. WOR Radio 25 Year Anniversary Gold Tie Tack,**
1950s. Gold Tie Tack with diamond set in radio mike. - **$150**

RAD-74

RAD-75

❑ **RAD-74. "War of the Worlds" Album,**
1950s. Radio broadcast of the invasion from Mars. Album and record. - **$30 $50 $65**

❑ **RAD-75. "When Radio Was King" Album,**
1972. Features big-name radio stars, entertainment highlights, and news reports. Premium from Reader's Digest. RCA Custom Record. - **$25 $50 $100**

RAD-76

RAD-77

❑ **RAD-76. "Radio Super Heroes At War" Album,**
1975. - **$15 $25 $50**

❑ **RAD-77. "Mallard Stern" Bean Bag,**
1998. Famous Meanies series with tag. - **$10**

## The Range Rider

**An early 1950s television weekly series, *The Range Rider* starred Jock Mahoney in the title role and Dick Jones as his youthful sidekick Dick West. The two wandered the West, apparently for the sole purpose of correcting local injustices. Both actors were accomplished stuntmen, a skill well displayed in each episode. The show was produced by Gene Autry's Flying A Productions and ran 1951-1953 on CBS-TV before syndication. Premiums were issued by bread companies in addition to non-premium coloring books and Dell comic books.**

RAN-1

❑ **RAN-1. "Range Rider" Picture,**
c. 1951. Issued by local sponsor Bueter's Butter-Krust Bread, Hannibal, Missouri. Color paper photo. - **$20 $50 $75**

RAN-2

RAN-3

❑ **RAN-2. Langendorf Bread Photo,**
c. 1951. - **$8 $15 $30**

❑ **RAN-3. Sunbeam Bread "Range Rider's Brand" Cello. Button,**
c. 1951. Pictures Jock Mahoney. - **$20 $50 $75**

RAN-4

RAN-5

❑ **RAN-4. "TV Guide Cowboy Album" Celluloid Covered Wall Plaque,**
1953. From series of TV Guide promotional plaques sent to stations. - **$50 $75 $150**

❑ **RAN-5. Cello. Button 2-1/4",**
1950s. Peter Pan Bread. - **$25 $65 $125**

RAN-6

❑ **RAN-6. "Range Rider" Pair Of Children's Cowboy Boots,**
1950s. Store item by Built-Wel Footwear. - **$50 $100 $150**

RAN-7

RAN-8

❑ **RAN-7. Bread Loaf End Paper,**
1950s. Issued by Langendorf Bread. Sepia photo on yellow background. - **$15 $40 $65**

❑ **RAN-8. "Range Rider" Bread Label Sheet,**
1950s. Bueter's Butterkrust Bread. Opens to 11x17" to hold 16 labels. - **$25 $60 $125**

RAN-9

RAN-10

❑ **RAN-9. Philadelphia TV Program Promotion Card,**
1950s. Pictures Jock Mahoney, Sally Starr and Gene Autry. Back has an offer for Oldsmobile "Wild West Fun And Game Booklet". - **$8 $15 $35**

❑ **RAN-10. "Range Rider's Brand" Cello. Button,**
1950s. No sponsor's names appear but there is space around the bottom rim for an imprint. 1-1/4" bw photo on dark red. - **$25 $60 $100**

RAN-11

RAN-12

❑ **RAN-11. ButterKrust Bread Label Folder,**
1950s. Opens to 11x17" for mounting 16 labels. - **$25 $60 $125**

❑ **RAN-12. "The Range Rider And Dick West" Mini-Flashlight,**
1950s. Store item by Bantam Lite. Metal case with plastic cap plus vinyl carrying cord. - **$15 $40 $75**

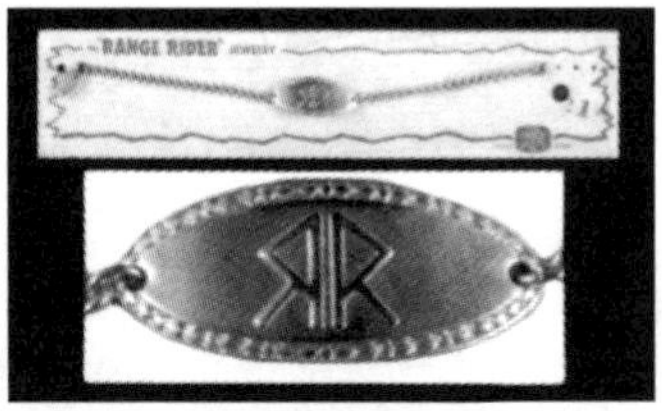
RAN-13

❑ **RAN-13. "Range Rider" Bracelet On Card,**
1950s. Store item. Carded - **$25 $50 $100**
Bracelet Only - **$15 $35 $60**

RAN-14

❑ **RAN-14. Member's Card,**
1950s. Peter Pan Peanut Butter. 2-1/2x3-3/4" lightly textured stiff brown paper identifying "Junior Range Rider" and with facsimile signature of "Dick West," the Range Rider's sidekick. - **$30 $75 $125**

# Ranger Joe

**Ranger Joe Honnies began in 1939, a creation of Jim Rex for the Philadelphia area. A new owner extended distribution throughout the east and south, operating as Ranger Joe, Inc. from Chester, Pennsylvania, a suburb southwest of Philadelphia. Despite this limited Western exposure, the cereal box depicted him as an authentic cowboy with horse; glassware premiums of "Ranch Mug" and cereal bowl repeated his image plus cowboy scenes. The other known Ranger Joe premium is a wood and cardboard gun designed for shooting rubber bands. Product and premiums were apparently tied into local telecasts of *Ranger Joe*, a 1951-1952 NBC-TV Saturday morning adventure show for youngsters.**

**Rice Honnies joined the original Wheat Honnies product in 1951 and both are considered among the forerunners of coated cereals. Nabisco bought the company in 1954 replacing Ranger Joe with Buffalo Bee, changing Honnies to Honeys and initiating national distribution.**

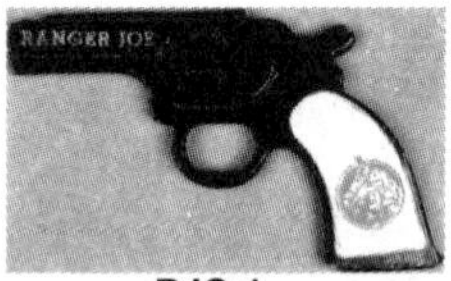

RJO-1

RJO-2

❑ **RJO-1. Rubber Band Cardboard Gun,**
c. 1940s. - **$25 $75 $150**

❑ **RJO-2. "Ranger Joe Honeyville Air Field Hangar" Cereal Box Back,**
c. 1950. Complete Box - **$25 $60 $100**
Back Panel Uncut - **$5 $15 $25**
Each Plastic Plane - **$3 $5 $10**

RJO-3

❑ **RJO-3. Cereal Ad Poster,**
1951. 12x16-1/2" in navy blue. - **$15 $30 $50**

RJO-4

RJO-5

❑ **RJO-4. "Ranger Joe's Western Manual,"**
1951. Promotes "Ranger Joe Popped Wheat" product. - **$15 $25 $40**

❑ **RJO-5. Fan Card,**
c. 1951. - **$8 $12 $25**

RJO-6

RJO-7

❑ **RJO-6. Glass Cup,**
c. 1951. Blue & red. - **$5 $10 $15**

❑ **RJO-7. Glass Cereal Bowl,**
c. 1951. Blue & red. - **$8 $15 $25**

RJO-8

RJO-9

❑ **RJO-8. "Ranger Joe & Topaz" Patch,**
1951. - **$20 $50 $85**

❑ **RJO-9. "Ranger Joe Ranch Money" Premium Currency Bill,**
1952. Ranger Joe Cereal. Box insert to be accumulated for ordering premiums pictured on reverse. - **$5 $8 $15**

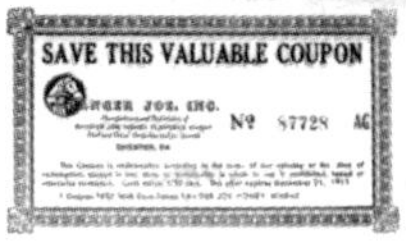

RJO-10

RJO-11

❑ **RJO-10. Free Gift Coupon,**
1952. - **$5 $8 $15**

❑ **RJO-11. "Wheat Honnies" Cereal Box,**
1950s. Complete Box - **$35 $65 $130**

# Red Ryder

**Artist Fred Harman created the *Red Ryder* comic strip as a Sunday feature in 1938 and added a daily version the following year. The strip, which ran until the late 1960s, told the story of rancher Ryder and his Navajo ward Little Beaver as they ranged the West of the 1890s, battling bandits and rustlers and settling frontier quarrels. Comic book reprints first appeared in 1939 and continued through most of the 1950s, and more than 20 "B" Westerns from Hollywood chronicled the popular hero's adventures. A radio series aired on the Mutual network--primarily on the West Coast--from early 1942 to 1949, sponsored by Langendorf bread and other bakeries. A television adaptation was syndicated in 1956. The Red Ryder character was used extensively for many years to promote Daisy air rifles.**

RYD-1

❑ **RYD-1. Red Ryder Target Game with Box,**
1939. Store item. - **$75 $200 $400**

RYD-2

❑ **RYD-2. "Red Ryder And Little Beaver On Hoofs Of Thunder" Better Little Book,**
1939. Whitman #1400. - **$15 $40 $90**

RYD-3

❑ **RYD-3. "Daisy Air Rifles" Catalogue,**
1940. Near Mint In Mailer - **$300**
Loose - **$50 $125 $200**

RYD-4

❑ **RYD-4. "Red Ryder And Western Border Guns" Better Little Book,**
1942. Whitman #1450. - **$15 $50 $100**

RYD-5 RYD-6

❑ **RYD-5. Victory Patrol Member Card,**
1943. Included in membership kit. Back has Red Ryder radio listings. - **$20 $50 $90**

❑ **RYD-6. Victory Patrol Magic V-Badge,**
1943. Scarce. Luminous cardboard badge. Ordered by sending coupon from membership kit. - **$50 $150 $350**

RYD-7

❑ **RYD-7. Membership Kit Promotion Sheet for Magic V-Badge,**
1943. Example shown has coupon to order and membership card trimmed off the bottom.
As Shown - **$20 $50 $90**

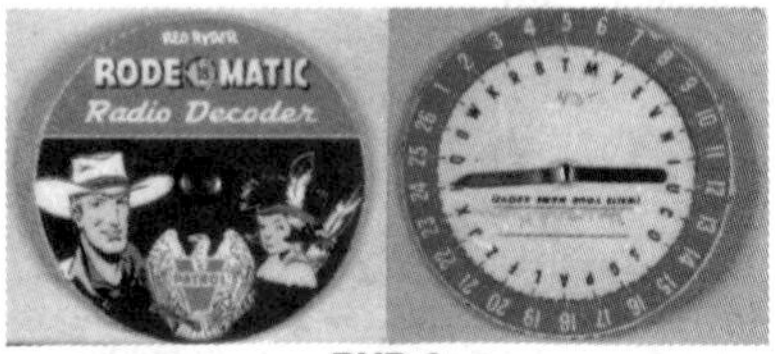


RYD-8

❑ **RYD-8. "Rodeomatic Radio Decoder",**
c. 1943. Rare. Cut out and assembled from "Victory Patrol" kit.
Assembled - **$200 $400 $600**

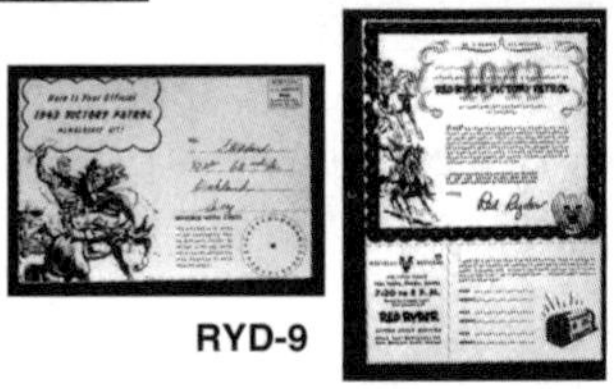

RYD-9

❑ **RYD-9. Victory Patrol Membership Kit With Comic,**
1943. Langendorf Bread. Scarce. Includes cut-out "Rodeomatic" decoder, order coupon for "Magic V-Badge", cut-out membership card and membership certificate, comic book.
Complete - **$421 $1475 $4200**

RYD-10

RYD-11

❑ **RYD-10. "Victory Patrol" Paper Store Signs,**
1944. Scarce. Langendorf Bread. Larger sign 7x15", smaller oval 4x5".
Picture Sign - **$50 $150 $250**
Oval Sign - **$20 $65 $100**

❑ **RYD-11. "Red Ryder Victory Patrol" Copper Luster Metal Badge,**
1944. - **$40 $100 $200**

RYD-12

❑ **RYD-12. Victory Patrol Membership Kit With Comic,**
1944. Scarce. Includes membership card, map, comic book, code card and regular cards. Complete - **$400 $1400 $4200**

RYD-13

RYD-14

❑ **RYD-13. Postcard,**
1944. Langendorf Bread. Promotes Red Ryder Victory Patrol comic book and shows how to get other premiums. - **$25 $50 $75**

❑ **RYD-14. "Bobby Blake/Little Beaver" Dixie Ice Cream Picture,**
1945. - **$25 $40 $75**

RYD-15

RYD-16

❑ **RYD-15. "War On The Range" BLB,**
1945. Better Little Book #1473. - **$10 $40 $90**

❑ **RYD-16. "Red Ryder and the Squaw-Tooth Rustlers" BLB,**
1946. Big Little Book #1414. - **$10 $40 $90**

RYD-17

RYD-18

❑ **RYD-17. "Red Ryder and Circus Luck" BLB,**
1947. Big Little Book #1466. - **$10 $40 $90**

❑ **RYD-18. "Red Ryder and the Rimrock Killer" BLB,**
1948. Big Little Book #1443. - **$10 $40 $90**

RYD-19

RYD-20

❑ **RYD-19. "Red Ryder and the Secret Canyon" BLB,**
1948. Big Little Book #1454. Harman art. - **$10 $40 $90**

❑ **RYD-20. Air Rifle Safety Litho. Button,** c. 1948. Daisy Mfg. Co. Given with Red Ryder rifle and handbook. - **$10 $18 $30**

RYD-21

❑ **RYD-21. "Daisy Handbook No. 2",**
1948. - **$35 $125 $275**

RYD-22

❑ **RYD-22. "Red Ryder Secret Pocket Billfold" Box,**
1949. Box - **$20 $40 $75**
Wallet (Not Shown) - **$35 $75 $100**

RYD-23

❑ **RYD-23. Pocketknife,**
1940s. Store item by Camco USA. Steel with plastic grips. - **$75 $150 $250**

RYD-24

RYD-25

❑ **RYD-24. "Red Ryder Fighting Cowboy" Certificate,**
c. 1940s. Wells Lamont Corp., maker of Red Ryder gloves. Text details 10 qualities of character for youthful members. - **$30 $75 $125**

❑ **RYD-25. Salesman's Fiberboard Glove Case,**
1940s. Wells-Lamont Co. - **$100 $225 $325**

RYD-26

RYD-27

❑ **RYD-26. Radio Sponsor Handbill,**
1940s. N.B.C. Bread, probably others. Imprint includes local broadcast times. - **$35 $60 $125**

❑ **RYD-27. "Red Ryder" Cello. Button,**
1940s. - **$15 $40 $75**

RYD-28

RYD-29

RYD-30

❑ **RYD-28. "Little Beaver" Cello. Button,**
1940s. - **$15 $35 $65**

❑ **RYD-29. "Red Ryder Patrol" Silvered Metal Badge,**
1940s. - **$30 $85 $150**

❑ **RYD-30. "I Have Entered The Red Ryder Pony Contest" Litho. Button,**
1940s. - **$8 $15 $25**

RYD-31

RYD-32

RYD-33

❑ **RYD-31. Penney's "Red Ryder Lucky Coin",**
1940s. J. C. Penney Co. Brass, holed for key-chain. Back slogan "Penney's For Super Value". - **$8 $12 $20**

❑ **RYD-32. "Red Ryder Gloves" Silvered Tin Whistle,**
1940s. Wells-Lamont Co. - **$35 $75 $150**

❑ **RYD-33. "Red Ryder Gloves/Red Ryder Sheriff" Silvered Metal Star Badge,**
1940s. Probable Wells-Lamont Co. - **$60 $150 $250**

RYD-34

❑ **RYD-34. Red Ryder/Little Beaver Fan Card,**
c. 1950. Fred Harman art. - **$10 $20 $40**

RYD-35

❑ **RYD-35. "Howdy Compadre" Photo and Letter,**
1950. Langendorf Bread. 5x7" photo with "Dear Compadre" letter as a thank-you for promising to eat Langendorf Bread.
Mailer - **$5 $15 $25**
Letter - **$15 $30 $50**
Photo - **$25 $50 $75**

RYD-36

❑ **RYD-36. "Little Beaver Buffalo Gun" Toy,**
c. 1950. Daisy Mfg. Co. 19" long. - **$35 $85 $150**

RYD-37

❑ **RYD-37. Trading Cards Sheet,**
1952. Wells-Lamont Corp.
Uncut. - **$15 $35 $65**

RYD-38

❑ **RYD-38. "Daisy Gun Book",**
1955. Daisy Mfg. Co. - **$25 $100 $175**

RYD-39

❑ **RYD-39. "Little Beaver's Complete 3 Game Set For Boys & Girls",**
1956. Store item by Red Ryder Enterprises. 6x11" box holds single board with three games plus accessories of six punch-out markers and pair of dice. - **$20 $40 $75**

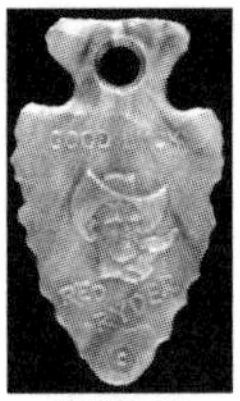

RYD-40

RYD-41

❑ **RYD-40. "Good Luck/Red Ryder" Plastic Arrowhead Keychain Charm,**
1955. Daisy Mfg. Co. - **$35 $80 $160**

❑ **RYD-41. Contest Prize Figure Set,**
1956. One of 100 second place prizes in Wells Lamont contest for selling Red Ryder gloves. Plastic horse has "Red Ryder" name on each side of red saddle blanket and "Wells Lamont Co." on inner side of horse's rear leg. Indian also has company name on seat with design identical to Chief Thunderbird figure by Hartland Plastics Co. Includes accessories of war bonnet, tomahawk and knife.
Figure Complete - **$50 $125 $175**
Generic Mailing Box - **$15 $25 $50**

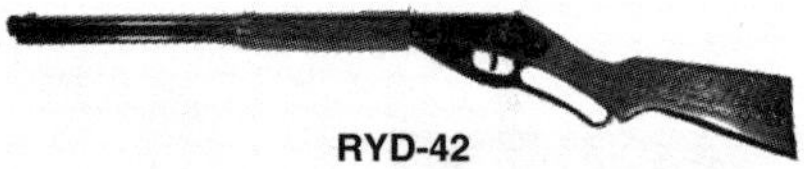

RYD-42

❑ **RYD-42. "Daisy Red Ryder BB Gun",**
1950s. - **$75 $175 $350**

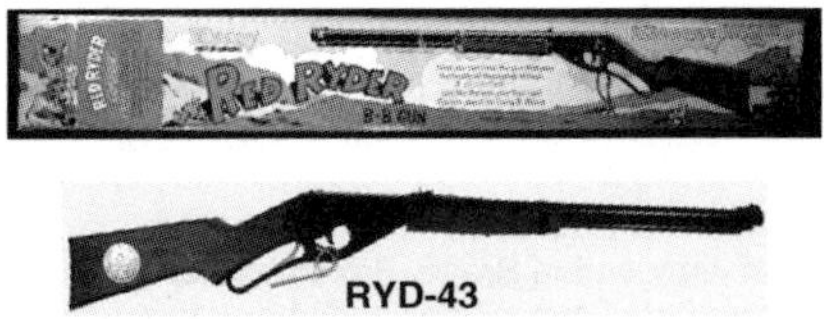

RYD-43

❑ **RYD-43. "Daisy Red Ryder Commemorative BB Gun with Box",**
1990s. Gun has medal in the stock. Set includes reprint of the Red Ryder comic book's first issue. - **$150**

RYD-44

❑ **RYD-44. "Daisy Red Ryder Commemorative BB Gun with Box",**
2000. Model commemorates old issue of rifle. Has flat snub nose which is different than old model. New box design. - **$100**

# Reddy Kilowatt

**The friendly little fellow with a lightbulb for a nose and a lightning-bolt torso was created in 1926 by A.B. Collins of the Alabama Power Company. Designed to personify the electric power industry, Reddy was licensed freely to**

**local power companies for promotional use, and his image has adorned a wide variety of items from ashtrays to soap, pinback buttons to comic books. A competing figure, Willie Wiredhand, was created in 1951 by the National Rural Electric Cooperative.**

**RKL-1**

❑ **RKL-1. Counter Display Early Figure,**
c. 1935. 12" tall wood. - **$100 $200 $300**

**RKL-2**

**RKL-3**

❑ **RKL-2. Early Silvered Metal Badge With Red Accent,**
c. 1938. - **$50 $100 $150**

❑ **RKL-3. Glass Bubble Bank With Wood Base,**
c. 1940. 6" diameter glass dome holds diecut thick cardboard figure of Reddy. Base reads "Reddy Kilowatt Says: Bank On Electric Cooking To Save Your Money." - **$150 $300 $500**

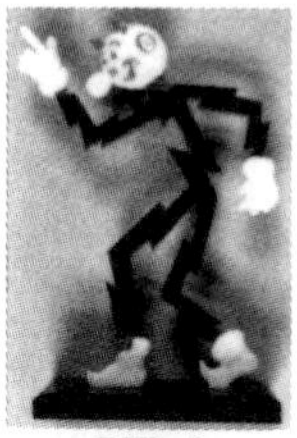

**RKL-4**

**RKL-5**

❑ **RKL-4. Translucent Plastic Figure,**
1940s. Earliest design style.
Pink - **$85 $150 $250**
1950s-60s design style.
Red - **$75 $125 $200**

❑ **RKL-5. "25th Anniversary Public Service" Cello. Button,**
1951. Public Service Co. of New Hampshire. - **$20 $40 $75**

**RKL-6**

❑ **RKL-6. "Your Favorite Pin-Up" Enameled Brass Pin On Card,**
1952. On Card - **$10 $15 $20**
Loose - **$3 $5 $10**

**RKL-7**

**RKL-8**

❑ **RKL-7. "Light's Diamond Jubilee" Cello. Button,**
1954. - **$25 $65 $100**

❑ **RKL-8. Cuff Links,**
c. 1950s. Color image under glass dome with brass frame and shaft. - **$20 $40 $85**

**RKL-9**

**RKL-10**

❑ **RKL-9. Fabric 8-1/2x11" Jacket Patch,**
1950s. Diecut flannel with stitched fabric image of Reddy Kilowatt as bowler. - **$35 $75 $125**

❑ **RKL-10. Cello. Button,**
c. 1950s. Canadian. - **$20 $50 $80**

**RKL-11**

❑ **RKL-11. Plastic Cookie Cutter With Card,**
c. 1950s. Boxed - **$10 $20 $35**
Loose - **$5 $15 $20**

**RKL-12**

❑ **RKL-12. "The Mighty Atom" Comic Book,**
1950s. Back cover may designate sponsoring electric utility company. - **$2 $6 $20**

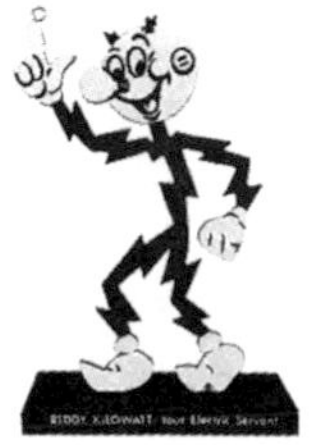

**RKL-13**

**RKL-14**

❑ **RKL-13. Service Counter Figure,**
c. 1950s. 11" tall jigsawed wood figure in finished image both sides and wire spring clip on raised fingertip for holding card or leaflet. - **$125 $250 $400**

❑ **RKL-14. Figural Vinyl Bank,**
c. 1960. 3-1/2x5-1/2" tall by 6-1/2" wide 3-D image of him dashing through clouds with coin slot in rear, trap in bottom.
Near Mint With Both Plastic Lightning Bolt Head Accents - **$1000**
Missing Accents - **$150 $300 $500**

**RKL-15**

**RKL-16**

**RKL-17**

❑ **RKL-15. Glow-In-The-Dark Plastic Figure,**
1961. 1961 copyright on base. - **$50 $85 $135**

❑ **RKL-16. "Reddy" Composition Bobbing Head,**
1960s. - **$250 $400 $750**

❑ **RKL-17. Employee Bowling Trophy,**
1960s. Metal figure and award plate on wood base. - **$250 $450 $750**

**RKL-18**

❑ **RKL-18. Night Light,**
1960s. Relief image of Reddy with miniature light bulb nose. - **$15 $25 $50**

RKL-19

RKL-20

❑ **RKL-19. "Courteous Personal Attention To Every Customer" Litho. Button,**
1960s. - **$15 $25 $50**

❑ **RKL-20. Hard Plastic Electric Alarm Clock,**
1960s. Inscribed "Compliments of Philadelphia Light and Electric." - **$35 $85 $175**

RKL-21

RKL-22

❑ **RKL-21. "Inspectors Club Big Rock Point Nuclear Plant",**
1970s. Consumers Power Company. -
**$10 $15 $25**

❑ **RKL-22. "Mod Power" Litho. Tin Button,**
1970s. About 1-3/8" green and white on fuchsia background. - **$15 $30 $50**

RKL-23

❑ **RKL-23. Wacky Wobbler Figure,**
2000. Boxed. - **$25**

## Renfrew of the Mounted

**Inspector Douglas Renfrew of the Royal Canadian Mounties, the hero of a dozen adventure novels by Laurie York Erskine, came to CBS radio in 1936. Sponsored by Wonder bread for two years, the series then moved to the Blue network, where it was sustained until it went off the air in 1940. Renfrew movies, produced by Grand National Pictures and Monogram in the late 1930s and early 1940s, were edited into 30-minute tales for television syndication in 1953. While he lasted, the strong, silent Renfrew always got his man.**

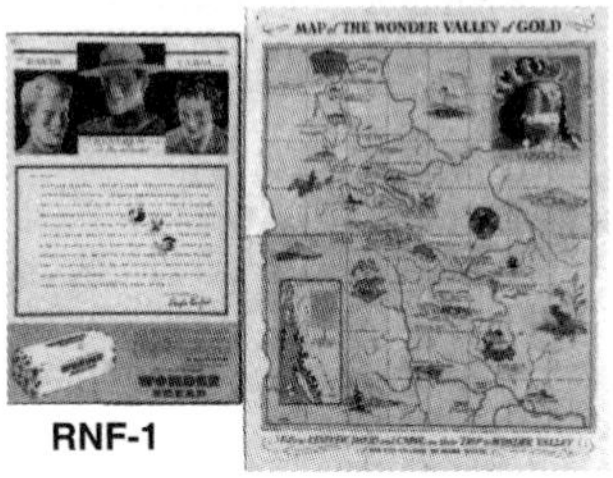


RNF-1

❑ **RNF-1. "Renfrew Of The Mounted" 17x22" Premium Map,**
1936. Wonder Bread. - **$40 $75 $140**

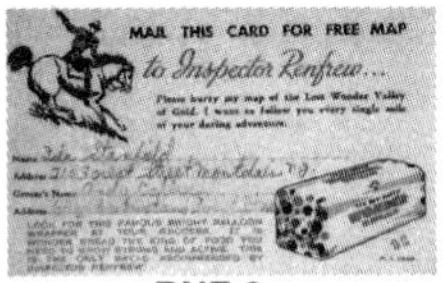


RNF-2

RNF-3

❑ **RNF-2. "Lost Wonder Valley Of Gold" Map Order Postcard,**
1936. Wonder Bread. Used to order previous item. - **$10 $20 $35**

❑ **RNF-3. "Around The Camp Fire With Carol And David" Leaflet,**
c. 1936. Wonder Bread. Illustrated magic tricks including "Tricks That Fooled Renfrew". -
**$12 $20 $35**

RNF-4

❑ **RNF-4. Renfrew Sign 9 1/2 x 20",**
1936. Wonder Bread. Promotes radio show. -
**$50 $100 $200**

RNF-5

❑ **RNF-5. Renfrew Radio Sponsor Folder,**
c. 1936. Wonder Bread. Four-page ad leaflet with mention on back for daily radio show. -
**$10 $15 $25**

RNF-6

❑ **RNF-6. Fan Postcard,**
c. 1936. Wonder Bread. - **$20 $40 $65**

RNF-7

❑ **RNF-7. Renfrew Adventure Store Window Signs,**
c. 1936. Wonder Bread. Paper "Wanted" and "Missing" posters, each 11x17" from radio episode "The Sunken City Of The Arctic."
Each - **$15 $40 $85**

RNF-8

❑ **RNF-8. Radio Program Debut Folder,**
c. 1936. Columbia Broadcasting System. Four-page leaflet previewing "Coming Thrills" plus mention of premium map and member badge.
Card Only - **$25 $50 $85**

RNF-9

RNF-10

❑ **RNF-9. Wonder Bread Radio Show Paper Sign 10x17",**
c. 1936. - **$50 $140 $275**

❑ **RNF-10. "Renfrew Of The Mounted" Cello. Button,**
c. 1936. Wonder Bread. - **$3 $6 $12**

RNF-11

❑ **RNF-11. One-Sheet Movie Poster,**
1940. Criterion Pictures. 27x41" showing James Newill as Renfrew. - **$75 $125 $200**

## Rin-Tin-Tin

**The Wonder Dog was introduced to the world by Warner Brothers in 1923 and the talented German shepherd, an instant success, proved to be the studio's first major film star. There were a number of Rintys over the years, but the canine hero consistently battled villains and the elements, rescued those in danger, preserved his good name, turned into a noteworthy "actor"--and saved the studio from bankruptcy. Rinty starred in 19 films for Warner Brothers between 1923 and 1930, and went on to make a series of chapter plays for the Mascot studios.**

**On radio, *Rin-Tin-Tin* aired on the Blue network (1930-1933) and CBS (1933-1934), sponsored by Ken-L-Ration, and returned for a season on the Mutual network in 1955, sponsored by Milk Bone.**

**On television, Rinty joined young Corporal Rusty and the troopers of the 101st Cavalry, the Fighting Blue Devils, in maintaining law and order in the West of the 1880s. The hit series, sponsored by the National Biscuit Company, aired in prime time on ABC from 1954 to 1959 and was the source of a wide variety of premiums and licensed products. Reruns were broadcast on ABC (1959 to 1961) and CBS (1962 to 1964), and sepia-tinted episodes were offered briefly for syndication in 1976. Comic books appeared during most of the 1950s and early 1960s.**

RIN-1

RIN-2

❑ **RIN-1. "King Of Canines" Button,**
c. 1930. 1-1/2" black and white with title applying to his fame rather than a movie title. - **$15 $35 $75**

❑ **RIN-2. Movie Promotional Button,**
1930. 7/8" brown on yellow. - **$10 $25 $50**

RIN-3

RIN-4

❑ **RIN-3. "The Lone Defender" Cello. Button,**
1930. For Mascot Pictures 12-chapter movie serial. - **$15 $35 $75**

❑ **RIN-4. "The Lightning Warrior" Movie Serial Cello. Button,**
1931. Mascot Pictures. Comes in 7/8" or 1-1/4" sizes. - **$15 $25 $50**

RIN-5

RIN-6

❑ **RIN-5. Fan Club Pin-Back,**
1931. Warner Bros. 1-1/4" with color portrait plus diecut cardboard attachment forming his body. Complete - **$40 $75 $125**
Pin-Back Only, No Body - **$20 $40 $75**

❑ **RIN-6. "Rin-Tin-Tin In An All Talking Serial The Lightning Warrior" Movie Herald,**
1931. - **$10 $20 $40**

RIN-7

RIN-8

❑ **RIN-7. Ken-L-Ration Photo,**
1931. - **$8 $12 $25**

❑ **RIN-8. Fan Club Notice,**
1931. Flyer for button premium - **$20 $40 $65**

RIN-9

RIN-10

❑ **RIN-9. Photo With Mailer,**
1931. Fan Club movie premium. Photo of two dogs. - **$15 $30 $60**

❑ **RIN-10. "What Every Dog Should Know" Booklet,**
c. 1931. Ken-L-Ration. - **$12 $20 $40**

RIN-11

RIN-12

❑ **RIN-11. Advertising Litho. Button,**
1930s. Atwater Kent Radios. - **$25 $50 $85**

❑ **RIN-12. Rin Tin Tin III Postcard,**
1940s. Premium promotes Camp Haan Training Center. - **$10 $20 $35**

RIN-13

❑ **RIN-13. Club Membership Kit,**
1954. Nabisco. Includes fabric banner, membership card, white metal badge.
Complete Near Mint - **$400**
Banner - **$60 $100 $200**
Card - **$10 $25 $50**
Badge - **$20 $60 $85**

RIN-14

RIN-15

❑ **RIN-14. Shredded Wheat Box,**
1954. Nabisco. Lt. Rip Masters on front. Offers insignia patch. Back of box shows picture of all seven patches. - **$50 $100 $175**

❑ **RIN-15. Shredded Wheat Box,**
1954. Nabisco. Shows Rin Tin Tin and Rusty on front. Back shows cast and promotes radio and TV show. - **$50 $100 $175**

RIN-16

RIN-17

❑ **RIN-16. Nabisco "Wonda-Scope",**
c. 1954. Components include compass, mirror, magnifying lenses. Dial marked "Rin-Tin-Tin". - **$20 $40 $75**

❑ **RIN-17. "Bugle Calls" Vinyl Cardboard Record,**
c. 1954. Nabisco. Came with plastic bugle premium. - **$15 $25 $40**

RIN-18

❑ **RIN-18. Stereo Cards With Viewer,**
1954. Nabisco. Set of 24 cards.
Viewer - **$10 $20 $35**
Card Set - **$30 $50 $80**

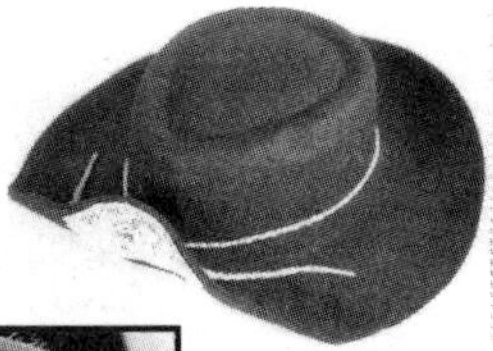

RIN-19

❑ **RIN-19. Felt Cavalry Hat,**
c. 1954. Nabisco. Fabric patch on brim front. - **$50 $115 $175**

RIN-20

❑ **RIN-20. Magic Brass Ring,**
c. 1954. Nabisco. Portrait cover opens over two miniature felt pads. Came with magic pencil and chemically treated paper strips.
Complete - **$200 $350 $600**
Ring Only - **$50 $100 $200**
Magic Pencil Only - **$40 $105 $170**
Instructions Only - **$110 $135 $150**

RIN-21

RIN-22

❑ **RIN-21. Nabisco Plastic Rings,**
1955. Set of 12: Cochise, Cpl. Boone, Fort Apache, Geronimo, Lt. Rip Masters, Major Swanson, Rin-Tin-Tin (front view), Rin-Tin-Tin (side view), Rinty & Rusty, Rusty, Rusty's Horse, and Sgt. Biff O'Hara.
Each - **$10 $15 $25**

❑ **RIN-22. Nabisco Cast Photo,**
c. 1955. - **$10 $20 $35**

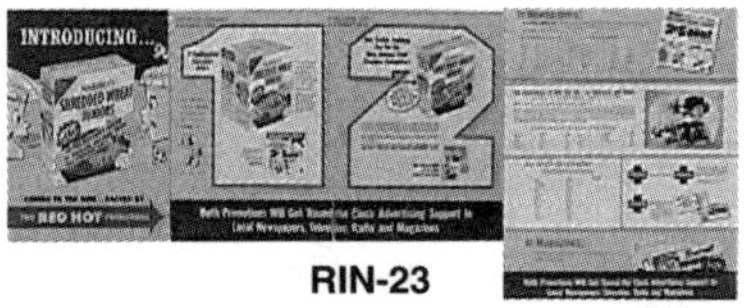


RIN-23

❑ **RIN-23. Nabisco Cereal Promotion Folder,**
c. 1955. 9x12-3/4" folder opens to 18x23" printed largely in yellow, red, white and blue. Urges grocer participation in publicity program tied to Rin-Tin-Tin popularity. Shows example window poster and shelf card picturing the Rin-Tin-Tin plastic premium rings. Gordon Gold Archives. - **$50 $75 $150**

RIN-24

❑ **RIN-24. Cereal Box With Plastic Rings Offer,**
1955. Gordon Gold Archives.
Used Complete - **$50 $150 $300**

RIN-25

❑ **RIN-25. "Rusty's Golden Bugle" Box With Bugle And Attachment,**
1955. Store item by Spec-Toy-Culars. Set includes "Bugle Book" instructions.
Near Mint Complete - **$300**

RIN-26

❑ **RIN-26. "Rusty" Boxed Costume,**
c. 1955. Store item by Ben Cooper.
Near Mint Boxed - **$150**
Mask And Costume Only - **$25 $50 $100**

RIN-27

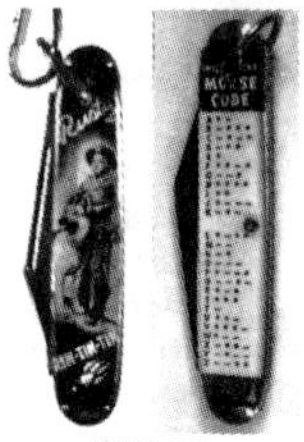

RIN-28

❑ **RIN-27. Jack Knife Store Display Card,**
1955. - **$40 $75 $150**

❑ **RIN-28. Plastic On Steel Pocketknife,**
c. 1955. Store item. - **$25 $70 $150**

(BOARD)

RIN-29

❑ **RIN-29. "Adventures of RinTinTin" Game,**
1956. Transogram Product. Has colorful board and pieces. - **$50 $100 $150**

RIN-30

RIN-31

❑ **RIN-30. English Postcard,**
c. 1955. - **$10 $20 $30**

❑ **RIN-31. "Rusty" Tin/Plastic Palm Puzzle,**
1956. From "Nabisco Juniors" set of 12: Army Wagon, Cochise, Conestoga Wagon, Fighting Blue Devils 101st Cavalry, Geronimo, Lt. Rip Masters, 101st Cavalry Trooper, Rinty & Rusty, RIn-Tin-Tin (close-up portrait), Rin-Tin-Tin (full body portrait), Rusty ("Go Rinty!"), and Sgt. Biff O'Hara. Each - **$7 $12 $20**

RIN-32

❑ **RIN-32. Cereal Box With Cut-Out Mask,**
1956. This is "Series 1" from a set of six to be cut from box back panels.
Each Used Complete Box - **$50 $125 $175**

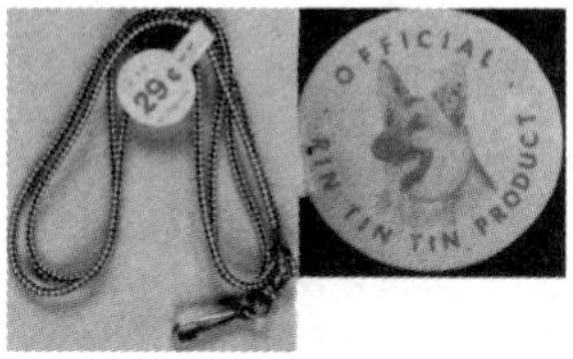


RIN-33

❑ **RIN-33. "Rin-Tin-Tin" Dog Leash,**
1956. Store item. - **$10 $25 $40**

RIN-34

❑ **RIN-34. Sweatshirt With Box Insert Offer Card,**
1956. Heavy cotton with 6x9-1/2" image area. Card insert is green ink on gray cardboard offering shirt for one box top plus $1.
Shirt - **$75 $200 $350**
Card - **$3 $6 $12**

RIN-35

RIN-36

❑ **RIN-35. Club Member's Cello. Button,**
c. 1956. Dairy Fresh. 1-1/2" black on cream. - **$25 $65 $100**

❑ **RIN-36. Gun And Holster,**
1956. Nabisco. Includes gun and leather holster with belt and buckle. Belt - **$20 $40 $75**
Holster - **$30 $80 $175**
Gun - **$75 $250 $400**

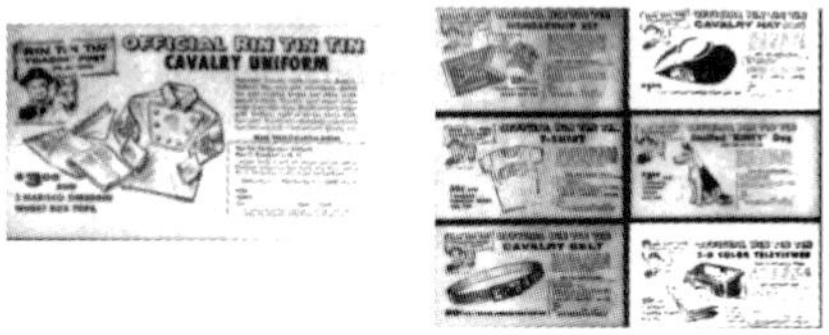


RIN-37

❑ **RIN-37. Nabisco Box Insert Cards,**
1956. At least 12 different examples.
Each - **$3 $6 $12**

RIN-38

❑ **RIN-38. "Rin-Tin-Tin At Fort Apache" Playset,**
1956. Store item by Marx Toys.
Complete - **$100 $300 $600**

RIN-39

❑ **RIN-39. Leather Belt With Metal Buckle,**
1956. Complete - **$20 $40 $100**
Buckle Only - **$10 $20 $40**

RIN-40

❑ **RIN-40. Cavalry Rifle Ballpoint Pen,**
1956. Nabisco. Near Mint In Mailer - **$50**
Rifle Pen Only - **$8 $15 $25**

(box front)

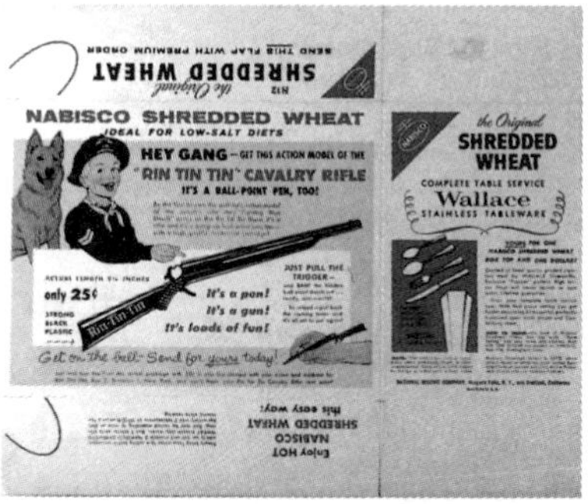


(back of box - enlarged)

RIN-41

❑ **RIN-41. Shredded Wheat Cereal 12 oz. Box Flat with Cavalry Rifle Ballpoint Pen Offer,**
1956. Nabisco. 12 oz. box. - **$50 $100 $175**

RIN-42

❑ **RIN-42. Shredded Wheat Cereal 6 oz. Box Flat with Cavalry Rifle Ballpoint Pen Offer,**
1956. Nabisco. 6 oz. box is much scarcer.
Box is 7 1/2" high by 4 1/2" - **$75 $185 $310**

RIN-43

RIN-44

❑ **RIN-43. Plastic Mug,**
1956. - **$15 $30 $60**

❑ **RIN-44. Plastic Cup,**
1956. - **$15 $25 $50**

RIN-45

RIN-46

❑ **RIN-45. Cast Member Photo,**
c. 1956. - **$8 $12 $25**

❑ **RIN-46. Color Litho. Button,**
c. 1956. Sent to participants in Nabisco's 'Name The Puppy Contest.' - **$5 $12 $25**

RIN-47

❑ **RIN-47. "Telegraph Key" Cereal Box Flat,**
1956. Plastic premium came in the package and back panel includes listing of proper clicks for 10 different messages. Gordon Gold Archives.
Near Mint Flat - **$200**
Used Complete - **$35 $75 $125**

RIN-48

RIN-49

❑ **RIN-48. Miniature Plastic Telegraph Set,**
c. 1956. Nabisco. Tapper key makes clicking sound. - **$10 $15 $25**

❑ **RIN-49. "101st Cavalry" Plastic Canteen With Strap,**
1957. Nabisco. - **$10 $20 $50**

RIN-50

❑ **RIN-50. Litho. Button,**
1957. Probable vending machine issue. 7/8" with browntone photo on various single-color backgrounds. From a larger set of western TV stars, probably totaling 14 different. -
**$10 $25 $40**

RIN-51

❑ **RIN-51. Cereal Box With Coloring Panel,**
c. 1958. Nabisco Shredded Wheat. -
**$40 $75 $150**

RIN-52

❑ **RIN-52. Totem Pole Plastic Punch-Outs,**
1958. Nabisco. Set of eight.
Each Unpunched - **$10 $20 $35**

RIN-53

❑ **RIN-53. Insignia Patch,**
1958. Nabisco, paper peel-off stickers. Set of seven: Cochise, Fort Apache, Lt. Rip Masters, Major Swanson, Rin Tin Tin, Rusty, and Sgt. O'Hara. Each Unused - **$5 $12 $20**

RIN-54

❑ **RIN-54. Plush And Vinyl Toy Dog,**
1959. Smile Novelty Co. Store item, about 15" long. - **$40 $80 $160**

RIN-55

❑ **RIN-55. "Indian Totem Pole" Cereal Box,**
1958. Gordon Gold Archives.
Near Mint Flat - **$250**
Used Complete - **$50 $100 $175**

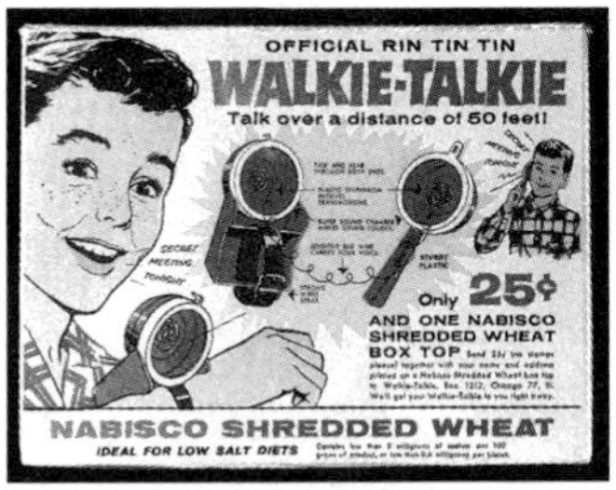


RIN-56

❑ **RIN-56. Cereal Box,**
1950s. Nabisco Shredded Wheat premium. Shows walkie talkie offer for 25¢ and box top. -
**$50 $125 $250**

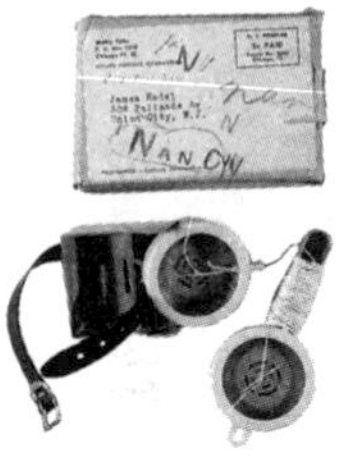

RIN-57

RIN-58

❑ **RIN-57. Walkie Talkies And Mailer,**
1950s. Nabisco Shredded Wheat premium. Also enclosed plastic belt for wrist to hold walkie-talkies - **$75 $150 $300**

❑ **RIN-58. Cast Photo,**
1950s. Movie premium. - **$25 $50 $75**

**RIN-59**

❑ **RIN-59. Cereal Box With Medal Ads,**
1960. Nabisco Wheat Honeys. Front and back panels picture and describe "Indian Wars Medal" and "Frontier Hero" medals offered as box inserts. - **$25 $50 $100**

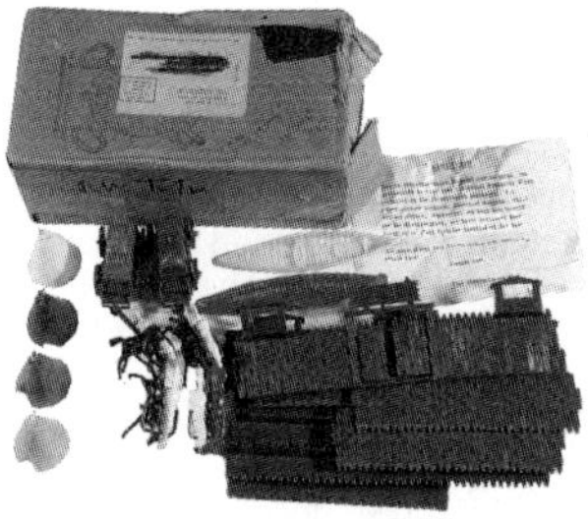

**RIN-60**

❑ **RIN-60. Fort Set,**
1960. Honeycomb Cereal premium. Plastic Ft. Apache with horses, wagons, teepees, canoes, instruction letter and box. Has printed name mistake at top on front of plastic fort. Says Fort Boone instead of Fort Apache. - **$50 $140 $225**

**RIN-61**

❑ **RIN-61. Rin-Tin-Tin Related Vacuum-Form Medals,**
c. 1960. Nabisco Rice Honeys and Wheat Honeys. Believed to have been offered while Nabisco sponsored the show but no reference to Rin-Tin-Tin on items or cereal box. Set of eight with four in "Indian Wars" series from Wheat Honeys, four in "Frontier Hero" series from Rice Honeys. Each - **$5 $12 $25**

# Rings Misc.

**Kids love to wear rings, and the sponsors of radio programs and their merchandisers, particularly cereal makers, learned that offering a ring related to their heroes was sure to bring in a flood of box tops. Hardly a radio character in the 1930s and 1940s could get through a season without a special ring premium offer. There were rings with secret compartments, glow-in-the-dark rings, flashlight rings, magnifying-glass rings, whistle rings, saddle rings, compass rings, magnet rings, rocket rings, decoder rings, baseball rings, movie rings, microscope rings, treasure rings, cannon rings, weather rings, and membership rings, along with rings bearing photos, faces, and logos. Collecting premium rings has become a specialty of its own. (For more information, refer to *The Overstreet Toy Ring Price Guide*, 3rd edition.)**

**RGS-1**

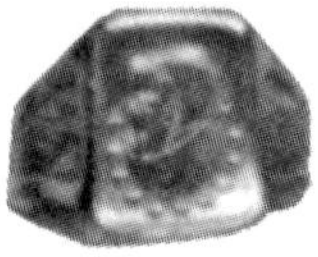

**RGS-2**

❑ **RGS-1. "Kewpie" Sterling Silver Ring,**
c. 1920s. Store item. Depicts single Kewpie with raised hands and kicking one foot. - **$75 $110 $150**

❑ **RGS-2. "Rosalie Gimple" Brass Ring,**
1936. Rare. Pabst-ett cheese food. Depicts air hostess. - **$200 $400 $575**

**RGS-3**

**(Cover)**

**RGS-4**

**(Inside)**

❑ **RGS-3. "Huskies Club" Brass Ring,**
1937. Post's Huskies Cereal. Top depicts discus thrower, bands picture various sports equipment. - **$150 $300 $550**

❑ **RGS-4. "Huskies Club" Brochure,**
1937. Post's Huskies Cereal. Lou Gehrig photo on cover. Inside displays prizes and athletes. - **$75 $100 $150**

**RGS-5**

**RGS-6**

❑ **RGS-5. "Murray-Go-Round" Brass Spinner Ring,**
1937. Fleischmann's Yeast for Arthur Murray Dance Studios. Disk pictures male dancer on one side, female on other. They appear to unite in dance when disk is spun. - **$25 $50 $75**

❑ **RGS-6. "Murray-Go-Round Ring" Folder,**
1937. Radio sponsor Fleischmann's Yeast. - **$10 $20 $30**

**RGS-8**

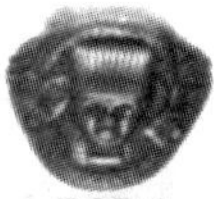

**RGS-9**

**RGS-7**

❑ **RGS-7. "Base Ball Centennial" Brass Ring,**
1939. Quaker Puffed Rice. Also offered in 1938 by General Mills as Jack Armstrong premium from July 27, 1938 to October 28, 1938 with company recording 46,501 responses. Quaker offered manufacturer's remainder in 1939. - **$250 $500 $750**

❑ **RGS-8. Chicago "Cubs" Gold Luster Metal Ring,**
1930s. Cubs name accented in blue, bands have baseball motifs. - **$50 $100 $150**

❑ **RGS-9. Lucky Sheik Brass Ring,**
1930s. Catalogue item from Johnson & Smith Novelty Co. Coiled snake design around Pharoh's head plus tiny accent stones. - **$40 $125 $225**

**RGS-10**

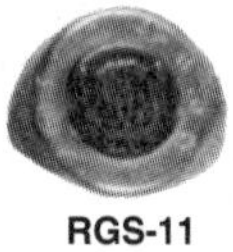

**RGS-11**

**RGS-12**

❑ **RGS-10. "Junior Broadcasters Club" Brass Ring,**
1930s. Top depicts radio microphone, bands depict radio transmission towers. -
**$25 $50 $75**

❑ **RGS-11. Kool-Aid "Treasure Hunt" Brass Ring,**
1940. - **$75 $150 $200**

❑ **RGS-12. Sky Birds Army Air Corps Ring,**
1941. Sky Birds Bubble Gum by Goudey. Brass insignia on silver luster base with adjustable bands. - **$30 $50 $100**

**(closed)** **(open)**

**RGS-13**

❑ **RGS-13. Viking Magnifying Ring,**
1941. Rare. Kellogg's All Rye Flakes. Brass with magnifying glass to view Prince "Valric Of The Vikings". Very limited distribution. -
**$1750 $3500 $7800**

**RGS-14**

❑ **RGS-14. Kix Pilot's Ring,**
1945. Brass secret compartment ring with slide-off top. Also issued in 1942 as Capt. Midnight ring. See item CMD-42.
Envelope - **$10 $25 $50**
Ring - **$75 $115 $200**

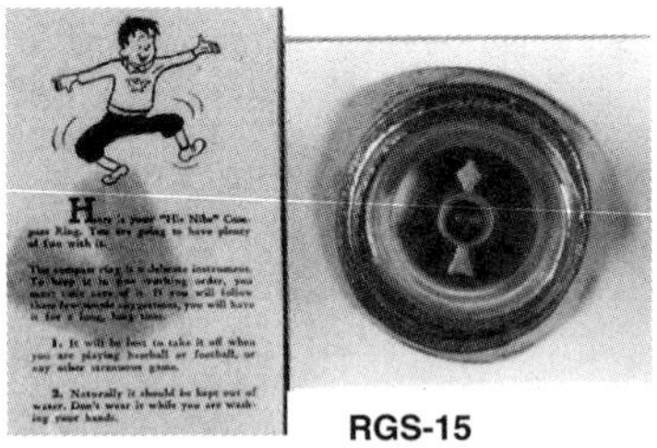

**RGS-15**

❑ **RGS-15. "His Nibs Compass Ring" On Card,**
1947. Nabisco. Ring - **$15 $25 $60**
Card - **$20 $40 $60**

**RGS-16**

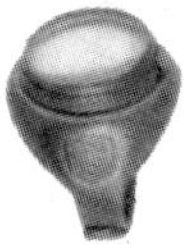

**RGS-17**

❑ **RGS-16. Roger Wilco Rescue Ring,**
1948. Power House Candy. Brass base with glow-in-dark plastic top which fits over brass whistle. - **$75 $150 $250**

❑ **RGS-17. Roger Wilco Magni-Ray Brass Ring,**
1948. Power House candy bar. Paper insert under hinged cover glows in dark. -
**$30 $60 $100**

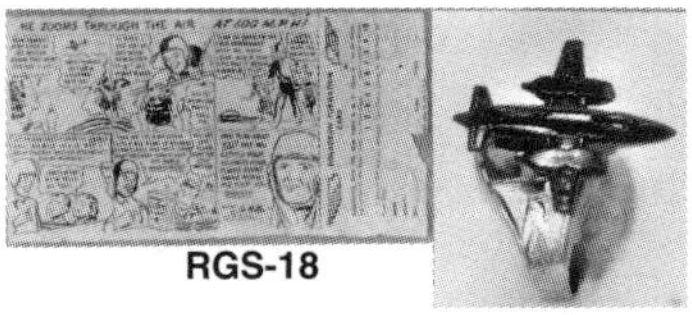

**RGS-18**

❑ **RGS-18. F-87 Super Jet Plane Ring.**
1948. Kellogg's Corn Flakes. Black plastic plane on nickel-plated ring. Advertised on Superman radio program but no other association.
Ring - **$125 $190 $260**
Instructions - **$125 $135 $150**

**RGS-19**

**RGS-20**

❑ **RGS-19. Jet Plane Ring,**
1948. Kellogg's Pep. Brass bands, metal airplane shoots off ring by spring lever. Advertised on Superman radio program but no other association. - **$125 $190 $260**

❑ **RGS-20. Fireball Twigg Explorer's Ring,**
1948. Post Cereals. Brass bands hold glow-in-dark plastic sundial under clear plastic dome. -
**$25 $50 $100**

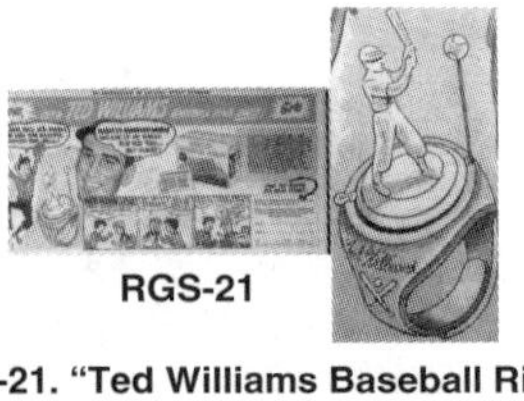

**RGS-21**

❑ **RGS-21. "Ted Williams Baseball Ring" Newspaper Ad,**
1948. Nabisco Shredded Wheat. - **$10 $20 $35**

**RGS-22**

❑ **RGS-22. "Ted Williams' Action Baseball Ring" Sign,**
1948. 10-1/4x12". - **$150 $250 $500**

**RGS-23**

**RGS-24**

❑ **RGS-23. "Ted Williams" Mechanical Ring,**
1948. Nabisco. Plastic batter figure moves by spring in brass base. - **$300 $550 $850**

❑ **RGS-24. "Andy Pafko" Baseball Scorer Brass Ring,**
1949. Muffetts cereal. Named for Chicago Cubs star, top has three turning wheels for counting balls, outs, strikes. - **$50 $110 $160**

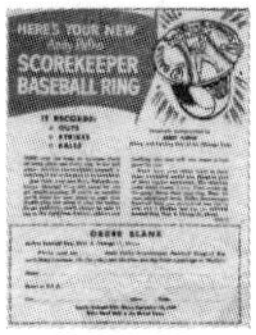


**RGS-25**

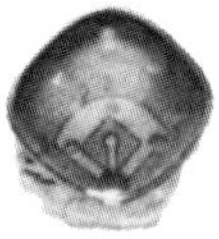

**RGS-26**

❑ **RGS-25. "Scorekeeper Baseball Ring" Order Blank,**
1949. Mechanical ring featuring Andy Pafko of Chicago Cubs. - **$25 $40 $75**

❑ **RGS-26. Baseball Game Mechanical Ring,**
1949. Kellogg's. Silvered metal capped by diamond-shaped plastic compartment with lever action for game of miniature palm puzzle nature. -
**$50 $150 $250**

**RGS-27**

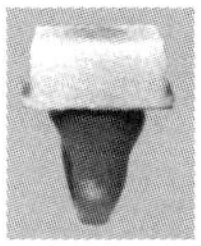

**RGS-28**

❑ **RGS-27. Your Name Ring,**
1949. Kellogg's Rice Krispies. Brass bands with good luck symbols hold plastic dome over paper with personalized first name designated by orderer. - **$20 $35 $50**

❑ **RGS-28. Glow-In-Dark "Flying Tigers Rescue Ring",**
c. 1949. Red or yellow plastic base with glow-in-dark top featuring secret compartment holding tiny brass whistle. - **$115 $225 $325**

RGS-29

RGS-30

❑ **RGS-29. "Flying Tiger Rescue Ring" Leaflet,**
c. 1949. Power House candy bar. -
**$20 $40 $60**

❑ **RGS-30. "Billy West Club" Silvered Brass Ring,**
1940s. Depicts cowboy on horseback. -
**$25 $50 $125**

RGS-31

RGS-32

RGS-33

❑ **RGS-31. Cap-Firing Brass Ring,**
1940s. Store item. Cover snaps down to fire single cap. On Card - **$65**
Loose - **$12 $15 $20**

❑ **RGS-32. Glow-In-Dark Whistle Ring,**
c. 1940s. Rare. Probable candy sponsor. Very similar to Kix atom bomb ring but varies by glow white plastic cap, whistle element is aluminum. - **$600 $1350 $2800**

❑ **RGS-33. "Arthur Murray" Watch Ring,**
c. 1940s. Brass bands pronged at top to hold actual miniature watch in brass case. -
**$100 $200 $300**

RGS-34

RGS-35

RGS-36

❑ **RGS-34. Indian Chewing Gum Ring,**
1940s. Goudey Gum Co. Silver luster with adjustable bands. - **$15 $30 $60**

❑ **RGS-35. Basketball Action Brass Ring,**
1940s. Scarce. Holds back board with tiny hoop and chained basketball to throw through it. -
**$75 $150 $300**

❑ **RGS-36. "Red Goose Shoes" Glow-In-Dark Secret Compartment Ring,**
c. 1940s. Metal and plastic with swing-out disk over paper lapel in glow compartment. -
**$115 $170 $225**

RGS-37

RGS-38

❑ **RGS-37. "Joe DiMaggio Sports Club" Member Card,**
1940s. M&M's Candies. Probably came with club ring. - **$25 $75 $150**

❑ **RGS-38. "Joe DiMaggio Sports Club" Brass Ring,**
1940s. Scarce. M & M's candies. Bands have club name and picture sports equipment. -
**$300 $700 $1000**

(closed) (open)

RGS-39

RGS-40

❑ **RGS-39. Knights Of Columbus Secret Compartment Glow-In-Dark Metal Ring,**
1940s. Rare. Same base as Green Hornet version except initials "GH" altered to "HG" (Holy Ghost). - **$750 $2500 $4600**

❑ **RGS-40. Skelly Oil Co. Red Checkmark Brass Ring,**
1940s. Top has stamped-in red enameled checkmark, possible Captain Midnight association but no documentation
seen. - **$75 $165 $325**

RGS-41

RGS-42

❑ **RGS-41. Sundial Brass Ring,**
c. 1950. Sundial Shoes. Top has plastic dome over sundial. - **$30 $45 $60**

❑ **RGS-42. "Magno-Power '50 Ford Mystery Control" Ring With Instruction Slip,**
1950. Kellogg's Pep. Magnetized plastic ring and car. Ring - **$100 $150 $250**
Instructions - **$75 $90 $100**

RGS-43

RGS-44

❑ **RGS-43. Ralston Wheat Chex "Magic Pup" Ring,**
1951. Magnet ring moves pup's magnetized head.
Complete - **$30 $50 $75**

❑ **RGS-44. "Western Saddle Ring" Offer Ad,**
1951. Smith Brothers Cough Drops. Comic book ad for finely detailed replica saddle expansion ring. Ad - **$1 $3 $5**
Ring - **$12 $25 $50**

RGS-45

RGS-46

❑ **RGS-45. "The Range Rider" Aluminum Ring With Paper Tag,**
c. 1951. Tag names TV show title produced by Autry Flying A Productions.
Near Mint With Tag - **$350**
No Tag - **$75 $135 $200**

❑ **RGS-46. Rocket-To-The-Moon Ring,**
1951. Kix Cereal. Brass bands with plastic top for launching three glow-in-dark rockets.
Ring Only - **$50 $100 $300**
Each Rocket Near Mint - **$150**

RGS-47

❑ **RGS-47. "Rocket-To-The-Moon Ring" Instruction Sheet,**
1951. Kix Cereal. - **$50 $100 $150**

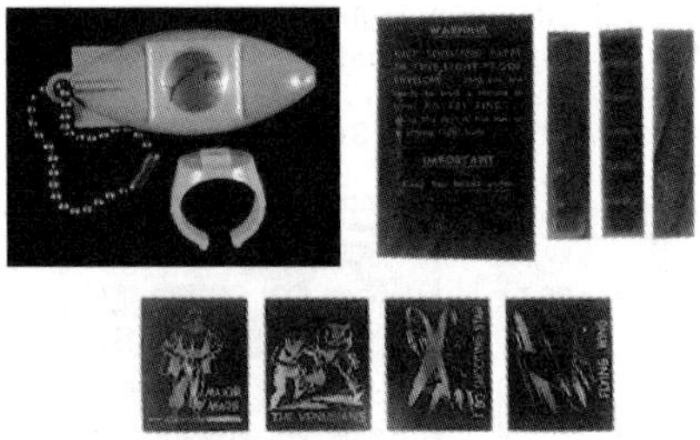

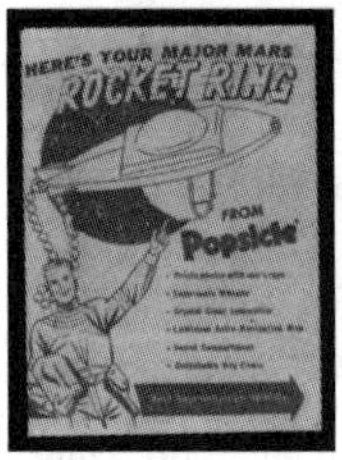


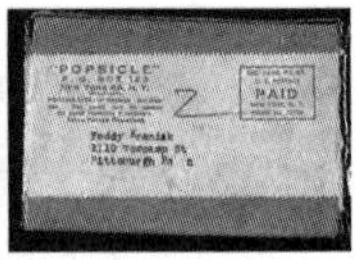

RGS-48

❑ **RGS-48. "Major Mars Rocket Ring" Kit,**
1952. Popsicle. Mailer holds plastic rocket with brass chain, ring base, instruction folder, strip with four negatives, envelope with 12 light-sensitive paper strips. A strip of four different negatives, 24 papers could be ordered separately.
Near Mint Complete - **$1600**
Rocket With Base - **$300 $600 $1000**
Rocket Without Base - **$200 $400 $600**

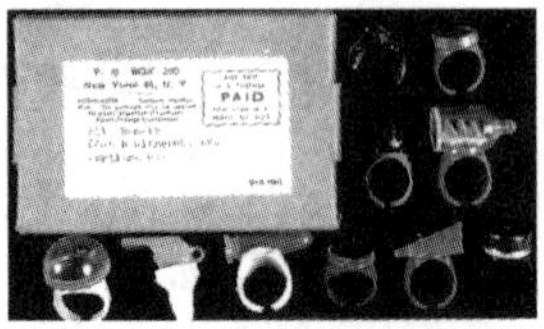

RGS-49

RGS-50

❑ **RGS-49. "Steve Donovan Western Marshal" Aluminum Ring,**
1955. Sponsor unknown. For syndicated western TV show. - **$75 $150 $225**

❑ **RGS-50. Quaker Cereals "Crazy Rings" Set,**
1957. Set of 10 plastic rings of assorted nature.
Near Mint In Mailer - **$250**
Each - **$10 $15 $20**

RGS-51

RGS-52

RGS-53

❑ **RGS-51. (Buffalo) Bill Jr. Brass Ring,**
1950s. Sides depict bucking horse and holster gun with buffalo on top. Probably from Mars Candy. - **$30 $45 $60**

❑ **RGS-52. Bazooka Joe Initial Ring,**
1950s. Topps Chewing Gum. Gold luster metal expansion ring with personalized single initial. Issued as late as 1966. - **$50 $100 $150**

❑ **RGS-53. "Smile" Orange Flavor Drink Ring,**
1950s. Brass with adjustable bands. -
**$15 $30 $50**

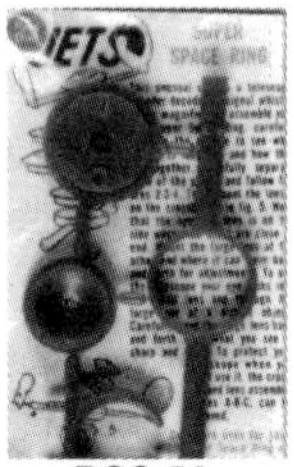


RGS-54

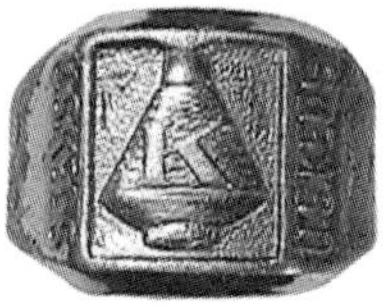

RGS-55

❑ **RGS-54. "Jets Super Space Ring",**
c. 1950s. Ball-Band. One of the few rings that actually decodes. Near Mint In Package - **$40**
Assembled - **$12 $20 $30**

❑ **RGS-55. "U.S. Keds" Space Symbols Silvered Brass Ring,**
c. 1962. Keds footwear. Depicts "K" space capsule, band has atomic symbol. - **$60 $90 $120**

RGS-56

RGS-57

❑ **RGS-56. Bazooka Joe Brass Initial Ink Stamp Ring,**
1962. Bazooka Joe Gum. Personalized by rubber stamp single initial designated by orderer. -
**$60 $120 $185**

❑ **RGS-57. "Smokey Stover" Assembly Ring,**
1964. Sugar Jets Cereal and Cracker Jack. From plastic series including Kayo, Smilin' Jack, Terry and the Pirates, others.
Each Near Mint On Tree - **$100**
Each Assembled - **$15 $25 $50**

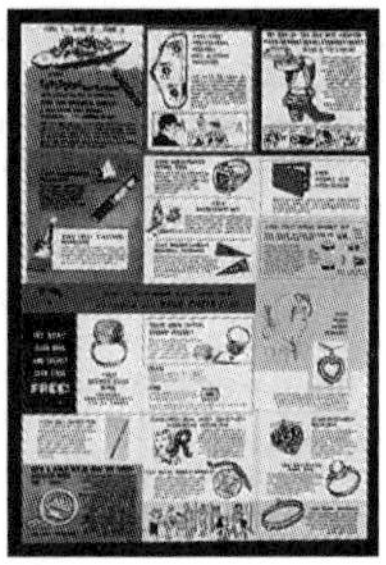

RGS-58

❑ **RGS-58. Bazooka Comics Premium Order Sheet,**
1966. Topps Chewing Gum. Paper folder opening to 9x14" picturing total of more than 30 items on both sides including Bazooka Joe Magic Circle Initial Stamp Club Ring, Gold-Plated Initial Ring and Cowboy Boot Ring. - **$10 $20 $40**

RGS-59

❑ **RGS-59. Old West Trail Club Kit,**
1968. Old West Trail Foundation. Includes map, member card, ring. Complete Near Mint - **$125**
Ring Only - **$25 $50 $80**

RGS-60

RGS-61

❑ **RGS-60. "Cousin Eerie" Brass Ring,**
1969. Warren Publishing Co., publisher of Eerie Comics. - **$30 $60 $100**

❑ **RGS-61. "Uncle Creepy" Gold Finish Metal Ring,**
1969. Warren Publishing Co., publisher of Eerie Comics. - **$100 $150 $225**

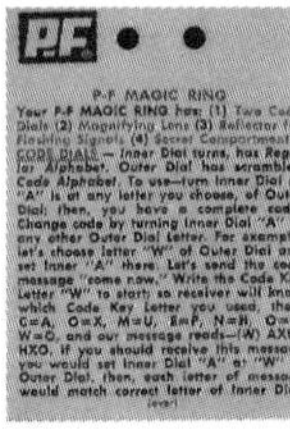

RGS-62

❑ **RGS-62. P.F. Magic Decoder Ring With Card,**
1960s. P.F. footwear. Also used as Jonny Quest premium. Gold plastic ring with several functions. Card - **$10 $20 $30**
Ring - **$25 $45 $70**

RGS-63

❑ **RGS-63. "Kolonel Keds Space Patrol" Decoder Card And Ring,**
1960s. Issued by U.S. Keds.
Card - **$15 $25 $50**
Ring - **$50 $100 $150**

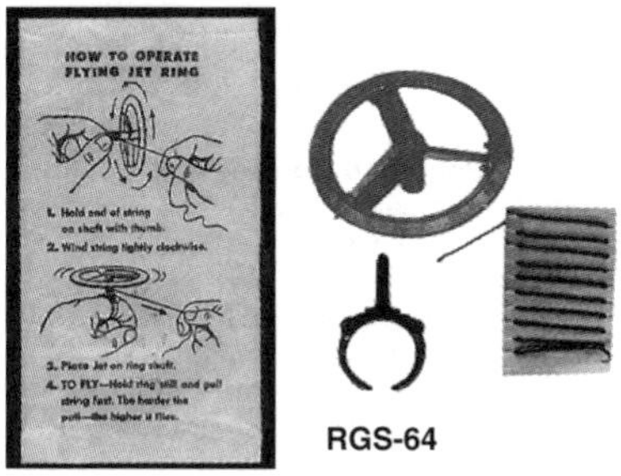


RGS-64

❑ **RGS-64. Flying Jet Ring With Envelope And Instructions,**
1960s. Cereal premium by unknown issuer.
Near Mint In Envelope - **$50**
Ring Only - **$15 $22 $30**

RGS-65

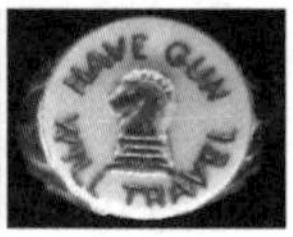


RGS-66

RGS-67

❑ **RGS-65. "Miss Dairylea" Plastic Ring,**
1960s. Dairylea Products. Domed plastic trademark girl image. - **$20 $30 $40**

❑ **RGS-66. "Have Gun Will Travel" Ring,**
1960s. Issuer unknown, may have come with costume or cap gun set. Version with silver plastic base and white plastic top with gold design. - **$20 $40 $75**

❑ **RGS-67. "Have Gun Will Travel" Ring,**
1960s. Same as previous item but version with top piece in black plastic. - **$20 $40 $75**

RGS-68

RGS-69

❑ **RGS-68. Ralston "Chex's Agent" Decoder Ring,**
c. 1960s. Plastic base topped by two cardboard dials. - **$8 $12 $20**

❑ **RGS-69. Large Plastic Decoder Ring,**
c. 1970s. Station "WABX." Call letters of Detroit station. Mostly red and green plastic with large 2" diameter decoding wheel on top. - **$20 $40 $75**

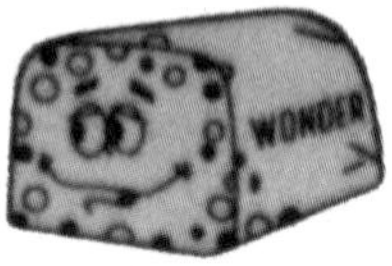


RGS-70

RGS-71

❑ **RGS-70. "Wonder" Bread Loaf Plastic Ring,**
c. 1970s. - **$5 $7 $10**

❑ **RGS-71. Tekno Comix Logo Secret Compartment Ring,**
1994. Silvery-gray metal. - **$5 $10 $15**

## Ripley's Believe It or Not!

***Robert L. Ripley's Believe It or Not!* started life as a newspaper cartoon for the *New York Globe* in 1919 and was ultimately syndicated in as many as 300 newspapers. The focus was on bizarre or freakish events and people and human oddities, all of which, Ripley (1893-1949) claimed, could be substantiated. In 1930 he took the show to radio, where it aired in various formats on NBC or CBS for 18 years. Sponsors included Colonial Oil, Esso, General Foods, Royal Crown Cola and Pall Mall cigarettes. A television version ran on NBC in 1949-1950, with other hosts after Ripley's death and resurfaced on CBS in 1982 with Jack Palance as host. Collections were published in book form around 1930 and as comic books in the 1960s.**

RPY-1

❑ **RPY-1. "Disk-O-Knowledge" Cardboard Diecut Mechanical Wheel,**
1932. Oddities appear in diecut openings on both sides. - **$10 $20 $40**

RPY-2

❑ **RPY-2. "Electric Flash" Game,**
1933. Store item by Meccano Co. of America. Battery operated game flashes miniature light bulb for correct response to question of Ripley nature. - **$40 $85 $150**

RPY-3

❑ **RPY-3. "Odditorium" Exhibit Souvenir,**
1936. From Texas Centennial exposition. Booklet and 12 postcards. Set - **$25 $50 $100**

RPY-4

RPY-5

❑ **RPY-4. Oddities Fabric Bandanna,**
1930s. - **$8 $15 $30**

❑ **RPY-5. "Believe It Or Not/Ripley" Diecut Metal Miniature Charm,**
1930s. Usually in green antiqued copper finish. - **$10 $20 $40**

RPY-6

❑ **RPY-6. Pair Of Hankies,**
1930s. Each is 5x7-1/4" in brown, green and white. Each - **$5 $10 $25**

RPY-7

**❏ RPY-7. Oddities Fold-Out Card,**
1940. Various local sponsors as Christmas premium. Opens to 13x19" sheet illustrated on both sides. - **$15 $35 $60**

RPY-8

RPY-9

**❏ RPY-8. Cardboard Ink Blotters,**
1948. Various local sponsors. Examples from monthly series dated October, November, December. Each - **$5 $10 $20**

**❏ RPY-9. Stamp,**
1940s. Scarce. Royal Crown Cola radio premium. - **$25 $40 $50**

RPY-10

**❏ RPY-10. Card Set,**
1962. Set of 45 large size 3-1/4x5-1/4" cards issued by Dynamic Toy Inc. Set - **$20 $50 $75**

## Rocky Jones, Space Ranger

**This early television space opera was two years in preparation and survived only one season of 39 episodes before it was syndicated. The series premiered in December 1953 on KNXT in Los Angeles, in February 1954 on WNBT in New York, and late in 1954 on WBKB in Chicago. Richard Crane played Rocky, chief of a 21st century security patrol force charged with maintaining peace in the galaxies. Silvercup Bread was a sponsor, and Space Ranger toys, uniforms, and comic books were licensed to promote the series.**

RKJ-1

**❏ RKJ-1. Two Stills,**
c. 1954. Each - **$5 $15 $30**

RKJ-2

**❏ RKJ-2. Cast Photo,**
1954. TV still of key cast members. - **$8 $20 $35**

RKJ-3

RKJ-4

**❏ RKJ-3. Color Photo,**
c. 1954. Possible school tablet cover. - **$10 $20 $30**

**❏ RKJ-4. "Official Space-Ranger" Metal Wings Pin On Card,**
c. 1954. Space Rangers Enterprises.
On Card - **$12 $30 $50**
Loose - **$8 $12 $20**

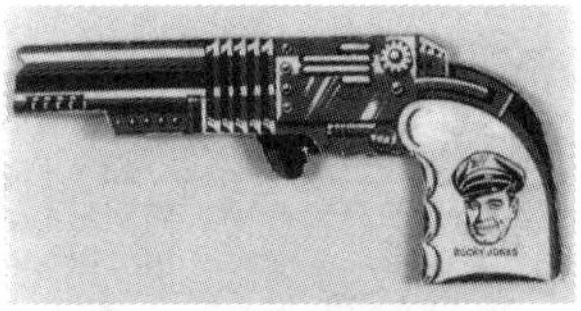

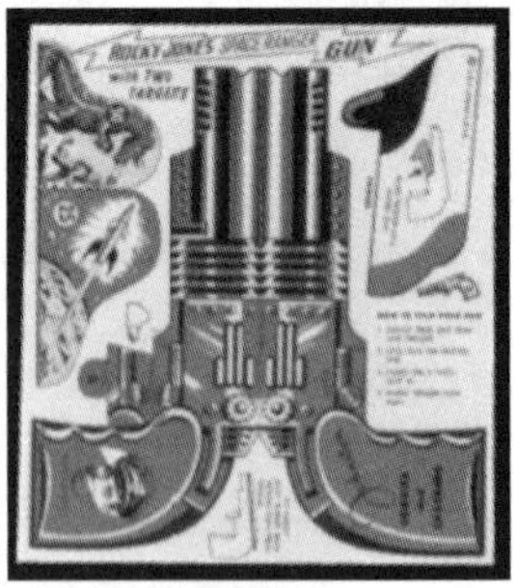

RKJ-5

**❏ RKJ-5. Cardboard Rubber Band Gun,**
c. 1954. Johnston Cookies And Crackers.
Near Mint Unpunched - **$125**
Punched - **$15 $30 $75**

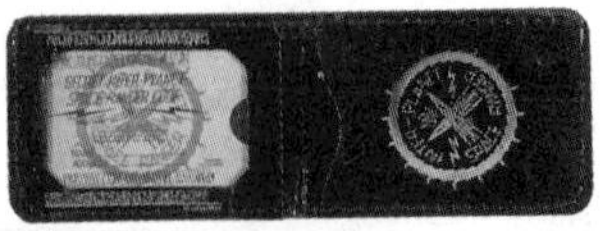

RKJ-6

**❏ RKJ-6. "Rocky Jones, Space Ranger" Billfold,**
1954. Space Ranger Secret code card & billfold with seal on right. - **$25 $50 $85**

RKJ-7

**❏ RKJ-7. Code Card,**
1954. Mickelberry's Meats. - **$30 $75 $135**

RKJ-8

RKJ-9

RKJ-10

**❏ RKJ-8. "Johnston Cookies" Litho. Button,**
c. 1954. Also comes with "Silvercup Bread" imprint. - **$10 $20 $35**

**❏ RKJ-9. Silvercup Bread Litho. Button,**
c. 1954. - **$10 $20 $35**

**❏ RKJ-10. "Rocky Jones-Space Ranger" Cello. Button,**
c. 1954. - **$10 $25 $50**

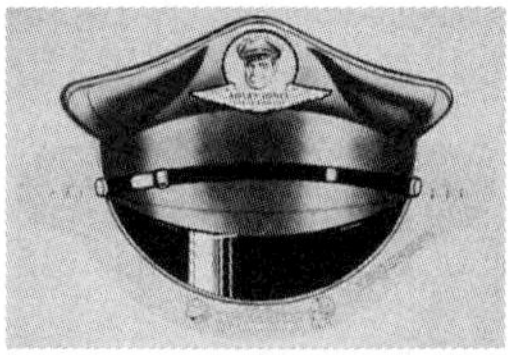

RKJ-11

**❏ RKJ-11. Punch-Out Hat Premium,**
c. 1954. Pied Piper Line, one of the bread companies sponsoring the show. 9x12-1/2" thin cardboard in blue, black and white. Gordon Gold Archives. Unpunched - **$30 $60 $125**

RKJ-12

**❏ RKJ-12. "Rocky Jones And The Space Pirates" Record,**
1953. 78 rpm issued by Columbia. - **$20 $40 $70**

## Rocky Lane

Harold Albershart (1904-1973), as Allan Rocky Lane, was a longtime actor in adventure films. He made dozens of "B" Westerns, Royal Mountie serials, and jungle epics for Republic Pictures between 1938 and 1961. Lane took over the film role of Red Ryder around 1944 and continued as a star for the studio into the 1950s. *Rocky Lane* comic books were published between 1949 and 1959, and Lane was the television voice of Mr. Ed, the talking horse, from 1961 to 1965.

RLN-1

RLN-2

❏ **RLN-1. "Alan Rocky Lane And His Stallion Black Jack" Dixie Picture,**
c. 1950. - **$15 $25 $50**

❏ **RLN-2. "Alan Rocky Lane" Dixie Picture,**
c. 1950. - **$15 $25 $50**

RLN-3

RLN-4

RLN-5

❏ **RLN-3. Cello. Button,**
c. 1950. 1-1/4" black and white on orange. - **$15 $25 $50**

❏ **RLN-4. "Allan 'Rocky' Lane" Cello. Button,**
c. 1950. Store item. - **$10 $20 $30**

❏ **RLN-5. "Rocky Lane Posse" Cello. Button,**
1950. Carnation Malted Milk. - **$50 $100 $175**

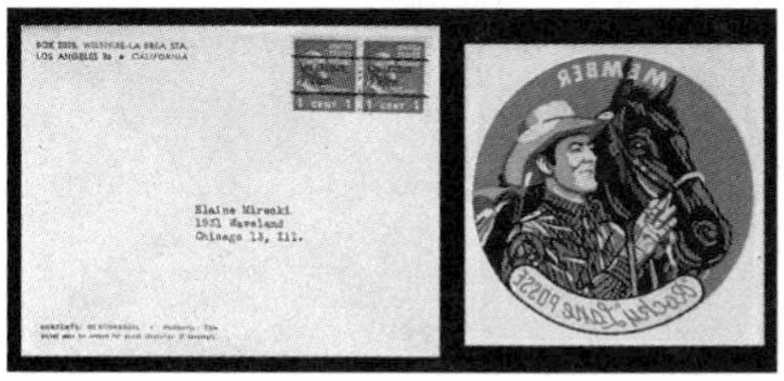


RLN-6

❏ **RLN-6. "Member 'Rocky' Lane Posse" Decal Club Patch,**
1950. Rare. Carnation Malted Milk.
Patch - **$50 $275 $375**
Mailer - **$25 $50 $100**

RLN-7

RLN-8

❏ **RLN-7. "Posse Shoulder Patch" Premium Offer Ad,**
1950. Carnation Malted Milk. Comic book page ad for clothing patch available until January 30, 1951. - **$3 $5 $10**

❏ **RLN-8. "Explorer's Sun Watch" Ad,**
1951. Carnation Malted Milk. Comic book page ad with product endorsement by "Rocky" Lane. - **$3 $5 $10**

RLN-9

RLN-10

❏ **RLN-9. Dixie Ice Cream Picture,**
c. 1952. - **$20 $40 $75**

❏ **RLN-10. "Thundering Caravans" Movie Poster,**
1952. Republic Pictures. 27x41". - **$30 $65 $100**

RLN-11

❏ **RLN-11. "Rocky Lane Western Comic" English Annual,**
1960. #4 in series by L. Miller & Co. Ltd. - **$10 $25 $50**

## Rootie Kazootie

Who is the lad who makes you feel so glad? He was Rootie Kazootie, the little puppet hero who became a giant hit in children's television. The series, known initially as *The Rootie Tootie Club* when it debuted locally in New York in 1950, changed its name to *The Rootie Kazootie Club* and was broadcast nationally on NBC (1951-1952) and ABC (1952-1954). Other puppet charcters were Polka Dottie, El Squeako Mouse, the villainous Poison Zoomack, and the pup Little Nipper, who became Gala Poochie when RCA dropped out as a sponsor. Todd Russell served as host, and Mr. Deetle Doodle, the silent policeman, was the only other human to appear. Sponsors, in addition to RCA, included Coca-Cola, Power House candy, and Silvercup bread. *Rootie Kazootie* comic books were published in the early 1950s.

ROO-1

ROO-2

❏ **ROO-1. "Rootie Kazootie Stars" Puppet Punch-Outs,**
c. 1952. Coca-Cola. Set of five. Each Unpunched - **$12 $20 $45**

❏ **ROO-2. "Rootie Kazootie Stars" Animated Punch-Outs,**
c. 1952. Coca-Cola. Set of five. Each Unpunched - **$12 $20 $45**

ROO-3

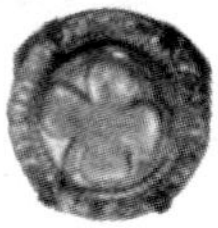

ROO-4

ROO-5

❏ **ROO-3. Club Member Litho. Button,**
c. 1952. Color (6 characters) or black/white (5 characters) versions. Each - **$10 $20 $45**

❏ **ROO-4. "Rootie Kazootie's Lucky Spot" Embossing Ring,**
c. 1952. Designed to emboss title and four-leaf clover image on paper. - **$150 $350 $600**

❏ **ROO-5. "Rootie Kazootie Rooter" Glow-In-Dark Plastic Disk,**
c. 1952. Back has pin fastener. - **$20 $35 $75**

ROO-6

❑ **ROO-6. "Rootie Kazootie Rooters Club" Membership Card,**
c. 1952. - **$10 $25 $60**

ROO-7

ROO-8

❑ **ROO-7. Flicker Ring,**
c. 1952. Premium issue probably from Power House Candy. - **$30 $65 $125**

❑ **ROO-8. "Rootie Kazootie Word Game,"**
1953. Store item by Ed-U-Cards. - **$8 $15 $25**

ROO-9

ROO-10

❑ **ROO-9. Hand Puppet,**
1950s. 9" tall. - **$50 $100 $150**

❑ **ROO-10. Hand Puppet,**
1950s. Store item. 10" tall with soft vinyl head and plain red fabric body. - **$50 $100 $150**

ROO-11

❑ **ROO-11. Picture Puzzles Set,**
1950s. Store item by E. E. Fairchild Corp. Three-puzzle set featuring Rootie, Polka Dottie, Gala Poochie. Boxed Set - **$30 $65 $110**

## Roscoe Turner

**A real-life aviator hero and successful aviation entrepeneur, Col. Roscoe Turner (1895-1970) was idolized in the 1930s much like cowboy fans adored Tom Mix. Turner was a barnstormer flyer and stunt performer of the 1920s following the start of his air career in the Balloon Service during World War I. He was the major test pilot for the DC-2 (Douglas Commercial) first passenger transport aircraft in 1934. In the latter 1930s, his frequent winning of the Thompson Trophy and Bendix Trophy for speed events at annual National Air Races enthralled a nation of speed fans. His enterprises included a passenger run from Los Angeles to Reno to Las Vegas and return, called by some the "Alimony Special" circuit due to frequent use by movie stars. Turner's popularity promoted premiums by several sponsors, notably Gilmore Oil, H. J. Heinz and Wonder Bread (see Sky Blazers). Probably his best remembered gimmick was for Gilmore Oil Co. An actual African lion--a Gilmore trademark lookalike--was acquired and flew with Turner throughout the United States, Canada and Mexico. Despite insistence by humane agencies that the lion be equipped with a parachute, Turner and his lion were welcomed everywhere until the lion died of old age and natural causes.**

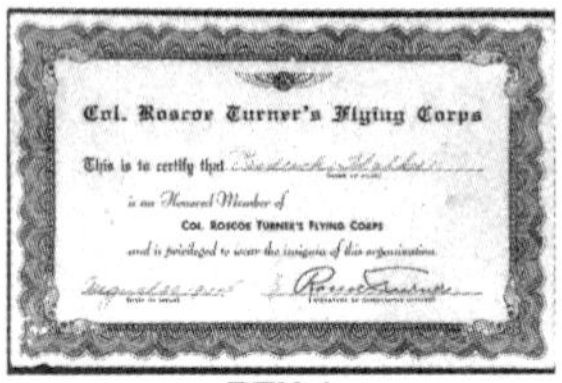

RTU-1

❑ **RTU-1. Flying Corps Certificate,**
1934. Heinz Rice Flakes. - **$20 $45 $75**

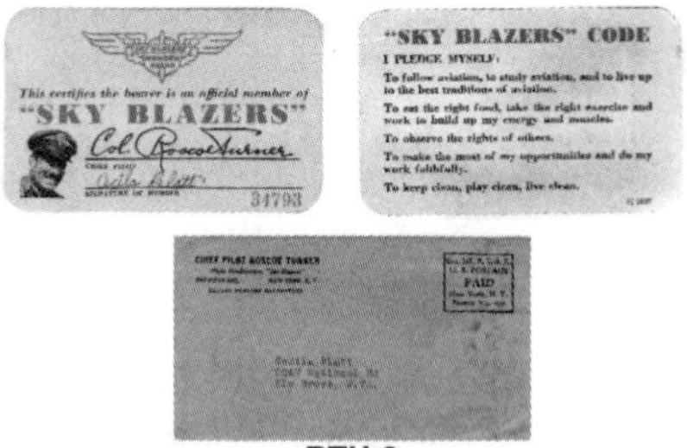

RTU-2

❑ **RTU-2. Membership Card with Mailer,**
c. 1934. Heinz Rice Flakes. - **$20 $75 $100**
Mailer - **$15 $30 $50**

RTU-3

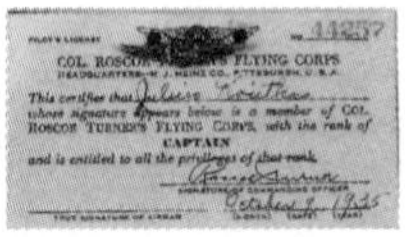

RTU-4

❑ **RTU-3. "Flying Corps" Bronze Wings Badge On Card,**
1934. Heinz Co. "Lieutenant" version.
Card - **$10 $25 $40**
Badge - **$10 $25 $40**

❑ **RTU-4. "Flying Corps" Silver Wings Badge On Card,**
1934. Heinz Co. "Captain" version.
Card - **$15 $30 $45**
Badge - **$15 $30 $45**

RTU-5

❑ **RTU-5. "Flying Corps" Gold Wings Badge On Card,**
1934. Heinz Co. "Major" version.
Card - **$20 $35 $60**
Badge - **$20 $35 $60**

RTU-6

❑ **RTU-6. "Beginning Col. Roscoe Turner's Flying Adventures,"**
1934. Full page in May 27 Sunday comic section sponsored by H. J. Heinz Co. -
**$10 $20 $30**

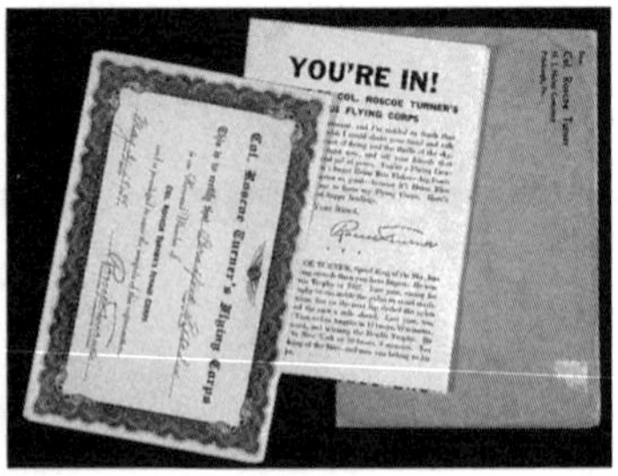


RTU-7

❑ **RTU-7. Certificate With Booklet and Mailer,**
1934. Mailer for Flying Corp Certificate.
Mailer - **$15 $30 $45**
Booklet - **$15 $30 $45**
Certificate - **$20 $45 $75**

RTU-8

❑ **RTU-8. Thompson Trophy Race "Winner" Color Print,**
c. 1939. Thompson Products. 13-1/4x14-1/2" beautiful color print with art by Charles H. Hubbel surrounded by black border with photo inset of pilot below. Total number of prints in the set is unknown but Turner is pictured as winner of the 1934, 1938 and 1939 air races held in Cleveland.
Each Print Picturing Turner - **$10 $25 $50**

RTU-9

RTU-10

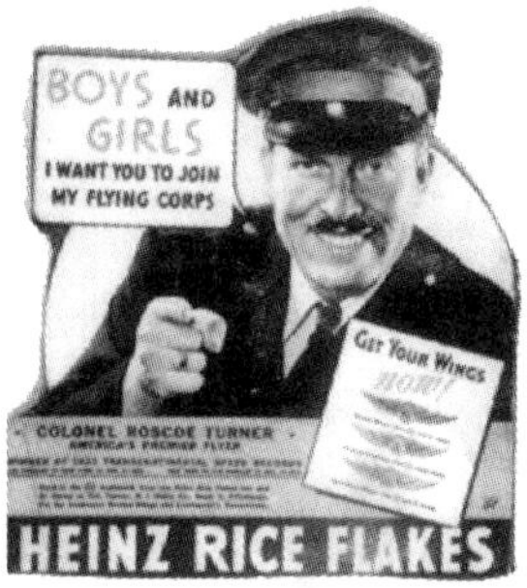


RTU-11

❑ **RTU-9. "Roscoe Turner" Photo,**
1930s. Heinz Rice Flakes. - **$10 $ 25 $40**

❑ **RTU-10. "Col. Roscoe Turner" Cello. Button,**
c. 1930s. For "Corinth Airport Dedication". - **$10 $20 $40**

❑ **RTU-11. "I Want You To Join My Flying Corps" 20x23" Cardboard Store Sign,**
1930s. Heinz Rice Flakes. - **$100 $250 $350**

# Roy Rogers

**Singing, movies, radio, records, comic books, comic strips, television, rodeos, personal appearances, merchandising--Roy Rogers (1911-1998) did it all, with style and huge success. Born Leonard Slye in Ohio in 1911, he started out organizing cowboy bands and singing in a hillbilly group, and made his first movies--in bit roles or as a member of the Sons of the Pioneers--as Slye or as Dick Weston in the mid-1930s.**

**His first film as Rogers was Republic Pictures' *Under Western Stars* (1938). He changed his name legally to Roy Rogers in 1942, and went on to make more than 80 Westerns for Republic, pursuing the Happy Trails to stardom as "King of the Cowboys," riding his palomino Trigger ("The Smartest Horse in the Movies") and accompanied by wife Dale Evans ("Queen of the West") on her steed Buttermilk. Evans died in 2001.**

**On radio, *The Roy Rogers Show* aired on the Mutual or NBC networks from 1944 to 1955, initially as a musical variety show with Dale, the Sons of the Pioneers, and a movie sidekick Gabby Hayes, later as a Western thriller with Pat Brady replacing Hayes. The show was sponsored by Goodyear Tire (1944-1945), Miles Laboratories (1946-1947), Quaker Oats and Mother's Oats (1948-1951), Post Sugar Crisp (1951-1953), and Dodge automobiles (1954-1955).**

***Roy Rogers* comic books were first published in 1944 and continued well into the 1960s, and daily and Sunday strips syndicated by King Features appeared from 1949 to 1961.**

**On television, *The Roy Rogers Show* was seen on NBC from 1951 to 1957, sponsored by Post cereals. The series was then syndicated for six years, sponsored by Nestle's from 1958 to 1964 and co-sponsored by Ideal Novelty & Toy Corp. from 1961 to 1964. Further syndication followed in 1976. The programs continued the successful mix of adventure, music, and comedy of the Rogers movies, with the usual cast, including Pat Brady and his trick jeep Nellybelle, and Bullet the Wonder Dog. *The Roy Rogers & Dale Evans Show,* a musical variety hour, had a brief run on ABC in 1962.**

**Merchandising of the Roy Rogers empire and sponsor premiums peaked during the radio and television years. At one point some 400 products were franchised by Roy Rogers Enterprises, earning millions for manufacturers and for the endorsers. A chain of family restaurants opened in the 1960s.**

**The Roy Rogers Museum in California displays the stuffed remains of Trigger, Buttermilk, Bullet; plus Nellybelle and other relics and memorabilia.**

ROY-1

❑ **ROY-1. "The Sons Of The Pioneers" Photo Ad Card With Roy,**
c. 1934. Radio KQV, Pittsburgh, Pa. 8-1/4x11-1/4" stiff paper advertising daily noon radio program. Photo identifies Roy by his actual name "Len Slye." Photo captions on the item are both misplaced and in some cases spelled incorrectly. Actually pictured from left to right are Hugh Farr, Bob Nolan, Lloyd Perryman, Len Slye. Karl Farr is not pictured. - **$75 $175 $275**

ROY-2

❑ **ROY-2. Sons Of Pioneers Photo Card With Roy,**
1935. One of earliest items to picture Roy. Text on reverse. - **$50 $150 $225**

ROY-3

ROY-4

❑ **ROY-3. Dixie Ice Cream Picture,**
1938. - **$40 $75 $150**

❑ **ROY-4. "Broadway Journal" 12x16" Publicity Newspaper,**
1938. Republic Studios. "Special Roy Rogers Edition" for July 16 appearances in New York City. - **$75 $135 $225**

ROY-5

ROY-6

❑ **ROY-5. "Republic's Singing Western Star" Cello. Button,**
c. 1938. Republic Studios. 1-1/4" with bluetone photo on dark beige background. Probably issued in conjunction with his first Republic film "Under Western Stars." - **$75 $150 $300**

❑ **ROY-6. Movie Promo Picture with Frame,**
1938. Republic Pictures. From the movie "Shine On Harvest Moon" starring Roy Rogers and Gabby Hayes. - **$25 $50 $75**

ROY-7

❑ **ROY-7. Dale Evans Early Sheet Music,**
1939. Store item by Calumet Music Co. Front cover reads "Dale Evans Over W.B.B.M.-Chicago/Columbia Broadcasting System." - **$10 $15 $30**

ROY-8

ROY-9

❑ **ROY-8. Photo,**
1930s. Republic Pictures. Color photo of Roy. - **$10 $25 $40**

❑ **ROY-9. Button With Early Portrait,**
1930s. Black and white 1-1/4" with photo of young Roy smiling and wearing floral pattern shirt. - **$40 $100 $175**

ROY-10

ROY-11

❑ **ROY-10. Dixie Ice Cream Picture,**
1940. - **$60 $100 $150**

❑ **ROY-11. Dixie Ice Cream Picture,**
1942. Reverse has scenes from "Man From Cheyenne." - **$50 $125 $250**

ROY-12

ROY-13

❑ **ROY-12. "Roy Rogers King Of The Cowboys" Dixie Lid,**
c. 1942. - **$8 $15 $30**

❑ **ROY-13. "Roy Rogers Robin Hood Of The Range" Better Little Book,**
1942. Whitman #1460. - **$25 $50 $125**

ROY-14

❑ **ROY-14. Los Angeles Rodeo Souvenir Program,**
1944. - **$65 $150 $250**

ROY-15

❑ **ROY-15. "The Roy Rogers Show" Radio Announcement Brochure,**
c. 1944. Goodyear Tire & Rubber Co. Press kit folder promoting radio series on Mutual Broadcasting System including listing of 67 radio stations. Complete - **$100 $225 $325**

ROY-16

ROY-17

❑ **ROY-16. "Roy Rogers And Trigger" Dixie Ice Cream Picture,**
1945. - **$75 $150 $300**

❑ **ROY-17. "Dale Evans" Dixie Ice Cream Picture,**
1945. - **$30 $75 $150**

ROY-18

ROY-19

❑ **ROY-18. "Roy Rogers at Crossed Feathers Ranch" Big Little Book #1494,**
1945. - **$15 $40 $90**

❑ **ROY-19. "My Pal Trigger" 13x19" Contest Paper Poster,**
1946. Republic Pictures for local theaters. - **$50 $175 $300**

ROY-20

❑ **ROY-20. "World's Championship Rodeo" Program,**
c. 1947. 8-1/2x11" with 20 pages. - **$25 $50 $75**

ROY-21

❑ **ROY-21. "Roy Rogers And His Trick Lasso" Photo,**
1947. Store item packaged with trick lasso. - **$15 $25 $50**

ROY-22

❑ **ROY-22. "Roy Rogers Trick Lasso",**
1947. Store item. Came with photo (see item ROY-21) and game book. Cellophane wrapper very fragile. Wrapper - **$10 $25 $60**
Lasso - **$10 $15 $35**
Game Book - **$25 $75 $125**

ROY-23

ROY-24

❑ **ROY-23. "Roy Rogers and the Dwarf-Cattle Ranch" Big Little Book #1421,**
1947. 352 pages. - **$15 $40 $90**

❑ **ROY-24. "Roy Rogers and the Deadly Treasure" Big Little Book #1437,**
1947. - **$15 $40 $90**

ROY-25

❑ **ROY-25. First Issue "Dale Evans Comics",**
1948. National Comics Publications. Issue #1 for September-October. - **$100 $300 $1100**

ROY-26

❑ **ROY-26. Quaker Oats Contest Store Poster,**
1948. 16x22" in full color announcing prizes for "Naming This Son Of Trigger" with grand prize of "Win A Vacation With Me In Hollywood." Gordon Gold Archives. - **$400 $800 $1300**

ROY-27

ROY-28

❑ **ROY-27. "Roy Rogers and the Mystery of the Howling Mesa" Big Little Book #1448,**
1948. - **$12 $35 $85**

❑ **ROY-28. "Roy Rogers in Robbers' Roost" Big Little Book #1452,**
1948. - **$12 $35 $85**

ROY-29

❑ **ROY-29. "Roy Rogers And His World Championship Rodeo" Program,**
1948. - **$25 $60 $125**

ROY-30

❑ **ROY-30. Product Box With "Branding Iron" Ring Offer,**
1948. - **$75 $100 $125**

ROY-31

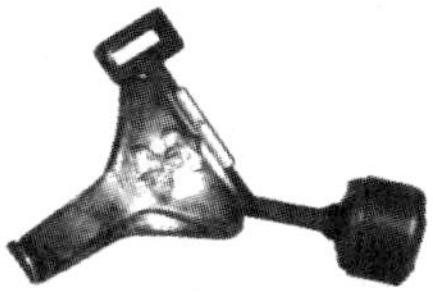

ROY-32

❑ **ROY-31. Dixie Ice Cream Picture,**
1948. - **$35 $75 $110**

❑ **ROY-32. Branding Iron/Initial Brass Ring With Black Cap,**
1948. Quaker Cereals. Plastic stamper under brass cover with ink pad was personalized with any requested initial. - **$75 $150 $250**

ROY-33

ROY-34

❑ **ROY-33. Contest Card,**
1948. Quaker Oats. - **$10 $20 $40**

❑ **ROY-34. Sterling Silver Saddle Ring,**
1948. Store item by W. G. Simpson Co., Phoenix, Az. Facsimile signature on saddle seat. - **$225 $350 $475**

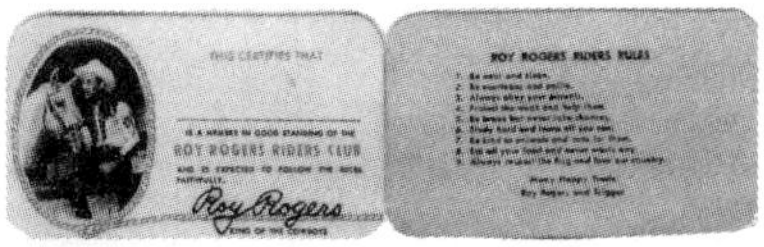


ROY-35

❑ **ROY-35. "Roy Rogers Riders Club" Membership Card,**
c. 1948. - **$20 $60 $100**

ROY-36

❑ **ROY-36. "Tattoo Transfers" Kit,**
c. 1948. Pack #7 with Fawcett Publications copyright, two sheets with 22 transfers. - **$30 $70 $150**

ROY-37

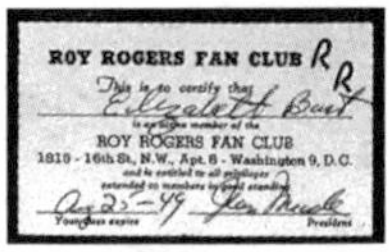


ROY-38

❑ **ROY-37. Quaker Contest Postcard,**
1949. - **$10 $15 $35**

❑ **ROY-38. Fan Club Membership Card,**
1949. Washington DC chapter. - **$10 $20 $35**

ROY-39

❑ **ROY-39. Microscope Ring/Saddle Ring Newspaper Ad,**
1949. Quaker Oats. - **$15 $30 $50**

ROY-40

❑ **ROY-40. "March Of Comics" #47,**
1949. Various sponsors. Pictured example for Sears merchandise. - **$23 $69 $195**

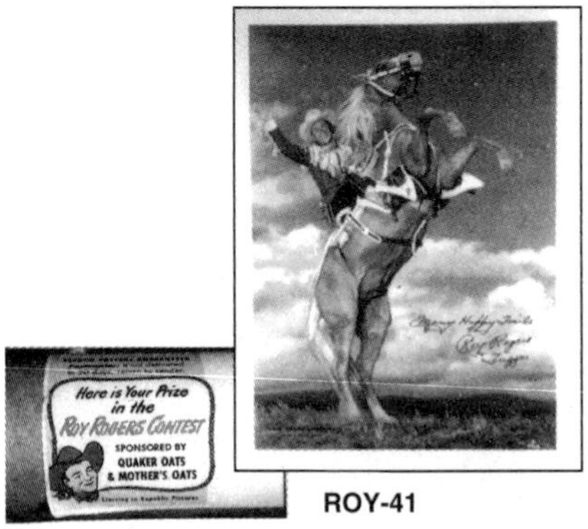


ROY-41

❑ **ROY-41. Quaker Contest Prize 19x26" Poster With Mailer,**
1949. Rare.
Near Mint With Label On Tube - **$2000**
Poster Only - **$300 $850 $1700**

ROY-42

ROY-43

❑ **ROY-42. Quaker Microscope Ring,**
1949. - **$50 $80 $175**

❑ **ROY-43. Mother's Oats Container with Offer for Roy Rogers Microscope Ring,**
1949. Quaker Oats.
Large Container - **$50 $100 $175**
Small Container - **$35 $85 $125**

ROY-44

ROY-45

❑ **ROY-44. "Roy Rogers and the Mystery of the Lazy M" Big Little Book #1462,**
1949. - **$15 $40 $90**

❑ **ROY-45. "Roy Rogers And Trigger" Dixie Ice Cream Picture,**
c. 1949. Reverse has photo montage and titles of seven movies from 1947-1949 era. - **$75 $150 $250**

ROY-46

❑ **ROY-46. Portrait Pinback,**
1940s. 1-3/4" black & white pinback. Scarce. - **$50 $100 $200**

ROY-47

❑ **ROY-47. Large Photo Portrait,**
1940s. 29-1/2x37" color photo on rigid cardboard. Likely for theater lobby or record store display. Marked only "Sign And Pictorial Local 230" at lower right. - **$100 $200 $400**

ROY-48

ROY-49

❑ **ROY-48. RCA Victor 18x24" Cardboard Store Sign,**
c. 1940s. - **$200 $375 $550**

❑ **ROY-49. Fan Club Membership Card,**
1940s. - **$20 $40 $75**

ROY-50

ROY-51

❑ **ROY-50. Rodeo Souvenir Cello. Button,**
1940s. Various attachments. - **$15 $50 $90**

❑ **ROY-51. Republic Studios Photo,**
c. 1940s. - **$10 $25 $40**

ROY-52

ROY-53

❑ **ROY-52. Republic Studios Photo,**
c. 1940s. Includes facsimile signature. - **$10 $25 $40**

❑ **ROY-53. Riders Club Card,**
1940s. Scarce. Vertical card with 24 marked stars around card. - **$30 $75 $140**

ROY-54

ROY-55

❑ **ROY-54. Movie Card,**
1940s. Roy's picture on a King card, symbolizing his trademark "King of the Cowboys." - **$10 $20 $35**

❑ **ROY-55. Roy Rogers & Trigger Glove Set,**
1940s. Gloves have a red jewel and silver colored studs. - **$125 $250 $375**

ROY-56

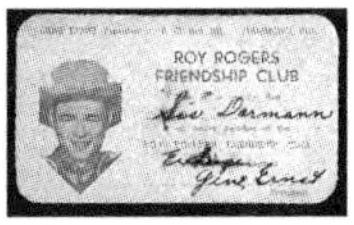


ROY-57

❑ **ROY-56. Postcard,**
1940s. Quaker Oats. Radio premium announcing free signed photo. - **$10 $20 $30**

❑ **ROY-57. Friendship Club Card,**
1940's. Hammond, Ind. Picture of Roy on left Red on white. - **$15 $40 $75**

ROY-58

ROY-59

❑ **ROY-58. Photo,**
1940s. Quaker Oats. Color photo of Roy on Trigger. - **$20 $40 $65**

❑ **ROY-59. Photo,**
1940s. Movie premium of Roy and the Sons of the Pioneers. - **$25 $50 $75**

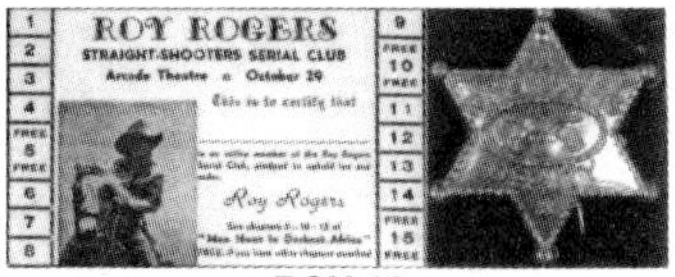


ROY-60

❑ **ROY-60. Movie Serial Club Card/Ticket With Metal Badge,**
1940s. Badge designated "Roy Rogers Deputy".
Card - **$20 $50 $75**
Badge - **$15 $30 $60**

ROY-61

ROY-62

❑ **ROY-61. "Roy Rogers" Sterling Silver Child's Ring,**
c. 1940s. Store item. Image of Roy on rearing Trigger, bands have branding iron design. - **$100 $200 $325**

❑ **ROY-62. "Dale Evans Fan Club" Cello. Button,**
1940s. - **$35 $70 $135**

ROY-63

❑ **ROY-63. Plastic Mug,**
1950. Quaker Oats. - **$10 $20 $50**

ROY-64

❑ **ROY-64. "Roy Rogers Riders Club" Member's Pack,**
1950. Package includes two cover letters, six cards, litho. button on card.
Near Mint In Mailer - **$330**
Each Card - **$10 $20 $35**
Loose Button - **$8 $12 $20**

ROY-65

❑ **ROY-65. Quaker Brass Badge With Sheet And Mailer,**
1950. Near Mint Boxed - **$175**
Badge Only - **$25 $60 $100**

ROY-66

ROY-67

❑ **ROY-66. "Souvenir Cup" 15x20" Paper Store Sign,**
1950. Quaker Oats. - **$100 $250 $425**

❑ **ROY-67. Quaker Canister With "Souvenir Cup" Offer,**
1950. - **$35 $85 $125**

ROY-68

ROY-69

❑ **ROY-68. Record Album 12x12" Cardboard Store Sign,**
c. 1950. RCA Victor. - **$50 $100 $150**

❑ **ROY-69. "Roy Rogers And Trigger" Dixie Ice Cream Picture,**
c. 1950. Reverse has montage of five photos plus titles of four movies from 1949 or 1950. - **$75 $150 $250**

ROY-70

❑ **ROY-70. "Thrill Circus" Felt Pennant,**
c. 1950. - **$35 $75 $150**

ROY-71

ROY-72

❑ **ROY-71. "Roy Rogers & Trigger" Lamp With Shade,**
c. 1950. 8" tall figural plaster on 3-1/4x5" base.
Near Mint With Shade **- $350**
Lamp Only - **$75 $150 $250**

❑ **ROY-72. "Dale Evans" Lamp With Shade,**
c. 1950. 8" tall figural plaster on 3-1/4x5" base.
Near Mint With Shade **- $300**
Lamp Only - **$65 $125 $200**

ROY-73

ROY-74

❑ **ROY-73. "Roy Rogers Range Detective" New Better Little Book,**
1950. Whitman. 3-1/4x5-1/2" vertical format. - **$20 $50 $95**

❑ **ROY-74. "Roy Rogers" Vinyl Notebook,**
c. 1950. Store item. 10-1/2x13". - **$100 $250 $400**

ROY-75

ROY-76

❑ **ROY-75. Roy and Dale Cut Out Book**
1950. Large cut out of Trigger on back cover. - **$50 $150 $300**

❑ **ROY-76. "Roy Rogers Birthday Club" Button,**
c. 1950. Times Newspapers. Large 2-1/2" button in black and white and various shades of red. Rare. - **$100 $225 $375**

ROY-77

❑ **ROY-77. "Sheriffs' Annual 'World's Championship Rodeo'" Program,**
1950. Sheriffs' Relief Assn. of Los Angeles County. Issued for single day event August 27, 1950. Inside back cover has Roy ad sponsored by Quaker Oats. - **$75 $150 $300**

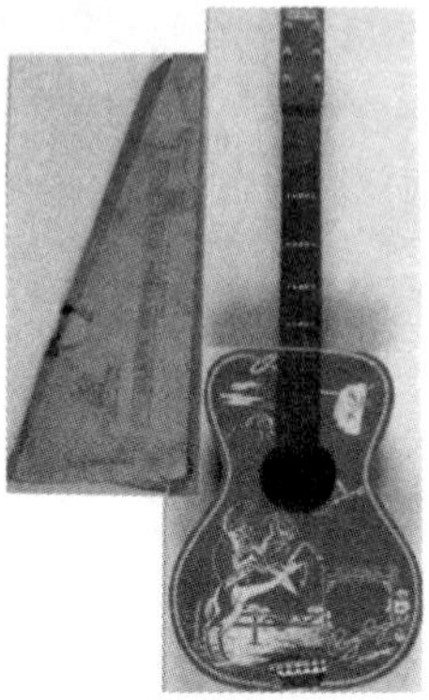

ROY-78

❑ **ROY-78. "Roy Rogers" Guitar With Carton,**
c. 1950. Store item by Range Rhythm Toys. 30" tall guitar. Box - **$25 $50 $75**
Guitar **- $40 $80 $135**

ROY-79

ROY-80

❑ **ROY-79. Dixie Ice Cream Picture,**
1951. - **$40 $65 $100**

❑ **ROY-80. Wrist Watch With Deputy Badge,**
1951. Mini "Western belt"-type strap. In box with clear mylar top and instructions. - **$500**
Watch only - **$60 $130 $250**

ROY-81

❑ **ROY-81. Newspaper Strips Promo,**
1951. Rare. Large & colorful. - **$125 $250 $500**

ROY-82

ROY-83

❑ **ROY-82. Quaker "Roy Rogers Cookies" Box,**
1951. One side panel pictures his gun belt.
Complete - **$200 $400 $650**

❑ **ROY-83. Quaker "Roy Rogers Cookies" Newspaper Ad,**
1951. Offers Humming Lariat premium. - **$15 $35 $60**

ROY-84

❑ **ROY-84. Roy Rogers' Cookies "Crackin' Good" Paper Pop Gun,**
1951. - **$15 $30 $65**

ROY-85

❑ **ROY-85. Bubble Gum Album,**
1951. Designed to hold two sets of 24 cards for movies "In Old Amarillo" and "South Of Caliente." Album
Complete - **$50 $125 $200**
Album Empty - **$25 $50 $75**

ROY-86

ROY-87

❑ **ROY-86. Quaker Cereal Box Puzzle Panel,**
1951. Back Panel Uncut - **$15 $30 $60**

❑ **ROY-87. "March Of Comics" Sears Christmas Book #77,**
1951. - **$18 $54 $150**

ROY-88

❑ **ROY-88. "Sears Christmas Trading Cards,"**
1951. Sears Happi-Time Toy Town. 10x10-1/2" punch-out sheet with card of Roy, Dale and six with Christmas theme. Gordon Gold archives.
Near Mint Unpunched **- $200**
Roy Card Loose - **$10 $25 $40**
Dale Card Loose - **$8 $15 $25**
Others Loose - **$1 $3 $5**

ROY-89

❑ **ROY-89. "Roy Rogers Cookies Wild West Action Toy" Store Sign And Punch-out Card,**
1951. Sign is 13x16-3/4". Shown with 5-1/4x7" punch-out carton insert premium. Gordon Gold Archives. Sign **- $100 $250 $350**
Unpunched Premium **- $15 $30 $50**

ROY-90

ROY-91

❑ **ROY-90. "Roy Rogers Riders Club Comics",**
1952. From membership kit. - **$40 $160 $350**

❑ **ROY-91. "Pop Out Card" Post's Box Wrapper,**
1952. Post's 40% Bran Flakes. Waxed paper wrapper offering set of 36 cards issued 1952-1955. Wrapper - **$150 $300 $700**

ROY-92

❑ **ROY-92. Pony Contest Entry Paper,**
1952. Post's Krinkles. For four consecutive weekly contests offering first prize pony each week plus other Roy merchandise prizes. - **$10 $20 $30**

ROY-93

ROY-94

❑ **ROY-93. "Trick Lasso Contestant" Transfer Sheet,**
1952. Issued for national lasso contest. - **$25 $50 $85**

❑ **ROY-94. Gun And Holster Premium Offer Sheet,**
1952. Post's Cereals. 6x7" red on white sheet for "Big Chrome Gun" and "Embossed Steer Hide Holster With Chrome Trappings And Bullets In Gun Belt." Expiration date of July 31. - **$20 $50 $85**

ROY-95

ROY-96

❑ **ROY-95. Litho. Tin Tab,**
1952. Roy Rogers Riders Club. Came with club comic book. - **$20 $40 $85**

❑ **ROY-96. Post Cereals Pop-Out Card #22,**
1952. From numbered set of 36 issued into 1955. Each Unpunched - **$8 $15 $30**

ROY-97

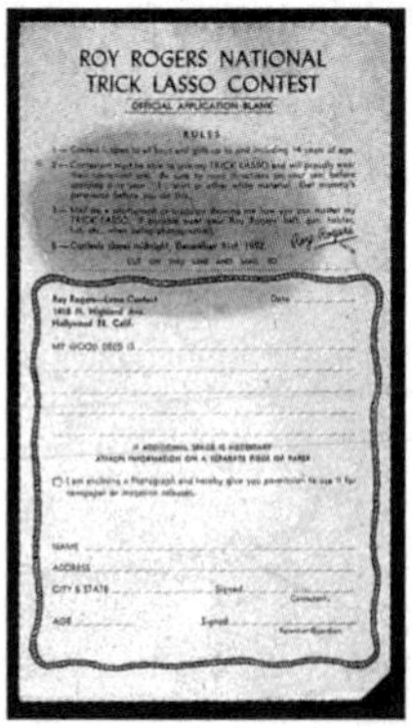

ROY-98

❑ **ROY-97. Grape Nuts Flakes Wrapper Flat,**
1952. Promotes pop-out cards. Gordon Gold Archives. - **$150 $300 $700**

❑ **ROY-98. Lasso Application,**
1952. National Trick Lasso contest application. - **$10 $20 $35**

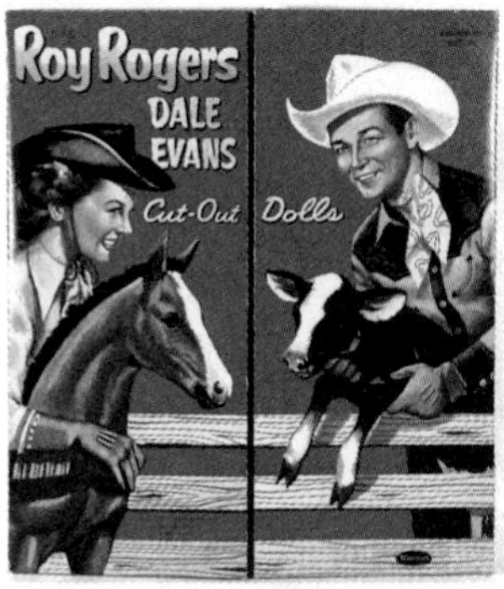

ROY-99

❑ **ROY-99. Roy Rogers and Dale Evans Cut-Out Dolls Book**
1953. With outfits. - **$75 $125 $250**

ROY-100

ROY-101

ROY-102

❑ **ROY-100. Knife in Sheath with Compass,**
1953. Knife handle shows Roy and Trigger. -
**$50 $140 $300**

❑ **ROY-101. "Western Ring" Post's Box Wrapper,**
1953. Post's Raisin Bran. Waxed paper wrapper offering set of 12 litho. tin rings. Gordon Gold Archives. Wrapper - **$150 $300 $700**

❑ **ROY-102. "Roy Rogers Western Medals" 17x24" Store Sign,**
1953. Post's Raisin Bran. Diecut cardboard with easel back. Pictures six example litho. tin tabs from set of 27 offered as box inserts. Gordon Gold Archives. - **$300 $650 $1000**

(ENLARGED VIEW)

ROY-103

❑ **ROY-103. "Post's Grape-Nuts Flakes" Store Window Display,**
c. 1953. 18x24" clear thin plastic with brightly colored inscriptions and box art featuring 3x4" Roy image. Top and bottom margins are banded by narrow peel-off adhesive strip for window mounting. Gordon Gold Archives. -
**$75 $200 $450**

(AD)

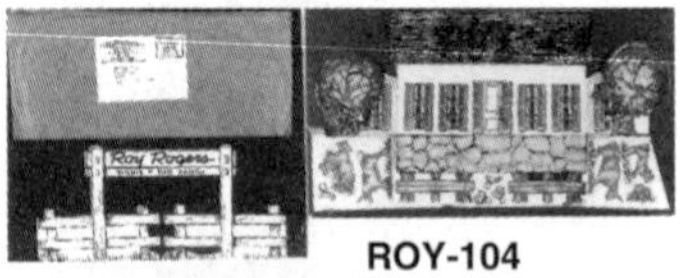

ROY-104

❑ **ROY-104. Post Cereals "Roy Rogers Ranch" Set,**
1953. Twenty-three piece set with plastic figures of Roy, Dale, Pat, Trigger, Buttermilk and Bullet. Set also included metal Nellybelle jeep and cardboard punch-outs of ranch house, gate, trees and ranch animals.
Complete - **$100 $250 $400**

ROY-105

❑ **ROY-105. Post Cardboard Sign 13x18",**
1953. Scarce. Pictures all 12 Raisin Bran rings. Gordon Gold Archives. - **$200 $450 $650**

ROY-106

❑ **ROY-106. "Bullet" Post's Raisin Bran Litho. Tin Ring,**
1953. This and the next 11 rings comprise a set of 12. The Near Mint price is for unbent examples with no rust. - **$10 $40 $100**

ROY-107

❑ **ROY-107. "Dale Evans" Post's Raisin Bran Litho. Tin Ring,**
1953. - **$10 $55 $125**

ROY-108

❑ **ROY-108. "Dale's Brand" Post's Raisin Bran Litho. Tin Ring,**
1953. - **$10 $30 $60**

ROY-109

❑ **ROY-109. "Deputy Sheriff" Post's Raisin Bran Litho. Tin Ring,**
1953. - **$10 $35 $70**

ROY-110

❑ **ROY-110. "Roy Rogers" Post's Raisin Bran Litho. Tin Ring,**
1953. - **$10 $55 $125**

ROY-111

❑ **ROY-111. "Roy's Boots" Post's Raisin Bran Litho. Tin Ring,**
1953. - **$10 $30 $60**

ROY-112

❑ **ROY-112. "Roy's Brand" Post's Raisin Bran Litho. Tin Ring,**
1953. - **$10 $30 $60**

ROY-113

❑ **ROY-113. "Roy's Gun" Post's Raisin Bran Litho. Tin Ring,**
1953. - **$10 $30 $60**

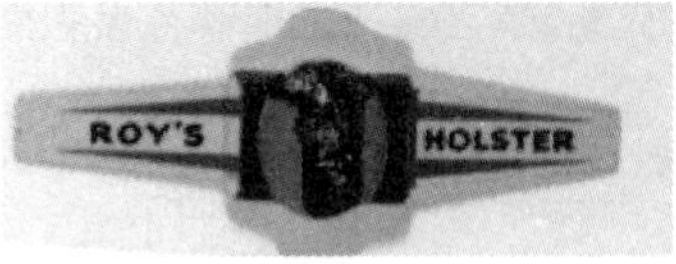


ROY-114

❑ **ROY-114. "Roy's Holster" Post's Raisin Bran Litho. Tin Ring,**
1953. - **$10 $30 $60**

ROY-115

❑ **ROY-115. "Roy's Saddle" Post's Raisin Bran Litho. Tin Ring,**
1953. - **$10 $30 $60**

ROY-116

❑ **ROY-116. "Sheriff" Post's Raisin Bran Litho. Tin Ring,**
1953. - **$10 $30 $60**

ROY-117

❑ **ROY-117. "Trigger" Post's Raisin Bran Litho. Tin Ring,**
1953. - **$10 $40 $100**

ROY-118

❑ **ROY-118. "Double R Bar Ranch" Cut-Outs,**
c. 1953. Post Grape-Nuts Flakes. Canadian Box, three in set. Each Box - **$100 $225 $425**

ROY-119 ROY-120

❑ **ROY-119. "King Of The Cowboys/Roy Rogers" Litho. Button,**
1953. Comes in 1-5/8" and 1-1/8" sizes. The 1-5/8" size comes with and without the Post's name on the reverse and was used as the "extra large" button in the U.S.A. along with fifteen 7/8" buttons to make a set of 16. The 1-1/8" button has not been seen with Post's name on the reverse but may have been used at a later time as the "extra large" button in both the U.S.A. and Canadian sets. Each - **$10 $25 $40**

❑ **ROY-120. "Queen Of The West/Dale Evans" Litho. Button,**
1953. Seen in 1-1/8" size only. Design matches ROY-119, but seen only with blank reverse. No documentation known indicates this is part of U.S.A. or Canadian set of 16 Post's buttons. - **$15 $25 $40**

ROY-121

❑ **ROY-121. Roy Rogers Western Medal Litho. Tin Tab,**
1953. Post's Raisin Bran. From set of 27. Each - **$5 $12 $25**

ROY-122

❑ **ROY-122. 3-D Photos,**
1953. Post's Sugar Crisp. Four photo folder with 3-D glasses, numbered series.
Intact - **$8 $15 $35**

ROY-123

❑ **ROY-123. Litho. Tin Button Set,**
1953. Post's Grape-Nuts Flakes and Rogers copyright text appears on reverse but also issued with blank reverses. Fifteen buttons are 7/8" and "extra large" portrait button inscribed "King of the Cowboys" in 1-5/8" or 1-1/8" size makes 16 in set. Each 7/8" - **$5 $10 $20**
"King of the Cowboys"-1-5/8" or 1-1/8" - **$10 $25 $40**

ROY-124

❑ **ROY-124. Canadian Litho. Tin Button Set,**
1953. Post's Canadian version of American set with different designs and smaller size. Fifteen small buttons are 3/4". The sixteenth button to complete the set is described as "extra large" and was likely the 1-1/8" version of the "King of the Cowboys" button pictured as ROY-123.
Each 3/4" - **$15 $30 $50**
Extra Large - **$10 $25 $40**

ROY-125

❑ **ROY-125. "March Of Comics" #105,**
1953. Various sponsors. Pictured example for Sears Christmas give-away. - **$10 $30 $85**

ROY-126

❑ **ROY-126. Post Grape-Nut Flakes Box With Roy Billboard,**
c. 1953. - **$40 $75 $175**

ROY-127

❑ **ROY-127. Roy Rogers Watch in Box,**
1953. With die-cut display. Box has a mylar top. Watch is the deluxe model with the metal band.
Boxed - **$700**
Watch only - **$100 $225 $375**

ROY-128

❑ **ROY-128. Dale Evans Watch in Box,**
1953. With die-cut display. Box has a mylar top. From Bradley Time Corp. Dale's watch is rarer than Roy's. Boxed - **$725**
Watch only - **$100 $225 $385**

ROY-129

ROY-130

❑ **ROY-129. Merchandise Promotion Button,**
c. 1953. Black and white photo on red background 1-3/4" seen with various imprints but this example promoted sales of merchandise in a special department of the Sears stores. -
**$25 $65 $100**

❑ **ROY-130. "Western Medals" Store Sign,**
1953. Full color about 17x24". Roy pictured only on the example medal. Gordon Gold Archives. -
**$200 $400 $600**

ROY-131

❑ **ROY-131. "Roy Rogers 3-D Pictures" Promotional Folder,**
1953. 8-1/2x11" full color stiff paper folder sent to grocery stores promoting 3-D pictures packaged with Post's Sugar Crisp cereal. Folder shows six of 48 photos and has attached envelope with 3-D glasses so store owner may view cards. Upper left has actual 3-D card glued in place while other images are replicas. Gordon Gold Archives. - **$200 $400 $600**

ROY-132

❑ **ROY-132. "3 Dimension Pictures" Offer On Waxed Wrapper Cereal Box,**
1953. Promotes set of 48 pictures. Each box held folder consisting of three-dimensional eyeglasses joined to a pair of picture cards with a separate picture on each side of the two cards. Gordon Gold Archives.
Used Complete - **$200 $425 $625**

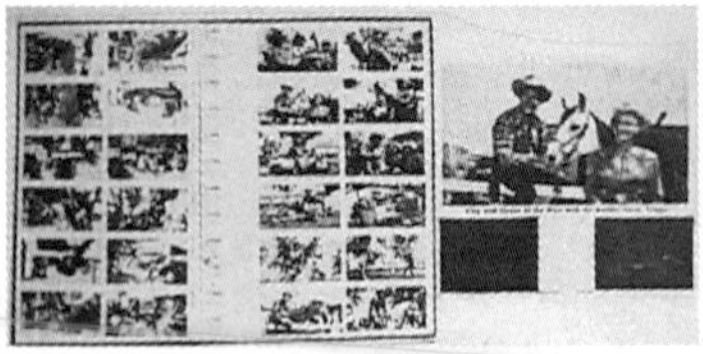
ROY-133

❑ **ROY-133. 3-D Premium Pictures Uncut Sheet With Viewer,**
1953. Post's Sugar Crisp. 16-1/2x21-1/2" single sheet showing 24 of the 48 different 3-D pictures. Gordon Gold Archives.
Sheet - **$150 $300 $500**
Glasses - **$5 $10 $15**

ROY-134

❑ **ROY-134. "Free! Roy Rogers Medals" Store Sign,**
1953. 8x9-1/8" diecut stiff paper designed like badge and holding actual litho. tin example "Roy Rogers." Gordon Gold Archives. -
**$100 $300 $500**

ROY-135

❑ **ROY-135. "Free! Buttons" Store Poster,**
1953. 18x24" full color picturing all 15 litho. tin pin-backs packaged in Grape-Nuts Flakes. Gordon Gold Archives. - **$250 $500 $800**

ROY-136

❑ **ROY-136. "King Of The Cowboys Roy Rogers Super Beanie" Complete Premium,**
1953. Mailer is 6x9" with red accent art with coupon on back to "Get The Entire Series Of 15 Roy Rogers Buttons." Green felt beanie is uninscribed. Button is full color 1-1/2" litho. Gordon Gold Archives.
Mailer And Beanie - **$200 $400 $700**
Button - **$10 $25 $40**

ROY-137

❑ **ROY-137. Cereal Box Wrapper With "Pin-On Button" Offer,**
1953. Includes offer for "Super Beanie! With Jumbo Roy Rogers Button" for 20 cents and one box top. Gordon Gold Archives.
Used Complete - **$300 $600 $900**

ROY-138

❑ **ROY-138. Cereal Box Wrapper With "Western Medal" Offer,**
1953. Gordon Gold Archives.
Used Complete - **$100 $300 $700**

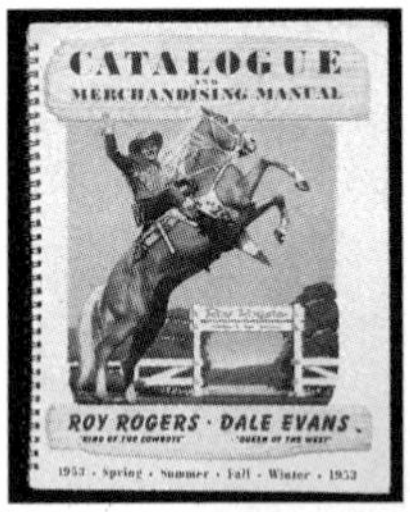

1953

1954-55

1955-56

ROY-139

❑ **ROY-139. Merchandise Manuals (all rare),**
1953 - **$125 $350 $725**
1954-1955 - **$100 $300 $625**
1955-1956 - **$75 $250 $525**

ROY-140

❑ **ROY-140. Paint By Number Set,**
1954. Post's Sugar Crisp. Three sets, each with two pictures. Each - **$25 $65 $120**

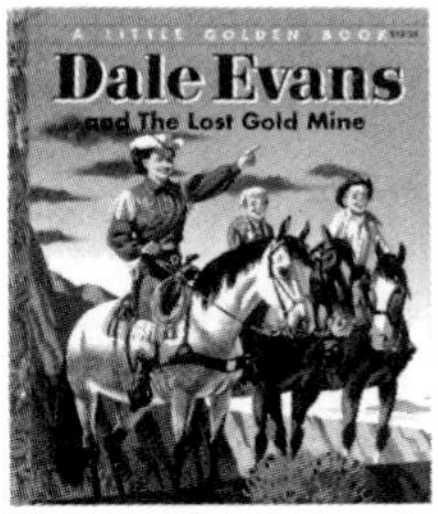


ROY-141

❑ **ROY-141. Dale Evans and the Lost Gold Mine" Golden Book,**
1954. - **$8 $20 $40**

ROY-143

ROY-142

❑ **ROY-142. Wrist Watch For Boys,**
1954. Deluxe watch with metal elastic band. On die-cut card in box with grey cardboard slipcase.
Boxed - **$650**
Watch with Metal Band - **$100 $200 $325**

❑ **ROY-143. "Roy Rogers Ranch Set" 21x22" Store Poster,**
1955. Post Cereals. Advertises the 18 piece all-cardboard set. - **$50 $175 $300**

ROY-144

❑ **ROY-144. "Roy Rogers Ranch" Cardboard Set,**
1955. Post Cereals. This 18 piece set was sent as a cardboard folder. - **$40 $75 $125**

ROY-145

❑ **ROY-145. Roy & Dale Golden Records Set With Mail Envelope,**
1955. Post's Sugar Crisp "Special Premium" offer not available at retail. Set of two.
Near Mint In Mailer - **$150**
Each Record - **$15 $30 $50**

ROY-146 (AD)

❑ **ROY-146. Dodge Motors Comic Booklet,**
1955. Ad story "Roy Rogers And The Man From Dodge City". - **$20 $50 $110**

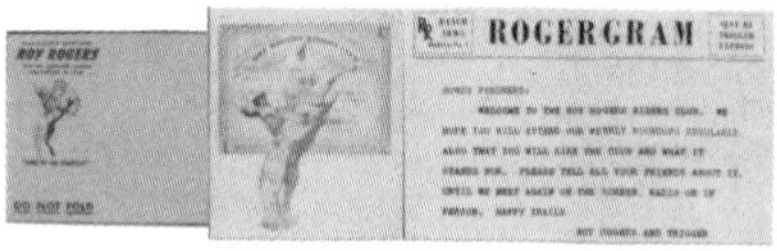


ROY-147

❑ **ROY-147. "Roy Rogers Riders Club" Theater Exhibitor Kit,**
c. 1955. Includes two cover letters, packet of eight pages with club information, "Rogergram" 14x20" poster. Complete **- $100 $200 $300**

ROY-148

ROY-149

❑ **ROY-148. March of Comics #136,**
1955. Various sponsors. - **$10 $30 $75**

❑ **ROY-149. "San Antonio World Championship Rodeo" Cello. Button,**
1955. Admittance serial number. -
**$60 $100 $150**

ROY-150

ROY-151

❑ **ROY-150. "Tracard" Photo Cards #2-3,**
c. 1955. American Tract Society. Examples from Christian message set. Each - **$5 $10 $15**

❑ **ROY-151. Sheathed Rubber Knife,**
1955. Knife has painted red handle. Leather belt loop holder has imprint of Roy. Very hard to find in nice condition. - **$75 $200 $375**

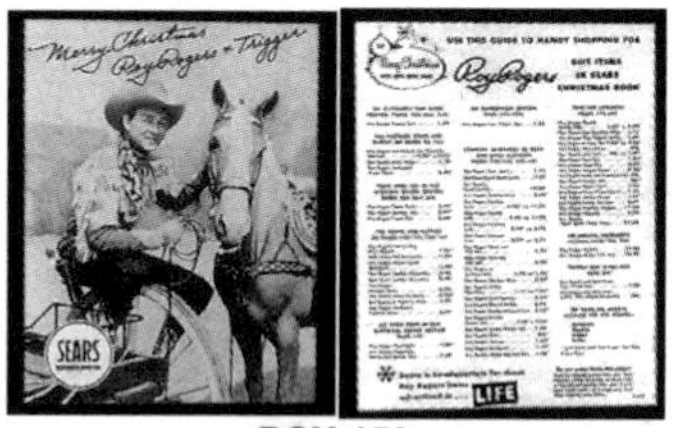


ROY-152

❑ **ROY-152. Roy/Sears Merchandise Handbill,**
c. 1955. Sears, Roebuck & Co. Single sheet with black and white photo plus listing on reverse of more than 60 Roy and/or Dale Evans gift items in Sears Christmas catalogue. - **$15 $50 $85**

ROY-153

❑ **ROY-153. Cereal Box Wrapper With "Ranch Set" Offer,**
1955. Waxed wrapper offering 18-piece set available for four box tops. Gordon Gold Archives. - **$200 $400 $750**

ROY-154

❑ **ROY-154. Roy Rogers Retail Card With "Western Blinkin' Blue Bolo Tie" ,**
c. 1955. Store item by Putnam Products Company. - **$50 $125 $225**

ROY-155

ROY-156

❑ **ROY-155. "Roy Rogers Riders" Cello. Button,**
c. 1955. Scarce variety with imprint of local "Mt. Ephraim Theatre." - **$50 $100 $200**

❑ **ROY-156. Advertising Calendar,**
1956. Sundial Shoes. 10x17" stiff paper with tipped-on 8-1/2x10-1/2" full color glossy photo with facsimile signature. - **$35 $75 $125**

ROY-157

❑ **ROY-157. "March Of Comics" #146 Booklet,**
1956. Printed for Sears, Roebuck. - **$15 $40 $85**

ROY-158

ROY-159

❑ **ROY-158. Schwinn Bicycles Catalogue With Roy And Others,**
1956. Folder opening to 18x24" printed on both sides including endorsement photos by Roy Rogers, Bill Williams as TV's Kit Carson, Gail Davis as TV's Annie Oakley. - **$35 $75 $150**

❑ **ROY-159. Roy Rogers, Dale Evans and Dusty Cut Out Doll Book,**
1957. Photo cover. - **$50 $100 $200**

ROY-160

❑ **ROY-160. Post Cereal Puzzles,**
1957. Set of six. Each - **$8 $15 $25**

ROY-161

❑ **ROY-161. Jig Saw Puzzle Wax Wrapper Cereal Box,**
1957. Six puzzles in set, inserted one per box. Gordon Gold Archives.
Used Complete - **$125 $250 $450**

ROY-162

❑ **ROY-162. "Roy Rogers March Of Comics" #161,**
1957. - **$10 $30 $65**

ROY-163

ROY-164

❑ **ROY-163. Harley-Davidson Motorcycle Monthly Magazine,**
1958. 9x12" with eight pages from October showing Roy on "Sportster" model at Wisconsin State Fairgrounds. - **$30 $75 $125**

❑ **ROY-164. "Guns" Magazine Monthly Issue,**
1958. 8-1/2x11" with 68 pages from August. - **$10 $20 $40**

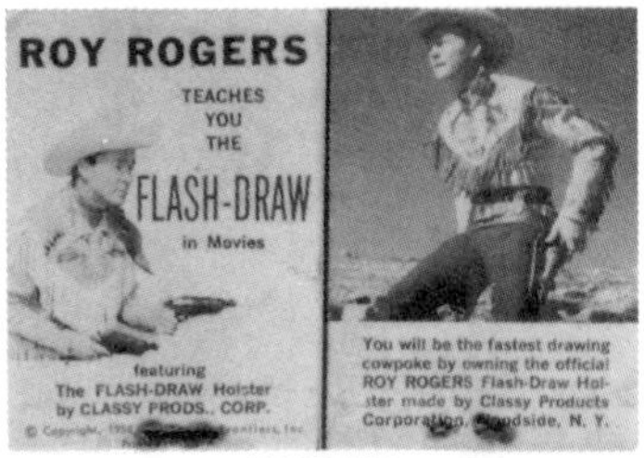


ROY-165

❑ **ROY-165. "Flash-Draw" Flip Booklet,**
1958. Classy Products Corp. Sequence photo "Movies" pages, came with cap gun set. - **$30 $75 $150**

ROY-166

❑ **ROY-166. "Roy Rogers Ranch Calendar",**
1959. Unmarked probably Nestle Quik. - **$50 $125 $175**

ROY-167

ROY-168

❑ **ROY-167. "Roy Rogers Stop Watch" Box,**
1959. Store item by Bradley Time. - **$100 $275 $500**

❑ **ROY-168. "Roy Rogers & Trigger" Pocketwatch,**
1959. Store item by Bradley. Also functions as a stopwatch. Beware of reproductions with color photocopy dial. - **$200 $325 $500**

ROY-169

ROY-170

❑ **ROY-169. "Roy Rogers Trick Lasso" 15x24" Cardboard Store Display,**
1950s. Scarce. Equipped with rope lasso on spring wire at center. - **$400 $1100 $2200**

❑ **ROY-170. Lariat Flashlight On Store Display Card,**
1950s. Bantamlite Inc.
Carded - **$75 $150 $325**
Light Only - **$15 $40 $95**

ROY-171

❑ **ROY-171. Promo Folder with Premium Record,**
1950s. Scarce. Sugar Crisp Cereal. - **$175 $300 $475**

ROY-172

❑ **ROY-172. "Double R Bar Ranch News" Club Newspaper,**
1950s. Issued bi-monthly. - **$25 $50 $85**

ROY-173

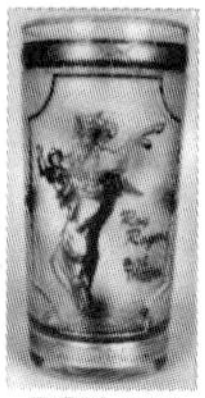
ROY-174

❑ **ROY-173. "Roy Rogers Riders" Metal/Plastic Harmonica,**
1950s. Store item by Harmonic Reed Corp. Also inscribed "King Of The Cowboys".
Boxed - **$40 $75 $125**
Loose - **$10 $20 $40**

❑ **ROY-174. Frosted Glass Tumbler With Gold Image,**
c. 1950s. Probable store item. On old glass, Trigger's front legs overlap. On Roy Rogers Museum new glass, Trigger's front legs each show without overlap.
Old - **$25 $60 $125**
New - **$3 $5 $8**

ROY-175

❑ **ROY-175 Western Clock,**
1950s. Electric clock with metal lasso rope that revolves as clock runs. - **$50 $100 $175**

(AD)

ROY-176

❑ **ROY-176. Trigger with Horseshoe Clock,**
1950s. These were used as prizes and sometimes sold at stores generically. - **$50 $100 $200**

ROY-177

❑ **ROY-177 Flash Camera With Papers And Box,**
1950s. Includes camera club card, press pass card.
Near Mint Boxed - **$350**
Unboxed With Flash - **$40 $75 $125**
Unboxed, No Flash - **$20 $50 $100**
Each Card - **$10 $20 $30**

ROY-178

ROY-179

❑ **ROY-178. "Riders Club" Membership Card,**
1950s. Back has club rules. - **$10 $30 $65**

❑ **ROY-179. "Roy Rogers Riders" Cello. Club Button,**
1950s. - **$15 $35 $75**

ROY-180

ROY-181

ROY-182

❑ **ROY-180. Fan Club Response Card,**
1950s. Club Headquarters. Back includes offer for View-Master reels plus name of TV sponsor Post Cereals. - **$15 $30 $50**

❑ **ROY-181. Fan Club Response Card,**
1950s. Club Headquarters. Back includes ad for store item decals plus name of TV sponsor Post Cereals. - **$15 $30 $50**

❑ **ROY-182. English Candy Cigarette Box,**
c. 1950s. - **$40 $75 $150**

ROY-183

❑ **ROY-183. "Wild West Action Toy" Punch-Out Sheet,**
1950s. Roy Rogers Cookies.
Unpunched - **$35 $60 $100**

ROY-184

ROY-185

❑ **ROY-184. "Roy Rogers Riders Lucky Piece",**
1950s. 1" brass medalet holed as made for key fob with Roy pictured facing right. - **$5 $15 $25**

❑ **ROY-185. "Roy Rogers Riders Lucky Piece",**
1950s. 1-1/16" brass medalet holed as made for key fob w/Roy pictured facing straight ahead. - **$7 $18 $28**

ROY-186

ROY-187

❑ **ROY-186. "Roy Rogers Riders Lucky Piece",**
1950s. 1" brass medalet with Roy pictured looking upward and facing slightly left. - **$10 $20 $30**

❑ **ROY-187. "Roy Rogers Riders Lucky Piece",**
1950s. 1-3/16" brass medalet picturing Roy with broad smile facing left. - **$12 $22 $35**

ROY-188

ROY-189

❑ **ROY-188. "Roy Rogers Riders Lucky Piece",**
1950s. 1-1/8" white metal with copper luster medalet picturing Roy facing straight ahead. Design is in much higher relief than other medalets with same inscription. - **$12 $22 $35**

❑ **ROY-189. English Club Member's Cello. Button,**
1950s. 1-1/4" with b&w photo on white and bright yellow rim. - **$100 $300 $450**

ROY-190

ROY-191

❑ **ROY-190. Deputy Tin Star Badge,**
1950s. Issued by Post's, Popsicle, and probably others. Comes in copper, yellow brass, or silver finish. - **$10 $20 $35**

❑ **ROY-191. Glass,**
1950s. Probably held dairy product. - **$50 $80 $150**

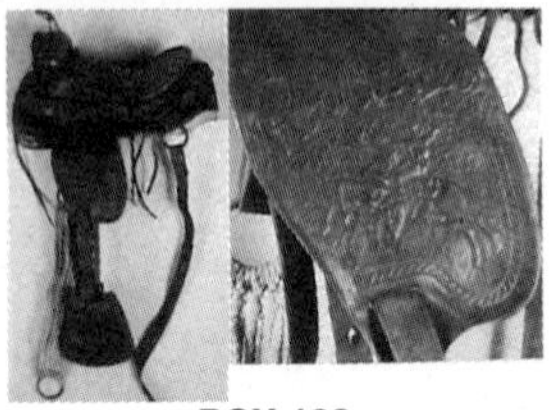

ROY-192

❑ **ROY-192. "Roy Rogers" Child's Leather Saddle,**
1950s. Store item. Well made brown leather western saddle with each side panel inscribed "Roy Rogers" in rope script above image of him on rearing Trigger. - **$400 $800 $1500**

ROY-193

❑ **ROY-193. Deputy Badge On Store Display Card,**
1950s. Post Cereals with seven varieties shown on card. 5x6-1/4" diecut stiff paper with actual example of copper finish badge mounted at center. Display - **$150 $300 $500**
Badge Only - **$10 $20 $35**

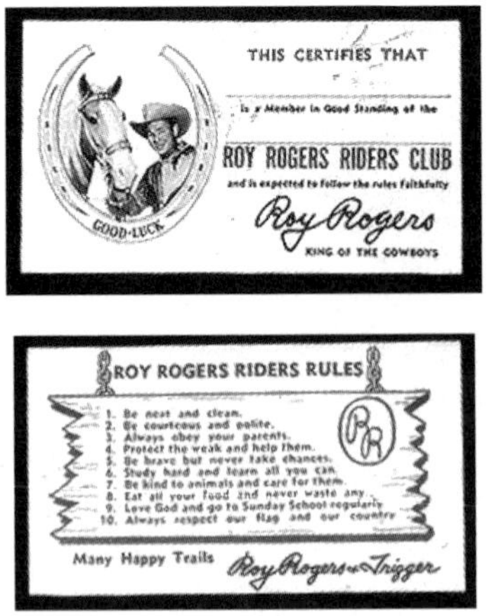


ROY-194

❑ **ROY-194. "Roy Rogers Riders Club" Membership Card,**
1950s. Version in red, white and blue front and black, blue and white reverse. - **$10 $40 $85**

ROY-195

ROY-196

❑ **ROY-195. "Roy Rogers Rodeo" 13x21" Cardboard Poster,**
1950s. - **$75 $150 $275**

❑ **ROY-196. "Roy Rogers Sweaters" Store Postcard,**
1950s. - **$10 $20 $35**

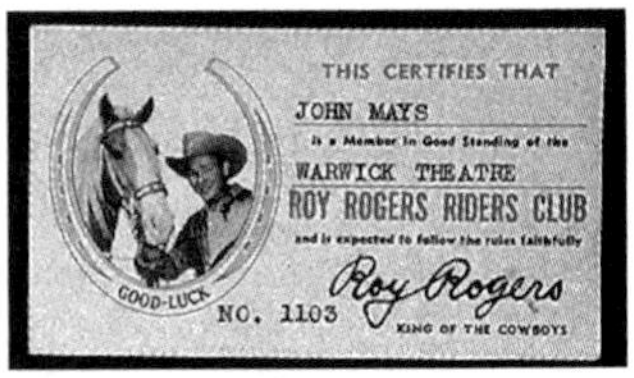


ROY-197

❑ **ROY-197. Riders Club Membership Card,**
1950s. Movie premium from Warwick Theater. - **$10 $40 $85**

ROY-198

❑ **ROY-198. Dale Evans Wristwatch,**
1950. - **$125 $250 $400**

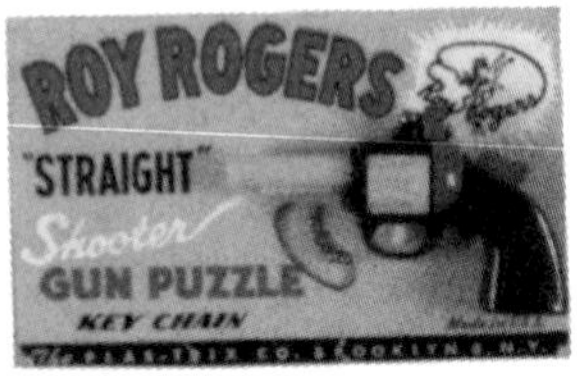


ROY-199

❑ **ROY-199. "Roy Rogers Gun Puzzle" On Card,**
1950s. Store item by Plas-Trix Co.
Carded - **$35 $75 $150**

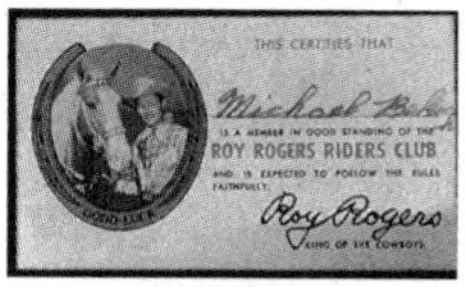


ROY-200

ROY-201

❑ **ROY-200. Riders Club Card,**
1950s. Yellow card. Movie premium. -
**$15 $40 $85**

❑ **ROY-201. Photo,**
1950s. Movie premium. Black & white photo featuring Roy and Gabby Hayes. - **$10 $20 $40**

ROY-202

ROY-203

❑ **ROY-202. Photo,**
1950s. Movie premium. Black & white photo of Roy and his gun. - **$10 $20 $30**

❑ **ROY-203. Photo,**
1950s. Movie premium. Black & white photo of Roy with two Deputy Sheriffs. - **$10 $20 $30**

ROY-204

❑ **ROY-204. "Best Wishes Roy Rogers, Dale Evans & Trigger" Picture,**
1950s. Issued by Nestle's Quik. 8x9-1/2". -
**$10 $20 $40**

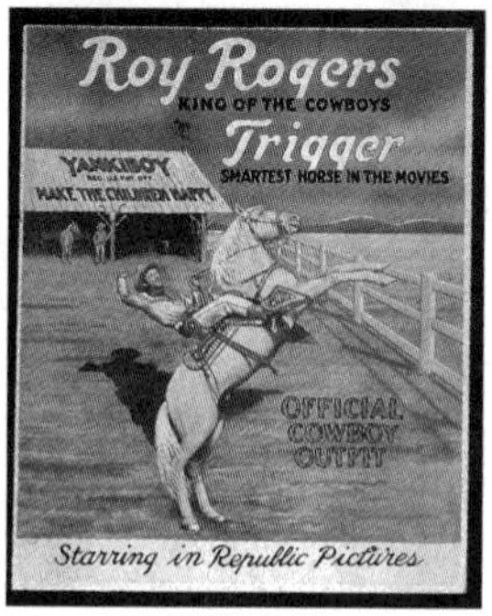


ROY-205

❑ **ROY-205. Official Cowboy Outfit In Box,**
1950s. Shirt, cloth chaps, marked Roy and Trigger, gun, holster, lariat, and belt. Republic Pictures promoted on colorful box. -
**$80 $200 $425**

ROY-206

❑ **ROY-206. Dell Comics Photo Strip Folder,**
1950s. - **$40 $75 $135**

ROY-207

❑ **ROY-207. "Nestle's Quik" Canister With Premium Offer,**
1960. Back offers 3-D plastic plaque set with expiration date June 30. - **$50 $150 $225**

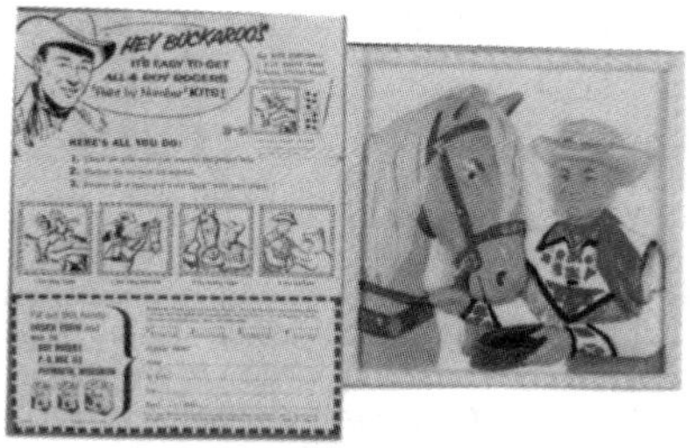


ROY-208

❑ **ROY-208. Roy Feeding Trigger Hand-Painted Relief Picture With Order Form,**
1960. 8-7/8x8-7/8" molded thin plastic issued by Nestle's Quik for 50 cents each and lid from can. Order Form - **$20 $40 $60**
Each Picture Unpainted Or Nicely Painted - **$65**

ROY-209

❑ **ROY-209. "Roy Rogers Chevy Show" Pair Of "NBC" Transcription Records,**
1960. Songs include Happy Trails.
Pair - **$50 $125 $225**

ROY-210

ROY-211

❑ **ROY-210. "Roy Rogers Ranch Calendar",**
1960. Nestle's Quik. - **$50 $125 $200**

❑ **ROY-211. "Roy Rogers Ranch Calendar",**
1961. Nestle's Quik. - **$50 $125 $200**

ROY-212

ROY-213

❑ **ROY-212. Quick Shooter Hat in Box,**
1961. - **$100 $250 $450**

❑ **ROY-213. Litho. Soda Can,**
c. 1960s. Continental Beverage Corp., La Jolla, California. - **$60 $130 $200**

ROY-214

❑ **ROY-214. Nestle Candy Coupon,**
1961. - **$15 $30 $50**

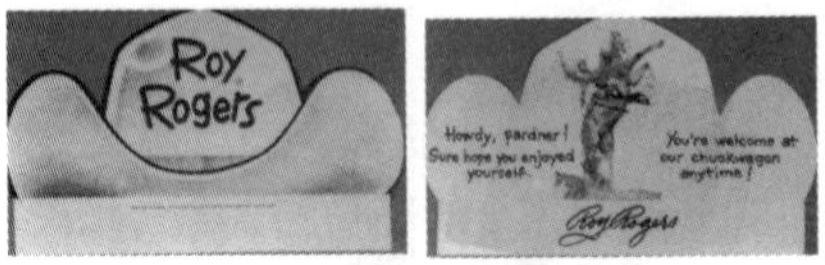


ROY-215

❑ **ROY-215. Paper Hat,**
c. 1970s. Roy Rogers Restaurants. -
**$5 $10 $20**

ROY-216

ROY-217

❑ **ROY-216. Life-Sized 75" Tall Cardboard Standee,**
c. 1980. Thousand Trails Campgrounds. -
**$100 $225 $400**

❑ **ROY-217. "Roy Rogers Family Restaurants" 2" Litho. Button,**
1980s. Various locations, pictured example from Maryland. - **$3 $6 $12**

(Gun)

(Box)

ROY-218

❑ **ROY-218. Daisy Limited Edition BB Gun,**
1995. With commemorative scarf and box with instructions. Only 2,500 produced. A medal with the edition number is embedded in the stock of the gun. Includes a certificate of authenticity. Complete - **$275**

ROY-219

❑ **ROY-219. Limited Edition Cookie Jar,**
1996. Edition of 2,500. - **$550**

ROY-220

ROY-221

❑ **ROY-220. "King of the Cowboys" Guitar,**
2000. Commemorates his life (1911-1998). - **$30**

❑ **ROY-221. Two Coin Proof Set,**
2000. From the Legends of the American West series. Authorized coins by the Republic of Liberia. Happy Trails coin was limited to 1,000. Set in box with certificate - **$75**

## Rudolph the Red-Nosed Reindeer

**Rudolph originated as a 1939 story created by Robert L. May for use by Montgomery Ward & Company. The company printed 2,400,000 copies to give away. The character achieved even greater recognition in 1949 when Johnny Marks wrote a song based on the story and the Gene Autry recording went off the charts. Over the years, in excess of ten million copies have sold, making it Autry's greatest hit.**

**DC Comics published thirteen comic books between 1950 and Winter 1962-63. Rudolph came to life first as a 1944 Max Fleischer animated cartoon and later as a 1964 "Dynamation" TV special produced by Rankin-Bass Productions and aired annually over twenty years, becoming one of the most popular holiday TV specials ever produced. In the last few years a restored print of the special with restored footage that was cut over the years has been aired several times.**

**Rankin-Bass' Rudolph went on to star in the television special *Rudolph's Shiny New Year* (1976) and the feature-length *Rudolph and Frosty's Christmas in July* (1979), with Ethel Merman offering her own unique rendition of Rudolph's theme song. Johnny Marks composed many additional songs for the various Rudolph productions, and a resurgence in the original special's popularity has led to a flood of new merchandise, from beanbag characters to Christmas tree ornaments, all in the Rankin-Bass style. A new animated film by another production company was released to video in recent years as well, but did not capture the level of attention and popularity that Rankin-Bass' version did.**

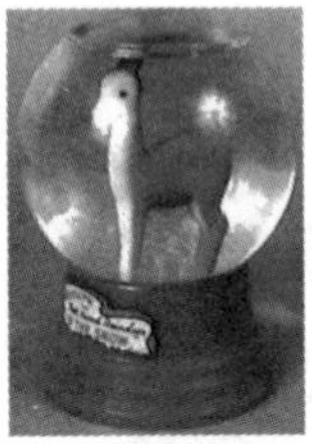

RUD-1

RUD-2

❑ **RUD-1. Snow Dome,**
c. 1950. Store item. Driss Co., Chicago. 4" tall on green plastic base with red and black name decal. - **$25 $50 $85**

❑ **RUD-2. Figural Plastic Light-Up Bank,**
c. 1950. Store item. 5-1/2" long. Inserted coin hits brass tab and should light the red bulb nose. - **$15 $40 $75**

RUD-3

❑ **RUD-3. "Rudolph's 32 Page Fun Book" Original Art Prototype,**
c. 1950. Presentation piece for Montgomery Ward stores. 8x10-1/2" with 32 pages of original art. Gordon Gold Archives. Unique - **$1050**

RUD-4

❑ **RUD-4. "Yearling" Litho. Tin Wind-Up Toy,**
c. 1950. Store item with box marked "Made In Occupied Japan" and toy marked "Made In Japan." 5-1/4" tall unlicensed but with red nose obviously inspired by Rudolph. Has leather ears.
Box - **$10 $20 $50**
Toy - **$20 $40 $70**

RUD-5

❑ **RUD-5. Classic Song Record By Gene Autry,**
1951. Store item by Columbia Records. 45 rpm with jacket. - **$10 $20 $30**

RUD-6

❑ **RUD-6. Classic Song Record By Gene Autry,**
1951. Store item by Columbia Records. 78 rpm with 10x10" jacket. - **$20 $40 $60**

RUD-7

❑ **RUD-7. Alvin And The Chipmunks 45 RPM Record,**
1961. Store item by Liberty. - **$5 $12 $25**

RUD-8

RUD-9

❑ **RUD-8. Plastic Mug With Flicker Eye,**
1960s. Store item. Eagle, U.S.A. 4-1/4" tall with brown and red art, black and white flicker eye. - **$10 $20 $40**

❑ **RUD-9. Rudolph Bean Figure,**
1998. 1st series. The set of 12 was available exclusively at CVS Pharmacies. - **$20**

RUD-10

RUD-11

❑ **RUD-10. Santa Claus Bean Figure,**
1998. 1st series. - **$20**

❑ **RUD-11. Clarice Bean Figure,**
1998. 1st series. Mouth is larger than 2nd series figure. - **$12**

RUD-12

RUD-13

RUD-14

❑ **RUD-12. Herbie Bean Figure,**
1998. 1st series. - **$10**

❑ **RUD-13. Sam the Snowman Bean Figure,**
1998. 1st series. - **$15**

❑ **RUD-14. Yukon Cornelius Bean Figure,**
1998. 1st series. No snowshoes, unlike 2nd series version. - **$12**

RUD-15

RUD-16

❑ **RUD-15. Misfit Train Bean Toy,**
1998. 1st series. From the Land of Misfit Toys.- **$12**

❑ **RUD-16. Misfit Doll Bean Figure,**
1998. 1st series. - **$12**

RUD-17

RUD-18

RUD-19

❑ **RUD-17. Spotted Elephant Bean Figure,**
1998. 1st series. - **$12**

❑ **RUD-18. King Moonracer Bean Figure,**
1998. 1st series. - **$12**

❑ **RUD-19. Charlie-in-the Box Bean Figure,**
1998. 1st series. - **$15**

RUD-20

RUD-21

❑ **RUD-20. Rudolph Bean Figure,**
1999. 2nd series. This 2nd set of 12 was also sold at CVS Pharmacies. - **$15**

❑ **RUD-21. Santa Bean Figure,**
1999. 2nd series. - **$10**

RUD-22

RUD-23

❑ **RUD-22. Clarice Bean Figure,**
1999. 2nd series. This Clarice has a smaller mouth than the 1st series figure. - **$12**

❑ **RUD-23. Reindeer Coach Comet Figure,**
1999. 2nd series. - **$10**

RUD-24

RUD-25

RUD-26

❑ **RUD-24. Boss Elf Bean Figure,**
1999. 2nd series. - **$10**

❑ **RUD-25. Tall Elf Bean Figure,**
1999. 2nd series. - **$10**

❑ **RUD-26. Sam the Snowman Bean Figure,**
1999. 2nd series. - **$12**

RUD-27

RUD-28

RUD-29

❑ **RUD-27. Yukon Cornelius Bean Figure,**
1999. 2nd series. This version has snowshoes unlike 1st series. - **$10**

❑ **RUD-28. Misfit Water Pistol Bean Figure,**
1999. 2nd series. - **$10**

❑ **RUD-29. Misfit Plane Bean Figure,**
1999. 2nd series. - **$10**

RUD-30

RUD-31

❑ **RUD-30. Frosty the Snowman Bean Figure,**
1999. Modeled after the cartoon character. Set of 4 figures sold at CVS. - **$12**

❑ **RUD-31. Karen Bean Figure,**
1999. Frosty series. - **$10**

RUD-32

RUD-33

❑ **RUD-32. Professor Hinkle Bean Figure,**
1999. Frosty series. - **$10**

❑ **RUD-33. Traffic Cop Bean Figure,**
1999. Frosty series. - **$10**

RUD-34

❑ **RUD-34. Abominable Snowman Bean Figure,**
1999. 16" tall. "Land of Misfit Toys" series. Released at the end of 1999 to celebrate New Year's 2000. Hard to find on the secondary market. - **$50**

RUD-35

❑ **RUD-35. Rudolph Lunch Box,**
2000. - **$25**

## Sally Starr

**Sally Starr, born in Kansas City, Mo., in 1923, was singing on a CBS country radio show at the age of 12. She worked as a radio disc jockey, and in 1950 became hostess of *Popeye Theater* on Channel 6, WFIL, in Philadelphia. Dressed as a cowgirl and calling herself Our Gal Sal, she showed cartoons and *Three Stooges* shorts, read original stories, and chatted with show business visitors. The program became Philadelphia's highest rated children's show and ran until 1972. In the mid-1980s Sal made personal appearances in the tri-state area and in 1993 she was named Grand Marshal of the 84th Annual Baby Parade in Ocean City, New Jersey. She continues to be a weekly radio show hostess at the outset of 2000.**

SAL-1

SAL-2

❑ **SAL-1. Full Color 3-1/2" Cello. Button,**
1950s. - **$10 $20 $40**

❑ **SAL-2. "Sally Starr" Outfitted Doll,**
1950s. 10" tall vinyl doll with fabric cowgirl outfit patterned after actual performance outfit. - **$25 $70 $125**

SAL-3

❑ **SAL-3. "Cowgirl Outfit" With Photo,**
1950s. Store item by Herman Iskin & Co. 8x10" photo accompanies youngster's denim and suede-like fabric colorful jacket and skirt.
Near Mint Boxed - **$140**
Photo Only - **$5 $10 $20**
Outfit Only - **$30 $50 $85**

SAL-4

❑ **SAL-4. Performance Ticket With Record Offer,**
1950s. Photo ticket with reverse offer for child's Easter song record by her. - **$5 $10 $15**

SAL-5

❑ **SAL-5. Cowgirl Doll Outfit,**
1950s. Store item by Dandee Doll Mfg. Co. Scaled for 10-1/2" dolls. - **$25 $60 $110**

SAL-6

❑ **SAL-6. TV Show Photo,**
1950s. 5x7" issued by "Gold Square Trading Stamps." **$15 $25 $50**

## Scoop Ward

**Laddie Seaman, alias Scoop Ward, narrated dramatizations of the news for his teenage audience in *News of Youth* on CBS radio from late 1935 to 1937. The program was sponsored by Ward's Soft Bun bread and Silver Queen pound cake.**

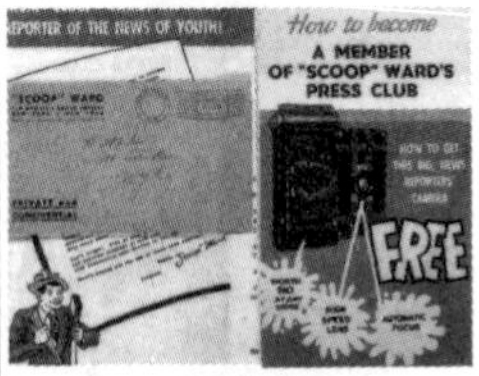


SCW-1

SCW-2

❑ **SCW-1. Club Newsletter With Envelope,**
1936. Ward's Bread and Silver Queen Pound Cake. Mailer - **$3 $5 $10**
Newsletter - **$10 $25 $60**

❑ **SCW-2. "Official Reporter" Brass Shield Badge,**
1936. Ward's Soft Bun Bread. - **$5 $12 $25**

SCW-3

❑ **SCW-3. Member Recruitment Brochure With Typewriter Offer,**
c. 1936. Ward's Bread/Silver Queen Pound Cake. - **$10 $25 $60**

## Seckatary Hawkins

**This children's program was developed from a comic strip of the same name by Robert F. Schulkers. Hawkins was the leader of a boys' club that spent its time helping to round up bad boys. The club's motto was "Fair and Square." The radio series, sponsored by Ralston Purina, was broadcast on NBC in 1932-1933.**

SKH-1

❑ **SKH-1. Club Kit,**
1929. With pin, card, and mailer.
Set - **$25 $50 $80**

SKH-2

SKH-3

❑ **SKH-2. Birthday Card,**
1929. Newspaper premium from the Milwaukee Journal. - **$12 $20 $30**

❑ **SKH-3. Birthday Card Mailer,**
1929. Premium mailer for card. - **$5 $10 $15**

SKH-4

SKH-5

SKH-6

❑ **SKH-4. "Fair And Square" Member's Cello. Button,**
1932. 7/8" size. Red rim. - **$5 $12 $20**

❑ **SKH-5. "Fair And Square" Cello. Club Button,**
1932. 7/8" size. Blue rim. - **$4 $8 $12**

❑ **SKH-6. "Fair And Square" Litho. Club Button,**
1932. 3/4" size. - **$5 $12 $20**

SKH-7

SKH-8

SKH-9

❑ **SKH-7. "Fair And Square" Ralston Club Enameled Brass Spinner,**
1932. Spinner disk forms club slogan when spun. - **$20 $50 $75**

❑ **SKH-8. "Sunday Baltimore American" Cello. Club Button,**
c. 1932. - **$10 $20 $30**

❑ **SKH-9. Figure Of Hollow Pressed Cardboard,**
c. 1932. About 12" tall. - **$35 $60 $100**

SKH-10

SKH-11

❑ **SKH-10. The Ghost of Lake Tapako Book,**
1932. Ralston. - **$10 $35 $75**

❑ **SKH-11. Good Luck Fair and Square Coin,**
1960s. Scarce. - **$15 $30 $50**

## Secret Agent X-9

**Written by Dashiell Hammett and drawn by Alex Raymond, *Secret Agent X-9* was introduced by King Features in January 1934. X-9 is a loner who fights urban criminals by seeming to become part of their evil world. Hammett and Raymond went on to other things in 1935, and the strip was continued by an assortment of writers and artists, evolving in 1967 to *Secret Agent Corrigan*. Comic book reprints of the first eight months of the strip were published in 1934. There was a short-lived radio program, and Universal Pictures made two *Secret Agent X-9* chapter plays, one in 1937 starring Scott Kolk; the other, with Lloyd Bridges starring, in 1945.**

SCX-1

❑ **SCX-1. Daily Comic Strip Book,**
1934. Store item. - **$40 $150 $350**

SCX-2

❑ **SCX-2. Secret Agent X-9 Original Comic Strip Art By Alex Raymond,**
1935. 7x27" three-panel comic strip art for publication September 19. Examples Of Similar Age And Content - **$500 $650 $1100**

SCX-3

SCX-4

❑ **SCX-3. Big Little Book #1144,**
1936. - **$15 $60 $100**

❑ **SCX-4. Movie Serial Cello. Button,**
1937. Universal. 1-1/4" red, black and white naming stars "Scott Kolk-Jean Rogers." - **$75 $175 $300**

SCX-5

SCX-6

❑ **SCX-5. Club Membership Card With Envelope,**
1930s. With Envelope - **$12 $40 $70**
Card Only - **$8 $20 $50**

❑ **SCX-6. "Secret Agent X-9/Chicago Herald And Examiner" Silvered Metal Badge,**
1930s. - **$15 $25 $50**

SCX-7

SCX-8

❑ **SCX-7. Cello. Button,**
1940s. - **$20 $50 $100**

❑ **SCX-8. Water Gun,**
1950s. Irwin. Store item. Billy club serves as water tank. - **$15 $50 $85**

SCX-9

❑ **SCX-9. Secret Agent X-9 Pair Of Original Daily Strips,**
1960. Art by Paul Norris, assistant to main artist Mel Graff.
Examples Of Similar Age And Content Each - **$10 $25 $40**

## The Secret 3

**Murray McLean starred in this serial detective drama sponsored by 3-Minute Oat Flakes and apparently broadcast only regionally in the 1930s. Premiums included a membership badge, a Confidential Code Book, and a variety of generic crime-fighting paraphernalia. The show's main characters were: Ben Potter, Chief of Detectives; Jack Williams, 1st Lieutenant; Mary Lou Davis, 2nd Lieutenant.**

SCT-1

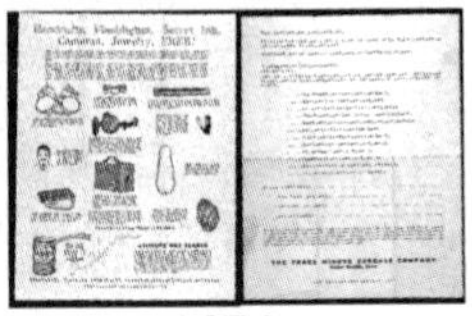

SCT-2

❑ **SCT-1. Silvered Brass Badge,**
1930s. Rare. - **$50 $110 $175**

❑ **SCT-2. Secret 3 Premium List,**
1930s. 3-Minute Oat Flakes Cereal premium. Shows color picture of 12 pieces of equipment on back. Front side lists premiums and how to get them. - **$10 $25 $50**

SCT-3

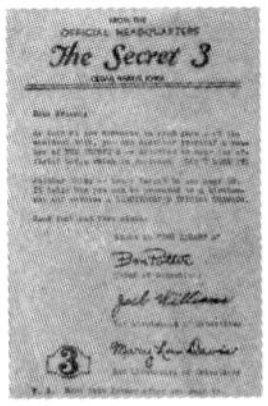


SCT-4

❑ **SCT-3. Club Member Code/Rule Book,**
1930s. Rare. 3-Minute Oat Flakes. Includes two pages of detective premiums. - **$25 $125 $200**

❑ **SCT-4. Club Headquarters Cover Letter,**
1930s. Scarce. P.S. notation on letter is "Burn this letter after you read it." - **$10 $35 $50**

SCT-5

❑ **SCT-5. "Lieutenant" Rank Pin,**
1930s. 3-Minute Oat Flakes premium.
1.25" wide. - **$50 $100 $150**

## Sergeant Preston of the Yukon

**Under its original title, *Challenge of the Yukon*, this adventure series of the Royal Canadian Mounties during the gold-rush days of the 1890s was heard initially on Detroit radio station WXYZ from 1938 to 1947. Created by George W. Trendle and Fran Striker after their success with *The Lone Ranger* and *The Green Hornet*, the program centered on the crime-fighting exploits of Sgt. Frank Preston and his malamute partner Yukon King, "the swiftest and strongest lead dog of the Northwest." The series moved to the ABC network in 1947 and then to Mutual in 1950, where it remained until 1955. Quaker Puffed Wheat and Rice were the long-term sponsors. In 1951 the program changed its name officially to *Sergeant Preston of the Yukon*, although it was also popularly known as Yukon King, a reflection of the dog's central role in Preston's always getting his man.**

**On television, the series was broadcast on CBS from 1955 to 1958, sponsored by Quaker Oats and Mother's Oats. Richard Simmons starred in the title role, riding his black stallion Rex and assisted, as always by Yukon King. Reruns were seen on NBC during the 1963-1964 season.**

***Sergeant Preston* comic books were published between 1951 and 1959, including a set of four giveaways in two sizes from Quaker cereals in 1956. The cereal company also offered a great variety of other premiums, notably a 1955 in-package deed to a one-square-inch tract of land in the Yukon.**

SGT-1

SGT-2

❑ **SGT-1. Autographed Photo,**
c. 1947. Believed to picture Paul Sutton radio voice of Sgt. Preston. - **$75 $135 $225**

❑ **SGT-2. Fan Photo,**
1947. - **$20 $30 $70**

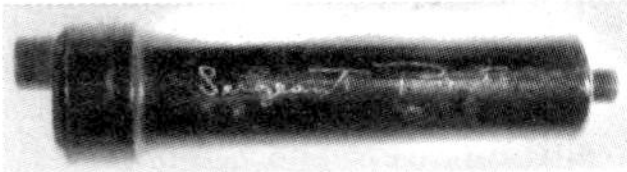

SGT-3

❑ **SGT-3. 2-Way Signal Flashlight,**
1949. Plastic disk produces red or green light. - **$25 $60 $125**

SGT-4

SGT-5

❑ **SGT-4. Dog Cards,**
1949. Set of 35. Each - **$2 $4 $6**

❑ **SGT-5. Club Photo,**
1949. Radio premium. - **$50 $75 $100**

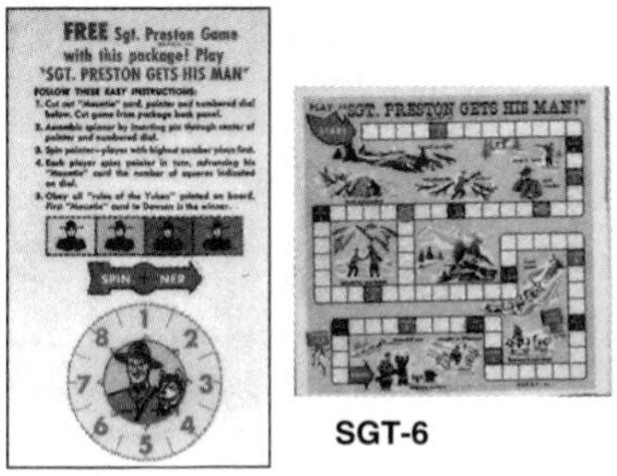

SGT-6

❑ **SGT-6. "Sergeant Preston Gets His Man" Game,**
1949. Game board and playing pieces from Quaker cereal boxes.
Cut But Complete - **$20 $40 $65**
Complete Box - **$75 $150 $250**

SGT-7

SGT-8

❑ **SGT-7. "Dog Sled Race" Quaker Box Back,**
1949. From series of three games offered.
Complete Box - **$75 $150 $250**
Uncut Box Back With Side Parts Panel - **$20 $40 $65**

❑ **SGT-8. "Great Yukon River Canoe Race" Quaker Box Back,**
1949. From series of three games offered.
Complete With Markers - **$20 $40 $65**

SGT-9

SGT-10

❑ **SGT-9. Sgt. Preston Autographed Photo,**
1949. 8x10" glossy signed with character name probably by Paul Sutton, one of the radio voices of Sgt. Preston. - **$50 $135 $225**

❑ **SGT-10. "Official Seal" Litho. Button,**
c. 1949. Rare.1-3/8" black and red on yellow background. Four known. - **$500 $1200 $2500**

SGT-11

SGT-12

❑ **SGT-11. Mountie Badge,**
1940s. Canada. No documentation as Sgt. Preston item. Came with Toy Clicker Gun Set. - **$25 $50 $85**

❑ **SGT-12. Rectangular Bar,**
1940s. Canada. No documentation as Sgt. Preston item. Came with Toy Clicker Gun Set. - **$25 $50 $85**

SGT-13

❑ **SGT-13. "Yukon Trail" Quaker Puffed Wheat Box Back,**
1950. Set of eight.
Complete Box - **$100 $200 $350**
Each Uncut Box Back - **$25 $50 $80**

SGT-14

SGT-15

❑ **SGT-14. "Sergeant Preston Yukon Adventure Picture Cards",**
1950. Set of 36. Each - **$2 $4 $6**
Complete Set With Mailer - **$240**

❑ **SGT-15. Quaker Contest Entrant Acknowledgement Postcard,**
1950. - **$15 $25 $50**

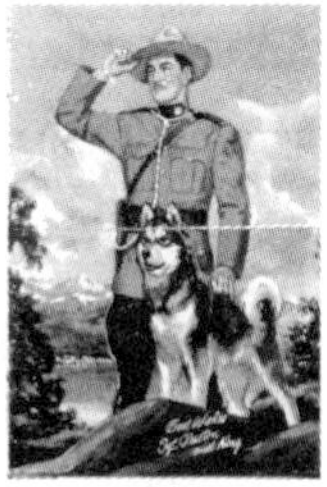
SGT-16

SGT-17

❑ **SGT-16. Dog-Naming Contest 19x25-1/2" Award Poster,**
1950. Scarce. - **$200 $400 $800**

❑ **SGT-17. Mailing Tube For Dog-Naming Contest Award Poster,**
1950. Rare. - **$25 $65 $125**

SGT-18

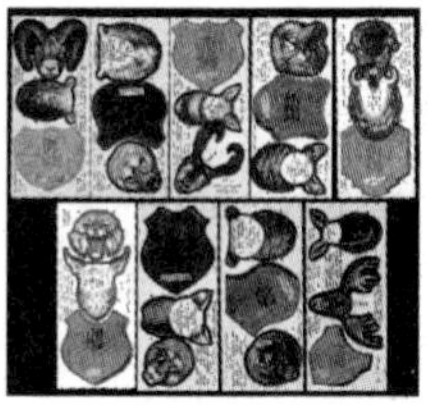
SGT-19

❑ **SGT-18. Award Poster Small Version,**
1950. - **$20 $35 $75**

❑ **SGT-19. Trophies,**
1950. 9 different punch-outs of animal heads.
Each - **$5 $10 $20**

SGT-20

❑ **SGT-20. Cereal Box With "Yukon Adventure" Cards Offer,**
1950. Cards were issued two per box for set of 36. Gordon Gold Archives.
Used Complete - **$75 $150 $250**

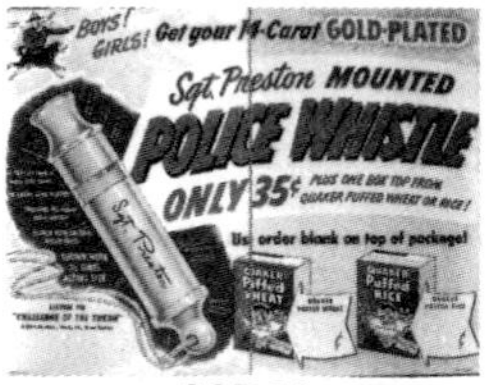

SGT-21

SGT-22

❑ **SGT-21. Police Whistle 17x22" Paper Store Sign,**
1950. - **$100 $250 $400**

❑ **SGT-22. Brass Whistle,**
1950. Facsimile signature on side. - **$20 $30 $60**

SGT-23

SGT-24

❏ **SGT-23. Portrait Photo,**
c. 1950 Probably a Quaker premium. -
**$20 $35 $70**

❏ **SGT-24. "Quaker Camp Stove" With Folder,**
1952. Scarce. Metal items are firebox & cover, oven, tongs. Set - **$35 $150 $300**
Folder - **$25 $35 $60**

SGT-25

❏ **SGT-25. Trading Card/Records Offer Cereal Box,**
1952. Quaker Puffed Rice. Back panel offers record series including theme song from TV series. Complete Box - **$50 $125 $200**

SGT-26

❏ **SGT-26. "Electronic Ore Detector" With Instructions And Box,**
1952. Plastic battery operated detector, black variety. Near Mint Boxed - **$250**
Detector Only - **$50 $100 $200**

SGT-27

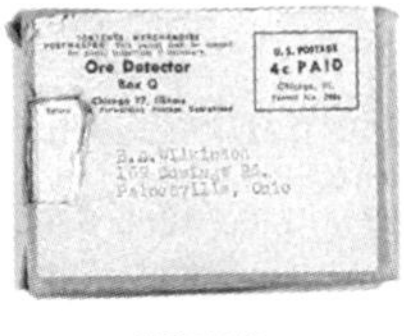

SGT-28

❏ **SGT-27. Electronic Ore Detector, Red Variety,**
1952. Near Mint Boxed - **$325**
Detector Only - **$65 $145 $250**

❏ **SGT-28. Ore Detector Mailer,**
1952. Quaker Puffed Wheat premium. -
**$20 $40 $75**

SGT-29

❏ **SGT-29. Wood Totem Poles,**
1952. Set of five. Named in order pictured left to right: Thunderbird, The Fight With the Land Otters, Burial Pole, Killer Whale, Sun and Raven. Each - **$10 $20 $45**

SGT-30

SGT-31

❏ **SGT-30. Aluminum Pedometer,**
1952. - **$20 $40 $75**

❏ **SGT-31. "Sgt. Preston Trail Goggles" Quaker Cereal Box Cut-Out,**
1952. - Complete Box - **$75 $150 $250**
Cut-out - **$10 $20 $40**

SGT-32

SGT-33

❏ **SGT-32. "The Case That Made Preston A Sergeant" Decca Record #1,**
1952. - **$20 $40 $75**

❏ **SGT-33. "The Case Of The Indian Rebellion" Decca Record #3,**
1952. - **$20 $40 $75**

SGT-34

❏ **SGT-34. Picture To Color Cereal Box Panel,**
1952. From a series of three boxes with different "Action Pictures."
Back Panel Only - **$10 $25 $50**
Used Complete Box - **$50 $100 $200**

SGT-35

❏ **SGT-35. Cereal Box With Ore Detector Offer,**
1952. Gordon Gold Archives.
Used Complete - **$75 $150 $250**

SGT-36

SGT-37

❏ **SGT-36. "Distance Finder",**
1954. Metal and paper insert distance gauge. -
**$20 $40 $60**

❏ **SGT-37. Distance Finder Instructions,**
1955. Quaker Puffed Wheat premium. -
**$15 $25 $35**

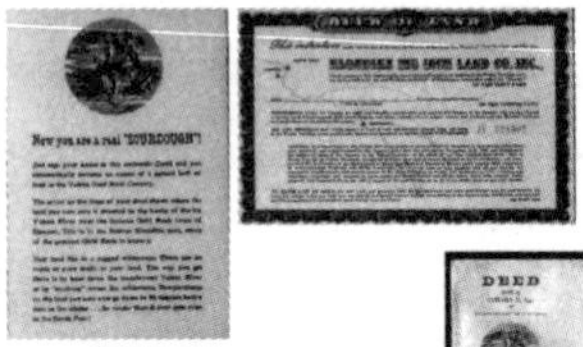
SGT-38

SGT-39

❑ **SGT-38. "Klondike Big Inch Land Deed" Certificate With Cover Sheet,**
1955. Deed - **$10 $15 $20**
Sheet - **$5 $10 $15**

❑ **SGT-39. Deed Mailer,**
1955. Radio premium. - **$100 $150 $200**

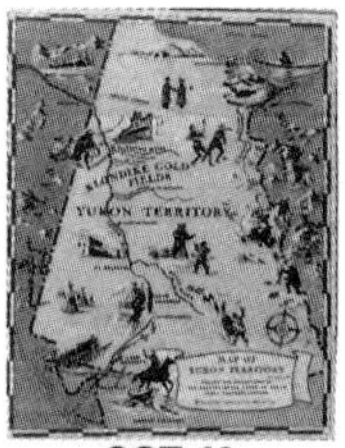


SGT-40

❑ **SGT-40. "Map Of Yukon Territory" 8x10",**
1955. Quaker Cereals box insert. -
**$15 $30 $60**

SGT-41

❑ **SGT-41. "Prospector's Pouch Order Blank",**
1955. - **$15 $30 $60**

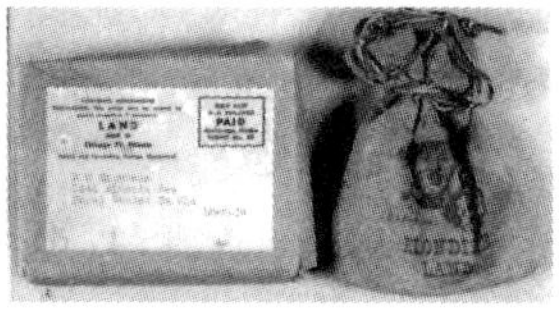

SGT-42

❑ **SGT-42. "Klondike Land" Pouch,**
1955.
Near Mint Boxed With Klondike Dirt Still In Pouch - **$300**
Pouch Only (pouch is generally cracked) -
**$50 $100 $200**

SGT-43

SGT-44

❑ **SGT-43. Order Form,**
1955. Order form for prospector's pouch & 1 oz. of Klondike land & deed to 1 square inch of gold rush land. **- $20 $40 $65**

❑ **SGT-44. Official Seal Cello. Button,**
1956. Full color 1-1/4". White rim. Scarce. -
**$250 $750 $1500**

SGT-45

❑ **SGT-45. "How He Found Yukon King" Comic Booklet,**
1956. Quaker box insert. Set of four, each 5" or 7" long. - **$10 $30 $85**

SGT-46

❑ **SGT-46. "How Yukon King Saved Him From The Wolves" Comic Booklet,**
1956. Quaker box insert. Set of four, each 5" or 7" long. - **$10 $30 $85**

SGT-47

❑ **SGT-47. "How He Became A Mountie" Comic Booklet,**
1956. Quaker box insert. Set of four, each 5" or 7" long. - **$10 $30 $85**

SGT-48

❑ **SGT-48. "The Case That Made Him A Sergeant" Comic Booklet,**
1956. Quaker box insert. Set of four, each 5" or 7" long. - **$10 $30 $85**

SGT-49

SGT-50

❑ **SGT-49. Quaker Cereals T-Shirt,**
c. 1956. Scarce. - **$75 $150 $300**

❑ **SGT-50. Official Seal Tin Badge,**
c. 1956. Seen in copper, silver or brass luster, all rare. - **$200 $500 $800**

SGT-51

SGT-52

❑ **SGT-51. Official Seal White Metal Badge With Insert Paper Photo,**
c. 1956. Photo is yellow/black. -
**$100 $250 $400**

❑ **SGT-52. Quaker Cereals Coloring Contest Letter And Photo,**
1957. Near Mint In Envelope - **$175**
Photo Only - **$35 $75 $100**

SGT-53

SGT-54

❑ **SGT-53. "Sergeant Preston 10-In-1 Trail Kit,"**
1958. 6" plastic pen/flashlight/sundial/compass/whistle including Sgt. Preston and King image on mouthpiece.
Box - **$15 $20 $40**
Instructions - **$30 $60 $90**
Device - **$75 $150 $325**

❑ **SGT-54. "Richard Simmons" Pencil Tablet,**
1950s. Store item. - **$10 $30 $60**

SGT-55

❑ **SGT-55. Sergeant Preston Pencil Tablet,**
1950s. Store item**. - $10 $30 $60**

## Seth Parker

***Seth Parker* was an early radio creation of Phillips H. Lord, who was later to create *Gang Busters* and other adventure programs. In contrast, Seth Parker combined the story of a gentle, kindly Maine philosopher with lots of hymn singing, and it was immensely successful. Also known as *Sunday at Seth Parker* and *Sunday Evenings at Seth Parker*, the series was sustained on NBC from 1929 to 1933, and sponsored by Frigidaire as *Cruise of the Seth Parker* in 1933-1934. It later aired from 1935 to 1939, sponsored by Vick Chemical for its final three years.**

SET-1

❑ **SET-1. Schooner 11x15" Paper Print,**
c. 1934. Frigidaire Corp. Pictures world cruise ship used by Phillips H. Lord, creator and radio voice of Seth Parker. - **$12 $20 $35**

SET-2

SET-3

❑ **SET-2. "Aboard The Seth Parker" Booklet,**
1934. Frigidaire Corp. Includes drawings of the various rooms of global sailing boat. -
**$5 $10 $15**

❑ **SET-3. "Seth Parker's Two-Year Almanac And Party Book",**
1939. Vicks Chemical Co. Hardcover edition for 1939-1940. - **$5 $10 $15**

SET-4

SET-5

❑ **SET-4. "Seth Parker's Scrapbook",**
1930s. Collection of folksy, small-town humor and wisdom. - **$10 $20 $30**

❑ **SET-5. Cast Member Fan Photo,**
1930s. Pictures family in a parlor hymn sing. -
**$5 $8 $15**

## The Shadow

**The Shadow, alias Lamont Cranston, was born in the 1930s, both as a character in Street & Smith publications and by radio sponsor Blue Coal. Written by Walter B. Gibson under the pen name Maxwell Grant, the Shadow fought crime and clouded men's minds not only in the pulps and on the radio but also, along with the lovely Margot Lane, in the movies, in comic books, and in a comic strip.**

**The Shadow debuted as the announcer of the *Detective Story* radio program in 1930, which became *The Shadow* in 1932. The show aired on CBS, NBC, or Mutual from 1932 to 1954, and the programs were resurrected and syndicated in the 1960s and 1970s. There were a number of regional or national sponsors: Blue Coal for most of the years between 1932 and 1949, along with Perfect-O-Lite (1932), Goodrich tires (1938-1939), Grove Laboratories (1949-1950), the Army Air Force (1950-1951), Wildroot Cream Oil (1951-1953), Carey Salt Company, and Bromo Quinine cold tablets. Both Blue Coal (in 1941) and Carey Salt (in 1945) offered glow-in-the-dark premium rings, and *The Shadow Magazine* offered a club membership lapel emblem and other items.**

**A *Shadow* comic strip appeared in newspapers from 1938 to 1942, and comic books were published from 1940 to 1950, in 1964-1965 (with the Shadow as costumed superhero), and in 1973-1975. The Shadow made a number of low-budget film appearances in the 1930s and 1940s, notably in a 15-episode chapter play from Columbia Pictures in 1940 with Victor Jory in the title role. In 1994 Alec Baldwin played the lead in a Universal film. "Who knows what evil lurks in the hearts of men?"**

SHA-1

SHA-2

❑ **SHA-1. "Eyes Of The Shadow" 7x11" Ad Card,**
c. 1931. For Maxwell Grant novel. -
**$50 $125 $250**

❑ **SHA-2. Perfect-O-Lite Radio Broadcast Promotion Folder,**
1932. For Perfect-O-Lite sales people. 11x17" folder that opens to 17x22" promoting new radio sponsorship over 29 stations of Columbia net-

SHA-3

❑ **SHA-3. "The Shadow" Cover Photo On Radio Schedule Magazine,**
1932. Subscription publication by Radio Log Company, Boston, Mass. 5-1/4x8-1/4" with 36 pages for week of December 11. -
**$50 $125 $175**

SHA-4

❑ **SHA-4. Radio Broadcasts Schedule Folder With Envelope,**
1932. Perfect-O-Lite (automotive accessory). Lists 27 stations in three time zones.
Envelope - **$25 $60 $85**
Folder - **$60 $150 $325**

SHA-5

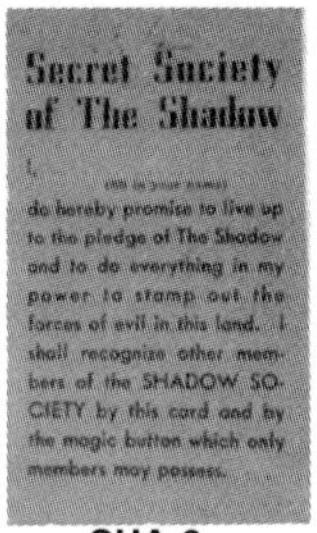
Secret Society of The Shadow
I, (fill in your name) do hereby promise to live up to the pledge of The Shadow and to do everything in my power to stamp out the forces of evil in this land. I shall recognize other members of the SHADOW SOCIETY by this card and by the magic button which only members may possess.

SHA-6

❑ **SHA-5. "The Shadow" 11x14" Cardboard Window Poster,**
c. 1934. Blue Coal, Shadow magazine. Promotes Monday and Wednesday radio broadcasts on Columbia network. - **$400 $1000 $1850**

❑ **SHA-6. "Secret Society Of The Shadow" Club Card,**
1939. Pledge card originally holding glow-in-dark "Magic Button". - **$100 $250 $375**

SHA-7

SHA-8

❑ **SHA-7. "The Shadow" Glow-In-Dark Cello. Magic Button,**
1939. Rare not cracked or stained. -
**$300 $800 $2000**

❑ **SHA-8. Blue Coal Portrait Photo,**
1930s. Shows Frank Readick Jr., the second Shadow radio program narrator. -
**$75 $225 $400**

SHA-9

❑ **SHA-9. The Shadow Unmasked Pulp Magazine Photo,**
1930s. Image on thin matte finish cardboard. Later re-issued by Carey's Salt as glossy photo. See SHA-35. - **$200 $400 $850**

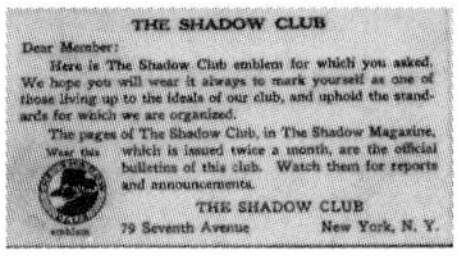
THE SHADOW CLUB
Dear Member:
Here is The Shadow Club emblem for which you asked. We hope you will wear it always to mark yourself as one of those living up to the ideals of our club, and uphold the standards for which we are organized.
The pages of The Shadow Club, in The Shadow Magazine, which is issued twice a month, are the official bulletins of this club. Watch them for reports and announcements.
THE SHADOW CLUB
79 Seventh Avenue New York, N. Y.

SHA-10

SHA-11

❑ **SHA-10. The Shadow Club Card,**
1930s. Street & Smith Publishers. Originally held Shadow lapel stud.
Card - **$100 $250 $425**
Mailer (Pictures The Shadow) - **$150 $300 $400**

❑ **SHA-11. "The Shadow Club" Silvered Brass Lapel Emblem,**
1930s. Lapel Stud - **$100 $200 $350**
Girl's Version With Pin - **$125 $300 $425**

SHA-12

SHA-13

❑ **SHA-12. "The Shadow Strikes Again" Paper Folder,**
1930s. Blue Coal. Includes listing of radio stations and broadcast times. - **$75 $175 $325**

❑ **SHA-13. The Shadow Large Enamel Pin,**
1930s. After auctioning an example of this 2-1/8" tall black enamel on 1/16" thick brass pin we were told the pin was used by members of the Shadow radio cast. Rare. -
**$150 $250 $500**

SHA-14

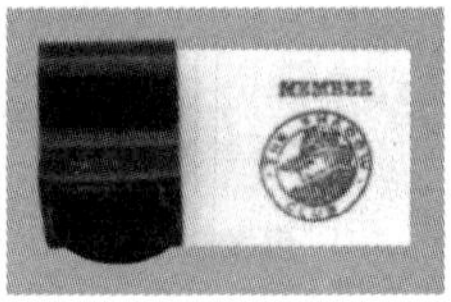

SHA-15

❑ **SHA-14. "The Shadow Hypno-Coin" Brass Medalet,**
1930s. About 1-1/4". Inscribed "Compliments Of Your Blue Coal Dealer." Rare. - **$150 $325 $525**

❑ **SHA-15. "Member/The Shadow Club" Rubber On Wood Stamp Block,**
1930s. Picture example includes ink stamp image from the block. Offered only from April 1, 1934 until the end of August 1934. - **$250 $600 $900**

SHA-16

SHA-17

❑ **SHA-16. "Thrilling Radio Program" Match Cover,**
1930s. Williams Coal Co. and others.
Near Mint Complete - **$100**
Used - **$25 $50 $75**

❑ **SHA-17. "Protect Your Home" Match Cover,**
1930s. Steward B. Rex and others.
Near Mint Unused - **$135**
Used - **$30 $60 $85**

SHA-18

❑ **SHA-18. "Tune In On-The Shadow" Paper Gummed Back Sticker,**
1930s. - **$35 $100 $150**

SHA-19

❑ **SHA-19. "The Shadow On The Air" Gummed Back Paper Sticker,**
1930s. - **$35 $100 $150**

SHA-20

SHA-21

❑ **SHA-20. "The Shadow Is Back On The Air" Paper Gummed Back Sticker,**
1930s. - **$35 $100 $150**

❑ **SHA-21. Pulp Magazine Ad Sticker,**
1930s. - **$50 $110 $175**

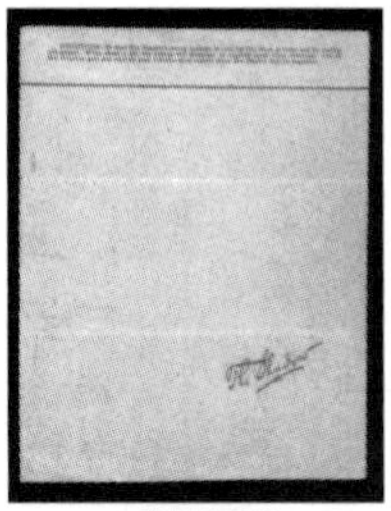

SHA-22

SHA-23

❑ **SHA-22. "The Shadow's Secret Message" Sheet,**
1930s. The Shadow pulp magazine. 8-1/2x11" yellow paper sheet treated to reveal message when dipped in water and then disappears when sheet is dry. Rare. - **$125 $250 $425**

❑ **SHA-23. "The Shadow and the Living Death" Better Little Book #1430,**
1940. - **$50 $150 $300**

SHA-24

❑ **SHA-24."The Shadow" Movie Poster,**
c. 1940 Australian insert poster for 15-chapter Columbia serial. 13-1/2x30". Most likely for first Australian release. - **$50 $150 $250**

SHA-25

❑ **SHA-25. Boxed Board Game,**
1940. Store item by Toy Creations. -
**$250 $650 $1100**
Board Only - **$75 $200 $350**

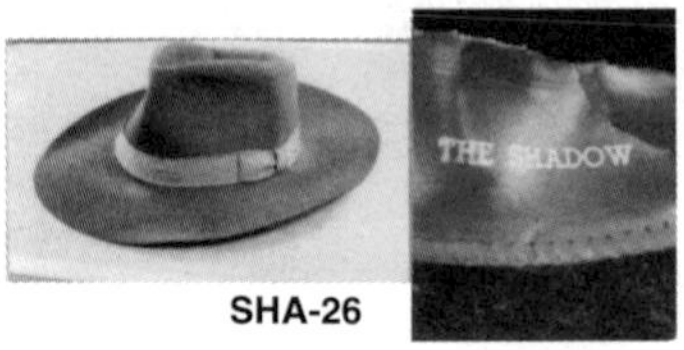


SHA-26

❑ **SHA-26. "The Shadow" Brown Felt Fabric Hat,**
1940. Adult size, offered by The Shadow Magazine. - **$150 $275 $525**

SHA-27

❑ **SHA-27. "The Shadow Movie Club" Member's Cello. Button,**
1940. 7/8" black on green. One of three examples found wrapped in a paper in the desk of Walter B. Gibson as his estate was prepared for auction. Possibly produced as samples but never used to promote the club tie-in with the Columbia Pictures 1940s serial. -
**$750 $1600 $2600**

SHA-28

❑ **SHA-28. Shadow Magazine Costume,**
c. 1940. Street & Smith Publishers. Consists of hat, mask and cape. Pocket of cape has image of the Shadow with text above "The Shadow Knows" and text below "The Shadow Magazine." Set - **$500 $1000 $2000**

SHA-29

❑ **SHA-29. Blue Coal Ink Blotter,**
1940. - **$25 $50 $75**

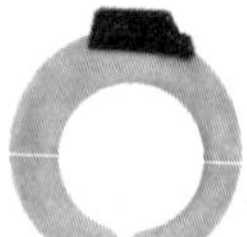

SHA-30

SHA-31

❑ **SHA-30. Blue Coal Ring,**
1941. Glows in the dark. - **$100 $275 $450**

❑ **SHA-31. "Blue Coal" Ring Instruction Sheet With Mailer Envelope,**
1941. Rare. Envelope - **$300 $600 $800**
Instruction Sheet - **$300 $600 $800**

SHA-32

❑ **SHA-32. Cardboard 11x16" Ad Wall Calendar,**
1942. Picture example shows calendar and corner detail from it. - **$150 $250 $500**

SHA-33

SHA-34

❑ **SHA-33. "The Shadow and the Ghost Makers" Better Little Book #1495,**
1942. - **$50 $150 $300**

❑ **SHA-34. Magic Ring,**
1945. Carey Salt. Black plastic stone, base glows in dark. - **$300 $750 $1200**

SHA-35

❑ **SHA-35. The Shadow Unmasked Photo,**
1945. Rare. Carey's Salt. Illustrated in the sales portfolio used by company salesmen. 8x10 glossy photo. See earlier pulp magazine issue, SHA-9. - **$175 $350 $800**

SHA-36

❏ **SHA-36. Dealer's Promotional Campaign Book,**
1945. Carey Salt. 10-1/2x16" spiral-bound covers plus 20 pages in red, white and blue including glued-in color covers of Shadow comics (Vol. 5 #8, September 1945) and The Shadow pulp magazine October 1945. About 75 produced and used by Carey Salt salesmen. - **$2500 $5000 $7500**

SHA-37

SHA-38

❏ **SHA-37. Blue Coal Sticker,**
1940s. - **$50 $100 $175**

❏ **SHA-38. Matchbook Cover,**
1940s. Inside cover has diecut hinged tab that lowers to expose jail cell view.
With Matches - **$40 $80 $150**
Empty - **$30 $60 $100**

SHA-39

SHA-40

❏ **SHA-39. Blotter,**
1940s. Blue Coal. - **$20 $40 $65**

❏ **SHA-40. Blotter,**
1940s. Blue Coal. - **$20 $40 $65**

SHA-41

❏ **SHA-41. Blotter,**
1940s. Blue Coal. - **$15 $35 $60**

SHA-42

❏ **SHA-42. Blotter,**
1940s. 8" man shows 2 bags of coal on front. - **$25 $50 $85**

SHA-43

SHA-44

❏ **SHA-43. Blotter,**
1940s. 8" photo of man on right talks about warm home. - **$25 $50 $85**

❏ **SHA-44. Full Figure Blotter,**
1940s. Scarce. Radio premium. 5" picture of Shadow in middle. - **$50 $125 $175**

SHA-45

SHA-46

❏ **SHA-45. Blotter,**
1940s. Blue Coal. - **$25 $50 $85**

❏ **SHA-46. Blotter,**
1940s. Blue Coal. - **$30 $60 $100**

SHA-47

SHA-48

❏ **SHA-47. Blotter,**
1940s. Blue Coal. - **$30 $70 $135**

❏ **SHA-48. Canadian Ink Blotter,**
1940s. Various coal companies. - **$30 $70 $135**

SHA-49

❏ **SHA-49. High Quality Glazed Ceramic Figure,**
c. 1940s. Store item with maker's mark under base of "K" with a crown above. Beautifully colored and designed 7" tall figurine depicting The Shadow in classic pose holding a dagger. - **$250 $500 $1000**

SHA-50

❏ **SHA-50. "The Shadow" Boxed Costume,**
1973. Store item by Collegeville. Holds thin plastic mask with red fabric panel at lower half. Comes with black rayon cape with large silk screen design which includes his classic question "Who Knows..." Near Mint Boxed - **$150**
Complete Unboxed - **$25 $50 $75**

SHA-51

SHA-52

❏ **SHA-51. Shadow Radio Broadcast Album,**
1974. Plays original Shadow radio shows. - **$15 $25 $50**

❏ **SHA-52. Crime Fighter Copter,**
1976. Battery operated. In original box. - **$25 $75 $135**

SHA-53

❑ **SHA-53. Pre-Release Promo Flyers,**
c. 1983. Universal. Pair of 8-1/2x11" glossy sheets. Each - **$3 $6 $12**

SHA-54

SHA-55

❑ **SHA-54. The Shadow Hologram Plastic Ring,**
1994. Coupon offer from Kenner Toys.
Ring - **$10 $20 $35**
Coupon - **$1 $2 $3**

❑ **SHA-55. Movie Giveaway Badge,**
1994. - **$2 $4 $10**

SHA-56

❑ **SHA-56. "The Shadow Club" Kit,**
1994. Promotes the movie. Includes pinback, photo, club card, mailer and newsletter.
Complete - **$75**

SHA-57

SHA-58

❑ **SHA-57. "The Shadow " 9" Bust,**
1994. Graphitti Designs. Limited to 2500, then reduced to 1500. - **$175**

❑ **SHA-58. "The Shadow " 6 1/2" Figurine,**
1994. Made from wood-like substance. Produced for promotion of the movie. Less than 125 made. Given out at Toy Fair.- **$175**

SHA-59

SHA-60

❑ **SHA-59. "The Shadow " Action Figure,**
1994. Lightning Draw. With Silver Heat 45s.
On card. - **$8**

❑ **SHA-60. "The Shadow " Action Figure,**
1994. Ambush Shadow with Quick Draw Action.
On card. - **$8**

SHA-61

SHA-62

❑ **SHA-61. "Transforming Lamont Cranston" Action Figure,**
1994. With snap-on armor. On card. - **$8**

❑ **SHA-62. "Ninja Shadow " Action Figure,**
1994. On card. - **$8**

SHA-63

SHA-64

❑ **SHA-63. Shiwan Khan Action Figure,**
1994. With Rapid Strike Chopping Action.
On card. - **$8**

❑ **SHA-64. Dr. MocQuino Action Figure,**
1994. On card. - **$8**

SHA-65

❑ **SHA-65. Action Figure Collector's Case,**
1994. - **$55**

(BOX FRONT) (BOX BACK)

SHA-66

❑ **SHA-66. "The Shadow" Nightmist Cycle,**
1994. In original box. - **$15**

SHA-67

❑ **SHA-67. "The Shadow" Mirage SX-100 Action Vehicle,**
1994. In original box. - **$40**

SHA-68

❑ **SHA-68. "The Shadow" Thunder Cab Action Vehicle,**
1994. With firing cannons and side-swiping swords. In original box. - **$45**

(BOX FRONT) (BOX BACK)

SHA-69

❑ **SHA-69. Shiwan Khan Serpent Bike,**
1994. In original box. - **$22**

SHA-70

❑ **SHA-70. Electronic Video Game on Card,**
1994. This is the hardest item to find on all the Shadow products produced to support the movie. - **$20 $50 $100**

SHA-71

❑ **SHA-71. "The Shadow" Board Game,**
1994. In original box. - **$50**

## Sherlock Holmes

**The world's most famous detective made his debut in 1887 in Arthur Conan Doyle's story *A Study in Scarlet*. Since then millions of fans have followed the adventures of the brilliant Holmes and his trusted chronicler Dr. John Watson in books, on stage, on the radio, on television, and in numerous films. Holmes solved cases in radio series from 1930 to 1936 and from 1939 to 1950, on various networks, with different sponsors, and through multiple cast changes. Best remembered are Basil Rathbone and Nigel Bruce, who played the radio leads from 1939 to 1946, as well as portraying the characters in a series of films. G. Washington coffee was an early sponsor (1930-1935), followed by Household Finance Corporation (1936), Bromo-Quinine cold tablets (1939-1942), Petri wine (1943-1946 and 1949-1950), and others. Holmes also made scattered comic book appearances from the 1940s to the 1970s. A popular series of one-hour shows and feature-length films from Britain's Granada Television (shown in the US on PBS) starred the late Jeremy Brett as Holmes and won accolades for their attention to detail, setting and performance. "Elementary, my dear Watson."**

SHL-1

❑ **SHL-1. Sherlock Holmes Game,**
1904. Store item by Parker Brothers. -
**$40 $100 $175**

SHL-2

❑ **SHL-2. Sherlock Holmes Map,**
1930s. Rare. Household Finance. -
**$100 $350 $500**

SHL-3

❑ **SHL-3. "Mutual" Radio "Thriller Dillers" Sign,**
c. 1945. WFBR, Baltimore, Md. 10-1/2x27-1/2" orange, black and white cardboard sign with photos of stars from "Return Of Nick Carter, Adventures Of Bulldog Drummond, Sherlock Holmes." - **$75 $150 $300**

SHL-4

❑ **SHL-4. "Sherlock Holmes' London" Prototype Map,**
1955. Prepared for TV show's producer Motion Pictures for Television, Inc. 16-1/2x22". Gordon Gold Archives. Unique. - **$1600**

SHL-5

❑ **SHL-5. Syndicated TV Show Promotional Folder,**
1955. Motion Pictures for Television Inc. 8-1/2x11" with black and white photos and magazine article reprints. Gordon Gold Archives. - **$50 $100 $175**

SHL-6

❑ **SHL-6. "Baker Street" Stage Production Postcard,**
c. 1970s. Broadway Theater, New York City. -
**$15 $30 $60**

SHL-7

❑ **SHL-7. "Sherlock Holmes Game Of Mystery",**
c. 1970s. English store item by Tri-Ang. Contains 16x16" board, clue cards, cardboard "Newspaper Clippings" folders and diecut playing pieces of Holmes, Dr. Watson and policeman. - **$25 $50 $100**

## Shield G-Man Club

**Joe Higgins, alias the Shield, was one of the most popular comic book heroes of the 1940s, fighting to protect the American way of life with truth, justice, patriotism, and courage--and a costume that made him invulnerable. He debuted in *Pep Comics* #1 in 1940 and, despite some changes in character, lasted until *Pep* #65 in 1948. Between 1940 and 1944 he also appeared in *Shield-Wizard Comics*. The *Shield G-Man Club*, which offered pins and a membership card, had a short life before becoming the *Archie Club*.**

SGM-1

SGM-2

❑ **SGM-1. Club Member Card,**
1940. Pep Comics, M.L.J. Magazines.
Card - **$100 $175 $350**
Mailer - **$10 $30 $60**

❑ **SGM-2. "Shield G-Man Club" Cello. Button (blue border),**
c. 1940. Rare. 1-3/4" version. -
**$250 $850 $1300**

SGM-3

❑ **SGM-3. "The Shield" Cardboard Movie Projector,**
c. 1941. Shield Wizard Comics. Filmstrips cut from comic book page by reader to produce "film." Pictured example has replaced viewing tube. - **$200 $450 $875**

(badge)

(button)

SGM-4

❑ **SGM-4. Club Member's Cello. Badge and Button,**
c. 1943. Bar pin behind top folded edge. Also issued as 1-1/4" circular cello. button.
Badge - **$15 $30 $60**
Button (no border) - **$100 $350 $625**

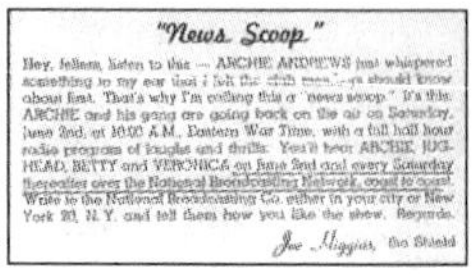
"News Scoop."

Hey, fellows, listen to this — ARCHIE ANDREWS just whispered something in my ear that [illegible] should know about first. That's why I'm calling this a "news scoop." It's this: ARCHIE and his gang are going back on the air on Saturday, June 2nd, at 10:00 A.M., Eastern War Time, with a full half hour radio program of laughs and thrills. You'll hear ARCHIE, JUGHEAD, BETTY and VERONICA on June 2nd and every Saturday thereafter over the National Broadcasting Network, coast to coast. Write to the National Broadcasting Co. either in your city or New York 20, N.Y. and tell them how you like the show. Regards.

Joe Higgins, the Shield

SGM-5

❑ **SGM-5. The Shield "News Scoop" Postcard,**
c. 1945. Announcement of Archie Andrews and his gang returning to radio on Saturday, June 2, Eastern War Time with facsimile signature of Joe Higgins as The Shield. - **$40 $65 $125**

## Shirley Temple

**America's dimpled sweetheart, the world's darling, Shirley Temple was probably the most popular child prodigy actress ever to come out of Hollywood. Born in 1928, she sang, danced, and acted in 30 movies by the age of 13, was a top box-office star, and charmed the nation. Merchandising during the 1930s was extensive, including Shirley Temple dresses, hats, underwear, mugs, soap, and an estimated 1.5 million Shirley Temple dolls from Ideal Novelty & Toy Corp. She made further films as a teen and as an adult, but could not sustain her immense popularity. There were several short-lived ventures on CBS radio: *Shirley Temple Time* (1939), the *Shirley Temple Variety Show*, sponsored by Elgin watches (1941), and *Junior Miss* (1942). On television, *Shirley Temple's Story Book* was seen in 1958-1959 and *The Shirley Temple Show* aired in 1960-1961.**

**Married from 1945-49 to actor John Agar, she remarried in 1960, to TV executive Charles Black. In 1967, as Shirley Temple Black, she lost a primary race for a California Congressional seat, but was appointed as a U.S. representative to the United Nations. From 1974 to 1976, Black served as U.S. Ambassador to Ghana, then became Chief of Protocol. She then took the appointment of Ambassador to Czechoslovakia in 1989. She has also authored an autobiography, *Child Star*, in 1988.**

SHR-1

SHR-2

SHR-3

❑ **SHR-1. Patriotic Hair Bow,**
c. 1935. Store item. - **$50 $125 $225**

❑ **SHR-2. "Shirley Temple" Quaker Cereal Box,**
c. 1935. Complete - **$100 $225 $375**

❑ **SHR-3. Drawing Set With Coloring Book,**
1935. 10x13x1" deep boxed Saalfield kit. -
**$125 $300 $450**

SHR-4

SHR-5

❑ **SHR-4. Cello. Covered Pocket Mirror,**
1935. Curl has copyright date and "Fox Film Corp." - **$15 $25 $45**

❑ **SHR-5. Cello. Button Off Doll,**
c. 1936. Ideal Novelty and Toy Co. 1-1/4" with white border surrounding browntone photo. There are two versions in darker and lighter brown, both with orange accent on her hair ribbon but only the lighter version seems to also have orange accent on her dress strap. Original issues have metal plate covering the reverse holding a straight pin anchored at one side which snaps under a metal tab at the opposite side. Each Version - **$35 $75 $125**

SHR-6

SHR-7

❑ **SHR-6. Theater Club Cello. Button Scarcer Variety,**
1936. 1-1/4" black and white real photo button without dot pattern and made as a standard celluloid button rather than the other variety which uses a brass rim to hold the button parts into a single unit. - **$65 $125 $200**

❑ **SHR-7. Theatre Club Cello. Button,**
c. 1936. Also inscribed for WFBR Radio, Baltimore. Beaded brass rim. Similar to SHR-6. -
**$35 $100 $150**

SHR-8

SHR-9

❑ **SHR-8. "The American Girl" Scout Magazine With Doll Ad,**
1936. Doll offered as premium for four subscriptions. - **$8 $10 $20**

❑ **SHR-9. Shirley Temple Pair Of Painted Salt Figures,**
c. 1936 Store items. Much scarcer than white salt uncolored version.
Each Colored - **$35 $75 $135**
Each White - **$15 $30 $75**

SHR-10

❑ **SHR-10. Doll Contest Newspaper Advertisement,**
1936. - **$15 $30 $50**

SHR-11

SHR-12

❑ **SHR-11. 15" Tall Composition Doll,**
c. 1936. Store item by Ideal Toy Co. Dress based on 1934 "Bright Eyes" movie costume. - **$200 $400 $800**

❑ **SHR-12. Wheaties Box Back Panels,**
c. 1936. Set of 12. Each - **$10 $20 $40**

SHR-13

SHR-14

❑ **SHR-13. Enameled Brass Figural Pin,**
c. 1936. Probable store item. - **$75 $150 $250**

❑ **SHR-14. "Shirley Temple's Pet/Rowdy" Enameled Brass Pin,**
c. 1936. Pictures her pet dog. Probably store item. - **$75 $150 $250**

SHR-15

SHR-16

❑ **SHR-15. "Chicago Times Shirley Temple Club" Litho. Button,**
c. 1936. - **$50 $100 $175**

❑ **SHR-16. Cello. Button Off Doll,**
c. 1936. Ideal Novelty And Toy Co. 1-1/4" with pink border. Many non-authentic doll button designs made in the 1970s-1990s exist. On original, reverse has metal plate holding a horizontal bar pin in fixed position. - **$30 $65 $100**

SHR-17

SHR-18

❑ **SHR-17. Photo,**
1936. Philadelphia Record newspaper premium. - **$12 $20 $40**

❑ **SHR-18. "Shirley Temple League" Enameled Brass English Pin,**
c. 1937. Sunday Referee newspaper. - **$40 $75 $125**

SHR-19

❑ **SHR-19. "The Toy Trumpet" Song Sheet,**
1938. From her movie "Rebecca of Sunnybrook Farm." - **$10 $20 $40**

SHR-20

❑ **SHR-20. Swimsuit Cardboard String Tag,**
1930s. Forest Mills. Various photos. - **$20 $40 $70**

SHR-21

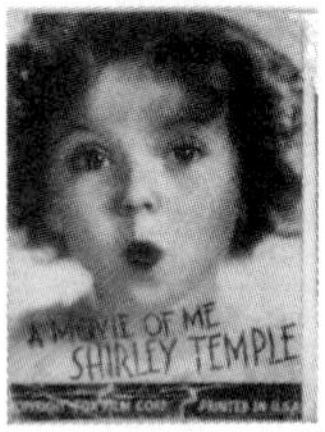


SHR-22

❑ **SHR-21. Portrait Picture,**
1930s. Probably store or theater give-away. - **$15 $25 $40**

❑ **SHR-22. "A Movie Of Me" Flip Book,**
1930s. Probably Quaker Cereals. - **$50 $100 $200**

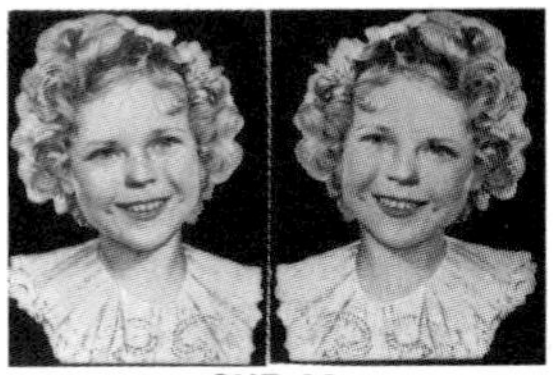

SHR-23

❑ **SHR-23. Diecut 12x16" Cardboard Hanger Sign For Theater Lobby,**
1930s. Color portrait each side. - **$75 $150 $250**

SHR-24

SHR-25

❑ **SHR-24. Photo,**
1930s. Sealtest Milk. Promotes the movie "Just Around The Corner" on back of photo. - **$25 $50 $75**

❑ **SHR-25. Shirley Temple Box Of Books,**
1940. Saalfield Publishing. Six storybooks and two paperdoll books. Set - **$400 $750 $1200**

SHR-26

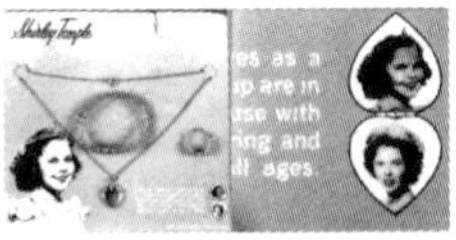

SHR-27

❑ **SHR-26. Cardboard Advertising Fan,**
1944. Royal Crown Cola. Inscribed for her 1944 movie "I'll Be Seeing You". - **$25 $50 $80**

❑ **SHR-27. "Picture Locket Jewelry" On Card,**
1940s. Store item. Heart-shaped symbol on ring, bracelet, locket. Set - **$75 $150 $250**

SHR-28

SHR-29

❑ **SHR-28. Vendor Card,**
1950s. - **$10 $20 $35**

❑ **SHR-29. Photo Guide,**
1960. TV Guide from St. Louis Post Digest. 52 pages. - **$20 $40 $60**

SHR-30

SHR-31

❑ **SHR-30. "Shirley Temple Black" Campaign Issues Position Card,**
1967. Issued for special election (November 14) Congressional camp aign in California to fill 11th District seat in U.S. Congress. Shirley lost a December 12 run-off election to Paul McCloskey. - **$15 $30 $60**

❑ **SHR-31. "Shirley Temple" Boxed Doll,**
1973. Store item by Ideal. 16" tall jointed vinyl. Near Mint Boxed - **$100**

## Shock Gibson

***Speed Comics* began in October 1939 with the origin and first appearance of Shock Gibson in issue #1. Gibson was the cover feature and lead character of the first 15 issues. *Speed Comics* continued through issue #44 in 1947.**

SHK-1

SHK-2

❑ **SHK-1. Volunteers Club Membership Card,**
c. 1939. Brookwood Publishing/Speed Publishing. - **$50 $150 $200**

❑ **SHK-2. Volunteers Club Cello. Button,**
c. 1939. - **$100 $300 $500**

SHK-3

❑ **SHK-3. Mask With Envelope,**
1940. Starched black linen generic mask in envelope from "Shock Gibson Volunteers" with New York City address.
With Envelope - **$50 $125 $175**

## Silver Dollar Brady

***Silver Dollar Brady* was a character created to promote Seagram's alcohol. Hoppy, Roy and Gene refused to support projects that used alcohol or cigarettes as sponsors. As a result of this dilemma, these companies had to create their own cowboy heroes. Silver Dollar Brady is a classic example of using in-house characters for this type of advertising. The premium listed was designed to test whether or not you had too much to drink and were off on your own "happy trails."**

SIL-1

❑ **SIL-1. Test Your Eye Card,**
1940s. Includes three different thin metal silver dollar sized play coins with Brady pictured on obverse.
Mailer - **$20 $40 $60**
Card - **$15 $30 $45**
Each Play Dollar - **$10 $20 $40**

## Silver Streak

**Magazine publisher Arthur Bernhard entered the comic book market with *Silver Streak Comics* #1 in December 1939. Jack Cole, later the creator of Plastic Man and a popular Playboy cartoonist, was brought in as artist/editor and drew the first Silver Streak story for issue #3, March 1940. Silver Streak became the second super-speed hero introduced that year, following the debut of The Flash just weeks earlier. The title is notable not only for Silver Streak but for the first appearance of Daredevil and the villainous Claw in issue #6. With issue #22 the title was changed to *Crime Does Not Pay*. Arthur Bernhard sold out to Lev Gleason shortly afterwards and Gleason continued to build a modest success based on the crime comics genre.**

SLV-1

❑ **SLV-1. Photo,**
c. 1941. Rare. - **$100 $300 $500**

SLV-2

❑ **SLV-2. Award Card From "Daredevil And Crimebuster" With Facsimile Charles Biro Signature,**
1944. Daredevil Comics. Daredevil made his first appearance in Silver Streak #6. Has recipient's name written in ink. - **$400 $700 $950**

# The Simpsons

In 1987, a series of 30-second animated shorts appeared on the new Fox network's *The Tracey Ullman Show.* Created by cartoonist Matt Groening, until then best known for his *Life in Hell* comic strip of 1980-1990, these short features would soon grow into a pop-culture phenomenon. On December 17, 1989, *The Simpsons* premiered with their own show on Fox as a half-hour Christmas special, soon followed by a regular series that debuted on January 14, 1990. After becoming Fox's #1 show for children under 17 and #4 for adults 18 to 34, and garnering critical praise and numerous awards including Emmys and a Peabody, *The Simpsons*, in February 1997, dethroned *The Flintstones* as the longest running animated series.

*The Simpsons*, like *The Flintstones*, concerns the exploits of a family: Homer—the dim-witted father; Marge—the loving wife and mother; Bart—the 10-year old trouble-making son; Lisa—the angst-ridden, intelligent sister; and Maggie—the toddler who communicates via pacifier. Also highlighted on the show are the citizens of Springfield, The Simpsons' hometown, plus guest appearances by a supporting cast of hundreds, voiced by many of Hollywood's top stars, including Dustin Hoffman, Michael Jackson, Mel Brooks, Leonard Nimoy, David Duchovny, Gillian Anderson, Meryl Streep, Mel Gibson, and many others.

Taking advantage of the popularity of his creations, Groening turned *The Simpsons* into a licensing empire, including comics, videos, CDs, and a string of best selling books. *The Simpsons* continue to be seen in syndication across the country in addition to new episodes airing on Fox. Most items are copyright Twentieth Century Fox or Matt Groening Productions. "D'oh!"

SIM-1

SIM-2

SIM-3

❑ **SIM-1. Simpsons Sofa and Boob Tube,**
1990. Mattel. Near Mint Boxed - **$80**

❑ **SIM-2. Bart Poseable Figure,**
1990. Mattel. Near Mint On Card - **$25**

❑ **SIM-3. Bartman Poseable Figure,**
1990. Mattel. Near Mint On Card - **$25**

SIM-4

❑ **SIM-4. Simpsons 3-D Chess Set,**
1991. Near Mint Boxed - **$55**

SIM-5

SIM-6

❑ **SIM-5. Simpsons Shampoo,**
1991. Cosrich. Each - **$10**

❑ **SIM-6. Anti-Dan Quayle Political Button,**
1992. 1-3/4" with black and white photo of Quayle against black background plus yellow cartoon of Bart. - **$3 $8 $12**

SIM-7

❑ **SIM-7. Roller Toys,**
1992. From UK Burger King. Each - **$5 $8**

SIM-8

❑ **SIM-8. Bongo Comics Promotional Badges,**
1993. Each - **$5**

SIM-9

SIM-10

❑ **SIM-9. Simpsons Series 1 Trading Cards,**
1993. Skybox. Metal storage container available by mail-order only. - **$15**

❑ **SIM-10. Simpsons 3-D Checker Set,**
1994. Near Mint Boxed - **$35**

SIM-11

❑ **SIM-11. Bongo Comics Promotional Badges,**
1994. Each - **$5**

SIM-12

❑ **SIM-12. Bongo Comics Promotional Badges,**
1995. Each - **$5**

SIM-13

❑ **SIM-13. Bongo Comics Promotional Badges,**
1996. Each - **$5**

SIM-14

❑ **SIM-14. "Puffa Pal" Asthma Inhaler Cover,**
1996. From Oddball in Australia. Lisa, Homer and Bart produced.
Each on unpunched card - **$15**
Each on punched card - **$7**

SIM-15

❑ **SIM-15. Simpsons Babies,**
1996. Mexican. Bart and Lisa. Made of Plaster of Paris standing 6" tall. Each - **45**

SIM-16

❑ **SIM-16. Bongo Comics Promotional Badges,**
1997. Each - **$5**

SIM-17

❑ **SIM-17. Squirt Rings,**
1997. United Kingdom Kellogg's Corn Pops premium. Bart (2 different versions), Homer, Lisa, Maggie, Mr. Burns. Total 6 different.
Near Mint Complete Wrapped Set - **$150**
Near Mint Complete Unwrapped Set - **$75**
Box - **$5 $10 $15**

SIM-18

❑ **SIM-18. Simpsons at the Beach Squirt Set,**
1998. Australian. 4 pieces. - **$15**

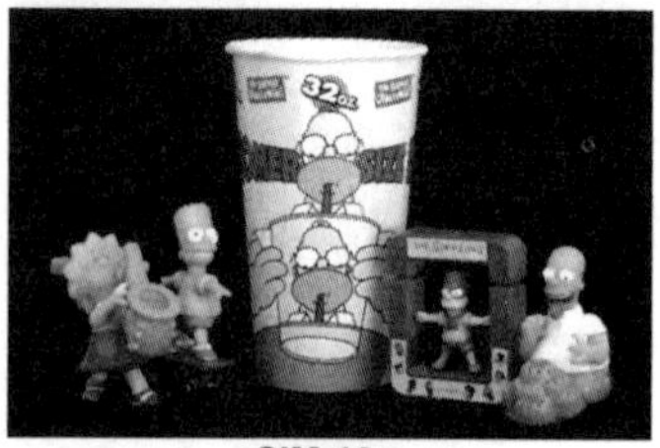

SIM-19

❑ **SIM-19. Subway Giveaways,**
1998. Set of 4. Set - **$16**

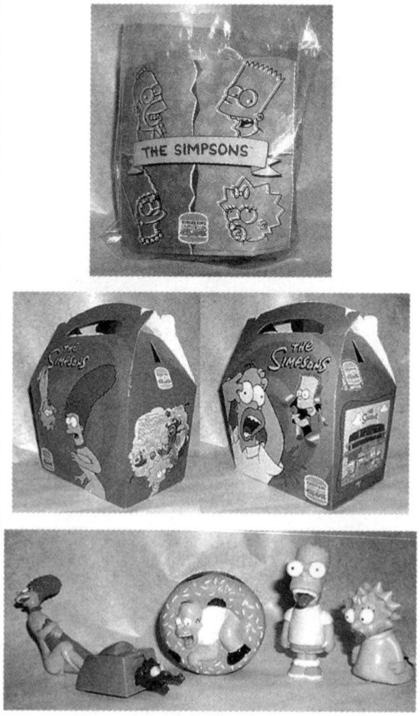


SIM-20

❑ **SIM-20. Burger King Figures,**
1998. From England. Marge, Homer, Bart and Maggie in Kid's Club bags or boxes.
Full set in bags - **$10**
Box - $3

SIM-21

❑ **SIM-21. Russian Nesting Dolls,**
1999. 7 dolls in all. - **$45**

SIM-22

SIM-23

❑ **SIM-22. Apu Coffee Mug,**
1999. - **$15**

❑ **SIM-23. Moe Mug,**
1999. Beer stein. - **$15**

SIM-24

SIM-25

❑ **SIM-24. Prototype Ring,**
1999. - **$50**

❑ **SIM-25. Electronic LCD Game,**
1999. In plastic package. - **$20**

SIM-26

❑ **SIM-26. Ceramic Figures,**
1999. Feves from France. 1" tall ceramic figures typically baked into cakes as a surprise. Set of 9. Set - **$50**

SIM-27

❑ **SIM-27. Plush Animal Figures,**
1999. Plushes of the show's animal characters: Itchy, Scratchy, Snowball II, Santa's Little Helper, and Blinky the 3-Eyed Fish. 4"-6" tall. From Giftware International PLC. Before importation to the U.S., the manufacturer was made to obliterate the word "Beanie" from the tag.
Each with tag - **$15**
Each without tag - **$7.50**

SIM-28

❑ **SIM-28. Panini Figures,**
1999. Set of 8 from Panini of Italy. 1-1/2" tall hard plastic figures. Set - **$15**

SIM-29

❑ **SIM-29. Plastic Family Set,**
1990s. Kinder Egg Germany. 1" tall. Set - **$30**

SIM-30

❑ **SIM-30. Winchells Donuts Figures,**
1990s. Winchells Donuts. Bart and Homer with changeable word balloons in Spanish and English. Each Figure - **$8**

SIM-31

❑ **SIM-31. Lucky Dip Set and Cards,**
1990s. Australian. 8 pieces with 15 cards.
Eight Piece Set - **$45**
With Cards - **$65**

SIM-32

❑ **SIM-32. Gum Containers,**
1990s. Each - **$5**

SIM-33

SIM-34

❑ **SIM-33. Bart Figural Cookie Jar,**
1990s. Extinct Collectibles. Near Mint - **$45**

❑ **SIM-34. Homer Figural Cookie Jar,**
1990s. Extinct Collectibles. Near Mint - **$50**

SIM-35

❑ **SIM-35. Bart & Lisa Salt & Pepper Set,**
1990s. Extinct Collectibles. Bart & Lisa watching TV. 3 piece set. Near Mint - **$25**

SIM-36

SIM-37

❑ **SIM-36. Bart Simpson Pez,**
1990s. 5 different. Each - **$2**

❑ **SIM-37. Homer & Marge Salt & Pepper Set,**
1990s. Extinct Collectibles. Homer & Marge with Maggie on couch. Near Mint - **$30**

SIM-38

❑ **SIM-38. Burger King Giveaways,**
1990s. Each - **$3**
With Backgrounds, Each - **$10**

SIM-39

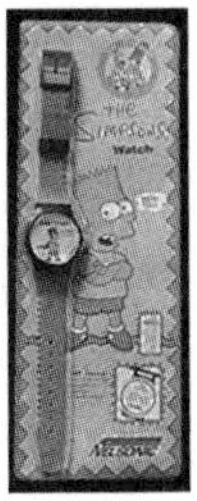

SIM-40

❑ **SIM-39. Simpsons Toy Display,**
1990s. Subway promotion with 4 toys.
Near Mint - **$60**

❑ **SIM-40. Bartman Watch,**
1990s. Nelsonic. Near Mint On Card - **$30**

SIM-41

❑ **SIM-41. Panini Figures,**
2000. Set of 12 from Panini of Italy. 3/4"-1" tall hard plastic figures. Set - **$20**
Bag - **$2**

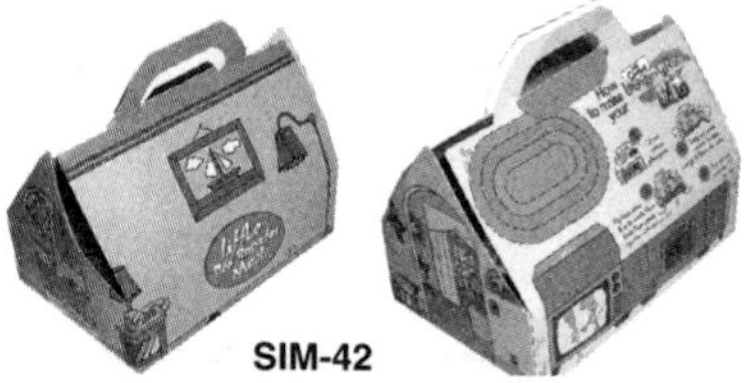

SIM-42

❑ **SIM-42. Lounge-A-Rama Set,**
2000. Set of 4 figures plus the couch from Little Red Rooster restaurant of Australia. 2-1/2"-5" tall plastic figures. Came in decorative box.
Set with box - **$15**

(BOX)

SIM-43

❑ **SIM-43. Dinner Table and Bar-B-Que Set,**
2000. 2 sets of 5 figures from Sabritas of Mexico. 1-1/2"-2" tall plastic figures. Came in decorative box.
10 figures bagged with box - **$30**
Set Unbagged - **$15**

SIM-44

❑ **SIM-44. "Radioactive Homer" Action Figure in Box,**
2000. A Toyfare magazine mail-order exclusive from the World of Springfield Interactive set. The figure glows in the dark. - **$150**

(PACKAGING)

(FIGURE WITH PLASTIC EGG FOUND IN CANDY)

SIM-45

❑ **SIM-45. Italian Candy Figure Set,**
2000. Set of 6 figures from Dolcerie Veneziane of Italy. Plastic figures came in plastic eggs found inside chocolate candy.
Set - **$30**

(COMIC BOOK)

(BAG)

SIM-46

❑ **SIM-46. Global Fanfest Figure Set,**
2000. From Burger King UK Global Fanfest Kid's Meal. Set of 10 soft plastic figures 5"-6" tall and a comic book in a decorative bag.
Each figure bagged with tag - **$5**
Each figure without bag or tag - **$3**
Carry bag - **$5**
Comic Book - **$3**

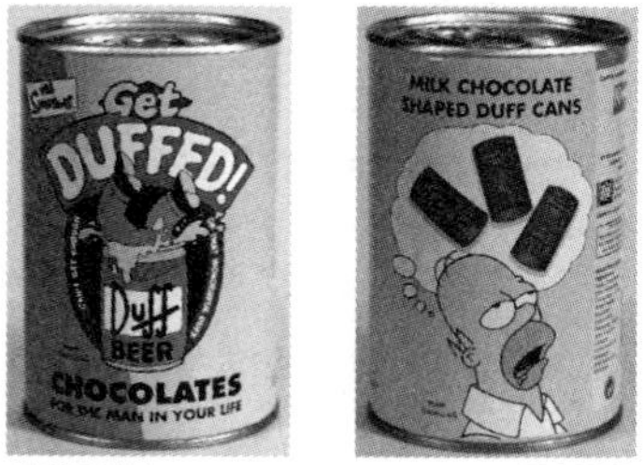


(FRONT) SIM-47 (BACK)

❑ **SIM-47. "Get Duffed" Chocolates,**
2000. Can contains milk chocolates shaped like Duff Beer cans. From England.
Unopened - **$5 $10 $15**

SIM-48 SIM-49

❑ **SIM-48. Krusty the Clown Action Figure on Card,**
2000. From the World of Springfield Interactive set. - **$7**

❑ **SIM-49. Barney Christmas Ornament,**
2001. In box. - **$5**

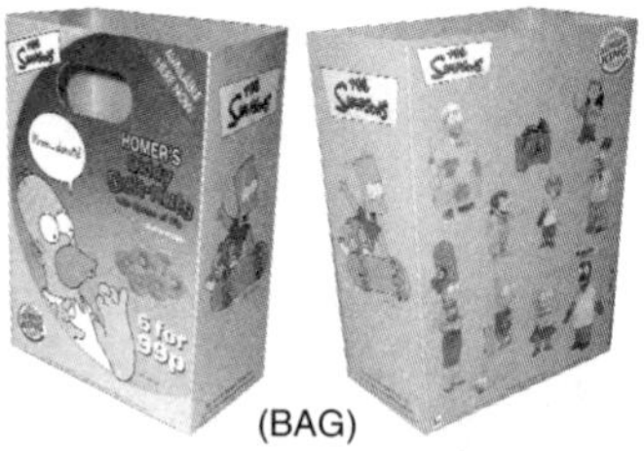

(BAG)

SIM-50

❑ **SIM-50. Diddy Doh-nuts Figure Set,**
2001. From Burger King UK Diddy Doh-nuts. Set of 11 soft plastic figures 5"-6" tall in a decorative box.
Each figure bagged with tag - **$5**
Mumu Homer bagged with tag - **$8**
Each figure without bag or tag - **$3**
Burger King box - **$5**

**SIM-51**

❑ **SIM-51. "Pin Pal Burns" Action Figure in Box,**
2001. A Toyfare magazine mail-order exclusive from the World of Springfield Interactive set. The episode "Team Homer" has Mr. Burns replacing star bowler Otto on the Pin Pals team, threatening the team's championship dreams with his poor athletic ability. - **$90**

PUNCHOUTS

**SIM-52** (BACKGROUND)

❑ **SIM-52. "Pop-Out People" Punchouts,**
2001. Cardboard punchouts of characters with background. - **$3**

**SIM-53**

❑ **SIM-53. "Woo-hoo!" Homer Sculpture,**
2001. From the "Misadventures of Homer Sculpture Collection. The Hamilton Collection.
In box - **$25**

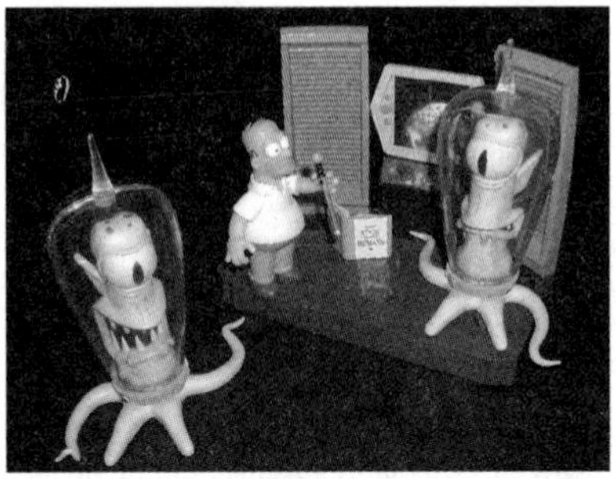

**SIM-54**

❑ **SIM-54. "Treehouse of Horror II" Action Figure Set,**
2001. Toys 'R' Us exclusive. Limited edition of 20,000 sets.
In box - **$65**

(ACTIVITY BOOK)

**SIM-55**

❑ **SIM-55. "Spooky Light-Ups" Figure Set,**
2001. Burger King Halloween. Set of 15 figures, 4" tall. Came with a 4-page Spooky Adventures 8-1/2"x 11" activity book.
Each figure in packaging - **$3**
Each figure loose - **$1**
Spooky Adventures activity book - **$5**

**SIM-56**

❑ **SIM-56. "Spooky Light-Ups" Promotional Poster,**
2001. Burger King Halloween. 26" x 39" paper poster. - **$20**

**SIM-57**

❑ **SIM-57. "Spooky Light-Ups" Promotional Poster,**
2001. Burger King Halloween. 19-1/2" x 19-1/2" cardboard poster. Some posters have a paste-over sticker changing the program air date from Oct. 30th to Nov. 6th. - **$5**

**SIM-58**

❑ **SIM-58. "Spooky Light-Ups" Window Cling,**
2001. Burger King Halloween. 17" x 24" plastic static window cling. Some have a paste-over sticker changing the program air date from Oct. 30th to Nov. 6th. - **$10**

# Sinclair Oil

**Harry F. Sinclair (1876-1956) founded the Sinclair Oil & Refining Corporation in 1916, and the company soon grew to become one of the nation's largest integrated oil companies. (Sinclair himself was caught up in the Teapot Dome oil-lease scandal and served a prison term in 1929 for contempt of the Senate.) The company started using dinosaurs in its advertising in 1930 to illustrate its theme that Sinclair oil was mellowed a hundred million years, and by 1931 had fixed on the brontosaurus as its symbol. Dino was put on signs and oil cans, the company sponsored dinosaur exhibits at the 1933 Century of Progress Exposition in Chicago and Dinoland at the 1964 New York World's Fair, funded dinosaur exploration, and in 1935 started giving out dinosaur stamps and albums at gas stations. Over the years Sinclair issued a number of dinosaur toys and other brontosaurus-oriented promotional items. In 1973 the company became part of the Atlantic Richfield Company, now ARCO.**

SNC-1

❑ **SNC-1. "Big News" Chicago World's Fair Sinclair Newspaper,**
1933. 11x16" photo feature eight-page publication devoted largely to the dinosaurs exhibit. Pictured example is "Second Edition" front and back cover. - **$15 $30 $60**

SNC-2

❑ **SNC-2. Dinosaur Stamp Album,**
1935. Holds 24 stamps.
Complete - **$25 $65 $125**

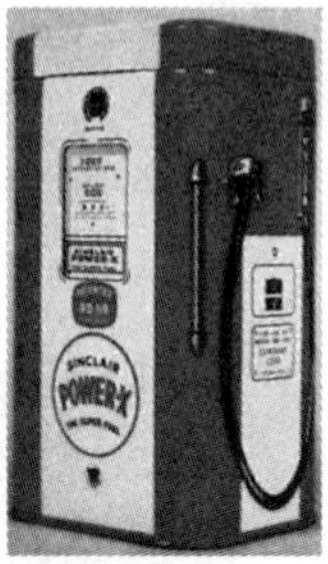

SNC-3 SNC-4

❑ **SNC-3. "Picture News" Issue,**
c. 1938. 11x16" monthly four-page news and human interest photo feature publication imprinted on top front and bottom rear page for local Sinclair dealer. - **$10 $25 $35**

❑ **SNC-4. "Sinclair Power-X" Litho. Tin Bank,**
c. 1950s. 4" tall with gauge showing price per gallon of 33 cents. - **$25 $70 $125**

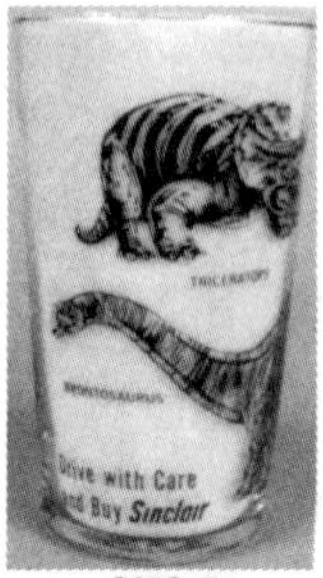

SNC-5

❑ **SNC-5. Dinosaurs Glass,**
1950s. 4-3/4" tall with images in green. -
**$10 $20 $30**

SNC-6

SNC-7

❑ **SNC-6. Coloring Book,**
1963. 8x10-3/4" with 32 pages including two which depict "Sinclair Dinoland" at 1964-65 New York World's Fair. - **$15 $25 $50**

❑ **SNC-7. "Dinoland" New York World's Fair Glass Tumbler,**
1964. Pictures symbolic twins at exhibit. -
**$10 $20 $30**

SNC-8

❑ **SNC-8. "Sinclair Dinoland" New York World's Fair Souvenir Booklet,**
1964. Twelve-page picture summary from life-sized dinosaur exhibit. Pictured are front and back cover. - **$10 $20 $35**

SNC-9

❑ **SNC-9. "Sinclair Dinoland" New York World's Fair Figure,**
1965. 9" long waxy-plastic dinosaur with inscriptions for Sinclair and second year of the fair. From series of various replicas purchased at the exhibit. Each - **$10 $20 $35**

SNC-10

❑ **SNC-10. Dinosaur Vinyl Bank,**
1960s. 9" long figure in green hard plastic unmarked but believed Sinclair issue. -
**$8 $15 $20**

SNC-11

SNC-12

❑ **SNC-11. Dinosaur Toy Pack,**
1960s. Six miniature plastic replica figures in cellophane packet naming each plus Sinclair Oil's logo. Near Mint Packaged - **$20**

❑ **SNC-12. "Drive With Care" Applique,**
c. 1960s. Molded thin shell plastic sign with peel-off adhesive strips on reverse. No Sinclair markings but obvious dinosaur symbol. -
**$10 $20 $30**

SNC-13

❑ **SNC-13. Inflatable Dinosaur Toy/Hanger Display,**
c. 1970s. Made by Alvimar. 48" long. -
**$10 $20 $35**

## The Singing Lady

**Ireene Wicker was the Singing Lady, and for 13 years (1932-1945) she told fairy tales and sang to the nation's children on a highly popular network radio program called *The Singing Story Lady*. The show, loved by parents as well as children, won many major broadcasting awards, including a Peabody. Kellogg's cereals, the long-term sponsor, offered a number of premiums, mostly song and story booklets designed by Vernon Grant. *The Singing Lady* moved to ABC television (1948-1950) with a similar format, using puppets to illustrate fairy tales and historical sketches. In 1953-1954, with Kellogg's again sponsoring, the program returned as *Story Time*.**

SNG-1

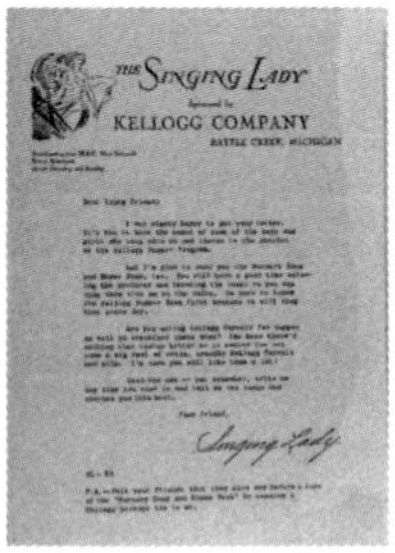

SNG-2

❑ **SNG-1. "Singing Lady Song Book",**
1931. Has coloring book pages. - **$8 $25 $50**

❑ **SNG-2. Singing Lady Promo Letter,**
1931. Kellogg's. Suggests you eat Kellogg's cereals for breakfast **and** supper. - **$5 $20 $35**

SNG-3

SNG-4

❑ **SNG-3. "Singing Lady Song Book",**
c. 1932. Art by Vernon Grant. - **$15 $25 $50**

❑ **SNG-4. Singing Lady Punchouts,**
1932. Kellogg's. Three cardboard pages of punchouts. Unpunched - **$25 $75 $100**

SNG-5

❑ **SNG-5. Kellogg's "Mother Goose" Booklet,**
1933. Cover art by Vernon Grant. -
**$15 $30 $50**

SNG-6

SNG-7

❑ **SNG-6. "Mother Goose" Booklet,**
1935. Kellogg's Rice Krispies. Subtitled "Mother Goose As Told By Kellogg's Singing Lady" with artwork over 16 pages by Vernon Grant. -
**$10 $20 $40**

❑ **SNG-7. Film Stories,**
1935. Kellogg's Rice Krispies. Promotes radio show. Has movie film cut-outs that can be played with by running through attached toy theatre. Features Mother Goose stories. -
**$20 $40 $60**

SNG-8

❑ **SNG-8. Punch-Out Paper "Party Kit",**
1936. Near Mint With Mailer - **$150**
Book Only - **$20 $50 $120**

SNG-9

❑ **SNG-9. "Mother Goose Action Circus" Punch-Out Book With Mailer Envelope,**
1936. Six sheets of Vernon Grant illustrations.
Mailer - **$10 $20 $30**
Punch-Out Book - **$100 $250 $350**

SNG-10

SNG-11

❑ **SNG-10. "Kellogg's Rice Krispies" Box Flat With Vernon Grant Art,**
1937. Has ad for Singing Lady Mother Goose Action Circus Book. Near Mint Flat - **$125**
Used Complete - **$15 $30 $75**

❑ **SNG-11. "Ireene Wicker" Fan Postcard,**
1940. National Broadcasting Co. for her "Musical Stories" radio broadcasts on Blue Network. - **$5 $20 $40**

## The Six Million Dollar Man

**Based on a Martin Caidin novel, *Cyborg*, this TV series, which ran from 1973 to 1978, followed the adventures of Steve Austin, a former test pilot and astronaut who is rebuilt with the latest technology after a freak accident ("better, stronger, faster"). He is given replacement limbs which heighten his strength, and a telescopic eye. As the series became a '70s phenomenon, the Bond-like**

**missions of the early episodes gave way to more cartoonish, comic-book adventures, involving stock Arab terrorists, dangerous space probes, and in several memorable episodes, aliens from outer space and a huge robot Bigfoot. A wide variety of toys and action figures were available.**

***The Bionic Woman*, a spin-off based on a story that aired on *The Six Million Dollar Man* in 1975, debuted in 1976 and ran until 1978. Lindsay Wagner played Jamie Summers, Steve's on-and-off girlfriend, and another enhanced government agent working for OSI. When *The Bionic Woman* switched networks, Richard Anderson and Martin E. Brooks (who played Goldman and bionics scientist Rudy Wells) made history as the first actors to play the same characters simultaneously on two different networks. There have been three reunion TV-movies: *Return of the Six-Million Dollar Man and the Bionic Woman* (1987), *Bionic Showdown: The Six-Million Dollar Man and the Bionic Woman* (1989), featuring a young Sandra Bullock, and *Bionic Ever After?* (1994), in which Steve and Jamie were finally wed. Persistent rumors of new incarnations of this popular series continue to pop up, but nothing concrete has happened as of this writing. Most items are copyright Universal City Studios.**

SXM-1

❑ **SXM-1. Lunch Box,**
1974. Aladdin Industries, Inc.
Box - **$15 $25 $50**
Thermos - **$10 $15 $25**
Complete - **$25 $40 $75**

SXM-2

❑ **SXM-2. Boxed Game,**
1975. Store item by Parker Brothers. - **$5 $10 $25**

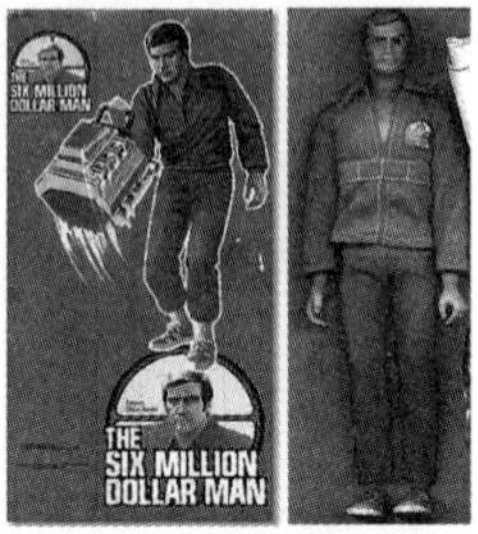

SXM-3

❑ **SXM-3. Six Million Dollar Man Action Figure,**
1975. 13" doll by Kenner. Figure was released in two versions. The first, with telescopic vision and bionic lifting arm with removable modules, came with an engine block. The second featured bionic gripping action and came with an orange I-beam. Box art for first version also shown.Boxed - **$35 $50 $85**

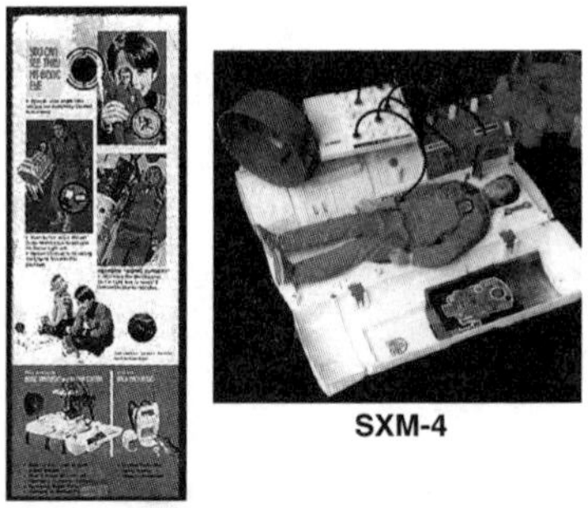
SXM-4

❑ **SXM-4. Bionic Transport and Repair Station,**
1975. Kenner. Side panel of box also shown. - **$25 $30 $60**

SXM-5

❑ **SXM-5. Venus Space Probe,**
1975. Kenner. Pictured with Steve Austin action figure (see SXM-2). - **$35 $40 $60**

SXM-6

❑ **SXM-6. "The Bionic Woman Action Club Kit,"**
1975. Issued by Kenner. Jamie Sommers portrait, membership card and certificate.
Complete **- $15 $35 $60**

SXM-7

❑ **SXM-7. Bionic Action Club Kit,**
1975. The kit included a mailing envelope (not pictured), a certificate, wallet card, logo sticker and portrait photo. A comic book ad with a coupon to join the club is also pictured.
Complete Kit - **$20 $35 $60**

SXM-8

❑ **SXM-8. The Six Million Dollar Man Record,**
1975. Peter Pan Industries. Four stories, including "Birth of the Bionic Man," "The Iron Heart," "The Man From the Future," and "Bionic Berserker." - **$5 $10 $20**

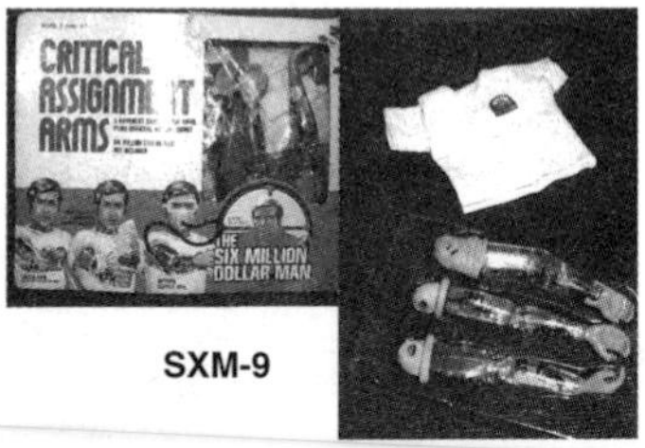

SXM-9

❑ **SXM-9. Critical Assignment Arms,**
1976. Accessories for the action figure. Set comes with three arms (laser, neutralizer, and oxygen supply) and a white T-shirt.
Boxed - **$20 $30 $50**

SXM-10

❑ **SXM-10. "Maskatron Six Million Dollar Man's Enemy" Action Figure,**
1976. Store item by Kenner. Figure is 13" tall.
Near Mint Boxed - **$165**
Loose Complete - **$20 $40 $75**

SXM-11

❑ **SXM-11. "O.S.I. Headquarters" Boxed Set,**
1977. Store item by Kenner.
Near Mint Boxed - **$85**
Loose Complete - **$15 $25 $50**

SXM-12

❑ **SXM-12. "The Six Million Dollar Man Bionic Mission Vehicle,"**
1977. Store item by Kenner.
Near Mint Boxed - **$75**
Loose Complete - **$15 $25 $45**

SXM-13

SXM-14

❑ **SXM-13. "6 Million Dollar Man Club" Cello. Button,**
1977. - **$10 $20 $30**

❑ **SXM-14. The Six Million Dollar Man Activity Book,**
1977. Rand McNally & Co. - **$10 $15 $20**

SXM-15

❑ **SXM-15. Book & Record Set,**
1977. Peter Pan Industries. Includes "Birth of the Bionic Man" and "The Man From the Future." - **$5 $10 $20**

SXM-16

❑ **SXM-16. "Hear 4 Exciting Christmas Adventures" Record,**
1978. Peter Pan Industries. Includes "The Toymaker," "Christmas Lights," "The Kris Kringle Caper," and "Elves Revolt." - **$5 $10 $20**

SXM-17

❑ **SXM-17. "The Six Million Dollar Man Venus Space Probe,"**
1978. Scarcest accessory in the Kenner series.
Complete Boxed - **$250 $500 $750**

## Skeezix

**The central character of the meandering continuity comic strip *Gasoline Alley*, Skeezix was an exception to the traditional comic style in that he aged accordingly as the strip continued over the years. Skeezix was a doorstep infant foundling left by unknown parents in 1921. He served in World War II and returned to continue his small town, middle-class life so readily identifiable to mass readership. Skeezix was an adult and father in the 1960s but the vast majority of related premiums are from his 1930s happy childhood years with guardian Uncle Walt surrounded by the extensive assortment of relatives, friends and neighbors created by cartoonist Frank King (1883-1969).**

SKX-1

❑ **SKX-1. Diecut Cardboard Standee For Cartoon Film,**
c. 1920. Capital Film Co. Inc., Chicago. About 7x7" full color. - **$75 $175 $325**

SKX-2

❑ **SKX-2. Uncle Walt And Skeezix Blotter,**
c. 1922. Various sponsor imprints. - **$10 $25 $60**

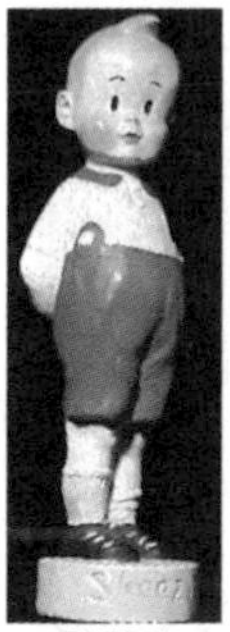
SKX-3

SKX-4

❑ **SKX-3. Large Plaster Statue,**
c. 1923. Store item by Live Long Toys, Chicago. 14-1/2" tall with realistic facial paint and red pants. - **$125 $275 $525**

❑ **SKX-4. "Handkerchiefs For Tiny Tots" Boxed Set,**
c. 1924. Store item. 6x6" box which held three.
Box - **$50 $125 $175**
Each Hanky - **$10 $20 $35**

SKX-5

SKX-6

**❑ SKX-5. "Party Invitations" Boxed,**
c. 1924. Store item. About a dozen full color in full color 4x6" box. Box - **$30 $60 $125**
Each Invitation - **$5 $10 $15**

**❑ SKX-6. Napkin Holder Boxed,**
c. 1926. Store item. 5x5" color box holding diecut flat wood figure of Pal the dog designed as napkin ring. Box - **$30 $60 $125**
Figure - **$35 $75 $125**

SKX-7

**❑ SKX-7. Toothbrush Holder Box,**
c. 1926. Full color 3x6-1/4".
Box Only - **$40 $100 $175**

SKX-8

**❑ SKX-8. "Skeezix Crayons With Pictures To Color" Boxed Set,**
c. 1930. Store item by Milton Bradley. Art includes Corky, born in 1928. - **$25 $60 $100**

SKX-9

**❑ SKX-9. "Walt & Skeezix Gasoline Alley Game,"**
c. 1932. Store item by Milton Bradley Co. -
**$40 $100 $165**

SKX-10

**❑ SKX-10. "The Skeezix Game,"**
c. 1936. Store item by Milton Bradley Co. -
**$35 $85 $150**

SKX-11

**❑ SKX-11. Celluloid Spinning Top,**
1930s. Skeezix Shoes. - **$25 $65 $100**

SKX-12

SKX-13

**❑ SKX-12. Skeezix Clothes Cello. Button,**
1930s. Braverman's Children's Shop. 1-1/4" full color. - **$20 $40 $75**

**❑ SKX-13. Skeezix' Clothes Cello. Button,**
1930s. Joseph Spiess Company. Full color 1-1/4". - **$20 $35 $70**

SKX-14

**❑ SKX-14. Card Game,**
1930s. Milton Bradley. Two varieties.
Black, White, Red Cards - **$20 $40 $60**
Full Color Cards - **$25 $50 $75**

SKX-15

SKX-16

**❑ SKX-15. Uncle Walt Ceramic Toothbrush Holder,**
1930s. Store item. Full color 5-1/2" tall. -
**$30 $75 $125**

**❑ SKX-16. "Skeezix At Military School" Premium Book,**
1930s. Pan-Am Gasoline. - **$35 $85 $175**

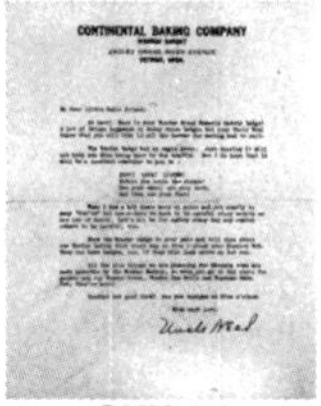

SKX-17

SKX-18

**❑ SKX-17. Club Letter,**
1930s. Wonder Bread. - **$10 $20 $40**

**❑ SKX-18. Skeezix Badge,**
1930s. Wonder Bread. - **$25 $50 $100**

SKX-19

SKX-20

**❑ SKX-19. Litho. Tin Toothbrush Holder,**
1930s. Pro-phy-lac-tic Listerine. -
**$40 $125 $225**

**❑ SKX-20. Birthstone Design "I Wear Skeezix Shoes" 2-1/4" Cello. Pocket Mirror,**
1930s. - **$20 $40 $75**

SKX-21

SKX-22

❑ **SKX-21. "I Wear Skeezix Shoes" Cello. Button,**
1930s. Unidentified sponsor. Added slogan is "Outgrown Before Outworn." - **$20 $40 $65**

❑ **SKX-22. "I Like Skeezix Sweaters" Cello. Button,**
1930s. - **$15 $25 $45**

SKX-23

❑ **SKX-23. "Skeezix" Cello. Button,**
1930s. Scarce variety. - **$30 $50 $100**

SKX-24

SKX-25

❑ **SKX-24. "Skeezix Loves Red Cross Macaroni" Cello. Button,**
1930s. - **$15 $35 $65**

❑ **SKX-25. "Buffalo Evening News" Cello. Button,**
1930s. From series of newspaper contest buttons, match number to win prize. - **$15 $30 $60**

SKX-26

SKX-27

❑ **SKX-26. "Skeezix" All Pictures Comic,**
1941. On his own in the big city. - **$10 $40 $85**

❑ **SKX-27. Clovia Doll Button,**
1949. About 2" diameter green and white. Character was "Born" May 15, 1949 and doll followed shortly after. - **$15 $25 $50**

SKX-28

❑ **SKX-28. "Skeezix Mask",**
1940s. Wheaties box panel.
Box Back Mask Uncut - **$15 $30 $45**
Cut Mask - **$5 $10 $15**

## Skippy

**Artist Percy Crosby (1891-1964) created the cartoon Skippy Skinner for the old *Life* humor magazine in the early 1920s and began syndicating the strip in 1925. Dressed in shorts, long jacket, and a checked hat, Skippy was the neighborhood pessimist, with a cynical view of the adult world, his humor shadowed by sadness and defeat. Even so, the strip was a popular one and ran until 1943, when Crosby became too ill to continue it. Comic book collections and illustrated Skippy novels appeared in the 1920s and 1930s, and there were two 1931 movies, *Skippy* and *Sooky*, both starring Jackie Cooper. A radio series aired on NBC (1932) and CBS (1932-1935), sponsored first by Wheaties (1932-1933), then by Phillips Magnesia toothpaste (1933-1935). Premiums included membership in *Skippy's Secret Service Society* and the *Skippy Mystic Circle Club*.**

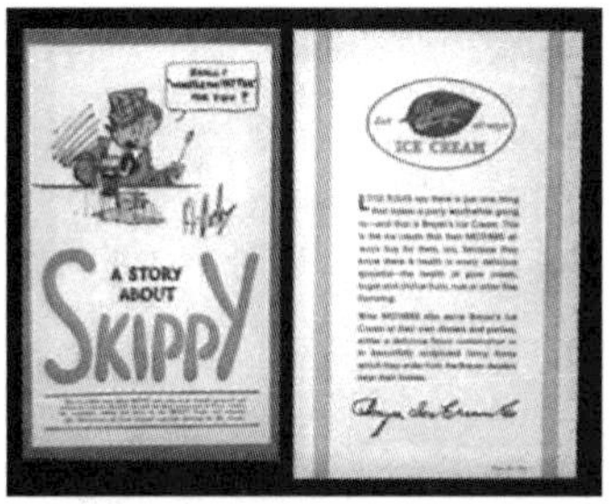

SKP-1

❑ **SKP-1. "A Story About Skippy" Booklet,**
c. 1930. Breyer's Ice Cream. 6x9-1/8" with 16 pages of specialty art by Crosby. -
**$35 $75 $125**

SKP-2

❑ **SKP-2. "Skippy" Handkerchief,**
1930. - **$8 $15 $30**

SKP-3

SKP-4

❑ **SKP-3. Skippy Plate - Boxed,**
1931. Large silver plate Skippy plate with price coupon. Store bought. Near Mint Boxed - **$250**
Plate Only - **$40 $100 $175**

❑ **SKP-4. Wheaties 9x18" Club Application and Information,**
1932. Rare with three perforated pieces intact.
Near Mint Intact - **$300**
Each Piece Loose - **$20 $40 $60**

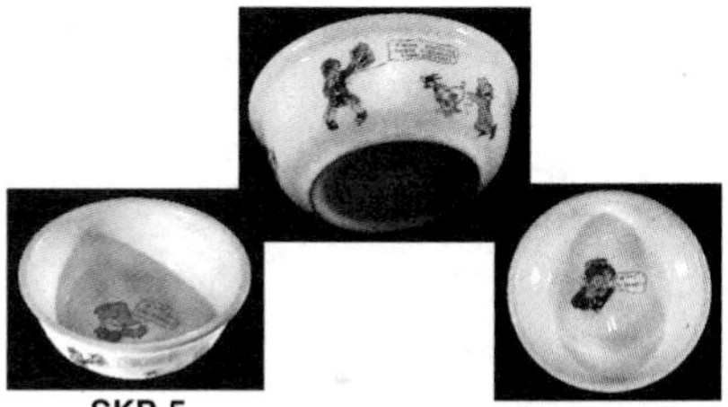
SKP-5 SKP-6

❑ **SKP-5. Wheaties Ceramic Bowl (Sooky),**
c. 1932. Rare. Same side view shown for both. Sooky pictured in bottom. - **$75 $135 $300**

❑ **SKP-6. Wheaties Ceramic Bowl (Skippy),**
c. 1932. Rare. Skippy pictured in bottom. -
**$50 $150 $250**

SKP-7

SKP-8

❑ **SKP-7. Plastic Bowl,**
1932. Beetleware bowl premium from Wheaties. Comes in green and orange.
Each - **$15 $30 $45**

❑ **SKP-8. Wheaties Cello. Club Button,**
1932. Initialed for Skippy's Secret Service Society. - **$5 $10 $15**

SKP-9

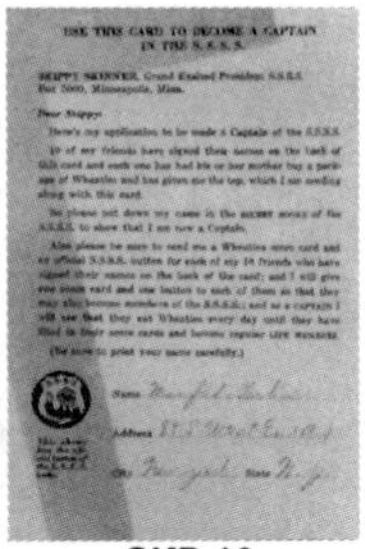

SKP-10

**❑ SKP-9. Life Membership,**
1932. Certificate for the Secret Service Society, plus 4 page secret code. - **$30 $60 $100**

**❑ SKP-10. Captain Application Form,**
c. 1932. Wheaties. - **$5 $10 $20**

SKP-11

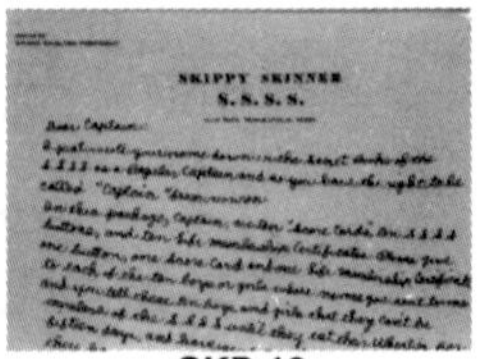


SKP-12

**❑ SKP-11. Wheaties "Captain" Cello. Rank Button,**
1932. For highest club rank. - **$20 $50 $75**

**❑ SKP-12. Wheaties Skippy Letter,**
c. 1932. "Dear Captain" form letter in simulated Skippy handwriting certifying rank attained by eating Wheaties "According To The Regulations And Rules". - **$8 $15 $30**

SKP-13

SKP-14

**❑ SKP-13. Wheaties "Captain's Commission" Certificate,**
c. 1932. Paper award for proven Wheaties consumption. - **$20 $50 $100**

**❑ SKP-14. Wheaties "Skippy Racer Club" Cello. Button,**
c. 1932. - **$20 $50 $85**

SKP-15

**❑ SKP-15. Skippy Cards,**
1933. Wheaties premium. Set of 12 different, 6 pictured. Each - **$10 $20 $35**

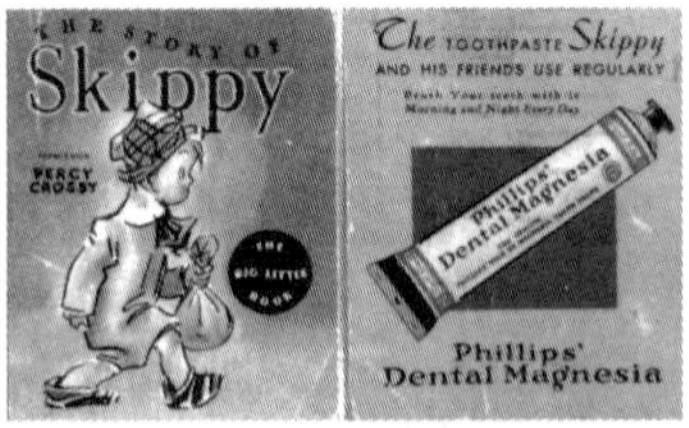


SKP-16

**❑ SKP-16. "The Story Of Skippy" BLB,**
1934. Phillips' Dental Magnesia Toothpaste. - **$15 $40 $90**

SKP-17

**❑ SKP-17. "Skippy" Big Little Book,**
1934. Whitman #781. - **$20 $60 $125**

SKP-18

**❑ SKP-18. Christmas Card,**
c. 1935. Phillips Dental Magnesia. - **$10 $25 $50**

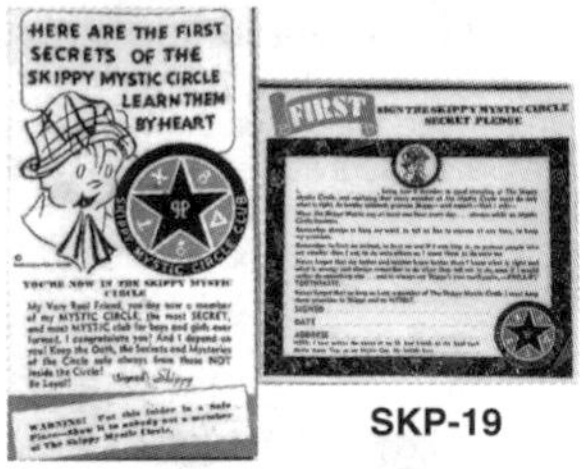


SKP-19

**❑ SKP-19. Mystic Circle Club Folder,**
c. 1935. Phillips Toothpaste. Folder opens to 16" length. - **$20 $40 $85**

SKP-20

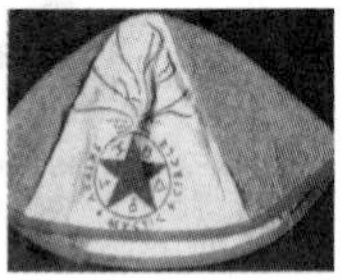

SKP-21

**❑ SKP-20. "Skippy Mystic Circle Club" Member Card,**
c. 1935. Phillips Dental Magnesia. - **$10 $35 $60**

**❑ SKP-21. "Skippy Mystic Circle" Felt Fabric Beanie,**
c. 1935. Phillips Dental Magnesia. - **$25 $75 $150**

SKP-22

**❑ SKP-22. "Skippy Puritan Blouses" Promo. Button,**
c. 1935. 1 1/4" diameter, orange background with black print. Parisian Novelty Company product, Chicago. - **$25 $55 $90**

SKP-23

SKP-24

SKP-25

**❑ SKP-23. "The Atlanta Georgian's Silver Anniversary" Litho. Button,**
1937. Named newspaper. From set of various characters. - **$35 $65 $125**

**❑ SKP-24. "Stories Of Interesting People Who Wear Glasses Booklet,**
1937. Manual for "Skippy Good Eyesight Brigade". - **$15 $20 $40**

**❑ SKP-25. Skippy Good Eyes Brigade Silvered Badge,**
1937. Scarce. - **$30 $80 $150**

(Movable Arms)

(Green Base)

SKP-26

(Celluloid Figure)

❑ **SKP-26. Bisque and Celluloid Figures,**
1930s. Store item, several versions.
Movable Arms, No Base - **$60 $125 $250**
One Arm Moves, Green Base - **$50 $90 $185**
Celluloid Figure - **$75 $200 $400**

SKP-27

SKP-28

❑ **SKP-27. "Fire Siren" Whistle Toy,**
1930s. Wooden tube 1-3/8" long with black image on red background. - **$15 $30 $50**

❑ **SKP-28. Skippy Cello. Button From Effanbee Doll,**
1930s. - **$20 $40 $75**

SKP-29

SKP-30

❑ **SKP-29. Skippy Mazda Lamps Sign,**
1930s. 15" by 26". - **$150 $350 $650**

❑ **SKP-30. "Fro-Joy Ice Cream" 24x36" Cardboard Store Sign,**
1930s. - **$100 $225 $350**

SKP-31

SKP-32

❑ **SKP-31. Paper Mask,**
1930s. Socony Oil. From set of "Five Free Funny Faces". - **$10 $35 $50**

❑ **SKP-32. Fabric Patch,**
1930s. Probably Wheaties. Orange/blue/white stitched design. - **$20 $50 $100**

SKP-33

SKP-34

SKP-35

❑ **SKP-33. Cello. Button,**
1930s. Includes artist's name "P. L. Crosby". - **$20 $40 $65**

❑ **SKP-34. "Saturday Chicago American" Litho. Button,**
1930s. From newspaper "16 Pages Of Comics" series of 10 known characters including two Skippy versions. - **$10 $20 $35**

❑ **SKP-35. "Sunday Examiner" Litho. Button,**
1930s. From "50 Comics" set of various newspaper characters, match number to win prize. - **$10 $25 $45**

## The Sky Blazers

***The Sky Blazers*, a radio series that dramatized episodes in the history of aviation, aired on CBS for a season (1939-1940), sponsored by Wonder bread. The show was created by Phillips H. Lord and hosted and narrated by Colonel Roscoe Turner, an early aviation hero and holder of various speed records. Each show closed with Turner interviewing the subject of that night's episode. Two issues of a *Sky Blazers* comic book appeared in 1940.**

SBZ-1

❑ **SBZ-1. Balsa Airplane In Tube,**
c. 1939. - **$60 $200 $300**

SBZ-2

❑ **SBZ-2. "'Sky Blazers' Wonder Bread" Brass Wings Pin,**
c. 1939. - **$15 $30 $65**

SBZ-3

❑ **SBZ-3. Paper Plane,**
1939. Wonder Bread premium. Two pieces. - **$30 $70 $100**

SBZ-4

❑ **SBZ-4. "Sky Blazers" Badge,**
1940. Silvered brass with red enamel paint. - **$60 $125 $175**

SBZ-5

SBZ-6

❑ **SBZ-5. Comic Book #1,**
Sept. 1940. - **$61 $182 $675**

❑ **SBZ-6. "Sky Blazers/Roscoe Turner" Photo,**
1940. Wonder Bread. From Sponsor Day Kit at New York World's Fair. - **$15 $25 $40**

SBZ-7

❑ **SBZ-7. Wonder Bread 8x12" Diecut Paper Sign,**
1940. Scarce. Promotes 7:00 P.M. CBS radio show. - **$50 $150 $250**

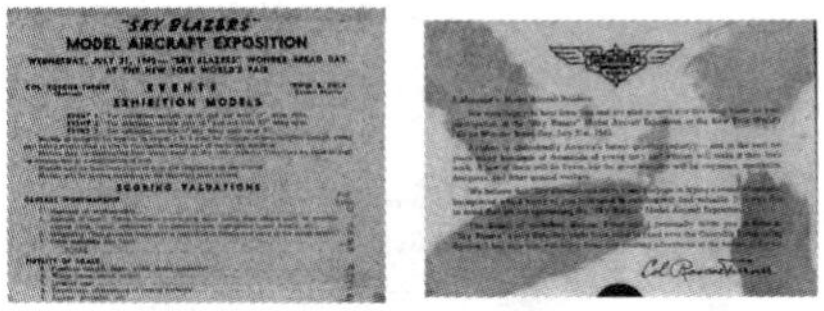


SBZ-8

❑ **SBZ-8. "Sky Blazers Model Aircraft Exposition/Roscoe Turner" Contest Registration Folder,**
1940. Wonder Bread. For Sponsor Day at New York World's Fair. - **$10 $25 $40**

SBZ-9

❑ **SBZ-9. "Sky Blazers/Roscoe Turner" Waxed Paper Bread Loaf Inserts,**
c. 1940. Wonder Bread. Each - **$10 $25 $40**

## Sky Climbers

**The Sky Climbers of America was an aviation-related club sponsored by boys' clothing stores around 1929. Members could qualify as Oiler, Mechanic, Pilot or Ace. The Flight Leader was reserved for the head of a club, like a Patrol Leader in Scouts. The "Chief" was the head of the sales department at the store. The symbol of the club was a youthful aviator type known as Pete Weet.**

SCL-1

❑ **SCL-1. "Sky Climbers Of America" Club Manual,**
1929. - **$30 $75 $100**

SCL-2

SCL-3

❑ **SCL-2. Fabric Patch,**
1929. - **$20 $60 $100**

❑ **SCL-3. Club Member Card,**
1929. - **$20 $50 $80**

SCL-4

SCL-5

❑ **SCL-4. Club Water Transfer Paper Picture,**
1929. Rare. - **$30 $90 $150**

❑ **SCL-5. "The Sky Climbers" Cello. Button,**
1929. - **$10 $20 $50**

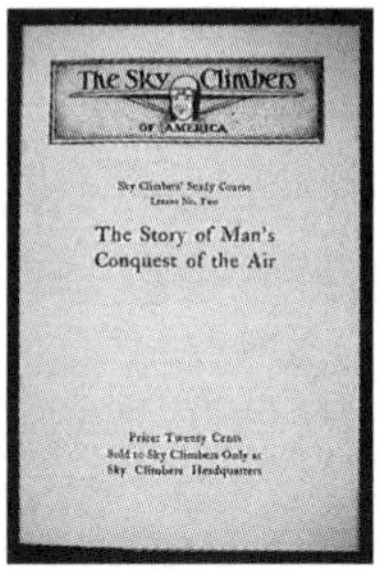


SCL-6

❑ **SCL-6. "Sky Climbers' Study Course Lesson No. Two" Booklet,**
1929. 5x7-1/2" booklet with 16 pages.
Each In Series - **$8 $15 $30**

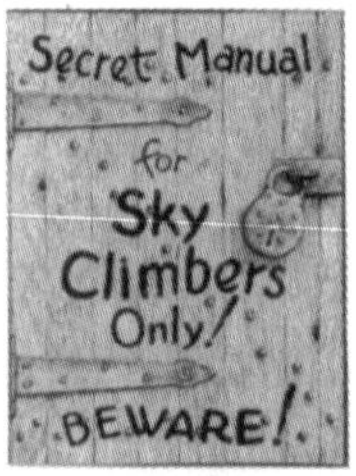


SCL-7

❑ **SCL-7. "The Sky Climbers Of America" Secret Manual,**
c. 1929. 4-1/4x6" with 12 pages. -
**$30 $75 $100**

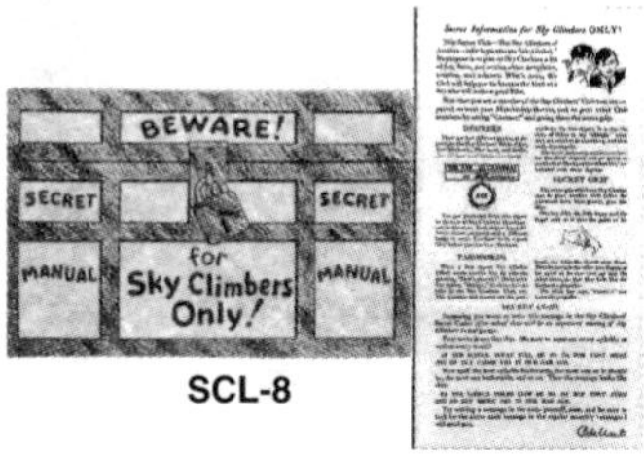


SCL-8

❑ **SCL-8. "Secret Manual For Sky Climbers Only!",**
c. 1930. - **$30 $75 $100**

SCL-9

SCL-10

❑ **SCL-9. "Pilot/The Sky Climbers Of America" Brass Bar And Pendant Badge,**
c. 1930. "Pilot" designation on pendant. The third degree in the club. - **$25 $60 $125**

❑ **SCL-10. "Ace/The Sky Climbers Of America" Brass Bar And Pendant Badge,**
c. 1930. "Ace" designation on pendant is for the highest degree in the club. - **$35 $75 $150**

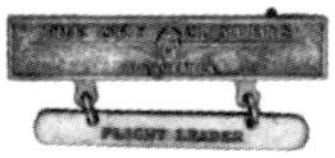

SCL-11

SCL-12

❑ **SCL-11. "The Sky Climbers Of America/Flight Leader" Brass Award Bar Badge,**
c. 1930. The Flight Leader was the person who ran each local club, like a Patrol Leader in Scouts. Each Flight Leader was appointed. -
**$60 $115 $165**

❑ **SCL-12. "Chief Sky Climber/The Sky Climbers Of America" Brass Bar and Pendant Badge,**
c. 1930. The Chief Sky Climber was the head of the clothing store that helped promote the club. -
**$65 $125 $175**

SCL-13

❑ **SCL-13. Last Club Manual,**
c. 1930. - **$30 $75 $100**

## Sky King

**America's favorite flying cowboy, Sky King aired on ABC radio from 1946 to 1950 and on Mutual from 1950 to 1954, sponsored starting in 1947 by Peter Pan peanut butter. The series centered on the crime-fighting exploits of rancher-pilot Schuyler King and his niece Penny and nephew Clipper. King's Flying Crown Ranch had an airstrip from which he and his young sidekicks flew off in his plane The Songbird to bring criminals to justice. The program made a successful transition to television as *Sky King Theater*, airing on NBC (1951-1952) and ABC (1952-1954), with Peter Pan again sponsoring. A new television series titled *Sky King* was syndicated from 1956 to 1958, then aired on CBS from 1959 to 1966, sponsored by Nabisco. Kirby Grant played King and Gloria Winters was Penny. Both Peter Pan and Nabisco issued program-related premiums, usually copyrighted by Jack Chertok Productions.**

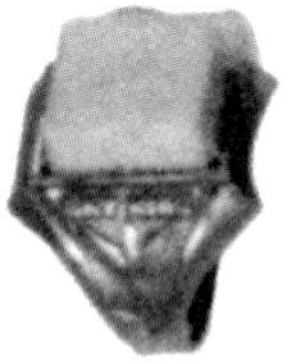

SKY-1

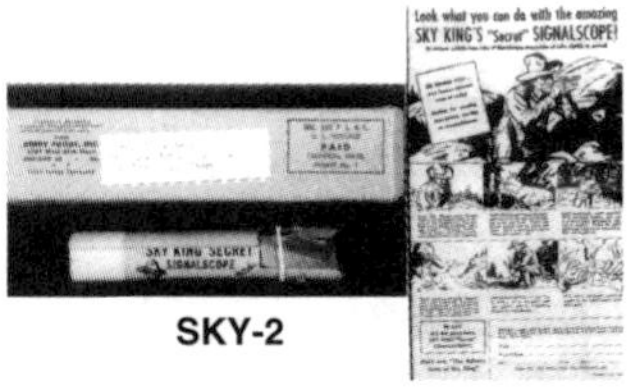


SKY-2

❑ **SKY-1. Radar Signal Ring,**
1946. Top glows in dark. - **$75 $150 $250**

❑ **SKY-2. "Secret Signalscope" With Instructions,**
1947. Whistle/magnifier held in scope tube.
Near Mint In Mailer - **$200**
Scope - **$35 $75 $125**

SKY-3

❑ **SKY-3. Sky King Secret Compartment Belt Buckle,**
1948. Prototype designed by Orin Armstrong for Robbins Co. Unique - **$6000**

SKY-4

SKY-5

SKY-6

❑ **SKY-4. "Mystery Picture Ring" Instruction Sheet,**
1948. - **$75 $90 $135**

❑ **SKY-5. Mystery Picture Ring,**
1948. Faint image on rectangular plastic sheet under gray plastic top has almost always disappeared. Complete No Image - **$125 $200 $300**
Near Mint With Image - **$1000**

❑ **SKY-6. Magni-Glo Writing Ring,**
1949. - **$20 $45 $125**

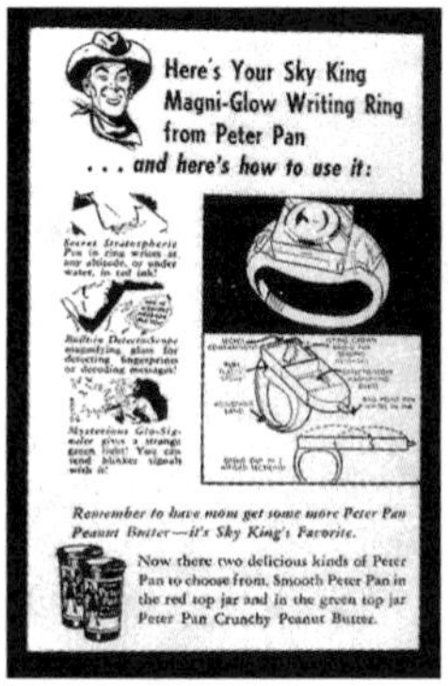


SKY-7

❑ **SKY-7. "Magni-Glow Writing Ring" Instruction Paper,**
1949. Peter Pan Peanut Butter. - **$25 $50 $75**

SKY-8

❑ **SKY-8. Electronic Television Picture Ring,**
1949. Brass and plastic, came with photo strip to be developed and cut showing Jim, Penny, Clipper, Martha. See SKY-10.
Ring Only - **$40 $75 $150**
Photo Set - **$75 $90 $100**

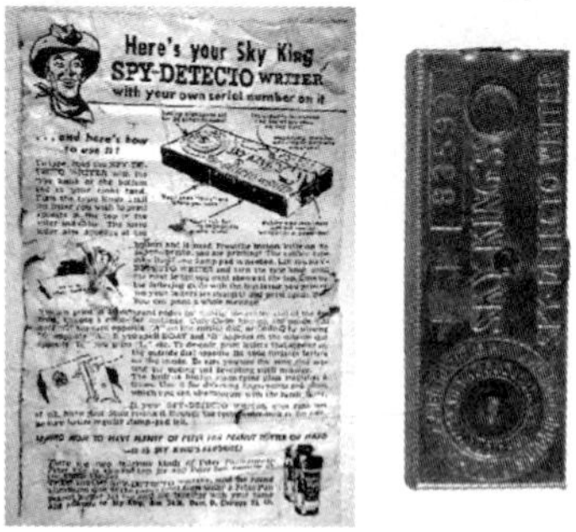


SKY-9

❑ **SKY-9. "Spy Detecto Writer",**
1949. Elaborate premium that includes decoder. Comes in all brass or brass/aluminum versions.
Writer - **$50 $90 $150**
Instruction Sheet - **$15 $35 $70**

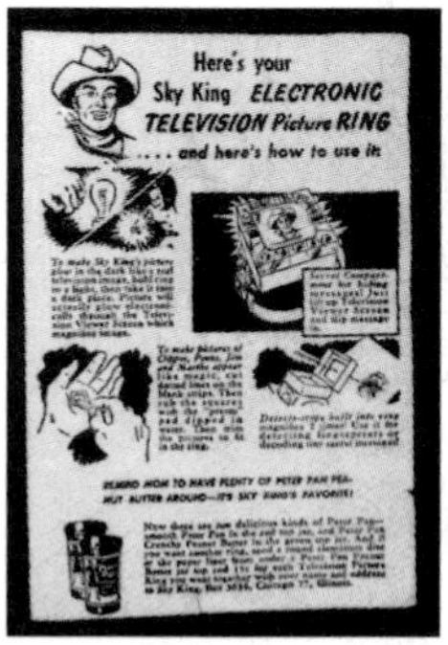


SKY-10

❑ **SKY-10. "Electronic Television Picture Ring" Instruction Sheet,**
1949. Peter Pan Peanut Butter. See SKY-8. - **$50 $60 $85**

SKY-11

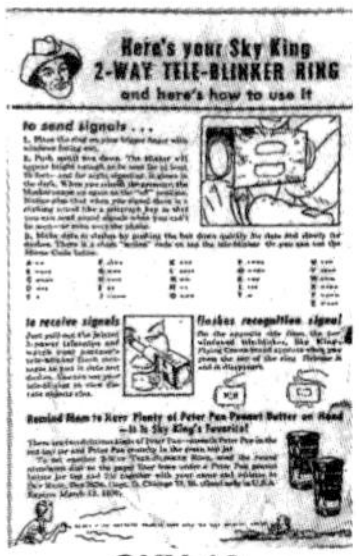


SKY-12

❑ **SKY-11. Tele-Blinker Ring,**
1949. Brass and other metals signal ring. When pressed, ring sides reveal cut-out panels with glow-in-dark inserts. - **$75 $120 $175**

❑ **SKY-12. "2-Way Tele-Blinker Ring" Instruction Sheet,**
1949. Peter Pan Peanut Butter. Sheet includes ring order coupon expiring March 13, 1950. - **$35 $50 $85**

SKY-13

SKY-14

❑ **SKY-13. Navajo Treasure Ring,**
1950. - **$50 $85 $150**

❑ **SKY-14. "Safety Is No Accident" Litho. Button,**
c. 1950. - **$30 $60 $125**

SKY-15

❑ **SKY-15. Kaleidoscope Prototype Ring,**
c. 1950. Large brass and other metals viewer ring developed in prototype design by Orin Armstrong but never actually offered as premium. Unique - **$12500**

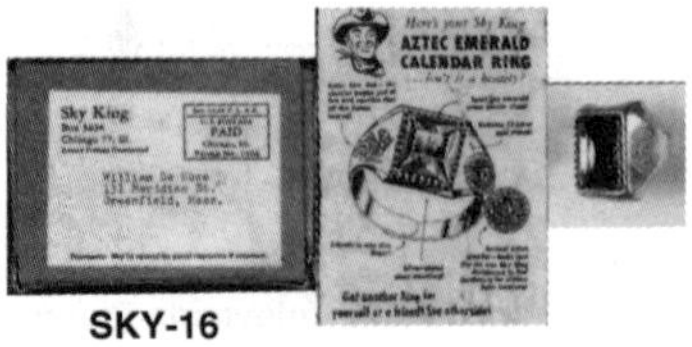

SKY-16

❑ **SKY-16. "Aztec Emerald Calendar Ring" With Instruction Sheet,**
1951. Mint Boxed With Instructions - **$1200**
Ring - **$200 $600 $1000**
Instructions - **$125 $135 $150**

SKY-17

❑ **SKY-17. "Detecto-Microscope" With Accessories,**
1952. Cardboard stand and four specimens not shown, map glows in dark.
Near Mint Complete - **$500**
Plastic Tube Only - **$25 $50 $75**
Map - **$20 $40 $60**

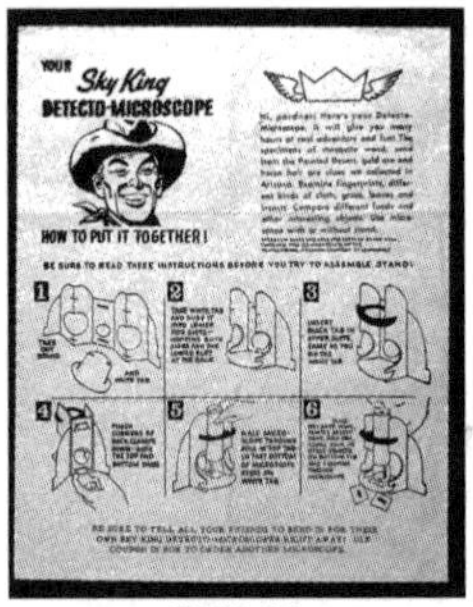


SKY-18

❑ **SKY-18. Detecto Instructions,**
1952. Six step instruction sheet for Detecto-Microscope. - **$20 $40 $60**

SKY-19

❑ **SKY-19. "Stamping Kit" Newspaper Ad,**
1953. - **$8 $15 $20**

SKY-20

SKY-21

❑ **SKY-20. "Stamping Kit" Order Blank,**
1953. - **$15 $25 $60**

❑ **SKY-21. Stamping Kit,**
1953. Tin container holding ink pad and personalized rubber stamp. Ink often rusts the tin. - **$20 $40 $85**

SKY-22

❑ **SKY-22. Figure Set,**
1956. Nabisco Wheat & Rice Honeys. Soft plastic in various colors. Sky King, Clipper, Penny, Sheriff, Songbird (plane), Yellow Fury (horse).
Each - **$15 $25 $50**

SKY-23

SKY-24

❑ **SKY-23. Nabisco Fan Postcard,**
c. 1956. - **$10 $20 $40**

❑ **SKY-24. "TV Eye" Cover Article,**
1956. Weekly television supplement to June 24 newspaper with color cover photo plus one-page Sky King article including three other bw photos. - **$15 $35 $60**

SKY-25

❑ **SKY-25. Kirby Grant Contest Photo,**
1957. McGowan Studios. Note on back about search for look-alike to play Kirby's twin in upcoming film. - **$15 $30 $60**

SKY-26

❑ **SKY-26. Fan Club Nabisco Contest Postcard,**
1959. Oversized 5-1/2x7" card. - **$20 $50 $90**

SKY-27

❑ **SKY-27. "Sky King Fan Club" Folder,**
1959. Nabisco. 3x5" closed but opens to five panels printed on both sides. Example shown is missing one panel. Includes membership card, good conduct rules, cut-out photos of Sky and Penny plus more. Came with litho. tin tab (SKY-28). Folder Complete - **$40 $75 $135**

SKY-28

❑ **SKY-28. Nabisco "Sky King Fan Club" Litho. Tin Tab Wings,**
1959. - **$40 $100 $150**

SKY-29

❑ **SKY-29. "Sky King" TV Promotion Sign,**
1959. Sponsored by Nabisco. 11"x28" sign shows photo of Sky King. - **$50 $150 $250**

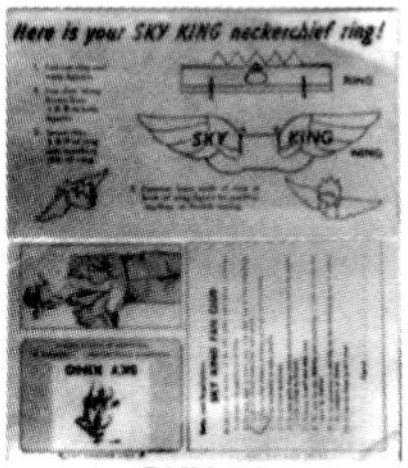

SKY-30 SKY-31

❑ **SKY-30. Nabisco Fan Club Member Kit,**
c. 1959. Includes cut-out Sky King neckerchief ring plus membership card. - **$35 $70 $150**

❑ **SKY-31. Autographed Photo,**
1950s. - **$20 $40 $75**

SKY-32

❑ **SKY-32. "Sky King And Penny" Autographed Photo,**
1950s. Issued by Zembo Shrine Circus. Signed in blue ink. Signed - **$35 $60 $100**
Unsigned - **$10 $25 $50**

SKY-33

SKY-34

❑ **SKY-33. "Cook Out With Sky King" Recipe Folder,**
1950s. Nabisco. - **$30 $60 $100**

❑ **SKY-34. Cowboy Tie With Envelope,**
1950s. Near Mint In Mailer - **$125**
Tie Only - **$15 $30 $60**

SKY-35 SKY-36

❑ **SKY-35. Autographed Photo,**
1950s. Carson & Barnes Circus. 8x10" black and white. Signed - **$25 $50 $75**
Unsigned - **$10 $25 $50**

❑ **SKY-36. "Runaway Train" Premium Comic Book,**
1964. Nabisco. 7x10" with 16 color pages. Reverse has ad for Sky King TV show. - **$20 $50 $75**

## Skyriders

**Skyriders was a 1930s aviation-themed club sponsored by Belle Meade Shoe Co., a division of General Shoe Corporation, located in Nashville, Tennessee. Their Pilot's Handbook invited youngsters to write to John Ball, Transport Pilot No. 20390, to obtain a Skyriders Pilot's Examination, which if passed secured the applicant a Skyriders Pilot's License. The club operated through much of the 1930s and was advertised in model airplane magazines of the era.**

SRD-1

❑ **SRD-1. Club Knife,**
1930. Scarce. - **$60 $125 $200**

SRD-2

SRD-3

❑ **SRD-2. "Skyrider Pilot's Club/Certified Pilot" Cello. Button,**
1930s. - **$20 $40 $75**

❑ **SRD-3. "Sky Riders Club" Member Cello. Button,**
1930s. - **$20 $40 $75**

SRD-4

❑ **SRD-4. "Lieutenant/Member Skyriders Club" Brass Wings Badge,**
1930s. Bronze luster. - **$20 $35 $50**

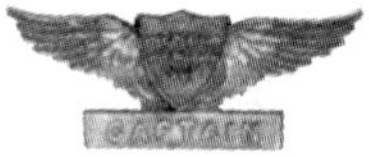

SRD-5 SRD-6

❑ **SRD-5. "Captain/Member Skyriders Club" Brass Wings Badge,**
1930s. Dark gold luster. - **$20 $40 $65**

❑ **SRD-6. "Colonel/Member Skyriders Club" Brass Wings Badge,**
1930s. Bronze luster. - **$20 $45 $85**

SRD-7 SRD-8

❑ **SRD-7. "General" Brass Wings Badge,**
1930s. Highest rank club badge. - **$30 $50 $110**

❑ **SRD-8. "Lieutenant" Litho. Tin Rank Badge,**
1930s. - **$15 $35 $60**

SRD-9

SRD-10

❑ **SRD-9. "Royal Order Of Sky Riders",**
1930s. 3/4" blue on cream member's button. - **$10 $20 $40**

❑ **SRD-10. "Skyriders Pilot's Hand Book",**
1930s. Example issued by H. Leh & Co., Allentown, Pa. Details history of flight and encourages youngster to write for Skyriders Pilot's Examination which if passed, results in Skyriders Pilot's License. - **$10 $20 $40**

SRD-11

❑ **SRD-11. "Captain" Litho. Tin Rank Badge,**
1930s. - **$20 $40 $70**

SRD-12

❑ **SRD-12. Brass Wings Badge With Celluloid Bar,**
1930s. Brass reads "Member Sky Riders Club" with small rivet holding red, white and blue diecut celluloid award for advancement to "Lieutenant." - **$20 $45 $75**

## Sky Roads

**This pioneer aviation comic strip was created in 1929 by two former World War I pilots, Dick Calkins (who gained fame with Buck Rogers) and Lester J. Maitland. The strip was distributed by the John F. Dille company. Zack Mosley, later creator of Smilin' Jack, and Russell Keaton, later creator of Flyin' Jenny, did the artwork, with Keaton taking over and signing the strip after 1933. Over the years the strip featured a variety of daredevil pilots dealing with many perils and romantic adventures. A children's club, the Flying Legion, offered readers metal badges for Pilot, Lieutenant, Captain, Major, Colonel, and Ace. Additional "intermediate ranks" of Aviation Mechanic, Stunt Flyer, and Combat Flyer were awarded, probably by letter, but not accompanied by metal badges. Reprints of the strip appeared in *Famous Funnies* comic books in the early 1940s and some early episodes were reprinted in a paperback in 1966. The strip ended in 1942.**

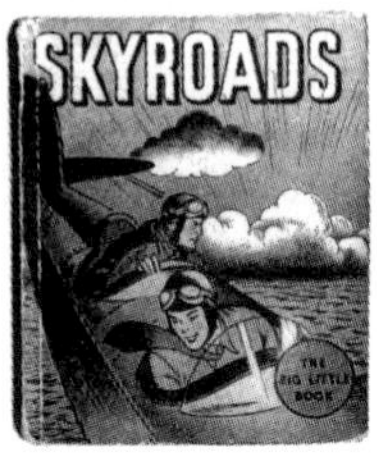

SRO-1

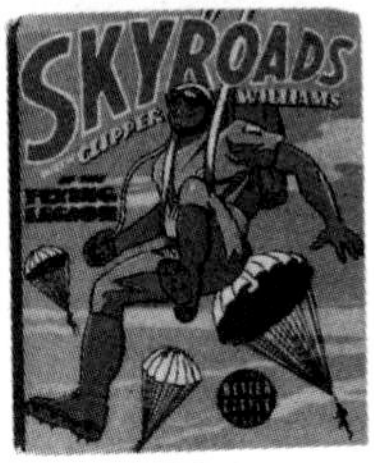

SRO-2

❑ **SRO-1. Skyroads Big Little Book,**
1936. Whitman #1127. - **$15 $50 $125**

❑ **SRO-2. "Skyroads With Clipper Williams Of The Flying Legion" BTLB,**
1938. Store item. Whitman Better Little Book #1439. - **$15 $50 $125**

SRO-3

SRO-4

❑ **SRO-3. "Sky Roads" Cello. Button,**
1930s. Buffalo Evening News. From series of newspaper contest buttons, match number to win prize. - **$20 $40 $75**

❑ **SRO-4. "Hurricane Hawk Flying Club" Membership Card,**
1930s. Certifies "Aerial Machine Gunner" with Skyroads emblem. - **$20 $50 $75**

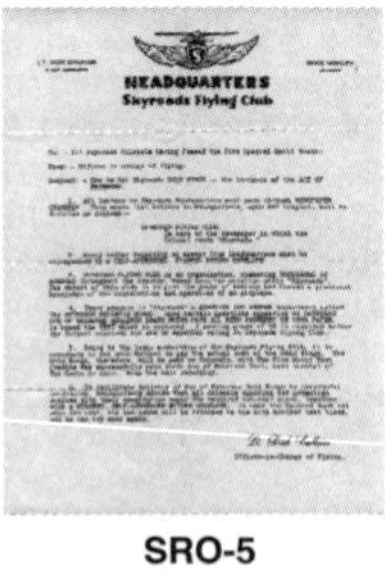

SRO-5

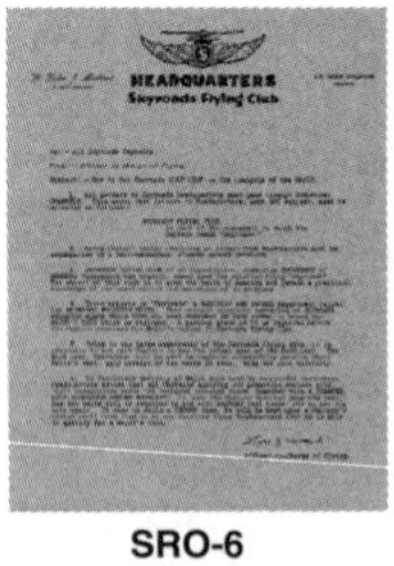

SRO-6

❑ **SRO-5. Skyroads "Gold Wings" Certificate,**
1930s. - **$10 $25 $40**

❑ **SRO-6. Skyroads "Gold Leaf" Certificate,**
1930s. - **$10 $25 $40**

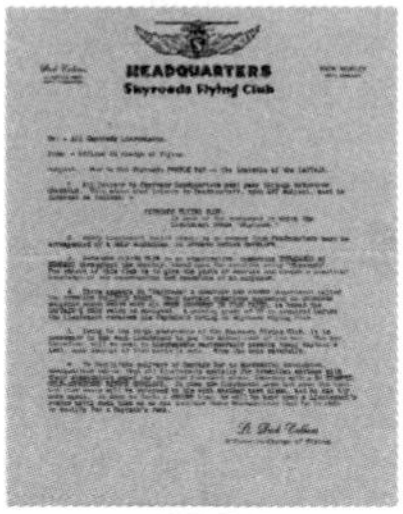

SRO-7

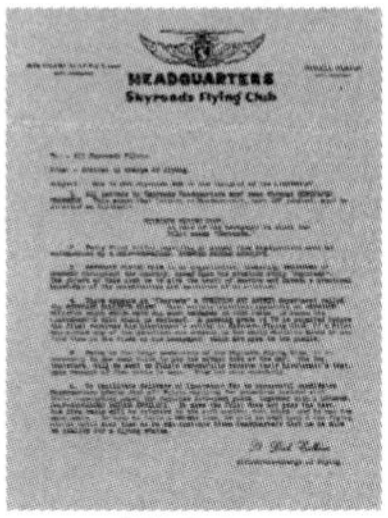

SRO-8

❑ **SRO-7. Skyroads "Captain Double Bar" Certificate,**
1930s. - **$10 $25 $40**

❑ **SRO-8. Skyroads "Lieutenant Bar" Certificate,**
1930s. - **$10 $25 $40**

SRO-9

❑ **SRO-9. "Skyroads Flying Club" Member Card,**
1941. Certified member to be "Flying Cadet." Club offered progressions in rank entitling member to officer pins pictured in next six examples. - **$25 $65 $100**

SRO-10

SRO-11

❑ **SRO-10. Skyroads Cadet Litho. Button,**
1941. - **$10 $30 $60**

❑ **SRO-11. Skyroads Cadet Litho. Button,**
1941. Has "Cleveland News" printed on bottom of pin. - **$15 $35 $70**

SRO-12

SRO-13

SRO-14

❑ **SRO-12. Skyroads Pilot Metal Wings Pin,**
1941. - **$20 $40 $85**

❑ **SRO-13. Skyroads Lieutenant Metal Bar Pin,**
1941. - **$20 $40 $85**

❑ **SRO-14. Skyroads Captain Metal Bar Pin,**
1941. - **$30 $60 $100**

SRO-15

SRO-16

❏ **SRO-15. Skyroads Major Oak Leaf Metal Pin,**
1941. - **$40 $75 $120**

❏ **SRO-16. Skyroads Colonel Metal Pin,**
1941. Highest rank eagle insignia. -
**$50 $100 $175**

SRO-17

❏ **SRO-17. Skyroads Combat Plane Metal Pin,**
1941. Rare. - **$50 $100 $175**

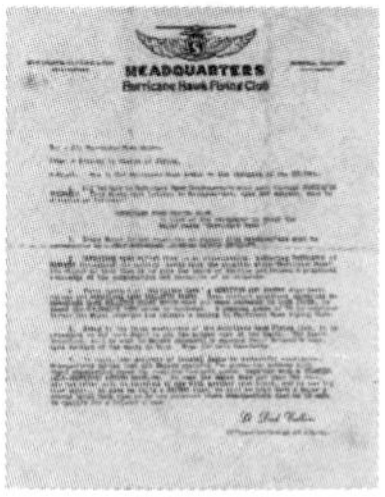


SRO-18

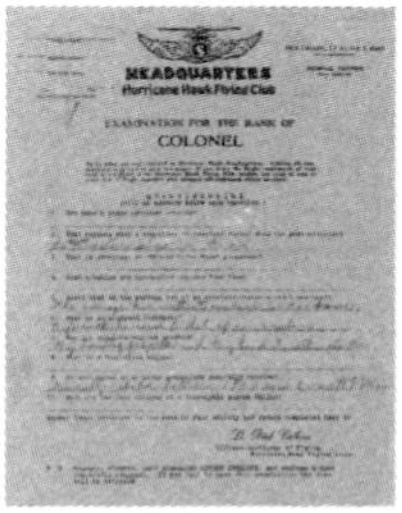


SRO-19

❏ **SRO-18. "Colonel" Hurricane Hawk's Eagle Instructions,**
1940s. - **$15 $30 $45**

❏ **SRO-19. "Colonel" Examination Sheet,**
1940s. A written test which had to be completed and sent with 10¢ and a self-addressed stamped envelope to get your promotion. -
**$15 $30 $50**

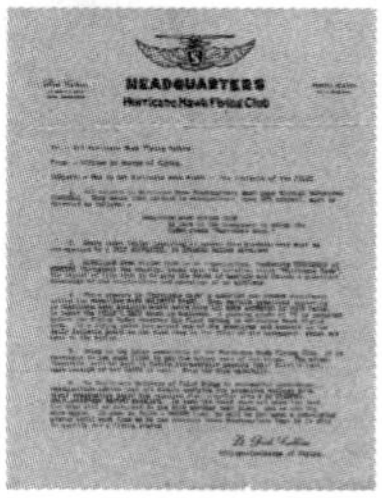


SRO-20

❏ **SRO-20. "Pilot" Hurricane Hawk's Wing Instructions,**
1940s. Club was set up to support the newspaper strip. Hurricane Hawk was one of the main stars of the Skyroads strip. - **$10 $25 $40**

# Small Soldiers

**The movie *Small Soldiers* hit the screen in 1998 to mixed reviews. The film had an interesting twist - the good guys, the Argonites, were the monsters and the soldiers, the Commando Elite ended up being the bad guys. The plot of the movie centered around two young inventors who were hired by a "hot shot" promoter to create "aggressive" toys quickly. In order to meet an impossible deadline, the inventors take a short-cut by purchasing computer chips from the government. What they didn't realize was that the chips gave the toys their own personalities and made them uncontrollable. The Commandos were programmed to destroy the Argonites, and they took their mission seriously. They developed weapons to destroy anyone in their path. The Argonites were programmed to lose, and their personalities were marked with low self-esteem. This drew the sympathies of the movie's audience. A set of the Argonites is delivered to a young boy, who instantly takes a liking to "Archer," the leader of the Argonites. The boy soon learns that Archer can talk and think on his own. Archer reveals that his wish is to help his fellow Argonites find a home where they can live safely in peace. The Commandos stand in the way, and a violent battle ensues. By the end, the Argonites have defeated the bad guys. Many film critics felt the violence of the film was too intense for children who were not accustomed to seeing their toys behave in such ways.**

**Since the video was released and the movie was shown on cable, Small Soldiers has gained a solid following. The toys that were produced for the film were of the highest quality and packaged well. Because of the mixed reviews, the box office numbers were disappointing and some of the toys were discounted at the stores. However, now that more people have seen the movie, the toys are gaining the interest of collectors.**

SMA-1

SMA-2

❏ **SMA-1. "Talking Chip Hazard" 12" Figure,**
1998. In box. - **$35**

❏ **SMA-2. "Talking Archer" 12" Figure,**
1998. In colorful box. With punching action, electronic lights and sounds. Harder to find than Chip Hazard Talking Figure. - **$50**

SMA-3

❏ **SMA-3. "Archer" String Shooting Gun,**
1998. Includes can of string fluid in box. - **$20**

SMA-4

❏ **SMA-4. "Slam Fist" Figure in Box,**
1998. Giant with boulder-throwing fist. - **$20**

SMA-5

❏ **SMA-5. "Punch-It" With Firing Assault Cannon in Box,**
1998. - **$18**

SMA-6 SMA-7 SMA-8

❏ **SMA-6. "Archer" Pop Candy Figure,**
1998. - **$6**

❏ **SMA-7. "Chip Hazard" Pop Candy Figure,**
1998. - **$6**

❏ **SMA-8. "Archer" Figure on Card,**
1998. - **$12**

SMA-9

SMA-10

❑ **SMA-9. "Insaniac" Figure on Card,**
1998. - **$15**

❑ **SMA-10. "Freakenstein" Figure on Card,**
1998. - **$15**

SMA-15

SMA-16

❑ **SMA-15. "Chip Hazard" Figure on Card,**
1998. Comes with Combat Blaster. - **$10**

❑ **SMA-16. "Electro-Charged Chip Hazard" Figure on Card,**
1998. Comes with Combat Blaster. - **$7**

SMA-21

SMA-22

❑ **SMA-21. "Action Car" on Card,**
1998. Promotes Shell Oil. - **$10 $20 $30**

❑ **SMA-22. War Games Activity Set,**
1998. - **$15**

SMA-11

SMA-12

❑ **SMA-11. "Witchdoctor Insaniac" Figure on Card,**
1998. - **$12**

❑ **SMA-12. "Archer's Battle Headquarters,"**
1998. With 3 Small Figures on Card. - **$5**

SMA-17

SMA-18

❑ **SMA-17. "Battle Damage Chip Hazard" Figure on Card,**
1998. Comes with Blow-Apart Legs. - **$7**

❑ **SMA-18. "Brick Bazooka" Figure on Card,**
1998. - **$15**

SMA-23

SMA-24

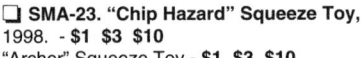

❑ **SMA-23. "Chip Hazard" Squeeze Toy,**
1998. - **$1 $3 $10**
"Archer" Squeeze Toy - **$1 $3 $10**
"Slam Fist" Squeeze Toy - **$1 $3 $10**

❑ **SMA-24. "Archer" Burger King Figure,**
1998. With working bow and arrow. - **$1 $3 $7**

SMA-13

SMA-14

❑ **SMA-13. "Punch-It's Battle Headquarters,"** 1998. With 3 Small Figures on Card. - **$5**

❑ **SMA-14. "Chip Hazard's Battle Headquarters,"**
1998. With 3 Small Figures on Card. - **$5**

SMA-19

SMA-20

❑ **SMA-19. "Battle Changing Kip" Figure on Card,**
1998. - **$15**

❑ **SMA-20. "Nick Nitro" Figure on Card,**
1998. With Launching Dual Missile Pack. - **$15**

SMA-25

SMA-26

❑ **SMA-25. "Ocula" Burger King Figure,**
1998. - **$1 $3 $7**

❑ **SMA-26. "Witchdoctor Insaniac" Burger King Figure,**
1998. - **$1 $3 $7**

SMA-27

SMA-28

❑ **SMA-27. "Freakenstein" Burger King Figure,**
1998. Attacking and riding a soldier figure. - **$1 $3 $7**

❑ **SMA-28. "Punch-It" Burger King Figure,**
1998. - **$1 $3 $7**

SMA-29

SMA-30

❑ **SMA-29. "Chip Hazard" Burger King Figure,**
1998. - **$1 $3 $7**

❑ **SMA-30. Burger King Figure,**
1998. With binoculars. - **$1 $3 $7**

SMA-31

SMA-32

❑ **SMA-31. "Brick Bazooka" Burger King Figure,**
1998. On toaster vehicle. - **$1 $3 $7**

❑ **SMA-32. "Nick Nitro" Burger King Figure,**
1998. On wind-up motorcycle. - **$1 $3 $7**

SMA-33

❑ **SMA-33. Buzzsaw Tank in Box,**
1998. With Ocala figure. - **$15**

SMA-34

❑ **SMA-34. "Archer's Crossbow" in Box,**
1998. Space Shooter Target Game. - **$30**

SMA-35

❑ **SMA-35. "Archer" Radio Control Cycle,**
1998. - **$40**

SMA-36

❑ **SMA-36. Power Drill Cycle,**
1998. With Scratch-It figure. - **$4 $8 $20**

SMA-37

❑ **SMA-37. Ground Assault Vehicle,**
1998. With "Missile Blastin' Action." - **$20**

(FRONT)

(BACK)

SMA-38

❑ **SMA-38. "Attack Zones" Micro Playset,**
1998. With 4 action figures. - **$15**

(FRONT)

(BACK)

SMA-39

❑ **SMA-39. Big Battle Game,**
1998. With 12 action figures. - **$35**

(FRONT)

(BACK)

SMA-40

❑ **SMA-40. Globotech Battle Command Case,**
1998. With accessories. - **$15**

(FRONT)

(BACK)

SMA-41

❑ **SMA-41. Secret Decoder Activity Case,**
1998. With accessories. - **$12**

SMA-42

SMA-43

❑ **SMA-42. Hand To Hand Combat Game,**
1998. Electronic game on card. - **$5 $15 $35**

❑ **SMA-43. Colorforms Play Set,**
1998. With 23 colorforms. - **$12**

SMA-44

SMA-45

❑ **SMA-44. Color Chrome Valentines,**
1998. With 32 valentines and 48 stickers. - **$5**

❑ **SMA-45. Clear Treat Bags,**
1998. In wrapper. - **$5**

SMA-46

❑ **SMA-46. Fun Bags,**
1998. 15 bags in package. - **$3**

SMA-47

SMA-48

❑ **SMA-47. Color and Activity Book,**
1998. Series 2. Nick Nitro on cover. - **$5**

❑ **SMA-48. Color and Activity Book,**
1998. Series 2. Punch-It on cover. - **$5**

SMA-49

SMA-50

❑ **SMA-49. Sticker Book,**
1998. Series 3. Freakenstein on cover. - **$10**

❑ **SMA-50. Sticker Book,**
1998. Series 3. Brick Bazooka on cover. - **$10**

SMA-51

SMA-52

❑ **SMA-51. "Archer" Ringed Notebook,**
1998. - **$8**

❑ **SMA-52. "Slam Fist" Ringed Notebook,**
1998. - **$8**

SMA-53

SMA-54

❑ **SMA-53. "Archer" Study Kit,**
1998. - **$8**

❑ **SMA-54. Black Ink Pen Set,**
1998. Features picture of Archer and Chip. - **$5**

SMA-55

❑ **SMA-55. "Punch-It and Brick Bazooka" 60 Piece Puzzle,**
1998. - **$8**

SMA-56

❑ **SMA-56. "Slam Fist" 60 Piece Puzzle,**
1998. - **$12**

SMA-57

❑ **SMA-57. "Witchdoctor Insaniac" 60 Piece Puzzle,**
1998. - **$8**

SMA-58

SMA-59

❑ **SMA-58. Personal Tape Player,**
1998. Boxed - **$35**

❑ **SMA-59. "Small Soldiers" Pocket Pops,**
1998. Archer and Chip character busts on lollipop. Each - **$5**

SMA-60

SMA-61

❑ **SMA-60. "Small Soldiers" Wrist Watch,**
1998. With 5 interchangable lenses. - **$20**

❑ **SMA-61. "Small Soldiers" Wrist Watch,**
1998. With interchangable Archer and Chip dial tops. On card. - **$20**

## Smiley Burnette

**Lester Smiley Burnette (1911-1967), a bluegrass singer and comic, starred in one movie, Republic's *Call of the Rockies* in 1944, but in floppy black hat and checkered shirt he provided comic relief as Frog Millhouse in a series of "B" Westerns with his pal Gene Autry. Burnette also appeared in a number of chapter plays in the 1930s, and he had his own syndicated radio show in 1950-1953. Smiley Burnette Western comic books were published in 1950.**

SMY-1

SMY-2

❑ **SMY-1. Fan Club Photo,**
c. 1940s. Black and white image of him and horse "Black Eyed Nellie" with club pledge on bottom margin. - **$10 $20 $40**

❑ **SMY-2. "Frog" Autographed Photo,**
c. 1940s. Personally signed by nickname only. - **$15 $25 $50**

SMY-3

❑ **SMY-3. "Smiley Burnette" Dixie Ice Cream Pictures,** 1940s. Back of each includes text for 1940 or 1941 Gene Autry movie.
Each - **$15 $25 $40**

SMY-4

❑ **SMY-4. "Checkered Shirt Drive-In Sandwich Shops" Folder,**
1955. Self-mailer sheet opening to 11x16" printed on both sides by whimsey art and text seeking individual investors for franchise endorsed by Burnette. - **$15 $25 $40**

SMY-5

SMY-6

❑ **SMY-5. "Checkered Shirt Drive-In Sandwich Shops" Signed Letter,**
1955. Art letterhead stationery with typewritten information on shop investment venture franchise, personally signed "Smiley." -
**$30 $50 $75**

❑ **SMY-6. "Checkered Shirt Drive-In Sandwich Shop" Invitation,**
1955. Card for grand opening of second shop endorsed franchise by Burnette. - **$5 $10 $15**

SMY-7

❑ **SMY-7. Premium Mask Sheet,**
1957. Bardahl Motor Oil. 11x14" stiff paper with large black, white and fleshtone mask of "TV's Ole Frog." Upper right has small photo of him with Autry. - **$20 $40 $75**

SMY-8

❑ **SMY-8. "$ellebrity Cash Phoney Money" Currency Bill,**
c. 1950s. Hiland Dairy Products. "Auction Points" paper bill picturing him on one side with his product endorsement on reverse. -
**$5 $10 $15**

## Smilin' Ed McConnell

**Ed McConnell (1892-1954), singer and banjo picker, moved from vaudeville to local radio in 1922, then to the networks from 1932 to 1941, doing his musical variety shows for a number of sponsors. In 1944 McConnell teamed with Buster Brown shoes to create a children's program combining dramatic tales, music, and listeners' letters. Known variously as *Smilin' Ed's Buster Brown Gang, The Smilin' Ed McConnell Show, The Buster Brown Gang*, or *The Buster Brown Show*, the program aired on NBC radio until 1953 and meantime made a successful move to television in 1950, appearing on all three networks: NBC (1950-1951), CBS (1951-1953), and ABC (1953-1955). The imaginary cast starred Froggy the Gremlin, along with Squeeky the Mouse, Midnight the Cat, and Old Grandie the Piano. Items are normally copyrighted J. Ed. McConnell. After McConnell's death, Andy Devine took over and the show was renamed *Andy's Gang.***

SMI-1

SMI-2

❑ **SMI-1. Photo,**
1920s. Radio premium. - **$15 $25 $50**

❑ **SMI-2. "Smilin' Ed McConnell" Autographed Photo,**
1932. First year of CBS radio show. -
**$25 $50 $85**

SMI-3

SMI-4

❑ **SMI-3. "Under His Wing" Theme Song Folder,**
1939. Taystee Bread. - **$20 $40 $75**

❑ **SMI-4. "Smilin' Ed McConnell/Bill Stewart" Fan Card,**
1930s. - **$8 $12 $25**

SMI-5

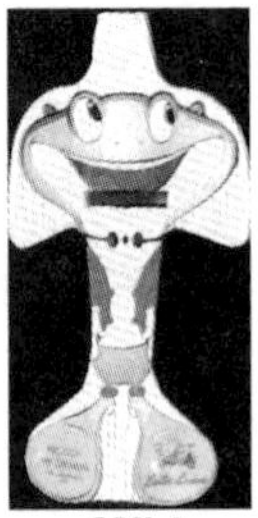
SMI-6

❑ **SMI-5. "Smilin' Ed McConnell" Advertising Calendar Card,**
1940. Taystee Bread, Purity Bakeries Service Corp. 12x17-1/2" color cardboard calendar from series issued on monthly basis. -
**$50 $100 $150**

❑ **SMI-6. Buster Brown Shoe Store Premium Paper Glider,**
1946. 4" wide by 7" long diecut paper with smiling image of Froggy. Photo example may be missing a cardboard tube and small tip from top edge of item. - **$35 $75 $125**

SMI-7

SMI-8

❑ **SMI-7. Froggy Paper Mask,**
1946. - **$20 $50 $75**

❑ **SMI-8. "Froggy" Litho. Tin Tab,**
1946. From radio show. - **$20 $45 $75**

SMI-9

SMI-10

SMI-11

❑ **SMI-9. "Member Buster Brown Gang" Litho. Tin Tab,**
1946. From radio show. - **$15 $30 $50**

❑ **SMI-10. "Member Buster Brown Gang/Squeeky" Litho. Tin Tab,**
1946. From radio show. - **$10 $20 $30**

❑ **SMI-11. "Midnight" Litho. Tin Tab,**
1946. From radio show. - **$10 $20 $30**

SMI-12

SMI-13

❑ **SMI-12. "Smilin' Ed McConnell" Letter**
1946. - **$8 $12 $20**

❑ **SMI-13. "Smilin' Ed McConnell" Picture**
1946. - **$10 $20 $30**

SMI-14

❑ **SMI-14. "Smilin' Ed McConnell" Picture**
1946. - **$10 $20 $30**

SMI-15

❑ **SMI-15. "Smilin' Ed McConnell" Picture**
1946. - **$10 $20 $30**

SMI-16

❑ **SMI-16. Squeeze Toy,**
1948. Store item by Rempel Mfg. Co.
Small 5" Size - **$75 $165 $300**
Large 9-1/2" Size - **$100 $250 $400**

SMI-17

❑ **SMI-17. "Smilin' Ed's Buster Brown Comics" #13,**
1948. Buster Brown Shoes. Issued between 1945 and 1959. First Issue - **$62 $187 $600**
Second Issue - **$19 $58 $170**
Others - (See *The Overstreet Comic Book Price Guide*)

SMI-18

SMI-19

❑ **SMI-18. Buster Brown Paddle Ball Game,**
c. 1948. - **$40 $100 $175**

❑ **SMI-19. Buster Brown Gang Brass Ring,**
c. 1948. Pictures him and Tige with Froggy and Squeeky on bands. - **$25 $50 $75**

SMI-20

❑ **SMI-20. "Buster Brown Gang" Card With Brass Badge,**
c. 1948. Card - **$15 $25 $50**
Badge - **$10 $20 $35**

SMI-21

❑ **SMI-21. "Smilin' Ed McConnell's Buster Brown Gang" Bandanna,**
c. 1948. - **$25 $50 $85**

SMI-22

SMI-23

❑ **SMI-22. "Buster Brown T.V. Theatre" Flicker Card,**
c. 1950. Screen area has movement image of Froggy jumping up and down. - **$30 $100 $125**

❑ **SMI-23. "Buster Brown Gang" Card With Litho. Button,**
1953. Card - **$10 $30 $50**
Button - **$10 $15 $25**

SMI-24

❑ **SMI-24. "Treasure Hunt Game" Shoe Box,**
c. 1950s. - **$25 $50 $85**

SMI-25

❑ **SMI-25. "Buster Brown Shoes" Periscope,**
1950s. 17" long cardboard and mirror lenses toy with design art including images of Smilin' Ed and various Buster Brown Gang members. - **$40 $100 $140**

## Smokey Bear

**Smokey was created for a U.S. Forest Service poster in 1944 to warn of the dangers--and the threat to the country's wartime lumber supply--of forest fires. Since then the brown bear with the ranger hat has become the beloved symbol of the Forest Service and spokesbear for the nation's trees. Smokey has been given special trademark status, had his own zip code, appeared on a postage stamp in 1984, and in balloon form has floated in Macy's Thanksgiving Day Parade since 1968. "Remember--only you can prevent forest fires!" dates from 1947. In 1950 a four-pound black bear cub that survived a forest fire in New Mexico was given the name Smokey, nursed back to health, and sent to live at the National Zoo in Washington, D.C. That Smokey died in 1976 but he was promptly replaced to continue as a symbol of conservation.**

***The Smokey Bear Show*, a half-hour animated cartoon series, was broadcast on ABC from 1969 to 1971, stressing the importance of saving natural resources and protecting wildlife. Smokey comic books appeared from 1950 into the 1970s, and in 1994 a traveling exhibition and party on the Mall in Washington celebrated Smokey's golden anniversary.**

SMO-1

❑ **SMO-1. Smokey Bear Poster,**
c. 1947. 18-1/4x24-3/4". - **$40 $85 $160**

SMO-2

❑ **SMO-2. Slogan Litho. Button,**
c. 1950. - **$10 $15 $30**

SMO-3

SMO-4

❑ **SMO-3. "Prevent Woods Fires" 12x14" Cardboard Sign,**
1955. - **$30 $60 $100**

❑ **SMO-4. Calendar,**
1956. - **$8 $15 $30**

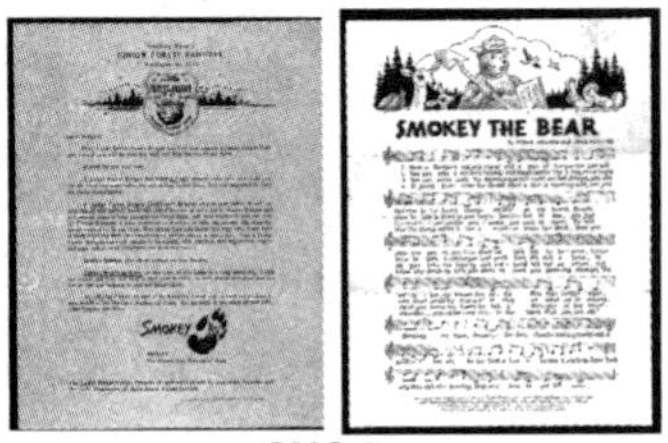

SMO-5

❑ **SMO-5. Letter,**
1957. Letter explains Kit, with song sheet on back - **$10 $35 $50**

SMO-6

SMO-7

❑ **SMO-6. "Forest Fire Prevention" Award Certificate,**
1950s. - **$15 $30 $50**

❑ **SMO-7. Cloth Doll With Plastic Hat And Badge,**
c. 1950s. Store item by Ideal Toy Corp. - **$25 $50 $85**

SMO-8

SMO-9

❑ **SMO-8. Fabric Patch,**
c. 1950s. - **$5 $10 $20**

❑ **SMO-9. "Picnics Are Fun" Hanky,**
1950s. Probable store item, no markings. Very colorful 8" square. - **$10 $20 $40**

SMO-10

SMO-11

❑ **SMO-10. "Join Smokey Ranger Club" Litho. Tin Tab,**
1950s. - **$15 $30 $60**

❑ **SMO-11. Biographical Card,**
1965. U.S. Department Of Agriculture-Forest Service. - **$5 $10 $20**

SMO-12

SMO-13

❑ **SMO-12. "Soaky" Plastic Soap Bottle,**
c. 1965. Colgate-Palmolive Co. - **$10 $20 $30**

❑ **SMO-13. Ceramic Salt & Pepper Shakers,**
c. 1960s. Store item. - **$15 $30 $50**

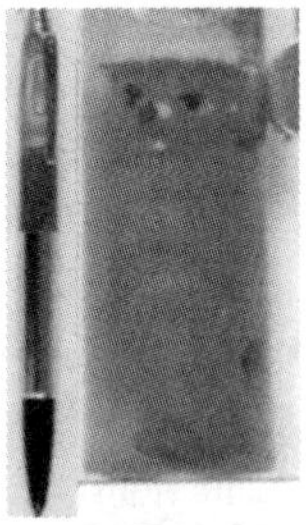
SMO-14

❑ **SMO-14. "Sign Up With Smokey" Ballpoint Pen With Floating Figure,**
1960s. USA otherwise unmarked. - **$20 $40 $65**

SMO-15

SMO-16

❑ **SMO-15. Fabric Patch,**
c. 1960s. U.S. Forest Service. 4" tall in shades of browns and greens on yellow background. - **$10 $20 $30**

❑ **SMO-16. Plastic Coin Bank,**
1960s. Store item. 4" diameter in copper-colored plastic. - **$10 $20 $30**

SMO-17

❑ **SMO-17.Boxed Game,**
1960s. Milton Bradley store item #4932. - **$20 $40 $75**

SMO-18

SMO-19

❑ **SMO-18. Wristwatch,**
c. 1960s. Store item. Boxed - **$60 $90 $125**
Loose - **$25 $40 $75**

❑ **SMO-19. Plastic Bank,**
c. 1960s. Store item. - **$15 $30 $60**

SMO-20

SMO-21

❑ **SMO-20. Composition Bobbing Head,**
1960s. Store item. - **$75 $150 $225**
Wooden handle on shovel - **$100 $200 $300**

❑ **SMO-21. "Junior Forest Ranger/Prevent Forest Fires" Tin Badge,**
1960s. Either silver, brass or copper luster. - **$5 $10 $20**

SMO-22

SMO-23

❏ **SMO-22. "Smokey's Reading Club" Litho. Button,** 1960s. Also says "Keep California Green & Golden." - **$10 $20 $40**

❏ **SMO-23. "March Of Comics #383",** 1973. Various Advertisers. - **$1 $4 $10**

SMO-24

SMO-25

❏ **SMO-24. Smokey Bear Book and Bear Set,** 1996. Plush doll and book in box. It's official, but Smokey's facial expression makes you wonder. - **$30**

❏ **SMO-25. "Smokey" Ring,** 1990s. No sponsor. Silver luster finish thin embossed metal expansion ring with name inscription on hat. - **$1 $3 $5**

SMO-26

❏ **SMO-26. Smokey Bear Wacky Wobbler,** 2000. In box. - **$15**

## Snap, Crackle, Pop

**The Kellogg Company introduced Snap, Crackle, and Pop in 1933 to personify the lively sounds made when a bowl of its Rice Krispies meets cold milk. Originally drawn by Vernon Grant, the cartoon trio has survived to this day on cereal boxes and in advertising, singing and dancing and crackling and popping for kids everywhere.**

SNP-1

❏ **SNP-1. Paper Masks,** 1933. Kellogg's copyright with unsigned Vernon Grant art. Each - **$35 $75 $135**

SNP-2

❏ **SNP-2. Booklet,** 1933. Six pages of Vernon Grant art and combination picture game. - **$25 $50 $75**

SNP-3

❏ **SNP-3. Comic,** 1933. Vernon Grant art on 8 pages plus 2 pages of premiums for Singing Lady. - **$15 $30 $50**

SNP-4

❏ **SNP-4. Blotter,** 1930s. Vernon Grant art. - **$15 $25 $35**

SNP-5

❏ **SNP-5. "Snap/Pop" China Salt & Pepper Shakers,** 1930s. - **$10 $20 $30**

SNP-6

SNP-7

❏ **SNP-6. Cloth Pattern Doll,** 1947. Issued as late as 1954.
Uncut - **$20 $40 $60**
Mailer - **$10 $20 $40**

❏ **SNP-7. Cloth Pattern Doll,** 1947. Issued as late as 1954.
Uncut - **$20 $40 $60**
Mailer - **$10 $20 $40**

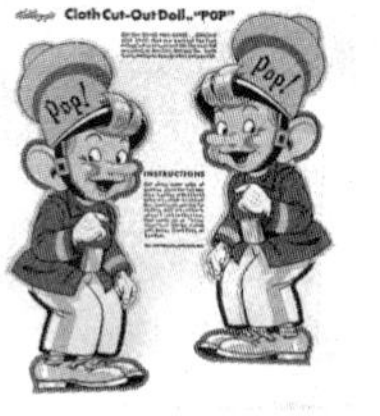

SNP-8

SNP-9

❏ **SNP-8. Cloth Pattern Doll,** 1947. Issued as late as 1954.
Uncut - **$20 $40 $60**
Mailer - **$10 $20 $40**

❏ **SNP-9. Cloth Dolls Store Sign,** c. 1947. 16x20". Gordon Gold Archives. - **$50 $110 $200**

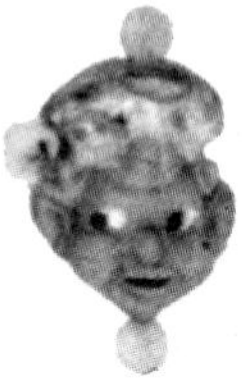
SNP-10

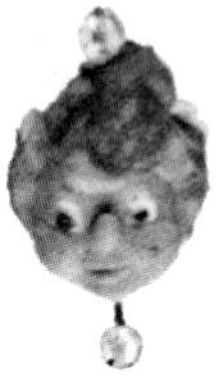
SNP-11

SNP-12

❑ **SNP-10. "Snap" Face Ring,**
1952. Brass bands holding soft rubber head that changes expressions by turning small knobs. - **$75 $175 $350**

❑ **SNP-11. "Crackle" Face Ring,**
1952. Brass bands holding soft rubber head that changes expressions by turning small knobs. - **$50 $100 $250**

❑ **SNP-12. "Pop" Face Ring,**
1952. Brass bands holding soft rubber head that changes expressions by turning small knobs. - **$100 $250 $500**

SNP-13

❑ **SNP-13. "Pop" Rice Krispies Hand Puppet,**
1950s. Kellogg's copyright on neck. From set of three. Each - **$20 $40 $65**

SNP-14

❑ **SNP-14. Friendly Folk Wood & Fabric Figure Set,**
1972. Frosted Mini-Wheats. Accent by simulated hair or fur. Each - **$3 $5 $8**

SNP-15

❑ **SNP-15. Vinyl Figure Set,**
1975. Each - **$12 $25 $50**

SNP-16

❑ **SNP-16. Glow Plastic Figures,**
c. 1980. Snap, Crackle, Pop, Tony, Tony Jr., Toucan Sam, Dig 'Em, Tusk (elephant). Each - **$2 $3 $5**

SNP-17

SNP-18

❑ **SNP-17. "Snap" Rubber Doll,**
1984. In box with mini comic. - **$20 $35 $50**

❑ **SNP-18. "Crackle" Rubber Doll,**
1984. In box with mini comic. - **$20 $35 $50**

SNP-19

SNP-20

❑ **SNP-19. "Pop" Rubber Doll,**
1984. In box with mini comic. - **$20 $35 $50**

❑ **SNP-20. "Pop" Bean Bag Figure,**
1997. With tag. - **$12**

SNP-21

SNP-22

❑ **SNP-21. "Snap" Bean Bag Figure,**
1997. With tag. - **$12**

❑ **SNP-22. "Crackle" Bean Bag Figure,**
1997. With tag. - **$12**

## Snow White & the Seven Dwarfs

**Disney's first full-length animated feature, *Snow White and the Seven Dwarfs* was both a cinematic masterpiece and a box office smash. The film, a retelling of the Grimm brothers' 19th century fairy tale, premiered in December 1937 and went on to break attendance records in the U.S. and throughout the world. Manufacturers rushed to jump on the bandwagon, producing a wealth of licensed items that elevated Dopey, Grumpy, Doc, Bashful, Sleepy, Happy, and Sneezy, as well as Snow White, to the level of Mickey and other earlier Disney characters as merchandising phenomena. Toys, dolls, games, costumes, storybooks, comic books, clothing, umbrellas, food and drink, watches and clocks, lamps and radios, jewelry, furniture--the list of Snow White items is virtually endless.**

SNO-1

❑ **SNO-1. Board Game,**
1937. Johnson & Johnson Tek Toothbrushes. Board edge held perforated playing pieces.
Complete With Slip Case Wrapper -
**$35 $75 $150**
Board Only - **$20 $50 $75**

SNO-2

SNO-3

❑ **SNO-2. Snow White Mask,**
1937. Procter And Gamble. At least nine, including Dwarfs and Witch issued by Procter and Gamble and others.
Snow White - **$20 $40 $75**

❑ **SNO-3. Dopey Mask,**
1937. Procter and Gamble. From Snow White series. - **$20 $40 $75**

SNO-4

SNO-5

SNO-6

❑ **SNO-4. Grumpy Mask,**
1937. Procter and Gamble. From Snow White series. - **$20 $40 $75**

❑ **SNO-5. Doc Mask,**
1937. Procter and Gamble. From Snow White series. - **$20 $40 $75**

❑ **SNO-6. "The Witch" Mask,**
1937. Procter and Gamble. From Snow White series. - **$20 $40 $75**

SNO-7

❑ **SNO-7. Movie Herald,**
1938. Various theaters. - **$10 $15 $30**

SNO-8

❑ **SNO-8. "Snow White" Promo Poster,**
1938. Rare. 28" x 22". - **$500 $750 $900**

SNO-9

❑ **SNO-9. "Snow White's Spice Roll" Recipe Folder,**
1938. Texas Electric Service Co. Four-page leaflet featuring her and Happy. - **$10 $20 $40**

SNO-10

❑ **SNO-10. Mechanical Valentine Set,**
1938. Near Mint Set - **$400**
Each - **$15 $25 $50**

SNO-11

SNO-12

❑ **SNO-11. Movie Herald,**
1938. 6x9" opens to 9x12". - **$25 $60 $100**

❑ **SNO-12. "Snow White" Sand Pail,**
1938. Store item by Ohio Art. 4-1/4" tall tin litho. - **$150 $300 $500**

SNO-13

SNO-14

❑ **SNO-13. "Snow White and the Seven Dwarfs" Big Little Book #1460,**
1938. - **$25 $75 $150**

❑ **SNO-14. "Snow White And The Seven Dwarfs" Celluloid Baby Rattle,**
1938. Store item. - **$75 $175 $325**

SNO-15

❑ **SNO-15. Ice Cream Advertising Store Sign,**
1938. Sealtest Velvet Brand Ice Cream. 11x35-1/4" glossy full color titled "Playing Here All Summer." - **$100 $250 $400**

SNO-16

❑ **SNO-16. "Pepsodent Moving Picture Machine" Mailer,**
1938. See SNO-20. - **$25 $50 $75**

SNO-17

❑ **SNO-17. First Ever Original Movie Soundtrack Record Set,**
1938. Store item by Victor Records. 10-1/2x10-3/4" sleeve holds set of three 78 rpm records. - **$60 $125 $250**

SNO-18

SNO-19

❑ **SNO-18. Gum Wrapper,**
1938. Dietz Gum Co. Also see item SNO-26. - **$30 $50 $80**

❑ **SNO-19. Dairy Glasses,**
1938. Various sponsors. Set of eight. Several sets with small height differences.
Each - **$10 $15 $30**

SNO-20

❑ **SNO-20. "Moving Picture Machine",**
1938. Pepsodent toothpaste. See SNO-16.
Assembled With All 56 Pictures -
**$125 $250 $375**
Unpunched - **$150 $375 $550**

SNO-21

SNO-22

❑ **SNO-21. "Jingle Club" Membership Request Card,**
1938. Various retailers. Offers Jingle Book and membership button. - **$20 $40 $75**

❑ **SNO-22. "Jingle Book" With Mailer Envelope,**
1938. Various retailers. Album for bread company pictures. Envelope - **$8 $15 $25**
Book - **$25 $50 $90**

SNO-23

❑ **SNO-23. Souvenir Album,**
1938. 50 pages. Features music and pictures from the movie. Has 2-page ad for Mickey Mouse Silly Symphony and Birthday Party song sheets. - **$35 $70 $140**

SNO-24

SNO-25

❑ **SNO-24. "Snow White Jingle Club Member" Cello. Button,**
1938. 1-1/4" size, widely distributed by businesses sponsoring the club. - **$10 $20 $30**

❑ **SNO-25. "Snow White Jingle Club" 3-1/2" Cello. Button,**
1938. Large version for employee of store participating in club advertising promotion. - **$175 $325 $750**

SNO-26

❑ **SNO-26. Dietz Gum Co. Box,**
1938. Held 100 packages. Also see item SNO-18. - **$75 $200 $325**

SNO-27

❑ **SNO-27. Milk Glass Cereal Bowl,**
1938. Post's Huskies Whole Wheat Flakes. - **$20 $40 $75**

SNO-28

SNO-29

❑ **SNO-28. "Dopey" Wind-Up,**
1938. 8" tall store item by Marx. - **$125 $250 $500**

❑ **SNO-29. Happy Store Display Figure,**
c. 1938. 23" tall hollow composition, probable Christmas display for toy department made by Old King Cole. - **$250 $400 $750**

SNO-30

❑ **SNO-30. Grape-Nuts Cereal Sign,**
1938. Scarce. - **$75 $200 $375**

SNO-31

❑ **SNO-31. Palmolive Cut-Out Sheets,**
c. 1938. European issue, set of 12 sheets. Uncut Set - **$100 $200 $300**

SNO-32

❑ **SNO-32. Post Toasties Box Back With Cut-Outs,**
c. 1938. Back Panel - **$10 $20 $30**

SNO-33

❑ **SNO-33. "Dopey's Christmas Tree" Book,**
c. 1938. Various department stores. - **$25 $50 $100**

SNO-34

SNO-35

❑ **SNO-34. Sleepy Beanie,**
1938. - **$30 $75 $125**

❑ **SNO-35. Snow White Paddle,**
1938. Rare. Kraft premium. - **$30 $75 $150**

SNO-36

❑ **SNO-36. Bracelet - Painted,**
1938. Small figure charms of Snow White and the Seven Dwarfs. Store bought. -
**$35 $60 $125**

SNO-37

❑ **SNO-37. Boxed Cut-Outs By Whitman,**
1938. Store item. Unused Near Mint - **$250**
Boxed and Cut - **$50 $100 $150**

SNO-38

❑ **SNO-38. Paper Doll Book,**
1938. Rare. Little Orphan Annie radio premium. Large red version was made to replace regular paper doll give-away book. See LAN-83 and 87.
Unpunched Book - **$300 $750 $1100**

SNO-39

❑ **SNO-39. Department Store 18x25" Paper Hanger Sign,**
c. 1938. Various stores. Same image both sides for Christmas toy departments. -
**$100 $225 $350**

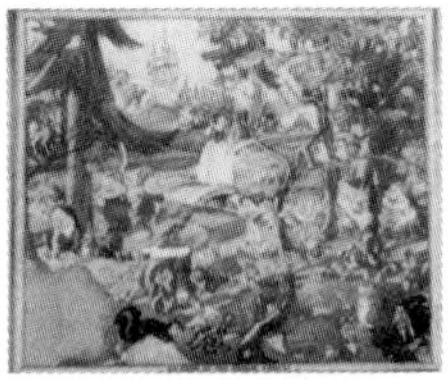
SNO-40

❑ **SNO-40. "Guards Of The Magic Forest" 18x20" Paper Mounting Chart For Bread Premium Pictures,**
c. 1938. Unidentified bread company. Holds 36 cut-out pictures completing forest scene.
Unused - **$100 $200 $300**
Completed - **$150 $300 $450**

SNO-41

❑ **SNO-41. Snow White Wood Case Radio,**
c. 1939. Store item by Emerson. Dials are acorn-shaped knobs. - **$800 $1500 $2500**

SNO-42

SNO-43

❑ **SNO-42. "All Star Parade" Glass,**
1939. From a set of dairy product containers picturing various Disney characters. -
**$10 $25 $50**

❑ **SNO-43. Dopey Studio Fan Card,**
c. 1939. - **$20 $40 $75**

SNO-44

❑ **SNO-44. "Snow White And Seven Dwarfs Crocus Bulbs" With Folder And Mailer,**
1948. Bab-O Cleanser of B. T. Babbitt, Inc. Folder describes proper measures for successful growth of actual crocus flowers from enclosed bulbs. Near Mint Complete - **$100**
Mailer - **$20 $30 $50**
Folder - **$10 $25 $40**

SNO-45

❑ **SNO-45. "Dopey Bubble Gum Club" Secret Code Folder,**
1940s. Yankee Doodle Gum Co. - **$20 $40 $75**

SNO-46

❑ **SNO-46. Bendix Washing Machines Comic,**
1952. - **$15 $35 $80**

SNO-47

❑ **SNO-47. "Snow White And The Seven Dwarfs Playtime Statuettes" Boxed Set,**
1952. Store item by Whitman. - **$50 $100 $175**

SNO-48

SNO-49

❑ **SNO-48. "The Milky Way" Comic Booklet,**
1955. American Dairy Association. -
**$15 $35 $80**

❑ **SNO-49. "Dairy Recipes" Booklet,**
1955. American Dairy Association. -
**$10 $20 $40**

SNO-50

SNO-51

❑ **SNO-50. "Mystery Of The Missing Magic" Comic,**
1958. Various advertisers. - **$10 $25 $50**

❑ **SNO-51. Bread Labels,**
1950s. Eight designs shown from set of sixteen. Each - **$3 $8 $12**

SNO-52

SNO-53

❑ **SNO-52. Bread Label Picture,**
1950s. Various sponsors. Holds 16 label cut-outs.
Completed - **$30 $100 $150**
Blank - **$20 $50 $100**

❑ **SNO-53. "Dopey" Soaky Figure,**
1965. - **$10 $30 $60**

SNO-54

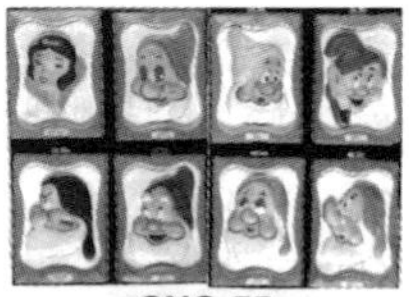

SNO-55

❑ **SNO-54. "Snow White" Paper Game,**
1960s. Royal Gelatin. Complete - **$15 $40 $80**

❑ **SNO-55. Thin Plastic Wall Plaques,**
1960s. Reynolds Wrap. Set. - **$10 $20 $40**

SNO-56

❑ **SNO-56. "Having Dinner With Snow White and the Seven Dwarfs" Sculpture,**
1984. Disney Capodimonte by master sculptor Enzo Arzenton. Edition of 1000. - **$3000**

SNO-57

❑ **SNO-57. "Snow White" 50th Anniversary Mobile with Captain Eo Sign,**
1987. Premium from Epcot Center Theme Park. - **$10 $25 $60**

SNO-58

SNO-59

❑ **SNO-58. "Snow White" Doll in Box,**
1980s. - **$20**

❑ **SNO-59. "The Prince" Doll in Box,**
1980s. - **$10**

SNO-60

SNO-61

❑ **SNO-60. "The Queen" Doll in Box,**
1980s. - **$20**

❑ **SNO-61. "The Witch" Doll in Box,**
1980s. - **$20**

SNO-62

SNO-63

❑ **SNO-62. "Happy" Doll in Box,**
1980s. - **$15**

❑ **SNO-63. "Grumpy" Doll in Box,**
1980s. - **$15**

SNO-64

SNO-65

❑ **SNO-64. "Bashful" Doll in Box,**
1980s. - **$15**

❑ **SNO-65. "Sneezy" Doll in Box,**
1980s. - **$15**

SNO-66

SNO-67

❑ **SNO-66. "Sleepy" Doll in Box,**
1980s. - **$15**

❑ **SNO-67. "Dopey" Doll in Box,**
1980s. - **$20**

SNO-68

SNO-69

❑ **SNO-68. "Doc" Doll in Box,**
1980s. - **$15**

❑ **SNO-69. McDonald's Acrylic On Metal Pin,**
1980s. - **$8 $15 $25**

SNO-70

SNO-71

❑ **SNO-70. "Old Witch with Apple" Figure,**
1995-96. From the Walt Disney Classics Collection. Made in Thailand. Has to rank as one of the best of the old hag figures. - **$350**

❑ **SNO-71. "Snow White" Video Promo Pinback,**
1990s. 4" x 4" pin from Wal-Mart. - **$2 $4 $10**

SNO-72

❑ **SNO-72. "Wedding Snow White" Doll in Box,**
2001. - **$40**

(Front) SNO-73 (Back)

❑ **SNO-73. Kellogg's Corn Flakes Commemorative Edition Cereal Box,**
2001. 18 oz. box promotes the Oct, 2001 release of the movie on DVD. - **$1 $3 $5**
Queen Version Box - **$1 $3 $5**

# Soupy Sales

**Born Milton "Soupbone" Hines in North Carolina in 1926, Soupy Sales grew up to become television's long-term clown and master of wacky pie-in-your-face humor. Wearing a battered top hat and giant polka-dot bow tie, his slapstick shows combined corny jokes, puns, zany conversations with animal puppets such as White Fang and Black Tooth, and the inevitable cream pies. After local television outings in Detroit in 1953, *The Soupy Sales Show* went national on ABC in 1955, again in 1959-1961, and in 1962 sponsored by Jell-O, and to syndication in 1965. *The New Soupy Sales Show* was syndicated in 1979-1980. Sales also hosted game shows and teen dance programs and made countless guest appearances on a number of variety programs. In the 1960s he created a popular dance called The Mouse. *The Official Soupy Sales Comic Book* was published in 1965. Items are usually copyrighted Soupy Sales--W.M.C. (Weston Merchandising Corp.)**

SOU-1

SOU-2

SOU-3

❑ **SOU-1. "Soupy Sales Society" 3-1/2" Cello. Button,**
1950s. - **$8 $15 $30**

❑ **SOU-2. "Soupy Sales Society Charter Member" 3-1/2" Cello. Button,**
1965. - **$5 $10 $20**

❑ **SOU-3. "SSS" 3-1/2" Cello. Button,**
c. 1965. - **$5 $10 $20**

SOU-4

SOU-5

❑ **SOU-4. "Soupy Sez" 3-1/2" Cello. Button,**
c. 1965. - **$10 $20 $35**

❑ **SOU-5. "Soupy Sales" 3" Litho. Button,**
1965. - **$15 $25 $40**

SOU-6

❑ **SOU-6. Autograph And Order Blanks,**
1965. Shown are: 3x5" signed index card, 3x4" order blank for 6' "Super Soupy" poster from Clark Gum and 3-1/4x5-1/4" "Burry's Soupy Sales Scooter-Pies Sweepstakes Entry Blank." Each - **$5 $10 $15**

SOU-7

❑ **SOU-7. Souvenir Program,**
c. 1965. The Paramount Theater, New York. Sixteen pages with photos and text on Soupy and music performers that were in the show including Little Richard and The Hollies. - **$10 $15 $30**

SOU-8

❑ **SOU-8. "Op-Yop" Toy Promotion Store Sign,**
1968. Paper banner 11x34" for "Op-Yop Funtastic Spinning Toy" by Kramer Designs. - **$35 $60 $100**

SOU-9

❑ **SOU-9. "Wallet-Size Photos" Display Box,**
1960s. Topps Gum. Countertop box originally holding gum/photo card packs.
Empty Box - **$25 $50 $75**

SOU-10

SOU-11

❑ **SOU-10. Miniature License Plate,**
1960s. Marx Toys of Great Britain. 2-1/4x4" litho. tin possible prototype or probable limited issue example. - **$10 $20 $30**

❑ **SOU-11. Advertising Litho. Button,**
1960s. United Dairies. 1-5/16" with bluetone photo and lettering plus logo in red. -
**$15 $30 $60**

## Space Misc.

**The mysteries of the stars have always fascinated earth-bound humans, with poets and scientists alike dreaming of soaring into space and exploring the planets. In the 20th century, even before Yuri Gagarin's historic flight in 1961, there were Buck Rogers and Flash Gordon and Captain Video. These and other comic strip, film, and television heroes, along with toy manufacturers, accounted for countless space-oriented premiums and novelties--spaceships, rockets, exotic space guns, games, puzzles, and robots. In addition, many items have been issued to commemorate events in the ongoing official program of space exploration.**

SPA-1

SPA-2

❑ **SPA-1. "John Carter of Mars" BLB #1402,**
1940. - **$40 $150 $300**

❑ **SPA-2. "Strat-O-Flier" Kite,**
1951. Classic design. - **$25 $50 $75**

SPA-3

❑ **SPA-3. Archer "Space Men",**
1952. Listed under a number of different names. Sold with or without clear plastic helmets. The figures were made in a number of different poses and colors.
Each 3-3/4" Space Man - **$5 $10 $20**
With helmet add **$5**

SPA-4

❑ **SPA-4. "Captain Space" Figures,**
1952. By Ajax. 3-1/4" tall. Sold with or without clear plastic helmets. The figures were made in a number of different poses and colors.
Each 3-1/4" Space Man - **$5 $10 $20**
With helmet add **$5**

SPA-5

SPA-6

❑ **SPA-5. Membership Card,**
c. 1953. Issuer unknown. 2-1/2x4" gray card for CBS-TV program starring Cliff Robertson which aired from April 1953 to May 1954. Pledge printed on reverse. - **$10 $20 $50**

❑ **SPA-6. "Starr Of Space" Record,**
c. 1953. Produced and recorded by Al Gannaway for Bill Brody Company. 7x7" sleeve holds 78 rpm record featuring original cast of 1953-1954 radio series. - **$15 $30 $50**

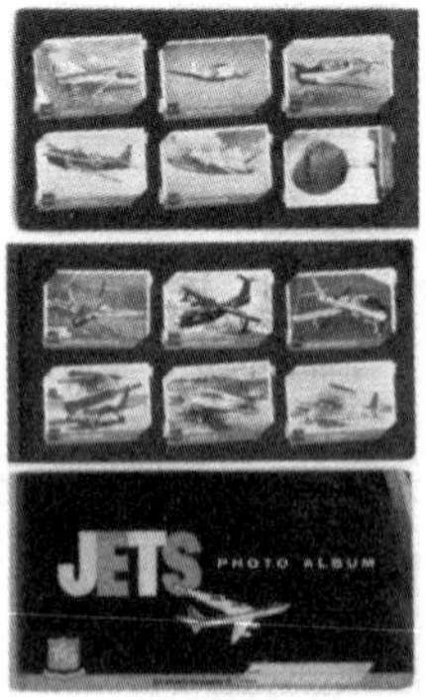


SPA-7

❑ **SPA-7. Topps "Jets" Cards and Albums,**
1956. A set of 240 cards was issued. They fit into 2 photo albums.
Photo Albums each - **$10 $20 $30**
Each card - **$2 $4 $8**

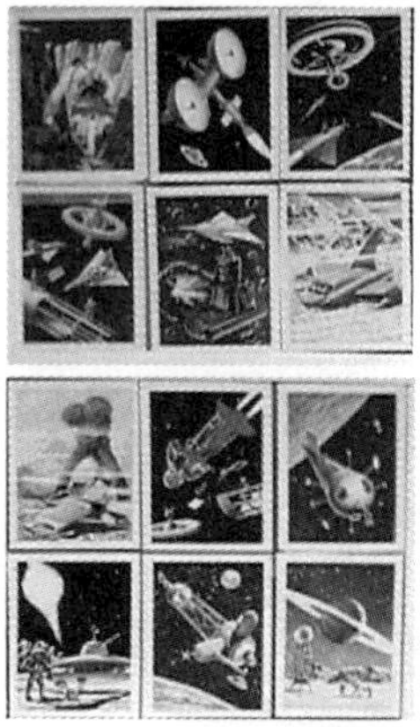

SPA-8

❑ **SPA-8. "Swift's Space Trading Card" Set,**
c. 1958. Swift's Premium Meats. Set of 12, each 2-1/4x3". Gordon Gold Archives.
Each - **$10 $20 $30**

SPA-9

❑ **SPA-9. Store Sign With Space Premiums Offer,**
c. 1958. Swift's Premium Meats. 21-1/2x30" paper sign promoting trading cards, celestial map, space guides and booklets. Sign was mailed in folded size of 8x11". Gordon Gold Archives. - **$150 $300 $500**

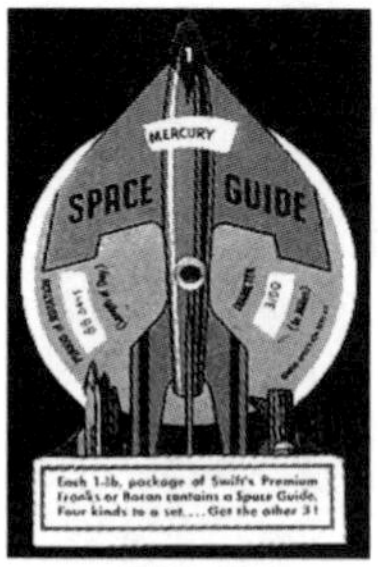


SPA-10

SPA-11

SPA-12

❑ **SPA-10. "Space Guide" Mechanical Card,**
1958. Swift's Premium franks and bacon. Diecut cardboard with revolving disks to provide planetary information. - **$10 $20 $35**

❑ **SPA-11. "Dan Dare" Cello. Button,**
1950s. English issue for popular space hero of comics and radio. - **$15 $25 $40**

❑ **SPA-12. "Dan Dare" Cello. Button,**
1950s. English issue depicting him in space helmet. - **$15 $25 $40**

SPA-13

❑ **SPA-13. Space Fantasy Scene Card,**
1950s. Bond Bread. 3-1/2x6-1/4" ink blotter. - **$5 $10 $20**

SPA-14

❑ **SPA-14. Nabisco Shredded Wheat Box with Sound-Jet Space Ship Glider,**
1950s. Glider is pictured on back and found in cereal box. - **$25 $75 $160**

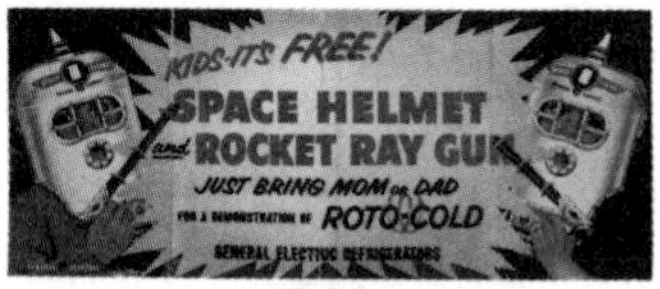


SPA-15

❑ **SPA-15. "Space Helmet And Rocket Ray Gun" Paper Poster,**
1950s. General Electric refrigerators. Colorful 21x49" poster offer for space toys to youngsters bringing parents to "Roto-Cold" refrigerator demonstration. - **$100 $250 $400**

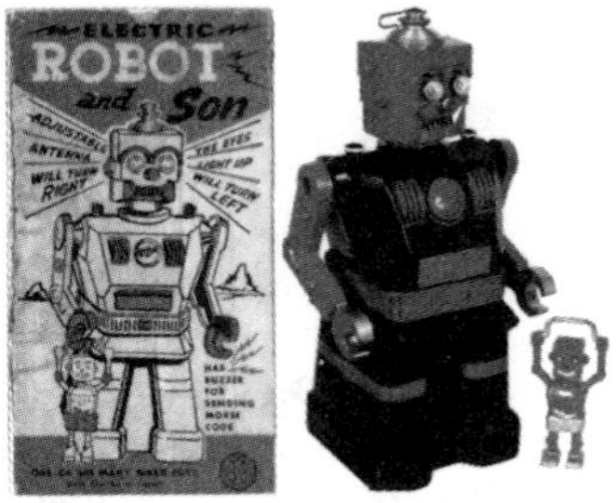


SPA-16

❑ **SPA-16. "Marx Electric Robot and Son" Battery Toy,**
1950s. Marx Toys. 16-1/2" tall box holds 14" tall red and black hard plastic robot and his matching 5" tall "son." Many functions. One of the classic '50s robot toys.
Box - **$75 $175 $350**
Toy - **$125 $225 $400**

SPA-17

❑ **SPA-17. "Speedy Spaceman" Toy With Cereal Box,**
c. 1960. Nabisco Rice Honeys. Plastic figure activated by loss of air from attached balloon following inflation.
Box - **$50 $75 $100**
Toy - **$10 $20 $30**

SPA-18

❑ **SPA-18. "Mystery Gyro Space Ship in Box,**
1961. Louis Marx product was heavily promoted on television. Comes with parts and instructions.
Boxed - **$75 $200 $350**

SPA-19

❑ **SPA-19. "America's Astronauts-Men Of The Year" Trigate Button,**
1962. 3-1/2" cello. Scarce. - **$25 $50 $100**

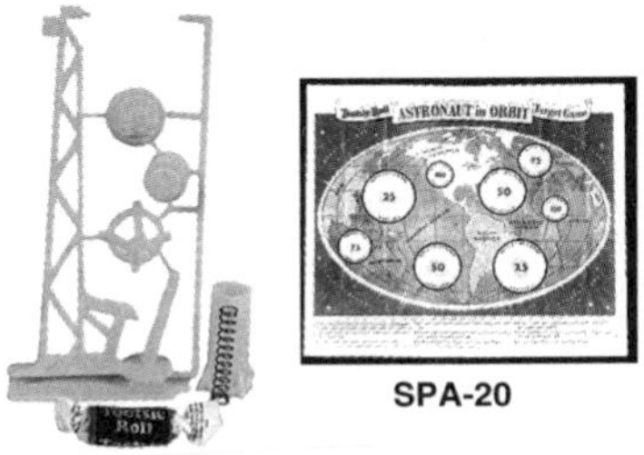


SPA-20

❑ **SPA-20. Astronaut In Orbit Target Game, Map And Parts,**
1963. Tootsie Roll. Plastic launcher assembly parts and 17x20" paper target map in mailer box.
Near Mint Boxed Unassembled - **$125**
Assembled With Target - **$20 $40 $60**

SPA-21

❑ **SPA-21. Crater Critters,**
1968. Kellogg's Apple Jacks. Pictured are five of the eight vinyl figures, each about 3/4" to 1-1/4" tall. Each - **$5 $10 $20**

SPA-22

❑ **SPA-22. Cereal Box Flat With Crater Critters Ad,**
1968. Kellogg's Apple Jacks. - **$150 $300 $550**

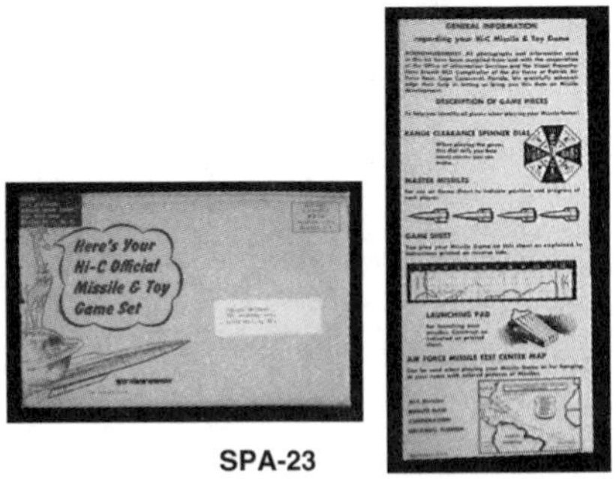


SPA-23

❑ **SPA-23. "Hi-C Official Missile & Toy Game Set",**
1969. Minute Maid. Consists of instruction sheet, 8-1/2x21" punch-out sheet, 4-1/2x21-1/2" game sheet picturing Cape Canaveral and target area ascension island, Cape Canaveral information booklet and 20x25" Air Force Missile Test Center Map. - **$25 $50 $75**

SPA-24

❑ **SPA-24. "Bubble Beanie With Satellite Spire" Space Novelty,**
1960s. Store item by F. M. Crump & Co.
Near Mint Boxed - **$85**
Toy Only - **$15 $30 $50**

SPA-25

❑ **SPA-25. "Buitoni" Macaroni Box,**
1960s. Promotes their product "Space Men." Cut outs of Rocket and Space Men on back. - **$15 $30 $60**

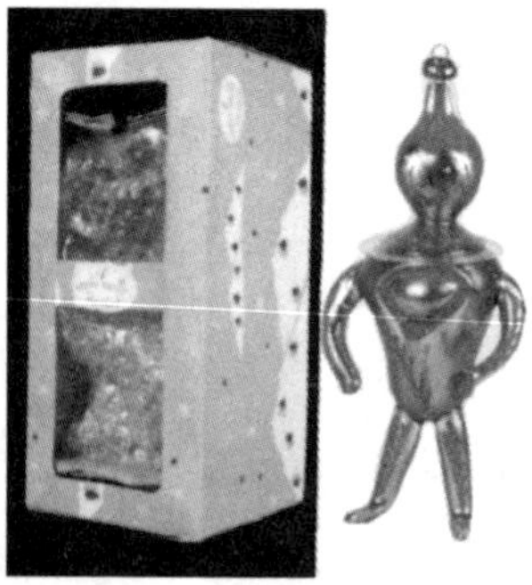
SPA-26

❑ **SPA-26. Martian Figural Christmas Ornament,**
1960s. Store item. Near Mint Boxed - **$120**
Ornament Only - **$25 $50 $75**

SPA-27

SMC-28

❑ **SPA-27. "Captain Jet" Cello. Button,**
1960s. "Channel 2" sponsorship includes CBS-TV logo. - **$12 $20 $30**

❑ **SPA-28. "Billy Blastoff" Toys Booklet,**
1970s. Eldon Toys. Full color 16-page comic story booklet illustrating space, scuba and other toys in "Billy Blastoff" series. - **$5 $10 $15**

SPA-29

SPA-30

❑ **SPA-29. "Magic Stars" Cereal Box,**
1992. With watch premium. - **$3 $8 $15**

❑ **SPA-30. "Blast Off 2000" Doll,**
2000. Madame Alexander product with 2 tags. Great example of space-themed collectible for the year 2000. - **$80**

SPA-31

❑ **SPA-31. "Robot 2000" with Box,**
2000. The Millennium Robot comes with blinking lights and a shooting gun behind its chest doors. - **$40**

## Space Patrol

**High adventure in the wild, vast reaches of space! Missions of daring in the name of interplanetary justice! Led by Commander Buzz Corry, the crew of the spaceship Terra policed the galaxies for the United Planets of the 30th century, traveling through time and battling crazed scientists, space pirates, and weird creatures.**

***Space Patrol* was first broadcast locally on KECA-TV in Los Angeles in March 1950. Six months later it went national on the ABC television and radio networks, where it aired until 1955. Corry, played by Ed Kemmer, was accompanied by young Cadet Happy (Smokin' rockets!), played by Lyn Osborne, and lovely Carol Karlyle, played by Virginia Hewitt, as they triumphed over such villains as Mr. Proteus, Captain Dagger, the Space Spider, and the evil Black Falcon, alias Prince Baccarratti.**
**The shows were sponsored by Ralston cereals (1951-1954) and Nestle foods (1954-1955), and dozens of program-related items were created for premium use and retail sales. Space suits, helmets, communicators, signal flashlights, a miniature spaceport, a rocket cockpit, Paralyzer Ray Gun, Cosmic Smoke Gun, trading cards, comic books and club membership material were among the available merchandise.**

**Many licensed items were sold by the May Stores on the west coast, but national distribution was limited. In 1952-1953, a wide variety of merchandise could be purchased through catalog flier order blanks from "Space Headquarters" Hollywood, California. In 1954 Ralston awarded a $30,000 replica of Buzz's spaceship to a young contest winner. Items are normally copyrighted Mike Moser Enterprises.**

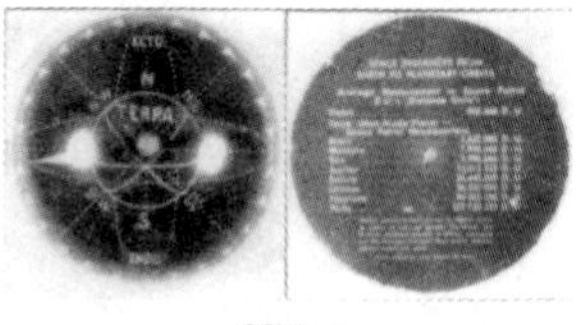
SPC-1

❑ **SPC-1. Plastic Dome Compass,**
1951. Store item. Came with boxed wristwatch by US Time. - **$25 $50 $85**

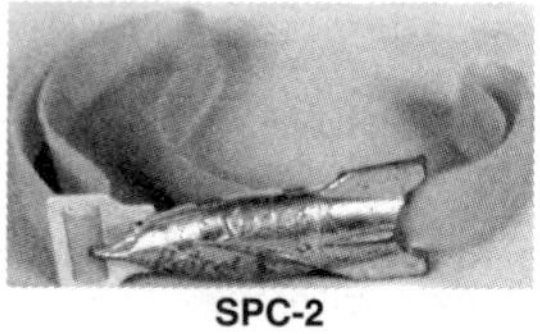
SPC-2

❑ **SPC-2. "Space Patrol" Metal Buckle On "Jet-Glow" Belt,**
1951. Decoder on back of buckle, belts usually no longer glow. Complete - **$75 $175 $300**
Buckle Only - **$40 $75 $150**

SPC-3

SPC-4

❑ **SPC-3. Membership Card,**
1952. - **$30 $85 $150**

❑ **SPC-4. Official Catalogue,**
1952. Shows 22 items priced for sale. - **$35 $75 $125**

SPC-5

❑ **SPC-5. Space Patrol Blood Boosters Booklet,**
1952. Ralston. Back cover reads "...Presented In Behalf Of The National Blood Program..." - **$75 $150 $300**

SPC-6

SPC-7

❑ **SPC-6. Wheat Chex Cereal Box - 12 oz.,**
1952. "Jet Glow" code belt and cosmic smoke gun pictured on back. Membership kit offer. Shows badge. - **$75 $250 $400**

❑ **SPC-7. "TV Digest" With Cover Article,**
1952. Weekly issue for October 11 with two-page article including photos. - **$20 $40 $75**

SPC-8

❑ **SPC-8. Ralston Club Membership Kit,**
1952. Letter, handbook, photo, envelope.
Complete Near Mint - **$325**
Handbook - **$50 $75 $150**
Others, Each - **$10 $20 $35**

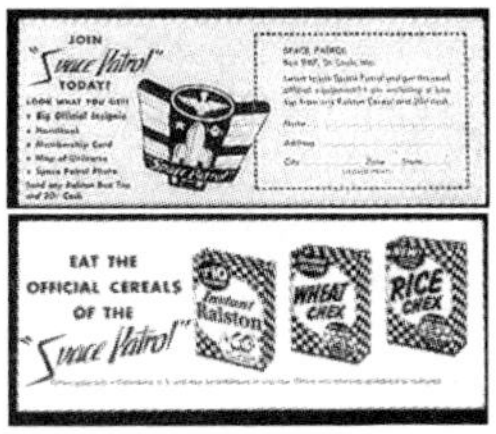


SPC-9

❑ **SPC-9. Space Patrol Premium Offer Sheet,**
c. 1952. Ralston Cereals. Instruction for Cosmic Smoke Gun plus offer of member insignia and kit. - **$10 $20 $30**

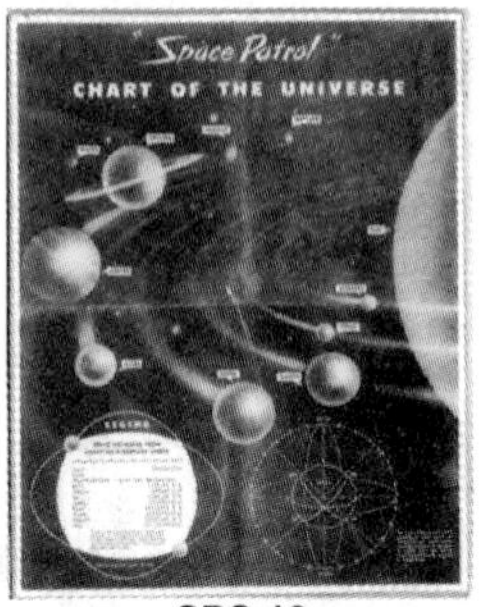


SPC-10

❑ **SPC-10. "Chart Of The Universe" 8x11",**
1952. - **$50 $100 $185**

SPC-11

❑ **SPC-11. "Space Patrol" Comic Book V.1 #1,**
1952. Back cover premium ad. - **$87 $261 $960**

SPC-12

❑ **SPC-12. "Space Patrol" Inlaid Puzzle,**
1952. With paper sleeve which went over the puzzle. Cast is pictured.
Sleeve - **$30 $60 $80**
Puzzle - **$40 $80 $120**

SPC-13

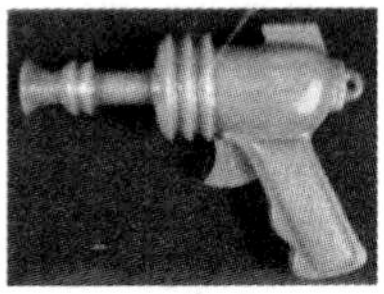

SPC-14

❑ **SPC-13. "Space Patrol" Vol. 1 #2 Comic Book,**
Oct.-Nov. 1952. Store item by Approved Comics. - **$62 $186 $685**

❑ **SPC-14. Cosmic Smoke Gun,**
1952. Smaller 4-1/2" size in red plastic. - **$75 $150 $265**

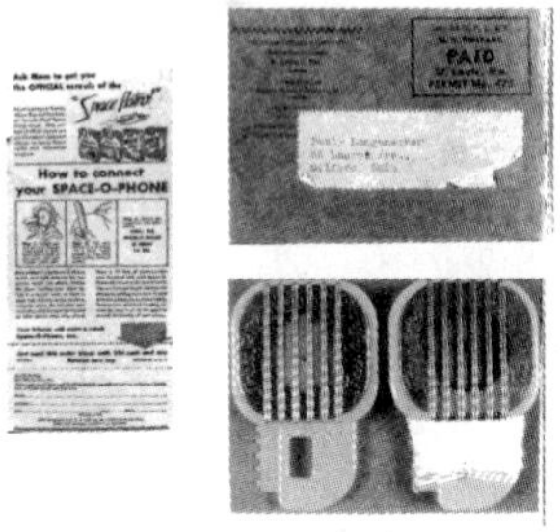


SPC-15

❑ **SPC-15. Space-O-Phone Set,**
1952. Boxed - **$50 $75 $150**
Phones Only - **$25 $50 $75**

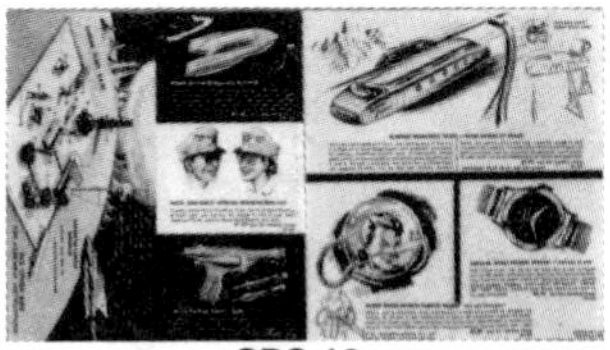

SPC-16

❑ **SPC-16. "Lunar Fleet Base" Instruction Sheet/Premium Catalogue,**
1952. - **$50 $150 $200**

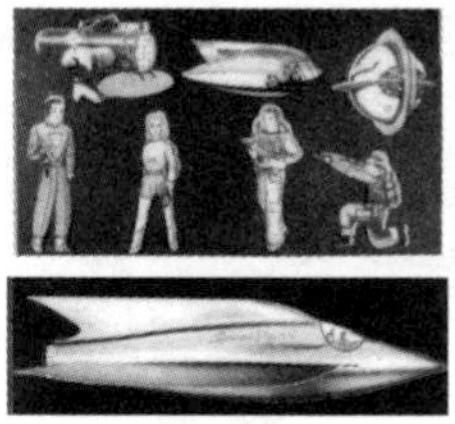

SPC-17

❑ **SPC-17. Ralston "Lunar Fleet Base",**
1952. Rare. Plastic parts shown, set also includes cardboard buildings, etc.
Near Mint In Mailer - **$3500**
Complete Used - **$500 $1200 $2000**

SPC-18

SPC-19

❑ **SPC-18. Plastic Badge,**
1952. Metallic red, blue, and silver finish. -
**$75 $175 $325**

❑ **SPC-19. Cosmic Glow Rocket Ring,**
1952. Unmarked Space Patrol premium plastic holding glow-in-dark powder in viewer. -
**$450 $900 $1500**

SPC-20

SPC-21

❑ **SPC-20. "Space Patrol Blood Boosters" Litho. Tin Tab,**
1952. - **$35 $75 $150**

❑ **SPC-21. "Outer Space Plastic Helmet",**
1952. Store item and also used as a contest prize. Includes inflatable vinyl piece that fits around neck.
Near Mint Boxed - **$1100**
Helmet Only - **$150 $300 $500**

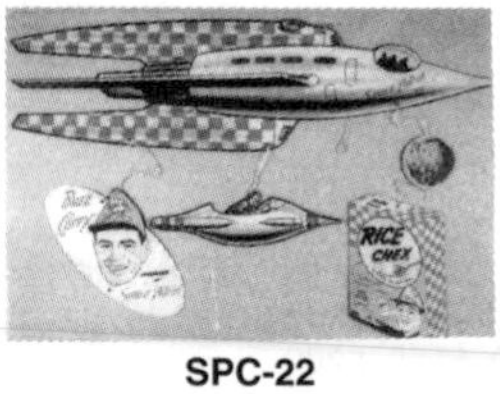

SPC-22

❑ **SPC-22. Rice Chex Cardboard Hanging Mobile Store Display,**
1953. Scarce. Each part printed identically on both sides, largest part is 27" wide. -
**$300 $1000 $1600**

SPC-23

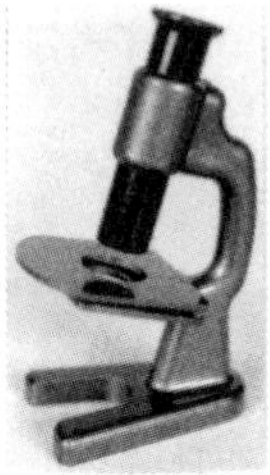

SPC-24

❑ **SPC-23. "Magic Space Pictures" Five-Part Diecut Cardboard Store Ceiling Mobile,**
1953. Scarce. Ralston Wheat Chex. Hanger display with 20" wide upper title part. -
**$300 $1000 $1600**

❑ **SPC-24. Plastic Microscope,**
1953. Came with plastic slides.
Complete - **$60 $100 $160**

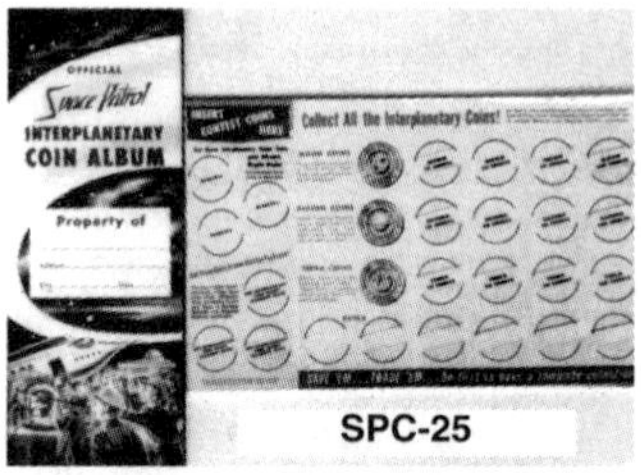


SPC-25

❑ **SPC-25. "Interplanetary Coin Album",**
1953. Schwinn Bicycles, others. Slotted for 24-coin set plus supplemental Schwinn coins. -
**$60 $150 $200**

SPC-26

SPC-27

❑ **SPC-26. "Interplanetary Space Patrol Credits" Plastic Coin,**
1953. Four denominations each for Moon, Saturn, Terra in gold, blue, black or silver (most common). Silver - **$5 $12 $20**
Other Colors - **$10 $20 $30**

❑ **SPC-27. "Terra V" Rocket Film Projector,**
1953. Also known as the Project-O-Scope. Four strips with six frames each.
Projector - **$75 $175 $325**
Film - **$35 $90 $125**
Instructions - **$30 $60 $90**

SPC-28

SPC-29

❑ **SPC-28. Magic Space Picture,**
1953. Set of 24. Each - **$15 $30 $60**

❑ **SPC-29. Binoculars,**
1953. Green plastic store issue, black plastic premium issue. Each - **$50 $85 $150**

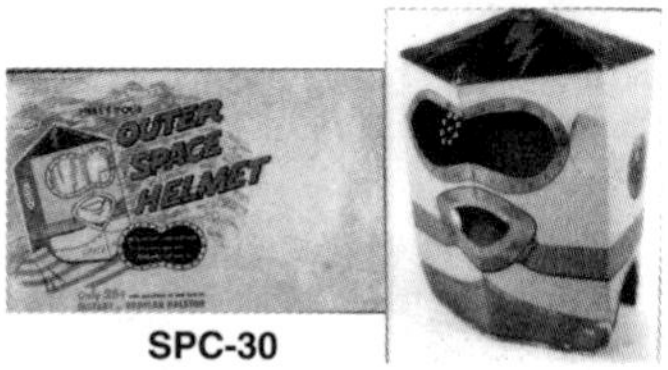


SPC-30

❑ **SPC-30. Ralston Cardboard "Outer Space Helmet",**
1953. Includes one-way viewing panel.
Near Mint With Mailer - **$200**
Complete Helmet - **$60 $80 $150**

SPC-31

❑ **SPC-31. Wheat Chex Cereal Box - 12 oz.,**
1953. Cadet Happy and magic space picture offer shown on front. Microscope kit offer on side. - **$100 $250 $400**

SPC-32

❑ **SPC-32. Christmas Catalogue Mailing Folder,**
c. 1953. Shows 13 items priced for sale. -
**$40 $100 $150**

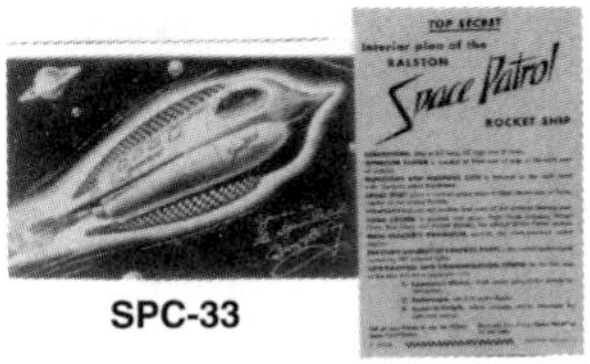


SPC-33

❑ **SPC-33. "Ralston Rocket" Card,**
c. 1953. - **$40 $90 $150**

SPC-34

❑ **SPC-34. Ralston "Buzz Corry Color Book",**
c. 1953. Example picture shows both covers. - **$30 $75 $125**

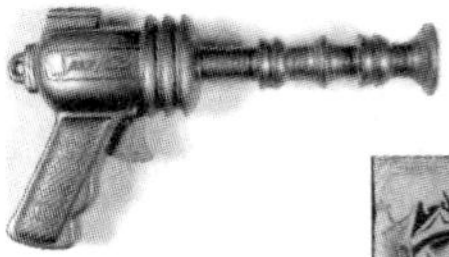

SPC-35

SPC-36

❑ **SPC-35. Smoke Gun,**
c. 1953. 6" green metallic. Came on card with smoke packets "Good For 10,000 Safe Shots".
Gun Only - **$100 $275 $325**
On Card - **$200 $450 $600**

❑ **SPC-36. Man-From-Mars Totem Head,**
1954. Includes silvered one-way plastic sheet for viewing.
In Envelope - **$40 $75 $150**
Assembled - **$25 $50 $75**

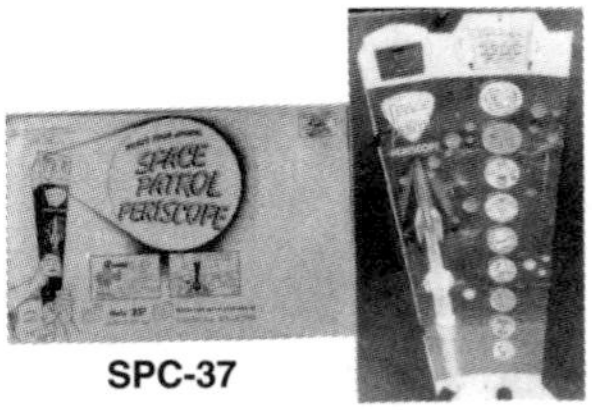


SPC-37

❑ **SPC-37. Periscope Cardboard Assembly Kit In Mailer Envelope,**
1954. Near Mint In Envelope - **$500**
Assembled - **$75 $200 $350**

SPC-38

SPC-39

❑ **SPC-38. Hydrogen Ray Gun Ring,**
1954. - **$75 $175 $275**

❑ **SPC-39. Ralston Trading Card,**
1950s. Wheat and Rice Chex. One card insert per box, set of 40.
Star And Planets Series (13) - **$8 $20 $35**
Rockets, Jets And Weapons Series (14) - **$8 $20 $35**
Space Heroes Series (13) - **$10 $25 $40**
Except Buzz Corry-Cadet Happy Each - **$25 $50 $100**

SPC-40

❑ **SPC-40. Cast Photos Folder,**
1950s. Dr. Ross dog & cat food. Front cover has photo, back cover facsimile signatures. - **$75 $150 $300**

SPC-41

SPC-42

❑ **SPC-41. Plastic Frame Character Charms,**
1950s. Unsure if Ralston premium or vending machine issue. Each - **$20 $40 $65**

❑ **SPC-42. "Space Patrol" Title Printer Plastic Ring,**
1950s. Top has "Space Patrol" printed backwards for correct stamped image after inking from included tiny ink pad.
Complete -**$350 $500 $750**
Missing Ink Pad - **$125 $200 $350**

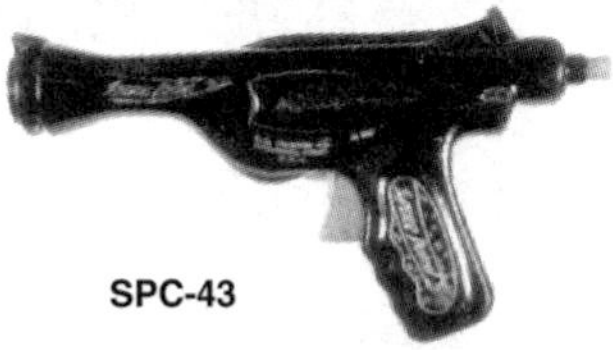

SPC-43

❑ **SPC-43. Plastic Dart Gun,**
1950s. Store item and premium. Came with two darts. Black plastic is store item; red plastic is premium. Complete - **$75 $125 $200**
Gun Only - **$50 $100 $175**

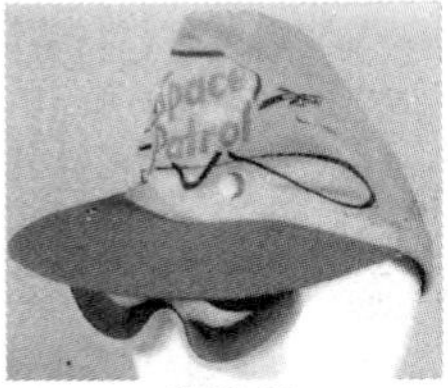


SPC-44

❑ **SPC-44. Fabric "Cosmic Cap",**
1950s. Store item by Bailey of Hollywood. - **$100 $250 $500**

SPC-45

❑ **SPC-45. "Space Patrol" Child's Shirt,**
1950s. Store item. Gray with red accents issued by Don Rancho Jr. - **$100 $200 $300**

SPC-46

SPC-47

❑ **SPC-46. "Space Patrol Napkins,"**
1950s. Store item by Reed with 32 napkins.
Near Mint Sealed - **$25**

❑ **SPC-47. "Space Patrol Party Plates,"**
1950s. Store item by Reed. Set of eight.
Near Mint Sealed - **$25**

SPC-48

❑ **SPC-48. "Giant Balloon" Mailing Envelope,**
1950s. Ralston. 10 cents with Wheat or Rice Chex purchase. Balloon usually disintegrated.
Envelope Only (8-1/2x11") - **$50 $100 $150**

SPC-49

❑ **SPC-49. Gun & Holster Set,**
1950s. Holster has rare silver Space Patrol Cadet badge on top of flap. Blue telescope gun is unmarked & has whistle on butt of gun.
Holster With Badge - **$100 $250 $500**
Blue Gun - **$15 $25 $50**

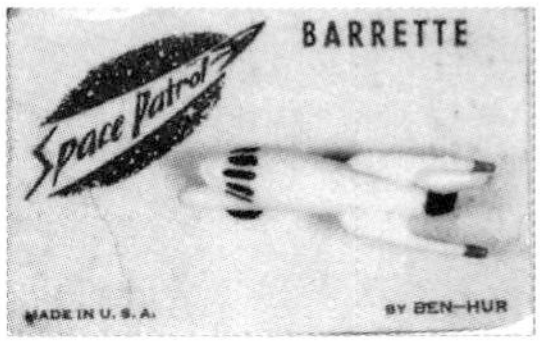


SPC-50

❑ **SPC-50. Plastic Rocketship Barrette,**
1950s. Store item by Ben-Hur.
On Card - **$40 $100 $150**

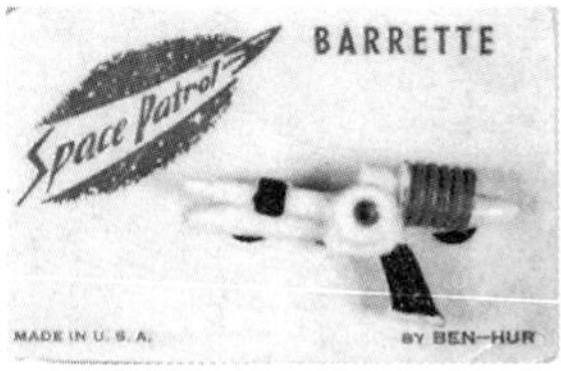


SPC-51

❑ **SPC-51. Plastic Gun Barrette,**
1950s. Store item by Ben-Hur.
On Card - **$40 $100 $150**

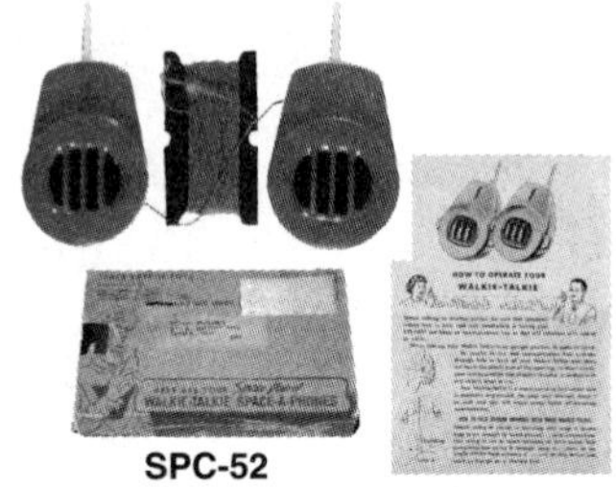

SPC-52

❑ **SPC-52. Premium Walkie Talkies With Box & Instructions,**
1950s. Scarce. Communication line with two plastic red walkie talkies. Rare Space Patrol premium box has Space graphics on back with Commander Cory on front.
Complete - **$150 $375 $525**

SPC-53

❑ **SPC-53. Plastic "Emergency Kit",**
1950s. Store item by Regis Space Toys. Handle contains flashlight.
Complete - **$400 $800 $1750**
Box and Yellow Insert - **$150 $300 $550**

SPC-54

❑ **SPC-54. "Commander" Vinyl Rain Hat With Cardboard Tag,**
1950s. Store item by Marketon Co. with license of Space Patrol Enterprises.
Hat - **$50 $125 $200**
Tag - **$20 $50 $100**

SPC-55

❑ **SPC-55. "United Planets Treasury Department Top Secret Diplomatic Pouch" Set,**
early 1950s. 11-1/2x11-1/2" portfolio holding Space Patrol stationery, United Planets currency bills, full color United Planets stamps, 16-page color stamp album, United Planets plastic coins and coin album.
Complete - **$75 $125 $225**

SPC-56

❑ **SPC-56. "Space Patrol Cadet" Silvered Metal Badge,**
1950s. Made in Japan.
Near Mint On Card - **$400**
Badge Only - **$75 $175 $275**

## Speed Gibson of the I.S.P.

**Young Speed Gibson, at the age of 15, was an ace pilot and member of the International Secret Police in this radio adventure series that was syndicated briefly in 1937-1938. Speed, along with his uncle, top agent Clint Barlow, and pilot Barney Dunlap, circled the globe in their ship The Flying Clipper on the trail of the criminal Octopus gang. "Suffering whang-doodles, Speed."**

SGB-1

SGB-2

❑ **SGB-1. Code Book Manual,**
c. 1937. Dreikorn's Orange Wrap Bread. Also seen with Stroehmann's Prize Winner Bread imprint. Includes membership card and oath to sign. - **$40 $125 $200**

❑ **SGB-2. Portrait Cello. Button,**
c. 1937. Winter's Bread. 1-1/2" with black and white photo on red. - **$35 $75 $140**

SGB-3

❑ **SGB-3. Textured Cardboard Card Holder With Photo,**
c. 1937. Buttercup Bread. 3-1/2x5" which opens to reveal storage pocket on right while left holds sepia photo with facsimile signature. Text inside reads "Property Of I.S.P. Operator Confidential Information." - **$30 $75 $175**

SGB-4

❑ **SGB-4. Adventure Map With Promotion Record And Envelope,**
c. 1937. Peter Pan Bakery and others.
Map - **$50 $175 $275**
Promotion Record - **$15 $40 $50**
Envelope - **$5 $20 $25**

SGB-5

❑ **SGB-5. "African Adventure And Clue Hunt" Map,**
c. 1937. Brown's Bread Ltd. (Canada). - **$100 $275 $350**

SGB-6

❑ **SGB-6. "Wings" Newspaper #1,**
c. 1937. Cote's Master Loaf Bread. - **$20 $75 $125**

SGB-7

❑ **SGB-7. Bread "Prize Winner" Cello. Badges,**
c. 1937. Various sponsors.
Berdan's Kew-Bee Bread (rare) - **$20 $40 $80**
Dreikorn's Bread (scarce) - **$18 $36 $72**
Le Stourgeon's Bread - **$15 $30 $60**
Remar Bread - **$15 $30 $60**
Stroehmann's Imprint - **$12 $20 $35**
Winter's Bread (scarce) - **$18 $36 $72**

SGB-8

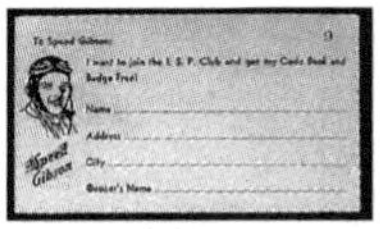

SGB-9

❑ **SGB-8. "Speed Gibson's Bread" Store Sign,**
c. 1937. Paper poster 10x17" including club membership offer text plus local imprint for radio station. - **$50 $125 $200**

❑ **SGB-9. I.S.P. Club Membership Application Postcard,**
c. 1937. Offers free Code Book and Badge for submission of grocer's name. - **$10 $20 $30**

SGB-10

❑ **SGB-10. "Rocket-Gyro X-3" Balsa/Cardboard Flying Toy With Mailer,**
c. 1937. "Hikes" chocolate-coated wheat cereal. Assembled toy flown by rubber band.
Near Mint With Mailer - **$175**
Without Mailer - **$25 $75 $125**

SGB-11

SGB-12

SGB-13

❑ **SGB-11. "Secret Police I.S.P." Litho. Club Member Button,**
c. 1937. - **$10 $25 $35**

❑ **SGB-12. Member's Small Blue/Silvered Brass Button,**
c. 1937. Phil A. Halle. - **$15 $45 $75**

❑ **SGB-13. Gorman's Bread "Speed Gibson Flying Police" Enameled Brass Badge,**
c. 1937. - **$25 $50 $85**

SGB-14

SGB-15

❑ **SGB-14. "Speed Gibson/Secret Police I.S.P." Canadian Cello. Button,**
c. 1937. Made by Shaw Mfg. Co., Toronto. - **$25 $60 $125**

❑ **SGB-15. "Speed Gibson's Great Clue Hunt" Paper Sheet,**
1938. Unidentified bread company. Pencil activity sheet for following radio broadcasts. Rare. - **$65 $250 $375**

SGB-16

SGB-17

❑ **SGB-16. Badge,**
1937. Dreikorn's Bread. Flying Police Badge, shaped like a shield. - **$25 $50 $85**

❑ **SGB-17. Badge,**
1937. Promote's Cote's Master Loaf Bread. Rare. - **$50 $100 $150**

SGB-18

❑ **SGB-18. Badge,**
1937. Dreikorn's Bread. Long Flying Police Badge, with two stars on it. - **$60 $125 $200**

SGB-19

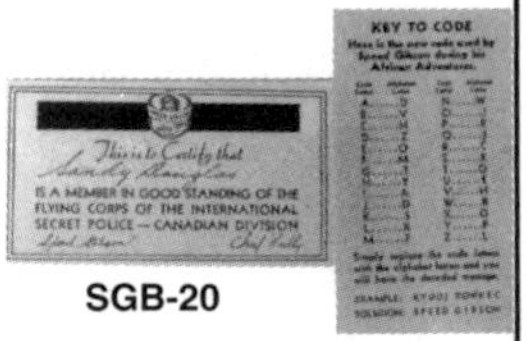


SGB-20

❑ **SGB-19. "Speed Gibson Flying Corps I.S.P." Brass Badge,**
c. 1937. Pictures him in aviator helmet above airplane. - **$75 $150 $300**

❑ **SGB-20. I.S.P. "Canadian Division" Club Card,**
c. 1937. Back has code used during Speed Gibson African adventures. - **$25 $75 $125**

SGB-21

❑ **SGB-21. Fan Postcard,**
1938. Gorman's Bread. Browntone photo. - **$25 $50 $85**

## Speedy Alka-Seltzer

**Alka-Seltzer, an antacid/analgesic combination tablet, was first marketed in 1931 by Miles Laboratories of Elkhart, Indiana. From 1951 to 1964 product promotion featured a perky little fellow with a prominent forelock and a tablet for a hat. Originally called Sparky, Speedy evolved into a popular spokesfigure in television commercials and in promotional items issued by the manufacturer. Speedy is translated as Pron-Tito in Spanish.**

SAS-1

SAS-2

❑ **SAS-1. Bank 5-1/2" Rubber Figure,**
1950s. Earliest version with word "Bank" below coin slot on top of hat, later version without word.
First Version - **$65 $200 $300**
Later Version - **$50 $175 $250**

❑ **SAS-2. Variant of Bank 5-1/2" Figure,**
1950s. Blonde haired variant of later version of SAS-1 figure. Scarce. - **$65 $200 $300**

SAS-3

SAS-4

❑ **SAS-3. Cardboard Store Display,**
1950s. - **$75 $150 $225**

❑ **SAS-4. "Speedy Alka-Seltzer" Enameled Brass Figural Pin,**
c. 1950s. Back has threaded post fastener for lapel or button hole. - **$20 $40 $60**

SAS-5

❑ **SAS-5. "Pron-Tito" Spanish Translation Sign,**
1962. Cardboard 21x28" with full color art. - **$50 $85 $150**

SAS-6

SAS-7

❑ **SAS-6. Store Display 8" Vinyl Figure,**
1960s. - **$200 $600 $1000**

❑ **SAS-7. "Pron-Tito" Spanish Litho. Tray,**
1960s. - **$50 $100 $150**

SAS-8

❑ **SAS-8. Visor Cap,**
1960s. Diecut thin cardboard. - **$10 $20 $35**

SAS-9

SAS-10

❑ **SAS-9. Small Flicker Sheet,**
1960s. About 1-1/2" square with "Pron Tito" name on his hat. He holds magician's wand and when tilted, a glass of the product appears. - **$15 $40 $60**

❑ **SAS-10. Paper Cup,**
1977. Miles Laboratories. - **$20 $40 $75**

SAS-11

❑ **SAS-11. "Speedy Alka-Seltzer" Bean Bag,**
1999. With tag. - **$25**

## The Spider

**Created by pulp author R.T.M. Scott in the 1930s, the Spider was actually Richard Wentworth, a wealthy New York crime fighter who divided his time between battling master criminals and hiding his true identity from the police. In the 1933 tale *Spider Strikes* and in the pulps into the 1940s, Wentworth's symbol, the drawing of a red spider, marked the foreheads of his vanquished and deceased criminal opponents. The same symbol appears on the pulp magazine club ring.**

SPD-1

**❑ SPD-1. Spider Enamel and Silver Luster Metal Ring,**
1934. First offered in "The Spider" pulp magazine #6, March 1934. Later used as 1941 "The Spider Returns" movie premium. The latest date of issue would be 1943, when the magazine ceased publication. The ring has a silver non-adjustable band, and examples prior to about 1940 are stamped on the inner band only with the maker's logo, an arrow through a letter "U" to represent "Uncas." Around 1940, because of increasing world conflict, the words "Made in USA" were also stamped on the inner band. Reported known: five in Good grade, ten in Very Good, five in Fine, five in Very Fine and three in Near Mint.
Good - **$800**
Fine - **$2500**
Very Fine - **$4500**
Near Mint - **$8000**

❑ An authorized modern reproduction exists in a limited edition run of 250 (originally sold for $55) with the spider image in red paint instead of red translucent enamel and a gold adjustable band.

Warning: A crude fake exists and can be identified by a visible seam running inside and on top of the ring.

SPD-2

**❑ SPD-2. Membership Card,**
1938. Columbia Pictures. Rare. First serial premium from "The Spider Web," based on "The Spider Magazine" stories. - **$100 $325 $500**

SPD-3

**❑ SPD-3. Movie Theater Club Member Card,**
1938. Columbia Pictures. Rare. For 15-episode serial "The Spider Web" based on "The Spider Magazine" stories. - **$125 $350 $600**

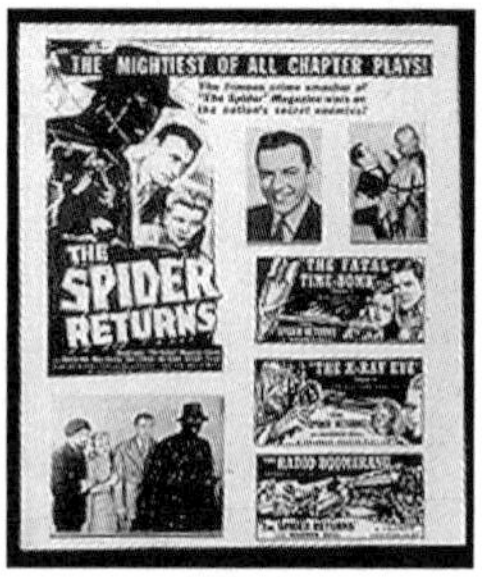


SPD-4

**❑ SPD-4. "The Spider Returns" Movie Serial 9x10-1/2" Handbill,**
1941. Columbia Pictures. - **$25 $60 $100**

SPD-5 SPD-6

**❑ SPD-5. "The Spider Returns" Movie Serial 9x12" Handbill,**
1941. Columbia Pictures for local theater imprint. - **$35 $75 $125**

**❑ SPD-6. "The Spider Returns" Movie Pressbook,**
1941. Columbia Pictures. Contents show ring, example of pulp cover, club card, mask. - **$125 $250 $450**

(cap on)

(cap off)

(close-up of eraser)

SPD-7

**❑ SPD-7. Cello. Mechanical Pencil With "The Spider" Eraser,**
c. 1942. Rare. The Spider pulp magazine. End cap covers rubber eraser with image on top surface. Succeeded Spider ring as premium, produced in very limited quantity. - **$600 $1600 $2500**

## Spider-Man

**Writer Stan Lee and artist Steve Ditko created *Spider-Man* for the Marvel Comics Group in the 1960s and the superhero has been battling for justice ever since. *Spider-Man* debuted in *Amazing Fantasy* #15 in August 1962. Six months later he appeared in his own comic book, the start of a series that continues to this day. (A syndicated newspaper strip started publication in 1979.) Teenage Peter Parker, who acquired his superhuman powers after being bitten by a radioactive spider, takes on a variety of villains and criminals, all the while working as a photographer for the New York *Daily Bugle* and struggling with the problems of a typical 1962 adolescent. In recent years, Peter has taken on the added responsibility of marriage to his long-time girlfriend Mary Jane.**

**On television an animated *Spider-Man* series aired on ABC from 1967 to 1970, and *Spider-Man and His Amazing Friends* appeared on NBC in 1981. A 1977 live-action CBS special with Nicholas Hammond was followed by a brief prime-time series in 1978 and scattered repeats for a year. The character was also featured on *The Electric Company*, speaking only in word balloons visible on the screen. In 1995 Ralston Foods introduced Spider-Man sweetened rice cereal, complete with trading cards inside specially marked boxes. Fox television launched an animated version of the popular character in 1994 with Christopher Daniel Barnes voicing Peter Parker/Spider-Man. Like Fox's (now WB's) *Batman* series, the guest voices were supplied by a veritable who's who of Hollywood. Ed Asner played J. Jonah Jameson, Martin Landau voiced the Scorpion, Roscoe Lee Brown supplied the voice for the Kingpin, and Mark Hamill (*Batman*'s Joker) voiced Hobgoblin. *Spider-Man* ended its original run of episodes in February 1998. In the last few years, numerous Spider-toys have appeared, chiefly from Toy Biz.**

**In 2002, after years of anxious anticipation from fans, a feature film adaptation of the wall-crawler's adventures hit theaters in May. Starring Tobey Maguire as Peter Parker/Spider-Man, Kirsten Dunst as Mary Jane, and Willem Dafoe as Norman Osborn/The Green Goblin, the film was directed by Sam Raimi.**

**Merchandised items are usually copyrighted Marvel Comics.**

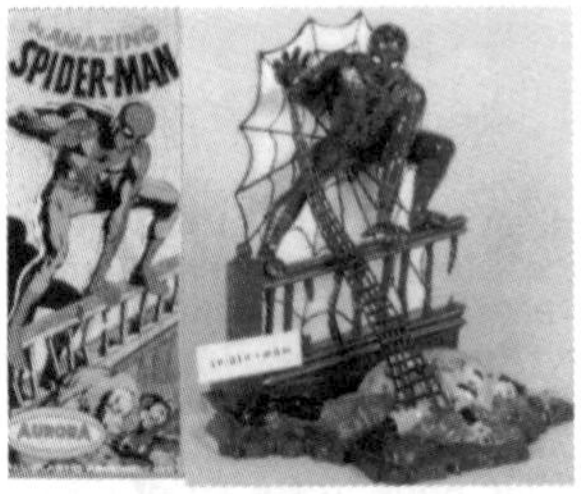
SPM-1

**❑ SPM-1. Aurora Model Kit,**
1966. Near Mint Boxed - **$400**
Built - **$35 $75 $125**

SPM-3

SPM-2

SPM-4

**❑ SPM-2. "The Amazing Spider-Man" 3-1/2" Cello. Button,**
1966. Store item. #6 from numbered series.
Near Mint Bagged - **$50**
Loose - **$10 $15 $30**

**❑ SPM-3. Litho. Metal Bicycle Attachment Plate,**
1967. Store item by Marx Toys. - **$12 $25 $60**

**❑ SPM-4. "Hong Kong" Vending Machine Aluminum Ring,**
1960s. - **$15 $30 $60**

SPM-5

SPM-6

**❑ SPM-5. "The Amazing Spider-Man" Boxed Action Figure,**
1972. Store item by Mego. 8" tall figure. Near Mint Boxed - **$175**

**❑ SPM-6. "The Amazing Spider-Man" Button Varieties,**
1975. Marvel Comics promotional button. Comes as 2" diameter celluloid or 7/8" litho.
Celluloid - **$5 $10 $15**
Litho. - **$2 $4 $6**

SPM-7

SPM-8

**❑ SPM-7. Spider-Man Vitamins Ring,**
1976. Hudson Pharmaceutical Co. -
**$30 $45 $85**

**❑ SPM-8. Spider-Man Talking View-Master Gift Pak,**
1976. Battery operated. Also features Captain America and Thor. Six reels included. -
**$75 $150 $225**

SPM-9

SPM-10

**❑ SPM-9. Spidey Super Stories Record,**
1977. Peter Pan Records and Children's Television Workshop. Features Electric Company cast in "Spider-Man is Born" and 7 other stories. Narrated by Morgan Freeman. - **$3 $5 $8**

**❑ SPM-10. Plastic Magnetic Compass,**
1978. - **$5 $10 $15**

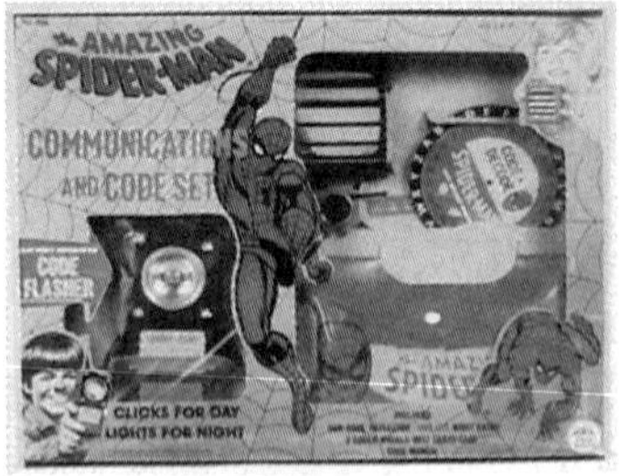

SPM-11

**❑ SPM-11. "Communications And Code Set",**
1978. Store item by HG Toys. Includes plastic battery operated Code Flasher and Sun Code Reflector, simulated wrist radio, vinyl belt carrying case and pair of cardboard code wheels with instruction card. Near Mint Complete - **$175**
Decoder Only - **$30 $60 $125**

SPM-12

SPM-13

**❑ SPM-12. "Spider-Man" 2-1/4" Cello. Button,**
1978. Store item by Rainbow Designs. -
**$3 $8 $12**

**❑ SPM-13. "Make Mine Marvel" Cello. Button,**
c. 1970s. Marvel Comics promotion featuring Spider-Man image. - **$10 $20 $30**

SPM-14

SPM-15

**❑ SPM-14. Newspaper Comic Strip Litho. Button,**
1970s. Miami Herald. 1-5/8" red, white and blue. Limited distribution. - **$30 $75 $125**

**❑ SPM-15. Advertising Button,**
1984. 2" black on bright yellow. - **$5 $10 $15**

SPM-16

SPM-17

**❑ SPM-16. Spider-Man Sunglasses,**
1980s. On card. - **$20**

**❑ SPM-17. Spider-Man Calculator,**
1995. 5" long. Copyright Marvel.- **$5 $15 $20**

SPM-18

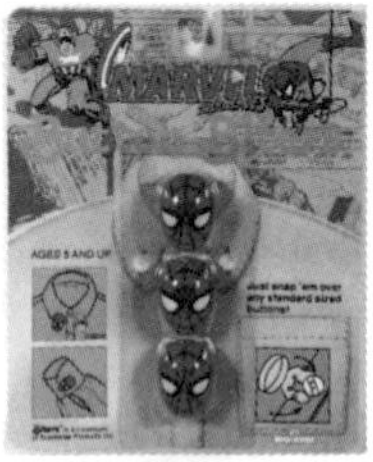

SPM-19

❑ **SPM-18. Dr. Strange Action Figure on Card,**
1996. From the Spider Wars set from the animated series. Comes with collector pin. - **$10**

❑ **SPM-19. Spider-Man Button Biters,**
1990s. On card. - **$5**

SPM-20

SPM-21

❑ **SPM-20. Spider-Man Cereal Box,**
1990s. Has offer of trading card in box. Five cards in the set. Box - **$10**
Each card - **$2**

❑ **SPM-21. Cookie Crisp Cereal Box,**
1990s. Has offer of trading card in box. Six cards in the set. Box - **$5**
Each card - **$1**

(STRAP)

(EXTRA STRINGS AND PICKS)

SPM-21

(CASE, SHOWN SMALLER IN RELATIVE SIZE)

(DETAIL SHOWING BODY DESIGN & STAN LEE AUTOGRAPH ABOVE PICK-UP)

❑ **SPM-22. "Web-Slinger" Limited Edition Signed Gibson Electric Guitar**
2000. Released in a limited run of 150. The first 75 were signed on the body by Stan Lee, the last 75 by the designer, John Romita Sr. The guitar came in a hardshell case with blue velvet lining. The case also included a certificate of authenticity, a plastic envelope with extra strings and plastic picks all featuring unique Spider-Man design touches, and a fabric strap with a white webbing pattern. Near Mint in Case With All Contents - **$4000**

SPM-23

❑ **SPM-23. Spider Racer in Box,**
2000. 1/18 scale with remote and includes 5" multi-jointed Spider-Man figure. - **$30**

SPM-24

❑ **SPM-24. Spider-Man Face Silver Ring,**
2000. 3,000 made. Sterling silver. Boxed - **$85**

SPM-25

❑ **SPM-25. Spider-Man Mini-Bust in Box,**
2001. Randy Bowen product. Limited to 12,000. - **$30**

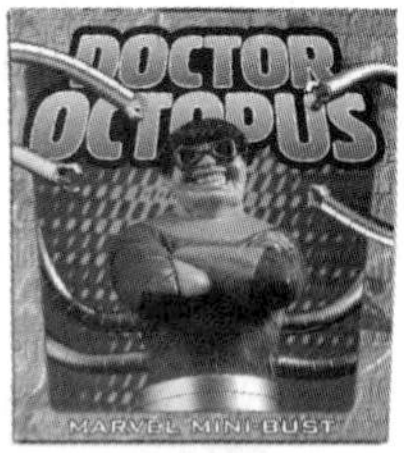


SPM-26

❑ **SPM-26. "Doctor Octopus" Mini-Bust,**
2001. Fully painted 5 1/2" tall bust sculpted by John Dennent. Limited to 6,000. Boxed - **$45**

SPM-27

❑ **SPM-27. "Rhino" Mini-Bust,**
2001. Fully painted 5 1/2" tall bust sculpted by Randy Bowen. Limited to 6,000. Boxed - **$40**

SPM-28

SPM-29

❑ **SPM-28. Peter Parker, The Amazing Spider-Man Mini-Bust in Box,**
2001. By Randy Bowen. Limited to 6,000. - **$45**

❑ **SPM-29. Green Goblin Mini-Bust in Box,**
2001. Limited to 10,000. - **$40**

## The Spirit

***The Spirit* was created by Will Eisner in 1940 in the unusual form of a comic book insert to be included with the comic sections of Sunday newspapers. The feature, distributed by the Register and Tribune Syndicate, survived until 1952, accompanied by a daily strip from 1941 to 1944. *The Spirit*--actually Denny Colt, a Central City crime fighter in a meager eye mask--has become a strip classic. There have been numerous comic book reprints from the 1940s into the 1990s, and a TV series pilot was broadcast in 1987. A brand new comic book series, *The Spirit--The New Adventures*, debuted in 1998 from Kitchen Sink Press with creator Eisner supervising some of the most popular modern comic book professionals.**

SPR-1

❑ **SPR-1. "Paper Mask",**
c. 1942. Various newspapers for Sunday comic book supplement beginning June 1940. -
**$100 $275 $500**

SPR-2

SPR-3

❑ **SPR-2. "Star Journal" Cello. Button,**
c. 1942. Various newspapers. For Sunday comic book supplement. - **$85 $175 $350**

❑ **SPR-3. "Minneapolis Morning Tribune" Cello. Button,**
c. 1942. Announcement for daily comic strip. -
**$100 $200 $400**

SPR-4

❑ **SPR-4. "The Spirit" Example Of Weekly Newspaper Comic Insert,**
1940s. Various newspapers 1940-1952. Prices vary widely by issue date, artist, condition. Consult *The Overstreet Comic Book Price Guide.*

SPR-5

❑ **SPR-5. "The Spirit" Resin Figure,**
2000. 11 3/4" high. Limited to 1,000.
With Box - **$195**

SPR-6

SPR-7

❑ **SPR-6. "The Spirit" Pinback Giveaway,**
2000. DC Comics promotion for the Spirit Archive reprint series by Will Eisner. - **$1-2**

❑ **SPR-7. Action Figure ,**
2001. From the Millennium Series. Comes with interchangeable head. - **$15**

SPR-8

❑ **SPR-8. "The Spirit" Lunch Box,**
2001. - **$20**

## Spy Smasher

**Playboy Alan Armstrong took on the identity of *Spy Smasher* to battle America's domestic enemies for Fawcett Publications during World War II. The caped crusader made his debut in *Whiz Comics* #1 in 1940, had his own comic book from 1941 to 1943, made a brief appearance as *Crime Smasher* in 1948, and finally was allowed to expire in 1953. Republic Pictures released a 12-episode chapter play in 1942 starring Kane Richmond in a life-and-death struggle against Nazi agents. Like Captain Marvel, the Marvel Family and the rest of the Fawcett Characters, Spy Smasher is now the property of DC Comics. He resurfaced on the cover of *The Power of Shazam* #24 (1997).**

SPY-1

SPY-2

❑ **SPY-1. Fawcett Picture,**
c. 1941. Title inscription "Hero Of Whiz Comics And Spy Smasher Comics". - **$75 $175 $275**

❑ **SPY-2. "I Am A Spy Smasher" Litho. Button,**
c. 1941. For comic book club member. - **$15 $25 $50**

SPY-3

SPY-4

❑ **SPY-3. "Spy Smasher" Argentine 27x41" Movie Serial Paper Poster,**
1942. - **$50 $125 $225**

❑ **SPY-4. "Spy Smasher" 27x41" Movie Serial Poster,**
1942. Republic Pictures. - **$200 $400 $800**

SPY-5

❑ **SPY-5. Movie Three-Sheet,**
1942. Republic Pictures serial. - **$2000 $5000 $7500**

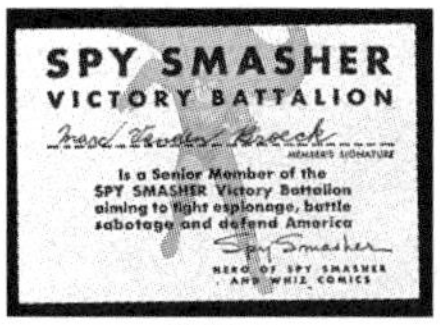


SPY-6

❑ **SPY-6. "Victory Batallion" Member Card,**
c. 1942. Fawcett Publications. - **$75 $150 $275**

SPY-7

❑ **SPY-7. "Spy Smasher" Lobby Cards,**
1942. Republic Pictures. Pair of 11x14" cards in greentone, one for Chapter 2 and the other for Chapter 11. Each - **$15 $25 $50**

# Star Trek

**The *Star Trek* phenomenon originated with the futuristic TV series created by Gene Roddenberry (1921-1991) that aired on NBC from 1966 to 1969, and has grown over the years into an international community of devoted fans, generating four additional TV series, eight movies, dozens of books, comic books, an animated cartoon, countless Trekkie conventions, and millions of dollars in licensed merchandise.**

**On television *Star Trek* was followed by *Star Trek: The Animated Series* (1973), *Star Trek: The Next Generation* (1987), *Star Trek: Deep Space Nine* (1993), *Star Trek: Voyager* (1995), and *Enterprise* (2001). The first movie--*Star Trek-The Motion Picture* (1979)--was followed by *Star Trek II: The Wrath of Khan* (1982), *Star Trek III: The Search for Spock* (1984), *Star Trek IV: The Voyage Home* (1986), *Star Trek V: The Final Frontier* (1989), *Star Trek VI: The Undiscovered Country* (1991), *Star Trek: Generations* (1994), *Star Trek: First Contact* (1996), and *Star Trek: Insurrection* (1998). Captain Kirk (William Shatner) has been succeeded by Captain Picard (Patrick Stewart), Captain Sisko (Avery Brooks), Captain Janeway (Kate Mulgrew), and Captain Archer (Scott Bakula). Spock (Leonard Nimoy) and the rest of the original crew may be gone, but the U.S.S. Enterprise and the U.S.S. Voyager continue to boldly cruise the galaxies, where no one has gone before, well into the future. Paramount Pictures holds the copyright.**

STR-1

❑ **STR-1. "Star Trek Rapid-Fire Tracer Gun,"**
1967. Store item by Ray Plastic Inc.
Carded - **$15 $30 $60**

STR-2

❑ **STR-2. Game,**
1967. Store item by Ideal. - **$40 $75 $150**

STR-3

STR-4

❑ **STR-3. "TV Guide" Weekly Issue,**
1967. Volume 15 #9 from March 4.
Without Mailing Label - **$15 $30 $60**
With Mailing Label - **$10 $25 $40**

❑ **STR-4. Pencil Tablet,**
c. 1967. Store item. 8x10" with glossy color cover. - **$10 $20 $35**

STR-5

❑ **STR-5. Domed Metal Lunch Box,**
1968. Store item by Aladdin. Came with lunch bottle not shown. Box - **$300 $650 $1100**
Bottle - **$100 $200 $325**

STR-6

❑ **STR-6. "Star Trek View-Master" Set,**
1968. Complete With Booklet - **$15 $30 $50**

STR-7

❑ **STR-7. Colorforms Adventure Set,**
1975. Store item. 8x12-1/2x1" deep box with thin diecut vinyl pieces for creating scenes. - **$12 $25 $50**

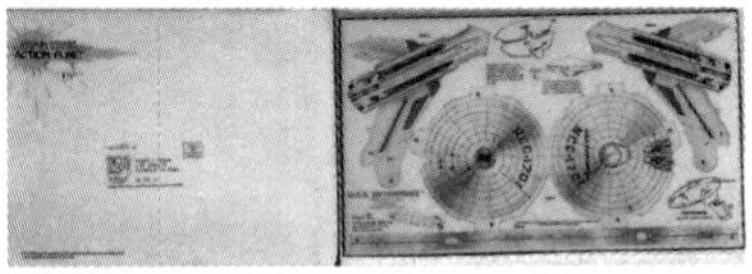
STR-8

❑ **STR-8. Action Fleet Punch-Out Mobile,**
1978. M&M/Mars Inc. Includes six punch-out sheets, instruction sheet, poster.
In Envelope - **$20 $35 $60**

STR-9

❑ **STR-9. "Star Trek The Motion Picture" Card And Sticker Set,**
1979. Store item by Topps Gum. Set of 88 cards and 22 unused stickers.
Near Mint Complete - **$30**

STR-10

❑ **STR-10. "Star Trek The Motion Picture" Premium Card Set,**
1979. Same cards as in standard set of this title but only 33 and these were offered by various bread companies. This example has "Rainbo." Backs feature text and repeated cast photo, none with puzzle backs. Near Mint Set - **$20**

STR-11

STR-12

❑ **STR-11. "The Bridge" McDonald's Meal Box,**
1979. Two versions: Reverse panel pictures Mr. Spock or Dr. McCoy. Unused/Flat - **$5 $12 $25**

❑ **STR-12. "Spacesuit" McDonald's Meal Box,**
1979. Unused/Flat - **$5 $12 $25**

STR-13

STR-14

❑ **STR-13. "Klingons" McDonald's Meal Box,**
1979. Unused/Flat - **$5 $12 $25**

❑ **STR-14. "Transporter" McDonald's Meal Box,**
1979. Unused Flat - **$5 $12 $25**

STR-15

STR-16

❑ **STR-15. "United Federation Of Planets" McDonald's Meal Box,**
1979. Unused/Flat - **$5 $12 $25**

❑ **STR-16. McDonald's Plastic Secret Compartment Ring,**
1979. Set of four: Kirk, Spock, U.S.S. Enterprise, insignia. Each - **$20 $40 $60**

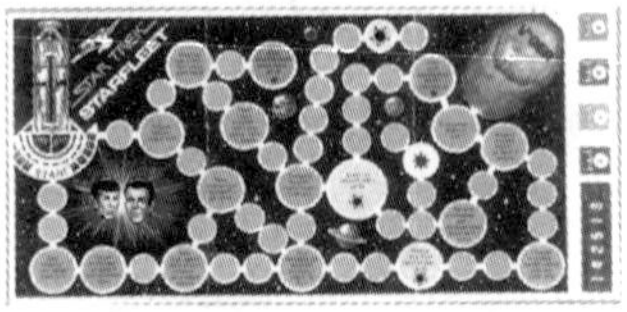

STR-17

❑ **STR-17. Star Fleet Game,**
1979. McDonald's. - **$5 $8 $12**

STR-18

❑ **STR-18. Matches,**
1979. Promo for *Star Trek-The Motion Picture.* Premium offer inside. - **$5 $10 $15**

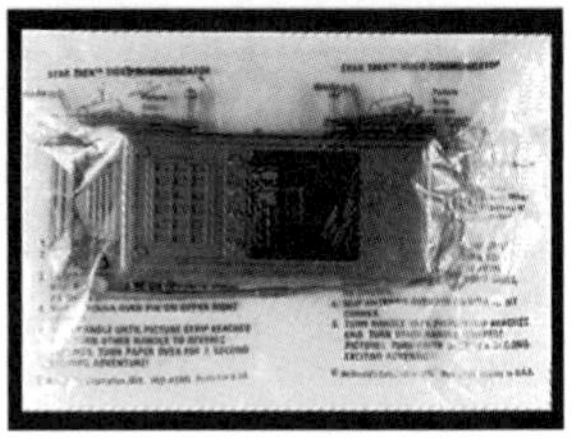
STR-19

❑ **STR-19. "Star Trek Video Communicator" Packaged Toy,**
1979. McDonald's Happy Meals. Unopened packet contains 4" plastic toy with full color picture strip from series of five.
Each Sealed - **$3 $6 $10**
Each Loose - **$1 $3 $5**

STR-20

❑ **STR-20. "Star Trek Navigation Bracelet" Toy,**
1979. McDonald's Happy Meals. Unopened packet containing 9" plastic bracelet plus sheet with color portrait stickers, paper scene strip for bracelet viewer. Sealed - **$3 $6 $10**
Loose - **$1 $3 $5**

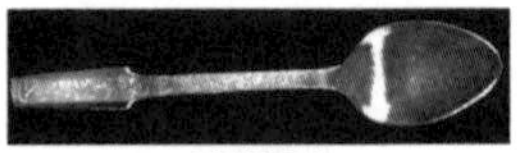
STR-21

❑ **STR-21. Spoon Premium,**
1970s. - **$30 $40 $60**

STR-22

STR-23

**❑ STR-22. Twentieth Anniversary 3" Plastic Badge,**
1986. - **$5 $10 $15**

**❑ STR-23. Pocket Books 2-1/4" Tin Tab,**
1986. - **$10 $15 $25**

STR-24

**❑ STR-24. Cheerios Box With First Promotion For Star Trek The Next Generation,**
1987. Boxes contained six different sticker portraits to determine winners of 75,000 replicas of Enterprise (4" pale blue vinyl) by Galoob.
Box - **$30 $75 $150**
Each Sticker - **$5 $10 $20**
Replica - **$75 $150 $250**

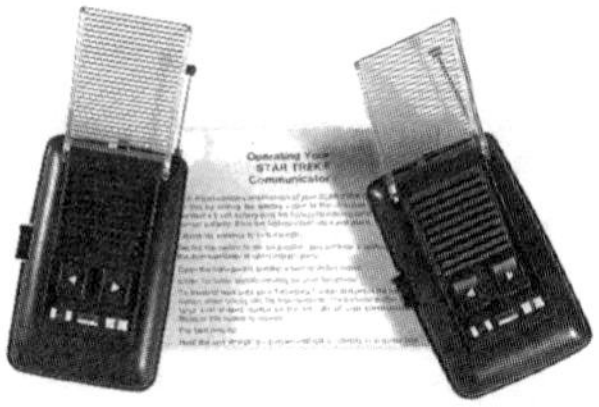

STR-25

**❑ STR-25. Walkie-Talkie Communicators,**
1989. P.J. McNerney & Associates. *Star Trek V* film tie-in offered by Procter & Gamble. Also came with instruction sheet. - **$25 $85 $110**

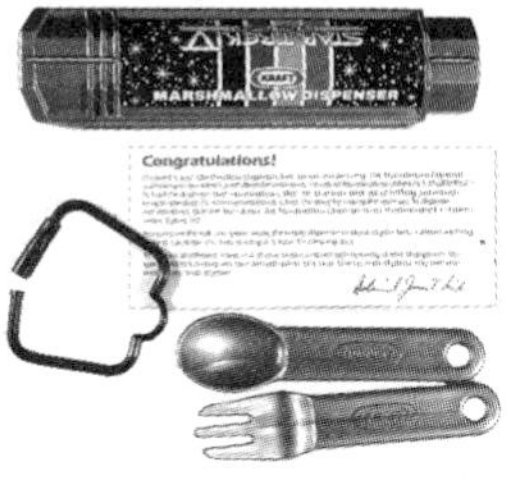


STR-26

**❑ STR-26. Marshmallow Dispenser and Utensils,**
1989. Kraft premium offered in conjunction with *Star Trek V*. Includes plastic dispenser, fork, spoon, and belt hook. Letter signed by "Admiral James T. Kirk" congratulates recipient. -
**$10 $20 $60**

STR-27

**❑ STR-27. Sign,**
1991. Space exploration stamp promo. Also promotes *Star Trek VI*. - **$25 $50 $85**

STR-28

STR-29

**❑ STR-28. Deep Space 9 Figural Premium Ink Stamps,**
1993. Canadian issued by Nabisco Shreddies. Stamps are: Odo, Cardassian, Quark and Kira.
Set - **$8 $15 $25**

**❑ STR-29. Movie Promo I.D. Pass,**
1997. - **$5 $10 $20**

STR-30

STR-31

**❑ STR-30. "Andorian" Bean Bag Alien,**
1998. With tag. - **$10**

**❑ STR-31. "Ferengi" Bean Bag Alien,**
1998. With tag. - **$10**

STR-32

STR-33

**❑ STR-32. "Gorn" Bean Bag Alien,**
1998. With tag. - **$10**

**❑ STR-33. "Mugato" Bean Bag Alien,**
1998. With tag. - **$15**

STR-34

STR-35

**❑ STR-34. "Romulan" Bean Bag Alien,**
1998. With tag. - **$10**

**❑ STR-35. "Targ" Bean Bag Alien,**
1998. Klingon pet. With tag. - **$10**

STR-36

**❑ STR-36. Star Trek Monopoly Game,**
2000. Limited Edition version. 8 pewter figures included. - **$45**

STR-37

**❑ STR-37. Movie Giveaway Badge,**
1998. - **$2 $4 $10**

## Star Wars

**George Lucas' movie trilogy--*Star Wars* (1977), *The Empire Strikes Back* (1980), and *Return of the Jedi* (1983)--chronicles the battle between good and evil a long time ago in a galaxy far, far away. Luke Skywalker (Mark Hamill), Princess Leia (Carrie Fisher), and Han Solo (Harrison Ford), along with Chewbacca the Wookiee and the droids C-3PO and R2D2, lead the Rebel Alliance in their epic struggle against Darth Vader and the Imperial Forces of the Empire. The phenomenal success of the films has spawned a world of merchandised items--action figures,**

comic books, novels, video games, trading cards, etc. An audio adaptation was broadcast on National Public Radio in 1980.

The movies were digitally remastered for home video in 1995, and enhanced versions of the films were re-released theatrically as "Special Editions" in 1997, with additional scenes and all-new special effects. These releases were the prelude to the first new Star Wars films in fifteen years--"Episode I" of the Star Wars saga debuted in May 1999 to huge box office success, with two sequels to follow (the original trilogy serves as Episodes IV-VI). The new trilogy will chronicle the rise and fall of Luke's father, Anakin, fated to transform into the evil Darth Vader. If the first trilogy is any indication, these prequels should spawn a whole new interest in the series, with plenty of new merchandise to collect and enjoy.

STW-1

❑ **STW-1. Lucky Charms Box,**
1977. General Mills. Offers four "Character Stick-ons". - **$10 $20 $50**

STW-2

❑ **STW-2. Cocoa Puffs Box,**
1977. General Mills. Offers four "Robot" stick-ons. - **$10 $20 $50**

STW-3

❑ **STW-3. Trix Box,**
1977. General Mills. Offers four "Creature" stick-ons. - **$10 $20 $50**

STW-4

❑ **STW-4. Cantina Adventure Set,**
1977. Store item by Kenner. Sears Exclusive with blue Snaggletooth figure. -
**$100 $250 $350**

STW-5

❑ **STW-5. Boxed Ring Set,**
1977. Store item. 20th Century Fox Film Corp. copyright depicting R2-D2, Darth Vader, C-3PO.
Near Mint Boxed Set - **$20**
Each - **$2 $3 $5**

STW-6

❑ **STW-6. "Star Wars 16 Trading Cards" Signs,**
1977. Wonder Bread. 12x16" poster sign and 5-1/2x18" shelf sign for cards packaged in bread loaves. Poster - **$30 $75 $125**
Shelf Card - **$10 $25 $50**

STW-7 STW-8

❑ **STW-7. "Star Wars" First Series Card Set With Box,**
1977. Store item by Topps. Cards #1-66 and stickers #1-11. Box - **$3 $5 $10**
Near Mint Cards And Sticker Set - **$50**

❑ **STW-8. "Star Wars" Second Series Card Set,**
1977. Store item by Topps. Cards are #67-132 and stickers are #12-22.
Box (Not Shown) - **$3 $5 $10**
Near Mint Cards And Sticker Set - **$50**

STW-9 STW-10

❑ **STW-9. "Star Wars" Third Series Card Set,**
1977. Store item by Topps. Cards are #133-198 and stickers are #23-33. Box - **$3 $5 $10**
Near Mint Cards And Sticker Set - **$40**

❑ **STW-10. "Star Wars" Fourth Series Card Set,**
1977. Store item by Topps. Cards are #199-264 and stickers are #33-44. Box - **$3 $5 $10**
Near Mint Cards And Sticker Set - **$40**

STW-12

STW-11

❑ **STW-11. "Star Wars" Fifth Series Card Set,**
1977. Store item by Topps. Cards are #265-330 and stickers are #45-55. Box - **$3 $5 $10**
Near Mint Cards And Sticker Set - **$30**

❑ **STW-12. C-3PO Model Kit,**
1977. Store item by MPC.
Near Mint Boxed - **$60**

STW-13

STW-14

❑ **STW-13. R2-D2 Model Kit,**
1977. Store item by MPC.
Near Mint Boxed - **$60**

❑ **STW-14. "Star Wars Gredo" Action Figure,**
1977. Store item by Kenner. Card is 21 back.
Carded **- $50 $100 $165**

STW-15

❑ **STW-15. Luke Skywalker Large Action Figure,**
1978. Store item by Kenner. Poseable figure is 12" tall. Near Mint Boxed - **$350**
Loose Complete - **$50 $100 $150**

STW-16 STW-17

❑ **STW-16. Chewbacca Large Action Figure,**
1978. Store item by Kenner. 12" tall.
Near Mint Boxed - **$200**
Loose Complete - **$25 $50 $75**

❑ **STW-17. Princess Leia Organa Large Size Action Figure,**
1978. Store item by Kenner. Box holds 12" poseable figure. Near Mint Boxed - **$250**
Loose Complete - **$30 $60 $100**

STW-18

❑ **STW-18. Darth Vader Large Action Figure,**
1978. Store item by Kenner. 15" tall poseable figure. Near Mint Boxed - **$250**
Loose - **$30 $60 $100**

STW-19

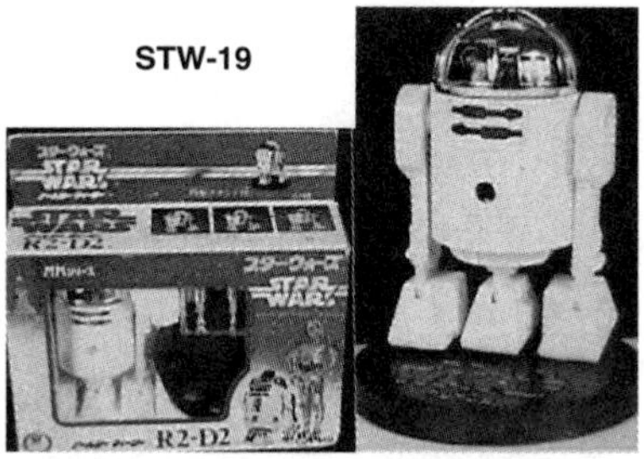

❑ **STW-19. "Star Wars R2-D2" Missile-Firing Japanese Figure,**
1978. Store item issued only in Japan by "Takara." 3" tall die cast metal and plastic figure with plastic sprue holding three missiles. Comes with sheet of accent stickers.
Near Mint Boxed - **$350**
Used Complete - **$75 $150 $250**

STW-20

❑ **STW-20. Lucky Charms Cereal Box With Hang Gliders Offer,**
1978. Boxes included four different punch-outs.
Box - **$50 $75 $150**
Punch-Outs Each - **$10 $20 $40**

STW-21

❑ **STW-21. "Star Wars Weekly" Vol. 1 #1,**
February 8, 1978. English edition by Marvel Comics International. - **$5 $10 $15**

STW-22

❑ **STW-22. "Official Star Wars Fan Club" Button Set,**
1978. 20th Century Fox. Set of 14, each 1-1/2", picturing 12 characters, George Lucas and title design. Each - **$5 $15 $25**

STW-23

❑ **STW-23. Procter & Gamble 19x20" Paper Posters,**
1978. Set of three. Set - **$10 $20 $40**

STW-24

❑ **STW-24. Creature Cantina Action Playset,**
1979. Store item by Kenner.
Near Mint Boxed - **$150**
Complete Unboxed - **$15 $30 $60**

STW-25 STW-26

❑ **STW-25. Ben Kenobi Large Action Figure,**
1979. 12" tall poseable figure store item by Kenner. Near Mint Boxed - **$350**
Loose Complete - **$175**

❑ **STW-26. Boba Fett Large Action Figure,**
1979. Store item by Kenner. 13" tall poseable figure. Near Mint Boxed - **$500**
Loose - **$75 $125 $250**

STW-27 STW-28

❑ **STW-27. Jawa Large Action Figure,**
1979. Store item by Kenner. 8" tall poseable figure. Near Mint Boxed - **$225**
Loose - **$25 $50 $100**

❑ **STW-28. "Stormtrooper" Large Size Action Figure,**
1979. Store item by Kenner. Figure is 12" tall.
Near Mint Boxed - **$250**
Loose - **$30 $60 $100**

STW-29

❑ **STW-29. "The Empire Strikes Back" Cards,**
1980. Burger King. Set of 36.
Set - **$10 $20 $30**

STW-30

❑ **STW-30. Droid Factory,**
1980. Store item by Kenner.
Near Mint Boxed - **$150**
Complete Unboxed - **$15 $30 $50**

STW-31

❑ **STW-31. Official Wrist Watch,**
1980. Store item by Bradley.
Near Mint Boxed - **$75**
Loose - **$10 $20 $30**

STW-32

STW-33

❑ **STW-32. Radio Promotion Cello. Button,**
1981. National Public Radio/KBPS. Lucasfilms copyright. - **$10 $15 $30**

❑ **STW-33. Record Tote,**
1982. Includes seal inside with index card. - **$10 $20 $35**

STW-34

❑ **STW-34. "3-D Electronic Quartz Clock",**
1982. Store item by Bradley.
Near Mint Boxed - **$100**
Loose - **$10 $20 $50**

STW-35

❑ **STW-35. "Star Wars IG-88" Action Figure,**
1982. Kenner. Card is 48 back variety with front and back stickers advertising "Revenge Of The Jedi" Admiral Ackbar mail offer figure.
Near Mint On Card - **$300**

STW-36

❑ **STW-36. Ewok Combat Glider,**
1983. Store item by Kenner.
Near Mint Boxed - **$35**
Near Mint Loose - **$15**

STW-37

❑ **STW-37. "Return of the Jedi" Poster,**
1983. 17-1/2x22" premium promotional poster from Oral B Star Wars Toothbrush. Shows set of six at bottom with coupons. Poster With Coupons - **$10 $20 $50**
Without Coupons - **$5 $10 $20**

STW-38 STW-39

❑ **STW-38. Cookie Box,**
1983. Pepperidge Farms.
Complete - **$10 $20 $40**

❑ **STW-39. "Return of the Jedi" Soundtrack,**
1983. Original soundtrack with 16 page color souvenir photo book. Complete - **$25**

**STW-40**

❑ **STW-40. "C-3PO's" Cereal Box with Star Wars C-3PO Mask,**
1984. - **$10 $30 $50**

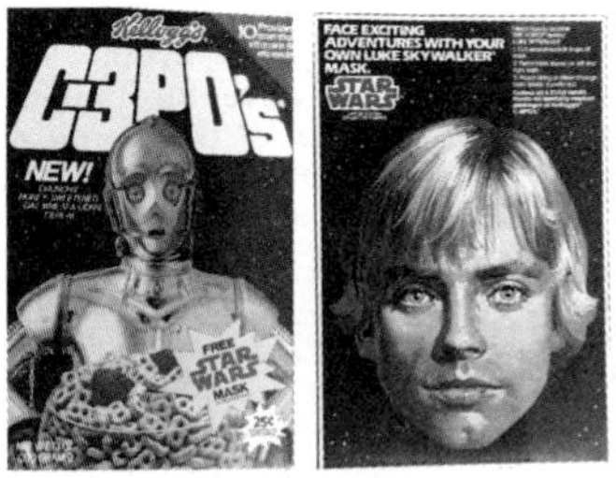

**STW-41**

❑ **STW-41. "C-3PO's" Cereal Box with Star Wars Luke Skywalker Mask,**
1984. - **$10 $30 $50**

**STW-42**

❑ **STW-42. "C-3PO's" Cereal Box with Star Wars Stormtrooper Mask,**
1984. - **$10 $30 $50**

**STW-43**

❑ **STW-43. "Sci-Fi Channel Star Wars" Limited Edition Watch,**
1992. Given to executives for the launch of the Sci-Fi Channel on 9/24/92 which premiered with the showing of Star Wars. Case reverse is marked "Manufactured By Fantasma."
Near Mint Boxed - **$125**

**STW-44**

❑ **STW-44. "Apple Jacks" Cereal Box with Star Wars Droids Comic Strip on Back,**
1995. Dark Horse Comics. - **$5 $8 $20**

**STW-45**

❑ **STW-45. "Froot Loops" Cereal Box with Star Wars Action Figure Offer on Back,**
1995. Han Solo as Stormtrooper. - **$2 $4 $15**

**STW-46**

❑ **STW-46. "Raisin Bran" Cereal Box with Star Wars Videos Rebate Offer on Back,**
1995. Original movie versions. - **$5 $8 $20**

**STW-47**

❑ **STW-47. "Star Wars" Pop-Up Book,**
1995. - **$8 $16 $30**

**STW-48**

❑ **STW-48. "Star Wars" Monopoly Game,**
1997. Limited colector's edition. - **$40**

**STW-50**

**STW-49**

❑ **STW-49. "C-3PO" Bean Figure with Tag,**
1997. Series 1. - **$20**

❑ **STW-50. "R2-D2" Bean Figure with Tag,**
1997. Series 1. - **$20**

**STW-51** **STW-52**

❑ **STW-51. "Yoda" Bean Figure with Tag,**
1997. Series 1. - **$20**

❑ **STW-52. "Chewbacca" Bean Figure with Tag,**
1997. Series 1. Figure has brown belt. - **$15**

STW-53

STW-54

❑ **STW-53. "Salacious Crumb" Bean Figure with Tag,**
1997. Series 1. - **$10**

❑ **STW-54. "Jabba the Hutt" Bean Figure with Tag,**
1997. Series 1. - **$15**

STW-55

STW-56

❑ **STW-55. "Jawa" Bean Figure with Tag,**
1997. Series 1. - **$15**

❑ **STW-56. "Wampa" Bean Figure with Tag,**
1997. Series 1. - **$15**

STW-57

STW-58

❑ **STW-57. "Wicket the Ewok" Bean Figure with Tag,**
1997. Series 1. - **$15**

❑ **STW-58. "D'An" Bean Figure with Tag,**
1998. Series 1. - **$12**

STW-59

STW-60

❑ **STW-59. "Qui-Gon Jinn" Episode 1 Bean Figure with Tag,**
1999. Series 2. - **$10**

❑ **STW-60. "Jar Jar Binks" Episode 1 Bean Figure with Tag,**
1999. Series 2. - **$10**

STW-61

STW-62

❑ **STW-61. "Obi-Wan Kenobi" Episode 1 Bean Figure with Tag,**
1999. Series 2. - **$10**

❑ **STW-62. "Darth Maul" Episode 1 Bean Figure with Tag,**
1999. Series 2. - **$10**

STW-63

STW-64

❑ **STW-63. "Padmé Naberrie" Episode 1 Bean Figure with Tag,**
1999. Series 2. - **$8**

❑ **STW-64. "Watto" Episode 1 Bean Figure with Tag,**
1999. Series 2. - **$10**

STW-65

❑ **STW-65. "Watto" Pepsi Standee,**
1999. Watto was a popular character in *Episode I*, making this standee eagerly sought when it appeared in grocery stores. Hard to find on the secondary market. - **$120**

STW-66

❑ **STW-66. Rebel Command Assault and Communications Set,**
2001. Includes laser guns, targets and walkie talkies. - **$30 $60 $90**

## Steve Canyon

**Following his success with *Terry and the Pirates*, Milton Caniff (1907-1988) created his *Steve Canyon* comic strip for distribution by Field Enterprises in 1947. Canyon, who runs a small airline, finds adventure and exotic women in all corners of the globe as he fights criminals and international spies. As the Cold War progresses, he sees service in Korea, Vietnam, and other hot spots, frequently doing battle with dangerous women. Comic books appeared in the late 1940s and 1950s, a radio adaptation with Barry Sullivan was syndicated in 1948, and a TV series with Dean Fredericks aired on NBC in 1958-1959 and was rerun on ABC in 1960. The newspaper strip ended publication in 1988. Items are copyrighted Field Enterprises Inc.**

STV-1

STV-2

❑ **STV-1. "Steve Canyon" Newspaper Club Cello. Button,**
c. 1947. New Journal Comic. - **$20 $45 $85**

❑ **STV-2. "Copper Calhoon With Steve Canyon" Newspaper Club Cello. Button,**
c. 1947. New Journal Comic. From same series as preceding item with "Calhoon" name as spelled. - **$15 $35 $75**

STV-3

STV-4

❑ **STV-3. "P.I." Cello. Button,**
c. 1947. - **$40 $75 $125**

❑ **STV-4. "Daily Record/Sunday Advertiser" Cello. Button,**
c. 1950. Various newspapers. - **$50 $115 $185**

STV-5

❑ **STV-5. "Steve Canyon" Boxed Game,**
1959. Store item by Lowell Toy Mfg. Corp. - **$20 $50 $100**

STV-6

❑ **STV-6. Chesterfield Cigarettes "Meet Steve Canyon-NBC TV" 21x22" Cardboard Store Poster,**
1950s. - **$35 $75 $125**

STV-7

STV-8

❑ **STV-7. "Steve Canyon's Airagers" Wings Litho. Tab,**
1950s. - **$15 $30 $45**

❑ **STV-8. Space Goggles On Picture Card,**
1950s. Store item by Rock Industries. Gold finish slitted plastic goggles of similar nature to sunglasses.
Carded - **$20 $40 $75**

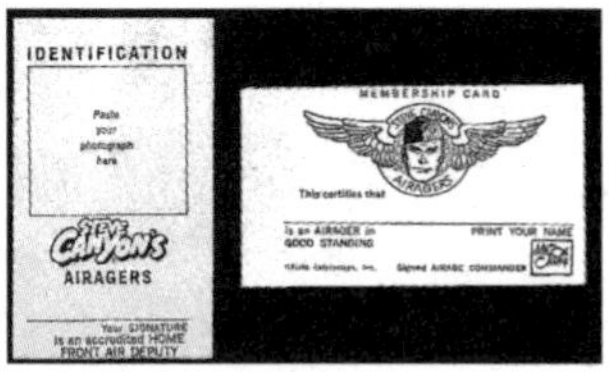


STV-9

❑ **STV-9. "Airager" Membership Card,**
1950s. Reverse has area for member's photograph. - **$15 $25 $45**

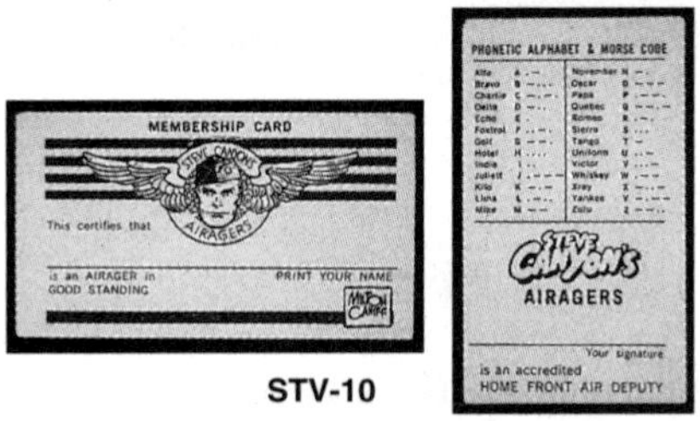


STV-10

❑ **STV-10. Airagers Membership Card,**
1950s. Variety with "Phonetic Alphabet & Morse Code" on reverse. - **$20 $30 $50**

## Straight Arrow

***Straight Arrow* was a Western adventure radio series that was broadcast from 1948 to 1951, first on the Don Lee network on the west coast, and starting in 1949 on the Mutual network nationally. The series was created for the National Biscuit Company as a means of promoting Nabisco shredded wheat. Boxtop premiums, on-package items, and retail products were offered in impressive quantities, all related to his scripted adventures.**

**Straight Arrow was actually young Steve Adams, owner of the Broken Bow Ranch, until innocent people were threatened or evil-doers plotted against justice. Then Adams would ride to his secret cave, mount his golden palomino Fury, and gallop out of the darkness as Straight Arrow, a Comanche warrior ready to fight for law and order. Howard Culver played Adams, and Fred Howard was his sidekick Packy McCloud.**

**Among the *Straight Arrow* premiums were several rings, a Mystic Wrist Kit containing an arrowhead and cowrie shell, an arrowhead flashlight, Indian war drum, bandanna, patch, and feathered headband. Sets of Injun-Uity cards, originally packaged in the cereal boxes, were later reissued as bound volumes.**

***Straight Arrow* comic books with sales reaching one million per month, were published from 1950 to 1956, many containing advertisements for the program's premiums and other merchandise. A daily newspaper strip distributed by the Bell Syndicate appeared from 1950 to 1952. "Kaneewah, Fury!"**

STA-1

❑ **STA-1. Large 20x36" Diecut Cardboard Store Sign,**
c. 1948. Promotes radio series on Mutual Network. - **$600 $1500 $2500**

STA-2

❑ **STA-2. Two-Red Feathered Headband With Mailer,**
1948. Includes two feathers. A second version has a 1949 copyright and says "Nabisco Shredded Wheat" under portrait.
Near Mint In Mailer - **$175**
Headband Only - **$50 $80 $135**

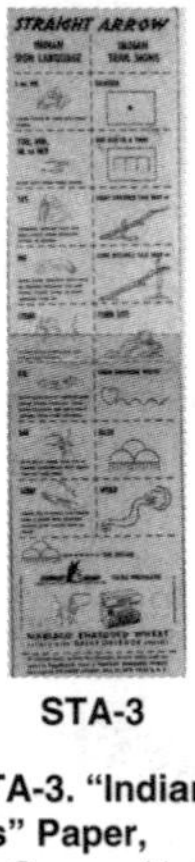


STA-3

STA-4

❑ **STA-3. "Indian Sign Language/Indian Trail Signs" Paper,**
1948. Came with headband. - **$25 $50 $100**

❑ **STA-4. Standee,**
1948. 5' 7" tall. Promotes Mutual Network Radio show. - **$800 $1700 $2800**

STA-5

❑ **STA-5. Radio Broadcast Reminder 12x15" Cardboard Store Sign,**
1949. Diecut to extend feathers at top edge. -
**$125 $250 $400**

STA-6

❑ **STA-6. Store Display Framed Picture,**
1949. Nabisco. Display promotion for set of 12 jigsaw puzzles of matching illustrations to the framed pictures. Example pictured is titled "Straight Arrow With Packy And Fury, To The Rescue." - **$40 $70 $135**

STA-7

STA-8

❑ **STA-7. "Book One" Box Insert Cards,**
1949. Set of 36. Each - **$1 $2 $3**

❑ **STA-8. Bandanna,**
1949. - **$20 $35 $65**

(TOP VIEW)

STA-9

❑ **STA-9. Bandanna Gold Plastic Slide,**
1949. - **$20 $40 $60**

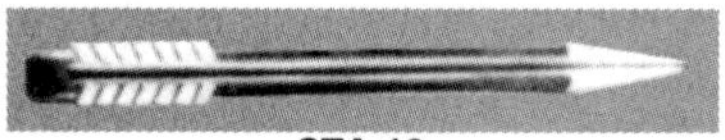

STA-10

❑ **STA-10. Gold Luster Metal Spring Tie Clip,**
1949. Scarce. Bar image of arrow. -
**$75 $200 $325**

STA-11

❑ **STA-11. War Drum,**
1949. Complete Boxed - **$50 $150 $200**
Drum Only - **$25 $50 $100**

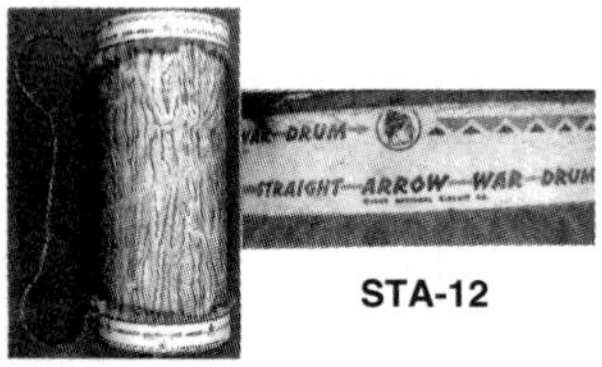


STA-12

❑ **STA-12. War Drum,**
1949. 12" tall cardboard/thin rubber with beater stick. Complete - **$65 $125 $200**

STA-13

❑ **STA-13. Jigsaw Puzzle,**
1949. Set of 12.
Each In Envelope - **$15 $25 $50**
Loose - **$5 $15 $25**
Box For 10 Puzzles (Rare) - **$50 $150 $250**

STA-14

STA-15

❑ **STA-14. Nabisco Shredded Wheat 4x10" Cardboard Display Sign,**
c. 1949. - **$150 $250 $400**

❑ **STA-15. Radio/Comic Strip Pressbook,**
1950. Rare. Contains comic strips, list of premiums, sales information. - **$200 $650 $825**

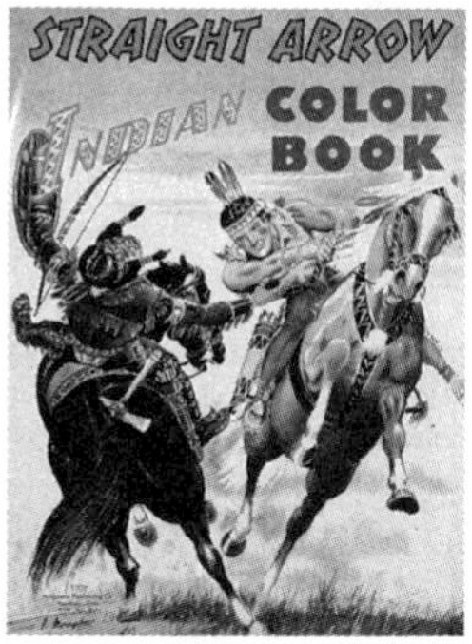


STA-16

❑ **STA-16. Straight Arrow Coloring Book,**
1950. Premium and store item. -
**$40 $125 $200**

STA-17

STA-18

❑ **STA-17. Mystic Wrist Kit Instructions,**
1950. Instructions on how to use kit also explains hidden secret word on bottom. - **$15 $30 $60**

❑ **STA-18. Mystic Wrist Kit,**
1950. Gold plastic bracelet with container holding arrowhead and cowrie shell.
Near Mint Boxed - **$225**
Bracelet and Parts - **$50 $100 $150**
Insert - **$10 $20 $30**

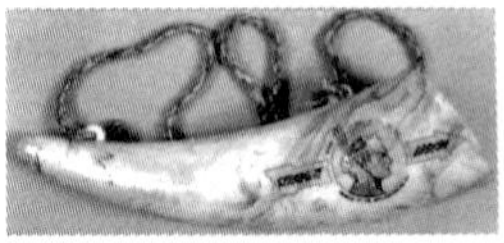

STA-19

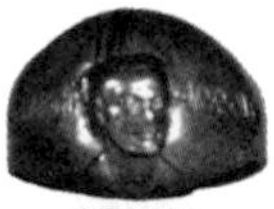

STA-20

❑ **STA-19. Plastic Powder Horn With String Cord,**
1950. - **$50 $150 $300**

❑ **STA-20. Brass Portrait Ring,**
1950. - **$20 $40 $75**

STA-21

STA-22

❑ **STA-21. Golden Nugget Picture Ring,**
1950. Gold plastic with view lens holding picture scene within cave interior, also known as "Cave Ring". Shows Straight Arrow, his horse Fury and his assistant Packy McCloud. Some versions show black and white photo of child that ordered the ring. - **$75 $150 $275**

❑ **STA-22. "Book 2" Box Insert Cards,**
1950. Set of 36. Each - **$1 $2 $3**

STA-23

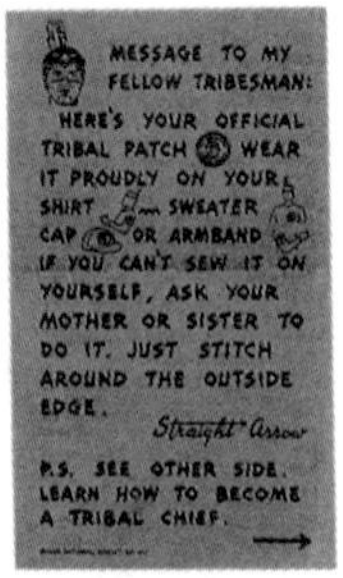


STA-24

❑ **STA-23. Tribal Shoulder Patch,**
1950. - **$10 $20 $40**

❑ **STA-24. Patch Instructions,**
1950. Rare. Tells about patch and how to become a big chief. - **$30 $60 $90**

STA-25

❑ **STA-25. Target Game with Box,**
1950. Store item. Metal target with bow-like launcher to fire "magnetic arrows." - **$75 $200 $350**

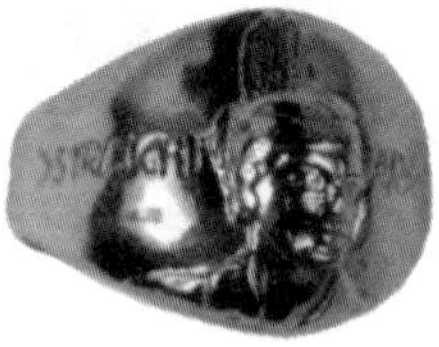

STA-26

❑ **STA-26. Gold Plated Portrait Ring,**
1950. Apparently the Robbins Co. produced a small number of the standard brass rings with a gold plated finish as the three examples we know of have all been traced back to Nabisco Co. executives. Near Mint **- $350**

STA-27

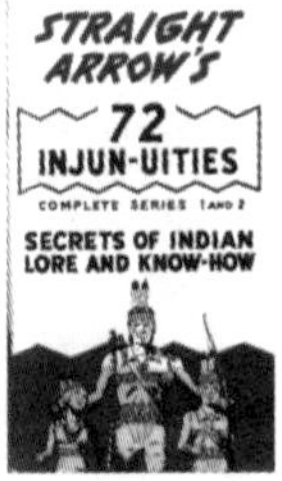


STA-28

❑ **STA-27. "Injun-Uities" 21x27" Store Announcement Poster,**
1951. Scarce. Pictures 12 "Injun-Uities" Nabisco cards from first series. - **$150 $575 $825**

❑ **STA-28. "Straight Arrow Injun-Uities Manual",**
1951. Series 1 and 2 box inserts in book format. - **$15 $25 $40**

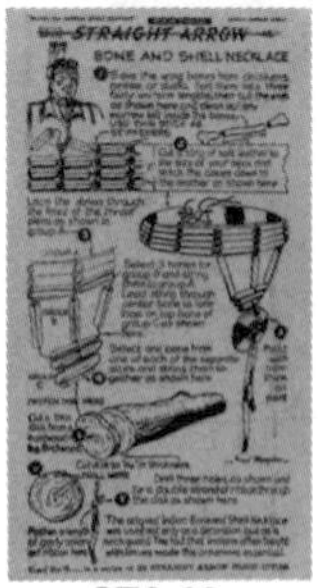


STA-29

STA-30

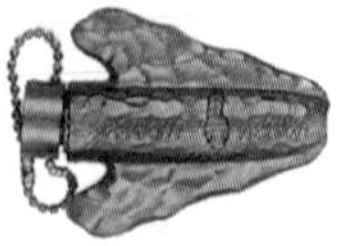

STA-31

❑ **STA-29. "Book Three" Box Insert Cards,**
1951. Set of 36. Each - **$1 $2 $3**

❑ **STA-30. "Rite-A-Lite" Order Form,**
1951. - **$15 $30 $50**

❑ **STA-31. Rite-A-Lite Arrowhead With Cap On Bottom,**
1951. Scarce. Gold heavy plastic battery operated light. Discontinued because of use of material for Korean War. - **$200 $500 $750**
Without End Cap - **$60 $90 $150**

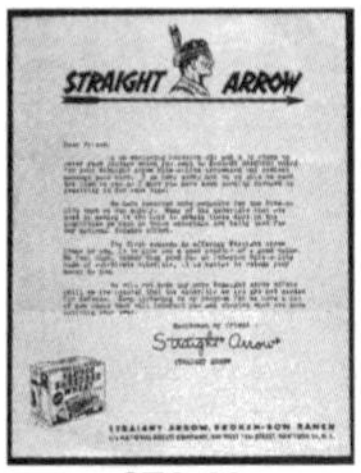


STA-32

❑ **STA-32. Rite-A-Lite Arrowhead Cancellation Letter,**
1951. Rare. - **$100 $175 $250**

STA-33

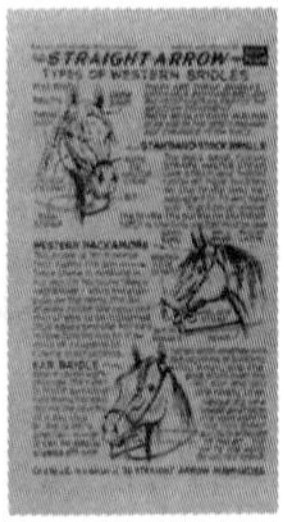


STA-34

❑ **STA-33. Glow-In-Dark Membership Card,**
1951. - **$35 $150 $225**

❑ **STA-34. "Book Four" Box Insert Cards,**
1952. Set of 36. Each - **$2 $3 $4**

STA-35

❑ **STA-35. Nabisco Shredded Wheat Box with Straight Arrow Finger Puppet Offer,**
1952. Package becomes paper toy TV set.- **$50 $125 $175**

STA-36

❑ **STA-36. Punch-Out Puppets Sheet,**
c. 1952. Comes with instruction card and two play script cards. See next item.
Unpunched - **$12 $20 $30**

STA-37

❑ **STA-37. Props,**
1952. Nabisco. Two pieces. For TV Puppet Theater. Goes with STA-36. Each - **$5 $10 $15**

## Strombecker Models Club

**A model kit maker (principally aviation) from the 1930s onward, Strombecker Co. sponsored a model building club with a code book and series of badges to denote club ranks based on model building expertise. A similar club was sponsored by competitor Megow Co.**

SMC-1

❑ **SMC-1. Club Manual,**
1930s. Includes secret code, photos of famous adult club members, photos of airplane and locomotive models. - **$15 $25 $50**

SMC-2

SMC-3

❑ **SMC-2. "Apprentice" Bronze Finish Badge,**
1930s. - **$8 $15 $25**

❑ **SMC-3. "First Class" Bronze Finish Badge,**
1930s. Awarded for building four models in four categories. - **$12 $20 $40**

SMC-4

❑ **SMC-4. "Airman 1st Class" Club Rank 3" Metal Wings Badge,**
1930s. Silver finish with red shield, one star. - **$10 $20 $35**

SMC-5

❑ **SMC-5. "Wing Leader" Club Rank 3" Metal Wings Badge,**
1930s. Gold finish, blue shield, two stars. - **$10 $20 $35**

SMC-6

❑ **SMC-6. "Captain" Club Rank Metal Wings Badge,**
1930s. Brass finish, green shield, three stars for highest rank. - **$15 $25 $50**

SMC-7

❑ **SMC-7. Club Application Folder,**
c. late 1940s. Features "Captain 'Jet'" and pictures "Air Man 1st Class" tin badge to be received. Folder - **$5 $12 $25**
Badge - **$10 $20 $35**

SMC-8

❑ **SMC-8. "Captain 'Jet' And The Strombecker Model-Makers Club" Comic,**
1953. 3-1/4x7-1/4" combination comic book and catalogue with 16 pages. - **$15 $25 $50**

## Sunset Carson

**Michael Harrison (1920-1990) took his cowboy name for a supporting role in the 1944 film *Call of the Rockies*. Carson starred in about 20 "B" Westerns for Republic Pictures from the mid-1940s to 1950, but his cowboy skills were demonstrated to greater advantage as an international rodeo star and trick rider in the Tom Mix Circus. Several Sunset Carson comic books were published in 1951, and adaptations of his films appeared in a number of issues of *Cowboy Western Comics* in the early 1950s.**

SUN-1

❑ **SUN-1. "Republic Pictures" Felt Pennant,**
1940s. - **$20 $40 $90**

SUN-2

❑ **SUN-2. "Sunset Carson" Cello. Button,**
1940s. - **$15 $40 $75**

SUN-3

❑ **SUN-3. Sunset Carson Autographed "Sharpshooting" Brochure,**
c. 1950. Has photos of Carson with illustrations for Remington ammunition, likely sponsor.
Signed **- $20 $40 $75**
Unsigned **- $10 $20 $30**

SUN-4

❑ **SUN-4. Sunset Carson/Monte Hale Records Offer,**
c. 1950. Illinois Merchandise Mart. Paper sheet offering recorded adventures "Sunset Carson And The Black Bandit" and "Monte Hale And The Flaming Arrow." - **$10 $20 $40**

## Super Circus

**What started out as a kids' radio quiz program in Chicago became one of television's highest-rated children's shows. *Super Circus*, a weekly variety spectacular, aired on ABC-TV from 1949 to 1956. Claude Kirchner acted as ringmaster, Mary Hartline--with dazzling blonde hair and miniskirt--twirled her baton, and clowns Cliffy, Nicky, and Scampy took care of the slapstick. Among the sponsors were Weather Bird shoes, Canada Dry, Kellogg's cereals, Quaker Oats, Mars candy, and Sunkist. Also, Mary Hartline Enterprises marketed a line of dolls, toys, children's clothes, food products, records, and books. The show moved to New York in 1955, and Jerry Colonna and Sandy Wirth replaced Kirchner and Hartline for the final season. *Super Circus* comic books appeared between 1951 and 1956.**

SUC-1

❑ **SUC-1. "Super Circus Action Toy" Punch-Out Kit With Envelope,**
1950. Canada Dry. Set of 10 punch-out sheets.
Unused In Mailer - **$40 $100 $200**

SUC-2

SUC-3

❑ **SUC-2. "Weather-Bird Shoes" Photos,**
c. 1950. From a set. Each - **$8 $12 $25**

❑ **SUC-3. "Mary Hartline" Hand Puppet,**
c. 1950. Three Musketeers. - **$15 $40 $60**

SUC-4

❑ **SUC-4. "Super Circus Side Show" Punch-Out Kit With Envelope,**
c. 1950. Milky Way candy bars. Punch-out sheet opens to 11x34".
Complete In Mailer - **$50 $125 $200**

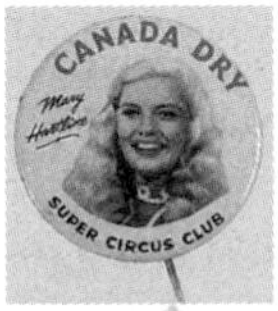


SUC-5

SUC-6

❑ **SUC-5. "Super Circus Club" Member's Litho. Button,**
1951. Canada Dry. - **$5 $20 $35**

❑ **SUC-6. Spiral-Bound Photo Book,**
1951. - **$25 $75 $110**

SUC-7

SUC-8

❑ **SUC-7. Weather Bird Shoes Comic Book Vol. 1 #1,**
1951. - **$4 $26 $40**

❑ **SUC-8. Iron-On Transfer Sheets,**
1951. Weather-Bird shoes. Four tissue sheets in reverse image picturing Mary, Scampy, Nicky, Cliffy. Each - **$3 $6 $12**

SUC-9

❑ **SUC-9. "Super Circus Snickers Shack" Punch-Out With Mailer,**
c. 1951. Mars, Inc. Punch sheet opens to 11-1/2 x17". Complete In Mailer - **$50 $100 $175**

SUC-10

❑ **SUC-10. "Super Circus Television Color Show" Boxed Set,**
1953. Store item by E. C. Kropp Co. -
**$20 $40 $75**

SUC-11

SUC-12

❑ **SUC-11. "TV Guide" With Cover Article,**
1953. Weekly issue for August 21 with color photo cover of Mary Hartline and Claude Kirchner plus two-page article. - **$15 $25 $40**

❑ **SUC-12. Mary Hartline Magic Doll,**
1955-56. Rare. Kellogg's premium from the show's last season. Has paper doll, cut-out dresses, stand, application and mailer. Ordered for 25¢ and 1 box top from Frosted Flakes or Sugar Smacks. Complete - **$100 $210 $320**

SUC-13

❑ **SUC-13. "Squeezem" Action Cards,**
1950s. Store item. Each is 3x4-1/2".
Each - **$5 $10 $20**

SUC-14

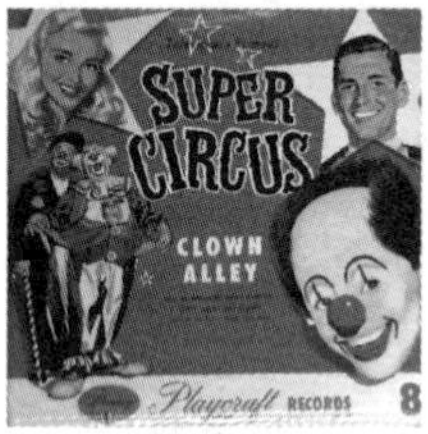

SUC-15

❑ **SUC-14. Punch-Out Puppets With Envelope,**
1950s. Snickers Candy Bars.
Unused In Mailer - **$30 $90 $150**

❑ **SUC-15. Clown Alley Record Album,**
1950s. Mercury Playcraft Records. With dust jacket. 78 RPM. Rare. - **$30 $60 $120**

SUC-16

SUC-17

❑ **SUC-16. Hard Plastic Doll,**
1950s. Mars Candy and store item. Seen marked "Ideal" or "Lingerie Lou Doll." -
**$35 $125 $200**
Picture Box - **$20 $40 $60**

❑ **SUC-17. Postcard,**
1950s. Premium from TV show, pictures 6 cast members - **$20 $35 $60**

# Superman

**Clark Kent's secret identity might just be the worst-kept secret ever. Consistently certified as one of the most recognized characters in the world, Superman is the very definition of a superhero (in fact, he's probably the reason for the word superhero). Not only was he dynamic and unlike anything anyone had seen before, but the marketing plan built around and executed for Superman was virtually a "how to" road map for future marketing executives.**

**When writer Jerry Siegel and artist Joe Shuster created Superman in 1933, they probably had no idea of the tremendous force they would unleash on an unsuspecting public. It wasn't until five years later, though, that *Action Comics* #1 (June 1938) launched Superman into comic books and captured the attention of children. The daily newspaper strip first appeared seven months later (January 1939) and adults began to take notice. A companion comic, *Superman*, followed that summer and included the first mention of Supermen of America, the official Superman fan club. The club's first contest began December 1, 1939 and ended January 28, 1940; the prize became one of the most sought-after Superman collectibles ever, the Supermen of America patch (see entry in this section). Two weeks later, February 12, 1940, the *Superman* radio show took to the airwaves for the first time and captured the imagination of entire families. Before long, characters Clark Kent and Lois Lane (and thanks to the radio show, several others) became fast friends with America's reading and listening public. The phenomenon had begun.**

**There have been thousands of Superman comic books, and daily and Sunday comic strips appeared from 1939 to 1967. On radio *The Adventures of Superman* aired from 1940 to 1951, on the Mutual network from 1940 to 1949, then on ABC. Bud Collyer starred as Superman from 1940 to 1949. Force cereal sponsored in 1940, followed by Kellogg's Pep from 1943 to 1947. The series moved successfully to prime-time television syndication (1953-1958), mainly on ABC outlets, with George Reeves in the lead and Kellogg's Sugar Frosted Flakes as sponsor. October 2001 marked Superman's return to television in a one hour drama on the WB network entitled *Smallville.* Tom Welling stars as the teenaged Clark Kent in a series that focuses on angst rather than adventure.**

**The first Superman cartoons were 17 six-minute theatrical shorts made by the Fleischer Studios for Paramount Pictures in 1941-1943. Television cartoons, with Bud Collyer returning as the voice of Superman, aired on CBS in the late 1960s under various titles: *The New Adventures of Superman* (1966-1967), *The Superman/Aquaman Hour of Adventure* (1967-1968), and *The Batman/Superman Hour* (1968-1969). Superman was also part of the *Superfriends* animated series on ABC in the 1970s, and a musical show, *It's a Bird...It's a Plane...It's Superman*, had a brief run on Broadway in 1966 and was shown on ABC-TV in 1975. Superman returned to the cartoon airwaves in 1996 on the WB network and now airs as part of *The New Batman/Superman Adventures.***

**Superman's movie career began with two 15-episode chapter plays from Columbia Pictures, *Superman* (1948) and *Atom Man vs. Superman* (1950), with Kirk Alyn (1911-1999) in the lead roles. *Superman and the Mole Men*, with George Reeves (1914-1959) starring, was released in 1951 and later served as a pilot for the TV series. *Superman - The Movie* (1978), with Christopher Reeve and Margot Kidder--a box office smash--was followed by *Superman II* (1981), *Superman III* (1983), and *Superman IV: The Quest for Peace* (1987). *Lois and Clark: The New Adventures of Superman* ran on ABC-TV from 1993 to 1997 and presently airs in re-runs on the TNT cable network with Dean Cain as Clark/Superman and Teri Hatcher as Lois Lane.**

**Superman marked his 60th anniversary in June 1998. As of 2002, he is presently published in four monthly titles, *Action Comics*, *Adventures of Superman*, *Superman*, and *Superman: The Man of Steel.* A cartoon companion comic, *Superman Adventures*, ran for 66 issues, and the character appears from time to time in many other DC titles.**

**In 2001, the 1978 feature film was released on DVD, including enhanced special effects, additional scenes, and some minor edits (including the impressive task of making the costume look the right color under the wide variety of lighting conditions in the movie). The release brought renewed interest to the '70s and '80s series. Superman presently appears on the Cartoon Network's *Justice League* animated series. Over the course of his career he's been transformed, transmogrified and even killed, but Superman keeps coming back in his never-ending battle for truth, justice and the American way. Items are typically copyrighted National Comics Publications, Inc., National Periodical Publications, Inc. or DC Comics.**

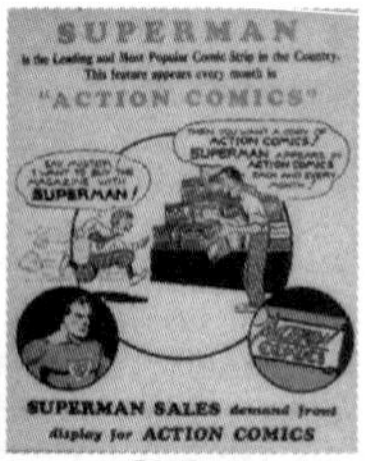

SUP-1

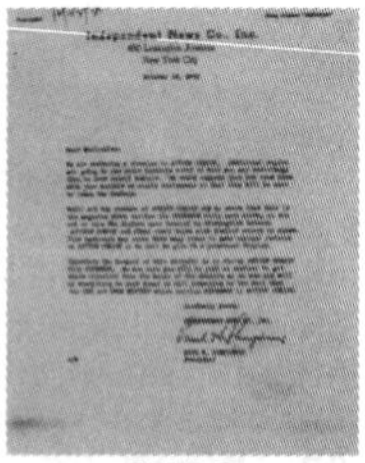
SUP-2

❑ **SUP-1. "Action Comics" Flier,**
1939. Sent to magazine wholesalers requesting they inform retailers Superman strip appears only in "Action Comics". - **$325 $800 $1600**

❑ **SUP-2. "Action Comics" Cover Letter,**
1939. Came with flier above. - **$250 $500 $750**

SUP-3

❑ **SUP-3. Action Comics "Superman" Litho. Button,**
1939. Back inscription "Read Superman/Action Comics Magazine". - **$50 $125 $200**

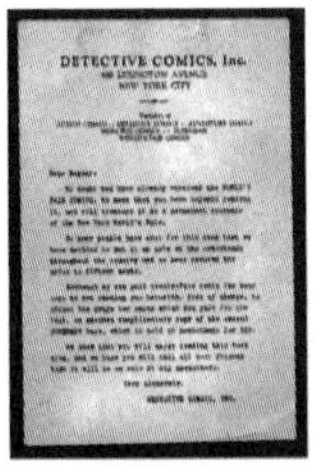


SUP-4

SUP-5

❑ **SUP-4. Letter,**
1939. N. Y. World's Fair. - **$150 $350 $600**

❑ **SUP-5. Action Comics Club Certificate, First Version,**
1939. Note bottom margin inscribed "Copyright 1939 by Detective Comics, Inc." - **$100 $250 $500**

SUP-6

❑ **SUP-6. Superman Contest Prize Ring,**
1940. Scarce. Inscribed "Supermen Of America, Member." Issued by DC Comics promoted in Superman and Action Comics. Believed to have been given away with candy and gum programs as well. Silver base, gold luster image, red accent on logo and around lettering. Reported 17 known: two in Poor grade, six in Good, two in Very Good, three in Fine, three in Very Fine, and one in Mint.
Good - **$6000**
Fine - **$20000**
Very Fine - **$45000**

SUP-7

SUP-8

❑ **SUP-7. Candy & Surprise Cut-Out Panels,**
1940. Set of 36. Superman member ring offered for 10 coupons and 10 cents or 75 coupons.
Cut Box Front With Coupon - **$20 $40 $60**
Cut Back With Card - **$20 $40 $60**

❑ **SUP-8. "Superman Adventure" Poster,**
1940. Macy's department store. 7x17" in red, white and blue promoting their "Toyland-Fifth Floor" performance in which Superman "Comes Alive." - **$225 $400 $750**

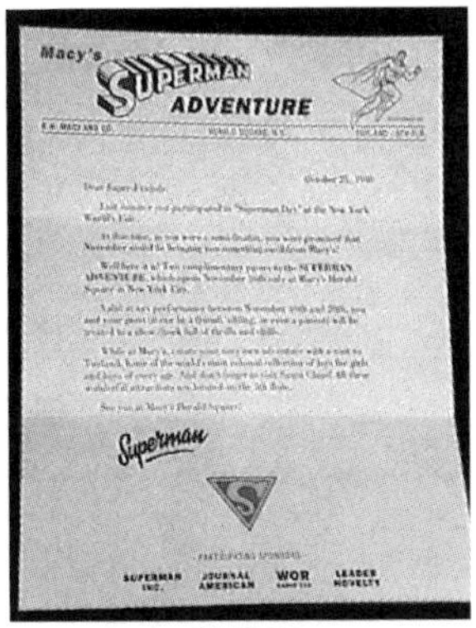


SUP-9

❑ **SUP-9. "Superman Adventure" Letter To "Dear Super-Friends",**
1940. Macy's. Letter to participant semi-finalist in "Superman Day" at the New York World's Fair which was accompanied by two passes to the "Superman Adventure" event opening November 16. Letter lists participating sponsors as Superman Inc., Journal American, WOR Radio 710, Leader Novelty. - **$200 $350 $500**

SUP-10

❑ **SUP-10. Superman Thanksgiving Day Parade Ad Card,**
1940. Similar in size to a postcard, promoted Macy's effort at Thanksgiving Day Parade. The Superman display was the largest balloon featured in the 1940 parade. - **$150 $300 $400**

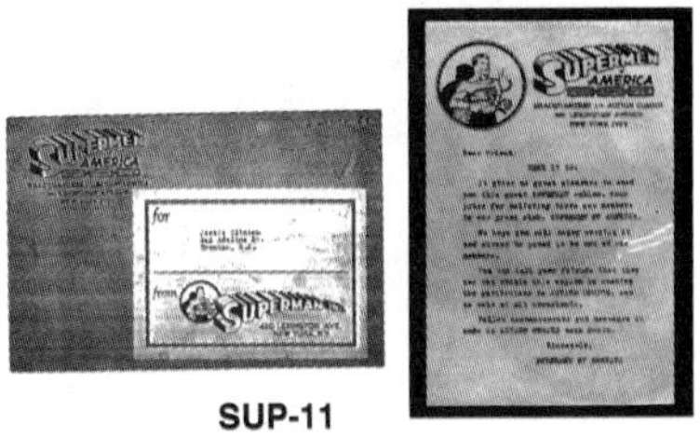

SUP-11

❑ **SUP-11. Letter and Mailer,**
1940. Came with Action Comics Patch.
Each - **$500 $1400 $2500**

SUP-12

❑ **SUP-12. Patch,**
1940. Scarce. Has "Action Comics" at bottom of front side. - **$1500 $6000 $8500**

SUP-13

❑ **SUP-13. Patch,**
1940. Rare. Prize same as the above Supermen of America Patch except has word "Leader" at bottom. - **$2000 $8000 $14000**

SUP-14

❑ **SUP-14. Candy Patch,**
1940. - **$600 $3000 $7500**

SUP-15

❑ **SUP-15. Handkerchief,**
1940. - **$600 $1500 $3000**

SUP-16

❑ **SUP-16. Marx Wind-Up Tin Tank**
1940. Store item. - **$200 $400 $1000**

SUP-17

❑ **SUP-17. Large Candy Box,**
1940. - **$400 $1500 $3500**

SUP-18

❑ **SUP-18. "Superman In Movie Style" Boxed Viewer And Film Set,**
1940. Store item by Acme Plastic Toys Inc. - **$100 $250 $500**

SUP-19

❑ **SUP-19. Superman Cut-Out Book,**
1940. Produced by Saalfield Publishing Company of Akron, Ohio. There were two editions; one had a red cover and the other was blue. Each - **$750 $1800 $3000**

SUP-20

❑ **SUP-20. Figural Brass Pin Serially Numbered,**
c. 1940. Sponsor unknown. 1" tall with red and blue enamel paint. - **$200 $500 $1000**

SUP-21

❑ **SUP-21. "Superman's Magic Flight" Cardboard Mechanical Toy,**
1940. - **$400 $750 $1500**

(front)

(back)

SUP-22

❑ **SUP-22. "Superman's Christmas Adventure" Comic Book,**
1940. First superhero premium comic book. First issue, various stores. - **$600 $2500 $5000**

SUP-23

❑ **SUP-23. "Superman" Enameled Brass Badge,**
1940. Sponsor not known. Possibly a Canadian premium. - **$400 $1250 $2500**

SUP-24

❑ **SUP-24. Rectangular Fabric Patch,**
1940. Scarce. - **$750 $3000 $6000**

SUP-25

❑ **SUP-25. "Macy's Superman Adventure" Gummed Sticker,**
1940. Macy's department store, applied to purchased items. - **$100 $200 $600**

SUP-26

❑ **SUP-26. "Krypto-Raygun" With Box,**
1940. Store item by Daisy Mfg. Co. Came with seven filmstrips.
Complete Boxed - **$400 $1000 $2500**
Gun Only - **$100 $200 $300**
Filmstrip - **$5 $15 $25**

SUP-27 SUP-28

❑ **SUP-27. Wood And Composition Jointed Doll,**
1940. Store item by Ideal Toys. Includes cloth cape. - **$300 $900 $1800**
Near Mint With Box - **$7500**

❑ **SUP-28. Superman Die-Cut Ad,**
1940. Promotes radio show on WHP radio station. About 4-1/2" high. Other ads feature different stations. - **$75 $150 $250**

SUP-29

❑ **SUP-29. Superman Bubble Gum Club Prizes Folder,**
1940. Gum, Inc. Shows 15 items, most also available in stores, available for cash and Superman Gum labels or free of charge for securing new club members. The "Superman American" brass club badge was 10¢ and 5 wrappers or 10 new members. -
**$175 $400 $800**

SUP-31

SUP-30

❑ **SUP-30. Bowman Bubble Gum Box,**
1940. Sold for **$7500** in 1998. Probably unique.

❑ **SUP-31. "Democrat" Newspaper Cello. Button,**
1940. Rare newspaper premium. -
**$600 $1200 $2000**

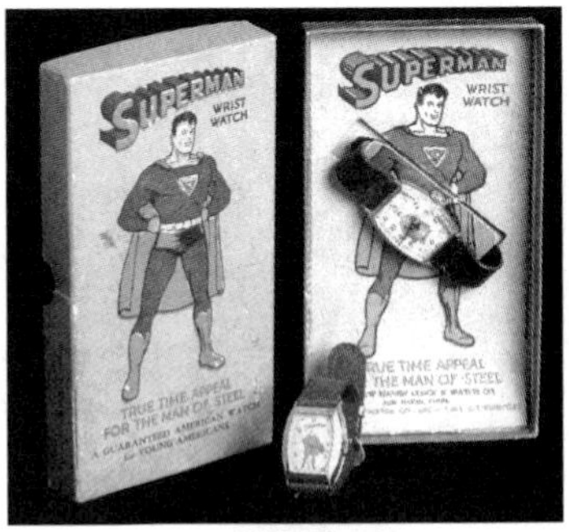


SUP-32

❑ **SUP-32. Superman Wristwatch in Box,**
1940. Made by New Haven Clock Co. and distributed by the Everbright Watch Company. Two different bands shown (brown band at bottom, black band at top). Boxed - **$750 $1500 $2500**
Box and Insert Only - **$350 $750 $1000**

SUP-33

❑ **SUP-33. Superman Christmas Adventure Ticket,**
1940. Admission ticket to Macy's Christmas Adventure play. This ticket has sponsor radio station WOR on the front. Other sponsors include Superman, Inc., Leader Novelty, and American Journal. Each - **$125 $250 $400**

SUP-34

SUP-35

❑ **SUP-34. Plaster "Carnival" Statue,**
1940. 1st of 4 varieties shown. With red and blue costume. - **$100 $250 $350**

❑ **SUP-35. Plaster "Carnival" Statue,**
1940. 2nd of 4 varieties shown. With red and green costume. - **$75 $225 $325**

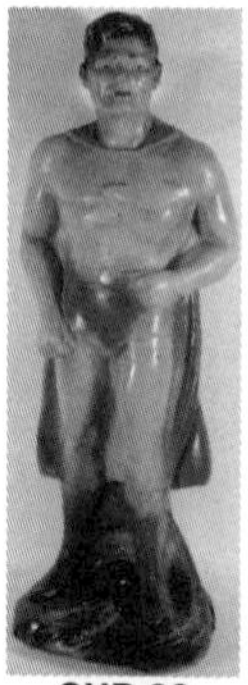

SUP-36

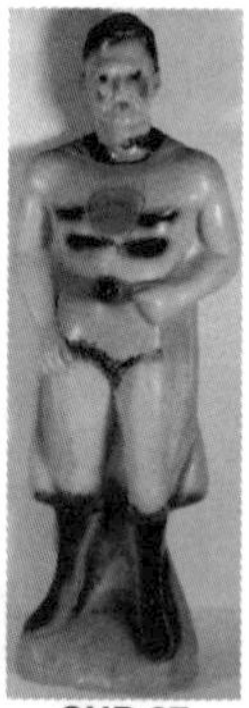

SUP-37

SUP-38

❑ **SUP-36. Plaster "Carnival" Statue,**
1940. 3rd of 4 varieties shown. With yellow and black costume. - **$75 $225 $325**

❑ **SUP-37. Plaster "Carnival" Statue,**
1940. 4th of 4 varieties shown. With red, yellow and black costume with emblem on chest. - **$75 $225 $325**

❑ **SUP-38. "Superman/American" Brass Figural Badge,**
1940. Gum Inc. for Superman Bubble Gum Club members - **$40 $75 $150**

SUP-39

❑ **SUP-39. Superman Valentine,**
1940. Valentine created by Quality Art Novelty Company in February, 1940. Many different. Each - **$30 $65 $125**

SPECIAL ADMISSION 10¢ SPECIAL ADMISSION
SUPERMAN ADVENTURE
This voucher entitles the holder to a repeat visit at the special admission price.
VALID JANUARY 2, 1941 TO CLOSING
5th Floor MACY'S Herald Square

SUP-40

❑ **SUP-40. "Superman Adventure Special Admission 10 Cent" Voucher,**
1940. Macy's. 4x4-1/2" card for repeat visit at special price beginning January 2, 1941 to closing. - **$100 $200 $400**

SUP-41

❑ **SUP-41. Cartoon Movie 6' Standee,**
1941. From Fleischer cartoon film. - **$10000 $25000 $40000**

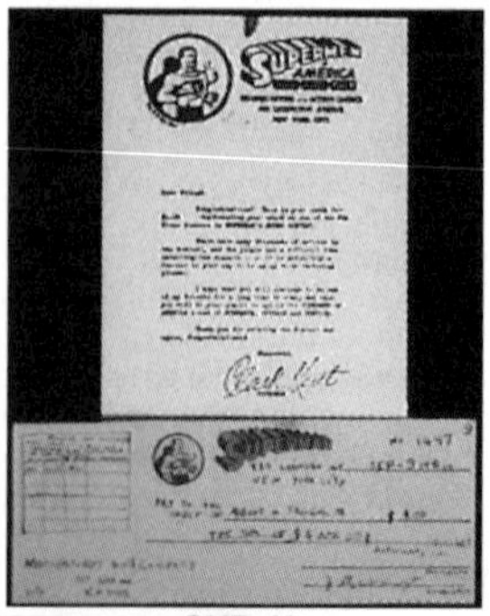

SUP-42

❑ **SUP-42. Contest Letter With Check Replica,**
1941. 7-1/4x10-1/2" letter congratulates winner of "Check For - $4 Representing Your Award As One Of The 8 Prize Winners In Superman's Super Contest." Original owner handmade a replica of the check prior to cashing it.
Letter Only - **$150 $300 $600**

SUP-43

SUP-44

❑ **SUP-43. Superman Secret Chamber Initial Brass Ring,**
1941. Produced by Ostby & Barton, Rhode Island. Sponsoring milk company's inital on top cover. First version with red/white/blue image of Superman glued on top of ring base, under the lift-off cover. Ring offered in conjunction with Defense Club Milk Program. Available for 2 bottle caps and 10¢. Ring must include the paper to obtain grade. 27 reported known: 4 in Good grade, 5 in Very Good, 5 in Fine, 5 in Very Fine and 3 in Near Mint. Five incomplete w/o paper. -
Good - **$1000**
Fine - **$4000**
Very Fine - **$9000**
Near Mint - **$15000**

❑ **SUP-44. Superman Secret Chamber Brass Ring With Superman Image on Top,**
1941. Produced by Ostby & Barton, Rhode Island. Pictures Superman, lightning bolt and letter "S". Top snaps off, Superman image was restamped over mystic eye on top, therefore rubbing exists on all rings. No Superman image under top. Ring offered in conjunction with Defense Club Milk Program. Available for 2 bottle caps and 10¢. 9 reported known: 4 in Good grade, 4 in Fine, 1 in Very Fine.
Good - **$1500**
Fine - **$7500**
Very Fine - **$18000**

SUP-45

❑ **SUP-45. Superman Defense Club Milk Bottle Lids,**
1941. Each cardboard lid contains a number and a pledge. These lids were collected and redeemable with the milkman for a Superman American pin. These lids are rare; a complete set does not exist. Each - **$75 $150 $250**

SUP-46

❑ **SUP-46. Superman Defense Club Milk Membership Card,**
1941. Roberts Milk sponsor. At the same time the Superman Junior Defense League of America bread campaign was going on, Superman was also promoting milk under this club name. Note the word "Junior" is deleted and "League" is changed to "Defense."
With Green Tab Notice Intact -
**$100 $225 $350**

SUP-47

❑ **SUP-47. Superman Defense Club Badge,**
1941. Same as SUP-38; 1940 badge offered again in conjunction with Defense Club milk program. Not to be confused with the Superman Junior Defense League bread program badge (see SUP-48). - **$40 $75 $150**

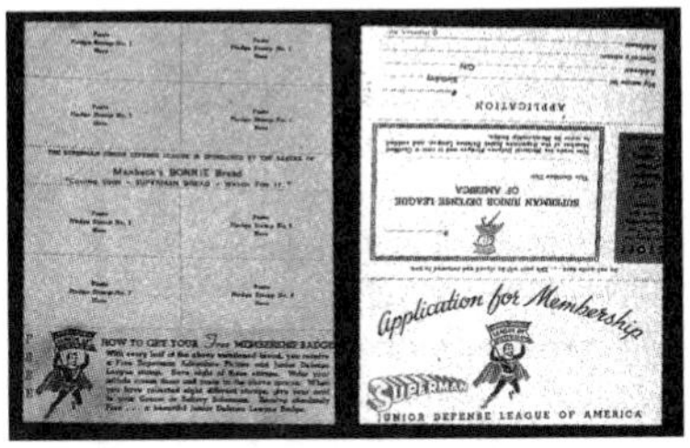


SUP-48

❑ **SUP-48. Superman Junior Defense League Bread Membership Folder,**
1941. Includes membership card and holder on back to paste membership pledge stamps. When the card was filled with eight stamps, it was redeemable at the local grocer for a Superman Junior Defense League pin.
Folder Complete - **$200 $400 $600**
Membership Card Only - **$100 $200 $300**
Superman Sticker Stamps Glued Each -
**$10 $20 $30**

SUP-49

❑ **SUP-49. Superman Junior Defense League Bread Badge,**
1941. Premium for complete folder with stickers glued to back. - **$60 $90 $160**

SUP-50

❑ **SUP-50. Superman Adventure Cards With Stamps,**
1941. Rare. 24 adventure picture cards were issued in 1941 for the Superman bread campaign. The pledge stamps were detachable in order to paste them on the folder and receive the Junior Defense League pin. These cards are rare with the stamps still intact. Less than 25 exist. Each - **$150 $250 $450**

SUP-51

❑ **SUP-51. Bread Certificate,**
1941. Used to promote Junior Defense League of America. - **$200 $450 $700**

SUP-52

❑ **SUP-52. Cardboard Shield Badge,**
c. 1941. Rare. Badge for the promotion of Superman Bread. Worn by the grocery clerks and managers. - **$300 $750 $1500**

SUP-53

❑ **SUP-53. Bread Loaf Paper,**
c. 1941. Stroehmann's Bread. 4" tall diecut glossy paper, probably a loaf wrapper sticker listing call letters and broadcast times for "The Adventures Of Superman" radio program. -
**$150 $300 $450**

SUP-54

❑ **SUP-54. "The Adventures Of Superman" Hardcover With Dust Jacket,**
1942. Store item published by Random House. 6x9-1/4" with 216 pages of text and black and white illustrations along with four color plates. Illustrations are by Joe Shuster, story is by George Lowther.
With Wrapper - **$200 $350 $750**
Without Wrapper - **$100 $200 $300**

SUP-55

**❑ SUP-55. "Schools At War/Help Smash The Axis" Poster,**
1942. Includes text "This Program Approved And Initiated By The U. S. Treasury Department And The U.S. Office Of Education." Red, white and blue 11x17". - **$400 $900 $1500**

SUP-56 SUP-57

**❑ SUP-56. Syroco-Style 5-1/2" Figure,**
1942. Wood composition in brown with red accents on logo and red cape. Promotional item from DC Comics for Superman comic books to distributors and retailers. Lois Boring, the wife of Superman artist Wayne Boring, states that Wayne told her he designed this figure for Detective Comics. - **$1000 $3000 $4000**

**❑ SUP-57. Syroco-Style 5-1/2" Painted Figure,**
1942. Full color, made of cellulose nitrate. See previous item. - **$1000 $3000 $5000**

SUP-58

**❑ SUP-58. "The Adventures Of Superman" Comic Booklet,**
c. 1942. Py-Co-Pay tooth powder. Eight-page color booklet. - **$100 $300 $700**

SUP-59

SUP-60

**❑ SUP-59. "The Adventures Of Superman/Armed Services Edition" Book,**
1942. Superman Inc. Paperback edition. - **$75 $125 $250**

**❑ SUP-60. DC Comics Portrait Sheet,**
c. 1942. Reverse shows covers of "Superman" #14, "World's Finest" #5, "Action Comics" #47. - **$75 $200 $300**

SUP-61 SUP-62

**❑ SUP-61. "Superman-Tim Club" Litho. Button,**
c. 1942. Back slogan "Member In Good Standing". - **$15 $25 $50**

**❑ SUP-62. "Superman-Tim Club" Litho. Button,**
c. 1942. - **$20 $35 $75**

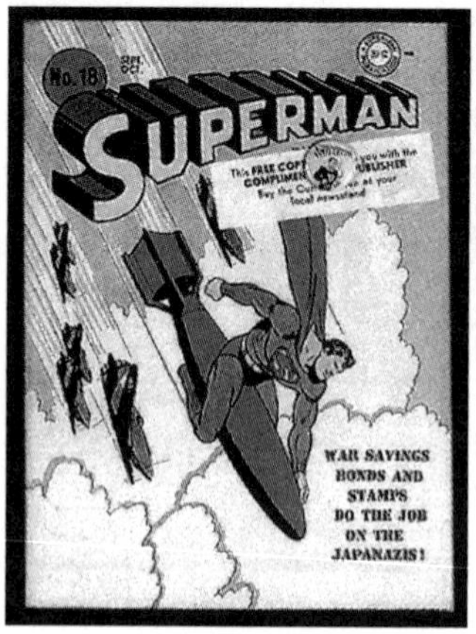


SUP-63

**❑ SUP-63. Superman #18 With Pinback on Cover,**
1942. Premium pinback (SUP-64) was pinned to *Superman* #18 to promote *Action Comics*, the other Superman title.
Comic only - **$300 $600 $1600**

SUP-64

**❑ SUP-64. Action Comics "Superman" Litho. Button,**
1942. Back inscription "Read Superman Action Comics Magazine". - **$45 $115 $175**

SUP-65

**❑ SUP-65. "Superman Overseas Cap,"**
c. 1942. Issued by Skippy Peanut Butter. 5-1/4x11" fabric promoting also station KECA. - **$1000 $2000 $3500**

SUP-66

**❑ SUP-66. "Salvage Speeds Victory" Sign,**
1942. 3 known. 18" x 12" sign has red, blue, black and yellow on white. - **$750 $1500 $3000**

SUP-67

**❑ SUP-67. "Third War Loan" Card,**
1943. Rare. 11" x 11". - **$750 $1500 $2500**

SUP-68

❑ **SUP-68. Decoder Folder,**
1943. Scarce. Similar to one used in club kit. Pictures comics on the reverse. Given away at theaters. - **$100 $200 $350**

SUP-69

❑ **SUP-69. Superman-Tim Birthday Postcards,**
1943. Various designs. Each - **$25 $65 $95**

SUP-70

❑ **SUP-70. "Superman Special Edition U.S. Navy" Comic Book,**
1944. Similar to Superman Comic Book #33 but with alterations to the cover plus additional contents. - **$100 $250 $500**

SUP-71

❑ **SUP-71. "Superman Transfers" Pack,**
1944. Detective Comics. Store packet containing "A Whole Flock Of Honest-To-Goodness" water transfer pictures. - **$100 $250 $500**

SUP-72

❑ **SUP-72. "Superman's Christmas Adventure" Comic Book,**
1944. Various stores. Example photo shows cover and first page. - **$125 $450 $1000**

SUP-73

SUP-74

❑ **SUP-73. "Superman's Christmas Play Book" Comic Book,**
1944. Various stores. Candy cane and Superman cover. - **$100 $400 $900**

❑ **SUP-74. "Sincerely, Superman" Charity Reply Postcard,**
1944. Response card for March of Dimes contribution. - **$100 $200 $400**

SUP-75

❑ **SUP-75. "Superman-Tim Club" Felt Patch,**
1945. Various stores. Six different known. Each - **$250 $750 $1500**

SUP-76

❑ **SUP-76. Superman/Tim "Franco Club" Patch,**
1946. "Franco" is likely name of boys' clothing store. - **$400 $800 $1200**

SUP-77

❑ **SUP-77. Superman Glow-In-The-Dark Picture,**
c. 1945. Probable store item, at least four different known. Each - **$100 $200 $300**

SUP-78

❑ **SUP-78. Metal Hood Ornament,**
c. 1946. Store item by L. W. Lee Mfg. Co.
6-1/2" Chrome Finish - **$1300 $2600 $5000**
4-1/2" Chrome Or Gold Finish -
**$1400 $3100 $6000**

SUP-79

❑ **SUP-79. "Superman-Tim Press Card",**
c. 1946. Opens to 9" to hold 12 poster stamps.
No Stamps - **$50 $120 $200**
Each Stamp Add $10

SUP-80

SUP-81

❑ **SUP-80. Pep Calendar Sign,**
1946. - **$100 $300 $500**

❑ **SUP-81. Grocer's Calendar Card,**
1947. Kellogg's Pep. Very colorful 4-1/2x9-1/2" monthly card urging stock and display of cereal featuring Superman endorsement. Pictured example is for September. - **$500 $1000 $1500**

SUP-82

❑ **SUP-82. Kellogg's Pep Box Back,**
1947. #3 of at least 12. Text below story reads: For further exciting Adventures of Superman, read the backs of other Pep packages and follow the Superman radio program on the Mutual Network. Each Cut Panel - **$20 $60 $80**

SUP-83

SUP-84

❑ **SUP-83. Sterling Silver Full-Dimensional Charm,**
1947. Del Weston. Only 1-1/8" tall with red enamel painted cape. - **$100 $220 $450**

❑ **SUP-84. "Superman-Tim Club Membership Card",**
1947. Various clothing stores. - **$30 $75 $100**

SUP-85

❑ **SUP-85. Magic Record Set,**
1947. With color folder that holds records. - **$50 $100 $125**

SUP-86

SUP-87

❑ **SUP-86. "Superman-Tim" Gummed Album Stamp,**
May 1947. Various participating stores. Issued monthly 1947-1950 to mount in club magazine. Each - **$25 $60 $100**

❑ **SUP-87. Australian Newspaper Superman Club Stickpin,**
1947. The Argus. 7/8" brass luster disk has embossed image of Superman in red along with newspaper name while below is a green panel surrounding inscription "Superman Club." - **$100 $250 $550**

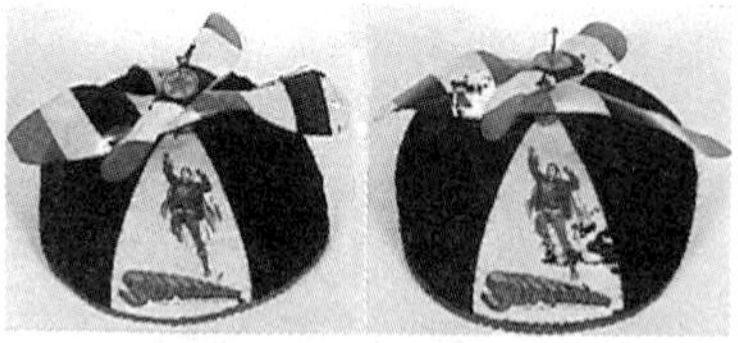
SUP-88

❑ **SUP-88. "Superman" Felt Beanie With Plastic Propellers,**
1948. Apparent store item with copyright of Nat'l Comics Pub. Inc. 7" diameter with alternating felt and leatherette panels plus metal rod at top holding three thin plastic propellers with small plastic star disk. Photo example is missing one propeller. - **$800 $1600 $2800**

SUP-89

❑ **SUP-89. "Radio Quiz Master Games With Model Microphone" With Mailer Envelope,**
1948. National Comics. Superman name on envelope and game but no picture. Includes punch-out cardboard microphone.
Mailer - **$10 $35 $60**
Game - **$30 $100 $180**

SUP-90

❑ **SUP-90. DC Comics Picture,**
1948. Back pictures comic book covers. - **$50 $125 $175**

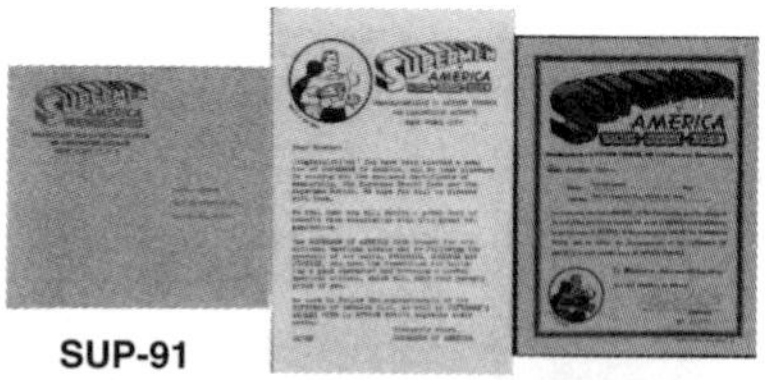
SUP-91

❑ **SUP-91. Membership Kit,**
1948. DC Comics. Includes envelope, letter, certificate, code folder, cello. button.
Complete With Envelope - **$150 $225 $400**
Letter - **$20 $40 $60**
Certificate - **$60 $80 $120**
Code Folder - **$20 $30 $60**
Button - **$20 $35 $60**

SUP-92

❑ **SUP-92. "Gilbert Hall Of Science" Catalogue,**
1948. A. C. Gilbert Co. - **$40 $100 $150**

SUP-93

❑ **SUP-93. "Superman-Tim Store" Birthday Postcard,**
1948. - **$25 $50 $100**

SUP-94

❑ **SUP-94. "Superman" Enameled Brass Shield,**
1949. Fo-Lee Gum Corp., Philadelphia. Reverse has two brass tabs to fold rather than bar pin. - **$1000 $2600 $5500**

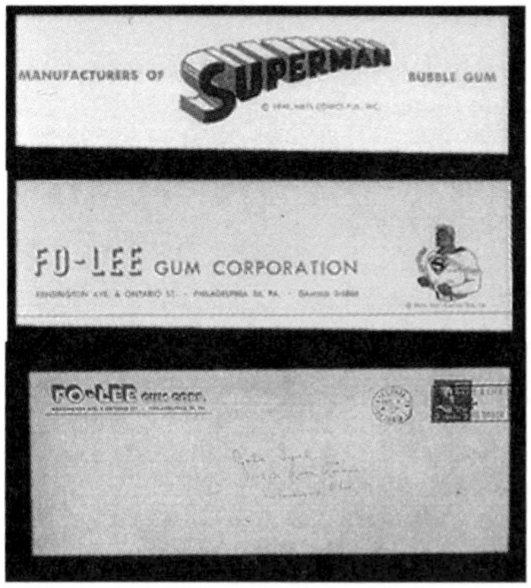

SUP-95

❑ **SUP-95. "Superman Bubble Gum" Maker's Stationery With Envelope,**
1949. Fo-Lee Gum Corp., Philadelphia. Stationery letterhead pictures Superman, bottom margin includes his name.
Envelope - **$50 $100 $200**
Stationery - **$75 $130 $300**

SUP-96

❑ **SUP-96. "Kellogg's Pep Real Photos" 22x32" Poster,**
1949. Folder that opens from 11x16" picturing movie and sports stars miniature photos offered individually as box inserts and in enlarged size as mail premiums. Superman image is pictured in two details. - **$200 $400 $600**

SUP-97

❑ **SUP-97. Superman Book Cover,**
1949. Nat'l Comics Pub. Inc. Distributed by Institute For American Democracy, Inc. 12x18" black on tan paper with text calling negative talk about religion, race or national origin "Un-American." - **$75 $150 $250**

SUP-98

❑ **SUP-98. Sunny Boy Cereal Code Premium,**
1940s. Scarce. Canadian issue. - **$100 $300 $600**

SUP-99

❑ **SUP-99. Comic Book Rack Promo Photo,**
1940s. Central Wire Frame Co. 5-1/2x8-1/2" showing example books for Superman, King Comics, Feature Comics, Whiz Comics, Target Comics. - **$35 $65 $100**

SUP-100

❑ **SUP-100. Superman-Tim Bracelet,**
1940s. Scarce. - **$350 $800 $1500**

SUP-101

SUP-102

❑ **SUP-101. "Superman-Tim" Magazine,**
1940s. One of two examples shown. Issued monthly August 1942-May 1950. See next item for prices.

❑ **SUP-102. "Superman-Tim Magazine,**
1940s. Issued monthly August 1942-May 1950.
First Issue - **$200 $800 $1500**
Typical Other Issues - **$40 $150 $300**

SUP-103

❑ **SUP-103. War Savings Bond Poster,**
1940s. 12-1/2"x19-1/2". **$3500 $9000 $18000**

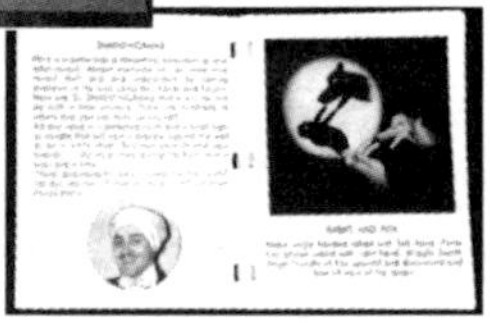

SUP-104

❑ **SUP-104. Superman-Tim Shadow-Grams Booklet,**
Late 1940s. Giveaway book pictures 30 shadow puppets by the master of illusion Prince Hara. - **$150 $325 $500**

SUP-105

❑ **SUP-105. Metal Figural Pin,**
c. 1940s. Probable store item. 1-3/4" tall with painted features in fleshtone with small black and red accents and with traditional red and blue outfit. No markings. - **$100 $250 $500**

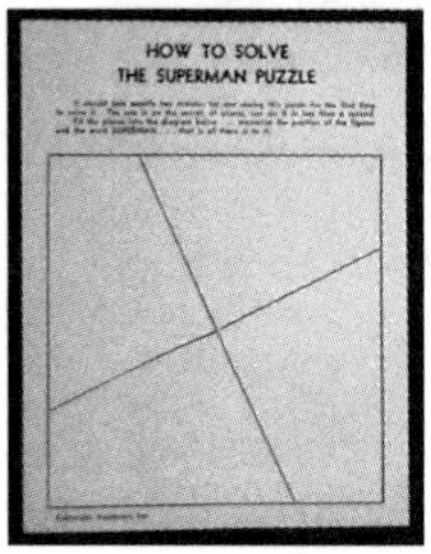

SUP-106

❑ **SUP-106. "Superman Magic Square Puzzle" Salesman's Sample Premium,**
1940s. Made by "Stunts! Inc." with blank area on envelope captioned "Imprint Here." Contains four cut puzzle pieces printed on both sides along with 5x6-1/4" diagram showing how to solve the puzzle by forming a square. Gordon Gold Archives. - **$600 $1200 $2400**

SUP-107

❑ **SUP-107. "Superman" Zippered Leather Billfold,**
1940s. Store item by Pioneer. -
**$75 $175 $300**

SUP-108

❑ **SUP-108. "Supermen Of Canada" Felt Patch,**
1940s. Issuer unknown. 3-1/2" diameter blue on white. - **$400 $800 $1500**

SUP-109

❑ **SUP-109. Superman-Tim Club Card,**
1940s. Red, white and blue with Secret Code chart on reverse. - **$30 $55 $100**

SUP-110

SUP-111

❑ **SUP-110. Superman-Tim Celluloid Pin,**
1940s. - **$500 $1000 $1600**

❑ **SUP-111. Superman-Tim "Press Card",**
1940s. Reverse blocks for 12 code stamps.
Card - **$75 $125 $225**
Each Stamp Mounted - **$5 $8 $12**

SUP-112

❑ **SUP-112. Superman-Tim Silvered Brass Store Ring,**
1940s. Depicts Superman flying above initials "S T". 25 reported known: 2 in Good grade, 15 in Very Good, 5 in Fine, 2 in Very Fine and 1 in Near Mint. Good - **$500**
Fine - **$2000**
Very Fine - **$4000**

SUP-113

❑ **SUP-113. Kellogg's "Superman Crusader" Silvered Brass Ring,**
1940s. - **$65 $150 $225**

SUP-114

SUP-115

❑ **SUP-114. "Superman-Tim" Felt Pennant,**
1940s. Scarce. Various clothing stores. Seen in yellow or red. Each - **$250 $600 $1000**

❑ **SUP-115. Superman-Tim "Redback" Currency Bills,**
1940s. Each - **$5 $8 $15**

SUP-116

❑ **SUP-116. "Superman-Tim Club" Bat Toy,**
1940s. Various participating stores imprinted on back. Diecut masonite with litho. paper art from set that included rubber darts to strike at. - **$50 $150 $250**

SUP-117

❑ **SUP-117. "Superman-Tim Club" Bat Toy,**
1940s. Various participating department stores imprinted on back. Diecut masonite with litho. paper design. - **$50 $150 $250**

SUP-118

❑ **SUP-118. Superman Belt in Box,**
1940s. Belt by Pioneer has metal circular buckle with Superman on front and graphics on leather strap. Boxed - **$100 $200 $300**
Belt and Buckle - **$75 $100 $200**
Buckle Only - **$35 $65 $100**

SUP-119

❑ **SUP-119. Superman Pep Box,**
1940s. Promotes Pep comic character pinbacks. - **$150 $350 $450**

SUP-120

SUP-121

❑ **SUP-120. "Supermen Of America" Color Variety Cello. Button,**
1940s. DC Comics. Pictures him in white shirt with red/yellow chest symbol, rare variety from DC files, apparently for test purposes. - **$200 $500 $800**

❑ **SUP-121. "Supermen Of America" Club Cello. Button,**
1940s. Scarce 7/8" size in full color. - **$150 $300 $500**

SUP-122

❑ **SUP-122. "Atom Man vs. Superman" 6' Movie Standee,**
1950. Columbia serial. - **$3000 $9000 $18000**

SUP-123

❑ **SUP-123. One-Sheet,**
1950. Promotes *Atom Man vs. Superman* serial. - **$600 $900 $1500**

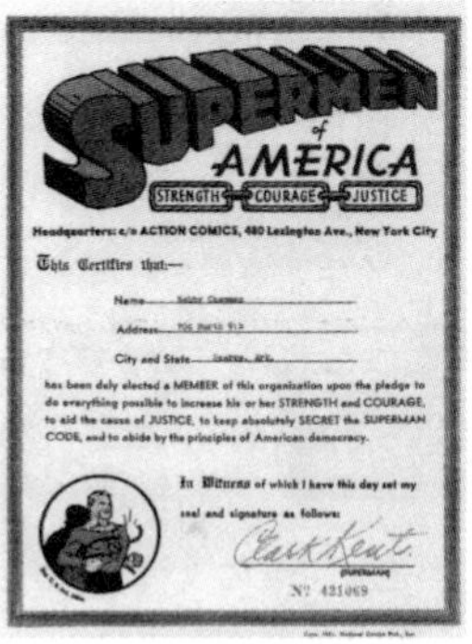


SUP-124

❑ **SUP-124 Superman Certificate,**
1951. - **$60 $80 $120**

SUP-126

SUP-125

❑ **SUP-125. Superman TV Guide,**
September 25, 1953. Featured George Reeves on the cover as Clark Kent and Superman. Inside was a story about the popular TV show. - **$250 $500 $750**

❑ **SUP-126. "Superman Muscle Building Club" Litho. Button,**
1954. Store item. Came with child's exercise set. - **$40 $100 $165**

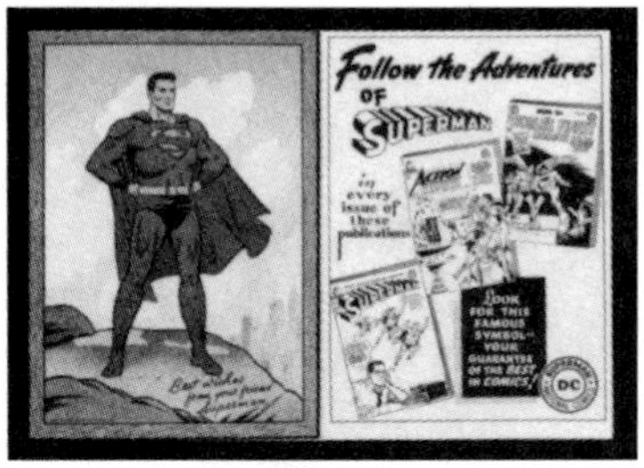


SUP-127

❑ **SUP-127. "Superman" Premium Picture,**
1954. Issued by National Comics Publications. 4-7/8x6-7/8". - **$50 $125 $200**

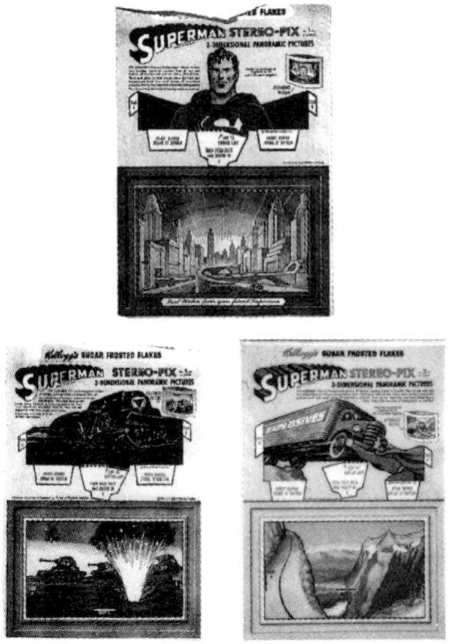


SUP-128

❑ **SUP-128. Kellogg's Stereo-Pix Box Back,**
1954. Sugar Frosted Flakes. Backs #1, #2, and #3 from series of 3-D assembly panels.
Uncut Box Back - **$30 $60 $100**

(FRONT) SUP-129 (BACK)

❑ **SUP-129. Kellogg's Sugar Smacks Cereal Box with Comic Book Offer,**
1955. Rare classic 1950's box which promotes free Superman comics inside the box. The above flat sold for $5,000 in 2001. Comic books shown as **SUP 130, 131, 132.**

SUP-130

❑ **SUP-130. "The Superman Time Capsule" Comic Book,**
1955. Kellogg's Sugar Smacks. From set of three. Art by Win Mortimer. - **$50 $150 $300**

SUP-131

❑ **SUP-131. "Duel In Space" Comic Book,**
1955. Kellogg's Sugar Smacks. From set of three. - **$50 $150 $300**

SUP-132

❑ **SUP-132. "The Supershow Of Metropolis" Comic Booklet,**
1955. Kellogg's Sugar Smacks. From set of three. - **$50 $150 $300**

SUP-133

❑ **SUP-133. Sales Promotion Folder,**
1955. National Comics Publications Inc. 8-3/4x11-3/4" four-page glossy stiff paper folder with Superman appearing on three pages along with list of "12 Top Manufacturers" of Superman merchandise. Gordon Gold Archives. -
**$250 $500 $900**

SUP-134

❑ **SUP-134. Kellogg's "Flying Superman" Toy Offer Box,**
1955. Complete Box - **$125 $375 $650**

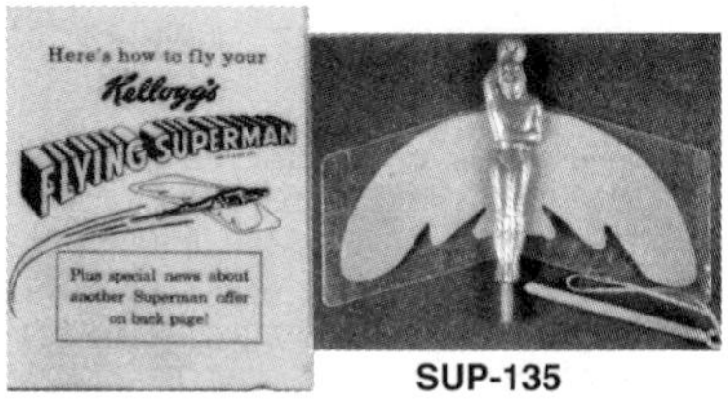


SUP-135

❑ **SUP-135. Kellogg's "Flying Superman" Thin Plastic Toy With Instruction Leaflet,**
1955. Fragile premium flown by rubber band.
Instructions - **$50 $100 $125**
Figure And Plastic Stick - **$125 $200 $400**

SUP-136

❑ **SUP-136. Kellogg's Corn Flakes Cereal Box with Krypton Hydro-Jet Rocket Offer,**
1955. 12 ounce box with Norman Rockwell art on front. - **$125 $375 $650**

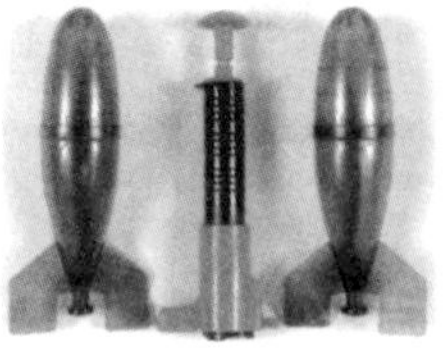

SUP-137

SUP-138

❑ **SUP-137. "Krypton Rocket" Plastic Set With Launcher,**
1955. Kellogg's. Rockets in red, blue, or green plastic with Superman logo.
Each Rocket - **$10 $40 $60**
Launcher - **$25 $75 $150**

❑ **SUP-138. Kellogg's Belt And Buckle,**
1955. Aluminum buckle with plastic belt.
Buckle - **$40 $75 $150**
With Belt - **$75 $150 $300**

SUP-139

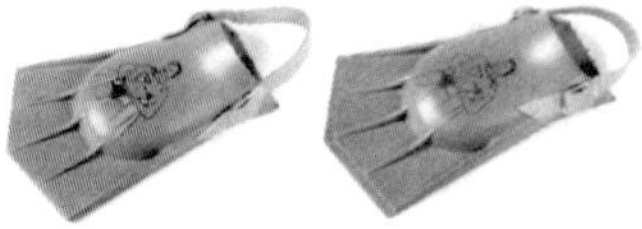

**❑ SUP-139. Superman Kiddie Paddlers in Box,**
1955. The popularity of the TV program prompted Super Swim Inc. to feature Superman on the packaging of this product. The boxes represent some of the best graphics produced in the 1950s. Each box also contained a Safety Swim Club membership card.
Complete - **$70 $165 $255**
Box - **$50 $125 $175**
Kiddie Paddlers - **$20 $40 $80**

SUP-140

**❑ SUP-140. "Sports Club" Membership Card,**
c. 1955. Store item. Came with swim fins or goggles. - **$10 $20 $35**

SUP-141

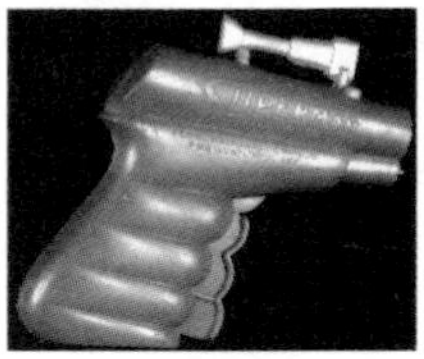

SUP-142

**❑ SUP-141. Kellogg's Dangle-Dandy Box Back,**
1955. Uncut Box Back - **$25 $50 $80**
Trimmed Out Figure - **$15 $30 $60**

**❑ SUP-142. Kellogg's "Space Satellite Launcher Set",**
1956. Came with two plastic spinners.
Complete With Spinners - **$200 $500 $750**
Box And Instructions - **$25 $50 $100**

SUP-143

**❑ SUP-143. Cereal Box With "Superman's Space Satellite Launcher" Offer,**
1956. "King Size" box advertising "Superman's Flying Space Satellite Launcher Set" for 25 cents and one box top. Gordon Gold Archives.
Used Complete - **$125 $375 $650**

SUP-144

**❑ SUP-144. Merchandiser's Guide,**
1956. Glossy black and white sheet, 10 3/4 x 13" with 4 Superman images and 3 logos for use on products. Gordon Gold Archives. - **$75 $150 $300**

SUP-145

**❑ SUP-145. "Superman Candy & Toy" Box,**
1950s. Novel Packaging Corp. From same series as SUP-149 showing Superman. Photo shows back panel "Play Card." - **$125 $250 $500**

SUP-146

**❑ SUP-146. Life-Size Cardboard Store Display,**
1956. Kellogg's Corn Flakes. Top diecut to hold jumbo display cereal box. Promotes Superman TV series.
Display Without Box - **$650 $2000 $4000**
Display Box Only - **$100 $200 $400**

SUP-147

**❑ SUP-147. "Superman" Hot Iron Transfer,**
1950s. 8-3/4x9-1/4" tissue paper sheet. Gordon Gold Archives. - **$35 $65 $100**

SUP-148

**❑ SUP-148. "Kellogg's Fun Catalog",**
1950s. - **$25 $50 $100**

SUP-149

❏ **SUP-149. "Superman Candy & Toy" Box,**
1950s. Novel Package Corp. 1x2-1/2x4" long cardboard with "Play Card" back panel. Also see SUP-145. - **$150 $300 $700**

SUP-150

❏ **SUP-150. Playsuit Mailing Folder,**
1950s. Promotion to retailers from Funtime Playwear, Inc. - **$75 $150 $250**

SUP-151

❏ **SUP-151. Fan Club Card,**
1950s. Probably came with playsuit by Funtime Playwear. - **$20 $35 $70**

SUP-152

❏ **SUP-152. George Reeves Fan Card,**
1950s. DC Comics. - **$35 $75 $150**

SUP-153

SUP-154

❏ **SUP-153. Toy Watch,**
1950s. Store item by Esco, West Germany. - **$50 $125 $250**

❏ **SUP-154. "Supermen Of America" Cello. Button,**
1950s. DC Comics. - **$20 $40 $60**

SUP-155

SUP-156

❏ **SUP-155. "Supermen Of America" Color Variety Cello. Button,**
1950s. DC Comics. Pictured in white shirt rather than blue with red/yellow chest symbol. Rare variety from DC files, apparently for test purposes. - **$200 $500 $800**

❏ **SUP-156. "Supermen Of America" Cello. Button,**
1961. National Periodical Publications. Final version of series with 1961 copyright on rim edge. Same dated bottom was used for 1965 kit. - **$15 $25 $50**

SUP-157

SUP-158

❏ **SUP-157. "Initiative Award" Poster 11x14",**
c. 1963. Independent News Co. Inc. given to comic book retailers. - **$15 $30 $50**

❏ **SUP-158. DC Publisher Response Letter To Fan Letter,** 1964. National Periodical Publications Inc. Mentions upcoming Superboy television program and 80-page Giant DC Annuals. - **$20 $35 $60**

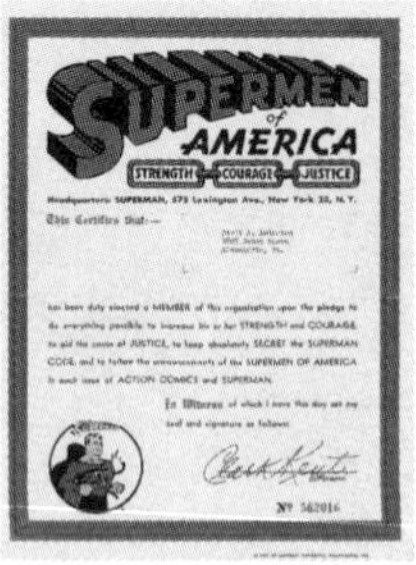


SUP-159

❏ **SUP-159. Superman Membership Certificate,**
1965. Last year for the Club. May be the rarest of all varieties of Superman Certificates since their beginning in 1939. Lack of participation in the Club was probably due to the strong market for Marvel Heroes which diverted interest from the DC Heroes. - **$175 $300 $425**

SUP-160

SUP-161

SUP-162

❏ **SUP-160. Superman Club 3-1/2" Cello. Button With Retail Box,**
1966. Store item. Box originally held quantity of buttons. Button - **$5 $10 $25**
Empty Box - **$25 $50 $100**

❏ **SUP-161. Superman Litho. Button,**
1966. N.P.P. Inc. Vending machine issue, set of eight. Each - **$10 $15 $30**

❏ **SUP-162. "New Adventures Of Superman" Gummed Paper Sticker,**
1966. CBS-TV. For introduction of Saturday morning animated series beginning September 10. Unused - **$10 $20 $40**

SUP-163

❏ **SUP-163. "Superman Golden Records" Boxed Set,**
1966. N.P.P. Inc. Includes comic book, LP record, iron-on patch, membership card with secret code, Supermen Of America litho. button. Complete - **$25 $65 $150**

SUP-164

**SUP-164. Superman Pennant,**
1966. 29" long. - **$75 $150 $250**

SUP-165

SUP-166

❑ **SUP-165. "Superman" Rare Flicker Ring,**
c. 1966. Issuer unknown. Has tiny copyright symbol and word "Eppy." Gold plastic base holds flicker with yellow background showing standing figure of Superman and flying image of him with his name below. - **$200 $400 $600**

❑ **SUP-166. Eating Set,**
1966. Knife and fork, store bought.
On Card - **$50 $75 $150**
Each Utensil Loose - **$5 $10 $15**

SUP-167

**SUP-167. Superman Plastic Identification Label,**
1960s. These were logo ads attached to comic book racks in the early '60s.
Each - **$50 $75 $125**

SUP-168

SUP-169

❑ **SUP-168. "All Star Dairy Foods" Plastic Truck Bank,**
1960s. - **$35 $75 $125**

❑ **SUP-169. Vending Machine Header Card,**
c. 1971. Includes Marvel and DC characters in form of magnet, sticker, rubber figures and Wonder Woman/Diana Prince flicker picture. - **$50 $100 $175**

SUP-170

❑ **SUP-170. Record,**
1972. Coca-Cola premium. - **$15 $35 $75**

SUP-171

❑ **SUP-171. "Original Radio Broadcast" Vol. 1 Record Album,**
1974. Kellogg's Corn Flakes. Issued as set of four.
Each - **$5 $30 $50**

SUP-172

❑ **SUP-172. Superman 1 ounce Silver Ingot,**
1974. Ingot proof. Copyright National Periodical Publications. - **$30 $50 $75**

SUP-173

❑ **SUP-173. Kellogg's Corn Flakes Cereal Box - 12 oz.,**
1976. Offers record album. Superman appears on front and back of box - **$40 $100 $175**

SUP-174

❑ **SUP-174. Post Sugar Crisp Cereal Box - 12 oz.,**
1975. Offers mini comic books. Superman appears on front; Superman, Batman, Robin, and Wonder Woman on back of box -
**$40 $100 $175**

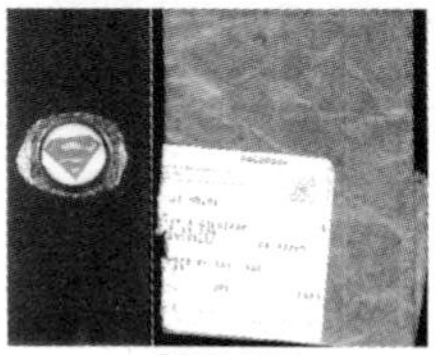
SUP-175

SUP-176

❑ **SUP-175. Nestle's Domed Ring With Mailer,**
1976. Near Mint With Mailer - **$65**
Ring Only - **$20 $40 $60**

❑ **SUP-176. "I Saw Superman" 3-1/2" Cello. Button,**
1976. Issued for Albright-Knox Art Gallery exhibit. - **$15 $30 $60**

SUP-177

SUP-178

❑ **SUP-177. Movie Sheet Music,**
1978. "Can You Read My Mind?" love theme. - **$15 $30 $45**

❑ **SUP-178. Drake's Trading Cards 23x32" Store Sign,**
1978. - **$15 $30 $50**

SUP-179

❑ **SUP-179. "Super Heroes Fun Book And Check List",**
1978. Various bread companies. Check list for sticker set. See next item. - **$15 $30 $50**

SUP-180

SUP-181

❑ **SUP-180. Super Hero Stickers,**
1978. Various bread companies. Set of 30. See SUP-166. Each Unused - **$1 $2 $3**

❑ **SUP-181. "Superbank" 3-1/2" Cello. Button,**
1970s. Garden State National Bank, probably others. - **$15 $25 $45**

SUP-182

❑ **SUP-182. Post Honey-Comb Cereal Box,**
1970s. Superman appears on front; offers Superman poster - setof 4 on back of box - **$50 $100 $175**

SUP-183

❑ **SUP-183. "Superman Peanut Butter" 7x11" Paper Store Sign,**
1981. Includes pad of t-shirt order forms. - **$25 $40 $60**

SUP-184

❑ **SUP-184. Super Powers Standee,**
1984. 1st standee to promote Superboy. - **$100 $225 $350**

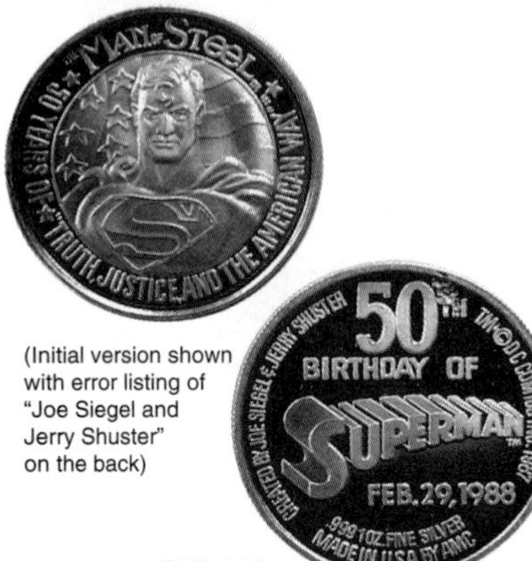


(Initial version shown with error listing of "Joe Siegel and Jerry Shuster" on the back)

SUP-185

❑ **SUP-185. Superman 50th Birthday Coin,**
1988. From a series devoted to different cartoon characters. When the coin was initially struck, the first names of Superman creators Jerry Siegel and Joe Shuster had been reversed. The error was fixed and the coin was struck properly.
Silver 1 oz. round with error - **$50 $75**
Silver 1 oz. round with correct names - **$15 $25**

SUP-186

❑ **SUP-186. "Supergirl" Motion Picture Soundtrack Album,**
1984. - **$10 $20 $35**

SUP-187

SUP-188

❑ **SUP-187. Super Powers Clark Kent Mail-In Action Figure,**
1986. Available only by mail with five proof-of-purchase seals from Super Powers figures.
Figure - $15 $30 $60
Generic Mailer Box - **$5 $10 $20**

❑ **SUP-188. Kryptonite Ring,**
1990. Toy Biz. Came packaged with Superman action figure. - **$10 $20 $30**

SUP-189

❑ **SUP-189. Superman Resin Figure,**
1993. Limited to 6,100. Shown many times on the "Seinfeld" TV show, causing great demand in the secondary market. Boxed - **$475**

SUP-190

❑ **SUP-190. Superman Statue,**
1993. By Ron Lee, limited to 750. Comes with tag. Statue and base are 12" high. - **$150**

SUP-191

❑ **SUP-191. Reign of the Supermen Watch,**
1993. Limited to 15,000. With instructions, insert and watch. Complete - **$150**

SUP-192

SUP-193

❑ **SUP-192. Syroco-Style Limited Edition Figure,**
1995. 4" tall, 250 made. Mint - **$75**

❑ **SUP-193. Superman Paper Tablecloth,**
1996. 54" x 84". Promotes animated TV show. - **$2 $4 $10**

(FRONT OF BOX)

(OPENED BOX)

SUP-194

❑ **SUP-194. "The History of Superman" Action Figure Collection,**
1996. Three action figures from different eras, in colorful display box. Boxed - **$120**

SUP-195

SUP-196

❑ **SUP-195. "I Hate Superman" Hardback Children's Book,**
1996. Unusual presentation. - **$5 $10 $20**

❑ **SUP-196. Superman Costume Kit in Box,**
1996. - **$5 $10 $20**

SUP-197

❑ **SUP-197. Burger King Standee,**
1997. Six foot tall standee promoting cartoon TV show. - **$50 $75 $125**

SUP-198

❑ **SUP-198. Hallmark Resin Figure,**
1997. Golden Age style. Limited edition of 1,450. Boxed - **$125**

SUP-199

SUP-200

❑ **SUP-199. Hallmark Resin Figure,**
1997. Figure is flying over the Daily Planet. Great example of Superman with long hair. Boxed - **$90**

❑ **SUP-200. Bean Bag Figure,**
1998. Warner Bros. store exclusive. - **$8**

SUP-201

❑ **SUP-201. Kingdom Come Resin Statue,**
1998. Sculpted by Alex Ross. Silver color. Limited to 5,000. Boxed - **$250**

SUP-202

SUP-203

❑ **SUP-202. Superman Radio,**
1999. Clock has the art deco style of the 1930s. Boxed. - **$100**

❑ **SUP-203. Resin Figure,**
1999. Warner Bros. store exclusive. - **$85**

SUP-204

❑ **SUP-204. Stamp Collecting Promotional Standee,**
1998. U.S. Postal Service. About five feet tall titled "Celebrate The Century/Collect A Century In Stamps." - **$125**

SUP-205

❑ **SUP-205. Stamp Collecting Standee With Brochures,**
1998. U.S. Postal Service. 15-1/2" tall standee designed to hold giveaway brochures.
Standee - **$85**
Brochure - **$1 $2 $5**

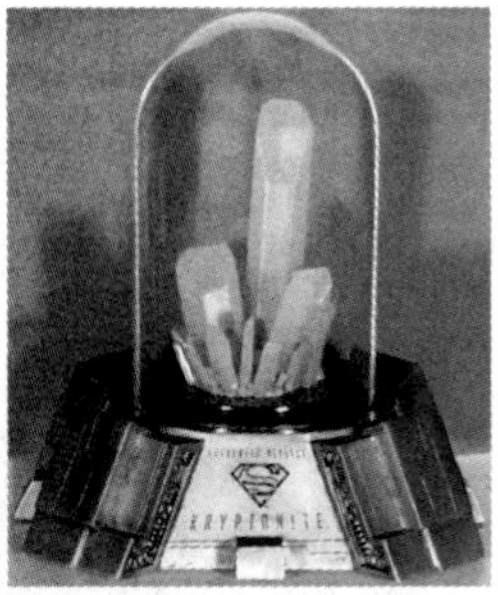

SUP-206

❑ **SUP-206. Kryptonite Prop,**
1999. Limited edition of 1,100. Mounted on base. Kryptonite glows green when the glass dome is lifted. - **$175**

SUP-207

❑ **SUP-207. Promo Sign for Burger King Toys,**
1990s. Shows 5 premium toys based on the animated series, given away at Burger King .-
**$10 $25 $60**

SUP-208

❑ **SUP-208. Lunch Box with Thermos,**
2000. - **$20**

SUP-209 (2nd view with lights on)

❑ **SUP-209. "Bottle City of Kandor" Prop,**
2000. Has mini-buildings inside that light up. Limited to 1,435. - **$200**

SUP-210

❑ **SUP-210. Superman Classic Rocket,**
2001. Plastic rocket holding baby Kal-El. In a graphic-filled box - **$20**

SUP-211

❑ **SUP-211. Superman Tin Carousel,**
2001. Superman circling the Daily Planet. In a graphic-filled box - **$25**

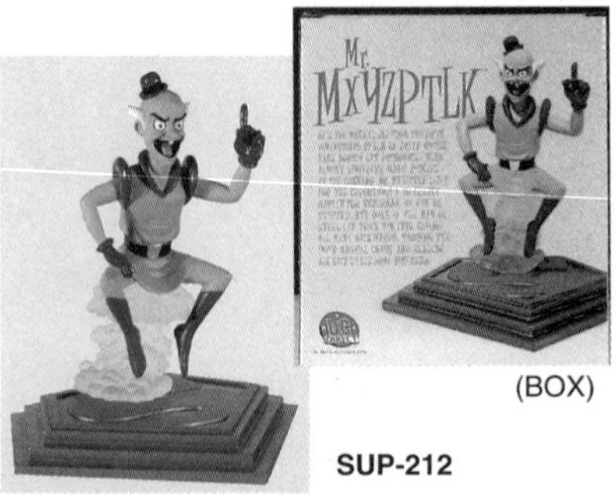


(BOX)

SUP-212

❑ **SUP-212. Mr. Mxyzptlk Statue,**
2001. The imp's cloud pedestal is resting on a Superman S-shield base. - **$50**

SUP-213

❑ **SUP-213. Supergirl's Arrival Statue,**
2001. Edition of 2,000. Resin re-creation of cover image from Action Comics #252, the first appearance of Supergirl. - **$195**

SUP-214

SUP-215

❑ **SUP-214. "Krypto" Soft Toy,**
2001. DC Direct. Plush figure of the Superdog. Boxed. - **$25**

❑ **SUP-215. Kingdom Come Full Color Statue,**
2001. Fully painted version of SUP-201. - **$150**

## Syroco Figures

**Adolph Holstein, a skilled European immigrant woodcarver, founded the Syracuse Ornamental Company in 1890, specializing in making hand-carved decorative components for the furniture industry. Demand for the company's intricate products soon exceeded production capacity, so Holstein developed a process to mass-produce replicas of the carvings by compressing a mixture of wood flour, waxes, and resins into molds. In the 1930s and 1940s the company changed its name to Syroco Inc. and manufactured a line of novelty items--cigarette boxes, pipe racks, plates, serving trays, and figurines of popular entertainers, comic strip characters and public personalities, for sale in roadside souvenir shops. Syroco Inc. continues in business to this day, but production of the figures was discontinued by about 1950.**

**Syroco products of greatest interest to premium collectors are the 1941 Great American Series of historic personalities (about 6" tall) and the 1944 series of King Features Syndicate comic strip characters (about 4-5" tall). There are 24 known characters. Pillsbury Mills, Inc. offered the following 12**

as premiums in 1944 each for 25¢ and a Pillsbury Enriched Farina box top: Alexander, Annie Rooney, Archie, Barney Google, Blondie, Cookie, Dagwood, Jiggs, Little King, Popeye, Tim Tyler, Wimpy.

Similar wood composition figures are pictured in sections on Captain Marvel, Pinocchio and Superman. While these are also generically known as "syroco" figures, the 1945 Captain Marvel figure and the Pinocchio character figures are attributed to Multi Products, Chicago. This inscription appears on the Pinocchio figures.

In 2000, Dark Horse Comics initiated its Syroco-like Classic Comic Characters line with Krazy Kat. Each of the figures depicts a famous character, thus far exclusively newspaper comic strips such as Li'l Abner, Blondie, and Terry and the Pirates. Each of the pieces is numbered, packaged in attractive custom tins, and comes with a descriptive booklet and a pin-back. The figures are sculpted by Craig Yoe of Yoe Studios.

Collectors have been highly receptive to the program, which Dark Horse indicates they envision as a ten-year plan, with one notable exception: The figures were initially offered editions of 550, but after the phenomenal early success the edition size was increased to 750. It was increased again 950, and then finally reduced to 600 copies, beginning with Felix the Cat.

SYR-1 SYR-2 SYR-3 SYR-4

❑ **SYR-1. Ben Franklin,**
1941. Great American Series. - **$40 $100 $225**

❑ **SYR-2. George Washington,**
1941. Great American Series. - **$40 $100 $225**

❑ **SYR-3. Will Rogers,**
1941. Great American Series. - **$50 $120 $275**

❑ **SYR-4. Buffalo Bill,**
1941.Great American series. - **$75 $150 $300**

SYR-5 SYR-6 SYR-7 SYR-8

❑ **SYR-5. "Stuyvesant,"**
1941. Great American series. - **$40 $100 $225**

❑ **SYR-6. Alexander Syroco Figure,**
1944. This and the following 23 figures comprise a set of 24 King Features Syndicate characters, all from 1944. - **$20 $40 $100**

❑ **SYR-7. Annie Rooney,**
1944. - **$30 $100 $150**

❑ **SYR-8. Archie In Uniform,**
1944. - **$30 $100 $150**

SYR-9 SYR-10 SYR-11 SYR-12

❑ **SYR-9. Barney Google In Navy Uniform,**
1944. - **$25 $75 $125**

❑ **SYR-10. Blondie,**
1944. Scarce. - **$60 $150 $375**

❑ **SYR-11. Captain,**
1944. - **$30 $100 $150**

❑ **SYR-12. Casper,**
1944. - **$20 $85 $125**

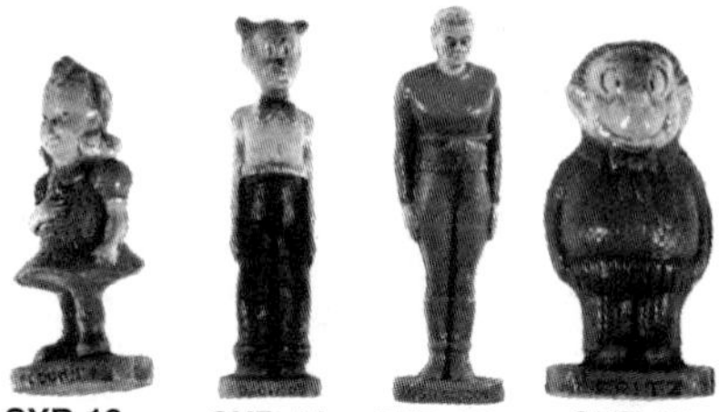


SYR-13 SYR-14 SYR-15 SYR-16

❑ **SYR-13. Cookie,**
1944. - **$20 $40 $100**

❑ **SYR-14. Dagwood,**
1944. - **$30 $100 $150**

❑ **SYR-15. Flash Gordon,**
1944. Scarce. - **$200 $600 $1200**

❑ **SYR-16. Fritz,**
1944. - **$25 $75 $125**

SYR-17 SYR-18 SYR-19

❑ **SYR-17. Hans,**
1944. - **$25 $75 $125**

❑ **SYR-18. Jiggs,**
1944. - **$40 $85 $125**

❑ **SYR-19. Little King,**
1944. - **$40 $150 $250**

SYR-20 SYR-21 SYR-22

❑ **SYR-20. Maggie,**
1944. Scarce. - **$125 $200 $400**

❑ **SYR-21. Rosie,**
1944. Rare. - **$200 $400 $525**

❑ **SYR-22. Olive Oyl,**
1944. - **$125 $200 $400**

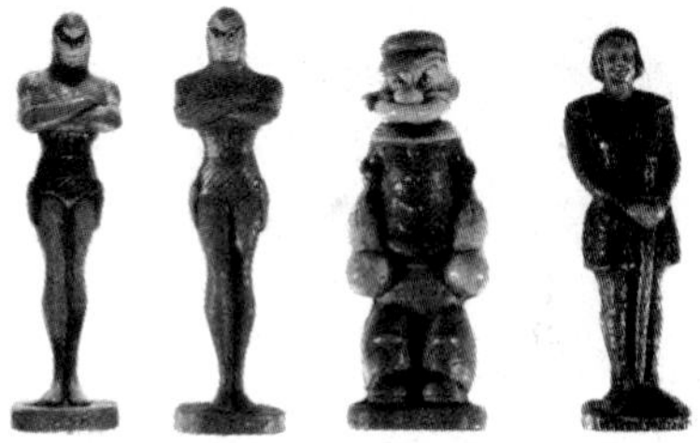

SYR-23 SYR-24 SYR-25

❑ **SYR-23. Phantom,**
1944. Scarce. A Cream of Wheat premium available for 10¢.
Brown Costume - **$300 $800 $1800**
Purple Costume - **$250 $600 $1350**

❑ **SYR-24. Popeye,**
1944. - $50 **$120 $225**

❑ **SYR-25. Prince Valiant,**
1944. - **$75 $200 $450**

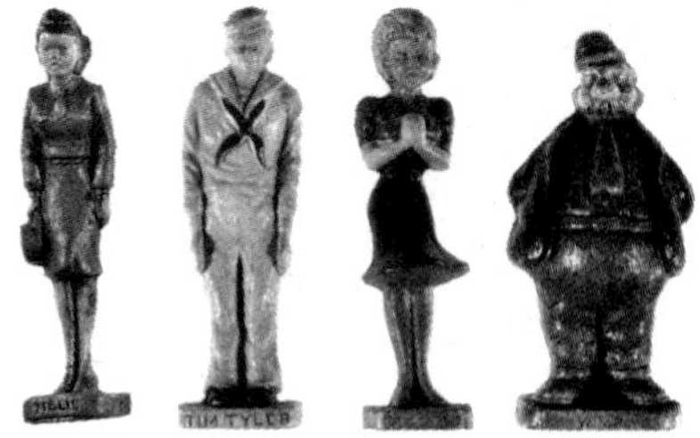


SYR-26 SYR-27 SYR-28 SYR-29

❑ **SYR-26. Tillie In Uniform,**
1944. Scarce. - **$200 $350 $525**

❑ **SYR-27. Tim Tyler In Navy Uniform,**
1944. - **$20 $75 $125**

❑ **SYR-28. Toots,**
1944. Scarce. - **$200 $350 $525**

❑ **SYR-29. Wimpy,**
1944. - **$40 $80 $150**

SYR-30

❑ **SYR-30. Comic Character Statuettes Ad,**
1945. Pillsbury Farina Cereal. Sunday comic section ad offering figures of Dagwood, Cookie, Alexander, Blondie, Popeye, Wimpy, Tim Tyler, Archie, Jiggs, Little King, Annie Rooney, Barney Google. - **$35 $75 $150**

SYR-31

SYR-32

SYR-33

❑ **SYR-31. Krazy Kat Figure,**
2000. From Dark Horse. Limited to 550. - **$75**

❑ **SYR-32. Ignatz Figure,**
2000. From Dark Horse. Limited to 750. - **$50**

❑ **SYR-33. Prince Valiant Figure,**
2000. From Dark Horse. Limited to 550. - **$75**

SYR-34

SYR-35

SYR-36

❑ **SYR-34. Popeye Figure,**
2000. From Dark Horse. Limited to 550. - **$75**

❑ **SYR-35. Olive Oyl Figure,**
2000. From Dark Horse. Limited to 750. - **$60**

❑ **SYR-36. The Phantom Figure,**
2000. From Dark Horse. Limited to 750. - **$60**

SYR-37

SYR-38

SYR-39

❑ **SYR-37. Mandrake Figure,**
2000. From Dark Horse. Limited to 750. - **$50**

❑ **SYR-38. Li'l Abner Figure,**
2000. From Dark Horse. Limited to 950. - **$50**

❑ **SYR-39. Daisy Mae Figure,**
2000. From Dark Horse. Limited to 950. - **$50**

SYR-40

SYR-41

SYR-42

❑ **SYR-40. Dick Tracy Figure,**
2000. From Dark Horse. Limited to 950. - **$50**

❑ **SYR-41. Beetle Bailey Figure,**
2000. From Dark Horse. Limited to 950. - **$50**

❑ **SYR-42. Sarge Figure,**
2000. From Dark Horse. Limited to 950. - **$50**

SYR-43

SYR-44

SYR-45

❑ **SYR-43. Little Orphan Annie Figure,**
2000. From Dark Horse. Limited to 950. - **$50**

❑ **SYR-44. Flash Gordon Figure,**
2000. From Dark Horse. Limited to 950. - **$50**

❑ **SYR-45. Terry (and the Pirates) Figure,**
2000. From Dark Horse. Limited to 950. - **$50**

SYR-46

SYR-47

❑ **SYR-46. Dragon Lady Figure,**
2000. From Dark Horse. Limited to 950. - **$50**

❑ **SYR-47. Blondie and Dagwood Figures,**
2001. From Dark Horse. Limited to 600.
Each - **$60**

SYR-48

SYR-49

SYR-50

❑ **SYR-48. Fearless Fosdick Figure,**
2001. From Dark Horse. Limited to 950. - **$50**

❑ **SYR-49. Felix the Cat Figure,**
2001. From Dark Horse. Limited to 600. - **$75**

❑ **SYR-50. Smokey Stover Figure,**
2001. From Dark Horse. Limited to 600. - **$50**

SYR-51

SYR-52

SYR-53

❑ **SYR-51. Bluto Figure,**
2001. From Dark Horse. Limited to 600. - **$50**

❑ **SYR-52. Nancy Figure,**
2001. From Dark Horse. Sculpted by Yoe Studio. Limited to 600. - **$50**

❑ **SYR-53. Sluggo Figure,**
2001. From Dark Horse. Sculpted by Yoe Studio. Limited to 600. - **$50**

SYR-54

SYR-55

SYR-56

❑ **SYR-54. Albert Figure,**
2001. From Dark Horse. Limited. - **$50**

❑ **SYR-55. Alley Oop Figure,**
2002. From Dark Horse. Limited. - **$50**

❑ **SYR-56. Little Nemo Figure,**
2002. From Dark Horse. Limited. - **$50**

## Tales of the Texas Rangers

**With stories said to be based on the files of the Texas Rangers between the 1830s and the 1950s, this series aired on NBC radio from 1950 to 1952, with Joel McCrea as Ranger Jace Pearson. A television version was broadcast from 1955 to 1957 on CBS and from 1957 to 1959 on ABC, with Willard Parker and Harry Lauter as the leading lawmen. General Mills sponsored the radio series and Tootsie Rolls candy joined the cereal company in sponsoring the TV version. *Texas Ranger* and *Jace Pearson* comic books appeared in the 1950s. Items may be copyrighted Screen Gems Inc.**

TXS-1

❑ **TXS-1. Membership Kit,**
c. 1955. Curtiss Candy.
Box Or Card - **$10 $25 $35**
Silvered Metal Badge - **$20 $45 $60**
Ring - **$25 $50 $90**

TXS-2

TXS-3

❑ **TXS-2. Candy Display Card,**
c. 1955. Curtiss Candy Co. - **$25 $50 $85**

❑ **TXS-3. Jace Pearson Fan Photo,**
c. 1955. - **$8 $12 $20**

TXS-4

TXS-5

❑ **TXS-4. "Baby Ruth" Candy Bar Box,**
c. 1955. Curtiss Candy Company. Pictured and named are stars Jace Pearson and Clay Morgan. 8x9-1/2x2" deep originally holding 24 bars. - **$25 $70 $100**

❑ **TXS-5. RCA 78 RPM Record With Sleeve,**
c. 1955. Store item. 10x10". - **$20 $40 $80**

## Tarzan

**Between 1911 and 1944 Edgar Rice Burroughs (1875-1950) wrote some 26 Tarzan novels, creating a world of adventure where justice and fair play triumph in the hands of an English orphan raised by apes in the African jungle. One of the most popular fictional characters of all time, Tarzan has thrilled readers and viewers throughout the world in print, in comics, in feature films and chapter plays, on radio, and on television. Tarzan's first appearance was in *All Story Magazine* in October, 1912.**

**The first Tarzan movie was the 1918 silent *Tarzan of the Apes*, starring Elmo Lincoln, but the best remembered apeman is undoubtedly Olympic hero Johnny Weissmuller (1904-1984), who originated the abiding victory cry and made a dozen Tarzan films between 1932 and 1948. Notable among the many other cinema Tarzans: Buster Crabbe (1933), Lex Barker (1949-1953), and Gordon Scott (1955-1966). Including the silents and chapter plays, there have been more than 40 Lord of the Jungle movies.**

**The *Tarzan* comic strip, distributed by Metropolitan Newspaper Service, debuted in 1929 and lasted until 1973. A Sunday version from United Feature Syndicate appeared in 1931. There have been numerous *Tarzan* comic books, with reprints of the strips starting in 1929 and original material starting in the late 1940s.**

**There have been two series of *Tarzan* radio programs, the first (1932-1936) syndicated by WOR in New York with the Signal Oil Company as a sponsor until 1934, the second (1952-1953) on CBS, sponsored by Post Toasties. Premiums from the 1930s series include membership material in a Tarzan Club and a number of items from such sponsors as Foulds macaroni, Kolynos toothpaste, Bursley coffee, Hormel foods, and the dairy industry.**

**A live-action TV adaptation starring Ron Ely was aired on NBC in 1966-1968 and rerun on CBS in 1969, and animated versions from Filmation studios were broadcast on CBS from 1976 to 1981. The University of Louisville in Kentucky maintains an extensive Burroughs Memorial Collection of printed material and memorabilia.**

**Dark Horse Comics published *Tarzan: The Lost Adventure*, a previously unreleased Burrough's manuscript completed by author Joe R. Lansdale, in both serialized and novel formats. They have also produced a comic book mini-series, *Tarzan vs. Predator at the Earth's Core*, as well as an ongoing *Tarzan* comic. Most recently, Tarzan was seen in a weekly syndicated TV show, *Tarzan: The Epic Adventures,* running for 21 episodes from 1996-1997.**

TRZ-1

TRZ-2

❑ **TRZ-1. Movie Premium,**
1918. Photo of Tarzan actor Elmo Lincoln. - **$25 $65 $125**

❑ **TRZ-2. "The Son Of Tarzan/The Mystic Order Of The Jungle" Early Serial Cello. Button,**
1920. National Film Corp. 1-1/4" real photo partially tinted in yellow with surrounding pale blue rim. Tarzan was played by P. Dempsey Tabler. Also issued as a 2-1/4" pocket mirror.
Each - **$500 $1500 $2500**

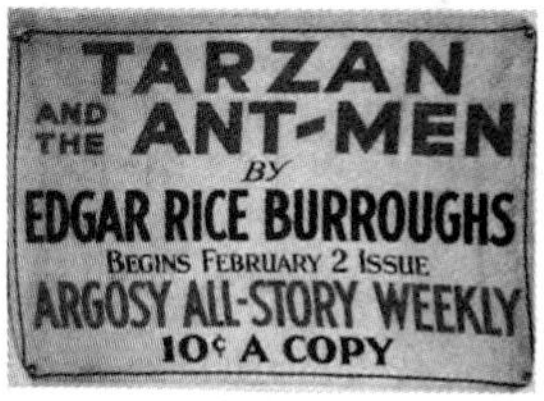


TRZ-3

❑ **TRZ-3. Tarzan Story Fabric Store Banner,**
c. 1920. Argosy All-Story Weekly. 29x40" banner with metal grommets at each corner and typed in red and blue on white background. Burroughs' first story appeared in this publication in 1912. - **$750 $1500 $2500**

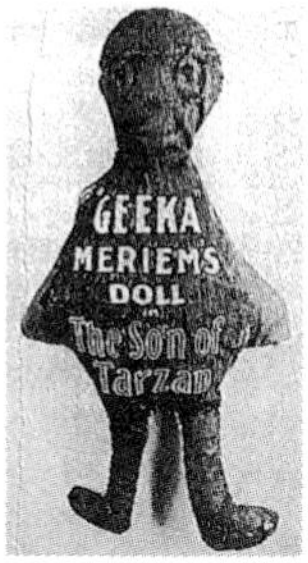


TRZ-4

TRZ-5

❑ **TRZ-4. "The Son Of Tarzan" Movie Serial Pattern Doll,**
1920. National Film Corporation. "Geeka" doll is pictured in the campaign book for the serial but an actual example is unknown to us. Doll was to be cut out, stuffed with cotton or sawdust and then sewn into shape. - **$750 $1500 $2500**

❑ **TRZ-5. "Elmo Lincoln In Adventures Of Tarzan" Movie Serial Paper Mask,**
1921. Great Western Producing Co. 15-chapter serial imprinted on back for local theaters. - **$150 $350 $600**

TRZ-6

❑ **TRZ-6. "The Tarzan Twins" Book,**
1927. Store item. - **$60 $250 $450**

TRZ-7

TRZ-8

❑ **TRZ-7. "Tarzan The Mighty Universal's Gigantic Chapter Play" Cello. Button,**
1928. Universal. Probably issued one button per serial chapter for a total of 15 but examples known depict coiled snake, giraffe, lion.
Each - **$50 $100 $150**

❑ **TRZ-8. "Tarzan The Tiger" Movie Serial Cello. Button,**
1929. Universal. Probably 15 in set, each depicting an animal or bird. Known buttons are: Armadillo, Bird on Branch, Crocodile, Dodo, Giraffe, Lion, Monkey, Ram, Tiger, and Zebra.
Each - **$45 $90 $140**

TRZ-9

❑ **TRZ-9. "The Illustrated Tarzan Book No. 1" Hardcover First Edition,**
1929. Store item by Grosset & Dunlap. 7x8-3/4" with 80 pages reprinting the first daily strips by Hal Foster.
With Dust Jacket - **$100 $350 $600**
Without Dust Jacket - **$40 $150 $250**

TRZ-10

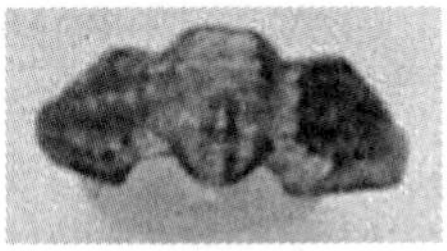

TRZ-11

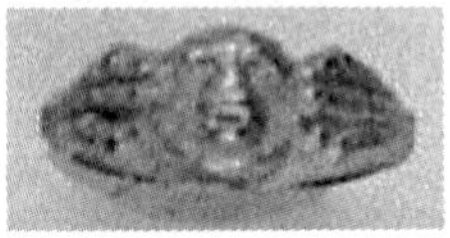

TRZ-12

❑ **TRZ-10. Cardboard Bookmark,**
c. 1920s. Grosset & Dunlap, publisher of Edgar Rice Burroughs novels. - **$15 $25 $50**

❑ **TRZ-11. Tarzan Face Ring,**
1920s-1930s. Issuer unknown. Non-adjustable white metal ring with silvery metallic finish. - **$125 $275 $425**

❑ **TRZ-12. Kon-Gah The Ape Ring,**
1920s-1930s. A mate to the Tarzan ring. Non-adjustable white metal with silvery metallic luster. - **$100 $225 $375**

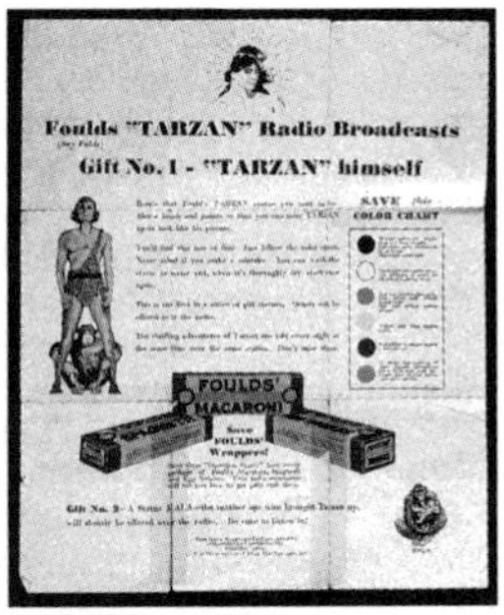


TRZ-13

❑ **TRZ-13. Gift #1 And #2 Promo,**
1932. Foulds Products. Radio premium printed on unstapled paper. - **$100 $150 $225**

TRZ-14

❑ **TRZ-14. Promo**
1932. Toddy Malted Drink. Premium gift sheet for statues. Printed on unstapled paper. - **$100 $150 $225**

TRZ-15

❑ **TRZ-15. Plaster Statues,**
1932. Made by Gem Clay Forming Co. for distribution by both sponsors of the Tarzan radio show and others. The basic set of ten includes Tarzan with Cheetah, Kala holding the baby Tarzan, Jane Porter, Numa the lion, Sheeta the panther, Witch doctor, Pirate sitting on treasure chest, Lt. D'Arnot, Cannibal Warrior, and three monkeys (counted as a single item). See next item.
Set Painted - **$200 $400 $600**
Set Unpainted - **$250 $600 $800**

TRZ-16

❑ **TRZ-16. Fould's Background For Plaster Statues,**
1932. Scarce. - **$1500 $3000 $5000**
Offer Blank - **$20 $40 $60**

TRZ-17

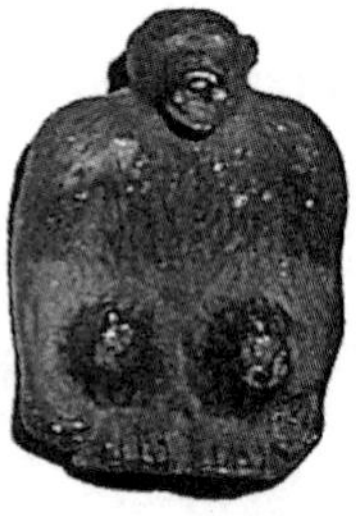

TRZ-18

❑ **TRZ-17. Plaster Statue Set Additions Order Coupons,**
c. 1932. Foulds' Macaroni, Spaghetti or Egg Noodles. Box insert papers for "Leopard Of Opar" and "Princess La, High Priestess Of Opar", later additions to the earlier set of ten.
Each Order Form - **$50 $125 $200**
Each Statue Painted - **$75 $125 $250**
Each Statue Unpainted - **$100 $200 $300**

❑ **TRZ-18. Kerchak Plaster Figure,**
c. 1932. A later addition to the earlier set of ten. Kerchak was the ape leader when Tarzan was adopted into the ape tribe. Later, Tarzan killed Kerchak to become King of the Apes. In addition to Foulds, these figures were given away by The Adlerika Co., Collin County Mill & Elevator, Grainger Bros., Heinz Foods, and Toddy, Inc.
Painted - **$75 $125 $250**
Unpainted - **$100 $200 $300**

**TRZ-19**

❑ **TRZ-19. "Signal Tarzan Club" Member Card,**
1932. Signal gasoline. Qualifies recipient as "Charter Member Of The Tribe Of Tarzan". - **$100 $300 $400**

**TRZ-20**

**TRZ-21**

❑ **TRZ-20. "Signal Tarzan Club" Cello. Button,**
1932. Signal Oil Co. - **$30 $65 $110**

❑ **TRZ-21. "Tarzan Of The Apes" Jigsaw Puzzle,**
c. 1932. Screen Book Magazine.
In Envelope, Sealed - **$650**
Near Mint With Envelope - **$450**
Loose - **$25 $80 $175**

**TRZ-22**

**TRZ-23**

❑ **TRZ-22. "Tarzan The Fearless" 9x14" Cardboard Sign,**
1933. Rare. - **$75 $150 $300**

❑ **TRZ-23. "Tarzan The Fearless" Cardboard Sign,**
1933. Two-sided, shows photo of Buster Crabbe as Tarzan. - **$250 $500 $750**

**TRZ-24**

❑ **TRZ-24. Northern Paper Mills Color Poster For Masks,**
1933. - **$300 $850 $1500**

**TRZ-25**

❑ **TRZ-25. Paper Masks,**
1933. Northern Paper Mills. Set of three picturing Tarzan, Numa the Lion, Akut the Ape.
Tarzan - **$50 $120 $200**
Each Animal - **$30 $80 $150**

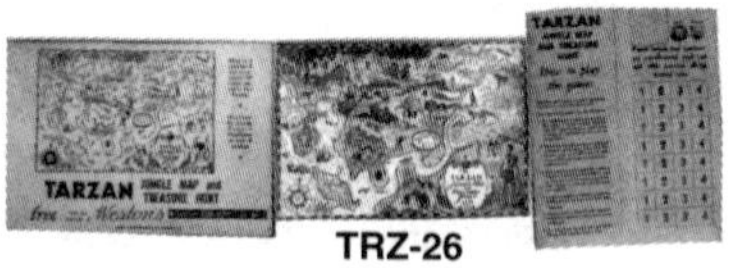

**TRZ-26**

❑ **TRZ-26. "Tarzan Jungle Map And Treasure Hunt" Game With Mailer Envelope,**
1933. Rare. Canadian version has "W" above logo for Weston's English Quality Biscuits. U.S. version has "T" above logo. Australian version has sponsor name of Pepsodent Toothpaste. Playing pieces printed on envelope back, except Australian version, which has separate sheet with perforated pieces.
Canada Near Mint In Mailer - **$750**
Canada Map Only - **$100 $300 $550**
U.S. Near Mint In Mailer - **$850**
U.S. Map Only - **$125 $400 $700**
Australia Near Mint In Mailer - **$650**
Australia Map Only - **$115 $225 $500**
Australia Parts Sheet Only - **$25 $50 $100**

**TRZ-27**

❑ **TRZ-27. Paper Film,**
1933. Scarce. Hormel Soups. - **$100 $350 $500**

**TRZ-28**

❑ **TRZ-28. Tarzan Cup Magic Picture Cutouts,**
1933. Rare. Complete Uncut - **$250 $500 $750**

**TRZ-29**

❑ **TRZ-29. "Notebook Filler" Paper Wrapper Band,**
c. 1933. Store item. Reverse pictures Mickey Mouse Ingersoll watch offered for saved bands. - **$10 $25 $50**

**TRZ-30**

**TRZ-31**

❑ **TRZ-30. Johnny Weissmuller Picture,**
1933. Rare. Wheaties premium for Jack Armstrong program. - **$50 $175 $250**

❑ **TRZ-31. Johnny Weissmuller Sport Kings Gum Card #21,**
1933. From same year that Wheaties issued his photo as Tarzan for the 1st Jack Armstrong premium. - **$150 $450 $1500**

**TRZ-32**

❑ **TRZ-32. Advertising Flip Booklet,**
c. 1933. Thom McAn shoes. Pages flipped one direction show Tarzan spearing an ape, reverse page sequence shows grateful child getting Thom McAn shoes from dad. - **$50 $125 $200**

TRZ-33

❑ **TRZ-33. "Tarzan 'Rescue'" Puzzle Game,**
1934. Store item by Einson-Freeman Co. - **$150 $350 $650**

TRZ-34

❑ **TRZ-34. "Tarzan and His Mate" Movie Theater Window Card,**
1934. Untrimmed card measures 21 1/2" x 14". Features Johnny Weissmuller and Maureen O'Sullivan. Scarce. - **$400 $850 $1200**

TRZ-35

❑ **TRZ-35. "Drink More Milk" Bracelet,**
1934. Rare. Radio premium. Also issued inscribed "Tarzan Radio Club/Bursley Coffee." Each - **$800 $2000 $3200**

TRZ-36

TRZ-37

❑ **TRZ-36. Tarzan of the Air Promo with Mailer,**
1934. - **$50 $125 $180**

❑ **TRZ-37. "The Tarzan Twins" Big Little Book,**
1934 (1st printing). Rare. - **$100 $300 $500**
1935 version is the same except for date listed. - **$35 $100 $175**

TRZ-38

❑ **TRZ-38. "Tarzan Of The Apes" Book,**
1935. Various advertisers. - **$50 $125 $275**

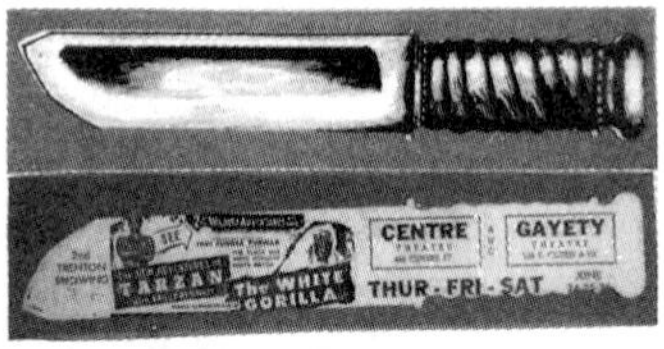


TRZ-39

❑ **TRZ-39. "The New Adventures Of Tarzan" Cardboard Knife Movie Give-Away,**
c. 1935. Various theaters. - **$20 $50 $100**

TRZ-40

TRZ-41

❑ **TRZ-40. "Tarzan" Ice Cream Premium Booklet,**
1935. 3 1/2" x 4" soft cover book. Pictured is a Whitman File copy. Rare. - **$100 $325 $775**

❑ **TRZ-41. "Tarzan And His Jungle Friends" Booklet #1,**
1936. Tarzan Ice Cream Cup. First of listed series of 12. - **$100 $175 $350**

TRZ-42

TRZ-43

❑ **TRZ-42. "Tarzan" Big Big Book,**
1936. Whitman #4056. - **$75 $150 $350**

❑ **TRZ-43. "Tarzan Escapes" Premium Card,**
1936. Promo for the MGM movie. The task was to identify animals and receive free tickets to movies. Rare. - **$175 $225 $275**

TRZ-44

TRZ-45

❑ **TRZ-44. "Tarzan Escapes" Big Little Book #1182,**
1936. Johnny Weissmuller photo cover. Has scenes from the MGM movie. - **$20 $80 $165**

❑ **TRZ-45. "The Beasts of Tarzan" Big Little Book #1410,**
1937. 432 pages. - **$20 $65 $135**

TRZ-46

❑ **TRZ-46. "Tarzan: Gift Picture No. 1 Of A Series",**
1937. "Tarzan Appears Each Month In Tip Top Comics Magazine Copyright 1937 By United Feature Syndicate Inc." Art by Rex Maxon. - **$100 $225 $325**

TRZ-47

❑ **TRZ-47. "Tarzan And A Daring Rescue" Booklet,**
1938. Pan-Am gasoline and motor oils. Title page offers bow and arrow set plus school bag premiums. - **$75 $225 $375**

TRZ-48

❑ **TRZ-48. "Tip Top Comics" 11x14" Store Sign,**
c. 1938. - **$125 $250 $350**

TRZ-49

TRZ-50

❑ **TRZ-49. "Tarzan Series Tablet/ Composition Books/Notebooks/Fillers" Salesman's Sample Portfolio,**
1939. Issued by Big Chief. 10x12-1/4". Has tipped-in fold-out poster, various tipped-in tablet covers. - **$700 $1250 $2500**

❑ **TRZ-50. Clans Manual,**
1939. Tarzan Clans of America, Tarzana, California. Complete procedures and rituals for organizing and running a clan. -
**$75 $150 $300**

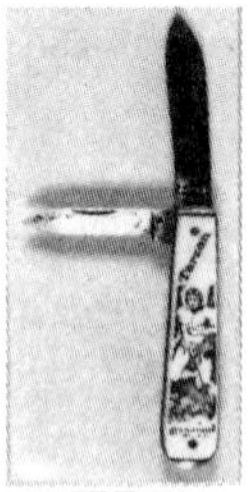
TRZ-51

❑ **TRZ-51. Celluloid Pocketknife With Steel Blades,**
1930s. Store item made by Imperial. There are four different knives with the same image:
Single Blade - **$100 $300 $750**
Two Blades - **$125 $350 $800**
Three Blades - **$150 $400 $1000**
Boy Scout Version with Multiple Utilitarian Blades - **$175 $500 $1200**

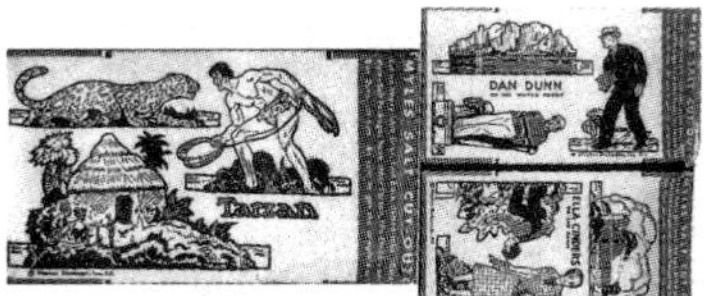

TRZ-52

❑ **TRZ-52. "Myles Salt Cut-Outs" Boxes,**
1930s. Panels picture Tarzan, Dan Dunn, Ella Cinders. Tarzan Box Uncut - **$50 $125 $200**
Others Uncut Each - **$20 $35 $60**

TRZ-53

❑ **TRZ-53. Safety Club Cards,**
1930s. Various radio sponsors. Two cards printed each side, originally joined by perforation. One card to order badge, one card of safety pledges. Pair - **$100 $350 $500**

TRZ-54 TRZ-55

❑ **TRZ-54. School Paper Supplies 10x14" Cardboard Store Sign,**
1930s. Birmingham Paper Co. -
**$100 $225 $350**

❑ **TRZ-55. "Tarzan Cups" 12x18" Paper Store Poster,**
1930s. - **$100 $250 $375**

TRZ-56

TRZ-57

❑ **TRZ-56. "Tarzan Ice Cream Cup" 10x20" Paper Store Poster,**
1930s. - **$100 $250 $400**

❑ **TRZ-57. "Tarzan And The Crystal Vault Of Isis" Card #18,**
1930s. Schutter-Johnson Candies. Card title "The Electric Menace" from numbered set of 50. Each - **$10 $30 $60**

TRZ-58

❑ **TRZ-58. "Tarzan Cups" 6x19" Paper Store Poster,**
1930s. Offers premiums for lids saved. -
**$85 $175 $350**

TRZ-59 TRZ-60

❑ **TRZ-59. "Tarzan Te Puro" Tea Canister With Lid,**
1930s. Litho. tin Spanish issue from Uruguay. -
**$35 $60 $100**

❑ **TRZ-60. "Tarzan" Club Cello. Button Variety,**
1930s. 1-1/4" size but no sponsor name and without words "Safety Club." See TRZ-65 and TRZ-66. - **$125 $300 $600**

TRZ-61

❑ **TRZ-61. "The Son Of Tarzan" Movie Serial Cardboard Ad Blotter,**
1930s. Scarce. - **$50 $150 $250**

TRZ-62

TRZ-63

❑ **TRZ-62. "Tarzan Radio Club/Bursley Coffees" Enameled Brass Badge,**
1930s. Scarce. - **$300 $750 $1500**

❑ **TRZ-63. "Tarzan Radio Club/Drink More Milk" Enameled Brass Badge,**
1930s. Scarce. - **$300 $750 $1500**

TRZ-64

TRZ-65

TRZ-66

❑ **TRZ-64. "Vita Hearts" Litho. Club Button,**
1930s. - **$275 $700 $1400**

❑ **TRZ-65. "Tarzan Safety Club" Cello. Button,**
1930s. 7/8" version. See TRZ-60. - **$80 $200 $400**

❑ **TRZ-66. "Feldman's Tarzan Safety Club" Cello. Button,**
1930s. 1-1/4" version of previous button with sponsor's name. - **$125 $400 $600**

TRZ-67

TRZ-68

TRZ-69

❑ **TRZ-67. "The Nielen Tarzan Club" Member's Cello. Button,**
1930s. - **$175 $500 $850**

❑ **TRZ-68. Club Member Cello. Button,**
1930s. Gano Downs Boys & Girls Shops. - **$175 $500 $850**

❑ **TRZ-69. "Sons Of Tarzan Club" Cello. Button,**
1930s. Facsimile Johnny Weissmuller signature. Theater contest issue, match number to win prize. - **$50 $100 $200**

TRZ-70

TRZ-71

TRZ-72

❑ **TRZ-70. "Sons Of Tarzan Club" Second Variety Cello. Button,**
1930s. 1-1/4" green on yellow the same as the preceding item except without a contest serial number. - **$75 $100 $300**

❑ **TRZ-71. "Tarzan's Grip" Australian Cello. Button,**
1930s. - **$50 $125 $250**

❑ **TRZ-72. "Tarzan Club" Cello. Button,**
1930s. K.L.S. Royal Bakers. 15/16" red, white and yellow with call letters of Salt Lake City, Utah radio station and company sponsor name. Scarce. - **$500 $1500 $2500**

TRZ-73

❑ **TRZ-73. Composition Figures,**
1930s. Store item by Belgian company Durso. Two Tarzan figures and Jane are about 2-1/2" tall, elephant is 3-1/2" tall and lion is 1-1/4" tall. Group As Pictured Near Mint - **$700**

TRZ-74

❑ **TRZ-74. "Tarzan's New York Adventure" Spanish Movie Herald,**
1942. M-G-M. 3-1/2x5-1/4". - **$10 $20 $40**

TRZ-75

❑ **TRZ-75. "Tarzan And The Golden Lion" Better Little Book,**
1943. Whitman #1448. - **$20 $50 $125**

TRZ-76

TRZ-77

❑ **TRZ-76. "Tarzan and the Ant Men" Big Little Book #1444,**
1945. - **$20 $60 $135**

❑ **TRZ-77. "Tarzan Lord of the Jungle" Big Little Book #1407,**
1946. - **$15 $50 $100**

TRZ-78

❑ **TRZ-78. Big Little Book Original Cover Art,**
1949. For #1467, *Tarzan in the Land of the Giant Apes*. - **$5000**

TRZ-79

❑ **TRZ-79. "I'm A Tarzan Fan" Valentine,**
c. 1940s. Store item with no copyright or maker's name. 4-1/2" tall diecut stiff paper. - **$50 $175 $275**

TRZ-80

❑ **TRZ-80. Dell Publishing Co. Pictures,**
1950. One sheet consisting of five photos.
Near Mint In Mailer - **$150**
Loose - **$25 $50 $100**

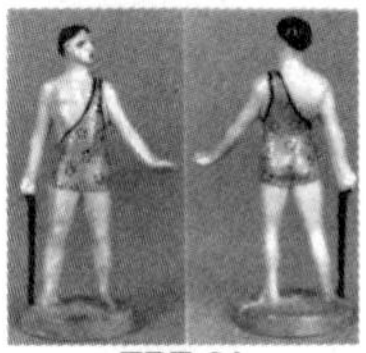

**TRZ-81**

❑ **TRZ-81. French Cello. Figure,**
1959. 2-1/2" tall marked "F Clairet". From a set of 15 figures, all marked "F. Clairet." The figures are: Tarzan, two apes holding sticks on a platform, one male lion, three female lions, tiger, adult elephant, baby elephant, black panther, zebra, ostrich, mountain goat, and kangaroo.
Tarzan - **$200 $400 $600**

**TRZ-82**

**TRZ-83**

❑ **TRZ-82. "Tarzan of the Apes" Hardcover Book with Ape-English Dictionary,**
1964. 285 pages. Tells story of Tarzan's birth and his growing up in Africa. Jesse Marsh art. - **$50 $100 $175**

❑ **TRZ-83. "Tarzan and the Lost Safari" Hardcover Book,**
1966. Adapted from the movie. - **$25 $50 $75**
1957 edition with photo/art cover featuring Gordon Scott - **$30 $60 $85**

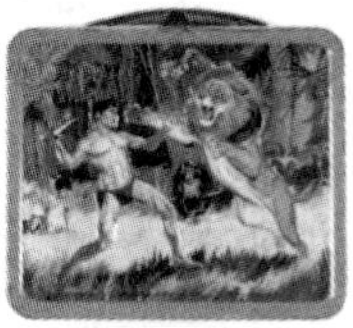

**TRZ-84**

**TRZ-85**

❑ **TRZ-84. "Tarzan" Lunch Box,**
1966. Store item by Aladdin. - **$75 $150 $250**

❑ **TRZ-85. "Tarzan/NBC" Promotional Book,**
1966. Advance information for 1966-1967 programming. - **$50 $100 $150**

**TRZ-86**

❑ **TRZ-86. P.F. Flyer Store Display,**
1960s. Cardboard 20-1/2x28". Die-cut pieces create 3-D appearance.
Standee - **$100 $250 $400**

**TRZ-87**

❑ **TRZ-87. Plastic Flicker Picture Rings,**
1960s. Set of six. Gold plastic bases.
Each - **$10 $15 $20**

**TRZ-88**

❑ **TRZ-88. "Tarzan" Model Kit,**
1974. Store item by Aurora.
Unused Near Mint - **$40**

**TRZ-89**

❑ **TRZ-89. Tarzan Resin Statue,**
1997. Last product worked on by the late Burne Hogarth. Limited to only 500.
Boxed - **$295**

## Teenage Mutant Ninja Turtles

**Donatello, Leonardo, Michaelangelo, and Raphael burst upon the scene in 1984 in issue #1 of *Teenage Mutant Ninja Turtles*. The pizza-loving sewer dwellers and their ninja master thrived not only in comic books but in a 1988 animated TV series, movies in 1990, 1991, and 1993, millions of premiums from Burger King, a concert tour sponsored by Pizza Hut, merchandising, and licensing to promote hundreds of products. After a waning of interest, a recent attempt to revitalize the characters with the addition of a female Turtle has proven moderately successful. "Cowabunga!"**

**TMT-1**

❑ **TMT-1. Fan Club Kit Ad and Coupon,**
1988. Playmates Toy Co. - **$10 $20 $30**

**TMT-2**

❑ **TMT-2. Fan Club Kit,**
1988. Playmates Toy Co. Envelope with bandanna, letter, story comic, sticker, charter member certificate with perforated membership card.
Set - **$40 $65 $90**

**TMT-3**

**TMT-4**

❑ **TMT-3. Movie Promotion 2-1/8" Cello. Button,**
1990. Mirage Studios. - **$3 $5 $10**

❑ **TMT-4. Nabisco Shreddies Canadian Cereal Box,**
1990. Box offers first four of eight "Power Rings". Complete Box - **$150**
Turtles Rings - **$5 $10 $15**
Other Character Rings - **$8 $12 $20**

TMT-5

❑ **TMT-5. Animated Television Cel,**
c. 1990. Store item sold through retailers such as K-Mart in a bag with header card or through galleries in other formats. Backgrounds are usually color laser copies. Near Mint - **$25**
Higher Values May Apply Depending On Image And Background

TMT-6

❑ **TMT-6. Nabisco Shreddies Canadian Cereal Box,**
1991. Box offers last four of eight rings.
Complete Box - **$200**
Turtles Rings - **$5 $10 $15**
Other Character Rings - **$8 $12 $20**

TMT-7

❑ **TMT-7. Technodrome Scout Vehicle,**
1998. With box. - **$20**

## Television Misc.

**Television, only an experimental and isolated technical dream through the 1930s, would likely have erupted sooner if not for the World War II years. But erupt it did in the late 1940s to present day norm of scarcely any household in the United States without at least one TV set. Early TV programming could be much more easily sponsored by a single sponsor per show. It has been estimated that an early sponsor could well finance an entire season or more for the current cost, in equal dollars, of a 30-second advertising spot during recent Super Bowl telecasts. The basic cost of TV advertising, of course, is a prior consideration to the supplemental cost of premiums; thus the noticeable lack of mail premium offers so prevalent in the radio and earliest TV eras. Premiums associated to TV characters or shows are now most likely found as part of a retail item if indeed offered at all. This book section depicts a sampling of premium collectibles from a wide variety of shows.**

TEL-1

TEL-2

❑ **TEL-1. Dumont "Small Fry Club" Cello. Button,**
1947. Dumont television network, hosted by Big Brother Bob Emory. - **$20 $35 $60**

❑ **TEL-2. Big Brother "Small Fry Marionette",**
1948. Small Fry Club. "Small Fry Girl" in box. "Big Brother Show" was on radio and converted over to TV. It was one of the first marionette TV shows. Boxed - **$50 $100 $175**

TEL-3

❑ **TEL-3. "Beany And His Pals" Cast Photo,**
1949. Tea Time Candies. 8x10" glossy black and white. - **$20 $50 $100**

TEL-4

❑ **TEL-4. "The Garry Moore Show" Cast Photo,**
1949. Shows Ken Carson, Garry Moore, Denise Lor and Durward Kirby. - **$25 $50 $75**

TEL-5

TEL-6

❑ **TEL-5. Jackie Gleason Photo Card,**
1940s. NBC TV premium. - **$20 $40 $50**

❑ **TEL-6. "Crosley's House Of Fun" Comic Booklet,**
1950. Crosley Appliances. - **$5 $10 $15**

TEL-7

TEL-8

❑ **TEL-7. Early Version Beany Hand Puppet,**
c. 1950. Sears store item. From era of KTLA-TV (Los Angeles) show "Time For Beany". - **$75 $200 $350**

❑ **TEL-8. "4 Norge TV Comic Masks" With Envelope,**
1951. Norge Appliances. Paper masks of Ed Wynn, Jack Carson, Danny Thomas, Jimmy Durante.
Unpunched In Envelope - **$30 $50 $80**

TEL-9

TEL-10

❑ **TEL-9. "Kit Carson" Tie With Clasp,**
c. 1951. 15" bolo tie with 1" brass slide clasp with TV portrayer Bill Williams portrait flanked by image of single Coca-Cola bottle. -
**$40 $80 $125**

❑ **TEL-10. "Adventures of Kit Carson" Premium Pinback,**
Early 1950s. Probably sponsored Snyder's Potato Chips. Scarce. - **$25 $75 $140**

TEL-11

TEL-12

❑ **TEL-11. "TV Guide" 8x11" Vending Rack Insert Card,**
c. 1952. Design based on Sgt. Joe Friday of Dragnet police TV series. - **$15 $30 $60**

❑ **TEL-12. Jack Webb "Dragnet" Sponsor Endorsement Sign,**
c. 1952. Fatima Cigarettes. Diecut cardboard countertop sign 16x16" with easel back. -
**$50 $150 $225**

TEL-13

❑ **TEL-13. "Beany" Boxed Hand Puppet,**
1952. Store item by Zany Toys.
Box - **$25 $50 $75**
Puppet - **$40 $75 $125**

TEL-14

❑ **TEL-14. TV Guide #3,**
1953. April 17, 1953 cover features the stars of the top 4 shows of that time. - **$50 $100 $150**

TEL-15

TEL-16

❑ **TEL-15. "Kit Carson Kerchief" 16x24" Cardboard Store Poster,**
1953. Coca-Cola. - **$25 $75 $150**

❑ **TEL-16. "Kit Carson" Fabric Kerchief,**
1953. Picturing Bill Williams, TV series star. -
**$15 $25 $50**

TEL-17

❑ **TEL-17. "See Kit Carson TV Show" Store Window Card,**
1953. Coca-Cola Co. 16x24" cardboard. -
**$25 $65 $125**

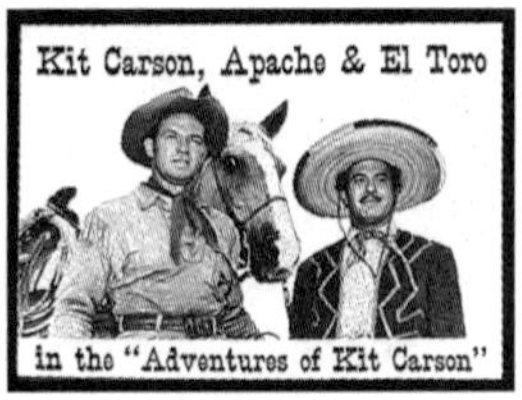

TEL-18

❑ **TEL-18. TV Promo,**
1953. Four page Coca Cola premium. Tells about Old West and Kit Carson background. Talks about design of Kit Carson Kerchief premium. Promotes TV show "Adventures of Kit Carson." - **$15 $40 $75**

TEL-19

❑ **TEL-19. Stagecoach,**
1953. Coca Cola TV premium. In mailer w/ complete instructions. - **$50 $100 $150**

TEL-20

❑ **TEL-20. "Jerry Lester 'Bean Bag' Club" Kit,**
1953. Genesee Beer & Ale. Includes membership card, button, message card. Complete -
**$10 $20 $30**

TEL-21

❑ **TEL-21. This is Your Life - Book Shaped Locket,**
1953. With coupon and ad.
Complete - **$50 $100 $175**
Locket Only - **$10 $20 $40**

TEL-22

TEL-23

❑ **TEL-22. "Rocket Ranger March" Record,**
c. 1953. Store item. From 1953-1954 CBS-TV show "Rod Brown Of The Rocket Rangers" on Columbia label. - **$10 $20 $40**

❑ **TEL-23. "The Adventures Of Ozzie And Harriet" Fan Photo,**
c. 1953. H. J. Heinz Co. Nelson family photo including sons David and Ricky for show newly sponsored by Heinz over ABC network. -
**$10 $20 $30**

TEL-24

TEL-25

TEL-26

❑ **TEL-24. Sid Caesar "Your Show of Shows" Cardboard Sign,**
1953. 10-1/2x13-1/2". - **$40 $80 $150**

❑ **TEL-25. "Groucho Marx" Fan Postcard,**
1954. Back ad for "You Bet Your Life" NBC-TV show. - **$20 $40 $65**

❑ **TEL-26. "Father Knows Best" Cast Photo Postcard,**
c. 1954. Oversized 5-1/2x7" card picturing Anderson family of TV series. - **$5 $12 $20**

TEL-27

❑ **TEL-27. "The Garry Moore Show" Ticket,**
1954. Unused ticket for CBS Studios show. - **$20 $40 $60**

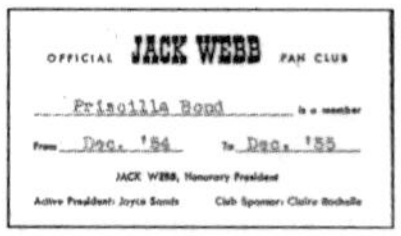


TEL-28

TEL-29

❑ **TEL-28. "Jack Webb Fan Club" Membership Card,**
1954. For star of Dragnet TV series. - **$8 $12 $20**

❑ **TEL-29. "Dragnet Code Chart" Cardboard Decoder,**
1955. Sponsor unknown. - **$10 $20 $30**

TEL-30

❑ **TEL-30. "Dragnet" Cap Gun,**
1955. Smoking gun in a decorative open box. Jack Webb picture on box. Has cut out I.D. card on back. Near Mint Boxed - **$200**
Loose - **$25 $50 $75**

TEL-31

TEL-32

❑ **TEL-31. "Dragnet" Water Gun with Refill Container,**
1955. Harder to find than regular gun. Jack Webb picture on box. Has cut out I.D. card on back. Boxed - **$125**

❑ **TEL-32. "Dragnet 714 Club" Metal Badge, Card and Case,**
1955. Store item. - **$15 $25 $50**

TEL-33

❑ **TEL-33. "Dragnet Whistle" 20x20" Cardboard Store Sign,**
1955. Kellogg's Corn Flakes.
Sign - **$50 $100 $150**
Whistle - **$1 $3 $5**

TEL-34

TEL-35

❑ **TEL-34. Sgt. Bilko Cardboard Ad Fan,**
c. 1955. Amana Refrigeration. - **$10 $20 $50**

❑ **TEL-35. "Chester A. Riley" Fan Postcard,**
c. 1955. Cast photo of "Life Of Riley" series. - **$10 $20 $35**

TEL-36

❑ **TEL-36. "Robin Hood's Band Of Merry Men" Membership Card,**
c. 1955. Johnson & Johnson. Front depicts Richard Greene and reverse has "Sherwood" pledge. - **$10 $20 $40**

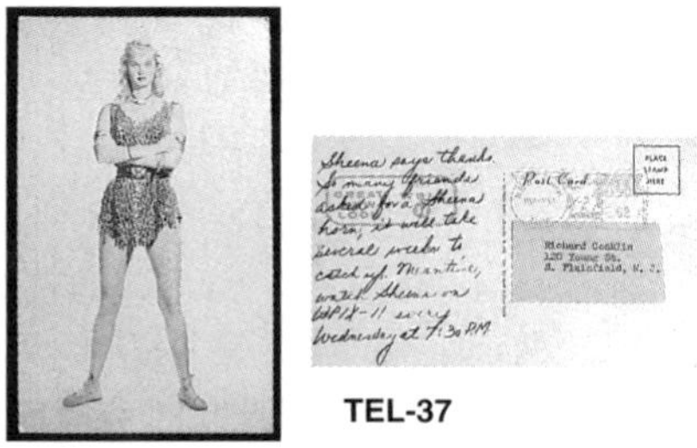

TEL-37

❑ **TEL-37. Sheena Queen Of The Jungle Postcard,**
1956. WPIX-TV, N.Y.C. Front is glossy bw picturing Irish McCalla. Reverse message says "Demand Will Delay Delivery Of The Sheena Horn Several Weeks." - **$25 $60 $95**

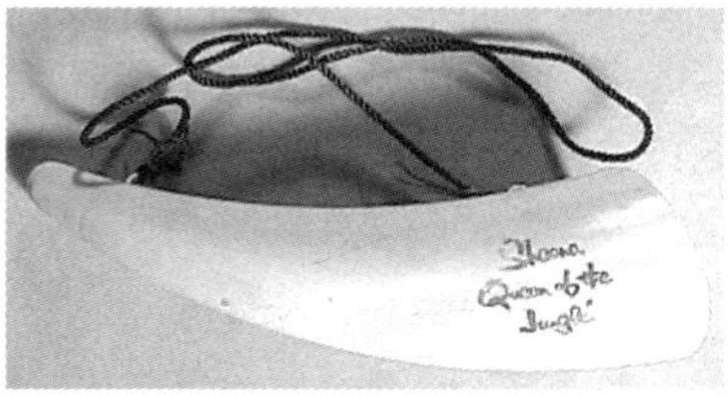

TEL-38

❑ **TEL-38. "Sheena Queen Of The Jungle" Plastic Horn With Cord,**
1956. WPIX-TV, N.Y.C. 8-1/2" long with green text on ivory plastic. - **$50 $115 $165**

TEL-39

TEL-40

❑ **TEL-39. Nelson Family Fan Photo,**
c. 1956. Pictures Ozzie, Harriet, Ricky, David with facsimile signatures. - **$10 $25 $40**

❑ **TEL-40. "'Kit Carson' Ranger" Membership Certificate,**
1956. Bar Bee meat products. 8-1/2x11" printed in black and white with gold engraving style inner border. - **$15 $30 $60**

TEL-41

❑ **TEL-41. "Win A Sgt. Bilko Money Tree" Contest Folder,**
1957. Joy liquid dishwashing soap. Contest expired October 15. - **$8 $15 $30**

TEL-42

TEL-43

❑ **TEL-42. "I'm An Eager Beaver And A U.S. Keds Kid" 3" Cello. Button,**
c. 1958. - **$30 $75 $125**

❑ **TEL-43. "The Adventures Of Ozzie & Harriet" Candy Box,**
c. 1958. Almond Joy candy bars of Peter Paul Candies. TV sponsorship also indicated for "Maverick" series. - **$35 $60 $80**

TEL-44

❑ **TEL-44. "Hawaiian Eye" Song Sheet,**
1959. Star Bob Conrad pictured. - **$15 $30 $45**

TEL-45

❑ **TEL-45. "Rinso Blue" Detergent Box Containing Paladin Trading Card,**
1959. Store item. Box is 8-3/4" tall in yellow, red, white and blue. See next item.
Near Mint Sealed - **$600**
Open - **$100 $200 $300**

TEL-46

❑ **TEL-46. Paladin Trading Card,**
1959. Rinso Blue. 2-1/4x3-5/8" black and white card which was in the product box. Unknown number in set but highest number card we know of is #22. See previous item.
Each - **$15 $30 $50**

TEL-47

TEL-48

TEL-49

❑ **TEL-47. TV Guide with "Cheyenne" Cover,**
1959. Features Clint Walker. - **$10 $20 $40**

❑ **TEL-48. "Cheyenne" Pinback,**
1950s. Australian. Very colorful. - **$20 $40 $85**

❑ **TEL-49. "Maverick" Book,**
1959. Whitman #1566; 5 1/2" x 7 3/4". Based on the Warner Bros. TV show. James Garner as Maverick pictured on the cover. 286 pages.
TV Edition. - **$10 $20 $45**

TEL-50

❑ **TEL-50. Jack Paar 12" Cardboard Standee,**
1950s. Schrafft's. - **$60 $90 $120**

TEL-51

TEL-52

❑ **TEL-51. Jack Paar Beech-Nut Gum Container,**
1950s. Held small free sample boxes. - **$30 $60 $90**

❑ **TEL-52. TV Cameraman Plastic Pull Toy,**
1950s. Kraft Foods. - **$25 $60 $100**

TEL-53

❑ **TEL-53. "RCA TV Coloring Book",**
1950s. - **$8 $15 $30**

TEL-54

TEL-55

❑ **TEL-54. "Crusader Rabbit Club" Member's Cello. Button,**
1950s. Celluloid 1-1/4" - **$25 $90 $150**
Litho. 1-1/8" - **$20 $65 $100**

❑ **TEL-55. Television Bread Loaf End Label,**
1950s. Pictured example from set depicts "Television Demonstrated" in 1927.
Each - **$8 $15 $30**

TEL-56

❑ **TEL-56. "Million Sellers" Record Album With Mary Tyler Moore Cover,**
1950s. Store item on Tops Records label. Cardboard sleeve holds 33-1/3 rpm record. - **$10 $25 $40**

TEL-57

❑ **TEL-57. "Pinky Lee Party Pack",**
1950s. Includes booklet, place mats, napkins, party hats, cardboard figures, "Pin The Hat On Pinky" poster with paper hats.
Near Mint In Envelope - **$100**

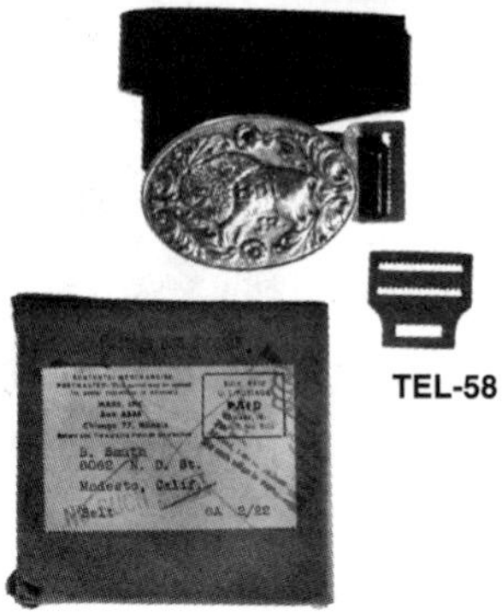

TEL-58

❑ **TEL-58. Buffalo Bill, Jr. Belt Buckle and Plastic Belt With Instructions,**
1950s. Milky Way. Near Mint Boxed - **$135**
Buckle Only - **$20 $30 $50**

TEL-59

TEL-60

❑ **TEL-59. Ding Dong School Bell,**
1950s. - **$20 $40 $75**

❑ **TEL-60. "Hollywood Off-Beat" TV Show Starring Melvyn Douglas - Dixie Cup Promo,**
1950s. - **$20 $40 $60**

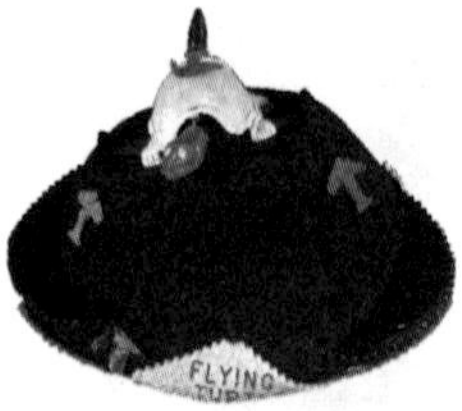

TEL-61

TEL-62

❑ **TEL-61. Flying Turtle Club Beany TV,**
1950s. - **$20 $40 $80**

❑ **TEL-62. I Led Three Lives Promo,**
1950s. Small cardboard tag. - **$20 $40 $60**

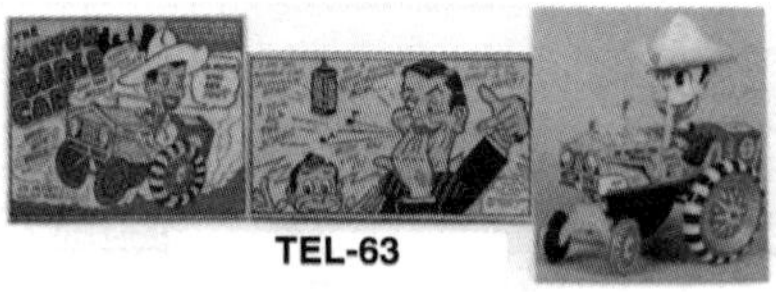

TEL-63

❑ **TEL-63. "The Milton Berle Car" Boxed Wind-Up,**
1950s. Store item by Marx. Tin litho.
Box - **$75 $125 $200**
Toy **$100 $250 $400**

TEL-64

❑ **TEL-64. "Winky Dink And You" TV Art Kit,**
1950s. Includes erasable "magic" window, crayons and erasing cloth. - **$40 $60 $125**

TEL-65

❑ **TEL-65. Nabisco Major Adams TV Sign 13x13",**
1950s. Promotes TV show, "Major Adams Trailmaster." Earlier TV program called Wagon Train. - **$50 $100 $175**

TEL-66

❑ **TEL-66. Dinah Shore Promo 2 1/2"x5",**
1950s. Chevrolet TV premium. - **$10 $25 $40**

TEL-67

❑ **TEL-67. Beat The Clock Brochure,**
1950s. Sylvania promo for TV program. 10x15". 12 pgs. of great graphics of stars. -
**$25 $50 $75**

TEL-68

❑ **TEL-68. Captain Kangaroo Puzzle Postcard,**
1950s. Kellogg's premium. 8 puzzle pieces. Prize for art drawing submitted to show. -
**$25 $50 $75**

TEL-69

TEL-70

❑ **TEL-69. "Captain Kangaroo" Cup,**
1950s. Colgate toothpaste. Figural plastic with inset flicker eyes. - **$8 $15 $30**

❑ **TEL-70. "TV Bank" Litho. Bank,**
1950s. Various companies. - **$10 $20 $30**

TEL-71

TEL-72

❑ **TEL-71. "Farfel" Ceramic Mug,**
1950s. - **$15 $25 $40**

❑ **TEL-72. "Gene London Club" 3" Cello. Button,**
1950s. Channel 10, Philadelphia TV station. -
**$5 $10 $15**

TEL-73

❑ **TEL-73. "Highway Patrol" Boxed Friction Toy,**
1950s. Store item by MS, Japan. 4x8-1/2x2-1/2" tall. Box - **$25 $50 $125**
Car - **$40 $75 $150**

TEL-74

TEL-75

❑ **TEL-74. Robin Hood Hat,**
1950s. Store bought. - **$20 $40 $80**

❑ **TEL-75. "Jackie Gleason Fan Club" Cello. Button,**
1950s. - **$20 $35 $75**

TEL-76

TEL-77

TEL-78

❑ **TEL-76. Arthur Godfrey Sponsor Ad Photo,**
1950s. Snow Crop Frozen Foods. Pictured are Godfrey and Teddy Snow Crop symbol character. - **$8 $15 $30**

❑ **TEL-77. "Winky Dink" Litho. Button,**
1950s. - **$15 $30 $60**

❑ **TEL-78. "The Ghost Rider" Cello. Button,**
1950s. WCAU-TV (Philadelphia). - **$8 $15 $30**

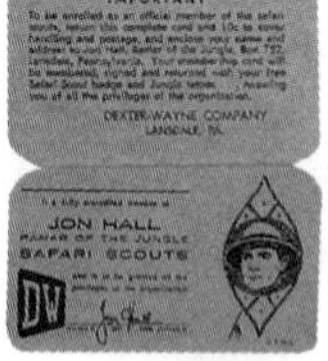
TEL-79

TEL-80

❑ **TEL-79. Jon Hall Ramar Of Jungle Membership Card,**
1950s. Rare. Membership card for Safari Scouts. 2 cards attached with code and order form for badge and tattoos. - **$25 $75 $110**

❑ **TEL-80. Jon Hall Ramar Safari Scout Pin,**
1950s. Yellow with red and brown lettering. - **$75 $140 $260**

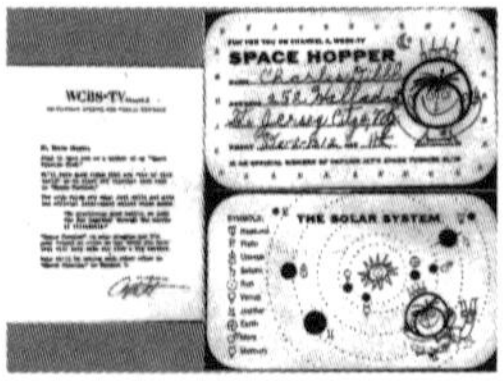

TEL-81

❑ **TEL-81. "Space Hopper" Club Letter & Card,**
c. 1960. WCBS-TV, New York City. Items for "Captain Jet" club. Letter - **$8 $15 $25**
Card - **$10 $15 $40**

TEL-82

❑ **TEL-82. "The Untouchables" Playset,**
1961. Marx #4676. Near Mint Boxed - **$1800**

TEL-83

❑ **TEL-83. Charlie Weaver Mechanical Bartender,**
1962. © Roy Rogers. Rosko Tested Toy. Boxed - **$75 $150 $250**

TEL-85

TEL-84

TEL-86

❑ **TEL-84. "New! Beany & Cecil In '62!" Cello. Button,**
1962. Mattel Toys with Bob Clampett copyright. Probably from industry toy show. - **$35 $75 $125**

❑ **TEL-85. "The Munsters Theatre" Gum Card Box,**
1964. Leaf Gum. - **$60 $100 $150**

❑ **TEL-86. "Chipmunks/Soaky" Cardboard Record,**
1964. Colgate-Palmolive. - **$5 $8 $12**

TEL-87

TEL-88

❑ **TEL-87. "Mr. Ed March Of Comics" #260,**
1964. Various sponsors. - **$10 $20 $35**

❑ **TEL-88. "Jimmy Nelson's Instant Ventriloquism" Record Album,**
1964. Album also pictures Danny O'Day and Farfel. - **$8 $12 $25**

TEL-89

❑ **TEL-89. Addams Family Button Set,**
c. 1964. Filmways TV Productions. Each is 15/16" litho. Issued with various background colors as set of 12. Fester not shown.
Each - **$12 $20 $30**

TEL-90

❑ **TEL-90. "The Addams Family View-Master" Set,**
1965. - **$20 $40 $85**

TEL-91

❑ **TEL-91. "Get Smart The Exploding Time Bomb Game,"**
1965. Store item by Ideal. - **$35 $75 $150**

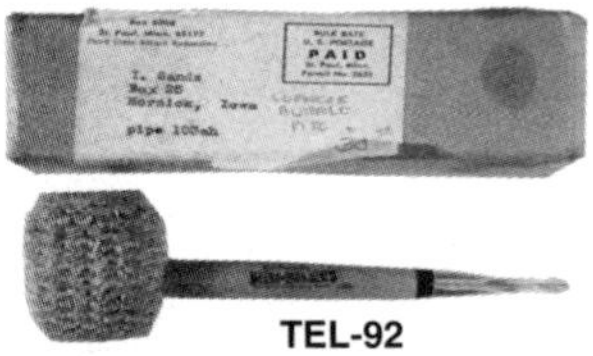

TEL-92

❑ **TEL-92. Beverly Hillbillies Pipe With Mailer,**
1965. TV premium. Corncob top pipe blows bubbles. - **$10 $25 $40**

TEL-93

❑ **TEL-93. J. Fred Muggs 'Autographed' Photo,**
1965. Autographed inscription includes names of apparent owners/trainers "Bud Roy & Jerry." 8x10" black and white glossy signed to a restaurant "Where Show Folks Can Enjoy Good Food..." Similar Example - **$15 $25 $40**

TEL-94

TEL-95

❑ **TEL-94. "Mrs. Beasley" Talking Doll,**
1966. Store item by Mattel. Includes plastic glasses. Talking - **$75 $175 $275**
Not Talking - **$40 $80 $150**

❑ **TEL-95. Munsters Flicker Picture Rings,**
c. 1966. Vending machine issue. Set of four plastic rings in either silver or blue base.
Silver Base Each - **$35 $60 $85**
Blue Base Each - **$15 $35 $55**

TEL-96

❑ **TEL-96. Flipper "Magic Whistle" 5"x24" Paper Store Sign,**
c. 1966. P.F. Flyers footwear of B.F. Goodrich. - **$15 $25 $60**

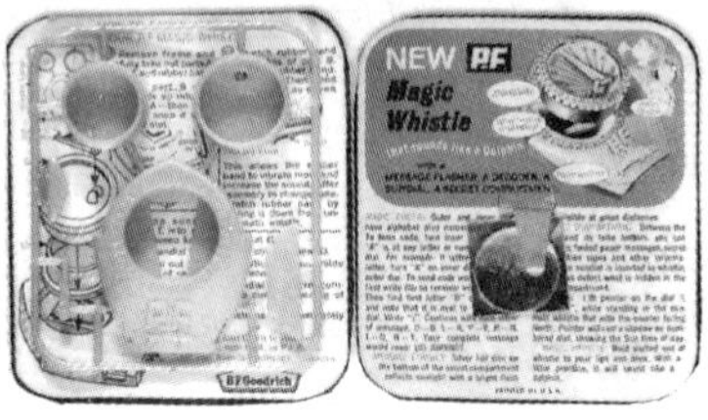


TEL-97

❑ **TEL-97. Dolphin "Magic Whistle" Plastic Assembly Parts On Card,**
c. 1966. P.F. footwear of B.F. Goodrich. "Flipper" not named but card pictures dolphin, assembled whistle is to produce tone "That Sounds Like A Dolphin".
Unassembled With Card - **$15 $30 $50**
Assembled - **$8 $15 $25**

TEL-98

❑ **TEL-98. Captain Scarlet Pinback on Card,**
1967. - **$50 $100 $150**

TEL-99

❑ **TEL-99. Captain Scarlet 12" Figure in Box,**
1967. Pedigree product. Much rarer than Captain Action doll of same period.
Boxed - **$1300**
Figure without box - **$350**

TEL-100

❑ **TEL-100. Vulture Squadron Set Of Soft Rubber Figures,**
1969. Kellogg's Froot Loops. Typically about 1-1/2" tall. Each - **$5 $12 $20**

TEL-101

❑ **TEL-101. "Dastardly And Muttley" Kite Safety Booklet,**
1969. Color comic produced in association with Reddy Kilowatt with 16 pages of comics and activities involving electricity. - **$4 $12 $40**

TEL-102

❑ **TEL-102. "ABC Super Saturday Club" Membership Kit,**
1969. Contains 11 pieces. Club letter, litho tin buttons (2), 4" stickers (2), plastic membership card, iron-on transfer, stamp sheet (8-1/4x10-1/2"), stamp card, 11x16" poster and color booklet. Near Mint Complete **- $175**

TEL-103

❑ **TEL-103. Addams Family Plastic Ring Figures,**
1960s. Store item. Set of four, originally on card also holding attachment ring.
Each Ring With Base - **$1 $3 $5**

TEL-104

TEL-105

TEL-106

❏ **TEL-104. "Maynard" G. Krebs Composition Bobbing Head,**
1960s. Store item. - **$100 $250 $400**

❏ **TEL-105. "Dr. Ben Casey M.D." Composition Bobbing Head,**
1960s. - **$50 $100 $175**

❏ **TEL-106. "Dr. Kildare" Composition Bobbing Head,**
1960s. - **$75 $125 $250**

TEL-107

TEL-108

❏ **TEL-107. Danny Thomas Flicker Small Sign,**
1960s. Post Corn Flakes. - **$50 $100 $125**

❏ **TEL-108. Gumby Flexible Plastic Ring,**
1960s. - **$4 $6 $10**

TEL-109

❏ **TEL-109. "Wonderful World of Color" Wooden Blocks Set,**
1960s. Used to promote Disney's TV show. Box shows cartoon host Ludwig Von Drake.
Blocks in box - **$50 $100 $150**

TEL-110

❏ **TEL-110. Elroy Jetson Pull Toy,**
1960s. Marked "Elroy" but no other markings. Plastic. 11" long by 12" tall. - **$75 $150 $250**

TEL-111

❏ **TEL-111. "Family Affair/Mrs. Beasley" Pin On Card,**
1970. From series of "Buffy Jewelry" by Werthley. Near Mint Carded **- $300**
Card Only **- $15 $30 $50**
Pin Only **- $35 $75 $150**

TEL-112

TEL-113

❏ **TEL-112. "Dark Shadows/Josette's Music Box",**
1970. Store item by Dan Curtis Productions Inc. 2-1/2" diameter hard plastic with wind-up key on the underside and music box which plays Josette's Theme. - **$75 $125 $250**

❏ **TEL-113. "The Age of Television" Record Album with 32 Page Book,**
1972. RCA. A chronicle of the first 25 years of television, hosted by Milton Berle, Hugh Downs and the late Arlene Francis.
Album - **$30**
Book - **$20**

TEL-114

❏ **TEL-114. "Flipper" Fan Postcard,**
1975. - **$10 $20 $35**

TEL-115

❏ **TEL-115. "I Dream Of Jeannie" Doll,**
1977. Store item by Remco. 6-1/2" tall version.
Boxed - **$75 $150 $250**
Loose - **$50 $125 $200**

TEL-116

❏ **TEL-116. "Battlestar Galactica Space Station Kit",**
1978. General Mills. Includes manual, punch-out control center, headset, activator card, patch, 11 mission cards, poster, four iron-on transfers.
Near Mint In Mailer - **$125**

TEL-117

❏ **TEL-117. Gilda Radner Cut-Out Doll Book,**
1979. Scarce. 11 pages of cut-outs and a card-board punch-out of Gilda. - **$25 $50 $75**

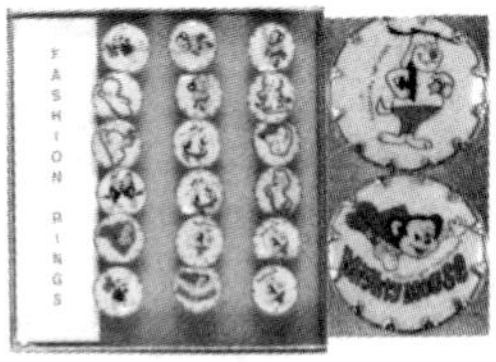

TEL-118

❏ **TEL-118. Animated TV Show Set Of 18 Character Rings In Box,**
c. 1980. Store item. Each has 7/8" diameter litho top. Various images of Mighty Mouse, Casper, Spooky, Wendy, Midnight, Heckle & Jeckle, Deputy Dawg. Near Mint Boxed - **$200**

TEL-119

TEL-120

❏ **TEL-119. "Smurf Glass" Promotion Button,**
1982. Hardee's Restaurants. 3" litho worn by employees to promote first series, set of eight glasses. - **$5 $10 $15**

❏ **TEL-120. "V" 45'er Pistol and Holster,**
1984. On card. - **$75**

TEL-121

TEL-122

❏ **TEL-121. "V" Enemy Visitor Figure,**
1984. With human mask, sunglasses and laser gun. In box. - **$50**

❏ **TEL-122. "V" Bop Bag in Box,**
1984. Copyright Warner Bros. - **$50**

TEL-123

❏ **TEL-123. Smurf-Berry Crunch Cereal Box with Campaign Button Ad and Buttons,**
1984. Box - **$15 $25 $40**
Each Button - **$2 $4 $10**

TEL-124

❏ **TEL-124. "Trans Formers" Cookie Jar with Original Box,**
1984. This product was discontinued because of the ease of damage to top of jar. Boxed - **$410**

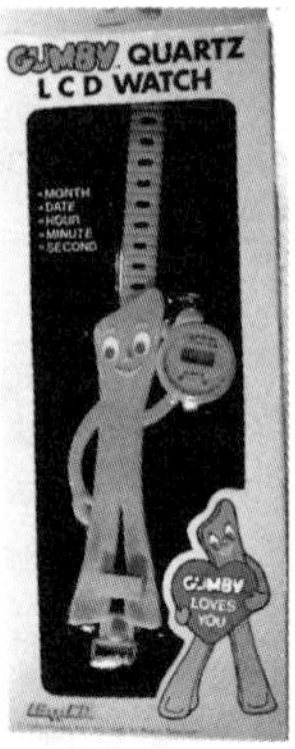


TEL-125

❏ **TEL-125. "Gumby" Quartz Watch with Box,**
1985. In colorful box with insert. - **$20 $40 $80**

TEL-126

(SAME BOX FOR BOTH DOLLS)

TEL-127

❏ **TEL-126. "Honeymooners" Jackie Gleason as Ralph Kramden Doll with Box,**
1986. From Effanbee. Boxed with 2 tags- **$150**

❏ **TEL-127. "Honeymooners" Art Carney as Ed Norton Doll with Box,**
1986. From Effanbee. Boxed with 2 tags- **$150**

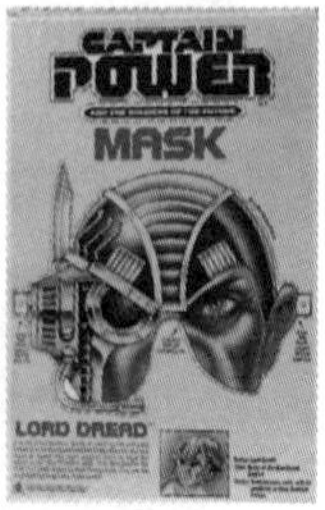


TEL-128

❏ **TEL-128. Kellogg's Corn Flakes Cereal Box with "Captain Power" Mask of Lord Dread,**
1987. Cut out mask on back. - **$10 $22 $40**

TEL-129

❏ **TEL-129. Talking Cryptkeeper Doll,**
1994. In box. - **$25**

TEL-130

TEL-131

❏ **TEL-130. "Man Eating" Cow Figure,**
1995. From "The Tick". - **$48**

❏ **TEL-131. Gumby Ceramic Bank,**
1996. Made in Taiwan. - **$40**

TEL-132

TEL-133

❑ **TEL-132. "Mr. Bill" Beanie,**
1998. 9" tall. TM Dreamsite Prod., Inc. - **$10**

❑ **TEL-133. Evel Knievel X-2 Replica on Card,**
1998. - **$10**

TEL-134

❑ **TEL-134. "South Park" Wristwatch in Metal Box,**
1998. Features the kids on box. - **$15 $40 $75**

TEL-135

❑ **TEL-135. "South Park" Plush Doll Boxed Sets,**
1998. Each has two characters- Kenny and Kyle, or Cartman and Stan.
Each box - **$15**
Each Beanie - **$10**

TEL-136

TEL-137

❑ **TEL-136. "Crush Me Phil" Toonsylvania Toy in Box,**
1998. From Steven Spielberg's animated series. - **$50**

❑ **TEL-137. "Taunt Me Igor" Toonsylvania Toy in Box,**
1998. - **$50**

TEL-138

❑ **TEL-138. "Nickelodeon" Blimp Premium,**
1999. From Burger King. - **$2 $4 $6**

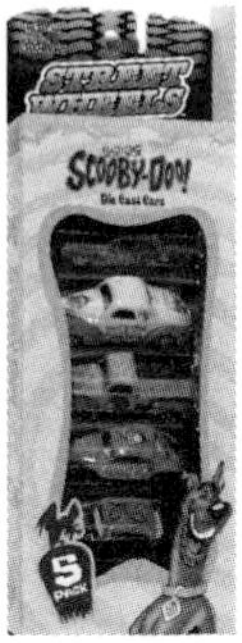

TEL-139

TEL-140

❑ **TEL-139. "Scooby-Doo" Street Wheels,**
1999. 5 die cast cars in box. - **$15**

❑ **TEL-140. "I Dream of Jeannie" Matchbox Car on Card,**
1999. - **$7**

TEL-141

TEL-142

❑ **TEL-141. "Digimon" Pop-Up Ring Set,**
2000. Set of 3 pop-up rings. - **$20**

❑ **TEL-142. "Pee Wee Herman" Bobbing Head Doll,**
2000. - **$15**

(Box) (Figure inside box)

TEL-143

❑ **TEL-143. "Bender" Robot Action Toy,**
2000. From the animated series "Futurama." - **$16**

(Box) (Figure inside box)

TEL-144

❑ **TEL-144. "Nibbler" Robot Action Toy,**
2000. From the animated series "Futurama." - **$16**

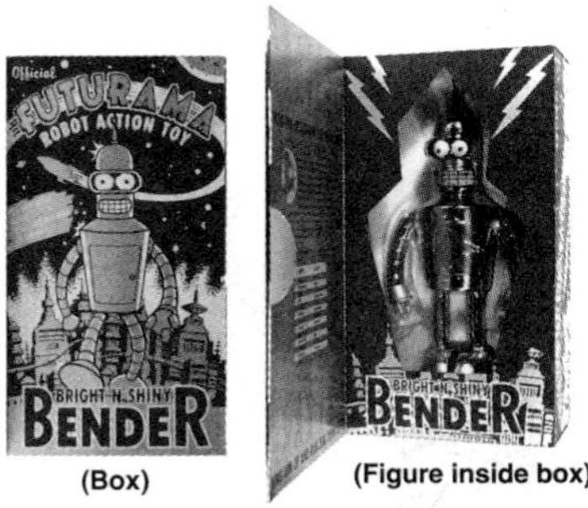


(Box) (Figure inside box)

TEL-145

❑ **TEL-145. "Bright 'N' Shiny Bender" Robot Action Toy with Box,**
2001. From the animated series "Futurama." - **$24**

TEL-146

❑ **TEL-146. Futurama "Bender" Mask,**
2001. 18" tall, 7 1/4" wide. - **$6**

Punchouts

TEL-147

Background

❑ **TEL-147. Futurama "Pop-Out People" Punchouts,**
2001. Cardboard punchouts of characters with background. - **$3**

TEL-148

❑ **TEL-148. "Battlestar Galactica" Lunch Box with Thermos,**
2001. - **$20**

TEL-149

❑ **TEL-149. "General Lee" 1:18 Scale Car,**
2001. From the show "The Dukes of Hazzard." Die cast metal 1969 Charger in box. - **$25**

TEL-150

❑ **TEL-150. "Muttley" Plush Doll,**
2001. From the show "Wacky Races." Includes glasses and tag. - **$20**

TEL-151

TEL-152

❑ **TEL-151. "Partridge Family" Bus Model,**
2001. Die-cast bus from the Johnny Lightning series. - **$5**

❑ **TEL-152. "The Jetsons" Car Set,**
2001. Five pack set of die cast cars in box. Each family member is featured on a car. - **$20**

## Tennessee Jed

**The frontier adventures of Jed Sloan aired on ABC radio from 1945 to 1947. Acting as an undercover agent for General Grant in the period just after the Civil War, Sloan was a deadly marksman who daily did away with cattle rustlers and other villains of the Western Plains. Tip-Top bread and cakes was the sponsor. A single issue of a give-away comic book was published in 1945.**

TEN-1

❑ **TEN-1. Exhibit Card And Cardboard Dexterity Puzzle With Envelope,**
1945. Tip-Top Bread.
Near Mint In Mailer - **$95**
Card - **$5 $20 $35**
Puzzle - **$10 $30 $45**

TEN-2

TEN-3

❑ **TEN-2. Oversized Cardboard Ear For Radio Broadcasts,**
1945. Tip-Top Bread. 3x5" with attachment tabs. - **$12 $35 $55**

❑ **TEN-3. Tip-Top Bread Comic Book,**
1945. Inside has adventure map keyed to radio broadcasts. - **$30 $100 $200**

TEN-4

**TEN-4. Tip-Top "Horse Puzzle" Cards With Envelope,**
c. 1945. Three-card picture placement puzzle with solution on envelope back. - **$20 $50 $80**

TEN-5

❑ **TEN-5. Pumpkin Mask,**
1945. Tip-Top Bread. - **$30 $75 $150**

TEN-6 TEN-7

❑ **TEN-6. "Tennessee Jed Magic Tricks" Booklet,**
1940s. Tip-Top Bread. Sixteen pages of illustrated tricks using household products. -
**$15 $25 $40**

❑ **TEN-7. Picture Card,**
1946. Tip-Top Bread. Radio premium. Jed kneeling on one knee. - **$10 $20 $35**

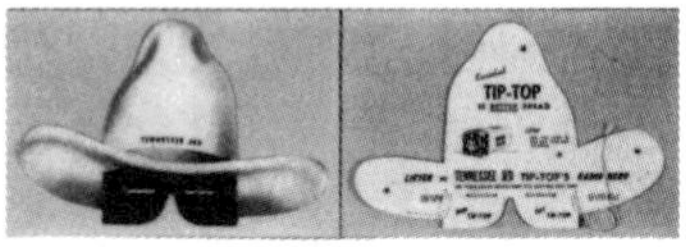


TEN-8

❑ **TEN-8. Paper Mask,**
1946. - **$20 $50 $85**

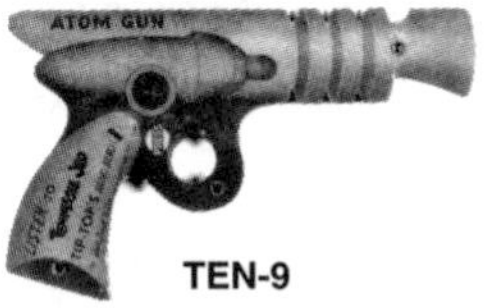


TEN-9

❑ **TEN-9. "Atom Gun" Cardboard Clicker,**
1946. Ward's Tip-Top Bread. - **$30 $85 $140**

TEN-10

❑ **TEN-10. Cardboard Ink Blotter,**
c. 1946. - **$10 $25 $40**

TEN-11 TEN-12

❑ **TEN-11. Magnet Ring,**
c. 1946. Brass base with diecut arrowhead designs holding top magnet. - **$125 $250 $525**

❑ **TEN-12. Look-Around Brass Ring,**
c. 1946. - **$100 $325 $600**

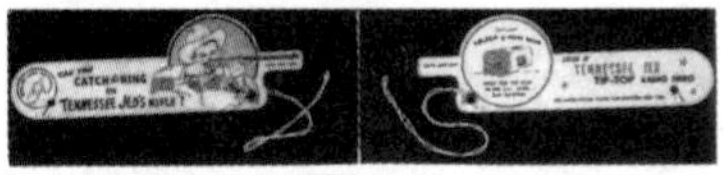

TEN-13

❑ **TEN-13. "Catch The Ring" Toy,**
1947. Cardboard with attached string and metal ring. - **$10 $30 $40**

## Terry and the Pirates

**Milton Caniff (1907-1988) created his *Terry and the Pirates* adventure comic strip in 1934 for the Chicago Tribune-New York News Syndicate. The scene of the action was China, and young Terry Lee and his pal Pat Ryan were to come up against a variety of evil-doers and exotic women, notably the infamous Dragon Lady. During World War II Terry became an Air Force pilot and, along with Colonel Flip Corkin, battled the Axis. The strip ceased publication in 1973. A number of *Terry and the Pirates* comic books were published between 1939 and 1955, including giveaways from Sears & Roebuck, Buster Brown, Canada Dry, Libby Foods, Weather Bird shoes and others.**

**Radio adaptations aired on NBC from 1937 to 1939, sponsored by Dari-Rich chocolate drink, and on ABC from 1943 to 1948, sponsored by Quaker Oats, Puffed Wheat, and Puffed Rice. A 15-episode chapter play was released by Columbia Pictures in 1940 with William Tracy as Terry, and a syndicated television series aired in New York in 1952-1953 and had continued distribution through the 1950s.**

TER-1

❑ **TER-1. "Terry And The Pirates" Book,**
1935. Published by Whitman. 3-3/8x5-5/8" soft-cover format. - **$50 $100 $150**

TER-2

❑ **TER-2. "Terry And The Pirates Meet Again",**
1936. Tarzan Ice Cream Cups. Booklet #10 from series of various character titles. - **$30 $85 $165**

TER-3

TER-4

❑ **TER-3. "Terry And The Pirates" Game,**
1937. "Find the Hidden Treasure Game" from Whitman Publishing. - **$75 $175 $350**

❑ **TER-4. Quaker Puffed Wheat Comic Book,**
1938. 1938 strips, but issued in the 1940s. - **$3 $8 $12**

TER-5

❑ **TER-5. "Terry And The Pirates Ashore In Singapore" Book,**
1938. Whitman BLB format with imprint for Stern & Co. - **$40 $85 $150**

TER-6

❑ **TER-6. "The Adventures Of Terry And The Pirates" Big Big Book,**
1938. Whitman #4073. - **$50 $125 $275**

TER-7 TER-8

❑ **TER-7. "Adventures Of Terry And The Pirates" Booklet,**
1938. From Whitman Penny Books series with inside ad for "Super-Comics" and "Crackajack Funnies" comic books. - **$15 $25 $40**

❑ **TER-8. "Terry And The Pirates" Big Little Book #1412,**
1938. Milton Caniff art. - **$15 $50 $90**

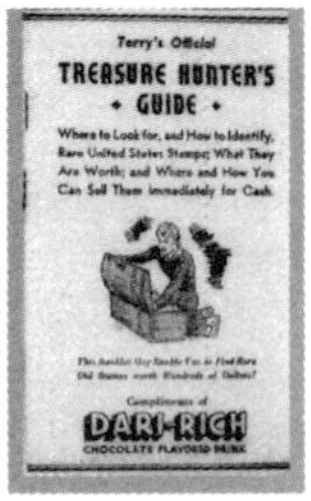

TER-9 TER-10

❑ **TER-9. "Treasure Hunter's Guide" Booklet,**
1938. Dari-Rich Chocolate Drink. Contents basically about stamp collecting. - **$20 $50 $75**

❑ **TER-10. "Terry And The Pirates And The Giant's Vengeance" Better Little Book,**
1939. Whitman #1446. - **$20 $60 $125**

TER-11

❑ **TER-11. "Terry And The Pirates in the Mountain Stronghold" Big Little Book #1499,**
1941. - **$15 $50 $90**

TER-12

❑ **TER-12. "Ruby Of Genghis Khan" Comic Activity Book,**
1941. Rare. Libby's fruit and vegetable juices. Contents include pencil puzzles, games, coloring pages, magic tricks, cut-out dolls. - **$300 $800 $1500**

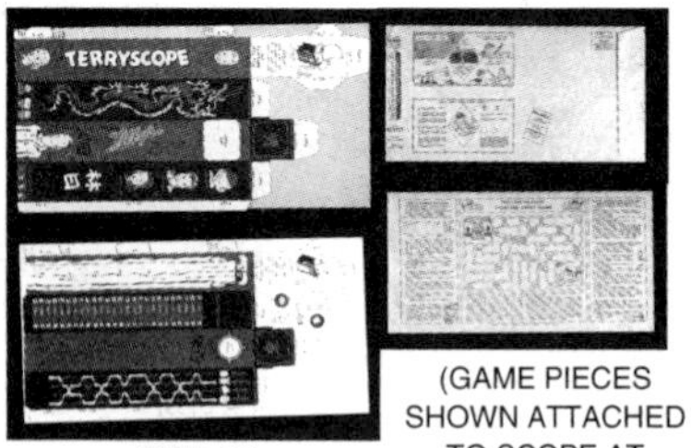


TER-13

(GAME PIECES SHOWN ATTACHED TO SCOPE AT BOTTOM LEFT)

❑ **TER-13. "Terryscope" Cardboard Assembly Kit,**
1941. Rare. Libby, McNeill & Libby. Pictures six characters, one side features secret code. Game pieces came attached on side of unassembled Terryscope.
Near Mint Terryscope Unassembled - **$650**
Terryscope Assembled - **$100 $300 $480**
Game Pieces (Four Different) - **$80**
Mailer - **$30 $60 $100**

TER-14

❑ **TER-14. Libby's Display Sign,**
1942. Shows Terry showing how to get plane spotter premium. 3 known. Gordon Gold Archives. - **$500 $1000 $1500**

TER-15

TER-16

TER-17

❑ **TER-15. "Victory Airplane Spotter" Cardboard Mechanical Disk With Envelope,**
1942. Libby, McNeill & Libby. Pictures Terry, Pat, April, Burma, Connie plus identifies 16 warplane silhouettes. - **$75 $175 $350**

❑ **TER-16. Quaker Oats B-25 Mascot Plane Photo,**
1943. - **$20 $50 $75**

❑ **TER-17. "Pilot's Mascot" Wooden Button,**
1943. Wire loop reverse for wearing with a safety pin. Came with Quaker Cereals B-25 airplane picture. - **$10 $25 $50**

TER-18

❑ **TER-18. Flip Corkin Picture,**
1944. Quaker Oats. Set of six.
Each - **$15 $30 $65**

TER-19

❑ **TER-19. Quaker Oats Pictures,**
c. 1944. Set of six. Pat Ryan, Burma, Terry, Phil Corkin, Dragon Lady, Connie. Near Mint In Mailer - **$525**
Each - **$20 $60 $75**

TER-20

❑ **TER-20. Quaker "Wings Of Victory" Box,**
c. 1945. Set of 12 warplane back pictures.
Each Complete Box - **$50 $175 $300**
Each Cut Picture Panel - **$5 $20 $25**

(PUZZLE BOX)

TER-21 (PUZZLE IMAGE)

❑ **TER-21. Jig Saw Puzzle in Box,**
1946. - **$50 $125 $200**

TER-22

❑ **TER-22. Quaker Cereals "Sparkies Jingle Contest" Postcard,**
1946. - **$20 $35 $50**

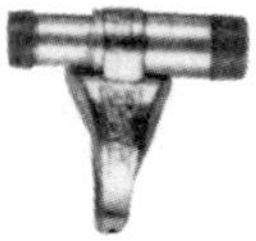

TER-23

TER-24

❑ **TER-23. Pirate's Gold Ore Detector Ring,**
1947. Quaker Cereals. Brass with aluminum/plastic telescope viewer holding tiny gold flakes. Documented by radio show episode titled "Quaker Puffed Wheat and Quaker Puffed Rice bring you Terry and the Pirates - the new and exciting adventure of Terry Lee and the Pirate Gold Detector Ring." The episode begins with Terry speaking about his long search for this ring. - **$50 $125 $175**

❑ **TER-24. "Tattoo Transfers" Set In Envelope,**
c. 1948. Coco-Wheats cereal. 22 water transfer pictures on two sheets, "Pack No. 9". - **$25 $50 $85**

TER-25

❑ **TER-25. Artist George Wunder Personal Christmas Card,**
c. 1948. - **$20 $40 $70**

TER-26

❑ **TER-26. Terry & The Pirates Four Color Code-Writer,**
1940s. Libby McNeill & Libby. Partially used example is 2-3/4" long with silver luster metal cap holding red and yellow wood pencil with the lead a combination of four distinct colors. - **$100 $200 $400**

TER-27

❑ **TER-27. Character Stamps For Contest Entry,**
1940s. Quaker Oats. Awarded to entrants in bicycle contest announced in part by radio broadcasts. - **$30 $60 $100**

TER-28

TER-29

❑ **TER-28. "Terry Jingle" Contest Postcard,**
1940s. Quaker Puffed Wheat and Rice Sparkies. Acknowledgement card for entrant. - **$20 $35 $50**

❑ **TER-29. "Canada Dry" 13x17" Cardboard Ad Sign,**
1953. (Has 1952 copyright.) Offered a comic book with purchase of every carton of soda. - **$100 $175 $300**

TER-30

❑ **TER-30. "Hot Shot Charlie Flies Again" No. 1 Comic Book,**
1953. Canada Dry. From set of three. - **$20 $45 $100**

TER-31

TER-32

❑ **TER-31. "Terry And The Pirates In Forced Landing" Comic Book #2,**
1953. Canada Dry. Third book in set "Dragon Lady In Distress". Each - **$20 $45 $100**

❑ **TER-32. Canada Dry "Chop-Stick-Joe" Litho. Button,**
1953. From set of five also including Terry, Burma, Dragon Lady, Hot Shot Charlie. Each - **$10 $20 $30**

TER-33

❑ **TER-33. "See Terry On TV" 3" Flicker Button,**
c. 1953. Canada Dry. - **$30 $50 $85**

TER-34

❑ **TER-34. Prototype for "Hot Shot Charlie" Mask Ad,**
1953. Original art from the Gordon Gold Archives. Shown framed. - **$600**

TER-35

TER-36

❑ **TER-35. Ad for Canada Dry Contest,**
1953. Promotes TV show. - **$5 $15 $20**

❑ **TER-36. Comic Book Ad,**
1950s. Canada Dry. - **$10 $20 $30**

## Three Little Pigs

**The story for Disney's *Three Little Pigs* was based on a Grimm brothers fairy tale. The pigs--Fifer, Fiddler, and Practical--defended their homes against a Big Bad Wolf (and later against three little wolves.) When the *Three Little Pigs* cartoon was released in 1933, it was a smash hit. The theme song *Who's Afraid of the Big Bad Wolf* was equally popular, climbing to the top of the charts.**

**The many fans of the film and song felt that if the pigs could overcome such a threat, then they could also handle the worst economic Depression the U.S. had ever seen. Disney saw the connection and released a sequel in 1934 called *The Big Bad Wolf.* In 1935, the song and all the products released to promote the film further enhanced the cry *Who's Afraid of the Depression.* The defeat of *The Big Bad Wolf* symbolized Americans' confidence that the Depression could similarly be vanquished.**

**In 1936, another sequel was released titled *The Three Little Wolves.* Disney decided to give the Wolf three pint-sized accomplices, so the four wolves could put the pigs in greater peril. The pigs won out again, this time relying on the help of a "Monkey Wrench." By 1938 the worst of the Depression had passed and Disney released another cartoon *The Practical Pig.***

**Let's take a look back and see why *The Big Bad Wolf*'s popularity couldn't have come at a better time.**

TLP-1

❑ **TLP-1. Three Little Pigs Paper Mask,**
1933. Lord & Taylor (and others), publisher is Einson-Freeman Co. Each - **$15 $30 $65**

TLP-2

❑ **TLP-2. Walt Disney Studio Christmas Card,**
1933. - **$200 $350 $750**

TLP-3

TLP-4

TLP-5

❑ **TLP-3. Practical Pig Bisque Largest Size,**
c. 1933. Store item. 4-1/2" tall. From set of three. Each **- $15 $30 $60**
Smaller Sizes **- $12 $20 $45**

❑ **TLP-4. Big Bad Wolf Bisque,**
c. 1933. Store item. 3-1/2" tall with "S258" on back**. - $20 $50 $85**

❑ **TLP-5. Big Bad Wolf Miniature Bisque,**
c. 1933. Japan 1-3/4" tall**. - $15 $40 $75**

TLP-6

TLP-7

❑ **TLP-6. "Who's Afraid Of The Big Bad Wolf" Sheet Music,**
1933. Store item. Words and music to song "From The Walt Disney Silly Symphony The Three Little Pigs." - **$15 $30 $60**

❑ **TLP-7. Ceramic Mug,**
1933. Promotes the cartoon and song. - **$75 $150 $225**

TLP-8

❑ **TLP-8. Ingersoll Animated Pocketwatch With Box,**
1934. Store item. Wolf's eye winks, red color on dial often faded. Near Mint Boxed - **$2000**
Watch - **$300 $600 $1000**

TLP-9

TLP-10

❑ **TLP-9. "Who's Afraid Of The Big Bad Wolf" Cello. Button,**
c. 1935. Pictured as give-away in Disney merchandise catalogs of the time. - **$50 $75 $150**

❑ **TLP-10. "1st Little Pig" Glass,**
c. 1936. Probable dairy product container. From a series of at least three different with small image on center front rather than image extending from top to bottom of glass.
Each - **$20 $40 $60**

TLP-11

❑ **TLP-11. Ink Blotter,**
1938. Issued by Sun-Heat Furnace Oil. **- $75 $125 $250**

TLP-12

TLP-13

❑ **TLP-12. "Who's Afraid Of The Big Bad Wolf" Tin Toy Watch With Moving Hands,**
1930s. Store item. Finished in four colors. - **$75 $125 $200**

❑ **TLP-13. Three Little Pigs Ceramic Ashtray,**
1930s. Store item. - **$40 $85 $165**

TLP-14

❑ **TLP-14. Three Little Pigs Ceramic Ashtray,**
1930s. Scarce version. - **$60 $120 $180**

TLP-15

❑ **TLP-15. China Compartment Dish,**
1930s. Store item also used as premium. - **$50 $115 $165**

TLP-16

❑ **TLP-16. Three Little Pigs Enameled Brass Matchbox Holder,**
1930s. Store item. - **$20 $50 $85**

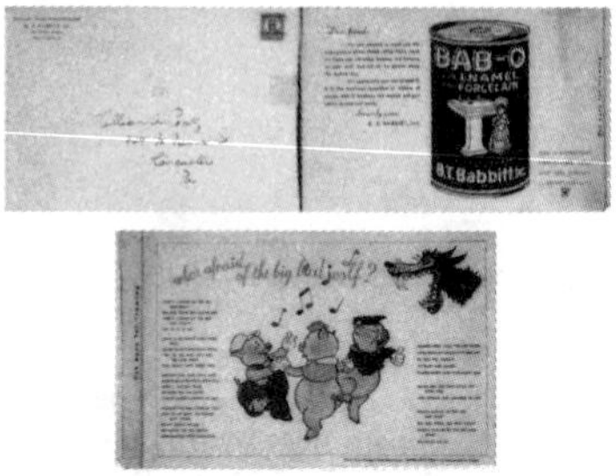


TLP-17

❑ **TLP-17. Bab-O Folder With Three Pigs Picture,**
1930s. - **$25 $50 $75**

TLP-18

❑ **TLP-18. "Who's Afraid Of The Big Bad Wolf" Pocketknife,**
1930s. Scarce. Store item by Geo. Schrade Co. Steel with silvered brass and enamel paint grips. - **$50 $125 $200**

TLP-19

TLP-20

❑ **TLP-19. "Who's Afraid Of The Big Bad Wolf" Enameled Brass Badge,**
1930s. Pig at piano. - **$50 $125 $225**

❑ **TLP-20. "Three Little Pigs/Who's Afraid Of The Big Bad Wolf" Enameled Brass Badge,**
1930s. Version pictures Fiddler Pig. - **$50 $125 $225**

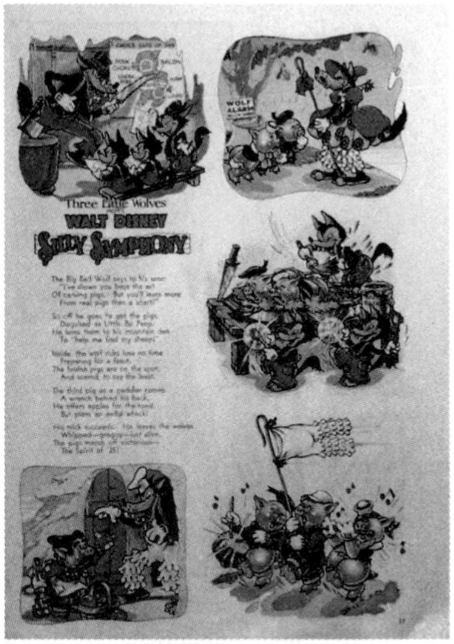


TLP-21

❑ **TLP-21. Three Little Wolves Ad Page,**
1935. From Good Housekeeping Magazine. Ad was released in 1935 to promote the 1936 film. - **$10 $20 $35**

TLP-22

❑ **TLP-22. Lil Bad Wolf Glass Tumbler,**
1985. Fanta soda. For German distribution with inscriptions mostly in German. - **$8 $12 $25**

TLP-23

TLP-24

❑ **TLP-23. Fiddler Pig Hand Puppet,**
1987. Product from France. - **$25 $50 $75**

❑ **TLP-24. Fifer Pig Hand Puppet,**
1987. Product from France. - **$25 $50 $75**

TLP-25

TLP-26

❑ **TLP-25. Practical Pig Hand Puppet,**
1987. Product from France. - **$25 $50 $75**

❑ **TLP-26. Big Bad Wolf Hand Puppet,**
1987. Product from France. - **$25 $50 $70**

TLP-27

(side view)

❑ **TLP-27. Big Bad Wolf Statue,**
1995. Walt Disney Classic series. Commemorates 60th anniversary of the Three Little Pigs series. Limited to 7,500 - **$400**

TLP-28

TLP-29

❑ **TLP-28. Fiddler Plush Doll with Tag,**
1999. From "Three Little Pigs" series sold only at Disneyworld. - **$22**

❑ **TLP-29. Fifer Plush Doll with Tag,**
1999. From "Three Little Pigs" series sold only at Disneyworld. - **$22**

TLP-30

TLP-31

❑ **TLP-30. Practical Pig Plush Doll with Tag,**
1999. From "Three Little Pigs" series sold only at Disneyworld. - **$24**

❑ **TLP-31. Big Bad Wolf Plush Doll with Tag,**
1999. From "Three Little Pigs" series sold only at Disneyworld. - **$32**

TLP-32

❑ **TLP-32. Disney Classic Edition Set,**
1990s. Set - **$180**

# Three Stooges

**Slapstick and comic mayhem were the wacky hallmarks of the Three Stooges in their two dozen feature films and almost 200 two-reelers made between 1930 and 1965. The original trio--Moe Howard, his brother Curly, and Larry Fine--went from success in vaudeville to cult status in Hollywood and later to enduring popularity via television reruns in the late 1950s. (Another brother, Shemp, took over when Curly died; Joe Besser replaced Shemp on his death; and Joe DeRita later replaced Besser.) Animated cartoon series produced by Hanna-Barbera were syndicated on television--*The Three Stooges* in 1965 and *The Three Robonic Stooges* in 1978. Comic books appeared from the late 1940s to the 1970s. Will the Stooges' brand of comedy continue into the future? "Soitenly!"**

THR-1

❑ **THR-1. "Moving Picture Machine" Newspaper Ad,**
1937. Pillsbury's Farina. - **$25 $75 $125**

THR-2

❑ **THR-2. "Moving Picture Machine" Cardboard Punch-Out Kit,**
1937. Pillsbury's Farina. Came with films #5 and #6 based on actual movie "False Alarms," others available by purchasing more Farina.
Scarce. Unpunched - **$350 $1000 $2000**
Assembled - **$150 $500 $800**

THR-3

THR-4

❑ **THR-3. Photo With Ad Reverse,**
c. 1937. Pillsbury's Farina. Back offer is tied to Columbia Pictures promotion. - **$75 $150 $300**

❑ **THR-4. "Three Stooges" 3-D Comic V. 1 #2,**
1953. St. John Publishing Co. - **$47 $142 $380**

THR-5

❑ **THR-5. "Fan Club Of America" Membership Kit,**
1959. Includes envelope, cover letter, sheet of stamps, "fan club franchise" certificate, sheet of four membership cards and two 5"x7" black and white photos.
Complete - **$50 $125 $225**

THR-6

❑ **THR-6. Vending Machine Display Paper For Picture Rings,**
1959. Same design on box which held rings.
Paper - **$15 $25 $45**
Empty Box - **$150 $300 $500**

THR-7

❑ **THR-7. "Magic Re-Color Book",**
1959. Store item by Fun Bilt Toys. 9x10-1/2" spiral-bound stiff cardboard covers and pages. - **$50 $125 $200**

THR-8

THR-9

❑ **THR-8. "Three Stooges/I'm Curly" Ring,**
1959. Gold plastic base with two flicker portraits. Also issued with Moe and Larry.
Each - **$10 $17 $25**

❑ **THR-9. Plastic Finger Puppets Set,**
c. 1950s. Probable store item. Each stands 3-3/4" tall. Each - **$25 $60 $115**

THR-10

❑ **THR-10. "The Nonsense Song Book" Record Album,**
1950s. 33-1/3 rpm on Coral label. - **$25 $60 $100**

THR-11

❑ **THR-11. Home Movie Film,**
c. 1950s. Store item by Excel Movie Products Inc. 4" square box holds 16mm black and white silent film of about 100' titled "All Hashed Up." - **$12 $25 $50**

THR-12

THR-13

❑ **THR-12. Group Portrait 2-1/4" Cello. Button,**
c. 1960s. No sponsor, made by St. Louis Badge Co. - **$15 $30 $50**

❑ **THR-13. Movie/Fan Club Photo Card,**
1964. Black and white picturing them from movie "The 3 Stooges Go Around The World In A Daze" with facsimile signatures. -
**$10 $20 $30**
Each Real Autograph Add - **$25 $50 $75**

THR-14

❑ **THR-14. Triple Image Ceramic Bank,**
c. 1960s. Store item. - **$200 $400 $800**

THR-15

THR-16

❑ **THR-15. Happy Birthday Record,**
1960s. Possible premium, personalized to individual first name. - **$10 $20 $35**

❑ **THR-16. "Clark/Collector Cups" 3" Cello. Button,**
1993. - **$5 $10 $20**

BOX FRONT

THR-17

❑ **THR-17. "The Three Little Beers" Doll Set,**
1997. 3 Dolls commemorate the 1935 movie. Boxed - **$120**

THR-18

❑ **THR-18. "The Three Little Beers" Resin Figures,**
1998. Classic golfing pose commemorates the 1935 movie. Set - **$80**

THR-19

❑ **THR-19. Bean Bear Set with Photo Tags,**
1990s. Bears each have embroidered names and pictures on chest and photo tags. Set - **$60**

THR-20

❑ **THR-20. Three Stooges Lunch Box,**
2000. - **$30**

THR-21

THR-22

❑ **THR-21. "Larry Fine" Die-cast Metal Car,**
2000. From Team Lightning. - **$5**

❑ **THR-22. "Moe Howard" Die-cast Metal Car,**
2000. From Team Lightning. - **$5**

# Thurston, the Magician

**Howard Thurston (1869-1936) was a master magician who made a triumphant world tour in the early years of the 20th century, performing before royalty and notables. Thurston's exploits and adventures were dramatized in a short-lived radio series on the NBC Blue network in 1932-1933. The program, known as *Thurston, the Magician* or *Howard Thurston, the Magician*, was sponsored by Swift & Co.**

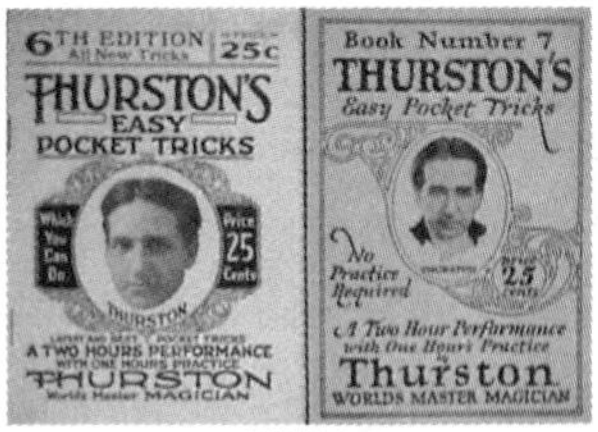


THU-1

❑ **THU-1. "Thurston's Easy Pocket Tricks" Instructional Booklets,**
1918, 1923. Each 5x7-1/2" paperback has 48 pages. One is identified as "6th Edition" from 1918 and the other is "Book Number 7" from 1923. Each - **$5 $15 $30**

THU-2

THU-3

❑ **THU-2. "Good Luck/Thurston" Cello. Button,**
c. 1920. - **$35 $75 $140**

❑ **THU-3. "Good Luck" Card,**
c. 1920s. - **$5 $10 $20**

THU-4

❑ **THU-4. Magician Coin,**
1928. Good Luck Charm premium. Says "Thurston The Magician" on front. -
**$20 $40 $60**

THU-5

THU-6

❑ **THU-5. Magician Coin,**
1929. Rare. Says "Thurston The Magician" on front. - **$30 $60 $130**

❑ **THU-6. "Thurston's Dream Book",**
c. 1920s. 32-page dream interpretation booklet sold for 25 cents through Thurston's Mystic Palace, Beechurst, Long Island, New York. -
**$15 $25 $40**

THU-7

THU-8

❑ **THU-7. "Thurston's Book Of Magic #1",**
1932. Swift & Company. Shows illustrations and explains how to do different tricks. -
**$15 $35 $50**

❑ **THU-8. "Thurston's Book Of Magic #2",**
1932. Swift & Company. Shows illustrations and explains how to do different tricks. -
**$15 $35 $50**

THU-9

THU-10

❑ **THU-9. "Thurston's Book Of Magic #3",**
1932. Swift & Company. Shows illustrations and explains how to do different tricks. -
**$15 $35 $50**

❑ **THU-10. "Thurston's Book Of Magic #4",**
1932. Swift & Company. Shows illustrations and explains how to do different tricks. -
**$15 $35 $50**

THU-11

THU-12

❑ **THU-11. "Thurston's Book Of Magic #5",**
1932. Swift & Company. Shows illustrations and explains how to do different tricks. -
**$15 $35 $50**

❑ **THU-12. Trick Packets,**
c. 1932. Swift & Co. At least 11 in set.
Each - **$3 $10 $25**

## Tim Club

**This club, headed by "Tim," a cartoon image lad with no surname, existed as early as 1929. Membership loosely consisted of youngsters that patronized clothing stores electing to join the "Tim" endorsement theme. Premiums included code books, stamp albums and pin-backs related to "Pie Eater" activities. Tim's merchandising clout was revitalized beginning in the early 1940s by addition of a super partner, Superman to be exact. Tim carried on his tradition but became the second banana in the new "Superman-Tim Store" promotion. Premiums continued, apparently free, including a monthly mailer newsletter/clothing catalogue/activities manual imprinted by local store name. Superman was prominently featured in each. Additional premiums were pin-back buttons, pennants, album stamps, Secret Code and other membership items. Superman-Tim currency was also available. The Club was still officially licensed to Tim Promotions, Inc. of New York City.**

TIM-1

TIM-2

❑ **TIM-1. "Tim's Trip To Mars" Booklet,**
c. 1929. Tim's Store for Boys. 3-3/4x6-3/4" with 16 pages. - **$8 $12 $25**

❑ **TIM-2. Code Books,**
c. 1930. Participating Tim stores. Pictured examples are for 1929, 1930, 1933.
Each - **$8 $12 $25**

TIM-3

TIM-4

❑ **TIM-3. "The Knicker" Magazine,**
1930. Monthly publication, pictured example is for October. Each contains 12 pages with local store imprint on back cover.
Each Issue - **$5 $12 $20**

❑ **TIM-4. Tim Rancho Code Book,**
1935. Pie Eater's Club premium. 16 pages. -
**$5 $12 $20**

TIM-5

TIM-6

❑ **TIM-5. 1938 Franco Club Patch,**
1938. - **$50 $100 $150**

❑ **TIM-6. Tim Patch,**
1930s. Scarce. Comes in red, grey and brown. -
**$15 $40 $75**

TIM-7

TIM-8

❑ **TIM-7. Pie-Eater Club Member Happy Birthday Letter,**
1930s. Metropolitan (clothing) store. Invites recipient to pick up free pie. - **$10 $15 $30**

❑ **TIM-8. “Tim's Official Stamps”,**
1930s. Participating stores. For mounting in album supplied by store. Each - **$3 $10 $20**

TIM-9

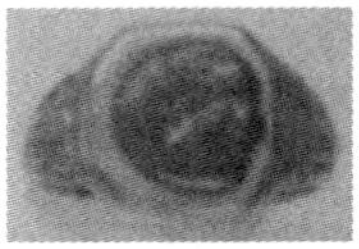
TIM-10

❑ **TIM-9. Cello. Club Button,**
1930s. Red, white, blue and gold. - **$8 $15 $30**

❑ **TIM-10. Silvered Metal Portrait Ring,**
1930s. Raised portrait with dog portrait on each band, possibly sterling. - **$50 $125 $250**

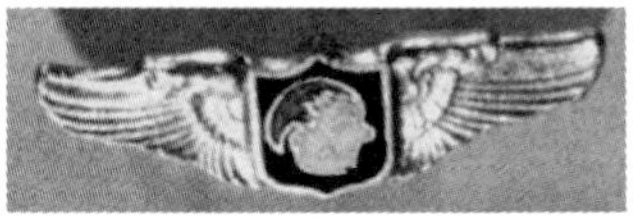
TIM-11

❑ **TIM-11. Tim Wings,**
1930s. Scarce. Store premium. - **$30 $110 $170**

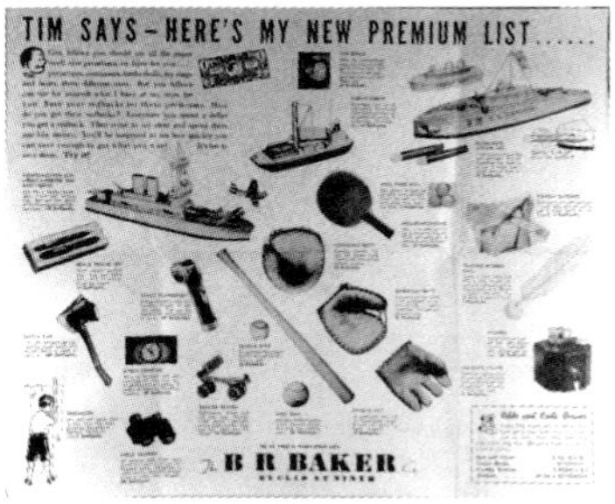

TIM-12

❑ **TIM-12. Premium Offer Display Poster,**
1930s. 14” x 17” poster features “Tim” ring and shows other items you can buy using special “redbacks” - play money received as a bonus for store purchases. - **$50 $100 $150**

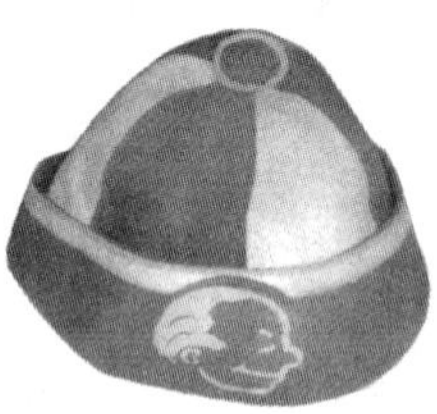
TIM-13

TIM-14

❑ **TIM-13. Felt Beanie,**
c. 1930s. - **$50 $125 $200**

❑ **TIM-14. Membership Card,**
c. 1940. - **$10 $20 $40**

TIM-15

TIM-16

❑ **TIM-15. “Tim's Magazine”,**
1940. Participating stores. Issued monthly. Each - **$5 $10 $15**

❑ **TIM-16. Tim's “Redback” Currency,**
1940s. Various stores. Various denominations. Each - **$2 $5 $8**

TIM-17

TIM-18

TIM-19

❑ **TIM-17. “Pie Eaters Club/Tim” Litho. Button,**
c. 1940s. - **$3 $6 $10**

❑ **TIM-18. “Tim's Store For Boys” Cello. Button,**
c. 1940s. - **$5 $10 $20**

❑ **TIM-19. “Tim's Official Pie Eaters Club” Cello. Button,**
c. 1940s. - **$3 $10 $15**

TIM-20

TIM-21

TIM-22

❑ **TIM-20. “Pie Eaters Club/Tim” Cello. Button,**
c. 1940s. - **$3 $10 $15**

❑ **TIM-21. “Tim's Lucky Coin”,**
c. 1940s. Front portrait, back inscription “From Tim's Official Store”. Brass. - **$10 $20 $50**

❑ **TIM-22. "Tim's Club For Boys" Litho. Button,**
1940s. - **$10 $25 $40**

## Tim Tyler

**Cartoonist Lyman Young created *Tim Tyler's Luck* for the King Features Syndicate as a daily strip in 1928 and as a Sunday page in 1931. Tim's adventures took him to Africa, where he joined the Ivory Patrol to help maintain law and order. A syndicated radio program aired in 1936-1937, a series of comic books appeared in the 1940s, and Universal Pictures released a 12-episode chapter play, also called *Tim Tyler's Luck*, in 1937, with Frankie Thomas as Tim.**

TYL-1

TYL-2

❑ **TYL-1. “Tim Tyler's Luck/Ivory Patrol Club” Cello. Button,**
1937. Universal Pictures. For 12-chapter movie serial. - **$30 $85 $165**

❑ **TYL-2. “Tim Tyler Ivory Patrol Club/Viva” Cello. Button,**
c. 1937. - **$75 $150 $300**

TYL-3

TYL-4

❑ **TYL-3. “Tim Tyler's Luck And The Plot Of The Exile King” Better Little Book,**
1939. Whitman #1479. - **$20 $50 $125**

❑ **TYL-4. “Tim Tyler” Newspaper Contest Cello. Button,**
1930s. New York Evening Journal. 1-1/4” in black and cream with shades of red. -
**$15 $30 $60**

# Tom and Jerry

**The classic helter-skelter cat-and-mouse rivalry between Tom and Jerry was brought to life in 114 theatrical cartoons created by the Hanna-Barbera team for MGM between 1939 and 1957. The animated superstars, with Tom generally chasing Jerry and with hardly ever a word of dialogue, won seven Oscars between 1943 and 1952. MGM produced additional *Tom & Jerry* series in 1961-1962 and in 1963-1967. *Tom & Jerry: The Movie* ("They talk!") was released in 1993.**

**The cartoon stars debuted on television when the Hanna-Barbera shorts aired on CBS Saturday mornings from 1965 to 1972. A made-for-TV series under a variety of names appeared starting in 1975. *Tom & Jerry Kids* premiered on the Fox Children's Network in 1990. The mischievous duo continues to win fans to this day. Licensing and merchandising of the characters has been extensive.**

TMJ-1

❑ **TMJ-1. Movie Flip Booklets,**
1949. Grape-Nuts Flakes. Box inserts from series of 12 based on M-G-M or Walter Lantz cartoon characters. Each - **$5 $12 $25**

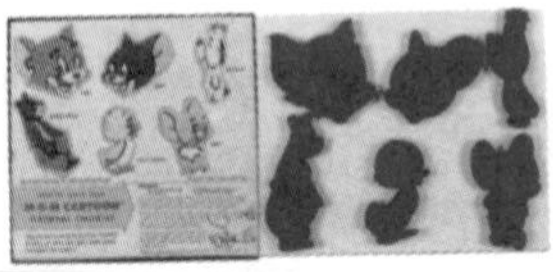

TMJ-2

❑ **TMJ-2. "M-G-M Cartoon Cookie Cutters" With Mailer,**
1956. Issued by Quaker Oats. Contains six different plastic figural cookie cutters.
Cutter Set - **$10 $20 $40**
Instructions - **$5 $10 $15**

TMJ-3

TMJ-4

❑ **TMJ-3. "Tom & Jerry Go For Stroehmann's Bread" Litho. Button,**
1950s. - **$10 $20 $30**

❑ **TMJ-4. "ABC Minors/M.G.M.'s Tom And Jerry" Cello. Button,**
c. 1960s. English Issue. - **$10 $15 $25**

TMJ-5

TMJ-6

❑ **TMJ-5. Glazed Ceramic English Mug,**
1960s. Store item. - **$15 $25 $50**

❑ **TMJ-6. "March Of Comics" Booklet,**
1970. Child Life Shoes. Issue #345 reprinting 1970 comic book story. - **$5 $10 $15**

TMJ-7

❑ **TMJ-7. Scooter Friction Drive Toy With Box,**
1972. Store item by Marx Toys. Plastic toy in image of Tom as operator and Jerry as sidecar passenger. Near Mint Boxed - **$100**
Loose - **$15 $30 $65**

TMJ-8

❑ **TMJ-8. "Tom Pulling Jerry's Cart" Plastic Wind-Up Toy,**
1977. Store item by Marx, Great Britain. 4-1/4" long. Near Mint Boxed - **$75**
Unboxed - **$15 $30 $50**

TMJ-9

❑ **TMJ-9. Boxed Vinyl Figure Banks,**
1978. Store item authorized figures packaged individually in matching "Money Box" cartons.
Near Mint Each Boxed - **$50**
Each Loose - **$8 $15 $30**

TMJ-10

❑ **TMJ-10. Ceramic Pencil Holder,**
1981. Store item made for Gorham Products. - **$10 $20 $45**

TMJ-11

❑ **TMJ-11. Tom and Jerry Figures,**
1989. 9" Tom and 5" Jerry. This set has Tom with a closed mouth grin. Set in box - **$40**

TMJ-12

❑ **TMJ-12. Tom and Jerry Figures,**
1989. 9" Tom and 5" Jerry. This set has Tom with an open mouth smile. Set in box - **$35**

TMJ-13

❑ **TMJ-13. Spike and Tyke Figures with Box,**
1989. 9" Spike and 5 3/4" Tyke. Set in box - **$35**

TMJ-15

TMJ-14

❑ **TMJ-14. "Tom" Bean Bag with Tag,**
1998. - **$12**

❑ **TMJ-15. "Jerry" Bean Bag with Tag,**
1998. - **$12**

## Tom Corbett, Space Cadet

**Set in the 24th century, this television space adventure followed the exploits of three young cadets as they trained in their spaceship Polaris to become officers of the Solar Guards. The series, based on Robert Heinlein's 1948 novel *Space Cadet* and scripted with the technical advice of rocket scientist Willy Ley, was distinguished by scientific accuracy and innovative camera effects. Corbett's unit at the Space Academy included Roger Manning (So what happens now, space heroes?) and Astro, a quick-tempered Venusian youth. Veteran actor Frankie Thomas played the part of Corbett.**

***Tom Corbett, Space Cadet* was one of the few series to appear on all four commercial TV networks, and on two of them simultaneously. The show, which was broadcast live, debuted on CBS in 1950, moved to ABC in 1951-1952, appeared on NBC in the summer of 1951, on the Dumont network in 1953-1954, and again on NBC in 1954-1955. Sponsors were Kellogg's cereals (1950-1952), Red Goose shoes (1953-1954), and Kraft Foods (1954-1955). The series also ran on ABC radio for six months in 1952, featuring the same cast as sponsored by Kellogg, and as a simulcast on NBC in 1954-1955, sponsored by Kraft.**

**In print, a Corbett comic strip distributed by the Field Newspaper Syndicate appeared from 1951 to 1953, comic books between 1952 and 1955, and a series of Corbett novels from Grosset & Dunlap between 1952 and 1956.**

**Merchandising of Tom Corbett material was extensive, including toys, a watch, lunch boxes, space goggles, and helmets. Kellogg's promoted a Space Academy membership club that offered badges, rings, patches, a cardboard decoder, ID cards, and autographed photos. Items are normally copyrighted Rockhill Productions.**

TCO-1

TCO-2

TCO-3

❑ **TCO-1. Membership Kit Cast Photo,**
1951. - **$15 $40 $80**

❑ **TCO-2. "Space Cadet" 2-1/8" Cello. Button,**
1951. Part of club membership kit. -
**$50 $150 $200**

❑ **TCO-3. Fabric Patch,**
1951. Part of member's kit. - **$20 $40 $75**

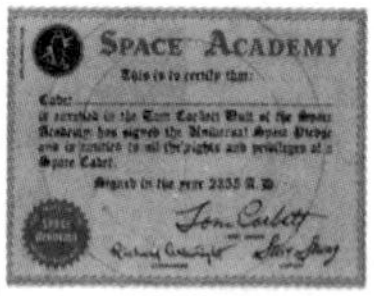


TCO-4

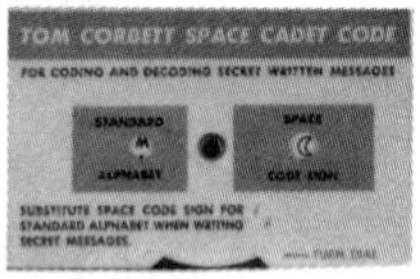


TCO-5

❑ **TCO-4. Certificate,**
1951. Part of member's kit. - **$20 $45 $85**

❑ **TCO-5. Kellogg's Cardboard Decoder,**
1951. Came with membership kit. -
**$35 $90 $160**

TCO-6

❑ **TCO-6. "Tom Corbett Space Cadet News" Vol. 1 #1,**
1951. Kellogg's. Part of member's kit. -
**$35 $115 $165**

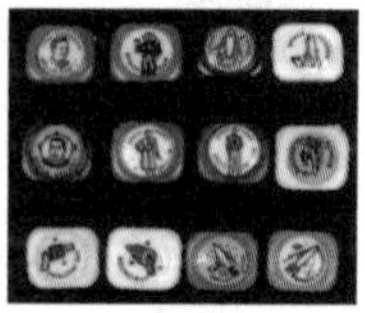

TCO-7

TCO-8

❑ **TCO-7. "Rocket Rings" Comic Book Ad,**
1951. Kellogg's Pep cereal. - **$2 $4 $6**

❑ **TCO-8. Kellogg's Plastic Rings With Insert Pictures,**
1951. Set of 12. Near Mint Set - **$200**
Each - **$5 $10 $15**

TCO-9

❑ **TCO-9. Cereal Box With "Tom Corbett Space Cadet Squadron" Back,**
1951. Also pictures "Rocket Launching Plane Catapulting Aircraft Carrier".
Complete Box - **$150 $300 $500**

TCO-10

❑ **TCO-10. Kellogg's "Space Cadet Rocketship" Action Picture Coin,**
1951. Plastic flicker disk from series picturing various Tom Corbett (and other) scenes. -
**$8 $12 $25**

TCO-11

❑ **TCO-11. "Space Cadet Song and March" Record Album with Sleeve,**
1951. Golden Record. - **$20 $40 $60**

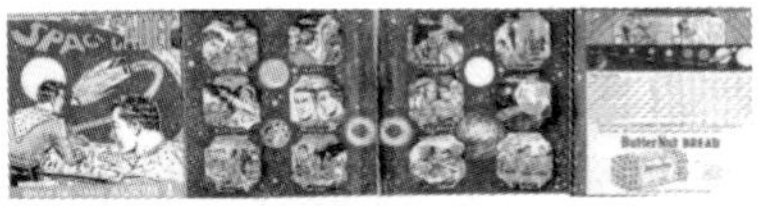

TCO-12

❑ **TCO-12. Butter-Nut Bread End Label Album #1,**
1952. Various sponsor imprints. Complete with 24 bread labels. Album #2 was also issued with additional set of 24 labels.
Near Mint Complete - **$625**
Album Only - **$30 $80 $125**
Each Label - **$10 $15 $25**

TCO-13

❑ **TCO-13. Fischer's Buttercup Bread End Label Album No. 2,**
1952. Various sponsors. Holds labels #25-48.
Near Mint Complete - **$625**
Album Only - **$30 $80 $125**
Each Label - **$10 $15 $25**

TCO-14

TCO-15

TCO-16

❑ **TCO-14. "Tom Corbett/Space Cadet" Silvered Metal Ring,**
c. 1952. - **$50 $85 $135**

❑ **TCO-15. Rocket Ring,**
c. 1952. Silvered brass and white gold luster metal inscribed on underside "Space Cadet/Tom Corbett Unit". - **$125 $225 $400**

❑ **TCO-16. "TV Digest" With Cover Article,**
1952. Weekly issue for August 23 with two-page article including photos. Front cover also pictures songstress Patti Page. - **$15 $30 $50**

TCO-17

❑ **TCO-17. Cereal Box With "Tom Corbett Space Goggles" Offer,**
1952. Gordon Gold Archives.
Used Complete - **$150 $300 $500**

TCO-18

❑ **TCO-18. Cereal Box With Back Panel For Pin-Up Or For Mask,**
1952. Mask in full color with text promoting both radio and TV shows.
Used Complete - **$150 $300 $500**

TCO-19

❑ **TCO-19. Kellogg's Pep Flat - 8 oz. Cereal Box,**
1952. Astro "Space Cadet" pictured on back. Also promotes Tom Corbett TV show. -
**$150 $300 $500**

TCO-20

TCO-21

❑ **TCO-20. Metal Badge,**
c. 1952. - **$25 $65 $150**

❑ **TCO-21. "Electronic Inter-Planet 2-Way Phone",**
1953. Store item. Cardboard box holding pair of plastic phones and coil of wire.
Boxed Set - **$100 $200 $300**
Each Phone - **$25 $50 $75**

TCO-22

❑ **TCO-22. "Tom Corbett Tru-Vue Stereo Film Card,"**
1954. Card is titled "The Secret From Space The Moon Pyramid." Near Mint Packet - **$40**
Loose - **$5 $10 $20**

TCO-23

❑ **TCO-23. View-Master Set,**
1954. Store item. - **$15 $25 $40**

TCO-24

❑ **TCO-24. Rocket-Lite Squadron Club Card,**
1950s. Reverse instructions for Space Cadet pin-on rocket light. - **$10 $30 $50**

TCO-25

**❏ TCO-25. Rocket-Lite Plastic Pin,**
1950s. Store item by Usalite. Battery operated. - **$25 $50 $100**

TCO-26

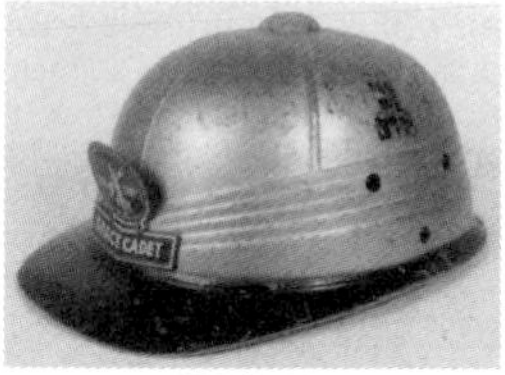

TCO-27

**❏ TCO-26. Die-Cut Metal Pin,**
1954. In Sears catalogue, came with purchase of Corbett flashlight. - **$20 $85 $165**
On Card **- $300**

**❏ TCO-27. Fiberboard Helmet,**
1950s. Scarce. Probable store item. Includes plastic badge on front. - **$75 $150 $225**

TCO-28

TCO-29

**❏ TCO-28. Metallic Silver Fabric Cap with Sunglasses,**
1950s. Scarce. Probable premium. - **$75 $150 $225**

**❏ TCO-29. Official Hat,**
1950s. Scarce. Probable store item. Includes plastic badge on front. - **$75 $150 $325**

TCO-30

**❏ TCO-30. "Tom Corbett Kellogg's Corn Flakes" Cereal Box,**
1950s. From a 1950s series of boxes that featured cut-out "Space Cadet Equipment."
Complete **- $75 $150 $400**

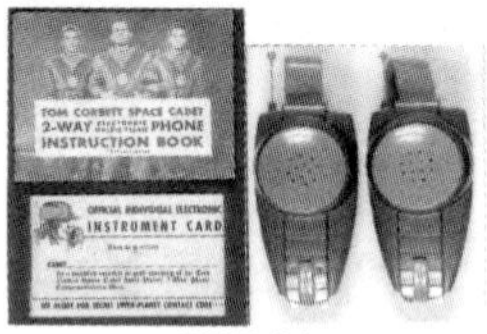

TCO-31

**❏ TCO-31. "Two-Way Electronic Walkie-Talkie Phone" Set,**
1950s. Store item by Remco.
Phone Set - **$30 $60 $100**
Instructions - **$15 $30 $50**
Code Card - **$15 $30 $50**

TCO-32

**❏ TCO-32. Visor,**
1950s. Cardboard cut-out from cereal box. - **$15 $25 $35**

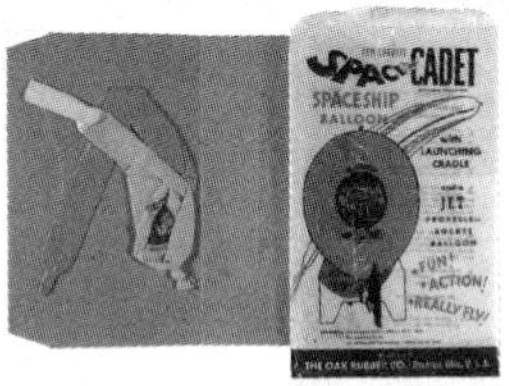


TCO-33

**❏ TCO-33. Spaceship Balloon With Mailer,**
1950s. Comes with unpunched cardboard base & two balloons. Probably store bought. - **$75 $125 $250**

TCO-34

TCO-35

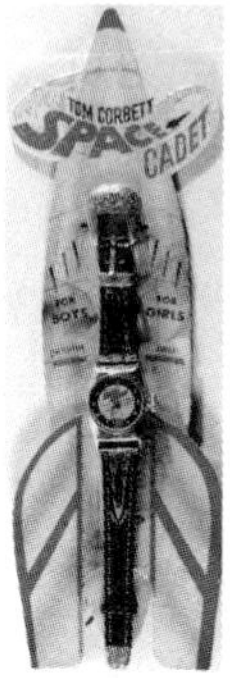


TCO-36

**❏ TCO-34. Space Cadet Patch,**
1950s. Cereal premium. One of several different. Each - **$20 $40 $60**

**❏ TCO-35. Pinback,**
1950s. Metallic silver center with very bright blue outer border. Rare. - **$75 $125 $225**

**❏ TCO-36. Watch on Die Cut Rocket Card,**
1950s. Ingraham.
Watch on card - **$425**
Watch only - **$75 $125 $200**

TCO-37

**❏ TCO-37. Model Craft Set,**
1950s. Box, powder, can, glue, paint set and 8 rubber molds. You could send off 10¢ for each extra mold. You could collect up to 350 different. Features molds for 7 Tom Corbett Space Cadet cast consisting of Tom, Roger, Astro, Captain Strong, Dr. Dale, and a Vesuvian as well as the logo for the TV show. - **$150 $350 $550**

TCO-38

**❏ TCO-38. Autographed Cast Photo,**
1990s. Signatures are of Jan Merlin, Al Markim, Frankie Thomas, Ed Bryce. Also signed by narrator Jackson Beck and director George Gould.
Near Mint - **$125**

## Tom Mix

**Tom Mix (1880-1940), the greatest Western film star of the silent era, was born and grew up in rural DuBois, Pennsylvania. He enlisted in the Army at the outbreak of the Spanish-American war in 1898 and achieved the rank of first sergeant. His overseas military adventures are part of the legend, not reality, as he never left the United States. After leaving the Army in 1902 he moved to Oklahoma and found work as a drum major, bartender, and part-time ranch hand. In 1904 he attended the St. Louis World's Fair as a member of the Oklahoma Cavalry Band. In 1905 he went to work as a "cowboy" for the Miller Brothers' 101 Real Wild West Ranch, barnstormed in other Wild West shows, and served as a deputy sheriff and night marshal.**

**Tom Mix's movie career began in 1909 for the Selig Polyscope Company, first as an**

advisor and troubleshooter, then doubling as a stunt man, and ultimately starring in, writing, and directing some 64 silent shorts. By 1917, when he was hired by William Fox Productions, he was a star, and by 1921 he was one of the country's 10 top box office attractions. Over a period of 10 years he made 78 silent features for Fox, most of them as an idealized Western hero, doing his own stunts and riding his chestnut steed, Tony the Wonder Horse, to fame and fortune. He made another six silent features in 1928-1929 for the Film Booking Office, then left Hollywood to tour and star in Sells Floto Circus from 1929 to 1931.

Returning to films, he and Tony Jr. made his first talkies, nine features for Universal Pictures in 1931-1932, and his last movie, *The Miracle Rider*, a 15-episode chapter play, for Mascot Pictures in 1935. That same year he bought a circus, and from 1935 to 1938 the Tom Mix Circus toured the country and performed for crowds of admirers. In 1940 he was killed in an automobile accident in Arizona.

The Tom Mix radio program aired from 1933 to 1950, on NBC until 1944, then on the Mutual network. Ralston cereal was the exclusive radio program sponsor. Various actors played Tom in what was billed as a Western detective program. Tom and the Ralston Straight Shooters operated out of the T-M Bar Ranch, solving mysteries, crusading for justice, finding water for the cattle, even fighting saboteurs during the war years. Helping out, along with Tony, were young Jimmy and Jane, the Old Wrangler, Sheriff Mike Shaw, Wash the cook, and Pecos Williams, a singing sidekick played by Joe "Curley" Bradley until he took over the role of Tom in 1940.

Ralston offered hundreds of Tom Mix premiums--rings, flashlights, magnifiers, whistles, sirens, spurs, telescopes, wooden guns, comic books, photo albums, badges, anything that could carry the familiar Ralston checkerboard design or the T-M Bar brand. Tom's first comic book appearance was in issue #1 of *The Comics* in 1937, and he had his own books in the 1940s and 1950s. Ralston briefly revived the Straight Shooters in 1982-1983 as a 50th anniversary tribute, offering a comic book, patch, cereal bowl and watch in exchange for box tops. The Tom Mix Museum in Dewey, Oklahoma, opened in 1968. An annual "National Tom Mix Festival" in DuBois, Pennsylvania, began in 1980.

TMX-1

TMX-2

❑ **TMX-1. "Tom Mix Fox Western Star" Pencil Tablet,**
c. 1925. Store item by Kay Co. Inc., New York City. 8x9-1/2". - **$25 $65 $125**

❑ **TMX-2. Coming Attractions Movie Theater Glass Slide,**
1927. For the movie "Tom Mix And Tony The Wonder Horse In The Arizona Wildcat." - **$35 $75 $125**

TMX-3

❑ **TMX-3. "Complete Novel Magazine" With Movie Story,**
1928. Pulp issue #35 for March featuring Tom Mix novel based on William Fox Production silent film "Daredevil's Reward." - **$75 $175 $325**

TMX-4

TMX-5

❑ **TMX-4. "Home Of Tom Mix" Postcard,**
c. 1929. Pacific Novelty Company. - **$10 $20 $35**

❑ **TMX-5. Photo Cover - Fox Trot Song Book,**
1929. Four pages. Store bought - **$25 $50 $100**

TMX-6

TMX-7

❑ **TMX-6. "Sells Floto Circus" Cello. Button,**
c. 1929. Word "Sells" is part of circus proper name. Mix toured with circus 1929-1931. - **$20 $50 $85**

❑ **TMX-7. "Tom Mix For Sheriff" Cello. Button,**
c. 1930. - **$200 $500 $900**

TMX-8

❑ **TMX-8. "State Theater" Contest Coupons,**
c. 1930. Series of 1-1/4x3-1/2" coupons inscribed with a single letter meant to be collected to spell out the phrase "Tom Mix Tickets" to obtain free admission. A free "Tom Mix Punching Ball" was awarded for a complete coupon set. Each Coupon - **$10 $20 $35**

TMX-9

❑ **TMX-9. "Thank You" Card With Dated Envelope,**
1931. 4-3/4x6-1/4". Text includes "...with the help of God and all my friends pullin' me by the boot straps I'm almost out again and will soon be feelin' right smart." - **$75 $150 $250**

TMX-10

TMX-11

❑ **TMX-10. "Tom Mix With Tony/Universal Pictures" Cello. Button,**
1932. From his 1932-1933 years at Universal. - **$65 $150 $300**

❑ **TMX-11. Chewing Gum Wrapper With Deputy Ring Offer,**
1933. National Chicle Co. Product copyright is 1933. Ring offer expired June 30, 1935. - **$80 $100 $150**

TMX-12

❑ **TMX-12. "Tom Mix Deputy Ring" Cardboard Mailing Holder,**
1933. National Chicle Gum. 2-5/8x8-1/8" red on cream. Designates ring owner as "a real Tom Mix Deputy." - **$100 $250 $500**

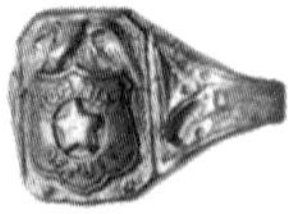

TMX-13

TMX-14

❑ **TMX-13. "Tom Mix Deputy" Gold And Silver Finish Brass Ring,**
1933. National Chicle Gum. Required 75 certificates clipped from gum wrappers. Offer expired June 30, 1935. See TMX-11, 12, and 18. - **$1000 $3000 $5000**

❑ **TMX-14. "The Life Of Tom Mix" First Club Manual,**
1933. Near Mint With Mailer - **$200**
Loose - **$50 $85 $150**

TMX-15

TMX-16

❑ **TMX-15. "Tom Mix Straight Shooters" Sheet Music,**
1933. Store item published by Shapiro, Bernstein & Co., New York. Shows two men, one in fancy outfit obviously representing Tom Mix along with young girl and young boy flanking "NBC" microphone. - **$15 $35 $60**

❑ **TMX-16. Exhibit Card,**
1933. - **$10 $20 $40**

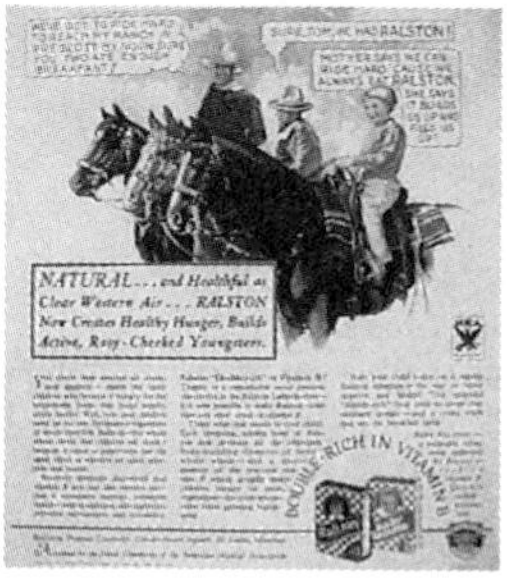

TMX-17

❑ **TMX-17. Premium Insert,**
1933. 5-3/4x6-1/4" full color insert included with the earliest premiums. - **$15 $25 $40**

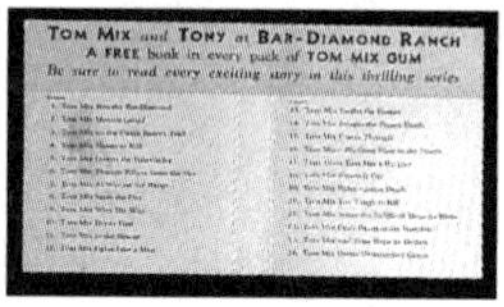


TMX-18

❑ **TMX-18. "Tom Mix Gum" Advertising Folder Designed Like A Book,**
1933. National Chicle Co. 6x10-1/2" yellow, black and white stiff cardboard which folds to front and back covers with a 1" wide spine. Inside lists all 24 titles in the series of free booklets given with the gum and reverse promotes the "Deputy Ring." Probably packed in gum packet boxes for use as dealer display. Rare. - **$125 $325 $525**

TMX-19

❑ **TMX-19. "Straight Shooters" Fabric Patch,**
1933. See TMX-32. - **$20 $50 $90**

TMX-20

TMX-21

❑ **TMX-20. Club Manual "Enlarged Edition",**
1933. Near Mint With Mailer - **$150**
Loose - **$40 $75 $125**

❑ **TMX-21. Premium Catalogue Sheet,**
1933. - **$20 $40 $75**

TMX-22

TMX-23

❑ **TMX-22. Tom Mix & Tony Photo,**
1933. Sent with both 1933 club manuals. - **$15 $25 $45**

❑ **TMX-23. Paper Lario With Tricks And Stunts Sheet,**
1933. Tricks Sheet - **$35 $80 $135**
Lario - **$50 $125 $225**

TMX-24

TMX-25

❑ **TMX-24. Cigar Box Label,**
1933. - **$10 $25 $50**

❑ **TMX-25. Cigar Box Label,**
1933. - **$15 $35 $60**

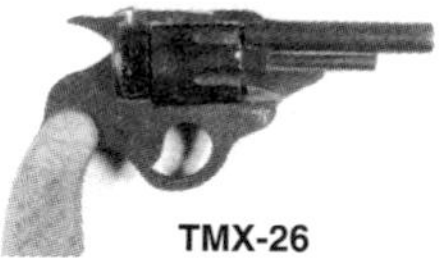

TMX-26

TMX-27

❑ **TMX-26. Wooden Revolver,**
1933. Earliest gun, opens and cylinder revolves. - **$50 $100 $165**

❑ **TMX-27. "Lucky Pocket Piece" Brass Medalet,**
c. 1933 "Exhibit Supply Company/Chicago" on reverse inside with horseshoe design. - **$25 $50 $100**

TMX-28

❑ **TMX-28. Cowboy Hat,**
1933. Rare premium. Name is not on inside. - **$250 $600 $1100**

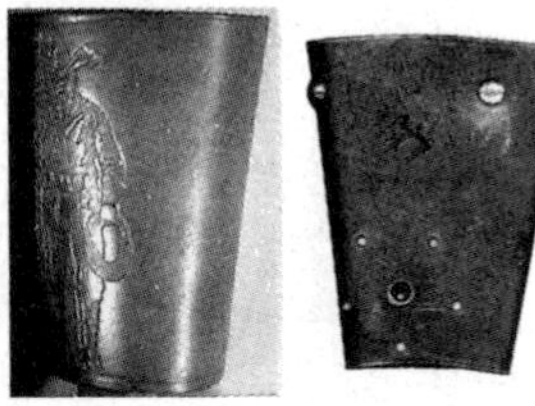

TMX-29

❑ **TMX-29. Leather Wrist Cuffs,**
1933. Shown at left, no Mix identification, depicts cowboy with lariat.
Set of Two - **$60 $150 $250**
With Mix Identification and Star (shown at right)
Set of Two Near Mint - **$350**

TMX-30

❑ **TMX-30. Metal Spurs With Leather Straps,**
1933. No Mix identification, horse head on top strap. Rubber rowels each have two metal jangle weights. - **$100 $200 $300**

TMX-31

TMX-32

❑ **TMX-31. Fabric Bandanna,**
1933. - **$30 $75 $150**

❑ **TMX-32. Second Version "Straight Shooters" Fabric Patch,**
1933. The 1933 patch TMX-19 is 2-1/4x2-1/4" of woven fabric. This example, which appears to be of the same time era, is 2-1/2x2-1/2" with the design printed on the fabric rather than woven into it. - **$65 $125 $200**

TMX-33

TMX-34

TMX-35

❑ **TMX-33. "Good Luck/TM" Spinner,**
1933. - **$20 $40 $75**

❑ **TMX-34. Horseshoe Nail Ring,**
1933. Generic horseshoe nail with silver luster. No Tom Mix markings. - **$20 $30 $40**

❑ **TMX-35. "TM" Spinner Ring,**
1933. Rare. Possibly a circus souvenir. - **$1000 $2000 $3600**

TMX-36

TMX-37

❑ **TMX-36. Radio Program 15x24" Cardboard Sign,**
c. 1933. Printed both sides. - **$100 $250 $450**

❑ **TMX-37. "Tom Mix" Bisque 5" Figurine,**
c. 1933. Rare. Store item. Only figural Mix item known. Made in Germany, marked #3509. - **$1000 $2750 $5250**

TMX-38

❑ **TMX-38. "Tom Mix In The Texas Bad Man" Movie Book,**
1934. Five Star Library book. 4-1/4x5" format. - **$35 $85 $175**

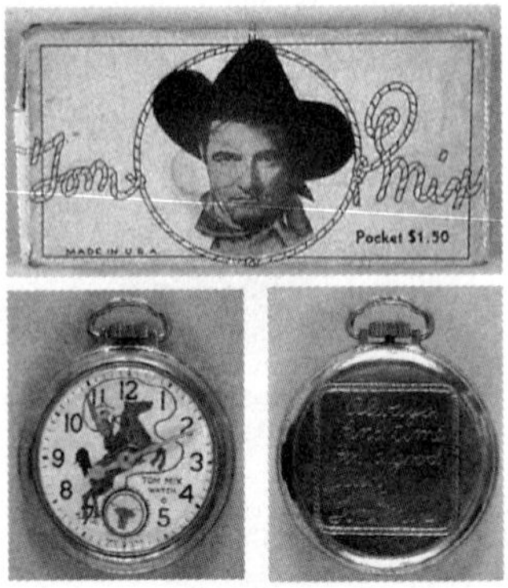


TMX-39

❑ **TMX-39. Tom Mix Pocket Watch With Box,**
1934. Store item by Ingersoll. Black and white box holds watch with color image of Tom on Tony. Hands are in yellow and reverse has inscription surrounded by rope design "Always Find Time For A Good Deed/Tom Mix."
Box - **$900 $1500 $2200**
Watch - **$1000 $2500 $4000**

TMX-40

❑ **TMX-40. Rodeorope And Full Color Box,**
1934. Store item. - **$200 $400 $700**

TMX-41

TMX-42

❑ **TMX-41. National Chicle Co. Gum Booklet #2 Example,**
1934. 48 numbered booklets.
Each - **$10 $25 $45**

❑ **TMX-42. Ralston Radio Ad Cardboard Sign,**
1934. Diecut cardboard 20x32" urging listenership over NBC Red Network. - **$250 $500 $900**

TMX-43

❑ **TMX-43. Press Book,**
1934. Rare. Elaborate 12 page book which features Tom Mix's first serial, "The Miracle Rider." Talks about Tom Mix's radio audience reaching 25 million listeners, his product line, and how to get premiums. Shows all 15 chapter lobby cards and posters. 16x 21" - **$400 $900 $1200**

TMX-44

❑ **TMX-44. Premiums Catalogue Folder Sheet,**
1934. Catalogue designated C 135 G. -
**$20 $35 $60**

TMX-45

❑ **TMX-45. "Official Commission/Ranch Boss" Certificate,**
1934. Promotion certification with facsimile signature of Tom Mix and "The Old Wrangler" as witness. - **$100 $250 $400**

TMX-46

❑ **TMX-46. Paper Mask,**
1934. Scarce. - **$250 $550 $850**

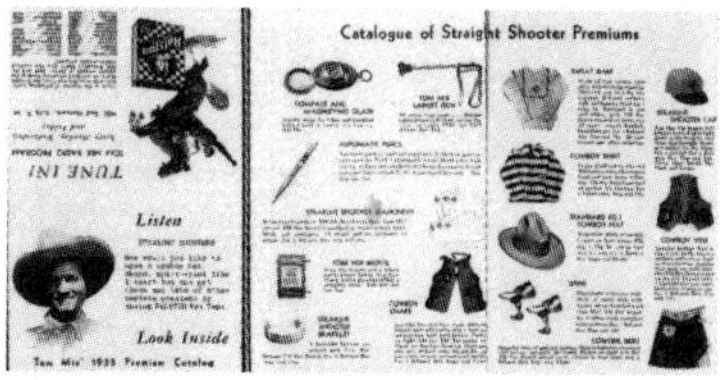


TMX-47

❑ **TMX-47. Premiums Catalogue Folder Sheet,**
1934. Catalogue designated C 135 O. -
**$15 $30 $50**

TMX-48

❑ **TMX-48. "Series A" Photo Set,**
1934. Set of five.
Each Photo Or Mailer - **$10 $25 $50**

TMX-49

❑ **TMX-49. "Series B" Photo Set With Envelope,**
1934. Set of five photos.
Each Photo Or Mailer - **$10 $25 $50**

TMX-50

❑ **TMX-50. "Tom Mix And Tony Jr. In Terror Trail" Photoplay Big Little Book,**
1934. Whitman #762. - **$25 $60 $150**

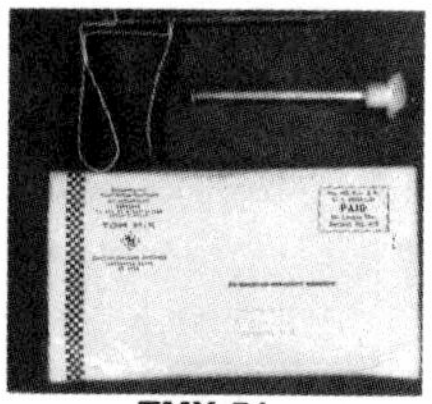

TMX-51

TMX-52

❑ **TMX-51. Zyp Gun With Mailer Envelope,**
1934. Scarce. Metal spring gun with rubber cup dart. Also known as Tom Mix Target Gun.
Gun With Dart - **$200 $550 $800**
Mailer - **$15 $35 $50**

❑ **TMX-52. "TM" Ralston Logo Brass Ring,**
1935. Named in ads "Tom Mix Lucky Ring". -
**$60 $90 $140**

TMX-53

❑ **TMX-53. "Tom Mix In Flaming Guns" Movie Edition Book,**
1935. Five Star Library Engle-Van Wiseman store item in BLB format with photos from Universal film. Scarce title. - **$125 $250 $400**

TMX-54

❑ **TMX-54. Tom Mix Big Little Book Puzzles (Boxed),**
1935. Store item. - **$100 $300 $450**

TMX-55

❑ **TMX-55. "Tom Mix Plays A Lone Hand" Big Little Book,**
1935. Whitman #1173. - **$20 $60 $150**

TMX-56

❑ **TMX-56. "Miracle Riders" Picture Folio,**
1935. Holds 15 bw numbered photo pages apparently corresponding to 15 serial chapters. Distributed by theaters, sponsored by Tootsie Rolls. Set - **$150 $300 $500**

TMX-57

TMX-58

❑ **TMX-57. "Miracle Rider" Serial Club Cello. Button,**
1935. Mascot. - **$150 $400 $800**

❑ **TMX-58. Paint Book,**
1935. Store item. - **$100 $250 $500**

TMX-59

❑ **TMX-59. "Shooting Gallery" Cardboard Target With Box,**
1935. Store item by Parker Brothers. Includes rubber band gun. - **$75 $250 $500**

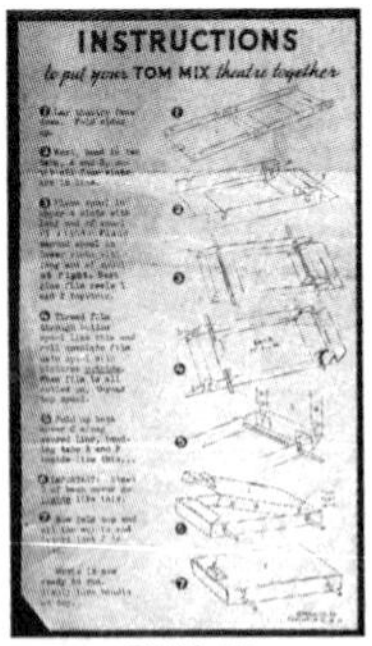


TMX-60

TMX-61

❑ **TMX-60. Theater Instructions,**
1935. 7-step instruction sheet. - **$15 $25 $45**

❑ **TMX-61. Litho. Portrait Button,**
1935. Canvas Products Co., St. Louis. Five buttons given with purchase of Tom Mix tent. - **$35 $100 $175**

TMX-62

TMX-63

❑ **TMX-62. Western Song Book,**
1935.Sixty-eight page book shows photos of Tom Mix and promotes his films. Includes letter from Tom Mix. - **$50 $100 $200**

❑ **TMX-63. "The Trail Of The Terrible 6" Booklet,**
1935. - **$25 $65 $150**

TMX-64

❑ **TMX-64. Premium Insert Folder,**
1935. 3-1/4x6" color folder for "Mother!" - **$8 $15 $30**

TMX-65

❑ **TMX-65. Sunday Comics Color Ad For "2 In 1 Compass",**
1935. This example of the ad has expiration date of March 6, 1937. See TMX-85. - **$8 $15 $25**

TMX-66

TMX-67

❑ **TMX-66. Tom Mix Wristwatch,**
1935. Store item by Ingersoll. Same dial design as pocket watch but no reverse inscription. Came with metal link bands and the largest two closest to the case have black on silver luster portraits of Tom. - **$1000 $2200 $4000**

❑ **TMX-67. Dixie Ice Cream Picture,**
1935. Reverse has four scenes from Mascot serial "The Miracle Rider." - **$30 $75 $135**

TMX-68

❑ **TMX-68. Ralston Promotional Store Window Transfer,**
1935. 8-1/4x8-1/2" backing sheet holds superb color gummed front decal for placement on inner surface of window or door. Rare. - **$150 $300 $600**

TMX-69

❑ **TMX-69. "Tom Mix And Tony" Wood/Metal Riding Toy,**
c. 1935. Store item by Mengel Co. Inc. 5-3/4x17x16" tall. - **$125 $300 $600**

TMX-70

TMX-71

❑ **TMX-70. "Western Movie" Cardboard Mechanical Viewer,**
1935. Film scenes from "The Miracle Rider" Mascot Pictures serial. - **$65 $175 $275**

❑ **TMX-71. "Western Movie" Cardboard Box Viewer,**
1935. Film scenes from "Rustlers Roundup". - **$65 $175 $275**

**TMX-72**

❑ **TMX-72. "Miracle Rider" Dixie Ice Cream Lid,**
1935. - **$10 $20 $30**

**TMX-73**

❑ **TMX-73. Promo,**
1935. Premium insert to promote Tom Mix film "The Miracle Rider." - **$15 $30 $50**

**TMX-74**

❑ **TMX-74. Spinning Rope,**
1935. Red, white and blue twine with Mix Ralston endorsement on wooden grip. - **$40 $80 $165**

(ENLARGED VIEW)
**TMX-75**

❑ **TMX-75. Suede Leather Chaps,**
1935. - **$50 $175 $400**

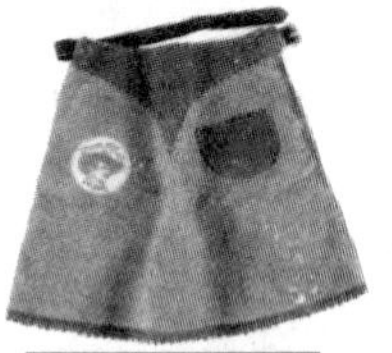

(ENLARGED VIEW)
**TMX-76**

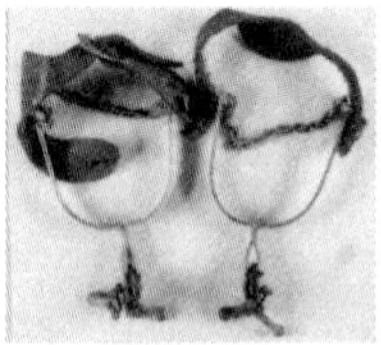
**TMX-77**

❑ **TMX-76. Suede Leather Cowgirl Skirt,**
1935. - **$60 $175 $400**

❑ **TMX-77. Metal Spurs With Leather Straps,**
1935. Straps have TM Bar Ranch symbol. - **$75 $175 $300**

**TMX-78**

❑ **TMX-78. Leather Wrist Cuffs,**
1935. - **$60 $150 $300**

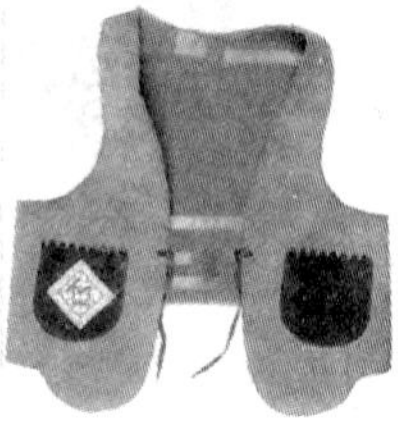
**TMX-79**

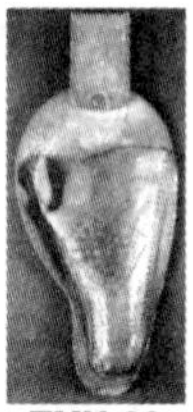
**TMX-80**

**TMX-81**

❑ **TMX-79. Suede Vest,**
1935. - **$60 $150 $200**

❑ **TMX-80. Brown Leather Holster,**
1935. Cover panel has Tom Mix Ralston logo. - **$75 $200 $300**

❑ **TMX-81. Leather Bracelet With Foil On Brass Title Plate,**
1935. Tom Mix or Ralston markings on both front and back. Named in ads "Lucky Wrist Band".
Complete - **$35 $75 $150**
No Strap - **$20 $40 $75**

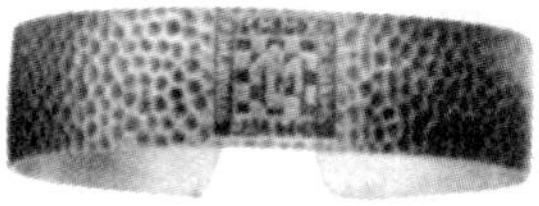
**TMX-82**

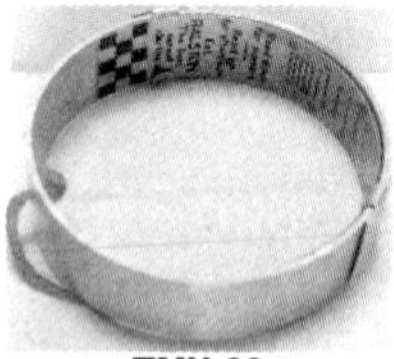
**TMX-83**

❑ **TMX-82. Straight Shooter Bracelet With Checkerboard Logo,**
1935. Silvered brass. - **$150 $250 $500**

❑ **TMX-83. Sun Watch,**
1935. - **$20 $40 $90**

**TMX-85**

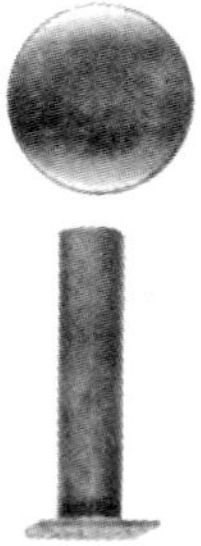
**TMX-84**

**TMX-86**

❑ **TMX-84. Bar Brand Branding Iron With Ink Pad Tin,**
1935. Brass stamper has TM initials and checkerboard design.
Branding Iron - **$25 $50 $85**
Ink Tin - **$30 $65 $100**

❑ **TMX-85. Compass With Magnifier,**
1935. Unmarked Ralston premium. Aluminum case with eyelet. See TMX-65. - **$15 $25 $40**

❑ **TMX-86. Lucky Charm Sterling Silver Horseshoe,**
1935. - **$90 $175 $300**

**TMX-87**

❑ **TMX-87. Premium Catalogue Folder,**
1936. - **$15 $30 $50**

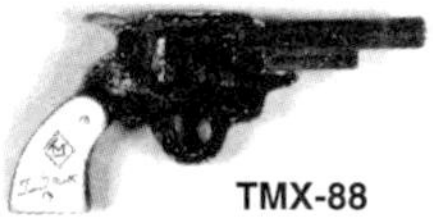
**TMX-88**

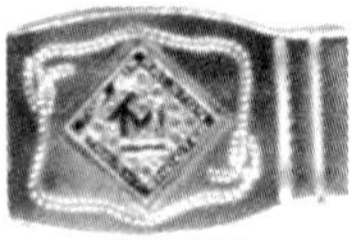
**TMX-89**

❑ **TMX-88. Wood Gun With Cardboard Handles,**
1936. Cylinder revolves but gun doesn't open. - **$75 $150 $225**

❑ **TMX-89. Championship Cowboy Belt Buckle,**
1936. Brass with foil paper insert, also came with belt. Buckle Only - **$35 $75 $125**
Buckle And Belt - **$50 $125 $200**

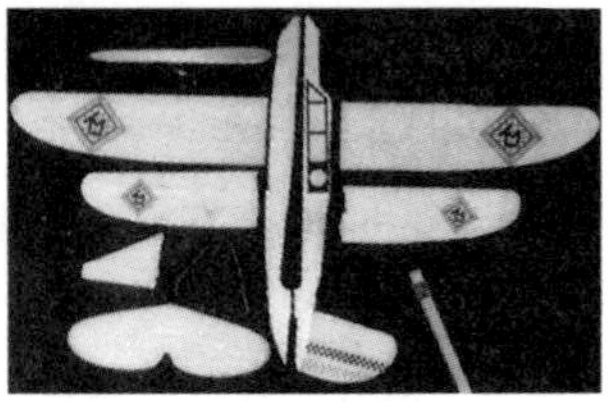
**TMX-90**

❑ **TMX-90. Flying Model Airplane Kit,**
1936. Scarce. Balsa wood with Ralston logo decals. - **$150 $300 $500**

**TMX-91**

❑ **TMX-91. "Rocket Parachute",**
1936. Consists of balsa and cardboard launcher, wood stick with rubber band, metal figure string joined to paper parachute.
Boxed - **$50 $100 $200**
Loose - **$35 $60 $100**

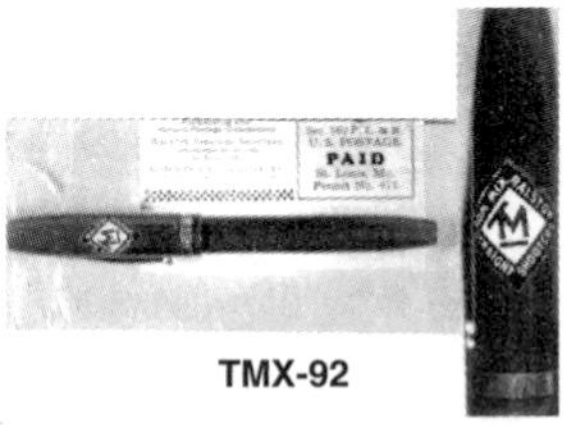

**TMX-92**

❑ **TMX-92. Fountain Pen With Mailer Envelope,**
1936. Pen cap has Tom Mix ranch brand symbol decal. Pen - **$40 $80 $150**
Mailer - **$8 $12 $20**

**TMX-93**

❑ **TMX-93. Girl's Brass Dangle Charm Bracelet,**
1936. Scarce. Charms depict ranch symbol, Tom on Tony, steer head, six-shooter. Also called "Championship Cowgirl Bracelet". - **$200 $600 $900**

**TMX-94**

❑ **TMX-94. "Tom Mix Circus" Season Tour Summary,**
1936. 7x10" with 24 pages issued "in-house" for employees. Rare. - **$75 $200 $300**

**TMX-95**

❑ **TMX-95. "Tom Mix Circus And Wild West" Poster,**
c. 1936. About 28x42". - **$75 $150 $275**

**TMX-96**

❑ **TMX-96. Signet Ring Newspaper Advertisement,**
1936. - **$10 $20 $30**

**TMX-97**

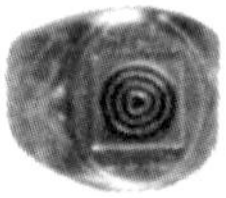
**TMX-98**

❑ **TMX-97. Lucky Signet Ring,**
1936. Brass bands topped by raised personalized single initial designated by orderer. Ad mentions onyx-like black background around initial but ring was issued both with and without black background. - **$100 $200 $300**

❑ **TMX-98. "Marlin Guns" Brass Target Ring,**
1937. Marlin Firearms Co. Tom Mix endorsed a Marlin rifle called the "Tom Mix Special .22 Caliber Rifle." The actual rifle is inscribed with his name. Mix appeared in Marlin ads promoting the rifle. The same ads offered a "simulated gold Military Type Ring" and a booklet by the National Rifle Association titled "How To Set Up A Rifle Range" for ten cents. Later, the rings were also offered as a "Gold Bull's Eye Ring" available to boys in lots of ten or more at 6 cents each with the suggestion that the rings be resold for 10 cents each and used as an insignia for members of a Marlin Club. Still later, in the 1950s, Marlin gave away the ring from their booths at National Rifle Association meetings and exhibits. - **$100 $175 $300**

**TMX-99**

❑ **TMX-99. Premium Catalogue Folder,**
1937. Pictured premiums include Signet Ring. - **$60 $70 $80**

**TMX-100**

**TMX-101**

❑ **TMX-100. "Ralston Straight Shooter News" Vol. 1 #1 Issue,**
1937. - **$35 $75 $150**

❑ **TMX-101. "Ralston Straight Shooter News" #2,**
1937. - **$25 $65 $125**

**TMX-102**

❑ **TMX-102. Baby Turtle Newspaper Advertisement,**
1937. Premium was a real live baby turtle with Mix decal on its shell. - **$10 $15 $30**

TMX-103

❑ **TMX-103. Movie Make-Up Kit With Paper,**
1937. Five tins with TM brand and words Clown, Indian, Chink, Mexican, Negro.
Complete - **$50 $100 $175**
Each Tin - **$8 $12 $25**

TMX-104

❑ **TMX-104. "Tom Mix Circus" 9x23" Felt Pennant,**
1937. - **$150 $300 $500**

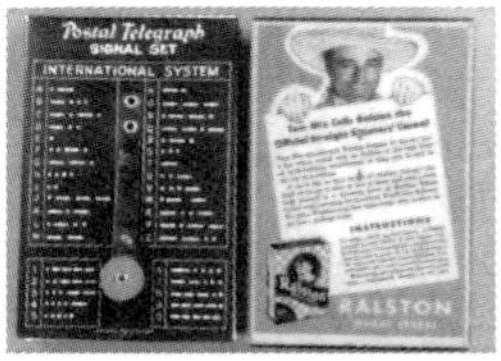


TMX-105

❑ **TMX-105. "Postal Telegraph Signal Set",**
1937. Cardboard box with metal tapper key. - **$50 $100 $175**

TMX-106 TMX-107

❑ **TMX-106. "Tom Mix And The Hoard Of Montezuma" Big Little Book,**
1937. Whitman #1462. - **$15 $50 $125**

❑ **TMX-107. "Tom Mix And The Scourge Of Paradise Valley" Book,**
1937. Whitman Big Big Book #4068. - **$50 $125 $300**

TMX-108

❑ **TMX-108. "Tom Mix In The Range War" Big Little Book,**
1937. Whitman #1166. - **$20 $50 $125**

TMX-109

❑ **TMX-109. Silver Frame Photo,**
1937. Photo is personalized by recipient first name. - **$35 $65 $135**

TMX-110

❑ **TMX-110. Straight Shooters Badge Offer Flyer,**
1937. A three-fold sheet 5x7-3/4" that includes coupon. Scarce as these were typically sent into Ralston with one box top to acquire the badge. Has 1934 copyright but not used until 1937. Text refers to "silver plated" version of the badge. - **$75 $150 $300**

TMX-111 TMX-112

❑ **TMX-111. Straight Shooter Metal Badge With Foil Paper Insert,**
1937. Silver luster. - **$25 $75 $140**

❑ **TMX-112. Straight Shooter Brass Badge,**
1937. Foil paper symbol. - **$35 $85 $160**

TMX-113 TMX-114

❑ **TMX-113. Straight Shooter Badge Lead Proof,**
c. 1937. Unique - **$800**

❑ **TMX-114. Prototype "Ranch Boss" Enameled Brass Badge,**
c. 1937. Trial design for Ralston approval by Robbins Co., Massachusetts with enamel emblem rather than foil paper. Unique - **$5000**

TMX-115

❑ **TMX-115. Prototype "Tom Mix Ralston Straight Shooters" Star Brass Badge,**
c. 1937. Trial design for Ralston approval by Robbins Co., Massachusetts. Unique - **$5000**

TMX-116

❑ **TMX-116. "Big Little Book" Cards,**
1937. Cards are 2-7/16x2-7/8" with 32 picturing Tom Mix although these are a subset from a larger set totaling seven different characters.
Each Tom Mix Card - **$25 $60 $85**

TMX-117

❑ **TMX-117. Second Variety Wrangler Badge Folder,**
1938. Item has 1934 Ralston copyright, but not used until 1938. 4x6" folder opens to 6x12" with slot for holding "Wrangler's Badge" which we believe refers to the version picturing him frontally rather than in partial profile. Includes offer to obtain "Ranch Boss" badge. See TMX-125 and 127. - **$50 $100 $175**

TMX-118

TMX-119

❑ **TMX-118. Premium Catalogue Sheet,**
1938. - **$15 $25 $50**

❑ **TMX-119. "Wrangler" Prototype Badge By Robbins,**
1938. Prototype brass badge resembling the badge issued in 1938 but the badge actually issued has a foil paper depicting the Ralston checkerboard while on this prototype there is no foil and the red color along with the "TM" initials in blue are applied directly to the brass. Rare and only one other example known with identical coloring. Near Mint - **$1000**

TMX-120

❑ **TMX-120. Secret Ink Writing Kit,**
1938. Includes: manual, cardboard decoder, two glass vials of ink and developer.
Manual - **$50 $125 $300**
Decoder - **$15 $50 $100**
Each Vial - **$10 $40 $60**

TMX-121

TMX-122

❑ **TMX-121. Metal Telescope,**
1938. Near Mint With Mailer - **$175**
Loose - **$35 $75 $125**

❑ **TMX-122. Bullet Flashlight,**
1938. 3" silvered brass tube with plastic end cap holding bulb. - **$50 $85 $150**

TMX-123

❑ **TMX-123. Telephone Set,**
1938. Litho. tin transmitter and receiver units joined by string. - **$30 $75 $100**

TMX-124

❑ **TMX-124. Wrangler Badge Folder,**
1938. - **$40 $100 $175**

TMX-125

TMX-126

❑ **TMX-125. "Wrangler" Brass Badge,**
1938. - **$50 $125 $200**

❑ **TMX-126. Wrangler Badge Lead Proof,**
c. 1938. Unique - **$1000**

TMX-127

TMX-128

❑ **TMX-127. "Wrangler" Metal Badge With Foil Paper Insert,**
1938. Version pictures him frontally rather than partial profile. Issued in either silver or gold luster. Either Version - **$75 $175 $325**

❑ **TMX-128. "Ranch Boss" Brass Rank Badge,**
1938. Centered by foil paper emblem. - **$125 $325 $650**

TMX-129

TMX-130

❑ **TMX-129. Ranch Boss Badge Lead Proof,**
c. 1938. Unique - **$2500**

❑ **TMX-130. Look-In Mystery Ring,**
1938. Brass with tiny view hole for inside portrait photo of Tom with Tony. - **$100 $200 $425**

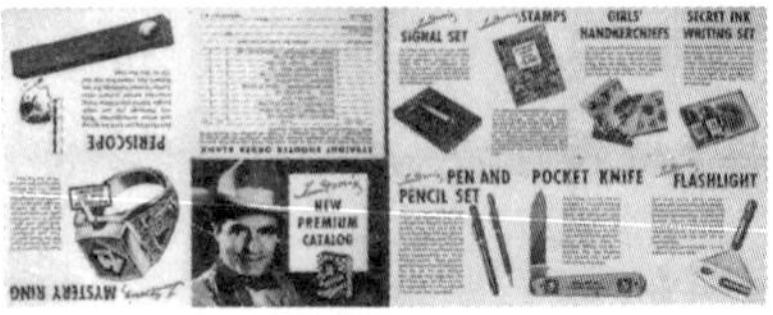

TMX-131

❑ **TMX-131. Premium Catalogue Folder Sheet,**
1939. - **$20 $30 $50**

TMX-132

❑ **TMX-132. Premium Catalogue,**
1939. 4x5" brown and white folded sheet. Contents picture three Tom Mix premiums plus generic premiums for adults. - **$10 $20 $35**

TMX-133

TMX-134

❑ **TMX-133. Wood Gun,**
1939. No moving parts. - **$65 $125 $175**

❑ **TMX-134. Streamline Parachute Plane,**
1939. Scarce. Balsa wood with designs in red and blue. Metal hinged wings. Came with parachutist and parachute. See next item.
Plane Only - **$125 $300 $450**

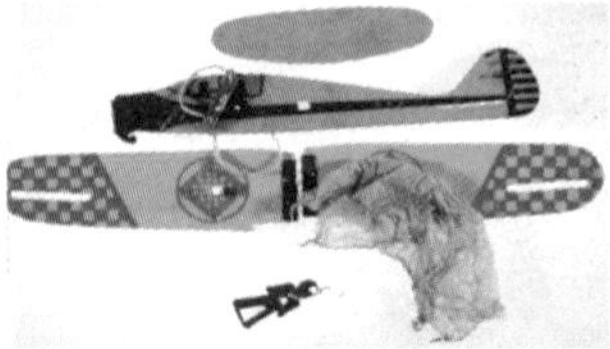

TMX-135

❑ **TMX-135. Streamline Plane Parachutist And Parachute,**
1939. Rare. Came with previous item. Metal figure smaller than 1936 Rocket Parachute and parachute is green or red. - **$75 $165 $250**

TMX-136

❑ **TMX-136. Signal Flashlight,**
1939. 3" metal tube with lens disk for red, green or clear light. Lens often missing and plastic end cap often cracked. Complete - **$30 $75 $150**

TMX-137

❑ **TMX-137. Cardboard Periscope,**
1939. Blue Tube - **$25 $50 $90**
Black Tube - **$50 $100 $150**

TMX-138 TMX-139 TMX-140

❑ **TMX-138. "Straight Shooters" Pocketknife,**
1939. - **$30 $75 $125**

❑ **TMX-139. Brass Compass And Magnifier,**
1939. Magnifying lens swings out. -
**$20 $40 $85**

❑ **TMX-140. Pinback,**
1930s. Black and white 1 1/4". - **$75 $150 $250**

TMX-141

❑ **TMX-141. Leather Belt With "Tom Mix" Buckle,**
1930s. Store item. - **$75 $125 $200**

TMX-142

❑ **TMX-142. Wooden Gun Delay Card,**
1930s. Ralston. 4x8" with art of Tom in workshop sweating over gun saying "Gosh I'm Sorry To Be So Late With This Gun, But How'd I Know Everyone In America Was Gonna Want One Of 'Em!" Which of three premium guns this applied to is unspecified. - **$50 $125 $175**

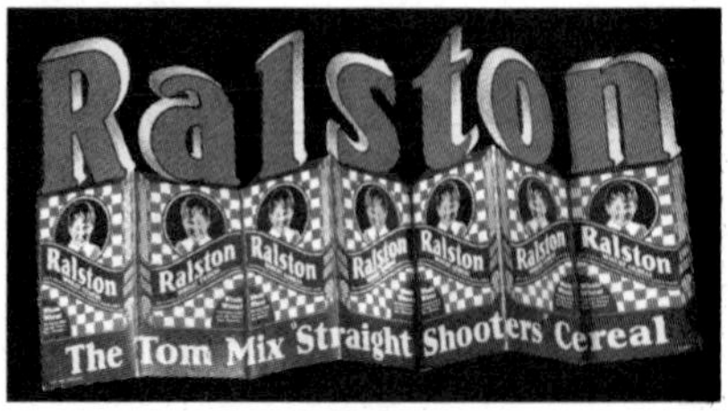


TMX-143

❑ **TMX-143. Ralston Diecut Accordion Fold Display Sign,**
1930s. Rare. - **$500 $1350 $2000**

TMX-144

TMX-145

❑ **TMX-144. Cinema Star Card #7,**
1930s. England. Wills Cigarettes premium. -
**$10 $20 $30**

❑ **TMX-145. Event Cello. Button,**
1930s. Issuer unknown. Blue on white, 1 1/4". -
**$20 $60 $100**

TMX-146

TMX-147

❑ **TMX-146. Hollywood Gum Card,**
1930s. - **$20 $40 $60**

❑ **TMX-147. "Wild West Club" Member Cello. Button,**
1930s. Rare. - **$250 $750 $1200**

TMX-148 TMX-149 TMX-150

❑ **TMX-148. "Toledo Paramount Theater" Movie Cello. Button,**
1930s. Scarce issue from a single theater in Ohio. - **$150 $425 $650**

❑ **TMX-149. "Yankiboy Play Clothes" Cello. Button,**
1930s. Yellow rim 1-3/4" size. - **$40 $85 $140**

❑ **TMX-150. "Yankiboy Play Clothes" 2" Cello. Button,**
1930s. Orange rim. - **$30 $55 $80**

**TMX-151**

❑ **TMX-151. "Rodeo Box" Cardboard Pencil Case,**
1930s. Probably a store item or circus souvenir. Inscribed for "Tom Mix & Tony" with rodeo generic art. - **$35 $85 $150**

**TMX-152** **TMX-153**

❑ **TMX-152. "My Own Confection" Candy Box,**
1930s. Casey Concession Co. Cardboard box for "Rare Sunshine Vitamin D" Candy probably sold at Tom Mix live performances. -
**$35 $100 $200**

❑ **TMX-153. Cello./Steel Pocketknife,**
1930s. Store item by Imperial. - **$40 $100 $175**

**TMX-154**

❑ **TMX-154. Pocketknife 6x24" Paper Store Sign,**
1930s. Scarce. - **$150 $275 $425**

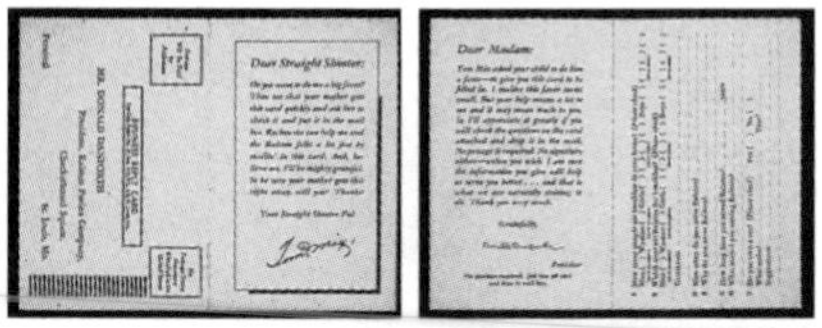


**TMX-155**

❑ **TMX-155. Ralston Purina Survey Folder,**
1930s. Perforated folder consisting of message from Tom asking child to pass the folder on to mother along with message addressed "Dear Madam" from company president Donald Danforth plus survey card on back of postpaid postcard. Complete - **$20 $30 $60**

**TMX-156**

❑ **TMX-156. Personal Christmas Card,**
1930s. 7x9" greeting card with front cover art of Indian blanket inscribed "A Blanket Message From The Mixes." Example we have seen was signed but not by Tom Mix.
With Mix Signature - **$150 $300 $450**
Secretarial Signature Or Unsigned -
**$75 $125 $225**

**TMX-157**

❑ **TMX-157. "Radio Rifle" Promotional Brochure,**
1930s. Made by Rock-Ola. 8-3/4x11-1/2" four-sided folder in red, black and white aimed at "Operators." This large coin-operated device retailed for - $434.50. A licensed item although Tom's name does not appear on the artist renditions of the device. Folder - **$65 $125 $175**

**TMX-158**

❑ **TMX-158. Rexall Toothpaste Puzzle,**
1930s. In Envelope - **$50 $100 $165**
Loose - **$25 $50 $85**

**TMX-159**

❑ **TMX-159. Cardboard Headband With Feathers,**
1930s. Realto Theater and probably others. Total length of 18" marked "Made In Germany." -
**$75 $165 $275**

**TMX-160** **TMX-161**

❑ **TMX-160. "Capturing Outlaws In The Bad Lands",**
1930s. Compliments Ralston Corn Flakes. Paper photo with facsimile Mix inscription and signature. Reverse has short story "As Told By The Old Wrangler". - **$50 $90 $150**

❑ **TMX-161. Book And Album,**
1930s. Autograph book and birthday album. Theater premium, 20 pages. Has write-up on Tom Mix and promotes film "The Best Bad Man." - **$50 $100 $150**

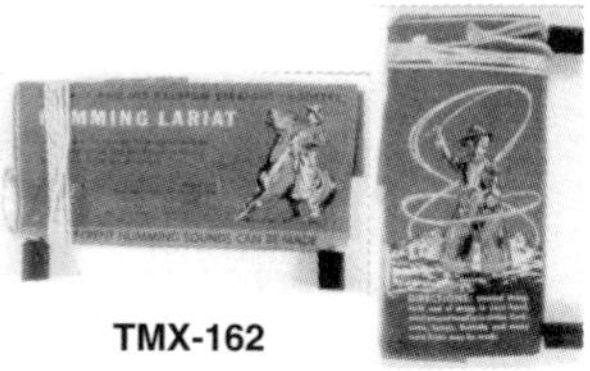

**TMX-162**

❑ **TMX-162. Humming Lariat**
1930s. Store item. - **$50 $125 $200**

**TMX-163**

❑ **TMX-163. "Purina Bread" Handbill,**
1930s. For various groceries. - **$35 $70 $100**

**TMX-164** **TMX-165**

❏ **TMX-164. "Tom Mix Comics Book 1",**
1940. Ralston premium sent via mail so rarely found in top condition. Eleven additional issued between 1940-1942. - **$350 $1750 $3600**

❏ **TMX-165. "Tom Mix Comics Book 2",**
1940. - **$106 $319 $1000**

**TMX-166**

❏ **TMX-166. "Stars Of Our Radio Program" Fan Card,**
1940. Back has form message for sending verses to contest song. - **$50 $100 $175**

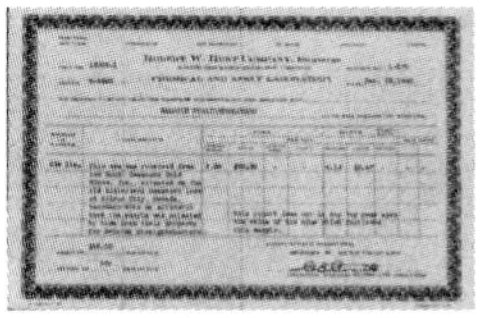

**TMX-167**

**TMX-168**

❏ **TMX-167. Gold Ore Assayer's Certificate,**
1940. Came folded with watch fob. - **$35 $75 $150**

❏ **TMX-168. Gold Ore Watch Fob,**
1940. - **$20 $50 $75**

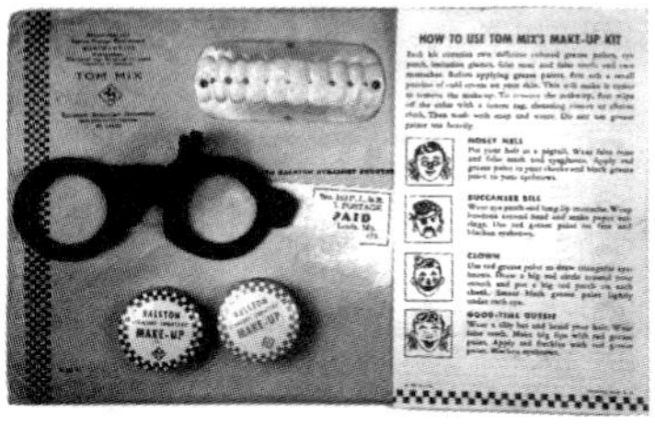


**TMX-169**

❏ **TMX-169. Tom Mix's Make-Up Kit,**
1940. Greasepaint in tin canisters of red or black checkerboard design. Other contents are instruction sheet, eye patch, imitation glasses, false nose and false teeth, and two moustaches.
Near Mint With Mailer - **$300**
Each Tin - **$8 $12 $20**
Nose or Teeth - **$15 $25 $50**
Other Pieces - **$5 $12 $20**

**TMX-170**

❏ **TMX-170. Indian Blow Gun Target Printer's Engraving Plate,**
1940. Unique - **$1200**

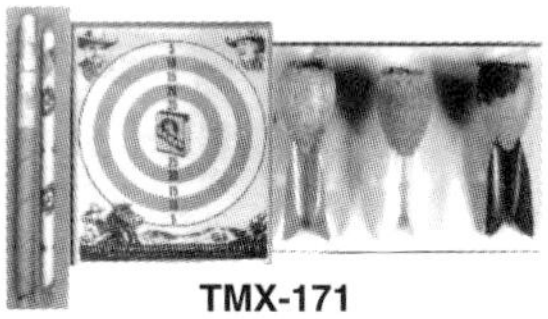

**TMX-171**

❏ **TMX-171. Indian Blow Gun Set,**
1940. Scarce. With paper target, four darts, mailer tube. Near Mint With Mailer - **$600**
Target - **$50 $100 $150**
Blow Gun - **$50 $100 $150**
Each Dart - **$15 $30 $50**

**TMX-172**

❏ **TMX-172. Telegraph Set With Box Mailer,**
1940. Cardboard with metal tapper key.
Telegraph - **$35 $75 $125**
Box - **$10 $20 $40**

**TMX-173**

**TMX-174**

❏ **TMX-173. Straight Shooters Manual,**
1941. - **$20 $50 $85**

❏ **TMX-174. "Tom Mix Comics" #3,**
1941. - **$66 $197 $650**

**TMX-175**

**TMX-176**

❏ **TMX-175. "Tom Mix Comics" #4,**
1941. - **$66 $197 $650**

❏ **TMX-176. "Tom Mix Comics" #5,**
1941. - **$66 $197 $650**

**TMX-177**

**TMX-178**

❏ **TMX-177. "Tom Mix Comics" #6,**
1941. - **$66 $197 $650**

❏ **TMX-178. "Tom Mix Comics" #7,**
1941. - **$66 $197 $650**

**TMX-179**

**TMX-180**

❏ **TMX-179. Six-Gun Brass Decoder Badge,**
1941. Gun turns brass pointer on reverse to one of nine code words. - **$40 $75 $140**

❏ **TMX-180. "Captain" Silvered Brass Spur Badge,**
1941. - **$60 $135 $200**

**TMX-181**

**TMX-182**

❏ **TMX-181. "Tom Mix Comics" #8,**
1942. - **$66 $197 $650**

❏ **TMX-182. "Tom Mix Comics" #9,**
1942. - **$66 $197 $650**

TMX-183

❑ **TMX-183. "Tom Mix Commandos Comics" Book #10,**
1942. - **$55 $165 $550**

TMX-184

TMX-185

❑ **TMX-184. "Tom Mix Commandos" Comic Book #11,**
1942. - **$55 $165 $550**

❑ **TMX-185. "Tom Mix Commandos" Comic Book #12,**
1942. - **$55 $165 $550**

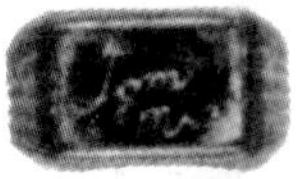
TMX-186

TMX-187

TMX-188

❑ **TMX-186. "Tom Mix" Signature Ring,**
1942. Brass with sterling silver top plate. - **$100 $200 $300**

❑ **TMX-187. Siren Ring,**
1944. Brass with enclosed siren disk wheel for blowing. - **$25 $75 $125**

❑ **TMX-188. "Secret Manual",**
1944. - **$25 $60 $100**

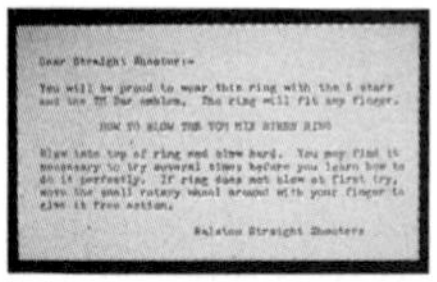
TMX-189

❑ **TMX-189. Siren Ring Instruction Flyer,**
1944. - **$15 $25 $50**

TMX-190

❑ **TMX-190. "Curley Bradley" Photo With Mailer,**
1945. 8x10" glossy black and white with facsimile signature and title "The Tom Mix Of Radio."
Mailer - **$15 $25 $40**
Photo - **$50 $125 $175**

TMX-191

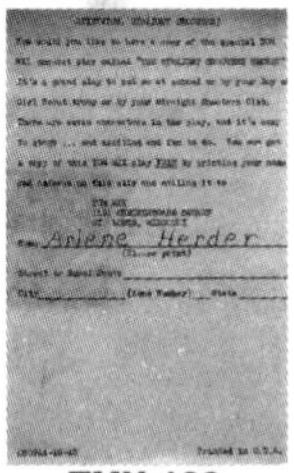
TMX-192

❑ **TMX-191. "Tom Mix Straight Shooters Album" Manual,**
1945. Near Mint With Envelope - **$150**
Manual Only - **$25 $60 $90**

❑ **TMX-192. "One-Act Play" Offer Sheet,**
1945. Offered script for play titled "The Straight Shooters Secret," issued with 1945 manual. No copy of the script is known. - **$20 $35 $60**

TMX-193

TMX-194

❑ **TMX-193. Cloth Patch,**
1945. Issued with 1945 club manual. Red flocking on white fabric. - **$25 $50 $100**

❑ **TMX-194. Straight Shooters Service Ribbon And Medal,**
1945. Fabric over metal bar pin suspending glow-in-dark plastic medal. - **$30 $100 $175**

TMX-195

❑ **TMX-195. "Curley Bradley The Tom Mix Of Radio" 78 RPM Three-Record Album,**
c. 1945. Universal Recording Corp. -
**$50 $125 $225**

TMX-196

❑ **TMX-196. Fabric Patch No Flocking,**
1945. Scarce version also likely issued with 1945 club manual. - **$50 $100 $175**

TMX-197

TMX-198

❑ **TMX-197. Tom Mix And Tony "Last Picture" Photo,**
1946. Black and white photo card captioned "This is the last picture taken of Tom and Tony together" prior to Mix death in 1940. Ralston premium with publication date on reverse of May, 1946. - **$40 $85 $150**

❑ **TMX-198. Curley Bradley Fan Photo Card,**
1946. Radio portrayer of Tom Mix, back has Safety Code. - **$30 $60 $100**

TMX-199

❑ **TMX-199. Glow Belt With Secret Compartment Buckle,**
1946. Complete - **$50 $100 $175**
Buckle Only - **$25 $60 $90**

TMX-200

**TMX-200. Decoder Buttons With Card,**
1946. Set of five litho. buttons.
Complete Near Mint - **$150**
Each Button - **$8 $12 $20**

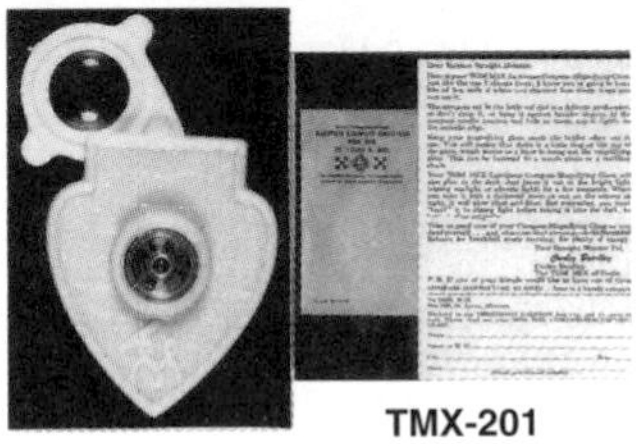

TMX-201

❑ **TMX-201. "Luminous Compass-Magnifying Glass",**
1946. Near Mint In Mailer - **$200**
Loose - **$20 $60 $100**

TMX-202

TMX-203

❑ **TMX-202. Dobie County Sheriff Siren Badge,**
1946. - **$20 $60 $100**

❑ **TMX-203. Folder Mailed With Siren Badge,**
1946. - **$15 $30 $75**

TMX-204

❑ **TMX-204. "Look-Around" Ring,**
1946. Near Mint In Mailer - **$175**
Ring Only - **$40 $75 $125**

TMX-205

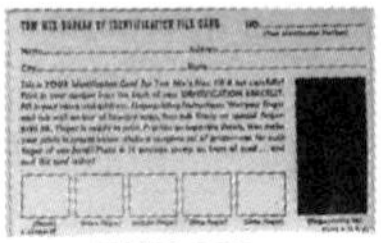

TMX-206

TMX-207

❑ **TMX-205. "Rocket Parachute" Version #2 Re-issue With Box,**
1947. Similar to original 1936 item with portrait added on mailer box. Boxed - **$75 $125 $200**

❑ **TMX-206. "Tom Mix Bureau Of Identification File Card",**
1947. Scarce as card was meant to be returned with member's fingerprints and ID bracelet number. - **$35 $75 $125**

❑ **TMX-207. Identification Bracelet,**
1947. Personalized by single initial designated by orderer. - **$15 $30 $60**

TMX-208

TMX-209

❑ **TMX-208. Magnet Ring,**
1947. Brass with silver finish magnet. - **$20 $45 $90**

❑ **TMX-209. "Magnet Ring" Paper Slip,**
1947. - **$25 $45 $65**

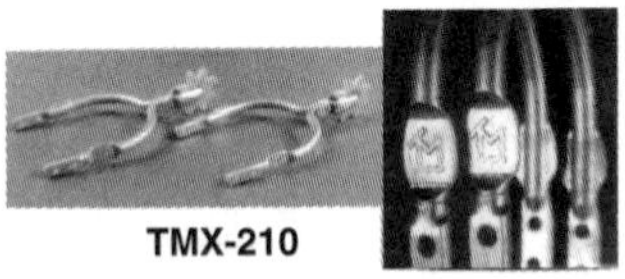

TMX-210

❑ **TMX-210. Cowboy Spurs,**
1947. Aluminum with glow in dark rowels. - **$40 $75 $125**

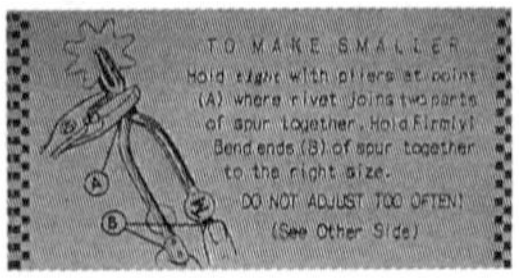


TMX-211

❑ **TMX-211. Spurs Size Adjustment Instruction Flyer,**
1947. 2-1/4x4-1/4" black on green. Reverse tells how to make spurs larger. - **$10 $20 $30**

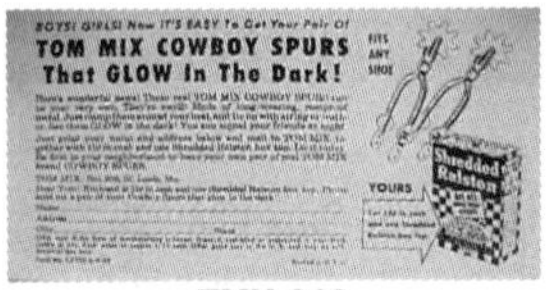


TMX-212

❑ **TMX-212. Spurs Offer Flyer,**
1947. 3x6". This example has coded date of April 1948. - **$10 $20 $40**

TMX-213

❑ **TMX-213. "Super-Magnetic Compass Gun And Signal Whistle" Instruction Sheet,**
1948. Reverse offers five other premiums. - **$15 $30 $45**

TMX-214

TMX-215

❑ **TMX-214. "Compass Gun" Dealer's Promotional Sheet,**
1948. 8-1/2x11" sheet describing premium and advertising it receives on radio show as incentive for grocer to stock Ralston Cereals. - **$75 $150 $225**

❑ **TMX-215. Super Magnetic Compass Gun And Whistle,**
1948. Both gun and arrowhead whistle glow in dark. - **$50 $100 $175**

TMX-216

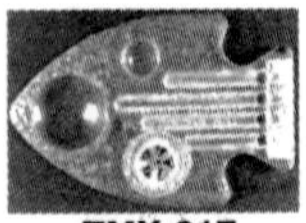

TMX-217

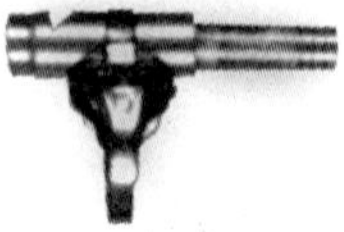

TMX-218

❑ **TMX-216. "Tom Mix Safety Story" Poster,**
1948. Yankee Network Station. Opens to 17x22". - **$15 $35 $65**

❑ **TMX-217. "Signal Arrowhead" Plastic Whistle/Siren/ Magnifier,**
1949. - **$30 $75 $125**

❑ **TMX-218. Musical Ring,**
1949. Aluminum slide whistle on brass base. - **$40 $85 $140**

TMX-219

❑ **TMX-219. "RCA Victor" Miniature TV Film Viewer,**
1949. Brass back includes Tom Mix name. - **$20 $30 $50 (**Add $10 Per Mix Film Disk)

TMX-220

❑ **TMX-220. "Tom Mix Straight Shooter" T-Shirt,**
1940s. Probable premium by Ralston**. -**
**$125 $250 $500**

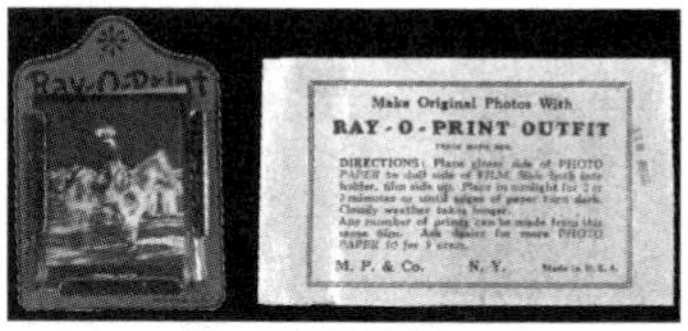


TMX-221

❑ **TMX-221. Ray O Print Outfit,**
1940s. With tin holder for negative and photo paper with envelope. - **$50 $125 $175**

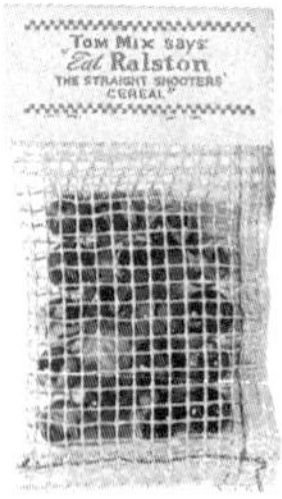

TMX-223

TMX-222

❑ **TMX-222. Marbles,**
1940s. Ralston premium with 18 marbles in bag. -
**$25 $50 $75**

❑ **TMX-223. Premiums Catalogue Sheet,**
1950. Came with 1950 model TV and Tiger-Eye Ring as single package. - **$10 $20 $35**

TMX-224 TMX-225

❑ **TMX-224. "RCA Victor" Miniature TV Film Viewer,**
1950. Version without Mix name on reverse. -
**$20 $35 $50 (**Add $10 Per Mix Film Disk)

❑ **TMX-225. Miniature Gold-Plated TV Viewer,**
1950. Scarce. Only 200 made for executives. -
**$65 $150 $250**

TMX-226

TMX-227

❑ **TMX-226. "2 For 1" Ralston Premium Offer Ad,**
1950. Comic book page picturing miniature RCA Victor television set and Magic-Light Tiger-Eye Ring as joint mail premiums. - **$1 $3 $5**

❑ **TMX-227. "Toy Television Set" Instruction Sheet,**
1950. - **$15 $25 $50**

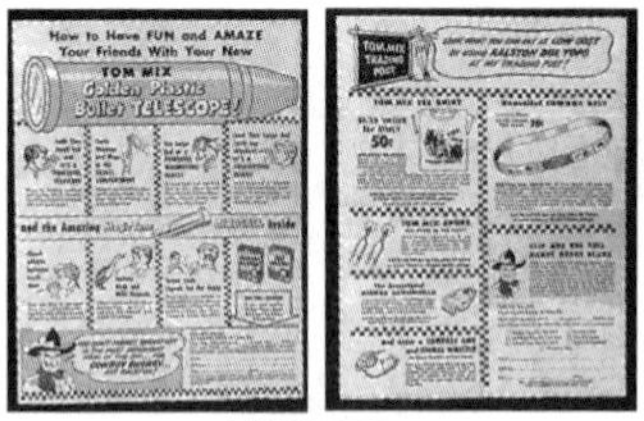


TMX-228

❑ **TMX-228. "Golden Plastic Bullet Telescope" Instruction Sheet,**
1950. Reverse side offers five other premiums. -
**$10 $20 $40**

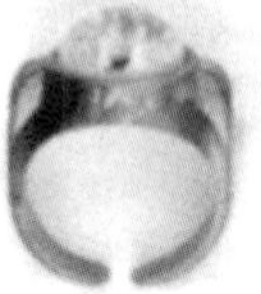

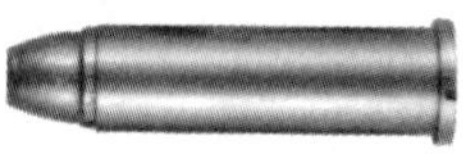

TMX-230

TMX-229

❑ **TMX-229. Magic-Light Tiger-Eye Ring,**
1950. Plastic with glow in the dark top. -
**$100 $200 $325**

❑ **TMX-230. Golden Plastic Bullet Telescope & Birdcall,**
1950. Gold plastic holding inside bird call whistle. Complete - **$25 $50 $75**
Without Whistle - **$10 $20 $40**

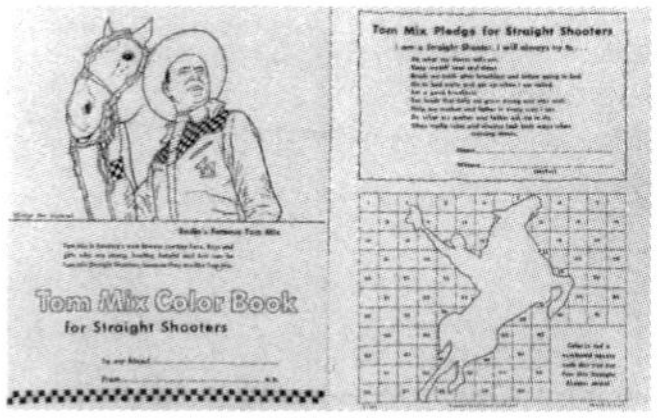


TMX-231

❑ **TMX-231. "Tom Mix Color Book",**
1950. - **$10 $20 $35**

TMX-232

❑ **TMX-232. "Tom Mix Ralston Straight Shooters Club" Revival Membership Kit,**
1982. 50-year membership card, fabric patch, comic booklet, early years photo reprint, current premium photo sheet.
Each - **$3 $5 $10**

TMX-233

❑ **TMX-233. "Tom Mix Ralston Straight Shooters" Revival Cereal Bowl,**
1982. - **$10 $15 $30**

TMX-234 TMX-235

❑ **TMX-234. Revival Wristwatch,**
1982. - **$50 $100 $250**

❑ **TMX-235. Tom Mix Festival Glass Mug,**
1982. Issued at 3rd annual festival in DuBois, PA. -
**$10 $20 $35**

## Tony the Tiger

**Kellogg's, preparing to launch its new Sugar Frosted Flakes into the 1952 market, called on the Leo Burnett advertising agency to devise a quartet of appealing animals as spokescreatures. The agency's account executive, Jack Baxter, plus art director Jack Tolzein and copywriter John Matthews, are credited as the trio who created Tony the Tiger and his since-forgotten sidekicks Katy the Kangaroo, Elmo the Elephant and Newt the Gnu. Tolzein had Martin and Alice Provensen in mind to develop the characters, but their work on Golden Books prevented this and Tolzein gave the job to Pheobe Moore, a Chicago freelancer. Jack Baxter is credited as the first to growl Tony's signature slogan, "Sugar Frosted Flakes are GR-R-R-REAT!" Tony and his one-liner endorsement roar have been with us ever since, voiced mostly by basso singer and Kellogg employee Thurl Ravenscroft.**

**Tony himself has undergone some changes over the years, including adaptations to animation, live-action support by entertainment stars, and dozens of plastic figural premiums, but he remains your basic smiling, lip-smacking tiger icon.**

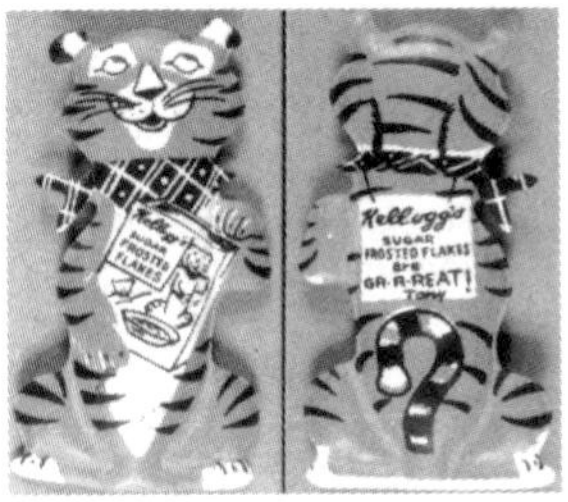


TNY-1

❑ **TNY-1. Vinyl Inflated Figure,**
1953. - **$20 $35 $70**

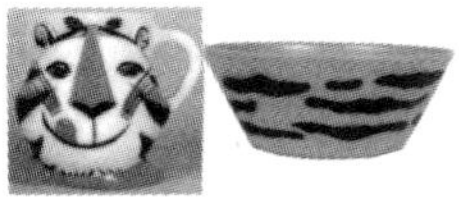

TNY-2

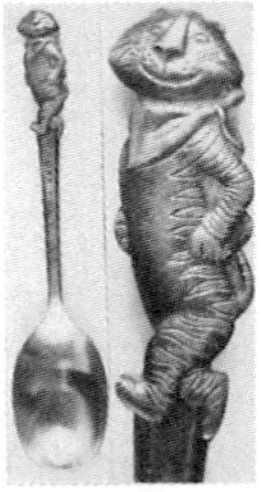

TNY-3

❑ **TNY-2. Tony The Tiger Mug And Bowl Set,**
1964. Kellogg's. Made by F&F Mold.
Each - **$5 $10 $30**

❑ **TNY-3. Kellogg's Premium Cereal Spoon,**
1965. Silver finish marked "Old Company Plate" on reverse. - **$5 $10 $20**

TNY-4

❑ **TNY-4. Noisemaker Attachment,**
1966. Hard plastic with attachment bracket for bicycle handlebar. Top disk wheel produces growling sound when turned. - **$15 $40 $80**

TNY-5

❑ **TNY-5. Cereal Box With "Tony The Tiger Beanie" Offer,**
1967. Beanie has image of Tony's face with attached 10" long tail. Gordon Gold Archives.
Used Complete - **$75 $125 $200**

TNY-6

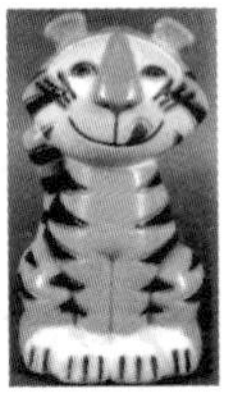

TNY-7

❑ **TNY-6. Tony The Tiger Swimmer Figure,**
1967. Kellogg's. 7-1/2" tall three-dimensional hard plastic with rubber bands holding arms which can be wound to make him swim. - **$50 $100 $150**

❑ **TNY-7. Plastic Bank,**
1968. - **$30 $45 $75**

TNY-8

❑ **TNY-8. Hard Plastic Cookie Jar With Box,**
1968. Jar Only - **$25 $50 $100**
Boxed - **$40 $75 $115**

TNY-9

❑ **TNY-9. Cereal Box With "Dick Dastardly Airplane-Telescope" Premium Offer,**
1969. Gordon Gold Archives.
Used Complete - **$100 $200 $300**

TNY-10

TNY-11

❑ **TNY-10. "Astronaut Breakfast Game" Litho. Button,**
1960s. White or blue background. - **$3 $8 $12**

❑ **TNY-11. "Astronaut Breakfast Game" Score Card,**
1960s. Multi-page scorecard - **$5 $10 $20**

TNY-12

TNY-13

❑ **TNY-12. Plush And Cloth Doll,**
1970. - **$15 $25 $40**

❑ **TNY-13. Vinyl Doll With Movable Head,**
c. 1974. - **$20 $45 $90**

TNY-14

❑ **TNY-14. Frosted Flakes TV Commercial Cel,**
1970s. Image is on pair of 10-1/2x12-1/2" acetate sheets. - **$35 $75 $100**

TNY-15

TNY-16

❑ **TNY-15. Plastic Radio,**
1980. Battery operated. Boxed - **$30 $40 $65**
Loose - **$10 $20 $40**

❑ **TNY-16. Stainless Steel Cereal Spoon,**
1983. - **$5 $10 $15**

TNY-17

❑ **TNY-17. Frosted Flakes Canadian Issue Box,**
1990. Offers Spider-Man and Tony The Tiger comic in English/French. Box - **$25 $40 $85**
Comic - **$10 $20 $40**

TNY-18

❑ **TNY-18. Large Stuffed Doll With Tag,**
1997. Sold at grocery stores. - **$5 $15 $25**

TNY-19

❑ **TNY-19. Cereal and Plush Doll Pack,**
1998. Large display with 2 boxes of cereal and a Tony the Tiger plush premium doll packaged in the center. - **$25**

TNY-20

❑ **TNY-20. Ring on Card,**
1998. Enameled. Copyright Kellogg's. - **$20**

## Toonerville Folks

**The comic cartoon panels of Fontaine Fox (1884-1964) apparently began appearing in newspapers in 1915. The following year the Toonerville Trolley was introduced, and in 1920 the Bell Syndicate began distributing Fox's Sunday page as *Toonerville Folks.* The ramshackle trolley and its Skipper, along with such Toonerville denizens as Mickey (Himself) McGuire, the Powerful Katrinka, and the Terrible-Tempered Mr. Bang, delighted millions of readers for 40 years. Several collections of reprints were published in the early years, a series of two-reel live-action film comedies were released in the 1920s, and Burt Gillett produced Toonerville animated shorts in 1936. The strip survived until 1955.**

TOO-1

❑ **TOO-1. "F. Fox's Funny Folks Cartoons" Toonerville Trolley Cartoon Book,**
1917. 8x10" hardcover published by George H. Duran Co. Probably the first Toonerville reprint book. - **$125 $200 $350**

TOO-2

TOO-3

❑ **TOO-2. Cartoon Book,**
1921. Store item published by Cupples & Leon Co. - **$65 $225 $400**

❑ **TOO-3. Litho. Tin Wind-Up Toy,**
1922. Store item by Nifty marked "Made In Germany." - **$400 $800 $1250**

TOO-4

❑ **TOO-4. Coca-Cola Ad Folder,**
1931. - **$20 $40 $70**

TOO-5

❑ **TOO-5. Cracker Box,**
1931. Uneeda Crackers by Nabisco. -
**$100 $225 $350**

TOO-6

❑ **TOO-6. Toonerville Character Bisques,**
c. 1931. Mickey Maguire, Powerful Katrinka, The Skipper. Mickey 2-1/2", others 3".
Each - **$25 $60 $85**

TOO-7

❑ **TOO-7. Toonerville Trolley Bisque Figure,**
c. 1931. 3-1/2" tall. Japan #5096. -
**$50 $115 $175**

TOO-8

❑ **TOO-8. "The Day The Big Wind Hit Toonerville" Magic Picture Folder,**
1930s. Johnson & Johnson Red Cross products. Came with translucent red sheet for viewing bottom portion of scene in center of folder.
With Sheet - **$35 $60 $100**
No Sheet - **$20 $35 $60**

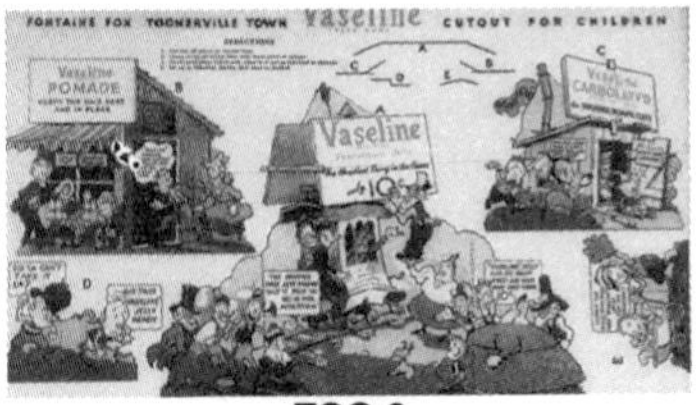

TOO-9

❑ **TOO-9. Vaseline Petroleum Jelly Cut-Out Sheet,**
1930s. Uncut - **$40 $100 $175**

TOO-10

❑ **TOO-10. Paper Masks,**
1930s. Westinghouse Mazda Lamps. Examples from set. Also seen with "Super Shell" gasoline ad on reverse.
Each - **$20 $40 $70**

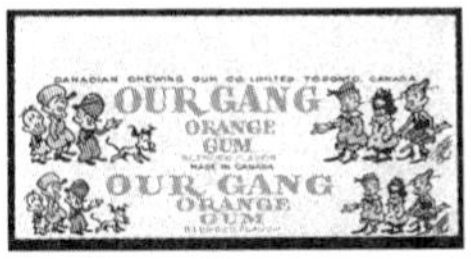

TOO-11

TOO-12

❑ **TOO-11. Comic Gum Wrapper,**
1930s. Our Gang gum wrapper from Canada. Art by Fontaine Fox. - **$20 $45 $80**

❑ **TOO-12. Mickey McGuire Bisque,**
1930s. Store item, German made. -
**$25 $75 $115**

TOO-13

TOO-14

❑ **TOO-13. "Mickey McGuire Club" Cello. Button,**
1930s. Probably a newspaper issue. Pictured is traditional derby hat with frayed crown. -
**$20 $40 $75**

❑ **TOO-14. "The Terrible Tempered Mr. Bang" Ad Poster,**
1930s. Eveready Mazda automobile lamps. Paper is 20x30". - **$75 $175 $300**

TOO-15

❑ **TOO-15. "Mickey And His Pal" Premium Photo,**
1930s. Issuer unknown. About 5x7" black and white photo depicting Mickey Rooney as Mickey McGuire with derby apparently shredded by his dog. - **$15 $30 $60**

## Toy Guns

**It often amazes us when magazines and TV shows list the top 100 toys, guns are never mentioned. If you were a boy born between the mid 1930s through the 1950s you know generally the last plaything you would part with would be your toy gun. Children's guns have been very popular for the last 150 years. Boys and girls loved to play Cowboys and Indians and every once in a while enjoyed being a detective, pirate, army man or space guy as well. These toys were constantly played with and unfortunately many were dropped and broken. It is quite surprising that any survived in high grade much less in the original box. The biggest problem with this important segment of the toy market is supply. The high-grade, unused guns in the box have virtually disappeared off the market. Each time they appear it seems like a new record is set. Holster sets, generic or character related, are in high demand. New toy guns are starting to turn up at department stores and are selling well. Listed are prime examples of toy guns, we will continue to add more items with each update of our guide.**

TGN-1

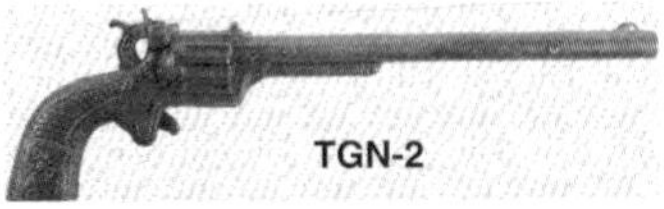
TGN-2

❑ **TGN-1. J. & E. Stevens Cap Gun,**
1870s. Cast iron. Rare. - **$200 $500 $700**

❑ **TGN-2. "Buffalo Bill" Cap Pistol,**
1890s. 11 3/4". Cast iron. - **$200 $425 $550**

TGN-3

❑ **TGN-3. "American Boy" Pistol and Box,**
1919. With instructions. Rare.
Boxed - **$125 $275 $400**

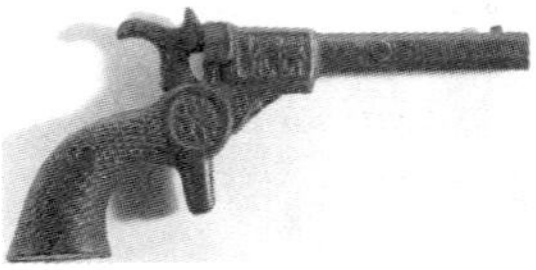
TGN-4

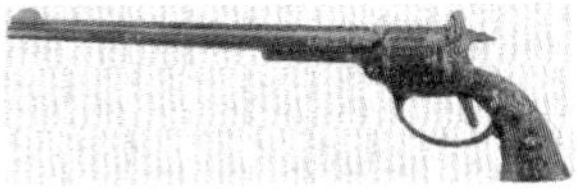
TGN-5

❑ **TGN-4. The "Victor" Cap Gun,**
1920s. Cast iron. - **$150 $200 $300**

❑ **TGN-5. "Longboy" Cap Pistol,**
1920s. 11". Cast iron. - **$150 $225 $325**

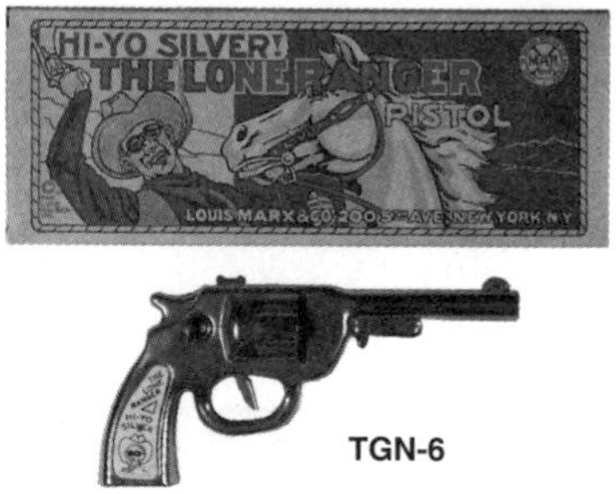

TGN-6

❑ **TGN-6. "Lone Ranger" Clicker Pistol,** 1938. Louis Marx gun. Was used as a giveaway on radio shows and sold at stores. Box is smaller than box for TGN-7. Scarce.
Pistol - **$100 $175 $275**
Box - **$75 $150 $225**

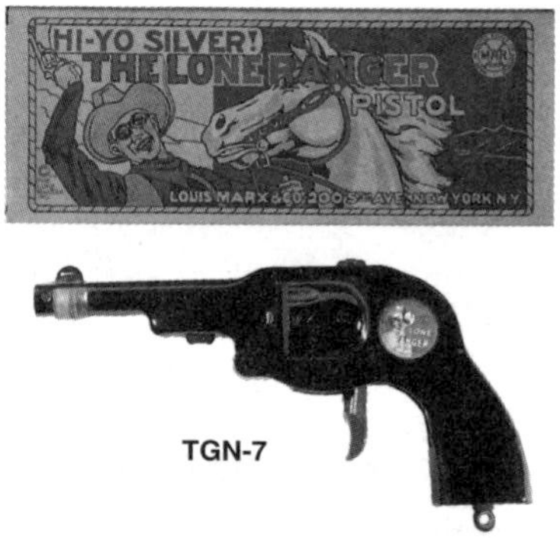

TGN-7

❑ **TGN-7. "Lone Ranger" Clicker Pistol,** 1938. Louis Marx gun. Gun is shiny black with silver trigger and clip on barrel. Colorful picture of the Lone Ranger above handle on side. Gun smokes when clicked. Powder was inserted inside gun. Box is 9 1/2" long.
Box Near Mint - **$225**
Pistol - **$100 $175 $300**

TGN-8

❑ **TGN-8. Bang-O Repeating Cap Pistol,** 1930s. J. & E. Stevens product. With white tenite grips with red jewel on each side and scroll barrel. Cowboy pictured on one side, a horse on the other.
Pistol - **$50 $120 $225**
Box Near Mint - **$85**

TGN-9

❑ **TGN-9. Bang-O Repeating Cap Pistol,** 1938. J. & E. Stevens product. Dark grey finish with white tenite grips. Box is orange colored with black print.
Pistol - **$30 $90 $160**
Box Near Mint - **$85**

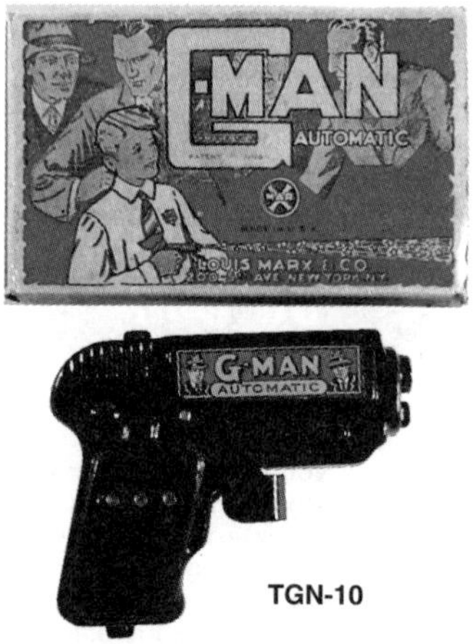

TGN-10

❑ **TGN-10. G-Man Automatic Sparkler Gun,** 1938. Louis Marx Co. Metal gun with 4 3/4" box.
Boxed Near Mint - **$150**
Pistol - **$25 $50 $100**

TGN-11

❑ **TGN-11. "G-Man" Gun with Siren Alarm,** 1930s. Louis Marx & Co. Colorful box.
Boxed Near Mint - **$350**

TGN-12

❑ **TGN-12. "Dick Tracy" Click Pistol,** 1930s. Louis Marx product in box.
Pistol - **$150**
Box Near Mint - **$40**

TGN-13

❑ **TGN-13. 25 Jr. Repeating Cap Pistol,** 1930s. J. & E. Stevens product in box. Bright silver-plate finish. Boxed Near Mint - **$135**

TGN-14

❑ **TGN-14. Flash Gordon Radio Repeater,** 1930s.
Gun - **$250 $500 $750**
Box - **$75 $200 $275**

TGN-15

❑ **TGN-15. "Popeye" Pirate Pistol in Box,** 1930s. Marx product. Tin clicker gun in colorful box.
Gun - **$150 $350 $550**
Box - **$75 $175 $250**

TGN-16 TGN-17

❑ **TGN-16. "Dick" Cap Pistol with Box,**
1940s. Hubley product.
Boxed - **$50 $75 $125**

❑ **TGN-17. "Spit Fire" Toy Pistol with Box,**
1940s. Stevens 50 shot repeating pistol. Has two color-embossed tenite grips. Bright silver finish. Boxed Near Mint - **$200**

TGN-18 TGN-19

❑ **TGN-18. "G-Boy" Cap Pistol with Box,**
1940s. Rapid firing. White grips. Acme Novelty.
Boxed Near Mint - **$200**

❑ **TGN-19. "Army 45" 50 Shot Repeater in Box,**
1940s. By Hubley. Boxed Near Mint - **$275**

TGN-20 TGN-21

❑ **TGN-20. "Pow'r Pop" Pistol with Box,**
1940s. Comes with 5 corks.
Complete - **$50 $125 $175**

❑ **TGN-21. "Squirt-O- Matic" Water and Noise Pistol with Box,**
1940s. Double-barreled 8 1/2" metal water gun and noise pistol. Daisy No. 72 with box.
Gun - **$50 $150 $200**
Box - **$30 $50 $75**

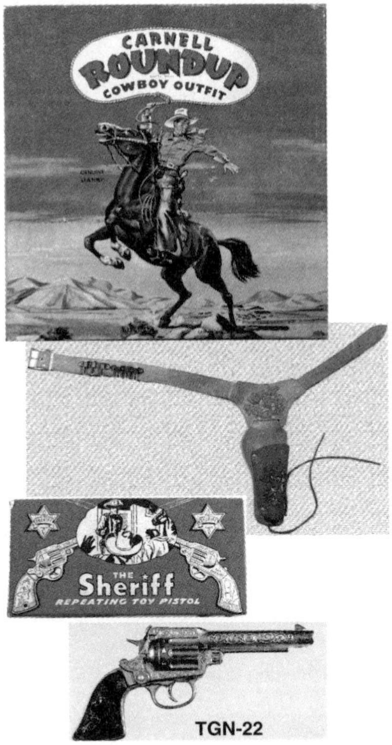


TGN-22

❑ **TGN-22. "Carnell Roundup" Cowboy Outfit and "The Sheriff" Packaged Pistol in Box,**
1940s. Roundup holster with six silver bullets. Has one "The Sheriff" pistol in red box. Gun has black handle with a red jewel on each side. This model gun is scarcer than the white handled model shown in TGN-23.
Outfit Box - **$25 $50 $75**
Holster - **$50 $100 $150**
Boxed Black Handled Gun - **$250**
Complete Near Mint - **$525**

TGN-23

❑ **TGN-23. "The Sheriff" Repeating Toy Cap Pistol in Box,**
1940s. Similar to TGN-22 model gun but has white grips with a red jewel on each side.
Boxed Near Mint - **$225**

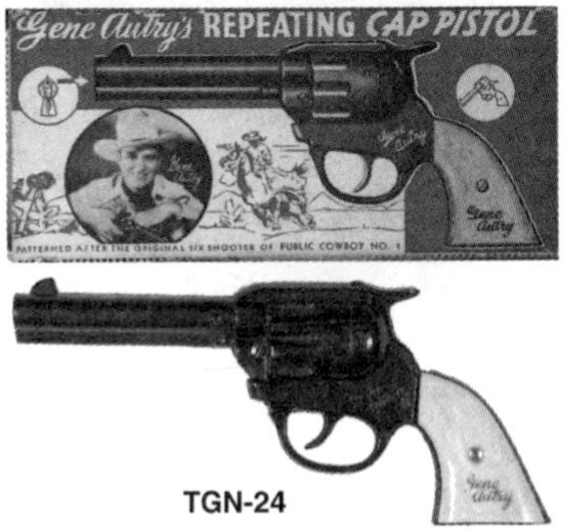


TGN-24

❑ **TGN-24. "Public Cowboy #1" Gene Autry Cap Pistol,**
1940s. Patterned after the movie gun.
Gun - **$135 $300 $400**
Box - **$100 $150 $200**

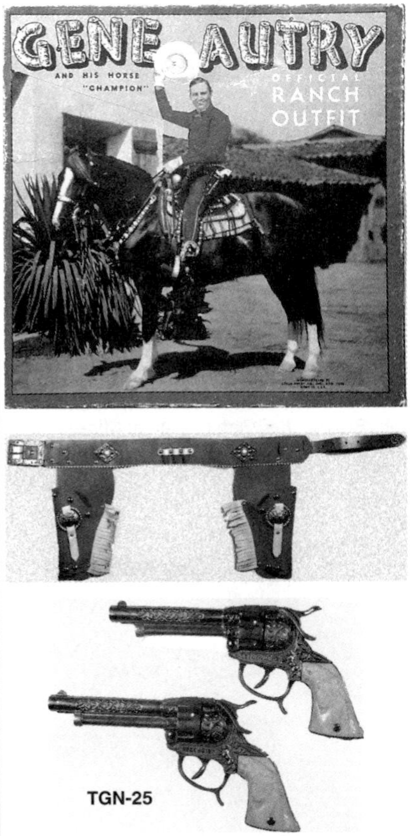


TGN-25

❑ **TGN-25. Gene Autry Double Holster Set,**
1940s. Guns are Leslie Stevens nickel-finish models with white grips embossed with a horse.
Box - **$100 $150 $200**
Double Holster - **$75 $150 $250**
Each Gun - **$85 $175 $350**
Complete Near Mint- **$1150**

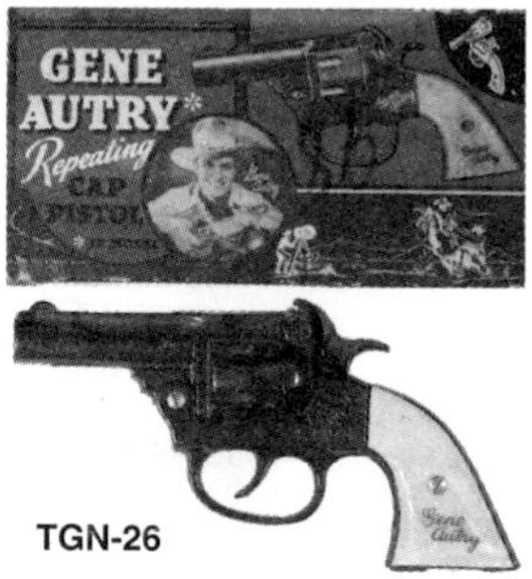


TGN-26

❑ **TGN-26. Gene Autry Cap Pistol -Jr. Model,**
1940s. Black with white grips.
Gun - **$110 $200 $300**
Box - **$100 $125 $175**

TGN-27

❑ **TGN-27. Gene Autry Grey Cap Pistol,**
1940s. Grey with white grips.- **$110 $200 $300**

TGN-28

❑ **TGN-28. "Red Ranger" Metal Clicker Gun,**
1940s. 8" Wyandotte Toy. - **$50 $100 $150**

TGN-29

TGN-30

❑ **TGN-29. "Teddy" Cap Gun,**
1940s. Hubley. Cast iron. - **$25 $50 $100**

❑ **TGN-30. "Hub" Cap Gun,**
1940s. Hubley. Grey cast iron. - **$25 $50 $100**

TGN-31

❑ **TGN-31. "Trooper" Cap Pistol in Box,**
1940s. Hubley. Dull silver finish with black handle and red star. Box is darker red lettering on brown paper. Boxed Near Mint - **$225**

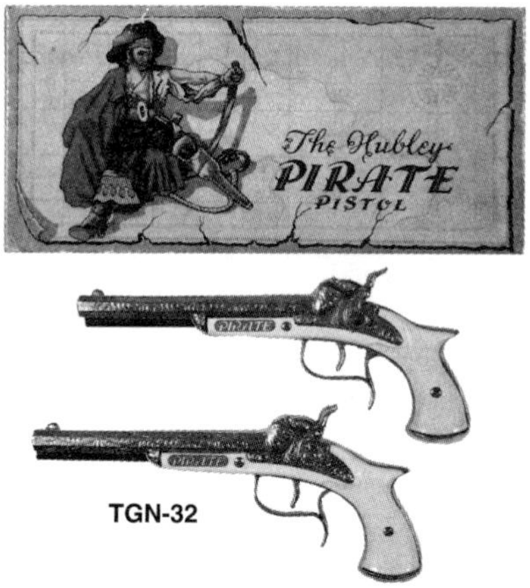


TGN-32

❑ **TGN-32. "Pirate" Pistol in Original Box,**
1940s. Hubley. Box is scarce.
Box - **$100 $150 $200**
Each Gun Pictured- **$90 $175 $250**

TGN-33

❑ **TGN-33. "Buffalo Bill" Repeating Toy Cap Pistol in Box,**
1940s. J. & E. Stevens product in box. With tenite embossed grips with red jewels. Has a cowboy design on one side, a horse on other.
Boxed Near Mint - **$325**

TGN-34

❑ **TGN-34. "Ranger" Repeating Toy Cap Pistol in Box,**
1940s. Kilgore product in box. Cast iron model. Bright silver color finish and scarce red grips.
Box - **$50 $75 $100**
Gun - **$125 $200 $300**

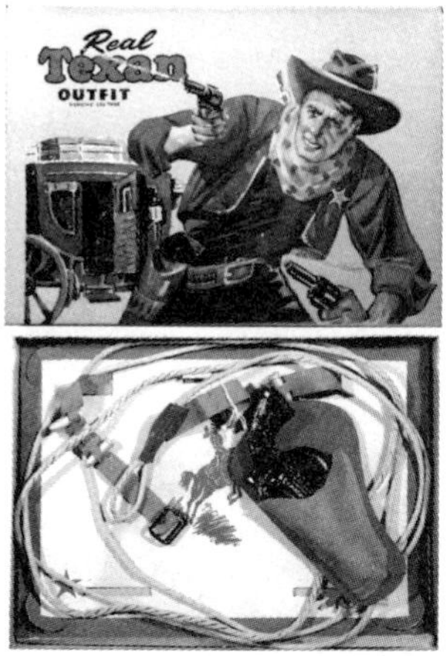


TGN-35

❑ **TGN-35. "Real Texan" Outfit in Box,**
1940s. "V" gun holster set with gun, lasso and belt. World War II era product.
Boxed Near Mint - **$250**

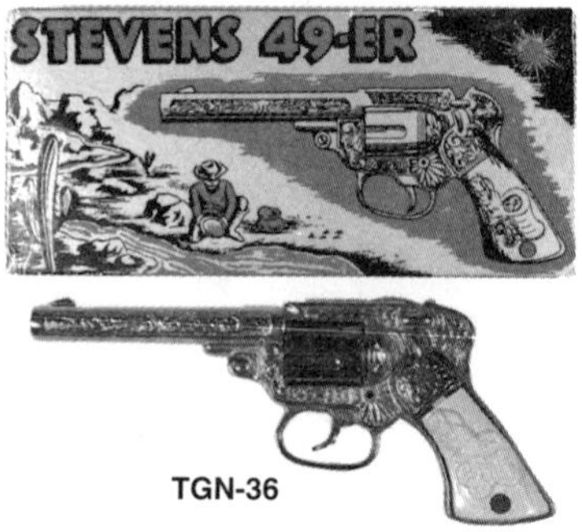


TGN-36

❑ **TGN-36. Stevens "49er" Cap Gun,**
1940s. Gold finish.
Box - **$85 $125 $150**
Gun - **$125 $250 $375**

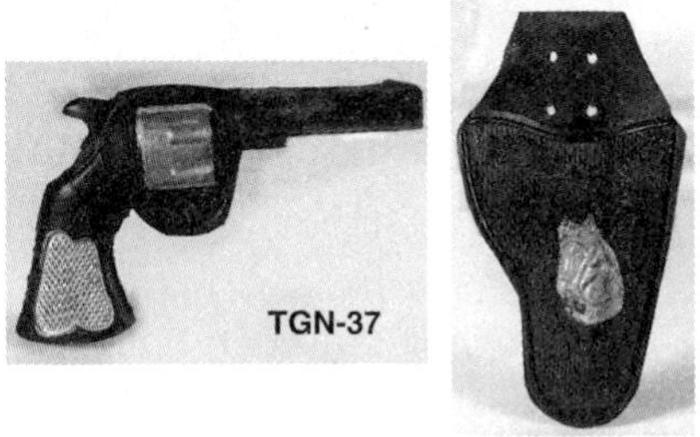


❑ **TGN-37. Rubber Gun and Holster Set,** 1940s. Made in Japan. - **$10 $15 $30**

❑ **TGN-38. "Texan Jr. Smoking" Toy Cap Pistol in Box,**
1940s. Hubley product. White grips. Nickel-like finish, not shiny. Smokes when caps are used. Cylinder does not rotate.
Boxed Near Mint - **$225**

❑ **TGN-39. "Texan Jr. " Gold Plated Pistol in Box,**
1950s. Hubley product. Black grips.
Boxed Near Mint - **$275**

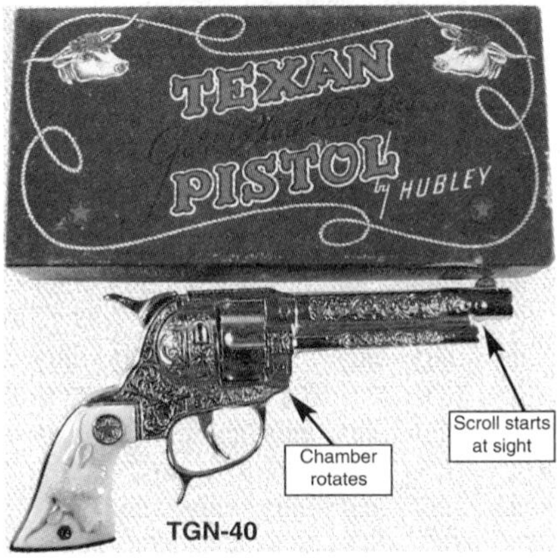


❑ **TGN-40. "Texan" Gold Plated Deluxe Pistol in Box,**
1950s. Hubley product. White grips.
Boxed Near Mint - **$400**

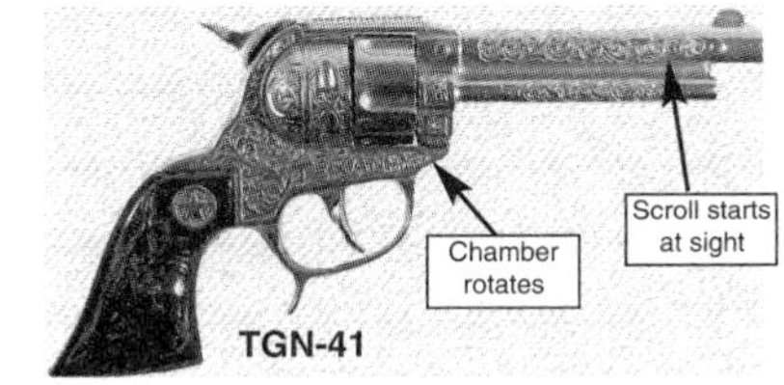


❑ **TGN-41. "Texan" Silver Plated Pistol,**
1950s. Hubley product. Black plastic grips.
Gun only - **$175**

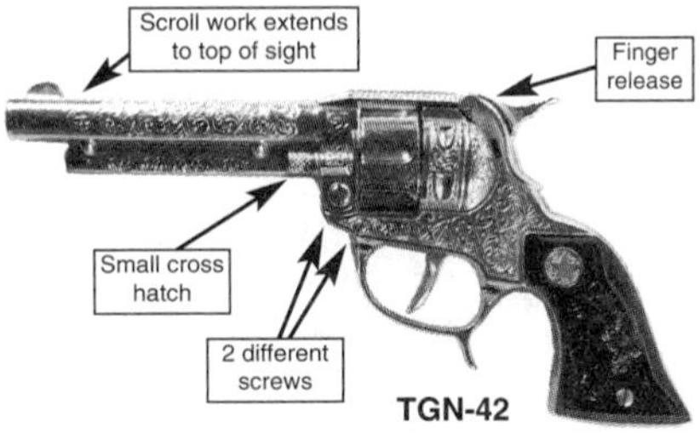


❑ **TGN-42. "Texan" Gold Plated Deluxe Pistol,**
Early 1950s. Hubley product. Black grips. Revolving cylinder.
Gun only - **$85 $160 $300**

❑ **TGN-43. Smoking "Tex" Pistol in Box,**
Early 1950s. With black grips. Shoots puff of smoke when caps are used.
Gun - **$25 $50 $100**
Box - **$25 $50 $75**

❑ **TGN-44. "Cowboy" Repeating Cap Pistol,**
May, 1950. Dull silver finish with white grips and black steer head on grips. Also comes in shiny finish with white grips and white steer head on grips (not pictured.)
Box - **$60 $85 $120**
Gun - **$100 $150 $250**

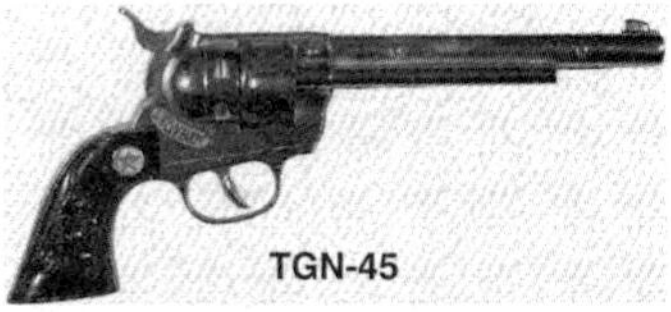


❑ **TGN-45. "Cowboy" Repeating Cap Pistol,**
1950s. Gold color with black grips. Scarce version of silver/white model.
Gun only - **$150 $300 $500**

❑ **TGN-46. "Buck'n Bronc Shoot'n Iron" 50 Shot Cap Gun,**
1950s. Schmidt product.
Gun - **$90 $175 $300**
Box - **$60 $100 $150**

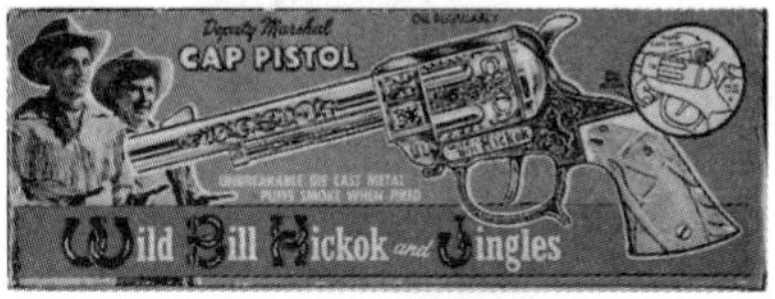


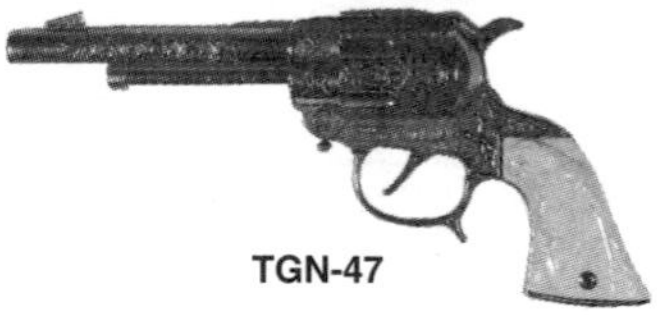

TGN-47

❑ **TGN-47. "Wild Bill Hickok" Cap Gun,**
1952. Bright silver finish with white grips. Toy produced to support popular TV series which began in 1951.
Box - **$100 $175 $225**
Gun - **$100 $225 $350**

(BOX FRONT) (SIDE OF BOX)

TGN-48

❑ **TGN-48. Roy Rogers Holster Set,**
1950-53. Belt holds 6 silver colored bullets. Roy's face and name printed at center of belt. "RR" embossed on each silver button and discs. Comes with official box with photo of Roy. Box has "Life Magazine" logo in upper left corner, distinguishing it from a similar box found with the TGN-52 set from 1954. Comes with 2 Schmidt cap guns each marked with Roy's name above the trigger. Guns have bronze colored grips and "RR & DE" embossed on barrel.
Double Holster - **$300 $425 $500**
Each Gun - **$175 $250 $500**
Box - **$175 $250 $375**
Boxed Complete- **$1825**

TGN-49

❑ **TGN-49. "Dale Evans Queen of the West" Cap Gun,**
1953. D-26 model. With initials in butterfly symbol on grips. If you have read any literature on toy guns, you know this item is highly sought after by collectors. Manufactured by George Schmidt. Very rare box included. Hammer and trigger are black and handle is gold colored.
Box - **$300 $500 $600**
Gun - **$300 $600 $1000**
Complete Unfired in Box - **$1600**

TGN-50

❑ **TGN-50. "Roy Rogers" Shootin' Iron,**
1953. Gold colored grips and polished nickel appearance. Comes in card with Roy's picture.
Gun on Card Near Mint - **$1000**

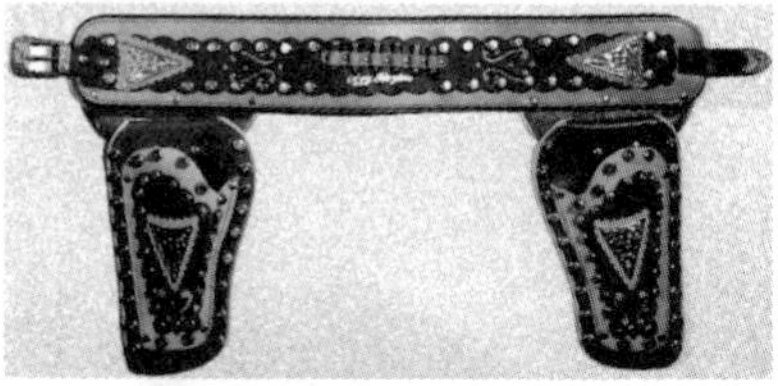

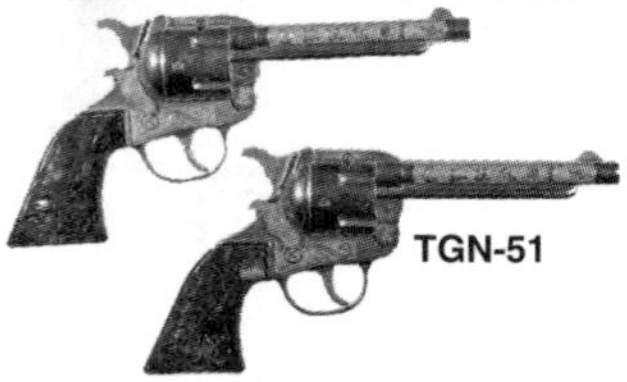

TGN-51

❑ **TGN-51. Roy Rogers Double Holster Set,**
1954. Belt holds 6 silver colored bullets. Belt is light brown and dark brown with many silver colored metal decorations and 2 red jewels. Comes with 2 Kilgore guns. Guns' grips are brown with caramel colored swirls and "RR" embossed on each grip. Each gun is marked with Roy's name above the trigger. Guns have "RR & DE" embossed on barrel.
Double Holster - **$300 $425 $650**
Each Gun - **$85 $175 $300**
Complete- **$1250**

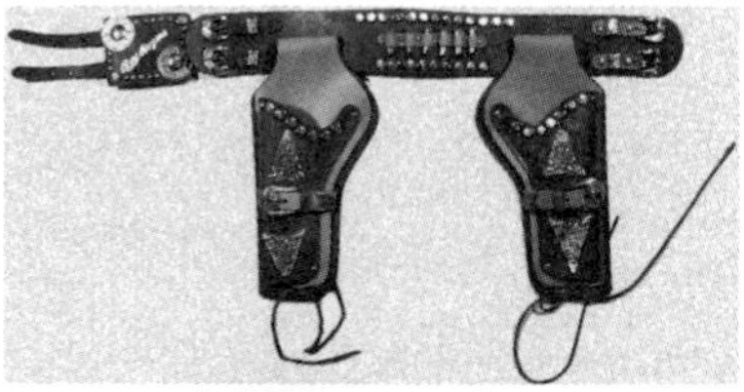

(SIDE OF BOX)

(BOX FRONT)

TGN-52

❑ **TGN-52. Roy Rogers Double Holster Set,**
1954. Dark brown belt holds 6 silver colored bullets. Roy's name printed on leather belt buckle with silver colored discs. Belt has silver colored decorations, no jewels, with "RR" embossed on silver triangular ornaments. Comes with official box with photo of Roy. Comes with 2 Kilgore cap guns each with dark brown horse head grips. Double Holster Set - **$250 $375 $600**
Each Gun - **$85 $175 $300**
Box - **$175 $250 $325**
Boxed Near Mint Complete - **$1525**

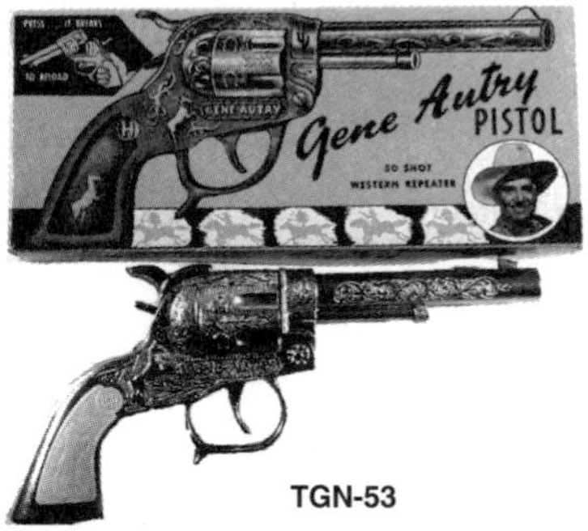


TGN-53

❑ **TGN-53. Gene Autry "50 Shot Western Repeater" Cap Gun,**
1950s. Leslie Henry model. Has white grips and a bright silver finish. Boxed Near Mint - **$400**

TGN-54

❑ **TGN-54. Gene Autry "50 Shot Western Repeater" Cap Gun,**
1950s. Leslie Henry model. Has white grips and a bright gold finish. Scarcer than silver finish model. Boxed Near Mint - **$500**

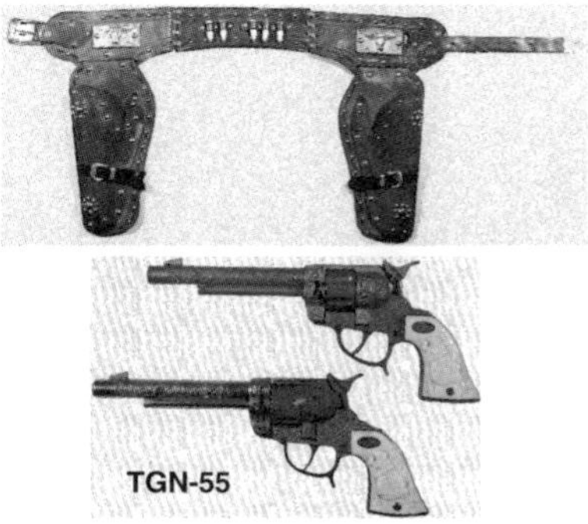

TGN-55

❑ **TGN-55. Gene Autry "Flying A" Double Holster Set,**
1950s. Has "Flying A" emblem pictured on each holster. Gene Autry's name is at the top of the emblem. Belt has 5 silver colored bullets. Set includes 2 "44" Leslie Henry cap guns with white horse head grips.
Holster - **$250 $400 $600**
Each Gun - **$125 $250 $400**
Complete - **$1400**

TGN-56

❑ **TGN-56. Gene Autry "50 Shot Western Repeater" Cap Gun with Box,**
1950s. Leslie Henry model. Puffs smoke.
Box - **$85 $175 $225**
Gun - **$85 $175 $300**

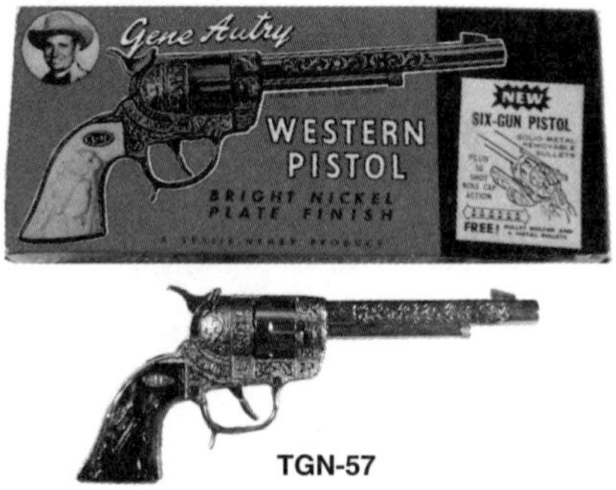


TGN-57

❑ **TGN-57. Gene Autry "Western Pistol" Cap Gun with Box,**
1950s. Rare 11" Box is colorful with photo of Gene on front. Gun is Leslie Henry model with nickel-plated finish. Comes with 6 removable copper bullets. See-through grips are copper colored. Box - **$350**
Gun with Bullets - **$150 $350 $600**

TGN-58

❑ **TGN-58. Set of Gene Autry Cast Iron Cap Guns,**
1950s. Engraving on guns was only used on later issues. Reddish grips. Scarce.
Each - **$275 $525 $900**

TGN-59

❑ **TGN-59. "Rodeo" Pistol with Box,**
1950s. Hubley product. Single shot cap shooting with double action.
Boxed Near Mint - **$125**

TGN-60

❑ **TGN-60. "Rodeo" Pistol with Box,**
1950s. Hubley product. Single shot repeating.
Boxed - **$20 $40 $125**

TGN-61

❑ **TGN-61. "Rodeo" Pistol with Box,**
1950s. Hubley product.
Boxed Near Mint - **$125**

TGN-62

❑ **TGN-62. Hopalong Cassidy Gun Box,**
1950s. Wyandotte product. - **$300 $500 $700**

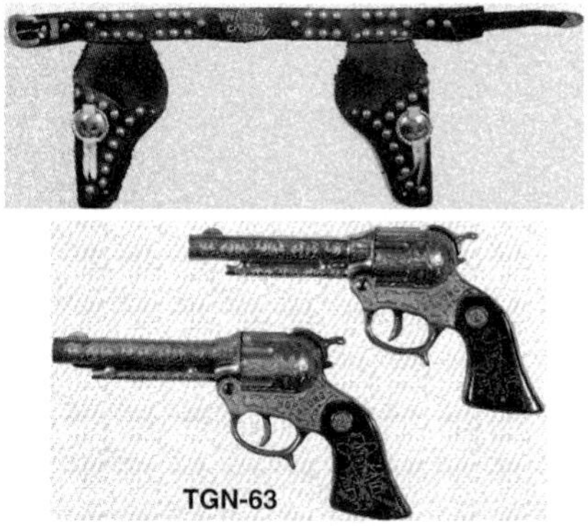

TGN-63

❑ **TGN-63. Hopalong Cassidy Double Holster Set with Guns,**
1950s. Wyandotte product. Guns are gold colored with black grips.
Double Holster - **$125 $175 $225**
Each Gun - **$250 $450 $750**
Complete Set - **$1725**

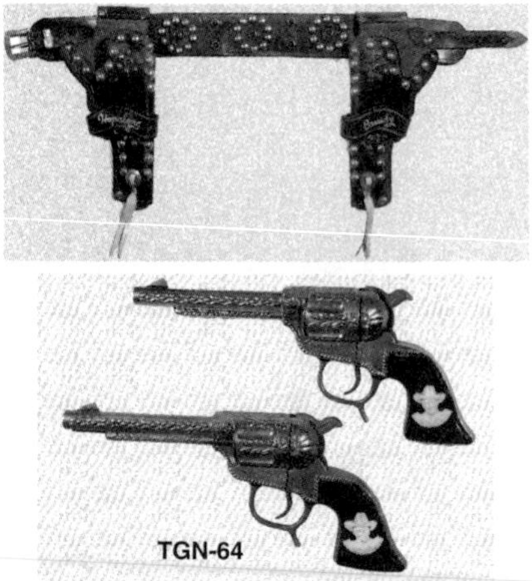

TGN-64

❑ **TGN-64. Hopalong Cassidy Variant Double Holster Set with Guns,**
1950s. Belt is decorated with red and blue jewels. 2 Schmidt guns have black grips with white Hoppy embossed face on each handle.
Double Holster - **$350 $550 $800**
Each Gun - **$200 $375 $550**
Complete Set - **$1900**

TGN-65 TGN-66

❑ **TGN-65. "Hawkeye" 50 Shot Cap Pistol with Box,**
1950s. Kilgore product. Boxed Near Mint - **$75**

❑ **TGN-66. "Mountie" 50 Shot Repeating Cap Pistol with Box,**
1950s. Kilgore product. Boxed Near Mint - **$60**

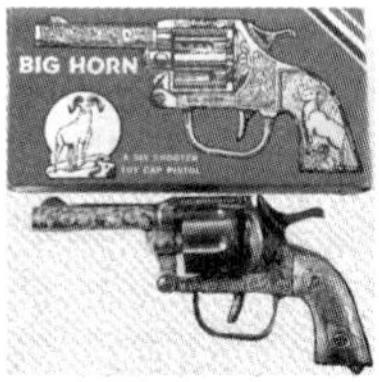


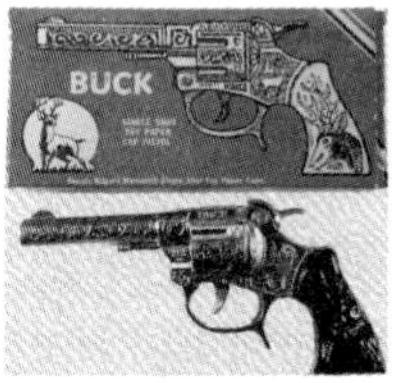


TGN-67 TGN-68

❑ **TGN-67. "Big Horn" Six Shooter with Box,**
1950s. Kilgore product #217. Silver metal grips.
Boxed Near Mint - **$175**

❑ **TGN-68. "Buck" Single Shot Pistol in Box,**
1950s. Kilgore product #407.
Boxed - **$70 $100 $150**

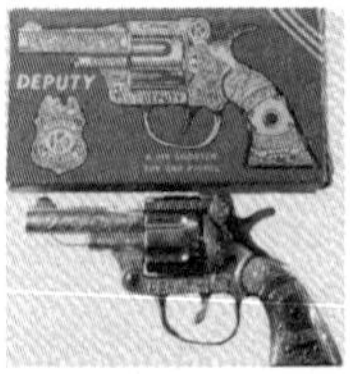


TGN-69 TGN-70

❑ **TGN-69. "Bronco" Six Shooter with Box,**
1950s. Kilgore product. Boxed Near Mint - **$175**

❑ **TGN-70. "Deputy Sheriff" Pistol in Box,**
1950s. Kilgore product #216. Boxed Near Mint - **$175**

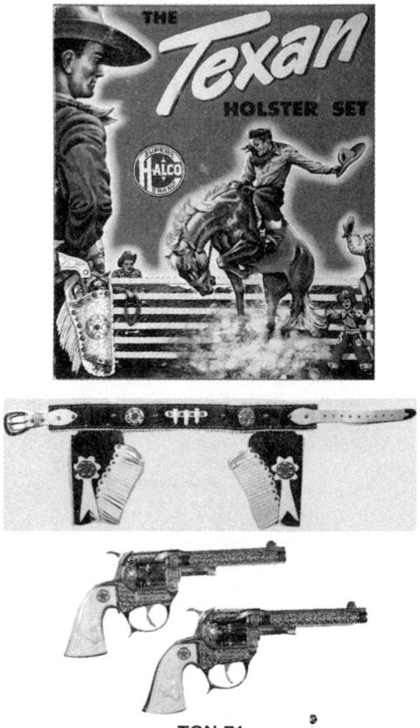


TGN-71

❑ **TGN-71. "Texan" Holster Set with Box,**
1950s. Halco. Includes 2 scarce Smokey Joe gold colored cap guns with white grips .
Box - **$25 $50 $75**
Double Holster - **$75 $150 $225**
Each gun - **$60 $120 $250**
Complete - **$800**

TGN-72

❑ **TGN-72. "Frontier Smoker" Cap Gun with Smoke Powder Packet in Box,**
1950s. Box is colorful.
Boxed Near Mint - **$200**

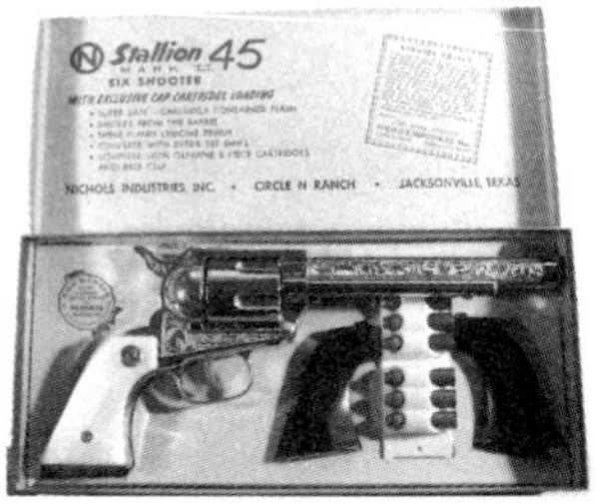


TGN-73

❑ **TGN-73. "Stallion 45 Mark II" Pistol with Box,**
1950s. Box and gun are silver color with 6 toy bullets in whote holder. Box is 12 1/2" long. There are white gun grips and extra black grips. Boxed Near Mint - **$450**

TGN-74

❑ **TGN-74. "Red Ranger Jr." Die Cast Cap Pistol in Box,**
1950s. Wyandotte product. Bright silver color. Boxed Near Mint - **$135**

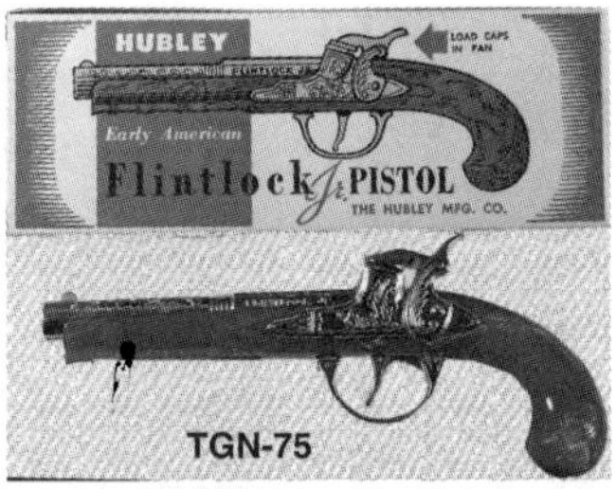

TGN-75

❑ **TGN-75. "Flintlock Jr." Cap Pistol in Box,**
1950s. Hubley product.
Boxed Near Mint - **$75**

TGN-76

❑ **TGN-76. "Kit Carson" Cap Gun on Card,**
1950s. Kilgore. - **$165**

TGN-77

❑ **TGN-77. "Cisco Kid" 100 Shot Repeater in Box,**
1950s. Lone Star made in England. Has Cisco Kid name on barrel. Boxed Near Mint - **$450**

TGN-78

❑ **TGN-78. "Stallion 38" Pistol with Box,**
1950s. Nichols six shooter cap pistol with cap cartridge loading. Boxed Near Mint - **$225**

TGN-79

❑ **TGN-79. "Stallion 41-40" Pistol with Box,**
1950s. Nichols cap pistol with flip cylinder which holds 6 bullets. Boxed Near Mint - **$500**

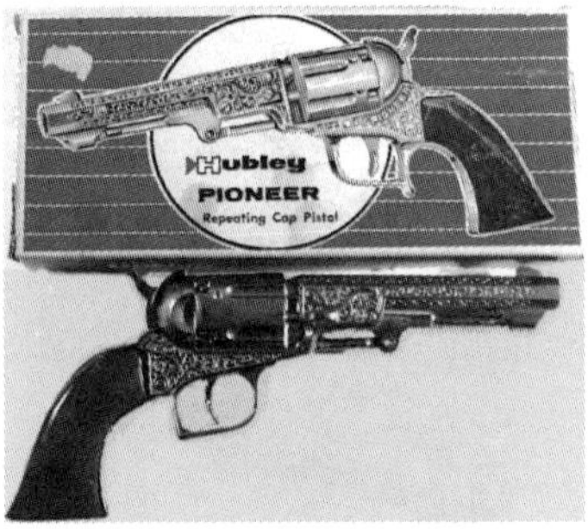

TGN-80

❑ **TGN-80. "Pioneer" Cap Pistol in Box,**
1950s. Hubley product. 9 1/2" gun has light brown plastic see-thru grips. Boxed Near Mint - **$200**

TGN-81

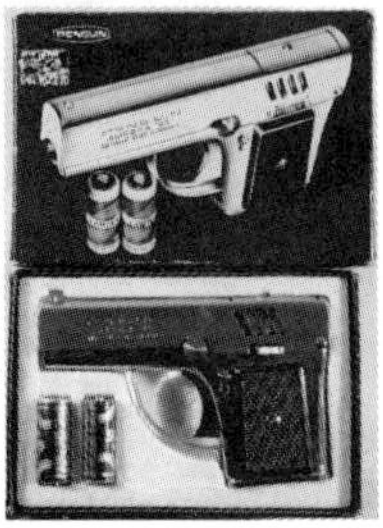
TGN-82

❑ **TGN-81. "Trooper" Cap Pistol with Box,**
1950s. Hubley product. Extremely bright silver finish with red star on handle. Gun is 6 3/4" long. Box is mostly bright red with white highlights.
Box - **$50**
Gun - **$100**

❑ **TGN-82. "Penguin Aurora 45" Butane Gas Lighter/Flashlight in Box,**
1950s.With 2 batteries. Boxed - **$15 $50 $100**

TGN-83

❑ **TGN-83. "Secret Agent" Hideaway Pistol in Box,**
1950s. Hamilton Specialties. Pistol has blue handle. Back of the box has a cut out Secret Agent I.D. card. Boxed Near Mint - **$75**

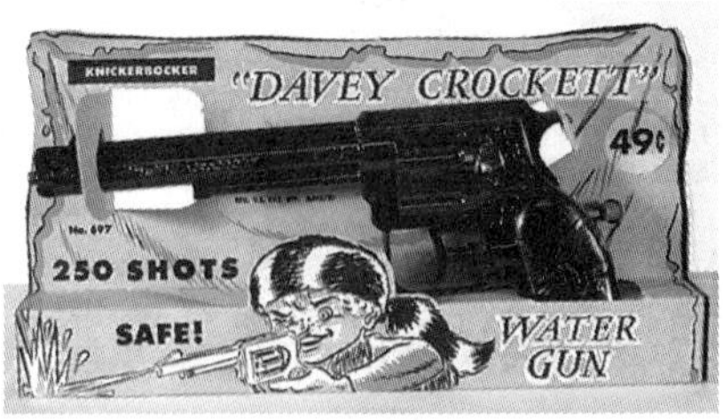

TGN-84

❑ **TGN-84. "Davey Crockett" Water Gun,**
1950s. By Knickerbocker. On card - **$25 $50 $85**

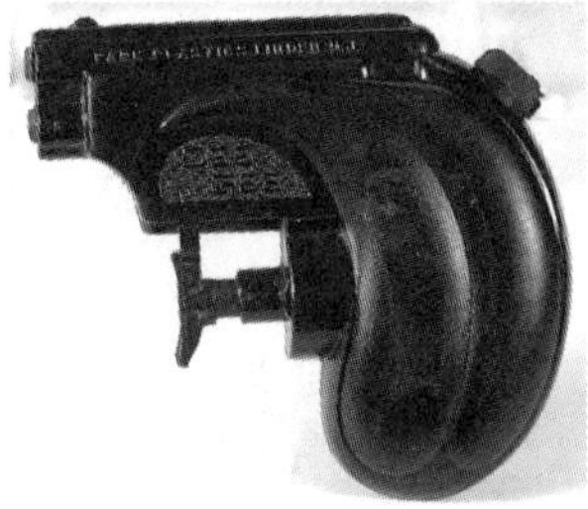
TGN-85

❑ **TGN-85. "Dee Gee" Water Gun,**
1950s. One of the most popular water guns from the 1950s fad. They're hard to find today. Water guns from the 40s and 50s all had metal tips on the end from where the water was forced. Later issues had plastic tips. - **$15 $30 $45**

TGN-86

❑ **TGN-86. Ideal Water Pistol in Box,**
1950s. Luger style. - **$15 $30 $45**

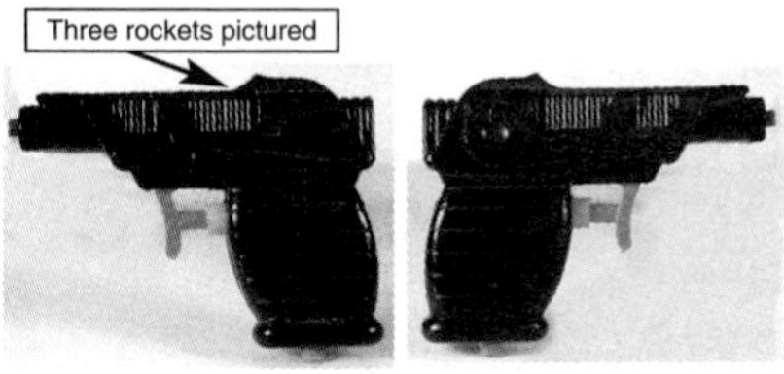


TGN-87

❑ **TGN-87. "Space Jet" Water Gun,**
1950s. By Knickerbocker. Gun has metal tip. Three rockets are pictured on one side. Rare. - **$20 $35 $50**

TGN-88

❑ **TGN-88. "Wee Gee" Salesman Sample Water Gun,**
1950s. The most popular water gun of the 1950s. Regular issue made in black and red. Must have metal tip.
Salesman sample (see-through red plastic) - **$50 $100 $125**
Regular black - **$15 $25 $35**
Regular red - **$20 $30 $40**

TGN-89

❑ **TGN-89. Rocket Dart Pistol in Box,**
1950s. Daisy product. Comes with 2 suction darts (1 green, 1 white) on colorful open box display. Box is 8 1/4" long and 6" high.
Metal Gun with 2 Darts - **$60 $120 $250**
Box - **$200**

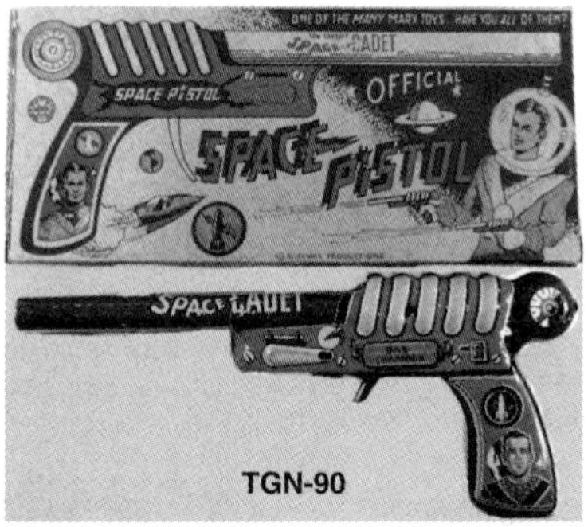


TGN-90

❑ **TGN-90. "Tom Corbett Space Cadet" Space Pistol in Box,**
1950s. Rockhill Productions.
Boxed Near Mint - **$800**

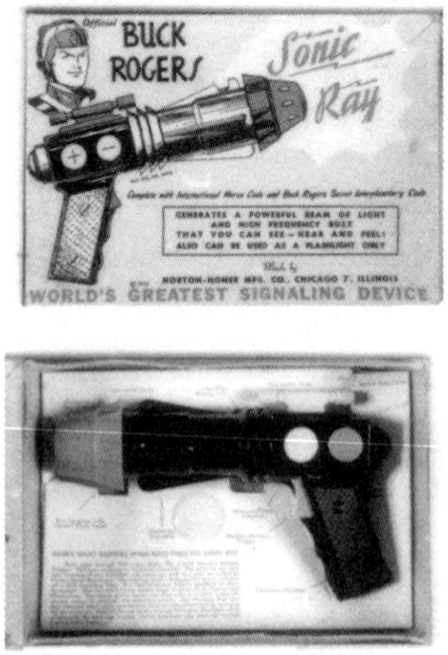


TGN-91

❑ **TGN-91. "Buck Rogers" Sonic Ray Gun in Box,**
1950s. Flashlight gun. In box with instructions.
Boxed - **$100 $300 $450**

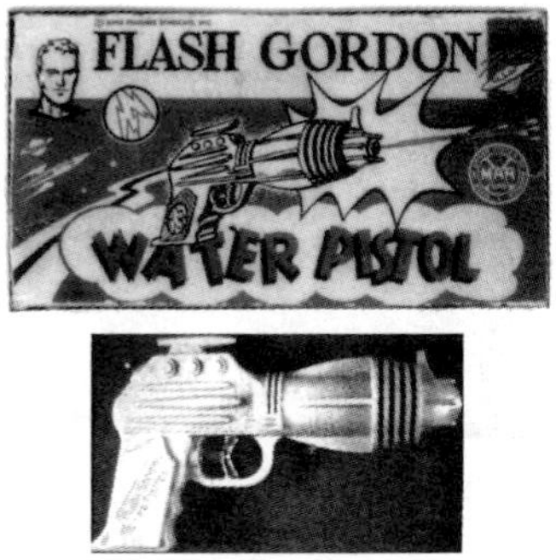


TGN-92

❑ **TGN-92. "Flash Gordon" Water Pistol in Box,**
1950s. Boxed - **$100 $275 $500**

TGN-93

TGN-94

❑ **TGN-93. "Coyote" Cap Pistol on Card,**
1950s. Hubley product #237. Black handle.
Unfired on Card - **$150**

❑ **TGN-94. "Wyatt Earp Buntline Special" Cap Pistol on Card,**
1957. Card features Hugh O'Brian as TV's Wyatt Earp. On Card - **$85 $225 $400**

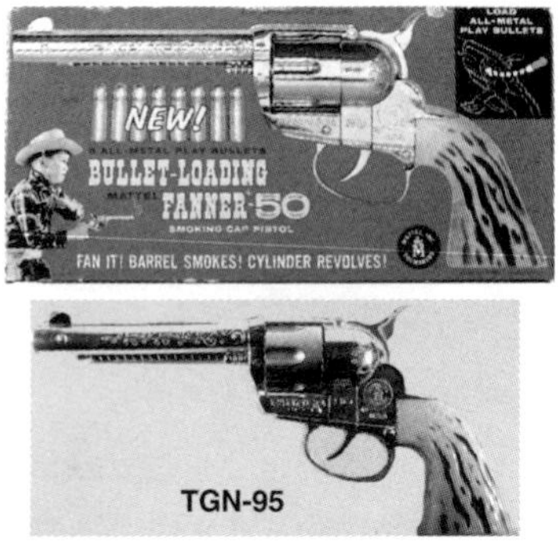


TGN-95

❑ **TGN-95. "Fanner-50" Pistol with Box,**
1950s. Mattel product. Has 8 all-metal play bullets. Boxed Near Mint - **$550**

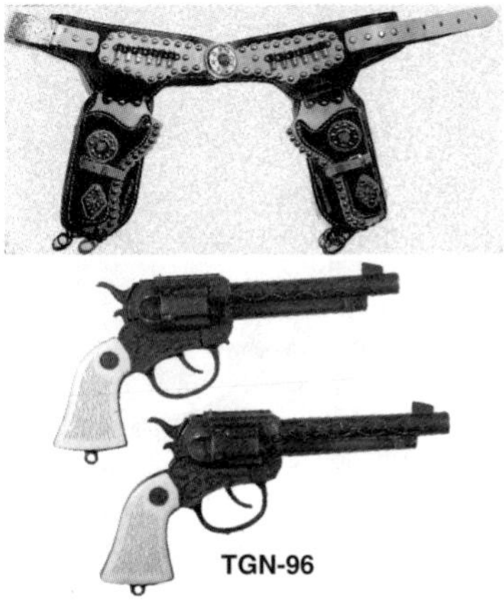

TGN-96

**❑ TGN-96. "Lone Ranger" Double Holster Set with Cap Pistols,**
Late 1950s. Belt holds 12 silver colored bullets. Lone Ranger name appears on each side of holsters. Belt and holster are decorated with red jewels. Guns are bronze colored with white grips. Grips have small loops at bottom.
Double Holster - **$125 $250 $400**
Each Gun - **$95 $180 $300**
Complete - **$1000**

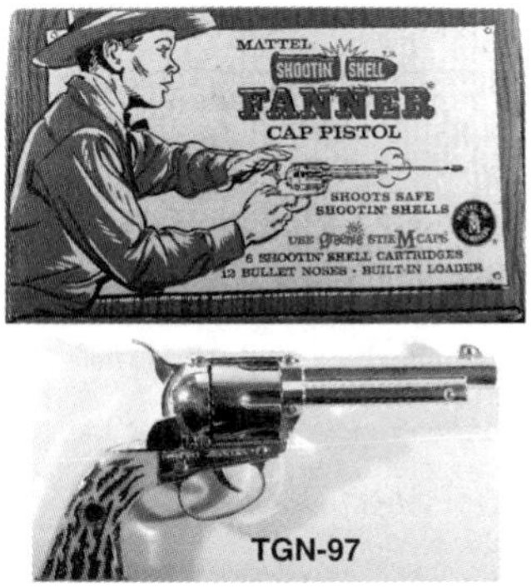


TGN-97

**❑ TGN-97. "Shootin' Shell Fanner" Pistol with Box,**
1960s. Mattel product. Boxed Near Mint - **$325**

TGN-98

**❑ TGN-98. "Wyatt Earp Buntline Special" Cap Pistol in Box,**
1960s. From Crescent Toys in England. Gun is bright silver with red grips. Box is 9 1/4" long.
Box Near Mint - **$100**
Gun - **$25 $75 $150**

TGN-99

**❑ TGN-99. Kilgore's "Champion Fast Draw" Pistol with Box,**
1960s. Box is 11" long and very colorful. Has instructions for reading timer on back. Gun has bright silver finish and black handle.
Box - **$100**
Gun - **$50 $90 $175**

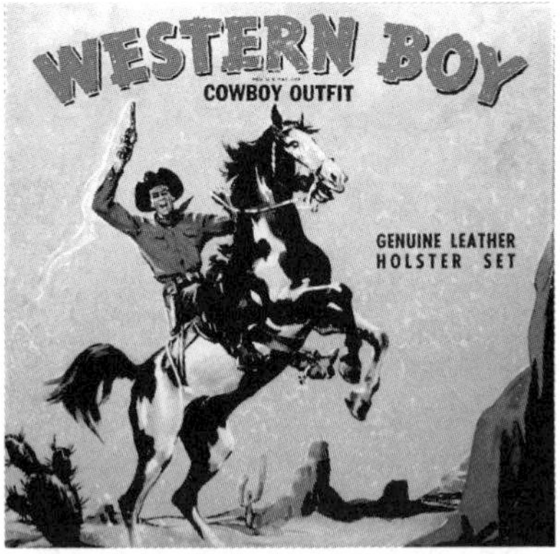


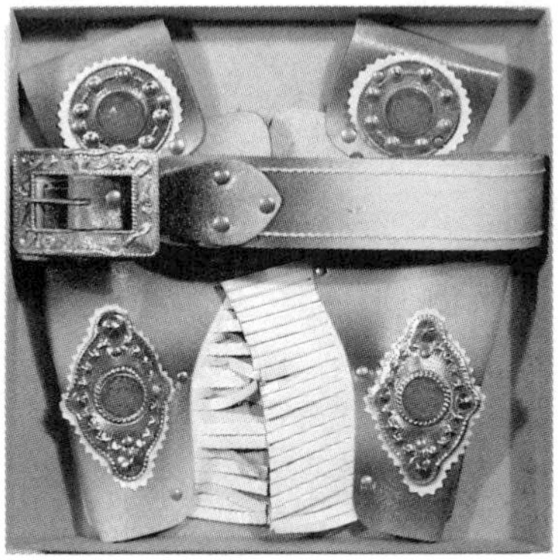

TGN-100

**❑ TGN-100. "Western Boy" Double Holster in Box,**
1960s. Grey and white with red jewels and silver colored buckles. No guns included.
Box - **$20 $30 $50**
Double Holster - **$50 $110 $175**
Complete - **$225**

TGN-101

**❑ TGN-101. "Six Gun" with Bullets in Box,**
1960s. Plastic six shooter which actually shot soft lightweight bullets. Set of 25 bullets came with the gun. Due to the popularity of the gun, most sets are now usually missing some or all of the bullets and the guns usually no longer work. There's also a target with a hole on the back of the box. Box - **$100**
Gun - **$25 $50 $100**
Set of 25 Bullets - **$50**

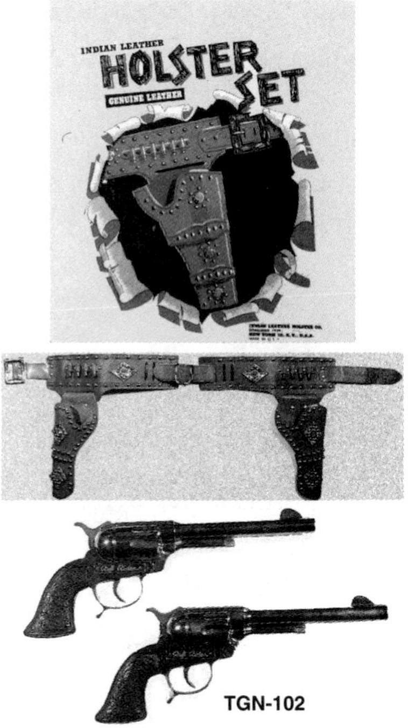


TGN-102

**❑ TGN-102. "Indian Leather" Holster Set with "Ruf Rider" Cap Pistols and Box,**
1960s. Belt and holsters have red jewels. Belt holds 8 silver colored bullets. Set comes with 2 guns which are die cast with bright chrome finish. "Ruf Rider" is embossed on guns.
Box - **$35 $60 $80**
Double Holster - **$75 $150 $225**
Each Gun - **$60 $120 $200**
Complete - **$705**

TGN-103

❑ **TGN-103. "2 Guns in 1" Cap Pistol with Box,**
1960s. Boxed - **$20 $50 $110**

TGN-104

❑ **TGN-104. "Deputy" Gun and Badge with Box,**
1960s. Hubley product. Box - **$25 $50 $75**
Gun and Badge - **$75 $100 $150**

TGN-105

❑ **TGN-105. "State Ranger" Holster Set with "Cowpoke" Cap Pistols and Box,**
1960s. Belt holds 6 red bullets and a single holster. "Cowpoke" cap gun is brightly silver plated with plastic grips. Box - **$20 $40 $60**
Holster - **$50 $100 $150**
Gun - **$50 $100 $150**
Complete - **$360**

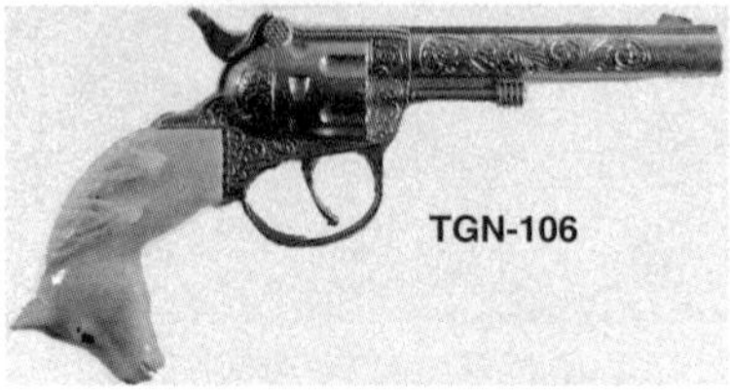

TGN-106

TGN-107

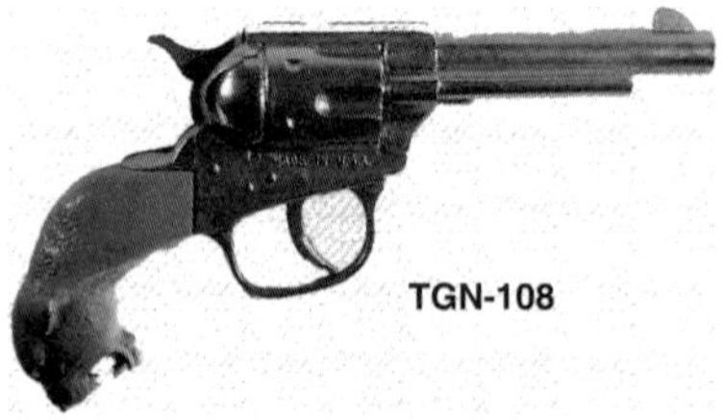

TGN-108

❑ **TGN-106. Cap Gun with Horse Head Grip,**
1960s. Hubley product. Horse is yellow with white mane. Unfired - **$160**

❑ **TGN-107. Cap Gun with Panther Head Grip,**
1960s. 6 1/2" Hubley product. Metal grip is black with white teeth and eyes. Prototype - **$400**

❑ **TGN-108. Cap Gun with Puma Head Grip,**
1960s. 7" Hubley product. Metal grip is tan with red eyes and mouth, and white teeth. Prototype - **$400**

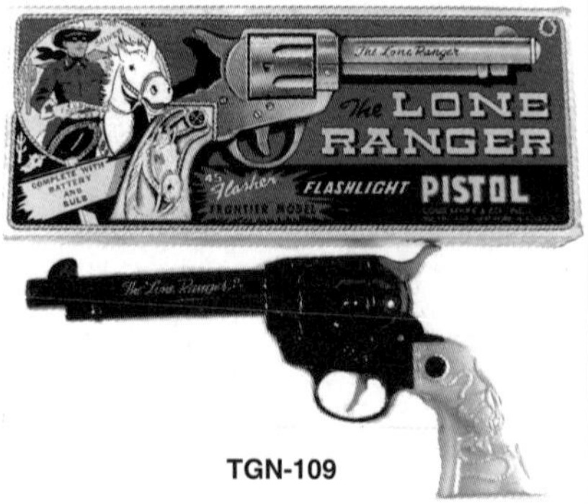


TGN-109

❑ **TGN-109. "Lone Ranger 45 Flasher" Frontier Model Flashlight Gun and Box,**
1960s. Complete with battery and bulb in box. Boxed - **$400**

TGN-110

❑ **TGN-110. "S-Bar-M" Double Holster Set with "Western" Cap Pistols and Box,**
1960s. Belt holds 12 gold colored bullets. Holster has red and yellow jewels. Black and green designs on white. "Western" cap guns have black steer design on white grips.
Box - **$20 $50 $70**
Double Holster - **$75 $150 $225**
Each Gun - **$50 $100 $175**
Complete with unfired guns - **$645**

TGN-111

❑ **TGN-111. "Bonanza" Holster and Gun Set,**
1960s. Rayo product from Mexico. Plastic holster has 6 plastic bullets and cast photo buckle.
Gun and Holster - **$100**

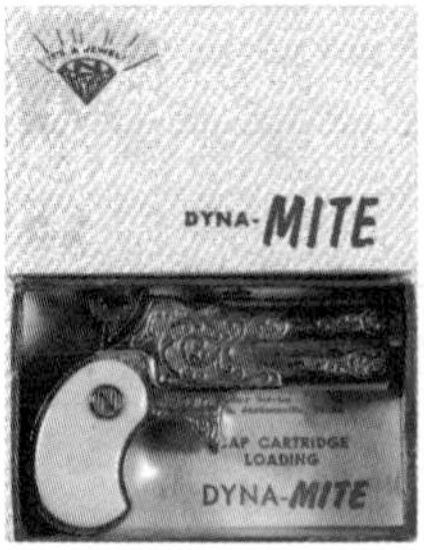


TGN-112

TGN-113

❑ **TGN-112. "Dyna-Mite" 3 1/2" Derringer,**
1960s. Nichols product. - **$20 $40 $100**

❑ **TGN-113. "Texas Ranger" Smoking Cap Gun on Card,**
1960s. Leslie Henry product. Die cast. - **$75**

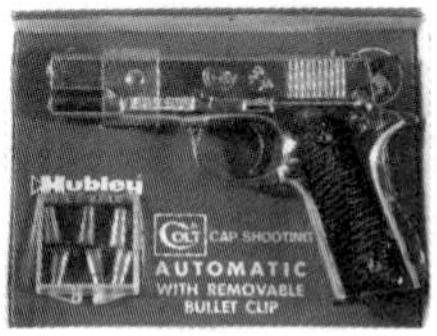


TGN-114

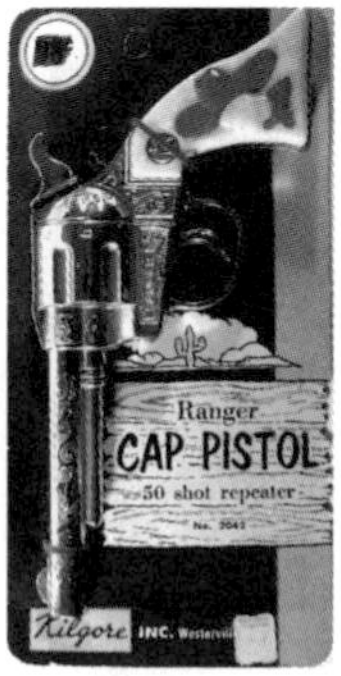


TGN-115

❑ **TGN-114. "Colt" Automatic Cap Pistol in Box,**
1960s. Hubley product. With toy bullets in box
Complete - **$15 $30 $60**

❑ **TGN-115. "Ranger" Cap Pistol on Card,**
1960s. Kilgore. 50 shot repeater has large white grips trimmed in red.
Carded - **$125**

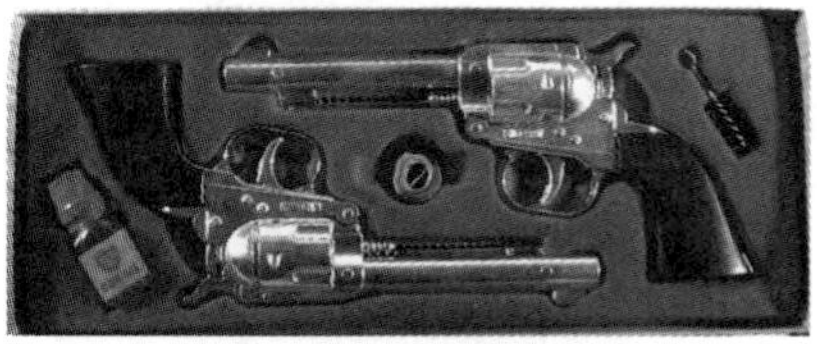

TGN-116

❑ **TGN-116. Set of "Kid MK II" Cap Guns with Gun Oil and Cleaner Brush in Box,**
1960s. BCM product from England. Guns have bright silver platings and specially-made brown grips. Box has insert.
Box - **$5 $10 $20**
Each Gun - **$10 $25 $45**
Complete - **$120**

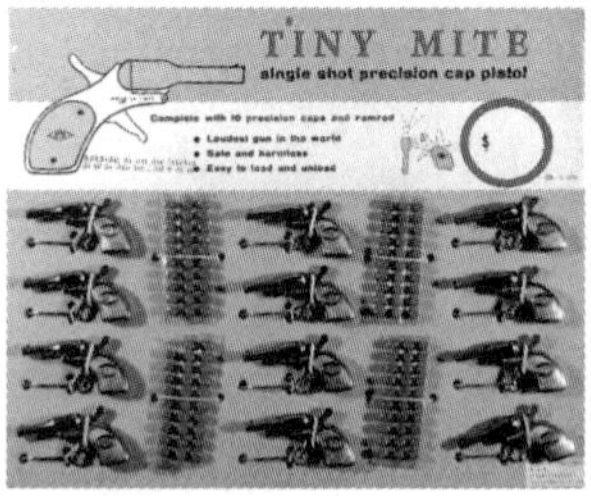


TGN-117

❑ **TGN-117. "Tiny Mite" Gun Set on Card,**
1960s. Made in Italy. 12 single shot precision guns per card.
Complete with Caps - **$90**
Each Gun with Caps - **$6**

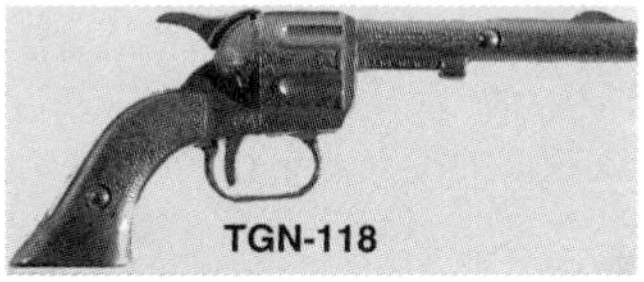

TGN-118

❑ **TGN-118. "Pal" Cap Pistol,**
1960s. - **$10 $20 $40**

TGN-119

❑ **TGN-119. "Mustang" Cap Pistols,**
1960s. Kilgore product. Set of gold plated cap guns in beautiful presentation box. Guns are referred to as "Tophand Twins." Deluxe gold finish with cameo grips. Each gun is approximately 9" long. Presentation box is cardboard made to look like wood. Insert is blue with felt-like finish. Gold finish on guns easily wears off.
Box - **$175**
Each Gun- **$50 $125 $225**

TGN-120

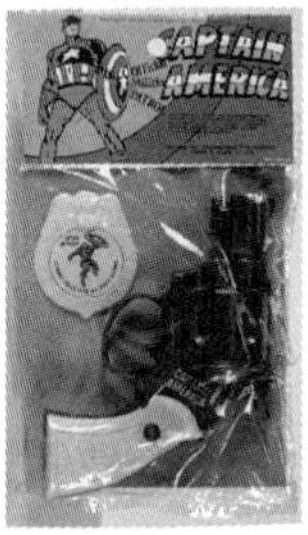


TGN-121

❑ **TGN-120. "Private Eye" Snub Nose Cap Gun on Card,**
1974. Kilgore product. Die cast metal.
On card - **$20 $60 $80**

❑ **TGN-121. "Captain America" Gun and Badge Set,**
1974. In display package. - **$15 $25 $35**

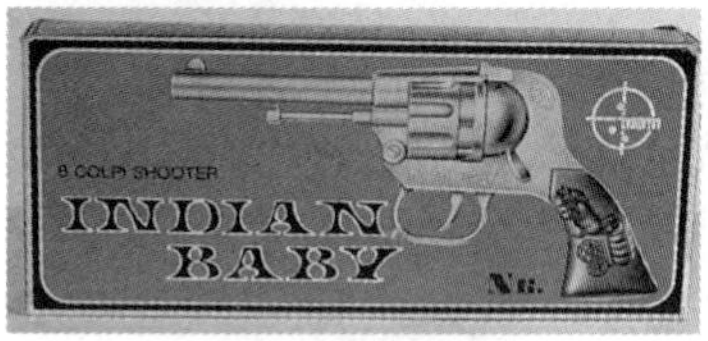


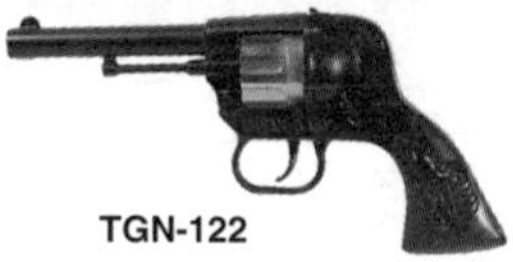

TGN-122

❑ **TGN-122. "Indian Baby" 8-Shot Toy Pistol in Box,**
1970s. Uses plastic cartridges. A smoker gun made in Italy. - **$25 $50 $75**

TGN-123

TGN-124

❑ **TGN-123. "Lost Frontier" Die Cast Metal Cap Gun on Card,**
1990. Esquire/Nichols product.
On Card - **$4 $8 $20**

❑ **TGN-124. "Masked Marshal" Set on Card,**
1990. Imperial product. Includes mask, badge, gun and bullets.
On Card - **$2 $4 $10**

TGN-125

TGN-126

❑ **TGN-125. "Range Rider" Bounty Hunter Set on Card,**
1992. Includes clicker gun, shot gun and handcuffs on open card. - **$4 $8 $20**

❑ **TGN-126. "Texan" Holster and Pistol Set on Card,**
1992. 50 shot roll cap pistol. Die cast metal.
On Card - **$4 $8 $20**

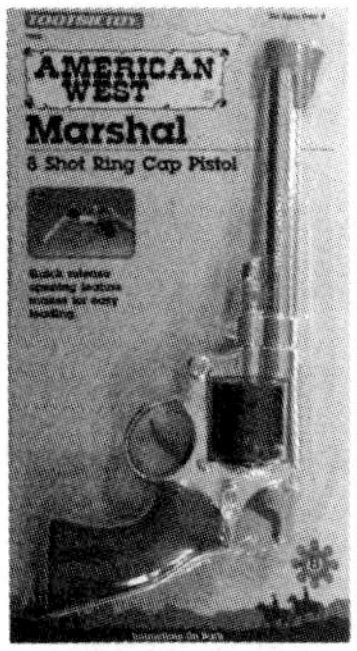


TGN-127

TGN-128

**❑ TGN-127. "Marshal" Cap Pistol on Card,**
1994. 8 shot cap pistol. Card is 6.75" x 12.75". - **$2 $5 $12**

**❑ TGN-128. "American West" Single Holster Set in Box,**
1995. Die cast metal cap gun in genuine leather holster. Boxed - **$2 $4 $10**

TGN-129

**❑ TGN-129. "American West" Brown Double Holster Set in Box,**
1995. With 2 die cast metal cap guns in brown holster. Boxed - **$5 $10 $30**

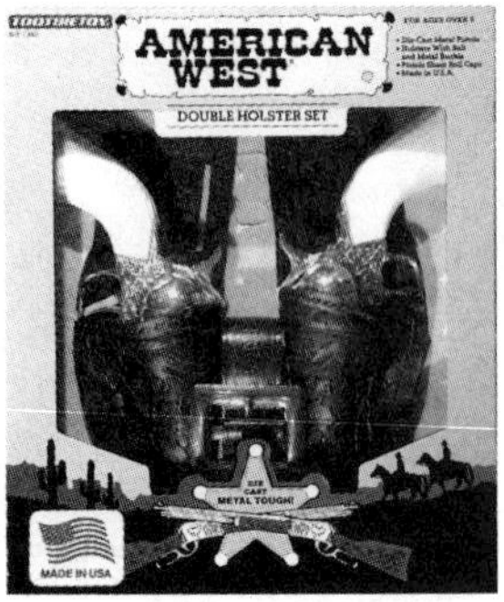


TGN-130

**❑ TGN-130. "American West" Black Double Holster Set in Box,**
1995. With 2 die cast metal cap guns in black holster. Boxed - **$5 $10 $30**

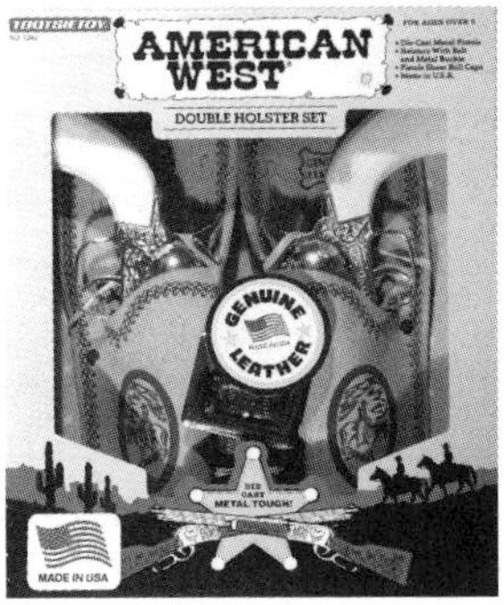


TGN-131

**❑ TGN-131. "American West" Leather Double Holster Set in Box,**
1995. With 2 die cast metal cap guns in leather holster. Boxed - **$5 $10 $30**

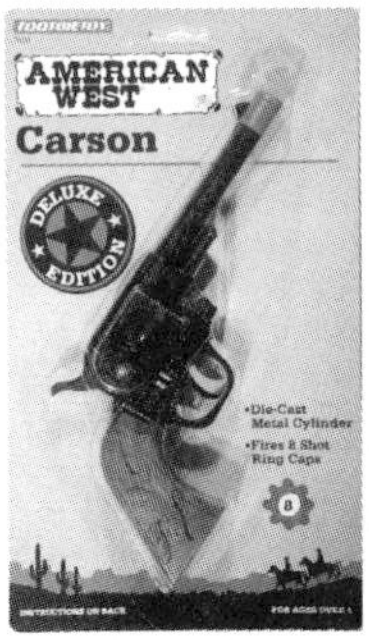

TGN-132 TGN-133

**❑ TGN-132. "American West" Carson Cap Gun on Card,**
1996. Die cast cylinder cap gun shoots 8 shot ring caps. On Card - **$2 $4 $10**

**❑ TGN-133. "American West" Snake Cap Gun on Card,**
1996. Die cast cylinder cap gun shoots strip caps. On Card - **$2 $4 $10**

TGN-134

**❑ TGN-134. "Electronic" Six Shooter in Box,**
1996. Western Gear product. What a kid wouldn't give for one of these in the 1950s. Has real sound and flashing barrel. Comes in black and brown grips. Boxed - **$2 $4 $12**

TGN-135 TGN-136

**❑ TGN-135. "Shiloh Kid" Double Gun and Holster Set on Card,**
1996. Die cast metal guns, holsters and belt. On Card - **$5 $10 $16**

**❑ TGN-136. "Cowboy Trail" Clicker Gun and Badge on Card,**
1997. On Card - **$2 $5 $12**

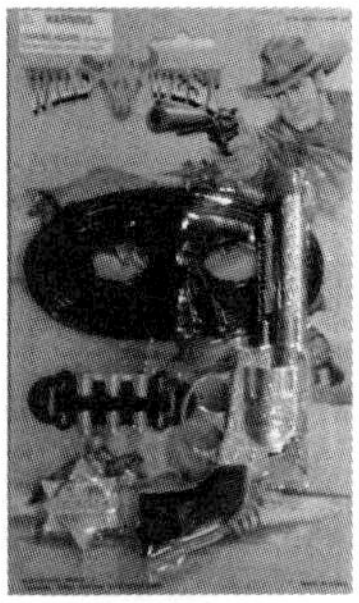

TGN-137 TGN-138

**❑ TGN-137. "Wild West" Gun and Knife Set on Card,**
1990s. Gun, 3 bullets, rubber knife and badge. On Card - **$2 $4 $10**

**❑ TGN-138. "Wild West" Gun and Mask Set on Card,**
1990s. Gun, 3 bullets, mask and badge. On Card - **$2 $4 $10**

TGN-139

**❑ TGN-139. "Electronic" Six Shooter with Holster in Box,**
2000. America Frontier product. Boxed - **$10**

# Toy Story

The success of the two *Toy Story* films is not surprising. For years, collectors have always joked that when they go to bed at night their toys come to life. Several cartoons from the past have also used this idea. *The Tin Soldier* is a good case in point. What makes the *Toy Story* plot so interesting is that it revisits the age-old rivalry between the popularity of cowboys and spacemen. In the late 1920s and early 1930s, cowboys were king until *Buck Rogers* and *Flash Gordon* hit the scene. *Captain Video* and *Space Patrol* ruled the early days of TV, only to be gunned down by *Paladin*, *The Rifleman*, *Sugarfoot*, *Maverick* and a host of others.

Even after *Star Wars* returned science fiction to the forefront, western movies like Clint Eastwood's *Unforgiven* were the ones winning Academy Awards. It only seems fair that spaceman Buzz Lightyear gets in his shots against cowboy Woody in 1996 and 1999. The big surprise of the new film's release is the unbelievable box office success. Estimates show that *Toy Story 2* will gross over $300 million and is racking up spectacular numbers internationally. As a collector, you had to love the plot of the second film. Woody discovers he was a big 1950s TV star, and since he's still in top-notch shape, he would bring big money. Of course the buyer is from Japan and Woody doesn't want to leave his friends. If you have seen the film, you know the rest.

The irony of all this is that items produced to support the films have become highly sought after. It is clear that several sequels will prevail and the toys produced in the future will only increase the number of collectors.

TYS-1

TYS-2

❑ **TYS-1. "Woody" Burger King Premium,**
1995. 6 1/2" tall in bag. - **$15**

❑ **TYS-2. "Mr. Potato Head" in Box,**
1995. Contains over 20 parts. - **$8 $12 $25**

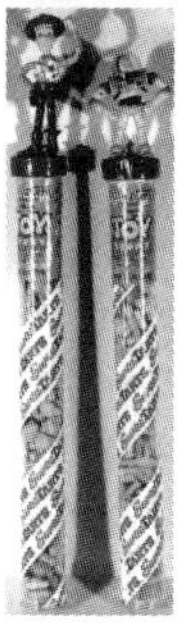

TYS-3

TYS-4

❑ **TYS-3. "Woody and Buzz" Candy Tubes,**
1995. Figures on top of tube of Sweet Tarts. Each - **$2 $3 $5**

❑ **TYS-4. Army Men Burger King Premium,**
1995. Bags contains 4 soldiers. - **$2 $4 $10**

TYS-5

❑ **TYS-5. Toy Story Animated Flip Book,**
1995. - **$2 $4 $10**

TYS-6

TYS-7

❑ **TYS-6. "Woody with Lasso" Burger King Premium in Bag,**
1995. Supports video release. - **$2 $4 $10**

❑ **TYS-7. "Buzz Lightyear" Burger King Premium in Bag,**
1995. Supports video release. Has plastic head and torso, cloth arms and legs. - **$2 $4 $12**

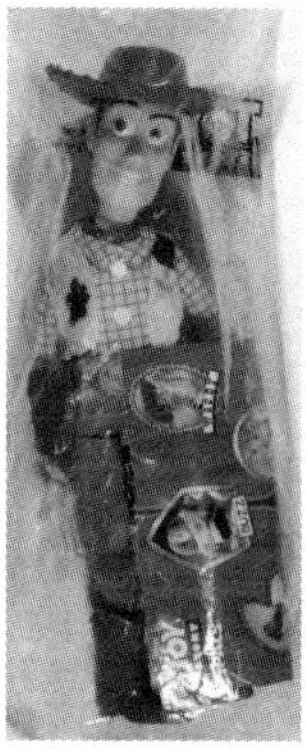

TYS-8

TYS-9

❑ **TYS-8. 11" "Woody" Burger King Premium in Bag,**
1996. Toy Story Pals set. - **$20**

❑ **TYS-9. "Woody" Burger King Premium in Bag,**
1996. Comes with literature. - **$15**

TYS-10

TYS-11

❑ **TYS-10. "Buzz" Burger King Figure,**
1996. With original bag. - **$15**

❑ **TYS-11. "Buzz" Burger King Figure,**
1996. 9" Toy Story Pal with literature. - **$20**

TYS-12

TYS-13

❑ **TYS-12. "Woody" Figure on Card,**
1996. Sheriff star base. - **$5**

❑ **TYS-13. "Hamm" Figure on Card,**
1996. - **$5**

TYS-14

TYS-15

❑ **TYS-14. "Woody" Watch in Tin,**
1996. Fossil. Comes in box inside colorful tin. Limited edition. - **$100**

❑ **TYS-15. "Buzz" Watch in Tin,**
1996. Fossil. Comes in box inside colorful tin. Limited edition. - **$100**

TYS-16 TYS-17

❑ **TYS-16. "Woody" Star Bean Figure,**
1996. 10 1/2" tall. With tag. - **$20**

❑ **TYS-17. "Buzz" Star Bean Figure,**
1996. 8 1/2" tall. With tag. - **$20**

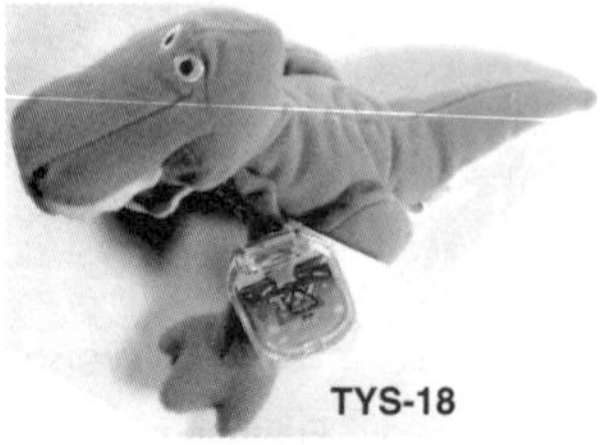

TYS-18

❑ **TYS-18. "Rex" Star Bean Figure,**
1996. With tag. - **$20**

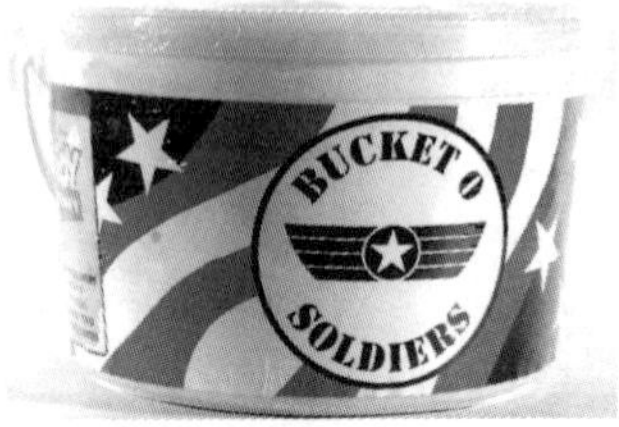


TYS-19

❑ **TYS-19. "Bucket O Soldiers",**
1996. 72 soldiers in plastic bucket with Toy Story logo on top of shrink wrap. Complete. - **$35**

TYS-20 TYS-21

❑ **TYS-20. "Woody" Squeeze Bottle,**
1996. Premium from Minute Maid. - **$40**

❑ **TYS-21. "Rex" Squeeze Bottle,**
1996. Premium from Minute Maid. - **$40**

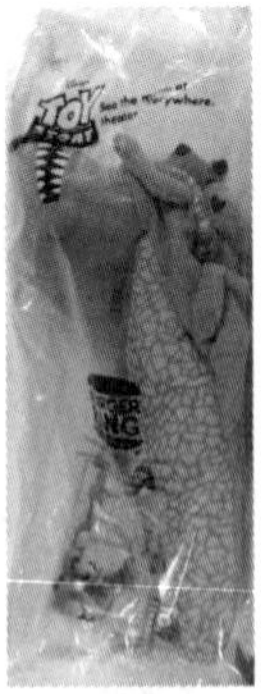

TYS-22

TYS-23

❑ **TYS-22. "Rex" Burger King Premium in Bag,**
1996. Comes with literature. - **$15**

❑ **TYS-23. Movie Promotion Badge,**
1996. Giveaway featuring Buzz. - **$2 $4 $10**

TYS-24

❑ **TYS-24. Musical Snow Globe,**
1996. - **$90**

TYS-25

❑ **TYS-25. "Cookie Crisp" Cereal Box,**
1996. Has Yo-Yo offer.
Box - **$2 $4 $6**
Yo-Yo - **$10**

TYS-26 TYS-27

❑ **TYS-26. "Cheerios" Cereal Box,**
1996. Has Toy Story video tape rebate offer. With Mr. Potato cut-outs on back.
Box - **$2 $4 $8**

❑ **TYS-27. "Trix" Cereal Box,**
1996. Has Toy Story figure offer. Five different figures pictured on box front
Box - **$2 $4 $8**

TYS-28

❏ **TYS-28. "Cinnamon Toast Crunch" Cereal Box and Flip Book Premium,**
1996. 2 different flip books.
Box - **$2 $4 $8**
Each Flip Book - **$10**

TYS-29

❏ **TYS-29. "Mrs. Potato Head" Hallmark Keepsake Ornament in Box,**
1998. - **$15**

TYS-30

❏ **TYS-30. "Holiday Hero Woody" Doll,**
1999. In Santa outfit. Talking figure in box. - **$35**

TYS-31

TYS-32

❏ **TYS-31. "Woody" Bean Bag Figure with Sound,**
1999. From Toy Story 2. Has two tags. - **$12**

❏ **TYS-32. 9 1/2" "Buzz" Bean Bag Figure with Sound,**
1999. From Toy Story 2. Has two tags. - **$10**

TYS-33

TYS-34

❏ **TYS-33. "Rex" Bean Figure with Tag,**
1999. 7" long. - **$12**

❏ **TYS-34. "Bullseye" Bean Figure with Tag,**
1999. 8" long. Disney Store exclusive. - **$10**

TYS-35

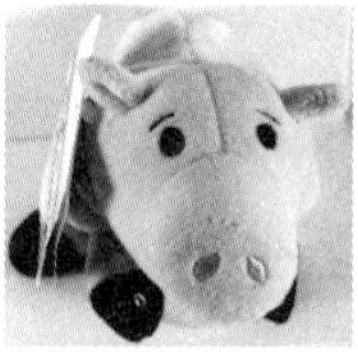

TYS-36

❏ **TYS-35. "Buzz" Bean Figure with Tag,**
1999. 8" tall. - **$20**

❏ **TYS-36. "Hamm" Bean Figure with Tag,**
1999. 9" tall. - **$12**

TYS-37

TYS-38

❏ **TYS-37. 20" "Woody" Doll with Tags,**
1999. From Toy Story 2. Has two tags. - **$25**

❏ **TYS-38. 18" "Buzz" Bean Bag Figure,**
1999. From Toy Story 2. Has two tags. First version has a $20 tag. - **$45**

TYS-39

❏ **TYS-39. "Jessie" 12" Doll in Box,**
1999. - **$15**

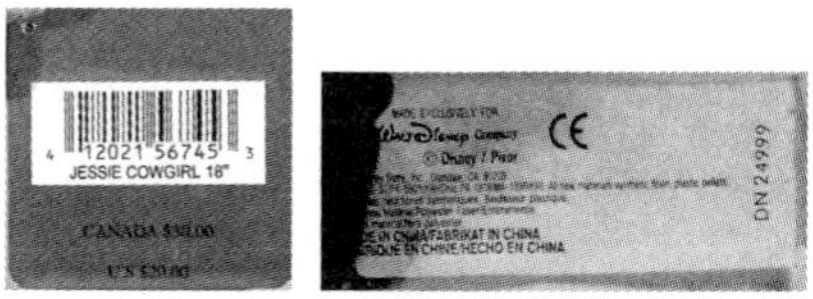

**(TAGS FOR 1999 MODEL)**

TYS-40

TYS-41

**(Figure is identical for both 1999 and 2000. Only tags differ)**

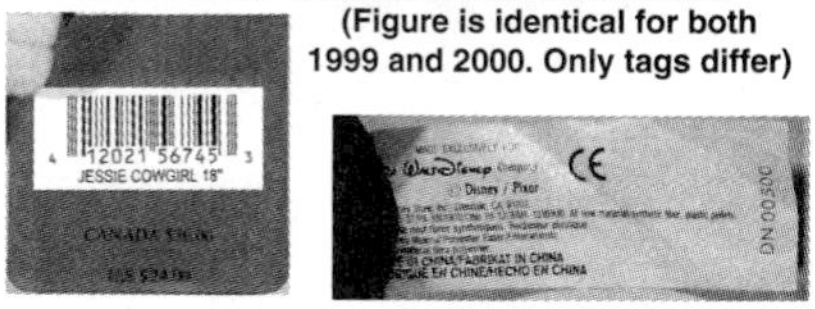

**(TAGS FOR 2000 MODEL)**

❏ **TYS-40. "Jessie Cowgirl" 18" Bean Figure with Tags,**
1999. Disney Store exclusive. One of the hot 1999 Christmas toys, it quickly sold out. Store price was $20 for this first edition. Has felt hat and 2 tags. - **$50**

❏ **TYS-41. Reissued "Jessie Cowgirl" 18" Bean Figure with New Tags,**
2000. Disney Store exclusive. Doll has same felt hat and 2 different tags. Store price was $24 for this second edition. - **$24**

TYS-42

TYS-43

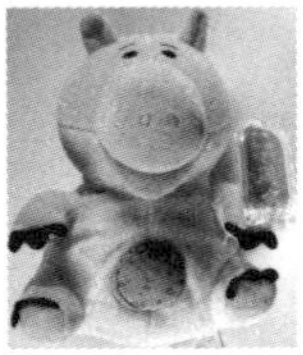

TYS-44

❑ **TYS-42. Large "Bullseye" Horse Beanie with Tags,**
1999. 13" x 14". Has 2 Disney Store tags. - **$30**

❑ **TYS-43. "Emperor Zerg" Bean Bag Figure,**
1999. From Toy Story 2. Has two tags. - **$10**

❑ **TYS-44. "Hamm" Bean Bag Figure,**
1999. From Toy Story 2. With tags. - **$10**

TYS-45

TYS-46

❑ **TYS-45. "The Prospector" Bean Figure with Tags,**
1999. 8" tall with a cloth hat. Has 2 Disney Store tags. - **$10**

❑ **TYS-46. "The Prospector" Star Bean Figure,**
1999. Hat easily chips at edges. - **$10**

TYS-47

TYS-48

❑ **TYS-47. Space Alien Figurine Eraser,**
1999. Space alien character was prominent in ads for Toy Story 2. - **$5**

❑ **TYS-48. "Buzz" Yo-Yo on Card,**
1999. Monogram product. - **$3 $5 $10**

TYS-49

TYS-50

❑ **TYS-49. "Buzz" Yo-Yo in Package,**
1999. Mattel product. - **$3 $5 $10**

❑ **TYS-50. "Woody" Yo-Yo in Package,**
1999. Mattel product. - **$3 $5 $10**

TYS-51

❑ **TYS-51. Hot Wheels Action Pack,**
1999. Includes miniature figures and car. Promotes Al's Toy Barn featured in *Toy Story 2*. - **$15**

TYS-52

❑ **TYS-52. "Woody" and "Buzz" Figures on Candy,**
1999. Pocket Pops. Each - **$2**

TYS-53

TYS-54

❑ **TYS-53. "Jessie" Gumball Machine,**
1999. - **$5**

❑ **TYS-54. "Jessie" Candy Dispenser,**
1999. Tart N Tinys candy. - **$5**

TYS-55

❑ **TYS-55. "Woody"Candy Dispenser in Bag,**
1999. McDonald's premium. Horse collapses when bottom is pushed. - **$5 $10 $30**

TYS-56

TYS-57

❑ **TYS-56. "Buzz"Candy Dispenser in Bag,**
1999. McDonald's premium. - **$20**

❑ **TYS-57. "Rex"Candy Dispenser in Bag,**
1999. McDonald's premium. - **$20**

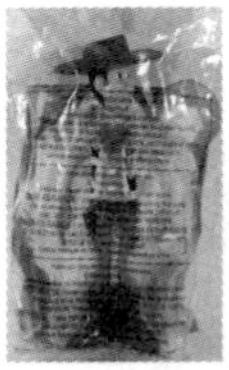

TYS-58

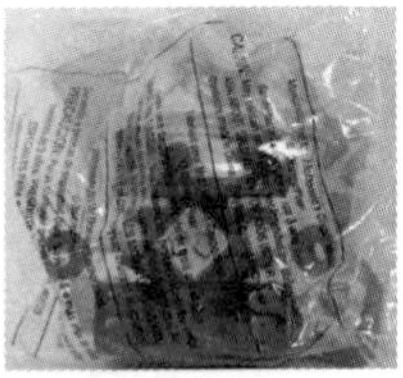

TYS-59

❑ **TYS-58. "Woody" 5 3/4" Toy in Bag,**
1999. McDonald's premium. - **$8**

❑ **TYS-59. "Robot" Mobile Toy in Bag,**
1999. McDonald's premium. - **$5**

TYS-60

TYS-61

❑ **TYS-60. "Mr. Potato Head" 4 3/4" Toy in Bag,**
1999. McDonald's premium. Has parts to change to Mrs. Potato Head. - **$5**

❑ **TYS-61. "Slinky Dog" Mobile Toy in Bag,**
1999. McDonald's premium. - **$5**

TYS-62

TYS-63

TYS-64

❑ **TYS-62. Cereal Box with Secret Compartment Spoon Premium Ad,**
1999. - **$1 $2 $4**

❑ **TYS-63. "Jessie the Cowgirl" Secret Compartment Spoon in Wrapper,**
1999. Cereal premium. - **$5**

❑ **TYS-64. "Bullseye" Premium Spoon in Wrapper,**
1999. Cereal premium. - **$5**

TYS-65

TYS-66

❑ **TYS-65. "Tour Guide Barbie" in Box,**
1999. - **$25**

❑ **TYS-66. "Woody and Bo Peep Gift Set",**
1999. In box. - **$30**

(ENLARGED VIEW OF TOY WINDOW)

TYS-67

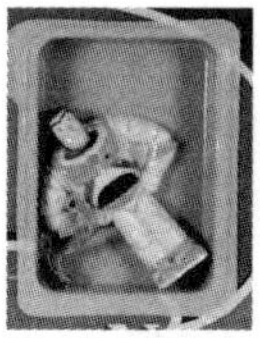

TYS-68

TYS-69

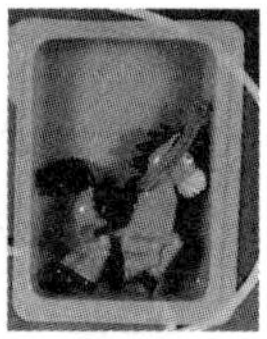

TYS-70

❑ **TYS-67. "Honey Nut Cheerios" Cereal Box with Woody Figure in Window,**
1999. Free dangler figurine is behind clear plastic window of front of box. - **$1 $3 $5**

❑ **TYS-68. "Honey Nut Cheerios" Cereal Box with Buzz Figure in Window,**
1999. - **$1 $3 $5**

❑ **TYS-69. "Honey Nut Cheerios" Cereal Box with Jessie Figure in Window,**
1999. - **$2 $4 $7**

❑ **TYS-70. "Honey Nut Cheerios" Cereal Box with Bullseye Figure in Window,**
1999. - **$1 $3 $5**

TYS-71

TYS-72

❑ **TYS-71. "Jessie the Cowgirl" Figure,**
1999. Base has rollers. - **$2 $4 $8**

❑ **TYS-72. "Honey Nut Cheerios" Cereal Box with Buzz Lightyear Clock Offer,**
1999. - **$1 $3 $5**

TYS-73

TYS-74

❑ **TYS-73. "Cocoa Puffs" Cereal Box with Yo-Yo Offer,**
1999. Box - **$1 $3 $5**
Yo-Yo - **$10**

❑ **TYS-74. "Kix" Cereal Box with Book Offer,**
1999. Box - **$1 $3 $5**
Each Book - **$10**

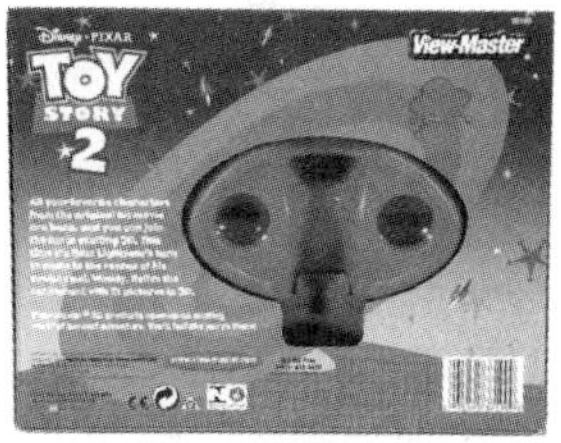


TYS-75

❑ **TYS-75. View-Master With 3-D Pictures,**
1999. Includes 21 photos. - **$20**

TYS-76

❑ **TYS-76. "Woody" Sprinkler in Box,**
1999. - **$25**

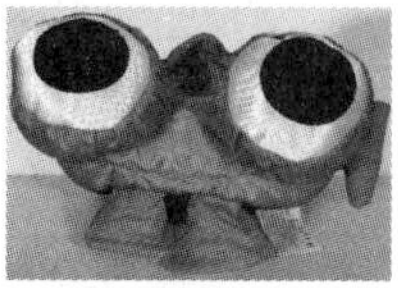

TYS-77

TYS-78

❑ **TYS-77. "Lenny" Bean Figure with Tags,**
2000. - **$10**

❑ **TYS-78. Bear Critter Bean Bag Figure,**
2000. Star Bean. - **$10**

TYS-79

❑ **TYS-79. Cookie Jar,**
2000. - **$35**

TYS-80 TYS-81 TYS-82

❑ **TYS-80. "Buzz" Push Puppet,**
2000. Wonka Candy. - **$3**

❑ **TYS-81. "Woody" Push Puppet,**
2000. Wonka Candy. - **$3**

❑ **TYS-82. "Jessie the Cowgirl" 7" Bean Figure with Tags,**
2000. Smaller than other versions. - **$8**

TYS-83 TYS-84

❑ **TYS-83. "Jessie and Buzz" Beanbags,**
2000. In box. - **$25**

❑ **TYS-84. "Jessie" Doll with Country Blossom Outfit,**
2000. - **$15**

TYS-85 TYS-86

❑ **TYS-85. "Jessie and Critters" Poseable Figures,**
2000. Mattel product on card. - **$15**

❑ **TYS-86. "Jessie" Talking Model Kit,**
2000. In box. - **$30**

TYS-87

❑ **TYS-87. "Hot Wheels" Cars,**
2000. NASCAR 2000 set has 3 cars in box. - **$25**

TYS-88

❑ **TYS-88. Aliens Shoe Accessories,**
2000. Two 3-eyed aliens on card. - **$15**

TYS-89

❑ **TYS-89. Buzz Lightyear Blaster in Box,**
2000. Produces cosmic lights and sounds. - **$20**

## Trix

**General Mills introduced Trix fruit-flavored corn puffs around 1955, and the distinctive Trix-loving rabbit made his debut on the cereal boxes and in animated television comercials in 1959. The original rabbit was a hand puppet that appeared in the introduction to *Rocky and His Friends, Captain Kangaroo*, and other General Mills-sponsored programs. "Silly rabbit, Trix are for kids."**

TRX-1

❑ **TRX-1. "Walky Squawky Talky" Cardboard Units In Envelope,**
1965. With Envelope - **$20 $35 $70**
Loose - **$10 $20 $30**

TRX-2

❑ **TRX-2. Cereal Box Flat With "Walkie-Squawky Talkies" Offer,**
1965. Gordon Gold Archives.
Near Mint Flat - **$225**
Used Complete - **$35 $75 $125**

TRX-3

❑ **TRX-3. "The Leaping Trix Rabbit" Box Flat,**
1969. Box contained 3" tall hard plastic premium of Rabbit figure and spring-loaded "Launching Tree Stump." Near Mint Flat - **$225**
Used Complete - **$35 $75 $125**
Complete Premium - **$10 $20 $40**

TRX-4

❑ **TRX-4. Tiddly Wink Miniature Plastic Game,**
c. 1960s. Lidded container holding small dexterity game featuring disks picturing Trix Rabbit. - **$8 $15 $20**

TRX-5

❑ **TRX-5. Harlem Globetrotters Premiums Cereal Box,**
1970. Back panel promotes series of four "Hot Shot Basketball Player" premiums. Gordon Gold Archives. Near Mint Flat - **$275**
Used Complete - **$50 $125 $200**

TRX-6

❑ **TRX-6. Vinyl Squeaker Figure,**
1978. - **$15 $25 $50**

TRX-7

❑ **TRX-7. Cereal Box Flat With "Rabbit Racer" Offer,**
1970s. Gordon Gold Archives.
Near Mint Flat - **$400**
Used Complete - **$50 $150 $250**

TRX-8

TRX-9

❑ **TRX-8. Club Stickers,**
c. 1970s. Set Of Five - **$5 $10 $25**

❑ **TRX-9. Plastic Ramp Toy,**
1970s. Designed to walk on inclined surface. - **$15 $30 $50**

TRX-10

TRX-11

Dear Friend,

Thank you for sending in your vote. I see that you voted no – you must really believe that Trix are for kids! However, enough children voted yes so that I was able to eat a whole bowl of fruity, delicious Trix! I hope you are enjoying your Trix as much as I did. Thanks again, my friend!

Your Pal,

The Trix Rabbit

TRX-12

❑ **TRX-10. "Yes! Let The Rabbit Eat Trix!" 2-1/4" Litho. Button,**
1970s. For affirmative voter in contest, back has metal clip. - **$5 $15 $25**

❑ **TRX-11. "No! Trix Are For Kids!" 2-1/4" Litho. Button,**
1970s. For negative voter in contest, back has metal clip. - **$5 $15 $25**

❑ **TRX-12. Contest Vote Thank-You Letter,**
1970s. Accompaniment letter to litho. buttons for entrant in contest to determine if Trix Rabbit should be allowed to eat Trix cereal. - **$5 $10 $20**

TRX-13

❑ **TRX-13. "Trix Rabbit" Premium Doll With Mailer,**
1987. Issued by General Mills. Plush doll is 16" tall. Mailer - **$1 $3 $5**
Doll - **$5 $15 $30**

## Twenty Thousand Years in Sing-Sing

**This was a series of dramatized prison stories related by Sing-Sing Prison Warden Lewis E. Lawes. The show was sponsored by Sloan's Liniment and heard on the Blue Network from 1933 until 1939. The title was based on some 2,000 inmates each incarcerated for one year or more. Lawes, one of the era's more lenient wardens, related human interest stories, most with a positive theme, about men who overcame obstacles and returned to society to lead successful lives.**

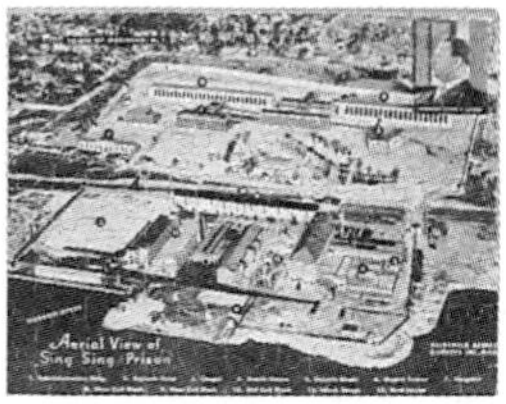


TWY-1

❑ **TWY-1. "Aerial View Of Sing-Sing Prison" Puzzle,**
1930s. Sloan's Liniment. 8x10" blue and white puzzle with inset black and white photo of Warden Lawes at top right.
Mailer (Not Shown) - **$5 $10 $15**
Puzzle - **$15 $30 $60**

TWY-2

❑ **TWY-2. "Strange Stories From Sing Sing!" Booklet,**
1930s. Has diecut front cover simulating jail bars. - **$15 $35 $60**

## Uncle Don

**Between 1928 and 1949, broadcasting regionally from New York radio station WOR, Uncle Don Carney entertained kids with stories, poems, jokes, songs, birthday announcements, and advice on health and behavior. Carney, whose real name was Howard Rice, started in vaudeville as a trick**

pianist and turned his air time into a classic children's program. Along with nonsense syllables, pig latin, and made-up words, Uncle Don promoted a number of "clubs" related to the products of his many commercial sponsors. The show was aired on the Mutual network for one season (1939-1940), sponsored by Maltex cereal. Uncle Don also read the comics on the air on Sunday mornings, and narrated *The Adventures of Terry and Ted* on CBS radio in 1935-1936. The often-told tale that Carney, after signing off one night, said "I guess that'll hold the little bastards" with the microphone still on, apparently never happened.

UDN-1

❑ **UDN-1. Engineers Club Cello. Button,**
1929. Lionel trains. 1-1/4" multicolor. -
**$75 $150 $300**

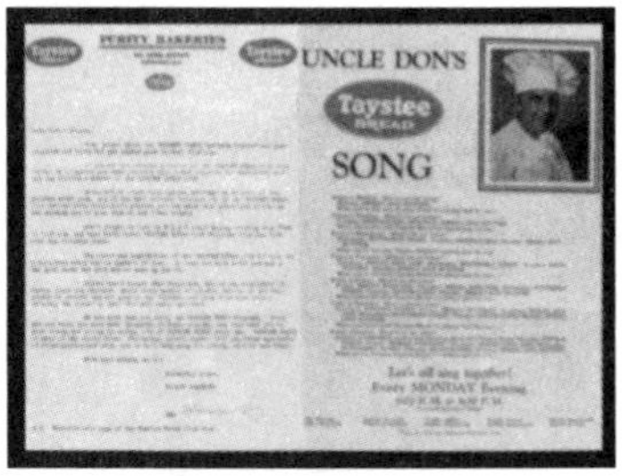


UDN-2

❑ **UDN-2. Letter And Song Sheet,**
1929. Taystee Bread, Chicago.
Letter **- $5 $12 $25**
Song **- $5 $12 $25**

UDN-4

UDN-3

❑ **UDN-3. Uncle Don Bank,**
1920s. Two types. Each **- $10 $40 $65**

❑ **UDN-4. "Lionel Engineers Club" Cello. Button,**
1930. **- $75 $150 $300**

UDN-5

❑ **UDN-5. Uncle Don's "Earnest Saver Club" Tin Bank,**
c. 1938. Various banks. Wrapper design of character with "Bank Book" body. **- $10 $40 $65**

UDN-6

UDN-7

UDN-8

❑ **UDN-6. "Maltex 100% Breakfast Club" Litho. Button,**
c. 1939. **- $3 $5 $10**

❑ **UDN-7. Uncle Don Letter and Mailer,**
1930s. Savings Club. **- $20 $40 $60**

❑ **UDN-8. Uncle Don's "Terry And Ted And Major Campbell" 12x19" Map,**
1930s. Bond Bread. Map follows route of trio in their "Land Cruiser" pictured at bottom. -
**$40 $100 $175**

UDN-9

UDN-10

❑ **UDN-9. "Terry And Ted On The Trail Of The Secret Formula" Booklet,**
1930s. Bond Bread. Story told by Uncle Don with color pictures. **- $5 $12 $20**

❑ **UDN-10. Autogiro Theme Photo,**
1930s. Popsicle. Pictures Uncle Don as aviator with facsimile signature inscription for Popsicles. -
**$5 $10 $20**

UDN-11

UDN-12

❑ **UDN-11. "Borden Health Club" Cello. Button,**
1930s. **- $10 $15 $25**

❑ **UDN-12. "Ice Cream Club/Borden" Cello. Button,**
1930s. **- $10 $15 $25**

UDN-14

UDN-13

❑ **UDN-13. "Borden's Health Club Honor Prize",**
1930s. "Uncle Don" brass bar holding cloth ribbon suspending cello. pendant with reverse image of Borden milk bottle. **- $10 $20 $40**

❑ **UDN-14. "Bosco Club" Cello. Button,**
1930s. Pictured holding jar of chocolate drink syrup product. **- $12 $25 $40**

UDN-15 UDN-16 UDN-17

❑ **UDN-15. "Good Humor/G.H.H.C." Cello. Button,**
1930s. Pictured in Good Humor Ice Cream uniform. **- $15 $35 $60**

❑ **UDN-16. "I.V.C. Club" Cello. Button,**
1930s. **- $5 $10 $20**

❑ **UDN-17. "Mutual Grocery Club" Cello. Button,**
1930s. **- $8 $12 $20**

UDN-18 UDN-19 UDN-20

❑ **UDN-18. "Castles Ice Cream Club" Cello. Button,** 1930s. - **$10 $18 $30**

❑ **UDN-19. "Remitypers" Cello. Button,** 1930s. Remington Typewriters. - **$12 $25 $35**

❑ **UDN-20. "Taystee Bread Club" Cello. Button,**
1930s. - **$10 $15 $25**

UDN-21

❑ **UDN-21. "Song Game And Paint Book",** 1940. Store item by Melrose Music Corp., New York. 8-7/8x11-7/8" with 68 pages. Back cover promotes "Uncle Don" reading comics over the Mutual System on Sunday mornings and shows 17 King Features Syndicate characters all commenting on the show. Major characters shown are Phantom, Popeye, Jiggs and Maggie, Blondie and Dagwood. - **$15 $25 $50**

## Uncle Scrooge

**Uncle Scrooge made his first appearance on December 1947 in the Donald Duck comic *Four Color* #178. The story was titled "Christmas on Bear Mountain." Uncle Scrooge's role in the story paralleled that of another fictitious character Ebenezer Scrooge who had a similar role in the favorite holiday story "A Christmas Carol." Uncle Scrooge was drawn by the famous artist Carl Barks (1901-2000). Carl made Uncle Scrooge into a ruthless character in the first story. In one panel Uncle Scrooge says, "me-I'm different! Everybody hates me, and I hate everybody." Shortly after this story, Barks started to include a role for Scrooge in more Donald Duck stories. As Scrooge evolved he became more friendly, less complex and famous among readers for his incredible wealth.**

**In 1952 Barks interrupted his role with the Donald Duck line of comics and worked most of the time on the newly titled Uncle Scrooge comic books until 1967. Strangely, the success of Uncle Scrooge did not follow the Disney Marketing scheme of developing a line of products to support the popularity of the character in the comic book. Rumors persisted that Disney himself did not want the character to be popular with the belief that people might see Disney as the real Scrooge. While these rumors were never proven, one had to wonder why so few Scrooge products were made in the fifties and sixties.**

**Without Carl's wonderful stories or a product line, Scrooge's fame started to fade in the early '70s. He was only remembered by those loyal fans who had read Carl's great one-shot stories and collected old Disney comic books. Many of Carl Barks' supporters were not happy with the demise of Uncle Scrooge and his faithful companions. Several important players in comic fandom made overtures to the staff at Disney to produce new products to support the interest of collectors of Disney comic books. After a difficult struggle with Disney executives, The Colonel and others worked out a deal to develop a wonderful product line of paintings, books, lithos and eventually figurines that brought Carl's character back to life.**

**Finally, in the 1980s old Scrooge got another break. The Disney company launched a new TV series called "Duck Tales" and the star became the one and only Uncle Scrooge. Disney launched some new inexpensive products to support the TV show and Scrooge was on the comeback trail. Today, Scrooge is as popular as he ever was, and recently he appeared on the front cover of a Disney store catalog as the chief spokesman for the company's new line of character toys.**

USC-1

❑ **USC-1. "Uncle Scrooge Color Book,"** 1955. Issued by Dell Publishing Co. - **$20 $45 $75**

USC-2

❑ **USC-2. Ceramic Figure with Bill and Card,** 1956. Ceramic figure from Hagen-Renaker Potteries is possibly the first Uncle Scrooge toy. Extremely rare to find on card with paper dollar bill. Near Mint With Card and Bill - **$450**
Figure Only - **$50 $100 $150**

USC-3

❑ **USC-3. "Uncle Scrooge The Lemonade King" Book,**
1960. Pencils by Carl Barks, finished art adapted by Norman McGary. 32 pages. -
**$100 $400 $800**

(Box)

(Front)

USC-4

(Side View)

❑ **USC-4. "Uncle Scrooge" Bank with Box,**
1961. Don Brechner exclusive.
Bank - **$50 $100 $150**
Box - **$10 $30 $100**

USC-5 (Green candy box)

(Blue display box)

(Lt. purple wood-grain box)

❑ **USC-5. "Uncle Scrooge" Disneykin,**
1961. Miniature figures (1 3/4" tall) were first released in 1961, followed by a second series marketed as "New Disneykins." Only some of the 34 Disney characters were available after 1962. There were also various solid color unpainted Mexican versions produced.
Figure with green candy box - **$40 $125 $200**
Figure with "TV Scenes" box - **$50 $150 $400**
Figure with blue display box with cellophane window - **$50 $150 $250**

**USC-6** (Disneykin figure)

❑ **USC-6. "Uncle Scrooge" DisneyKid,**
Early 1960s. Even smaller (1 1/4" tall) figure than Disneykins. These figures remain an enigma in the Disneykin collecting world. It is not known why or when these were produced. No official product paperwork or packaging has come to light. It is assumed that they first appeared in the early 1960s, around the same time as their slightly larger Disneykin second series counterparts. Even the name "DisneyKids" is assumed; collectors had to call them something to differentiate them from their larger cousins. - **$25 $75 $250**

**USC-7**

❑ **USC-7. "Uncle Scrooge" Dell Bank,**
1963. Soft rubber premium from Dell Comics. There may be variations in the nephews' sweater colors. - **$15 $45 $90**

**USC-8**

❑ **USC-8. "Uncle Scrooge" Bank,**
1963. English version of the Dell Bank. A soaky-type toy with a screw-top black hat. Colored differently from the U.S. version. - **$20 $60 $100**

**USC-9**

❑ **USC-9. "Uncle Scrooge" Premium Comic,**
1973. - **$1 $3 $5**

**USC-10**

**USC-11**

❑ **USC-10. "Uncle Scrooge" Patch on Card,**
1970s. Tough to find. - **$45**

❑ **USC-11. "Uncle Scrooge" Bank,**
1970s. Made in Korea by Walt Disney Prods. 8" tall and very colorful. - **$50 $100 $175**

**USC-12**

❑ **USC-12. "Uncle Scrooge" Ceramic Bank,**
1970s. - **$25 $50 $75**

**USC-13**

**USC-14**

❑ **USC-13. Premium Coca Cola Glass,**
1982. Scroge pictured from "Mickey's Christmas Carol." - **$25**

❑ **USC-14. "Bah Humbug" Pinback,**
1983. With flicker lights. Issued to promote "Mickey's Christmas Carol." - **$5 $10 $20**

**USC-15**

**USC-16**

❑ **USC-15. "Duck Tales" Stickers,**
1986. Promotes TV show. - **$8 $16 $32**

❑ **USC-16. "Duck Tales" Crayons,**
1986. 16 pack with Scrooge on box. Promotes TV show. - **$9 $18 $27**

**USC-17**

**USC-18**

❑ **USC-17. "Duck Tales" 3-D Puzzle,**
1986. Promotes TV show. - **$10 $25 $50**

❑ **USC-18. "Duck Tales" Party Candles,**
1986. On card - **$25**

**USC-19**

❑ **USC-19. "Uncle Scrooge" Figure,**
1986. 2 3/4" tall painted red rubber figure. Bully product. - **$5 $10 $20**

USC-20 USC-21

❑ **USC-20. Ceramic Figure,**
1986. - **$15 $30 $50**

❑ **USC-21. "Uncle Scrooge" Figure,**
1986. Figure with removable cane. Made by Applause to promote Duck Tales TV show. - **$15 $30 $50**

USC-22 USC-23

❑ **USC-22. "Uncle Scrooge" Figure,**
1986. 2 1/2" rubber figure made by Applause. - **$5 $10 $25**

❑ **USC-23. "Uncle Scrooge" Figure,**
1986. 2 1/2" rubber figure made by Applause. - **$5 $10 $25**

USC-24 USC-25

❑ **USC-24. "Uncle Scrooge" Pock-It,**
1989. Promotes Duck Tales TV show. - **$25**

❑ **USC-25. "Uncle Scrooge" Plush Doll,**
1980s. Fast Food premium promotes "Mickey's Christmas Carol" movie. - **$20**

USC-26 USC-27

❑ **USC-26. "Uncle Scrooge" 4" Figure,**
1980s. With cane and outfit. - **$10 $20 $35**

❑ **USC-27. "Uncle Scrooge" Rubber Figure Bank,**
1980s. - **$10 $20 $45**

USC-28 USC-29

❑ **USC-28. "Uncle Scrooge" Ceramic Music Box,**
1980s. Promotes "Mickey's Christmas Carol." Chair rocks as music plays. - **$25 $60 $100**

❑ **USC-29. "Uncle Scrooge" Figure,**
1980s. Figure has crystal tummy and glasses. Plated in 14K gold. 2 1/2" tall. Limited edition from Austria. Hard to find. - **$35 $65 $90**

USC-30 USC-31

❑ **USC-30. "Uncle Scrooge" Bisque Figure,**
1980s. 3" Christmas ornament. - **$10 $20 $30**

❑ **USC-31. "Uncle Scrooge" Ceramic Figure,**
1980s. 5 1/2" tall. From Japan. - **$10 $25 $40**

USC-32

❑ **USC-32. Uncle Scrooge Porcelain Figure,**
1991. Limited edition from the Franklin Mint. Figure has metal glasses, felt clothing and a wooden cane. 14" tall. - **$75 $175 $300**

USC-33

❑ **USC-33. "Rice Krispies" Cereal Box with Duck Tales Figures Offer,**
1991. Back of box has offer for set of 4 Duck Tales figures. - **$5 $10 $25**

USC-34

❑ **USC-34. "Fruity Marshmallow Krispies" Cereal Box with Duck Tales Figures Offer,**
1992. Back of box has offer for set of 4 Duck Tales figures as part of set of 16 Disney figures. - **$4 $8 $20**

USC-35

❑ **USC-35. "Sport of Tycoons" Bronze Sculpture,**
1994. Limited edition of 100. Sculpted by Paul Vought. Signed by Carl Barks. - **$4500**

USC-36

USC-37

❑ **USC-36. Uncle Scrooge Door Hanger,**
1998. From Disney's Christmas Collection. -
**$10 $20 $35**

❑ **USC-37. Uncle Scrooge Plush Doll,**
1998. With patch and money sack. -
**$10 $20 $40**

USC-38

USC-39

❑ **USC-38. Uncle Scrooge Ceramic Bank,**
1998. High quality product. Made in France. -
**$100**

❑ **USC-39. Uncle Scrooge Star Bean Figure,**
1998. With tag. - **$20**

USC-40

❑ **USC-40. "This Dollar Saved My Life at Whitehorse" Capodimonte Sculpture,**
1999. Limited edition of 250. - **$3600**

USC-41

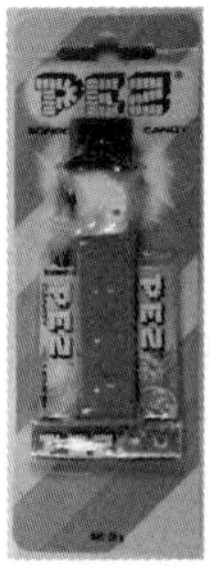


USC-42

❑ **USC-41. Uncle Scrooge Bean Bag,**
1999. Promotes Christmas Carol film. -
**$5 $10 $15**

❑ **USC-42. Uncle Scrooge Pez Dispenser,**
1990s. With candy on card. - **$5 $10 $20**

USC-43

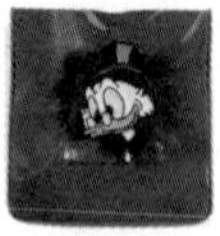

USC-44

USC-45

❑ **USC-43. Uncle Scrooge Pin on Card,**
1990s. From collection of 10 pins from Germany. - **$25**

❑ **USC-44. Uncle Scrooge Pin on Holder,**
1990s. From Germany. - **$25**

❑ **USC-45. Uncle Scrooge Clock,**
1990s. Top closes to give the impression of a safe. - **$32 $60 $95**

USC-46

❑ **USC-46. "The 1st Cent of Uncle Scrooge" Coin Display Book and Coin,**
1990s. Red felt book with snap closure holds coin. Coin is mounted inside a capsule.
Book - **$10 $25 $50**
Coin - **$10 $25 $50**

USC-47

❑ **USC-47. Uncle Scrooge Boxed Puzzle,**
1990s. Limited edition boxed 1000 piece puzzle. Shows Carl Barks painting "Rich Finds at Inventory Time." Made in Japan. - **$75**

USC-48

❑ **USC-48. Uncle Scrooge Porcelain Card,**
1990s. Prototype card (only 6 made) shows oil painting "Always Another Rainbow." - **$150**

USC-49

❑ **USC-49. Uncle Scrooge Water Globe,**
2000. Plays the tune "Pennies From Heaven." - **$30**

USC-50

❑ **USC-50. Uncle Scrooge Figure,**
2001. 18" tall x 15" wide Disneyland Park exclusive. - **$125**

USC-51

❑ **USC-51. Monopoly Disney Edition,**
2001. Features Uncle Scrooge rightfully leading the group. Boxed - **$35**

## Uncle Wiggily

**Uncle Wiggily Longears, an elderly rabbit in a tailcoat, was created by writer Howard R. Garis (1873-1962) for a nationally syndicated newspaper column of bedtime stories that began appearing in 1910. Drawings were added for a Sunday page that ran from 1919 through the 1920s, and a daily comic strip appeared in the mid-1920s, illustrated by various artists. Wiggily comic books were published between 1942 and 1954, and there have been dozens of *Uncle Wiggily* story books. On radio, Albert Goris was Wiggily, telling bedtime stories to his young audience.**

**Uncle Wiggily may be the most underated character in comic character history today! The newspaper strip and the great stories told in books about the Bunny Rabbit Gentleman are legendary. Uncle Wiggly features were one of the first to include real name villains. What a line-up he had to face. First this was the "Skillery Scallery Alligator" followed by the "Pipsisewak" and his mean buddy "Skeezicks." Other villains were the bad old "Skuddlemagoon" and the Fox and Wolf known as the "Bad Chaps", "Old Bazumbers" and the "Bob Cat", these villians were always after one thing, Uncle Wiggley's ears which were referred to by these scoundrels as "souse."**

**What made Uncle Wiggily stories so interesting was the direct tie-in with children and adults use of personal free time. The author would place the bunny in natural settings like a picnic, fishing trip, at the beach swimming, visit to the farm, holiday trips, sports activities and others. On each trip he would run into the scheming bad guys and of course escaped the impossible traps set by each villain.**

**Uncle Wiggily also had a great supporting cast of friends that joined him on his great adventures. These included Nurse Jane Fuzzy Wuzzy, Sammie and Suzie Littletail, Jackie and Peetie Bow Wow, Johnnie and Billie Bushytail, Grandpa Goosey Gander, Nannie and Billy Wagtail, Mrs. Wibblewobble and her son Jimmie, curly and Floppy Twistytail, Kittie Kat and a host of others.**

UWG-1

❑ **UWG-1. "Put A Hat On Uncle Wiggily" Party Game Kit,**
1919. Store item by Milton Bradley. Game sheet is 22x27". Uncut In Envelope - **$150**

UWG-2

UWG-3

❑ **UWG-2. "Uncle Wiggily's Travels" Book,**
1922. No. 6 in a series of 28 of which only 7 books feature Uncle Wiggily. Many colored pictures with text. Scarce. - **$75 $150 $250**

❑ **UWG-3. "Uncle Wiggily's Fortune" Book,**
1922. No. 8 in the same series as UWG-2. Scarce. - **$75 $150 $250**

UWG-4

UWG-5

❑ **UWG-4. "Uncle Wiggily and the Pirates",**
1922. - **$20 $60 $100**

❑ **UWG-5. "Uncle Wiggily's Apple Roast",**
1922. - **$20 $60 $100**

UWG-6

UWG-7

UWG-8

❑ **UWG-6. "Uncle Wiggily's Holidays",**
1922. - **$20 $60 $100**

❑ **UWG-7. "Uncle Wiggily's June Bug Friends",**
1922. - **$20 $60 $100**

❑ **UWG-8. "Uncle Wiggily's Picnic",**
1922. - **$20 $60 $100**

UWG-9

UWG-10

UWG-11

❑ **UWG-9. China Mug,**
Copyright 1924. House named "Ovaltine House". Also came without name.
With Name - **$20 $80 $130**
No Name - **$35 $100 $175**
Two Handle Version - **$60 $150 $250**

❑ **UWG-10. China Plate,**
1924. Scarce. Store item by Sebring Pottery Co. Design matches mug. - **$50 $200 $300**

❑ **UWG-11. China Bowl With Silverplate Trim,**
1924. Rare store item by Sebring Pottery Co. Matches mug and plate. - **$100 $250 $425**

UWG-12

❑ **UWG-12. Boxed Game,**
c. 1920s. Milton Bradley #4817. - **$30 $60 $100**

UWG-13

UWG-14

❑ **UWG-13. "Hollow Stump Bungalow" Pressed Cardboard Toy With Figures,**
1920s. Store item by Androscoggin Pulp Co. 3-D residence and 10 diecut thin cardboard characters, each on wooden base.
Bungalow - **$75 $175 $275**
Each Figure - **$10 $20 $35**

❑ **UWG-14. "Animal Story Library" Box Set,**
1939. Box for 16 books, 8 of which were Uncle Wiggily. Books are 12 pages; 8" high and 6 7/8" wide. Other titles in the set are: Reddy Fox, Peter Rabbit (2), Babbling Coon, Flash the Deer, Three Little Bears, Paddy and Robber the Rat. Box - **$75 $150 $200**
Uncle Wiggily Books each - **$15 $25 $40**
Peter Rabbit Books each - **$10 $20 $30**
Other books each - **$5 $10 $20**

UWG-15

❑ **UWG-15. "Uncle Wiggily's Adventures" Boxed Set Of Storybooks,**
1939. Store item by Platt & Munk Co. with art by George Carlson. Set - **$25 $60 $100**

(PUZZLE BOX)

Puzzle #1 shows some of the villains chasing Uncle Wiggily. The plot of many of his stories involved Wiggily's escapades with various villains who wanted to eat him, especially his ears.

Puzzle #2 shows Uncle Wiggily with many of his friends on a camping trip.

Puzzle #3 shows Uncle Wiggily with many of his friends at the beach.

UWG-16

❑ **UWG-16. "Uncle Wiggily" Picture Puzzles,**
1940. Scarce. Box contained three puzzles shown above. Box - **$25 $50 $100**
Each Puzzle- **$10 $20 $40**

UWG-17

UWG-18

❑ **UWG-17. Stuffed Doll,**
1943. Store item licensed by Georgine Averill. 20" tall stuffed cloth doll with fabric outfit including hat stitched to left hand. - **$200 $400 $600**

❑ **UWG-18. "Uncle Wiggily and the Red Monkey" Book,**
1943. From a series of 9 books, also used as a coloring book. There were 2 different sets- one with a slick cover and blank back cover and insides; the other had stiff cardboard covers, some with designs inside, some blank. Books measured 8 1/2" x 11". Each - **$5 $15 $30**

UWG-19

UWG-20

❑ **UWG-19. "Hollow Stump Club" Cello. Button,**
1946. WNJR Radio, Newark, New Jersey established by Newark Evening News. After Howard Garis retired from the newspaper, he read Uncle Wiggily stories over the air. Club membership and button distribution reached about 9,000 boys and girls. - **$35 $100 $200**

❑ **UWG-20. "Uncle Wiggily's Adventures" All Pictures Comics #1405,**
1946. - **$15 $50 $110**

## Uncle Wip

**Philadelphia radio station WIP, owned and operated by Gimbel's department store, started broadcasting in March 1922. Uncle Wip's Kiddie Club was a late-afternoon children's program organized by the store in the 1930s, probably as early as 1936.**

UWP-1

UWP-2

❑ **UWP-1. "Uncle Wip And His Friends/Their Bed-Time Stories" Book,**
1923. - **$10 $50 $85**

❑ **UWP-2. "Uncle Wip's Kiddie Club" Certificate,**
1930s. Rare. - **$30 $75 $100**

UWP-3

UWP-4

UWP-5

❑ **UWP-3. "See Me At Gimbels" Cello. Button,**
1930s. Gimbels department store, Philadelphia. - **$20 $40 $75**

❑ **UWP-4. "Uncle Wip's Kiddie Club At Gimbels" Cello. Button,**
1930s. Gimbels department store, Philadelphia. - **$10 $20 $35**

❑ **UWP-5. "Uncle Wip's Kiddie Club/Listen In 6.45 P.M." Cello. Button,**
1930s. Gimbels department store, Philadelphia. - **$10 $20 $30**

**UWP-6**

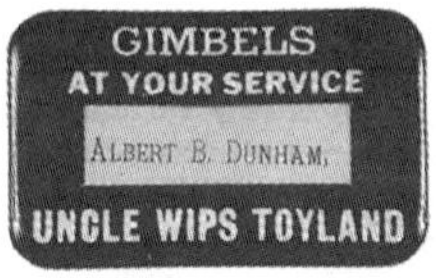


**UWP-8**

**UWP-7**

❑ **UWP-6. "Kiddie Klub/Gimbels" Cello. Button,**
1930s. Gimbels department store, Philadelphia. - **$5 $10 $15**

❑ **UWP-7. "Uncle Wip's Radio Girls" Cello. Buttons,** 1930s. - **$10 $20 $30**

❑ **UWP-8. "Uncle Wip's Toyland" Clerk Badge,**
1930s. Gimbels department store. 1-3/4x2-3/4" cello. slotted in rear for insertion of clerk's name paper. - **$15 $35 $75**

## Underdog

**Loveable, humble canine Shoeshine Boy was in actuality plucky superhero Underdog, whose magic cape and energy pills gave him the power to overcome mad scientists and villains, such as Simon Bar Sinister and Riff Raff, and rescue Sweet Polly Purebred, ace TV reporter. This animated series, with Wally Cox providing the voice of Underdog, aired on NBC from 1964 to 1966, moved to CBS from 1966 to 1968, then went back to NBC from 1968 to 1973. *Underdog* comic books appeared in the early 1970s. Items are normally copyrighted Leonardo Productions.**

**UND-1**

❑ **UND-1. "The Underdog Theme Song" Record With Sleeve,**
1965. LTY Records EP #1001. - **$10 $20 $40**

**UND-2**

**UND-3**

❑ **UND-2. "Super Saturday Cavalcade" Cartoons Promotional Photo,**
1966. CBS-TV. Pictures stars of new Saturday morning lineup of animated color cartoons including Underdog. - **$8 $15 $25**

❑ **UND-3. Dakin Co. Vinyl Figure,**
1960s. Store item. Comes with blue felt cape. - **$35 $125 $200**
Near Mint Boxed - **$275**

**UND-4**

**UND-5**

❑ **UND-4. Underdog Mug,**
1960s. Rare. Parents Magazine premium. - **$50 $100 $200**

❑ **UND-5. Underdog Club Ring,**
1970. Charlton Comics. Silvered plastic expansion band with black on red paper picture. - **$20 $40 $60**

**UND-6**

**UND-7**

❑ **UND-6. Fan Club Membership Card,**
1970. Charlton Comics. Part of fan club kit. - **$5 $10 $15**

❑ **UND-7. T-Shirt,**
1970. Charlton Comics. - **$35 $75 $125**

**UND-8**

**UND-9**

❑ **UND-8. Sweatshirt,**
1970. Charlton Comics. - **$50 $100 $150**

❑ **UND-9. Color-Your-Own Giant Posters,**
1970. Charlton Comics. Set of six B&W 17x22" posters sent folded. Offered as "3 Good Guys/3 Funny Bad Guys" with pairs consisting of Underdog/Simon & Cad; Dudley Do-Right/ Snidely Whiplash; Bullwinkle & Rocky/Boris & Natasha. Each Uncolored - **$10 $25 $40**
Each Colored - **$5 $10 $15**

**UND-10**

❑ **UND-10. Wristwatch,**
1973. Store item by Lafayette with gold-tone case. Working - **$35 $75 $150**

**UND-11**

**UND-12**

❑ **UND-11. Premium Offer Poster,**
1974. Pacific Gas and Electric. 16x21". - **$20 $45 $75**

❑ **UND-12. "Kite Fun Book",**
1974. Pacific Gas and Electric. - **$5 $10 $20**

UND-13

UND-14

❑ **UND-13. Simon Bar Sinister Plastic Ring,** 1975. Vending machine. - **$25 $50 $75**

❑ **UND-14. "Saturday Cartoon Magnets",** 1975. Breaker Confections, Division of Sunline Inc., St. Louis. Set of four including Rocky, Bullwinkle, Speedy Gonzales, Underdog.
Order Folder - **$5 $12 $25**
Each Magnet - **$3 $8 $18**

UND-15

❑ **UND-15. Hard Vinyl Bank,** 1970s. Store item by Play Pal Plastics. 7-1/4" tall. - **$15 $35 $75**

UND-16

UND-17

❑ **UND-16. Pepsi Glass,** c. 1970s. One of 5 Leonardo TTV characters in 16 oz. size. This one comes with and without Pepsi logo. - **$5 $10 $20**

❑ **UND-17. Plastic Cup And Bowl,** 1970s. Store item. Each - **$5 $10 $20**

UND-18

UND-19

❑ **UND-18. "Underdog" Plastic Ring,** 1970s. Vending machine item. Image in slight raised relief. - **$75 $125 $200**

❑ **UND-19. Underdog Rings Vending Machine Card,** 1970s. 5x7" insert display card diecut to hold six example plastic character image rings. - **$10 $15 $20**

UND-20

UND-21

❑ **UND-20. "March Of Comics" Issue,** 1981. No sponsor imprint on pictured example. Issue #479 by Western Publishing Co. - **$5 $12 $20**

❑ **UND-21. "Macy's Thanksgiving Day Parade" Souvenir 3" Cello. Button,** 1981. Pictures parade balloon figures of Underdog and Bullwinkle. - **$10 $20 $30**

UND-22

UND-23

❑ **UND-22. Figures with Ring in Box,** 1998. - **$15 $25 $50**

❑ **UND-23. Underdog Wacky Wobbler,** 2000. - **$15**

## Universal Monsters

It began in 1931 with the release of *Dracula*, starring Bela Lugosi as the magnetic monster with a blood fetish. Universal had an enormous hit with the film version of Hamilton Deane's stage play based on Bram Stoker's novel. Originally intended for Lon Chaney, the film went to Lugosi after Chaney's death. *Frankenstein* followed that same year, directed by James Whale and featuring the macabre mastery of Boris Karloff acting under heavy makeup designed by Jack Pierce. From these two films would spring an entire franchise of horror heroes who would reshape pop culture and make being scared something fun and exciting for generations of wide-eyed viewers.

As conflict around the globe escalated and America came closer to entering World War II, audiences turned increasingly to escapist fantasy in the theaters to embody and then vanquish their worst fears, and the Universal monsters were there to provide the catharsis. Universal launched a series based on *The Mummy* (again played by Karloff in its original appearance), blending Egyptian lore with fictional material. In 1941, Lon Chaney Jr. portrayed the last of the major Universal monsters to be introduced, *The Wolf Man*. Universal then teamed these characters up in later installments to keep the excitement at a fever pitch and movie-goers in the theaters. *Frankenstein Meets the Wolf Man* (1943) brought Lugosi (now reduced to playing Frankenstein's monster after originally refusing the role) and Chaney Jr. together, and the final films in the Universal monster movie canon, *House of Frankenstein* (1944) and *House of Dracula* (1945), brought together all the major monsters and even resolved the Wolf Man's long-standing curse, allowing him to walk away with the girl at the end.

By the end of the 1940s, Universal Studios had established an extensive universe of scary stars who dominated the matinees and sparked a fan following that would insure their immortality in the years to come (through the later publication of magazines like Forrest J. Ackerman's *Famous Monsters of Filmland*). Even when played for laughs, in movies like *Abbott and Costello Meet Frankenstein* (1948) (with Frankenstein, Dracula and the Wolf Man, also featuring Vincent Price in a closing Invisible Man cameo voice-over), or on television in guest appearances and parodies, the essential power of these characters did not diminish, and new generations of fans continued to discover the films.

By the 1950s, Frankenstein and the Wolf Man gave way to the Cold War and aliens from afar (none too subtle Communist metaphors invoked in many sci-fi and horror films). The era of the Universal monster appeared to be over, but Universal had a few more tricks up their sleeve with the release of the classic sci-fi film, *This Island Earth* (1954), featuring the Metaluna Mutat. *Creature From the Black Lagoon* (also 1954) brought us face to face with the misunderstood Gill-Man, an evolutionary throwback discovered in the Amazon and brought back in two sequels.

Decades later, countless reruns of all the old films on local television have made all the Universal monsters into cultural icons that remain potent and entertaining to this day. In the last few years, Sideshow Toys has sparked a renewal of collector interest in the venerable stars of the silver scream with an extensive line of merchandise, from action figures to polystone sculptures. Most items are copyright Universal Studios.

(COMPLETED PUZZLE)

(MAILER) UVM-1

❑ **UVM-1. "King Kong" Jig Saw Puzzle,**
1933. With mailer. RKO Radio Picture Product. 21-3/4" high x 10-1/2" wide. Rare. - **$750 $1500 $3000**

UVM-2

❑ **UVM-2. "Frankenstein" Early Movie Theater Giveaway Photo,**
1930s. 4x5-1/8" with inscription "I'll Be Scaring You-Frankenstein At Capitol Theater Newark N.J." - **$100 $250 $400**

UVM-3

❑ **UVM-3. Wolfman Model Kit,**
1962. Store item by Aurora.
Near Mint Boxed - **$450**
Built Unboxed - **$20 $40 $60**

UVM-4

❑ **UVM-4. Dracula Model Kit,**
1962. Store item by Aurora.
Near Mint Boxed - **$300**
Built No Box - **$15 $30 $60**

UVM-5

❑ **UVM-5. "The Witch" Model Kit,**
1963. Store item by Aurora.
Near Mint Boxed - **$350**
Built No Box - **$25 $50 $75**

UVM-6

❑ **UVM-6. "The Mummy" Model Kit,**
1963. Store item by Aurora.
Near Mint Boxed - **$400**
Built No Box - **$10 $25 $50**

UVM-7

❑ **UVM-7. "Dracula's Dragster" Model Kit,**
1964. Store item by Aurora.
Near Mint Boxed - **$500**
Built No Box - **$75 $100 $150**

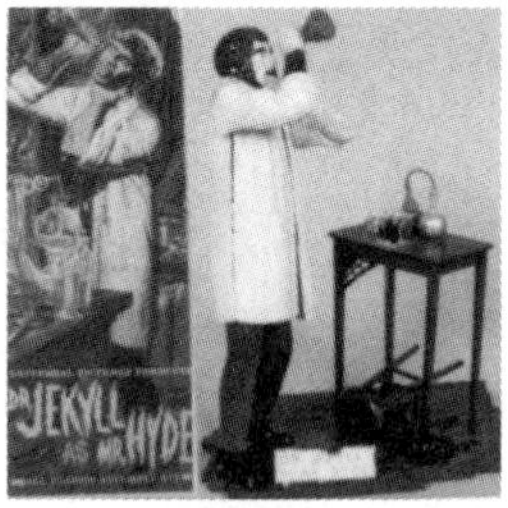


UVM-8

❑ **UVM-8. "Dr. Jekyll As Mr. Hyde" Model Kit,**
1964. Aurora. Near Mint Boxed - **$350**
Built No Box - **$20 $40 $60**

UVM-9 UVM-10

❑ **UVM-9. "Bride Of Frankenstein/A Book-Box Paperdoll,"**
1964. Store item by Merry Mfg. Co. Includes 15" tall diecut paperdoll. - **$30 $60 $100**

❑ **UVM-10. Large Buttons,**
c. 1965. Elwar Ltd. 3-1/2" full color button. Set includes Dracula, Frankenstein, Mummy, Wolfman, Creature From Black Lagoon.
Each - **$20 $50 $75**

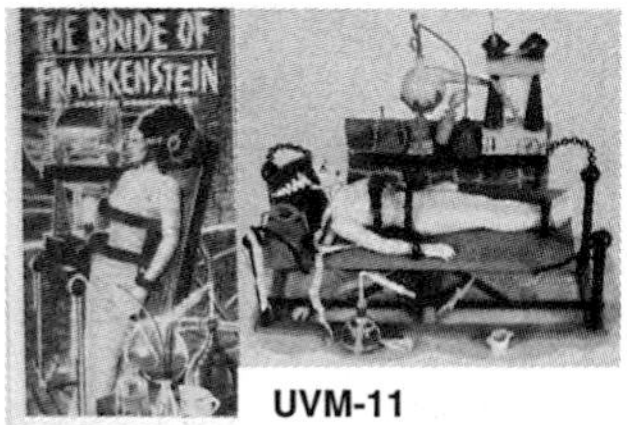


UVM-11

❑ **UVM-11. The Bride Of Frankenstein Model Kit,**
1965. Store item by Aurora.
Near Mint Boxed - **$1200**
Built No Box - **$100 $200 $300**

UVM-12 UVM-13

❑ **UVM-12 Soaky Bubble Bath Bottle,**
c. 1965. Store item by Colgate-Palmolive. Also issued were Wolfman, The Mummy, The Creature From The Black Lagoon.
The Creature - **$30 $75 $125**
Others - **$25 $60 $90**

❑ **UVM-13. Universal Monster Flicker Rings,**
1960s. Vending machine issues. Each ring has two images of the character. Of those we've seen, all are black and white on green background except for the Mummy which is black and white on red background. Prices are for examples on silver plastic bases unmarked or marked "Hong Kong," not for flickers mounted

on bases marked "China."
Dracula - **$50 $100 $175**
Frankenstein - **$50 $100 $175**
Wolfman - **$75 $150 $250**
Mummy - **$50 $100 $175**
Phantom - **$50 $100 $175**

UVM-14

❑ **UVM-14. Monster Figures By Palmer Plastics,**
1960s. Store item, unmarked. 3" tall in single color soft plastic. Pictured are: Creature From The Black Lagoon, Frankenstein, Wolfman, Dracula, Creature from It Came From Outer Space. Each - **$5 $15 $25**

UVM-15

❑ **UVM-15. Universal Monsters Flicker Rings,**
1960s. Probable vending machine issue. Soft plastic base with full color flicker featuring images taken from Don Post Universal Monster masks. Two images per ring: Creature From The Black Lagoon/Mr. Hyde, Phantom Of The Opera/Wolfman, Mummy/Hunchback.
Each - **$15 $25 $40**

UVM-16

❑ **UVM-16. Universal Monster Figures,**
1960s. Lot of four from Palmer Plastics series. Each is about 3" tall. Each - **$10 $20 $40**

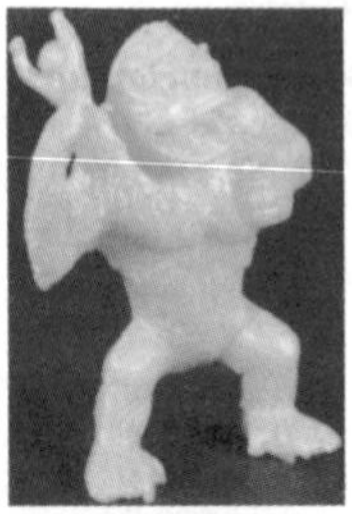

UVM-17

❑ **UVM-17. King Kong Figure With Woman,**
1960s. 3" tall unmarked but issued by Palmer Plastics. - **$40 $75 $150**

UVM-18

❑ **UVM-18. "Universal's Movie Monsters" Lunch Box With Thermos,**
1979. Store item by Aladdin.
Box - **$75 $150 $300**
Bottle - **$25 $50 $100**

UVM-19

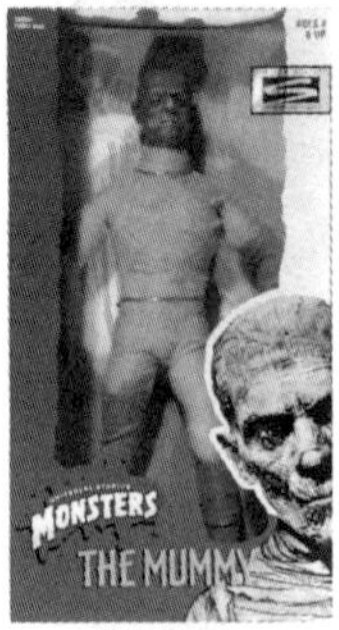


UVM-20

❑ **UVM-19. Ball Puzzle Party Favors,**
1991. 8 ball puzzles featuring Frankenstein, Dracula, Wolfman and the Mummy on card.
Complete - **$50**
Each puzzle - **$5**

❑ **UVM-20. "The Mummy" Figure in Box,**
1998. Hasbro. - **$5 $15 $25**

UVM-21

UVM-22

❑ **UVM-21. "Frankenstein" Figure in Box,**
1998. Hasbro. - **$5 $15 $25**

❑ **UVM-22. "The Bride of Frankenstein" Figure in Box,**
1998. Hasbro. - **$5 $15 $25**

UVM-23

❑ **UVM-23. Collector Beans Box,**
1999. Green colored box for holding the limited edition bean bag figures. Box only - **$25**

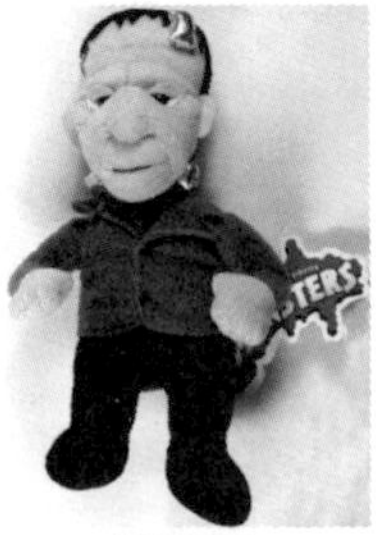

UVM-24

UVM-25

❑ **UVM-24. "Frankenstein" Bean Figure,**
1999. Limited edition figure with tag. - **$10**

❑ **UVM-25. "The Bride of Frankenstein" Bean Figure,**
1999. Limited edition figure with tag. - **$10**

UVM-26

UVM-27

❑ **UVM-26. "Dracula" Bean Figure,**
1999. Limited edition figure with tag. - **$10**

❑ **UVM-27. "The Mummy" Bean Figure,**
1999. Limited edition figure with tag. - **$10**

UVM-28

UVM-29

❑ **UVM-28. "The Wolfman" Bean Figure,**
1999. Limited edition figure with tag. - **$10**

❑ **UVM-29. "The Creature From the Black Lagoon" Bean Figure,**
1999. Limited edition figure with tag. - **$10**

UVM-30

UVM-31

❑ **UVM-30. "The Hunchback" Bean Figure,**
1999. Limited edition figure with tag. - **$10**

❑ **UVM-31. "The Phantom of the Opera" Bean Figure,**
1999. Limited edition figure with tag. - **$10**

UVM-32

UVM-33

❑ **UVM-32. "Sweet Crispers" Cookie Box,**
1999. Promotes Universal Monsters Prize trip to Universal Studios in Florida. Features the Creature on box front. Dracula is on the side of the box. - **$1 $2 $3**

❑ **UVM-33. "Monsters Cookies" Box,**
1999. Promotes Universal Studios in Florida. The main monsters are on the box. - **$1 $2 $3**

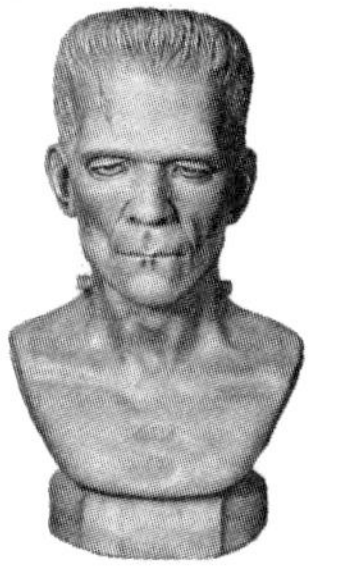

UVM-34

UVM-35

❑ **UVM-34. "Frankenstein" Bust,**
1990s. Very heavy 17 1/2" tall bust is an incredible likeness of Boris Karloff as the Monster. Limited edition of 50 from Karloff Studios. Production was supervised by Karloff's daughter. - **$500**

❑ **UVM-35. "The Mummy" Bust,**
1990s. Very heavy 17 1/2" tall bust is an incredible likeness of Boris Karloff as the Mummy. Limited edition of 50 from Karloff Studios. Production was supervised by Karloff's daughter. - **$500**

(Close-up of Creature face)

UVM-36

❑ **UVM-36. "The Creature" Bolo Tie,**
1990s. Only 10 made. By Randy Bowen. - **$250**

UVM-37

❑ **UVM-37. "Classic Movie Monsters" Boxed Set,**
2001. Features Frankenstein, the Mummy and the Wolfman. - **$15 $30 $50**

UVM-38

❑ **UVM-38. Monster Figures Boxed Set,**
2001. 9 small figures boxed. - **$10 $20 $35**

## U.S. Jones

**Defender of democracy in the all-American way, U.S. Jones had a brief comic book life at the outset of World War II. Jones made his first appearance in issue #28 of *Wonderworld Comics* in August 1941, and two issues of his own book appeared in 1941 and 1942. U.S. Jones Cadets received a decoder, a pinback button, and other membership material.**

USJ-1

❑ **USJ-1. "U.S. Jones Cadets" Comic Book Club Cello. Button,**
1941. Rare. Part of member's kit. -
**$1000 $3000 $4800**

USJ-2

USJ-3

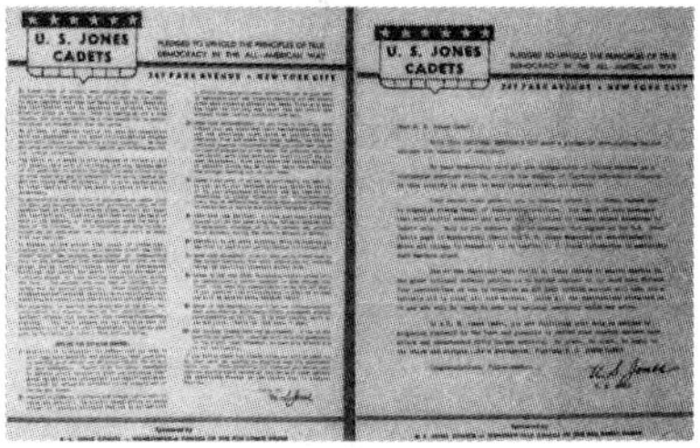

USJ-4

❑ **USJ-2. Secret Code Card,**
1941. Rare. Part of member's kit. Has instructions for use of 26 different code keys. -
**$125 $500 $675**

❑ **USJ-3. Cadets Membership Card,**
1941. Rare. Part of member's kit. -
**$100 $250 $400**

❑ **USJ-4. Cadet Cover Letter And Cadet Civil Defense Sheet,**
1941. Rare. Part of member's kit. Explains kit and duties with pledge text.
Each - **$75 $150 $200**

USJ-5

❑ **USJ-5. U.S. Jones #1 Comic Book Ad,**
1941. Inside cover ad shown. - **$25 $50 $100**

## Vic and Sade

**Considered by many to be one of the greatest radio shows ever, *Vic and Sade* has been called a true original and the best American humor of its day. The series told of events in the daily lives of radio's home folks--Victor Gook, his wife Sade, their son Rush, and Sade's Uncle Fletcher--who lived in the little house halfway up in the next block in the town of Crooper, Illinois. Written by Paul Rhyer, *Vic and Sade* aired on the NBC, CBS, and Mutual networks from 1932 to 1946. The program was supported by local advertisers the first two years until Crisco took over as longterm sponsor. Fitch's Cocoanut Shampoo sponsored in 1946.**

VAS-1

❑ **VAS-1. Hometown Paper Map With Mailer Envelope,**
c. 1942. Rare. Procter & Gamble. 14x16" map of "Crooper, Illinois/40 Miles From Peoria" with cast member pictures at lower corner. Also issued on cardboard.
Envelope - **$15 $25 $50**
Map - **$100 $300 $600**

## Wheaties Misc.

**Wheaties, the Breakfast of Champions, was the result of a kitchen accident in 1921 when some gruel spilled on a hot stove and turned into crispy flakes. The Washburn Crosby Company in Minneapolis developed the cereal and began marketing it regionally in 1924. Advertising on radio, including the world's first singing commercial, proved successful and by 1928, when Washburn Crosby joined with other grain millers to form General Mills, Wheaties was an established product. Over the years sponsorship of such popular radio programs as *Jack Armstrong* and *Skippy*, as well as continuing promotion that linked the product to major figures in sports and the movies, has kept Wheaties an all-American favorite breakfast food. This section shows an assortment of their baseball and non-character premiums.**

WHE-1

WHE-2

❑ **WHE-1. "Earl Averill" Box Back,**
1937. From a series of baseball stars described by their 1936 season statistics. - **$15 $25 $50**
Complete Box - **$80 $160 $320**

❑ **WHE-2. Knothole Drilling Insect 2-1/2" Cello. Button,**
c. 1930s. - **$15 $30 $60**

WHE-3

WHE-4

❑ **WHE-3. "Champs" Of The U.S.A. Box Back #1 Stamp Set,**
1930s. Shows 3 different cut-out stamps of Charles Ruffing, Lynn Patrick, and Leo Durocher. - **$10 $25 $40**

❑ **WHE-4. "Champs" Of The U.S.A. Box Back #2 Stamp Set,**
1930s. Shows 3 different cut-out stamps of Joe Dimaggio, Mel Ott, and Ellsworth Vines. - **$25 $50 $85**

WHE-5

WHE-6

❑ **WHE-5. "Champs" Of The U.S.A. Box Back #3 Stamp Set,**
1930s. Shows 3 different cut-out stamps of Jimmie Foxx, Bernie Bierman, and Bill Dickey. - **$15 $30 $60**

❑ **WHE-6. "Champs" Of The U.S.A. Box Back #5 Stamp Set,**
1930s. Shows 3 different cut-out stamps of Joe Medwick, Madison "Matty" Bell, and Ab Jenkins. - **$5 $10 $25**

WHE-7

WHE-8

❑ **WHE-7. "Champs" Of The U.S.A. Box Back #6 Stamp Set,**
1930s. Shows 3 different cut-out stamps of John Mize, Davey O'Brien, and Ralph Guldahl. - **$5 $10 $25**

❑ **WHE-8. "Champs" Of The U.S.A. Box Back #7 Stamp Set,**
1930s. Shows 3 different cut-out stamps of Joe Cronin, Cecil Isbell, and Byron Nelson. - **$5 $15 $30**

WHE-9

WHE-10

❑ **WHE-9. "Champs" Of The U.S.A. Box Back #8 Stamp Set,**
1930s. Shows 3 different cut-out stamps of Paul Derringer, Ernie Lombardi, and George I. Myers. - **$5 $15 $30**

❑ **WHE-10. "Champs" Of The U.S.A. Box Back #12 Stamp Set,**
1930s. Shows 3 different cut-out stamps of Hugh McManus, Luke Appling, and Stanley Hack. - **$5 $15 $30**

WHE-11

❑ **WHE-11. "Funny Stuff" Comic,**
1946. Books were taped to boxes.
Good - **$170**
Fine - **$475**

WHE-12

❑ **WHE-12. Miniature Metal License Plates With Mailer,**
1953. Offered in four sets of 12 plus bonus District of Columbia if all ordered at same time. Each License - **$3 $8 $12**

WHE-13

❑ **WHE-13. Box Flat - 1 oz.,**
1953. Has rare George Mikan basketball card on back - the key to the set. - **$50 $125 $250**

WHE-14

❑ **WHE-14. Box Back With Sports Cards,**
1950s. Has 7 sports cards. - **$120**

WHE-15

❑ **WHE-15. "Wheaties 6 Power Microscope" Store Display Sign, Shelf Stickers And Premium,**
1950s. Sign is 13-1/2x13-1/2". Gordon Gold Archives. Display - **$35 $75 $125**
Sticker Sheet - **$8 $12 $25**
Microscope - **$5 $10 $20**

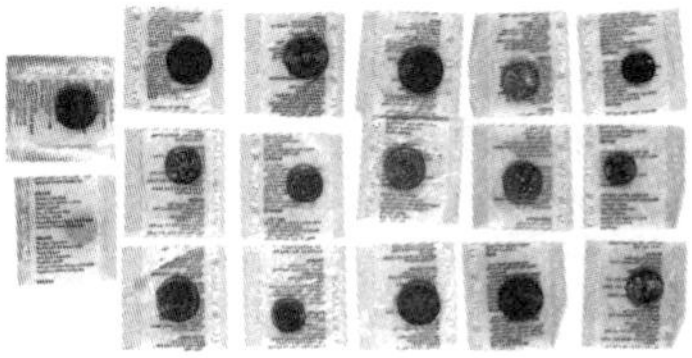
WHE-16

❑ **WHE-16. Wrapped Coins,**
1955. 17 international coins pictured with Wheaties wrapper. Each wrapper explains coin and facts about each country. Coin with wrapper was a premium given away in each box of Wheaties. Each - **$8 $15 $30**

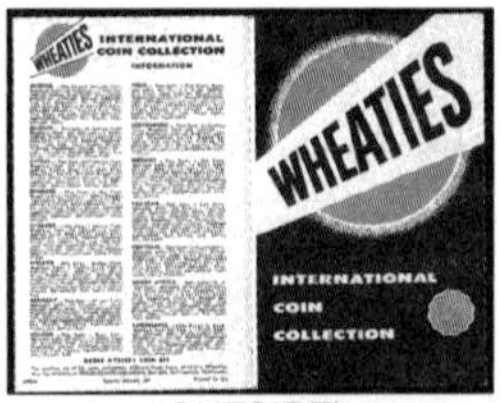

(OUTSIDE)

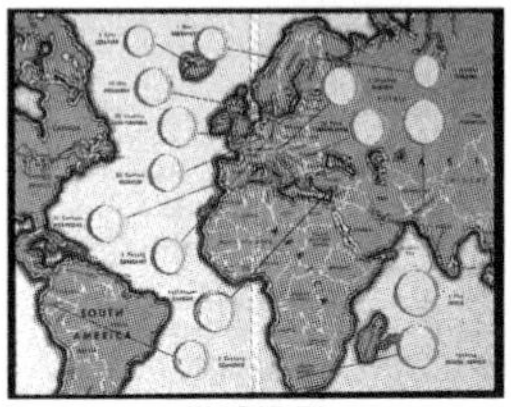

(INSIDE)
WHE-17

❑ **WHE-17. Coin Card,**
1955. Holder for 15 coins. International set. - **$20 $40 $60**

WHE-18

❑ **WHE-18. Cereal Box Featuring Champy And Mr. Fox Hand Puppets,**
1957. Side panel has order coupon for both puppets and the puppet theater. Gordon Gold Archives. Used Complete - **$75 $125 $200**

WHE-19

❑ **WHE-19. "Champy's Theatre" With Hand Puppets,**
1957. 17x44" theater assembly sheet offered as part of mail purchase of Champy and Mr. Fox puppets based on creation by Bill Baird for Mickey Mouse Club TV show.
Theater - **$15 $30 $50**
Each Puppet - **$10 $30 $60**

WHE-20

❑ **WHE-20. "Auto Emblems" Box,**
1950s. Shows all 31 emblems offered. Complete - **$25 $100 $150**

WHE-21

WHE-22

❑ **WHE-21. Hike-O-Meter,**
1950s. Pedometer with aluminum rim. - **$10 $18 $30**

❑ **WHE-22. Rare Rock Card,**
1950s. With 11 different rocks in descriptive mailers.
Display Card with Mailer - **$10 $35 $50**
Rocks in Mailer each - **$20**

WHE-23

❑ **WHE-23. Airline Stickers,**
1950s. Offered in each box of Wheaties. Stickers were 3"x3-1/2". 15 in the set. Each - **$5 $10 $20**

WHE-24

WHE-25

❑ **WHE-24. British Auto Metal Emblems,**
1950s. Set of 10, Bentley and MG not shown.
Each - **$3 $10 $20**

❑ **WHE-25. Continental Auto Metal Emblems,**
1950s. Set of 10. Volkswagen, Citroen, Bugati not shown. Each - **$3 $10 $20**

WHE-26

❑ **WHE-26. Auto Emblems,**
1950s. Ten different tin U.S. car emblems, mailer and instructions. Each - **$3 $6 $15**

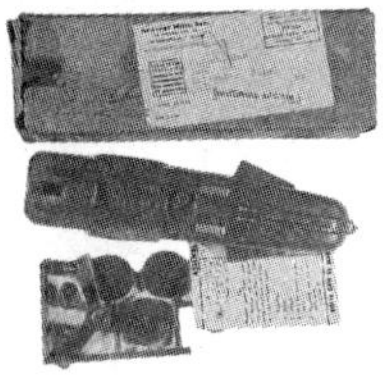

WHE-27

WHE-28

❑ **WHE-27. Land And Water Rover,**
1950s. General Mills. Red plastic car with propeller. Runs on land and water.
Complete - **$35 $75 $150**

❑ **WHE-28. Red Records,**
1950s. Cereal premiums. Various popular folk, sea & traditional songs on labels.
Each - **$12 $25 $40**

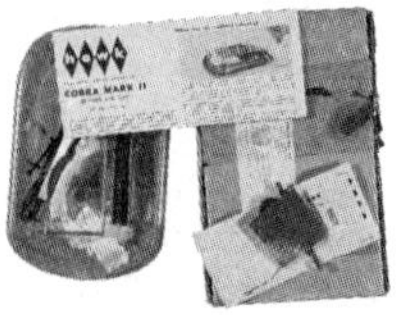

WHE-29

WHE-30

❑ **WHE-29. Flying Air Car,**
1960. Rare. General Mills. Large, wide, Cobra Mark II battery powered car.
With Instructions and Mailer. - **$50 $100 $150**

❑ **WHE-30. Miniature Reflective Paper License Plates With Mailer,**
1963. Wheaties Bran With Raisin Flakes. Probable set of 25 for scattered states in reflective flocked surface with peel-off back.
Each License - **$2 $4 $6**

WHE-31

❑ **WHE-31. Cereal Box With "Baseball Stamp Album" Offer,**
c. 1966. Gordon Gold Archives.
Near Mint Flat - **$150**
Used Complete - **$25 $50 $75**

WHE-32

❑ **WHE-32. Walter Payton Box,**
c. 1990. Complete Near Mint - **$20**

WHE-33

WHE-34

❑ **WHE-33. Christmas Ornament in Box,**
1994. In original box. - **$15**

❑ **WHE-34. Special Walter Payton Box,**
1998. "Great Moments in Sports" box salutes Walter Payton, the NFL career rushing leader. They called him "Sweetness" and he was a great man in and out of sports. A special tribute for the late Walter Payton because everything about him was sweet. - **$2 $4 $15**

## Wild Bill Hickok

**James Butler "Wild Bill" Hickok (1837-1876) was a U.S. Marshal in Kansas after the Civil War with a reputation as a marksman and a deadly lawman. Hollywood produced a number of fictionalized versions of the Hickok legend as portrayed by such stars as William S. Hart, Bill Elliott, Roy Rogers, Bruce Cabot, and Gary Cooper. In 1951, with Guy Madison (1922-1996) as Hickok and Andy Devine (1905-1977) as his sidekick Jingles, *The Adventures of Wild Bill Hickok* came to television and radio. The television series, sponsored by Kellogg's Sugar Corn Pops, aired until 1958, first in syndication, then on CBS (1955-1958), and on ABC (1957-1958). The radio version lasted until 1956, with Kellogg also sponsoring until 1954. Hickok comic books appeared from the late 1940s to the late 1950s. "Hey, Wild Bill, wait for me!"**

WLD-1

❑ **WLD-1. "Andy Devine" Dixie Picture,**
1948. - **$10 $20 $45**

WLD-2

❑ **WLD-2. "Sincerely Guy Madison" Studio Fan Postcard,**
c. 1948. Movie magazine promo. - **$5 $12 $25**

WLD-3

WLD-4

❑ **WLD-3. Kellogg's Breakfast Game Score Card,**
c. 1952. One side printed by game chart for entering daily breakfast diet over one-month period to be certified by school teacher and then presented to parents. - **$10 $20 $30**

❑ **WLD-4. Cereal Mini-Box,**
c. 1952. 4" tall "Kel-Bowl-Pac" one ounce individual serving box of Sugar Corn Pops with front panel art. - **$65 $140 $200**

WLD-5

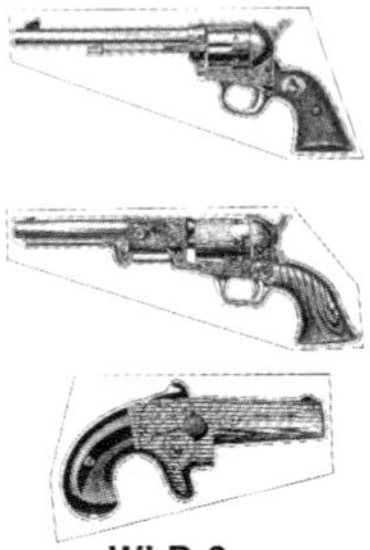

WLD-6

❑ **WLD-5. Kellogg's Sugar Pops Cereal Box With Cut-Outs,**
1952. Features Jingles and promotes "Famous Gun Series Cut-Outs." Back shows Wild Bill's gun "The Peacemaker."
Each Box - **$75 $150 $225**
Box Back Only - **$50**

❑ **WLD-6. Original Art For "Famous Gun Series" Cut-Outs,**
1952. 3 different shown. Each - **$100**

WLD-7

❑ **WLD-7. Cereal Display Box,**
c. 1952. Kellogg of Canada. - **$50 $250 $450**

WLD-8

❑ **WLD-8. "Secret Treasure Guide" And Treasure Map 25x36",**
1952. Kellogg's Sugar Corn Pops.
Near Mint In Mailer - **$125**
Treasure Guide Booklet - **$10 $20 $35**
Treasure Map - **$20 $40 $75**

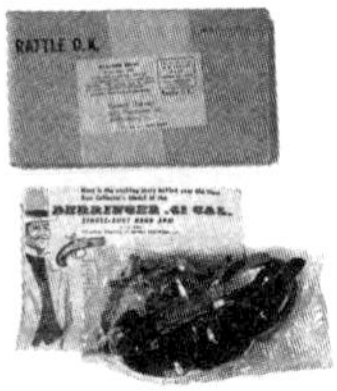

WLD-9

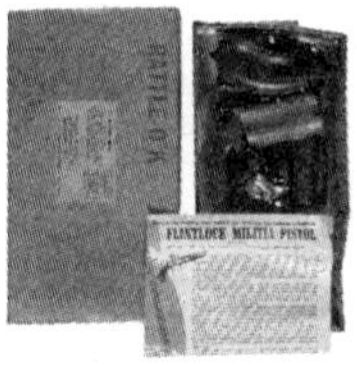

WLD-10

❑ **WLD-9. Kellogg's "Old-Time Gun Series,"**
1954. Kellogg's Sugar Corn Pops. Plastic old time gun series. Derringer, 41 cal.brown handle. With instructions and mailer. - **$25 $60 $100**

❑ **WLD-10. Kellogg's "Old-Time Gun Series,"**
1954. Kellogg's Sugar Corn Pops. Plastic old time guns. Flintlock Militia Pistol was originally offered for 1 box top and 50¢. That was a lot of money in those days, so the guns are all rare. With instructions and mailer. - **$25 $60 $100**

(front) (back)

WLD-11

❑ **WLD-11. Kellogg's Sugar Pops Cereal Box Flat - 5 oz.,**
1954. Jingles and his horse Joker pictured on front. Stereo-pix cut-out of the West on back. #1 of series. - **$75 $175 $275**

WLD-12

WLD-13

❑ **WLD-12. Hickok/Guy Madison Fan Postcard,**
1954. - **$10 $15 $25**

❑ **WLD-13. "Jingles" Cello. Button With Attachment,**
c. 1954. Fabric ribbon holds miniature metal six-shooter. - **$10 $25 $60**

(FRONT) (BACK)

WLD-14

❑ **WLD-14. Kellogg's Rice Krispies Cereal Box Flat with TV Promotion,**
1954. Bilingual Canadian box. Contest awards a part in his TV show. - **$75 $175 $325**

WLD-15

WLD-16

❑ **WLD-15. Deputy Marshal Certificate,**
1955. Probably a Kellogg's Sugar Corn Pops premium. - **$20 $50 $100**

❑ **WLD-16. Deputy Marshal Certificate,**
1955. Wild Bill & Jingles pictured. -
**$20 $50 $100**

(FRONT) (BACK)

WLD-17

❑ **WLD-17. Kellogg's Sugar Pops Cereal Box with Badge Promotion,**
1956. Collection of 6 badges offered inside box. See WLD-18-20.
Box - **$85 $200 $325**

WLD-18

WLD-19

WLD-20

❑ **WLD-18. "Special Deputy" Copper Luster Tin Star Badge,**
1956. Kellogg's Sugar Pops. Set of six. Others without character name are: Deputy Marshall (sic), Deputy Sheriff, Junior Ranger, Sheriff.
Each - **$10 $15 $25**

❑ **WLD-19. Kellogg's "Jingles/Deputy" 2-1/4" Copper Luster Tin Badge,**
1956. From Sugar Pops set of six, see previous item. - **$12 $20 $30**

❑ **WLD-20. Kellogg's "Wild Bill Hickok/ Deputy Marshal" 2-1/4" Silvered Tin Star Badge,**
c. 1956. Similar to but not part of previous set. Finished in silver luster, not copper. - **$12 $20 $30**

WLD-21

❑ **WLD-21. Cereal Box With "Deputy Badge" Offer,**
1956. Gordon Gold Archives. Jingles pictured on front.
Used Complete - **$75 $175 $275**

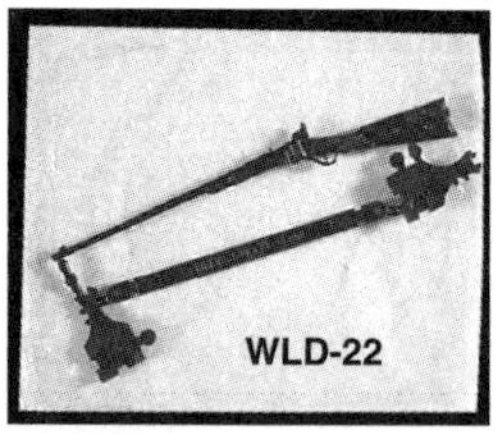
WLD-22

❑ **WLD-22. Rifle Series,**
1956. Sugar Corn Pops premium. Buffalo Sharps rifle in original package promoted by Jingles. Six different miniature rifles offered.
Each - **$10 $25 $40**

WLD-23

❑ **WLD-23. "Chris-Craft Speed Boat And Surfboard" Offer Cereal Box,**
1956. Gordon Gold Archives.
Used Complete - **$75 $175 $250**

WLD-24

❑ **WLD-24. Litho. Buttons,**
1957. Probable vending machine issue. 7/8" with browntone photo on single-color background. Part of a western TV star set probably totaling 14 different.
Wild Bill Or Jingles Each - **$10 $20 $35**

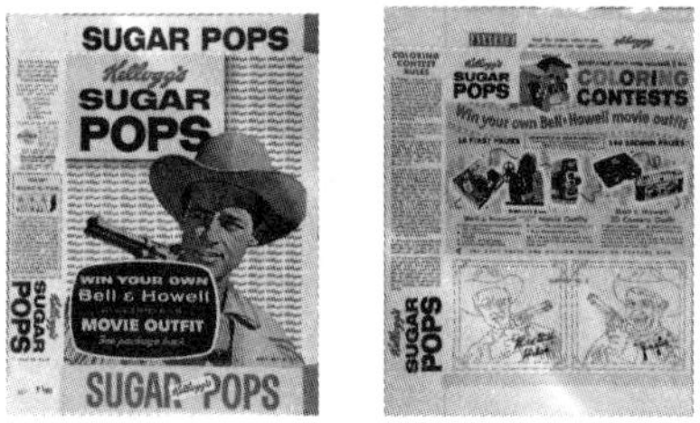

(front) (back)

WLD-25

❑ **WLD-25. Kellogg's Sugar Pops Cereal Box Flat with Movie Outfit Promotion,**
1958. 8 oz. box has coloring contest to win a movie projector or 3-D camera.
Box - **$75 $175 $325**

WLD-26

❑ **WLD-26. "Kellogg's Sugar Corn Pops" Cereal Box,**
1950s. 16 "Famous Indian" drawings on back panels. Complete Box - **$75 $175 $275**

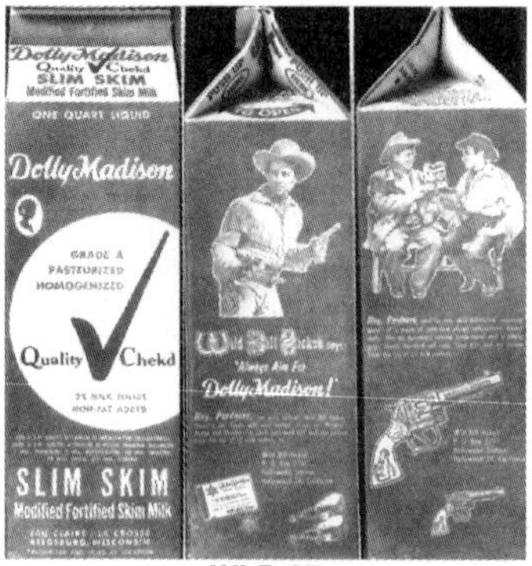

WLD-27

❑ **WLD-27. Hickok/Jingles Waxed Cardboard Milk Carton,**
1950s. Various dairies. - **$20 $50 $100**

WLD-28

WLD-29

❑ **WLD-28. "Drink Milk" Vinyl Tumbler,**
1950s. Various sponsors. -**$20 $50 $75**

❑ **WLD-29. Promo Press Kit & 10 Photos,**
1950s. Rare. - **$50 $125 $200**

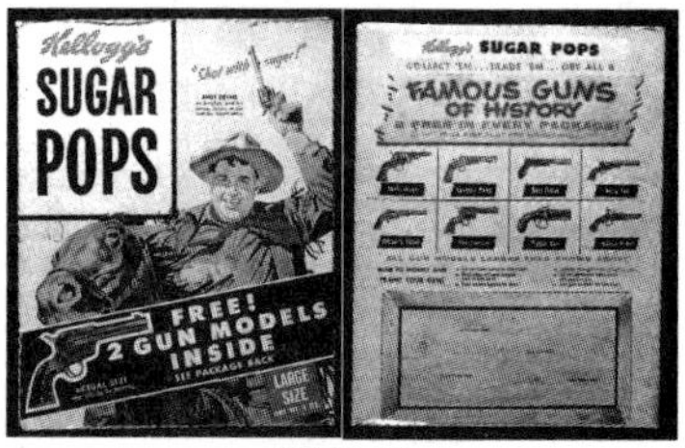

WLD-30

❑ **WLD-30. Kellogg's Sugar Pops Cereal Box,**
1950s. The "Famous Guns of History" series is featured. Small plastic guns in each package. Box back was used for mounting guns. Eight guns pictured on back of box. Jingles pictured on front. Also offered generically in Pep cereal.
Complete Box - **$75 $175 $275**
Box Back Only - **$60**

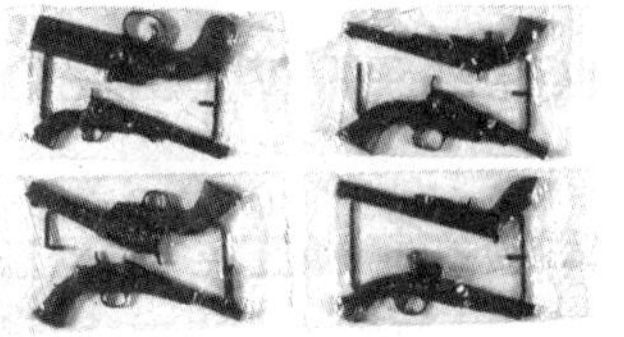
WLD-31

❑ **WLD-31. Kellogg's "Famous Guns of History" Series,**
1950s. Kellogg's Sugar Corn Pops. Four packages shown.
Each Package (Two Guns) - **$10 $20 $40**

WLD-32

WLD-33

❑ **WLD-32. Color Photo Litho. Button,**
1950s. - **$20 $50 $75**

❑ **WLD-33. Hickok & Jingles "We're Pardners" Litho. Button,**
1950s. - **$15 $35 $60**

WLD-34

WLD-35

❑ **WLD-34. "Wild Bill Hickok/Marshal" 2-1/4" Silvered Brass Badge,**
1950s. With insert paper photo, came with wallet and club member card.
Badge Only - **$15 $40 $80**
Three Piece Set - **$50 $100 $200**

❑ **WLD-35. "Marshal Wild Bill Hickok" Silvered Brass Badge On Metal Clip,**
1950s. Came with related wallet. - **$15 $30 $60**

## Willie Wiredhand

**The National Rural Electric Cooperative Association was formed in 1942 as a support group for public power and rural electrification. In 1951 the association created the figure of Willie Wiredhand to personify and characterize its aims. The smiling little fellow with an electric plug and cord for a torso has appeared on mugs, towels, Christmas ornaments, water bottles, magnets, pinback buttons, etc., and is still doing his job after almost 50 years.**

WWH-1

❑ **WWH-1. "All-Electric Farm" Sign,**
1955. 9-1/2x13-1/2" tin litho. Issued by National Rural Electric Cooperative Assn. -
**$35 $75 $125**

WWH-2

WWH-3

❑ **WWH-2. Willie Wiredhand Cello. Button,**
1950s. Designated for "Director" of Rural Electrification program. - **$15 $25 $40**

❑ **WWH-3. Willie Wiredhand Cello. Button,**
1950s. For "Member" of Rural Electrification program. - **$10 $15 $20**

WWH-4

WWH-5

❑ **WWH-4. Willie Wiredhand Oval Cello. Button,**
1950s. - **$20 $40 $60**

❑ **WWH-5. Anniversary Event Button,**
1967. National Rural Electrical Cooperative Assn. About 2-1/2" issued for 25th annual meeting. - **$5 $10 $20**

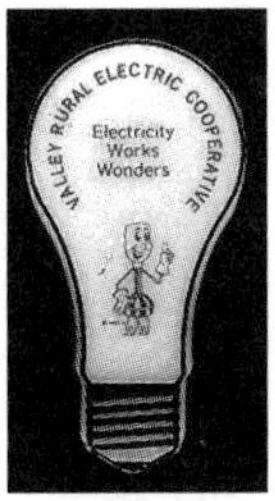

WWH-6

WWH-7

❑ **WWH-6. Willy Wiredhand Night Light,**
1960s. National Rural Electric Cooperative Association. Plastic replica bulb with flat plane back pronged for insertion in household receptacle. Inscribed for local cooperative with initials copyright "NRECA." - **$15 $30 $50**

❑ **WWH-7. Glass Ashtray,**
c. 1960s. Dark translucent glass centered by figure image surrounded by other images of his household benefits. Imprinted for a local sponsoring company. - **$35 $75 $125**

WWH-8

WWH-9

❑ **WWH-8. Patriotic Cap,**
1960s. Flattened 4x12" garrison-style cardboard cap captioned "Minutemen For Rural Electrification." - **$10 $20 $35**

❑ **WWH-9. Iowa Rural Electric Co-Op Cello. Button,**
1970s. Colorful 2-1/4". - **$5 $10 $20**

## Winnie the Pooh

**A.A. Milne (1882-1956) published his classic children's stories *Winnie-the-Pooh* in 1926 and *The House at Pooh Corner* in 1928. A short-lived radio adaptation aired on NBC in 1935, but the Disney Studios gave new life to the beloved characters in a series of 30-minute animated films. *Winnie the Pooh and the Honey Tree* (1965), *Winnie the Pooh and the Blustery Day* (1968), and *Winnie the Pooh and Tigger Too* (1974) were produced for theatrical release and later telecast as prime-time specials on NBC, sponsored by Sears, Roebuck & Company. A fourth short, *Winnie the Pooh and a Day for Eeyore*, was broadcast on the Disney Channel in 1986. The cartoons were true to the Milne originals, with Pooh, Eeyore, Kanga and baby Roo, Wol the Owl, Tigger, Piglet, and the other characters joining Christopher Robin in a variety of woodland adventures. Disney also released a number of Pooh comic books between 1977 and 1984. A feature length animated film *The Tigger Movie* was released in 2000.**

WIN-1

❑ **WIN-1. "Winnie The Pooh/Talking Pooh" Boxed Doll,**
1964. Store item by Sears.
Near Mint Boxed - **$125**
Unboxed, Working - **$20 $50 $75**

WIN-2

❑ **WIN-2. Canadian Breakfast Buddies Set,**
1965. Nabisco premium. Six in set rather than seven as in U.S.A. Christopher and Owl are not in the Canadian set but Tigger is in this set (and not in U.S.A. set). Tigger - **$10 $20 $30**
Others - **$5 $10 $15**

WIN-3

❑ **WIN-3. Spoon Sitter Vinyl Figures,**
1965. Nabisco. Seven in set, Christopher Robin not shown. Each - **$10 $20 $30**

WIN-4

❑ **WIN-4. Cereal Box With Example "Wiggly" Figure Premium,**
1965. Quaker Oats Co. of Canada. The four different figures are Winnie The Pooh, Kanga, Tigger and Eeyore, each 2-1/2" tall. Gordon Gold Archives.
Used Complete Box - **$125 $250 $400**
Each Figure - **$15 $30 $50**

WIN-5

❑ **WIN-5. Honey Munch Cereal Retailer's Promotional Folder,**
1965. Quaker Oats Co. of Canada. 8-1/2x16" stiff cardboard diecut folder with product and ad campaign information. Gordon Gold Archives. - **$50 $100 $150**

WIN-6

❑ **WIN-6. Felt Doll in Seated Position,**
1966. Store item by Gund. 5-1/4" tall. - **$15 $30 $50**

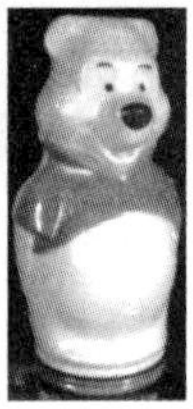

WIN-7

WIN-8

WIN-9

❑ **WIN-7. "Puppets Wheat Puffs Cereal" Plastic Container,**
1966. Nabisco. Metal lid bottom.
With Lid - **$20 $40 $60**

❑ **WIN-8. "Pooh For Peace" Anti-Vietnam War Cello. Button,**
c. 1960s. Unauthorized use of character on button of the type sold in counter-culture stores. 1-1/2" black on lt. purple. - **$25 $60 $100**

❑ **WIN-9. "Now We Are Fifty" Cello. Button,**
c. 1976. Publisher is Eagle Regalia Co., New York City, for apparent anniversary of character creation by A. A. Milne although picturing Piglet and Pooh in unauthorized but Disney image. - **$10 $20 $30**

WIN-10

WIN-11

❑ **WIN-10. "Winnie-The-Pooh And Friends" Glass Tumbler,**
1970s. Sears, Roebuck & Co. Set of three.
Each - **$3 $6 $10**

❑ **WIN-11. "Wardrobe Gets My Vote!" 3x4" Cello. Rectangle Button,**
1980. - **$10 $20 $40**

WIN-12

WIN-13

❑ **WIN-12. "Grad Nite '81" 3-1/2" Cello. Button,**
1981. From Disneyland graduation series of early 1980s picturing various characters. - **$3 $5 $8**

❑ **WIN-13. Watch in Box,**
1992. Lorus product. On a clear disk that rotates with the seconds, there are bees that appear to circle the honey pot. Leather watch band has bee designs. Comes in grey box with top. - **$50**

WIN-14

WIN-15

❑ **WIN-14. Yo-Yo in Package,**
1999. - **$2 $4 $6**

❑ **WIN-15. Video Promo Badge,**
1999. Premium badge promotes upcoming video of "Sing a Song With Pooh Bear." - **$5**

WIN-16

WIN-17

❑ **WIN-16. Hockey Pooh Bean Figure,**
1999. Disney Store exclusive. With tag - **$20**

❑ **WIN-17. Oktoberfest Pooh Bean Figure,**
1999. 8" tall figure with tag. - **$20**

WIN-18

WIN-19

WIN-20

❑ **WIN-18. Baseball Pooh Bean Figure,**
1999. 8" tall figure with tag. - **$20**

❑ **WIN-19. Choo Choo Pooh Bean Figure,**
1999. 8" tall figure with tag. - **$20**

❑ **WIN-20. Pilgrim Pooh Bean Figure,**
1999. - **$20**

WIN-21 WIN-22 WIN-23

❑ **WIN-21. Nautical Pooh Bean Figure,**
1999. 8" tall figure with tag. - **$20**

❑ **WIN-22. Choir Angel Pooh Bean Figure,**
2000. 8" tall figure with tag. - **$15**

❑ **WIN-23. Pirate Pooh Figure,**
2000. Star Bean figure with tag. - **$20**

WIN-24 WIN-25 WIN-26

❑ **WIN-24. "Prisoner of Love" Pooh Figure,**
2001. 8" tall figure with tag. - **$15**

❑ **WIN-25. "Robin Hood Pooh" Bean Figure,**
2001. 8" tall figure with tag. - **$15**

❑ **WIN-26. "Super Pooh" Bean Figure,**
2001. With tag. - **$7**

WIN-27 WIN-28

❑ **WIN-27. Winnie the Pooh Pinback Set,**
2001. 6 different pinbacks on card. - **$5**

❑ **WIN-28. Tigger Pinback Set,**
2001. 6 different pinbacks on card. - **$5**

## The Wizard of Oz

**L. Frank Baum (1856-1919) wrote 14 Oz books, but it was the first, *The Wonderful Wizard of Oz*, published in 1900, that served as the basis of MGM's 1939 Technicolor spectacular, *The Wizard of Oz*. (A musical theatrical adaptation ran on Broadway in 1903, a silent film was made in 1925, and a radio version sponsored by Jell-O aired on NBC in 1933-1934.) The 1939 film, with an all-star cast headed by Judy Garland, has proved to be an enduring classic, repeated annually on television for millions of viewers since the 1950s. There have also been Oz theme parks and resorts, an exhibit at the Smithsonian, appearances in Macy's Thanksgiving Day parade, comic books, and extensive licensing in dozens of categories.**

WIZ-1

❑ **WIZ-1. Music Supplement Newspaper Insert,**
1903. New York American and Journal. Four-page folder dated May 10, 1903 picturing singer Lottie Faust from New York's Majestic Theater. - **$50 $125 $225**

WIZ-2

WIZ-3

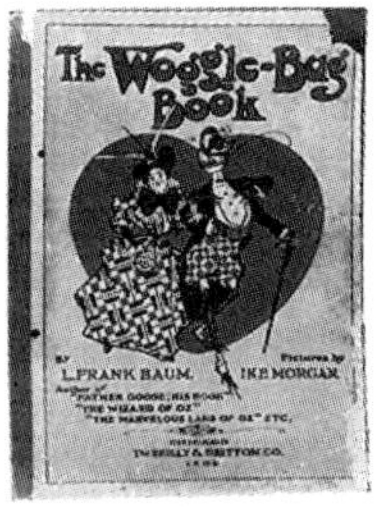


WIZ-4

❑ **WIZ-2. "What Did The Woggle Bug Say?" Cello. Button,**
1904. Book advertising button. - **$20 $60 $140**

❑ **WIZ-3. Woggle Bug Cello. Button,**
1904. Book advertising button. Colors on coat vary from yellow to green. - **$20 $60 $140**

❑ **WIZ-4. "The Woggle-Bug Book,"**
1905. Store item. 11x15" 48-page storybook by L. Frank Baum illustrated by Ike Morgan, published by Reilly & Britton Co., Chicago. - **$250 $500 $1000**

WIZ-5

WIZ-6

❑ **WIZ-5. Magazine Story Poster 13x22",**
1905. For issue of St. Nicholas magazine with art by F. Richardson for Baum serial story "Queen Zixi Of Ix". - **$150 $300 $600**

❑ **WIZ-6. "Read The New Baum Book/The Scarecrow Of Oz" Cello. Button,**
1915. Early and rare book advertising release. - **$500 $1000 $2000**

WIZ-7

WIZ-8

❑ **WIZ-7. "The Scarecrow Of Oz Answers Questions By Radio" Book Promotional Leaflet,**
1924. J. B. Carroll Company, Chicago. Book sellers' give-away advertising the Oz books, incorporating a metal arrow and interior magnetic dial to ask and respond to questions. - **$200 $450 $650**

❑ **WIZ-8. "Wonderland Of Oz" Map 16x22",**
1932. Philadelphia Evening Bulletin newspaper. - **$200 $650 $900**

WIZ-9

WIZ-10

❑ **WIZ-9. Jackpumpkinhead And The Sawhorse,**
1933. Jell-O softbound book. - **$40 $100 $150**

❑ **WIZ-10. Tik Tok And The Nome King,**
1933. Jell-O softbound book. - **$40 $100 $150**

(FRONT) WIZ-11 (BACK)

❑ **WIZ-11. Ozma And The Little Wizard,**
1933. Jell-O softbound book. - **$40 $100 $150**

(FRONT) WIZ-12 (BACK)

❑ **WIZ-12. The Scarecrow And The Tin Woodman,**
1933. Jell-O softbound book. - **$40 $100 $150**

WIZ-13

❑ **WIZ-13. The Laughing Dragon of Oz,**
1934. Big Little Book #1126. Rare. 432 pages by Frank Baum. - **$50 $150 $300**

WIZ-14

WIZ-15

❑ **WIZ-14. Movie Advertising Cello. Button,**
1939. Scarce. Seen with "Loew's" (theater) and "Hecht's" (Baltimore department store) imprints. - **$200 $400 $750**

❑ **WIZ-15. Dorothy Mask,**
1939. Distributed by department stores and others. - **$20 $40 $75**

WIZ-16

WIZ-17

❑ **WIZ-16. Scarecrow Mask,**
1939. Distributed by department stores and others. - **$20 $40 $75**

❑ **WIZ-17. Cowardly Lion Mask,**
1939. Distributed by department stores and others. - **$20 $40 $75**

WIZ-18

WIZ-19

❑ **WIZ-18. Tin Woodman Mask,**
1939. Distributed by department stores and others. - **$20 $40 $75**

❑ **WIZ-19. Wizard Mask,**
1939. Distributed by department stores and others. - **$20 $40 $75**

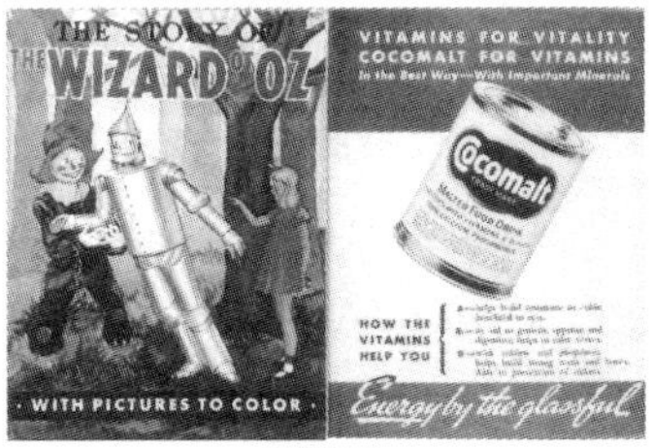


WIZ-20

❑ **WIZ-20. "The Story Of The Wizard Of Oz" Coloring Book,**
1939. Cocomalt. Premium Version -
**$15 $30 $70**
Store Version Without Cocomalt Ad -
**$12 $25 $60**

WIZ-21

❑ **WIZ-21. Pictorial Fabric Scarf,**
1939. Store item. Two different designs with numerous color variations. - **$75 $150 $300**

WIZ-22

❑ **WIZ-22. "The Wizard Of Oz" Movie Songs Folio,**
1939. Store item with 24 miniature illustrations for M-G-M film. - **$25 $60 $85**

WIZ-23

❑ **WIZ-23. "The Wizard Of Oz" Movie Score Record Album,**
c. 1939. Decca Records. 10-1/2x12" with four records including "The Jitterbug" song that was cut from the movie. - **$35 $75 $150**

WIZ-24

❑ **WIZ-24. "Wizard of Oz" Boxed Board Game,**
1939. Store item by Whitman Publishing Co. Board in linen on 13x19" cardboard. Parts are wood die and four markers each in a single color. - **$200 $450 $750**

WIZ-25

WIZ-26

❑ **WIZ-25. Dorothy Glass,**
1939. Sealtest Cottage Cheese. Seven known: Dorothy, Toto, Scarecrow, Tin Woodman, The Cowardly Lion, The Good Witch, The Bad Witch. The Wizard is unknown.
Each - **$60 $125 $200**

❑ **WIZ-26. Movie 3" Cello. Button,**
1939. M-G-M Studio. - **$50 $175 $350**

WIZ-27

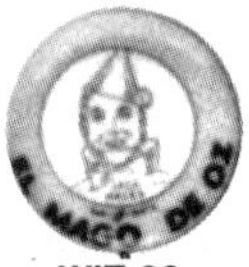


WIZ-28

❑ **WIZ-27. "Frank Morgan" Movie Contest Cello. Button,**
1939. M-G-M Studios. 1-1/4" size, set of five also includes Judy Garland, Ray Bolger, Jack Haley, Bert Lahr. This size has serial number to match for winning prize.
Judy Garland - **$250 $600 $1200**
Others - **$200 $500 $1000**

❑ **WIZ-28. Title in Spanish Cello. Button,**
1939. From 7/8" series of five characters with Oz film title in Spanish.
Judy Garland - **$250 $500 $1000**
Other Four - **$50 $125 $250**

WIZ-29

WIZ-30

❑ **WIZ-29. Full Color Paper Seal,**
1939. W. L. Stensgaard & Associates, Inc. 2-1/2" square designed for the Christmas 1939 department store promotion of the movie inscribed "Merry Christmas from The Merry Old Land of Oz." - **$100 $225 $350**

❑ **WIZ-30. Movie Premiere Souvenir Program,**
1939. Metro-Goldwyn-Mayer. Oversized 10-1/8x13-3/4" program titled "The Wizard of Oz Comes to Life," available only at the premiere screening held at Graumann's Chinese Theatre on August 15, 1939. - **$600 $1600 $2750**

WIZ-31

WIZ-32

❑ **WIZ-31. Scarecrow Valentine,**
1940 Store item. From set of 12 picturing various characters by American Colortype Co.
Each - **$25 $65 $125**

❑ **WIZ-32. "Magic Sand" Packet Envelope,**
c. 1940. Various theaters. Contains sand "From Along The Yellow Brick Road.." -
**$125 $275 $600**

WIZ-33

❑ **WIZ-33. "S & Co." Glass Tumblers,**
1953. Swift Peanut Butter. Six designs with wavy, plain or fluted bases. Characters depicted are Dorothy, Toto, Scarecrow, Cowardly Lion, Tinman, and the Wizard. Each - **$12 $20 $30**

(FRONT)

(BACK)

WIZ-34

❑ **WIZ-34. "The Wizard Of Oz Coloring Book",**
1955. Swift & Company. Twelve page booklet retelling the Baum story and advertising Oz Peanut Butter tumblers on inside front and back covers. - **$25 $60 $125**

WIZ-35

❑ **WIZ-35. "Wizard Of Oz" Movie Soundtrack Album,**
1956. M-G-M. - **$15 $25 $50**

WIZ-36

❑ **WIZ-36. Dorothy And Scarecrow Boxed Marionettes,**
1950s. Store item by Hazelle's Marionettes. Each is 13" tall. No Oz license but obvious likenesses. Each Boxed - **$40 $75 $150**
Each UnBoxed - **$20 $40 $75**

WIZ-37

❑ **WIZ-37. Oz Peanut Butter Mobile,**
c. 1960. Swift & Company. Thin cardboard punch-out of the Baum characters, advertising Oz Peanut Butter.
Unpunched - **$75 $150 $300**
Assembled - **$50 $100 $150**

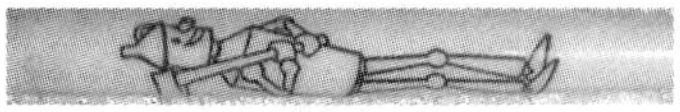

(CLOSE-UP)

WIZ-38

❑ **WIZ-38. "Swift's Oz Peanut Butter" Ballpoint Pen,**
c. 1960. Plastic advertising pen issued in colors of red, beige, blue or yellow with lettering and Tin Man image in black. Also issued as a black pen with writing and Tin Man image printed in silver. - **$50 $75 $150**

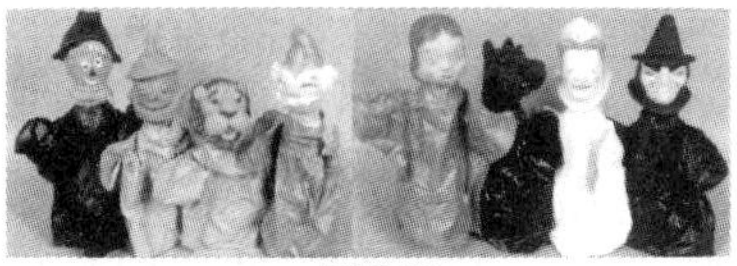

WIZ-39

❑ **WIZ-39. Vinyl Hand Puppets,**
1965. Procter & Gamble. Eight in set. Cardboard theater also issued.
Each Puppet - **$5 $12 $25**
Theater - **$20 $45 $75**

WIZ-40

❑ **WIZ-40. "Free Wizard Of Oz Hand Puppets" Store Display,**
1966. Procter & Gamble. Diecut standing display about five feet tall with plastic-bubble compartment at base holding seven samples of the eight available hand puppets. In 1966 the puppets were premiums for Top Job, Zest and Downy. When the promotion repeated in 1969, the products were Ivory Snow, Oxydol and Joy (the display was adjusted accordingly). Originally the Wizard puppet was available only with the cardboard Emerald City theater as a mail-away premium.
Near Mint With Seven Puppets - **$2000**
Display Without Puppets - **$500 $1000 $1800**

WIZ-41

❑ **WIZ-41. Oz Character Flicker Ring Set,**
c. 1967. Made by Vari-Vue and likely dispensed in vending machines. Set of 12 with two blue plastic rings for these characters: Cowardly Lion, Dorothy, Scarecrow, Tin Woodman, Witch, Wizard. One variety of the Lion ring and one of the Wizard ring includes inscription "Off To See The Wizard." Each - **$10 $20 $35**

WIZ-42

❑ **WIZ-42. Set Of 12 Litho. Buttons,**
1967. Samson Products. Vending machine distribution. Each - **$5 $10 $15**

WIZ-43

❑ **WIZ-43. "Magic Kit",**
1967. Store item by Fun Inc. - **$25 $40 $75**

WIZ-44

WIZ-45

❑ **WIZ-44. Iron-On Transfers,**
1967. Available through Morton Foods, Kitty Clover and others. Depicts images of Chuck Jones cartoon characters from the 1967-68 TV show, "Off to See the Wizard," issued in cellophane packets as a set of five (four main characters; the fifth was either "Wizard" or "Wicked Witch"). Each - **$15 $30 $50**

❑ **WIZ-45. "Wizard Of Oz Coloring Book",**
1968. Procter & Gamble. Captioned "Free! When You Buy One Regular-Size Bottle Of Top Job." - **$25 $60 $110**

WIZ-46

❑ **WIZ-46. Oz Characters Ceramic Music Box,**
c. 1969. Store item plays "Somewhere Over The Rainbow." **$40 $90 $150**

WIZ-47

WIZ-48

❑ **WIZ-47. Oz Promotional Wristwatch,**
1989. Macy's department store. 9-1/2" long plastic hinged case holds watch issued for 50th anniversary of original movie. 1-1/4" dial has color illustration of Dorothy and friends headed to Emerald City. Near Mint Boxed - **$75**
Unboxed - **$10 $25 $50**

❑ **WIZ-48. "It's Oz Time At Macy's" Store Clerk Button,**
1989. Macy's department store. 3" diameter beautifully colored cello. button used in conjunction with promotion for 50th year movie anniversary. - **$15 $30 $60**

WIZ-49

WIZ-50

WIZ-51

WIZ-52

❑ **WIZ-49. "Dorothy" Bean Bag with Tag,**
1998. Warner Brothers Studio Store. - **$15**

❑ **WIZ-50. "Cowardly Lion" Bean Bag with Tag,**
1998. Warner Brothers Studio Store. - **$12**

❑ **WIZ-51. "Scarecrow" Bean Bag with Tag,**
1998. Warner Brothers Studio Store. - **$15**

❑ **WIZ-52. "Tin Man" Bean Bag with Tag,**
1998. Warner Brothers Studio Store. - **$12**
Other bean bag figures exist for Glinda the Good Witch, Wicked Witch of the West, Lollipop Girl, Munchkin Boy, Flying Monkey and the Wizard -**$10-15 each**

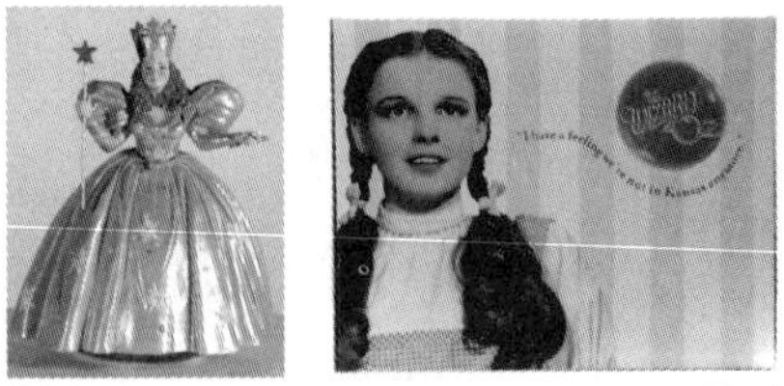

(Figure) WIZ-53 (Box)

❑ **WIZ-53. "Glinda the Good Witch" Bobber Figure,**
2000. - **$20**

# Wonder Woman

*Wonder Woman* was created by psychologist/writer William Moulton Marston (1893-1947; pen name, Charles Moulton). The comics' first major female superhero debuted in issue #8 of *All Star Comics* in December 1941 and had her own comic book by the next summer. Wonder Woman came from mysterious Paradise Island (no men allowed) to America as Diana Prince to help fight World War II. Over the years she has also battled aliens and terrorists, lost her flag-like costume and superpowers, regained them, dabbled in I Ching, and fallen in and out of love. A comic strip appearance in 1944 had a short life, and a hardback anthology was published in 1972. There have been two TV movies--*Wonder Woman* (1974) with Cathy Lee Crosby, and *The New, Original Wonder Woman* (1975) with Lynda Carter--and a TV series, also starring Carter, that aired on ABC (1976-1977) and CBS (1977-1979). The character was also featured in the *Superfriends* cartoon that aired on ABC in the 1970s, and the current *Justice League* animated series on the Cartoon Network. Items are usually copyrighted DC Comics or Warner Bros. TV.

WON-1

❑ **WON-1. "Sensation Comics" Litho. Button,**
1942. Rare. Offered in May issue of Sensation Comics. - **$400 $1200 $2500**

WON-2

❑ **WON-2. WWII Infantile Paralysis Comic Book Postcard Premium,**
1940s. Rare. - **$100 $400 $600**

WON-3

WON-4

❑ **WON-3. Valentine Card,**
1940s. Store item. Diecut stiff paper folder with inner message "For You, Valentine, I'd Move Heaven And Earth!" - **$25 $50 $100**

❑ **WON-4. "Wonder Woman" 3-1/2" Cello. Button,**
1966. Store item. #14 from series.
Near Mint Bagged - **$50**
Loose - **$12 $20 $40**

WON-5

WON-6

❑ **WON-5. Boxed Board Game,**
1967. Store item by Hasbro. Also features other Justice League of America characters. - **$25 $75 $150**

❑ **WON-6. Proof Ingot,**
1974. Used as incentive to promote other DC Comics character ingots. Only 300 made.
Near Mint - **$200**

WON-7

WON-8

❑ **WON-7. "Wonder Woman" 2-1/4" Cello. Button,**
1975. Store item by Rainbow Designs. DC Comics copyright. - **$5 $10 $15**

❑ **WON-8. Metal Ring With Cello. Portrait,**
1976. N.P.P. Inc. Brass finish with copyright on underside. - **$75 $100 $150**

WON-9

WON-10

❑ **WON-9. TV Guide Weekly Issue,**
1977. Volume 25 #5 for week of January 29.
Without Mailing Label - **$8 $15 $20**
With Mailing Label - **$5 $10 $15**

❑ **WON-10. Vinyl Lunch Box,**
1977. Store item by Aladdin Industries Inc. - **$40 $85 $150**

WON-11

❑ **WON-11. Lynda Carter Autographed Photo,**
c. 1977. Glossy black and white. - **$10 $20 $45**

WON-12

❑ **WON-12. "Wonder Woman" Boxed Marionette,**
1977. Store item by Madison Ltd.
Near Mint Boxed - **$150**
Loose - **$25 $50 $75**

WON-13

❑ **WON-13. Watch,**
1977. Store item by Dabs.
Near Mint Boxed - **$175**
Loose - **$35 $75 $125**

WON-14

WON-15

❑ **WON-14. Pepsi Glass,**
1978. - **$5 $10 $15**

❑ **WON-15. "See The Superheroes At Sea World" Photo,**
1970s. Sea World appearance souvenir. Batman and Wonder Woman pictured with facsimile signatures. - **$10 $20 $30**

WON-16

❑ **WON-16. Resin Statue in Box,**
1995. Limited edition of 3000. Produced by Graphitti. Boxed - **$200**

WON-17

WON-18

❑ **WON-17. Hallmark Figure,**
1996. From DC Superheroes set. - **$50**

❑ **WON-18. Hallmark Figure,**
1996. 6" tall with base. - **$75**

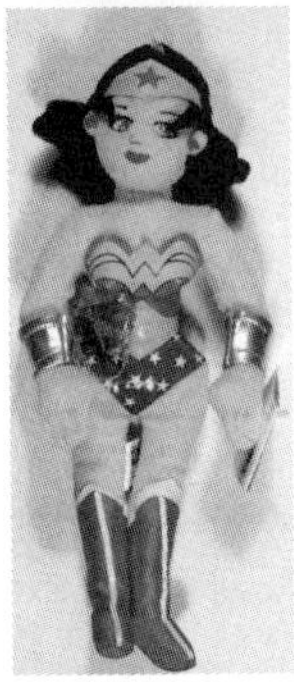

WON-18

WON-20

❑ **WON-18. Bean Bag Figure,**
1998. Warner Bros store exclusive. - **$8**

❑ **WON-20. Action Figure,**
1999. Variant with helmet and spear. - **$25**

WON-21

❑ **WON-21. Resin Figure,**
1999. Warner Bros store exclusive. - **$75**

WON-22

❑ **WON-22. Wonder Woman Statue,**
2000. DC Direct product. Hand painted, 9 1/2" tall. Limited to 5,000. - **$195**

WON-23

❑ **WON-23. "Spirit Of Truth" Graphic Novel,**
2001. Art by Alex Ross. - **$10**

WON-24

(Inside of bracelet is engraved)

(Box)

❑ **WON-24. Wonder Woman Prop Set,**
2001. DC Direct product. Set includes tiara, bracelets and earrings with a decorative base. Display base has a clear plastic removable lid. Limited to 1,200. Boxed - **$195**

WON-25

❑ **WON-25. Pocket Super Heroes Figure,**
2002. Golden Age Wonder Woman figure was a retailer preview promotion. Also available in different packaging with a Solomon Grundy figure.
Figure in Promotional package - **$8**
Figure in Grundy box - **$5**

## Woody Woodpecker

**Between 1940 and 1972 Walter Lantz (1900-1994) created more than 200 animated shorts featuring the hyperactive woodpecker with the raucous laugh (supplied by Lantz's wife). Over the years Woody evolved from a multi-colored lunatic into an appealing red-haired imp. His musical theme, *The Woody Woodpecker Song,* was nominated for an Academy Award in 1948. *The Woody Woodpecker Show* aired on the Mutual radio network in 1952-1954 and came to ABC television for the 1957-1958 season, then to NBC in 1971-1972 and 1976-1977. Woody made a number of comic book appearances starting in 1942. Items are normally copyrighted Walter Lantz Productions.**

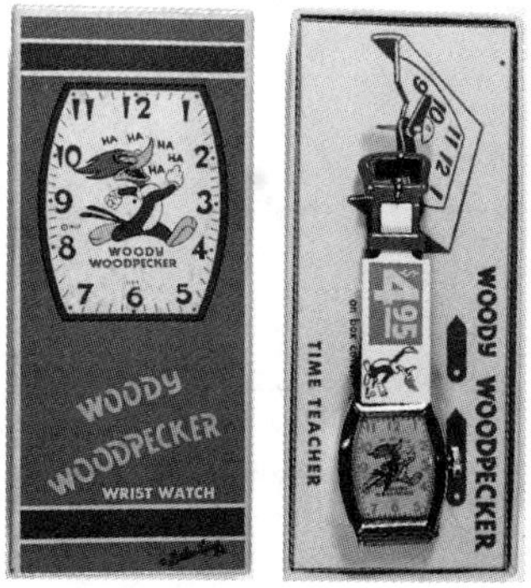


WDY-1

❑ **WDY-1. Wrist Watch with Box,**
1940s. Scarce.
Near Mint With Insert and Price Tag - **$750**
Watch only - **$75 $150 $275**

WDY-2

WDY-3

❑ **WDY-2. Albers Quick Oats Container,**
1940s. Rare. Shows how to draw Woody and has a model sheet on back. Andy Panda is also featured. - **$150 $375 $475**

❑ **WDY-3. Promo,**
1951. Scarce. 6 pages (4 pages of comics). - **$100 $250 $400**

WDY-4

❑ **WDY-4. Cards With Folder,**
1953. Carnation Corn Flakes. Eighteen Walter Lantz cards. Set - **$75 $125 $180**

WDY-5

WDY-6

❑ **WDY-5. "Hi Pal!" Cello. Button,**
1957. Came on store bought doll. - **$15 $30 $60**

❑ **WDY-6. Premium Booklet,**
1958. Kellogg's Rice Krispies. 4 pages of recipes and a 1958 quarter. - **$25 $50 $75**

WDY-7

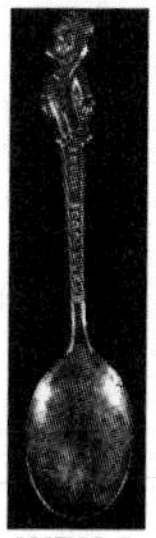

WDY-8

❑ **WDY-7. Premium Comic Chevrolet,**
1950s. - **$25 $65 $150**

❑ **WDY-8. Spoon,**
1950s. Cereal premium. - **$10 $20 $30**

WDY-9

WDY-10

❑ **WDY-9. Comic,**
1950s. Scotch Tape sponsor. - **$20 $60 $175**

❑ **WDY-10. Movie Label,**
1950s. - **$10 $20 $30**

WDY-11

❑ **WDY-11. Woody/Winnie Glazed Ceramic Salt And Pepper Set,**
1950s. Store item marked "Napco Originals By Guildcraft." Each is 3-7/8" tall from a series of pairs featuring Woody Woodpecker characters and other Lantz characters.
Each Pair - **$65 $125 $200**

(FRONT) (BACK)

WDY-12

❑ **WDY-12. Kellogg's Rice Krispies Cereal Box Flat with Fruit Promotion,**
1960. Woody fruit offer on back. Huck and Yogi spoon offer on side.
Box - **$40 $90 $170**

(FRONT) (BACK)

**WDY-13**

❑ **WDY-13. Kellogg's Raisin Bran Cereal Box Flat with Mug and Bowl Promotion,**
1963. Promotes mug and cereal bowl WDY-14.
Box - **$40 $90 $170**

**WDY-14**

❑ **WDY-14. Kellogg's Plastic Mug And Cereal Bowl,**
1963. Bowl image of log trough.
Set - **$25 $40 $70**

**WDY-15**

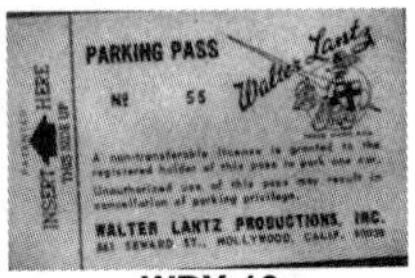


**WDY-16**

❑ **WDY-15. Swimming Figure,**
1962. Kellogg's Cereals. Plastic jointed toy propelled by rubber band. Near Mint Boxed - **$125**
Unboxed - **$30 $65 $90**

❑ **WDY-16. Parking Pass,**
c. 1963. Lantz Studios. - **$30 $60 $90**

(FRONT) (BACK)

**WDY-17**

❑ **WDY-17. Kellogg's Rice Krispies 10 oz. Cereal Box Flat with Kazoo Promotion,**
1963. Promotes kazoo on back of box.
Box - **$40 $90 $170**

(FRONT) (BACK)

**WDY-18**

❑ **WDY-18. Kellogg's Rice Krispies 10 oz. Cereal Box Flat with Woody Crossword Puzzle,**
1963. Sports crossword on back of box.
Box - **$40 $90 $170**

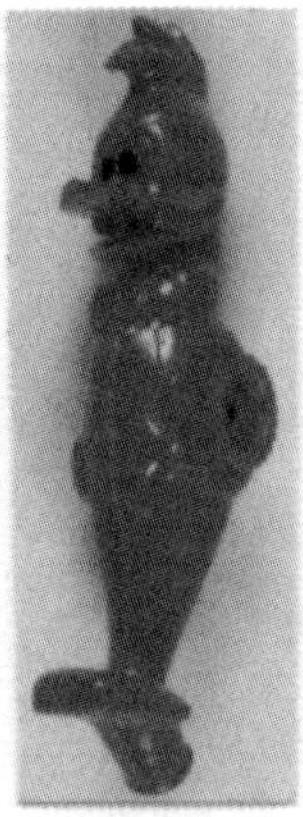

**WDY-19**

❑ **WDY-19. Figural Plastic Kazoo,**
c. 1965. 6-1/2" tall red plastic issued by Kellogg's. - **$10 $20 $40**

**WDY-20**

❑ **WDY-20. Kellogg's Plastic Door Knocker Assembly Kit,**
1966. Canadian issue. Boxed - **$20 $40 $60**
Built - **$15 $25 $40**

(FRONT) **WDY-21** (BACK)

❑ **WDY-21. Rice Krispies Stuffed Toy Offer,**
1966. Cereal box flat. - **$40 $80 $130**

(FRONT) **WDY-22** (BACK)

❑ **WDY-22. Stars Cereal Swimmer Offer,**
1967. Cereal box flat. - **$40 $80 $130**

**WDY-23**

**WDY-24**

❑ **WDY-23. Gum Box Display Card,**
1968. Fleer Gum. - **$8 $12 $25**

❑ **WDY-24. Figural Harmonica,**
c. 1960s. Possible Kellogg's premium. Plastic full figure with harmonica reed formed in tail.-
**$15 $30 $50**

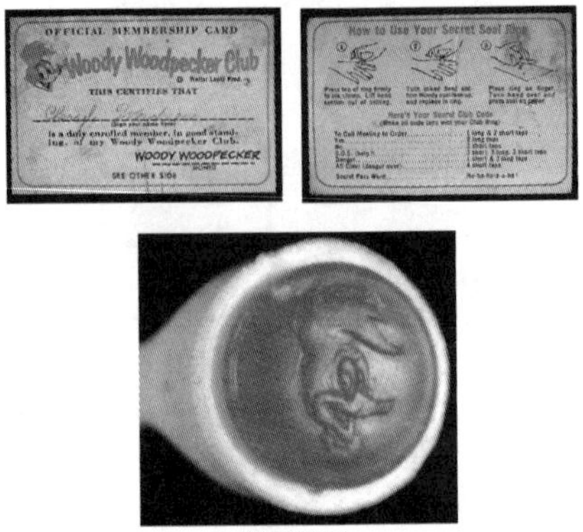


**WDY-25**

❑ **WDY-25. Club Card And "Secret Seal Ring",**
1960s. Kellogg's. Plastic ring in two color varieties has interior ink pad to stamp image of Woody. Card - **$10 $20 $35**
Ring - **$40 $75 $125**

**WDY-26**

❑ **WDY-26. "Woody's Cafe" Alarm Clock Varieties,**
c. 1970. Store item by Westclox, made in Hong Kong. This version has diecut hole on tree trunk to show alarm numerals. The original 1959 version by Columbia Time has a dial showing alarm numerals. Westclox - **$25 $50 $100**
Columbia - **$75 $150 $300**

**WDY-27**

❑ **WDY-27. Woody And Winnie Woodpecker "Love" Leather Lunch Box,**
c. 1970s. Store item, maker unknown. Dark green leather with full color illustration on flap. Includes Walter Lantz Productions copyright. - **$150 $300 $500**

**WDY-28**

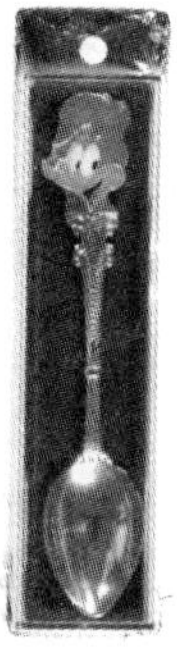

**WDY-29**

❑ **WDY-28. Plastic Portrait Ring,**
c. 1970s. Vending machine issue. - **$5 $8 $12**

❑ **WDY-29. Spoon,**
1970s. Store bought. - **$10 $25 $35**

**WDY-30**

**WDY-31**

❑ **WDY-30. Replica Race Car on Card,**
1997. Revell diecast Wally Dallenbach car commemorates Universal Studios sponsorship of NASCAR Suzuka 100 held in Suzuka, Japan on Nov. 3, 1997. First in a series of proposed animated characters that Universal plans to feature on NASCAR Winston Cup cars. - **$30**

❑ **WDY-31. Valentine Kit,**
1999. Includes cards, stickers and envelopes. - **$2**

**WDY-32**

**WDY-33**

❑ **WDY-32. Premium Yo-Yo,**
1990s. Promotes new cartoons on the FOX Kids Network. Comes in yellow and blue.
Each - **$10 $20 $50**

❑ **WDY-33. Bobbing Head Figure,**
1990s. Boxed - **$60**

## World War

**Memorabilia was produced by various entities during World War I (1914-1919), setting a precedent for the huge volume of collectibles produced during World War II (1938-1945). American involvement in WWII was intense on the home front as well as the war zones. With millions of young men and women in uniform and far from home between early 1942 and 1945, family members and loved ones wanted to follow events as they occurred in Europe and in the Pacific. A number of advertisers answered the call by offering war maps and atlases and other print material that brought home details of the military movements and battles. V-E Day (Victory-Europe) was commonly celebrated on May 8, 1945, and V-J Day (Victory-Japan) on August 15, 1945.**

**WWII-1**

❑ **WWII-1. Pre-WWII Anti-War Button And Booklet,**
1936. Emergency Peace Campaign.
Button - **$5 $10 $20**
Booklet - **$10 $20 $35**

**WWII-2**

**WWII-3**

❑ **WWII-2. "Pat Nelson Ace of Test Pilots" BLB #1445,**
1937. - **$10 $25 $65**

❑ **WWII-3. "Barney Baxter In The Air With The Eagle Squadron" BLB #1459,**
1938. - **$10 $25 $65**

**WWII-4**

❑ **WWII-4. "Brad Turner In Transatlantic Flight" BLB #1425,**
1939. - **$10 $25 $65**

**WWII-5**

**WWII-6**

❑ **WWII-5. "Don O'Dare Finds War" BLB #1438,**
1940. - **$10 $25 $65**

❑ **WWII-6. "Wings of the U.S.A." BLB #1401,**
1940. - **$10 $25 $65**

WWII-7

❑ **WWII-7. "Super-Defense Paper-Buster Gun,"**
c. 1940. Store item by Langson Mfg. Co. Metal gun is 6-1/4" long. Box - **$25 $50 $100**
Gun - **$25 $50 $100**

WWII-8 WWII-9

❑ **WWII-8. "Allen Pike of the Parachute Squad" BLB #1481,**
1941. - **$10 $25 $65**

❑ **WWII-9. "Air Fighters of America" BLB #1448,**
1941. - **$12 $30 $75**

WWII-10 WWII-11

❑ **WWII-10. "Pilot Pete Dive Bomber" BLB #1466,**
1941. - **$10 $25 $65**

❑ **WWII-11. "Uncle Sam's Sky Defenders" BLB #1461,**
1941. - **$12 $30 $75**

WWII-12

❑ **WWII-12. License Plate Attachment,**
c. 1942. George Goode Garage and others. 5-1/2x10" metal finished in red, white and blue. - **$50 $125 $250**

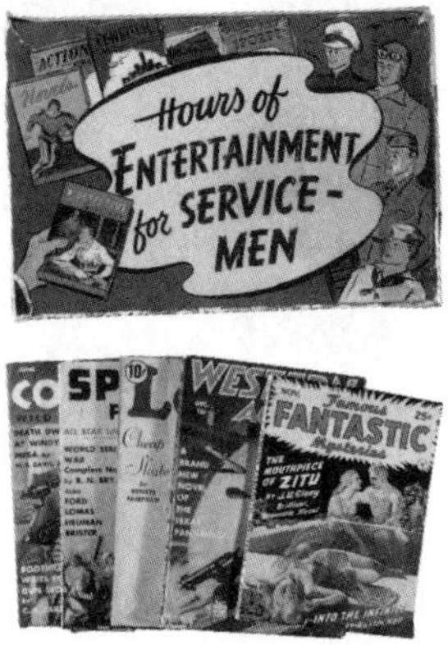


WWII-13

❑ **WWII-13. Reading Kit - Boxed,**
1942. Says "Hours of entertainment for service men", included 5 different pulp magazines. - **$100 $200 $350**

WWII-14 WWII-15

❑ **WWII-14. Atlas Map,**
1942. Pure Oil premium. 16 pages. Edited by H. V. Kaltenborn. - **$20 $30 $45**

❑ **WWII-15. Atlas Map - 2nd Edition,**
1942. Pure Oil premium. 16 pages. - **$20 $30 $45**

WWII-16 WWII-17

❑ **WWII-16. H. V. Kaltenborn Photo,**
1942. Radio premium with Kaltenborn in uniform with "C" on sleeve for news correspondent. - **$10 $20 $35**

❑ **WWII-17. "Eat To Beat The Devil" Booklet,**
1942. Servel refrigerators. 32-page listing of health and nutrition tips with front cover caricature art of Hitler as the devil. - **$10 $20 $40**

WWII-18

❑ **WWII-18. Uncle Sam Punch Board,**
c. 1942. Issued by Hamilton Mfg. Co. 10x17". - **$50 $85 $150**

WWII-19

❑ **WWII-19. "Keep 'Em Flying! USA For America's Defense" Better Little Book #1420,**
1943. Whitman #1420. - **$12 $30 $75**

WWII-20 WWII-21

❑ **WWII-20. Anti-Mussolini Plaster Ashtray With Sticker Label,**
1943. - **$60 $100 $150**

❑ **WWII-21. "Kool Cigarettes" Poster,**
c. 1943. Issued by Brown & Williamson Tobacco Co. 12x18". - **$35 $75 $150**

WWII-22

❑ **WWII-22. "7UP" Calendar for 1943,**
1943. The 12" x 7" calendar features a drawn pin-up of General MacArthur. - **$25 $50 $85**

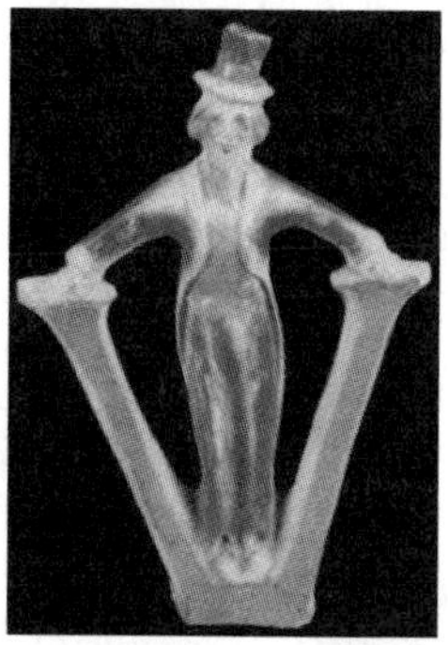

WWII-23

❑ **WWII-23. Uncle Sam Victory Statuette,**
c. 1943. 12-1/2" tall plaster store item by Turiddi Art. - **$75 $150 $250**

WWII-24

❑ **WWII-24. Anti-Hitler Matchbook Cover,**
c. 1943. Seat of Hitler is brown sandpaper for striking surface. Issued by Monogram.
Full Pack - **$25 $50 $75**
Cover Only - **$20 $40 $65**

WWII-25

❑ **WWII-25. "Fatso-Ratso-Japso" Anti-Axis Easel Poster,**
c. 1943. 15-1/4x18" rigid cardboard. -
**$150 $250 $350**

WWII-26

❑ **WWII-26. "Girls In Uniform" Paperdoll Kit,**
1943. Store item by D. A. Pachter Co., Chicago. Unpunched - **$125 $250 $350**

WWII-27

❑ **WWII-27. "Capt. Ben Dix" Comic Book,**
1943. Bendix Aviation Corp. - **$8 $24 $60**

WWII-28

WWII-29

❑ **WWII-28. "Radio At War Picture Book",**
c. 1943. Various sponsors. Depicts programs and stars of "Blue Network." - **$15 $25 $45**

❑ **WWII-29. Atlas Map - Victory Edition,**
1943. Pure Oil premium. 20 pages. -
**$25 $35 $50**

WWII-30

WWII-31

❑ **WWII-30. Flying Cadets Coloring Book,**
1943. Classic World War II cover by Fredric C. Madan. Book is filled with many pictures of U.S. planes. - **$50 $100 $150**

❑ **WWII-31. U.S. Marines Coloring Book,**
1943. Classic World War II cover by Fredric C. Madan. - **$50 $100 $150**

WWII-32

❑ **WWII-32. Submarine Coloring Book,**
1943. Cover by Fredric C. Madan. -
**$50 $100 $150**

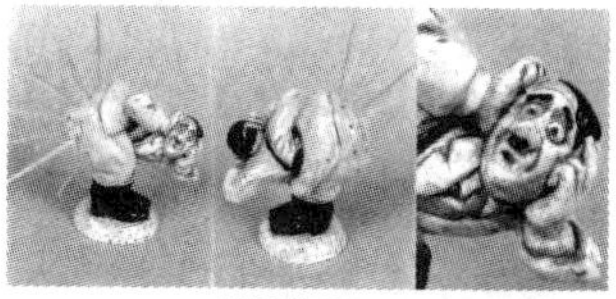

WWII-33

❑ **WWII-33. Anti-Hitler Plaster Toothpick Holder,**
c. 1943. - **$100 $200 $350**

WWII-34

WWII-35

❑ **WWII-34. Hitler Plaster Pin Cushion,**
c. 1943. Large Size - **$100 $175 $300**
Smaller "Hotzi Notzi" Size - **$65 $100 $150**

❑ **WWII-35. "Target Tokyo" Cardboard Wheel Game,**
1944. Tip-Top Bread. - **$15 $25 $60**

WWII-36

WWII-37

❑ **WWII-36. Flying Forts Coloring Book,**
1944. Spectacular cover by Fredric C. Madan. Mentions loading eggs (bombs) heading for Hitler and Hirohito. - **$75 $125 $200**

❑ **WWII-37. Planes of Tomorrow Coloring Book,**
1944. Incredible look into the future. 50 different planes are shown, many of which look familiar 56 years later. It also talks about rocket ships going to the moon. - **$75 $125 $200**

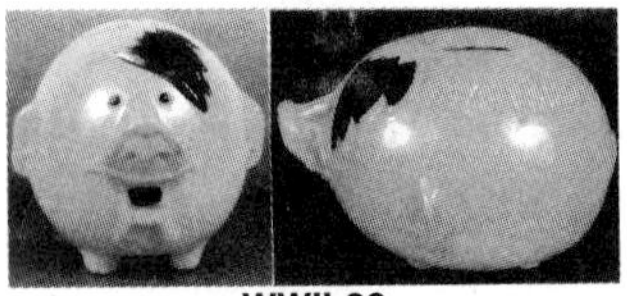
WWII-38

❑ **WWII-38. Anti-Hitler Composition Pig Bank,**
c. 1944. Squeaking mechanism rarely works. Not Working - **$75 $150 $300**

WWII-39

❑ **WWII-39. "Sky Heroes" Stamp Album,**
c. 1944. Sinclair Oil Corp. Twenty stamps in set. Complete - **$25 $50 $120**

WWII-40

❑ **WWII-40. Christmas Card,**
1944. Christmas card from the United States Army in Italy. - **$5 $10 $20**

WWII-41

❑ **WWII-41. Pacific Map,**
1944. Pure Oil premium. Folds out to show battle areas in Pacific. - **$25 $35 $50**

WWII-42

WWII-43

❑ **WWII-42. Victory Map Set,**
1944. Pure Oil Co. Two sections fold out into huge wall map. - **$30 $60 $90**

❑ **WWII-43. Hitler Skunk,**
c. 1944. Ceramic composition. - **$60 $125 $200**

WWII-44

❑ **WWII-44. "Victory Star Tumblers" Glasses Set,**
c. 1944. Pillsbury's Flour. Set - **$25 $60 $90**

WWII-45

❑ **WWII-45. "Exide Batteries At War" Book,**
1946. Illustrations similar to Dixie Ice Cream series. - **$20 $50 $100**

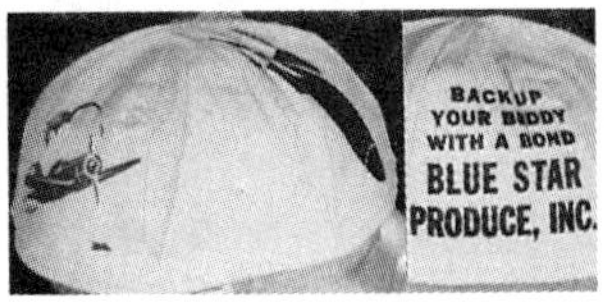

WWII-46

❑ **WWII-46. Bond Promotion Skull Cap,**
1940s. Blue Star Produce and others. Blue on white fabric reading "Backup Your Buddy With A Bond." - **$15 $30 $60**

WWII-47

❑ **WWII-47. War Bonds Dairy Milk Bottle,**
1940s. Fraim's Dairies and others. 9-1/2" tall glass quart bottle with image in maroon. - **$25 $50 $75**

WWII-48

❑ **WWII-48. Esso War Maps,**
1940s. Periodic revisions in war years. Each - **$5 $12 $20**

WWII-49

WWII-50

❑ **WWII-49. Lowell Thomas NBC War Map 16x20",**
1940s. Radio premium. Two sided colorful map of the World. - **$30 $65 $100**

❑ **WWII-50. Kaltenborn Campaign Book,**
1940s. Pure Oil premium. News editor for Roosevelt vs. Willkie election. - **$15 $30 $50**

WWII-51

WWII-52

❑ **WWII-51. Photo,**
1940s. H. V. Kaltenborn . Edits the news. No uniform. - **$5 $10 $20**

❑ **WWII-52. Radio Sign,**
1940s. Features Uncle Sam telling people to listen to updates on the War. - **$25 $50 $100**

WWII-53

❑ **WWII-53. Coca-Cola Air Insignia Cello. Buttons,**
1940s. Each is a full color 1" cello. from a believed set of 24. Manner of distribution is unknown. The numbered reverse back paper identifies the squadron and reads "Drink Coca-Cola." Each - **$10 $25 $50**

**WWII-54**

❑ **WWII-54. Cartoon Slogan Matchbook,**
1940s. Topps Gum. Cover includes security slogan illustrated by cartoonist O. Soglow, creator of The Little King comic strip.
Complete - **$15 $30 $50**

**WWII-55**

**WWII-56**

❑ **WWII-55. Bill Henry's Presidential Election Map,**
1940s. - **$25 $35 $50**

❑ **WWII-56. "Wanted for Murder" Hitler Pinback,**
1940s. - **$20 $45 $85**

# World's Fairs

**International expositions blossomed into creative and technical spectacles in the 19th century, first in Europe and then in the United States, providing a mix of fine arts, industrial progress, and nationalist emotions. In addition to promoting international understanding, world's fairs produced an abundance of collectible souvenirs. Major American fairs include the Centennial Exposition (Philadelphia, 1876), World's Columbian Exposition (Chicago, 1893), Cotton Centennial (New Orleans, 1894), Pan-American (Buffalo, 1901), Louisiana Purchase (St. Louis, 1904), Panama-Pacific (San Francisco, 1915), Sesquicentennial (Philadelphia, 1926) Century of Progress (Chicago, 1933-1934), California Pacific International (San Diego, 1935-1936), Great Lakes (Cleveland, 1936-1937), Golden Gate International (San Francisco, 1939-1940), World of Tomorrow (New York, 1939-1940), Seattle Expo (1962), New York World's Fair (1964-1965), Expo '67 (Montreal 1967), Expo '74 (Spokane 1974), Knoxville World's Fair (1982), and Expo '86 (Vancouver, British Columbia 1986).**

**WFA-1**

❑ **WFA-1. U.S. Centennial Pennant,**
1876. 18x24" vertical swallow-tail linen fabric including border design of 38 stars representing states admitted to the Union as of celebration year. - **$75 $135 $225**

**WFA-2**

❑ **WFA-2. Spoon ,**
1893. World's Fair spoon shows picture of Columbus and Administration Building. Sold at Fair. - **$10 $20 $35**

**WFA-3**

❑ **WFA-3. Giveaway Comic Booklet,**
1893. Features the story of "Bill an' Me" and their trip from Baltimore to Chicago to visit the Fair. Sponsored by Emerson's Bromo Seltzer. - **$25 $50 $85**

**WFA-4**

❑ **WFA-4. Ticket - Chicago 1893,**
1893. Unused 1893 child's ticket for World's Fair in Chicago. Children dreamed of the chance of attending the World's Columbian Exhibition in 1893. It is very rare to find an unused ticket that was bought at the Fair.
Complete - **$15 $30 $60**

**WFA-5**

**WFA-6**

**WFA-7**

❑ **WFA-5. Pan-American Exposition "Swift & Company" Cello. Button,**
1901. Caricature art for meat products. - **$15 $25 $50**

❑ **WFA-6. Pan-American Exposition Cello. Button,**
1901. Pictured is establishment and proprietor of "Cheyenne Joe's Rocky Mountain Tavern." - **$20 $50 $75**

❑ **WFA-7. Pan-American Exposition Cello. Button,**
1901. Full color 1-1/4" based on theme of North and South American continents joining hands, although depicting monkeys rather than the traditional two ladies of the official theme art design. - **$30 $65 $115**

**WFA-8**

**WFA-9**

**WFA-10**

❑ **WFA-8. St. Louis World's Fair Cello. Button,**
1904. Full color 1-3/4" depicting "The Home Of Jefferson." - **$20 $50 $85**

❑ **WFA-9. St. Louis World's Fair Cello. Button,**
1904. Pictured is Thomas Jefferson under alternate title of the fair "Universal Exposition." - **$10 $25 $45**

❑ **WFA-10. Sesquicentennial Cello. Button,**
1926. Mostly red, white and blue with bronze image of bell, 1-1/4". - **$10 $20 $30**

**WFA-11**

**WFA-12**

❑ **WFA-11. Sky Ride Promo ,**
1933. Chicago World's Fair premium came with Frank Buck Club material. - **$25 $50 $75**

❑ **WFA-12. Puzzle - Boxed ,**
1933. Chicago World's Fair 11x16" puzzle sold at Fair. - **$15 $30 $60**

WFA-13

❑ **WFA-13. Notebook and Pen ,**
1934. Chicago World's Fair premium from the Curtiss Candy Co. - **$20 $40 $60**
Mailer - **$10 $20 $30**

WFA-14

WFA-15

❑ **WFA-14. Salt And Pepper Shakers ,**
1934. Chicago World's Fair - Hall of Science pictured on each shaker. Sold at Fair. - **$20 $40 $60**

❑ **WFA-15. "Sears, Roebuck & Co." Chicago World's Fair Key Holder,**
1933. Cello. and brass 3" key case dated for opening year of the fair. - **$25 $50 $75**

WFA-16

WFA-17

WFA-18

❑ **WFA-16. New York World's Fair Enameled Brass Star Badge,**
1939. Souvenir issue for youthful "Safety Monitor." - **$60 $140 $200**

❑ **WFA-17. New York World's Fair "Westinghouse" Robot Pin,**
1939. Diecut thin brass figural pin of Robot Elektro giant mechanical man of Westinghouse Exhibit. - **$10 $20 $40**

❑ **WFA-18. New York World's Fair "Westinghouse" Robot Cello. Button,**
1939. Images of robot and robot dog "Elektro And Sparko." - **$30 $75 $125**

WFA-19

❑ **WFA-19. New York World's Fair Posterette,**
1939. 7x10-1/2" issued by Grinnell Litho Company. - **$25 $65 $110**

WFA-20

WFA-21

❑ **WFA-20. New York World's Fair "Abbott & Costello" Cello. Button,**
1939. Nomination of Costello for mayor and Abbott for "Commissioner Of Laffs" of "World's Fair Midway." - **$35 $75 $150**

❑ **WFA-21. "Guernseys" New York World's Fair Cello. Button,**
1939. Blue, white and brown 1-1/4" believed from exhibit by Guernsey Breeders Assn. - **$15 $30 $65**

WFA-22

❑ **WFA-22. Penny Bracelet 1939,**
1939. Boxed. 14 KT gold plated. Sold at the World's Fair. - **$25 $50 $75**

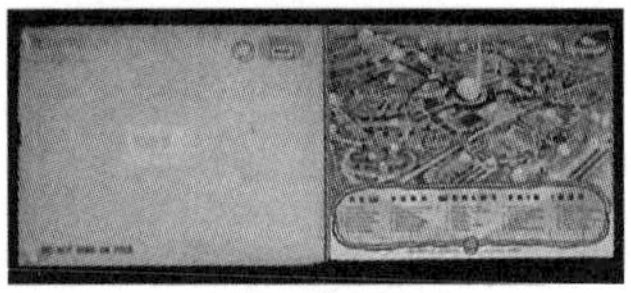

WFA-23

❑ **WFA-23. Jigsaw Puzzle Premium With Mailer,**
1939. Sloan's Liniment. 10-1/2x12-1/2" mailer holds 100-piece puzzle with color aerial view of the grounds identifying exhibit buildings by a numbered legend across the bottom.
Mailer - **$5 $10 $20**
Puzzle - **$20 $50 $75**

WFA-24

❑ **WFA-24. New York World's Fair Lunch Box And Bottle,**
1939. Store item by American Thermos Bottle Co. Both pieces are dark blue steel with the exposition logo in bright orange. The box was issued with a leather carrying strap.
Box - **$150 $250 $500**
Bottle - **$75 $150 $250**

WDY-25

❑ **WFA-25. "Today At The Fair" New York World's Fair Schedule Newspaper,** 1939. Daily edition #118 for Monday, August 28 with eight pages of either daily or continuous events. Back page includes photo of "Elektro," the seven-foot tall robot of Westinghouse exhibit. - **$25 $50 $75**

WFA-26

❑ **WFA-26. "Wonder Bread" New York World's Fair Sticker Signs,** 1939. 11x18" and 9" diameter full color signs gummed on front for store window application. Both include image of "Wonder Bakery" exhibit building.
Each - **$10 $25 $40**

WFA-27

WFA-28

❑ **WFA-27. Bike Product New York World's Fair Ad Poster,**
1939. New Departure Coaster Brake. Photo endorsement by Grover Whalen, fair director, on 16x25" poster. - **$25 $50 $75**

❑ **WFA-28. "108 World's Fair Recipes" Booklet,**
1939. Souvenir of Borden Exhibit of New York World's Fair with 32 pages of recipes and Elsie illustrations. - **$10 $25 $50**

**WFA-29**

**WFA-30**

❑ **WFA-29. "Either World's Fair" Contest Paper Poster,**
1939. 16x25" by unidentifed sponsor offering prize of free trips for boys and girls to either Golden Gate Exposition of San Francisco or New York World's Fair. - **$75 $150 $250**

❑ **WFA-30. New York World's Fair Clown Doll,**
1939. 15" tall wood and composition doll in orange and blue fabric outfit. - **$100 $250 $350**

**WFA-31**

❑ **WFA-31. Fabric Flag With Logo,**
1939. Linen-like fabric in orange and blue with logo in white, 11x16". - **$40 $90 $150**

**WFA-32**

❑ **WFA-32. Classic Die-Cut Sign,**
1939. 15"x19-1/2" sign features the skyline of New York City and the Golden Gate Bridge. Issued by Colgate-Palmolive Co. Promotes the "Golden Gate International" and "World of Tomorrow" Worlds' Fairs. Rare . - **$150 $250 $350**

**WFA-33**

❑ **WFA-33. "Boys' Life" Cover Article,**
1940. May issue with article "Scout Camp At The World's Fair." - **$5 $15 $25**

**WFA-34**

❑ **WFA-34. NYWF Banking Employee Jacket,**
1940. Has bakelite-like plastic chest buttons with relief images of Trylon and Perisphere. - **$50 $100 $175**

**WFA-35**

❑ **WFA-35. New York World's Fair Closing Day Pennant,**
1940. 4x9" felt fabric inscribed for visit on final day October 27th. - **$10 $25 $50**

**WFA-36**

❑ **WFA-36. "Futurama" Exhibit Booklet From Second Season,**
1940. General Motors. 7x8k-1/4" with 24 pages of black and white photos showing "The World Of Tomorrow." - **$10 $25 $50**

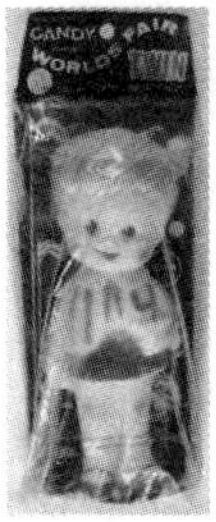


**WFA-37**

**WFA-38**

❑ **WFA-37. "Candy World's Fair Twin" Squeaker Doll,**
1964. 8-1/2" tall soft rubber made by Sun Rubber Co. Near Mint Packaged - **$150**
Loose - **$20 $40 $75**

❑ **WFA-38. New York World's Fair Flicker Ring,**
1964. Silvered plastic base topped by alternating image of Unisphere and souvenir text. - **$8 $12 $20**

**WFA-39**

**WFA-40**

❑ **WFA-39. Schaefer Center Sign,**
1964. Schaefer Beer. 15-1/2x18-1/2" full color stiff cardboard. - **$15 $30 $60**

❑ **WFA-40. Eastman Kodak Exhibit Glass,**
1964. Yellow and white images on 5-1/4" tall clear glass tumbler. - **$8 $15 $25**

**WFA-41**

❑ **WFA-41. "Sinclair Dinoland" Injection Molded Vinyl Dinosaur,**
1964. Sinclair Exhibit. From a series of at least six different, each about 5" to 9" long and produced in various single colors from a coin vending molding machine within the pavilion.
Each - **$10 $20 $30**

**WFA-42**

❑ **WFA-42. "World's Fair Twins" Kissing Bobbing Head Set,**
1965. Pair of composition symbolic twins with spring-mounted heads and inner magnet behind pursed lips. Boxed - **$50 $100 $200**
Loose - **$35 $70 $150**

## Wyatt Earp

**Legendary gunfighter and lawman Wyatt Earp (1848-1929) has been portrayed in at least two dozen Hollywood Westerns by such stars as George O'Brien, Randolph Scott, Richard Dix, Henry Fonda, Joel McCrea, Burt Lancaster and Kevin Costner. On television *The Life and Legend of Wyatt Earp* starred Hugh O'Brian in a serial drama that aired on ABC from 1955 to 1961. The series followed the romanticized adventures of Earp as a frontier marshal in Ellsworth and Dodge City, Kansas, and Tombstone, Arizona. Comic books appeared from 1955 on. Most licensed items came from the TV series and are copyrighted Wyatt Earp Ent. Inc.**

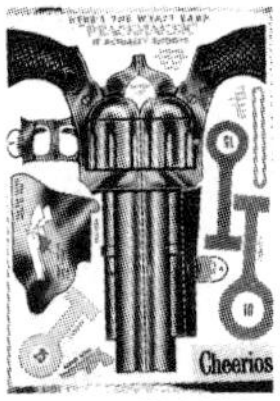


(FRONT) WYT-1 (BACK)

❑ **WYT-1. Cheerios Box,**
1955. Back panel has cut-out parts for "Peacemaker" gun on 10-1/2 oz. box; "Paterson" gun on 7 oz. box. A "Dragoon" gun was also issued. Each Complete Box - **$75 $200 $300**

WYT-2

❑ **WYT-2. "Buntline Special" Gun On Card,**
c. 1955. Store item. 6x20" card holds 18" long plastic clicker replica gun popularized on TV series.
Carded - **$75 $125 $250**
Uncarded Gun - **$50 $100 $175**

WYT-3

❑ **WYT-3. Response Postcard To Fan With Real Photo,**
1956. Example shown has autograph.
Signed - **$20 $40 $75**
Unsigned - **$5 $15 $25**

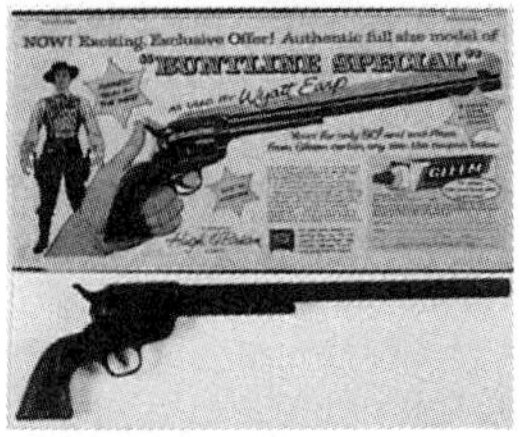


WYT-4

❑ **WYT-4. "Wyatt Earp Buntline Special" Plastic Pistol With Sunday Comic Ad Offer,**
1957. Gleem Toothpaste. 18" long black plastic clicker gun and newspaper ad dated February 3, 1957. Ad - **$5 $10 $15**
Gun - **$75 $150 $200**

WYT-5

❑ **WYT-5. Photo Puzzle,**
1958. Large puzzle of Hugh O'Brien as Wyatt Earp. - **$25 $50 $75**

WYT-6 WYT-7

❑ **WYT-6. "Marshal Wyatt Earp" Sterling Silver Initial Ring,**
1958. Cheerios. Engraved personal initial, TV show copyright. - **$40 $60 $80**

❑ **WYT-7. "Marshal Wyatt Earp" Metal Badge On Card,**
c. 1958. Store item.
On Card - **$15 $25 $40**
Loose - **$8 $10 $20**

WYT-8

❑ **WYT-8. "TV's Wyatt Earp" Hugh O'Brian Record Album,**
c. 1958. 33-1/3 rpm. - **$10 $20 $35**

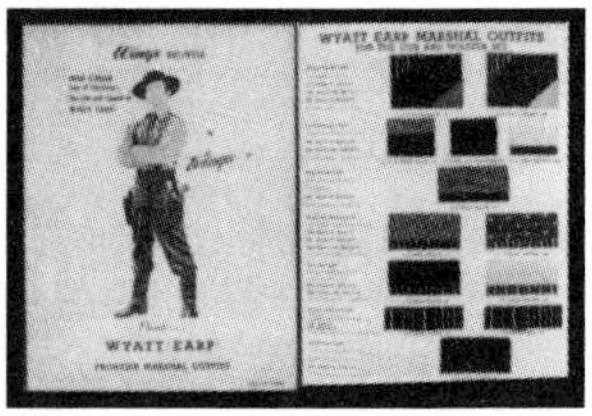


WYT-9

❑ **WYT-9. "Wyatt Earp Frontier Marshal Outfit" Fabric Selection Brochure,**
c. 1958. Issued by Wings Boyswear. 11x15" folder holds 34 different fabric swatches. - **$50 $100 $150**

WYT-10

WYT-11

❑ **WYT-10. TV Guide with "Wyatt Earp" Cover,**
1959. Hugh O'Brian featured. - **$10 $20 $45**

❑ **WYT-11. "Wyatt Earp" Pinback,**
1950s. Australian issue. Very colorful. - **$25 $50 $85**

## X-Men

**Stan Lee and Jack Kirby created the X-Men, a band of superpower teenage mutant fighters crusading for justice and the acceptance of mutants in an increasingly prejudiced society. Introduced in issue #1 of *X-Men* in 1963, Cyclops, The Angel, The Beast, and Marvel Girl joined with Professor X to foil the evil schemes of arch-enemy Magneto. The book was suspended briefly in 1970, then revived with reprints and, starting in 1975, new adventures and new characters were introduced, sparking a run that has proliferated into numerous other titles and a huge surge in popularity. Including Specials and Annuals, Marvel has published well over 300 *X-Men* comic books. An animated version debuted on the Fox Children's Network in 1992, and a live-action feature film opened in July, 2000.**

XMN-1

XMN-2

❑ **XMN-1. X-Men #1,**
Sept. 1963. Marvel Comics. Origin and first appearance of the X-Men. -
**$560 $1680 $10000**

❑ **XMN-2. Plastic Badge With Reverse Needle Post/Clutch,**
1988. Marvel. - **$2 $4 $6**

XMN-3

XMN-4

❑ **XMN-3. Gold Ring,**
1993. Diamond Comics Distribution seminar giveaway. 25 made. - **$750**

❑ **XMN-4. Silver Ring,**
1993. Diamond Comics Distribution seminar giveaway. - **$125**

(TOP) **XMN-5** (SIDE)

❑ **XMN-5. Xavier Institute Class Ring,**
1994. 10k gold. - **$400**
Sterling Silver Version - **$75**
Bronze Finished Pewter Version - **$20**

(FRONT) **XMN-6** (BACK)

❑ **XMN-6. "Berry Berry Kix" Cereal Box with X-Men Overpower Card Promotion,**
1995. Game offer on back. - **$2 $4 $10**

(FRONT) **XMN-7** (BACK)

❑ **XMN-7. "Cookie Crisp" Cereal Box with X-Men Trading Card Promotion,**
1994. Fleer trading card inside box and poster by Andy Kubert on back. - **$2 $4 $12**

**XMN-8**

**XMN-9**

❑ **XMN-8. Gambit and the Shadow King Book,**
1994. Has a hologram on the front cover. -
**$3 $8 $20**

❑ **XMN-9. Xavier Institute Class Ring,**
2000. 1,000 made. Sterling silver. Boxed - **$195**

**XMN-10**

❑ **XMN-10. Electronic X-Jet in Box,**
2000. From the movie. - **$40**

**XMN-11**

❑ **XMN-11. "Wolverine" in Debut Costume Mini-Bust,**
2000. Limited to 2,000. - **$85**

## The Yellow Kid

***The Yellow Kid,* created by Richard F. Outcault (1863-1925), is generally considered to be the first true comic strip. After appearances as a minor character in the *Hogan's Alley* gag panels in the *New York World* in 1895, the bald, jug-eared kid in a nightshirt grew in popularity and, by the beginning of 1896, his nightshirt was yellow. Although Outcault named him Mickey Dugan, readers referred to him as the yellow kid. William Randolph Hearst hired Outcault for his *New York Journal* later that year and titled his panels *McFadden's Flats*. Outcault dropped the strip in 1898 and went on to other work, but the Kid made licensing history in promoting a wide range of products such as chewing gum, candy, cookies, games, puzzles, cigarettes, soap, bicycles, highchairs, and whiskey.**

**YLW-1**

❑ **YLW-1. Yellow Kid And Lady 18x24" Paper Announcement Poster For New York Journal's Colored Sunday Supplement,**
1896. Scarce. Also reads "Wait For It-It Is Coming" including artists' names Archie Gunn and R. F. Outcault. - **$1500 $2500 $4500**

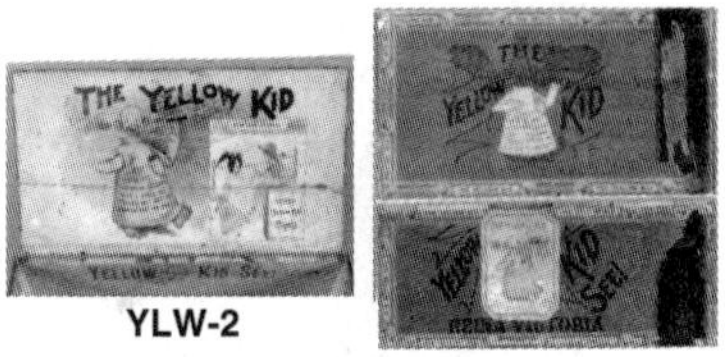

**YLW-2**

❑ **YLW-2. Wooden Cigar Box,**
1896. - **$200 $400 $750**

**YLW-3**

**YLW-4**

❑ **YLW-3. Advertising Card,**
1896. Sweet Wheat Chewing Gum. -
**$125 $225 $400**
Version without gum ad - **$100 $200 $300**

❑ **YLW-4. Gum Card #11 Example,**
1896. Adams' Yellow Kid Chewing Gum. Set of 25, two styles: small number or large number (see YLW-8.)
Small Numbers Each - **$15 $30 $75**

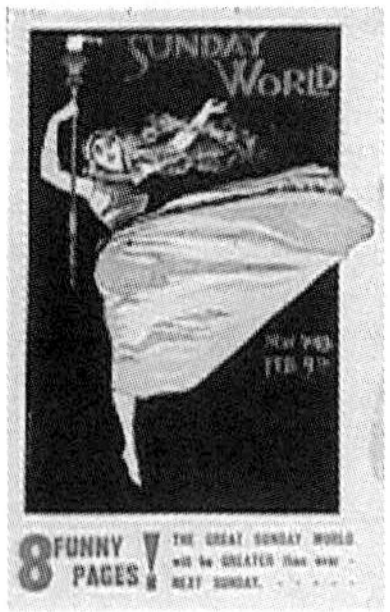


YLW-5

❑ **YLW-5. "Sunday World 8 Funny Pages!" Newspaper Advertising Poster,**
1896. 11x18-1/2" promoting the Sunday February 9th issue with facsimile signature of Outcault at lower left. A historic poster issued for what we believe was the first eight-page, color Sunday section. An unknown quantity of these were discovered about 1995. Over that time we've become aware of seven examples. - **$75 $150 $300**

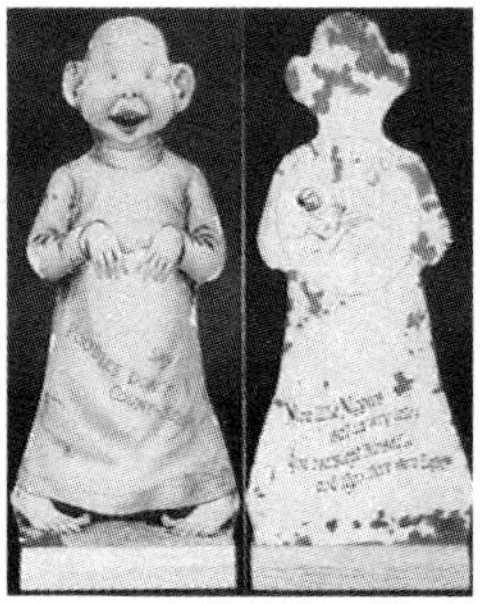

YLW-6

❑ **YLW-6. Diecut Wooden Target Figure,**
1896. Store item. 10-1/4" tall paper on wood part of a set. Each - **$125 $250 $500**

YLW-7

YLW-8

❑ **YLW-7. Soap Figure,**
c. 1896. Store item by D. S. Brown & Co.
Near Mint Boxed - **$500**
Loose - **$100 $200 $300**

❑ **YLW-8. Gum Cards #6 and #21,**
1896. Adams' Yellow Kid Chewing Gum. Examples from set of 25 with large numbers. Each - **$15 $30 $75**

YLW-9

YLW-10

YLW-11

❑ **YLW-9. Yellow Kid First Button In Set,**
1896. High Admiral cigarettes. The first 39 buttons in the set are the most frequently found. Each - **$15 $30 $50**

❑ **YLW-10. Cello. Button #35,**
1896. Buttons #40-94 become scarcer as the button number becomes higher. #90-94 are the scarcest. #95-100 were never issued. - **$35 $50 $85**

❑ **YLW-11. Yellow Kid With Various Flags Cello. Button,**
1896. High Admiral Cigarette. Buttons numbered 101-160 depict him holding some type of flag, usually with the name of a country. Each - **$30 $50 $85**

YLW-12

YLW-13

❑ **YLW-12. Theatrical Production Cello. Button,**
1896. - **$20 $40 $75**

❑ **YLW-13. Yellow Kid For President McKinley Enameled Brass Lapel Stud,**
1896. Small figure inscribed "Hogan's Alley Is Out Fer McKinley". - **$125 $400 $750**

YLW-14

❑ **YLW-14. "The Latest And The Greatest" Sheet Music Clipping From Newspaper,**
c. 1896. Rare. - **$75 $250 $500**

YLW-15

YLW-16

❑ **YLW-15. "The Original Yell-er Kid" Cello. Button,**
c. 1896. - **$150 $350 $600**

❑ **YLW-16. Miniature Painted White Metal Figure Stickpin,**
c. 1896. - **$25 $60 $100**

YLW-17

YLW-18

YLW-19

❑ **YLW-17. Pewter Candy Mold,**
c. 1896. - **$50 $100 $175**

❑ **YLW-18. Trade Card,**
c. 1896. Various advertisers. - **$30 $60 $125**

❑ **YLW-19. Chocolate Ad Paper Bookmark,**
c. 1896. Hawley & Hoops Breakfast Cocoa. Pictured are penny chocolate pieces in figural images including Yellow Kid. - **$20 $60 $125**

YLW-20

❑ **YLW-20. Toy Sand Pail,**
1896. 3-1/2" tall by 4-1/2" diameter full color litho tin including four perimeter cartoon images copyright by R. F. Outcault. - **$600 $1200 $2400**

YLW-21

❑ **YLW-21. Flip Movie Book,**
1897. Has copyright by H. H. Willc. 1-1/2x2-1/4" with 84 pages printed on one side in black and white with his nightshirt in yellow against black background. Color page reads "Living Photograph Draw Thumb Over Top Edge And Pictures Appear As Alive." - **$125 $250 $400**

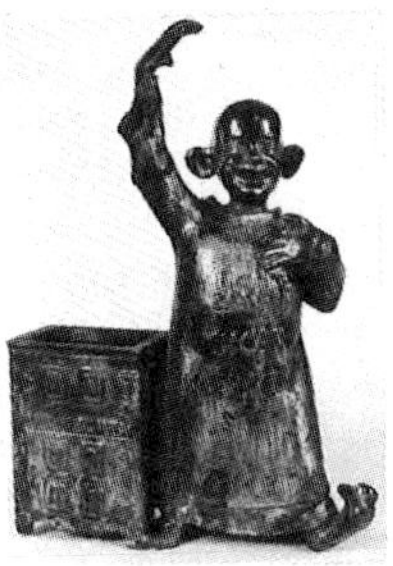

YLW-22

❑ **YLW-22. Advertising Figure With Refrigerator White Metal Match Holder,**
c. 1898. Ranny-Refrigerator Co., Greenville, Mich. 1-3/4x4-3/4x6-1/2" tall heavy metal with brass luster. Text on shirt says "Say! Now I Can Keep Cool See." Front of refrigerator has additional product text. - **$250 $500 $800**

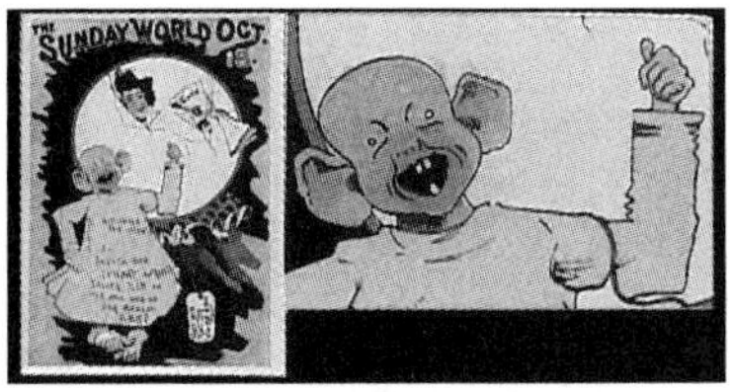

YLW-23

❑ **YLW-23. "The Sunday World Oct. 18" Newspaper Poster,**
1890s. 12x16" with color portrait of Yellow Kid along with his dialogue promoting himself as the original Yellow Kid. Unsigned but art is probably by George Luks. At this time Outcault was drawing the Yellow Kid for the New York Journal. - **$500 $1000 $2500**

YLW-24

❑ **YLW-24. "The Burr McIntosh-Monthly" Magazine With Yellow Kid As William Jennings Bryan,**
1904. January issue, Vol. 3 #10. Shows Yellow Kid as William Jennings Bryan about to throw snowball at snowman of smiling Theodore Roosevelt in front of White House. - **$25 $50 $100**

YLW-25

❑ **YLW-25. Ad Printing Blocks in Box,**
1910. Box with four blocks & four ad flyers. -
Box - **$40 $60 $80**
Each Block - **$50 $100 $150**
Each Ad - **$10 $20 $30**

YLW-26

YLW-27

❑ **YLW-26. Cigarette Giveaway Button With Art By Tad,**
c. 1912. Has back paper from either Hassen cigarette or Tokio cigarette. One of the scarcest buttons in the "I'm The Guy" series. - **$25 $50 $100**

❑ **YLW-27. Calendar Postcard,**
January 1914. Various advertisers. Series of monthly calendar cards with 1911 Outcault copyright. Each - **$35 $70 $125**

YLW-28

❑ **YLW-28. Ink Blotter,**
Early 1900s. Rare. - **$75 $200 $300**

YLW-29

❑ **YLW-29. "Big Bubble Chewing Gum" Cello. Button,**
c. 1930. Full inscription "There Is Only One Yellow Kid Big Bubble Chewing Gum". - **$25 $50 $85**

(ENLARGED VIEW)

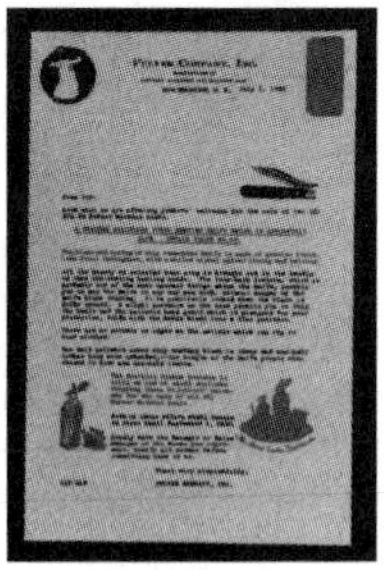

YLW-30

❑ **YLW-30. Pulver Gum Co. With Yellow Kid Logo,**
1930. 8-1/2x13" stationery sheet with typewritten message dated July 1 to Pulver salesmen offering prizes for sale of gum machines. Yellow Kid symbol is upper left. - **$15 $30 $50**

YLW-31

❑ **YLW-31. "Confectioner's Machinery And Tools" Catalogue,**
1930. Pictures candy molds and shapers including one with Yellow Kid candy pattern. Thos. Mills & Brothers. - **$20 $40 $75**

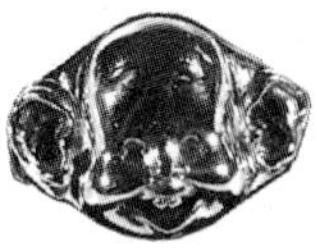

YLW-32

❑ **YLW-32. Richard Outcault's Yellow Kid Bronze Statue, Collectors' Ring & Lithograph,**
1995. Sculpted and produced by Randy Bowen. Limited edition of 100. The ring is complete with blue stones for eyes and fully articulated ears.
Complete - **$2000**
Ring only - **$800**
Lithograph - **$200**

YLW-33

❑ **YLW-33. Richard Outcault's Yellow Kid Gold Edition Statue,**
1995. Sculpted and produced by Randy Bowen. Limited edition of 25. Gold is 23 kt. Comes with a framed limited edition print.
Complete - **$3500**

## Yogi Bear

**Hanna-Barbera's Yogi Bear, a TV cartoon and merchandising superstar, was introduced in 1959 on *The Huckleberry Hound Show* and two years later was starring in his own series. The genial bear in a pork-pie hat, trailed by his diminutive pal Boo Boo, spent his time panhandling and swiping picnic baskets from visitors to Jellystone Park. Yogi's love interest was Cindy Bear (Ah do declare!). *The Yogi Bear Show* was syndicated from 1961 to 1963, sponsored by Kellogg cereals; *Yogi's Gang* with Yogi leaving the Park to crusade for the environment, was broadcast on ABC from 1973 to 1975; and *Yogi's Space Race* appeared on NBC from 1978 to 1979. Yogi has also appeared teamed with other Hanna-Barbera characters and in several TV specials. Yogi comic books began publication in 1959. His popularity continues to this day. Items are normally copyrighted Hanna-Barbera Productions.**

YOG-1

YOG-2

❑ **YOG-1. Vinyl And Plush Doll,**
1960. Store item and Kellogg's premium. 19" tall. - **$20 $50 $75**

❑ **YOG-2. Ceramic Figurine,**
c. 1960. Store item. - **$20 $40 $75**

YOG-3

YOG-4

❑ **YOG-3. "Hey There, It's Yogi Bear" Litho. Button,**
c. 1960. - **$10 $20 $35**

❑ **YOG-4. Plastic Bank,**
c. 1960. Store item by Knickerbocker. - **$20 $30 $50**

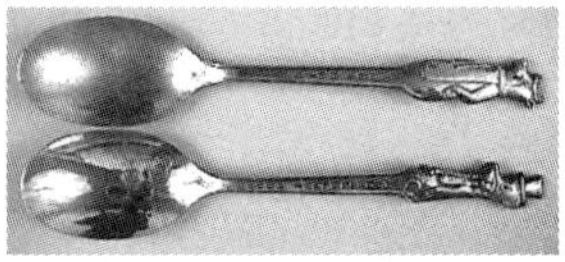

YOG-5

❑ **YOG-5. Cereal Spoon Set,**
1960. Kellogg's. Available for 50 cents and two box tops. Each - **$3 $8 $15**

YOG-6

YOG-7

❑ **YOG-6. "Yogi's Mystery Message De-Coder" Newspaper Ad,**
1961. Kellogg's. Ad pictures cereal box and describes cut-out mechanical de-coder printed on box back.
Used Complete Box - **$60 $150 $250**
Assembled Decoder - **$15 $40 $75**
Advertisement - **$1 $2 $3**

❑ **YOG-7. Huck And Yogi Sweater Pins,**
1962. Kellogg's. Silver luster figures are joined by a chain and were advertised as "Pin-Mates" on the cereal box. - **$10 $20 $30**

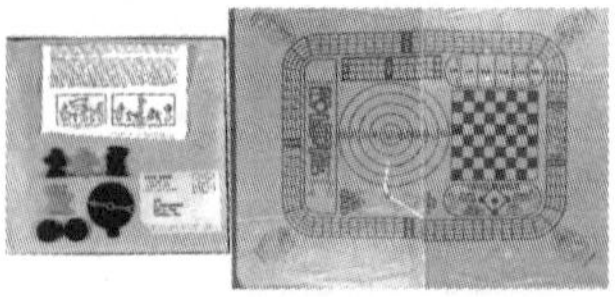

YOG-8

❑ **YOG-8. Yogi Bear Game Cloth,**
1962. Kellogg's Corn Flakes. 35x45" vinyl sheet; markers of Yogi, Huck, Quick Draw, Mr. Jinks; spinner; instructions; 24 red or black checkers picturing Yogi or Huck.
Near Mint In Mailer - **$50**
Complete/Loose - **$10 $20 $35**

YOG-9

❑ **YOG-9. Cereal Box With Printing Press Premium Offer,**
1963. Gordon Gold Archives.
Used Complete - **$100 $250 $375**

YOG-10

❑ **YOG-10. Movie Associated Premium Record,**
1964. Kellogg's. Features music and story from the feature length movie "Hey There It's Yogi Bear!" Came in illustrated mailer.
Mailer - **$5 $10 $15**
Record Jacket - **$5 $10 $15**
Record - **$5 $10 $15**

YOG-11

YOG-12

❑ **YOG-11. "Yogi Bear For President" Litho. Button,**
1964. Hanna-Barbera copyright. Comes in 2-1/4" or 3-1/2" size. Small - **$20 $30 $65**
Large - **$25 $35 $75**

❑ **YOG-12. "Yogi Bear For President" 3" Litho. Button,**
1964. - **$15 $30 $65**

YOG-13

YOG-14

❑ **YOG-13. Purex Bottle Bank With Wrapper,**
1967. Near Mint With Wrapper - **$75**
Bottle Only - **$15 $30 $55**

❑ **YOG-14. "Yogi Bear's Honey Fried Chicken" Restaurant Punch-Out Puzzle,**
c. 1969. - **$5 $10 $15**

YOG-15

YOG-16

❑ **YOG-15. Stamped Image Plastic Ring,**
1960s. Unknown sponsor. Hanna-Barbera copyright. - **$15 $40 $75**

❑ **YOG-16. Newspaper Strip Promotion Cello. Button,**
1960s. Sunday Tribune, possibly Chicago. - **$20 $50 $90**

YOG-17

❑ **YOG-17. "Yogi Bear" Vinyl Lunch Box,**
1960s. Store item. - **$125 $300 $600**

YOG-18

❑ **YOG-18. Yogi Bear Hat,**
1960s. Kellogg's premium. - **$20 $30 $40**

YOG-19

YOG-20

❑ **YOG-19. Yogi Bear Cereal Box,**
1960s. - **$100 $250 $375**

❑ **YOG-20. "Procter & Gamble Dividend Day '85" 2-1/4" Cello. Button,**
1985. Used by employees at amusement park outing. - **$5 $10 $20**

YOG-21

YOG-22

❑ **YOG-21. Yogi Bear Bean Bag with Tag,**
1999. - **$10**

❑ **YOG-22. Yogi Bear Plush on Card,**
1999. With Cartoon Network tag. - **$2 $4 $10**

## Young Forty-Niners

**Colgate's Ribbon Dental Cream sponsored this radio serial in the early 1930s, relating adventures in the California Gold Rush of 1849. Premiums included a map of the gold territory and punch-out versions of an Indian encampment and a wagon train. The program was apparently broadcast only regionally.**

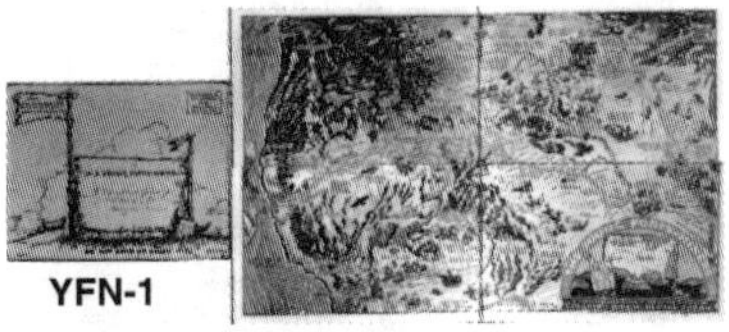

YFN-1

❑ **YFN-1. United States Adventure Map With Envelope,**
c. 1932. Colgate-Palmolive-Peet. Map opens to 20x31". Envelope - **$10 $25 $30**
Map - **$40 $125 $200**

YFN-2

YFN-3

❑ **YFN-2. Capt. Sam's Wagon Cardboard Punch-Out Folder,**
c. 1932. Rare. Colgate-Palmolive-Peet. Sheet opens to 19x37". Unpunched - **$60 $150 $225**

❑ **YFN-3. Indian Village,**
c. 1932. Rare. Colgate-Palmolive-Peet. Sheet opens to 19"x37". Unpunched - **$60 $150 $225**

## Zorro

**Don Diego de la Vega, alter ego of Zorro, the fox, was created by author Johnston McCulley in serialized magazine stories around 1919. In the tradition of *The Scarlet Pimpernel*, Don Diego posed as an effete dandy until it was time to defend the oppressed; then out came the black cape, mask, and sword. Zorro has a long film history, ranging from the 1920 silent *The Mark of Zorro*, starring Douglas Fairbanks Sr., to the 1981 spoof *Zorro, the Gay Blade,* with George Hamilton (and George Hamilton; it was a dual role). On television Guy Williams played the flashy 19th century fencer in the popular Disney series that aired on ABC from 1957 to 1959. Some 24 years later Disney produced a comic version, *Zorro and Son,* that lasted less than two months on CBS in 1983. Zorro comic books appeared from 1949 to 1961, 1966 to 1968, and 1990-1991. The original TV series generated a wide variety of related merchandise, copyrighted by Walt Disney Productions. A new 1998 feature film, *The Mask of Zorro*, starred Antonio Banderas as the masked avenger, with Anthony Hopkins as his swash-buckling predecessor.**

ZOR-1

ZOR-2

ZOR-3

❑ **ZOR-1. "Don Q/Son Of Zorro" Cello. Button,**
1925. Pictures movie title star Douglas Fairbanks, Sr. - **$60 $150 $275**

❑ **ZOR-2. 7up Litho. Ad Button,**
1957. 1-3/8" size. The 1-1/8" litho. variety appeared about 1990. Unsure if reproduction or quantity find-it is extremely common.
1-3/8" Size - **$8 $15 $30**
1-1/8" Size - **$1 $2 $3**

❑ **ZOR-3. 7up Litho. Tin Advertising Tab,**
1957. Also marked "ABC/TV". - **$12 $25 $60**

ZOR-4

ZOR-5

❑ **ZOR-4. Cardboard Matchbook,**
1957. 7up. Top edge of pack reads "2 New Hits!" Complete - **$10 $20 $30**
Used - **$5 $10 $15**

❑ **ZOR-5. "Zorro Candy And Toy" Box,**
c. 1958. Store item by Super Novelty Candy Co. From a series with different black and white comic panel stories on reverse.
Each - **$15 $30 $60**

ZOR-6

ZOR-7

❑ **ZOR-6. T.V. Promo Pinback,**
1958. 3-1/2". - **$10 $25 $60**

❑ **ZOR-7. Walt Disney Magazine,**
1958. Vol III, #6. Features a photo cover of Guy Williams as Zorro. - **$15 $50 $75**

ZOR-8

ZOR-9

❑ **ZOR-8. Fan Postcard,**
c. 1958. - **$10 $15 $30**

❑ **ZOR-9. Plastic Boot Mug,**
c. 1958. Store item. - **$20 $50 $75**

ZOR-10

❑ **ZOR-10.Daisy Rifle,**
c. 1958. 25" long pressed steel with wood stock. Produces "pop" sound. - **$100 $200 $300**

ZOR-11

ZOR-12

❑ **ZOR-11. TV Station Litho. Tin Tab,**
c. 1958. - **$15 $25 $60**

❑ **ZOR-12. "Zorro Candy" Display Box,**
c. 1958. Super Novelty Candy Co. Held multiple packages. - **$50 $100 $175**

ZOR-13

❑ **ZOR-13."Zorro" Figurine With Tag,**
c. 1958. Store item by Enesco. 5-3/4" tall glazed ceramic. - **$50 $125 $200**

ZOR-14

❑ **ZOR-14. "Walt Disney's Zorro" Jigsaw Puzzle,**
1958. Jaymar product in box. - **$20 $40 $80**

ZOR-15

ZOR-16

❑ **ZOR-15. Paper 23x36" Dry Cleaning Bag Cut-Out Costume,**
1950s. Various sponsors. - **$20 $30 $50**

❑ **ZOR-16. "Official Ring" Ad Paper,**
1950s. - **$20 $30 $40**

ZOR-17

ZOR-18

ZOR-19

❑ **ZOR-17. Plastic Ring,**
1950s. Silver band with black top and name in gold. - **$15 $30 $50**

❑ **ZOR-18. Plastic Ring,**
1950s. Entirely black except name in gold. - **$15 $30 $50**

❑ **ZOR-19. English Plastic Lapel Stud,**
1950s. Quaker Puffed Wheat. - **$20 $40 $75**

ZOR-20

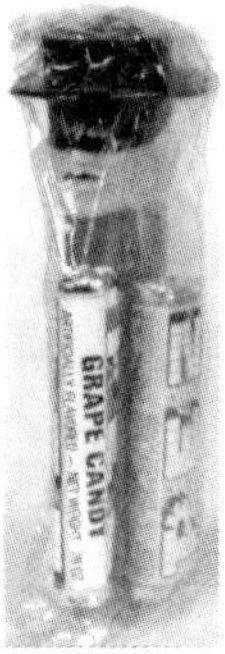


ZOR-21

❑ **ZOR-20. U.S. Time Boxed Wristwatch,**
1950s. Store item. Box - **$50 $100 $200**
Watch (Not Shown) - **$50 $100 $200**

❑ **ZOR-21. Sealed Pez Dispenser,**
1960s. Variety with red stem and "Pez" logo plus mask going straight over nose.
Near Mint Sealed - **$150**

ZOR-22

❑ **ZOR-22. Hat with Mask,**
1960s. Store item. - **$30 $60 $85**

ZOR-23

ZOR-24

❑ **ZOR-23. Zorro Hand Puppet,**
1987. High quality from France. - **$25 $50 $75**

❑ **ZOR-24. Zorro #0 Premium Comic**
1993. - **$2**

ZOR-25

❑ **ZOR-25. Zorro #1 Preview Edition**
1993. - **$2**

ZOR-26

❑ **ZOR-26. Don Diego Zorro Figure on Card,**
1997. With Slashing Sword Action. - **$10**

ZOR-27

ZOR-28

❑ **ZOR-27. Classic Zorro Figure on Card,**
1997. With Slashing Sword Action. - **$10**

❑ **ZOR-28. Cold Steel Zorro Figure on Card,**
1997. With 3 daggers. - **$10**

ZOR-29

❑ **ZOR-29. Barbed Wire Zorro Figure on Card,**
1997. With Punishing Punching Action. - **$10**

ZOR-30

❑ **ZOR-30. Chain Mail Zorro Figure on Card,**
1997. With Whip Cracking Action. - **$10**

ZOR-31

❑ **ZOR-31. Evil Machete Figure on Card,**
1997. With Spring-Fired Arrow Action. - **$10**

ZOR-32

❑ **ZOR-32. Evil Ramon Figure on Card,**
1997. With Slashing Sword Action. - **$10**

ZOR-33

❑ **ZOR-33. Zorro & Tornado Figure Set,**
1997. - **$20**

This index covers the subject histories and listed items in all category sections. Actual people are entered alphabetically by last name. All other entries are alphabetical by the first word, disregarding articles A, An, and The.

## A



## B

## C

## G

## H

## M

## T

## U

## ADVERTISERS' DIRECTORY

Aikins, Larry. *Pictorial Price Guide to Metal Lunch Boxes & Thermoses.* Gas City, IN: L-W Book Sales, 1999.
Aikins, Larry. *Pictorial Price Guide to Vinyl & Plastic Lunch Boxes & Thermoses.* Gas City, IN: L-W Book Sales, 1992.
Bordman, Gerald. *American Musical Theatre.* New York: Oxford University Press, 1978.
Brooks, Tim & Marsh, Earle. *The Complete Directory to Prime Time Network TV Shows.* 3rd ed. NY: Ballantine Books, 1985.
Brown, Hy. *Comic Character Timepieces: Seven Decades of Memories.* West Chester, PA: Schiffer Publishing, Ltd. 1992.
Bruce, Scott. *Cereal Box Bonanza: The 1950s.* Paducah, KY: Collector Books, 1995.
Bruce, Scott. *Cereal Boxes & Prizes 1960s.* Cambridge, MA: Flake World Publishing, 1998.
Bruce, Scott & Crawford, Bill. *Cerealizing America.* Boston: Faber & Faber, 1995.
Bruce, Scott. *Flake: The Breakfast Nostalgia Magazine.* Cambridge, MA: 1990-1995.
Bruegman, Bill. *The Aurora History and Price Guide.* Akron, OH: Cap'n Penny Productions, 1992.
Claggett, Tom, ed. *The Premium Exchange*. St. Clair Shores, MI: December 1976-January 1978.
Davis, Stephen. *Say Kids! What Time Is It? Notes From The Peanut Gallery.* Boston: Little, Brown and Company, 1987.
Dinan, John A. *The Pulp Western.* San Bernardino, CA: Borgo Press, 1983.
Douglas, George H. *The Early Days of Radio Broadcasting.* Jefferson, NC: McFarland & Co., 1987.
Dunning, John. *Tune in Yesterday.* Englewood Cliffs, NJ: Prentice-Hall, 1976.
Erickson, Hal. *Television Cartoon Shows: An Illustrated Encyclopedia 1949 Through 1993.* Jefferson, NC: McFarland & Co., 1995.
Fenin, George N. & Everson, William K. *The Western.* New York: Orion Press, 1962.
Fischer, Stuart. *Kids' TV: The First 25 Years.* New York: Facts on File, 1983.
Geissman, Grant. *Collectibly Mad: The Mad And EC Collectibles Guide.* Northhampton, MA: Kitchen Sink Press, 1995.
Goulart, Ron. *Cheap Thrills.* New Rochelle, NY: Arlington House, 1972.
Goulart, Ron, ed. *Encyclopedia of American Comics.* New York: Facts on File, 1990.
Goulart, Ron. *Great History of Comic Books.* Chicago: Contemporary Books, 1986.
Grossman, Gary H. *Saturday Morning TV.* New York: Dell, 1981.
Hake, Ted. *Hake's Americana & Collectibles Auction Catalogues Nos. 17-164.* York, PA: 1971-2001.
Hake, Ted. *Hake's Guide to Advertising Collectibles.* Radnor, PA: Wallace-Homestead, 1992.
Hake, Ted. *Hake's Guide to Comic Character Collectibles.* Radnor, PA: Wallace-Homestead, 1993.
Hake, Ted. *Hake's Guide to Cowboy Character Collectibles.* Radnor, PA: Wallace-Homestead, 1994.
Hake, Ted. *Hake's Guide to TV Collectibles.* Radnor, PA: Wallace-Homestead, 1990.
Hake, Ted & King, Russell. *Collectible Pin-Back Buttons 1896-1986.* Radnor PA: Wallace-Homestead, 1991.
Halliwell, Leslie. *Halliwell's Film Guide.* 7th ed. New York: Harper & Row, 1990.
Hamilton, Bruce, ed. *Mickey Mouse in Color*. New York: Another Rainbow. 1988.
Heide, Robert & Gilman, John. *Cartoon Collectibles.* Garden City, NY: Doubleday, 1983.
Hickerson, Jay. *The Ultimate History of Network Radio Programming and Guide to All Circulating Shows.* 2nd ed. Hamden, CT: Presto Print II, 1992.
Hirschhorn, Clive. *The Warner Bros. Story.* New York: Crown, 1979.
Horn, Maurice, ed. *The World Encyclopedia of Comics.* New York: Avon Books, 1977.
Inman, David. *The TV Encyclopedia.* New York: Putnam, 1991.
Jacobs, Larry. *Big Little Books: A Collector's Reference & Value Guide.* Paducah, KY: Collector Books, 1996.
Keaton, Russell. *The Aviation Art of Russell Keaton.* Northampton, MA: Kitchen Sink Press, 1995.
Lenburg, Jeff. *The Encyclopedia of Animated Cartoon Series.* Westport, CT: Arlington House, 1981.
Levin, Marshall N. and Hake, Theodore L. *Buttons In Sets 1896-1972.* York PA: Hake's Americana & Collectibles Press, 1984.
Maltin, Leonard. *Of Mice and Magic.* New York: McGraw-Hill, 1980.
Maltin, Leonard. *TV Movies and Video Guide.* 1991 ed. New York: Penguin, 1990.
Mandelowitz, Hy. *The Premium Guide.* New York: November 1977-August 1979.
Matetsky, Amanda Murrah. *The Adventures Of Superman Collecting.* West Plains, MO: Russ Cochran, Ltd., 1988.
Melcher, Jack, ed. *Radio Premium Collectors Newsletter.* Waukegan, IL: January 1973-September 1975.
Miller, Francis. *Lindbergh–His Story in Pictures*. New York: Knickerbocker Press, 1929.
Milne, Tom and Willeman, Paul. *The Encyclopedia of Horror Movies.* New York: Harper & Row, Publishers, 1986.
Mix, Paul E. *The Life and Legend of Tom Mix.* South Brunswick & NY: A.S. Barnes, 1972.
Morgan, Hal. *Symbols of America.* New York: Viking Penguin, 1986.
Moskowitz, Milton, Levering, Robert & Katz, Michael. *Everybody's Business.* New York: Doubleday, 1990.
Murray, John J. & Bruce R. Fox. *The Fisher-Price 1931-1963 Toy Book*. Florence, AL: Books Americana, 1996. 3rd Edition.
Norris, M.G. "Bud." *The Tom Mix Book.* Waynesville, NC: The World Of Yesterday, 1989.
O'Brien, Richard. *Collecting Toys No. 8.* Florence, AL: Books Americana, 1997.
Olson, Richard D., ed. *Little Orphan Annie Reader.* New Orleans, LA: 1979-1980.
Olson, Richard D., ed. *The R.F. Outcault Reader: The Official Newsletter Of The R.F. Outcault Society.* Slidell, LA:1993.
Overstreet, Robert M. *The Overstreet Comic Book Price Guide.* 31st ed. Timonium, MD: Gemstone Publishing, Inc. 2001.
Overstreet, Robert M. *The Overstreet Toy Ring Price Guide.* 3rd ed. Timonium, MD: Gemstone Publishing, Inc. 1997.
Paquin, Mike. "Put on a 'Funny Face,'" *Collecting Figures*, pp. 74-75, June, 1995.
Penzler, Otto, Steinbrunner, Chris & Lachman, Marvin, eds. *Detectionary.* Woodstock, N.: Overlook Press, 1977.
Pinsky, Maxine A. *Marx Toys: Robots, Space, Comic, Disney & TV Characters.* Atglen, PA: Schiffer Publishing, 1996.
Rinker, Harry L. *Hopalong Cassidy King Of The Cowboy Merchandisers.* Atglen, PA: Schiffer Publishing, Ltd., 1995.
Santelmo, Vincent. *The Official 30th Anniversary Salute To GI Joe 1964-1994.* Iola, WI: Krause Publications, 1994.
Sarno, Joe, ed. *Space Academy Newsletter.* Chicago: July 1978-October, 1981.
Scarfone, Jay and Stillman, William. *The Wizard of Oz Collector's Treasury.* West Chester, PA: Schiffer Publishing, Ltd. 1992.
Selitzer, Ralph. *The Dairy Industry in America.* New York: Magazines for Industry, 1976.
Smilgis, Joel, ed. *Box Top Bonanza.* Moline, IL: December 1983-No. 49, 1991.
Stedman, Raymond William. *The Serials.* 2nd ed. Norman, OK: University of Oklahoma Press, 1977.
Swartz, Jon D. & Reinehr, Robert C. *Handbook of Old-Time Radio.* Metuchen, NJ: Scarecrow Press, 1993.
Terrace, Vincent. *Radio's Golden Years.* San Diego, CA: A.S. Barnes, 1981.
Thompson, Steve. *The Walt Kelly Collector's Guide: A Bibliography and Price Guide.* Richfield, MN: Spring Hollow Books.
Tumbusch, Tom. *Tomart's Price Guide to Radio Premium and Cereal Box Collectibles.* Dayton, OH: Tomart Publications, 1991.
Weiss, Ken & Goodgold, ed. *To Be Continued....* New York: Bonanza Books, 1972.
White, Larry. *Cracker Jack Toys.* Atglen, PA: Schiffer Publishing, Ltd. 1997.
Woolery, George W. *Animated TV Specials*. Metuchen, NJ: Scarecrow Press, 1989.
Woolery, George W. *Children's Television: The First Thirty-Five Years, 1946-1981. Part I.* Metuchen, NJ: Scarecrow Press, 1983.
Woolery, George W. *Children's Television: The First Thirty-Five Years, 1946-1981. Part II.* Metuchen, NJ: Scarecrow Press, 1985.

# COLOR gallery

# PRESIDENT'S NOTE

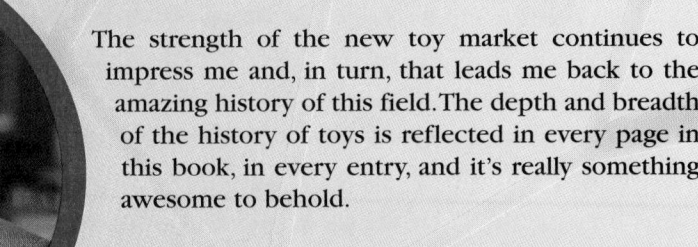

The strength of the new toy market continues to impress me and, in turn, that leads me back to the amazing history of this field.The depth and breadth of the history of toys is reflected in every page in this book, in every entry, and it's really something awesome to behold.

I've seen first-hand the phenomenal growth in comic character collectibles over the past few years. It's hard to watch that kind of growth and not wonder increasingly about where it came from-how it all came about.That's what's so great, if you'll indulge my pride, about this book. Once again there are literally thousands of new items listed in this volume.Through the process of documenting them and updating our previous listings (no small undertaking!), we are truly exploring the history of popular culture.The items and the characters they represent include those most sought-after in terms of both importance and collectability, and they help define specific moments in our personal and shared experiences.

Ted Hake, his staff, and our staff at Gemstone Publishing have outdone themselves in researching and updating every item in this book. Done correctly, it's an incredibly painstaking process...and believe me,Ted has done it correctly. Nowhere is this more manifest than in our biggest, most breathtaking, new color section yet.You'll see a spectacular mix of new and old, and in these amazing images you'll see a veritable cross-section of toy history.

Please write to us and let us know what you think. Our hobby works best when everyone participates!

Sincerely,

Stephen A. Geppi

Stephen A. Geppi
President and
Chief Executive Officer

5¢
IN THE COMICS · BUCK ROGERS ON THE RADIO · AT THE MOVIES
Popsicle
REFRESHING
SAVE BAGS—ASK FOR GIFT LIST

**BRG-126**
**Diecut Standup of Buck and Wilma**
**1939**

# ARMAGEDDON – 2419 A.D.

*By Philip Francis Nowlan*

**Foreword**

ELSEWHERE I have set down, for whatever interest they have in this, the 25th Century, my personal recollections of the 20th Century.

Now it occurs to me that my memoirs of the 25th Century may have an equal interest 500 years from now—particularly in view of that unique perspective from which I have seen the 25th Century, entering it as I did, in one leap across a gap of 492 years.

This statement requires elucidation. There are still many in the world who are not familiar with my unique experience. Five centuries from now there may be many more, especially if civilization is fated to endure any worse convulsions than those which have occurred between 1975 A.D. and the present time.

I should state therefore, that I, Anthony Rogers, am, so far as I know, the only man alive whose normal span of eighty-one years of life has been spread over a period of 573 years. To be precise, I lived the first twenty-nine years of my life between 1898 and 1927; the other fifty-two since 2419. The gap between these two, a period of nearly five hundred years, I spent in a state of suspended animation, free from the ravages of katabolic processes, and without any apparent effect on my physical or mental faculties.

When I began my long sleep, man had just begun his real conquest of the air in a sudden series of transoceanic flights in airplanes driven by internal combustion motors. He had barely begun to speculate on the possibilities of harnessing sub-atomic forces, and had made no further practical penetration into the field of ethereal pulsations than the primitive radio and television of that day. The United States of America was the most powerful nation in the world, its political, financial, industrial and scientific influence being supreme; and in the arts also it was rapidly climbing into leadership.

I awoke to find the America I knew a total wreck—to find Americans a hunted race in their own land, hiding in the dense forests that covered the shattered and leveled ruins of their once magnificent cities, desperately preserving, and struggling to develop in their secret retreats, the remnants of their culture and science—and the undying flame of their sturdy independence.

World domination was in the hands of Mongolians and the center of world power lay in inland China, with Americans one of the few races of mankind unsubdued—and it must be admitted in fairness to the truth, not worth the trouble of subduing in the eyes of the Han Airlords who ruled North America as titular tributaries of the Most Magnificent.

For they needed not the forests in which the Americans lived, nor the resources of the vast territories these forests covered. With the perfection to which they had reduced the synthetic production of necessities and luxuries, their remarkable development of scientific processes and mechanical accomplishment of work, they had no economic need for the forests, and no economic desire for the enslaved labor of an unruly race.

They had all they needed for their magnificently luxurious and degraded scheme of civilization within the walls of the fifteen cities of sparkling glass they had flung skyward on the sites of ancient American centers, into the bowels of the earth underneath them, and with relatively small surrounding areas of agriculture.

Complete domination of the air rendered communication between these centers a matter of ease and safety. Occasional destructive raids on the waste lands were considered all that was necessary to keep the "wild" Americans on the run within the shelter of their forests, and prevent their becoming a menace to the Han civilization.

But nearly three hundred years of easily maintained security, the last century of which had been nearly sterile in scientific, social and economic progress, had softened and devitalized the Hans.

It had likewise developed, beneath the protecting foliage of the forest, the growth of a vigorous new American civilization, remarkable in the mobility and flexibility of its organization, in its conquest of almost insuperable obstacles, in the development and guarding of its industrial and scientific resources, all in anticipation of that "Day of Hope" to which it had been looking forward for generations, when it would be strong enough to burst from the green chrysalis of the forests, soar into the upper air lanes and destroy the yellow incubus.

At the time I awoke, the "Day of Hope" was almost at hand. I shall not attempt to set forth a detailed history of the Second War of Independence, for that has

*HERE, once more, is a real scientifiction story plus. It is a story which will make the heart of many readers leap with joy.*

*We have rarely printed a story in this magazine that for scientific interest, as well as suspense, could hold its own with this particular story. We prophesy that this story will become more valuable as the years go by. It certainly holds a number of interesting prophecies, of which no doubt, many will come true. For wealth of science, it will be hard to beat for some time to come. It is one of those rare stories that will bear reading and re-reading many times.*

*This story has impressed us so favorably, that we hope the author may be induced to write a sequel to it soon.*

422

**BRG-1**

**"Amazing Stories" Pulp Magazine With First Buck Rogers Story**

**1928**

MCK-47
Litho. Button
c. 1935

MCK-3
Movie Club Cello. Button
1930

MCK-118
Southern Dairies
Ice Cream
Cello. Button
1930s

MCK-122
Mickey Mouse
Undies
Cello. Button
1930s

MCK-100
"Mickey Mouse Club"
Cello. Button
1930s

MCK-61
Atlanta Georgian's
Silver Anniversary
Cello. Button
1937

MCK-46
"Mickey Mouse Hose"
Cello. Button
1930s

MCK-4
"Mickey Mouse Club"
Cello. Button
1930

MCK-6
Mickey in
Santa Outfit
Cello. Button
c. 1930

Mickey Mouse made his first appearance in 1928 in thirty-six storyboard drawings on six pages for a silent cartoon titled **Plane Crazy**. Shown are the first six drawn by Ub Iwerks. The story was inspired by Charles Lindbergh and his 1927 flight across the Atlantic.

BKJ-41
Club Cello. Button
1930s

BKJ-6
"Rangers' Club of America"
Cello. Button
c. 1931

BKJ-7
"Rangers' Club of America"
Cello. Button
c. 1931

BKJ-37
Chicago Stadium Rodeo
Cello. Button
1930s

BKJ-48
"Riders of Death Valley
Club" Cello. Button
1941

BKJ-38
Australian Issue
Movie Cello. Button
1930s

BKJ-18
"The Red Rider" Cello. Button
1934

KAT-9 Kate Smith
1930s

LUM-18 Lum and Abner
1940s

MOV-98 George Raft
1940s

MUS-5 Frank Sinatra
1940s

KEN-11 Ken Maynard
1930

LON-325 Lone Ranger
1950s

HOP-25 Hopalong Cassidy
1950

BKJ-16 White Eagle
(Buck Jones) 1932

ROY-54 Roy Rogers
1940s

MOV-97 Humphrey Bogart
1940s

GAB-1 Gabby Hayes
Early 1940s

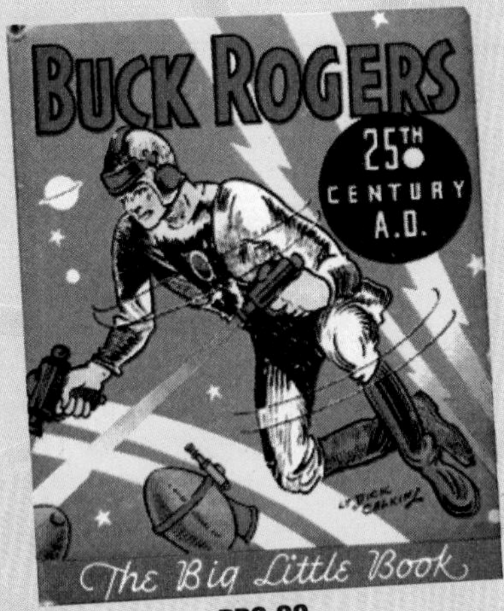


BRG-20
"Buck Rogers 25th Century A.D." Hardcover
1933

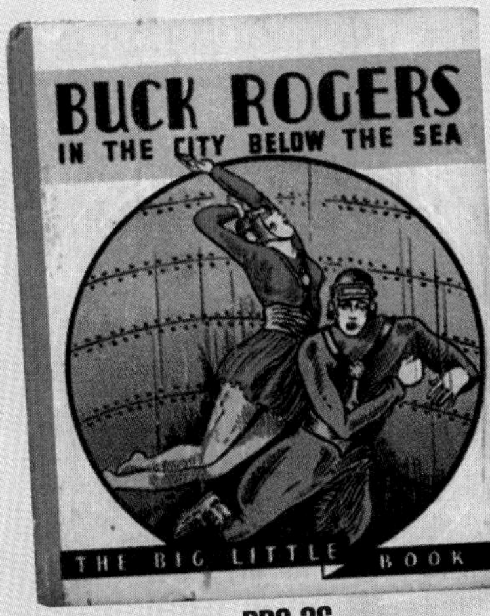


BRG-36
"Buck Rogers In The City Below The Sea"
1934

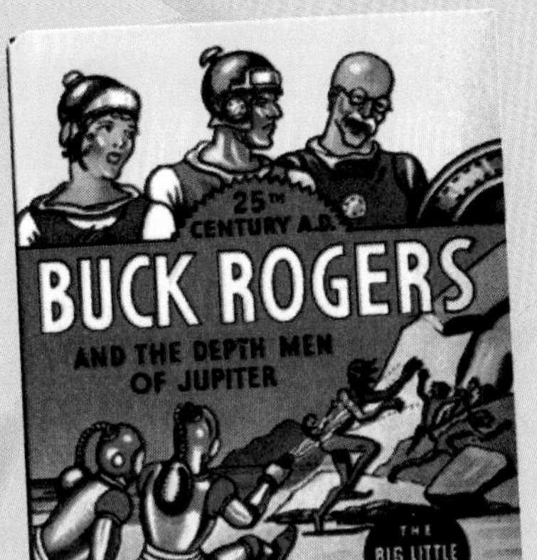


BRG-54
"Buck Rogers And The Depth Men Of Jupiter"
BLB #1169
1935

BRG-38
"Buck Rogers On The Moons Of Saturn"
BLB #1143
1934

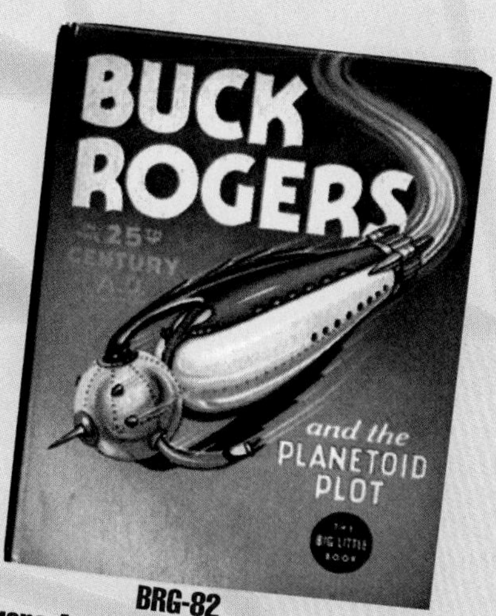


BRG-82
"Buck Rogers And The Planetoid Plot" BLB #1197
1936

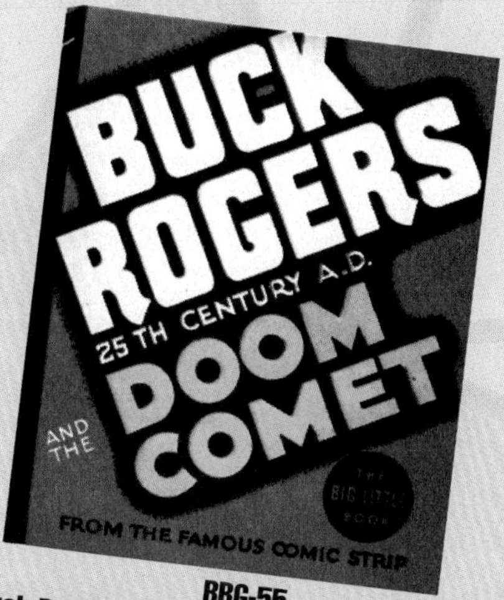


BRG-55
"Buck Rogers And The Doom Comet" BLB #1178
1935

BRG-143
"Buck Rogers And The Overturned World"
Better Little Book #1474
1941

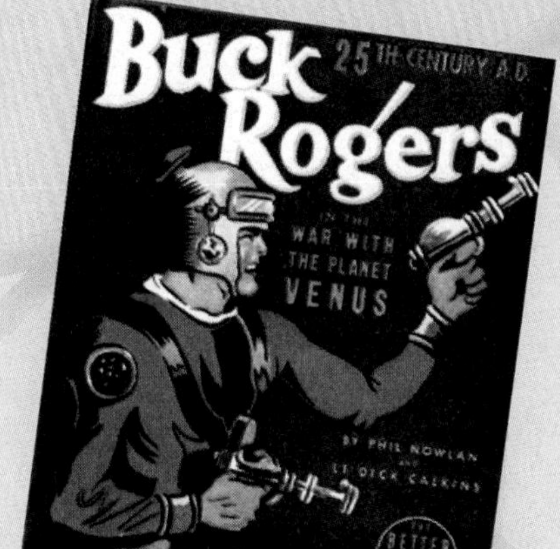


BRG-113
"Buck Rogers In The War With The Planet Venus"
Better Little Book #1437
1938

ADV-55
Earl Ortman's Model Planes
Die Cut Standee
1930s

KEL-16
Die Cut Aeroplane Sign
1930s

FLX-13
Felix the Cat
1930s

DUN-11
Dan Dunn
1930s

NES-10
Connie
1930s

PPY-49
Wimpy and Popeye
1930s

NES-11
Harold Teen
1930s

NES-12
Bobby Thatcher
1930s

NES-13
Babe Bunting
1930s

MCK-120
Mickey Mouse
1930s

MCK-121
Minnie Mouse
1930s

NES-14
Smitty
1930s

NES-9
2 Relentless Rudolph Pins
1930s

CMR-109
Captain Marvel Play Cape
1940s

CMR-118
Captain Marvel
English Club Button
1940s

CMR-119
Captain Marvel
Shirt
1940s

("Warning" Label)

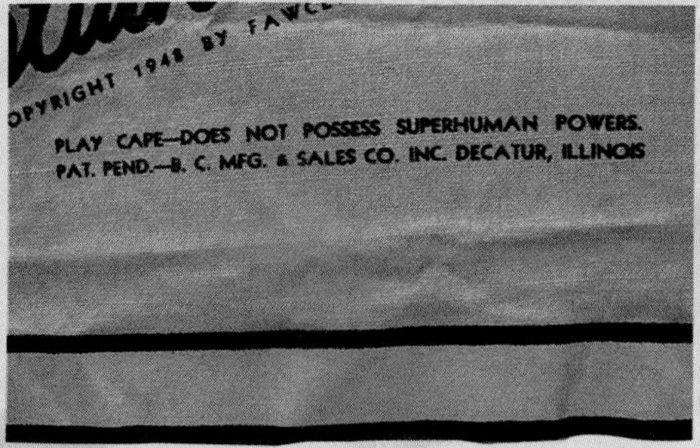


CMR-6
Serial 6" Blotter
1941

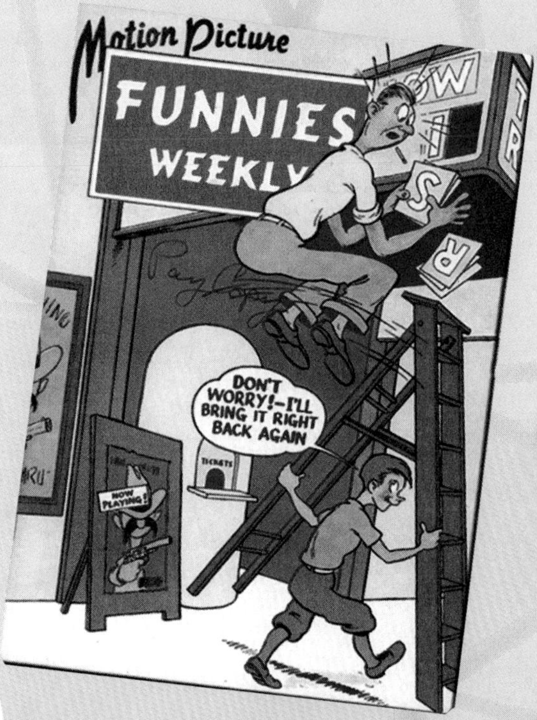


**MOV-46**
**Motion Picture Funnies Weekly**
**Comic Book Promo**
**1939**

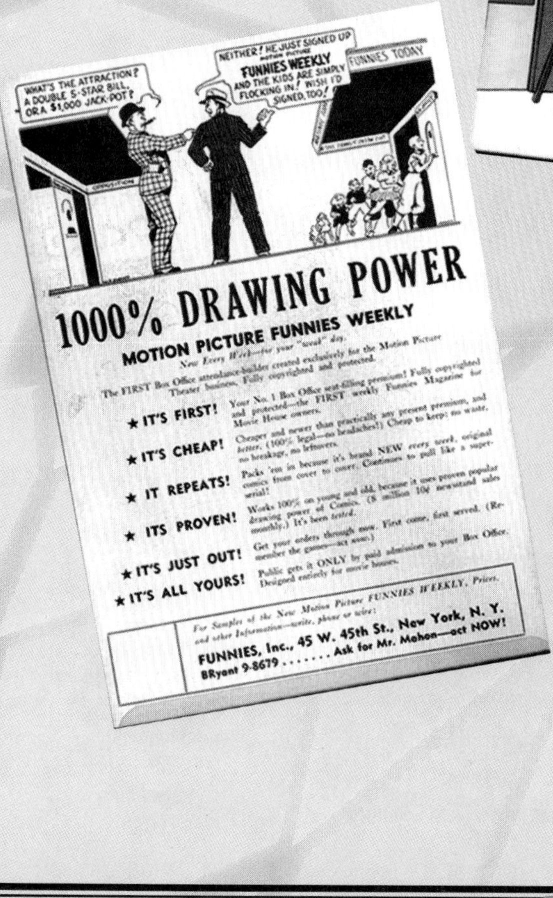


**(Back cover)**

**An assortment of litho. and cello. buttons**

CMR-15
Captain Marvel Club/Shazam!
1942

WON-1
Wonder Woman Sensation Comics
1942

GRN-11
The Green Hornet Adventure Club
1940

SPY-2
"I Am A Spy Smasher"
c. 1941

SGM-1
Shield G-Man Club
c. 1940

SUP-3
Action Comics "Superman"
1939

SUP-126
Superman Muscle Building Club
1954

EAG-1
The Eagle Member's Pin
1942

BAT-11
Batman "Crimefighter" 1 3/8"
1966

FLA-1
The Flash/Fastest Man Alive
1942

PHN-11
The Phantom's Club Member
1940s

SUP-161
Superman
1966

**LON-64**
**Lone Ranger**
**Tin Litho. Wind-Up and Box**
**1938**

LAN-45
Brass Decoder
1935

LAN-55
Secret Compartment Brass Decoder
1936

LAN-66
Sunburst Brass Decoder Badge
1937

LAN-76
Telematic Brass Decoder Badge
1938

LAN-91
"Mysto-Matic" Brass Decoder Badge
1942

LAN-119
Speed-O-Matic Brass Decoder Badge
1940

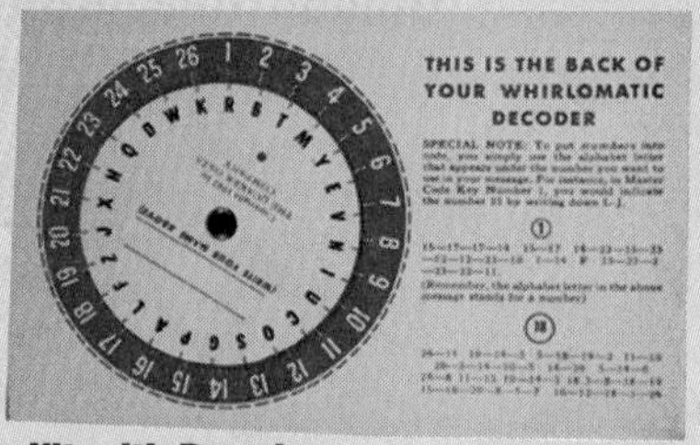


LAN-160
"Safety Guard" Membership Kit with Decoder
1942

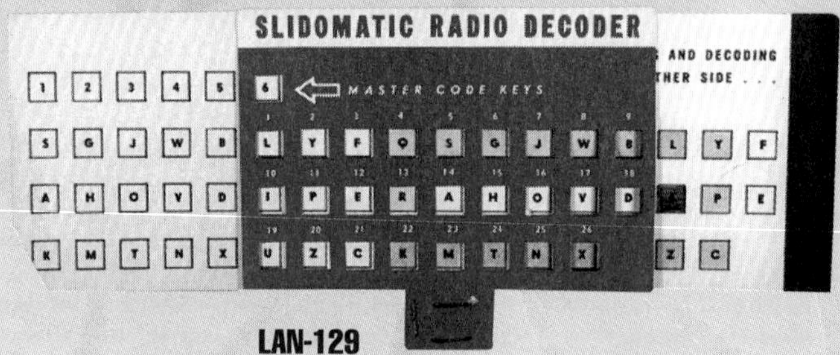


LAN-129
Slidomatic Radio Decoder
1941

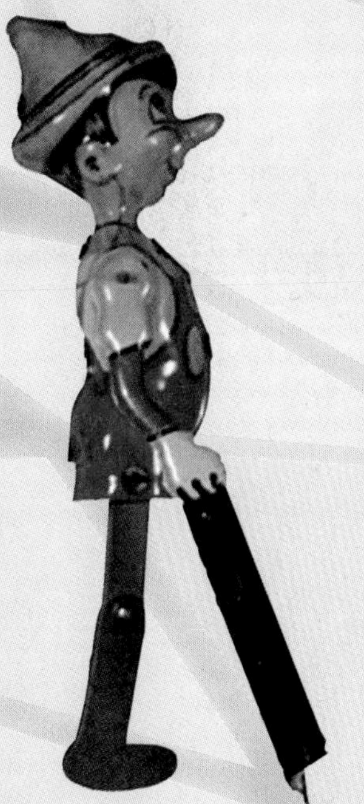

PCC-29
Victor Records
Cello. Button
1940

PCC-61
Disney Artist
Promotional Pin
2000

PCC-13
"Pinocchio the Acrobat!"
Litho. Tin Wind-Up Toy
1939

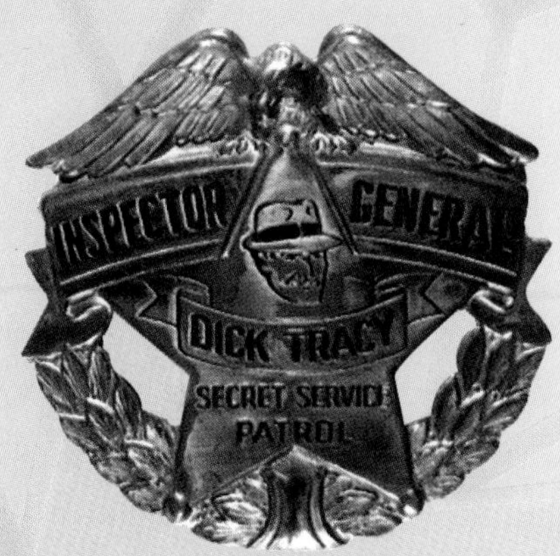


**DCY-32**
**Dick Tracy Inspector General**
**2 1/2" Brass Badge**
**1938**

**DTC-3**
**Detectives Black & Blue**
**"Folger's Coffee" Brass Badge**
**c. 1932**

**DTC-2**
**Detectives Black & Blue**
**"Iodent Toothpaste" Brass Badge**
**c. 1932**

**COU-4**
**Counterspy**
**Junior Agent Glow-In-Dark**
**Brass Badge**
**1949**

**DST-6**
**"Dick Steel News Service/**
**Special Police Reporter"**
**Brass Badge**
**c. 1934**

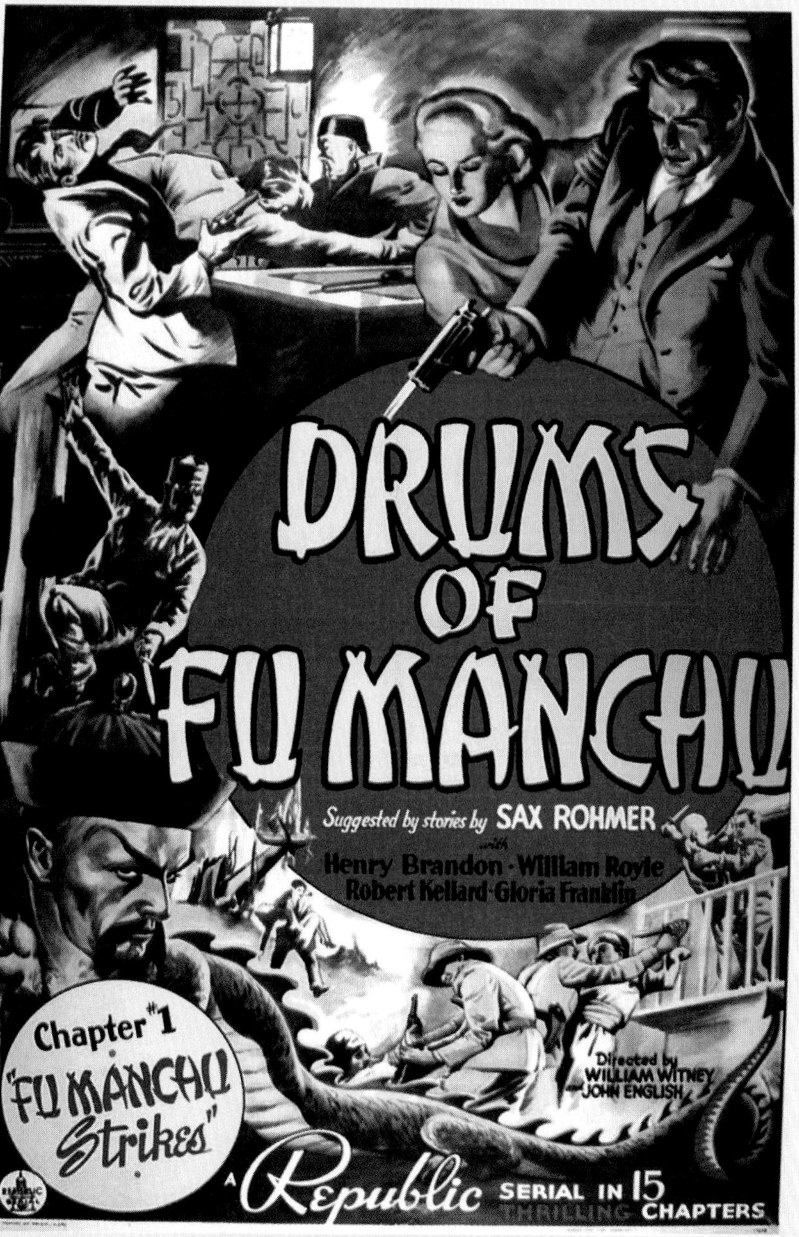


**FUM-10**
**"Drums of Fu Manchu" 27x41"**
**One Sheet Poster**
**1940**

ADC-3
"Special Operator"
Cello. Button
c. 1939

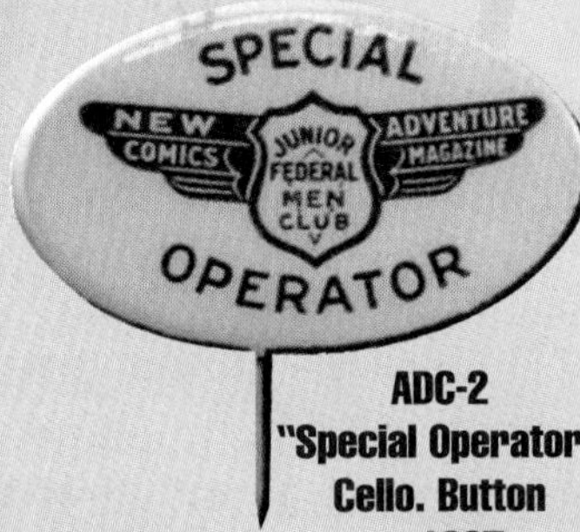


ADC-2
"Special Operator"
Cello. Button
c. 1937

ADC-1
"Special Operator"
Cello. Button
c. 1937

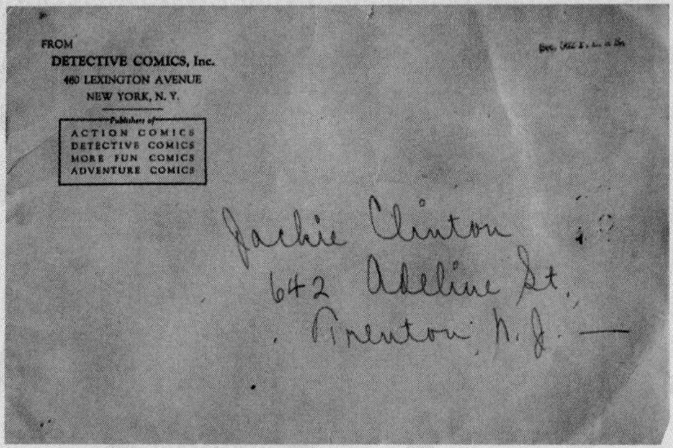
FROM
DETECTIVE COMICS, Inc.
480 LEXINGTON AVENUE
NEW YORK, N. Y.

Publishers of
ACTION COMICS
DETECTIVE COMICS
MORE FUN COMICS
ADVENTURE COMICS

Jackie Clinton
642 Adeline St.
Trenton, N. J.

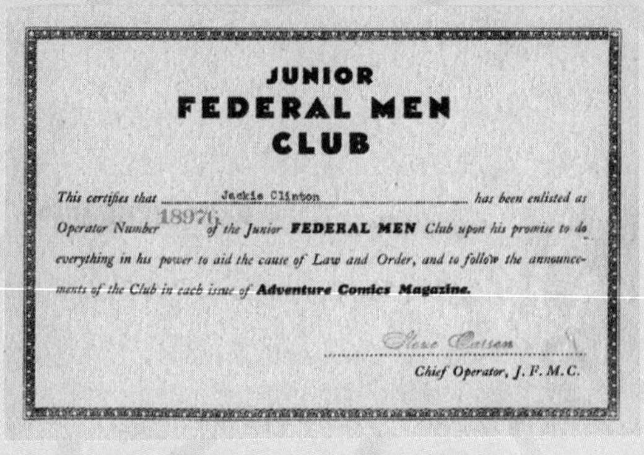
JUNIOR
FEDERAL MEN
CLUB

*This certifies that* Jackie Clinton *has been enlisted as Operator Number* 18976 *of the Junior* **FEDERAL MEN** *Club upon his promise to do everything in his power to aid the cause of Law and Order, and to follow the announcements of the Club in each issue of* **Adventure Comics Magazine.**

Steve Carson
*Chief Operator, J. F. M. C.*

ADC-4
"Junior Federal Men Club"
Member Certificate
and Mailer
c. 1939

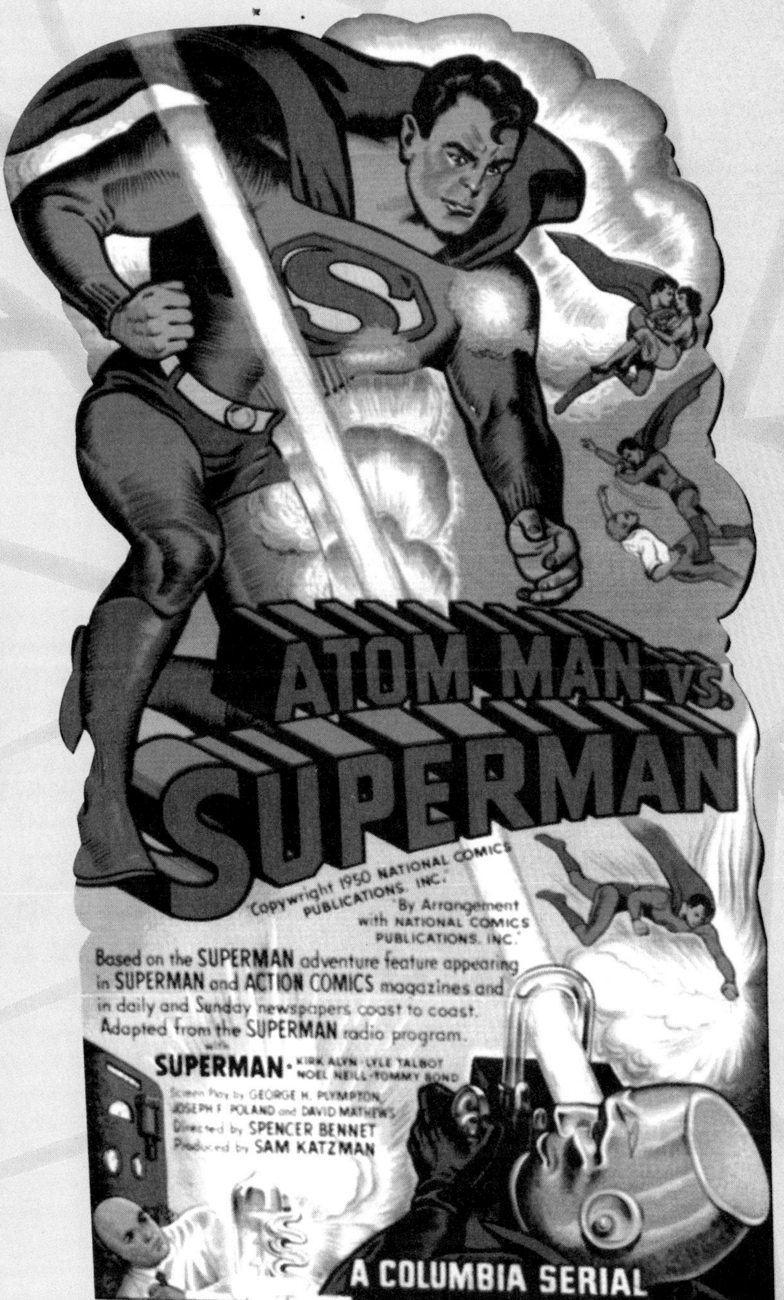


**SUP-122**
**"Atom Man vs. Superman"**
**6' Movie Standee**
**1950**

COM-23
3 versions of the
Marx Merrymakers Band
1931

**Young Sky Birds Pin**
**Compare price to COM-40**
**Tailspin Tommy Pin**
**1930s**

**HWN-14**
**Howie Wing Australian Club**
**Member's Aluminum Wings Pin**
**1930s**

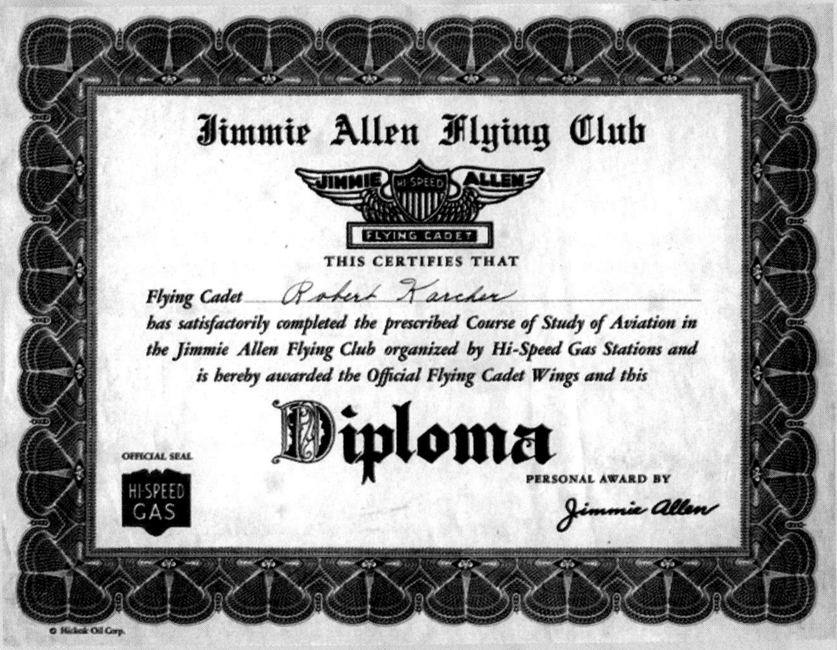

Jimmie Allen Flying Club

JIMMIE HI-SPEED ALLEN
FLYING CADET

THIS CERTIFIES THAT

*Flying Cadet* Robert Karcher
*has satisfactorily completed the prescribed Course of Study of Aviation in the Jimmie Allen Flying Club organized by Hi-Speed Gas Stations and is hereby awarded the Official Flying Cadet Wings and this*

Diploma

OFFICIAL SEAL
HI-SPEED GAS

PERSONAL AWARD BY
Jimmie Allen

© Hickok Oil Corp.

**JMA-91**
**Jimmie Allen Flying Club Diploma**
**1930s**

**SRD-12**
**Skyriders Brass Wings Badge**
**with Celluloid Bar**
**1930s**

**AIR-5**
**Air Juniors Air Scouts**
**Member's Brass Pin**
**c. 1929**

**AIR-2**
**Air Juniors**
**Club Member Pin**
**1929**

MLV-6
"Junior G-Man Corps" Brass Badge
1936

MLV-24
"Captain" Brass Rank Badge
1937

MLV-23
"Lieutenant" Brass Rank Badge
1937

MLV-25
"Secret Operator/ Girls Division"
Brass Badge
1937

MLV-1
Melvin Purvis Premium Photo
1936

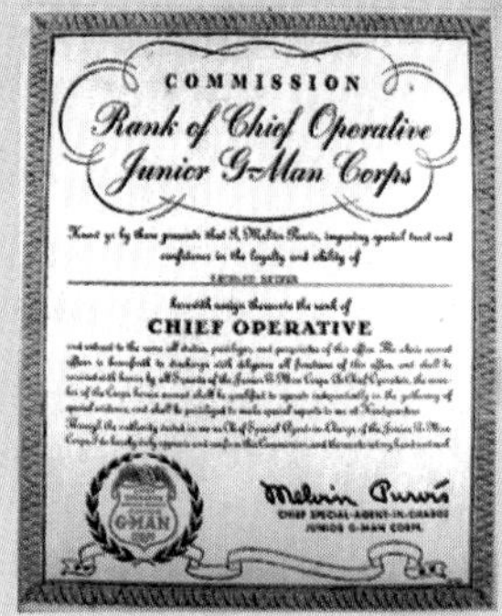


MLV-4
Chief
Operative
Certificate
1937

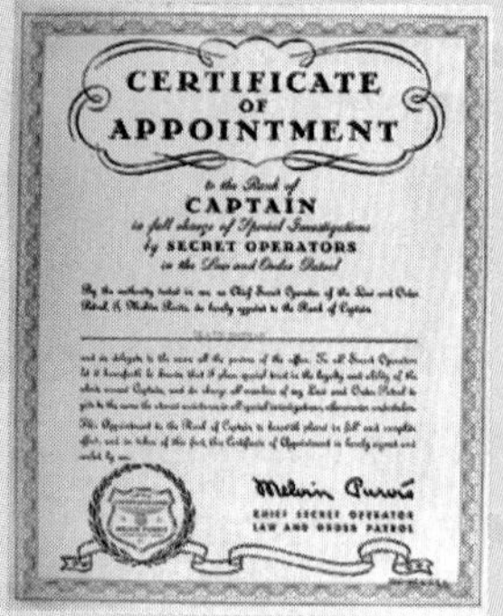


MLV-18
"Certificate of Appointment"
1937

MLV-31
"G-Man Squad" Gun
1937

DNL-94
"Walt Disney's Donald Duck Duet"
Tin Wind-Up Toy
1950s

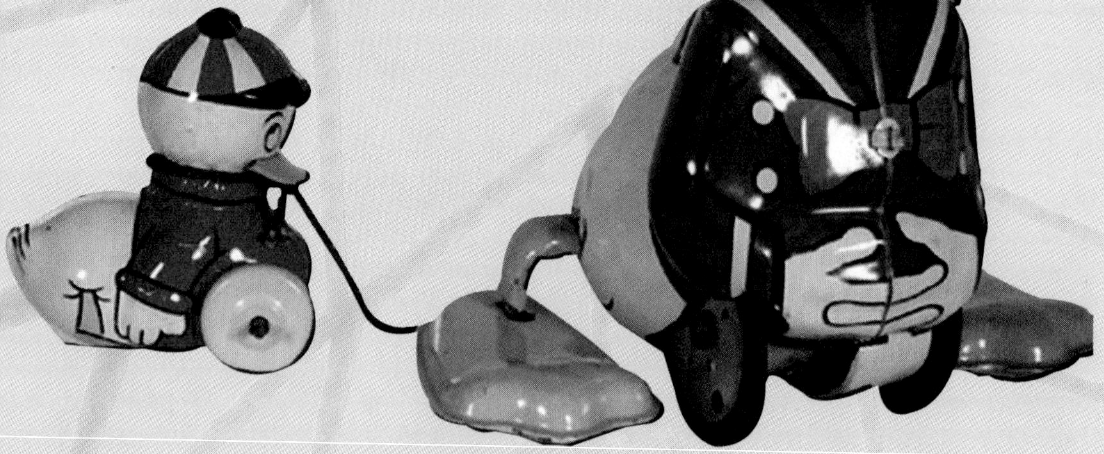

**DNL-93**
**"Donald Duck with Huey and Voice"**
**Tin Toy**
**1950s**

**DIS-40**
**"Pluto the Drum Major"**
**Wind-Up Toy**
**1950s**

# GALAXY GUARDIANS

TCO-35
"Tom Corbett Space Cadet"
Pinback
1950s

RKJ-9
"Rocky Jones Silvercup Bread"
Litho. Button
c. 1954

BRG-49
"Buck Rogers in the 25th
Century" Cello. Pinback
1935

FGR-3
"Dale Arden" Litho. Button
1934

FGR-19
Chicago Herald and
Examiner Litho. Button
1930s

CVD-1
Captain Video
Picture Ring
c. 1950

RKJ-10
"Rocky Jones Space Ranger"
Cello. Button
c. 1954

FGR-2
"Flash Gordon" Litho. Button
1934

BRG-107
Canadian Club Member
Cello Button
1934

TCO-2
Tom Corbett "Space Cadet"
2 1/8" Cello. Button
1951

BRG-97
"25th Century Accousticon Jr."
2 1/4" Cello. Button
1936

SPC-18
Space Patrol
Plastic Badge
1952

TRZ-37
"The Tarzan Twins"
Big Little Book
1934

PUP-19
"The New Adventures of Tarzan"
Pop-Up Book
1935

TRZ-40
"Tarzan"
Ice Cream
Premium Booklet
1935

TRZ-23
"Tarzan the Fearless"
Cardboard Sign
1933

TER-3
"Terry and the Pirates"
Board Game
1937

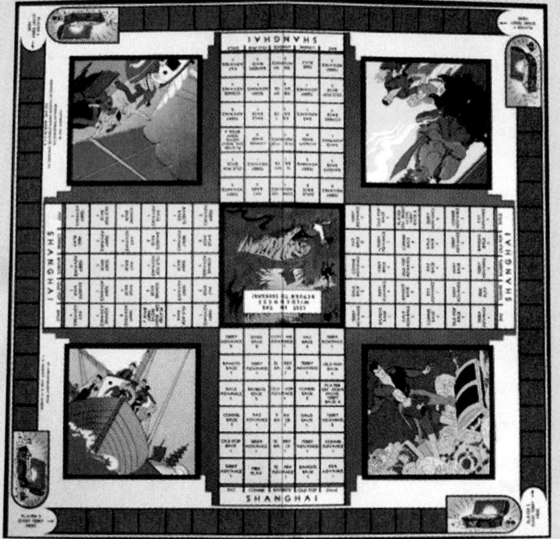


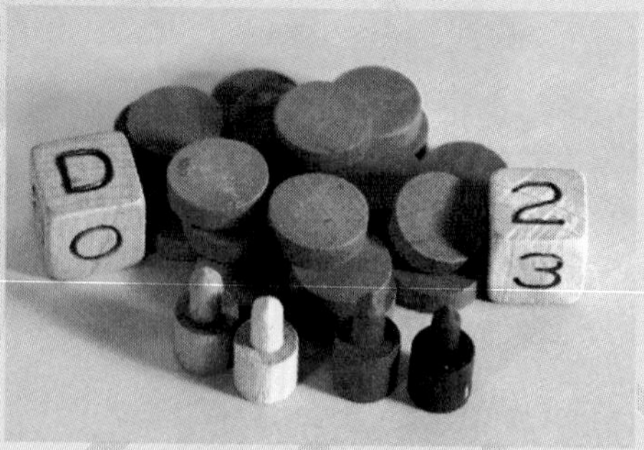

SNO-5
"Doc" Mask
1937

SNO-3
"Dopey" Mask
1937

SNO-6
"The Witch" Mask
1937

DCY-142
"Dick Tracy" Mask
1950s

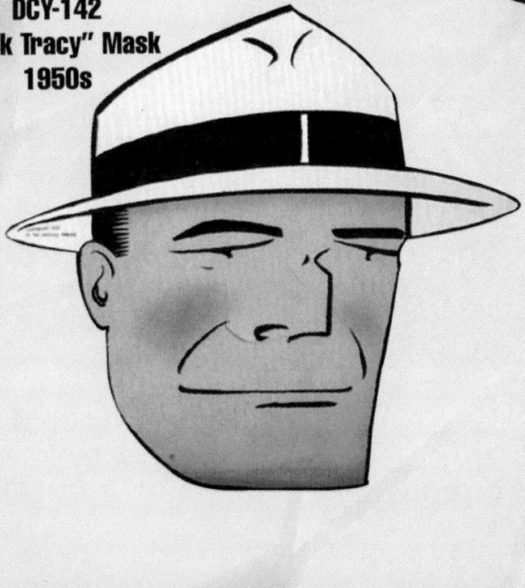

CPN-20
"The Great Dictator"
Movie Promotion
Mask
1940

RJO-8
"Ranger Joe & Topaz"
Patch
1951

OPN-6 (Open Road For Boys)
"Open Road Pioneers" 4 1/2" Fabric Patch
1930s

HPH-6
Hop Harrigan Club
Fabric Patch
c. 1942

JRB-12
Junior Birdmen of America
Felt Fabric Emblem
1930s

TIM-5
Tim Club "Franco Club"
Patch
1938

JMA-54
Jimmie Allen
Air Corps" Patch
1930s

SMO-15
Smokey Bear
Fabric Patch
c. 1960s

SCL-2
Sky Climber Fabric Patch
1929

FAC-12
"Flying Aces" Large Cloth Patch
1930s

JMA-54
"Flying Cadet Be-Square
Air Corps" Felt Patch
1930s

**KEL-53**
**Pep Comic Character**
**Litho. Button Set**
**1945**

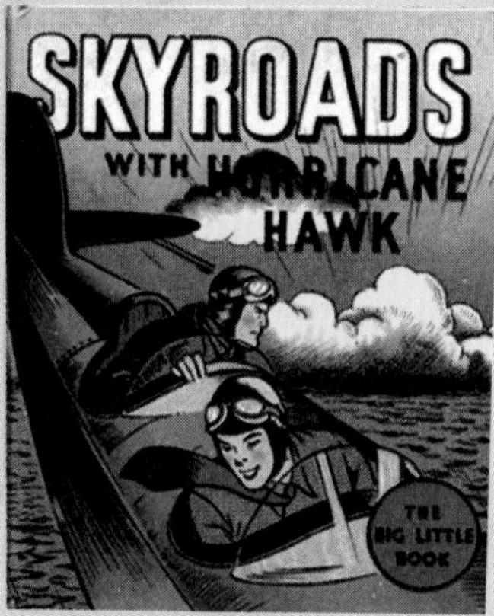

SRO-1
Big Little Book #1127 1936

WWII-8
Better Little Book #1481
1941

COM-35
Big Little Book #747 1933

WWII-11
Big Little Book #1461 1941

WWII-4
Better Little Book #1425
1939

WWII-6
Better Little Book #1401
1940

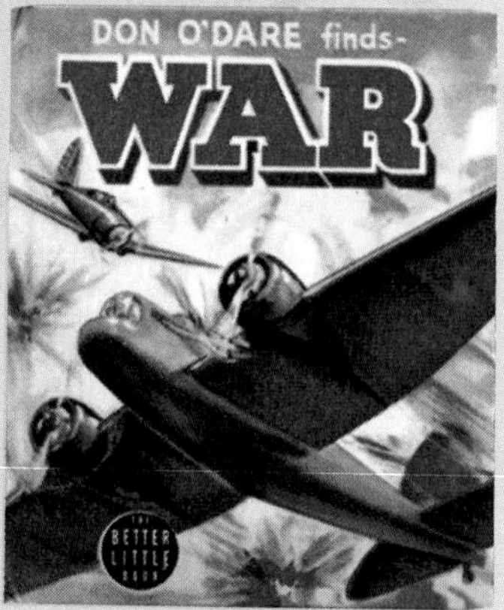

WWII-5
Better Little Book #1438
1940

WWII-9
Better Little Book #1448
1941

WWII-2
Big Little Book #1445
1937

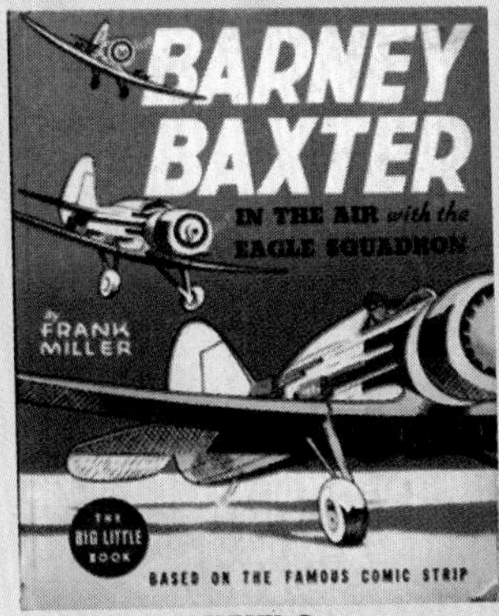


WWII-3
Big Little Book #1459
1938

WWII-10
Better Little Book #1466
1941

CFH-15
Big Little Book #1444
1938

WWII-19
Better Little Book #1420
1943

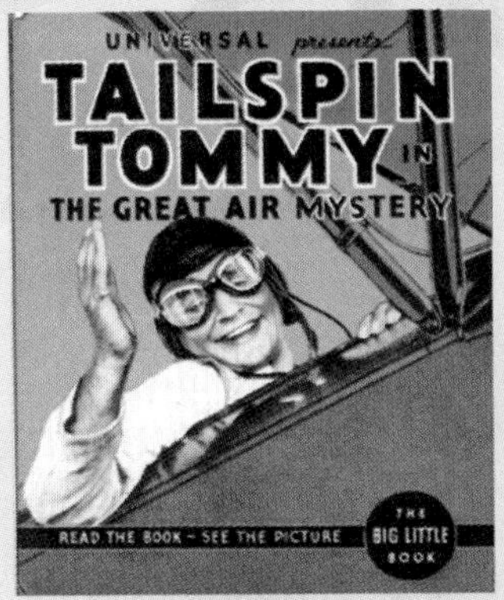


COM-39
Big Little Book #1184
1936

JKR-15
"The Jackie Robinson Story"
Hardback Book
1963

JKR-4
Metal Bust Bank
1950

JKR-1
"Rookie of the Year"
Pinback
1947

JKR-16
Commemorative Coin
1997

JKR-10
Dime Bank
1950

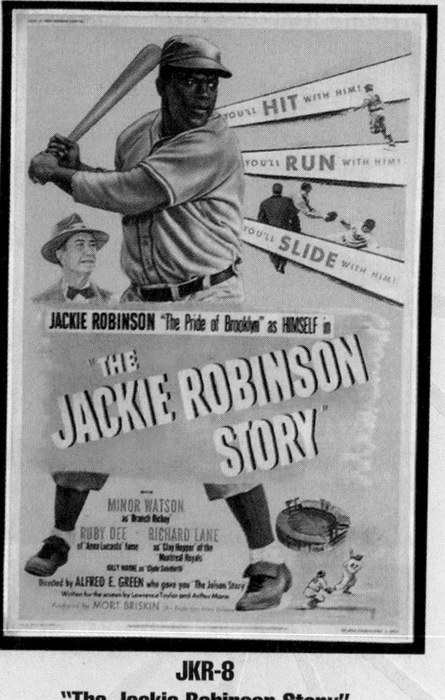


JKR-8
"The Jackie Robinson Story"
Movie Poster
1950

JKR-3
"Jackie Robinson
Baseball Hero"
Comic Book #1
1950

**AMO-21**
**Radio Episode Script**
**1935**

**AMO-29**
**Bisque Figurines**
**1930s**

**AMO-10**
**Pencil Tablet**
**c. 1930**

**AMO-21**
**Cast Photo**
**1929**

**AMO-22**
**Radio Theme Song**
**Sheet Music**
**1935**

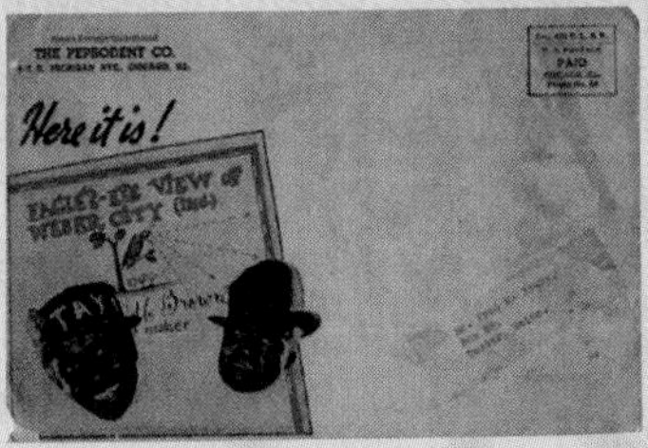


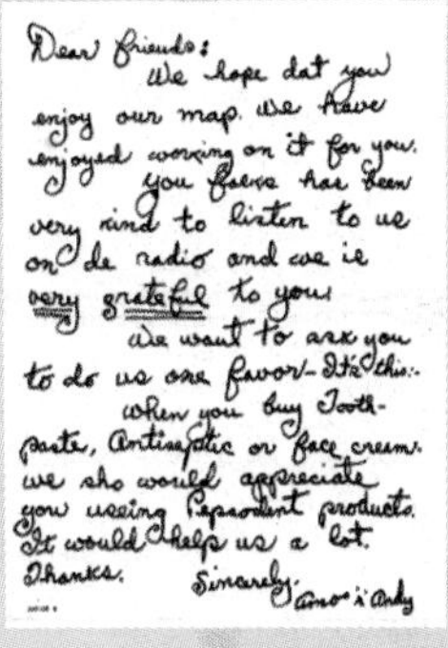
Dear Friends:
We hope dat you enjoy our map. We have enjoyed working on it for you. You folks has been very kind to listen to us on de radio and we is very grateful to you.
We want to ask you to do us one favor- It's this:-
When you buy Tooth-paste, Antiseptic or face cream. we sho would appreciate you useing Pepsodent products. It would help us a lot.
Thanks. Sincerely, Amos 'n' Andy

**AMO-46**
**"The Best of Amos 'N' Andy"**
**CD Box Set**
**2001**

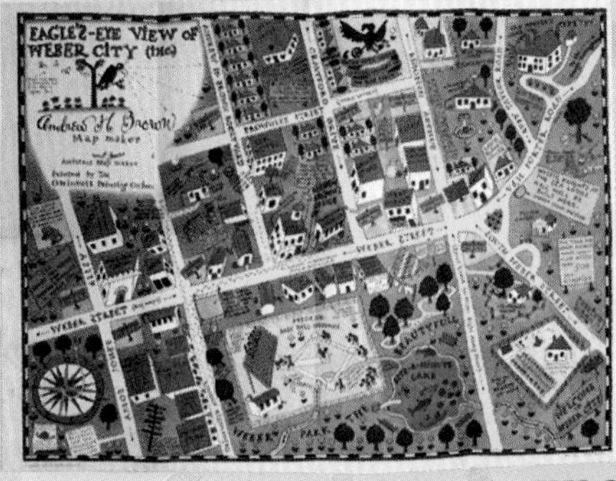


**AMO-23**
**"Eagle's Eye View of Weber City (Inc.)" Map, Letter and Mailer**
**1935**

MRP-28
Vending Machine
1999

MRP-24
Stuffed Doll
1997

MRP-23
Peanut Butter Maker
1996

**MUH-9**
**Mr. Toothdecay Pinback**
**1974**

**MUH-29**
**Starting Lineup**
**"Timeless Legend"**
**Figure in Box**
**1998**

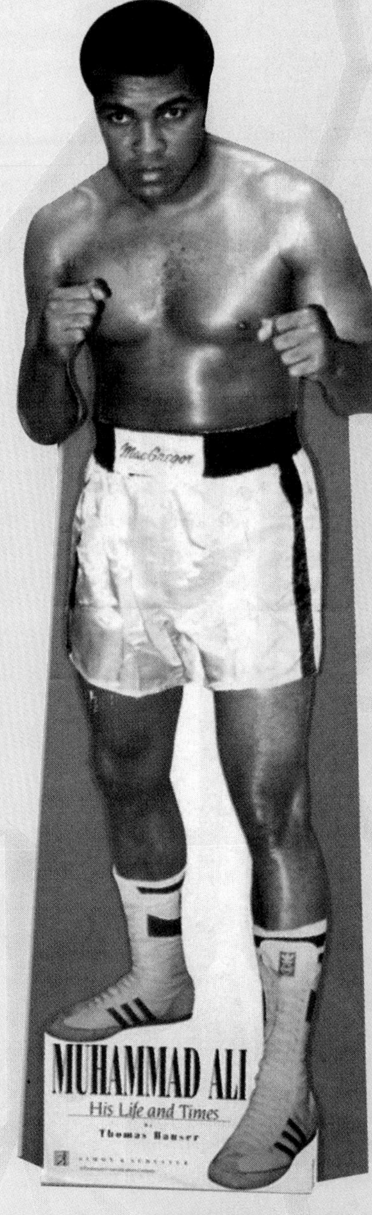


**MUH-26**
**Promotional Standee**
**1992**

**MUH-27**
**Starting Lineup**
**Figure on Card**
**1998**

TGN-121
"Captain America"
Gun & Badge Set
1974

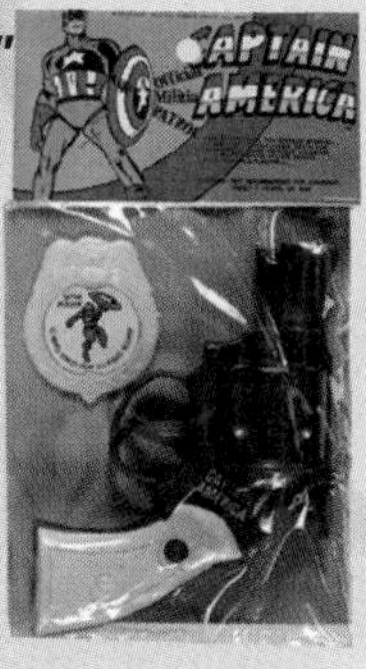

TGN-84
"Davey Crockett" Water Gun
1950s

TGN-88
Wee Gee
Salesman Sample
Water Gun
1950s

TGN-87
"Space Jet"
Water Gun
1950s

TGN-85
"Dee Gee" Water Gun
1950s

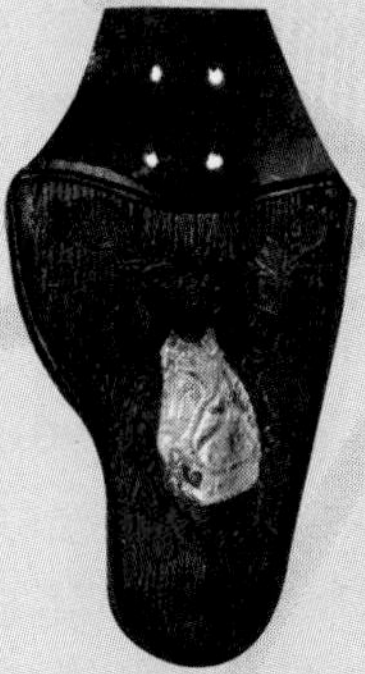

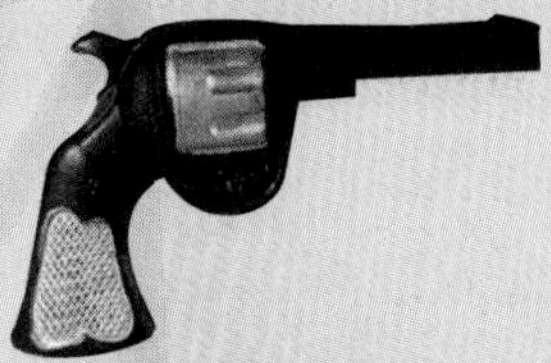

TGN-122
"Indian Baby" 8-Shot
Toy Pistol in Box
1970s

TGN-37
Rubber Gun and Holster Set
1940s

TGN-86
Ideal Water Pistol Box
1950s

UVM-1
"King Kong" Jig Saw Puzzle
1933

FGR-31
"Flash Gordon" Inlaid Puzzle
1952

BOZ-19
Bozo Block Puzzle
1997

JDN-15
James Dean
Photo Puzzle
1995

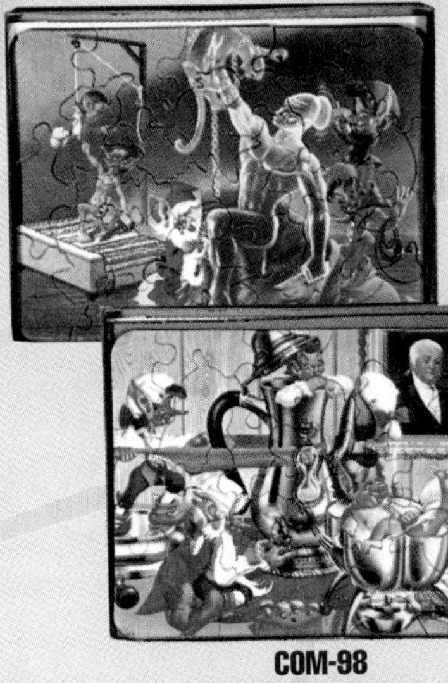

COM-98
Children's Puzzles
1950

MCK-14
Mickey Mouse Puzzle Set
1933

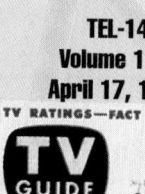

**LUC-4**
**Volume 1 #1**
**Little Ricky (I Love Lucy)**
**April 3, 1953**

**TEL-14**
**Volume 1 #3**
**April 17, 1953**

**SUC-11**
**Super Circus**
**August 21, 1953**

**SUP-125**
**George Reeves**
**as Superman**
**September 25, 1953**

**KUK-5**
**Kukla, Fran and Ollie**
**October 30, 1953**

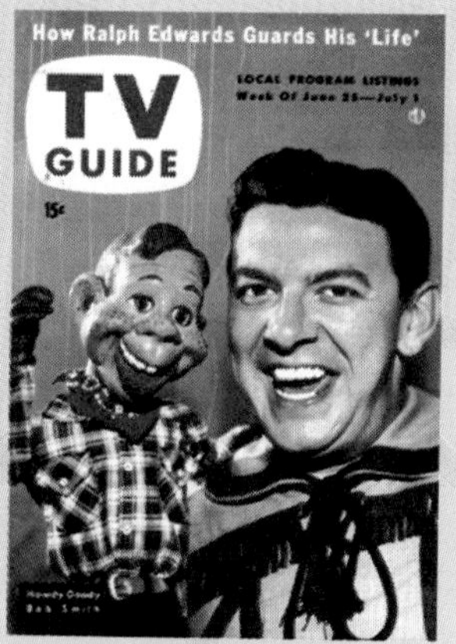


**HOW-47**
**Howdy Doody and**
**Buffalo Bob**
**June 25, 1954**

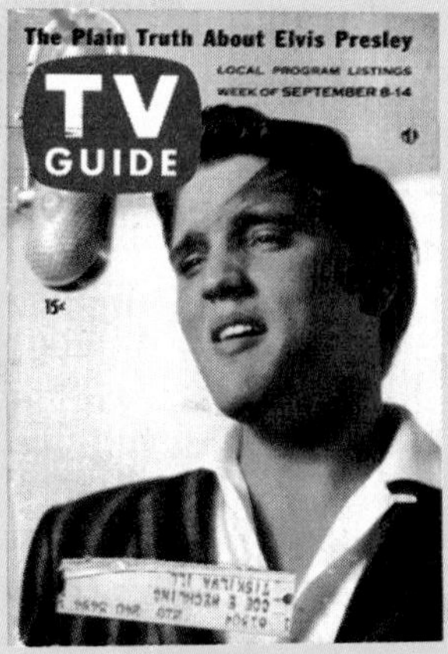


**ELV-8**
**Elvis Presley**
**September 8, 1956**

LIL-21
Bank on Card
1949

LIL-21
Bank on Card
1949

LIL-21
Bank on Card
1949

LIL-12
Utility Bag
1948-49

LIL-21
Bank on Card
1949

LIL-14
Small Pin
1949

LIL-20
Shmoo Pocketbook
1949

LIL-11
Carnival Bank
1948

LIL-32
Pet Shmoo 6 in 1 Figure 1940s

BAB-30
Babe Ruth Plastic Ring
c. 1950

BAB-40
Raisin Bran Cereal Box
2001

BAB-17
Quaker "Babe Ruth Champions"
Brass Club Badge
1935

BAB-10
Quaker Cello.
Club Button
1934

BAB-38
Baseball in Box
1999

BAB-39
Figure on Card
Late 1990s

BAB-35
Commemorative Bank Car
1995

BAB-14
"Ask Me" 3" Cello. Button
c. 1934

CAL-9
Figure with Bass Fiddle
1988

CAL-11
Valentine Girl Figure
1988

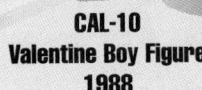

CAL-10
Valentine Boy Figure
1988

CAL-8
Girl Figure with Tambourine
1988

CAL-4
Figure Keychain
1987

FLN-25
Fred Flintstone Bank Statue
1993

FLN-26
Barney Rubble
Bank Statue
1993

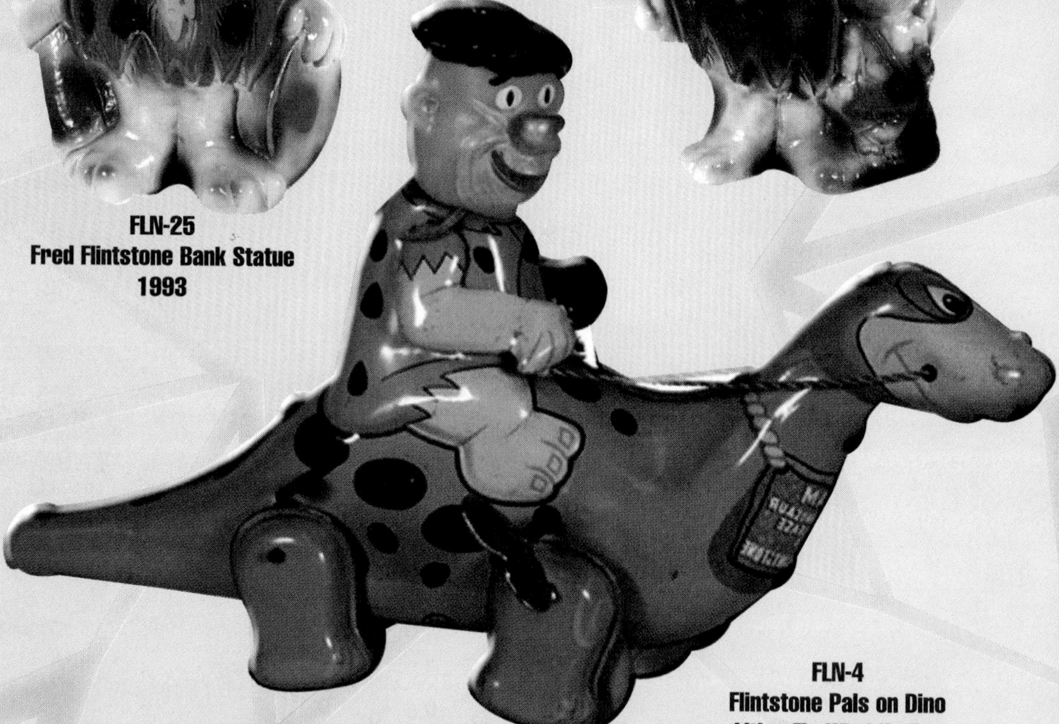

FLN-4
Flintstone Pals on Dino
Litho. Tin Wind-Up Toy
1962

MAD-30
"Alfred E. Neuman"
Cookie Jar
2001

# MOVIE BUTTONS

TRZ-2
Tarzan
Early Serial
Cello. Button
1920

WIZ-14
"Wizard of Oz"
Movie Advertising
Cello. Button
1939

STW-22
"Official Star Wars
Fan Club" Button
1978

RLN-3
Rocky Lane
Cello. Button
c. 1950

WLD-24
"Wild Bill Hickok"
Litho. Button
1957

HGB-5
Hoot Gibson
Cello. Button
1930s

TMX-148
Tom Mix "Toledo
Paramount Theater"
Movie Cello. Button
1930s

SUN-2
"Sunset Carson"
Cello. Button
1940s

SHR-7
Theater Club
Cello. Button
c. 1936

MOV-23
"Freaks"
Cello. Button
1932

CPN-19
"Modern Times"
Movie Button
1936

RIN-4
"The Lightning Warrior"
Movie Serial Cello. Button
1931

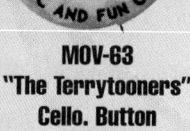

MOV-63
"The Terrytooners"
Cello. Button
1930s

HOW-131
Howdy Doody
2000

SUP-208
Superman
2000

RUD-35
Rudolph
2000

MOV-203
Harry Potter
2001

MOV-198
Beetlejuice
2001

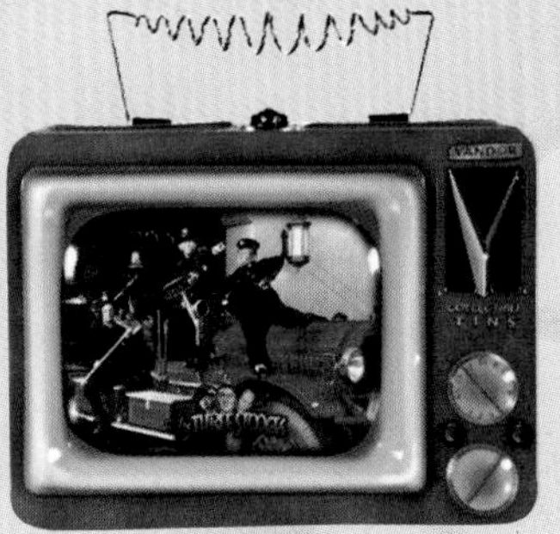


THR-20
Three Stooges
2000

MUS-58
Janis Joplin
2000

MGH-20
Mighty Mouse
2001

DMB-19
Dumbo
1999

DIS-73
"Slue Foot Sue" Statue
1990s

DIS-72
"Pecos Bill" Statue
1990s

DIS-66
"Minnie on the Beach" Figure
1993

DIS-75
"The Tortoise and the Hare" Movie Figures
2000

BOZ-21 2001

GEN-37 2001

FLX-30 2000

GEN-38 2001

TEL-142 2000

PEZ-63 2000

PEZ-61 2000

PEZ-62 2000

ADV-149 2001

UND-23 2000

BTY-18 2000

BIG-26 1999

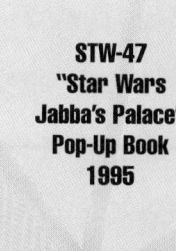

**STW-47**
**"Star Wars Jabba's Palace" Pop-Up Book**
**1995**

**(Poster came with Pop-Up Book)**

**STW-38**
**"Star Wars" Cookies Box**
**1983**

PEPPERIDGE FARM
STAR WARS
COOKIES
Pepperidge Farm is pleased to offer you your favorite Star Wars characters in your favorite cookie flavors!
R2-D2,™ C-3PO,™ and Chewbacca™ team up with the support of Admiral Ackbar™ and Max Rebo™ to help the Rebel cause. Now you can try these characters in a delicious peanut butter cookie, Wookiee™ Cookie and all!
FREE STAR WARS®* TUMBLERS!
We'll send you a set of 4-10 oz. STAR WARS PLASTIC TUMBLERS when you buy three packages of PEPPERIDGE FARM STAR WARS COOKIES!
Now you can enjoy your favorite beverage with our delicious cookies! Mail this completed certificate, along with the ingredient panel from any three packages of Pepperidge Farm STAR WARS COOKIES, to:
Star Wars Tumblers Offer P.O. Box 4108 Reidsville, N.C. 27322-4108
NAME
ADDRESS
CITY ST ZIP
Offer expires midnight, December 31, 1983. Offer void if taxed, restricted or forbidden by law. Limit one set of 4 Star Wars Tumblers per household. Good only in USA. Wisconsin residents - facsimile ingredient panels only. Allow 4-6 weeks for delivery. Offer good only while supply lasts.
PEPPERIDGE FARM
NEW
STAR WARS®
COOKIES
PEANUT BUTTER
R2-D2
CHEWBACCA
THE REBEL ALLIANCE II
NET WT. 8 OZ. (227g)

**STW-66**
**Rebel Command Assault and Communications Set**
**2001**

DIZ-71
Cinderella
1990s

PCC-62
Pinocchio
2000

BAM-17
Bambi Musical Water Globe
1999

DIS-70
Disney Villains
1999

DIS-69
Roger Rabbit
1999

DSA-52
Family Reunion Pin
2001

DSA-53
Cloth Holder
with Badge
2001

DSA-48
"It's A Small World"
Badge with Pin Hanging
2000

DSA-47
Flicker Badge
2000

DSA-2
"1st Convention"
Pin on Card
1992

DNL-114
Tokyo Disneyland
Patch
1983

DSA-51
Family Reunion Pin
2001

DSA-49
Convention Pin
2000

MOV-195
"Talos" Statue
2000

MOV-194
"Cyclops" Statue
2000

MOV-192
"Kali" Statue
2000

MOV-193
"Minotaur" Statue
2000

MOV-191
"Ymir" Statue
2000

BUL-36
Bullwinkle series
1998

BUL-36
Bullwinkle series
1998

BUL-36
Bullwinkle series
1998

GRN-50
Green Hornet's Black Beauty
2001

JBD-42
James Bond
1998

JBD-41
James Bond
1998

COM-132
"Father Time" Dragster
1998

SUP-201
Kingdom Come
Resin Statue
1998

SUP-213
"Supergirl's
Arrival" Statue
2001

BAT-154
Batgirl
Resin Statue
2001

SUP-210
Superman Classic Rocket
2001

BAT-153
Batman Beyond
Batmobile
2000

SUP-211
Superman Tin Carousel
2001

SUP-212
Mr. Mxyzptlk Statue
2001

JUN-31
Justice Society of America Bookends
2001

**DSU-40**
**"The Grinch" Lunch Box**
**2000**

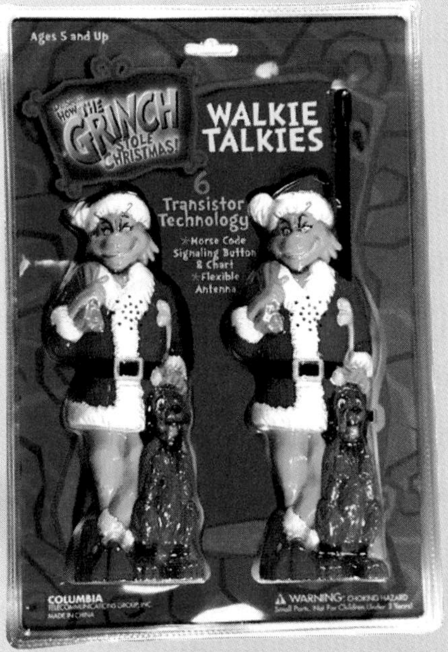


**DSU-38**
**"The Grinch"**
**Walkie Talkies**
**2000**

**DSU-39**
**"The Grinch"**
**Wacky Wobbler**
**2000**

**DSU-37**
**"Cindy Lou Who" Doll**
**2000**

**DSU-36**
**"The Grinch"**
**Talking Doll**
**2000**

**DSU-41**
**"Whoville-opoly" Board Game**
**2000**

MAR-43
"The Vision" Bust
2000

SPM-28
"Peter Parker,
The Amazing
Spider-Man"
Bust
2001

XMN-11
"Wolverine in
Debut Costume"
Bust
2000

SPM-26
"Dr. Octopus"
Bust
2001

MAR-41
"Scarlet Witch"
Bust
2000

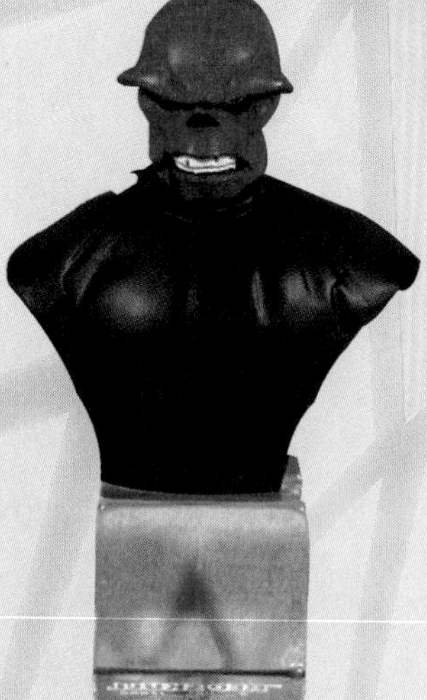

CAP-28
"Red Skull" Bust
1999

SPM-29
"Green Goblin" Bust
2001

PEZ-52
"Wolverine"
Dispenser
1990s

PEZ-52
"Webby"
Dispenser
2000

PEZ-44
Crystal
Elephant
Dispenser
1999

PEZ-69
"Giant Pez"
Candy Roll
Dispenser
2001

PEZ-41
"Roman"
Dispenser
1997

PEZ-43
Crystal Pumpkin
Head Dispenser
1999

SIM-36
"Bart Simpson"
Dispenser
1990s

PEZ-57
Eyewear Case
2000

PEZ-39
Pez Promo Decal
1980s

PEZ-56
Eyewear Case
2000

PEZ-58
Valentine's
Dispenser
2000

PEZ-40
Müeslix
Dispenser
2000

PEZ-54
Gyro Gearloose
Dispenser
2000

PEZ-45
Crystal Hippo
Dispenser
1999

PEZ-65
Smiley Face
Dispenser
1999

**BAT-152**
**Batman 24″ Statue on Base**
**2000**

**DCM-38**
**Golden Age Green Lantern Bust with Removable Power Ring**
**2001**

**WON-22**
**Wonder Woman Statue**
**2000**

**DCM-43**
**Green Arrow Resin Statue**
**2002**

**SUP-215**
**Kingdom Come Full Color Resin Statue**
**2001**

**BAT-156**
**Poison Ivy Porcelain Statue**
**2001**

**BAR-27**
**Samantha from Bewitched**
**2001**

**BAR-26**
**Wonder Woman**
**2000**

**SNO-72**
**"Wedding Snow White"**
**2001**

**BAR-24**
**Becky the Paralympic Champion**
**2000**

**TYS-65 (Toy Story 2)**
**Tour Guide Barbie**
**1999**

**BAR-19**
**Space Camp Barbie**
**1998**

# FANTASTIC FOUR FIGURES

MAR-49
"Mr. Fantastic" Statue
2001

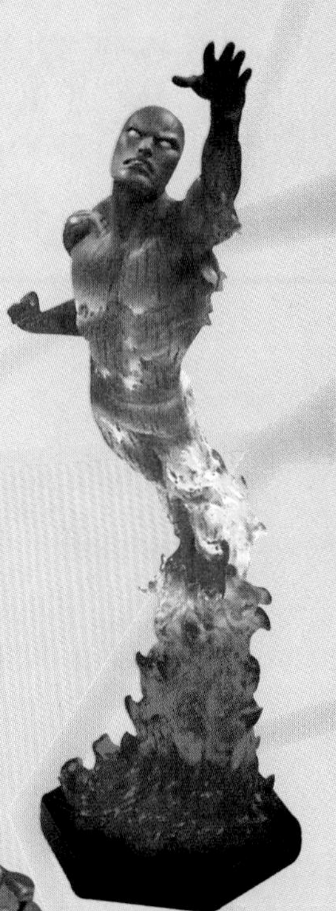

MAR-50
"The Human Torch"
Statue
2001

MAR-45
"The Thing" Statue
2000

MAR-48
"The Invisible Woman" Statue
2001

COM-167
10th Anniversary Figure with Comic
2001

COM-120
"Fone Bone" Resin Figure
1994

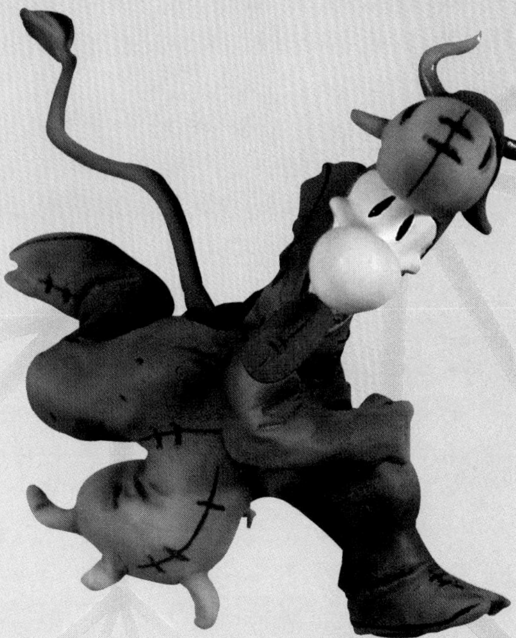

COM-130
"Smiley Bone" Resin Figure
1997

DCM-37
Green Lantern
2000

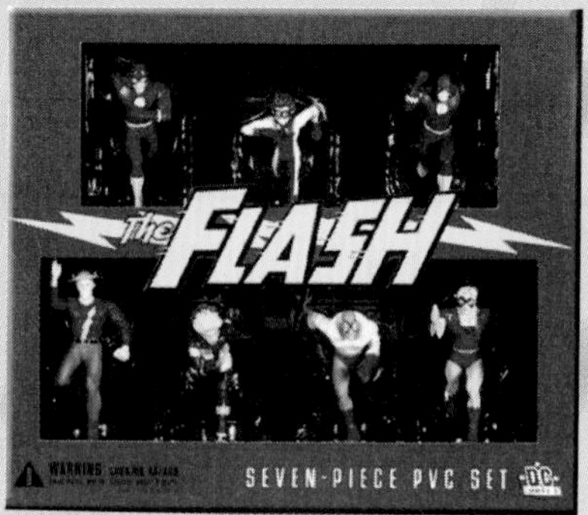


FLA-10
The Flash Seven-Piece Set
2000

COM-164
Beetle Bailey
2000

JUN-30
Justice Society
of America
Series 2
2000

DCM-34
"The New
Teen Titans"
2000

MOV-200
"Shrek" Doll in Box
2001

TEL-136
"Crush Me Phil" Toonsylvania Toy in Box
1998

MOV-201
"Shrek" Donkey Figure in Box
2001

TEL-137
"Taunt Me Igor" Toonsylvania Toy in Box
1998

**MAR-32**
**"Sparkling Gun"**
**1991**

**MAR-31**
**"Ball Blaster"**
**1990**

**MAR-33**
**"Flying Props" Toy Gun**
**1991**

**MAR-29**
**"Disc Shooter Target Set"**
**1990**

**MAR-30**
**"Soft Darts Target Set"**
**1990**

USC-50
Uncle Scrooge Figure
2001

CARL BARKS
THIS DOLLAR SAVED MY
LIFE AT WHITEHORSE

USC-40
"This Dollar Saved My Life at Whitehorse"
Capodimonte Sculpture
1999

BRG-10
Buck Rogers
"Earth to Mars"
Contest Cards
1933

FGR-32 (Flash Gordon)
Solar Command Set
1952

CVD-15
Captain Video
Spaceship Set
1951

TCO-34
Space Cadet
Patch
1950s

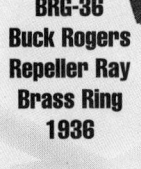

BRG-36
Buck Rogers
Repeller Ray
Brass Ring
1936

FGR-16
Flash Gordon Movie Poster
1938

TCO-15
Tom Corbett Rocket Ring
1952

SPA-26
Martian
Ornament
1960s

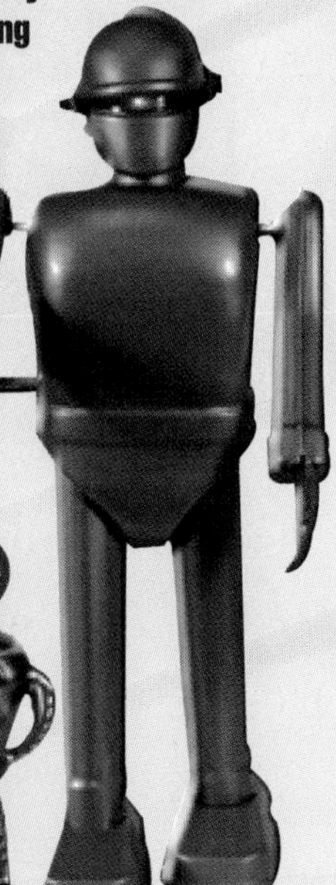

MOV-199
"Gort" Wind-Up Toy
2001

SPA-4
"Captain Space" Figures
1952

MOV-139
Robby the Robot
1984

WIN-23
Pirate Pooh
Bean Figure
2000

WIN-19
Choo Choo Pooh
Bean Figure
1999

WIN-18
Baseball Pooh
Bean Figure
2000

WIN-22
Choir Angel Pooh
Bean Figure
2000

WIN-17
Oktoberfest Pooh
Bean Figure
1999

WIN-20
Pilgrim Pooh
Bean Figure
1999

WIN-16
Hockey Pooh Bean Figure
1999

TEL-54
Crusader Rabbit
1950s

CIS-48
Cisco Kid
1950s

SUC-5
Super Circus
1951

TEL-75
Jackie Gleason Fan Club
1950s

DVY-31
Davy Crockett
1950s

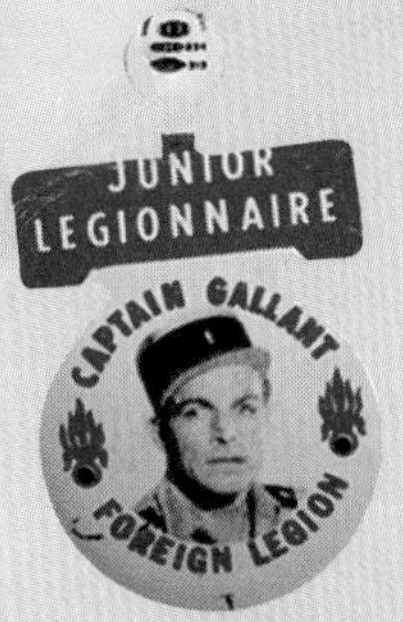


CGL-7
Captain Gallant
1950s

HOW-85
Howdy Doody
1950s

WLD-32
Wild Bill Hickok & Jingles
1950s

TEL-78
The Ghost Rider
1950s

ANN-5
Annie Oakley
c. 1955

TEL-77
Winky Dink
1950s

LAS-14
Lassie
1950s

BON-1
Bonanza
c. 1960

SKY-14
Sky King
c. 1950

DNS-7
Dennis the Menace
1968

ROO-3
Rootie Kazootie
c. 1952

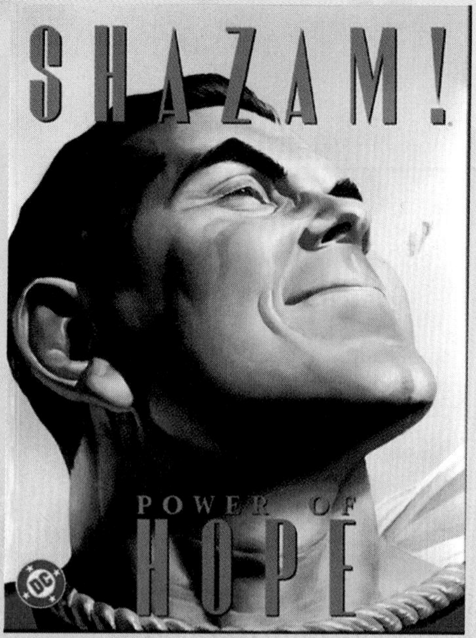

2000

1998

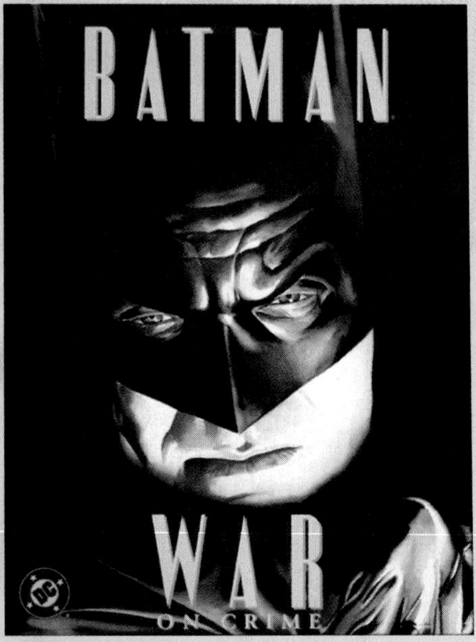

1999

2001

SYR-41
Beetle Bailey
2000

SYR-42
Sarge
2000

SYR-45
Terry (and the Pirates)
2000

SYR-46
Dragon Lady
2000

SYR-56
Little Nemo
2002

SYR-34
Popeye
2000

SYR-35
Olive Oyl
2000

SYR-51
Bluto
2001

SYR-50
Smokey Stover
2001

SYR-55
Alley Oop
2002

SYR-38
Li'l Abner
2000

SYR-39
Daisy Mae
2000

SYR-40
Dick Tracy
2000

SYR-48
Fearless Fosdick
2000

SYR-36
The Phantom
2000

SYR-37
Mandrake
2000

SYR-33
Prince Valiant
2000

SYR-44
Flash Gordon
2000

**UVM-13
Monster Figures
Boxed Set
2001**

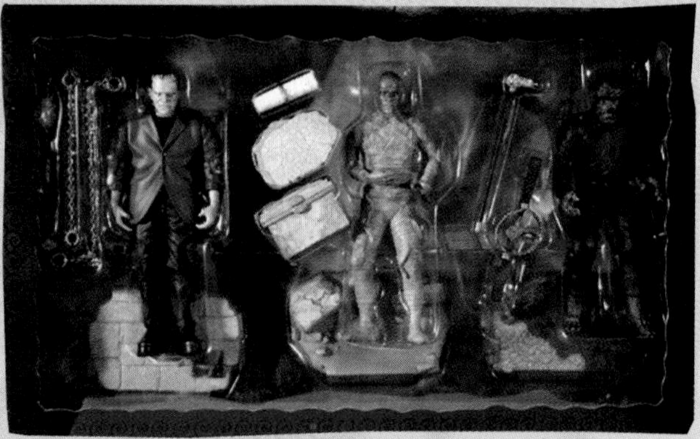

**UVM-37
"Classic
Movie Monsters"
Boxed Set
2001**

# ACADEMY AWARDS POSTER

**2002 Academy Awards Commemorative Poster by Alex Ross**

# DOCTOR WHO PINBALL MACHINE

**DWH-13**
**Bally Pinball Machine**
**1991**

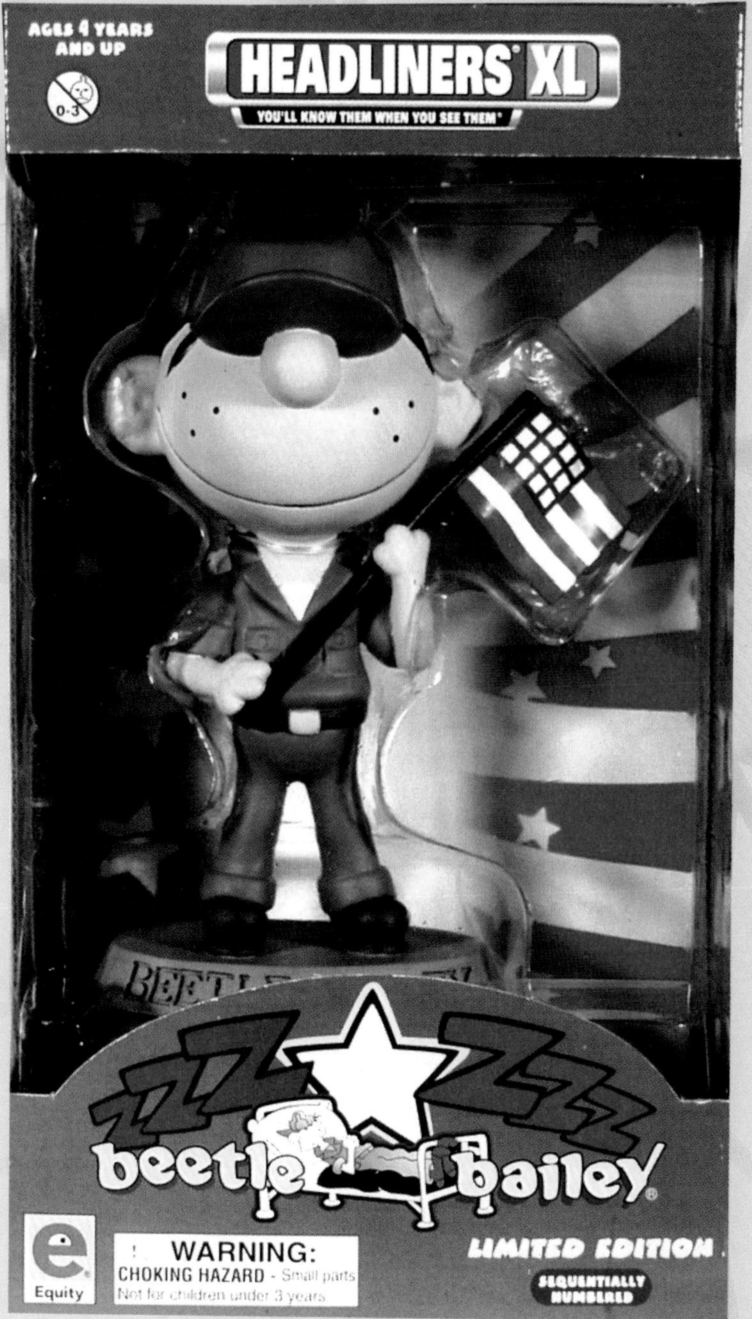


**COM-165**
**Beetle Bailey Resin Figure with Flag**
**2000**

METROPOLIS
COLLECTIBLES
873 Broadway, Suite 201
New York, NY 10003
BUYING
ACTION COMICS
BATMAN
Fantastic Four
SHOWCASE
FLASH
Absolutely
no other comic dealer
buys or sells more
Golden and Silver Age
comic books than
METROPOLIS
1. We pay more because we sell more!
2. We travel anywhere to buy your books!
3. We have millions of dollars to spend!
4. We offer a toll-free phone number!
5. We offer a free appraisal service!
6. We offer immediate payment!
7. We have over 25 years experience!
CALL TOLL-FREE
1-800-229-6387
tel 212-260-4147
fax 212-260-4304
email us at:
buying@metropoliscomics.com
visit us on the web at:
www.metropoliscomics.com
COMICS GUARANTY, LLC
Charter
Member Dealer